Peterson's Two-Year Colleges 2014

PETERSON'S

About Peterson's

Peterson's provides the accurate, dependable, high-quality education content and guidance you need to succeed. No matter where you are on your academic or professional path, you can rely on Peterson's print and digital publications for the most up-to-date education exploration data, expert test-prep tools, and top-notch career success resources—everything you need to achieve your goals.

Visit us online at www.petersonsbooks.com and let Peterson's help you achieve your goals.

For more information, contact Peterson's Publishing, 3 Columbia Circle, Suite 205, Albany, NY 12203-5158; 800-338-3282 Ext. 54229; or find us on the World Wide Web at www.petersonsbooks.com.

© 2013 Peterson's, a Nelnet company

Previous editions published as Peterson's Annual Guide to Undergraduate Study © 1970, 1971, 1972, 1973, 1974, 1975, 1976, 1977, 1978, 1979, 1980, 1981, 1982 and as Peterson's Two-Year Colleges © 1983, 1984, 1985, 1986, 1987, 1988, 1989, 1990, 1991, 1992, 1993, 1994, 1995, 1996, 1997, 1998, 1999, 2000, 2001, 2002, 2003, 2004, 2005, 2006, 2007, 2008, 2009, 2010, 2011, 2012

Bernadette Webster, Managing Editor; Jill C. Schwartz, Editor; John Wells, Research Project Manager; Jim Bonar, Research Operations Data Analyst; Amanda Ortiz, Research Associate; Phyllis Johnson, Software Engineer; Ray Golaszewski, Publishing Operations Manager; Linda M. Williams, Composition Manager; Carrie Hansen, Christine Lucht, Kiele Nowak, Bailey Williams, Fulfillment Coordinators

ISSN 0894-9328
ISBN: 978-0-7689-3756-5

Printed in the United States of America

10 9 8 7 6 5 4 3 2 1   15 14 13

Forty-fourth Edition

Sustainability—Its Importance to Peterson's

What does sustainability mean to Peterson's? As a leading publisher, we are aware that our business has a direct impact on vital resources—most especially the trees that are used to make our books. Peterson's is proud that its products are certified by the Sustainable Forestry Initiative (SFI) chain-of-custody standard and that all of its books are printed on paper that is 40% post-consumer waste using vegetable-based ink.

Being a part of the Sustainable Forestry Initiative (SFI) means that all of our vendors—from paper suppliers to printers—have undergone rigorous audits to demonstrate that they are maintaining a sustainable environment.

Peterson's continuously strives to find new ways to incorporate sustainability throughout all aspects of its business.

Contents

A Note from the Peterson's Editors

For more than 40 years, Peterson's has given students and parents the most comprehensive, up-to-date information on undergraduate institutions in the United States. Peterson's researches the data published in *Peterson's Two-Year Colleges* each year. The information is furnished by the colleges and is accurate at the time of publishing.

This guide also features advice and tips on the college search and selection process, such as how to decide if a two-year college is right for you, how to approach transferring between colleges, and what's in store for adults returning to college. If you seem to be getting more, not less, anxious about choosing and getting into the right college, *Peterson's Two-Year Colleges* provides just the right help, giving you the information you need to make important college decisions and ace the admission process.

Opportunities abound for students, and this guide can help you find what you want in a number of ways:

"What You Need to Know About Two-Year Colleges" outlines the basic features and advantages of two-year colleges. "Surviving Standardized Tests" gives an overview of the common examinations students take prior to attending college. "Who's Paying for This? Financial Aid Basics" provides guidelines for financing your college education. "Frequently Asked Questions About Transferring" takes a look at the two-year college scene from the perspective of a student who is looking toward the day when he or she may pursue additional education at a four-year institution. "Returning to School: Advice for Adult Students" is an analysis of the pros and cons (mostly pros) of returning to college after already having begun a professional career. "What International Students Need to Know About Admission to U.S. Colleges and Universities" is an article written particularly for students overseas who are considering a U.S. college education. "Community Colleges and the New Green Economy" offers information on some exciting "green" programs at community colleges throughout the United States, as well as two insightful essays by Mary F. T. Spilde, President, Lane Community College and James DeHaven, V.P. of Economic and Business Development, Kalamazoo Valley Community College. Finally, "How to Use This Guide"

gives details on the data in this guide: what terms mean and why they're here.

- If you already have specifics in mind, such as a particular institution or major, turn to the easy-to-use **Two-Year Colleges At-a-Glance Chart** or **Indexes.** You can look up a particular feature—location and programs offered—or use the alphabetical index and immediately find the colleges that meet your criteria.

- For information about particular colleges, turn to the **Profiles of Two-Year Colleges** section. Here, our comprehensive college profiles are arranged alphabetically by state. They provide a complete picture of need-to-know information about every accredited two-year college—from admission to graduation, including expenses, financial aid, majors, and campus safety. All the information you need to apply is placed together at the conclusion of each college **Profile.** Display ads, which appear near some of the institutions' profiles, have been provided and paid for by those colleges or universities that wished to supplement their profile data with additional information about their institution.

- In addition, two-page narrative descriptions, which appear as **College Close-Ups,** are paid for and written by college officials and offer great detail about each college. They are edited to provide a consistent format across entries for your ease of comparison.

Peterson's publishes a full line of books—education exploration, test prep, financial aid, and career preparation. Peterson's publications can be found at high school guidance offices, college libraries and career centers, and your local bookstore and library. Peterson's books are now also available as eBooks and online at www.petersonsbooks.com.

We welcome any comments or suggestions you may have about this publication. Your feedback will help us make educational dreams possible for you—and others like you.

Colleges will be pleased to know that Peterson's helped you in your selection. Admissions staff members are more than happy to answer questions, address specific problems and help in any way they can. The editors at Peterson's wish you great success in your college search.

The College Admissions Process: An Overview

What You Need to Know About Two-Year Colleges

David R. Pierce

Two-year colleges—better known as community colleges—are often called "the people's colleges." With their open-door policies (admission is open to individuals with a high school diploma or its equivalent), community colleges provide access to higher education for millions of Americans who might otherwise be excluded from higher education. Community college students are diverse and of all ages, races, and economic backgrounds. While many community college students enroll full-time, an equally large number attend on a part-time basis so they can fulfill employment and family commitments as they advance their education.

Community colleges can also be referred to as either technical or junior colleges, and they may either be under public or independent control. What unites two-year colleges is that they are regionally accredited, postsecondary institutions, whose highest credential awarded is the associate degree. With few exceptions, community colleges offer a comprehensive curriculum, which includes transfer, technical, and continuing education programs.

IMPORTANT FACTORS IN A COMMUNITY COLLEGE EDUCATION

The student who attends a community college can count on receiving high-quality instruction in a supportive learning community. This setting frees the student to pursue his or her own goals, nurture special talents, explore new fields of learning, and develop the capacity for lifelong learning.

From the student's perspective, four characteristics capture the essence of community colleges:

1. They are community-based institutions that work in close partnership with high schools, community groups, and employers in extending high-quality programs at convenient times and places.

2. Community colleges are cost effective. Annual tuition and fees at public community colleges average approximately half those at public four-year colleges and less than 15 percent of private four-year institutions. In addition, since most community colleges are generally close to their students' homes, these students can also save a significant amount of money on the room, board, and transportation expenses traditionally associated with a college education.

3. Community colleges provide a caring environment, with faculty members who are expert instructors, known for excellent teaching and meeting students at the point of their individual needs, regardless of age, sex, race, current job status, or previous academic preparation. Community colleges join a strong curriculum with a broad range of counseling and career services that are intended to assist students in making the most of their educational opportunities.

4. Many offer comprehensive programs, including transfer curricula in such liberal arts programs as chemistry, psychology, and business management, that lead directly to a baccalaureate degree and career programs that prepare students for employment or assist those already employed in upgrading their skills. For those students who need to strengthen their academic skills, community colleges also offer a wide range of developmental programs in mathematics, languages, and learning skills, designed to prepare the student for success in college studies.

GETTING TO KNOW YOUR TWO-YEAR COLLEGE

The first step in determining the quality of a community college is to check the status of its accreditation. Once you have established that a community college is appropriately accredited, find out as much as you can about the programs and services it has to offer. Much of that information can be found in materials the college provides. However, the best way to learn about a college is to visit in person.

During a campus visit, be prepared to ask a lot of questions. Talk to students, faculty members, administrators, and counselors about the college and its programs, particularly those in which you have a special interest. Ask about available certificates and associate degrees. Don't be shy. Do what you can to dig below the surface. Ask college officials about the transfer rate to four-year colleges. If a college emphasizes student services, find out what particular assistance is offered, such as educational or career guidance. Colleges are eager to provide you with the information you need to make informed decisions.

COMMUNITY COLLEGES CAN SAVE YOU MONEY

If you are able to live at home while you attend college, you will certainly save money on room and board, but it does cost something to commute. Many two-year colleges offer you instruction in your own home through online learning programs or through home study courses that can save both time and money. Look into all the options, and be sure to add up all the costs of attending various colleges before deciding which is best for you.

FINANCIAL AID

Many students who attend community colleges are eligible for a range of federal financial aid programs, state aid, and on-campus jobs. Your high school counselor or the financial aid officer at a community college will also be able to help you. It is in your interest to apply for financial aid months in advance of the date you intend to start your college program, so find out early what assistance is available to you. While many community colleges are able to help students who make a last-minute decision to attend college, either through short-term loans or emergency grants, if you are considering entering college and think you might need financial aid, it is best to find out as much as you can as early as you can.

WORKING AND GOING TO SCHOOL

Many two-year college students maintain full-time or part-time employment while they earn their degrees. Over the years, a steadily growing number of students have chosen to attend community colleges while they fulfill family and employment responsibilities. To enable these students to balance the demands of home, work, and school, most community colleges offer classes at night and on weekends.

For the full-time student, the usual length of time it takes to obtain an associate degree is two years. However, your length of study will depend on the course load you take: the fewer credits you earn each term, the longer it will take you to earn a degree. To assist you in moving more quickly toward earning your degree, many community colleges now award credit through examination or for equivalent knowledge gained through relevant life experiences. Be certain to find out the credit options that are available to you at the college in which you are interested. You may discover that it will take less time to earn a degree than you first thought.

PREPARATION FOR TRANSFER

Studies have repeatedly shown that students who first attend a community college and then transfer to a four-year college or university do at least as well academically as the students who entered the four-year institutions as freshmen. Most community colleges have agreements with nearby four-year institutions to make transfer of credits easier. If you are thinking of transferring, be sure to meet with a counselor or faculty adviser before choosing your courses. You will want to map out a course of study with transfer in mind. Make sure you also find out the credit-transfer requirements of the four-year institution you might want to attend.

ATTENDING A TWO-YEAR COLLEGE IN ANOTHER REGION

Although many community colleges serve a specific county or district, they are committed (to the extent of their ability) to the goal of equal educational opportunity without regard to economic status, race, creed, color, sex, or national origin. Independent two-year colleges recruit from a much broader geographical area—throughout the United States and, increasingly, around the world.

Although some community colleges do provide on-campus housing for their students, most do not. However, even if on-campus housing is not available, most colleges do have housing referral services.

NEW CAREER OPPORTUNITIES

Community colleges realize that many entering students are not sure about the field in which they want to focus their studies or the career they would like to pursue. Often, students discover fields and careers they never knew existed. Community colleges have the resources to help students identify areas of career interest and to set challenging occupational goals.

Once a career goal is set, you can be confident that a community college will provide job-relevant, technical education. About half of the students who take courses for credit at community colleges do so to prepare for employment or to acquire or upgrade skills for their current job. Especially helpful in charting a career path is the assistance of a counselor or a faculty adviser, who can discuss job opportunities in your chosen field and help you map out your course of study.

In addition, since community colleges have close ties to their communities, they are in constant contact with leaders in business, industry, organized labor, and public life. Community colleges work with these individuals and their organizations to prepare students for direct entry into the world of work. For example, some community colleges have established partnerships with local businesses and industries to provide specialized training programs. Some also provide the academic portion of apprenticeship training, while others offer extensive job-shadowing and cooperative education opportunities. Be sure to examine all of the career-preparation opportunities offered by the community colleges in which you are interested.

David R. Pierce is the former President of the American Association of Community Colleges.

Surviving Standardized Tests

WHAT ARE STANDARDIZED TESTS?

Colleges and universities in the United States use tests to help evaluate applicants' readiness for admission or to place them in appropriate courses. The tests that are most frequently used by colleges are the ACT of American College Testing, Inc., and the College Board's SAT. In addition, the Educational Testing Service (ETS) offers the TOEFL test, which evaluates the English-language proficiency of nonnative speakers. The tests are offered at designated testing centers located at high schools and colleges throughout the United States and U.S. territories and at testing centers in various countries throughout the world.

Upon request, special accommodations for students with documented visual, hearing, physical, or learning disabilities are available. Examples of special accommodations include tests in Braille or large print and such aids as a reader, recorder, magnifying glass, or sign language interpreter. Additional testing time may be allowed in some instances. Contact the appropriate testing program or your guidance counselor for details on how to request special accommodations.

THE ACT

The ACT is a standardized college entrance examination that measures knowledge and skills in English, mathematics, reading, and science reasoning and the application of these skills to future academic tasks. The ACT consists of four multiple-choice tests.

Test 1: English
- 75 questions, 45 minutes
- Usage and mechanics
- Rhetorical skills

Test 2: Mathematics
- 60 questions, 60 minutes
- Pre-algebra
- Elementary algebra
- Intermediate algebra
- Coordinate geometry
- Plane geometry
- Trigonometry

Test 3: Reading
- 40 questions, 35 minutes
- Prose fiction
- Humanities
- Social studies
- Natural sciences

Test 4: Science
- 40 questions, 35 minutes
- Data representation
- Research summary
- Conflicting viewpoints

Each section is scored from 1 to 36 and is scaled for slight variations in difficulty. Students are not penalized for incorrect responses. The composite score is the average of the four scaled scores. The ACT Plus Writing includes the four multiple-choice tests and a writing test, which measures writing skills emphasized in high school English classes and in entry-level college composition courses.

To prepare for the ACT, ask your guidance counselor for a free guidebook called "Preparing for the ACT." Besides providing general test-preparation information and additional test-taking strategies, this guidebook describes the content and format of the four ACT subject area tests, summarizes test administration procedures followed at ACT test centers, and includes a practice test. Peterson's publishes *The Real ACT Prep Guide* that includes five official ACT tests.

THE SAT

The SAT measures developed critical reading and mathematical reasoning abilities as they relate to successful performance in college. It is intended to supplement the secondary school record and other information about the student in assessing readiness for college. There is one unscored, experimental section on the exam, which is used for equating and/or pretesting purposes and can cover either the mathematics or critical reading area.

Critical Reading
- 67 questions, 70 minutes
- Sentence completion
- Passage-based reading

DON'T FORGET TO . . .

- ❑ Take the SAT or ACT before application deadlines.
- ❑ Note that test registration deadlines precede test dates by about six weeks.
- ❑ Register to take the TOEFL test if English is not your native language and you are planning on studying at a North American college.
- ❑ Practice your test-taking skills with *Peterson's Master the SAT, The Real ACT Prep Guide* (published by Peterson's).
- ❑ Contact the College Board or American College Testing, Inc., in advance if you need special accommodations when taking tests.

Mathematics
- 54 questions, 70 minutes
- Multiple-choice
- Student-produced response (grid-ins)

Writing
- 49 questions plus essay, 60 minutes
- Identifying sentence errors
- Improving paragraphs
- Improving sentences
- Essay

Students receive one point for each correct response and lose a fraction of a point for each incorrect response (except for student-produced responses). These points are totaled to produce the raw scores, which are then scaled to equalize the scores for slight variations in difficulty for various editions of the test. The critical reading, writing, and mathematics scaled scores range from 200–800 per section. The total scaled score range is from 600–2400.

SAT SUBJECT TESTS

Subject Tests are required by some institutions for admission and/or placement in freshman-level courses. Each Subject Test measures one's knowledge of a specific subject and the ability to apply that knowledge. Students should check with each institution for its specific requirements. In general, students are required to take three Subject Tests (one English, one mathematics, and one of their choice).

Subject Tests are given in the following areas: biology, chemistry, Chinese, French, German, Italian, Japanese, Korean, Latin, literature, mathematics, modern Hebrew, physics, Spanish, U.S. history, and world history. These tests are 1 hour long and are primarily multiple-choice tests. Three Subject Tests may be taken on one test date.

Scored like the SAT, students gain a point for each correct answer and lose a fraction of a point for each incorrect answer. The raw scores are then converted to scaled scores that range from 200 to 800.

THE TOEFL INTERNET-BASED TEST (IBT)

The Test of English as a Foreign Language Internet-Based Test (TOEFL iBT) is designed to help assess a student's grasp of English if it is not the student's first language. Performance on the TOEFL test may help interpret scores on the critical reading sections of the SAT. The test consists of four integrated sections: speaking, listening, reading, and writing. The TOEFL iBT emphasizes integrated skills. The paper-based versions of the TOEFL will continue to be administered in certain countries where the Internet-based version has not yet been introduced. For further information, visit www.toefl.org.

WHAT OTHER TESTS SHOULD I KNOW ABOUT?

The AP Program

This program allows high school students to try college-level work and build valuable skills and study habits in the process. Subject matter is explored in more depth in AP courses than in other high school classes. A qualifying score on an AP test—which varies from school to school—can earn you college credit or advanced placement. Getting qualifying grades on enough exams can even earn you a full year's credit and sophomore standing at more than 1,500 higher-education institutions. There are more than thirty AP courses across multiple subject areas, including art history, biology, and computer science. Speak to your guidance counselor for information about your school's offerings.

College-Level Examination Program (CLEP)

The CLEP enables students to earn college credit for what they already know, whether it was learned in school, through independent study, or through other experiences outside of the classroom. More than 2,900 colleges and universities now award credit for qualifying scores on one or more of the 33 CLEP exams. The exams, which are 90 minutes in length and are primarily multiple choice, are administered at participating colleges and universities. For more information, check out the Web site at www.collegeboard.com/clep.

WHAT CAN I DO TO PREPARE FOR THESE TESTS?

Know what to expect. Get familiar with how the tests are structured, how much time is allowed, and the directions for each type of question. Get plenty of rest the night before the test and eat breakfast that morning.

There are a variety of products, from books to software to videos, available to help you prepare for most standardized tests. Find the learning style that suits you best. As for which products to buy, there are two major categories— those created by the test makers and those created by private companies. The best approach is to talk to someone who has been through the process and find out which product or products he or she recommends.

Some students report significant increases in scores after participating in coaching programs. Longer-term programs (40 hours) seem to raise scores more than short-term programs (20 hours), but beyond 40 hours, score gains are minor. Math scores appear to benefit more from coaching than critical reading scores.

Resources

There is a variety of ways to prepare for standardized tests—find a method that fits your schedule and your budget. But you should definitely prepare. Far too many students walk into these tests cold, either because they find standardized tests frightening or annoying or they just haven't found the time to study. The key is that these exams are standardized. That means these tests are largely the same from administration to administration; they always test the same concepts. They have to, or else you couldn't compare the scores of people who took the tests on different dates. The numbers or words may change, but the underlying content doesn't.

So how do you prepare? At the very least, you should review relevant material, such as math formulas and commonly used vocabulary words, and know the directions for each question type or test section. You should take at least one practice test and review your mistakes so you don't make them again on the test day. Beyond that, you know best how much preparation you need. You'll also find lots of material in libraries or bookstores to help you: books and software from the test makers and from other publishers (including Peterson's) or live courses that range from national test-preparation companies to teachers at your high school who offer classes.

Top 10 Ways Not to Take the Test
10. Cramming the night before the test.
9. Not becoming familiar with the directions before you take the test.
8. Not becoming familiar with the format of the test before you take it.
7. Not knowing how the test is graded.
6. Spending too much time on any one question.
5. Second-guessing yourself.
4. Not checking spelling, grammar, and sentence structure in essays.
3. Writing a one-paragraph essay.
2. Forgetting to take a deep breath to keep from—
1. Losing It!

Who's Paying for This?
Financial Aid Basics

A college education can be expensive—costing more than $150,000 for four years at some of the higher priced private colleges and universities. Even at the lower cost state colleges and universities, the cost of a four-year education can approach $60,000. Determining how you and your family will come up with the necessary funds to pay for your education requires planning, perseverance, and learning as much as you can about the options that are available to you. But before you get discouraged, College Board statistics show that 53 percent of full-time students attend four-year public and private colleges with tuition and fees less than $9000, while 20 percent attend colleges that have tuition and fees more than $36,000. College costs tend to be less in the western states and higher in New England.

Paying for college should not be looked at as a four-year financial commitment. For many families, paying the total cost of a student's college education out of current income and savings is usually not realistic. For families that have planned ahead and have financial savings established for higher education, the burden is a lot easier. But for most, meeting the cost of college requires the pooling of current income and assets and investing in longer-term loan options. These family resources, together with financial assistance from state, federal, and institutional sources, enable millions of students each year to attend the institution of their choice.

FINANCIAL AID PROGRAMS

There are three types of financial aid:

1. Gift-aid—Scholarships and grants are funds that do not have to be repaid.

2. Loans—Loans must be repaid, usually after graduation; the amount you have to pay back is the total you've borrowed plus any accrued interest. This is considered a source of self-help aid.

3. Student employment—Student employment is a job arranged for you by the financial aid office. This is another source of self-help aid.

The federal government has four major grant programs—the Federal Pell Grant, the Federal Supplemental Educational Opportunity Grant, Academic Competitiveness Grants (ACG), and SMART grants. ACG and SMART grants are limited to students who qualify for a Pell grant and are awarded to a select group of students. Overall, these grants are targeted to low-to-moderate income families with significant financial need. The federal government also sponsors a student employment program called the Federal Work-Study Program, which offers jobs both on and off campus, and several loan programs, including those for students and for parents of undergraduate students.

There are two types of student loan programs: subsidized and unsubsidized. The subsidized Federal Direct Loan and the Federal Perkins Loan are need-based, government-subsidized loans. Students who borrow through these programs do not have to pay interest on the loan until after they graduate or leave school. The unsubsidized Federal Direct Loan and the Federal Direct PLUS Loan Program are not based on need, and borrowers are responsible for the interest while the student is in school. These loans are administered by different methods. Once you choose your college, the financial aid office will guide you through this process.

After you've submitted your financial aid application and you've been accepted for admission, each college will send you a letter describing your financial aid award. Most award letters show estimated college costs, how much you and your family are expected to contribute, and the amount and types of aid you have been awarded. Most students are awarded aid from a combination of sources and programs. Hence, your award is often called a financial aid "package."

SOURCES OF FINANCIAL AID

Millions of students and families apply for financial aid each year. Financial aid from all sources exceeds $143 billion per year. The largest single source of aid is the federal government, which will award more than $100 billion this year.

The next largest source of financial aid is found in the college and university community. Most of this aid is awarded to students who have a demonstrated need based on the Federal Methodology. Some institutions use a different formula, the Institutional Methodology (IM), to award their own funds in conjunction with other forms of aid. Institutional aid may be either need-based or non-need based. Aid that is not based on need is usually awarded for a student's academic performance (merit awards), specific talents or abilities, or to attract the type of students a college seeks to enroll.

Another source of financial aid is from state government. All states offer grant and/or scholarship aid, most of which is need-based. However, more and more states are offering substantial merit-based aid programs. Most state programs award aid only to students attending college in their home state.

Other sources of financial aid include:

- Private agencies
- Foundations
- Corporations

- Clubs
- Fraternal and service organizations
- Civic associations
- Unions
- Religious groups that award grants, scholarships, and low-interest loans
- Employers that provide tuition reimbursement benefits for employees and their children

More information about these different sources of aid is available from high school guidance offices, public libraries, college financial aid offices, directly from the sponsoring organizations, and on the Web at www.petersons.com and www.finaid.org.

HOW NEED-BASED FINANCIAL AID IS AWARDED

When you apply for aid, your family's financial situation is analyzed using a government-approved formula called the Federal Methodology. This formula looks at five items:

1. Demographic information of the family
2. Income of the parents
3. Assets of the parents
4. Income of the student
5. Assets of the student

This analysis determines the amount you and your family are expected to contribute toward your college expenses, called your Expected Family Contribution or EFC. If the EFC is equal to or more than the cost of attendance at a particular college, then you do not demonstrate financial need. However, even if you don't have financial need, you may still qualify for aid, as there are grants, scholarships, and loan programs that are not need-based.

If the cost of your education is greater than your EFC, then you do demonstrate financial need and qualify for assistance. The amount of your financial need that can be met varies from school to school. Some are able to meet your full need, while others can only cover a certain percentage of need. Here's the formula:

Cost of Attendance
− Expected Family Contribution
= Financial Need

The EFC remains constant, but your need will vary according to the costs of attendance at a particular college. In general, the higher the tuition and fees at a particular college, the higher the cost of attendance will be. Expenses for books and supplies, room and board, transportation, and other miscellaneous items are included in the overall cost of attendance. It is important to remember that you do not have to be "needy" to qualify for financial aid. Many middle and upper-middle income families qualify for need-based financial aid.

APPLYING FOR FINANCIAL AID

Every student must complete the Free Application for Federal Student Aid (FAFSA) to be considered for financial aid. The FAFSA is available from your high school guidance office, many public libraries, colleges in your area, or directly from the U.S. Department of Education.

Students are encouraged to apply for federal student aid on the Web. The electronic version of the FAFSA can be accessed at http://www.fafsa.ed.gov. Both the student and at least one parent must apply for a federal PIN at http:// www.pin.ed.gov. The PIN serves as your electronic signature when applying for aid on the Web.

To award their own funds, some colleges require an additional application, the CSS/Financial Aid PROFILE® form. The PROFILE asks supplemental questions that some colleges and awarding agencies feel provide a more accurate assessment of the family's ability to pay for college. It is up to the college to decide whether it will use only the FAFSA or both the FAFSA and the PROFILE. PROFILE applications are available from the high school guidance office and on the Web. Both the paper application and the Web site list those colleges and programs that require the PROFILE application.

If Every College You're Applying to for Fall 2014 Requires the FAFSA

. . . then it's pretty simple: Complete the FAFSA after January 1, 2014, being certain to send it in before any college-imposed deadlines. (You are not permitted to send in the 2014–15 FAFSA before January 1, 2014.) Most college FAFSA application deadlines are in February or early March. It is easier if you have all your financial records for the previous year available, but if that is not possible, you are strongly encouraged to use estimated figures.

After you send in your FAFSA, either with the paper application or electronically, you'll receive a Student Aid Report (SAR) that includes all of the information you reported and shows your EFC. If you provided an e-mail address, the SAR is sent to you electronically; otherwise, you will receive a paper copy in the mail. Be sure to review the SAR, checking to see if the information you reported is accurately represented. If you used estimated numbers to complete the FAFSA, you may have to resubmit the SAR with any corrections to the data. The college(s) you have designated on the FAFSA will receive the information you reported and will use that data to make their decision. In many instances, the colleges to which you've applied will ask you to send copies of your and your parents' federal income tax returns for 2012, plus any other documents needed to verify the information you reported.

If a College Requires the PROFILE

Step 1: Register for the CSS/Financial Aid PROFILE in the fall of your senior year in high school. You can apply for the PROFILE online at http://profileonline.collegeboard.com/prf/index.jsp. Registration information with a list of the colleges that require the PROFILE is available in most high school guidance offices. There is a fee for using the Financial Aid

PROFILE application ($25 for the first college, which includes the $9 application fee, and $16 for each additional college). You must pay for the service by credit card when you register. If you do not have a credit card, you will be billed. A limited number of fee waivers are automatically granted to first-time applicants based on the financial information provided on the PROFILE.

Step 2: Fill out your customized CSS/Financial Aid PROFILE. Once you register, your application will be immediately available online and will have questions that all students must complete, questions which must be completed by the student's parents (unless the student is independent and the colleges or programs selected do not require parental information), and *may* have supplemental questions needed by one or more of your schools or programs. If required, those will be found in Section Q of the application.

In addition to the PROFILE application you complete online, you may also be required to complete a Business/ Farm Supplement via traditional paper format. Completion of this form is not a part of the online process. If this form is required, instructions on how to download and print the supplemental form are provided. If your biological or adoptive parents are separated or divorced and your colleges and programs require it, your noncustodial parent may be asked to complete the Noncustodial PROFILE.

Once you complete and submit your PROFILE application, it will be processed and sent directly to your requested colleges and programs.

IF YOU DON'T QUALIFY FOR NEED-BASED AID

If you are not eligible for need-based aid, you can still find ways to lessen your burden.

Here are some suggestions:

- Search for merit scholarships. You can start at the initial stages of your application process. College merit awards are increasingly important as more and more colleges award these to students they especially want to attract. As a result, applying to a college at which your qualifications put you at the top of the entering class may give you a larger merit award. Another source of aid to look for is private scholarships that are given for special skills and talents. Additional information can be found at and at www.finaid.org.

- Seek employment during the summer and the academic year. The student employment office at your college can help you locate a school-year job. Many colleges and local businesses have vacancies remaining after they have hired students who are receiving Federal Work-Study Program financial aid.

- Borrow through the unsubsidized Federal Direct Loan program. This is generally available to all students. The terms and conditions are similar to the subsidized loans. The biggest difference is that the borrower is responsible for the interest while still in college, although the government permits students to delay paying the interest right away and add the accrued interest to the total amount owed. You must file the FAFSA to be considered.

- After you've secured what you can through scholarships, working, and borrowing, you and your parents will be expected to meet your share of the college bill (the Expected Family Contribution). Many colleges offer monthly payment plans that spread the cost over the academic year. If the monthly payments are too high, parents can borrow through the Federal Direct PLUS Loan Program, through one of the many private education loan programs available, or through home equity loans and lines of credit. Families seeking assistance in financing college expenses should inquire at the financial aid office about what programs are available at the college. Some families seek the advice of professional financial advisers and tax consultants.

Frequently Asked Questions About Transferring

Muriel M. Shishkoff

Among the students attending two-year colleges are a large number who began their higher education knowing they would eventually transfer to a four-year school to obtain their bachelor's degree. There are many reasons why students go this route. Upon graduating from high school, some simply do not have definite career goals. Although they don't want to put their education on hold, they prefer not to pay exorbitant amounts in tuition while trying to "find themselves." As the cost of a university education escalates—even in public institutions—the option of spending the freshman and sophomore years at a two-year college looks attractive to many students. Others attend a two-year college because they are unable to meet the initial entrance standards—a specified grade point average (GPA), standardized test scores, or knowledge of specific academic subjects—required by the four-year school of their choice. Many such students praise the community college system for giving them the chance to be, academically speaking, "born again." In addition, students from other countries often find that they can adapt more easily to language and cultural changes at a two-year school before transferring to a larger, more diverse four-year college.

If your plan is to attend a two-year college with the ultimate goal of transferring to a four-year school, you will be pleased to know that the increased importance of the community college route to a bachelor's degree is recognized by all segments of higher education. As a result, many two-year schools have revised their course outlines and established new courses in order to comply with the programs and curricular offerings of the universities. Institutional improvements to make transferring easier have also proliferated at both the two-and four-year levels. The generous transfer policies of the Pennsylvania, New York, and Florida state university systems, among others, reflect this attitude; these systems accept all credits from students who have graduated from accredited community colleges.

If you are interested in moving from a two-year college to a four-year school, the sooner you make up your mind that you are going to make the switch, the better position you will be in to transfer successfully (that is, without having wasted valuable time and credits). The ideal point at which to make such a decision is **before** you register for classes at your two-year school; a counselor can help you plan your course work with an eye toward fulfilling the requirements needed for your major course of study.

Naturally, it is not always possible to plan your transferring strategy that far in advance, but keep in mind that the key to a successful transfer is **preparation,** and preparation takes time—time to think through your objectives and time to plan the right classes to take.

As students face the prospect of transferring from a two-year to a four-year school, many thoughts and concerns about this complicated and often frustrating process race through their minds. Here are answers to the questions that are most frequently asked by transferring students.

Q Does every college and university accept transfer students?

A Most four-year institutions accept transfer students, but some do so more enthusiastically than others. Graduating from a community college is an advantage at, for example, Arizona State University and the University of Massachusetts Boston; both accept more community college transfer students than traditional freshmen. At the State University of New York at Albany, graduates of two-year transfer programs within the State University of New York System are given priority for upper-division (i.e., junior- and senior-level) vacancies.

Schools offering undergraduate work at the upper division only are especially receptive to transfer applications. On the other hand, some schools accept only a few transfer students; others refuse entrance to sophomores or those in their final year. Princeton University requires an "excellent academic record and particularly compelling reasons to transfer." Check the catalogs of several colleges for their transfer requirements before you make your final choice.

Q Do students who go directly from high school to a four-year college do better academically than transfer students from community colleges?

A On the contrary: some institutions report that transfers from two-year schools who persevere until graduation do *better* than those who started as freshmen in a four-year college.

Q Why is it so important that my two-year college be accredited?

A Four-year colleges and universities accept transfer credits only from schools formally recognized by a regional, national, or professional educational agency. This accreditation signifies that an institution or program of study meets or exceeds a minimum level of educational quality necessary for meeting stated educational objectives.

Q After enrolling at a four-year school, may I still make up necessary courses at a community college?

A Some institutions restrict credit after transfer to their own facilities. Others allow students to take a limited number of transfer courses after matriculation, depending on the subject matter. A few provide opportunities for cross-registration or dual enrollment, which means taking classes on more than one campus.

Q What do I need to do to transfer?

A First, send for your high school and college transcripts. Having chosen the school you wish to transfer to, check its admission requirements against your transcripts. If you find that you are admissible, file an application as early as possible before the deadline. Part of the process will be asking your former schools to send official transcripts to the admission office, i.e., not the copies you used in determining your admissibility.

Plan your transfer program with the head of your new department as soon as you have decided to transfer. Determine the recommended general education pattern and necessary preparation for your major. At your present school, take the courses you will need to meet transfer requirements for the new school.

Q What qualifies me for admission as a transfer student?

A Admission requirements for most four-year institutions vary. Depending on the reputation or popularity of the school and program you wish to enter, requirements may be quite selective and competitive. Usually, you will need to show satisfactory test scores, an academic record up to a certain standard, and completion of specific subject matter.

Transfer students can be eligible to enter a four-year school in a number of ways: by having been eligible for admission directly upon graduation from high school, by making up shortcomings in grades (or in subject matter not covered in high school) at a community college, or by satisfactory completion of necessary courses or credit hours at another postsecondary institution. Ordinarily, students coming from a community college or from another four-year institution must meet or exceed the receiving institution's standards for freshmen and show appropriate college-level course work taken since high school. Students who did not graduate from high school can present proof of proficiency through results on the General Educational Development (GED) test.

Q Are exceptions ever made for students who don't meet all the requirements for transfer?

A Extenuating circumstances, such as disability, low family income, refugee or veteran status, or athletic talent, may permit the special enrollment of students who would not otherwise be eligible but who demonstrate the potential for academic success. Consult the appropriate office—the Educational Opportunity Program, the disabled students' office, the athletic department, or the academic dean—to see whether an exception can be made in your case.

Q How far in advance do I need to apply for transfer?

A Some schools have a rolling admission policy, which means that they process transfer applications as they are received, all year long. With other schools, you must apply during the priority filing period, which can be up to a year before you wish to enter. Check the date with the admission office at your prospective campus.

Q Is it possible to transfer courses from several different institutions?

A Institutions ordinarily accept the courses that they consider transferable, regardless of the number of accredited schools involved. However, there is the danger of exceeding the maximum number of credit hours that can be transferred from all other schools or earned through credit by examination, extension courses, or correspondence courses. The limit placed on transfer credits varies from school to school, so read the catalog carefully to avoid taking courses you won't be able to use. To avoid duplicating courses, keep attendance at different campuses to a minimum.

Q What is involved in transferring from a semester system to a quarter or trimester system?

A In the semester system, the academic calendar is divided into two equal parts. The quarter system is more aptly named trimester, since the academic calendar is divided into three equal terms (not counting a summer session). To convert semester units into quarter units or credit hours, simply multiply the semester units by one and a half. Conversely, multiply quarter units by two thirds to come up with semester units. If you are used to a semester system of fifteen- to sixteen-week courses, the ten-week courses of the quarter system may seem to fly by.

Q Why might a course be approved for transfer credit by one four-year school but not by another?

A The beauty of postsecondary education in the United States lies in its variety. Entrance policies and graduation requirements are designed to reflect and serve each institution's mission. Because institutional policies vary so widely, schools may interpret the subject matter of a course from quite different points of view. Given that the granting of transfer credit indicates that a course is viewed as being, in effect, parallel to one offered by the receiving institution, it is easy to see how this might be the case at one university and not another.

Q Must I take a foreign language to transfer?

A Foreign language proficiency is often required for admission to a four-year institution; such proficiency also often figures in certain majors or in the general education pattern. Often, two or three years of a single language in high school will do the trick. Find out if scores received on Advanced Placement (AP) examinations, placement examinations given by the foreign language department, or SAT Subject Tests will be accepted in lieu of college course work.

Q Will the school to which I'm transferring accept pass/ no pass, pass/fail, or credit/no credit grades in lieu of letter grades?

A Usually, a limit is placed on the number of these courses you can transfer, and there may be other restrictions as well. If you want to use other-than-letter grades for the fulfillment of general education requirements or lower-division (freshman and sophomore) preparation for the major, check with the receiving institution.

Q Which is more important for transfer—my grade point average or my course completion pattern?

A Some schools believe that your past grades indicate academic potential and overshadow prior preparation for a specific degree program. Others require completion of certain introductory courses before transfer to prepare you for upper-division work in your major. In any case, appropriate course selection will cut down the time to graduation and increase your chances of making a successful transfer.

Q What happens to my credits if I change majors?

A If you change majors after admission, your transferable course credit should remain fairly intact. However, because you may need extra or different preparation for your new major, some of the courses you've taken may now be useful only as electives. The need for additional lower-level preparation may mean you're staying longer at your new school than you originally planned. On the other hand, you may already have taken courses that count toward your new major as part of the university's general education pattern.

Excerpted from *Transferring Made Easy: A Guide to Changing Colleges Successfully,* by Muriel M. Shishkoff, © 1991 by Muriel M. Shishkoff (published by Peterson's).

Returning to School: Advice for Adult Students

Sandra Cook, Ph.D.
Assistant Vice President for Academic Affairs, Enrollment Services, San Diego State University

Many adults think for a long time about returning to school without taking any action. One purpose of this article is to help the "thinkers" finally make some decisions by examining what is keeping them from action. Another purpose is to describe not only some of the difficulties and obstacles that adult students may face when returning to school but also tactics for coping with them.

If you have been thinking about going back to college, and believing that you are the only person your age contemplating college, you should know that approximately 7 million adult students are currently enrolled in higher education institutions. This number represents 50 percent of total higher education enrollments. The majority of adult students are enrolled at two-year colleges.

There are many reasons why adult students choose to attend a two-year college. Studies have shown that the three most important criteria that adult students consider when choosing a college are location, cost, and availability of the major or program desired. Most two-year colleges are public institutions that serve a geographic district, making them readily accessible to the community. Costs at most two-year colleges are far less than at other types of higher education institutions. For many students who plan to pursue a bachelor's degree, completing their first two years of college at a community college is an affordable means to that end. If you are interested in an academic program that will transfer to a four-year institution, most two-year colleges offer the "general education" courses that compose most freshman and sophomore years. If you are interested in a vocational or technical program, two-year colleges excel in providing this type of training.

SETTING THE STAGE

There are three different "stages" in the process of adults returning to school. The first stage is uncertainty. Do I really want to go back to school? What will my friends or family think? Can I compete with those 18-year-old whiz kids? Am I too old? The second stage is choice. Once the decision to return has been made, you must choose where you will attend. There are many criteria to use in making this decision. The third stage is support. You have just added another role to your already-too-busy life. There are, however, strategies that

will help you accomplish your goals—perhaps not without struggle, but with grace and humor nonetheless. Let's look at each of these stages.

UNCERTAINTY

Why are you thinking about returning to school? Is it to

- fulfill a dream that had to be delayed?
- become more educationally well-rounded?
- fill an intellectual void in your life?

These reasons focus on personal growth.

If you are returning to school to

- meet people and make friends
- attain and enjoy higher social status and prestige among friends, relatives, and associates
- understand/study a cultural heritage
- have a medium in which to exchange ideas

You are interested in social and cultural opportunities.

If you are like most adult students, you want to

- qualify for a new occupation
- enter or reenter the job market
- increase earnings potential
- qualify for a more challenging position in the same field of work

You are seeking career growth.

Understanding the reasons why you want to go back to school is an important step in setting your educational goals and will help you to establish some criteria for selecting a college. However, don't delay your decision because you have not been able to clearly define your motives. Many times, these aren't clear until you have already begun the process, and they may change as you move through your college experience.

Assuming you agree that additional education will benefit you, what is it that keeps you from returning to school? You may have a litany of excuses running through your mind:

- I don't have time.
- I can't afford it.
- I'm too old to learn.
- My friends will think I'm crazy.

- I'll be older than the teachers and other students.
- My family can't survive without me to take care of them every minute.
- I'll be X years old when I finish.
- I'm afraid.
- I don't know what to expect.

And that is just what these are—excuses. You can make school, like anything else in your life, a priority or not. If you really want to return, you can. The more you understand your motivation for returning to school and the more you understand what excuses are keeping you from taking action, the easier your task will be.

If you think you don't have time: The best way to decide how attending class and studying can fit into your schedule is to keep track of what you do with your time each day for several weeks. Completing a standard time-management grid (each day is plotted out by the half hour) is helpful for visualizing how your time is spent. For each 3-credit-hour class you take, you will need to find 3 hours for class plus 6 to 9 hours for reading-studying-library time. This study time should be spaced evenly throughout the week, not loaded up on one day. It is not possible to learn or retain the material that way. When you examine your grid, see where there are activities that could be replaced with school and study time. You may decide to give up your bowling league or some time in front of the TV. Try not to give up sleeping, and don't cut out every moment of free time. Here are some suggestions that have come from adults who have returned to school:

- Enroll in a time-management workshop. It helps you rethink how you use your time.
- Don't think you have to take more than one course at a time. You may eventually want to work up to taking more, but consider starting with one. (It is more than you are taking now!)
- If you have a family, start assigning to them those household chores that you usually do—and don't redo what they do.
- Use your lunch hour or commuting time for reading.

If you think you cannot afford it: As mentioned earlier, two-year colleges are extremely affordable. If you cannot afford the tuition, look into the various financial aid options. Most federal and state funds are available to full- and part-time students. Loans are also available. While many people prefer not to accumulate a debt for school, these same people will think nothing of taking out a loan to buy a car. After five or six years, which is the better investment? Adult students who work should look into whether their company has a tuition-reimbursement policy. There are also private scholarships, available through foundations, service organizations, and clubs, that are focused on adult learners. Your public library, the Web, and a college financial aid adviser are three excellent sources for reference materials regarding financial aid.

If you think you are too old to learn: This is pure myth. A number of studies have shown that adult learners perform as well as, or better than, traditional-age students.

If you are afraid your friends will think you're crazy: Who cares? Maybe they will, maybe they won't. Usually, they will admire your courage and be just a little jealous of your ambition (although they'll never tell you that). Follow your dreams, not theirs.

If you are concerned because the teachers or students will be younger than you: Don't be. The age differences that may be apparent in other settings evaporate in the classroom. If anything, an adult in the classroom strikes fear into the hearts of some 18-year-olds because adults have been known to be prepared, ask questions, be truly motivated, and be there to learn!

If you think your family will have a difficult time surviving while you are in school: If you have done everything for them up to now, they might struggle. Consider this an opportunity to help them become independent and self-sufficient. Your family can only make you feel guilty if you let them. You are not abandoning them; you are becoming an educational role model. When you are happy and working toward your goals, everyone benefits. Admittedly, it sometimes takes time for them to realize this. For single parents, there are schools that offer support groups, child care, and cooperative babysitting.

If you're appalled at the thought of being X years old when you graduate in Y years: How old will you be in Y years if you don't go back to school?

If you are afraid or don't know what to expect: Know that these are natural feelings when one encounters any new situation. Adult students find that their fears usually dissipate once they begin classes. Fear of trying is usually the biggest roadblock to the reentry process.

No doubt you have dreamed up a few more reasons for not making the decision to return to school. Keep in mind that what you are doing is making up excuses, and you are using these excuses to release you from the obligation to make a decision about your life. The thought of returning to college can be scary. Anytime anyone ventures into unknown territory, there is a risk, but taking risks is a necessary component of personal and professional growth. It is your life, and you alone are responsible for making the decisions that determine its course. Education is an investment in your future.

CHOICE

Once you have decided to go back to school, your next task is to decide where to go. If your educational goals are well defined (e.g., you want to pursue a degree in order to change careers), then your task is a bit easier. But even if your educational goals are still evolving, do not defer your return. Many students who enter higher education with a specific major in mind change that major at least once.

Most students who attend a public two-year college choose the community college in the district in which they live. This is generally the closest and least expensive option if the school offers the programs you want. If you are planning to begin your education at a two-year college and then transfer to a four-year school, there are distinct advantages to choosing your four-year school early. Many community and four-year colleges have "articulation" agreements that designate what credits from the two-year school will transfer to the four-year college and how. Some four-year institutions accept an associate degree as equivalent to the freshman and sophomore years, regardless of the courses you have taken. Some four-year schools accept two-year college work only on a course-by-course basis. If you can identify which school you will transfer to, you can know in advance exactly how your two-year credits will apply, preventing an unexpected loss of credit or time.

Each institution of higher education is distinctive. Your goal in choosing a college is to come up with the best student-institution fit—matching your needs with the offerings and characteristics of the school. The first step in choosing a college is to determine what criteria are most important to you in attaining your educational goals. Location, cost, and program availability are the three main factors that influence an adult student's college choice. In considering location, don't forget that some colleges have conveniently located branch campuses. In considering cost, remember to explore your financial aid options before ruling out an institution because of its tuition. Program availability should include not only the major in which you are interested, but also whether or not classes in that major are available when you can take them.

Some additional considerations beyond location, cost, and programs are:

- Does the school have a commitment to adult students and offer appropriate services, such as child care, tutoring, and advising?

- Are classes offered at times when you can take them?

- Are there academic options for adults, such as credit for life or work experience, credit by examination (including CLEP), credit for military service, or accelerated programs?

- Is the faculty sensitive to the needs of adult learners?

Once you determine which criteria are vital in your choice of an institution, you can begin to narrow your choices. There are myriad ways for you to locate the information you desire. Many newspapers publish a "School Guide" several times a year in which colleges and universities advertise to an adult student market. In addition, schools themselves publish catalogs, class schedules, and promotional materials that contain much of the information you need, and they are yours for the asking. Many colleges sponsor information sessions and open houses that allow you to visit the campus and ask questions. An appointment with an adviser is a good way to assess the fit

between you and the institution. Be sure to bring your questions with you to your interview.

SUPPORT

Once you have made the decision to return to school and have chosen the institution that best meets your needs, take some additional steps to ensure your success during your crucial first semester. Take advantage of institutional support and build some social support systems of your own. Here are some ways of doing just that:

- Plan to participate in any orientation programs. These serve the threefold purpose of providing you with a great deal of important information, familiarizing you with the campus and its facilities, and giving you the opportunity to meet and begin networking with other students.

- Take steps to deal with any academic weaknesses. Take mathematics and writing placement tests if you have reason to believe you may need some extra help in these areas. It is not uncommon for adult students to need a math refresher course or a program to help alleviate math anxiety. Ignoring a weakness won't make it go away.

- Look into adult reentry programs. Many institutions offer adults workshops focusing on ways to improve study skills, textbook reading, test-taking, and time-management skills.

- Build new support networks by joining an adult student organization, making a point of meeting other adult students through workshops, or actively seeking out a "study buddy" in each class—that invaluable friend who shares and understands your experience.

- Incorporate your new status as "student" into your family life. Doing your homework with your children at a designated "homework time" is a valuable family activity and reinforces the importance of education.

- Make sure you take a reasonable course load in your first semester. It is far better to have some extra time on your hands and to succeed magnificently than to spend the entire semester on the brink of a breakdown. Also, whenever possible, try to focus your first courses not only on requirements, but also on areas of personal interest.

- Faculty members, advisers, and student affairs personnel are there to help you during difficult times—let them assist you as often as necessary.

After completing your first semester, you will probably look back in wonder at why you thought going back to school was so imposing. Certainly, it's not without its occasional exasperations. But, as with life, keeping things in perspective and maintaining your sense of humor make the difference between just coping and succeeding brilliantly.

What International Students Need to Know About Admission to U.S. Colleges and Universities

Kitty M. Villa

There are two principles to remember about admission to a university in the United States. First, applying is almost never a one-time request for admission but an ongoing process that may involve several exchanges of information between applicant and institution. "Admission process" or "application process" means that a "yes" or "no" is usually not immediate, and requests for additional information are to be expected. To successfully manage this process, you must be prepared to send additional information when requested and then wait for replies. You need a thoughtful balance of persistence to communicate regularly and effectively with your selected universities and patience to endure what can be a very long process.

The second principle involves a marketplace analogy. The most successful applicants are alert to opportunities to create a positive impression that sets them apart from other applicants. They are able to market themselves to their target institution. Institutions are also trying to attract the highest-quality student that they can. The admissions process presents you with the opportunity to analyze your strengths and weaknesses as a student and to look for ways to present yourself in the most marketable manner.

FIRST STEP—SELECTING INSTITUTIONS

With thousands of institutions of higher education in the United States, how do you begin to narrow your choices down to the institutions that are best for you? There are many factors to consider, and you must ultimately decide which factors are most important to you.

Location

You may spend several years studying in the United States. Do you prefer an urban or rural campus? Large or small metropolitan area? If you need to live on campus, will you be unhappy at a university where most students commute from off-campus housing? How do you feel about extremely hot summers or cold winters? Eliminating institutions that do not match your preferences in terms of location will narrow your choices.

Recommendations from Friends, Professors, or Others

There are valid academic reasons to consider the recommendations of people who know you well and have firsthand knowledge about particular institutions. Friends and contacts may be able to provide you with "inside information" about the campus or its academic programs to which published sources have no access. You should carefully balance anecdotal information with your own research and your own impressions. However, current and former students, professors, and others may provide excellent information during the application process.

Your Own Academic and Career Goals

Consideration of your academic goals is more complex than it may seem at first glance. All institutions do not offer the same academic programs. The application form usually provides a definitive listing of the academic programs offered by an institution. A course catalog describes the degree program and all the courses offered. In addition to printed sources, there is a tremendous amount of institutional information available on the Web. Program descriptions, even course descriptions and course syllabi, are often available to peruse online.

You may be interested in the rankings of either the university or of a program of study. Keep in mind, however, that rankings usually assume that quality is quantifiable. Rankings are usually based on presumptions about how data relate to quality and are likely to be unproven. It is important to carefully consider the source and the criteria of any ranking information before believing and acting upon it.

Your Own Educational Background

You may be concerned about the interpretation of your educational credentials, since your country's degree nomenclature and the grading scale may differ from those in the United States. Universities use reference books about the educational systems of other countries to help them understand specific educational credentials. Generally, these credentials are interpreted by each institution; there is not a single interpretation that applies to every institution. The lack of uniformity is good news for most students, since it means that students from a wide variety of educational backgrounds can find a U.S. university that is appropriate to their needs.

To choose an appropriate institution, you can and should do an informal self-evaluation of your educational background. This self-analysis involves three important questions:

1. How Many Years of Study Have You Completed?

Completion of secondary school with at least twelve total years of education usually qualifies students to apply for undergraduate (bachelor's) degree programs. Completion of a university degree program that involves at least sixteen years of total education qualifies one to apply for admission to graduate (master's) degree programs in the United States.

2. Does the Education That You Have Completed in Your Country Provide Access to Further Study in the United States?

Consider the kind of institution where you completed your previous studies. If educational opportunities in your country are limited, it may be necessary to investigate many U.S. institutions and programs in order to find a match.

3. Are Your Previous Marks or Grades Excellent, Average, or Poor?

Your educational record influences your choice of U.S. institutions. If your grades are average or poor, it may be advisable to apply to several institutions with minimally difficult or non-competitive entrance levels.

YOU are one of the best sources of information about the level and quality of your previous studies. Awareness of your educational assets and liabilities will serve you well throughout the application process.

SECOND STEP—PLANNING AND ASSEMBLING THE APPLICATION

Planning and assembling a university application can be compared to the construction of a building. First, you must start with a solid foundation, which is the application form itself. The application, often available online as well as in paper form, usually contains a wealth of useful information, such as deadlines, fees, and degree programs available at that institution. To build a solid application, it is best to begin well in advance of the application deadline.

How to Obtain the Application Form

Application forms and links to institutional Web sites may also be available at a U.S. educational advising center associated with the American Embassy or Consulate in your country. These centers are excellent resources for international students and provide information about standardized test administration, scholarships, and other matters to students who are interested in studying in the United States. Your local U.S. Embassy or Consulate can guide you to the nearest educational advising center.

What Are the Key Components of a Complete Application?

Institutional requirements vary, but the standard components of a complete application include the following:

- Transcript
- Required standardized examination scores
- Evidence of financial support
- Letters of recommendation
- Application fee

Transcript

A complete academic record or transcript includes all courses completed, grades earned, and degrees awarded. Most universities require an official transcript to be sent directly from the school or university. In many other countries, however, the practice is to issue official transcripts and degree certificates directly to the student. If you have only one official copy of your transcript, it may be a challenge to get additional certified copies that are acceptable to U.S. universities. Some institutions will issue additional official copies for application purposes.

If your institution does not provide this service, you may have to seek an alternate source of certification. As a last resort, you may send a photocopy of your official transcript, explain that you have only one original, and ask the university for advice on how to deal with this situation.

Required Standardized Examination Scores

Arranging to take standardized examinations and earning the required scores seem to cause the most anxiety for international students.

The university application form usually indicates which examinations are required. The standardized examination required most often for undergraduate admission is the Test of English as a Foreign Language (TOEFL). Institutions may also require the SAT of undergraduate applicants. These standardized examinations are administered by the Educational Testing Service (ETS).

These examinations are offered in almost every country of the world. It is advisable to begin planning for standardized examinations at least six months prior to the application deadline of your desired institutions. Test centers fill up quickly, so it is important to register as soon as possible. Information about the examinations is available at U.S. educational advising centers associated with embassies or consulates.

Most universities require that the original test scores, not a student copy, be sent directly by the testing service. When you register for the test, be sure to indicate that the testing service should send the test scores directly to the universities.

You should begin your application process before you receive your test scores. Delaying submission of your application until the test scores arrive may cause you to miss deadlines and negatively affect the outcome of your application. If you want to know your scores in order to assess your chances of admission to an institution with rigorous admission standards, you should take the tests early.

Many universities in the United States set minimum required scores on the TOEFL or other standardized examinations. Test scores are an important factor, but most institutions also look at a number of other factors in their consideration of a candidate for admission.

For More Information

Questions about test formats, locations, dates, and registration may be addressed to:

ETS Corporate Headquarters
Rosedale Road
Princeton, New Jersey 08541
Web sites: http://www.ets.org
http://www.ets.org/toefl/
Phone: 609-921-9000
Fax: 609-734-5410

Evidence of Financial Support

Evidence of financial support is required to issue immigration documents to admitted students. This is part of a complete application package but usually plays no role in determining admission. Most institutions make admissions decisions without regard to the source and amount of financial support.

Letters of Recommendation

Most institutions require one or more letters of recommendation. The best letters are written by former professors, employers, or others who can comment on your academic achievements or professional potential.

Some universities provide a special form for the letters of recommendation. If possible, use the forms provided. If you are applying to a large number of universities, however, or if your recommenders are not available to complete several forms, it may be necessary for you to duplicate a general recommendation letter.

Application Fee

Most universities also require an application fee, ranging from $25 to $100, which must be paid to initiate consideration of the application.

Completing the Application Form

Whether sent by mail or electronically, the application form must be neat and thoroughly filled out. Although parts of the application may not seem to apply to you or your situation, do your best to answer all the questions.

Remember that this is a process. You provide information, and your proposed university then may request clarification and further information. If you have questions, it is better to initiate the entire process by submitting the application form rather than asking questions before you apply. The university will be better able to respond to you after it has your application. Always complete as much as you can. Do not permit uncertainty about the completion of the application form to cause unnecessary delays.

THIRD STEP—DISTINGUISH YOUR APPLICATION

To distinguish your application—to market yourself successfully—is ultimately the most important part of the application process. As you select your prospective universities, begin to analyze your strengths and weaknesses as a prospective student. As you complete your application, you should strive to create a positive impression and set yourself apart from other applicants, to highlight your assets and bring these qualities to the attention of the appropriate university administrators and professors. Applying early is a very easy way to distinguish your application.

Deadline or Guideline?

The application deadline is the last date that an application for a given semester will be accepted. Often, the application will specify that all required documents and information be submitted before the deadline date. To meet the deadlines, start the application process early. This also gives you more time to take—and perhaps retake and improve—the required standardized tests.

Admissions deliberations may take several weeks or months. In the meantime, most institutions accept additional information, including improved test scores, after the posted deadline.

Even if your application is initially rejected, you may be able to provide additional information to change the decision. You can request reconsideration based on additional information, such as improved test scores, strong letters of recommendation, or information about your class rank. Applying early allows more time to improve your application. Also, some students may decide not to accept their offers of admission, leaving room for offers to students on a waiting list. Reconsideration of the admission decisions can occur well beyond the application deadline.

Think of the deadline as a guideline rather than an impermeable barrier. Many factors—the strength of the application, your research interests, the number of spaces available at the proposed institution—can override the enforcement of an application deadline. So, if you lack a test score or transcript by the official deadline, you may still be able to apply and be accepted.

Statement of Purpose

The statement of purpose is your first and perhaps best opportunity to present yourself as an excellent candidate for admission. Whether or not a personal history essay or statement of purpose is required, always include a carefully written statement of purpose with your applications. A compelling statement of purpose does not have to be lengthy, but it should include some basic components:

- Part One—Introduce yourself and describe your educational background. This is your opportunity to describe any facet of your educational experience that you wish to emphasize. Perhaps you attended a highly ranked secondary school or university in your home country. Mention the name and any noteworthy characteristics of the secondary school or university from which you graduated. Explain the grading scale used at your university. Do not forget to mention your rank in your graduating class and any honors you may have received. This is not the time to be modest.

- Part Two—Describe your current academic and career interests and goals. Think about how these will fit into those of the institution to which you are applying, and mention the reasons why you have selected that institution.

- Part Three—Describe your long-term goals. When you finish your program of study, what do you plan to do next? If you already have a job offer or a career plan, describe it. Give some thought to how you'll demonstrate that studying in the United States. will ultimately benefit others.

Use Personal Contacts When Possible

Appropriate and judicious use of your own network of contacts can be very helpful. Friends, former professors, former students of your selected institutions, and others may be willing to advise you during the application process and provide you with introductions to key administrators or professors. If suggested, you may wish to contact certain professors or administrators by mail, phone, or e-mail. A personal visit to discuss your interest in the institution may be appropriate. Whatever your choice of communication, try to make the encounter pleasant and personal. Your goal is to make a positive impression, not to rush the admission decision.

There is no single right way to be admitted to U.S. universities. The same characteristics that make the educational choice in the United States so difficult—the number of institutions and the variety of programs of study—are the same attributes that allow so many international students to find the institution that's right for them.

_____

Kitty M. Villa is the former Assistant Director, International Office, at The University of Texas at Austin.

Community Colleges and the New Green Economy

Community colleges are a focal point for state and national efforts to create a green economy and workforce. As the United States transforms its economy into a "green" one, community colleges are leading the way—filling the need for both educated technicians whose skills can cross industry lines as well as those technicians who are able to learn new skills as technologies evolve.

Community colleges have been at the heart of the Obama administration's economic recovery strategy, with $12 billion allocated over this decade. President Obama has extolled community colleges as "the unsung heroes of America's education system," essential to our country's success in the "global competition to lead in the growth of industries of the twenty-first century." With the support of state governments, and, more importantly, local and international business partners, America's community colleges are rising to meet the demands of the new green economy. Community colleges are training individuals to work in fields such as renewable energy, energy efficiency, wind energy, green building, and sustainability. The programs are as diverse as the campuses housing them.

Here is a quick look at just some of the exciting "green" programs available at community colleges throughout the United States.

At Mesalands Community College in Tucumcari, New Mexico, the North American Wind Research and Training Center provides state-of-the-art facilities for research and training qualified technicians in wind energy technology to help meet the need for an estimated 170,000 new positions in the industry by 2030. The Center includes a facility for applied research in collaboration with Sandia National Laboratories—the first-ever such partnership between a national laboratory and a community college. It also provides associate degree training for wind energy technicians, meeting the fast-growing demand for "windsmiths" in the western part of the country—jobs that pay $45,000–$60,000 per year. For more information, visit http://www.mesalands.edu.

Cape Cod Community College (CCCC) in Massachusetts has become one of the nation's leading colleges in promoting and integrating sustainability and green practices throughout all campus operations and technical training programs. Ten years ago, Cape Wind Associates, Cape Cod's first wind farm, provided $50,000 to jumpstart CCCC's wind technician program—considered a state model for community-based clean energy workforce development and education. In addition, hundreds of CCCC students have earned associate degrees in environmental technology and environmental studies, as well as certificate programs in coastal zone management, environmental site assessment, solar thermal tech-

nology, and more. Visit http://www.capecod.edu/web/natsci/env/programs for more information.

At Oakland Community College in Michigan, more than 350 students are enrolled in the college's Renewable Energies and Sustainable Living program and its related courses. Students gain field experience refurbishing public buildings with renewable materials, performing energy audits for the government, and working with small businesses and hospitals to reduce waste and pollution. To learn more, visit http://www.oaklandcc.edu/est/.

In 2007, Columbia Gorge Community College in Oregon became the first community college in the Pacific Northwest to offer training programs for the windpower generation industry. The college offers a one-year certificate and a two-year Associate of Applied Science (A.A.S.) degree in renewable energy technology. The Renewable Energy Technology program was designed in collaboration with industry partners from the wind energy industry and the power generation industry. Students are prepared for employment in a broad range of industries, including hydro-generation, wind-generation, automated manufacturing, and engineering technology, and the College plans to add solar array technology to this list as well. For more information, visit http://www.cgcc.cc.or.us/Academics/WindTechnologyPage.cfm.

Central Carolina Community College (CCCC) in Pittsboro, North Carolina, has been leading the way in "green" programs for more than a decade. It offered a sustainable agriculture class at its Chatham campus in 1996 and soon became the first community college in the nation to offer an Associate in Applied Science degree in sustainable agriculture and the first in North Carolina to offer an associate degree in biofuels. In addition, it was the first North Carolina community college to offer a North American Board of Certified Energy Practitioners (NABCEP)–approved solar PV panel installation course as part of its green building/renewable energy program. In 2010, CCCC added an associate degree in sustainable technology and launched its new Natural Chef culinary arts program. The College also offers an ecotourism certificate as well as certificates in other green programs. For more information about Central Carolina Community College's green programs, visit http://www.cccc.edu/green.

The Green Jobs Academy at Bucks County Community College in Pennsylvania is an exciting new venture that includes a variety of academic and private industry partners that include Gamesa, Lockheed Martin, Dow, Veterans Green Jobs, and PECO, an Excelon Company. The Green Jobs Academy provides both long- and short-term training programs that are geared toward workers, who are looking for new skill sets in the green and sustainability industries. Courses include Hazardous Site Remediation & Preliminary Assessments, PV Solar Design, NABCEP (*North American Board of Certified Energy Practitioners*) PV Solar Entry Level Program (40 hours), Electric Vehicle Conversion Workshop, Wind Energy Apprentice, Certified Green Supply Chain Professional, Certified Indoor Air Quality Manager, a Veterans' Weatherization Training Program, and many others. For details, visit http://www.bucks.edu/academics/cwd/green/.

At Cascadia Community College in Bothell, Washington, thanks to a grant from Puget Sound Energy (PSE), students in the Energy Informatics class designed a kiosk screen that shows the energy usage and solar generation at the local 21 Acres Center for Local Food and Sustainable Living. The PSE grant supports the classroom materials for renewable energy education and the Web-based monitoring software that allows students and interested community members to track how much energy is being generated as the weather changes. For more information, visit http://www.cascadia.edu/Default.aspx.

At Grand Rapids Community College, the federally funded Pathways to Prosperity program has successfully prepared low-income residents for jobs in fields such as renewable energy. More than 200 people have completed the program, which began in 2010 thanks to a $4-million grant from the Department of Labor, and found jobs in industries ranging from energy-efficient building construction to alternative energy and sustainable manufacturing. For additional information, check out http://cms.grcc.edu/workforce-training/pathways-prosperity.

Linn-Benton Community College (LBCC) in Albany, Oregon, is now offering training for the Oregon Green Technology Certificate. Oregon Green Tech is a federally funded program that is designed to prepare entry-level workers with foundational skills for a variety of industries associated with or in support of green jobs. Students learn skills in green occupations that include green energy production; manufacturing, construction, installation, monitoring, and repair of equipment for solar, wind, wave, and bio-energy; building retro-fitting; process recycling; hazardous materials removal work; and more. LBCC is one of ten Oregon community colleges to provide training for the Green Technology Certificate, offered through the Oregon Consortium and Oregon Workforce Alliance. Visit http://www.linnbenton.edu for additional information.

The Santa Fe Community College Sustainable Technology Center in New Mexico offers several green jobs training programs along with various noncredit courses. It also provides credit programs from certificates in green building systems, environmental technology training, and solar energy training as well as an Associate in Applied Science (A.A.S.) degree in environmental technology. For more information, go online to http://www.sfcc.edu/sustainable_technologies_center.

In Colorado, Red Rocks Community College (RRCC) offers degree and certificate programs in renewable energy (solar photovoltaic, solar thermal, and wind energy technology),

energy and industrial maintenance, energy operations and process technology, environmental technology, water quality management, and energy audit. RRCC has made a commitment to the national challenge of creating and sustaining a green workforce and instructs students about the issues of energy, environmental stewardship, and renewable resources across the college curriculum. For more information, visit http://www.rrcc.edu/green/.

Next you'll find two essays about other green community college programs. The first essay was written by the president of Lane Community College in Eugene, Oregon, about the role Lane and other community colleges are playing in creating a workforce for the green economy. Then, read a first-hand account of the new Wind Turbine Training Program at Kalamazoo Valley Community College in Kalamazoo, Michigan—a program that has more applicants than spaces and one whose students are being hired BEFORE they even graduate. It's clear that there are exciting "green" programs at community colleges throughout the United States.

The Role of Community Colleges in Creating a Workforce for the Green Economy

by Mary F.T. Spilde, President
Lane Community College

Community colleges are expected to play a leadership role in educating and training the workforce for the green economy. Due to close connections with local and regional labor markets, colleges assure a steady supply of skilled workers by developing and adapting programs to respond to the needs of business and industry. Further, instead of waiting for employers to create job openings, many colleges are actively engaged in local economic development to help educate potential employers to grow their green business opportunities and to participate in the creation of the green economy.

As the green movement emerges there has been confusion about what constitutes a green job. It is now clear that many of the green jobs span several economic sectors such as renewable energy, construction, manufacturing, transportation and agriculture. It is predicted that there will be many middle skill jobs requiring more than a high school diploma but less than a bachelor's degree. This is precisely the unique role that community colleges play. Community colleges develop training programs, including pre-apprenticeship, that ladder the curriculum to take lower skilled workers through a relevant and sequenced course of study that provides a clear pathway to career track jobs. As noted in *Going Green: The Vital Role of Community Colleges in Building a Sustainable Future and Green Workforce* by the National Council for Workforce Education and the Academy for Educational Development, community colleges are strategically positioned to work with employers to redefine skills and competencies needed by the green workforce and to create the framework for new and expanded green career pathways.

While there will be new occupations such as solar and wind technologists, the majority of the jobs will be in the energy management sector—retrofitting the built environment. For example, President Obama called for retrofitting more than 75 percent of federal buildings and more than 2 million homes to make them more energy-efficient. The second major area for growth will be the "greening" of existing jobs as they evolve to incorporate green practices. Both will require new knowledge, skills and abilities. For community colleges, this means developing new programs that meet newly created industry standards and adapting existing programs and courses to integrate green skills. The key is to create a new talent pool of environmentally conscious, highly skilled workers.

These two areas show remarkable promise for education and training leading to high wage/high demand jobs:

- Efficiency and energy management: There is a need for auditors and energy efficiency experts to retrofit existing buildings. Consider how much built environment we have in this country, and it's not difficult to see that this is where the vast amount of jobs are now and will be in the future.

- Greening of existing jobs: There are few currently available jobs that environmental sustainability will not impact. Whether it is jobs in construction, such as plumbers, electricians, heating and cooling technicians, painters, and building supervisors, or chefs, farmers, custodians, architects, automotive technicians and interior designers, all will need to understand how to lessen their impact on the environment.

Lane Community College offers a variety of degree and certificate programs to prepare students to enter the energy efficiency fields. Lane has offered an Energy Management program since the late 1980s—before it was hip to be green! Students in this program learn to apply basic principles of physics and analysis techniques to the description and measurement of energy in today's building systems, with the goal of evaluating and recommending alternative energy solutions that will result in greater energy efficiency and energy cost savings. Students gain a working understanding of energy systems in today's built environment and the tools to analyze and quantify energy efficiency efforts. The program began with an emphasis in residential energy efficiency/solar energy systems and has evolved to include commercial energy efficiency and renewable energy system installation technology.

The Renewable Energy Technician program is offered as a second-year option within the Energy Management program. Course work prepares students for employment designing and installing solar electric and domestic hot water systems. Renewable Energy students, along with Energy Management students, take a first-year curriculum in commercial energy efficiency giving them a solid background that includes residential energy efficiency, HVAC systems, lighting, and physics and math. In the second year, Renewable Energy students diverge from the Energy Management curriculum and take course work that starts with two courses in electricity fundamentals and one course in energy economics. In the following terms, students learn to design, install, and develop a thorough

understanding of photovoltaics and domestic hot water systems.

Recent additions to Lane's offerings are Sustainability Coordinator and Water Conservation Technician degrees. Both programs were added to meet workforce demand.

Lane graduates find employment in a wide variety of disciplines and may work as facility managers, energy auditors, energy program coordinators, or control system specialists, for such diverse employers as engineering firms, public and private utilities, energy equipment companies, and departments of energy and as sustainability leaders within public and private sector organizations.

Lane Community College also provides continuing education for working professionals. The Sustainable Building Advisor (SBA) Certificate Program is a nine-month, specialized training program for working professionals. Graduate are able to advise employers or clients on strategies and tools for implementing sustainable building practices. Benefits from participating in the SBA program often include saving long-term building operating costs; improving the environmental, social, and economic viability of the region; and reducing environmental impacts and owner liability—not to mention the chance to improve one's job skills in a rapidly growing field.

The Building Operators Certificate is a professional development program created by The Northwest Energy Efficiency Council. It is offered through the Northwest Energy Education Institute at Lane. The certificate is designed for operations and maintenance staff working in public or private commercial buildings. It certifies individuals in energy and resource-efficient operation of building systems at two levels: Level I–Building System Maintenance and Level II–Equipment Troubleshooting and Maintenance.

Lane Community College constantly scans the environment to assess workforce needs and develop programs that provide highly skilled employees. Lane, like most colleges, publishes information in its catalog on workforce demand and wages so that students can make informed decisions about program choice.

Green jobs will be a large part of a healthy economy. Opportunities will abound for those who take advantage of programs with a proven record of connecting with employers and successfully educating students to meet high skills standards.

Establishing a World-Class Wind Turbine Technician Academy

by James DeHaven, Vice President of Economic & Business Development
Kalamazoo Valley Community College

When Kalamazoo Valley Community College (KVCC) decided it wanted to become involved in the training of utility-grade technicians for wind-energy jobs, early on the choice was made to avoid another "me too" training course.

Our program here in Southwest Michigan, 30 miles from Lake Michigan, had to meet industry needs and industry standards.

It was also obvious from the start that the utility-grade or large wind industry had not yet adopted any uniform training standards in the United States.

Of course, these would come, but why should the college wait when European standards were solidly established and working well in Germany, France, Denmark and Great Britain?

As a result, in 2009, KVCC launched its Wind Turbine Technician Academy, the first of its kind in the United States. The noncredit academy runs 8 hours a day, five days a week, for twenty-six weeks of intense training in electricity, mechanics, wind dynamics, safety, and climbing. The college developed this program rather quickly—in eight months—to fast-track individuals into this emerging field.

KVCC based its program on the training standards forged by the Bildungszentrum fur Erneuerebare Energien (BZEE)—the Renewable Energy Education Center. Located in Husum, Germany, the BZEE was created and supported by major wind-turbine manufacturers, component makers, and enterprises that provide operation and maintenance services.

As wind-energy production increased throughout Europe, the need for high-quality, industry-driven, international standards emerged. The BZEE has become the leading trainer for wind-turbine technicians across Europe and now in Asia.

With the exception of one college in Canada, the standards are not yet available in North America. When Kalamazoo Valley realized it could be the first college or university in the United States to offer this training program—that was enough motivation to move forward.

For the College to become certified by the BZEE, it needed to hire and send an electrical instructor and a mechanical instructor to Germany for six weeks of "train the trainer." The instructors not only had to excel in their respective fields, they also needed to be able to climb the skyscraper towers supporting megawatt-class turbines—a unique combination of skills to possess. Truly, individuals who fit this job description don't walk through the door everyday—but we found them! Amazingly, we found a top mechanical instructor who was a part-time fireman and comfortable with tall ladder rescues and a skilled electrical instructor who used to teach rappelling off the Rockies to the Marine Corps.

In addition to employing new instructors, the College needed a working utility-grade nacelle that could fit in its training lab that would be located in the KVCC Michigan Technical Education Center. So one of the instructors traveled to Denmark and purchased a 300-kilowatt turbine.

Once their own training was behind them and the turbine was on its way from the North Sea, the instructors quickly turned to crafting the curriculum necessary for our graduates to earn both an academy certificate from KVCC and a certification from the BZEE.

Promoting the innovative program to qualified potential students across the country was the next step. News releases were published throughout Michigan, and they were also picked up on the Internet. Rather quickly, KVCC found itself with more than 500 requests for applications for a program built for 16 students.

Acceptance into the academy includes a medical release, a climbing test, reading and math tests, relevant work experience, and, finally, an interview. Students in the academy's pioneer class, which graduated in spring 2010, ranged in age from their late teens to early 50s. They hailed from throughout Michigan, Indiana, Ohio, and Illinois as well as from Puerto Rico and Great Britain.

The students brought with them degrees in marketing, law, business, science, and architecture, as well as entrepreneurial experiences in several businesses, knowledge of other languages, military service, extensive travel, and electrical, computer, artistic, and technical/mechanical skills.

Kalamazoo Valley's academy has provided some high-value work experiences for the students in the form of two collaborations with industry that has allowed them to maintain and/or repair actual utility-grade turbines, including those at the 2.5 megawatt size. This hands-on experience will add to the attractiveness of the graduates in the market place. Potential employers were recently invited to an open house where they could see the lab and meet members of this pioneer class.

The College's Turbine Technician Academy has also attracted a federal grant for $550,000 to expand its program through additional equipment purchases. The plan is to erect our own climbing tower. Climbing is a vital part of any valid program, and yet wind farms cannot afford to shut turbines down just for climb-training.

When the students are asked what best distinguishes the Kalamazoo Valley program, their answers point to the experienced instructors and the working lab, which is constantly changing to offer the best training experiences.

Industry continues to tell us that community colleges need to offer fast-track training programs of this caliber if the nation is to reach the U.S. Department of Energy's goal of 20 percent renewable energy by 2030. This would require more than 1,500 new technicians each year.

With that in mind, KVCC plans to host several BZEE orientation programs for other community colleges in order to encourage them to consider adopting the European training standards and start their own programs.

Meanwhile, applications are continuing to stream in from across the country for the next Wind Turbine Technician Academy program at Kalamazoo Valley Community College. For more information about the program, visit http://groves-center.kvcc.edu/career/wtta/.

How to Use This Guide

eterson's Two-Year Colleges 2014 contains a wealth of information for anyone interested in colleges offering associate degrees. This section details the criteria that institutions must meet to be included in this guide and provides information about research procedures used by Peterson's.

QUICK-REFERENCE CHART

The **Two-Year Colleges At-a-Glance Chart** is a geographically arranged table that lists colleges by name and city within the state, or country in which they are located. Areas listed include the United States, Canada, and other countries; the institutions are included because they are accredited by recognized U.S. accrediting bodies (see **Criteria for Inclusion** section).

The At-a-Glance chart contains basic information that enables you to compare institutions quickly according to broad characteristics such as degrees awarded, enrollment, application requirements, financial aid availability, and numbers of sports and majors offered. A dagger (†) after the institution's name indicates that an institution has an entry in the **College Close-Ups** section.

Column 1: Degrees Awarded

C= *college transfer associate degree:* the degree awarded after a "university-parallel" program, equivalent to the first two years of a bachelor's degree.

T= *terminal associate degree:* the degree resulting from a one- to three-year program providing training for a specific occupation.

B= *bachelor's degree (baccalaureate):* the degree resulting from a liberal arts, science, professional, or preprofessional program normally lasting four years, although in some cases an accelerated program can be completed in three years.

M= *master's degree:* the first graduate (postbaccalaureate) degree in the liberal arts and sciences and certain professional fields, usually requiring one to two years of full-time study.

D= *doctoral degree* (research/scholarship, professional practice, or other)

Column 2: Institutional Control

Private institutions are designated as one of the following:

Ind = *independent* (nonprofit)

I-R = *independent-religious:* nonprofit; sponsored by or affiliated with a particular religious group or having a nondenominational or interdenominational religious orientation.

Prop = *proprietary* (profit-making)

Public institutions are designated by the source of funding, as follows:

Fed = *federal*

St = *state*

Comm = *commonwealth* (Puerto Rico)

Terr = *territory* (U.S. territories)

Cou = *county*

Dist = *district:* an administrative unit of public education, often having boundaries different from units of local government.

City = *city*

St-L = *state and local:* local may refer to county, district, or city.

St-R = *state-related:* funded primarily by the state but administratively autonomous.

Column 3: Student Body

M= *men only* (100% of student body)

PM = *coed, primarily men*

W= *women only* (100% of student body)

PW = *coed, primarily women*

M/W = *coeducational*

Column 4: Undergraduate Enrollment

The figure shown represents the number of full-time and part-time students enrolled in undergraduate degree programs as of fall 2012.

Columns 5–7: Enrollment Percentages

Figures are shown for the percentages of the fall 2012 undergraduate enrollment made up of students attending part-time (column 5) and students 25 years of age or older (column 6). Also listed is the percentage of students in the last graduating class who completed a college-transfer associate program and went directly on to four-year colleges (column 7).

For columns 8 through 15, the following letter codes are used: Y = yes; N = no; R = recommended; S = for some.

Columns 8–10: Admission Policies

The information in these columns shows whether the college has an open admission policy (column 8) whereby virtually all applicants are accepted without regard to standardized test scores, grade average, or class rank; whether a high school equivalency certificate is accepted in place of a high school diploma for admission consideration (column 9); and whether a high school transcript (column 10) is required as part of the application process. In column 10, the combination of the codes R and S indicates that a high school transcript is recommended for all applicants (R) or required for some (S).

Columns 11–12: Financial Aid

These columns show which colleges offer the following types of financial aid: need-based aid (column 11) and part-time jobs (column 12), including those offered through the federal government's Federal Work-Study program.

Columns 13–15: Services and Facilities

These columns show which colleges offer the following: career counseling (column 13) on either an individual or group basis, job placement services (column 14) for individual students, and college-owned or -operated housing facilities (column 16) for noncommuting students.

Column 16: Sports

This figure indicates the number of sports that a college offers at the intramural and/or intercollegiate levels.

Column 17: Majors

This figure indicates the number of major fields of study in which a college offers degree programs.

PROFILES OF TWO-YEAR COLLEGES AND SPECIAL MESSAGES

The **Profiles of Two-Year Colleges** contain basic data in capsule form for quick review and comparison. The following outline of the **Profile** format shows the section headings and the items that each section covers. Any item that does not apply to a particular college or for which no information was supplied is omitted from that college's **Profile.** Display ads, which appear near some of the institution's profiles, have been provided and paid for by those colleges that chose to supplement their profile with additional information.

Bulleted Highlights

The bulleted highlights section features important information, for quick reference and comparison. The number of possible bulleted highlights that an ideal **Profile** would have if all questions were answered in a timely manner follow. However, not every institution provides all of the information necessary to fill out every bulleted line. In such instances, the line will not appear.

First Bullet

Institutional control: Private institutions are designated as independent (nonprofit), proprietary (profit-making), or independent, with a specific religious denomination or affiliation. Nondenominational or interdenominational religious orientation is possible and would be indicated.

Public institutions are designated by the source of funding. Designations include federal, state, province, commonwealth (Puerto Rico), territory (U.S. territories), county, district (an administrative unit of public education, often having boundaries different from units of local government), city, state and local (local may refer to county, district, or city), or state-related (funded primarily by the state but administratively autonomous).

Religious affiliation is also noted here.

Institutional type: Each institution is classified as one of the following:

> *Primarily two-year college:* Awards baccalaureate degrees, but the vast majority of students are enrolled in two-year programs.
>
> *Four-year college:* Awards baccalaureate degrees; may also award associate degrees; does not award graduate (postbaccalaureate) degrees.
>
> *Upper-level institution:* Awards baccalaureate degrees, but entering students must have at least two years of previous college-level credit; may also offer graduate degrees.
>
> *Comprehensive institution:* Awards baccalaureate degrees; may also award associate degrees; offers graduate degree programs, primarily at the master's, specialist's, or professional level, although one or two doctoral programs may be offered.
>
> *University:* Offers four years of undergraduate work plus graduate degrees through the doctorate in more than two academic or professional fields.

Founding date: If the year an institution was chartered differs from the year when instruction actually began, the earlier date is given.

System or administrative affiliation: Any coordinate institutions or system affiliations are indicated. An institution that has separate colleges or campuses for men and women but shares facilities and courses is termed a coordinate institution. A formal administrative grouping of institutions, either private or public, of which the college is a part, or the name of a single institution with which the college is administratively affiliated, is a system.

Second Bullet

Setting: Schools are designated as urban (located within a major city), suburban (a residential area within commuting distance of a major city), small-town (a small but compactly settled area not within commuting distance of a major city), or rural (a remote and sparsely populated area). The phrase *easy access to...* indicates that the campus is within an hour's drive of the nearest major metropolitan area that has a population greater than 500,000.

Third Bullet

Endowment: The total dollar value of funds and/or property donated to the institution or the multicampus educational system of which the institution is a part.

Fourth Bullet

Student body: An institution is coed (coeducational—admits men and women), primarily (80 percent or more) women, primarily men, women only, or men only.

Undergraduate students: Represents the number of full-time and part-time students enrolled in undergraduate degree programs as of fall 2012. The percentage of full-time undergraduates and the percentages of men and women are given.

Category Overviews

Undergraduates

For fall 2012, the number of full- and part-time undergraduate students is listed. This list provides the number of states and U.S. territories, including the District of Columbia and Puerto Rico (or for Canadian institutions, provinces and territories), and other countries from which undergraduates come. Percentages of undergraduates who are part-time or full-time students; transfers in; live on campus; out-of-state; Black or African American, non-Hispanic/Latino; Hispanic/Latino; Asian, non-Hispanic/Latino; Native Hawaiian or other Pacific Islander, non-Hispanic/Latino; American Indian or Alaska Native, non-Hispanic/Latino are given.

Retention: The percentage of freshmen (or, for upper-level institutions, entering students) who returned the following year for the fall term.

Freshmen

Admission: Figures are given for the number of students who applied for fall 2012 admission, the number of those who were admitted, and the number who enrolled. Freshman statistics include the average high school GPA; the percentage of freshmen who took the SAT and received critical reading, writing, and math scores above 500, above 600, and above 700; as well as the percentage of freshmen taking the ACT who received a composite score of 18 or higher.

Faculty

Total: The total number of faculty members; the percentage of full-time faculty members as of fall 2012; and the percentage of full-time faculty members who hold doctoral/first professional/ terminal degrees.

Student-faculty ratio: The school's estimate of the ratio of matriculated undergraduate students to faculty members teaching undergraduate courses.

Majors

This section lists the major fields of study offered by the college.

Academics

Calendar: Most colleges indicate one of the following: 4-1-4, 4-4-1, or a similar arrangement (two terms of equal length plus an abbreviated winter or spring term, with the numbers referring to months); semesters; trimesters; quarters; 3-3 (three courses for each of three terms); modular (the academic year is divided into small blocks of time; courses of varying lengths are assembled according to individual programs); or standard year (for most Canadian institutions).

Degrees: This names the full range of levels of certificates, diplomas, and degrees, including prebaccalaureate, graduate, and professional, that are offered by this institution:

Associate degree: Normally requires at least two but fewer than four years of full-time college work or its equivalent.

Bachelor's degree (baccalaureate): Requires at least four years but not more than five years of full-time college-level work or its equivalent. This includes all bachelor's degrees in which the normal four years of work are completed in three years and bachelor's degrees conferred in a five-year cooperative (work-study plan) program. A cooperative plan provides for alternate class attendance and employment in business, industry, or government. This allows students to combine actual work experience with their college studies.

Master's degree: Requires the successful completion of a program of study of at least the full-time equivalent of one but not more than two years of work beyond the bachelor's degree.

Doctoral degree (doctorate; research/scholarship, professional, or other): The highest degree in graduate study. The doctoral degree classification includes Doctor of Education, Doctor of Juridical Science, Doctor of Public Health, Doctor of Philosophy, Doctor of Podiatry, Doctor of Veterinary Medicine, and many more.

Post-master's certificate: Requires completion of an organized program of study of 24 credit hours beyond the master's degree but does not meet the requirements of academic degrees at the doctoral level.

Special study options: Details are next given here on study options available at each college:

Accelerated degree program: Students may earn a bachelor's degree in three academic years.

Academic remediation for entering students: Instructional courses designed for students deficient in the general competencies necessary for a regular postsecondary curriculum and educational setting.

Adult/continuing education programs: Courses offered for nontraditional students who are currently working or are returning to formal education.

Advanced placement: Credit toward a degree awarded for acceptable scores on College Board Advanced Placement (AP) tests.

Cooperative (co-op) education programs: Formal arrangements with off-campus employers allowing students to combine work and study in order to gain degree-related experience, usually extending the time required to complete a degree.

Distance learning: For-credit courses that can be accessed off-campus via cable television, the Internet, satellite, DVD, correspondence course, or other media.

Double major: A program of study in which a student concurrently completes the requirements of two majors.

English as a second language (ESL): A course of study designed specifically for students whose native language is not English.

External degree programs: A program of study in which students earn credits toward a degree through a combination of independent study, college courses, proficiency examinations, and personal experience. External degree programs require minimal or no classroom attendance.

Freshmen honors college: A separate academic program for talented freshmen.

Honors programs: Any special program for very able students offering the opportunity for educational enrichment, independent study, acceleration, or some combination of these.

Independent study: Academic work, usually undertaken outside the regular classroom structure, chosen or designed by the student with departmental approval and instructor supervision.

Internships: Any short-term, supervised work experience usually related to a student's major field, for which the student earns academic credit. The work can be full- or part-time, on or off-campus, paid or unpaid.

Off-campus study: A formal arrangement with one or more domestic institutions under which students may take courses at the other institution(s) for credit.

Part-time degree program: Students may earn a degree through part-time enrollment in regular session (daytime) classes or evening, weekend, or summer classes.

Self-designed major: Program of study based on individual interests, designed by the student with the assistance of an adviser.

Services for LD students: Special help for learning-disabled students with resolvable difficulties, such as dyslexia.

Study abroad: An arrangement by which a student completes part of the academic program studying in another country. A college may operate a campus abroad or it may have a cooperative agreement with other U.S. institutions or institutions in other countries.

Summer session for credit: Summer courses through which students may make up degree work or accelerate their program.

Tutorials: Undergraduates can arrange for special in-depth academic assignments (not for remediation)

working with faculty members one-on-one or in small groups.

ROTC: Army, Naval, or Air Force Reserve Officers' Training Corps programs offered either on campus, at a branch campus [designated by a (b)], or at a cooperating host institution [designated by (c)].

Unusual degree programs: Nontraditional programs such as a 3-2 degree program, in which three years of liberal arts study is followed by two years of study in a professional field at another institution (or in a professional division of the same institution), resulting in two bachelor's degrees or a bachelor's and a master's degree.

Student Life

Housing options: The institution's policy about whether students are permitted to live off-campus or are required to live on campus for a specified period; whether freshmen-only, coed, single-sex, cooperative, and disabled student housing options are available; whether campus housing is leased by the school and/or provided by a third party; whether freshman applicants are given priority for college housing. The phrase *college housing not available* indicates that no college-owned or -operated housing facilities are provided for undergraduates and that noncommuting students must arrange for their own accommodations.

Activities and organizations: Lists information on drama-theater groups, choral groups, marching bands, student-run campus newspapers, student-run radio stations, and social organizations (sororities, fraternities, eating clubs, etc.) and how many are represented on campus.

Campus security: Campus safety measures including 24-hour emergency response devices (telephones and alarms) and patrols by trained security personnel, student patrols, late-night transport-escort service, and controlled dormitory access (key, security card, etc.).

Student services: Information provided indicates services offered to students by the college, such as legal services, health clinics, personal-psychological counseling, and women's centers.

Athletics

Membership in one or more of the following athletic associations is indicated by initials.

NCAA: National Collegiate Athletic Association

NAIA: National Association of Intercollegiate Athletics

NCCAA: National Christian College Athletic Association

NJCAA: National Junior College Athletic Association

USCAA: United States Collegiate Athletic Association

CIS: Canadian Interuniversity Sports

The overall NCAA division in which all or most intercollegiate teams compete is designated by a roman numeral I, II, or

III. All teams that do not compete in this division are listed as exceptions.

Sports offered by the college are divided into two groups: intercollegiate (**M** or **W** following the name of each sport indicates that it is offered for men or women) and intramural. An **s** in parentheses following an **M** or **W** for an intercollegiate sport indicates that athletic scholarships (or grants-in-aid) are offered for men or women in that sport, and a c indicates a club team as opposed to a varsity team.

Standardized Tests

The most commonly required standardized tests are the ACT, SAT, and SAT Subject Tests. These and other standardized tests may be used for selective admission, as a basis for counseling or course placement, or for both purposes. This section notes if a test is used for admission or placement and whether it is required, required for some, or recommended.

In addition to the ACT and SAT, the following standardized entrance and placement examinations are referred to by their initials:

ABLE: Adult Basic Learning Examination

ACT ASSET: ACT Assessment of Skills for Successful Entry and Transfer

ACT PEP: ACT Proficiency Examination Program

CAT: California Achievement Tests

CELT: Comprehensive English Language Test

CPAt: Career Programs Assessment

CPT: Computerized Placement Test

DAT: Differential Aptitude Test

LSAT: Law School Admission Test

MAPS: Multiple Assessment Program Service

MCAT: Medical College Admission Test

MMPI: Minnesota Multiphasic Personality Inventory

OAT: Optometry Admission Test

PAA: Prueba de Aptitud Académica (Spanish-language version of the SAT)

PCAT: Pharmacy College Admission Test

PSAT/NMSQT: Preliminary SAT National Merit Scholarship Qualifying Test

SCAT: Scholastic College Aptitude Test

SRA: Scientific Research Association (administers verbal, arithmetical, and achievement tests)

TABE: Test of Adult Basic Education

TASP: Texas Academic Skills Program

TOEFL: Test of English as a Foreign Language (for international students whose native language is not English)

WPCT: Washington Pre-College Test

Costs

Costs are given for the 2013–14 academic year or for the 2012–13 academic year if 2013–14 figures were not yet available. Annual expenses may be expressed as a comprehensive fee (including full-time tuition, mandatory fees, and college room and board) or as separate figures for full-time tuition, fees, room and board, or room only. For public institutions where tuition differs according to residence, separate figures are given for area or state residents and for nonresidents. Part-time tuition is expressed in terms of a per-unit rate (per credit, per semester hour, etc.) as specified by the institution.

The tuition structure at some institutions is complex in that freshmen and sophomores may be charged a different rate from that for juniors and seniors, a professional or vocational division may have a different fee structure from the liberal arts division of the same institution, or part-time tuition may be prorated on a sliding scale according to the number of credit hours taken. Tuition and fees may vary according to academic program, campus/location, class time (day, evening, weekend), course/credit load, course level, degree level, reciprocity agreements, and student level. Room and board charges are reported as an average for one academic year and may vary according to the board plan selected, campus/location, type of housing facility, or student level. If no college-owned or -operated housing facilities are offered, the phrase *college housing not available* will appear in the Housing section of the Student Life paragraph.

Tuition payment plans that may be offered to undergraduates include tuition prepayment, installment payments, and deferred payment. A tuition prepayment plan gives a student the option of locking in the current tuition rate for the entire term of enrollment by paying the full amount in advance rather than year by year. Colleges that offer such a prepayment plan may also help the student to arrange financing.

The availability of full or partial undergraduate tuition waivers to minority students, children of alumni, employees or their children, adult students, and senior citizens may be listed.

Financial Aid

The number of Federal Work Study and/or part-time jobs and average earnings are listed. Financial aid deadlines are given as well.

Applying

Application and admission options include the following:

Early admission: Highly qualified students may matriculate before graduating from high school.

Early action plan: An admission plan that allows students to apply and be notified of an admission decision well in advance of the regular notification dates. If accepted, the candidate is not committed to enroll; students may reply to the offer under the college's regular reply policy.

Early decision plan: A plan that permits students to apply and be notified of an admission decision (and financial aid offer, if applicable) well in advance of the regular notification date. Applicants agree to accept an offer of admission and to withdraw their applications from other colleges. Candidates who are not accepted under early decision are automatically considered with the regular applicant pool, without prejudice.

Deferred entrance: The practice of permitting accepted students to postpone enrollment, usually for a period of one academic term or year.

Application fee: The fee required with an application is noted. This is typically nonrefundable, although under certain specified conditions it may be waived or returned.

Requirements: Other application requirements are grouped into three categories: required for all, required for some, and recommended. They may include an essay, standardized test scores, a high school transcript, a minimum high school grade point average (expressed as a number on a scale of 0 to 4.0, where 4.0 equals A, 3.0 equals B, etc.), letters of recommendation, an interview on campus or with local alumni, and, for certain types of schools or programs, special requirements such as a musical audition or an art portfolio.

Application deadlines and notification dates: Admission application deadlines and dates for notification of acceptance or rejection are given either as specific dates or as **rolling** and **continuous.** Rolling means that applications are processed as they are received, and qualified students are accepted as long as there are openings. Continuous means that applicants are notified of acceptance or rejection as applications are processed up until the date indicated or the actual beginning of classes. The application deadline and the notification date for transfers are given if they differ from the dates for freshmen. Early decision and early action application deadlines and notification dates are also indicated when relevant.

Admissions Contact

The name, title, and phone number of the person to contact for application information are given at the end of the Profile. The admission office address is listed in most cases. Toll-free phone numbers may also be included. The admission office fax number and e-mail address, if available, are listed, provided the school wanted them printed for use by prospective students. Finally, the URL of the institution's Web site is provided.

Additional Information

Each college that has a **College Close-Up** in the guide will have a cross-reference appended to the Profile, referring you directly to that **College Close-Up.**

COLLEGE CLOSE-UPS

These narrative descriptions provide an inside look at certain colleges, shifting the focus to a variety of other factors that should also be considered. The descriptions provide a wealth of statistics that are crucial components in the college decision-making equation—components such as tuition, financial aid, and major fields of study. Prepared exclusively by college officials, the descriptions are designed to help give students a better sense of the individuality of each institution, in terms that include campus environment, student activities, and lifestyle. Such quality-of-life intangibles can be the deciding factors in the college selection process. The absence of any college or university does not constitute an editorial decision on the part of Peterson's. In essence, these descriptions are an open forum for colleges, on a voluntary basis, to communicate their particular message to prospective college students. The colleges included have paid a fee to Peterson's to provide this information. The **College Close-Ups** are edited to provide a consistent format across entries for your ease of comparison.

INDEXES

2012–13 Changes in Institutions

Here you will find an alphabetical listing of institutions that have recently closed, merged with other institutions, or changed their name or status.

Associate Degree Programs at Two-and Four-Year Colleges

These indexes present hundreds of undergraduate fields of study that are currently offered most widely according to the colleges' responses on *Peterson's Annual Survey of Undergraduate Institutions*. The majors appear in alphabetical order, each followed by an alphabetical list of the schools that offer an associate-level program in that field. Liberal Arts and Studies indicates a general program with no specified major. The terms used for the majors are those of the U.S. Department of Education Classification of Instructional Programs (CIPs). Many institutions, however, use different terms. Readers should refer to the **College Close-Up** in this book for the school's exact terminology. In addition, although the term "major" is used in this guide, some colleges may use other terms, such as "concentration," "program of study," or "field."

DATA COLLECTION PROCEDURES

The data contained in the **Profiles** of Two-Year Colleges and **Indexes** were researched in winter and spring 2013 through *Peterson's Annual Survey of Undergraduate Institutions*. Questionnaires were sent to the more than 1,800 colleges that meet the outlined inclusion criteria. All data included in this edition have been submitted by officials (usually admission and financial aid officers, registrars, or institutional research personnel) at the colleges themselves. All usable information received in time for publication has been included. The omission of any particular item from the **Profiles** of Two-Year Colleges and **Indexes** listing signifies either that the item is not applicable to that institution or that data were not available. Because of the comprehensive editorial review that takes place in our offices and because all material comes directly from college officials, Peterson's has every reason to believe that the information presented in this guide is accurate at the time of printing. However, students should check with a specific college or university at the time of application to verify such figures as tuition and fees, which may have changed since the publication of this volume.

CRITERIA FOR INCLUSION IN THIS BOOK

Peterson's Two-Year Colleges 2014 covers accredited institutions in the United States, U.S. territories, and other countries that award the associate degree as their most popular undergraduate offering (a few also offer bachelor's, master's, or doctoral degrees). The term two-year college is the commonly used designation for institutions that grant the associate degree, since two years is the normal duration of the traditional associate degree program. However, some programs may be completed in one year, others require three years, and, of course, part-time programs may take a considerably longer period. Therefore, "two-year college" should be understood as a conventional term that accurately describes most of the institutions included in this guide but which should not be taken literally in all cases. Also included are some non-degree-granting institutions, usually branch campuses of a multicampus system, which offer the equivalent of the first two years of a bachelor's degree, transferable to a bachelor's degree–granting institution.

To be included in this guide, an institution must have full accreditation or be a candidate for accreditation (preaccreditation) status by an institutional or specialized accrediting body recognized by the U.S. Department of Education or the Council for Higher Education Accreditation (CHEA). Institutional accrediting bodies, which review each institution as a whole, include the six regional associations of schools and colleges (Middle States, New England, North Central, Northwest, Southern, and Western), each of which is responsible for a specified portion of the United States and its territories. Other institutional accrediting bodies are national in scope and accredit specific kinds of institutions (e.g., Bible colleges, independent colleges, and rabbinical and Talmudic schools). Program registration by the New York State Board of Regents is considered to be the equivalent of institutional accreditation, since the board requires that all programs offered by an institution meet its standards before recognition is granted. This guide also includes institutions outside the United States that are accredited by these U.S. accrediting bodies. There are recognized specialized or professional accrediting bodies in more than forty different fields, each of which is authorized to accredit institutions or specific programs in its particular field. For specialized institutions that offer programs in one field only, we designate this to be the equivalent of institutional accreditation. A full explanation of the accrediting process and complete information on recognized, institutional (regional and national), and specialized accrediting bodies can be found online at www.chea.org or at www.ed.gov/admins/finaid/accred/index.html.

Quick-Reference Chart

Two-Year Colleges At-a-Glance

This chart includes the names and locations of accredited two-year colleges in the United States, Canada, and other countries and shows institutions' responses to the *Peterson's Annual Survey of Undergraduate Institutions*. If an institution submitted incomplete data, one or more columns opposite the institution's name is blank. A dagger after the school name indicates that the institution has one or more entries in the *College Close-Ups* section. If a school does not appear, it did not report any of the information.

Key: Y—Yes; N—No; R—Recommended; S—For Some

Column headings: Degrees Awarded — College Transfer Associate (C), Terminal Associate (T), Bachelor's (B), Master's (M), Doctoral (D)

Name	Location	Degrees Awarded	Inst. Control	Student Body	Undergrad Enroll.	% Part-Time	% 25+	% Grads to 4-Yr	HS Equiv. Accepted	Open Admissions	HS Transcript Req.	Need-Based Aid	Part-Time Jobs	Career Counseling	Job Placement	College Housing	# Sports	# Majors
UNITED STATES																		
Alabama																		
Bevill State Community College	Jasper	C,T	St	M/W	4,069	45	36		Y	Y		Y		Y	Y	Y		13
Chattahoochee Valley Community College	Phenix City	C,T	St	M/W	1,697	44												
Community College of the Air Force	Maxwell Gunter Air Force Base	T	Fed	PM	314,962		64		Y		Y	Y		Y	Y		15	49
Gadsden State Community College	Gadsden	C,T	St	M/W	5,882	46	37	19	Y	Y		Y		Y	Y	Y	5	23
H. Councill Trenholm State Technical College	Montgomery	T	St	M/W	1,721													
ITT Technical Institute	Bessemer	T,B	Prop	M/W														
ITT Technical Institute	Madison	T,B	Prop	M/W														
ITT Technical Institute	Mobile	T,B	Prop	M/W														
Jefferson State Community College	Birmingham	C,T	St	M/W	8,878	66	37		Y	Y	S			Y	Y	N		19
J. F. Drake State Technical College	Huntsville	C,T	St	M/W	1,258	40	57		Y	Y	Y			Y	Y	N		21
Lawson State Community College	Birmingham	C,T	St	M/W	3,419	43	35	2	Y	Y	Y			Y	Y	Y	4	14
Lurleen B. Wallace Community College	Andalusia	C,T	St	M/W	1,646	39	28		Y	Y	Y			Y		N	3	13
Northeast Alabama Community College	Rainsville	C,T	St	M/W	3,294	45												
Northwest-Shoals Community College	Muscle Shoals	C	St	M/W	3,717	48	28	12	Y		Y			Y	Y	N	4	15
Reid State Technical College	Evergreen	T	St	M/W	495	37	13		Y		Y	Y		Y	Y	N		3
Shelton State Community College	Tuscaloosa	C,T	St	M/W	5,104	47	24		Y		Y	Y		Y	Y	N	5	18
Alaska																		
University of Alaska Anchorage, Kenai Peninsula College	Soldotna	C,T,B	St	M/W	2,733				Y	Y	Y				Y			9
University of Alaska Anchorage, Kodiak College	Kodiak	C,T	St	M/W	479													
Arizona																		
Arizona Western College	Yuma	C,T	St-L	M/W	7,854	65	27		Y			Y		Y	Y	Y	7	55
Carrington College–Mesa	Mesa	T	Prop	M/W	685		46		N		Y					N		5
Carrington College–Phoenix	Phoenix	T	Prop	M/W	560		30			Y	Y				Y	N		6
Carrington College–Phoenix Westside	Phoenix	T	Prop	M/W	542		64		Y	Y	Y					N		6
Carrington College–Tucson	Tucson	T	Prop	M/W	399		43		N	Y	Y					N		2
Chandler-Gilbert Community College	Chandler	C,T	St-L	M/W	14,030	68												
Cochise College	Sierra Vista	C,T	St-L	M/W	4,516	67	46	61	Y		R			Y		Y	3	53
CollegeAmerica–Flagstaff	Flagstaff	T,B	Priv	M/W	200		0		Y	Y								3
Eastern Arizona College	Thatcher	C,T	St-L	M/W	6,997	69												
GateWay Community College	Phoenix	C,T	St-L	M/W	716	73												
Glendale Community College	Glendale	C,T	St-L	M/W	20,154	65			Y		S			Y	Y	N	11	32
ITT Technical Institute	Phoenix	T,B	Prop	M/W														
ITT Technical Institute	Phoenix	T,B	Prop	M/W														
ITT Technical Institute	Tucson	T,B	Prop	M/W														
Mesa Community College	Mesa	C,T	St-L	M/W	23,000				Y					Y	Y	N	11	36
Mohave Community College	Kingman	C,T	St	M/W	5,220	73	51		Y							N		34
Phoenix College	Phoenix	C,T	Cou	M/W	12,565				Y					Y	Y	N	10	56
Pima Community College	Tucson	C,T	St-L	M/W	36,969	63			Y							N		
Scottsdale Community College	Scottsdale	C,T	St-L	M/W	10,895	68	30		Y							N	13	25
Arkansas																		
Arkansas State University–Mountain Home	Mountain Home	T	St	M/W					Y	Y	Y			Y	Y	N		14
College of the Ouachitas	Malvern	C,T	St	M/W	1,407	58												
Cossatot Community College of the University of Arkansas	De Queen	C,T	St	M/W	1,542		33		Y	Y	R			Y	Y	N		11
ITT Technical Institute	Little Rock	T,B	Prop	M/W														
NorthWest Arkansas Community College	Bentonville	C,T	St-L	M/W	8,341	63	47		Y	Y	Y			Y	Y	N	6	24
Ozarka College	Melbourne	C,T	St	M/W	1,600		43		Y	Y	Y			Y	Y	N		8
Southeast Arkansas College	Pine Bluff	C,T	St	M/W	2,190	47												
University of Arkansas Community College at Morrilton	Morrilton	C,T	St	M/W	2,139	41	36		Y	Y	Y			Y	Y	N	5	16
California																		
Bakersfield College	Bakersfield	C,T	St-L	M/W	15,001		50		Y					Y	Y	N	11	76
Berkeley City College	Berkeley	C,T	St-L	M/W	7,645	65		0						Y	Y	N		32
Butte College	Oroville	C,T	Dist	M/W	12,719	36			Y		S			Y	Y	N	9	55
Carrington College California–Pleasant Hill	Pleasant Hill	T	Prop	M/W	346		45			Y	Y					N		16
Carrington College California–San Jose	San Jose	T	Prop	M/W	646		44			Y	Y					N		19
Carrington College California–San Leandro	San Leandro	T	Prop	M/W	471		35			Y	Y					N		10
Carrington College of California–Antioch	Antioch	T	Prop	M/W	318		37			Y	Y					N		9
Carrington College of California–Citrus Heights	Citrus Heights	T	Prop	M/W	412		43			Y	Y					N		10
Carrington College of California–Sacramento	Sacramento	T	Prop	M/W	1,392		55				Y							11
College of Marin	Kentfield	C,T	St-L	M/W	7,000				Y					Y	Y	N	8	55
College of the Canyons	Santa Clarita	C,T	St-L	M/W	16,844	69			Y		R			Y	Y	N	11	52
College of the Desert	Palm Desert	C,T	St-L	M/W	10,099		37		Y	Y				Y	Y	N	11	61
De Anza College	Cupertino	C,T	St-L	M/W			52							Y	Y	N	13	63
Deep Springs College	Deep Springs	C	Ind	CM	26		0	75			Y				Y	Y	13	1
FIDM/The Fashion Institute of Design & Merchandising, Los Angeles Campus†	Los Angeles	C,T,B	Prop	M/W	3,743	12			N	Y	Y			Y	Y	Y		10

35

This chart includes the names and locations of accredited two-year colleges in the United States, Canada, and other countries and shows institutions' responses to the *Peterson's Annual Survey of Undergraduate Institutions*. If an institution submitted incomplete data, one or more columns opposite the institution's name is blank. A dagger after the school name indicates that the institution has one or more entries in the *College Close-Ups* section. If a school does not appear, it did not report any of the information.

Key: Y—Yes; N—No; R—Recommended; S—For Some

Degrees Awarded: College Transfer Associate (C); Terminal Associate (T); Bachelor's (B); Master's (M), Doctoral (D)

Institution	Location	Degrees Awarded	Institutional Control	Student Body	Undergraduate Enrollment	Percent Attending Part-Time	Percent of Grads Going on to Four-Year Colleges	Percent 25 Years of Age or Older	High School Equivalency Certificate Accepted	High School Transcript Required	Open Admissions	Need-Based Aid Available	Part-Time Jobs Available	Career Counseling Available	Job Placement Services Available	College Housing Available	Number of Sports Offered	Number of Majors Offered
FIDM/The Fashion Institute of Design & Merchandising, Orange County Campus	Irvine	C,T	Prop	PW	293	2	6				N	Y	Y	Y	Y	Y		9
FIDM/The Fashion Institute of Design & Merchandising, San Diego Campus	San Diego	C,T	Prop	PW	183	5					N	Y	Y	Y	Y	Y		7
FIDM/The Fashion Institute of Design & Merchandising, San Francisco Campus	San Francisco	C,T	Prop	M/W	753	14					N	Y	Y	Y	Y	N		8
Foothill College	Los Altos Hills	C,T	St-L	M/W	15,765				Y		R			Y	Y	N	8	55
Gavilan College	Gilroy	C,T	St-L	M/W	8,382													
ITT Technical Institute	Culver City	T,B	Prop	M/W														
ITT Technical Institute	Lathrop	T,B	Prop	M/W														
ITT Technical Institute	Oakland	T,B	Prop	M/W														
ITT Technical Institute	Orange	T,B	Prop	M/W														
ITT Technical Institute	Oxnard	C,T,B	Prop	M/W														
ITT Technical Institute	Rancho Cordova	T,B	Prop	M/W														
ITT Technical Institute	San Bernardino	T,B	Prop	M/W														
ITT Technical Institute	San Diego	T,B	Prop	M/W														
ITT Technical Institute	San Dimas	T,B	Prop	M/W														
ITT Technical Institute	Sylmar	T,B	Prop	M/W														
ITT Technical Institute	Torrance	T,B	Prop	M/W														
ITT Technical Institute	West Covina	T,B	Prop	M/W														
Kaplan College, Bakersfield Campus	Bakersfield	T	Prop	M/W														
Kaplan College, Chula Vista Campus	Chula Vista	T	Prop	M/W														
Kaplan College, Fresno Campus	Clovis	T	Prop	M/W														
Kaplan College, Modesto Campus	Salida	T	Prop	PW														
Kaplan College, Palm Springs Campus	Palm Springs	T	Prop	M/W														
Kaplan College, Riverside Campus	Riverside	T	Prop	M/W														
Kaplan College, Sacramento Campus	Sacramento	T	Prop	M/W														
Kaplan College, San Diego Campus	San Diego	T	Prop	M/W														
Kaplan College, Vista Campus	Vista	T	Prop	M/W														
Los Angeles Harbor College	Wilmington	C,T	St-L	M/W	10,181	72												
Mendocino College	Ukiah	C,T	St-L	M/W	3,614	64	40	30	Y			Y		Y	Y	N	8	34
Moreno Valley College	Moreno Valley	C,T	St-L	M/W	10,413													
Mt. San Antonio College	Walnut	C,T	Dist	M/W	28,036	62			Y		S			Y	Y	N	15	77
MTI College	Sacramento	C,T	Prop	M/W	900													
Norco College	Norco	C,T	St-L	M/W	9,674													
Orange Coast College	Costa Mesa	C,T	St-L	M/W	24,239	58	70		Y					Y	Y	N	14	99
Oxnard College	Oxnard	C	St	M/W	7,060	73	55		Y	Y	R					N	4	35
Pasadena City College	Pasadena	C,T	St-L	M/W	22,859	65	28		Y					Y	Y	N	13	76
Reedley College	Reedley	C,T	St-L	M/W	14,573													
Riverside City College	Riverside	T	St-L	M/W	18,586													
San Diego City College	San Diego	C	St-L	M/W	17,681			61	Y		S				Y	N	16	66
San Diego Mesa College	San Diego	C	St-L	M/W	25,464		38		Y		S				Y	N	19	55
San Joaquin Valley College	Bakersfield	T	Prop	M/W	541													
San Joaquin Valley College	Fresno	T	Prop	M/W	675													
San Joaquin Valley College	Hanford		Prop	M/W														
San Joaquin Valley College	Hesperia		Prop	M/W														
San Joaquin Valley College	Rancho Cordova	T	Prop	M/W	619													
San Joaquin Valley College	Salida	T	Prop	M/W	254													
San Joaquin Valley College	Temecula		Prop	M/W														
San Joaquin Valley College	Visalia	T	Ind	M/W	895													
San Joaquin Valley College–Fresno Aviation Campus	Fresno	T	Prop	M/W	59													
San Joaquin Valley College–Online	Visalia	T	Prop	M/W	887													
Santa Monica College	Santa Monica	C,T	St-L	M/W	31,138	64												
Santa Rosa Junior College	Santa Rosa	C,T	St-L	M/W	21,878		54		Y						Y	N	15	76
Sierra College	Rocklin	C,T	St	M/W	19,416	72	32		Y			Y		Y	Y	N	13	61
Taft College	Taft	C,T	St-L	M/W	9,500	95	47		Y	Y	S			Y	Y	Y	5	23
Victor Valley College	Victorville	C,T	St	M/W	6,790	61	34		Y					Y	Y	N	12	41
Colorado																		
Arapahoe Community College	Littleton	C,T	St	M/W	9,963	73	53		Y					Y	Y	N	15	24
Colorado Northwestern Community College	Rangely	C,T	St	M/W	1,291	61	47		Y					Y	Y	Y	11	14
Colorado School of Trades	Lakewood	T	Prop	PW	134		4					Y		Y				1
Front Range Community College	Westminster	C,T	St	M/W	20,092	63												
Institute of Business & Medical Careers	Fort Collins	T	Priv	M/W	302													
ITT Technical Institute	Aurora	T,B	Prop	M/W														
ITT Technical Institute	Westminster	T,B	Prop	M/W														
Northeastern Junior College	Sterling	C,T	St	M/W	1,486	34	22		Y						Y	Y	15	58
Otero Junior College	La Junta	C,T	St	M/W	1,660	48												
Red Rocks Community College	Lakewood	C,T	St	M/W	9,028	68	53		Y					Y	Y	N		51
Connecticut																		
Gateway Community College	New Haven	C,T	St	M/W	7,261	66												
Goodwin College	East Hartford	C,T,B	Ind	M/W	3,317	85	65		Y		Y	Y		Y	Y	N	4	24
Housatonic Community College	Bridgeport	C,T	St	M/W	6,097				Y		Y	Y		Y	Y	N		24
Manchester Community College	Manchester	C,T	St	M/W	7,692	65	32		Y		Y	Y				N	4	31
Northwestern Connecticut Community College	Winsted	C,T	St	M/W	1,701	70												
Norwalk Community College	Norwalk	C,T	St	M/W	6,810	67	37	35	Y		Y	Y		Y	Y	N		35
Three Rivers Community College	Norwich	C,T	St	M/W	5,154	68			Y		Y	Y		Y	Y	N		23
Tunxis Community College	Farmington	C,T	St	M/W	4,764	63	38		Y		Y	Y		Y	Y	N		23

This chart includes the names and locations of accredited two-year colleges in the United States, Canada, and other countries and shows institutions' responses to the *Peterson's Annual Survey of Undergraduate Institutions*. If an institution submitted incomplete data, one or more columns opposite the institution's name is blank. A dagger after the school name indicates that the institution has one or more entries in the *College Close-Ups* section. If a school does not appear, it did not report any of the information.

Y—Yes; N—No; R—Recommended; S—For Some

Institution	Location	Degrees Awarded	Institutional Control	Student Body	Undergraduate Enrollment	Percent Attending Part-Time	Percent 25 Years of Age or Older	Percent of Grads Going on to Four-Year Colleges	High School Equivalency Certificate Accepted	High School Transcript Required	Open Admissions	Need-Based Aid Required	Part-Time Jobs Available	Career Counseling Available	Job Placement Services Available	College Housing Available	Number of Sports Offered	Number of Majors Offered
Delaware																		
Delaware Technical & Community College, Jack F. Owens Campus	Georgetown	C,T	St	M/W	4,611	57	57		Y	Y	S					N	4	52
Delaware Technical & Community College, Stanton/Wilmington Campus	Newark	C,T	St	M/W	7,216	64	35		Y	Y	S					N	5	64
Delaware Technical & Community College, Terry Campus	Dover	C,T	St	M/W	3,107	54	39		Y	Y	S					N	3	44
Florida																		
Chipola College	Marianna	C,T,B	St	M/W	2,292	58	37		Y	Y	Y			Y	Y	N	4	19
College of Business and Technology	Miami	C,B	Prop	M/W	1,098													
College of Central Florida	Ocala	C,T,B	St-L	M/W	8,766	58												
Daytona State College	Daytona Beach	C,T,B	St	M/W	15,708	59	40	75	Y	Y	Y			Y	Y	N	12	52
Florida Gateway College	Lake City	C,T,B	St	M/W	3,073	66	35		Y	Y	S			Y	Y			18
Florida State College at Jacksonville	Jacksonville	C,T,B	St	M/W	30,863	65												
Gulf Coast State College	Panama City	C,T,B	St	M/W	6,436	62												
Hillsborough Community College	Tampa	C,T	St	M/W	27,754	56	38		Y	Y	Y			Y	Y	Y	5	41
ITT Technical Institute	Bradenton	T,B	Prop	M/W														
ITT Technical Institute	Fort Lauderdale	T,B	Prop	M/W														
ITT Technical Institute	Fort Myers	T,B	Prop	M/W														
ITT Technical Institute	Jacksonville	T,B	Prop	M/W														
ITT Technical Institute	Lake Mary	T,B	Prop	M/W														
ITT Technical Institute	Miami	T,B	Prop	M/W														
ITT Technical Institute	Orlando	T,B	Prop	M/W														
ITT Technical Institute	St. Petersburg	T,B	Prop	M/W														
ITT Technical Institute	Tallahassee	T,B	Prop	M/W														
ITT Technical Institute	Tampa	T,B	Prop	M/W														
Kaplan College, Jacksonville Campus	Jacksonville	T	Prop	M/W														
Miami Dade College	Miami	C,T,B	St-L	M/W	66,701	61	36		Y	Y	Y			Y	Y	N	4	142
Northwest Florida State College	Niceville	C,T,B	St-L	M/W	10,317													
Pasco-Hernando Community College	New Port Richey	C,T	St	M/W	10,795	64	35		Y	Y	Y			Y		N	6	18
Pensacola State College	Pensacola	C,T,B	St	M/W	11,862	59	39		Y	Y	Y			Y	Y	N	16	101
Rasmussen College Fort Myers	Fort Myers	C,T,B	Prop	M/W	798		84			Y	Y			Y	Y	N		23
Rasmussen College New Port Richey	New Port Richey	C,T,B	Prop	M/W	893		84			Y	Y			Y	Y	N		23
Rasmussen College Ocala	Ocala	C,T,B	Prop	PW	1,266		84		Y	Y	Y			Y	Y	N		22
Seminole State College of Florida	Sanford	C,T,B	St-L	M/W	19,450	61	42		Y	Y	Y			Y	Y	N	3	50
Tallahassee Community College	Tallahassee	C,T	St-L	M/W	14,237	52	24		Y	Y	Y			Y	Y	N	6	30
Georgia																		
Albany Technical College	Albany	T	St	M/W	4,918	42												
Altamaha Technical College	Jesup	T	St	M/W	1,499	73												
Athens Technical College	Athens	T	St	M/W	5,323	71												
Atlanta Technical College	Atlanta	T	St	M/W	4,779	69												
Augusta Technical College	Augusta	T	St	M/W	4,631	66												
Bainbridge College	Bainbridge	C,T	St	M/W	2,938			57		Y	S			Y	Y	N	2	33
Central Georgia Technical College	Macon	T	St	M/W	6,187	57												
Chattahoochee Technical College	Marietta	T	St	M/W	12,158	69												
Columbus Technical College	Columbus	T	St	M/W	4,164	71												
Darton State College	Albany	C,T,B	St	M/W	6,396	51	47		Y	Y	S			Y	Y	Y	14	67
Emory University, Oxford College	Oxford	C,B	I-R	M/W	936													
Georgia Highlands College	Rome	C,T	St	M/W	5,532	50	28		N	Y	Y			Y		N	12	36
Georgia Military College	Milledgeville	C	St-L	M/W	8,071	33	37		Y	Y	S				Y		7	22
Georgia Northwestern Technical College	Rome	T	St	M/W	6,506	63												
Georgia Piedmont Technical College	Clarkston	T	St	M/W	4,544	75												
Gordon State College	Barnesville	C,T,B	St	M/W	4,171		16		Y	Y	Y			Y		Y	5	42
Gwinnett Technical College	Lawrenceville	T	St	M/W	6,787	63												
ITT Technical Institute	Atlanta	T,B	Prop	M/W														
ITT Technical Institute	Duluth	T,B	Prop	M/W														
ITT Technical Institute	Kennesaw	T,B	Prop	M/W														
Lanier Technical College	Oakwood	T	St	M/W	3,722	75												
Middle Georgia Technical College	Warner Robbins	T	St	M/W	4,045	68												
Moultrie Technical College	Moultrie	T	St	M/W	2,308	59												
North Georgia Technical College	Clarkesville	T	St	M/W	2,670	57												
Oconee Fall Line Technical College–North Campus	Sandersville	T	St	M/W	1,934	68												
Ogeechee Technical College	Statesboro	T	St	M/W	2,298	60												
Okefenokee Technical College	Waycross	T	St	M/W	1,432	70												
Savannah Technical College	Savannah	T	St	M/W	4,998	67												
Southeastern Technical College	Vidalia	T	St	M/W	1,910	70												
Southern Crescent Technical College	Griffin	T	St	M/W	5,381	62												
South Georgia Technical College	Americus	T	St	M/W	2,361	53												
Southwest Georgia Technical College	Thomasville	T	St	M/W	1,871	78												
West Georgia Technical College	Waco	T	St	M/W	7,845	73												
Wiregrass Georgia Technical College	Valdosta	T	St	M/W	4,743	60												
Idaho																		
Carrington College–Boise	Boise	T	Prop	M/W	508		65		N	Y	Y			Y	Y	N		9
Eastern Idaho Technical College	Idaho Falls	T	St	M/W	702	60	62	0	Y	Y	Y			Y	Y	N		17
ITT Technical Institute	Boise	T,B	Prop	M/W														
Illinois																		
City Colleges of Chicago, Harry S. Truman College	Chicago	C,T	St-L	M/W	13,174													

This chart includes the names and locations of accredited two-year colleges in the United States, Canada, and other countries and shows institutions' responses to the *Peterson's Annual Survey of Undergraduate Institutions*. If an institution submitted incomplete data, one or more columns opposite the institution's name is blank. A dagger after the school name indicates that the institution has one or more entries in the *College Close-Ups* section. If a school does not appear, it did not report any of the information.

Column key for Degrees Awarded: College Transfer Associate (C), Terminal Associate (T), Bachelor's (B), Master's (M), Doctoral (D).
Mark key: Y—Yes; N—No; R—Recommended; S—For Some

Institution	Location	Degrees	Control	Student Body	Undergrad Enroll	% Part-Time	% Grads to 4-Yr	% 25+	HS Equiv Accepted	Open Adm	HS Transcript Req	Need-Based Aid	PT Jobs	Career Counsel	Job Placement	College Housing	# Sports	# Majors
College of DuPage	Glen Ellyn	C,T	St-L	M/W	26,209	64												
College of Lake County	Grayslake	C,T	Dist	M/W	17,577	72		43	Y			S		Y	Y	N	9	40
Elgin Community College	Elgin	C,T	St-L	M/W	11,554	66		42	Y			S		Y	Y	N	8	35
Fox College	Bedford Park	T	Priv	M/W	447											N		8
Harper College	Palatine	C,T	St-L	M/W	14,673	62		38	Y			Y		Y	Y	N	12	66
Highland Community College	Freeport	C,T	St-L	M/W	2,064	49		39	Y	Y		R,S		Y		N	6	22
Illinois Central College	East Peoria	C,T	St-L	M/W	11,125	63		38	Y			Y		Y	Y	Y	7	68
Illinois Eastern Community Colleges, Frontier Community College	Fairfield	C,T	St-L	M/W	2,597	89		60	Y	Y		Y		Y	Y	N		15
Illinois Eastern Community Colleges, Lincoln Trail College	Robinson	C,T	St-L	M/W	1,055	59		38	Y	Y		Y		Y	Y	N	3	12
Illinois Eastern Community Colleges, Olney Central College	Olney	C,T	St-L	M/W	1,477	53		41	Y	Y		Y		Y	Y	N	3	13
Illinois Eastern Community Colleges, Wabash Valley College	Mount Carmel	C,T	St-L	M/W	4,706	88		52	Y	Y		Y		Y	Y	N	3	19
Illinois Valley Community College	Oglesby	C,T	Dist	M/W	4,355	57												
ITT Technical Institute	Mount Prospect	T,B	Prop	M/W														
ITT Technical Institute	Oak Brook	T,B	Prop	M/W														
ITT Technical Institute	Orland Park	T,B	Prop	M/W														
John Wood Community College	Quincy	C,T	Dist	M/W	2,390	51												
Kankakee Community College	Kankakee	C,T	St-L	M/W	3,913	59	26	42	Y	Y		Y		Y	Y	N	5	42
Kaskaskia College	Centralia	C,T	St-L	M/W	5,104	61		40	Y	Y		Y		Y	Y	N	9	36
Lincoln Land Community College	Springfield	C,T	Dist	M/W	7,193	58		44	Y			R		Y	Y	N	5	40
McHenry County College	Crystal Lake	C,T	St-L	M/W	5,618	58		33	Y			R			Y	N	6	24
Moraine Valley Community College	Palos Hills	C,T	St-L	M/W	16,650	58	88	30	Y	Y		R		Y		N	9	38
Oakton Community College	Des Plaines	C,T	Dist	M/W	10,406	48			Y	Y		R		Y		N	10	30
Parkland College	Champaign	C,T	Dist	M/W	9,368	63		34	Y	Y		R		Y	Y	N	7	60
Rasmussen College Aurora	Aurora	C,T,B	Prop	M/W	366	82						Y		Y	Y			14
Rasmussen College Rockford	Rockford	C,T,B	Prop	M/W	713	85						Y		Y	Y			14
Rock Valley College	Rockford	C,T	Dist	M/W	8,849	51												
Shawnee Community College	Ullin	C,T	St-L	M/W	2,139	67		33	Y	Y		Y		Y	Y	N	4	31
South Suburban College	South Holland	C,T	St-L	M/W	6,211	52			Y	Y		Y		Y		N	5	23
Southwestern Illinois College	Belleville	C,T	Dist	M/W	12,779	59												
Spoon River College	Canton	C,T	St	M/W	1,966	56		41	Y	Y		Y		Y	Y	N	5	47
Vet Tech Institute at Fox College	Tinley Park	T	Priv	M/W	148							Y				N		1
Waubonsee Community College	Sugar Grove	C,T	Dist	M/W	11,146	67		34	Y							N	11	41
Indiana																		
Ancilla College	Donaldson	C,T	I-R	M/W	440	33		38	Y	Y		Y		Y		N	7	14
International Business College	Indianapolis	T	Priv	M/W	413						Y				Y			11
ITT Technical Institute	Fort Wayne	T,B	Prop	M/W														
ITT Technical Institute	Merrillville	T,B	Prop	M/W														
ITT Technical Institute	Newburgh	T,B	Prop	M/W														
Ivy Tech Community College–Bloomington	Bloomington	C,T	St	M/W	5,822	54		46	Y			Y		Y	Y			27
Ivy Tech Community College–Central Indiana	Indianapolis	C,T	St	M/W	21,407	66		53	Y			Y		Y	Y	N	6	42
Ivy Tech Community College–Columbus	Columbus	C,T	St	M/W	4,140	64		50	Y			Y		Y	Y	N		32
Ivy Tech Community College–East Central	Muncie	C,T	St	M/W	7,471	52		49	Y			Y		Y	Y	N		38
Ivy Tech Community College–Kokomo	Kokomo	C,T	St	M/W	4,649	61		60	Y			Y		Y	Y	N		31
Ivy Tech Community College–Lafayette	Lafayette	C,T	St	M/W	6,666	56		43	Y			Y		Y	Y	N		42
Ivy Tech Community College–North Central	South Bend	C,T	St	M/W	7,852	71		60	Y			Y		Y	Y	N		42
Ivy Tech Community College–Northeast	Fort Wayne	C,T	St	M/W	9,883	62		54	Y			Y		Y	Y	N		39
Ivy Tech Community College–Northwest	Gary	C,T	St	M/W	9,813	61		56	Y			Y		Y	Y	N		42
Ivy Tech Community College–Richmond	Richmond	C,T	St	M/W	3,233	65		61	Y			Y		Y	Y	N	1	30
Ivy Tech Community College–Southeast	Madison	C,T	St	M/W	2,778	60		51	Y			Y		Y	Y	N		18
Ivy Tech Community College–Southern Indiana	Sellersburg	C,T	St	M/W	5,283	71		58	Y			Y		Y	Y	N		31
Ivy Tech Community College–Southwest	Evansville	C,T	St	M/W	5,731	64		56	Y			Y		Y	Y	N		42
Ivy Tech Community College–Wabash Valley	Terre Haute	C,T	St	M/W	5,544	60		50	Y			Y		Y	Y	N	2	44
Kaplan College, Hammond Campus	Hammond	T	Prop	M/W														
Kaplan College, Southeast Indianapolis Campus	Indianapolis	T	Prop	M/W														
Vet Tech Institute at International Business College	Fort Wayne	T	Priv	M/W	125											Y		1
Vet Tech Institute at International Business College	Indianapolis	T	Priv	M/W	111						Y					Y		1
Vincennes University	Vincennes	C,T,B	St	M/W	17,530	65			Y	Y		Y				Y	8	125
Iowa																		
Hawkeye Community College	Waterloo	C,T	St-L	M/W	5,971	55		30	Y			Y		Y	Y	N	8	34
Iowa Lakes Community College	Estherville	C,T	St-L	M/W	3,102	46												
ITT Technical Institute	Cedar Rapids	T,B	Prop	M/W														
ITT Technical Institute	Clive	T,B	Prop	M/W														
Northeast Iowa Community College	Calmar	C,T	St-L	M/W	5,018	59		24	Y			R		Y		N	7	29
St. Luke's College	Sioux City	T	Ind	M/W	203	19		27	N			Y		Y	Y	N		3
Southeastern Community College	West Burlington	C	St-L	M/W	3,112	48		30	Y			Y		Y		Y	6	29
Western Iowa Tech Community College	Sioux City	C,T	St	M/W	6,425	58		42	Y			Y			R	Y	8	36
Kansas																		
Barton County Community College	Great Bend	C,T	St-L	M/W					Y	Y		R		Y	Y	Y	14	101
Colby Community College	Colby	C,T	St-L	M/W	1,451	50		12	Y	Y		Y		Y	Y	Y	10	24
Cowley County Community College and Area Vocational–Technical School	Arkansas City	C,T	St-L	M/W	4,328	46		13	Y	Y		Y			Y	Y	10	43
Garden City Community College	Garden City	C,T	Cou	M/W	2,059	50		24	Y	Y		Y		Y	Y	Y	16	42

This chart includes the names and locations of accredited two-year colleges in the United States, Canada, and other countries and shows institutions' responses to the *Peterson's Annual Survey of Undergraduate Institutions*. If an institution submitted incomplete data, one or more columns opposite the institution's name is blank. A dagger after the school name indicates that the institution has one or more entries in the *College Close-Ups* section. If a school does not appear, it did not report any of the information.

Y—Yes; N—No; R—Recommended; S—For Some

Column key — **Degrees Awarded:** College Transfer Associate (C), Terminal Associate (T), Bachelor's (B), Master's (M), Doctoral (D). **Institutional Control:** County District (Cou), State and Local (St-L), Federal, State and Local, State (St), District (Dist), Independent (Ind), Independent-Religious, Proprietary (Prop). **Student Body:** Men, Primarily Men (PM), Women, Primarily Women (PW), Coed (M/W).

Institution	Location	Degrees Awarded	Institutional Control	Student Body	Undergrad Enrollment	% Part-Time	% 25+	% to 4-Yr	Open Admissions	HS Equiv Cert Accepted	HS Transcript Required	Need-Based Aid	Part-Time Jobs	Job Placement Services	Career Counseling	College Housing	# Sports	# Majors
Hutchinson Community College and Area Vocational School	Hutchinson	C,T	St-L	M/W	6,159	58	36	70	Y	Y	S				Y		13	49
Kansas City Kansas Community College	Kansas City	C,T	St-L	M/W	7,555	62												
Kentucky																		
Bluegrass Community and Technical College	Lexington	C,T	St	M/W	11,596	52												
Gateway Community and Technical College	Florence	C	St	M/W	4,648				Y	Y	Y			Y		N		14
ITT Technical Institute	Louisville	T,B	Prop	M/W														
Owensboro Community and Technical College	Owensboro	C,T	St	M/W	4,768	58	31		Y	Y	Y			Y	Y			21
Spencerian College	Louisville	T	Prop	PW	696	38			Y	Y	Y			Y	Y	Y		11
Sullivan College of Technology and Design	Louisville	C,T,B	Prop	M/W	457	31	45	29	N	Y	Y	Y	Y	Y	Y			45
West Kentucky Community and Technical College	Paducah	C,T	St	M/W	5,785	59	54		Y	Y	S			Y	Y	N	4	14
Louisiana																		
Bossier Parish Community College	Bossier City	C,T	St	M/W	7,855	38	38		Y	Y	Y			Y	Y	N	10	21
Career Technical College	Monroe	T	Prop	M/W	558	18	56		N	Y	Y			Y	Y	N		12
Elaine P. Nunez Community College	Chalmette	C,T	St	M/W	2,302	65	49		Y		S			Y	Y	N	2	19
ITI Technical College	Baton Rouge	T	Prop	PM	585		50	1	Y	Y	Y			Y	Y	N		7
ITT Technical Institute	Baton Rouge	T,B	Prop	M/W														
ITT Technical Institute	St. Rose	T,B	Prop	M/W														
Maine																		
Central Maine Community College	Auburn	C,T	St	M/W	2,905	51	41		N	Y	Y			Y	Y	Y	7	23
Central Maine Medical Center College of Nursing and Health Professions	Lewiston	T	Ind	M/W	217	70	76		N	Y	Y				Y			3
Kennebec Valley Community College	Fairfield	C,T	St	M/W	2,470	71	44		Y	Y	Y			Y	Y	N	7	32
Southern Maine Community College	South Portland	C,T	St	M/W	7,574	59	41		Y	Y				Y	Y	Y	10	33
York County Community College	Wells	C,T	St	M/W	1,524	65	46		Y	Y	Y			Y	Y	N	8	16
Maryland																		
Anne Arundel Community College	Arnold	C,T	St-L	M/W	17,650	71	40		Y					Y	Y	N	8	49
Carroll Community College	Westminster	C,T	St-L	M/W	4,103	61	30		Y		Y			Y	Y	N	2	33
Cecil College	North East	C	Cou	M/W	2,641	66	32	10	Y		R			Y	Y	N	7	42
College of Southern Maryland	La Plata	C,T	St-L	M/W	9,210	63	35		Y		R			Y	Y	N	7	33
The Community College of Baltimore County	Baltimore	C,T	Cou	M/W	25,188	67				Y	Y			Y		N	8	58
Garrett College	McHenry	C,T	St-L	M/W	873	21	19		Y	Y	Y			Y		Y	9	13
Hagerstown Community College	Hagerstown	C,T	St-L	M/W	5,005	72	39		Y		S			Y		N	12	30
Harford Community College	Bel Air	C,T	St-L	M/W	7,226	61	32	47	Y					Y		N	13	65
Howard Community College	Columbia	C,T	St-L	M/W	10,152				Y		S			Y	Y	N	6	52
ITT Technical Institute	Owings Mills	T,B	Prop	M/W														
Montgomery College	Rockville	C,T	St-L	M/W	27,453	64	31	58	Y		R			Y	Y		10	45
TESST College of Technology	Baltimore	T	Prop	M/W														
TESST College of Technology	Beltsville	T	Prop	M/W														
TESST College of Technology	Towson	T	Prop	M/W														
Massachusetts																		
Bay State College †	Boston	C,T,B	Ind	M/W	1,153		43		N	Y	Y			Y	Y	Y		12
Berkshire Community College	Pittsfield	C,T	St	M/W	2,503	63	42	33	Y	Y	Y			Y	Y	N		20
Bunker Hill Community College	Boston	C,T	St	M/W	12,934	65												
Greenfield Community College	Greenfield	C,T	St	M/W	2,437	62	42		Y	Y	S			Y		N		35
Holyoke Community College	Holyoke	C,T	St	M/W	7,164	51	12		Y				Y	Y		N	7	22
ITT Technical Institute	Norwood	T,B	Prop	M/W														
ITT Technical Institute	Wilmington	T,B	Prop	M/W														
Massachusetts Bay Community College	Wellesley Hills	C,T	St	M/W	5,427	62	39		Y	Y				Y	Y	N	9	30
Middlesex Community College	Bedford	C,T	St	M/W	9,664		35		Y	Y	S			Y	Y	N	3	33
Mount Wachusett Community College	Gardner	C,T	St	M/W	4,755	58												
Northern Essex Community College	Haverhill	C,T	St	M/W	7,312	64	51		Y	Y	Y			Y	Y	N	10	58
North Shore Community College	Danvers	C,T	St	M/W	7,912	61	41	45	Y	Y	S			Y	Y	N	2	40
Quinsigamond Community College	Worcester	C,T	St	M/W	8,991	56	40		Y	Y	Y			Y	Y	N	6	43
Springfield Technical Community College	Springfield	C,T	St	M/W	7,011	56	45		Y	Y	Y			Y	Y	N	8	60
Michigan																		
Alpena Community College	Alpena	C,T	St-L	M/W	1,950		40		Y		R			Y	Y	Y	7	29
Grand Rapids Community College	Grand Rapids	C,T	Dist	M/W	17,448	64	35		Y	Y	Y			Y		N	6	37
ITT Technical Institute	Canton	T,B	Prop	M/W														
ITT Technical Institute	Dearborn	T,B	Prop	M/W														
ITT Technical Institute	Swartz Creek	C,B	Prop	M/W														
ITT Technical Institute	Troy	T,B	Prop	M/W														
ITT Technical Institute	Wyoming	T,B	Prop	M/W														
Jackson College	Jackson	C,T	Cou	M/W	6,337	59	56		Y					Y	Y	Y	7	26
Kirtland Community College	Roscommon	C,T	Dist	M/W	1,807	62	45		Y	Y				Y	Y	N	3	30
Lake Michigan College	Benton Harbor	C,T	Dist	M/W	4,548	67	37	44	Y					Y		N	4	63
Lansing Community College	Lansing	C,T	St-L	M/W	19,123	63	40		Y		S			Y	Y	N	6	114
Macomb Community College	Warren	C,T	Dist	M/W	23,729	68	36		Y					Y	Y	N	11	72
Mid Michigan Community College	Harrison	C,T	St-L	M/W	4,885	55												
Monroe County Community College	Monroe	C,T	Cou	M/W			45		Y					Y	Y	N	2	42
Montcalm Community College	Sidney	C,T	St-L	M/W	2,011	66	56		Y		R			Y		N	1	23
Mott Community College	Flint	C,T	Dist	M/W	9,968	68	47		Y					Y	Y	N	7	48
Muskegon Community College	Muskegon	C,T	St-L	M/W	5,579	66												
Oakland Community College	Bloomfield Hills	C,T	St-L	M/W	27,296	68	49	52	Y		R			Y	Y	N	5	98
St. Clair County Community College	Port Huron	C,T	St-L	M/W	4,547	59	32		Y					Y	Y	N	5	29

This chart includes the names and locations of accredited two-year colleges in the United States, Canada, and other countries and shows institutions' responses to the *Peterson's Annual Survey of Undergraduate Institutions*. If an institution submitted incomplete data, one or more columns opposite the institution's name is blank. A dagger after the school name indicates that the institution has one or more entries in the *College Close-Ups* section. If a school does not appear, it did not report any of the information.

Y—Yes; N—No; R—Recommended; S—For Some

Name	Location	Degrees Awarded	Institutional Control	Student Body	Undergrad Enrollment	% Part-Time	% 25 or Older	% Grads to 4-Year	HS Equiv. Accepted	Open Admissions	HS Transcript Req.	Need-Based Aid Req.	Part-Time Jobs Avail.	Career Counseling Avail.	Job Placement Avail.	College Housing Avail.	Sports Offered	Majors Offered
Schoolcraft College	Livonia	C,T	Dist	M/W	12,522	63			Y	Y	R,S			Y	Y	N	5	58
Southwestern Michigan College	Dowagiac	C,T	St-L	M/W	2,639	50	34		Y	Y	Y					Y	9	35
Minnesota																		
Alexandria Technical and Community College	Alexandria	C,T	St	M/W	2,877		24		Y	Y	Y			Y	Y	N	4	42
Anoka-Ramsey Community College	Coon Rapids	C,T	St	M/W	7,773		27		Y	Y	S			Y	Y	N	10	23
Anoka-Ramsey Community College, Cambridge Campus	Cambridge	C,T	St	M/W	2,545		30		Y	Y	S			Y	Y	N	7	22
Century College	White Bear Lake	C,T	St	M/W	10,422	57	44		Y	Y	Y			Y	Y	N	8	38
Dunwoody College of Technology	Minneapolis	T,B	Ind	PM	1,131	22	51		N	Y	Y			Y	Y	N		24
The Institute of Production and Recording	Minneapolis	C,T	Prop	M/W	456	15												
Itasca Community College	Grand Rapids	C,T	St	M/W	1,299													
ITT Technical Institute	Brooklyn Center	T,B	Prop	M/W														
ITT Technical Institute	Eden Prairie	T,B	Prop	M/W														
Lake Superior College	Duluth	C,T	St	M/W	4,627	54	36		Y		S			Y	Y	N		36
Minneapolis Business College	Roseville	T	Priv	PW	373									Y		Y		9
Minneapolis Community and Technical College	Minneapolis	C,T	St	M/W	9,991	62												
Minnesota School of Business–Brooklyn Center	Brooklyn Center	C,T,B	Prop	M/W	620	77												
Minnesota School of Business–Plymouth	Minneapolis	C,T,B	Prop	M/W	487	77												
Minnesota School of Business–Richfield	Richfield	T,B	Prop	M/W	1,738	70												
Minnesota School of Business–St. Cloud	Waite Park	C,T,B	Prop	M/W	921	49												
Minnesota School of Business–Shakopee	Shakopee	C,T,B	Prop	M/W	390	61												
Minnesota State College–Southeast Technical	Winona	C,T	St	M/W	2,237	40												
Minnesota West Community and Technical College	Pipestone	C,T	St	M/W	3,467	62			Y	Y	Y					Y	7	42
Normandale Community College	Bloomington	C,T	St	M/W	9,790	56			Y	Y	S			Y		N	10	23
North Hennepin Community College	Brooklyn Park	C,T	St	M/W	7,657	70	49		Y	Y	R			Y	Y	N	14	31
Northwest Technical College	Bemidji	T	St	M/W	1,168	63	53		Y	Y						Y		16
Rainy River Community College	International Falls	C,T	St	M/W	344													
Rasmussen College Bloomington	Bloomington	C,T,B	Prop	M/W	546		88				Y		Y	Y	Y	N		21
Rasmussen College Brooklyn Park	Brooklyn Park	C,T,B	Prop	M/W	892		89				Y		Y	Y	Y	N		22
Rasmussen College Eagan	Eagan	C,T,B	Prop	PW	883		88				Y		Y	Y	Y	N		21
Rasmussen College Lake Elmo/Woodbury	Lake Elmo	C,T,B	Prop	M/W	682		87				Y		Y	Y	Y	N		22
Rasmussen College Mankato	Mankato	C,T,B	Prop	PW	745		84				Y		Y	Y	Y	N		22
Rasmussen College Moorhead	Moorhead	C,T,B	Prop	M/W	420		83				Y		Y	Y	Y	N		21
Rasmussen College St. Cloud	St. Cloud	C,T,B	Prop	PW	845		86				Y		Y	Y	Y	N		23
St. Cloud Technical & Community College	St. Cloud	C,T	St	M/W	4,883	44												
Mississippi																		
Copiah-Lincoln Community College	Wesson	C,T	St-L	M/W	3,436	20		20	Y	Y	Y			Y	Y	Y	8	45
Southwest Mississippi Community College	Summit	C,T	St-L	M/W	2,053	13												
Missouri																		
Anthem College–Maryland Heights	Maryland Heights	T	Prop	M/W	281													
Crowder College	Neosho	C,T	St-L	M/W	5,576	55		12	Y	Y	Y			Y	Y	Y	4	35
Culinary Institute of St. Louis at Hickey College	St. Louis	T	Priv	M/W	103									Y				1
ITT Technical Institute	Arnold	T,B	Prop	M/W														
ITT Technical Institute	Earth City	T,B	Prop	M/W														
ITT Technical Institute	Kansas City	T,B	Prop	M/W														
Jefferson College	Hillsboro	C,T	Dist	M/W	5,494	46		25	Y	Y	Y			Y	Y	Y	6	26
Linn State Technical College	Linn	T	St	PM	1,168	14												
Metropolitan Community College–Kansas City	Lee's Summit	C,T	St-L	M/W	20,141	62		39	Y					Y	Y	N	6	53
Mineral Area College	Park Hills	C,T	Dist	M/W	3,784	38		34	Y		Y			Y	Y	Y	5	33
Missouri State University–West Plains	West Plains	C,T	St	M/W	2,102	40		37	Y	Y	S			Y	Y	Y	2	21
Ozarks Technical Community College	Springfield	C,T	Dist	M/W	15,179	51		39	Y	Y	Y			Y	Y	Y		34
St. Louis Community College at Forest Park	St. Louis	C,T	Dist	M/W	7,991	65		61	Y	Y	S			Y	Y	N	5	29
St. Louis Community College at Meramec	Kirkwood	C,T	Dist	M/W	10,432	55		40	Y	Y	S			Y	Y	N	5	20
Southeast Missouri Hospital College of Nursing and Health Sciences	Cape Girardeau	C,T	Ind	M/W	196	87												
Vet Tech Institute at Hickey College	St. Louis	T	Priv	M/W	134									Y				1
Montana																		
Dawson Community College	Glendive	C,T	St-L	M/W	603	53												
Flathead Valley Community College	Kalispell	C,T	St-L	M/W	2,395	51	49	68	Y	Y	R,S			Y	Y	Y	7	28
Great Falls College Montana State University	Great Falls	C,T	St	M/W	1,835	50	50	58	Y	Y	Y			Y				24
Miles Community College	Miles City	C,T	St-L	M/W	441	37	0		Y	Y	Y			Y	Y	Y	9	25
The University of Montana–Helena College of Technology	Helena	C,T	St	M/W	1,679	52												
Nebraska																		
Central Community College–Columbus Campus	Columbus	C,T	St-L	M/W	2,872	82												
Central Community College–Grand Island Campus	Grand Island	C,T	St-L	M/W	3,469	88												
Central Community College–Hastings Campus	Hastings	C,T	St-L	M/W	2,966	66												
ITT Technical Institute	Omaha	T,B	Prop	M/W														
Mid-Plains Community College	North Platte	C,T	Dist	M/W	2,591	62	36		Y	Y	Y			Y	Y	Y	5	18
Northeast Community College	Norfolk	C,T	St-L	M/W	5,161	58												
Nevada																		
Carrington College–Las Vegas	Las Vegas	T	Prop	M/W	182		68						Y	Y		N		2
Carrington College–Reno	Reno	T	Prop	M/W	315		69						Y	Y		N		1
ITT Technical Institute	Henderson	T,B	Prop	M/W														
ITT Technical Institute	North Las Vegas	T,B	Prop	M/W														
Kaplan College, Las Vegas Campus	Las Vegas	T	Prop	M/W														
Truckee Meadows Community College	Reno	C,T	St	M/W	12,587	72												

This chart includes the names and locations of accredited two-year colleges in the United States, Canada, and other countries and shows institutions' responses to the *Peterson's Annual Survey of Undergraduate Institutions.* If an institution submitted incomplete data, one or more columns opposite the institution's name is blank. A dagger after the school name indicates that that institution has one or more entries in the *College Close-Ups* section. If a school does not appear, it did not report any of the information.

Y—Yes; N—No; R—Recommended; S—For Some

Institution	City	Degrees Awarded	Institutional Control	Student Body	Undergraduate Enrollment	Percent Attending Part-Time	Percent 25 Years of Age or Older	Percent of Grads Going on to Four-Year Colleges	High School Equivalency Certificate Accepted	High School Transcript Required	Open Admissions	Need-Based Aid Required	Part-Time Jobs Available	Career Counseling Available	Job Placement Services Available	College Housing Available	Number of Sports Offered	Number of Majors Offered
New Hampshire																		
Hesser College, Concord	Concord	T,B	Prop	M/W														
Hesser College, Manchester	Manchester	T,B	Prop	M/W														
Hesser College, Nashua	Nashua	T,B	Prop	M/W														
Hesser College, Portsmouth	Portsmouth	T,B	Prop	M/W														
Hesser College, Salem	Salem	T,B	Prop	M/W														
White Mountains Community College	Berlin	C,T	St	M/W	922	62												
New Jersey																		
Burlington County College	Pemberton	C,T	Cou	M/W	10,071	49	35		Y	Y	R			Y	Y	N	6	58
County College of Morris	Randolph	C,T	Cou	M/W	8,679		23		Y		Y					N	12	30
Essex County College	Newark	C,T	Cou	M/W	11,979	45	41	52	Y			Y		Y	Y	N	6	47
ITT Technical Institute	Marlton	T	Prop	M/W														
Ocean County College	Toms River	C,T	Cou	M/W	10,048	48	28	53	Y			S			Y	N	12	19
Raritan Valley Community College	Branchburg	C,T	St-L	M/W	8,398	56	27	67	Y	Y		Y		Y	Y	N	5	57
Salem Community College	Carneys Point	C,T	Cou	M/W	1,321													
Union County College	Cranford	C,T	St-L	M/W	12,146	52	43		Y			Y		Y	Y	N	6	50
New Mexico																		
Carrington College–Albuquerque	Albuquerque	T	Prop	M/W	628		61					Y						3
Central New Mexico Community College	Albuquerque	C,T	St	M/W	28,323	67	48		Y					Y	Y	N		43
Do&nna Ana Community College	Las Cruces	C,T	St-L	M/W	8,891	55												
ITT Technical Institute	Albuquerque	T,B	Prop	M/W														
New Mexico State University–Alamogordo	Alamogordo	C,T	St	M/W	3,371	70												
San Juan College	Farmington	C,T	St	M/W	9,463	67	58		Y	Y	Y			Y	Y	N	13	53
Southwestern Indian Polytechnic Institute	Albuquerque	C,T	Fed	M/W	480	15												
New York																		
Adirondack Community College	Queensbury	C,T	St-L	M/W	3,987	43	31		Y	Y				Y	Y	Y	9	27
American Academy of Dramatic Arts–New York	New York	T	Ind	M/W	258		7		N	Y	Y			Y		Y		1
The Art Institute of New York City†	New York	C,T	Prop	M/W														
Borough of Manhattan Community College of the City University of New York	New York	C,T	St-L	M/W	24,537	34	24		Y	Y	Y			Y		N	5	25
Cayuga County Community College	Auburn	C,T	St-L	M/W	4,619	50	34		Y	Y	Y			Y	Y	Y	7	34
Clinton Community College	Plattsburgh	C,T	St-L	M/W	2,240		25	31	Y	Y	Y			Y	Y	Y	5	17
Corning Community College	Corning	C,T	St-L	M/W	4,957	54	35		Y	Y	Y			Y	Y*		8	64
Dutchess Community College	Poughkeepsie	C,T	St-L	M/W	10,316	51	23		Y	Y	Y			Y	Y	Y	8	28
Ellis School of Nursing	Schenectady	C,T	Ind	PW	132	66	65				Y			Y				1
Elmira Business Institute	Elmira	C,T	Priv	PW	235	18	70		Y	Y	Y			Y	Y	N		4
Erie Community College	Buffalo	C,T	St-L	M/W	3,333	26	41		Y	Y	Y			Y	Y	N	11	15
Erie Community College, North Campus	Williamsville	C,T	St-L	M/W	6,561	35	36		Y	Y	Y			Y	Y	N	11	27
Erie Community College, South Campus	Orchard Park	C,T	St-L	M/W	4,096	40	25		Y	Y	Y			Y	Y	N	11	16
Fashion Institute of Technology†	New York	C,T,B,M	St-L	PW	9,848	27	22		N	Y	Y			Y	Y	Y	8	20
Finger Lakes Community College	Canandaigua	C,T	St-L	M/W	6,539	45	32		Y	Y	Y			Y	Y	N	9	51
Fiorello H. LaGuardia Community College of the City University of New York	Long Island City	C,T	St-L	M/W	17,468	44	29	45	Y	Y	Y			Y		N	8	42
Genesee Community College	Batavia	C,T	St-L	M/W	6,965	50	36		Y	Y	Y			Y		Y	13	38
Institute of Design and Construction	Brooklyn	C,T	Ind	PM	127	57	42	0	Y	Y	Y			Y	Y	N		4
Island Drafting and Technical Institute	Amityville	C,T	Prop	M/W	116													
ITT Technical Institute	Albany	T	Prop	M/W														
ITT Technical Institute	Getzville	T	Prop	M/W														
ITT Technical Institute	Liverpool	T	Prop	M/W														
Jamestown Business College	Jamestown	T,B	Prop	M/W	294	2	47		N	Y	Y			Y	Y	N	8	4
Jamestown Community College	Jamestown	C,T	St-L	M/W	3,582	29	30	59	Y	Y	Y			Y	Y	N	10	29
Jefferson Community College	Watertown	C,T	St-L	M/W	4,143	47			N	Y	Y			Y	Y	N	6	35
Kingsborough Community College of the City University of New York	Brooklyn	C,T	St-L	M/W	19,261	42												
Long Island Business Institute	Flushing	C	Prop	PW	513	26	66	0	Y	Y	Y			Y	Y	N		7
Mohawk Valley Community College	Utica	C,T	St-L	M/W	7,445	38	34		Y			S		Y	Y	Y	13	52
Monroe Community College	Rochester	C,T	St-L	M/W	17,296	39	41		Y	Y		S		Y	Y	Y	17	67
Nassau Community College	Garden City	C,T	St-L	M/W	23,079	38	23		Y	Y	Y			Y	Y	N	18	53
New York Career Institute	New York	T	Prop	PW	702				N	Y				Y		N		3
Niagara County Community College	Sanborn	C,T	St-L	M/W	6,743	38	27		Y	Y	Y			Y	Y	Y	12	42
Onondaga Community College	Syracuse	C,T	St-L	M/W	12,991	48	29		Y	Y	Y			Y	Y	Y	13	39
Rockland Community College	Suffern	C,T	St-L	M/W	7,986	40												
St. Elizabeth College of Nursing	Utica	T	Ind	M/W	217	33												
St. Joseph's College of Nursing	Syracuse	T	I-R	M/W	273	39												
State University of New York College of Environmental Science and Forestry, Ranger School	Wanakena	C,T	St	PM	58													
State University of New York College of Technology at Alfred	Alfred	C,T,B	St	M/W	3,527	9	15		N	Y	R			Y	Y	Y	17	79
Sullivan County Community College	Loch Sheldrake	C,T	St-L	M/W	1,614	36	25	19	Y	Y	Y			Y	Y	Y	14	34
Tompkins Cortland Community College	Dryden	C,T	St-L	M/W	5,663	48			Y	Y	Y			Y	Y	Y	22	34
Westchester Community College	Valhalla	C,T	St-L	M/W	13,997	46	28		Y	Y	Y			Y	N	N	11	50
Wood Tobe–Coburn School	New York	T	Priv	PW	617				N	Y						N		9
North Carolina																		
Alamance Community College	Graham	C,T	St	M/W	4,739		44		Y	Y	S			Y	Y	N	4	28
Beaufort County Community College	Washington	C,T	St	M/W	1,933				Y	Y	S			Y	N	N		18
Cape Fear Community College	Wilmington	C,T	St	M/W	9,559	50	31		Y	Y	S			Y	Y	N	6	35
Carolinas College of Health Sciences	Charlotte	T	Pub	M/W	438	87	61		N	Y	S			Y	Y	Y		3

This chart includes the names and locations of accredited two-year colleges in the United States, Canada, and other countries and shows institutions' responses to the *Peterson's Annual Survey of Undergraduate Institutions*. If an institution submitted incomplete data, one or more columns opposite the institution's name is blank. A dagger after the school name indicates that the institution has one or more entries in the *College Close-Ups* section. If a school does not appear, it did not report any of the information.

Y—Yes; N—No; R—Recommended; S—For Some

Institution	Location	Degrees Awarded	Institutional Control	Student Body	Undergrad Enrollment	% Part-Time	% 25 or Older	% to 4-Year	HS Equiv Cert Accepted	HS Transcript Required	Open Admissions	Need-Based Aid	Part-Time Jobs	Career Counseling	Job Placement	College Housing	Sports Offered	Majors Offered
Catawba Valley Community College	Hickory	C,T	St-L	M/W	5,099	63	42		Y	Y	Y			Y	Y	N	4	35
Central Carolina Community College	Sanford	C,T	St-L	M/W	4,900	56	53		Y	Y	Y			Y	Y	N	5	29
Cleveland Community College	Shelby	C,T	St	M/W	3,398	49			Y	Y	Y			Y	Y	N		32
Fayetteville Technical Community College	Fayetteville	C,T	St	M/W	12,594	59	74	10	Y	Y		S		Y	Y	N	7	49
Forsyth Technical Community College	Winston-Salem	C,T	St	M/W	9,941	53	46					S		Y	Y	N		49
Guilford Technical Community College	Jamestown	C,T	St-L	M/W	14,793	47	42		Y	Y		S		Y	Y	N	4	54
Halifax Community College	Weldon	C,T	St-L	M/W	1,142		53		Y	Y	Y	Y		Y	Y	N		24
Harrison College	Morrisville	C,T	Prop	M/W	192	14	65		N		Y	Y		Y	Y	N		
ITT Technical Institute	Cary	T,B	Prop	M/W														
ITT Technical Institute	Charlotte	T,B	Prop	M/W														
ITT Technical Institute	High Point	T,B	Prop	M/W														
James Sprunt Community College	Kenansville	C,T	St	M/W	1,572	45	49	1	Y	Y	Y			Y		N	2	17
Johnston Community College	Smithfield	C,T	St	M/W	4,216	51	45		Y	Y	Y			Y	Y	N	4	23
Kaplan College, Charlotte Campus	Charlotte	T	Prop	M/W														
King's College	Charlotte	T	Priv	M/W	529										Y			10
Living Arts College	Raleigh	T,B	Prop	M/W	578		25		N	Y	Y	Y		Y	Y	Y		6
Montgomery Community College	Troy	C,T	St	M/W	837	54	44		Y	Y	Y			Y		N		11
Piedmont Community College	Roxboro	C,T	St	M/W	1,805	55			Y	Y	S			Y	Y	N	1	24
Randolph Community College	Asheboro	C,T	St	M/W	2,894	63	36	53	Y	Y						N	4	31
Robeson Community College	Lumberton	C,T	St	M/W	2,869				Y	Y	Y			Y		N		12
Rockingham Community College	Wentworth	C,T	St	M/W	2,631	54												
Tri-County Community College	Murphy	C,T	St	M/W	1,353		65		Y	Y	Y			Y	Y	N		11
Wilson Community College	Wilson	C,T	St	M/W	1,837	51	49		Y	Y	Y			Y	Y	N		26
North Dakota																		
Bismarck State College	Bismarck	C,T,B	St	M/W	4,109	41			Y	Y	Y	Y		Y	Y	Y		35
Dakota College at Bottineau	Bottineau	C,T	St	M/W	773	55	23		Y	Y	Y	Y		Y	Y	Y	9	72
Lake Region State College	Devils Lake	C,T	St	M/W	1,974	73	19		Y	Y	S			Y	Y	Y	4	15
North Dakota State College of Science	Wahpeton	C,T	St	M/W	3,066	41	18		Y	Y	S	Y		Y	Y	Y	6	44
Rasmussen College Bismarck	Bismarck	C,T,B	Prop	M/W	222		87			Y	Y			Y	Y	N		20
Rasmussen College Fargo	Fargo	C,T,B	Prop	M/W	400		86			Y	Y			Y	Y	N		18
Ohio																		
The Art Institute of Ohio–Cincinnati	Cincinnati	C,T,B	Prop	M/W														
Bowling Green State University-Firelands College	Huron	C,T,B	St	M/W	2,397	46	48		Y	Y	Y							26
Bradford School	Columbus	T	Priv	PW	603				N		Y				Y			14
The Christ College of Nursing and Health Sciences	Cincinnati	T	Priv	M/W	346	42												
Clark State Community College	Springfield	C,T	St	M/W			48		Y	Y	R			Y		N	5	37
Cleveland Institute of Electronics	Cleveland	T	Prop	PM	1,675		85		Y	Y	Y				Y			3
Columbus Culinary Institute at Bradford School	Columbus	T	Priv	M/W	204													1
Cuyahoga Community College	Cleveland	C,T	St-L	M/W	30,065	65	54		Y			S		Y	Y	N	8	32
Edison Community College	Piqua	C,T	St	M/W	3,168	67	54	62	Y	Y		S		Y	Y	N	3	35
ETI Technical College of Niles	Niles	T	Prop	M/W	212	33												
Good Samaritan College of Nursing and Health Science	Cincinnati	T	Prop	M/W	313	58												
International College of Broadcasting	Dayton	C,T	Priv	M/W	77		35		Y	Y	Y			Y	Y	N		1
ITT Technical Institute	Akron	T,B	Prop	M/W														
ITT Technical Institute	Columbus	T,B	Prop	M/W														
ITT Technical Institute	Dayton	T,B	Prop	M/W														
ITT Technical Institute	Hilliard	T,B	Prop	M/W														
ITT Technical Institute	Maumee	T,B	Prop	M/W														
ITT Technical Institute	Norwood	C,B	Prop	M/W														
ITT Technical Institute	Strongsville	T,B	Prop	M/W														
ITT Technical Institute	Warrensville Heights	T,B	Prop	M/W														
ITT Technical Institute	Youngstown	T,B	Prop	M/W														
James A. Rhodes State College	Lima	C,T	St	M/W	3,883	60	45		Y		Y			Y	Y	N	7	29
Kaplan Career Institute, Cleveland Campus	Brooklyn	T	Prop	M/W														
Kaplan College, Dayton Campus	Dayton	T	Prop	M/W														
Kent State University at Ashtabula	Ashtabula	C,B	St	M/W	2,511	50	57		Y	Y	Y			Y	Y	Y		25
Kent State University at East Liverpool	East Liverpool	C,B	St	M/W	1,504	46	50		Y	Y	Y			Y	Y	Y		14
Kent State University at Salem	Salem	C,B	St	M/W	1,878	33	46		Y	Y	Y			Y	Y	N	5	21
Kent State University at Trumbull	Warren	C,B	St	M/W	3,103	39	51		Y	Y	Y			Y	Y	N		26
Kent State University at Tuscarawas	New Philadelphia	C,B	St	M/W	2,983	50	46		Y	Y	Y			Y	Y	N	2	25
Lakeland Community College	Kirtland	C,T	St-L	M/W	9,283	63			Y	Y	Y			Y	Y	N	6	39
Lorain County Community College	Elyria	C,T	St-L	M/W	12,656	69	42		Y	Y	Y		S	Y	Y	N	6	72
Northwest State Community College	Archbold	C,T	St	M/W	4,244	79	64		Y	Y	Y			Y	Y	N	5	62
The Ohio State University Agricultural Technical Institute	Wooster	C,T	St	M/W	730		10		Y	Y	Y			Y	Y	Y		35
Owens Community College	Toledo	C,T	St	M/W	16,993	64	51		Y			R		Y	Y	N	11	55
Southern State Community College	Hillsboro	C,T	St	M/W	2,806	54		25	Y		Y	R		Y	Y	N	4	31
Stark State College	North Canton	C,T	St-R	M/W	15,536	65	54		Y			R		Y		N		49
Terra State Community College	Fremont	C,T	St	M/W	3,172	61			Y	Y	Y	Y		Y	Y	N	6	67
The University of Akron–Wayne College	Orrville	C,T,B	St	M/W	2,415	51	30		Y	Y	S			Y	Y	N	4	8
Vet Tech Institute at Bradford School	Columbus	T	Priv	M/W	167										Y			1
Oklahoma																		
Carl Albert State College	Poteau	C,T	St	M/W	2,460	44	35		Y			Y		Y	Y	Y	6	29
Clary Sage College	Tulsa	T	Prop	PW					Y	Y	Y			Y		N		3
Community Care College	Tulsa	T	Prop	PW	942													
ITT Technical Institute	Tulsa	T,B	Prop	M/W														
Murray State College	Tishomingo	C,T	St	M/W	2,674													
Oklahoma City Community College	Oklahoma City	C,T	St	M/W	14,163	66	44		Y		S			Y	Y	N	7	72
Oklahoma State University, Oklahoma City	Oklahoma City	C,T,B	St	M/W	7,585	67	51		Y	Y	Y			Y	Y	N		46

This chart includes the names and locations of accredited two-year colleges in the United States, Canada, and other countries and shows institutions' responses to the *Peterson's Annual Survey of Undergraduate Institutions*. If an institution submitted incomplete data, one or more columns opposite the institution's name is blank. A dagger after the school name indicates that the institution has one or more entries in the *College Close-Ups* section. If a school does not appear, it did not report any of the information.

Y—Yes; N—No; R—Recommended; S—For Some

Institution	Location	Degrees Awarded	Institutional Control	Student Body	Undergraduate Enrollment	Percent Attending Part-Time	Percent of Grads Going on to Four-Year Colleges	Percent 25 Years of Age or Older	Open Admissions	High School Equivalency Certificate Accepted	High School Transcript Required	Need-Based Aid Available	Part-Time Jobs Available	Career Counseling Available	Job Placement Services Available	College Housing Available	Number of Sports Offered	Number of Majors Offered
Oklahoma Technical College	Tulsa	T	Prop	PM						Y	Y	Y		Y	Y	N		5
Southwestern Oklahoma State University at Sayre	Sayre	C,T	St-L	M/W	643	60												
Oregon																		
Carrington College–Portland	Portland	T	Prop	M/W														1
Central Oregon Community College	Bend	C,T	Dist	M/W	7,132	55	48		Y	Y					Y	Y	Y	11	56
Chemeketa Community College	Salem	C,T	St-L	M/W	12,371	50	52					S		Y	Y	N	6	48
Columbia Gorge Community College	The Dalles	C,T	St	M/W	1,245	56												
ITT Technical Institute	Portland	T,B	Prop	M/W														
Klamath Community College	Klamath Falls	C,T	St	M/W	1,148	66	52	47	Y	Y		Y		Y	Y			14
Oregon Coast Community College	Newport	C,T	Pub	M/W	536	65	54	32	Y					Y		N		5
Rogue Community College	Grants Pass	C,T	St-L	M/W	5,556	58	52		Y					Y	Y		5	25
Umpqua Community College	Roseburg	C,T	St-L	M/W	3,233	46												
Pennsylvania																		
Antonelli Institute	Erdenheim	T	Prop	M/W	183					Y					Y			2
The Art Institute of York–Pennsylvania	York	T,B	Prop	M/W														
Bradford School	Pittsburgh	T	Priv	M/W	441					Y					Y			11
Bucks County Community College	Newtown	C,T	Cou	M/W	10,252	67	31	42	Y	Y		Y		Y	Y	N	10	61
Career Training Academy	Pittsburgh	T	Prop	M/W	70	49	0		N	Y	Y		Y	Y				3
Community College of Allegheny County	Pittsburgh	C,T	Cou	M/W	18,913	62	46					Y		R		N	15	115
Community College of Beaver County	Monaca	C,T	St	M/W	2,779	33			Y			R		S		N		71
Community College of Philadelphia	Philadelphia	C,T	St-L	M/W	39,500	53	71		Y	Y		S		Y		N	8	38
Consolidated School of Business	York	T	Prop	PW	176													
Delaware County Community College	Media	C,T	St-L	M/W	13,248													
Harrisburg Area Community College	Harrisburg	C,T	St-L	M/W	21,945	69	43	55	Y			S				N	5	86
ITT Technical Institute	Dunmore	T	Prop	M/W														
ITT Technical Institute	Harrisburg	T	Prop	M/W														
ITT Technical Institute	Levittown	T	Prop	M/W														
ITT Technical Institute	Pittsburgh	T	Prop	M/W														
ITT Technical Institute	Plymouth Meeting	T	Prop	M/W														
ITT Technical Institute	Tarentum	T	Prop	M/W														
JNA Institute of Culinary Arts	Philadelphia	T	Prop	M/W	65													1
Kaplan Career Institute, Broomall Campus	Broomall	T	Prop	M/W														
Kaplan Career Institute, Franklin Mills Campus	Philadelphia	T	Prop	M/W														
Kaplan Career Institute, Harrisburg Campus	Harrisburg	T	Prop	M/W														
Kaplan Career Institute, Philadelphia Campus	Philadelphia	T	Prop	M/W														
Kaplan Career Institute, Pittsburgh Campus	Pittsburgh	T	Prop	M/W														
Lancaster General College of Nursing & Health Sciences	Lancaster	T,B	Ind	M/W	1,375	63	52			Y		S		Y		N	2	11
Lehigh Carbon Community College	Schnecksville	C,T	St-L	M/W	8,880	69	39	48	Y			S		Y	Y	N	7	60
Luzerne County Community College	Nanticoke	C,T	Cou	M/W	6,579	49	36		Y			R		Y	Y	N	10	74
Manor College	Jenkintown	C,T	I-R	M/W	926		50		N	Y	Y			Y		Y	2	18
McCann School of Business & Technology	Pottsville	C,T	Prop	M/W	1,657		53	33	Y	Y	Y		Y	Y		N		12
Montgomery County Community College	Blue Bell	C,T	Cou	M/W	13,645	63	36	65	Y	Y		Y		Y		N	13	59
Northampton Community College	Bethlehem	C,T	St-L	M/W	11,018	58	35	68	Y	Y		R,S		Y	Y	Y	8	59
Orleans Technical Institute	Philadelphia	C,T	Ind	M/W	533	25												
Pennco Tech	Bristol	T	Prop	M/W	400	39												
Penn State Beaver	Monaca	C,T,B	St-R	M/W	759	16	12		N	Y	Y					Y	10	118
Penn State Brandywine	Media	C,T,B	St-R	M/W	1,581	15	12		N	Y	Y					N	10	120
Penn State DuBois	DuBois	C,T,B	St-R	M/W	704	21	27		N	Y	Y					N	7	127
Penn State Fayette, The Eberly Campus	Uniontown	C,T,B	St-R	M/W	867	22	29		N	Y	Y					N	11	124
Penn State Greater Allegheny	McKeesport	C,T,B,M	St-R	M/W	635	8	11		N	Y	Y					Y	12	119
Penn State Hazleton	Hazleton	C,T,B	St-R	M/W	1,060	6	9		N	Y	Y					Y	8	125
Penn State Lehigh Valley	Fogelsville	C,T,B	St-R	M/W	907	20	14		N	Y	Y			Y	Y	N	13	119
Penn State Mont Alto	Mont Alto	C,T,B	St-R	M/W	1,106	25	22		N	Y	Y					Y	10	120
Penn State New Kensington	New Kensington	C,T,B,M	St-R	M/W	715	22	22		N	Y	Y						13	124
Penn State Schuylkill	Schuylkill Haven	C,T,B	St-R	M/W	867	20	16		N	Y	Y						8	124
Penn State Wilkes-Barre	Lehman	C,T,B	St-R	M/W	617	13	9		N	Y	Y					N	11	122
Penn State Worthington Scranton	Dunmore	C,T,B	St-R	M/W	1,234	20	22		N	Y	Y					N	10	119
Penn State York	York	C,T,B,M	St-R	M/W	1,155	28	25		N	Y	Y					N		126
Pittsburgh Technical Institute	Oakdale	T	Prop	M/W	1,792		20		Y	Y	Y		Y	Y	Y		5	13
The Restaurant School at Walnut Hill College	Philadelphia	T,B	Prop	M/W	402													
University of Pittsburgh at Titusville	Titusville	C,T	St-R	M/W	388	19	14					Y		Y	Y	Y	12	13
Vet Tech Institute	Pittsburgh	T	Priv	M/W	340							Y			Y			1
Westmoreland County Community College	Youngwood	C,T	Cou	M/W	6,571	55	40		Y					Y	Y	N	10	72
YTI Career Institute–York	York	T	Priv	M/W	680													
Rhode Island																		
Community College of Rhode Island	Warwick	C,T	St	M/W	17,884	67	39		Y	Y		Y		Y		N	8	47
South Carolina																		
Aiken Technical College	Aiken	C,T	St-L	M/W	3,045	57												
Central Carolina Technical College	Sumter	C,T	St	M/W	4,522	64												
Denmark Technical College	Denmark	C,T	St	M/W	2,003	9	41		Y	Y	Y		Y	Y	Y	2	8	
Forrest College	Anderson	C,T	Prop	M/W	120	28	62				Y		Y	Y	N		10	
ITT Technical Institute	Columbia	T,B	Prop	M/W														
ITT Technical Institute	Greenville	T,B	Prop	M/W														
ITT Technical Institute	Myrtle Beach	T,B	Prop	M/W														
ITT Technical Institute	North Charleston	T,B	Prop	M/W														
Spartanburg Community College	Spartanburg	C,T	St	M/W	6,036	52	36		Y	Y	Y		Y	Y	N		25
Technical College of the Lowcountry	Beaufort	C,T	St	M/W	2,511						Y				N		19

This chart includes the names and locations of accredited two-year colleges in the United States, Canada, and other countries and shows institutions' responses to the *Peterson's Annual Survey of Undergraduate Institutions*. If an institution submitted incomplete data, one or more columns opposite the institution's name is blank. A dagger after the school name indicates that the institution has one or more entries in the *College Close-Ups* section. If a school does not appear, it did not report any of the information.

Y—Yes; N—No; R—Recommended; S—For Some

Column key (left to right): Degrees Awarded [College Transfer Associate (C); Bachelor's (B); Master's (M), Doctoral (D); Terminal Associate (T)] · Institutional Control · Student Body · Undergraduate Enrollment · Percent Attending Part-Time · Percent of Grads Going on to Four-Year Colleges · Percent 25 Years of Age or Older · Open Admissions · High School Equivalency Certificate Accepted · High School Transcript Required · Need-Based Aid Required · Part-Time Jobs Available · Career Counseling Available · Job Placement Services Available · College Housing Available · Number of Sports Offered · Number of Majors Offered

Institution	Location	Deg	Ctrl	Body	Enroll	%PT	%→4yr	%25+	Open	HS Eq	HS Tr	Need	PT Job	Career	Job Pl	Hous	Sports	Majors
Trident Technical College	Charleston	C,T	St-L	M/W	17,224	56	44		Y	Y	S			Y	Y	N		39
University of South Carolina Union	Union	C	St	M/W	500	50	33		N	Y					S	N	1	2
South Dakota																		
Kilian Community College	Sioux Falls	C,T	Ind	M/W	294	87	57		Y	Y	Y			Y		N		16
Lake Area Technical Institute	Watertown	T	St	M/W	1,600					N	Y		Y	Y	Y	N	3	33
Mitchell Technical Institute	Mitchell	T	St	M/W	1,089	20	25		Y	Y	Y	Y	Y	Y	Y	Y	6	26
Southeast Technical Institute	Sioux Falls	T	St	M/W	2,632	28	27		N	Y	Y		Y	Y	Y	Y	3	51
Western Dakota Technical Institute	Rapid City	T	St	M/W	1,019	23	45		Y	Y	Y			Y	Y	N		18
Tennessee																		
Chattanooga State Community College	Chattanooga	C,T	St	M/W	10,438	54												
Cleveland State Community College	Cleveland	C,T	St	M/W	3,640	47	36	35	Y	Y				Y	Y	N	8	13
Dyersburg State Community College	Dyersburg	C,T	St	M/W	3,590	55	45	62		Y	Y			Y		N	6	14
Fountainhead College of Technology	Knoxville	C,T,B	Prop	M/W	230					Y	Y		Y	Y	Y	N		8
ITT Technical Institute	Chattanooga	T,B	Prop	M/W														
ITT Technical Institute	Cordova	T,B	Prop	M/W														
ITT Technical Institute	Johnson City	T,B	Prop	M/W														
ITT Technical Institute	Knoxville	T,B	Prop	M/W														
ITT Technical Institute	Nashville	T,B	Prop	M/W														
Jackson State Community College	Jackson	C,T	St	M/W	5,109		37	80	Y	Y	S			Y	Y		3	15
John A. Gupton College	Nashville	C,T	Ind	M/W	138	51	32		N	Y	Y			Y	Y	Y		1
Kaplan Career Institute, Nashville Campus	Nashville	T	Prop	M/W														
Motlow State Community College	Tullahoma	C,T	St	M/W	4,580	61	28		Y	Y	Y			Y	Y	N	8	7
Nossi College of Art	Goodlettsville	C,T,B	Ind	M/W	478		9		N	Y	Y			Y	Y	Y		5
Volunteer State Community College	Gallatin	C,T	St	M/W	8,177	56	33		Y	Y	Y			Y	Y	N	3	17
Texas																		
Alvin Community College	Alvin	C,T	St-L	M/W	5,794	73	35		Y	Y	S			Y	Y	Y	3	33
Amarillo College	Amarillo	C,T	St-L	M/W			36		Y		Y			Y	Y	N	5	83
Austin Community College	Austin	C,T	St-L	M/W	43,315		41		Y	Y	Y			Y		N	5	90
Brookhaven College	Farmers Branch	C,T	Cou	M/W	13,705	79	50		Y		Y			Y	Y	N	5	26
Collin County Community College District	McKinney	C,T	St-L	M/W	27,424	64	35	25	Y	Y	Y			Y	Y	N	3	49
Culinary Institute LeNotre	Houston	T	Prop	M/W	403		55				Y			Y	Y	N		2
Dallas Institute of Funeral Service	Dallas	C,T	Ind	M/W	141													
El Centro College	Dallas	C,T	Cou	M/W	10,101	77	46		Y	Y	S			Y		N		37
El Paso Community College	El Paso	C,T	Cou	M/W	30,723	61												
Hallmark College of Technology	San Antonio	T,B,M	Ind	M/W	356		49			Y	Y			Y	Y	N		13
Hallmark Institute of Aeronautics	San Antonio	T	Priv	M/W	227		54			Y	Y			Y	Y	N		2
Houston Community College System	Houston	C,T	St-L	M/W	58,476	68	43		Y	Y	S			Y	Y	N		61
ITT Technical Institute	Arlington	T,B	Prop	M/W														
ITT Technical Institute	Austin	T,B	Prop	M/W														
ITT Technical Institute	DeSoto	T,B	Prop	M/W														
ITT Technical Institute	Houston	T,B	Prop	M/W														
ITT Technical Institute	Houston	T,B	Prop	M/W														
ITT Technical Institute	Richardson	T,B	Prop	M/W														
ITT Technical Institute	San Antonio	T,B	Prop	M/W														
ITT Technical Institute	Waco	T,B	Prop	M/W														
ITT Technical Institute	Webster	T,B	Prop	M/W														
Kaplan College, Arlington Campus	Arlington	T	Prop	M/W														
Kaplan College, Beaumont Campus	Beaumont	T	Prop	M/W														
Kaplan College, Brownsville Campus	Brownsville	T	Prop	M/W														
Kaplan College, Corpus Christi Campus	Corpus Christi	T	Prop	M/W														
Kaplan College, Dallas Campus	Dallas	T	Prop	M/W														
Kaplan College, El Paso Campus	El Paso	T	Prop	M/W														
Kaplan College, Fort Worth Campus	Fort Worth	T	Prop	M/W														
Kaplan College, Laredo Campus	Laredo	T	Prop	M/W														
Kaplan College, Lubbock Campus	Lubbock	T	Prop	M/W														
Kaplan College, San Antonio Campus	San Antonio	T	Prop	M/W														
Kaplan College, San Antonio–San Pedro Area Campus	San Antonio	T	Prop	M/W														
KD Studio	Dallas	T	Prop	M/W	177													
Kilgore College	Kilgore	C,T	St-L	M/W	6,231	54	33		Y	Y	Y			Y	Y	Y	6	69
Lone Star College–CyFair	Cypress	C,T	St-L	M/W	18,906	67	33		Y	Y				Y		N		42
Lone Star College–Kingwood	Kingwood	C,T	St-L	M/W	11,947	65	41		Y	Y				Y		N	1	46
Lone Star College–Montgomery	Conroe	C,T	St-L	M/W	13,250	65	39		Y	Y				Y	Y	N		50
Lone Star College–North Harris	Houston	C,T	St-L	M/W	18,756	69	43		Y	Y				Y	Y		15	61
Lone Star College–Tomball	Tomball	C,T	St-L	M/W	9,454	68	37		Y	Y				Y	Y	N		41
Panola College	Carthage	C,T	St-L	M/W	2,562	56	34		Y	Y	R,S			Y	Y	Y	7	14
Paris Junior College	Paris	C,T	St-L	M/W	5,513	53	31		Y	Y	Y			Y	Y	Y	11	24
St. Philip's College	San Antonio	C,T	Dist	M/W	10,710	79	44		Y	Y	Y			Y	Y	N	5	68
San Jacinto College District	Pasadena	C,T	St-L	M/W	28,721	70	30		Y	Y	Y			Y	Y	N	13	101
South Plains College	Levelland	C,T	St-L	M/W	9,444	54	39	95	Y	Y	Y			Y	Y	Y	11	58
Tarrant County College District	Fort Worth	C,T	Cou	M/W	50,062	65	37		Y					Y	Y	N	6	42
Temple College	Temple	C,T	Dist	M/W	5,547	61	38	44	Y	Y	R,S			Y	Y	Y	5	20
Texarkana College	Texarkana	C,T	St-L	M/W	4,111				Y	Y	Y			Y	Y	Y	3	37
Texas School of Business, Friendswood Campus	Friendswood	T	Prop	M/W														
Texas School of Business, Houston North Campus	Houston	T	Prop	M/W														
Texas State Technical College Harlingen	Harlingen	C,T	St	M/W	5,509	57	33		Y	Y	Y			Y	Y	Y	11	34
Tyler Junior College	Tyler	C,T	St-L	M/W	11,374	44	28		Y	Y	Y			Y	Y	Y	9	56
Vet Tech Institute of Houston	Houston	T	Priv	M/W	239											N		1

This chart includes the names and locations of accredited two-year colleges in the United States, Canada, and other countries and shows institutions' responses to the *Peterson's Annual Survey of Undergraduate Institutions.* If an institution submitted incomplete data, one or more columns opposite the institution's name is blank. A dagger after the school name indicates that the institution has one or more entries in the *College Close-Ups* section. If a school does not appear, it did not report any of the information.

Y—Yes; N—No; R—Recommended; S—For Some

Institution	City	Degrees Awarded	Institutional Control	Student Body	Undergraduate Enrollment	Percent Attending Part-Time	Percent 25 Years of Age or Older	Percent of Grads Going on to Four-Year Colleges	High School Equivalency Certificate Accepted	Open Admissions	High School Transcript Required	Need-Based Aid Available	Part-Time Career Jobs Available	Career Counseling Available	Job Placement Services Available	College Housing Available	Number of Sports Offered	Number of Majors Offered
Utah																		
ITT Technical Institute	Murray	T,B	Prop	M/W														
LDS Business College	Salt Lake City	C,T	I-R	M/W	2,191	27	21		Y	Y	Y			Y	Y	N	15	69
Salt Lake Community College	Salt Lake City	C,T	St	M/W	28,967	69	47		Y					Y	Y	N	6	69
Snow College	Ephraim	C,T	St	M/W	4,465	34												
Vermont																		
Community College of Vermont	Montpelier	C,T	St	M/W	6,908		50	26	Y	Y				Y		N		25
Virginia																		
Dabney S. Lancaster Community College	Clifton Forge	C,T	St	M/W	1,538	69	28				R			Y	Y	N	4	17
Eastern Shore Community College	Melfa	C,T	St	M/W	1,332				Y	Y	Y			Y	Y	N		9
ITT Technical Institute	Chantilly	T,B	Prop	M/W														
ITT Technical Institute	Norfolk	T,B	Prop	M/W														
ITT Technical Institute	Richmond	T,B	Prop	M/W														
ITT Technical Institute	Salem	T,B	Prop	M/W														
ITT Technical Institute	Springfield	T,B	Prop	M/W														
John Tyler Community College	Chester	C,T	St	M/W	10,145	72			Y		R			Y	Y	N		28
J. Sargeant Reynolds Community College	Richmond	C,T	St	M/W	13,370	70												
Paul D. Camp Community College	Franklin	C,T	St	M/W	1,579		40		Y	Y	Y					N		10
Piedmont Virginia Community College	Charlottesville	C,T	St	M/W	5,693	79	46		Y		S			Y	Y	N	8	16
Rappahannock Community College	Glenns	C,T	St-L	M/W	3,711		42		Y					Y	Y	N	2	11
Southwest Virginia Community College	Richlands	C,T	St	M/W	2,766	58	33		Y	Y	Y			Y	Y	N		12
Thomas Nelson Community College	Hampton	C,T	St	M/W	10,942				Y		R			Y	Y	N	3	28
Virginia Western Community College	Roanoke	C,T	St	M/W	8,440	70	38	61	Y	Y	R,S			Y	Y	N	2	25
Wytheville Community College	Wytheville	C,T	St	M/W	3,792		33		Y					Y	Y	N	3	21
Washington																		
The Art Institute of Seattle†	Seattle	T,B	Prop	M/W														
Big Bend Community College	Moses Lake	C,T	St	M/W	1,946	29	35		Y		S			Y	Y	Y	4	15
Carrington College–Spokane	Spokane	T	Prop	M/W	448		50			Y				Y	Y	N		3
Cascadia Community College	Bothell	C,T	St	M/W	2,834	46	20		Y							N		3
Clark College	Vancouver	C,T	St	M/W	12,314		41									N	8	37
Highline Community College	Des Moines	C,T	St	M/W	6,743	42												
ITT Technical Institute	Everett	T,B	Prop	M/W														
ITT Technical Institute	Seattle	T,B	Prop	M/W														
ITT Technical Institute	Spokane Valley	T,B	Prop	M/W														
Lower Columbia College	Longview	C,T	St	M/W	4,252	39	55	55	Y		R			Y		N	5	20
North Seattle Community College	Seattle	C,T	St	M/W	6,303	69												
Olympic College	Bremerton	C,T,B	St	M/W	8,260		49		Y		S				Y	N	10	17
Peninsula College	Port Angeles	C,T,B	St	M/W	3,321													
Pierce College at Puyallup	Puyallup	C,T	St	M/W	13,294		56		Y					Y	Y	N	5	17
South Puget Sound Community College	Olympia	C,T	St	M/W	4,955	46	42	19	Y					Y	Y	N	3	23
West Virginia																		
Blue Ridge Community and Technical College	Martinsburg	C,T	St	M/W	4,317	73	57		Y	Y	Y			Y	Y	N		13
ITT Technical Institute	Huntington	T	Prop	M/W														
Potomac State College of West Virginia University	Keyser	C,T,B	St	M/W	1,781	19	14		Y	Y	Y				Y		6	53
West Virginia Junior College–Bridgeport	Bridgeport	C,T	Prop	M/W	507		30		Y	Y	R				Y	N		8
West Virginia Northern Community College	Wheeling	C,T	St	M/W	2,505	54	50		Y	Y	S			Y	Y	N		22
Wisconsin																		
Blackhawk Technical College	Janesville	C,T	Dist	M/W	2,967	56	53	0	Y	Y	Y			Y	Y	N		29
Chippewa Valley Technical College	Eau Claire	C,T	Dist	M/W	6,086	57	44		Y	Y	S			Y	Y	N		28
Fox Valley Technical College	Appleton	T	St-L	M/W	10,948	73	48		Y	Y	Y			Y	Y	N	6	48
Gateway Technical College	Kenosha	T	St-L	M/W	8,720	80	55		Y					Y		N		48
ITT Technical Institute	Green Bay	T,B	Prop	M/W														
ITT Technical Institute	Greenfield	T,B	Prop	M/W														
ITT Technical Institute	Madison	T,B	Prop	M/W														
Moraine Park Technical College	Fond du Lac	C,T	Dist	M/W	6,074	82	70		Y	Y	Y			Y	Y	N		37
Rasmussen College Green Bay	Green Bay	C,T,B	Prop	M/W	582	91				Y	Y			Y	Y	N		22
University of Wisconsin–Fox Valley	Menasha	C,T	St	M/W	1,797	42	25	70				Y		Y		N	6	1
University of Wisconsin–Richland	Richland Center	C	St	M/W	519	44	16					Y		Y	Y	N	9	2
University of Wisconsin–Waukesha	Waukesha	C	St	M/W	2,115	58	28					N		Y	Y	N	10	1
Waukesha County Technical College	Pewaukee	T	St-L	M/W	10,286	80	51		Y						Y	N		37
Wisconsin Indianhead Technical College	Shell Lake	T	Dist	M/W	3,596	56	54									N		21
Wyoming																		
Casper College	Casper	C,T	St-L	M/W	4,207	54	36	40	Y					Y	Y	Y	10	101
Central Wyoming College	Riverton	C,T	St-L	M/W	2,164	61	40	49	Y		R			Y	Y	Y	15	62
Laramie County Community College	Cheyenne	C,T	Dist	M/W	5,115	59	42	64	Y	Y	S			Y	Y	Y	11	62
Northwest College	Powell	C,T	St-L	M/W	2,047	41	27		Y	Y				Y	Y	Y	10	62
Sheridan College	Sheridan	C,T	St-L	M/W	4,236	65	34		Y		R,S				Y	Y	10	49
INTERNATIONAL																		
Palau																		
Palau Community College	Koror	C,T	Terr	M/W	694	33												

Profiles
of Two-Year
Colleges

Creativity is all around you, and so is opportunity. We can help you prepare for it with a focused education in programs in the areas of design, media arts, fashion, or culinary. We'll guide your learning as you prepare to enter the job market with a strong set of professional skills and the portfolio to prove it to employers. The world is your canvas. Together, we can fill it in.

create.artinstitutes.edu
1.800.894.5793

DESIGN   MEDIA ARTS   FASHION   CULINARY

CREATE TOMORROW

U.S. AND U.S. TERRITORIES

ALABAMA

Alabama Southern Community College
Monroeville, Alabama

Director of Admissions Ms. Jana S. Horton, Registrar, Alabama Southern Community College, PO Box 2000, Monroeville, AL 36461. *Phone:* 251-575-3156 Ext. 252. *E-mail:* jhorton@ascc.edu.
Website: http://www.ascc.edu/.

Bevill State Community College
Jasper, Alabama

- **State-supported** 2-year, founded 1969, part of Alabama College System
- **Rural** 245-acre campus with easy access to Birmingham
- **Endowment** $142,934
- **Coed,** 4,069 undergraduate students, 55% full-time, 64% women, 36% men

Undergraduates 2,258 full-time, 1,811 part-time. 16% Black or African American, non-Hispanic/Latino; 1% Hispanic/Latino; 0.5% Asian, non-Hispanic/Latino; 0.3% American Indian or Alaska Native, non-Hispanic/Latino; 1% Two or more races, non-Hispanic/Latino; 2% Race/ethnicity unknown; 0.0% international.
Freshmen *Admission:* 993 enrolled.
Faculty *Total:* 337, 34% full-time, 13% with terminal degrees. *Student/faculty ratio:* 16:1.
Majors Administrative assistant and secretarial science; child-care and support services management; computer and information sciences; drafting and design technology; electrician; emergency medical technology (EMT paramedic); general studies; heating, ventilation, air conditioning and refrigeration engineering technology; industrial electronics technology; legal assistant/paralegal; liberal arts and sciences/liberal studies; registered nursing/registered nurse; tool and die technology.
Academics *Calendar:* semesters. *Degree:* certificates and associate. *Special study options:* academic remediation for entering students, adult/continuing education programs, advanced placement credit, cooperative education, distance learning, honors programs, off-campus study, part-time degree program, services for LD students, summer session for credit.
Library 141,434 titles, 23,905 serial subscriptions, an OPAC, a Web page.
Student Life *Housing Options:* coed. Campus housing is university owned. *Activities and Organizations:* choral group, Student Government Association, Campus Ministries, Circle K, Outdoors men Club, Students Against Destructive Decisions. *Campus security:* 24-hour emergency response devices.
Costs (2012–13) *Tuition:* state resident $2616 full-time, $109 per credit hour part-time; nonresident $5232 full-time, $218 per credit hour part-time. Full-time tuition and fees vary according to course load and program. Part-time tuition and fees vary according to course load and program. *Required fees:* $711 full-time, $29 per credit hour part-time. *Room and board:* $2695. Room and board charges vary according to board plan and location. *Payment plan:* installment. *Waivers:* employees or children of employees.
Financial Aid Of all full-time matriculated undergraduates who enrolled in 2011, 88 Federal Work-Study jobs (averaging $1807).
Applying *Options:* electronic application, early admission, deferred entrance. *Required:* high school transcript. *Application deadlines:* rolling (freshmen), rolling (transfers).
Freshman Application Contact Bevill State Community College, 1411 Indiana Avenue, Jasper, AL 35501. *Phone:* 205-387-0511 Ext. 5813.
Website: http://www.bscc.edu/.

Bishop State Community College
Mobile, Alabama

Freshman Application Contact Bishop State Community College, 351 North Broad Street, Mobile, AL 36603-5898. *Phone:* 251-405-7000. *Toll-free phone:* 800-523-7235.
Website: http://www.bishop.edu/.

Brown Mackie College–Birmingham
Birmingham, Alabama

Freshman Application Contact Brown Mackie College–Birmingham, 105 Vulcan Road, Suite 400, Birmingham, AL 35209.

Phone: 205-909-1500. *Toll-free phone:* 888-299-4699.
Website: http://www.brownmackie.edu/birmingham.

See display on next page and page 350 for the College Close-Up.

Calhoun Community College
Decatur, Alabama

Freshman Application Contact Admissions Office, Calhoun Community College, PO Box 2216, Decatur, AL 35609-2216. *Phone:* 256-306-2593. *Toll-free phone:* 800-626-3628. *Fax:* 256-306-2941. *E-mail:* admissions@calhoun.edu.
Website: http://www.calhoun.edu/.

Central Alabama Community College
Alexander City, Alabama

Freshman Application Contact Ms. Donna Whaley, Central Alabama Community College, 1675 Cherokee Road, Alexander City, AL 35011-0699. *Phone:* 256-234-6346 Ext. 6232. *Toll-free phone:* 800-634-2657.
Website: http://www.cacc.edu/.

Chattahoochee Valley Community College
Phenix City, Alabama

- **State-supported** 2-year, founded 1974, part of Alabama College System
- **Small-town** 103-acre campus
- **Coed**

Undergraduates 944 full-time, 753 part-time. 42% Black or African American, non-Hispanic/Latino; 4% Hispanic/Latino; 1% Asian, non-Hispanic/Latino; 0.2% Native Hawaiian or other Pacific Islander, non-Hispanic/Latino; 0.5% American Indian or Alaska Native, non-Hispanic/Latino; 0.6% Two or more races, non-Hispanic/Latino; 2% Race/ethnicity unknown; 16% transferred in. *Retention:* 54% of full-time freshmen returned.
Faculty *Student/faculty ratio:* 20:1.
Academics *Calendar:* semesters. *Degree:* certificates and associate. *Special study options:* academic remediation for entering students, adult/continuing education programs, advanced placement credit, distance learning, honors programs, off-campus study, part-time degree program, services for LD students, student-designed majors, summer session for credit.
Student Life *Campus security:* 24-hour emergency response devices and patrols.
Athletics Member NJCAA.
Applying *Options:* early admission. *Required:* high school transcript.
Freshman Application Contact Chattahoochee Valley Community College, 2602 College Drive, Phenix City, AL 36869-7928. *Phone:* 334-291-4929.
Website: http://www.cv.edu/.

Community College of the Air Force
Maxwell Gunter Air Force Base, Alabama

- **Federally supported** 2-year, founded 1972, part of Air University
- **Suburban** campus
- **Coed, primarily men,** 314,962 undergraduate students, 100% full-time, 18% women, 82% men

Undergraduates 314,962 full-time.
Freshmen *Admission:* 29,486 applied, 29,486 admitted, 29,486 enrolled.
Faculty *Total:* 6,293, 100% full-time.
Majors Aeronautics/aviation/aerospace science and technology; airframe mechanics and aircraft maintenance technology; air traffic control; apparel and textile marketing management; atmospheric sciences and meteorology; automobile/automotive mechanics technology; avionics maintenance technology; biomedical technology; cardiovascular technology; clinical/medical laboratory technology; commercial and advertising art; communications technology; construction engineering technology; criminal justice/law enforcement administration; dental assisting; dental laboratory technology; dietetics; educational/instructional technology; educational leadership and administration; electrical, electronic and communications engineering technology; environmental health; environmental studies; finance; fire science/firefighting; health/health-care administration; hematology technology; hotel/motel administration; human resources management; industrial technology; legal assistant/paralegal; logistics, materials, and supply chain management; management information systems; medical radiologic technology;

49

mental health counseling; metallurgical technology; music performance; nuclear medical technology; occupational safety and health technology; office management; ophthalmic laboratory technology; parks, recreation and leisure; pharmacy technician; physical therapy technology; physiology; public relations/image management; purchasing, procurement/acquisitions and contracts management; security and loss prevention; social work; surgical technology.

Academics *Calendar:* continuous. *Degrees:* certificates and associate (courses conducted at 125 branch locations worldwide for members of the U.S. Air Force). *Special study options:* academic remediation for entering students, adult/continuing education programs, advanced placement credit, distance learning, independent study, internships.

Library Air Force Library Service with 5.0 million titles, 56,654 serial subscriptions, an OPAC, a Web page.

Student Life *Housing:* on-campus residence required for freshman year. *Options:* coed. Campus housing is university owned, leased by the school and is provided by a third party. Freshman applicants given priority for college housing. *Campus security:* 24-hour emergency response devices and patrols. *Student services:* health clinic, personal/psychological counseling, legal services.

Athletics *Intramural sports:* badminton M/W, baseball M, basketball M/W, bowling M/W, cross-country running M/W, football M, golf M/W, racquetball M/W, softball M/W, squash M/W, table tennis M/W, tennis M/W, track and field M/W, volleyball M/W, weight lifting M/W.

Standardized Tests *Required:* Armed Services Vocational Aptitude Battery (for admission).

Applying *Options:* electronic application. *Required:* high school transcript, interview, military physical, good character, criminal background check. *Application deadlines:* rolling (freshmen), rolling (transfers). *Notification:* continuous (freshmen), continuous (transfers).

Freshman Application Contact Ms. Teresa Amatuzzi, Director of Enrollment Management/Registrar, Community College of the Air Force, 100 South Turner Blvd., Maxwell Air Force Base, Maxwell - Gunter AFB, AL 36114-3011. *Phone:* 334-649-5080. *Fax:* 334-649-5015. *E-mail:* teresa.amatuzzi@maxwell.af.mil.

Website: http://www.au.af.mil/au/ccaf/.

Enterprise State Community College

Enterprise, Alabama

Director of Admissions Mr. Gary Deas, Associate Dean of Students/Registrar, Enterprise State Community College, PO Box 1300, Enterprise, AL 36331-1300.

Phone: 334-347-2623 Ext. 2233. *E-mail:* gdeas@eocc.edu. *Website:* http://www.escc.edu/.

Gadsden State Community College

Gadsden, Alabama

- **State-supported** 2-year, founded 1965, part of Alabama Community College System
- **Small-town** 275-acre campus with easy access to Birmingham
- **Coed,** 5,882 undergraduate students, 54% full-time, 62% women, 38% men

Undergraduates 3,158 full-time, 2,724 part-time. Students come from 17 states and territories; 60 other countries; 1% are from out of state; 20% Black or African American, non-Hispanic/Latino; 2% Hispanic/Latino; 0.5% Asian, non-Hispanic/Latino; 0.1% Native Hawaiian or other Pacific Islander, non-Hispanic/Latino; 0.5% American Indian or Alaska Native, non-Hispanic/Latino; 2% Two or more races, non-Hispanic/Latino; 5% Race/ethnicity unknown; 1% international; 6% transferred in; 2% live on campus.

Freshmen *Admission:* 1,319 enrolled.

Faculty *Total:* 345, 45% full-time. *Student/faculty ratio:* 19:1.

Majors Accounting technology and bookkeeping; administrative assistant and secretarial science; child-care and support services management; civil engineering technology; clinical/medical laboratory technology; communication and journalism related; computer and information sciences; court reporting; criminal justice/police science; drafting and design technology; electrical, electronic and communications engineering technology; emergency medical technology (EMT paramedic); general studies; heating, ventilation, air conditioning and refrigeration engineering technology; industrial mechanics and maintenance technology; legal assistant/paralegal; liberal arts and sciences/liberal studies; manufacturing engineering technology; radiologic technology/science; registered nursing/registered nurse; sales, distribution, and marketing operations; substance abuse/addiction counseling; tool and die technology.

Academics *Calendar:* semesters. *Degree:* certificates and associate. *Special study options:* academic remediation for entering students, adult/continuing education programs, advanced placement credit, cooperative education, distance learning, English as a second language, external degree program, honors programs, internships, part-time degree program, services for LD students, study abroad, summer session for credit. *ROTC:* Army (b).

Library Meadows Library with 115,901 titles, 144 serial subscriptions, 7,080 audiovisual materials, an OPAC, a Web page.

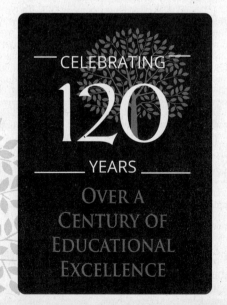

Student Life *Housing Options:* coed. Campus housing is university owned. *Activities and Organizations:* drama/theater group, choral group, National Society of Leadership and Success, Student Government Association, Circle K, International Club, Cardinal Spirit Club. *Campus security:* 24-hour patrols. *Student services:* personal/psychological counseling.

Athletics Member NJCAA. *Intercollegiate sports:* baseball M(s), basketball M(s)/W(s), softball W(s), tennis M(s), volleyball W(s).

Costs (2012–13) *Tuition:* state resident $3270 full-time, $109 per credit hour part-time; nonresident $6540 full-time, $218 per credit hour part-time. Full-time tuition and fees vary according to reciprocity agreements. Part-time tuition and fees vary according to reciprocity agreements. *Required fees:* $684 full-time, $19 per credit hour part-time. *Room and board:* $3200. *Waivers:* minority students, adult students, senior citizens, and employees or children of employees.

Applying *Options:* electronic application, early admission, deferred entrance. *Required:* high school transcript. *Application deadlines:* rolling (freshmen), rolling (transfers).

Freshman Application Contact Mrs. Jennie Dobson, Admissions and Records, Gadsden State Community College, Allen Hall, Gadsden, AL 35902-0227. *Phone:* 256-549-8210. *Toll-free phone:* 800-226-5563. *Fax:* 256-549-8205. *E-mail:* info@gadsdenstate.edu. *Website:* http://www.gadsdenstate.edu/.

George Corley Wallace State Community College
Selma, Alabama

Director of Admissions Ms. Sunette Newman, Registrar, George Corley Wallace State Community College, PO Box 2530, Selma, AL 36702. *Phone:* 334-876-9305. *Website:* http://www.wccs.edu/.

George C. Wallace Community College
Dothan, Alabama

Freshman Application Contact Mr. Keith Saulsberry, Director, Enrollment Services/Registrar, George C. Wallace Community College, 1141 Wallace Drive, Dothan, AL 36303. *Phone:* 334-983-3521 Ext. 2470. *Toll-free phone:* 800-543-2426. *Fax:* 334-983-3600. *E-mail:* ksaulsberry@wallace.edu. *Website:* http://www.wallace.edu/.

H. Councill Trenholm State Technical College
Montgomery, Alabama

- **State-supported** 2-year, founded 1962, part of Alabama Department of Postsecondary Education
- **Urban** 81-acre campus
- **Coed**

Undergraduates Students come from 2 states and territories; 1% are from out of state; 62% Black or African American, non-Hispanic/Latino; 0.6% Hispanic/Latino; 0.8% Asian, non-Hispanic/Latino; 0.3% American Indian or Alaska Native, non-Hispanic/Latino; 0.1% Two or more races, non-Hispanic/Latino; 1% Race/ethnicity unknown. *Retention:* 50% of full-time freshmen returned.

Faculty *Student/faculty ratio:* 10:1.

Academics *Calendar:* semesters. *Degree:* certificates, diplomas, and associate. *Special study options:* academic remediation for entering students, adult/continuing education programs, advanced placement credit, cooperative education, distance learning, external degree program, independent study, internships, part-time degree program, services for LD students, summer session for credit.

Student Life *Campus security:* 24-hour emergency response devices and patrols, late-night transport/escort service.

Standardized Tests *Required for some:* ACT (for admission).

Costs (2012–13) *Tuition:* state resident $2784 full-time, $116 per unit part-time; nonresident $5568 full-time, $232 per unit part-time. *Required fees:* $456 full-time, $19 per unit part-time.

Applying *Options:* early admission. *Required:* high school transcript.

Freshman Application Contact Mrs. Tennie McBryde, Registrar, H. Councill Trenholm State Technical College, Montgomery, AL 36108. *Phone:* 334-420-4306. *Toll-free phone:* 866-753-4544. *Fax:* 334-420-4201. *E-mail:* tmcbryde@trenholmstate.edu. *Website:* http://www.trenholmstate.edu/.

ITT Technical Institute
Bessemer, Alabama

- **Proprietary** primarily 2-year, founded 1994, part of ITT Educational Services, Inc.
- **Suburban** campus
- **Coed**

Academics *Calendar:* quarters. *Degrees:* associate and bachelor's.
Student Life *Campus security:* 24-hour emergency response devices.
Freshman Application Contact Director of Recruitment, ITT Technical Institute, 6270 Park South Drive, Bessemer, AL 35022. *Phone:* 205-497-5700. *Toll-free phone:* 800-488-7033. *Website:* http://www.itt-tech.edu/.

ITT Technical Institute
Madison, Alabama

- **Proprietary** primarily 2-year, part of ITT Educational Services, Inc.
- **Coed**

Academics *Degrees:* associate and bachelor's.
Freshman Application Contact Director of Recruitment, ITT Technical Institute, 9238 Madison Boulevard, Suite 500, Madison, AL 35758. *Phone:* 256-542-2900. *Toll-free phone:* 877-628-5960. *Website:* http://www.itt-tech.edu/.

ITT Technical Institute
Mobile, Alabama

- **Proprietary** primarily 2-year, part of ITT Educational Services, Inc.
- **Coed**

Academics *Degrees:* associate and bachelor's.
Freshman Application Contact Director of Recruitment, ITT Technical Institute, Office Mall South, 3100 Cottage Hill Road, Building 3, Mobile, AL 36606. *Phone:* 251-472-4760. *Toll-free phone:* 877-327-1013. *Website:* http://www.itt-tech.edu/.

James H. Faulkner State Community College
Bay Minette, Alabama

Freshman Application Contact Ms. Carmelita Mikkelsen, Director of Admissions and High School Relations, James H. Faulkner State Community College, 1900 Highway 31 South, Bay Minette, AL 36507. *Phone:* 251-580-2213. *Toll-free phone:* 800-231-3752. *Fax:* 251-580-2285. *E-mail:* cmikkelsen@faulknerstate.edu. *Website:* http://www.faulknerstate.edu/.

Jefferson Davis Community College
Brewton, Alabama

Director of Admissions Ms. Robin Sessions, Registrar, Jefferson Davis Community College, PO Box 958, Brewton, AL 36427-0958. *Phone:* 251-867-4832. *Website:* http://www.jdcc.edu/.

Jefferson State Community College
Birmingham, Alabama

- **State-supported** 2-year, founded 1965, part of Alabama Community College System
- **Suburban** 351-acre campus
- **Endowment** $1.1 million
- **Coed,** 8,878 undergraduate students, 34% full-time, 61% women, 39% men

Undergraduates 3,062 full-time, 5,816 part-time. 21% Black or African American, non-Hispanic/Latino; 3% Hispanic/Latino; 2% Asian, non-Hispanic/Latino; 0.2% American Indian or Alaska Native, non-Hispanic/Latino; 3% Two or more races, non-Hispanic/Latino; 0.2% Race/ethnicity unknown; 0.7% international; 48% transferred in.

Freshmen *Admission:* 4,046 applied, 4,046 admitted, 1,592 enrolled. *Average high school GPA:* 2.87.

Faculty *Total:* 405, 32% full-time, 14% with terminal degrees. *Student/faculty ratio:* 26:1.

Majors Accounting technology and bookkeeping; administrative assistant and secretarial science; child-care and support services management; clinical/medical laboratory technology; computer and information sciences; construction engineering technology; criminal justice/police science; emergency medical technology (EMT paramedic); engineering technology; fire services administration; funeral service and mortuary science; general studies; hospitality administration; liberal arts and sciences/liberal studies; office management; physical therapy technology; radiologic technology/science; registered nursing/registered nurse; veterinary/animal health technology.

Academics *Calendar:* semesters. *Degree:* certificates and associate. *Special study options:* academic remediation for entering students, adult/continuing education programs, advanced placement credit, distance learning, English as a second language, honors programs, independent study, internships, part-time degree program, services for LD students, summer session for credit. *ROTC:* Army (c), Air Force (c).

Library Jefferson State Libraries plus 4 others with 217,609 titles, 301 serial subscriptions, 1,478 audiovisual materials, an OPAC, a Web page.

Student Life *Housing:* college housing not available. *Activities and Organizations:* choral group, Student Government Association, Phi Theta Kappa, Sigma Kappa Delta, Jefferson State Ambassadors, Students in Free Enterprise (SIFE). *Campus security:* 24-hour patrols.

Costs (2012–13) *Tuition:* state resident $4200 full-time, $140 per semester hour part-time; nonresident $7470 full-time, $249 per semester hour part-time. Full-time tuition and fees vary according to course load. Part-time tuition and fees vary according to course load. *Waivers:* senior citizens and employees or children of employees.

Financial Aid Of all full-time matriculated undergraduates who enrolled in 2011, 189 Federal Work-Study jobs (averaging $1926).

Applying *Options:* electronic application, early admission, early action, deferred entrance. *Required for some:* high school transcript. *Application deadline:* rolling (freshmen). *Notification:* continuous (freshmen), continuous (transfers).

Freshman Application Contact Mrs. Lillian Owens, Director of Admissions and Retention, Jefferson State Community College, 2601 Carson Road, Birmingham, AL 35215-3098. *Phone:* 205-853-1200 Ext. 7990. *Toll-free phone:* 800-239-5900. *Fax:* 205-856-6070. *E-mail:* lowens@jeffstateonline.com.
Website: http://www.jeffstateonline.com/.

J. F. Drake State Technical College
Huntsville, Alabama

- **State-supported** 2-year, founded 1961, part of Alabama Community College System of the Alabama Department of Postsecondary Education
- **Urban** 6-acre campus
- **Coed,** 1,258 undergraduate students, 60% full-time, 55% women, 45% men

Undergraduates 754 full-time, 504 part-time. Students come from 1 other state; 2 other countries; 4% are from out of state; 23% transferred in.
Freshmen *Admission:* 1,010 applied, 699 admitted, 347 enrolled.
Faculty *Total:* 72, 35% full-time, 7% with terminal degrees. *Student/faculty ratio:* 17:1.
Majors Accounting; accounting technology and bookkeeping; administrative assistant and secretarial science; automobile/automotive mechanics technology; automotive engineering technology; commercial and advertising art; computer and information sciences; cosmetology; culinary arts; drafting and design technology; electrical, electronic and communications engineering technology; electrician; heating, ventilation, air conditioning and refrigeration engineering technology; industrial electronics technology; industrial mechanics and maintenance technology; information science/studies; licensed practical/vocational nurse training; machine tool technology; medical/clinical assistant; multi/interdisciplinary studies related; tool and die technology.
Academics *Calendar:* semesters. *Degree:* certificates and associate. *Special study options:* academic remediation for entering students, cooperative education, internships, part-time degree program, services for LD students.
Library S.C. O'Neal Library Technology Center with 24,676 titles, 150 serial subscriptions, 2,247 audiovisual materials, an OPAC, a Web page.
Student Life *Housing:* college housing not available. *Activities and Organizations:* Phi Beta Lambda, SKILLS - USA. *Campus security:* 24-hour patrols.
Costs (2012–13) *Tuition:* state resident $3270 full-time, $109 per credit hour part-time; nonresident $6540 full-time, $218 per credit hour part-time. *Required fees:* $720 full-time, $24 per credit hour part-time. *Waivers:* senior citizens and employees or children of employees.
Applying *Options:* electronic application, deferred entrance. *Required:* high school transcript. *Application deadlines:* rolling (freshmen), rolling (transfers). *Notification:* continuous (freshmen), continuous (transfers).
Freshman Application Contact Mrs. Kristin Treadway, Pre-Admissions Coordinator, J. F. Drake State Technical College, Huntsville, AL 35811. *Phone:* 256-551-3111 Ext. 704. *Toll-free phone:* 888-413-7253. *E-mail:* sudeall@drakestate.edu.
Website: http://www.drakestate.edu/.

Lawson State Community College
Birmingham, Alabama

- **State-supported** 2-year, founded 1949, part of Alabama Community College System
- **Urban** 30-acre campus
- **Coed,** 3,419 undergraduate students, 57% full-time, 60% women, 40% men

Undergraduates 1,957 full-time, 1,462 part-time. Students come from 14 states and territories; 1 other country; 1% are from out of state; 75% Black or African American, non-Hispanic/Latino; 0.9% Hispanic/Latino; 0.6% Asian, non-Hispanic/Latino; 0.1% Native Hawaiian or other Pacific Islander, non-Hispanic/Latino; 0.1% American Indian or Alaska Native, non-Hispanic/Latino; 0.4% Two or more races, non-Hispanic/Latino; 8% Race/ethnicity unknown; 0.2% international; 6% transferred in; 1% live on campus. *Retention:* 51% of full-time freshmen returned.
Freshmen *Admission:* 1,596 applied, 1,311 admitted, 771 enrolled.
Faculty *Total:* 223, 39% full-time. *Student/faculty ratio:* 18:1.
Majors Accounting technology and bookkeeping; administrative assistant and secretarial science; automotive engineering technology; building/construction finishing, management, and inspection related; business administration and management; child-care and support services management; computer and information sciences; criminal justice/police science; drafting and design technology; general studies; industrial electronics technology; liberal arts and sciences/liberal studies; registered nursing/registered nurse; social work.
Academics *Calendar:* semesters. *Degree:* certificates and associate. *Special study options:* academic remediation for entering students, adult/continuing education programs, advanced placement credit, cooperative education, distance learning, internships, part-time degree program, services for LD students, summer session for credit.
Library Lawson State Library with 51,627 titles, 261 serial subscriptions, an OPAC.
Student Life *Housing Options:* coed. Campus housing is university owned. *Activities and Organizations:* choral group, Student Government Association, Phi Theta Kappa, Kappa Beta Delta Honor Society, Phi Beta Lambda, Social Work Club. *Campus security:* 24-hour emergency response devices and patrols, controlled dormitory access. *Student services:* personal/psychological counseling.
Athletics Member NJCAA. *Intercollegiate sports:* baseball M, basketball M/W, volleyball W. *Intramural sports:* weight lifting M.
Costs (2013–14) *Tuition:* state resident $3360 full-time; nonresident $3720 full-time. *Required fees:* $850 full-time. *Room and board:* $4000; room only: $3000. *Payment plan:* installment. *Waivers:* senior citizens and employees or children of employees.
Financial Aid Of all full-time matriculated undergraduates who enrolled in 2011, 91 Federal Work-Study jobs (averaging $3000).
Applying *Options:* electronic application. *Required:* high school transcript. *Application deadlines:* rolling (freshmen), rolling (transfers). *Notification:* continuous (freshmen), continuous (transfers).
Freshman Application Contact Mr. Jeff Shelley, Director of Admissions and Records, Lawson State Community College, 3060 Wilson Road, SW, Birmingham, AL 35221-1798. *Phone:* 205-929-6361. *Fax:* 205-923-7106. *E-mail:* jshelley@lawsonstate.edu.
Website: http://www.lawsonstate.edu/.

Lurleen B. Wallace Community College
Andalusia, Alabama

- **State-supported** 2-year, founded 1969, part of Alabama Community College System
- **Small-town** 200-acre campus
- **Coed,** 1,646 undergraduate students, 61% full-time, 63% women, 37% men

Undergraduates 1,000 full-time, 646 part-time. 4% are from out of state; 22% Black or African American, non-Hispanic/Latino; 0.6% Hispanic/Latino; 1% Asian, non-Hispanic/Latino; 0.4% American Indian or Alaska Native, non-Hispanic/Latino; 0.1% Two or more races, non-Hispanic/Latino; 0.6% Race/ethnicity unknown; 5% transferred in.
Freshmen *Admission:* 392 enrolled.
Faculty *Total:* 91, 70% full-time, 9% with terminal degrees. *Student/faculty ratio:* 17:1.
Majors Accounting technology and bookkeeping; administrative assistant and secretarial science; child-care and support services management; computer and information sciences; diagnostic medical sonography and ultrasound technology; drafting and design technology; electrician; emergency medical technology (EMT paramedic); forest technology; general studies; industrial electronics technology; liberal arts and sciences/liberal studies; registered nursing/registered nurse.

Academics *Calendar:* semesters. *Degree:* certificates and associate. *Special study options:* academic remediation for entering students, cooperative education, distance learning, honors programs, independent study, part-time degree program, summer session for credit.

Library Lurleen B. Wallace Library plus 2 others with 40,088 titles, 2,345 audiovisual materials, an OPAC, a Web page.

Student Life *Housing:* college housing not available. *Activities and Organizations:* drama/theater group, choral group, Student Government Association, Student Ambassadors, Interclub Council, Campus Civitan, Christian Student Ministries. *Student services:* personal/psychological counseling.

Athletics Member NJCAA. *Intercollegiate sports:* baseball M(s), basketball M(s)/W(s), softball W(s).

Costs (2012–13) *Tuition:* state resident $3270 full-time, $109 per credit hour part-time; nonresident $6540 full-time, $218 per credit hour part-time. Full-time tuition and fees vary according to course load. Part-time tuition and fees vary according to course load. *Required fees:* $690 full-time. *Waivers:* senior citizens and employees or children of employees.

Financial Aid Of all full-time matriculated undergraduates who enrolled in 2010, 903 were judged to have need.

Applying *Required:* high school transcript. *Application deadlines:* rolling (freshmen), rolling (transfers).

Freshman Application Contact Lurleen B. Wallace Community College, PO Box 1418, Andalusia, AL 36420-1418. *Phone:* 334-881-2273. *Website:* http://www.lbwcc.edu/.

Marion Military Institute
Marion, Alabama

Director of Admissions Director of Admissions, Marion Military Institute, 1101 Washington Street, Marion, AL 36756. *Phone:* 800-664-1842 Ext. 306. *Toll-free phone:* 800-664-1842.
Website: http://www.marionmilitary.edu/.

Northeast Alabama Community College
Rainsville, Alabama

- **State-supported** 2-year, founded 1963, part of Alabama Community College System
- **Rural** 117-acre campus
- **Coed**

Undergraduates 1,805 full-time, 1,489 part-time. 2% Black or African American, non-Hispanic/Latino; 4% Hispanic/Latino; 0.4% Asian, non-Hispanic/Latino; 0.1% Native Hawaiian or other Pacific Islander, non-Hispanic/Latino; 3% American Indian or Alaska Native, non-Hispanic/Latino; 0.3% Two or more races, non-Hispanic/Latino; 0.4% international. *Retention:* 58% of full-time freshmen returned.

Faculty *Student/faculty ratio:* 24:1.

Academics *Calendar:* quarters. *Degree:* certificates and associate. *Special study options:* academic remediation for entering students, accelerated degree program, adult/continuing education programs, advanced placement credit, distance learning, double majors, English as a second language, honors programs, part-time degree program, services for LD students, summer session for credit.

Student Life *Campus security:* 24-hour emergency response devices and patrols, late-night transport/escort service.

Costs (2012–13) *Tuition:* state resident $3270 full-time, $109 per credit hour part-time; nonresident $6540 full-time, $218 per credit hour part-time. *Required fees:* $870 full-time, $29 per credit hour part-time.

Financial Aid Of all full-time matriculated undergraduates who enrolled in 2011, 40 Federal Work-Study jobs (averaging $2500).

Freshman Application Contact Northeast Alabama Community College, PO Box 159, Rainsville, AL 35986-0159. *Phone:* 256-228-6001 Ext. 2325. *Website:* http://www.nacc.edu/.

Northwest-Shoals Community College
Muscle Shoals, Alabama

- **State-supported** 2-year, founded 1963, part of Alabama Department of Postsecondary Education
- **Small-town** 210-acre campus
- **Endowment** $311,484
- **Coed**, 3,717 undergraduate students, 52% full-time, 57% women, 43% men

Undergraduates 1,915 full-time, 1,802 part-time. Students come from 7 states and territories; 1 other country; 1% are from out of state; 10% Black or African American, non-Hispanic/Latino; 3% Hispanic/Latino; 0.4% Asian, non-Hispanic/Latino; 0.1% Native Hawaiian or other Pacific Islander, non-Hispanic/Latino; 0.6% American Indian or Alaska Native, non-Hispanic/Latino; 0.5% Two or more races, non-Hispanic/Latino; 0.1% Race/ethnicity unknown; 5% transferred in.

Freshmen *Admission:* 860 enrolled.

Faculty *Total:* 156, 48% full-time, 12% with terminal degrees. *Student/faculty ratio:* 22:1.

Majors Administrative assistant and secretarial science; child-care and support services management; child development; computer and information sciences; criminal justice/police science; drafting and design technology; emergency medical technology (EMT paramedic); environmental engineering technology; general studies; industrial electronics technology; industrial mechanics and maintenance technology; liberal arts and sciences/liberal studies; medical/clinical assistant; multi/interdisciplinary studies related; registered nursing/registered nurse.

Academics *Calendar:* semesters. *Degree:* certificates and associate. *Special study options:* academic remediation for entering students, accelerated degree program, adult/continuing education programs, advanced placement credit, cooperative education, distance learning, honors programs, independent study, part-time degree program, services for LD students, summer session for credit.

Library Larry W. McCoy Learning Resource Center and James Glasgow Library with 70,248 titles, 50 serial subscriptions, 1,499 audiovisual materials, an OPAC.

Student Life *Housing:* college housing not available. *Activities and Organizations:* choral group, Student Government Association, Science Club, Phi Theta Kappa, Baptist Campus Ministry, Northwest-Shoals Singers. *Campus security:* 24-hour emergency response devices. *Student services:* personal/psychological counseling.

Athletics *Intramural sports:* basketball M/W, softball M/W, table tennis M/W, tennis M/W.

Standardized Tests *Required:* COMPASS Placement Test for English and Math (for admission).

Costs (2013–14) *Tuition:* state resident $3270 full-time, $109 per credit hour part-time; nonresident $6540 full-time, $218 per credit hour part-time. *Required fees:* $810 full-time, $27 per credit hour part-time. *Waivers:* senior citizens and employees or children of employees.

Financial Aid Of all full-time matriculated undergraduates who enrolled in 2012, 46 Federal Work-Study jobs (averaging $1605). *Financial aid deadline:* 6/1.

Applying *Options:* electronic application. *Required:* high school transcript. *Application deadlines:* rolling (freshmen), rolling (transfers). *Notification:* continuous (transfers).

Freshman Application Contact Mr. Charles Taylor, Associate Dean of Student Development Services, Northwest-Shoals Community College, PO Box 2545, Muscle Shoals, AL 35662. *Phone:* 256-331-5462. *Toll-free phone:* 800-645-8967. *Fax:* 256-331-5366. *E-mail:* taylor@nwscc.edu. *Website:* http://www.nwscc.edu/.

Prince Institute of Professional Studies
Montgomery, Alabama

Freshman Application Contact Kellie Brescia, Director of Admissions, Prince Institute of Professional Studies, 7735 Atlanta Highway, Montgomery, AL 35117. *Phone:* 334-271-1670. *Toll-free phone:* 877-853-5569. *Fax:* 334-271-1671. *E-mail:* admissions@princeinstitute.edu. *Website:* http://www.princeinstitute.edu/.

Reid State Technical College
Evergreen, Alabama

- **State-supported** 2-year, founded 1966, part of Alabama Community College System
- **Rural** 26-acre campus
- **Coed**, 495 undergraduate students, 63% full-time, 60% women, 40% men

Undergraduates 312 full-time, 183 part-time. Students come from 2 states and territories; 1% are from out of state; 53% Black or African American, non-Hispanic/Latino; 0.4% Hispanic/Latino; 0.2% Native Hawaiian or other Pacific Islander, non-Hispanic/Latino; 0.4% American Indian or Alaska Native, non-Hispanic/Latino; 0.4% Two or more races, non-Hispanic/Latino; 0.2% Race/ethnicity unknown.

Freshmen *Admission:* 122 applied, 122 admitted, 95 enrolled.

Faculty *Total:* 37, 73% full-time, 11% with terminal degrees. *Student/faculty ratio:* 12:1.

Majors Administrative assistant and secretarial science; child-care and support services management; electrical, electronic and communications engineering technology.

Academics *Calendar:* semesters. *Degree:* certificates, diplomas, and associate. *Special study options:* academic remediation for entering students, adult/continuing education programs, double majors, independent study, internships, part-time degree program, services for LD students, summer session for credit.

Library Edith A. Gray Library with 4,157 titles, 99 serial subscriptions, 298 audiovisual materials, a Web page.

Student Life *Housing:* college housing not available. *Activities and Organizations:* Student Government Association, Phi Beta Lambda, National Vocational-Technical Society, Ambassadors, Who's Who. *Campus security:* 24-hour emergency response devices, day and evening security guard. *Student services:* personal/psychological counseling.

Costs (2013–14) *Tuition:* state resident $3270 full-time, $109 per credit hour part-time; nonresident $6540 full-time, $218 per credit hour part-time. Full-time tuition and fees vary according to course load and program. Part-time tuition and fees vary according to course load and program. *Required fees:* $930 full-time, $30 per credit hour part-time. *Waivers:* senior citizens and employees or children of employees.

Financial Aid Of all full-time matriculated undergraduates who enrolled in 2011, 35 Federal Work-Study jobs (averaging $1500).

Applying *Options:* early admission. *Required:* high school transcript. *Application deadlines:* rolling (freshmen), rolling (transfers).

Freshman Application Contact Dr. Alesia Stuart, Public Relations/Marketing/Associate Dean of Workforce Development, Reid State Technical College, Evergreen, AL 36401-0588. *Phone:* 251-578-1313 Ext. 108. *E-mail:* akstuart@rstc.edu.
Website: http://www.rstc.edu/.

Remington College–Mobile Campus
Mobile, Alabama

Freshman Application Contact Remington College–Mobile Campus, 828 Downtowner Loop West, Mobile, AL 36609-5404. *Phone:* 251-343-8200. *Toll-free phone:* 800-560-6192.
Website: http://www.remingtoncollege.edu/.

Shelton State Community College
Tuscaloosa, Alabama

- **State-supported** 2-year, founded 1979, part of Alabama Community College System
- **Small-town** 202-acre campus with easy access to Birmingham
- **Coed,** 5,104 undergraduate students, 53% full-time, 57% women, 43% men

Undergraduates 2,699 full-time, 2,405 part-time. 3% are from out of state; 34% Black or African American, non-Hispanic/Latino; 0.9% Hispanic/Latino; 1% Asian, non-Hispanic/Latino; 0.2% American Indian or Alaska Native, non-Hispanic/Latino; 1% Two or more races, non-Hispanic/Latino; 8% Race/ethnicity unknown; 0.2% international; 9% transferred in. *Retention:* 53% of full-time freshmen returned.

Freshmen *Admission:* 1,209 enrolled.

Faculty *Total:* 254, 38% full-time. *Student/faculty ratio:* 24:1.

Majors Administrative assistant and secretarial science; business/commerce; culinary arts; diesel mechanics technology; drafting and design technology; electrical, electronic and communications engineering technology; electrician; general studies; heating, ventilation, air conditioning and refrigeration engineering technology; industrial electronics technology; liberal arts and sciences/liberal studies; machine tool technology; medical administrative assistant and medical secretary; precision metal working related; registered nursing/registered nurse; respiratory care therapy; tool and die technology; welding technology.

Academics *Calendar:* semesters. *Degree:* certificates, diplomas, and associate. *Special study options:* academic remediation for entering students, accelerated degree program, adult/continuing education programs, advanced placement credit, cooperative education, distance learning, double majors, part-time degree program, services for LD students, summer session for credit. *ROTC:* Army (c), Air Force (c).

Library Brooks-Cork Library plus 1 other with an OPAC, a Web page.

Student Life *Housing:* college housing not available. *Activities and Organizations:* drama/theater group, choral group, Phi Theta Kappa, Student Government Association, African American Cultural Association, Red Cross Club. *Campus security:* 24-hour emergency response devices and patrols.

Athletics Member NJCAA. *Intercollegiate sports:* baseball M(s), basketball M(s)/W(s), cheerleading M(s)/W(s), softball W(s). *Intramural sports:* fencing M/W.

Costs (2013–14) *Tuition:* state resident $3270 full-time, $109 per credit part-time; nonresident $6450 full-time, $218 per credit part-time. Full-time tuition and fees vary according to course load and reciprocity agreements. Part-time tuition and fees vary according to course load and reciprocity agreements.

Required fees: $870 full-time, $18 per credit part-time. *Waivers:* senior citizens and employees or children of employees.

Applying *Options:* electronic application. *Required:* high school transcript. *Application deadlines:* rolling (freshmen), rolling (transfers).

Freshman Application Contact Ms. Loretta Jones, Assistant to the Dean of Students, Shelton State Community College, 9500 Old Greensboro Road, Tuscaloosa, AL 35405. *Phone:* 205-391-2236. *Fax:* 205-391-3910. *E-mail:* ljones@sheltonstate.edu.
Website: http://www.sheltonstate.edu/.

Snead State Community College
Boaz, Alabama

Freshman Application Contact Dr. Greg Chapman, Director of Instruction, Snead State Community College, PO Box 734, Boaz, AL 35957-0734. *Phone:* 256-840-4111. *Fax:* 256-593-7180. *E-mail:* gchapman@snead.edu.
Website: http://www.snead.edu/.

Southern Union State Community College
Wadley, Alabama

Freshman Application Contact Admissions Office, Southern Union State Community College, PO Box 1000, Roberts Street, Wadley, AL 36276. *Phone:* 256-395-5157. *E-mail:* info@suscc.edu.
Website: http://www.suscc.edu/.

Virginia College in Huntsville
Huntsville, Alabama

Freshman Application Contact Director of Admission, Virginia College in Huntsville, 2021 Drake Avenue SW, Huntsville, AL 35801. *Phone:* 256-533-7387. *Fax:* 256-533-7785.
Website: http://www.vc.edu/.

Wallace State Community College
Hanceville, Alabama

Director of Admissions Ms. Linda Sperling, Director of Admissions, Wallace State Community College, PO Box 2000, 801 Main Street, Hanceville, AL 35077-2000. *Phone:* 256-352-8278. *Toll-free phone:* 866-350-9722.
Website: http://www.wallacestate.edu/.

ALASKA

Charter College
Anchorage, Alaska

Director of Admissions Ms. Lily Sirianni, Vice President, Charter College, 2221 East Northern Lights Boulevard, Suite 120, Anchorage, AK 99508. *Phone:* 907-277-1000. *Toll-free phone:* 888-200-9942.
Website: http://www.chartercollege.edu/.

Ilisagvik College
Barrow, Alaska

Freshman Application Contact Janelle Everett, Recruiter, Ilisagvik College, UIC/Narl, Barrow, AK 99723. *Phone:* 907-852-1799. *Toll-free phone:* 800-478-7337. *E-mail:* janelle.everett@ilisagvik.edu.
Website: http://www.ilisagvik.edu/.

University of Alaska Anchorage, Kenai Peninsula College
Soldotna, Alaska

- **State-supported** primarily 2-year, founded 1964, part of University of Alaska System
- **Rural** 360-acre campus
- **Coed,** 2,733 undergraduate students

Majors Business administration and management; digital communication and media/multimedia; early childhood education; elementary education; emergency medical technology (EMT paramedic); human services; liberal arts and sciences/liberal studies; occupational safety and health technology; psychology.

Academics *Calendar:* semesters. *Degrees:* certificates, associate, and bachelor's. *Special study options:* academic remediation for entering students, adult/continuing education programs, advanced placement credit, cooperative education, distance learning, English as a second language, part-time degree program, services for LD students.

Library Kenai Peninsula College Library.

Student Life *Housing Options:* coed. *Campus security:* 24-hour emergency response devices. *Student services:* health clinic.

Standardized Tests *Required:* ACT, SAT or ACCUPLACER scores (for admission).

Financial Aid Of all full-time matriculated undergraduates who enrolled in 2011, 50 Federal Work-Study jobs (averaging $3000). 50 state and other part-time jobs (averaging $3000).

Applying *Options:* electronic application. *Application fee:* $40. *Required:* high school transcript. *Application deadlines:* rolling (freshmen), rolling (transfers).

Freshman Application Contact Ms. Shelly Love Blatchford, Admission and Registration Coordinator, University of Alaska Anchorage, Kenai Peninsula College, 156 College Road, Soldotna, AK 99669-9798. *Phone:* 907-262-0311. *Toll-free phone:* 877-262-0330. *Website:* http://www.kpc.alaska.edu/.

University of Alaska Anchorage, Kodiak College
Kodiak, Alaska

- **State-supported** 2-year, founded 1968, part of University of Alaska System
- **Rural** 68-acre campus
- **Coed**

Undergraduates 148 full-time, 331 part-time. Students come from 18 states and territories; 3 other countries; 2% Black or African American, non-Hispanic/Latino; 8% Hispanic/Latino; 6% Asian, non-Hispanic/Latino; 0.8% Native Hawaiian or other Pacific Islander, non-Hispanic/Latino; 12% American Indian or Alaska Native, non-Hispanic/Latino; 6% Two or more races, non-Hispanic/Latino; 4% Race/ethnicity unknown; 2% international.

Faculty *Student/faculty ratio:* 13:1.

Academics *Calendar:* semesters. *Degree:* certificates and associate. *Special study options:* academic remediation for entering students, adult/continuing education programs, advanced placement credit, distance learning, double majors, part-time degree program, study abroad, summer session for credit.

Standardized Tests *Required:* ACCUPLACER (for admission).

Costs (2012–13) *Tuition:* state resident $4320 full-time, $144 per credit part-time; nonresident $13,450 full-time, $580 per credit part-time. *Required fees:* $340 full-time, $8 per credit part-time, $5 per term part-time.

Applying *Options:* electronic application. *Application fee:* $40. *Required for some:* high school transcript.

Freshman Application Contact University of Alaska Anchorage, Kodiak College, 117 Benny Benson Drive, Kodiak, AK 99615-6643. *Phone:* 907-486-1235. *Toll-free phone:* 800-486-7660. *Website:* http://www.koc.alaska.edu/.

University of Alaska Anchorage, Matanuska-Susitna College
Palmer, Alaska

Freshman Application Contact Ms. Sandra Gravley, Student Services Director, University of Alaska Anchorage, Matanuska-Susitna College, PO Box 2889, Palmer, AK 99645-2889. *Phone:* 907-745-9712. *Fax:* 907-745-9747. *E-mail:* info@matsu.alaska.edu. *Website:* http://www.matsu.alaska.edu/.

University of Alaska, Prince William Sound Community College
Valdez, Alaska

Freshman Application Contact Mr. Nathan J. Platt, Director of Student Services, University of Alaska, Prince William Sound Community College, PO Box 97, Valdez, AK 99686-0097. *Phone:* 907-834-1631. *Toll-free phone:* 800-478-8800. *E-mail:* studentservices@pwscc.edu. *Website:* http://www.pwscc.edu/.

University of Alaska Southeast, Ketchikan Campus
Ketchikan, Alaska

Freshman Application Contact Admissions Office, University of Alaska Southeast, Ketchikan Campus, 2600 7th Avenue, Ketchikan, AK 99901-5798. *Phone:* 907-225-6177. *Toll-free phone:* 888-550-6177. *Fax:* 907-225-3895. *E-mail:* ketch.info@uas.alaska.edu. *Website:* http://www.ketch.alaska.edu/.

University of Alaska Southeast, Sitka Campus
Sitka, Alaska

Freshman Application Contact Cynthia Rogers, Coordinator of Admissions, University of Alaska Southeast, Sitka Campus, 1332 Seward Avenue, Sitka, AK 99835-9418. *Phone:* 907-747-7705. *Toll-free phone:* 800-478-6653. *Fax:* 907-747-7793. *E-mail:* cynthia.rogers@uas.alaska.edu. *Website:* http://www.uas.alaska.edu/.

AMERICAN SAMOA

American Samoa Community College
Pago Pago, American Samoa

Director of Admissions Sifagatogo Tuitasi, Admissions, American Samoa Community College, PO Box 2609, Pago Pago, AS 96799-2609. *Phone:* 684-699-1141. *E-mail:* admissions@amsamoa.edu. *Website:* http://www.amsamoa.edu/.

ARIZONA

Anthem College–Phoenix
Phoenix, Arizona

Freshman Application Contact Mr. Glen Husband, Vice President of Admissions, Anthem College–Phoenix, 1515 East Indian School Road, Phoenix, AZ 85014-4901. *Phone:* 602-279-9700. *Toll-free phone:* 855-331-7767. *Website:* http://anthem.edu/phoenix-arizona/.

Arizona Automotive Institute
Glendale, Arizona

Director of Admissions Director of Admissions, Arizona Automotive Institute, 6829 North 46th Avenue, Glendale, AZ 85301-3597. *Phone:* 623-934-7273 Ext. 211. *Toll-free phone:* 800-321-5861 (in-state); 800-321-5961 (out-of-state). *Fax:* 623-937-5000. *E-mail:* info@azautoinst.com. *Website:* http://www.aai.edu/.

Arizona College
Glendale, Arizona

Freshman Application Contact Admissions Department, Arizona College, 4425 West Olive Avenue, Suite 300, Glendale, AZ 85302-3843. *Phone:* 602-222-9300. *E-mail:* lhicks@arizonacollege.edu. *Website:* http://www.arizonacollege.edu/.

Arizona Western College
Yuma, Arizona

- **State and locally supported** 2-year, founded 1962, part of Arizona State Community College System
- **Rural** 640-acre campus
- **Coed**, 7,854 undergraduate students, 35% full-time, 57% women, 43% men

Undergraduates 2,725 full-time, 5,129 part-time. Students come from 37 states and territories; 31 other countries; 3% are from out of state; 3% Black or African American, non-Hispanic/Latino; 63% Hispanic/Latino; 1% Asian, non-Hispanic/Latino; 0.3% Native Hawaiian or other Pacific Islander, non-Hispanic/Latino; 1% American Indian or Alaska Native, non-Hispanic/Latino;

0.1% Two or more races, non-Hispanic/Latino; 3% Race/ethnicity unknown; 8% international; 3% live on campus.

Freshmen *Admission:* 1,789 enrolled.

Faculty *Total:* 444, 26% full-time. *Student/faculty ratio:* 20:1.

Majors Accounting; agricultural business and management; agriculture; architectural technology; biology/biological sciences; business administration and management; business/commerce; carpentry; chemistry; civil engineering technology; computer and information sciences; computer graphics; construction trades related; criminal justice/law enforcement administration; crop production; data entry/microcomputer applications; dramatic/theater arts; early childhood education; electrical/electronics equipment installation and repair; elementary education; emergency medical technology (EMT paramedic); engineering; English; environmental science; fine/studio arts; fire science/firefighting; general studies; geology/earth science; health services/allied health/health sciences; heating, air conditioning, ventilation and refrigeration maintenance technology; history; hospitality administration; industrial technology; legal administrative assistant/secretary; logistics, materials, and supply chain management; marketing/marketing management; massage therapy; mass communication/media; mathematics; music; office management; parks, recreation and leisure facilities management; philosophy; physics; plumbing technology; political science and government; prenursing studies; radio and television broadcasting technology; radiologic technology/science; secondary education; social sciences; solar energy technology; Spanish; welding technology; work and family studies.

Academics *Calendar:* semesters. *Degree:* certificates and associate. *Special study options:* academic remediation for entering students, adult/continuing education programs, advanced placement credit, cooperative education, distance learning, English as a second language, honors programs, independent study, part-time degree program, services for LD students, summer session for credit.

Library Arizona Western College Library with 109,016 titles, 290 serial subscriptions, 5,109 audiovisual materials, an OPAC, a Web page.

Student Life *Housing Options:* coed. Campus housing is university owned. *Activities and Organizations:* drama/theater group, student-run newspaper, radio and television station, choral group, Student Government Association, Spirit Squad, Dance Team, Students in Free Enterprise (SIFE), International Students Team, national fraternities, national sororities. *Campus security:* 24-hour emergency response devices and patrols, student patrols, late-night transport/escort service. *Student services:* health clinic, personal/psychological counseling.

Athletics Member NJCAA. *Intercollegiate sports:* baseball M(s), basketball M(s)/W(s), football M(s), soccer M(s), softball W(s), volleyball W(s). *Intramural sports:* cheerleading M(c)/W(c).

Standardized Tests *Required for some:* SAT or ACT (for admission).

Costs (2013–14) *Tuition:* state resident $1776 full-time, $74 per credit hour part-time; nonresident $7224 full-time, $301 per credit hour part-time. Full-time tuition and fees vary according to course load and program. Part-time tuition and fees vary according to course load and program. *Room and board:* $5828; room only: $2152. Room and board charges vary according to board plan. *Payment plan:* installment. *Waivers:* senior citizens and employees or children of employees.

Financial Aid Of all full-time matriculated undergraduates who enrolled in 2011, 350 Federal Work-Study jobs (averaging $1500). 100 state and other part-time jobs (averaging $1800).

Applying *Options:* electronic application, early admission, deferred entrance. *Application deadlines:* rolling (freshmen), rolling (out-of-state freshmen), rolling (transfers).

Freshman Application Contact Amy Pignatore, Director of Admissions/Registrar, Arizona Western College, PO Box 929, Yuma, AZ 85366. *Phone:* 928-317-7600. *Toll-free phone:* 888-293-0392. *Fax:* 928-344-7712. *E-mail:* amy.pignatore@azwestern.edu. *Website:* http://www.azwestern.edu/.

Brown Mackie College–Phoenix

Phoenix, Arizona

Freshman Application Contact Brown Mackie College–Phoenix, 13430 North Black Canyon Highway, Suite 190, Phoenix, AZ 85029. *Phone:* 602-337-3044. *Toll-free phone:* 866-824-4793. *Website:* http://www.brownmackie.edu/phoenix/.

See display below and page 384 for the College Close-Up.

Brown Mackie College–Tucson

Tucson, Arizona

Freshman Application Contact Brown Mackie College–Tucson, 4585 East Speedway, Suite 204, Tucson, AZ 85712. *Phone:* 520-319-3300. *Website:* http://www.brownmackie.edu/tucson/.

See display below and page 396 for the College Close-Up.

The Bryman School of Arizona
Phoenix, Arizona

Freshman Application Contact Admissions Office, The Bryman School of Arizona, 2250 West Peoria Avenue, Phoenix, AZ 85029. *Phone:* 602-274-4300. *Toll-free phone:* 866-381-6383 (in-state); 866-391-6383 (out-of-state). *Fax:* 602-248-9087.
Website: http://www.brymanschool.edu/.

Carrington College–Mesa
Mesa, Arizona

- **Proprietary** 2-year, founded 1977, part of Carrington Colleges Group, Inc.
- **Suburban** campus
- **Coed,** 685 undergraduate students, 100% full-time, 81% women, 19% men

Undergraduates 685 full-time. 7% Black or African American, non-Hispanic/Latino; 24% Hispanic/Latino; 0.9% Asian, non-Hispanic/Latino; 0.9% Native Hawaiian or other Pacific Islander, non-Hispanic/Latino; 11% American Indian or Alaska Native, non-Hispanic/Latino; 3% Two or more races, non-Hispanic/Latino; 3% Race/ethnicity unknown.
Freshmen *Admission:* 78 enrolled.
Faculty *Total:* 45, 42% full-time. *Student/faculty ratio:* 25:1.
Majors Dental hygiene; medical office management; physical therapy technology; respiratory care therapy; respiratory therapy technician.
Academics *Calendar:* semesters. *Degree:* certificates and associate.
Student Life *Housing:* college housing not available.
Standardized Tests *Required:* Entrance test administered by Carrington College (for admission).
Applying *Required:* essay or personal statement, high school transcript, interview.
Freshman Application Contact Carrington College–Mesa, 1001 West Southern Avenue, Suite 130, Mesa, AZ 85210.
Website: http://carrington.edu/.

Carrington College–Phoenix
Phoenix, Arizona

- **Proprietary** 2-year, founded 1976, part of Carrington Colleges Group, Inc.
- **Urban** campus
- **Coed,** 560 undergraduate students, 100% full-time, 85% women, 15% men

Undergraduates 560 full-time. 5% Black or African American, non-Hispanic/Latino; 47% Hispanic/Latino; 1% Asian, non-Hispanic/Latino; 0.7% Native Hawaiian or other Pacific Islander, non-Hispanic/Latino; 9% American Indian or Alaska Native, non-Hispanic/Latino; 2% Two or more races, non-Hispanic/Latino; 2% Race/ethnicity unknown.
Freshmen *Admission:* 160 enrolled.
Faculty *Total:* 27, 59% full-time. *Student/faculty ratio:* 28:1.
Majors Massage therapy; medical office management; occupational therapy; radiologic technology/science; registered nursing/registered nurse; respiratory care therapy.
Academics *Calendar:* continuous. *Degree:* certificates and associate.
Student Life *Housing:* college housing not available.
Standardized Tests *Required:* Entrance test administered by Carrington College (for admission).
Applying *Required:* essay or personal statement, high school transcript, interview.
Freshman Application Contact Carrington College–Phoenix, 8503 North 27th Avenue, Phoenix, AZ 85051.
Website: http://carrington.edu/.

Carrington College–Phoenix Westside
Phoenix, Arizona

- **Proprietary** 2-year, part of Carrington Colleges Group, Inc.
- **Urban** campus
- **Coed,** 542 undergraduate students, 100% full-time, 63% women, 37% men

Undergraduates 542 full-time. 8% Black or African American, non-Hispanic/Latino; 28% Hispanic/Latino; 3% Asian, non-Hispanic/Latino; 0.4% Native Hawaiian or other Pacific Islander, non-Hispanic/Latino; 4% American Indian or Alaska Native, non-Hispanic/Latino; 1% Two or more races, non-Hispanic/Latino; 2% Race/ethnicity unknown.
Freshmen *Admission:* 13 enrolled.

Faculty *Total:* 40, 40% full-time. *Student/faculty ratio:* 23:1.
Majors Clinical/medical laboratory technology; hospital and health-care facilities administration; medical radiologic technology; occupational therapist assistant; registered nursing/registered nurse; respiratory therapy technician.
Academics *Calendar:* semesters. *Degree:* certificates and associate.
Student Life *Housing:* college housing not available.
Standardized Tests *Required:* Entrance test administered by Carrington College (for admission).
Applying *Required:* essay or personal statement, high school transcript, interview. *Application deadlines:* rolling (freshmen), rolling (transfers). *Notification:* continuous (freshmen), continuous (transfers).
Freshman Application Contact Carrington College–Phoenix Westside, 2701 West Bethany Home Road, Phoenix, AZ 85017.
Website: http://carrington.edu/.

Carrington College–Tucson
Tucson, Arizona

- **Proprietary** 2-year, founded 1984, part of Carrington Colleges Group, Inc.
- **Suburban** campus
- **Coed,** 399 undergraduate students, 100% full-time, 79% women, 21% men

Undergraduates 399 full-time. 3% Black or African American, non-Hispanic/Latino; 57% Hispanic/Latino; 0.5% Asian, non-Hispanic/Latino; 5% American Indian or Alaska Native, non-Hispanic/Latino; 0.5% Two or more races, non-Hispanic/Latino; 4% Race/ethnicity unknown.
Freshmen *Admission:* 77 enrolled.
Faculty *Total:* 16, 56% full-time. *Student/faculty ratio:* 35:1.
Majors Clinical/medical laboratory technology; medical office management.
Academics *Calendar:* semesters modular courses are offered. *Degree:* certificates and associate.
Student Life *Housing:* college housing not available. *Student services:* personal/psychological counseling, legal services.
Standardized Tests *Required:* Entrance test administered by Carrington College (for admission).
Applying *Required:* essay or personal statement, high school transcript, interview.
Freshman Application Contact Carrington College–Tucson, 3550 North Oracle Road, Tucson, AZ 85705.
Website: http://carrington.edu/.

Central Arizona College
Coolidge, Arizona

Freshman Application Contact Dr. James Moore, Dean of Records and Admissions, Central Arizona College, 8470 North Overfield Road, Coolidge, AZ 85128. *Phone:* 520-494-5261. *Toll-free phone:* 800-237-9814. *Fax:* 520-426-5083. *E-mail:* james.moore@centralaz.edu.
Website: http://www.centralaz.edu/.

Chandler-Gilbert Community College
Chandler, Arizona

- **State and locally supported** 2-year, founded 1985, part of Maricopa County Community College District System
- **Suburban** 80-acre campus with easy access to Phoenix
- **Coed**

Undergraduates 4,424 full-time, 9,606 part-time. Students come from 38 states and territories; 37 other countries; 2% are from out of state; 4% Black or African American, non-Hispanic/Latino; 19% Hispanic/Latino; 5% Asian, non-Hispanic/Latino; 0.3% Native Hawaiian or other Pacific Islander, non-Hispanic/Latino; 1% American Indian or Alaska Native, non-Hispanic/Latino; 2% Two or more races, non-Hispanic/Latino; 11% Race/ethnicity unknown; 0.5% international; 4% transferred in. *Retention:* 61% of full-time freshmen returned.
Faculty *Student/faculty ratio:* 25:1.
Academics *Calendar:* semesters. *Degree:* certificates, diplomas, and associate. *Special study options:* academic remediation for entering students, advanced placement credit, English as a second language, freshman honors college, honors programs, independent study, part-time degree program, services for LD students, study abroad, summer session for credit.
Student Life *Campus security:* 24-hour emergency response devices and patrols, late-night transport/escort service.
Athletics Member NJCAA.
Costs (2012–13) *Tuition:* area resident $1824 full-time, $76 per credit hour part-time; state resident $7200 full-time, $300 per credit hour part-time; non-resident $7608 full-time, $317 per credit hour part-time. Full-time tuition and fees vary according to reciprocity agreements. Part-time tuition and fees vary

according to reciprocity agreements. *Required fees:* $30 full-time, $15 per term part-time. *Payment plans:* installment, deferred payment.

Applying *Options:* electronic application.

Freshman Application Contact Ryan Cain, Coordinator of Enrollment Services, Chandler-Gilbert Community College, 2626 East Pecos Road, Chandler, AZ 85225-2479. *Phone:* 480-732-7044. *E-mail:* ryan.cain@ cgcmail.maricopa.edu.
Website: http://www.cgc.maricopa.edu/.

Cochise College
Sierra Vista, Arizona

- **State and locally supported** 2-year, founded 1977
- **Small-town** 518-acre campus with easy access to Tucson
- **Coed,** 4,516 undergraduate students, 33% full-time, 54% women, 46% men

Undergraduates 1,507 full-time, 3,009 part-time. Students come from 40 states and territories; 2 other countries; 9% are from out of state; 6% Black or African American, non-Hispanic/Latino; 43% Hispanic/Latino; 2% Asian, non-Hispanic/Latino; 0.6% Native Hawaiian or other Pacific Islander, non-Hispanic/Latino; 0.8% American Indian or Alaska Native, non-Hispanic/Latino; 2% Two or more races, non-Hispanic/Latino; 2% Race/ethnicity unknown; 0.2% international; 20% transferred in; 3% live on campus. *Retention:* 55% of full-time freshmen returned.

Freshmen *Admission:* 1,758 applied, 1,758 admitted, 724 enrolled. *Average high school GPA:* 2.75.

Faculty *Total:* 349, 25% full-time.

Majors Administrative assistant and secretarial science; adult and continuing education; agricultural business and management; air and space operations technology; airline pilot and flight crew; anthropology; art; art teacher education; automobile/automotive mechanics technology; avionics maintenance technology; biology/biological sciences; building construction technology; business administration and management; chemistry; computer and information systems security; computer programming; computer science; computer systems networking and telecommunications; criminal justice/police science; culinary arts; data processing and data processing technology; dramatic/theater arts; early childhood education; economics; electrical, electronic and communications engineering technology; elementary education; emergency medical technology (EMT paramedic); engineering; English; English/language arts teacher education; fire science/firefighting; foreign language teacher education; general studies; health and physical education/fitness; history; history teacher education; humanities; information science/studies; intelligence; journalism; logistics, materials, and supply chain management; mathematics; music; philosophy; physics; political science and government; psychology; registered nursing/registered nurse; respiratory care therapy; social work; sociology; speech communication and rhetoric; welding technology.

Academics *Calendar:* semesters. *Degree:* certificates and associate. *Special study options:* academic remediation for entering students, adult/continuing education programs, advanced placement credit, cooperative education, distance learning, English as a second language, honors programs, independent study, internships, part-time degree program, services for LD students, summer session for credit.

Library Charles DiPeso and Andrea Cracchiolo Libraries with 101,262 titles, 6,364 serial subscriptions, 3,508 audiovisual materials, an OPAC, a Web page.

Student Life *Housing Options:* coed, disabled students. Campus housing is university owned. *Activities and Organizations:* drama/theater group, student-run newspaper, choral group, Student Nurses, Phi Theta Kappa, Strong Oak. *Campus security:* 24-hour emergency response devices and patrols. *Student services:* personal/psychological counseling.

Athletics Member NJCAA. *Intercollegiate sports:* baseball M(s), basketball M(s)/W(s), soccer W(s).

Costs (2013–14) *Tuition:* state resident $2190 full-time, $73 per credit hour part-time; nonresident $7500 full-time, $250 per credit hour part-time. Full-time tuition and fees vary according to course load, program, and reciprocity agreements. Part-time tuition and fees vary according to course load, program, and reciprocity agreements. *Room and board:* $6160. Room and board charges vary according to housing facility. *Payment plan:* installment. *Waivers:* senior citizens and employees or children of employees.

Financial Aid Of all full-time matriculated undergraduates who enrolled in 2011, 1,174 applied for aid, 1,065 were judged to have need. In 2011, 19 non-need-based awards were made. *Average financial aid package:* $5486. *Average need-based loan:* $3130. *Average need-based gift aid:* $3341. *Average non-need-based aid:* $1353.

Applying *Options:* electronic application, deferred entrance. *Recommended:* high school transcript. *Application deadlines:* rolling (freshmen), rolling (out-of-state freshmen), rolling (transfers). *Notification:* continuous (freshmen), continuous (out-of-state freshmen), continuous (transfers).

Freshman Application Contact Ms. Debbie Quick, Director of Admissions and Records, Cochise College, 901 North Colombo Avenue, Sierra Vista, AZ 85635-2317. *Phone:* 520-515-3640. *Toll-free phone:* 800-593-9567. *Fax:* 520-515-5452. *E-mail:* quickd@cochise.edu.
Website: http://www.cochise.edu/.

Coconino Community College
Flagstaff, Arizona

Freshman Application Contact Miss Veronica Hipolito, Director of Student Services, Coconino Community College, 2800 South Lone Tree Road, Flagstaff, AZ 86001. *Phone:* 928-226-4334 Ext. 4334. *Toll-free phone:* 800-350-7122. *Fax:* 928-226-4114. *E-mail:* veronica.hipolito@coconino.edu.
Website: http://www.coconino.edu/.

CollegeAmerica–Flagstaff
Flagstaff, Arizona

- **Private** primarily 2-year
- **Coed,** 200 undergraduate students

Majors Computer systems networking and telecommunications; health/healthcare administration; medical/health management and clinical assistant.

Academics *Degrees:* associate and bachelor's.

Library Main Library plus 1 other.

Freshman Application Contact CollegeAmerica–Flagstaff, 3012 East Route 66, Flagstaff, AZ 86004. *Phone:* 928-213-6060 Ext. 1402. *Toll-free phone:* 800-622-2894.
Website: http://www.collegeamerica.edu/.

Diné College
Tsaile, Arizona

Freshman Application Contact Mrs. Louise Litzin, Registrar, Diné College, PO Box 67, Tsaile, AZ 86556. *Phone:* 928-724-6633. *Toll-free phone:* 877-988-DINE. *Fax:* 928-724-3349. *E-mail:* loulse@dinecollege.edu.
Website: http://www.dinecollege.edu/.

Eastern Arizona College
Thatcher, Arizona

- **State and locally supported** 2-year, founded 1888, part of Arizona State Community College System
- **Small-town** campus
- **Endowment** $3.6 million
- **Coed**

Undergraduates 2,154 full-time, 4,843 part-time. Students come from 34 states and territories; 25 other countries; 5% are from out of state; 4% Black or African American, non-Hispanic/Latino; 19% Hispanic/Latino; 1% Asian, non-Hispanic/Latino; 0.1% Native Hawaiian or other Pacific Islander, non-Hispanic/Latino; 7% American Indian or Alaska Native, non-Hispanic/Latino; 0.6% Two or more races, non-Hispanic/Latino; 0.3% Race/ethnicity unknown; 0.6% international; 2% transferred in; 5% live on campus.

Faculty *Student/faculty ratio:* 25:1.

Academics *Calendar:* semesters. *Degree:* certificates and associate. *Special study options:* academic remediation for entering students, adult/continuing education programs, advanced placement credit, cooperative education, distance learning, double majors, independent study, internships, part-time degree program, services for LD students, study abroad, summer session for credit.

Student Life *Campus security:* 24-hour emergency response devices, late-night transport/escort service, controlled dormitory access, 20-hour patrols by trained security personnel.

Athletics Member NJCAA.

Costs (2012–13) *Tuition:* state resident $1760 full-time; nonresident $8360 full-time. *Room and board:* $5390. Room and board charges vary according to board plan.

Financial Aid Of all full-time matriculated undergraduates who enrolled in 2010, 1,610 applied for aid, 1,468 were judged to have need, 72 had their need fully met. In 2010, 133. *Average percent of need met:* 56. *Average financial aid package:* $5999. *Average need-based gift aid:* $5241. *Average non-need-based aid:* $3122.

Applying *Options:* electronic application, early admission, deferred entrance. *Recommended:* high school transcript.

Freshman Application Contact Erline Norton, Records Assistant, Eastern Arizona College, 615 North Stadium Avenue, Thatcher, AZ 85552-0769. *Phone:* 928-428-8250. *Toll-free phone:* 800-678-3808. *Fax:* 928-428-2578. *E-mail:* admissions@eac.edu.
Website: http://www.eac.edu/.

Estrella Mountain Community College

Avondale, Arizona

Freshman Application Contact Estrella Mountain Community College, 3000 North Dysart Road, Avondale, AZ 85392. *Phone:* 623-935-8812. *Website:* http://www.emc.maricopa.edu/.

Everest College

Phoenix, Arizona

Freshman Application Contact Mr. Jim Askins, Director of Admissions, Everest College, 10400 North 25th Avenue, Suite 190, Phoenix, AZ 85021. *Phone:* 602-942-4141. *Toll-free phone:* 888-741-4270. *Fax:* 602-943-0960. *E-mail:* jaskins@cci.edu. *Website:* http://www.everest.edu/.

GateWay Community College

Phoenix, Arizona

- **State and locally supported** 2-year, founded 1968, part of Maricopa County Community College District System
- **Urban** 20-acre campus
- **Coed**

Undergraduates 191 full-time, 525 part-time. 11% Black or African American, non-Hispanic/Latino; 26% Hispanic/Latino; 4% Asian, non-Hispanic/Latino; 0.2% Native Hawaiian or other Pacific Islander, non-Hispanic/Latino; 4% American Indian or Alaska Native, non-Hispanic/Latino; 9% Race/ethnicity unknown; 1% international.

Faculty *Student/faculty ratio:* 18:1.

Academics *Calendar:* semesters. *Degree:* certificates, diplomas, and associate. *Special study options:* academic remediation for entering students, accelerated degree program, adult/continuing education programs, advanced placement credit, cooperative education, distance learning, double majors, English as a second language, freshman honors college, honors programs, independent study, internships, off-campus study, part-time degree program, services for LD students, study abroad, summer session for credit. *ROTC:* Army (c), Air Force (c).

Student Life *Campus security:* 24-hour emergency response devices and patrols, student patrols, late-night transport/escort service.

Athletics Member NJCAA.

Costs (2012–13) *Tuition:* state resident $1824 full-time, $76 per credit hour part-time; nonresident $7608 full-time, $317 per credit hour part-time. *Required fees:* $30 full-time. *Payment plans:* installment, deferred payment.

Applying *Options:* electronic application, early admission, deferred entrance. *Required for some:* high school transcript, interview.

Freshman Application Contact Director of Admissions and Records, GateWay Community College, 108 North 40th Street, Phoenix, AZ 85034. *Phone:* 602-286-8200. *Fax:* 602-286-8200. *E-mail:* enroll@gatewaycc.edu. *Website:* http://www.gatewaycc.edu/.

Glendale Community College

Glendale, Arizona

- **State and locally supported** 2-year, founded 1965, part of Maricopa County Community College District System
- **Suburban** 222-acre campus with easy access to Phoenix
- **Endowment** $1.2 million
- **Coed,** 20,154 undergraduate students, 35% full-time, 54% women, 46% men

Undergraduates 7,126 full-time, 13,028 part-time. Students come from 51 states and territories; 92 other countries; 8% are from out of state; 7% transferred in. *Retention:* 64% of full-time freshmen returned.

Freshmen *Admission:* 3,423 enrolled.

Faculty *Student/faculty ratio:* 24:1.

Majors Accounting technology and bookkeeping; administrative assistant and secretarial science; architectural drafting and CAD/CADD; automobile/automotive mechanics technology; behavioral sciences; biotechnology; business administration and management; business/commerce; CAD/CADD drafting/design technology; cinematography and film/video production; commercial and advertising art; computer and information sciences; computer and information systems security; computer systems analysis; computer systems networking and telecommunications; criminal justice/safety; data entry/microcomputer applications; early childhood education; educational leadership and administration; emergency medical technology (EMT paramedic); engineering technology; family and community services; fire science/firefighting; graphic

design; homeland security, law enforcement, firefighting and protective services related; kinesiology and exercise science; marketing/marketing management; music management; public relations/image management; recording arts technology; registered nursing/registered nurse; web page, digital/multimedia and information resources design.

Academics *Calendar:* semesters. *Degree:* certificates and associate. *Special study options:* academic remediation for entering students, adult/continuing education programs, advanced placement credit, cooperative education, distance learning, double majors, English as a second language, freshman honors college, honors programs, internships, off-campus study, part-time degree program, services for LD students, study abroad, summer session for credit. *ROTC:* Army (c), Air Force (c).

Library Library/Media Center plus 1 other with 97,768 titles, 30,094 serial subscriptions, 6,032 audiovisual materials, an OPAC, a Web page.

Student Life *Housing:* college housing not available. *Activities and Organizations:* drama/theater group, student-run newspaper, choral group, marching band, Phi Theta Kappa, M.E.Ch.A. (Movimiento Estudiantil Chicano de Aztlan), Associated Student Government, Biotechnology Club, Compass. *Campus security:* 24-hour patrols, student patrols, late-night transport/escort service. *Student services:* personal/psychological counseling, legal services.

Athletics Member NJCAA. *Intercollegiate sports:* baseball M(s), basketball M(s)/W(s), cross-country running M(s)/W(s), football M(s), golf M(s), soccer M(s)/W(s), softball W(s), tennis M(s)/W(s), track and field M(s)/W(s), volleyball W(s). *Intramural sports:* golf M, racquetball M/W, softball W, tennis M/W, volleyball W.

Costs (2012–13) *Tuition:* state resident $1824 full-time, $76 per semester hour part-time; nonresident $7608 full-time, $317 per semester hour part-time. Full-time tuition and fees vary according to program and reciprocity agreements. Part-time tuition and fees vary according to course load, program, and reciprocity agreements. *Required fees:* $30 full-time, $15 per term part-time. *Payment plan:* installment. *Waivers:* employees or children of employees.

Financial Aid Of all full-time matriculated undergraduates who enrolled in 2011, 350 Federal Work-Study jobs (averaging $1700).

Applying *Options:* electronic application. *Required for some:* high school transcript. *Application deadlines:* 8/20 (freshmen), 8/20 (transfers). *Notification:* continuous until 8/20 (freshmen), continuous until 8/20 (transfers).

Freshman Application Contact Ms. Mary Blackwell, Dean of Enrollment Services, Glendale Community College, 6000 West Olive Avenue, Glendale, AZ 85302. *Phone:* 623-435-3305. *Fax:* 623-845-3303. *E-mail:* info@gc.maricopa.edu. *Website:* http://www.gc.maricopa.edu/.

Golf Academy of America

Chandler, Arizona

Admissions Office Contact Golf Academy of America, 2031 N. Arizona Avenue, Suite 2, Chandler, AZ 85225. *Website:* http://www.golfacademy.edu/.

ITT Technical Institute

Phoenix, Arizona

- **Proprietary** primarily 2-year, founded 1972, part of ITT Educational Services, Inc.
- **Urban** campus
- **Coed**

Academics *Calendar:* quarters. *Degrees:* associate and bachelor's.

Financial Aid Of all full-time matriculated undergraduates who enrolled in 2011, 10 Federal Work-Study jobs (averaging $4000).

Freshman Application Contact Director of Recruitment, ITT Technical Institute, 10220 North 25th Avenue, Suite 100, Phoenix, AZ 85021. *Phone:* 602-749-7900. *Toll-free phone:* 877-221-1132. *Website:* http://www.itt-tech.edu/.

ITT Technical Institute

Phoenix, Arizona

- **Proprietary** primarily 2-year, part of ITT Educational Services, Inc.
- **Coed**

Academics *Calendar:* quarters. *Degrees:* associate and bachelor's.

Freshman Application Contact Director of Recruitment, ITT Technical Institute, 1840 N. 95th Avenue, Suite 132, Phoenix, AZ 85037. *Phone:* 623-474-7900. *Toll-free phone:* 800-210-1178. *Website:* http://www.itt-tech.edu/.

ITT Technical Institute

Tucson, Arizona

- **Proprietary** primarily 2-year, founded 1984, part of ITT Educational Services, Inc.
- **Urban** campus
- **Coed**

Academics *Calendar:* quarters. *Degrees:* associate and bachelor's.

Freshman Application Contact Director of Recruitment, ITT Technical Institute, 1455 West River Road, Tucson, AZ 85704. *Phone:* 520-408-7488. *Toll-free phone:* 800-870-9730.
Website: http://www.itt-tech.edu/.

Le Cordon Bleu College of Culinary Arts in Scottsdale

Scottsdale, Arizona

Director of Admissions Le Cordon Bleu College of Culinary Arts in Scottsdale, 8100 East Camelback Road, Suite 1001, Scottsdale, AZ 85251-3940. *Toll-free phone:* 888-557-4222.
Website: http://www.chefs.edu/SCOTTSDALE.

Mesa Community College

Mesa, Arizona

- **State and locally supported** 2-year, founded 1965, part of Maricopa County Community College District System
- **Urban** 160-acre campus with easy access to Phoenix
- **Coed,** 23,000 undergraduate students

Majors Accounting; administrative assistant and secretarial science; agricultural business and management; agricultural mechanization; agronomy and crop science; art; automobile/automotive mechanics technology; biology/biological sciences; business administration and management; child development; criminal justice/law enforcement administration; data processing and data processing technology; drafting and design technology; electrical, electronic and communications engineering technology; engineering technology; family and consumer sciences/human sciences; fashion merchandising; finance; fire science/firefighting; heavy equipment maintenance technology; horticultural science; industrial technology; insurance; interior design; liberal arts and sciences/liberal studies; library and information science; marketing/marketing management; mathematics; medical administrative assistant and medical secretary; music; ornamental horticulture; pre-engineering; quality control technology; real estate; registered nursing/registered nurse; teacher assistant/aide.

Academics *Calendar:* semesters. *Degree:* certificates and associate. *Special study options:* academic remediation for entering students, adult/continuing education programs, advanced placement credit, cooperative education, distance learning, English as a second language, freshman honors college, honors programs, independent study, off-campus study, part-time degree program, services for LD students, student-designed majors, study abroad, summer session for credit. *ROTC:* Army (c), Air Force (c).

Library Information Commons with an OPAC, a Web page.

Student Life *Housing:* college housing not available. *Activities and Organizations:* drama/theater group, student-run newspaper, choral group, MECHA, International Student Association, American Indian Association, Asian/Pacific Islander Club. *Campus security:* 24-hour emergency response devices and patrols, student patrols. *Student services:* personal/psychological counseling, legal services.

Athletics Member NJCAA. *Intercollegiate sports:* baseball M, basketball M/W, cross-country running M, football M, golf M/W, soccer M/W, softball W, tennis M/W, track and field M/W, volleyball W, wrestling M. *Intramural sports:* basketball M/W, cross-country running M, football M/W, tennis M/W, track and field M/W, volleyball M/W, wrestling M/W.

Costs (2013–14) *Tuition:* area resident $1944 full-time; state resident $7608 full-time; nonresident $7728 full-time. Full-time tuition and fees vary according to course load and reciprocity agreements. Part-time tuition and fees vary according to course load and reciprocity agreements. *Payment plan:* installment. *Waivers:* employees or children of employees.

Applying *Options:* electronic application, early admission, deferred entrance. *Application deadlines:* 8/22 (freshmen), 8/22 (transfers). *Notification:* continuous (freshmen).

Freshman Application Contact Mr. Stephen Gerlock, Director, Admissions and Records, Mesa Community College, 1833 West Southern Avenue, Mesa, AZ 85202-4866. *Phone:* 480-461-7400. *Toll-free phone:* 866-532-4983. *Fax:* 480-844-3117. *E-mail:* admissionsandrecords@mesacc.edu.
Website: http://www.mesacc.edu/.

Mohave Community College

Kingman, Arizona

- **State-supported** 2-year, founded 1971
- **Small-town** 160-acre campus
- **Coed,** 5,220 undergraduate students, 27% full-time, 65% women, 35% men

Undergraduates 1,412 full-time, 3,808 part-time. Students come from 16 states and territories; 4% are from out of state; 1% Black or African American, non-Hispanic/Latino; 18% Hispanic/Latino; 2% Asian, non-Hispanic/Latino; 0.7% Native Hawaiian or other Pacific Islander, non-Hispanic/Latino; 2% American Indian or Alaska Native, non-Hispanic/Latino; 2% Two or more races, non-Hispanic/Latino; 1% Race/ethnicity unknown.

Freshmen *Admission:* 912 enrolled.

Faculty *Total:* 400, 20% full-time. *Student/faculty ratio:* 16:1.

Majors Accounting; art; automobile/automotive mechanics technology; building/construction finishing, management, and inspection related; business administration and management; computer and information sciences related; computer programming (specific applications); computer science; criminal justice/police science; culinary arts; dental assisting; dental hygiene; drafting and design technology; education; emergency medical technology (EMT paramedic); English; fire science/firefighting; heating, air conditioning, ventilation and refrigeration maintenance technology; history; information technology; legal assistant/paralegal; liberal arts and sciences/liberal studies; mathematics; medical/clinical assistant; personal and culinary services related; pharmacy technician; physical therapy technology; psychology; registered nursing/registered nurse; sociology; substance abuse/addiction counseling; surgical technology; truck and bus driver/commercial vehicle operation/instruction; welding technology.

Academics *Calendar:* semesters. *Degree:* certificates and associate. *Special study options:* academic remediation for entering students, adult/continuing education programs, cooperative education, distance learning, English as a second language, independent study, part-time degree program, summer session for credit.

Library Mohave Community College Library with 45,849 titles, 476 serial subscriptions, an OPAC, a Web page.

Student Life *Housing:* college housing not available. *Activities and Organizations:* Art Club, Phi Theta Kappa, Computer Club (MC4), Science Club, Student government. *Campus security:* late-night transport/escort service.

Costs (2013–14) *Tuition:* state resident $2340 full-time, $78 per credit hour part-time; nonresident $9360 full-time, $312 per credit hour part-time. Full-time tuition and fees vary according to program. Part-time tuition and fees vary according to program. *Required fees:* $210 full-time, $7 per credit hour part-time. *Payment plans:* installment, deferred payment. *Waivers:* employees or children of employees.

Applying *Options:* electronic application, early admission, deferred entrance. *Application deadlines:* rolling (freshmen), rolling (transfers). *Notification:* continuous (freshmen), continuous (transfers).

Freshman Application Contact Ms. Ana Masterson, Dean of Student Services, Mohave Community College, 1971 Jagerson Ave, Kingman, AZ 86409. *Phone:* 928-757-0803. *Toll-free phone:* 888-664-2832. *Fax:* 928-757-0808. *E-mail:* amasterson@mohave.edu.
Website: http://www.mohave.edu/.

Northland Pioneer College

Holbrook, Arizona

Freshman Application Contact Ms. Suzette Willis, Coordinator of Admissions, Northland Pioneer College, PO Box 610, Holbrook, AZ 86025. *Phone:* 928-536-6271. *Toll-free phone:* 800-266-7845. *Fax:* 928-536-6212.
Website: http://www.npc.edu/.

Paradise Valley Community College

Phoenix, Arizona

Freshman Application Contact Paradise Valley Community College, 18401 North 32nd Street, Phoenix, AZ 85032-1200. *Phone:* 602-787-7020.
Website: http://www.pvc.maricopa.edu/.

The Paralegal Institute, Inc.

Phoenix, Arizona

Freshman Application Contact Patricia Yancy, Director of Admissions, The Paralegal Institute, Inc., 2933 West Indian School Road, Drawer 11408, Phoenix, AZ 85061-1408. *Phone:* 602-212-0501. *Toll-free phone:* 800-354-1254. *Fax:* 602-212-0502. *E-mail:* paralegalinst@mindspring.com.
Website: http://www.theparalegalinstitute.edu/.

Phoenix College

Phoenix, Arizona

- **County-supported** 2-year, founded 1920, part of Maricopa County Community College District System
- **Urban** 52-acre campus
- **Coed,** 12,565 undergraduate students, 28% full-time, 62% women, 38% men

Undergraduates 3,498 full-time, 9,067 part-time. 12% Black or African American, non-Hispanic/Latino; 38% Hispanic/Latino; 3% Asian, non-Hispanic/Latino; 0.1% Native Hawaiian or other Pacific Islander, non-Hispanic/Latino; 4% American Indian or Alaska Native, non-Hispanic/Latino; 1% Two or more races, non-Hispanic/Latino; 11% Race/ethnicity unknown; 0.4% international.

Faculty *Total:* 718, 23% full-time. *Student/faculty ratio:* 18:1.

Majors Accounting; administrative assistant and secretarial science; architectural drafting and CAD/CADD; art; banking and financial support services; building/home/construction inspection; business administration and management; business/commerce; child-care and support services management; civil engineering technology; clinical/medical laboratory technology; commercial and advertising art; commercial photography; computer and information sciences; computer graphics; computer systems analysis; construction management; criminal justice/safety; culinary arts; dental assisting; dental hygiene; dramatic/theater arts; elementary education; emergency medical technology (EMT paramedic); family and community services; family and consumer sciences/human sciences; fashion/apparel design; fashion merchandising; fine/studio arts; fire science/firefighting; food service systems administration; forensic science and technology; general studies; graphic design; health information/medical records technology; histologic technology/histotechnologist; human services; interior design; legal assistant/paralegal; liberal arts and sciences/liberal studies; marketing/marketing management; massage therapy; medical/clinical assistant; medical office assistant; music management; natural sciences; organizational behavior; parks, recreation and leisure; physical sciences; recording arts technology; registered nursing/registered nurse; sign language interpretation and translation; surveying technology; teacher assistant/aide; visual and performing arts; web page, digital/multimedia and information resources design.

Academics *Calendar:* semesters. *Degree:* certificates, diplomas, and associate. *Special study options:* academic remediation for entering students, adult/continuing education programs, advanced placement credit, cooperative education, distance learning, English as a second language, freshman honors college, honors programs, independent study, internships, off-campus study, part-time degree program, services for LD students, study abroad, summer session for credit. *ROTC:* Army (c), Navy (c), Air Force (c).

Library Fannin Library with 67,370 titles, 210 serial subscriptions, 7,667 audiovisual materials, an OPAC, a Web page.

Student Life *Housing:* college housing not available. *Activities and Organizations:* drama/theater group, choral group, Student Leadership Council (SLC), MEChA Movimiento Estudiantil Chicanos de Aztlan, ALE Asociacion Latina Estudiantil, Rainbow Spectrum - Gay, Straight, Whatever alliance, International Club. *Campus security:* 24-hour emergency response devices and patrols, student patrols, late-night transport/escort service. *Student services:* personal/psychological counseling.

Athletics Member NCAA, NJCAA. All NCAA Division II. *Intercollegiate sports:* baseball M(s), basketball M(s)/W(s), cross-country running M(s)/W(s), football M(s), golf M(s)/W(s), soccer M/W, softball W(s), tennis M(s)/W(s), track and field M(s)/W(s), volleyball W(s).

Costs (2013–14) *Tuition:* area resident $912 full-time; state resident $3804 full-time; nonresident $3804 full-time. *Required fees:* $30 full-time.

Financial Aid Of all full-time matriculated undergraduates who enrolled in 2011, 220 Federal Work-Study jobs (averaging $4800).

Applying *Options:* electronic application, early admission, deferred entrance. *Application deadlines:* rolling (freshmen), rolling (out-of-state freshmen), rolling (transfers). *Notification:* continuous (freshmen), continuous (out-of-state freshmen), continuous (transfers).

Freshman Application Contact Ms. Brenda Stark, Director of Admissions, Registration, and Records, Phoenix College, 1202 West Thomas Road, Phoenix, AZ 85013. *Phone:* 602-285-7503. *Fax:* 602-285-7813. *E-mail:* kathy.french@pcmail.maricopa.edu. *Website:* http://www.pc.maricopa.edu/.

Pima Community College

Tucson, Arizona

- **State and locally supported** 2-year, founded 1966
- **Urban** 486-acre campus with easy access to Tucson, Arizona
- **Endowment** $4.3 million
- **Coed**

Undergraduates 13,730 full-time, 23,239 part-time. Students come from 53 states and territories; 63 other countries; 3% are from out of state; 5% Black or African American, non-Hispanic/Latino; 35% Hispanic/Latino; 3% Asian, non-Hispanic/Latino; 0.3% Native Hawaiian or other Pacific Islander, non-Hispanic/Latino; 3% American Indian or Alaska Native, non-Hispanic/Latino; 3% Two or more races, non-Hispanic/Latino; 4% Race/ethnicity unknown; 1% international; 7% transferred in. *Retention:* 60% of full-time freshmen returned.

Faculty *Student/faculty ratio:* 29:1.

Academics *Calendar:* semesters. *Degrees:* certificates, diplomas, associate, and postbachelor's certificates. *Special study options:* academic remediation for entering students, adult/continuing education programs, advanced placement credit, cooperative education, distance learning, English as a second language, honors programs, independent study, internships, off-campus study, part-time degree program, services for LD students, student-designed majors, summer session for credit. *ROTC:* Army (c), Navy (c), Air Force (c).

Student Life *Campus security:* 24-hour emergency response devices and patrols, late-night transport/escort service.

Athletics Member NJCAA.

Costs (2012–13) *Tuition:* state resident $1524 full-time, $64 per credit hour part-time; nonresident $7656 full-time, $106 per credit hour part-time. Full-time tuition and fees vary according to course load and program. Part-time tuition and fees vary according to course load and program. *Required fees:* $128 full-time, $5 per credit hour part-time, $10 per term part-time. *Payment plans:* installment, deferred payment.

Applying *Options:* electronic application.

Freshman Application Contact Terra Benson, Director of Admissions and Registrar, Pima Community College, 4905B East Broadway Boulevard, Tucson, AZ 85709-1120. *Phone:* 520-206-4640. *Fax:* 520-206-4790. *E-mail:* tbenson@pima.edu. *Website:* http://www.pima.edu/.

Pima Medical Institute

Mesa, Arizona

Freshman Application Contact Pima Medical Institute, 2160 S. Power Road, Mesa, AZ 85209. *Phone:* 480-898-9898. *Website:* http://www.pmi.edu/.

Pima Medical Institute

Mesa, Arizona

Freshman Application Contact Admissions Office, Pima Medical Institute, 957 South Dobson Road, Mesa, AZ 85202. *Phone:* 480-644-0267 Ext. 225. *Toll-free phone:* 800-477-PIMA (in-state); 888-477-PIMA (out-of-state). *Website:* http://www.pmi.edu/.

Pima Medical Institute

Tucson, Arizona

Freshman Application Contact Admissions Office, Pima Medical Institute, 3350 East Grant Road, Tucson, AZ 85716. *Phone:* 520-326-1600 Ext. 5112. *Toll-free phone:* 800-477-PIMA (in-state); 888-477-PIMA (out-of-state). *Website:* http://www.pmi.edu/.

The Refrigeration School

Phoenix, Arizona

Freshman Application Contact Ms. Heather Haskell, The Refrigeration School, 4210 East Washington Street. *Phone:* 602-275-7133. *Toll-free phone:* 888-943-4822. *Fax:* 602-267-4811. *E-mail:* heather@rsiaz.edu. *Website:* http://www.refrigerationschool.com/.

Rio Salado College

Tempe, Arizona

Freshman Application Contact Laurel Redman, Director, Instruction Support Services and Student Development, Rio Salado College, 2323 West 14th Street, Tempe 85281. *Phone:* 480-517-8563. *Toll-free phone:* 800-729-1197. *Fax:* 480-517-8199. *E-mail:* admission@riomail.maricopa.edu. *Website:* http://www.rio.maricopa.edu/.

Scottsdale Community College

Scottsdale, Arizona

- **State and locally supported** 2-year, founded 1969, part of Maricopa County Community College District System
- **Urban** 160-acre campus with easy access to Phoenix
- **Coed,** 10,895 undergraduate students, 32% full-time, 52% women, 48% men

Undergraduates 3,468 full-time, 7,427 part-time. Students come from 56 states and territories; 42 other countries; 1% are from out of state; 5% Black or African American, non-Hispanic/Latino; 15% Hispanic/Latino; 2% Asian, non-Hispanic/Latino; 0.4% Native Hawaiian or other Pacific Islander, non-Hispanic/Latino; 5% American Indian or Alaska Native, non-Hispanic/Latino; 2% Two or more races, non-Hispanic/Latino; 8% Race/ethnicity unknown; 1% international; 72% transferred in.

Faculty *Total:* 681, 24% full-time, 14% with terminal degrees. *Student/faculty ratio:* 18:1.

Majors Accounting; administrative assistant and secretarial science; business administration and management; criminal justice/law enforcement administration; culinary arts; dramatic/theater arts; electrical, electronic and communications engineering technology; emergency medical technology (EMT paramedic); environmental design/architecture; equestrian studies; fashion merchandising; finance; fire science/firefighting; hospitality administration; hotel/motel administration; information science/studies; interior design; kindergarten/preschool education; mathematics; medical administrative assistant and medical secretary; photography; public administration; real estate; registered nursing/registered nurse; special products marketing.

Academics *Calendar:* semesters. *Degree:* certificates, diplomas, and associate. *Special study options:* academic remediation for entering students, adult/continuing education programs, advanced placement credit, cooperative education, English as a second language, honors programs, internships, off-campus study, part-time degree program, services for LD students, study abroad, summer session for credit.

Library Scottsdale Community College Library with an OPAC, a Web page.

Student Life *Housing:* college housing not available. *Activities and Organizations:* drama/theater group, student-run newspaper, radio station, choral group, Student Leadership Forum, International Community Club, Phi Theta Kappa, Music Industry Club, SCC ASID-Interior Design group. *Campus security:* 24-hour emergency response devices and patrols, student patrols, late-night transport/escort service, 24-hour automatic surveillance cameras. *Student services:* personal/psychological counseling.

Athletics Member NCAA, NJCAA. All NCAA Division II. *Intercollegiate sports:* baseball M, basketball M/W, cross-country running M/W, football M, golf M/W, soccer M/W, softball W, tennis M/W, track and field M/W, volleyball W. *Intramural sports:* archery M/W, badminton M/W, basketball M/W, racquetball M/W, track and field M/W, volleyball M/W.

Costs (2012–13) *Tuition:* area resident $2280 full-time, $76 per credit part-time; state resident $8550 full-time, $285 per credit part-time; nonresident $9510 full-time, $317 per credit part-time. Full-time tuition and fees vary according to program and reciprocity agreements. Part-time tuition and fees vary according to program and reciprocity agreements. *Required fees:* $30 full-time. *Payment plan:* deferred payment. *Waivers:* employees or children of employees.

Financial Aid Of all full-time matriculated undergraduates who enrolled in 2011, 75 Federal Work-Study jobs (averaging $2000). *Financial aid deadline:* 7/15.

Applying *Options:* electronic application, early admission. *Application deadline:* rolling (freshmen). *Notification:* continuous (freshmen).

Freshman Application Contact Ms. Fran Watkins, Director of Admissions and Records, Scottsdale Community College, 9000 East Chaparral Road, Scottsdale, AZ 85256. *Phone:* 480-423-6133. *Fax:* 480-423-6200. *E-mail:* fran.watkins@scottsdalecc.edu.
Website: http://www.scottsdalecc.edu/.

Sessions College for Professional Design

Tempe, Arizona

Freshman Application Contact Admissions, Sessions College for Professional Design, 398 South MIll Avenue, Suite 300, Tempe, AZ 85281. *Phone:* 480-212-1704. *Toll-free phone:* 800-258-4115. *E-mail:* admissions@sessions.edu.
Website: http://www.sessions.edu/.

South Mountain Community College

Phoenix, Arizona

Director of Admissions Dean of Enrollment Services, South Mountain Community College, 7050 South Twenty-fourth Street, Phoenix, AZ 85040. *Phone:* 602-243-8120.
Website: http://www.southmountaincc.edu/.

Southwest Institute of Healing Arts

Tempe, Arizona

Director of Admissions Katie Yearous, Student Advisor, Southwest Institute of Healing Arts, 1100 East Apache Boulevard, Tempe, AZ 85281. *Phone:* 480-994-9244. *Toll-free phone:* 888-504-9106. *E-mail:* joannl@swiha.net. *Website:* http://www.swiha.org/.

Tohono O'odham Community College

Sells, Arizona

Freshman Application Contact Admissions, Tohono O'odham Community College, PO Box 3129, Sells, AZ 85634. *Phone:* 520-383-8401. *E-mail:* info@tocc.cc.az.us.
Website: http://www.tocc.cc.az.us/.

Universal Technical Institute

Avondale, Arizona

Freshman Application Contact Director of Admission, Universal Technical Institute, 10695 West Pierce Street, Avondale, AZ 85323. *Phone:* 623-245-4600. *Toll-free phone:* 800-510-5072. *Fax:* 623-245-4601.
Website: http://www.uti.edu/.

Yavapai College

Prescott, Arizona

Freshman Application Contact Mrs. Sheila Jarrell, Admissions, Registration, and Records Manager, Yavapai College, 1100 East Sheldon Street, Prescott, AZ 86301-3297. *Phone:* 928-776-2107. *Toll-free phone:* 800-922-6787. *Fax:* 928-776-2151. *E-mail:* registration@yc.edu.
Website: http://www.yc.edu/.

ARKANSAS

Arkansas Northeastern College

Blytheville, Arkansas

Freshman Application Contact Mrs. Leslie Wells, Admissions Counselor, Arkansas Northeastern College, PO Box 1109, Blytheville, AR 72316. *Phone:* 870-762-1020 Ext. 1118. *Fax:* 870-763-1654. *E-mail:* lwells@anc.edu.
Website: http://www.anc.edu/.

Arkansas State University–Beebe

Beebe, Arkansas

Freshman Application Contact Mr. Ronald Hudson, Coordinator of Student Recruitment, Arkansas State University–Beebe, PO Box 1000, Beebe, AR 72012. *Phone:* 501-882-8860. *Toll-free phone:* 800-632-9985. *E-mail:* rdhudson@asub.edu.
Website: http://www.asub.edu/.

Arkansas State University–Mountain Home

Mountain Home, Arkansas

- **State-supported** 2-year, founded 2000, part of Arkansas State University System
- **Small-town** 136-acre campus
- **Coed**

Majors Administrative assistant and secretarial science; business/commerce; criminal justice/law enforcement administration; criminal justice/police science; early childhood education; education (multiple levels); emergency medical technology (EMT paramedic); forensic science and technology; funeral service and mortuary science; information science/studies; liberal arts and sciences/liberal studies; middle school education; respiratory care therapy; welding technology.

Academics *Calendar:* semesters. *Degree:* certificates and associate. *Special study options:* academic remediation for entering students, advanced placement credit, cooperative education, distance learning, English as a second language, honors programs, independent study, internships, part-time degree program, services for LD students, summer session for credit. *ROTC:* Army (b).

Library Norma Wood Library with an OPAC, a Web page.

Student Life *Housing:* college housing not available. *Activities and Organizations:* Phi Theta Kappa, Circle K, Criminal Justice Club, Mortuary Science Club, Student Ambassadors. *Campus security:* during operation hours security is present and available as needed.

Standardized Tests *Recommended:* SAT or ACT (for admission), COMPASS, ASSET.

Costs (2013–14) *Tuition:* state resident $2112 full-time, $88 per credit hour part-time; nonresident $3600 full-time, $150 per credit hour part-time. Full-time tuition and fees vary according to course load. Part-time tuition and fees vary according to course load. *Required fees:* $504 full-time, $21 per credit hour part-time. *Payment plan:* installment. *Waivers:* children of alumni, senior citizens, and employees or children of employees.

Financial Aid Of all full-time matriculated undergraduates who enrolled in 2012, 645 applied for aid, 608 were judged to have need, 45 had their need fully met. 14 Federal Work-Study jobs (averaging $3500). In 2012, 10 non-need-based awards were made. *Average percent of need met:* 62%. *Average financial aid package:* $8217. *Average need-based loan:* $3154. *Average need-based gift aid:* $4308. *Average non-need-based aid:* $1772.

Applying *Options:* electronic application. *Required:* high school transcript. *Recommended:* placement scores, GED scores accepted. *Notification:* continuous (freshmen).

Freshman Application Contact Ms. Delba Parrish, Admissions Coordinator, Arkansas State University–Mountain Home, 1600 South College Street, Mountain Home, AR 72653. *Phone:* 870-508-6180. *Fax:* 870-508-6287. *E-mail:* dparrish@asumh.edu.
Website: http://www.asumh.edu/.

Arkansas State University–Newport
Newport, Arkansas

Director of Admissions Robert Summers, Director of Admissions/Registrar, Arkansas State University–Newport, 7648 Victory Boulevard, Newport, AR 72112. *Phone:* 870-512-7800. *Toll-free phone:* 800-976-1676. *Fax:* 870-512-7825. *E-mail:* robert.summers@asun.edu.
Website: http://www.asun.edu/.

Black River Technical College
Pocahontas, Arkansas

Director of Admissions Director of Admissions, Black River Technical College, 1410 Highway 304 East, Pocahontas, AR 72455. *Phone:* 870-892-4565.
Website: http://www.blackrivertech.edu/.

College of the Ouachitas
Malvern, Arkansas

- **State-supported** 2-year, founded 1972
- **Small-town** 11-acre campus
- **Coed**

Undergraduates 592 full-time, 815 part-time. 12% Black or African American, non-Hispanic/Latino; 3% Hispanic/Latino; 0.4% Asian, non-Hispanic/Latino; 0.1% Native Hawaiian or other Pacific Islander, non-Hispanic/Latino; 0.4% American Indian or Alaska Native, non-Hispanic/Latino; 3% Two or more races, non-Hispanic/Latino; 0.2% international.

Academics *Calendar:* semesters. *Degree:* certificates and associate. *Special study options:* academic remediation for entering students, accelerated degree program, advanced placement credit, cooperative education, distance learning, double majors, independent study, internships, part-time degree program, services for LD students, summer session for credit.

Student Life *Campus security:* 24-hour patrols.

Standardized Tests *Recommended:* SAT or ACT (for admission), ACT COMPASS or ASSET.

Costs (2012–13) *Tuition:* state resident $1950 full-time, $65 per credit hour part-time; nonresident $3900 full-time, $130 per credit hour part-time. Full-time tuition and fees vary according to program. Part-time tuition and fees vary according to program. No tuition increase for student's term of enrollment. *Required fees:* $557 full-time, $17 per credit part-time, $16 per credit part-time.

Financial Aid Of all full-time matriculated undergraduates who enrolled in 2011, 18 Federal Work-Study jobs (averaging $2400).

Applying *Options:* electronic application, early admission, deferred entrance. *Required:* high school transcript.

Freshman Application Contact Kathy Lazenby, Counselor, College of the Ouachitas, One College Circle, Malvern, AR 72104. *Phone:* 501-337-5000 Ext. 1103. *Toll-free phone:* 800-337-0266. *Fax:* 501-337-9382. *E-mail:* klazenby@coto.edu.
Website: http://www.coto.edu/.

Cossatot Community College of the University of Arkansas
De Queen, Arkansas

- **State-supported** 2-year, founded 1991, part of University of Arkansas System
- **Rural** 30-acre campus
- **Endowment** $108,167
- **Coed,** 1,542 undergraduate students

Undergraduates Students come from 6 states and territories; 1 other country; 2% are from out of state; 13% Black or African American, non-Hispanic/Latino; 16% Hispanic/Latino; 1% Asian, non-Hispanic/Latino; 0.3% Native Hawaiian or other Pacific Islander, non-Hispanic/Latino; 2% American Indian or Alaska Native, non-Hispanic/Latino.

Faculty *Total:* 74, 46% full-time, 3% with terminal degrees. *Student/faculty ratio:* 14:1.

Majors Automobile/automotive mechanics technology; business administration and management; criminal justice/law enforcement administration; early childhood education; forensic science and technology; general studies; liberal arts and sciences/liberal studies; management information systems; medical/clinical assistant; middle school education; multi/interdisciplinary studies related.

Academics *Calendar:* semesters. *Degree:* certificates and associate. *Special study options:* academic remediation for entering students, accelerated degree program, adult/continuing education programs, advanced placement credit, cooperative education, distance learning, double majors, independent study, internships, off-campus study, part-time degree program, services for LD students, summer session for credit.

Library Kimbell Library.

Student Life *Housing:* college housing not available. *Activities and Organizations:* student-run radio station, Students 4 Students, Phi Theta Kappa, ALPNA, VICA (Vocational Industrial Clubs of America). *Student services:* personal/psychological counseling.

Financial Aid Of all full-time matriculated undergraduates who enrolled in 2011, 14 Federal Work-Study jobs (averaging $2700).

Applying *Options:* electronic application. *Recommended:* high school transcript.

Freshman Application Contact Cossatot Community College of the University of Arkansas, DeQueen, AR 71832. *Phone:* 870-584-4471 Ext. 1143. *Toll-free phone:* 800-844-4471.
Website: http://www.cccua.edu/.

Crowley's Ridge College
Paragould, Arkansas

Freshman Application Contact Amanda Drake, Director of Admissions, Crowley's Ridge College, 100 College Drive, Paragould, AR 72450-9731. *Phone:* 870-236-6901. *Toll-free phone:* 800-264-1096. *Fax:* 870-236-7748. *E-mail:* njoneshi@crc.pioneer.paragould.ar.us.
Website: http://www.crc.edu/.

East Arkansas Community College
Forrest City, Arkansas

Freshman Application Contact Ms. DeAnna Adams, Director of Enrollment Management/Institutional Research, East Arkansas Community College, 1700 Newcastle Road, Forrest City, AR 72335-2204. *Phone:* 870-633-4480. *Toll-free phone:* 877-797-3222. *Fax:* 870-633-3840. *E-mail:* dadams@eacc.edu.
Website: http://www.eacc.edu/.

ITT Technical Institute
Little Rock, Arkansas

- **Proprietary** primarily 2-year, founded 1993, part of ITT Educational Services, Inc.
- **Urban** campus
- **Coed**

Academics *Calendar:* quarters. *Degrees:* associate and bachelor's.

Freshman Application Contact Director of Recruitment, ITT Technical Institute, 12200 Westhaven Drive, Little Rock, AR 72211. *Phone:* 501-565-5550. *Toll-free phone:* 800-359-4429.
Website: http://www.itt-tech.edu/.

Mid-South Community College
West Memphis, Arkansas

Freshman Application Contact Jeremy Reece, Director of Admissions, Mid-South Community College, 2000 West Broadway, West Memphis, AR 72301. *Phone:* 870-733-6786. *Toll-free phone:* 866-733-6722. *Fax:* 870-733-6719. *E-mail:* jreece@midsouthcc.edu.
Website: http://www.midsouthcc.edu/.

National Park Community College
Hot Springs, Arkansas

Director of Admissions Dr. Allen B. Moody, Director of Institutional Services/Registrar, National Park Community College, 101 College Drive, Hot Springs, AR 71913. *Phone:* 501-760-4222. *E-mail:* bmoody@npcc.edu.
Website: http://www.npcc.edu/.

North Arkansas College
Harrison, Arkansas

Freshman Application Contact Mrs. Charla Jennings, Director of Admissions, North Arkansas College, 1515 Pioneer Drive, Harrison, AR 72601. *Phone:* 870-391-3221. *Toll-free phone:* 800-679-6622. *Fax:* 870-391-3339. *E-mail:* charlam@northark.edu.
Website: http://www.northark.edu/.

NorthWest Arkansas Community College
Bentonville, Arkansas

- State and locally supported 2-year, founded 1989
- Urban 77-acre campus
- Coed, 8,341 undergraduate students, 37% full-time, 57% women, 43% men

Undergraduates 3,095 full-time, 5,246 part-time. Students come from 21 states and territories; 2% are from out of state; 9% transferred in. *Retention:* 55% of full-time freshmen returned.
Freshmen *Admission:* 1,509 enrolled. *Average high school GPA:* 2.8. *Test scores:* ACT scores over 18: 74%; ACT scores over 24: 17%; ACT scores over 30: 1%.
Faculty *Total:* 491, 29% full-time. *Student/faculty ratio:* 19:1.
Majors Accounting; administrative assistant and secretarial science; business administration and management; commercial and advertising art; computer programming; criminal justice/law enforcement administration; criminal justice/safety; culinary arts; data processing and data processing technology; drafting and design technology; early childhood education; education; electrical, electronic and communications engineering technology; emergency medical technology (EMT paramedic); environmental science; finance; fire services administration; homeland security, law enforcement, firefighting and protective services related; legal assistant/paralegal; liberal arts and sciences/liberal studies; occupational safety and health technology; physical therapy; registered nursing/registered nurse; respiratory care therapy.
Academics *Calendar:* semesters. *Degree:* certificates and associate. *Special study options:* academic remediation for entering students, accelerated degree program, adult/continuing education programs, advanced placement credit, cooperative education, distance learning, double majors, English as a second language, honors programs, independent study, internships, part-time degree program, services for LD students, student-designed majors, summer session for credit. *ROTC:* Army (c), Air Force (c).
Library Library Resource Center plus 1 other with 15,500 titles, 159 serial subscriptions, an OPAC, a Web page.
Student Life *Housing:* college housing not available. *Activities and Organizations:* drama/theater group, student-run newspaper, choral group, Student Advisory Activity Council, Gamma Beta Phi, Phi Beta Lambda, Student Nurses Association, Students in Free Enterprise (SIFE). *Campus security:* 24-hour emergency response devices and patrols. *Student services:* personal/psychological counseling.
Athletics *Intramural sports:* basketball M(c)/W(c), bowling M(c)/W(c), golf M(c), soccer M(c)/W(c), softball M(c)/W(c), volleyball W(c).
Costs (2012–13) *Tuition:* area resident $2250 full-time, $75 per credit hour part-time; state resident $3675 full-time, $123 per credit hour part-time; nonresident $5250 full-time, $175 per credit hour part-time. *Required fees:* $665

full-time, $19 per credit hour part-time, $55 per term part-time. *Payment plan:* installment. *Waivers:* senior citizens and employees or children of employees.
Applying *Options:* electronic application. *Application fee:* $10. *Required:* high school transcript. *Application deadline:* rolling (freshmen). *Notification:* continuous (freshmen).
Freshman Application Contact NorthWest Arkansas Community College, One College Drive, Bentonville, AR 72712. *Phone:* 479-636-9222. *Toll-free phone:* 800-995-6922. *Fax:* 479-619-4116. *E-mail:* admissions@nwacc.edu.
Website: http://www.nwacc.edu/.

Ozarka College
Melbourne, Arkansas

- State-supported 2-year, founded 1973
- Rural 40-acre campus
- Coed, 1,600 undergraduate students

Undergraduates 1% are from out of state.
Faculty *Total:* 71, 44% full-time, 4% with terminal degrees. *Student/faculty ratio:* 20:1.
Majors Automobile/automotive mechanics technology; business automation/technology/data entry; criminal justice/law enforcement administration; culinary arts; health information/medical records technology; information science/studies; liberal arts and sciences/liberal studies; middle school education.
Academics *Calendar:* semesters. *Degree:* certificates and associate. *Special study options:* academic remediation for entering students, advanced placement credit, distance learning, external degree program, internships, services for LD students, summer session for credit.
Library Ozarka College Library with 10,500 titles, 4,000 serial subscriptions, an OPAC.
Student Life *Housing:* college housing not available. *Activities and Organizations:* drama/theater group, VICA (Vocational Industrial Clubs of America), Phi Beta Lambda, Drama Club, HOSA, Phi Theta Kappa. *Campus security:* security patrols after business hours. *Student services:* personal/psychological counseling.
Applying *Options:* electronic application, deferred entrance. *Required:* high school transcript. *Required for some:* essay or personal statement, interview. *Recommended:* minimum 2.0 GPA. *Application deadlines:* 8/19 (freshmen), 8/15 (transfers).
Freshman Application Contact Ms. Dylan Mowery, Director of Admissions, Ozarka College, PO Box 10, Melbourne, AR 72556. *Phone:* 870-368-7371 Ext. 2013. *Toll-free phone:* 800-821-4335. *E-mail:* dmmowery@ozarka.edu.
Website: http://www.ozarka.edu/.

Phillips Community College of the University of Arkansas
Helena, Arkansas

Director of Admissions Mr. Lynn Boone, Registrar, Phillips Community College of the University of Arkansas, PO Box 785, Helena, AR 72342-0785. *Phone:* 870-338-6474.
Website: http://www.pccua.edu/.

Pulaski Technical College
North Little Rock, Arkansas

Freshman Application Contact Mr. Clark Atkins, Director of Admissions, Pulaski Technical College, 3000 West Scenic Drive, North Little Rock, AR 72118. *Phone:* 501-812-2734. *Fax:* 501-812-2316. *E-mail:* catkins@pulaskitech.edu.
Website: http://www.pulaskitech.edu/.

Remington College–Little Rock Campus
Little Rock, Arkansas

Director of Admissions Brian Maggio, Director of Recruitment, Remington College–Little Rock Campus, 19 Remington Drive, Little Rock, AR 72204. *Phone:* 501-312-0007. *Fax:* 501-225-3819. *E-mail:* brian.maggio@remingtoncollege.edu.
Website: http://www.remingtoncollege.edu/.

Rich Mountain Community College
Mena, Arkansas

Director of Admissions Dr. Steve Rook, Dean of Students, Rich Mountain Community College, 1100 College Drive, Mena, AR 71953. *Phone:* 479-394-

7622 Ext. 1400.
Website: http://www.rmcc.edu/.

South Arkansas Community College

El Dorado, Arkansas

Freshman Application Contact Mr. Dean Inman, Director of Enrollment Services, South Arkansas Community College, PO Box 7010, El Dorado, AR 71731-7010. *Phone:* 870-864-7142. *Toll-free phone:* 800-955-2289. *Fax:* 870-864-7109. *E-mail:* dinman@southark.edu. *Website:* http://www.southark.edu/.

Southeast Arkansas College

Pine Bluff, Arkansas

- **State-supported** 2-year, founded 1991
- **Urban** campus with easy access to Little Rock
- **Coed**

Undergraduates 1,157 full-time, 1,033 part-time. Students come from 3 states and territories; 58% Black or African American, non-Hispanic/Latino; 0.9% Hispanic/Latino; 0.4% Asian, non-Hispanic/Latino; 0.2% Native Hawaiian or other Pacific Islander, non-Hispanic/Latino; 0.5% American Indian or Alaska Native, non-Hispanic/Latino; 2% transferred in. *Retention:* 31% of full-time freshmen returned.

Faculty *Student/faculty ratio:* 16:1.

Academics *Calendar:* semesters. *Degree:* certificates and associate. *Special study options:* academic remediation for entering students, accelerated degree program, advanced placement credit, cooperative education, distance learning, double majors, honors programs, independent study, internships, part-time degree program, services for LD students, summer session for credit.

Student Life *Campus security:* 24-hour patrols.

Standardized Tests *Required:* ACT (for admission). *Recommended:* SAT or ACT (for admission), SAT and SAT Subject Tests or ACT (for admission), SAT Subject Tests (for admission), Compass.

Applying *Options:* early admission. *Required:* high school transcript.

Freshman Application Contact Ms. Barbara Dunn, Director of Admissions, Southeast Arkansas College, 1900 Hazel Street, Pine Bluff, AR 71603. *Phone:* 870-543-5957. *Toll-free phone:* 888-SEARK TC (in-state); 888-SEARC TC (out-of-state). *Fax:* 870-543-5957. *E-mail:* bdunn@seark.edu. *Website:* http://www.seark.edu/.

Southern Arkansas University Tech

Camden, Arkansas

Freshman Application Contact Mrs. Beverly Ellis, Admissions Analyst, Southern Arkansas University Tech, PO Box 3499, Camden, AR 71711-1599. *Phone:* 870-574-4558. *Fax:* 870-574-4478. *E-mail:* bellis@sautech.edu. *Website:* http://www.sautech.edu/.

University of Arkansas Community College at Batesville

Batesville, Arkansas

Freshman Application Contact Ms. Sharon Gage, Admissions Coordinator, University of Arkansas Community College at Batesville, PO Box 3350, Batesville, AR 72503. *Phone:* 870-612-2042. *Toll-free phone:* 800-508-7878. *Fax:* 870-612-2129. *E-mail:* sgage@uaccb.edu. *Website:* http://www.uaccb.edu/.

University of Arkansas Community College at Hope

Hope, Arkansas

Freshman Application Contact University of Arkansas Community College at Hope, PO Box 140, Hope, AR 71802. *Phone:* 870-772-8174. *Website:* http://www.uacch.edu/.

University of Arkansas Community College at Morrilton

Morrilton, Arkansas

- **State-supported** 2-year, founded 1961, part of University of Arkansas System
- **Rural** 79-acre campus
- **Coed,** 2,139 undergraduate students, 59% full-time, 58% women, 42% men

Undergraduates 1,267 full-time, 872 part-time. Students come from 5 states and territories; 1 other country; 0.5% are from out of state; 10% Black or African American, non-Hispanic/Latino; 5% Hispanic/Latino; 0.8% Asian, non-Hispanic/Latino; 0.1% Native Hawaiian or other Pacific Islander, non-Hispanic/Latino; 0.4% American Indian or Alaska Native, non-Hispanic/Latino; 4% Two or more races, non-Hispanic/Latino; 0.7% Race/ethnicity unknown; 2% international; 8% transferred in.

Freshmen *Admission:* 1,405 applied, 895 admitted, 554 enrolled. *Average high school GPA:* 2.78. *Test scores:* ACT scores over 18: 77%; ACT scores over 24: 23%; ACT scores over 30: 1%.

Faculty *Total:* 98, 63% full-time, 11% with terminal degrees. *Student/faculty ratio:* 21:1.

Majors Autobody/collision and repair technology; automobile/automotive mechanics technology; business/commerce; child development; commercial and advertising art; computer technology/computer systems technology; criminal justice/law enforcement administration; drafting and design technology; education (multiple levels); forensic science and technology; general studies; heating, air conditioning, ventilation and refrigeration maintenance technology; liberal arts and sciences/liberal studies; petroleum technology; registered nursing/registered nurse; surveying technology.

Academics *Calendar:* semesters. *Degree:* certificates and associate. *Special study options:* academic remediation for entering students, advanced placement credit, distance learning, double majors, internships, part-time degree program, services for LD students, summer session for credit.

Library E. Allen Gordon Library with 18,365 titles, 55 serial subscriptions, 1,602 audiovisual materials, an OPAC, a Web page.

Student Life *Housing:* college housing not available. *Activities and Organizations:* drama/theater group, choral group, Student Government Association, Phi Beta Lambda, Student Practical Nurses Organization, Computer Information Systems Organization, Early Childhood Development Organization. *Campus security:* 24-hour emergency response devices, campus alert system through mass e-mail. *Student services:* personal/psychological counseling.

Athletics *Intramural sports:* basketball M/W, football M/W, table tennis M/W, ultimate Frisbee M/W, volleyball M/W.

Standardized Tests *Recommended:* SAT or ACT (for admission), ACT COMPASS.

Costs (2012–13) *Tuition:* area resident $2340 full-time, $78 per credit hour part-time; state resident $2550 full-time, $85 per credit hour part-time; nonresident $3660 full-time, $122 per credit hour part-time. Full-time tuition and fees vary according to course load and program. Part-time tuition and fees vary according to course load and program. *Required fees:* $810 full-time, $26 per credit hour part-time, $15 per term part-time. *Payment plan:* installment. *Waivers:* senior citizens and employees or children of employees.

Financial Aid Of all full-time matriculated undergraduates who enrolled in 2012, 1,446 applied for aid, 1,266 were judged to have need, 79 had their need fully met. 28 Federal Work-Study jobs (averaging $1537). In 2012, 110 non-need-based awards were made. *Average percent of need met:* 54%. *Average financial aid package:* $5998. *Average need-based loan:* $2692. *Average need-based gift aid:* $4047. *Average non-need-based aid:* $1561. *Financial aid deadline:* 7/1.

Applying *Options:* electronic application, early admission, deferred entrance. *Required:* high school transcript. *Required for some:* immunization records and prior college transcript(s). *Application deadlines:* rolling (freshmen), rolling (transfers). *Notification:* continuous (freshmen), continuous (transfers).

Freshman Application Contact Ms. Rachel Mullins, Coordinator of Recruitment, University of Arkansas Community College at Morrilton, 1537 University Boulevard, Morrilton, AR 72110. *Phone:* 501-977-2174. *Toll-free phone:* 800-264-1094. *Fax:* 501-977-2123. *E-mail:* mullins@uaccm.edu. *Website:* http://www.uaccm.edu/.

CALIFORNIA

Academy of Couture Art

West Hollywood, California

Admissions Office Contact Academy of Couture Art, Pacific Design Center, 8687 Melrose Avenue, Suite G520, West Hollywood, CA 90069.
Website: http://www.academyofcoutureart.edu/.

Allan Hancock College

Santa Maria, California

Freshman Application Contact Ms. Adela Esquivel Swinson, Director of Admissions and Records, Allan Hancock College, 800 South College Drive, Santa Maria, CA 93454-6399. *Phone:* 805-922-6966 Ext. 3272. *Toll-free phone:* 866-342-5242. *Fax:* 805-922-3477.
Website: http://www.hancockcollege.edu/.

American Academy of Dramatic Arts

Hollywood, California

Freshman Application Contact American Academy of Dramatic Arts, 1336 North La Brea Avenue, Hollywood, CA 90028. *Phone:* 800-463-8990. *Toll-free phone:* 800-222-2867.
Website: http://www.aada.org/.

American Career College

Anaheim, California

Director of Admissions Susan Pailet, Senior Executive Director of Admission, American Career College, 1200 North Magnolia Avenue, Anaheim, CA 92801. *Phone:* 714-952-9066. *Toll-free phone:* 877-832-0790. *E-mail:* info@americancareer.com.
Website: http://americancareercollege.edu/.

American Career College

Los Angeles, California

Director of Admissions Tamra Adams, Director of Admissions, American Career College, 4021 Rosewood Avenue, Los Angeles, CA 90004-2932. *Phone:* 323-668-7555. *Toll-free phone:* 877-832-0790. *E-mail:* info@americancareer.com.
Website: http://americancareercollege.edu/.

American Career College

Ontario, California

Director of Admissions Juan Tellez, Director of Admissions, American Career College, 3130 East Sedona Court, Ontario, CA 91764. *Phone:* 951-739-0788. *Toll-free phone:* 877-832-0790. *E-mail:* info@amerciancareer.com.
Website: http://americancareercollege.edu/.

American River College

Sacramento, California

Freshman Application Contact American River College, 4700 College Oak Drive, Sacramento, CA 95841-4286. *Phone:* 916-484-8171.
Website: http://www.arc.losrios.edu/.

Antelope Valley College

Lancaster, California

Freshman Application Contact Welcome Center, Antelope Valley College, 3041 West Avenue K, Lancaster, CA 93536-5426. *Phone:* 661-722-6331.
Website: http://www.avc.edu/.

Anthem College–Sacramento

Sacramento, California

Freshman Application Contact Admissions Office, Anthem College–Sacramento, 9738 Lincoln Village Drive, Suite 100, Sacramento, CA 95827. *Phone:* 916-929-9700. *Toll-free phone:* 855-331-7768.
Website: http://anthem.edu/sacramento-california/.

Applied Professional Training, Inc.

Carlsbad, California

Director of Admissions Monica Hoffman, Director of Admissions/Registrar, Applied Professional Training, Inc., 5751 Palmer Way, Suite D, PO Box 131717, Carlsbad, CA 92013. *Phone:* 800-431-8488. *Toll-free phone:* 800-431-8488. *Fax:* 888-431-8588. *E-mail:* aptc@aptc.com.
Website: http://www.aptc.edu/.

Aviation & Electronic Schools of America

Colfax, California

Freshman Application Contact Admissions Office, Aviation & Electronic Schools of America, 111 South Railroad Street, PO Box 1810, Colfax, CA 95713-1810. *Phone:* 530-346-6792. *Toll-free phone:* 800-345-2742. *Fax:* 530-346-8466. *E-mail:* aesa@aesa.com.
Website: http://www.aesa.com/.

Bakersfield College

Bakersfield, California

- **State and locally supported** 2-year, founded 1913, part of California Community College System
- **Urban** 175-acre campus
- **Coed,** 15,001 undergraduate students

Majors Accounting; administrative assistant and secretarial science; agricultural business and management; agriculture; animal sciences; anthropology; architectural engineering technology; art; art teacher education; automobile/automotive mechanics technology; biology/biological sciences; broadcast journalism; business administration and management; carpentry; chemistry; child development; computer science; corrections; cosmetology; criminal justice/law enforcement administration; criminal justice/police science; culinary arts; data processing and data processing technology; dental hygiene; developmental and child psychology; dietetics; drafting and design technology; dramatic/theater arts; economics; electrical, electronic and communications engineering technology; emergency medical technology (EMT paramedic); engineering; English; environmental engineering technology; family and consumer economics related; finance; fire science/firefighting; foods, nutrition, and wellness; forestry; French; geography; geology/earth science; German; history; horticultural science; hotel/motel administration; human services; industrial radiologic technology; industrial technology; information science/studies; interior design; journalism; legal administrative assistant/secretary; liberal arts and sciences/liberal studies; machine tool technology; marketing/marketing management; mathematics; music; ornamental horticulture; parks, recreation and leisure; petroleum technology; philosophy; photography; physical education teaching and coaching; physics; pipefitting and sprinkler fitting; political science and government; psychology; real estate; registered nursing/registered nurse; rhetoric and composition; sociology; Spanish; surveying technology; welding technology; wood science and wood products/pulp and paper technology.

Academics *Calendar:* semesters. *Degree:* associate. *Special study options:* academic remediation for entering students, accelerated degree program, adult/continuing education programs, advanced placement credit, cooperative education, English as a second language, internships, part-time degree program, services for LD students, summer session for credit.

Library Grace Van Dyke Bird Library with 93,500 titles, 298 serial subscriptions, an OPAC, a Web page.

Student Life *Housing:* college housing not available. *Activities and Organizations:* drama/theater group, student-run newspaper, radio station, choral group. *Campus security:* 24-hour patrols, late-night transport/escort service. *Student services:* health clinic, women's center.

Athletics *Intercollegiate sports:* baseball M, basketball M/W, cross-country running M/W, football M, golf M, soccer W, softball W, tennis M/W, track and field M/W, volleyball W, wrestling M.

Financial Aid Of all full-time matriculated undergraduates who enrolled in 2011, 300 Federal Work-Study jobs (averaging $2500). 15 state and other part-time jobs (averaging $2500).

Applying *Application deadline:* rolling (freshmen).

Freshman Application Contact Bakersfield College, 1801 Panorama Drive, Bakersfield, CA 93305-1299. *Phone:* 661-395-4301.
Website: http://www.bakersfieldcollege.edu/.

Barstow Community College

Barstow, California

Director of Admissions Heather Caldon, Manager of Admissions and Records, Barstow Community College, 2700 Barstow Road, Barstow, CA

92311-6699. *Phone:* 760-252-2411 Ext. 7236. *Fax:* 760-252-6754. *E-mail:* hcaldon@barstow.edu. *Website:* http://www.barstow.edu/.

Berkeley City College
Berkeley, California

- **State and locally supported** 2-year, founded 1974, part of California Community College System
- **Urban** campus with easy access to San Francisco
- **Coed,** 7,645 undergraduate students

Undergraduates 1% are from out of state; 18% Black or African American, non-Hispanic/Latino; 12% Hispanic/Latino; 16% Asian, non-Hispanic/Latino; 0.5% Native Hawaiian or other Pacific Islander, non-Hispanic/Latino; 0.5% American Indian or Alaska Native, non-Hispanic/Latino; 3% Two or more races, non-Hispanic/Latino; 31% Race/ethnicity unknown.
Faculty *Total:* 287, 22% full-time. *Student/faculty ratio:* 35:1.
Majors Accounting; accounting and business/management; American Sign Language (ASL); art; biology/biotechnology laboratory technician; business administration and management; business administration, management and operations related; business/commerce; business, management, and marketing related; computer and information sciences; computer and information sciences related; computer and information systems security; computer graphics; computer software and media applications related; creative writing; data entry/microcomputer applications related; English; fine/studio arts; general studies; liberal arts and sciences/liberal studies; medical administrative assistant and medical secretary; office management; psychology; public health education and promotion; public health related; sign language interpretation and translation; social sciences related; social work related; sociology; Spanish; web page, digital/multimedia and information resources design; writing.
Academics *Calendar:* semesters. *Degree:* certificates and associate. *Special study options:* academic remediation for entering students, adult/continuing education programs, cooperative education, distance learning, double majors, English as a second language, independent study, internships, off-campus study, part-time degree program, services for LD students, student-designed majors, study abroad, summer session for credit.
Library Susan A. Duncan Library plus 1 other with an OPAC, a Web page.
Student Life *Housing:* college housing not available. *Activities and Organizations:* student-run newspaper, choral group, Civic Engagement Club, Global Studies Club, Indigenous Student Alliance, The National Society of Leadership and Success, The Digital Arts Club (DAC). *Campus security:* 24-hour patrols. *Student services:* health clinic, personal/psychological counseling.
Standardized Tests *Required:* Matriculating students must take a math and English assessment test (for admission).
Costs (2013–14) *Tuition:* state resident $1380 full-time, $46 per unit part-time; nonresident $7080 full-time, $236 per unit part-time. Full-time tuition and fees vary according to class time, course load, and program. Part-time tuition and fees vary according to class time, course load, and program. *Required fees:* $170 full-time, $46 per unit part-time, $690 per term part-time. *Waivers:* minority students, children of alumni, adult students, senior citizens, and employees or children of employees.
Financial Aid Of all full-time matriculated undergraduates who enrolled in 2012, 45 Federal Work-Study jobs (averaging $3000).
Applying *Required:* Berkeley City College requires an assessment test in Math and English for Matriculating students. *Recommended:* high school transcript.
Freshman Application Contact Dr. May Kuang-chi Chen, Vice President of Student Services, Berkeley City College, 2050 Center Street, Berkeley, CA 94704. *Phone:* 510-981-2820. *Fax:* 510-841-7333. *E-mail:* mrivas@peralta.edu. *Website:* http://www.berkeleycitycollege.edu/.

Bryan College
Gold River, California

Freshman Application Contact Bryan College, 2317 Gold Meadow Way, Gold River, CA 95670. *Phone:* 916-649-2400. *Toll-free phone:* 866-649-2400. *Website:* http://www.bryancollege.edu/.

Butte College
Oroville, California

- **District-supported** 2-year, founded 1966, part of California Community College System
- **Rural** 900-acre campus
- **Coed,** 12,719 undergraduate students

Majors Accounting; administrative assistant and secretarial science; agribusiness; agricultural mechanics and equipment technology; agriculture; art; automobile/automotive mechanics technology; biology/biological sciences; business administration and management; ceramic arts and ceramics; chemistry; child development; computer science; cosmetology; criminal justice/police science; data entry/microcomputer applications related; digital communication and media/multimedia; drafting and design technology; emergency medical technology (EMT paramedic); engineering; engineering technologies and engineering related; English language and literature related; environmental science; family and consumer sciences/human sciences; fire science/firefighting; foods, nutrition, and wellness; graphic design; hazardous materials management and waste technology; health and physical education/fitness; horticultural science; information technology; interior design; journalism; legal administrative assistant/secretary; liberal arts and sciences/liberal studies; licensed practical/vocational nurse training; mathematics; medical administrative assistant and medical secretary; natural resources management and policy; network and system administration; parks, recreation and leisure facilities management; photography; physical sciences; physics; radio and television; real estate; registered nursing/registered nurse; respiratory care therapy; retailing; sales, distribution, and marketing operations; small business administration; social sciences; substance abuse/addiction counseling; tourism and travel services management; welding technology.
Academics *Calendar:* semesters. *Degree:* certificates and associate. *Special study options:* academic remediation for entering students, accelerated degree program, adult/continuing education programs, advanced placement credit, cooperative education, distance learning, double majors, English as a second language, honors programs, independent study, internships, part-time degree program, services for LD students, study abroad, summer session for credit.
Library 50,000 titles, 300 serial subscriptions, an OPAC, a Web page.
Student Life *Housing:* college housing not available. *Activities and Organizations:* drama/theater group, student-run newspaper. *Campus security:* 24-hour emergency response devices and patrols, student patrols. *Student services:* health clinic, personal/psychological counseling.
Athletics *Intercollegiate sports:* baseball M, basketball M/W, cross-country running M/W, football M, golf M/W, soccer M/W, softball W, track and field M/W, volleyball W.
Costs (2013–14) *Tuition:* state resident $1104 full-time, $46 per unit part-time; nonresident $5904 full-time, $246 per unit part-time. Full-time tuition and fees vary according to course level, course load, location, and program. Part-time tuition and fees vary according to course level, course load, location, and program. *Required fees:* $252 full-time, $126 per term part-time. *Payment plans:* installment, deferred payment.
Applying *Options:* electronic application, early admission, deferred entrance. *Required for some:* high school transcript. *Application deadlines:* rolling (freshmen), rolling (transfers).
Freshman Application Contact Mr. Brad Zuniga, Director of Recruitment, Outreach, and New Student Orientation, Butte College, 3536 Butte Campus Drive, Oroville, CA 95965-8399. *Phone:* 530-895-2948. *Website:* http://www.butte.edu/.

Cabrillo College
Aptos, California

Freshman Application Contact Tama Bolton, Director of Admissions and Records, Cabrillo College, 6500 Soquel Drive, Aptos, CA 95003-3194. *Phone:* 831-477-3548. *Fax:* 831-479-5782. *E-mail:* tabolton@cabrillo.edu. *Website:* http://www.cabrillo.edu/.

California Culinary Academy
San Francisco, California

Director of Admissions Ms. Nancy Seyfert, Vice President of Admissions, California Culinary Academy, 625 Polk Street, San Francisco, CA 94102-3368. *Phone:* 800-229-2433 Ext. 275. *Toll-free phone:* 800-229-2433 (in-state); 800-BAYCHEF (out-of-state). *Website:* http://www.baychef.com/.

Cambridge Junior College
Yuba City, California

Freshman Application Contact Admissions Office, Cambridge Junior College, 990-A Klamath Lane, Yuba City, CA 95993. *Phone:* 530-674-9199. *Fax:* 530-671-7319. *Website:* http://cambridge.edu/.

Cañada College
Redwood City, California

Freshman Application Contact Cañada College, 4200 Farm Hill Boulevard, Redwood City, CA 94061-1099. *Phone:* 650-306-3125. *Website:* http://www.canadacollege.edu/.

Carrington College California–Pleasant Hill

Pleasant Hill, California

- **Proprietary** 2-year, founded 1997, part of Carrington Colleges Group, Inc.
- **Coed,** 346 undergraduate students, 100% full-time, 75% women, 25% men

Undergraduates 346 full-time. 8% Black or African American, non-Hispanic/Latino; 24% Hispanic/Latino; 15% Asian, non-Hispanic/Latino; 3% Native Hawaiian or other Pacific Islander, non-Hispanic/Latino; 1% American Indian or Alaska Native, non-Hispanic/Latino; 3% Two or more races, non-Hispanic/Latino; 0.6% Race/ethnicity unknown; 0.3% international.
Freshmen *Admission:* 30 enrolled.
Faculty *Total:* 15, 53% full-time. *Student/faculty ratio:* 33:1.
Majors Accounting technology and bookkeeping; business administration and management; criminal justice/police science; criminal justice/safety; dental assisting; graphic communications related; health and medical administrative services related; health/health-care administration; health information/medical records technology; massage therapy; medical/clinical assistant; medical insurance/medical billing; pharmacy technician; physical therapy technology; respiratory therapy technician; veterinary/animal health technology.
Academics *Calendar:* semesters. *Degree:* certificates and associate.
Student Life *Housing:* college housing not available.
Applying *Required:* essay or personal statement, high school transcript, interview.
Freshman Application Contact Carrington College California–Pleasant Hill, 380 Civic Drive, Suite 300, Pleasant Hill, CA 94523.
Website: http://carrington.edu/.

Carrington College California–San Jose

San Jose, California

- **Proprietary** 2-year, founded 1999, part of Carrington Colleges Group, Inc.
- **Coed,** 646 undergraduate students, 100% full-time, 85% women, 15% men

Undergraduates 646 full-time. 4% Black or African American, non-Hispanic/Latino; 44% Hispanic/Latino; 15% Asian, non-Hispanic/Latino; 3% Native Hawaiian or other Pacific Islander, non-Hispanic/Latino; 0.3% American Indian or Alaska Native, non-Hispanic/Latino; 5% Two or more races, non-Hispanic/Latino; 2% Race/ethnicity unknown; 0.3% international. *Retention:* 64% of full-time freshmen returned.
Freshmen *Admission:* 36 enrolled.
Faculty *Total:* 56, 30% full-time. *Student/faculty ratio:* 22:1.
Majors Accounting technology and bookkeeping; allied health and medical assisting services related; architectural drafting and CAD/CADD; biology/biotechnology laboratory technician; business administration and management; computer graphics; criminal justice/safety; dental assisting; dental hygiene; drafting and design technology; health/health-care administration; licensed practical/vocational nurse training; massage therapy; medical/clinical assistant; medical insurance/medical billing; medical office management; pharmacy technician; surgical technology; veterinary/animal health technology.
Academics *Calendar:* semesters. *Degree:* certificates and associate.
Student Life *Housing:* college housing not available.
Standardized Tests *Required:* Entrance test administered by Carrington College California (for admission).
Applying *Required:* essay or personal statement, high school transcript, interview.
Freshman Application Contact Carrington College California–San Jose, 6201 San Ignacio Avenue, San Jose, CA 95119.
Website: http://carrington.edu/.

Carrington College California–San Leandro

San Leandro, California

- **Proprietary** 2-year, founded 1986, part of Carrington Colleges Group, Inc.
- **Coed,** 471 undergraduate students, 100% full-time, 89% women, 11% men

Undergraduates 471 full-time. 23% Black or African American, non-Hispanic/Latino; 39% Hispanic/Latino; 11% Asian, non-Hispanic/Latino; 3% Native Hawaiian or other Pacific Islander, non-Hispanic/Latino; 0.2% American Indian or Alaska Native, non-Hispanic/Latino; 4% Two or more races, non-Hispanic/Latino; 2% Race/ethnicity unknown.
Freshmen *Admission:* 37 enrolled.
Faculty *Total:* 22, 55% full-time. *Student/faculty ratio:* 31:1.
Majors Accounting technology and bookkeeping; business administration and management; dental assisting; health and medical administrative services related; health/health-care administration; massage therapy; medical/clinical assistant; medical insurance/medical billing; pharmacy technician; veterinary/animal health technology.
Academics *Calendar:* semesters. *Degree:* certificates and associate.
Student Life *Housing:* college housing not available.
Standardized Tests *Required:* Entrance test administered by Carrington Colleges California (for admission).
Applying *Required:* essay or personal statement, high school transcript, interview.
Freshman Application Contact Carrington College California–San Leandro, 15555 East 14th Street, Suite 500, San Leandro, CA 94578.
Website: http://carrington.edu/.

Carrington College of California–Antioch

Antioch, California

- **Proprietary** 2-year, founded 1997, part of Carrington Colleges Group, Inc.
- **Coed,** 318 undergraduate students, 100% full-time, 81% women, 19% men

Undergraduates 318 full-time. 27% Black or African American, non-Hispanic/Latino; 30% Hispanic/Latino; 3% Asian, non-Hispanic/Latino; 3% Native Hawaiian or other Pacific Islander, non-Hispanic/Latino; 0.3% American Indian or Alaska Native, non-Hispanic/Latino; 5% Two or more races, non-Hispanic/Latino; 3% Race/ethnicity unknown; 0.6% international.
Freshmen *Admission:* 43 enrolled.
Faculty *Total:* 18, 61% full-time. *Student/faculty ratio:* 24:1.
Majors Criminal justice/safety; dental assisting; health/health-care administration; licensed practical/vocational nurse training; massage therapy; medical/clinical assistant; medical insurance/medical billing; medical office management; pharmacy technician.
Academics *Calendar:* continuous. *Degree:* certificates and associate.
Student Life *Housing:* college housing not available.
Standardized Tests *Required:* Entrance exam administered by Carrington College California (for admission).
Applying *Required:* essay or personal statement, high school transcript, interview. *Required for some:* essay or personal statement. *Notification:* continuous (freshmen), continuous (transfers).
Freshman Application Contact Carrington College of California–Antioch, 2157 Country Hills Drive, Antioch, CA 94509.
Website: http://carrington.edu/.

Carrington College of California–Citrus Heights

Citrus Heights, California

- **Proprietary** 2-year, part of Carrington Colleges Group, Inc.
- **Coed,** 412 undergraduate students, 100% full-time, 84% women, 16% men

Undergraduates 412 full-time. Students come from 4 states and territories; 1% are from out of state; 5% Black or African American, non-Hispanic/Latino; 12% Hispanic/Latino; 2% Asian, non-Hispanic/Latino; 1% Native Hawaiian or other Pacific Islander, non-Hispanic/Latino; 2% American Indian or Alaska Native, non-Hispanic/Latino; 1% Two or more races, non-Hispanic/Latino; 36% Race/ethnicity unknown.
Freshmen *Admission:* 22 enrolled.
Faculty *Total:* 16, 63% full-time. *Student/faculty ratio:* 34:1.
Majors Accounting technology and bookkeeping; business administration and management; criminal justice/safety; dental assisting; health/health-care administration; medical/clinical assistant; medical insurance/medical billing; pharmacy technician; surgical technology; veterinary/animal health technology.
Academics *Degree:* certificates and associate.
Student Life *Housing:* college housing not available.
Standardized Tests *Required:* Entrance test administered by Carrington College California (for admission).
Applying *Required:* essay or personal statement, high school transcript, interview.
Freshman Application Contact Carrington College of California–Citrus Heights, 7301 Greenback Lane, Suite A, Citrus Heights, CA 95621.
Website: http://carrington.edu/.

Carrington College of California–Emeryville

Emeryville, California

Freshman Application Contact Admissions Office, Carrington College of California–Emeryville, 6001 Shellmound Street, Suite 145, Emeryville, CA 94608. *Phone:* 510-601-0133. *Fax:* 510-623-9822.
Website: http://carrington.edu/.

Carrington College of California–Sacramento

Sacramento, California

- **Proprietary** 2-year, founded 1967, part of Carrington Colleges Group, Inc.
- **Coed,** 1,392 undergraduate students, 100% full-time, 85% women, 15% men

Undergraduates 1,392 full-time. 24% are from out of state; 17% Black or African American, non-Hispanic/Latino; 20% Hispanic/Latino; 9% Asian, non-Hispanic/Latino; 2% Native Hawaiian or other Pacific Islander, non-Hispanic/Latino; 1% American Indian or Alaska Native, non-Hispanic/Latino; 6% Two or more races, non-Hispanic/Latino; 4% Race/ethnicity unknown; 0.1% international.

Freshmen *Admission:* 124 enrolled.

Faculty *Total:* 97, 24% full-time. *Student/faculty ratio:* 29:1.

Majors Dental assisting; dental hygiene; health/health-care administration; licensed practical/vocational nurse training; massage therapy; medical/clinical assistant; medical insurance/medical billing; medical office management; pharmacy technician; registered nursing/registered nurse; veterinary/animal health technology.

Academics *Calendar:* semesters. *Degree:* certificates and associate.

Standardized Tests *Required:* Entrance test administered by Carrington College California (for admission).

Applying *Required:* essay or personal statement, high school transcript, interview.

Freshman Application Contact Carrington College of California–Sacramento, 8909 Folsom Boulevard, Sacramento, CA 95826.
Website: http://carrington.edu/.

Cerritos College

Norwalk, California

Director of Admissions Ms. Stephanie Murguia, Director of Admissions and Records, Cerritos College, 11110 Alondra Boulevard, Norwalk, CA 90650-6298. *Phone:* 562-860-2451. *E-mail:* smurguia@cerritos.edu.
Website: http://www.cerritos.edu/.

Cerro Coso Community College

Ridgecrest, California

Freshman Application Contact Mrs. Heather Ootash, Counseling/Matriculation Coordinator, Cerro Coso Community College, 3000 College Heights Boulevard, Ridgecrest, CA 93555. *Phone:* 760-384-6291. *Fax:* 760-375-4776. *E-mail:* hostash@cerrocoso.edu.
Website: http://www.cerrocoso.edu/.

Chabot College

Hayward, California

Director of Admissions Paulette Lino, Director of Admissions and Records, Chabot College, 25555 Hesperian Boulevard, Hayward, CA 94545-5001. *Phone:* 510-723-6700.
Website: http://www.chabotcollege.edu/.

Chaffey College

Rancho Cucamonga, California

Freshman Application Contact Erlinda Martinez, Coordinator of Admissions, Chaffey College, 5885 Haven Avenue, Rancho Cucamonga, CA 91737-3002. *Phone:* 909-652-6610. *E-mail:* erlinda.martinez@chaffey.edu.
Website: http://www.chaffey.edu/.

Citrus College

Glendora, California

Freshman Application Contact Admissions and Records, Citrus College, Glendora, CA 91741-1899. *Phone:* 626-914-8511. *Fax:* 626-914-8613. *E-mail:* admissions@citruscollege.edu.
Website: http://www.citruscollege.edu/.

City College of San Francisco

San Francisco, California

Freshman Application Contact Ms. Mary Lou Leyba-Frank, Dean of Admissions and Records, City College of San Francisco, 50 Phelan Avenue, San Francisco, CA 94112-1821. *Phone:* 415-239-3291. *Fax:* 415-239-3936. *E-mail:* mleyba@ccsf.edu.
Website: http://www.ccsf.edu/.

Coastline Community College

Fountain Valley, California

Freshman Application Contact Jennifer McDonald, Director of Admissions and Records, Coastline Community College, 11460 Warner Avenue, Fountain Valley, CA 92708-2597. *Phone:* 714-241-6163.
Website: http://www.coastline.edu/.

Coleman University

San Marcos, California

Director of Admissions Senior Admissions Officer, Coleman University, 1284 West San Marcos Boulevard, San Marcos, CA 92078. *Phone:* 760-747-3990. *Fax:* 760-752-9808.
Website: http://www.coleman.edu/.

College of Alameda

Alameda, California

Freshman Application Contact College of Alameda, 555 Ralph Appezzato Memorial Parkway, Alameda, CA 94501-2109. *Phone:* 510-748-2204.
Website: http://alameda.peralta.edu/.

College of Marin

Kentfield, California

- **State and locally supported** 2-year, founded 1926, part of California Community College System
- **Suburban** 410-acre campus with easy access to San Francisco
- **Coed,** 7,000 undergraduate students

Faculty *Total:* 330.

Majors Accounting technology and bookkeeping; animation, interactive technology, video graphics and special effects; architectural technology; art; autobody/collision and repair technology; automobile/automotive mechanics technology; biological and physical sciences; biology/biological sciences; business administration and management; business/commerce; chemistry; child-care provision; cinematography and film/video production; computer science; computer systems networking and telecommunications; court reporting; criminal justice/police science; dance; data modeling/warehousing and database administration; dental assisting; design and visual communications; dramatic/theater arts; engineering; engineering technology; English; ethnic, cultural minority, gender, and group studies related; film/cinema/video studies; foreign languages and literatures; French; geography; geology/earth science; health and physical education/fitness; history; humanities; interior design; international relations and affairs; landscaping and groundskeeping; liberal arts and sciences/liberal studies; machine tool technology; mass communication/media; mathematics; medical administrative assistant and medical secretary; medical/clinical assistant; music; office management; physical sciences; physics; plant nursery management; political science and government; psychology; real estate; registered nursing/registered nurse; social sciences; Spanish; speech communication and rhetoric.

Academics *Calendar:* semesters. *Degree:* certificates and associate. *Special study options:* academic remediation for entering students, advanced placement credit, cooperative education, distance learning, English as a second language, part-time degree program, services for LD students, summer session for credit.

Library Main Library plus 1 other.

Student Life *Housing:* college housing not available. *Activities and Organizations:* drama/theater group, student-run newspaper. *Campus security:* 24-hour emergency response devices and patrols. *Student services:* health clinic, personal/psychological counseling.

Athletics *Intercollegiate sports:* baseball M, basketball M/W, soccer M/W, softball W, swimming and diving M/W, track and field M/W, volleyball W, water polo M/W.

Costs (2013–14) *Tuition:* state resident $0 full-time; nonresident $7568 full-time, $251 per unit part-time. Full-time tuition and fees vary according to course load. Part-time tuition and fees vary according to course load. *Required fees:* $1418 full-time, $46 per unit part-time. *Payment plan:* installment.

Applying *Options:* electronic application, early admission. *Application deadlines:* rolling (freshmen), rolling (transfers).

Freshman Application Contact College of Marin, 835 College Avenue, Kentfield, CA 94904. *Phone:* 415-485-9414. *Website:* http://www.marin.edu/.

College of San Mateo
San Mateo, California

Director of Admissions Mr. Henry Villareal, Dean of Admissions and Records, College of San Mateo, 1700 West Hillsdale Boulevard, San Mateo, CA 94402-3784. *Phone:* 650-574-6590. *E-mail:* csmadmission@smccd.edu. *Website:* http://www.collegeofsanmateo.edu/.

College of the Canyons
Santa Clarita, California

- **State and locally supported** 2-year, founded 1969, part of California Community College System
- **Suburban** 224-acre campus with easy access to Los Angeles
- **Coed,** 16,844 undergraduate students, 31% full-time, 48% women, 52% men

Undergraduates 5,285 full-time, 11,559 part-time. 4% are from out of state; 5% Black or African American, non-Hispanic/Latino; 40% Hispanic/Latino; 9% Asian, non-Hispanic/Latino; 0.2% Native Hawaiian or other Pacific Islander, non-Hispanic/Latino; 0.3% American Indian or Alaska Native, non-Hispanic/Latino; 4% Two or more races, non-Hispanic/Latino; 0.8% Race/ethnicity unknown.

Freshmen *Admission:* 2,698 enrolled.

Faculty *Total:* 703, 25% full-time. *Student/faculty ratio:* 35:1.

Majors Accounting technology and bookkeeping; administrative assistant and secretarial science; animation, interactive technology, video graphics and special effects; architectural drafting and CAD/CADD; art; athletic training; automobile/automotive mechanics technology; biological and physical sciences; building/construction site management; business administration and management; child-care provision; computer science; computer systems networking and telecommunications; criminal justice/police science; dramatic/theater arts; English; fire prevention and safety technology; French; graphic design; health and physical education/fitness; history; hospitality administration; hotel/motel administration; humanities; interior design; intermedia/multimedia; journalism; landscaping and groundskeeping; legal assistant/paralegal; liberal arts and sciences/liberal studies; library and archives assisting; manufacturing engineering technology; mathematics; music; parks, recreation and leisure; photographic and film/video technology; photography; pre-engineering; psychology; radio and television; real estate; registered nursing/registered nurse; restaurant, culinary, and catering management; sales, distribution, and marketing operations; sign language interpretation and translation; small business administration; social sciences; sociology; Spanish; surveying technology; water quality and wastewater treatment management and recycling technology; welding technology.

Academics *Calendar:* semesters. *Degree:* certificates and associate. *Special study options:* academic remediation for entering students, accelerated degree program, adult/continuing education programs, advanced placement credit, cooperative education, distance learning, double majors, English as a second language, honors programs, internships, part-time degree program, services for LD students, summer session for credit.

Library College of the Canyons Library with an OPAC, a Web page.

Student Life *Housing:* college housing not available. *Activities and Organizations:* drama/theater group, choral group, Gamma Beta Phi, Phi Theta Kappa, Welding Club, Communication Studies Club, Ice Hockey Club, Psychology Club. *Campus security:* 24-hour emergency response devices, late-night transport/escort service. *Student services:* health clinic, personal/psychological counseling, women's center.

Athletics *Intercollegiate sports:* baseball M, basketball M/W, cross-country running M/W, football M, golf M/W, ice hockey M(c), soccer M/W, softball W, swimming and diving M/W, track and field M/W, volleyball W.

Costs (2013–14) *Tuition:* state resident $1152 full-time, $46 per unit part-time; nonresident $5450 full-time, $225 per unit part-time. *Required fees:* $50 full-time.

Applying *Options:* electronic application, early admission. *Recommended:* high school transcript. *Application deadlines:* rolling (freshmen), rolling (transfers). *Notification:* continuous (freshmen), continuous (transfers).

Freshman Application Contact Ms. Jasmine Ruys, Director, Admissions and Records and Online Services, College of the Canyons, 26455 Rockwell Canyon Road, Santa Clarita, CA 91355. *Phone:* 661-362-3280. *Fax:* 661-254-7996. *E-mail:* jasmine.ruys@canyons.edu. *Website:* http://www.canyons.edu/.

College of the Desert
Palm Desert, California

- **State and locally supported** 2-year, founded 1959, part of California Community College System
- **Small-town** 160-acre campus
- **Coed,** 10,099 undergraduate students

Undergraduates 4% Black or African American, non-Hispanic/Latino; 65% Hispanic/Latino; 4% Asian, non-Hispanic/Latino; 0.8% Native Hawaiian or other Pacific Islander, non-Hispanic/Latino; 0.4% American Indian or Alaska Native, non-Hispanic/Latino; 2% Two or more races, non-Hispanic/Latino; 2% Race/ethnicity unknown.

Faculty *Total:* 403, 26% full-time. *Student/faculty ratio:* 30:1.

Majors Agribusiness; agriculture; anthropology; applied horticulture/horticulture operations; architectural technology; art; automobile/automotive mechanics technology; biological and physical sciences; biology/biological sciences; building/construction site management; business administration and management; business/commerce; chemistry; child-care and support services management; computer graphics; computer science; creative writing; criminal justice/police science; crop production; culinary arts; dietetic technology; drafting and design technology; dramatic/theater arts; economics; English; environmental science; environmental studies; fire science/firefighting; French; geography; geology/earth science; health and physical education/fitness; heating, air conditioning, ventilation and refrigeration maintenance technology; history; hospitality administration; humanities; information technology; Italian; journalism; liberal arts and sciences/liberal studies; licensed practical/vocational nurse training; mass communication/media; mathematics; multi/interdisciplinary studies related; music; natural resources/conservation; office management; parks, recreation and leisure facilities management; philosophy; physics; political science and government; psychology; registered nursing/registered nurse; resort management; social sciences; sociology; Spanish; speech communication and rhetoric; substance abuse/addiction counseling; turf and turfgrass management; vehicle maintenance and repair technologies.

Academics *Calendar:* semesters. *Degree:* certificates, diplomas, and associate. *Special study options:* academic remediation for entering students, adult/continuing education programs, distance learning, English as a second language, freshman honors college, honors programs, part-time degree program, services for LD students, summer session for credit.

Library College of the Desert Library plus 1 other with an OPAC, a Web page.

Student Life *Housing:* college housing not available. *Activities and Organizations:* drama/theater group, student-run newspaper, radio station, choral group, Student Nursing Association, Phi Theta Kappa, Dramatic Arts Company, International Club, World Beat. *Campus security:* 24-hour emergency response devices and patrols, late-night transport/escort service. *Student services:* health clinic, personal/psychological counseling.

Athletics Member NJCAA. *Intercollegiate sports:* baseball M, basketball M/W, cross-country running M/W, fencing M/W, football M, golf M/W, soccer M/W, softball W, tennis M/W, track and field M/W, volleyball W.

Costs (2012–13) *Tuition:* state resident $1288 full-time, $46 per unit part-time; nonresident $6496 full-time, $232 per unit part-time. Full-time tuition and fees vary according to course load and program. Part-time tuition and fees vary according to course load and program. *Required fees:* $37 full-time, $0 per unit part-time, $15 per term part-time. *Payment plan:* installment.

Applying *Options:* electronic application, early admission. *Application deadlines:* rolling (freshmen), rolling (transfers). *Notification:* continuous (freshmen), continuous (transfers).

Freshman Application Contact College of the Desert, 43-500 Monterey Avenue, Palm Desert, CA 92260-9305. *Phone:* 760-346-8041 Ext. 7441. *Website:* http://www.collegeofthedesert.edu/.

College of the Redwoods
Eureka, California

Freshman Application Contact Director of Enrollment Management, College of the Redwoods, 7351 Tompkins Hill Road, Eureka, CA 95501-9300. *Phone:* 707-476-4100. *Toll-free phone:* 800-641-0400. *Fax:* 707-476-4400. *Website:* http://www.redwoods.edu/.

College of the Sequoias
Visalia, California

Freshman Application Contact Ms. Lisa Hott, Director for Admissions, College of the Sequoias, 915 South Mooney Boulevard, Visalia, CA 93277-2234. *Phone:* 559-737-4844. *Fax:* 559-737-4820.
Website: http://www.cos.edu/.

College of the Siskiyous
Weed, California

Freshman Application Contact Recruitment and Admissions, College of the Siskiyous, 800 College Avenue, Weed, CA 96094-2899. *Phone:* 530-938-5555. *Toll-free phone:* 888-397-4339. *E-mail:* admissions-weed@siskyous.edu.
Website: http://www.siskiyous.edu/.

Columbia College
Sonora, California

Freshman Application Contact Admissions Office, Columbia College, 11600 Columbia College Drive, Sonora, CA 95370. *Phone:* 209-588-5231. *Fax:* 209-588-5337. *E-mail:* ccadmissions@yosemite.edu.
Website: http://www.gocolumbia.edu/.

Community Christian College
Redlands, California

Freshman Application Contact Enrique D. Melendez, Assistant Director of Admissions, Community Christian College, 251 Tennessee Street, Redlands, CA 92373. *Phone:* 909-222-9556. *Fax:* 909-335-9101. *E-mail:* emelendez@cccollege.edu.
Website: http://www.cccollege.edu/.

Concorde Career College
Garden Grove, California

Freshman Application Contact Chris Becker, Director, Concorde Career College, 12951 Euclid Street, Suite 101, Garden Grove, CA 92840. *Phone:* 714-703-1900. *Fax:* 714-530-4737. *E-mail:* cbecker@concorde.edu.
Website: http://www.concorde.edu/.

Concorde Career College
North Hollywood, California

Freshman Application Contact Madeline Volker, Director, Concorde Career College, 12412 Victory Boulevard, North Hollywood, CA 91606. *Phone:* 818-766-8151. *Fax:* 818-766-1587. *E-mail:* mvolker@concorde.edu.
Website: http://www.concorde.edu/.

Contra Costa College
San Pablo, California

Freshman Application Contact Admissions and Records Office, Contra Costa College, San Pablo, CA 94806. *Phone:* 510-235-7800 Ext. 7500. *Fax:* 510-412-0769. *E-mail:* A&R@contracosta.edu.
Website: http://www.contracosta.edu/.

Copper Mountain College
Joshua Tree, California

Freshman Application Contact Dr. Laraine Turk, Associate Dean of Student Services, Copper Mountain College, 6162 Rotary Way, Joshua Tree, CA 92252. *Phone:* 760-366-5290. *Toll-free phone:* 866-366-3791.
Website: http://www.cmccd.edu/.

Cosumnes River College
Sacramento, California

Freshman Application Contact Admissions and Records, Cosumnes River College, 8401 Center Parkway, Sacramento, CA 95823-5799. *Phone:* 916-691-7411.
Website: http://www.crc.losrios.edu/.

Crafton Hills College
Yucaipa, California

Director of Admissions Larry Aycock, Admissions and Records Coordinator, Crafton Hills College, 11711 Sand Canyon Road, Yucaipa, CA 92399-1799. *Phone:* 909-389-3663. *E-mail:* laycock@craftonhills.edu.
Website: http://www.craftonhills.edu/.

Cuesta College
San Luis Obispo, California

Freshman Application Contact Cuesta College, PO Box 8106, San Luis Obispo, CA 93403-8106. *Phone:* 805-546-3130 Ext. 2262.
Website: http://www.cuesta.edu/.

Cuyamaca College
El Cajon, California

Freshman Application Contact Ms. Susan Topham, Dean of Admissions and Records, Cuyamaca College, 900 Rancho San Diego Parkway, El Cajon, CA 92019-4304. *Phone:* 619-660-4302. *Fax:* 619-660-4575. *E-mail:* susan.topham@gcccd.edu.
Website: http://www.cuyamaca.net/.

Cypress College
Cypress, California

Freshman Application Contact Admissions Office, Cypress College, 9200 Valley View, Cypress, CA 90630-5897. *Phone:* 714-484-7346. *Fax:* 714-484-7446. *E-mail:* admissions@cypresscollege.edu.
Website: http://www.cypresscollege.edu/.

De Anza College
Cupertino, California

- **State and locally supported** 2-year, founded 1967, part of California Community College System
- **Suburban** 112-acre campus with easy access to San Francisco, San Jose
- **Coed**

Undergraduates 5% Black or African American, non-Hispanic/Latino; 22% Hispanic/Latino; 37% Asian, non-Hispanic/Latino; 0.8% Native Hawaiian or other Pacific Islander, non-Hispanic/Latino; 0.7% American Indian or Alaska Native, non-Hispanic/Latino; 5% Race/ethnicity unknown.
Faculty *Total:* 794, 38% full-time. *Student/faculty ratio:* 36:1.
Majors Accounting; administrative assistant and secretarial science; art; art history, criticism and conservation; automobile/automotive mechanics technology; behavioral sciences; biology/biological sciences; business administration and management; business machine repair; ceramic arts and ceramics; child development; commercial and advertising art; computer graphics; computer programming; computer science; construction engineering technology; corrections; criminal justice/law enforcement administration; criminal justice/police science; developmental and child psychology; drafting/design engineering technologies related; dramatic/theater arts; drawing; economics; engineering; engineering technology; English; environmental studies; film/cinema/video studies; history; humanities; industrial technology; information science/studies; international relations and affairs; journalism; legal assistant/paralegal; liberal arts and sciences/liberal studies; licensed practical/vocational nurse training; machine tool technology; marketing/marketing management; mass communication/media; mathematics; medical/clinical assistant; music; philosophy; photography; physical education teaching and coaching; physical therapy; physics; political science and government; pre-engineering; printmaking; professional, technical, business, and scientific writing; psychology; purchasing, procurement/acquisitions and contracts management; radio and television; real estate; registered nursing/registered nurse; rhetoric and composition; sculpture; social sciences; sociology; Spanish.
Academics *Calendar:* quarters. *Degree:* certificates, diplomas, and associate. *Special study options:* academic remediation for entering students, adult/continuing education programs, advanced placement credit, cooperative education, distance learning, English as a second language, external degree program, honors programs, independent study, internships, part-time degree program, services for LD students, student-designed majors, study abroad, summer session for credit. *ROTC:* Army (c), Air Force (c).
Library A. Robert DeHart Learning Center with 80,000 titles, 927 serial subscriptions, an OPAC, a Web page.
Student Life *Housing:* college housing not available. *Activities and Organizations:* drama/theater group, student-run newspaper, choral group, Student Nurses Association, Phi Theta Kappa, Automotive Club, Vietnamese Club, Filipino Club. *Campus security:* 24-hour emergency response devices, student

patrols, late-night transport/escort service. *Student services:* health clinic, personal/psychological counseling, legal services.

Athletics Member NCAA. All Division II. *Intercollegiate sports:* baseball M, basketball M/W, cross-country running M/W, football M, golf M/W, soccer M/W, softball W, swimming and diving M/W, tennis M/W, track and field M/W, volleyball M/W, water polo M. *Intramural sports:* badminton M/W, basketball M, soccer M/W, swimming and diving M/W, volleyball M/W.

Costs (2012–13) *Tuition:* state resident $1116 full-time; nonresident $6084 full-time. Full-time tuition and fees vary according to course load. Part-time tuition and fees vary according to course load. *Required fees:* $167 full-time. *Payment plan:* installment. *Waivers:* minority students and adult students.

Freshman Application Contact De Anza College, 21250 Stevens Creek Boulevard, Cupertino, CA 95014-5793. *Phone:* 408-864-8292.
Website: http://www.deanza.fhda.edu/.

Deep Springs College
Deep Springs, California

- **Independent** 2-year, founded 1917
- **Rural** 3000-acre campus
- **Endowment** $18.0 million
- **Men only,** 26 undergraduate students, 100% full-time

Undergraduates 26 full-time. Students come from 18 states and territories; 3 other countries; 80% are from out of state; 62% transferred in; 100% live on campus. *Retention:* 100% of full-time freshmen returned.

Freshmen *Admission:* 26 enrolled. *Average high school GPA:* 3.87. *Test scores:* SAT critical reading scores over 500: 100%; SAT math scores over 500: 100%; SAT writing scores over 500: 100%; SAT critical reading scores over 600: 100%; SAT math scores over 600: 95%; SAT writing scores over 600: 100%; SAT critical reading scores over 700: 95%; SAT math scores over 700: 80%; SAT writing scores over 700: 80%.

Faculty *Total:* 8, 38% full-time, 100% with terminal degrees. *Student/faculty ratio:* 5:1.

Majors Liberal arts and sciences/liberal studies.

Academics *Calendar:* 6 seven-week terms. *Degree:* associate. *Special study options:* advanced placement credit, distance learning, freshman honors college, honors programs, independent study, internships, services for LD students, summer session for credit.

Library Mossner Library of Deep Springs with 20,000 titles, 60 serial subscriptions.

Student Life *Housing:* on-campus residence required through sophomore year. *Options:* men-only. Campus housing is university owned. Freshman campus housing is guaranteed. *Activities and Organizations:* drama/theater group, choral group, Student Self-Government, Labor Program, Applications Committee, Review Committee, Curriculum Committee. *Campus security:* 24-hour emergency response devices, late-night transport/escort service. *Student services:* personal/psychological counseling, legal services.

Athletics *Intramural sports:* archery M, basketball M, cross-country running M, equestrian sports M, football M, riflery M, rock climbing M, soccer M, swimming and diving M, table tennis M, ultimate Frisbee M, water polo M, weight lifting M.

Standardized Tests *Required:* SAT and SAT Subject Tests or ACT (for admission).

Costs (2013–14) *Comprehensive fee:* includes mandatory fees ($800). Every student accepted to Deep Springs receives a scholarship covering tuition, room, and board.

Applying *Required:* essay or personal statement, high school transcript, interview.

Freshman Application Contact David Neidorf, President, Deep Springs College, HC 72, Box 45001, Dyer, NV 89010-9803. *Phone:* 760-872-2000 Ext. 45. *Fax:* 760-874-0314. *E-mail:* apcom@deepsprings.edu.
Website: http://www.deepsprings.edu/.

Diablo Valley College
Pleasant Hill, California

Freshman Application Contact Ileana Dorn, Director of Admissions and Records, Diablo Valley College, Pleasant Hill, CA 94523-1529. *Phone:* 925-685-1230 Ext. 2330. *Fax:* 925-609-8085. *E-mail:* idorn@dvc.edu.
Website: http://www.dvc.edu/.

East Los Angeles College
Monterey Park, California

Freshman Application Contact Mr. Jeremy Allred, Associate Dean of Admissions, East Los Angeles College, 1301 Avenida Cesar Chavez, Monterey Park, CA 91754. *Phone:* 323-265-8801. *Fax:* 323-265-8688. *E-mail:* allredjp@elac.edu.
Website: http://www.elac.edu/.

El Camino College
Torrance, California

Director of Admissions Mr. William Mulrooney, Director of Admissions, El Camino College, 16007 Crenshaw Boulevard, Torrance, CA 90506-0001. *Phone:* 310-660-3418. *Toll-free phone:* 866-ELCAMINO. *Fax:* 310-660-6779. *E-mail:* wmulrooney@elcamino.edu.
Website: http://www.elcamino.edu/.

Empire College
Santa Rosa, California

Freshman Application Contact Ms. Dahnja Barker, Admissions Officer, Empire College, 3035 Cleveland Avenue, Santa Rosa, CA 95403. *Phone:* 707-546-4000. *Toll-free phone:* 877-395-8535.
Website: http://www.empcol.edu/.

Everest College
City of Industry, California

Freshman Application Contact Admissions Office, Everest College, 12801 Crossroads Parkway South, City of Industry, CA 91746. *Phone:* 562-908-2500. *Toll-free phone:* 888-741-4270. *Fax:* 562-908-7656.
Website: http://www.everest.edu/.

Everest College
Ontario, California

Freshman Application Contact Admissions Office, Everest College, 1819 South Excise Avenue, Ontario, CA 91761. *Phone:* 909-484-4311. *Toll-free phone:* 888-741-4270. *Fax:* 909-484-1162.
Website: http://www.everest.edu/.

Evergreen Valley College
San Jose, California

Freshman Application Contact Evergreen Valley College, 3095 Yerba Buena Road, San Jose, CA 95135-1598. *Phone:* 408-270-6423.
Website: http://www.evc.edu/.

Feather River College
Quincy, California

Freshman Application Contact Leslie Mikesell, Interim Director of Admissions and Records, Feather River College, 570 Golden Eagle Avenue, Quincy, CA 95971-9124. *Phone:* 530-283-0202 Ext. 600. *Toll-free phone:* 800-442-9799. *E-mail:* lmikesell@frc.edu.
Website: http://www.frc.edu/.

FIDM/The Fashion Institute of Design & Merchandising, Los Angeles Campus
Los Angeles, California

- **Proprietary** primarily 2-year, founded 1969, part of The Fashion Institute of Design and Merchandising/FIDM
- **Urban** campus
- **Coed,** 3,743 undergraduate students, 88% full-time, 89% women, 11% men

Undergraduates 3,288 full-time, 455 part-time. 6% Black or African American, non-Hispanic/Latino; 23% Hispanic/Latino; 12% Asian, non-Hispanic/Latino; 1% Native Hawaiian or other Pacific Islander, non-Hispanic/Latino; 0.3% American Indian or Alaska Native, non-Hispanic/Latino; 3% Two or more races, non-Hispanic/Latino; 9% Race/ethnicity unknown; 12% international. *Retention:* 91% of full-time freshmen returned.

Freshmen *Admission:* 1,777 applied, 1,009 admitted, 638 enrolled. *Average high school GPA:* 2.75.

Faculty *Total:* 326, 21% full-time. *Student/faculty ratio:* 21:1.

Majors Apparel and accessories marketing; apparel and textiles; business administration and management; commercial and advertising art; consumer merchandising/retailing management; design and visual communications; fashion/apparel design; fashion merchandising; interior design; metal and jewelry arts.

Academics *Calendar:* quarters. *Degrees:* associate and bachelor's (also includes Orange County Campus). *Special study options:* academic remediation for entering students, adult/continuing education programs, advanced placement credit, cooperative education, distance learning, English as a second language, independent study, internships, part-time degree program, services for LD students, study abroad, summer session for credit.

Library FIDM Los Angeles Campus Library plus 1 other with 39,205 titles, 243 serial subscriptions, 6,243 audiovisual materials, an OPAC.

Student Life *Activities and Organizations:* student-run newspaper, ASID (student chapter), Design Council, Phi Theta Kappa Honor Society, Student Council, MODE. *Campus security:* 24-hour emergency response devices and patrols, late-night transport/escort service. *Student services:* personal/psychological counseling.

Standardized Tests *Recommended:* SAT or ACT (for admission).

Costs (2013–14) *Tuition:* $23,965 full-time. Full-time tuition and fees vary according to degree level and program. *Required fees:* $225 full-time.

Financial Aid Of all full-time matriculated undergraduates who enrolled in 2011, 88 Federal Work-Study jobs (averaging $2935).

Applying *Options:* electronic application, deferred entrance. *Application fee:* $225. *Required:* essay or personal statement, high school transcript, minimum 2.0 GPA, 3 letters of recommendation, interview, major-determined project. *Application deadlines:* rolling (freshmen), rolling (out-of-state freshmen), rolling (transfers).

Freshman Application Contact Ms. Susan Aronson, Director of Admissions, FIDM/The Fashion Institute of Design & Merchandising, Los Angeles Campus, Los Angeles, CA 90015. *Phone:* 213-624-1201. *Toll-free phone:* 800-624-1200. *Fax:* 213-624-4799. *E-mail:* saronson@fidm.com. *Website:* http://www.fidm.edu/.

See display below and page 404 for the College Close-Up.

FIDM/The Fashion Institute of Design & Merchandising, Orange County Campus

Irvine, California

- **Proprietary** 2-year, founded 1981, part of The Fashion Institute of Design and Merchandising/FIDM
- **Coed, primarily women,** 293 undergraduate students, 98% full-time, 91% women, 9% men

Undergraduates 286 full-time, 7 part-time. Students come from 8 states and territories; 1 other country; 11% are from out of state; 2% Black or African American, non-Hispanic/Latino; 31% Hispanic/Latino; 13% Asian, non-Hispanic/Latino; 2% Native Hawaiian or other Pacific Islander, non-Hispanic/Latino; 0.7% American Indian or Alaska Native, non-Hispanic/Latino; 3% Two or more races, non-Hispanic/Latino; 8% Race/ethnicity unknown; 3% international; 31% transferred in.

Freshmen *Admission:* 376 applied, 260 admitted, 166 enrolled. *Average high school GPA:* 2.75.

Faculty *Total:* 33, 24% full-time. *Student/faculty ratio:* 21:1.

Majors Apparel and textiles; commercial and advertising art; consumer merchandising/retailing management; fashion/apparel design; fashion merchandising; fiber, textile and weaving arts; industrial technology; interior design; marketing/marketing management.

Academics *Calendar:* quarters. *Degree:* associate. *Special study options:* academic remediation for entering students, adult/continuing education programs, advanced placement credit, cooperative education, distance learning, English as a second language, independent study, internships, part-time degree program, services for LD students, study abroad, summer session for credit.

Library FIDM Orange County Campus Library plus 1 other with 7,300 titles, 84 serial subscriptions, 3,010 audiovisual materials.

Student Life *Activities and Organizations:* student-run newspaper, ASID (student chapter), Design Council, Association of Manufacturing Students. *Campus security:* 24-hour emergency response devices, late-night transport/escort service. *Student services:* personal/psychological counseling.

Costs (2013–14) *Tuition:* $23,965 full-time. Full-time tuition and fees vary according to program. *Required fees:* $225 full-time.

Applying *Options:* deferred entrance. *Application fee:* $225. *Required:* essay or personal statement, high school transcript, minimum 2.0 GPA, 3 letters of recommendation, interview, entrance requirement project. *Application deadlines:* rolling (freshmen), rolling (out-of-state freshmen), rolling (transfers). *Notification:* continuous (freshmen), continuous (out-of-state freshmen), continuous (transfers).

Freshman Application Contact Admissions, FIDM/The Fashion Institute of Design & Merchandising, Orange County Campus, 17590 Gillette Avenue, Irvine, CA 92614-5610. *Phone:* 949-851-6200. *Toll-free phone:* 888-974-3436. *Fax:* 949-851-6808. *Website:* http://www.fidm.edu/.

Fashion Institute of Design & Merchandising

It's more than a college, it's FIDM.

- 2-year & 4-year co-educational college
- Associate of Arts, Bachelor's and Advanced Study Degree programs
- Accredited by WASC & NASAD
- Extensive industry job placement
- Faculty of industry professionals
- 22 professionally-based majors
- Unparalleled industry partnerships
- A powerful network of 52,000 alumni working worldwide
- 4 California campuses: Los Angeles, San Francisco, Orange County & San Diego

FiDM

Visit fidm.edu or call 800.624.1200

FIDM/The Fashion Institute of Design & Merchandising, San Diego Campus

San Diego, California

- **Proprietary** 2-year, founded 1985, part of The Fashion Institute of Design and Merchandising/FIDM
- **Urban** campus
- **Coed, primarily women,** 183 undergraduate students, 95% full-time, 90% women, 10% men

Undergraduates 174 full-time, 9 part-time. 4% Black or African American, non-Hispanic/Latino; 37% Hispanic/Latino; 12% Asian, non-Hispanic/Latino; 4% Native Hawaiian or other Pacific Islander, non-Hispanic/Latino; 1% American Indian or Alaska Native, non-Hispanic/Latino; 5% Two or more races, non-Hispanic/Latino; 7% Race/ethnicity unknown; 4% international.

Freshmen *Admission:* 353 applied, 245 admitted, 74 enrolled. *Average high school GPA:* 2.75. *Test scores:* ACT scores over 18: 100%; ACT scores over 24: 40%; ACT scores over 30: 10%.

Faculty *Total:* 27, 11% full-time. *Student/faculty ratio:* 15:1.

Majors Apparel and accessories marketing; commercial and advertising art; consumer merchandising/retailing management; design and visual communications; fashion/apparel design; fashion merchandising; interior design.

Academics *Calendar:* quarters. *Degree:* associate. *Special study options:* academic remediation for entering students, adult/continuing education programs, advanced placement credit, cooperative education, distance learning, English as a second language, independent study, internships, part-time degree program, services for LD students, study abroad, summer session for credit.

Library FIDM San Diego Campus Library plus 1 other with 10,145 titles, 124 serial subscriptions, 3,497 audiovisual materials, an OPAC.

Student Life *Activities and Organizations:* Student Council, Phi Theta Kappa. *Campus security:* 24-hour emergency response devices and patrols. *Student services:* personal/psychological counseling.

Standardized Tests *Recommended:* SAT or ACT (for admission).

Costs (2013–14) *Tuition:* $22,965 full-time. Full-time tuition and fees vary according to program. *Required fees:* $225 full-time.

Applying *Options:* electronic application, deferred entrance. *Application fee:* $225. *Required:* essay or personal statement, high school transcript, minimum 2.0 GPA, 3 letters of recommendation, interview, major-determined project. *Application deadlines:* rolling (freshmen), rolling (out-of-state freshmen), rolling (transfers).

Freshman Application Contact Ms. Susan Aronson, Director of Admissions, FIDM/The Fashion Institute of Design & Merchandising, San Diego Campus, San Diego, CA 92101. *Phone:* 213-624-1200 Ext. 5400. *Toll-free phone:* 800-243-3436. *Fax:* 619-232-4322. *E-mail:* info@fidm.com. *Website:* http://www.fidm.edu/.

FIDM/The Fashion Institute of Design & Merchandising, San Francisco Campus

San Francisco, California

- **Proprietary** 2-year, founded 1973, part of The Fashion Institute of Design and Merchandising/FIDM
- **Urban** campus
- **Coed,** 753 undergraduate students, 86% full-time, 91% women, 9% men

Undergraduates 651 full-time, 102 part-time. 7% Black or African American, non-Hispanic/Latino; 22% Hispanic/Latino; 2% Asian, non-Hispanic/Latino; 2% Native Hawaiian or other Pacific Islander, non-Hispanic/Latino; 0.3% American Indian or Alaska Native, non-Hispanic/Latino; 4% Two or more races, non-Hispanic/Latino; 7% Race/ethnicity unknown; 4% international.

Freshmen *Admission:* 316 applied, 199 admitted, 130 enrolled. *Average high school GPA:* 2.75. *Test scores:* ACT scores over 18: 100%; ACT scores over 24: 40%; ACT scores over 30: 10%.

Faculty *Total:* 74, 12% full-time. *Student/faculty ratio:* 20:1.

Majors Apparel and accessories marketing; apparel and textiles; commercial and advertising art; consumer merchandising/retailing management; design and visual communications; fashion/apparel design; fashion merchandising; interior design.

Academics *Calendar:* quarters. *Degree:* associate. *Special study options:* academic remediation for entering students, adult/continuing education programs, advanced placement credit, cooperative education, distance learning, English as a second language, honors programs, independent study, internships, off-campus study, part-time degree program, services for LD students, study abroad, summer session for credit.

Library FIDM San Francisco Library plus 1 other with 12,540 titles, 175 serial subscriptions, 3,500 audiovisual materials, an OPAC.

Student Life *Housing:* college housing not available. *Activities and Organizations:* ASID (student chapter), Student Council, Premiere Marketing Group,

Phi Theta Kappa. *Campus security:* 24-hour emergency response devices and patrols. *Student services:* personal/psychological counseling.

Standardized Tests *Recommended:* SAT or ACT (for admission).

Costs (2013–14) *Tuition:* $23,965 full-time. Full-time tuition and fees vary according to degree level and program. *Required fees:* $225 full-time.

Applying *Options:* electronic application, deferred entrance. *Application fee:* $225. *Required:* essay or personal statement, high school transcript, 3 letters of recommendation, interview, major-determined project. *Application deadlines:* rolling (freshmen), rolling (out-of-state freshmen), rolling (transfers).

Freshman Application Contact Ms. Susan Aronson, Director of Admissions, FIDM/The Fashion Institute of Design & Merchandising, San Francisco Campus, San Francisco, CA 94108. *Phone:* 213-624-1201. *Toll-free phone:* 800-422-3436. *Fax:* 415-296-7299. *E-mail:* info@fidm.com. *Website:* http://www.fidm.edu/.

Folsom Lake College

Folsom, California

Freshman Application Contact Admissions Office, Folsom Lake College, 10 College Parkway, Folsom, CA 95630. *Phone:* 916-608-6500. *Website:* http://www.flc.losrios.edu/.

Foothill College

Los Altos Hills, California

- **State and locally supported** 2-year, founded 1958, part of Foothill-DeAnza Community College District
- **Suburban** 122-acre campus with easy access to San Jose
- **Endowment** $15.0 million
- **Coed,** 15,765 undergraduate students, 33% full-time, 51% women, 49% men

Undergraduates 5,191 full-time, 10,574 part-time. Students come from 16 states and territories; 109 other countries; 1% are from out of state; 4% Black or African American, non-Hispanic/Latino; 19% Hispanic/Latino; 22% Asian, non-Hispanic/Latino; 1% Native Hawaiian or other Pacific Islander, non-Hispanic/Latino; 0.3% American Indian or Alaska Native, non-Hispanic/Latino; 4% Two or more races, non-Hispanic/Latino; 3% Race/ethnicity unknown; 6% international.

Freshmen *Admission:* 5,697 applied, 5,697 admitted.

Faculty *Total:* 538, 34% full-time. *Student/faculty ratio:* 45:1.

Majors Accounting; American studies; anthropology; art; art history, criticism and conservation; athletic training; biology/biological sciences; business administration and management; chemistry; child development; classics and classical languages; communication; comparative literature; computer science; dental assisting; dental hygiene; diagnostic medical sonography and ultrasound technology; dramatic/theater arts; economics; electrical, electronic and communications engineering technology; emergency medical technology (EMT paramedic); English; fine/studio arts; geography; graphic design; history; international business/trade/commerce; Japanese; liberal arts and sciences/liberal studies; mathematics; medical radiologic technology; music; music technology; nanotechnology; natural sciences; ornamental horticulture; pharmacy technician; philosophy; photography; physical education teaching and coaching; physician assistant; physics; political science and government; pre-law studies; psychology; radiologic technology/science; real estate; respiratory care therapy; social sciences; sociology; Spanish; special education (administration); theater design and technology; veterinary/animal health technology; women's studies.

Academics *Calendar:* quarters. *Degree:* certificates and associate. *Special study options:* academic remediation for entering students, accelerated degree program, adult/continuing education programs, advanced placement credit, cooperative education, distance learning, English as a second language, honors programs, independent study, internships, off-campus study, part-time degree program, services for LD students, student-designed majors, study abroad, summer session for credit. *ROTC:* Army (c), Air Force (c).

Library Hubert H. Semans Library with 70,000 titles, 450 serial subscriptions, 5,150 audiovisual materials, an OPAC, a Web page.

Student Life *Housing:* college housing not available. *Activities and Organizations:* drama/theater group, student-run newspaper, radio station, choral group. *Campus security:* 24-hour emergency response devices and patrols, late-night transport/escort service. *Student services:* health clinic, personal/psychological counseling, legal services.

Athletics Member NJCAA. *Intercollegiate sports:* basketball M/W, football M, soccer M/W, softball W, swimming and diving M/W, tennis M/W, volleyball W, water polo W. *Intramural sports:* basketball M/W, football M/W, softball M/W, volleyball M/W.

Costs (2013–14) *Tuition:* state resident $1224 full-time; nonresident $6192 full-time. Full-time tuition and fees vary according to course load. Part-time tuition and fees vary according to course load. *Waivers:* employees or children of employees.

Financial Aid Of all full-time matriculated undergraduates who enrolled in 2011, 80 Federal Work-Study jobs (averaging $1300). 210 state and other part-time jobs.

Applying *Options:* electronic application. *Recommended:* high school transcript. *Application deadlines:* rolling (freshmen), rolling (out-of-state freshmen), rolling (transfers). *Notification:* continuous (freshmen), continuous (out-of-state freshmen), continuous (transfers).

Freshman Application Contact Ms. Shawna Aced, Registrar, Foothill College, Admissions and Records, 12345 El Monte Road, Los Altos Hills, CA 94022. *Phone:* 650-949-7771. *E-mail:* acedshawna@hda.edu. *Website:* http://www.foothill.edu/.

Fresno City College
Fresno, California

Freshman Application Contact Office Assistant, Fresno City College, 1101 East University Avenue, Fresno, CA 93741-0002. *Phone:* 559-442-4600 Ext. 8604. *Fax:* 559-237-4232. *E-mail:* fcc.admissions@fresnocitycollege.edu. *Website:* http://www.fresnocitycollege.edu/.

Fullerton College
Fullerton, California

Director of Admissions Mr. Albert Abutin, Dean of Admissions and Records, Fullerton College, 321 East Chapman Avenue, Fullerton, CA 92832-2095. *Phone:* 714-992-7076. *Fax:* 714-992-9903. *E-mail:* aabutin@fullcoll.edu. *Website:* http://www.fullcoll.edu/.

Gavilan College
Gilroy, California

- **State and locally supported** 2-year, founded 1919, part of California Community College System
- **Rural** 150-acre campus with easy access to San Jose
- **Coed**

Undergraduates 5% Black or African American, non-Hispanic/Latino; 43% Hispanic/Latino; 4% Asian, non-Hispanic/Latino; 2% Native Hawaiian or other Pacific Islander, non-Hispanic/Latino; 1% American Indian or Alaska Native, non-Hispanic/Latino; 10% Race/ethnicity unknown. *Retention:* 70% of full-time freshmen returned.

Faculty *Student/faculty ratio:* 30:1.

Academics *Calendar:* semesters. *Degree:* certificates, diplomas, and associate. *Special study options:* academic remediation for entering students, adult/continuing education programs, advanced placement credit, cooperative education, distance learning, English as a second language, honors programs, independent study, internships, part-time degree program, services for LD students, study abroad, summer session for credit.

Student Life *Campus security:* 24-hour emergency response devices.

Costs (2012–13) *Tuition:* state resident $36 per unit part-time; nonresident $216 per unit part-time. Full-time tuition and fees vary according to course load. Part-time tuition and fees vary according to course load. *Required fees:* $36 per unit part-time.

Financial Aid Of all full-time matriculated undergraduates who enrolled in 2011, 50 Federal Work-Study jobs (averaging $2000). *Financial aid deadline:* 6/30.

Freshman Application Contact Gavilan College, 5055 Santa Teresa Boulevard, Gilroy, CA 95020-9599. *Phone:* 408-848-4754. *Website:* http://www.gavilan.edu/.

Glendale Community College
Glendale, California

Freshman Application Contact Ms. Sharon Combs, Dean, Admissions, and Records, Glendale Community College, 1500 North Verdugo Road, Glendale, CA 91208. *Phone:* 818-240-1000 Ext. 5910. *E-mail:* scombs@glendale.edu. *Website:* http://www.glendale.edu/.

Golden West College
Huntington Beach, California

Freshman Application Contact Golden West College, PO Box 2748, 15744 Golden West Street, Huntington Beach, CA 92647-2748. *Phone:* 714-892-7711 Ext. 58196. *Website:* http://www.goldenwestcollege.edu/.

Golf Academy of America
Carlsbad, California

Director of Admissions Ms. Deborah Wells, Admissions Coordinator, Golf Academy of America, 1950 Camino Vida Roble, Suite 125, Carlsbad, CA 92008. *Phone:* 760-414-1501. *Toll-free phone:* 800-342-7342. *E-mail:* sdga@sdgagolf.com. *Website:* http://www.golfacademy.edu/.

Grossmont College
El Cajon, California

Freshman Application Contact Admissions Office, Grossmont College, 8800 Grossmont College Drive, El Cajon, CA 92020-1799. *Phone:* 619-644-7186. *Website:* http://www.grossmont.edu/.

Hartnell College
Salinas, California

Director of Admissions Director of Admissions, Hartnell College, 411 Central Avenue, Salinas, CA 93901. *Phone:* 831-755-6711. *Fax:* 831-759-6014. *Website:* http://www.hartnell.edu/.

Heald College–Concord
Concord, California

Freshman Application Contact Director of Admissions, Heald College–Concord, 5130 Commercial Circle, Concord, CA 94520. *Phone:* 925-288-5800. *Toll-free phone:* 800-88-HEALD. *Fax:* 925-288-5896. *E-mail:* concordinfo@heald.edu. *Website:* http://www.heald.edu/.

Heald College–Fresno
Fresno, California

Freshman Application Contact Director of Admissions, Heald College–Fresno, 255 West Bullard Avenue, Fresno, CA 93704-1706. *Phone:* 559-438-4222. *Toll-free phone:* 800-88-HEALD. *Fax:* 559-438-0948. *E-mail:* fresnoinfo@heald.edu. *Website:* http://www.heald.edu/.

Heald College–Hayward
Hayward, California

Freshman Application Contact Director of Admissions, Heald College–Hayward, 25500 Industrial Boulevard, Hayward, CA 94545. *Phone:* 510-783-2100. *Toll-free phone:* 800-88-HEALD. *Fax:* 510-783-3287. *E-mail:* harwardinfo@heald.edu. *Website:* http://www.heald.edu/.

Heald College–Modesto
Salida, California

Admissions Office Contact Heald College–Modesto, 5260 Pirrone Court, Salida, CA 95368. *Website:* http://www.heald.edu/.

Heald College–Rancho Cordova
Rancho Cordova, California

Freshman Application Contact Director of Admissions, Heald College–Rancho Cordova, 2910 Prospect Park Drive, Rancho Cordova, CA 95670-6005. *Phone:* 916-638-1616. *Toll-free phone:* 800-88-HEALD. *Fax:* 916-638-1580. *E-mail:* ranchocordovainfo@heald.edu. *Website:* http://www.heald.edu/.

Heald College–Roseville
Roseville, California

Freshman Application Contact Director of Admissions, Heald College–Roseville, 7 Sierra Gate Plaza, Roseville, CA 95678. *Phone:* 916-789-8600. *Toll-free phone:* 800-88-HEALD. *Fax:* 916-789-8606. *E-mail:* rosevilleinfo@heald.edu. *Website:* http://www.heald.edu/.

Heald College–Salinas

Salinas, California

Freshman Application Contact Director of Admissions, Heald College–Salinas, 1450 North Main Street, Salinas, CA 93906. *Phone:* 831-443-1700. *Toll-free phone:* 800-88-HEALD. *Fax:* 831-443-1050. *E-mail:* salinasinfo@heald.edu.
Website: http://www.heald.edu/.

Heald College–San Francisco

San Francisco, California

Freshman Application Contact Director of Admissions, Heald College–San Francisco, 350 Mission Street, San Francisco, CA 94105. *Phone:* 415-808-3000. *Toll-free phone:* 800-88-HEALD. *Fax:* 415-808-3005. *E-mail:* sanfranciscoinfo@heald.edu.
Website: http://www.heald.edu/.

Heald College–San Jose

Milpitas, California

Freshman Application Contact Director of Admissions, Heald College–San Jose, 341 Great Mall Parkway, Milpitas, CA 95035. *Phone:* 408-934-4900. *Toll-free phone:* 800-88-HEALD. *Fax:* 408-934-7777. *E-mail:* sanjoseinfo@heald.edu.
Website: http://www.heald.edu/.

Heald College–Stockton

Stockton, California

Freshman Application Contact Director of Admissions, Heald College–Stockton, 1605 East March Lane, Stockton, CA 95210. *Phone:* 209-473-5200. *Toll-free phone:* 800-88-HEALD. *Fax:* 209-477-2739. *E-mail:* stocktoninfo@heald.edu.
Website: http://www.heald.edu/.

ICDC College

Los Angeles, California

Admissions Office Contact ICDC College, 5422 West Sunset Boulevard, Los Angeles, CA 90027.
Website: http://icdccollege.edu/.

Imperial Valley College

Imperial, California

Director of Admissions Dawn Chun, Associate Dean of Admissions and Records, Imperial Valley College, 380 East Aten Road, PO Box 158, Imperial, CA 92251-0158. *Phone:* 760-352-8320 Ext. 200.
Website: http://www.imperial.edu/.

Irvine Valley College

Irvine, California

Director of Admissions Mr. John Edwards, Director of Admissions, Records, and Enrollment Services, Irvine Valley College, 5500 Irvine Center Drive, Irvine, CA 92618. *Phone:* 949-451-5416.
Website: http://www.ivc.edu/.

ITT Technical Institute

Culver City, California

- **Proprietary** primarily 2-year, part of ITT Educational Services, Inc.
- **Coed**

Academics *Calendar:* quarters. *Degrees:* associate and bachelor's.
Freshman Application Contact Director of Recruitment, ITT Technical Institute, 6101 W. Centinela Avenue, Suite 180, Culver City, CA 90230. *Phone:* 310-417-5800. *Toll-free phone:* 800-215-6151.
Website: http://www.itt-tech.edu/.

ITT Technical Institute

Lathrop, California

- **Proprietary** primarily 2-year, founded 1997, part of ITT Educational Services, Inc.
- **Coed**

Academics *Calendar:* quarters. *Degrees:* associate and bachelor's.
Freshman Application Contact Director of Recruitment, ITT Technical Institute, 16916 South Harlan Road, Lathrop, CA 95330. *Phone:* 209-858-0077. *Toll-free phone:* 800-346-1786.
Website: http://www.itt-tech.edu/.

ITT Technical Institute

Oakland, California

- **Proprietary** primarily 2-year, part of ITT Educational Services, Inc.
- **Coed**

Academics *Calendar:* quarters. *Degrees:* associate and bachelor's.
Freshman Application Contact Director of Recruitment, ITT Technical Institute, 7901 Oakport Street, Suite 3000, Oakland, CA 94621. *Phone:* 510-553-2800. *Toll-free phone:* 877-442-5833.
Website: http://www.itt-tech.edu/.

ITT Technical Institute

Orange, California

- **Proprietary** primarily 2-year, founded 1982, part of ITT Educational Services, Inc.
- **Suburban** campus
- **Coed**

Academics *Calendar:* quarters. *Degrees:* associate and bachelor's.
Financial Aid Of all full-time matriculated undergraduates who enrolled in 2011, 20 Federal Work-Study jobs (averaging $5000).
Freshman Application Contact Director of Recruitment, ITT Technical Institute, 4000 West Metropolitan Drive, Suite 100, Orange, CA 92868. *Phone:* 714-941-2400.
Website: http://www.itt-tech.edu/.

ITT Technical Institute

Oxnard, California

- **Proprietary** primarily 2-year, founded 1993, part of ITT Educational Services, Inc.
- **Urban** campus
- **Coed**

Academics *Calendar:* quarters. *Degrees:* associate and bachelor's.
Freshman Application Contact Director of Recruitment, ITT Technical Institute, 2051 Solar Drive, Suite 150, Oxnard, CA 93036. *Phone:* 805-988-0143. *Toll-free phone:* 800-530-1582.
Website: http://www.itt-tech.edu/.

ITT Technical Institute

Rancho Cordova, California

- **Proprietary** primarily 2-year, founded 1954, part of ITT Educational Services, Inc.
- **Urban** campus
- **Coed**

Academics *Calendar:* quarters. *Degrees:* associate and bachelor's.
Freshman Application Contact Director of Recruitment, ITT Technical Institute, 10863 Gold Center Drive, Rancho Cordova, CA 95670-6034. *Phone:* 916-851-3900. *Toll-free phone:* 800-488-8466.
Website: http://www.itt-tech.edu/.

ITT Technical Institute

San Bernardino, California

- **Proprietary** primarily 2-year, founded 1987, part of ITT Educational Services, Inc.
- **Urban** campus
- **Coed**

Academics *Calendar:* quarters. *Degrees:* associate and bachelor's.
Freshman Application Contact Director of Recruitment, ITT Technical Institute, 670 East Carnegie Drive, San Bernardino, CA 92408. *Phone:* 909-806-4600. *Toll-free phone:* 800-888-3801.
Website: http://www.itt-tech.edu/.

ITT Technical Institute
San Diego, California
- **Proprietary** primarily 2-year, founded 1981, part of ITT Educational Services, Inc.
- **Suburban** campus
- **Coed**

Academics *Calendar:* quarters. *Degrees:* associate and bachelor's.
Freshman Application Contact Director of Recruitment, ITT Technical Institute, 9680 Granite Ridge Drive, San Diego, GA 92123. *Phone:* 858-571-8500. *Toll-free phone:* 800-883-0380.
Website: http://www.itt-tech.edu/.

ITT Technical Institute
San Dimas, California
- **Proprietary** primarily 2-year, founded 1982, part of ITT Educational Services, Inc.
- **Suburban** campus
- **Coed**

Academics *Calendar:* quarters. *Degrees:* associate and bachelor's.
Financial Aid Of all full-time matriculated undergraduates who enrolled in 2011, 20 Federal Work-Study jobs (averaging $4500).
Freshman Application Contact Director of Recruitment, ITT Technical Institute, 650 West Cienega Avenue, San Dimas, CA 91773. *Phone:* 909-971-2300. *Toll-free phone:* 800-414-6522.
Website: http://www.itt-tech.edu/.

ITT Technical Institute
Sylmar, California
- **Proprietary** primarily 2-year, founded 1982, part of ITT Educational Services, Inc.
- **Urban** campus
- **Coed**

Academics *Calendar:* quarters. *Degrees:* associate and bachelor's.
Freshman Application Contact Director of Recruitment, ITT Technical Institute, 12669 Encinitas Avenue, Sylmar, CA 91342-3664. *Phone:* 818-364-5151. *Toll-free phone:* 800-363-2086 (in-state); 800-636-2086 (out-of-state).
Website: http://www.itt-tech.edu/.

ITT Technical Institute
Torrance, California
- **Proprietary** primarily 2-year, founded 1987, part of ITT Educational Services, Inc.
- **Urban** campus
- **Coed**

Academics *Calendar:* quarters. *Degrees:* associate and bachelor's.
Financial Aid Of all full-time matriculated undergraduates who enrolled in 2011, 6 Federal Work-Study jobs (averaging $4000).
Freshman Application Contact Director of Recruitment, ITT Technical Institute, 2555 West 190th Street, Suite 125, Torrance, CA 90504. *Phone:* 310-965-5900.
Website: http://www.itt-tech.edu/.

ITT Technical Institute
West Covina, California
- **Proprietary** primarily 2-year, part of ITT Educational Services, Inc.
- **Coed**

Academics *Calendar:* quarters. *Degrees:* associate and bachelor's.
Freshman Application Contact Director of Recruitment, ITT Technical Institute, 1530 W. Cameron Avenue, West Covina, CA 91790. *Phone:* 626-813-3681. *Toll-free phone:* 877-480-2766.
Website: http://www.itt-tech.edu/.

Kaplan College, Bakersfield Campus
Bakersfield, California
- **Proprietary** 2-year
- **Coed**

Academics *Degree:* diplomas and associate.
Freshman Application Contact Kaplan College, Bakersfield Campus, 1914 Wible Road, Bakersfield, CA 93304. *Phone:* 661-836-6300. *Toll-free phone:* 800-935-1857.
Website: http://bakersfield.kaplancollege.com/.

Kaplan College, Chula Vista Campus
Chula Vista, California
- **Proprietary** 2-year
- **Coed**

Academics *Degree:* diplomas and associate.
Freshman Application Contact Kaplan College, Chula Vista Campus, 555 Broadway, Chula Vista, CA 91910. *Phone:* 877-473-3052. *Toll-free phone:* 800-935-1857.
Website: http://chulavista.kaplancollege.com/.

Kaplan College, Fresno Campus
Clovis, California
- **Proprietary** 2-year
- **Coed**

Academics *Degree:* diplomas and associate.
Freshman Application Contact Kaplan College, Fresno Campus, 44 Shaw Avenue, Clovis, CA 93612. *Phone:* 559-325-5100. *Toll-free phone:* 800-935-1857.
Website: http://fresno.kaplancollege.com/.

Kaplan College, Modesto Campus
Salida, California
- **Proprietary** 2-year
- **Coed, primarily women**

Academics *Calendar:* semesters. *Degree:* diplomas and associate.
Freshman Application Contact Kaplan College, Modesto Campus, 5172 Kiernan Court, Salida, CA 95368. *Phone:* 209-543-7000. *Toll-free phone:* 800-935-1857.
Website: http://modesto.kaplancollege.com/.

Kaplan College, Palm Springs Campus
Palm Springs, California
- **Proprietary** 2-year
- **Coed**

Academics *Degree:* diplomas and associate.
Freshman Application Contact Kaplan College, Palm Springs Campus, 2475 East Tahquitz Canyon Way, Palm Springs, CA 92262. *Phone:* 760-778-3540. *Toll-free phone:* 800-935-1857.
Website: http://palm-springs.kaplancollege.com/.

Kaplan College, Riverside Campus
Riverside, California
- **Proprietary** 2-year
- **Coed**

Academics *Degree:* diplomas and associate.
Freshman Application Contact Kaplan College, Riverside Campus, 4040 Vine Street, Riverside, CA 92507. *Phone:* 951-276-1704. *Toll-free phone:* 800-935-1857.
Website: http://riverside.kaplancollege.com/.

Kaplan College, Sacramento Campus
Sacramento, California
- **Proprietary** 2-year
- **Coed**

Academics *Calendar:* semesters. *Degree:* diplomas and associate.
Freshman Application Contact Kaplan College, Sacramento Campus, 4330 Watt Avenue, Suite 400, Sacramento, CA 95821. *Phone:* 916-649-8168. *Toll-free phone:* 800-935-1857.
Website: http://sacramento.kaplancollege.com/.

Kaplan College, San Diego Campus
San Diego, California
- **Proprietary** 2-year, founded 1976
- **Urban** campus
- **Coed**

Academics *Calendar:* semesters. *Degrees:* diplomas and associate (also includes Vista campus).

Freshman Application Contact Kaplan College, San Diego Campus, 9055 Balboa Avenue, San Diego, CA 92123. *Phone:* 858-279-4500. *Toll-free phone:* 800-935-1857.
Website: http://san-diego.kaplancollege.com/.

Kaplan College, Vista Campus
Vista, California

- **Proprietary** 2-year
- **Coed**

Academics *Degree:* diplomas and associate.
Freshman Application Contact Kaplan College, Vista Campus, 2022 University Drive, Vista, CA 92083. *Phone:* 760-630-1555. *Toll-free phone:* 800-935-1857.
Website: http://vista.kaplancollege.com/.

Lake Tahoe Community College
South Lake Tahoe, California

Freshman Application Contact Office of Admissions and Records, Lake Tahoe Community College, One College Drive, South Lake Tahoe, CA 96150. *Phone:* 530-541-4660 Ext. 211. *Fax:* 530-541-7852. *E-mail:* admissions@ltcc.edu.
Website: http://www.ltcc.edu/.

Laney College
Oakland, California

Freshman Application Contact Mrs. Barbara Simmons, District Admissions Officer, Laney College, 900 Fallon Street, Oakland, CA 94607-4893. *Phone:* 510-466-7369.
Website: http://www.laney.edu/.

Las Positas College
Livermore, California

Director of Admissions Mrs. Sylvia R. Rodriguez, Director of Admissions and Records, Las Positas College, 3000 Campus Hill Drive, Livermore, CA 94551. *Phone:* 925-373-4942.
Website: http://www.laspositascollege.edu/.

Lassen Community College District
Susanville, California

Freshman Application Contact Mr. Chris J. Alberico, Registrar, Lassen Community College District, Highway 139, PO Box 3000, Susanville, CA 96130. *Phone:* 530-257-6181.
Website: http://www.lassencollege.edu/.

Le Cordon Bleu College of Culinary Arts in Los Angeles
Pasadena, California

Director of Admissions Nora Sandoval, Registrar, Le Cordon Bleu College of Culinary Arts in Los Angeles, 521 East Green Street, Pasadena, CA 91101. *Phone:* 626-229-1300. *Fax:* 626-204-3905. *E-mail:* nsandoval@la.chefs.edu.
Website: http://www.chefs.edu/Los-Angeles.

Long Beach City College
Long Beach, California

Director of Admissions Mr. Ross Miyashiro, Dean of Admissions and Records, Long Beach City College, 4901 East Carson Street, Long Beach, CA 90808-1780. *Phone:* 562-938-4130.
Website: http://www.lbcc.edu/.

Los Angeles City College
Los Angeles, California

Freshman Application Contact Elaine Geismar, Director of Student Assistance Center, Los Angeles City College, 855 North Vermont Avenue, Los Angeles, CA 90029-3590. *Phone:* 323-953-4340.
Website: http://www.lacitycollege.edu/.

Los Angeles County College of Nursing and Allied Health
Los Angeles, California

Freshman Application Contact Admissions Office, Los Angeles County College of Nursing and Allied Health, 1237 North Mission Road, Los Angeles, CA 90033. *Phone:* 323-226-4911.
Website: http://www.ladhs.org/wps/portal/CollegeOfNursing.

Los Angeles Film School
Hollywood, California

Admissions Office Contact Los Angeles Film School, 6363 Sunset Boulevard, Hollywood, CA 90028. *Toll-free phone:* 877-952-3456.
Website: http://www.lafilm.edu/.

Los Angeles Harbor College
Wilmington, California

- **State and locally supported** 2-year, founded 1949, part of Los Angeles Community College District System
- **Suburban** 80-acre campus with easy access to Los Angeles
- **Coed**

Undergraduates 2,812 full-time, 7,369 part-time. Students come from 14 states and territories; 15 other countries.
Faculty *Student/faculty ratio:* 47:1.
Academics *Calendar:* semesters. *Degree:* certificates and associate. *Special study options:* academic remediation for entering students, accelerated degree program, adult/continuing education programs, advanced placement credit, cooperative education, distance learning, double majors, English as a second language, freshman honors college, honors programs, independent study, off-campus study, part-time degree program, services for LD students, study abroad, summer session for credit.
Student Life *Campus security:* 24-hour emergency response devices and patrols, late-night transport/escort service.
Costs (2012–13) *Tuition:* state resident $1380 full-time, $46 per unit part-time; nonresident $7080 full-time, $236 per unit part-time. *Required fees:* $24 full-time, $12 per term part-time.
Financial Aid Of all full-time matriculated undergraduates who enrolled in 2011, 100 Federal Work-Study jobs (averaging $1800).
Applying *Options:* electronic application, early admission, deferred entrance.
Freshman Application Contact Los Angeles Harbor College, 1111 Figueroa Place, Wilmington, CA 90744-2397. *Phone:* 310-233-4091.
Website: http://www.lahc.edu/.

Los Angeles Mission College
Sylmar, California

Freshman Application Contact Ms. Angela Merrill, Admissions Supervisor, Los Angeles Mission College, 13356 Eldridge Avenue, Sylmar, CA 91342-3245. *Phone:* 818-364-7658.
Website: http://www.lamission.edu/.

Los Angeles Pierce College
Woodland Hills, California

Director of Admissions Ms. Shelley L. Gerstl, Dean of Admissions and Records, Los Angeles Pierce College, 6201 Winnetka Avenue, Woodland Hills, CA 91371-0001. *Phone:* 818-719-6448.
Website: http://www.piercecollege.edu/.

Los Angeles Southwest College
Los Angeles, California

Director of Admissions Dan W. Walden, Dean of Academic Affairs, Los Angeles Southwest College, 1600 West Imperial Highway, Los Angeles, CA 90047-4810. *Phone:* 323-242-5511.
Website: http://www.lasc.edu/.

Los Angeles Trade-Technical College
Los Angeles, California

Director of Admissions Dr. Raul Cardoza, Los Angeles Trade-Technical College, 400 West Washington Boulevard, Los Angeles, CA 90015-4108. *Phone:* 213-763-5301. *E-mail:* CardozaRJ@lattc.edu.
Website: http://www.lattc.edu/.

Los Angeles Valley College

Van Nuys, California

Director of Admissions Mr. Florentino Manzano, Associate Dean, Los Angeles Valley College, 5800 Fulton Avenue, Van Nuys, CA 91401-4096. *Phone:* 818-947-2353. *E-mail:* manzanf@lavc.edu. *Website:* http://www.lavc.cc.ca.us/.

Los Medanos College

Pittsburg, California

Freshman Application Contact Ms. Gail Newman, Director of Admissions and Records, Los Medanos College, 2700 East Leland Road, Pittsburg, CA 94565-5197. *Phone:* 925-439-2181 Ext. 7500. *Website:* http://www.losmedanos.net/.

Mendocino College

Ukiah, California

- **State and locally supported** 2-year, founded 1973, part of California Community College System
- **Rural** 127-acre campus
- **Endowment** $6.4 million
- **Coed**, 3,614 undergraduate students, 36% full-time, 60% women, 40% men

Undergraduates 1,296 full-time, 2,318 part-time. Students come from 16 states and territories; 2 other countries; 3% Black or African American, non-Hispanic/Latino; 23% Hispanic/Latino; 3% Asian, non-Hispanic/Latino; 0.6% Native Hawaiian or other Pacific Islander, non-Hispanic/Latino; 5% American Indian or Alaska Native, non-Hispanic/Latino; 3% Race/ethnicity unknown; 4% transferred in.

Freshmen *Admission:* 660 applied, 660 admitted, 384 enrolled.

Faculty *Total:* 294, 17% full-time, 3% with terminal degrees. *Student/faculty ratio:* 16:1.

Majors Accounting; administrative assistant and secretarial science; agriculture; art; automobile/automotive mechanics technology; biology/biological sciences; business administration and management; chemistry; child development; criminal justice/law enforcement administration; criminal justice/police science; data processing and data processing technology; developmental and child psychology; dramatic/theater arts; English; fiber, textile and weaving arts; finance; French; health professions related; human services; information science/studies; kindergarten/preschool education; liberal arts and sciences/liberal studies; mathematics; music; ornamental horticulture; physical education teaching and coaching; physical sciences; psychology; real estate; rhetoric and composition; social sciences; Spanish; substance abuse/addiction counseling.

Academics *Calendar:* semesters. *Degree:* certificates and associate. *Special study options:* academic remediation for entering students, adult/continuing education programs, advanced placement credit, cooperative education, distance learning, English as a second language, honors programs, independent study, internships, part-time degree program, services for LD students, summer session for credit.

Library Lowery Library with 27,441 titles, 275 serial subscriptions, a Web page.

Student Life *Housing:* college housing not available. *Activities and Organizations:* drama/theater group, student-run radio station, choral group. *Campus security:* late-night transport/escort service, security patrols 6 pm to 10 pm.

Athletics Member NJCAA. *Intercollegiate sports:* baseball M, basketball M/W, football M, soccer W, softball W, volleyball W. *Intramural sports:* table tennis M/W, tennis M/W.

Costs (2013–14) *Tuition:* state resident $1380 full-time; nonresident $7380 full-time. Full-time tuition and fees vary according to course load. Part-time tuition and fees vary according to course load. *Required fees:* $32 full-time.

Financial Aid *Financial aid deadline:* 5/20.

Applying *Options:* electronic application, early admission, deferred entrance. *Required:* high school transcript. *Application deadlines:* rolling (freshmen), rolling (transfers). *Notification:* continuous (freshmen), continuous (transfers).

Freshman Application Contact Mendocino College, 1000 Hensley Creek Road, Ukiah, CA 95482-0300. *Phone:* 707-468-3103. *Website:* http://www.mendocino.edu/.

Merced College

Merced, California

Freshman Application Contact Ms. Cherie Davis, Associate Registrar, Merced College, 3600 M Street, Merced, CA 95348-2898. *Phone:* 209-384-

6188. *Fax:* 209-384-6339. *Website:* http://www.mccd.edu/.

Merritt College

Oakland, California

Freshman Application Contact Ms. Barbara Simmons, District Admissions Officer, Merritt College, 12500 Campus Drive, Oakland, CA 94619-3196. *Phone:* 510-466-7369. *E-mail:* hperdue@peralta.cc.ca.us. *Website:* http://www.merritt.edu/.

MiraCosta College

Oceanside, California

Freshman Application Contact Director of Admissions, MiraCosta College, One Barnard Drive, Oceanside, CA 92056-3899. *Phone:* 760-795-6620. *Toll-free phone:* 888-201-8480. *E-mail:* admissions@miracosta.edu. *Website:* http://www.miracosta.edu/.

Mission College

Santa Clara, California

Director of Admissions Daniel Sanidad, Dean of Student Services, Mission College, 3000 Mission College Boulevard, Santa Clara, CA 95054-1897. *Phone:* 408-855-5139. *Website:* http://www.missioncollege.org/.

Modesto Junior College

Modesto, California

Freshman Application Contact Ms. Susie Agostini, Dean of Matriculation, Admissions, and Records, Modesto Junior College, 435 College Avenue, Modesto, CA 95350. *Phone:* 209-575-6470. *Fax:* 209-575-6859. *E-mail:* mjcadmissions@mail.yosemite.cc.ca.us. *Website:* http://www.mjc.edu/.

Monterey Peninsula College

Monterey, California

Director of Admissions Ms. Vera Coleman, Registrar, Monterey Peninsula College, 980 Fremont Street, Monterey, CA 93940-4799. *Phone:* 831-646-4007. *E-mail:* vcoleman@mpc.edu. *Website:* http://www.mpc.edu/.

Moorpark College

Moorpark, California

Freshman Application Contact Ms. Katherine Colborn, Registrar, Moorpark College, 7075 Campus Road, Moorpark, CA 93021-2899. *Phone:* 805-378-1415. *Website:* http://www.moorparkcollege.edu/.

Moreno Valley College

Moreno Valley, California

- **State and locally supported** 2-year, founded 2010
- **Suburban** campus
- **Coed**

Academics *Degree:* associate. *Special study options:* academic remediation for entering students, distance learning, English as a second language, honors programs.

Student Life *Campus security:* late-night transport/escort service.

Costs (2012–13) *Tuition:* state resident $1380 full-time, $46 per unit part-time; nonresident $6660 full-time, $222 per unit part-time. Full-time tuition and fees vary according to course load. Part-time tuition and fees vary according to course load.

Applying *Options:* electronic application.

Freshman Application Contact Jamie Clifton, Director, Enrollment Services, Moreno Valley College, 16130 Lasselle Street, Moreno Valley, CA 92551. *Phone:* 951-571-6293. *E-mail:* admissions@mvc.edu. *Website:* http://www.rcc.edu/morenovalley/index.cfm.

Mt. San Antonio College

Walnut, California

- **District-supported** 2-year, founded 1946, part of California Community College System
- **Suburban** 421-acre campus with easy access to Los Angeles
- **Coed,** 28,036 undergraduate students, 38% full-time, 51% women, 49% men

Undergraduates 10,749 full-time, 17,287 part-time. Students come from 21 states and territories; 139 other countries; 1% are from out of state; 5% Black or African American, non-Hispanic/Latino; 56% Hispanic/Latino; 18% Asian, non-Hispanic/Latino; 0.4% Native Hawaiian or other Pacific Islander, non-Hispanic/Latino; 0.2% American Indian or Alaska Native, non-Hispanic/Latino; 3% Two or more races, non-Hispanic/Latino; 2% Race/ethnicity unknown; 2% international. *Retention:* 79% of full-time freshmen returned.

Freshmen *Admission:* 4,163 enrolled.

Faculty *Total:* 1,191, 33% full-time.

Majors Accounting; administrative assistant and secretarial science; advertising; agricultural business and management; agriculture; airframe mechanics and aircraft maintenance technology; airline pilot and flight crew; air traffic control; animal sciences; apparel and textiles; architectural engineering technology; avionics maintenance technology; biological and physical sciences; building/construction finishing, management, and inspection related; business administration and management; business teacher education; child development; civil engineering technology; commercial and advertising art; computer and information sciences; computer engineering technology; computer graphics; computer science; corrections; criminal justice/police science; dairy science; data processing and data processing technology; drafting and design technology; drafting/design engineering technologies related; electrical, electronic and communications engineering technology; emergency medical technology (EMT paramedic); engineering technology; English language and literature related; family and consumer sciences/human sciences; fashion merchandising; finance; fire science/firefighting; forest technology; health and physical education/fitness; heating, air conditioning, ventilation and refrigeration maintenance technology; horticultural science; hotel/motel administration; humanities; industrial and product design; industrial radiologic technology; interior design; journalism; kindergarten/preschool education; landscape architecture; legal administrative assistant/secretary; legal assistant/paralegal; machine tool technology; marketing/marketing management; materials science; mathematics; medical administrative assistant and medical secretary; mental health counseling; music; occupational safety and health technology; ornamental horticulture; parks, recreation and leisure; parks, recreation and leisure facilities management; photography; physical sciences related; pre-engineering; quality control technology; radio and television; real estate; registered nursing/registered nurse; respiratory care therapy; sign language interpretation and translation; social sciences; surveying technology; transportation and materials moving related; visual and performing arts; welding technology; wildlife, fish and wildlands science and management.

Academics *Calendar:* semesters. *Degree:* certificates, diplomas, and associate. *Special study options:* academic remediation for entering students, adult/continuing education programs, advanced placement credit, cooperative education, distance learning, double majors, English as a second language, honors programs, independent study, part-time degree program, services for LD students, study abroad, summer session for credit. *ROTC:* Army (b), Air Force (b).

Library Learning Resources Center with 97,996 titles, 986 serial subscriptions, 9,933 audiovisual materials, an OPAC, a Web page.

Student Life *Housing:* college housing not available. *Activities and Organizations:* drama/theater group, student-run radio station, choral group, Alpha Gamma Sigma, Muslim Student Association, student government, Asian Student Association, Kasama-Filipino Student Organization. *Campus security:* 24-hour emergency response devices and patrols, late-night transport/escort service. *Student services:* health clinic, personal/psychological counseling, women's center.

Athletics *Intercollegiate sports:* badminton W, baseball M, basketball M/W, cheerleading M/W, cross-country running M/W, football M, golf M/W, soccer M/W, softball W, swimming and diving M/W, tennis M/W, track and field M/W, volleyball M/W, water polo M/W, wrestling M.

Costs (2013–14) *Tuition:* state resident $1104 full-time; nonresident $6000 full-time. Full-time tuition and fees vary according to course load and program. Part-time tuition and fees vary according to course load and program. *Required fees:* $60 full-time.

Applying *Options:* electronic application, early admission, deferred entrance. *Required for some:* high school transcript. *Notification:* continuous (freshmen), continuous (transfers).

Freshman Application Contact Dr. George Bradshaw, Dean of Enrollment Management, Mt. San Antonio College, Walnut, CA 91789. *Phone:* 909-594-5611 Ext. 4505.
Website: http://www.mtsac.edu/.

Mt. San Jacinto College

San Jacinto, California

Freshman Application Contact Mt. San Jacinto College, 1499 North State Street, San Jacinto, CA 92583-2399. *Phone:* 951-639-5212.
Website: http://www.msjc.edu/.

MTI College

Sacramento, California

- **Proprietary** 2-year, founded 1965
- **Suburban** 5-acre campus with easy access to Sacramento
- **Coed**
- 62% of applicants were admitted

Faculty *Student/faculty ratio:* 15:1.

Academics *Calendar:* continuous. *Degree:* diplomas and associate.

Standardized Tests *Required:* MTI Assessment (for admission).

Financial Aid Of all full-time matriculated undergraduates who enrolled in 2011, 35 Federal Work-Study jobs (averaging $1722).

Applying *Application fee:* $50. *Required:* essay or personal statement, high school transcript, interview.

Freshman Application Contact Director of Admissions, MTI College, 5221 Madison Avenue, Sacramento, CA 95841. *Phone:* 916-339-1500. *Fax:* 916-339-0305.
Website: http://www.mticollege.edu/.

Napa Valley College

Napa, California

Director of Admissions Mr. Oscar De Haro, Vice President of Student Services, Napa Valley College, 2277 Napa-Vallejo Highway, Napa, CA 94558-6236. *Phone:* 707-253-3000. *Toll-free phone:* 800-826-1077. *E-mail:* odeharo@napavalley.edu.
Website: http://www.napavalley.edu/.

Norco College

Norco, California

- **State and locally supported** 2-year, founded 2010
- **Urban** 141-acre campus with easy access to Los Angeles
- **Coed**

Academics *Degree:* associate. *Special study options:* academic remediation for entering students, distance learning, English as a second language, honors programs.

Costs (2012–13) *Tuition:* state resident $1380 full-time, $46 per unit part-time; nonresident $6660 full-time, $222 per unit part-time. Full-time tuition and fees vary according to course load. Part-time tuition and fees vary according to course load.

Applying *Options:* electronic application.

Freshman Application Contact Mark DeAsis, Director, Enrollment Services, Norco College, 2001 Third Street, Norco, CA 92860. *E-mail:* admissionsnorco@norcocollege.edu.
Website: http://www.rcc.edu/norco/index.cfm.

Ohlone College

Fremont, California

Freshman Application Contact Christopher Williamson, Director of Admissions and Records, Ohlone College, 43600 Mission Boulevard, Fremont, CA 94539-5884. *Phone:* 510-659-6518. *Fax:* 510-659-7321. *E-mail:* cwilliamson@ohlone.edu.
Website: http://www.ohlone.edu/.

Orange Coast College

Costa Mesa, California

- **State and locally supported** 2-year, founded 1947, part of Coast Community College District System
- **Suburban** 164-acre campus with easy access to Los Angeles
- **Endowment** $10.8 million
- **Coed,** 24,239 undergraduate students, 42% full-time, 49% women, 51% men

Undergraduates 10,094 full-time, 14,145 part-time. Students come from 52 states and territories; 69 other countries; 2% are from out of state; 2% Black or African American, non-Hispanic/Latino; 25% Hispanic/Latino; 23% Asian, non-Hispanic/Latino; 0.5% Native Hawaiian or other Pacific Islander, non-Hispanic/Latino; 0.4% American Indian or Alaska Native, non-Hispanic/Latino; 3% Two or more races, non-Hispanic/Latino; 3% Race/ethnicity unknown; 3% international; 8% transferred in. *Retention:* 79% of full-time freshmen returned.

Freshmen *Admission:* 4,205 enrolled.

Faculty *Total:* 758, 28% full-time. *Student/faculty ratio:* 34:1.

Majors Accounting; administrative assistant and secretarial science; aeronautics/aviation/aerospace science and technology; airline pilot and flight crew; anthropology; architectural engineering technology; art; athletic training; avionics maintenance technology; behavioral sciences; biology/biological sciences; building/home/construction inspection; business administration and management; cardiovascular technology; chemistry; child-care and support services management; child-care provision; cinematography and film/video production; clinical laboratory science/medical technology; commercial and advertising art; communications technology; computer engineering technology; computer graphics; computer programming; computer programming (specific applications); computer typography and composition equipment operation; construction engineering technology; culinary arts; dance; data entry/microcomputer applications related; data processing and data processing technology; dental hygiene; dietetics; drafting and design technology; dramatic/theater arts; economics; electrical and power transmission installation; electrical, electronic and communications engineering technology; electrical/electronics equipment installation and repair; emergency medical technology (EMT paramedic); engineering; English; family and consumer economics related; family and consumer sciences/human sciences; fashion merchandising; film/cinema/video studies; food science; foods, nutrition, and wellness; food technology and processing; French; geography; geology/earth science; German; health professions related; heating, air conditioning, ventilation and refrigeration maintenance technology; history; horticultural science; hotel/motel administration; housing and human environments; human development and family studies; humanities; industrial and product design; industrial radiologic technology; information science/studies; interior design; journalism; kindergarten/preschool education; kinesiology and exercise science; liberal arts and sciences/liberal studies; machine shop technology; machine tool technology; marine maintenance and ship repair technology; marketing/marketing management; mass communication/media; mathematics; medical administrative assistant and medical secretary; medical/clinical assistant; music; musical instrument fabrication and repair; music management; natural sciences; nuclear medical technology; ornamental horticulture; philosophy; photography; physical education teaching and coaching; physics; political science and government; religious studies; respiratory care therapy; restaurant, culinary, and catering management; retailing; selling skills and sales; social sciences; sociology; Spanish; special products marketing; welding technology; word processing.

Academics *Calendar:* semesters plus summer session. *Degree:* certificates and associate. *Special study options:* academic remediation for entering students, adult/continuing education programs, advanced placement credit, cooperative education, distance learning, double majors, English as a second language, external degree program, freshman honors college, honors programs, internships, off-campus study, part-time degree program, services for LD students, student-designed majors, study abroad, summer session for credit. *ROTC:* Army (c), Air Force (c).

Library Library with 112,276 titles, 210 serial subscriptions, 3,462 audiovisual materials, an OPAC, a Web page.

Student Life *Housing:* college housing not available. *Activities and Organizations:* drama/theater group, student-run newspaper, choral group, Architecture Club, Circle K, Doctors of Tomorrow, Speech, Theater, and Debate, Vietnamese Student Association. *Campus security:* 24-hour emergency response devices and patrols, student patrols, late-night transport/escort service. *Student services:* health clinic, personal/psychological counseling, legal services.

Athletics *Intercollegiate sports:* baseball M, basketball M/W, bowling M(c)/W(c), crew M/W, cross-country running M/W, football M, golf M/W, soccer M/W, softball W, swimming and diving M/W, tennis M/W, track and field M/W, volleyball W, water polo M/W.

Costs (2013–14) *Tuition:* state resident $1112 full-time, $36 per unit part-time; nonresident $6992 full-time, $232 per unit part-time. *Required fees:* $902 full-time, $61 per unit part-time.

Financial Aid Of all full-time matriculated undergraduates who enrolled in 2011, 108 Federal Work-Study jobs (averaging $3000). *Financial aid deadline:* 5/28.

Applying *Options:* electronic application. *Application deadlines:* rolling (freshmen), rolling (transfers). *Notification:* continuous (freshmen), continuous (transfers).

Freshman Application Contact Efren Galvan, Director of Admissions, Records and Enrollment Technology, Orange Coast College, 2701 Fairview Road, Costa Mesa, CA 92926. *Phone:* 714-432-5774. *E-mail:* egalvan@

occ.cccd.edu.
Website: http://www.orangecoastcollege.edu/.

Oxnard College
Oxnard, California

- **State-supported** 2-year, founded 1975, part of Ventura County Community College District System
- **Urban** 119-acre campus
- **Endowment** $1.7 million
- **Coed,** 7,060 undergraduate students, 27% full-time, 56% women, 44% men

Undergraduates 1,920 full-time, 5,140 part-time. 3% Black or African American, non-Hispanic/Latino; 69% Hispanic/Latino; 6% Asian, non-Hispanic/Latino; 0.4% Native Hawaiian or other Pacific Islander, non-Hispanic/Latino; 0.4% American Indian or Alaska Native, non-Hispanic/Latino; 2% Two or more races, non-Hispanic/Latino; 0.7% Race/ethnicity unknown; 12% transferred in. *Retention:* 56% of full-time freshmen returned.

Freshmen *Admission:* 989 enrolled.

Faculty *Total:* 184, 48% full-time.

Majors Administrative assistant and secretarial science; anthropology; art; autobody/collision and repair technology; automobile/automotive mechanics technology; biology/biological sciences; business administration and management; child development; computer and information systems security; computer systems networking and telecommunications; culinary arts; dental hygiene; economics; English; environmental engineering technology; family and community services; fine/studio arts; fire prevention and safety technology; fire science/firefighting; fire services administration; heating, air conditioning, ventilation and refrigeration maintenance technology; history; hotel/motel administration; legal assistant/paralegal; marketing/marketing management; mathematics; philosophy; political science and government; psychology; radio and television; restaurant/food services management; sociology; Spanish; substance abuse/addiction counseling; web page, digital/multimedia and information resources design.

Academics *Calendar:* semesters. *Degree:* certificates, diplomas, and associate. *Special study options:* academic remediation for entering students, accelerated degree program, advanced placement credit, distance learning, double majors, English as a second language, honors programs, independent study, part-time degree program, services for LD students, summer session for credit.

Library Oxnard College Library with 31,500 titles, 107 serial subscriptions, an OPAC, a Web page.

Student Life *Housing:* college housing not available. *Activities and Organizations:* drama/theater group, student-run television station. *Campus security:* 24-hour patrols. *Student services:* health clinic, personal/psychological counseling, women's center.

Athletics *Intercollegiate sports:* baseball M, cross-country running M/W, soccer M/W, softball W.

Financial Aid Of all full-time matriculated undergraduates who enrolled in 2011, 80 Federal Work-Study jobs (averaging $3000).

Applying *Options:* electronic application, early admission. *Recommended:* high school transcript. *Application deadlines:* rolling (freshmen), rolling (transfers). *Notification:* continuous (freshmen), continuous (transfers).

Freshman Application Contact Mr. Joel Diaz, Registrar, Oxnard College, 4000 South Rose Avenue, Oxnard, CA 93033-6699. *Phone:* 805-986-5843. *Fax:* 805-986-5943. *E-mail:* jdiaz@vcccd.edu.
Website: http://www.oxnardcollege.edu/.

Palomar College
San Marcos, California

Freshman Application Contact Mr. Herman Lee, Director of Enrollment Services, Palomar College, 1140 West Mission Road, San Marcos, CA 92069-1487. *Phone:* 760-744-1150 Ext. 2171. *Fax:* 760-744-2932. *E-mail:* admissions@palomar.edu.
Website: http://www.palomar.edu/.

Palo Verde College
Blythe, California

Freshman Application Contact Diana Rodriguez, Vice President of Student Services, Palo Verde College, 1 College Drive, Blythe, CA 92225. *Phone:* 760-921-5428. *Fax:* 760-921-3608. *E-mail:* diana.rodriguez@paloverde.edu.
Website: http://www.paloverde.edu/.

Pasadena City College
Pasadena, California

- **State and locally supported** 2-year, founded 1924, part of California Community College System
- **Urban** 55-acre campus with easy access to Los Angeles
- **Coed,** 22,859 undergraduate students, 35% full-time, 51% women, 49% men

Undergraduates 8,092 full-time, 14,767 part-time. Students come from 1 other state; 271 other countries; 4% Black or African American, non-Hispanic/Latino; 42% Hispanic/Latino; 25% Asian, non-Hispanic/Latino; 0.2% Native Hawaiian or other Pacific Islander, non-Hispanic/Latino; 0.2% American Indian or Alaska Native, non-Hispanic/Latino; 3% Two or more races, non-Hispanic/Latino; 4% Race/ethnicity unknown; 4% international; 4% transferred in. *Retention:* 80% of full-time freshmen returned.

Freshmen *Admission:* 6,853 applied, 6,702 admitted, 3,556 enrolled.

Faculty *Total:* 1,014, 37% full-time. *Student/faculty ratio:* 22:1.

Majors Accounting; accounting technology and bookkeeping; administrative assistant and secretarial science; animation, interactive technology, video graphics and special effects; anthropology; architecture; art; art history, criticism and conservation; audiology and speech-language pathology; automobile/automotive mechanics technology; biochemistry; bioethics/medical ethics; biological and physical sciences; biology/biological sciences; broadcast journalism; building/home/construction inspection; business administration and management; business automation/technology/data entry; chemistry; child development; cinematography and film/video production; classics and classical languages; computer/information technology services administration related; computer science; computer technology/computer systems technology; construction trades; cosmetology; cosmetology, barber/styling, and nail instruction; criminal justice/law enforcement administration; dance; data entry/microcomputer applications related; dental assisting; dental hygiene; dental laboratory technology; desktop publishing and digital imaging design; digital communication and media/multimedia; drafting and design technology; dramatic/theater arts; electrical and electronic engineering technologies related; electrical and electronics engineering; engineering technology; fashion/apparel design; fashion merchandising; fire prevention and safety technology; food service and dining room management; graphic and printing equipment operation/production; graphic design; history; hospitality administration; humanities; industrial electronics technology; international business/trade/commerce; international/global studies; legal assistant/paralegal; liberal arts and sciences/liberal studies; library science related; licensed practical/vocational nurse training; machine shop technology; marketing/marketing management; mathematics; mechanical engineering; medical/clinical assistant; medical insurance/medical billing; medical office assistant; photography; photojournalism; psychology; radio and television; radio and television broadcasting technology; radiologic technology/science; registered nursing/registered nurse; sociology; Spanish; speech communication and rhetoric; theater design and technology; welding technology.

Academics *Calendar:* semesters. *Degree:* certificates and associate. *Special study options:* academic remediation for entering students, adult/continuing education programs, advanced placement credit, distance learning, double majors, English as a second language, honors programs, independent study, internships, part-time degree program, services for LD students, study abroad, summer session for credit.

Library Pasadena City College Library plus 1 other with 137,945 titles, 19,326 serial subscriptions, 12,079 audiovisual materials, an OPAC, a Web page.

Student Life *Housing:* college housing not available. *Activities and Organizations:* drama/theater group, student-run newspaper, choral group, marching band. *Campus security:* 24-hour emergency response devices and patrols, late-night transport/escort service, cadet patrols. *Student services:* health clinic, personal/psychological counseling.

Athletics *Intercollegiate sports:* badminton M/W, baseball M, basketball M/W, cheerleading W(c), cross-country running M/W, football M, soccer M/W, softball W, swimming and diving M/W, tennis M/W, track and field M/W, volleyball W, water polo W. *Intramural sports:* water polo M(c).

Costs (2013–14) *Tuition:* state resident $1152 full-time; nonresident $6120 full-time. *Required fees:* $48 full-time.

Applying *Options:* electronic application. *Application deadlines:* rolling (freshmen), rolling (transfers). *Notification:* continuous (freshmen), continuous (transfers).

Freshman Application Contact Pasadena City College, 1570 East Colorado Boulevard, Pasadena, CA 91106-2041. *Phone:* 626-585-7284. *Fax:* 626-585-7915.
Website: http://www.pasadena.edu/.

Pima Medical Institute
Chula Vista, California

Freshman Application Contact Admissions Office, Pima Medical Institute, 780 Bay Boulevard, Suite 101, Chula Vista, CA 91910. *Phone:* 619-425-3200. *Toll-free phone:* 800-477-PIMA (in-state); 888-477-PIMA (out-of-state). *Website:* http://www.pmi.edu/.

Platt College
Alhambra, California

Director of Admissions Mr. Detroit Whiteside, Director of Admissions, Platt College, 1000 South Fremont A9W, Alhambra, CA 91803. *Phone:* 323-258-8050. *Toll-free phone:* 888-866-6697 (in-state); 888-80-PLATT (out-of-state). *Website:* http://www.plattcollege.edu/.

Platt College
Ontario, California

Director of Admissions Ms. Jennifer Abandonato, Director of Admissions, Platt College, 3700 Inland Empire Boulevard, Suite 400, Ontario, CA 91764. *Phone:* 909-941-9410. *Toll-free phone:* 888-80-PLATT.
Website: http://www.plattcollege.edu/.

Porterville College
Porterville, California

Director of Admissions Ms. Judy Pope, Director of Admissions and Records/Registrar, Porterville College, 100 East College Avenue, Porterville, CA 93257-6058. *Phone:* 559-791-2222.
Website: http://www.pc.cc.ca.us/.

Professional Golfers Career College
Temecula, California

Freshman Application Contact Mr. Mark Bland, Director of Admissions, Professional Golfers Career College, 26109 Ynez Road, Temecula, CA 92591. *Phone:* 951-719-2994. *Toll-free phone:* 800-877-4380. *Fax:* 951-719-1643. *E-mail:* Mark@golfcollege.edu.
Website: http://www.golfcollege.edu/.

Reedley College
Reedley, California

- **State and locally supported** 2-year, founded 1926, part of State Center Community College District System
- **Rural** 350-acre campus
- **Coed**

Undergraduates Students come from 15 states and territories; 2% Black or African American, non-Hispanic/Latino; 41% Hispanic/Latino; 5% Asian, non-Hispanic/Latino; 0.1% American Indian or Alaska Native, non-Hispanic/Latino; 21% Race/ethnicity unknown.

Academics *Calendar:* semesters. *Degree:* certificates, diplomas, and associate. *Special study options:* academic remediation for entering students, adult/continuing education programs, advanced placement credit, cooperative education, distance learning, English as a second language, freshman honors college, honors programs, independent study, part-time degree program, services for LD students, study abroad, summer session for credit. *ROTC:* Air Force (c).

Student Life *Campus security:* 24-hour emergency response devices, late-night transport/escort service, 24-hour on-campus police dispatcher.

Applying *Required:* high school transcript.

Freshman Application Contact Admissions and Records Office, Reedley College, 995 North Reed Avenue, Reedley, CA 93654. *Phone:* 559-638-0323. *Fax:* 559-637-2523.
Website: http://www.reedleycollege.edu/.

Rio Hondo College
Whittier, California

Director of Admissions Ms. Judy G. Pearson, Director of Admissions and Records, Rio Hondo College, 3600 Workman Mill Road, Whittier, CA 90601-1699. *Phone:* 562-692-0921 Ext. 3153.
Website: http://www.riohondo.edu/.

Riverside City College

Riverside, California

- **State and locally supported** 2-year, founded 1916, part of California Community College System
- **Suburban** 108-acre campus with easy access to Los Angeles
- **Coed**

Academics *Calendar:* semesters. *Degree:* certificates and associate. *Special study options:* academic remediation for entering students, distance learning, English as a second language, honors programs, study abroad.

Student Life *Campus security:* late-night transport/escort service.

Costs (2012–13) *Tuition:* state resident $1380 full-time, $46 per unit part-time; nonresident $6660 full-time, $222 per unit part-time. Full-time tuition and fees vary according to course load. Part-time tuition and fees vary according to course load.

Applying *Options:* electronic application.

Freshman Application Contact Joy Chambers, Dean of Enrollment Services, Riverside City College, Riverside, CA 92506. *Phone:* 951-222-8600. *Fax:* 951-222-8037. *E-mail:* admissionsriverside@rcc.edu.

Website: http://www.rcc.edu/.

Sacramento City College

Sacramento, California

Director of Admissions Mr. Sam T. Sandusky, Dean, Student Services, Sacramento City College, 3835 Freeport Boulevard, Sacramento, CA 95822-1386. *Phone:* 916-558-2438.

Website: http://www.scc.losrios.edu/.

Saddleback College

Mission Viejo, California

Freshman Application Contact Admissions Office, Saddleback College, 28000 Marguerite Parkway, Mission Viejo, CA 92692. *Phone:* 949-582-4555. *Fax:* 949-347-8315. *E-mail:* earaiza@saddleback.edu.

Website: http://www.saddleback.edu/.

Sage College

Moreno Valley, California

Admissions Office Contact Sage College, 12125 Day Street, Building L, Moreno Valley, CA 92557-6720. *Toll-free phone:* 888-755-SAGE.

Website: http://www.sagecollege.edu/.

The Salvation Army College for Officer Training at Crestmont

Rancho Palos Verdes, California

Freshman Application Contact Capt. Kevin Jackson, Director of Curriculum, The Salvation Army College for Officer Training at Crestmont, 30840 Hawthorne Boulevard, Rancho Palos Verdes, CA 90275. *Phone:* 310-544-6442. *Fax:* 310-265-6520.

Website: http://www.crestmont.edu/.

San Bernardino Valley College

San Bernardino, California

Director of Admissions Ms. Helena Johnson, Director of Admissions and Records, San Bernardino Valley College, 701 South Mount Vernon Avenue, San Bernardino, CA 92410-2748. *Phone:* 909-384-4401.

Website: http://www.valleycollege.edu/.

San Diego City College

San Diego, California

- **State and locally supported** 2-year, founded 1914, part of San Diego Community College District System
- **Urban** 60-acre campus with easy access to San Diego, Tijuana
- **Endowment** $166,270
- **Coed,** 17,681 undergraduate students

Undergraduates 12% Black or African American, non-Hispanic/Latino; 46% Hispanic/Latino; 9% Asian, non-Hispanic/Latino; 0.5% Native Hawaiian or other Pacific Islander, non-Hispanic/Latino; 0.4% American Indian or Alaska Native, non-Hispanic/Latino; 8% Race/ethnicity unknown.

Faculty *Total:* 803, 21% full-time, 16% with terminal degrees. *Student/faculty ratio:* 35:1.

Majors Accounting; administrative assistant and secretarial science; African American/Black studies; anthropology; art; artificial intelligence; automobile/automotive mechanics technology; behavioral sciences; biology/biological sciences; business administration and management; carpentry; commercial and advertising art; computer engineering technology; consumer services and advocacy; cosmetology; court reporting; data processing and data processing technology; developmental and child psychology; drafting and design technology; dramatic/theater arts; electrical, electronic and communications engineering technology; emergency medical technology (EMT paramedic); engineering technology; English; environmental engineering technology; fashion merchandising; finance; graphic and printing equipment operation/production; Hispanic-American, Puerto Rican, and Mexican-American/Chicano studies; hospitality administration; industrial technology; insurance; interior design; journalism; labor and industrial relations; Latin American studies; legal administrative assistant/secretary; legal assistant/paralegal; liberal arts and sciences/liberal studies; licensed practical/vocational nurse training; machine tool technology; marketing/marketing management; mathematics; modern languages; music; occupational safety and health technology; parks, recreation and leisure; photography; physical education teaching and coaching; physical sciences; political science and government; pre-engineering; psychology; radio and television; real estate; registered nursing/registered nurse; rhetoric and composition; social sciences; social work; sociology; special products marketing; teacher assistant/aide; telecommunications technology; tourism and travel services management; transportation and materials moving related; welding technology.

Academics *Calendar:* semesters. *Degree:* certificates and associate. *Special study options:* academic remediation for entering students, adult/continuing education programs, cooperative education, distance learning, English as a second language, external degree program, honors programs, independent study, off-campus study, part-time degree program, services for LD students, student-designed majors, summer session for credit. *ROTC:* Air Force (c).

Library San Diego City College Library with 88,000 titles, 191 serial subscriptions, 950 audiovisual materials, an OPAC.

Student Life *Housing:* college housing not available. *Activities and Organizations:* drama/theater group, student-run newspaper, radio station, choral group, Alpha Gamma Sigma, Association of United Latin American Students, MECHA, Afrikan Student Union, Student Nurses Association. *Campus security:* 24-hour emergency response devices and patrols, late-night transport/escort service. *Student services:* health clinic, personal/psychological counseling.

Athletics *Intercollegiate sports:* baseball M, basketball M/W, cross-country running M/W, football M, golf M/W, soccer M/W, softball W, tennis M/W, track and field M/W, volleyball M/W. *Intramural sports:* archery M/W, badminton M/W, baseball M, basketball M/W, bowling M/W, racquetball M/W, soccer M/W, softball W, swimming and diving M/W, tennis M/W, track and field M/W, volleyball M/W, weight lifting M/W.

Costs (2013–14) *Tuition:* state resident $1380 full-time, $46 per unit part-time; nonresident $6870 full-time, $229 per unit part-time. Full-time tuition and fees vary according to course load. Part-time tuition and fees vary according to course load. *Required fees:* $38 full-time.

Financial Aid Of all full-time matriculated undergraduates who enrolled in 2010, 90 Federal Work-Study jobs (averaging $3844). 19 state and other part-time jobs (averaging $2530).

Applying *Options:* electronic application. *Required for some:* high school transcript. *Application deadlines:* rolling (freshmen), rolling (transfers).

Freshman Application Contact Ms. Lou Humphries, Registrar/Supervisor of Admissions, Records, Evaluations and Veterans, San Diego City College, 1313 Park Boulevard, San Diego, CA 92101-4787. *Phone:* 619-388-3474. *Fax:* 619-388-3505. *E-mail:* lhumphri@sdccd.edu.

Website: http://www.sdcity.edu/.

San Diego Mesa College

San Diego, California

- **State and locally supported** 2-year, founded 1964, part of San Diego Community College District System
- **Suburban** 104-acre campus
- **Coed,** 25,464 undergraduate students, 100% full-time, 52% women, 48% men

Undergraduates 25,464 full-time. 7% Black or African American, non-Hispanic/Latino; 31% Hispanic/Latino; 16% Asian, non-Hispanic/Latino; 0.7% Native Hawaiian or other Pacific Islander, non-Hispanic/Latino; 0.4% American Indian or Alaska Native, non-Hispanic/Latino; 9% Race/ethnicity unknown.

Faculty *Total:* 723, 28% full-time.

Majors Accounting; administrative assistant and secretarial science; African American/Black studies; architectural engineering technology; architecture; art; biology/biological sciences; business administration and management; chemistry; child-care provision; clinical/medical laboratory technology; computer and information sciences; computer programming related; computer programming (specific applications); computer science; computer software and media applications related; construction engineering technology; data entry/microcomputer applications related; dental assisting; engineering; English; fashion/apparel design; fashion merchandising; foods and nutrition related; foods, nutrition, and wellness; French; geography; health information/medical records administration; Hispanic-American, Puerto Rican, and Mexican-American/Chicano studies; hospitality and recreation marketing; hotel/motel administration; industrial radiologic technology; interior design; intermedia/multimedia; landscape architecture; legal administrative assistant/secretary; liberal arts and sciences/liberal studies; marketing/marketing management; marketing research; mathematics; medical/clinical assistant; music; physical education teaching and coaching; physical sciences; physical therapy technology; physics; psychology; real estate; rhetoric and composition; social sciences; sociology; Spanish; tourism and travel services management; tourism and travel services marketing; veterinary/animal health technology.

Academics *Calendar:* semesters. *Degree:* certificates, diplomas, and associate. *Special study options:* academic remediation for entering students, adult/continuing education programs, English as a second language, external degree program, honors programs, independent study, part-time degree program, services for LD students, summer session for credit.

Library Learning Resource Center- Library with 99,806 titles, 104 serial subscriptions, 1,923 audiovisual materials, an OPAC.

Student Life *Housing:* college housing not available. *Activities and Organizations:* drama/theater group, student-run newspaper, television station, choral group, Alpha Gamma Sigma, Black Student Union, MECHA, Associated Student Government, Vietnamese Student Association. *Campus security:* 24-hour emergency response devices and patrols, late-night transport/escort service. *Student services:* health clinic, personal/psychological counseling.

Athletics *Intercollegiate sports:* baseball M, basketball M/W, cross-country running M/W,· football M, soccer M/W, softball W, swimming and diving M/W, tennis M/W, track and field M/W, volleyball M/W, water polo M/W. *Intramural sports:* badminton M/W, basketball M/W, bowling M/W, fencing M/W, football M, golf M/W, gymnastics M/W, racquetball M/W, skiing (downhill) M, soccer M/W, softball M/W, swimming and diving M/W, tennis M/W, volleyball M/W, weight lifting M/W.

Costs (2013–14) *Tuition:* state resident $552 full-time, $46 per unit part-time; nonresident $2196 full-time, $229 per unit part-time. *Required fees:* $1104 full-time. *Room and board:* $10,962.

Financial Aid Of all full-time matriculated undergraduates who enrolled in 2011, 115 Federal Work-Study jobs (averaging $5000). *Financial aid deadline:* 6/30.

Freshman Application Contact Ms. Cheri Sawyer, Admissions Supervisor, San Diego Mesa College, 7250 Mesa College Drive, San Diego, CA 92111. *Phone:* 619-388-2686. *Fax:* 619-388-2960. *E-mail:* csawyer@sdccd.edu. *Website:* http://www.sdmesa.edu/.

San Diego Miramar College

San Diego, California

Freshman Application Contact Ms. Dana Andras, Admissions Supervisor, San Diego Miramar College, 10440 Black Mountain Road, San Diego, CA 92126-2999. *Phone:* 619-536-7854. *E-mail:* dmaxwell@sdccd.cc.ca.us. *Website:* http://www.sdmiramar.edu/.

San Joaquin Delta College

Stockton, California

Freshman Application Contact Ms. Catherine Mooney, Registrar, San Joaquin Delta College, 5151 Pacific Avenue, Stockton, CA 95207. *Phone:* 209-954-5635. *Fax:* 209-954-5769. *E-mail:* admissions@deltacollege.edu. *Website:* http://www.deltacollege.edu/.

San Joaquin Valley College

Bakersfield, California

- **Proprietary** 2-year, founded 1977, part of San Joaquin Valley College
- **Coed**

Undergraduates 541 full-time. Students come from 6 states and territories; 2 other countries; 1% are from out of state.
Faculty *Student/faculty ratio:* 12:1.
Academics *Degree:* associate.
Costs (2012–13) *Tuition:* $29,750 per degree program part-time. No tuition increase for student's term of enrollment.
Applying *Required for some:* essay or personal statement, interview.
Freshman Application Contact Enrollment Services Director, San Joaquin Valley College, 201 New Stine Road, Bakersfield, CA 93309. *Phone:* 661-834-0126. *Toll-free phone:* 866-544-7898. *Fax:* 661-834-8124. *E-mail:*

admissions@sjvc.edu.
Website: http://www.sjvc.edu/.

San Joaquin Valley College

Fresno, California

- **Proprietary** 2-year, part of San Joaquin Valley College
- **Coed**

Undergraduates 675 full-time. Students come from 4 states and territories; 3% are from out of state.
Faculty *Student/faculty ratio:* 10:1.
Academics *Degree:* certificates and associate.
Costs (2012–13) *Tuition:* $15,500 full-time. Full-time tuition and fees vary according to location and program. *Payment plans:* tuition prepayment, installment.
Applying *Required for some:* essay or personal statement, 1 letter of recommendation, interview.
Freshman Application Contact Enrollment Services Director, San Joaquin Valley College, 295 East Sierra Avenue, Fresno, CA 93710. *Phone:* 559-448-8282. *Fax:* 559-448-8250. *E-mail:* admissions@sjvc.edu.
Website: http://www.sjvc.edu/.

San Joaquin Valley College

Hanford, California

- **Proprietary** 2-year
- **Coed**

Academics *Degree:* certificates.
Costs (2012–13) *Tuition:* $29,750 per degree program part-time.
Freshman Application Contact San Joaquin Valley College, 215 West 7th Street, Hanford, CA 93230.
Website: http://www.sjvc.edu/.

San Joaquin Valley College

Hesperia, California

- **Proprietary** 2-year
- **Coed**

Costs (2012–13) *Tuition:* $31,950 per degree program part-time.
Freshman Application Contact San Joaquin Valley College, 9331 Mariposa Road, Hesperia, CA 92344.
Website: http://www.sjvc.edu/.

San Joaquin Valley College

Rancho Cordova, California

- **Proprietary** 2-year, part of San Joaquin Valley College
- **Coed**

Undergraduates 619 full-time.
Faculty *Student/faculty ratio:* 17:1.
Academics *Degree:* certificates and associate.
Costs (2012–13) *Tuition:* $21,560 full-time. Full-time tuition and fees vary according to location and program. *Payment plans:* tuition prepayment, installment.
Applying *Required for some:* essay or personal statement, 1 letter of recommendation, interview.
Freshman Application Contact Enrollment Services Director, San Joaquin Valley College, 11050 Olson Drive, Suite 100, Rancho Cordova, CA 95670. *Phone:* 916-638-7582. *Fax:* 916-638-7553. *E-mail:* admissions@sjvc.edu.
Website: http://www.sjvc.edu/.

San Joaquin Valley College

Rancho Cucamonga, California

Freshman Application Contact Enrollment Services Director, San Joaquin Valley College, 10641 Church Street, Rancho Cucamonga, CA 91730. *Phone:* 909-948-7582. *Fax:* 909-948-3860. *E-mail:* admissions@sjvc.edu.
Website: http://www.sjvc.edu/.

San Joaquin Valley College

Salida, California

- **Proprietary** 2-year, part of San Joaquin Valley College
- **Coed**

Undergraduates 254 full-time. Students come from 3 states and territories; 3% are from out of state.
Faculty *Student/faculty ratio:* 18:1.
Academics *Degree:* certificates and associate.

Costs (2012–13) *Tuition:* $15,500 full-time. Full-time tuition and fees vary according to location and program. *Payment plans:* tuition prepayment, installment.

Applying *Required for some:* essay or personal statement, 1 letter of recommendation, interview.

Freshman Application Contact Enrollment Services Director, San Joaquin Valley College, 5380 Pirrone Road, Salida, CA 95368. *Phone:* 209-543-8800. *Fax:* 209-543-8320. *E-mail:* admissions@sjvc.edu. *Website:* http://www.sjvc.edu/.

San Joaquin Valley College
Temecula, California

- **Proprietary** 2-year
- **Coed**

Costs (2012–13) *Tuition:* $31,950 per degree program part-time.

Freshman Application Contact San Joaquin Valley College, 27270 Madison Avenue, Suite 305, Temecula, CA 92590. *Website:* http://www.sjvc.edu/.

San Joaquin Valley College
Visalia, California

- **Independent** 2-year, founded 1977, part of San Joaquin Valley College
- **Small-town** campus
- **Coed**

Undergraduates 895 full-time. Students come from 17 states and territories; 2% are from out of state.

Faculty *Student/faculty ratio:* 9:1.

Academics *Calendar:* semesters. *Degree:* certificates and associate. *Special study options:* academic remediation for entering students.

Student Life *Campus security:* late-night transport/escort service, full-time security personnel.

Costs (2012–13) *Tuition:* $29,750 per degree program part-time. No tuition increase for student's term of enrollment.

Applying *Required for some:* essay or personal statement, high school transcript, interview.

Freshman Application Contact Enrollment Services Director, San Joaquin Valley College, 8400 West Mineral King Boulevard, Visalia, CA 93291. *Phone:* 559-651-2500. *Fax:* 559-734-9048. *E-mail:* admissions@sjvc.edu. *Website:* http://www.sjvc.edu/.

San Joaquin Valley College–Fresno Aviation Campus
Fresno, California

- **Proprietary** 2-year, part of San Joaquin Valley College
- **Coed**

Undergraduates 59 full-time.

Faculty *Student/faculty ratio:* 12:1.

Academics *Degree:* associate.

Costs (2012–13) *Tuition:* $27,265 per degree program part-time. No tuition increase for student's term of enrollment.

Applying *Required for some:* essay or personal statement, interview.

Freshman Application Contact Enrollment Services Coordinator, San Joaquin Valley College–Fresno Aviation Campus, 4985 East Anderson Avenue, Fresno, CA 93727. *Phone:* 559-453-0123. *Fax:* 599-453-0133. *E-mail:* admissions@sjvc.edu. *Website:* http://www.sjvc.edu/.

San Joaquin Valley College–Online
Visalia, California

- **Proprietary** 2-year, part of San Joaquin Valley College
- **Suburban** campus with easy access to Fresno
- **Coed**

Undergraduates 887 full-time. Students come from 14 states and territories; 31% are from out of state. *Retention:* 77% of full-time freshmen returned.

Faculty *Student/faculty ratio:* 21:1.

Academics *Degree:* certificates and associate.

Costs (2012–13) *Tuition:* $30,800 per degree program part-time. No tuition increase for student's term of enrollment.

Applying *Options:* electronic application. *Required for some:* essay or personal statement, interview.

Freshman Application Contact Enrollment Services Director, San Joaquin Valley College–Online, 801 S. Akers Street, Suite 150, Visalia, CA 93277. *E-mail:* admissions@sjvc.edu. *Website:* http://www.sjvc.edu/campus/SJVC_Online/.

San Jose City College
San Jose, California

Freshman Application Contact Mr. Carlo Santos, Director of Admissions/Registrar, San Jose City College, 2100 Moorpark Avenue, San Jose, CA 95128-2799. *Phone:* 408-288-3707. *Fax:* 408-298-1935. *Website:* http://www.sjcc.edu/.

Santa Ana College
Santa Ana, California

Freshman Application Contact Mrs. Christie Steward, Admissions Clerk, Santa Ana College, 1530 West 17th Street, Santa Ana, CA 92706-3398. *Phone:* 714-564-6053. *Website:* http://www.sac.edu/.

Santa Barbara City College
Santa Barbara, California

Freshman Application Contact Ms. Allison Curtis, Director of Admissions and Records, Santa Barbara City College, Santa Barbara, CA 93109. *Phone:* 805-965-0581 Ext. 2352. *Fax:* 805-962-0497. *E-mail:* admissions@sbcc.edu. *Website:* http://www.sbcc.edu/.

Santa Monica College
Santa Monica, California

- **State and locally supported** 2-year, founded 1929, part of California Community College System
- **Urban** 40-acre campus with easy access to Los Angeles
- **Coed**

Undergraduates 11,160 full-time, 19,978 part-time. 10% Black or African American, non-Hispanic/Latino; 32% Hispanic/Latino; 12% Asian, non-Hispanic/Latino; 0.3% Native Hawaiian or other Pacific Islander, non-Hispanic/Latino; 0.3% American Indian or Alaska Native, non-Hispanic/Latino; 3% Two or more races, non-Hispanic/Latino; 4% Race/ethnicity unknown; 10% international.

Academics *Calendar:* semester plus optional winter and summer terms. *Degree:* certificates and associate. *Special study options:* academic remediation for entering students, adult/continuing education programs, advanced placement credit, cooperative education, distance learning, English as a second language, honors programs, independent study, internships, part-time degree program, services for LD students, study abroad, summer session for credit. *ROTC:* Army (c).

Student Life *Campus security:* 24-hour emergency response devices and patrols, student patrols, late-night transport/escort service.

Costs (2012–13) *Tuition:* state resident $1080 full-time, $36 per unit part-time; nonresident $8250 full-time, $275 per unit part-time. Full-time tuition and fees vary according to course load. Part-time tuition and fees vary according to course load. *Required fees:* $49 full-time.

Financial Aid Of all full-time matriculated undergraduates who enrolled in 2011, 450 Federal Work-Study jobs (averaging $3000).

Applying *Options:* early admission. *Required:* high school transcript.

Freshman Application Contact Santa Monica College, 1900 Pico Boulevard, Santa Monica, CA 90405-1628. *Phone:* 310-434-4774. *Website:* http://www.smc.edu/.

Santa Rosa Junior College
Santa Rosa, California

- **State and locally supported** 2-year, founded 1918, part of California Community College System
- **Urban** 100-acre campus with easy access to San Francisco
- **Endowment** $35.5 million
- **Coed**, 21,878 undergraduate students, 31% full-time, 55% women, 45% men

Undergraduates 6,733 full-time, 15,145 part-time. Students come from 40 other countries; 2% are from out of state; 2% Black or African American, non-Hispanic/Latino; 22% Hispanic/Latino; 4% Asian, non-Hispanic/Latino; 1% Native Hawaiian or other Pacific Islander, non-Hispanic/Latino; 0.8% American Indian or Alaska Native, non-Hispanic/Latino; 11% Two or more races, non-Hispanic/Latino; 5% Race/ethnicity unknown.

Freshmen *Admission:* 5,474 applied, 5,474 admitted.

Faculty *Total:* 1,188, 23% full-time, 12% with terminal degrees. *Student/faculty ratio:* 23:1.

Majors Agricultural business and management; agricultural communication/journalism; agroecology and sustainable agriculture; American Sign Language (ASL); animal sciences; anthropology; art; art history, criticism and conservation; automobile/automotive mechanics technology; behavioral sciences; biology/biological sciences; business administration and management; chemistry; child development; civil engineering technology; communication; community health services counseling; computer science; criminal justice/law enforcement administration; culinary arts; dance; dental hygiene; diesel mechanics technology; dietetic technology; digital communication and media/multimedia; dramatic/theater arts; early childhood education; economics; electrical, electronic and communications engineering technology; emergency medical technology (EMT paramedic); engineering; English; environmental studies; fashion/apparel design; fashion merchandising; fire science/firefighting; floriculture/floristry management; French; graphic design; health and physical education/fitness; history; horse husbandry/equine science and management; humanities; human resources management; human services; interior design; jazz/jazz studies; kinesiology and exercise science; landscaping and groundskeeping; Latin American studies; legal assistant/paralegal; liberal arts and sciences/liberal studies; licensed practical/vocational nurse training; mathematics; medical/clinical assistant; music related; natural resources/conservation; natural sciences; nutrition sciences; parks, recreation and leisure facilities management; pharmacy technician; philosophy; physics; political science and government; psychology; radiologic technology/science; real estate; registered nursing/registered nurse; religious studies; restaurant/food services management; social sciences; sociology; Spanish; surveying technology; viticulture and enology; women's studies.

Academics *Calendar:* semesters. *Degree:* certificates and associate. *Special study options:* academic remediation for entering students, adult/continuing education programs, advanced placement credit, cooperative education, distance learning, English as a second language, independent study, internships, off-campus study, part-time degree program, services for LD students, study abroad, summer session for credit.

Library Doyle Library plus 1 other with 185,461 titles, 29,932 serial subscriptions, 18,173 audiovisual materials, an OPAC, a Web page.

Student Life *Housing:* college housing not available. *Activities and Organizations:* drama/theater group, student-run newspaper, choral group, AG Ambassadors, MECHA, Alpha Gamma Sigma, Phi Theta Kappa, Puente. *Campus security:* 24-hour emergency response devices and patrols, student patrols. *Student services:* health clinic, personal/psychological counseling.

Athletics Member NJCAA. *Intercollegiate sports:* baseball M, basketball M/W, cross-country running M/W, football M, golf M, ice hockey M(c), rugby M(c), soccer M/W, softball W, swimming and diving M/W, tennis M/W, track and field M/W, volleyball W, water polo M/W, wrestling M.

Costs (2013–14) *One-time required fee:* $38. *Tuition:* state resident $0 full-time; nonresident $4728 full-time, $197 per unit part-time. Full-time tuition and fees vary according to course load. Part-time tuition and fees vary according to course load. *Required fees:* $1104 full-time, $46 per unit part-time, $19 per term part-time. *Payment plans:* installment, deferred payment.

Financial Aid Of all full-time matriculated undergraduates who enrolled in 2009, 135 Federal Work-Study jobs (averaging $2210). 43 state and other part-time jobs (averaging $7396).

Applying *Options:* electronic application, early admission. *Application deadlines:* rolling (freshmen), rolling (out-of-state freshmen), rolling (transfers). *Notification:* continuous (freshmen), continuous (out-of-state freshmen), continuous (transfers).

Freshman Application Contact Ms. Diane Traversi, Director of Enrollment Services, Santa Rosa Junior College, 1501 Mendocino Avenue, Santa Rosa, CA 95401. *Phone:* 707-527-4510. *Fax:* 707-527-4798. *E-mail:* admininfo@santarosa.edu.
Website: http://www.santarosa.edu/.

Santiago Canyon College
Orange, California

Freshman Application Contact Denise Pennock, Admissions and Records, Santiago Canyon College, 8045 East Chapman Avenue, Orange, CA 92869. *Phone:* 714-564-4000.
Website: http://www.sccollege.edu/.

School of Urban Missions
Oakland, California

Freshman Application Contact Admissions, School of Urban Missions, 735 105th Avenue, Oakland, CA 94603. *Phone:* 510-567-6174. *Toll-free phone:* 888-567-6174. *Fax:* 510-568-1024.
Website: http://www.sum.edu/.

Shasta College
Redding, California

Director of Admissions Dr. Kevin O'Rorke, Dean of Enrollment Services, Shasta College, PO Box 496006, 11555 Old Oregon Trail, Redding, CA 96049-6006. *Phone:* 530-242-7669.
Website: http://www.shastacollege.edu/.

Sierra College
Rocklin, California

- **State-supported** 2-year, founded 1936, part of California Community College System
- **Suburban** 327-acre campus with easy access to Sacramento
- **Coed,** 19,416 undergraduate students, 28% full-time, 57% women, 43% men

Undergraduates 5,355 full-time, 14,061 part-time. 1% are from out of state; 4% transferred in; 1% live on campus.

Freshmen *Admission:* 24,000 applied, 24,000 admitted, 2,112 enrolled.

Faculty *Total:* 870, 18% full-time. *Student/faculty ratio:* 25:1.

Majors Accounting; administrative assistant and secretarial science; agriculture; American Sign Language (ASL); animal/livestock husbandry and production; apparel and textile manufacturing; apparel and textile marketing management; applied horticulture/horticulture operations; architectural drafting and CAD/CADD; art; automobile/automotive mechanics technology; biological and physical sciences; biology/biological sciences; business administration and management; business/commerce; cabinetmaking and millwork; chemistry; child development; commercial photography; computer and information sciences and support services related; computer installation and repair technology; computer programming; computer systems networking and telecommunications; construction trades; corrections; criminal justice/police science; data entry/microcomputer applications; digital communication and media/multimedia; electrical/electronics equipment installation and repair; engineering; English; equestrian studies; fire science/firefighting; forestry; general studies; geology/earth science; graphic design; hazardous materials management and waste technology; health and physical education/fitness; industrial electronics technology; information technology; liberal arts and sciences/liberal studies; licensed practical/vocational nurse training; manufacturing engineering technology; mathematics; mechanical drafting and CAD/CADD; music; network and system administration; parks, recreation and leisure; philosophy; physics; psychology; real estate; registered nursing/registered nurse; rhetoric and composition; sales, distribution, and marketing operations; small business administration; social sciences; visual and performing arts; web page, digital/multimedia and information resources design; women's studies.

Academics *Calendar:* semesters. *Degree:* certificates and associate. *Special study options:* academic remediation for entering students, accelerated degree program, advanced placement credit, distance learning, double majors, English as a second language, honors programs, independent study, internships, off-campus study, part-time degree program, services for LD students, study abroad, summer session for credit.

Library Leary Resource Center plus 1 other with 69,879 titles, 189 serial subscriptions, an OPAC, a Web page.

Student Life *Housing Options:* coed. Campus housing is university owned. *Activities and Organizations:* drama/theater group, student-run newspaper, choral group, Drama Club, student government, Art Club, band, Aggie Club. *Campus security:* 24-hour emergency response devices and patrols, late-night transport/escort service. *Student services:* health clinic, personal/psychological counseling.

Athletics *Intercollegiate sports:* baseball M, basketball M/W, football M, golf M/W, soccer W, softball W, swimming and diving M/W, tennis M/W, volleyball W, water polo M/W, wrestling M. *Intramural sports:* archery M/W, badminton M/W, basketball M/W, tennis M/W, volleyball M/W.

Financial Aid Of all full-time matriculated undergraduates who enrolled in 2011, 150 Federal Work-Study jobs (averaging $2340).

Applying *Options:* electronic application, early admission. *Application deadline:* rolling (freshmen). *Notification:* continuous (freshmen), continuous (transfers).

Freshman Application Contact Sierra College, 5000 Rocklin Road, Rocklin, CA 95677-3397. *Phone:* 916-660-7341.
Website: http://www.sierracollege.edu/.

Skyline College
San Bruno, California

Freshman Application Contact Terry Stats, Admissions Office, Skyline College, 3300 College Drive, San Bruno, CA 94066-1698. *Phone:* 650-738-4251. *E-mail:* stats@smccd.net.
Website: http://skylinecollege.net/.

Solano Community College

Fairfield, California

Freshman Application Contact Solano Community College, 4000 Suisun Valley Road, Fairfield, CA 94534. *Phone:* 707-864-7000 Ext. 4313. *Website:* http://www.solano.edu/.

South Coast College

Orange, California

Director of Admissions South Coast College, 2011 West Chapman Avenue, Orange, CA 92868. *Toll-free phone:* 877-568-6130. *Website:* http://www.southcoastcollege.com/.

Southwestern College

Chula Vista, California

Freshman Application Contact Director of Admissions and Records, Southwestern College, 900 Otay Lakes Road, Chula Vista, CA 91910-7299. *Phone:* 619-421-6700 Ext. 5215. *Fax:* 619-482-6489. *Website:* http://www.swc.edu/.

Stanbridge College

Irvine, California

Admissions Office Contact Stanbridge College, 2041 Business Center Drive, Irvine, CA 92612. *Website:* http://www.stanbridge.edu/.

Taft College

Taft, California

- **State and locally supported** 2-year, founded 1922, part of California Community College System
- **Small-town** 15-acre campus
- **Endowment** $14,405
- **Coed,** 9,500 undergraduate students, 5% full-time, 20% women, 80% men

Undergraduates 505 full-time, 8,995 part-time. Students come from 1 other country; 5% are from out of state; 3% transferred in; 6% live on campus.
Freshmen *Admission:* 812 applied, 812 admitted, 324 enrolled.
Faculty *Total:* 91, 41% full-time, 9% with terminal degrees.
Majors Accounting; administrative assistant and secretarial science; art; automobile/automotive mechanics technology; biology/biological sciences; business administration and management; computer science; criminal justice/law enforcement administration; data processing and data processing technology; dental hygiene; drafting and design technology; electrical, electronic and communications engineering technology; English; general studies; journalism; kindergarten/preschool education; liberal arts and sciences/liberal studies; mathematics; parks, recreation and leisure; physical education teaching and coaching; physical sciences; pre-engineering; social sciences.
Academics *Calendar:* semesters. *Degree:* certificates and associate. *Special study options:* academic remediation for entering students, adult/continuing education programs, advanced placement credit, distance learning, English as a second language, honors programs, independent study, part-time degree program, services for LD students, summer session for credit.
Library Taft College Library with 28,500 titles, 150 serial subscriptions, 1,500 audiovisual materials, an OPAC, a Web page.
Student Life *Housing Options:* coed, disabled students. Campus housing is university owned. *Activities and Organizations:* student-run newspaper, International Club, Alpha Gamma Sigma, Rotaract, ASB Club. *Campus security:* 24-hour emergency response devices, controlled dormitory access, parking lot security. *Student services:* personal/psychological counseling.
Athletics *Intercollegiate sports:* baseball M, basketball W, soccer M, softball W, volleyball W.
Costs (2013–14) *Tuition:* state resident $0 full-time; nonresident $7080 full-time, $190 per unit part-time. Full-time tuition and fees vary according to course load and program. Part-time tuition and fees vary according to course load. *Required fees:* $1380 full-time, $46 per unit part-time. *Room and board:* Room and board charges vary according to board plan and housing facility. *Waivers:* minority students, children of alumni, adult students, senior citizens, and employees or children of employees.
Applying *Options:* electronic application. *Required for some:* high school transcript. *Application deadlines:* rolling (freshmen), 8/1 (transfers).
Freshman Application Contact Nichole Cook, Admissions/Counseling Technician, Taft College, 29 Emmons Park Drive, Taft, CA 93268-2317. *Phone:* 661-763-7790. *Fax:* 661-763-7758. *E-mail:* ncook@taftcollege.edu. *Website:* http://www.taftcollege.edu/.

Unitek College

Fremont, California

Admissions Office Contact Unitek College, 4670 Auto Mall Parkway, Fremont, CA 94538. *Website:* http://www.unitekcollege.edu/.

Ventura College

Ventura, California

Freshman Application Contact Ms. Susan Bricker, Registrar, Ventura College, 4667 Telegraph Road, Ventura, CA 93003-3899. *Phone:* 805-654-6456. *Fax:* 805-654-6357. *E-mail:* sbricker@vcccd.net. *Website:* http://www.venturacollege.edu/.

Victor Valley College

Victorville, California

- **State-supported** 2-year, founded 1961, part of California Community College System
- **Small-town** 253-acre campus with easy access to Los Angeles
- **Coed,** 6,790 undergraduate students, 39% full-time, 55% women, 45% men

Undergraduates 2,668 full-time, 4,122 part-time. 3% are from out of state; 1% Black or African American, non-Hispanic/Latino; 0.5% Hispanic/Latino; 0.1% Asian, non-Hispanic/Latino; 0.3% Native Hawaiian or other Pacific Islander, non-Hispanic/Latino; 44% American Indian or Alaska Native, non-Hispanic/Latino; 33% Two or more races, non-Hispanic/Latino; 4% Race/ethnicity unknown; 14% international; 6% transferred in. *Retention:* 66% of full-time freshmen returned.
Freshmen *Admission:* 1,372 enrolled.
Faculty *Total:* 565, 22% full-time. *Student/faculty ratio:* 27:1.
Majors Administrative assistant and secretarial science; agricultural teacher education; art; automobile/automotive mechanics technology; biological and physical sciences; biology/biological sciences; building/construction finishing, management, and inspection related; business administration and management; business/commerce; child-care and support services management; child development; computer and information sciences; computer programming (specific applications); computer science; construction engineering technology; criminal justice/police science; dramatic/theater arts; electrical, electronic and communications engineering technology; fire prevention and safety technology; fire science/firefighting; food technology and processing; horticultural science; humanities; information science/studies; kindergarten/preschool education; liberal arts and sciences/liberal studies; management information systems; mathematics; music; natural sciences; ornamental horticulture; physical sciences; real estate; registered nursing/registered nurse; respiratory care therapy; science technologies related; social sciences; teacher assistant/aide; trade and industrial teacher education; vehicle maintenance and repair technologies related; welding technology.
Academics *Calendar:* semesters. *Degree:* certificates, diplomas, and associate. *Special study options:* academic remediation for entering students, accelerated degree program, advanced placement credit, cooperative education, distance learning, double majors, English as a second language, honors programs, independent study, internships, off-campus study, part-time degree program, services for LD students, study abroad, summer session for credit.
Library Learning Resource Center with an OPAC, a Web page.
Student Life *Housing:* college housing not available. *Activities and Organizations:* drama/theater group, student-run newspaper, choral group, Black Student Union, Drama Club, rugby, Phi Theta Kappa. *Campus security:* 24-hour emergency response devices and patrols, late-night transport/escort service, part-time trained security personnel. *Student services:* health clinic, personal/psychological counseling.
Athletics Member NCAA, NJCAA. *Intercollegiate sports:* baseball M, basketball M/W, cross-country running M/W, football M, golf M, soccer M/W, softball W, tennis M/W, track and field M/W, volleyball W, wrestling M. *Intramural sports:* rock climbing M/W.
Costs (2013–14) *Tuition:* state resident $1104 full-time; nonresident $4296 full-time.
Financial Aid *Average need-based loan:* $6168. *Average need-based gift aid:* $3707.
Applying *Application deadline:* rolling (freshmen). *Notification:* continuous (freshmen).
Freshman Application Contact Ms. Greta Moon, Director of Admissions and Records (Interim), Victor Valley College, 18422 Bear Valley Road, Victorville, CA 92395. *Phone:* 760-245-4271. *Fax:* 760-843-7707. *E-mail:* moong@vvc.edu. *Website:* http://www.vvc.edu/.

West Hills Community College

Coalinga, California

Freshman Application Contact Sandra Dagnino, West Hills Community College, 300 Cherry Lane, Coalinga, CA 93210-1399. *Phone:* 559-934-3203. *Toll-free phone:* 800-266-1114. *Fax:* 559-934-2830. *E-mail:* sandradagnino@ westhillscollege.com.
Website: http://www.westhillscollege.com/.

West Los Angeles College

Culver City, California

Director of Admissions Mr. Len Isaksen, Director of Admissions, West Los Angeles College, 9000 Overland Avenue, Culver City, CA 90230-3519. *Phone:* 310-287-4255.
Website: http://www.lacolleges.net/.

West Valley College

Saratoga, California

Freshman Application Contact Ms. Barbara Ogilive, Supervisor, Admissions and Records, West Valley College, 14000 Fruitvale Avenue, Saratoga, CA 95070-5698. *Phone:* 408-741-4630. *E-mail:* barbara_ogilvie@westvalley.edu.
Website: http://www.westvalley.edu/.

Woodland Community College

Woodland, California

Admissions Office Contact Woodland Community College, 2300 East Gibson Road, Woodland, CA 95776.
Website: http://www.yccd.edu/woodland/.

WyoTech Fremont

Fromont, California

Freshman Application Contact Admissions Department, WyoTech Fremont, 200 Whitney Place, Fremont, CA 94539-7663. *Phone:* 510-580-3507. *Toll-free phone:* 888-577-7559. *Fax:* 510-490-8599.
Website: http://www.wyotech.edu/.

WyoTech Long Beach

Long Beach, California

Freshman Application Contact Admissions Office, WyoTech Long Beach, 2161 Technology Place, Long Beach, CA 90810. *Phone:* 562-624-9530. *Toll-free phone:* 888-577-7559. *Fax:* 562-437-8111.
Website: http://www.wyotech.edu/.

WyoTech Sacramento

West Sacramento, California

Freshman Application Contact Admissions Office, WyoTech Sacramento, 980 Riverside Parkway, West Sacramento, CA 95605-1507. *Phone:* 916-376-8888. *Toll-free phone:* 888-577-7559. *Fax:* 916-617-2059.
Website: http://www.wyotech.edu/.

Yuba College

Marysville, California

Director of Admissions Dr. David Farrell, Dean of Student Development, Yuba College, 2088 North Beale Road, Marysville, CA 95901-7699. *Phone:* 530-741-6705.
Website: http://www.yccd.edu/.

COLORADO

Aims Community College

Greeley, Colorado

Freshman Application Contact Ms. Susie Gallardo, Admissions Technician, Aims Community College, Box 69, 5401 West 20th Street, Greeley, CO 80632-0069. *Phone:* 970-330-8008 Ext. 6624. *E-mail:* wgreen@ chiron.aims.edu.
Website: http://www.aims.edu/.

Anthem College–Aurora

Aurora, Colorado

Director of Admissions Amy Marshall, Director of Admissions, Anthem College–Aurora, 350 Blackhawk Street, Aurora, CO 80011. *Phone:* 720-859-7900. *Toll-free phone:* 855-268-4363.
Website: http://www.anthem.edu/aurora-colorado/.

Arapahoe Community College

Littleton, Colorado

- **State-supported** 2-year, founded 1965, part of Colorado Community College and Occupational Education System
- **Suburban** 52-acre campus with easy access to Denver
- **Coed,** 9,963 undergraduate students, 27% full-time, 59% women, 41% men

Undergraduates 2,644 full-time, 7,319 part-time. Students come from 38 states and territories; 54 other countries; 8% are from out of state; 4% Black or African American, non-Hispanic/Latino; 10% Hispanic/Latino; 3% Asian, non-Hispanic/Latino; 0.4% Native Hawaiian or other Pacific Islander, non-Hispanic/Latino; 2% American Indian or Alaska Native, non-Hispanic/Latino; 0.4% Two or more races, non-Hispanic/Latino; 10% Race/ethnicity unknown; 0.9% international; 7% transferred in. *Retention:* 55% of full-time freshmen returned.

Freshmen *Admission:* 2,389 applied, 2,389 admitted, 1,004 enrolled. *Average high school GPA:* 2.6.

Faculty *Total:* 473, 20% full-time. *Student/faculty ratio:* 18:1.

Majors Accounting technology and bookkeeping; architectural engineering technology; automobile/automotive mechanics technology; banking and financial support services; business administration and management; civil engineering technology; clinical/medical laboratory technology; computer and information sciences; computer and information sciences and support services related; criminal justice/law enforcement administration; electrical, electronic and communications engineering technology; emergency medical technology (EMT paramedic); engineering technology; funeral service and mortuary science; graphic design; health and physical education/fitness; health information/medical records technology; interior design; legal assistant/paralegal; liberal arts and sciences/liberal studies; medical office management; physical therapy technology; registered nursing/registered nurse; system, networking, and LAN/WAN management.

Academics *Calendar:* semesters. *Degree:* certificates, diplomas, and associate. *Special study options:* academic remediation for entering students, accelerated degree program, adult/continuing education programs, advanced placement credit, cooperative education, distance learning, double majors, English as a second language, honors programs, independent study, internships, off-campus study, part-time degree program, services for LD students, student-designed majors, study abroad, summer session for credit. *ROTC:* Army (c), Navy (c), Air Force (c).

Library Weber Center for Learning Resources plus 1 other with 48,693 titles, 194 serial subscriptions, an OPAC, a Web page.

Student Life *Housing:* college housing not available. *Activities and Organizations:* drama/theater group, student-run newspaper, choral group, History Club, Science Club, Phi Theta Kappa, Outdoor Club, Frisbee Golf. *Campus security:* 24-hour emergency response devices and patrols, late-night transport/escort service. *Student services:* personal/psychological counseling.

Athletics *Intercollegiate sports:* baseball M, softball W. *Intramural sports:* baseball M(c)/W, basketball M, football M, ice hockey M, rock climbing M/W, skiing (cross-country) M/W, skiing (downhill) M/W, soccer M/W, softball M/W, swimming and diving M/W, table tennis M/W, tennis M/W, ultimate Frisbee M/W, volleyball M/W, weight lifting M.

Standardized Tests *Recommended:* ACT (for admission), SAT or ACT (for admission).

Costs (2013–14) *Tuition:* state resident $1449 full-time, $175 per hour part-time; nonresident $5647 full-time, $463 per hour part-time. *Required fees:* $182 full-time. *Payment plans:* installment, deferred payment. *Waivers:* senior citizens.

Financial Aid Of all full-time matriculated undergraduates who enrolled in 2011, 100 Federal Work-Study jobs (averaging $4200). 200 state and other part-time jobs (averaging $4200).

Applying *Options:* electronic application, early admission, deferred entrance. *Application deadlines:* rolling (freshmen), rolling (out-of-state freshmen), rolling (transfers). *Notification:* continuous (freshmen), continuous (out-of-state freshmen), continuous (transfers).

Freshman Application Contact Arapahoe Community College, 5900 South Santa Fe Drive, PO Box 9002, Littleton, CO 80160-9002. *Phone:* 303-797-5623.
Website: http://www.arapahoe.edu/.

Bel–Rea Institute of Animal Technology
Denver, Colorado

Director of Admissions Ms. Paulette Kaufman, Director, Bel–Rea Institute of Animal Technology, 1681 South Dayton Street, Denver, CO 80247. *Phone:* 303-751-8700. *Toll-free phone:* 800-950-8001. *E-mail:* admissions@bel-rea.com.
Website: http://www.bel-rea.com/.

Boulder College of Massage Therapy
Boulder, Colorado

Freshman Application Contact Admissions Office, Boulder College of Massage Therapy, 6255 Longbow Drive, Boulder, CO 80301. *Phone:* 303-530-2100. *Toll-free phone:* 800-442-5131. *Fax:* 303-530-2204. *E-mail:* admissions@bcmt.org.
Website: http://www.bcmt.org/.

CollegeAmerica–Colorado Springs
Colorado Springs, Colorado

Freshman Application Contact CollegeAmerica–Colorado Springs, 3645 Citadel Drive South, Colorado Springs, CO 80909. *Phone:* 719-637-0600. *Toll-free phone:* 800-622-2894.
Website: http://www.collegeamerica.edu/.

CollegeAmerica–Denver
Denver, Colorado

Freshman Application Contact Admissions Office, CollegeAmerica–Denver, 1385 South Colorado Boulevard, Denver, CO 80222. *Phone:* 303-300-8740. *Toll-free phone:* 800-622-2894.
Website: http://www.collegeamerica.edu/.

CollegeAmerica–Fort Collins
Fort Collins, Colorado

Director of Admissions Ms. Anna DiTorrice-Mull, Director of Admissions, CollegeAmerica–Fort Collins, 4601 South Mason Street, Fort Collins, CO 80525-3740. *Phone:* 970-223-6060 Ext. 8002. *Toll-free phone:* 800-622-2894.
Website: http://www.collegeamerica.edu/.

Colorado Northwestern Community College
Rangely, Colorado

- **State-supported** 2-year, founded 1962, part of Colorado Community College and Occupational Education System
- **Rural** 150-acre campus
- **Coed,** 1,291 undergraduate students, 39% full-time, 58% women, 42% men

Undergraduates 504 full-time, 787 part-time. Students come from 17 states and territories; 3 other countries; 38% are from out of state; 5% Black or African American, non-Hispanic/Latino; 9% Hispanic/Latino; 2% Asian, non-Hispanic/Latino; 0.1% Native Hawaiian or other Pacific Islander, non-Hispanic/Latino; 2% American Indian or Alaska Native, non-Hispanic/Latino; 4% Two or more races, non-Hispanic/Latino; 6% Race/ethnicity unknown; 0.5% international; 5% transferred in. *Retention:* 51% of full-time freshmen returned.
Freshmen *Admission:* 1,009 applied, 1,009 admitted, 189 enrolled.
Faculty *Total:* 92, 36% full-time. *Student/faculty ratio:* 14:1.
Majors Accounting; aircraft powerplant technology; airline pilot and flight crew; banking and financial support services; cosmetology; dental hygiene; early childhood education; emergency medical technology (EMT paramedic); equestrian studies; general studies; liberal arts and sciences/liberal studies; natural resources/conservation; registered nursing/registered nurse; small business administration.
Academics *Calendar:* semesters. *Degree:* certificates and associate. *Special study options:* academic remediation for entering students, adult/continuing education programs, advanced placement credit, distance learning, double majors, independent study, internships, part-time degree program, services for LD students, student-designed majors, summer session for credit.
Library Colorado Northwestern Community College Library plus 1 other with 20,063 titles, 230 serial subscriptions, 3,559 audiovisual materials, an OPAC.
Student Life *Housing:* on-campus residence required for freshman year. *Options:* coed. Campus housing is university owned. Freshman applicants given priority for college housing. *Activities and Organizations:* student-run newspaper, choral group. *Campus security:* student patrols, late-night transport/escort service. *Student services:* personal/psychological counseling.
Athletics Member NJCAA. *Intercollegiate sports:* baseball M(s), basketball M(s)/W(s), softball W(s), volleyball W(s). *Intramural sports:* basketball M/W, football M/W, golf M/W, racquetball M/W, skiing (cross-country) M/W, skiing (downhill) M/W, softball M/W, table tennis M/W, tennis M/W, volleyball M/W.
Standardized Tests *Recommended:* ACT (for admission).
Costs (2013–14) *Tuition:* state resident $2540 full-time, $106 per credit hour part-time; nonresident $5035 full-time, $210 per credit hour part-time. Full-time tuition and fees vary according to program. Part-time tuition and fees vary according to program. *Required fees:* $200 full-time. *Room and board:* $5988; room only: $2306. Room and board charges vary according to board plan and housing facility. *Payment plan:* installment.
Applying *Options:* electronic application, early admission, deferred entrance. *Required:* high school transcript. *Required for some:* essay or personal statement, 3 letters of recommendation, interview. *Application deadlines:* rolling (freshmen), rolling (out-of-state freshmen), rolling (transfers). *Notification:* continuous (freshmen), continuous (out-of-state freshmen), continuous (transfers).
Freshman Application Contact Colorado Northwestern Community College, 500 Kennedy Drive, Rangely, CO 81648-3598. *Phone:* 970-675-3285. *Toll-free phone:* 800-562-1105.
Website: http://www.cncc.edu/.

Colorado School of Healing Arts
Lakewood, Colorado

Freshman Application Contact Colorado School of Healing Arts, 7655 West Mississippi Avenue, Suite 100, Lakewood, CO 80220. *Phone:* 303-986-2320. *Toll-free phone:* 800-233-7114. *Fax:* 303-980-6594.
Website: http://www.csha.net/.

Colorado School of Trades
Lakewood, Colorado

- **Proprietary** 2-year, founded 1947
- **Suburban** campus
- **Coed,** 134 undergraduate students, 100% full-time, 1% women, 99% men
- 87% of applicants were admitted

Undergraduates 134 full-time. 88% are from out of state.
Freshmen *Admission:* 174 applied, 152 admitted, 30 enrolled.
Faculty *Total:* 10. *Student/faculty ratio:* 12:1.
Majors Gunsmithing.
Academics *Degree:* associate.
Costs (2012–13) *Tuition:* $18,900 full-time. No tuition increase for student's term of enrollment. *Payment plan:* installment.
Applying *Application fee:* $25. *Required:* essay or personal statement, high school transcript, interview.
Freshman Application Contact Colorado School of Trades, 1575 Hoyt Street, Lakewood, CO 80215-2996. *Phone:* 303-233-4697 Ext. 44. *Toll-free phone:* 800-234-4594.
Website: http://www.schooloftrades.com/.

Community College of Aurora
Aurora, Colorado

Freshman Application Contact Community College of Aurora, 16000 East Centre Tech Parkway, Aurora, CO 80011-9036. *Phone:* 303-360-4701.
Website: http://www.ccaurora.edu/.

Community College of Denver
Denver, Colorado

Freshman Application Contact Mr. Michael Rusk, Dean of Students, Community College of Denver, PO Box 173363, Campus Box 201, Denver, CO 80127-3363. *Phone:* 303-556-6325. *Fax:* 303-556-2431. *E-mail:* enrollment_services@ccd.edu.
Website: http://www.ccd.edu/.

Everest College
Aurora, Colorado

Freshman Application Contact Everest College, 14280 East Jewell Avenue, Suite 100, Aurora, CO 80014. *Phone:* 303-745-6244. *Toll-free phone:* 888-

741-4270.
Website: http://www.everest.edu/.

Everest College
Colorado Springs, Colorado

Director of Admissions Director of Admissions, Everest College, 1815 Jet Wing Drive, Colorado Springs, CO 80916. *Phone:* 719-630-6580. *Toll-free phone:* 888-741-4270. *Fax:* 719-638-6818.
Website: http://www.everest.edu/.

Everest College
Thornton, Colorado

Freshman Application Contact Admissions Office, Everest College, 9065 Grant Street, Thornton, CO 80229-4339. *Phone:* 303-457-2757. *Toll-free phone:* 888-741-4270. *Fax:* 303-457-4030.
Website: http://www.everest.edu/.

Front Range Community College
Westminster, Colorado

- **State-supported** 2-year, founded 1968, part of Community Colleges of Colorado System
- **Suburban** 90-acre campus with easy access to Denver
- **Endowment** $294,302
- **Coed**

Undergraduates 7,445 full-time, 12,647 part-time. Students come from 44 states and territories; 26 other countries; 2% are from out of state; 2% Black or African American, non-Hispanic/Latino; 13% Hispanic/Latino; 3% Asian, non-Hispanic/Latino; 0.4% Native Hawaiian or other Pacific Islander, non-Hispanic/Latino; 0.9% American Indian or Alaska Native, non-Hispanic/Latino; 1% Two or more races, non-Hispanic/Latino; 10% Race/ethnicity unknown; 1% international; 9% transferred in. *Retention:* 43% of full-time freshmen returned.
Faculty *Student/faculty ratio:* 23:1.
Academics *Calendar:* semesters. *Degree:* certificates and associate. *Special study options:* academic remediation for entering students, advanced placement credit, cooperative education, distance learning, double majors, English as a second language, freshman honors college, honors programs, independent study, internships, off-campus study, part-time degree program, services for LD students, student-designed majors, study abroad, summer session for credit. *ROTC:* Army (c), Air Force (c).
Student Life *Campus security:* 24-hour patrols, late-night transport/escort service.
Financial Aid Of all full-time matriculated undergraduates who enrolled in 2011, 165 Federal Work-Study jobs (averaging $1316). 277 state and other part-time jobs (averaging $1635).
Applying *Options:* electronic application, early admission, deferred entrance. **Freshman Application Contact** Ms. Yolanda Espinoza, Registrar, Front Range Community College, Westminster, CO 80031. *Phone:* 303-404-5000. *Fax:* 303-439-2614. *E-mail:* yolanda.espinoza@frontrange.edu.
Website: http://www.frontrange.edu/.

Heritage College
Denver, Colorado

Freshman Application Contact Admissions Office, Heritage College, 12 Lakeside Lane, Denver, CO 80212-7413.
Website: http://www.heritage-education.com/.

Institute of Business & Medical Careers
Fort Collins, Colorado

- **Private** 2-year, founded 1987
- **Suburban** campus with easy access to Denver
- **Coed**
- **100% of applicants were admitted**

Undergraduates 302 full-time. Students come from 1 other state; 2% are from out of state. *Retention:* 69% of full-time freshmen returned.
Faculty *Student/faculty ratio:* 14:1.
Academics *Calendar:* continuous. *Degree:* certificates, diplomas, and associate. *Special study options:* accelerated degree program, cooperative education, honors programs, internships.
Costs (2012–13) *Tuition:* $11,340 full-time. Full-time tuition and fees vary according to course load and program. Part-time tuition and fees vary accord-

ing to course load and program. No tuition increase for student's term of enrollment. *Payment plans:* tuition prepayment, installment.
Financial Aid Of all full-time matriculated undergraduates who enrolled in 2011, 826 applied for aid, 786 were judged to have need, 655 had their need fully met. 36 Federal Work-Study jobs (averaging $2220). *Average percent of need met:* 73. *Average financial aid package:* $7500. *Average need-based loan:* $3500. *Average need-based gift aid:* $3205.
Applying *Application fee:* $75. *Required:* high school transcript, interview.
Freshman Application Contact Mr. Kevin McNeil, Regional Director of Admissions, Institute of Business & Medical Careers, 3842 South Mason Street, Fort Collins, CO 80525. *Phone:* 970-223-2669 Ext. 1105. *Toll-free phone:* 800-495-2669. *E-mail:* kmcneil@ibmc.edu.
Website: http://www.ibmc.edu/.

IntelliTec College
Colorado Springs, Colorado

Director of Admissions Director of Admissions, IntelliTec College, 2315 East Pikes Peak Avenue, Colorado Springs, CO 80909-6030. *Phone:* 719-632-7626. *Toll-free phone:* 800-748-2282.
Website: http://www.intelliteccollege.edu/.

IntelliTec College
Grand Junction, Colorado

Freshman Application Contact Admissions, IntelliTec College, 772 Horizon Drive, Grand Junction, CO 81506. *Phone:* 970-245-8101. *Toll-free phone:* 800-748-2282. *Fax:* 970-243-8074.
Website: http://www.intelliteccollege.edu/.

IntelliTec Medical Institute
Colorado Springs, Colorado

Director of Admissions Michelle Squibb, Admissions Representative, IntelliTec Medical Institute, 2345 North Academy Boulevard, Colorado Springs, CO 80909. *Phone:* 719-596-7400. *Toll-free phone:* 800-748-2282.
Website: http://www.intelliteccollege.edu/.

ITT Technical Institute
Aurora, Colorado

- **Proprietary** primarily 2-year
- **Coed**

Academics *Degrees:* associate and bachelor's.
Freshman Application Contact Director of Recruitment, ITT Technical Institute, 12500 East Iliff Avenue, Suite 100, Aurora, CO 80014. *Phone:* 303-695-6317. *Toll-free phone:* 877-832-8460.
Website: http://www.itt-tech.edu/.

ITT Technical Institute
Westminster, Colorado

- **Proprietary** primarily 2-year, founded 1984, part of ITT Educational Services, Inc.
- **Suburban** campus
- **Coed**

Academics *Calendar:* quarters. *Degrees:* associate and bachelor's.
Freshman Application Contact Director of Recruitment, ITT Technical Institute, 8620 Wolff Court, Suite 100, Westminster, CO 80031. *Phone:* 303-288-4488. *Toll-free phone:* 800-395-4488.
Website: http://www.itt-tech.edu/.

Lamar Community College
Lamar, Colorado

Freshman Application Contact Director of Admissions, Lamar Community College, 2401 South Main Street, Lamar, CO 81052-3999. *Phone:* 719-336-1592. *Toll-free phone:* 800-968-6920. *E-mail:* admissions@lamarcc.edu.
Website: http://www.lamarcc.edu/.

Lincoln College of Technology
Denver, Colorado

Director of Admissions Jennifer Hash, Assistant Director of Admissions, Lincoln College of Technology, 11194 East 45th Avenue, Denver, CO 80239. *Phone:* 800-347-3232 Ext. 43032.
Website: http://www.lincolnedu.com/campus/denver-co/.

Morgan Community College

Fort Morgan, Colorado

Freshman Application Contact Ms. Kim Maxwell, Morgan Community College, 920 Barlow Road, Fort Morgan, CO 80701-4399. *Phone:* 970-542-3111. *Toll-free phone:* 800-622-0216. *Fax:* 970-867-6608. *E-mail:* kim.maxwell@morgancc.edu.
Website: http://www.morgancc.edu/.

Northeastern Junior College

Sterling, Colorado

- **State-supported** 2-year, founded 1941, part of Colorado Community College and Occupational Education System
- **Small-town** 65-acre campus
- **Endowment** $5.6 million
- **Coed,** 1,486 undergraduate students, 66% full-time, 58% women, 42% men

Undergraduates 979 full-time, 507 part-time. Students come from 26 states and territories; 4 other countries; 5% are from out of state; 6% Black or African American, non-Hispanic/Latino; 9% Hispanic/Latino; 0.6% Asian, non-Hispanic/Latino; 0.2% Native Hawaiian or other Pacific Islander, non-Hispanic/Latino; 1% American Indian or Alaska Native, non-Hispanic/Latino; 2% Two or more races, non-Hispanic/Latino; 13% Race/ethnicity unknown; 0.7% international; 56% transferred in; 37% live on campus. *Retention:* 48% of full-time freshmen returned.
Freshmen *Admission:* 1,290 applied, 1,290 admitted, 408 enrolled. *Average high school GPA:* 2.83.
Faculty *Total:* 98, 49% full-time, 4% with terminal degrees. *Student/faculty ratio:* 18:1.
Majors Accounting; agricultural business and management; agricultural economics; agricultural mechanization; agricultural teacher education; agriculture; agronomy and crop science; anatomy; animal sciences; applied mathematics; art; art teacher education; automobile/automotive mechanics technology; biological and physical sciences; biology/biological sciences; business administration and management; business teacher education; child development; clinical laboratory science/medical technology; computer engineering technology; computer science; corrections; cosmetology; criminal justice/police science; dramatic/theater arts; drawing; economics; education; elementary education; emergency medical technology (EMT paramedic); English; equestrian studies; family and consumer sciences/human sciences; farm and ranch management; fine/studio arts; health professions related; history; humanities; journalism; kindergarten/preschool education; legal administrative assistant/secretary; liberal arts and sciences/liberal studies; licensed practical/vocational nurse training; marketing/marketing management; mathematics; medical administrative assistant and medical secretary; music; music teacher education; natural sciences; physical education teaching and coaching; physical sciences; pre-engineering; psychology; registered nursing/registered nurse; social sciences; social work; trade and industrial teacher education; zoology/animal biology.
Academics *Calendar:* semesters. *Degree:* certificates and associate. *Special study options:* academic remediation for entering students, accelerated degree program, adult/continuing education programs, advanced placement credit, cooperative education, distance learning, double majors, English as a second language, honors programs, independent study, internships, part-time degree program, services for LD students, summer session for credit.
Library Monahan Library with 96,871 titles, 116 serial subscriptions, an OPAC, a Web page.
Student Life *Housing:* on-campus residence required for freshman year. *Options:* coed, women-only. Campus housing is university owned. Freshman campus housing is guaranteed. *Activities and Organizations:* drama/theater group, choral group, Associated Student Government, Post Secondary Agriculture (PAS), Crossroads, Students in Free Enterprise (SIFE), NJC Ambassadors. *Campus security:* 24-hour emergency response devices, late-night transport/escort service, controlled dormitory access. *Student services:* health clinic, personal/psychological counseling.
Athletics Member NCAA, NJCAA. All NCAA Division I. *Intercollegiate sports:* baseball M(s), basketball M(s)/W(s), equestrian sports M(s)/W(s), golf M(s)/W(s), soccer M(s), softball W(s), volleyball W(s). *Intramural sports:* badminton M/W, baseball M/W, basketball M/W, bowling M/W, cheerleading M/W, football M, golf M/W, racquetball M/W, soccer M/W, softball M/W, tennis M/W, ultimate Frisbee M/W, volleyball M/W, weight lifting M/W.
Costs (2012–13) *Tuition:* state resident $3383 full-time, $113 per credit hour part-time; nonresident $11,099 full-time, $370 per credit hour part-time. Full-time tuition and fees vary according to course load. Part-time tuition and fees vary according to course load. *Required fees:* $596 full-time, $22 per credit hour part-time, $12 per term part-time. *Room and board:* $6190; room only:

$2732. Room and board charges vary according to board plan and housing facility. *Payment plan:* installment. *Waivers:* senior citizens and employees or children of employees.
Applying *Options:* electronic application, early admission, deferred entrance. *Required:* high school transcript. *Application deadlines:* rolling (freshmen), rolling (out-of-state freshmen), rolling (transfers). *Notification:* continuous until 8/1 (freshmen), continuous (out-of-state freshmen), continuous until 8/1 (transfers).
Freshman Application Contact Mr. Andy Long, Director of Admissions, Northeastern Junior College, 100 College Avenue, Sterling, CO 80751-2399. *Phone:* 970-521-7000. *Toll-free phone:* 800-626-4637. *E-mail:* andy.long@njc.edu.
Website: http://www.njc.edu/.

Otero Junior College

La Junta, Colorado

- **State-supported** 2-year, founded 1941, part of Colorado Community College System
- **Rural** 40-acre campus
- **Coed**

Undergraduates 870 full-time, 790 part-time. 17% live on campus.
Academics *Calendar:* semesters. *Degree:* certificates and associate. *Special study options:* academic remediation for entering students, adult/continuing education programs, advanced placement credit, distance learning, external degree program, internships, part-time degree program, summer session for credit.
Student Life *Campus security:* 24-hour patrols, late-night transport/escort service.
Athletics Member NJCAA.
Costs (2012–13) *Tuition:* state resident $2706 full-time; nonresident $5362 full-time. *Required fees:* $263 full-time. *Room and board:* $5536. Room and board charges vary according to board plan and housing facility. *Payment plans:* installment, deferred payment.
Financial Aid Of all full-time matriculated undergraduates who enrolled in 2011, 30 Federal Work-Study jobs (averaging $2000). 100 state and other part-time jobs (averaging $2000).
Applying *Options:* electronic application, early admission. *Recommended:* high school transcript.
Freshman Application Contact Mr. Jeff Paolucci, Vice President for Student Services, Otero Junior College, 1802 Colorado Avenue, La Junta, CO 81050-3415. *Phone:* 719-384-6833. *Fax:* 719-384-6933. *E-mail:* jan.schiro@ojc.edu.
Website: http://www.ojc.edu/.

Pikes Peak Community College

Colorado Springs, Colorado

Freshman Application Contact Pikes Peak Community College, 5675 South Academy Boulevard, Colorado Springs, CO 80906-5498. *Phone:* 719-540-7041. *Toll-free phone:* 866-411-7722.
Website: http://www.ppcc.edu/.

Pima Medical Institute

Colorado Springs, Colorado

Freshman Application Contact Pima Medical Institute, 3770 Citadel Drive North, Colorado Springs, CO 80909. *Phone:* 719-482-7462.
Website: http://www.pmi.edu/.

Pima Medical Institute

Denver, Colorado

Freshman Application Contact Admissions Office, Pima Medical Institute, 7475 Dakin Street, Denver, CO 80221. *Phone:* 303-426-1800. *Toll-free phone:* 800-477-PIMA (in-state); 888-477-PIMA (out-of-state).
Website: http://www.pmi.edu/.

Prince Institute–Rocky Mountains Campus

Westminster, Colorado

Director of Admissions Director of Admissions, Prince Institute–Rocky Mountains Campus, 9051 Harlan Street, Unit 20, Westminster, CO 80031. *Phone:* 303-427-5292. *Toll-free phone:* 866-712-2425.
Website: http://www.princeinstitute.edu/.

Pueblo Community College

Pueblo, Colorado

Freshman Application Contact Ms. Barbara Benedict, Assistant Director of Admissions and Records, Pueblo Community College, 900 West Orman Avenue, Pueblo, CO 81004. *Phone:* 719-549-3039. *Toll-free phone:* 888-642-6017. *Fax:* 719-549-3012.
Website: http://www.pueblocc.edu/.

Red Rocks Community College

Lakewood, Colorado

- **State-supported** 2-year, founded 1969, part of Colorado Community College and Occupational Education System
- **Urban** 141-acre campus with easy access to Denver
- **Coed,** 9,028 undergraduate students, 32% full-time, 50% women, 50% men

Undergraduates 2,854 full-time, 6,174 part-time. Students come from 38 states and territories; 27 other countries; 6% are from out of state; 2% Black or African American, non-Hispanic/Latino; 13% Hispanic/Latino; 2% Asian, non-Hispanic/Latino; 0.3% Native Hawaiian or other Pacific Islander, non-Hispanic/Latino; 1% American Indian or Alaska Native, non-Hispanic/Latino; 3% Two or more races, non-Hispanic/Latino; 7% Race/ethnicity unknown; 1% international; 22% transferred in.

Freshmen *Admission:* 3,258 applied, 3,258 admitted, 1,352 enrolled.

Faculty *Total:* 511, 18% full-time. *Student/faculty ratio:* 23:1.

Majors Accounting technology and bookkeeping; animation, interactive technology, video graphics and special effects; autobody/collision and repair technology; automobile/automotive mechanics technology; building construction technology; business administration and management; business administration, management and operations related; cinematography and film/video production; computer programming; computer systems networking and telecommunications; construction trades; cosmetology; criminal justice/police science; culinary arts; data modeling/warehousing and database administration; diagnostic medical sonography and ultrasound technology; digital communication and media/multimedia; drafting and design technology; early childhood education; educational/instructional technology; electrician; electromechanical and instrumentation and maintenance technologies related; emergency medical technology (EMT paramedic); energy management and systems technology; fire science/firefighting; game and interactive media design; general studies; holistic health; homeland security, law enforcement, firefighting and protective services related; industrial technology; interior design; liberal arts and sciences and humanities related; liberal arts and sciences/liberal studies; machine shop technology; management information systems; manufacturing engineering technology; medical office management; motorcycle maintenance and repair technology; parks, recreation and leisure; parts and warehousing operations and maintenance technology; photography; radiologic technology/science; real estate; science technologies related; theater design and technology; vehicle maintenance and repair technologies; water quality and wastewater treatment management and recycling technology; web/multimedia management and webmaster; web page, digital/multimedia and information resources design; welding technology; woodworking.

Academics *Calendar:* semesters. *Degree:* certificates and associate. *Special study options:* academic remediation for entering students, adult/continuing education programs, cooperative education, distance learning, English as a second language, honors programs, off-campus study, part-time degree program, services for LD students, study abroad, summer session for credit. *ROTC:* Army (c), Air Force (c).

Library Marvin Buckels Library with 38,204 titles, 84 serial subscriptions, 4,098 audiovisual materials, an OPAC, a Web page.

Student Life *Housing:* college housing not available. *Activities and Organizations:* drama/theater group. *Campus security:* 24-hour emergency response devices and patrols. *Student services:* health clinic, personal/psychological counseling.

Costs (2013–14) *Tuition:* state resident $3383 full-time, $115 per credit hour part-time; nonresident $13,877 full-time, $465 per credit hour part-time. Full-time tuition and fees vary according to program and reciprocity agreements. Part-time tuition and fees vary according to program and reciprocity agreements. *Required fees:* $285 full-time, $11 per credit hour part-time, $35 per term part-time. *Payment plans:* installment, deferred payment. *Waivers:* employees or children of employees.

Financial Aid Of all full-time matriculated undergraduates who enrolled in 2011, 21 Federal Work-Study jobs (averaging $5000). 95 state and other part-time jobs (averaging $5000).

Applying *Options:* electronic application, early admission. *Application deadlines:* rolling (freshmen), rolling (out-of-state freshmen), rolling (transfers).

Notification: continuous (freshmen), continuous (out-of-state freshmen), continuous (transfers).

Freshman Application Contact Admissions Office, Red Rocks Community College, 13300 West 6th Avenue, Lakewood, CO 80228-1255. *Phone:* 303-914-6360. *Fax:* 303-914-6919. *E-mail:* admissions@rrcc.edu.
Website: http://www.rrcc.edu/.

Redstone College–Denver

Broomfield, Colorado

Freshman Application Contact Redstone College–Denver, 10851 West 120th Avenue, Broomfield, CO 80021. *Phone:* 303-466-7383. *Toll-free phone:* 877-801-1025.
Website: http://www.redstone.edu/.

Trinidad State Junior College

Trinidad, Colorado

Freshman Application Contact Dr. Sandra Veltri, Vice President of Student/Academic Affairs, Trinidad State Junior College, 600 Prospect Street, Trinidad, CO 81082. *Phone:* 719-846-5559. *Toll-free phone:* 800-621-8752. *Fax:* 719-846-5620. *E-mail:* sandy.veltri@trinidadstate.edu.
Website: http://www.trinidadstate.edu/.

CONNECTICUT

Asnuntuck Community College

Enfield, Connecticut

Freshman Application Contact Timothy St. James, Director of Admissions, Asnuntuck Community College, 170 Elm Street, Enfield, CT 06082-3800. *Phone:* 860-253-3087. *Fax:* 860-253-3014. *E-mail:* tstjames@acc.commnet.edu.
Website: http://www.acc.commnet.edu/.

Capital Community College

Hartford, Connecticut

Freshman Application Contact Ms. Jackie Phillips, Director of the Welcome and Advising Center, Capital Community College, 950 Main Street, Hartford, CT 06103. *Phone:* 860-906-5078. *Toll-free phone:* 800-894-6126. *E-mail:* jphillips@ccc.commnet.edu.
Website: http://www.ccc.commnet.edu/.

Gateway Community College

New Haven, Connecticut

- **State-supported** 2-year, founded 1992, part of Connecticut Community–Technical College System
- **Urban** 5-acre campus with easy access to New York City
- **Coed**

Undergraduates 2,490 full-time, 4,771 part-time.

Faculty *Student/faculty ratio:* 20:1.

Academics *Calendar:* semesters. *Degree:* certificates and associate. *Special study options:* academic remediation for entering students, adult/continuing education programs, advanced placement credit, distance learning, English as a second language, external degree program, independent study, internships, off-campus study, part-time degree program, services for LD students, summer session for credit.

Student Life *Campus security:* late-night transport/escort service.

Athletics Member NJCAA.

Costs (2012–13) *Tuition:* state resident $3168 full-time, $132 per credit part-time; nonresident $9504 full-time, $396 per credit part-time. *Required fees:* $402 full-time.

Applying *Options:* early admission, deferred entrance. *Application fee:* $20. *Required:* high school transcript. *Required for some:* essay or personal statement, interview.

Freshman Application Contact Ms. Kim Shea, Director of Admissions, Gateway Community College, New Haven, CT 06511. *Phone:* 203-789-7043. *Toll-free phone:* 800-390-7723. *Fax:* 203-285-2018. *E-mail:* gateway_ctc@commnet.edu.
Website: http://www.gwcc.commnet.edu/.

Goodwin College
East Hartford, Connecticut

- **Independent** primarily 2-year, founded 1999
- **Suburban** 660-acre campus with easy access to Hartford
- **Endowment** $3.4 million
- **Coed,** 3,317 undergraduate students, 15% full-time, 83% women, 17% men

Undergraduates 495 full-time, 2,822 part-time. 2% are from out of state; 22% Black or African American, non-Hispanic/Latino; 19% Hispanic/Latino; 2% Asian, non-Hispanic/Latino; 0.4% American Indian or Alaska Native, non-Hispanic/Latino; 3% Two or more races, non-Hispanic/Latino; 0.2% Race/ethnicity unknown; 0.1% international; 15% transferred in. *Retention:* 57% of full-time freshmen returned.
Freshmen *Admission:* 604 applied, 604 admitted, 370 enrolled.
Faculty *Total:* 275, 23% full-time. *Student/faculty ratio:* 11:1.
Majors Accounting technology and bookkeeping; business administration and management; business/commerce; child-care and support services management; child development; criminal justice/law enforcement administration; entrepreneurship; environmental studies; health services/allied health/health sciences; homeland security; homeland security, law enforcement, firefighting and protective services related; human resources management; human services; liberal arts and sciences/liberal studies; medical administrative assistant and medical secretary; medical/clinical assistant; medical insurance coding; medical insurance/medical billing; nonprofit management; occupational therapist assistant; office management; organizational behavior; registered nursing/registered nurse; respiratory care therapy.
Academics *Calendar:* semesters. *Degrees:* certificates, associate, and bachelor's. *Special study options:* academic remediation for entering students, adult/continuing education programs, advanced placement credit, distance learning, double majors, English as a second language, internships, off-campus study, part-time degree program, services for LD students, summer session for credit.
Library Hoffman Family Library with an OPAC.
Student Life *Housing:* college housing not available. *Activities and Organizations:* student-run newspaper, choral group. *Campus security:* 24-hour emergency response devices, evening security patrolman. *Student services:* personal/psychological counseling.
Athletics *Intramural sports:* basketball M, football M/W, soccer M/W, softball M/W.
Costs (2013–14) *Tuition:* $18,900 full-time, $590 per credit hour part-time. Full-time tuition and fees vary according to course load and program. Part-time tuition and fees vary according to course load and program. *Required fees:* $500 full-time. *Payment plan:* installment. *Waivers:* employees or children of employees.
Financial Aid Of all full-time matriculated undergraduates who enrolled in 2011, 76 Federal Work-Study jobs (averaging $2878).
Applying *Options:* electronic application, early admission, early decision, early action, deferred entrance. *Application fee:* $50. *Required:* essay or personal statement, high school transcript, minimum 2.0 GPA, medical exam. *Recommended:* 2 letters of recommendation, interview. *Application deadlines:* rolling (freshmen), rolling (transfers), 6/1 (early action). *Early decision deadline:* 3/1. *Notification:* continuous (freshmen), continuous (transfers), 3/15 (early decision), 6/15 (early action).
Freshman Application Contact Mr. Nicholas Lentino, Director of Admissions, Goodwin College, One Riverside Drive, East Hartford, CT 06118. *Phone:* 860-727-6765. *Toll-free phone:* 800-889-3282. *Fax:* 860-291-9550. *E-mail:* nlantino@goodwin.edu.
Website: http://www.goodwin.edu/.

Housatonic Community College
Bridgeport, Connecticut

- **State-supported** 2-year, founded 1965, part of Connecticut Community Colleges and State Universities Board of Regents
- **Urban** 4-acre campus with easy access to New York City
- **Coed,** 6,097 undergraduate students

Undergraduates 30% Black or African American, non-Hispanic/Latino; 2% Asian, non-Hispanic/Latino; 0.1% Native Hawaiian or other Pacific Islander, non-Hispanic/Latino; 1% American Indian or Alaska Native, non-Hispanic/Latino; 2% Two or more races, non-Hispanic/Latino; 3% Race/ethnicity unknown.
Faculty *Total:* 377, 18% full-time. *Student/faculty ratio:* 16:1.
Majors Accounting; administrative assistant and secretarial science; art; avionics maintenance technology; business administration and management; child development; clinical/medical laboratory technology; commercial and advertising art; computer typography and composition equipment operation; criminal justice/law enforcement administration; data processing and data processing technology; environmental studies; humanities; human services;

journalism; liberal arts and sciences/liberal studies; mathematics; mental health counseling; physical therapy; pre-engineering; public administration; registered nursing/registered nurse; social sciences; substance abuse/addiction counseling.
Academics *Calendar:* semesters. *Degree:* certificates and associate. *Special study options:* academic remediation for entering students, adult/continuing education programs, advanced placement credit, cooperative education, distance learning, double majors, English as a second language, honors programs, independent study, internships, part-time degree program, services for LD students, summer session for credit. *ROTC:* Army (c). *Unusual degree programs:* nursing with Bridgeport Hospital.
Library Housatonic Community College Library with 30,000 titles, 300 serial subscriptions, an OPAC, a Web page.
Student Life *Housing:* college housing not available. *Activities and Organizations:* drama/theater group, student-run newspaper, Student Senate, Association of Latin American Students, Community Action Network, Drama Club. *Campus security:* 24-hour emergency response devices, late-night transport/escort service. *Student services:* health clinic, personal/psychological counseling, women's center.
Costs (2012–13) *Tuition:* state resident $3598 full-time; nonresident $10,754 full-time. Full-time tuition and fees vary according to program. *Payment plan:* installment. *Waivers:* senior citizens and employees or children of employees.
Financial Aid Of all full-time matriculated undergraduates who enrolled in 2011, 70 Federal Work-Study jobs (averaging $2850).
Applying *Options:* electronic application, deferred entrance. *Application fee:* $20. *Required:* high school transcript. *Required for some:* interview. *Application deadlines:* rolling (freshmen), rolling (transfers). *Notification:* continuous (freshmen), continuous (transfers).
Freshman Application Contact Ms. Delores Y. Curtis, Director of Admissions, Housatonic Community College, 900 Lafayette Boulevard, Bridgeport, CT 06604-4704. *Phone:* 203-332-5102.
Website: http://www.hctc.commnet.edu/.

Lincoln College of New England
Suffield, Connecticut

Freshman Application Contact Director of Admissions, Lincoln College of New England, 1760 Mapleton Avenue, Suffield, CT 06078. *Phone:* 860-628-4751. *Toll-free phone:* 800-825-0087. *E-mail:* admissions@lincolncollegene.edu.
Website: http://www.lincolncollegene.edu/.

Manchester Community College
Manchester, Connecticut

- **State-supported** 2-year, founded 1963, part of Connecticut Community–Technical College System
- **Small-town** campus
- **Coed,** 7,692 undergraduate students, 35% full-time, 53% women, 47% men

Undergraduates 2,721 full-time, 4,971 part-time. 15% Black or African American, non-Hispanic/Latino; 15% Hispanic/Latino; 4% Asian, non-Hispanic/Latino; 0.1% Native Hawaiian or other Pacific Islander, non-Hispanic/Latino; 0.1% American Indian or Alaska Native, non-Hispanic/Latino; 2% Two or more races, non-Hispanic/Latino; 6% Race/ethnicity unknown; 0.5% international; 16% transferred in. *Retention:* 64% of full-time freshmen returned.
Freshmen *Admission:* 2,874 applied, 2,862 admitted, 1,685 enrolled.
Faculty *Total:* 509, 20% full-time. *Student/faculty ratio:* 18:1.
Majors Accounting; administrative assistant and secretarial science; business administration and management; clinical/medical laboratory technology; commercial and advertising art; criminal justice/law enforcement administration; dramatic/theater arts; engineering science; fine/studio arts; general studies; hotel/motel administration; human services; industrial engineering; industrial technology; information science/studies; journalism; kindergarten/preschool education; legal administrative assistant/secretary; legal assistant/paralegal; liberal arts and sciences/liberal studies; management information systems; marketing/marketing management; medical administrative assistant and medical secretary; music; occupational therapist assistant; physical therapy technology; respiratory care therapy; social work; speech communication and rhetoric; surgical technology; teacher assistant/aide.
Academics *Calendar:* semesters. *Degree:* certificates and associate. *Special study options:* adult/continuing education programs, part-time degree program.
Student Life *Housing:* college housing not available.
Athletics Member NJCAA. *Intercollegiate sports:* baseball M, basketball M/W, soccer M/W, softball W.
Costs (2013–14) *Tuition:* state resident $3598 full-time; nonresident $10,754 full-time. *Required fees:* $406 full-time. *Payment plan:* installment. *Waivers:* senior citizens and employees or children of employees.

Financial Aid Of all full-time matriculated undergraduates who enrolled in 2011, 1,934 applied for aid, 1,562 were judged to have need. *Financial aid deadline:* 8/13.
Applying *Options:* electronic application. *Application fee:* $20. *Required:* high school transcript. *Application deadlines:* rolling (freshmen), rolling (transfers). *Notification:* continuous (freshmen), continuous (transfers).
Freshman Application Contact Director of Admissions, Manchester Community College, PO Box 1046, Manchester, CT 06045-1046. *Phone:* 860-512-3210. *Fax:* 860-512-3221.
Website: http://www.mcc.commnet.edu/.

Middlesex Community College
Middletown, Connecticut

Freshman Application Contact Mensimah Shabazz, Director of Admissions, Middlesex Community College, Middletown, CT 06457-4889. *Phone:* 860-343-5742. *Fax:* 860-344-3055. *E-mail:* mshabazz@mxcc.commnet.edu.
Website: http://www.mxcc.commnet.edu/.

Naugatuck Valley Community College
Waterbury, Connecticut

Freshman Application Contact Ms. Lucretia Sveda, Director of Enrollment Services, Naugatuck Valley Community College, Waterbury, CT 06708. *Phone:* 203-575-8016. *Fax:* 203-596-8766. *E-mail:* lsveda@nvcc.commnet.edu.
Website: http://www.nvcc.commnet.edu/.

Northwestern Connecticut Community College
Winsted, Connecticut

- **State-supported** 2-year, founded 1965, part of Connecticut State Colleges and Universities
- **Small-town** 5-acre campus with easy access to Hartford
- **Coed**

Undergraduates 511 full-time, 1,190 part-time. Students come from 3 states and territories; 0.5% are from out of state; 2% Black or African American, non-Hispanic/Latino; 7% Hispanic/Latino; 0.9% Asian, non-Hispanic/Latino; 0.1% Native Hawaiian or other Pacific Islander, non-Hispanic/Latino; 2% Two or more races, non-Hispanic/Latino; 4% Race/ethnicity unknown; 0.2% international; 10% transferred in. *Retention:* 60% of full-time freshmen returned.
Academics *Calendar:* semesters. *Degree:* certificates and associate. *Special study options:* academic remediation for entering students, adult/continuing education programs, advanced placement credit, cooperative education, distance learning, double majors, English as a second language, independent study, internships, part-time degree program, services for LD students, summer session for credit.
Student Life *Campus security:* evening security patrols.
Applying *Options:* deferred entrance. *Application fee:* $20.
Freshman Application Contact Admissions Office, Northwestern Connecticut Community College, Park Place East, Winsted, CT 06098-1798. *Phone:* 860-738-6330. *Fax:* 860-738-6437. *E-mail:* admissions@nwcc.commnet.edu.
Website: http://www.nwcc.commnet.edu/.

Norwalk Community College
Norwalk, Connecticut

- **State-supported** 2-year, founded 1961, part of Connecticut Community–Technical College System
- **Suburban** 30-acre campus with easy access to New York City
- **Coed,** 6,810 undergraduate students, 33% full-time, 59% women, 41% men

Undergraduates 2,267 full-time, 4,543 part-time. Students come from 6 states and territories; 44 other countries; 4% are from out of state; 17% Black or African American, non-Hispanic/Latino; 30% Hispanic/Latino; 4% Asian, non-Hispanic/Latino; 0.2% Native Hawaiian or other Pacific Islander, non-Hispanic/Latino; 0.2% American Indian or Alaska Native, non-Hispanic/Latino; 1% Two or more races, non-Hispanic/Latino; 7% Race/ethnicity unknown; 2% international; 6% transferred in.
Freshmen *Admission:* 2,162 applied, 2,162 admitted, 1,063 enrolled.
Faculty *Total:* 428, 24% full-time. *Student/faculty ratio:* 16:1.
Majors Accounting; administrative assistant and secretarial science; architectural engineering technology; art; business administration and management; commercial and advertising art; computer and information systems security; computer systems networking and telecommunications; construction engineering technology; criminal justice/law enforcement administration; early child-

hood education; engineering science; finance; fine/studio arts; fire science/firefighting; general studies; graphic design; hotel/motel administration; human services; information science/studies; information technology; interior design; kinesiology and exercise science; legal assistant/paralegal; liberal arts and sciences/liberal studies; marketing/marketing management; medical office management; parks, recreation and leisure; psychology; registered nursing/registered nurse; respiratory care therapy; restaurant/food services management; speech communication and rhetoric; web page, digital/multimedia and information resources design; women's studies.
Academics *Calendar:* semesters. *Degree:* certificates and associate. *Special study options:* academic remediation for entering students, adult/continuing education programs, advanced placement credit, cooperative education, distance learning, English as a second language, honors programs, independent study, internships, part-time degree program, services for LD students, summer session for credit.
Library Everett I. L. Baker Library with 64,878 titles, 120 serial subscriptions, 10,704 audiovisual materials, an OPAC, a Web page.
Student Life *Housing:* college housing not available. *Activities and Organizations:* drama/theater group, student-run newspaper, choral group, Student World Assembly, Archaeology Club, Literature Club, Art Club, Phi Theta Kappa. *Campus security:* late-night transport/escort service, all buildings are secured each evening; there are foot patrols and vehicle patrols by security from 8am to 11pm. *Student services:* personal/psychological counseling, women's center.
Costs (2013–14) *Tuition:* state resident $3360 full-time; nonresident $10,080 full-time. *Required fees:* $426 full-time, $70 per contact hour part-time, $25 per term part-time. *Payment plan:* installment. *Waivers:* senior citizens and employees or children of employees.
Financial Aid Of all full-time matriculated undergraduates who enrolled in 2012, 53 Federal Work-Study jobs (averaging $2800). 20 state and other part-time jobs (averaging $2800).
Applying *Options:* electronic application, deferred entrance. *Application fee:* $20. *Required:* high school transcript. *Application deadlines:* rolling (freshmen), rolling (transfers). *Notification:* continuous (freshmen), continuous (transfers).
Freshman Application Contact Mr. Curtis Antrum, Admissions Counselor, Norwalk Community College, 188 Richards Avenue, Norwalk, CT 06854-1655. *Phone:* 203-857-7060. *Fax:* 203-857-3335. *E-mail:* admissions@ncc.commnet.edu.
Website: http://www.ncc.commnet.edu/.

Quinebaug Valley Community College
Danielson, Connecticut

Freshman Application Contact Dr. Toni Moumouris, Director of Admissions, Quinebaug Valley Community College, 742 Upper Maple Street, Danielson, CT 06239. *Phone:* 860-774-1130 Ext. 318. *Fax:* 860-774-7768. *E-mail:* qu_isd@commnet.edu.
Website: http://www.qvcc.commnet.edu/.

St. Vincent's College
Bridgeport, Connecticut

Freshman Application Contact Mr. Joseph Marrone, Director of Admissions and Recruitment Marketing, St. Vincent's College, 2800 Main Street, Bridgeport, CT 06606-4292. *Phone:* 203-576-5515. *Toll-free phone:* 800-873-1013. *Fax:* 203-576-5893. *E-mail:* jmarrone@stvincentscollege.edu.
Website: http://www.stvincentscollege.edu/.

Three Rivers Community College
Norwich, Connecticut

- **State-supported** 2-year, founded 1963, part of Connecticut Community–Technical College System
- **Suburban** 40-acre campus with easy access to Hartford
- **Coed**

Undergraduates 1,650 full-time, 3,504 part-time. 1% are from out of state; 8% Black or African American, non-Hispanic/Latino; 13% Hispanic/Latino; 3% Asian, non-Hispanic/Latino; 0.2% Native Hawaiian or other Pacific Islander, non-Hispanic/Latino; 0.8% American Indian or Alaska Native, non-Hispanic/Latino; 3% Two or more races, non-Hispanic/Latino; 5% Race/ethnicity unknown; 0.1% international; 7% transferred in.
Faculty *Student/faculty ratio:* 18:1.
Academics *Calendar:* semesters. *Degrees:* certificates and associate (engineering technology programs are offered on the Thames Valley Campus; liberal arts, transfer and career programs are offered on the Mohegan Campus). *Special study options:* adult/continuing education programs, part-time degree program.

Student Life *Campus security:* 24-hour emergency response devices, late-night transport/escort service, 14-hour patrols by trained security personnel.

Costs (2012–13) *Tuition:* state resident $3192 full-time, $133 per credit hour part-time; nonresident $10,348 full-time, $399 per credit hour part-time. Full-time tuition and fees vary according to course load and reciprocity agreements. Part-time tuition and fees vary according to course load and reciprocity agreements. *Required fees:* $386 full-time, $78 per course part-time.

Financial Aid Of all full-time matriculated undergraduates who enrolled in 2010, 1,135 applied for aid, 967 were judged to have need, 266 had their need fully met. *Average percent of need met:* 48. *Average financial aid package:* $2631. *Average need-based loan:* $3308. *Average need-based gift aid:* $2409.

Applying *Options:* electronic application, early admission, deferred entrance. *Required for some:* minimum 3.0 GPA. *Recommended:* high school transcript.

Freshman Application Contact Ms. Aida Garcia, Admissions and Recruitment Counselor, Three Rivers Community College, 574 New London Turnpike, Norwich, CT 06360. *Phone:* 860-383-5268. *Fax:* 860-885-1684. *E-mail:* admissions@trcc.commnet.edu. *Website:* http://www.trcc.commnet.edu/.

Tunxis Community College

Farmington, Connecticut

- **State-supported** 2-year, founded 1969, part of Connecticut State Colleges and Universities (ConnSCU), Board of Regents for Higher Education
- **Suburban** 12-acre campus with easy access to Hartford
- **Coed,** 4,764 undergraduate students, 37% full-time, 57% women, 43% men

Undergraduates 1,783 full-time, 2,981 part-time. Students come from 6 states and territories; 2% are from out of state; 7% Black or African American, non-Hispanic/Latino; 14% Hispanic/Latino; 3% Asian, non-Hispanic/Latino; 0.1% Native Hawaiian or other Pacific Islander, non-Hispanic/Latino; 0.2% American Indian or Alaska Native, non-Hispanic/Latino; 5% Race/ethnicity unknown; 0.5% international. *Retention:* 61% of full-time freshmen returned.

Freshmen *Admission:* 820 enrolled.

Faculty *Total:* 239, 28% full-time, 12% with terminal degrees. *Student/faculty ratio:* 19:1.

Majors Accounting; administrative assistant and secretarial science; art; business administration and management; commercial and advertising art; corrections; criminal justice/law enforcement administration; data processing and data processing technology; dental hygiene; design and applied arts related; engineering; engineering technology; fashion merchandising; forensic science and technology; human services; information science/studies; kindergarten/preschool education; legal administrative assistant/secretary; liberal arts and sciences/liberal studies; marketing/marketing management; medical administrative assistant and medical secretary; physical therapy; substance abuse/addiction counseling.

Academics *Calendar:* semesters. *Degree:* certificates and associate. *Special study options:* academic remediation for entering students, adult/continuing education programs, cooperative education, distance learning, double majors, English as a second language, honors programs, independent study, internships, part-time degree program, services for LD students, summer session for credit.

Library Tunxis Community College Library with 33,866 titles, 285 serial subscriptions, an OPAC.

Student Life *Housing:* college housing not available. *Activities and Organizations:* drama/theater group, student-run newspaper, Phi Theta Kappa, Student American Dental Hygiene Association (SADHA), Human Services Club, student newspaper, Criminal Justice Club. *Campus security:* 24-hour emergency response devices.

Costs (2012–13) *Tuition:* state resident $3192 full-time, $133 per credit hour part-time; nonresident $9576 full-time, $399 per credit hour part-time. *Required fees:* $446 full-time, $114 per term part-time, $332 per term part-time. *Payment plan:* installment. *Waivers:* senior citizens and employees or children of employees.

Applying *Options:* deferred entrance. *Application fee:* $20. *Required:* high school transcript. *Application deadlines:* rolling (freshmen), rolling (transfers).

Freshman Application Contact Ms. Allison McCarthy, Interim Director of Admissions, Tunxis Community College, 271 Scott Swamp Road, Farmington, CT 06032. *Phone:* 860-255-3550. *Fax:* 860-255-3559. *E-mail:* pmccluskey@tunxis.edu. *Website:* http://www.tunxis.commnet.edu/.

DELAWARE

Delaware College of Art and Design

Wilmington, Delaware

Freshman Application Contact Ms. Allison Gullo, Delaware College of Art and Design, 600 North Market Street, Wilmington, DE 19801. *Phone:* 302-622-8867 Ext. 111. *Fax:* 302-622-8870. *E-mail:* agullo@dcad.edu. *Website:* http://www.dcad.edu/.

Delaware Technical & Community College, Jack F. Owens Campus

Georgetown, Delaware

- **State-supported** 2-year, founded 1967, part of Delaware Technical and Community College System
- **Small-town** campus
- **Coed,** 4,611 undergraduate students, 43% full-time, 63% women, 37% men

Undergraduates 1,979 full-time, 2,632 part-time. 17% Black or African American, non-Hispanic/Latino; 7% Hispanic/Latino; 2% Asian, non-Hispanic/Latino; 0.1% Native Hawaiian or other Pacific Islander, non-Hispanic/Latino; 0.3% American Indian or Alaska Native, non-Hispanic/Latino; 2% Two or more races, non-Hispanic/Latino; 0.6% Race/ethnicity unknown; 2% international; 4% transferred in. *Retention:* 59% of full-time freshmen returned.

Freshmen *Admission:* 1,627 applied, 1,627 admitted, 883 enrolled.

Majors Accounting; aeronautical/aerospace engineering technology; agricultural business and management; agricultural production; applied horticulture/horticulture operations; architectural engineering technology; automobile/automotive mechanics technology; biology/biological sciences; biology/biotechnology laboratory technician; business automation/technology/data entry; business/commerce; civil engineering technology; clinical/medical laboratory assistant; computer and information sciences; computer technology/computer systems technology; construction management; criminal justice/law enforcement administration; criminal justice/police science; customer service support/call center/teleservice operation; diagnostic medical sonography and ultrasound technology; drafting and design technology; early childhood education; e-commerce; education (multiple levels); electrical, electronic and communications engineering technology; elementary education; emergency medical technology (EMT paramedic); energy management and systems technology; entrepreneurship; heating, air conditioning, ventilation and refrigeration maintenance technology; human services; kindergarten/preschool education; legal administrative assistant/secretary; licensed practical/vocational nurse training; management information systems; marketing/marketing management; mathematics teacher education; mechanical drafting and CAD/CADD; medical/clinical assistant; middle school education; nuclear engineering technology; occupational therapist assistant; office management; physical therapy technology; poultry science; radiologic technology/science; registered nursing/registered nurse; respiratory therapy technician; surveying technology; turf and turfgrass management; veterinary/animal health technology; water quality and wastewater treatment management and recycling technology.

Academics *Calendar:* semesters. *Degree:* certificates, diplomas, and associate. *Special study options:* part-time degree program.

Library Stephen J. Betze Library.

Student Life *Housing:* college housing not available. *Campus security:* 24-hour emergency response devices, late-night transport/escort service.

Athletics Member NJCAA. *Intercollegiate sports:* baseball M(s), golf M, softball W(s). *Intramural sports:* football M/W.

Financial Aid Of all full-time matriculated undergraduates who enrolled in 2011, 250 Federal Work-Study jobs (averaging $2000).

Applying *Options:* electronic application, early admission, deferred entrance. *Application fee:* $10. *Required for some:* high school transcript. *Application deadline:* rolling (freshmen). *Notification:* continuous (freshmen).

Freshman Application Contact Ms. Claire McDonald, Admissions Counselor, Delaware Technical & Community College, Jack F. Owens Campus, PO Box 610, Georgetown, DE 19947. *Phone:* 302-856-5400. *Fax:* 302-856-9461. *Website:* http://www.dtcc.edu/.

Delaware Technical & Community College, Stanton/Wilmington Campus
Newark, Delaware

- **State-supported** 2-year, founded 1968, part of Delaware Technical and Community College System
- **Urban** campus
- **Coed,** 7,216 undergraduate students, 36% full-time, 60% women, 40% men

Undergraduates 2,600 full-time, 4,616 part-time. 25% Black or African American, non-Hispanic/Latino; 9% Hispanic/Latino; 4% Asian, non-Hispanic/Latino; 0.2% Native Hawaiian or other Pacific Islander, non-Hispanic/Latino; 0.2% American Indian or Alaska Native, non-Hispanic/Latino; 11% Two or more races, non-Hispanic/Latino; 1% Race/ethnicity unknown; 2% international; 4% transferred in. *Retention:* 62% of full-time freshmen returned.

Freshmen *Admission:* 2,806 applied, 2,806 admitted, 1,201 enrolled.

Majors Accounting; agricultural business and management; architectural engineering technology; automobile/automotive mechanics technology; biology/biological sciences; biology/biotechnology laboratory technician; business administration and management; business automation/technology/data entry; business/commerce; CAD/CADD drafting/design technology; cardiovascular technology; chemical technology; civil drafting and CAD/CADD; computer and information sciences; computer engineering technology; computer systems networking and telecommunications; construction management; criminal justice/law enforcement administration; criminal justice/police science; culinary arts; customer service management; customer service support/call center/teleservice operation; dental hygiene; diagnostic medical sonography and ultrasound technology; drafting and design technology; early childhood education; education (multiple levels); electrical, electronic and communications engineering technology; electrocardiograph technology; elementary education; emergency care attendant (EMT ambulance); emergency medical technology (EMT paramedic); energy management and systems technology; engineering/industrial management; fire prevention and safety technology; fire science/firefighting; fire services administration; heating, ventilation, air conditioning and refrigeration engineering technology; histologic technology/histotechnologist; hotel/motel administration; human services; kindergarten/preschool education; kinesiology and exercise science; management information systems; management science; manufacturing engineering technology; marketing/marketing management; mathematics teacher education; mechanical engineering/mechanical technology; medical/clinical assistant; middle school education; nuclear engineering technology; nuclear medical technology; occupational therapist assistant; office management; operations research; physical therapy technology; radiologic technology/science; registered nursing/registered nurse; respiratory therapy technician; restaurant, culinary, and catering management; science technologies related; substance abuse/addiction counseling; surveying technology.

Academics *Calendar:* semesters. *Degree:* certificates, diplomas, and associate. *Special study options:* part-time degree program. *ROTC:* Air Force (c).

Library Stanton Campus Library and John Eugene Derrickson Memorial Library.

Student Life *Housing:* college housing not available. *Campus security:* 24-hour emergency response devices, late-night transport/escort service.

Athletics Member NJCAA. *Intercollegiate sports:* basketball M(s)/W(s), soccer M(s), softball W(s). *Intramural sports:* basketball M/W, football M/W, softball W, volleyball M/W.

Applying *Options:* electronic application, early admission, deferred entrance. *Application fee:* $10. *Required for some:* high school transcript. *Application deadlines:* rolling (freshmen), rolling (transfers). *Notification:* continuous (freshmen), continuous (transfers).

Freshman Application Contact Ms. Rebecca Bailey, Admissions Coordinator, Wilmington, Delaware Technical & Community College, Stanton/Wilmington Campus, 333 Shipley Street, Wilmington, DE 19713. *Phone:* 302-571-5343. *Fax:* 302-577-2548.
Website: http://www.dtcc.edu/.

Delaware Technical & Community College, Terry Campus
Dover, Delaware

- **State-supported** 2-year, founded 1972, part of Delaware Technical and Community College System
- **Small-town** campus
- **Coed,** 3,107 undergraduate students, 46% full-time, 64% women, 36% men

Undergraduates 1,436 full-time, 1,671 part-time. 28% Black or African American, non-Hispanic/Latino; 5% Hispanic/Latino; 3% Asian, non-Hispanic/Latino; 0.2% Native Hawaiian or other Pacific Islander, non-His-

panic/Latino; 0.3% American Indian or Alaska Native, non-Hispanic/Latino; 3% Two or more races, non-Hispanic/Latino; 2% Race/ethnicity unknown; 1% international; 5% transferred in. *Retention:* 56% of full-time freshmen returned.

Freshmen *Admission:* 1,235 applied, 1,235 admitted, 619 enrolled.

Majors Accounting; agricultural business and management; architectural engineering technology; bilingual and multilingual education; biomedical technology; business administration and management; business automation/technology/data entry; business/commerce; civil engineering technology; commercial and advertising art; computer and information sciences; computer engineering technology; computer systems networking and telecommunications; computer technology/computer systems technology; construction management; criminal justice/law enforcement administration; criminal justice/police science; culinary arts; digital communication and media/multimedia; drafting and design technology; early childhood education; e-commerce; education (multiple levels); electrical, electronic and communications engineering technology; electromechanical technology; elementary education; emergency medical technology (EMT paramedic); energy management and systems technology; entrepreneurship; hotel/motel administration; human resources management; human services; interior design; kindergarten/preschool education; legal administrative assistant/secretary; management information systems; marketing/marketing management; mathematics teacher education; medical/clinical assistant; middle school education; office management; photography; registered nursing/registered nurse; substance abuse/addiction counseling.

Academics *Calendar:* semesters. *Degree:* certificates, diplomas, and associate. *Special study options:* part-time degree program. *ROTC:* Air Force (c).

Student Life *Housing:* college housing not available. *Campus security:* 24-hour emergency response devices, late-night transport/escort service.

Athletics Member NJCAA. *Intercollegiate sports:* lacrosse M(s), soccer M(s)/W(s), softball W(s).

Financial Aid Of all full-time matriculated undergraduates who enrolled in 2011, 50 Federal Work-Study jobs (averaging $1500).

Applying *Options:* electronic application, early admission, deferred entrance. *Application fee:* $10. *Required for some:* high school transcript. *Application deadline:* rolling (freshmen). *Notification:* continuous (freshmen).

Freshman Application Contact Mrs. Maria Harris, Admissions Officer, Delaware Technical & Community College, Terry Campus, 100 Campus Drive, Dover, DE 19904. *Phone:* 302-857-1020. *Fax:* 302-857-1296. *E-mail:* terry-info@dtcc.edu.
Website: http://www.dtcc.edu/.

FLORIDA

Anthem College–Orlando
Orlando, Florida

Freshman Application Contact Admissions Office, Anthem College–Orlando, 3710 Maguire Boulevard, Orlando, FL 32803. *Toll-free phone:* 855-824-0055.
Website: http://anthem.edu/orlando-florida/.

ATI Career Training Center
Fort Lauderdale, Florida

Director of Admissions Director of Admissions, ATI Career Training Center, 2890 NW 62nd Street, Fort Lauderdale, FL 33309. *Phone:* 954-973-4760. *Toll-free phone:* 888-209-8264.
Website: http://www.aticareertraining.edu/.

ATI College of Health
Miami, Florida

Director of Admissions Admissions, ATI College of Health, 1395 NW 167th Street, Suite 200, Miami, FL 33169-5742. *Phone:* 305-628-1000. *Toll-free phone:* 888-209-8264. *Fax:* 305-628-1461. *E-mail:* admissions@atienterprises.edu.
Website: http://www.aticareertraining.edu/.

Brevard Community College
Cocoa, Florida

Freshman Application Contact Ms. Stephanie Burnette, Registrar, Brevard Community College, Cocoa, FL 32922-6597. *Phone:* 321-433-7271. *Fax:* 321-433-7172. *E-mail:* cocoaadmissions@brevardcc.edu.
Website: http://www.brevardcc.edu/.

Broward College

Fort Lauderdale, Florida

Freshman Application Contact Willie J. Alexander, Associate Vice President for Student Affairs/College Registrar, Broward College, 225 East Las Olas Boulevard, Fort Lauderdale, FL 33301. *Phone:* 954-201-7471. *Fax:* 954-201-7466. *E-mail:* walexand@broward.edu.
Website: http://www.broward.edu/.

Brown Mackie College–Miami

Miami, Florida

Freshman Application Contact Brown Mackie College–Miami, 3700 Lakeside Drive, Miramar, Florida 33027-3264. *Phone:* 305-341-6600. *Toll-free phone:* 866-505-0335.
Website: http://www.brownmackie.edu/miami/.

See display below and page 374 for the College Close-Up.

Cambridge Institute of Allied Health and Technology

Delray Beach, Florida

Admissions Office Contact Cambridge Institute of Allied Health and Technology, 5150 Linton Boulevard, Suite 340, Delray Beach, FL 33484.
Website: http://www.cambridgehealth.edu/.

Central Florida Institute

Palm Harbor, Florida

Director of Admissions Carol Bruno, Director of Admissions, Central Florida Institute, 30522 US Highway 19 North, Suite 300, Palm Harbor, FL 34684. *Phone:* 727-786-4707. *Toll-free phone:* 888-831-8303.
Website: http://www.cfinstitute.com/.

Centura Institute

Orlando, Florida

Director of Admissions John DiBenedetto, Director of Admissions, Centura Institute, 6359 Edgewater Drive, Orlando, FL 32810. *Phone:* 407-275-9696.

Toll-free phone: 888-312-1320. *Fax:* 407-275-4499. *E-mail:* admcircorl@centura.edu.
Website: http://www.centurainstitute.edu/.

Chipola College

Marianna, Florida

- **State-supported** primarily 2-year, founded 1947
- **Rural** 105-acre campus
- **Coed,** 2,292 undergraduate students, 42% full-time, 63% women, 37% men

Undergraduates 964 full-time, 1,328 part-time. Students come from 7 states and territories; 6 other countries; 8% are from out of state; 17% Black or African American, non-Hispanic/Latino; 3% Hispanic/Latino; 1% Asian, non-Hispanic/Latino; 0.6% American Indian or Alaska Native, non-Hispanic/Latino; 2% Two or more races, non-Hispanic/Latino; 0.1% Race/ethnicity unknown; 6% transferred in.
Freshmen *Admission:* 247 enrolled. *Average high school GPA:* 2.5. *Test scores:* SAT critical reading scores over 500: 16%; SAT math scores over 500: 36%; ACT scores over 18: 81%; SAT critical reading scores over 600: 4%; SAT math scores over 600: 12%; ACT scores over 24: 25%; ACT scores over 30: 3%.
Faculty *Total:* 127, 31% full-time, 13% with terminal degrees. *Student/faculty ratio:* 24:1.
Majors Accounting; agriculture; agronomy and crop science; art; biological and physical sciences; business administration and management; clinical laboratory science/medical technology; computer and information sciences related; computer science; education; finance; liberal arts and sciences/liberal studies; mass communication/media; mathematics teacher education; pre-engineering; registered nursing/registered nurse; science teacher education; secondary education; social work.
Academics *Calendar:* semesters. *Degrees:* certificates, associate, and bachelor's. *Special study options:* academic remediation for entering students, adult/continuing education programs, advanced placement credit, distance learning, honors programs, independent study, part-time degree program, services for LD students, summer session for credit.
Library Chipola Library with 37,740 titles, 226 serial subscriptions.
Student Life *Housing:* college housing not available. *Activities and Organizations:* drama/theater group, student-run newspaper, choral group, Drama/Theater Group. *Campus security:* night security personnel.
Athletics Member NJCAA. *Intercollegiate sports:* baseball M(s), basketball M(s)/W(s), softball W(s).

Costs (2012–13) *Tuition:* state resident $3060 full-time, $102 per semester hour part-time; nonresident $8891 full-time, $296 per semester hour part-time. Full-time tuition and fees vary according to degree level. Part-time tuition and fees vary according to degree level. *Required fees:* $40 full-time.

Applying *Options:* early admission. *Required:* high school transcript. *Application deadlines:* rolling (freshmen), rolling (transfers). *Notification:* continuous (freshmen), continuous (transfers).

Freshman Application Contact Mrs. Kathy L. Rehberg, Registrar, Chipola College, 3094 Indian Circle, Marianna, FL 32446-3065. *Phone:* 850-718-2233. *Fax:* 850-718-2287. *E-mail:* rehbergk@chipola.edu. *Website:* http://www.chipola.edu/.

City College

Almonte Springs, Florida

Director of Admissions Ms. Kimberly Bowden, Director of Admissions, City College, 177 Montgomery Road, Almonte Springs, FL 32714. *Phone:* 352-335-4000. *Fax:* 352-335-4303. *E-mail:* kbowden@citycollege.edu. *Website:* http://www.citycollege.edu/.

City College

Fort Lauderdale, Florida

Freshman Application Contact City College, 2000 West Commercial Boulevard, Suite 200, Fort Lauderdale, FL 33309. *Phone:* 954-492-5353. *Toll-free phone:* 866-314-5681. *Website:* http://www.citycollege.edu/.

City College

Gainesville, Florida

Freshman Application Contact Admissions Office, City College, 7001 Northwest 4th Boulevard, Gainesville, FL 32607. *Phone:* 352-335-4000. *Website:* http://www.citycollege.edu/.

City College

Miami, Florida

Freshman Application Contact Admissions Office, City College, 9300 South Dadeland Boulevard, Suite PH, Miami, FL 33156. *Phone:* 305-666-9242. *Fax:* 305-666-9243. *Website:* http://www.citycollege.edu/.

College of Business and Technology

Miami, Florida

- **Proprietary** primarily 2-year, founded 1988
- **Coed**

Undergraduates 1,098 full-time. Students come from 4 states and territories; 11% Black or African American, non-Hispanic/Latino; 85% Hispanic/Latino; 0.1% Asian, non-Hispanic/Latino; 0.1% Native Hawaiian or other Pacific Islander, non-Hispanic/Latino; 0.7% American Indian or Alaska Native, non-Hispanic/Latino; 0.2% Two or more races, non-Hispanic/Latino; 0.8% Race/ethnicity unknown; 3% transferred in.

Faculty *Student/faculty ratio:* 15:1.

Academics *Calendar:* semesters. *Degrees:* certificates, diplomas, associate, and bachelor's. *Special study options:* academic remediation for entering students, accelerated degree program, adult/continuing education programs, advanced placement credit, cooperative education, distance learning, double majors, English as a second language, honors programs, independent study, internships, off-campus study, part-time degree program, services for LD students, summer session for credit.

Costs (2012–13) *Tuition:* $10,920 full-time. *Required fees:* $1400 full-time.

Applying *Options:* electronic application. *Application fee:* $25. *Required:* essay or personal statement, high school transcript, minimum 2.6 GPA, 2 letters of recommendation, interview.

Freshman Application Contact Ms. Ivis Delgado, Admissions Representative, College of Business and Technology, 8230 West Flagler Street, Miami, FL 33144. *Phone:* 305-273-4499 Ext. 2204. *Toll-free phone:* 866-626-8842. *Fax:* 305-485-4411. *E-mail:* admissions@cbt.edu. *Website:* http://www.cbt.edu/.

College of Central Florida

Ocala, Florida

- **State and locally supported** primarily 2-year, founded 1957, part of Florida Community College System
- **Small-town** 139-acre campus
- **Endowment** $40.1 million
- **Coed**

Undergraduates 3,666 full-time, 5,100 part-time.

Faculty *Student/faculty ratio:* 18:1.

Academics *Calendar:* semesters. *Degrees:* certificates, diplomas, associate, and bachelor's. *Special study options:* academic remediation for entering students, adult/continuing education programs, advanced placement credit, cooperative education, distance learning, English as a second language, freshman honors college, honors programs, independent study, internships, part-time degree program, services for LD students, summer session for credit.

Student Life *Campus security:* 24-hour emergency response devices and patrols, student patrols, late-night transport/escort service.

Athletics Member NJCAA.

Standardized Tests *Recommended:* SAT (for admission), ACT (for admission), SAT or ACT (for admission), SAT and SAT Subject Tests or ACT (for admission), SAT Subject Tests (for admission).

Costs (2012–13) *Tuition:* state resident $2388 full-time, $80 per credit hour part-time; nonresident $9552 full-time, $422 per credit hour part-time. Full-time tuition and fees vary according to course level, degree level, and program. Part-time tuition and fees vary according to course level, degree level, and program. *Required fees:* $765 full-time, $26 per credit hour part-time.

Financial Aid Of all full-time matriculated undergraduates who enrolled in 2011, 85 Federal Work-Study jobs (averaging $1505).

Applying *Options:* early admission. *Application fee:* $30. *Required:* high school transcript.

Freshman Application Contact Ms. Devona Sewell, Registrar, Admission and Records, College of Central Florida, 3001 SW College Road, Ocala, FL 34474. *Phone:* 352-237-2111 Ext. 1398. *Fax:* 352-873-5882. *E-mail:* sewelld@cf.edu. *Website:* http://www.cf.edu/.

Daytona State College

Daytona Beach, Florida

- **State-supported** primarily 2-year, founded 1958, part of Florida Community College System
- **Suburban** 100-acre campus with easy access to Orlando
- **Endowment** $9.4 million
- **Coed,** 15,708 undergraduate students, 41% full-time, 60% women, 40% men

Undergraduates 6,429 full-time, 9,279 part-time. Students come from 51 states and territories; 130 other countries; 4% are from out of state; 13% Black or African American, non-Hispanic/Latino; 11% Hispanic/Latino; 2% Asian, non-Hispanic/Latino; 0.1% Native Hawaiian or other Pacific Islander, non-Hispanic/Latino; 0.5% American Indian or Alaska Native, non-Hispanic/Latino; 1% Two or more races, non-Hispanic/Latino; 0.9% Race/ethnicity unknown; 7% transferred in.

Freshmen *Admission:* 4,684 applied, 4,629 admitted, 1,769 enrolled.

Faculty *Total:* 931, 35% full-time, 16% with terminal degrees. *Student/faculty ratio:* 26:1.

Majors Accounting; administrative assistant and secretarial science; architectural engineering technology; automobile/automotive mechanics technology; biology teacher education; business administration and management; child development; communications technology; computer and information sciences related; computer engineering; computer engineering related; computer graphics; computer/information technology services administration related; computer programming; computer programming (specific applications); computer science; computer systems networking and telecommunications; computer technology/computer systems technology; criminal justice/law enforcement administration; criminal justice/police science; culinary arts; dental hygiene; drafting and design technology; electrical, electronic and communications engineering technology; elementary education; emergency medical technology (EMT paramedic); engineering; fire science/firefighting; health information/medical records administration; hospitality administration; hotel/motel administration; human services; industrial radiologic technology; industrial technology; information technology; interior design; kindergarten/preschool education; legal assistant/paralegal; machine shop technology; mathematics teacher education; medical administrative assistant and medical secretary; occupational therapist assistant; photographic and film/video technology; physical therapy; plastics and polymer engineering technology; radio and television; registered nursing/registered nurse; respiratory care therapy; robotics technology; secondary education; special education–early childhood; tourism and travel services management.

Academics *Calendar:* semesters. *Degrees:* certificates, diplomas, associate, bachelor's, and postbachelor's certificates. *Special study options:* academic remediation for entering students, adult/continuing education programs, advanced placement credit, cooperative education, distance learning, double majors, English as a second language, external degree program, freshman honors college, honors programs, independent study, internships, off-campus study, part-time degree program, services for LD students, study abroad, summer session for credit. *ROTC:* Army (c), Air Force (c).

Library Mary Karl Memorial Learning Resources Center plus 1 other with 91,000 titles, 735 serial subscriptions, 5,000 audiovisual materials, an OPAC, a Web page.

Student Life *Housing:* college housing not available. *Activities and Organizations:* drama/theater group, student-run newspaper, choral group, Florida Student Nursing Association, Phi Theta Kappa, Mu Rho Chapter, Student Government Association, Campus Crusade for Christ, Student Paralegal Association, national fraternities, national sororities. *Campus security:* 24-hour emergency response devices and patrols, late-night transport/escort service. *Student services:* personal/psychological counseling, women's center.

Athletics Member NJCAA. *Intercollegiate sports:* baseball M(s), basketball M(s)/W(s), golf W(s), softball W(s), swimming and diving M(s)/W(s), volleyball W. *Intramural sports:* basketball M/W, cheerleading M/W, football M/W, golf M/W, racquetball M/W, soccer M/W, table tennis M/W, tennis M/W, volleyball M/W.

Financial Aid Of all full-time matriculated undergraduates who enrolled in 2011, 212 Federal Work-Study jobs (averaging $1479). 1 state and other part-time job (averaging $2373). In 2011, 525 non-need-based awards were made. *Average need-based loan:* $2704. *Average need-based gift aid:* $1580. *Average non-need-based aid:* $1222.

Applying *Options:* electronic application, early admission, deferred entrance. *Required:* high school transcript. *Application deadlines:* rolling (freshmen), rolling (transfers). *Notification:* continuous (freshmen), continuous (transfers). **Freshman Application Contact** Dr. Karen Sanders, Director of Admissions and Recruitment, Daytona State College, 1200 International Speedway Boulevard, Daytona Beach, FL 32114. *Phone:* 386-506-3050. *E-mail:* sanderk@daytonastate.edu. *Website:* http://www.daytonastate.edu/.

Edison State College
Fort Myers, Florida

Freshman Application Contact Lauren Willison, Admissions Specialist, Edison State College, 8099 College Parkway, Fort Myers, FL 33919. *Phone:* 239-489-9257. *Toll-free phone:* 800-749-2ECC. *E-mail:* Lauren.Willison@edison.edu. *Website:* http://www.edison.edu/.

Everest Institute
Fort Lauderdale, Florida

Freshman Application Contact Admissions Office, Everest Institute, 1040 Bayview Drive, Fort Lauderdale, FL 33304. *Phone:* 954-630-0066. *Toll-free phone:* 888-741-4270. *Website:* http://www.everest.edu/.

Everest Institute
Hialeah, Florida

Director of Admissions Director of Admissions, Everest Institute, 530 West 49th Street, Hialeah, FL 33012. *Phone:* 305-558-9500. *Toll-free phone:* 888-741-4270. *Fax:* 305-558-4419. *Website:* http://www.everest.edu/.

Everest Institute
Miami, Florida

Director of Admissions Director of Admissions, Everest Institute, 111 Northwest 183rd Street, Second Floor, Miami, FL 33169. *Phone:* 305-949-9500. *Toll-free phone:* 888-741-4270. *Website:* http://www.everest.edu/.

Everest Institute
Miami, Florida

Freshman Application Contact Director of Admissions, Everest Institute, 9020 Southwest 137th Avenue, Miami, FL 33186. *Phone:* 305-386-9900. *Toll-free phone:* 888-741-4270. *Fax:* 305-388-1740. *Website:* http://www.everest.edu/.

Everest University
Orange Park, Florida

Freshman Application Contact Admissions Office, Everest University, 805 Wells Road, Orange Park, FL 32073. *Phone:* 904-264-9122. *Website:* http://www.everest.edu/.

Florida Career College
Miami, Florida

Director of Admissions Mr. David Knobel, President, Florida Career College, 1321 Southwest 107 Avenue, Suite 201B, Miami, FL 33174. *Phone:* 305-553-6065. *Toll-free phone:* 888-852-7272. *Website:* http://www.careercollege.edu/.

Florida College of Natural Health
Bradenton, Florida

Freshman Application Contact Admissions Office, Florida College of Natural Health, 616 67th Street Circle East, Bradenton, FL 34208. *Phone:* 941-744-1244. *Toll-free phone:* 800-966-7117. *Fax:* 941-744-1242. *Website:* http://www.fcnh.com/.

Florida College of Natural Health
Maitland, Florida

Freshman Application Contact Admissions Office, Florida College of Natural Health, 2600 Lake Lucien Drive, Suite 140, Maitland, FL 32751. *Phone:* 407-261-0319. *Toll-free phone:* 800-393-7337. *Website:* http://www.fcnh.com/.

Florida College of Natural Health
Miami, Florida

Director of Admissions Admissions Coordinator, Florida College of Natural Health, 7925 Northwest 12th Street, Suite 201, Miami, FL 33126. *Phone:* 305-597-9599. *Toll-free phone:* 800-599-9599. *Fax:* 305-597-9110. *Website:* http://www.fcnh.com/.

Florida College of Natural Health
Pompano Beach, Florida

Freshman Application Contact Admissions Office, Florida College of Natural Health, 2001 West Sample Road, Suite 100, Pompano Beach, FL 33064. *Phone:* 954-975-6400. *Toll-free phone:* 800-541-9299. *Website:* http://www.fcnh.com/.

Florida Gateway College
Lake City, Florida

- **State-supported** primarily 2-year, founded 1962, part of Florida Community College System
- **Small-town** 132-acre campus with easy access to Jacksonville
- **Coed,** 3,073 undergraduate students, 34% full-time, 65% women, 35% men

Undergraduates 1,040 full-time, 2,033 part-time. Students come from 4 states and territories; 10% Black or African American, non-Hispanic/Latino; 4% Hispanic/Latino; 0.9% Asian, non-Hispanic/Latino; 0.4% American Indian or Alaska Native, non-Hispanic/Latino; 0.4% Two or more races, non-Hispanic/Latino; 0.5% Race/ethnicity unknown; 0.1% international; 4% transferred in.

Freshmen *Admission:* 279 enrolled.

Faculty *Total:* 179, 38% full-time, 8% with terminal degrees. *Student/faculty ratio:* 16:1.

Majors Child development; computer and information sciences; computer programming; corrections; criminal justice/law enforcement administration; emergency medical technology (EMT paramedic); graphic design; health information/medical records administration; health services administration; information technology; landscaping and groundskeeping; liberal arts and sciences/liberal studies; natural resources/conservation; office management; physical therapy technology; registered nursing/registered nurse; turf and turfgrass management; veterinary/animal health technology.

Academics *Calendar:* semesters. *Degrees:* certificates, diplomas, associate, and bachelor's. *Special study options:* academic remediation for entering students, adult/continuing education programs, advanced placement credit, cooperative education, distance learning, English as a second language, independent study, internships, off-campus study, part-time degree program, services for LD students, summer session for credit.

Library Wilson S. Rivers Library and Media Center with 43,811 titles, 180 serial subscriptions, an OPAC, a Web page.

Student Life *Housing:* college housing not available. *Activities and Organizations:* drama/theater group, choral group. *Campus security:* 24-hour emergency response devices and patrols. *Student services:* personal/psychological counseling.

Costs (2012–13) *Tuition:* state resident $2480 full-time, $103 per credit hour part-time; nonresident $11,747 full-time, $392 per credit hour part-time. Full-time tuition and fees vary according to course level, course load, degree level, program, and reciprocity agreements. Part-time tuition and fees vary according to course level, course load, degree level, program, and reciprocity agreements. *Required fees:* $731 full-time, $24 per credit hour part-time. *Payment plan:* deferred payment. *Waivers:* employees or children of employees.

Applying *Required for some:* high school transcript. *Application deadlines:* rolling (freshmen), rolling (transfers). *Notification:* continuous (freshmen), continuous (transfers).

Freshman Application Contact Admissions, Florida Gateway College, 149 SE College Place, Lake City, FL 32025-8703. *Phone:* 386-755-4236. *E-mail:* admissions@fgc.edu.
Website: http://www.fgc.edu/.

Florida Keys Community College

Key West, Florida

Director of Admissions Ms. Cheryl A. Malsheimer, Director of Admissions and Records, Florida Keys Community College, 5901 College Road, Key West, FL 33040-4397. *Phone:* 305-296-9081 Ext. 201.
Website: http://www.fkcc.edu/.

The Florida School of Traditional Midwifery

Gainseville, Florida

Freshman Application Contact Admissions Office, The Florida School of Traditional Midwifery, 810 East University Avenue, 2nd Floor, Gainesville, FL 32601. *Phone:* 352-338-0766. *Fax:* 352-338-2013. *E-mail:* info@midwiferyschool.org.
Website: http://www.midwiferyschool.org/.

Florida State College at Jacksonville

Jacksonville, Florida

- **State-supported** primarily 2-year, founded 1963, part of Florida College System
- **Urban** 825-acre campus
- **Endowment** $28.8 million
- **Coed**

Undergraduates 10,778 full-time, 20,085 part-time. 28% Black or African American, non-Hispanic/Latino; 4% Hispanic/Latino; 3% Asian, non-Hispanic/Latino; 0.6% Native Hawaiian or other Pacific Islander, non-Hispanic/Latino; 0.5% American Indian or Alaska Native, non-Hispanic/Latino; 1% Two or more races, non-Hispanic/Latino; 15% Race/ethnicity unknown; 0.8% international; 7% transferred in. *Retention:* 36% of full-time freshmen returned.

Faculty *Student/faculty ratio:* 29:1.

Academics *Calendar:* semesters. *Degrees:* certificates, diplomas, associate, and bachelor's. *Special study options:* academic remediation for entering students, accelerated degree program, adult/continuing education programs, advanced placement credit, cooperative education, distance learning, double majors, English as a second language, honors programs, independent study, internships, off-campus study, part-time degree program, services for LD students, study abroad, summer session for credit. *ROTC:* Navy (c).

Student Life *Campus security:* 24-hour emergency response devices and patrols, late-night transport/escort service.

Athletics Member NJCAA.

Applying *Options:* electronic application, early admission, deferred entrance. *Application fee:* $25. *Required:* high school transcript.

Freshman Application Contact Dr. Peter Biegel, AVP, Enrollment Management, Florida State College at Jacksonville, 501 West State Street, Jacksonville, FL 32202. *Phone:* 904-632-3131. *Toll-free phone:* 888-873-1145. *Fax:* 904-632-5105. *E-mail:* pbiegel@fscj.edu.
Website: http://www.fscj.edu/.

Florida Technical College

DeLand, Florida

Freshman Application Contact Mr. Bill Atkinson, Director, Florida Technical College, 1199 South Woodland Boulevard, 3rd Floor, DeLand, FL 32720. *Phone:* 386-734-3303. *Fax:* 386-734-5150.
Website: http://www.ftccollege.edu/.

Florida Technical College

Orlando, Florida

Director of Admissions Ms. Jeanette E. Muschlitz, Director of Admissions, Florida Technical College, 12900 Challenger Parkway, Orlando, FL 32826. *Phone:* 407-678-5600.
Website: http://www.ftccollege.edu/.

Fortis College

Largo, Florida

Admissions Office Contact Fortis College, 6565 Ulmerton Road, Largo, FL 33771.
Website: http://www.fortis.edu/.

Fortis College

Tampa, Florida

Freshman Application Contact Admissions Office, Fortis College, 3910 US Highway 301 North, Suite 200, Tampa, FL 33619-1259. *Phone:* 813-620-1446. *Toll-free phone:* 855-4-FORTIS. *Fax:* 813-620-1641.
Website: http://www.fortis.edu/.

Fortis College

Winter Park, Florida

Freshman Application Contact Admissions Office, Fortis College, 1573 West Fairbanks Avenue, Suite 100, Winter Park, FL 32789. *Phone:* 407-843-3984. *Toll-free phone:* 855-4-FORTIS. *Fax:* 407-843-9828.
Website: http://www.fortis.edu/.

Golf Academy of America

Apopka, Florida

Admissions Office Contact Golf Academy of America, 510 South Hunt Club Boulevard, Apopka, FL 32703.
Website: http://www.golfacademy.edu/.

Gulf Coast State College

Panama City, Florida

- **State-supported** primarily 2-year, founded 1957
- **Suburban** 80-acre campus
- **Endowment** $25.9 million
- **Coed**

Undergraduates 2,414 full-time, 4,022 part-time. Students come from 21 states and territories; 6% are from out of state; 11% Black or African American, non-Hispanic/Latino; 8% Hispanic/Latino; 2% Asian, non-Hispanic/Latino; 0.2% Native Hawaiian or other Pacific Islander, non-Hispanic/Latino; 0.5% American Indian or Alaska Native, non-Hispanic/Latino; 3% Two or more races, non-Hispanic/Latino; 2% Race/ethnicity unknown; 0.6% international; 4% transferred in.

Faculty *Student/faculty ratio:* 21:1.

Academics *Calendar:* semesters. *Degrees:* certificates, associate, and bachelor's. *Special study options:* academic remediation for entering students, accelerated degree program, adult/continuing education programs, advanced placement credit, cooperative education, distance learning, double majors, English as a second language, external degree program, honors programs, independent study, off-campus study, part-time degree program, services for LD students, summer session for credit.

Student Life *Campus security:* late-night transport/escort service, patrols by trained security personnel during campus hours.

Athletics Member NJCAA.

Costs (2012–13) *One-time required fee:* $20. *Tuition:* state resident $2370 full-time, $99 per credit hour part-time; nonresident $8635 full-time, $360 per credit hour part-time. Full-time tuition and fees vary according to degree level. Part-time tuition and fees vary according to degree level.

Financial Aid Of all full-time matriculated undergraduates who enrolled in 2011, 145 Federal Work-Study jobs (averaging $3200). 60 state and other part-time jobs (averaging $2600).

Applying *Options:* electronic application, early admission, deferred entrance. *Application fee:* $20. *Required:* high school transcript.

Freshman Application Contact Mrs. Jackie Kuczenski, Administrative Secretary of Admissions, Gulf Coast State College, 5230 West U.S. Highway 98, Panama City, FL 32401. *Phone:* 850-769-1551 Ext. 4892. *Fax:* 850-913-

3308. *E-mail:* jkuczenski@gulfcoast.edu.
Website: http://www.gulfcoast.edu/.

Hillsborough Community College

Tampa, Florida

- **State-supported** 2-year, founded 1968, part of Florida College System
- **Urban** campus with easy access to Tampa, Clearwater, St. Petersburg
- **Coed,** 27,754 undergraduate students, 44% full-time, 57% women, 43% men

Undergraduates 12,098 full-time, 15,656 part-time. Students come from 43 states and territories; 133 other countries; 0.8% are from out of state; 18% Black or African American, non-Hispanic/Latino; 25% Hispanic/Latino; 3% Asian, non-Hispanic/Latino; 0.2% Native Hawaiian or other Pacific Islander, non-Hispanic/Latino; 0.4% American Indian or Alaska Native, non-Hispanic/Latino; 2% Two or more races, non-Hispanic/Latino; 11% Race/ethnicity unknown; 2% international; 24% transferred in.

Freshmen *Admission:* 5,194 enrolled.

Faculty *Total:* 1,613, 17% full-time, 13% with terminal degrees. *Student/faculty ratio:* 24:1.

Majors Accounting technology and bookkeeping; aquaculture; architectural engineering technology; biology/biotechnology laboratory technician; biomedical technology; building/construction site management; business administration and management; child-care and support services management; cinematography and film/video production; computer/information technology services administration related; computer programming (specific applications); computer systems analysis; computer technology/computer systems technology; criminal justice/law enforcement administration; dental hygiene; diagnostic medical sonography and ultrasound technology; dietitian assistant; electrical, electronic and communications engineering technology; emergency medical technology (EMT paramedic); engineering technology; environmental control technologies related; executive assistant/executive secretary; fire prevention and safety technology; hospitality administration; landscaping and groundskeeping; legal assistant/paralegal; liberal arts and sciences/liberal studies; management information systems; management information systems and services related; medical radiologic technology; nuclear medical technology; operations management; opticianry; optometric technician; psychiatric/mental health services technology; radio and television broadcasting technology; registered nursing/registered nurse; respiratory care therapy; restaurant, culinary, and catering management; restaurant/food services management; veterinary/animal health technology.

Academics *Calendar:* semesters. *Degree:* certificates and associate. *Special study options:* academic remediation for entering students, advanced placement credit, cooperative education, distance learning, English as a second language, honors programs, independent study, internships, off-campus study, part-time degree program, services for LD students, study abroad, summer session for credit. *ROTC:* Army (c), Air Force (c).

Library Dale Mabry plus 4 others with 170,615 titles, 1,283 serial subscriptions, 50,000 audiovisual materials, an OPAC, a Web page.

Student Life *Housing Options:* Campus housing is provided by a third party. *Activities and Organizations:* drama/theater group, student-run newspaper, radio station, choral group, Student Government Association, Student Nursing Association, Phi Theta Kappa, International Students. *Campus security:* 24-hour emergency response devices and patrols, late-night transport/escort service, Emergency call boxes. *Student services:* personal/psychological counseling.

Athletics Member NJCAA. *Intercollegiate sports:* baseball M(s), basketball M(s)/W(s), softball W(s), tennis W(s), volleyball W(s).

Standardized Tests *Required:* Entrance exams are required for assessing student readiness for college level courses. Florida's Postsecondary Education Readiness Test (PERT) is the primary entrance exam used. Hillsborough Community College is an open-access institution (for admission).

Costs (2012–13) *Tuition:* state resident $2505 full-time, $104 per credit hour part-time; nonresident $9112 full-time, $380 per credit hour part-time. *Payment plan:* installment. *Waivers:* senior citizens and employees or children of employees.

Applying *Options:* electronic application, early admission. *Required:* high school transcript. *Application deadlines:* rolling (freshmen), rolling (out-of-state freshmen), rolling (transfers).

Freshman Application Contact Ms. Katherine Durkee, College Registrar, Hillsborough Community College, PO Box 31127, Tampa, FL 33631-3127. *Phone:* 813-259-6565. *E-mail:* kdurkee@hccfl.edu. *Website:* http://www.hccfl.edu/.

ITT Technical Institute

Bradenton, Florida

- **Proprietary** primarily 2-year, part of ITT Educational Services, Inc.
- **Coed**

Academics *Calendar:* quarters. *Degrees:* associate and bachelor's.

Freshman Application Contact Director of Recruitment, ITT Technical Institute, 8039 Cooper Creek Boulevard, Bradenton, FL 34201. *Phone:* 941-309-9200. *Toll-free phone:* 800-342-8684. *Website:* http://www.itt-tech.edu/.

ITT Technical Institute

Fort Lauderdale, Florida

- **Proprietary** primarily 2-year, founded 1991, part of ITT Educational Services, Inc.
- **Suburban** campus
- **Coed**

Academics *Calendar:* quarters. *Degrees:* associate and bachelor's.

Freshman Application Contact Director of Recruitment, ITT Technical Institute, 3401 South University Drive, Fort Lauderdale, FL 33328-2021. *Phone:* 954-476-9300. *Toll-free phone:* 800-488-7797. *Website:* http://www.itt-tech.edu/.

ITT Technical Institute

Fort Myers, Florida

- **Proprietary** primarily 2-year
- **Coed**

Academics *Degrees:* associate and bachelor's.

Freshman Application Contact Director of Recruitment, ITT Technical Institute, 13500 Powers Court, Suite 100, Fort Myers, FL 33912. *Phone:* 239-603-8700. *Toll-free phone:* 877-485-5313. *Website:* http://www.itt-tech.edu/.

ITT Technical Institute

Jacksonville, Florida

- **Proprietary** primarily 2-year, founded 1991, part of ITT Educational Services, Inc.
- **Urban** campus
- **Coed**

Academics *Calendar:* quarters. *Degrees:* associate and bachelor's.

Financial Aid Of all full-time matriculated undergraduates who enrolled in 2011, 5 Federal Work-Study jobs.

Freshman Application Contact Director of Recruitment, ITT Technical Institute, 7011 A.C. Skinner Parkway, Suite 140, Jacksonville, FL 32256. *Phone:* 904-573-9100. *Toll-free phone:* 800-318-1264. *Website:* http://www.itt-tech.edu/.

ITT Technical Institute

Lake Mary, Florida

- **Proprietary** primarily 2-year, founded 1989, part of ITT Educational Services, Inc.
- **Suburban** campus
- **Coed**

Academics *Calendar:* quarters. *Degrees:* associate and bachelor's.

Freshman Application Contact Director of Recruitment, ITT Technical Institute, 1400 South International Parkway, Lake Mary, FL 32746. *Phone:* 407-660-2900. *Toll-free phone:* 866-489-8441. *Fax:* 407-660-2566. *Website:* http://www.itt-tech.edu/.

ITT Technical Institute

Miami, Florida

- **Proprietary** primarily 2-year, founded 1996, part of ITT Educational Services, Inc.
- **Coed**

Academics *Calendar:* quarters. *Degrees:* associate and bachelor's.

Freshman Application Contact Director of Recruitment, ITT Technical Institute, 7955 NW 12th Street, Suite 119, Miami, FL 33126. *Phone:* 305-477-3080. *Website:* http://www.itt-tech.edu/.

ITT Technical Institute

Orlando, Florida

- **Proprietary** primarily 2-year, part of ITT Educational Services, Inc.
- **Coed**

Academics *Calendar:* quarters. *Degrees:* associate and bachelor's.

Freshman Application Contact Director of Recruitment, ITT Technical Institute, 8301 Southpark Circle, Suite 100, Orlando, FL 32819. *Phone:* 407-371-6000. *Toll-free phone:* 877-201-4367.
Website: http://www.itt-tech.edu/.

ITT Technical Institute

St. Petersburg, Florida

- **Proprietary** primarily 2-year, part of ITT Educational Services, Inc.
- **Coed**

Academics *Degrees:* associate and bachelor's.

Freshman Application Contact Director of Recruitment, ITT Technical Institute, 877 Executive Center Drive W., Suite 100, St. Petersburg, FL 33702. *Phone:* 727-209-4700. *Toll-free phone:* 866-488-5084.
Website: http://www.itt-tech.edu/.

ITT Technical Institute

Tallahassee, Florida

- **Proprietary** primarily 2-year
- **Coed**

Academics *Degrees:* associate and bachelor's.

Freshman Application Contact Director of Recruitment, ITT Technical Institute, 2639 North Monroe Street, Building A, Suite 100, Tallahassee, FL 32303. *Phone:* 850-422-6300. *Toll-free phone:* 877-230-3559.
Website: http://www.itt-tech.edu/.

ITT Technical Institute

Tampa, Florida

- **Proprietary** primarily 2-year, founded 1981, part of ITT Educational Services, Inc.
- **Suburban** campus
- **Coed**

Academics *Calendar:* quarters. *Degrees:* associate and bachelor's.

Freshman Application Contact Director of Recruitment, ITT Technical Institute, 4809 Memorial Highway, Tampa, FL 33634-7151. *Phone:* 813-885-2244. *Toll-free phone:* 800-825-2831.
Website: http://www.itt-tech.edu/.

Kaplan College, Jacksonville Campus

Jacksonville, Florida

- **Proprietary** 2-year
- **Coed**

Academics *Degree:* diplomas and associate.

Freshman Application Contact Director of Admissions, Kaplan College, Jacksonville Campus, 7450 Beach Boulevard, Jacksonville, FL 32216. *Phone:* 904-855-2405.
Website: http://jacksonville.kaplancollege.com/.

Key College

Dania Beach, Florida

Director of Admissions Mr. Ronald H. Dooley, President and Director of Admissions, Key College, 225 East Dania Beach Boulevard, Dania Beach, FL 33004. *Phone:* 954-581-2223 Ext. 23. *Toll-free phone:* 800-581-8292.
Website: http://www.keycollege.edu/.

Lake-Sumter State College

Leesburg, Florida

Freshman Application Contact Ms. Bonnie Yanick, Enrollment Specialist, Lake-Sumter State College, 9501 U.S. Highway 441, Leesburg, FL 34788-8751. *Phone:* 352-365-3561. *Fax:* 352-365-3553. *E-mail:* admissinquiry@lscc.edu.
Website: http://www.lscc.edu/.

Le Cordon Bleu College of Culinary Arts in Orlando

Orlando, Florida

Admissions Office Contact Le Cordon Bleu College of Culinary Arts in Orlando, 8511 Commodity Circle, Suite 100, Orlando, FL 32819. *Toll-free phone:* 888-793-3222.
Website: http://www.chefs.edu/Orlando.

Le Cordon Bleu College of Culinary Arts, Miami

Miramar, Florida

Freshman Application Contact Admissions Office, Le Cordon Bleu College of Culinary Arts, Miami, 3221 Enterprise Way, Miramar, FL 33025. *Phone:* 954-628-4000. *Toll-free phone:* 888-569-3222.
Website: http://www.miamiculinary.com/.

Lincoln College of Technology

West Palm Beach, Florida

Director of Admissions Mr. Kevin Cassidy, Director of Admissions, Lincoln College of Technology, 2410 Metrocentre Boulevard, West Palm Beach, FL 33407. *Phone:* 561-842-8324 Ext. 117. *Fax:* 561-842-9503.
Website: http://www.lincolnedu.com/.

Lincoln Technical Institute

Fern Park, Florida

Admissions Office Contact Lincoln Technical Institute, 7275 Estapona Circle, Fern Park, FL 32730.
Website: http://www.lincolnedu.com/.

MedVance Institute

Palm Springs, Florida

Director of Admissions Campus Director, MedVance Institute, 1630 South Congress Avenue, Palm Springs, FL 33461. *Phone:* 561-304-3466. *Toll-free phone:* 877-606-3382. *Fax:* 561-304-3471.
Website: http://www.medvance.edu/.

Meridian College

Sarasota, Florida

Admissions Office Contact Meridian College, 7020 Professional Parkway East, Sarasota, FL 34240.
Website: http://www.meridian.edu/.

Miami Dade College

Miami, Florida

- **State and locally supported** primarily 2-year, founded 1960, part of Florida College System
- **Urban** campus
- **Endowment** $165.5 million
- **Coed,** 66,701 undergraduate students, 39% full-time, 58% women, 42% men

Undergraduates 26,211 full-time, 40,490 part-time. Students come from 43 states and territories; 185 other countries; 1% are from out of state; 17% Black or African American, non-Hispanic/Latino; 70% Hispanic/Latino; 1% Asian, non-Hispanic/Latino; 0.1% Native Hawaiian or other Pacific Islander, non-Hispanic/Latino; 0.1% American Indian or Alaska Native, non-Hispanic/Latino; 0.3% Two or more races, non-Hispanic/Latino; 3% Race/ethnicity unknown; 2% international; 3% transferred in.

Freshmen *Admission:* 10,575 applied, 10,575 admitted, 12,224 enrolled.

Faculty *Total:* 2,558, 28% full-time, 18% with terminal degrees. *Student/faculty ratio:* 30:1.

Majors Accounting technology and bookkeeping; administrative assistant and secretarial science; aeronautics/aviation/aerospace science and technology; agriculture; airline pilot and flight crew; air traffic control; American studies; anthropology; architectural drafting and CAD/CADD; architectural engineering technology; art; Asian studies; audiology and speech-language pathology; aviation/airway management; behavioral sciences; biology/biological sciences; biology teacher education; biomedical technology; biotechnology; business administration and management; business administration, management and operations related; chemistry; chemistry teacher education; child development; cinematography and film/video production; civil engineering technology; clinical/medical laboratory technology; commercial and advertising art; comparative literature; computer engineering technology; computer graphics; computer programming; computer science; computer software technology; computer technology/computer systems technology; construction engineering technology; cooking and related culinary arts; court reporting; criminal justice/law enforcement administration; criminal justice/police science; culinary arts; dance; data processing and data processing technology; dental hygiene; diagnostic medical sonography and ultrasound technology; dietetics; dietetic technology; drafting and design technology; dramatic/theater arts; economics; education; education related; electrical and electronic engineering technologies related; electrical, electronic and communications engineering technology; elementary education; emergency medical technology (EMT paramedic); engineering; engineering related; engineering technology; English; environmental engineering technology; finance; fire science/firefighting; food science; forestry; French; funeral service and mortuary science; general studies; geology/earth science; German; health information/medical records administration; health/medical preparatory programs related; health professions related; health services/allied health/health sciences; heating, air conditioning, ventilation and refrigeration maintenance technology; heating, ventilation, air conditioning and refrigeration engineering technology; histologic technician; history; homeland security, law enforcement, firefighting and protective services related; horticultural science; hospitality administration; humanities; human services; industrial technology; information science/studies; interior design; international relations and affairs; Italian; journalism; kindergarten/preschool education; landscaping and groundskeeping; Latin American studies; legal administrative assistant/secretary; legal assistant/paralegal; management information systems; marketing/marketing management; mass communication/media; mathematics; mathematics teacher education; medical/clinical assistant; middle school education; music; music performance; music teacher education; natural sciences; nonprofit management; nuclear medical technology; ophthalmic technology; ornamental horticulture; parks, recreation and leisure; philosophy; photographic and film/video technology; photography; physical education teaching and coaching; physical sciences; physical therapy technology; physics; physics teacher education; plant nursery management; political science and government; Portuguese; pre-engineering; psychology; public administration; radio and television; radio and television broadcasting technology; radiologic technology/science; recording arts technology; registered nursing/registered nurse; respiratory care therapy; respiratory therapy technician; science teacher education; sign language interpretation and translation; social sciences; social work; sociology; Spanish; special education; substance abuse/addiction counseling; teacher assistant/aide; telecommunications technology; tourism and travel services management.

Academics *Calendar:* 16-16-6-6. *Degrees:* certificates, associate, bachelor's, and postbachelor's certificates. *Special study options:* academic remediation for entering students, accelerated degree program, adult/continuing education programs, advanced placement credit, cooperative education, distance learning, English as a second language, freshman honors college, honors programs, independent study, internships, off-campus study, part-time degree program, services for LD students, study abroad, summer session for credit. *ROTC:* Army (b), Air Force (b).

Library Miami Dade College Learning Resources plus 8 others with 367,687 titles, 750 serial subscriptions, 32,428 audiovisual materials, an OPAC, a Web page.

Student Life *Housing:* college housing not available. *Activities and Organizations:* drama/theater group, student-run newspaper, radio and television station, choral group, Student Government Association, Phi Theta Kappa, Phi Beta Lambda (Business), Future Educators of America Professional, Kappa Delta Pi Honor Society (Education), national fraternities. *Campus security:* 24-hour emergency response devices and patrols, mass communication emergency notification systems. *Student services:* personal/psychological counseling.

Athletics Member NCAA, NJCAA. All NCAA Division I. *Intercollegiate sports:* baseball M(s), basketball M(s)/W(s), softball W(s), volleyball W(s).

Costs (2012–13) *One-time required fee:* $30. *Tuition:* state resident $2483 full-time, $83 per credit hour part-time; nonresident $9933 full-time, $331 per credit hour part-time. Full-time tuition and fees vary according to course load, degree level, and program. Part-time tuition and fees vary according to course load, degree level, and program. *Required fees:* $883 full-time, $29 per credit hour part-time. *Waivers:* employees or children of employees.

Financial Aid Of all full-time matriculated undergraduates who enrolled in 2011, 800 Federal Work-Study jobs (averaging $5000). 125 state and other part-time jobs (averaging $5000).

Applying *Options:* electronic application, early admission. *Application fee:* $30. *Required:* high school transcript. *Required for some:* Some programs such as Honors College and Medical programs have additional admissions requirements. *Application deadlines:* rolling (freshmen), rolling (out-of-state freshmen), rolling (transfers). *Notification:* continuous (freshmen), continuous (out-of-state freshmen), continuous (transfers).

Freshman Application Contact Mrs. Dulce Beltran, College Registrar, Miami Dade College, 11011 SW 104th Street, Miami, FL 33176. *Phone:* 305-237-2206. *Fax:* 305-237-2532. *E-mail:* dbeltran@mdc.edu. *Website:* http://www.mdc.edu/.

North Florida Community College
Madison, Florida

Freshman Application Contact Mr. Bobby Scott, North Florida Community College, 325 Northwest Turner Davis Drive, Madison, FL 32340. *Phone:* 850-973-9450. *Toll-free phone:* 866-937-6322. *Fax:* 850-973-1697. *Website:* http://www.nfcc.edu/.

Northwest Florida State College
Niceville, Florida

- **State and locally supported** primarily 2-year, founded 1963, part of Florida College System
- **Small-town** 264-acre campus
- **Endowment** $28.6 million
- **Coed**

Undergraduates Students come from 18 states and territories.
Faculty *Student/faculty ratio:* 15:1.
Academics *Calendar:* semesters plus summer sessions. *Degrees:* certificates, associate, and bachelor's. *Special study options:* academic remediation for entering students, accelerated degree program, adult/continuing education programs, advanced placement credit, distance learning, English as a second language, independent study, part-time degree program, services for LD students, summer session for credit. *ROTC:* Army (b).
Athletics Member NJCAA.
Standardized Tests *Required for some:* ACT, SAT I, ACT ASSET, MAPS, or Florida College Entry Placement Test are used for placement not admission.
Costs (2012–13) *One-time required fee:* $30. *Tuition:* state resident $3234 full-time, $108 per credit part-time; nonresident $11,604 full-time, $387 per credit part-time. Full-time tuition and fees vary according to course level, course load, degree level, and reciprocity agreements. Part-time tuition and fees vary according to course level, course load, degree level, and reciprocity agreements. *Payment plans:* tuition prepayment, installment, deferred payment.
Applying *Options:* electronic application. *Required:* high school transcript.
Freshman Application Contact Ms. Christine Bishop, Dean Enrollment Services, Northwest Florida State College, 100 College Boulevard, Niceville, FL 32578. *Phone:* 850-729-5373. *Fax:* 850-729-5323. *E-mail:* registrar@nwfsc.edu.
Website: http://www.nwfsc.edu/.

Pasco-Hernando Community College
New Port Richey, Florida

- **State-supported** 2-year, founded 1972, part of Florida College System
- **Suburban** 142-acre campus with easy access to Tampa
- **Endowment** $35.2 million
- **Coed,** 10,795 undergraduate students, 36% full-time, 62% women, 38% men

Undergraduates 3,893 full-time, 6,902 part-time. Students come from 6 states and territories; 51 other countries; 1% are from out of state; 5% Black or African American, non-Hispanic/Latino; 14% Hispanic/Latino; 3% Asian, non-Hispanic/Latino; 1% American Indian or Alaska Native, non-Hispanic/Latino; 2% Race/ethnicity unknown; 0.2% international; 3% transferred in. *Retention:* 60% of full-time freshmen returned.
Freshmen *Admission:* 661 applied, 1,628 enrolled.
Faculty *Total:* 377, 33% full-time, 8% with terminal degrees. *Student/faculty ratio:* 29:1.
Majors Business administration and management; computer programming related; computer programming (specific applications); computer systems networking and telecommunications; computer technology/computer systems technology; criminal justice/law enforcement administration; dental hygiene; drafting and design technology; e-commerce; emergency medical technology (EMT paramedic); human services; information technology; legal assistant/paralegal; liberal arts and sciences/liberal studies; marketing/marketing management; radiologic technology/science; registered nursing/registered nurse; web page, digital/multimedia and information resources design.
Academics *Calendar:* semesters. *Degree:* certificates, diplomas, and associate. *Special study options:* academic remediation for entering students, accelerated degree program, adult/continuing education programs, advanced placement credit, cooperative education, distance learning, double majors, honors programs, independent study, internships, off-campus study, part-time degree program, services for LD students, summer session for credit. *ROTC:* Army (c).
Library Alric Pottberg Library plus 3 others with an OPAC, a Web page.

Student Life *Housing:* college housing not available. *Activities and Organizations:* drama/theater group, choral group, Student Government Association, Phi Theta Kappa, Phi Beta Lambda, Human Services, PHCC Cares. *Campus security:* late-night transport/escort service. *Student services:* personal/psychological counseling.

Athletics Member NJCAA. *Intercollegiate sports:* baseball M(s), basketball M(s), cross-country running W(s), softball W(s), volleyball W(s). *Intramural sports:* cheerleading M/W.

Standardized Tests *Recommended:* SAT and SAT Subject Tests or ACT (for admission), CPT.

Costs (2013–14) *Tuition:* state resident $101 per credit hour part-time; nonresident $385 per credit hour part-time. Full-time tuition and fees vary according to program. Part-time tuition and fees vary according to program. *Payment plan:* installment.

Financial Aid Of all full-time matriculated undergraduates who enrolled in 2011, 83 Federal Work-Study jobs (averaging $3201).

Applying *Options:* electronic application. *Application fee:* $25. *Required:* high school transcript. *Application deadlines:* rolling (freshmen), rolling (out-of-state freshmen), rolling (transfers). *Notification:* continuous (freshmen), continuous (out-of-state freshmen), continuous (transfers).

Freshman Application Contact Ms. Estela Carrion, Director of Admissions and Student Records, Pasco-Hernando Community College, 10230 Ridge Road, New Port Richey, FL 34654-5199. *Phone:* 727-816-3261. *Toll-free phone:* 877-TRY-PHCC. *Fax:* 727-816-3389. *E-mail:* carrioe@phcc.edu. *Website:* http://www.phcc.edu/.

Pensacola State College

Pensacola, Florida

- **State-supported** primarily 2-year, founded 1948, part of Florida College System
- **Urban** 130-acre campus
- **Coed,** 11,862 undergraduate students, 41% full-time, 61% women, 39% men

Undergraduates 4,865 full-time, 6,997 part-time. Students come from 25 states and territories; 1% are from out of state; 13% Black or African American, non-Hispanic/Latino; 5% Hispanic/Latino; 3% Asian, non-Hispanic/Latino; 0.4% Native Hawaiian or other Pacific Islander, non-Hispanic/Latino; 0.9% American Indian or Alaska Native, non-Hispanic/Latino; 4% Two or more races, non-Hispanic/Latino; 1% Race/ethnicity unknown; 0.4% international; 6% transferred in.

Freshmen *Admission:* 1,843 enrolled.

Faculty *Total:* 632, 30% full-time, 6% with terminal degrees. *Student/faculty ratio:* 25:1.

Majors Accounting; accounting technology and bookkeeping; administrative assistant and secretarial science; agriculture; art; art teacher education; automobile/automotive mechanics technology; banking and financial support services; biochemistry; biology/biological sciences; botany/plant biology; building/property maintenance; business administration and management; business administration, management and operations related; business/commerce; chemical technology; chemistry; child-care and support services management; child-care provision; cinematography and film/video production; civil engineering; civil engineering technology; commercial and advertising art; communications technology; computer and information sciences; computer and information sciences related; computer engineering; computer programming; computer programming (specific applications); computer science; computer systems analysis; construction engineering technology; consumer services and advocacy; cooking and related culinary arts; criminal justice/law enforcement administration; dental hygiene; diagnostic medical sonography and ultrasound technology; dietetics; drafting and design technology; dramatic/theater arts; early childhood education; education; electrical and electronics engineering; electrical, electronic and communications engineering technology; elementary education; emergency medical technology (EMT paramedic); engineering; English; executive assistant/executive secretary; fire prevention and safety technology; fire science/firefighting; food service systems administration; foods, nutrition, and wellness; forest resources production and management; forestry; forest technology; geology/earth science; graphic design; hazardous materials management and waste technology; health information/medical records administration; history; hospitality administration; hospitality and recreation marketing; information science/studies; journalism; landscaping and groundskeeping; legal administrative assistant/secretary; legal assistant/paralegal; liberal arts and sciences/liberal studies; management information systems; management information systems and services related; management science; manufacturing engineering technology; mathematics; medical radiologic technology; music; music teacher education; natural resources management and policy; nursing science; office management; operations management; ornamental horticulture; philosophy; photographic and film/video technology; physical education teaching and coaching; physical therapy technology; physics; pre-dentistry studies; pre-law studies; premedical studies; prenursing studies; pre-pharmacy studies; pre-veterinary studies; psy-

chology; registered nursing/registered nurse; religious studies; restaurant, culinary, and catering management; sociology; special education; speech communication and rhetoric; zoology/animal biology.

Academics *Calendar:* semesters. *Degrees:* certificates, diplomas, associate, and bachelor's. *Special study options:* academic remediation for entering students, adult/continuing education programs, advanced placement credit, cooperative education, distance learning, double majors, English as a second language, external degree program, honors programs, independent study, part-time degree program, services for LD students, summer session for credit. *ROTC:* Army (b).

Library Edward M. Chadbourne Library plus 4 others with 116,312 titles, 93 serial subscriptions, 7,702 audiovisual materials, an OPAC, a Web page.

Student Life *Housing:* college housing not available. *Activities and Organizations:* drama/theater group, student-run newspaper, choral group. *Campus security:* 24-hour emergency response devices and patrols, late-night transport/escort service. *Student services:* health clinic, personal/psychological counseling, women's center.

Athletics Member NJCAA. *Intercollegiate sports:* baseball M(s), basketball M(s)/W(s), softball W(s), volleyball W. *Intramural sports:* archery M/W, badminton M/W, basketball M/W, bowling M/W, cross-country running M/W, gymnastics M/W, racquetball M/W, sailing M/W, swimming and diving M/W, tennis M/W, track and field M/W, volleyball M/W, weight lifting M/W, wrestling M.

Costs (2012–13) *One-time required fee:* $30. *Tuition:* state resident $2510 full-time, $105 per credit hour part-time; nonresident $10,075 full-time, $420 per credit hour part-time. Full-time tuition and fees vary according to degree level. Part-time tuition and fees vary according to degree level. *Waivers:* senior citizens and employees or children of employees.

Financial Aid Of all full-time matriculated undergraduates who enrolled in 2011, 120 Federal Work-Study jobs (averaging $3000).

Applying *Options:* electronic application, early admission. *Application fee:* $30. *Required:* high school transcript. *Application deadlines:* 8/30 (freshmen), 8/30 (transfers). *Notification:* continuous until 8/30 (freshmen), continuous until 8/30 (transfers).

Freshman Application Contact Ms. Martha Caughey, Registrar, Pensacola State College, 1000 College Boulevard, Pensacola, FL 32504-8998. *Phone:* 850-484-1600. *Fax:* 850-484-1829. *Website:* http://www.pensacolastate.edu/.

Rasmussen College Fort Myers

Fort Myers, Florida

- **Proprietary** primarily 2-year, part of Rasmussen College System
- **Suburban** campus
- **Coed,** 798 undergraduate students

Faculty *Student/faculty ratio:* 22:1.

Majors Accounting; accounting and business/management; business administration and management; computer and information systems security; computer science; computer software engineering; corrections and criminal justice related; early childhood education; graphic communications related; health/health-care administration; health information/medical records administration; health information/medical records technology; human resources management; human services; information resources management; legal assistant/paralegal; management information systems and services related; marketing/marketing management; medical administrative assistant and medical secretary; medical/clinical assistant; pharmacy technician; registered nursing/registered nurse; web page, digital/multimedia and information resources design.

Academics *Degrees:* certificates, diplomas, associate, and bachelor's. *Special study options:* academic remediation for entering students, accelerated degree program, adult/continuing education programs, distance learning, double majors, internships, part-time degree program, summer session for credit.

Library Rasmussen College Library - Fort Myers with 2,367 titles, 17 serial subscriptions, 155 audiovisual materials, an OPAC, a Web page.

Student Life *Housing:* college housing not available.

Standardized Tests *Required:* Internal Exam (for admission).

Costs (2013–14) *Tuition:* $12,600 full-time. Full-time tuition and fees vary according to course level, course load, degree level, location, and program. Part-time tuition and fees vary according to course level, course load, degree level, location, and program. *Required fees:* $1800 full-time. *Payment plans:* installment, deferred payment. *Waivers:* employees or children of employees.

Applying *Options:* electronic application, early admission, deferred entrance. *Required:* high school transcript, minimum 2.0 GPA. *Required for some:* interview. *Application deadlines:* rolling (freshmen), rolling (transfers).

Freshman Application Contact Susan Hammerstrom, Director of Admissions, Rasmussen College Fort Myers, 9160 Forum Corporate Parkway, Suite 100, Fort Myers, FL 33905. *Phone:* 239-477-2100. *Toll-free phone:* 888-549-6755. *E-mail:* susan.hammerstrom@rasmussen.edu. *Website:* http://www.rasmussen.edu/.

Rasmussen College New Port Richey
New Port Richey, Florida

- **Proprietary** primarily 2-year, part of Rasmussen College System
- **Suburban** campus
- **Coed,** 893 undergraduate students

Faculty *Student/faculty ratio:* 22:1.

Majors Accounting; accounting and business/management; business administration and management; computer and information systems security; computer science; computer software engineering; corrections and criminal justice related; early childhood education; graphic communications related; health/health-care administration; health information/medical records administration; health information/medical records technology; human resources management; human services; information resources management; legal assistant/paralegal; management information systems and services related; marketing/marketing management; medical administrative assistant and medical secretary; medical/clinical assistant; pharmacy technician; registered nursing/registered nurse; web page, digital/multimedia and information resources design.

Academics *Degrees:* certificates, diplomas, associate, and bachelor's. *Special study options:* academic remediation for entering students, accelerated degree program, adult/continuing education programs, distance learning, double majors, internships, part-time degree program, summer session for credit.

Library Rasmussen College Library - New Port Richey with 2,228 titles, 16 serial subscriptions, 87 audiovisual materials, an OPAC, a Web page.

Student Life *Housing:* college housing not available.

Standardized Tests *Required:* Internal Exam (for admission).

Costs (2013–14) *Tuition:* $12,600 full-time. Full-time tuition and fees vary according to course level, course load, degree level, location, and program. Part-time tuition and fees vary according to course level, course load, degree level, location, and program. *Required fees:* $1800 full-time. *Payment plans:* installment, deferred payment. *Waivers:* employees or children of employees.

Financial Aid Of all full-time matriculated undergraduates who enrolled in 2011, 6 Federal Work-Study jobs.

Applying *Options:* electronic application, early admission, deferred entrance. *Required:* high school transcript, minimum 2.0 GPA. *Required for some:* interview. *Application deadlines:* rolling (freshmen), rolling (transfers).

Freshman Application Contact Susan Hammerstrom, Director of Admissions, Rasmussen College New Port Richey, 8661 Citizens Drive, New Port Richey, FL 34654. *Phone:* 727-942-0069. *Toll-free phone:* 888-549-6755. *E-mail:* susan.hammerstrom@rasmussen.edu. *Website:* http://www.rasmussen.edu/.

Rasmussen College Ocala
Ocala, Florida

- **Proprietary** primarily 2-year, founded 1984, part of Rasmussen College System
- **Suburban** campus with easy access to Orlando
- **Coed, primarily women,** 1,266 undergraduate students

Faculty *Student/faculty ratio:* 22:1.

Majors Accounting; accounting and business/management; business administration and management; computer and information systems security; computer science; computer software engineering; corrections and criminal justice related; early childhood education; graphic communications related; health/health-care administration; health information/medical records administration; health information/medical records technology; human resources management; human services; information resources management; legal assistant/paralegal; management information systems and services related; marketing/marketing management; medical administrative assistant and medical secretary; medical/clinical assistant; pharmacy technician; web page, digital/multimedia and information resources design.

Academics *Calendar:* quarters. *Degrees:* certificates, diplomas, associate, and bachelor's. *Special study options:* academic remediation for entering students, accelerated degree program, adult/continuing education programs, distance learning, double majors, internships, part-time degree program, summer session for credit.

Library Rasmussen College Library - Ocala with 1,868 titles, 6 serial subscriptions, 159 audiovisual materials, an OPAC, a Web page.

Student Life *Housing:* college housing not available.

Standardized Tests *Required:* Internal Exam (for admission).

Costs (2013–14) *Tuition:* $12,600 full-time. Full-time tuition and fees vary according to course level, course load, degree level, location, and program. Part-time tuition and fees vary according to course level, course load, degree level, location, and program. *Required fees:* $1800 full-time. *Payment plans:* installment, deferred payment. *Waivers:* employees or children of employees.

Applying *Options:* electronic application, early admission, deferred entrance. *Required:* high school transcript, minimum 2.0 GPA. *Required for some:* interview. *Application deadlines:* rolling (freshmen), rolling (transfers).

Freshman Application Contact Susan Hammerstrom, Director of Admissions, Rasmussen College Ocala, 4755 SW 46th Court, Ocala, FL 34471. *Phone:* 352-629-1941. *Toll-free phone:* 888-549-6755. *E-mail:* susan.hammerstrom@rasmussen.edu. *Website:* http://www.rasmussen.edu/.

Remington College–Tampa Campus
Tampa, Florida

Freshman Application Contact Remington College–Tampa Campus, 6302 E. Dr. Martin Luther King, Jr. Boulevard, Suite 400, Tampa, FL 33619. *Phone:* 813-932-0701. *Toll-free phone:* 800-560-6192. *Website:* http://www.remingtoncollege.edu/.

St. Johns River State College
Palatka, Florida

Director of Admissions Dean of Admissions and Records, St. Johns River State College, 5001 Saint Johns Avenue, Palatka, FL 32177-3897. *Phone:* 386-312-4032. *Fax:* 386-312-4289. *Website:* http://www.sjrstate.edu/.

Sanford-Brown Institute
Fort Lauderdale, Florida

Director of Admissions Scott Nelowet, Sanford-Brown Institute, 1201 West Cypress Creek Road, Fort Lauderdale, FL 33309. *Phone:* 904-363-6221. *Toll-free phone:* 888-742-0333. *Fax:* 904-363-6824. *E-mail:* snelowet@sbjacksonville.com. *Website:* http://www.sanfordbrown.edu/Fort-Lauderdale.

Sanford-Brown Institute
Jacksonville, Florida

Freshman Application Contact Denise Neal, Assistant Director of Admissions, Sanford-Brown Institute, 10255 Fortune Parkway, Suite 501. *Phone:* 904-380-2912. *Toll-free phone:* 888-577-5333. *Fax:* 904-363-6824. *E-mail:* dneal@sbjacksonville.com. *Website:* http://www.sanfordbrown.edu/Jacksonville.

Sanford-Brown Institute
Tampa, Florida

Admissions Office Contact Sanford-Brown Institute, 5701 East Hillsborough Avenue, Tampa, FL 33610. *Toll-free phone:* 888-450-0333. *Website:* http://www.sanfordbrown.edu/Tampa.

Seminole State College of Florida
Sanford, Florida

- **State and locally supported** primarily 2-year, founded 1966
- **Small-town** 200-acre campus with easy access to Orlando
- **Endowment** $12.5 million
- **Coed,** 19,450 undergraduate students, 39% full-time, 59% women, 41% men

Undergraduates 7,559 full-time, 11,891 part-time. Students come from 88 other countries; 0.5% are from out of state; 18% Black or African American, non-Hispanic/Latino; 22% Hispanic/Latino; 3% Asian, non-Hispanic/Latino; 0.3% Native Hawaiian or other Pacific Islander, non-Hispanic/Latino; 0.3% American Indian or Alaska Native, non-Hispanic/Latino; 3% Two or more races, non-Hispanic/Latino; 0.8% Race/ethnicity unknown; 2% international; 6% transferred in.

Freshmen *Admission:* 9,901 applied, 9,901 admitted, 2,721 enrolled.

Faculty *Total:* 795, 30% full-time, 16% with terminal degrees. *Student/faculty ratio:* 27:1.

Majors Accounting; administrative assistant and secretarial science; architectural engineering technology; automobile/automotive mechanics technology; banking and financial support services; building/construction finishing, management, and inspection related; business administration and management; child development; civil engineering technology; computer and information sciences and support services related; computer and information sciences related; computer and information systems security; computer engineering related; computer engineering technology; computer graphics; computer hardware engineering; computer/information technology services administration related; computer programming; computer programming related; computer programming (specific applications); computer programming (vendor/product certification); computer software and media applications related; computer software engineering; computer systems networking and telecommunications;

construction engineering technology; criminal justice/law enforcement administration; data entry/microcomputer applications; data entry/microcomputer applications related; data modeling/warehousing and database administration; data processing and data processing technology; drafting and design technology; electrical, electronic and communications engineering technology; emergency medical technology (EMT paramedic); finance; fire science/firefighting; industrial technology; information science/studies; information technology; interior design; legal assistant/paralegal; liberal arts and sciences/liberal studies; marketing/marketing management; network and system administration; physical therapy; registered nursing/registered nurse; respiratory care therapy; telecommunications technology; web/multimedia management and webmaster; web page, digital/multimedia and information resources design; word processing.

Academics *Calendar:* semesters. *Degrees:* certificates, diplomas, associate, and bachelor's. *Special study options:* academic remediation for entering students, accelerated degree program, adult/continuing education programs, advanced placement credit, cooperative education, distance learning, double majors, English as a second language, external degree program, honors programs, independent study, internships, part-time degree program, services for LD students, study abroad, summer session for credit. *ROTC:* Army (b).

Library Seminole State College Library - SLM plus 8 others with 110,331 titles, 245 serial subscriptions, 7,401 audiovisual materials, an OPAC, a Web page.

Student Life *Housing:* college housing not available. *Activities and Organizations:* drama/theater group, student-run newspaper, choral group, Phi Beta Lambda, Phi Theta Kappa, Student Government Association, Sigma Phi Gamma, Hispanic Student Association. *Campus security:* 24-hour emergency response devices and patrols. *Student services:* personal/psychological counseling.

Athletics Member NJCAA. *Intercollegiate sports:* baseball M(s), golf W(s), softball W(s).

Standardized Tests *Required:* CPT, PERT (for admission). *Recommended:* ACT (for admission).

Costs (2013–14) *Tuition:* state resident $3131 full-time; nonresident $11,456 full-time. Full-time tuition and fees vary according to degree level and program. Part-time tuition and fees vary according to degree level and program. *Payment plan:* deferred payment. *Waivers:* senior citizens and employees or children of employees.

Applying *Options:* electronic application, early admission, deferred entrance. *Required:* high school transcript, minimum 2.0 GPA. *Application deadlines:* rolling (freshmen), rolling (transfers). *Notification:* continuous (freshmen), continuous (transfers).

Freshman Application Contact Ms. Pamela Mennechey, Associate Vice President - Student Recruitment and Enrollment, Seminole State College of Florida, Sanford, FL 32773-6199. *Phone:* 407-708-2050. *Fax:* 407-708-2395. *E-mail:* admissions@scc-fl.edu.
Website: http://www.seminolestate.edu/.

Southeastern College–Greenacres

Greenacres, Florida

Freshman Application Contact Admissions Office, Southeastern College–Greenacres, 6812 Forest Hill Boulevard, Suite D-1, Greenacres, FL 33413. *Website:* http://www.sec.edu/.

Southeastern College–Miami Lakes

Miami Lakes, Florida

Freshman Application Contact Admissions Office, Southeastern College–Miami Lakes, 17395 NW 59th Avenue, Miami Lakes, FL 33015. *Website:* http://www.sec.edu/.

Southeastern College–St. Petersburg

St. Petersburg, Florida

Admissions Office Contact Southeastern College–St. Petersburg, 11208 Blue Heron Boulevard, Suite A, St. Petersburg, FL 33716. *Website:* http://www.sec.edu/.

Southern Technical College

Auburndale, Florida

Director of Admissions Mr. Charles Owens, Admissions Office, Southern Technical College, 298 Havendale Boulevard, Auburndale, FL 33823. *Phone:* 863-967-8822.
Website: http://www.southerntech.edu/.

Southern Technical College

Orlando, Florida

Admissions Office Contact Southern Technical College, 1485 Florida Mall Avenue, Orlando, FL 32809. *Toll-free phone:* 407-438-6005.
Website: http://www.southerntech.edu/.

South Florida State College

Avon Park, Florida

Director of Admissions Ms. Annie Alexander-Harvey, Dean of Student Services, South Florida State College, 600 West College Drive, Avon Park, FL 33825-9356. *Phone:* 863-453-6661 Ext. 7107.
Website: http://www.southflorida.edu/.

Southwest Florida College

Tampa, Florida

Director of Admissions Admissions, Southwest Florida College, 3910 Riga Boulevard, Tampa, FL 33619. *Phone:* 813-630-4401. *Toll-free phone:* 877-493-5147.
Website: http://www.swfc.edu/.

Tallahassee Community College

Tallahassee, Florida

- **State and locally supported** 2-year, founded 1966, part of Florida College System
- **Suburban** 258-acre campus
- **Endowment** $7.9 million
- **Coed,** 14,237 undergraduate students, 48% full-time, 53% women, 47% men

Undergraduates 6,840 full-time, 7,397 part-time. 7% are from out of state; 33% Black or African American, non-Hispanic/Latino; 9% Hispanic/Latino; 1% Asian, non-Hispanic/Latino, 0.1% Native Hawaiian or other Pacific Islander, non-Hispanic/Latino; 0.2% American Indian or Alaska Native, non-Hispanic/Latino; 3% Two or more races, non-Hispanic/Latino; 3% Race/ethnicity unknown; 0.9% international; 8% transferred in.

Freshmen *Admission:* 2,628 applied, 2,628 admitted, 2,177 enrolled.

Faculty *Total:* 868, 22% full-time, 18% with terminal degrees. *Student/faculty ratio:* 23:1.

Majors Accounting technology and bookkeeping; administrative assistant and secretarial science; business administration and management; civil engineering technology; computer and information sciences; computer graphics; computer programming; computer programming (specific applications); computer systems networking and telecommunications; construction engineering technology; criminal justice/law enforcement administration; data processing and data processing technology; dental hygiene; emergency medical technology (EMT paramedic); engineering; film/cinema/video studies; finance; health information/medical records technology; kindergarten/preschool education; legal administrative assistant/secretary; legal assistant/paralegal; liberal arts and sciences/liberal studies; management information systems; marketing/marketing management; network and system administration; parks, recreation and leisure; public administration; registered nursing/registered nurse; respiratory care therapy; word processing.

Academics *Calendar:* semesters. *Degree:* certificates and associate. *Special study options:* academic remediation for entering students, accelerated degree program, adult/continuing education programs, advanced placement credit, distance learning, English as a second language, external degree program, honors programs, independent study, off-campus study, part-time degree program, services for LD students, study abroad, summer session for credit. *ROTC:* Army (c), Navy (c), Air Force (c).

Library Tallahassee Community College Library with 126,904 titles, 7,965 audiovisual materials, an OPAC.

Student Life *Housing:* college housing not available. *Activities and Organizations:* drama/theater group, student-run newspaper, choral group, Student Government Association, International Student Organization, Phi Theta Kappa, Model United Nations, Honors Council. *Campus security:* 24-hour emergency response devices and patrols, late-night transport/escort service. *Student services:* personal/psychological counseling.

Athletics Member NJCAA. *Intercollegiate sports:* baseball M(s), basketball M(s)/W(s), softball W(s). *Intramural sports:* basketball M/W, football M/W, soccer M/W, softball M/W, volleyball M/W.

Costs (2012–13) *Tuition:* state resident $2518 full-time, $97 per credit hour part-time; nonresident $9724 full-time, $373 per credit hour part-time. Full-time tuition and fees vary according to course load. Part-time tuition and fees vary according to course load. No tuition increase for student's term of enrollment. *Payment plan:* installment. *Waivers:* employees or children of employees.

Financial Aid Of all full-time matriculated undergraduates who enrolled in 2011, 187 Federal Work-Study jobs (averaging $2408).

Applying *Options:* electronic application, early admission, deferred entrance. *Required:* high school transcript. *Application deadlines:* 8/1 (freshmen), 8/1 (transfers).

Freshman Application Contact Student Success Center, Tallahassee Community College, 444 Appleyard Drive, Tallahassee, FL 32304-2895. *Phone:* 850-201-8555. *E-mail:* admissions@tcc.fl.edu. *Website:* http://www.tcc.fl.edu/.

GEORGIA

Albany Technical College

Albany, Georgia

- **State-supported** 2-year, founded 1961, part of Technical College System of Georgia
- **Coed**

Undergraduates 2,863 full-time, 2,055 part-time. 0.3% are from out of state; 81% Black or African American, non-Hispanic/Latino; 0.8% Hispanic/Latino; 0.3% Asian, non-Hispanic/Latino; 0.1% American Indian or Alaska Native, non-Hispanic/Latino; 0.6% Two or more races, non-Hispanic/Latino; 0.3% Race/ethnicity unknown. *Retention:* 59% of full-time freshmen returned.

Academics *Calendar:* quarters. *Degree:* certificates, diplomas, and associate. *Special study options:* distance learning.

Applying *Options:* early admission. *Application fee:* $23. *Required:* high school transcript.

Freshman Application Contact Albany Technical College, 1704 South Slappey Boulevard, Albany, GA 31701. *Phone:* 229-430-3520. *Toll-free phone:* 877-261-3113. *Website:* http://www.albanytech.edu/.

Altamaha Technical College

Jesup, Georgia

- **State-supported** 2-year, part of Technical College System of Georgia
- **Coed**

Undergraduates 399 full-time, 1,100 part-time. 30% Black or African American, non-Hispanic/Latino; 2% Hispanic/Latino; 0.5% Asian, non-Hispanic/Latino; 0.5% American Indian or Alaska Native, non-Hispanic/Latino; 2% Race/ethnicity unknown. *Retention:* 66% of full-time freshmen returned.

Academics *Calendar:* quarters. *Degree:* certificates, diplomas, and associate. *Special study options:* distance learning.

Applying *Options:* early admission. *Application fee:* $24. *Required:* high school transcript.

Freshman Application Contact Altamaha Technical College, 1777 West Cherry Street, Jesup, GA 31545. *Phone:* 912-427-1958. *Toll-free phone:* 800-645-8284. *Website:* http://www.altamahatech.edu/.

Andrew College

Cuthbert, Georgia

Freshman Application Contact Ms. Bridget Kurkowski, Director of Admission, Andrew College, 413 College Street, Cuthbert, GA 39840. *Phone:* 229-732-5986. *Toll-free phone:* 800-664-9250. *Fax:* 229-732-2176. *E-mail:* admissions@andrewcollege.edu. *Website:* http://www.andrewcollege.edu/.

Anthem College–Atlanta

Atlanta, Georgia

Director of Admissions Frank Webster, Office Manager, Anthem College–Atlanta, 2450 Piedmont Road NE, Atlanta, GA 30324. *Phone:* 770-988-9877. *Toll-free phone:* 855-268-4360. *Fax:* 770-988-8824. *E-mail:* ckusema@hightechschools.com. *Website:* http://anthem.edu/atlanta-georgia/.

Athens Technical College

Athens, Georgia

- **State-supported** 2-year, founded 1958, part of Technical College System of Georgia
- **Suburban** campus
- **Coed**

Undergraduates 1,560 full-time, 3,763 part-time. 0.3% are from out of state; 23% Black or African American, non-Hispanic/Latino; 3% Hispanic/Latino; 4% Asian, non-Hispanic/Latino; 0.3% American Indian or Alaska Native, non-Hispanic/Latino; 0.2% Two or more races, non-Hispanic/Latino; 8% Race/ethnicity unknown. *Retention:* 56% of full-time freshmen returned.

Academics *Calendar:* quarters. *Degree:* certificates, diplomas, and associate. *Special study options:* distance learning.

Financial Aid Of all full-time matriculated undergraduates who enrolled in 2011, 34 Federal Work-Study jobs (averaging $3090).

Applying *Options:* early admission. *Application fee:* $20. *Required:* high school transcript.

Freshman Application Contact Athens Technical College, 800 US Highway 29 North, Athens, GA 30601-1500. *Phone:* 706-355-5008. *Website:* http://www.athenstech.edu/.

Atlanta Metropolitan State College

Atlanta, Georgia

Freshman Application Contact Ms. Audrey Reid, Director, Office of Admissions, Atlanta Metropolitan State College, 1630 Metropolitan Parkway, SW, Atlanta, GA 30310-4498. *Phone:* 404-756-4004. *Fax:* 404-756-4407. *E-mail:* admissions@atlm.edu. *Website:* http://www.atlm.edu/.

Atlanta Technical College

Atlanta, Georgia

- **State-supported** 2-year, founded 1945, part of Technical College System of Georgia
- **Coed**

Undergraduates 1,463 full-time, 3,316 part-time. 0.2% are from out of state; 94% Black or African American, non-Hispanic/Latino; 1% Hispanic/Latino; 0.8% Asian, non-Hispanic/Latino; 0.1% American Indian or Alaska Native, non-Hispanic/Latino; 0.7% Race/ethnicity unknown. *Retention:* 50% of full-time freshmen returned.

Academics *Calendar:* quarters. *Degree:* certificates, diplomas, and associate. *Special study options:* distance learning, study abroad.

Applying *Options:* early admission. *Application fee:* $20. *Required:* high school transcript.

Freshman Application Contact Atlanta Technical College, 1560 Metropolitan Parkway, SW, Atlanta, GA 30310. *Phone:* 404-225-4455. *Website:* http://www.atlantatech.edu/.

Augusta Technical College

Augusta, Georgia

- **State-supported** 2-year, founded 1961, part of Technical College System of Georgia
- **Urban** campus
- **Coed**

Undergraduates 1,596 full-time, 3,035 part-time. 2% are from out of state; 52% Black or African American, non-Hispanic/Latino; 2% Hispanic/Latino; 2% Asian, non-Hispanic/Latino; 0.3% American Indian or Alaska Native, non-Hispanic/Latino; 0.1% Two or more races, non-Hispanic/Latino; 2% Race/ethnicity unknown. *Retention:* 49% of full-time freshmen returned.

Academics *Calendar:* quarters. *Degree:* certificates, diplomas, and associate. *Special study options:* distance learning.

Applying *Options:* early admission. *Application fee:* $20. *Required:* high school transcript.

Freshman Application Contact Augusta Technical College, 3200 Augusta Tech Drive, Augusta, GA 30906. *Phone:* 706-771-4150. *Website:* http://www.augustatech.edu/.

Bainbridge College
Bainbridge, Georgia

- **State-supported** 2-year, founded 1972, part of University System of Georgia
- **Small-town** 160-acre campus
- **Coed,** 2,938 undergraduate students, 51% full-time, 71% women, 29% men

Undergraduates 1,511 full-time, 1,427 part-time. Students come from 5 states and territories; 2% are from out of state; 56% Black or African American, non-Hispanic/Latino; 0.9% Hispanic/Latino; 0.3% Asian, non-Hispanic/Latino; 0.2% American Indian or Alaska Native, non-Hispanic/Latino; 0.7% Two or more races, non-Hispanic/Latino; 2% Race/ethnicity unknown.

Freshmen *Admission:* 1,030 applied, 688 admitted.

Faculty *Total:* 179, 41% full-time, 16% with terminal degrees.

Majors Accounting; administrative assistant and secretarial science; agriculture; art; biology/biological sciences; business administration and management; business teacher education; chemistry; criminal justice/law enforcement administration; data processing and data processing technology; drafting and design technology; dramatic/theater arts; education; electrical, electronic and communications engineering technology; elementary education; English; family and consumer sciences/human sciences; forestry; health teacher education; history; information science/studies; journalism; kindergarten/preschool education; liberal arts and sciences/liberal studies; licensed practical/vocational nurse training; marketing/marketing management; mathematics; political science and government; psychology; registered nursing/registered nurse; rhetoric and composition; sociology; welding technology.

Academics *Calendar:* semesters. *Degree:* certificates and associate. *Special study options:* academic remediation for entering students, adult/continuing education programs, advanced placement credit, distance learning, double majors, independent study, part-time degree program, services for LD students, study abroad, summer session for credit.

Library Bainbridge College Library with 45,366 titles, 83 serial subscriptions, 3,958 audiovisual materials, an OPAC.

Student Life *Housing:* college housing not available. *Activities and Organizations:* drama/theater group, choral group, Honors Club, Alpha Beta Gamma, Sigma Kappa Delta, History Club, Student Government Association. *Campus security:* 24-hour patrols. *Student services:* personal/psychological counseling.

Athletics *Intramural sports:* table tennis M/W, volleyball M/W.

Standardized Tests *Required for some:* SAT or ACT (for admission), ACT COMPASS.

Costs (2012–13) *Tuition:* state resident $2026 full-time, $84 per credit hour part-time; nonresident $7666 full-time, $319 per credit hour part-time. Full-time tuition and fees vary according to course load. Part-time tuition and fees vary according to course load. *Required fees:* $888 full-time, $444 per term part-time. *Waivers:* senior citizens and employees or children of employees.

Applying *Options:* electronic application, early admission. *Required for some:* high school transcript, minimum 1.8 GPA, 3 letters of recommendation, interview, immunizations/waivers, medical records and criminal. *Application deadlines:* rolling (freshmen), rolling (transfers). *Notification:* continuous (freshmen), continuous (transfers).

Freshman Application Contact Mr. Spencer Stewart, Director of Admissions and Records, Bainbridge College, 2500 East Shotwell Street, Bainbridge, GA 39819. *Phone:* 229-248-2504. *Toll-free phone:* 866-825-1715 (in-state); 888-825-1715 (out-of-state). *Fax:* 229-248-2525. *E-mail:* sstewart@bainbridge.edu.

Website: http://www.bainbridge.edu/.

Brown Mackie College–Atlanta
Atlanta, Georgia

Freshman Application Contact Brown Mackie College–Atlanta, 4370 Peachtree Road, NE, Atlanta, GA 30319. *Phone:* 404-799-4500.

Website: http://www.brownmackie.edu/atlanta/.

See display below and page 348 for the College Close-Up.

Central Georgia Technical College
Macon, Georgia

- **State-supported** 2-year, founded 1966, part of Technical College System of Georgia
- **Suburban** campus
- **Coed**

Undergraduates 2,685 full-time, 3,502 part-time. 64% Black or African American, non-Hispanic/Latino; 0.8% Hispanic/Latino; 0.7% Asian, non-Hispanic/Latino; 0.3% American Indian or Alaska Native, non-Hispanic/Latino; 0.4% Two or more races, non-Hispanic/Latino; 0.9% Race/ethnicity unknown. *Retention:* 43% of full-time freshmen returned.

Academics *Calendar:* quarters. *Degree:* certificates, diplomas, and associate. *Special study options:* distance learning.

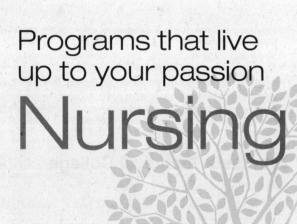

Financial Aid Of all full-time matriculated undergraduates who enrolled in 2011, 175 Federal Work-Study jobs (averaging $2000). *Financial aid deadline:* 9/1.

Applying *Options:* early admission. *Application fee:* $15. *Required:* high school transcript.

Freshman Application Contact Central Georgia Technical College, 3300 Macon Tech Drive, Macon, GA 31206. *Phone:* 770-531-6332. *Toll-free phone:* 866-430-0135.

Website: http://www.centralgatech.edu/.

Chattahoochee Technical College

Marietta, Georgia

- **State-supported** 2-year, founded 1961, part of Technical College System of Georgia
- **Suburban** campus
- **Coed**

Undergraduates 3,731 full-time, 8,427 part-time. 0.1% are from out of state; 33% Black or African American, non-Hispanic/Latino; 6% Hispanic/Latino; 2% Asian, non-Hispanic/Latino; 0.2% Native Hawaiian or other Pacific Islander, non-Hispanic/Latino; 0.4% American Indian or Alaska Native, non-Hispanic/Latino; 2% Two or more races, non-Hispanic/Latino; 1% Race/ethnicity unknown; 0.4% international. *Retention:* 49% of full-time freshmen returned.

Academics *Calendar:* quarters. *Degree:* certificates, diplomas, and associate. *Special study options:* distance learning.

Financial Aid Of all full-time matriculated undergraduates who enrolled in 2011, 40 Federal Work-Study jobs (averaging $2500).

Applying *Options:* early admission. *Application fee:* $15. *Required:* high school transcript.

Freshman Application Contact Chattahoochee Technical College, 980 South Cobb Drive, SE, Marietta, GA 30060. *Phone:* 770-757-3408.

Website: http://www.chattahoocheetech.edu/.

Columbus Technical College

Columbus, Georgia

- **State-supported** 2-year, founded 1961, part of Technical College System of Georgia
- **Urban** campus
- **Coed**

Undergraduates 1,188 full-time, 2,976 part-time. 14% are from out of state; 45% Black or African American, non-Hispanic/Latino; 7% Hispanic/Latino; 2% Asian, non-Hispanic/Latino; 0.3% Native Hawaiian or other Pacific Islander, non-Hispanic/Latino; 0.4% American Indian or Alaska Native, non-Hispanic/Latino; 1% Two or more races, non-Hispanic/Latino; 2% Race/ethnicity unknown; 0.1% international. *Retention:* 45% of full-time freshmen returned.

Academics *Calendar:* quarters. *Degree:* certificates, diplomas, and associate. *Special study options:* distance learning.

Financial Aid Of all full-time matriculated undergraduates who enrolled in 2011, 6 Federal Work-Study jobs (averaging $2000).

Applying *Options:* early admission. *Application fee:* $25. *Required:* high school transcript.

Freshman Application Contact Columbus Technical College, 928 Manchester Expressway, Columbus, GA 31904-6572. *Phone:* 706-649-1901.

Website: http://www.columbustech.edu/.

Darton State College

Albany, Georgia

- **State-supported** primarily 2-year, founded 1965, part of University System of Georgia
- **Urban** 185-acre campus
- **Endowment** $978,169
- **Coed,** 6,396 undergraduate students, 49% full-time, 70% women, 30% men

Undergraduates 3,137 full-time, 3,259 part-time. Students come from 33 states and territories; 46 other countries; 7% are from out of state; 45% Black or African American, non-Hispanic/Latino; 2% Hispanic/Latino; 0.9% Asian, non-Hispanic/Latino; 0.2% Native Hawaiian or other Pacific Islander, non-Hispanic/Latino; 0.4% American Indian or Alaska Native, non-Hispanic/Latino; 0.3% Two or more races, non-Hispanic/Latino; 0.6% Race/ethnicity unknown; 1% international; 15% transferred in. *Retention:* 53% of full-time freshmen returned.

Freshmen *Admission:* 1,251 enrolled. *Average high school GPA:* 2.73. *Test scores:* SAT critical reading scores over 500: 25%; SAT math scores over 500:

23%; SAT writing scores over 500: 17%; ACT scores over 18: 42%; SAT critical reading scores over 600: 6%; SAT math scores over 600: 4%; SAT writing scores over 600: 3%; ACT scores over 24: 5%; SAT critical reading scores over 700: 1%.

Faculty *Total:* 282, 43% full-time. *Student/faculty ratio:* 21:1.

Majors Accounting; agriculture; anthropology; art; art teacher education; behavioral aspects of health; biological and biomedical sciences related; biology/biological sciences; business administration and management; business teacher education; cardiovascular technology; chemistry; clinical laboratory science/medical technology; computer and information sciences; computer and information sciences and support services related; computer science; criminal justice/law enforcement administration; dance; dental hygiene; diagnostic medical sonography and ultrasound technology; drama and dance teacher education; dramatic/theater arts; economics; emergency medical technology (EMT paramedic); engineering technology; English; English/language arts teacher education; environmental studies; foreign languages and literatures; forensic science and technology; forestry; general studies; geography; health and physical education/fitness; health information/medical records administration; health information/medical records technology; health/medical preparatory programs related; histologic technician; history; history teacher education; journalism; mathematics; mathematics teacher education; middle school education; music; music teacher education; nuclear medical technology; occupational therapist assistant; philosophy; physical therapy technology; physics; political science and government; pre-dentistry studies; pre-engineering; pre-law studies; premedical studies; pre-pharmacy studies; pre-veterinary studies; psychology; registered nursing/registered nurse; respiratory care therapy; science teacher education; social work; sociology; special education; speech teacher education; trade and industrial teacher education.

Academics *Calendar:* semesters. *Degrees:* certificates, associate, bachelor's, and postbachelor's certificates. *Special study options:* academic remediation for entering students, accelerated degree program, adult/continuing education programs, advanced placement credit, cooperative education, distance learning, double majors, English as a second language, honors programs, independent study, off-campus study, part-time degree program, services for LD students, student-designed majors, study abroad, summer session for credit. *ROTC:* Army (c).

Library Weatherbee Learning Resources Center with 101,612 titles, 125 serial subscriptions, 5,182 audiovisual materials, an OPAC, a Web page.

Student Life *Housing Options:* coed. Campus housing is university owned. *Activities and Organizations:* drama/theater group, choral group, Cultural Exchange Club, Democratic, Independent, & Republican Team (D.I.R.T.), Human Services Club, Outdoor Adventure Club (OAC), Music Club. *Campus security:* 24-hour emergency response devices and patrols, student patrols, late-night transport/escort service, controlled dormitory access. *Student services:* health clinic, personal/psychological counseling.

Athletics Member NJCAA. *Intercollegiate sports:* baseball M(s), basketball W(s), cross-country running M(s)/W(s), golf M(s), soccer M(s)/W(s), softball W(s), swimming and diving M(s)/W(s), wrestling M. *Intramural sports:* badminton M/W, basketball M/W, bowling M/W, football M, racquetball M/W, table tennis M, volleyball M/W.

Standardized Tests *Required:* non-traditional students must take the COMPASS test (for admission). *Required for some:* SAT or ACT (for admission), SAT Subject Tests (for admission). *Recommended:* SAT or ACT (for admission), SAT Subject Tests (for admission).

Costs (2012–13) *Tuition:* state resident $2026 full-time, $84 per credit hour part-time; nonresident $7666 full-time, $319 per credit hour part-time. *Required fees:* $1144 full-time, $395 per course part-time. *Room and board:* $8730. Room and board charges vary according to board plan and housing facility. *Waivers:* senior citizens and employees or children of employees.

Financial Aid Of all full-time matriculated undergraduates who enrolled in 2011, 60 Federal Work-Study jobs.

Applying *Options:* electronic application, deferred entrance. *Application fee:* $20. *Required:* minimum 2.0 GPA, proof of immunization. *Required for some:* high school transcript. *Application deadlines:* 7/20 (freshmen), 7/20 (transfers). *Notification:* continuous until 7/27 (freshmen), continuous until 7/27 (transfers).

Freshman Application Contact Darton State College, 2400 Gillionville Road, Albany, GA 31707-3098. *Phone:* 229-430-6740. *Toll-free phone:* 866-775-1214.

Website: http://www.darton.edu/.

East Georgia State College

Swainsboro, Georgia

Freshman Application Contact East Georgia State College, 131 College Circle, Swainsboro, GA 30401-2699. *Phone:* 478-289-2017.

Website: http://www.ega.edu/.

Emory University, Oxford College

Oxford, Georgia

- **Independent Methodist** primarily 2-year, founded 1836
- **Small-town** 150-acre campus with easy access to Atlanta
- **Endowment** $39.0 million
- **Coed**

Undergraduates 936 full-time. Students come from 45 states and territories; 29 other countries; 61% are from out of state; 14% Black or African American, non-Hispanic/Latino; 6% Hispanic/Latino; 29% Asian, non-Hispanic/Latino; 0.1% Native Hawaiian or other Pacific Islander, non-Hispanic/Latino; 0.3% American Indian or Alaska Native, non-Hispanic/Latino; 3% Two or more races, non-Hispanic/Latino; 4% Race/ethnicity unknown; 15% international; 99% live on campus. *Retention:* 90% of full-time freshmen returned.
Faculty *Student/faculty ratio:* 14:1.
Academics *Calendar:* semesters. *Degrees:* associate and bachelor's. *Special study options:* advanced placement credit, double majors, independent study, internships, off-campus study, services for LD students, study abroad, summer session for credit. *ROTC:* Army (c), Navy (c), Air Force (c). *Unusual degree programs:* 3-2 engineering with Georgia Institute of Technology.
Student Life *Campus security:* 24-hour emergency response devices and patrols, student patrols, late-night transport/escort service, controlled dormitory access.
Athletics Member NJCAA.
Standardized Tests *Required:* SAT or ACT (for admission). *Required for some:* SAT Subject Tests (for admission).
Costs (2012–13) *Comprehensive fee:* $47,054 includes full-time tuition ($36,100), mandatory fees ($478), and room and board ($10,476). Part-time tuition: $1504 per contact hour. *Room and board:* college room only: $7196.
Financial Aid Of all full-time matriculated undergraduates who enrolled in 2011, 225 Federal Work-Study jobs (averaging $1600).
Applying *Options:* electronic application, early admission, early action, deferred entrance. *Application fee:* $50. *Required:* essay or personal statement, high school transcript, 1 letter of recommendation. *Required for some:* interview. *Recommended:* minimum 3.0 GPA, 2 letters of recommendation.
Freshman Application Contact Emory University, Oxford College, 100 Hamill Street, PO Box 1328, Oxford, GA 30054. *Phone:* 770-784-8328. *Toll-free phone:* 800-723-8328.
Website: http://oxford.emory.edu/.

Georgia Highlands College

Rome, Georgia

- **State-supported** 2-year, founded 1970, part of University System of Georgia
- **Suburban** 226-acre campus with easy access to Atlanta
- **Endowment** $31,769
- **Coed,** 5,532 undergraduate students, 50% full-time, 63% women, 37% men

Undergraduates 2,756 full-time, 2,776 part-time. Students come from 10 states and territories; 48 other countries; 1% are from out of state; 17% Black or African American, non-Hispanic/Latino; 7% Hispanic/Latino; 1% Asian, non-Hispanic/Latino; 0.2% Native Hawaiian or other Pacific Islander, non-Hispanic/Latino; 0.2% American Indian or Alaska Native, non-Hispanic/Latino; 2% Two or more races, non-Hispanic/Latino; 0.7% Race/ethnicity unknown; 9% transferred in. *Retention:* 56% of full-time freshmen returned.
Freshmen *Admission:* 1,044 enrolled. *Average high school GPA:* 2.7.
Faculty *Total:* 245, 56% full-time, 20% with terminal degrees. *Student/faculty ratio:* 22:1.
Majors Agriculture; art; biological and physical sciences; business administration and management; chemistry; clinical laboratory science/medical technology; communication and journalism related; computer and information sciences; criminal justice/police science; criminal justice/safety; dental hygiene; economics; education related; English; foreign languages and literatures; general studies; geology/earth science; health information/medical records administration; history; human services; journalism; liberal arts and sciences/liberal studies; marketing/marketing management; mathematics and statistics related; philosophy; physician assistant; physics; political science and government; pre-occupational therapy; pre-pharmacy studies; pre-physical therapy; psychology; registered nursing/registered nurse; respiratory therapy technician; secondary education; sociology.
Academics *Calendar:* semesters. *Degree:* associate. *Special study options:* academic remediation for entering students, advanced placement credit, cooperative education, distance learning, double majors, honors programs, independent study, part-time degree program, services for LD students, study abroad, summer session for credit.

Library Georgia Highlands College Library - Floyd Campus plus 1 other with 139,861 titles, 102 serial subscriptions, 9,247 audiovisual materials, an OPAC, a Web page.
Student Life *Housing:* college housing not available. *Activities and Organizations:* drama/theater group, student-run newspaper, Highlands Association of Nursing Students, Green Highlands, Black Awareness Society, Political Science Association, Phi Theta Kappa. *Campus security:* 24-hour emergency response devices and patrols, emergency phone/email alert system. *Student services:* personal/psychological counseling.
Athletics Member NJCAA. *Intercollegiate sports:* baseball M(s)/W(s), basketball M(s)/W(s), softball M(s)/W(s). *Intramural sports:* basketball M/W, cheerleading M/W, football M/W, golf M/W, skiing (downhill) M/W, table tennis M/W, tennis M/W, ultimate Frisbee M/W, volleyball M/W, weight lifting M/W.
Costs (2013–14) *Tuition:* state resident $2532 full-time, $84 per credit hour part-time; nonresident $9582 full-time, $319 per credit hour part-time. Full-time tuition and fees vary according to course load. Part-time tuition and fees vary according to course load. *Required fees:* $934 full-time, $467 per term part-time. *Waivers:* senior citizens.
Financial Aid Of all full-time matriculated undergraduates who enrolled in 2011, 50 Federal Work-Study jobs (averaging $3500).
Applying *Options:* electronic application, deferred entrance. *Application fee:* $20. *Required:* high school transcript, minimum 2.0 GPA. *Required for some:* minimum 2.2 GPA. *Application deadlines:* rolling (freshmen), rolling (out-of-state freshmen), rolling (transfers). *Notification:* continuous (freshmen), continuous (out-of-state freshmen), continuous (transfers).
Freshman Application Contact Sandra Davis, Director of Admissions, Georgia Highlands College, 3175 Cedartown Highway, Rome, GA 30161. *Phone:* 706-295-6339. *Toll-free phone:* 800-332-2406. *Fax:* 706-295-6341. *E-mail:* sdavis@highlands.edu.
Website: http://www.highlands.edu/.

Georgia Military College

Milledgeville, Georgia

- **State and locally supported** 2-year, founded 1879, part of Georgia Independent College Association (GICA)
- **Small-town** campus
- **Endowment** $12.8 million
- **Coed,** 8,071 undergraduate students, 67% full-time, 61% women, 39% men

Undergraduates 5,384 full-time, 2,687 part-time. Students come from 8 states and territories; 1% are from out of state; 43% Black or African American, non-Hispanic/Latino; 5% Hispanic/Latino; 1% Asian, non-Hispanic/Latino; 1% American Indian or Alaska Native, non-Hispanic/Latino; 0.7% Two or more races, non-Hispanic/Latino; 9% Race/ethnicity unknown; 14% transferred in; 10% live on campus. *Retention:* 55% of full-time freshmen returned.
Freshmen *Admission:* 1,748 enrolled.
Faculty *Total:* 429, 29% full-time. *Student/faculty ratio:* 25:1.
Majors Army ROTC/military science; biology/biological sciences; business administration and management; criminal justice/law enforcement administration; early childhood education; education; general studies; health services/allied health/health sciences; health teacher education; history; homeland security, law enforcement, firefighting and protective services related; human development and family studies; information technology; international relations and affairs; legal assistant/paralegal; logistics, materials, and supply chain management; mass communication/media; prenursing studies; psychology; public health education and promotion; secondary education; social sciences.
Academics *Calendar:* quarters. *Degree:* associate. *Special study options:* academic remediation for entering students, advanced placement credit, cooperative education, distance learning, double majors, independent study, off-campus study, part-time degree program, services for LD students, student-designed majors, study abroad, summer session for credit. *ROTC:* Army (b).
Library an OPAC, a Web page.
Student Life *Housing:* on-campus residence required through sophomore year. *Options:* coed. Campus housing is university owned. *Activities and Organizations:* drama/theater group, student-run newspaper, choral group, Student Government Association, Alpha Phi Omega National Service Fraternity, Phi Theta Kappa, Drama Club, Biology Club. *Campus security:* 24-hour emergency response devices and patrols, controlled dormitory access. *Student services:* health clinic.
Athletics Member NJCAA. *Intercollegiate sports:* cheerleading M/W, cross-country running M/W, football M(s), golf M, riflery M(s)/W(s), soccer M(s)/W(s), softball W(s). *Intramural sports:* soccer M/W, softball M/W.
Financial Aid Of all full-time matriculated undergraduates who enrolled in 2011, 4,394 applied for aid, 4,394 were judged to have need, 4,292 had their need fully met. In 2011, 1414 non-need-based awards were made. *Average percent of need met:* 54%. *Average financial aid package:* $6285. *Average need-based loan:* $3510. *Average need-based gift aid:* $6826. *Average non-need-based aid:* $15,237.

Applying *Options:* electronic application, early admission, deferred entrance. *Application fee:* $35. *Required for some:* essay or personal statement, high school transcript, interview. *Application deadlines:* rolling (freshmen), rolling (out-of-state freshmen), rolling (transfers).

Freshman Application Contact Georgia Military College, 201 East Greene Street, Old Capitol Building, Milledgeville, GA 31061-3398. *Phone:* 478-387-4948. *Toll-free phone:* 800-342-0413.
Website: http://www.gmc.cc.ga.us/.

Georgia Northwestern Technical College

Rome, Georgia

- **State-supported** 2-year, founded 1962, part of Technical College System of Georgia
- **Coed**

Undergraduates 2,411 full-time, 4,095 part-time. 0.9% are from out of state; 11% Black or African American, non-Hispanic/Latino; 4% Hispanic/Latino; 0.5% Asian, non-Hispanic/Latino; 0.1% Native Hawaiian or other Pacific Islander, non-Hispanic/Latino; 0.2% American Indian or Alaska Native, non-Hispanic/Latino; 1% Two or more races, non-Hispanic/Latino; 0.1% Race/ethnicity unknown. *Retention:* 49% of full-time freshmen returned.

Academics *Calendar:* quarters. *Degree:* certificates, diplomas, and associate. *Special study options:* distance learning.

Applying *Options:* early admission. *Application fee:* $15. *Required:* high school transcript.

Freshman Application Contact Georgia Northwestern Technical College, One Maurice Culberson Drive, Rome, GA 30161. *Phone:* 706-295-6933. *Toll-free phone:* 866-983-GNTC.
Website: http://www.gntc.edu/.

Georgia Perimeter College

Decatur, Georgia

Freshman Application Contact Georgia Perimeter College, 3251 Panthersville Road, Decatur, GA 30034-3897. *Phone:* 678-891-3250. *Toll-free phone:* 888-696-2780.
Website: http://www.gpc.edu/.

Georgia Piedmont Technical College

Clarkston, Georgia

- **State-supported** 2-year, founded 1961, part of Technical College System of Georgia
- **Suburban** campus
- **Coed**

Undergraduates 1,140 full-time, 3,404 part-time. 1% are from out of state; 77% Black or African American, non-Hispanic/Latino; 2% Hispanic/Latino; 2% Asian, non-Hispanic/Latino; 0.1% Native Hawaiian or other Pacific Islander, non-Hispanic/Latino; 0.2% American Indian or Alaska Native, non-Hispanic/Latino; 0.9% Two or more races, non-Hispanic/Latino; 0.8% Race/ethnicity unknown; 0.2% international. *Retention:* 46% of full-time freshmen returned.

Academics *Calendar:* quarters. *Degree:* certificates, diplomas, and associate. *Special study options:* distance learning.

Financial Aid Of all full-time matriculated undergraduates who enrolled in 2010, 7,200 applied for aid, 7,100 were judged to have need. 145 Federal Work-Study jobs (averaging $4000). *Average financial aid package:* $4500. *Average need-based gift aid:* $4500.

Applying *Options:* early admission. *Application fee:* $25. *Required:* high school transcript.

Freshman Application Contact Georgia Piedmont Technical College, 495 North Indian Creek Drive, Clarkston, GA 30021-2397. *Phone:* 404-297-9522 Ext. 1229.
Website: http://www.gptc.edu/.

Gordon State College

Barnesville, Georgia

- **State-supported** primarily 2-year, founded 1852, part of University System of Georgia
- **Small-town** 125-acre campus with easy access to Atlanta
- **Endowment** $7.5 million
- **Coed**, 4,171 undergraduate students

Undergraduates Students come from 9 states and territories; 1 other country; 0.1% are from out of state.

Freshmen *Admission:* 2,871 applied, 1,222 admitted.

Faculty *Total:* 207, 60% full-time, 52% with terminal degrees. *Student/faculty ratio:* 24:1.

Majors Art; astronomy; biological and biomedical sciences related; biology teacher education; business administration and management; chemistry; communication; computer science; criminal justice/safety; dental services and allied professions related; dramatic/theater arts; early childhood education; elementary education; English; English as a second/foreign language (teaching); English/language arts teacher education; environmental science; foreign languages and literatures; forestry; general studies; health and physical education/fitness; health/medical preparatory programs related; history; history teacher education; information technology; liberal arts and sciences/liberal studies; mathematics; mathematics teacher education; middle school education; music; physics; political science and government; pre-engineering; pre-occupational therapy; pre-pharmacy studies; pre-physical therapy; psychology; radiologic technology/science; registered nursing/registered nurse; secondary education; social work; sociology.

Academics *Calendar:* semesters. *Degrees:* certificates, associate, and bachelor's. *Special study options:* academic remediation for entering students, accelerated degree program, adult/continuing education programs, advanced placement credit, cooperative education, honors programs, internships, off-campus study, part-time degree program, study abroad, summer session for credit.

Library Hightower Library with 150,062 titles, 55,588 serial subscriptions, 5,037 audiovisual materials, an OPAC, a Web page.

Student Life *Housing:* on-campus residence required for freshman year. *Options:* coed. Campus housing is university owned. Freshman applicants given priority for college housing. *Activities and Organizations:* drama/theater group, student-run newspaper, choral group, Campus Activity Board, Student Government Association, Earth wind fire (Science Club), Student African American Brotherhood (SAAB), Swazi Step Team. *Campus security:* 24-hour emergency response devices and patrols, student patrols, late-night transport/escort service, controlled dormitory access, RA's and RDs (housing) and Parking Patrol (Public Safety). *Student services:* health clinic, personal/psychological counseling.

Athletics Member NJCAA. *Intercollegiate sports:* baseball M, basketball M, soccer M/W, softball M/W, track and field M/W.

Financial Aid Of all full-time matriculated undergraduates who enrolled in 2011, 75 Federal Work-Study jobs (averaging $1850).

Applying *Options:* electronic application, early admission, deferred entrance. *Application fee:* $20. *Required:* high school transcript. *Application deadlines:* rolling (freshmen), rolling (transfers).

Freshman Application Contact Gordon State College, 419 College Drive, Barnesville, GA 30204-1762. *Phone:* 678-359-5021. *Toll-free phone:* 800-282-6504.
Website: http://www.gordonstate.edu/.

Gupton-Jones College of Funeral Service

Decatur, Georgia

Freshman Application Contact Ms. Beverly Wheaton, Registrar, Gupton-Jones College of Funeral Service, 5141 Snapfinger Woods Drive, Decatur, GA 30035-4022. *Phone:* 770-593-2257. *Toll-free phone:* 800-848-5352.
Website: http://www.gupton-jones.edu/.

Gwinnett Technical College

Lawrenceville, Georgia

- **State-supported** 2-year, founded 1984, part of Technical College System of Georgia
- **Suburban** campus
- **Coed**

Undergraduates 2,514 full-time, 4,273 part-time. 0.1% are from out of state; 34% Black or African American, non-Hispanic/Latino; 10% Hispanic/Latino; 6% Asian, non-Hispanic/Latino; 0.1% Native Hawaiian or other Pacific Islander, non-Hispanic/Latino; 0.3% American Indian or Alaska Native, non-Hispanic/Latino; 2% Two or more races, non-Hispanic/Latino; 3% Race/ethnicity unknown. *Retention:* 51% of full-time freshmen returned.

Academics *Calendar:* quarters. *Degree:* certificates, diplomas, and associate. *Special study options:* distance learning.

Financial Aid Of all full-time matriculated undergraduates who enrolled in 2011, 20 Federal Work-Study jobs (averaging $2100).

Applying *Options:* early admission. *Application fee:* $20. *Required:* high school transcript.

Freshman Application Contact Gwinnett Technical College, 5150 Sugarloaf Parkway, Lawrenceville, GA 30043-5702. *Phone:* 678-762-7580 Ext. 434.
Website: http://www.gwinnetttech.edu/.

Interactive College of Technology
Chamblee, Georgia

Freshman Application Contact Director of Admissions, Interactive College of Technology, 5303 New Peachtree Road, Chamblee, GA 30341. *Phone:* 770-216-2960. *Toll-free phone:* 800-447-2011. *Fax:* 770-216-2988. *Website:* http://www.ict-ils.edu/.

ITT Technical Institute
Atlanta, Georgia

- **Proprietary** primarily 2-year, part of ITT Educational Services, Inc.
- **Coed**

Academics *Degrees:* associate and bachelor's.

Freshman Application Contact Director of Recruitment, ITT Technical Institute, 485 Oak Place, Suite 800, Atlanta, GA 30349. *Phone:* 404-765-4600. *Toll-free phone:* 877-488-6102 (in-state); 877-788-6102 (out-of-state). *Website:* http://www.itt-tech.edu/.

ITT Technical Institute
Duluth, Georgia

- **Proprietary** primarily 2-year, founded 2003, part of ITT Educational Services, Inc.
- **Coed**

Academics *Calendar:* quarters. *Degrees:* associate and bachelor's.

Freshman Application Contact Director of Recruitment, ITT Technical Institute, 10700 Abbotts Bridge Road, Duluth, GA 30097. *Phone:* 678-957-8510. *Toll-free phone:* 866-489-8818. *Website:* http://www.itt-tech.edu/.

ITT Technical Institute
Kennesaw, Georgia

- **Proprietary** primarily 2-year, founded 2004, part of ITT Educational Services, Inc.
- **Coed**

Academics *Calendar:* quarters. *Degrees:* associate and bachelor's.

Freshman Application Contact Director of Recruitment, ITT Technical Institute, 2065 ITT Tech Way NW, Kennesaw, GA 30144. *Phone:* 770-426-2300. *Toll-free phone:* 877-231-6415 (in-state); 800-231-6415 (out-of-state). *Website:* http://www.itt-tech.edu/.

Lanier Technical College
Oakwood, Georgia

- **State-supported** 2-year, founded 1964, part of Technical College System of Georgia
- **Coed**

Undergraduates 932 full-time, 2,790 part-time. 2% are from out of state; 10% Black or African American, non-Hispanic/Latino; 7% Hispanic/Latino; 2% Asian, non-Hispanic/Latino; 0.6% American Indian or Alaska Native, non-Hispanic/Latino; 0.7% Two or more races, non-Hispanic/Latino; 0.6% Race/ethnicity unknown; 0.1% international. *Retention:* 50% of full-time freshmen returned.

Academics *Calendar:* quarters. *Degree:* certificates, diplomas, and associate. *Special study options:* distance learning.

Applying *Options:* early admission. *Application fee:* $15. *Required:* high school transcript.

Freshman Application Contact Lanier Technical College, 2990 Landrum Education Drive, PO Box 58, Oakwood, GA 30566. *Phone:* 770-531-6332. *Website:* http://www.laniertech.edu/.

Le Cordon Bleu College of Culinary Arts, Atlanta
Tucker, Georgia

Freshman Application Contact Admissions Office, Le Cordon Bleu College of Culinary Arts, Atlanta, 1957 Lakeside Parkway, Tucker, GA 30084. *Toll-free phone:* 888-549-8222. *Website:* http://www.atlanticculinary.com/.

Middle Georgia Technical College
Warner Robbins, Georgia

- **State-supported** 2-year, founded 1973, part of Technical College System of Georgia
- **Coed**

Undergraduates 1,305 full-time, 2,740 part-time. 2% are from out of state; 42% Black or African American, non-Hispanic/Latino; 3% Hispanic/Latino; 1% Asian, non-Hispanic/Latino; 0.1% Native Hawaiian or other Pacific Islander, non-Hispanic/Latino; 0.3% American Indian or Alaska Native, non-Hispanic/Latino; 1% Two or more races, non-Hispanic/Latino; 2% Race/ethnicity unknown. *Retention:* 64% of full-time freshmen returned.

Academics *Calendar:* quarters. *Degree:* certificates, diplomas, and associate. *Special study options:* distance learning.

Applying *Options:* early admission. *Application fee:* $15. *Required:* high school transcript.

Freshman Application Contact Middle Georgia Technical College, 80 Cohen Walker Drive, Warner Robbins, GA 31088. *Phone:* 478-988-6800. *Toll-free phone:* 800-474-1031. *Website:* http://www.middlegatech.edu/.

Moultrie Technical College
Moultrie, Georgia

- **State-supported** 2-year, founded 1964, part of Technical College System of Georgia
- **Coed**

Undergraduates 948 full-time, 1,360 part-time. 0.5% are from out of state; 37% Black or African American, non-Hispanic/Latino; 4% Hispanic/Latino; 0.3% Asian, non-Hispanic/Latino; 0.3% American Indian or Alaska Native, non-Hispanic/Latino; 0.3% Two or more races, non-Hispanic/Latino; 2% Race/ethnicity unknown. *Retention:* 52% of full-time freshmen returned.

Academics *Calendar:* quarters. *Degree:* certificates, diplomas, and associate. *Special study options:* distance learning.

Applying *Options:* early admission. *Application fee:* $20. *Required:* high school transcript.

Freshman Application Contact Moultrie Technical College, 800 Veterans Parkway North, Moultrie, GA 31788. *Phone:* 229-528-4581. *Website:* http://www.moultrietech.edu/.

North Georgia Technical College
Clarkesville, Georgia

- **State-supported** 2-year, founded 1943, part of Technical College System of Georgia
- **Coed**

Undergraduates 1,138 full-time, 1,532 part-time. 7% Black or African American, non-Hispanic/Latino; 2% Hispanic/Latino; 0.9% Asian, non-Hispanic/Latino; 0.4% American Indian or Alaska Native, non-Hispanic/Latino; 1% Two or more races, non-Hispanic/Latino; 0.8% Race/ethnicity unknown. *Retention:* 53% of full-time freshmen returned.

Academics *Calendar:* quarters. *Degree:* certificates, diplomas, and associate. *Special study options:* distance learning.

Applying *Options:* early admission. *Application fee:* $15. *Required:* high school transcript.

Freshman Application Contact North Georgia Technical College, 1500 Georgia Highway 197, North, PO Box 65, Clarkesville, GA 30523. *Phone:* 706-754-7724. *Website:* http://www.northgatech.edu/.

Oconee Fall Line Technical College–North Campus
Sandersville, Georgia

- **State-supported** 2-year, part of Technical College System of Georgia
- **Coed**

Undergraduates 628 full-time, 1,306 part-time. 46% Black or African American, non-Hispanic/Latino; 1% Hispanic/Latino; 0.3% Asian, non-Hispanic/Latino; 0.2% American Indian or Alaska Native, non-Hispanic/Latino; 0.7% Two or more races, non-Hispanic/Latino; 0.6% Race/ethnicity unknown. *Retention:* 34% of full-time freshmen returned.

Academics *Calendar:* quarters. *Degree:* certificates, diplomas, and associate. *Special study options:* distance learning.

Applying *Options:* early admission. *Application fee:* $20. *Required:* high school transcript.

Freshman Application Contact Oconee Fall Line Technical College–North Campus, 1189 Deepstep Road, Sandersville, GA 31082. *Phone:* 478-553-

2050. *Toll-free phone:* 877-399-8324.
Website: http://www.oftc.edu/.

Oconee Fall Line Technical College– South Campus

Dublin, Georgia

Freshman Application Contact Oconee Fall Line Technical College–South Campus, 560 Pinehill Road, Dublin, GA 31021. *Phone:* 478-274-7837. *Toll-free phone:* 800-200-4484.
Website: http://www.oftc.edu/.

Ogeechee Technical College

Statesboro, Georgia

- **State-supported** 2-year, founded 1989, part of Technical College System of Georgia
- **Small-town** campus
- **Coed**

Undergraduates 914 full-time, 1,384 part-time. 36% Black or African American, non-Hispanic/Latino; 2% Hispanic/Latino; 0.7% Asian, non-Hispanic/Latino; 0.2% American Indian or Alaska Native, non-Hispanic/Latino; 1% Two or more races, non-Hispanic/Latino; 0.3% Race/ethnicity unknown. *Retention:* 50% of full-time freshmen returned.
Academics *Calendar:* quarters. *Degree:* certificates, diplomas, and associate. *Special study options:* distance learning.
Applying *Options:* early admission. *Application fee:* $25. *Required:* high school transcript.
Freshman Application Contact Ogeechee Technical College, One Joe Kennedy Boulevard, Statesboro, GA 30458. *Phone:* 912-871-1600. *Toll-free phone:* 800-646-1316.
Website: http://www.ogeecheetech.edu/.

Okefenokee Technical College

Waycross, Georgia

- **State-supported** 2-year, part of Technical College System of Georgia
- **Small-town** campus
- **Coed**

Undergraduates 429 full-time, 1,003 part-time. 0.1% are from out of state; 25% Black or African American, non-Hispanic/Latino; 3% Hispanic/Latino; 0.4% Asian, non-Hispanic/Latino; 0.6% American Indian or Alaska Native, non-Hispanic/Latino; 0.3% Two or more races, non-Hispanic/Latino; 0.4% Race/ethnicity unknown. *Retention:* 47% of full-time freshmen returned.
Academics *Calendar:* quarters. *Degree:* certificates, diplomas, and associate. *Special study options:* distance learning.
Applying *Options:* early admission. *Application fee:* $20. *Required:* high school transcript.
Freshman Application Contact Okefenokee Technical College, 1701 Carswell Avenue, Waycross, GA 31503. *Phone:* 912-338-5251. *Toll-free phone:* 877-ED-AT-OTC.
Website: http://www.okefenokeetech.edu/.

Savannah Technical College

Savannah, Georgia

- **State-supported** 2-year, founded 1929, part of Technical College System of Georgia
- **Urban** campus
- **Coed**

Undergraduates 1,648 full-time, 3,350 part-time. 2% are from out of state; 46% Black or African American, non-Hispanic/Latino; 6% Hispanic/Latino; 2% Asian, non-Hispanic/Latino; 0.2% Native Hawaiian or other Pacific Islander, non-Hispanic/Latino; 0.5% American Indian or Alaska Native, non-Hispanic/Latino; 2% Two or more races, non-Hispanic/Latino; 0.4% Race/ethnicity unknown; 1% international. *Retention:* 42% of full-time freshmen returned.
Academics *Calendar:* quarters. *Degree:* certificates, diplomas, and associate. *Special study options:* distance learning.
Applying *Options:* early admission. *Application fee:* $20. *Required:* high school transcript.
Freshman Application Contact Savannah Technical College, 5717 White Bluff Road, Savannah, GA 31405. *Phone:* 912-443-5711. *Toll-free phone:* 800-769-6362.
Website: http://www.savannahtech.edu/.

Southeastern Technical College

Vidalia, Georgia

- **State-supported** 2-year, founded 1989, part of Technical College System of Georgia
- **Coed**

Undergraduates 576 full-time, 1,334 part-time. 1% are from out of state; 34% Black or African American, non-Hispanic/Latino; 3% Hispanic/Latino; 0.1% Asian, non-Hispanic/Latino; 0.4% American Indian or Alaska Native, non-Hispanic/Latino; 0.2% Two or more races, non-Hispanic/Latino; 0.1% Race/ethnicity unknown; 0.1% international. *Retention:* 55% of full-time freshmen returned.
Academics *Calendar:* quarters. *Degree:* certificates, diplomas, and associate. *Special study options:* distance learning.
Applying *Options:* early admission. *Application fee:* $20. *Required:* high school transcript.
Freshman Application Contact Southeastern Technical College, 3001 East First Street, Vidalia, GA 30474. *Phone:* 912-538-3121.
Website: http://www.southeasterntech.edu/.

Southern Crescent Technical College

Griffin, Georgia

- **State-supported** 2-year, founded 1965, part of Technical College System of Georgia
- **Small-town** campus
- **Coed**

Undergraduates 2,058 full-time, 3,323 part-time. 0.1% are from out of state; 42% Black or African American, non-Hispanic/Latino; 3% Hispanic/Latino; 1% Asian, non-Hispanic/Latino; 0.1% Native Hawaiian or other Pacific Islander, non-Hispanic/Latino; 0.2% American Indian or Alaska Native, non-Hispanic/Latino; 2% Two or more races, non-Hispanic/Latino; 0.2% Race/ethnicity unknown. *Retention:* 53% of full-time freshmen returned.
Academics *Calendar:* quarters. *Degree:* certificates, diplomas, and associate. *Special study options:* distance learning.
Applying *Options:* early admission. *Application fee:* $15. *Required:* high school transcript.
Freshman Application Contact Southern Crescent Technical College, 501 Varsity Road, Griffin, GA 30223. *Phone:* 770-646-6160.
Website: http://www.sctech.edu/.

South Georgia State College

Douglas, Georgia

Freshman Application Contact South Georgia State College, 100 West College Park Drive, Douglas, GA 31533-5098. *Phone:* 912-260-4419. *Toll-free phone:* 800-342-6364.
Website: http://www.sgc.edu/.

South Georgia State College

Waycross, Georgia

Freshman Application Contact South Georgia State College, 2001 South Georgia Parkway, Waycross, GA 31503-9248. *Phone:* 912-449-7600.
Website: http://www.waycross.edu/.

South Georgia Technical College

Americus, Georgia

- **State-supported** 2-year, founded 1948, part of Technical College System of Georgia
- **Coed**

Undergraduates 1,102 full-time, 1,259 part-time. 1% are from out of state; 58% Black or African American, non-Hispanic/Latino; 1% Hispanic/Latino; 0.7% Asian, non-Hispanic/Latino; 0.2% American Indian or Alaska Native, non-Hispanic/Latino; 1% Race/ethnicity unknown. *Retention:* 47% of full-time freshmen returned.
Academics *Calendar:* quarters. *Degree:* certificates, diplomas, and associate. *Special study options:* distance learning.
Applying *Options:* early admission. *Application fee:* $20. *Required:* high school transcript.
Freshman Application Contact South Georgia Technical College, 900 South Georgia Tech Parkway, Americus, GA 31709. *Phone:* 229-931-2299.
Website: http://www.southgatech.edu/.

Southwest Georgia Technical College

Thomasville, Georgia

- **State-supported** 2-year, founded 1963, part of Technical College System of Georgia
- **Coed**

Undergraduates 405 full-time, 1,466 part-time. 2% are from out of state; 35% Black or African American, non-Hispanic/Latino; 2% Hispanic/Latino; 0.6% Asian, non-Hispanic/Latino; 0.1% Native Hawaiian or other Pacific Islander, non-Hispanic/Latino; 0.5% American Indian or Alaska Native, non-Hispanic/Latino; 0.4% Two or more races, non-Hispanic/Latino; 0.6% Race/ethnicity unknown. *Retention:* 56% of full-time freshmen returned.

Academics *Calendar:* quarters. *Degree:* certificates, diplomas, and associate. *Special study options:* distance learning.

Applying *Options:* electronic application, early admission. *Application fee:* $20. *Required:* high school transcript.

Freshman Application Contact Southwest Georgia Technical College, 15689 US 19 North, Thomasville, GA 31792. *Phone:* 229-225-5089. *Website:* http://www.southwestgatech.edu/.

Virginia College in Macon

Macon, Georgia

Admissions Office Contact Virginia College in Macon, 1901 Paul Walsh Drive, Macon, GA 31206. *Website:* http://www.vc.edu/.

West Georgia Technical College

Waco, Georgia

- **State-supported** 2-year, founded 1966, part of Technical College System of Georgia
- **Coed**

Undergraduates 2,082 full-time, 5,763 part-time. 3% are from out of state; 29% Black or African American, non-Hispanic/Latino; 3% Hispanic/Latino; 0.8% Asian, non-Hispanic/Latino; 0.1% Native Hawaiian or other Pacific Islander, non-Hispanic/Latino; 0.5% American Indian or Alaska Native, non-Hispanic/Latino; 2% Race/ethnicity unknown. *Retention:* 52% of full-time freshmen returned.

Academics *Calendar:* quarters. *Degree:* certificates, diplomas, and associate. *Special study options:* distance learning.

Financial Aid Of all full-time matriculated undergraduates who enrolled in 2011, 68 Federal Work-Study jobs (averaging $800).

Applying *Options:* early admission. *Application fee:* $25. *Required:* high school transcript.

Freshman Application Contact West Georgia Technical College, 176 Murphy Campus Boulevard, Waco, GA 30182. *Phone:* 770-537-5719. *Website:* http://www.westgatech.edu/.

Wiregrass Georgia Technical College

Valdosta, Georgia

- **State-supported** 2-year, founded 1963, part of Technical College System of Georgia
- **Suburban** campus
- **Coed**

Undergraduates 1,894 full-time, 2,849 part-time. 1% are from out of state; 37% Black or African American, non-Hispanic/Latino; 2% Hispanic/Latino; 0.6% Asian, non-Hispanic/Latino; 0.1% Native Hawaiian or other Pacific Islander, non-Hispanic/Latino; 0.4% American Indian or Alaska Native, non-Hispanic/Latino; 0.6% Two or more races, non-Hispanic/Latino; 1% Race/ethnicity unknown. *Retention:* 48% of full-time freshmen returned.

Academics *Calendar:* quarters. *Degree:* certificates, diplomas, and associate. *Special study options:* distance learning.

Applying *Options:* early admission. *Application fee:* $15. *Required:* high school transcript.

Freshman Application Contact Wiregrass Georgia Technical College, 4089 Val Tech Road, Valdosta, GA 31602. *Phone:* 229-468-2278. *Website:* http://www.wiregrass.edu/.

GUAM

Guam Community College

Barrigada, Guam

Freshman Application Contact Mr. Patrick L. Clymer, Registrar, Guam Community College, PO Box 23069, Sesame Street, Barrigada, GU 96921. *Phone:* 671-735-5561. *Fax:* 671-735-5531. *E-mail:* patrick.clymer@guamcc.edu. *Website:* http://www.guamcc.net/.

HAWAII

Hawaii Community College

Hilo, Hawaii

Director of Admissions Mrs. Tammy M. Tanaka, Admissions Specialist, Hawaii Community College, 200 West Kawili Street, Hilo, HI 96720-4091. *Phone:* 808-974-7661. *Website:* http://www.hawcc.hawaii.edu/.

Hawaii Tokai International College

Honolulu, Hawaii

Freshman Application Contact Ms. Morna Dexter, Director, Student Services, Hawaii Tokai International College, 2241 Kapiolani Boulevard, Honolulu, HI 96826. *Phone:* 808-983-4187. *Fax:* 808-983-4173. *E-mail:* studentservices@tokai.edu. *Website:* http://www.hawaiitokai.edu/.

Heald College–Honolulu

Honolulu, Hawaii

Freshman Application Contact Director of Admissions, Heald College–Honolulu, 1500 Kapiolani Boulevard, Honolulu, HI 96814. *Phone:* 808-955-1500. *Toll-free phone:* 800-88-HEALD. *Fax:* 808-955-6964. *E-mail:* honoluluinfo@heald.edu. *Website:* http://www.heald.edu/.

Honolulu Community College

Honolulu, Hawaii

Freshman Application Contact Ms. Grace Funai, Admissions Office, Honolulu Community College, 874 Dillingham Boulevard, Honolulu, HI 96817. *Phone:* 808-845-9129. *E-mail:* honcc@hawaii.edu. *Website:* http://www.honolulu.hawaii.edu/.

Kapiolani Community College

Honolulu, Hawaii

Freshman Application Contact Kapiolani Community College, 4303 Diamond Head Road, Honolulu, HI 96816-4421. *Phone:* 808-734-9555. *Website:* http://kapiolani.hawaii.edu/page/home.

Kauai Community College

Lihue, Hawaii

Freshman Application Contact Mr. Leighton Oride, Admissions Officer and Registrar, Kauai Community College, 3-1901 Kaumualii Highway, Lihue, HI 96766. *Phone:* 808-245-8225. *Fax:* 808-245-8297. *E-mail:* arkauai@hawaii.edu. *Website:* http://kauai.hawaii.edu/.

Leeward Community College

Pearl City, Hawaii

Freshman Application Contact Ms. Anna Donald, Office Assistant, Leeward Community College, 96-045 Ala Ike, Pearl City, HI 96782-3393. *Phone:* 808-455-0642. *Website:* http://www.lcc.hawaii.edu/.

Remington College–Honolulu Campus

Honolulu, Hawaii

Director of Admissions Louis LaMair, Director of Recruitment, Remington College–Honolulu Campus, 1111 Bishop Street, Suite 400, Honolulu, HI 96813. *Phone:* 808-942-1000. *Fax:* 808-533-3064. *E-mail:* louis.lamair@ remingtoncollege.edu.
Website: http://www.remingtoncollege.edu/.

University of Hawaii Maui College

Kahului, Hawaii

Freshman Application Contact Mr. Stephen Kameda, Director of Admissions and Records, University of Hawaii Maui College, 310 Kaahumanu Avenue, Kahului, HI 96732. *Phone:* 808-984-3267. *Toll-free phone:* 800-479-6692. *Fax:* 808-242-9618. *E-mail:* kameda@hawaii.edu.
Website: http://maui.hawaii.edu/.

Windward Community College

Kaneohe, Hawaii

Director of Admissions Geri Imai, Registrar, Windward Community College, 45-720 Keaahala Road, Kaneohe, HI 96744-3528. *Phone:* 808-235-7430. *E-mail:* gerii@hawaii.edu.
Website: http://www.wcc.hawaii.edu/.

IDAHO

Brown Mackie College–Boise

Boise, Idaho

Freshman Application Contact Brown Mackie College–Boise, 9050 West Overland Road, Suite 100, Boise, ID 83709. *Phone:* 208-321-8800.
Website: http://www.brownmackie.edu/boise/.

See display below and page 352 for the College Close-Up.

Carrington College–Boise

Boise, Idaho

- **Proprietary** 2-year, founded 1980, part of Carrington Colleges Group, Inc.
- **Coed,** 508 undergraduate students, 100% full-time, 82% women, 18% men

Undergraduates 508 full-time. 2% Black or African American, non-Hispanic/Latino; 13% Hispanic/Latino; 3% Asian, non-Hispanic/Latino; 0.8% Native Hawaiian or other Pacific Islander, non-Hispanic/Latino; 1% American Indian or Alaska Native, non-Hispanic/Latino; 2% Two or more races, non-Hispanic/Latino; 0.8% Race/ethnicity unknown.

Freshmen *Admission:* 37 enrolled.

Faculty *Total:* 45, 42% full-time. *Student/faculty ratio:* 18:1.

Majors Dental assisting; dental hygiene; massage therapy; medical/clinical assistant; medical insurance/medical billing; medical office management; pharmacy technician; physical therapy technology; registered nursing/registered nurse.

Academics *Calendar:* semesters. *Degree:* certificates and associate.

Library an OPAC.

Student Life *Housing:* college housing not available.

Applying *Required:* essay or personal statement, high school transcript, interview, Entrance test administered by Carrington College.

Freshman Application Contact Carrington College–Boise, 1122 North Liberty Street, Boise, ID 83704.
Website: http://carrington.edu/.

College of Southern Idaho

Twin Falls, Idaho

Freshman Application Contact Director of Admissions, Registration, and Records, College of Southern Idaho, PO Box 1238, Twin Falls, ID 83303-1238. *Phone:* 208-732-6232. *Toll-free phone:* 800-680-0274. *Fax:* 208-736-3014.
Website: http://www.csi.edu/.

College of Western Idaho
Nampa, Idaho

Admissions Office Contact College of Western Idaho, 2407 Caldwell Boulevard, Nampa, ID 83651.
Website: http://cwidaho.cc/.

Eastern Idaho Technical College
Idaho Falls, Idaho

- **State-supported** 2-year, founded 1970
- **Small-town** 40-acre campus
- **Endowment** $789,503
- **Coed,** 702 undergraduate students, 40% full-time, 64% women, 36% men

Undergraduates 278 full-time, 424 part-time. Students come from 2 states and territories; 1 other country; 0.4% Black or African American, non-Hispanic/Latino; 11% Hispanic/Latino; 1% Asian, non-Hispanic/Latino; 1% Native Hawaiian or other Pacific Islander, non-Hispanic/Latino; 0.7% American Indian or Alaska Native, non-Hispanic/Latino; 0.6% Two or more races, non-Hispanic/Latino; 8% Race/ethnicity unknown; 1% international; 22% transferred in.
Freshmen *Admission:* 527 applied, 265 admitted, 60 enrolled.
Faculty *Total:* 68, 59% full-time. *Student/faculty ratio:* 13:1.
Majors Accounting; administrative assistant and secretarial science; automobile/automotive mechanics technology; computer systems networking and telecommunications; dental assisting; desktop publishing and digital imaging design; diesel mechanics technology; fire science/firefighting; legal assistant/paralegal; licensed practical/vocational nurse training; marketing/marketing management; medical/clinical assistant; nuclear and industrial radiologic technologies related; registered nursing/registered nurse; surgical technology; truck and bus driver/commercial vehicle operation/instruction; welding technology.
Academics *Calendar:* semesters. *Degree:* certificates and associate. *Special study options:* academic remediation for entering students, adult/continuing education programs, advanced placement credit, English as a second language, part-time degree program, services for LD students, summer session for credit.
Library Richard and Lila Jordan Library plus 1 other with 18,000 titles, 125 serial subscriptions, 150 audiovisual materials, an OPAC, a Web page.
Student Life *Housing:* college housing not available. *Campus security:* 24-hour patrols. *Student services:* personal/psychological counseling.
Standardized Tests *Required:* COMPASS (for admission).
Costs (2012–13) *Tuition:* state resident $1932 full-time, $90 per credit part-time; nonresident $7078 full-time, $180 per credit part-time. *Required fees:* $15 per term part-time. *Waivers:* employees or children of employees.
Financial Aid Of all full-time matriculated undergraduates who enrolled in 2011, 37 Federal Work-Study jobs (averaging $1176). 11 state and other part-time jobs (averaging $1619).
Applying *Options:* deferred entrance. *Application fee:* $10. *Required:* high school transcript, interview. *Required for some:* essay or personal statement. *Application deadline:* rolling (freshmen).
Freshman Application Contact Annalea Avery, Director of Admissions, Eastern Idaho Technical College, 1600 South 25th East, Idaho Falls, ID 83404. *Phone:* 208-524-3000 Ext. 3337. *Toll-free phone:* 800-662-0261. *Fax:* 208-524-0429. *E-mail:* Annalea.avery@my.eitc.edu. *Website:* http://www.eitc.edu/.

ITT Technical Institute
Boise, Idaho

- **Proprietary** primarily 2-year, founded 1906, part of ITT Educational Services, Inc.
- **Urban** campus
- **Coed**

Academics *Calendar:* quarters. *Degrees:* associate and bachelor's.
Financial Aid Of all full-time matriculated undergraduates who enrolled in 2011, 9 Federal Work-Study jobs (averaging $5500).
Freshman Application Contact Director of Recruitment, ITT Technical Institute, 12302 West Explorer Drive, Boise, ID 83713. *Phone:* 208-322-8844. *Toll-free phone:* 800-666-4888. *Fax:* 208-322-0173. *Website:* http://www.itt-tech.edu/.

North Idaho College
Coeur d'Alene, Idaho

Freshman Application Contact North Idaho College, 1000 West Garden Avenue, Coeur d Alene, ID 83814-2199. *Phone:* 208-769-3303. *Toll-free*
phone: 877-404-4536 Ext. 3311. *E-mail:* admit@nic.edu. *Website:* http://www.nic.edu/.

ILLINOIS

Benedictine University at Springfield
Springfield, Illinois

Freshman Application Contact Kevin Hinkle, Associate Director of Admissions, Benedictine University at Springfield, 1500 North Fifth Street, Springfield, IL 62702. *Phone:* 217-525-1420 Ext. 321. *Toll-free phone:* 800-635-7289. *Fax:* 217-525-1497. *E-mail:* khinkle@sci.edu. *Website:* http://www1.ben.edu/springfield/.

Black Hawk College
Moline, Illinois

Freshman Application Contact Ms. Vashti Berry, College Recruiter, Black Hawk College, 6600-34th Avenue, Moline, IL 61265. *Phone:* 309-796-5341. *Toll-free phone:* 800-334-1311. *E-mail:* berryv@bhc.edu. *Website:* http://www.bhc.edu/.

Carl Sandburg College
Galesburg, Illinois

Director of Admissions Ms. Carol Kreider, Dean of Student Support Services, Carl Sandburg College, 2400 Tom L. Wilson Boulevard, Galesburg, IL 61401-9576. *Phone:* 309-341-5234. *Website:* http://www.sandburg.edu/.

City Colleges of Chicago, Harold Washington College
Chicago, Illinois

Freshman Application Contact Admissions Office, City Colleges of Chicago, Harold Washington College, 30 East Lake Street, Chicago, IL 60601-2449. *Phone:* 312-553-6010. *Website:* http://hwashington.ccc.edu/.

City Colleges of Chicago, Harry S. Truman College
Chicago, Illinois

- **State and locally supported** 2-year, founded 1956, part of City Colleges of Chicago
- **Urban** 5-acre campus
- **Coed**

Faculty *Student/faculty ratio:* 34:1.
Academics *Calendar:* semesters. *Degree:* certificates, diplomas, and associate. *Special study options:* academic remediation for entering students, adult/continuing education programs, advanced placement credit, cooperative education, distance learning, English as a second language, honors programs, internships, part-time degree program, services for LD students, summer session for credit.
Student Life *Campus security:* 24-hour patrols, late-night transport/escort service.
Athletics Member NJCAA.
Financial Aid Of all full-time matriculated undergraduates who enrolled in 2011, 150 Federal Work-Study jobs (averaging $3000).
Applying *Options:* early admission, deferred entrance.
Freshman Application Contact City Colleges of Chicago, Harry S. Truman College, 1145 West Wilson Avenue, Chicago, IL 60640-5616. *Phone:* 773-907-4000 Ext. 1112. *Website:* http://www.trumancollege.edu/.

City Colleges of Chicago, Kennedy-King College
Chicago, Illinois

Freshman Application Contact Admissions Office, City Colleges of Chicago, Kennedy-King College, 6301 South Halstead Street, Chicago, IL 60621. *Phone:* 773-602-5062. *Fax:* 773-602-5055. *Website:* http://kennedyking.ccc.edu/.

City Colleges of Chicago, Malcolm X College
Chicago, Illinois

Freshman Application Contact Ms. Kimberly Hollingsworth, Dean of Student Services, City Colleges of Chicago, Malcolm X College, 1900 West Van Buren Street, Chicago, IL 60612-3145. *Phone:* 312-850-7120. *Fax:* 312-850-7119. *E-mail:* khollingsworth@ccc.edu. *Website:* http://malcolmx.ccc.edu/.

City Colleges of Chicago, Olive-Harvey College
Chicago, Illinois

Freshman Application Contact City Colleges of Chicago, Olive-Harvey College, 10001 South Woodlawn Avenue, Chicago, IL 60628-1645. *Phone:* 773-291-6362. *Website:* http://oliveharvey.ccc.edu/.

City Colleges of Chicago, Richard J. Daley College
Chicago, Illinois

Freshman Application Contact City Colleges of Chicago, Richard J. Daley College, 7500 South Pulaski Road, Chicago, IL 60652-1242. *Phone:* 773-838-7606. *Website:* http://daley.ccc.edu/.

City Colleges of Chicago, Wilbur Wright College
Chicago, Illinois

Freshman Application Contact Ms. Amy Aiello, Assistant Dean of Student Services, City Colleges of Chicago, Wilbur Wright College, Chicago, IL 60634. *Phone:* 773-481-8207. *Fax:* 773-481-8185. *E-mail:* aaiello@ccc.edu. *Website:* http://wright.ccc.edu/.

College of DuPage
Glen Ellyn, Illinois

- **State and locally supported** 2-year, founded 1967
- **Suburban** 297-acre campus with easy access to Chicago
- **Endowment** $7.4 million
- **Coed**

Undergraduates 9,464 full-time, 16,745 part-time. Students come from 24 states and territories; 1% are from out of state; 7% Black or African American, non-Hispanic/Latino; 22% Hispanic/Latino; 9% Asian, non-Hispanic/Latino; 0.2% American Indian or Alaska Native, non-Hispanic/Latino; 2% Two or more races, non-Hispanic/Latino; 1% Race/ethnicity unknown; 0.4% international; 13% transferred in. *Retention:* 60% of full-time freshmen returned.
Faculty *Student/faculty ratio:* 21:1.
Academics *Calendar:* semesters. *Degree:* certificates and associate. *Special study options:* academic remediation for entering students, accelerated degree program, adult/continuing education programs, advanced placement credit, cooperative education, distance learning, double majors, English as a second language, external degree program, honors programs, independent study, internships, off-campus study, part-time degree program, services for LD students, student-designed majors, study abroad, summer session for credit.
Student Life *Campus security:* 24-hour emergency response devices and patrols, student patrols, late-night transport/escort service.
Athletics Member NJCAA.
Standardized Tests *Recommended:* ACT (for admission).
Costs (2012–13) *Tuition:* area resident $4080 full-time, $136 per credit hour part-time; state resident $9690 full-time, $323 per credit hour part-time; nonresident $11,790 full-time, $393 per credit hour part-time. Full-time tuition and fees vary according to program. Part-time tuition and fees vary according to program. *Payment plans:* installment, deferred payment.
Financial Aid Of all full-time matriculated undergraduates who enrolled in 2011, 424 Federal Work-Study jobs (averaging $4135).
Applying *Options:* early admission, deferred entrance. *Application fee:* $20.
Freshman Application Contact College of DuPage, IL. *E-mail:* admissions@cod.edu. *Website:* http://www.cod.edu/.

College of Lake County
Grayslake, Illinois

- **District-supported** 2-year, founded 1967, part of Illinois Community College Board
- **Suburban** 226-acre campus with easy access to Chicago, Milwaukee
- **Coed,** 17,577 undergraduate students, 28% full-time, 55% women, 45% men

Undergraduates 4,945 full-time, 12,632 part-time. Students come from 42 other countries; 1% are from out of state; 9% Black or African American, non-Hispanic/Latino; 29% Hispanic/Latino; 5% Asian, non-Hispanic/Latino; 0.1% Native Hawaiian or other Pacific Islander, non-Hispanic/Latino; 0.2% American Indian or Alaska Native, non-Hispanic/Latino; 1% Two or more races, non-Hispanic/Latino; 7% Race/ethnicity unknown.
Freshmen *Admission:* 1,860 enrolled.
Faculty *Total:* 1,032, 20% full-time, 16% with terminal degrees. *Student/faculty ratio:* 17:1.
Majors Accounting technology and bookkeeping; administrative assistant and secretarial science; architectural drafting and CAD/CADD; art; automobile/automotive mechanics technology; biological and physical sciences; business administration and management; business automation/technology/data entry; chemical technology; child-care provision; civil engineering technology; computer installation and repair technology; computer programming (specific applications); computer systems networking and telecommunications; construction engineering technology; criminal justice/police science; dental hygiene; electrical, electronic and communications engineering technology; electrician; engineering; fire prevention and safety technology; heating, air conditioning, ventilation and refrigeration maintenance technology; industrial mechanics and maintenance technology; landscaping and groundskeeping; liberal arts and sciences/liberal studies; machine shop technology; mechanical engineering/mechanical technology; medical office management; medical radiologic technology; music; music teacher education; natural resources management and policy; ornamental horticulture; professional, technical, business, and scientific writing; registered nursing/registered nurse; restaurant, culinary, and catering management; selling skills and sales; social work; substance abuse/addiction counseling; turf and turfgrass management.
Academics *Calendar:* semesters. *Degree:* certificates and associate. *Special study options:* academic remediation for entering students, adult/continuing education programs, advanced placement credit, cooperative education, distance learning, double majors, English as a second language, honors programs, independent study, internships, off-campus study, part-time degree program, services for LD students, student-designed majors, study abroad, summer session for credit.
Library College of Lake County Library plus 1 other with 99,037 titles, 457 serial subscriptions, an OPAC, a Web page.
Student Life *Housing:* college housing not available. *Activities and Organizations:* drama/theater group, student-run newspaper, radio station, choral group, Latino Alliance, Men of Vision, Asian Student Alliance, Student Government Association, Anime. *Campus security:* 24-hour emergency response devices and patrols, late-night transport/escort service. *Student services:* health clinic, personal/psychological counseling, women's center.
Athletics Member NJCAA. *Intercollegiate sports:* baseball M(s), basketball M(s)/W(s), cross-country running M(s)/W(s), golf M(s), soccer M(s)/W(s), softball W(s), tennis M(s)/W(s), volleyball W(s). *Intramural sports:* cheerleading W, golf M/W.
Costs (2013–14) *Tuition:* area resident $2790 full-time, $93 per credit hour part-time; state resident $7200 full-time, $240 per credit hour part-time; nonresident $9705 full-time, $324 per credit hour part-time. *Required fees:* $570 full-time, $19 per credit hour part-time. *Payment plan:* installment. *Waivers:* senior citizens and employees or children of employees.
Financial Aid Of all full-time matriculated undergraduates who enrolled in 2011, 98 Federal Work-Study jobs (averaging $1311).
Applying *Options:* electronic application, early admission, deferred entrance. *Required for some:* high school transcript, interview. *Application deadlines:* rolling (freshmen), rolling (transfers). *Notification:* continuous (freshmen), continuous (transfers).
Freshman Application Contact Director, Student Recruitment, College of Lake County, Grayslake, IL 60030-1198. *Phone:* 847-543-2383. *Fax:* 847-543-3061. *Website:* http://www.clcillinois.edu/.

The College of Office Technology
Chicago, Illinois

Director of Admissions Mr. William Bolton, Director of Admissions, The College of Office Technology, 1520 West Division Street, Chicago, IL 60622. *Phone:* 773-278-0042. *Toll-free phone:* 800-953-6161. *E-mail:* bbolton@cot.edu. *Website:* http://www.cot.edu/.

Danville Area Community College
Danville, Illinois

Freshman Application Contact Danville Area Community College, 2000 East Main Street, Danville, IL 61832-5199. *Phone:* 217-443-8803. *Website:* http://www.dacc.edu/.

Elgin Community College
Elgin, Illinois

- **State and locally supported** 2-year, founded 1949, part of Illinois Community College Board
- **Suburban** 145-acre campus with easy access to Chicago
- **Coed,** 11,554 undergraduate students, 34% full-time, 55% women, 45% men

Undergraduates 3,910 full-time, 7,644 part-time. Students come from 4 states and territories; 15 other countries; 0.2% are from out of state; 5% Black or African American, non-Hispanic/Latino; 36% Hispanic/Latino; 7% Asian, non-Hispanic/Latino; 0.1% Native Hawaiian or other Pacific Islander, non-Hispanic/Latino; 0.3% American Indian or Alaska Native, non-Hispanic/Latino; 3% Race/ethnicity unknown; 0.7% international; 4% transferred in.
Freshmen *Admission:* 1,295 enrolled.
Faculty *Total:* 598, 22% full-time, 13% with terminal degrees. *Student/faculty ratio:* 23:1.
Majors Accounting; administrative assistant and secretarial science; animation, interactive technology, video graphics and special effects; automobile/automotive mechanics technology; baking and pastry arts; biological and physical sciences; biology/biotechnology laboratory technician; business administration and management; CAD/CADD drafting/design technology; clinical/medical laboratory technology; computer and information systems security; criminal justice/police science; culinary arts; data entry/microcomputer applications; design and visual communications; engineering; entrepreneurship; executive assistant/executive secretary; fine/studio arts; fire science/firefighting; graphic design; health and physical education/fitness; heating, air conditioning, ventilation and refrigeration maintenance technology; industrial mechanics and maintenance technology; legal assistant/paralegal; liberal arts and sciences/liberal studies; machine tool technology; marketing/marketing management; music; physical therapy technology; radiologic technology/science; registered nursing/registered nurse; restaurant, culinary, and catering management; retailing; social work.
Academics *Calendar:* semesters. *Degree:* certificates, diplomas, and associate. *Special study options:* academic remediation for entering students, accelerated degree program, advanced placement credit, cooperative education, distance learning, double majors, English as a second language, honors programs, independent study, internships, off-campus study, part-time degree program, services for LD students, study abroad, summer session for credit.
Library Renner Learning Resource Center with an OPAC, a Web page.
Student Life *Housing:* college housing not available. *Activities and Organizations:* drama/theater group, student-run newspaper, choral group, Phi Theta Kappa Honor Society, Organization of Latin American Students, Asian Filipino Club, Amnesty International, Student Government. *Campus security:* grounds are patrolled Sunday-Saturday 7am-11pm during the academic year. *Student services:* personal/psychological counseling, legal services.
Athletics Member NJCAA. *Intercollegiate sports:* baseball M(s), basketball M(s)/W(s), cross-country running M(s)/W(s), golf M(s), soccer M(s)/W(s), softball W(s), tennis M(s)/W(s), volleyball W(s).
Applying *Options:* electronic application. *Required for some:* high school transcript, some academic programs have additional departmental admission requirements that students must meet. *Application deadlines:* rolling (freshmen), rolling (transfers). *Notification:* continuous (freshmen), continuous (transfers).
Freshman Application Contact Admissions, Recruitment, and Student Life, Elgin Community College, 1700 Spartan Drive, Elgin, IL 60123. *Phone:* 847-214-7414. *E-mail:* admissions@elgin.edu.
Website: http://www.elgin.edu/.

Fox College
Bedford Park, Illinois

- **Private** 2-year, founded 1932
- **Suburban** campus
- **Coed,** 447 undergraduate students
- **62%** of applicants were admitted

Freshmen *Admission:* 1,071 applied, 667 admitted.
Majors Accounting technology and bookkeeping; administrative assistant and secretarial science; graphic design; hotel/motel administration; medical/clinical assistant; physical therapy technology; retailing; veterinary/animal health technology.

Academics *Degree:* diplomas and associate. *Special study options:* accelerated degree program, internships.
Student Life *Housing:* college housing not available.
Freshman Application Contact Admissions Office, Fox College, 6640 South Cicero, Bedford Park, IL 60638. *Phone:* 708-444-4500.
Website: http://www.foxcollege.edu/.

Gem City College
Quincy, Illinois

Director of Admissions Admissions Director, Gem City College, PO Box 179, Quincy, IL 62301. *Phone:* 217-222-0391.
Website: http://www.gemcitycollege.com/.

Harper College
Palatine, Illinois

- **State and locally supported** 2-year, founded 1965, part of Illinois Community College Board
- **Suburban** 200-acre campus with easy access to Chicago
- **Endowment** $4.0 million
- **Coed,** 14,673 undergraduate students, 38% full-time, 56% women, 44% men

Undergraduates 5,550 full-time, 9,123 part-time. Students come from 9 states and territories; 1% are from out of state; 4% Black or African American, non-Hispanic/Latino; 18% Hispanic/Latino; 9% Asian, non-Hispanic/Latino; 0.2% American Indian or Alaska Native, non-Hispanic/Latino; 6% Race/ethnicity unknown; 4% transferred in. *Retention:* 67% of full-time freshmen returned.
Freshmen *Admission:* 3,274 applied, 3,274 admitted, 1,592 enrolled. *Test scores:* ACT scores over 18: 73%; ACT scores over 24: 22%; ACT scores over 30: 3%.
Faculty *Total:* 827, 25% full-time. *Student/faculty ratio:* 19:1.
Majors Accounting; administrative assistant and secretarial science; architectural drafting and CAD/CADD; architectural engineering technology; art; banking and financial support services; biology/biological sciences; business administration and management; cardiovascular technology; chemistry; childcare provision; computer and information sciences; computer programming; computer programming (specific applications); computer science; criminal justice/law enforcement administration; cyber/computer forensics and counterterrorism; dental hygiene; diagnostic medical sonography and ultrasound technology; dietetics; dietetic technology; early childhood education; electrical, electronic and communications engineering technology; elementary education; emergency medical technology (EMT paramedic); engineering; English; environmental studies; fashion and fabric consulting; fashion/apparel design; fashion merchandising; finance; fine/studio arts; fire science/firefighting; food service systems administration; health teacher education; heating, air conditioning, ventilation and refrigeration maintenance technology; history; homeland security; hospitality administration; humanities; human services; interior design; international business/trade/commerce; legal administrative assistant/secretary; legal assistant/paralegal; liberal arts and sciences/liberal studies; marketing/marketing management; mathematics; medical administrative assistant and medical secretary; medical/clinical assistant; music; nanotechnology; philosophy; physical education teaching and coaching; physical sciences; psychology; public relations, advertising, and applied communication related; radiologic technology/science; registered nursing/registered nurse; sales, distribution, and marketing operations; small business administration; sociology and anthropology; speech communication and rhetoric; theater/theater arts management; web page, digital/multimedia and information resources design.
Academics *Calendar:* semesters. *Degree:* certificates and associate. *Special study options:* academic remediation for entering students, accelerated degree program, adult/continuing education programs, advanced placement credit, cooperative education, distance learning, English as a second language, honors programs, independent study, internships, part-time degree program, services for LD students, study abroad, summer session for credit.
Library Harper College Library with 128,068 titles, 242 serial subscriptions, 17,540 audiovisual materials, an OPAC, a Web page.
Student Life *Housing:* college housing not available. *Activities and Organizations:* drama/theater group, student-run newspaper, radio station, choral group, Student Radio Station, Program Board, Student Senate, Nursing Club, Phi Theta Kappa. *Campus security:* 24-hour emergency response devices and patrols, late-night transport/escort service. *Student services:* health clinic, personal/psychological counseling, women's center, legal services.
Athletics Member NJCAA. *Intercollegiate sports:* baseball M, basketball M/W, cross-country running M/W, football M, soccer M/W, softball W, track and field M/W, volleyball W, wrestling M. *Intramural sports:* baseball M, basketball M, football M, racquetball M/W, softball M/W, table tennis M/W, tennis M/W, volleyball M/W.
Costs (2013–14) *Tuition:* area resident $3255 full-time, $109 per credit hour part-time; state resident $10,965 full-time, $366 per credit hour part-time; non-

resident $13,230 full-time, $441 per credit hour part-time. Full-time tuition and fees vary according to course load and program. Part-time tuition and fees vary according to course load and program. No tuition increase for student's term of enrollment. *Payment plans:* installment, deferred payment. *Waivers:* senior citizens and employees or children of employees.

Financial Aid Of all full-time matriculated undergraduates who enrolled in 2011, 85 Federal Work-Study jobs (averaging $1210).

Applying *Options:* electronic application, early admission, deferred entrance. *Application fee:* $25. *Required:* high school transcript. *Application deadlines:* rolling (freshmen), rolling (transfers). *Notification:* continuous (freshmen), continuous (transfers).

Freshman Application Contact Admissions Office, Harper College, 1200 West Algonquin Road, Palatine, IL 60067. *Phone:* 847-925-6700. *Fax:* 847-925-6044. *E-mail:* admissions@harpercollege.edu. *Website:* http://goforward.harpercollege.edu/.

Heartland Community College

Normal, Illinois

Freshman Application Contact Ms. Candace Brownlee, Director of Student Recruitment, Heartland Community College, 1500 West Raab Road, Normal, IL 61761. *Phone:* 309-268-8041. *Fax:* 309-268-7992. *E-mail:* candace.brownlee@heartland.edu. *Website:* http://www.heartland.edu/.

Highland Community College

Freeport, Illinois

- **State and locally supported** 2-year, founded 1962, part of Illinois Community College Board
- **Rural** 240-acre campus
- **Coed,** 2,064 undergraduate students, 51% full-time, 62% women, 38% men

Undergraduates 1,062 full-time, 1,002 part-time. 3% are from out of state; 10% Black or African American, non-Hispanic/Latino; 2% Hispanic/Latino; 0.7% Asian, non-Hispanic/Latino; 0.1% Native Hawaiian or other Pacific Islander, non-Hispanic/Latino; 2% American Indian or Alaska Native, non-Hispanic/Latino; 3% Two or more races, non-Hispanic/Latino; 2% Race/ethnicity unknown; 4% transferred in.

Freshmen *Admission:* 710 applied, 710 admitted, 463 enrolled.

Faculty *Total:* 140, 32% full-time, 6% with terminal degrees. *Student/faculty ratio:* 18:1.

Majors Accounting; agricultural business and management; autobody/collision and repair technology; automobile/automotive mechanics technology; biological and physical sciences; child-care provision; early childhood education; emergency medical technology (EMT paramedic); engineering; general studies; graphic design; health information/medical records technology; heavy equipment maintenance technology; horse husbandry/equine science and management; industrial technology; information technology; liberal arts and sciences/liberal studies; mathematics teacher education; medical/clinical assistant; registered nursing/registered nurse; special education; teacher assistant/aide.

Academics *Calendar:* semesters. *Degree:* certificates and associate. *Special study options:* academic remediation for entering students, adult/continuing education programs, advanced placement credit, cooperative education, distance learning, English as a second language, external degree program, honors programs, independent study, internships, part-time degree program, services for LD students, student-designed majors, summer session for credit.

Library Clarence Mitchell Library with 71 serial subscriptions, 6,843 audiovisual materials, an OPAC, a Web page.

Student Life *Housing:* college housing not available. *Activities and Organizations:* drama/theater group, student-run newspaper, radio station, choral group, Phi Theta Kappa, Royal Scots, Prairie Wind, intramurals, Collegiate Choir. *Campus security:* 24-hour emergency response devices and patrols. *Student services:* personal/psychological counseling.

Athletics Member NJCAA. *Intercollegiate sports:* baseball M(s), basketball M(s)/W(s), bowling M(s)/W(s), golf M(s)/W(s), softball W(s), volleyball W(s). *Intramural sports:* basketball M/W, volleyball M/W.

Costs (2012–13) *Tuition:* area resident $3150 full-time, $105 per credit hour part-time; state resident $4530 full-time, $151 per credit hour part-time; nonresident $5250 full-time, $175 per credit hour part-time. Full-time tuition and fees vary according to program and reciprocity agreements. Part-time tuition and fees vary according to program and reciprocity agreements. *Required fees:* $270 full-time, $9 per credit hour part-time. *Payment plans:* installment, deferred payment. *Waivers:* minority students, senior citizens, and employees or children of employees.

Financial Aid Of all full-time matriculated undergraduates who enrolled in 2011, 955 applied for aid, 841 were judged to have need, 1 had their need fully met. 53 Federal Work-Study jobs (averaging $1540). In 2011, 28 non-need-based awards were made. *Average percent of need met:* 41%. *Average financial aid package:* $6313. *Average need-based loan:* $3330. *Average need-based gift aid:* $5751. *Average non-need-based aid:* $3907.

Applying *Options:* electronic application, early admission, deferred entrance. *Required for some:* high school transcript, 1 letter of recommendation. *Recommended:* high school transcript. *Application deadlines:* rolling (freshmen), rolling (transfers).

Freshman Application Contact Mr. Jeremy Bradt, Director, Enrollment and Records, Highland Community College, 2998 West Pearl City Road, Freeport, IL 61032. *Phone:* 815-235-6121 Ext. 3500. *Fax:* 815-235-6130. *E-mail:* jeremy.bradt@highland.edu. *Website:* http://www.highland.edu/.

Illinois Central College

East Peoria, Illinois

- **State and locally supported** 2-year, founded 1967, part of Illinois Community College Board
- **Suburban** 430-acre campus
- **Coed,** 11,125 undergraduate students, 37% full-time, 57% women, 43% men

Undergraduates 4,123 full-time, 7,002 part-time. Students come from 31 states and territories; 4 other countries; 1% are from out of state; 12% Black or African American, non-Hispanic/Latino; 4% Hispanic/Latino; 2% Asian, non-Hispanic/Latino; 0.1% Native Hawaiian or other Pacific Islander, non-Hispanic/Latino; 0.3% American Indian or Alaska Native, non-Hispanic/Latino; 3% Two or more races, non-Hispanic/Latino; 4% Race/ethnicity unknown; 2% transferred in. *Retention:* 59% of full-time freshmen returned.

Freshmen *Admission:* 4,829 applied, 1,961 admitted, 967 enrolled.

Faculty *Total:* 633, 29% full-time, 8% with terminal degrees. *Student/faculty ratio:* 18:1.

Majors Accounting; accounting technology and bookkeeping; administrative assistant and secretarial science; agricultural business and management; agricultural/farm supplies retailing and wholesaling; agricultural mechanics and equipment technology; agricultural production; animal/livestock husbandry and production; animation, interactive technology, video graphics and special effects; applied horticulture/horticulture operations; automobile/automotive mechanics technology; banking and financial support services; business administration and management; child-care provision; clinical/medical laboratory technology; communications technology; community health services counseling; computer programming; computer systems networking and telecommunications; construction engineering; construction engineering technology; corrections; criminal justice/police science; crop production; culinary arts; data entry/microcomputer applications; data processing and data processing technology; dental hygiene; diesel mechanics technology; electrical, electronic and communications engineering technology; emergency medical technology (EMT paramedic); energy management and systems technology; engineering; fire science/firefighting; forensic science and technology; general studies; graphic design; health and physical education/fitness; heating, air conditioning, ventilation and refrigeration maintenance technology; home furnishings and equipment installation; hospital and health-care facilities administration; industrial electronics technology; industrial technology; legal assistant/paralegal; liberal arts and sciences/liberal studies; library and archives assisting; manufacturing engineering technology; mechanical engineering/mechanical technology; mental health counseling; occupational therapist assistant; physical therapy technology; platemaking/imaging; psychiatric/mental health services technology; radiologic technology/science; real estate; registered nursing/registered nurse; respiratory care therapy; retailing; robotics technology; security and loss prevention; selling skills and sales; sign language interpretation and translation; substance abuse/addiction counseling; surgical technology; teacher assistant/aide; web/multimedia management and webmaster; web page, digital/multimedia and information resources design; welding technology.

Academics *Calendar:* semesters. *Degree:* certificates and associate. *Special study options:* academic remediation for entering students, adult/continuing education programs, advanced placement credit, English as a second language, honors programs, independent study, internships, part-time degree program, services for LD students, summer session for credit.

Library Illinois Central College Library plus 2 others with 92,550 titles, 5,341 audiovisual materials, an OPAC, a Web page.

Student Life *Housing Options:* Campus housing is provided by a third party. *Activities and Organizations:* drama/theater group, student-run newspaper, radio station, choral group. *Campus security:* 24-hour emergency response devices and patrols, late-night transport/escort service. *Student services:* health clinic, personal/psychological counseling.

Athletics Member NJCAA. *Intercollegiate sports:* baseball M, basketball M/W, cross-country running M, golf M, soccer M/W, softball W, volleyball W.

Costs (2013–14) *Tuition:* area resident $2760 full-time, $115 per credit hour part-time; state resident $6120 full-time, $255 per credit hour part-time; nonresident $6120 full-time, $255 per credit hour part-time. Full-time tuition and fees vary according to course load. Part-time tuition and fees vary according to course load. *Room and board:* Room and board charges vary according to housing facility. *Payment plan:* installment. *Waivers:* senior citizens and employees or children of employees.

Financial Aid Of all full-time matriculated undergraduates who enrolled in 2011, 6,521 applied for aid, 5,525 were judged to have need.

Applying *Options:* electronic application, early admission. *Required:* high school transcript. *Application deadlines:* rolling (freshmen), rolling (out-of-state freshmen), rolling (transfers). *Notification:* continuous (freshmen), continuous (out-of-state freshmen), continuous (transfers).

Freshman Application Contact Angela Dreessen, Illinois Central College, East Peoria, IL. *Phone:* 309-694-5353.
Website: http://www.icc.edu/.

Illinois Eastern Community Colleges, Frontier Community College

Fairfield, Illinois

- **State and locally supported** 2-year, founded 1976, part of Illinois Eastern Community College System
- **Rural** 8-acre campus
- **Coed,** 2,597 undergraduate students, 11% full-time, 64% women, 36% men

Undergraduates 278 full-time, 2,319 part-time. 1% are from out of state; 0.7% Black or African American, non-Hispanic/Latino; 0.8% Hispanic/Latino; 0.4% Asian, non-Hispanic/Latino; 0.3% American Indian or Alaska Native, non-Hispanic/Latino; 0.1% Race/ethnicity unknown.

Freshmen *Admission:* 110 enrolled.

Faculty *Total:* 218, 3% full-time. *Student/faculty ratio:* 21:1.

Majors Administrative assistant and secretarial science; automobile/automotive mechanics technology; biological and physical sciences; business automation/technology/data entry; construction trades; corrections; emergency care attendant (EMT ambulance); engineering; fire science/firefighting; general studies; health information/medical records technology; information technology; liberal arts and sciences/liberal studies; quality control technology; registered nursing/registered nurse.

Academics *Calendar:* semesters. *Degree:* certificates and associate. *Special study options:* academic remediation for entering students, adult/continuing education programs, advanced placement credit, cooperative education, distance learning, double majors, English as a second language, external degree program, independent study, part-time degree program, services for LD students, student-designed majors, summer session for credit.

Library 19,244 titles, 96 serial subscriptions, 2,659 audiovisual materials.

Student Life *Housing:* college housing not available.

Costs (2013–14) *Tuition:* area resident $2464 full-time, $77 per semester hour part-time; state resident $7840 full-time, $245 per semester hour part-time; nonresident $9920 full-time, $310 per semester hour part-time. *Required fees:* $490 full-time, $15 per semester hour part-time, $5 per term part-time. *Waivers:* senior citizens and employees or children of employees.

Applying *Options:* early admission, deferred entrance. *Required:* high school transcript. *Application deadlines:* rolling (freshmen), rolling (transfers). *Notification:* continuous (freshmen), continuous (transfers).

Freshman Application Contact Ms. Mary Atkins, Coordinator of Registration and Records, Illinois Eastern Community Colleges, Frontier Community College, Frontier Drive, Fairfield, IL 62837. *Phone:* 618-842-3711 Ext. 4111. *Fax:* 618-842-6340. *E-mail:* atkinsm@iecc.edu.
Website: http://www.iecc.edu/fcc/.

Illinois Eastern Community Colleges, Lincoln Trail College

Robinson, Illinois

- **State and locally supported** 2-year, founded 1969, part of Illinois Eastern Community College System
- **Rural** 120-acre campus
- **Coed,** 1,055 undergraduate students, 41% full-time, 59% women, 41% men

Undergraduates 436 full-time, 619 part-time. 4% are from out of state; 2% Black or African American, non-Hispanic/Latino; 1% Hispanic/Latino; 1% Asian, non-Hispanic/Latino; 0.1% American Indian or Alaska Native, non-Hispanic/Latino.

Freshmen *Admission:* 142 enrolled.

Faculty *Total:* 81, 22% full-time. *Student/faculty ratio:* 18:1.

Majors Biological and physical sciences; business automation/technology/data entry; computer systems networking and telecommunications; construction trades; corrections; general studies; health information/medical records administration; liberal arts and sciences/liberal studies; mechanical engineering/mechanical technology; quality control technology; teacher assistant/aide; telecommunications technology.

Academics *Calendar:* semesters. *Degree:* certificates and associate. *Special study options:* academic remediation for entering students, adult/continuing education programs, advanced placement credit, cooperative education, distance learning, double majors, English as a second language, external degree program, independent study, internships, part-time degree program, services for LD students, student-designed majors, summer session for credit.

Library Eagleton Learning Resource Center plus 1 other with 15,563 titles, 34 serial subscriptions, 652 audiovisual materials.

Student Life *Housing:* college housing not available. *Activities and Organizations:* drama/theater group, choral group, national fraternities.

Athletics Member NJCAA. *Intercollegiate sports:* baseball M(s), basketball M(s)/W(s), softball W(s). *Intramural sports:* baseball M, basketball M, softball W.

Costs (2013–14) *Tuition:* area resident $2464 full-time, $77 per semester hour part-time; state resident $7840 full-time, $245 per semester hour part-time; nonresident $9920 full-time, $310 per semester hour part-time. *Required fees:* $490 full-time, $15 per semester hour part-time, $5 per term part-time. *Waivers:* senior citizens and employees or children of employees.

Applying *Options:* early admission, deferred entrance. *Required:* high school transcript. *Application deadlines:* rolling (freshmen), rolling (transfers). *Notification:* continuous (freshmen), continuous (transfers).

Freshman Application Contact Ms. Becky Mikeworth, Director of Admissions, Illinois Eastern Community Colleges, Lincoln Trail College, 11220 State Highway 1, Robinson, IL 62454. *Phone:* 618-544-8657 Ext. 1137. *Fax:* 618-544-7423. *E-mail:* mikeworthb@iecc.edu.
Website: http://www.iecc.edu/ltc/.

Illinois Eastern Community Colleges, Olney Central College

Olney, Illinois

- **State and locally supported** 2-year, founded 1962, part of Illinois Eastern Community College System
- **Rural** 128-acre campus
- **Coed,** 1,477 undergraduate students, 47% full-time, 67% women, 33% men

Undergraduates 692 full-time, 785 part-time. 2% are from out of state; 2% Black or African American, non-Hispanic/Latino; 0.7% Hispanic/Latino; 1% Asian, non-Hispanic/Latino; 0.2% American Indian or Alaska Native, non-Hispanic/Latino.

Freshmen *Admission:* 283 enrolled.

Faculty *Total:* 108, 39% full-time. *Student/faculty ratio:* 16:1.

Majors Accounting; administrative assistant and secretarial science; autobody/collision and repair technology; automobile/automotive mechanics technology; biological and physical sciences; business automation/technology/data entry; engineering; general studies; industrial mechanics and maintenance technology; liberal arts and sciences/liberal studies; medical administrative assistant and medical secretary; medical radiologic technology; registered nursing/registered nurse.

Academics *Calendar:* semesters. *Degree:* certificates and associate. *Special study options:* academic remediation for entering students, adult/continuing education programs, advanced placement credit, cooperative education, distance learning, double majors, English as a second language, external degree program, independent study, internships, part-time degree program, services for LD students, student-designed majors, summer session for credit.

Library Anderson Learning Resources Center plus 1 other with 21,020 titles, 22 serial subscriptions, 1,156 audiovisual materials.

Student Life *Housing:* college housing not available. *Activities and Organizations:* drama/theater group, student-run newspaper, choral group.

Athletics Member NJCAA. *Intercollegiate sports:* baseball M(s), basketball M(s)/W(s), softball W(s). *Intramural sports:* baseball M, basketball M/W, softball W.

Costs (2013–14) *Tuition:* area resident $2464 full-time, $77 per semester hour part-time; state resident $7840 full-time, $245 per semester hour part-time; nonresident $9920 full-time, $310 per semester hour part-time. *Required fees:* $490 full-time, $15 per semester hour part-time, $5 per term part-time. *Waivers:* senior citizens and employees or children of employees.

Applying *Options:* early admission, deferred entrance. *Required:* high school transcript. *Application deadlines:* rolling (freshmen), rolling (transfers). *Notification:* continuous (freshmen), continuous (transfers).

Freshman Application Contact Ms. Chris Webber, Assistant Dean for Student Services, Illinois Eastern Community Colleges, Olney Central College, 305 North West Street, Olney, IL 62450. *Phone:* 618-395-7777 Ext. 2005. *Fax:* 618-392-5212. *E-mail:* webberc@iecc.edu.
Website: http://www.iecc.edu/occ/.

Illinois Eastern Community Colleges, Wabash Valley College

Mount Carmel, Illinois

- **State and locally supported** 2-year, founded 1960, part of Illinois Eastern Community College System
- **Rural** 40-acre campus
- **Coed,** 4,706 undergraduate students, 12% full-time, 42% women, 58% men

Undergraduates 585 full-time, 4,121 part-time. 4% are from out of state; 4% Black or African American, non-Hispanic/Latino; 0.8% Hispanic/Latino; 1% Asian, non-Hispanic/Latino; 0.3% American Indian or Alaska Native, non-Hispanic/Latino; 0.3% Race/ethnicity unknown.
Freshmen *Admission:* 347 enrolled.
Faculty *Total:* 120, 29% full-time. *Student/faculty ratio:* 43:1.
Majors Administrative assistant and secretarial science; agricultural business and management; agricultural production; biological and physical sciences; business administration and management; business automation/technology/data entry; child development; diesel mechanics technology; energy management and systems technology; engineering; general studies; industrial technology; legal assistant/paralegal; liberal arts and sciences/liberal studies; machine tool technology; manufacturing engineering technology; mining technology; radio and television; social work.
Academics *Calendar:* semesters. *Degree:* certificates and associate. *Special study options:* academic remediation for entering students, adult/continuing education programs, advanced placement credit, cooperative education, distance learning, double majors, English as a second language, external degree program, independent study, internships, part-time degree program, services for LD students, student-designed majors, summer session for credit.
Library Bauer Media Center plus 1 other with 32,811 titles, 21,649 serial subscriptions, 1,480 audiovisual materials.
Student Life *Housing:* college housing not available. *Activities and Organizations:* drama/theater group, student-run newspaper, radio and television station, choral group.
Athletics Member NJCAA. *Intercollegiate sports:* baseball M(s), basketball M(s)/W(s), softball W(s). *Intramural sports:* baseball M, basketball M/W, softball W.
Costs (2013–14) *Tuition:* area resident $2464 full-time, $77 per semester hour part-time; state resident $7840 full-time, $245 per semester hour part-time; nonresident $9920 full-time, $310 per semester hour part-time. *Required fees:* $490 full-time, $15 per semester hour part-time, $5 per term part-time. *Waivers:* senior citizens and employees or children of employees.
Applying *Options:* early admission, deferred entrance. *Required:* high school transcript. *Application deadlines:* rolling (freshmen), rolling (transfers). *Notification:* continuous (freshmen), continuous (transfers).
Freshman Application Contact Mrs. Diana Spear, Assistant Dean for Student Services, Illinois Eastern Community Colleges, Wabash Valley College, 2200 College Drive, Mt. Carmel, IL 62863. *Phone:* 618-262-8641 Ext. 3101. *Fax:* 618-262-8641. *E-mail:* speard@iecc.edu.
Website: http://www.iecc.edu/wvc/.

Illinois Valley Community College

Oglesby, Illinois

- **District-supported** 2-year, founded 1924, part of Illinois Community College Board
- **Rural** 410-acre campus with easy access to Chicago
- **Endowment** $3.7 million
- **Coed**

Undergraduates 1,881 full-time, 2,474 part-time. Students come from 1 other state; 1% are from out of state; 2% Black or African American, non-Hispanic/Latino; 9% Hispanic/Latino; 1% Asian, non-Hispanic/Latino; 0.3% American Indian or Alaska Native, non-Hispanic/Latino; 0.2% Two or more races, non-Hispanic/Latino; 53% Race/ethnicity unknown; 37% transferred in. *Retention:* 52% of full-time freshmen returned.
Faculty *Student/faculty ratio:* 18:1.
Academics *Calendar:* semesters. *Degree:* certificates and associate. *Special study options:* academic remediation for entering students, advanced placement credit, distance learning, English as a second language, honors programs, independent study, internships, off-campus study, part-time degree program, services for LD students, student-designed majors, study abroad, summer session for credit.
Student Life *Campus security:* 24-hour emergency response devices and patrols, late-night transport/escort service.
Athletics Member NJCAA.
Standardized Tests *Recommended:* ACT (for admission).
Costs (2012–13) *Tuition:* area resident $2720 full-time, $84 per credit part-time; state resident $7808 full-time, $244 per credit part-time; nonresident $8720 full-time, $273 per credit part-time. Full-time tuition and fees vary according to course load. Part-time tuition and fees vary according to course load. *Required fees:* $247 full-time, $7 per credit hour part-time, $5 part-time.
Financial Aid Of all full-time matriculated undergraduates who enrolled in 2011, 81 Federal Work-Study jobs (averaging $955).
Applying *Options:* electronic application, early admission, deferred entrance. *Required:* high school transcript.
Freshman Application Contact Mr. Mark Grzybowski, Director of Admissions and Records, Illinois Valley Community College, Oglesby, IL 61348. *Phone:* 815-224-0437. *Fax:* 815-224-3033. *E-mail:* mark_grzybowski@ivcc.edu.
Website: http://www.ivcc.edu/.

ITT Technical Institute

Mount Prospect, Illinois

- **Proprietary** primarily 2-year, founded 1986, part of ITT Educational Services, Inc.
- **Suburban** campus
- **Coed**

Academics *Calendar:* quarters. *Degrees:* associate and bachelor's.
Freshman Application Contact Director of Recruitment, ITT Technical Institute, 1401 Feehanville Drive, Mount Prospect, IL 60056. *Phone:* 847-375-8800.
Website: http://www.itt-tech.edu/.

ITT Technical Institute

Oak Brook, Illinois

- **Proprietary** primarily 2-year, founded 1998, part of ITT Educational Services, Inc.
- **Coed**

Academics *Calendar:* quarters. *Degrees:* associate and bachelor's.
Freshman Application Contact Director of Recruitment, ITT Technical Institute, 800 Jorie Boulevard, Suite 100, Oak Brook, IL 60523. *Phone:* 630-472-7000. *Toll-free phone:* 877-488-0001.
Website: http://www.itt-tech.edu/.

ITT Technical Institute

Orland Park, Illinois

- **Proprietary** primarily 2-year, founded 1993, part of ITT Educational Services, Inc.
- **Suburban** campus
- **Coed**

Academics *Calendar:* quarters. *Degrees:* associate and bachelor's.
Financial Aid Of all full-time matriculated undergraduates who enrolled in 2011, 6 Federal Work-Study jobs (averaging $4000).
Freshman Application Contact Director of Recruitment, ITT Technical Institute, 11551 184th Place, Orland Park, IL 60467. *Phone:* 708-326-3200.
Website: http://www.itt-tech.edu/.

John A. Logan College

Carterville, Illinois

Director of Admissions Mr. Terry Crain, Dean of Student Services, John A. Logan College, 700 Logan College Road, Carterville, IL 62918-9900. *Phone:* 618-985-3741 Ext. 8382. *Fax:* 618-985-4433. *E-mail:* terrycrain@jalc.edu.
Website: http://www.jalc.edu/.

John Wood Community College

Quincy, Illinois

- **District-supported** 2-year, founded 1974, part of Illinois Community College Board
- **Small-town** campus
- **Coed**

Undergraduates 1,178 full-time, 1,212 part-time. Students come from 18 states and territories; 7% are from out of state; 4% Black or African American, non-Hispanic/Latino; 0.8% Hispanic/Latino; 0.6% Asian, non-Hispanic/Latino; 0.1% Native Hawaiian or other Pacific Islander, non-Hispanic/Latino; 0.4% American Indian or Alaska Native, non-Hispanic/Latino; 1% Two or more races, non-Hispanic/Latino; 4% Race/ethnicity unknown; 9% transferred in.
Faculty *Student/faculty ratio:* 13:1.
Academics *Calendar:* semesters. *Degree:* certificates and associate. *Special study options:* academic remediation for entering students, accelerated degree program, adult/continuing education programs, advanced placement credit, cooperative education, distance learning, English as a second language, exter-

nal degree program, independent study, internships, off-campus study, part-time degree program, services for LD students, student-designed majors, study abroad, summer session for credit.

Student Life *Campus security:* 24-hour emergency response devices, late-night transport/escort service, campus police department, 911-enhanced phone system.

Athletics Member NJCAA.

Standardized Tests *Recommended:* ACT (for admission).

Costs (2012–13) *Tuition:* area resident $3690 full-time, $123 per credit hour part-time; state resident $6900 full-time, $233 per credit hour part-time; non-resident $6990 full-time, $233 per credit hour part-time. Full-time tuition and fees vary according to program and reciprocity agreements. Part-time tuition and fees vary according to program and reciprocity agreements. *Required fees:* $300 full-time, $10 per credit hour part-time.

Applying *Options:* electronic application, early admission. *Required:* high school transcript.

Freshman Application Contact Mr. Lee Wibbell, Director of Admissions, John Wood Community College, Quincy, IL 62305-8736. *Phone:* 217-641-4339. *Fax:* 217-224-4208. *E-mail:* admissions@jwcc.edu.

Website: http://www.jwcc.edu/.

Joliet Junior College
Joliet, Illinois

Freshman Application Contact Ms. Jennifer Kloberdanz, Director of Admissions and Recruitment, Joliet Junior College, 1215 Houbolt Road, Joliet, IL 60431. *Phone:* 815-729-9020 Ext. 2414. *E-mail:* admission@jjc.edu. *Website:* http://www.jjc.edu/.

Kankakee Community College
Kankakee, Illinois

- **State and locally supported** 2-year, founded 1966, part of Illinois Community College Board
- **Small-town** 178-acre campus with easy access to Chicago
- **Endowment** $4.5 million
- **Coed,** 3,913 undergraduate students, 41% full-time, 62% women, 38% men

Undergraduates 1,613 full-time, 2,300 part-time. Students come from 14 states and territories; 6 other countries; 1% are from out of state; 18% Black or African American, non-Hispanic/Latino; 8% Hispanic/Latino; 1% Asian, non-Hispanic/Latino; 0.2% Native Hawaiian or other Pacific Islander, non-Hispanic/Latino; 0.5% American Indian or Alaska Native, non-Hispanic/Latino; 0.5% Two or more races, non-Hispanic/Latino; 0.7% Race/ethnicity unknown; 47% transferred in. *Retention:* 59% of full-time freshmen returned.

Freshmen *Admission:* 1,765 applied, 366 enrolled. *Average high school GPA:* 3.04.

Faculty *Total:* 198, 36% full-time, 7% with terminal degrees. *Student/faculty ratio:* 17:1.

Majors Administrative assistant and secretarial science; agriculture; applied horticulture/horticulture operations; art; automobile/automotive mechanics technology; biology/biological sciences; business administration and management; chemistry; clinical/medical laboratory technology; construction management; criminal justice/law enforcement administration; criminal justice/police science; desktop publishing and digital imaging design; drafting and design technology; early childhood education; education; elementary education; emergency medical technology (EMT paramedic); engineering; English; general studies; heating, air conditioning, ventilation and refrigeration maintenance technology; history; industrial electronics technology; legal assistant/paralegal; mathematics; mathematics teacher education; medical/clinical assistant; medical office assistant; physical therapy technology; physics; political science and government; psychology; radiologic technology/science; registered nursing/registered nurse; respiratory care therapy; secondary education; sociology; special education; teacher assistant/aide; visual and performing arts; welding technology.

Academics *Calendar:* semesters. *Degrees:* certificates, diplomas, and associate (also offers continuing education program with significant enrollment not reflected in profile). *Special study options:* academic remediation for entering students, advanced placement credit, distance learning, English as a second language, honors programs, independent study, internships, off-campus study, part-time degree program, services for LD students, student-designed majors, study abroad, summer session for credit. *ROTC:* Army (c).

Library Kankakee Community College Learning Resource Center with 35,308 titles, 120 serial subscriptions, 2,299 audiovisual materials, an OPAC, a Web page.

Student Life *Housing:* college housing not available. *Activities and Organizations:* drama/theater group, Phi Theta Kappa, Hort, Student Nursing, Gay Straight Alliance, Student Advisory Council. *Campus security:* 24-hour patrols, late-night transport/escort service.

Athletics Member NJCAA. *Intercollegiate sports:* baseball M(s), basketball M(s)/W(s), soccer M(s), softball W(s), volleyball W(s).

Costs (2013–14) *Tuition:* area resident $3000 full-time; state resident $5681 full-time; nonresident $13,600 full-time. *Required fees:* $390 full-time. *Payment plan:* installment. *Waivers:* senior citizens and employees or children of employees.

Financial Aid Of all full-time matriculated undergraduates who enrolled in 2011, 70 Federal Work-Study jobs (averaging $1100). *Financial aid deadline:* 10/1.

Applying *Options:* electronic application, early admission. *Required:* high school transcript. *Application deadlines:* rolling (freshmen), rolling (out-of-state freshmen), rolling (transfers). *Notification:* continuous (freshmen), continuous (out-of-state freshmen), continuous (transfers).

Freshman Application Contact Mrs. Oshunda Carpenter-Williams, Kankakee Community College, 100 College Drive, Kankakee, IL 60901. *Phone:* 815-802-8513. *Fax:* 815-802-8521. *E-mail:* ocarpenterwilliams@kcc.edu.

Website: http://www.kcc.edu/.

Kaskaskia College
Centralia, Illinois

- **State and locally supported** 2-year, founded 1966, part of Illinois Community College Board
- **Rural** 195-acre campus with easy access to St. Louis
- **Endowment** $5.1 million
- **Coed,** 5,104 undergraduate students, 39% full-time, 61% women, 39% men

Undergraduates 2,006 full-time, 3,098 part-time. Students come from 10 states and territories; 3 other countries; 1% are from out of state; 7% Black or African American, non-Hispanic/Latino; 2% Hispanic/Latino; 0.7% Asian, non-Hispanic/Latino; 0.4% American Indian or Alaska Native, non-Hispanic/Latino; 2% Two or more races, non-Hispanic/Latino; 0.3% Race/ethnicity unknown; 0.2% international; 36% transferred in.

Freshmen *Admission:* 284 applied, 284 admitted, 452 enrolled.

Faculty *Total:* 253, 30% full-time, 7% with terminal degrees. *Student/faculty ratio:* 21:1.

Majors Accounting; agriculture; applied horticulture/horticulture operations; architectural drafting and CAD/CADD; autobody/collision and repair technology; automobile/automotive mechanics technology; biological and physical sciences; business automation/technology/data entry; business/commerce; carpentry; child-care provision; clinical/medical laboratory technology; criminal justice/law enforcement administration; culinary arts; electrical, electronic and communications engineering technology; emergency medical technology (EMT paramedic); engineering; executive assistant/executive secretary; general studies; health information/medical records technology; industrial mechanics and maintenance technology; information science/studies; juvenile corrections; liberal arts and sciences/liberal studies; mathematics teacher education; music; network and system administration; occupational therapist assistant; physical therapy technology; radiologic technology/science; registered nursing/registered nurse; respiratory care therapy; teacher assistant/aide; veterinary/animal health technology; web/multimedia management and webmaster; welding technology.

Academics *Calendar:* semesters. *Degree:* certificates and associate. *Special study options:* academic remediation for entering students, accelerated degree program, adult/continuing education programs, cooperative education, distance learning, double majors, English as a second language, honors programs, independent study, internships, off-campus study, part-time degree program, services for LD students, study abroad, summer session for credit.

Library Kaskaskia College Library with 19,007 titles, 77 serial subscriptions, 545 audiovisual materials, an OPAC, a Web page.

Student Life *Housing:* college housing not available. *Activities and Organizations:* drama/theater group, student-run newspaper, choral group, Student Nurse Organization, Student Practical Nurses, Student Radiology Club, Agriculture Club, Cosmetology Club. *Campus security:* 24-hour emergency response devices and patrols, late-night transport/escort service. *Student services:* personal/psychological counseling.

Athletics Member NJCAA. *Intercollegiate sports:* baseball M(s), basketball M(s)/W(s), cheerleading M(s)/W(s), cross-country running M(s)/W(s), golf M(s)/W(s), soccer W(s), softball W(s), tennis M(s), volleyball W(s).

Standardized Tests *Recommended:* ACT (for admission).

Costs (2012–13) *Tuition:* area resident $2944 full-time, $92 per credit hour part-time; state resident $5728 full-time, $179 per credit hour part-time; nonresident $12,480 full-time, $390 per credit hour part-time. Full-time tuition and fees vary according to program. Part-time tuition and fees vary according to program. *Required fees:* $384 full-time, $12 per credit hour part-time. *Payment plan:* installment. *Waivers:* senior citizens and employees or children of employees.

Financial Aid Of all full-time matriculated undergraduates who enrolled in 2011, 1,191 applied for aid, 926 were judged to have need, 231 had their need fully met. 81 Federal Work-Study jobs (averaging $3208). 94 state and other part-time jobs (averaging $4480). In 2011, 145 non-need-based awards were made. *Average percent of need met:* 62%. *Average financial aid package:* $5345. *Average need-based gift aid:* $4571. *Average non-need-based aid:* $2357.

Applying *Options:* electronic application, early admission, deferred entrance. *Required:* high school transcript. *Required for some:* interview. *Application deadlines:* rolling (freshmen), rolling (transfers). *Notification:* continuous (freshmen), continuous (transfers).

Freshman Application Contact Jan Ripperda, Manager of Records and Registration, Kaskaskia College, 27210 College Road, Centralia, IL 62801. *Phone:* 618-545-3041. *Toll-free phone:* 800-642-0859. *Fax:* 618-532-1990. *E-mail:* jripperda@kaskaskia.edu. *Website:* http://www.kaskaskia.edu/.

Kishwaukee College

Malta, Illinois

Freshman Application Contact Ms. Sally Misciasci, Admission Analyst, Kishwaukee College, 21193 Malta Road, Malta, IL 60150. *Phone:* 815-825-2086 Ext. 400. *Website:* http://www.kishwaukeecollege.edu/.

Lake Land College

Mattoon, Illinois

Freshman Application Contact Mr. Jon VanDyke, Dean of Admission Services, Lake Land College, Mattoon, IL 61938-9366. *Phone:* 217-234-5378. *E-mail:* admissions@lakeland.cc.il.us. *Website:* http://www.lakelandcollege.edu/.

Le Cordon Bleu College of Culinary Arts in Chicago

Chicago, Illinois

Freshman Application Contact Mr. Matthew Verratti, Vice President of Admissions and Marketing, Le Cordon Bleu College of Culinary Arts in Chicago, 361 West Chestnut, Chicago, IL 60610. *Phone:* 312-873-2064. *Toll-free phone:* 888-295-7222. *Fax:* 312-798-2903. *E-mail:* mverratti@chicnet.org. *Website:* http://www.chefs.edu/chicago/.

Lewis and Clark Community College

Godfrey, Illinois

Freshman Application Contact Lewis and Clark Community College, 5800 Godfrey Road, Godfrey, IL 62035-2466. *Phone:* 618-468-5100. *Toll-free phone:* 800-YES-LCCC. *Website:* http://www.lc.edu/.

Lincoln College

Lincoln, Illinois

Director of Admissions Gretchen Bree, Director of Admissions, Lincoln College, 300 Keokuk Street, Lincoln, IL 62656-1699. *Phone:* 217-732-3155 Ext. 256. *Toll-free phone:* 800-569-0558. *E-mail:* gbree@lincolncollege.edu. *Website:* http://www.lincolncollege.edu/.

Lincoln Land Community College

Springfield, Illinois

- **District-supported** 2-year, founded 1967, part of Illinois Community College Board
- **Suburban** 441-acre campus
- **Endowment** $2.6 million
- **Coed,** 7,193 undergraduate students, 42% full-time, 58% women, 42% men

Undergraduates 3,047 full-time, 4,146 part-time. Students come from 12 states and territories; 9% Black or African American, non-Hispanic/Latino; 2% Hispanic/Latino; 2% Asian, non-Hispanic/Latino; 0.1% Native Hawaiian or other Pacific Islander, non-Hispanic/Latino; 0.2% American Indian or Alaska Native, non-Hispanic/Latino; 0.5% Two or more races, non-Hispanic/Latino; 5% Race/ethnicity unknown; 0.1% international; 1% transferred in. *Retention:* 50% of full-time freshmen returned.

Freshmen *Admission:* 1,359 enrolled. *Test scores:* ACT scores over 18: 68%; ACT scores over 24: 19%; ACT scores over 30: 1%.

Faculty *Total:* 382, 34% full-time, 12% with terminal degrees. *Student/faculty ratio:* 21:1.

Majors Accounting; administrative assistant and secretarial science; agricultural production; airframe mechanics and aircraft maintenance technology; architectural drafting and CAD/CADD; autobody/collision and repair technology; automobile/automotive mechanics technology; aviation/airway management; biological and physical sciences; building/property maintenance; business automation/technology/data entry; business/commerce; child-care provision; computer programming; computer programming (specific applications); computer systems networking and telecommunications; construction engineering technology; criminal justice/police science; early childhood education; electrical, electronic and communications engineering technology; emergency medical technology (EMT paramedic); engineering; fine/studio arts; fire science/firefighting; general studies; graphic design; hospitality administration; industrial electronics technology; industrial technology; landscaping and groundskeeping; legal administrative assistant/secretary; liberal arts and sciences/liberal studies; medical office assistant; music; occupational therapist assistant; radiologic technology/science; registered nursing/registered nurse; special education; surgical technology; teacher assistant/aide.

Academics *Calendar:* semesters. *Degree:* certificates and associate. *Special study options:* academic remediation for entering students, accelerated degree program, adult/continuing education programs, advanced placement credit, distance learning, English as a second language, external degree program, honors programs, independent study, internships, off-campus study, part-time degree program, services for LD students, study abroad, summer session for credit.

Library Learning Resource Center with 64,916 titles, 2,860 serial subscriptions, 2,057 audiovisual materials, an OPAC, a Web page.

Student Life *Housing:* college housing not available. *Activities and Organizations:* drama/theater group, student-run newspaper, choral group, Student Government Association, Phi Theta Kappa, Agriculture Club, Epicurean Club, Veteran's Club. *Campus security:* 24-hour emergency response devices and patrols, late-night transport/escort service. *Student services:* health clinic, personal/psychological counseling.

Athletics Member NJCAA. *Intercollegiate sports:* baseball M(s), basketball M(s)/W(s), soccer M(s), softball W(s), volleyball W(s).

Costs (2012–13) *Tuition:* area resident $2304 full-time, $96 per credit hour part-time; state resident $4608 full-time, $192 per credit hour part-time; nonresident $6912 full-time, $288 per credit hour part-time. Full-time tuition and fees vary according to program. Part-time tuition and fees vary according to program. *Required fees:* $264 full-time, $11 per credit hour part-time. *Payment plans:* installment, deferred payment. *Waivers:* senior citizens and employees or children of employees.

Applying *Options:* electronic application, early admission, deferred entrance. *Recommended:* high school transcript. *Application deadlines:* rolling (freshmen), rolling (transfers). *Notification:* continuous (freshmen), continuous (transfers).

Freshman Application Contact Mr. Ron Gregoire, Executive Director of Admissions and Records, Lincoln Land Community College, 5250 Shepherd Road, PO Box 19256, Springfield, IL 62794-9256. *Phone:* 217-786-2243. *Toll-free phone:* 800-727-4161. *Fax:* 217-786-2492. *E-mail:* ron.gregoire@llcc.edu. *Website:* http://www.llcc.edu/.

MacCormac College

Chicago, Illinois

Director of Admissions Mr. David Grassi, Director of Admissions, MacCormac College, 506 South Wabash Avenue, Chicago, IL 60605-1667. *Phone:* 312-922-1884 Ext. 102. *Website:* http://www.maccormac.edu/.

McHenry County College

Crystal Lake, Illinois

- **State and locally supported** 2-year, founded 1967, part of Illinois Community College Board
- **Suburban** 168-acre campus with easy access to Chicago
- **Endowment** $856,341
- **Coed,** 5,618 undergraduate students, 42% full-time, 55% women, 45% men

Undergraduates 2,375 full-time, 3,243 part-time. 0.6% are from out of state; 2% Black or African American, non-Hispanic/Latino; 10% Hispanic/Latino; 2% Asian, non-Hispanic/Latino; 0.2% Native Hawaiian or other Pacific Islander, non-Hispanic/Latino; 0.4% American Indian or Alaska Native, non-Hispanic/Latino; 9% Race/ethnicity unknown; 0.2% international.

Freshmen *Admission:* 2,630 applied, 2,630 admitted, 1,040 enrolled. *Average high school GPA:* 2.25.

Faculty *Total:* 401, 25% full-time. *Student/faculty ratio:* 18:1.

Majors Accounting; administrative assistant and secretarial science; animation, interactive technology, video graphics and special effects; applied horticulture/horticulture operations; automobile/automotive mechanics technology; biological and physical sciences; building/home/construction inspection; business administration and management; child-care provision; computer and information systems security; criminal justice/police science; electrical, electronic and communications engineering technology; emergency medical technology (EMT paramedic); engineering; fine/studio arts; fire science/firefighting; general studies; health and physical education/fitness; information technology; liberal arts and sciences/liberal studies; music; operations management; registered nursing/registered nurse; selling skills and sales.

Academics *Calendar:* semesters. *Degree:* certificates and associate. *Special study options:* academic remediation for entering students, accelerated degree program, adult/continuing education programs, advanced placement credit, cooperative education, distance learning, English as a second language, honors programs, independent study, internships, part-time degree program, services for LD students, study abroad, summer session for credit.

Library McHenry County College Library with 60,000 titles, 125 serial subscriptions, 5,042 audiovisual materials, an OPAC, a Web page.

Student Life *Housing:* college housing not available. *Activities and Organizations:* drama/theater group, student-run newspaper, choral group, Phi Theta Kappa, Student Senate, Equality Club, Writer's Block, Latinos Unidos. *Campus security:* 24-hour emergency response devices and patrols, late-night transport/escort service. *Student services:* personal/psychological counseling.

Athletics Member NJCAA. *Intercollegiate sports:* baseball M(s), basketball M(s)/W(s), soccer M(s), softball W(s), tennis M(s)/W(s), volleyball W(s).

Costs (2013–14) *Tuition:* area resident $2700 full-time, $90 per credit hour part-time; state resident $8010 full-time, $267 per credit hour part-time; nonresident $9780 full-time, $326 per credit hour part-time. Full-time tuition and fees vary according to course load. Part-time tuition and fees vary according to course load. *Required fees:* $229 full-time, $9 per credit hour part-time, $7 per credit hour part-time. *Payment plan:* installment. *Waivers:* senior citizens and employees or children of employees.

Financial Aid Of all full-time matriculated undergraduates who enrolled in 2011, 200 Federal Work-Study jobs (averaging $3700). 130 state and other part-time jobs (averaging $2000).

Applying *Options:* electronic application, early admission, deferred entrance. *Application fee:* $15. *Recommended:* high school transcript. *Application deadlines:* rolling (freshmen), rolling (out-of-state freshmen), rolling (transfers). *Notification:* continuous (freshmen), continuous (out-of-state freshmen), continuous (transfers).

Freshman Application Contact Anne Weaver, New Student Enrollment Specialist, McHenry County College, 8900 US Highway 14, Crystal Lake, IL 60012-2761. *Phone:* 815-455-7782. *E-mail:* admissions@mchenry.edu. *Website:* http://www.mchenry.edu/.

Moraine Valley Community College
Palos Hills, Illinois

- **State and locally supported** 2-year, founded 1967, part of Illinois Community College Board
- **Suburban** 294-acre campus with easy access to Chicago
- **Endowment** $13.5 million
- **Coed,** 16,650 undergraduate students, 42% full-time, 53% women, 47% men

Undergraduates 6,983 full-time, 9,667 part-time. Students come from 3 states and territories; 39 other countries; 0.1% are from out of state; 10% Black or African American, non-Hispanic/Latino; 17% Hispanic/Latino; 2% Asian, non-Hispanic/Latino; 0.2% American Indian or Alaska Native, non-Hispanic/Latino; 1% Two or more races, non-Hispanic/Latino; 9% Race/ethnicity unknown; 2% international; 7% transferred in. *Retention:* 58% of full-time freshmen returned.

Freshmen *Admission:* 2,139 enrolled. *Test scores:* ACT scores over 18: 59%; ACT scores over 24: 18%; ACT scores over 30: 2%.

Faculty *Total:* 812, 26% full-time, 8% with terminal degrees. *Student/faculty ratio:* 25:1.

Majors Administrative assistant and secretarial science; automobile/automotive mechanics technology; biological and physical sciences; business administration and management; business/commerce; child-care provision; computer and information systems security; criminal justice/police science; emergency medical technology (EMT paramedic); fire prevention and safety technology; fire science/firefighting; graphic design; health information/medical records technology; heating, air conditioning, ventilation and refrigeration maintenance technology; hospitality administration; human resources management; industrial electronics technology; instrumentation technology; liberal arts and sciences/liberal studies; management information systems; mathematics teacher education; mechanical engineering/mechanical technology; movement and mind-body therapies and education related; parks, recreation and leisure facilities management; radiologic technology/science; registered nursing/registered nurse; respiratory care therapy; restaurant, culinary, and catering man-

agement; retailing; science teacher education; small business administration; special education; substance abuse/addiction counseling; system, networking, and LAN/WAN management; teacher assistant/aide; tourism and travel services management; visual and performing arts; web/multimedia management and webmaster.

Academics *Calendar:* semesters. *Degree:* certificates and associate. *Special study options:* academic remediation for entering students, accelerated degree program, adult/continuing education programs, advanced placement credit, cooperative education, distance learning, double majors, English as a second language, honors programs, independent study, internships, off-campus study, part-time degree program, services for LD students, study abroad, summer session for credit.

Library Library with 70,878 titles, 412 serial subscriptions, 8,076 audiovisual materials, an OPAC, a Web page.

Student Life *Housing:* college housing not available. *Activities and Organizations:* drama/theater group, student-run newspaper, choral group, student newspaper, Speech Team, Alliance of Latin American Students, Phi Theta Kappa, Arab Student Union. *Campus security:* 24-hour emergency response devices and patrols, late-night transport/escort service, safety and security programs. *Student services:* personal/psychological counseling, women's center.

Athletics Member NJCAA. *Intercollegiate sports:* baseball M(s), basketball M(s)/W(s), cross-country running M(s)/W(s), golf M(s), soccer M(s)/W(s), softball W(s), tennis M(s)/W(s), volleyball W(s). *Intramural sports:* basketball M/W, football M, soccer M/W, volleyball M/W.

Costs (2012–13) *Tuition:* area resident $3120 full-time, $104 per credit part-time; state resident $7740 full-time, $258 per hour part-time; nonresident $9060 full-time, $302 per hour part-time. *Required fees:* $516 full-time, $17 per credit hour part-time, $3 per term part-time. *Payment plan:* installment. *Waivers:* senior citizens and employees or children of employees.

Financial Aid Of all full-time matriculated undergraduates who enrolled in 2011, 50 Federal Work-Study jobs (averaging $2155). 298 state and other part-time jobs (averaging $2444).

Applying *Options:* electronic application, early admission, deferred entrance. *Recommended:* high school transcript. *Application deadlines:* rolling (freshmen), rolling (transfers). *Notification:* continuous (freshmen), continuous (transfers).

Freshman Application Contact Ms. Claudia Roselli, Director, Admissions and Recruitment, Moraine Valley Community College, 9000 West College Parkway, Palos Hills, IL 60465-0937. *Phone:* 708-974-5357. *Fax:* 708-974-0681. *E-mail:* roselli@morainevalley.edu. *Website:* http://www.morainevalley.edu/.

Morrison Institute of Technology
Morrison, Illinois

Freshman Application Contact Mrs. Tammy Pruis, Admission Secretary, Morrison Institute of Technology, 701 Portland Avenue, Morrison, IL 61270. *Phone:* 815-772-7218. *Fax:* 815-772-7584. *E-mail:* admissions@morrison.tec.il.us. *Website:* http://www.morrisontech.edu/.

Morton College
Cicero, Illinois

Freshman Application Contact Morton College, 3801 South Central Avenue, Cicero, IL 60804-4398. *Phone:* 708-656-8000 Ext. 401. *Website:* http://www.morton.edu/.

Northwestern College
Rosemont, Illinois

Freshman Application Contact Northwestern College, 9700 West Higgins Road, Suite 750, Rosemont, IL 60018. *Phone:* 773-481-3730. *Toll-free phone:* 888-205-2283. *Website:* http://www.northwesterncollege.edu/.

Oakton Community College
Des Plaines, Illinois

- **District-supported** 2-year, founded 1969, part of Illinois Community College Board
- **Suburban** 193-acre campus with easy access to Chicago
- **Coed,** 10,406 undergraduate students

Majors Accounting technology and bookkeeping; administrative assistant and secretarial science; architectural drafting and CAD/CADD; automobile/automotive mechanics technology; banking and financial support services; biological and physical sciences; building/construction finishing, management, and inspection related; child-care provision; clinical/medical laboratory technology; computer programming; criminal justice/police science; electrical, electronic and communications engineering technology; engineering; fire science/firefighting; graphic design; health information/medical records administration; heating, ventilation, air conditioning and refrigeration engineering technology; information technology; liberal arts and sciences/liberal studies; manufacturing engineering technology; marketing/marketing management; mechanical engineering/mechanical technology; music; operations management; physical therapy technology; real estate; registered nursing/registered nurse; sales, distribution, and marketing operations; social work; substance abuse/addiction counseling.

Academics *Calendar:* semesters. *Degree:* certificates and associate. *Special study options:* academic remediation for entering students, adult/continuing education programs, advanced placement credit, distance learning, English as a second language, honors programs, independent study, part-time degree program, services for LD students, study abroad, summer session for credit.

Library Oakton Community College Library plus 1 other with 92,000 titles, 586 serial subscriptions, 10,500 audiovisual materials, an OPAC, a Web page.

Student Life *Housing:* college housing not available. *Activities and Organizations:* drama/theater group, student-run newspaper, choral group. *Campus security:* 24-hour emergency response devices and patrols, student patrols, late-night transport/escort service. *Student services:* health clinic, personal/psychological counseling.

Athletics Member NJCAA. *Intercollegiate sports:* baseball M, basketball M/W, cross-country running M/W, soccer M/W, softball W, tennis M/W, track and field M/W, volleyball W. *Intramural sports:* basketball M/W, cheerleading W, soccer M, table tennis M/W, volleyball M/W.

Costs (2013–14) *Tuition:* area resident $2288 full-time, $95 per semester hour part-time; state resident $6909 full-time, $288 per semester hour part-time; nonresident $8881 full-time, $370 per semester hour part-time. *Required fees:* $167 full-time.

Applying *Options:* electronic application. *Application fee:* $25. *Required for some:* interview. *Recommended:* high school transcript. *Application deadlines:* rolling (freshmen), rolling (transfers). *Notification:* continuous (freshmen), continuous (transfers).

Freshman Application Contact Mr. Dale Cohen, Admissions Specialist, Oakton Community College, 1600 East Golf Road, Des Plaines, IL 60016-1268. *Phone:* 847-635-1703. *Fax:* 847-635-1890. *E-mail:* dcohen@oakton.edu.

Website: http://www.oakton.edu/.

Parkland College
Champaign, Illinois

- **District-supported** 2-year, founded 1967, part of Illinois Community College Board
- **Suburban** 233-acre campus
- **Coed,** 9,368 undergraduate students, 37% full-time, 54% women, 46% men

Undergraduates 3,432 full-time, 5,936 part-time. 1% are from out of state; 16% Black or African American, non-Hispanic/Latino; 4% Hispanic/Latino; 3% Asian, non-Hispanic/Latino; 0.1% Native Hawaiian or other Pacific Islander, non-Hispanic/Latino; 0.5% American Indian or Alaska Native, non-Hispanic/Latino; 0.1% Two or more races, non-Hispanic/Latino; 19% Race/ethnicity unknown; 1% international; 4% transferred in.

Freshmen *Admission:* 6,780 applied, 6,780 admitted, 1,343 enrolled. *Test scores:* ACT scores over 18: 61%; ACT scores over 24: 16%; ACT scores over 30: 1%.

Faculty *Total:* 521, 33% full-time.

Majors Accounting technology and bookkeeping; administrative assistant and secretarial science; advertising; agricultural business and management; agricultural mechanization; art; art teacher education; autobody/collision and repair technology; automobile/automotive mechanics technology; biological and physical sciences; biomedical technology; building/construction finishing, management, and inspection related; business administration and management; business automation/technology/data entry; child-care provision; computer and information sciences; computer and information sciences and support services related; computer graphics; computer/information technology services administration related; computer programming; computer programming (specific applications); computer programming (vendor/product certification); computer science; computer software and media applications related; computer systems networking and telecommunications; consumer merchandising/retailing management; criminal justice/safety; data entry/microcomputer applications; dental hygiene; design and visual communications; electroneurodiagnostic/electroencephalographic technology; elementary education; engineering science; English; general studies; graphic design; history; human services; industrial technology; information science/studies; kindergarten/preschool education; landscaping and groundskeeping; liberal arts and sciences/liberal studies; mass communication/media; medical radiologic technology; music performance; music teacher education; network and system administration; occupational therapist assistant; radio and television; radio and television broadcasting technology; registered nursing/registered nurse; respi-

ratory care therapy; sales and marketing/marketing and distribution teacher education; secondary education; speech-language pathology; surgical technology; theater/theater arts management; veterinary/animal health technology; web page, digital/multimedia and information resources design.

Academics *Calendar:* semesters. *Degree:* certificates and associate. *Special study options:* academic remediation for entering students, accelerated degree program, adult/continuing education programs, advanced placement credit, cooperative education, distance learning, double majors, English as a second language, honors programs, independent study, internships, off-campus study, part-time degree program, services for LD students, student-designed majors, study abroad, summer session for credit. *ROTC:* Army (c), Navy (c), Air Force (c).

Library Parkland College Library with an OPAC, a Web page.

Student Life *Housing:* college housing not available. *Activities and Organizations:* drama/theater group, student-run newspaper, radio and television station, choral group. *Campus security:* 24-hour emergency response devices and patrols, late-night transport/escort service. *Student services:* personal/psychological counseling.

Athletics Member NJCAA. *Intercollegiate sports:* baseball M(s), basketball M(s)/W(s), golf M(s), soccer M(s)/W(s), softball W(s), volleyball W(s). *Intramural sports:* basketball M/W, bowling M/W, softball M/W, volleyball M/W.

Standardized Tests *Required for some:* ACT (for admission).

Financial Aid Of all full-time matriculated undergraduates who enrolled in 2009, 2,359 applied for aid, 2,164 were judged to have need, 391 had their need fully met. 84 Federal Work-Study jobs (averaging $1825). *Average percent of need met:* 71%. *Average financial aid package:* $7296. *Average need-based gift aid:* $7296. *Average indebtedness upon graduation:* $7762.

Applying *Options:* deferred entrance. *Recommended:* high school transcript. *Application deadlines:* rolling (freshmen), rolling (transfers). *Notification:* continuous (freshmen), continuous (transfers).

Freshman Application Contact Admissions Representative, Parkland College, Champaign, IL 61821-1899. *Phone:* 217-351-2482. *Toll-free phone:* 800-346-8089. *Fax:* 217-351-2640.

Website: http://www.parkland.edu/.

Prairie State College
Chicago Heights, Illinois

Freshman Application Contact Jaime Miller, Director of Admissions, Prairie State College, 202 South Halsted Street, Chicago Heights, IL 60411. *Phone:* 708-709-3513. *E-mail:* jmmiller@prairiestate.edu.

Website: http://www.prairiestate.edu/.

Rasmussen College Aurora
Aurora, Illinois

- **Proprietary** primarily 2-year, part of Rasmussen College System
- **Suburban** campus
- **Coed,** 366 undergraduate students

Faculty *Student/faculty ratio:* 22:1.

Majors Accounting; business administration and management; corrections and criminal justice related; early childhood education; graphic communications related; health/health-care administration; health information/medical records administration; health information/medical records technology; legal assistant/paralegal; management information systems and services related; medical administrative assistant and medical secretary; medical/clinical assistant; pharmacy technician; web page, digital/multimedia and information resources design.

Academics *Degrees:* certificates, diplomas, associate, and bachelor's. *Special study options:* academic remediation for entering students, accelerated degree program, adult/continuing education programs, distance learning, double majors, internships, part-time degree program, summer session for credit.

Library Rasmussen College Library - Aurora with 2,543 titles, 4 serial subscriptions, 322 audiovisual materials, an OPAC, a Web page.

Student Life *Housing:* college housing not available.

Standardized Tests *Required:* Internal Exam (for admission).

Costs (2013–14) *Tuition:* $12,600 full-time. Full-time tuition and fees vary according to course level, course load, degree level, location, and program. Part-time tuition and fees vary according to course level, course load, degree level, location, and program. *Required fees:* $1800 full-time. *Payment plans:* installment, deferred payment. *Waivers:* employees or children of employees.

Applying *Options:* electronic application, early admission, deferred entrance. *Required:* high school transcript, minimum 2.0 GPA. *Required for some:* interview. *Application deadlines:* rolling (freshmen), rolling (transfers).

Freshman Application Contact Susan Hammerstrom, Director of Admissions, Rasmussen College Aurora, 2363 Sequoia Drive, Aurora, IL 60506. *Phone:* 630-888-3500. *Toll-free phone:* 888-549-6755. *E-mail:* susan.hammerstrom@rasmussen.edu.

Website: http://www.rasmussen.edu/.

Rasmussen College Rockford

Rockford, Illinois

- **Proprietary** primarily 2-year, part of Rasmussen College System
- **Suburban** campus
- **Coed**, 713 undergraduate students

Faculty *Student/faculty ratio:* 22:1.

Majors Accounting; business administration and management; corrections and criminal justice related; early childhood education; graphic communications related; health/health-care administration; health information/medical records administration; health information/medical records technology; legal assistant/paralegal; management information systems and services related; medical administrative assistant and medical secretary; medical/clinical assistant; pharmacy technician; web page, digital/multimedia and information resources design.

Academics *Degrees:* certificates, diplomas, associate, and bachelor's. *Special study options:* academic remediation for entering students, accelerated degree program, adult/continuing education programs, distance learning, double majors, internships, part-time degree program, summer session for credit.

Library Rasmussen College Library - Rockford with 2,343 titles, 6 serial subscriptions, 195 audiovisual materials, an OPAC, a Web page.

Student Life *Housing:* college housing not available.

Standardized Tests *Required:* Internal Exam (for admission).

Costs (2013–14) *Tuition:* $12,600 full-time. Full-time tuition and fees vary according to course level, course load, degree level, location, and program. Part-time tuition and fees vary according to course level, course load, degree level, location, and program. *Required fees:* $1800 full-time. *Payment plans:* installment, deferred payment. *Waivers:* employees or children of employees.

Applying *Options:* electronic application, early admission, deferred entrance. *Required:* high school transcript, minimum 2.0 GPA. *Required for some:* interview. *Application deadlines:* rolling (freshmen), rolling (transfers).

Freshman Application Contact Susan Hammerstrom, Director of Admissions, Rasmussen College Rockford, 6000 East State Street, Fourth Floor, Rockford, IL 61108-2513. *Phone:* 815-316-4800. *Toll-free phone:* 888-549-6755. *E-mail:* susan.hammerstrom@rasmussen.edu.
Website: http://www.rasmussen.edu/.

Rend Lake College

Ina, Illinois

Freshman Application Contact Mr. Jason Swann, Recruiter, Rend Lake College, 468 North Ken Gray Parkway, Ina, IL 62846-9801. *Phone:* 618-437-5321 Ext. 1265. *Toll-free phone:* 800-369-5321. *Fax:* 618-437-5677. *E-mail:* swannj@rlc.edu.
Website: http://www.rlc.edu/.

Richland Community College

Decatur, Illinois

Freshman Application Contact Ms. JoAnn Wirey, Director of Admissions and Records, Richland Community College, Decatur, IL 62521. *Phone:* 217-875-7200 Ext. 284. *Fax:* 217-875-7783. *E-mail:* jwirey@richland.edu.
Website: http://www.richland.edu/.

Rockford Career College

Rockford, Illinois

Director of Admissions Ms. Barbara Holliman, Director of Admissions, Rockford Career College, 1130 South Alpine Road, Suite 100, Rockford, IL 61108. *Phone:* 815-965-8616 Ext. 16.
Website: http://www.rockfordcareercollege.edu/.

Rock Valley College

Rockford, Illinois

- **District-supported** 2-year, founded 1964, part of Illinois Community College Board
- **Suburban** 217-acre campus with easy access to Chicago
- **Coed**

Undergraduates 4,308 full-time, 4,541 part-time. Students come from 2 states and territories; 3 other countries; 2% are from out of state; 10% Black or African American, non-Hispanic/Latino; 9% Hispanic/Latino; 1% Asian, non-Hispanic/Latino; 0.1% Native Hawaiian or other Pacific Islander, non-Hispanic/Latino; 0.3% American Indian or Alaska Native, non-Hispanic/Latino; 2% Two or more races, non-Hispanic/Latino; 0.7% Race/ethnicity unknown; 0.2% international. *Retention:* 66% of full-time freshmen returned.

Faculty *Student/faculty ratio:* 24:1.

Academics *Calendar:* semesters. *Degree:* certificates and associate. *Special study options:* academic remediation for entering students, adult/continuing education programs, advanced placement credit, cooperative education, distance learning, English as a second language, honors programs, independent study, internships, part-time degree program, services for LD students, student-designed majors, study abroad, summer session for credit.

Student Life *Campus security:* 24-hour emergency response devices and patrols, late-night transport/escort service.

Athletics Member NJCAA.

Costs (2012–13) *Tuition:* area resident $2490 full-time, $83 per credit part-time; state resident $7920 full-time, $264 per credit part-time; nonresident $13,950 full-time, $456 per credit part-time. Full-time tuition and fees vary according to course load. Part-time tuition and fees vary according to course load. *Required fees:* $314 full-time. *Payment plans:* installment, deferred payment.

Financial Aid Of all full-time matriculated undergraduates who enrolled in 2011, 120 Federal Work-Study jobs (averaging $1800).

Applying *Required:* high school transcript.

Freshman Application Contact Mr. Patrick Peyer, Director, Student Retention and Success, Rock Valley College, 3301 North Mulford Rd, Rockford, IL 61008. *Phone:* 815-921-4103. *Toll-free phone:* 800-973-7821. *E-mail:* p.peyer@rockvalleycollege.edu.
Website: http://www.rockvalleycollege.edu/.

Sauk Valley Community College

Dixon, Illinois

Freshman Application Contact Sauk Valley Community College, 173 Illinois Route 2, Dixon, IL 61021. *Phone:* 815-288-5511 Ext. 378.
Website: http://www.svcc.edu/.

Shawnee Community College

Ullin, Illinois

- **State and locally supported** 2-year, founded 1967, part of Illinois Community College Board
- **Rural** 163-acre campus
- **Coed**, 2,139 undergraduate students, 33% full-time, 62% women, 38% men

Undergraduates 701 full-time, 1,438 part-time. Students come from 5 states and territories; 2 other countries; 2% are from out of state; 17% Black or African American, non-Hispanic/Latino; 2% Hispanic/Latino; 0.4% Asian, non-Hispanic/Latino; 0.1% Native Hawaiian or other Pacific Islander, non-Hispanic/Latino; 0.6% American Indian or Alaska Native, non-Hispanic/Latino; 0.1% Race/ethnicity unknown.

Freshmen *Admission:* 771 applied, 771 admitted, 191 enrolled. *Test scores:* ACT scores over 18: 61%; ACT scores over 24: 15%.

Faculty *Total:* 169, 24% full-time, 4% with terminal degrees. *Student/faculty ratio:* 13:1.

Majors Accounting; administrative assistant and secretarial science; agricultural business and management; agriculture; agronomy and crop science; animal sciences; automobile/automotive mechanics technology; biological and physical sciences; business administration and management; business automation/technology/data entry; child development; clinical/medical laboratory technology; computer graphics; computer systems networking and telecommunications; cosmetology; criminal justice/police science; electrical, electronic and communications engineering technology; health information/medical records technology; horticultural science; human services; information science/studies; legal administrative assistant/secretary; liberal arts and sciences/liberal studies; medical administrative assistant and medical secretary; occupational therapist assistant; registered nursing/registered nurse; social work; substance abuse/addiction counseling; veterinary/animal health technology; welding technology; wildlife, fish and wildlands science and management.

Academics *Calendar:* semesters. *Degree:* certificates, diplomas, and associate. *Special study options:* academic remediation for entering students, accelerated degree program, adult/continuing education programs, advanced placement credit, cooperative education, distance learning, double majors, English as a second language, external degree program, independent study, internships, off-campus study, part-time degree program, services for LD students, summer session for credit.

Library Shawnee Community College Library with 46,313 titles, 148 serial subscriptions, 1,842 audiovisual materials, an OPAC, a Web page.

Student Life *Housing:* college housing not available. *Activities and Organizations:* drama/theater group, choral group, Phi Theta Kappa, Phi Beta Lambda, Music Club, Student Senate, Future Teachers Organization. *Campus security:* 24-hour patrols. *Student services:* personal/psychological counseling.

Athletics Member NJCAA. *Intercollegiate sports:* baseball M(s), basketball M(s)/W(s), softball W(s). *Intramural sports:* weight lifting M/W.

Standardized Tests *Required for some:* ACT (for admission). *Recommended:* ACT (for admission).

Costs (2013–14) *Tuition:* area resident $2208 full-time, $92 per credit hour part-time; state resident $3312 full-time, $138 per credit hour part-time; non-resident $3696 full-time, $154 per credit hour part-time. *Payment plans:* installment, deferred payment. *Waivers:* senior citizens and employees or children of employees.

Financial Aid Of all full-time matriculated undergraduates who enrolled in 2011, 60 Federal Work-Study jobs (averaging $2000). 50 state and other part-time jobs (averaging $2000).

Applying *Options:* electronic application, early admission, deferred entrance. *Required:* high school transcript. *Application deadlines:* rolling (freshmen), rolling (out-of-state freshmen), rolling (transfers). *Notification:* continuous (freshmen), continuous (out-of-state freshmen), continuous (transfers).

Freshman Application Contact Mrs. Erin King, Recruiter/Advisor, Shawnee Community College, 8364 Shawnee College Road, Ullin, IL 62992. *Phone:* 618-634-3200. *Toll-free phone:* 800-481-2242. *Fax:* 618-634-3300. *E-mail:* erink@shawneecc.edu.
Website: http://www.shawneecc.edu/.

Solex College
Wheeling, Illinois

Freshman Application Contact Solex College, 350 East Dundee Road, Wheeling, IL 60090.
Website: http://www.solex.edu/.

Southeastern Illinois College
Harrisburg, Illinois

Freshman Application Contact Dr. David Nudo, Director of Counseling, Southeastern Illinois College, 3575 College Road, Harrisburg, IL 62946-4925. *Phone:* 618-252-5400 Ext. 2430. *Toll-free phone:* 866-338-2742. *Website:* http://www.sic.edu/.

South Suburban College
South Holland, Illinois

- **State and locally supported** 2-year, founded 1927, part of Illinois Community College Board
- **Suburban** campus with easy access to Chicago
- **Coed,** 6,211 undergraduate students, 42% full-time, 69% women, 31% men

Undergraduates 2,583 full-time, 3,628 part-time. 6% are from out of state; 68% Black or African American, non-Hispanic/Latino; 9% Hispanic/Latino; 0.2% Asian, non-Hispanic/Latino; 2% American Indian or Alaska Native, non-Hispanic/Latino; 0.7% Two or more races, non-Hispanic/Latino; 1% Race/ethnicity unknown; 0.8% international. *Retention:* 58% of full-time freshmen returned.

Freshmen *Admission:* 873 applied, 873 admitted. *Average high school GPA:* 2.33.

Faculty *Total:* 364, 32% full-time. *Student/faculty ratio:* 17:1.

Majors Accounting; accounting technology and bookkeeping; architectural drafting and CAD/CADD; biological and physical sciences; building/home/construction inspection; CAD/CADD drafting/design technology; child-care provision; construction engineering technology; court reporting; criminal justice/safety; electrical, electronic and communications engineering technology; executive assistant/executive secretary; fine/studio arts; information technology; kinesiology and exercise science; legal assistant/paralegal; liberal arts and sciences/liberal studies; nursing administration; occupational therapist assistant; office management; radiologic technology/science; small business administration; social work.

Academics *Calendar:* semesters. *Degree:* certificates and associate. *Special study options:* academic remediation for entering students, adult/continuing education programs, advanced placement credit, cooperative education, distance learning, English as a second language, honors programs, internships, off-campus study, part-time degree program, services for LD students, study abroad, summer session for credit.

Library South Suburban College Library with 28,500 titles, 55 serial subscriptions, an OPAC, a Web page.

Student Life *Housing:* college housing not available. *Activities and Organizations:* drama/theater group, choral group. *Campus security:* 24-hour emergency response devices and patrols.

Athletics Member NJCAA. *Intercollegiate sports:* baseball M, basketball M/W, soccer M/W, softball W, volleyball W.

Costs (2013–14) *Tuition:* area resident $3300 full-time; state resident $8640 full-time; nonresident $10,290 full-time. Full-time tuition and fees vary according to course load and reciprocity agreements. Part-time tuition and fees vary according to course load and reciprocity agreements. *Required fees:* $473

full-time. *Payment plan:* installment. *Waivers:* senior citizens and employees or children of employees.

Financial Aid Of all full-time matriculated undergraduates who enrolled in 2011, 121 Federal Work-Study jobs (averaging $1750).

Applying *Options:* early admission, deferred entrance. *Required:* high school transcript. *Required for some:* essay or personal statement. *Recommended:* essay or personal statement, minimum 2.0 GPA. *Application deadlines:* rolling (freshmen), rolling (transfers). *Notification:* continuous (freshmen), continuous (transfers).

Freshman Application Contact Ms. Tiffane Jones, Admissions, South Suburban College, 15800 South State Street, South Holland, IL 60473. *Phone:* 708-596-2000 Ext. 2158. *E-mail:* admissionsquestions@ssc.edu. *Website:* http://www.ssc.edu/.

Southwestern Illinois College
Belleville, Illinois

- **District-supported** 2-year, founded 1946, part of Illinois Community College Board
- **Suburban** 341-acre campus with easy access to St. Louis
- **Endowment** $5.2 million
- **Coed**

Undergraduates 5,276 full-time, 7,503 part-time. Students come from 12 states and territories; 1% are from out of state; 23% Black or African American, non-Hispanic/Latino; 2% Hispanic/Latino; 1% Asian, non-Hispanic/Latino; 0.4% Native Hawaiian or other Pacific Islander, non-Hispanic/Latino; 0.4% American Indian or Alaska Native, non-Hispanic/Latino; 5% Race/ethnicity unknown; 4% transferred in.

Faculty *Student/faculty ratio:* 23:1.

Academics *Calendar:* semesters. *Degree:* certificates, diplomas, and associate. *Special study options:* academic remediation for entering students, accelerated degree program, adult/continuing education programs, advanced placement credit, cooperative education, distance learning, double majors, English as a second language, internships, off-campus study, part-time degree program, services for LD students, study abroad, summer session for credit. *ROTC:* Army (c), Air Force (c).

Student Life *Campus security:* 24-hour emergency response devices and patrols, late-night transport/escort service.

Athletics Member NJCAA.

Standardized Tests *Required for some:* ACT (for admission), ACT ASSET or ACT COMPASS.

Costs (2012–13) *Tuition:* area resident $3120 full-time, $99 per credit hour part-time; state resident $7440 full-time, $243 per credit hour part-time; nonresident $11,100 full-time, $365 per credit hour part-time. Full-time tuition and fees vary according to course load. Part-time tuition and fees vary according to course load. *Required fees:* $150 full-time, $4 per credit hour part-time.

Financial Aid Of all full-time matriculated undergraduates who enrolled in 2011, 170 Federal Work-Study jobs (averaging $1537). 179 state and other part-time jobs (averaging $1004).

Applying *Options:* early admission, deferred entrance. *Required:* high school transcript.

Freshman Application Contact Michelle Birk, Dean of Enrollment Services, Southwestern Illinois College, 2500 Carlyle Road, Belleville, IL 62221. *Phone:* 618-235-2700 Ext. 5400. *Toll-free phone:* 866-942-SWIC. *Fax:* 618-222-9768. *E-mail:* michelle.birk@swic.edu. *Website:* http://www.southwestern.cc.il.us/.

Spoon River College
Canton, Illinois

- **State-supported** 2-year, founded 1959, part of Illinois Community College Board
- **Rural** 160-acre campus
- **Endowment** $1.4 million
- **Coed,** 1,966 undergraduate students, 44% full-time, 59% women, 41% men

Undergraduates 872 full-time, 1,094 part-time. 5% Black or African American, non-Hispanic/Latino; 2% Hispanic/Latino; 0.9% Asian, non-Hispanic/Latino; 0.5% American Indian or Alaska Native, non-Hispanic/Latino; 0.3% Two or more races, non-Hispanic/Latino; 11% transferred in. *Retention:* 58% of full-time freshmen returned.

Freshmen *Admission:* 605 applied, 605 admitted, 301 enrolled. *Test scores:* ACT scores over 18: 68%; ACT scores over 24: 16%.

Faculty *Total:* 116, 30% full-time. *Student/faculty ratio:* 17:1.

Majors Accounting; administrative assistant and secretarial science; agricultural business and management; agricultural mechanics and equipment technology; agricultural mechanization; agricultural teacher education; art; biological and physical sciences; biology/biological sciences; botany/plant biology; business administration and management; business teacher education;

chemistry; child development; computer and information systems security; computer programming (specific applications); criminal justice/law enforcement administration; criminal justice/police science; dramatic/theater arts; education; electrical, electronic and communications engineering technology; English; finance; general studies; graphic design; health professions related; history; industrial technology; information science/studies; kindergarten/preschool education; legal administrative assistant/secretary; liberal arts and sciences/liberal studies; mass communication/media; mathematics; medical administrative assistant and medical secretary; physical education teaching and coaching; physical sciences; physics; political science and government; preengineering; psychology; registered nursing/registered nurse; rhetoric and composition; social sciences; sociology; truck and bus driver/commercial vehicle operation/instruction; web page, digital/multimedia and information resources design.

Academics *Calendar:* semesters. *Degree:* certificates and associate. *Special study options:* academic remediation for entering students, accelerated degree program, adult/continuing education programs, advanced placement credit, distance learning, English as a second language, freshman honors college, honors programs, internships, part-time degree program, services for LD students, summer session for credit. *ROTC:* Army (b).

Library Library/Learning Resource Center with 74,252 titles, 121 serial subscriptions, 2,285 audiovisual materials, an OPAC, a Web page.

Student Life *Housing:* college housing not available. *Activities and Organizations:* drama/theater group, student-run newspaper, Student Government Association, PEEPS, Intramural Athletics, Habitat for Humanity, Drama Club. *Campus security:* 24-hour emergency response devices. *Student services:* personal/psychological counseling.

Athletics Member NJCAA. *Intercollegiate sports:* baseball M(s), cross-country running M(s)/W(s), golf M(s)/W(s), softball W(s), track and field M(s)/W(s).

Costs (2013–14) *Tuition:* area resident $3390 full-time, $113 per semester hour part-time; state resident $7470 full-time, $249 per semester hour part-time; nonresident $8550 full-time, $285 per semester hour part-time. Full-time tuition and fees vary according to course load and program. Part-time tuition and fees vary according to course load and program. *Required fees:* $450 full-time. *Room and board:* $4830. *Payment plan:* deferred payment. *Waivers:* senior citizens and employees or children of employees.

Applying *Options:* electronic application, early admission, deferred entrance. *Required:* high school transcript. *Application deadlines:* rolling (freshmen), rolling (transfers). *Notification:* continuous (freshmen), continuous (transfers).

Freshman Application Contact Ms. Missy Wilkinson, Dean of Student Services, Spoon River College, 23235 North County 22, Canton, IL 61520-9801. *Phone:* 309-649-6305. *Toll-free phone:* 800-334-7337. *Fax:* 309-649-6235. *E-mail:* info@spoonrivercollege.edu. *Website:* http://www.src.edu/.

Taylor Business Institute

Chicago, Illinois

Director of Admissions Mr. Rashed Jahangir, Taylor Business Institute, 318 West Adams, Chicago, IL 60606. *Website:* http://www.tbiil.edu/.

Triton College

River Grove, Illinois

Freshman Application Contact Ms. Mary-Rita Moore, Dean of Admissions, Triton College, 2000 Fifth Avenue, River Grove, IL 60171. *Phone:* 708-456-0300 Ext. 3679. *Fax:* 708-583-3162. *E-mail:* mpatrice@triton.edu. *Website:* http://www.triton.edu/.

Vet Tech Institute at Fox College

Tinley Park, Illinois

- **Private** 2-year, founded 2006
- **Suburban** campus
- **Coed,** 148 undergraduate students
- 56% of applicants were admitted

Freshmen *Admission:* 475 applied, 266 admitted.

Majors Veterinary/animal health technology.

Academics *Degree:* associate. *Special study options:* accelerated degree program, internships.

Student Life *Housing:* college housing not available.

Freshman Application Contact Admissions Office, Vet Tech Institute at Fox College, 18020 South Oak Park Avenue, Tinley Park, IL 60477. *Phone:* 888-884-3694. *Toll-free phone:* 888-884-3694. *Website:* http://www.vettechinstitute.edu/chicago.

Waubonsee Community College

Sugar Grove, Illinois

- **District-supported** 2-year, founded 1966, part of Illinois Community College Board
- **Small-town** 243-acre campus with easy access to Chicago
- **Coed,** 11,146 undergraduate students, 33% full-time, 56% women, 44% men

Undergraduates 3,666 full-time, 7,480 part-time. Students come from 21 states and territories; 8% Black or African American, non-Hispanic/Latino; 26% Hispanic/Latino; 2% Asian, non-Hispanic/Latino; 0.1% Native Hawaiian or other Pacific Islander, non-Hispanic/Latino; 0.2% American Indian or Alaska Native, non-Hispanic/Latino; 2% Two or more races, non-Hispanic/Latino; 3% Race/ethnicity unknown; 3% transferred in.

Freshmen *Admission:* 2,405 applied, 2,405 admitted, 1,391 enrolled.

Faculty *Total:* 720, 16% full-time, 7% with terminal degrees.

Majors Accounting; autobody/collision and repair technology; automobile/automotive mechanics technology; biological and physical sciences; business administration and management; business automation/technology/data entry; CAD/CADD drafting/design technology; child-care provision; community health services counseling; computer programming; construction management; criminal justice/police science; electrical, electronic and communications engineering technology; electrician; emergency care attendant (EMT ambulance); engineering; executive assistant/executive secretary; fine/studio arts; fire science/firefighting; general studies; graphic design; health and physical education/fitness; health information/medical records technology; heating, air conditioning, ventilation and refrigeration maintenance technology; human resources management; industrial mechanics and maintenance technology; industrial technology; liberal arts and sciences/liberal studies; library and archives assisting; massage therapy; music; radio and television broadcasting technology; registered nursing/registered nurse; retailing; sign language interpretation and translation; small business administration; social work; surveying technology; teacher assistant/aide; web page, digital/multimedia and information resources design; welding technology.

Academics *Calendar:* semesters. *Degree:* certificates and associate. *Special study options:* academic remediation for entering students, accelerated degree program, advanced placement credit, distance learning, English as a second language, honors programs, independent study, internships, off-campus study, part-time degree program, services for LD students, study abroad, summer session for credit. *ROTC:* Army (c).

Library Todd Library plus 3 others with 81,282 titles, 384 serial subscriptions, 3,248 audiovisual materials, an OPAC, a Web page.

Student Life *Housing:* college housing not available. *Activities and Organizations:* drama/theater group, student-run newspaper, choral group, Phi Theta Kappa, Otaku Gamers Society, Waubonsee Student Education Association (WSEA), Business Club, Latinos Unidos. *Campus security:* 24-hour emergency response devices and patrols, late-night transport/escort service.

Athletics Member NJCAA. *Intercollegiate sports:* baseball M, basketball M(s)/W(s), cheerleading M/W, cross-country running M(s)/W(s), golf M(s), soccer M(s)/W(s), softball W(s), tennis M(s)/W(s), volleyball W(s), wrestling M. *Intramural sports:* basketball M/W, table tennis M/W, volleyball M/W.

Financial Aid Of all full-time matriculated undergraduates who enrolled in 2011, 23 Federal Work-Study jobs (averaging $2000).

Applying *Options:* electronic application. *Application deadlines:* rolling (freshmen), rolling (transfers). *Notification:* continuous (freshmen), continuous (transfers).

Freshman Application Contact Joy Sanders, Admissions Manager, Waubonsee Community College, Route 47 at Waubonsee Drive, Sugar Grove, IL 60554. *Phone:* 630-466-7900 Ext. 5756. *Fax:* 630-466-6663. *E-mail:* admissions@waubonsee.edu. *Website:* http://www.waubonsee.edu/.

Worsham College of Mortuary Science

Wheeling, Illinois

Director of Admissions President, Worsham College of Mortuary Science, 495 Northgate Parkway, Wheeling, IL 60090-2646. *Phone:* 847-808-8444. *Website:* http://www.worshamcollege.com/.

INDIANA

Ancilla College

Donaldson, Indiana

- **Independent Roman Catholic** 2-year, founded 1937
- **Rural** 63-acre campus with easy access to Chicago
- **Endowment** $3.7 million
- **Coed,** 440 undergraduate students, 67% full-time, 64% women, 36% men

Undergraduates 294 full-time, 146 part-time. Students come from 9 states and territories; 3 other countries; 7% are from out of state; 7% Black or African American, non-Hispanic/Latino; 6% Hispanic/Latino; 0.5% American Indian or Alaska Native, non-Hispanic/Latino; 2% Two or more races, non-Hispanic/Latino; 1% Race/ethnicity unknown; 0.5% international; 10% transferred in. *Retention:* 46% of full-time freshmen returned.

Freshmen *Admission:* 547 applied, 303 admitted, 120 enrolled. *Average high school GPA:* 2.36.

Faculty *Total:* 39, 54% full-time, 26% with terminal degrees. *Student/faculty ratio:* 16:1.

Majors Behavioral sciences; biological and physical sciences; business administration and management; criminal justice/safety; early childhood education; elementary education; general studies; health and physical education related; health services/allied health/health sciences; history; logistics, materials, and supply chain management; mass communication/media; registered nursing/registered nurse; secondary education.

Academics *Calendar:* semesters. *Degree:* certificates and associate. *Special study options:* academic remediation for entering students, accelerated degree program, adult/continuing education programs, advanced placement credit, cooperative education, distance learning, double majors, independent study, internships, part-time degree program, services for LD students, student-designed majors, summer session for credit.

Library Ball Library with 25,313 titles, 97 serial subscriptions, 1,009 audiovisual materials, an OPAC, a Web page.

Student Life *Housing:* college housing not available. *Activities and Organizations:* Student Government Association, Student Nursing Organization, Ancilla Student Ambassadors, Phi Theta Kappa. *Campus security:* 24-hour patrols, late-night transport/escort service. *Student services:* personal/psychological counseling.

Athletics Member NJCAA. *Intercollegiate sports:* baseball M(s), basketball M(s)/W(s), cheerleading M(s)/W(s), golf M(s)/W(s), soccer M(s), softball W(s), volleyball W(s).

Standardized Tests *Recommended:* SAT or ACT (for admission).

Costs (2013–14) *Tuition:* $13,650 full-time, $455 per credit part-time. Full-time tuition and fees vary according to course load and program. Part-time tuition and fees vary according to course load and program. *Required fees:* $230 full-time. *Payment plan:* installment. *Waivers:* employees or children of employees.

Financial Aid Of all full-time matriculated undergraduates who enrolled in 2012, 391 applied for aid, 391 were judged to have need. 21 Federal Work-Study jobs (averaging $2473). *Financial aid deadline:* 3/1.

Applying *Options:* electronic application. *Required:* high school transcript. *Application deadlines:* rolling (freshmen), rolling (out-of-state freshmen), rolling (transfers).

Freshman Application Contact Ms. Sarah Lawrence, Assistant Director of Admissions, Ancilla College, 9601 Union Road, Donaldson, IN 46513. *Phone:* 574-936-8898 Ext. 396. *Toll-free phone:* 866-ANCILLA. *Fax:* 574-935-1773. *E-mail:* admissions@ancilla.edu. *Website:* http://www.ancilla.edu/.

Aviation Institute of Maintenance–Indianapolis

Indianapolis, Indiana

Freshman Application Contact Admissions Office, Aviation Institute of Maintenance–Indianapolis, 7251 West McCarty Street, Indianapolis, IN 46241. *Toll-free phone:* 888-349-5387. *Website:* http://www.aviationmaintenance.edu/.

Brown Mackie College–Fort Wayne

Fort Wayne, Indiana

Freshman Application Contact Brown Mackie College–Fort Wayne, 3000 East Coliseum Boulevard, Fort Wayne, IN 46805. *Phone:* 260-484-4400. *Toll-free phone:* 866-433-2289. *Website:* http://www.brownmackie.edu/fortwayne/.

See display below and page 360 for the College Close-Up.

Brown Mackie College–Indianapolis

Indianapolis, Indiana

Freshman Application Contact Brown Mackie College–Indianapolis, 1200 North Meridian Street, Suite 100, Indianapolis, IN 46204. *Phone:* 317-554-8301. *Toll-free phone:* 866-255-0279.
Website: http://www.brownmackie.edu/indianapolis/.

See display below and page 366 for the College Close-Up.

Brown Mackie College–Merrillville

Merrillville, Indiana

Freshman Application Contact Brown Mackie College–Merrillville, 1000 East 80th Place, Suite 205S, Merrillville, IN 46410. *Phone:* 219-769-3321. *Toll-free phone:* 800-258-3321.
Website: http://www.brownmackie.edu/merrillville/.

See display below and page 372 for the College Close-Up.

Brown Mackie College–Michigan City

Michigan City, Indiana

Freshman Application Contact Brown Mackie College–Michigan City, 325 East US Highway 20, Michigan City, IN 46360. *Phone:* 219-877-3100. *Toll-free phone:* 800-519-2416.
Website: http://www.brownmackie.edu/michigancity/.

See display below and page 376 for the College Close-Up.

Brown Mackie College–South Bend

South Bend, Indiana

Freshman Application Contact Brown Mackie College–South Bend, 3454 Douglas Road, South Bend, IN 46635. *Phone:* 574-237-0774. *Toll-free phone:* 800-743-2447.
Website: http://www.brownmackie.edu/southbend/.

See display below and page 394 for the College Close-Up.

College of Court Reporting

Hobart, Indiana

Freshman Application Contact Ms. Nicky Rodriquez, Director of Admissions, College of Court Reporting, 111 West Tenth Street, Suite 111, Hobart, IN 46342. *Phone:* 219-942-1459 Ext. 222. *Toll-free phone:* 866-294-3974. *Fax:* 219-942-1631. *E-mail:* nrodriquez@ccr.edu.
Website: http://www.ccr.edu/.

International Business College

Indianapolis, Indiana

- **Private** 2-year, founded 1889
- **Suburban** campus
- **Coed,** 413 undergraduate students
- 73% of applicants were admitted

Freshmen *Admission:* 1,054 applied, 768 admitted.

Majors Accounting technology and bookkeeping; administrative assistant and secretarial science; computer programming; computer systems networking and telecommunications; dental assisting; graphic design; hotel/motel administration; legal administrative assistant/secretary; legal assistant/paralegal; medical/clinical assistant; veterinary/animal health technology.

Academics *Calendar:* semesters. *Degree:* diplomas and associate. *Special study options:* accelerated degree program, internships.

Freshman Application Contact Admissions Office, International Business College, 7205 Shadeland Station, Indianapolis, IN 46256. *Phone:* 317-813-2300. *Toll-free phone:* 800-589-6500.
Website: http://www.ibcindianapolis.edu/.

ITT Technical Institute

Fort Wayne, Indiana

- **Proprietary** primarily 2-year, founded 1967, part of ITT Educational Services, Inc.
- **Coed**

Academics *Calendar:* quarters. *Degrees:* associate and bachelor's.

Freshman Application Contact Director of Recruitment, ITT Technical Institute, 2810 Dupont Commerce Court, Fort Wayne, IN 46825. *Phone:* 260-497-6200. *Toll-free phone:* 800-866-4488. *Fax:* 260-497-6299.
Website: http://www.itt-tech.edu/.

ITT Technical Institute

Merrillville, Indiana

- **Proprietary** primarily 2-year
- **Coed**

Academics *Degrees:* associate and bachelor's.

Freshman Application Contact Director of Recruitment, ITT Technical Institute, 8488 Georgia Street, Merrillville, IN 46410. *Phone:* 219-738-6100. *Toll-free phone:* 877-418-8134.

Website: http://www.itt-tech.edu/.

ITT Technical Institute

Newburgh, Indiana

- **Proprietary** primarily 2-year, founded 1966, part of ITT Educational Services, Inc.
- **Coed**

Academics *Calendar:* quarters. *Degrees:* associate and bachelor's.

Freshman Application Contact Director of Recruitment, ITT Technical Institute, 10999 Stahl Road, Newburgh, IN 47630-7430. *Phone:* 812-858-1600. *Toll-free phone:* 800-832-4488.

Website: http://www.itt-tech.edu/.

Ivy Tech Community College– Bloomington

Bloomington, Indiana

- **State-supported** 2-year, founded 2001, part of Ivy Tech Community College System
- **Coed,** 5,822 undergraduate students, 46% full-time, 57% women, 43% men

Undergraduates 2,705 full-time, 3,117 part-time. 1% are from out of state; 4% Black or African American, non-Hispanic/Latino; 2% Hispanic/Latino; 2% Asian, non-Hispanic/Latino; 0.6% American Indian or Alaska Native, non-Hispanic/Latino; 2% Two or more races, non-Hispanic/Latino; 10% Race/ethnicity unknown; 6% transferred in. *Retention:* 45% of full-time freshmen returned.

Freshmen *Admission:* 2,141 applied, 2,141 admitted, 1,041 enrolled.

Faculty *Total:* 356, 22% full-time. *Student/faculty ratio:* 22:1.

Majors Accounting technology and bookkeeping; building/property maintenance; business administration and management; business automation/technology/data entry; cabinetmaking and millwork; child-care and support services management; computer and information sciences; criminal justice/safety; early childhood education; electrical, electronic and communications engineering technology; electrician; emergency medical technology (EMT paramedic); executive assistant/executive secretary; general studies; heating, air conditioning, ventilation and refrigeration maintenance technology; human services; industrial technology; legal assistant/paralegal; liberal arts and sciences/liberal studies; library and archives assisting; machine tool technology; mechanic and repair technologies related; mechanics and repair; pipefitting and sprinkler fitting; psychiatric/mental health services technology; registered nursing/registered nurse; tool and die technology.

Academics *Calendar:* semesters. *Degree:* certificates and associate. *Special study options:* academic remediation for entering students, adult/continuing education programs, advanced placement credit, distance learning, external degree program, internships, part-time degree program, services for LD students, summer session for credit.

Library 5,516 titles, 97 serial subscriptions, 1,281 audiovisual materials, an OPAC, a Web page.

Student Life *Activities and Organizations:* student government, Phi Theta Kappa. *Campus security:* late-night transport/escort service.

Costs (2012–13) *Tuition:* state resident $3335 full-time, $111 per credit hour part-time; nonresident $7182 full-time, $239 per credit hour part-time. *Required fees:* $120 full-time, $60 per term part-time. *Payment plans:* installment, deferred payment. *Waivers:* senior citizens and employees or children of employees.

Financial Aid Of all full-time matriculated undergraduates who enrolled in 2011, 51 Federal Work-Study jobs (averaging $3259).

Applying *Options:* electronic application, deferred entrance. *Required:* high school transcript. *Required for some:* interview. *Application deadlines:* rolling (freshmen), rolling (transfers). *Notification:* continuous (freshmen), continuous (transfers).

Freshman Application Contact Mr. Neil Frederick, Assistant Director of Admissions, Ivy Tech Community College–Bloomington, 200 Daniels Way, Bloomington, IN 47404. *Phone:* 812-330-6026. *Toll-free phone:* 888-IVY-LINE. *Fax:* 812-332-8147. *E-mail:* nfrederi@ivytech.edu.

Website: http://www.ivytech.edu/.

Ivy Tech Community College–Central Indiana

Indianapolis, Indiana

- **State-supported** 2-year, founded 1963, part of Ivy Tech Community College System
- **Urban** 10-acre campus
- **Coed,** 21,407 undergraduate students, 34% full-time, 58% women, 42% men

Undergraduates 7,203 full-time, 14,204 part-time. 2% are from out of state; 28% Black or African American, non-Hispanic/Latino; 5% Hispanic/Latino; 2% Asian, non-Hispanic/Latino; 0.4% American Indian or Alaska Native, non-Hispanic/Latino; 2% Two or more races, non-Hispanic/Latino; 4% Race/ethnicity unknown; 5% transferred in. *Retention:* 46% of full-time freshmen returned.

Freshmen *Admission:* 4,000 enrolled.

Faculty *Total:* 859, 22% full-time. *Student/faculty ratio:* 29:1.

Majors Accounting technology and bookkeeping; automobile/automotive mechanics technology; biotechnology; building/property maintenance; business administration and management; business automation/technology/data entry; cabinetmaking and millwork; carpentry; child-care and support services management; child development; computer and information sciences; criminal justice/safety; design and visual communications; drafting and design technology; early childhood education; electrical, electronic and communications engineering technology; electrician; executive assistant/executive secretary; general studies; heating, air conditioning, ventilation and refrigeration maintenance technology; hospitality administration related; human services; industrial production technologies related; industrial technology; legal assistant/paralegal; liberal arts and sciences/liberal studies; machine shop technology; machine tool technology; masonry; mechanics and repair; medical/clinical assistant; medical radiologic technology; occupational safety and health technology; occupational therapist assistant; painting and wall covering; pipefitting and sprinkler fitting; psychiatric/mental health services technology; registered nursing/registered nurse; respiratory care therapy; sheet metal technology; surgical technology; tool and die technology.

Academics *Calendar:* semesters. *Degree:* certificates and associate. *Special study options:* academic remediation for entering students, adult/continuing education programs, advanced placement credit, cooperative education, distance learning, English as a second language, internships, off-campus study, part-time degree program, services for LD students, summer session for credit.

Library 20,247 titles, 138 serial subscriptions, 2,135 audiovisual materials, an OPAC, a Web page.

Student Life *Housing:* college housing not available. *Activities and Organizations:* student-run newspaper, student government, Phi Theta Kappa, Human Services Club, Administrative Office Assistants Club, Radiology Club. *Campus security:* 24-hour emergency response devices and patrols, late-night transport/escort service. *Student services:* personal/psychological counseling.

Athletics *Intramural sports:* baseball M, basketball M/W, cheerleading W, golf M/W, softball W, volleyball M/W.

Costs (2012–13) *Tuition:* state resident $3335 full-time, $111 per credit hour part-time; nonresident $7182 full-time, $239 per credit hour part-time. *Required fees:* $120 full-time, $60 per term part-time. *Payment plans:* installment, deferred payment. *Waivers:* senior citizens and employees or children of employees.

Financial Aid Of all full-time matriculated undergraduates who enrolled in 2011, 92 Federal Work-Study jobs (averaging $3766).

Applying *Options:* electronic application, early admission, deferred entrance. *Required:* high school transcript. *Required for some:* interview. *Application deadlines:* rolling (freshmen), rolling (transfers). *Notification:* continuous (freshmen), continuous (transfers).

Freshman Application Contact Ms. Tracy Funk, Director of Admissions, Ivy Tech Community College–Central Indiana, 50 West Fall Creek Parkway North Drive, Indianapolis, IN 46208-4777. *Phone:* 317-921-4371. *Toll-free phone:* 888-IVYLINE. *Fax:* 317-917-5919. *E-mail:* tfunk@ivytech.edu.

Website: http://www.ivytech.edu/.

Ivy Tech Community College– Columbus

Columbus, Indiana

- **State-supported** 2-year, founded 1963, part of Ivy Tech Community College System
- **Small-town** campus with easy access to Indianapolis
- **Coed,** 4,140 undergraduate students, 36% full-time, 66% women, 34% men

Undergraduates 1,509 full-time, 2,631 part-time. 1% are from out of state; 2% Black or African American, non-Hispanic/Latino; 2% Hispanic/Latino; 0.9% Asian, non-Hispanic/Latino; 0.2% American Indian or Alaska Native, non-Hispanic/Latino; 0.9% Two or more races, non-Hispanic/Latino; 14% Race/ethnicity unknown; 3% transferred in. *Retention:* 48% of full-time freshmen returned.

Freshmen *Admission:* 749 enrolled.

Faculty *Total:* 275, 20% full-time. *Student/faculty ratio:* 19:1.

Majors Accounting technology and bookkeeping; automobile/automotive mechanics technology; building/property maintenance; business administration and management; business automation/technology/data entry; cabinet-making and millwork; child-care and support services management; computer and information sciences; design and visual communications; drafting and design technology; early childhood education; electrical and power transmission installation; electrical, electronic and communications engineering technology; executive assistant/executive secretary; general studies; heating, air conditioning, ventilation and refrigeration maintenance technology; human services; industrial technology; legal assistant/paralegal; liberal arts and sciences/liberal studies; library and archives assisting; machine tool technology; masonry; mechanic and repair technologies related; mechanics and repair; medical/clinical assistant; medical radiologic technology; pipefitting and sprinkler fitting; psychiatric/mental health services technology; robotics technology; surgical technology; tool and die technology.

Academics *Calendar:* semesters. *Degree:* certificates and associate. *Special study options:* academic remediation for entering students, adult/continuing education programs, advanced placement credit, distance learning, internships, part-time degree program, services for LD students, summer session for credit.

Library 7,855 titles, 13,382 serial subscriptions, 989 audiovisual materials, an OPAC, a Web page.

Student Life *Housing:* college housing not available. *Activities and Organizations:* student government, Phi Theta Kappa, LPN Club. *Campus security:* late-night transport/escort service, trained evening security personnel, escort service.

Costs (2012–13) *Tuition:* state resident $3335 full-time, $111 per credit hour part-time; nonresident $7182 full-time, $239 per credit hour part-time. *Required fees:* $120 full-time, $60 per term part-time. *Payment plans:* installment, deferred payment. *Waivers:* senior citizens and employees or children of employees.

Financial Aid Of all full-time matriculated undergraduates who enrolled in 2011, 26 Federal Work-Study jobs (averaging $1694).

Applying *Options:* electronic application, early admission, deferred entrance. *Required:* high school transcript. *Required for some:* interview. *Application deadlines:* rolling (freshmen), rolling (transfers). *Notification:* continuous (freshmen), continuous (transfers).

Freshman Application Contact Alisa Deck, Director of Admissions, Ivy Tech Community College–Columbus, 4475 Central Avenue, Columbus, IN 47203-1868. *Phone:* 812-374-5129. *Toll-free phone:* 888-IVY-LINE. *Fax:* 812-372-0331. *E-mail:* adeck@ivytech.edu. *Website:* http://www.ivytech.edu/.

Ivy Tech Community College–East Central

Muncie, Indiana

- **State-supported** 2-year, founded 1968, part of Ivy Tech Community College System
- **Suburban** 15-acre campus with easy access to Indianapolis
- **Coed,** 7,471 undergraduate students, 48% full-time, 63% women, 37% men

Undergraduates 3,589 full-time, 3,882 part-time. 8% Black or African American, non-Hispanic/Latino; 2% Hispanic/Latino; 0.7% Asian, non-Hispanic/Latino; 0.4% American Indian or Alaska Native, non-Hispanic/Latino; 2% Two or more races, non-Hispanic/Latino; 5% Race/ethnicity unknown; 4% transferred in. *Retention:* 42% of full-time freshmen returned.

Freshmen *Admission:* 1,644 enrolled.

Faculty *Total:* 548, 22% full-time. *Student/faculty ratio:* 19:1.

Majors Accounting technology and bookkeeping; automobile/automotive mechanics technology; building/property maintenance; business administration and management; business automation/technology/data entry; cabinet-making and millwork; carpentry; child-care and support services management; computer and information sciences; construction trades; construction trades related; criminal justice/safety; early childhood education; electrical, electronic and communications engineering technology; electrician; executive assistant/executive secretary; general studies; heating, air conditioning, ventilation and refrigeration maintenance technology; hospitality administration; hospitality administration related; human services; industrial mechanics and maintenance technology; industrial production technologies related; industrial technology; legal assistant/paralegal; liberal arts and sciences/liberal studies; library and archives assisting; machine tool technology; masonry; medical/clinical assistant; medical radiologic technology; painting and wall covering; physical therapy technology; pipefitting and sprinkler fitting;

psychiatric/mental health services technology; registered nursing/registered nurse; surgical technology; tool and die technology.

Academics *Calendar:* semesters. *Degree:* certificates and associate. *Special study options:* academic remediation for entering students, adult/continuing education programs, advanced placement credit, distance learning, internships, part-time degree program, services for LD students.

Library 5,779 titles, 145 serial subscriptions, 6,266 audiovisual materials, an OPAC, a Web page.

Student Life *Housing:* college housing not available. *Activities and Organizations:* Business Professionals of America, Skills USA - VICA, student government, Phi Theta Kappa, Human Services Club.

Costs (2012–13) *Tuition:* state resident $3335 full-time, $111 per credit hour part-time; nonresident $7182 full-time, $239 per credit hour part-time. *Required fees:* $120 full-time, $60 per term part-time. *Payment plans:* installment, deferred payment. *Waivers:* senior citizens and employees or children of employees.

Financial Aid Of all full-time matriculated undergraduates who enrolled in 2011, 65 Federal Work-Study jobs (averaging $2666).

Applying *Options:* electronic application, early admission, deferred entrance. *Required:* high school transcript. *Required for some:* interview. *Application deadlines:* rolling (freshmen), rolling (transfers). *Notification:* continuous (freshmen), continuous (transfers).

Freshman Application Contact Ms. Mary Lewellen, Ivy Tech Community College–East Central, 4301 South Cowan Road, Muncie, IN 47302-9448. *Phone:* 765-289-2291 Ext. 1391. *Toll-free phone:* 888-IVY-LINE. *Fax:* 765-289-2292. *E-mail:* mlewelle@ivytech.edu. *Website:* http://www.ivytech.edu/.

Ivy Tech Community College–Kokomo

Kokomo, Indiana

- **State-supported** 2-year, founded 1968, part of Ivy Tech Community College System
- **Small-town** 20-acre campus with easy access to Indianapolis
- **Coed,** 4,649 undergraduate students, 39% full-time, 64% women, 36% men

Undergraduates 1,821 full-time, 2,828 part-time. 6% Black or African American, non-Hispanic/Latino; 3% Hispanic/Latino; 0.5% Asian, non-Hispanic/Latino; 0.8% American Indian or Alaska Native, non-Hispanic/Latino; 1% Two or more races, non-Hispanic/Latino; 4% Race/ethnicity unknown; 3% transferred in. *Retention:* 50% of full-time freshmen returned.

Freshmen *Admission:* 849 enrolled.

Faculty *Total:* 364, 20% full-time. *Student/faculty ratio:* 16:1.

Majors Accounting technology and bookkeeping; automobile/automotive mechanics technology; building/property maintenance; business administration and management; business automation/technology/data entry; cabinet-making and millwork; child-care and support services management; computer and information sciences; construction trades related; criminal justice/safety; drafting and design technology; early childhood education; electrical, electronic and communications engineering technology; electrician; emergency medical technology (EMT paramedic); executive assistant/executive secretary; general studies; heating, air conditioning, ventilation and refrigeration maintenance technology; human services; industrial technology; legal assistant/paralegal; liberal arts and sciences/liberal studies; library and archives assisting; machine tool technology; mechanic and repair technologies related; mechanics and repair; medical/clinical assistant; pipefitting and sprinkler fitting; psychiatric/mental health services technology; surgical technology; tool and die technology.

Academics *Calendar:* semesters. *Degree:* certificates and associate. *Special study options:* academic remediation for entering students, adult/continuing education programs, advanced placement credit, distance learning, internships, part-time degree program, services for LD students, summer session for credit.

Library 5,177 titles, 99 serial subscriptions, 772 audiovisual materials, an OPAC, a Web page.

Student Life *Housing:* college housing not available. *Activities and Organizations:* student-run newspaper, student government, Collegiate Secretaries International, Licensed Practical Nursing Club, Phi Theta Kappa. *Campus security:* 24-hour emergency response devices, late-night transport/escort service. *Student services:* personal/psychological counseling.

Costs (2012–13) *Tuition:* state resident $3335 full-time, $111 per credit hour part-time; nonresident $7182 full-time, $239 per credit hour part-time. *Required fees:* $120 full-time, $60 per term part-time. *Payment plans:* installment, deferred payment. *Waivers:* senior citizens and employees or children of employees.

Financial Aid Of all full-time matriculated undergraduates who enrolled in 2011, 45 Federal Work-Study jobs (averaging $1829).

Applying *Options:* electronic application, early admission. *Required:* high school transcript. *Required for some:* interview. *Application deadlines:* rolling (freshmen), rolling (transfers). *Notification:* continuous (freshmen), continuous (transfers).

Freshman Application Contact Mr. Mike Federspill, Director of Admissions, Ivy Tech Community College–Kokomo, 1815 East Morgan Street, Kokomo, IN 46903-1373. *Phone:* 765-459-0561 Ext. 233. *Toll-free phone:* 888-IVY-LINE. *Fax:* 765-454-5111. *E-mail:* mfedersp@ivytech.edu. *Website:* http://www.ivytech.edu/.

Ivy Tech Community College–Lafayette

Lafayette, Indiana

- **State-supported** 2-year, founded 1968, part of Ivy Tech Community College System
- **Suburban** campus with easy access to Indianapolis
- **Coed,** 6,666 undergraduate students, 44% full-time, 56% women, 44% men

Undergraduates 2,933 full-time, 3,733 part-time. 1% are from out of state; 4% Black or African American, non-Hispanic/Latino; 6% Hispanic/Latino; 2% Asian, non-Hispanic/Latino; 0.5% American Indian or Alaska Native, non-Hispanic/Latino; 1% Two or more races, non-Hispanic/Latino; 8% Race/ethnicity unknown; 5% transferred in. *Retention:* 49% of full-time freshmen returned.

Freshmen *Admission:* 1,229 enrolled.

Faculty *Total:* 412, 25% full-time.

Majors Accounting; accounting technology and bookkeeping; automobile/automotive mechanics technology; biotechnology; building/property maintenance; business administration and management; business automation/technology/data entry; cabinetmaking and millwork; carpentry; child-care and support services management; computer and information sciences; drafting and design technology; early childhood education; electrical, electronic and communications engineering technology; electrician; executive assistant/executive secretary; general studies; heating, air conditioning, ventilation and refrigeration maintenance technology; human services; industrial production technologies related; industrial technology; ironworking; legal assistant/paralegal; liberal arts and sciences/liberal studies; library and archives assisting; lineworker; machine tool technology; masonry; mechanic and repair technologies related; mechanics and repair; medical/clinical assistant; painting and wall covering; pipefitting and sprinkler fitting; psychiatric/mental health services technology; quality control and safety technologies related; quality control technology; registered nursing/registered nurse; respiratory care therapy; robotics technology; sheet metal technology; surgical technology; tool and die technology.

Academics *Calendar:* semesters. *Degree:* certificates and associate. *Special study options:* academic remediation for entering students, advanced placement credit, distance learning, internships, part-time degree program, services for LD students, summer session for credit.

Library 8,043 titles, 200 serial subscriptions, 2,234 audiovisual materials, an OPAC, a Web page.

Student Life *Housing:* college housing not available. *Activities and Organizations:* student-run newspaper, student government, Phi Theta Kappa, LPN Club, Accounting Club, Student Computer Technology Association. *Student services:* personal/psychological counseling.

Costs (2012–13) *Tuition:* state resident $3335 full-time, $111 per credit hour part-time; nonresident $7182 full-time, $239 per credit hour part-time. *Required fees:* $120 full-time, $60 per term part-time. *Payment plans:* installment, deferred payment. *Waivers:* senior citizens and employees or children of employees.

Financial Aid Of all full-time matriculated undergraduates who enrolled in 2011, 65 Federal Work-Study jobs (averaging $2222). 1 state and other part-time job (averaging $2436).

Applying *Options:* electronic application. *Required:* high school transcript. *Required for some:* interview. *Application deadlines:* rolling (freshmen), rolling (transfers). *Notification:* continuous (freshmen), continuous (transfers).

Freshman Application Contact Mr. Ivan Hernanadez, Director of Admissions, Ivy Tech Community College–Lafayette, 3101 South Creasy Lane, PO Box 6299, Lafayette, IN 47903. *Phone:* 765-269-5116. *Toll-free phone:* 888-IVY-LINE. *Fax:* 765-772-9293. *E-mail:* ihernand@ivytech.edu. *Website:* http://www.ivytech.edu/.

Ivy Tech Community College–North Central

South Bend, Indiana

- **State-supported** 2-year, founded 1968, part of Ivy Tech Community College System
- **Suburban** 4-acre campus
- **Coed,** 7,852 undergraduate students, 29% full-time, 62% women, 38% men

Undergraduates 2,290 full-time, 5,562 part-time. 2% are from out of state; 18% Black or African American, non-Hispanic/Latino; 9% Hispanic/Latino; 1% Asian, non-Hispanic/Latino; 0.6% American Indian or Alaska Native, non-Hispanic/Latino; 2% Two or more races, non-Hispanic/Latino; 4% Race/ethnicity unknown; 6% transferred in. *Retention:* 44% of full-time freshmen returned.

Freshmen *Admission:* 1,449 enrolled.

Faculty *Total:* 423, 26% full-time. *Student/faculty ratio:* 19:1.

Majors Accounting technology and bookkeeping; automobile/automotive mechanics technology; biotechnology; building/property maintenance; business administration and management; business automation/technology/data entry; cabinetmaking and millwork; carpentry; child-care and support services management; clinical/medical laboratory technology; computer and information sciences; criminal justice/safety; design and visual communications; early childhood education; educational/instructional technology; electrical, electronic and communications engineering technology; electrician; emergency medical technology (EMT paramedic); executive assistant/executive secretary; general studies; heating, air conditioning, ventilation and refrigeration maintenance technology; hospitality administration; human services; industrial production technologies related; industrial technology; interior design; ironworking; legal assistant/paralegal; liberal arts and sciences/liberal studies; library and archives assisting; machine tool technology; masonry; mechanic and repair technologies related; mechanics and repair; medical/clinical assistant; painting and wall covering; pipefitting and sprinkler fitting; registered nursing/registered nurse; robotics technology; sheet metal technology; telecommunications technology; tool and die technology.

Academics *Calendar:* semesters. *Degree:* certificates and associate. *Special study options:* academic remediation for entering students, adult/continuing education programs, advanced placement credit, distance learning, English as a second language, internships, off-campus study, part-time degree program, services for LD students, summer session for credit.

Library 6,246 titles, 90 serial subscriptions, 689 audiovisual materials, an OPAC, a Web page.

Student Life *Housing:* college housing not available. *Activities and Organizations:* Phi Theta Kappa, student government, LPN Club. *Campus security:* 24-hour emergency response devices and patrols, late-night transport/escort service, security during open hours. *Student services:* personal/psychological counseling, women's center.

Costs (2012–13) *Tuition:* state resident $3335 full-time, $111 per credit hour part-time; nonresident $7182 full-time, $239 per credit hour part-time. *Required fees:* $120 full-time, $60 per term part-time. *Payment plans:* installment, deferred payment. *Waivers:* senior citizens and employees or children of employees.

Financial Aid Of all full-time matriculated undergraduates who enrolled in 2011, 100 Federal Work-Study jobs (averaging $1538).

Applying *Options:* electronic application, early admission, deferred entrance. *Required:* high school transcript. *Required for some:* interview. *Application deadlines:* rolling (freshmen), rolling (transfers). *Notification:* continuous (freshmen), continuous (transfers).

Freshman Application Contact Ms. Janice Austin, Director of Admissions, Ivy Tech Community College–North Central, 220 Dean Johnson Boulevard, South Bend, IN 46601-3415. *Phone:* 574-289-7001 Ext. 5326. *Toll-free phone:* 888-IVY-LINE. *Fax:* 574-236-7177. *E-mail:* jaustin@ivytech.edu. *Website:* http://www.ivytech.edu/.

Ivy Tech Community College–Northeast

Fort Wayne, Indiana

- **State-supported** 2-year, founded 1969, part of Ivy Tech Community College System
- **Urban** 22-acre campus
- **Coed,** 9,883 undergraduate students, 38% full-time, 59% women, 41% men

Undergraduates 3,738 full-time, 6,145 part-time. 3% are from out of state; 16% Black or African American, non-Hispanic/Latino; 5% Hispanic/Latino; 2% Asian, non-Hispanic/Latino; 0.5% American Indian or Alaska Native, non-Hispanic/Latino; 2% Two or more races, non-Hispanic/Latino; 3% Race/ethnicity unknown; 6% transferred in. *Retention:* 42% of full-time freshmen returned.

Freshmen *Admission:* 1,860 enrolled.

Faculty *Total:* 506, 26% full-time. *Student/faculty ratio:* 22:1.

Majors Accounting technology and bookkeeping; automobile/automotive mechanics technology; building/property maintenance; business administration and management; business automation/technology/data entry; cabinet-making and millwork; child-care and support services management; computer and information sciences; construction trades; construction trades related; drafting and design technology; early childhood education; electrical, electronic and communications engineering technology; electrician; executive assistant/executive secretary; general studies; heating, air conditioning, ventilation and refrigeration maintenance technology; hospitality administration; hospitality administration related; human services; industrial production technologies related; industrial technology; ironworking; legal assistant/paralegal; liberal arts and sciences/liberal studies; library and archives assisting; machine tool technology; masonry; massage therapy; mechanics and repair; medical/clinical assistant; occupational safety and health technology; painting and wall covering; pipefitting and sprinkler fitting; psychiatric/mental health services technology; respiratory care therapy; robotics technology; sheet metal technology; tool and die technology.

Academics *Calendar:* semesters. *Degree:* certificates and associate. *Special study options:* adult/continuing education programs, advanced placement credit, distance learning, English as a second language, internships, part-time degree program, services for LD students, summer session for credit.

Library 18,389 titles, 110 serial subscriptions, 3,397 audiovisual materials, an OPAC, a Web page.

Student Life *Housing:* college housing not available. *Activities and Organizations:* student-run newspaper, student government, LPN Club, Phi Theta Kappa. *Campus security:* 24-hour emergency response devices and patrols, late-night transport/escort service.

Costs (2012–13) *Tuition:* state resident $3335 full-time, $111 per credit hour part-time; nonresident $7182 full-time, $239 per credit hour part-time. *Required fees:* $120 full-time, $60 per term part-time. *Payment plans:* installment, deferred payment. *Waivers:* senior citizens and employees or children of employees.

Financial Aid Of all full-time matriculated undergraduates who enrolled in 2011, 40 Federal Work-Study jobs (averaging $4041).

Applying *Options:* early admission. *Required:* high school transcript. *Required for some:* interview. *Application deadlines:* rolling (freshmen), rolling (transfers). *Notification:* continuous (freshmen), continuous (transfers).

Freshman Application Contact Robyn Boss, Director of Admissions, Ivy Tech Community College–Northeast, 3800 North Anthony Boulevard, Ft. Wayne, IN 46805-1489. *Phone:* 260-480-4211. *Toll-free phone:* 888-IVY-LINE. *Fax:* 260-480-2053. *E-mail:* rboss1@ivytech.edu. *Website:* http://www.ivytech.edu/.

Ivy Tech Community College–Northwest
Gary, Indiana

- **State-supported** 2-year, founded 1963, part of Ivy Tech Community College System
- **Urban** 13-acre campus with easy access to Chicago
- **Coed,** 9,813 undergraduate students, 39% full-time, 60% women, 40% men

Undergraduates 3,807 full-time, 6,006 part-time. 2% are from out of state; 26% Black or African American, non-Hispanic/Latino; 11% Hispanic/Latino; 0.7% Asian, non-Hispanic/Latino; 0.3% American Indian or Alaska Native, non-Hispanic/Latino; 1% Two or more races, non-Hispanic/Latino; 8% Race/ethnicity unknown; 7% transferred in. *Retention:* 47% of full-time freshmen returned.

Freshmen *Admission:* 2,115 enrolled.

Faculty *Total:* 482, 26% full-time. *Student/faculty ratio:* 24:1.

Majors Accounting technology and bookkeeping; automobile/automotive mechanics technology; building/construction finishing, management, and inspection related; building/property maintenance; business administration and management; business automation/technology/data entry; cabinetmaking and millwork; carpentry; child-care and support services management; computer and information sciences; construction trades; criminal justice/safety; drafting and design technology; early childhood education; electrical, electronic and communications engineering technology; electrician; executive assistant/executive secretary; funeral service and mortuary science; general studies; heating, air conditioning, ventilation and refrigeration maintenance technology; hospitality administration; human services; industrial technology; ironworking; legal assistant/paralegal; liberal arts and sciences/liberal studies; library and archives assisting; machine tool technology; masonry; mechanic and repair technologies related; mechanics and repair; medical/clinical assistant; occupational safety and health technology; painting and wall covering; pipefitting and

sprinkler fitting; psychiatric/mental health services technology; registered nursing/registered nurse; respiratory care therapy; sheet metal technology; surgical technology; telecommunications technology; tool and die technology.

Academics *Calendar:* semesters. *Degree:* certificates and associate. *Special study options:* academic remediation for entering students, adult/continuing education programs, advanced placement credit, distance learning, internships, part-time degree program, services for LD students, summer session for credit.

Library 13,805 titles, 160 serial subscriptions, 4,295 audiovisual materials, an OPAC, a Web page.

Student Life *Housing:* college housing not available. *Activities and Organizations:* Phi Theta Kappa, LPN Club, Computer Club, student government, Business Club. *Campus security:* 24-hour emergency response devices, late-night transport/escort service.

Financial Aid Of all full-time matriculated undergraduates who enrolled in 2011, 74 Federal Work-Study jobs (averaging $2131).

Applying *Options:* electronic application, deferred entrance. *Required:* high school transcript. *Required for some:* interview. *Application deadlines:* rolling (freshmen), rolling (transfers). *Notification:* continuous (freshmen), continuous (transfers).

Freshman Application Contact Ms. Twilla Lewis, Associate Dean of Student Affairs, Ivy Tech Community College–Northwest, 1440 East 35th Avenue, Gary, IN 46409-499. *Phone:* 219-981-1111 Ext. 2273. *Toll-free phone:* 888-IVY-LINE. *Fax:* 219-981-4415. *E-mail:* tlewis@ivytech.edu. *Website:* http://www.ivytech.edu/.

Ivy Tech Community College–Richmond
Richmond, Indiana

- **State-supported** 2-year, founded 1963, part of Ivy Tech Community College System
- **Small-town** 23-acre campus with easy access to Indianapolis
- **Coed,** 3,233 undergraduate students, 35% full-time, 65% women, 35% men

Undergraduates 1,117 full-time, 2,116 part-time. 8% are from out of state; 5% Black or African American, non-Hispanic/Latino; 1% Hispanic/Latino; 0.3% Asian, non-Hispanic/Latino; 0.6% American Indian or Alaska Native, non-Hispanic/Latino; 1% Two or more races, non-Hispanic/Latino; 2% Race/ethnicity unknown; 3% transferred in. *Retention:* 38% of full-time freshmen returned.

Freshmen *Admission:* 488 enrolled.

Faculty *Total:* 196, 21% full-time. *Student/faculty ratio:* 20:1.

Majors Accounting technology and bookkeeping; automobile/automotive mechanics technology; building/property maintenance; business administration and management; business automation/technology/data entry; cabinet-making and millwork; child-care and support services management; computer and information sciences; construction trades; construction trades related; early childhood education; electrical, electronic and communications engineering technology; electrician; executive assistant/executive secretary; general studies; heating, air conditioning, ventilation and refrigeration maintenance technology; human services; industrial production technologies related; industrial technology; legal assistant/paralegal; liberal arts and sciences/liberal studies; library and archives assisting; machine tool technology; mechanics and repair; medical/clinical assistant; pipefitting and sprinkler fitting; psychiatric/mental health services technology; registered nursing/registered nurse; robotics technology; tool and die technology.

Academics *Calendar:* semesters. *Degree:* certificates and associate. *Special study options:* academic remediation for entering students, adult/continuing education programs, advanced placement credit, distance learning, independent study, internships, off-campus study, part-time degree program, services for LD students, summer session for credit.

Student Life *Housing:* college housing not available. *Activities and Organizations:* student-run newspaper, student government, Phi Theta Kappa, LPN Club, CATS 2000, Business Professionals of America. *Campus security:* 24-hour emergency response devices, late-night transport/escort service. *Student services:* personal/psychological counseling.

Athletics *Intramural sports:* softball M/W.

Costs (2012–13) *Tuition:* state resident $3335 full-time, $111 per credit hour part-time; nonresident $7182 full-time, $239 per credit hour part-time. *Required fees:* $120 full-time, $60 per term part-time. *Payment plans:* installment, deferred payment. *Waivers:* senior citizens and employees or children of employees.

Financial Aid Of all full-time matriculated undergraduates who enrolled in 2011, 14 Federal Work-Study jobs (averaging $3106). 1 state and other part-time job (averaging $3380).

Applying *Options:* electronic application, early admission. *Required:* high school transcript. *Required for some:* interview. *Application deadlines:* rolling (freshmen), rolling (transfers). *Notification:* continuous (freshmen), continuous (transfers).

Freshman Application Contact Christine Seger, Director of Admissions, Ivy Tech Community College–Richmond, 2325 Chester Boulevard, Richmond, IN 47374-1298. *Phone:* 765-966-2656 Ext. 1212. *Toll-free phone:* 888-IVY-LINE. *Fax:* 765-962-8741. *E-mail:* crethlake@ivytech.edu. *Website:* http://www.ivytech.edu/richmond/.

Ivy Tech Community College–Southeast

Madison, Indiana

- **State-supported** 2-year, founded 1963, part of Ivy Tech Community College System
- **Small-town** 5-acre campus with easy access to Louisville
- **Coed,** 2,778 undergraduate students, 40% full-time, 69% women, 31% men

Undergraduates 1,106 full-time, 1,672 part-time. 4% are from out of state; 0.7% Black or African American, non-Hispanic/Latino; 1% Hispanic/Latino; 0.3% Asian, non-Hispanic/Latino; 0.3% American Indian or Alaska Native, non-Hispanic/Latino; 0.6% Two or more races, non-Hispanic/Latino; 11% Race/ethnicity unknown; 3% transferred in. *Retention:* 54% of full-time freshmen returned.

Freshmen *Admission:* 508 enrolled.

Faculty *Total:* 200, 23% full-time. *Student/faculty ratio:* 17:1.

Majors Accounting technology and bookkeeping; business administration and management; business automation/technology/data entry; child-care and support services management; computer and information sciences; early childhood education; electrical, electronic and communications engineering technology; executive assistant/executive secretary; general studies; human services; industrial technology; legal assistant/paralegal; liberal arts and sciences/liberal studies; library and archives assisting; licensed practical/vocational nurse training; medical/clinical assistant; psychiatric/mental health services technology; registered nursing/registered nurse.

Academics *Calendar:* semesters. *Degree:* certificates and associate. *Special study options:* academic remediation for entering students, advanced placement credit, distance learning, internships, part-time degree program, services for LD students, summer session for credit.

Library 9,027 titles, 14,299 serial subscriptions, 1,341 audiovisual materials, an OPAC, a Web page.

Student Life *Housing:* college housing not available. *Activities and Organizations:* student government, Phi Theta Kappa, LPN Club. *Campus security:* 24-hour emergency response devices.

Costs (2012–13) *Tuition:* state resident $3335 full-time, $111 per credit hour part-time; nonresident $7182 full-time, $239 per credit hour part-time. *Required fees:* $120 full-time, $60 per term part-time. *Payment plans:* installment, deferred payment. *Waivers:* senior citizens and employees or children of employees.

Financial Aid Of all full-time matriculated undergraduates who enrolled in 2011, 26 Federal Work-Study jobs (averaging $1696).

Applying *Options:* electronic application. *Required:* high school transcript. *Required for some:* interview. *Application deadlines:* rolling (freshmen), rolling (transfers). *Notification:* continuous (freshmen), continuous (transfers).

Freshman Application Contact Ms. Cindy Hutcherson, Assistant Director of Admission/Career Counselor, Ivy Tech Community College–Southeast, 590 Ivy Tech Drive, Madison, IN 47250-1881. *Phone:* 812-265-2580 Ext. 4142. *Toll-free phone:* 888-IVY-LINE. *Fax:* 812-265-4028. *E-mail:* chutcher@ivytech.edu. *Website:* http://www.ivytech.edu/.

Ivy Tech Community College–Southern Indiana

Sellersburg, Indiana

- **State-supported** 2-year, founded 1968, part of Ivy Tech Community College System
- **Small-town** 63-acre campus with easy access to Louisville
- **Coed,** 5,283 undergraduate students, 29% full-time, 56% women, 44% men

Undergraduates 1,554 full-time, 3,729 part-time. 8% are from out of state; 8% Black or African American, non-Hispanic/Latino; 2% Hispanic/Latino; 0.8% Asian, non-Hispanic/Latino; 0.5% American Indian or Alaska Native, non-Hispanic/Latino; 1% Two or more races, non-Hispanic/Latino; 5% Race/ethnicity unknown; 6% transferred in. *Retention:* 45% of full-time freshmen returned.

Freshmen *Admission:* 1,043 enrolled.

Faculty *Total:* 240, 25% full-time. *Student/faculty ratio:* 23:1.

Majors Accounting technology and bookkeeping; automobile/automotive mechanics technology; building/property maintenance; business administration and management; business automation/technology/data entry; cabinet-making and millwork; carpentry; child-care and support services management; computer and information sciences; design and visual communications; early childhood education; electrical, electronic and communications engineering technology; electrician; executive assistant/executive secretary; general studies; heating, air conditioning, ventilation and refrigeration maintenance technology; human services; industrial technology; legal assistant/paralegal; liberal arts and sciences/liberal studies; library and archives assisting; machine tool technology; masonry; mechanics and repair; medical/clinical assistant; pipefitting and sprinkler fitting; psychiatric/mental health services technology; registered nursing/registered nurse; respiratory care therapy; sheet metal technology; tool and die technology.

Academics *Calendar:* semesters. *Degree:* certificates and associate. *Special study options:* academic remediation for entering students, adult/continuing education programs, advanced placement credit, cooperative education, distance learning, internships, part-time degree program, services for LD students, summer session for credit.

Library 7,634 titles, 66 serial subscriptions, 648 audiovisual materials, an OPAC, a Web page.

Student Life *Housing:* college housing not available. *Activities and Organizations:* Phi Theta Kappa, Practical Nursing Club, Medical Assistant Club, Accounting Club, student government. *Campus security:* late-night transport/escort service.

Costs (2012–13) *Tuition:* state resident $3335 full-time, $111 per credit hour part-time; nonresident $7182 full-time, $239 per credit hour part-time. *Required fees:* $60 per term part-time. *Payment plans:* installment, deferred payment. *Waivers:* senior citizens and employees or children of employees.

Financial Aid Of all full-time matriculated undergraduates who enrolled in 2011, 20 Federal Work-Study jobs (averaging $5007). 1 state and other part-time job (averaging $6080).

Applying *Options:* electronic application, early admission, deferred entrance. *Required:* high school transcript. *Required for some:* interview. *Application deadlines:* rolling (freshmen), rolling (transfers). *Notification:* continuous (freshmen), continuous (transfers).

Freshman Application Contact Ben Harris, Director of Admissions, Ivy Tech Community College–Southern Indiana, 8204 Highway 311, Sellersburg, IN 47172-1897. *Phone:* 812-246-3301 Ext. 4137. *Toll-free phone:* 888-IVY-LINE. *Fax:* 812-246-9905. *E-mail:* bharris88@ivytech.edu. *Website:* http://www.ivytech.edu/.

Ivy Tech Community College–Southwest

Evansville, Indiana

- **State-supported** 2-year, founded 1963, part of Ivy Tech Community College System
- **Suburban** 15-acre campus
- **Coed,** 5,731 undergraduate students, 36% full-time, 55% women, 45% men

Undergraduates 2,066 full-time, 3,665 part-time. 3% are from out of state; 10% Black or African American, non-Hispanic/Latino; 2% Hispanic/Latino; 0.5% Asian, non-Hispanic/Latino; 0.4% American Indian or Alaska Native, non-Hispanic/Latino; 1% Two or more races, non-Hispanic/Latino; 3% Race/ethnicity unknown; 5% transferred in. *Retention:* 45% of full-time freshmen returned.

Freshmen *Admission:* 901 enrolled.

Faculty *Total:* 341, 25% full-time. *Student/faculty ratio:* 19:1.

Majors Accounting technology and bookkeeping; automobile/automotive mechanics technology; boilermaking; building/property maintenance; business administration and management; business automation/technology/data entry; cabinetmaking and millwork; carpentry; child-care and support services management; computer and information sciences; construction/heavy equipment/earthmoving equipment operation; criminal justice/safety; design and visual communications; early childhood education; electrical, electronic and communications engineering technology; electrician; emergency medical technology (EMT paramedic); executive assistant/executive secretary; general studies; graphic design; heating, air conditioning, ventilation and refrigeration maintenance technology; human services; industrial production technologies related; industrial technology; interior design; ironworking; legal assistant/paralegal; liberal arts and sciences/liberal studies; library and archives assisting; machine tool technology; masonry; mechanic and repair technologies related; mechanics and repair; medical/clinical assistant; painting and wall covering; pipefitting and sprinkler fitting; psychiatric/mental health services technology; registered nursing/registered nurse; robotics technology; sheet metal technology; surgical technology; tool and die technology.

Academics *Calendar:* semesters. *Degree:* certificates and associate. *Special study options:* academic remediation for entering students, advanced placement credit, cooperative education, distance learning, independent study, internships, part-time degree program, services for LD students, summer session for credit.

Library 7,082 titles, 107 serial subscriptions, 1,755 audiovisual materials, an OPAC, a Web page.

Student Life *Housing:* college housing not available. *Activities and Organizations:* student government, Phi Theta Kappa, LPN Club, National Association of Industrial Technology, Design Club. *Campus security:* late-night transport/escort service.

Costs (2012–13) *Tuition:* state resident $3335 full-time, $111 per credit hour part-time; nonresident $7182 full-time, $239 per credit hour part-time. *Required fees:* $120 full-time, $60 per term part-time. *Payment plans:* installment, deferred payment. *Waivers:* senior citizens and employees or children of employees.

Financial Aid Of all full-time matriculated undergraduates who enrolled in 2011, 65 Federal Work-Study jobs (averaging $2264).

Applying *Options:* electronic application, early admission, deferred entrance. *Required:* high school transcript. *Required for some:* interview. *Application deadlines:* rolling (freshmen), rolling (transfers). *Notification:* continuous (freshmen), continuous (transfers).

Freshman Application Contact Ms. Denise Johnson-Kincade, Director of Admissions, Ivy Tech Community College–Southwest, 3501 First Avenue, Evansville, IN 47710-3398. *Phone:* 812-429-1430. *Toll-free phone:* 888-IVY-LINE. *Fax:* 812-429-9878. *E-mail:* ajohnson@ivytech.edu. *Website:* http://www.ivytech.edu/.

Ivy Tech Community College–Wabash Valley

Terre Haute, Indiana

- **State-supported** 2-year, founded 1966, part of Ivy Tech Community College System
- **Suburban** 55-acre campus with easy access to Indianapolis
- **Coed,** 5,544 undergraduate students, 40% full-time, 56% women, 44% men

Undergraduates 2,224 full-time, 3,320 part-time. 5% are from out of state; 4% Black or African American, non-Hispanic/Latino; 1% Hispanic/Latino; 0.5% Asian, non-Hispanic/Latino; 0.3% American Indian or Alaska Native, non-Hispanic/Latino; 1% Two or more races, non-Hispanic/Latino; 10% Race/ethnicity unknown; 6% transferred in. *Retention:* 48% of full-time freshmen returned.

Freshmen *Admission:* 842 enrolled.

Faculty *Total:* 267, 35% full-time. *Student/faculty ratio:* 22:1.

Majors Accounting technology and bookkeeping; airframe mechanics and aircraft maintenance technology; allied health diagnostic, intervention, and treatment professions related; automobile/automotive mechanics technology; building/property maintenance; business administration and management; cabinetmaking and millwork; carpentry; child-care and support services management; clinical/medical laboratory technology; computer and information sciences; construction/heavy equipment/earthmoving equipment operation; criminal justice/safety; design and visual communications; early childhood education; electrical, electronic and communications engineering technology; electrician; emergency medical technology (EMT paramedic); executive assistant/executive secretary; general studies; heating, air conditioning, ventilation and refrigeration maintenance technology; human services; industrial production technologies related; industrial technology; ironworking; legal assistant/paralegal; liberal arts and sciences/liberal studies; library and archives assisting; machine tool technology; masonry; mechanics and repair; medical/clinical assistant; medical radiologic technology; occupational safety and health technology; office management; painting and wall covering; pipefitting and sprinkler fitting; psychiatric/mental health services technology; quality control and safety technologies related; registered nursing/registered nurse; robotics technology; sheet metal technology; surgical technology; tool and die technology.

Academics *Calendar:* semesters. *Degree:* certificates and associate. *Special study options:* academic remediation for entering students, adult/continuing education programs, advanced placement credit, distance learning, internships, part-time degree program, services for LD students, summer session for credit.

Library 4,403 titles, 77 serial subscriptions, 406 audiovisual materials, an OPAC, a Web page.

Student Life *Housing:* college housing not available. *Activities and Organizations:* student government, Phi Theta Kappa, LPN Club, National Association of Industrial Technology. *Campus security:* 24-hour emergency response devices. *Student services:* personal/psychological counseling, women's center.

Athletics *Intramural sports:* basketball M/W, volleyball M/W.

Costs (2012–13) *Tuition:* state resident $3335 full-time, $111 per credit hour part-time; nonresident $7182 full-time, $239 per credit hour part-time.

Required fees: $120 full-time, $60 per term part-time. *Payment plans:* installment, deferred payment. *Waivers:* senior citizens and employees or children of employees.

Financial Aid Of all full-time matriculated undergraduates who enrolled in 2011, 51 Federal Work-Study jobs (averaging $2110). 1 state and other part-time job (averaging $2963).

Applying *Options:* electronic application, early admission, deferred entrance. *Required:* high school transcript. *Required for some:* interview. *Application deadlines:* rolling (freshmen), rolling (transfers). *Notification:* continuous (freshmen), continuous (transfers).

Freshman Application Contact Mr. Michael Fisher, Director of Admissions, Ivy Tech Community College–Wabash Valley, 7999 U.S. Highway 41 South, Terre Haute, IN 47802-4898. *Phone:* 812-298-2300. *Toll-free phone:* 888-IVY-LINE. *Fax:* 812-298-2291. *E-mail:* mfisher@ivytech.edu. *Website:* http://www.ivytech.edu/.

Kaplan College, Hammond Campus

Hammond, Indiana

- **Proprietary** 2-year, founded 1962
- **Suburban** campus
- **Coed**

Academics *Calendar:* quarters. *Degree:* diplomas and associate.

Freshman Application Contact Kaplan College, Hammond Campus, 7833 Indianapolis Boulevard, Hammond, IN 46324. *Phone:* 219-844-0100. *Toll-free phone:* 800-935-1857. *Website:* http://hammond.kaplancollege.com/.

Kaplan College, Southeast Indianapolis Campus

Indianapolis, Indiana

- **Proprietary** 2-year
- **Coed**

Academics *Degree:* diplomas and associate.

Freshman Application Contact Director of Admissions, Kaplan College, Southeast Indianapolis Campus, 4200 South East Street, Indianapolis, IN 46227. *Phone:* 317-782-0315. *Website:* http://www.seindianapolis.kaplancollege.com/.

Lincoln College of Technology

Indianapolis, Indiana

Director of Admissions Ms. Cindy Ryan, Director of Admissions, Lincoln College of Technology, 7225 Winton Drive, Building 128, Indianapolis, IN 46268. *Phone:* 317-632-5553. *Website:* http://www.lincolnedu.com/.

MedTech College

Ft. Wayne, Indiana

Admissions Office Contact MedTech College, 7230 Engle Road, Ft. Wayne, IN 46804. *Website:* http://www.medtechcollege.edu/.

MedTech College

Greenwood, Indiana

Admissions Office Contact MedTech College, 1500 American Way, Greenwood, IN 46143. *Website:* http://www.medtechcollege.edu/.

Mid-America College of Funeral Service

Jeffersonville, Indiana

Freshman Application Contact Mr. Richard Nelson, Dean of Students, Mid-America College of Funeral Service, 3111 Hamburg Pike, Jeffersonville, IN 47130-9630. *Phone:* 812-288-8878. *Toll-free phone:* 800-221-6158. *Fax:* 812-288-5942. *E-mail:* macfs@mindspring.com. *Website:* http://www.mid-america.edu/.

Vet Tech Institute at International Business College

Fort Wayne, Indiana

- **Private** 2-year, founded 2005
- **Suburban** campus
- **Coed,** 125 undergraduate students
- 48% of applicants were admitted

Freshmen *Admission:* 360 applied, 173 admitted.

Majors Veterinary/animal health technology.

Academics *Degree:* associate. *Special study options:* accelerated degree program, internships.

Freshman Application Contact Admissions Office, Vet Tech Institute at International Business College, 5699 Coventry Lane, Fort Wayne, IN 46804. *Phone:* 800-589-6363. *Toll-free phone:* 800-589-6363. *Website:* http://www.vettechinstitute.edu/.

Vet Tech Institute at International Business College

Indianapolis, Indiana

- **Private** 2-year, founded 2007
- **Suburban** campus
- **Coed,** 111 undergraduate students
- 45% of applicants were admitted

Freshmen *Admission:* 418 applied, 190 admitted.

Majors Veterinary/animal health technology.

Academics *Degree:* associate. *Special study options:* accelerated degree program, internships.

Freshman Application Contact Admissions Office, Vet Tech Institute at International Business College, 7205 Shadeland Station, Indianapolis, IN 46256. *Phone:* 800-589-6500. *Toll-free phone:* 877-835-7297. *Website:* http://www.vettechinstitute.edu/indianapolis.

Vincennes University

Vincennes, Indiana

- **State-supported** primarily 2-year, founded 1801
- **Small-town** 100-acre campus
- **Coed,** 17,530 undergraduate students, 35% full-time, 45% women, 55% men

Undergraduates 6,199 full-time, 11,331 part-time. 11% Black or African American, non-Hispanic/Latino; 2% Hispanic/Latino; 0.4% Asian, non-Hispanic/Latino; 0.2% Native Hawaiian or other Pacific Islander, non-Hispanic/Latino; 0.3% American Indian or Alaska Native, non-Hispanic/Latino; 1% Two or more races, non-Hispanic/Latino; 11% Race/ethnicity unknown; 0.6% international. *Retention:* 69% of full-time freshmen returned.

Freshmen *Admission:* 2,644 enrolled.

Faculty *Total:* 1,614, 15% full-time. *Student/faculty ratio:* 14:1.

Majors Accounting technology and bookkeeping; administrative assistant and secretarial science; agricultural business and management; agricultural engineering; agriculture; aircraft powerplant technology; airline pilot and flight crew; American Sign Language (ASL); anthropology; applied horticulture/horticulture operations; architectural drafting and CAD/CADD; art; art teacher education; art therapy; autobody/collision and repair technology; automobile/automotive mechanics technology; behavioral sciences; biochemistry; biological and biomedical sciences related; biological and physical sciences; biology/biological sciences; biotechnology; building/home/construction inspection; business administration and management; business/commerce; chemistry; chemistry related; chemistry teacher education; child-care and support services management; child-care provision; civil engineering; commercial and advertising art; communications technology; computer and information sciences; computer/information technology services administration related; computer programming; computer science; computer systems networking and telecommunications; construction trades; corrections; corrections and criminal justice related; cosmetology; criminal justice/police science; culinary arts; design and applied arts related; diesel mechanics technology; dietetics; dramatic/theater arts; early childhood education; economics; education; electrical, electronic and communications engineering technology; elementary education; emergency medical technology (EMT paramedic); engineering technology; English; English/language arts teacher education; family and consumer sciences/home economics teacher education; family and consumer sciences/human sciences; fashion merchandising; finance; fire science/firefighting; food science; foreign languages and literatures; foreign languages related; funeral service and mortuary science; geology/earth science; graphic and printing equipment operation/production; health and physi-

cal education/fitness; health information/medical records technology; history; hospitality administration; hotel/motel administration; industrial technology; journalism; legal assistant/paralegal; liberal arts and sciences/liberal studies; manufacturing engineering technology; marketing/marketing management; massage therapy; mathematics; mathematics teacher education; mechanical drafting and CAD/CADD; mechanical engineering/mechanical technology; medical radiologic technology; music; music teacher education; natural resources/conservation; nuclear medical technology; ophthalmic and optometric support services and allied professions related; parks, recreation and leisure; pharmacy technician; philosophy; photojournalism; physical education teaching and coaching; physical sciences; physical therapy technology; political science and government; pre-dentistry studies; premedical studies; pre-pharmacy studies; pre-veterinary studies; psychology; public relations/image management; radio and television broadcasting technology; recording arts technology; registered nursing/registered nurse; restaurant, culinary, and catering management; robotics technology; science teacher education; secondary education; securities services administration; security and loss prevention; sheet metal technology; social work; sociology; special education; sport and fitness administration/management; surgical technology; surveying technology; teacher assistant/aide; theater design and technology; tool and die technology; web/multimedia management and webmaster; woodworking.

Academics *Calendar:* semesters. *Degrees:* certificates, associate, and bachelor's. *Special study options:* academic remediation for entering students, adult/continuing education programs, advanced placement credit, distance learning, double majors, English as a second language, external degree program, honors programs, off-campus study, part-time degree program, services for LD students, summer session for credit. *ROTC:* Army (c), Air Force (c).

Library Shake Learning Resource Center.

Student Life *Housing:* on-campus residence required for freshman year. *Options:* coed, men-only, women-only, disabled students. Campus housing is university owned. Freshman campus housing is guaranteed. *Activities and Organizations:* drama/theater group, student-run newspaper, radio and television station, choral group, national fraternities, national sororities. *Campus security:* 24-hour emergency response devices and patrols, student patrols, late-night transport/escort service, controlled dormitory access, surveillance cameras. *Student services:* health clinic, personal/psychological counseling.

Athletics Member NJCAA. *Intercollegiate sports:* baseball M, basketball M/W, bowling M, cross-country running M/W, golf M, tennis M, track and field M/W, volleyball W.

Costs (2012–13) *Tuition:* state resident $4882 full-time, $2013 per year part-time; nonresident $11,542 full-time, $4580 per year part-time. Full-time tuition and fees vary according to course level, course load, location, and program. Part-time tuition and fees vary according to course level, course load, location, and program. *Room and board:* $8152. Room and board charges vary according to board plan, gender, and housing facility.

Financial Aid Of all full-time matriculated undergraduates who enrolled in 2011, 220 Federal Work-Study jobs (averaging $1072).

Applying *Options:* electronic application, early admission, deferred entrance. *Application fee:* $20. *Required:* high school transcript. *Required for some:* interview. *Application deadlines:* rolling (freshmen), rolling (transfers). *Notification:* continuous until 8/1 (freshmen), continuous (transfers).

Freshman Application Contact Vincennes University, 1002 North First Street, Vincennes, IN 47591-5202. *Phone:* 812-888-4313. *Toll-free phone:* 800-742-9198. *Website:* http://www.vinu.edu/.

Vincennes University Jasper Campus

Jasper, Indiana

Freshman Application Contact Ms. Louann Gilbert, Admissions Director, Vincennes University Jasper Campus, 850 College Avenue, Jasper, IN 47546-9393. *Phone:* 812-482-3030. *Toll-free phone:* 800-809-VUJC. *Fax:* 812-481-5960. *E-mail:* lagilbert@vinu.edu. *Website:* http://vujc.vinu.edu/.

IOWA

Brown Mackie College–Quad Cities

Bettendorf, Iowa

Freshman Application Contact Brown Mackie College–Quad Cities, 2119 East Kimberly Road, Bettendorf, IA 52722. *Phone:* 309-762-2100. *Toll-free phone:* 888-420-1652. *Website:* http://www.brownmackie.edu/quad-cities/.

See display on next page and page 386 for the College Close-Up.

Clinton Community College

Clinton, Iowa

Freshman Application Contact Mr. Gary Mohr, Executive Director of Enrollment Management and Marketing, Clinton Community College, 1000 Lincoln Boulevard, Clinton, IA 52732-6299. *Phone:* 563-336-3322. *Toll-free phone:* 800-462-3255. *Fax:* 563-336-3350. *E-mail:* gmohr@eicc.edu. *Website:* http://www.eicc.edu/ccc/.

Des Moines Area Community College

Ankeny, Iowa

Freshman Application Contact Mr. Michael Lentsch, Director of Enrollment Management, Des Moines Area Community College, 2006 South Ankeny Boulevard, Ankeny, IA 50021-8995. *Phone:* 515-964-6216. *Toll-free phone:* 800-362-2127. *Fax:* 515-964-6391. *E-mail:* mjleutsch@dmacc.edu. *Website:* http://www.dmacc.edu/.

Ellsworth Community College

Iowa Falls, Iowa

Director of Admissions Mrs. Nancy Walters, Registrar, Ellsworth Community College, 1100 College Avenue, Iowa Falls, IA 50126-1199. *Phone:* 641-648-4611. *Toll-free phone:* 800-ECC-9235. *Website:* http://www.iavalley.cc.ia.us/ecc/.

Hawkeye Community College

Waterloo, Iowa

- **State and locally supported** 2-year, founded 1966
- **Rural** 320-acre campus
- **Endowment** $1.9 million
- **Coed,** 5,971 undergraduate students, 45% full-time, 56% women, 44% men

Undergraduates 2,683 full-time, 3,288 part-time. 1% are from out of state; 8% Black or African American, non-Hispanic/Latino; 3% Hispanic/Latino; 1% Asian, non-Hispanic/Latino; 0.1% Native Hawaiian or other Pacific Islander, non-Hispanic/Latino; 0.3% American Indian or Alaska Native, non-Hispanic/Latino; 1% Two or more races, non-Hispanic/Latino; 0.2% international; 33% transferred in.

Freshmen *Admission:* 2,186 applied, 3,378 admitted, 1,712 enrolled. *Test scores:* ACT scores over 18: 53%; ACT scores over 24: 15%.

Faculty *Total:* 346, 34% full-time, 8% with terminal degrees. *Student/faculty ratio:* 20:1.

Majors Accounting; agricultural/farm supplies retailing and wholesaling; agricultural power machinery operation; animal/livestock husbandry and production; applied horticulture/horticulture operations; autobody/collision and repair technology; automobile/automotive mechanics technology; child-care provision; civil engineering technology; clinical/medical laboratory technology; commercial photography; computer/information technology services administration related; computer systems networking and telecommunications; criminal justice/police science; dental hygiene; diesel mechanics technology; electrical, electronic and communications engineering technology; energy management and systems technology; executive assistant/executive secretary; graphic communications; human resources management; interior design; liberal arts and sciences/liberal studies; machine tool technology; manufacturing engineering technology; medical administrative assistant and medical secretary; multi/interdisciplinary studies related; natural resources management and policy; occupational therapist assistant; physical therapy technology; registered nursing/registered nurse; respiratory care therapy; sales, distribution, and marketing operations; web page, digital/multimedia and information resources design.

Academics *Calendar:* semesters. *Degree:* certificates, diplomas, and associate. *Special study options:* academic remediation for entering students, accelerated degree program, adult/continuing education programs, advanced placement credit, cooperative education, distance learning, English as a second language, external degree program, part-time degree program, services for LD students, study abroad, summer session for credit. *ROTC:* Army (c).

Library Hawkeye Community College Library with 125,194 titles, 220 serial subscriptions, 1,800 audiovisual materials, an OPAC, a Web page.

Student Life *Housing:* college housing not available. *Activities and Organizations:* Student Senate, Phi Theta Kappa, Student Ambassadors, Nursing, IAAP. *Campus security:* 24-hour patrols. *Student services:* health clinic, personal/psychological counseling, women's center.

Athletics *Intramural sports:* badminton M/W, basketball M/W, bowling M/W, cross-country running M/W, golf M/W, soccer M/W, table tennis M/W, volleyball M/W.

Standardized Tests *Required:* COMPASS or the equivalent from ACT or accredited college course(s) (for admission). *Required for some:* ACT (for admission).

Costs (2012–13) *Tuition:* state resident $3836 full-time, $137 per credit hour part-time; nonresident $4536 full-time, $162 per credit hour part-time. Full-time tuition and fees vary according to course load and program. Part-time tuition and fees vary according to course load and program. *Required fees:* $168 full-time, $6 per credit hour part-time. *Payment plans:* installment, deferred payment. *Waivers:* employees or children of employees.

Applying *Options:* electronic application, deferred entrance. *Required:* high school transcript. *Application deadlines:* rolling (freshmen), rolling (out-of-state freshmen), rolling (transfers). *Notification:* continuous (freshmen), continuous (out-of-state freshmen), continuous (transfers).

Freshman Application Contact Ms. Holly Grimm-See, Associate Director, Admissions and Recruitment, Hawkeye Community College, PO Box 8015, Waterloo, IA 50704-8015. *Phone:* 319-296-4277. *Toll-free phone:* 800-670-4769. *Fax:* 319-296-2505. *E-mail:* holly.grimm-see@hawkeyecollege.edu. *Website:* http://www.hawkeyecollege.edu/.

Indian Hills Community College

Ottumwa, Iowa

Freshman Application Contact Mrs. Jane Sapp, Admissions Officer, Indian Hills Community College, 525 Grandview Avenue, Building #1, Ottumwa, IA 52501-1398. *Phone:* 641-683-5155. *Toll-free phone:* 800-726-2585. *Website:* http://www.ihcc.cc.ia.us/.

Iowa Central Community College

Fort Dodge, Iowa

Freshman Application Contact Mrs. Deb Bahls, Coordinator of Admissions, Iowa Central Community College, 330 Avenue M, Fort Dodge, IA 50501-5798. *Phone:* 515-576-0099 Ext. 2402. *Toll-free phone:* 800-362-2793. *Fax:* 515-576-7724. *E-mail:* bahls@iowacentral.com. *Website:* http://www.iccc.cc.ia.us/.

Iowa Lakes Community College

Estherville, Iowa

- **State and locally supported** 2-year, founded 1967, part of Iowa Community College System
- **Small-town** 20-acre campus
- **Endowment** $6.5 million
- **Coed**

Undergraduates 1,663 full-time, 1,439 part-time. Students come from 33 states and territories; 6 other countries; 3% Black or African American, non-Hispanic/Latino; 3% Hispanic/Latino; 1% Asian, non-Hispanic/Latino; 0.4% Native Hawaiian or other Pacific Islander, non-Hispanic/Latino; 0.4% American Indian or Alaska Native, non-Hispanic/Latino; 0.4% Two or more races, non-Hispanic/Latino; 4% Race/ethnicity unknown; 0.6% international; 37% live on campus. *Retention:* 59% of full-time freshmen returned.

Faculty *Student/faculty ratio:* 24:1.

Academics *Calendar:* semesters. *Degree:* certificates, diplomas, and associate. *Special study options:* academic remediation for entering students, accelerated degree program, adult/continuing education programs, advanced placement credit, cooperative education, distance learning, English as a second language, honors programs, independent study, internships, part-time degree program, services for LD students, summer session for credit.

Student Life *Campus security:* 24-hour emergency response devices, student patrols.

Athletics Member NJCAA.

Applying *Options:* electronic application. *Required for some:* interview.

Freshman Application Contact Ms. Anne Stansbury Johnson, Director of Admission, Iowa Lakes Community College, 3200 College Drive, Emmetsburg, IA 50536. *Phone:* 712-852-3554 Ext. 5254. *Toll-free phone:* 800-521-5054. *Fax:* 712-852-2152. *E-mail:* info@iowalakes.edu. *Website:* http://www.iowalakes.edu/.

Iowa Western Community College

Council Bluffs, Iowa

Freshman Application Contact Ms. Tori Christie, Director of Admissions, Iowa Western Community College, 2700 College Road, Box 4-C, Council Bluffs, IA 51502. *Phone:* 712-325-3288. *Toll-free phone:* 800-432-5852. *E-mail:* admissions@iwcc.edu. *Website:* http://www.iwcc.edu/.

ITT Technical Institute

Cedar Rapids, Iowa

- **Proprietary** primarily 2-year
- **Coed**

Academics *Degrees:* associate and bachelor's.

Freshman Application Contact Director of Recruitment, ITT Technical Institute, 3735 Queen Court SW, Cedar Rapids, IA 52404. *Phone:* 319-297-3400. *Toll-free phone:* 877-320-4625. *Website:* http://www.itt-tech.edu/.

ITT Technical Institute

Clive, Iowa

- **Proprietary** primarily 2-year, part of ITT Educational Services, Inc.
- **Coed**

Academics *Degrees:* associate and bachelor's.

Freshman Application Contact Director of Recruitment, ITT Technical Institute, 1860 Northwest 118th Street, Suite 110, Clive, IA 50325. *Phone:* 515-327-5500. *Toll-free phone:* 877-526-7312. *Website:* http://www.itt-tech.edu/.

Kaplan University, Cedar Falls

Cedar Falls, Iowa

Freshman Application Contact Kaplan University, Cedar Falls, 7009 Nordic Drive, Cedar Falls, IA 50613. *Phone:* 319-277-0220. *Toll-free phone:* 866-527-5268 (in-state); 800-527-5268 (out-of-state). *Website:* http://www.cedarfalls.kaplanuniversity.edu/.

Kaplan University, Cedar Rapids

Cedar Rapids, Iowa

Freshman Application Contact Kaplan University, Cedar Rapids, 3165 Edgewood Parkway, SW, Cedar Rapids, IA 52404. *Phone:* 319-363-0481. *Toll-free phone:* 866-527-5268 (in-state); 800-527-5268 (out-of-state). *Website:* http://www.cedarrapids.kaplanuniversity.edu/.

Kaplan University, Council Bluffs

Council Bluffs, Iowa

Freshman Application Contact Kaplan University, Council Bluffs, 1751 Madison Avenue, Council Bluffs, IA 51503. *Phone:* 712-328-4212. *Toll-free phone:* 866-527-5268 (in-state); 800-527-5268 (out-of-state). *Website:* http://www.councilbluffs.kaplanuniversity.edu/.

Kaplan University, Des Moines

Urbandale, Iowa

Freshman Application Contact Kaplan University, Des Moines, 4655 121st Street, Urbandale, IA 50323. *Phone:* 515-727-2100. *Toll-free phone:* 866-527-5268 (in-state); 800-527-5268 (out-of-state). *Website:* http://www.desmoines.kaplanuniversity.edu/.

Kirkwood Community College

Cedar Rapids, Iowa

Freshman Application Contact Kirkwood Community College, PO Box 2068, Cedar Rapids, IA 52406-2068. *Phone:* 319-398-5517. *Toll-free phone:* 800-332-2055. *Website:* http://www.kirkwood.edu/.

Marshalltown Community College

Marshalltown, Iowa

Freshman Application Contact Ms. Deana Inman, Director of Admissions, Marshalltown Community College, 3700 South Center Street, Marshalltown, IA 50158-4760. *Phone:* 641-752-7106. *Toll-free phone:* 866-622-4748. *Fax:* 641-752-8149. *Website:* http://www.marshalltowncommunitycollege.com/.

Muscatine Community College

Muscatine, Iowa

Freshman Application Contact Gary Mohr, Executive Director of Enrollment Management and Marketing, Muscatine Community College, 152 Colorado Street, Muscatine, IA 52761-5396. *Phone:* 563-336-3322. *Toll-free phone:* 800-351-4669. *Fax:* 563-336-3350. *E-mail:* gmohr@eicc.edu. *Website:* http://www.eicc.edu/general/muscatine/.

Northeast Iowa Community College

Calmar, Iowa

- **State and locally supported** 2-year, founded 1966, part of Iowa Area Community Colleges System
- **Rural** 210-acre campus
- **Coed,** 5,018 undergraduate students, 41% full-time, 61% women, 39% men

Undergraduates 2,066 full-time, 2,952 part-time. 10% are from out of state; 3% Black or African American, non-Hispanic/Latino; 2% Hispanic/Latino; 0.4% Asian, non-Hispanic/Latino; 0.1% Native Hawaiian or other Pacific Islander, non-Hispanic/Latino; 0.2% American Indian or Alaska Native, non-Hispanic/Latino; 0.5% Two or more races, non-Hispanic/Latino; 3% Race/ethnicity unknown; 7% transferred in. *Retention:* 50% of full-time freshmen returned.

Freshmen *Admission:* 1,227 applied, 960 admitted, 756 enrolled.

Faculty *Total:* 348, 31% full-time, 7% with terminal degrees. *Student/faculty ratio:* 16:1.

Majors Accounting; administrative assistant and secretarial science; agribusiness; agricultural and food products processing; agricultural power machinery operation; agricultural production; automobile/automotive mechanics technology; business administration and management; business automation/technology/data entry; clinical/medical laboratory technology; computer programming (specific applications); construction trades; cosmetology; crop production; dairy husbandry and production; desktop publishing and digital imaging design; electrical, electronic and communications engineering technology; electrician; emergency medical technology (EMT paramedic); energy management and systems technology; fire science/firefighting; health information/medical records technology; liberal arts and sciences/liberal studies; plumbing technology; radiologic technology/science; registered nursing/registered nurse; respiratory care therapy; sales, distribution, and marketing operations; social work.

Academics *Calendar:* semesters. *Degree:* certificates, diplomas, and associate. *Special study options:* academic remediation for entering students, adult/continuing education programs, advanced placement credit, cooperative education, distance learning, double majors, external degree program, honors programs, internships, off-campus study, part-time degree program, services for LD students, summer session for credit.

Library Wilder Resource Center & Burton Payne Library plus 2 others with 44,835 titles, 341 serial subscriptions, 7,326 audiovisual materials, an OPAC, a Web page.

Student Life *Housing:* college housing not available. *Activities and Organizations:* student-run newspaper, choral group, national fraternities, national sororities. *Campus security:* security personnel on weeknights. *Student services:* personal/psychological counseling.

Athletics *Intramural sports:* basketball M/W, bowling M/W, football M, golf M/W, skiing (downhill) M/W, softball M/W, volleyball M/W.

Applying *Options:* electronic application. *Recommended:* high school transcript. *Application deadlines:* rolling (freshmen), rolling (out-of-state freshmen), rolling (transfers). *Notification:* continuous (freshmen), continuous (out-of-state freshmen), continuous (transfers).

Freshman Application Contact Ms. Brynn McConnell, Admissions Representative, Northeast Iowa Community College, Calmar, IA 52132. *Phone:* 563-562-3263 Ext. 307. *Toll-free phone:* 800-728-CALMAR. *Fax:* 563-562-4369. *E-mail:* mcconnellb@nicc.edu.
Website: http://www.nicc.edu/.

North Iowa Area Community College

Mason City, Iowa

Freshman Application Contact Ms. Rachel McGuire, Director of Admissions, North Iowa Area Community College, 500 College Drive, Mason City, IA 50401. *Phone:* 641-422-4104. *Toll-free phone:* 888-GO NIACC Ext. 4245. *Fax:* 641-422-4385. *E-mail:* request@niacc.edu.
Website: http://www.niacc.edu/.

Northwest Iowa Community College

Sheldon, Iowa

Director of Admissions Ms. Lisa Story, Director of Enrollment Management, Northwest Iowa Community College, 603 West Park Street, Sheldon, IA 51201-1046. *Phone:* 712-324-5061 Ext. 115. *Toll-free phone:* 800-352-4907. *E-mail:* lstory@nwicc.edu.
Website: http://www.nwicc.edu/.

St. Luke's College

Sioux City, Iowa

- **Independent** 2-year, founded 1967, part of St. Luke's Regional Medical Center
- **Rural** 3-acre campus with easy access to Omaha
- **Endowment** $981,282
- **Coed,** 203 undergraduate students, 81% full-time, 86% women, 14% men

Undergraduates 165 full-time, 38 part-time. Students come from 14 states and territories; 2 other countries; 43% are from out of state; 0.5% Black or African American, non-Hispanic/Latino; 8% Hispanic/Latino; 4% Asian, non-Hispanic/Latino; 0.5% Native Hawaiian or other Pacific Islander, non-Hispanic/Latino; 1% American Indian or Alaska Native, non-Hispanic/Latino; 1% Two or more races, non-Hispanic/Latino; 7% transferred in. *Retention:* 90% of full-time freshmen returned.

Freshmen *Admission:* 35 applied, 12 admitted, 6 enrolled. *Average high school GPA:* 2.95. *Test scores:* ACT scores over 18: 92%; ACT scores over 24: 25%; ACT scores over 30: 2%.

Faculty *Total:* 36, 61% full-time, 8% with terminal degrees. *Student/faculty ratio:* 8:1.

Majors Radiologic technology/science; registered nursing/registered nurse; respiratory care therapy.

Academics *Calendar:* semesters. *Degree:* certificates and associate. *Special study options:* advanced placement credit, cooperative education, summer session for credit.

Library St. Luke's College with 2,418 titles, 100 serial subscriptions, 249 audiovisual materials, an OPAC, a Web page.

Student Life *Housing:* college housing not available. *Campus security:* 24-hour emergency response devices and patrols, late-night transport/escort service. *Student services:* health clinic, personal/psychological counseling.

Standardized Tests *Required:* SAT or ACT (for admission).

Costs (2013–14) *Tuition:* $16,740 full-time, $465 per credit hour part-time. Full-time tuition and fees vary according to course load, degree level, and program. Part-time tuition and fees vary according to course load, degree level, and program. *Required fees:* $1050 full-time, $1050 per year part-time. *Payment plans:* installment, deferred payment.

Financial Aid Of all full-time matriculated undergraduates who enrolled in 2012, 109 applied for aid, 109 were judged to have need, 20 had their need fully met. 5 Federal Work-Study jobs (averaging $1500). 4 state and other part-time jobs (averaging $2000). *Average percent of need met:* 75%. *Average financial aid package:* $7500. *Average need-based loan:* $9000. *Average need-based gift aid:* $5692. *Average indebtedness upon graduation:* $17,701.

Applying *Options:* electronic application. *Application fee:* $50. *Required:* essay or personal statement, high school transcript, minimum 2.5 GPA, interview. *Application deadline:* 8/1 (freshmen). *Notification:* continuous (transfers).

Freshman Application Contact Ms. Sherry McCarthy, Admissions Coordinator, St. Luke's College, 2720 Stone Park Boulevard, Sioux City, IA 51104. *Phone:* 712-279-3149. *Toll-free phone:* 800-352-4660 Ext. 3149. *Fax:* 712-233-8017. *E-mail:* mccartsj@stlukes.org.
Website: http://stlukescollege.edu/.

Scott Community College

Bettendorf, Iowa

Freshman Application Contact Mr. Gary Mohr, Executive Director of Enrollment Management and Marketing, Scott Community College, 500 Belmont Road, Bettendorf, IA 52722-6804. *Phone:* 563-336-3322. *Toll-free phone:* 800-895-0811. *Fax:* 563-336-3350. *E-mail:* gmohr@eicc.edu.
Website: http://www.eicc.edu/scc/.

Southeastern Community College

West Burlington, Iowa

- **State and locally supported** 2-year, founded 1968, part of Iowa Department of Education Division of Community Colleges
- **Small-town** 160-acre campus
- **Coed,** 3,112 undergraduate students, 52% full-time, 61% women, 39% men

Undergraduates 1,621 full-time, 1,491 part-time. 15% are from out of state; 4% Black or African American, non-Hispanic/Latino; 4% Hispanic/Latino; 1% Asian, non-Hispanic/Latino; 0.1% Native Hawaiian or other Pacific Islander, non-Hispanic/Latino; 0.8% American Indian or Alaska Native, non-Hispanic/Latino; 2% Two or more races, non-Hispanic/Latino; 2% Race/ethnicity unknown; 0.5% international; 3% transferred in; 3% live on campus.

Freshmen *Admission:* 716 applied, 441 admitted, 358 enrolled. *Average high school GPA:* 2.76. *Test scores:* ACT scores over 18: 66%; ACT scores over 24: 16%; ACT scores over 30: 1%.

Faculty *Total:* 168, 46% full-time, 5% with terminal degrees. *Student/faculty ratio:* 20:1.

Majors Accounting; administrative assistant and secretarial science; agricultural business and management; agronomy and crop science; artificial intelligence; automobile/automotive mechanics technology; biomedical technology; business administration and management; child development; computer programming; construction engineering technology; cosmetology; criminal justice/law enforcement administration; drafting and design technology; electrical, electronic and communications engineering technology; emergency medical technology (EMT paramedic); engineering related; industrial radiologic technology; information science/studies; liberal arts and sciences/liberal studies; licensed practical/vocational nurse training; machine tool technology; mechanical engineering/mechanical technology; medical/clinical assistant; registered nursing/registered nurse; respiratory care therapy; substance abuse/addiction counseling; trade and industrial teacher education; welding technology.

Academics *Calendar:* semesters. *Degree:* certificates, diplomas, and associate. *Special study options:* adult/continuing education programs, part-time degree program.

Library Yohe Memorial Library.

Student Life *Housing Options:* coed, men-only, disabled students. Campus housing is university owned. *Campus security:* controlled dormitory access, night patrols by trained security personnel.

Athletics Member NJCAA. *Intercollegiate sports:* baseball M(s), basketball M(s), softball W(s), volleyball W(s). *Intramural sports:* basketball M, bowling M/W, softball M/W, volleyball M/W, weight lifting M/W.

Costs (2013–14) *Tuition:* state resident $4260 full-time, $142 per credit hour part-time; nonresident $4410 full-time, $147 per credit hour part-time. Full-time tuition and fees vary according to course load, program, and reciprocity agreements. Part-time tuition and fees vary according to course load, program, and reciprocity agreements. *Room and board:* $5800. Room and board charges vary according to board plan and housing facility. *Payment plan:* installment. *Waivers:* employees or children of employees.

Financial Aid Of all full-time matriculated undergraduates who enrolled in 2011, 1,378 applied for aid, 1,269 were judged to have need. In 2011, 34 non-need-based awards were made. *Average financial aid package:* $6299. *Average need-based loan:* $3049. *Average need-based gift aid:* $4283. *Average non-need-based aid:* $2035.

Applying *Options:* early admission, deferred entrance. *Application deadlines:* rolling (freshmen), rolling (transfers). *Notification:* continuous (freshmen).

Freshman Application Contact Ms. Stacy White, Admissions, Southeastern Community College, 1500 West Agency Road, West Burlington, IA 52655-0180. *Phone:* 319-752-2731 Ext. 8137. *Toll-free phone:* 866-722-4692. *E-mail:* admoff@scciowa.edu. *Website:* http://www.scciowa.edu/.

Southwestern Community College

Creston, Iowa

Freshman Application Contact Ms. Lisa Carstens, Admissions Coordinator, Southwestern Community College, 1501 West Townline Street, Creston, IA 50801. *Phone:* 641-782-7081 Ext. 453. *Toll-free phone:* 800-247-4023. *Fax:* 641-782-3312. *E-mail:* carstens@swcciowa.edu. *Website:* http://www.swcciowa.edu/.

Vatterott College

Des Moines, Iowa

Freshman Application Contact Mr. Henry Franken, Co-Director, Vatterott College, 7000 Fleur Drive, Suite 290, Des Moines, IA 50321. *Phone:* 515-309-9000. *Toll-free phone:* 888-553-6627. *Fax:* 515-309-0366. *Website:* http://www.vatterott.edu/.

Western Iowa Tech Community College

Sioux City, Iowa

- **State-supported** 2-year, founded 1966, part of Iowa Department of Education Division of Community Colleges
- **Suburban** 143-acre campus
- **Endowment** $1.0 million
- **Coed,** 6,425 undergraduate students, 42% full-time, 58% women, 42% men

Undergraduates 2,685 full-time, 3,740 part-time. Students come from 25 states and territories; 4 other countries; 18% are from out of state; 4% Black or African American, non-Hispanic/Latino; 12% Hispanic/Latino; 2% Asian, non-Hispanic/Latino; 0.2% Native Hawaiian or other Pacific Islander, non-Hispanic/Latino; 3% American Indian or Alaska Native, non-Hispanic/Latino; 0.5% Two or more races, non-Hispanic/Latino; 8% Race/ethnicity unknown; 0.1% international; 20% transferred in; 5% live on campus. *Retention:* 41% of full-time freshmen returned.

Freshmen *Admission:* 716 enrolled. *Test scores:* ACT scores over 18: 74%; ACT scores over 24: 12%; ACT scores over 30: 1%.

Faculty *Total:* 373, 21% full-time, 8% with terminal degrees. *Student/faculty ratio:* 22:1.

Majors Accounting; administrative assistant and secretarial science; agricultural/farm supplies retailing and wholesaling; animation, interactive technology, video graphics and special effects; autobody/collision and repair technology; automobile/automotive mechanics technology; business administration and management; business automation/technology/data entry; childcare provision; cinematography and film/video production; commercial photography; computer/information technology services administration related; criminal justice/police science; dental hygiene; desktop publishing and digital imaging design; emergency medical technology (EMT paramedic); energy management and systems technology; finance; fire science/firefighting; human resources management; interior design; legal assistant/paralegal; liberal arts and sciences/liberal studies; mechanical drafting and CAD/CADD; medical administrative assistant and medical secretary; medical office management; motorcycle maintenance and repair technology; multi/interdisciplinary studies related; musical instrument fabrication and repair; physical therapy technology; recording arts technology; registered nursing/registered nurse; sales, distribution, and marketing operations; surgical technology; telecommunications technology; web page, digital/multimedia and information resources design.

Academics *Calendar:* semesters. *Degree:* certificates, diplomas, and associate. *Special study options:* academic remediation for entering students, accelerated degree program, advanced placement credit, cooperative education, distance learning, double majors, English as a second language, honors programs, independent study, internships, off-campus study, part-time degree program, services for LD students, student-designed majors, study abroad, summer session for credit.

Library Western Iowa Tech Community College Library Services plus 1 other with 26,598 titles, 210 serial subscriptions, 5,376 audiovisual materials, an OPAC, a Web page.

Student Life *Housing Options:* coed. Campus housing is university owned. *Activities and Organizations:* drama/theater group, choral group, Shakespeare Overseas Traveling Club, Habitat for Humanity, Anime Club, Leadership Academy, Police Science Club. *Campus security:* 24-hour emergency response devices and patrols, controlled dormitory access. *Student services:* personal/psychological counseling.

Athletics *Intramural sports:* basketball M/W, bowling M/W, football M/W, rugby M/W, soccer M/W, softball M/W, volleyball M/W, wrestling M/W.

Standardized Tests *Recommended:* ACT (for admission), SAT or ACT (for admission).

Costs (2013–14) *Tuition:* state resident $3072 full-time, $128 per credit hour part-time; nonresident $3192 full-time, $133 per credit hour part-time. Full-time tuition and fees vary according to class time and program. Part-time tuition and fees vary according to class time and program. *Required fees:* $372 full-time, $16 per credit hour part-time. *Room and board:* Room and board charges vary according to housing facility. *Payment plan:* installment. *Waivers:* employees or children of employees.

Financial Aid Of all full-time matriculated undergraduates who enrolled in 2011, 148 Federal Work-Study jobs (averaging $1000). 2 state and other part-time jobs (averaging $2500).

Applying *Options:* electronic application, early admission, deferred entrance. *Recommended:* high school transcript. *Application deadlines:* rolling (freshmen), rolling (out-of-state freshmen), rolling (transfers). *Notification:* continuous (freshmen), continuous (out-of-state freshmen), continuous (transfers).

Freshman Application Contact Lora VanderZwaag, Director of Admissions, Western Iowa Tech Community College, 4647 Stone Avenue, PO Box 5199, Sioux City, IA 51102-5199. *Phone:* 712-274-6400. *Toll-free phone:* 800-352-4649 Ext. 6403. *Fax:* 712-274-6441. *Website:* http://www.witcc.edu/.

KANSAS

Allen Community College

Iola, Kansas

Freshman Application Contact Rebecca Bilderback, Director of Admissions, Allen Community College, 1801 North Cottonwood, Iola, KS 66749. *Phone:* 620-365-5116 Ext. 267. *Fax:* 620-365-7406. *E-mail:* bilderback@allencc.edu. *Website:* http://www.allencc.edu/.

Barton County Community College
Great Bend, Kansas

- **State and locally supported** 2-year, founded 1969, part of Kansas Board of Regents
- **Rural** 140-acre campus
- **Coed**

Undergraduates 8% live on campus.
Faculty *Total:* 206, 33% full-time. *Student/faculty ratio:* 23:1.
Majors Accounting; administrative assistant and secretarial science; agricultural business and management; agriculture; anthropology; architecture; art; athletic training; automobile/automotive mechanics technology; banking and financial support services; biology/biological sciences; business administration and management; chemistry; child-care and support services management; chiropractic assistant; clinical/medical laboratory technology; computer/information technology services administration related; computer programming (specific applications); computer science; computer systems networking and telecommunications; corrections; criminal justice/police science; crop production; cytotechnology; dance; dental hygiene; dietitian assistant; dramatic/theater arts; early childhood education; economics; elementary education; emergency care attendant (EMT ambulance); emergency medical technology (EMT paramedic); engineering technology; English; financial planning and services; fire science/firefighting; forestry; funeral service and mortuary science; general studies; geology/earth science; graphic design; hazardous materials management and waste technology; health aides/attendants/orderlies related; health and medical administrative services related; health information/medical records administration; history; home health aide/home attendant; homeland security, law enforcement, firefighting and protective services related; human resources management; human resources management and services related; industrial production technologies related; information science/studies; journalism; kinesiology and exercise science; liberal arts and sciences/liberal studies; licensed practical/vocational nurse training; livestock management; logistics, materials, and supply chain management; marketing/marketing management; mathematics; medical administrative assistant and medical secretary; medical/clinical assistant; medical insurance coding; medical office assistant; medical transcription; medication aide; military studies; modern languages; music; nursing assistant/aide and patient care assistant/aide; occupational therapy; optometric technician; pharmacy; pharmacy technician; philosophy; phlebotomy technology; physical education teaching and coaching; physical sciences; physical therapy; physical therapy technology; physician assistant; physics; political science and government; pre-dentistry studies; pre-engineering; pre-law studies; premedical studies; pre-veterinary studies; psychology; public administration; radiologic technology/science; registered nursing/registered nurse; religious studies; respiratory care therapy; secondary education; social work; sociology; speech communication and rhetoric; sport and fitness administration/management; wildlife, fish and wildlands science and management.
Academics *Calendar:* semesters. *Degree:* certificates and associate. *Special study options:* academic remediation for entering students, accelerated degree program, adult/continuing education programs, advanced placement credit, cooperative education, distance learning, double majors, English as a second language, external degree program, honors programs, independent study, internships, part-time degree program, services for LD students, summer session for credit. *ROTC:* Army (b).
Library Barton County Community College Library with an OPAC, a Web page.
Student Life *Housing Options:* coed, disabled students. Campus housing is university owned. Freshman campus housing is guaranteed. *Activities and Organizations:* drama/theater group, student-run newspaper, choral group, Danceline, Business Professionals, Psychology Club, Agriculture Club, Cougarettes. *Campus security:* 24-hour emergency response devices and patrols. *Student services:* health clinic, personal/psychological counseling.
Athletics Member NJCAA. *Intercollegiate sports:* baseball M(s), basketball M(s)/W(s), cheerleading M(s)/W(s), cross-country running M(s)/W(s), golf M(s)/W(s), soccer M(s)/W(s), softball W(s), tennis M(s)/W(s), track and field M(s)/W(s), volleyball W(s). *Intramural sports:* basketball M/W, bowling M/W, football M/W, golf M/W, softball M/W, swimming and diving M/W, table tennis M/W, tennis M/W, track and field M/W, volleyball M/W.
Costs (2013–14) *Tuition:* state resident $1770 full-time, $59 per credit hour part-time; nonresident $2700 full-time, $90 per credit hour part-time. Full-time tuition and fees vary according to course load. Part-time tuition and fees vary according to course load. *Required fees:* $960 full-time, $32 per credit hour part-time. *Room and board:* Room and board charges vary according to board plan. *Payment plans:* installment, deferred payment. *Waivers:* senior citizens and employees or children of employees.
Applying *Options:* electronic application, early admission. *Recommended:* high school transcript. *Application deadlines:* rolling (freshmen), rolling (transfers).
Freshman Application Contact Ms. Tana Cooper, Director of Admissions and Promotions, Barton County Community College, 245 Northeast 30th Road, Great Bend, KS 67530. *Phone:* 620-792-9241. *Toll-free phone:* 800-722-6842. *Fax:* 620-786-1160. *E-mail:* admissions@bartonccc.edu. *Website:* http://www.bartonccc.edu/.

Brown Mackie College–Kansas City
Lenexa, Kansas

Freshman Application Contact Brown Mackie College–Kansas City, 9705 Lenexa Drive, Lenexa, KS 66215. *Phone:* 913-768-1900. *Toll-free phone:* 800-635-9101.
Website: http://www.brownmackie.edu/kansascity/.

See display on next page and page 368 for the College Close-Up.

Brown Mackie College–Salina
Salina, Kansas

Freshman Application Contact Brown Mackie College–Salina, 2106 South 9th Street, Salina, KS 67401-2810. *Phone:* 785-825-5422. *Toll-free phone:* 800-365-0433.
Website: http://www.brownmackie.edu/salina/.

See display on next page and page 390 for the College Close-Up.

Butler Community College
El Dorado, Kansas

Freshman Application Contact Mr. Glenn Lygrisse, Interim Director of Enrollment Management, Butler Community College, 901 South Haverhill Road, El Dorado, KS 67042. *Phone:* 316-321-2222. *Fax:* 316-322-3109. *E-mail:* admissions@butlercc.edu.
Website: http://www.butlercc.edu/.

Cloud County Community College
Concordia, Kansas

Director of Admissions Kim Reynolds, Director of Admissions, Cloud County Community College, 2221 Campus Drive, PO Box 1002, Concordia, KS 66901-1002. *Phone:* 785-243-1435 Ext. 214. *Toll-free phone:* 800-729-5101.
Website: http://www.cloud.edu/.

Coffeyville Community College
Coffeyville, Kansas

Freshman Application Contact Stacia Meek, Admissions Counselor/Marketing Event Coordinator, Coffeyville Community College, 400 West 11th Street, Coffeyville, KS 67337-5063. *Phone:* 620-252-7100. *Toll-free phone:* 877-51-RAVEN. *E-mail:* staciam@coffeyville.edu.
Website: http://www.coffeyville.edu/.

Colby Community College
Colby, Kansas

- **State and locally supported** 2-year, founded 1964, part of Kansas State Board of Education
- **Small-town** 80-acre campus
- **Endowment** $3.4 million
- **Coed,** 1,451 undergraduate students, 50% full-time, 65% women, 35% men

Undergraduates 723 full-time, 728 part-time. Students come from 15 states and territories; 5 other countries; 30% are from out of state; 7% Black or African American, non-Hispanic/Latino; 7% Hispanic/Latino; 2% Asian, non-Hispanic/Latino; 0.5% Native Hawaiian or other Pacific Islander, non-Hispanic/Latino; 0.6% American Indian or Alaska Native, non-Hispanic/Latino; 5% international; 6% transferred in; 30% live on campus.
Freshmen *Admission:* 1,016 applied, 1,016 admitted, 219 enrolled. *Average high school GPA:* 2.96. *Test scores:* ACT scores over 18: 67%; ACT scores over 24: 12%; ACT scores over 30: 2%.
Faculty *Total:* 153, 38% full-time, 11% with terminal degrees. *Student/faculty ratio:* 11:1.
Majors Administrative assistant and secretarial science; agribusiness; agricultural business and management; agricultural teacher education; agronomy and crop science; broadcast journalism; business administration and management; child-care and support services management; child development; computer and information sciences; computer and information sciences related; criminal justice/law enforcement administration; criminal justice/police science; dental hygiene; engineering related; farm and ranch management; horse husbandry/equine science and management; liberal arts and sciences/liberal stud-

ies; licensed practical/vocational nurse training; physical therapy technology; radio and television; registered nursing/registered nurse; substance abuse/addiction counseling; veterinary/animal health technology.

Academics *Calendar:* semesters. *Degree:* certificates, diplomas, and associate. *Special study options:* academic remediation for entering students, adult/continuing education programs, advanced placement credit, cooperative education, distance learning, double majors, honors programs, internships, part-time degree program, services for LD students, student-designed majors, summer session for credit.

Library Davis Library with 34,000 titles, 463 serial subscriptions, 600 audiovisual materials, an OPAC.

Student Life *Housing:* on-campus residence required for freshman year. *Options:* coed, men-only, women-only. Campus housing is university owned. *Activities and Organizations:* drama/theater group, student-run newspaper, radio and television station, choral group, KSNEA, Physical Therapist Assistants Club, Block and Bridle, SVTA, COPNS. *Campus security:* 24-hour emergency response devices and patrols. *Student services:* health clinic, personal/psychological counseling.

Athletics Member NJCAA. *Intercollegiate sports:* baseball M(s), basketball M(s)/W(s), cheerleading M(s)/W(s), cross-country running M(s)/W(s), equestrian sports M/W, golf M(s)/W(s), softball W(s), track and field M(s)/W(s), volleyball W(s), wrestling M(s). *Intramural sports:* basketball M/W, softball M/W, volleyball M/W.

Standardized Tests *Required:* COMPASS or ASSET (for admission). *Recommended:* SAT or ACT (for admission).

Costs (2013–14) *Tuition:* state resident $1920 full-time, $60 per credit part-time; nonresident $3648 full-time, $114 per credit part-time. Full-time tuition and fees vary according to course load and program. Part-time tuition and fees vary according to course load and program. *Required fees:* $1140 full-time, $38 per credit part-time, $38 per credit part-time. *Room and board:* $6090. Room and board charges vary according to board plan and housing facility. *Payment plan:* installment. *Waivers:* senior citizens and employees or children of employees.

Financial Aid Of all full-time matriculated undergraduates who enrolled in 2011, 737 applied for aid, 615 were judged to have need, 88 had their need fully met. In 2011, 73 non-need-based awards were made. *Average percent of need met:* 73%. *Average financial aid package:* $6385. *Average need-based loan:* $2439. *Average need-based gift aid:* $4685. *Average non-need-based aid:* $1633.

Applying *Options:* electronic application, early admission, deferred entrance. *Required:* high school transcript. *Required for some:* interview. *Application deadlines:* rolling (freshmen), rolling (out-of-state freshmen), rolling (transfers). *Notification:* continuous (freshmen), continuous (out-of-state freshmen), continuous (transfers).

Freshman Application Contact Ms. Nikol Nolan, Admissions Director, Colby Community College, Colby, KS 67701-4099. *Phone:* 785-462-3984 Ext. 5496. *Toll-free phone:* 888-634-9350. *Fax:* 785-460-4691. *E-mail:* admissions@colbycc.edu. *Website:* http://www.colbycc.edu/.

Cowley County Community College and Area Vocational–Technical School

Arkansas City, Kansas

- **State and locally supported** 2-year, founded 1922, part of Kansas State Board of Education
- **Small-town** 19-acre campus
- **Endowment** $4.7 million
- **Coed,** 4,328 undergraduate students, 54% full-time, 62% women, 38% men

Undergraduates 2,328 full-time, 2,000 part-time. 10% are from out of state; 12% live on campus. *Retention:* 58% of full-time freshmen returned.

Freshmen *Admission:* 1,010 applied, 1,010 admitted, 1,010 enrolled. *Average high school GPA:* 2.94. *Test scores:* ACT scores over 18: 72%; ACT scores over 24: 20%; ACT scores over 30: 1%.

Faculty *Total:* 253, 19% full-time. *Student/faculty ratio:* 26:1.

Majors Accounting; administrative assistant and secretarial science; agriculture; art; automobile/automotive mechanics technology; biology/biological sciences; business administration and management; chemistry; child-care and support services management; child development; computer and information sciences; computer and information systems security; computer graphics; computer programming (specific applications); computer science; cosmetology; criminal justice/law enforcement administration; criminal justice/police science; dietetics and clinical nutrition services related; drafting and design technology; dramatic/theater arts; education; electromechanical and instrumentation and maintenance technologies related; elementary education; emergency medical technology (EMT paramedic); engineering technology; entrepreneurship; hotel/motel administration; industrial radiologic technology; journalism; legal administrative assistant/secretary; liberal arts and sciences/liberal studies; machine tool technology; marketing/marketing management; medical insurance coding; medical transcription; music; physical and

biological anthropology; pre-engineering; religious studies; social work; technology/industrial arts teacher education; welding technology.

Academics *Calendar:* semesters. *Degree:* certificates, diplomas, and associate. *Special study options:* academic remediation for entering students, accelerated degree program, adult/continuing education programs, advanced placement credit, cooperative education, distance learning, external degree program, independent study, off-campus study, part-time degree program, services for LD students, summer session for credit.

Library Renn Memorial Library with 27,000 titles, 12,000 serial subscriptions, 1,000 audiovisual materials, an OPAC, a Web page.

Student Life *Housing Options:* coed, men-only, women-only. Campus housing is university owned. *Activities and Organizations:* drama/theater group, student-run newspaper, choral group, Cowley Activity Awareness Team (CAAT), Academic Civic Engagement through Service (ACES), Phi Theta Kappa, Cowley College Student Senate, Creative Claws. *Campus security:* 24-hour emergency response devices and patrols, student patrols, late-night transport/escort service, controlled dormitory access, residence hall entrances are locked at night. *Student services:* health clinic, personal/psychological counseling.

Athletics Member NJCAA. *Intercollegiate sports:* baseball M(s), basketball M(s)/W(s), cross-country running M(s)/W(s), soccer M(s)/W(s), softball W(s), tennis M(s)/W(s), track and field M(s)/W(s), volleyball W(s). *Intramural sports:* basketball M/W, bowling M/W, football M, softball M/W, tennis M/W, volleyball M/W.

Standardized Tests *Recommended:* ACT (for admission).

Costs (2012–13) *Tuition:* area resident $1568 full-time, $49 per credit hour part-time; state resident $1888 full-time, $59 per credit hour part-time; nonresident $3392 full-time, $106 per credit hour part-time. *Required fees:* $864 full-time, $27 per credit hour part-time. *Room and board:* $4475. Room and board charges vary according to board plan. *Payment plan:* installment. *Waivers:* employees or children of employees.

Financial Aid Of all full-time matriculated undergraduates who enrolled in 2012, 2,204 applied for aid, 2,023 were judged to have need. 88 Federal Work-Study jobs (averaging $1191). 135 state and other part-time jobs (averaging $888). *Average financial aid package:* $3508. *Average need-based loan:* $3554. *Average need-based gift aid:* $4554.

Applying *Options:* electronic application, early admission. *Required:* high school transcript. *Application deadlines:* rolling (freshmen), rolling (out-of-state freshmen), rolling (transfers). *Notification:* continuous (freshmen), continuous (out-of-state freshmen), continuous (transfers).

Freshman Application Contact Ms. Lory West, Director of Admissions, Cowley County Community College and Area Vocational–Technical School, PO Box 1147, Arkansas City, KS 67005. *Phone:* 620-441-5594. *Toll-free phone:* 800-593-CCCC. *Fax:* 620-441-5350. *E-mail:* admissions@cowley.edu. *Website:* http://www.cowley.edu/.

Dodge City Community College

Dodge City, Kansas

Freshman Application Contact Dodge City Community College, 2501 North 14th Avenue, Dodge City, KS 67801-2399. *Phone:* 620-225-1321. *Website:* http://www.dc3.edu/.

Donnelly College

Kansas City, Kansas

Freshman Application Contact Mr. Edward Marquez, Director of Admissions, Donnelly College, 608 North 18th Street, Kansas City, KS 66102. *Phone:* 913-621-8713. *Fax:* 913-621-8719. *E-mail:* admissions@donnelly.edu. *Website:* http://www.donnelly.edu/.

Flint Hills Technical College

Emporia, Kansas

Freshman Application Contact Admissions Office, Flint Hills Technical College, 3301 West 18th Avenue, Emporia, KS 66801. *Phone:* 620-341-1325. *Toll-free phone:* 800-711-6947. *Website:* http://www.fhtc.edu/.

Fort Scott Community College

Fort Scott, Kansas

Director of Admissions Mrs. Mert Barrows, Director of Admissions, Fort Scott Community College, 2108 South Horton, Fort Scott, KS 66701. *Phone:* 620-223-2700 Ext. 353. *Toll-free phone:* 800-874-3722. *Website:* http://www.fortscott.edu/.

Garden City Community College

Garden City, Kansas

- **County-supported** 2-year, founded 1919, part of Kansas Board of Regents
- **Rural** 63-acre campus
- **Coed,** 2,059 undergraduate students, 50% full-time, 53% women, 47% men

Undergraduates 1,038 full-time, 1,021 part-time. Students come from 41 states and territories; 6 other countries; 15% are from out of state; 6% Black or African American, non-Hispanic/Latino; 31% Hispanic/Latino; 3% Asian, non-Hispanic/Latino; 0.8% American Indian or Alaska Native, non-Hispanic/Latino; 0.5% Race/ethnicity unknown; 4% international; 4% transferred in.

Freshmen *Admission:* 558 applied, 558 admitted, 563 enrolled. *Average high school GPA:* 2.99.

Majors Administrative assistant and secretarial science; agricultural and food products processing; agricultural mechanization; agricultural production; architecture related; automobile/automotive mechanics technology; biology/biological sciences; business administration and management; computer science; computer systems networking and telecommunications; cosmetology; criminal justice/police science; drafting and design technology; education; emergency medical technology (EMT paramedic); engineering; English; family and consumer sciences/human sciences; fire science/firefighting; general studies; health and physical education related; health services/allied health/health sciences; humanities; liberal arts and sciences/liberal studies; manufacturing engineering technology; mathematics; physical sciences; pre-law studies; premedical studies; prenursing studies; pre-pharmacy studies; pre-veterinary studies; psychology; registered nursing/registered nurse; retailing; social sciences; social work; speech communication and rhetoric; substance abuse/addiction counseling; visual and performing arts; welding technology; zoology/animal biology.

Academics *Calendar:* semesters. *Degree:* certificates and associate. *Special study options:* academic remediation for entering students, adult/continuing education programs, advanced placement credit, distance learning, English as a second language, external degree program, part-time degree program, services for LD students, student-designed majors, summer session for credit.

Library Saffell Library with 15,984 titles, 31 serial subscriptions, 428 audiovisual materials, an OPAC, a Web page.

Student Life *Housing Options:* coed. Campus housing is university owned. *Activities and Organizations:* drama/theater group, student-run newspaper, choral group, HALO (Hispanic Student Leadership Organization), GC3 Media, Criminal Justice/Tau Epsilon Lambda, SGA (Student Government Association), PTK (Phi Theta Kappa). *Campus security:* 24-hour emergency response devices and patrols, student patrols, late-night transport/escort service, controlled dormitory access. *Student services:* health clinic, personal/psychological counseling.

Athletics Member NJCAA. *Intercollegiate sports:* baseball M(s), basketball M(s)/W(s), cheerleading M(s)/W(s), cross-country running M(s)/W(s), football M(s), soccer M/W, softball W(s), track and field M(s)/W(s), volleyball W(s). *Intramural sports:* basketball M/W, bowling M/W, football M/W, golf M/W, racquetball M/W, riflery M/W, soccer M/W, softball M/W, table tennis M/W, tennis M/W, track and field M/W, ultimate Frisbee M/W, volleyball M/W.

Standardized Tests *Required:* ACT COMPASS (for admission). *Recommended:* ACT (for admission).

Financial Aid Of all full-time matriculated undergraduates who enrolled in 2011, 90 Federal Work-Study jobs (averaging $1000). 100 state and other part-time jobs (averaging $900).

Applying *Required:* high school transcript. *Application deadlines:* rolling (freshmen), rolling (transfers).

Freshman Application Contact Office of Admissions, Garden City Community College, 801 Campus Drive, Garden City, KS 67846. *Phone:* 620-276-9531. *Toll-free phone:* 800-658-1696. *Fax:* 620-276-9650. *E-mail:* admissions@gcccks.edu. *Website:* http://www.gcccks.edu/.

Hesston College

Hesston, Kansas

Freshman Application Contact Joel Kauffman, Vice President of Admissions, Hesston College, Hesston, KS 67062. *Phone:* 620-327-8222. *Toll-free phone:* 800-995-2757. *Fax:* 620-327-8300. *E-mail:* admissions@hesston.edu. *Website:* http://www.hesston.edu/.

Highland Community College

Highland, Kansas

Director of Admissions Ms. Cheryl Rasmussen, Vice President of Student Services, Highland Community College, 606 West Main Street, Highland, KS 66035. *Phone:* 785-442-6020. *Fax:* 785-442-6106. *Website:* http://www.highlandcc.edu/.

Hutchinson Community College and Area Vocational School

Hutchinson, Kansas

- **State and locally supported** 2-year, founded 1928, part of Kansas Board of Regents
- **Small-town** 47-acre campus
- **Coed,** 6,159 undergraduate students, 42% full-time, 56% women, 44% men

Undergraduates 2,586 full-time, 3,573 part-time. Students come from 46 states and territories; 6 other countries; 7% are from out of state; 7% Black or African American, non-Hispanic/Latino; 8% Hispanic/Latino; 0.7% Asian, non-Hispanic/Latino; 1% American Indian or Alaska Native, non-Hispanic/Latino; 2% Two or more races, non-Hispanic/Latino; 6% Race/ethnicity unknown; 0.4% international; 8% transferred in; 7% live on campus. *Retention:* 57% of full-time freshmen returned.

Freshmen *Admission:* 1,373 applied, 1,373 admitted, 909 enrolled. *Average high school GPA:* 3. *Test scores:* ACT scores over 18: 73%; ACT scores over 24: 20%; ACT scores over 30: 1%.

Faculty *Total:* 500, 24% full-time, 4% with terminal degrees. *Student/faculty ratio:* 15:1.

Majors Administrative assistant and secretarial science; agricultural mechanics and equipment technology; agriculture; architectural drafting and CAD/CADD; autobody/collision and repair technology; automobile/automotive mechanics technology; biology/biological sciences; biotechnology; business and personal/financial services marketing; business/commerce; carpentry; child-care and support services management; communications technology; computer and information sciences; computer systems analysis; computer systems networking and telecommunications; criminal justice/police science; design and visual communications; drafting and design technology; education; electrical, electronic and communications engineering technology; electrical/electronics equipment installation and repair; emergency medical technology (EMT paramedic); engineering; English; family and consumer sciences/human sciences; farm and ranch management; fire science/firefighting; foreign languages and literatures; health information/medical records technology; legal assistant/paralegal; liberal arts and sciences/liberal studies; machine tool technology; manufacturing engineering technology; mathematics; mechanical drafting and CAD/CADD; medical radiologic technology; pharmacy technician; physical sciences; physical therapy technology; psychology; registered nursing/registered nurse; respiratory therapy technician; retailing; social sciences; speech communication and rhetoric; visual and performing arts; web page, digital/multimedia and information resources design; welding technology.

Academics *Calendar:* semesters. *Degree:* certificates and associate. *Special study options:* academic remediation for entering students, adult/continuing education programs, advanced placement credit, cooperative education, distance learning, double majors, English as a second language, honors programs, independent study, internships, part-time degree program, services for LD students, student-designed majors, summer session for credit. *ROTC:* Army (c).

Library John F. Kennedy Library plus 1 other with 41,510 titles, 132 serial subscriptions, 2,238 audiovisual materials, an OPAC, a Web page.

Student Life *Housing Options:* men-only, women-only. Campus housing is university owned. *Activities and Organizations:* drama/theater group, student-run newspaper, choral group, Black Leadership League, Hispanic American Leadership Organization, Campus Crusade for Christ, Circle K, Block and Bridle Club. *Campus security:* 24-hour emergency response devices and patrols, student patrols, late-night transport/escort service, controlled dormitory access. *Student services:* health clinic, personal/psychological counseling.

Athletics Member NJCAA. *Intercollegiate sports:* baseball M(s), basketball M(s)/W(s), cheerleading M(s)/W(s), cross-country running M(s)/W(s), football M(s), golf M(s), soccer W(s), softball W(s), track and field M(s)/W(s), volleyball W(s). *Intramural sports:* badminton M/W, basketball M/W, football M/W, racquetball M/W, soccer M/W, tennis M/W, track and field M/W, volleyball M/W.

Costs (2012–13) *Tuition:* state resident $2144 full-time, $67 per hour part-time; nonresident $3136 full-time, $98 per hour part-time. *Required fees:* $544 full-time, $17 per hour part-time. *Room and board:* $5150. Room and board charges vary according to board plan. *Payment plan:* installment. *Waivers:* employees or children of employees.

Applying *Options:* electronic application, early admission, deferred entrance. *Required for some:* high school transcript, interview. *Application deadlines:*

rolling (freshmen), rolling (transfers). *Notification:* continuous (freshmen), continuous (transfers).

Freshman Application Contact Mr. Corbin Strobel, Director of Admissions, Hutchinson Community College and Area Vocational School, 1300 North Plum, Hutchinson, KS 67501. *Phone:* 620-665-3536. *Toll-free phone:* 888-GO-HUTCH. *Fax:* 620-665-3301. *E-mail:* strobelc@hutchcc.edu. *Website:* http://www.hutchcc.edu/.

Independence Community College

Independence, Kansas

Freshman Application Contact Ms. Sally A. Ciufulescu, Director of Admissions, Independence Community College, Brookside Drive and College Avenue, PO Box 708, Independence, KS 67301-0708. *Phone:* 620-332-5400. *Toll-free phone:* 800-842-6063. *Fax:* 620-331-0946. *E-mail:* sciufulescu@indycc.edu. *Website:* http://www.indycc.edu/.

Johnson County Community College

Overland Park, Kansas

Director of Admissions Dr. Charles J. Carlsen, President, Johnson County Community College, 12345 College Boulevard, Overland Park, KS 66210-1299. *Phone:* 913-469-8500 Ext. 3806. *Website:* http://www.johnco.cc.ks.us/.

Kansas City Kansas Community College

Kansas City, Kansas

- **State and locally supported** 2-year, founded 1923
- **Urban** 148-acre campus
- **Endowment** $1.1 million
- **Coed**

Undergraduates 2,903 full-time, 4,652 part-time. Students come from 27 states and territories; 13 other countries; 5% are from out of state; 29% Black or African American, non-Hispanic/Latino; 10% Hispanic/Latino; 2% Asian, non-Hispanic/Latino; 0.2% Native Hawaiian or other Pacific Islander, non-Hispanic/Latino; 0.6% American Indian or Alaska Native, non-Hispanic/Latino; 2% Two or more races, non-Hispanic/Latino; 5% Race/ethnicity unknown; 2% international; 4% transferred in.

Faculty *Student/faculty ratio:* 17:1.

Academics *Calendar:* semesters. *Degree:* certificates, diplomas, and associate. *Special study options:* academic remediation for entering students, adult/continuing education programs, advanced placement credit, cooperative education, distance learning, English as a second language, external degree program, freshman honors college, honors programs, independent study, internships, part-time degree program, services for LD students, summer session for credit.

Student Life *Campus security:* 24-hour emergency response devices and patrols, student patrols, late-night transport/escort service.

Athletics Member NJCAA.

Financial Aid Of all full-time matriculated undergraduates who enrolled in 2011, 125 Federal Work-Study jobs (averaging $3000).

Applying *Options:* electronic application. *Required:* high school transcript.

Freshman Application Contact Dr. Denise McDowell, Dean of Enrollment Management/Registrar, Kansas City Kansas Community College, Admissions Office, 7250 State Avenue, Kansas City, KS 66112. *Phone:* 913-288-7694. *Fax:* 913-288-7648. *E-mail:* dmcdowell@kckcc.edu. *Website:* http://www.kckcc.edu/.

Labette Community College

Parsons, Kansas

Freshman Application Contact Ms. Tammy Fuentez, Director of Admission, Labette Community College, 200 South 14th Street, Parsons, KS 67357-4299. *Phone:* 620-421-6700. *Toll-free phone:* 888-522-3883. *Fax:* 620-421-0180. *Website:* http://www.labette.edu/.

Manhattan Area Technical College

Manhattan, Kansas

Freshman Application Contact Mr. Rick Smith, Coordinator of Admissions and Recruitment, Manhattan Area Technical College, 3136 Dickens Avenue, Manhattan, KS 66503. *Phone:* 785-587-2800 Ext. 104. *Toll-free phone:* 800-352-7575. *Fax:* 913-587-2804. *Website:* http://www.matc.net/.

National American University

Overland Park, Kansas

Freshman Application Contact Admissions Office, National American University, 10310 Mastin, Overland Park, KS 66212.
Website: http://www.national.edu/.

Neosho County Community College

Chanute, Kansas

Freshman Application Contact Ms. Lisa Last, Dean of Student Development, Neosho County Community College, 800 West 14th Street, Chanute, KS 66720. *Phone:* 620-431-2820 Ext. 213. *Toll-free phone:* 800-729-6222. *Fax:* 620-431-0082. *E-mail:* llast@neosho.edu.
Website: http://www.neosho.edu/.

North Central Kansas Technical College

Beloit, Kansas

Freshman Application Contact Ms. Judy Heidrick, Director of Admissions, North Central Kansas Technical College, PO Box 507, 3033 US Highway 24, Beloit, KS 67420. *Toll-free phone:* 800-658-4655. *E-mail:* jheidrick@ncktc.tec.ks.us.
Website: http://www.ncktc.edu/.

Northwest Kansas Technical College

Goodland, Kansas

Admissions Office Contact Northwest Kansas Technical College, PO Box 668, 1209 Harrison Street, Goodland, KS 67735. *Toll-free phone:* 800-316-4127.
Website: http://www.nwktc.edu/.

Pratt Community College

Pratt, Kansas

Freshman Application Contact Ms. Theresa Zjehr, Office Assistant, Student Services, Pratt Community College, 348 Northeast State Road 61, Pratt, KS 67124. *Phone:* 620-450-2217. *Toll-free phone:* 800-794-3091. *Fax:* 620-672-5288. *E-mail:* theresaz@prattcc.edu.
Website: http://www.prattcc.edu/.

Seward County Community College and Area Technical School

Liberal, Kansas

Director of Admissions Dr. Gerald Harris, Dean of Student Services, Seward County Community College and Area Technical School, PO Box 1137, Liberal, KS 67905-1137. *Phone:* 620-624-1951 Ext. 617. *Toll-free phone:* 800-373-9951.
Website: http://www.sccc.edu/.

Wichita Area Technical College

Wichita, Kansas

Freshman Application Contact Ms. Jessica Ross, Dean, Enrollment Management, Wichita Area Technical College, Wichita, KS 67211-2099. *Phone:* 316-677-9400. *Fax:* 316-677-9555. *E-mail:* info@watc.edu.
Website: http://www.wichitatech.com/.

Wright Career College

Overland Park, Kansas

Admissions Office Contact Wright Career College, 10700 Metcalf Avenue, Overland Park, KS 66210.
Website: http://www.wrightcareercollege.com/.

KENTUCKY

Ashland Community and Technical College

Ashland, Kentucky

Freshman Application Contact Ashland Community and Technical College, 1400 College Drive, Ashland, KY 41101-3683. *Phone:* 606-326-2008. *Toll-free phone:* 800-928-4256.
Website: http://www.ashland.kctcs.edu/.

ATA College

Louisville, Kentucky

Freshman Application Contact Admissions Office, ATA College, 10180 Linn Station Road, Suite A200, Louisville, KY 40223. *Phone:* 502-371-8330. *Fax:* 502-371-8598.
Website: http://www.ata.edu/.

Beckfield College

Florence, Kentucky

Freshman Application Contact Mrs. Leah Boerger, Director of Admissions, Beckfield College, 16 Spiral Drive, Florence, KY 41042. *Phone:* 859-371-9393. *E-mail:* lboerger@beckfield.edu.
Website: http://www.beckfield.edu/.

Big Sandy Community and Technical College

Prestonsburg, Kentucky

Director of Admissions Jimmy Wright, Director of Admissions, Big Sandy Community and Technical College, One Bert T. Combs Drive, Prestonsburg, KY 41653-1815. *Phone:* 606-886-3863. *Toll-free phone:* 888-641-4132. *E-mail:* jimmy.wright@kctcs.edu.
Website: http://www.bigsandy.kctcs.edu/.

Bluegrass Community and Technical College

Lexington, Kentucky

- **State-supported** 2-year, founded 1965, part of Kentucky Community and Technical College System
- **Urban** 10-acre campus
- **Endowment** $967,117
- **Coed**

Undergraduates 5,539 full-time, 6,057 part-time. Students come from 16 states and territories; 26 other countries; 13% Black or African American, non-Hispanic/Latino; 3% Hispanic/Latino; 1% Asian, non-Hispanic/Latino; 0.1% Native Hawaiian or other Pacific Islander, non-Hispanic/Latino; 0.3% American Indian or Alaska Native, non-Hispanic/Latino; 2% Two or more races, non-Hispanic/Latino; 2% Race/ethnicity unknown; 0.5% international; 4% transferred in; 3% live on campus.
Faculty *Student/faculty ratio:* 18:1.
Academics *Calendar:* semesters. *Degree:* certificates, diplomas, and associate. *Special study options:* academic remediation for entering students, accelerated degree program, adult/continuing education programs, advanced placement credit, cooperative education, distance learning, double majors, English as a second language, honors programs, part-time degree program, services for LD students, summer session for credit. *ROTC:* Army (c), Air Force (c).
Student Life *Campus security:* 24-hour emergency response devices and patrols, late-night transport/escort service.
Costs (2012–13) *Tuition:* state resident $3360 full-time, $140 per credit part-time; nonresident $11,760 full-time, $490 per credit part-time. *Required fees:* $60 full-time, $30 per term part-time.
Applying *Options:* electronic application, early admission. *Application fee:* $20. *Required for some:* high school transcript. *Recommended:* high school transcript.
Freshman Application Contact Mrs. Shelbie Hugle, Director of Admission Services, Bluegrass Community and Technical College, 470 Cooper Drive, Lexington, KY 40506. *Phone:* 859-246-6216. *Toll-free phone:* 800-744-4872 (in-state); 866-744-4872 (out-of-state). *E-mail:* shelbie.hugle@kctcs.edu.
Website: http://www.bluegrass.kctcs.edu/.

Bowling Green Technical College

Bowling Green, Kentucky

Director of Admissions Mark Garrett, Chief Student Affairs Officer, Bowling Green Technical College, 1845 Loop Drive, Bowling Green, KY 42101. *Phone:* 270-901-1114. *Toll-free phone:* 800-790-0990. *Website:* http://www.bowlinggreen.kctcs.edu/.

Brown Mackie College–Hopkinsville

Hopkinsville, Kentucky

Freshman Application Contact Brown Mackie College–Hopkinsville, 4001 Fort Cambell Boulevard, Hopkinsville, KY 42240. *Phone:* 270-886-1302. *Toll-free phone:* 800-359-4753. *Website:* http://www.brownmackie.edu/Hopkinsville/.

See display below and page 364 for the College Close-Up.

Brown Mackie College–Louisville

Louisville, Kentucky

Freshman Application Contact Brown Mackie College–Louisville, 3605 Fern Valley Road, Louisville, KY 40219. *Phone:* 502-968-7191. *Toll-free phone:* 800-999-7387. *Website:* http://www.brownmackie.edu/louisville/.

See display below and page 370 for the College Close-Up.

Brown Mackie College–Northern Kentucky

Fort Mitchell, Kentucky

Freshman Application Contact Brown Mackie College–Northern Kentucky, 309 Buttermilk Pike, Fort Mitchell, KY 41017-2191. *Phone:* 859-341-5627. *Toll-free phone:* 800-888-1445. *Website:* http://www.brownmackie.edu/northernkentucky/.

See display below and page 380 for the College Close-Up.

Daymar College

Bellevue, Kentucky

Freshman Application Contact Cathy Baird, Director of Admissions, Daymar College, 119 Fairfield Avenue, Bellevue, KY 41073. *Phone:* 859-291-0800. *Toll-free phone:* 877-258-7796. *Fax:* 859-491-7500. *Website:* http://www.daymarcollege.edu/.

Daymar College

Bowling Green, Kentucky

Freshman Application Contact Mrs. Traci Henderson, Admissions Director, Daymar College, 2421 Fitzgerald Industrial Drive, Bowling Green, KY 42101. *Phone:* 270-843-6750. *Toll-free phone:* 877-258-7796. *E-mail:* thenderson@daymarcollege.edu. *Website:* http://www.daymarcollege.edu/.

Daymar College

Louisville, Kentucky

Director of Admissions Mr. Patrick Carney, Director of Admissions, Daymar College, 4112 Fern Valley Road, Louisville, KY 40219. *Toll-free phone:* 877-258-7796. *Website:* http://www.daymarcollege.edu/.

Daymar College

Owensboro, Kentucky

Freshman Application Contact Ms. Vickie McDougal, Director of Admissions, Daymar College, 3361 Buckland Square, Owensboro, KY 42301. *Phone:* 270-926-4040. *Toll-free phone:* 877-258-7796. *Fax:* 270-685-4090. *E-mail:* info@daymarcollege.edu. *Website:* http://www.daymarcollege.edu/.

Daymar College

Paducah, Kentucky

Freshman Application Contact Daymar College, 509 South 30th Street, Paducah, KY 42001. *Phone:* 270-444-9950. *Toll-free phone:* 877-258-7796. *Website:* http://www.daymarcollege.edu/.

Elizabethtown Community and Technical College

Elizabethtown, Kentucky

Freshman Application Contact Elizabethtown Community and Technical College, 620 College Street Road, Elizabethtown, KY 42701. *Phone:* 270-706-8800. *Toll-free phone:* 877-246-2322.
Website: http://www.elizabethtown.kctcs.edu/.

Gateway Community and Technical College

Florence, Kentucky

- **State-supported** 2-year, founded 1961, part of Kentucky Community and Technical College System
- **Suburban** campus with easy access to Cincinnati
- **Coed,** 4,648 undergraduate students, 31% full-time, 54% women, 46% men

Undergraduates 1,451 full-time, 3,197 part-time. 10% Black or African American, non-Hispanic/Latino; 2% Hispanic/Latino; 0.8% Asian, non-Hispanic/Latino; 0.1% Native Hawaiian or other Pacific Islander, non-Hispanic/Latino; 0.3% American Indian or Alaska Native, non-Hispanic/Latino; 1% Two or more races, non-Hispanic/Latino; 2% Race/ethnicity unknown.

Freshmen *Average high school GPA:* 2.35.

Faculty *Total:* 291, 31% full-time. *Student/faculty ratio:* 16:1.

Majors Accounting technology and bookkeeping; business administration and management; CAD/CADD drafting/design technology; criminal justice/law enforcement administration; early childhood education; engineering technology; fire science/firefighting; general studies; health professions related; industrial technology; information technology; manufacturing engineering technology; office occupations and clerical services; registered nursing/registered nurse.

Academics *Calendar:* semesters. *Degree:* certificates, diplomas, and associate. *Special study options:* academic remediation for entering students, cooperative education, distance learning, internships, part-time degree program, services for LD students, summer session for credit.

Library Main Library plus 3 others.

Student Life *Housing:* college housing not available. *Activities and Organizations:* Multi-Cultural Student Organization, Student Government Association, Speech Team, American Criminal Justice Association, Phi Theta Kappa. *Student services:* personal/psychological counseling.

Standardized Tests *Required:* ACT or ACT COMPASS (for admission).

Costs (2012–13) *Tuition:* state resident $3360 full-time, $140 per credit hour part-time; nonresident $11,760 full-time, $490 per credit hour part-time. Full-time tuition and fees vary according to course load. Part-time tuition and fees vary according to course load. *Required fees:* $40 part-time. *Payment plan:* installment. *Waivers:* senior citizens and employees or children of employees.

Applying *Options:* electronic application, early admission, deferred entrance. *Required:* high school transcript. *Application deadlines:* rolling (freshmen), rolling (out-of-state freshmen), rolling (transfers). *Notification:* continuous (freshmen), continuous (out-of-state freshmen), continuous (transfers).

Freshman Application Contact Gateway Community and Technical College, 500 Technology Way, Florence, KY 41042. *Phone:* 859-441-4500. *E-mail:* andre.washington@kctcs.edu.
Website: http://www.gateway.kctcs.edu/.

Hazard Community and Technical College

Hazard, Kentucky

Freshman Application Contact Director of Admissions, Hazard Community and Technical College, 1 Community College Drive, Hazard, KY 41701-2403. *Phone:* 606-487-3102. *Toll-free phone:* 800-246-7521.
Website: http://www.hazard.kctcs.edu/.

Henderson Community College

Henderson, Kentucky

Freshman Application Contact Ms. Teresa Hamiton, Admissions Counselor, Henderson Community College, 2660 South Green Street, Henderson, KY 42420-4623. *Phone:* 270-827-1867 Ext. 354. *Toll-free phone:* 800-696-9958.
Website: http://www.henderson.kctcs.edu/.

Hopkinsville Community College

Hopkinsville, Kentucky

Freshman Application Contact Ms. Janet Level, Student Records, Hopkinsville Community College, Room 135, English Education Center, 202 Bastogne Avenue, Fort Campbell, KY. *Phone:* 270-707-3918. *Toll-free phone:* 866-534-2224. *Fax:* 270-707-3973. *E-mail:* janet.level@kctcs.edu.
Website: http://hopkinsville.kctcs.edu/.

ITT Technical Institute

Louisville, Kentucky

- **Proprietary** primarily 2-year, founded 1993, part of ITT Educational Services, Inc.
- **Suburban** campus
- **Coed**

Academics *Calendar:* quarters. *Degrees:* associate and bachelor's.

Freshman Application Contact Director of Recruitment, ITT Technical Institute, 9500 Ormsby Station Road, Suite 100, Louisville, KY 40223. *Phone:* 502-327-7424. *Toll-free phone:* 888-790-7427.
Website: http://www.itt-tech.edu/.

Jefferson Community and Technical College

Louisville, Kentucky

Freshman Application Contact Ms. Melanie Vaughan-Cooke, Admissions Coordinator, Jefferson Community and Technical College, Louisville, KY 40202. *Phone:* 502-213-4000. *Fax:* 502-213-2540.
Website: http://www.jefferson.kctcs.edu/.

Lincoln College of Technology

Florence, Kentucky

Freshman Application Contact Director of Admission, Lincoln College of Technology, 8095 Connector Drive, Florence, KY 41042. *Phone:* 859-282-9999.
Website: http://www.lincolnedu.com/.

Madisonville Community College

Madisonville, Kentucky

Director of Admissions Mr. Jay Parent, Registrar, Madisonville Community College, 2000 College Drive, Madisonville, KY 42431-9185. *Phone:* 270-821-2250.
Website: http://www.madcc.kctcs.edu/.

Maysville Community and Technical College

Maysville, Kentucky

Director of Admissions Ms. Patee Massie, Registrar, Maysville Community and Technical College, 1755 US 68, Maysville, KY 41056. *Phone:* 606-759-7141. *Fax:* 606-759-5818. *E-mail:* ccsmayrg@ukcc.uky.edu.
Website: http://www.maysville.kctcs.edu/.

Maysville Community and Technical College

Morehead, Kentucky

Director of Admissions Patee Massie, Registrar, Maysville Community and Technical College, 609 Viking Drive, Morehead, KY 40351. *Phone:* 606-759-7141 Ext. 66184.
Website: http://www.maysville.kctcs.edu/.

MedTech College

Lexington, Kentucky

Admissions Office Contact MedTech College, 1648 McGrathiana Parkway, Suite 200, Lexington, KY 40511.
Website: http://www.medtechcollege.edu/.

National College

Danville, Kentucky

Director of Admissions James McGuire, Campus Director, National College, 115 East Lexington Avenue, Danville, KY 40422. *Phone:* 859-236-6991. *Toll-free phone:* 888-9-JOBREADY.
Website: http://www.national-college.edu/.

National College

Florence, Kentucky

Director of Admissions Mr. Terry Kovacs, Campus Director, National College, 7627 Ewing Boulevard, Florence, KY 41042. *Phone:* 859-525-6510. *Toll-free phone:* 888-9-JOBREADY.
Website: http://www.national-college.edu/.

National College

Lexington, Kentucky

Director of Admissions Kim Thomasson, Campus Director, National College, 2376 Sir Barton Way, Lexington, KY 40509. *Phone:* 859-253-0621. *Toll-free phone:* 888-9-JOBREADY.
Website: http://www.national-college.edu/.

National College

Louisville, Kentucky

Director of Admissions Vincent C. Tinebra, Campus Director, National College, 4205 Dixie Highway, Louisville, KY 40216. *Phone:* 502-447-7634. *Toll-free phone:* 888-9-JOBREADY.
Website: http://www.national-college.edu/.

National College

Pikeville, Kentucky

Director of Admissions Tammy Riley, Campus Director, National College, 50 National College Boulevard, Pikeville, KY 41501. *Phone:* 606-478-7200. *Toll-free phone:* 888-9-JOBREADY.
Website: http://www.national-college.edu/.

National College

Richmond, Kentucky

Director of Admissions Ms. Keeley Gadd, Campus Director, National College, 125 South Killarney Lane, Richmond, KY 40475. *Phone:* 859-623-8956. *Toll-free phone:* 888-9-JOBREADY.
Website: http://www.national-college.edu/.

Owensboro Community and Technical College

Owensboro, Kentucky

- **State-supported** 2-year, founded 1986, part of Kentucky Community and Technical College System
- **Suburban** 102-acre campus
- **Coed,** 4,768 undergraduate students, 42% full-time, 57% women, 43% men

Undergraduates 1,979 full-time, 2,789 part-time. Students come from 11 states and territories; 4% are from out of state; 3% Black or African American, non-Hispanic/Latino; 1% Hispanic/Latino; 0.2% Asian, non-Hispanic/Latino; 0.1% Native Hawaiian or other Pacific Islander, non-Hispanic/Latino; 0.2% American Indian or Alaska Native, non-Hispanic/Latino; 1% Two or more races, non-Hispanic/Latino; 4% Race/ethnicity unknown. *Retention:* 59% of full-time freshmen returned.
Freshmen *Admission:* 697 enrolled.
Faculty *Total:* 206, 49% full-time, 8% with terminal degrees. *Student/faculty ratio:* 21:1.
Majors Agriculture; biotechnology; business administration and management; computer and information sciences; computer/information technology services administration related; criminal justice/police science; data entry/microcomputer applications; diagnostic medical sonography and ultrasound technology; electrical, electronic and communications engineering technology; executive assistant/executive secretary; fire science/firefighting; human services; information technology; kindergarten/preschool education; liberal arts and sciences/liberal studies; medical radiologic technology; network and system administration; precision production trades; registered nursing/registered nurse; social work; word processing.

Academics *Calendar:* semesters. *Degree:* certificates, diplomas, and associate. *Special study options:* academic remediation for entering students, adult/continuing education programs, advanced placement credit, cooperative education, distance learning, double majors, English as a second language, external degree program, honors programs, independent study, off-campus study, part-time degree program, services for LD students, student-designed majors, study abroad, summer session for credit.
Library Learning Resource Center with 81,096 titles, 2,463 audiovisual materials, an OPAC, a Web page.
Student Life *Activities and Organizations:* drama/theater group, student-run television station, choral group, Student Government Association. *Campus security:* 24-hour emergency response devices, late-night transport/escort service.
Standardized Tests *Recommended:* SAT or ACT (for admission).
Costs (2012–13) *Tuition:* state resident $4200 full-time, $140 per credit part-time; nonresident $14,700 full-time, $490 per credit part-time. Full-time tuition and fees vary according to course load and reciprocity agreements. Part-time tuition and fees vary according to course load and reciprocity agreements. *Payment plan:* installment. *Waivers:* senior citizens and employees or children of employees.
Financial Aid Of all full-time matriculated undergraduates who enrolled in 2011, 48 Federal Work-Study jobs (averaging $5760). *Financial aid deadline:* 4/1.
Applying *Options:* electronic application. *Required:* high school transcript. *Application deadlines:* rolling (freshmen), rolling (transfers). *Notification:* continuous (freshmen), continuous (transfers).
Freshman Application Contact Ms. Barbara Tipmore, Admissions Counselor, Owensboro Community and Technical College, 4800 New Hartford Road, Owensboro, KY 42303. *Phone:* 270-686-4530. *Toll-free phone:* 866-755-6282. *E-mail:* barb.tipmore@kctcs.edu.
Website: http://www.octc.kctcs.edu/.

Somerset Community College

Somerset, Kentucky

Freshman Application Contact Director of Admission, Somerset Community College, 808 Monticello Street, Somerset, KY 42501-2973. *Phone:* 606-451-6630. *Toll-free phone:* 877-629-9722. *E-mail:* somerset-admissions@kctcs.edu.
Website: http://www.somerset.kctcs.edu/.

Southeast Kentucky Community and Technical College

Cumberland, Kentucky

Freshman Application Contact Southeast Kentucky Community and Technical College, 700 College Road, Cumberland, KY 40823-1099. *Phone:* 606-589-2145 Ext. 13018. *Toll-free phone:* 888-274-SECC.
Website: http://www.southeast.kctcs.edu/.

Spencerian College

Louisville, Kentucky

- **Proprietary** 2-year, founded 1892
- **Urban** 10-acre campus
- **Coed, primarily women,** 696 undergraduate students, 62% full-time, 85% women, 15% men

Undergraduates 429 full-time, 267 part-time. 21% Black or African American, non-Hispanic/Latino; 2% Hispanic/Latino; 0.3% Asian, non-Hispanic/Latino; 0.1% Native Hawaiian or other Pacific Islander, non-Hispanic/Latino; 0.1% American Indian or Alaska Native, non-Hispanic/Latino; 12% Two or more races, non-Hispanic/Latino; 1% Race/ethnicity unknown; 1% live on campus.
Freshmen *Admission:* 117 enrolled.
Faculty *Total:* 101, 47% full-time, 5% with terminal degrees. *Student/faculty ratio:* 11:1.
Majors Accounting technology and bookkeeping; cardiovascular technology; clinical/medical laboratory technology; massage therapy; medical insurance coding; medical insurance/medical billing; office management; radiologic technology/science; registered nursing/registered nurse; respiratory care therapy; surgical technology.
Academics *Calendar:* quarters. *Degree:* certificates, diplomas, and associate. *Special study options:* distance learning, summer session for credit.
Library Spencerian College Learning Resource Center with 1,585 titles, 300 audiovisual materials, an OPAC, a Web page.
Student Life *Housing Options:* coed. Campus housing is university owned.
Applying *Application fee:* $100. *Required:* high school transcript. *Required for some:* essay or personal statement, interview, Some medical programs have

specific selective admission criteria. *Notification:* continuous (freshmen), continuous (out-of-state freshmen), continuous (transfers).

Freshman Application Contact Spencerian College, 4627 Dixie Highway, Louisville, KY 40216. *Phone:* 502-447-1000 Ext. 7808. *Toll-free phone:* 800-264-1799.

Website: http://www.spencerian.edu/.

Spencerian College–Lexington

Lexington, Kentucky

Freshman Application Contact Spencerian College–Lexington, 1575 Winchester Road, Lexington, KY 40505. *Phone:* 859-223-9608 Ext. 5430. *Toll-free phone:* 800-456-3253.

Website: http://www.spencerian.edu/.

Sullivan College of Technology and Design

Louisville, Kentucky

- **Proprietary** primarily 2-year, founded 1961, part of The Sullivan University System, Inc.
- **Suburban** 10-acre campus with easy access to Louisville
- **Coed,** 457 undergraduate students, 69% full-time, 32% women, 68% men

Undergraduates 316 full-time, 141 part-time. Students come from 5 states and territories; 1 other country; 11% are from out of state; 18% Black or African American, non-Hispanic/Latino; 5% Hispanic/Latino; 1% Asian, non-Hispanic/Latino; 0.2% American Indian or Alaska Native, non-Hispanic/Latino; 8% Two or more races, non-Hispanic/Latino; 18% transferred in; 7% live on campus.

Freshmen *Admission:* 83 enrolled.

Faculty *Total:* 65, 46% full-time. *Student/faculty ratio:* 12:1.

Majors Animation, interactive technology, video graphics and special effects; architectural drafting and CAD/CADD; architectural engineering technology; architecture related; artificial intelligence; CAD/CADD drafting/design technology; civil drafting and CAD/CADD; computer and information sciences; computer and information sciences and support services related; computer and information systems security; computer engineering technology; computer graphics; computer hardware engineering; computer hardware technology; computer installation and repair technology; computer programming (vendor/product certification); computer systems networking and telecommunications; computer technology/computer systems technology; desktop publishing and digital imaging design; digital communication and media/multimedia; drafting and design technology; drafting/design engineering technologies related; electrical and electronic engineering technologies related; electrical, electronic and communications engineering technology; electrical/electronics equipment installation and repair; electrical/electronics maintenance and repair technology related; electromechanical and instrumentation and maintenance technologies related; engineering technologies and engineering related; engineering technology; graphic and printing equipment operation/production; graphic communications; graphic communications related; graphic design; heating, ventilation, air conditioning and refrigeration engineering technology; housing and human environments; industrial electronics technology; industrial mechanics and maintenance technology; information technology; interior design; manufacturing engineering technology; mechanical drafting and CAD/CADD; mechanical engineering/mechanical technology; network and system administration; robotics technology; web page, digital/multimedia and information resources design.

Academics *Calendar:* quarters. *Degrees:* associate and bachelor's. *Special study options:* academic remediation for entering students, accelerated degree program, adult/continuing education programs, advanced placement credit, double majors, independent study, internships, part-time degree program, services for LD students, summer session for credit.

Library Sullivan College of Technology and Design Library plus 1 other with 3,035 titles, 66 serial subscriptions, 370 audiovisual materials, an OPAC, a Web page.

Student Life *Housing Options:* coed. Campus housing is university owned and leased by the school. Freshman applicants given priority for college housing. *Activities and Organizations:* ASID, IIDA, ADDA, ADFED, Skills USA. *Campus security:* late-night transport/escort service, controlled dormitory access, telephone alarm device during hours school is open; patrols by trained security personnel while classes are in session.

Standardized Tests *Required:* Career Performance Assessment Test (CPAt) or ACT or SAT Language and Math scores in place of CPAt results (for admission). *Recommended:* SAT or ACT (for admission).

Costs (2013–14) *One-time required fee:* $100. *Comprehensive fee:* $27,560 includes full-time tuition ($17,340), mandatory fees ($1400), and room and board ($8820). Full-time tuition and fees vary according to course load, degree

level, and program. Part-time tuition: $425 per quarter hour. Part-time tuition and fees vary according to course load, degree level, and program. No tuition increase for student's term of enrollment. *Room and board:* Room and board charges vary according to board plan. *Payment plan:* installment. *Waivers:* employees or children of employees.

Applying *Options:* electronic application, deferred entrance. *Application fee:* $100. *Required:* high school transcript, interview, CPAT Exam or ACT/SAT Scores. *Application deadlines:* rolling (freshmen), rolling (out-of-state freshmen), rolling (transfers). *Notification:* continuous (freshmen), continuous (out-of-state freshmen), continuous (transfers).

Freshman Application Contact Mr. Aamer Z. Chauhdri, Director of Admissions, Sullivan College of Technology and Design, 3901 Atkinson Square Drive, Louisville, KY 40218. *Phone:* 502-456-6509 Ext. 8220. *Toll-free phone:* 800-884-6528. *Fax:* 502-456-2341. *E-mail:* achauhdri@sctd.edu. *Website:* http://www.sctd.edu/.

West Kentucky Community and Technical College

Paducah, Kentucky

- **State-supported** 2-year, founded 1932, part of Kentucky Community and Technical College System
- **Small-town** 117-acre campus
- **Coed,** 5,785 undergraduate students, 41% full-time, 58% women, 42% men

Undergraduates 2,398 full-time, 3,387 part-time. Students come from 26 states and territories; 1 other country; 8% are from out of state; 7% Black or African American, non-Hispanic/Latino; 2% Hispanic/Latino; 0.4% Asian, non-Hispanic/Latino; 0.1% Native Hawaiian or other Pacific Islander, non-Hispanic/Latino; 0.3% American Indian or Alaska Native, non-Hispanic/Latino; 1% Two or more races, non-Hispanic/Latino; 7% Race/ethnicity unknown; 0.1% international; 4% transferred in. *Retention:* 56% of full-time freshmen returned.

Freshmen *Admission:* 777 enrolled. *Test scores:* ACT scores over 18: 91%; ACT scores over 24: 37%; ACT scores over 30: 7%.

Majors Accounting; business administration and management; computer and information sciences; court reporting; criminal justice/law enforcement administration; culinary arts; diagnostic medical sonography and ultrasound technology; electrician; fire science/firefighting; machine shop technology; physical therapy technology; registered nursing/registered nurse; respiratory care therapy; surgical technology.

Academics *Calendar:* semesters. *Degree:* certificates, diplomas, and associate. *Special study options:* academic remediation for entering students, adult/continuing education programs, cooperative education, distance learning, English as a second language, honors programs, independent study, internships, part-time degree program, study abroad.

Library WKCTC Matheson Library with 74,676 titles, 155 serial subscriptions, 5,043 audiovisual materials, an OPAC, a Web page.

Student Life *Housing:* college housing not available. *Activities and Organizations:* drama/theater group, choral group. *Campus security:* late-night transport/escort service, 14-hour patrols by trained security personnel.

Athletics *Intramural sports:* basketball M/W, golf M/W, soccer M/W, volleyball M/W.

Standardized Tests *Required:* SAT or ACT (for admission). *Recommended:* ACT (for admission).

Financial Aid Of all full-time matriculated undergraduates who enrolled in 2011, 50 Federal Work-Study jobs (averaging $1650).

Applying *Options:* early admission. *Required for some:* high school transcript. *Application deadlines:* rolling (freshmen), rolling (transfers).

Freshman Application Contact Ms. Debbie Smith, Admissions Counselor, West Kentucky Community and Technical College, 4810 Alben Barkley Drive, Paducah, KY 42002-7380. *Phone:* 270-554-3266. *E-mail:* Debbie.Smith@kctcs.edu.

Website: http://www.westkentucky.kctcs.edu/.

LOUISIANA

Baton Rouge Community College

Baton Rouge, Louisiana

Director of Admissions Nancy Clay, Interim Executive Director for Enrollment Services, Baton Rouge Community College, 5310 Florida Boulevard, Baton Rouge, LA 70806. *Phone:* 225-216-8700. *Toll-free phone:* 800-601-4558.

Website: http://www.mybrcc.edu/.

Baton Rouge School of Computers
Baton Rouge, Louisiana

Freshman Application Contact Admissions Office, Baton Rouge School of Computers, 10425 Plaza Americana, Baton Rouge, LA 70816. *Phone:* 225-923-2524. *Toll-free phone:* 888-920-BRSC. *Fax:* 225-923-2979. *E-mail:* admissions@brsc.net.
Website: http://www.brsc.edu/.

Blue Cliff College–Lafayette
Lafayette, Louisiana

Freshman Application Contact Admissions Office, Blue Cliff College–Lafayette, 100 Asma Boulevard, Suite 350, Lafayette, LA 70508-3862. *Toll-free phone:* 800-514-2609.
Website: http://www.bluecliffcollege.com/.

Blue Cliff College–Shreveport
Shreveport, Louisiana

Freshman Application Contact Blue Cliff College–Shreveport, 8731 Park Plaza Drive, Shreveport, LA 71105. *Toll-free phone:* 800-516-6597.
Website: http://www.bluecliffcollege.com/.

Bossier Parish Community College
Bossier City, Louisiana

- **State-supported** 2-year, founded 1967, part of Louisiana Community and Technical College System
- **Urban** 64-acre campus
- **Coed,** 7,855 undergraduate students, 62% full-time, 64% women, 36% men

Undergraduates 4,866 full-time, 2,989 part-time. 3% are from out of state; 32% Black or African American, non-Hispanic/Latino; 15% Hispanic/Latino; 0.6% Asian, non-Hispanic/Latino; 0.1% Native Hawaiian or other Pacific Islander, non-Hispanic/Latino; 0.6% American Indian or Alaska Native, non-Hispanic/Latino; 14% Two or more races, non-Hispanic/Latino; 14% transferred in. *Retention:* 49% of full-time freshmen returned.
Freshmen *Admission:* 3,205 applied, 3,110 admitted, 1,564 enrolled.
Faculty *Total:* 322, 41% full-time, 40% with terminal degrees. *Student/faculty ratio:* 31:1.
Majors Administrative assistant and secretarial science; business/commerce; construction engineering; criminal justice/safety; culinary arts; drafting and design technology; dramatic/theater arts; education; educational/instructional technology; emergency medical technology (EMT paramedic); foods, nutrition, and wellness; general studies; industrial mechanics and maintenance technology; information science/studies; liberal arts and sciences/liberal studies; medical/clinical assistant; music; pharmacy technician; physical therapy; recording arts technology; respiratory care therapy.
Academics *Calendar:* semesters. *Degree:* certificates, diplomas, and associate. *Special study options:* academic remediation for entering students, adult/continuing education programs, advanced placement credit, distance learning, double majors, part-time degree program, services for LD students, summer session for credit.
Library Bossier Parish Community College Library with 29,600 titles, 384 serial subscriptions, an OPAC.
Student Life *Housing:* college housing not available. *Activities and Organizations:* drama/theater group, student-run newspaper, choral group. *Campus security:* student patrols. *Student services:* personal/psychological counseling.
Athletics Member NJCAA. *Intercollegiate sports:* baseball M(s), basketball M(s), soccer W, softball W(s). *Intramural sports:* badminton M/W, bowling M/W, football M, racquetball M, softball M, table tennis M/W, volleyball M/W.
Costs (2013–14) *Tuition:* state resident $2608 full-time, $159 per credit hour part-time; nonresident $5834 full-time, $293 per credit hour part-time. Full-time tuition and fees vary according to course load and program. Part-time tuition and fees vary according to course load and program. *Required fees:* $540 full-time. *Payment plan:* deferred payment. *Waivers:* employees or children of employees.
Financial Aid Of all full-time matriculated undergraduates who enrolled in 2011, 3,624 applied for aid, 3,317 were judged to have need, 87 had their need fully met. In 2011, 1 non-need-based awards were made. *Average percent of need met:* 35%. *Average financial aid package:* $11,694. *Average need-based loan:* $3165. *Average need-based gift aid:* $2544. *Average non-need-based aid:* $500.
Applying *Options:* early admission. *Application fee:* $15. *Required:* high school transcript. *Application deadlines:* 8/10 (freshmen), 8/10 (transfers).
Freshman Application Contact Ms. Ann Jampole, Director of Admissions, Bossier Parish Community College, 6220 East Texas Street, Bossier City, LA

71111. *Phone:* 318-678-6166. *Fax:* 318-742-8664.
Website: http://www.bpcc.edu/.

Camelot College
Baton Rouge, Louisiana

Freshman Application Contact Camelot College, 2618 Wooddale Boulevard, Suite A, Baton Rouge, LA 70805. *Phone:* 225-928-3005. *Toll-free phone:* 800-470-3320.
Website: http://www.camelotcollege.com/.

Cameron College
New Orleans, Louisiana

Admissions Office Contact Cameron College, 2740 Canal Street, New Orleans, LA 70119.
Website: http://www.cameroncollege.com/.

Capital Area Technical College–Baton Rouge Campus
Baton Rouge, Louisiana

Freshman Application Contact Ms. Amber Aguillard, Admissions Officer, Capital Area Technical College–Baton Rouge Campus, 3250 North Acadian Thruway, East, Baton Rouge, LA 70805. *Phone:* 225-359-9263. *Fax:* 225-359-9354. *E-mail:* aaguillard@ltc.edu.
Website: http://region2.ltc.edu/.

Career Technical College
Monroe, Louisiana

- **Proprietary** 2-year, founded 1985, part of Delta Career Education Corporation
- **Small-town** campus with easy access to Shreveport
- **Coed,** 558 undergraduate students, 82% full-time, 79% women, 21% men

Undergraduates 455 full-time, 103 part-time. Students come from 2 states and territories; 1% are from out of state; 64% Black or African American, non-Hispanic/Latino; 2% Hispanic/Latino; 0.4% Asian, non-Hispanic/Latino; 0.2% Native Hawaiian or other Pacific Islander, non-Hispanic/Latino; 0.2% American Indian or Alaska Native, non-Hispanic/Latino; 2% Two or more races, non-Hispanic/Latino; 0.2% Race/ethnicity unknown. *Retention:* 90% of full-time freshmen returned.
Freshmen *Admission:* 558 enrolled.
Faculty *Total:* 35, 57% full-time. *Student/faculty ratio:* 16:1.
Majors Administrative assistant and secretarial science; business administration and management; computer and information sciences and support services related; corrections and criminal justice related; legal administrative assistant/secretary; management science; massage therapy; medical/clinical assistant; medical office management; radiologic technology/science; respiratory therapy technician; surgical technology.
Academics *Calendar:* quarters. *Degree:* diplomas and associate. *Special study options:* academic remediation for entering students, adult/continuing education programs, advanced placement credit, cooperative education, double majors, independent study, internships.
Library Library & Information Resources Network.
Student Life *Housing:* college housing not available. *Activities and Organizations:* Medical Assisting Club, Surgical Technology Club, Criminal Justice Club, Rad Tech Club, Management/Information Processing Club. *Campus security:* 24-hour emergency response devices, late-night transport/escort service, evening security guard.
Standardized Tests *Required:* SLE-Wonderlic Scholastic Level Exam; Math Proficiency Exam; English Proficiency Exam (for admission).
Costs (2013–14) *One-time required fee:* $120. *Tuition:* $11,376 full-time. Full-time tuition and fees vary according to course load and program. Part-time tuition and fees vary according to course load and program. No tuition increase for student's term of enrollment. *Required fees:* $1275 full-time. *Payment plans:* tuition prepayment, installment. *Waivers:* employees or children of employees.
Applying *Options:* deferred entrance. *Application fee:* $40. *Required:* high school transcript, interview. *Application deadlines:* rolling (freshmen), rolling (out-of-state freshmen), rolling (transfers). *Notification:* continuous (freshmen), continuous (out-of-state freshmen), continuous (transfers).
Freshman Application Contact Mrs. Susan Boudreaux, Admissions Office, Career Technical College, 2319 Louisville Avenue, Monroe, LA 71201. *Phone:* 318-323-2889. *Toll-free phone:* 800-923-1947. *Fax:* 318-324-9883. *E-mail:* susan.boudreaux@careertc.edu.
Website: http://www.careertc.edu/.

Delgado Community College

New Orleans, Louisiana

Freshman Application Contact Ms. Gwen Boute, Director of Admissions, Delgado Community College, 501 City Park Avenue, New Orleans, LA 70119-4399. *Phone:* 504-671-5010. *Fax:* 504-483-1895. *E-mail:* enroll@dcc.edu. *Website:* http://www.dcc.edu/.

Delta College of Arts and Technology

Baton Rouge, Louisiana

Freshman Application Contact Ms. Beulah Laverghe-Brown, Admissions Director, Delta College of Arts and Technology, 7380 Exchange Place, Baton Rouge, LA 70806-3851. *Phone:* 225-928-7770. *Fax:* 225-927-9096. *E-mail:* bbrown@deltacollege.com. *Website:* http://www.deltacollege.com/.

Delta School of Business & Technology

Lake Charles, Louisiana

Freshman Application Contact Jeffery Tibodeaux, Director of Admissions, Delta School of Business & Technology, 517 Broad Street, Lake Charles, LA 70601. *Phone:* 337-439-5765. *Website:* http://www.deltatech.edu/.

Elaine P. Nunez Community College

Chalmette, Louisiana

- **State-supported** 2-year, founded 1992, part of Louisiana Community and Technical College System
- **Suburban** 20-acre campus with easy access to New Orleans
- **Endowment** $1.2 million
- **Coed,** 2,302 undergraduate students, 35% full-time, 66% women, 34% men

Undergraduates 804 full-time, 1,498 part-time. Students come from 2 states and territories. *Retention:* 49% of full-time freshmen returned.

Freshmen *Admission:* 245 enrolled. *Average high school GPA:* 2.17.

Faculty *Total:* 79, 51% full-time. *Student/faculty ratio:* 29:1.

Majors Administrative assistant and secretarial science; business/commerce; carpentry; child-care provision; culinary arts; education; emergency medical technology (EMT paramedic); general studies; health information/medical records administration; heating, air conditioning, ventilation and refrigeration maintenance technology; industrial technology; information science/studies; kindergarten/preschool education; legal assistant/paralegal; liberal arts and sciences and humanities related; liberal arts and sciences/liberal studies; medical office management; nursing assistant/aide and patient care assistant/aide; welding technology.

Academics *Calendar:* semesters. *Degree:* certificates, diplomas, and associate. *Special study options:* academic remediation for entering students, adult/continuing education programs, advanced placement credit, cooperative education, distance learning, double majors, independent study, internships, off-campus study, part-time degree program, services for LD students, student-designed majors, summer session for credit.

Library Nunez Community College Library with 72,500 titles, 2,500 serial subscriptions, 3,128 audiovisual materials, an OPAC, a Web page.

Student Life *Housing:* college housing not available. *Activities and Organizations:* drama/theater group, student-run newspaper, Nunez Environmental Team, national fraternities. *Campus security:* 24-hour emergency response devices, late-night transport/escort service, security cameras. *Student services:* personal/psychological counseling.

Athletics *Intramural sports:* basketball M, football M/W.

Standardized Tests *Recommended:* ACT (for admission).

Financial Aid Of all full-time matriculated undergraduates who enrolled in 2011, 70 Federal Work-Study jobs (averaging $1452).

Applying *Options:* electronic application, early admission, deferred entrance. *Application fee:* $10. *Required for some:* high school transcript. *Application deadlines:* rolling (freshmen), rolling (transfers).

Freshman Application Contact Mrs. Becky Maillet, Elaine P. Nunez Community College, 3710 Paris Road, Chalmette, LA 70043. *Phone:* 504-278-6477. *E-mail:* bmaillet@nunez.edu. *Website:* http://www.nunez.edu/.

Fletcher Technical Community College

Schriever, Louisiana

Director of Admissions Admissions Office, Fletcher Technical Community College, 1407 Highway 311, Schriever, LA 70395. *Phone:* 985-857-3659. *Website:* http://www.fletcher.edu/.

Fortis College

Baton Rouge, Louisiana

Director of Admissions Ms. Sheri Kirley, Associate Director of Admissions, Fortis College, 9255 Interline Avenue, Baton Rouge, LA 70809. *Phone:* 225-248-1015. *Website:* http://www.fortis.edu/.

ITI Technical College

Baton Rouge, Louisiana

- **Proprietary** 2-year, founded 1973
- **Suburban** 10-acre campus
- **Coed, primarily men,** 585 undergraduate students, 100% full-time, 15% women, 85% men

Undergraduates 585 full-time. Students come from 3 states and territories; 1% are from out of state; 38% Black or African American, non-Hispanic/Latino; 2% Hispanic/Latino; 0.7% Asian, non-Hispanic/Latino; 0.9% American Indian or Alaska Native, non-Hispanic/Latino; 0.7% Two or more races, non-Hispanic/Latino. *Retention:* 81% of full-time freshmen returned.

Freshmen *Admission:* 174 applied, 172 admitted, 142 enrolled.

Faculty *Total:* 51, 47% full-time, 49% with terminal degrees. *Student/faculty ratio:* 15:1.

Majors Chemical technology; computer technology/computer systems technology; drafting and design technology; electrical, electronic and communications engineering technology; information technology; instrumentation technology; office occupations and clerical services.

Academics *Calendar:* continuous. *Degree:* certificates and associate. *Special study options:* internships.

Library ITI Technical College Library with 1,260 titles.

Student Life *Housing:* college housing not available. *Campus security:* electronic alarm devices are activated during non-business hours and security cameras monitor campus 24 hours.

Applying *Required:* high school transcript, interview.

Freshman Application Contact Mrs. Marcia Stevens, Admissions Director, ITI Technical College, 13944 Airline Highway, Baton Rouge, LA 70817. *Phone:* 225-752-4230 Ext. 261. *Toll-free phone:* 888-211-7165. *Fax:* 225-756-0903. *E-mail:* mstevens@iticollege.edu. *Website:* http://www.iticollege.edu/.

ITT Technical Institute

Baton Rouge, Louisiana

- **Proprietary** primarily 2-year
- **Coed**

Academics *Degrees:* associate and bachelor's.

Freshman Application Contact Director of Recruitment, ITT Technical Institute, 14111 Airline Highway, Suite 101, Baton Rouge, LA 70817. *Phone:* 225-754-5800. *Toll-free phone:* 800-295-8485. *Website:* http://www.itt-tech.edu/.

ITT Technical Institute

St. Rose, Louisiana

- **Proprietary** primarily 2-year, founded 1998, part of ITT Educational Services, Inc.
- **Coed**

Academics *Calendar:* quarters. *Degrees:* associate and bachelor's.

Freshman Application Contact Director of Recruitment, ITT Technical Institute, 140 James Drive East, St. Rose, LA 70087. *Phone:* 504-463-0338. *Toll-free phone:* 866-463-0338. *Website:* http://www.itt-tech.edu/.

Louisiana Delta Community College

Monroe, Louisiana

Admissions Office Contact Louisiana Delta Community College, 7500 Millhaven Road, Monroe, LA 71203. *Toll-free phone:* 866-500-LDCC. *Website:* http://www.ladelta.edu/.

Louisiana State University at Eunice

Eunice, Louisiana

Freshman Application Contact Ms. Gracie Guillory, Director of Financial Aid, Louisiana State University at Eunice, PO Box 1129, Eunice, LA 70535-1129. *Phone:* 337-550-1282. *Toll-free phone:* 888-367-5783. *Website:* http://www.lsue.edu/.

Northeast Louisiana Technical College–Northeast Campus

Winnsboro, Louisiana

Director of Admissions Admissions Office, Northeast Louisiana Technical College–Northeast Campus, 1710 Warren Street, Winnsboro, LA 71295. *Phone:* 318-435-2163. *Toll-free phone:* 877-842-6956. *Website:* http://www.ltc.edu/.

Northshore Technical Community College–Florida Parishes Campus

Greensburg, Louisiana

Director of Admissions Mrs. Sharon G. Hornsby, Campus Dean, Northshore Technical Community College–Florida Parishes Campus, 948 Highway 1042, Greensburg, LA 70441. *Phone:* 225-222-4251. *Toll-free phone:* 800-827-9750. *Website:* http://www.ltc.edu/.

Remington College–Baton Rouge Campus

Baton Rouge, Louisiana

Director of Admissions Monica Butler-Johnson, Director of Recruitment, Remington College–Baton Rouge Campus, 10551 Coursey Boulevard, Baton Rouge, LA 70816. *Phone:* 225-236-3200. *Fax:* 225-922-3250. *E-mail:* monica.johnson@remingtoncollege.edu. *Website:* http://www.remingtoncollege.edu/.

Remington College–Lafayette Campus

Lafayette, Louisiana

Freshman Application Contact Remington College–Lafayette Campus, 303 Rue Louis XIV, Lafayette, LA 70508. *Phone:* 337-981-4010. *Toll-free phone:* 800-560-6192. *Website:* http://www.remingtoncollege.edu/.

Remington College–Shreveport

Shreveport, Louisiana

Freshman Application Contact Marc Wright, Remington College–Shreveport, 2106 Bert Kouns Industrial Loop, Shreveport, LA 71118. *Phone:* 318-671-4000. *Website:* http://www.remingtoncollege.edu/.

River Parishes Community College

Sorrento, Louisiana

Director of Admissions Ms. Allison Dauzat, Dean of Students and Enrollment Management, River Parishes Community College, PO Box 310, Sorrento, LA 70778. *Phone:* 225-675-8270. *Fax:* 225-675-5478. *E-mail:* adauzat@rpcc.cc.la.us. *Website:* http://www.rpcc.edu/.

South Central Louisiana Technical College–Young Memorial Campus

Morgan City, Louisiana

Director of Admissions Ms. Melanie Henry, Admissions Office, South Central Louisiana Technical College–Young Memorial Campus, 900 Youngs Road, Morgan City, LA 70381. *Phone:* 504-380-2436. *Fax:* 504-380-2440. *Website:* http://www.ltc.edu/.

Southern University at Shreveport

Shreveport, Louisiana

Freshman Application Contact Ms. Juanita Johnson, Acting Admissions Records Technician, Southern University at Shreveport, 3050 Martin Luther King, Jr. Drive, Shreveport, LA 71107. *Phone:* 318-674-3342. *Toll-free phone:* 800-458-1472. *Website:* http://www.susla.edu/.

South Louisiana Community College

Lafayette, Louisiana

Freshman Application Contact Metilda Wilson, Dean of Student Services, South Louisiana Community College, 320 Devalcourt, Lafayette, LA 70506. *Phone:* 337-521-8909. *Website:* http://www.southlouisiana.edu/.

Sowela Technical Community College

Lake Charles, Louisiana

Director of Admissions Admissions Office, Sowela Technical Community College, 3820 J. Bennett Johnston Avenue, Lake Charles, LA 70616-6950. *Phone:* 337-491-2698. *Website:* http://www.sowela.edu/.

Virginia College in Baton Rouge

Baton Rouge, Louisiana

Admissions Office Contact Virginia College in Baton Rouge, 9501 Cortana Place, Baton Rouge, LA 70815. *Website:* http://www.vc.edu/.

MAINE

Beal College

Bangor, Maine

Freshman Application Contact Admissions Assistant, Beal College, 99 Farm Road, Bangor, ME 04401. *Phone:* 207-947-4591. *Toll-free phone:* 800-660-7351. *Fax:* 207-947-0208. *E-mail:* admissions@bealcollege.edu. *Website:* http://www.bealcollege.edu/.

Central Maine Community College

Auburn, Maine

- **State-supported** 2-year, founded 1964, part of Maine Community College System
- **Small-town** 135-acre campus
- **Endowment** $530,000
- **Coed,** 2,905 undergraduate students, 49% full-time, 54% women, 46% men

Undergraduates 1,426 full-time, 1,479 part-time. Students come from 9 states and territories; 5 other countries; 8% are from out of state; 2% Black or African American, non-Hispanic/Latino; 1% Hispanic/Latino; 0.7% Asian, non-Hispanic/Latino; 0.5% American Indian or Alaska Native, non-Hispanic/Latino; 0.7% Two or more races, non-Hispanic/Latino; 18% Race/ethnicity unknown; 0.3% international; 3% transferred in; 8% live on campus.

Freshmen *Admission:* 2,070 applied, 714 admitted, 602 enrolled. *Test scores:* SAT critical reading scores over 500: 22%; SAT math scores over 500: 22%; SAT writing scores over 500: 18%; SAT critical reading scores over 600: 3%; SAT math scores over 600: 3%; SAT writing scores over 600: 3%; SAT writing scores over 700: 1%.

Faculty *Total:* 233, 21% full-time, 1% with terminal degrees. *Student/faculty ratio:* 13:1.

Majors Accounting technology and bookkeeping; administrative assistant and secretarial science; architectural engineering technology; automobile/automotive mechanics technology; building construction technology; business administration and management; child development; communications systems installation and repair technology; computer installation and repair technology; construction engineering technology; construction trades related; criminal justice/law enforcement administration; electromechanical technology; graphic and printing equipment operation/production; human services; liberal arts and sciences/liberal studies; licensed practical/vocational nurse training; machine tool technology; medical/clinical assistant; multi/interdisciplinary studies related; registered nursing/registered nurse; teacher assistant/aide; vehicle maintenance and repair technologies related.

Academics *Calendar:* semesters. *Degree:* certificates, diplomas, and associate. *Special study options:* academic remediation for entering students, accelerated degree program, adult/continuing education programs, advanced placement credit, cooperative education, distance learning, English as a second language, independent study, internships, part-time degree program, services for LD students, summer session for credit.

Library Central Maine Community College Library with 15,914 titles, 200 serial subscriptions, 2 audiovisual materials, an OPAC, a Web page.

Student Life *Housing Options:* coed, men-only, women-only. Campus housing is university owned. Freshman applicants given priority for college housing. *Activities and Organizations:* drama/theater group. *Campus security:* 24-hour emergency response devices, student patrols, controlled dormitory access, night patrols by police.

Athletics Member USCAA. *Intercollegiate sports:* baseball M, basketball M/W, golf M/W, lacrosse M, soccer M/W, softball W, volleyball M/W.

Standardized Tests *Recommended:* SAT (for admission).

Financial Aid Of all full-time matriculated undergraduates who enrolled in 2011, 89 Federal Work-Study jobs (averaging $1200). *Financial aid deadline:* 8/1.

Applying *Options:* electronic application, deferred entrance. *Application fee:* $20. *Required:* high school transcript. *Application deadlines:* rolling (freshmen), rolling (transfers). *Notification:* continuous (freshmen), continuous (transfers).

Freshman Application Contact Ms. Joan Nichols, Admissions Assistant, Central Maine Community College, 1250 Turner Street, Auburn, ME 04210. *Phone:* 207-755-5273. *Toll-free phone:* 800-891-2002. *Fax:* 207-755-5493. *E-mail:* enroll@cmcc.edu. *Website:* http://www.cmcc.edu/.

Central Maine Medical Center College of Nursing and Health Professions
Lewiston, Maine

- **Independent** 2-year, founded 1891.
- **Urban** campus
- **Coed,** 217 undergraduate students, 30% full-time, 78% women, 22% men

Undergraduates 66 full-time, 151 part-time. Students come from 2 states and territories; 1% are from out of state; 2% live on campus.

Freshmen *Admission:* 3 enrolled.

Faculty *Student/faculty ratio:* 10:1.

Majors Nuclear medical technology; radiologic technology/science; registered nursing/registered nurse.

Academics *Calendar:* semesters. *Degree:* associate. *Special study options:* advanced placement credit, off-campus study, services for LD students, summer session for credit.

Library Gerrish True Health Sciences Library plus 1 other with 1,975 titles, 339 serial subscriptions, an OPAC, a Web page.

Student Life *Housing Options:* coed. Campus housing is university owned. *Activities and Organizations:* Student Communication Council, student government, Student Nurses Association. *Campus security:* 24-hour emergency response devices and patrols, late-night transport/escort service, controlled dormitory access. *Student services:* health clinic, personal/psychological counseling.

Standardized Tests *Required:* SAT or ACT (for admission), Accuplacer Entrance Exam (for admission).

Costs (2013–14) *Tuition:* $7665 full-time. *Required fees:* $1885 full-time. *Room only:* $2350. *Waivers:* employees or children of employees.

Financial Aid Of all full-time matriculated undergraduates who enrolled in 2010, 5 applied for aid, 4 were judged to have need. *Average financial aid package:* $17,200. *Average need-based loan:* $4000. *Average need-based gift aid:* $7700.

Applying *Application fee:* $40. *Required:* essay or personal statement, high school transcript, Entrance exam, SAT or ACT, high school or college level algebra, second math, biology, chemistry, high school transcript or GED. *Application deadline:* 1/15 (freshmen). *Notification:* 3/15 (freshmen).

Freshman Application Contact Ms. Dagmar Jenison, Assistant Registrar, Central Maine Medical Center College of Nursing and Health Professions, 70 Middle Street, Lewiston, ME 04240. *Phone:* 207-795-2843. *Fax:* 207-795-2849. *E-mail:* jenisod@cmhc.org. *Website:* http://www.cmmccollege.edu/.

Eastern Maine Community College
Bangor, Maine

Freshman Application Contact Mr. W. Gregory Swett, Director of Admissions, Eastern Maine Community College, 354 Hogan Road, Bangor, ME 04401. *Phone:* 207-974-4680. *Toll-free phone:* 800-286-9357. *Fax:* 207-974-4683. *E-mail:* admissions@emcc.edu. *Website:* http://www.emcc.edu/.

Kaplan University
Lewiston, Maine

Freshman Application Contact Kaplan University, 475 Lisbon Street, Lewiston, ME 04240. *Phone:* 207-333-3300. *Toll-free phone:* 866-527-5268 (in-state); 800-527-5268 (out-of-state). *Website:* http://lewiston.kaplanuniversity.edu/.

Kaplan University
South Portland, Maine

Freshman Application Contact Kaplan University, 265 Western Avenue, South Portland, ME 04106. *Phone:* 207-774-6126. *Toll-free phone:* 866-527-5268 (in-state); 800-527-5268 (out-of-state). *Website:* http://portland.kaplanuniversity.edu/.

Kennebec Valley Community College
Fairfield, Maine

- **State-supported** 2-year, founded 1970, part of Maine Community College System
- **Small-town** 61-acre campus
- **Coed,** 2,470 undergraduate students, 29% full-time, 67% women, 33% men

Undergraduates 714 full-time, 1,756 part-time. Students come from 9 states and territories; 1% are from out of state; 0.7% Black or African American, non-Hispanic/Latino; 1% Hispanic/Latino; 0.7% Asian, non-Hispanic/Latino; 0.6% American Indian or Alaska Native, non-Hispanic/Latino; 0.3% Two or more races, non-Hispanic/Latino; 10% Race/ethnicity unknown; 0.1% international; 8% transferred in.

Freshmen *Admission:* 1,851 applied, 838 admitted, 310 enrolled.

Faculty *Total:* 47, 100% full-time.

Majors Accounting technology and bookkeeping; biology/biotechnology laboratory technician; child development; diagnostic medical sonography and ultrasound technology; drafting/design engineering technologies related; electrical, electronic and communications engineering technology; electrical/electronics maintenance and repair technology related; electrician; emergency medical technology (EMT paramedic); executive assistant/executive secretary; finance; health information/medical records technology; heating, ventilation, air conditioning and refrigeration engineering technology; industrial mechanics and maintenance technology; legal administrative assistant/secretary; liberal arts and sciences and humanities related; liberal arts and sciences/liberal studies; lineworker; machine tool technology; management information systems; marketing/marketing management; massage therapy; medical administrative assistant and medical secretary; medical/clinical assistant; mental and social health services and allied professions related; occupational therapist assistant; physical therapy technology; radiologic technology/science; registered nursing/registered nurse; respiratory care therapy; teacher assistant/aide; wood science and wood products/pulp and paper technology.

Academics *Calendar:* semesters. *Degree:* certificates, diplomas, and associate. *Special study options:* academic remediation for entering students, accelerated degree program, adult/continuing education programs, advanced placement credit, distance learning, external degree program, independent study, internships, part-time degree program, services for LD students, summer session for credit.

Library Lunder Library plus 1 other with 19,316 titles, 188 serial subscriptions, 2,955 audiovisual materials, an OPAC, a Web page.

Student Life *Housing:* college housing not available. *Activities and Organizations:* choral group, Phi Theta Kappa, National Society for Leadership & Success, Student Senate, Respiratory Therapy Club, KV Federal Nurses Association. *Campus security:* evening security patrol. *Student services:* personal/psychological counseling.

Athletics *Intercollegiate sports:* ice hockey M/W. *Intramural sports:* basketball M/W, bowling M/W, golf M/W, soccer M/W, softball M/W, volleyball M/W.

Standardized Tests *Required for some:* HESI nursing exam, HOBET for Allied Health programs, ACCUPLACER. *Recommended:* SAT or ACT (for admission).

Costs (2012–13) *One-time required fee:* $30. *Tuition:* state resident $2580 full-time, $86 per credit hour part-time; nonresident $5160 full-time, $172 per credit hour part-time. *Required fees:* $606 full-time, $3 per credit hour part-time. *Payment plan:* installment. *Waivers:* senior citizens and employees or children of employees.

Financial Aid Of all full-time matriculated undergraduates who enrolled in 2011, 34 Federal Work-Study jobs (averaging $1207).

Applying *Options:* electronic application, deferred entrance. *Application fee:* $20. *Required:* essay or personal statement, high school transcript. *Required for some:* interview. *Application deadlines:* rolling (freshmen), rolling (transfers). *Notification:* continuous (freshmen), continuous (transfers).

Freshman Application Contact Mr. Jim Bourgoin, Director of Admissions, Kennebec Valley Community College, Fairfield, ME 04937-1367. *Phone:* 207-453-5035. *Toll-free phone:* 800-528-5882. *Fax:* 207-453-5011. *E-mail:* admissions@kvcc.me.edu. *Website:* http://www.kvcc.me.edu/.

Northern Maine Community College
Presque Isle, Maine

Freshman Application Contact Ms. Nancy Gagnon, Admissions Secretary, Northern Maine Community College, 33 Edgemont Drive, Presque Isle, ME 04769-2016. *Phone:* 207-768-2785. *Toll-free phone:* 800-535-6682. *Fax:* 207-768-2848. *E-mail:* ngagnon@nmcc.edu. *Website:* http://www.nmcc.edu/.

Southern Maine Community College
South Portland, Maine

- **State-supported** 2-year, founded 1946, part of Maine Community College System
- **Urban** 80-acre campus
- **Coed,** 7,574 undergraduate students, 41% full-time, 48% women, 52% men

Undergraduates 3,086 full-time, 4,488 part-time. Students come from 24 states and territories; 41 other countries; 3% are from out of state; 4% Black or African American, non-Hispanic/Latino; 2% Hispanic/Latino; 2% Asian, non-Hispanic/Latino; 0.1% Native Hawaiian or other Pacific Islander, non-Hispanic/Latino; 0.7% American Indian or Alaska Native, non-Hispanic/Latino; 2% Two or more races, non-Hispanic/Latino; 8% Race/ethnicity unknown; 0.4% international; 35% transferred in; 5% live on campus. *Retention:* 53% of full-time freshmen returned.

Freshmen *Admission:* 1,391 enrolled.

Faculty *Total:* 482, 23% full-time. *Student/faculty ratio:* 20:1.

Majors Applied horticulture/horticulture operations; architectural drafting and CAD/CADD; automobile/automotive mechanics technology; biotechnology; business administration and management; cardiovascular technology; computer engineering technology; construction trades; criminal justice/police science; culinary arts; dietetic technology; digital communication and media/multimedia; early childhood education; electrical, electronic and communications engineering technology; emergency medical technology (EMT paramedic); environmental engineering technology; fire science/firefighting; health information/medical records technology; heating, air conditioning, ventilation and refrigeration maintenance technology; hotel/motel administration; liberal arts and sciences and humanities related; machine tool technology; marine biology and biological oceanography; materials engineering; medical/clinical assistant; medical radiologic technology; mental and social health services and allied professions related; plumbing technology; pre-engineering; radiologic technology/science; registered nursing/registered nurse; respiratory care therapy; surgical technology.

Academics *Calendar:* semesters. *Degree:* certificates and associate. *Special study options:* academic remediation for entering students, advanced placement credit, distance learning, double majors, English as a second language, honors programs, independent study, internships, off-campus study, part-time degree program, services for LD students, study abroad, summer session for credit.

Library Southern Maine Community College Library with an OPAC, a Web page.

Student Life *Housing Options:* coed. Campus housing is university owned. *Activities and Organizations:* drama/theater group, student-run newspaper, choral group, Student Senate. *Campus security:* 24-hour emergency response devices and patrols, student patrols, late-night transport/escort service, controlled dormitory access. *Student services:* personal/psychological counseling.

Athletics Member USCAA. *Intercollegiate sports:* baseball M, basketball M/W, golf M/W, soccer M/W, softball W. *Intramural sports:* cheerleading M(c)/W, cross-country running M(c)/W(c), ice hockey M(c), rock climbing M(c)/W(c), soccer M/W, volleyball M/W.

Standardized Tests *Recommended:* SAT or ACT (for admission), ACCUPLACER.

Financial Aid Of all full-time matriculated undergraduates who enrolled in 2011, 130 Federal Work-Study jobs (averaging $1500).

Applying *Options:* electronic application. *Application fee:* $20. *Required:* high school transcript or proof of high school graduation. *Application dead-*

lines: rolling (freshmen), rolling (out-of-state freshmen), rolling (transfers). *Notification:* continuous (freshmen), continuous (out-of-state freshmen), continuous (transfers).

Freshman Application Contact Amy Lee, Associate Dean for Enrollment Services, Southern Maine Community College, 2 Fort Road, South, Portland, ME 04106. *Phone:* 207-741-5800. *Toll-free phone:* 877-282-2182. *Fax:* 207-741-5760. *E-mail:* alee@smccme.edu. *Website:* http://www.smccme.edu/.

Washington County Community College
Calais, Maine

Director of Admissions Mr. Kent Lyons, Admissions Counselor, Washington County Community College, One College Drive, Calais, ME 04619. *Phone:* 207-454-1000. *Toll-free phone:* 800-210-6932. *Website:* http://www.wccc.me.edu/.

York County Community College
Wells, Maine

- **State-supported** 2-year, founded 1994, part of Maine Community College System
- **Small-town** 84-acre campus with easy access to Boston
- **Endowment** $804,057
- **Coed,** 1,524 undergraduate students, 35% full-time, 65% women, 35% men

Undergraduates 532 full-time, 992 part-time. Students come from 7 states and territories; 1 other country; 2% are from out of state; 0.8% Black or African American, non-Hispanic/Latino; 2% Hispanic/Latino; 1% Asian, non-Hispanic/Latino; 0.9% American Indian or Alaska Native, non-Hispanic/Latino; 2% Two or more races, non-Hispanic/Latino; 6% Race/ethnicity unknown; 0.3% international; 5% transferred in. *Retention:* 52% of full-time freshmen returned.

Freshmen *Admission:* 296 enrolled.

Faculty *Total:* 136, 13% full-time, 9% with terminal degrees. *Student/faculty ratio:* 15:1.

Majors Accounting; architectural drafting and CAD/CADD; business administration and management; business/corporate communications; child development; construction trades related; criminal justice/safety; culinary arts; design and visual communications; education; health information/medical records technology; health services/allied health/health sciences; liberal arts and sciences and humanities related; management information systems; medical/clinical assistant; multi/interdisciplinary studies related.

Academics *Calendar:* semesters. *Degree:* certificates and associate. *Special study options:* academic remediation for entering students, accelerated degree program, adult/continuing education programs, advanced placement credit, cooperative education, distance learning, internships, part-time degree program, services for LD students, summer session for credit.

Library Library and Learning Resource Center plus 1 other with 14,000 titles, 93 serial subscriptions, 1,926 audiovisual materials, an OPAC, a Web page.

Student Life *Housing:* college housing not available. *Activities and Organizations:* Student Senate, Phi Theta Kappa, Photography Club, Culinary Arts Club. *Campus security:* 24-hour emergency response devices, late-night transport/escort service.

Athletics *Intramural sports:* basketball M/W, bowling M/W, cross-country running M/W, football M/W, ice hockey M/W, skiing (downhill) M/W, softball M/W, ultimate Frisbee M/W.

Costs (2013–14) *Tuition:* state resident $2580 full-time, $86 per credit part-time; nonresident $5160 full-time, $172 per credit part-time. *Required fees:* $606 full-time. *Payment plan:* installment. *Waivers:* employees or children of employees.

Financial Aid Of all full-time matriculated undergraduates who enrolled in 2012, 580 applied for aid, 480 were judged to have need, 13 had their need fully met. 28 Federal Work-Study jobs (averaging $1350). In 2012, 27 non-need-based awards were made. *Average percent of need met:* 42%. *Average financial aid package:* $5943. *Average need-based loan:* $2919. *Average need-based gift aid:* $4769. *Average non-need-based aid:* $1297.

Applying *Options:* electronic application. *Required:* high school transcript, interview. *Application deadlines:* rolling (freshmen), rolling (transfers).

Freshman Application Contact Fred Quistgard, Director of Admissions, York County Community College, 112 College Drive, Wells, ME 04090. *Phone:* 207-216-4406 Ext. 311. *Toll-free phone:* 800-580-3820. *Fax:* 207-641-0837. *Website:* http://www.yccc.edu/.

MARSHALL ISLANDS

College of the Marshall Islands
Majuro, Marshall Islands, Marshall Islands

Freshman Application Contact Ms. Rosita Capelle, Director of Admissions and Records, College of the Marshall Islands, PO Box 1258, Majuro, MH 96960, Marshall Islands. *Phone:* 692-625-6823. *Fax:* 692-625-7203. *E-mail:* cmiadmissions@cmi.edu.
Website: http://www.cmi.edu/.

MARYLAND

Allegany College of Maryland
Cumberland, Maryland

Freshman Application Contact Ms. Cathy Nolan, Director of Admissions and Registration, Allegany College of Maryland, Cumberland, MD 21502. *Phone:* 301-784-5000 Ext. 5202. *Fax:* 301-784-5220. *E-mail:* cnolan@allegany.edu.
Website: http://www.allegany.edu/.

Anne Arundel Community College
Arnold, Maryland

- **State and locally supported** 2-year, founded 1961
- **Suburban** 230-acre campus with easy access to Baltimore and Washington, DC
- **Coed,** 17,650 undergraduate students, 29% full-time, 60% women, 40% men

Undergraduates 5,098 full-time, 12,552 part-time. Students come from 34 states and territories; 18% Black or African American, non-Hispanic/Latino; 5% Hispanic/Latino; 4% Asian, non-Hispanic/Latino; 0.3% Native Hawaiian or other Pacific Islander, non-Hispanic/Latino; 0.5% American Indian or Alaska Native, non-Hispanic/Latino; 2% Two or more races, non-Hispanic/Latino; 8% Race/ethnicity unknown; 0.8% international.
Freshmen *Admission:* 2,968 enrolled. *Test scores:* SAT critical reading scores over 500: 51%; SAT math scores over 500: 69%; ACT scores over 18: 75%; SAT critical reading scores over 600: 16%; SAT math scores over 600: 27%; ACT scores over 24: 25%; SAT critical reading scores over 700: 3%; SAT math scores over 700: 3%.
Faculty *Total:* 1,194, 22% full-time, 10% with terminal degrees. *Student/faculty ratio:* 16:1.
Majors Accounting technology and bookkeeping; architectural drafting and CAD/CADD; biology/biological sciences; business administration and management; business administration, management and operations related; business/commerce; chemistry teacher education; child-care and support services management; clinical/medical laboratory technology; communications technologies and support services related; computer and information sciences; computer and information systems security; computer/information technology services administration related; computer software and media applications related; computer systems networking and telecommunications; criminal justice/law enforcement administration; criminal justice/police science; early childhood education; electrical and electronics engineering; electrical, electronic and communications engineering technology; elementary education; engineering; English/language arts teacher education; entrepreneurship; fire prevention and safety technology; graphic design; health and physical education/fitness; health information/medical records technology; hotel/motel administration; legal assistant/paralegal; liberal arts and sciences and humanities related; liberal arts and sciences/liberal studies; management information systems; management information systems and services related; mathematics; mathematics teacher education; medical administrative assistant and medical secretary; medical radiologic technology; occupational safety and health technology; parks, recreation, leisure, and fitness studies related; physical therapy technology; physics teacher education; pre-law studies; psychiatric/mental health services technology; public health; registered nursing/registered nurse; Spanish language teacher education; substance abuse/addiction counseling; surgical technology.
Academics *Calendar:* semesters. *Degree:* certificates and associate. *Special study options:* academic remediation for entering students, accelerated degree program, adult/continuing education programs, advanced placement credit, cooperative education, distance learning, English as a second language, freshman honors college, honors programs, independent study, internships, part-time degree program, services for LD students, summer session for credit.
ROTC: Army (c), Air Force (c).

Library Andrew G. Truxal Library plus 1 other with 175,000 titles, 215 serial subscriptions, 3,130 audiovisual materials, an OPAC, a Web page.
Student Life *Housing:* college housing not available. *Activities and Organizations:* drama/theater group, student-run newspaper, choral group, Drama Club, Student Association, Black Student Union, International Student Association, Chemistry Club. *Campus security:* 24-hour emergency response devices and patrols, student patrols, late-night transport/escort service. *Student services:* health clinic, personal/psychological counseling.
Athletics Member NJCAA. *Intercollegiate sports:* baseball M(s), basketball M(s)/W(s), cross-country running M(s)/W(s), golf M, lacrosse M(s)/W(s), soccer M(s)/W(s), softball W(s), volleyball W.
Costs (2012–13) *Tuition:* area resident $2700 full-time; state resident $5190 full-time; nonresident $9180 full-time. Full-time tuition and fees vary according to course load. Part-time tuition and fees vary according to course load. *Required fees:* $500 full-time. *Payment plan:* installment. *Waivers:* senior citizens and employees or children of employees.
Financial Aid Of all full-time matriculated undergraduates who enrolled in 2011, 104 Federal Work-Study jobs (averaging $1900). 55 state and other part-time jobs (averaging $1740).
Applying *Options:* electronic application, early admission, deferred entrance. *Application deadlines:* rolling (freshmen), rolling (out-of-state freshmen), rolling (transfers). *Notification:* continuous (freshmen), continuous (out-of-state freshmen), continuous (transfers).
Freshman Application Contact Mr. Thomas McGinn, Director of Enrollment Development and Admissions, Anne Arundel Community College, 101 College Parkway, Arnold, MD 21012-1895. *Phone:* 410-777-2240. *Fax:* 410-777-2246. *E-mail:* 4info@aacc.edu.
Website: http://www.aacc.edu/.

Baltimore City Community College
Baltimore, Maryland

Freshman Application Contact Baltimore City Community College, 2901 Liberty Heights Avenue, Baltimore, MD 21215-7893. *Phone:* 410-462-8311. *Toll-free phone:* 888-203-1261.
Website: http://www.bccc.edu/.

Carroll Community College
Westminster, Maryland

- **State and locally supported** 2-year, founded 1993, part of Maryland Higher Education Commission
- **Suburban** 80-acre campus with easy access to Baltimore
- **Endowment** $4.2 million
- **Coed,** 4,103 undergraduate students, 39% full-time, 61% women, 39% men

Undergraduates 1,614 full-time, 2,489 part-time. Students come from 7 states and territories; 18 other countries; 2% are from out of state; 3% Black or African American, non-Hispanic/Latino; 3% Hispanic/Latino; 1% Asian, non-Hispanic/Latino; 0.1% Native Hawaiian or other Pacific Islander, non-Hispanic/Latino; 0.2% American Indian or Alaska Native, non-Hispanic/Latino; 1% Two or more races, non-Hispanic/Latino; 1% Race/ethnicity unknown; 0.2% international; 8% transferred in.
Freshmen *Admission:* 854 applied, 854 admitted, 854 enrolled.
Faculty *Total:* 293, 26% full-time, 3% with terminal degrees. *Student/faculty ratio:* 16:1.
Majors Accounting; architectural drafting and CAD/CADD; art; business administration and management; chemistry teacher education; child-care and support services management; computer and information sciences; computer engineering; computer graphics; criminal justice/police science; early childhood education; education; electrical and electronics engineering; elementary education; emergency care attendant (EMT ambulance); English/language arts teacher education; forensic science and technology; general studies; health information/medical records technology; health professions related; kindergarten/preschool education; kinesiology and exercise science; legal studies; liberal arts and sciences/liberal studies; management information systems; mathematics teacher education; multi/interdisciplinary studies related; music; physical therapy technology; psychology; registered nursing/registered nurse; Spanish language teacher education; theater design and technology.
Academics *Calendar:* semesters plus winter session. *Degree:* certificates and associate. *Special study options:* academic remediation for entering students, advanced placement credit, distance learning, English as a second language, honors programs, independent study, internships, part-time degree program, services for LD students, summer session for credit.
Library Random House Learning Resources Center with 124,578 titles, 181 serial subscriptions, 3,878 audiovisual materials, an OPAC, a Web page.
Student Life *Housing:* college housing not available. *Activities and Organizations:* drama/theater group, student-run newspaper, Student Government Organization, Carroll Student Art Society, Campus Activities Board, Service

Learning Club, Academic Communities (Creativity, Education, Great Ideas, Health and Wellness). *Campus security:* 24-hour emergency response devices, late-night transport/escort service.

Athletics *Intramural sports:* basketball M/W, soccer M/W.

Costs (2012–13) *Tuition:* area resident $3912 full-time, $130 per credit hour part-time; state resident $5676 full-time, $189 per credit hour part-time; nonresident $7944 full-time, $265 per credit hour part-time. *Payment plan:* deferred payment. *Waivers:* senior citizens and employees or children of employees.

Financial Aid Of all full-time matriculated undergraduates who enrolled in 2011, 30 Federal Work-Study jobs (averaging $2289).

Applying *Options:* electronic application. *Required:* high school transcript. *Application deadlines:* rolling (freshmen), rolling (out-of-state freshmen), rolling (transfers). *Notification:* continuous (freshmen), continuous (out-of-state freshmen), continuous (transfers).

Freshman Application Contact Ms. Candace Edwards, Director of Admissions, Carroll Community College, 1601 Washington Road, Westminster, MD 21157. *Phone:* 410-386-8405. *Toll-free phone:* 888-221-9748. *Fax:* 410-386-8446. *E-mail:* cedwards@carrollcc.edu. *Website:* http://www.carrollcc.edu/.

Cecil College
North East, Maryland

- **County-supported** 2-year, founded 1968
- **Small-town** 159-acre campus with easy access to Baltimore
- **Coed,** 2,641 undergraduate students, 34% full-time, 62% women, 38% men

Undergraduates 886 full-time, 1,755 part-time. Students come from 13 states and territories; 16 other countries; 10% are from out of state; 10% Black or African American, non-Hispanic/Latino; 4% Hispanic/Latino; 1% Asian, non-Hispanic/Latino; 0.1% Native Hawaiian or other Pacific Islander, non-Hispanic/Latino; 0.7% American Indian or Alaska Native, non-Hispanic/Latino; 2% Two or more races, non-Hispanic/Latino; 0.5% Race/ethnicity unknown; 0.2% international; 0.1% transferred in.

Freshmen *Admission:* 672 applied, 672 admitted, 711 enrolled.

Faculty *Total:* 251, 19% full-time, 4% with terminal degrees. *Student/faculty ratio:* 13:1.

Majors Administrative assistant and secretarial science; aeronautics/aviation/aerospace science and technology; air traffic control; animation, interactive technology, video graphics and special effects; applied horticulture/horticulture operations; biology/biological sciences; biotechnology; business administration and management; business/commerce; business/corporate communications; chemistry; child-care and support services management; commercial photography; criminal justice/police science; design and visual communications; drawing; education; electrical, electronic and communications engineering technology; elementary education; emergency medical technology (EMT paramedic); English/language arts teacher education; financial planning and services; fine/studio arts; fire science/firefighting; general studies; health services/allied health/health sciences; horse husbandry/equine science and management; human resources management; liberal arts and sciences/liberal studies; logistics, materials, and supply chain management; management information systems; marketing/marketing management; mathematics; office management; photography; physics; purchasing, procurement/acquisitions and contracts management; registered nursing/registered nurse; secondary education; transportation and materials moving related; transportation/mobility management; web page, digital/multimedia and information resources design.

Academics *Calendar:* semesters. *Degree:* certificates and associate. *Special study options:* academic remediation for entering students, accelerated degree program, adult/continuing education programs, advanced placement credit, cooperative education, distance learning, double majors, English as a second language, independent study, internships, off-campus study, part-time degree program, services for LD students, summer session for credit.

Library Cecil County Veterans Memorial Library with 57,776 titles, 42 serial subscriptions, 834 audiovisual materials, an OPAC, a Web page.

Student Life *Housing:* college housing not available. *Activities and Organizations:* drama/theater group, Student Government, Non-traditional Student Organization, Student Nurses Association, national fraternities. *Campus security:* 24-hour emergency response devices, late-night transport/escort service. *Student services:* personal/psychological counseling, women's center.

Athletics Member NJCAA. *Intercollegiate sports:* baseball M(s), basketball M(s)/W(s), cheerleading W, soccer M(s)/W(s), softball W(s), tennis W(s), volleyball W(s).

Costs (2012–13) *Tuition:* area resident $2850 full-time, $95 per credit hour part-time; state resident $5550 full-time, $185 per credit hour part-time; nonresident $6900 full-time, $230 per credit hour part-time. *Required fees:* $362 full-time. *Payment plan:* deferred payment. *Waivers:* senior citizens and employees or children of employees.

Applying *Options:* electronic application, early admission, deferred entrance. *Required:* high school transcript. *Application deadlines:* rolling (freshmen), rolling (out-of-state freshmen), rolling (transfers). *Notification:* continuous (freshmen), continuous (out-of-state freshmen), continuous (transfers).

Freshman Application Contact Dr. Diane Lane, Cecil College, One Seahawk Drive, North East, MD 21901-1999. *Phone:* 410-287-1002. *Fax:* 410-287-1001. *E-mail:* dlane@cecil.edu. *Website:* http://www.cecil.edu/.

Chesapeake College
Wye Mills, Maryland

Freshman Application Contact Randy Holliday, Director of Student Recruitment and Outreach, Chesapeake College, PO Box 8, Wye Mills, MD 21679-0008. *Phone:* 410-822-5400. *Fax:* 410-827-5875. *E-mail:* rholliday@chesapeake.edu. *Website:* http://www.chesapeake.edu/.

College of Southern Maryland
La Plata, Maryland

- **State and locally supported** 2-year, founded 1958
- **Rural** 175-acre campus with easy access to Washington, DC
- **Coed,** 9,210 undergraduate students, 37% full-time, 62% women, 38% men

Undergraduates 3,405 full-time, 5,805 part-time. 25% Black or African American, non-Hispanic/Latino; 5% Hispanic/Latino; 2% Asian, non-Hispanic/Latino; 0.5% Native Hawaiian or other Pacific Islander, non-Hispanic/Latino; 0.6% American Indian or Alaska Native, non-Hispanic/Latino; 4% Two or more races, non-Hispanic/Latino; 1% Race/ethnicity unknown; 0.4% international; 6% transferred in.

Freshmen *Admission:* 2,007 enrolled.

Faculty *Total:* 529, 24% full-time, 12% with terminal degrees. *Student/faculty ratio:* 20:1.

Majors Accounting; accounting technology and bookkeeping; building/construction finishing, management, and inspection related; business administration and management; business/commerce; child-care and support services management; clinical/medical laboratory technology; computer and information sciences; computer programming; criminal justice/law enforcement administration; early childhood education; education; electrician; elementary education; emergency medical technology (EMT paramedic); engineering; engineering technologies and engineering related; environmental engineering technology; fire prevention and safety technology; fire science/firefighting; health and physical education related; hospitality administration; information technology; legal assistant/paralegal; liberal arts and sciences and humanities related; liberal arts and sciences/liberal studies; licensed practical/vocational nurse training; lineworker; massage therapy; mental and social health services and allied professions related; multi/interdisciplinary studies related; physical therapy technology; registered nursing/registered nurse.

Academics *Calendar:* semesters. *Degree:* certificates and associate. *Special study options:* academic remediation for entering students, accelerated degree program, adult/continuing education programs, advanced placement credit, cooperative education, distance learning, honors programs, internships, part-time degree program, services for LD students, study abroad, summer session for credit.

Library College of Southern Maryland Library with 44,896 titles, 166 serial subscriptions, an OPAC, a Web page.

Student Life *Housing:* college housing not available. *Activities and Organizations:* drama/theater group, student-run newspaper, television station, choral group, Spanish Club, Nursing Student Association, Science Club, Black Student Union, BACCHUS. *Campus security:* 24-hour emergency response devices and patrols. *Student services:* personal/psychological counseling, women's center.

Athletics Member NJCAA. *Intercollegiate sports:* baseball M, basketball M/W, golf M, soccer M/W, softball W, tennis M, volleyball W.

Costs (2012–13) *Tuition:* area resident $4096 full-time, $111 per credit part-time; state resident $7085 full-time, $192 per credit part-time; nonresident $9151 full-time, $248 per credit hour part-time. Full-time tuition and fees vary according to course load. Part-time tuition and fees vary according to course load. *Payment plan:* deferred payment. *Waivers:* senior citizens and employees or children of employees.

Financial Aid Of all full-time matriculated undergraduates who enrolled in 2011, 25 Federal Work-Study jobs (averaging $1200).

Applying *Options:* electronic application, early admission, deferred entrance. *Recommended:* high school transcript. *Application deadlines:* rolling (freshmen), rolling (transfers). *Notification:* continuous (freshmen), continuous (transfers).

Freshman Application Contact Information Center Coordinator, College of Southern Maryland, PO Box 910, La Plata, MD 20646-0910. *Phone:* 301-934-

7520 Ext. 7765. *Toll-free phone:* 800-933-9177. *Fax:* 301-934-7698. *E-mail:* info@csmd.edu.
Website: http://www.csmd.edu/.

The Community College of Baltimore County

Baltimore, Maryland

- **County-supported** 2-year, founded 1957
- **Suburban** 350-acre campus
- **Coed,** 25,188 undergraduate students, 33% full-time, 62% women, 38% men

Undergraduates 8,373 full-time, 16,815 part-time. 39% Black or African American, non-Hispanic/Latino; 4% Hispanic/Latino; 5% Asian, non-Hispanic/Latino; 0.2% Native Hawaiian or other Pacific Islander, non-Hispanic/Latino; 0.3% American Indian or Alaska Native, non-Hispanic/Latino; 3% Two or more races, non-Hispanic/Latino; 0.8% Race/ethnicity unknown; 3% international.
Freshmen *Admission:* 4,879 enrolled.
Faculty *Total:* 1,379, 31% full-time, 8% with terminal degrees.
Majors Accounting technology and bookkeeping; administrative assistant and secretarial science; aeronautics/aviation/aerospace science and technology; applied horticulture/horticulture operations; architectural drafting and CAD/CADD; automobile/automotive mechanics technology; biological and physical sciences; building/construction finishing, management, and inspection related; building/construction site management; business administration and management; business administration, management and operations related; business/commerce; chemistry teacher education; child-care and support services management; clinical/medical laboratory technology; commercial and advertising art; computer and information sciences; computer and information systems security; computer graphics; computer systems networking and telecommunications; criminal justice/police science; dental hygiene; early childhood education; education; elementary education; emergency medical technology (EMT paramedic); engineering; engineering technologies and engineering related; funeral service and mortuary science; geography; heating, ventilation, air conditioning and refrigeration engineering technology; hotel/motel administration; hydraulics and fluid power technology; labor and industrial relations; legal assistant/paralegal; liberal arts and sciences and humanities related; liberal arts and sciences/liberal studies; management information systems; massage therapy; mathematics teacher education; medical administrative assistant and medical secretary; medical informatics; medical radiologic technology; occupational safety and health technology; occupational therapy; parks, recreation and leisure; parks, recreation, leisure, and fitness studies related; physics teacher education; psychiatric/mental health services technology; registered nursing/registered nurse; respiratory care therapy; science technologies related; sign language interpretation and translation; Spanish language teacher education; substance abuse/addiction counseling; surveying technology; veterinary/animal health technology; visual and performing arts.
Academics *Calendar:* semesters. *Degree:* certificates and associate. *Special study options:* academic remediation for entering students, advanced placement credit, cooperative education, distance learning, English as a second language, honors programs, independent study, internships, off-campus study, services for LD students, study abroad, summer session for credit.
Student Life *Housing:* college housing not available. *Campus security:* 24-hour emergency response devices and patrols, late-night transport/escort service.
Athletics Member NJCAA. *Intercollegiate sports:* baseball M(s), basketball M(s)/W(s), cross-country running W(s), lacrosse M(s)/W(s), soccer M(s)/W(s), softball W(s), track and field W(s), volleyball W(s).
Standardized Tests *Recommended:* SAT or ACT (for admission).
Applying *Required:* high school transcript. *Application deadlines:* rolling (freshmen), rolling (out-of-state freshmen), rolling (transfers).
Freshman Application Contact Ms. Diane Drake, Director of Admissions, The Community College of Baltimore County, 7201 Rossville Boulevard, Baltimore, MD 21228. *Phone:* 443-840-4392. *E-mail:* ddrake@ccbcmd.edu.
Website: http://www.ccbcmd.edu/.

Frederick Community College

Frederick, Maryland

Freshman Application Contact Ms. Lisa A. Freel, Director of Admissions, Frederick Community College, 7932 Opossumtown Pike, Frederick, MD 21702. *Phone:* 301-846-2468. *Fax:* 301-624-2799. *E-mail:* admissions@frederick.edu.
Website: http://www.frederick.edu/.

Garrett College

McHenry, Maryland

- **State and locally supported** 2-year, founded 1966
- **Rural** 62-acre campus
- **Coed,** 873 undergraduate students, 79% full-time, 52% women, 48% men

Undergraduates 687 full-time, 186 part-time. 23% Black or African American, non-Hispanic/Latino; 3% Hispanic/Latino; 0.3% Asian, non-Hispanic/Latino; 0.5% Native Hawaiian or other Pacific Islander, non-Hispanic/Latino; 0.2% American Indian or Alaska Native, non-Hispanic/Latino; 0.9% Two or more races, non-Hispanic/Latino; 2% international; 6% transferred in; 19% live on campus.
Freshmen *Admission:* 1,463 applied, 1,320 admitted, 230 enrolled. *Average high school GPA:* 2.38. *Test scores:* SAT critical reading scores over 500: 33%; SAT math scores over 500: 42%; SAT writing scores over 500: 25%; ACT scores over 18: 71%; SAT critical reading scores over 600: 13%; SAT math scores over 600: 10%; SAT writing scores over 600: 5%; ACT scores over 24: 6%.
Faculty *Total:* 81, 27% full-time. *Student/faculty ratio:* 17:1.
Majors Business administration and management; business automation/technology/data entry; business/commerce; corrections; early childhood education; education; electrical and electronics engineering; elementary education; liberal arts and sciences and humanities related; liberal arts and sciences/liberal studies; management information systems; sport and fitness administration/management; wildlife, fish and wildlands science and management.
Academics *Calendar:* semesters. *Degree:* certificates and associate. *Special study options:* academic remediation for entering students, adult/continuing education programs, advanced placement credit, cooperative education, distance learning, double majors, external degree program, honors programs, independent study, internships, part-time degree program, services for LD students, summer session for credit.
Library Learning Resource Center with 56,588 titles, 73 serial subscriptions, 3,397 audiovisual materials, an OPAC, a Web page.
Student Life *Housing Options:* coed, disabled students. Campus housing is university owned and leased by the school. *Activities and Organizations:* drama/theater group, SGA, Theatre Club. *Campus security:* 24-hour emergency response devices and patrols, controlled dormitory access. *Student services:* health clinic, personal/psychological counseling.
Athletics Member NJCAA. *Intercollegiate sports:* baseball M(s), basketball M(s)/W(s), cross-country running M/W, golf M, softball W, volleyball W. *Intramural sports:* basketball M/W, football M/W, rock climbing M/W, ultimate Frisbee M/W.
Standardized Tests *Recommended:* SAT or ACT (for admission).
Costs (2013–14) *Tuition:* area resident $2632 full-time, $94 per credit hour part-time; state resident $6048 full-time, $216 per credit hour part-time; non-resident $7140 full-time, $255 per credit hour part-time. Full-time tuition and fees vary according to reciprocity agreements. Part-time tuition and fees vary according to reciprocity agreements. *Required fees:* $758 full-time, $26 per credit hour part-time, $15 per semester part-time. *Room and board:* $7640; room only: $5400. Room and board charges vary according to board plan and housing facility. *Payment plans:* installment, deferred payment. *Waivers:* senior citizens and employees or children of employees.
Financial Aid Of all full-time matriculated undergraduates who enrolled in 2011, 552 applied for aid, 496 were judged to have need, 30 had their need fully met. In 2011, 6 non-need-based awards were made. *Average percent of need met:* 34%. *Average financial aid package:* $4907. *Average need-based loan:* $1860. *Average need-based gift aid:* $3383. *Average non-need-based aid:* $179.
Applying *Options:* early admission, deferred entrance. *Required:* high school transcript. *Application deadlines:* rolling (freshmen), rolling (out-of-state freshmen), rolling (transfers). *Notification:* continuous (freshmen), continuous (out-of-state freshmen), continuous (transfers).
Freshman Application Contact Mrs. Rachelle Davis, Director of Admissions, Garrett College, 687 Mosser Road, McHenry, MD 21541. *Phone:* 301-387-3044. *Toll-free phone:* 866-55-GARRETT. *E-mail:* admissions@garrettcollege.edu.
Website: http://www.garrettcollege.edu/.

Hagerstown Community College

Hagerstown, Maryland

- **State and locally supported** 2-year, founded 1946
- **Suburban** 319-acre campus with easy access to Baltimore and Washington, DC
- **Coed,** 5,005 undergraduate students, 28% full-time, 62% women, 38% men

Undergraduates 1,382 full-time, 3,623 part-time. Students come from 11 states and territories; 3 other countries; 20% are from out of state; 10% Black or African American, non-Hispanic/Latino; 4% Hispanic/Latino; 2% Asian, non-Hispanic/Latino; 0.2% Native Hawaiian or other Pacific Islander, non-Hispanic/Latino; 0.4% American Indian or Alaska Native, non-Hispanic/Latino; 3% Two or more races, non-Hispanic/Latino; 2% Race/ethnicity unknown; 0.3% international; 7% transferred in. *Retention:* 62% of full-time freshmen returned.

Freshmen *Admission:* 916 enrolled.

Faculty *Total:* 265, 30% full-time, 6% with terminal degrees. *Student/faculty ratio:* 18:1.

Majors Accounting technology and bookkeeping; animation, interactive technology, video graphics and special effects; biology/biotechnology laboratory technician; business administration and management; business/commerce; child-care and support services management; commercial and advertising art; computer and information sciences; computer and information systems security; criminal justice/police science; dental hygiene; early childhood education; education; elementary education; emergency medical technology (EMT paramedic); engineering; engineering technologies and engineering related; English/language arts teacher education; health information/medical records administration; industrial technology; instrumentation technology; liberal arts and sciences and humanities related; liberal arts and sciences/liberal studies; management information systems; mechanical engineering/mechanical technology; medical radiologic technology; psychiatric/mental health services technology; registered nursing/registered nurse; transportation/mobility management; web page, digital/multimedia and information resources design.

Academics *Calendar:* semesters. *Degree:* certificates and associate. *Special study options:* academic remediation for entering students, accelerated degree program, adult/continuing education programs, advanced placement credit, cooperative education, distance learning, English as a second language, honors programs, independent study, internships, off-campus study, part-time degree program, services for LD students, summer session for credit.

Library William Brish Library with an OPAC, a Web page.

Student Life *Housing:* college housing not available. *Activities and Organizations:* drama/theater group, student-run newspaper, choral group, Phi Theta Kappa, Robinwood Players Theater Club, Association of Nursing Students, Radiography Club, Art and Design Club. *Campus security:* 24-hour patrols, student patrols. *Student services:* personal/psychological counseling.

Athletics Member NJCAA. *Intercollegiate sports:* baseball M(s), basketball M(s)/W(s), cross-country running M(s)/W(s), golf M/W, soccer M(s)/W, softball W(s), track and field M(s)/W(s), volleyball W(s). *Intramural sports:* cheerleading M/W, golf M/W, lacrosse M/W, table tennis M/W, tennis M/W.

Financial Aid Of all full-time matriculated undergraduates who enrolled in 2011, 27 Federal Work-Study jobs (averaging $2955).

Applying *Options:* electronic application, early admission, deferred entrance. *Required for some:* high school transcript, selective admissions for RN, LPN, EMT, and radiography programs. *Application deadlines:* rolling (freshmen), rolling (out-of-state freshmen), rolling (transfers). *Notification:* continuous (freshmen), continuous (out-of-state freshmen), continuous (transfers).

Freshman Application Contact Assistant Director, Admissions, Records and Registration, Hagerstown Community College, 11400 Robinwood Drive, Hagerstown, MD 21742-6514. *Phone:* 240-500-2338. *Fax:* 301-791-9165. *E-mail:* admissions@hagerstowncc.edu.
Website: http://www.hagerstowncc.edu/.

Harford Community College
Bel Air, Maryland

- **State and locally supported** 2-year, founded 1957
- **Small-town** 331-acre campus with easy access to Baltimore
- **Coed,** 7,226 undergraduate students, 39% full-time, 59% women, 41% men

Undergraduates 2,830 full-time, 4,396 part-time. 15% Black or African American, non-Hispanic/Latino; 4% Hispanic/Latino; 2% Asian, non-Hispanic/Latino; 0.2% Native Hawaiian or other Pacific Islander, non-Hispanic/Latino; 0.3% American Indian or Alaska Native, non-Hispanic/Latino; 3% Two or more races, non-Hispanic/Latino; 0.6% Race/ethnicity unknown; 0.5% international.

Freshmen *Admission:* 1,454 enrolled. *Test scores:* SAT critical reading scores over 500: 99%; SAT math scores over 500: 99%; SAT critical reading scores over 600: 38%; SAT math scores over 600: 45%; SAT critical reading scores over 700: 4%; SAT math scores over 700: 2%.

Faculty *Total:* 391, 27% full-time, 14% with terminal degrees. *Student/faculty ratio:* 22:1.

Majors Accounting; accounting technology and bookkeeping; advertising; agricultural business and management; anthropology; biology/biological sciences; business administration and management; business/commerce; CAD/CADD drafting/design technology; chemistry; chemistry teacher education; computer and information sciences; computer and information systems security; computer science; criminal justice/police science; design and visual communications; digital arts; early childhood education; economics; education; electroneurodiagnostic/electroencephalographic technology; elementary

education; engineering; engineering technology; English; English/language arts teacher education; entrepreneurship; environmental science; environmental studies; equestrian studies; fine/studio arts; general studies; golf course operation and grounds management; graphic design; history; human resources management; interior design; landscaping and groundskeeping; legal assistant/paralegal; legal studies; liberal arts and sciences/liberal studies; licensed practical/vocational nurse training; marketing/marketing management; mass communication/media; mathematics; mathematics teacher education; medical/clinical assistant; medical office assistant; multi/interdisciplinary studies related; music; philosophy; photography; physics; physics teacher education; political science and government; psychology; registered nursing/registered nurse; science technologies; secondary education; social work; sociology; Spanish language teacher education; theater design and technology; turf and turfgrass management; visual and performing arts.

Academics *Calendar:* semesters. *Degree:* certificates, diplomas, and associate. *Special study options:* academic remediation for entering students, adult/continuing education programs, advanced placement credit, cooperative education, distance learning, double majors, English as a second language, honors programs, independent study, internships, part-time degree program, services for LD students, student-designed majors, study abroad, summer session for credit.

Library Harford Community College Library with 52,069 titles, 129 serial subscriptions, 4,224 audiovisual materials, an OPAC, a Web page.

Student Life *Activities and Organizations:* drama/theater group, student-run newspaper, radio station, choral group, Student Association, Paralegal Club, Multi-National Students Association, Student Nurses Association, Gamers Guild. *Campus security:* 24-hour patrols, late-night transport/escort service. *Student services:* personal/psychological counseling.

Athletics Member NJCAA. *Intercollegiate sports:* baseball M(s), basketball M(s)/W(s), cross-country running M(s)/W(s), golf M(s), lacrosse M(s)/W(s), soccer M(s)/W(s), softball W(s), tennis M(s)/W(s), volleyball W(s). *Intramural sports:* badminton M/W, basketball M/W, cheerleading M(c)/W(c), football M/W, soccer M/W, softball M/W, swimming and diving M/W, tennis M/W, volleyball M/W.

Costs (2013–14) *Tuition:* area resident $2610 full-time, $87 per credit hour part-time; state resident $5220 full-time, $174 per credit hour part-time; nonresident $7830 full-time, $261 per credit hour part-time. *Required fees:* $313 full-time. *Waivers:* senior citizens and employees or children of employees.

Financial Aid Of all full-time matriculated undergraduates who enrolled in 2011, 1,561 applied for aid, 1,192 were judged to have need. 69 Federal Work-Study jobs (averaging $2423).

Applying *Options:* electronic application. *Application deadlines:* rolling (freshmen), rolling (transfers). *Notification:* continuous (transfers).

Freshman Application Contact Ms. Jennifer Starkey, Enrollment Services Associate - Admissions, Harford Community College, 401 Thomas Run Road, Bel Air, MD 21015-1698. *Phone:* 443-412-2311. *Fax:* 443-412-2169. *E-mail:* sendinfo@harford.edu.
Website: http://www.harford.edu/.

Howard Community College
Columbia, Maryland

- **State and locally supported** 2-year, founded 1966
- **Suburban** 122-acre campus with easy access to Baltimore and Washington, DC
- **Coed,** 10,152 undergraduate students, 36% full-time, 57% women, 43% men

Undergraduates 3,705 full-time, 6,447 part-time. 28% Black or African American, non-Hispanic/Latino; 9% Hispanic/Latino; 13% Asian, non-Hispanic/Latino; 0.3% Native Hawaiian or other Pacific Islander, non-Hispanic/Latino; 0.3% American Indian or Alaska Native, non-Hispanic/Latino; 3% Two or more races, non-Hispanic/Latino; 1% Race/ethnicity unknown. *Retention:* 59% of full-time freshmen returned.

Faculty *Total:* 724, 24% full-time. *Student/faculty ratio:* 19:1.

Majors Accounting; architecture; art; biological and physical sciences; biomedical technology; biotechnology; business administration and management; cardiovascular technology; child development; clinical laboratory science/medical technology; computer and information sciences related; computer graphics; computer/information technology services administration related; computer science; computer systems networking and telecommunications; criminal justice/law enforcement administration; design and applied arts related; diagnostic medical sonography and ultrasound technology; dramatic/theater arts; electrical, electronic and communications engineering technology; elementary education; emergency medical technology (EMT paramedic); engineering; environmental studies; financial planning and services; general studies; health teacher education; information science/studies; information technology; kindergarten/preschool education; legal administrative assistant/secretary; liberal arts and sciences/liberal studies; licensed practical/vocational nurse training; medical administrative assistant and medical secretary; music; nuclear medical technology; office management; photography; physical sciences; physical therapy technology; pre-dentistry studies; pre-medical studies; pre-pharmacy studies; pre-veterinary studies; psychology; registered nursing/registered nurse; secondary education; social sciences; sport and fitness administration/management; substance abuse/addiction counseling; telecommunications technology; theater design and technology.

Academics *Calendar:* semesters. *Degree:* certificates and associate. *Special study options:* academic remediation for entering students, adult/continuing education programs, advanced placement credit, cooperative education, distance learning, double majors, English as a second language, external degree program, freshman honors college, honors programs, off-campus study, part-time degree program, services for LD students, study abroad, summer session for credit.

Library Howard Community College Library with 45,707 titles, 39,910 serial subscriptions, 2,636 audiovisual materials, an OPAC, a Web page.

Student Life *Housing:* college housing not available. *Activities and Organizations:* drama/theater group, student-run newspaper, radio station, choral group, Phi Theta Kappa, Nursing Club, Black Leadership Organization, student newspaper, Student Government Association. *Campus security:* 24-hour emergency response devices and patrols, late-night transport/escort service. *Student services:* personal/psychological counseling.

Athletics Member NJCAA. *Intercollegiate sports:* basketball M/W, cross-country running M/W, lacrosse M/W, soccer M/W, track and field M/W, volleyball W. *Intramural sports:* basketball M/W.

Standardized Tests *Required for some:* SAT or ACT (for admission).

Costs (2012–13) *Tuition:* area resident $3690 full-time, $123 per credit hour part-time; state resident $6180 full-time, $206 per credit hour part-time; non-resident $7530 full-time, $251 per credit hour part-time. *Required fees:* $618 full-time, $21 per credit hour part-time. *Payment plan:* installment. *Waivers:* senior citizens and employees or children of employees.

Financial Aid Of all full-time matriculated undergraduates who enrolled in 2012, 342 applied for aid, 298 were judged to have need, 1 had their need fully met. In 2012, 15 non-need-based awards were made. *Average percent of need met:* 20%. *Average financial aid package:* $3221. *Average need-based gift aid:* $3162. *Average non-need-based aid:* $817.

Applying *Options:* electronic application, early admission, deferred entrance. *Application fee:* $25. *Required for some:* essay or personal statement, high school transcript, 2 letters of recommendation. *Application deadlines:* rolling (freshmen), rolling (out-of-state freshmen), rolling (transfers). *Notification:* continuous (freshmen), continuous (out-of-state freshmen), continuous (transfers).

Freshman Application Contact Ms. Christy Thomson, Associate Director of Admissions, Howard Community College, Columbia, MD 21044-3197. *Phone:* 443-518-4599. *Fax:* 443-518-4589. *E-mail:* admissions@howardcc.edu.
Website: http://www.howardcc.edu/.

ITT Technical Institute

Owings Mills, Maryland

- **Proprietary** primarily 2-year, founded 2005
- **Coed**

Academics *Calendar:* quarters. *Degrees:* associate and bachelor's.

Freshman Application Contact Director of Recruitment, ITT Technical Institute, 11301 Red Run Boulevard, Owings Mills, MD 21117. *Phone:* 443-394-7115. *Toll-free phone:* 877-411-6782.
Website: http://www.itt-tech.edu/.

Kaplan University, Hagerstown Campus

Hagerstown, Maryland

Freshman Application Contact Kaplan University, Hagerstown Campus, 18618 Crestwood Drive, Hagerstown, MD 21742-2797. *Phone:* 301-739-2680 Ext. 217. *Toll-free phone:* 866-527-5268 (in-state); 800-527-5268 (out-of-state).
Website: http://www.ku-hagerstown.com/.

Montgomery College

Rockville, Maryland

- **State and locally supported** 2-year, founded 1946
- **Suburban** 333-acre campus with easy access to Washington, DC
- **Endowment** $17.8 million
- **Coed,** 27,453 undergraduate students, 36% full-time, 53% women, 47% men

Undergraduates 9,888 full-time, 17,565 part-time. Students come from 26 states and territories; 162 other countries; 3% are from out of state; 25% Black or African American, non-Hispanic/Latino; 20% Hispanic/Latino; 12% Asian,

non-Hispanic/Latino; 0.3% Native Hawaiian or other Pacific Islander, non-Hispanic/Latino; 0.3% American Indian or Alaska Native, non-Hispanic/Latino; 2% Two or more races, non-Hispanic/Latino; 0.1% Race/ethnicity unknown; 10% international; 5% transferred in.

Freshmen *Admission:* 10,756 applied, 10,756 admitted, 4,277 enrolled.

Faculty *Total:* 1,569, 34% full-time, 29% with terminal degrees. *Student/faculty ratio:* 18:1.

Majors Accounting technology and bookkeeping; American Sign Language (ASL); animation, interactive technology, video graphics and special effects; applied horticulture/horticulture operations; architectural drafting and CAD/CADD; art; automobile/automotive mechanics technology; biology/biotechnology laboratory technician; building/construction finishing, management, and inspection related; business/commerce; chemistry teacher education; child-care provision; commercial and advertising art; commercial photography; communications technologies and support services related; computer and information sciences; computer and information systems security; computer technology/computer systems technology; criminal justice/police science; crisis/emergency/disaster management; data entry/microcomputer applications; diagnostic medical sonography and ultrasound technology; early childhood education; elementary education; engineering; English/language arts teacher education; fire prevention and safety technology; geography; health information/medical records technology; hotel/motel administration; interior design; legal assistant/paralegal; liberal arts and sciences and humanities related; liberal arts and sciences/liberal studies; management information systems and services related; mathematics teacher education; medical radiologic technology; physical therapy technology; physics teacher education; psychiatric/mental health services technology; registered nursing/registered nurse; Spanish language teacher education; speech communication and rhetoric; surgical technology; web page, digital/multimedia and information resources design.

Academics *Calendar:* semesters. *Degree:* certificates and associate. *Special study options:* academic remediation for entering students, accelerated degree program, adult/continuing education programs, advanced placement credit, cooperative education, distance learning, double majors, English as a second language, external degree program, honors programs, independent study, internships, off-campus study, part-time degree program, services for LD students, study abroad, summer session for credit. *ROTC:* Air Force (c).

Library Montgomery College Library plus 1 other with 402,499 titles, 58,386 serial subscriptions, 29,507 audiovisual materials, an OPAC, a Web page.

Student Life *Activities and Organizations:* drama/theater group, student-run newspaper, choral group, Math Club, International Club, Anime Society Club, Animation & Video Game Club, Soccer, basketball, Rugby, Cricket, Tennis, Lacrosse and Swim Clubs. *Campus security:* 24-hour emergency response devices and patrols, late-night transport/escort service. *Student services:* personal/psychological counseling, women's center.

Athletics Member NJCAA. *Intercollegiate sports:* baseball M, basketball M/W, soccer M/W, softball W, tennis M/W, track and field M/W, volleyball W. *Intramural sports:* baseball M, basketball M/W, cheerleading W, cross-country running M, football M, soccer M/W, softball W, tennis M/W, track and field M/W, volleyball W.

Costs (2012–13) *One-time required fee:* $25. *Tuition:* area resident $2688 full-time, $112 per credit part-time; state resident $5496 full-time, $229 per credit part-time; nonresident $7536 full-time, $314 per credit part-time. Full-time tuition and fees vary according to course load. Part-time tuition and fees vary according to course load. *Required fees:* $874 full-time, $36 per credit part-time. *Payment plans:* installment, deferred payment. *Waivers:* senior citizens and employees or children of employees.

Financial Aid Of all full-time matriculated undergraduates who enrolled in 2011, 26,000 applied for aid, 15,000 were judged to have need. 223 Federal Work-Study jobs (averaging $3000). In 2011, 1000 non-need-based awards were made. *Average percent of need met:* 75%. *Average financial aid package:* $7500. *Average need-based loan:* $3000. *Average need-based gift aid:* $4500. *Average non-need-based aid:* $1500.

Applying *Options:* electronic application, early admission, deferred entrance. *Application fee:* $25. *Recommended:* high school transcript, interview. *Application deadlines:* rolling (freshmen), rolling (out-of-state freshmen), rolling (transfers). *Notification:* continuous (freshmen), continuous (out-of-state freshmen), continuous (transfers).

Freshman Application Contact Montgomery College, 51 Mannakee Street, Rockville, MD 20850. *Phone:* 240-567-5036.
Website: http://www.montgomerycollege.edu/.

Prince George's Community College

Largo, Maryland

Freshman Application Contact Ms. Vera Bagley, Director of Admissions and Records, Prince George's Community College, 301 Largo Road, Largo, MD 20774-2199. *Phone:* 301-322-0801. *Fax:* 301-322-0119. *E-mail:* enrollmentservices@pgcc.edu.
Website: http://www.pgcc.edu/.

TESST College of Technology

Baltimore, Maryland

- **Proprietary** 2-year, founded 1956
- **Coed**

Academics *Calendar:* quarters. *Degree:* certificates and associate.
Freshman Application Contact TESST College of Technology, 1520 South Caton Avenue, Baltimore, MD 21227. *Phone:* 410-644-6400. *Toll-free phone:* 800-935-1857.
Website: http://www.baltimore.tesst.com/.

TESST College of Technology

Beltsville, Maryland

- **Proprietary** 2-year, founded 1967
- **Coed**

Academics *Calendar:* quarters. *Degree:* certificates and associate.
Applying *Application fee:* $20.
Freshman Application Contact TESST College of Technology, 4600 Powder Mill Road, Beltsville, MD 20705. *Phone:* 301-937-8448. *Toll-free phone:* 800-935-1857.
Website: http://www.beltsville.tesst.com/.

TESST College of Technology

Towson, Maryland

- **Proprietary** 2-year, founded 1992
- **Coed**

Academics *Calendar:* quarters. *Degree:* certificates and associate.
Freshman Application Contact TESST College of Technology, 803 Glen Eagles Court, Towson, MD 21286. *Phone:* 410-296-5350. *Toll-free phone:* 800-935-1857.
Website: http://www.towson.tesst.com/.

Wor-Wic Community College

Salisbury, Maryland

Freshman Application Contact Mr. Richard Webster, Director of Admissions, Wor-Wic Community College, 32000 Campus Drive, Salisbury, MD 21804. *Phone:* 410-334-2895. *Fax:* 410-334-2954. *E-mail:* admissions@worwic.edu. *Website:* http://www.worwic.edu/.

MASSACHUSETTS

Bay State College

Boston, Massachusetts

- **Independent** primarily 2-year, founded 1946
- **Urban** campus
- **Coed,** 1,153 undergraduate students

Undergraduates 14% are from out of state. *Retention:* 76% of full-time freshmen returned.
Freshmen *Admission:* 1,761 applied, 1,045 admitted.
Faculty *Student/faculty ratio:* 16:1.
Majors Accounting; animation, interactive technology, video graphics and special effects; business administration and management; child-care and support services management; criminal justice/safety; education; fashion merchandising; medical/clinical assistant; medical office management; merchandising, sales, and marketing operations related (specialized); physical therapy technology; tourism and travel services marketing.
Academics *Calendar:* semesters. *Degrees:* diplomas, associate, and bachelor's. *Special study options:* academic remediation for entering students, adult/continuing education programs, advanced placement credit, cooperative education, English as a second language, independent study, internships, part-time degree program.
Library Bay State College Library with 6,000 titles, 80 serial subscriptions, an OPAC.
Student Life *Housing Options:* coed, women-only. Campus housing is provided by a third party. *Campus security:* late-night transport/escort service, controlled dormitory access, 14-hour patrols by trained security personnel. *Student services:* personal/psychological counseling.
Standardized Tests *Recommended:* SAT or ACT (for admission).
Financial Aid Of all full-time matriculated undergraduates who enrolled in 2011, 20 Federal Work-Study jobs (averaging $2600).
Applying *Options:* early admission. *Application fee:* $40. *Required:* high school transcript, minimum 2.3 GPA. *Recommended:* interview. *Application deadlines:* rolling (freshmen), rolling (transfers).
Freshman Application Contact Julia Croft, Director of Admissions, Bay State College, 122 Commonwealth Avenue, Boston, MA 02116. *Phone:* 617-217-9115. *Toll-free phone:* 800-81-LEARN. *Fax:* 617-536-1735. *E-mail:* admissions@baystate.edu. *Website:* http://www.baystate.edu/.

See display below and page 342 for the College Close-Up.

not your typical
social network

At Bay State College, networking means more than adding friends or followers. It means access to instructors actively working in their fields who want to share their experiences—and connections—with you.

- Day, evening and online class options.
- Personal financial aid advisors.
- Conveniently located in the Back Bay.

Get started today at
choosebaystate.com

Bay State College

Benjamin Franklin Institute of Technology

Boston, Massachusetts

Freshman Application Contact Ms. Brittainy Johnson, Associate Director of Admissions, Benjamin Franklin Institute of Technology, Boston, MA 02116. *Phone:* 617-423-4630 Ext. 122. *Toll-free phone:* 877-400-BFIT. *Fax:* 617-482-3706. *E-mail:* bjohnson@bfit.edu.
Website: http://www.bfit.edu/.

Berkshire Community College

Pittsfield, Massachusetts

- **State-supported** 2-year, founded 1960, part of Massachusetts Public Higher Education System
- **Rural** 180-acre campus with easy access to Hartford, CT and Albany, NY
- **Endowment** $7.1 million
- **Coed,** 2,503 undergraduate students, 37% full-time, 60% women, 40% men

Undergraduates 922 full-time, 1,581 part-time. Students come from 6 states and territories; 8 other countries; 3% are from out of state; 6% Black or African American, non-Hispanic/Latino; 6% Hispanic/Latino; 2% Asian, non-Hispanic/Latino; 0.1% Native Hawaiian or other Pacific Islander, non-Hispanic/Latino; 0.4% American Indian or Alaska Native, non-Hispanic/Latino; 2% Two or more races, non-Hispanic/Latino; 2% Race/ethnicity unknown; 0.3% international; 46% transferred in. *Retention:* 35% of full-time freshmen returned.

Freshmen *Admission:* 683 applied, 496 admitted, 496 enrolled. *Average high school GPA:* 2.81.

Faculty *Total:* 216, 24% full-time, 73% with terminal degrees. *Student/faculty ratio:* 15:1.

Majors Business administration and management; business automation/technology/data entry; business/commerce; community organization and advocacy; computer and information sciences; criminal justice/safety; electrical, electronic and communications engineering technology; engineering; environmental studies; fire science/firefighting; health professions related; hospitality administration; human services; international/global studies; liberal arts and sciences/liberal studies; medical insurance coding; physical therapy technology; registered nursing/registered nurse; respiratory care therapy; visual and performing arts.

Academics *Calendar:* semesters. *Degree:* certificates and associate. *Special study options:* academic remediation for entering students, accelerated degree program, adult/continuing education programs, advanced placement credit, cooperative education, distance learning, double majors, English as a second language, honors programs, independent study, internships, off-campus study, part-time degree program, services for LD students, summer session for credit.

Library Jonathan Edwards Library plus 1 other with 76,918 titles, 241 serial subscriptions, 13,227 audiovisual materials, an OPAC, a Web page.

Student Life *Housing:* college housing not available. *Activities and Organizations:* drama/theater group, student-run newspaper, choral group, Mass PIRG, Student Nurse Organization, Student Senate, Diversity Club, LPN Organization. *Campus security:* 24-hour emergency response devices and patrols, late-night transport/escort service. *Student services:* personal/psychological counseling.

Costs (2012–13) *One-time required fee:* $10. *Tuition:* state resident $624 full-time, $26 per credit part-time; nonresident $6240 full-time, $260 per credit part-time. Full-time tuition and fees vary according to class time, course load, program, and reciprocity agreements. Part-time tuition and fees vary according to class time, course load, program, and reciprocity agreements. *Required fees:* $4980 full-time, $166 per credit part-time. *Payment plan:* installment. *Waivers:* senior citizens and employees or children of employees.

Financial Aid Of all full-time matriculated undergraduates who enrolled in 2011, 1,985 applied for aid, 1,859 were judged to have need. 174 Federal Work-Study jobs (averaging $955). 25 state and other part-time jobs (averaging $341). In 2011, 142 non-need-based awards were made. *Average financial aid package:* $4344. *Average need-based loan:* $2675. *Average need-based gift aid:* $3556. *Average non-need-based aid:* $1058.

Applying *Options:* deferred entrance. *Application fee:* $10. *Required:* high school transcript. *Recommended:* interview. *Application deadlines:* rolling (freshmen), rolling (out-of-state freshmen), rolling (transfers). *Notification:* continuous (freshmen), continuous (out-of-state freshmen), continuous (transfers).

Freshman Application Contact Ms. Tina Schettini, Enrollment Services, Berkshire Community College, 1350 West Street, Pittsfield, MA 01201-5786. *Phone:* 413-236-1635. *Toll-free phone:* 800-816-1233. *Fax:* 413-496-9511. *E-mail:* tschetti@berkshirecc.edu.
Website: http://www.berkshirecc.edu/.

Bristol Community College

Fall River, Massachusetts

Freshman Application Contact Mr. Rodney S. Clark, Dean of Admissions, Bristol Community College, 777 Elsbree Street, Fall River, MA 02720. *Phone:* 508-678-2811 Ext. 2177. *Fax:* 508-730-3265. *E-mail:* rodney.clark@bristolcc.edu.
Website: http://www.bristolcc.edu/.

Bunker Hill Community College

Boston, Massachusetts

- **State-supported** 2-year, founded 1973
- **Urban** 21-acre campus
- **Endowment** $2.4 million
- **Coed**

Undergraduates 4,486 full-time, 8,448 part-time. Students come from 78 other countries; 19% Black or African American, non-Hispanic/Latino; 24% Hispanic/Latino; 10% Asian, non-Hispanic/Latino; 0.5% American Indian or Alaska Native, non-Hispanic/Latino; 12% Two or more races, non-Hispanic/Latino; 9% Race/ethnicity unknown; 6% international; 7% transferred in.

Faculty *Student/faculty ratio:* 19:1.

Academics *Calendar:* semesters. *Degree:* certificates and associate. *Special study options:* academic remediation for entering students, advanced placement credit, cooperative education, distance learning, English as a second language, external degree program, honors programs, independent study, internships, part-time degree program, services for LD students, study abroad, summer session for credit.

Student Life *Campus security:* 24-hour emergency response devices and patrols, late-night transport/escort service.

Athletics Member NJCAA.

Costs (2012–13) *Tuition:* state resident $576 full-time, $24 per credit hour part-time; nonresident $5520 full-time, $230 per credit hour part-time. Full-time tuition and fees vary according to course load, program, and reciprocity agreements. Part-time tuition and fees vary according to course load, program, and reciprocity agreements. *Required fees:* $2808 full-time, $117 per credit hour part-time.

Financial Aid Of all full-time matriculated undergraduates who enrolled in 2010, 135 Federal Work-Study jobs (averaging $2376).

Applying *Options:* deferred entrance. *Application fee:* $10. *Required:* high school transcript.

Freshman Application Contact Mr. William Sakamoto, Associate Vice President of Academic Affairs and Enrollment Services, Bunker Hill Community College, 250 New Rutherford Avenue, Boston, MA 02129. *Phone:* 617-228-2346. *Fax:* 617-228-2082.
Website: http://www.bhcc.mass.edu/.

Cape Cod Community College

West Barnstable, Massachusetts

Freshman Application Contact Director of Admissions, Cape Cod Community College, 2240 Iyannough Road, West Barnstable, MA 02668-1599. *Phone:* 508-362-2131 Ext. 4311. *Toll-free phone:* 877-846-3672. *Fax:* 508-375-4089. *E-mail:* admiss@capecod.edu.
Website: http://www.capecod.edu/.

Dean College

Franklin, Massachusetts

Freshman Application Contact Mr. James Fowler, Dean College, 99 Main Street, Franklin, MA 02038. *Phone:* 508-541-1547. *Toll-free phone:* 877-TRY-DEAN. *Fax:* 508-541-8726. *E-mail:* jfowler@dean.edu.
Website: http://www.dean.edu/.

FINE Mortuary College, LLC

Norwood, Massachusetts

Freshman Application Contact Dean Marsha Wise, Admissions Office, FINE Mortuary College, LLC, 150 Kerry Place, Norwood, MA 02062. *Phone:* 781-762-1211. *Fax:* 781-762-7177. *E-mail:* mwise@fine-ne.com.
Website: http://www.fine-ne.com/.

Greenfield Community College
Greenfield, Massachusetts

- **State-supported** 2-year, founded 1962, part of Commonwealth of Massachusetts Department of Higher Education
- **Small-town** 120-acre campus
- **Coed**, 2,437 undergraduate students, 38% full-time, 59% women, 41% men

Undergraduates 920 full-time, 1,517 part-time. Students come from 14 states and territories; 11 other countries; 10% are from out of state; 3% Black or African American, non-Hispanic/Latino; 5% Hispanic/Latino; 3% Asian, non-Hispanic/Latino; 0.1% Native Hawaiian or other Pacific Islander, non-Hispanic/Latino; 0.7% American Indian or Alaska Native, non-Hispanic/Latino; 3% Two or more races, non-Hispanic/Latino; 2% Race/ethnicity unknown; 6% transferred in. *Retention:* 60% of full-time freshmen returned.
Freshmen *Admission:* 944 applied, 944 admitted, 432 enrolled.
Faculty *Total:* 183, 34% full-time. *Student/faculty ratio:* 14:1.
Majors Accounting technology and bookkeeping; acting; administrative assistant and secretarial science; American studies; art; business administration and management; business/commerce; community health services counseling; computer and information sciences; computer and information sciences and support services related; criminal justice/police science; crop production; dance; early childhood education; economics; education; engineering science; English; environmental science; film/video and photographic arts related; fine/studio arts; fire prevention and safety technology; food science; health professions related; hospitality administration; international relations and affairs; liberal arts and sciences/liberal studies; massage therapy; music performance; natural resources/conservation related; registered nursing/registered nurse; sales, distribution, and marketing operations; social sciences; social sciences related; women's studies.
Academics *Calendar:* semesters. *Degree:* certificates and associate. *Special study options:* academic remediation for entering students, adult/continuing education programs, advanced placement credit, cooperative education, distance learning, double majors, English as a second language, independent study, internships, part-time degree program, services for LD students, summer session for credit.
Library Greenfield Community College Library with 69,974 titles, 106 serial subscriptions, 1,158 audiovisual materials, an OPAC, a Web page.
Student Life *Housing:* college housing not available. *Activities and Organizations:* drama/theater group, choral group, Student Senate, Art Club, Permaculture Club, VetNet, International Students Club. *Campus security:* 24-hour emergency response devices and patrols, late-night transport/escort service. *Student services:* personal/psychological counseling, women's center.
Standardized Tests *Required for some:* Psychological Corporation Practical Nursing Entrance Examination.
Applying *Options:* electronic application. *Required for some:* high school transcript, interview. *Application deadlines:* rolling (freshmen), rolling (transfers).
Freshman Application Contact Ms. Colleen Kucinski, Assistant Director of Admission, Greenfield Community College, 1 College Drive, Greenfield, MA 01301-9739. *Phone:* 413-775-1000. *Fax:* 413-773-5129. *E-mail:* admission@gcc.mass.edu.
Website: http://www.gcc.mass.edu/.

Holyoke Community College
Holyoke, Massachusetts

- **State-supported** 2-year, founded 1946, part of Massachusetts Public Higher Education System
- **Small-town** 135-acre campus
- **Endowment** $9.0 million
- **Coed**, 7,164 undergraduate students, 49% full-time, 62% women, 38% men

Undergraduates 3,488 full-time, 3,676 part-time. Students come from 16 states and territories; 1% are from out of state; 7% Black or African American, non-Hispanic/Latino; 21% Hispanic/Latino; 2% Asian, non-Hispanic/Latino; 0.7% American Indian or Alaska Native, non-Hispanic/Latino; 2% Two or more races, non-Hispanic/Latino; 2% Race/ethnicity unknown; 0.2% international; 8% transferred in.
Freshmen *Admission:* 1,645 admitted, 1,645 enrolled.
Faculty *Total:* 531, 24% full-time, 19% with terminal degrees. *Student/faculty ratio:* 18:1.
Majors Accounting technology and bookkeeping; administrative assistant and secretarial science; art; business administration and management; child-care and support services management; computer programming (specific applications); criminal justice/safety; engineering; environmental control technologies related; geography; health and physical education/fitness; hospitality administration related; liberal arts and sciences and humanities related; liberal arts and sciences/liberal studies; medical radiologic technology; music; opticianry; registered nursing/registered nurse; retailing; social work; sport and fitness administration/management; veterinary/animal health technology.
Academics *Calendar:* semesters. *Degree:* certificates and associate. *Special study options:* academic remediation for entering students, adult/continuing education programs, advanced placement credit, cooperative education, distance learning, double majors, English as a second language, external degree program, honors programs, independent study, internships, off-campus study, part-time degree program, services for LD students, student-designed majors, study abroad, summer session for credit. *ROTC:* Army (c), Air Force (c).
Library Holyoke Community College Library plus 1 other with 98,569 titles, 49,591 serial subscriptions, 13,146 audiovisual materials, an OPAC, a Web page.
Student Life *Housing:* college housing not available. *Activities and Organizations:* drama/theater group, student-run newspaper, radio station, Drama Club, Japanese Anime Club, Student Senate, LISA Club, STRIVE. *Campus security:* 24-hour emergency response devices and patrols, late-night transport/escort service. *Student services:* health clinic, personal/psychological counseling, women's center.
Athletics Member NJCAA. *Intercollegiate sports:* baseball M, basketball M/W, cross-country running M/W, golf M/W, soccer M/W, softball W, volleyball W.
Costs (2012–13) *Tuition:* state resident $576 full-time, $141 per credit part-time; nonresident $5520 full-time, $347 per credit part-time. Full-time tuition and fees vary according to course load. Part-time tuition and fees vary according to course load. *Required fees:* $2998 full-time, $95 per term part-time. *Payment plan:* installment. *Waivers:* senior citizens and employees or children of employees.
Applying *Options:* electronic application, early admission, deferred entrance. *Required:* high school transcript. *Recommended:* interview. *Application deadlines:* rolling (freshmen), rolling (transfers). *Notification:* continuous (freshmen), continuous (transfers).
Freshman Application Contact Ms. Marcia Rosbury-Henne, Director of Admissions and Transfer Affairs, Holyoke Community College, Admission Office, Holyoke, MA 01040. *Phone:* 413-552-2321. *Fax:* 413-552-2045. *E-mail:* admissions@hcc.edu.
Website: http://www.hcc.edu/.

ITT Technical Institute
Norwood, Massachusetts

- **Proprietary** primarily 2-year, founded 1990, part of ITT Educational Services, Inc.
- **Suburban** campus
- **Coed**

Academics *Calendar:* quarters. *Degrees:* associate and bachelor's.
Freshman Application Contact Director of Recruitment, ITT Technical Institute, 333 Providence Highway, Norwood, MA 02062. *Phone:* 781-278-7200. *Toll-free phone:* 800-879-8324.
Website: http://www.itt-tech.edu/.

ITT Technical Institute
Wilmington, Massachusetts

- **Proprietary** primarily 2-year, founded 2000, part of ITT Educational Services, Inc.
- **Coed**

Academics *Calendar:* quarters. *Degrees:* associate and bachelor's.
Freshman Application Contact Director of Recruitment, ITT Technical Institute, 200 Ballardvale Street, Suite 200, Wilmington, MA 01887. *Phone:* 978-658-2636. *Toll-free phone:* 800-430-5097.
Website: http://www.itt-tech.edu/.

Labouré College
Boston, Massachusetts

Director of Admissions Ms. Gina M. Morrissette, Director of Admissions, Labouré College, 2120 Dorchester Avenue, Boston, MA 02124-5698. *Phone:* 617-296-8300.
Website: http://www.laboure.edu/.

Marian Court College
Swampscott, Massachusetts

Director of Admissions Bryan Boppert, Director of Admissions, Marian Court College, 35 Little's Point Road, Swampscott, MA 01907-2840. *Phone:* 781-309-5230. *Fax:* 781-309-5286.
Website: http://www.mariancourt.edu/.

Massachusetts Bay Community College

Wellesley Hills, Massachusetts

- **State-supported** 2-year, founded 1961
- **Suburban** 84-acre campus with easy access to Boston
- **Coed,** 5,427 undergraduate students, 38% full-time, 55% women, 45% men

Undergraduates 2,058 full-time, 3,369 part-time. Students come from 12 states and territories; 100 other countries; 2% are from out of state; 17% Black or African American, non-Hispanic/Latino; 13% Hispanic/Latino; 4% Asian, non-Hispanic/Latino; 0.1% Native Hawaiian or other Pacific Islander, non-Hispanic/Latino; 0.5% American Indian or Alaska Native, non-Hispanic/Latino; 9% Race/ethnicity unknown; 2% international; 5% transferred in. *Retention:* 55% of full-time freshmen returned.

Freshmen *Admission:* 2,017 applied, 2,015 admitted, 1,244 enrolled.

Faculty *Total:* 382, 23% full-time. *Student/faculty ratio:* 17:1.

Majors Accounting; automotive engineering technology; biological and physical sciences; biology/biotechnology laboratory technician; business administration and management; business/commerce; chemical technology; child-care and support services management; computer and information sciences; computer engineering technology; computer science; criminal justice/law enforcement administration; drafting and design technology; engineering technology; environmental engineering technology; forensic science and technology; general studies; hospitality administration; human services; information science/studies; international relations and affairs; legal assistant/paralegal; liberal arts and sciences/liberal studies; mechanical engineering/mechanical technology; medical radiologic technology; physical therapy technology; registered nursing/registered nurse; respiratory care therapy; social sciences; speech communication and rhetoric.

Academics *Calendar:* semesters. *Degree:* certificates and associate. *Special study options:* academic remediation for entering students, adult/continuing education programs, advanced placement credit, cooperative education, distance learning, honors programs, internships, part-time degree program, services for LD students, summer session for credit.

Library Perkins Library with 51,429 titles, 280 serial subscriptions, 4,780 audiovisual materials, an OPAC, a Web page.

Student Life *Housing:* college housing not available. *Activities and Organizations:* drama/theater group, student-run newspaper, Student Government Association, Latino Student Organization, New World Society Club, Mass Bay Players, Student Occupational Therapy Association. *Campus security:* 24-hour emergency response devices and patrols. *Student services:* health clinic, personal/psychological counseling.

Athletics Member NJCAA. *Intercollegiate sports:* baseball M, basketball M/W, cross-country running M/W, golf M/W, soccer M/W, softball W, tennis M/W, volleyball W. *Intramural sports:* ice hockey M, soccer M/W.

Costs (2013–14) *Tuition:* state resident $576 full-time, $24 per credit part-time; nonresident $5520 full-time, $230 per credit part-time. Full-time tuition and fees vary according to program and reciprocity agreements. Part-time tuition and fees vary according to program and reciprocity agreements. *Required fees:* $3680 full-time, $130 per credit part-time, $20 per term part-time. *Payment plan:* installment. *Waivers:* senior citizens and employees or children of employees.

Financial Aid Of all full-time matriculated undergraduates who enrolled in 2011, 59 Federal Work-Study jobs (averaging $1840).

Applying *Options:* electronic application, deferred entrance. *Application fee:* $20. *Application deadlines:* rolling (freshmen), rolling (transfers). *Notification:* continuous (freshmen), continuous (transfers).

Freshman Application Contact Ms. Donna Raposa, Director of Admissions, Massachusetts Bay Community College, 50 Oakland Street, Wellesley Hills, MA 02481. *Phone:* 781-239-2500. *Fax:* 781-239-1047. *E-mail:* info@massbay.edu.
Website: http://www.massbay.edu/.

Massasoit Community College

Brockton, Massachusetts

Freshman Application Contact Michelle Hughes, Director of Admissions, Massasoit Community College, 1 Massasoit Boulevard, Brockton, MA 02302-3996. *Phone:* 508-588-9100. *Toll-free phone:* 800-CAREERS.
Website: http://www.massasoit.mass.edu/.

Middlesex Community College

Bedford, Massachusetts

- **State-supported** 2-year, founded 1970, part of Massachusetts Public Higher Education System
- **Suburban** 200-acre campus with easy access to Boston
- **Coed,** 9,664 undergraduate students

Majors Aircraft powerplant technology; art; biology/biological sciences; biology/biotechnology laboratory technician; business administration and management; commercial and advertising art; computer and information sciences; computer and information sciences and support services related; computer engineering technology; computer programming; criminal justice/law enforcement administration; dental assisting; dental hygiene; dental laboratory technology; diagnostic medical sonography and ultrasound technology; electrical, electronic and communications engineering technology; electrical/electronics drafting and CAD/CADD; elementary education; engineering technologies and engineering related; fashion merchandising; fire science/firefighting; general studies; hotel/motel administration; kindergarten/preschool education; legal assistant/paralegal; liberal arts and sciences/liberal studies; medical/clinical assistant; medical radiologic technology; office occupations and clerical services; physical sciences; psychiatric/mental health services technology; registered nursing/registered nurse; web page, digital/multimedia and information resources design.

Academics *Calendar:* semesters. *Degree:* certificates and associate. *Special study options:* academic remediation for entering students, accelerated degree program, adult/continuing education programs, advanced placement credit, cooperative education, distance learning, English as a second language, honors programs, independent study, internships, off-campus study, part-time degree program, services for LD students, study abroad, summer session for credit. *ROTC:* Air Force (c).

Library Main Library plus 1 other with 52,960 titles, 538 serial subscriptions, an OPAC, a Web page.

Student Life *Housing:* college housing not available. *Activities and Organizations:* drama/theater group, student-run newspaper. *Campus security:* 24-hour emergency response devices and patrols. *Student services:* health clinic, personal/psychological counseling, legal services.

Athletics *Intramural sports:* basketball M/W, table tennis M/W, volleyball M/W.

Standardized Tests *Required for some:* CPT.

Costs (2012–13) *Tuition:* state resident $4224 full-time; nonresident $9168 full-time. Full-time tuition and fees vary according to course load and reciprocity agreements. Part-time tuition and fees vary according to course load and reciprocity agreements. *Required fees:* $50 full-time. *Payment plan:* installment. *Waivers:* senior citizens and employees or children of employees.

Financial Aid Of all full-time matriculated undergraduates who enrolled in 2011, 68 Federal Work-Study jobs (averaging $2200).

Applying *Options:* electronic application, early admission. *Required for some:* essay or personal statement, high school transcript, 3 letters of recommendation, interview. *Application deadlines:* rolling (freshmen), rolling (transfers). *Notification:* continuous (freshmen), continuous (transfers).

Freshman Application Contact Middlesex Community College, Springs Road, Bedford, MA 01730-1655. *Phone:* 978-656-3207. *Toll-free phone:* 800-818-3434.
Website: http://www.middlesex.mass.edu/.

Mount Wachusett Community College

Gardner, Massachusetts

- **State-supported** 2-year, founded 1963, part of Massachusetts Public Higher Education System
- **Small-town** 270-acre campus with easy access to Boston
- **Endowment** $3.4 million
- **Coed**

Undergraduates 2,016 full-time, 2,739 part-time. Students come from 10 states and territories; 4% are from out of state; 7% Black or African American, non-Hispanic/Latino; 13% Hispanic/Latino; 2% Asian, non-Hispanic/Latino; 0.1% Native Hawaiian or other Pacific Islander, non-Hispanic/Latino; 0.4% American Indian or Alaska Native, non-Hispanic/Latino; 2% Two or more races, non-Hispanic/Latino; 3% Race/ethnicity unknown; 0.9% international; 6% transferred in. *Retention:* 54% of full-time freshmen returned.

Faculty *Student/faculty ratio:* 23:1.

Academics *Calendar:* semesters. *Degree:* certificates and associate. *Special study options:* academic remediation for entering students, accelerated degree program, adult/continuing education programs, advanced placement credit, cooperative education, distance learning, double majors, English as a second language, honors programs, independent study, internships, part-time degree program, services for LD students, study abroad, summer session for credit.

Student Life *Campus security:* 24-hour emergency response devices and patrols.

Standardized Tests *Required for some:* SAT (for admission). *Recommended:* SAT (for admission), ACT (for admission), SAT or ACT (for admission), SAT and SAT Subject Tests or ACT (for admission), SAT Subject Tests (for admission).

Financial Aid Of all full-time matriculated undergraduates who enrolled in 2011, 47 Federal Work-Study jobs (averaging $2228).

Applying *Options:* electronic application, early admission. *Application fee:* $10. *Required:* high school transcript. *Required for some:* 2 letters of recommendation. *Recommended:* interview.

Freshman Application Contact Mr. Ryan Forsythe, Director of Admissions, Mount Wachusett Community College, 444 Green Street, Gardner, MA 01440-1000. *Phone:* 978-632-6600 Ext. 110. *Fax:* 978-630-9554. *E-mail:* admissions@mwcc.mass.edu.
Website: http://www.mwcc.mass.edu/.

Northern Essex Community College
Haverhill, Massachusetts

- **State-supported** 2-year, founded 1960
- **Suburban** 106-acre campus with easy access to Boston
- **Endowment** $4.5 million
- **Coed,** 7,312 undergraduate students, 36% full-time, 62% women, 38% men

Undergraduates 2,596 full-time, 4,716 part-time. Students come from 6 states and territories; 17% are from out of state; 4% Black or African American, non-Hispanic/Latino; 34% Hispanic/Latino; 2% Asian, non-Hispanic/Latino; 0.6% Native Hawaiian or other Pacific Islander, non-Hispanic/Latino; 0.2% American Indian or Alaska Native, non-Hispanic/Latino; 1% Two or more races, non-Hispanic/Latino; 3% Race/ethnicity unknown; 0.5% international; 5% transferred in. *Retention:* 61% of full-time freshmen returned.

Freshmen *Admission:* 3,000 applied, 2,800 admitted, 1,441 enrolled.

Faculty *Total:* 657, 16% full-time. *Student/faculty ratio:* 22:1.

Majors Accounting; administrative assistant and secretarial science; biological and physical sciences; business administration and management; business teacher education; civil engineering technology; commercial and advertising art; computer and information sciences; computer engineering technology; computer graphics; computer programming; computer programming related; computer programming (specific applications); computer science; computer systems networking and telecommunications; computer typography and composition equipment operation; criminal justice/law enforcement administration; dance; data processing and data processing technology; dental assisting; dramatic/theater arts; education; electrical, electronic and communications engineering technology; elementary education; engineering science; finance; general studies; health information/medical records administration; history; hotel/motel administration; human services; industrial radiologic technology; international relations and affairs; journalism; kindergarten/preschool education; legal assistant/paralegal; liberal arts and sciences/liberal studies; machine tool technology; marketing/marketing management; materials science; medical administrative assistant and medical secretary; medical transcription; mental health counseling; music; parks, recreation and leisure; physical education teaching and coaching; political science and government; radiologic technology/science; real estate; registered nursing/registered nurse; respiratory care therapy; respiratory therapy technician; sign language interpretation and translation; telecommunications technology; tourism and travel services management; web/multimedia management and webmaster; web page, digital/multimedia and information resources design; women's studies.

Academics *Calendar:* semesters. *Degree:* certificates and associate. *Special study options:* academic remediation for entering students, adult/continuing education programs, advanced placement credit, cooperative education, distance learning, double majors, English as a second language, freshman honors college, honors programs, independent study, internships, off-campus study, part-time degree program, services for LD students, study abroad, summer session for credit. *ROTC:* Air Force (c).

Library Bentley Library with 61,120 titles, 598 serial subscriptions, an OPAC.

Student Life *Housing:* college housing not available. *Activities and Organizations:* drama/theater group, student-run newspaper. *Campus security:* 24-hour emergency response devices and patrols. *Student services:* health clinic, personal/psychological counseling, women's center.

Athletics Member NJCAA. *Intercollegiate sports:* baseball M, basketball M/W, cross-country running M/W, volleyball M/W. *Intramural sports:* basketball M/W, cross-country running M/W, football M/W, golf M/W, racquetball M/W, skiing (cross-country) M/W, skiing (downhill) M/W, weight lifting M/W.

Standardized Tests *Required:* Psychological Corporation Aptitude Test for Practical Nursing (for admission).

Financial Aid Of all full-time matriculated undergraduates who enrolled in 2011, 74 Federal Work-Study jobs (averaging $1759).

Applying *Options:* early admission. *Application fee:* $25. *Required:* high school transcript. *Application deadlines:* rolling (freshmen), rolling (transfers). *Notification:* continuous (freshmen), continuous (transfers).

Freshman Application Contact Ms. Laurie Dimitrov, Director of Admissions, Northern Essex Community College, Haverhill, MA 01830. *Phone:* 978-556-3616. *Fax:* 978-556-3155.
Website: http://www.necc.mass.edu/.

North Shore Community College
Danvers, Massachusetts

- **State-supported** 2-year, founded 1965
- **Suburban** campus with easy access to Boston
- **Endowment** $5.5 million
- **Coed,** 7,912 undergraduate students, 39% full-time, 61% women, 39% men

Undergraduates 3,064 full-time, 4,848 part-time. Students come from 9 states and territories; 8 other countries; 2% are from out of state; 9% Black or African American, non-Hispanic/Latino; 19% Hispanic/Latino; 4% Asian, non-Hispanic/Latino; 0.1% Native Hawaiian or other Pacific Islander, non-Hispanic/Latino; 0.3% American Indian or Alaska Native, non-Hispanic/Latino; 2% Two or more races, non-Hispanic/Latino; 3% Race/ethnicity unknown; 0.2% international; 8% transferred in.

Freshmen *Admission:* 4,760 applied, 3,988 admitted, 1,501 enrolled.

Faculty *Total:* 486, 28% full-time, 18% with terminal degrees. *Student/faculty ratio:* 17:1.

Majors Accounting; administrative assistant and secretarial science; airline pilot and flight crew; biology/biotechnology laboratory technician; business administration and management; child development; computer and information sciences related; computer engineering technology; computer graphics; computer programming; computer programming (specific applications); computer science; criminal justice/law enforcement administration; culinary arts; data entry/microcomputer applications; engineering science; fire science/firefighting; foods, nutrition, and wellness; gerontology; health professions related; hospitality administration; information science/studies; interdisciplinary studies; kindergarten/preschool education; legal administrative assistant/secretary; legal assistant/paralegal; liberal arts and sciences/liberal studies; marketing/marketing management; medical administrative assistant and medical secretary; medical radiologic technology; mental health counseling; occupational therapy; physical therapy technology; pre-engineering; registered nursing/registered nurse; respiratory care therapy; substance abuse/addiction counseling; tourism and travel services management; veterinary/animal health technology; web page, digital/multimedia and information resources design.

Academics *Calendar:* semesters. *Degree:* certificates and associate. *Special study options:* academic remediation for entering students, accelerated degree program, adult/continuing education programs, advanced placement credit, cooperative education, distance learning, English as a second language, honors programs, independent study, internships, part-time degree program, services for LD students, summer session for credit.

Library Learning Resource Center plus 2 others with 68,035 titles, 257 serial subscriptions, 4,213 audiovisual materials, an OPAC, a Web page.

Student Life *Housing:* college housing not available. *Activities and Organizations:* drama/theater group, student-run newspaper, Program Council, student government, performing arts, student newspaper, Phi Theta Kappa, national fraternities. *Campus security:* 24-hour emergency response devices and patrols, late-night transport/escort service. *Student services:* health clinic, personal/psychological counseling, women's center.

Athletics *Intramural sports:* basketball M/W, soccer M/W.

Costs (2013–14) *Tuition:* state resident $600 full-time, $25 per credit hour part-time; nonresident $6168 full-time, $257 per credit hour part-time. *Required fees:* $3456 full-time, $144 per credit hour part-time. *Payment plan:* installment. *Waivers:* senior citizens and employees or children of employees.

Financial Aid Of all full-time matriculated undergraduates who enrolled in 2009, 1,658 applied for aid, 1,438 were judged to have need, 23 had their need fully met. 123 Federal Work-Study jobs (averaging $1359). In 2009, 11 non-need-based awards were made. *Average percent of need met:* 18%. *Average financial aid package:* $6856. *Average need-based loan:* $1639. *Average need-based gift aid:* $2522. *Average non-need-based aid:* $614.

Applying *Options:* electronic application, early admission, deferred entrance. *Required for some:* essay or personal statement, high school transcript, interview. *Application deadlines:* rolling (freshmen), rolling (transfers). *Notification:* continuous (freshmen), continuous (transfers).

Freshman Application Contact Ms. Lisa Barrett, Academic Counselor, North Shore Community College, Danvers, MA 01923. *Phone:* 978-762-4000 Ext. 6225. *Fax:* 978-762-4015. *E-mail:* lbarrett@northshore.edu.
Website: http://www.northshore.edu/.

Quincy College
Quincy, Massachusetts

Freshman Application Contact Paula Smith, Dean, Enrollment Services, Quincy College, 34 Coddington Street, Quincy, MA 02169-4522. *Phone:* 617-

984-1700. *Toll-free phone:* 800-698-1700. *Fax:* 617-984-1779. *E-mail:* psmith@quincycollege.edu.
Website: http://www.quincycollege.edu/.

Quinsigamond Community College

Worcester, Massachusetts

- **State-supported** 2-year, founded 1963, part of Massachusetts System of Higher Education
- **Urban** 57-acre campus with easy access to Boston
- **Endowment** $390,167
- **Coed,** 8,991 undergraduate students, 44% full-time, 58% women, 42% men

Undergraduates 3,943 full-time, 5,048 part-time. Students come from 11 states and territories; 34 other countries; 0.8% are from out of state; 12% Black or African American, non-Hispanic/Latino; 15% Hispanic/Latino; 4% Asian, non-Hispanic/Latino; 0.1% Native Hawaiian or other Pacific Islander, non-Hispanic/Latino; 0.4% American Indian or Alaska Native, non-Hispanic/Latino; 2% Two or more races, non-Hispanic/Latino; 6% Race/ethnicity unknown; 0.3% international.

Freshmen *Admission:* 4,327 applied, 2,331 admitted, 1,897 enrolled.

Faculty *Total:* 580, 23% full-time, 11% with terminal degrees. *Student/faculty ratio:* 20:1.

Majors Alternative and complementary medicine related; American Sign Language (ASL); automobile/automotive mechanics technology; bioengineering and biomedical engineering; biomedical technology; biotechnology; business administration and management; business/commerce; computer and information systems security; computer engineering technology; computer graphics; computer programming (specific applications); computer science; computer systems analysis; criminal justice/police science; data modeling/warehousing and database administration; dental hygiene; dental services and allied professions related; electrical, electronic and communications engineering technology; electromechanical technology; elementary education; emergency medical technology (EMT paramedic); energy management and systems technology; engineering technologies and engineering related; executive assistant/executive secretary; fire services administration; general studies; health services/allied health/health sciences; hospitality administration; human services; kindergarten/preschool education; liberal arts and sciences/liberal studies; manufacturing engineering technology; medical administrative assistant and medical secretary; occupational therapist assistant; occupational therapy; pre-pharmacy studies; radiologic technology/science; registered nursing/registered nurse; respiratory care therapy; restaurant/food services management; telecommunications technology; web page, digital/multimedia and information resources design.

Academics *Calendar:* semesters. *Degree:* certificates and associate. *Special study options:* academic remediation for entering students, accelerated degree program, advanced placement credit, cooperative education, distance learning, double majors, English as a second language, honors programs, independent study, internships, off-campus study, part-time degree program, services for LD students, summer session for credit. *ROTC:* Army (c).

Library Alden Library with 95,000 titles, 140 serial subscriptions, 1,500 audiovisual materials, an OPAC, a Web page.

Student Life *Housing:* college housing not available. *Activities and Organizations:* drama/theater group, student-run newspaper, Phi Theta Kappa, academic-related clubs, Student Senate, Chess Club, Business Club. *Campus security:* 24-hour emergency response devices and patrols, late-night transport/escort service. *Student services:* personal/psychological counseling.

Athletics Member NJCAA. *Intercollegiate sports:* baseball M, basketball M/W, softball W. *Intramural sports:* basketball M/W, soccer M/W, ultimate Frisbee M/W, volleyball M/W.

Costs (2012–13) *Tuition:* state resident $576 full-time, $24 per credit hour part-time; nonresident $5520 full-time, $230 per credit hour part-time. Full-time tuition and fees vary according to course load and program. Part-time tuition and fees vary according to course load and program. *Required fees:* $4518 full-time, $157 per credit hour part-time, $280 per term part-time. *Payment plan:* installment. *Waivers:* senior citizens and employees or children of employees.

Applying *Options:* electronic application. *Application fee:* $20. *Required:* high school transcript. *Required for some:* interview. *Application deadlines:* rolling (freshmen), rolling (out-of-state freshmen), rolling (transfers). *Notification:* continuous (freshmen), continuous (out-of-state freshmen), continuous (transfers).

Freshman Application Contact Quinsigamond Community College, 670 West Boylston Street, Worcester, MA 01606-2092. *Phone:* 508-854-4260. *Website:* http://www.qcc.edu/.

Roxbury Community College
Roxbury Crossing, Massachusetts

Director of Admissions Mr. Milton Samuels, Director, Admissions, Roxbury Community College, 1234 Columbus Avenue, Roxbury Crossing, MA 02120-3400. *Phone:* 617-541-5310.
Website: http://www.rcc.mass.edu/.

Salter College
Chicopee, Massachusetts

Admissions Office Contact Salter College, 645 Shawinigan Drive, Chicopee, MA 01020.
Website: http://www.saltercollege.com/.

Springfield Technical Community College
Springfield, Massachusetts

- **State-supported** 2-year, founded 1967
- **Urban** 34-acre campus
- **Coed,** 7,011 undergraduate students, 44% full-time, 58% women, 42% men

Undergraduates 3,104 full-time, 3,907 part-time. Students come from 12 states and territories; 15 other countries; 3% are from out of state; 16% Black or African American, non-Hispanic/Latino; 24% Hispanic/Latino; 3% Asian, non-Hispanic/Latino; 0.1% Native Hawaiian or other Pacific Islander, non-Hispanic/Latino; 0.6% American Indian or Alaska Native, non-Hispanic/Latino; 2% Two or more races, non-Hispanic/Latino; 4% Race/ethnicity unknown; 0.7% international; 9% transferred in.

Freshmen *Admission:* 3,279 applied, 2,872 admitted, 1,394 enrolled.

Faculty *Total:* 398, 37% full-time. *Student/faculty ratio:* 19:1.

Majors Accounting; administrative assistant and secretarial science; animation, interactive technology, video graphics and special effects; automotive engineering technology; biology/biological sciences; biotechnology; building/construction finishing, management, and inspection related; business administration and management; business/commerce; chemistry; civil engineering technology; clinical/medical laboratory technology; commercial and advertising art; commercial photography; computer and information systems security; computer engineering technology; computer programming (specific applications); computer science; criminal justice/police science; data processing and data processing technology; dental hygiene; diagnostic medical sonography and ultrasound technology; early childhood education; electrical, electronic and communications engineering technology; electromechanical technology; elementary education; engineering; executive assistant/executive secretary; finance; fine/studio arts; fire prevention and safety technology; general studies; heating, ventilation, air conditioning and refrigeration engineering technology; landscaping and groundskeeping; laser and optical technology; liberal arts and sciences/liberal studies; marketing/marketing management; massage therapy; mathematics; mechanical engineering/mechanical technology; medical administrative assistant and medical secretary; medical/clinical assistant; medical insurance coding; network and system administration; nuclear medical technology; occupational therapist assistant; physical therapy technology; physics; premedical studies; radio and television broadcasting technology; radiologic technology/science; recording arts technology; registered nursing/registered nurse; respiratory care therapy; secondary education; small business administration; sport and fitness administration/management; surgical technology; telecommunications technology; web page, digital/multimedia and information resources design.

Academics *Calendar:* semesters. *Degree:* certificates and associate. *Special study options:* academic remediation for entering students, adult/continuing education programs, advanced placement credit, cooperative education, distance learning, English as a second language, honors programs, independent study, internships, off-campus study, part-time degree program, services for LD students, summer session for credit.

Library Springfield Technical Community College Library with 58,950 titles, 323 serial subscriptions, 15,031 audiovisual materials, an OPAC, a Web page.

Student Life *Housing:* college housing not available. *Activities and Organizations:* Phi Theta Kappa, Campus Civitian Club, Tech Times (student newspaper), Dental Hygiene Club, Landscape Design Club. *Campus security:* 24-hour emergency response devices and patrols, late-night transport/escort service. *Student services:* health clinic, personal/psychological counseling.

Athletics Member NJCAA. *Intercollegiate sports:* basketball M/W, golf M, soccer M/W, wrestling M. *Intramural sports:* basketball M/W, cross-country running M/W, golf M/W, skiing (cross-country) M/W, volleyball M/W, weight lifting M/W.

Standardized Tests *Required for some:* SAT (for admission).

Costs (2012–13) *Tuition:* state resident $750 full-time, $25 per credit part-time; nonresident $7260 full-time, $242 per credit part-time. Full-time tuition and fees vary according to course load and reciprocity agreements. Part-time tuition and fees vary according to course load and reciprocity agreements. No tuition increase for student's term of enrollment. *Required fees:* $4356 full-time, $138 per credit part-time, $108 per term part-time. *Payment plan:* installment. *Waivers:* senior citizens and employees or children of employees.

Financial Aid Of all full-time matriculated undergraduates who enrolled in 2011, 124 Federal Work-Study jobs (averaging $2400).

Applying *Options:* electronic application. *Application fee:* $10. *Required:* high school transcript. *Required for some:* interview. *Application deadlines:* rolling (freshmen), rolling (transfers).

Freshman Application Contact Mr. Ray Blair, Springfield Technical Community College, Springfield, MA 01105. *Phone:* 413-781-7822 Ext. 4868. *E-mail:* rblair@stcc.edu.

Website: http://www.stcc.edu/.

Urban College of Boston

Boston, Massachusetts

Director of Admissions Dr. Henry J. Johnson, Director of Enrollment Services/Registrar, Urban College of Boston, 178 Tremont Street, Boston, MA 02111. *Phone:* 617-348-6353.

Website: http://www.urbancollege.edu/.

MICHIGAN

Alpena Community College

Alpena, Michigan

- **State and locally supported** 2-year, founded 1952
- **Small-town** 700-acre campus
- **Endowment** $3.3 million
- **Coed,** 1,950 undergraduate students

Undergraduates Students come from 4 states and territories; 2% live on campus. *Retention:* 55% of full-time freshmen returned.

Freshmen *Admission:* 1,050 applied, 1,050 admitted. *Average high school GPA:* 2.67.

Faculty *Total:* 125, 44% full-time, 3% with terminal degrees. *Student/faculty ratio:* 17:1.

Majors Accounting; administrative assistant and secretarial science; automobile/automotive mechanics technology; biology/biological sciences; business administration and management; business automation/technology/data entry; chemical engineering; chemistry; computer and information sciences; computer/information technology services administration related; computer systems networking and telecommunications; corrections; criminal justice/police science; data processing and data processing technology; drafting and design technology; elementary education; English; general studies; information science/studies; liberal arts and sciences/liberal studies; licensed practical/vocational nurse training; manufacturing engineering technology; mathematics; medical office assistant; office management; operations management; pre-engineering; registered nursing/registered nurse; secondary education.

Academics *Calendar:* semesters. *Degree:* certificates and associate. *Special study options:* academic remediation for entering students, advanced placement credit, distance learning, double majors, internships, part-time degree program, services for LD students, summer session for credit.

Library Stephen Fletcher Library with 29,000 titles, 183 serial subscriptions, an OPAC, a Web page.

Student Life *Housing Options:* coed, men-only, women-only. Campus housing is provided by a third party. *Activities and Organizations:* drama/theater group, choral group, Nursing Association, Student Senate, Phi Theta Kappa, Law Enforcement Club. *Campus security:* 24-hour emergency response devices. *Student services:* personal/psychological counseling.

Athletics Member NJCAA. *Intercollegiate sports:* basketball M(s)/W(s), cross-country running M, softball W(s), volleyball W(s). *Intramural sports:* basketball M/W, bowling M/W, football M, soccer M, softball M/W, volleyball M/W.

Costs (2013–14) *Tuition:* area resident $3180 full-time, $106 per contact hour part-time; state resident $3660 full-time, $122 per contact hour part-time; nonresident $3660 full-time, $122 per contact hour part-time. *Required fees:* $600 full-time, $16 per hour part-time, $30 per term part-time. *Room and board:* $3500.

Financial Aid Of all full-time matriculated undergraduates who enrolled in 2011, 80 Federal Work-Study jobs (averaging $1200). 20 state and other part-time jobs (averaging $800).

Applying *Options:* electronic application, early admission, deferred entrance. *Recommended:* high school transcript. *Application deadlines:* rolling (freshmen), rolling (transfers). *Notification:* continuous (freshmen), continuous (transfers).

Freshman Application Contact Mr. Mike Kollien, Director of Admissions, Alpena Community College, 665 Johnson, Alpena, MI 49707. *Phone:* 989-358-7339. *Toll-free phone:* 888-468-6222. *Fax:* 989-358-7540. *E-mail:* kollienm@alpenacc.edu.

Website: http://www.alpenacc.edu/.

Bay de Noc Community College

Escanaba, Michigan

Freshman Application Contact Bay de Noc Community College, 2001 North Lincoln Road, Escanaba, MI 49829-2511. *Phone:* 906-786-5802 Ext. 1276. *Toll-free phone:* 800-221-2001.

Website: http://www.baycollege.edu/.

Bay Mills Community College

Brimley, Michigan

Freshman Application Contact Ms. Elaine Lehre, Admissions Officer, Bay Mills Community College, 12214 West Lakeshore Drive, Brimley, MI 49715. *Phone:* 906-248-3354. *Toll-free phone:* 800-844-BMCC. *Fax:* 906-248-3351.

Website: http://www.bmcc.edu/.

Delta College

University Center, Michigan

Freshman Application Contact Mr. Gary Brasseur, Associate Director of Admissions, Delta College, 1961 Delta Road, University Center, MI 48710. *Phone:* 989-686-9590. *Fax:* 989-667-2202. *E-mail:* admit@delta.edu.

Website: http://www.delta.edu/.

Glen Oaks Community College

Centreville, Michigan

Freshman Application Contact Ms. Beverly M. Andrews, Director of Admissions/Registrar, Glen Oaks Community College, 62249 Shimmel Road, Centreville, MI 49032-9719. *Phone:* 269-467-9945 Ext. 248. *Toll-free phone:* 888-994-7818.

Website: http://www.glenoaks.edu/.

Gogebic Community College

Ironwood, Michigan

Freshman Application Contact Ms. Jeanne Graham, Director of Admissions, Gogebic Community College, E4946 Jackson Road, Ironwood, MI 49938. *Phone:* 906-932-4231 Ext. 306. *Toll-free phone:* 800-682-5910. *Fax:* 906-932-2339. *E-mail:* jeanneg@gogebic.edu.

Website: http://www.gogebic.edu/.

Grand Rapids Community College

Grand Rapids, Michigan

- **District-supported** 2-year, founded 1914, part of Michigan Department of Education
- **Urban** 35-acre campus
- **Endowment** $30.5 million
- **Coed,** 17,448 undergraduate students, 36% full-time, 53% women, 47% men

Undergraduates 6,264 full-time, 11,184 part-time. Students come from 8 states and territories; 23 other countries; 1% are from out of state; 12% Black or African American, non-Hispanic/Latino; 8% Hispanic/Latino; 3% Asian, non-Hispanic/Latino; 0.8% American Indian or Alaska Native, non-Hispanic/Latino; 0.3% Two or more races, non-Hispanic/Latino; 8% Race/ethnicity unknown; 0.1% international; 9% transferred in. *Retention:* 55% of full-time freshmen returned.

Freshmen *Admission:* 11,571 applied, 3,601 enrolled. *Average high school GPA:* 2.9. *Test scores:* ACT scores over 18: 67%; ACT scores over 24: 18%; ACT scores over 30: 1%.

Faculty *Total:* 847, 30% full-time, 10% with terminal degrees. *Student/faculty ratio:* 22:1.

Majors Architectural engineering technology; architecture; art; automobile/automotive mechanics technology; business administration and management; chemistry; child-care and support services management; computer engineering technology; computer programming; computer science; corrections; criminal justice/law enforcement administration; criminal justice/police science; culinary arts; dental hygiene; drafting and design technology; electrical, electronic and communications engineering technology; elementary education; engineering; English; fashion merchandising; foreign languages and literatures; forestry; geology/earth science; heating, air conditioning, ventilation and refrigeration maintenance technology; industrial technology; landscaping and groundskeeping; liberal arts and sciences/liberal studies; library and information science; licensed practical/vocational nurse training; mass communication/media; medical administrative assistant and medical secretary; music; plastics and polymer engineering technology; quality control technology; registered nursing/registered nurse; welding technology.

Academics *Calendar:* semesters. *Degree:* certificates and associate. *Special study options:* academic remediation for entering students, adult/continuing education programs, advanced placement credit, cooperative education, distance learning, English as a second language, honors programs, independent study, internships, off-campus study, part-time degree program, services for LD students, study abroad, summer session for credit.

Library Arthur Andrews Memorial Library with 161,263 titles, 33,064 serial subscriptions, 3,200 audiovisual materials, an OPAC, a Web page.

Student Life *Housing:* college housing not available. *Activities and Organizations:* drama/theater group, student-run newspaper, choral group, Student Congress, Phi Theta Kappa, Hispanic Student Organization, Student Gamers Association, Foreign Affairs Club. *Campus security:* 24-hour emergency response devices, late-night transport/escort service. *Student services:* personal/psychological counseling.

Athletics Member NJCAA. *Intercollegiate sports:* baseball M(s), basketball M(s)/W(s), golf M(s), softball W(s), tennis M(s)/W(s), volleyball W(s).

Standardized Tests *Recommended:* SAT or ACT (for admission).

Costs (2012–13) *Tuition:* area resident $2940 full-time, $98 per contact hour part-time; state resident $6450 full-time, $215 per contact hour part-time; nonresident $9660 full-time, $322 per contact hour part-time. Full-time tuition and fees vary according to course load. Part-time tuition and fees vary according to course load. *Required fees:* $459 full-time, $6 per contact hour part-time, $125 per term part-time. *Payment plan:* installment. *Waivers:* employees or children of employees.

Financial Aid Of all full-time matriculated undergraduates who enrolled in 2008, 6,142 applied for aid, 4,896 were judged to have need, 1,012 had their need fully met. In 2008, 96 non-need-based awards were made. *Average financial aid package:* $4850. *Average need-based loan:* $2764. *Average need-based gift aid:* $3984. *Average non-need-based aid:* $1051.

Applying *Options:* electronic application, early admission, deferred entrance. *Required:* high school transcript. *Application deadline:* 8/30 (freshmen). *Notification:* continuous (freshmen), continuous (transfers).

Freshman Application Contact Ms. Diane Patrick, Director of Admissions, Grand Rapids Community College, Grand Rapids, MI 49503-3201. *Phone:* 616-234-4100. *Fax:* 616-234-4005. *E-mail:* dpatrick@grcc.edu. *Website:* http://www.grcc.edu/.

Henry Ford Community College

Dearborn, Michigan

Freshman Application Contact Admissions Office, Henry Ford Community College, 5101 Evergreen Road, Dearborn, MI 48128-1495. *Phone:* 313-845-6403. *Toll-free phone:* 800-585-HFCC. *Fax:* 313-845-6464. *E-mail:* enroll@hfcc.edu. *Website:* http://www.hfcc.edu/.

ITT Technical Institute

Canton, Michigan

- **Proprietary** primarily 2-year, founded 2002, part of ITT Educational Services, Inc.
- **Coed**

Academics *Calendar:* quarters. *Degrees:* associate and bachelor's.

Freshman Application Contact Director of Recruitment, ITT Technical Institute, 1905 South Haggerty Road, Canton, MI 48188-2025. *Phone:* 784-397-7800. *Toll-free phone:* 800-247-4477. *Website:* http://www.itt-tech.edu/.

ITT Technical Institute

Dearborn, Michigan

- **Proprietary** primarily 2-year, part of ITT Educational Services, Inc.
- **Coed**

Academics *Calendar:* quarters. *Degrees:* associate and bachelor's.

Freshman Application Contact Director of Recruitment, ITT Technical Institute, 19855 W. Outer Drive, Suite L10W, Dearborn, MI 48124. *Phone:* 313-278-5208. *Toll-free phone:* 800-605-0801. *Website:* http://www.itt-tech.edu/.

ITT Technical Institute

Swartz Creek, Michigan

- **Proprietary** primarily 2-year, founded 2005, part of ITT Educational Services, Inc.
- **Coed**

Academics *Calendar:* quarters. *Degrees:* associate and bachelor's.

Freshman Application Contact Director of Recruitment, ITT Technical Institute, 6359 Miller Road, Swartz Creek, MI 48473. *Phone:* 810-628-2500. *Toll-free phone:* 800-514-6564. *Website:* http://www.itt-tech.edu/.

ITT Technical Institute

Troy, Michigan

- **Proprietary** primarily 2-year, founded 1987, part of ITT Educational Services, Inc.
- **Coed**

Academics *Calendar:* quarters. *Degrees:* associate and bachelor's.

Freshman Application Contact Director of Recruitment, ITT Technical Institute, 1522 East Big Beaver Road, Troy, MI 48083-1905. *Phone:* 248-524-1800. *Toll-free phone:* 800-832-6817. *Fax:* 248-524-1965. *Website:* http://www.itt-tech.edu/.

ITT Technical Institute

Wyoming, Michigan

- **Proprietary** primarily 2-year, part of ITT Educational Services, Inc.
- **Coed**

Academics *Calendar:* quarters. *Degrees:* associate and bachelor's.

Freshman Application Contact Director of Recruitment, ITT Technical Institute, 1980 Metro Court SW, Wyoming, MI 49519. *Phone:* 616-406-1200. *Toll-free phone:* 800-632-4676. *Website:* http://www.itt-tech.edu/.

Jackson College

Jackson, Michigan

- **County-supported** 2-year, founded 1928
- **Suburban** 580-acre campus with easy access to Detroit
- **Coed,** 6,337 undergraduate students, 41% full-time, 61% women, 39% men

Undergraduates 2,598 full-time, 3,739 part-time. 0.1% are from out of state; 8% Black or African American, non-Hispanic/Latino; 4% Hispanic/Latino; 0.6% Asian, non-Hispanic/Latino; 0.8% American Indian or Alaska Native, non-Hispanic/Latino; 2% Two or more races, non-Hispanic/Latino; 8% Race/ethnicity unknown; 0.1% international; 2% live on campus.

Freshmen *Admission:* 1,236 enrolled.

Faculty *Total:* 488, 18% full-time. *Student/faculty ratio:* 17:1.

Majors Accounting and finance; administrative assistant and secretarial science; airline pilot and flight crew; automobile/automotive mechanics technology; business administration and management; computer and information sciences and support services related; construction trades related; corrections; criminal justice/law enforcement administration; data processing and data processing technology; diagnostic medical sonography and ultrasound technology; early childhood education; electrical, electronic and communications engineering technology; emergency medical technology (EMT paramedic); executive assistant/executive secretary; general studies; graphic design; heating, ventilation, air conditioning and refrigeration engineering technology; liberal arts and sciences/liberal studies; licensed practical/vocational nurse training; marketing/marketing management; medical/clinical assistant; medical insurance/medical billing; medical radiologic technology; medical transcription; registered nursing/registered nurse.

Academics *Calendar:* semesters. *Degree:* certificates and associate. *Special study options:* academic remediation for entering students, accelerated degree program, adult/continuing education programs, advanced placement credit, cooperative education, distance learning, double majors, English as a second language, freshman honors college, honors programs, independent study, internships, part-time degree program, services for LD students, summer session for credit.

Library Atkinson Learning Resources Center plus 1 other.

Student Life *Housing Options:* coed. Campus housing is university owned. *Activities and Organizations:* drama/theater group, choral group. *Campus security:* 24-hour emergency response devices and patrols, student patrols, late-night transport/escort service, controlled dormitory access. *Student services:* health clinic.

Athletics Member NJCAA. *Intercollegiate sports:* baseball M(s), basketball M(s)/W(s), cross-country running M(s)/W(s), golf M(s)/W(s), soccer M(s)/W(s), softball W(s), volleyball W(s).
Standardized Tests *Required for some:* ACT (for admission). *Recommended:* ACT (for admission).
Costs (2012–13) *Tuition:* area resident $2544 full-time, $106 per contact hour part-time; state resident $3816 full-time, $159 per contact hour part-time; non-resident $5088 full-time, $212 per contact hour part-time. Full-time tuition and fees vary according to location. Part-time tuition and fees vary according to location. *Required fees:* $768 full-time, $32 per contact hour part-time, $32 per contact part-time. *Room and board:* room only: $5150. *Payment plans:* installment, deferred payment. *Waivers:* senior citizens and employees or children of employees.
Applying *Options:* electronic application. *Required:* Minimum ACT of 16 is required for housing admission. *Required for some:* minimum #### GPA. *Application deadlines:* rolling (freshmen), rolling (out-of-state freshmen), rolling (transfers). *Notification:* continuous (freshmen), continuous (out-of-state freshmen), continuous (transfers).
Freshman Application Contact Mr. Daniel Vainner, Registrar, Jackson College, 2111 Emmons Road, Jackson, MI 49201. *Phone:* 517-796-8425. *Toll-free phone:* 888-522-7344. *Fax:* 517-796-8446. *E-mail:* admissions@jccmi.edu.
Website: http://www.jccmi.edu/.

Kalamazoo Valley Community College
Kalamazoo, Michigan
Freshman Application Contact Kalamazoo Valley Community College, PO Box 4070, Kalamazoo, MI 49003-4070. *Phone:* 269-488-4207.
Website: http://www.kvcc.edu/.

Kellogg Community College
Battle Creek, Michigan
Freshman Application Contact Ms. Denise Newman, Director of Enrollment Services, Kellogg Community College, 450 North Avenue, Battle Creek, MI 49017. *Phone:* 269-965-3931 Ext. 2620. *Fax:* 269-965-4133. *E-mail:* harriss@kellogg.edu.
Website: http://www.kellogg.edu/.

Keweenaw Bay Ojibwa Community College
Baraga, Michigan
Freshman Application Contact Megan Shanahan, Admissions Officer, Keweenaw Bay Ojibwa Community College, 111 Beartown Road, Baraga, MI 49908. *Phone:* 909-353-4600. *E-mail:* megan@kbocc.org.
Website: http://www.kbocc.org/.

Kirtland Community College
Roscommon, Michigan
- **District-supported** 2-year, founded 1966
- **Rural** 180-acre campus
- **Coed,** 1,807 undergraduate students, 38% full-time, 64% women, 36% men
Undergraduates 690 full-time, 1,117 part-time. Students come from 4 states and territories; 4 other countries; 0.9% Black or African American, non-Hispanic/Latino; 2% Hispanic/Latino; 0.3% Asian, non-Hispanic/Latino; 0.1% Native Hawaiian or other Pacific Islander, non-Hispanic/Latino; 1% American Indian or Alaska Native, non-Hispanic/Latino; 0.8% Two or more races, non-Hispanic/Latino; 6% Race/ethnicity unknown; 0.4% international.
Freshmen *Admission:* 414 applied, 414 admitted, 288 enrolled. *Test scores:* ACT scores over 18: 70%; ACT scores over 24: 9%; ACT scores over 30: 1%.
Faculty *Total:* 124, 31% full-time. *Student/faculty ratio:* 18:1.
Majors Administrative assistant and secretarial science; animation, interactive technology, video graphics and special effects; art; automobile/automotive mechanics technology; business administration and management; cardiovascular technology; computer systems analysis; corrections; cosmetology; criminal justice/law enforcement administration; electrical, electronic and communications engineering technology; electromechanical technology; general studies; graphic design; health information/medical records technology; heating, air conditioning, ventilation and refrigeration maintenance technology; industrial and product design; information science/studies; legal administrative assistant/secretary; liberal arts and sciences/liberal studies; licensed practical/vocational nurse training; management information systems; medical administrative assistant and medical secretary; pharmacy technician; registered nursing/registered nurse; robotics technology; surgical technology; teacher

assistant/aide; web/multimedia management and webmaster; welding technology.
Academics *Calendar:* semesters. *Degree:* certificates and associate. *Special study options:* academic remediation for entering students, adult/continuing education programs, advanced placement credit, cooperative education, distance learning, English as a second language, honors programs, independent study, internships, part-time degree program, services for LD students, summer session for credit.
Library Kirtland Community College Library with 33,000 titles, 321 serial subscriptions, an OPAC.
Student Life *Housing:* college housing not available. *Campus security:* 24-hour emergency response devices, student patrols, late-night transport/escort service, campus warning siren, uniformed armed police officers, RAVE alert system (text, email, voice).
Athletics Member NJCAA. *Intercollegiate sports:* basketball M(s)/W(s), cross-country running M(s)/W(s), golf M(s)/W(s).
Standardized Tests *Recommended:* ACT (for admission).
Costs (2012–13) *Tuition:* area resident $2760 full-time, $92 per contact hour part-time; state resident $3840 full-time, $128 per contact hour part-time; non-resident $6360 full-time, $212 per contact hour part-time. *Required fees:* $475 full-time, $14 per contact hour part-time, $35 per term part-time. *Payment plan:* installment. *Waivers:* minority students, senior citizens, and employees or children of employees.
Financial Aid Of all full-time matriculated undergraduates who enrolled in 2011, 50 Federal Work-Study jobs (averaging $1253). 28 state and other part-time jobs (averaging $1647).
Applying *Options:* electronic application. *Application deadlines:* rolling (freshmen), rolling (transfers). *Notification:* continuous until 8/22 (freshmen), continuous until 8/22 (transfers).
Freshman Application Contact Ms. Michelle Vyskocil, Dean of Student Services, Kirtland Community College, 10775 North Saint Helen Road, Roscommon, MI 48653. *Phone:* 989-275-5000 Ext. 248. *Fax:* 989-275-6789. *E-mail:* registrar@kirtland.edu.
Website: http://www.kirtland.edu/.

Lake Michigan College
Benton Harbor, Michigan
- **District-supported** 2-year, founded 1946, part of Michigan Department of Education
- **Small-town** 260-acre campus
- **Endowment** $6.4 million
- **Coed,** 4,548 undergraduate students, 33% full-time, 60% women, 40% men
Undergraduates 1,508 full-time, 3,040 part-time. Students come from 5 states and territories; 50 other countries; 2% are from out of state; 21% Black or African American, non-Hispanic/Latino; 6% Hispanic/Latino; 1% Asian, non-Hispanic/Latino; 0.4% Native Hawaiian or other Pacific Islander, non-Hispanic/Latino; 0.8% American Indian or Alaska Native, non-Hispanic/Latino; 2% Two or more races, non-Hispanic/Latino; 5% Race/ethnicity unknown; 6% transferred in. *Retention:* 42% of full-time freshmen returned.
Freshmen *Admission:* 1,580 applied, 1,490 admitted, 806 enrolled. *Average high school GPA:* 2.8.
Faculty *Total:* 327, 18% full-time, 11% with terminal degrees. *Student/faculty ratio:* 17:1.
Majors Accounting; administrative assistant and secretarial science; agricultural and horticultural plant breeding; applied horticulture/horticulture operations; art; biology/biological sciences; business administration and management; casino management; chemistry; communication; computer and information sciences; corrections; criminal justice/law enforcement administration; dental assisting; diagnostic medical sonography and ultrasound technology; drafting and design technology; dramatic/theater arts; early childhood education; elementary education; emergency medical technology (EMT paramedic); energy management and systems technology; English; environmental science; foreign languages and literatures; forensic science and technology; general studies; geography; geology/earth science; graphic design; health and physical education/fitness; health/medical preparatory programs related; history; hospitality administration; humanities; industrial technology; landscaping and groundskeeping; legal administrative assistant/secretary; liberal arts and sciences/liberal studies; machine tool technology; magnetic resonance imaging (MRI) technology; manufacturing engineering; marketing/marketing management; mathematics; medical administrative assistant and medical secretary; medical radiologic technology; music; philosophy; physical sciences; physics; political science and government; precision production related; pre-dentistry studies; pre-engineering; pre-law studies; premedical studies; pre-pharmacy studies; pre-veterinary studies; psychology; radiologic technology/science; registered nursing/registered nurse; secondary education; sociology; turf and turfgrass management.
Academics *Calendar:* semesters. *Degree:* certificates and associate. *Special study options:* academic remediation for entering students, adult/continuing

education programs, cooperative education, distance learning, English as a second language, honors programs, independent study, off-campus study, part-time degree program, services for LD students, student-designed majors, summer session for credit.

Library William Hessel Library with 98,682 titles, 23,943 serial subscriptions, 3,837 audiovisual materials, an OPAC, a Web page.

Student Life *Housing:* college housing not available. *Activities and Organizations:* drama/theater group, choral group, Cheer Team, Phi Theta Kappa, Student Senate, Movie Club, LMC Sky Kings (Sky Diving Club). *Campus security:* 24-hour emergency response devices, contracted campus security force.

Athletics Member NJCAA. *Intercollegiate sports:* baseball M(s), basketball M(s)/W(s), softball W(s), volleyball W(s).

Costs (2013–14) *Tuition:* area resident $2490 full-time, $83 per contact hour part-time; state resident $3840 full-time, $128 per contact hour part-time; non-resident $5070 full-time, $169 per contact hour part-time. *Required fees:* $1170 full-time, $39 per contact hour part-time. *Payment plans:* installment, deferred payment. *Waivers:* senior citizens and employees or children of employees.

Applying *Options:* electronic application. *Required:* high school transcript. *Required for some:* interview. *Application deadlines:* rolling (freshmen), rolling (transfers). *Notification:* continuous (freshmen), continuous (transfers).

Freshman Application Contact Mr. Louis Thomas, Lead Admissions Specialist, Lake Michigan College, 2755 East Napier Avenue, Benton Harbor, MI 49022-1899. *Phone:* 269-927-6584. *Toll-free phone:* 800-252-1LMC. *Fax:* 269-927-6718. *E-mail:* thomas@lakemichigancollege.edu. *Website:* http://www.lakemichigancollege.edu/.

Lansing Community College
Lansing, Michigan

- **State and locally supported** 2-year, founded 1957, part of Michigan Department of Education
- **Urban** 28-acre campus
- **Endowment** $7.3 million
- **Coed,** 19,123 undergraduate students, 37% full-time, 55% women, 45% men

Undergraduates 7,133 full-time, 11,990 part-time. Students come from 17 states and territories; 37 other countries; 0.2% are from out of state; 11% Black or African American, non-Hispanic/Latino; 2% Hispanic/Latino; 3% Asian, non-Hispanic/Latino; 0.3% Native Hawaiian or other Pacific Islander, non-Hispanic/Latino; 0.7% American Indian or Alaska Native, non-Hispanic/Latino; 3% Two or more races, non-Hispanic/Latino; 10% Race/ethnicity unknown; 2% international; 2% transferred in.

Freshmen *Admission:* 5,095 admitted, 5,095 enrolled. *Test scores:* SAT critical reading scores over 500: 21%; ACT scores over 18: 64%; ACT scores over 24: 17%; ACT scores over 30: 1%.

Faculty *Total:* 2,047, 11% full-time. *Student/faculty ratio:* 13:1.

Majors Accounting related; accounting technology and bookkeeping; administrative assistant and secretarial science; African American/Black studies; agricultural business and management; aircraft powerplant technology; airframe mechanics and aircraft maintenance technology; airline pilot and flight crew; American studies; animation, interactive technology, video graphics and special effects; anthropology; architectural engineering technology; architectural technology; art; art history, criticism and conservation; autobody/collision and repair technology; automobile/automotive mechanics technology; avionics maintenance technology; banking and financial support services; biology/biological sciences; biotechnology; business administration and management; business/commerce; carpentry; chemical technology; chemistry; child-care provision; cinematography and film/video production; civil engineering technology; community organization and advocacy; computer and information sciences; computer programming (specific applications); computer systems networking and telecommunications; computer technology/computer systems technology; construction/heavy equipment/earthmoving equipment operation; construction management; corrections; criminal justice/police science; customer service support/call center/teleservice operation; data modeling/warehousing and database administration; dental hygiene; diagnostic medical sonography and ultrasound technology; dramatic/theater arts; e-commerce; economics; electrical and power transmission installation; electrician; electromechanical technology; elementary education; emergency medical technology (EMT paramedic); energy management and systems technology; engineering; engineering physics/applied physics; English; environmental engineering technology; fashion merchandising; fine/studio arts; fire science/firefighting; foreign languages and literatures; French; geography; Germanic languages; graphic design; health and physical education/fitness; heating, air conditioning, ventilation and refrigeration maintenance technology; higher education/higher education administration; histologic technician; history; hotel/motel administration; humanities; human resources management; industrial production technologies related; interior design; international business/trade/commerce; international relations and affairs; Japanese; juvenile

corrections; legal assistant/paralegal; liberal arts and sciences/liberal studies; licensed practical/vocational nurse training; machine tool technology; magnetic resonance imaging (MRI) technology; management information systems; mathematics; mechanical drafting and CAD/CADD; music; music performance; office management; philosophy; photography; political science and government; premedical studies; psychology; radio and television broadcasting technology; radiologic technology/science; real estate; registered nursing/registered nurse; religious studies; sales, distribution, and marketing operations; secondary education; selling skills and sales; sign language interpretation and translation; social sciences; sociology; Spanish; speech communication and rhetoric; surgical technology; surveying technology; teacher assistant/aide; theater design and technology; tourism and travel services management; veterinary/animal health technology; web page, digital/multimedia and information resources design; welding technology.

Academics *Calendar:* semesters. *Degree:* certificates and associate. *Special study options:* academic remediation for entering students, adult/continuing education programs, advanced placement credit, cooperative education, distance learning, double majors, English as a second language, external degree program, honors programs, independent study, internships, part-time degree program, services for LD students, study abroad, summer session for credit. *ROTC:* Army (c), Air Force (c).

Library Lansing Community College Library with 340,420 titles, 164 serial subscriptions, 7,455 audiovisual materials, an OPAC, a Web page.

Student Life *Housing:* college housing not available. *Activities and Organizations:* drama/theater group, student-run newspaper, choral group, American Marketing Association, Phi Theta Kappa, Future Teachers' Club, Health Career Related Clubs (Dental Hygiene, Nurses), Gay-Straight Alliance, national fraternities, national sororities. *Campus security:* 24-hour emergency response devices and patrols, student patrols, late-night transport/escort service. *Student services:* personal/psychological counseling, women's center.

Athletics Member NJCAA. *Intercollegiate sports:* baseball M(s), basketball M(s)/W(s), cross-country running M(s)/W(s), softball W(s), track and field M/W, volleyball W(s).

Costs (2012–13) *Tuition:* area resident $2430 full-time, $81 per credit hour part-time; state resident $4860 full-time, $162 per credit hour part-time; non-resident $7290 full-time, $243 per credit hour part-time. *Required fees:* $200 full-time, $5 per credit hour part-time, $25 per term part-time. *Room and board:* $7100. *Payment plan:* installment. *Waivers:* senior citizens and employees or children of employees.

Financial Aid Of all full-time matriculated undergraduates who enrolled in 2011, 125 Federal Work-Study jobs (averaging $2636). 122 state and other part-time jobs (averaging $2563).

Applying *Options:* electronic application, early admission, deferred entrance. *Required for some:* essay or personal statement, high school transcript, 2 letters of recommendation, interview, Special requirements for health, aviation, music, police academy, and fire academy program admissions. *Application deadlines:* 8/7 (freshmen), 8/7 (transfers).

Freshman Application Contact Ms. Tammy Grossbauer, Director of Admissions/Registrar, Lansing Community College, 1121 - Enrollment Services, PO BOX 40010, Lansing, MI 48901. *Phone:* 517-483-1200. *Toll-free phone:* 800-644-4LCC. *Fax:* 517-483-1170. *E-mail:* grossbt@lcc.edu. *Website:* http://www.lcc.edu/.

Macomb Community College
Warren, Michigan

- **District-supported** 2-year, founded 1954, part of Michigan Public Community College System
- **Suburban** 384-acre campus with easy access to Detroit
- **Endowment** $16.4 million
- **Coed,** 23,729 undergraduate students, 32% full-time, 53% women, 47% men

Undergraduates 7,624 full-time, 16,105 part-time. Students come from 4 states and territories; 11% Black or African American, non-Hispanic/Latino; 2% Hispanic/Latino; 3% Asian, non-Hispanic/Latino; 0.1% Native Hawaiian or other Pacific Islander, non-Hispanic/Latino; 0.6% American Indian or Alaska Native, non-Hispanic/Latino; 1% Two or more races, non-Hispanic/Latino; 9% Race/ethnicity unknown; 1% international. *Retention:* 56% of full-time freshmen returned.

Freshmen *Admission:* 1,529 enrolled.

Faculty *Total:* 1,102, 21% full-time, 10% with terminal degrees. *Student/faculty ratio:* 27:1.

Majors Accounting; administrative assistant and secretarial science; agriculture; architectural drafting and CAD/CADD; automobile/automotive mechanics technology; automotive engineering technology; biology/biological sciences; business administration and management; business automation/technology/data entry; business/commerce; cabinetmaking and millwork; chemistry; child-care and support services management; civil engineering technology; commercial and advertising art; computer programming; computer programming (specific applications); construction engineering technology; criminal justice/law enforcement administration; criminal justice/police science; culinary arts; drafting and design technology; drafting/design engineering technologies related; electrical, electronic and communications engineering technology; electrical/electronics equipment installation and repair; electromechanical technology; emergency medical technology (EMT paramedic); energy management and systems technology; engineering related; finance; fire prevention and safety technology; forensic science and technology; general studies; graphic and printing equipment operation/production; heating, air conditioning, ventilation and refrigeration maintenance technology; heating, ventilation, air conditioning and refrigeration engineering technology; industrial mechanics and maintenance technology; industrial technology; international/global studies; legal assistant/paralegal; legal studies; liberal arts and sciences/liberal studies; machine tool technology; manufacturing engineering technology; marketing/marketing management; mathematics; mechanical drafting and CAD/CADD; mechanical engineering/mechanical technology; mechanic and repair technologies related; medical/clinical assistant; mental health counseling; metallurgical technology; music performance; occupational therapist assistant; operations management; physical therapy technology; plastics and polymer engineering technology; plumbing technology; pre-engineering; quality control and safety technologies related; quality control technology; registered nursing/registered nurse; respiratory care therapy; robotics technology; sheet metal technology; social psychology; speech communication and rhetoric; surgical technology; surveying technology; tool and die technology; veterinary/animal health technology; welding technology.

Academics *Calendar:* semesters. *Degree:* certificates and associate. *Special study options:* academic remediation for entering students, adult/continuing education programs, advanced placement credit, cooperative education, English as a second language, honors programs, internships, off-campus study, part-time degree program, services for LD students, student-designed majors, summer session for credit.

Library Library of South Campus, Library of Center Campus with 159,226 titles, 4,240 serial subscriptions, an OPAC.

Student Life *Housing:* college housing not available. *Activities and Organizations:* drama/theater group, Phi Beta Kappa, Adventure Unlimited, Alpha Rho Rho, SADD. *Campus security:* 24-hour emergency response devices and patrols, late-night transport/escort service, security phones in parking lots, surveillance cameras. *Student services:* health clinic, personal/psychological counseling.

Athletics Member NJCAA. *Intercollegiate sports:* baseball M(s), basketball M(s), cross-country running M(s)/W(s), soccer M(s), softball W(s), track and field M(s)/W(s), volleyball W(s). *Intramural sports:* baseball M, basketball M, bowling M/W, cross-country running M/W, football M/W, skiing (cross-country) M/W, skiing (downhill) M/W, volleyball M/W.

Costs (2012–13) *Tuition:* area resident $2666 full-time, $86 per credit hour part-time; state resident $4061 full-time, $131 per credit hour part-time; nonresident $5270 full-time, $170 per credit hour part-time. Full-time tuition and fees vary according to course load. Part-time tuition and fees vary according to course load. *Required fees:* $100 full-time, $50 per term part-time. *Waivers:* senior citizens and employees or children of employees.

Applying *Options:* early admission, deferred entrance. *Application deadlines:* rolling (freshmen), rolling (transfers).

Freshman Application Contact Mr. Brian Bouwman, Coordinator of Admissions and Transfer Credit, Macomb Community College, G312, 14500 East 12 Mile Road, Warren, MI 48088-3896. *Phone:* 586-445-7246. *Toll-free phone:* 866-MACOMB1. *Fax:* 586-445-7140. *E-mail:* stevensr@macomb.edu. *Website:* http://www.macomb.edu/.

Mid Michigan Community College

Harrison, Michigan

- **State and locally supported** 2-year, founded 1965, part of Michigan Department of Education
- **Rural** 560-acre campus
- **Coed**

Undergraduates 2,193 full-time, 2,692 part-time. 0.5% are from out of state; 3% Black or African American, non-Hispanic/Latino; 3% Hispanic/Latino; 0.2% Asian, non-Hispanic/Latino; 0.4% Native Hawaiian or other Pacific Islander, non-Hispanic/Latino; 2% American Indian or Alaska Native, non-Hispanic/Latino; 0.1% Two or more races, non-Hispanic/Latino; 7% Race/ethnicity unknown; 0.6% international; 4% transferred in. *Retention:* 43% of full-time freshmen returned.

Faculty *Student/faculty ratio:* 26:1.

Academics *Calendar:* semesters. *Degree:* certificates and associate. *Special study options:* academic remediation for entering students, adult/continuing education programs, advanced placement credit, cooperative education, distance learning, honors programs, independent study, internships, part-time degree program, services for LD students, summer session for credit.

Student Life *Campus security:* 24-hour emergency response devices.

Costs (2012–13) *Tuition:* area resident $2600 full-time, $93 per contact hour part-time; state resident $4748 full-time, $182 per contact hour part-time; nonresident $8396 full-time, $334 per contact hour part-time. Full-time tuition and fees vary according to course load. Part-time tuition and fees vary according to course load. *Required fees:* $10 per contact hour part-time, $45 per term part-time.

Financial Aid Of all full-time matriculated undergraduates who enrolled in 2011, 50 Federal Work-Study jobs (averaging $3600). 50 state and other part-time jobs (averaging $3600).

Applying *Options:* electronic application, early admission. *Recommended:* high school transcript.

Freshman Application Contact Jennifer Casebeer, Admissions Specialist, Mid Michigan Community College, 1375 South Clare Avenue, Harrison, MI 48625-9447. *Phone:* 989-386-6661. *E-mail:* apply@midmich.edu. *Website:* http://www.midmich.edu/.

Monroe County Community College

Monroe, Michigan

- **County-supported** 2-year, founded 1964, part of Michigan Department of Education
- **Small-town** 150-acre campus with easy access to Detroit, Toledo
- **Coed**

Undergraduates Students come from 3 other countries; 4% are from out of state.

Freshmen *Admission:* 1,700 applied, 1,698 admitted. *Average high school GPA:* 2.5.

Faculty *Total:* 196, 28% full-time.

Majors Accounting; administrative assistant and secretarial science; architectural engineering technology; art; biology/biological sciences; business administration and management; child development; clinical laboratory science/medical technology; computer and information sciences related; computer engineering technology; computer graphics; computer programming (specific applications); criminal justice/police science; criminal justice/safety; culinary arts; data processing and data processing technology; drafting and design technology; electrical, electronic and communications engineering technology; elementary education; English; finance; funeral service and mortuary science; industrial technology; information technology; journalism; legal administrative assistant/secretary; liberal arts and sciences/liberal studies; marketing/marketing management; mass communication/media; mathematics; medical administrative assistant and medical secretary; physical therapy; pre-engineering; psychology; registered nursing/registered nurse; respiratory care therapy; rhetoric and composition; social work; web/multimedia management and webmaster; web page, digital/multimedia and information resources design; welding technology; word processing.

Academics *Calendar:* semesters. *Degree:* certificates and associate. *Special study options:* academic remediation for entering students, advanced placement credit, distance learning, independent study, part-time degree program, services for LD students, summer session for credit.

Library Campbell Learning Resource Center with 47,352 titles, 321 serial subscriptions, an OPAC.

Student Life *Housing:* college housing not available. *Activities and Organizations:* drama/theater group, student-run newspaper, choral group, student government, Society of Auto Engineers, Oasis, Nursing Students Organization. *Campus security:* police patrols during open hours.

Athletics *Intramural sports:* soccer M/W, volleyball M/W.

Standardized Tests *Required:* ACT, ACT COMPASS (for admission). *Required for some:* ACT (for admission). *Recommended:* ACT (for admission).

Costs (2013–14) *Tuition:* area resident $2316 full-time; state resident $3726 full-time; nonresident $4110 full-time. *Payment plan:* installment. *Waivers:* senior citizens and employees or children of employees.

Applying *Options:* early admission, deferred entrance. *Required:* high school transcript, Baseline cut scores on ACT or COMPASS. *Application deadline:* rolling (transfers). *Notification:* continuous (freshmen), continuous (transfers).

Freshman Application Contact Mr. Mark V. Hall, Director of Admissions and Guidance Services, Monroe County Community College, 1555 South Raisinville Road, Monroe, MI 48161. *Phone:* 734-384-4261. *Toll-free phone:* 877-YES-MCCC. *Fax:* 734-242-9711. *E-mail:* mhall@monroeccc.edu. *Website:* http://www.monroeccc.edu/.

Montcalm Community College

Sidney, Michigan

- **State and locally supported** 2-year, founded 1965, part of Michigan Department of Education
- **Rural** 240-acre campus with easy access to Grand Rapids
- **Endowment** $4.7 million
- **Coed,** 2,011 undergraduate students, 34% full-time, 65% women, 35% men

Undergraduates 680 full-time, 1,331 part-time. 0.2% Black or African American, non-Hispanic/Latino; 2% Hispanic/Latino; 0.2% Asian, non-Hispanic/Latino; 0.2% American Indian or Alaska Native, non-Hispanic/Latino; 1% Two or more races, non-Hispanic/Latino; 28% Race/ethnicity unknown; 19% transferred in.
Freshmen *Admission:* 244 applied, 244 admitted, 244 enrolled.
Faculty *Total:* 114, 25% full-time, 7% with terminal degrees.
Majors Accounting; administrative assistant and secretarial science; automobile/automotive mechanics technology; business administration and management; child-care and support services management; child-care provision; computer installation and repair technology; corrections; cosmetology; criminal justice/law enforcement administration; data processing and data processing technology; drafting and design technology; electrical, electronic and communications engineering technology; emergency medical technology (EMT paramedic); entrepreneurship; general studies; industrial engineering; industrial technology; liberal arts and sciences/liberal studies; medical administrative assistant and medical secretary; registered nursing/registered nurse; teacher assistant/aide; welding technology.
Academics *Calendar:* semesters. *Degree:* certificates and associate. *Special study options:* academic remediation for entering students, adult/continuing education programs, advanced placement credit, cooperative education, distance learning, double majors, independent study, internships, off-campus study, part-time degree program, services for LD students, study abroad, summer session for credit.
Library Montcalm Community College Library with 29,848 titles, 3,670 serial subscriptions, an OPAC, a Web page.
Student Life *Housing:* college housing not available. *Activities and Organizations:* drama/theater group, choral group, Nursing Club, Native American Club, Phi Theta Kappa, Business Club, Judo Club. *Student services:* personal/psychological counseling.
Athletics *Intramural sports:* volleyball M/W.
Costs (2013–14) *Tuition:* $87 per credit hour part-time; state resident $164 per credit hour part-time; nonresident $244 per credit hour part-time. *Payment plan:* installment. *Waivers:* senior citizens and employees or children of employees.
Financial Aid *Average indebtedness upon graduation:* $2600.
Applying *Options:* electronic application, early admission, deferred entrance. *Recommended:* high school transcript. *Application deadlines:* rolling (freshmen), rolling (transfers). *Notification:* continuous (freshmen), continuous (transfers).
Freshman Application Contact Ms. Debra Alexander, Associate Dean of Student Services, Montcalm Community College, 2800 College Drive, SW, Sidney, MI 48885. *Phone:* 989-328-1276. *Toll-free phone:* 877-328-2111. *E-mail:* admissions@montcalm.edu.
Website: http://www.montcalm.edu/.

Mott Community College

Flint, Michigan

- **District-supported** 2-year, founded 1923, part of Michigan Workforce Programs/Postsecondary Services/Community College Services
- **Urban** 32-acre campus with easy access to Detroit
- **Endowment** $35.3 million
- **Coed,** 9,968 undergraduate students, 32% full-time, 59% women, 41% men

Undergraduates 3,140 full-time, 6,828 part-time. Students come from 15 states and territories; 19% Black or African American, non-Hispanic/Latino; 4% Hispanic/Latino; 0.4% Asian, non-Hispanic/Latino; 0.1% Native Hawaiian or other Pacific Islander, non-Hispanic/Latino; 1% American Indian or Alaska Native, non-Hispanic/Latino; 2% Two or more races, non-Hispanic/Latino; 13% Race/ethnicity unknown; 0.2% international; 2% transferred in.
Freshmen *Admission:* 572 enrolled.
Faculty *Total:* 517, 28% full-time, 11% with terminal degrees. *Student/faculty ratio:* 20:1.
Majors Accounting technology and bookkeeping; administrative assistant and secretarial science; architectural engineering technology; automobile/automotive mechanics technology; baking and pastry arts; biology/biological sciences; business administration and management; business/commerce; child-care provision; cinematography and film/video production; communications technology; community health services counseling; computer programming;

computer programming (specific applications); computer systems networking and telecommunications; criminal justice/police science; culinary arts; dental assisting; dental hygiene; drafting and design technology; early childhood education; electrical, electronic and communications engineering technology; emergency medical technology (EMT paramedic); engineering technologies and engineering related; entrepreneurship; fire prevention and safety technology; food service systems administration; general studies; graphic design; health information/medical records technology; heating, ventilation, air conditioning and refrigeration engineering technology; histologic technician; liberal arts and sciences/liberal studies; manufacturing engineering technology; marketing/marketing management; mechanical engineering/mechanical technology; medical informatics; medical radiologic technology; occupational therapist assistant; photography; physical therapy technology; precision production related; registered nursing/registered nurse; respiratory care therapy; salon/beauty salon management; sign language interpretation and translation; visual and performing arts; web page, digital/multimedia and information resources design.
Academics *Calendar:* semesters. *Degree:* certificates and associate. *Special study options:* academic remediation for entering students, accelerated degree program, adult/continuing education programs, advanced placement credit, cooperative education, distance learning, double majors, English as a second language, honors programs, independent study, internships, part-time degree program, services for LD students, summer session for credit.
Library Charles Stewart Mott Library with 66,741 titles, 165 serial subscriptions, 89 audiovisual materials, an OPAC, a Web page.
Student Life *Housing:* college housing not available. *Activities and Organizations:* student-run newspaper, choral group, Otaku Club, Gay, Straight Alliance (GSA), Student Veteran's Services (SVA), American Sign Language (ASL), Dental Hygiene Club. *Campus security:* 24-hour emergency response devices and patrols, student patrols, late-night transport/escort service. *Student services:* health clinic, personal/psychological counseling.
Athletics Member NJCAA. *Intercollegiate sports:* baseball M(s), basketball M(s)/W(s), cross-country running M(s)/W(s), golf M(s), softball W(s), volleyball W(s). *Intramural sports:* cheerleading W(c).
Costs (2013–14) *Tuition:* area resident $2813 full-time, $117 per contact hour part-time; state resident $4102 full-time, $171 per contact hour part-time; nonresident $5832 full-time, $243 per contact hour part-time. Full-time tuition and fees vary according to course load. Part-time tuition and fees vary according to course load. *Required fees:* $396 full-time, $7 per contact hour part-time, $117 per term part-time. *Payment plan:* installment. *Waivers:* senior citizens and employees or children of employees.
Financial Aid Of all full-time matriculated undergraduates who enrolled in 2011, 16,668 applied for aid, 15,858 were judged to have need, 810 had their need fully met. 7,449 Federal Work-Study jobs (averaging $6303). In 2011, 95 non-need-based awards were made. *Average percent of need met:* 79%. *Average financial aid package:* $21,292. *Average need-based loan:* $3019. *Average need-based gift aid:* $3471. *Average non-need-based aid:* $2356.
Applying *Options:* electronic application, early admission, deferred entrance. *Required:* high school transcript. *Application deadline:* 8/31 (freshmen). *Notification:* continuous (transfers).
Freshman Application Contact Ms. Regina Broomfield, Supervisor of Admissions Operations, Mott Community College, 1401 East Court Street, Flint, MI 48503. *Phone:* 810-762-0358. *Toll-free phone:* 800-852-8614. *Fax:* 810-232-9442. *E-mail:* regina.broomfield@mcc.edu.
Website: http://www.mcc.edu/.

Muskegon Community College

Muskegon, Michigan

- **State and locally supported** 2-year, founded 1926, part of Michigan Department of Education
- **Small-town** 112-acre campus with easy access to Grand Rapids
- **Coed**

Undergraduates 1,886 full-time, 3,693 part-time. 9% Black or African American, non-Hispanic/Latino; 4% Hispanic/Latino; 0.7% Asian, non-Hispanic/Latino; 0.1% Native Hawaiian or other Pacific Islander, non-Hispanic/Latino; 1% American Indian or Alaska Native, non-Hispanic/Latino; 2% Two or more races, non-Hispanic/Latino; 19% Race/ethnicity unknown; 0.1% international.
Faculty *Student/faculty ratio:* 20:1.
Academics *Calendar:* semesters. *Degree:* associate. *Special study options:* academic remediation for entering students, adult/continuing education programs, cooperative education, honors programs, part-time degree program, student-designed majors, summer session for credit.
Student Life *Campus security:* 24-hour emergency response devices, on-campus security officer.
Athletics Member NJCAA.
Costs (2012–13) *Tuition:* area resident $1980 full-time, $86 per credit hour part-time; state resident $3432 full-time, $153 per credit hour part-time; non-

resident $4704 full-time, $210 per credit hour part-time. *Required fees:* $10 per contact hour part-time.

Financial Aid Of all full-time matriculated undergraduates who enrolled in 2011, 250 Federal Work-Study jobs (averaging $2500). 50 state and other part-time jobs (averaging $2500).

Applying *Options:* electronic application, early admission, deferred entrance. *Required:* high school transcript.

Freshman Application Contact Ms. Darlene Peklar, Enrollment Generalist, Muskegon Community College, 221 South Quarterline Road, Muskegon, MI 49442-1493. *Phone:* 231-777-0366. *Toll-free phone:* 866-711-4622. *E-mail:* Dalene.Peklar@muskegoncc.edu. *Website:* http://www.muskegoncc.edu/.

North Central Michigan College

Petoskey, Michigan

Director of Admissions Ms. Julieanne Tobin, Director of Enrollment Management, North Central Michigan College, 1515 Howard Street, Petoskey, MI 49770-8717. *Phone:* 231-439-6511. *Toll-free phone:* 888-298-6605. *E-mail:* jtobin@ncmich.edu. *Website:* http://www.ncmich.edu/.

Northwestern Michigan College

Traverse City, Michigan

Freshman Application Contact Mr. James Bensley, Coordinator of Admissions, Northwestern Michigan College, 1701 East Front Street, Traverse City, MI 49686-3061. *Phone:* 231-995-1034. *Toll-free phone:* 800-748-0566. *Fax:* 616-955-1339. *E-mail:* welcome@nmc.edu. *Website:* http://www.nmc.edu/.

Oakland Community College

Bloomfield Hills, Michigan

- **State and locally supported** 2-year, founded 1964
- **Suburban** 540-acre campus with easy access to Detroit
- **Endowment** $1.2 million
- **Coed,** 27,296 undergraduate students, 32% full-time, 57% women, 43% men

Undergraduates 8,662 full-time, 18,634 part-time. Students come from 11 states and territories; 47 other countries; 0.1% are from out of state; 29% Black or African American, non-Hispanic/Latino; 3% Hispanic/Latino; 2% Asian, non-Hispanic/Latino; 0.1% Native Hawaiian or other Pacific Islander, non-Hispanic/Latino; 0.6% American Indian or Alaska Native, non-Hispanic/Latino; 2% Two or more races, non-Hispanic/Latino; 3% Race/ethnicity unknown; 4% international. *Retention:* 44% of full-time freshmen returned.

Freshmen *Admission:* 10,336 applied, 10,336 admitted, 2,489 enrolled.

Faculty *Total:* 986, 25% full-time. *Student/faculty ratio:* 30:1.

Majors Accounting and business/management; accounting technology and bookkeeping; adult development and aging; architectural engineering technology; art; biotechnology; business administration and management; business automation/technology/data entry; carpentry; ceramic arts and ceramics; childcare and support services management; commercial and advertising art; community health services counseling; computer and information sciences and support services related; computer and information systems security; computer hardware technology; computer/information technology services administration related; computer programming; computer systems analysis; computer technology/computer systems technology; construction management; corrections; cosmetology; court reporting; criminalistics and criminal science; criminal justice/law enforcement administration; criminal justice/police science; culinary arts; data processing and data processing technology; dental hygiene; diagnostic medical sonography and ultrasound technology; drafting and design technology; dramatic/theater arts and stagecraft related; electrical, electronic and communications engineering technology; electrician; electromechanical technology; electroneurodiagnostic/electroencephalographic technology; emergency medical technology (EMT paramedic); engineering; entrepreneurship; fashion merchandising; film/cinema/video studies; fire science/firefighting; general studies; graphic design; health/health-care administration; health professions related; heating, ventilation, air conditioning and refrigeration engineering technology; histologic technician; histologic technology/histotechnologist; hotel/motel administration; illustration; industrial production technologies related; industrial technology; interior design; international business/trade/commerce; international/global studies; kinesiology and exercise science; landscaping and groundskeeping; legal assistant/paralegal; liberal arts and sciences and humanities related; liberal arts and sciences/liberal studies; library and archives assisting; machine tool technology; management information systems; manufacturing engineering technology; massage therapy; mechanical drafting and CAD/CADD; mechanics and repair; medical/clinical assistant; medical radiologic technology; medical transcription; music perfor-

mance; music theory and composition; nanotechnology; nuclear medical technology; occupational therapist assistant; office management; pharmacy technician; photographic and film/video technology; photography; physical therapy technology; pipefitting and sprinkler fitting; precision metal working related; radio and television broadcasting technology; registered nursing/registered nurse; respiratory care therapy; restaurant/food services management; retail management; robotics technology; salon/beauty salon management; science technologies related; sign language interpretation and translation; surgical technology; tool and die technology; veterinary/animal health technology; voice and opera; welding technology.

Academics *Calendar:* semesters. *Degree:* certificates and associate. *Special study options:* academic remediation for entering students, adult/continuing education programs, advanced placement credit, cooperative education, distance learning, English as a second language, internships, off-campus study, part-time degree program, services for LD students, study abroad, summer session for credit.

Library Main Library plus 5 others with 263,563 titles, 1,159 serial subscriptions, 8,835 audiovisual materials, an OPAC, a Web page.

Student Life *Housing:* college housing not available. *Activities and Organizations:* drama/theater group, choral group, Phi Theta Kappa, Gamers Guild, BELIEVERS, Criminal Justice Student Organization, Student Government. *Campus security:* 24-hour emergency response devices, late-night transport/escort service. *Student services:* personal/psychological counseling, women's center.

Athletics Member NJCAA. *Intercollegiate sports:* basketball M(s)/W(s), cross-country running M(s)/W(s), golf M(s), softball W(s), volleyball W(s).

Costs (2012–13) *Tuition:* area resident $2142 full-time, $71 per credit hour part-time; state resident $3760 full-time, $125 per credit hour part-time; nonresident $5275 full-time, $176 per credit hour part-time. Full-time tuition and fees vary according to course load and reciprocity agreements. Part-time tuition and fees vary according to course load and reciprocity agreements. *Required fees:* $70 full-time, $35 per term part-time. *Waivers:* senior citizens and employees or children of employees.

Financial Aid Of all full-time matriculated undergraduates who enrolled in 2012, 3,703 applied for aid, 3,227 were judged to have need, 2 had their need fully met. 204 Federal Work-Study jobs (averaging $4186). In 2012, 43 non-need-based awards were made. *Average percent of need met:* 42%. *Average financial aid package:* $4609. *Average need-based loan:* $732. *Average need-based gift aid:* $4864. *Average non-need-based aid:* $1480.

Applying *Options:* electronic application, deferred entrance. *Recommended:* high school transcript, interview. *Application deadlines:* rolling (freshmen), rolling (transfers). *Notification:* continuous (freshmen), continuous (transfers).

Freshman Application Contact Stephan M. Linden, Registrar, Oakland Community College, 2480 Opdyke Road, Bloomfield Hills, MI 48304-2266. *Phone:* 248-341-2192. *Fax:* 248-341-2099. *E-mail:* smlinden@oaklandcc.edu. *Website:* http://www.oaklandcc.edu/.

Saginaw Chippewa Tribal College

Mount Pleasant, Michigan

Freshman Application Contact Ms. Tracy Reed, Admissions Officer/Registrar/Financial Aid, Saginaw Chippewa Tribal College, 2274 Enterprise Drive, Mount Pleasant, MI 48858. *Phone:* 989-775-4123. *Fax:* 989-775-4528. *E-mail:* treed@sagchip.org. *Website:* http://www.sagchip.edu/.

St. Clair County Community College

Port Huron, Michigan

- **State and locally supported** 2-year, founded 1923, part of Michigan Department of Education
- **Small-town** 25-acre campus with easy access to Detroit
- **Coed,** 4,547 undergraduate students, 41% full-time, 59% women, 41% men

Undergraduates 1,853 full-time, 2,694 part-time. 4% Black or African American, non-Hispanic/Latino; 3% Hispanic/Latino; 0.5% Asian, non-Hispanic/Latino; 0.1% Native Hawaiian or other Pacific Islander, non-Hispanic/Latino; 1% American Indian or Alaska Native, non-Hispanic/Latino; 0.8% Two or more races, non-Hispanic/Latino; 3% Race/ethnicity unknown; 0.3% international; 21% transferred in. *Retention:* 60% of full-time freshmen returned.

Freshmen *Admission:* 841 enrolled.

Faculty *Total:* 251, 29% full-time. *Student/faculty ratio:* 20:1.

Majors Accounting technology and bookkeeping; architectural engineering technology; business/commerce; commercial and advertising art; computer programming; criminal justice/police science; data processing and data processing technology; electrical, electronic and communications engineering technology; energy management and systems technology; engineering; executive assistant/executive secretary; health information/medical records technology; industrial production technologies related; journalism; kindergarten/preschool education; landscaping and groundskeeping; liberal arts and sciences/liberal studies; marketing/marketing management; massage therapy; mechanical drafting and CAD/CADD; medical administrative assistant and medical secretary; medical/clinical assistant; office management; radio and television broadcasting technology; robotics technology; teacher assistant/aide; transportation and materials moving related; web/multimedia management and webmaster; welding technology.

Academics *Calendar:* semesters. *Degree:* certificates and associate. *Special study options:* academic remediation for entering students, adult/continuing education programs, advanced placement credit, cooperative education, distance learning, honors programs, independent study, part-time degree program, summer session for credit.

Library Library plus 1 other with an OPAC, a Web page.

Student Life *Housing:* college housing not available. *Activities and Organizations:* drama/theater group, student-run newspaper, radio station, Phi Theta Kappa, Zombie Defense Council, Marketing and Management Club, Gay-Straight Alliance, Criminal Justice Club. *Campus security:* 24-hour emergency response devices, late-night transport/escort service, patrols by security until 10 pm. *Student services:* personal/psychological counseling.

Athletics Member NJCAA. *Intercollegiate sports:* baseball M(s), basketball M(s)/W(s), golf M, softball W(s), volleyball W(s).

Costs (2012–13) *Tuition:* area resident $2835 full-time, $95 per contact hour part-time; state resident $5520 full-time, $184 per contact hour part-time; non-resident $8040 full-time, $268 per contact hour part-time. Full-time tuition and fees vary according to course load and location. Part-time tuition and fees vary according to course load and location. *Required fees:* $418 full-time, $10 per contact hour part-time. *Payment plan:* deferred payment. *Waivers:* senior citizens and employees or children of employees.

Applying *Options:* electronic application, early admission. *Required:* high school transcript. *Application deadlines:* rolling (freshmen), rolling (transfers).

Freshman Application Contact St. Clair County Community College, 323 Erie Street, PO Box 5015, Port Huron, MI 48061-5015. *Phone:* 810-989-5501. *Toll-free phone:* 800-553-2427.

Website: http://www.sc4.edu/.

Schoolcraft College
Livonia, Michigan

- **District-supported** 2-year, founded 1961, part of Michigan Department of Education
- **Suburban** 183-acre campus with easy access to Detroit
- **Coed,** 12,522 undergraduate students, 37% full-time, 56% women, 44% men

Undergraduates 4,654 full-time, 7,868 part-time. 15% Black or African American, non-Hispanic/Latino; 3% Hispanic/Latino; 3% Asian, non-Hispanic/Latino; 0.2% Native Hawaiian or other Pacific Islander, non-Hispanic/Latino; 0.8% American Indian or Alaska Native, non-Hispanic/Latino; 2% Two or more races, non-Hispanic/Latino; 9% Race/ethnicity unknown; 1% international. *Retention:* 57% of full-time freshmen returned.

Freshmen *Admission:* 1,766 enrolled.

Faculty *Total:* 514, 18% full-time. *Student/faculty ratio:* 29:1.

Majors Accounting; accounting technology and bookkeeping; administrative assistant and secretarial science; baking and pastry arts; biomedical technology; business administration and management; business automation/technology/data entry; business/commerce; child development; commercial and advertising art; computer graphics; computer programming; computer programming (specific applications); computer systems networking and telecommunications; computer technology/computer systems technology; criminal justice/police science; culinary arts; data processing and data processing technology; drafting and design technology; education; electrical, electronic and communications engineering technology; electrical/electronics equipment installation and repair; electromechanical technology; emergency medical technology (EMT paramedic); engineering; entrepreneurship; environmental engineering technology; executive assistant/executive secretary; fire science/firefighting; general studies; health information/medical records technology; health services/allied health/health sciences; homeland security, law enforcement, firefighting and protective services related; industrial technology; liberal arts and sciences/liberal studies; licensed practical/vocational nurse training; manufacturing engineering technology; marketing/marketing management; massage therapy; mechanical engineering/mechanical technology; medical insurance/medical billing; medical office assistant; medical transcription; metallurgical technology; music teacher education; nursing assistant/aide and patient care assistant/aide; phlebotomy technology; physical sciences related; pre-pharmacy studies; radio and television broadcasting technology; recording arts technology; registered nursing/registered nurse; robotics technology; salon/beauty salon management; sculpture; small business administration; web page, digital/multimedia and information resources design; welding technology.

Academics *Calendar:* semesters. *Degree:* certificates and associate. *Special study options:* academic remediation for entering students, adult/continuing education programs, advanced placement credit, distance learning, English as a second language, honors programs, internships, part-time degree program, services for LD students, study abroad, summer session for credit.

Library Bradner Library with an OPAC.

Student Life *Housing:* college housing not available. *Activities and Organizations:* drama/theater group, student-run newspaper, choral group, Student Activities Board, Ski Club, Student newspaper, Music Club, Phi Theta Kappa, national fraternities. *Campus security:* 24-hour emergency response devices and patrols, late-night transport/escort service. *Student services:* health clinic, personal/psychological counseling, women's center, legal services.

Athletics Member NJCAA. *Intercollegiate sports:* basketball M(s)/W(s), cross-country running W(s), golf M(s)/W(s), soccer M(s)/W(s), volleyball W(s).

Financial Aid Of all full-time matriculated undergraduates who enrolled in 2011, 42 Federal Work-Study jobs (averaging $1722).

Applying *Options:* early admission, deferred entrance. *Required for some:* high school transcript. *Recommended:* high school transcript. *Application deadlines:* rolling (freshmen), rolling (transfers).

Freshman Application Contact Ms. Cheryl Hagen, Dean of Student Services, Schoolcraft College, 18600 Haggerty Road, Livonia, MI 48152-2696. *Phone:* 734-462-4426. *Fax:* 734-462-4553. *E-mail:* admissions@schoolcraft.edu. *Website:* http://www.schoolcraft.edu/.

Southwestern Michigan College
Dowagiac, Michigan

- **State and locally supported** 2-year, founded 1964
- **Rural** 240-acre campus
- **Coed,** 2,639 undergraduate students, 50% full-time, 61% women, 39% men

Undergraduates 1,312 full-time, 1,327 part-time. Students come from 9 states and territories; 12 other countries; 11% are from out of state; 10% Black or African American, non-Hispanic/Latino; 3% Hispanic/Latino; 0.8% Asian, non-Hispanic/Latino; 1% American Indian or Alaska Native, non-Hispanic/Latino; 4% Two or more races, non-Hispanic/Latino; 4% Race/ethnicity unknown; 0.6% international; 35% transferred in; 10% live on campus. *Retention:* 52% of full-time freshmen returned.

Freshmen *Admission:* 2,029 applied, 2,006 admitted, 629 enrolled.

Faculty *Total:* 171, 30% full-time, 19% with terminal degrees. *Student/faculty ratio:* 19:1.

Majors Accounting technology and bookkeeping; administrative assistant and secretarial science; automation engineer technology; automobile/automotive mechanics technology; business administration and management; carpentry; computer and information sciences and support services related; computer programming; computer support specialist; computer systems networking and telecommunications; drafting and design technology; early childhood education; electrical, electronic and communications engineering technology; emergency medical technology (EMT paramedic); engineering technology; executive assistant/executive secretary; fire science/firefighting; general studies; graphic design; health information/medical records technology; hotel/motel administration; industrial mechanics and maintenance technology; industrial production technologies related; liberal arts and sciences/liberal studies; machine tool technology; medical/clinical assistant; meeting and event planning; prenursing studies; professional, technical, business, and scientific writing; registered nursing/registered nurse; social work; teacher assistant/aide; theater design and technology; tool and die technology; welding technology.

Academics *Calendar:* semesters. *Degree:* certificates and associate. *Special study options:* academic remediation for entering students, accelerated degree program, adult/continuing education programs, advanced placement credit, cooperative education, distance learning, double majors, English as a second language, independent study, internships, part-time degree program, services for LD students, summer session for credit.

Library Fred L. Mathews Library with 29,157 titles, 19,757 serial subscriptions, 3,001 audiovisual materials, an OPAC, a Web page.

Student Life *Housing Options:* coed. Campus housing is university owned. *Activities and Organizations:* drama/theater group, choral group, Dionysus Drama Club, Rock Climbing Club, SMC Community of Veterans, Alpha Kappa Omega, SMC Green Club. *Campus security:* 24-hour emergency response devices and patrols, controlled dormitory access, day and evening police patrols.

Athletics *Intramural sports:* basketball M/W, football M/W, golf M/W, racquetball M/W, rock climbing M/W, soccer M/W, softball M/W, tennis M/W, volleyball M/W.

Costs (2012–13) *Tuition:* area resident $2711 full-time, $104 per contact hour part-time; state resident $3504 full-time, $135 per contact hour part-time; non-resident $3816 full-time, $147 per contact hour part-time. *Required fees:* $1034 full-time, $40 per contact hour part-time. *Room and board:* $7715;

room only: $5465. *Payment plan:* installment. *Waivers:* employees or children of employees.

Financial Aid Of all full-time matriculated undergraduates who enrolled in 2011, 125 Federal Work-Study jobs (averaging $1000). 75 state and other part-time jobs (averaging $1000).

Applying *Options:* electronic application, deferred entrance. *Required:* high school transcript. *Required for some:* interview. *Application deadlines:* rolling (freshmen), rolling (transfers). *Notification:* continuous (freshmen), continuous (transfers).

Freshman Application Contact Ms. Angela Palsak, Dean of Students, Southwestern Michigan College, Dowagiac, MI 49047. *Phone:* 269-782-1000 Ext. 1310. *Toll-free phone:* 800-456-8675. *Fax:* 269-782-1331. *E-mail:* apalsak@swmich.edu.
Website: http://www.swmich.edu/.

Washtenaw Community College
Ann Arbor, Michigan

Freshman Application Contact Washtenaw Community College, 4800 East Huron River Drive, PO Box D-1, Ann Arbor, MI 48106. *Phone:* 734-973-3315.
Website: http://www.wccnet.edu/.

Wayne County Community College District
Detroit, Michigan

Freshman Application Contact Office of Enrollment Management and Student Services, Wayne County Community College District, 801 West Fort Street, Detroit, MI 48226-9975. *Phone:* 313-496-2634. *E-mail:* caafjh@wccc.edu.
Website: http://www.wcccd.edu/.

West Shore Community College
Scottville, Michigan

Freshman Application Contact Wendy Fought, Director of Admissions, West Shore Community College, PO Box 277, 3000 North Stiles Road, Scottville, MI 49454-0277. *Phone:* 231-843-5503. *Fax:* 231-845-3944. *E-mail:* admissions@westshore.edu.
Website: http://www.westshore.edu/.

MICRONESIA

College of Micronesia–FSM
Kolonia Pohnpei, Federated States of Micronesia, Micronesia

Freshman Application Contact Rita Hinga, Student Services Specialist, College of Micronesia–FSM, PO Box 159, Kolonia Pohnpei, FM 96941-0159, Micronesia. *Phone:* 691-320-3795 Ext. 15. *E-mail:* rhinga@comfsm.fm.
Website: http://www.comfsm.fm/.

MINNESOTA

Alexandria Technical and Community College
Alexandria, Minnesota

- **State-supported** 2-year, founded 1961, part of Minnesota State Colleges and Universities System
- **Small-town** 98-acre campus
- **Coed,** 2,877 undergraduate students, 54% full-time, 51% women, 49% men

Undergraduates 1,546 full-time, 1,331 part-time. Students come from 22 states and territories; 1 other country; 3% are from out of state; 1% Black or African American, non-Hispanic/Latino; 1% Hispanic/Latino; 0.5% Asian, non-Hispanic/Latino; 1% American Indian or Alaska Native, non-Hispanic/Latino; 4% Race/ethnicity unknown.
Faculty *Total:* 108, 62% full-time, 4% with terminal degrees. *Student/faculty ratio:* 24:1.

Majors Accounting; automation engineer technology; business administration and management; carpentry; child-care and support services management; child-care provision; child development; clinical/medical laboratory technology; commercial and advertising art; computer and information sciences; computer and information systems security; computer systems networking and telecommunications; credit management; criminal justice/police science; customer service management; diesel mechanics technology; farm and ranch management; fashion merchandising; geographic information science and cartography; health and physical education/fitness; hospitality administration; human services; industrial mechanics and maintenance technology; information science/studies; interior design; legal administrative assistant/secretary; legal assistant/paralegal; liberal arts and sciences/liberal studies; licensed practical/vocational nurse training; machine tool technology; manufacturing engineering technology; marine maintenance and ship repair technology; marketing/marketing management; mechanical drafting and CAD/CADD; medical administrative assistant and medical secretary; multi/interdisciplinary studies related; office management; operations management; physical fitness technician; registered nursing/registered nurse; sales, distribution, and marketing operations; small engine mechanics and repair technology.
Academics *Calendar:* semesters. *Degree:* certificates, diplomas, and associate. *Special study options:* academic remediation for entering students, advanced placement credit, distance learning, double majors, independent study, internships, part-time degree program, services for LD students, student-designed majors, summer session for credit.
Library Learning Resource Center with 23,886 titles, 1,995 serial subscriptions, 1,378 audiovisual materials, an OPAC, a Web page.
Student Life *Housing:* college housing not available. *Activities and Organizations:* choral group, Skills USA, Business Professionals of America, Delta Epsilon Chi, Student Senate, Phi Theta Kappa. *Campus security:* student patrols, late-night transport/escort service, security cameras inside and outside. *Student services:* personal/psychological counseling.
Athletics *Intramural sports:* basketball M/W, football M/W, softball M/W, volleyball M/W.
Financial Aid Of all full-time matriculated undergraduates who enrolled in 2011, 94 Federal Work-Study jobs (averaging $1871).
Applying *Options:* electronic application, early admission, deferred entrance. *Application fee:* $20. *Required:* high school transcript. *Required for some:* interview. *Application deadlines:* rolling (freshmen), rolling (out-of-state freshmen), rolling (transfers). *Notification:* continuous (freshmen), continuous (out-of-state freshmen), continuous (transfers).
Freshman Application Contact Janet Dropik, Admissions Receptionist, Alexandria Technical and Community College, 1601 Jefferson Street, Alexandria, MN 56308. *Phone:* 320-762-4520. *Toll-free phone:* 888-234-1222. *Fax:* 320-762-4603. *E-mail:* admissionsrep@alextech.edu.
Website: http://www.alextech.edu/.

Anoka-Ramsey Community College
Coon Rapids, Minnesota

- **State-supported** 2-year, founded 1965, part of Minnesota State Colleges and Universities System
- **Suburban** 100-acre campus with easy access to Minneapolis-St. Paul
- **Coed,** 7,773 undergraduate students

Undergraduates 4% are from out of state; 8% Black or African American, non-Hispanic/Latino; 5% Hispanic/Latino; 4% Asian, non-Hispanic/Latino; 0.1% Native Hawaiian or other Pacific Islander, non-Hispanic/Latino; 0.5% American Indian or Alaska Native, non-Hispanic/Latino; 4% Two or more races, non-Hispanic/Latino; 1% Race/ethnicity unknown; 0.3% international. *Retention:* 52% of full-time freshmen returned.
Freshmen *Admission:* 2,884 applied, 1,515 admitted.
Faculty *Total:* 227, 49% full-time. *Student/faculty ratio:* 39:1.
Majors Accounting; accounting technology and bookkeeping; bioengineering and biomedical engineering; biology/biological sciences; biomedical technology; business administration and management; business/commerce; community health and preventive medicine; computer science; computer systems networking and telecommunications; dramatic/theater arts; environmental science; fine/studio arts; health services/allied health/health sciences; holistic health; human resources management; liberal arts and sciences/liberal studies; multi/interdisciplinary studies related; music; physical therapy technology; pre-engineering; registered nursing/registered nurse; sales, distribution, and marketing operations.
Academics *Calendar:* semesters. *Degree:* certificates and associate. *Special study options:* academic remediation for entering students, accelerated degree program, advanced placement credit, cooperative education, distance learning, double majors, honors programs, independent study, internships, off-campus study, part-time degree program, services for LD students, study abroad, summer session for credit. *ROTC:* Air Force (c).
Library Coon Rapids Campus Library with 41,992 titles, 157 serial subscriptions, 2,003 audiovisual materials, an OPAC, a Web page.

Student Life *Housing:* college housing not available. *Activities and Organizations:* drama/theater group, student-run newspaper, choral group, student government, Phi Theta Kappa, Multicultural Club, CRU (Campus Christian group), Salmagundi (student newspaper). *Campus security:* 24-hour emergency response devices, late-night transport/escort service. *Student services:* personal/psychological counseling.

Athletics Member NJCAA. *Intercollegiate sports:* baseball M, basketball M/W, soccer M/W, softball W, volleyball W. *Intramural sports:* basketball M/W, bowling M/W, football M/W, golf M/W, ice hockey M/W, soccer M/W, softball M/W, tennis M/W, volleyball M/W.

Costs (2012–13) *Tuition:* state resident $4349 full-time, $145 per credit part-time; nonresident $4349 full-time, $145 per credit part-time. Full-time tuition and fees vary according to course load and program. Part-time tuition and fees vary according to course load and program. *Required fees:* $639 full-time, $21 per credit part-time. *Payment plans:* installment, deferred payment. *Waivers:* senior citizens and employees or children of employees.

Financial Aid Of all full-time matriculated undergraduates who enrolled in 2012, 2,375 applied for aid, 2,281 were judged to have need, 1,655 had their need fully met. In 2012, 15 non-need-based awards were made. *Average percent of need met:* 94%. *Average financial aid package:* $4852. *Average need-based loan:* $1925. *Average need-based gift aid:* $2262. *Average non-need-based aid:* $795.

Applying *Options:* electronic application, early admission, deferred entrance. *Application fee:* $20. *Required for some:* high school transcript. *Application deadlines:* rolling (freshmen), rolling (out-of-state freshmen), rolling (transfers). *Notification:* continuous (freshmen), continuous (out-of-state freshmen), continuous (transfers).

Freshman Application Contact Admissions Department, Anoka-Ramsey Community College, 11200 Mississippi Boulevard NW, Coon Rapids, MN 55433-3470. *Phone:* 763-433-1300. *Fax:* 763-433-1521. *E-mail:* admissions@anokaramsey.edu.

Website: http://www.anokaramsey.edu/.

Anoka-Ramsey Community College, Cambridge Campus

Cambridge, Minnesota

- **State-supported** 2-year, founded 1965, part of Minnesota State Colleges and Universities System
- **Small-town** campus
- **Coed,** 2,545 undergraduate students

Undergraduates 4% are from out of state; 1% Black or African American, non-Hispanic/Latino; 3% Hispanic/Latino; 1% Asian, non-Hispanic/Latino; 0.2% Native Hawaiian or other Pacific Islander, non-Hispanic/Latino; 0.5% American Indian or Alaska Native, non-Hispanic/Latino; 3% Two or more races, non-Hispanic/Latino; 1% Race/ethnicity unknown; 0.1% international. *Retention:* 47% of full-time freshmen returned.

Freshmen *Admission:* 695 applied, 351 admitted.

Faculty *Total:* 60, 50% full-time. *Student/faculty ratio:* 36:1.

Majors Accounting; accounting technology and bookkeeping; bioengineering and biomedical engineering; biology/biological sciences; biomedical technology; business administration and management; business/commerce; community health and preventive medicine; computer science; computer systems networking and telecommunications; dramatic/theater arts; environmental science; fine/studio arts; health services/allied health/health sciences; holistic health; human resources management; liberal arts and sciences/liberal studies; multi/interdisciplinary studies related; music; pre-engineering; registered nursing/registered nurse; sales, distribution, and marketing operations.

Academics *Calendar:* semesters. *Degree:* certificates and associate. *Special study options:* academic remediation for entering students, accelerated degree program, advanced placement credit, cooperative education, distance learning, double majors, honors programs, independent study, internships, off-campus study, part-time degree program, services for LD students, study abroad, summer session for credit. *ROTC:* Air Force (c).

Library Cambridge Campus Library with 17,406 titles, 131 serial subscriptions, 1,240 audiovisual materials, an OPAC, a Web page.

Student Life *Housing:* college housing not available. *Activities and Organizations:* drama/theater group, student-run newspaper, choral group. *Campus security:* 24-hour emergency response devices, late-night transport/escort service. *Student services:* personal/psychological counseling.

Athletics Member NJCAA. *Intercollegiate sports:* baseball M, basketball M/W, soccer M/W, softball W, volleyball W. *Intramural sports:* bowling M/W, golf M/W, volleyball M/W.

Costs (2012–13) *Tuition:* state resident $4349 full-time, $145 per credit part-time; nonresident $4349 full-time, $145 per credit part-time. Full-time tuition and fees vary according to course load and program. Part-time tuition and fees vary according to course load and program. *Required fees:* $632 full-time, $21 per credit part-time. *Payment plans:* installment, deferred payment. *Waivers:* senior citizens and employees or children of employees.

Applying *Options:* electronic application, early admission, deferred entrance. *Application fee:* $20. *Required for some:* high school transcript. *Application deadlines:* rolling (freshmen), rolling (out-of-state freshmen), rolling (transfers). *Notification:* continuous (freshmen), continuous (out-of-state freshmen), continuous (transfers).

Freshman Application Contact Admissions Department, Anoka-Ramsey Community College, Cambridge Campus, 300 Spirit River Drive South, Cambridge, MN 55008-5706. *Phone:* 763-433-1300. *Fax:* 763-433-1841. *E-mail:* admissions@anokaramsey.edu.

Website: http://www.anokaramsey.edu/.

Anoka Technical College

Anoka, Minnesota

Director of Admissions LeAnn Brown, Director of Admissions, Anoka Technical College, 1355 West Highway 10, Anoka, MN 55303. *Phone:* 763-576-4784. *E-mail:* lbrown@anokatech.edu.

Website: http://www.anokatech.edu/.

Anthem College–St. Louis Park

St. Louis Park, Minnesota

Freshman Application Contact Admissions Office, Anthem College–St. Louis Park, 5100 Gamble Drive, St. Louis Park, MN 55416. *Toll-free phone:* 855-331-7769.

Website: http://anthem.edu/minneapolis-minnesota/.

Brown College

Mendota Heights, Minnesota

Freshman Application Contact Mr. Mark Fredrichs, Registrar, Brown College, 1440 Northland Drive, Mendota Heights, MN 55120. *Phone:* 651-905-3400. *Toll-free phone:* 866-551-0049. *Fax:* 651-905-3550.

Website: http://www.browncollege.edu/.

Central Lakes College

Brainerd, Minnesota

Freshman Application Contact Ms. Rose Tretter, Central Lakes College, 501 West College Drive, Brainerd, MN 56401-3904. *Phone:* 218-855-8036. *Toll-free phone:* 800-933-0346. *Fax:* 218-855-8220. *E-mail:* cdanicls@clcmn.cdu.

Website: http://www.clcmn.edu/.

Century College

White Bear Lake, Minnesota

- **State-supported** 2-year, founded 1970, part of Minnesota State Colleges and Universities System
- **Suburban** 170-acre campus with easy access to Minneapolis-St. Paul
- **Coed,** 10,422 undergraduate students, 43% full-time, 55% women, 45% men

Undergraduates 4,490 full-time, 5,932 part-time. Students come from 35 states and territories; 50 other countries; 6% are from out of state; 11% Black or African American, non-Hispanic/Latino; 6% Hispanic/Latino; 16% Asian, non-Hispanic/Latino; 0.2% Native Hawaiian or other Pacific Islander, non-Hispanic/Latino; 0.5% American Indian or Alaska Native, non-Hispanic/Latino; 5% Two or more races, non-Hispanic/Latino; 0.5% Race/ethnicity unknown; 1% international; 44% transferred in.

Freshmen *Admission:* 3,310 applied, 3,310 admitted, 1,435 enrolled.

Faculty *Total:* 389, 58% full-time. *Student/faculty ratio:* 23:1.

Majors Accounting; administrative assistant and secretarial science; building/property maintenance; business administration and management; CAD/CADD drafting/design technology; computer and information systems security; computer science; computer systems networking and telecommunications; computer technology/computer systems technology; cosmetology; criminalistics and criminal science; criminal justice/police science; criminal justice/safety; dental assisting; dental hygiene; digital communication and media/multimedia; emergency medical technology (EMT paramedic); energy management and systems technology; fine/studio arts; greenhouse management; health services/allied health/health sciences; heating, air conditioning, ventilation and refrigeration maintenance technology; homeland security, law enforcement, firefighting and protective services related; horticultural science; human services; interior design; landscaping and groundskeeping; language interpretation and translation; liberal arts and sciences/liberal studies; marketing/marketing management; medical administrative assistant and medical secretary; multi/interdisciplinary studies related; music; orthotics/prosthetics; radiologic technology/science; registered nursing/registered nurse; substance abuse/addiction counseling; teacher assistant/aide.

Academics *Calendar:* semesters. *Degree:* certificates, diplomas, and associate. *Special study options:* academic remediation for entering students, advanced placement credit, distance learning, double majors, English as a second language, honors programs, internships, part-time degree program, services for LD students, summer session for credit. *ROTC:* Air Force (c).

Library Century College Library with 105,530 titles, 289 serial subscriptions, 13,992 audiovisual materials, an OPAC.

Student Life *Housing:* college housing not available. *Activities and Organizations:* drama/theater group, student-run newspaper, choral group, Asian Student Association, Intercultural Club, Student Senate, Phi Theta Kappa, Planning Activities Committee. *Campus security:* late-night transport/escort service, day patrols. *Student services:* personal/psychological counseling.

Athletics Member NJCAA. *Intercollegiate sports:* baseball M, soccer M/W, softball W. *Intramural sports:* badminton M/W, basketball M/W, bowling M/W, soccer M/W, softball M/W, table tennis M/W, volleyball M/W.

Costs (2012–13) *Tuition:* state resident $4818 full-time, $161 per semester hour part-time; nonresident $4818 full-time, $161 per semester hour part-time. Full-time tuition and fees vary according to class time, program, and reciprocity agreements. Part-time tuition and fees vary according to class time, program, and reciprocity agreements. *Required fees:* $539 full-time, $18 per credit hour part-time. *Payment plan:* installment. *Waivers:* senior citizens and employees or children of employees.

Financial Aid Of all full-time matriculated undergraduates who enrolled in 2011, 81 Federal Work-Study jobs (averaging $2763). 85 state and other part-time jobs (averaging $2646).

Applying *Options:* electronic application, deferred entrance. *Application fee:* $20. *Required:* high school transcript. *Application deadlines:* rolling (freshmen), rolling (transfers).

Freshman Application Contact Ms. Christine Paulos, Admissions Director, Century College, 3300 Century Avenue North, White Bear Lake, MN 55110. *Phone:* 651-779-2619. *Toll-free phone:* 800-228-1978. *Fax:* 651-773-1796. *E-mail:* admissions@century.edu. *Website:* http://www.century.edu/.

Dakota County Technical College
Rosemount, Minnesota

Freshman Application Contact Mr. Patrick Lair, Admissions Director, Dakota County Technical College, 1300 East 145th Street, Rosemount, MN 55068. *Phone:* 651-423-8399. *Toll-free phone:* 877-YES-DCTC. *Fax:* 651-423-8775. *E-mail:* admissions@dctc.mnscu.edu. *Website:* http://www.dctc.edu/.

Duluth Business University
Duluth, Minnesota

Freshman Application Contact Mr. Mark Traux, Director of Admissions, Duluth Business University, 4724 Mike Colalillo Drive, Duluth, MN 55807. *Phone:* 218-722-4000. *Toll-free phone:* 800-777-8406. *Fax:* 218-628-2127. *E-mail:* markt@dbumn.edu. *Website:* http://www.dbumn.edu/.

Dunwoody College of Technology
Minneapolis, Minnesota

- **Independent** primarily 2-year, founded 1914
- **Urban** 12-acre campus with easy access to Minneapolis, Minnesota
- **Coed, primarily men,** 1,131 undergraduate students, 78% full-time, 13% women, 87% men

Undergraduates 881 full-time, 250 part-time. 3% are from out of state; 6% Black or African American, non-Hispanic/Latino; 2% Hispanic/Latino; 5% Asian, non-Hispanic/Latino; 0.2% Native Hawaiian or other Pacific Islander, non-Hispanic/Latino; 0.7% American Indian or Alaska Native, non-Hispanic/Latino; 5% Two or more races, non-Hispanic/Latino; 15% Race/ethnicity unknown. *Retention:* 67% of full-time freshmen returned.

Freshmen *Admission:* 494 applied, 286 admitted, 202 enrolled. *Average high school GPA:* 2.42.

Faculty *Total:* 130, 60% full-time, 5% with terminal degrees. *Student/faculty ratio:* 10:1.

Majors Architectural drafting and CAD/CADD; architectural technology; autobody/collision and repair technology; automobile/automotive mechanics technology; building/construction site management; business administration and management; CAD/CADD drafting/design technology; computer systems networking and telecommunications; construction management; desktop publishing and digital imaging design; electrical, electronic and communications engineering technology; electrical/electronics drafting and CAD/CADD; electrician; graphic design; heating, air conditioning, ventilation and refrigeration maintenance technology; heating, ventilation, air conditioning and refrigeration engineering technology; industrial technology; interior design; medical

radiologic technology; printing press operation; robotics technology; tool and die technology; web page, digital/multimedia and information resources design; welding technology.

Academics *Calendar:* quarters. *Degrees:* diplomas, associate, and bachelor's. *Special study options:* academic remediation for entering students, distance learning, independent study, internships, study abroad, summer session for credit.

Library Learning Resource Center with 8,000 titles, 115 serial subscriptions, 250 audiovisual materials, an OPAC, a Web page.

Student Life *Housing:* college housing not available. *Activities and Organizations:* Student Government, Historic Green. *Campus security:* 24-hour emergency response devices, late-night transport/escort service. *Student services:* personal/psychological counseling, women's center.

Standardized Tests *Recommended:* SAT or ACT (for admission).

Costs (2013–14) *Tuition:* $17,077 full-time. *Required fees:* $1437 full-time. *Payment plans:* installment, deferred payment.

Financial Aid Of all full-time matriculated undergraduates who enrolled in 2011, 1,068 applied for aid, 959 were judged to have need, 41 had their need fully met. 24 Federal Work-Study jobs (averaging $4601). 17 state and other part-time jobs (averaging $3206). In 2011, 45 non-need-based awards were made. *Average percent of need met:* 41%. *Average financial aid package:* $11,546. *Average need-based loan:* $4532. *Average need-based gift aid:* $8624. *Average non-need-based aid:* $2518. *Average indebtedness upon graduation:* $9937.

Applying *Options:* electronic application. *Application fee:* $50. *Required:* essay or personal statement, high school transcript, minimum 2.5 GPA, interview. *Required for some:* minimum 3.0 GPA, . *Application deadline:* rolling (freshmen). *Notification:* continuous (freshmen).

Freshman Application Contact Bonney Bielen, Director of Admissions and Student Services, Dunwoody College of Technology, 818 Dunwoody Boulevard, Minneapolis, MN 55403. *Phone:* 612-374-5800. *Toll-free phone:* 800-292-4625. *Website:* http://www.dunwoody.edu/.

Fond du Lac Tribal and Community College
Cloquet, Minnesota

Freshman Application Contact Kathie Jubie, Admissions Representative, Fond du Lac Tribal and Community College, 2101 14th Street, Cloquet, MN 55720. *Phone:* 218-879-0808. *Toll-free phone:* 800-657-3712. *E-mail:* admissions@fdltcc.edu. *Website:* http://www.fdltcc.edu/.

Hennepin Technical College
Brooklyn Park, Minnesota

Freshman Application Contact Hennepin Technical College, 9000 Brooklyn Boulevard, Brooklyn Park, MN 55445. *Phone:* 763-488-2415. *Toll-free phone:* 800-345-4655 (in-state); 800-645-4655 (out-of-state). *Website:* http://www.hennepintech.edu/.

Herzing University
Minneapolis, Minnesota

Freshman Application Contact Ms. Shelly Larson, Director of Admissions, Herzing University, 5700 West Broadway, Minneapolis, MN 55428. *Phone:* 763-231-3155. *Toll-free phone:* 800-596-0724. *Fax:* 763-535-9205. *E-mail:* info@mpls.herzing.edu. *Website:* http://www.herzing.edu/minneapolis.

Hibbing Community College
Hibbing, Minnesota

Freshman Application Contact Admissions, Hibbing Community College, 1515 East 25th Street, Hibbing, MN 55746. *Phone:* 218-262-7200. *Toll-free phone:* 800-224-4HCC. *Fax:* 218-262-6717. *E-mail:* admissions@hibbing.edu.. *Website:* http://www.hcc.mnscu.edu/.

The Institute of Production and Recording
Minneapolis, Minnesota

- **Proprietary** 2-year, part of Globe Education Network (GEN) which is composed of Globe University, Minnesota School of Business,

Broadview University, The Institute of Production and Recording and Minnesota School of Cosmetology
- **Urban** 4-acre campus with easy access to Minneapolis-St. Paul
- **Coed**

Undergraduates 389 full-time, 67 part-time. Students come from 28 states and territories; 6% are from out of state; 8% Black or African American, non-Hispanic/Latino; 5% Hispanic/Latino; 2% Asian, non-Hispanic/Latino; 0.2% Native Hawaiian or other Pacific Islander, non-Hispanic/Latino; 0.9% American Indian or Alaska Native, non-Hispanic/Latino; 5% Two or more races, non-Hispanic/Latino; 9% Race/ethnicity unknown; 16% transferred in.
Faculty *Student/faculty ratio:* 10:1.
Academics *Degree:* associate. *Special study options:* academic remediation for entering students, accelerated degree program, adult/continuing education programs, advanced placement credit, internships, part-time degree program, services for LD students, summer session for credit.
Student Life *Campus security:* 24-hour emergency response devices, late-night transport/escort service.
Standardized Tests *Required:* ACCUPLACER is required of all applicants unless documentation of a minimum ACT composite score of 21 or documentation of a minimum composite score of 1485 on the SAT is presented (for admission).
Costs (2012–13) *Tuition:* $16,560 full-time, $460 per credit part-time. Full-time tuition and fees vary according to course load, degree level, and program. Part-time tuition and fees vary according to course load, degree level, and program. *Required fees:* $1548 full-time, $43 per credit part-time.
Applying *Options:* electronic application. *Application fee:* $50. *Required:* high school transcript, interview, high school transcript or GED. *Required for some:* essay or personal statement, 2 letters of recommendation.
Freshman Application Contact The Institute of Production and Recording, 312 Washington Avenue North, Minneapolis, MN 55401. *Phone:* 612-375-1900.
Website: http://www.ipr.edu/.

Inver Hills Community College

Inver Grove Heights, Minnesota

Freshman Application Contact Mr. Casey Carmody, Admissions Representative, Inver Hills Community College, 2500 East 80th Street, Inver Grove Heights, MN 55076-3224. *Phone:* 651-450-3589. *Fax:* 651-450-3677. *E-mail:* admissions@inverhills.edu.
Website: http://www.inverhills.edu/.

Itasca Community College

Grand Rapids, Minnesota

- **State-supported** 2-year, founded 1922, part of Minnesota State Colleges and Universities System, Northeastern Higher Education District
- **Rural** 24-acre campus
- **Endowment** $4.0 million
- **Coed**

Undergraduates 983 full-time, 316 part-time. Students come from 2 other countries; 4% are from out of state; 3% Black or African American, non-Hispanic/Latino; 0.4% Hispanic/Latino; 0.5% Asian, non-Hispanic/Latino; 0.2% Native Hawaiian or other Pacific Islander, non-Hispanic/Latino; 4% American Indian or Alaska Native, non-Hispanic/Latino; 3% Race/ethnicity unknown; 10% live on campus. *Retention:* 53% of full-time freshmen returned.
Faculty *Student/faculty ratio:* 17:1.
Academics *Calendar:* semesters. *Degree:* certificates, diplomas, and associate. *Special study options:* academic remediation for entering students, adult/continuing education programs, advanced placement credit, cooperative education, double majors, independent study, internships, off-campus study, part-time degree program, services for LD students, study abroad, summer session for credit.
Student Life *Campus security:* student patrols, late-night transport/escort service, controlled dormitory access, evening patrols by trained security personnel.
Athletics Member NJCAA.
Costs (2012–13) *Tuition:* state resident $4729 full-time; nonresident $5911 full-time. *Required fees:* $578 full-time. *Room and board:* room only: $3480.
Financial Aid Of all full-time matriculated undergraduates who enrolled in 2011, 1,132 applied for aid. 71 Federal Work-Study jobs (averaging $1176). 156 state and other part-time jobs (averaging $1524).
Applying *Options:* electronic application. *Required:* high school transcript.
Freshman Application Contact Ms. Candace Perry, Director of Enrollment Services, Itasca Community College, Grand Rapids, MN 55744. *Phone:* 218-322-2340. *Toll-free phone:* 800-996-6422. *Fax:* 218-327-4350. *E-mail:* iccinfo@itascacc.edu.
Website: http://www.itascacc.edu/.

ITT Technical Institute

Brooklyn Center, Minnesota

- **Proprietary** primarily 2-year, part of ITT Educational Services, Inc.
- **Coed**

Academics *Calendar:* quarters. *Degrees:* associate and bachelor's.
Freshman Application Contact Director of Recruitment, ITT Technical Institute, 6120 Earle Brown Drive, Suite 100, Brooklyn Center, MN 55430. *Phone:* 763-549-5900. *Toll-free phone:* 800-216-8883.
Website: http://www.itt-tech.edu/.

ITT Technical Institute

Eden Prairie, Minnesota

- **Proprietary** primarily 2-year, founded 2003, part of ITT Educational Services, Inc.
- **Coed**

Academics *Calendar:* quarters. *Degrees:* associate and bachelor's.
Freshman Application Contact Director of Recruitment, ITT Technical Institute, 8911 Columbine Road, Eden Prairie, MN 55347. *Phone:* 952-914-5300. *Toll-free phone:* 888-488-9646.
Website: http://www.itt-tech.edu/.

Lake Superior College

Duluth, Minnesota

- **State-supported** 2-year, founded 1995, part of Minnesota State Colleges and Universities System
- **Urban** 105-acre campus
- **Coed,** 4,627 undergraduate students, 46% full-time, 57% women, 43% men

Undergraduates 2,122 full-time, 2,505 part-time. Students come from 29 states and territories; 3 other countries; 12% are from out of state; 4% Black or African American, non-Hispanic/Latino; 2% Hispanic/Latino; 1% Asian, non-Hispanic/Latino; 0.2% Native Hawaiian or other Pacific Islander, non-Hispanic/Latino; 2% American Indian or Alaska Native, non-Hispanic/Latino; 4% Two or more races, non-Hispanic/Latino; 1% Race/ethnicity unknown; 0.1% international; 41% transferred in. *Retention:* 48% of full-time freshmen returned.
Freshmen *Admission:* 990 applied, 990 admitted, 701 enrolled.
Faculty *Total:* 235, 44% full-time, 6% with terminal degrees. *Student/faculty ratio:* 22:1.
Majors Accounting; airline pilot and flight crew; architectural drafting and CAD/CADD; automobile/automotive mechanics technology; building construction technology; business administration and management; business automation/technology/data entry; CAD/CADD drafting/design technology; civil engineering technology; clinical/medical laboratory technology; computer support specialist; computer systems networking and telecommunications; computer technology/computer systems technology; dental hygiene; electrical, electronic and communications engineering technology; electrician; fine/studio arts; fire prevention and safety technology; health services/allied health/health sciences; legal administrative assistant/secretary; legal assistant/paralegal; liberal arts and sciences/liberal studies; machine tool technology; management information systems; mechanical drafting and CAD/CADD; medical administrative assistant and medical secretary; multi/interdisciplinary studies related; network and system administration; office management; physical therapy technology; radiologic technology/science; registered nursing/registered nurse; respiratory care therapy; sheet metal technology; surgical technology; web page, digital/multimedia and information resources design.
Academics *Calendar:* semesters. *Degree:* certificates, diplomas, and associate. *Special study options:* academic remediation for entering students, advanced placement credit, distance learning, double majors, independent study, internships, part-time degree program, services for LD students, study abroad, summer session for credit.
Library Harold P. Erickson Library with an OPAC, a Web page.
Student Life *Housing:* college housing not available. *Activities and Organizations:* choral group. *Campus security:* late-night transport/escort service. *Student services:* personal/psychological counseling.
Financial Aid Of all full-time matriculated undergraduates who enrolled in 2011, 72 Federal Work-Study jobs (averaging $2720). 103 state and other part-time jobs (averaging $2720).
Applying *Options:* electronic application. *Application fee:* $20. *Required:* Transcripts from high school, GED, or HSED and official transcripts from all previous post-secondary institutions attended. *Required for some:* high school transcript. *Application deadlines:* rolling (freshmen), rolling (transfers). *Notification:* continuous (freshmen), continuous (transfers).
Freshman Application Contact Ms. Melissa Leno, Director of Admissions, Lake Superior College, 2101 Trinity Road, Duluth, MN 55811. *Phone:* 218-

733-5903. *Toll-free phone:* 800-432-2884. *E-mail:* enroll@lsc.edu. *Website:* http://www.lsc.edu/.

Le Cordon Bleu College of Culinary Arts

Saint Paul, Minnesota

Freshman Application Contact Admissions Office, Le Cordon Bleu College of Culinary Arts, 1315 Mendota Heights Road, Saint Paul, MN 55120. *Phone:* 651-675-4700. *Toll-free phone:* 888-348-5222. *Website:* http://www.chefs.edu/Minneapolis-St-Paul/.

Leech Lake Tribal College

Cass Lake, Minnesota

Freshman Application Contact Ms. Shelly Braford, Recruiter, Leech Lake Tribal College, PO Box 180, 6945 Littlewolf Road NW, Cass Lake, MN 56633. *Phone:* 218-335-4200 Ext. 4270. *Fax:* 218-335-4217. *E-mail:* shelly.braford@lltc.edu. *Website:* http://www.lltc.edu/.

Mesabi Range Community and Technical College

Virginia, Minnesota

Freshman Application Contact Ms. Brenda Kochevar, Enrollment Services Director, Mesabi Range Community and Technical College, Virginia, MN 55792. *Phone:* 218-749-0314. *Toll-free phone:* 800-657-3860. *Fax:* 218-749-0318. *E-mail:* b.kochevar@mr.mnscu.edu. *Website:* http://www.mesabirange.edu/.

Minneapolis Business College

Roseville, Minnesota

- **Private** 2-year, founded 1874
- **Suburban** campus with easy access to Minneapolis-St. Paul
- **Coed, primarily women,** 373 undergraduate students
- 88% of applicants were admitted

Freshmen *Admission:* 565 applied, 498 admitted.

Majors Accounting technology and bookkeeping; administrative assistant and secretarial science; computer programming; computer systems networking and telecommunications; graphic design; hotel/motel administration; legal administrative assistant/secretary; legal assistant/paralegal; medical/clinical assistant.

Academics *Degree:* diplomas and associate. *Special study options:* accelerated degree program, internships.

Freshman Application Contact Admissions Office, Minneapolis Business College, 1711 West County Road B, Roseville, MN 55113. *Phone:* 651-636-7406. *Toll-free phone:* 800-279-5200. *Website:* http://www.minneapolisbusinesscollege.edu/.

Minneapolis Community and Technical College

Minneapolis, Minnesota

- **State-supported** 2-year, founded 1965, part of Minnesota State Colleges and Universities System
- **Urban** 22-acre campus
- **Coed**

Undergraduates 3,758 full-time, 6,233 part-time. Students come from 31 states and territories; 31% Black or African American, non-Hispanic/Latino; 8% Hispanic/Latino; 5% Asian, non-Hispanic/Latino; 0.1% Native Hawaiian or other Pacific Islander, non-Hispanic/Latino; 2% American Indian or Alaska Native, non-Hispanic/Latino; 8% Two or more races, non-Hispanic/Latino; 1% Race/ethnicity unknown; 2% international; 12% transferred in.

Faculty *Student/faculty ratio:* 27:1.

Academics *Calendar:* semesters. *Degree:* certificates, diplomas, and associate. *Special study options:* academic remediation for entering students, accelerated degree program, adult/continuing education programs, advanced placement credit, distance learning, English as a second language, honors programs, independent study, internships, off-campus study, part-time degree program, services for LD students, study abroad, summer session for credit.

Student Life *Campus security:* 24-hour emergency response devices and patrols, late-night transport/escort service.

Costs (2012–13) *Tuition:* state resident $4523 full-time; nonresident $4523 full-time. *Required fees:* $669 full-time.

Applying *Options:* electronic application, early admission, deferred entrance. *Application fee:* $20. *Required:* high school transcript.

Freshman Application Contact Minneapolis Community and Technical College, 1501 Hennepin Avenue, Minneapolis, MN 55403. *Phone:* 612-659-6200. *Toll-free phone:* 800-247-0911. *E-mail:* admissions.office@minneapolis.edu. *Website:* http://www.minneapolis.edu/.

Minneapolis Media Institute

Edina, Minnesota

Admissions Office Contact Minneapolis Media Institute, 4100 West 76th Street, Edina, MN 55435. *Toll-free phone:* 800-236-4997. *Website:* http://www.mediainstitute.edu/.

Minnesota School of Business–Brooklyn Center

Brooklyn Center, Minnesota

- **Proprietary** primarily 2-year, founded 1989, part of Globe Education Network (GEN) which is composed of Globe University, Minnesota School of Business, Broadview University, The Institute of Production and Recording and Minnesota School of Cosmetology
- **Suburban** 4-acre campus with easy access to Minneapolis-St. Paul
- **Coed**
- 68% of applicants were admitted

Undergraduates 145 full-time, 475 part-time. Students come from 2 states and territories; 0.2% are from out of state; 22% Black or African American, non-Hispanic/Latino; 1% Hispanic/Latino; 7% Asian, non-Hispanic/Latino; 1% American Indian or Alaska Native, non-Hispanic/Latino; 2% Two or more races, non-Hispanic/Latino; 40% Race/ethnicity unknown; 14% transferred in. *Retention:* 38% of full-time freshmen returned.

Faculty *Student/faculty ratio:* 10:1.

Academics *Calendar:* quarters. *Degrees:* diplomas, associate, and bachelor's. *Special study options:* academic remediation for entering students, accelerated degree program, adult/continuing education programs, advanced placement credit, internships, part-time degree program, services for LD students, summer session for credit.

Student Life *Campus security:* 24-hour emergency response devices, late-night transport/escort service.

Standardized Tests *Required:* ACCUPLACER is required of all applicants unless documentation of a minimum ACT composite score of 21 or documentation of a minimum composite score of 1485 on the SAT is presented (for admission).

Costs (2012–13) *Tuition:* $15,300 full-time, $460 per credit part-time. Full-time tuition and fees vary according to course load, degree level, location, and program. Part-time tuition and fees vary according to course load, degree level, location, and program. *Required fees:* $1548 full-time, $43 per credit part-time.

Applying *Options:* electronic application. *Application fee:* $50. *Required:* high school transcript, interview, High school transcript or GED. *Required for some:* essay or personal statement, 2 letters of recommendation.

Freshman Application Contact Minnesota School of Business–Brooklyn Center, 5910 Shingle Creek Parkway, Brooklyn Center, MN 55430. *Phone:* 763-566-7777. *Website:* http://www.msbcollege.edu/.

Minnesota School of Business–Plymouth

Minneapolis, Minnesota

- **Proprietary** primarily 2-year, founded 2002, part of Globe Education Network (GEN) which is composed of Globe University, Minnesota School of Business, Broadview University, The Institute of Production and Recording and Minnesota School of Cosmetology
- **Suburban** 7-acre campus with easy access to Minneapolis-St. Paul
- **Coed**

Undergraduates 114 full-time, 373 part-time. Students come from 1 other state; 6% Black or African American, non-Hispanic/Latino; 2% Hispanic/Latino; 0.8% Asian, non-Hispanic/Latino; 0.2% Native Hawaiian or other Pacific Islander, non-Hispanic/Latino; 0.8% American Indian or Alaska Native, non-Hispanic/Latino; 2% Two or more races, non-Hispanic/Latino; 11% Race/ethnicity unknown; 14% transferred in. *Retention:* 44% of full-time freshmen returned.

Faculty *Student/faculty ratio:* 21:1.

Academics *Calendar:* quarters. *Degrees:* diplomas, associate, and bachelor's. *Special study options:* academic remediation for entering students, accelerated degree program, adult/continuing education programs, advanced placement credit, internships, part-time degree program, services for LD students, summer session for credit.

Student Life *Campus security:* 24-hour emergency response devices, late-night transport/escort service.

Standardized Tests *Required:* ACCUPLACER is required of all applicants unless documentation of a minimum ACT composite score of 21 or documentation of a minimum composite score of 1485 on the SAT is presented (for admission).

Costs (2012–13) *Tuition:* $15,300 full-time, $460 per credit part-time. Full-time tuition and fees vary according to course load, degree level, location, and program. Part-time tuition and fees vary according to course load, degree level, location, and program. *Required fees:* $1548 full-time, $43 per credit part-time.

Applying *Options:* electronic application. *Application fee:* $50. *Required:* high school transcript, interview, High school transcript or GED required of all applicants. *Required for some:* essay or personal statement, 2 letters of recommendation.

Freshman Application Contact Minnesota School of Business–Plymouth, Plymouth, MN 55447. *Phone:* 763-476-2000. *Fax:* 763-476-1000. *Website:* http://www.msbcollege.edu/.

Minnesota School of Business–Richfield

Richfield, Minnesota

- **Proprietary** primarily 2-year, founded 1877, part of Globe Education Network (GEN) which is composed of Globe University, Minnesota School of Business, Broadview University, The Institute of Production and Recording and Minnesota School of Cosmetology
- **Urban** 3-acre campus with easy access to Minneapolis-St. Paul
- **Coed**

Undergraduates 524 full-time, 1,214 part-time. Students come from 9 states and territories; 1% are from out of state; 9% Black or African American, non-Hispanic/Latino; 2% Hispanic/Latino; 3% Asian, non-Hispanic/Latino; 0.1% Native Hawaiian or other Pacific Islander, non-Hispanic/Latino; 1% American Indian or Alaska Native, non-Hispanic/Latino; 2% Two or more races, non-Hispanic/Latino; 12% Race/ethnicity unknown; 0.2% international; 18% transferred in. *Retention:* 28% of full-time freshmen returned.

Faculty *Student/faculty ratio:* 16:1.

Academics *Calendar:* quarters. *Degrees:* diplomas, associate, and bachelor's. *Special study options:* academic remediation for entering students, accelerated degree program, adult/continuing education programs, advanced placement credit, internships, part-time degree program, services for LD students, summer session for credit.

Student Life *Campus security:* 24-hour emergency response devices, late-night transport/escort service.

Standardized Tests *Required:* ACCUPLACER is required of all applicants unless documentation of a minimum ACT composite score of 21 or documentation of a minimum composite score of 1485 on the SAT is presented (for admission).

Costs (2012–13) *Tuition:* $15,300 full-time, $460 per credit part-time. Full-time tuition and fees vary according to course load, degree level, location, and program. Part-time tuition and fees vary according to course load, degree level, location, and program. *Required fees:* $1548 full-time, $43 per credit part-time.

Applying *Options:* electronic application. *Application fee:* $50. *Required:* high school transcript, interview, High school transcript or GED required of all applicants. Application fee for Nursing Program is $100. *Required for some:* essay or personal statement, 2 letters of recommendation.

Freshman Application Contact Minnesota School of Business–Richfield, 1401 West 76th Street, Suite 500, Richfield, MN 55423. *Phone:* 612-861-2000. *Toll-free phone:* 800-752-4223. *Website:* http://www.msbcollege.edu/.

Minnesota School of Business–St. Cloud

Waite Park, Minnesota

- **Proprietary** primarily 2-year, founded 2004, part of Globe Education Network (GEN) which is composed of Globe University, Minnesota School of Business, Broadview University, The Institute of Production and Recording and Minnesota School of Cosmetology
- **Small-town** 2-acre campus
- **Coed**

Undergraduates 468 full-time, 453 part-time. Students come from 1 other state; 2% Black or African American, non-Hispanic/Latino; 1% His-

panic/Latino; 1% Asian, non-Hispanic/Latino; 0.8% American Indian or Alaska Native, non-Hispanic/Latino; 0.8% Two or more races, non-Hispanic/Latino; 7% Race/ethnicity unknown; 0.1% international; 16% transferred in. *Retention:* 47% of full-time freshmen returned.

Faculty *Student/faculty ratio:* 22:1.

Academics *Calendar:* quarters. *Degrees:* diplomas, associate, and bachelor's. *Special study options:* academic remediation for entering students, accelerated degree program, adult/continuing education programs, advanced placement credit, internships, part-time degree program, services for LD students, summer session for credit.

Student Life *Campus security:* 24-hour emergency response devices, late-night transport/escort service.

Standardized Tests *Required:* ACCUPLACER is required of all applicants unless documentation of a minimum ACT composite score of 21 or documentation of a minimum composite score of 1485 on the SAT is presented (for admission).

Costs (2012–13) *Tuition:* $15,300 full-time, $460 per credit part-time. Full-time tuition and fees vary according to course level, course load, degree level, location, and program. Part-time tuition and fees vary according to course level, course load, degree level, location, and program. *Required fees:* $1548 full-time, $43 per credit part-time.

Applying *Options:* electronic application. *Application fee:* $50. *Required:* high school transcript, interview, High school transcript or GED required of all applicants. *Required for some:* essay or personal statement, 2 letters of recommendation.

Freshman Application Contact Minnesota School of Business–St. Cloud, 1201 2nd Street South, Waite Park, MN 56387. *Phone:* 320-257-2000. *Toll-free phone:* 866-403-3333. *Website:* http://www.msbcollege.edu/.

Minnesota School of Business–Shakopee

Shakopee, Minnesota

- **Proprietary** primarily 2-year, founded 2004, part of Globe Education Network (GEN) which is composed of Globe University, Minnesota School of Business, Broadview University, The Institute of Production and Recording and Minnesota School of Cosmetology
- **Suburban** 1-acre campus
- **Coed**

Undergraduates 154 full-time, 236 part-time. Students come from 1 other state; 2% Black or African American, non-Hispanic/Latino; 3% Hispanic/Latino; 4% Asian, non-Hispanic/Latino; 1% American Indian or Alaska Native, non-Hispanic/Latino; 1% Two or more races, non-Hispanic/Latino; 9% Race/ethnicity unknown; 0.8% international; 14% transferred in. *Retention:* 20% of full-time freshmen returned.

Faculty *Student/faculty ratio:* 15:1.

Academics *Calendar:* quarters. *Degrees:* diplomas, associate, and bachelor's. *Special study options:* academic remediation for entering students, accelerated degree program, adult/continuing education programs, advanced placement credit, internships, part-time degree program, services for LD students, summer session for credit.

Student Life *Campus security:* 24-hour emergency response devices, late-night transport/escort service.

Standardized Tests *Required:* ACCUPLACER is required of all applicants unless documentation of a minimum ACT composite score of 21 or documentation of a minimum composite score of 1485 on the SAT is presented (for admission).

Applying *Options:* electronic application. *Application fee:* $50. *Required:* high school transcript, interview, High school transcript or GED required of all applicants. *Required for some:* essay or personal statement, 2 letters of recommendation.

Freshman Application Contact Minnesota School of Business–Shakopee, 1200 Shakopee Town Square, Shakopee, MN 55379. *Phone:* 952-345-1200. *Toll-free phone:* 866-766-1200. *Website:* http://www.msbcollege.edu/.

Minnesota State College–Southeast Technical

Winona, Minnesota

- **State-supported** 2-year, founded 1992, part of Minnesota State Colleges and Universities System
- **Small-town** 132-acre campus with easy access to Minneapolis-St. Paul
- **Coed**

Undergraduates 1,350 full-time, 887 part-time. 27% are from out of state; 4% Black or African American, non-Hispanic/Latino; 1% Hispanic/Latino; 2% Asian, non-Hispanic/Latino; 0.1% Native Hawaiian or other Pacific Islander, non-Hispanic/Latino; 0.8% American Indian or Alaska Native, non-Hispanic/Latino; 0.1% Race/ethnicity unknown; 0.4% international; 49% transferred in.

Faculty *Student/faculty ratio:* 19:1.

Academics *Calendar:* semesters. *Degree:* certificates, diplomas, and associate. *Special study options:* distance learning, double majors, internships.

Student Life *Campus security:* 24-hour emergency response devices, late-night transport/escort service.

Applying *Options:* electronic application. *Application fee:* $20. *Required:* high school transcript. *Recommended:* interview.

Freshman Application Contact Admissions, SE Technical, Minnesota State College–Southeast Technical, 1250 Homer Road, PO Box 409, Winona, MN 55987. *Phone:* 877-853-8324. *Toll-free phone:* 800-372-8164. *Fax:* 507-453-2715. *E-mail:* enrollmentservices@southeastmn.edu. *Website:* http://www.southeastmn.edu/.

Minnesota State Community and Technical College

Fergus Falls, Minnesota

Freshman Application Contact Ms. Carrie Brimhall, Dean of Enrollment Management, Minnesota State Community and Technical College, Fergus Falls, MN 56537-1009. *Phone:* 218-736-1528. *Toll-free phone:* 877-450-3322. *E-mail:* carrie.brimhall@minnesota.edu. *Website:* http://www.minnesota.edu/.

Minnesota State Community and Technical College–Detroit Lakes

Detroit Lakes, Minnesota

Director of Admissions Mr. Dale Westley, Enrollment Manager, Minnesota State Community and Technical College–Detroit Lakes, 900 Highway 34, E, Detroit Lakes, MN 56501. *Phone:* 218-846-3777. *Toll-free phone:* 800-492-4836. *Website:* http://www.minnesota.edu/.

Minnesota State Community and Technical College–Moorhead

Moorhead, Minnesota

Director of Admissions Laurie McKeever, Enrollment Manager, Minnesota State Community and Technical College–Moorhead, 1900 28th Avenue, South, Moorhead, MN 56560. *Phone:* 218-299-6583. *Toll-free phone:* 800-426-5603. *Fax:* 218-299-6810. *Website:* http://www.minnesota.edu/.

Minnesota State Community and Technical College–Wadena

Wadena, Minnesota

Director of Admissions Mr. Paul Drange, Enrollment Manager, Minnesota State Community and Technical College–Wadena, 405 Colfax Avenue, SW, PO Box 566, Wadena, MN 56482. *Phone:* 218-631-7818. *Toll-free phone:* 800-247-2007. *Website:* http://www.minnesota.edu/.

Minnesota West Community and Technical College

Pipestone, Minnesota

- **State-supported** 2-year, founded 1967, part of Minnesota State Colleges and Universities System
- **Rural** campus
- **Coed,** 3,467 undergraduate students, 38% full-time, 57% women, 43% men

Undergraduates 1,316 full-time, 2,151 part-time. Students come from 30 states and territories; 3 other countries; 11% are from out of state; 4% Black or African American, non-Hispanic/Latino; 5% Hispanic/Latino; 2% Asian, non-Hispanic/Latino; 0.1% Native Hawaiian or other Pacific Islander, non-Hispanic/Latino; 1% American Indian or Alaska Native, non-Hispanic/Latino; 2% Two or more races, non-Hispanic/Latino; 5% Race/ethnicity unknown; 0.2% international; 0.8% transferred in. *Retention:* 54% of full-time freshmen returned.

Freshmen *Admission:* 3,301 applied, 425 enrolled. *Average high school GPA:* 2.62.

Faculty *Total:* 95, 88% full-time. *Student/faculty ratio:* 13:1.

Majors Accounting; administrative assistant and secretarial science; agribusiness; agricultural and food products processing; agricultural/farm supplies retailing and wholesaling; agricultural production; agriculture; agronomy and crop science; automobile/automotive mechanics technology; biology/biotechnology laboratory technician; business administration and management; business/commerce; child-care and support services management; clinical/medical laboratory technology; computer and information systems security; computer engineering technology; computer science; computer systems networking and telecommunications; computer technology/computer systems technology; criminal justice/police science; dental assisting; diesel mechanics technology; electrical and power transmission installation; electrical and power transmission installation related; electrician; energy management and systems technology; heating, air conditioning, ventilation and refrigeration maintenance technology; hospital and health-care facilities administration; human services; hydraulics and fluid power technology; information technology; liberal arts and sciences and humanities related; liberal arts and sciences/liberal studies; lineworker; manufacturing engineering technology; medical administrative assistant and medical secretary; medical/clinical assistant; medical insurance coding; plumbing technology; radiologic technology/science; registered nursing/registered nurse; robotics technology.

Academics *Calendar:* semesters. *Degrees:* certificates, diplomas, and associate (profile contains information from Canby, Granite Falls, Jackson, and Worthington campuses). *Special study options:* academic remediation for entering students, advanced placement credit, cooperative education, distance learning, double majors, external degree program, honors programs, independent study, internships, part-time degree program, services for LD students, summer session for credit.

Library Library and Academic Resource Center plus 4 others with 44,078 titles, 213 serial subscriptions, 4,253 audiovisual materials, an OPAC, a Web page.

Student Life *Housing Options:* Campus housing is university owned. *Activities and Organizations:* choral group.

Athletics Member NJCAA. *Intercollegiate sports:* baseball M, basketball M/W, cheerleading W, football M, softball W, volleyball W, wrestling M.

Standardized Tests *Required:* Accuplacer (for admission).

Costs (2013–14) *Tuition:* state resident $172 per credit part-time. Full-time tuition and fees vary according to course load, program, and reciprocity agreements. Part-time tuition and fees vary according to course load, program, and reciprocity agreements. *Required fees:* $17 per credit hour part-time. *Room and board:* Room and board charges vary according to location. *Payment plan:* installment. *Waivers:* senior citizens and employees or children of employees.

Applying *Options:* electronic application. *Application fee:* $20. *Required:* high school transcript. *Application deadlines:* rolling (freshmen), rolling (transfers).

Freshman Application Contact Ms. Crystal Strouth, College Registrar, Minnesota West Community and Technical College, 1450 Collegeway, Worthington, MN 56187. *Phone:* 507-372-3451. *Toll-free phone:* 800-658-2330. *Fax:* 507-372-5803. *E-mail:* crystal.strouth@mnwest.edu. *Website:* http://www.mnwest.edu/.

National American University

Bloomington, Minnesota

Freshman Application Contact Ms. Jennifer Michaelson, Admissions Assistant, National American University, 321 Kansas City Street, Rapid City, SD 57201. *Phone:* 605-394-4827. *Toll-free phone:* 866-628-6387. *E-mail:* jmichaelson@national.edu. *Website:* http://www.national.edu/.

National American University

Brooklyn Center, Minnesota

Freshman Application Contact Admissions Office, National American University, 6200 Shingle Creek Parkway, Suite 130, Brooklyn Center, MN 55430. *Website:* http://www.national.edu/.

Normandale Community College

Bloomington, Minnesota

- **State-supported** 2-year, founded 1968, part of Minnesota State Colleges and Universities System
- **Suburban** 90-acre campus with easy access to Minneapolis-St. Paul
- **Coed,** 9,790 undergraduate students, 44% full-time, 55% women, 45% men

Undergraduates 4,279 full-time, 5,511 part-time. 17% Black or African American, non-Hispanic/Latino; 4% Hispanic/Latino; 9% Asian, non-Hispanic/Latino; 0.3% Native Hawaiian or other Pacific Islander, non-His-

panic/Latino; 0.8% American Indian or Alaska Native, non-Hispanic/Latino; 2% Race/ethnicity unknown. *Retention:* 53% of full-time freshmen returned.
Freshmen *Admission:* 1,544 applied, 1,544 admitted, 2,224 enrolled. *Average high school GPA:* 3.15.
Faculty *Total:* 358, 54% full-time.
Majors Computer science; computer technology/computer systems technology; creative writing; criminal justice/police science; criminal justice/safety; dental hygiene; dietetic technology; dramatic/theater arts; elementary education; fine/studio arts; food science; hospitality administration; liberal arts and sciences/liberal studies; management information systems; manufacturing engineering technology; marketing/marketing management; medical office computer specialist; multi/interdisciplinary studies related; music; pre-engineering; registered nursing/registered nurse; special education; theater design and technology.
Academics *Calendar:* semesters. *Degree:* certificates and associate. *Special study options:* academic remediation for entering students, adult/continuing education programs, advanced placement credit, cooperative education, distance learning, English as a second language, external degree program, independent study, internships, off-campus study, part-time degree program, services for LD students, student-designed majors, study abroad, summer session for credit.
Library Library plus 1 other with 93,000 titles, 600 serial subscriptions, 40,000 audiovisual materials, an OPAC, a Web page.
Student Life *Housing:* college housing not available. *Activities and Organizations:* drama/theater group, student-run newspaper, choral group, Program Board (NPB), Student Senate, Phi Theta Kappa, Inter-Varsity Christian Fellowship, Latino Student Club. *Campus security:* 24-hour emergency response devices, student patrols, late-night transport/escort service. *Student services:* personal/psychological counseling.
Athletics *Intramural sports:* archery M/W, badminton M/W, basketball M/W, ice hockey M/W, soccer M/W, softball M/W, table tennis M/W, tennis M/W, volleyball M/W, weight lifting M/W.
Costs (2012–13) *Tuition:* state resident $161 per credit hour part-time; nonresident $161 per credit hour part-time. Full-time tuition and fees vary according to program and reciprocity agreements. Part-time tuition and fees vary according to program and reciprocity agreements. *Required fees:* $28 per credit hour part-time. *Payment plan:* installment. *Waivers:* senior citizens and employees or children of employees.
Applying *Options:* electronic application, deferred entrance. *Application fee:* $20. *Required for some:* high school transcript, GED is also accepted for admission. *Application deadlines:* rolling (freshmen), rolling (transfers). *Notification:* continuous (freshmen), continuous (transfers).
Freshman Application Contact Admissions Office, Normandale Community College, Normandy Community College, 9700 France Avenue South, Bloomington, MN 55431. *Phone:* 952-358-8201. *Toll-free phone:* 866-880-8740. *Fax:* 952-358-8230. *E-mail:* information@normandale.edu.
Website: http://www.normandale.edu/.

North Hennepin Community College
Brooklyn Park, Minnesota

- **State-supported** 2-year, founded 1966, part of Minnesota State Colleges and Universities System
- **Suburban** 80-acre campus
- **Endowment** $697,321
- **Coed,** 7,657 undergraduate students, 30% full-time, 56% women, 44% men

Undergraduates 2,260 full-time, 5,397 part-time. Students come from 18 states and territories; 47 other countries; 0.3% are from out of state; 20% Black or African American, non-Hispanic/Latino; 5% Hispanic/Latino; 11% Asian, non-Hispanic/Latino; 0.4% American Indian or Alaska Native, non-Hispanic/Latino; 5% Two or more races, non-Hispanic/Latino; 2% Race/ethnicity unknown; 1% international; 14% transferred in. *Retention:* 56% of full-time freshmen returned.
Freshmen *Admission:* 3,192 applied, 2,094 admitted, 925 enrolled.
Faculty *Total:* 248, 42% full-time, 6% with terminal degrees. *Student/faculty ratio:* 31:1.
Majors Accounting; biology/biological sciences; building/construction site management; building/home/construction inspection; business administration and management; chemistry; clinical/medical laboratory technology; computer science; construction management; creative writing; criminal justice/law enforcement administration; criminal justice/police science; criminal justice/safety; dramatic/theater arts; engineering; finance; fine/studio arts; graphic design; histologic technology/histotechnologist; history; legal assistant/paralegal; liberal arts and sciences/liberal studies; management information systems; marketing/marketing management; mathematics; multi/interdisciplinary studies related; music; physical education teaching and coaching; pre-engineering; registered nursing/registered nurse; small business administration.
Academics *Calendar:* semesters. *Degree:* certificates and associate. *Special study options:* academic remediation for entering students, accelerated degree

program, adult/continuing education programs, advanced placement credit, distance learning, double majors, English as a second language, external degree program, honors programs, independent study, internships, off-campus study, part-time degree program, services for LD students, student-designed majors, study abroad, summer session for credit. *ROTC:* Army (c), Navy (c), Air Force (c).
Library Learning Resource Center with 52,849 titles, 8,000 serial subscriptions, 3,244 audiovisual materials, an OPAC, a Web page.
Student Life *Housing:* college housing not available. *Activities and Organizations:* drama/theater group, choral group, Muslim Student Association, Phi Theta Kappa, Student Anime Game Club, Multicultural Club. *Campus security:* 24-hour emergency response devices, student patrols, late-night transport/escort service. *Student services:* personal/psychological counseling.
Athletics *Intramural sports:* badminton M/W, basketball M/W, bowling M/W, cross-country running M/W, football M/W, golf M/W, ice hockey M/W, rock climbing M/W, soccer M/W, softball M/W, table tennis M/W, tennis M/W, volleyball M/W, weight lifting M/W.
Costs (2013–14) *Tuition:* state resident $4952 full-time, $206 per credit part-time; nonresident $4952 full-time, $21 per credit part-time. Full-time tuition and fees vary according to course load, location, and program. Part-time tuition and fees vary according to course load, location, and program. *Required fees:* $495 full-time. *Payment plan:* installment. *Waivers:* senior citizens and employees or children of employees.
Financial Aid Of all full-time matriculated undergraduates who enrolled in 2011, 125 Federal Work-Study jobs, 200 state and other part-time jobs.
Applying *Options:* electronic application, early admission, deferred entrance. *Application fee:* $20. *Recommended:* high school transcript. *Application deadlines:* rolling (freshmen), rolling (transfers). *Notification:* continuous (freshmen), continuous (transfers).
Freshman Application Contact Ms. Alison Leintz, Admissions Specialist, North Hennepin Community College, 7411 85th Ave N., Brooklyn Park, MN 55445. *Phone:* 763-424-0722. *Toll-free phone:* 800-818-0395. *Fax:* 763-424-0929. *E-mail:* aleintz@nhcc.edu.
Website: http://www.nhcc.edu/.

Northland Community and Technical College–Thief River Falls & East Grand Forks
Thief River Falls, Minnesota

Freshman Application Contact Mr. Eugene Klinke, Director of Enrollment Management and Multicultural Services, Northland Community and Technical College–Thief River Falls & East Grand Forks, 1101 Highway One East, Thief River Falls, MN 56701. *Phone:* 218-683-8554. *Toll-free phone:* 800-959-6282. *Fax:* 218-683-8980. *E-mail:* eugene.klinke@northlandcollege.edu.
Website: http://www.northlandcollege.edu/.

Northwest Technical College
Bemidji, Minnesota

- **State-supported** 2-year, founded 1993, part of Minnesota State Colleges and Universities System
- **Small-town** campus
- **Coed,** 1,168 undergraduate students, 37% full-time, 69% women, 31% men

Undergraduates 435 full-time, 733 part-time. 7% are from out of state; 4% Black or African American, non-Hispanic/Latino; 2% Hispanic/Latino; 0.6% Asian, non-Hispanic/Latino; 0.1% Native Hawaiian or other Pacific Islander, non-Hispanic/Latino; 1% American Indian or Alaska Native, non-Hispanic/Latino; 4% Two or more races, non-Hispanic/Latino; 1% Race/ethnicity unknown; 0.1% international; 19% transferred in; 3% live on campus. *Retention:* 39% of full-time freshmen returned.
Freshmen *Admission:* 279 admitted, 129 enrolled.
Faculty *Total:* 67, 46% full-time. *Student/faculty ratio:* 16:1.
Majors Accounting; administrative assistant and secretarial science; automobile/automotive mechanics technology; business administration and management; child-care and support services management; computer systems networking and telecommunications; dental assisting; energy management and systems technology; engine machinist; industrial safety technology; industrial technology; licensed practical/vocational nurse training; manufacturing engineering technology; medical administrative assistant and medical secretary; registered nursing/registered nurse; sales, distribution, and marketing operations.
Academics *Calendar:* semesters. *Degree:* certificates, diplomas, and associate. *Special study options:* part-time degree program.
Library Northwest Technical College Learning Enrichment Center.
Student Life *Housing Options:* coed, disabled students. Campus housing is provided by a third party.

Costs (2012–13) *Tuition:* state resident $5190 full-time, $173 per credit part-time; nonresident $5190 full-time, $173 per credit part-time. Full-time tuition and fees vary according to program. Part-time tuition and fees vary according to program. *Required fees:* $292 full-time, $10 per credit part-time. *Room and board:* $6970; room only: $4380. Room and board charges vary according to board plan and housing facility. *Payment plan:* installment. *Waivers:* senior citizens and employees or children of employees.

Applying *Options:* electronic application. *Application fee:* $20. *Required:* high school transcript. *Application deadlines:* rolling (freshmen), rolling (transfers). *Notification:* continuous (freshmen), continuous (transfers).

Freshman Application Contact Ms. Kari Kantack-Miller, Diversity and Enrollment Representative, Northwest Technical College, 905 Grant Avenue, Southeast, Bemidji, MN 56601. *Phone:* 218-333-6645. *Toll-free phone:* 800-942-8324. *Fax:* 218-333-6694. *E-mail:* kari.kantack@ntcmn.edu. *Website:* http://www.ntcmn.edu/.

Northwest Technical Institute
Eagan, Minnesota

Freshman Application Contact Northwest Technical Institute, 950 Blue Gentian Road, Suite 500, Eagan, MN 55121. *Phone:* 952-944-0080 Ext. 103. *Toll-free phone:* 800-443-4223.
Website: http://www.nti.edu/.

Pine Technical College
Pine City, Minnesota

Freshman Application Contact Pine Technical College, 900 4th Street SE, Pine City, MN 55063. *Phone:* 320-629-5100. *Toll-free phone:* 800-521-7463. *Website:* http://www.pinetech.edu/.

Rainy River Community College
International Falls, Minnesota

- **State-supported** 2-year, founded 1967, part of Minnesota State Colleges and Universities System
- **Small-town** 80-acre campus
- **Coed**

Undergraduates 268 full-time, 76 part-time. 13% Black or African American, non-Hispanic/Latino; 0.9% Hispanic/Latino; 1% Asian, non-Hispanic/Latino; 5% American Indian or Alaska Native, non-Hispanic/Latino; 8% international.
Faculty *Student/faculty ratio:* 15:1.
Academics *Calendar:* semesters. *Degree:* certificates, diplomas, and associate. *Special study options:* academic remediation for entering students, adult/continuing education programs, advanced placement credit, cooperative education, honors programs, independent study, internships, part-time degree program, services for LD students, summer session for credit.
Student Life *Campus security:* 24-hour emergency response devices, late-night transport/escort service, controlled dormitory access.
Athletics Member NJCAA.
Costs (2012–13) *Tuition:* state resident $4729 full-time; nonresident $5911 full-time. Full-time tuition and fees vary according to program and reciprocity agreements. Part-time tuition and fees vary according to program and reciprocity agreements. *Required fees:* $594 full-time. *Room and board:* room only: $2950. Room and board charges vary according to housing facility.
Applying *Options:* electronic application, early admission, deferred entrance. *Application fee:* $20. *Recommended:* high school transcript.
Freshman Application Contact Ms. Berta Hagen, Registrar, Rainy River Community College, 1501 Highway 71, International Falls, MN 56649. *Phone:* 218-285-2207. *Toll-free phone:* 800-456-3996. *Fax:* 218-285-2314. *E-mail:* bhagen@rrcc.mnscu.edu.
Website: http://www.rrcc.mnscu.edu/.

Rasmussen College Bloomington
Bloomington, Minnesota

- **Proprietary** primarily 2-year, founded 1904, part of Rasmussen College System
- **Suburban** campus with easy access to Minneapolis/St. Paul
- **Coed,** 546 undergraduate students

Faculty *Student/faculty ratio:* 22:1.
Majors Accounting; business administration and management; computer and information systems security; computer science; computer software engineering; corrections and criminal justice related; criminal justice/police science; early childhood education; graphic communications related; health/health-care administration; health information/medical records administration; health information/medical records technology; human resources management; human services; legal assistant/paralegal; management information systems and services related; marketing/marketing management; medical administra-

tive assistant and medical secretary; medical/clinical assistant; pharmacy technician; web page, digital/multimedia and information resources design.
Academics *Calendar:* quarters. *Degrees:* certificates, diplomas, associate, and bachelor's. *Special study options:* academic remediation for entering students, accelerated degree program, adult/continuing education programs, distance learning, double majors, internships, part-time degree program, summer session for credit.
Library Rasmussen College Library - Bloomington with 2,259 titles, 29 serial subscriptions, 296 audiovisual materials, an OPAC, a Web page.
Student Life *Housing:* college housing not available.
Standardized Tests *Required:* Internal Exam (for admission).
Costs (2013–14) *Tuition:* $14,220 full-time. Full-time tuition and fees vary according to course level, course load, degree level, location, and program. Part-time tuition and fees vary according to course level, course load, degree level, location, and program. *Required fees:* $1800 full-time. *Payment plans:* installment, deferred payment. *Waivers:* employees or children of employees.
Financial Aid Of all full-time matriculated undergraduates who enrolled in 2011, 3 state and other part-time jobs (averaging $4338).
Applying *Options:* electronic application, early admission, deferred entrance. *Required:* high school transcript, minimum 2.0 GPA. *Required for some:* interview. *Application deadlines:* rolling (freshmen), rolling (transfers).
Freshman Application Contact Susan Hammerstrom, Director of Admissions, Rasmussen College Bloomington, 4400 West 78th Street, Bloomington, MN 55305. *Phone:* 952-545-2000. *Toll-free phone:* 888-549-6755.
Website: http://www.rasmussen.edu/.

Rasmussen College Brooklyn Park
Brooklyn Park, Minnesota

- **Proprietary** primarily 2-year, part of Rasmussen College System
- **Suburban** campus
- **Coed,** 892 undergraduate students

Faculty *Student/faculty ratio:* 22:1.
Majors Accounting; business administration and management; computer and information systems security; computer science; computer software engineering; corrections and criminal justice related; criminal justice/police science; early childhood education; graphic communications related; health/health-care administration; health information/medical records administration; health information/medical records technology; human resources management; human services; legal assistant/paralegal; management information systems and services related; marketing/marketing management; medical administrative assistant and medical secretary; medical/clinical assistant; pharmacy technician; surgical technology; web page, digital/multimedia and information resources design.
Academics *Degrees:* certificates, diplomas, associate, and bachelor's. *Special study options:* academic remediation for entering students, accelerated degree program, adult/continuing education programs, distance learning, double majors, internships, part-time degree program, summer session for credit.
Library Rasmussen College Library - Brooklyn Park with 2,563 titles, 22 serial subscriptions, 387 audiovisual materials, an OPAC, a Web page.
Student Life *Housing:* college housing not available.
Standardized Tests *Required:* Internal Exam (for admission).
Costs (2013–14) *Tuition:* $14,220 full-time. Full-time tuition and fees vary according to course level, course load, degree level, location, and program. Part-time tuition and fees vary according to course level, course load, degree level, location, and program. *Required fees:* $1800 full-time. *Payment plans:* installment, deferred payment. *Waivers:* employees or children of employees.
Applying *Options:* electronic application, early admission, deferred entrance. *Required:* high school transcript, minimum 2.0 GPA. *Required for some:* interview. *Application deadlines:* rolling (freshmen), rolling (transfers).
Freshman Application Contact Susan Hammerstrom, Director of Admissions, Rasmussen College Brooklyn Park, 8301 93rd Avenue North, Brooklyn Park, MN 55445-1512. *Phone:* 763-493-4500. *Toll-free phone:* 888-549-6755. *E-mail:* susan.hammerstrom@rasmussen.edu.
Website: http://www.rasmussen.edu/.

Rasmussen College Eagan
Eagan, Minnesota

- **Proprietary** primarily 2-year, founded 1904, part of Rasmussen College System
- **Suburban** campus with easy access to Minneapolis/St. Paul
- **Coed, primarily women,** 883 undergraduate students

Faculty *Student/faculty ratio:* 22:1.
Majors Accounting; business administration and management; computer and information systems security; computer science; computer software engineering; corrections and criminal justice related; criminal justice/police science; early childhood education; graphic communications related; health/health-care

administration; health information/medical records administration; health information/medical records technology; human resources management; human services; legal assistant/paralegal; management information systems and services related; marketing/marketing management; medical administrative assistant and medical secretary; medical/clinical assistant; pharmacy technician; web page, digital/multimedia and information resources design.

Academics *Calendar:* quarters. *Degrees:* certificates, diplomas, associate, and bachelor's. *Special study options:* academic remediation for entering students, accelerated degree program, adult/continuing education programs, distance learning, double majors, internships, part-time degree program, summer session for credit.

Library Rasmussen College Library - Eagan with 2,542 titles, 19 serial subscriptions, 207 audiovisual materials, an OPAC, a Web page.

Student Life *Housing:* college housing not available.

Standardized Tests *Required:* Internal Exam (for admission).

Costs (2013–14) *Tuition:* $14,220 full-time. Full-time tuition and fees vary according to course level, course load, degree level, location, and program. Part-time tuition and fees vary according to course level, course load, degree level, location, and program. *Required fees:* $1800 full-time. *Payment plans:* installment, deferred payment. *Waivers:* employees or children of employees.

Applying *Options:* electronic application, early admission, deferred entrance. *Required:* high school transcript, minimum 2.0 GPA. *Required for some:* interview. *Application deadlines:* rolling (freshmen), rolling (transfers).

Freshman Application Contact Susan Hammerstrom, Director of Admissions, Rasmussen College Eagan, 3500 Federal Drive, Eagan, MN 55122-1346. *Phone:* 651-687-9000. *Toll-free phone:* 888-549-6755. *E-mail:* susan.hammerstrom@rasmussen.edu. *Website:* http://www.rasmussen.edu/.

Rasmussen College Lake Elmo/Woodbury

Lake Elmo, Minnesota

- **Proprietary** primarily 2-year, part of Rasmussen College System
- **Suburban** campus
- **Coed,** 682 undergraduate students

Faculty *Student/faculty ratio:* 22:1.

Majors Accounting; business administration and management; clinical/medical laboratory technology; computer and information systems security; computer science; computer software engineering; corrections and criminal justice related; criminal justice/police science; early childhood education; graphic communications related; health/health-care administration; health information/medical records administration; health information/medical records technology; human resources management; human services; legal assistant/paralegal; management information systems and services related; marketing/marketing management; medical administrative assistant and medical secretary; medical/clinical assistant; pharmacy technician; web page, digital/multimedia and information resources design.

Academics *Degrees:* certificates, diplomas, associate, and bachelor's. *Special study options:* academic remediation for entering students, accelerated degree program, adult/continuing education programs, distance learning, double majors, internships, part-time degree program, summer session for credit.

Library Rasmussen College Library - Lake Elmo with 2,981 titles, 22 serial subscriptions, 90 audiovisual materials, an OPAC, a Web page.

Student Life *Housing:* college housing not available.

Standardized Tests *Required:* Internal Exam (for admission).

Costs (2013–14) *Tuition:* $14,220 full-time. Full-time tuition and fees vary according to course level, course load, degree level, location, and program. Part-time tuition and fees vary according to course level, course load, degree level, location, and program. *Required fees:* $1800 full-time. *Payment plans:* installment, deferred payment. *Waivers:* employees or children of employees.

Applying *Options:* electronic application, early admission, deferred entrance. *Required:* high school transcript, minimum 2.0 GPA. *Required for some:* interview. *Application deadlines:* rolling (freshmen), rolling (transfers).

Freshman Application Contact Susan Hammerstrom, Director of Admissions, Rasmussen College Lake Elmo/Woodbury, 8565 Eagle Point Circle, Lake Elmo, MN 55042. *Phone:* 651-259-6600. *Toll-free phone:* 888-549-6755. *E-mail:* susan.hammerstrom@rasmussen.edu. *Website:* http://www.rasmussen.edu/.

Rasmussen College Mankato

Mankato, Minnesota

- **Proprietary** primarily 2-year, founded 1904, part of Rasmussen College System
- **Suburban** campus
- **Coed, primarily women,** 745 undergraduate students

Faculty *Student/faculty ratio:* 22:1.

Majors Accounting; business administration and management; clinical/medical laboratory technology; computer and information systems security; computer science; computer software engineering; corrections and criminal justice related; criminal justice/police science; early childhood education; graphic communications related; health/health-care administration; health information/medical records administration; health information/medical records technology; human resources management; human services; legal assistant/paralegal; management information systems and services related; marketing/marketing management; medical administrative assistant and medical secretary; medical/clinical assistant; pharmacy technician; web page, digital/multimedia and information resources design.

Academics *Calendar:* quarters. *Degrees:* certificates, diplomas, associate, and bachelor's. *Special study options:* academic remediation for entering students, accelerated degree program, adult/continuing education programs, distance learning, double majors, internships, part-time degree program, summer session for credit.

Library Rasmussen College Library - Mankato with 2,838 titles, 24 serial subscriptions, 261 audiovisual materials, an OPAC, a Web page.

Student Life *Housing:* college housing not available.

Standardized Tests *Required:* Internal Exam (for admission).

Costs (2013–14) *Tuition:* $14,220 full-time. Full-time tuition and fees vary according to course level, course load, degree level, location, and program. Part-time tuition and fees vary according to course level, course load, degree level, location, and program. *Required fees:* $1800 full-time. *Payment plans:* installment, deferred payment. *Waivers:* employees or children of employees.

Financial Aid Of all full-time matriculated undergraduates who enrolled in 2011, 15 Federal Work-Study jobs (averaging $4000). 13 state and other part-time jobs (averaging $4000).

Applying *Options:* electronic application, early admission, deferred entrance. *Required:* high school transcript, minimum 2.0 GPA. *Required for some:* interview. *Application deadlines:* rolling (freshmen), rolling (transfers).

Freshman Application Contact Susan Hammerstrom, Director of Admissions, Rasmussen College Mankato, 130 Saint Andrews Drive, Mankato, MN 56001. *Phone:* 507-625-6556. *Toll-free phone:* 888-549-6755. *E-mail:* susan.hammerstrom@rasmussen.edu. *Website:* http://www.rasmussen.edu/.

Rasmussen College Moorhead

Moorhead, Minnesota

- **Proprietary** primarily 2-year, part of Rasmussen College System
- **Suburban** campus
- **Coed,** 420 undergraduate students

Faculty *Student/faculty ratio:* 22:1.

Majors Accounting; business administration and management; clinical/medical laboratory technology; computer and information systems security; computer science; computer software engineering; corrections and criminal justice related; early childhood education; graphic communications related; health/health-care administration; health information/medical records administration; health information/medical records technology; human resources management; human services; legal assistant/paralegal; management information systems and services related; marketing/marketing management; medical administrative assistant and medical secretary; medical/clinical assistant; pharmacy technician; web page, digital/multimedia and information resources design.

Academics *Degrees:* certificates, diplomas, associate, and bachelor's. *Special study options:* academic remediation for entering students, accelerated degree program, adult/continuing education programs, distance learning, double majors, internships, part-time degree program, summer session for credit.

Library Rasmussen College Library - Moorhead with 624 titles, 12 serial subscriptions, 112 audiovisual materials, an OPAC, a Web page.

Student Life *Housing:* college housing not available.

Standardized Tests *Required:* Internal Exam (for admission).

Costs (2013–14) *Tuition:* $14,220 full-time. Full-time tuition and fees vary according to course level, course load, degree level, location, and program. Part-time tuition and fees vary according to course level, course load, degree level, location, and program. *Required fees:* $1800 full-time. *Payment plans:* installment, deferred payment. *Waivers:* employees or children of employees.

Applying *Options:* electronic application, early admission, deferred entrance. *Required:* high school transcript, minimum 2.0 GPA. *Required for some:* interview. *Application deadlines:* rolling (freshmen), rolling (transfers).

Freshman Application Contact Susan Hammerstrom, Director of Admissions, Rasmussen College Moorhead, 1250 29th Avenue South, Moorhead, MN 56560. *Phone:* 218-304-6200. *Toll-free phone:* 888-549-6755. *E-mail:* susan.hammerstrom@rasmussen.edu. *Website:* http://www.rasmussen.edu/.

Rasmussen College St. Cloud

St. Cloud, Minnesota

- **Proprietary** primarily 2-year, founded 1904, part of Rasmussen College System
- **Suburban** campus
- **Coed, primarily women,** 845 undergraduate students

Faculty *Student/faculty ratio:* 22:1.

Majors Accounting; blood bank technology; business administration and management; clinical/medical laboratory technology; computer and information systems security; computer science; computer software engineering; corrections and criminal justice related; criminal justice/police science; early childhood education; graphic communications related; health/health-care administration; health information/medical records administration; health information/medical records technology; human services; legal assistant/paralegal; management information systems and services related; marketing/marketing management; medical administrative assistant and medical secretary; medical/clinical assistant; pharmacy technician; surgical technology; web page, digital/multimedia and information resources design.

Academics *Calendar:* quarters. *Degrees:* certificates, diplomas, associate, and bachelor's. *Special study options:* academic remediation for entering students, accelerated degree program, adult/continuing education programs, distance learning, double majors, internships, part-time degree program, summer session for credit.

Library Rasmussen College Library - St. Cloud with 2,423 titles, 6 serial subscriptions, 397 audiovisual materials, an OPAC, a Web page.

Student Life *Housing:* college housing not available.

Standardized Tests *Required:* Internal Exam (for admission).

Costs (2013–14) *Tuition:* $14,220 full-time. Full-time tuition and fees vary according to course level, course load, degree level, location, and program. Part-time tuition and fees vary according to course level, course load, degree level, location, and program. *Required fees:* $1800 full-time. *Payment plans:* installment, deferred payment. *Waivers:* employees or children of employees.

Financial Aid Of all full-time matriculated undergraduates who enrolled in 2011, 34 Federal Work-Study jobs (averaging $866). 51 state and other part-time jobs (averaging $700).

Applying *Options:* electronic application, early admission, deferred entrance. *Required:* high school transcript, minimum 2.0 GPA. *Required for some:* interview. *Application deadlines:* rolling (freshmen), rolling (transfers).

Freshman Application Contact Susan Hammerstrom, Director of Admissions, Rasmussen College St. Cloud, 226 Park Avenue South, St. Cloud, MN 56301-3713. *Phone:* 320-251-5600. *Toll-free phone:* 888-549-6755. *E-mail:* susan.hammerstrom@rasmussen.edu. *Website:* http://www.rasmussen.edu/.

Ridgewater College

Willmar, Minnesota

Freshman Application Contact Ms. Linda Barron, Admissions Assistant, Ridgewater College, PO Box 1097, Willmar, MN 56201-1097. *Phone:* 320-222-5976. *Toll-free phone:* 800-722-1151. *E-mail:* linda.barron@ridgewater.edu. *Website:* http://www.ridgewater.edu/.

Riverland Community College

Austin, Minnesota

Freshman Application Contact Ms. Renee Njos, Admission Secretary, Riverland Community College, Austin, MN 55912. *Phone:* 507-433-0820. *Toll-free phone:* 800-247-5039. *Fax:* 507-433-0515. *E-mail:* admissions@riverland.edu. *Website:* http://www.riverland.edu/.

Rochester Community and Technical College

Rochester, Minnesota

Director of Admissions Mr. Troy Tynsky, Director of Admissions, Rochester Community and Technical College, 851 30th Avenue, SE, Rochester, MN 55904-4999. *Phone:* 507-280-3509. *Website:* http://www.rctc.edu/.

St. Cloud Technical & Community College

St. Cloud, Minnesota

- **State-supported** 2-year, founded 1948, part of Minnesota State Colleges and Universities System
- **Urban** 35-acre campus with easy access to Minneapolis-St. Paul
- **Coed**

Undergraduates 2,742 full-time, 2,141 part-time. Students come from 15 states and territories; 3 other countries; 1% are from out of state; 36% transferred in.

Faculty *Student/faculty ratio:* 23:1.

Academics *Calendar:* semesters. *Degree:* certificates, diplomas, and associate. *Special study options:* academic remediation for entering students, adult/continuing education programs, advanced placement credit, cooperative education, distance learning, English as a second language, independent study, internships, part-time degree program, services for LD students, summer session for credit.

Student Life *Campus security:* late-night transport/escort service.

Athletics Member NJCAA.

Financial Aid Of all full-time matriculated undergraduates who enrolled in 2011, 69 Federal Work-Study jobs (averaging $2177). 76 state and other part-time jobs (averaging $1850).

Applying *Options:* electronic application, early admission, deferred entrance. *Application fee:* $20. *Required:* high school transcript. *Required for some:* essay or personal statement, interview.

Freshman Application Contact Ms. Jodi Elness, Admissions Office, St. Cloud Technical & Community College, 1540 Northway Drive, St. Cloud, MN 56303. *Phone:* 320-308-5089. *Toll-free phone:* 800-222-1009. *Fax:* 320-308-5981. *E-mail:* jelness@sctcc.edu. *Website:* http://www.sctcc.edu/.

Saint Paul College–A Community & Technical College

St. Paul, Minnesota

Freshman Application Contact Ms. Sarah Carrico, Saint Paul College–A Community & Technical College, 235 Marshall Avenue, Saint Paul, MN 55102. *Phone:* 651-846-1424. *Toll-free phone:* 800-227-6029. *Fax:* 651-846-1703. *E-mail:* admissions@saintpaul.edu. *Website:* http://www.saintpaul.edu/.

South Central College

North Mankato, Minnesota

Freshman Application Contact Ms. Beverly Herda, Director of Admissions, South Central College, 1920 Lee Boulevard, North Mankato, MN 56003. *Phone:* 507-389-7334. *Fax:* 507-388-9951. *Website:* http://southcentral.edu/.

Vermilion Community College

Ely, Minnesota

Freshman Application Contact Mr. Todd Heiman, Director of Enrollment Services, Vermilion Community College, 1900 East Camp Street, Ely, MN 55731-1996. *Phone:* 218-365-7224. *Toll-free phone:* 800-657-3608. *Website:* http://www.vcc.edu/.

MISSISSIPPI

Antonelli College

Hattiesburg, Mississippi

Freshman Application Contact Mrs. Karen Gautreau, Director, Antonelli College, 1500 North 31st Avenue, Hattiesburg, MS 39401. *Phone:* 601-583-4100. *Fax:* 601-583-0839. *E-mail:* admissionsh@antonellicollege.edu. *Website:* http://www.antonellicollege.edu/.

Antonelli College

Jackson, Mississippi

Freshman Application Contact Antonelli College, 2323 Lakeland Drive, Jackson, MS 39232. *Phone:* 601-362-9991. *Website:* http://www.antonellicollege.edu/.

Coahoma Community College

Clarksdale, Mississippi

Freshman Application Contact Mrs. Wanda Holmes, Director of Admissions and Records, Coahoma Community College, Clarksdale, MS 38614-9799. *Phone:* 662-621-4205. *Toll-free phone:* 866-470-1CCC. *Website:* http://www.ccc.cc.ms.us/.

Copiah-Lincoln Community College

Wesson, Mississippi

- **State and locally supported** 2-year, founded 1928, part of Mississippi Community College Board
- **Rural** 525-acre campus with easy access to Jackson
- **Endowment** $2.5 million
- **Coed,** 3,436 undergraduate students, 80% full-time, 64% women, 36% men

Undergraduates 2,754 full-time, 682 part-time. Students come from 10 states and territories; 1 other country; 43% Black or African American, non-Hispanic/Latino; 0.7% Hispanic/Latino; 0.2% Asian, non-Hispanic/Latino; 0.1% American Indian or Alaska Native, non-Hispanic/Latino; 0.1% Two or more races, non-Hispanic/Latino; 1% Race/ethnicity unknown; 30% live on campus.

Freshmen *Admission:* 804 enrolled.

Faculty *Total:* 138.

Majors Accounting; agribusiness; agricultural business and management; agricultural business and management related; agricultural business technology; agricultural economics; agricultural/farm supplies retailing and wholesaling; agriculture; architecture; art teacher education; biological and physical sciences; biology/biological sciences; business administration and management; chemistry; child development; civil engineering technology; clinical/medical laboratory technology; computer programming; cosmetology; criminal justice/police science; data processing and data processing technology; drafting and design technology; economics; education; electrical, electronic and communications engineering technology; elementary education; engineering; English; family and consumer sciences/home economics teacher education; farm and ranch management; food technology and processing; forestry; French; health teacher education; history; industrial radiologic technology; journalism; liberal arts and sciences/liberal studies; library and information science; music teacher education; physical education teaching and coaching; registered nursing/registered nurse; special products marketing; trade and industrial teacher education; wood science and wood products/pulp and paper technology.

Academics *Calendar:* semesters. *Degree:* certificates and associate. *Special study options:* academic remediation for entering students, adult/continuing education programs, advanced placement credit, honors programs, part-time degree program, student-designed majors, summer session for credit.

Library Oswalt Memorial Library with 34,357 titles, 166 serial subscriptions.

Student Life *Housing Options:* Campus housing is university owned. *Activities and Organizations:* drama/theater group, student-run newspaper, radio station, choral group, marching band. *Campus security:* 24-hour patrols. *Student services:* health clinic, personal/psychological counseling.

Athletics Member NJCAA. *Intercollegiate sports:* baseball M(s), basketball M(s)/W(s), football M(s), golf M/W, softball W, tennis M/W, track and field M. *Intramural sports:* basketball M/W, football M, golf M/W, tennis M/W, volleyball M/W.

Costs (2012–13) *Tuition:* state resident $2100 full-time; nonresident $3900 full-time. *Room and board:* Room and board charges vary according to board plan. *Waivers:* senior citizens and employees or children of employees.

Financial Aid Of all full-time matriculated undergraduates who enrolled in 2011, 125 Federal Work-Study jobs (averaging $1000).

Applying *Options:* early admission. *Required:* high school transcript. *Application deadlines:* rolling (freshmen), rolling (transfers).

Freshman Application Contact Ms. Gay Langham, Student Records Manager, Copiah-Lincoln Community College, PO Box 649, Wesson, MS 39191-0457. *Phone:* 601-643-8307. *E-mail:* gay.langham@colin.edu. *Website:* http://www.colin.edu/.

Copiah-Lincoln Community College– Natchez Campus

Natchez, Mississippi

Freshman Application Contact Copiah-Lincoln Community College– Natchez Campus, 11 Co-Lin Circle, Natchez, MS 39120-8446. *Phone:* 601-442-9111 Ext. 224. *Website:* http://www.colin.edu/.

East Central Community College

Decatur, Mississippi

Director of Admissions Ms. Donna Luke, Director of Admissions, Records, and Research, East Central Community College, PO Box 129, Decatur, MS 39327-0129. *Phone:* 601-635-2111 Ext. 206. *Toll-free phone:* 877-462-3222. *Website:* http://www.eccc.edu/.

East Mississippi Community College

Scooba, Mississippi

Director of Admissions Ms. Melinda Sciple, Admissions Officer, East Mississippi Community College, PO Box 158, Scooba, MS 39358-0158. *Phone:* 662-476-5041. *Website:* http://www.eastms.edu/.

Hinds Community College

Raymond, Mississippi

Director of Admissions Ms. Ginger Turner, Director of Admissions and Records, Hinds Community College, PO Box 1100, Raymond, MS 39154-1100. *Phone:* 601-857-3280. *Toll-free phone:* 800-HINDSCC. *Fax:* 601-857-3539. *Website:* http://www.hindscc.edu/.

Holmes Community College

Goodman, Mississippi

Director of Admissions Dr. Lynn Wright, Dean of Admissions and Records, Holmes Community College, PO Box 369, Goodman, MS 39079-0369. *Phone:* 601-472-2312 Ext. 1023. *Toll-free phone:* 800-HOLMES-4. *Website:* http://www.holmescc.edu/.

Itawamba Community College

Fulton, Mississippi

Freshman Application Contact Mr. Larry Boggs, Director of Student Recruitment and Scholarships, Itawamba Community College, 602 West Hill Street, Fulton, MS 38843. *Phone:* 601-862-8252. *E-mail:* laboggs@iccms.edu. *Website:* http://www.iccms.edu/.

Jones County Junior College

Ellisville, Mississippi

Director of Admissions Mrs. Dianne Speed, Director of Admissions and Records, Jones County Junior College, 900 South Court Street, Ellisville, MS 39437-3901. *Phone:* 601-477-4025. *Website:* http://www.jcjc.edu/.

Meridian Community College

Meridian, Mississippi

Freshman Application Contact Ms. Angela Payne, Director of Admissions, Meridian Community College, 910 Highway 19 North, Meridian, MS 39307. *Phone:* 601-484-8357. *Toll-free phone:* 800-MCC-THE-1. *E-mail:* apayne@meridiancc.edu. *Website:* http://www.meridiancc.edu/.

Mississippi Delta Community College

Moorhead, Mississippi

Director of Admissions Mr. Joseph F. Ray Jr., Vice President of Admissions, Mississippi Delta Community College, PO Box 668, Highway 3 and Cherry Street, Moorhead, MS 38761-0668. *Phone:* 662-246-6308. *Website:* http://www.msdelta.edu/.

Mississippi Gulf Coast Community College

Perkinston, Mississippi

Freshman Application Contact Mr. Ladd Taylor, Director of Admissions, Mississippi Gulf Coast Community College, Perkinston, MS 39573. *Phone:* 601-928-6264. *Fax:* 601-928-6299. *E-mail:* ladd.taylor@mgccc.edu. *Website:* http://www.mgccc.edu/.

Northeast Mississippi Community College

Booneville, Mississippi

Freshman Application Contact Office of Enrollment Services, Northeast Mississippi Community College, 101 Cunningham Boulevard, Booneville, MS 38829. *Phone:* 662-720-7239. *Toll-free phone:* 800-555-2154. *E-mail:* admitme@nemcc.edu.
Website: http://www.nemcc.edu/.

Northwest Mississippi Community College

Senatobia, Mississippi

Director of Admissions Ms. Deanna Ferguson, Director of Admissions and Recruiting, Northwest Mississippi Community College, 4975 Highway 51 North, Senatobia, MS 38668-1701. *Phone:* 662-562-3222.
Website: http://www.northwestms.edu/.

Pearl River Community College

Poplarville, Mississippi

Freshman Application Contact Mr. J. Dow Ford, Director of Admissions, Pearl River Community College, 101 Highway 11 North, Poplarville, MS 39470. *Phone:* 601-403-1000. *E-mail:* dford@prcc.edu.
Website: http://www.prcc.edu/.

Southwest Mississippi Community College

Summit, Mississippi

- **State and locally supported** 2-year, founded 1918, part of Mississippi State Board for Community and Junior Colleges
- **Rural** 701-acre campus
- **Coed**

Undergraduates 1,785 full-time, 268 part-time. Students come from 8 states and territories; 1 other country; 6% are from out of state; 43% Black or African American, non-Hispanic/Latino; 0.3% Hispanic/Latino; 0.5% Asian, non-Hispanic/Latino; 0.4% American Indian or Alaska Native, non-Hispanic/Latino; 0.2% Two or more races, non-Hispanic/Latino; 0.2% Race/ethnicity unknown; 45% transferred in; 35% live on campus. *Retention:* 50% of full-time freshmen returned.

Faculty *Student/faculty ratio:* 24:1.

Academics *Calendar:* semesters. *Degree:* certificates and associate. *Special study options:* academic remediation for entering students, adult/continuing education programs, advanced placement credit, distance learning, part-time degree program, summer session for credit.

Student Life *Campus security:* 24-hour patrols.

Athletics Member NJCAA.

Financial Aid Of all full-time matriculated undergraduates who enrolled in 2011, 85 Federal Work-Study jobs (averaging $698). 6 state and other part-time jobs (averaging $550).

Applying *Required:* high school transcript.

Freshman Application Contact Mr. Matthew Calhoun, Vice President of Admissions and Records, Southwest Mississippi Community College, 1156 College Drive, Summit, MS 39666. *Phone:* 601-276-2001. *Fax:* 601-276-3888. *E-mail:* mattc@smcc.edu.
Website: http://www.smcc.cc.ms.us/.

Virginia College in Jackson

Jackson, Mississippi

Director of Admissions Director of Admissions, Virginia College in Jackson, 4795 Interstate 55 North, Jackson, MS 39206. *Phone:* 601-977-0960.
Website: http://www.vc.edu/.

MISSOURI

American College of Technology

Saint Joseph, Missouri

Director of Admissions Richard Lingle, Lead Admission Coordinator, American College of Technology, 2300 Frederick Avenue, Saint Joseph, MO 64506. *Phone:* 800-908-9329 Ext. 13. *Toll-free phone:* 800-908-9329. *E-mail:* ricahrd@acot.edu.
Website: http://www.acot.edu/.

Anthem College–Kansas City

Kansas City, Missouri

Freshman Application Contact Admissions Office, Anthem College–Kansas City, 9001 State Line Road, Kansas City, MO 64114. *Phone:* 816-444-4300. *Toll-free phone:* 855-464-2684. *Fax:* 816-444-4494.
Website: http://anthem.edu/kansas-city-missouri/.

Anthem College–Maryland Heights

Maryland Heights, Missouri

- **Proprietary** 2-year
- **Urban** 1-acre campus with easy access to St Louis
- **Coed**

Undergraduates 281 full-time. Students come from 1 other state; 1 other country; 43% Black or African American, non-Hispanic/Latino; 2% Hispanic/Latino; 0.7% Asian, non-Hispanic/Latino; 4% Two or more races, non-Hispanic/Latino; 1% Race/ethnicity unknown; 0.4% international.
Faculty *Student/faculty ratio:* 21:1.
Academics *Degree:* certificates and associate. *Special study options:* academic remediation for entering students, internships.
Student Life *Campus security:* 24-hour emergency response devices and patrols.
Applying *Application fee:* $20. *Required:* high school transcript, interview, Entrance Assessment Tests.
Freshman Application Contact Mr. Brad Coleman, Admissions Office, Anthem College–Maryland Heights, 13723 Riverport Drive, Maryland Heights, MO 63043. *Phone:* 314-595-3400. *Toll-free phone:* 855-526-8436. *Fax:* 314-739-5133.
Website: http://anthem.edu/maryland-heights-missouri/.

Aviation Institute of Maintenance–Kansas City

Kansas City, Missouri

Freshman Application Contact Aviation Institute of Maintenance–Kansas City, 4100 Raytown Road, Kansas City, MO 64129. *Phone:* 816-753-9920. *Toll-free phone:* 888-349-5387. *Fax:* 816-753-9941.
Website: http://www.aviationmaintenance.edu/.

Brown Mackie College–St. Louis

Fenton, Missouri

Freshman Application Contact Brown Mackie College–St. Louis, #2 Soccer Park Road, Fenton, MO 63026. *Phone:* 636-651-3290.
Website: http://www.brownmackie.edu/st-louis/.

See display on next page and page 388 for the College Close-Up.

Concorde Career College

Kansas City, Missouri

Freshman Application Contact Deborah Crow, Director, Concorde Career College, 3239 Broadway, Kansas City, MO 64111-2407. *Phone:* 816-531-5223. *Fax:* 816-756-3231. *E-mail:* dcrow@concorde.edu.
Website: http://www.concorde.edu/.

Cottey College

Nevada, Missouri

Freshman Application Contact Ms. Judi Steege, Director of Admission, Cottey College, 1000 West Austin Boulevard, Nevada, MO 64772. *Phone:* 417-667-8181. *Toll-free phone:* 888-526-8839. *Fax:* 417-667-8103. *E-mail:* enrollmgt@cottey.edu.
Website: http://www.cottey.edu/.

Crowder College

Neosho, Missouri

- **State and locally supported** 2-year, founded 1963, part of Missouri Coordinating Board for Higher Education
- **Rural** 608-acre campus
- **Coed,** 5,576 undergraduate students, 45% full-time, 64% women, 36% men

Undergraduates 2,516 full-time, 3,060 part-time. Students come from 19 states and territories; 25 other countries; 4% are from out of state; 2% Black or African American, non-Hispanic/Latino; 7% Hispanic/Latino; 1% Asian, non-Hispanic/Latino; 0.5% Native Hawaiian or other Pacific Islander, non-Hispanic/Latino; 2% American Indian or Alaska Native, non-Hispanic/Latino; 2% Two or more races, non-Hispanic/Latino; 2% Race/ethnicity unknown; 0.2% international; 0.7% transferred in; 10% live on campus.

Freshmen *Admission:* 1,097 enrolled.

Faculty *Total:* 436, 19% full-time, 7% with terminal degrees. *Student/faculty ratio:* 12:1.

Majors Administrative assistant and secretarial science; agribusiness; agriculture; art; biology/biological sciences; business administration and management; business automation/technology/data entry; computer systems networking and telecommunications; construction engineering technology; drafting and design technology; dramatic/theater arts; education; electrical, electronic and communications engineering technology; elementary education; environmental engineering technology; environmental health; executive assistant/executive secretary; farm and ranch management; fire science/firefighting; general studies; industrial technology; legal administrative assistant/secretary; liberal arts and sciences/liberal studies; mass communication/media; mathematics; mathematics and computer science; medical administrative assistant and medical secretary; music; physical education teaching and coaching; physical sciences; poultry science; pre-engineering; psychology; public relations/image management; registered nursing/registered nurse.

Academics *Calendar:* semesters. *Degree:* certificates and associate. *Special study options:* academic remediation for entering students, adult/continuing education programs, advanced placement credit, cooperative education, English as a second language, freshman honors college, honors programs, independent study, part-time degree program, student-designed majors, study abroad, summer session for credit.

Library Bill & Margot Lee Library with 42,996 titles, 183 serial subscriptions, 6,499 audiovisual materials, an OPAC, a Web page.

Student Life *Housing Options:* men-only, women-only. Campus housing is university owned. *Activities and Organizations:* drama/theater group, student-run newspaper, choral group, Phi Theta Kappa, Students in Free Enterprise (SIFE), Baptist Student Union, Student Senate, Student Ambassadors. *Campus security:* 24-hour patrols. *Student services:* personal/psychological counseling. **Athletics** Member NJCAA. *Intercollegiate sports:* baseball M(s), basketball W(s), soccer M(s).

Financial Aid Of all full-time matriculated undergraduates who enrolled in 2011, 150 Federal Work-Study jobs (averaging $1000).

Applying *Application fee:* $25. *Required:* high school transcript. *Application deadlines:* rolling (freshmen), rolling (transfers). *Notification:* continuous (freshmen).

Freshman Application Contact Mr. Jim Riggs, Admissions Coordinator, Crowder College, Neosho, MO 64850. *Phone:* 417-451-3223 Ext. 5466. *Toll-free phone:* 866-238-7788. *Fax:* 417-455-5731. *E-mail:* jimriggs@crowder.edu.
Website: http://www.crowder.edu/.

Culinary Institute of St. Louis at Hickey College

St. Louis, Missouri

- **Private** 2-year, founded 2009
- **Suburban** campus
- **Coed,** 103 undergraduate students

Majors Cooking and related culinary arts.

Academics *Degree:* associate.

Freshman Application Contact Admissions Office, Culinary Institute of St. Louis at Hickey College, 2700 North Lindbergh Boulevard, St. Louis, MO 63114. *Phone:* 314-434-2212.
Website: http://www.ci-stl.com/.

East Central College

Union, Missouri

Freshman Application Contact Miss Megen Poynter, Admissions Coordinator, East Central College, 1964 Prairie Dell Road, Union, MO 63084. *Phone:* 636-584-6564. *Fax:* 636-584-7347. *E-mail:* poynterm@eastcentral.edu.
Website: http://www.eastcentral.edu/.

Everest College
Springfield, Missouri

Freshman Application Contact Admissions Office, Everest College, 1010 West Sunshine, Springfield, MO 65807-2488. *Phone:* 417-864-7220. *Toll-free phone:* 888-741-4270. *Fax:* 417-864-5697.
Website: http://www.everest.edu/.

Heritage College
Kansas City, Missouri

Freshman Application Contact Admissions Office, Heritage College, 1200 East 104th Street, Suite 300, Kansas City, MO 64131. *Phone:* 816-942-5474. *Toll-free phone:* 888-334-7339. *E-mail:* info@heritage-education.com. *Website:* http://www.heritage-education.com/.

IHM Academy of EMS
St. Louis, Missouri

Freshman Application Contact Admissions Director, IHM Academy of EMS, 2500 Abbott Place, St. Louis, MO 63143. *Phone:* 314-768-1234. *Fax:* 314-768-1595. *E-mail:* info@ihmhealthstudies.edu.
Website: http://www.ihmacademyofems.net/.

ITT Technical Institute
Arnold, Missouri

- **Proprietary** primarily 2-year, founded 1997, part of ITT Educational Services, Inc.
- **Coed**

Academics *Calendar:* quarters. *Degrees:* associate and bachelor's.
Freshman Application Contact Director of Recruitment, ITT Technical Institute, 1930 Meyer Drury Drive, Arnold, MO 63010. *Phone:* 636-464-6600. *Toll-free phone:* 888-488-1082.
Website: http://www.itt-tech.edu/.

ITT Technical Institute
Earth City, Missouri

- **Proprietary** primarily 2-year, founded 1936, part of ITT Educational Services, Inc.
- **Suburban** campus
- **Coed**

Academics *Calendar:* quarters. *Degrees:* associate and bachelor's.
Freshman Application Contact Director of Recruitment, ITT Technical Institute, 3640 Corporate Trail Drive, Earth City, MO 63045. *Phone:* 314-298-7800. *Toll-free phone:* 800-235-5488.
Website: http://www.itt-tech.edu/.

ITT Technical Institute
Kansas City, Missouri

- **Proprietary** primarily 2-year, founded 2004, part of ITT Educational Services, Inc.
- **Coed**

Academics *Calendar:* quarters. *Degrees:* associate and bachelor's.
Freshman Application Contact Director of Recruitment, ITT Technical Institute, 9150 East 41st Terrace, Kansas City, MO 64133. *Phone:* 816-276-1400. *Toll-free phone:* 877-488-1442.
Website: http://www.itt-tech.edu/.

Jefferson College
Hillsboro, Missouri

- **District-supported** 2-year, founded 1963
- **Rural** 455-acre campus with easy access to St. Louis
- **Endowment** $681,575
- **Coed,** 5,494 undergraduate students, 54% full-time, 58% women, 42% men

Undergraduates 2,944 full-time, 2,550 part-time. 12% are from out of state; 2% Black or African American, non-Hispanic/Latino; 0.8% Hispanic/Latino; 0.6% Asian, non-Hispanic/Latino; 0.1% Native Hawaiian or other Pacific Islander, non-Hispanic/Latino; 0.5% American Indian or Alaska Native, non-Hispanic/Latino; 0.4% Two or more races, non-Hispanic/Latino; 4% Race/ethnicity unknown; 0.2% international.
Freshmen *Admission:* 1,160 enrolled.
Faculty *Total:* 360, 26% full-time, 11% with terminal degrees.

Majors Administrative assistant and secretarial science; automobile/automotive mechanics technology; business administration and management; business/commerce; child-care and support services management; computer systems networking and telecommunications; criminal justice/law enforcement administration; criminal justice/police science; culinary arts; education (specific levels and methods) related; electrical, electronic and communications engineering technology; emergency medical technology (EMT paramedic); engineering; fire prevention and safety technology; heating, air conditioning, ventilation and refrigeration maintenance technology; information technology; legal administrative assistant/secretary; liberal arts and sciences/liberal studies; licensed practical/vocational nurse training; machine tool technology; manufacturing engineering technology; medical administrative assistant and medical secretary; precision production related; registered nursing/registered nurse; veterinary/animal health technology; welding technology.
Academics *Calendar:* semesters. *Degree:* certificates, diplomas, and associate. *Special study options:* academic remediation for entering students, adult/continuing education programs, advanced placement credit, distance learning, English as a second language, freshman honors college, honors programs, internships, off-campus study, part-time degree program, services for LD students, summer session for credit.
Library Jefferson College Library plus 1 other with 71,576 titles, 60 serial subscriptions, 2,713 audiovisual materials, an OPAC, a Web page.
Student Life *Housing Options:* coed. Campus housing is university owned. *Activities and Organizations:* drama/theater group, student-run newspaper, television station, choral group, Student Senate, Nursing associations, Baptist Student Unit, Phi Beta Lambda, Phi Theta Kappa, national sororities. *Campus security:* 24-hour patrols. *Student services:* personal/psychological counseling.
Athletics Member NJCAA. *Intercollegiate sports:* baseball M(s), basketball W(s), cheerleading M(s)/W(s), soccer M(s), softball W(s), volleyball W(s).
Costs (2013–14) *One-time required fee:* $25. *Tuition:* area resident $2910 full-time; state resident $4260 full-time; nonresident $5610 full-time. *Required fees:* $90 full-time. *Room and board:* $5121; room only: $3240. Room and board charges vary according to housing facility. *Payment plan:* installment. *Waivers:* senior citizens and employees or children of employees.
Financial Aid Of all full-time matriculated undergraduates who enrolled in 2011, 2,778 applied for aid, 2,193 were judged to have need, 112 had their need fully met. 104 Federal Work-Study jobs (averaging $1205). 169 state and other part-time jobs (averaging $1522). In 2011, 159 non-need-based awards were made. *Average percent of need met:* 56%. *Average financial aid package:* $4969. *Average need-based loan:* $2874. *Average need-based gift aid:* $2501. *Average non-need-based aid:* $1801.
Applying *Options:* electronic application, early admission. *Application fee:* $25. *Required:* high school transcript. *Application deadlines:* rolling (freshmen), rolling (transfers).
Freshman Application Contact Ms. Kim Harvey, Director of Student Records and Admissions Services, Jefferson College, 1000 Viking Drive, Hillsboro, MO 63050-2441. *Phone:* 636-481-3217 Ext. 3217. *Fax:* 636-789-5103. *E-mail:* admissions@jeffco.edu.
Website: http://www.jeffco.edu/.

Linn State Technical College
Linn, Missouri

- **State-supported** 2-year, founded 1961
- **Rural** 249-acre campus
- **Coed, primarily men**
- 63% of applicants were admitted

Undergraduates 1,001 full-time, 167 part-time. Students come from 7 states and territories; 4% are from out of state; 2% Black or African American, non-Hispanic/Latino; 0.3% Hispanic/Latino; 0.3% Asian, non-Hispanic/Latino; 0.5% American Indian or Alaska Native, non-Hispanic/Latino; 0.3% Two or more races, non-Hispanic/Latino; 2% Race/ethnicity unknown; 14% transferred in; 15% live on campus. *Retention:* 77% of full-time freshmen returned.
Faculty *Student/faculty ratio:* 12:1.
Academics *Calendar:* semesters. *Degree:* certificates and associate. *Special study options:* academic remediation for entering students, adult/continuing education programs, cooperative education, distance learning, double majors, independent study, internships, off-campus study, part-time degree program, services for LD students, summer session for credit. *ROTC:* Army (c).
Student Life *Campus security:* 24-hour emergency response devices, student patrols, controlled dormitory access, indoor and outdoor surveillance cameras.
Standardized Tests *Required:* COMPASS (for admission). *Required for some:* ACT (for admission).
Financial Aid Of all full-time matriculated undergraduates who enrolled in 2011, 70 Federal Work-Study jobs (averaging $769).
Applying *Options:* electronic application. *Required:* high school transcript. *Required for some:* essay or personal statement, 1 letter of recommendation, interview, some require high school attendance, mechanical test.
Freshman Application Contact Linn State Technical College, One Technology Drive, Linn, MO 65051-9606. *Phone:* 573-897-5196. *Toll-free*

phone: 800-743-TECH.
Website: http://www.linnstate.edu/.

Metro Business College
Cape Girardeau, Missouri

Director of Admissions Ms. Kyla Evans, Admissions Director, Metro Business College, 1732 North Kingshighway, Cape Girardeau, MO 63701. *Phone:* 573-334-9181. *Toll-free phone:* 888-206-4545. *Fax:* 573-334-0617. *Website:* http://www.metrobusinesscollege.edu/.

Metro Business College
Jefferson City, Missouri

Freshman Application Contact Ms. Cheri Chockley, Campus Director, Metro Business College, 1407 Southwest Boulevard, Jefferson City, MO 65109. *Phone:* 573-635-6600. *Toll-free phone:* 888-206-4545. *Fax:* 573-635-6999. *E-mail:* cheri@metrobusinesscollege.edu. *Website:* http://www.metrobusinesscollege.edu/.

Metro Business College
Rolla, Missouri

Freshman Application Contact Admissions Office, Metro Business College, 1202 East Highway 72, Rolla, MO 65401. *Phone:* 573-364-8464. *Toll-free phone:* 888-206-4545. *Fax:* 573-364-8077. *E-mail:* inforolla@metrobusinesscollege.edu. *Website:* http://www.metrobusinesscollege.edu/.

Metropolitan Community College–Kansas City
Lee's Summit, Missouri

- **State and locally supported** 2-year, founded 1969, part of Metropolitan Community Colleges System
- **Suburban** 420-acre campus with easy access to Kansas City
- **Endowment** $3.4 million
- **Coed,** 20,141 undergraduate students, 38% full-time, 58% women, 42% men

Undergraduates 7,736 full-time, 12,405 part-time. Students come from 18 states and territories; 80 other countries; 1% are from out of state; 18% Black or African American, non-Hispanic/Latino; 7% Hispanic/Latino; 2% Asian, non-Hispanic/Latino; 0.4% Native Hawaiian or other Pacific Islander, non-Hispanic/Latino; 0.4% American Indian or Alaska Native, non-Hispanic/Latino; 6% Two or more races, non-Hispanic/Latino; 1% Race/ethnicity unknown; 0.1% international; 4% transferred in. *Retention:* 53% of full-time freshmen returned.
Freshmen *Admission:* 4,468 applied, 4,468 admitted, 4,468 enrolled.
Faculty *Total:* 1,147, 24% full-time, 2% with terminal degrees. *Student/faculty ratio:* 35:1.
Majors Accounting; agricultural mechanization; artificial intelligence; automobile/automotive mechanics technology; biological and physical sciences; biology/biological sciences; building/construction site management; business administration and management; carpentry; chemistry; child-care provision; commercial and advertising art; computer and information sciences related; computer graphics; computer programming; computer science; computer typography and composition equipment operation; corrections; criminal justice/law enforcement administration; criminal justice/police science; data processing and data processing technology; drafting and design technology; electrical, electronic and communications engineering technology; emergency medical technology (EMT paramedic); engineering; family and consumer sciences/human sciences; fashion/apparel design; fashion merchandising; fire science/firefighting; glazier; health information/medical records administration; heavy equipment maintenance technology; human services; information science/studies; information technology; kindergarten/preschool education; legal administrative assistant/secretary; liberal arts and sciences/liberal studies; machine shop technology; marketing/marketing management; masonry; medical administrative assistant and medical secretary; network and system administration; occupational therapy; physical therapy; pre-engineering; quality control technology; registered nursing/registered nurse; respiratory care therapy; special products marketing; system, networking, and LAN/WAN management; web/multimedia management and webmaster; web page, digital/multimedia and information resources design.
Academics *Calendar:* semesters. *Degree:* certificates and associate. *Special study options:* academic remediation for entering students, accelerated degree program, adult/continuing education programs, advanced placement credit, cooperative education, distance learning, English as a second language, honors programs, independent study, internships, off-campus study, part-time degree program, services for LD students, summer session for credit.
Library College Library with 10,098 titles, 288 serial subscriptions, 103 audiovisual materials, an OPAC.
Student Life *Housing:* college housing not available. *Activities and Organizations:* drama/theater group, student-run newspaper, choral group, student newspaper, student government, Phi Theta Kappa, Metropolitan Chorale of KC, Student Ambassadors, national fraternities. *Campus security:* 24-hour emergency response devices and patrols, late-night transport/escort service. *Student services:* personal/psychological counseling.
Athletics Member NJCAA. *Intercollegiate sports:* baseball M(s), basketball M(s)/W(s), cross-country running W(s), soccer M(s)/W(s), softball W(s), volleyball W(s).
Standardized Tests *Recommended:* ACT (for admission), Placement Testing for first-time freshman.
Applying *Options:* electronic application, early admission, deferred entrance. *Application deadlines:* rolling (freshmen), rolling (transfers). *Notification:* continuous (freshmen), continuous (transfers).
Freshman Application Contact Dr. Tuesday Stanley, Vice Chancellor of Student Development and Enrollment Services, Metropolitan Community College–Kansas City, 3200 Broadway, Kansas City, MO 64111-2429. *Phone:* 816-604-1253. *E-mail:* tuesday.stanley@mcckc.edu. *Website:* http://www.mcckc.edu/.

Midwest Institute
Fenton, Missouri

Freshman Application Contact Admissions Office, Midwest Institute, 964 S. Highway Drive, Fenton, MO 63026. *Toll-free phone:* 800-695-5550. *Website:* http://www.midwestinstitute.com/.

Midwest Institute
St. Louis, Missouri

Freshman Application Contact Admissions Office, Midwest Institute, 4260 Shoreline Drive, St. Louis, MO 63045. *Phone:* 314-344-4440. *Toll-free phone:* 800-695-5550. *Fax:* 314-344-0495. *Website:* http://www.midwestinstitute.com/.

Mineral Area College
Park Hills, Missouri

- **District-supported** 2-year, founded 1922, part of Missouri Coordinating Board for Higher Education
- **Rural** 240-acre campus with easy access to St. Louis
- **Coed,** 3,784 undergraduate students, 62% full-time, 62% women, 38% men

Undergraduates 2,342 full-time, 1,442 part-time. Students come from 13 states and territories; 7 other countries; 1% are from out of state; 2% Black or African American, non-Hispanic/Latino; 0.8% Hispanic/Latino; 0.3% Asian, non-Hispanic/Latino; 0.6% American Indian or Alaska Native, non-Hispanic/Latino; 4% Race/ethnicity unknown; 0.2% international; 5% transferred in. *Retention:* 66% of full-time freshmen returned.
Freshmen *Admission:* 920 enrolled.
Faculty *Total:* 335, 22% full-time. *Student/faculty ratio:* 11:1.
Majors Administrative assistant and secretarial science; agribusiness; applied horticulture/horticulture operations; autobody/collision and repair technology; automobile/automotive mechanics technology; business/commerce; carpentry; child-care provision; civil engineering technology; computer programming; criminal justice/police science; culinary arts; drafting and design technology; electrical, electronic and communications engineering technology; emergency medical technology (EMT paramedic); engineering technology; fire science/firefighting; general studies; graphic and printing equipment operation/production; health professions related; heating, ventilation, air conditioning and refrigeration engineering technology; heavy/industrial equipment maintenance technologies related; industrial technology; liberal arts and sciences/liberal studies; machine tool technology; operations management; precision production related; precision production trades; radio and television broadcasting technology; registered nursing/registered nurse; respiratory therapy technician; system, networking, and LAN/WAN management; technical teacher education.
Academics *Calendar:* semesters. *Degree:* certificates and associate. *Special study options:* academic remediation for entering students, advanced placement credit, distance learning, honors programs, internships, off-campus study, part-time degree program, services for LD students, summer session for credit.
Library C. H. Cozen Learning Resource Center with 32,228 titles, 214 serial subscriptions, 4,859 audiovisual materials, an OPAC, a Web page.

Student Life *Housing Options:* coed. Campus housing is university owned. *Activities and Organizations:* drama/theater group, choral group. *Campus security:* 24-hour patrols. *Student services:* personal/psychological counseling.
Athletics Member NJCAA. *Intercollegiate sports:* baseball M(s), basketball M(s)/W(s), golf M, softball W(s), volleyball W(s).
Costs (2013–14) *Tuition:* area resident $2760 full-time, $92 per semester hour part-time; state resident $3660 full-time, $122 per semester hour part-time; nonresident $4650 full-time, $155 per semester hour part-time. *Room and board:* room only: $3555. Room and board charges vary according to board plan and housing facility. *Payment plan:* installment. *Waivers:* senior citizens and employees or children of employees.
Financial Aid Of all full-time matriculated undergraduates who enrolled in 2011, 65 Federal Work-Study jobs (averaging $3708).
Applying *Options:* electronic application, early admission. *Application fee:* $15. *Required:* high school transcript. *Application deadlines:* rolling (freshmen), rolling (transfers). *Notification:* continuous (freshmen).
Freshman Application Contact Linda Huffman, Registrar, Mineral Area College, PO Box 1000, Park Hills, MO 63601-1000. *Phone:* 573-518-2130. *Fax:* 573-518-2166. *E-mail:* lhuffman@mineralarea.edu.
Website: http://www.mineralarea.edu/.

Missouri College
Brentwood, Missouri

Director of Admissions Mr. Doug Brinker, Admissions Director, Missouri College, 1405 South Hanley Road, Brentwood, MO 63117. *Phone:* 314-821-7700. *Toll-free phone:* 800-216-6732. *Fax:* 314-821-0891.
Website: http://www.missouricollege.edu/.

Missouri State University–West Plains
West Plains, Missouri

- **State-supported** 2-year, founded 1963, part of Missouri State University
- **Small-town** 20-acre campus
- **Endowment** $6.4 million
- **Coed,** 2,102 undergraduate students, 60% full-time, 59% women, 41% men

Undergraduates 1,260 full-time, 842 part-time. Students come from 27 states and territories; 3 other countries; 3% are from out of state; 2% Black or African American, non-Hispanic/Latino; 1% Hispanic/Latino; 1% Asian, non-Hispanic/Latino; 1% American Indian or Alaska Native, non-Hispanic/Latino; 5% Race/ethnicity unknown; 0.5% international; 4% transferred in; 4% live on campus. *Retention:* 45% of full-time freshmen returned.
Freshmen *Admission:* 1,027 applied, 782 admitted, 561 enrolled. *Average high school GPA:* 3.12. *Test scores:* ACT scores over 18: 71%; ACT scores over 24: 16%; ACT scores over 30: 1%.
Faculty *Total:* 110, 30% full-time, 9% with terminal degrees. *Student/faculty ratio:* 25:1.
Majors Accounting; agriculture; business administration and management; business/commerce; child-care and support services management; computer and information sciences related; computer graphics; computer programming (specific applications); criminal justice/law enforcement administration; criminal justice/police science; engineering; entrepreneurship; food science; general studies; horticultural science; industrial technology; information technology; legal assistant/paralegal; management information systems and services related; registered nursing/registered nurse; respiratory therapy technician.
Academics *Calendar:* semesters. *Degree:* certificates and associate. *Special study options:* academic remediation for entering students, adult/continuing education programs, advanced placement credit, cooperative education, distance learning, honors programs, internships, off-campus study, part-time degree program, services for LD students, study abroad, summer session for credit.
Library Garnett Library with 40,233 titles, 149 serial subscriptions, 1,280 audiovisual materials, an OPAC, a Web page.
Student Life *Housing Options:* men-only, women-only. Campus housing is university owned. *Activities and Organizations:* Student Government Association, Chi Alpha, Adult Students in Higher Education, Lambda Lambda Lambda, Programming Board. *Campus security:* access only with key. *Student services:* personal/psychological counseling, legal services.
Athletics Member NJCAA. *Intercollegiate sports:* basketball M(s), volleyball W(s).
Costs (2013–14) *Tuition:* state resident $3624 full-time, $111 per quarter hour part-time; nonresident $6954 full-time, $222 per quarter hour part-time. Full-time tuition and fees vary according to course load, location, and program. Part-time tuition and fees vary according to course load and location. *Required fees:* $294 full-time, $5 per quarter hour part-time, $72 per year part-time. *Room and board:* $5300. Room and board charges vary according to board plan. *Payment plan:* deferred payment. *Waivers:* senior citizens and employees or children of employees.

Financial Aid Of all full-time matriculated undergraduates who enrolled in 2011, 63 Federal Work-Study jobs (averaging $2000).
Applying *Options:* electronic application. *Application fee:* $15. *Required for some:* high school transcript. *Application deadlines:* 8/20 (freshmen), 8/20 (out-of-state freshmen), 8/20 (transfers). *Notification:* continuous (freshmen), continuous (out-of-state freshmen), continuous (transfers).
Freshman Application Contact Ms. Melissa Jett, Coordinator of Admissions, Missouri State University–West Plains, 128 Garfield, West Plains, MO 65775. *Phone:* 417-255-7955. *Toll-free phone:* 888-466-7897. *Fax:* 417-255-7959. *E-mail:* melissajett@missouristate.edu.
Website: http://wp.missouristate.edu/.

Moberly Area Community College
Moberly, Missouri

Freshman Application Contact Dr. James Grant, Dean of Student Services, Moberly Area Community College, Moberly, MO 65270-1304. *Phone:* 660-263-4110 Ext. 235. *Toll-free phone:* 800-622-2070. *Fax:* 660-263-2406. *E-mail:* info@macc.edu.
Website: http://www.macc.edu/.

North Central Missouri College
Trenton, Missouri

Freshman Application Contact Megan Goodin, Admissions Assistant, North Central Missouri College, Trenton, MO 64683. *Phone:* 660-359-3948 Ext. 1410. *E-mail:* megoodin@mail.ncmissouri.edu.
Website: http://www.ncmissouri.edu/.

Ozarks Technical Community College
Springfield, Missouri

- **District-supported** 2-year, founded 1990, part of Missouri Coordinating Board for Higher Education
- **Urban** campus
- **Coed,** 15,179 undergraduate students, 49% full-time, 58% women, 42% men

Undergraduates 7,447 full-time, 7,732 part-time. Students come from 31 states and territories; 2% are from out of state; 3% Black or African American, non-Hispanic/Latino; 2% Hispanic/Latino; 1% Asian, non-Hispanic/Latino; 0.2% Native Hawaiian or other Pacific Islander, non-Hispanic/Latino; 1% American Indian or Alaska Native, non-Hispanic/Latino; 2% Race/ethnicity unknown; 6% transferred in. *Retention:* 59% of full-time freshmen returned.
Freshmen *Admission:* 3,283 enrolled.
Faculty *Total:* 667, 28% full-time. *Student/faculty ratio:* 25:1.
Majors Accounting; administrative assistant and secretarial science; autobody/collision and repair technology; automobile/automotive mechanics technology; business administration and management; business machine repair; computer systems networking and telecommunications; construction engineering technology; culinary arts; diesel mechanics technology; electrical, electronic and communications engineering technology; emergency medical technology (EMT paramedic); fire science/firefighting; graphic and printing equipment operation/production; health information/medical records technology; heating, air conditioning, ventilation and refrigeration maintenance technology; heavy equipment maintenance technology; hotel/motel administration; industrial technology; information science/studies; instrumentation technology; kindergarten/preschool education; liberal arts and sciences/liberal studies; machine tool technology; management information systems; mechanical drafting and CAD/CADD; occupational therapist assistant; occupational therapy; physical sciences; physical therapy technology; radio and television broadcasting technology; respiratory care therapy; turf and turfgrass management; welding technology.
Academics *Calendar:* semesters. *Degree:* certificates, diplomas, and associate. *Special study options:* academic remediation for entering students, adult/continuing education programs, cooperative education, distance learning, double majors, English as a second language, honors programs, internships, off-campus study, part-time degree program, services for LD students, summer session for credit.
Library Library plus 1 other with 6,000 titles, 190 serial subscriptions, an OPAC, a Web page.
Student Life *Housing:* college housing not available. *Activities and Organizations:* student-run newspaper, Phi Theta Kappa. *Campus security:* 24-hour emergency response devices. *Student services:* personal/psychological counseling.
Costs (2013–14) *Tuition:* area resident $2184 full-time, $91 per credit hour part-time; state resident $3084 full-time, $129 per credit hour part-time; nonresident $4056 full-time, $169 per credit hour part-time. *Required fees:* $500 full-time. *Payment plans:* installment, deferred payment. *Waivers:* employees or children of employees.

Financial Aid Of all full-time matriculated undergraduates who enrolled in 2011, 201 Federal Work-Study jobs.

Applying *Options:* electronic application. *Required:* high school transcript. *Application deadlines:* rolling (freshmen), rolling (out-of-state freshmen), rolling (transfers). *Notification:* continuous (freshmen), continuous (out-of-state freshmen), continuous (transfers).

Freshman Application Contact Ozarks Technical Community College, 1001 E. Chestnut Expressway, Springfield, MO 65802.

Website: http://www.otc.edu/.

Pinnacle Career Institute

Kansas City, Missouri

Director of Admissions Ms. Ruth Matous, Director of Admissions, Pinnacle Career Institute, 1001 East 101st Terrace, Suite 325, Kansas City, MO 64131. *Phone:* 816-331-5700 Ext. 212. *Toll-free phone:* 877-241-3097.

Website: http://www.pcitraining.edu/.

Ranken Technical College

St. Louis, Missouri

Director of Admissions Ms. Elizabeth Keserauskis, Director of Admissions, Ranken Technical College, 4431 Finney Avenue, St. Louis, MO 63113. *Phone:* 314-371-0233 Ext. 4811. *Toll-free phone:* 866-4-RANKEN.

Website: http://www.ranken.edu/.

Saint Charles Community College

Cottleville, Missouri

Freshman Application Contact Ms. Kathy Brockgreitens-Gober, Director of Admissions/Registrar/Financial Assistance, Saint Charles Community College, 4601 Mid Rivers Mall Drive, Cottleville, MO 63376-0975. *Phone:* 636-922-8229. *Fax:* 636-922-8236. *E-mail:* regist@stchas.edu.

Website: http://www.stchas.edu/.

St. Louis College of Health Careers

St. Louis, Missouri

Freshman Application Contact Admissions Office, St. Louis College of Health Careers, 909 South Taylor Avenue, St. Louis, MO 63110-1511. *Phone:* 314-652-0300. *Toll-free phone:* 888-789-4820. *Fax:* 314-652-4825.

Website: http://www.slchc.com/.

St. Louis Community College at Florissant Valley

St. Louis, Missouri

Freshman Application Contact Ms. Brenda Davenport, Manager of Admissions and Registration, St. Louis Community College at Florissant Valley, 3400 Pershall Road, St. Louis, MO 63135-1499. *Phone:* 314-513-4248. *Fax:* 314-513-4724.

Website: http://www.stlcc.edu/.

St. Louis Community College at Forest Park

St. Louis, Missouri

- **District-supported** 2-year, founded 1962, part of St. Louis Community College System
- **Suburban** 34-acre campus
- **Endowment** $1.3 million
- **Coed,** 7,991 undergraduate students, 35% full-time, 62% women, 38% men

Undergraduates 2,765 full-time, 5,226 part-time. Students come from 17 states and territories; 75 other countries; 3% are from out of state; 56% Black or African American, non-Hispanic/Latino; 3% Hispanic/Latino; 3% Asian, non-Hispanic/Latino; 0.2% Native Hawaiian or other Pacific Islander, non-Hispanic/Latino; 0.4% American Indian or Alaska Native, non-Hispanic/Latino; 2% Two or more races, non-Hispanic/Latino; 3% Race/ethnicity unknown; 0.8% international; 10% transferred in. *Retention:* 40% of full-time freshmen returned.

Freshmen *Admission:* 1,219 enrolled.

Faculty *Total:* 452, 32% full-time. *Student/faculty ratio:* 19:1.

Majors Accounting technology and bookkeeping; automobile/automotive mechanics technology; baking and pastry arts; building/home/construction inspection; business automation/technology/data entry; child-care provision;

clinical/medical laboratory technology; communications technology; computer and information sciences; computer programming (specific applications); computer programming (vendor/product certification); computer systems networking and telecommunications; corrections; criminal justice/police science; culinary arts; data processing and data processing technology; dental hygiene; diesel mechanics technology; engineering technology; fire science/firefighting; funeral service and mortuary science; graphic design; health information/medical records technology; hospitality administration; human services; journalism; radiologic technology/science; registered nursing/registered nurse; respiratory care therapy.

Academics *Calendar:* semesters. *Degree:* certificates and associate. *Special study options:* academic remediation for entering students, accelerated degree program, adult/continuing education programs, advanced placement credit, distance learning, English as a second language, honors programs, independent study, internships, part-time degree program, services for LD students, study abroad, summer session for credit.

Library Forest Park Library with 74,861 titles, 284 serial subscriptions, 1,778 audiovisual materials, an OPAC, a Web page.

Student Life *Housing:* college housing not available. *Activities and Organizations:* student-run newspaper, Programming Board, Phi Theta Kappa, Radiology Club, Forest Park Business Club, Human Services Club. *Campus security:* 24-hour emergency response devices, late-night transport/escort service. *Student services:* personal/psychological counseling.

Athletics Member NJCAA. *Intercollegiate sports:* baseball M(s), basketball M(s)/W(s), soccer M(s)/W(s), softball W(s), volleyball W(s).

Standardized Tests *Recommended:* SAT or ACT (for admission).

Costs (2013–14) *Tuition:* area resident $2232 full-time, $93 per credit part-time; state resident $3336 full-time, $139 per credit part-time; nonresident $4536 full-time, $189 per credit part-time. Full-time tuition and fees vary according to course load. Part-time tuition and fees vary according to course load. *Payment plan:* installment. *Waivers:* senior citizens and employees or children of employees.

Financial Aid Of all full-time matriculated undergraduates who enrolled in 2011, 165 Federal Work-Study jobs (averaging $3000).

Applying *Options:* electronic application. *Required for some:* high school transcript, interview. *Application deadlines:* rolling (freshmen), rolling (out-of-state freshmen), rolling (transfers). *Notification:* continuous (freshmen), continuous (out-of-state freshmen), continuous (transfers).

Freshman Application Contact Director of Admissions, St. Louis Community College at Forest Park, 5600 Oakland Avenue, 200 Student Center, St. Louis, MO 63110. *Phone:* 314-644-9127. *Fax:* 314-644-9375. *E-mail:* fp-admissions@stlcc.edu.

Website: http://www.stlcc.edu/.

St. Louis Community College at Meramec

Kirkwood, Missouri

- **District-supported** 2-year, founded 1963, part of St. Louis Community College System
- **Suburban** 80-acre campus with easy access to St. Louis
- **Endowment** $1.3 million
- **Coed,** 10,432 undergraduate students, 45% full-time, 57% women, 43% men

Undergraduates 4,717 full-time, 5,715 part-time. Students come from 17 states and territories; 74 other countries; 1% are from out of state; 10% Black or African American, non-Hispanic/Latino; 3% Hispanic/Latino; 3% Asian, non-Hispanic/Latino; 0.1% Native Hawaiian or other Pacific Islander, non-Hispanic/Latino; 0.3% American Indian or Alaska Native, non-Hispanic/Latino; 3% Two or more races, non-Hispanic/Latino; 0.9% Race/ethnicity unknown; 1% international; 8% transferred in. *Retention:* 62% of full-time freshmen returned.

Freshmen *Admission:* 1,701 enrolled.

Faculty *Total:* 554, 34% full-time. *Student/faculty ratio:* 22:1.

Majors Accounting technology and bookkeeping; applied horticulture/horticulture operations; architectural technology; business administration and management; business automation/technology/data entry; child-care provision; comparative literature; computer programming; court reporting; criminal justice/police science; emergency medical technology (EMT paramedic); graphic design; human services; interior design; legal assistant/paralegal; liberal arts and sciences/liberal studies; occupational therapist assistant; physical therapy technology; registered nursing/registered nurse; system, networking, and LAN/WAN management.

Academics *Calendar:* semesters. *Degree:* certificates and associate. *Special study options:* academic remediation for entering students, accelerated degree program, adult/continuing education programs, advanced placement credit, distance learning, English as a second language, honors programs, independent study, internships, off-campus study, part-time degree program, services for LD students, study abroad, summer session for credit.

Library Meramec Library with 122,988 titles, 496 serial subscriptions, 11,538 audiovisual materials, an OPAC, a Web page.

Student Life *Housing:* college housing not available. *Activities and Organizations:* drama/theater group, student-run newspaper. *Campus security:* 24-hour emergency response devices, late-night transport/escort service. *Student services:* personal/psychological counseling.

Athletics Member NJCAA. *Intercollegiate sports:* baseball M(s), basketball M(s)/W(s), soccer M(s)/W(s), softball W(s), volleyball W(s).

Standardized Tests *Recommended:* SAT or ACT (for admission).

Costs (2013–14) *Tuition:* area resident $2232 full-time, $93 per credit part-time; state resident $3336 full-time, $139 per credit part-time; nonresident $4536 full-time, $189 per credit part-time. Full-time tuition and fees vary according to course load. Part-time tuition and fees vary according to course load. *Payment plan:* installment. *Waivers:* senior citizens and employees or children of employees.

Applying *Options:* electronic application. *Required for some:* high school transcript, interview. *Application deadlines:* rolling (freshmen), rolling (out-of-state freshmen), rolling (transfers). *Notification:* continuous (freshmen), continuous (out-of-state freshmen), continuous (transfers).

Freshman Application Contact Director of Admissions, St. Louis Community College at Meramec, 11333 Big Bend Road, 110 Clark Hall, Kirkwood, MO 63122. *Phone:* 314-984-7601. *Fax:* 314-984-7051. *E-mail:* mc-admissions@stlcc.edu.
Website: http://www.stlcc.edu/.

Southeast Missouri Hospital College of Nursing and Health Sciences
Cape Girardeau, Missouri

- **Independent** 2-year, founded 1928
- **Rural** 1-acre campus
- **Coed**

Undergraduates 25 full-time, 171 part-time. Students come from 3 states and territories; 5% are from out of state; 3% Black or African American, non-Hispanic/Latino; 0.5% Hispanic/Latino; 1% Asian, non-Hispanic/Latino; 0.5% Native Hawaiian or other Pacific Islander, non-Hispanic/Latino; 96% transferred in. *Retention:* 100% of full-time freshmen returned.

Faculty *Student/faculty ratio:* 5:1.

Academics *Calendar:* six 7-week terms per year. *Degrees:* certificates, associate, and postbachelor's certificates. *Special study options:* advanced placement credit.

Student Life *Campus security:* 24-hour emergency response devices and patrols, late-night transport/escort service, electronic campus access.

Standardized Tests *Required:* SAT or ACT (for admission), COMPASS and NLN also used for various programs and tracks (for admission).

Costs (2012–13) *Tuition:* $300 per credit part-time. Full-time tuition and fees vary according to course load and program. Part-time tuition and fees vary according to course load and program. *Required fees:* $21 per hour part-time.

Applying *Application fee:* $50. *Required:* high school transcript, minimum 2.0 GPA, 1 letter of recommendation, Bridge Program requirement is a minimum score of 75 on NLN exam. COMPASS exam minimum scores are required for the associate degree programs of 75 in writing, 85 in reading, and 46 in Pre-Algebra.

Freshman Application Contact Southeast Missouri Hospital College of Nursing and Health Sciences, 2001 William Street, Cape Girardeau, MO 63701. *Phone:* 573-334-6825 Ext. 12.
Website: http://www.southeastmissourihospitalcollege.edu/.

State Fair Community College
Sedalia, Missouri

Freshman Application Contact State Fair Community College, 3201 West 16th Street, Sedalia, MO 65301-2199. *Phone:* 660-596-7221. *Toll-free phone:* 877-311-7322.
Website: http://www.sfccmo.edu/.

Three Rivers Community College
Poplar Bluff, Missouri

Freshman Application Contact Ms. Marcia Fields, Director of Admissions and Recruiting, Three Rivers Community College, Poplar Bluff, MO 63901. *Phone:* 573-840-9675. *Toll-free phone:* 877-TRY-TRCC. *E-mail:* trytrcc@trcc.edu.
Website: http://www.trcc.edu/.

Vatterott College
Berkeley, Missouri

Director of Admissions Ann Farajallah, Director of Admissions, Vatterott College, 8580 Evans Avenue, Berkeley, MO 63134. *Phone:* 314-264-1020. *Toll-free phone:* 888-553-6627.
Website: http://www.vatterott.edu/.

Vatterott College
Kansas City, Missouri

Admissions Office Contact Vatterott College, 4131 N. Corrington Avenue, Kansas City, MO 64117. *Toll-free phone:* 888-553-6627.
Website: http://www.vatterott.edu/.

Vatterott College
St. Charles, Missouri

Director of Admissions Gertrude Bogan-Jones, Director of Admissions, Vatterott College, 3550 West Clay Street, St. Charles, MO 63301. *Phone:* 636-978-7488. *Toll-free phone:* 888-553-6627. *Fax:* 636-978-5121. *E-mail:* ofallon@vatterott-college.edu.
Website: http://www.vatterott.edu/.

Vatterott College
St. Joseph, Missouri

Director of Admissions Director of Admissions, Vatterott College, 3131 Frederick Avenue, St. Joseph, MO 64506. *Phone:* 816-364-5399. *Toll-free phone:* 888-553-6627. *Fax:* 816-364-1593.
Website: http://www.vatterott.edu/.

Vatterott College
Springfield, Missouri

Freshman Application Contact Mr. Scott Lester, Director of Admissions, Vatterott College, 3850 South Campbell Avenue, Springfield, MO 65807. *Phone:* 417-831-8116. *Toll-free phone:* 888-553-6627. *Fax:* 417-831-5099. *E-mail:* springfield@vatterott-college.edu.
Website: http://www.vatterott.edu/.

Vatterott College
Sunset Hills, Missouri

Director of Admissions Director of Admission, Vatterott College, 12900 Maurer Industrial Drive, Sunset Hills, MO 63127. *Phone:* 314-843-4200. *Toll-free phone:* 888-553-6627. *Fax:* 314-843-1709.
Website: http://www.vatterott.edu/.

Vet Tech Institute at Hickey College
St. Louis, Missouri

- **Private** 2-year, founded 2007
- **Suburban** campus
- **Coed,** 134 undergraduate students
- **59%** of applicants were admitted

Freshmen *Admission:* 420 applied, 246 admitted.

Majors Veterinary/animal health technology.

Academics *Degree:* associate. *Special study options:* accelerated degree program, internships.

Freshman Application Contact Admissions Office, Vet Tech Institute at Hickey College, 2780 North Lindbergh Boulevard, St. Louis, MO 63114. *Phone:* 888-884-1459. *Toll-free phone:* 888-884-1459.
Website: http://www.vettechinstitute.edu/.

Wentworth Military Academy and College
Lexington, Missouri

Freshman Application Contact Capt. Mike Bellis, College Admissions Director, Wentworth Military Academy and College, 1880 Washington Avenue, Lexington, MO 64067. *Phone:* 660-259-2221 Ext. 1351. *Fax:* 660-259-2677. *E-mail:* admissions@wma.edu.
Website: http://www.wma.edu/.

MONTANA

Aaniiih Nakoda College

Harlem, Montana

Director of Admissions Ms. Dixie Brockie, Registrar and Admissions Officer, Aaniiih Nakoda College, PO Box 159, Harlem, MT 59526-0159. *Phone:* 406-353-2607 Ext. 233. *Fax:* 406-353-2898. *E-mail:* dbrockie@mail.fbcc.edu. *Website:* http://www.fbcc.edu/.

Blackfeet Community College

Browning, Montana

Freshman Application Contact Ms. Deana M. McNabb, Registrar and Admissions Officer, Blackfeet Community College, PO Box 819, Browning, MT 59417-0819. *Phone:* 406-338-5421. *Toll-free phone:* 800-549-7457. *Fax:* 406-338-3272. *Website:* http://www.bfcc.edu/.

Chief Dull Knife College

Lame Deer, Montana

Freshman Application Contact Director of Admissions, Chief Dull Knife College, PO Box 98, 1 College Drive, Lame Deer, MT 59043-0098. *Phone:* 406-477-6215. *Website:* http://www.cdkc.edu/.

Dawson Community College

Glendive, Montana

- **State and locally supported** 2-year, founded 1940, part of Montana University System
- **Rural** 300-acre campus
- **Endowment** $344,944
- **Coed**

Undergraduates 284 full-time, 319 part-time.
Faculty *Student/faculty ratio:* 26:1.
Academics *Calendar:* semesters. *Degree:* certificates and associate. *Special study options:* academic remediation for entering students, adult/continuing education programs, distance learning, independent study, internships, part-time degree program, services for LD students, summer session for credit.
Student Life *Campus security:* 24-hour emergency response devices.
Athletics Member NJCAA.
Financial Aid Of all full-time matriculated undergraduates who enrolled in 2011, 45 Federal Work-Study jobs (averaging $1500). 17 state and other part-time jobs (averaging $1500).
Applying *Options:* deferred entrance. *Application fee:* $30. *Required:* high school transcript.
Freshman Application Contact Dawson Community College, 300 College Drive, PO Box 421, Glendive, MT 59330-0421. *Phone:* 406-377-3396 Ext. 410. *Toll-free phone:* 800-821-8320. *Website:* http://www.dawson.edu/.

Flathead Valley Community College

Kalispell, Montana

- **State and locally supported** 2-year, founded 1967, part of Montana University System
- **Small-town** 209-acre campus
- **Endowment** $5.4 million
- **Coed,** 2,395 undergraduate students, 49% full-time, 62% women, 38% men

Undergraduates 1,170 full-time, 1,225 part-time. Students come from 14 states and territories; 3% are from out of state; 0.3% Black or African American, non-Hispanic/Latino; 2% Hispanic/Latino; 0.9% Asian, non-Hispanic/Latino; 0.3% Native Hawaiian or other Pacific Islander, non-Hispanic/Latino; 4% American Indian or Alaska Native, non-Hispanic/Latino; 12% Race/ethnicity unknown; 7% transferred in; 1% live on campus. *Retention:* 52% of full-time freshmen returned.
Freshmen *Admission:* 409 enrolled.
Faculty *Total:* 197, 27% full-time, 6% with terminal degrees. *Student/faculty ratio:* 16:1.
Majors Accounting; administrative assistant and secretarial science; business administration and management; carpentry; child-care and support services management; computer/information technology services administration related; criminal justice/law enforcement administration; crisis/emergency/disaster management; culinary arts; electrician; emergency medical technology (EMT paramedic); hospitality and recreation marketing; human services; liberal arts and sciences/liberal studies; licensed practical/vocational nurse training; medical administrative assistant and medical secretary; medical/clinical assistant; medical insurance coding; medical radiologic technology; metal and jewelry arts; registered nursing/registered nurse; small business administration; substance abuse/addiction counseling; surgical technology; surveying technology; web/multimedia management and webmaster; welding technology; wildlife, fish and wildlands science and management.
Academics *Calendar:* semesters. *Degree:* certificates and associate. *Special study options:* academic remediation for entering students, adult/continuing education programs, advanced placement credit, cooperative education, distance learning, double majors, English as a second language, honors programs, independent study, internships, part-time degree program, services for LD students, study abroad, summer session for credit.
Library Flathead Valley Community College Library with 35,000 titles, 125 serial subscriptions, 514 audiovisual materials, an OPAC, a Web page.
Student Life *Housing Options:* coed. Campus housing is leased by the school. *Activities and Organizations:* drama/theater group, student-run newspaper, choral group, Forestry Club, Phi Theta Kappa. *Student services:* health clinic, personal/psychological counseling.
Athletics *Intramural sports:* basketball M/W, bowling M/W, cross-country running M/W, softball M/W, table tennis M/W, ultimate Frisbee M/W, volleyball M/W.
Standardized Tests *Required:* COMPASS Placement Test (for admission).
Costs (2013–14) *Tuition:* area resident $2761 full-time, $99 per credit hour part-time; state resident $4133 full-time, $148 per credit hour part-time; nonresident $9901 full-time, $354 per credit hour part-time. Full-time tuition and fees vary according to course load. Part-time tuition and fees vary according to course load. *Required fees:* $969 full-time, $35 per credit hour part-time. *Payment plans:* installment, deferred payment. *Waivers:* senior citizens and employees or children of employees.
Applying *Options:* early admission, deferred entrance. *Application fee:* $15. *Required:* high school transcript. *Application deadlines:* rolling (freshmen), rolling (transfers).
Freshman Application Contact Ms. Marlene C. Stoltz, Admissions/Graduation Coordinator, Flathead Valley Community College, 777 Grandview Drive, Kalispell, MT 59901-2622. *Phone:* 406-756-3846. *Toll-free phone:* 800-313-3822. *E-mail:* mstoltz@fvcc.cc.mt.us. *Website:* http://www.fvcc.edu/.

Fort Peck Community College

Poplar, Montana

Director of Admissions Mr. Robert McAnally, Vice President for Student Services, Fort Peck Community College, PO Box 398, Poplar, MT 59255-0398. *Phone:* 406-768-6329. *Website:* http://www.fpcc.edu/.

Great Falls College Montana State University

Great Falls, Montana

- **State-supported** 2-year, founded 1969, part of Montana University System
- **Small-town** 40-acre campus
- **Endowment** $11,300
- **Coed,** 1,835 undergraduate students, 50% full-time, 71% women, 29% men

Undergraduates 909 full-time, 926 part-time. Students come from 27 states and territories; 1 other country; 2% are from out of state; 1% Black or African American, non-Hispanic/Latino; 4% Hispanic/Latino; 1% Asian, non-Hispanic/Latino; 0.2% Native Hawaiian or other Pacific Islander, non-Hispanic/Latino; 6% American Indian or Alaska Native, non-Hispanic/Latino; 4% Two or more races, non-Hispanic/Latino; 0.9% Race/ethnicity unknown; 8% transferred in.
Freshmen *Admission:* 477 applied, 460 admitted, 363 enrolled. *Average high school GPA:* 2.8.
Faculty *Total:* 145, 32% full-time, 14% with terminal degrees. *Student/faculty ratio:* 15:1.
Majors Accounting technology and bookkeeping; business administration and management; computer systems networking and telecommunications; dental hygiene; dietetic technology; emergency medical technology (EMT paramedic); energy management and systems technology; entrepreneurship; fire science/firefighting; graphic design; health information/medical records technology; information technology; interior design; liberal arts and sciences and humanities related; licensed practical/vocational nurse training; medical/clinical assistant; medical insurance/medical billing; medical transcription; physical therapy technology; radiologic technology/science; respiratory care

therapy; surgical technology; web page, digital/multimedia and information resources design; welding technology.

Academics *Calendar:* semesters. *Degree:* certificates and associate. *Special study options:* academic remediation for entering students, advanced placement credit, distance learning, double majors, independent study, internships, off-campus study, part-time degree program, services for LD students, summer session for credit.

Library Weaver Library with 50,470 titles, 50,274 serial subscriptions, 1,294 audiovisual materials, an OPAC, a Web page.

Student Life *Activities and Organizations:* The Associated Students of Great Falls College Montana State University, Native American Students, Veteran's Club. *Campus security:* 24-hour emergency response devices.

Costs (2012–13) *Tuition:* state resident $2496 full-time, $104 per credit hour part-time; nonresident $8748 full-time, $364 per credit hour part-time. Full-time tuition and fees vary according to course load and program. Part-time tuition and fees vary according to course load and program. *Required fees:* $581 full-time, $20 per semester hour part-time, $50 per term part-time. *Payment plan:* deferred payment. *Waivers:* minority students, senior citizens, and employees or children of employees.

Financial Aid Of all full-time matriculated undergraduates who enrolled in 2011, 878 applied for aid, 792 were judged to have need, 22 had their need fully met. 39 Federal Work-Study jobs (averaging $2000). 37 state and other part-time jobs (averaging $2000). In 2011, 1 non-need-based awards were made. *Average percent of need met:* 66%. *Average financial aid package:* $9018. *Average need-based loan:* $3031. *Average need-based gift aid:* $5330. *Average non-need-based aid:* $250. *Average indebtedness upon graduation:* $16,557.

Applying *Options:* early admission. *Application fee:* $30. *Required:* high school transcript, proof of immunization. *Application deadlines:* rolling (freshmen), rolling (out-of-state freshmen), rolling (transfers). *Notification:* continuous (freshmen), continuous (out-of-state freshmen), continuous (transfers).

Freshman Application Contact Ms. Brittany Budeski, Admissions, Great Falls College Montana State University, 2100 16th Avenue South, Great Falls, MT 59405. *Phone:* 406-771-4300. *Toll-free phone:* 800-446-2698. *Fax:* 406-771-4329. *E-mail:* brittany.budeski@gfcmsu.edu.
Website: http://www.gfcmsu.edu/.

Little Big Horn College

Crow Agency, Montana

Freshman Application Contact Ms. Ann Bullis, Dean of Student Services, Little Big Horn College, Box 370, 1 Forest Lane, Crow Agency, MT 59022-0370. *Phone:* 406-638-2228 Ext. 50.
Website: http://www.lbhc.edu/.

Miles Community College

Miles City, Montana

- **State and locally supported** 2-year, founded 1939, part of Montana University System
- **Small-town** 8-acre campus
- **Coed,** 441 undergraduate students, 63% full-time, 61% women, 39% men

Undergraduates 280 full-time, 161 part-time. Students come from 24 states and territories; 4 other countries; 14% are from out of state; 2% Black or African American, non-Hispanic/Latino; 2% Hispanic/Latino; 1% Asian, non-Hispanic/Latino; 4% American Indian or Alaska Native, non-Hispanic/Latino; 0.7% Two or more races, non-Hispanic/Latino; 2% international; 11% transferred in; 32% live on campus.

Freshmen *Admission:* 319 applied, 319 admitted, 111 enrolled.

Faculty *Total:* 50, 48% full-time. *Student/faculty ratio:* 10:1.

Majors Agricultural business and management; agricultural production; animal health; automotive engineering technology; building/property maintenance; business/commerce; computer and information sciences; computer and information systems security; construction engineering technology; education; electrical, electronic and communications engineering technology; elementary education; engineering; equestrian studies; insurance; legal administrative assistant/secretary; liberal arts and sciences/liberal studies; livestock management; medical administrative assistant and medical secretary; physical education teaching and coaching; registered nursing/registered nurse; sales, distribution, and marketing operations; small business administration; special education; web page, digital/multimedia and information resources design.

Academics *Calendar:* semesters. *Degree:* certificates and associate. *Special study options:* academic remediation for entering students, accelerated degree program, adult/continuing education programs, advanced placement credit, cooperative education, distance learning, double majors, English as a second language, honors programs, independent study, internships, part-time degree program, services for LD students, summer session for credit.

Library Library Resource Center with 17,563 titles, 310 serial subscriptions, 174 audiovisual materials, an OPAC, a Web page.

Student Life *Housing:* on-campus residence required for freshman year. *Options:* coed. Campus housing is university owned. *Activities and Organizations:* drama/theater group. *Campus security:* 24-hour emergency response devices, Manual dormitory entrances locked all the time, only accessible with key. *Student services:* personal/psychological counseling.

Athletics Member NJCAA. *Intercollegiate sports:* baseball M(s), basketball M(s)/W(s), golf M(s)/W(s). *Intramural sports:* basketball M/W, bowling M/W, golf M/W, racquetball M/W, tennis M/W, track and field M/W, volleyball M/W, weight lifting M/W.

Financial Aid Of all full-time matriculated undergraduates who enrolled in 2011, 25 Federal Work-Study jobs (averaging $1400). 22 state and other part-time jobs (averaging $1300).

Applying *Options:* electronic application, early admission, deferred entrance. *Application fee:* $30. *Required:* high school transcript. *Application deadlines:* rolling (freshmen), rolling (transfers).

Freshman Application Contact Mr. Haley Anderson, Admissions Representative, Miles Community College, 2715 Dickinson Street, Miles City, MT 59301. *Phone:* 406-874-6178. *Toll-free phone:* 800-541-9281. *E-mail:* andersonh@milescc.edu.
Website: http://www.milescc.edu/.

Salish Kootenai College

Pablo, Montana

Freshman Application Contact Ms. Jackie Moran, Admissions Officer, Salish Kootenai College, PO Box 70, Pablo, MT 59855-0117. *Phone:* 406-275-4866. *Fax:* 406-275-4810. *E-mail:* jackie_moran@skc.edu.
Website: http://www.skc.edu/.

Stone Child College

Box Elder, Montana

Director of Admissions Mr. Ted Whitford, Director of Admissions/Registrar, Stone Child College, RR1, Box 1082, Box Elder, MT 59521. *Phone:* 406-395-4313 Ext. 110. *E-mail:* uanet337@quest.ocsc.montana.edu.
Website: http://www.stonechild.edu/.

The University of Montana–Helena College of Technology

Helena, Montana

- **State-supported** 2-year, founded 1939, part of Montana University System
- **Small-town** campus
- **Coed**

Undergraduates 813 full-time, 866 part-time. Students come from 10 states and territories; 2% are from out of state; 0.5% Black or African American, non-Hispanic/Latino; 3% Hispanic/Latino; 1% Asian, non-Hispanic/Latino; 5% American Indian or Alaska Native, non-Hispanic/Latino; 0.7% Two or more races, non-Hispanic/Latino; 6% Race/ethnicity unknown; 7% transferred in. *Retention:* 61% of full-time freshmen returned.

Faculty *Student/faculty ratio:* 15:1.

Academics *Calendar:* semesters. *Degree:* certificates and associate. *Special study options:* academic remediation for entering students, adult/continuing education programs, distance learning, double majors, internships, part-time degree program, services for LD students, summer session for credit.

Student Life *Campus security:* late-night transport/escort service.

Costs (2012–13) *Tuition:* state resident $3030 full-time; nonresident $8326 full-time. Full-time tuition and fees vary according to course load and reciprocity agreements. Part-time tuition and fees vary according to course load and reciprocity agreements. *Required fees:* $672 full-time.

Financial Aid Of all full-time matriculated undergraduates who enrolled in 2008, 445 applied for aid, 334 were judged to have need. 42 Federal Work-Study jobs (averaging $1549). 22 state and other part-time jobs (averaging $1476). In 2008, 37. *Average financial aid package:* $6368. *Average need-based loan:* $3428. *Average need-based gift aid:* $3111. *Average non-need-based aid:* $1769. *Average indebtedness upon graduation:* $14,068.

Applying *Options:* early admission, deferred entrance. *Application fee:* $30. *Required for some:* high school transcript.

Freshman Application Contact Mr. James Bisom, Admissions Representative/Recruiter, The University of Montana–Helena College of Technology, 1115 North Roberts Street, Helena, MT 59601. *Phone:* 406-444-5436. *Toll-free phone:* 800-241-4882.
Website: http://www.umhelena.edu/.

NEBRASKA

Central Community College–Columbus Campus

Columbus, Nebraska

- **State and locally supported** 2-year, founded 1968, part of Central Community College
- **Small-town** 90-acre campus
- **Coed**

Undergraduates 523 full-time, 2,349 part-time. Students come from 38 states and territories; 24 other countries; 2% Black or African American, non-Hispanic/Latino; 13% Hispanic/Latino; 0.8% Asian, non-Hispanic/Latino; 0.2% Native Hawaiian or other Pacific Islander, non-Hispanic/Latino; 0.2% American Indian or Alaska Native, non-Hispanic/Latino; 0.9% Two or more races, non-Hispanic/Latino; 4% Race/ethnicity unknown; 4% transferred in; 17% live on campus.

Academics *Calendar:* semesters plus six-week summer session. *Degree:* certificates, diplomas, and associate. *Special study options:* academic remediation for entering students, accelerated degree program, adult/continuing education programs, advanced placement credit, cooperative education, distance learning, English as a second language, external degree program, independent study, internships, off-campus study, part-time degree program, services for LD students, student-designed majors, summer session for credit.

Student Life *Campus security:* 24-hour emergency response devices and patrols, controlled dormitory access, night security.

Athletics Member NJCAA.

Applying *Options:* electronic application, early admission. *Required:* high school transcript. *Required for some:* 3 letters of recommendation, interview.

Freshman Application Contact Ms. Erica Leffler, Admissions/Recruiting Coordinator, Central Community College–Columbus Campus, PO Box 1027, Columbus, NE 68602-1027. *Phone:* 402-562-1296. *Toll-free phone:* 877-CCC-0780. *Fax:* 402-562-1201. *E-mail:* eleffler@cccneb.edu.
Website: http://www.cccneb.edu/.

Central Community College–Grand Island Campus

Grand Island, Nebraska

- **State and locally supported** 2-year, founded 1976, part of Central Community College
- **Small-town** 80-acre campus
- **Coed**

Undergraduates 423 full-time, 3,046 part-time. Students come from 24 other countries; 2% Black or African American, non-Hispanic/Latino; 13% Hispanic/Latino; 1% Asian, non-Hispanic/Latino; 0.2% Native Hawaiian or other Pacific Islander, non-Hispanic/Latino; 0.5% American Indian or Alaska Native, non-Hispanic/Latino; 1% Two or more races, non-Hispanic/Latino; 4% Race/ethnicity unknown; 3% transferred in; 10% live on campus.

Faculty *Student/faculty ratio:* 15:1.

Academics *Calendar:* semesters plus six-week summer session. *Degree:* certificates, diplomas, and associate. *Special study options:* academic remediation for entering students, accelerated degree program, adult/continuing education programs, advanced placement credit, cooperative education, distance learning, English as a second language, external degree program, independent study, internships, off-campus study, part-time degree program, services for LD students, student-designed majors, summer session for credit.

Applying *Options:* electronic application, early admission. *Required:* high school transcript. *Required for some:* 3 letters of recommendation, interview.

Freshman Application Contact Michelle Lubken, Admissions Director, Central Community College–Grand Island Campus, PO Box 4903, Grand Island, NE 68802-4903. *Phone:* 308-398-7406 Ext. 406. *Toll-free phone:* 877-CCC-0780. *Fax:* 308-398-7398. *E-mail:* mlubken@cccneb.edu.
Website: http://www.cccneb.edu/.

Central Community College–Hastings Campus

Hastings, Nebraska

- **State and locally supported** 2-year, founded 1966, part of Central Community College
- **Small-town** 644-acre campus
- **Coed**

Undergraduates 1,001 full-time, 1,965 part-time. Students come from 38 states and territories; 24 other countries; 0.7% Black or African American, non-Hispanic/Latino; 7% Hispanic/Latino; 0.9% Asian, non-Hispanic/Latino; 0.1% Native Hawaiian or other Pacific Islander, non-Hispanic/Latino; 0.4% American Indian or Alaska Native, non-Hispanic/Latino; 1% Two or more races, non-Hispanic/Latino; 5% Race/ethnicity unknown; 5% transferred in.

Faculty *Student/faculty ratio:* 15:1.

Academics *Calendar:* semesters plus six-week summer session. *Degree:* certificates, diplomas, and associate. *Special study options:* academic remediation for entering students, accelerated degree program, adult/continuing education programs, advanced placement credit, cooperative education, distance learning, English as a second language, external degree program, independent study, internships, off-campus study, part-time degree program, services for LD students, student-designed majors, summer session for credit.

Student Life *Campus security:* 24-hour emergency response devices and patrols, controlled dormitory access.

Financial Aid Of all full-time matriculated undergraduates who enrolled in 2011, 70 Federal Work-Study jobs (averaging $1200). 12 state and other part-time jobs (averaging $1250).

Applying *Options:* electronic application, early admission. *Required:* high school transcript. *Required for some:* 3 letters of recommendation, interview.

Freshman Application Contact Mr. Robert Glenn, Admissions and Recruiting Director, Central Community College–Hastings Campus, PO Box 1024, East Highway 6, Hastings, NE 68902-1024. *Phone:* 402-461-2428. *Toll-free phone:* 877-CCC-0780. *E-mail:* rglenn@ccneb.edu.
Website: http://www.cccneb.edu/.

ITT Technical Institute

Omaha, Nebraska

- **Proprietary** primarily 2-year, founded 1991, part of ITT Educational Services, Inc.
- **Urban** campus
- **Coed**

Academics *Calendar:* quarters. *Degrees:* associate and bachelor's.

Freshman Application Contact Director of Recruitment, ITT Technical Institute, 1120 North 103rd Plaza, Suite 200, Omaha, NE 68114. *Phone:* 402-331-2900. *Toll-free phone:* 800-677-9260.
Website: http://www.itt-tech.edu/.

Kaplan University, Lincoln

Lincoln, Nebraska

Freshman Application Contact Kaplan University, Lincoln, 1821 K Street, Lincoln, NE 68501-2826. *Phone:* 402-474-5315. *Toll-free phone:* 866-527-5268 (in-state); 800-527-5268 (out-of-state).
Website: http://www.lincoln.kaplanuniversity.edu/.

Kaplan University, Omaha

Omaha, Nebraska

Freshman Application Contact Kaplan University, Omaha, 5425 North 103rd Street, Omaha, NE 68134. *Phone:* 402-572-8500. *Toll-free phone:* 866-527-5268 (in-state); 800-527-5268 (out-of-state).
Website: http://www.omaha.kaplanuniversity.edu/.

Little Priest Tribal College

Winnebago, Nebraska

Director of Admissions Ms. Karen Kemling, Director of Admissions and Records, Little Priest Tribal College, PO Box 270, Winnebago, NE 68071. *Phone:* 402-878-2380.
Website: http://www.littlepriest.edu/.

Metropolitan Community College

Omaha, Nebraska

Freshman Application Contact Ms. Maria Vazquez, Associate Vice President for Student Affairs, Metropolitan Community College, PO Box 3777, Omaha, NE 69103-0777. *Phone:* 402-457-2430. *Toll-free phone:* 800-228-9553. *Fax:* 402-457-2238. *E-mail:* mvazquez@mccneb.edu.
Website: http://www.mccneb.edu/.

Mid-Plains Community College

North Platte, Nebraska

- **District-supported** 2-year, founded 1973
- **Small-town** campus
- **Endowment** $5.9 million
- **Coed,** 2,591 undergraduate students, 38% full-time, 59% women, 41% men

Undergraduates 980 full-time, 1,611 part-time. Students come from 39 states and territories; 13 other countries; 7% are from out of state; 4% Black or African American, non-Hispanic/Latino; 8% Hispanic/Latino; 0.3% Asian, non-Hispanic/Latino; 0.7% American Indian or Alaska Native, non-Hispanic/Latino; 2% Two or more races, non-Hispanic/Latino; 3% Race/ethnicity unknown; 1% international; 3% transferred in; 8% live on campus.

Freshmen *Admission:* 426 applied, 426 admitted, 536 enrolled.

Faculty *Total:* 311, 22% full-time, 2% with terminal degrees. *Student/faculty ratio:* 10:1.

Majors Administrative assistant and secretarial science; autobody/collision and repair technology; automobile/automotive mechanics technology; building/construction finishing, management, and inspection related; business administration and management; clinical/medical laboratory technology; commercial and advertising art; computer and information sciences; construction engineering technology; dental assisting; diesel mechanics technology; fire science/firefighting; heating, air conditioning, ventilation and refrigeration maintenance technology; liberal arts and sciences/liberal studies; licensed practical/vocational nurse training; registered nursing/registered nurse; transportation and materials moving related; welding technology.

Academics *Calendar:* semesters. *Degree:* certificates, diplomas, and associate. *Special study options:* academic remediation for entering students, accelerated degree program, adult/continuing education programs, advanced placement credit, cooperative education, distance learning, double majors, English as a second language, external degree program, independent study, internships, part-time degree program, services for LD students, summer session for credit.

Library McDonald-Belton Learning Resource Center (LRC) plus 1 other with 79,334 titles, 124 serial subscriptions, 1,803 audiovisual materials, an OPAC, a Web page.

Student Life *Housing Options:* coed, disabled students. Campus housing is university owned. *Activities and Organizations:* drama/theater group, student-run newspaper, choral group, Student Senate, Phi Theta Kappa, Phi Beta Lambda, Intercollegiate Athletics, MPCC Student Nurses Association, national fraternities, national sororities. *Campus security:* controlled dormitory access, patrols by trained security personnel.

Athletics Member NJCAA. *Intercollegiate sports:* baseball M(s), basketball M(s)/W(s), golf M(s), softball W(s), volleyball W(s). *Intramural sports:* baseball M, basketball M/W, softball W, volleyball W.

Standardized Tests *Required for some:* COMPASS. *Recommended:* ACT (for admission).

Costs (2013–14) *Tuition:* state resident $2310 full-time, $77 per credit hour part-time; nonresident $3450 full-time, $115 per credit hour part-time. Full-time tuition and fees vary according to reciprocity agreements. Part-time tuition and fees vary according to reciprocity agreements. *Required fees:* $450 full-time, $15 per credit hour part-time. *Room and board:* $5460. Room and board charges vary according to board plan, housing facility, and location. *Payment plan:* installment. *Waivers:* senior citizens and employees or children of employees.

Financial Aid Of all full-time matriculated undergraduates who enrolled in 2012, 1,022 applied for aid, 858 were judged to have need, 181 had their need fully met. 55 Federal Work-Study jobs (averaging $849). In 2012, 80 non-need-based awards were made. *Average percent of need met:* 66%. *Average financial aid package:* $6330. *Average need-based loan:* $2697. *Average need-based gift aid:* $4673. *Average non-need-based aid:* $1340. *Average indebtedness upon graduation:* $10,888.

Applying *Options:* electronic application, deferred entrance. *Required:* high school transcript. *Required for some:* 2 letters of recommendation, interview. *Application deadlines:* rolling (freshmen), rolling (transfers). *Notification:* continuous (freshmen), continuous (transfers).

Freshman Application Contact Mr. Michael Driskell, Area Recruiter, Mid-Plains Community College, 1101 Halligan Dr, North Platte, NE 69101. *Phone:* 308-535-3709. *Toll-free phone:* 800-658-4308 (in-state); 800-658-4348 (out-of-state). *Fax:* 308-534-5767. *E-mail:* driskellm@mpcc.edu. *Website:* http://www.mpcc.edu/.

Myotherapy Institute

Lincoln, Nebraska

Freshman Application Contact Admissions Office, Myotherapy Institute, 6020 South 58th Street, Lincoln, NE 68516. *Phone:* 402-421-7410. *Website:* http://www.myotherapy.edu/.

Nebraska College of Technical Agriculture

Curtis, Nebraska

Freshman Application Contact Kevin Martin, Assistant Admissions Coordinator, Nebraska College of Technical Agriculture, 404 East 7th Street, Curtis, NE 69025, NE 69025. *Phone:* 308-367-4124. *Toll-free phone:* 800-3CURTIS. *Website:* http://www.ncta.unl.edu/.

Nebraska Indian Community College

Macy, Nebraska

Director of Admissions Ms. Theresa Henry, Admission Counselor, Nebraska Indian Community College, PO Box 428, Macy, NE 68039-0428. *Phone:* 402-837-5078. *Website:* http://www.thenicc.edu/.

Northeast Community College

Norfolk, Nebraska

- **State and locally supported** 2-year, founded 1973, part of Nebraska Coordinating Commission for Postsecondary Education
- **Small-town** 205-acre campus
- **Coed**

Undergraduates 2,169 full-time, 2,992 part-time. 6% are from out of state; 1% Black or African American, non-Hispanic/Latino; 6% Hispanic/Latino; 0.3% Asian, non-Hispanic/Latino; 0.9% American Indian or Alaska Native, non-Hispanic/Latino; 0.7% Two or more races, non-Hispanic/Latino; 3% Race/ethnicity unknown; 0.6% international; 5% transferred in; 6% live on campus. *Retention:* 65% of full-time freshmen returned.

Faculty *Student/faculty ratio:* 16:1.

Academics *Calendar:* semesters. *Degree:* certificates, diplomas, and associate. *Special study options:* academic remediation for entering students, adult/continuing education programs, advanced placement credit, cooperative education, distance learning, double majors, English as a second language, internships, off-campus study, part-time degree program, services for LD students, summer session for credit.

Student Life *Campus security:* 24-hour patrols, controlled dormitory access.

Athletics Member NJCAA.

Financial Aid Of all full-time matriculated undergraduates who enrolled in 2011, 1,749 applied for aid, 1,491 were judged to have need, 164 had their need fully met. 70 Federal Work-Study jobs (averaging $1015). In 2011, 22. *Average percent of need met:* 68. *Average financial aid package:* $6400. *Average need-based loan:* $3196. *Average need-based gift aid:* $4641. *Average non-need-based aid:* $691. *Average indebtedness upon graduation:* $9952.

Applying *Options:* electronic application, early admission. *Required for some:* high school transcript, minimum 2.0 GPA, 3 letters of recommendation, interview. *Recommended:* high school transcript.

Freshman Application Contact Maureen Baker, Dean of Students, Northeast Community College, 801 East Benjamin Avenue, PO Box 469, Norfolk, NE 68702-0469. *Phone:* 402-844-7258. *Toll-free phone:* 800-348-9033 Ext. 7260. *Fax:* 402-844-7403. *E-mail:* admission@northeast.edu. *Website:* http://www.northeast.edu/.

Omaha School of Massage Therapy and Healthcare of Herzing University

Omaha, Nebraska

Admissions Office Contact Omaha School of Massage Therapy and Healthcare of Herzing University, 9748 Park Drive, Omaha, NE 68127. *Website:* http://www.osmhc.com/.

Southeast Community College, Beatrice Campus

Beatrice, Nebraska

Freshman Application Contact Admissions Office, Southeast Community College, Beatrice Campus, 4771 West Scott Road, Beatrice, NE 68310. *Phone:* 402-228-3468. *Toll-free phone:* 800-233-5027. *Fax:* 402-228-2218. *Website:* http://www.southeast.edu/.

Southeast Community College, Lincoln Campus

Lincoln, Nebraska

Freshman Application Contact Admissions Office, Southeast Community College, Lincoln Campus, 8800 O Street, Lincoln, NE 68520-1299. *Phone:* 402-471-3333. *Toll-free phone:* 800-642-4075. *Fax:* 402-437-2404.
Website: http://www.southeast.edu/.

Southeast Community College, Milford Campus

Milford, Nebraska

Freshman Application Contact Admissions Office, Southeast Community College, Milford Campus, 600 State Street, Milford, NE 68405. *Phone:* 402-761-2131. *Toll-free phone:* 800-933-7223. *Fax:* 402-761-2324.
Website: http://www.southeast.edu/.

Vatterott College

Omaha, Nebraska

Freshman Application Contact Admissions Office, Vatterott College, 11818 I Street, Omaha, NE 68137. *Phone:* 402-891-9411. *Toll-free phone:* 888-553-6627. *Fax:* 402-891-9413.
Website: http://www.vatterott.edu/.

Western Nebraska Community College

Sidney, Nebraska

Director of Admissions Mr. Troy Archuleta, Admissions and Recruitment Director, Western Nebraska Community College, 371 College Drive, Sidney, NE 69162. *Phone:* 308-635-6015. *Toll-free phone:* 800-222-9682. *E-mail:* rhovey@wncc.net.
Website: http://www.wncc.net/.

NEVADA

Anthem Institute–Las Vegas

Las Vegas, Nevada

Freshman Application Contact Admissions Office, Anthem Institute–Las Vegas, 2320 South Rancho Drive, Las Vegas, NV 89102. *Phone:* 702-385-6700. *Toll-free phone:* 855-331-7762.
Website: http://anthem.edu/las-vegas-nevada/.

Career College of Northern Nevada

Sparks, Nevada

Freshman Application Contact Ms. Laura Goldhammer, Director of Admissions, Career College of Northern Nevada, 1421 Pullman Drive, Sparks, NV 89434. *Phone:* 775-856-2266 Ext. 11. *Fax:* 775-856-0935. *E-mail:* lgoldhammer@ccnn4u.com.
Website: http://www.ccnn.edu/.

Carrington College–Las Vegas

Las Vegas, Nevada

- **Proprietary** 2-year, part of Carrington Colleges Group, Inc.
- **Coed,** 182 undergraduate students, 100% full-time, 61% women, 39% men

Undergraduates 182 full-time. 15% Black or African American, non-Hispanic/Latino; 13% Hispanic/Latino; 21% Asian, non-Hispanic/Latino; 8% Native Hawaiian or other Pacific Islander, non-Hispanic/Latino; 1% American Indian or Alaska Native, non-Hispanic/Latino; 3% Two or more races, non-Hispanic/Latino; 2% Race/ethnicity unknown.
Freshmen *Admission:* 9 enrolled.
Faculty *Total:* 15, 40% full-time. *Student/faculty ratio:* 20:1.
Majors Physical therapy technology; respiratory therapy technician.
Academics *Degree:* certificates and associate.
Student Life *Housing:* college housing not available.

Applying *Required:* essay or personal statement, high school transcript, interview, Entrance test administered by Carrington College.
Freshman Application Contact Carrington College–Las Vegas, 5740 South Eastern Avenue, Las Vegas, NV 89119.
Website: http://carrington.edu/.

Carrington College–Reno

Reno, Nevada

- **Proprietary** 2-year, part of Carrington Colleges Group, Inc.
- **Coed,** 315 undergraduate students, 100% full-time, 84% women, 16% men

Undergraduates 315 full-time. 2% Black or African American, non-Hispanic/Latino; 12% Hispanic/Latino; 3% Asian, non-Hispanic/Latino; 0.6% Native Hawaiian or other Pacific Islander, non-Hispanic/Latino; 0.6% American Indian or Alaska Native, non-Hispanic/Latino; 1% Two or more races, non-Hispanic/Latino; 0.3% Race/ethnicity unknown.
Freshmen *Admission:* 10 enrolled.
Faculty *Total:* 32, 56% full-time. *Student/faculty ratio:* 14:1.
Majors Registered nursing/registered nurse.
Academics *Degree:* associate.
Student Life *Housing:* college housing not available.
Applying *Required:* essay or personal statement, high school transcript, interview, Entrance test administered by Carrington College.
Freshman Application Contact Carrington College–Reno, 5580 Kietzke Lane, Reno, NV 89511. *Phone:* 775-335-2900.
Website: http://carrington.edu/.

College of Southern Nevada

North Las Vegas, Nevada

Freshman Application Contact Admissions and Records, College of Southern Nevada, 3200 East Cheyenne Avenue, North Las Vegas, NV 89030-4296. *Phone:* 702-651-4060.
Website: http://www.csn.edu/.

Everest College

Henderson, Nevada

Admissions Office Contact Everest College, 170 North Stephanie Street, 1st Floor, Henderson, NV 89074. *Toll-free phone:* 888-741-4270.
Website: http://www.everest.edu/.

Great Basin College

Elko, Nevada

Freshman Application Contact Ms. Janice King, Director of Admissions and Registrar, Great Basin College, 1500 College Parkway, Elko, NV 89801-3348. *Phone:* 775-753-2361. *Fax:* 775-753-2311. *E-mail:* janicek@gwmail.gbcnv.edu.
Website: http://www.gbcnv.edu/.

ITT Technical Institute

Henderson, Nevada

- **Proprietary** primarily 2-year, founded 1997, part of ITT Educational Services, Inc.
- **Coed**

Academics *Degrees:* associate and bachelor's.
Financial Aid Of all full-time matriculated undergraduates who enrolled in 2011, 6 Federal Work-Study jobs (averaging $5000).
Freshman Application Contact Director of Recruitment, ITT Technical Institute, 168 North Gibson Road, Henderson, NV 89014. *Phone:* 702-558-5404. *Toll-free phone:* 800-488-8459.
Website: http://www.itt-tech.edu/.

ITT Technical Institute

North Las Vegas, Nevada

- **Proprietary** primarily 2-year, part of ITT Educational Services, Inc.
- **Coed**

Academics *Calendar:* quarters. *Degrees:* associate and bachelor's.
Freshman Application Contact Director of Recruitment, ITT Technical Institute, 3825 W. Cheyenne Avenue, Suite 600, North Las Vegas, NV 89032. *Phone:* 702-240-0967. *Toll-free phone:* 877-832-8442.
Website: http://www.itt-tech.edu/.

Kaplan College, Las Vegas Campus

Las Vegas, Nevada

- **Proprietary** 2-year, founded 1990
- **Coed**

Academics *Degree:* diplomas and associate.

Freshman Application Contact Admissions Office, Kaplan College, Las Vegas Campus, 3535 West Sahara Avenue, Las Vegas, NV 89102. *Phone:* 702-368-2338. *Toll-free phone:* 800-935-1857.
Website: http://las-vegas.kaplancollege.com/.

Le Cordon Bleu College of Culinary Arts, Las Vegas

Las Vegas, Nevada

Freshman Application Contact Admissions Office, Le Cordon Bleu College of Culinary Arts, Las Vegas, 1451 Center Crossing Road, Las Vegas, NV 89144. *Toll-free phone:* 888-551-8222.
Website: http://www.vegasculinary.com/.

Pima Medical Institute

Las Vegas, Nevada

Freshman Application Contact Admissions Office, Pima Medical Institute, 3333 East Flamingo Road, Las Vegas, NV 89121. *Phone:* 702-458-9650 Ext. 202. *Toll-free phone:* 800-477-PIMA.
Website: http://www.pmi.edu/.

Truckee Meadows Community College

Reno, Nevada

- **State-supported** 2-year, founded 1971, part of Nevada System of Higher Education
- **Suburban** 63-acre campus
- **Endowment** $9.0 million
- **Coed**

Undergraduates 3,530 full-time, 9,057 part-time. Students come from 18 states and territories; 7% are from out of state; 3% Black or African American, non-Hispanic/Latino; 19% Hispanic/Latino; 5% Asian, non-Hispanic/Latino; 1% Native Hawaiian or other Pacific Islander, non-Hispanic/Latino; 2% American Indian or Alaska Native, non-Hispanic/Latino; 3% Two or more races, non-Hispanic/Latino; 1% Race/ethnicity unknown; 0.6% international; 5% transferred in. *Retention:* 62% of full-time freshmen returned.

Faculty *Student/faculty ratio:* 22:1.

Academics *Calendar:* semesters. *Degree:* certificates and associate. *Special study options:* academic remediation for entering students, accelerated degree program, adult/continuing education programs, advanced placement credit, distance learning, English as a second language, part-time degree program, services for LD students, summer session for credit. *ROTC:* Army (c).

Student Life *Campus security:* 24-hour emergency response devices and patrols, late-night transport/escort service.

Costs (2012–13) *Tuition:* state resident $2265 full-time, $76 per credit part-time; nonresident $8910 full-time, $159 per credit part-time. Full-time tuition and fees vary according to course load and program. Part-time tuition and fees vary according to course load and program. *Required fees:* $445 full-time, $15 per credit part-time. *Payment plans:* tuition prepayment, installment.

Financial Aid Of all full-time matriculated undergraduates who enrolled in 2011, 126 Federal Work-Study jobs (averaging $5000). 368 state and other part-time jobs (averaging $5000).

Applying *Options:* early admission, deferred entrance. *Application fee:* $10.

Freshman Application Contact Truckee Meadows Community College, 7000 Dandini Boulevard, Reno, NV 89512-3901. *Phone:* 775-3375616.
Website: http://www.tmcc.edu/.

Western Nevada College

Carson City, Nevada

Freshman Application Contact Admissions and Records, Western Nevada College, 2201 West College Parkway, Carson City, NV 89703. *Phone:* 775-445-2377. *Fax:* 775-445-3147. *E-mail:* wncc_aro@wncc.edu.
Website: http://www.wnc.edu/.

NEW HAMPSHIRE

Great Bay Community College

Portsmouth, New Hampshire

Freshman Application Contact Matt Thornton, Admissions Coordinator, Great Bay Community College, 320 Corporate Drive, Portsmouth, NH 03801. *Phone:* 603-427-7605. *Toll-free phone:* 800-522-1194. *E-mail:* askgreatbay@ccsnh.edu.
Website: http://www.greatbay.edu/.

Hesser College, Concord

Concord, New Hampshire

- **Proprietary** primarily 2-year
- **Coed**

Academics *Degrees:* diplomas, associate, and bachelor's.

Freshman Application Contact Hesser College, Concord, 16 Foundry Street, Concord, NH 03301. *Phone:* 603-225-9200. *Toll-free phone:* 800-935-1824.
Website: http://www.hesser.edu/.

Hesser College, Manchester

Manchester, New Hampshire

- **Proprietary** primarily 2-year, founded 1900
- **Urban** campus
- **Coed**

Academics *Calendar:* semesters. *Degrees:* diplomas, associate, and bachelor's.

Financial Aid Of all full-time matriculated undergraduates who enrolled in 2011, 700 Federal Work-Study jobs (averaging $1000).

Freshman Application Contact Hesser College, Manchester, 3 Sundial Avenue, Manchester, NH 03103. *Phone:* 603-668-6660. *Toll-free phone:* 800-935-1824.
Website: http://www.hesser.edu/.

Hesser College, Nashua

Nashua, New Hampshire

- **Proprietary** primarily 2-year
- **Coed**

Academics *Degrees:* diplomas, associate, and bachelor's.

Freshman Application Contact Hesser College, Nashua, 410 Amherst Street, Nashua, NH 03063. *Phone:* 603-883-0404. *Toll-free phone:* 800-935-1824.
Website: http://www.hesser.edu/.

Hesser College, Portsmouth

Portsmouth, New Hampshire

- **Proprietary** primarily 2-year
- **Coed**

Academics *Degrees:* diplomas, associate, and bachelor's.

Freshman Application Contact Hesser College, Portsmouth, 170 Commerce Way, Portsmouth, NH 03801. *Phone:* 603-436-5300. *Toll-free phone:* 800-935-1824.
Website: http://www.hesser.edu/.

Hesser College, Salem

Salem, New Hampshire

- **Proprietary** primarily 2-year
- **Coed**

Academics *Degrees:* diplomas, associate, and bachelor's.

Freshman Application Contact Hesser College, Salem, 11 Manor Parkway, Salem, NH 03079. *Phone:* 603-898-3480. *Toll-free phone:* 800-935-1824.
Website: http://www.hesser.edu/.

Lakes Region Community College

Laconia, New Hampshire

Director of Admissions Wayne Fraser, Director of Admissions, Lakes Region Community College, 379 Belmont Road, Laconia, NH 03246. *Phone:* 603-524-3207 Ext. 766. *Toll-free phone:* 800-357-2992. *E-mail:* wfraser@ccsnh.edu.
Website: http://www.lrcc.edu/.

Manchester Community College

Manchester, New Hampshire

Freshman Application Contact Ms. Jacquie Poirier, Coordinator of Admissions, Manchester Community College, 1066 Front Street, Manchester, NH 03102-8518. *Phone:* 603-668-6706 Ext. 283. *Toll-free phone:* 800-924-3445. *E-mail:* jpoirier@nhctc.edu.
Website: http://www.mccnh.edu/.

Nashua Community College

Nashua, New Hampshire

Freshman Application Contact Ms. Patricia Goodman, Vice President of Student Services, Nashua Community College, Nashua, NH 03063. *Phone:* 603-882-6923 Ext. 1529. *Fax:* 603-882-8690. *E-mail:* pgoodman@ccsnh.edu.
Website: http://www.nashuacc.edu/.

NHTI, Concord's Community College

Concord, New Hampshire

Freshman Application Contact Mr. Francis P. Meyer, Director of Admissions, NHTI, Concord's Community College, 31 College Drive, Concord, NH 03301-7412. *Phone:* 603-271-7131. *Toll-free phone:* 800-247-0179. *E-mail:* fmeyer@nhctc.edu.
Website: http://www.nhti.edu/.

River Valley Community College

Claremont, New Hampshire

Director of Admissions Charles Kusselow, Director of Admissions, River Valley Community College, 1 College Drive, Claremont, NH 03743. *Phone:* 603-542-7744 Ext. 5322. *Toll-free phone:* 800-837-0658. *Fax:* 603-543-1844. *E-mail:* ckusselow@ccsnh.edu.
Website: http://www.rivervalley.edu/.

White Mountains Community College

Berlin, New Hampshire

- **State-supported** 2-year, founded 1966, part of Community College System of New Hampshire
- **Rural** 325-acre campus
- **Coed**

Undergraduates 348 full-time, 574 part-time.

Academics *Calendar:* semesters. *Degree:* certificates, diplomas, and associate. *Special study options:* academic remediation for entering students, adult/continuing education programs, advanced placement credit, distance learning, double majors, external degree program, independent study, internships, part-time degree program, services for LD students, summer session for credit.

Standardized Tests *Required:* ACCUPLACER Placement Test, Pre National League of Nursing entrance exam (Nursing AS Degree) (for admission).

Costs (2012–13) *Tuition:* state resident $6300 full-time, $210 per credit part-time; nonresident $14,340 full-time, $478 per credit part-time. *Required fees:* $540 full-time, $18 per credit part-time.

Applying *Options:* electronic application, deferred entrance. *Application fee:* $20. *Required:* high school transcript, placement test. *Required for some:* essay or personal statement.

Freshman Application Contact Ms. Jamie Rivard, Program Assistant, White Mountains Community College, 2020 Riverside Drive, Berlin, NH 03570. *Phone:* 603-752-1113 Ext. 3000. *Toll-free phone:* 800-445-4525. *Fax:* 603-752-6335. *E-mail:* jrivard@ccsnh.edu.
Website: http://www.wmcc.edu/.

NEW JERSEY

Assumption College for Sisters

Mendham, New Jersey

Freshman Application Contact Sr. Gerardine Tantsits, Academic Dean/Registrar, Assumption College for Sisters, 350 Bernardsville Road, Mendham, NJ 07945-2923. *Phone:* 973-543-6528 Ext. 228. *Fax:* 973-543-1738. *E-mail:* deanregistrar@acs350.org.
Website: http://www.acs350.org/.

Atlantic Cape Community College

Mays Landing, New Jersey

Freshman Application Contact Mrs. Linda McLeod, Assistant Director, Admissions and College Recruitment, Atlantic Cape Community College, 5100 Black Horse Pike, Mays Landing, NJ 08330-2699. *Phone:* 609-343-5009. *Fax:* 609-343-4921. *E-mail:* accadmit@atlantic.edu.
Website: http://www.atlantic.edu/.

Bergen Community College

Paramus, New Jersey

Freshman Application Contact Admissions Office, Bergen Community College, 400 Paramus Road, Paramus, NJ 07652-1595. *Phone:* 201-447-7195. *E-mail:* admsoffice@bergen.edu.
Website: http://www.bergen.edu/.

Brookdale Community College

Lincroft, New Jersey

Director of Admissions Ms. Kim Toomey, Registrar, Brookdale Community College, 765 Newman Springs Road, Lincroft, NJ 07738-1597. *Phone:* 732-224-2268.
Website: http://www.brookdalecc.edu/.

Burlington County College

Pemberton, New Jersey

- **County-supported** 2-year, founded 1966
- **Suburban** 225-acre campus with easy access to Philadelphia
- **Coed,** 10,071 undergraduate students, 51% full-time, 58% women, 42% men

Undergraduates 5,129 full-time, 4,942 part-time. Students come from 17 states and territories; 1% are from out of state; 19% Black or African American, non-Hispanic/Latino; 9% Hispanic/Latino; 3% Asian, non-Hispanic/Latino; 0.2% Native Hawaiian or other Pacific Islander, non-Hispanic/Latino; 0.2% American Indian or Alaska Native, non-Hispanic/Latino; 3% Two or more races, non-Hispanic/Latino; 7% Race/ethnicity unknown; 2% international; 7% transferred in. *Retention:* 60% of full-time freshmen returned.

Freshmen *Admission:* 5,521 applied, 5,521 admitted, 2,283 enrolled.

Faculty *Total:* 657, 9% full-time. *Student/faculty ratio:* 26:1.

Majors Accounting; agribusiness; American Sign Language (ASL); animation, interactive technology, video graphics and special effects; art; automotive engineering technology; biological and physical sciences; biology/biological sciences; biotechnology; business administration and management; chemical engineering; chemistry; commercial and advertising art; communication disorders sciences and services related; computer graphics; computer science; construction engineering technology; criminal justice/police science; dental hygiene; drafting and design technology; dramatic/theater arts; education; electrical, electronic and communications engineering technology; engineering; engineering technologies and engineering related; English; environmental science; fashion/apparel design; fire science/firefighting; food service systems administration; geological and earth sciences/geosciences related; graphic and printing equipment operation/production; graphic design; health information/medical records technology; health services/allied health/health sciences; history; hospitality administration; human services; information technology; international/global studies; journalism; legal assistant/paralegal; liberal arts and sciences/liberal studies; management information systems; mathematics; medical radiologic technology; music; philosophy; physics; psychology; registered nursing/registered nurse; respiratory care therapy; restaurant/food services management; retailing; sales, distribution, and marketing operations; sign language interpretation and translation; social sciences; sociology.

Academics *Calendar:* semesters plus 2 summer terms. *Degree:* certificates and associate. *Special study options:* academic remediation for entering students, accelerated degree program, adult/continuing education programs, advanced placement credit, cooperative education, distance learning, double majors, English as a second language, honors programs, independent study, internships, part-time degree program, services for LD students, study abroad, summer session for credit.

Library Burlington County College Library plus 1 other with 92,400 titles, 1,750 serial subscriptions, an OPAC, a Web page.

Student Life *Housing:* college housing not available. *Activities and Organizations:* drama/theater group, student-run radio station, choral group, Student Government Association, Phi Theta Kappa, Creative Writing Guild. *Campus security:* 24-hour emergency response devices and patrols, late-night transport/escort service, electronic entrances to buildings and rooms, surveillance cameras. *Student services:* health clinic, personal/psychological counseling.

Athletics Member NJCAA. *Intercollegiate sports:* baseball M(s), basketball M(s)/W(s), golf M/W, soccer M/W, softball W. *Intramural sports:* archery M.

Costs (2013–14) *Tuition:* area resident $2760 full-time, $92 per credit hour part-time; state resident $3240 full-time, $108 per credit hour part-time; non-resident $5190 full-time, $173 per credit hour part-time. Full-time tuition and fees vary according to course load and program. Part-time tuition and fees vary according to course load and program. *Required fees:* $855 full-time, $92 per credit hour part-time. *Payment plans:* installment, deferred payment. *Waivers:* senior citizens and employees or children of employees.

Financial Aid Of all full-time matriculated undergraduates who enrolled in 2011, 100 Federal Work-Study jobs (averaging $1200). 100 state and other part-time jobs (averaging $2000).

Applying *Options:* electronic application, early admission, deferred entrance. *Application fee:* $20. *Recommended:* high school transcript. *Application deadlines:* rolling (freshmen), rolling (out-of-state freshmen), rolling (transfers). *Notification:* continuous (freshmen), continuous (out-of-state freshmen), continuous (transfers).

Freshman Application Contact Burlington County College, 601 Pemberton Browns Mills Road, Pemberton, NJ 08068. *Phone:* 609-894-9311 Ext. 1200. *Website:* http://www.bcc.edu/.

Camden County College

Blackwood, New Jersey

Freshman Application Contact Donald Delaney, Outreach Coordinator, School and Community Academic Programs, Camden County College, PO Box 200, Blackwood, NJ 08012-0200. *Phone:* 856-227-7200 Ext. 4371. *Fax:* 856-374-4916. *E-mail:* ddelaney@camdencc.edu. *Website:* http://www.camdencc.edu/.

See display on this page and page 400 for the College Close-Up.

County College of Morris

Randolph, New Jersey

- **County-supported** 2-year, founded 1966, part of New Jersey Commission on Higher Education
- **Suburban** 218-acre campus with easy access to New York City
- **Coed,** 8,679 undergraduate students, 53% full-time, 49% women, 51% men

Undergraduates 4,636 full-time, 4,043 part-time. Students come from 3 states and territories; 5% Black or African American, non-Hispanic/Latino; 18% Hispanic/Latino; 5% Asian, non-Hispanic/Latino; 0.1% Native Hawaiian or other Pacific Islander, non-Hispanic/Latino; 0.3% American Indian or Alaska Native, non-Hispanic/Latino; 1% Two or more races, non-Hispanic/Latino; 9% Race/ethnicity unknown.

Faculty *Total:* 885, 51% full-time. *Student/faculty ratio:* 10:1.

Majors Administrative assistant and secretarial science; agricultural business and management; airline pilot and flight crew; biology/biotechnology laboratory technician; business administration and management; business, management, and marketing related; chemical technology; criminal justice/police science; design and applied arts related; electrical, electronic and communications engineering technology; engineering science; fine/studio arts; fire prevention and safety technology; graphic design; hospitality and recreation marketing; kindergarten/preschool education; kinesiology and exercise science; liberal arts and sciences/liberal studies; management information systems; mechanical engineering/mechanical technology; multi/interdisciplinary studies related; music; photography; public administration; radiologic technology/science; registered nursing/registered nurse; respiratory care therapy; telecommunications technology; veterinary/animal health technology; web page, digital/multimedia and information resources design.

Academics *Calendar:* semesters. *Degree:* certificates and associate.

Student Life *Housing:* college housing not available.

Athletics Member NJCAA. *Intercollegiate sports:* baseball M(s), basketball M(s)/W(s), golf M, ice hockey M(s), soccer M/W, softball W(s), tennis M. *Intramural sports:* badminton M/W, basketball M/W, football M, soccer W, softball W, tennis M/W, volleyball M/W, weight lifting M/W, wrestling M/W.

Costs (2013–14) *Tuition:* area resident $3580 full-time, $117 per credit hour part-time; state resident $7160 full-time, $234 per credit hour part-time; non-resident $10,740 full-time, $251 per credit hour part-time. Full-time tuition and fees vary according to location and program. Part-time tuition and fees vary according to course load, location, and program. *Required fees:* $525 full-time, $18 per credit hour part-time. *Waivers:* senior citizens and employees or children of employees.

Financial Aid Of all full-time matriculated undergraduates who enrolled in 2011, 588 Federal Work-Study jobs (averaging $1947).

Applying *Application fee:* $30. *Required:* high school transcript. *Notification:* continuous (freshmen), continuous (transfers).

Freshman Application Contact County College of Morris, 214 Center Grove Road, Randolph, NJ 07869-2086. *Phone:* 973-328-5100. *Website:* http://www.ccm.edu/.

Cumberland County College
Vineland, New Jersey

Freshman Application Contact Ms. Anne Daly-Eimer, Director of Admissions and Registration, Cumberland County College, PO Box 1500, College Drive, Vineland, NJ 08362. *Phone:* 856-691-8986. *Website:* http://www.cccnj.edu/.

Essex County College
Newark, New Jersey

- **County-supported** 2-year, founded 1966, part of New Jersey Commission on Higher Education
- **Urban** 22-acre campus with easy access to New York City
- **Coed,** 11,979 undergraduate students, 55% full-time, 58% women, 42% men

Undergraduates 6,569 full-time, 5,410 part-time. Students come from 9 states and territories; 49 other countries; 1% are from out of state; 48% Black or African American, non-Hispanic/Latino; 24% Hispanic/Latino; 4% Asian, non-Hispanic/Latino; 0.1% Native Hawaiian or other Pacific Islander, non-Hispanic/Latino; 0.2% American Indian or Alaska Native, non-Hispanic/Latino; 0.5% Two or more races, non-Hispanic/Latino; 6% Race/ethnicity unknown; 8% international; 2% transferred in. *Retention:* 50% of full-time freshmen returned.

Freshmen *Admission:* 7,757 applied, 7,757 admitted, 2,222 enrolled.

Faculty *Total:* 601, 20% full-time. *Student/faculty ratio:* 29:1.

Majors Accounting; accounting technology and bookkeeping; administrative assistant and secretarial science; architectural engineering technology; art; biology/biological sciences; biotechnology; business administration and management; business teacher education; chemical technology; chemistry; civil engineering technology; communications technology; computer and information sciences; computer programming; computer programming (specific applications); computer science; criminal justice/police science; dental hygiene; education; educational/instructional technology; electrical, electronic and communications engineering technology; energy management and systems technology; engineering; engineering technologies and engineering related; health/health-care administration; health/medical preparatory programs related; health professions related; health services/allied health/health sciences; hotel/motel administration; human services; industrial production technologies related; information science/studies; kindergarten/preschool education; legal assistant/paralegal; liberal arts and sciences/liberal studies; manufacturing engineering technology; mathematics; medical radiologic technology; music; opticianry; physical education teaching and coaching; physical therapy technology; registered nursing/registered nurse; respiratory care therapy; social sciences; social work.

Academics *Calendar:* semesters. *Degree:* certificates and associate. *Special study options:* academic remediation for entering students, accelerated degree program, adult/continuing education programs, advanced placement credit, cooperative education, distance learning, double majors, English as a second language, independent study, internships, off-campus study, part-time degree program, services for LD students, summer session for credit. *ROTC:* Army (c).

Library Martin Luther King, Jr. Library with 91,000 titles, 639 serial subscriptions, an OPAC, a Web page.

Student Life *Housing:* college housing not available. *Activities and Organizations:* drama/theater group, student-run newspaper, choral group, Fashion Entertainment Board, Phi Theta Kappa, Latin Student Union, DECA, Black Student Association. *Campus security:* 24-hour emergency response devices and patrols. *Student services:* personal/psychological counseling, women's center.

Athletics Member NJCAA. *Intercollegiate sports:* basketball M(s)/W(s), cross-country running M(s)/W(s), soccer M, track and field M/W. *Intramural sports:* table tennis M, weight lifting M.

Costs (2012–13) *Tuition:* area resident $3255 full-time, $109 per credit hour part-time; state resident $6510 full-time, $217 per credit hour part-time; non-resident $6510 full-time, $217 per credit hour part-time. *Required fees:* $975 full-time, $33 per credit hour part-time. *Payment plan:* deferred payment. *Waivers:* employees or children of employees.

Financial Aid Of all full-time matriculated undergraduates who enrolled in 2009, 256 Federal Work-Study jobs (averaging $2488).

Applying *Options:* electronic application, deferred entrance. *Application fee:* $25. *Required:* high school transcript. *Application deadlines:* 8/15 (freshmen), rolling (transfers). *Notification:* continuous (freshmen), continuous (out-of-state freshmen), continuous (transfers).

Freshman Application Contact Ms. Marva Mack, Director of Admissions, Essex County College, 303 University Avenue, Newark, NJ 07102. *Phone:* 973-877-3119. *Fax:* 973-623-6449. *Website:* http://www.essex.edu/.

Gloucester County College
Sewell, New Jersey

Freshman Application Contact Ms. Judy Atkinson, Registrar/Admissions, Gloucester County College, 1400 Tanyard Road, Sewell, NJ 08080. *Phone:* 856-415-2209. *E-mail:* jatkinso@gccnj.edu. *Website:* http://www.gccnj.edu/.

Hudson County Community College
Jersey City, New Jersey

Director of Admissions Mr. Robert Martin, Assistant Dean of Admissions, Hudson County Community College, 25 Journal Square, Jersey City, NJ 07306. *Phone:* 201-714-2115. *Fax:* 201-714-2136. *E-mail:* martin@hccc.edu. *Website:* http://www.hccc.edu/.

ITT Technical Institute
Marlton, New Jersey

- **Proprietary** 2-year
- **Coed**

Academics *Degree:* associate.

Freshman Application Contact Director of Recruitment, ITT Technical Institute, 9000 Lincoln Drive East, Suite 100, Marlton, NJ 08053. *Phone:* 856-396-3500. *Toll-free phone:* 877-209-5410. *Website:* http://www.itt-tech.edu/.

Mercer County Community College
Trenton, New Jersey

Freshman Application Contact Dr. L. Campbell, Dean for Student and Academic Services, Mercer County Community College, 1200 Old Trenton Road, PO Box B, Trenton, NJ 08690-1004. *Phone:* 609-586-4800 Ext. 3222. *Toll-free phone:* 800-392-MCCC. *Fax:* 609-586-6944. *E-mail:* admiss@mccc.edu. *Website:* http://www.mccc.edu/.

Middlesex County College
Edison, New Jersey

Director of Admissions Mr. Peter W. Rice, Director of Admissions and Recruitment, Middlesex County College, 2600 Woodbridge Avenue, PO Box 3050, Edison, NJ 08818-3050. *Phone:* 732-906-4243. *Website:* http://www.middlesexcc.edu/.

Ocean County College
Toms River, New Jersey

- **County-supported** 2-year, founded 1964, part of New Jersey Higher Education
- **Suburban** 275-acre campus with easy access to Philadelphia
- **Coed,** 10,048 undergraduate students, 52% full-time, 57% women, 43% men

Undergraduates 5,232 full-time, 4,816 part-time. Students come from 23 states and territories; 13 other countries; 2% are from out of state; 5% Black or African American, non-Hispanic/Latino; 9% Hispanic/Latino; 2% Asian, non-Hispanic/Latino; 0.1% Native Hawaiian or other Pacific Islander, non-Hispanic/Latino; 0.5% American Indian or Alaska Native, non-Hispanic/Latino; 5% Race/ethnicity unknown; 1% international; 3% transferred in. *Retention:* 71% of full-time freshmen returned.

Freshmen *Admission:* 3,922 applied, 3,922 admitted, 2,304 enrolled.

Faculty *Total:* 536, 20% full-time, 27% with terminal degrees. *Student/faculty ratio:* 29:1.

Majors Administrative assistant and secretarial science; broadcast journalism; business administration and management; business/commerce; communications technologies and support services related; computer and information sciences; criminal justice/police science; dental hygiene; engineering; engineering technologies and engineering related; environmental science; fire prevention and safety technology; general studies; homeland security, law enforcement, firefighting and protective services related; human services; liberal arts and sciences/liberal studies; occupational therapist assistant; registered nursing/registered nurse; sign language interpretation and translation.

Academics *Calendar:* semesters. *Degree:* certificates, diplomas, and associate. *Special study options:* academic remediation for entering students, accelerated degree program, adult/continuing education programs, advanced placement credit, cooperative education, distance learning, English as a second language, honors programs, independent study, internships, part-time degree program, services for LD students, study abroad, summer session for credit.

Library Ocean County College Library with 75,809 titles, 287 serial subscriptions, 1,434 audiovisual materials, an OPAC, a Web page.

Student Life *Housing:* college housing not available. *Activities and Organizations:* drama/theater group, student-run newspaper, radio and television station, choral group, Student Activities Board, Student Government, OCC Vikings Cheerleaders, Speech and Theater Club, Veterans' Club. *Campus security:* 24-hour emergency response devices and patrols, late-night transport/escort service, security cameras in hallways and parking lots. *Student services:* personal/psychological counseling.

Athletics Member NJCAA. *Intercollegiate sports:* baseball M, basketball M/W, cross-country running M/W, golf M/W, soccer M/W, softball W, swimming and diving M/W, tennis M/W. *Intramural sports:* basketball M/W, cheerleading M(c)/W(c), ice hockey M, sailing M(c)/W(c), soccer M/W, softball W, volleyball M/W.

Standardized Tests *Required for some:* ACCUPLACER is required for degree seeking students. Waiver may be obtained by meeting institution's minimum ACT or SAT scores, or English and math transfer credits.

Costs (2013–14) *Tuition:* area resident $3030 full-time, $101 per credit part-time; state resident $3990 full-time, $133 per credit part-time; nonresident $6450 full-time, $215 per credit part-time. Full-time tuition and fees vary according to course load and program. Part-time tuition and fees vary according to program. *Required fees:* $960 full-time, $30 per credit part-time, $20 per term part-time. *Payment plan:* installment. *Waivers:* senior citizens and employees or children of employees.

Financial Aid Of all full-time matriculated undergraduates who enrolled in 2011, 76 Federal Work-Study jobs (averaging $1300). 45 state and other part-time jobs (averaging $850).

Applying *Options:* electronic application. *Required for some:* high school transcript, Accuplacer testing required for degree seeking students not meeting minimum ACT or SAT institutional requirements. Selective admissions for nursing students. Please see our website for details. *Application deadlines:* rolling (freshmen), rolling (out-of-state freshmen), rolling (transfers). *Notification:* continuous (freshmen), continuous (out-of-state freshmen), continuous (transfers).

Freshman Application Contact Ms. Elizabeth Clements, Associate Registrar, Ocean County College, College Drive, PO Box 2001, Toms River, NJ 08754-2001. *Phone:* 732-255-0400 Ext. 2377. *E-mail:* eclements@ocean.edu. *Website:* http://www.ocean.edu/.

Passaic County Community College
Paterson, New Jersey

Freshman Application Contact Mr. Patrick Noonan, Director of Admissions, Passaic County Community College, One College Boulevard, Paterson, NJ 07505-1179. *Phone:* 973-684-6304.
Website: http://www.pccc.cc.nj.us/.

Raritan Valley Community College
Branchburg, New Jersey

- **State and locally supported** 2-year, founded 1965
- **Suburban** 225-acre campus with easy access to New York City, Philadelphia
- **Endowment** $871,383
- **Coed,** 8,398 undergraduate students, 44% full-time, 53% women, 47% men

Undergraduates 3,712 full-time, 4,686 part-time. Students come from 13 states and territories; 1% are from out of state; 9% Black or African American, non-Hispanic/Latino; 15% Hispanic/Latino; 6% Asian, non-Hispanic/Latino; 0.3% Native Hawaiian or other Pacific Islander, non-Hispanic/Latino; 0.2% American Indian or Alaska Native, non-Hispanic/Latino; 2% Two or more races, non-Hispanic/Latino; 7% Race/ethnicity unknown; 2% international; 6% transferred in.

Freshmen *Admission:* 2,581 applied, 2,563 admitted, 1,499 enrolled. *Average high school GPA:* 2.74. *Test scores:* SAT critical reading scores over 500: 64%; SAT math scores over 500: 73%; SAT writing scores over 500: 57%; SAT critical reading scores over 600: 18%; SAT math scores over 600: 27%; SAT writing scores over 600: 13%; SAT critical reading scores over 700: 2%; SAT math scores over 700: 2%.

Faculty *Total:* 470, 25% full-time. *Student/faculty ratio:* 22:1.

Majors Accounting related; accounting technology and bookkeeping; administrative assistant and secretarial science; animation, interactive technology, video graphics and special effects; automotive engineering technology; bio-

technology; business administration and management; business/commerce; chemical technology; child-care provision; cinematography and film/video production; communication and media related; computer and information sciences and support services related; computer programming (vendor/product certification); computer systems networking and telecommunications; construction engineering technology; corrections; criminal justice/law enforcement administration; criminal justice/police science; critical incident response/special police operations; dance; dental assisting; dental hygiene; design and applied arts related; diesel mechanics technology; digital communication and media/multimedia; engineering science; engineering technologies and engineering related; English; financial planning and services; fine/studio arts; health and physical education/fitness; health information/medical records technology; health services/allied health/health sciences; heating, ventilation, air conditioning and refrigeration engineering technology; information technology; interior design; international business/trade/commerce; kindergarten/preschool education; kinesiology and exercise science; legal assistant/paralegal; liberal arts and sciences/liberal studies; lineworker; management information systems; manufacturing engineering technology; marketing/marketing management; medical/clinical assistant; meeting and event planning; multi/interdisciplinary studies related; music; opticianry; optometric technician; registered nursing/registered nurse; respiratory care therapy; restaurant, culinary, and catering management; small business administration; web page, digital/multimedia and information resources design.

Academics *Calendar:* semesters. *Degree:* certificates and associate. *Special study options:* academic remediation for entering students, adult/continuing education programs, advanced placement credit, cooperative education, distance learning, double majors, English as a second language, honors programs, independent study, internships, off-campus study, part-time degree program, services for LD students, summer session for credit. *ROTC:* Army (c), Air Force (c).

Library Evelyn S. Field Library with 143,559 titles, 26,810 serial subscriptions, 2,712 audiovisual materials, an OPAC, a Web page.

Student Life *Housing:* college housing not available. *Activities and Organizations:* drama/theater group, student-run radio station, choral group, Phi Theta Kappa, Orgullo Latino, Student Nurses Association, Business Club/SIFE, Environmental club. *Campus security:* 24-hour emergency response devices and patrols, late-night transport/escort service, 24-hour outdoor and indoor surveillance cameras; 24-hr mobile patrols; 24-hr communication center. *Student services:* personal/psychological counseling.

Athletics Member NJCAA. *Intercollegiate sports:* baseball M(s), basketball M(s)/W(s), golf M/W, soccer M/W, softball W(s).

Financial Aid Of all full-time matriculated undergraduates who enrolled in 2011, 12 Federal Work-Study jobs (averaging $2500).

Applying *Options:* electronic application. *Application fee:* $25. *Required:* high school transcript. *Application deadlines:* rolling (freshmen), rolling (transfers).

Freshman Application Contact Mr. Daniel Palubniak, Registrar, Enrollment Services, Raritan Valley Community College, 118 Lamington Road, Branchburg, NJ 08876-1265. *Phone:* 908-526-1200 Ext. 8206. *Fax:* 908-704-3442. *E-mail:* dpalubni@raritanval.edu.
Website: http://www.raritanval.edu/.

Salem Community College
Carneys Point, New Jersey

- **County-supported** 2-year, founded 1972
- **Small-town** campus with easy access to Philadelphia
- **Coed**

Undergraduates 17% are from out of state; 22% Black or African American, non-Hispanic/Latino; 3% Hispanic/Latino; 0.8% Asian, non-Hispanic/Latino; 0.1% American Indian or Alaska Native, non-Hispanic/Latino; 3% Two or more races, non-Hispanic/Latino; 10% Race/ethnicity unknown.

Faculty *Student/faculty ratio:* 20:1.

Academics *Calendar:* semesters. *Degree:* certificates and associate. *Special study options:* academic remediation for entering students, adult/continuing education programs, advanced placement credit, cooperative education, distance learning, double majors, English as a second language, independent study, off-campus study, part-time degree program, services for LD students, summer session for credit.

Student Life *Campus security:* 24-hour emergency response devices and patrols, late-night transport/escort service.

Athletics Member NJCAA.

Financial Aid Of all full-time matriculated undergraduates who enrolled in 2010, 756 applied for aid, 624 were judged to have need, 35 had their need fully met. 34 Federal Work-Study jobs (averaging $1137). In 2010, 39. *Average percent of need met:* 47. *Average financial aid package:* $4663. *Average need-based loan:* $2304. *Average need-based gift aid:* $4284. *Average non-need-based aid:* $1652.

Applying *Options:* electronic application, early admission, deferred entrance. *Application fee:* $27. *Required:* high school transcript, Basic Skills test or minimum SAT scores. Students with a minimum score of 530 in math and 540 in English on the SAT are exempt from placement testing. *Required for some:* essay or personal statement.

Freshman Application Contact Lynn Fishlock, Director of Enrollment and Transfer Services, Salem Community College, 460 Hollywood Avenue, Carneys Point, NJ 08069. *Phone:* 856-351-2701. *Fax:* 856-299-9193. *E-mail:* info@salemcc.edu.
Website: http://www.salemcc.edu/.

Sussex County Community College

Newton, New Jersey

Freshman Application Contact Mr. James Donohue, Director of Admissions and Registrar, Sussex County Community College, 1 College Hill Road, Newton, NJ 07860. *Phone:* 973-300-2219. *Fax:* 973-579-5226. *E-mail:* jdonohue@sussex.edu.
Website: http://www.sussex.edu/.

Union County College

Cranford, New Jersey

- **State and locally supported** 2-year, founded 1933, part of New Jersey Higher Education
- **Urban** 49-acre campus with easy access to New York City
- **Endowment** $9.0 million
- **Coed,** 12,146 undergraduate students, 48% full-time, 63% women, 37% men

Undergraduates 5,886 full-time, 6,260 part-time. Students come from 10 states and territories; 77 other countries; 3% are from out of state; 27% Black or African American, non-Hispanic/Latino; 31% Hispanic/Latino; 4% Asian, non-Hispanic/Latino; 0.4% Native Hawaiian or other Pacific Islander, non-Hispanic/Latino; 0.5% American Indian or Alaska Native, non-Hispanic/Latino; 0.4% Two or more races, non-Hispanic/Latino; 12% Race/ethnicity unknown; 3% international; 2% transferred in. *Retention:* 60% of full-time freshmen returned.

Freshmen *Admission:* 8,515 applied, 3,517 admitted, 1,142 enrolled.

Faculty *Total:* 519, 33% full-time, 18% with terminal degrees. *Student/faculty ratio:* 27:1.

Majors Accounting technology and bookkeeping; allied health diagnostic, intervention, and treatment professions related; American Sign Language (ASL); American Sign Language related; animation, interactive technology, video graphics and special effects; automobile/automotive mechanics technology; biology/biological sciences; business administration and management; business/commerce; chemistry; civil engineering technology; computer and information sciences and support services related; computer science; criminal justice/law enforcement administration; criminal justice/police science; customer service support/call center/teleservice operation; dental assisting; dental hygiene; diagnostic medical sonography and ultrasound technology; electromechanical technology; emergency medical technology (EMT paramedic); engineering; fire prevention and safety technology; hospitality administration; hotel/motel administration; human services; information science/studies; information technology; language interpretation and translation; legal assistant/paralegal; liberal arts and sciences/liberal studies; licensed practical/vocational nurse training; management information systems; manufacturing engineering technology; marketing/marketing management; mass communication/media; mathematics; mechanical engineering/mechanical technology; medical radiologic technology; nuclear medical technology; physical therapy technology; radiologic technology/science; recording arts technology; registered nursing/registered nurse; rehabilitation and therapeutic professions related; respiratory care therapy; security and loss prevention; sign language interpretation and translation; sport and fitness administration/management; telecommunications technology.

Academics *Calendar:* semesters. *Degree:* certificates, diplomas, and associate. *Special study options:* academic remediation for entering students, accelerated degree program, adult/continuing education programs, advanced placement credit, distance learning, English as a second language, honors programs, independent study, internships, off-campus study, part-time degree program, services for LD students, student-designed majors, summer session for credit. *ROTC:* Air Force (c).

Library MacKay Library plus 2 others with 137,731 titles, 20,938 serial subscriptions, 3,610 audiovisual materials, an OPAC, a Web page.

Student Life *Housing:* college housing not available. *Activities and Organizations:* drama/theater group, student-run newspaper, radio and television station, SIGN, Business Management Club, Art Society, La Sociedad Hispanica de UCC, Architecture Club. *Campus security:* 24-hour emergency response devices and patrols, late-night transport/escort service. *Student services:* personal/psychological counseling.

Athletics Member NJCAA. *Intercollegiate sports:* baseball M, basketball M/W(s), golf M/W, soccer M, volleyball W. *Intramural sports:* cheerleading W.

Costs (2012–13) *Tuition:* area resident $2688 full-time, $112 per credit part-time; state resident $5376 full-time, $224 per credit part-time; nonresident $5376 full-time, $224 per credit part-time. Full-time tuition and fees vary according to course load. Part-time tuition and fees vary according to course load. *Required fees:* $918 full-time, $38 per credit part-time. *Payment plan:* deferred payment. *Waivers:* senior citizens and employees or children of employees.

Financial Aid Of all full-time matriculated undergraduates who enrolled in 2011, 150 Federal Work-Study jobs (averaging $1700).

Applying *Options:* electronic application, early admission, deferred entrance. *Required:* high school transcript. *Required for some:* interview. *Application deadlines:* rolling (freshmen), rolling (transfers). *Notification:* continuous (freshmen), continuous (transfers).

Freshman Application Contact Ms. Nina Hernandez, Director of Admissions, Records, and Registration, Union County College, Cranford, NJ 07016. *Phone:* 908-709-7127. *Fax:* 908-709-7125. *E-mail:* hernandez@ucc.edu.
Website: http://www.ucc.edu/.

Warren County Community College

Washington, New Jersey

Freshman Application Contact Shannon Horwath, Associate Director of Admissions, Warren County Community College, 475 Route 57 West, Washington, NJ 07882-9605. *Phone:* 908-835-2300. *E-mail:* shorwath@warren.edu.
Website: http://www.warren.edu/.

NEW MEXICO

Brown Mackie College–Albuquerque

Albuquerque, New Mexico

Freshman Application Contact Brown Mackie College–Albuquerque, 10500 Copper Avenue NE, Albuquerque, NM 87123. *Phone:* 505-559-5200. *Toll-free phone:* 877-271-3488.
Website: http://www.brownmackie.edu/albuquerque/.

See display on next page and page 346 for the College Close-Up.

Carrington College–Albuquerque

Albuquerque, New Mexico

- **Proprietary** 2-year, part of Carrington Colleges Group, Inc.
- **Coed,** 628 undergraduate students, 100% full-time, 82% women, 18% men

Undergraduates 628 full-time. 3% Black or African American, non-Hispanic/Latino; 53% Hispanic/Latino; 2% Asian, non-Hispanic/Latino; 13% American Indian or Alaska Native, non-Hispanic/Latino; 1% Two or more races, non-Hispanic/Latino; 2% Race/ethnicity unknown.

Freshmen *Admission:* 61 enrolled.

Faculty *Total:* 54, 30% full-time. *Student/faculty ratio:* 22:1.

Majors Medical office management; physical therapy technology; registered nursing/registered nurse.

Academics *Degree:* certificates and associate.

Applying *Required:* essay or personal statement, high school transcript, interview, Entrance test administered by Carrington College.

Freshman Application Contact Carrington College–Albuquerque, 1001 Menaul Boulevard NE, Albuquerque, NM 87107.
Website: http://carrington.edu/.

Central New Mexico Community College

Albuquerque, New Mexico

- **State-supported** 2-year, founded 1965
- **Urban** 312-acre campus
- **Endowment** $1.6 million
- **Coed,** 28,323 undergraduate students, 33% full-time, 56% women, 44% men

Undergraduates 9,324 full-time, 18,999 part-time. Students come from 29 states and territories; 0.4% are from out of state; 3% Black or African American, non-Hispanic/Latino; 45% Hispanic/Latino; 2% Asian, non-Hispanic/Latino; 0.3% Native Hawaiian or other Pacific Islander, non-Hispanic/Latino; 7% American Indian or Alaska Native, non-Hispanic/Latino; 2% Two or more races, non-Hispanic/Latino; 4% Race/ethnicity unknown; 3% international; 5% transferred in. *Retention:* 58% of full-time freshmen returned.

Freshmen *Admission:* 6,818 applied, 6,818 admitted, 3,796 enrolled.

Faculty *Total:* 1,035, 31% full-time. *Student/faculty ratio:* 28:1.

Majors Accounting; administrative assistant and secretarial science; agriculture; architectural drafting and CAD/CADD; art; automotive engineering technology; banking and financial support services; biotechnology; building/construction finishing, management, and inspection related; business administration and management; child-care and support services management; clinical/medical laboratory technology; computer systems analysis; construction trades related; cosmetology; criminal justice/safety; culinary arts; data processing and data processing technology; diagnostic medical sonography and ultrasound technology; electrical, electronic and communications engineering technology; electrical/electronics drafting and CAD/CADD; elementary education; engineering; environmental/environmental health engineering; executive assistant/executive secretary; fire prevention and safety technology; general studies; health information/medical records administration; hospitality administration; information science/studies; international business/trade/commerce; laser and optical technology; legal assistant/paralegal; liberal arts and sciences/liberal studies; manufacturing engineering technology; medical radiologic technology; parks, recreation and leisure; registered nursing/registered nurse; respiratory care therapy; surveying technology; technology/industrial arts teacher education; vehicle maintenance and repair technologies related; veterinary/animal health technology.

Academics *Calendar:* trimesters. *Degree:* certificates and associate. *Special study options:* academic remediation for entering students, adult/continuing education programs, advanced placement credit, cooperative education, distance learning, English as a second language, honors programs, independent study, internships, part-time degree program, services for LD students, summer session for credit. *ROTC:* Army (c), Navy (c), Air Force (c).

Library Main Campus Library with 58,855 titles, 16,304 serial subscriptions, an OPAC, a Web page.

Student Life *Housing:* college housing not available. *Activities and Organizations:* student-run newspaper. *Campus security:* 24-hour emergency response devices and patrols, late-night transport/escort service. *Student services:* health clinic, personal/psychological counseling.

Applying *Options:* electronic application. *Application deadlines:* rolling (freshmen), rolling (out-of-state freshmen), rolling (transfers). *Notification:* continuous (freshmen), continuous (out-of-state freshmen), continuous (transfers).

Freshman Application Contact Mother Supr. Glenn Damiani, Sr. Director, Enrollment Services, Central New Mexico Community College, Albuquerque, NM 87106. *Phone:* 505-224-3223.
Website: http://www.cnm.edu/.

Clovis Community College
Clovis, New Mexico

Freshman Application Contact Ms. Rosie Corrie, Director of Admissions and Records/Registrar, Clovis Community College, Clovis, NM 88101-8381. *Phone:* 575-769-4962. *Toll-free phone:* 800-769-1409. *Fax:* 575-769-4190. *E-mail:* admissions@clovis.edu.
Website: http://www.clovis.edu/.

Doña Ana Community College
Las Cruces, New Mexico

- **State and locally supported** 2-year, founded 1973, part of New Mexico State University System
- **Urban** 15-acre campus with easy access to El Paso
- **Endowment** $18,682
- **Coed**

Undergraduates 4,037 full-time, 4,854 part-time. Students come from 14 states and territories; 1 other country; 12% are from out of state; 3% Black or African American, non-Hispanic/Latino; 65% Hispanic/Latino; 1% Asian, non-Hispanic/Latino; 2% American Indian or Alaska Native, non-Hispanic/Latino; 5% Race/ethnicity unknown; 2% international; 2% transferred in. *Retention:* 85% of full-time freshmen returned.

Faculty *Student/faculty ratio:* 21:1.

Academics *Calendar:* semesters. *Degree:* certificates and associate. *Special study options:* academic remediation for entering students, adult/continuing education programs, advanced placement credit, cooperative education, distance learning, English as a second language, freshman honors college, honors programs, internships, part-time degree program, services for LD students, summer session for credit. *ROTC:* Army (c), Air Force (c).

Student Life *Campus security:* 24-hour emergency response devices and patrols, late-night transport/escort service, controlled dormitory access.

Standardized Tests *Recommended:* ACT, ACT ASSET, or ACT COMPASS.

Financial Aid Of all full-time matriculated undergraduates who enrolled in 2011, 15 Federal Work-Study jobs (averaging $2800). 106 state and other part-time jobs (averaging $2800). *Financial aid deadline:* 6/30.
Applying *Options:* electronic application, deferred entrance. *Application fee:* $20. *Required:* high school transcript.
Freshman Application Contact Mrs. Ricci Montes, Admissions Advisor, Doña Ana Community College, MSC-3DA, Box 30001, 3400 South Espina Street, Las Cruces, NM 88003-8001. *Phone:* 575-527-7683. *Toll-free phone:* 800-903-7503. *Fax:* 575-527-7515.
Website: http://dabcc-www.nmsu.edu/.

Eastern New Mexico University–Roswell

Roswell, New Mexico

Freshman Application Contact Eastern New Mexico University–Roswell, PO Box 6000, Roswell, NM 88202-6000. *Phone:* 505-624-7142. *Toll-free phone:* 800-243-6687 (in-state); 800-624-7000 (out-of-state).
Website: http://www.roswell.enmu.edu/.

ITT Technical Institute

Albuquerque, New Mexico

- **Proprietary** primarily 2-year, founded 1989, part of ITT Educational Services, Inc.
- **Coed**

Academics *Calendar:* quarters. *Degrees:* associate and bachelor's.
Freshman Application Contact Director of Recruitment, ITT Technical Institute, 5100 Masthead Street, NE, Albuquerque, NM 87109. *Phone:* 505-828-1114. *Toll-free phone:* 800-636-1114.
Website: http://www.itt-tech.edu/.

Luna Community College

Las Vegas, New Mexico

Freshman Application Contact Ms. Henrietta Griego, Director of Admissions, Recruitment, and Retention, Luna Community College, PO Box 1510, Las Vegas, NM 87701. *Phone:* 505-454-2020. *Toll-free phone:* 800-588-7232 (in-state); 800-5888-7232 (out-of-state). *Fax:* 505-454-2588. *E-mail:* hgriego@luna.cc.nm.us.
Website: http://www.luna.edu/.

Mesalands Community College

Tucumcari, New Mexico

Director of Admissions Mr. Ken Brashear, Director of Enrollment Management, Mesalands Community College, 911 South Tenth Street, Tucumcari, NM 88401. *Phone:* 505-461-4413.
Website: http://www.mesalands.edu/.

National American University

Albuquerque, New Mexico

Freshman Application Contact Admissions Office, National American University, 10131 Coors Boulevard NW, Suite I-01, Albuquerque, NM 87114.
Website: http://www.national.edu/.

Navajo Technical College

Crownpoint, New Mexico

Director of Admissions Director of Admission, Navajo Technical College, PO Box 849, Crownpoint, NM 87313. *Phone:* 505-786-4100.
Website: http://www.navajotech.edu/.

New Mexico Junior College

Hobbs, New Mexico

Director of Admissions Mr. Robert Bensing, Dean of Enrollment Management, New Mexico Junior College, 5317 Lovington Highway, Hobbs, NM 88240-9123. *Phone:* 505-392-5092. *Toll-free phone:* 800-657-6260.
Website: http://www.nmjc.edu/.

New Mexico Military Institute

Roswell, New Mexico

Freshman Application Contact New Mexico Military Institute, Roswell, NM 88201-5173. *Phone:* 505-624-8050. *Toll-free phone:* 800-421-5376. *Fax:* 505-

624-8058. *E-mail:* admissions@nmmi.edu.
Website: http://www.nmmi.edu/.

New Mexico State University–Alamogordo

Alamogordo, New Mexico

- **State-supported** 2-year, founded 1958, part of New Mexico State University System
- **Small-town** 540-acre campus
- **Endowment** $147,086
- **Coed**

Undergraduates 1,005 full-time, 2,366 part-time. Students come from 26 states and territories; 15% are from out of state; 4% Black or African American, non-Hispanic/Latino; 38% Hispanic/Latino; 2% Asian, non-Hispanic/Latino; 0.1% Native Hawaiian or other Pacific Islander, non-Hispanic/Latino; 3% American Indian or Alaska Native, non-Hispanic/Latino; 1% Two or more races, non-Hispanic/Latino; 6% Race/ethnicity unknown; 2% international; 6% transferred in. *Retention:* 50% of full-time freshmen returned.
Faculty *Student/faculty ratio:* 20:1.
Academics *Calendar:* semesters. *Degree:* certificates and associate. *Special study options:* academic remediation for entering students, adult/continuing education programs, advanced placement credit, distance learning, double majors, honors programs, independent study, internships, off-campus study, part-time degree program, services for LD students, study abroad, summer session for credit.
Student Life *Campus security:* 24-hour emergency response devices.
Costs (2012–13) *Tuition:* area resident $1824 full-time, $76 per credit hour part-time; state resident $2160 full-time, $90 per credit hour part-time; nonresident $4872 full-time, $203 per credit hour part-time. Full-time tuition and fees vary according to course load. *Required fees:* $96 full-time, $4 per credit hour part-time. *Payment plans:* installment, deferred payment.
Financial Aid Of all full-time matriculated undergraduates who enrolled in 2011, 10 Federal Work-Study jobs (averaging $3300). 60 state and other part-time jobs (averaging $3300). *Financial aid deadline:* 5/1.
Applying *Options:* electronic application, early admission, deferred entrance. *Application fee:* $20. *Required:* high school transcript, minimum 2.0 GPA.
Freshman Application Contact Ms. Bobi McDonald, Coordinator of Admissions and Records, New Mexico State University–Alamogordo, 2400 North Scenic Drive, Alamogordo, NM 88311-0477. *Phone:* 575-439-3700. *E-mail:* advisor@nmsua.nmsu.edu.
Website: http://nmsua.edu/.

New Mexico State University–Carlsbad

Carlsbad, New Mexico

Freshman Application Contact Ms. Everal Shannon, Records Specialist, New Mexico State University–Carlsbad, 1500 University Drive, Carlsbad, NM 88220. *Phone:* 575-234-9222. *Fax:* 575-885-4951. *E-mail:* eshannon@nmsu.edu.
Website: http://www.cavern.nmsu.edu/.

New Mexico State University–Grants

Grants, New Mexico

Director of Admissions Ms. Irene Lutz, Campus Student Services Officer, New Mexico State University–Grants, 1500 3rd Street, Grants, NM 87020-2025. *Phone:* 505-287-7981.
Website: http://grants.nmsu.edu/.

Northern New Mexico College

Española, New Mexico

Freshman Application Contact Mr. Mike L. Costello, Registrar, Northern New Mexico College, 921 Paseo de Oñate, Española, NM 87532. *Phone:* 505-747-2193. *Fax:* 505-747-2191. *E-mail:* dms@nnmc.edu.
Website: http://www.nnmc.edu/.

Pima Medical Institute

Albuquerque, New Mexico

Freshman Application Contact Admissions Office, Pima Medical Institute, 4400 Cutler Avenue NE, Albuquerque, NM 87110. *Phone:* 505-881-1234. *Toll-free phone:* 800-477-PIMA (in-state); 888-477-PIMA (out-of-state). *Fax:*

505-881-5329.
Website: http://www.pmi.edu/.

Pima Medical Institute

Albuquerque, New Mexico

Freshman Application Contact Pima Medical Institute, RMTS 32, 8601 Golf Course Road, NW, Albuquerque, NM 87114. *Phone:* 505-816-0556. *Website:* http://www.pmi.edu/.

San Juan College

Farmington, New Mexico

- **State-supported** 2-year, founded 1958, part of New Mexico Higher Education Department
- **Small-town** 698-acre campus
- **Endowment** $10.5 million
- **Coed,** 9,463 undergraduate students, 33% full-time, 51% women, 49% men

Undergraduates 3,085 full-time, 6,378 part-time. Students come from 50 states and territories; 32 other countries; 23% are from out of state; 1% Black or African American, non-Hispanic/Latino; 14% Hispanic/Latino; 0.6% Asian, non-Hispanic/Latino; 0.2% Native Hawaiian or other Pacific Islander, non-Hispanic/Latino; 35% American Indian or Alaska Native, non-Hispanic/Latino; 0.9% Two or more races, non-Hispanic/Latino; 3% Race/ethnicity unknown; 0.6% international; 5% transferred in. *Retention:* 50% of full-time freshmen returned.

Freshmen *Admission:* 1,013 applied, 1,013 admitted, 1,013 enrolled.

Faculty *Total:* 406, 39% full-time. *Student/faculty ratio:* 25:1.

Majors Accounting technology and bookkeeping; administrative assistant and secretarial science; autobody/collision and repair technology; automobile/automotive mechanics technology; biology/biological sciences; business administration and management; carpentry; chemistry; child-care provision; clinical/medical laboratory technology; commercial and advertising art; cosmetology; criminal justice/police science; data processing and data processing technology; dental hygiene; diesel mechanics technology; drafting and design technology; electrical, electronic and communications engineering technology; elementary education; emergency medical technology (EMT paramedic); engineering; engineering technology; fire science/firefighting; general studies; geography; geology/earth science; health and physical education/fitness; health information/medical records technology; industrial mechanics and maintenance technology; industrial technology; instrumentation technology; landscaping and groundskeeping; legal assistant/paralegal; liberal arts and sciences/liberal studies; machine shop technology; mathematics; occupational safety and health technology; parks, recreation and leisure; physical sciences; physical therapy technology; physics; premedical studies; psychology; registered nursing/registered nurse; respiratory care therapy; secondary education; social work; solar energy technology; special education; surgical technology; theater design and technology; veterinary/animal health technology; welding technology.

Academics *Calendar:* semesters. *Degree:* certificates, diplomas, and associate. *Special study options:* academic remediation for entering students, adult/continuing education programs, advanced placement credit, cooperative education, distance learning, English as a second language, honors programs, independent study, internships, part-time degree program, services for LD students, summer session for credit.

Library San Juan College Library with 98,621 titles, 261 serial subscriptions, 5,021 audiovisual materials, an OPAC, a Web page.

Student Life *Housing:* college housing not available. *Activities and Organizations:* drama/theater group, student-run newspaper, radio station, choral group, national fraternities, national sororities. *Campus security:* 24-hour emergency response devices and patrols, late-night transport/escort service. *Student services:* personal/psychological counseling.

Athletics *Intramural sports:* badminton M/W, basketball M/W, cross-country running M/W, football M/W, golf M/W, rock climbing M/W, skiing (cross-country) M/W, skiing (downhill) M/W, soccer M/W, softball M/W, table tennis M/W, ultimate Frisbee M/W, volleyball M/W.

Costs (2013–14) *Tuition:* state resident $984 full-time, $41 per credit hour part-time; nonresident $2520 full-time, $105 per credit hour part-time. Full-time tuition and fees vary according to reciprocity agreements. *Required fees:* $288 full-time, $12 per credit hour part-time. *Payment plans:* tuition prepayment, installment. *Waivers:* senior citizens and employees or children of employees.

Financial Aid Of all full-time matriculated undergraduates who enrolled in 2011, 150 Federal Work-Study jobs (averaging $2500). 175 state and other part-time jobs (averaging $2500).

Applying *Options:* electronic application, early admission, deferred entrance. *Required:* high school transcript. *Application deadlines:* rolling (freshmen), rolling (transfers). *Notification:* continuous (freshmen), continuous (transfers).

Freshman Application Contact Ms. Skylar Maston, Enrollment Services Coordinator, San Juan College, 4601 College Blvd, Farmington, NM 87402. *Phone:* 505-566-3300. *Fax:* 505-566-3500. *E-mail:* mastons@sanjuancollege.edu. *Website:* http://www.sanjuancollege.edu/.

Santa Fe Community College

Santa Fe, New Mexico

Freshman Application Contact Ms. Rebecca Estrada, Director of Recruitment, Santa Fe Community College, 6401 Richards Ave, Santa Fe, NM 87508. *Phone:* 505-428-1604. *Fax:* 505-428-1468. *E-mail:* rebecca.estrada@sfcc.edu. *Website:* http://www.sfcc.edu/.

Southwestern Indian Polytechnic Institute

Albuquerque, New Mexico

- **Federally supported** 2-year, founded 1971
- **Suburban** 144-acre campus
- **Coed**

Undergraduates 406 full-time, 74 part-time. Students come from 21 states and territories; 60% live on campus.

Faculty *Student/faculty ratio:* 15:1.

Academics *Calendar:* trimesters. *Degree:* certificates and associate. *Special study options:* academic remediation for entering students, advanced placement credit, cooperative education, distance learning, double majors, internships, part-time degree program, services for LD students, summer session for credit.

Student Life *Campus security:* 24-hour emergency response devices and patrols, late-night transport/escort service.

Costs (2012–13) *Tuition:* state resident $675 full-time, $150 per term part-time; nonresident $675 full-time, $150 per term part-time. *Room and board:* $165.

Financial Aid Of all full-time matriculated undergraduates who enrolled in 2010, 351 applied for aid, 351 were judged to have need, 23 had their need fully met. 14 Federal Work-Study jobs (averaging $661). 36 state and other part-time jobs (averaging $726). *Average percent of need met:* 27. *Average financial aid package:* $2943. *Average need-based gift aid:* $2878.

Applying *Required:* high school transcript, Certificate of Indian Blood.

Freshman Application Contact Southwestern Indian Polytechnic Institute, 9169 Coors, NW, Box 10146, Albuquerque, NM 87184-0146. *Phone:* 505-346-2324. *Toll-free phone:* 800-586-7474. *Website:* http://www.sipi.edu/.

University of New Mexico–Gallup

Gallup, New Mexico

Director of Admissions Ms. Pearl A. Morris, Admissions Representative, University of New Mexico–Gallup, 200 College Road, Gallup, NM 87301-5603. *Phone:* 505-863-7576. *Website:* http://www.gallup.unm.edu/.

University of New Mexico–Los Alamos Branch

Los Alamos, New Mexico

Freshman Application Contact Mrs. Irene K. Martinez, Enrollment Representative, University of New Mexico–Los Alamos Branch, 4000 University Drive, Los Alamos, NM 87544-2233. *Phone:* 505-662-0332. *E-mail:* L65130@unm.edu. *Website:* http://www.la.unm.edu/.

University of New Mexico–Taos

Taos, New Mexico

Director of Admissions Vickie Alvarez, Student Enrollment Associate, University of New Mexico–Taos, 115 Civic Plaza Drive, Taos, NM 87571. *Phone:* 575-737-6425. *E-mail:* valvarez@unm.edu. *Website:* http://taos.unm.edu/.

University of New Mexico–Valencia Campus

Los Lunas, New Mexico

Director of Admissions Richard M. Hulett, Director of Admissions and Recruitment, University of New Mexico–Valencia Campus, 280 La Entrada, Los Lunas, NM 87031-7633. *Phone:* 505-277-2446. *E-mail:* mhulett@unm.edu.
Website: http://www.unm.edu/~unmvc/.

NEW YORK

Adirondack Community College

Queensbury, New York

- **State and locally supported** 2-year, founded 1960, part of State University of New York System
- **Small-town** 141-acre campus
- **Endowment** $2.9 million
- **Coed,** 3,987 undergraduate students, 57% full-time, 61% women, 39% men

Undergraduates 2,263 full-time, 1,724 part-time. Students come from 10 states and territories; 9 other countries; 0.6% are from out of state; 1% Black or African American, non-Hispanic/Latino; 2% Hispanic/Latino; 0.5% Asian, non-Hispanic/Latino; 0.3% American Indian or Alaska Native, non-Hispanic/Latino; 1% Two or more races, non-Hispanic/Latino; 2% Race/ethnicity unknown; 0.4% international; 5% transferred in. *Retention:* 59% of full-time freshmen returned.

Freshmen *Admission:* 1,236 applied, 1,222 admitted, 831 enrolled.

Faculty *Total:* 276, 32% full-time. *Student/faculty ratio:* 14:1.

Majors Accounting; accounting technology and bookkeeping; business administration and management; computer science; computer systems networking and telecommunications; cooking and related culinary arts; creative writing; criminal justice/police science; design and visual communications; electrical, electronic and communications engineering technology; electrician; engineering; food technology and processing; hospitality administration; information technology; liberal arts and sciences/liberal studies; marketing/marketing management; music; music performance; parks, recreation and leisure facilities management; radio and television broadcasting technology; radiologic technology/science; registered nursing/registered nurse; speech communication and rhetoric; sport and fitness administration/management; substance abuse/addiction counseling; tourism and travel services management.

Academics *Calendar:* semesters. *Degree:* certificates and associate. *Special study options:* academic remediation for entering students, accelerated degree program, adult/continuing education programs, advanced placement credit, cooperative education, distance learning, double majors, independent study, internships, part-time degree program, services for LD students, study abroad, summer session for credit.

Library SUNY Adirondack Library with 65,000 titles, 391 serial subscriptions, an OPAC, a Web page.

Student Life *Housing Options:* coed. *Activities and Organizations:* drama/theater group, student-run radio and television station, choral group. *Campus security:* late-night transport/escort service, patrols by trained security personnel 8 am to 10 pm. *Student services:* personal/psychological counseling.

Athletics Member NJCAA. *Intercollegiate sports:* baseball M, basketball M/W, bowling M/W, golf M/W, soccer M, softball W, tennis M/W, volleyball W. *Intramural sports:* badminton M/W, basketball M/W, volleyball M/W.

Costs (2012–13) *One-time required fee:* $75. *Tuition:* state resident $3664 full-time, $153 per credit hour part-time; nonresident $7328 full-time, $306 per credit hour part-time. Full-time tuition and fees vary according to course load and program. Part-time tuition and fees vary according to course load and program. *Required fees:* $309 full-time, $11 per credit hour part-time, $5 per term part-time. *Payment plan:* installment. *Waivers:* senior citizens and employees or children of employees.

Financial Aid Of all full-time matriculated undergraduates who enrolled in 2011, 98 Federal Work-Study jobs (averaging $462).

Applying *Options:* electronic application. *Application fee:* $35.

Freshman Application Contact Office of Admissions, Adirondack Community College, 640 Bay Road, Queensbury, NY 12804. *Phone:* 518-743-2264. *Toll-free phone:* 888-SUNY-ADK. *Fax:* 518-743-2200.
Website: http://www.sunyacc.edu/.

American Academy McAllister Institute of Funeral Service

New York, New York

Freshman Application Contact Mr. Norman Provost, Registrar, American Academy McAllister Institute of Funeral Service, 450 West 56th Street, New York, NY 10019-3602. *Phone:* 212-757-1190. *Toll-free phone:* 866-932-2264. *Website:* http://www.funeraleducation.org/.

American Academy of Dramatic Arts–New York

New York, New York

- **Independent** 2-year, founded 1884, part of AADA-New York has a branch campus: American Academy of Dramatic Arts - Los Angeles
- **Urban** campus
- **Endowment** $6.0 million
- **Coed,** 258 undergraduate students, 100% full-time, 59% women, 41% men

Undergraduates 258 full-time. Students come from 34 states and territories; 20 other countries; 86% are from out of state; 8% Black or African American, non-Hispanic/Latino; 7% Hispanic/Latino; 2% Asian, non-Hispanic/Latino; 38% international; 40% live on campus.

Freshmen *Admission:* 468 applied, 377 admitted. *Average high school GPA:* 2.88.

Faculty *Total:* 29, 28% full-time, 38% with terminal degrees. *Student/faculty ratio:* 9:1.

Majors Dramatic/theater arts.

Academics *Calendar:* continuous. *Degree:* certificates and associate. *Special study options:* academic remediation for entering students, honors programs.

Library Academy/CBS Library with 10,000 titles, 24 serial subscriptions, 670 audiovisual materials, an OPAC.

Student Life *Housing:* on-campus residence required for freshman year. *Options:* coed. Campus housing is leased by the school. Freshman applicants given priority for college housing. *Campus security:* 24-hour emergency response devices and patrols, controlled dormitory access, trained security guard during hours of operation and campus housing. *Student services:* personal/psychological counseling.

Costs (2013–14) *Tuition:* $29,900 full-time. *Required fees:* $750 full-time. *Room only:* Room and board charges vary according to housing facility. *Payment plan:* installment. *Waivers:* employees or children of employees.

Financial Aid Of all full-time matriculated undergraduates who enrolled in 2012, 240 applied for aid, 231 were judged to have need. 50 Federal Work-Study jobs (averaging $900). 50 state and other part-time jobs (averaging $2000). In 2012, 59 non-need-based awards were made. *Average percent of need met:* 67%. *Average financial aid package:* $18,150. *Average need-based loan:* $4500. *Average need-based gift aid:* $7000. *Average non-need-based aid:* $7000. *Average indebtedness upon graduation:* $15,000. *Financial aid deadline:* 5/15.

Applying *Options:* electronic application, deferred entrance. *Application fee:* $50. *Required:* essay or personal statement, high school transcript, minimum 2.0 GPA, 2 letters of recommendation, interview, audition. *Application deadlines:* rolling (freshmen), rolling (transfers). *Notification:* continuous (freshmen), continuous (transfers).

Freshman Application Contact Mrs. Barry Zucker, Assistant Director of Admissions, American Academy of Dramatic Arts–New York, 120 Madison Avenue, New York, NY 10016. *Phone:* -800-463-8990. *Toll-free phone:* 800-463-8990. *E-mail:* admissions@aada.org.
Website: http://www.aada.org/.

The Art Institute of New York City

New York, New York

- **Proprietary** 2-year, founded 1980, part of Education Management Corporation
- **Urban** campus
- **Coed**

Academics *Calendar:* quarters. *Degree:* associate.

Freshman Application Contact The Art Institute of New York City, 11 Beach Street, New York, NY 10013. *Phone:* 212-226-5500. *Toll-free phone:* 800-654-2433.
Website: http://www.artinstitutes.edu/newyork/.

See full-page display on page 48 and page 338 for the College Close-Up.

ASA The College For Excellence

Brooklyn, New York

Freshman Application Contact Admissions Office, ASA The College For Excellence, 81 Willoughby Street, Brooklyn, NY 11201. *Phone:* 718-522-9073. *Toll-free phone:* 877-679-8772.
Website: http://www.asa.edu/.

Berkeley College–Westchester Campus

White Plains, New York

Freshman Application Contact Director of Admissions, Berkeley College–Westchester Campus, White Plains, NY 10601. *Phone:* 914-694-1122. *Toll-free phone:* 800-446-5400. *Fax:* 914-328-9469. *E-mail:* info@berkeleycollege.edu.
Website: http://www.berkeleycollege.edu/.

Borough of Manhattan Community College of the City University of New York

New York, New York

- **State and locally supported** 2-year, founded 1963, part of City University of New York System
- **Urban** 5-acre campus
- **Coed,** 24,537 undergraduate students, 66% full-time, 57% women, 43% men

Undergraduates 16,151 full-time, 8,386 part-time. 2% are from out of state; 31% Black or African American, non-Hispanic/Latino; 40% Hispanic/Latino; 12% Asian, non-Hispanic/Latino; 0.2% American Indian or Alaska Native, non-Hispanic/Latino; 7% international; 4% transferred in.
Freshmen *Admission:* 24,888 admitted, 6,056 enrolled. *Test scores:* SAT critical reading scores over 500: 9%; SAT math scores over 500: 12%; SAT writing scores over 500: 6%; SAT critical reading scores over 600: 1%; SAT math scores over 600: 2%; SAT writing scores over 600: 1%.
Faculty *Total:* 1,559, 28% full-time, 33% with terminal degrees. *Student/faculty ratio:* 24:1.
Majors Accounting technology and bookkeeping; administrative assistant and secretarial science; biotechnology; business administration and management; community organization and advocacy; computer and information sciences; computer science; computer systems networking and telecommunications; criminal justice/police science; criminal justice/safety; emergency medical technology (EMT paramedic); engineering; English; forensic science and technology; health information/medical records technology; liberal arts and sciences/liberal studies; mathematics; physical sciences; radio and television broadcasting technology; registered nursing/registered nurse; respiratory therapy technician; small business administration; teacher assistant/aide; visual and performing arts; web page, digital/multimedia and information resources design.
Academics *Calendar:* semesters. *Degree:* certificates and associate. *Special study options:* academic remediation for entering students, adult/continuing education programs, advanced placement credit, cooperative education, distance learning, English as a second language, honors programs, independent study, internships, off-campus study, part-time degree program, services for LD students, study abroad, summer session for credit.
Library A. Philip Randolph Library with 342,000 titles, 250 serial subscriptions, an OPAC, a Web page.
Student Life *Housing:* college housing not available. *Activities and Organizations:* drama/theater group, student-run newspaper, choral group. *Campus security:* 24-hour patrols. *Student services:* health clinic, personal/psychological counseling, women's center.
Athletics Member NJCAA. *Intercollegiate sports:* baseball M, basketball M/W, soccer M/W, swimming and diving M/W, volleyball W.
Standardized Tests *Recommended:* SAT or ACT (for admission).
Applying *Options:* electronic application, deferred entrance. *Application fee:* $65. *Required:* high school transcript. *Application deadlines:* rolling (freshmen), rolling (transfers). *Notification:* continuous (freshmen), continuous (transfers).
Freshman Application Contact Dr. Eugenio Barrios, Director of Enrollment Management, Borough of Manhattan Community College of the City University of New York, 199 Chambers Street, Room S-310, New York, NY 10007. *Phone:* 212-220-1265. *Toll-free phone:* 866-583-5729 (in-state); 866-593-5729 (out-of-state). *Fax:* 212-220-2366. *E-mail:* admissions@bmcc.cuny.edu.
Website: http://www.bmcc.cuny.edu/.

Bramson ORT College

Forest Hills, New York

Freshman Application Contact Admissions Office, Bramson ORT College, 69-30 Austin Street, Forest Hills, NY 11375-4239. *Phone:* 718-261-5800. *Fax:* 718-575-5119. *E-mail:* admissions@bramsonort.edu.
Website: http://www.bramsonort.edu/.

Bronx Community College of the City University of New York

Bronx, New York

Freshman Application Contact Ms. Alba N. Cancetty, Admissions Officer, Bronx Community College of the City University of New York, 2155 University Avenue, Bronx, NY 10453. *Phone:* 718-289-5888. *E-mail:* admission@bcc.cuny.edu.
Website: http://www.bcc.cuny.edu/.

Broome Community College

Binghamton, New York

Freshman Application Contact Ms. Jenae Norris, Director of Admissions, Broome Community College, PO Box 1017, Upper Front Street, Binghamton, NY 13902. *Phone:* 607-778-5001. *Fax:* 607-778-5394. *E-mail:* admissions@sunybroome.edu.
Website: http://www.sunybroome.edu/.

Bryant & Stratton College - Albany Campus

Albany, New York

Freshman Application Contact Mr. Robert Ferrell, Director of Admissions, Bryant & Stratton College - Albany Campus, 1259 Central Avenue, Albany, NY 12205. *Phone:* 518-437-1802 Ext. 205. *Fax:* 518-437-1048.
Website: http://www.bryantstratton.edu/.

Bryant & Stratton College - Amherst Campus

Clarence, New York

Freshman Application Contact Mr. Brian K. Dioguardi, Director of Admissions, Bryant & Stratton College - Amherst Campus, Audubon Business Center, 40 Hazelwood Drive, Amherst, NY 14228. *Phone:* 716-691-0012. *Fax:* 716-691-0012. *E-mail:* bkdioguardi@bryantstratton.edu.
Website: http://www.bryantstratton.edu/.

Bryant & Stratton College - Buffalo Campus

Buffalo, New York

Freshman Application Contact Mr. Philip J. Struebel, Director of Admissions, Bryant & Stratton College - Buffalo Campus, 465 Main Street, Suite 400, Buffalo, NY 14203. *Phone:* 716-884-9120. *Fax:* 716-884-0091. *E-mail:* pjstruebel@bryantstratton.edu.
Website: http://www.bryantstratton.edu/.

Bryant & Stratton College - Greece Campus

Rochester, New York

Freshman Application Contact Bryant & Stratton College - Greece Campus, 150 Bellwood Drive, Rochester, NY 14606. *Phone:* 585-720-0660.
Website: http://www.bryantstratton.edu/.

Bryant & Stratton College - Henrietta Campus

Rochester, New York

Freshman Application Contact Bryant & Stratton College - Henrietta Campus, 1225 Jefferson Road, Rochester, NY 14623-3136. *Phone:* 585-292-5627 Ext. 101.
Website: http://www.bryantstratton.edu/.

Bryant & Stratton College - North Campus

Liverpool, New York

Freshman Application Contact Ms. Heather Macnik, Director of Admissions, Bryant & Stratton College - North Campus, 8687 Carling Road, Liverpool, NY 13090-1315. *Phone:* 315-652-6500.
Website: http://www.bryantstratton.edu/.

Bryant & Stratton College - Southtowns Campus

Orchard Park, New York

Freshman Application Contact Bryant & Stratton College - Southtowns Campus, 200 Redtail, Orchard Park, NY 14127. *Phone:* 716-677-9500.
Website: http://www.bryantstratton.edu/.

Bryant & Stratton College - Syracuse Campus

Syracuse, New York

Freshman Application Contact Ms. Dawn Rajkowski, Director of High School Enrollments, Bryant & Stratton College - Syracuse Campus, 953 James Street, Syracuse, NY 13203-2502. *Phone:* 315-472-6603 Ext. 248. *Fax:* 315-474-4383.
Website: http://www.bryantstratton.edu/.

Business Informatics Center, Inc.

Valley Stream, New York

Freshman Application Contact Admissions Office, Business Informatics Center, Inc., 134 South Central Avenue, Valley Stream, NY 11580-5431. *Phone:* 516-561-0050. *Fax:* 516-561-0074. *E-mail:* info@thecollegeforbusiness.com.
Website: http://www.thecollegeforbusiness.com/.

Cayuga County Community College

Auburn, New York

- **State and locally supported** 2-year, founded 1953, part of State University of New York System
- **Small-town** 50-acre campus with easy access to Rochester, Syracuse
- **Endowment** $6.3 million
- **Coed,** 4,619 undergraduate students, 50% full-time, 62% women, 38% men

Undergraduates 2,314 full-time, 2,305 part-time. 4% Black or African American, non-Hispanic/Latino; 2% Hispanic/Latino; 0.7% Asian, non-Hispanic/Latino; 0.6% American Indian or Alaska Native, non-Hispanic/Latino; 2% Two or more races, non-Hispanic/Latino; 13% Race/ethnicity unknown; 7% transferred in. *Retention:* 51% of full-time freshmen returned.
Freshmen *Admission:* 2,304 applied, 1,621 admitted, 736 enrolled.
Faculty *Total:* 275, 20% full-time. *Student/faculty ratio:* 24:1.
Majors Accounting technology and bookkeeping; art; business administration and management; child-care and support services management; communication and journalism related; communications systems installation and repair technology; computer and information sciences; computer and information sciences and support services related; corrections; criminal justice/police science; drafting and design technology; education (multiple levels); electrical, electronic and communications engineering technology; fine/studio arts; game and interactive media design; general studies; geography; graphic design; humanities; information science/studies; liberal arts and sciences/liberal studies; literature related; mathematics related; mechanical engineering; mechanical engineering/mechanical technology; music related; psychology related; radio, television, and digital communication related; registered nursing/registered nurse; science technologies related; sport and fitness administration/management; telecommunications technology; wine steward/sommelier; writing.
Academics *Calendar:* semesters. *Degree:* certificates and associate. *Special study options:* academic remediation for entering students, accelerated degree program, adult/continuing education programs, advanced placement credit, cooperative education, distance learning, double majors, honors programs, independent study, internships, off-campus study, part-time degree program, services for LD students, study abroad, summer session for credit. *ROTC:* Air Force (c).
Library Norman F. Bourke Memorial Library plus 2 others with 92,156 titles, 187 serial subscriptions, 5,240 audiovisual materials, an OPAC, a Web page.

Student Life *Housing Options:* coed. Campus housing is provided by a third party. *Activities and Organizations:* drama/theater group, student-run newspaper, radio and television station, choral group, Student Activity Board, Student Government, Criminal Justice Club, Tutor Club, Early Childhood Club. *Campus security:* security from 8 am to 9 pm. *Student services:* health clinic.
Athletics Member NJCAA. *Intercollegiate sports:* basketball M/W, bowling M/W, golf M/W, lacrosse M, soccer M/W, volleyball W. *Intramural sports:* basketball M/W, skiing (downhill) M/W, volleyball M/W.
Standardized Tests *Required for some:* SAT or ACT (for admission).
Costs (2012–13) *Tuition:* state resident $3950 full-time, $160 per credit hour part-time; nonresident $7990 full-time, $300 per credit hour part-time. Full-time tuition and fees vary according to course load. Part-time tuition and fees vary according to course load. *Required fees:* $376 full-time, $19 per credit part-time. *Room and board:* room only: $6500. *Payment plan:* installment. *Waivers:* senior citizens and employees or children of employees.
Financial Aid Of all full-time matriculated undergraduates who enrolled in 2011, 150 Federal Work-Study jobs (averaging $2000). 200 state and other part-time jobs (averaging $1000).
Applying *Options:* electronic application, deferred entrance. *Required:* high school transcript. *Required for some:* interview. *Application deadlines:* rolling (freshmen), rolling (transfers). *Notification:* continuous (freshmen), continuous (transfers).
Freshman Application Contact Cayuga County Community College, 197 Franklin Street, Auburn, NY 13021-3099. *Phone:* 315-255-1743 Ext. 2244. *Toll-free phone:* 866-598-8883.
Website: http://www.cayuga-cc.edu/.

Clinton Community College

Plattsburgh, New York

- **State and locally supported** 2-year, founded 1969, part of State University of New York System
- **Small-town** 100-acre campus
- **Coed,** 2,240 undergraduate students, 56% full-time, 52% women, 48% men

Undergraduates 1,257 full-time, 983 part-time. Students come from 7 states and territories; 19 other countries; 2% are from out of state; 10% live on campus. *Retention:* 52% of full-time freshmen returned.
Faculty *Total:* 163, 33% full-time. *Student/faculty ratio:* 9:1.
Majors Accounting; administrative assistant and secretarial science; biological and physical sciences; business administration and management; community organization and advocacy; computer/information technology services administration related; consumer merchandising/retailing management; criminal justice/law enforcement administration; criminal justice/police science; electrical, electronic and communications engineering technology; energy management and systems technology; humanities; industrial technology; liberal arts and sciences/liberal studies; physical education teaching and coaching; registered nursing/registered nurse; social sciences.
Academics *Calendar:* semesters. *Degree:* certificates and associate. *Special study options:* academic remediation for entering students, adult/continuing education programs, advanced placement credit, cooperative education, distance learning, English as a second language, external degree program, independent study, internships, off-campus study, part-time degree program, services for LD students, student-designed majors, summer session for credit.
Library Clinton Community College Learning Resource Center plus 1 other with 40,665 titles, 59,765 serial subscriptions, 1,687 audiovisual materials, an OPAC, a Web page.
Student Life *Housing Options:* coed, disabled students. Campus housing is provided by a third party. Freshman campus housing is guaranteed. *Activities and Organizations:* drama/theater group, student-run newspaper, choral group, Athletics, Future Human Services Professionals, PTK (Honor Society), Drama Club, Criminal Justice Club. *Campus security:* 24-hour emergency response devices and patrols, late-night transport/escort service, controlled dormitory access. *Student services:* health clinic, personal/psychological counseling.
Athletics Member NJCAA. *Intercollegiate sports:* baseball M, basketball M/W, soccer M/W, softball W. *Intramural sports:* volleyball M/W.
Costs (2012–13) *Tuition:* state resident $3620 full-time, $151 per credit part-time; nonresident $8500 full-time, $350 per credit part-time. Full-time tuition and fees vary according to program. Part-time tuition and fees vary according to course load and program. *Required fees:* $464 full-time, $16 per credit part-time, $10 per credit part-time. *Room and board:* $8250; room only: $4300. Room and board charges vary according to board plan. *Payment plan:* tuition prepayment.
Financial Aid Of all full-time matriculated undergraduates who enrolled in 2011, 45 Federal Work-Study jobs (averaging $1260).
Applying *Options:* electronic application, deferred entrance. *Required:* high school transcript. *Required for some:* essay or personal statement, 3 letters of recommendation, interview. *Application deadlines:* 8/26 (freshmen), 9/3 (transfers). *Notification:* continuous (freshmen), continuous (out-of-state freshmen), continuous (transfers).

Freshman Application Contact Clinton Community College, 136 Clinton Point Drive, Plattsburgh, NY 12901-9573. *Phone:* 518-562-4100. *Toll-free phone:* 800-552-1160.
Website: http://clintoncc.suny.edu/.

Cochran School of Nursing
Yonkers, New York

Freshman Application Contact Cochran School of Nursing, 967 North Broadway, Yonkers, NY 10701. *Phone:* 914-964-4606.
Website: http://www.cochranschoolofnursing.us/.

The College of Westchester
White Plains, New York

Freshman Application Contact Mr. Dale T. Smith, Vice President, The College of Westchester, 325 Central Avenue, PO Box 710, White Plains, NY 10602. *Phone:* 914-948-4442 Ext. 311. *Toll-free phone:* 800-660-7093. *Fax:* 914-948-5441. *E-mail:* admissions@cw.edu.
Website: http://www.cw.edu/.

Columbia-Greene Community College
Hudson, New York

Freshman Application Contact Director of Admissions, Columbia-Greene Community College, 4400 Route 23, Hudson, NY 12534-0327. *Phone:* 518-828-4181 Ext. 5513.
Website: http://www.sunycgcc.edu/.

Corning Community College
Corning, New York

- **State and locally supported** 2-year, founded 1956, part of State University of New York System
- **Rural** 500-acre campus
- **Endowment** $535,490
- **Coed,** 4,957 undergraduate students, 46% full-time, 58% women, 42% men

Undergraduates 2,298 full-time, 2,659 part-time. Students come from 7 states and territories; 19 other countries; 5% are from out of state; 4% Black or African American, non-Hispanic/Latino; 5% Hispanic/Latino; 0.9% Asian, non-Hispanic/Latino; 0.3% American Indian or Alaska Native, non-Hispanic/Latino; 2% Two or more races, non-Hispanic/Latino; 10% Race/ethnicity unknown; 0.1% international; 4% transferred in. *Retention:* 56% of full-time freshmen returned.
Freshmen *Admission:* 2,088 applied, 2,084 admitted, 915 enrolled.
Faculty *Total:* 245, 38% full-time, 11% with terminal degrees. *Student/faculty ratio:* 22:1.
Majors Accounting; art; autobody/collision and repair technology; automobile/automotive mechanics technology; business administration and management; CAD/CADD drafting/design technology; chemical technology; computer and information sciences; computer and information sciences and support services related; computer and information sciences related; computer/information technology services administration related; computer numerically controlled (CNC) machinist technology; computer science; computer support specialist; computer technology/computer systems technology; corrections and criminal justice related; criminal justice/police science; customer service management; digital arts; drafting/design engineering technologies related; early childhood education; education related; education (specific levels and methods) related; electrical and electronic engineering technologies related; electrical and electronics engineering; energy management and systems technology; engineering science; engineering technology; environmental science; fine arts related; fine/studio arts; graphic design; health and physical education/fitness; health and physical education related; health and wellness; health professions related; hospitality administration related; humanities; human services; information technology; liberal arts and sciences and humanities related; liberal arts and sciences/liberal studies; machine tool technology; manufacturing engineering technology; mathematics; mathematics related; mechanical drafting and CAD/CADD; mechanical engineering/mechanical technology; mechanical engineering technologies related; mechanic and repair technologies related; mechanics and repair; network and system administration; office management; office occupations and clerical services; outdoor education; parks, recreation and leisure; parks, recreation, leisure, and fitness studies related; pre-engineering; registered nursing/registered nurse; social sciences; substance abuse/addiction counseling; vehicle maintenance and repair technologies; vehicle maintenance and repair technologies related; web page, digital/multimedia and information resources design.
Academics *Calendar:* semesters. *Degree:* certificates and associate. *Special study options:* academic remediation for entering students, accelerated degree

program, adult/continuing education programs, advanced placement credit, cooperative education, distance learning, double majors, English as a second language, honors programs, independent study, internships, off-campus study, part-time degree program, services for LD students, student-designed majors, study abroad, summer session for credit.
Library Arthur A. Houghton, Jr. Library with 46,427 titles, 44,819 serial subscriptions, 1,107 audiovisual materials, an OPAC, a Web page.
Student Life *Housing Options:* coed, men-only, women-only, disabled students. Campus housing is university owned. *Activities and Organizations:* drama/theater group, student-run newspaper, radio station, choral group, Student Association, EQUAL, Nursing Society, Muse of Fire theatre group, WCEB radio station. *Campus security:* 24-hour emergency response devices and patrols, late-night transport/escort service, controlled dormitory access. *Student services:* health clinic, personal/psychological counseling.
Athletics Member NJCAA. *Intercollegiate sports:* baseball M, basketball M/W, bowling M/W, golf M/W, soccer M/W, softball W, volleyball W. *Intramural sports:* badminton M/W, basketball M/W, soccer M/W, softball W, volleyball M/W.
Costs (2013–14) *Tuition:* state resident $3950 full-time, $165 per credit hour part-time; nonresident $7900 full-time, $330 per credit hour part-time. Part-time tuition and fees vary according to course load. *Required fees:* $442 full-time, $9 per credit hour part-time. *Room and board:* $4250. *Payment plan:* installment. *Waivers:* senior citizens and employees or children of employees.
Financial Aid Of all full-time matriculated undergraduates who enrolled in 2011, 264 Federal Work-Study jobs (averaging $1128).
Applying *Options:* electronic application, early admission. *Application fee:* $25. *Required:* high school transcript. *Required for some:* interview. *Application deadlines:* rolling (freshmen), rolling (transfers). *Notification:* continuous (freshmen), continuous (transfers).
Freshman Application Contact Corning Community College, One Academic Drive, Corning, NY 14830-3297. *Phone:* 607-962-9427. *Toll-free phone:* 800-358-7171.
Website: http://www.corning-cc.edu/.

Crouse Hospital School of Nursing
Syracuse, New York

Freshman Application Contact Ms. Amy Graham, Enrollment Management Supervisor, Crouse Hospital School of Nursing, 736 Irving Avenue, Syracuse, NY 13210. *Phone:* 315-470-7481. *Fax:* 315-470-7925. *E-mail:* amygraham@crouse.org.
Website: http://www.crouse.org/nursing/.

Dorothea Hopfer School of Nursing at The Mount Vernon Hospital
Mount Vernon, New York

Director of Admissions Sandra Farrior, Coordinator of Student Services, Dorothea Hopfer School of Nursing at The Mount Vernon Hospital, 53 Valentine Street, Mount Vernon, NY 10550. *Phone:* 914-361-6472. *E-mail:* hopferadmissions@sshsw.org.
Website: http://www.ssmc.org/.

Dutchess Community College
Poughkeepsie, New York

- **State and locally supported** 2-year, founded 1957, part of State University of New York System
- **Suburban** 130-acre campus with easy access to New York City
- **Coed,** 10,316 undergraduate students, 49% full-time, 55% women, 45% men

Undergraduates 5,095 full-time, 5,221 part-time. 10% Black or African American, non-Hispanic/Latino; 13% Hispanic/Latino; 3% Asian, non-Hispanic/Latino; 0.1% Native Hawaiian or other Pacific Islander, non-Hispanic/Latino; 0.2% American Indian or Alaska Native, non-Hispanic/Latino; 2% Two or more races, non-Hispanic/Latino; 2% Race/ethnicity unknown; 0.5% international; 4% transferred in; 5% live on campus.
Freshmen *Admission:* 2,148 enrolled. *Average high school GPA:* 2.5.
Faculty *Total:* 551, 23% full-time, 5% with terminal degrees.
Majors Accounting; airline pilot and flight crew; architectural engineering technology; art; aviation/airway management; business administration and management; child-care and support services management; clinical/medical laboratory technology; commercial and advertising art; communications systems installation and repair technology; community health services counseling; computer and information sciences; computer/information technology services administration related; construction trades related; criminal justice/police science; electrical, electronic and communications engineering technology; emergency medical technology (EMT paramedic); engineering; fire services

administration; general studies; humanities; human services; information science/studies; legal assistant/paralegal; liberal arts and sciences and humanities related; liberal arts and sciences/liberal studies; physical education teaching and coaching; visual and performing arts.

Academics *Calendar:* semesters. *Degree:* certificates and associate. *Special study options:* academic remediation for entering students, adult/continuing education programs, advanced placement credit, distance learning, English as a second language, freshman honors college, honors programs, internships, off-campus study, part-time degree program, services for LD students, summer session for credit.

Library Dutchess Library with 173,128 titles, 255 serial subscriptions, 2,149 audiovisual materials, an OPAC, a Web page.

Student Life *Housing Options:* coed. Campus housing is university owned. *Activities and Organizations:* drama/theater group, student-run newspaper, radio station, choral group, Rap, Poetry & Music, Outdoor Adventure, Gamers Guild, Masquers Guild, Christian Fellowship. *Campus security:* 24-hour emergency response devices and patrols, late-night transport/escort service. *Student services:* health clinic, personal/psychological counseling.

Athletics Member NJCAA. *Intercollegiate sports:* baseball M, basketball M/W, bowling M/W, golf M, soccer M, softball W, tennis M/W, volleyball W.

Costs (2013–14) *Tuition:* state resident $3100 full-time, $129 per hour part-time; nonresident $6200 full-time, $258 per hour part-time. *Required fees:* $420 full-time, $10 per hour part-time, $13 per term part-time. *Room and board:* $8690. *Payment plan:* installment. *Waivers:* senior citizens and employees or children of employees.

Applying *Options:* early admission, deferred entrance. *Required:* high school transcript. *Application deadlines:* rolling (freshmen), rolling (transfers). *Notification:* continuous (freshmen), continuous (transfers).

Freshman Application Contact Dutchess Community College, 53 Pendell Road, Poughkeepsie, NY 12601-1595. *Phone:* 845-431-8010. *Website:* http://www.sunydutchess.edu/.

Ellis School of Nursing

Schenectady, New York

- **Independent** 2-year, founded 1906
- **Urban** campus
- **Coed, primarily women,** 132 undergraduate students, 34% full-time, 83% women, 17% men

Undergraduates 45 full-time, 87 part-time. Students come from 3 states and territories; 7% Black or African American, non-Hispanic/Latino; 8% Hispanic/Latino; 3% Asian, non-Hispanic/Latino; 2% American Indian or Alaska Native, non-Hispanic/Latino; 2% Race/ethnicity unknown.

Freshmen *Admission:* 3 enrolled. *Average high school GPA:* 3.2.

Faculty *Student/faculty ratio:* 6:1.

Majors Registered nursing/registered nurse.

Academics *Degree:* associate.

Standardized Tests *Recommended:* SAT or ACT (for admission).

Costs (2012–13) *Tuition:* $7863 full-time, $5181 per year part-time. *Required fees:* $903 full-time, $483 per year part-time.

Applying *Required:* essay or personal statement, high school transcript, minimum 3.0 GPA, 2 letters of recommendation.

Freshman Application Contact Carolyn Lansing, Student Services Coordinator, Ellis School of Nursing, 1101 Nott Street, Schenectady, NY 12308. *Phone:* 518-243-4471. *Fax:* 518-243-4470. *E-mail:* lansingc@ellismedicine.org. *Website:* http://www.ellismedicine.org/AboutEllis/SchoolofNursing.aspx.

Elmira Business Institute

Elmira, New York

- **Private** 2-year, founded 1858
- **Urban** campus
- **Coed, primarily women,** 235 undergraduate students, 82% full-time, 88% women, 12% men

Undergraduates 192 full-time, 43 part-time. 10% are from out of state.

Freshmen *Admission:* 79 enrolled.

Faculty *Student/faculty ratio:* 9:1.

Majors Accounting; administrative assistant and secretarial science; medical/clinical assistant; medical insurance coding.

Academics *Calendar:* semesters. *Degree:* certificates and associate. *Special study options:* academic remediation for entering students, advanced placement credit, internships, part-time degree program.

Library Elmira Business Institute Library plus 1 other.

Student Life *Housing:* college housing not available. *Campus security:* 24-hour emergency response devices.

Costs (2013–14) *Tuition:* $12,000 full-time, $400 per credit part-time. Full-time tuition and fees vary according to program. Part-time tuition and fees vary according to program. No tuition increase for student's term of enrollment. *Required fees:* $700 full-time. *Payment plan:* installment.

Financial Aid Of all full-time matriculated undergraduates who enrolled in 2011, 316 applied for aid, 306 were judged to have need. *Average percent of need met:* 85%. *Average financial aid package:* $30,450. *Average need-based loan:* $3500. *Average need-based gift aid:* $18,950. *Average indebtedness upon graduation:* $14,000.

Applying *Options:* electronic application. *Required:* high school transcript, interview. *Required for some:* essay or personal statement. *Application deadline:* rolling (freshmen).

Freshman Application Contact Mrs. Lisa Roan, Admissions Director, Elmira Business Institute, Elmira, NY 14901. *Phone:* 607-733-7178. *Toll-free phone:* 800-843-1812. *E-mail:* info@ebi-college.com. *Website:* http://www.ebi-college.com/.

Erie Community College

Buffalo, New York

- **State and locally supported** 2-year, founded 1971, part of State University of New York System
- **Urban** 1-acre campus
- **Coed,** 3,333 undergraduate students, 74% full-time, 61% women, 39% men

Undergraduates 2,483 full-time, 850 part-time. Students come from 14 states and territories; 6 other countries; 1% are from out of state; 31% Black or African American, non-Hispanic/Latino; 10% Hispanic/Latino; 1% Asian, non-Hispanic/Latino; 0.1% Native Hawaiian or other Pacific Islander, non-Hispanic/Latino; 0.5% American Indian or Alaska Native, non-Hispanic/Latino; 4% Two or more races, non-Hispanic/Latino; 3% Race/ethnicity unknown; 7% international; 7% transferred in.

Freshmen *Admission:* 3,540 applied, 2,387 admitted, 742 enrolled. *Test scores:* SAT critical reading scores over 500: 86%; SAT critical reading scores over 600: 13%; SAT critical reading scores over 700: 1%.

Faculty *Total:* 219, 35% full-time. *Student/faculty ratio:* 18:1.

Majors Building/property maintenance; business administration and management; child-care and support services management; community health services counseling; criminal justice/police science; culinary arts; humanities; legal assistant/paralegal; liberal arts and sciences/liberal studies; medical radiologic technology; middle school education; physical education teaching and coaching; public administration and social service professions related; registered nursing/registered nurse; substance abuse/addiction counseling.

Academics *Calendar:* semesters. *Degree:* certificates, diplomas, and associate. *Special study options:* academic remediation for entering students, adult/continuing education programs, advanced placement credit, cooperative education, distance learning, double majors, English as a second language, honors programs, independent study, internships, part-time degree program, services for LD students, student-designed majors, study abroad, summer session for credit. *ROTC:* Army (c).

Library Leon E. Butler Library with 22,876 titles, 95 serial subscriptions, 1,483 audiovisual materials, an OPAC, a Web page.

Student Life *Housing:* college housing not available. *Activities and Organizations:* drama/theater group, student-run newspaper, radio station, choral group. *Campus security:* 24-hour emergency response devices and patrols, late-night transport/escort service. *Student services:* health clinic, personal/psychological counseling, women's center.

Athletics Member NJCAA. *Intercollegiate sports:* baseball M, basketball M/W, bowling M/W, cheerleading W, football M, ice hockey M, lacrosse W, soccer M/W, softball W, swimming and diving M/W, volleyball W.

Costs (2012–13) *One-time required fee:* $75. *Tuition:* area resident $3900 full-time, $163 per credit hour part-time; state resident $7800 full-time, $326 per credit hour part-time; nonresident $7800 full-time, $326 per credit hour part-time. *Required fees:* $580 full-time, $15 per credit hour part-time, $60 per term part-time. *Payment plan:* installment. *Waivers:* senior citizens and employees or children of employees.

Applying *Options:* electronic application. *Application fee:* $25. *Required:* high school transcript. *Required for some:* interview. *Application deadlines:* rolling (freshmen), rolling (transfers). *Notification:* continuous (freshmen), continuous (transfers).

Freshman Application Contact Erie Community College, 121 Ellicott Street, Buffalo, NY 14203-2698. *Phone:* 716-851-1155. *Fax:* 716-270-2821. *Website:* http://www.ecc.edu/.

Erie Community College, North Campus

Williamsville, New York

- **State and locally supported** 2-year, founded 1946, part of State University of New York System
- **Suburban** 120-acre campus with easy access to Buffalo
- **Coed,** 6,561 undergraduate students, 65% full-time, 49% women, 51% men

Undergraduates 4,269 full-time, 2,292 part-time. Students come from 15 states and territories; 23 other countries; 0.5% are from out of state; 13% Black or African American, non-Hispanic/Latino; 5% Hispanic/Latino; 2% Asian, non-Hispanic/Latino; 0.5% American Indian or Alaska Native, non-Hispanic/Latino; 3% Two or more races, non-Hispanic/Latino; 4% Race/ethnicity unknown; 4% international; 10% transferred in.

Freshmen *Admission:* 5,675 applied, 4,143 admitted, 1,364 enrolled. *Test scores:* SAT critical reading scores over 500: 86%; SAT math scores over 500: 90%; SAT critical reading scores over 600: 13%; SAT math scores over 600: 20%; SAT critical reading scores over 700: 1%.

Faculty *Total:* 374, 40% full-time. *Student/faculty ratio:* 18:1.

Majors Business administration and management; civil engineering technology; clinical/medical laboratory technology; computer and information sciences; construction management; criminal justice/police science; culinary arts; dental hygiene; dietitian assistant; electrical, electronic and communications engineering technology; engineering; environmental science; geological and earth sciences/geosciences related; health information/medical records technology; humanities; industrial technology; information technology; liberal arts and sciences/liberal studies; mechanical engineering/mechanical technology; medical office management; occupational therapist assistant; office management; opticianry; physical education teaching and coaching; registered nursing/registered nurse; respiratory care therapy; restaurant, culinary, and catering management.

Academics *Calendar:* semesters plus summer sessions, winter intersession. *Degree:* certificates, diplomas, and associate. *Special study options:* academic remediation for entering students, adult/continuing education programs, advanced placement credit, cooperative education, distance learning, double majors, English as a second language, honors programs, independent study, internships, part-time degree program, services for LD students, student-designed majors, study abroad, summer session for credit. *ROTC:* Army (c).

Library Richard R. Dry Memorial Library with 52,846 titles, 285 serial subscriptions, 4,743 audiovisual materials, an OPAC, a Web page.

Student Life *Housing:* college housing not available. *Activities and Organizations:* drama/theater group, student-run newspaper, radio station, choral group. *Campus security:* 24-hour emergency response devices and patrols, late-night transport/escort service. *Student services:* health clinic, personal/psychological counseling, women's center.

Athletics Member NJCAA. *Intercollegiate sports:* baseball M, basketball M/W, bowling M/W, cheerleading W, football M, ice hockey M, lacrosse W, soccer M/W, softball W, swimming and diving M/W, volleyball W.

Costs (2012–13) *One-time required fee:* $75. *Tuition:* area resident $3900 full-time, $163 per credit hour part-time; state resident $7800 full-time, $326 per credit hour part-time; nonresident $7800 full-time, $326 per credit hour part-time. *Required fees:* $580 full-time, $15 per credit hour part-time, $60 per term part-time. *Payment plan:* installment. *Waivers:* senior citizens and employees or children of employees.

Applying *Options:* electronic application. *Application fee:* $25. *Required:* high school transcript. *Required for some:* interview. *Application deadlines:* rolling (freshmen), rolling (transfers). *Notification:* continuous (freshmen), continuous (transfers).

Freshman Application Contact Erie Community College, North Campus, 6205 Main Street, Williamsville, NY 14221-7095. *Phone:* 716-851-1455. *Fax:* 716-270-2961.
Website: http://www.ecc.edu/.

Erie Community College, South Campus

Orchard Park, New York

- **State and locally supported** 2-year, founded 1974, part of State University of New York System
- **Suburban** 110-acre campus with easy access to Buffalo
- **Coed,** 4,096 undergraduate students, 60% full-time, 45% women, 55% men

Undergraduates 2,441 full-time, 1,655 part-time. Students come from 16 states and territories; 5 other countries; 1% are from out of state; 6% Black or African American, non-Hispanic/Latino; 5% Hispanic/Latino; 0.5% Asian, non-Hispanic/Latino; 0.1% Native Hawaiian or other Pacific Islander, non-Hispanic/Latino; 0.8% American Indian or Alaska Native, non-Hispanic/Latino; 2% Two or more races, non-Hispanic/Latino; 4% Race/ethnicity unknown; 0.9% international; 6% transferred in.

Freshmen *Admission:* 2,427 applied, 1,944 admitted, 779 enrolled. *Test scores:* SAT critical reading scores over 500: 93%; SAT math scores over 500: 94%; SAT critical reading scores over 600: 11%; SAT math scores over 600: 18%; SAT critical reading scores over 700: 1%; SAT math scores over 700: 1%.

Faculty *Total:* 321, 30% full-time. *Student/faculty ratio:* 18:1.

Majors Architectural engineering technology; autobody/collision and repair technology; automobile/automotive mechanics technology; business administration and management; CAD/CADD drafting/design technology; communications systems installation and repair technology; computer technology/computer systems technology; criminal justice/police science; dental laboratory technology; emergency medical technology (EMT paramedic); fire services administration; graphic and printing equipment operation/production; humanities; liberal arts and sciences/liberal studies; physical education teaching and coaching; speech communication and rhetoric.

Academics *Calendar:* semesters plus summer sessions, winter intersession. *Degree:* certificates, diplomas, and associate. *Special study options:* academic remediation for entering students, adult/continuing education programs, advanced placement credit, cooperative education, distance learning, double majors, English as a second language, honors programs, independent study, internships, part-time degree program, services for LD students, student-designed majors, study abroad, summer session for credit. *ROTC:* Army (c).

Library 47,316 titles, 192 serial subscriptions, 1,368 audiovisual materials, an OPAC, a Web page.

Student Life *Housing:* college housing not available. *Activities and Organizations:* drama/theater group, student-run newspaper, radio station, choral group. *Campus security:* 24-hour emergency response devices and patrols, late-night transport/escort service. *Student services:* health clinic, personal/psychological counseling, women's center.

Athletics Member NJCAA. *Intercollegiate sports:* baseball M, basketball M/W, bowling M/W, cheerleading W, football M, ice hockey M, lacrosse W, soccer M/W, softball W, swimming and diving M/W, volleyball W.

Costs (2012–13) *One-time required fee:* $75. *Tuition:* area resident $3900 full-time, $163 per credit hour part-time; state resident $7800 full-time, $326 per credit hour part-time; nonresident $7800 full-time, $326 per credit hour part-time. *Required fees:* $580 full-time, $15 per credit hour part-time, $60 per term part-time. *Payment plan:* installment. *Waivers:* senior citizens and employees or children of employees.

Applying *Options:* electronic application. *Application fee:* $25. *Required:* high school transcript. *Required for some:* interview. *Application deadlines:* rolling (freshmen), rolling (transfers). *Notification:* continuous (freshmen), continuous (transfers).

Freshman Application Contact Erie Community College, South Campus, 4041 Southwestern Boulevard, Orchard Park, NY 14127-2199. *Phone:* 716-851-1655. *Fax:* 716-851-1687.
Website: http://www.ecc.edu/.

Eugenio María de Hostos Community College of the City University of New York

Bronx, New York

Freshman Application Contact Mr. Roland Velez, Director of Admissions, Eugenio María de Hostos Community College of the City University of New York, 120 149th Street, Bronx, NY 10451. *Phone:* 718-319-7968. *Fax:* 718-319-7919. *E-mail:* admissions@hostos.cuny.edu.
Website: http://www.hostos.cuny.edu/.

Everest Institute

Rochester, New York

Freshman Application Contact Deanna Pfluke, Director of Admissions, Everest Institute, 1630 Portland Avenue, Rochester, NY 14621. *Phone:* 585-266-0430. *Toll-free phone:* 888-741-4270. *Fax:* 585-266-8243.
Website: http://www.everest.edu/campus/rochester/.

Fashion Institute of Technology

New York, New York

- **State and locally supported** comprehensive, founded 1944, part of State University of New York System
- **Urban** 5-acre campus with easy access to New York City
- **Endowment** $25.9 million
- **Coed, primarily women,** 9,848 undergraduate students, 73% full-time, 85% women, 15% men

Undergraduates 7,154 full-time, 2,694 part-time. 35% are from out of state; 9% Black or African American, non-Hispanic/Latino; 15% Hispanic/Latino; 10% Asian, non-Hispanic/Latino; 0.4% Native Hawaiian or other Pacific Islander, non-Hispanic/Latino; 0.1% American Indian or Alaska Native, non-Hispanic/Latino; 3% Two or more races, non-Hispanic/Latino; 3% Race/ethnicity unknown; 13% international; 10% transferred in; 28% live on campus. *Retention:* 85% of full-time freshmen returned.

Freshmen *Admission:* 4,449 applied, 1,995 admitted, 1,233 enrolled.

Faculty *Total:* 977, 24% full-time. *Student/faculty ratio:* 17:1.

Majors Advertising; animation, interactive technology, video graphics and special effects; apparel and textile manufacturing; commercial and advertising art; commercial photography; entrepreneurial and small business related; fashion/apparel design; fashion merchandising; fashion modeling; fine and studio arts management; fine/studio arts; graphic design; illustration; industrial and product design; interior design; international marketing; marketing research; merchandising, sales, and marketing operations related (specialized); metal and jewelry arts; special products marketing.

Academics *Calendar:* semesters. *Degrees:* certificates, associate, bachelor's, and master's. *Special study options:* academic remediation for entering students, adult/continuing education programs, advanced placement credit, distance learning, English as a second language, honors programs, internships, part-time degree program, services for LD students, study abroad, summer session for credit.

Library Gladys Marcus Library.

Student Life *Housing Options:* coed, women-only. Campus housing is university owned. Freshman applicants given priority for college housing. *Activities and Organizations:* drama/theater group, student-run newspaper, radio and television station, choral group, Asian Student Network, Fashion Show Club, Black Student Union, Phi Theta Kappa, Gospel Choir. *Campus security:* 24-hour emergency response devices and patrols, late-night transport/escort service, controlled dormitory access. *Student services:* health clinic, personal/psychological counseling.

Athletics Member NJCAA. *Intercollegiate sports:* cross-country running M/W, soccer W, swimming and diving M/W, table tennis M/W, tennis W, track and field M/W, volleyball W. *Intramural sports:* archery M(c)/W(c).

Standardized Tests *Recommended:* SAT or ACT (for admission).

Costs (2012–13) *Tuition:* state resident $5768 full-time, $240 per credit hour part-time; nonresident $15,430 full-time, $643 per credit hour part-time. Full-time tuition and fees vary according to degree level. Part-time tuition and fees vary according to degree level. *Required fees:* $590 full-time, $8 per credit hour part-time, $170 per term part-time. *Room and board:* $12,598. Room and board charges vary according to board plan and housing facility. *Payment plan:* installment. *Waivers:* senior citizens and employees or children of employees.

Financial Aid Of all full-time matriculated undergraduates who enrolled in 2010, 5,019 applied for aid, 3,858 were judged to have need, 535 had their need fully met. In 2010, 95 non-need-based awards were made. *Average percent of need met:* 75%. *Average financial aid package:* $13,577. *Average need-based loan:* $4248. *Average need-based gift aid:* $5405. *Average non-need-based aid:* $894.

Applying *Options:* electronic application. *Application fee:* $50. *Required:* essay or personal statement, high school transcript. *Required for some:* portfolio for art and design programs. *Application deadlines:* 1/1 (freshmen), 1/1 (transfers). *Notification:* 4/1 (freshmen), 4/1 (transfers).

Freshman Application Contact Ms. Laura Arbogast, Director of Admissions and Strategic Recruitment, Fashion Institute of Technology, Seventh Avenue at 27th Street, New York, NY 10001-5992. *Phone:* 212-217-3760. *Fax:* 212-217-3761. *E-mail:* fitinfo@fitnyc.edu. *Website:* http://www.fitnyc.edu/.

See display below and page 402 for the College Close-Up.

Finger Lakes Community College

Canandaigua, New York

- **State and locally supported** 2-year, founded 1965, part of State University of New York System
- **Small-town** 300-acre campus with easy access to Rochester
- **Coed,** 6,539 undergraduate students, 55% full-time, 57% women, 43% men

Undergraduates 3,610 full-time, 2,929 part-time. Students come from 25 states and territories; 4 other countries; 0.7% are from out of state; 8% Black or African American, non-Hispanic/Latino; 5% Hispanic/Latino; 0.5% Asian, non-Hispanic/Latino; 0.4% American Indian or Alaska Native, non-His-

panic/Latino; 2% Two or more races, non-Hispanic/Latino; 7% Race/ethnicity unknown; 0.1% international; 5% transferred in.

Freshmen *Admission:* 4,712 admitted, 1,430 enrolled.

Faculty *Total:* 383, 31% full-time. *Student/faculty ratio:* 22:1.

Majors Accounting; administrative assistant and secretarial science; animation, interactive technology, video graphics and special effects; architectural engineering technology; biological and physical sciences; biology/biological sciences; biology/biotechnology laboratory technician; business administration and management; chemistry; commercial and advertising art; computer and information sciences; computer science; criminal justice/law enforcement administration; criminal justice/police science; data processing and data processing technology; digital communication and media/multimedia; drafting and design technology; dramatic/theater arts; early childhood education; e-commerce; emergency medical technology (EMT paramedic); engineering science; environmental studies; fine/studio arts; fishing and fisheries sciences and management; hotel/motel administration; humanities; human services; kindergarten/preschool education; legal assistant/paralegal; liberal arts and sciences/liberal studies; marketing/marketing management; mass communication/media; mathematics; mechanical engineering/mechanical technology; music; natural resources/conservation; natural resources management and policy; natural resources management and policy related; ornamental horticulture; physical education teaching and coaching; physics; political science and government; pre-engineering; psychology; recording arts technology; registered nursing/registered nurse; social sciences; sociology; substance abuse/addiction counseling; tourism and travel services management.

Academics *Calendar:* semesters. *Degree:* certificates and associate. *Special study options:* academic remediation for entering students, advanced placement credit, distance learning, honors programs, internships, off-campus study, part-time degree program, services for LD students, summer session for credit. *ROTC:* Air Force (c).

Library Charles Meder Library with 75,610 titles, 464 serial subscriptions, 6,954 audiovisual materials, an OPAC.

Student Life *Housing:* college housing not available. *Options:* Campus housing is provided by a third party. *Activities and Organizations:* drama/theater group, student-run radio station, choral group. *Campus security:* 24-hour emergency response devices and patrols, late-night transport/escort service. *Student services:* health clinic, personal/psychological counseling, legal services.

Athletics Member NJCAA. *Intercollegiate sports:* baseball M, basketball M/W, cross-country running M/W, lacrosse M, soccer M/W, softball W, track and field M/W, volleyball W. *Intramural sports:* basketball M/W, tennis M/W, volleyball M/W.

Costs (2012–13) *Tuition:* state resident $3654 full-time, $151 per credit hour part-time; nonresident $7308 full-time, $303 per credit hour part-time. Full-time tuition and fees vary according to course load. Part-time tuition and fees vary according to course load. *Required fees:* $414 full-time, $13 per credit hour part-time. *Payment plan:* installment. *Waivers:* senior citizens.

Financial Aid Of all full-time matriculated undergraduates who enrolled in 2011, 200 Federal Work-Study jobs (averaging $2200). 100 state and other part-time jobs (averaging $2200).

Applying *Options:* electronic application, early admission, deferred entrance. *Application fee:* $20. *Required:* high school transcript. *Application deadlines:* 8/23 (freshmen), 8/23 (transfers). *Notification:* continuous (freshmen), continuous (transfers).

Freshman Application Contact Ms. Bonnie B. Ritts, Director of Admissions, Finger Lakes Community College, 3325 Marvin Sands Drive, Canandaigua, NY 14424-8395. *Phone:* 585-785-1278. *Fax:* 585-785- 1734. *E-mail:* admissions@flcc.edu.
Website: http://www.flcc.edu/.

Fiorello H. LaGuardia Community College of the City University of New York

Long Island City, New York

- **State and locally supported** 2-year, founded 1970, part of City University of New York System
- **Urban** 6-acre campus with easy access to New York City
- **Coed,** 17,468 undergraduate students, 56% full-time, 58% women, 42% men

Undergraduates 9,752 full-time, 7,716 part-time. Students come from 15 states and territories; 160 other countries; 2% are from out of state; 16% Black or African American, non-Hispanic/Latino; 37% Hispanic/Latino; 13% Asian, non-Hispanic/Latino; 0.4% Native Hawaiian or other Pacific Islander, non-Hispanic/Latino; 0.3% American Indian or Alaska Native, non-Hispanic/Latino; 0.9% Two or more races, non-Hispanic/Latino; 13% Race/ethnicity unknown; 10% international; 8% transferred in.

Freshmen *Admission:* 6,624 applied, 6,624 admitted, 3,240 enrolled.

Faculty *Total:* 1,121, 29% full-time, 25% with terminal degrees. *Student/faculty ratio:* 21:1.

Majors Accounting technology and bookkeeping; administrative assistant and secretarial science; adult development and aging; biology/biological sciences; business administration and management; civil engineering; commercial photography; computer and information sciences and support services related; computer installation and repair technology; computer programming; computer science; criminal justice/safety; data entry/microcomputer applications; dietetic technology; digital arts; dramatic/theater arts; electrical and electronics engineering; emergency medical technology (EMT paramedic); English; environmental science; fine/studio arts; funeral service and mortuary science; industrial and product design; legal assistant/paralegal; liberal arts and sciences/liberal studies; licensed practical/vocational nurse training; mechanical engineering; medical radiologic technology; occupational therapist assistant; philosophy; physical therapy technology; psychiatric/mental health services technology; psychology; recording arts technology; registered nursing/registered nurse; restaurant/food services management; Spanish; speech communication and rhetoric; teacher assistant/aide; tourism and travel services management; veterinary/animal health technology; visual and performing arts.

Academics *Calendar:* enhanced semester. *Degree:* certificates and associate. *Special study options:* academic remediation for entering students, accelerated degree program, adult/continuing education programs, advanced placement credit, cooperative education, distance learning, double majors, English as a second language, honors programs, independent study, internships, off-campus study, part-time degree program, services for LD students, student-designed majors, study abroad, summer session for credit.

Library Fiorello H. LaGuardia Community College Library Media Resources Center plus 1 other with 342,977 titles, 531 serial subscriptions, 3,577 audiovisual materials, an OPAC, a Web page.

Student Life *Housing:* college housing not available. *Activities and Organizations:* drama/theater group, student-run newspaper, radio station, Bangladesh Student Association, Christian Club, Chinese Club, Web Radio, Black Student Union. *Campus security:* 24-hour emergency response devices and patrols, late-night transport/escort service. *Student services:* health clinic, personal/psychological counseling, women's center, legal services.

Athletics *Intramural sports:* basketball M/W, bowling M/W, football M, soccer M/W, softball M/W, swimming and diving M/W, table tennis M/W, volleyball M/W.

Costs (2012–13) *Tuition:* state resident $3900 full-time, $165 per credit part-time; nonresident $7800 full-time, $260 per credit part-time. *Required fees:* $366 full-time, $92 per term part-time. *Payment plan:* installment. *Waivers:* senior citizens and employees or children of employees.

Financial Aid Of all full-time matriculated undergraduates who enrolled in 2010, 7,674 applied for aid, 7,208 were judged to have need, 118 had their need fully met. 343 Federal Work-Study jobs (averaging $650). *Average percent of need met:* 51%. *Average financial aid package:* $6079. *Average need-based loan:* $4319. *Average need-based gift aid:* $4743.

Applying *Options:* electronic application, early admission, deferred entrance. *Application fee:* $65. *Required:* high school transcript. *Application deadlines:* rolling (freshmen), rolling (transfers). *Notification:* continuous (freshmen), continuous (transfers).

Freshman Application Contact Ms. LaVora Desvigne, Director of Admissions, Fiorello H. LaGuardia Community College of the City University of New York, RM-147, 31-10 Thomson Avenue, Long Island City, NY 11101. *Phone:* 718-482-5114. *Fax:* 718-482-5112. *E-mail:* admissions@lagcc.cuny.edu.
Website: http://www.lagcc.cuny.edu/.

Fulton-Montgomery Community College

Johnstown, New York

Freshman Application Contact Fulton-Montgomery Community College, 2805 State Highway 67, Johnstown, NY 12095-3790. *Phone:* 518-762-4651 Ext. 8301.
Website: http://www.fmcc.suny.edu/.

Genesee Community College

Batavia, New York

- **State and locally supported** 2-year, founded 1966, part of State University of New York System
- **Small-town** 256-acre campus with easy access to Buffalo, Rochester
- **Endowment** $3.0 million
- **Coed,** 6,965 undergraduate students, 50% full-time, 63% women, 37% men

Undergraduates 3,469 full-time, 3,496 part-time. Students come from 25 states and territories; 27 other countries; 4% are from out of state; 9% Black or African American, non-Hispanic/Latino; 3% Hispanic/Latino; 0.5% Asian, non-Hispanic/Latino; 0.1% Native Hawaiian or other Pacific Islander, non-Hispanic/Latino; 1% American Indian or Alaska Native, non-Hispanic/Latino; 0.9% Two or more races, non-Hispanic/Latino; 4% Race/ethnicity unknown; 3% international; 6% transferred in.

Freshmen *Admission:* 2,796 applied, 2,796 admitted, 1,210 enrolled.

Faculty *Total:* 369, 24% full-time, 3% with terminal degrees. *Student/faculty ratio:* 18:1.

Majors Accounting; administrative assistant and secretarial science; business administration and management; clinical/medical laboratory technology; computer and information sciences related; computer engineering technology; computer graphics; computer software and media applications related; criminal justice/law enforcement administration; criminology; drafting and design technology; dramatic/theater arts; education; electrical, electronic and communications engineering technology; elementary education; engineering science; fashion merchandising; gerontology; health professions related; hotel/motel administration; human services; information science/studies; kindergarten/preschool education; legal assistant/paralegal; liberal arts and sciences/liberal studies; marketing/marketing management; mass communication/media; mathematics; network and system administration; physical education teaching and coaching; physical therapy; polysomnography; psychology; registered nursing/registered nurse; respiratory care therapy; substance abuse/addiction counseling; tourism and travel services management; veterinary/animal health technology.

Academics *Calendar:* semesters. *Degree:* certificates and associate. *Special study options:* academic remediation for entering students, adult/continuing education programs, advanced placement credit, cooperative education, distance learning, double majors, English as a second language, honors programs, independent study, internships, part-time degree program, services for LD students, study abroad, summer session for credit.

Library Alfred C. OConnell Library with 81,811 titles, 180 serial subscriptions, 6,789 audiovisual materials, an OPAC, a Web page.

Student Life *Housing Options:* disabled students. Campus housing is university owned. *Activities and Organizations:* drama/theater group, student-run newspaper, radio station, choral group, Student Government Association, Phi Theta Kappa, DECA, Student Activities Council, Forum Players. *Campus security:* 24-hour emergency response devices and patrols, student patrols, late-night transport/escort service, controlled dormitory access. *Student services:* health clinic, personal/psychological counseling.

Athletics Member NJCAA. *Intercollegiate sports:* baseball M(s), basketball M(s)/W(s), cheerleading M/W, golf M/W, lacrosse M(s)/W, soccer M/W, softball W, swimming and diving M/W, volleyball W(s). *Intramural sports:* badminton M/W, basketball M/W, soccer M/W, tennis M/W, track and field M/W, volleyball M/W, water polo M/W.

Standardized Tests *Recommended:* ACT (for admission).

Costs (2012–13) *Tuition:* state resident $3550 full-time, $145 per credit hour part-time; nonresident $4150 full-time, $165 per credit hour part-time. Full-time tuition and fees vary according to course load. Part-time tuition and fees vary according to course load. *Required fees:* $350 full-time, $2 per credit hour part-time, $42 per term part-time. *Room and board:* room only: $5800. Room and board charges vary according to board plan and housing facility. *Payment plan:* installment. *Waivers:* senior citizens and employees or children of employees.

Financial Aid Of all full-time matriculated undergraduates who enrolled in 2011, 2,988 applied for aid, 2,675 were judged to have need, 993 had their need fully met. 160 Federal Work-Study jobs (averaging $1070). 120 state and other part-time jobs (averaging $1271). *Average percent of need met:* 72%. *Average financial aid package:* $4415. *Average need-based loan:* $3425. *Average need-based gift aid:* $2987. *Average indebtedness upon graduation:* $8872.

Applying *Options:* electronic application. *Required:* high school transcript. *Required for some:* 1 letter of recommendation. *Application deadlines:* rolling (freshmen), rolling (out-of-state freshmen), rolling (transfers). *Notification:* continuous (freshmen), continuous (out-of-state freshmen), continuous (transfers).

Freshman Application Contact Mrs. Tanya Lane-Martin, Director of Admissions, Genesee Community College, Batavia, NY 14020. *Phone:* 585-343-0055 Ext. 6413. *Toll-free phone:* 800-CALL GCC. *Fax:* 585-345-6892. *E-mail:* tmlanemartin@genesee.edu. *Website:* http://www.genesee.edu/.

Helene Fuld College of Nursing of North General Hospital

New York, New York

Freshman Application Contact Helene Fuld College of Nursing of North General Hospital, 24 East 120th Street, New York, NY 10035. *Phone:* 212-616-7271. *Website:* http://www.helenefuld.edu/.

Herkimer County Community College

Herkimer, New York

Director of Admissions Mr. Scott J. Hughes, Associate Dean for Enrollment Management, Herkimer County Community College, Reservoir Road, Herkimer, NY 13350. *Phone:* 315-866-0300 Ext. 278. *Toll-free phone:* 888-464-4222 Ext. 8278. *Website:* http://www.herkimer.edu/.

Hudson Valley Community College

Troy, New York

Freshman Application Contact Ms. Marie Claire Bauer, Director of Admissions, Hudson Valley Community College, 80 Vandenburgh Avenue, Troy, NY 12180-6096. *Phone:* 518-629-7309. *Toll-free phone:* 877-325-HVCC. *Website:* http://www.hvcc.edu/.

Institute of Design and Construction

Brooklyn, New York

- **Independent** 2-year, founded 1947
- **Urban** campus
- **Coed, primarily men,** 127 undergraduate students, 43% full-time, 16% women, 84% men

Undergraduates 55 full-time, 72 part-time. Students come from 3 states and territories; 2 other countries; 3% are from out of state; 39% Black or African American, non-Hispanic/Latino; 17% Hispanic/Latino; 9% Asian, non-Hispanic/Latino; 0.8% Two or more races, non-Hispanic/Latino; 2% international; 7% transferred in. *Retention:* 40% of full-time freshmen returned.

Freshmen *Admission:* 30 applied, 30 admitted, 20 enrolled.

Faculty *Total:* 22, 64% with terminal degrees. *Student/faculty ratio:* 10:1.

Majors Architectural engineering technology; construction engineering technology; drafting and design technology; interior architecture.

Academics *Calendar:* semesters. *Degree:* associate. *Special study options:* academic remediation for entering students, adult/continuing education programs, advanced placement credit, cooperative education, part-time degree program, summer session for credit.

Library Vito P. Battista Library plus 1 other with an OPAC.

Student Life *Housing:* college housing not available. *Student services:* personal/psychological counseling.

Costs (2012–13) *One-time required fee:* $30. *Tuition:* $7800 full-time, $325 per credit part-time. *Required fees:* $280 full-time, $140 per term part-time. *Payment plan:* installment.

Applying *Options:* electronic application, deferred entrance. *Application fee:* $30. *Required:* high school transcript. *Recommended:* interview. *Application deadline:* rolling (freshmen). *Notification:* continuous until 9/3 (freshmen).

Freshman Application Contact Ms. Elizabeth A. Battista, Director of Communications, Institute of Design and Construction, 141 Willoughby Street, Brooklyn, NV 11201. *Phone:* 718-855-3661. *Fax:* 718-852-5889. *E-mail:* ebattista@idc.edu. *Website:* http://www.idcbrooklyn.org/.

Island Drafting and Technical Institute

Amityville, New York

- **Proprietary** 2-year, founded 1957
- **Suburban** campus with easy access to New York City
- **Coed**

Undergraduates 116 full-time. Students come from 1 other state; 18% Black or African American, non-Hispanic/Latino; 21% Hispanic/Latino; 0.9% Asian, non-Hispanic/Latino; 0.9% Two or more races, non-Hispanic/Latino. *Retention:* 80% of full-time freshmen returned.

Faculty *Student/faculty ratio:* 15:1.

Academics *Calendar:* semesters. *Degree:* certificates, diplomas, and associate. *Special study options:* accelerated degree program, adult/continuing education programs, summer session for credit.

Costs (2012–13) *Tuition:* $15,300 full-time, $510 per credit hour part-time. No tuition increase for student's term of enrollment. *Required fees:* $350 full-time.

Applying *Options:* early admission. *Application fee:* $25. *Required:* interview. *Recommended:* high school transcript.

Freshman Application Contact John Olivio, Island Drafting and Technical Institute, Island Drafting and Technical Institute, 128 Broadway, Amityville, NY 11701. *Phone:* 631-691-8733 Ext. 14. *Fax:* 631-691-8738. *E-mail:* info@idti.edu. *Website:* http://www.idti.edu/.

ITT Technical Institute

Albany, New York

- **Proprietary** 2-year, founded 1998, part of ITT Educational Services, Inc.
- **Coed**

Academics *Calendar:* quarters. *Degree:* associate.

Freshman Application Contact Director of Recruitment, ITT Technical Institute, 13 Airline Drive, Albany, NY 12205. *Phone:* 518-452-9300. *Toll-free phone:* 800-489-1191.
Website: http://www.itt-tech.edu/.

ITT Technical Institute

Getzville, New York

- **Proprietary** 2-year, part of ITT Educational Services, Inc.
- **Coed**

Academics *Degree:* associate.

Freshman Application Contact Director of Recruitment, ITT Technical Institute, 2295 Millersport Highway, PO Box 327, Getzville, NY 14068. *Phone:* 716-689-2200. *Toll-free phone:* 800-469-7593.
Website: http://www.itt-tech.edu/.

ITT Technical Institute

Liverpool, New York

- **Proprietary** 2-year, founded 1998, part of ITT Educational Services, Inc.
- **Coed**

Academics *Calendar:* semesters. *Degree:* associate.

Freshman Application Contact Director of Recruitment, ITT Technical Institute, 235 Greenfield Parkway, Liverpool, NY 13088. *Phone:* 315-461-8000. *Toll-free phone:* 877-488-0011.
Website: http://www.itt-tech.edu/.

Jamestown Business College

Jamestown, New York

- **Proprietary** primarily 2-year, founded 1886
- **Small-town** 1-acre campus
- **Coed**, 294 undergraduate students, 98% full-time, 73% women, 27% men

Undergraduates 288 full-time, 6 part-time. Students come from 2 states and territories; 11% are from out of state; 2% Black or African American, non-Hispanic/Latino; 3% Hispanic/Latino; 0.7% Asian, non-Hispanic/Latino; 0.3% Native Hawaiian or other Pacific Islander, non-Hispanic/Latino; 2% American Indian or Alaska Native, non-Hispanic/Latino; 2% Two or more races, non-Hispanic/Latino; 2% Race/ethnicity unknown; 10% transferred in.

Freshmen *Admission:* 98 applied, 91 admitted, 70 enrolled.

Faculty *Total:* 24, 29% full-time, 8% with terminal degrees. *Student/faculty ratio:* 25:1.

Majors Administrative assistant and secretarial science; business administration and management; medical/clinical assistant; office management.

Academics *Calendar:* quarters. *Degrees:* certificates, associate, and bachelor's. *Special study options:* advanced placement credit, double majors, internships, part-time degree program, summer session for credit.

Library James Prendergast Library with 279,270 titles, 372 serial subscriptions, an OPAC, a Web page.

Student Life *Housing:* college housing not available. *Campus security:* 24-hour emergency response devices.

Athletics *Intramural sports:* basketball M(c)/W(c), racquetball M(c)/W(c), softball M(c)/W(c), swimming and diving M(c)/W(c), table tennis M(c)/W(c), tennis M(c)/W(c), volleyball M(c)/W(c), weight lifting M(c)/W(c).

Costs (2013–14) *One-time required fee:* $25. *Tuition:* $10,500 full-time, $292 per credit hour part-time. *Required fees:* $900 full-time, $150 per term part-time. *Waivers:* employees or children of employees.

Financial Aid Of all full-time matriculated undergraduates who enrolled in 2011, 311 applied for aid, 311 were judged to have need. *Average need-based loan:* $6049. *Average need-based gift aid:* $8254.

Applying *Application fee:* $25. *Required:* essay or personal statement, high school transcript, interview. *Application deadlines:* rolling (freshmen), rolling (transfers).

Freshman Application Contact Mrs. Brenda Salemme, Director of Admissions and Placement, Jamestown Business College, 7 Fairmount Avenue, Box 429, Jamestown, NY 14702-0429. *Phone:* 716-664-5100. *Fax:* 716-664-3144. *E-mail:* brendasalemme@jamestownbusinesscollege.edu.
Website: http://www.jbcny.org/.

Jamestown Community College

Jamestown, New York

- **State and locally supported** 2-year, founded 1950, part of State University of New York System
- **Small-town** 107-acre campus
- **Endowment** $8.1 million
- **Coed**, 3,582 undergraduate students, 71% full-time, 58% women, 42% men

Undergraduates 2,533 full-time, 1,049 part-time. Students come from 16 states and territories; 5 other countries; 9% are from out of state; 4% Black or African American, non-Hispanic/Latino; 6% Hispanic/Latino; 0.5% Asian, non-Hispanic/Latino; 0.1% Native Hawaiian or other Pacific Islander, non-Hispanic/Latino; 1% American Indian or Alaska Native, non-Hispanic/Latino; 3% Two or more races, non-Hispanic/Latino; 1% Race/ethnicity unknown; 0.1% international; 7% transferred in; 9% live on campus.

Freshmen *Admission:* 2,065 applied, 1,981 admitted, 1,072 enrolled. *Average high school GPA:* 3.18.

Faculty *Total:* 340, 21% full-time. *Student/faculty ratio:* 16:1.

Majors Accounting technology and bookkeeping; administrative assistant and secretarial science; biology/biological sciences; biology/biotechnology laboratory technician; business administration and management; commercial and advertising art; computer programming; criminal justice/police science; data processing and data processing technology; early childhood education; electrical, electronic and communications engineering technology; elementary education; engineering; fine/studio arts; fire prevention and safety technology; health information/medical records technology; humanities; human services; information technology; kindergarten/preschool education; liberal arts and sciences and humanities related; liberal arts and sciences/liberal studies; mechanical engineering/mechanical technology; music; occupational therapist assistant; physical education teaching and coaching; registered nursing/registered nurse; speech communication and rhetoric; welding technology.

Academics *Calendar:* semesters. *Degree:* certificates and associate. *Special study options:* academic remediation for entering students, adult/continuing education programs, advanced placement credit, distance learning, honors programs, independent study, internships, off-campus study, part-time degree program, services for LD students, study abroad, summer session for credit.

Library Hultquist Library with 88,767 titles, 334 serial subscriptions, 6,373 audiovisual materials, an OPAC, a Web page.

Student Life *Housing Options:* coed. Campus housing is university owned. *Activities and Organizations:* drama/theater group, student-run radio station, choral group, Nursing Club, InterVarsity Christian Fellowship, Anime Club, Student Occupational Therapy Assistant (SOTA) Club, InterWeave Gay-Straight Alliance. *Student services:* health clinic, personal/psychological counseling.

Athletics Member NJCAA. *Intercollegiate sports:* baseball M, basketball M/W, golf M/W, soccer M/W, softball W, swimming and diving M/W, volleyball W, wrestling M. *Intramural sports:* basketball M/W, bowling M/W, cross-country running M/W, softball M/W, volleyball M/W.

Costs (2012–13) *Tuition:* state resident $4050 full-time, $170 per credit hour part-time; nonresident $8100 full-time, $305 per credit hour part-time. Full-time tuition and fees vary according to course load and program. Part-time tuition and fees vary according to course load and program. *Required fees:* $445 full-time. *Room and board:* $9600; room only: $6600. Room and board charges vary according to board plan. *Payment plan:* installment. *Waivers:* employees or children of employees.

Financial Aid Of all full-time matriculated undergraduates who enrolled in 2011, 85 Federal Work-Study jobs (averaging $1500). 85 state and other part-time jobs (averaging $1300).

Applying *Options:* electronic application, deferred entrance. *Required:* high school transcript. *Required for some:* standardized test scores used for placement, GEDs accepted. TOEFL (or equivalent) required for international students. *Application deadlines:* rolling (freshmen), rolling (out-of-state freshmen), rolling (transfers). *Notification:* continuous (freshmen), continuous (out-of-state freshmen), continuous (transfers).

Freshman Application Contact Ms. Wendy Present, Director of Admissions and Recruitment, Jamestown Community College, 525 Falconer Street, PO Box 20, Jamestown, NY 14702-0020. *Phone:* 716-338-1001. *Toll-free phone:* 800-388-8557. *Fax:* 716-338-1450. *E-mail:* admissions@mail.sunyjcc.edu.
Website: http://www.sunyjcc.edu/.

Jefferson Community College

Watertown, New York

- **State and locally supported** 2-year, founded 1961, part of State University of New York System
- **Small-town** 90-acre campus with easy access to Syracuse
- **Coed,** 4,143 undergraduate students, 53% full-time, 61% women, 39% men

Undergraduates 2,204 full-time, 1,939 part-time. 5% Black or African American, non-Hispanic/Latino; 8% Hispanic/Latino; 1% Asian, non-Hispanic/Latino; 0.5% Native Hawaiian or other Pacific Islander, non-Hispanic/Latino; 0.7% American Indian or Alaska Native, non-Hispanic/Latino; 0.3% Two or more races, non-Hispanic/Latino; 8% Race/ethnicity unknown.

Freshmen *Admission:* 1,130 enrolled.

Faculty *Total:* 230, 35% full-time. *Student/faculty ratio:* 18:1.

Majors Accounting; accounting technology and bookkeeping; administrative assistant and secretarial science; animal/livestock husbandry and production; business administration and management; child-care and support services management; child development; community organization and advocacy; computer and information sciences; computer and information sciences and support services related; computer/information technology services administration related; computer science; computer technology/computer systems technology; criminal justice/law enforcement administration; early childhood education; emergency medical technology (EMT paramedic); engineering; engineering science; fire prevention and safety technology; fire services administration; forest technology; hospitality administration; humanities; human services; information science/studies; legal assistant/paralegal; liberal arts and sciences/liberal studies; mathematics; mechanical engineering technologies related; medical administrative assistant and medical secretary; office management; office occupations and clerical services; registered nursing/registered nurse; teacher assistant/aide; tourism promotion.

Academics *Calendar:* semesters. *Degree:* certificates and associate. *Special study options:* academic remediation for entering students, advanced placement credit, cooperative education, distance learning, double majors, honors programs, independent study, internships, part-time degree program, services for LD students, student-designed majors, summer session for credit.

Library Melvil Dewey Library with 172,262 titles, 144 serial subscriptions, 5,761 audiovisual materials, an OPAC, a Web page.

Student Life *Housing:* college housing not available. *Activities and Organizations:* student-run newspaper. *Campus security:* 24-hour emergency response devices and patrols. *Student services:* health clinic, personal/psychological counseling.

Athletics Member NJCAA. *Intercollegiate sports:* baseball M, basketball M/W, lacrosse M/W, soccer M/W, softball W, volleyball W.

Standardized Tests *Recommended:* SAT or ACT (for admission).

Costs (2012–13) *Tuition:* state resident $3744 full-time, $156 per credit hour part-time; nonresident $5394 full-time, $225 per credit hour part-time. Full-time tuition and fees vary according to course load, location, program, and reciprocity agreements. Part-time tuition and fees vary according to course load, location, program, and reciprocity agreements. *Required fees:* $533 full-time. *Payment plan:* installment. *Waivers:* senior citizens and employees or children of employees.

Financial Aid Of all full-time matriculated undergraduates who enrolled in 2009, 1,748 applied for aid. 98 Federal Work-Study jobs (averaging $1093).

Applying *Options:* electronic application, early admission, deferred entrance. *Required:* high school transcript. *Required for some:* interview. *Application deadlines:* 9/6 (freshmen), rolling (transfers). *Notification:* continuous (freshmen), continuous (transfers).

Freshman Application Contact Ms. Rosanne N. Weir, Director of Admissions, Jefferson Community College, 1220 Coffeen Street, Watertown, NY 13601. *Phone:* 315-786-2277. *Toll-free phone:* 888-435-6522. *Fax:* 315-786-2459. *E-mail:* admissions@sunyjefferson.edu. *Website:* http://www.sunyjefferson.edu/.

Kingsborough Community College of the City University of New York

Brooklyn, New York

- **State and locally supported** 2-year, founded 1963, part of City University of New York System
- **Urban** 72-acre campus with easy access to New York City
- **Coed**

Undergraduates 11,205 full-time, 8,056 part-time. Students come from 10 states and territories; 136 other countries; 1% are from out of state; 33% Black or African American, non-Hispanic/Latino; 16% Hispanic/Latino; 13% Asian, non-Hispanic/Latino; 0.2% American Indian or Alaska Native, non-Hispanic/Latino; 3% international; 9% transferred in. *Retention:* 66% of full-time freshmen returned.

Faculty *Student/faculty ratio:* 23:1.

Academics *Calendar:* semesters. *Degree:* associate. *Special study options:* academic remediation for entering students, adult/continuing education programs, advanced placement credit, distance learning, English as a second language, honors programs, independent study, internships, off-campus study, part-time degree program, services for LD students, summer session for credit.

Student Life *Campus security:* 24-hour emergency response devices and patrols.

Athletics Member NJCAA.

Costs (2012–13) *Tuition:* state resident $3610 full-time, $150 per credit part-time; nonresident $7200 full-time, $240 per credit part-time. *Required fees:* $350 full-time, $92 per term part-time.

Applying *Application fee:* $65. *Required:* high school transcript.

Freshman Application Contact Mr. Robert Ingenito, Director of Admissions Information Center, Kingsborough Community College of the City University of New York, 2001 Oriental Boulevard, Brooklyn, NY 11235. *Phone:* 718-368-4600. *Fax:* 718-368-5356. *E-mail:* info@kbcc.cuny.edu. *Website:* http://www.kbcc.cuny.edu/.

Long Island Business Institute

Flushing, New York

- **Proprietary** 2-year, founded 1968
- **Urban** campus with easy access to New York City
- **Coed, primarily women,** 513 undergraduate students, 74% full-time, 75% women, 25% men

Undergraduates 380 full-time, 133 part-time. Students come from 2 states and territories; 23 other countries; 1% are from out of state; 10% Black or African American, non-Hispanic/Latino; 23% Hispanic/Latino; 43% Asian, non-Hispanic/Latino; 0.4% Two or more races, non-Hispanic/Latino; 0.2% Race/ethnicity unknown; 5% international; 8% transferred in.

Freshmen *Admission:* 286 applied, 113 admitted, 111 enrolled.

Faculty *Total:* 90, 17% full-time, 2% with terminal degrees. *Student/faculty ratio:* 10:1.

Majors Accounting; business administration and management; business, management, and marketing related; court reporting; homeland security; hospitality administration related; medical office management.

Academics *Calendar:* semesters. *Degrees:* certificates and associate (information provided for Commack and Flushing campuses). *Special study options:* academic remediation for entering students, adult/continuing education programs, advanced placement credit, cooperative education, English as a second language, honors programs, independent study, part-time degree program, summer session for credit.

Library Flushing Main Campus Library, Commack Campus Library with 7,314 titles, 77 serial subscriptions, 1,209 audiovisual materials, an OPAC, a Web page.

Student Life *Housing:* college housing not available. *Activities and Organizations:* Small Business Club, Web Design Club, Investment Club, Court Reporting Alumni Association. *Campus security:* 24-hour emergency response devices.

Standardized Tests *Required:* COMPASS, CELSA (for admission).

Costs (2013–14) *Tuition:* $13,299 full-time, $375 per credit part-time. *Required fees:* $600 full-time, $200 per term part-time. *Payment plans:* installment, deferred payment.

Applying *Application fee:* $55. *Required:* essay or personal statement, high school transcript, interview. *Application deadlines:* rolling (freshmen), rolling (transfers).

Freshman Application Contact Mr. Chen Zhang, Associate Director of Admissions, Long Island Business Institute, 136-18 39th Avenue, Flushing, NY 11354. *Phone:* 718-939-5100. *Fax:* 718-939-9235. *E-mail:* czang@libi.edu. *Website:* http://www.libi.edu/.

Long Island College Hospital School of Nursing

Brooklyn, New York

Freshman Application Contact Ms. Barbara Evans, Admissions Assistant, Long Island College Hospital School of Nursing, 350 Henry Street, 7th Floor, Brooklyn, NY 11201. *Phone:* 718-780-1071. *Fax:* 718-780-1936. *E-mail:* bevans@chpnet.org. *Website:* http://www.futurenurselich.org/.

Memorial Hospital School of Nursing
Albany, New York

Freshman Application Contact Admissions Office, Memorial Hospital School of Nursing, 600 Northern Boulevard, Albany, NY 12204. *Website:* http://www.nehealth.com/son/.

Mildred Elley–New York City
New York, New York

Admissions Office Contact Mildred Elley–New York City, 25 Broadway, 16th Floor, New York, NY 10004-1010. *Website:* http://www.mildred-elley.edu/.

Mildred Elley School
Albany, New York

Director of Admissions Mr. Michael Cahalan, Enrollment Manager, Mildred Elley School, 855 Central Avenue, Albany, NY 12206. *Phone:* 518-786-3171 Ext. 227. *Toll-free phone:* 800-622-6327. *Website:* http://www.mildred-elley.edu/.

Mohawk Valley Community College
Utica, New York

- **State and locally supported** 2-year, founded 1946, part of State University of New York System
- **Suburban** 80-acre campus
- **Endowment** $3.8 million
- **Coed,** 7,445 undergraduate students, 62% full-time, 55% women, 45% men

Undergraduates 4,601 full-time, 2,844 part-time. Students come from 13 states and territories; 19 other countries; 8% Black or African American, non-Hispanic/Latino; 7% Hispanic/Latino; 3% Asian, non-Hispanic/Latino; 0.1% Native Hawaiian or other Pacific Islander, non-Hispanic/Latino; 0.5% American Indian or Alaska Native, non-Hispanic/Latino; 2% Two or more races, non-Hispanic/Latino; 0.2% Race/ethnicity unknown; 1% international; 5% transferred in; 7% live on campus.

Freshmen *Admission:* 4,760 applied, 3,627 admitted, 1,623 enrolled. *Average high school GPA:* 2.65.

Faculty *Total:* 488, 28% full-time, 10% with terminal degrees. *Student/faculty ratio:* 23:1.

Majors Accounting technology and bookkeeping; administrative assistant and secretarial science; advertising; airframe mechanics and aircraft maintenance technology; art; banking and financial support services; building/property maintenance; business administration and management; chemical technology; civil engineering technology; commercial and advertising art; commercial photography; communications systems installation and repair technology; community organization and advocacy; computer and information sciences; computer and information sciences and support services related; computer programming; computer science; criminal justice/law enforcement administration; design and applied arts related; drafting and design technology; dramatic/theater arts; electrical and electronic engineering technologies related; electrical, electronic and communications engineering technology; electrical/electronics maintenance and repair technology related; elementary education; emergency medical technology (EMT paramedic); engineering; entrepreneurship; fire services administration; food service systems administration; heating, ventilation, air conditioning and refrigeration engineering technology; hotel/motel administration; humanities; industrial production technologies related; liberal arts and sciences and humanities related; liberal arts and sciences/liberal studies; management information systems and services related; mechanical engineering/mechanical technology; mechanical engineering technologies related; medical/clinical assistant; medical radiologic technology; nutrition sciences; parks, recreation and leisure facilities management; public administration; registered nursing/registered nurse; respiratory care therapy; restaurant, culinary, and catering management; secondary education; sign language interpretation and translation; substance abuse/addiction counseling; surveying technology.

Academics *Calendar:* semesters. *Degree:* certificates and associate. *Special study options:* academic remediation for entering students, advanced placement credit, distance learning, double majors, English as a second language, honors programs, independent study, internships, off-campus study, part-time degree program, services for LD students, student-designed majors, summer session for credit. *ROTC:* Army (c), Air Force (c).

Library Mohawk Valley Community College Library plus 1 other with 127,254 titles, 32,838 serial subscriptions, 9,039 audiovisual materials, an OPAC, a Web page.

Student Life *Housing Options:* coed, men-only, women-only, disabled students. Campus housing is provided by a third party. Freshman applicants given priority for college housing. *Activities and Organizations:* drama/theater group, student-run newspaper, Student Congress, Student Nurses Organization (SNO), Photography Club, Recreation Club, Phi Theta Kappa. *Campus security:* 24-hour emergency response devices and patrols, late-night transport/escort service, controlled dormitory access. *Student services:* health clinic, personal/psychological counseling.

Athletics Member NJCAA. *Intercollegiate sports:* baseball M, basketball M/W, bowling M/W, cross-country running M/W, golf M/W, ice hockey M, lacrosse M/W, soccer M/W, softball W, tennis M/W, track and field M/W, volleyball W. *Intramural sports:* badminton M/W, basketball M/W, soccer M/W, tennis M/W, volleyball M/W.

Costs (2012–13) *Tuition:* state resident $3580 full-time, $130 per credit hour part-time; nonresident $7160 full-time, $260 per credit hour part-time. *Required fees:* $550 full-time, $7 per credit hour part-time, $40 per term part-time. *Room and board:* $9150; room only: $5500. Room and board charges vary according to board plan. *Payment plans:* installment, deferred payment. *Waivers:* senior citizens and employees or children of employees.

Financial Aid Of all full-time matriculated undergraduates who enrolled in 2011, 229 Federal Work-Study jobs (averaging $1750).

Applying *Options:* electronic application, deferred entrance. *Required for some:* high school transcript. *Recommended:* interview. *Application deadlines:* rolling (freshmen), rolling (out-of-state freshmen), rolling (transfers). *Notification:* continuous (freshmen), continuous (out-of-state freshmen), continuous (transfers).

Freshman Application Contact Mrs. Sandra Fiebiger, Data Processing Clerk, Admissions, Mohawk Valley Community College, Utica, NY 13501. *Phone:* 315-792-5640. *Toll-free phone:* 800-SEE-MVCC. *Fax:* 315-792-5527. *E-mail:* sfiebiger@mvcc.edu. *Website:* http://www.mvcc.edu/.

Monroe Community College
Rochester, New York

- **State and locally supported** 2-year, founded 1961, part of State University of New York System
- **Suburban** 314-acre campus with easy access to Buffalo
- **Coed,** 17,296 undergraduate students, 61% full-time, 54% women, 46% men

Undergraduates 10,554 full-time, 6,742 part-time. 19% Black or African American, non-Hispanic/Latino; 8% Hispanic/Latino; 3% Asian, non-Hispanic/Latino; 0.1% Native Hawaiian or other Pacific Islander, non-Hispanic/Latino; 0.3% American Indian or Alaska Native, non-Hispanic/Latino; 4% Two or more races, non-Hispanic/Latino; 0.3% Race/ethnicity unknown; 0.6% international. *Retention:* 61% of full-time freshmen returned.

Freshmen *Admission:* 4,089 enrolled. *Test scores:* SAT critical reading scores over 500: 33%; SAT math scores over 500: 22%; SAT writing scores over 500: 22%; ACT scores over 18: 76%; SAT critical reading scores over 600: 6%; SAT math scores over 600: 3%; SAT writing scores over 600: 3%; ACT scores over 24: 20%; SAT critical reading scores over 700: 1%; ACT scores over 30: 2%.

Faculty *Total:* 895, 36% full-time, 10% with terminal degrees. *Student/faculty ratio:* 25:1.

Majors Accounting; administrative assistant and secretarial science; art; automobile/automotive mechanics technology; behavioral sciences; biological and physical sciences; biology/biological sciences; biology/biotechnology laboratory technician; business administration and management; chemical engineering; chemistry; civil engineering technology; commercial and advertising art; computer and information sciences and support services related; computer and information sciences related; computer engineering related; computer engineering technology; computer science; construction engineering technology; consumer merchandising/retailing management; corrections; criminal justice/law enforcement administration; criminal justice/police science; data processing and data processing technology; dental hygiene; electrical, electronic and communications engineering technology; engineering science; environmental studies; family and consumer sciences/human sciences; fashion/apparel design; fashion merchandising; fire science/firefighting; food technology and processing; forestry; graphic and printing equipment operation/production; health information/medical records administration; heating, air conditioning, ventilation and refrigeration maintenance technology; history; hotel/motel administration; human services; industrial radiologic technology; industrial technology; information science/studies; information technology; instrumentation technology; interior design; international business/trade/commerce; landscape architecture; laser and optical technology; legal administrative assistant/secretary; liberal arts and sciences/liberal studies; marketing/marketing management; mass communication/media; mathematics; mechanical engineering/mechanical technology; music; parks, recreation and leisure; physical education teaching and coaching; physics; political science and government; pre-pharmacy studies; quality control technology; registered nursing/registered nurse; social sciences; special products marketing; telecommunications technology; tourism and travel services management.

Academics *Calendar:* semesters. *Degree:* certificates and associate. *Special study options:* academic remediation for entering students, accelerated degree program, adult/continuing education programs, advanced placement credit, cooperative education, English as a second language, honors programs, internships, off-campus study, part-time degree program, services for LD students, summer session for credit. *ROTC:* Army (c), Air Force (c).

Library LeRoy V. Good Library plus 1 other with 110,748 titles, 745 serial subscriptions, 4,100 audiovisual materials, an OPAC.

Student Life *Housing Options:* Campus housing is university owned. *Activities and Organizations:* drama/theater group, student-run newspaper, radio station, choral group, student newspaper, Phi Theta Kappa, student government. *Campus security:* 24-hour emergency response devices, late-night transport/escort service. *Student services:* health clinic, personal/psychological counseling.

Athletics Member NJCAA. *Intercollegiate sports:* baseball M(s), basketball M(s)/W(s), golf M, ice hockey M(s), lacrosse M(s), soccer M(s)/W(s), softball W, swimming and diving M(s)/W(s), tennis M/W, volleyball W. *Intramural sports:* archery M/W, basketball M/W, bowling M/W, cheerleading W, cross-country running M/W, lacrosse W, racquetball M/W, rugby M, skiing (cross-country) M/W, soccer M/W, softball M/W, swimming and diving M/W, tennis M/W, volleyball M/W.

Costs (2013–14) *Tuition:* state resident $3140 full-time, $131 per credit hour part-time; nonresident $6280 full-time, $262 per credit hour part-time. Full-time tuition and fees vary according to program. Part-time tuition and fees vary according to course load and program. *Required fees:* $13 full-time, $18 per year part-time. *Room and board:* $5800. Room and board charges vary according to housing facility. *Payment plan:* installment. *Waivers:* senior citizens and employees or children of employees.

Applying *Options:* electronic application, early admission. *Application fee:* $20. *Required:* high school transcript. *Application deadlines:* rolling (freshmen), rolling (transfers). *Notification:* continuous (freshmen), continuous (transfers).

Freshman Application Contact Mr. Andrew Freeman, Director of Admissions, Monroe Community College, 1000 East Henrietta Road, Rochester, NY 14623-5780. *Phone:* 585-292-2231. *Fax:* 585-292-3860. *E-mail:* admissions@monroecc.edu. *Website:* http://www.monroecc.edu/.

Nassau Community College
Garden City, New York

- **State and locally supported** 2-year, founded 1959, part of State University of New York System
- **Suburban** 225-acre campus with easy access to New York City
- **Coed,** 23,079 undergraduate students, 62% full-time, 50% women, 50% men

Undergraduates 14,306 full-time, 8,778 part-time. Students come from 19 states and territories; 69 other countries; 0.3% are from out of state; 22% Black or African American, non-Hispanic/Latino; 20% Hispanic/Latino; 6% Asian, non-Hispanic/Latino; 0.4% Native Hawaiian or other Pacific Islander, non-Hispanic/Latino; 0.3% American Indian or Alaska Native, non-Hispanic/Latino; 6% Race/ethnicity unknown; 1% international; 6% transferred in. *Retention:* 32% of full-time freshmen returned.

Freshmen *Admission:* 4,869 enrolled. *Average high school GPA:* 2.51.

Faculty *Total:* 1,474, 32% full-time, 33% with terminal degrees. *Student/faculty ratio:* 22:1.

Majors Accounting; accounting technology and bookkeeping; administrative assistant and secretarial science; African American/Black studies; art; business administration and management; civil engineering technology; clinical/medical laboratory technology; commercial and advertising art; computer and information sciences; computer and information sciences related; computer graphics; computer science; computer systems networking and telecommunications; criminal justice/law enforcement administration; criminal justice/safety; dance; data processing and data processing technology; design and visual communications; dramatic/theater arts; engineering; entrepreneurship; fashion/apparel design; fashion merchandising; funeral service and mortuary science; general studies; hotel/motel administration; instrumentation technology; insurance; interior design; kindergarten/preschool education; legal administrative assistant/secretary; legal assistant/paralegal; liberal arts and sciences/liberal studies; management information systems; marketing/marketing management; mass communication/media; mathematics; medical administrative assistant and medical secretary; medical radiologic technology; music performance; photography; physical therapy technology; real estate; registered nursing/registered nurse; rehabilitation and therapeutic professions related; respiratory care therapy; retailing; speech communication and rhetoric; surgical technology; theater design and technology; transportation and materials moving related; visual and performing arts.

Academics *Calendar:* semesters. *Degree:* certificates and associate. *Special study options:* academic remediation for entering students, adult/continuing education programs, advanced placement credit, cooperative education, dis-

tance learning, English as a second language, honors programs, internships, off-campus study, part-time degree program, services for LD students, summer session for credit.

Library A. Holly Patterson Library with 186,782 titles, 401 serial subscriptions, 18,903 audiovisual materials, an OPAC, a Web page.

Student Life *Housing:* college housing not available. *Activities and Organizations:* drama/theater group, student-run newspaper, radio station, choral group, Muslim Student Association, Make a Difference Club, Interact Club, Political Science Club, Investment Club. *Campus security:* 24-hour emergency response devices and patrols, late-night transport/escort service. *Student services:* personal/psychological counseling, women's center.

Athletics Member NJCAA. *Intercollegiate sports:* baseball M, basketball M/W, bowling M/W, cheerleading M/W, cross-country running M/W, football M, golf M/W, lacrosse M/W, soccer M/W, softball W, tennis M/W, track and field M/W, volleyball W, wrestling M. *Intramural sports:* badminton M/W, baseball M, basketball M/W, racquetball M/W, soccer M/W, softball M/W, swimming and diving M/W, table tennis M/W, tennis M/W, volleyball M/W.

Standardized Tests *Recommended:* SAT or ACT (for admission).

Costs (2013–14) *Tuition:* area resident $3990 full-time; state resident $7980 full-time. *Required fees:* $340 full-time.

Financial Aid Of all full-time matriculated undergraduates who enrolled in 2011, 400 Federal Work-Study jobs (averaging $3000).

Applying *Options:* electronic application, deferred entrance. *Application fee:* $40. *Required:* high school transcript. *Required for some:* minimum 3.0 GPA, interview. *Recommended:* minimum 2.0 GPA. *Application deadlines:* 8/7 (freshmen), 8/7 (transfers). *Notification:* continuous (freshmen), continuous (transfers).

Freshman Application Contact Mr. Craig Wright, Vice President of Enrollment Management, Nassau Community College, Garden City, NY 11530. *Phone:* 516-572-7345. *E-mail:* admissions@sunynassau.edu. *Website:* http://www.ncc.edu/.

New York Career Institute
New York, New York

- **Proprietary** 2-year, founded 1942
- **Urban** campus
- **Coed, primarily women,** 702 undergraduate students, 66% full-time, 90% women, 10% men

Undergraduates 461 full-time, 241 part-time. 25% Black or African American, non-Hispanic/Latino; 17% Hispanic/Latino; 2% Asian, non-Hispanic/Latino; 0.7% American Indian or Alaska Native, non-Hispanic/Latino; 3% Two or more races, non-Hispanic/Latino; 19% Race/ethnicity unknown.

Faculty *Total:* 42, 21% full-time.

Majors Court reporting; legal assistant/paralegal; medical office assistant.

Academics *Calendar:* trimesters (semesters for evening division). *Degree:* certificates and associate. *Special study options:* academic remediation for entering students, advanced placement credit, internships, part-time degree program, summer session for credit.

Library 5,010 titles, 23 serial subscriptions.

Student Life *Housing:* college housing not available.

Costs (2012–13) *Tuition:* $12,750 full-time, $400 per credit hour part-time. Full-time tuition and fees vary according to class time. Part-time tuition and fees vary according to class time. *Required fees:* $150 full-time, $50 per term part-time. *Payment plan:* installment.

Applying *Application fee:* $50. *Required:* high school transcript, interview. *Application deadlines:* 9/7 (freshmen), 9/7 (transfers). *Notification:* continuous (freshmen), continuous (transfers).

Freshman Application Contact Mr. Larry Stieglitz, Director of Admissions, New York Career Institute, 11 Park Place, New York, NY 10007. *Phone:* 212-962-0002 Ext. 115. *Fax:* 212-385-7574. *E-mail:* lstieglitz@nyci.edu. *Website:* http://www.nyci.com/.

Niagara County Community College
Sanborn, New York

- **State and locally supported** 2-year, founded 1962, part of State University of New York System
- **Rural** 287-acre campus with easy access to Buffalo
- **Endowment** $3.7 million
- **Coed,** 6,743 undergraduate students, 62% full-time, 57% women, 43% men

Undergraduates 4,202 full-time, 2,541 part-time. Students come from 11 states and territories; 5 other countries; 1% are from out of state; 9% Black or African American, non-Hispanic/Latino; 2% Hispanic/Latino; 1% Asian, non-Hispanic/Latino; 2% American Indian or Alaska Native, non-Hispanic/Latino; 4% Race/ethnicity unknown; 0.4% international; 4% transferred in; 4% live on campus.

Freshmen *Admission:* 2,455 applied, 2,455 admitted, 1,448 enrolled. *Average high school GPA:* 2.48.

Faculty *Total:* 382, 29% full-time, 10% with terminal degrees. *Student/faculty ratio:* 17:1.

Majors Accounting; administrative assistant and secretarial science; animal sciences; baking and pastry arts; biological and physical sciences; business administration and management; business, management, and marketing related; chemical technology; computer science; consumer merchandising/retailing management; criminal justice/law enforcement administration; culinary arts; design and applied arts related; drafting and design technology; drafting/design engineering technologies related; dramatic/theater arts; elementary education; fine/studio arts; general studies; hospitality administration; humanities; human services; information science/studies; liberal arts and sciences/liberal studies; massage therapy; mass communication/media; mathematics; medical/clinical assistant; medical radiologic technology; music; natural resources/conservation; occupational health and industrial hygiene; parks, recreation and leisure; physical education teaching and coaching; physical therapy technology; registered nursing/registered nurse; social sciences; sport and fitness administration/management; surgical technology; tourism and travel services management; web page, digital/multimedia and information resources design; wine steward/sommelier.

Academics *Calendar:* semesters. *Degree:* certificates and associate. *Special study options:* academic remediation for entering students, adult/continuing education programs, advanced placement credit, cooperative education, distance learning, double majors, honors programs, independent study, internships, off-campus study, part-time degree program, services for LD students, student-designed majors, study abroad, summer session for credit. *ROTC:* Army (c).

Library Henrietta G. Lewis Library with 99,210 titles, 345 serial subscriptions, 7,861 audiovisual materials, an OPAC, a Web page.

Student Life *Housing Options:* coed. Campus housing is provided by a third party. *Activities and Organizations:* drama/theater group, student-run newspaper, radio station, choral group, student radio station, Student Nurses Association, Phi Theta Kappa, Alpha Beta Gamma, Physical Education Club. *Campus security:* 24-hour emergency response devices and patrols, student patrols, late-night transport/escort service. *Student services:* health clinic, personal/psychological counseling.

Athletics Member NJCAA. *Intercollegiate sports:* baseball M, basketball M(s)/W(s), bowling M/W, golf M/W, lacrosse M/W, soccer M/W, softball W, volleyball W, wrestling M(s). *Intramural sports:* basketball M/W, racquetball M/W, soccer M/W, swimming and diving M/W, tennis M/W.

Costs (2012–13) *Tuition:* state resident $3696 full-time, $154 per credit hour part-time; nonresident $9240 full-time, $385 per credit hour part-time. Full-time tuition and fees vary according to course load and program. Part-time tuition and fees vary according to course load and program. *Required fees:* $344 full-time, $169 per term part-time. *Room and board:* $10,860; room only: $8360. Room and board charges vary according to housing facility. *Payment plan:* installment. *Waivers:* senior citizens and employees or children of employees.

Financial Aid Of all full-time matriculated undergraduates who enrolled in 2011, 5,027 applied for aid, 5,027 were judged to have need. 144 Federal Work-Study jobs (averaging $2845). 127 state and other part-time jobs (averaging $508). *Average percent of need met:* 70%. *Average financial aid package:* $5026. *Average need-based loan:* $4338. *Average need-based gift aid:* $1144.

Applying *Options:* electronic application, early admission. *Required:* high school transcript. *Required for some:* minimum 2.0 GPA. *Notification:* continuous until 8/31 (freshmen), continuous until 8/31 (transfers).

Freshman Application Contact Ms. Kathy Saunders, Director of Enrollment Services, Niagara County Community College, 3111 Saunders Settlement Road, Sanborn, NY 14132. *Phone:* 716-614-6200. *Fax:* 716-614-6820. *E-mail:* admissions@niagaracc.suny.edu. *Website:* http://www.niagaracc.suny.edu/.

North Country Community College
Saranac Lake, New York

Freshman Application Contact Enrollment Management Assistant, North Country Community College, 23 Santanoni Avenue, PO Box 89, Saranac Lake, NY 12983-0089. *Phone:* 518-891-2915 Ext. 686. *Toll-free phone:* 800-TRY-NCCC (in-state); 888-TRY-NCCC (out-of-state). *Fax:* 518-891-0898. *E-mail:* info@nccc.edu. *Website:* http://www.nccc.edu/.

Olean Business Institute
Olean, New York

Freshman Application Contact Olean Business Institute, 301 North Union Street, Olean, NY 14760-2691. *Phone:* 716-372-7978. *Website:* http://www.obi.edu/.

Onondaga Community College
Syracuse, New York

- **State and locally supported** 2-year, founded 1962, part of State University of New York System
- **Suburban** 280-acre campus
- **Endowment** $6.0 million
- **Coed,** 12,991 undergraduate students, 52% full-time, 52% women, 48% men

Undergraduates 6,704 full-time, 6,287 part-time. Students come from 22 states and territories; 23 other countries; 0.5% are from out of state; 12% Black or African American, non-Hispanic/Latino; 4% Hispanic/Latino; 2% Asian, non-Hispanic/Latino; 0.1% Native Hawaiian or other Pacific Islander, non-Hispanic/Latino; 2% American Indian or Alaska Native, non-Hispanic/Latino; 2% Two or more races, non-Hispanic/Latino; 6% Race/ethnicity unknown; 0.5% international; 49% transferred in; 6% live on campus.

Freshmen *Admission:* 8,099 applied, 5,643 admitted, 2,418 enrolled.

Faculty *Total:* 660, 27% full-time. *Student/faculty ratio:* 27:1.

Majors Accounting; accounting technology and bookkeeping; architectural engineering technology; architectural technology; art; automobile/automotive mechanics technology; business administration and management; business/commerce; computer engineering technology; computer science; computer systems networking and telecommunications; construction engineering technology; criminal justice/law enforcement administration; criminal justice/police science; design and applied arts related; education (multiple levels); electrical and electronic engineering technologies related; electrical, electronic and communications engineering technology; engineering science; environmental engineering technology; fire prevention and safety technology; general studies; health information/medical records technology; health professions related; homeland security, law enforcement, firefighting and protective services related; hospitality administration; humanities; interior design; liberal arts and sciences and humanities related; mechanical engineering/mechanical technology; music; parks, recreation and leisure; photography; physical therapy technology; public administration and social service professions related; radio and television; registered nursing/registered nurse; respiratory care therapy; speech communication and rhetoric.

Academics *Calendar:* semesters. *Degree:* certificates, diplomas, and associate. *Special study options:* academic remediation for entering students, accelerated degree program, adult/continuing education programs, advanced placement credit, cooperative education, distance learning, double majors, English as a second language, external degree program, honors programs, internships, part-time degree program, services for LD students, study abroad, summer session for credit. *ROTC:* Air Force (c).

Library Sidney B. Coulter Library with 114,481 titles, 277 serial subscriptions, 14,874 audiovisual materials, an OPAC, a Web page.

Student Life *Housing Options:* coed. Campus housing is provided by a third party. *Activities and Organizations:* drama/theater group, student-run newspaper, radio station, choral group. *Campus security:* 24-hour emergency response devices and patrols, controlled dormitory access. *Student services:* personal/psychological counseling.

Athletics Member NJCAA. *Intercollegiate sports:* baseball M, basketball M/W, cross-country running M/W, lacrosse M/W, soccer M/W, softball W, tennis M/W, volleyball W. *Intramural sports:* badminton M/W, basketball M/W, golf M/W, skiing (downhill) M/W, swimming and diving M/W, table tennis M/W, tennis M/W, volleyball M/W.

Costs (2012–13) *Tuition:* state resident $4050 full-time, $161 per credit hour part-time; nonresident $8100 full-time, $322 per credit hour part-time. Full-time tuition and fees vary according to program. Part-time tuition and fees vary according to course load and program. *Required fees:* $554 full-time, $115 per term part-time. *Room and board:* room only: $6200. Room and board charges vary according to board plan. *Payment plan:* installment. *Waivers:* senior citizens and employees or children of employees.

Financial Aid Of all full-time matriculated undergraduates who enrolled in 2012, 5,769 applied for aid, 5,188 were judged to have need, 287 had their need fully met. *Average percent of need met:* 57%. *Average financial aid package:* $6500. *Average need-based loan:* $3080. *Average need-based gift aid:* $5080.

Applying *Options:* electronic application. *Required:* high school transcript, some programs require specific prerequisite courses and/or tests to be admitted directly to the program; an alternate program is offered. *Required for some:* minimum 2.0 GPA, interview. *Application deadlines:* 8/12 (freshmen), 8/12 (transfers). *Notification:* continuous (freshmen), continuous (transfers).

Freshman Application Contact Mrs. Katherine Perry, Director of Admissions, Onondaga Community College, 4585 West Seneca Turnpike, Syracuse, NY 13215. *Phone:* 315-488-2602. *Fax:* 315-488-2107. *E-mail:* admissions@sunyocc.edu. *Website:* http://www.sunyocc.edu/.

Orange County Community College
Middletown, New York

Freshman Application Contact Michael Roe, Director of Admissions and Recruitment, Orange County Community College, 115 South Street, Middletown, NY 10940. *Phone:* 845-341-4205. *Fax:* 845-343-1228. *E-mail:* apply@sunyorange.edu.
Website: http://www.sunyorange.edu/.

Phillips Beth Israel School of Nursing
New York, New York

Freshman Application Contact Mrs. Bernice Pass-Stern, Assistant Dean, Phillips Beth Israel School of Nursing, 776 Sixth Avenue, 4th Floor, New York, NY 10010-6354. *Phone:* 212-614-6176. *Fax:* 212-614-6109. *E-mail:* bstern@chpnet.org.
Website: http://www.futurenursebi.org/.

Plaza College
Jackson Heights, New York

Freshman Application Contact Dean Rose Ann Black, Dean of Administration, Plaza College, 74-09 37th Avenue, Jackson Heights, NY 11372. *Phone:* 718-779-1430. *E-mail:* info@plazacollege.edu.
Website: http://www.plazacollege.edu/.

Queensborough Community College of the City University of New York
Bayside, New York

Freshman Application Contact Ms. Ann Tullio, Director of Registration, Queensborough Community College of the City University of New York, 222-05 56th Avenue, Bayside, NY 11364. *Phone:* 718-631-6307. *Fax:* 718-281-5189.
Website: http://www.qcc.cuny.edu/.

Rockland Community College
Suffern, New York

- **State and locally supported** 2-year, founded 1959, part of State University of New York System
- **Suburban** 150-acre campus with easy access to New York City
- **Coed**

Undergraduates 4,752 full-time, 3,234 part-time. 20% Black or African American, non-Hispanic/Latino; 19% Hispanic/Latino; 5% Asian, non-Hispanic/Latino; 0.4% American Indian or Alaska Native, non-Hispanic/Latino; 12% Race/ethnicity unknown; 2% international; 8% transferred in. *Retention:* 64% of full-time freshmen returned.
Faculty *Student/faculty ratio:* 20:1.
Academics *Calendar:* semesters. *Degree:* certificates and associate. *Special study options:* adult/continuing education programs, external degree program, part-time degree program.
Student Life *Campus security:* 24-hour emergency response devices and patrols, student patrols, late-night transport/escort service.
Athletics Member NJCAA.
Financial Aid Of all full-time matriculated undergraduates who enrolled in 2011, 68 Federal Work-Study jobs (averaging $2358). *Average need-based loan:* $4232. *Average need-based gift aid:* $3573.
Applying *Options:* early admission, deferred entrance. *Application fee:* $30. *Required:* high school transcript.
Freshman Application Contact Rockland Community College, 145 College Road, Suffern, NY 10901-3699. *Phone:* 845-574-4237. *Toll-free phone:* 800-722-7666.
Website: http://www.sunyrockland.edu/.

St. Elizabeth College of Nursing
Utica, New York

- **Independent** 2-year, founded 1904
- **Small-town** 1-acre campus with easy access to Syracuse
- **Coed**
- 60% of applicants were admitted

Undergraduates 145 full-time, 72 part-time. Students come from 4 states and territories; 1 other country; 1% are from out of state; 1% Black or African American, non-Hispanic/Latino; 1% Hispanic/Latino; 2% Asian, non-His-

panic/Latino; 0.9% American Indian or Alaska Native, non-Hispanic/Latino; 2% international; 42% transferred in. *Retention:* 75% of full-time freshmen returned.
Faculty *Student/faculty ratio:* 10:1.
Academics *Calendar:* semesters. *Degree:* associate. *Special study options:* academic remediation for entering students, advanced placement credit, off-campus study, part-time degree program, services for LD students.
Student Life *Campus security:* 24-hour emergency response devices and patrols.
Standardized Tests *Required:* SAT or ACT (for admission). *Recommended:* SAT or ACT (for admission).
Costs (2012–13) *Tuition:* $12,750 full-time, $375 per credit hour part-time. Full-time tuition and fees vary according to course load, location, program, and student level. Part-time tuition and fees vary according to course load, location, program, and student level. *Required fees:* $1000 full-time, $500 per term part-time.
Applying *Options:* electronic application. *Application fee:* $65. *Required:* high school transcript, 2 letters of recommendation. *Recommended:* minimum 3.0 GPA.
Freshman Application Contact Donna Ernst, Director of Recruitment, St. Elizabeth College of Nursing, 2215 Genesee Street, Utica, NY 13501. *Phone:* 315-798-8189. *E-mail:* dernst@secon.edu.
Website: http://www.secon.edu/.

St. Joseph's College of Nursing
Syracuse, New York

- **Independent Roman Catholic** 2-year, founded 1898
- **Urban** campus
- **Coed**

Undergraduates 166 full-time, 107 part-time. Students come from 2 states and territories; 20% live on campus.
Faculty *Student/faculty ratio:* 9:1.
Academics *Calendar:* semesters. *Degree:* associate. *Special study options:* academic remediation for entering students, adult/continuing education programs, advanced placement credit, cooperative education, internships, part-time degree program, services for LD students.
Student Life *Campus security:* 24-hour patrols.
Standardized Tests *Required:* SAT or ACT (for admission).
Costs (2012–13) *Tuition:* $16,592 full-time, $488 per credit hour part-time. Full-time tuition and fees vary according to course load. Part-time tuition and fees vary according to course load. *Required fees:* $200 full-time. *Room only:* $4400.
Applying *Options:* electronic application, deferred entrance. *Application fee:* $50. *Required:* essay or personal statement, high school transcript, minimum 3.0 GPA, 2 letters of recommendation, interview.
Freshman Application Contact Ms. Felicia Corp, Recruiter, St. Joseph's College of Nursing, 206 Prospect Avenue, Syracuse, NY 13203. *Phone:* 315-448-5040. *Fax:* 315-448-5745. *E-mail:* collegeofnursing@sjhsyr.org.
Website: http://www.sjhsyr.org/nursing/.

St. Paul's School of Nursing
Rego Park, New York

Director of Admissions Nancy Wolinski, Chairperson of Admissions, St. Paul's School of Nursing, 97-77 Queens Boulevard, Rego Park, NY 11374. *Phone:* 718-357-0500 Ext. 131. *E-mail:* nwolinski@svcmcny.org.
Website: http://www.stpaulsschoolofnursing.com/.

Samaritan Hospital School of Nursing
Troy, New York

Director of Admissions Ms. Jennifer Marrone, Student Services Coordinator, Samaritan Hospital School of Nursing, 2215 Burdett Avenue, Troy, NY 12180. *Phone:* 518-271-3734. *Fax:* 518-271-3303. *E-mail:* marronej@nehealth.com.
Website: http://www.nehealth.com/.

SBI Campus–an affiliate of Sanford-Brown
Melville, New York

Director of Admissions Ms. Cynthia Gamache, Director of Admissions, SBI Campus–an affiliate of Sanford-Brown, 320 South Service Road, Melville, NY 11747-3785. *Phone:* 631-370-3307.
Website: http://www.sbmelville.edu/.

Schenectady County Community College
Schenectady, New York

Freshman Application Contact Mr. David Sampson, Director of Admissions, Schenectady County Community College, 78 Washington Avenue, Schenectady, NY 12305-2294. *Phone:* 518-381-1370. *E-mail:* sampsodg@gw.sunysccc.edu.
Website: http://www.sunysccc.edu/.

Simmons Institute of Funeral Service
Syracuse, New York

Freshman Application Contact Ms. Vera Wightman, Director of Admissions, Simmons Institute of Funeral Service, 1828 South Avenue, Syracuse, NY 13207. *Phone:* 315-475-5142. *Toll-free phone:* 800-727-3536. *Fax:* 315-475-3817. *E-mail:* admissions@simmonsinstitute.com.
Website: http://www.simmonsinstitute.com/.

State University of New York College of Environmental Science and Forestry, Ranger School
Wanakena, New York

- **State-supported** 2-year, founded 1912, part of State University of New York
- **Rural** 2800-acre campus
- **Coed, primarily men**

Undergraduates 58 full-time. Students come from 1 other state; 2% Hispanic/Latino; 2% Asian, non-Hispanic/Latino; 60% transferred in; 100% live on campus.
Faculty *Student/faculty ratio:* 9:1.
Academics *Calendar:* semesters. *Degrees:* associate (The associate degrees offered at The Ranger School campus of SUNY-ESF are 1 + 1 programs enrolling students for the second year of study after they complete their first-year requirements at SUNY-ESF's Syracuse campus or the college of their choice). *Special study options:* advanced placement credit.
Student Life *Campus security:* 24-hour emergency response devices.
Standardized Tests *Required:* SAT or ACT (for admission).
Costs (2012–13) *Tuition:* state resident $5570 full-time, $220 per credit hour part-time; nonresident $15,180 full-time, $597 per credit hour part-time. Full-time tuition and fees vary according to course load and location. Part-time tuition and fees vary according to course load and location. *Required fees:* $1260 full-time. *Room and board:* $10,020; room only: $2720. Room and board charges vary according to housing facility.
Financial Aid Of all full-time matriculated undergraduates who enrolled in 2012, 44 applied for aid, 33 were judged to have need, 17 had their need fully met. 7 Federal Work-Study jobs (averaging $1686). In 2012, 3. *Average percent of need met:* 80. *Average financial aid package:* $10,071. *Average need-based loan:* $4101. *Average need-based gift aid:* $6452. *Average non-need-based aid:* $3667.
Applying *Options:* electronic application, deferred entrance. *Application fee:* $50. *Required:* essay or personal statement, high school transcript, minimum 2.5 GPA. *Recommended:* essay or personal statement, high school transcript, minimum 2.5 GPA, interview.
Freshman Application Contact Ms. Susan Sanford, Director of Admissions, State University of New York College of Environmental Science and Forestry, Ranger School, 1 Forestry Drive, Syracuse, NY 13210-2779. *Phone:* 315-470-6600. *Fax:* 315-470-6933. *E-mail:* esfinfo@esf.edu.
Website: http://www.esf.edu/rangerschool/default.asp.

State University of New York College of Technology at Alfred
Alfred, New York

- **State-supported** primarily 2-year, founded 1908, part of The State University of New York System
- **Rural** 1084-acre campus with easy access to Rochester, Buffalo
- **Endowment** $3.6 million
- **Coed,** 3,527 undergraduate students, 91% full-time, 38% women, 62% men

Undergraduates 3,211 full-time, 316 part-time. Students come from 35 states and territories; 19 other countries; 7% are from out of state; 9% Black or African American, non-Hispanic/Latino; 6% Hispanic/Latino; 2% Asian, non-Hispanic/Latino; 0.1% Native Hawaiian or other Pacific Islander, non-Hispanic/Latino; 0.3% American Indian or Alaska Native, non-His-

panic/Latino; 2% Two or more races, non-Hispanic/Latino; 5% Race/ethnicity unknown; 7% transferred in; 74% live on campus. *Retention:* 81% of full-time freshmen returned.
Freshmen *Admission:* 3,890 applied, 2,136 admitted, 1,109 enrolled. *Average high school GPA:* 2.9.
Faculty *Total:* 219, 83% full-time, 21% with terminal degrees. *Student/faculty ratio:* 18:1.
Majors Accounting technology and bookkeeping; agribusiness; agriculture; agroecology and sustainable agriculture; agronomy and crop science; animal sciences; architectural engineering technology; autobody/collision and repair technology; automotive engineering technology; baking and pastry arts; banking and financial support services; biology/biological sciences; business, management, and marketing related; CAD/CADD drafting/design technology; carpentry; community organization and advocacy; computer and information sciences; computer and information sciences and support services related; computer and information systems security; computer engineering technology; computer hardware technology; computer science; computer systems networking and telecommunications; construction engineering technology; construction trades related; cooking and related culinary arts; court reporting; culinary arts related; dairy science; data processing and data processing technology; design and applied arts related; diesel mechanics technology; digital arts; digital communication and media/multimedia; electrical, electronic and communications engineering technology; electrical/electronics equipment installation and repair; electrician; electromechanical technology; engineering; engineering technologies and engineering related; entrepreneurial and small business related; entrepreneurship; environmental science; finance; finance and financial management services related; financial planning and services; forensic science and technology; health information/medical records technology; heating, air conditioning, ventilation and refrigeration maintenance technology; heating, ventilation, air conditioning and refrigeration engineering technology; heavy equipment maintenance technology; humanities; human resources management; human services; industrial technology; information technology; interior architecture; interior design; liberal arts and sciences/liberal studies; machine tool technology; manufacturing engineering technology; marketing/marketing management; masonry; mechanical drafting and CAD/CADD; mechanical engineering/mechanical technology; merchandising, sales, and marketing operations related (general); network and system administration; plumbing technology; registered nursing/registered nurse; robotics technology; secondary education; sport and fitness administration/management; surveying technology; system, networking, and LAN/WAN management; urban forestry; vehicle maintenance and repair technologies related; veterinary/animal health technology; web/multimedia management and webmaster; welding technology.
Academics *Calendar:* semesters. *Degrees:* certificates, associate, and bachelor's. *Special study options:* academic remediation for entering students, adult/continuing education programs, advanced placement credit, cooperative education, distance learning, double majors, English as a second language, honors programs, independent study, internships, off-campus study, part-time degree program, services for LD students, student-designed majors, study abroad, summer session for credit. *ROTC:* Army (c).
Library Walter C. Hinkle Memorial Library plus 1 other with 61,639 titles, 68,689 serial subscriptions, 4,478 audiovisual materials, an OPAC, a Web page.
Student Life *Housing Options:* coed, men-only, women-only, disabled students. Campus housing is university owned. Freshman campus housing is guaranteed. *Activities and Organizations:* drama/theater group, student-run newspaper, radio station, choral group, Outdoor Recreation Club, International Club, intramural sports, Pioneer Woodsmen Team, Black Student Union. *Campus security:* 24-hour emergency response devices and patrols, late-night transport/escort service, controlled dormitory access, residence hall entrance guards. *Student services:* health clinic, personal/psychological counseling.
Athletics Member NJCAA. *Intercollegiate sports:* baseball M, basketball M(s)/W(s), cross-country running M/W, equestrian sports M/W, football M(s), lacrosse M(s), soccer M/W, softball W, swimming and diving M/W, track and field M/W, volleyball W, wrestling M. *Intramural sports:* basketball M/W, football M(c), golf M/W, ice hockey M(c)/W(c), lacrosse M(c)/W(c), rock climbing M/W, soccer M/W, softball M/W, swimming and diving M(c)/W(c), tennis M/W, ultimate Frisbee M/W, volleyball M/W.
Standardized Tests *Required for some:* SAT or ACT (for admission). *Recommended:* SAT or ACT (for admission).
Costs (2013–14) *One-time required fee:* $100. *Tuition:* state resident $5570 full-time, $232 per credit hour part-time; nonresident $9740 full-time, $406 per credit hour part-time. Full-time tuition and fees vary according to course load and degree level. Part-time tuition and fees vary according to course load and degree level. *Required fees:* $1304 full-time, $53 per credit hour part-time, $10 per credit hour part-time. *Room and board:* $11,160; room only: $6650. Room and board charges vary according to board plan and housing facility. *Payment plan:* installment. *Waivers:* employees or children of employees.
Financial Aid Of all full-time matriculated undergraduates who enrolled in 2010, 3,084 applied for aid, 2,722 were judged to have need, 256 had their

need fully met. 228 Federal Work-Study jobs (averaging $861). In 2010, 99 non-need-based awards were made. *Average percent of need met:* 57%. *Average financial aid package:* $9568. *Average need-based loan:* $3760. *Average need-based gift aid:* $5759. *Average non-need-based aid:* $4307. *Average indebtedness upon graduation:* $29,772.

Applying *Options:* electronic application. *Application fee:* $50. *Required:* high school transcript, minimum 2.0 GPA. *Recommended:* essay or personal statement, interview. *Application deadlines:* rolling (freshmen), rolling (out-of-state freshmen), rolling (transfers). *Notification:* continuous (freshmen), continuous (out-of-state freshmen), continuous (transfers).

Freshman Application Contact Mrs. Deborah Goodrich, Associate Vice President for Enrollment Management, State University of New York College of Technology at Alfred, Huntington Administration Building, 10 Upper College Drive, Alfred, NY 14802. *Phone:* 607-587-4215. *Toll-free phone:* 800-4-ALFRED. *Fax:* 607-587-4299. *E-mail:* admissions@alfredstate.edu. *Website:* http://www.alfredstate.edu/.

Suffolk County Community College
Selden, New York

Freshman Application Contact Suffolk County Community College, 533 College Road, Selden, NY 11784-2899. *Phone:* 631-451-4000. *Website:* http://www.sunysuffolk.edu/.

Sullivan County Community College
Loch Sheldrake, New York

- **State and locally supported** 2-year, founded 1962, part of State University of New York System
- **Rural** 405-acre campus
- **Endowment** $956,148
- **Coed,** 1,614 undergraduate students, 64% full-time, 57% women, 43% men

Undergraduates 1,040 full-time, 574 part-time. Students come from 8 states and territories; 6 other countries; 3% are from out of state; 21% Black or African American, non-Hispanic/Latino; 15% Hispanic/Latino; 1% Asian, non-Hispanic/Latino; 0.4% American Indian or Alaska Native, non-Hispanic/Latino; 15% Race/ethnicity unknown; 0.4% international; 5% transferred in; 22% live on campus.

Freshmen *Admission:* 1,775 applied, 1,717 admitted, 394 enrolled.

Faculty *Total:* 109, 44% full-time, 17% with terminal degrees. *Student/faculty ratio:* 18:1.

Majors Accounting; administrative assistant and secretarial science; baking and pastry arts; business administration and management; commercial and advertising art; computer graphics; computer programming (specific applications); consumer merchandising/retailing management; corrections; culinary arts; data entry/microcomputer applications; electrical, electronic and communications engineering technology; elementary education; environmental studies; hospitality administration; human services; information science/studies; kindergarten/preschool education; legal assistant/paralegal; liberal arts and sciences/liberal studies; marketing/marketing management; mathematics; medical/clinical assistant; photography; radio and television; radio, television, and digital communication related; registered nursing/registered nurse; respiratory care therapy; science technologies related; sport and fitness administration/management; substance abuse/addiction counseling; surveying technology; tourism and travel services management; web/multimedia management and webmaster.

Academics *Calendar:* 4-1-4. *Degree:* certificates and associate. *Special study options:* academic remediation for entering students, adult/continuing education programs, advanced placement credit, distance learning, double majors, honors programs, independent study, internships, part-time degree program, services for LD students, summer session for credit.

Library Hermann Memorial Library plus 1 other with 62,500 titles, 215 serial subscriptions, 8,275 audiovisual materials, an OPAC, a Web page.

Student Life *Housing Options:* coed. Campus housing is provided by a third party. Freshman applicants given priority for college housing. *Activities and Organizations:* student-run newspaper, radio station, Science Alliance, Black Student Union, Gay Straight Alliance, Dance Club, Honor Society. *Campus security:* 24-hour emergency response devices and patrols, student patrols, controlled dormitory access. *Student services:* health clinic, personal/psychological counseling, legal services.

Athletics Member NJCAA. *Intercollegiate sports:* basketball M/W, cheerleading W, cross-country running M/W, golf M, softball W, volleyball W. *Intramural sports:* basketball M/W, bowling M/W, cross-country running M/W, football M, golf M/W, racquetball M/W, skiing (downhill) M/W, soccer M/W, softball M/W, table tennis M/W, tennis M/W, volleyball M/W, weight lifting M/W.

Costs (2013–14) *Tuition:* state resident $4474 full-time, $174 per credit hour part-time; nonresident $8948 full-time, $230 per credit hour part-time. Full-time tuition and fees vary according to program and student level. Part-time tuition and fees vary according to program and student level. *Required fees:* $642 full-time, $67 per credit hour part-time. *Room and board:* $8620; room only: $5600. Room and board charges vary according to board plan and housing facility. *Payment plans:* installment, deferred payment. *Waivers:* senior citizens and employees or children of employees.

Financial Aid Of all full-time matriculated undergraduates who enrolled in 2011, 1,195 applied for aid, 1,195 were judged to have need, 1,192 had their need fully met. 71 Federal Work-Study jobs (averaging $862). 32 state and other part-time jobs (averaging $751). *Average percent of need met:* 100%. *Average financial aid package:* $5788. *Average need-based loan:* $4975. *Average need-based gift aid:* $5788.

Applying *Options:* electronic application, early admission, deferred entrance. *Application fee:* $20. *Required:* high school transcript. *Application deadlines:* rolling (freshmen), rolling (out-of-state freshmen), rolling (transfers). *Notification:* continuous (freshmen), continuous (out-of-state freshmen), continuous (transfers).

Freshman Application Contact Ms. Sari Rosenheck, Director of Admissions and Registration Services, Sullivan County Community College, 112 College Road, Loch Sheldrake, NY 12759. *Phone:* 845-434-5750 Ext. 4200. *Toll-free phone:* 800-577-5243. *Fax:* 845-434-4806. *E-mail:* sarir@sunysullivan.edu. *Website:* http://www.sullivan.suny.edu/.

TCI–The College of Technology
New York, New York

Freshman Application Contact Director of Admission, TCI–The College of Technology, 320 West 31st Street, New York, NY 10001-2705. *Phone:* 212-594-4000. *Toll-free phone:* 800-878-8246. *E-mail:* admissions@tcicollege.edu. *Website:* http://www.tcicollege.edu/.

Tompkins Cortland Community College
Dryden, New York

- **State and locally supported** 2-year, founded 1968, part of State University of New York System
- **Rural** 250-acre campus with easy access to Syracuse
- **Coed,** 5,663 undergraduate students, 52% full-time, 55% women, 45% men

Undergraduates 2,931 full-time, 2,732 part-time. 7% Black or African American, non-Hispanic/Latino; 7% Hispanic/Latino; 1% Asian, non-Hispanic/Latino; 0.1% Native Hawaiian or other Pacific Islander, non-Hispanic/Latino; 0.4% American Indian or Alaska Native, non-Hispanic/Latino; 2% Two or more races, non-Hispanic/Latino; 3% Race/ethnicity unknown; 2% international; 23% live on campus.

Freshmen *Admission:* 1,098 enrolled.

Faculty *Total:* 347, 20% full-time, 14% with terminal degrees. *Student/faculty ratio:* 19:1.

Majors Accounting technology and bookkeeping; administrative assistant and secretarial science; biotechnology; business administration and management; business, management, and marketing related; child-care and support services management; commercial and advertising art; community organization and advocacy; computer and information sciences; computer and information sciences and support services related; construction trades related; creative writing; criminal justice/law enforcement administration; early childhood education; electrical, electronic and communications engineering technology; engineering; forensic science and technology; hotel/motel administration; humanities; information science/studies; international business/trade/commerce; kindergarten/preschool education; legal assistant/paralegal; liberal arts and sciences/liberal studies; natural resources/conservation; parks, recreation and leisure facilities management; parks, recreation, leisure, and fitness studies related; photography; radio and television broadcasting technology; registered nursing/registered nurse; speech communication and rhetoric; sport and fitness administration/management; substance abuse/addiction counseling; web/multimedia management and webmaster.

Academics *Calendar:* semesters. *Degree:* certificates and associate. *Special study options:* academic remediation for entering students, adult/continuing education programs, advanced placement credit, cooperative education, distance learning, double majors, English as a second language, honors programs, independent study, internships, off-campus study, part-time degree program, services for LD students, study abroad, summer session for credit.

Library Gerald A. Barry Memorial Library plus 1 other with 65,386 titles, 200 serial subscriptions, 3,445 audiovisual materials, an OPAC, a Web page.

Student Life *Housing Options:* coed. Campus housing is provided by a third party. *Activities and Organizations:* drama/theater group, College Entertainment Board, Sport Management Club, Nursing Club, Media Club, Writer's Guild. *Campus security:* 24-hour patrols, late-night transport/escort service, controlled dormitory access, Armed peace officers. *Student services:* health clinic, personal/psychological counseling.

Athletics Member NJCAA. *Intercollegiate sports:* baseball M, basketball M/W, golf M/W, lacrosse M, soccer M/W, softball W, volleyball W. *Intramural sports:* archery M/W, badminton M/W, basketball M/W, bowling M/W, football M/W, golf M/W, lacrosse M/W, racquetball M/W, skiing (cross-country) M/W, skiing (downhill) M/W, soccer M/W, softball M/W, squash M/W, swimming and diving M/W, table tennis M/W, tennis M/W, ultimate Frisbee M/W, volleyball M/W, water polo M/W, weight lifting M/W, wrestling M/W.

Costs (2012–13) *Tuition:* state resident $4150 full-time, $147 per credit hour part-time; nonresident $8600 full-time, $304 per credit hour part-time. Part-time tuition and fees vary according to course load. *Required fees:* $721 full-time, $25 per credit hour part-time, $12 per year part-time. *Room and board:* $9290. Room and board charges vary according to board plan and housing facility. *Payment plans:* installment, deferred payment. *Waivers:* employees or children of employees.

Financial Aid Of all full-time matriculated undergraduates who enrolled in 2011, 150 Federal Work-Study jobs (averaging $1000). 150 state and other part-time jobs (averaging $1000).

Applying *Options:* electronic application, early admission, deferred entrance. *Application fee:* $15. *Required:* high school transcript. *Required for some:* essay or personal statement, interview. *Application deadlines:* rolling (freshmen), rolling (out-of-state freshmen), rolling (transfers). *Notification:* continuous (freshmen), continuous (out-of-state freshmen), continuous (transfers).

Freshman Application Contact Mr. Sandy Drumluk, Director of Admissions, Tompkins Cortland Community College, 170 North Street, PO Box 139, Dryden, NY 13053-0139. *Phone:* 607-844-6580. *Toll-free phone:* 888-567-8211. *Fax:* 607-844-6538. *E-mail:* admissions@tc3.edu. *Website:* http://www.TC3.edu/.

Trocaire College

Buffalo, New York

Freshman Application Contact Mrs. Theresa Horner, Director of Records, Trocaire College, 360 Choate Avenue, Buffalo, NY 14220-2094. *Phone:* 716-827-2459. *Fax:* 716-828-6107. *E-mail:* info@trocaire.edu. *Website:* http://www.trocaire.edu/.

Ulster County Community College

Stone Ridge, New York

Freshman Application Contact Admissions Office, Ulster County Community College, 491 Cottekill Road, Stone Ridge, NY 12484. *Phone:* 845-687-5022. *Toll-free phone:* 800-724-0833. *E-mail:* admissionsoffice@sunyulster.edu. *Website:* http://www.sunyulster.edu/.

Utica School of Commerce

Utica, New York

Freshman Application Contact Senior Admissions Coordinator, Utica School of Commerce, 201 Bleecker Street, Utica, NY 13501-2280. *Phone:* 315-733-2300. *Toll-free phone:* 800-321-4USC. *Fax:* 315-733-9281. *Website:* http://www.uscny.edu/.

Westchester Community College

Valhalla, New York

- **State and locally supported** 2-year, founded 1946, part of State University of New York System
- **Suburban** 218-acre campus with easy access to New York City
- **Coed,** 13,997 undergraduate students, 54% full-time, 53% women, 47% men

Undergraduates 7,618 full-time, 6,379 part-time. Students come from 13 states and territories; 40 other countries; 0.5% are from out of state; 21% Black or African American, non-Hispanic/Latino; 28% Hispanic/Latino; 5% Asian, non-Hispanic/Latino; 0.2% Native Hawaiian or other Pacific Islander, non-Hispanic/Latino; 0.7% American Indian or Alaska Native, non-Hispanic/Latino; 1% Two or more races, non-Hispanic/Latino; 7% Race/ethnicity unknown; 7% transferred in.

Freshmen *Admission:* 5,606 applied, 5,358 admitted, 2,715 enrolled.

Faculty *Total:* 1,069, 15% full-time. *Student/faculty ratio:* 18:1.

Majors Accounting; administrative assistant and secretarial science; apparel and textile manufacturing; business administration and management; child development; civil engineering technology; clinical laboratory science/medical technology; clinical/medical laboratory technology; community organization and advocacy; computer and information sciences; computer and information sciences and support services related; computer and information sciences related; computer and information systems security; computer science; computer systems networking and telecommunications; consumer merchandising/retailing management; corrections; culinary arts; dance; data processing and data processing technology; design and applied arts related; dietetics; education (multiple levels); electrical, electronic and communications engineering technology; emergency medical technology (EMT paramedic); energy management and systems technology; engineering science; engineering technology; environmental control technologies related; environmental science; environmental studies; film/video and photographic arts related; finance; fine/studio arts; food technology and processing; humanities; information science/studies; international business/trade/commerce; journalism; legal assistant/paralegal; liberal arts and sciences/liberal studies; marketing/marketing management; mass communication/media; mechanical engineering/mechanical technology; public administration; registered nursing/registered nurse; respiratory care therapy; social sciences; substance abuse/addiction counseling; veterinary/animal health technology.

Academics *Calendar:* semesters. *Degree:* certificates and associate. *Special study options:* academic remediation for entering students, adult/continuing education programs, advanced placement credit, cooperative education, distance learning, double majors, English as a second language, honors programs, independent study, internships, off-campus study, part-time degree program, services for LD students, student-designed majors, study abroad, summer session for credit.

Library Harold L. Drimmer Library plus 1 other with 225,654 titles, 253 serial subscriptions, 4,877 audiovisual materials, an OPAC, a Web page.

Student Life *Housing:* college housing not available. *Activities and Organizations:* drama/theater group, student-run newspaper, radio station, choral group, Deca Fashion Retail, Future Educators, Respiratory Club, Black Student Union, Diversity Action. *Campus security:* 24-hour emergency response devices and patrols, late-night transport/escort service. *Student services:* health clinic, personal/psychological counseling, women's center.

Athletics Member NJCAA. *Intercollegiate sports:* baseball M, basketball M/W, bowling M/W, golf M, soccer M, softball W, volleyball W. *Intramural sports:* badminton M/W, basketball M/W, softball M/W, swimming and diving M/W, tennis M/W, volleyball M/W, weight lifting M/W.

Costs (2013–14) *Tuition:* state resident $4280 full-time, $179 per credit part-time; nonresident $11,770 full-time, $493 per credit part-time. *Required fees:* $423 full-time, $98 per term part-time. *Payment plan:* installment.

Financial Aid Of all full-time matriculated undergraduates who enrolled in 2011, 200 Federal Work-Study jobs (averaging $1000).

Applying *Options:* early admission. *Application fee:* $35. *Required:* high school transcript. *Recommended:* interview. *Application deadlines:* rolling (freshmen), rolling (transfers). *Notification:* continuous until 2/2 (freshmen), continuous (transfers).

Freshman Application Contact Ms. Gloria Leon, Director of Admissions, Westchester Community College, 75 Grasslands Road, Administration Building, Valhalla, NY 10595-1698. *Phone:* 914-606-6735. *Fax:* 914-606-6540. *E-mail:* admissions@sunywcc.edu. *Website:* http://www.sunywcc.edu/.

Wood Tobe–Coburn School

New York, New York

- **Private** 2-year, founded 1879
- **Urban** campus
- **Coed, primarily women,** 617 undergraduate students
- **84%** of applicants were admitted

Freshmen *Admission:* 967 applied, 809 admitted.

Majors Accounting technology and bookkeeping; administrative assistant and secretarial science; computer programming; computer systems networking and telecommunications; fashion/apparel design; graphic design; hotel/motel administration; medical/clinical assistant; retailing.

Academics *Calendar:* semesters. *Degree:* diplomas and associate. *Special study options:* accelerated degree program, internships.

Student Life *Housing:* college housing not available.

Freshman Application Contact Admissions Office, Wood Tobe–Coburn School, 8 East 40th Street, New York, NY 10016. *Phone:* 212-686-9040. *Toll-free phone:* 800-394-9663. *Website:* http://www.woodtobecoburn.edu/.

NORTH CAROLINA

Alamance Community College

Graham, North Carolina

- **State-supported** 2-year, founded 1959, part of North Carolina Community College System
- **Small-town** 48-acre campus
- **Endowment** $2.9 million
- **Coed,** 4,739 undergraduate students, 55% full-time, 36% women, 64% men

Undergraduates 2,607 full-time, 2,132 part-time. Students come from 6 states and territories; 1% are from out of state; 21% Black or African American, non-Hispanic/Latino; 4% Hispanic/Latino; 2% Asian, non-Hispanic/Latino; 1% American Indian or Alaska Native, non-Hispanic/Latino.

Freshmen *Admission:* 646 applied, 646 admitted. *Average high school GPA:* 2.

Faculty *Total:* 435, 26% full-time, 3% with terminal degrees. *Student/faculty ratio:* 12:1.

Majors Accounting technology and bookkeeping; animal sciences; applied horticulture/horticulture operations; automobile/automotive mechanics technology; banking and financial support services; biotechnology; business administration and management; carpentry; clinical/medical laboratory technology; commercial and advertising art; criminal justice/safety; culinary arts; electrical, electronic and communications engineering technology; executive assistant/executive secretary; heating, ventilation, air conditioning and refrigeration engineering technology; information science/studies; kindergarten/preschool education; legal administrative assistant/secretary; liberal arts and sciences/liberal studies; machine tool technology; mechanical engineering/mechanical technology; medical administrative assistant and medical secretary; medical/clinical assistant; office occupations and clerical services; registered nursing/registered nurse; retailing; teacher assistant/aide; welding technology.

Academics *Calendar:* semesters. *Degree:* certificates, diplomas, and associate. *Special study options:* academic remediation for entering students, adult/continuing education programs, cooperative education, distance learning, double majors, English as a second language, independent study, off-campus study, part-time degree program, services for LD students, summer session for credit.

Library Learning Resources Center with 22,114 titles, 185 serial subscriptions, an OPAC, a Web page.

Student Life *Housing:* college housing not available. *Campus security:* 24-hour emergency response devices and patrols, student patrols, late-night transport/escort service. *Student services:* personal/psychological counseling.

Athletics *Intramural sports:* basketball M/W, bowling M/W, tennis M/W, volleyball M/W.

Costs (2012–13) *Tuition:* state resident $2070 full-time; nonresident $7830 full-time. Full-time tuition and fees vary according to course load. Part-time tuition and fees vary according to course load. *Required fees:* $30 full-time. *Waivers:* senior citizens.

Financial Aid Of all full-time matriculated undergraduates who enrolled in 2010, 4,000 applied for aid, 3,000 were judged to have need. 200 Federal Work-Study jobs. *Average percent of need met:* 30%. *Average financial aid package:* $4500. *Average need-based gift aid:* $4500. *Average indebtedness upon graduation:* $2500.

Applying *Options:* electronic application. *Required:* high school transcript. *Application deadlines:* rolling (freshmen), rolling (transfers). *Notification:* continuous (freshmen), continuous (transfers).

Freshman Application Contact Ms. Elizabeth Brehler, Director for Enrollment Management, Alamance Community College, Graham, NC 27253-8000. *Phone:* 336-506-4120. *Fax:* 336-506-4264. *E-mail:* brehlere@alamancecc.edu.
Website: http://www.alamancecc.edu/.

Asheville-Buncombe Technical Community College

Asheville, North Carolina

Freshman Application Contact Asheville-Buncombe Technical Community College, 340 Victoria Road, Asheville, NC 28801-4897. *Phone:* 828-254-1921 Ext. 7520.
Website: http://www.abtech.edu/.

Beaufort County Community College

Washington, North Carolina

- **State-supported** 2-year, founded 1967, part of North Carolina Community College System
- **Rural** 67-acre campus
- **Coed,** 1,933 undergraduate students

Undergraduates 32% Black or African American, non-Hispanic/Latino; 2% Hispanic/Latino; 0.2% Asian, non-Hispanic/Latino; 0.6% American Indian or Alaska Native, non-Hispanic/Latino; 3% Race/ethnicity unknown.

Freshmen *Admission:* 856 applied, 856 admitted.

Majors Accounting; administrative assistant and secretarial science; automobile/automotive mechanics technology; business administration and management; clinical/medical laboratory technology; computer programming; criminal justice/law enforcement administration; criminal justice/police science; drafting and design technology; electrical, electronic and communications engineering technology; heavy equipment maintenance technology; information science/studies; kindergarten/preschool education; liberal arts and sciences/liberal studies; mechanical engineering/mechanical technology; medical office management; registered nursing/registered nurse; welding technology.

Academics *Calendar:* semesters. *Degree:* certificates, diplomas, and associate. *Special study options:* academic remediation for entering students, advanced placement credit, cooperative education, distance learning, English as a second language, part-time degree program, services for LD students, summer session for credit.

Library Beaufort Community College Library with 25,734 titles, 214 serial subscriptions, an OPAC, a Web page.

Student Life *Housing:* college housing not available. *Activities and Organizations:* Student Government Association, Gamma Beta Phi, BECANS-Nursing. *Campus security:* 24-hour emergency response devices and patrols, late-night transport/escort service. *Student services:* personal/psychological counseling.

Standardized Tests *Required:* ACCUPLACER, COMPASS, ASSET (for admission). *Recommended:* SAT or ACT (for admission).

Applying *Options:* electronic application. *Required for some:* high school transcript. *Application deadlines:* rolling (freshmen), rolling (out-of-state freshmen), rolling (transfers).

Freshman Application Contact Mr. Gary Burbage, Director of Admissions, Beaufort County Community College, PO Box 1069, 5337 US Highway 264 East, Washington, NC 27889-1069. *Phone:* 252-940-6233. *Fax:* 252-940-6393. *E-mail:* garyb@beaufortccc.edu.
Website: http://www.beaufortccc.edu/.

Bladen Community College

Dublin, North Carolina

Freshman Application Contact Ms. Andrea Fisher, Enrollment Specialist, Bladen Community College, PO Box 266, Dublin, NC 28332. *Phone:* 910-879-5593. *Fax:* 910-879-5564. *E-mail:* acarterfisher@bladencc.edu.
Website: http://www.bladen.cc.nc.us/.

Blue Ridge Community College

Flat Rock, North Carolina

Freshman Application Contact Blue Ridge Community College, 180 West Campus Drive, Flat Rock, NC 28731. *Phone:* 828-694-1810.
Website: http://www.blueridge.edu/.

Brunswick Community College

Supply, North Carolina

Freshman Application Contact Admissions Counselor, Brunswick Community College, 50 College Road, PO Box 30, Supply, NC 28462-0030. *Phone:* 910-755-7300. *Toll-free phone:* 800-754-1050. *Fax:* 910-754-9609. *E-mail:* admissions@brunswickcc.edu.
Website: http://www.brunswickcc.edu/.

Caldwell Community College and Technical Institute

Hudson, North Carolina

Freshman Application Contact Carolyn Woodard, Director of Enrollment Management Services, Caldwell Community College and Technical Institute, 2855 Hickory Boulevard, Hudson, NC 28638. *Phone:* 828-726-2703. *Fax:* 828-726-2709. *E-mail:* cwoodard@cccti.edu.
Website: http://www.cccti.edu/.

Cape Fear Community College

Wilmington, North Carolina

- **State-supported** 2-year, founded 1959, part of North Carolina Community College System
- **Urban** 150-acre campus
- **Endowment** $5.3 million
- **Coed,** 9,559 undergraduate students, 50% full-time, 54% women, 46% men

Undergraduates 4,771 full-time, 4,788 part-time. Students come from 36 states and territories; 5 other countries; 4% are from out of state; 16% Black or African American, non-Hispanic/Latino; 4% Hispanic/Latino; 1% Asian, non-Hispanic/Latino; 0.9% American Indian or Alaska Native, non-Hispanic/Latino; 4% Race/ethnicity unknown; 8% transferred in.

Freshmen *Admission:* 4,924 applied, 2,404 admitted, 1,856 enrolled.

Faculty *Total:* 1,017, 29% full-time. *Student/faculty ratio:* 8:1.

Majors Accounting technology and bookkeeping; architectural engineering technology; automobile/automotive mechanics technology; building/property maintenance; business administration and management; chemical technology; cinematography and film/video production; computer systems networking and telecommunications; computer technology/computer systems technology; criminal justice/police science; culinary arts; dental hygiene; diagnostic medical sonography and ultrasound technology; early childhood education; electrical, electronic and communications engineering technology; electrical/electronics equipment installation and repair; electromechanical and instrumentation and maintenance technologies related; executive assistant/executive secretary; fire prevention and safety technology; hotel/motel administration; instrumentation technology; interior design; landscaping and groundskeeping; language interpretation and translation; liberal arts and sciences/liberal studies; machine shop technology; marine maintenance and ship repair technology; mechanical engineering/mechanical technology; medical office management; medical radiologic technology; nuclear/nuclear power technology; occupational therapist assistant; oceanography (chemical and physical); registered nursing/registered nurse; surgical technology.

Academics *Calendar:* semesters. *Degree:* certificates, diplomas, and associate. *Special study options:* academic remediation for entering students, adult/continuing education programs, advanced placement credit, cooperative education, distance learning, double majors, English as a second language, independent study, off-campus study, part-time degree program, services for LD students, summer session for credit.

Library Cape Fear Community College Library with 7,951 serial subscriptions, 16,682 audiovisual materials, an OPAC, a Web page.

Student Life *Housing:* college housing not available. *Activities and Organizations:* student-run newspaper, choral group, Nursing Club, Dental Hygiene Club, Pineapple Guild, Phi Theta Kappa, Occupational Therapy. *Campus security:* 24-hour emergency response devices and patrols, late-night transport/escort service, armed police officer. *Student services:* personal/psychological counseling.

Athletics Member NJCAA. *Intercollegiate sports:* basketball M/W, cheerleading M/W, golf M, soccer M/W, volleyball W. *Intramural sports:* basketball M/W, table tennis M/W.

Costs (2012–13) *Tuition:* state resident $2204 full-time, $69 per credit hour part-time; nonresident $8352 full-time, $261 per credit hour part-time. Full-time tuition and fees vary according to course load. Part-time tuition and fees vary according to course load. *Required fees:* $137 full-time. *Payment plans:* installment, deferred payment. *Waivers:* senior citizens.

Financial Aid Of all full-time matriculated undergraduates who enrolled in 2011, 118 Federal Work-Study jobs (averaging $1550).

Applying *Options:* electronic application, early admission. *Required for some:* high school transcript, interview, placement testing. *Application deadlines:* 8/20 (freshmen), rolling (transfers). *Notification:* continuous (freshmen), continuous (transfers).

Freshman Application Contact Ms. Linda Kasyan, Director of Enrollment Management, Cape Fear Community College, 411 North Front Street, Wilmington, NC 28401-3993. *Phone:* 910-362-7054. *Toll-free phone:* 877-799-2322. *Fax:* 910-362-7080. *E-mail:* admissions@cfcc.edu. *Website:* http://www.cfcc.edu/.

Carolinas College of Health Sciences

Charlotte, North Carolina

- **Public** 2-year, founded 1990
- **Urban** 3-acre campus with easy access to Charlotte
- **Endowment** $1.8 million
- **Coed,** 438 undergraduate students, 13% full-time, 86% women, 14% men

Undergraduates 58 full-time, 380 part-time. Students come from 4 states and territories; 6% are from out of state; 9% Black or African American, non-Hispanic/Latino; 4% Hispanic/Latino; 2% Asian, non-Hispanic/Latino; 0.7%

Native Hawaiian or other Pacific Islander, non-Hispanic/Latino; 0.5% American Indian or Alaska Native, non-Hispanic/Latino; 3% Two or more races, non-Hispanic/Latino; 3% Race/ethnicity unknown.

Freshmen *Admission:* 14 enrolled. *Average high school GPA:* 3.5.

Faculty *Total:* 71, 37% full-time. *Student/faculty ratio:* 11:1.

Majors Medical radiologic technology; radiologic technology/science; registered nursing/registered nurse.

Academics *Calendar:* semesters. *Degree:* certificates, diplomas, and associate. *Special study options:* advanced placement credit, distance learning, double majors, honors programs, independent study, services for LD students, summer session for credit.

Library AHEC Library with 9,810 titles, 503 serial subscriptions, an OPAC, a Web page.

Student Life *Housing Options:* Campus housing is provided by a third party. *Campus security:* 24-hour emergency response devices and patrols, late-night transport/escort service. *Student services:* health clinic, personal/psychological counseling.

Standardized Tests *Required for some:* SAT or ACT (for admission).

Costs (2013–14) *Tuition:* state resident $11,760 full-time, $308 per credit hour part-time; nonresident $11,760 full-time, $308 per credit hour part-time. Full-time tuition and fees vary according to course load and program. Part-time tuition and fees vary according to course load and program. *Required fees:* $1215 full-time, $125 per term part-time. *Waivers:* employees or children of employees.

Financial Aid Of all full-time matriculated undergraduates who enrolled in 2011, 11 Federal Work-Study jobs (averaging $4500).

Applying *Options:* electronic application. *Application fee:* $50. *Required:* minimum 2.5 GPA. *Required for some:* high school transcript, 1 letter of recommendation, interview, SAT or ACT Test Scores.

Freshman Application Contact Ms. Nicki Sabourin, Admissions Representative, Carolinas College of Health Sciences, 1200 Blythe Boulevard, Charlotte, NC 28203. *Phone:* 704-355-5043. *Fax:* 704-355-9336. *E-mail:* cchsinformation@carolinashealthcare.org. *Website:* http://www.carolinascollege.edu/.

Carteret Community College

Morehead City, North Carolina

Freshman Application Contact Ms. Margie Ward, Admissions Officer, Carteret Community College, 3505 Arendell Street, Morehead City, NC 28557-2989. *Phone:* 252-222-6155. *Fax:* 252-222-6265. *E-mail:* admissions@carteret.edu. *Website:* http://www.carteret.edu/.

Catawba Valley Community College

Hickory, North Carolina

- **State and locally supported** 2-year, founded 1960, part of North Carolina Community College System
- **Small-town** 50-acre campus with easy access to Charlotte
- **Endowment** $1.3 million
- **Coed,** 5,099 undergraduate students, 37% full-time, 59% women, 41% men

Undergraduates 1,910 full-time, 3,189 part-time. Students come from 9 states and territories; 9% Black or African American, non-Hispanic/Latino; 6% Hispanic/Latino; 8% Asian, non-Hispanic/Latino; 0.1% Native Hawaiian or other Pacific Islander, non-Hispanic/Latino; 0.7% American Indian or Alaska Native, non-Hispanic/Latino; 0.4% Two or more races, non-Hispanic/Latino; 3% Race/ethnicity unknown; 0.1% international; 25% transferred in.

Freshmen *Admission:* 1,867 applied, 1,842 admitted, 1,012 enrolled. *Average high school GPA:* 2.95.

Faculty *Total:* 542, 29% full-time. *Student/faculty ratio:* 10:1.

Majors Accounting technology and bookkeeping; applied horticulture/horticulture operations; architectural engineering technology; automobile/automotive mechanics technology; banking and financial support services; business administration and management; commercial and advertising art; computer engineering technology; computer programming; criminal justice/safety; customer service management; cyber/computer forensics and counterterrorism; dental hygiene; early childhood education; e-commerce; electrical, electronic and communications engineering technology; electromechanical and instrumentation and maintenance technologies related; electroneurodiagnostic/electroencephalographic technology; emergency medical technology (EMT paramedic); fire prevention and safety technology; forensic science and technology; general studies; health information/medical records technology; information technology; liberal arts and sciences/liberal studies; mechanical engineering/mechanical technology; medical office management; medical radiologic technology; office management; photographic and film/video technology; polysomnography; registered nursing/registered nurse; respiratory care therapy; system, networking, and LAN/WAN management; turf and turf-grass management.

Academics *Calendar:* semesters. *Degree:* certificates, diplomas, and associate. *Special study options:* academic remediation for entering students, adult/continuing education programs, advanced placement credit, cooperative education, distance learning, double majors, English as a second language, independent study, part-time degree program, services for LD students, student-designed majors, summer session for credit.

Library Learning Resource Center with 27,000 titles, 1,250 serial subscriptions, 700 audiovisual materials, an OPAC, a Web page.

Student Life *Housing:* college housing not available. *Activities and Organizations:* drama/theater group, choral group, Campus Crusade for Christ, Emerging Entrepreneur, Rotaract, Circle K, Skills USA. *Campus security:* 24-hour patrols. *Student services:* personal/psychological counseling.

Athletics Member NJCAA. *Intercollegiate sports:* baseball M, basketball M/W, cheerleading M/W, volleyball W.

Standardized Tests *Required:* COMPASS test series (for admission).

Costs (2012–13) *Tuition:* state resident $1656 full-time, $69 per credit hour part-time; nonresident $6264 full-time, $261 per credit part-time. Part-time tuition and fees vary according to course load. *Required fees:* $87 full-time, $5 per credit hour part-time, $11 per term part-time. *Payment plan:* installment. *Waivers:* senior citizens.

Applying *Options:* electronic application. *Required:* high school transcript. *Required for some:* 1 letter of recommendation. *Application deadlines:* rolling (freshmen), rolling (out-of-state freshmen), rolling (transfers). *Notification:* continuous (freshmen), continuous (out-of-state freshmen), continuous (transfers).

Freshman Application Contact Catawba Valley Community College, 2550 Highway 70 SE, Hickory, NC 28602-9699. *Phone:* 828-327-7000 Ext. 4618. *Website:* http://www.cvcc.edu/.

Central Carolina Community College
Sanford, North Carolina

- **State and locally supported** 2-year, founded 1962, part of North Carolina Community College System
- **Small-town** 41-acre campus
- **Endowment** $3.0 million
- **Coed,** 4,900 undergraduate students, 44% full-time, 66% women, 34% men

Undergraduates 2,138 full-time, 2,762 part-time. Students come from 36 states and territories; 6% are from out of state; 23% Black or African American, non-Hispanic/Latino; 9% Hispanic/Latino; 0.7% Asian, non-Hispanic/Latino; 0.1% Native Hawaiian or other Pacific Islander, non-Hispanic/Latino; 0.8% American Indian or Alaska Native, non-Hispanic/Latino; 1% Two or more races, non-Hispanic/Latino; 0.5% Race/ethnicity unknown; 0.4% international.

Freshmen *Admission:* 1,130 enrolled.

Faculty *Total:* 1,050, 35% full-time.

Majors Accounting; administrative assistant and secretarial science; automobile/automotive mechanics technology; business administration and management; computer/information technology services administration related; computer programming; computer programming (specific applications); computer systems networking and telecommunications; criminal justice/law enforcement administration; drafting and design technology; electrical, electronic and communications engineering technology; information science/studies; information technology; instrumentation technology; kindergarten/preschool education; laser and optical technology; legal administrative assistant/secretary; legal assistant/paralegal; liberal arts and sciences/liberal studies; marketing/marketing management; medical administrative assistant and medical secretary; medical/clinical assistant; operations management; quality control technology; radio and television; registered nursing/registered nurse; social work; telecommunications technology; veterinary/animal health technology.

Academics *Calendar:* semesters. *Degree:* certificates, diplomas, and associate. *Special study options:* academic remediation for entering students, adult/continuing education programs, advanced placement credit, distance learning, double majors, English as a second language, independent study, internships, part-time degree program, services for LD students, summer session for credit.

Library Library/Learning Resources Center plus 2 others with 50,479 titles, 240 serial subscriptions, 5,946 audiovisual materials, an OPAC, a Web page.

Student Life *Housing:* college housing not available. *Activities and Organizations:* student-run radio station. *Campus security:* 24-hour emergency response devices and patrols, student patrols, patrols by trained security personnel during operating hours. *Student services:* personal/psychological counseling.

Athletics Member NJCAA. *Intercollegiate sports:* basketball M/W, golf M/W, softball W, volleyball W. *Intramural sports:* bowling M/W, golf M/W, softball W, volleyball W.

Financial Aid Of all full-time matriculated undergraduates who enrolled in 2011, 70 Federal Work-Study jobs (averaging $1361). *Financial aid deadline:* 5/4.

Applying *Options:* electronic application, early admission, deferred entrance. *Required:* high school transcript. *Application deadlines:* rolling (freshmen), rolling (transfers). *Notification:* continuous (freshmen), continuous (transfers).

Freshman Application Contact Mrs. Jamie Tyson Childress, Dean of Enrollment/Registrar, Central Carolina Community College, 1105 Kelly Drive, Sanford, NC 27330-9000. *Phone:* 919-718-7239. *Toll-free phone:* 800-682-8353. *Fax:* 919-718-7380.
Website: http://www.cccc.edu/.

Central Piedmont Community College
Charlotte, North Carolina

Freshman Application Contact Ms. Linda McComb, Associate Dean, Central Piedmont Community College, PO Box 35009, Charlotte, NC 28235-5009. *Phone:* 704-330-6784. *Fax:* 704-330-6136.
Website: http://www.cpcc.edu/.

Cleveland Community College
Shelby, North Carolina

- **State-supported** 2-year, founded 1965, part of North Carolina Community College System
- **Small-town** 43-acre campus with easy access to Charlotte
- **Coed,** 3,398 undergraduate students, 51% full-time, 63% women, 37% men

Undergraduates 1,736 full-time, 1,662 part-time. 24% Black or African American, non-Hispanic/Latino; 2% Hispanic/Latino; 0.4% Asian, non-Hispanic/Latino; 0.4% American Indian or Alaska Native, non-Hispanic/Latino; 1% Two or more races, non-Hispanic/Latino; 2% Race/ethnicity unknown; 0.7% international.

Freshmen *Admission:* 4,355 applied, 4,297 admitted, 464 enrolled.

Faculty *Student/faculty ratio:* 10:1.

Majors Accounting; banking and financial support services; biology/biotechnology laboratory technician; business administration and management; computer and information systems security; computer systems networking and telecommunications; criminal justice/safety; early childhood education; electrical, electronic and communications engineering technology; electrician; elementary education; emergency medical technology (EMT paramedic); entrepreneurship; fire prevention and safety technology; general studies; information science/studies; information technology; language interpretation and translation; legal administrative assistant/secretary; liberal arts and sciences and humanities related; liberal arts and sciences/liberal studies; marketing/marketing management; mechanical drafting and CAD/CADD; medical/clinical assistant; medical office management; office management; operations management; pre-engineering; prenursing studies; radio and television broadcasting technology; radiologic technology/science; registered nursing/registered nurse.

Academics *Calendar:* semesters. *Degree:* certificates, diplomas, and associate. *Special study options:* academic remediation for entering students, adult/continuing education programs, advanced placement credit, cooperative education, distance learning, double majors, English as a second language, independent study, off-campus study, part-time degree program, summer session for credit.

Library Jim & Patsy Rose Library with an OPAC, a Web page.

Student Life *Housing:* college housing not available. *Activities and Organizations:* drama/theater group, student-run television station. *Campus security:* security personnel during open hours. *Student services:* personal/psychological counseling.

Costs (2013–14) *Tuition:* state resident $2128 full-time; nonresident $8272 full-time. *Required fees:* $94 full-time.

Financial Aid Of all full-time matriculated undergraduates who enrolled in 2011, 20 Federal Work-Study jobs.

Applying *Options:* electronic application, deferred entrance. *Required:* high school transcript. *Application deadlines:* rolling (freshmen), rolling (transfers). *Notification:* continuous (freshmen), continuous (transfers).

Freshman Application Contact Cleveland Community College, 137 South Post Road, Shelby, NC 28152. *Phone:* 704-669-4139.
Website: http://www.clevelandcc.edu/.

Coastal Carolina Community College
Jacksonville, North Carolina

Freshman Application Contact Ms. Heather Calihan, Counseling Coordinator, Coastal Carolina Community College, Jacksonville, NC 28546. *Phone:* 910-938-6241. *Fax:* 910-455-2767. *E-mail:* calihanh@

coastal.cc.nc.us.
Website: http://www.coastalcarolina.edu/.

College of The Albemarle
Elizabeth City, North Carolina

Freshman Application Contact Mr. Kenny Krentz, Director of Admissions and International Students, College of The Albemarle, PO Box 2327, Elizabeth City, NC 27906-2327. *Phone:* 252-335-0821. *Fax:* 252-335-2011. *E-mail:* kkrentz@albemarle.edu.
Website: http://www.albemarle.edu/.

Craven Community College
New Bern, North Carolina

Freshman Application Contact Ms. Millicent Fulford, Recruiter, Craven Community College, 800 College Court, New Bern, NC 28562-4984. *Phone:* 252-638-7232.
Website: http://www.cravencc.edu/.

Davidson County Community College
Lexington, North Carolina

Freshman Application Contact Davidson County Community College, PO Box 1287, Lexington, NC 27293-1287. *Phone:* 336-249-8186 Ext. 6715. *Fax:* 336-224-0240. *E-mail:* admissions@davidsonccc.edu.
Website: http://www.davidsonccc.edu/.

Durham Technical Community College
Durham, North Carolina

Director of Admissions Ms. Penny Augustine, Director of Admissions and Testing, Durham Technical Community College, 1637 Lawson Street, Durham, NC 27703-5023. *Phone:* 919-686-3619.
Website: http://www.durhamtech.edu/.

ECPI College of Technology
Charlotte, North Carolina

Admissions Office Contact ECPI College of Technology, 4800 Airport Center Parkway, Charlotte, NC 28208. *Toll-free phone:* 866-708-6167.
Website: http://www.ecpi.edu/.

ECPI College of Technology
Greensboro, North Carolina

Admissions Office Contact ECPI College of Technology, 7802 Airport Center Drive, Greensboro, NC 27409. *Toll-free phone:* 866-708-6170.
Website: http://www.ecpi.edu/.

Edgecombe Community College
Tarboro, North Carolina

Freshman Application Contact Ms. Jackie Heath, Admissions Officer, Edgecombe Community College, 2009 West Wilson Street, Tarboro, NC 27886-9399. *Phone:* 252-823-5166 Ext. 254.
Website: http://www.edgecombe.edu/.

Fayetteville Technical Community College
Fayetteville, North Carolina

- **State-supported** 2-year, founded 1961, part of North Carolina Community College System
- **Suburban** 209-acre campus with easy access to Raleigh
- **Endowment** $39,050
- **Coed,** 12,594 undergraduate students, 41% full-time, 61% women, 39% men

Undergraduates 5,197 full-time, 7,397 part-time. Students come from 45 states and territories; 43 other countries; 21% are from out of state; 44% Black or African American, non-Hispanic/Latino; 9% Hispanic/Latino; 1% Asian, non-Hispanic/Latino; 0.4% Native Hawaiian or other Pacific Islander, non-Hispanic/Latino; 3% American Indian or Alaska Native, non-Hispanic/Latino; 3% Two or more races, non-Hispanic/Latino; 3% Race/ethnicity unknown; 0.8% international; 21% transferred in.

Freshmen *Admission:* 4,263 applied, 4,263 admitted, 2,032 enrolled. *Average high school GPA:* 2.49.
Faculty *Total:* 496, 54% full-time, 8% with terminal degrees. *Student/faculty ratio:* 16:1.
Majors Accounting; applied horticulture/horticulture operations; architectural engineering technology; automobile/automotive mechanics technology; banking and financial support services; building/construction finishing, management, and inspection related; business administration and management; civil engineering technology; commercial and advertising art; computer and information systems security; computer programming; computer systems networking and telecommunications; corrections and criminal justice related; criminal justice/safety; crisis/emergency/disaster management; culinary arts; dental hygiene; early childhood education; electrical, electronic and communications engineering technology; electrician; elementary education; emergency medical technology (EMT paramedic); fire prevention and safety technology; forensic science and technology; funeral service and mortuary science; game and interactive media design; heating, air conditioning, ventilation and refrigeration maintenance technology; hotel, motel, and restaurant management; human resources management; information science/studies; information technology; legal assistant/paralegal; liberal arts and sciences and humanities related; liberal arts and sciences/liberal studies; machine shop technology; marketing/marketing management; medical office management; nuclear medical technology; office management; operations management; pharmacy technician; physical therapy technology; public administration; radiologic technology/science; registered nursing/registered nurse; respiratory care therapy; speech-language pathology assistant; surgical technology; surveying technology.
Academics *Calendar:* semesters. *Degree:* certificates, diplomas, and associate. *Special study options:* academic remediation for entering students, accelerated degree program, adult/continuing education programs, advanced placement credit, cooperative education, distance learning, double majors, English as a second language, independent study, internships, off-campus study, part-time degree program, services for LD students, summer session for credit.
Library Paul H. Thompson Library plus 1 other with 67,997 titles, 329 serial subscriptions, 594 audiovisual materials, an OPAC, a Web page.
Student Life *Housing:* college housing not available. *Activities and Organizations:* Parents for Higher Education, Early Childhood Club, Phi Beta Lambda, Association of Nursing Students, African/American Heritage Club. *Campus security:* 24-hour emergency response devices and patrols, late-night transport/escort service, Campus-wide emergency notification system. *Student services:* personal/psychological counseling.
Athletics *Intramural sports:* basketball M/W, bowling M/W, football M/W, soccer M/W, softball M/W, tennis M/W, volleyball M/W.
Standardized Tests *Required:* ACCUPLACER is required or ACT and SAT scores in lieu of ACCUPLACER if the scores are no more than 5 years old or ASSET and COMPASS scores are also accepted if they are no more than 3 years old (for admission).
Costs (2012–13) *One-time required fee:* $25. *Tuition:* state resident $2208 full-time, $69 per credit hour part-time; nonresident $8352 full-time, $261 per credit hour part-time. Full-time tuition and fees vary according to course load. Part-time tuition and fees vary according to course load. *Required fees:* $180 full-time, $90 per term part-time. *Payment plan:* installment. *Waivers:* senior citizens and employees or children of employees.
Financial Aid Of all full-time matriculated undergraduates who enrolled in 2011, 75 Federal Work-Study jobs (averaging $2000). *Financial aid deadline:* 6/1.
Applying *Options:* electronic application. *Required for some:* essay or personal statement, high school transcript, interview. *Application deadlines:* rolling (freshmen), rolling (out-of-state freshmen), rolling (transfers). *Notification:* continuous (freshmen), continuous (out-of-state freshmen), continuous (transfers).
Freshman Application Contact Ms. Melissa Ann Jones, Registrar/Curriculum, Fayetteville Technical Community College, 2201 Hull Road, Fayetteville, NC 28303. *Phone:* 910-678-8474. *Fax:* 910-678-0085. *E-mail:* jonesma@faytechcc.edu.
Website: http://www.faytechcc.edu/.

Forsyth Technical Community College
Winston-Salem, North Carolina

- **State-supported** 2-year, founded 1964, part of North Carolina Community College System
- **Suburban** 38-acre campus
- **Coed,** 9,941 undergraduate students, 47% full-time, 61% women, 39% men

Undergraduates 4,639 full-time, 5,302 part-time. 1% are from out of state; 26% transferred in.

Freshmen *Admission:* 1,711 enrolled.
Faculty *Total:* 729, 30% full-time. *Student/faculty ratio:* 17:1.
Majors Accounting; allied health diagnostic, intervention, and treatment professions related; animation, interactive technology, video graphics and special effects; applied horticulture/horticultural business services related; architectural engineering technology; automobile/automotive mechanics technology; biology/biotechnology laboratory technician; biophysics; business administration and management; cardiovascular science; cardiovascular technology; clinical/medical laboratory technology; communication sciences and disorders; computer and information sciences; computer engineering technology; computer hardware technology; computer programming; computer systems networking and telecommunications; criminal justice/safety; diagnostic medical sonography and ultrasound technology; early childhood education; e-commerce; electrical, electronic and communications engineering technology; emergency medical technology (EMT paramedic); fire prevention and safety technology; forensic science and technology; general studies; graphic design; health information/medical records administration; health professions related; human services; industrial technology; information science/studies; information technology; interior design; international business/trade/commerce; legal assistant/paralegal; liberal arts and sciences/liberal studies; logistics, materials, and supply chain management; machine shop technology; massage therapy; mechanical engineering/mechanical technology; medical/clinical assistant; medical office management; medical radiologic technology; nuclear medical technology; office management; radiologic technology/science; registered nursing/registered nurse.
Academics *Calendar:* semesters. *Degree:* certificates, diplomas, and associate. *Special study options:* academic remediation for entering students, adult/continuing education programs, advanced placement credit, cooperative education, distance learning, double majors, English as a second language, independent study, internships, part-time degree program, services for LD students, summer session for credit.
Library Forsyth Technical Community College Library plus 1 other with an OPAC, a Web page.
Student Life *Housing:* college housing not available. *Activities and Organizations:* student-run newspaper. *Campus security:* 24-hour emergency response devices and patrols, late-night transport/escort service. *Student services:* personal/psychological counseling, women's center.
Standardized Tests *Required:* COMPASS (for admission).
Costs (2012–13) *Tuition:* state resident $2208 full-time, $69 per credit hour part-time; nonresident $7952 full-time, $261 per credit hour part-time. Full-time tuition and fees vary according to course load. Part-time tuition and fees vary according to course load. *Required fees:* $30 full-time, $30 per term part-time. *Payment plan:* installment. *Waivers:* senior citizens.
Financial Aid Of all full-time matriculated undergraduates who enrolled in 2011, 42 Federal Work-Study jobs (averaging $2083).
Applying *Required:* high school transcript.
Freshman Application Contact Admissions Office, Forsyth Technical Community College, 2100 Silas Creek Parkway, Winston-Salem, NC 27103-5197. *Phone:* 336-734-7556. *E-mail:* admissions@forsythtech.edu. *Website:* http://www.forsythtech.edu/.

Gaston College

Dallas, North Carolina

Freshman Application Contact Terry Basier, Director of Enrollment Management and Admissions, Gaston College, 201 Highway 321 South, Dallas, NC 28034. *Phone:* 704-922-6214. *Fax:* 704-922-6443. *Website:* http://www.gaston.edu/.

Guilford Technical Community College

Jamestown, North Carolina

- **State and locally supported** 2-year, founded 1958, part of North Carolina Community College System
- **Urban** 158-acre campus with easy access to Raleigh, Charlotte, Greensboro
- **Coed,** 14,793 undergraduate students, 53% full-time, 57% women, 43% men

Undergraduates 7,903 full-time, 6,890 part-time. Students come from 10 states and territories; 98 other countries; 0.1% are from out of state; 46% Black or African American, non-Hispanic/Latino; 5% Hispanic/Latino; 3% Asian, non-Hispanic/Latino; 0.1% Native Hawaiian or other Pacific Islander, non-Hispanic/Latino; 0.8% American Indian or Alaska Native, non-Hispanic/Latino; 1% Two or more races, non-Hispanic/Latino; 3% Race/ethnicity unknown; 0.7% international; 9% transferred in. *Retention:* 52% of full-time freshmen returned.
Freshmen *Admission:* 9,181 applied, 9,181 admitted, 2,921 enrolled. *Average high school GPA:* 2.39.

Faculty *Total:* 1,044, 38% full-time, 6% with terminal degrees. *Student/faculty ratio:* 24:1.
Majors Accounting technology and bookkeeping; agricultural power machinery operation; airline pilot and flight crew; architectural engineering technology; automobile/automotive mechanics technology; avionics maintenance technology; biology/biotechnology laboratory technician; building/property maintenance; business administration and management; chemical technology; civil engineering technology; commercial and advertising art; computer programming; computer systems analysis; computer systems networking and telecommunications; cosmetology; criminal justice/safety; culinary arts; dental hygiene; early childhood education; education related; electrical, electronic and communications engineering technology; electrician; electromechanical technology; emergency medical technology (EMT paramedic); fire prevention and safety technology; general studies; heating, air conditioning, ventilation and refrigeration maintenance technology; hotel/motel administration; human resources management; industrial production technologies related; information science/studies; information technology; legal assistant/paralegal; liberal arts and sciences and humanities related; liberal arts and sciences/liberal studies; logistics, materials, and supply chain management; machine shop technology; mechanical engineering/mechanical technology; medical/clinical assistant; medical office management; office management; pharmacy technician; physical therapy technology; psychiatric/mental health services technology; recording arts technology; registered nursing/registered nurse; substance abuse/addiction counseling; surgical technology; surveying technology; system, networking, and LAN/WAN management; telecommunications technology; turf and turfgrass management; vehicle maintenance and repair technologies related.
Academics *Calendar:* semesters. *Degree:* certificates, diplomas, and associate. *Special study options:* academic remediation for entering students, adult/continuing education programs, advanced placement credit, cooperative education, distance learning, double majors, English as a second language, external degree program, independent study, internships, off-campus study, part-time degree program, services for LD students, student-designed majors, summer session for credit. *ROTC:* Army (c), Air Force (c).
Library M. W. Bell Library plus 2 others with 113,818 titles, 13,821 serial subscriptions, 4,723 audiovisual materials, an OPAC, a Web page.
Student Life *Housing:* college housing not available. *Activities and Organizations:* drama/theater group, International Students Association, Steppin' N Style, Surgical Technology, Rotaract, Fellowship of Christian Athletes, national sororities. *Campus security:* 24-hour emergency response devices and patrols, late-night transport/escort service. *Student services:* personal/psychological counseling.
Athletics Member NJCAA. *Intercollegiate sports:* baseball M(s), basketball M(s)/W(s), cheerleading M/W, volleyball W(s).
Costs (2013–14) *Tuition:* state resident $1656 full-time, $69 per credit hour part-time; nonresident $6264 full-time, $261 per credit hour part-time. Full-time tuition and fees vary according to course load and program. Part-time tuition and fees vary according to course load and program. *Required fees:* $167 full-time, $49 per term part-time. *Payment plan:* deferred payment. *Waivers:* senior citizens and employees or children of employees.
Applying *Options:* electronic application, early admission, deferred entrance. *Required for some:* high school transcript, interview. *Application deadlines:* rolling (freshmen), rolling (transfers). *Notification:* continuous (freshmen), continuous (transfers).
Freshman Application Contact Guilford Technical Community College, PO Box 309, Jamestown, NC 27282-0309. *Phone:* 336-334-4822 Ext. 50125. *Website:* http://www.gtcc.edu/.

Halifax Community College

Weldon, North Carolina

- **State and locally supported** 2-year, founded 1967, part of North Carolina Community College System
- **Rural** 109-acre campus
- **Endowment** $1.1 million
- **Coed,** 1,142 undergraduate students

Undergraduates 57% Black or African American, non-Hispanic/Latino; 2% Hispanic/Latino; 0.2% Asian, non-Hispanic/Latino; 2% American Indian or Alaska Native, non-Hispanic/Latino; 1% Two or more races, non-Hispanic/Latino; 2% Race/ethnicity unknown.
Majors Accounting; applied horticulture/horticulture operations; business administration and management; clinical/medical laboratory technology; clinical/medical social work; commercial and advertising art; computer systems networking and telecommunications; criminal justice/police science; dental hygiene; early childhood education; e-commerce; electrical, electronic and communications engineering technology; electromechanical and instrumentation and maintenance technologies related; elementary education; health professions related; information technology; interior design; legal assistant/paralegal; liberal arts and sciences and humanities related; liberal arts and sciences/liberal studies; medical administrative assistant and medical sec-

retary; office management; registered nursing/registered nurse; wood science and wood products/pulp and paper technology.

Academics *Calendar:* semesters. *Degree:* certificates, diplomas, and associate. *Special study options:* academic remediation for entering students, adult/continuing education programs, cooperative education, part-time degree program, summer session for credit.

Library Halifax Community College Library with 33,267 titles, 101 serial subscriptions, 2,195 audiovisual materials, an OPAC, a Web page.

Student Life *Housing:* college housing not available. *Campus security:* 12-hour patrols by trained security personnel.

Costs (2013–14) *Tuition:* state resident $1163 full-time, $69 per credit part-time; nonresident $4235 full-time, $261 per credit part-time.

Applying *Options:* deferred entrance. *Required:* high school transcript. *Application deadlines:* rolling (freshmen), rolling (transfers). *Notification:* continuous (freshmen), continuous (transfers).

Freshman Application Contact Halifax Community College, PO Drawer 809, Weldon, NC 27890-0809. *Phone:* 252-536-7220.
Website: http://www.halifaxcc.edu/.

Harrison College
Morrisville, North Carolina

- **Proprietary** 2-year, founded 2011, part of This campus is part of Harrison College, which has several campuses in Indiana and one in Ohio
- **Suburban** campus with easy access to Raleigh, NC
- **Coed,** 192 undergraduate students, 86% full-time, 49% women, 51% men

Undergraduates 165 full-time, 27 part-time. Students come from 2 states and territories; 0.5% are from out of state; 49% Black or African American, non-Hispanic/Latino; 6% Hispanic/Latino; 0.5% Asian, non-Hispanic/Latino; 0.5% Native Hawaiian or other Pacific Islander, non-Hispanic/Latino; 5% Two or more races, non-Hispanic/Latino; 2% Race/ethnicity unknown; 13% transferred in. *Retention:* 33% of full-time freshmen returned.

Freshmen *Admission:* 46 applied, 46 admitted, 24 enrolled.

Faculty *Total:* 19, 42% full-time. *Student/faculty ratio:* 16:1.

Academics *Degree:* associate. *Special study options:* adult/continuing education programs, advanced placement credit, cooperative education, distance learning, double majors, internships, off-campus study, part-time degree program, summer session for credit.

Library North Carolina Learning Resource Center.

Student Life *Housing:* college housing not available.

Standardized Tests *Required:* Wonderlic Scholastic Level Exam (SLE) (for admission).

Applying *Options:* electronic application. *Application fee:* $50. *Required:* high school transcript, interview. *Application deadlines:* rolling (freshmen), rolling (out-of-state freshmen), rolling (transfers). *Notification:* continuous (freshmen), continuous (out-of-state freshmen), continuous (transfers).

Freshman Application Contact Mr. Jason Howanec, Vice President of Enrollment, Harrison College, 500 N. Meridian St., Indianapolis, IN 46204. *Phone:* 800-919-2500. *E-mail:* Admissions@harrison.edu.
Website: http://www.harrison.edu/.

Haywood Community College
Clyde, North Carolina

Director of Admissions Ms. Debbie Rowland, Coordinator of Admissions, Haywood Community College, 185 Freedlander Drive, Clyde, NC 28721-9453. *Phone:* 828-627-4505. *Toll-free phone:* 866-GOTOHCC.
Website: http://www.haywood.edu/.

Isothermal Community College
Spindale, North Carolina

Freshman Application Contact Ms. Vickie Searcy, Enrollment Management Office, Isothermal Community College, PO Box 804, Spindale, NC 28160-0804. *Phone:* 828-286-3636 Ext. 251. *Fax:* 828-286-8109. *E-mail:* vsearcy@isothermal.edu.
Website: http://www.isothermal.edu/.

ITT Technical Institute
Cary, North Carolina

- **Proprietary** primarily 2-year, part of ITT Educational Services, Inc.
- **Coed**

Academics *Degrees:* associate and bachelor's.

Freshman Application Contact Director of Recruitment, ITT Technical Institute, 5520 Dillard Drive, Suite 100, Cary, NC 27518. *Phone:* 919-233-2520. *Toll-free phone:* 877-203-5533.
Website: http://www.itt-tech.edu/.

ITT Technical Institute
Charlotte, North Carolina

- **Proprietary** primarily 2-year
- **Coed**

Academics *Degrees:* associate and bachelor's.

Freshman Application Contact Director of Recruitment, ITT Technical Institute, 4135 Southstream Boulevard, Suite 200, Charlotte, NC 28217. *Phone:* 704-423-3100. *Toll-free phone:* 800-488-0173.
Website: http://www.itt-tech.edu/.

ITT Technical Institute
High Point, North Carolina

- **Proprietary** primarily 2-year, founded 2007, part of ITT Educational Services, Inc.
- **Coed**

Academics *Calendar:* quarters. *Degrees:* associate and bachelor's.

Freshman Application Contact Director of Recruitment, ITT Technical Institute, 4050 Piedmont Parkway, Suite 110, High Point, NC 27265. *Phone:* 336-819-5900. *Toll-free phone:* 877-536-5231.
Website: http://www.itt-tech.edu/.

James Sprunt Community College
Kenansville, North Carolina

- **State-supported** 2-year, founded 1964, part of North Carolina Community College System
- **Rural** 51-acre campus
- **Endowment** $1.1 million
- **Coed,** 1,572 undergraduate students, 55% full-time, 73% women, 27% men

Undergraduates 869 full-time, 703 part-time. Students come from 3 states and territories; 1% are from out of state; 38% Black or African American, non-Hispanic/Latino; 9% Hispanic/Latino; 0.2% Asian, non-Hispanic/Latino; 0.1% Native Hawaiian or other Pacific Islander, non-Hispanic/Latino; 0.4% American Indian or Alaska Native, non-Hispanic/Latino; 1% Two or more races, non-Hispanic/Latino; 13% transferred in.

Freshmen *Admission:* 585 applied, 291 admitted, 230 enrolled.

Faculty *Total:* 128, 47% full-time, 3% with terminal degrees. *Student/faculty ratio:* 14:1.

Majors Accounting; agribusiness; animal sciences; business administration and management; child development; commercial and advertising art; criminal justice/safety; early childhood education; elementary education; general studies; information technology; institutional food workers; liberal arts and sciences and humanities related; liberal arts and sciences/liberal studies; medical/clinical assistant; registered nursing/registered nurse; viticulture and enology.

Academics *Calendar:* semesters. *Degree:* certificates, diplomas, and associate. *Special study options:* academic remediation for entering students, accelerated degree program, advanced placement credit, cooperative education, distance learning, double majors, English as a second language, independent study, internships, part-time degree program, services for LD students, summer session for credit.

Library James Sprunt Community College Library with 25,268 titles, 92 serial subscriptions, 200 audiovisual materials, an OPAC, a Web page.

Student Life *Housing:* college housing not available. *Activities and Organizations:* student-run newspaper, Student Nurses Association, Art Club, Alumni Association, National Technical-Vocational Honor Society, Phi Theta Kappa, national sororities. *Campus security:* day, evening and Saturday trained security personnel. *Student services:* personal/psychological counseling.

Athletics *Intercollegiate sports:* softball M/W, volleyball M/W.

Costs (2013–14) *Tuition:* state resident $2208 full-time, $69 per semester hour part-time; nonresident $8352 full-time, $261 per semester hour part-time. Full-time tuition and fees vary according to course load. Part-time tuition and fees vary according to course load. *Required fees:* $70 full-time, $35 per term part-time. *Waivers:* senior citizens.

Financial Aid Of all full-time matriculated undergraduates who enrolled in 2011, 35 Federal Work-Study jobs (averaging $1057).

Applying *Options:* electronic application. *Required:* high school transcript. *Application deadlines:* rolling (freshmen), rolling (transfers). *Notification:* continuous (freshmen), continuous (transfers).

Freshman Application Contact Ms. Lea Matthews, Admissions Specialist, James Sprunt Community College, Highway 11 South, 133 James Sprunt Drive, Kenansville, NC 28349. *Phone:* 910-296-6078. *Fax:* 910-296-1222.

E-mail: lmatthews@jamessprunt.edu.
Website: http://www.jamessprunt.edu/.

Johnston Community College

Smithfield, North Carolina

- **State-supported** 2-year, founded 1969, part of North Carolina Community College System
- **Rural** 100-acre campus
- **Coed,** 4,216 undergraduate students, 49% full-time, 66% women, 34% men

Undergraduates 2,075 full-time, 2,141 part-time. 21% Black or African American, non-Hispanic/Latino; 7% Hispanic/Latino; 0.2% Asian, non-Hispanic/Latino; 0.2% Native Hawaiian or other Pacific Islander, non-Hispanic/Latino; 0.5% American Indian or Alaska Native, non-Hispanic/Latino; 0.7% Two or more races, non-Hispanic/Latino; 4% Race/ethnicity unknown; 0.8% international.

Freshmen *Admission:* 683 enrolled.

Faculty *Total:* 385, 37% full-time. *Student/faculty ratio:* 14:1.

Majors Accounting; accounting technology and bookkeeping; administrative assistant and secretarial science; business administration and management; commercial and advertising art; computer programming; criminal justice/police science; diesel mechanics technology; early childhood education; electrical, electronic and communications engineering technology; heating, air conditioning, ventilation and refrigeration maintenance technology; kindergarten/preschool education; landscaping and groundskeeping; legal assistant/paralegal; liberal arts and sciences/liberal studies; machine shop technology; machine tool technology; medical administrative assistant and medical secretary; medical/clinical assistant; medical office management; medical radiologic technology; office management; registered nursing/registered nurse.

Academics *Calendar:* semesters. *Degree:* certificates, diplomas, and associate. *Special study options:* academic remediation for entering students, adult/continuing education programs, advanced placement credit, cooperative education, distance learning, double majors, honors programs, independent study, part-time degree program, services for LD students, summer session for credit.

Library Johnston Community College Library plus 1 other with 36,889 titles, 156 serial subscriptions, 5,624 audiovisual materials, an OPAC, a Web page.

Student Life *Housing:* college housing not available. *Activities and Organizations:* choral group. *Campus security:* 24-hour patrols. *Student services:* personal/psychological counseling.

Athletics Member NJCAA. *Intercollegiate sports:* golf M/W, softball M/W, volleyball M/W. *Intramural sports:* basketball M/W.

Standardized Tests *Required:* ACCUPLACER (for admission). *Recommended:* SAT or ACT (for admission).

Costs (2013–14) *Tuition:* state resident $2208 full-time; nonresident $8352 full-time. *Required fees:* $32 full-time. *Room and board:* $3683.

Financial Aid Of all full-time matriculated undergraduates who enrolled in 2011, 35 Federal Work-Study jobs (averaging $1853).

Applying *Options:* electronic application. *Required:* high school transcript, interview. *Application deadlines:* rolling (freshmen), rolling (transfers). *Notification:* continuous (freshmen), continuous (transfers).

Freshman Application Contact Dr. Pamela J. Harrell, Vice President of Student Services, Johnston Community College, Smithfield, NC 27577-2350. *Phone:* 919-209-2048. *Fax:* 919-989-7862. *E-mail:* pjharrell@johnstoncc.edu. *Website:* http://www.johnstoncc.edu/.

Kaplan College, Charlotte Campus

Charlotte, North Carolina

- **Proprietary** 2-year
- **Coed**

Academics *Degree:* diplomas and associate.

Freshman Application Contact Director of Admissions, Kaplan College, Charlotte Campus, 6070 East Independence Boulevard, Charlotte, NC 28212. *Phone:* 704-567-3700. *Website:* http://charlotte.kaplancollege.com/.

King's College

Charlotte, North Carolina

- **Private** 2-year, founded 1901
- **Suburban** campus
- **Coed,** 529 undergraduate students
- 77% of applicants were admitted

Freshmen *Admission:* 1,157 applied, 886 admitted.

Majors Accounting and business/management; accounting technology and bookkeeping; administrative assistant and secretarial science; computer programming; computer systems networking and telecommunications; graphic design; hotel/motel administration; legal administrative assistant/secretary; legal assistant/paralegal; medical/clinical assistant.

Academics *Calendar:* quarters. *Degree:* diplomas and associate. *Special study options:* accelerated degree program, internships.

Freshman Application Contact Admissions Office, King's College, 322 Lamar Avenue, Charlotte, NC 28204-2436. *Phone:* 704-372-0266. *Toll-free phone:* 800-768-2255. *Website:* http://www.kingscollegecharlotte.edu/.

Lenoir Community College

Kinston, North Carolina

Freshman Application Contact Ms. Tammy Buck, Director of Enrollment Management, Lenoir Community College, PO Box 188, Kinston, NC 28502-0188. *Phone:* 252-527-6223 Ext. 309. *Fax:* 252-526-5112. *E-mail:* tbuck@lenoircc.edu. *Website:* http://www.lenoircc.edu/.

Living Arts College

Raleigh, North Carolina

- **Proprietary** primarily 2-year, founded 1992
- **Suburban** campus with easy access to Raleigh, NC
- **Coed,** 578 undergraduate students, 100% full-time, 57% women, 43% men

Undergraduates 578 full-time. Students come from 5 states and territories; 2 other countries; 3% are from out of state; 54% Black or African American, non-Hispanic/Latino; 5% Hispanic/Latino; 1% Asian, non-Hispanic/Latino; 0.3% American Indian or Alaska Native, non-Hispanic/Latino; 2% Two or more races, non-Hispanic/Latino; 3% Race/ethnicity unknown; 35% live on campus.

Freshmen *Admission:* 158 applied, 158 admitted, 158 enrolled.

Faculty *Total:* 30, 63% full-time, 37% with terminal degrees. *Student/faculty ratio:* 12:1.

Majors Animation, interactive technology, video graphics and special effects; cinematography and film/video production; interior design; photography; recording arts technology; web page, digital/multimedia and information resources design.

Academics *Calendar:* quarters. *Degrees:* certificates, diplomas, associate, and bachelor's. *Special study options:* cooperative education.

Student Life *Housing Options:* Campus housing is university owned. Freshman applicants given priority for college housing. *Activities and Organizations:* MODIV - student council, Student Ambassadors, Firebreathers Animation Studio, NVTHS-National Vocational Technical Honor Society. *Campus security:* controlled dormitory access.

Standardized Tests *Required:* Wonderlic aptitude test (for admission).

Costs (2013–14) *One-time required fee:* $275. *Tuition:* $23,968 full-time. No tuition increase for student's term of enrollment. *Room only:* $7100.

Applying *Options:* early admission, early decision, early action, deferred entrance. *Application fee:* $25. *Required:* essay or personal statement, high school transcript, interview, Portfolio for selected program. *Application deadlines:* rolling (freshmen), rolling (out-of-state freshmen). *Notification:* continuous (freshmen), continuous (out-of-state freshmen).

Freshman Application Contact Julie Wenta, Director of Admissions, Living Arts College, 3000 Wakefield Crossing Drive, Raleigh, NC 27614. *Phone:* 919-488-5902. *Toll-free phone:* 800-288-7442. *Fax:* 919-488-8490. *E-mail:* jwenta@living-arts-college.edu. *Website:* http://www.higherdigital.com/.

Louisburg College

Louisburg, North Carolina

Freshman Application Contact Mr. Jim Schlimmer, Vice President for Enrollment Management, Louisburg College, 501 North Main Street, Louisburg, NC 27549-2399. *Phone:* 919-497-3233. *Toll-free phone:* 800-775-0208. *Fax:* 919-496-1788. *E-mail:* admissions@louisburg.edu. *Website:* http://www.louisburg.edu/.

Martin Community College

Williamston, North Carolina

Freshman Application Contact Martin Community College, 1161 Kehukee Park Road, Williamston, NC 27892. *Phone:* 252-792-1521 Ext. 243. *Website:* http://www.martin.cc.nc.us/.

Mayland Community College

Spruce Pine, North Carolina

Director of Admissions Ms. Cathy Morrison, Director of Admissions, Mayland Community College, PO Box 547, Spruce Pine, NC 28777-0547. *Phone:* 828-765-7351 Ext. 224. *Toll-free phone:* 800-462-9526.
Website: http://www.mayland.edu/.

McDowell Technical Community College

Marion, North Carolina

Freshman Application Contact Mr. Rick L. Wilson, Director of Admissions, McDowell Technical Community College, 54 College Drive, Marion, NC 28752. *Phone:* 828-652-0632. *Fax:* 828-652-1014. *E-mail:* rickw@ mcdowelltech.edu.
Website: http://www.mcdowelltech.edu/.

Mitchell Community College

Statesville, North Carolina

Freshman Application Contact Mr. Doug Rhoney, Counselor, Mitchell Community College, 500 West Broad, Statesville, NC 28677-5293. *Phone:* 704-878-3280.
Website: http://www.mitchellcc.edu/.

Montgomery Community College

Troy, North Carolina

- **State-supported** 2-year, founded 1967, part of North Carolina Community College System
- **Rural** 159-acre campus
- **Coed,** 837 undergraduate students, 46% full-time, 64% women, 36% men

Undergraduates 381 full-time, 456 part-time. Students come from 10 states and territories; 1% are from out of state; 21% Black or African American, non-Hispanic/Latino; 7% Hispanic/Latino; 2% Asian, non-Hispanic/Latino; 0.4% American Indian or Alaska Native, non-Hispanic/Latino; 0.4% Two or more races, non-Hispanic/Latino; 0.1% international.
Freshmen *Admission:* 112 enrolled.
Faculty *Total:* 76, 47% full-time.
Majors Business administration and management; crafts, folk art and artisanry; criminal justice/safety; early childhood education; forest technology; heating, air conditioning, ventilation and refrigeration maintenance technology; legal administrative assistant/secretary; liberal arts and sciences/liberal studies; medical/clinical assistant; mental and social health services and allied professions related; office management.
Academics *Calendar:* semesters. *Degree:* certificates, diplomas, and associate. *Special study options:* academic remediation for entering students, advanced placement credit, distance learning, English as a second language, part-time degree program, services for LD students, summer session for credit.
Library Montgomery Community College Learning Resource Center with 23,000 titles, 100 serial subscriptions, 1,430 audiovisual materials, an OPAC, a Web page.
Student Life *Housing:* college housing not available. *Activities and Organizations:* Student Government Association, Nursing Club, Gunsmithing Society, Medical Assisting Club, Forestry Club. *Campus security:* 24-hour emergency response devices. *Student services:* personal/psychological counseling.
Costs (2013–14) *Tuition:* state resident $2208 full-time, $69 per credit part-time; nonresident $8352 full-time, $261 per credit part-time. Part-time tuition and fees vary according to course load. *Required fees:* $75 full-time, $75 per year part-time. *Payment plan:* installment.
Financial Aid Of all full-time matriculated undergraduates who enrolled in 2011, 24 Federal Work-Study jobs (averaging $500).
Applying *Options:* electronic application, early admission, deferred entrance. *Required:* high school transcript. *Application deadlines:* rolling (freshmen), rolling (transfers). *Notification:* continuous (freshmen), continuous (transfers).
Freshman Application Contact Montgomery Community College, 1011 Page Street, Troy, NC 27371. *Phone:* 910-576-6222 Ext. 240.
Website: http://www.montgomery.edu/.

Nash Community College

Rocky Mount, North Carolina

Freshman Application Contact Ms. Dorothy Gardner, Admissions Officer, Nash Community College, PO Box 7488, Rocky Mount, NC 27804. *Phone:* 252-451-8300. *E-mail:* dgardner@nashcc.edu.
Website: http://www.nashcc.edu/.

Pamlico Community College

Grantsboro, North Carolina

Director of Admissions Mr. Floyd H. Hardison, Admissions Counselor, Pamlico Community College, PO Box 185, Grantsboro, NC 28529-0185. *Phone:* 252-249-1851 Ext. 28.
Website: http://www.pamlico.cc.nc.us/.

Piedmont Community College

Roxboro, North Carolina

- **State-supported** 2-year, founded 1970, part of North Carolina Community College System
- **Small-town** 178-acre campus
- **Coed,** 1,805 undergraduate students, 45% full-time, 63% women, 37% men

Undergraduates 819 full-time, 986 part-time.
Freshmen *Admission:* 284 enrolled.
Majors Accounting; building/property maintenance; business administration and management; child-care and support services management; cinematography and film/video production; clinical/medical social work; computer programming (specific applications); computer systems networking and telecommunications; criminal justice/law enforcement administration; e-commerce; electrical and power transmission installation; electrician; electromechanical and instrumentation and maintenance technologies related; elementary education; general studies; graphic communications; health professions related; industrial technology; information technology; liberal arts and sciences and humanities related; liberal arts and sciences/liberal studies; medical administrative assistant and medical secretary; office management; registered nursing/registered nurse.
Academics *Calendar:* semesters. *Degree:* certificates, diplomas, and associate. *Special study options:* academic remediation for entering students, adult/continuing education programs, advanced placement credit, cooperative education, distance learning, double majors, English as a second language, off-campus study, part-time degree program, summer session for credit.
Library Learning Resource Center with 24,166 titles, 278 serial subscriptions.
Student Life *Housing:* college housing not available. *Activities and Organizations:* drama/theater group, choral group. *Campus security:* routine patrols by the local sheriff's department. *Student services:* personal/psychological counseling.
Athletics *Intramural sports:* volleyball M/W.
Financial Aid Of all full-time matriculated undergraduates who enrolled in 2011, 30 Federal Work-Study jobs (averaging $1500).
Applying *Options:* electronic application, early admission, deferred entrance. *Required for some:* high school transcript. *Application deadlines:* rolling (freshmen), rolling (transfers). *Notification:* continuous until 9/29 (freshmen), continuous until 9/29 (transfers).
Freshman Application Contact Piedmont Community College, PO Box 1197, Roxboro, NC 27573-1197. *Phone:* 336-599-1181 Ext. 2115.
Website: http://www.piedmont.cc.nc.us/.

Pitt Community College

Greenville, North Carolina

Freshman Application Contact Ms. Bev Webster, Interim Coordinator of Counseling, Pitt Community College, PO Drawer 7007, Greenville, NC 27835-7007. *Phone:* 252-493-7217. *Fax:* 252-321-4612. *E-mail:* pittadm@ pcc.pitt.cc.nc.us.
Website: http://www.pittcc.edu/.

Randolph Community College

Asheboro, North Carolina

- **State-supported** 2-year, founded 1962, part of North Carolina Community College System
- **Small-town** 40-acre campus with easy access to Greensboro, Winston-Salem, High Point
- **Endowment** $8.7 million
- **Coed,** 2,894 undergraduate students, 37% full-time, 66% women, 34% men

Undergraduates 1,066 full-time, 1,828 part-time. Students come from 5 states and territories; 10 other countries; 1% are from out of state; 9% Black or African American, non-Hispanic/Latino; 9% Hispanic/Latino; 1% Asian, non-Hispanic/Latino; 0.1% Native Hawaiian or other Pacific Islander, non-Hispanic/Latino; 0.9% American Indian or Alaska Native, non-Hispanic/Latino; 6% Race/ethnicity unknown; 17% transferred in. *Retention:* 56% of full-time freshmen returned.

Freshmen *Admission:* 2,792 applied, 2,792 admitted, 571 enrolled. *Average high school GPA:* 2.86.

Faculty *Total:* 252, 33% full-time. *Student/faculty ratio:* 11:1.

Majors Accounting; autobody/collision and repair technology; automobile/automotive mechanics technology; biology/biotechnology laboratory technician; business administration and management; commercial and advertising art; commercial photography; computer systems networking and telecommunications; cosmetology; criminal justice/safety; early childhood education; electrician; electromechanical and instrumentation and maintenance technologies related; funeral service and mortuary science; industrial electronics technology; information technology; interior design; liberal arts and sciences and humanities related; liberal arts and sciences/liberal studies; logistics, materials, and supply chain management; machine shop technology; medical/clinical assistant; medical office management; office management; photographic and film/video technology; photojournalism; physical therapy technology; pre-engineering; prenursing studies; radiologic technology/science; registered nursing/registered nurse.

Academics *Calendar:* semesters. *Degree:* certificates, diplomas, and associate. *Special study options:* academic remediation for entering students, adult/continuing education programs, advanced placement credit, cooperative education, distance learning, double majors, English as a second language, independent study, internships, off-campus study, part-time degree program, services for LD students, summer session for credit.

Library R. Alton Cox Learning Resources Center with 30,000 titles, 5,000 audiovisual materials, an OPAC, a Web page.

Student Life *Housing:* college housing not available. *Activities and Organizations:* Student Government Association, Phi Theta Kappa, Student Nurse Association, Phi Beta Lambda, Campus Crusaders. *Campus security:* 24-hour emergency response devices, security officer during open hours. *Student services:* personal/psychological counseling.

Athletics *Intramural sports:* basketball M/W, football M/W, golf M/W, volleyball M/W.

Costs (2013–14) *Tuition:* state resident $2208 full-time, $69 per credit part-time; nonresident $8352 full-time, $261 per credit part-time. *Required fees:* $88 full-time, $3 per credit part-time. *Payment plan:* installment. *Waivers:* senior citizens.

Applying *Options:* electronic application, deferred entrance. *Application deadlines:* rolling (freshmen), rolling (transfers). *Notification:* continuous (freshmen), continuous (transfers).

Freshman Application Contact Ms. Brandi F. Hagerman, Director of Enrollment Management/Registrar, Randolph Community College, 629 Industrial Park Avenue, Asheboro, NC 27205-7333. *Phone:* 336-633-0213. *Fax:* 336-629-9547. *E-mail:* bhagerman@randolph.edu. *Website:* http://www.randolph.edu/.

Richmond Community College

Hamlet, North Carolina

Freshman Application Contact Daphne Stancil, Director of Admissions/Registrar, Richmond Community College, PO Box 1189, Hamlet, NC 28345-1189. *Phone:* 910-410-1732. *Fax:* 910-582-7102. *E-mail:* daphnes@richmondcc.edu. *Website:* http://www.richmondcc.edu/.

Roanoke-Chowan Community College

Ahoskie, North Carolina

Director of Admissions Miss Sandra Copeland, Director, Counseling Services, Roanoke-Chowan Community College, 109 Community College Road, Ahoskie, NC 27910. *Phone:* 252-862-1225. *Website:* http://www.roanokechowan.edu/.

Robeson Community College

Lumberton, North Carolina

- **State-supported** 2-year, founded 1965, part of North Carolina Community College System
- **Small-town** 78-acre campus
- **Coed,** 2,869 undergraduate students

Faculty *Total:* 114, 39% full-time.

Majors Administrative assistant and secretarial science; business administration and management; computer and information sciences; computer and information sciences and support services related; computer systems networking and telecommunications; criminal justice/law enforcement administration; early childhood education; electrical, electronic and communications engineering technology; food technology and processing; industrial technology; registered nursing/registered nurse; respiratory care therapy.

Academics *Calendar:* semesters. *Degree:* associate. *Special study options:* academic remediation for entering students, cooperative education, distance learning, services for LD students.

Library 39,000 titles, 225 serial subscriptions.

Student Life *Housing:* college housing not available. *Student services:* personal/psychological counseling.

Applying *Options:* electronic application, early admission. *Required:* high school transcript. *Application deadlines:* rolling (freshmen), rolling (transfers). *Notification:* continuous (freshmen), continuous (transfers).

Freshman Application Contact Ms. Patricia Locklear, College Recruiter, Robeson Community College, PO Box 1420, Lumberton, NC 28359. *Phone:* 910-272-3356 Ext. 251. *Fax:* 910-618-5686. *E-mail:* plocklear@robeson.edu. *Website:* http://www.robeson.cc.nc.us/.

Rockingham Community College

Wentworth, North Carolina

- **State-supported** 2-year, founded 1964, part of North Carolina Community College System
- **Rural** 257-acre campus
- **Coed**

Undergraduates 1,216 full-time, 1,415 part-time. Students come from 10 states and territories; 8 other countries; 1% are from out of state; 25% Black or African American, non-Hispanic/Latino; 2% Hispanic/Latino; 0.5% Asian, non-Hispanic/Latino; 0.1% Native Hawaiian or other Pacific Islander, non-Hispanic/Latino; 0.6% American Indian or Alaska Native, non-Hispanic/Latino; 0.7% Two or more races, non-Hispanic/Latino; 1% Race/ethnicity unknown; 0.1% international; 18% transferred in.

Faculty *Student/faculty ratio:* 18:1.

Academics *Calendar:* semesters. *Degree:* certificates, diplomas, and associate. *Special study options:* academic remediation for entering students, adult/continuing education programs, advanced placement credit, cooperative education, part-time degree program, student-designed majors, summer session for credit.

Student Life *Campus security:* 24-hour emergency response devices and patrols.

Athletics Member NJCAA.

Costs (2012–13) *Tuition:* state resident $2128 full-time, $67 per credit part-time; nonresident $8272 full-time, $259 per credit part-time. Full-time tuition and fees vary according to course load. Part-time tuition and fees vary according to course load. *Required fees:* $116 full-time.

Financial Aid Of all full-time matriculated undergraduates who enrolled in 2011, 37 Federal Work-Study jobs (averaging $2300).

Applying *Options:* electronic application, early admission, deferred entrance.

Freshman Application Contact Mr. Derrick Satterfield, Director of Enrollment Services, Rockingham Community College, PO Box 38, Wentworth, NC 27375-0038. *Phone:* 336-342-4261 Ext. 2114. *Fax:* 336-342-1809. *E-mail:* admissions@rockinghamcc.edu. *Website:* http://www.rockinghamcc.edu/.

Rowan-Cabarrus Community College

Salisbury, North Carolina

Freshman Application Contact Mrs. Gail Cummins, Director of Admissions and Recruitment, Rowan-Cabarrus Community College, PO Box 1595, Salisbury, NC 28145-1595. *Phone:* 704-637-0760. *Fax:* 704-633-6804. *Website:* http://www.rccc.edu/.

Sampson Community College

Clinton, North Carolina

Director of Admissions Mr. William R. Jordan, Director of Admissions, Sampson Community College, PO Box 318, 1801 Sunset Avenue, Highway 24 West, Clinton, NC 28329-0318. *Phone:* 910-592-8084 Ext. 2022. *Website:* http://www.sampsoncc.edu/.

Sandhills Community College

Pinehurst, North Carolina

Freshman Application Contact Mr. Isai Robledo, Recruiter, Sandhills Community College, 3395 Airport Road, Pinehurst, NC 28374-8299. *Phone:* 910-246-5365. *Toll-free phone:* 800-338-3944. *Fax:* 910-695-3981. *E-mail:* robledoi@sandhills.edu. *Website:* http://www.sandhills.edu/.

South College–Asheville
Asheville, North Carolina

Freshman Application Contact Director of Admissions, South College–Asheville, 1567 Patton Avenue, Asheville, NC 28806. *Phone:* 828-277-5521. *Fax:* 828-277-6151.
Website: http://www.southcollegenc.edu/.

Southeastern Community College
Whiteville, North Carolina

Freshman Application Contact Ms. Sylvia Tart, Registrar, Southeastern Community College, PO Box 151, Whiteville, NC 28472. *Phone:* 910-642-7141 Ext. 249. *Fax:* 910-642-5658. *E-mail:* start@sccnc.edu.
Website: http://www.sccnc.edu/.

South Piedmont Community College
Polkton, North Carolina

Freshman Application Contact Ms. Jeania Martin, Admissions Coordinator, South Piedmont Community College, PO Box 126, Polkton, NC 28135-0126. *Phone:* 704-272-7635. *Toll-free phone:* 800-766-0319. *E-mail:* abaucom@vnet.net.
Website: http://www.spcc.edu/.

Southwestern Community College
Sylva, North Carolina

Freshman Application Contact Mr. Delos Monteith, Institutional Research and Planning Officer, Southwestern Community College, 447 College Drive, Sylva, NC 28779. *Phone:* 828-586-4091 Ext. 236. *Toll-free phone:* 800-447-4091 (in-state); 800-447-7091 (out-of-state). *Fax:* 828-586-3129. *E-mail:* delos@southwesterncc.edu.
Website: http://www.southwesterncc.edu/.

Stanly Community College
Albemarle, North Carolina

Freshman Application Contact Mrs. Denise B. Ross, Associate Dean, Admissions, Stanly Community College, 141 College Drive, Albemarle, NC 28001. *Phone:* 704-982-0121 Ext. 264. *Fax:* 704-982-0255. *E-mail:* dross7926@stanly.edu.
Website: http://www.stanly.edu/.

Surry Community College
Dobson, North Carolina

Freshman Application Contact Renita Hazelwood, Director of Admissions, Surry Community College, 630 South Main Street, Dobson, NC 27017. *Phone:* 336-386-3392. *Fax:* 336-386-3690. *E-mail:* hazelwoodr@surry.edu.
Website: http://www.surry.edu/.

Tri-County Community College
Murphy, North Carolina

- **State-supported** 2-year, founded 1964, part of North Carolina Community College System
- **Rural** 40-acre campus
- **Coed,** 1,353 undergraduate students

Freshmen *Average high school GPA:* 2.9.
Faculty *Total:* 80, 58% full-time, 5% with terminal degrees. *Student/faculty ratio:* 21:1.
Majors Accounting; automobile/automotive mechanics technology; business administration and management; early childhood education; electrical, electronic and communications engineering technology; engine machinist; information technology; liberal arts and sciences/liberal studies; medical/clinical assistant; registered nursing/registered nurse; welding technology.
Academics *Calendar:* semesters. *Degree:* certificates, diplomas, and associate. *Special study options:* academic remediation for entering students, adult/continuing education programs, distance learning, double majors, internships, part-time degree program, study abroad, summer session for credit.
Library 16,224 titles, 306 serial subscriptions.
Student Life *Housing:* college housing not available. *Student services:* personal/psychological counseling.
Standardized Tests *Recommended:* SAT and SAT Subject Tests or ACT (for admission).
Financial Aid Of all full-time matriculated undergraduates who enrolled in 2011, 11 Federal Work-Study jobs.

Applying *Options:* electronic application. *Required:* high school transcript. *Application deadlines:* rolling (freshmen), rolling (transfers). *Notification:* continuous (freshmen), continuous (transfers).
Freshman Application Contact Dr. Jason Chambers, Director of Student Services and Admissions, Tri-County Community College, 21 Campus Circle, Murphy, NC 28906-7919. *Phone:* 828-837-6810. *Fax:* 828-837-3266. *E-mail:* jchambers@tricountycc.edu.
Website: http://www.tricountycc.edu/.

Vance-Granville Community College
Henderson, North Carolina

Freshman Application Contact Ms. Kathy Kutl, Admissions Officer, Vance-Granville Community College, PO Box 917, State Road 1126, Henderson, NC 27536. *Phone:* 252-492-2061 Ext. 3265. *Fax:* 252-430-0460.
Website: http://www.vgcc.edu/.

Wake Technical Community College
Raleigh, North Carolina

Director of Admissions Ms. Susan Bloomfield, Director of Admissions, Wake Technical Community College, 9101 Fayetteville Road, Raleigh, NC 27603-5696. *Phone:* 919-866-5452. *E-mail:* srbloomfield@waketech.edu.
Website: http://www.waketech.edu/.

Wayne Community College
Goldsboro, North Carolina

Freshman Application Contact Ms. Jennifer Parker, Associate/Director of Admissions and Records, Wayne Community College, PO Box 8002, Goldsboro, NC 27533. *Phone:* 919-735-5151 Ext. 6721. *Fax:* 919-736-9425. *E-mail:* jbparker@waynecc.edu.
Website: http://www.waynecc.edu/.

Western Piedmont Community College
Morganton, North Carolina

Freshman Application Contact Susan Williams, Director of Admissions, Western Piedmont Community College, 1001 Burkemont Avenue, Morganton, NC 28655-4511. *Phone:* 828-438-6051. *Fax:* 828-438-6065. *E-mail:* swilliams@wpcc.edu.
Website: http://www.wpcc.edu/.

Wilkes Community College
Wilkesboro, North Carolina

Freshman Application Contact Mr. Mac Warren, Director of Admissions, Wilkes Community College, PO Box 120, Wilkesboro, NC 28697. *Phone:* 336-838-6141. *Fax:* 336-838-6547. *E-mail:* mac.warren@wilkescc.edu.
Website: http://www.wilkescc.edu/.

Wilson Community College
Wilson, North Carolina

- **State-supported** 2-year, founded 1958, part of North Carolina Community College System
- **Small-town** 35-acre campus with easy access to Raleigh
- **Coed,** 1,837 undergraduate students, 49% full-time, 68% women, 32% men

Undergraduates 897 full-time, 940 part-time. Students come from 3 states and territories; 45% Black or African American, non-Hispanic/Latino; 5% Hispanic/Latino; 0.7% Asian, non-Hispanic/Latino; 0.1% Native Hawaiian or other Pacific Islander, non-Hispanic/Latino; 0.9% American Indian or Alaska Native, non-Hispanic/Latino; 0.1% Two or more races, non-Hispanic/Latino; 2% Race/ethnicity unknown; 27% transferred in.
Freshmen *Admission:* 270 enrolled.
Faculty *Total:* 210, 25% full-time, 2% with terminal degrees. *Student/faculty ratio:* 12:1.
Majors Accounting; automobile/automotive mechanics technology; biology/biotechnology laboratory technician; business administration and management; computer and information systems security; computer systems networking and telecommunications; criminal justice/safety; culinary arts; early childhood education; electrician; elementary education; executive assistant/executive secretary; fire prevention and safety technology; game and interactive media design; general studies; heating, air conditioning, ventilation and refrigeration maintenance technology; information technology; legal assis-

tant/paralegal; liberal arts and sciences and humanities related; liberal arts and sciences/liberal studies; mechanical engineering/mechanical technology; medical office management; office management; registered nursing/registered nurse; sign language interpretation and translation; surgical technology.

Academics *Calendar:* semesters. *Degree:* certificates, diplomas, and associate. *Special study options:* academic remediation for entering students, advanced placement credit, cooperative education, distance learning, double majors, English as a second language, independent study, internships, part-time degree program, services for LD students, summer session for credit.

Library 38,466 titles, an OPAC.

Student Life *Housing:* college housing not available. *Campus security:* 11-hour patrols by trained security personnel; also have a certified sworn Law Enforcement Agency on campus.

Costs (2012–13) *Tuition:* state resident $2070 full-time, $69 per credit hour part-time; nonresident $7830 full-time, $261 per credit hour part-time. *Required fees:* $103 full-time, $1 per credit hour part-time, $31 per term part-time.

Financial Aid Of all full-time matriculated undergraduates who enrolled in 2011, 65 Federal Work-Study jobs (averaging $1500).

Applying *Options:* electronic application, deferred entrance. *Required:* high school transcript. *Application deadlines:* rolling (freshmen), rolling (transfers). *Notification:* continuous (freshmen), continuous (transfers).

Freshman Application Contact Mrs. Maegan Williams, Admissions Technician, Wilson Community College, Wilson, NC 27893-0305. *Phone:* 252-246-1275. *Fax:* 252-243-7148. *E-mail:* mwilliams@wilsoncc.edu. *Website:* http://www.wilsoncc.edu/.

NORTH DAKOTA

Bismarck State College
Bismarck, North Dakota

- **State-supported** primarily 2-year, founded 1939, part of North Dakota University System
- **Urban** 100-acre campus
- **Coed,** 4,109 undergraduate students, 59% full-time, 45% women, 55% men

Undergraduates 2,416 full-time, 1,693 part-time. 3% Black or African American, non-Hispanic/Latino; 2% Hispanic/Latino; 0.4% Asian, non-Hispanic/Latino; 0.2% Native Hawaiian or other Pacific Islander, non-Hispanic/Latino; 2% American Indian or Alaska Native, non-Hispanic/Latino; 2% Two or more races, non-Hispanic/Latino; 2% Race/ethnicity unknown; 0.5% international.

Freshmen *Admission:* 807 enrolled.

Faculty *Total:* 370, 34% full-time. *Student/faculty ratio:* 16:1.

Majors Administrative assistant and secretarial science; agricultural business and management; autobody/collision and repair technology; automobile/automotive mechanics technology; business automation/technology/data entry; business/commerce; carpentry; clinical/medical laboratory technology; commercial and advertising art; computer systems networking and telecommunications; criminal justice/safety; electrical, electronic and communications engineering technology; emergency medical technology (EMT paramedic); engineering technology; environmental control technologies related; farm and ranch management; heating, air conditioning, ventilation and refrigeration maintenance technology; human services; industrial mechanics and maintenance technology; industrial production technologies related; industrial technology; legal administrative assistant/secretary; liberal arts and sciences/liberal studies; licensed practical/vocational nurse training; lineworker; medical administrative assistant and medical secretary; nuclear engineering technology; operations management; public relations/image management; registered nursing/registered nurse; social work; surgical technology; surveying technology; web page, digital/multimedia and information resources design; welding technology.

Academics *Calendar:* semesters. *Degrees:* certificates, diplomas, associate, and bachelor's. *Special study options:* academic remediation for entering students, adult/continuing education programs, advanced placement credit, cooperative education, distance learning, internships, part-time degree program, study abroad, summer session for credit. *ROTC:* Army (c), Air Force (c).

Library Bismarck State College Library with an OPAC, a Web page.

Student Life *Housing Options:* men-only, women-only. Campus housing is university owned. *Activities and Organizations:* drama/theater group, student-run newspaper, radio station, choral group. *Campus security:* 24-hour emergency response devices and patrols, late-night transport/escort service, controlled dormitory access.

Athletics Member NJCAA.

Standardized Tests *Required:* SAT or ACT (for admission).

Financial Aid Of all full-time matriculated undergraduates who enrolled in 2011, 60 Federal Work-Study jobs (averaging $1367).

Applying *Options:* electronic application, early admission. *Application fee:* $35. *Required:* high school transcript. *Required for some:* interview. *Application deadlines:* rolling (freshmen), 8/1 (transfers). *Notification:* continuous (freshmen), continuous (transfers).

Freshman Application Contact Karen Erickson, Director of Admissions and Enrollment Services, Bismarck State College, PO Box 5587, Bismarck, ND 58506-5587. *Phone:* 701-224-5424. *Toll-free phone:* 800-445-5073. *Fax:* 701-224-5643. *E-mail:* karen.erickson@bismarckstate.edu. *Website:* http://www.bismarckstate.edu/.

Cankdeska Cikana Community College
Fort Totten, North Dakota

Director of Admissions Mr. Ermen Brown Jr., Registrar, Cankdeska Cikana Community College, PO Box 269, Fort Totten, ND 58335-0269. *Phone:* 701-766-1342. *Toll-free phone:* 888-783-1463. *Website:* http://www.littlehoop.edu/.

Dakota College at Bottineau
Bottineau, North Dakota

- **State-supported** 2-year, founded 1906, part of North Dakota University System
- **Rural** 35-acre campus
- **Coed,** 773 undergraduate students, 45% full-time, 52% women, 48% men

Undergraduates 348 full-time, 425 part-time. Students come from 37 states and territories; 4 other countries; 23% are from out of state; 6% Black or African American, non-Hispanic/Latino; 3% Hispanic/Latino; 1% Asian, non-Hispanic/Latino; 0.1% Native Hawaiian or other Pacific Islander, non-Hispanic/Latino; 3% American Indian or Alaska Native, non-Hispanic/Latino; 5% Two or more races, non-Hispanic/Latino; 24% Race/ethnicity unknown; 3% international.

Freshmen *Admission:* 551 enrolled.

Faculty *Total:* 94, 30% full-time, 11% with terminal degrees. *Student/faculty ratio:* 10:1.

Majors Accounting; accounting related; accounting technology and bookkeeping; administrative assistant and secretarial science; adult development and aging; advertising; agriculture; applied horticulture/horticultural business services related; applied horticulture/horticulture operations; biology/biological sciences; business administration and management; business automation/technology/data entry; chemistry; child-care and support services management; child-care provision; computer and information sciences; computer and information sciences and support services related; computer software and media applications related; computer technology/computer systems technology; crop production; education; entrepreneurial and small business related; environmental engineering technology; executive assistant/executive secretary; fishing and fisheries sciences and management; floriculture/floristry management; general studies; greenhouse management; health and physical education/fitness; health services/allied health/health sciences; history; horticultural science; hospitality and recreation marketing; humanities; information science/studies; information technology; landscaping and groundskeeping; land use planning and management; liberal arts and sciences and humanities related; liberal arts and sciences/liberal studies; licensed practical/vocational nurse training; marketing/marketing management; marketing related; mathematics; medical administrative assistant and medical secretary; medical/clinical assistant; medical insurance coding; medical office assistant; medical transcription; natural resources/conservation; network and system administration; office management; office occupations and clerical services; ornamental horticulture; parks, recreation and leisure; parks, recreation and leisure facilities management; parks, recreation, leisure, and fitness studies related; physical sciences; physical sciences related; premedical studies; prenursing studies; pre-veterinary studies; psychology; receptionist; registered nursing/registered nurse; science technologies related; small business administration; social sciences; teacher assistant/aide; urban forestry; wildlife, fish and wildlands science and management; zoology/animal biology.

Academics *Calendar:* semesters. *Degree:* certificates, diplomas, and associate. *Special study options:* academic remediation for entering students, advanced placement credit, cooperative education, distance learning, double majors, off-campus study, part-time degree program, services for LD students, summer session for credit.

Library Dakota College at Bottineau Library plus 1 other with 41,411 titles, 5,544 serial subscriptions, 1,339 audiovisual materials, an OPAC, a Web page.

Student Life *Housing:* on-campus residence required through sophomore year. *Options:* men-only, women-only. Campus housing is university owned. Freshman campus housing is guaranteed. *Activities and Organizations:* drama/theater group, student-run newspaper, Student Senate, Wildlife Club/Horticulture Club, Snowboarding Club, Phi Theta Kappa, Delta Epsilon Chi. *Campus security:* controlled dormitory access, security cameras. *Student services:* health clinic, personal/psychological counseling.

Athletics Member NJCAA. *Intercollegiate sports:* baseball M(s), basketball M(s)/W(s), football M(s), ice hockey M(s), softball W(s), volleyball W(s). *Intramural sports:* archery M/W, badminton M/W, basketball M/W, skiing (downhill) M/W, volleyball M/W.

Standardized Tests *Required:* SAT or ACT (for admission). *Recommended:* ACT (for admission).

Financial Aid Of all full-time matriculated undergraduates who enrolled in 2011, 50 Federal Work-Study jobs (averaging $1100).

Applying *Options:* electronic application, early admission, deferred entrance. *Application fee:* $35. *Required:* high school transcript, immunization records. *Application deadlines:* rolling (freshmen), rolling (out-of-state freshmen), rolling (transfers).

Freshman Application Contact Mrs. Luann Soland, Admissions Counselor, Dakota College at Bottineau, 105 Simrall Boulevard, Bottineau, ND 58318. *Phone:* 701-228-5487. *Toll-free phone:* 800-542-6866. *Fax:* 701-228-5499. *E-mail:* luann.soland@dakotacollege.edu. *Website:* http://www.dakotacollege.edu/.

Fort Berthold Community College
New Town, North Dakota

Freshman Application Contact Office of Admissions, Fort Berthold Community College, PO Box 490, 220 8th Avenue North, New Town, ND 58763-0490. *Phone:* 701-627-4738 Ext. 295. *Website:* http://www.fortbertholdcc.edu/.

Lake Region State College
Devils Lake, North Dakota

- **State-supported** 2-year, founded 1941, part of North Dakota University System
- **Small-town** 120-acre campus
- **Coed,** 1,974 undergraduate students, 27% full-time, 57% women, 43% men

Undergraduates 524 full-time, 1,450 part-time. Students come from 14 states and territories; 7 other countries; 19% are from out of state; 6% Black or African American, non-Hispanic/Latino; 3% Hispanic/Latino; 0.1% Asian, non-Hispanic/Latino; 5% American Indian or Alaska Native, non-Hispanic/Latino; 2% Two or more races, non-Hispanic/Latino; 1% Race/ethnicity unknown; 3% international; 4% transferred in; 10% live on campus. *Retention:* 45% of full-time freshmen returned.

Freshmen *Admission:* 265 applied, 255 admitted, 216 enrolled. *Test scores:* ACT scores over 18: 58%; ACT scores over 24: 12%; ACT scores over 30: 1%.

Faculty *Total:* 139, 23% full-time, 12% with terminal degrees. *Student/faculty ratio:* 14:1.

Majors Administrative assistant and secretarial science; agricultural business and management; business administration and management; child-care provision; criminal justice/police science; electrical and electronic engineering technologies related; electrical/electronics equipment installation and repair; language interpretation and translation; liberal arts and sciences/liberal studies; management information systems; merchandising, sales, and marketing operations related (general); office management; physical fitness technician; registered nursing/registered nurse; speech-language pathology.

Academics *Calendar:* semesters. *Degree:* certificates, diplomas, and associate. *Special study options:* academic remediation for entering students, cooperative education, distance learning, double majors, English as a second language, honors programs, internships, part-time degree program, summer session for credit.

Library Paul Hoghaug Library with 47,000 titles, 92 serial subscriptions, 2,000 audiovisual materials, an OPAC.

Student Life *Housing Options:* coed, men-only, women-only. Campus housing is university owned. *Activities and Organizations:* drama/theater group, choral group, marching band, Student Senate, Phi Theta Kappa, Delta Epsilon Chi, Phi Theta Lambda, Student Nurse Organization. *Campus security:* 24-hour emergency response devices, controlled dormitory access. *Student services:* personal/psychological counseling.

Athletics Member NJCAA. *Intercollegiate sports:* basketball M(s)/W(s), golf M/W, volleyball W(s). *Intramural sports:* basketball M/W, golf M/W, skiing (downhill) M/W, volleyball M/W.

Standardized Tests *Required for some:* SAT or ACT (for admission), COMPASS Test scores must be submitted to be fully admitted (unless exempt).

Costs (2013–14) *Tuition:* state resident $3065 full-time, $128 per credit hour part-time; nonresident $3065 full-time, $128 per credit hour part-time. Full-time tuition and fees vary according to course load, location, and program.

Part-time tuition and fees vary according to location and program. *Required fees:* $843 full-time, $28 per credit hour part-time. *Room and board:* $5316. Room and board charges vary according to board plan and housing facility. *Payment plan:* installment. *Waivers:* minority students, senior citizens, and employees or children of employees.

Financial Aid Of all full-time matriculated undergraduates who enrolled in 2012, 435 applied for aid, 358 were judged to have need, 177 had their need fully met. In 2012, 141 non-need-based awards were made. *Average percent of need met:* 56%. *Average financial aid package:* $9057. *Average need-based loan:* $4653. *Average need-based gift aid:* $4560. *Average non-need-based aid:* $680. *Average indebtedness upon graduation:* $11,084.

Applying *Options:* electronic application. *Application fee:* $35. *Required:* Immunizations records and college transcripts. *Required for some:* high school transcript, interview. *Application deadlines:* rolling (freshmen), rolling (transfers). *Notification:* continuous (freshmen), continuous (transfers).

Freshman Application Contact Samantha Cordrey, Administrative Assistant, Admissions Office, Lake Region State College, 1801 College Drive North, Devils Lake, ND 58301. *Phone:* 701-662-1514. *Toll-free phone:* 800-443-1313. *Fax:* 701-662-1581. *E-mail:* samantha.cordrey@lrsc.edu. *Website:* http://www.lrsc.edu/.

North Dakota State College of Science
Wahpeton, North Dakota

- **State-supported** 2-year, founded 1903, part of North Dakota University System
- **Rural** 125-acre campus
- **Endowment** $12.4 million
- **Coed,** 3,066 undergraduate students, 59% full-time, 45% women, 55% men

Undergraduates 1,807 full-time, 1,259 part-time. Students come from 32 states and territories; 5 other countries; 39% are from out of state; 5% Black or African American, non-Hispanic/Latino; 2% Hispanic/Latino; 0.8% Asian, non-Hispanic/Latino; 0.1% Native Hawaiian or other Pacific Islander, non-Hispanic/Latino; 2% American Indian or Alaska Native, non-Hispanic/Latino; 2% Two or more races, non-Hispanic/Latino; 1% Race/ethnicity unknown; 0.6% international; 57% transferred in; 51% live on campus.

Freshmen *Admission:* 1,322 applied, 974 admitted, 884 enrolled. *Test scores:* ACT scores over 18: 60%; ACT scores over 24: 12%; ACT scores over 30: 1%.

Faculty *Total:* 314, 36% full-time, 7% with terminal degrees. *Student/faculty ratio:* 12:1.

Majors Administrative assistant and secretarial science; agricultural business and management; agricultural mechanics and equipment technology; architectural engineering technology; autobody/collision and repair technology; automobile/automotive mechanics technology; biology/biotechnology laboratory technician; building construction technology; business administration and management; civil engineering technology; computer and information sciences; computer and information systems security; computer programming; computer support specialist; computer systems networking and telecommunications; construction engineering technology; culinary arts; data entry/microcomputer applications; dental assisting; dental hygiene; diesel mechanics technology; e-commerce; electrical and electronic engineering technologies related; emergency medical technology (EMT paramedic); energy management and systems technology; health information/medical records technology; heating, air conditioning, ventilation and refrigeration maintenance technology; heating, ventilation, air conditioning and refrigeration engineering technology; liberal arts and sciences/liberal studies; licensed practical/vocational nurse training; machine tool technology; manufacturing engineering technology; medical insurance coding; multi/interdisciplinary studies related; nanotechnology; occupational therapist assistant; pharmacy technician; plumbing technology; psychiatric/mental health services technology; registered nursing/registered nurse; small engine mechanics and repair technology; vehicle maintenance and repair technologies related; web page, digital/multimedia and information resources design; welding technology.

Academics *Calendar:* semesters. *Degree:* certificates, diplomas, and associate. *Special study options:* academic remediation for entering students, adult/continuing education programs, cooperative education, distance learning, double majors, English as a second language, independent study, internships, part-time degree program, services for LD students, student-designed majors, summer session for credit.

Library Mildred Johnson Library with 72,142 titles, 156 serial subscriptions, 4,488 audiovisual materials, an OPAC, a Web page.

Student Life *Housing:* on-campus residence required for freshman year. *Options:* coed, men-only, women-only, disabled students. Campus housing is university owned. Freshman campus housing is guaranteed. *Activities and Organizations:* drama/theater group, choral group, marching band, music, Drama Club, Inter-Varsity Christian Fellowship, Cultural Diversity, Habitat for

Humanity. *Campus security:* 24-hour emergency response devices and patrols, student patrols, late-night transport/escort service, controlled dormitory access. *Student services:* health clinic, personal/psychological counseling, legal services.

Athletics Member NJCAA. *Intercollegiate sports:* basketball M(s)/W(s), football M(s), softball W, volleyball W(s). *Intramural sports:* baseball M, basketball M/W, football M, racquetball M/W, softball M/W, volleyball M/W.

Standardized Tests *Required:* ACT (for admission).

Costs (2012–13) *Tuition:* state resident $4177 full-time, $137 per credit hour part-time; nonresident $10,175 full-time. Full-time tuition and fees vary according to program and reciprocity agreements. Part-time tuition and fees vary according to program and reciprocity agreements. *Room and board:* $5164. Room and board charges vary according to board plan and housing facility. *Payment plan:* installment. *Waivers:* minority students, children of alumni, and employees or children of employees.

Financial Aid Of all full-time matriculated undergraduates who enrolled in 2011, 1,554 applied for aid, 1,550 were judged to have need, 87 had their need fully met. In 2011, 301 non-need-based awards were made. *Average percent of need met:* 1%. *Average financial aid package:* $7090. *Average need-based loan:* $3857. *Average need-based gift aid:* $4209. *Average non-need-based aid:* $564. *Average indebtedness upon graduation:* $15,349. *Financial aid deadline:* 3/15.

Applying *Options:* electronic application, early admission. *Application fee:* $35. *Required:* high school transcript. *Application deadlines:* rolling (freshmen), rolling (out-of-state freshmen), rolling (transfers). *Notification:* continuous (freshmen), continuous (out-of-state freshmen), continuous (transfers).

Freshman Application Contact Ms. Karen Reilly, Director of Enrollment Services, North Dakota State College of Science, 800 North 6th Street, Wahpeton, ND 58076. *Phone:* 701-671-2189. *Toll-free phone:* 800-342-4325. *Fax:* 701-671-2332. *E-mail:* Karen.Reilly@ndscs.edu. *Website:* http://www.ndscs.nodak.edu/.

Rasmussen College Bismarck

Bismarck, North Dakota

- **Proprietary** primarily 2-year, part of Rasmussen College System
- **Suburban** campus
- **Coed,** 222 undergraduate students

Faculty *Student/faculty ratio:* 22:1.

Majors Accounting; business administration and management; clinical/medical laboratory technology; computer and information systems security; computer science; computer software engineering; corrections and criminal justice related; early childhood education; graphic communications related; health/health-care administration; health information/medical records administration; health information/medical records technology; human resources management; human services; legal assistant/paralegal; management information systems and services related; marketing/marketing management; medical administrative assistant and medical secretary; medical/clinical assistant; web page, digital/multimedia and information resources design.

Academics *Degrees:* certificates, diplomas, associate, and bachelor's. *Special study options:* academic remediation for entering students, accelerated degree program, adult/continuing education programs, distance learning, double majors, internships, part-time degree program, summer session for credit.

Library Rasmussen College Library - Bismarck with 1,953 titles, 20 serial subscriptions, 235 audiovisual materials, an OPAC, a Web page.

Student Life *Housing:* college housing not available.

Standardized Tests *Required:* Internal Exam (for admission).

Costs (2013–14) *Tuition:* $12,600 full-time. Full-time tuition and fees vary according to course level, course load, degree level, location, and program. Part-time tuition and fees vary according to course level, course load, degree level, location, and program. *Required fees:* $1800 full-time. *Payment plans:* installment, deferred payment. *Waivers:* employees or children of employees.

Applying *Options:* electronic application, early admission, deferred entrance. *Required:* high school transcript, minimum 2.0 GPA. *Required for some:* interview. *Application deadlines:* rolling (freshmen), rolling (transfers).

Freshman Application Contact Susan Hammerstrom, Director of Admissions, Rasmussen College Bismarck, 1701 East Century Avenue, Bismarck, ND 58503. *Phone:* 701-530-9600. *Toll-free phone:* 888-549-6755. *E-mail:* susan.hammerstrom@rasmussen.edu. *Website:* http://www.rasmussen.edu/.

Rasmussen College Fargo

Fargo, North Dakota

- **Proprietary** primarily 2-year, founded 1902, part of Rasmussen College System
- **Suburban** campus
- **Coed,** 400 undergraduate students

Faculty *Student/faculty ratio:* 22:1.

Majors Accounting; business administration and management; computer and information systems security; computer programming; computer science; computer software engineering; corrections and criminal justice related; early childhood education; graphic communications related; health/health-care administration; health information/medical records administration; human resources management; human services; legal assistant/paralegal; management information systems and services related; marketing/marketing management; medical administrative assistant and medical secretary; web page, digital/multimedia and information resources design.

Academics *Calendar:* quarters. *Degrees:* certificates, diplomas, associate, and bachelor's. *Special study options:* academic remediation for entering students, accelerated degree program, adult/continuing education programs, distance learning, double majors, internships, part-time degree program, summer session for credit.

Library Rasmussen College Library - Fargo with 1,477 titles, 20 serial subscriptions, 292 audiovisual materials, an OPAC, a Web page.

Student Life *Housing:* college housing not available.

Standardized Tests *Required:* Internal Exam (for admission).

Costs (2013–14) *Tuition:* $12,600 full-time. Full-time tuition and fees vary according to course level, course load, degree level, location, and program. Part-time tuition and fees vary according to course level, course load, degree level, location, and program. *Required fees:* $1800 full-time. *Payment plans:* installment, deferred payment. *Waivers:* employees or children of employees.

Applying *Options:* electronic application, early admission, deferred entrance. *Required:* high school transcript, minimum 2.0 GPA. *Required for some:* interview. *Application deadlines:* rolling (freshmen), rolling (transfers).

Freshman Application Contact Susan Hammerstrom, Director of Admissions, Rasmussen College Fargo, 4012 19th Avenue SW, Fargo, ND 58103. *Phone:* 701-277-3889. *Toll-free phone:* 888-549-6755. *E-mail:* susan.hammerstrom@rasmussen.edu. *Website:* http://www.rasmussen.edu/.

Sitting Bull College

Fort Yates, North Dakota

Director of Admissions Ms. Melody Silk, Director of Registration and Admissions, Sitting Bull College, 1341 92nd Street, Fort Yates, ND 58538-9701. *Phone:* 701-854-3864. *Fax:* 701-854-3403. *E-mail:* melodys@sbcl.edu. *Website:* http://www.sittingbull.edu/.

Turtle Mountain Community College

Belcourt, North Dakota

Director of Admissions Ms. Joni LaFontaine, Admissions/Records Officer, Turtle Mountain Community College, Box 340, Belcourt, ND 58316-0340. *Phone:* 701-477-5605 Ext. 217. *E-mail:* jlafontaine@tm.edu. *Website:* http://www.turtle-mountain.cc.nd.us/.

United Tribes Technical College

Bismarck, North Dakota

Freshman Application Contact Ms. Vivian Gillette, Director of Admissions, United Tribes Technical College, Bismarck, ND 58504. *Phone:* 701-255-3285 Ext. 1334. *Fax:* 701-530-0640. *E-mail:* vgillette@uttc.edu. *Website:* http://www.uttc.edu/.

Williston State College

Williston, North Dakota

Freshman Application Contact Ms. Jan Solem, Director for Admission and Records, Williston State College, PO Box 1326, Williston, ND 58802-1326. *Phone:* 701-774-4554. *Toll-free phone:* 888-863-9455. *Fax:* 701-774-4211. *E-mail:* wsc.admission@wsc.nodak.edu. *Website:* http://www.willistonstate.edu/.

NORTHERN MARIANA ISLANDS

Northern Marianas College

Saipan, Northern Mariana Islands

Freshman Application Contact Ms. Leilani M. Basa-Alam, Admission Specialist, Northern Marianas College, PO Box 501250, Saipan, MP 96950-1250. *Phone:* 670-234-3690 Ext. 1539. *Fax:* 670-235-4967. *E-mail:* leilanib@nmcnet.edu. *Website:* http://www.nmcnet.edu/.

OHIO

Akron Institute of Herzing University
Akron, Ohio

Admissions Office Contact Akron Institute of Herzing University, 1600 South Arlington Street, Suite 100, Akron, OH 44306. *Toll-free phone:* 800-311-0512.
Website: http://www.akroninstitute.com/.

Antonelli College
Cincinnati, Ohio

Freshman Application Contact Antonelli College, 124 East Seventh Street, Cincinnati, OH 45202. *Phone:* 513-241-4338. *Toll-free phone:* 877-500-4304.
Website: http://www.antonellicollege.edu/.

The Art Institute of Cincinnati
Cincinnati, Ohio

Director of Admissions Director of Admissions, The Art Institute of Cincinnati, 1171 East Kemper Road, Cincinnati, OH 45246. *Phone:* 513-751-1206. *Fax:* 513-751-1209.
Website: http://www.aic-arts.edu/.

The Art Institute of Ohio–Cincinnati
Cincinnati, Ohio

- **Proprietary** primarily 2-year, part of Education Management Corporation
- **Urban** campus
- **Coed**

Academics *Calendar:* continuous. *Degrees:* diplomas, associate, and bachelor's.
Freshman Application Contact The Art Institute of Ohio–Cincinnati, 8845 Governors Hill Drive, Cincinnati, OH 45249-3317. *Phone:* 513-833-2400. *Toll-free phone:* 866-613-5184.
Website: http://www.artinstitutes.edu/cincinnati/.

ATS Institute of Technology
Highland Heights, Ohio

Freshman Application Contact Admissions Office, ATS Institute of Technology, 325 Alpha Park, Highland Heights, OH 44143. *Phone:* 440-449-1700 Ext. 103. *E-mail:* info@atsinstitute.edu.
Website: http://www.atsinstitute.edu/cleveland/.

Belmont College
St. Clairsville, Ohio

Director of Admissions Michael Sterling, Director of Recruitment, Belmont College, 120 Fox Shannon Place, St. Clairsville, OH 43950-9735. *Phone:* 740-695-9500 Ext. 1563. *Toll-free phone:* 800-423-1188. *E-mail:* msterling@btc.edu.
Website: http://www.belmontcollege.edu/.

Bowling Green State University-Firelands College
Huron, Ohio

- **State-supported** primarily 2-year, founded 1968, part of Bowling Green State University System
- **Rural** 216-acre campus with easy access to Cleveland, Toledo
- **Coed,** 2,397 undergraduate students, 54% full-time, 65% women, 35% men

Undergraduates 1,285 full-time, 1,112 part-time. Students come from 2 states and territories; 7% Black or African American, non-Hispanic/Latino; 4% Hispanic/Latino; 0.6% Asian, non-Hispanic/Latino; 0.2% Native Hawaiian or other Pacific Islander, non-Hispanic/Latino; 0.5% American Indian or Alaska Native, non-Hispanic/Latino; 3% Two or more races, non-Hispanic/Latino; 3% Race/ethnicity unknown; 6% transferred in. *Retention:* 54% of full-time freshmen returned.
Freshmen *Admission:* 711 applied, 555 admitted, 393 enrolled. *Average high school GPA:* 2.69. *Test scores:* ACT scores over 18: 75%; ACT scores over 24: 15%; ACT scores over 30: 1%.

Faculty *Total:* 154, 36% full-time, 27% with terminal degrees. *Student/faculty ratio:* 19:1.
Majors Allied health and medical assisting services related; business administration and management; communications technologies and support services related; computer and information sciences and support services related; computer engineering technology; computer systems networking and telecommunications; criminal justice/safety; design and visual communications; diagnostic medical sonography and ultrasound technology; education; electrical, electronic and communications engineering technology; electromechanical technology; health information/medical records administration; health professions related; human services; industrial technology; interdisciplinary studies; kindergarten/preschool education; liberal arts and sciences/liberal studies; management information systems and services related; manufacturing engineering technology; mechanical engineering/mechanical technology; medical radiologic technology; registered nursing/registered nurse; respiratory care therapy; social work.
Academics *Calendar:* semesters. *Degrees:* certificates, associate, and bachelor's (also offers some upper-level and graduate courses). *Special study options:* academic remediation for entering students, adult/continuing education programs, advanced placement credit, distance learning, double majors, honors programs, independent study, internships, part-time degree program, services for LD students, student-designed majors, summer session for credit. *ROTC:* Army (c), Air Force (c).
Library BGSU Firelands College Library with 61,019 titles, 223 serial subscriptions, 1,958 audiovisual materials, an OPAC, a Web page.
Student Life *Housing:* college housing not available. *Activities and Organizations:* drama/theater group, Humanity Organized for Peace through Education-H.O.P.E., Science and Environment Club, Speech Activities Organization - Theatre, Visual Communication Technology Organization, intramurals. *Campus security:* 24-hour emergency response devices, late-night transport/escort service, patrols by trained security personnel.
Costs (2012–13) *Tuition:* state resident $4614 full-time, $192 per credit hour part-time; nonresident $11,922 full-time, $497 per credit hour part-time. Full-time tuition and fees vary according to location. Part-time tuition and fees vary according to location. *Required fees:* $236 full-time, $9 per credit hour part-time, $118 per term part-time. *Payment plan:* installment. *Waivers:* employees or children of employees.
Applying *Options:* electronic application, early admission, deferred entrance. *Application fee:* $45. *Required:* high school transcript. *Application deadlines:* 8/6 (freshmen), 8/6 (transfers). *Notification:* continuous (freshmen), continuous (transfers).
Freshman Application Contact Debralee Divers, Director of Admissions and Financial Aid, Bowling Green State University-Firelands College, One University Drive, Huron, OH 44839-9791. *Phone:* 419-433-5560. *Toll-free phone:* 800-322-4787. *Fax:* 419-372-0604. *E-mail:* divers@bgsu.edu.
Website: http://www.firelands.bgsu.edu/.

Bradford School
Columbus, Ohio

- **Private** 2-year, founded 1911
- **Suburban** campus
- **Coed, primarily women,** 603 undergraduate students
- **50% of applicants were admitted**

Freshmen *Admission:* 2,021 applied, 1,005 admitted.
Majors Accounting and business/management; accounting technology and bookkeeping; computer systems networking and telecommunications; cooking and related culinary arts; culinary arts; graphic design; hotel/motel administration; legal administrative assistant/secretary; legal assistant/paralegal; medical/clinical assistant; physical therapy technology; system, networking, and LAN/WAN management; tourism and travel services management; veterinary/animal health technology.
Academics *Calendar:* semesters. *Degree:* diplomas and associate. *Special study options:* accelerated degree program, internships.
Freshman Application Contact Admissions Office, Bradford School, 2469 Stelzer Road, Columbus, OH 43219. *Phone:* 614-416-6200. *Toll-free phone:* 800-678-7981.
Website: http://www.bradfordschoolcolumbus.edu/.

Brown Mackie College–Akron
Akron, Ohio

Freshman Application Contact Brown Mackie College–Akron, 755 White Pond Drive, Suite 101, Akron, OH 44320. *Phone:* 330-869-3600.
Website: http://www.brownmackie.edu/akron/.

See display on next page and page 344 for the College Close-Up.

Brown Mackie College–Cincinnati

Cincinnati, Ohio

Freshman Application Contact Brown Mackie College–Cincinnati, 1011 Glendale-Milford Road, Cincinnati, OH 45215. *Phone:* 513-771-2424. *Toll-free phone:* 800-888-1445.
Website: http://www.brownmackie.edu/cincinnati/.

See display below and on next page and page 354 for the College Close-Up.

Brown Mackie College–Findlay

Findlay, Ohio

Freshman Application Contact Brown Mackie College–Findlay, 1700 Fostoria Avenue, Suite 100, Findlay, OH 45840. *Phone:* 419-423-2211. *Toll-free phone:* 800-842-3687.
Website: http://www.brownmackie.edu/findlay/.

See display below and on next page and page 358 for the College Close-Up.

Brown Mackie College–North Canton

Canton, Ohio

Freshman Application Contact Brown Mackie College–North Canton, 4300 Munson Street NW, Canton, OH 44718-3674. *Phone:* 330-494-1214.
Website: http://www.brownmackie.edu/northcanton/.

See display below and on next page and page 378 for the College Close-Up.

Bryant & Stratton College - Eastlake Campus

Eastlake, Ohio

Freshman Application Contact Ms. Melanie Pettit, Director of Admissions, Bryant & Stratton College - Eastlake Campus, 35350 Curtis Boulevard, Eastlake, OH 44095. *Phone:* 440-510-1112.
Website: http://www.bryantstratton.edu/.

Bryant & Stratton College - Parma Campus

Parma, Ohio

Freshman Application Contact Bryant & Stratton College - Parma Campus, 12955 Snow Road, Parma, OH 44130-1013. *Phone:* 216-265-3151. *Toll-free phone:* 866-948-0571.
Website: http://www.bryantstratton.edu/.

Central Ohio Technical College

Newark, Ohio

Freshman Application Contact Jacqueline Stewart, Admissions Representative, Central Ohio Technical College, 1179 University Drive, Newark, OH 43055-1767. *Phone:* 740-366-9222. *Toll-free phone:* 800-9NEWARK. *Fax:* 740-366-5047.
Website: http://www.cotc.edu/.

Chatfield College

St. Martin, Ohio

Freshman Application Contact Chatfield College, 20918 State Route 251, St. Martin, OH 45118-9705. *Phone:* 513-875-3344 Ext. 137.
Website: http://www.chatfield.edu/.

The Christ College of Nursing and Health Sciences

Cincinnati, Ohio

- **Private** 2-year
- **Urban** campus with easy access to Cincinnati
- **Coed**
- 64% of applicants were admitted

Undergraduates 202 full-time, 144 part-time. 10% Black or African American, non-Hispanic/Latino; 1% Hispanic/Latino; 0.9% Asian, non-Hispanic/Latino; 0.9% Two or more races, non-Hispanic/Latino; 0.9% Race/ethnicity unknown; 22% transferred in.
Faculty *Student/faculty ratio:* 7:1.

Academics *Degree:* associate. *Special study options:* academic remediation for entering students, advanced placement credit, services for LD students, summer session for credit.

Student Life *Campus security:* 24-hour emergency response devices and patrols, late-night transport/escort service.

Standardized Tests *Required:* SAT or ACT (for admission).

Costs (2012–13) *Tuition:* $14,060 full-time, $370 per credit hour part-time. Full-time tuition and fees vary according to course load. Part-time tuition and fees vary according to course load. *Required fees:* $800 full-time.

Applying *Application fee:* $45. *Required:* high school transcript, minimum 2.8 GPA.

Freshman Application Contact Mr. Bradley Jackson, Admissions, The Christ College of Nursing and Health Sciences, 2139 Auburn Avenue, Cincinnati, OH 45219. *Phone:* 513-585-0016. *E-mail:* bradley.jackson@thechristcollege.edu. *Website:* http://www.thechristcollege.edu/.

Cincinnati State Technical and Community College
Cincinnati, Ohio

Freshman Application Contact Ms. Gabriele Boeckermann, Director of Admission, Cincinnati State Technical and Community College, Cincinnati, OH 45223-2690. *Phone:* 513-569-1550. *Toll-free phone:* 877-569-0115. *Fax:* 513-569-1562. *E-mail:* adm@cincinnatistate.edu. *Website:* http://www.cincinnatistate.edu/.

Clark State Community College
Springfield, Ohio

- **State-supported** 2-year, founded 1962, part of Ohio Board of Regents
- **Suburban** 60-acre campus with easy access to Columbus, Dayton
- **Endowment** $8.9 million
- **Coed**

Undergraduates Students come from 12 states and territories; 1% are from out of state; 15% Black or African American, non-Hispanic/Latino; 1% Hispanic/Latino; 0.8% Asian, non-Hispanic/Latino; 0.2% Native Hawaiian or other Pacific Islander, non-Hispanic/Latino; 0.4% American Indian or Alaska Native, non-Hispanic/Latino; 9% Race/ethnicity unknown; 0.3% international. *Retention:* 33% of full-time freshmen returned.

Freshmen *Admission:* 3,504 applied, 3,504 admitted.

Faculty *Total:* 552, 13% full-time, 4% with terminal degrees. *Student/faculty ratio:* 13:1.

Majors Accounting; administrative assistant and secretarial science; agricultural business and management; agricultural mechanization; agriculture; business administration and management; civil engineering technology; clinical/medical laboratory technology; commercial and advertising art; computer and information sciences and support services related; computer programming; computer programming related; computer systems networking and telecommunications; corrections; court reporting; criminal justice/law enforcement administration; criminal justice/police science; drafting and design technology; dramatic/theater arts; electrical, electronic and communications engineering technology; emergency medical technology (EMT paramedic); horticultural science; human services; industrial technology; information science/studies; information technology; kindergarten/preschool education; kinesiology and exercise science; landscaping and groundskeeping; legal assistant/paralegal; liberal arts and sciences/liberal studies; licensed practical/vocational nurse training; mechanical engineering/mechanical technology; medical administrative assistant and medical secretary; physical therapy; registered nursing/registered nurse; social work.

Academics *Calendar:* quarters. *Degree:* certificates and associate. *Special study options:* academic remediation for entering students, adult/continuing education programs, advanced placement credit, cooperative education, distance learning, double majors, honors programs, independent study, internships, off-campus study, part-time degree program, services for LD students, summer session for credit. *ROTC:* Army (c).

Library Clark State Community College Library with an OPAC, a Web page.

Student Life *Housing:* college housing not available. *Activities and Organizations:* drama/theater group, choral group, Student Senate, Gay Straight Alliance, Student Theatre Guild, Chi Alpha, Creative Writers Club. *Campus security:* late-night transport/escort service. *Student services:* health clinic, personal/psychological counseling.

Athletics Member NJCAA. *Intercollegiate sports:* baseball M, basketball M/W, softball W, volleyball W. *Intramural sports:* baseball M, basketball M/W, tennis M/W, volleyball M/W.

Applying *Options:* electronic application. *Application fee:* $15. *Recommended:* high school transcript. *Application deadlines:* rolling (freshmen), rolling (out-of-state freshmen), rolling (transfers). *Notification:* continuous (freshmen), continuous (out-of-state freshmen), continuous (transfers).

Freshman Application Contact Admissions Office, Clark State Community College, PO Box 570, Springfield, OH 45501-0570. *Phone:* 937-328-3858. *Fax:* 937-328-6133. *E-mail:* admissions@clarkstate.edu. *Website:* http://www.clarkstate.edu/.

Cleveland Institute of Electronics

Cleveland, Ohio

- **Proprietary** 2-year, founded 1934
- **Coed, primarily men,** 1,675 undergraduate students

Undergraduates Students come from 52 states and territories; 70 other countries; 97% are from out of state.

Faculty *Total:* 8, 50% full-time, 13% with terminal degrees.

Majors Computer/information technology services administration related; computer software engineering; electrical, electronic and communications engineering technology.

Academics *Calendar:* continuous. *Degrees:* diplomas and associate (offers only external degree programs conducted through home study). *Special study options:* accelerated degree program, adult/continuing education programs, distance learning, external degree program, independent study, part-time degree program.

Library 5,000 titles, 38 serial subscriptions.

Costs (2012–13) *Tuition:* $2075 per term part-time. No tuition increase for student's term of enrollment. *Payment plans:* tuition prepayment, installment.

Applying *Options:* electronic application, early admission. *Required:* high school transcript. *Application deadlines:* rolling (freshmen), rolling (out-of-state freshmen), rolling (transfers). *Notification:* continuous (freshmen), continuous (out-of-state freshmen), continuous (transfers).

Freshman Application Contact Mr. Scott Katzenmeyer, Registrar, Cleveland Institute of Electronics, Cleveland, OH 44114. *Phone:* 216-781-9400. *Toll-free phone:* 800-243-6446. *Fax:* 216-781-0331. *E-mail:* instruct@cie-wc.edu. *Website:* http://www.cie-wc.edu/.

Columbus Culinary Institute at Bradford School

Columbus, Ohio

- **Private** 2-year, founded 2006
- **Suburban** campus
- **Coed,** 204 undergraduate students
- 49% of applicants were admitted

Freshmen *Admission:* 811 applied, 394 admitted.

Majors Cooking and related culinary arts.

Academics *Calendar:* semesters. *Degree:* associate.

Freshman Application Contact Admissions Office, Columbus Culinary Institute at Bradford School, 2435 Stelzer Road, Columbus, OH 43219. *Phone:* 614-944-4200. *Toll-free phone:* 877-506-5006. *Website:* http://www.columbusculinary.com/.

Columbus State Community College

Columbus, Ohio

Freshman Application Contact Ms. Tari Blaney, Director of Admissions, Columbus State Community College, Box 1609, Columbus, OH 43216-1609. *Phone:* 614-287-2669. *Toll-free phone:* 800-621-6407 Ext. 2669. *Fax:* 614-287-6019. *E-mail:* tblaney@cscc.edu. *Website:* http://www.cscc.edu/.

Cuyahoga Community College

Cleveland, Ohio

- **State and locally supported** 2-year, founded 1963
- **Urban** campus
- **Endowment** $22.5 million
- **Coed,** 30,065 undergraduate students, 35% full-time, 62% women, 38% men

Undergraduates 10,590 full-time, 19,475 part-time. Students come from 32 states and territories; 27 other countries; 1% are from out of state; 28% Black or African American, non-Hispanic/Latino; 5% Hispanic/Latino; 2% Asian, non-Hispanic/Latino; 0.9% American Indian or Alaska Native, non-Hispanic/Latino; 0.2% Two or more races, non-Hispanic/Latino; 16% Race/ethnicity unknown; 1% international; 5% transferred in. *Retention:* 48% of full-time freshmen returned.

Freshmen *Admission:* 9,492 applied, 9,492 admitted, 2,633 enrolled.

Faculty *Total:* 1,673, 21% full-time, 14% with terminal degrees. *Student/faculty ratio:* 18:1.

Majors Accounting; administrative assistant and secretarial science; automobile/automotive mechanics technology; avionics maintenance technology; business administration and management; clinical laboratory science/medical technology; commercial and advertising art; computer engineering technology; computer typography and composition equipment operation; court reporting; criminal justice/police science; engineering technology; finance; fire science/firefighting; industrial radiologic technology; kindergarten/preschool

education; legal assistant/paralegal; liberal arts and sciences/liberal studies; marketing/marketing management; merchandising; opticianry; photography; physician assistant; quality control and safety technologies related; real estate; registered nursing/registered nurse; respiratory care therapy; restaurant, culinary, and catering management; sales, distribution, and marketing operations; selling skills and sales; surgical technology; veterinary/animal health technology.

Academics *Calendar:* semesters. *Degree:* certificates and associate. *Special study options:* adult/continuing education programs, advanced placement credit, cooperative education, distance learning, English as a second language, external degree program, independent study, part-time degree program, services for LD students, summer session for credit.

Library Metro Library plus 3 others with 177,767 titles, 1,135 serial subscriptions, an OPAC, a Web page.

Student Life *Housing:* college housing not available. *Activities and Organizations:* drama/theater group, student-run newspaper, choral group, Student Senate, Student Nursing Organization, Business Focus, Phi Theta Kappa. *Campus security:* 24-hour emergency response devices and patrols, late-night transport/escort service. *Student services:* health clinic, personal/psychological counseling.

Athletics Member NJCAA. *Intercollegiate sports:* baseball M(s), basketball M(s), cross-country running M(s)/W(s), soccer M(s), softball W(s). *Intramural sports:* basketball M, tennis M/W, track and field M/W, volleyball M/W.

Costs (2013–14) *Tuition:* area resident $2936 full-time, $98 per credit part-time; state resident $3753 full-time, $125 per credit part-time; nonresident $7268 full-time, $242 per credit part-time. *Room and board:* $5000. *Payment plan:* installment.

Financial Aid Of all full-time matriculated undergraduates who enrolled in 2011, 802 Federal Work-Study jobs (averaging $3300).

Applying *Options:* early admission, deferred entrance. *Required for some:* high school transcript. *Application deadlines:* rolling (freshmen), rolling (transfers). *Notification:* continuous (freshmen), continuous (transfers).

Freshman Application Contact Mr. Kevin McDaniel, Director of Admissions and Records, Cuyahoga Community College, Cleveland, OH 44115. *Phone:* 216-987-4030. *Toll-free phone:* 800-954-8742. *Fax:* 216-696-2567. *Website:* http://www.tri-c.edu/.

Davis College

Toledo, Ohio

Freshman Application Contact Ms. Dana Stern, Davis College, 4747 Monroe Street, Toledo, OH 43623-4307. *Phone:* 419-473-2700. *Toll-free phone:* 800-477-7021. *Fax:* 419-473-2472. *E-mail:* dstern@daviscollege.edu. *Website:* http://daviscollege.edu/.

Daymar College

Chillicothe, Ohio

Freshman Application Contact Admissions Office, Daymar College, 1410 Industrial Drive, Chillicothe, OH 45601. *Phone:* 740-774-6300. *Toll-free phone:* 877-258-7796. *Fax:* 740-774-6317. *Website:* http://www.daymarcollege.edu/.

Daymar College

Jackson, Ohio

Freshman Application Contact Admissions Office, Daymar College, 980 East Main Street, Jackson, OH 45640. *Phone:* 740-286-1554. *Toll-free phone:* 877-258-7796. *Fax:* 740-774-6317. *Website:* http://www.daymarcollege.edu/.

Daymar College

Lancaster, Ohio

Freshman Application Contact Holly Hankinson, Admissions Office, Daymar College, 1579 Victor Road, NW, Lancaster, OH 43130. *Phone:* 740-687-6126. *Toll-free phone:* 877-258-7796. *E-mail:* hhankinson@daymarcollege.edu. *Website:* http://www.daymarcollege.edu/.

Daymar College

New Boston, Ohio

Freshman Application Contact Mike Bell, Admissions Representative, Daymar College, 3879 Rhodes Avenue, New Boston, OH 45662. *Phone:* 740-456-4124. *Toll-free phone:* 877-258-7796. *Website:* http://www.daymarcollege.edu/.

Eastern Gateway Community College

Steubenville, Ohio

Freshman Application Contact Mrs. Kristen Taylor, Director of Admissions, Eastern Gateway Community College, 4000 Sunset Boulevard, Steubenville, OH 43952. *Phone:* 740-264-5591 Ext. 142. *Toll-free phone:* 800-68-COLLEGE. *Fax:* 740-266-2944. *E-mail:* kltaylor@egcc.edu. *Website:* http://www.egcc.edu/.

Edison Community College

Piqua, Ohio

- **State-supported** 2-year, founded 1973, part of Ohio Board of Regents' University System of Ohio
- **Small-town** 130-acre campus with easy access to Dayton, Columbus, Cincinnati
- **Endowment** $1.5 million
- **Coed,** 3,168 undergraduate students, 33% full-time, 65% women, 35% men

Undergraduates 1,036 full-time, 2,132 part-time. Students come from 8 states and territories; 4 other countries; 1% are from out of state; 3% Black or African American, non-Hispanic/Latino; 1% Hispanic/Latino; 0.8% Asian, non-Hispanic/Latino; 0.3% American Indian or Alaska Native, non-Hispanic/Latino; 1% Two or more races, non-Hispanic/Latino; 3% Race/ethnicity unknown; 0.2% international; 4% transferred in. *Retention:* 52% of full-time freshmen returned.

Freshmen *Admission:* 633 applied, 633 admitted, 531 enrolled. *Average high school GPA:* 2.75. *Test scores:* ACT scores over 18: 86%; ACT scores over 24: 14%.

Faculty *Total:* 221, 22% full-time, 9% with terminal degrees. *Student/faculty ratio:* 16:1.

Majors Accounting; art; business administration and management; child development; clinical/medical laboratory technology; commercial and advertising art; computer and information sciences; computer and information systems security; computer programming; computer systems networking and telecommunications; criminal justice/police science; dramatic/theater arts; education; electrical, electronic and communications engineering technology; electromechanical technology; executive assistant/executive secretary; health/medical preparatory programs related; heating, air conditioning, ventilation and refrigeration maintenance technology; human resources management; industrial technology; legal administrative assistant/secretary; legal assistant/paralegal; liberal arts and sciences/liberal studies; logistics, materials, and supply chain management; marketing/marketing management; mechanical drafting and CAD/CADD; mechanical engineering/mechanical technology; medical administrative assistant and medical secretary; medical/clinical assistant; medium/heavy vehicle and truck technology; physical therapy technology; prenursing studies; registered nursing/registered nurse; social work; speech communication and rhetoric.

Academics *Calendar:* semesters. *Degrees:* certificates, associate, and post-bachelor's certificates. *Special study options:* academic remediation for entering students, accelerated degree program, adult/continuing education programs, advanced placement credit, distance learning, double majors, English as a second language, honors programs, independent study, internships, off-campus study, part-time degree program, services for LD students, student-designed majors, summer session for credit.

Library Edison Community College Library with 27,433 titles, 75,282 serial subscriptions, 2,608 audiovisual materials, an OPAC, a Web page.

Student Life *Housing:* college housing not available. *Activities and Organizations:* drama/theater group, Campus Crusade for Christ, Student Ambassadors, Edison Stagelight Players, Writers Club, Edison Photo Society. *Campus security:* late-night transport/escort service, 18-hour patrols by trained security personnel. *Student services:* health clinic, personal/psychological counseling.

Athletics Member NJCAA. *Intercollegiate sports:* basketball M(s)/W(s), volleyball W(s). *Intramural sports:* baseball M(c).

Standardized Tests *Required:* ACT COMPASS (for admission).

Costs (2012–13) *One-time required fee:* $20. *Tuition:* state resident $4019 full-time, $134 per credit hour part-time; nonresident $7429 full-time, $248 per credit hour part-time. Full-time tuition and fees vary according to course load, program, and reciprocity agreements. Part-time tuition and fees vary according to course load, program, and reciprocity agreements. *Required fees:* $15 full-time. *Payment plans:* installment, deferred payment. *Waivers:* senior citizens and employees or children of employees.

Financial Aid Of all full-time matriculated undergraduates who enrolled in 2011, 42 Federal Work-Study jobs (averaging $3000).

Applying *Options:* electronic application. *Application fee:* $20. *Required:* high school transcript. *Application deadlines:* rolling (freshmen), rolling (out-of-state freshmen), rolling (transfers).

Freshman Application Contact Ms. Velina Bogart, Coordinator of Recruiting, Edison Community College, 1973 Edison Drive, Piqua, OH 45356. *Phone:* 937-778-7854. *Toll-free phone:* 800-922-3722. *Fax:* 937-778-4692. *E-mail:* vbogart@edisonohio.edu. *Website:* http://www.edisonohio.edu/.

ETI Technical College of Niles

Niles, Ohio

- **Proprietary** 2-year, founded 1989
- **Small-town** 1-acre campus with easy access to Cleveland, Pittsburgh
- **Coed**

Undergraduates 143 full-time, 69 part-time. Students come from 2 states and territories; 10% are from out of state; 8% transferred in.

Faculty *Student/faculty ratio:* 7:1.

Academics *Calendar:* semesters. *Degree:* diplomas and associate. *Special study options:* academic remediation for entering students, adult/continuing education programs, double majors, internships, part-time degree program, services for LD students.

Student Life *Campus security:* 24-hour emergency response devices.

Standardized Tests *Recommended:* SAT (for admission), ACT (for admission).

Costs (2012–13) *Tuition:* $7854 full-time, $281 per credit part-time. Full-time tuition and fees vary according to course load and program. Part-time tuition and fees vary according to course load and program. *Required fees:* $300 full-time, $400 per year part-time.

Financial Aid Of all full-time matriculated undergraduates who enrolled in 2009, 475 applied for aid, 370 were judged to have need, 450 had their need fully met. *Average percent of need met:* 100. *Average financial aid package:* $15,250. *Average need-based loan:* $3500. *Average need-based gift aid:* $5750.

Applying *Options:* early admission, deferred entrance. *Application fee:* $50. *Required:* high school transcript, interview.

Freshman Application Contact Ms. Diane Marsteller, Director of Admissions, ETI Technical College of Niles, 2076 Youngstown-Warren Road, Niles, OH 44446-4398. *Phone:* 330-652-9919 Ext. 16. *Fax:* 330-652-4399. *E-mail:* dianemarsteller@eticollege.edu. *Website:* http://eticollege.edu/.

Fortis College

Centerville, Ohio

Freshman Application Contact Fortis College, 555 East Alex Bell Road, Centerville, OH 45459. *Phone:* 937-433-3410. *Toll-free phone:* 855-4-FORTIS. *Website:* http://www.fortis.edu/.

Fortis College

Cuyahoga Falls, Ohio

Freshman Application Contact Admissions Office, Fortis College, 2545 Bailey Road, Cuyahoga Falls, OH 44221. *Phone:* 330-923-9959. *Fax:* 330-923-0886. *Website:* http://www.fortis.edu/.

Fortis College

Ravenna, Ohio

Freshman Application Contact Admissions Office, Fortis College, 653 Enterprise Parkway, Ravenna, OH 44266. *Toll-free phone:* 855-4-FORTIS. *Website:* http://www.fortis.edu/.

Gallipolis Career College

Gallipolis, Ohio

Freshman Application Contact Mr. Jack Henson, Director of Admissions, Gallipolis Career College, 1176 Jackson Pike, Suite 312, Gallipolis, OH 45631. *Phone:* 740-446-4367. *Toll-free phone:* 800-214-0452. *Fax:* 740-446-4124. *E-mail:* admissions@gallipoliscareercollege.com. *Website:* http://www.gallipoliscareercollege.com/.

Good Samaritan College of Nursing and Health Science

Cincinnati, Ohio

- **Proprietary** 2-year
- **Urban** campus with easy access to Cincinnati
- **Coed**

Undergraduates 131 full-time, 182 part-time. 7% are from out of state; 20% transferred in.

Faculty *Student/faculty ratio:* 7:1.

Academics *Degree:* associate.

Standardized Tests *Required:* SAT or ACT (for admission).

Financial Aid Of all full-time matriculated undergraduates who enrolled in 2010, 155 applied for aid, 149 were judged to have need. 8 state and other part-time jobs (averaging $750). In 2010, 8. *Average percent of need met:* 68. *Average financial aid package:* $7488. *Average need-based loan:* $3477. *Average need-based gift aid:* $4260. *Average non-need-based aid:* $1100.

Applying *Options:* electronic application. *Application fee:* $40. *Required:* high school transcript, minimum 2.5 GPA, Required average GPA 2.25 in these high school courses: English, Math (Algebra required), Science (Chemistry required), and Social Studies.

Freshman Application Contact Admissions Office, Good Samaritan College of Nursing and Health Science, 375 Dixmyth Avenue, Cincinnati, OH 45220. *Phone:* 513-862-2743. *Fax:* 513-862-3572.
Website: http://www.gscollege.edu/.

Herzing University

Toledo, Ohio

Admissions Office Contact Herzing University, 5212 Hill Avenue, Toledo, OH 43615. *Toll-free phone:* 800-596-0724.
Website: http://www.herzing.edu/toledo.

Hocking College

Nelsonville, Ohio

Director of Admissions Ms. Lyn Hull, Director of Admissions, Hocking College, 3301 Hocking Parkway, Nelsonville, OH 45764-9588. *Phone:* 740-753-3591 Ext. 2803. *Toll-free phone:* 877-462-5464. *E-mail:* hull_lyn@hocking.edu.
Website: http://www.hocking.edu/.

Hondros College

Westerville, Ohio

Director of Admissions Ms. Carol Thomas, Operations Manager, Hondros College, 4140 Executive Parkway, Westerville, OH 43081-3855. *Phone:* 614-508-7244. *Toll-free phone:* 888-HONDROS.
Website: http://www.hondros.edu/.

International College of Broadcasting

Dayton, Ohio

- **Private** 2-year, founded 1968
- **Urban** 1-acre campus with easy access to Dayton
- **Coed,** 77 undergraduate students

Faculty *Total:* 14, 43% full-time.

Majors Recording arts technology.

Academics *Calendar:* semesters. *Degree:* diplomas and associate. *Special study options:* academic remediation for entering students, internships, services for LD students.

Student Life *Housing:* college housing not available. *Activities and Organizations:* student-run radio station.

Standardized Tests *Required:* Wonderlic aptitude test (for admission).

Costs (2013–14) *Tuition:* $29,120 full-time. No tuition increase for student's term of enrollment. *Payment plan:* tuition prepayment.

Applying *Options:* early admission. *Application fee:* $100. *Required:* high school transcript, interview, Passing Wonderlic Test.

Freshman Application Contact International College of Broadcasting, 6 South Smithville Road, Dayton, OH 45431-1833. *Phone:* 937-258-8251. *Toll-free phone:* 800-517-7284.
Website: http://www.icbcollege.com/.

ITT Technical Institute

Akron, Ohio

- **Proprietary** primarily 2-year
- **Coed**

Academics *Degrees:* associate and bachelor's.

Freshman Application Contact Director of Recruitment, ITT Technical Institute, 3428 West Market Street, Akron, OH 44333. *Phone:* 330-865-8600. *Toll-free phone:* 877-818-0154.
Website: http://www.itt-tech.edu/.

ITT Technical Institute

Columbus, Ohio

- **Proprietary** primarily 2-year, part of ITT Educational Services, Inc.
- **Coed**

Academics *Calendar:* quarters. *Degrees:* associate and bachelor's.

Freshman Application Contact Director of Recruitment, ITT Technical Institute, 4717 Hilton Corporate Drive, Columbus, OH 43232. *Phone:* 614-868-2000. *Toll-free phone:* 877-233-8864.
Website: http://www.itt-tech.edu/.

ITT Technical Institute

Dayton, Ohio

- **Proprietary** primarily 2-year, founded 1935, part of ITT Educational Services, Inc.
- **Suburban** campus
- **Coed**

Academics *Calendar:* quarters. *Degrees:* associate and bachelor's.

Freshman Application Contact Director of Recruitment, ITT Technical Institute, 3325 Stop 8 Road, Dayton, OH 45414. *Phone:* 937-264-7700. *Toll-free phone:* 800-568-3241.
Website: http://www.itt-tech.edu/.

ITT Technical Institute

Hilliard, Ohio

- **Proprietary** primarily 2-year, founded 2003, part of ITT Educational Services, Inc.
- **Coed**

Academics *Calendar:* quarters. *Degrees:* associate and bachelor's.

Freshman Application Contact Director of Recruitment, ITT Technical Institute, 3781 Park Mill Run Drive, Hilliard, OH 43026. *Phone:* 614-771-4888. *Toll-free phone:* 888-483-4888.
Website: http://www.itt-tech.edu/.

ITT Technical Institute

Maumee, Ohio

- **Proprietary** primarily 2-year
- **Coed**

Academics *Degrees:* associate and bachelor's.

Freshman Application Contact Director of Recruitment, ITT Technical Institute, 1656 Henthorne Drive, Suite B, Maumee, OH 43537. *Phone:* 419-861-6500. *Toll-free phone:* 877-205-4639.
Website: http://www.itt-tech.edu/.

ITT Technical Institute

Norwood, Ohio

- **Proprietary** primarily 2-year, founded 1995, part of ITT Educational Services, Inc.
- **Coed**

Academics *Calendar:* quarters. *Degrees:* associate and bachelor's.

Freshman Application Contact Director of Recruitment, ITT Technical Institute, 4750 Wesley Avenue, Norwood, OH 45212. *Phone:* 513-531-8300. *Toll-free phone:* 800-314-8324.
Website: http://www.itt-tech.edu/.

ITT Technical Institute

Strongsville, Ohio

- **Proprietary** primarily 2-year, founded 1994, part of ITT Educational Services, Inc.
- **Coed**

Academics *Calendar:* quarters. *Degrees:* associate and bachelor's.

Freshman Application Contact Director of Recruitment, ITT Technical Institute, 14955 Sprague Road, Strongsville, OH 44136. *Phone:* 440-234-9091. *Toll-free phone:* 800-331-1488.
Website: http://www.itt-tech.edu/.

ITT Technical Institute
Warrensville Heights, Ohio

- **Proprietary** primarily 2-year, founded 2005
- **Coed**

Academics *Calendar:* quarters. *Degrees:* associate and bachelor's.
Freshman Application Contact Director of Recruitment, ITT Technical Institute, 4700 Richmond Road, Warrensville Heights, OH 44128. *Phone:* 216-896-6500. *Toll-free phone:* 800-741-3494.
Website: http://www.itt-tech.edu/.

ITT Technical Institute
Youngstown, Ohio

- **Proprietary** primarily 2-year, founded 1967, part of ITT Educational Services, Inc.
- **Suburban** campus
- **Coed**

Academics *Calendar:* quarters. *Degrees:* associate and bachelor's.
Financial Aid Of all full-time matriculated undergraduates who enrolled in 2011, 5 Federal Work-Study jobs (averaging $3979).
Freshman Application Contact Director of Recruitment, ITT Technical Institute, 1030 North Meridian Road, Youngstown, OH 44509-4098. *Phone:* 330-270-1600. *Toll-free phone:* 800-832-5001.
Website: http://www.itt-tech.edu/.

James A. Rhodes State College
Lima, Ohio

- **State-supported** 2-year, founded 1971
- **Small-town** 565-acre campus
- **Endowment** $1.7 million
- **Coed**, 3,883 undergraduate students, 40% full-time, 68% women, 32% men

Undergraduates 1,548 full-time, 2,335 part-time. Students come from 4 states and territories; 1% are from out of state; 8% Black or African American, non-Hispanic/Latino; 2% Hispanic/Latino; 0.6% Asian, non-Hispanic/Latino; 0.1% Native Hawaiian or other Pacific Islander, non-Hispanic/Latino; 0.4% American Indian or Alaska Native, non-Hispanic/Latino; 0.1% Two or more races, non-Hispanic/Latino; 0.9% Race/ethnicity unknown; 7% transferred in. *Retention:* 55% of full-time freshmen returned.
Freshmen *Admission:* 1,691 applied, 1,691 admitted, 544 enrolled. *Average high school GPA:* 2.98.
Faculty *Total:* 248, 42% full-time. *Student/faculty ratio:* 15:1.
Majors Accounting technology and bookkeeping; administrative assistant and secretarial science; business, management, and marketing related; child development; civil engineering technology; computer programming; computer technology/computer systems technology; corrections; criminal justice/police science; dental hygiene; drafting/design engineering technologies related; electrical, electronic and communications engineering technology; emergency medical technology (EMT paramedic); environmental control technologies related; finance; industrial technology; legal assistant/paralegal; marketing/marketing management; mechanical engineering/mechanical technology; medical/clinical assistant; medical radiologic technology; multi/interdisciplinary studies related; occupational therapist assistant; physical therapy; quality control technology; registered nursing/registered nurse; respiratory care therapy; robotics technology; social work.
Academics *Calendar:* quarters. *Degree:* certificates and associate. *Special study options:* academic remediation for entering students, adult/continuing education programs, advanced placement credit, cooperative education, distance learning, independent study, internships, off-campus study, part-time degree program, services for LD students, student-designed majors, summer session for credit.
Library Rhodes State/Ohio State Library with 80,000 titles, an OPAC.
Student Life *Housing:* college housing not available. *Options:* Campus housing is provided by a third party. *Activities and Organizations:* drama/theater group, student-run newspaper, choral group. *Campus security:* 24-hour emergency response devices and patrols, student patrols, late-night transport/escort service. *Student services:* personal/psychological counseling.
Athletics *Intercollegiate sports:* baseball M(c), basketball M(c)/W(c), golf M(c). *Intramural sports:* baseball M, basketball M/W, bowling M/W, football M/W, golf M/W, softball M/W, volleyball M/W.
Financial Aid Of all full-time matriculated undergraduates who enrolled in 2011, 110 Federal Work-Study jobs (averaging $1000).

Applying *Options:* electronic application, early admission, deferred entrance. *Application fee:* $25. *Required:* high school transcript. *Application deadlines:* rolling (freshmen), rolling (transfers). *Notification:* continuous until 8/15 (freshmen), continuous until 8/15 (transfers).
Freshman Application Contact Traci Cox, Director, Office of Admissions, James A. Rhodes State College, http://www.rhodesstate.edu/Admissions/Apply%20Now.aspx, Lima, OH 45804-3597. *Phone:* 419-995-8040. *E-mail:* cox.t@rhodesstate.edu.
Website: http://www.rhodesstate.edu/.

Kaplan Career Institute, Cleveland Campus
Brooklyn, Ohio

- **Proprietary** 2-year
- **Coed**

Academics *Degree:* diplomas and associate.
Freshman Application Contact Admissions Office, Kaplan Career Institute, Cleveland Campus, 8720 Brookpark Road, Brooklyn, OH 44129. *Toll-free phone:* 800-935-1857.
Website: http://cleveland.kaplancareerinstitute.com/.

Kaplan College, Dayton Campus
Dayton, Ohio

- **Proprietary** 2-year, founded 1971
- **Urban** campus
- **Coed**

Academics *Calendar:* quarters. *Degree:* diplomas and associate.
Freshman Application Contact Kaplan College, Dayton Campus, 2800 East River Road, Dayton, OH 45439. *Phone:* 937-294-6155. *Toll-free phone:* 800-935-1857.
Website: http://dayton.kaplancollege.com/.

Kent State University at Ashtabula
Ashtabula, Ohio

- **State-supported** primarily 2-year, founded 1958, part of Kent State University System
- **Small-town** 120-acre campus with easy access to Cleveland
- **Coed**, 2,511 undergraduate students, 50% full-time, 65% women, 35% men

Undergraduates 1,268 full-time, 1,243 part-time. Students come from 12 states and territories; 1 other country; 2% are from out of state; 5% Black or African American, non-Hispanic/Latino; 3% Hispanic/Latino; 0.6% Asian, non-Hispanic/Latino; 0.5% American Indian or Alaska Native, non-Hispanic/Latino; 1% Two or more races, non-Hispanic/Latino; 3% Race/ethnicity unknown; 0.2% international; 7% transferred in. *Retention:* 49% of full-time freshmen returned.
Freshmen *Admission:* 565 applied, 562 admitted, 348 enrolled. *Average high school GPA:* 2.74. *Test scores:* SAT critical reading scores over 500: 29%; ACT scores over 18: 67%; ACT scores over 24: 11%; ACT scores over 30: 2%.
Faculty *Total:* 126, 42% full-time. *Student/faculty ratio:* 22:1.
Majors Accounting; accounting technology and bookkeeping; administrative assistant and secretarial science; aerospace, aeronautical and astronautical/space engineering; biological and biomedical sciences related; business administration and management; business/commerce; computer programming (specific applications); criminal justice/safety; electrical and electronic engineering technologies related; English; general studies; health and medical administrative services related; health/medical preparatory programs related; hospitality administration; liberal arts and sciences and humanities related; medical radiologic technology; occupational therapist assistant; physical therapy technology; psychology; registered nursing/registered nurse; respiratory care therapy; sociology; speech communication and rhetoric; viticulture and enology.
Academics *Calendar:* semesters. *Degrees:* certificates, associate, and bachelor's (also offers some upper-level and graduate courses). *Special study options:* academic remediation for entering students, advanced placement credit, distance learning, double majors, independent study, internships, part-time degree program, services for LD students, student-designed majors, study abroad, summer session for credit. *ROTC:* Army (c), Navy (c), Air Force (c).
Library Kent State at Ashtabula Library with 51,884 titles, 225 serial subscriptions, 640 audiovisual materials, an OPAC, a Web page.
Student Life *Housing:* college housing not available. *Activities and Organizations:* student government, student veterans association, Student Nurses Association, Student Occupational Therapy Association (SOTA), Media Club. *Campus security:* 24-hour emergency response devices.

Standardized Tests *Required for some:* SAT or ACT (for admission). *Recommended:* SAT or ACT (for admission).

Financial Aid Of all full-time matriculated undergraduates who enrolled in 2012, 846 applied for aid, 814 were judged to have need, 169 had their need fully met. In 2012, 3 non-need-based awards were made. *Average percent of need met:* 42%. *Average financial aid package:* $7513. *Average need-based loan:* $3764. *Average need-based gift aid:* $4675. *Average non-need-based aid:* $1333.

Applying *Options:* electronic application, early admission, deferred entrance. *Application fee:* $30. *Required:* high school transcript. *Application deadlines:* rolling (freshmen), rolling (transfers). *Notification:* continuous (freshmen), continuous (transfers).

Freshman Application Contact Kent State University at Ashtabula, 3300 Lake Road West, Ashtabula, OH 44004-2299. *Phone:* 440-964-4217. *Website:* http://www.ashtabula.kent.edu/.

Kent State University at East Liverpool

East Liverpool, Ohio

- **State-supported** primarily 2-year, founded 1967, part of Kent State University System
- **Small-town** 4-acre campus with easy access to Pittsburgh
- **Coed,** 1,504 undergraduate students, 54% full-time, 69% women, 31% men

Undergraduates 818 full-time, 686 part-time. Students come from 8 states and territories; 2 other countries; 5% are from out of state; 4% Black or African American, non-Hispanic/Latino; 2% Hispanic/Latino; 0.6% Asian, non-Hispanic/Latino; 0.3% American Indian or Alaska Native, non-Hispanic/Latino; 1% Two or more races, non-Hispanic/Latino; 2% Race/ethnicity unknown; 0.1% international; 5% transferred in. *Retention:* 52% of full-time freshmen returned.

Freshmen *Admission:* 179 applied, 171 admitted, 130 enrolled. *Average high school GPA:* 2.89. *Test scores:* SAT math scores over 500: 50%; ACT scores over 18: 53%; ACT scores over 24: 7%.

Faculty *Total:* 75, 36% full-time. *Student/faculty ratio:* 24:1.

Majors Accounting technology and bookkeeping; biological and biomedical sciences related; business/commerce; computer programming (specific applications); criminal justice/safety; English; general studies; legal assistant/paralegal; liberal arts and sciences and humanities related; occupational therapist assistant; physical therapy technology; psychology; registered nursing/registered nurse; speech communication and rhetoric.

Academics *Calendar:* semesters. *Degrees:* certificates, associate, and bachelor's (also offers some upper-level and graduate courses). *Special study options:* academic remediation for entering students, accelerated degree program, adult/continuing education programs, advanced placement credit, distance learning, double majors, freshman honors college, honors programs, independent study, internships, part-time degree program, services for LD students, student-designed majors, study abroad, summer session for credit. *ROTC:* Army (c), Navy (c), Air Force (c).

Library Blair Memorial Library with 31,320 titles, 135 serial subscriptions, an OPAC, a Web page.

Student Life *Housing:* college housing not available. *Activities and Organizations:* student-run newspaper, Student Government, Student Nurses Association, Environmental Club, Occupational Therapist Assistant Club, Physical Therapist Assistant Club. *Campus security:* student patrols, late-night transport/escort service.

Standardized Tests *Required for some:* SAT or ACT (for admission). *Recommended:* SAT or ACT (for admission).

Financial Aid Of all full-time matriculated undergraduates who enrolled in 2012, 398 applied for aid, 372 were judged to have need, 97 had their need fully met. In 2012, 2 non-need-based awards were made. *Average percent of need met:* 45%. *Average financial aid package:* $7555. *Average need-based loan:* $3821. *Average need-based gift aid:* $4655. *Average non-need-based aid:* $750.

Applying *Options:* electronic application, early admission, deferred entrance. *Application fee:* $30. *Required:* high school transcript. *Application deadlines:* rolling (freshmen), rolling (transfers). *Notification:* continuous (freshmen), continuous (transfers).

Freshman Application Contact Kent State University at East Liverpool, OH. *Phone:* 330-385-3805. *Website:* http://www.eliv.kent.edu/.

Kent State University at Salem

Salem, Ohio

- **State-supported** primarily 2-year, founded 1966, part of Kent State University System
- **Rural** 98-acre campus
- **Coed,** 1,878 undergraduate students, 67% full-time, 70% women, 30% men

Undergraduates 1,266 full-time, 612 part-time. Students come from 11 states and territories; 4 other countries; 1% are from out of state; 3% Black or African American, non-Hispanic/Latino; 1% Hispanic/Latino; 0.6% Asian, non-Hispanic/Latino; 0.4% American Indian or Alaska Native, non-Hispanic/Latino; 1% Two or more races, non-Hispanic/Latino; 3% Race/ethnicity unknown; 0.1% international; 7% transferred in. *Retention:* 59% of full-time freshmen returned.

Freshmen *Admission:* 446 applied, 439 admitted, 262 enrolled. *Average high school GPA:* 2.92. *Test scores:* SAT math scores over 500: 50%; ACT scores over 18: 71%; ACT scores over 24: 13%.

Faculty *Total:* 123, 37% full-time. *Student/faculty ratio:* 20:1.

Majors Accounting technology and bookkeeping; administrative assistant and secretarial science; applied horticulture/horticulture operations; biological and biomedical sciences related; business administration and management; business/commerce; computer programming (specific applications); criminal justice/safety; early childhood education; education related; English; general studies; health and medical administrative services related; human development and family studies; insurance; liberal arts and sciences and humanities related; liberal arts and sciences/liberal studies; medical radiologic technology; psychology; registered nursing/registered nurse; speech communication and rhetoric.

Academics *Calendar:* semesters. *Degrees:* certificates, associate, and bachelor's (also offers some upper-level and graduate courses). *Special study options:* academic remediation for entering students, accelerated degree program, adult/continuing education programs, advanced placement credit, cooperative education, distance learning, double majors, freshman honors college, honors programs, independent study, internships, part-time degree program, services for LD students, student-designed majors, study abroad, summer session for credit. *ROTC:* Army (c), Air Force (c).

Library Kent State Salem Library with 19,000 titles, 163 serial subscriptions, 158 audiovisual materials, an OPAC, a Web page.

Student Life *Housing:* college housing not available. *Activities and Organizations:* choral group, Honors Club, Human Services Technology Club, Radiologic Technology Club, Student Government Organization, Students for Professional Nursing. *Campus security:* 24-hour emergency response devices, late-night transport/escort service. *Student services:* personal/psychological counseling.

Athletics *Intramural sports:* basketball M/W, skiing (downhill) M/W, table tennis M/W, tennis M/W, volleyball M/W.

Standardized Tests *Required for some:* SAT or ACT (for admission). *Recommended:* SAT or ACT (for admission).

Financial Aid Of all full-time matriculated undergraduates who enrolled in 2012, 889 applied for aid, 815 were judged to have need, 246 had their need fully met. In 2012, 9 non-need-based awards were made. *Average percent of need met:* 46%. *Average financial aid package:* $7145. *Average need-based loan:* $3786. *Average need-based gift aid:* $4536. *Average non-need-based aid:* $1448.

Applying *Options:* electronic application, early admission, deferred entrance. *Application fee:* $30. *Required:* high school transcript. *Required for some:* essay or personal statement. *Application deadlines:* rolling (freshmen), rolling (out-of-state freshmen), rolling (transfers). *Notification:* continuous (freshmen), continuous (out-of-state freshmen), continuous (transfers).

Freshman Application Contact Kent State University at Salem, 2491 State Route 45 South, Salem, OH 44460-9412. *Phone:* 330-382-7415. *Website:* http://www.salem.kent.edu/.

Kent State University at Trumbull

Warren, Ohio

- **State-supported** primarily 2-year, founded 1954, part of Kent State University System
- **Suburban** 200-acre campus with easy access to Cleveland
- **Coed,** 3,103 undergraduate students, 61% full-time, 63% women, 37% men

Undergraduates 1,892 full-time, 1,211 part-time. Students come from 16 states and territories; 3 other countries; 1% are from out of state; 10% Black or African American, non-Hispanic/Latino; 3% Hispanic/Latino; 0.5% Asian, non-Hispanic/Latino; 0.2% American Indian or Alaska Native, non-Hispanic/Latino; 2% Two or more races, non-Hispanic/Latino; 2% Race/ethnicity unknown; 0.4% international; 7% transferred in. *Retention:* 47% of full-time freshmen returned.

Freshmen *Admission:* 485 applied, 481 admitted, 375 enrolled. *Average high school GPA:* 2.69. *Test scores:* SAT critical reading scores over 500: 50%; SAT math scores over 500: 50%; SAT writing scores over 500: 25%; ACT scores over 18: 74%; ACT scores over 24: 10%; ACT scores over 30: 1%.

Faculty *Total:* 121, 48% full-time. *Student/faculty ratio:* 29:1.

Majors Accounting technology and bookkeeping; administrative assistant and secretarial science; biological and biomedical sciences related; business administration and management; business/commerce; computer/information technology services administration related; computer programming (specific applications); criminal justice/safety; electrical and electronic engineering technologies related; electrical, electronic and communications engineering technology; emergency medical technology (EMT paramedic); English; environmental engineering technology; general studies; health/health-care administration; industrial production technologies related; industrial technology; legal assistant/paralegal; liberal arts and sciences and humanities related; liberal arts and sciences/liberal studies; mechanical engineering/mechanical technology; nursing science; psychology; registered nursing/registered nurse; speech communication and rhetoric; urban forestry.

Academics *Calendar:* semesters. *Degrees:* certificates, associate, and bachelor's (also offers some upper-level and graduate courses). *Special study options:* academic remediation for entering students, adult/continuing education programs, advanced placement credit, distance learning, double majors, freshman honors college, honors programs, independent study, internships, part-time degree program, services for LD students, student-designed majors, study abroad, summer session for credit. *ROTC:* Army (c), Air Force (c).

Library Trumbull Campus Library with 65,951 titles, 759 serial subscriptions, an OPAC, a Web page.

Student Life *Housing:* college housing not available. *Activities and Organizations:* drama/theater group, National Student Nurses Association, Spot On Improv Group, ENACTUS, GLOW (Gay, Lesbian, or Whatever), If These Hands Could Talk - ASL. *Campus security:* 24-hour emergency response devices, late-night transport/escort service, patrols by trained security personnel during open hours. *Student services:* personal/psychological counseling.

Standardized Tests *Required for some:* SAT or ACT (for admission). *Recommended:* SAT or ACT (for admission).

Financial Aid Of all full-time matriculated undergraduates who enrolled in 2012, 1,119 applied for aid, 1,058 were judged to have need, 254 had their need fully met. In 2012, 7 non-need-based awards were made. *Average percent of need met:* 45%. *Average financial aid package:* $7497. *Average need-based loan:* $3869. *Average need-based gift aid:* $4614. *Average non-need-based aid:* $1500.

Applying *Options:* electronic application, deferred entrance. *Application fee:* $30. *Required:* high school transcript. *Application deadlines:* rolling (freshmen), rolling (out-of-state freshmen), rolling (transfers). *Notification:* continuous (freshmen), continuous (out-of-state freshmen), continuous (transfers).

Freshman Application Contact Kent State University at Trumbull, Warren, OH 44483. *Phone:* 330-675-8935.
Website: http://www.trumbull.kent.edu/.

Kent State University at Tuscarawas
New Philadelphia, Ohio

- **State-supported** primarily 2-year, founded 1962, part of Kent State University System
- **Small-town** 172-acre campus with easy access to Cleveland
- **Coed,** 2,983 undergraduate students, 50% full-time, 54% women, 46% men

Undergraduates 1,484 full-time, 1,499 part-time. 1% are from out of state; 2% Black or African American, non-Hispanic/Latino; 0.9% Hispanic/Latino; 0.6% Asian, non-Hispanic/Latino; 0.1% Native Hawaiian or other Pacific Islander, non-Hispanic/Latino; 0.1% American Indian or Alaska Native, non-Hispanic/Latino; 1% Two or more races, non-Hispanic/Latino; 3% Race/ethnicity unknown; 0.2% international; 6% transferred in. *Retention:* 59% of full-time freshmen returned.

Freshmen *Admission:* 470 applied, 448 admitted, 348 enrolled. *Average high school GPA:* 2.81. *Test scores:* SAT critical reading scores over 500: 25%; SAT math scores over 500: 50%; SAT writing scores over 500: 25%; ACT scores over 18: 77%; SAT critical reading scores over 600: 25%; ACT scores over 24: 19%; ACT scores over 30: 2%.

Faculty *Total:* 139, 37% full-time. *Student/faculty ratio:* 23:1.

Majors Accounting; accounting technology and bookkeeping; administrative assistant and secretarial science; biological and biomedical sciences related; business administration and management; business/commerce; computer programming (specific applications); criminal justice/police science; criminal justice/safety; early childhood education; education related; electrical and electronic engineering technologies related; engineering; engineering technologies and engineering related; engineering technology; English; general studies; industrial technology; liberal arts and sciences and humanities related; liberal arts and sciences/liberal studies; mechanical engineering/mechanical

technology; psychology; registered nursing/registered nurse; speech communication and rhetoric; veterinary/animal health technology.

Academics *Calendar:* semesters. *Degrees:* certificates, associate, and bachelor's (also offers some upper-level and graduate courses). *Special study options:* academic remediation for entering students, accelerated degree program, adult/continuing education programs, advanced placement credit, distance learning, double majors, freshman honors college, honors programs, independent study, internships, part-time degree program, services for LD students, student-designed majors, study abroad, summer session for credit.

Library Tuscarawas Campus Library with 63,880 titles, 208 serial subscriptions, 1,179 audiovisual materials, an OPAC, a Web page.

Student Life *Housing:* college housing not available. *Activities and Organizations:* drama/theater group, choral group, Society of Manufacturing Engineers, IEEE, Animation Imagineers, Justice Studies Club, Student Activities Council. *Campus security:* 24-hour emergency response devices.

Athletics *Intramural sports:* basketball M/W, volleyball M/W.

Standardized Tests *Required for some:* SAT or ACT (for admission). *Recommended:* SAT or ACT (for admission).

Financial Aid Of all full-time matriculated undergraduates who enrolled in 2012, 1,002 applied for aid, 928 were judged to have need, 262 had their need fully met. In 2012, 15 non-need-based awards were made. *Average percent of need met:* 47%. *Average financial aid package:* $7249. *Average need-based loan:* $3860. *Average need-based gift aid:* $4382. *Average non-need-based aid:* $1265.

Applying *Options:* electronic application, deferred entrance. *Application fee:* $30. *Required:* high school transcript. *Application deadlines:* rolling (freshmen), rolling (out-of-state freshmen), rolling (transfers). *Notification:* continuous (freshmen), continuous (out-of-state freshmen), continuous (transfers).

Freshman Application Contact Kent State University at Tuscarawas, Kent State University at Tuscarawas, 330 University Drive Northeast, New Philadelphia, OH 44663-9403. *Phone:* 330-339-3391 Ext. 47425. *Fax:* 330-339-3321. *E-mail:* info@tusc.kent.edu.
Website: http://www.tusc.kent.edu/.

Lakeland Community College
Kirtland, Ohio

- **State and locally supported** 2-year, founded 1967, part of Ohio Board of Regents
- **Suburban** 380-acre campus with easy access to Cleveland
- **Endowment** $354,544
- **Coed,** 9,283 undergraduate students, 37% full-time, 59% women, 41% men

Undergraduates 3,397 full-time, 5,886 part-time. Students come from 6 states and territories; 1% are from out of state; 16% Black or African American, non-Hispanic/Latino; 3% Hispanic/Latino; 1% Asian, non-Hispanic/Latino; 0.1% Native Hawaiian or other Pacific Islander, non-Hispanic/Latino; 0.3% American Indian or Alaska Native, non-Hispanic/Latino; 0.9% Two or more races, non-Hispanic/Latino; 4% Race/ethnicity unknown; 0.3% international; 5% transferred in. *Retention:* 51% of full-time freshmen returned.

Freshmen *Admission:* 1,246 enrolled.

Faculty *Total:* 673, 18% full-time. *Student/faculty ratio:* 18:1.

Majors Accounting; administrative assistant and secretarial science; biotechnology; business administration and management; child-care provision; civil engineering technology; clinical/medical laboratory technology; commercial and advertising art; computer engineering technology; computer programming (specific applications); computer systems analysis; computer systems networking and telecommunications; computer technology/computer systems technology; corrections; criminal justice/police science; dental hygiene; electrical, electronic and communications engineering technology; energy management and systems technology; fire prevention and safety technology; health professions related; homeland security, law enforcement, firefighting and protective services related; hospitality administration; instrumentation technology; legal assistant/paralegal; liberal arts and sciences/liberal studies; management information systems; marketing/marketing management; mechanical engineering/mechanical technology; medical radiologic technology; nuclear medical technology; ophthalmic technology; quality control technology; registered nursing/registered nurse; respiratory care therapy; restaurant, culinary, and catering management; sign language interpretation and translation; social work; surgical technology; tourism and travel services management.

Academics *Calendar:* semesters. *Degree:* certificates and associate. *Special study options:* academic remediation for entering students, adult/continuing education programs, advanced placement credit, cooperative education, distance learning, English as a second language, external degree program, independent study, internships, off-campus study, part-time degree program, services for LD students, study abroad, summer session for credit.

Library Lakeland Community College Library with 65,814 titles, 248 serial subscriptions, 4,212 audiovisual materials, an OPAC, a Web page.

Student Life *Housing:* college housing not available. *Activities and Organizations:* drama/theater group, student-run newspaper, radio station, choral group,

Campus Activities Board, Lakeland Student Government, Lakeland Signers, Thousand Shoes Skat Dance Team, Gamer's Guild. *Campus security:* 24-hour emergency response devices and patrols, student patrols, late-night transport/escort service. *Student services:* health clinic, personal/psychological counseling, women's center.

Athletics Member NJCAA. *Intercollegiate sports:* baseball M(s), basketball M(s)/W(s), golf M(s), soccer M(s), softball W(s), volleyball W(s).

Standardized Tests *Required:* Compass test is required (for admission).

Costs (2012–13) *Tuition:* area resident $3087 full-time, $103 per credit hour part-time; state resident $3936 full-time, $131 per credit hour part-time; non-resident $8573 full-time, $286 per credit hour part-time. Full-time tuition and fees vary according to course load. Part-time tuition and fees vary according to course load. *Required fees:* $29 full-time, $14 per term part-time. *Payment plan:* installment. *Waivers:* senior citizens and employees or children of employees.

Financial Aid Of all full-time matriculated undergraduates who enrolled in 2011, 3,429 applied for aid, 2,958 were judged to have need, 468 had their need fully met. 72 Federal Work-Study jobs (averaging $2936). *Average percent of need met:* 56%. *Average financial aid package:* $7026. *Average need-based loan:* $3232. *Average need-based gift aid:* $5251.

Applying *Options:* electronic application, early admission, deferred entrance. *Application fee:* $15. *Required:* high school transcript. *Application deadlines:* 9/1 (freshmen), 9/1 (transfers). *Notification:* continuous until 9/1 (freshmen), continuous until 9/1 (transfers).

Freshman Application Contact Lakeland Community College, 7700 Clocktower Drive, Kirtland, OH 44094-5198. *Phone:* 440-525-7230. *Toll-free phone:* 800-589-8520.
Website: http://www.lakeland.cc.oh.us/.

Lincoln College of Technology
Cincinnati, Ohio

Freshman Application Contact Director of Admission, Lincoln College of Technology, 149 Northland Boulevard, Cincinnati, OH 45246-1122. *Phone:* 513-874-0432. *Fax:* 513-874-1330.
Website: http://www.lincolnedu.com/.

Lincoln College of Technology
Dayton, Ohio

Director of Admissions William Furlong, Director of Admissions, Lincoln College of Technology, 111 West First Street, Dayton, OH 45402-3003. *Phone:* 937-224-0061.
Website: http://www.lincolnedu.com/.

Lorain County Community College
Elyria, Ohio

- **State and locally supported** 2-year, founded 1963, part of Ohio Board of Regents
- **Suburban** 280-acre campus with easy access to Cleveland
- **Endowment** $21.7 million
- **Coed**, 12,656 undergraduate students, 31% full-time, 64% women, 36% men

Undergraduates 3,918 full-time, 8,738 part-time. Students come from 17 states and territories; 28 other countries; 1% are from out of state; 11% Black or African American, non-Hispanic/Latino; 8% Hispanic/Latino; 1% Asian, non-Hispanic/Latino; 0.5% American Indian or Alaska Native, non-Hispanic/Latino; 2% Two or more races, non-Hispanic/Latino; 2% Race/ethnicity unknown; 0.7% international. *Retention:* 58% of full-time freshmen returned.

Freshmen *Admission:* 2,283 applied, 2,283 admitted, 2,283 enrolled.

Faculty *Total:* 752, 18% full-time. *Student/faculty ratio:* 20:1.

Majors Accounting; administrative assistant and secretarial science; art; artificial intelligence; athletic training; biological and physical sciences; biology/biological sciences; business administration and management; chemistry; civil engineering technology; clinical/medical laboratory technology; computer and information sciences related; computer engineering technology; computer programming; computer programming related; computer programming (specific applications); computer programming (vendor/product certification); computer science; computer systems networking and telecommunications; computer technology/computer systems technology; consumer merchandising/retailing management; corrections; cosmetology; cosmetology and personal grooming arts related; criminal justice/police science; data entry/microcomputer applications; data entry/microcomputer applications related; diagnostic medical sonography and ultrasound technology; drafting and design technology; drafting/design engineering technologies related; dramatic/theater arts; education; electrical, electronic and communications engineering technology; elementary education; engineering; engineering technology; finance; fire science/firefighting; history; human services; indus-

trial radiologic technology; industrial technology; information science/studies; information technology; journalism; kindergarten/preschool education; liberal arts and sciences/liberal studies; machine tool technology; marketing/marketing management; mass communication/media; mathematics; music; nuclear medical technology; pharmacy; physical education teaching and coaching; physical therapy technology; physics; plastics and polymer engineering technology; political science and government; pre-engineering; psychology; quality control technology; real estate; registered nursing/registered nurse; social sciences; social work; sociology; sport and fitness administration/management; surgical technology; tourism and travel services management; urban studies/affairs; word processing.

Academics *Calendar:* semesters. *Degree:* certificates and associate. *Special study options:* academic remediation for entering students, adult/continuing education programs, advanced placement credit, cooperative education, distance learning, double majors, English as a second language, external degree program, honors programs, independent study, internships, part-time degree program, services for LD students, student-designed majors, summer session for credit.

Library Learning Resource Center with 198,984 titles, 3,289 audiovisual materials, an OPAC.

Student Life *Housing:* college housing not available. *Activities and Organizations:* drama/theater group, student-run newspaper, radio station, choral group, Phi Beta Kappa, Black Progressives, Hispanic Club, national fraternities, national sororities. *Campus security:* 24-hour emergency response devices and patrols, late-night transport/escort service. *Student services:* health clinic, personal/psychological counseling, women's center, legal services.

Athletics *Intramural sports:* archery M/W, basketball M/W, softball M/W, volleyball M/W, weight lifting M/W, wrestling M.

Financial Aid Of all full-time matriculated undergraduates who enrolled in 2011, 100 Federal Work-Study jobs.

Applying *Options:* early admission, deferred entrance. *Required for some:* high school transcript. *Application deadlines:* rolling (freshmen), rolling (transfers). *Notification:* continuous (freshmen), continuous (transfers).

Freshman Application Contact Lorain County Community College, 1005 Abbe Road, North, Elyria, OH 44035. *Phone:* 440-366-7622. *Toll-free phone:* 800-995-5222 Ext. 4032.
Website: http://www.lorainccc.edu/.

Marion Technical College
Marion, Ohio

Freshman Application Contact Mr. Joel Liles, Dean of Enrollment Services, Marion Technical College, 1467 Mount Vernon Avenue, Marion, OH 43302. *Phone:* 740-389-4636 Ext. 249. *Fax:* 740-389-6136. *E-mail:* enroll@mtc.edu.
Website: http://www.mtc.edu/.

Miami-Jacobs Career College
Columbus, Ohio

Admissions Office Contact Miami-Jacobs Career College, 150 E. Gay Street, Columbus, OH 43215.
Website: http://www.miamijacobs.edu/.

Miami-Jacobs Career College
Dayton, Ohio

Director of Admissions Mary Percell, Vice President of Information Services, Miami-Jacobs Career College, 110 N. Patterson Boulevard, Dayton, OH 45402. *Phone:* 937-461-5174 Ext. 118.
Website: http://www.miamijacobs.edu/.

Miami-Jacobs Career College
Independence, Ohio

Freshman Application Contact Director of Admissions, Miami-Jacobs Career College, 6400 Rockside Road, Independence, OH 44131. *Phone:* 216-861-3222. *Toll-free phone:* 866-324-0142. *Fax:* 216-861-4517.
Website: http://www.miamijacobs.edu/.

Miami University–Middletown Campus
Middletown, Ohio

Freshman Application Contact Diane Cantonwine, Assistant Director of Admission and Financial Aid, Miami University–Middletown Campus, 4200 East University Boulevard, Middletown, OH 45042-3497. *Phone:* 513-727-3346. *Toll-free phone:* 866-426-4643. *Fax:* 513-727-3223. *E-mail:*

cantondm@muohio.edu.
Website: http://www.mid.muohio.edu/.

National College
Stow, Ohio

Admissions Office Contact National College, 3855 Fishcreek Road, Stow, OH 44224.
Website: http://www.national-college.edu/.

National College
Youngstown, Ohio

Admissions Office Contact National College, 3487 Belmont Avenue, Youngstown, OH 44505.
Website: http://www.national-college.edu/.

North Central State College
Mansfield, Ohio

Freshman Application Contact Ms. Nikia L. Fletcher, Director of Admissions, North Central State College, 2441 Kenwood Circle, PO Box 698, Mansfield, OH 44901-0698. *Phone:* 419-755-4813. *Toll-free phone:* 888-755-4899. *E-mail:* nfletcher@ncstatecollege.edu.
Website: http://www.ncstatecollege.edu/.

Northwest State Community College
Archbold, Ohio

- **State-supported** 2-year, founded 1968, part of Ohio Board of Regents
- **Rural** 80-acre campus with easy access to Toledo
- **Coed,** 4,244 undergraduate students, 21% full-time, 43% women, 57% men

Undergraduates 881 full-time, 3,363 part-time. Students come from 9 states and territories; 6 other countries; 0.2% are from out of state; 2% Black or African American, non-Hispanic/Latino; 6% Hispanic/Latino; 0.5% Asian, non-Hispanic/Latino; 0.2% American Indian or Alaska Native, non-Hispanic/Latino; 0.8% Two or more races, non-Hispanic/Latino; 16% Race/ethnicity unknown; 2% transferred in. *Retention:* 53% of full-time freshmen returned.
Freshmen *Admission:* 1,144 applied, 1,144 admitted, 721 enrolled. *Average high school GPA:* 2.85.
Faculty *Total:* 309, 14% full-time, 74% with terminal degrees. *Student/faculty ratio:* 15:1.
Majors Accounting; accounting related; administrative assistant and secretarial science; automotive engineering technology; banking and financial support services; business administration and management; business administration, management and operations related; business automation/technology/data entry; business/commerce; CAD/CADD drafting/design technology; child-care and support services management; child development; computer and information systems security; computer engineering; computer engineering technology; computer programming; corrections; corrections and criminal justice related; criminal justice/law enforcement administration; criminal justice/police science; criminal justice/safety; data entry/microcomputer applications; design and visual communications; education; electrical, electronic and communications engineering technology; energy management and systems technology; engineering/industrial management; engineering related; engineering technologies and engineering related; entrepreneurship; environmental control technologies related; executive assistant/executive secretary; history; human development and family studies related; industrial electronics technology; industrial mechanics and maintenance technology; industrial production technologies related; international business/trade/commerce; kindergarten/preschool education; legal administrative assistant/secretary; legal assistant/paralegal; liberal arts and sciences/liberal studies; logistics, materials, and supply chain management; machine tool technology; marketing/marketing management; mechanical engineering; mechanical engineering/mechanical technology; medical administrative assistant and medical secretary; medical/clinical assistant; merchandising, sales, and marketing operations related (general); network and system administration; nonprofit management; office management; plastics and polymer engineering technology; precision metal working related; quality control technology; registered nursing/registered nurse; sheet metal technology; social work; teacher assistant/aide; tool and die technology; web page, digital/multimedia and information resources design.
Academics *Calendar:* semesters. *Degree:* certificates and associate. *Special study options:* academic remediation for entering students, adult/continuing education programs, advanced placement credit, cooperative education, distance learning, double majors, external degree program, independent study, internships, off-campus study, part-time degree program, services for LD students, student-designed majors, summer session for credit.

Library Northwest State Community College Library with 30,596 titles, 124 serial subscriptions, 3,401 audiovisual materials, an OPAC, a Web page.
Student Life *Housing:* college housing not available. *Campus security:* 24-hour emergency response devices, security patrols. *Student services:* personal/psychological counseling.
Athletics *Intramural sports:* basketball M/W, bowling M/W, soccer M/W, table tennis M/W, volleyball M/W.
Costs (2013–14) *Tuition:* state resident $3504 full-time, $146 per credit part-time; nonresident $6864 full-time, $286 per credit part-time. Full-time tuition and fees vary according to course load. Part-time tuition and fees vary according to course load. *Required fees:* $60 full-time, $30 per term part-time. *Payment plan:* installment. *Waivers:* employees or children of employees.
Financial Aid Of all full-time matriculated undergraduates who enrolled in 2011, 43 Federal Work-Study jobs (averaging $1077).
Applying *Options:* electronic application, early admission, deferred entrance. *Application fee:* $20. *Required:* high school transcript. *Application deadlines:* rolling (freshmen), rolling (out-of-state freshmen), rolling (transfers). *Notification:* continuous (freshmen), continuous (out-of-state freshmen), continuous (transfers).
Freshman Application Contact Mr. Dennis Giacomino, Director of Admissions, Northwest State Community College, 22600 State Route 34, Archbold, OH 43502. *Phone:* 419-267-1356. *Fax:* 419-267-3688. *E-mail:* admissions@northweststate.edu.
Website: http://www.northweststate.edu/.

Ohio Business College
Hilliard, Ohio

Admissions Office Contact Ohio Business College, 4525 Trueman Boulevard, Hilliard, OH 43026.
Website: http://www.ohiobusinesscollege.edu/.

Ohio Business College
Sandusky, Ohio

Freshman Application Contact Ohio Business College, 5202 Timber Commons Drive, Sandusky, OH 44870. *Phone:* 419-627-8345. *Toll-free phone:* 888-627-8345.
Website: http://www.ohiobusinesscollege.edu/.

Ohio Business College
Sheffield Village, Ohio

Director of Admissions Mr. Jim Unger, Admissions Director, Ohio Business College, 5095 Waterford Drive, Sheffield Village, OH 44035. *Toll-free phone:* 888-514-3126.
Website: http://www.ohiobusinesscollege.edu/.

Ohio College of Massotherapy
Akron, Ohio

Director of Admissions Mr. John Atkins, Director of Admissions and Marketing, Ohio College of Massotherapy, 225 Heritage Woods Drive, Akron, OH 44321. *Phone:* 330-665-1084 Ext. 11. *Toll-free phone:* 888-888-4325. *E-mail:* johna@ocm.edu.
Website: http://www.ocm.edu/.

The Ohio State University Agricultural Technical Institute
Wooster, Ohio

- **State-supported** 2-year, founded 1971, part of Ohio State University System
- **Small-town** campus with easy access to Cleveland, Columbus
- **Endowment** $2.2 million
- **Coed,** 730 undergraduate students, 100% full-time, 43% women, 57% men

Undergraduates 730 full-time. Students come from 7 states and territories; 2% are from out of state; 5% transferred in. *Retention:* 68% of full-time freshmen returned.
Freshmen *Admission:* 636 applied, 581 admitted, 346 enrolled. *Test scores:* ACT scores over 18: 57%; ACT scores over 24: 11%.
Faculty *Total:* 70, 47% full-time, 33% with terminal degrees. *Student/faculty ratio:* 17:1.
Majors Agribusiness; agricultural business and management; agricultural business technology; agricultural communication/journalism; agricultural economics; agricultural mechanization; agricultural power machinery operation; agricultural teacher education; agronomy and crop science; animal/livestock

husbandry and production; animal sciences; biology/biotechnology laboratory technician; building/construction site management; clinical/medical laboratory technology; construction engineering technology; construction management; crop production; dairy husbandry and production; dairy science; environmental science; equestrian studies; floriculture/floristry management; greenhouse management; heavy equipment maintenance technology; horse husbandry/equine science and management; horticultural science; hydraulics and fluid power technology; industrial technology; landscaping and groundskeeping; livestock management; natural resources management and policy; natural resources management and policy related; plant nursery management; soil science and agronomy; turf and turfgrass management.

Academics *Calendar:* quarters. *Degree:* certificates, diplomas, and associate. *Special study options:* academic remediation for entering students, accelerated degree program, adult/continuing education programs, advanced placement credit, cooperative education, distance learning, double majors, independent study, internships, part-time degree program, services for LD students, student-designed majors, study abroad, summer session for credit. *ROTC:* Army (c), Navy (c), Air Force (c).

Library Agricultural Technical Institute Library with 9,000 titles, 260 serial subscriptions, 100 audiovisual materials, an OPAC, a Web page.

Student Life *Housing:* on-campus residence required for freshman year. *Options:* coed. Campus housing is university owned. *Activities and Organizations:* Hoof-n-Hide Club, Collegiate FFA, Campus Crusade for Christ, Phi Theta Kappa, Community Council. *Campus security:* 24-hour emergency response devices and patrols, controlled dormitory access. *Student services:* health clinic, personal/psychological counseling.

Athletics *Intramural sports:* basketball M/W, football M/W, racquetball M/W, soccer M/W, softball M/W, volleyball M/W.

Standardized Tests *Required for some:* SAT or ACT (for admission).

Financial Aid Of all full-time matriculated undergraduates who enrolled in 2010, 540 applied for aid, 474 were judged to have need, 25 had their need fully met. 64 Federal Work-Study jobs (averaging $2000). In 2010, 24 non-need-based awards were made. *Average percent of need met:* 44%. *Average financial aid package:* $6859. *Average need-based loan:* $3826. *Average need-based gift aid:* $4241. *Average non-need-based aid:* $2107.

Applying *Options:* electronic application. *Application fee:* $60. *Required:* high school transcript. *Application deadlines:* 7/1 (freshmen), 7/1 (out-of-state freshmen), 7/1 (transfers). *Notification:* continuous (freshmen).

Freshman Application Contact Ms. Julia Morris, Admissions Counselor, The Ohio State University Agricultural Technical Institute, 1328 Dover Road, Wooster, OH 44691. *Phone:* 330-287-1327. *Toll-free phone:* 800-647-8283 Ext. 1327. *Fax:* 330-287-1333. *E-mail:* morris.878@osu.edu. *Website:* http://www.ati.osu.edu/.

Ohio Technical College

Cleveland, Ohio

Director of Admissions Mr. Marc Brenner, President, Ohio Technical College, 1374 East 51st Street, Cleveland, OH 44103. *Phone:* 216-881-1700. *Toll-free phone:* 800-322-7000. *Fax:* 216-881-9145. *E-mail:* ohioauto@aol.com. *Website:* http://www.ohiotechnicalcollege.com/.

Ohio Valley College of Technology

East Liverpool, Ohio

Freshman Application Contact Mr. Scott S. Rogers, Director, Ohio Valley College of Technology, 16808 St. Clair Avenue, PO Box 7000, East Liverpool, OH 43920. *Phone:* 330-385-1070. *Website:* http://www.ovct.edu/.

Owens Community College

Toledo, Ohio

- **State-supported** 2-year, founded 1966
- **Suburban** 420-acre campus with easy access to Detroit
- **Endowment** $1.3 million
- **Coed,** 17,173 undergraduate students, 35% full-time, 50% women, 49% men

Undergraduates 6,061 full-time, 10,932 part-time. Students come from 21 states and territories; 28 other countries; 3% are from out of state; 14% Black or African American, non-Hispanic/Latino; 6% Hispanic/Latino; 0.7% Asian, non-Hispanic/Latino; 0.1% Native Hawaiian or other Pacific Islander, non-Hispanic/Latino; 0.4% American Indian or Alaska Native, non-Hispanic/Latino; 2% Two or more races, non-Hispanic/Latino; 2% Race/ethnicity unknown; 0.6% international; 0.6% transferred in.

Freshmen *Admission:* 11,378 applied, 11,378 admitted, 2,764 enrolled. *Average high school GPA:* 2.48. *Test scores:* SAT critical reading scores over 500: 24%; SAT math scores over 500: 32%; SAT writing scores over 500: 20%;

ACT scores over 18: 57%; SAT critical reading scores over 600: 8%; SAT math scores over 600: 8%; SAT writing scores over 600: 8%; ACT scores over 24: 8%.

Faculty *Total:* 1,582, 12% full-time, 8% with terminal degrees. *Student/faculty ratio:* 16:1.

Majors Accounting technology and bookkeeping; agricultural mechanization; architectural drafting and CAD/CADD; architectural engineering technology; automotive engineering technology; biomedical technology; business/commerce; commercial and advertising art; commercial photography; communications technology; computer and information systems security; computer engineering technology; computer programming (specific applications); construction engineering technology; corrections; criminal justice/law enforcement administration; criminal justice/police science; dental hygiene; diagnostic medical sonography and ultrasound technology; dietetics; early childhood education; education; electrical, electronic and communications engineering technology; energy management and systems technology; environmental engineering technology; executive assistant/executive secretary; fire prevention and safety technology; general studies; golf course operation and grounds management; health/health-care administration; health information/medical records technology; industrial and product design; industrial technology; information technology; international business/trade/commerce; landscaping and groundskeeping; manufacturing engineering technology; massage therapy; medical administrative assistant and medical secretary; medical/health management and clinical assistant; medical radiologic technology; music technology; nuclear medical technology; occupational therapist assistant; office management; operations management; physical therapy technology; public administration; quality control technology; registered nursing/registered nurse; restaurant/food services management; sales, distribution, and marketing operations; surgical technology; tool and die technology; welding technology.

Academics *Calendar:* semesters. *Degree:* certificates and associate. *Special study options:* academic remediation for entering students, accelerated degree program, adult/continuing education programs, advanced placement credit, cooperative education, distance learning, double majors, English as a second language, honors programs, independent study, internships, part-time degree program, services for LD students, study abroad, summer session for credit. *ROTC:* Army (c), Air Force (c).

Library Owens Community College Library plus 1 other with 36,770 titles, 9,612 serial subscriptions, 13,470 audiovisual materials, an OPAC, a Web page.

Student Life *Housing:* college housing not available. *Activities and Organizations:* drama/theater group, student-run newspaper, choral group, Student Government, Raising Awareness Club, Environmental Club, First Year Experience, Gamers. *Campus security:* 24-hour emergency response devices and patrols, student patrols, classroom doors that lock from the inside; campus alert system.

Athletics Member NJCAA. *Intercollegiate sports:* baseball M(s), basketball M(s)/W(s), golf M(s)/W, soccer M(s)/W(s), softball W(s), volleyball W(s). *Intramural sports:* basketball M/W, bowling M/W, football M, golf M/W, softball M/W, table tennis M/W, tennis M/W, volleyball M/W, weight lifting M.

Costs (2012–13) *Tuition:* state resident $3655 full-time, $131 per credit hour part-time; nonresident $7744 full-time, $277 per credit hour part-time. Full-time tuition and fees vary according to course load and reciprocity agreements. Part-time tuition and fees vary according to course load and reciprocity agreements. *Required fees:* $392 full-time, $16 per credit hour part-time, $10 per term part-time. *Payment plans:* installment, deferred payment. *Waivers:* senior citizens and employees or children of employees.

Financial Aid Of all full-time matriculated undergraduates who enrolled in 2012, 5,071 applied for aid, 4,575 were judged to have need, 240 had their need fully met. In 2012, 201 non-need-based awards were made. *Average percent of need met:* 59%. *Average financial aid package:* $7384. *Average need-based loan:* $7881. *Average need-based gift aid:* $4955. *Average non-need-based aid:* $1056.

Applying *Options:* electronic application, early admission. *Required for some:* minimum 2.0 GPA, interview. *Recommended:* high school transcript. *Application deadlines:* rolling (freshmen), rolling (out-of-state freshmen), rolling (transfers). *Notification:* continuous (freshmen), continuous (out-of-state freshmen), continuous (transfers).

Freshman Application Contact Mr. Cory Stine, Director, Admissions, Owens Community College, P.O. Box 10000, Toledo, OH 43699. *Phone:* 567-661-7515. *Toll-free phone:* 800-GO-OWENS. *Fax:* 567-661-7734. *E-mail:* cory_stine@owens.edu. *Website:* http://www.owens.edu/.

Professional Skills Institute

Toledo, Ohio

Director of Admissions Ms. Hope Finch, Director of Marketing, Professional Skills Institute, 1505 Holland Road, Maumee, Toledo, OH 43537. *Phone:* 419-

531-9610.
Website: http://www.proskills.com/.

Remington College–Cleveland Campus

Cleveland, Ohio

Director of Admissions Director of Recruitment, Remington College–Cleveland Campus, 14445 Broadway Avenue, Cleveland, OH 44125. *Phone:* 216-475-7520. *Fax:* 216-475-6055.
Website: http://www.remingtoncollege.edu/.

Remington College–Cleveland West Campus

North Olmstead, Ohio

Freshman Application Contact Remington College–Cleveland West Campus, 26350 Brookpark Road, North Olmstead, OH 44070. *Phone:* 440-777-2560.
Website: http://www.remingtoncollege.edu/.

Rosedale Bible College

Irwin, Ohio

Director of Admissions Mr. John Showalter, Director of Enrollment Services, Rosedale Bible College, 2270 Rosedale Road, Irwin, OH 43029-9501. *Phone:* 740-857-1311. *Fax:* 740-857-1577. *E-mail:* pweber@rosedale.edu.
Website: http://www.rosedale.edu/.

School of Advertising Art

Kettering, Ohio

Freshman Application Contact Ms. Abigail Heaney, Admissions, School of Advertising Art, 1725 East David Road, Kettering, OH 45440. *Phone:* 937-294-0592. *Toll-free phone:* 877-300-9866. *Fax:* 937-294-5869. *E-mail:* Abbie@saa.edu.
Website: http://www.saa.edu/.

Sinclair Community College

Dayton, Ohio

Freshman Application Contact Ms. Sara Smith, Director and Systems Manager, Outreach Services, Sinclair Community College, 444 West Third Street, Dayton, OH 45402-1460. *Phone:* 937-512-3060. *Toll-free phone:* 800-315-3000. *Fax:* 937-512-2393. *E-mail:* ssmith@sinclair.edu.
Website: http://www.sinclair.edu/.

Southern State Community College

Hillsboro, Ohio

- **State-supported** 2-year, founded 1975
- **Rural** 60-acre campus
- **Endowment** $1.9 million
- **Coed,** 2,806 undergraduate students, 46% full-time, 68% women, 32% men

Undergraduates 1,292 full-time, 1,514 part-time. Students come from 2 states and territories; 2% Black or African American, non-Hispanic/Latino; 0.5% Hispanic/Latino; 0.3% Asian, non-Hispanic/Latino; 0.1% Native Hawaiian or other Pacific Islander, non-Hispanic/Latino; 0.4% American Indian or Alaska Native, non-Hispanic/Latino; 1% Two or more races, non-Hispanic/Latino; 2% Race/ethnicity unknown.
Freshmen *Admission:* 443 applied, 443 admitted, 305 enrolled.
Faculty *Total:* 172, 35% full-time, 10% with terminal degrees. *Student/faculty ratio:* 17:1.
Majors Accounting technology and bookkeeping; administrative assistant and secretarial science; agricultural production; agriculture; business administration and management; business/commerce; CAD/CADD drafting/design technology; computer programming; computer programming (specific applications); computer systems analysis; computer technology/computer systems technology; corrections; criminal justice/law enforcement administration; criminal justice/police science; drafting and design technology; early childhood education; electrical, electronic and communications engineering technology; electromechanical technology; emergency medical technology (EMT paramedic); entrepreneurship; executive assistant/executive secretary; food technology and processing; human services; kindergarten/preschool education; liberal arts and sciences/liberal studies; medical/clinical assistant; real estate;

registered nursing/registered nurse; respiratory care therapy; substance abuse/addiction counseling; teacher assistant/aide.
Academics *Calendar:* quarters. *Degree:* certificates and associate. *Special study options:* academic remediation for entering students, advanced placement credit, cooperative education, distance learning, double majors, independent study, internships, off-campus study, part-time degree program, services for LD students, student-designed majors, summer session for credit.
Library Learning Resources Center plus 3 others with 83,421 titles, 271 serial subscriptions, 12,035 audiovisual materials, an OPAC, a Web page.
Student Life *Housing:* college housing not available. *Activities and Organizations:* drama/theater group, choral group, Student Government Association, Drama Club. *Student services:* personal/psychological counseling.
Athletics Member USCAA. *Intercollegiate sports:* basketball M(s)/W(s), soccer M(s), softball W(s), volleyball W(s).
Financial Aid Of all full-time matriculated undergraduates who enrolled in 2011, 3,082 applied for aid, 3,082 were judged to have need, 2,537 had their need fully met. 61 Federal Work-Study jobs (averaging $2030). In 2011, 754 non-need-based awards were made. *Average percent of need met:* 92%. *Average financial aid package:* $4570. *Average need-based loan:* $2247. *Average need-based gift aid:* $3560. *Average non-need-based aid:* $1675.
Applying *Options:* electronic application, early admission, deferred entrance. *Recommended:* high school transcript. *Application deadlines:* rolling (freshmen), rolling (transfers). *Notification:* continuous (freshmen), continuous (transfers).
Freshman Application Contact Ms. Wendy Johnson, Director of Admissions, Southern State Community College, Hillsboro, OH 45133. *Phone:* 937-393-3431 Ext. 2720. *Toll-free phone:* 800-628-7722. *Fax:* 937-393-6682. *E-mail:* wjohnson@sscc.edu.
Website: http://www.sscc.edu/.

Stark State College

North Canton, Ohio

- **State-related** 2-year, founded 1970, part of University System of Ohio
- **Suburban** 34-acre campus with easy access to Cleveland
- **Endowment** $2.8 million
- **Coed,** 15,536 undergraduate students, 35% full-time, 60% women, 40% men

Undergraduates 5,441 full-time, 10,095 part-time. Students come from 15 states and territories; 6 other countries; 0.8% are from out of state; 19% Black or African American, non-Hispanic/Latino; 0.8% Hispanic/Latino; 0.7% Asian, non-Hispanic/Latino; 0.1% Native Hawaiian or other Pacific Islander, non-Hispanic/Latino; 0.5% American Indian or Alaska Native, non-Hispanic/Latino; 2% Two or more races, non-Hispanic/Latino; 5% Race/ethnicity unknown; 5% transferred in. *Retention:* 45% of full-time freshmen returned.
Freshmen *Admission:* 3,067 enrolled. *Test scores:* ACT scores over 18: 48%; ACT scores over 24: 6%; ACT scores over 30: 1%.
Faculty *Total:* 730, 27% full-time. *Student/faculty ratio:* 23:1.
Majors Accounting; administrative assistant and secretarial science; architectural engineering technology; automobile/automotive mechanics technology; biomedical technology; business administration and management; child development; civil engineering technology; clinical/medical laboratory technology; computer and information sciences and support services related; computer and information sciences related; computer engineering related; computer hardware engineering; computer/information technology services administration related; computer programming; computer programming related; computer programming (specific applications); computer programming (vendor/product certification); computer software and media applications related; computer software engineering; computer systems networking and telecommunications; consumer merchandising/retailing management; court reporting; data entry/microcomputer applications; data entry/microcomputer applications related; dental hygiene; drafting and design technology; environmental studies; finance; fire science/firefighting; food technology and processing; health information/medical records administration; human services; industrial technology; information technology; international business/trade/commerce; legal administrative assistant/secretary; marketing/marketing management; mechanical engineering/mechanical technology; medical/clinical assistant; occupational therapy; operations management; physical therapy; registered nursing/registered nurse; respiratory care therapy; surveying technology; web/multimedia management and webmaster; web page, digital/multimedia and information resources design; word processing.
Academics *Calendar:* semesters. *Degree:* certificates and associate. *Special study options:* academic remediation for entering students, adult/continuing education programs, cooperative education, distance learning, double majors, external degree program, independent study, off-campus study, part-time degree program, services for LD students, student-designed majors, summer session for credit.
Library Learning Resource Center plus 1 other with 82,728 titles, 23,331 serial subscriptions, an OPAC, a Web page.

Student Life *Housing:* college housing not available. *Activities and Organizations:* student-run newspaper, Phi Theta Kappa, Business Student Club, Institute of Management Accountants, Stark State College Association of Medical Assistants, Student Health Information Management Association, national fraternities, national sororities. *Campus security:* late-night transport/escort service, Patrols by trained security personnel at anytime the campus is open. *Student services:* personal/psychological counseling.

Standardized Tests *Recommended:* SAT or ACT (for admission).

Costs (2012–13) *Tuition:* state resident $3495 full-time, $147 per credit hour part-time; nonresident $6225 full-time, $238 per credit hour part-time. Full-time tuition and fees vary according to course load and program. Part-time tuition and fees vary according to program. *Required fees:* $915 full-time. *Payment plan:* installment. *Waivers:* senior citizens and employees or children of employees.

Financial Aid Of all full-time matriculated undergraduates who enrolled in 2011, 194 Federal Work-Study jobs (averaging $2383).

Applying *Required:* high school transcript.

Freshman Application Contact Mr. Wallace Hoffer, Dean of Student Services, Stark State College, 6200 Frank Road, NW, Canton, OH 44720. *Phone:* 330-966-5450. *Toll-free phone:* 800-797-8275. *Fax:* 330-497-6313. *E-mail:* info@starkstate.edu. *Website:* http://www.starkstate.edu/.

Stautzenberger College
Brecksville, Ohio

Admissions Office Contact Stautzenberger College, 8001 Katherine Boulevard, Brecksville, OH 44141. *Toll-free phone:* 800-437-2997. *Website:* http://www.sctoday.edu/.

Stautzenberger College
Maumee, Ohio

Director of Admissions Ms. Karen Fitzgerald, Director of Admissions and Marketing, Stautzenberger College, 1796 Indian Wood Circle, Maumee, OH 43537. *Phone:* 419-866-0261. *Toll-free phone:* 800-552-5099. *Fax:* 419-867-9821. *E-mail:* klfitzgerald@stautzenberger.com. *Website:* http://www.sctoday.edu/maumee/.

Terra State Community College
Fremont, Ohio

- **State-supported** 2-year, founded 1968, part of Ohio Board of Regents
- **Small-town** 100-acre campus with easy access to Toledo
- **Coed,** 3,172 undergraduate students, 39% full-time, 57% women, 43% men

Undergraduates 1,252 full-time, 1,920 part-time. 5% Black or African American, non-Hispanic/Latino; 7% Hispanic/Latino; 0.5% Asian, non-Hispanic/Latino; 0.3% American Indian or Alaska Native, non-Hispanic/Latino; 0.9% Two or more races, non-Hispanic/Latino; 3% Race/ethnicity unknown; 0.2% international.

Freshmen *Admission:* 394 applied, 394 admitted, 475 enrolled.

Faculty *Total:* 220, 22% full-time, 5% with terminal degrees. *Student/faculty ratio:* 20:1.

Majors Accounting; agricultural business and management; animation, interactive technology, video graphics and special effects; architectural engineering technology; art history, criticism and conservation; automotive engineering technology; banking and financial support services; biological and physical sciences; biology/biological sciences; business administration and management; business/commerce; chemistry; commercial and advertising art; computer and information sciences; computer programming; computer systems networking and telecommunications; criminal justice/police science; data processing and data processing technology; desktop publishing and digital imaging design; economics; education; electrical and electronic engineering technologies related; electrical, electronic and communications engineering technology; engineering; English; executive assistant/executive secretary; fine/studio arts; general studies; health/health-care administration; health information/medical records administration; health information/medical records technology; health professions related; heating, ventilation, air conditioning and refrigeration engineering technology; history; hospitality administration; humanities; kindergarten/preschool education; language interpretation and translation; liberal arts and sciences/liberal studies; manufacturing engineering technology; marketing/marketing management; mathematics; mechanical engineering/mechanical technology; mechanical engineering technologies related; medical administrative assistant and medical secretary; medical/clinical assistant; medical/health management and clinical assistant; medical insurance coding; medical office assistant; music; music management; music performance; music related; nuclear/nuclear power technology; operations management; physics; plastics and polymer engineering technology; psychol-

ogy; real estate; registered nursing/registered nurse; robotics technology; sheet metal technology; social sciences; social work; teaching assistants/aides related; web page, digital/multimedia and information resources design; welding technology.

Academics *Calendar:* semesters. *Degree:* certificates, diplomas, and associate. *Special study options:* academic remediation for entering students, adult/continuing education programs, advanced placement credit, cooperative education, distance learning, double majors, independent study, internships, off-campus study, part-time degree program, services for LD students, student-designed majors, summer session for credit.

Library Learning Resource Center with 22,675 titles, 383 serial subscriptions, an OPAC, a Web page.

Student Life *Housing:* college housing not available. *Activities and Organizations:* choral group, Phi Theta Kappa, Student Activities Club, Society of Plastic Engineers, Koinonia, Student Senate. *Campus security:* 24-hour emergency response devices. *Student services:* personal/psychological counseling, legal services.

Athletics *Intramural sports:* basketball M/W, bowling M/W, football M, golf M/W, table tennis M/W, volleyball M/W.

Costs (2012–13) *Tuition:* state resident $3056 full-time, $127 per semester hour part-time; nonresident $4991 full-time, $208 per semester hour part-time. *Required fees:* $339 full-time, $14 per semester hour part-time. *Payment plan:* installment. *Waivers:* employees or children of employees.

Financial Aid Of all full-time matriculated undergraduates who enrolled in 2011, 57 Federal Work-Study jobs (averaging $1450).

Applying *Options:* electronic application, early admission, deferred entrance. *Required:* high school transcript. *Application deadlines:* rolling (freshmen), rolling (transfers).

Freshman Application Contact Ms. Kristen Taylor, Director of Admissions and Enrollment Services, Terra State Community College, 2830 Napoleon Road, Fremont, OH 43420. *Phone:* 419-559-2154. *Toll-free phone:* 866-AT-TERRA. *Fax:* 419-559-2352. *E-mail:* ktaylor01@terra.edu. *Website:* http://www.terra.edu/.

Trumbull Business College
Warren, Ohio

Director of Admissions Admissions Office, Trumbull Business College, 3200 Ridge Road, Warren, OH 44484. *Phone:* 330-369-6792. *Toll-free phone:* 888-766-1598. *E-mail:* admissions@tbc-trumbullbusiness.com. *Website:* http://www.tbc-trumbullbusiness.com/.

The University of Akron–Wayne College
Orrville, Ohio

- **State-supported** primarily 2-year, founded 1972, part of The University of Akron
- **Rural** 157-acre campus
- **Coed,** 2,415 undergraduate students, 49% full-time, 59% women, 41% men

Undergraduates 1,185 full-time, 1,230 part-time. Students come from 2 states and territories; 3% Black or African American, non-Hispanic/Latino; 1% Hispanic/Latino; 0.8% Asian, non-Hispanic/Latino; 0.3% American Indian or Alaska Native, non-Hispanic/Latino; 4% Two or more races, non-Hispanic/Latino; 3% Race/ethnicity unknown; 3% transferred in. *Retention:* 49% of full-time freshmen returned.

Freshmen *Admission:* 983 applied, 838 admitted, 394 enrolled. *Average high school GPA:* 2.97. *Test scores:* ACT scores over 18: 80%; ACT scores over 24: 20%; ACT scores over 30: 1%.

Faculty *Total:* 202, 13% full-time, 24% with terminal degrees. *Student/faculty ratio:* 19:1.

Majors Administrative assistant and secretarial science; business administration and management; general studies; liberal arts and sciences/liberal studies; medical office management; office management; social work; teacher assistant/aide.

Academics *Calendar:* semesters. *Degrees:* certificates, associate, and bachelor's. *Special study options:* academic remediation for entering students, adult/continuing education programs, advanced placement credit, cooperative education, distance learning, double majors, honors programs, independent study, internships, off-campus study, part-time degree program, services for LD students, summer session for credit. *ROTC:* Army (c), Air Force (c).

Library Wayne College Library with 19,810 titles, 109 serial subscriptions, 1,764 audiovisual materials, an OPAC, a Web page.

Student Life *Housing:* college housing not available. *Campus security:* 24-hour emergency response devices, late-night transport/escort service. *Student services:* personal/psychological counseling.

Athletics *Intercollegiate sports:* basketball M/W, cheerleading W, golf M, volleyball W. *Intramural sports:* basketball M/W, golf M, volleyball M/W.

Standardized Tests *Required for some:* SAT or ACT (for admission), ACT COMPASS. *Recommended:* SAT or ACT (for admission), ACT COMPASS.

Costs (2012–13) *Tuition:* state resident $5940 full-time, $248 per semester hour part-time; nonresident $14,281 full-time, $526 per semester hour part-time. Full-time tuition and fees vary according to course load and location. Part-time tuition and fees vary according to course load and location. *Required fees:* $176 full-time, $7 per semester hour part-time. *Payment plan:* installment. *Waivers:* employees or children of employees.

Financial Aid Of all full-time matriculated undergraduates who enrolled in 2011, 8 Federal Work-Study jobs (averaging $2200).

Applying *Options:* electronic application, early admission, deferred entrance. *Application fee:* $40. *Required for some:* high school transcript. *Application deadlines:* 8/13 (freshmen), 8/13 (transfers). *Notification:* continuous (freshmen), continuous (transfers).

Freshman Application Contact Ms. Alicia Broadus, Student Services Counselor, The University of Akron–Wayne College, Orrville, OH 44667. *Phone:* 800-221-8308 Ext. 8901. *Toll-free phone:* 800-221-8308. *Fax:* 330-684-8989. *E-mail:* wayneadmissions@uakron.edu.
Website: http://www.wayne.uakron.edu/.

University of Cincinnati Blue Ash
Cincinnati, Ohio

Freshman Application Contact Leigh Schlegal, Admission Counselor, University of Cincinnati Blue Ash, 9555 Plainfield Road, Cincinnati, OH 45236-1007. *Phone:* 513-745-5783. *Fax:* 513-745-5768.
Website: http://www.ucblueash.edu/.

University of Cincinnati Clermont College
Batavia, Ohio

Freshman Application Contact Mrs. Jamie Adkins, Records Management Officer, University of Cincinnati Clermont College, 4200 Clermont College Drive, Batavia, OH 45103. *Phone:* 513-732-5294. *Fax:* 513-732-5303. *E-mail:* jamie.adkins@uc.edu.
Website: http://www.ucclermont.edu/.

Vatterott College
Broadview Heights, Ohio

Director of Admissions Mr. Jack Chalk, Director of Admissions, Vatterott College, 5025 East Royalton Road, Broadview Heights, OH 44147. *Phone:* 440-526-1660. *Toll-free phone:* 888-553-6627.
Website: http://www.vatterott.edu/.

Vet Tech Institute at Bradford School
Columbus, Ohio

- **Private** 2-year, founded 2005
- **Suburban** campus
- **Coed,** 167 undergraduate students
- 33% of applicants were admitted

Freshmen *Admission:* 592 applied, 196 admitted.
Majors Veterinary/animal health technology.
Academics *Degree:* associate. *Special study options:* accelerated degree program, internships.
Freshman Application Contact Admissions Office, Vet Tech Institute at Bradford School, 2469 Stelzer Road, Columbus, OH 43219. *Phone:* 800-678-7981. *Toll-free phone:* 800-678-7981.
Website: http://www.vettechinstitute.edu/.

Virginia Marti College of Art and Design
Lakewood, Ohio

Freshman Application Contact Virginia Marti College of Art and Design, 11724 Detroit Avenue, PO Box 580, Lakewood, OH 44107-3002. *Phone:* 216-221-8584 Ext. 106.
Website: http://www.vmcad.edu/.

Washington State Community College
Marietta, Ohio

Freshman Application Contact Ms. Rebecca Peroni, Director of Admissions, Washington State Community College, 110 Coligate Drive, Marietta, OH 45750. *Phone:* 740-374-8716. *Fax:* 740-376-0257. *E-mail:* rperoni@
wscc.edu.
Website: http://www.wscc.edu/.

Wright State University, Lake Campus
Celina, Ohio

Freshman Application Contact Sandra Gilbert, Student Services Officer, Wright State University, Lake Campus, 7600 State Route 703, Celina, OH 45822-2921. *Phone:* 419-586-0324. *Toll-free phone:* 800-237-1477. *Fax:* 419-586-0358.
Website: http://www.wright.edu/lake/.

Zane State College
Zanesville, Ohio

Director of Admissions Mr. Paul Young, Director of Admissions, Zane State College, 1555 Newark Road, Zanesville, OH 43701-2626. *Phone:* 740-454-2501 Ext. 1225. *Toll-free phone:* 800-686-8324. *E-mail:* pyoung@zanestate.edu.
Website: http://www.zanestate.edu/.

OKLAHOMA

Brown Mackie College–Oklahoma City
Oklahoma City, Oklahoma

Admissions Office Contact Brown Mackie College–Oklahoma City, 7101 Northwest Expressway, Suite 800, Oklahoma City, OK 73132. *Toll-free phone:* 888-229-3280.
Website: http://www.brownmackie.edu/oklahoma-city/.

See display on next page and page 382 for the College Close-Up.

Brown Mackie College–Tulsa
Tulsa, Oklahoma

Freshman Application Contact Brown Mackie College–Tulsa, 4608 South Garnett, Suite 110, Tulsa, OK 74146. *Phone:* 918-628-3700. *Toll-free phone:* 888-794-8411.
Website: http://www.brownmackie.edu/tulsa/.

See display on next page and page 398 for the College Close-Up.

Carl Albert State College
Poteau, Oklahoma

- **State-supported** 2-year, founded 1934, part of Oklahoma State Regents for Higher Education
- **Small-town** 78-acre campus
- **Endowment** $5.7 million
- **Coed,** 2,460 undergraduate students, 56% full-time, 66% women, 34% men

Undergraduates 1,373 full-time, 1,087 part-time. Students come from 16 states and territories; 9 other countries; 12% live on campus.
Freshmen *Admission:* 733 applied, 733 admitted, 605 enrolled.
Faculty *Total:* 154, 33% full-time, 2% with terminal degrees. *Student/faculty ratio:* 16:1.
Majors Biology/biological sciences; business administration and management; business/commerce; child development; computer and information sciences; elementary education; engineering; engineering technologies and engineering related; English; film/cinema/video studies; fine arts related; foods, nutrition, and wellness; health professions related; health services/allied health/health sciences; hotel/motel administration; journalism; management information systems; mathematics; music related; physical education teaching and coaching; physical sciences; physical therapy technology; pre-law studies; radiologic technology/science; registered nursing/registered nurse; rhetoric and composition; secondary education; social sciences; telecommunications technology.
Academics *Calendar:* semesters. *Degree:* certificates and associate. *Special study options:* academic remediation for entering students, adult/continuing education programs, cooperative education, part-time degree program.
Library Joe E. White Library with 27,200 titles, 1,350 serial subscriptions, an OPAC.
Student Life *Housing Options:* men-only, women-only. Campus housing is university owned. *Activities and Organizations:* drama/theater group, student-

run newspaper, radio station, choral group, Student Government Association, Phi Theta Kappa, Baptist Student Union, BACCHUS, Student Physical Therapist Assistant Association. *Campus security:* security guards. *Student services:* health clinic, personal/psychological counseling.

Athletics Member NJCAA. *Intercollegiate sports:* baseball M; basketball M(s)/W(s), softball M. *Intramural sports:* tennis M/W, volleyball M/W, weight lifting M.

Costs (2013–14) *Tuition:* state resident $1234 full-time, $89 per credit hour part-time; nonresident $2643 full-time, $189 per credit hour part-time. *Required fees:* $450 per term part-time. *Room and board:* $1930; room only: $1650. Room and board charges vary according to board plan. *Waivers:* employees or children of employees.

Financial Aid Of all full-time matriculated undergraduates who enrolled in 2011, 112 Federal Work-Study jobs (averaging $2100).

Applying *Required:* high school transcript. *Application deadlines:* 8/13 (freshmen), 8/15 (transfers). *Notification:* continuous (freshmen), continuous (transfers).

Freshman Application Contact Admission Clerk, Carl Albert State College, 1507 South McKenna, Poteau, OK 74953-5208. *Phone:* 918-647-1300. *Fax:* 918-647-1306.

Website: http://www.carlalbert.edu/.

Clary Sage College

Tulsa, Oklahoma

- **Proprietary** 2-year, part of Dental Directions, Inc.
- **Urban** 6-acre campus with easy access to Tulsa, OK
- **Coed, primarily women**

Undergraduates Students come from 3 states and territories.

Faculty *Total:* 23, 100% full-time. *Student/faculty ratio:* 9:1.

Majors Cosmetology; fashion/apparel design; interior design.

Academics *Degree:* diplomas and associate. *Special study options:* adult/continuing education programs, distance learning, internships, part-time degree program.

Student Life *Housing:* college housing not available. *Activities and Organizations:* Student Ambassadors. *Campus security:* security guard during hours of operation. *Student services:* personal/psychological counseling.

Costs (2012–13) *Tuition:* $17,808 full-time. Full-time tuition and fees vary according to class time, course level, course load, degree level, location, program, and reciprocity agreements. Part-time tuition and fees vary according to class time, course level, location, and reciprocity agreements. *Required fees:* $2349 full-time. *Payment plans:* tuition prepayment, installment. *Waivers:* employees or children of employees.

Applying *Options:* electronic application. *Application fee:* $100. *Required:* essay or personal statement, high school transcript, interview. *Application deadlines:* rolling (freshmen), rolling (out-of-state freshmen), rolling (transfers). *Notification:* continuous (freshmen), continuous (out-of-state freshmen), continuous (transfers).

Freshman Application Contact Ms. Rebecca Banuelos, Director of Marketing, Clary Sage College, 3131 South Sheridan, Tulsa, OK 74145. *Phone:* 918-610-0027 Ext. 2002. *E-mail:* rbanuelos@communitycarecollege.edu.

Website: http://www.clarysagecollege.com/.

Community Care College

Tulsa, Oklahoma

- **Proprietary** 2-year, founded 1995, part of Dental Directions, Inc.
- **Urban** 6-acre campus
- **Coed, primarily women**

Undergraduates 942 full-time. Students come from 14 states and territories; 11% are from out of state; 17% Black or African American, non-Hispanic/Latino; 4% Hispanic/Latino; 2% Asian, non-Hispanic/Latino; 10% American Indian or Alaska Native, non-Hispanic/Latino; 0.1% Two or more races, non-Hispanic/Latino; 7% Race/ethnicity unknown.

Faculty *Student/faculty ratio:* 27:1.

Academics *Calendar:* continuous. *Degree:* diplomas and associate. *Special study options:* adult/continuing education programs, distance learning, independent study, internships, services for LD students.

Student Life *Campus security:* campus security personnel are available during school hours.

Costs (2012–13) *Tuition:* $22,084 full-time. Full-time tuition and fees vary according to class time, course level, course load, degree level, location, program, and reciprocity agreements. Part-time tuition and fees vary according to class time, course level, location, and reciprocity agreements. *Required fees:* $2680 full-time. *Payment plans:* tuition prepayment, installment.

Applying *Options:* electronic application. *Application fee:* $100. *Required:* essay or personal statement, high school transcript, interview. *Required for some:* 1 letter of recommendation.

Freshman Application Contact Ms. Teresa L. Knox, Chief Executive Officer, Community Care College, 4242 South Sheridan, Tulsa, OK 74145. *Phone:* 918-610-0027 Ext. 2005. *Fax:* 918-610-0029. *E-mail:* tknox@

communitycarecollege.edu.
Website: http://www.communitycarecollege.edu/.

Connors State College
Warner, Oklahoma

Freshman Application Contact Ms. Sonya Baker, Registrar, Connors State College, Route 1 Box 1000, Warner, OK 74469-9700. *Phone:* 918-463-6233. *Website:* http://www.connorsstate.edu/.

Eastern Oklahoma State College
Wilburton, Oklahoma

Freshman Application Contact Ms. Leah McLaughlin, Director of Admissions, Eastern Oklahoma State College, 1301 West Main, Wilburton, OK 74578-4999. *Phone:* 918-465-1811. *Toll-free phone:* 855-534-3672. *Fax:* 918-465-2431. *E-mail:* lmiller@eosc.edu. *Website:* http://www.eosc.edu/.

Heritage College
Oklahoma City, Oklahoma

Freshman Application Contact Admissions Office, Heritage College, 7100 I-35 Services Road, Suite 7118, Oklahoma City, OK 73149. *Phone:* 405-631-3399. *Toll-free phone:* 888-334-7339. *E-mail:* info@heritage-education.com. *Website:* http://www.heritage-education.com/.

ITT Technical Institute
Tulsa, Oklahoma

- **Proprietary** primarily 2-year, founded 2005
- **Coed**

Academics *Calendar:* quarters. *Degrees:* associate and bachelor's.
Freshman Application Contact Director of Recruitment, ITT Technical Institute, 4500 South 129th East Avenue, Suite 152, Tulsa, OK 74134. *Phone:* 918-615-3900. *Toll-free phone:* 800-514-6535. *Website:* http://www.itt-tech.edu/.

Murray State College
Tishomingo, Oklahoma

- **State-supported** 2-year, founded 1908, part of Oklahoma State Regents for Higher Education
- **Rural** 120-acre campus
- **Coed**

Undergraduates 1,317 full-time, 1,357 part-time. Students come from 19 states and territories; 9 other countries; 4% are from out of state; 5% Black or African American, non-Hispanic/Latino; 6% Hispanic/Latino; 0.3% Asian, non-Hispanic/Latino; 0.1% Native Hawaiian or other Pacific Islander, non-Hispanic/Latino; 13% American Indian or Alaska Native, non-Hispanic/Latino; 9% Two or more races, non-Hispanic/Latino; 2% Race/ethnicity unknown; 0.1% international; 11% live on campus. *Retention:* 49% of full-time freshmen returned.
Faculty *Student/faculty ratio:* 20:1.
Academics *Calendar:* semesters. *Degree:* associate. *Special study options:* academic remediation for entering students, advanced placement credit, distance learning, honors programs, internships, part-time degree program, services for LD students, summer session for credit.
Student Life *Campus security:* 24-hour patrols.
Athletics Member NJCAA.
Standardized Tests *Required:* SAT or ACT (for admission).
Costs (2012–13) *Tuition:* state resident $2940 full-time, $98 per credit hour part-time; nonresident $7650 full-time, $255 per credit hour part-time. Full-time tuition and fees vary according to course level, course load, location, and program. Part-time tuition and fees vary according to course level, course load, location, and program. *Required fees:* $695 full-time. *Room and board:* $5800. Room and board charges vary according to board plan and housing facility.
Financial Aid Of all full-time matriculated undergraduates who enrolled in 2011, 68 Federal Work-Study jobs (averaging $3354). 20 state and other part-time jobs (averaging $2516).
Applying *Options:* electronic application, early admission. *Required:* high school transcript.
Freshman Application Contact Murray State College, One Murray Campus, Tishomingo, OK 73460-3130. *Phone:* 580-371-2371 Ext. 171. *Website:* http://www.mscok.edu/.

Northeastern Oklahoma Agricultural and Mechanical College
Miami, Oklahoma

Freshman Application Contact Amy Ishmael, Vice President for Enrollment Management, Northeastern Oklahoma Agricultural and Mechanical College, 200 I Street, NE, Miami, OK 74354-6434. *Phone:* 918-540-6212. *Toll-free phone:* 800-464-6636. *Fax:* 918-540-6946. *E-mail:* neoadmission@neo.edu. *Website:* http://www.neo.edu/.

Northern Oklahoma College
Tonkawa, Oklahoma

Freshman Application Contact Ms. Sheri Snyder, Director of College Relations, Northern Oklahoma College, 1220 East Grand Avenue, PO Box 310, Tonkawa, OK 74653-0310. *Phone:* 580-628-6290. *Website:* http://www.north-ok.edu/.

Oklahoma City Community College
Oklahoma City, Oklahoma

- **State-supported** 2-year, founded 1969, part of Oklahoma State Regents for Higher Education
- **Urban** 143-acre campus
- **Endowment** $303,207
- **Coed,** 14,163 undergraduate students, 34% full-time, 58% women, 42% men

Undergraduates 4,825 full-time, 9,338 part-time. Students come from 23 states and territories; 41 other countries; 4% are from out of state; 10% Black or African American, non-Hispanic/Latino; 5% Hispanic/Latino; 5% Asian, non-Hispanic/Latino; 0.4% Native Hawaiian or other Pacific Islander, non-Hispanic/Latino; 7% American Indian or Alaska Native, non-Hispanic/Latino; 7% Race/ethnicity unknown.
Freshmen *Admission:* 5,407 applied, 5,407 admitted, 2,305 enrolled. *Test scores:* ACT scores over 18: 67%; ACT scores over 24: 14%; ACT scores over 30: 1%.
Faculty *Total:* 766, 20% full-time. *Student/faculty ratio:* 22:1.
Majors Accounting; administrative assistant and secretarial science; airframe mechanics and aircraft maintenance technology; American government and politics; animation, interactive technology, video graphics and special effects; architectural drafting and CAD/CADD; art; automobile/automotive mechanics technology; banking and financial support services; biology/biological sciences; biotechnology; broadcast journalism; business administration and management; business/commerce; chemistry; child development; cinematography and film/video production; commercial and advertising art; computer engineering technology; computer science; computer systems analysis; computer systems networking and telecommunications; cyber/electronic operations and warfare; design and applied arts related; design and visual communications; diagnostic medical sonography and ultrasound technology; diesel mechanics technology; digital communication and media/multimedia; drafting and design technology; dramatic/theater arts; electrical, electronic and communications engineering technology; elementary education; emergency medical technology (EMT paramedic); engineering technologies and engineering related; finance; fine/studio arts; foreign languages and literatures; game and interactive media design; general studies; geographic information science and cartography; graphic communications; health information/medical records administration; history; humanities; legal administrative assistant/secretary; liberal arts and sciences/liberal studies; literature; management information systems; manufacturing engineering technology; mass communication/media; mathematics; medical/clinical assistant; multi/interdisciplinary studies related; music; occupational therapy; orthotics/prosthetics; parks, recreation and leisure facilities management; philosophy; photographic and film/video technology; physical therapy; physics; political science and government; pre-engineering; psychology; public relations, advertising, and applied communication; registered nursing/registered nurse; respiratory care therapy; sociology; speech-language pathology assistant; surgical technology; system, networking, and LAN/WAN management; web/multimedia management and webmaster.
Academics *Calendar:* semesters. *Degree:* certificates and associate. *Special study options:* academic remediation for entering students, accelerated degree program, advanced placement credit, cooperative education, distance learning, double majors, English as a second language, honors programs, independent study, internships, part-time degree program, services for LD students, student-designed majors, summer session for credit.
Library Keith Leftwich Memorial Library with 135,739 titles, 20,329 serial subscriptions, 18,322 audiovisual materials, an OPAC, a Web page.
Student Life *Housing:* college housing not available. *Activities and Organizations:* drama/theater group, student-run newspaper, choral group, Health Professions Association, Black Student Association, Nursing Student Association,

Hispanic Organization Promoting Education (H.O.P.E). *Campus security:* 24-hour emergency response devices and patrols, late-night transport/escort service. *Student services:* personal/psychological counseling.

Athletics *Intramural sports:* basketball M/W, bowling M/W, football M/W, rock climbing M/W, soccer M(c)/W(c), volleyball M/W, weight lifting M/W.

Standardized Tests *Required for some:* ACT (for admission). *Recommended:* ACT (for admission), SAT or ACT (for admission).

Costs (2013–14) *One-time required fee:* $25. *Tuition:* state resident $2237 full-time, $75 per credit part-time; nonresident $6851 full-time, $228 per credit part-time. *Required fees:* $736 full-time, $24 per credit part-time. *Payment plan:* installment. *Waivers:* senior citizens and employees or children of employees.

Financial Aid Of all full-time matriculated undergraduates who enrolled in 2010, 4,062 applied for aid, 3,608 were judged to have need, 1,576 had their need fully met. 315 Federal Work-Study jobs (averaging $4800). 240 state and other part-time jobs (averaging $2502). In 2010, 321 non-need-based awards were made. *Average percent of need met:* 70%. *Average financial aid package:* $7351. *Average need-based loan:* $2801. *Average need-based gift aid:* $4769. *Average non-need-based aid:* $589.

Applying *Options:* electronic application. *Application fee:* $25. *Required:* Proof of English Proficiency, All college and university transcripts. *Required for some:* high school transcript. *Application deadlines:* rolling (freshmen), rolling (out-of-state freshmen), rolling (transfers). *Notification:* continuous (freshmen), continuous (out-of-state freshmen), continuous (transfers).

Freshman Application Contact Mr. Jon Horinek, Director of Recruitment and Admissions, Oklahoma City Community College, 7777 South May Avenue, Oklahoma City, OK 73159. *Phone:* 405-682-7743. *Fax:* 405-682-7817. *E-mail:* jhorinek@occc.edu.
Website: http://www.occc.edu/.

Oklahoma State University Institute of Technology

Okmulgee, Oklahoma

Freshman Application Contact Mary Graves, Director, Admissions, Oklahoma State University Institute of Technology, 1801 East Fourth Street, Okmulgee, OK 74447-3901. *Phone:* 918-293-5298. *Toll-free phone:* 800-722-4471. *Fax:* 918-293-4643. *E-mail:* mary.r.graves@okstate.edu.
Website: http://www.osuit.edu/.

Oklahoma State University, Oklahoma City

Oklahoma City, Oklahoma

- **State-supported** primarily 2-year, founded 1961, part of Oklahoma State University
- **Urban** 110-acre campus
- **Coed,** 7,585 undergraduate students, 33% full-time, 61% women, 39% men

Undergraduates 2,510 full-time, 5,075 part-time. Students come from 18 states and territories; 8 other countries; 2% are from out of state; 17% Black or African American, non-Hispanic/Latino; 8% Hispanic/Latino; 2% Asian, non-Hispanic/Latino; 4% American Indian or Alaska Native, non-Hispanic/Latino; 6% Two or more races, non-Hispanic/Latino; 2% Race/ethnicity unknown; 0.2% international; 11% transferred in. *Retention:* 40% of full-time freshmen returned.

Freshmen *Admission:* 562 applied, 562 admitted, 606 enrolled.

Faculty *Total:* 389, 22% full-time. *Student/faculty ratio:* 20:1.

Majors Accounting; American Sign Language (ASL); architectural engineering technology; art; building/home/construction inspection; business administration and management; civil engineering technology; construction engineering technology; construction management; construction trades; criminal justice/police science; drafting and design technology; early childhood education; economics; electrical and power transmission installation; electrical, electronic and communications engineering technology; electrocardiograph technology; emergency medical technology (EMT paramedic); engineering technology; fire prevention and safety technology; fire science/firefighting; general studies; health/health-care administration; history; horticultural science; humanities; human services; illustration; information science/studies; information technology; language interpretation and translation; occupational safety and health technology; physics; pre-engineering; prenursing studies; professional, technical, business, and scientific writing; psychology; public administration and social service professions related; radiologic technology/science; registered nursing/registered nurse; sign language interpretation and translation; substance abuse/addiction counseling; surveying technology; turf and turfgrass management; veterinary/animal health technology; web page, digital/multimedia and information resources design.

Academics *Calendar:* semesters. *Degrees:* certificates, associate, and bachelor's. *Special study options:* academic remediation for entering students, advanced placement credit, cooperative education, distance learning, double majors, honors programs, independent study, part-time degree program, services for LD students, study abroad, summer session for credit.

Library Oklahoma State University-Oklahoma City Campus Library with 15,000 titles, 300 serial subscriptions, an OPAC, a Web page.

Student Life *Housing:* college housing not available. *Activities and Organizations:* Phi Theta Kappa, Deaf/Hearing Social Club, American Criminal Justice Association, Horticulture Club, Vet-Tech Club. *Campus security:* 24-hour patrols, late-night transport/escort service.

Applying *Options:* electronic application, early admission. *Required:* high school transcript. *Application deadlines:* rolling (freshmen), rolling (transfers). *Notification:* continuous (freshmen), continuous (transfers).

Freshman Application Contact Mr. Kyle Williams, Director, Enrollment Management, Oklahoma State University, Oklahoma City, 900 North Portland, AD202, Oklahoma City, OK 73107. *Phone:* 405-945-9152. *Toll-free phone:* 800-560-4099. *E-mail:* wilkylw@osuokc.edu.
Website: http://www.osuokc.edu/.

Oklahoma Technical College

Tulsa, Oklahoma

- **Proprietary** 2-year, part of Dental Directions, Inc.
- **Urban** 9-acre campus with easy access to Tulsa, OK
- **Coed, primarily men**

Undergraduates Students come from 2 states and territories; 2% are from out of state.

Faculty *Total:* 11, 100% full-time. *Student/faculty ratio:* 8:1.

Majors Automobile/automotive mechanics technology; barbering; diesel mechanics technology; heating, ventilation, air conditioning and refrigeration engineering technology; welding technology.

Academics *Degree:* diplomas and associate. *Special study options:* adult/continuing education programs, distance learning, internships, services for LD students.

Student Life *Housing:* college housing not available. *Activities and Organizations:* Student Ambassadors. *Campus security:* Campus security is available during school hours. *Student services:* personal/psychological counseling.

Costs (2012–13) *Tuition:* $25,804 full-time. Full-time tuition and fees vary according to course load, degree level, location, and program. Part-time tuition and fees vary according to degree level. *Required fees:* $3280 full-time. *Payment plans:* tuition prepayment, installment. *Waivers:* employees or children of employees.

Applying *Options:* electronic application. *Application fee:* $100. *Required:* essay or personal statement, high school transcript, interview. *Required for some:* valid Oklahoma driver's license. *Application deadlines:* rolling (freshmen), rolling (out-of-state freshmen), rolling (transfers). *Notification:* continuous (freshmen), continuous (out-of-state freshmen), continuous (transfers).

Freshman Application Contact Ms. Rebecca Banuelos, Director of Marketing, Oklahoma Technical College, 4242 South Sheridan, Tulsa, OK 74145. *Phone:* 918-610-0027 Ext. 2002. *Fax:* 918-610-0029. *E-mail:* rbanuelos@communitycarecollege.edu.
Website: http://www.oklahomatechnicalcollege.com/.

Platt College

Moore, Oklahoma

Admissions Office Contact Platt College, 201 North Eastern Avenue, Moore, OK 73160.
Website: http://www.plattcolleges.edu/.

Platt College

Oklahoma City, Oklahoma

Freshman Application Contact Ms. Kim Lamb, Director of Admissions, Platt College, 309 South Ann Arbor, Oklahoma City, OK 73128. *Phone:* 405-946-7799. *Fax:* 405-943-2150. *E-mail:* klamb@plattcollege.org.
Website: http://www.plattcolleges.edu/.

Platt College

Tulsa, Oklahoma

Director of Admissions Mrs. Susan Rone, Director, Platt College, 3801 South Sheridan Road, Tulsa, OK 74145-111. *Phone:* 918-663-9000. *Fax:* 918-622-1240. *E-mail:* susanr@plattcollege.org.
Website: http://www.plattcolleges.edu/.

Redlands Community College

El Reno, Oklahoma

Director of Admissions Ms. Tricia Hobson, Director, Enrollment Management, Redlands Community College, 1300 South Country Club Road, El Reno, OK 73036-5304. *Phone:* 405-262-2552 Ext. 1263. *Toll-free phone:* 866-415-6367. *Fax:* 405-422-1239. *E-mail:* hobsont@redlandscc.edu. *Website:* http://www.redlandscc.edu/.

Rose State College

Midwest City, Oklahoma

Freshman Application Contact Ms. Mechelle Aitson-Roessler, Registrar and Director of Admissions, Rose State College, 6420 Southeast 15th Street, Midwest City, OK 73110-2799. *Phone:* 405-733-7308. *Toll-free phone:* 866-621-0987. *Fax:* 405-736-0203. *E-mail:* maitson@ms.rose.cc.ok.us. *Website:* http://www.rose.edu/.

Seminole State College

Seminole, Oklahoma

Freshman Application Contact Mr. Chris Lindley, Director of Enrollment Management, Seminole State College, PO Box 351, 2701 Boren Boulevard, Seminole, OK 74818-0351. *Phone:* 405-382-9272. *Fax:* 405-382-9524. *E-mail:* lindley_c@ssc.cc.ok.us. *Website:* http://www.sscok.edu/.

Southwestern Oklahoma State University at Sayre

Sayre, Oklahoma

- **State and locally supported** 2-year, founded 1938, part of Southwestern Oklahoma State University
- **Rural** 6-acre campus
- **Coed**

Undergraduates 258 full-time, 385 part-time. 2% Black or African American, non-Hispanic/Latino; 6% Hispanic/Latino; 0.6% Asian, non-Hispanic/Latino; 0.5% Native Hawaiian or other Pacific Islander, non-Hispanic/Latino; 5% American Indian or Alaska Native, non-Hispanic/Latino; 3% Two or more races, non-Hispanic/Latino.

Faculty *Student/faculty ratio:* 18:1.

Academics *Calendar:* semesters. *Degree:* diplomas and associate. *Special study options:* academic remediation for entering students, adult/continuing education programs, advanced placement credit, cooperative education, distance learning, independent study, part-time degree program, services for LD students, summer session for credit.

Standardized Tests *Required for some:* ACT (for admission).

Applying *Application fee:* $15. *Required:* high school transcript.

Freshman Application Contact Ms. Kim Seymour, Registrar, Southwestern Oklahoma State University at Sayre, 409 East Mississippi Avenue, Sayre, OK 73662. *Phone:* 580-928-5533 Ext. 101. *Fax:* 580-928-1140. *E-mail:* kim.seymour@swosu.edu. *Website:* http://www.swosu.edu/sayre/.

Spartan College of Aeronautics and Technology

Tulsa, Oklahoma

Freshman Application Contact Mr. Mark Fowler, Vice President of Student Records and Finance, Spartan College of Aeronautics and Technology, 8820 East Pine Street, PO Box 582833, Tulsa, OK 74158-2833. *Phone:* 918-836-6886. *Toll-free phone:* 800-331-1204 (in-state); 800-331-124 (out-of-state). *Website:* http://www.spartan.edu/.

Tulsa Community College

Tulsa, Oklahoma

Freshman Application Contact Ms. Leanne Brewer, Director of Admissions and Records, Tulsa Community College, 6111 East Skelly Drive, Tulsa, OK 74135. *Phone:* 918-595-7811. *Fax:* 918-595-7910. *E-mail:* lbrewer@tulsacc.edu. *Website:* http://www.tulsacc.edu/.

Tulsa Welding School

Tulsa, Oklahoma

Freshman Application Contact Mrs. Debbie Renee Burke, Vice President/Executive Director, Tulsa Welding School, 2545 East 11th Street, Tulsa, OK 74104. *Phone:* 918-587-6789 Ext. 2258. *Toll-free phone:* 888-765-5555. *Fax:* 918-295-6812. *E-mail:* dburke@twsweld.com. *Website:* http://www.weldingschool.com/.

Vatterott College

Tulsa, Oklahoma

Freshman Application Contact Mr. Terry Queeno, Campus Director, Vatterott College, 4343 South 118th East Avenue, Suite A, Tulsa, OK 74146. *Phone:* 918-836-6656. *Toll-free phone:* 888-553-6627. *Fax:* 918-836-9698. *E-mail:* tulsa@vatterott-college.edu. *Website:* http://www.vatterott.edu/.

Vatterott College

Warr Acres, Oklahoma

Freshman Application Contact Mr. Mark Hybers, Director of Admissions, Vatterott College, Oklahoma City, OK 73127. *Phone:* 405-945-0088 Ext. 4416. *Toll-free phone:* 888-553-6627. *Fax:* 405-945-0788. *E-mail:* mark.hybers@vatterott-college.edu. *Website:* http://www.vatterott.edu/.

Western Oklahoma State College

Altus, Oklahoma

Freshman Application Contact Dr. Larry W. Paxton, Director of Academic Services, Western Oklahoma State College, 2801 North Main, Altus, OK 73521. *Phone:* 580-477-7720. *Fax:* 580-477-7723. *E-mail:* larry.paxton@wosc.edu. *Website:* http://www.wosc.edu/.

OREGON

American College of Healthcare Sciences

Portland, Oregon

Freshman Application Contact ACHS Admissions, American College of Healthcare Sciences, 5940 SW Hood Avenue, Portland, OR 97239. *Phone:* 503-244-0726. *Toll-free phone:* 800-487-8839. *Fax:* 503-244-0727. *E-mail:* achs@achs.edu. *Website:* http://www.achs.edu/.

Blue Mountain Community College

Pendleton, Oregon

Director of Admissions Ms. Theresa Bosworth, Director of Admissions, Blue Mountain Community College, 2411 Northwest Carden Avenue, PO Box 100, Pendleton, OR 97801-1000. *Phone:* 541-278-5774. *E-mail:* tbosworth@bluecc.edu. *Website:* http://www.bluecc.edu/.

Carrington College–Portland

Portland, Oregon

- **Proprietary** 2-year
- **Coed**

Majors Medical radiologic technology.

Academics *Degree:* certificates and associate.

Freshman Application Contact Admissions Office, Carrington College–Portland, 2004 Lloyd Center, 3rd Floor, Portland, OR 97232. *Phone:* 503-761-6100. *Website:* http://carrington.edu/.

Central Oregon Community College

Bend, Oregon

- **District-supported** 2-year, founded 1949, part of Oregon Community College Association
- **Small-town** 193-acre campus
- **Endowment** $10.0 million
- **Coed,** 7,132 undergraduate students, 45% full-time, 56% women, 44% men

Undergraduates 3,184 full-time, 3,948 part-time. Students come from 10 states and territories; 4% are from out of state; 0.9% Black or African American, non-Hispanic/Latino; 7% Hispanic/Latino; 1% Asian, non-Hispanic/Latino; 0.4% Native Hawaiian or other Pacific Islander, non-Hispanic/Latino; 2% American Indian or Alaska Native, non-Hispanic/Latino; 1% Two or more races, non-Hispanic/Latino; 10% Race/ethnicity unknown; 1% live on campus. *Retention:* 53% of full-time freshmen returned.

Freshmen *Admission:* 1,481 applied, 1,481 admitted, 955 enrolled.

Faculty *Total:* 298, 40% full-time, 14% with terminal degrees. *Student/faculty ratio:* 25:1.

Majors Accounting; administrative assistant and secretarial science; airline pilot and flight crew; art; automobile/automotive mechanics technology; biological and physical sciences; biology/biological sciences; business administration and management; CAD/CADD drafting/design technology; child-care and support services management; computer and information sciences related; computer science; computer systems networking and telecommunications; cooking and related culinary arts; customer service management; dental assisting; dietetics; drafting and design technology; early childhood education; education; electrical, electronic and communications engineering technology; emergency medical technology (EMT paramedic); engineering; fire science/firefighting; fishing and fisheries sciences and management; foreign languages and literatures; forestry; forest technology; health and physical education/fitness; health information/medical records technology; hotel/motel administration; humanities; industrial technology; kinesiology and exercise science; liberal arts and sciences/liberal studies; licensed practical/vocational nurse training; management information systems; manufacturing engineering technology; marketing/marketing management; massage therapy; mathematics; medical/clinical assistant; natural resources/conservation; physical sciences; physical therapy; polymer/plastics engineering; pre-law studies; premedical studies; pre-pharmacy studies; radiologic technology/science; registered nursing/registered nurse; retailing; social sciences; speech communication and rhetoric; sport and fitness administration/management; substance abuse/addiction counseling.

Academics *Calendar:* quarters. *Degree:* certificates and associate. *Special study options:* academic remediation for entering students, cooperative education, distance learning, double majors, English as a second language, independent study, internships, part-time degree program, student-designed majors, study abroad, summer session for credit. *ROTC:* Army (c).

Library COCC Library plus 1 other with 76,421 titles, 329 serial subscriptions, 3,570 audiovisual materials, an OPAC, a Web page.

Student Life *Housing Options:* coed. Campus housing is university owned. *Activities and Organizations:* drama/theater group, student-run newspaper, choral group, club sports, student newspaper, Criminal Justice Club, Aviation Club. *Campus security:* 24-hour emergency response devices and patrols, late-night transport/escort service. *Student services:* personal/psychological counseling.

Athletics *Intercollegiate sports:* golf M/W. *Intramural sports:* baseball M, basketball M/W, cross-country running M/W, football M, skiing (cross-country) M/W, skiing (downhill) M/W, soccer M/W, track and field M/W, volleyball M/W, weight lifting M/W.

Financial Aid Of all full-time matriculated undergraduates who enrolled in 2011, 725 Federal Work-Study jobs (averaging $2130).

Applying *Options:* electronic application. *Application fee:* $25. *Application deadlines:* rolling (freshmen), rolling (transfers). *Notification:* continuous (freshmen), continuous (transfers).

Freshman Application Contact Central Oregon Community College, 2600 Northwest College Way, Bend, OR 97701-5998. *Phone:* 541-383-7500. *Website:* http://www.cocc.edu/.

Chemeketa Community College

Salem, Oregon

- **State and locally supported** 2-year, founded 1955
- **Urban** 72-acre campus with easy access to Portland, Oregon
- **Endowment** $3.7 million
- **Coed,** 12,371 undergraduate students, 50% full-time, 57% women, 43% men

Undergraduates 6,225 full-time, 6,146 part-time. Students come from 21 states and territories; 20 other countries; 5% are from out of state; 1% Black or African American, non-Hispanic/Latino; 18% Hispanic/Latino; 2% Asian, non-Hispanic/Latino; 0.8% Native Hawaiian or other Pacific Islander, non-Hispanic/Latino; 2% American Indian or Alaska Native, non-Hispanic/Latino; 4% Two or more races, non-Hispanic/Latino; 4% Race/ethnicity unknown; 0.6% international; 1% transferred in. *Retention:* 61% of full-time freshmen returned.

Freshmen *Admission:* 1,423 enrolled.

Faculty *Total:* 740, 25% full-time. *Student/faculty ratio:* 26:1.

Majors Accounting; accounting technology and bookkeeping; administrative assistant and secretarial science; agricultural business and management; applied horticulture/horticulture operations; automobile/automotive mechanics technology; building/home/construction inspection; business administration and management; CAD/CADD drafting/design technology; child-care and support services management; civil engineering technology; computer engineering technology; computer programming (specific applications); computer technology/computer systems technology; construction trades; criminal justice/safety; crop production; design and visual communications; electrical and electronics engineering; electrical, electronic and communications engineering technology; electromechanical and instrumentation and maintenance technologies related; emergency medical technology (EMT paramedic); executive assistant/executive secretary; fire prevention and safety technology; fire science/firefighting; general studies; graphic and printing equipment operation/production; graphic design; hospitality administration; hotel/motel administration; industrial mechanics and maintenance technology; juvenile corrections; liberal arts and sciences/liberal studies; machine shop technology; mechanical drafting and CAD/CADD; medical administrative assistant and medical secretary; medical office management; medical transcription; office management; pharmacy technician; registered nursing/registered nurse; social work; special education–individuals with speech/language impairments; substance abuse/addiction counseling; technical teacher education; tourism and travel services management; viticulture and enology; welding technology.

Academics *Calendar:* quarters. *Degree:* certificates, diplomas, and associate. *Special study options:* academic remediation for entering students, adult/continuing education programs, advanced placement credit, cooperative education, distance learning, double majors, English as a second language, independent study, internships, part-time degree program, services for LD students, study abroad, summer session for credit.

Library Chemeketa Community College Library (CCRLS) with 64,513 titles, 1,747 serial subscriptions, an OPAC, a Web page.

Student Life *Housing:* college housing not available. *Activities and Organizations:* drama/theater group, student-run newspaper, choral group, Student Center and Multicultural Center (the two largest), Phi Theta Kapa, Student Government, Juntos (promotes the Latin American culture, leadership development, community service, and higher education), Theater by Storm (all aspects of theater, including acting, technical theater, and management). *Campus security:* 24-hour emergency response devices and patrols, late-night transport/escort service. *Student services:* personal/psychological counseling, women's center.

Athletics *Intercollegiate sports:* baseball M(s), basketball M(s)/W(s), softball W(s), volleyball W(s). *Intramural sports:* soccer M/W, track and field M/W.

Costs (2013–14) *Tuition:* state resident $3690 full-time, $82 per quarter hour part-time; nonresident $10,980 full-time, $244 per quarter hour part-time. *Required fees:* $640 full-time, $14 per quarter hour part-time. *Payment plans:* installment, deferred payment. *Waivers:* senior citizens and employees or children of employees.

Applying *Required for some:* high school transcript, interview.

Freshman Application Contact Admissions Office, Chemeketa Community College, Chemeketa Community College, PO Box 14009. *Phone:* 503-399-5001. *E-mail:* admissions@chemeketa.edu. *Website:* http://www.chemeketa.edu/.

Clackamas Community College

Oregon City, Oregon

Freshman Application Contact Ms. Tara Sprehe, Registrar, Clackamas Community College, 19600 South Molalla Avenue, Oregon City, OR 97045. *Phone:* 503-657-6958 Ext. 2742. *Fax:* 503-650-6654. *E-mail:* pattyw@clackamas.edu. *Website:* http://www.clackamas.edu/.

Clatsop Community College

Astoria, Oregon

Freshman Application Contact Ms. Kristen Lee, Director, Enrollment Services, Clatsop Community College, 1653 Jerome Avenue, Astoria, OR 97103. *Phone:* 503-338-2326. *Toll-free phone:* 855-252-8767. *Fax:* 503-325-5738. *E-mail:* admissions@clatsopcc.edu. *Website:* http://www.clatsopcc.edu/.

Columbia Gorge Community College
The Dalles, Oregon

- **State-supported** 2-year, founded 1977
- **Small-town** 78-acre campus
- **Coed**

Undergraduates 542 full-time, 703 part-time. 0.6% Black or African American, non-Hispanic/Latino; 7% Hispanic/Latino; 0.8% Asian, non-Hispanic/Latino; 0.1% Native Hawaiian or other Pacific Islander, non-Hispanic/Latino; 5% American Indian or Alaska Native, non-Hispanic/Latino; 0.3% Two or more races, non-Hispanic/Latino; 17% Race/ethnicity unknown.
Academics *Calendar:* quarters. *Degree:* certificates, diplomas, and associate. *Special study options:* academic remediation for entering students, cooperative education, distance learning, English as a second language, honors programs, independent study, part-time degree program, services for LD students, summer session for credit.
Student Life *Campus security:* 24-hour emergency response devices.
Costs (2012–13) *Tuition:* state resident $2670 full-time, $89 per credit part-time; nonresident $2670 full-time, $89 per credit part-time. *Required fees:* $360 full-time. *Room and board:* $8610; room only: $3200. Room and board charges vary according to board plan.
Applying *Options:* electronic application.
Freshman Application Contact Columbia Gorge Community College, 400 East Scenic Drive, The Dalles, OR 97058. *Phone:* 541-506-6011.
Website: http://www.cgcc.cc.or.us/.

Everest College
Portland, Oregon

Freshman Application Contact Admissions Office, Everest College, 425 Southwest Washington Street, Portland, OR 97204. *Phone:* 503-222-3225. *Toll-free phone:* 888-741-4270. *Fax:* 503-228-6926.
Website: http://www.everest.edu/.

Heald College–Portland
Portland, Oregon

Freshman Application Contact Director of Admissions, Heald College–Portland, 6035 NE 78th Court, Portland, OR 97218. *Phone:* 503-229-0492. *Toll-free phone:* 800-88-HEALD. *Fax:* 503-229-0498. *E-mail:* portlandinfo@heald.edu.
Website: http://www.heald.edu/.

ITT Technical Institute
Portland, Oregon

- **Proprietary** primarily 2-year, founded 1971, part of ITT Educational Services, Inc.
- **Urban** campus
- **Coed**

Academics *Calendar:* quarters. *Degrees:* associate and bachelor's.
Financial Aid Of all full-time matriculated undergraduates who enrolled in 2011, 15 Federal Work-Study jobs (averaging $5000).
Freshman Application Contact Director of Recruitment, ITT Technical Institute, 9500 Northeast Cascades Parkway, Portland, OR 97220. *Phone:* 503-255-6500. *Toll-free phone:* 800-234-5488.
Website: http://www.itt-tech.edu/.

Klamath Community College
Klamath Falls, Oregon

- **State-supported** 2-year, founded 1996
- **Small-town** 58-acre campus
- **Endowment** $129,870
- **Coed,** 1,148 undergraduate students, 34% full-time, 60% women, 40% men

Undergraduates 385 full-time, 763 part-time. Students come from 2 states and territories; 0.1% are from out of state; 1% Black or African American, non-Hispanic/Latino; 13% Hispanic/Latino; 0.6% Asian, non-Hispanic/Latino; 0.2% Native Hawaiian or other Pacific Islander, non-Hispanic/Latino; 6% American Indian or Alaska Native, non-Hispanic/Latino; 0.7% Two or more races, non-Hispanic/Latino; 5% Race/ethnicity unknown; 14% transferred in. *Retention:* 58% of full-time freshmen returned.
Freshmen *Admission:* 202 enrolled.
Faculty *Total:* 129, 22% full-time, 8% with terminal degrees. *Student/faculty ratio:* 14:1.
Majors Accounting; administrative assistant and secretarial science; agriculture; automobile/automotive mechanics technology; business administration

and management; construction management; corrections; diesel mechanics technology; education; environmental studies; general studies; health services/allied health/health sciences; liberal arts and sciences/liberal studies; science technologies related.
Academics *Calendar:* quarters. *Degree:* certificates and associate. *Special study options:* academic remediation for entering students, advanced placement credit, cooperative education, distance learning, double majors, English as a second language, independent study, internships, services for LD students, student-designed majors, summer session for credit.
Library Learning Resource Center with an OPAC.
Student Life *Activities and Organizations:* Phi Beta Lambda, Hispanic Club, Future Farmers of America, Veterans Club, Business Club. *Campus security:* 24-hour emergency response devices. *Student services:* personal/psychological counseling.
Costs (2013–14) *Tuition:* state resident $2988 full-time, $83 per credit part-time; nonresident $5796 full-time, $161 per credit part-time. No tuition increase for student's term of enrollment. *Required fees:* $12 full-time, $12 per credit part-time. *Payment plan:* installment. *Waivers:* senior citizens and employees or children of employees.
Applying *Options:* electronic application. *Required:* high school transcript. *Application deadlines:* rolling (freshmen), rolling (out-of-state freshmen). *Notification:* continuous (freshmen), continuous (out-of-state freshmen).
Freshman Application Contact Tammi Garlock, Retention Coordinator, Klamath Community College, 7390 So. 6th St., Klamath Falls, OR 97603. *Phone:* 541-882-3521. *Fax:* 541-885-7758. *E-mail:* garlock@klamathcc.edu.
Website: http://www.klamathcc.edu/.

Lane Community College
Eugene, Oregon

Director of Admissions Ms. Helen Garrett, Director of Admissions/Registrar, Lane Community College, 4000 East 30th Avenue, Eugene, OR 97405-0640. *Phone:* 541-747-4501 Ext. 2686.
Website: http://www.lanecc.edu/.

Le Cordon Bleu College of Culinary Arts in Portland
Portland, Oregon

Admissions Office Contact Le Cordon Bleu College of Culinary Arts in Portland, 921 Southwest Morrison Street, Suite 400, Portland, OR 97205. *Toll-free phone:* 888-891-6222.
Website: http://www.wci.edu/.

Linn-Benton Community College
Albany, Oregon

Freshman Application Contact Ms. Christine Baker, Outreach Coordinator, Linn-Benton Community College, 6500 Pacific Boulevard, SW, Albany, OR 97321. *Phone:* 541-917-4813. *Fax:* 541-917-4838. *E-mail:* admissions@linnbenton.edu.
Website: http://www.linnbenton.edu/.

Mt. Hood Community College
Gresham, Oregon

Director of Admissions Dr. Craig Kolins, Associate Vice President of Enrollment Services, Mt. Hood Community College, 26000 Southeast Stark Street, Gresham, OR 97030-3300. *Phone:* 503-491-7265.
Website: http://www.mhcc.edu/.

Oregon Coast Community College
Newport, Oregon

- **Public** 2-year, founded 1987
- **Small-town** 24-acre campus
- **Coed,** 536 undergraduate students, 35% full-time, 60% women, 40% men

Undergraduates 188 full-time, 348 part-time. Students come from 2 states and territories; 1% are from out of state; 1% Black or African American, non-Hispanic/Latino; 2% Hispanic/Latino; 2% Asian, non-Hispanic/Latino; 0.4% Native Hawaiian or other Pacific Islander, non-Hispanic/Latino; 2% American Indian or Alaska Native, non-Hispanic/Latino; 9% Two or more races, non-Hispanic/Latino; 7% Race/ethnicity unknown; 12% transferred in. *Retention:* 53% of full-time freshmen returned.
Freshmen *Admission:* 93 applied, 93 admitted, 123 enrolled.
Faculty *Total:* 42, 24% full-time, 17% with terminal degrees. *Student/faculty ratio:* 15:1.

Majors Criminal justice/safety; general studies; liberal arts and sciences/liberal studies; marine biology and biological oceanography; registered nursing/registered nurse.

Academics *Calendar:* quarters. *Degree:* certificates and associate. *Special study options:* academic remediation for entering students, cooperative education, distance learning, English as a second language, honors programs, internships, part-time degree program, services for LD students, summer session for credit.

Library Oregon Coast Community College Library with 63,302 titles, 50 serial subscriptions, 2,079 audiovisual materials, an OPAC, a Web page.

Student Life *Housing:* college housing not available. *Activities and Organizations:* Psych club, Triangle club, Writing club, ASG. *Campus security:* 24-hour emergency response devices.

Standardized Tests *Required for some:* nursing entrance exam.

Costs (2013–14) *Tuition:* state resident $3564 full-time, $99 per credit part-time; nonresident $7704 full-time, $214 per credit part-time. Full-time tuition and fees vary according to course load and program. Part-time tuition and fees vary according to course load and program. *Required fees:* $252 full-time, $7 per credit part-time. *Payment plan:* deferred payment. *Waivers:* employees or children of employees.

Applying *Required for some:* essay or personal statement, 2 letters of recommendation, interview.

Freshman Application Contact Student Services, Oregon Coast Community College, 400 SE College Way, Newport, OR 97366. *Phone:* 541-265-2283. *Fax:* 541-265-3820. *E-mail:* webinfo@occc.cc.or.us. *Website:* http://www.oregoncoastcc.org.

Portland Community College

Portland, Oregon

Freshman Application Contact PCC Admissions and Registration Office, Portland Community College, PO Box 19000, Portland, OR 97280. *Phone:* 503-977-8888. *Website:* http://www.pcc.edu/.

Rogue Community College

Grants Pass, Oregon

- **State and locally supported** 2-year, founded 1970
- **Rural** 84-acre campus
- **Endowment** $6.4 million
- **Coed,** 5,556 undergraduate students, 42% full-time, 58% women, 42% men

Undergraduates 2,312 full-time, 3,244 part-time. Students come from 22 states and territories; 3 other countries; 2% are from out of state; 1% Black or African American, non-Hispanic/Latino; 12% Hispanic/Latino; 2% Asian, non-Hispanic/Latino; 0.5% Native Hawaiian or other Pacific Islander, non-Hispanic/Latino; 2% American Indian or Alaska Native, non-Hispanic/Latino; 3% Two or more races, non-Hispanic/Latino; 4% Race/ethnicity unknown; 0.1% international; 69% transferred in.

Freshmen *Admission:* 850 enrolled.

Faculty *Total:* 408, 19% full-time. *Student/faculty ratio:* 18:1.

Majors Accounting technology and bookkeeping; automobile/automotive mechanics technology; business administration and management; business/commerce; child-care and support services management; computer and information sciences; computer software technology; construction engineering technology; construction trades; criminal justice/police science; diesel mechanics technology; electrical and power transmission installation; electrical, electronic and communications engineering technology; emergency medical technology (EMT paramedic); fire prevention and safety technology; general studies; liberal arts and sciences/liberal studies; manufacturing engineering technology; marketing/marketing management; mechanics and repair; medical office computer specialist; registered nursing/registered nurse; social work; visual and performing arts; welding technology.

Academics *Calendar:* quarters. *Degree:* certificates and associate. *Special study options:* academic remediation for entering students, adult/continuing education programs, advanced placement credit, cooperative education, distance learning, double majors, English as a second language, independent study, internships, part-time degree program, services for LD students, study abroad, summer session for credit.

Library Rogue Community College Library with 33,000 titles, 275 serial subscriptions, an OPAC.

Student Life *Activities and Organizations:* drama/theater group, student-run newspaper, choral group. *Campus security:* 24-hour emergency response devices and patrols, late-night transport/escort service. *Student services:* personal/psychological counseling.

Athletics *Intramural sports:* badminton M/W, basketball M/W, soccer M/W, softball M/W, volleyball M/W.

Costs (2012–13) *Tuition:* state resident $3132 full-time, $87 per credit hour part-time; nonresident $3852 full-time, $107 per credit hour part-time. Full-time tuition and fees vary according to course load. Part-time tuition and fees vary according to course load. *Required fees:* $549 full-time, $4 per credit hour part-time, $135 per term part-time. *Payment plan:* installment. *Waivers:* employees or children of employees.

Financial Aid Of all full-time matriculated undergraduates who enrolled in 2012, 1,806 applied for aid, 1,599 were judged to have need, 59 had their need fully met. 85 Federal Work-Study jobs (averaging $2810). In 2012, 30 non-need-based awards were made. *Average percent of need met:* 80%. *Average financial aid package:* $10,078. *Average need-based loan:* $3558. *Average need-based gift aid:* $5568. *Average non-need-based aid:* $1439.

Applying *Options:* electronic application, early admission. *Application deadlines:* rolling (freshmen), rolling (out-of-state freshmen), rolling (transfers).

Freshman Application Contact Ms. Claudia Sullivan, Director of Enrollment Services, Rogue Community College, 3345 Redwood Highway, Grants Pass, OR 97527-9291. *Phone:* 541-956-7176. *Fax:* 541-471-3585. *E-mail:* csullivan@roguecc.edu. *Website:* http://www.roguecc.edu/.

Southwestern Oregon Community College

Coos Bay, Oregon

Freshman Application Contact Miss Lela Wells, Southwestern Oregon Community College, Student First Stop, 1988 Newmark Avenue, Coos Bay, OR 97420. *Phone:* 541-888-7611. *Toll-free phone:* 800-962-2838. *E-mail:* lwells@socc.edu. *Website:* http://www.socc.edu/.

Tillamook Bay Community College

Tillamook, Oregon

Freshman Application Contact Lori Gates, Tillamook Bay Community College, 4301 Third Street, Tillamook, OR 97141. *Phone:* 503-842-8222. *Fax:* 503-842-2214. *E-mail:* gates@tillamookbay.cc. *Website:* http://www.tbcc.cc.or.us/.

Treasure Valley Community College

Ontario, Oregon

Freshman Application Contact Ms. Candace Bell, Office of Admissions and Student Services, Treasure Valley Community College, 650 College Boulevard, Ontario, OR 97914. *Phone:* 541-881-8822 Ext. 239. *Fax:* 541-881-2721. *E-mail:* clbell@tvcc.cc. *Website:* http://www.tvcc.cc.or.us/.

Umpqua Community College

Roseburg, Oregon

- **State and locally supported** 2-year, founded 1964
- **Rural** 100-acre campus
- **Endowment** $6.1 million
- **Coed**

Undergraduates 1,735 full-time, 1,498 part-time. Students come from 5 states and territories; 2 other countries; 12% transferred in.

Faculty *Student/faculty ratio:* 30:1.

Academics *Calendar:* quarters. *Degree:* certificates and associate. *Special study options:* academic remediation for entering students, accelerated degree program, adult/continuing education programs, advanced placement credit, cooperative education, distance learning, English as a second language, honors programs, independent study, internships, part-time degree program, services for LD students, study abroad, summer session for credit.

Student Life *Campus security:* 24-hour emergency response devices and patrols.

Costs (2012–13) *Tuition:* state resident $4107 full-time, $75 per credit hour part-time; nonresident $9552 full-time, $196 per credit hour part-time. *Required fees:* $304 full-time, $10 per credit hour part-time, $101 per term part-time.

Financial Aid Of all full-time matriculated undergraduates who enrolled in 2011, 120 Federal Work-Study jobs (averaging $3000).

Applying *Options:* electronic application, early admission, deferred entrance. *Application fee:* $25. *Recommended:* high school transcript.

Freshman Application Contact Mr. Rich Robles, Recruiter, Umpqua Community College, PO Box 967, Roseburg, OR 97470-0226. *Phone:* 541-440-4600 Ext. 7661. *Fax:* 541-440-4612. *E-mail:* Richard.Robles@umpqua.edu. *Website:* http://www.umpqua.edu/.

PENNSYLVANIA

Antonelli Institute

Erdenheim, Pennsylvania

- **Proprietary** 2-year, founded 1938
- **Suburban** 15-acre campus with easy access to Philadelphia
- **Coed,** 183 undergraduate students
- 85% of applicants were admitted

Freshmen *Admission:* 270 applied, 229 admitted.

Majors Graphic design; photography.

Academics *Calendar:* semesters. *Degree:* associate. *Special study options:* adult/continuing education programs.

Financial Aid Of all full-time matriculated undergraduates who enrolled in 2011, 5 Federal Work-Study jobs (averaging $2000).

Freshman Application Contact Admissions Office, Antonelli Institute, 300 Montgomery Avenue, Erdenheim, PA 19038. *Phone:* 800-722-7871. *Toll-free phone:* 800-722-7871.
Website: http://www.antonelli.edu/.

The Art Institute of York–Pennsylvania

York, Pennsylvania

- **Proprietary** primarily 2-year, founded 1952, part of Education Management Corporation
- **Suburban** campus
- **Coed**

Academics *Calendar:* quarters. *Degrees:* associate and bachelor's.

Freshman Application Contact The Art Institute of York–Pennsylvania, 1409 Williams Road, York, PA 17402-9012. *Phone:* 717-755-2300. *Toll-free phone:* 800-864-7725.
Website: http://www.artinstitutes.edu/york/.

Berks Technical Institute

Wyomissing, Pennsylvania

Freshman Application Contact Mr. Allan Brussolo, Academic Dean, Berks Technical Institute, 2205 Ridgewood Road, Wyomissing, PA 19610-1168. *Phone:* 610-372-1722. *Toll-free phone:* 866-591-8384. *Fax:* 610-376-4684. *E-mail:* abrussolo@berks.edu.
Website: http://www.berks.edu/.

Bidwell Training Center

Pittsburgh, Pennsylvania

Freshman Application Contact Admissions Office, Bidwell Training Center, 1815 Metropolitan Street, Pittsburgh, PA 15233. *Phone:* 412-322-1773. *Toll-free phone:* 800-516-1800. *E-mail:* admissions@mcg-btc.org.
Website: http://www.bidwell-training.org/.

Bradford School

Pittsburgh, Pennsylvania

- **Private** 2-year, founded 1968
- **Urban** campus
- **Coed,** 441 undergraduate students
- 87% of applicants were admitted

Freshmen *Admission:* 915 applied, 794 admitted.

Majors Accounting technology and bookkeeping; administrative assistant and secretarial science; computer programming; computer systems networking and telecommunications; dental assisting; graphic design; hotel/motel administration; legal administrative assistant/secretary; legal assistant/paralegal; medical/clinical assistant; retailing.

Academics *Degree:* diplomas and associate. *Special study options:* accelerated degree program, internships.

Freshman Application Contact Admissions Office, Bradford School, 125 West Station Square Drive, Pittsburgh, PA 15219. *Phone:* 412-391-6710. *Toll-free phone:* 800-391-6810.
Website: http://www.bradfordpittsburgh.edu/.

Bucks County Community College

Newtown, Pennsylvania

- **County-supported** 2-year, founded 1964
- **Suburban** 200-acre campus with easy access to Philadelphia
- **Endowment** $4.6 million
- **Coed,** 10,252 undergraduate students, 33% full-time, 56% women, 44% men

Undergraduates 3,378 full-time, 6,874 part-time. Students come from 12 states and territories; 1% are from out of state; 5% Black or African American, non-Hispanic/Latino; 5% Hispanic/Latino; 3% Asian, non-Hispanic/Latino; 0.1% Native Hawaiian or other Pacific Islander, non-Hispanic/Latino; 1% American Indian or Alaska Native, non-Hispanic/Latino; 2% Two or more races, non-Hispanic/Latino; 12% Race/ethnicity unknown; 0.6% international; 76% transferred in.

Freshmen *Admission:* 4,963 applied, 4,852 admitted, 2,442 enrolled.

Faculty *Total:* 577, 30% full-time, 21% with terminal degrees. *Student/faculty ratio:* 21:1.

Majors Accounting technology and bookkeeping; American studies; baking and pastry arts; biology/biotechnology laboratory technician; biology teacher education; biotechnology; building/home/construction inspection; business administration and management; business/commerce; business, management, and marketing related; cabinetmaking and millwork; chemical technology; chemistry teacher education; child-care provision; cinematography and film/video production; commercial and advertising art; computer and information sciences; computer programming (specific applications); computer systems networking and telecommunications; corrections; criminal justice/law enforcement administration; criminal justice/safety; crisis/emergency/disaster management; culinary arts; dramatic/theater arts; early childhood education; education; engineering technology; environmental science; fire prevention and safety technology; food service systems administration; health professions related; historic preservation and conservation; history teacher education; human development and family studies; humanities; industrial technology; information science/studies; journalism; legal professions and studies related; liberal arts and sciences and humanities related; liberal arts and sciences/liberal studies; mathematics; mathematics teacher education; medical/clinical assistant; medical insurance coding; multi/interdisciplinary studies related; music; network and system administration; parks, recreation and leisure facilities management; physical education teaching and coaching; precision production trades; psychology; registered nursing/registered nurse; retailing; speech communication and rhetoric; sport and fitness administration/management; tourism and travel services management; visual and performing arts; web page, digital/multimedia and information resources design; women's studies.

Academics *Calendar:* semesters. *Degree:* certificates and associate. *Special study options:* academic remediation for entering students, adult/continuing education programs, advanced placement credit, cooperative education, distance learning, English as a second language, external degree program, independent study, internships, part-time degree program, services for LD students, student-designed majors, summer session for credit.

Library Bucks County Community College Library with 131,156 titles, 268 serial subscriptions, 1,828 audiovisual materials, an OPAC, a Web page.

Student Life *Housing:* college housing not available. *Activities and Organizations:* drama/theater group, student-run newspaper, television station, choral group, Phi Theta Kappa, Inter-Varsity Christian Fellowship, Drama Club, Habitat for Humanity, Future Teachers Organization. *Campus security:* 24-hour emergency response devices and patrols, late-night transport/escort service. *Student services:* personal/psychological counseling, women's center.

Athletics Member NJCAA. *Intercollegiate sports:* baseball M, basketball M/W, equestrian sports M/W, golf M/W, soccer M/W, tennis M/W, volleyball W. *Intramural sports:* basketball M/W, soccer M/W, softball M/W, table tennis M/W, tennis M/W, ultimate Frisbee M/W, volleyball W.

Costs (2012–13) *Tuition:* area resident $3510 full-time, $117 per credit hour part-time; state resident $7020 full-time, $234 per credit hour part-time; nonresident $10,530 full-time, $351 per credit hour part-time. Full-time tuition and fees vary according to program. Part-time tuition and fees vary according to program. *Required fees:* $1124 full-time, $63 per credit hour part-time. *Payment plans:* installment, deferred payment. *Waivers:* senior citizens and employees or children of employees.

Financial Aid Of all full-time matriculated undergraduates who enrolled in 2011, 162 Federal Work-Study jobs (averaging $2395).

Applying *Options:* electronic application, early admission. *Required:* high school transcript. *Required for some:* essay or personal statement, interview.

Freshman Application Contact Ms. Marlene Barlow, Director of Admissions, Bucks County Community College, Newtown, PA 18940. *Phone:* 215-968-8137. *Fax:* 215-968-8110. *E-mail:* barlowm@bucks.edu.
Website: http://www.bucks.edu/.

Peterson's Two-Year Colleges 2014

www.petersonsbooks.com **261**

Butler County Community College
Butler, Pennsylvania

Freshman Application Contact Ms. Patricia Bajuszik, Director of Admissions, Butler County Community College, College Drive, PO Box 1205, Butler, PA 16003-1203. *Phone:* 724-287-8711 Ext. 344. *Toll-free phone:* 888-826-2829. *Fax:* 724-287-4961. *E-mail:* pattie.bajoszik@bc3.edu. *Website:* http://www.bc3.edu/.

Cambria-Rowe Business College
Indiana, Pennsylvania

Freshman Application Contact Mrs. Stacey Bell-Leger, Representative at Indiana Campus, Cambria-Rowe Business College, 422 South 13th Street, Indiana, PA 15701. *Phone:* 724-483-0222. *Toll-free phone:* 800-NEW-CAREER. *Fax:* 724-463-7246. *E-mail:* sbell-leger@crbc.net. *Website:* http://www.crbc.net/.

Cambria-Rowe Business College
Johnstown, Pennsylvania

Freshman Application Contact Mrs. Amanda Artim, Director of Admissions, Cambria-Rowe Business College, 221 Central Avenue, Johnstown, PA 15902-2494. *Phone:* 814-536-5168. *Toll-free phone:* 800-NEWCAREER. *Fax:* 814-536-5160. *E-mail:* admissions@crbc.net. *Website:* http://www.crbc.net/.

Career Training Academy
Monroeville, Pennsylvania

Freshman Application Contact Career Training Academy, 4314 Old William Penn Highway, Suite 103, Monroeville, PA 15146. *Phone:* 412-372-3900. *Toll-free phone:* 866-673-7773. *Website:* http://www.careerta.edu/.

Career Training Academy
New Kensington, Pennsylvania

Freshman Application Contact Career Training Academy, 950 Fifth Avenue, New Kensington, PA 15068-6301. *Phone:* 724-337-1000. *Toll-free phone:* 866-673-7773. *Website:* http://www.careerta.edu/.

Career Training Academy
Pittsburgh, Pennsylvania

- **Proprietary** 2-year
- **Suburban** campus with easy access to Pittsburgh
- **Coed,** 70 undergraduate students, 100% full-time, 93% women, 7% men

Undergraduates 70 full-time. Students come from 1 other state; 33% Black or African American, non-Hispanic/Latino; 4% Hispanic/Latino; 1% Native Hawaiian or other Pacific Islander, non-Hispanic/Latino.
Freshmen *Admission:* 13 enrolled. *Average high school GPA:* 2.
Faculty *Total:* 9, 78% full-time. *Student/faculty ratio:* 9:1.
Majors Massage therapy; medical/clinical assistant; medical insurance coding.
Academics *Calendar:* continuous. *Degree:* diplomas and associate. *Special study options:* academic remediation for entering students, advanced placement credit, cooperative education, internships, services for LD students.
Library Career Training Academy.
Student Life *Housing:* college housing not available. *Campus security:* 24-hour emergency response devices, late-night transport/escort service.
Costs (2013–14) *Tuition:* $12,218 full-time. Full-time tuition and fees vary according to program. No tuition increase for student's term of enrollment. *Payment plans:* tuition prepayment, installment.
Applying *Application fee:* $30. *Required:* essay or personal statement, high school transcript, minimum 1.5 GPA, interview. *Application deadlines:* rolling (freshmen), rolling (out-of-state freshmen).
Freshman Application Contact Jaimie Vignone, Career Training Academy, 1500 Northway Mall, Suite 200, Pittsburgh, PA 15237. *Phone:* 412-367-4000. *Toll-free phone:* 866-673-7773. *Fax:* 412-369-7223. *E-mail:* admission3@careerta.edu. *Website:* http://www.careerta.edu/.

Commonwealth Technical Institute
Johnstown, Pennsylvania

Freshman Application Contact Ms. Rebecca Halza, Admissions Supervisor, Commonwealth Technical Institute, Hiram G. Andrews Center, 727 Goucher Street, Johnstown, PA 15905. *Phone:* 814-255-8200. *Toll-free phone:* 800-762-4211. *Fax:* 814-255-8283. *E-mail:* rhalza@state.pa.us. *Website:* http://www.portal.state.pa.us/portal/server.pt/community/commonwealth_technical_institute/10361.

Community College of Allegheny County
Pittsburgh, Pennsylvania

- **County-supported** 2-year, founded 1966
- **Urban** 242-acre campus
- **Coed,** 18,913 undergraduate students, 38% full-time, 59% women, 41% men

Undergraduates 7,101 full-time, 11,812 part-time. 2% are from out of state; 18% Black or African American, non-Hispanic/Latino; 0.9% Hispanic/Latino; 2% Asian, non-Hispanic/Latino; 0.1% Native Hawaiian or other Pacific Islander, non-Hispanic/Latino; 0.4% American Indian or Alaska Native, non-Hispanic/Latino; 0.7% Two or more races, non-Hispanic/Latino; 15% Race/ethnicity unknown; 0.1% international.
Freshmen *Admission:* 4,170 enrolled.
Faculty *Total:* 1,188, 22% full-time. *Student/faculty ratio:* 20:1.
Majors Accounting technology and bookkeeping; administrative assistant and secretarial science; airline pilot and flight crew; applied horticulture/horticulture operations; architectural drafting and CAD/CADD; art; athletic training; automotive engineering technology; aviation/airway management; banking and financial support services; biology/biological sciences; building/property maintenance; business administration and management; business automation/technology/data entry; business machine repair; carpentry; chemical technology; chemistry; child-care provision; child development; civil drafting and CAD/CADD; civil engineering technology; clinical/medical laboratory technology; commercial and advertising art; communications technologies and support services related; community health services counseling; computer engineering technology; computer systems networking and telecommunications; computer technology/computer systems technology; construction engineering technology; construction trades related; corrections; cosmetology and personal grooming arts related; court reporting; criminal justice/police science; culinary arts; diagnostic medical sonography and ultrasound technology; dietitian assistant; drafting and design technology; drafting/design engineering technologies related; dramatic/theater arts; education (specific levels and methods) related; education (specific subject areas) related; electrical, electronic and communications engineering technology; electroneurodiagnostic/electroencephalographic technology; energy management and systems technology; engineering technologies and engineering related; English; entrepreneurship; environmental engineering technology; fire prevention and safety technology; food service systems administration; foreign languages and literatures; general studies; greenhouse management; health and physical education/fitness; health information/medical records technology; health professions related; health unit coordinator/ward clerk; heating, air conditioning, ventilation and refrigeration maintenance technology; hotel/motel administration; housing and human environments related; human development and family studies related; humanities; human resources management; industrial technology; insurance; journalism; landscaping and groundskeeping; legal administrative assistant/secretary; legal assistant/paralegal; liberal arts and sciences/liberal studies; licensed practical/vocational nurse training; machine shop technology; management information systems; marketing/marketing management; mathematics; mechanical drafting and CAD/CADD; medical administrative assistant and medical secretary; medical/clinical assistant; medical radiologic technology; music; nuclear medical technology; nursing assistant/aide and patient care assistant/aide; occupational therapist assistant; office management; ornamental horticulture; perioperative/operating room and surgical nursing; pharmacy technician; physical therapy technology; physics; plant nursery management; psychiatric/mental health services technology; psychology; quality control technology; real estate; registered nursing/registered nurse; respiratory care therapy; restaurant, culinary, and catering management; retailing; robotics technology; science technologies related; sheet metal technology; sign language interpretation and translation; social sciences; social work; sociology; solar energy technology; substance abuse/addiction counseling; surgical technology; therapeutic recreation; tourism promotion; turf and turfgrass management; visual and performing arts related; welding technology.
Academics *Calendar:* semesters. *Degree:* certificates, diplomas, and associate. *Special study options:* part-time degree program.
Library Community College of Allegheny County Library.
Student Life *Housing:* college housing not available. *Campus security:* 24-hour emergency response devices and patrols, late-night transport/escort service.
Athletics Member NJCAA. *Intercollegiate sports:* baseball M, basketball M/W, bowling M/W, golf M/W, ice hockey M, softball W, table tennis M/W, tennis M/W, volleyball W. *Intramural sports:* badminton M/W, basketball

M/W, bowling M/W, cross-country running M/W, football M, golf M/W, lacrosse M, racquetball M/W, softball M/W, table tennis M/W, tennis M/W, volleyball M/W, weight lifting M/W.

Applying *Recommended:* high school transcript. *Application deadlines:* rolling (freshmen), rolling (transfers). *Notification:* continuous (freshmen), continuous (transfers).

Freshman Application Contact Admissions Office, Community College of Allegheny County, 808 Ridge Avenue, Pittsburgh, PA 15212. *Phone:* 412-237-2511.
Website: http://www.ccac.edu/.

Community College of Beaver County
Monaca, Pennsylvania

- **State-supported** 2-year, founded 1966
- **Small-town** 75-acre campus with easy access to Pittsburgh
- **Coed,** 2,779 undergraduate students

Undergraduates 2% are from out of state.

Faculty *Student/faculty ratio:* 16:1.

Majors Accounting technology and bookkeeping; administrative assistant and secretarial science; adult development and aging; aeronautical/aerospace engineering technology; airline pilot and flight crew; air traffic control; architectural drafting and CAD/CADD; autobody/collision and repair technology; automobile/automotive mechanics technology; aviation/airway management; banking and financial support services; biological and physical sciences; business administration and management; business/commerce; carpentry; chemical technology; chemistry; clinical/medical laboratory assistant; communication and journalism related; communications technologies and support services related; computer and information sciences; computer and information systems security; computer systems networking and telecommunications;,cosmetology; criminal justice/police science; culinary arts; diesel mechanics technology; digital communication and media/multimedia; education; education (multiple levels); electrical, electronic and communications engineering technology; electrician; engineering technology; entrepreneurship; environmental engineering technology; executive assistant/executive secretary; finance; fine/studio arts; general studies; health and medical administrative services related; health and physical education/fitness; heating, air conditioning, ventilation and refrigeration maintenance technology; humanities; human resources management; industrial production technologies related; journalism; liberal arts and sciences/liberal studies; machine tool technology; marketing/marketing management; masonry; materials engineering; mathematics; mechanical engineering technologies related; medical administrative assistant and medical secretary; medical radiologic technology; music; physics; plumbing technology; psychology; public relations, advertising, and applied communication related; registered nursing/registered nurse; security and loss prevention; small business administration; social sciences; sociology; speech communication and rhetoric; system, networking, and LAN/WAN management; teacher assistant/aide; tourism and travel services marketing; web/multimedia management and webmaster; welding technology.

Academics *Calendar:* semesters. *Degree:* certificates, diplomas, and associate. *Special study options:* academic remediation for entering students, adult/continuing education programs, advanced placement credit, cooperative education, distance learning, double majors, independent study, internships, off-campus study, part-time degree program, services for LD students, summer session for credit.

Library Community College of Beaver County Library.

Student Life *Housing:* college housing not available. *Campus security:* 24-hour emergency response devices and patrols, late-night transport/escort service.

Athletics Member NJCAA.

Applying *Options:* early admission. *Required:* interview. *Recommended:* high school transcript. *Application deadlines:* rolling (freshmen), rolling (transfers). *Notification:* continuous (freshmen), continuous (transfers).

Freshman Application Contact Enrollment Management, Community College of Beaver County, One Campus Drive, Monaca, PA 15061-2588. *Phone:* 724-480-3500. *Toll-free phone:* 800-335-0222. *E-mail:* admissions@ccbc.edu.
Website: http://www.ccbc.edu/.

Community College of Philadelphia
Philadelphia, Pennsylvania

- **State and locally supported** 2-year, founded 1964
- **Urban** 14-acre campus
- **Coed,** 39,500 undergraduate students

Undergraduates Students come from 50 other countries.

Faculty *Total:* 1,109, 39% full-time.

Majors Accounting; architectural engineering technology; art; automobile/automotive mechanics technology; business administration and management; chemical technology; clinical/medical laboratory technology; computer science; construction engineering technology; criminal justice/law enforcement administration; culinary arts; dental hygiene; drafting and design technology; education; engineering; engineering technology; facilities planning and management; finance; fire science/firefighting; forensic science and technology; health information/medical records administration; health professions related; hotel/motel administration; human services; kindergarten/preschool education; liberal arts and sciences/liberal studies; medical administrative assistant and medical secretary; medical radiologic technology; mental health counseling; music; occupational therapist assistant; photography; pre-engineering; psychology; recording arts technology; registered nursing/registered nurse; respiratory care therapy; sign language interpretation and translation.

Academics *Calendar:* semesters. *Degree:* certificates, diplomas, and associate. *Special study options:* academic remediation for entering students, accelerated degree program, ' adult/continuing education programs, advanced placement credit, cooperative education, distance learning, English as a second language, external degree program, honors programs, independent study, internships, off-campus study, part-time degree program, services for LD students, student-designed majors, study abroad, summer session for credit. *ROTC:* Army (c).

Library Main Campus Library plus 2 others with 110,000 titles, 420 serial subscriptions, an OPAC, a Web page.

Student Life *Housing:* college housing not available. *Activities and Organizations:* drama/theater group, student-run newspaper, choral group, Philadelphia L.E.A.D.S, Phi Theta Kappa, Student Government Association, Vanguard Student Newspaper, Fundraising Club. *Campus security:* 24-hour emergency response devices and patrols, phone/alert systems in classrooms/buildings. *Student services:* personal/psychological counseling, women's center.

Athletics *Intercollegiate sports:* baseball M, basketball M/W, cheerleading M/W, cross-country running M/W, soccer M, tennis M/W, track and field M/W, volleyball M/W. *Intramural sports:* basketball M/W, soccer M/W, tennis M/W, track and field M/W, volleyball M/W.

Costs (2012–13) *Tuition:* area resident $4980 full-time, $148 per credit hour part-time; state resident $8828 full-time, $296 per credit hour part-time; nonresident $12,676 full-time, $444 per credit hour part-time. Full-time tuition and fees vary according to program. Part-time tuition and fees vary according to program. *Payment plan:* installment. *Waivers:* senior citizens and employees or children of employees.

Applying *Options:* electronic application, early admission, deferred entrance. *Application fee:* $20. *Required for some:* high school transcript, allied health and nursing programs have specific entry requirements. *Application deadlines:* rolling (freshmen), rolling (transfers). *Notification:* continuous (freshmen), continuous (transfers).

Freshman Application Contact Community College of Philadelphia, 1700 Spring Garden Street, Philadelphia, PA 19130-3991. *Phone:* 215-751-8010. *Website:* http://www.ccp.edu/.

Consolidated School of Business
Lancaster, Pennsylvania

Freshman Application Contact Ms. Libby Paul, Admissions Representative, Consolidated School of Business, 2124 Ambassador Circle, Lancaster, PA 17603. *Phone:* 717-394-6211. *Toll-free phone:* 800-541-8298. *Fax:* 717-394-6213. *E-mail:* lpaul@csb.edu.
Website: http://www.csb.edu/.

Consolidated School of Business
York, Pennsylvania

- **Proprietary** 2-year, founded 1981
- **Suburban** 6-acre campus with easy access to Baltimore
- **Coed, primarily women**

Undergraduates 176 full-time.

Faculty *Student/faculty ratio:* 15:1.

Academics *Calendar:* continuous. *Degree:* diplomas and associate. *Special study options:* accelerated degree program, double majors, honors programs, independent study, internships, part-time degree program, services for LD students.

Applying *Options:* electronic application. *Required:* high school transcript, interview.

Freshman Application Contact Ms. Sandra Swanger, Admissions Representative, Consolidated School of Business, 1605 Clugston Road, York, PA 17404. *Phone:* 717-764-9550. *Toll-free phone:* 800-520-0691. *Fax:* 717-764-9469. *E-mail:* sswanger@csb.edu.
Website: http://www.csb.edu/.

Dean Institute of Technology
Pittsburgh, Pennsylvania

Director of Admissions Mr. Richard D. Ali, Admissions Director, Dean Institute of Technology, 1501 West Liberty Avenue, Pittsburgh, PA 15226-1103. *Phone:* 412-531-4433.
Website: http://www.deantech.edu/.

Delaware County Community College
Media, Pennsylvania

- **State and locally supported** 2-year, founded 1967
- **Suburban** 123-acre campus with easy access to Philadelphia
- **Endowment** $3.8 million
- **Coed**

Undergraduates 5,360 full-time, 7,888 part-time. Students come from 9 states and territories; 53 other countries; 1% are from out of state; 25% Black or African American, non-Hispanic/Latino; 2% Hispanic/Latino; 4% Asian, non-Hispanic/Latino; 0.1% Native Hawaiian or other Pacific Islander, non-Hispanic/Latino; 0.2% American Indian or Alaska Native, non-Hispanic/Latino; 2% Two or more races, non-Hispanic/Latino; 5% Race/ethnicity unknown. *Retention:* 61% of full-time freshmen returned.
Faculty *Student/faculty ratio:* 24:1.
Academics *Calendar:* semesters. *Degree:* certificates and associate. *Special study options:* academic remediation for entering students, adult/continuing education programs, advanced placement credit, cooperative education, distance learning, double majors, English as a second language, independent study, internships, part-time degree program, services for LD students, student-designed majors, summer session for credit.
Student Life *Campus security:* 24-hour emergency response devices and patrols, late-night transport/escort service.
Athletics Member NJCAA.
Financial Aid Of all full-time matriculated undergraduates who enrolled in 2011, 95 Federal Work-Study jobs (averaging $900).
Applying *Options:* early admission. *Application fee:* $25. *Required:* high school transcript.
Freshman Application Contact Ms. Hope Diehl, Director of Admissions and Enrollment Services, Delaware County Community College, 901 South Media Line Road, Media, PA 19063-1094. *Phone:* 610-359-5050. *Fax:* 610-723-1530. *E-mail:* admiss@dccc.edu.
Website: http://www.dccc.edu/.

Douglas Education Center
Monessen, Pennsylvania

Freshman Application Contact Ms. Sherry Lee Walters, Director of Enrollment Services, Douglas Education Center, 130 Seventh Street, Monessen, PA 15062. *Phone:* 724-684-3684 Ext. 2181. *Toll-free phone:* 800-413-6013.
Website: http://www.dec.edu/.

DuBois Business College
DuBois, Pennsylvania

Director of Admissions Mrs. Lisa Doty, Director of Admissions, DuBois Business College, 1 Beaver Drive, DuBois, PA 15801-2401. *Phone:* 814-371-6920. *Toll-free phone:* 800-692-6213. *Fax:* 814-371-3947. *E-mail:* dotylj@dbcollege.com.
Website: http://www.dbcollege.com/.

Erie Business Center, Main
Erie, Pennsylvania

Freshman Application Contact Erie Business Center, Main, 246 West Ninth Street, Erie, PA 16501-1392. *Phone:* 814-456-7504. *Toll-free phone:* 800-352-3743.
Website: http://www.eriebc.edu/.

Erie Business Center, South
New Castle, Pennsylvania

Freshman Application Contact Erie Business Center, South, 170 Cascade Galleria, New Castle, PA 16101-3950. *Phone:* 724-658-9066. *Toll-free phone:* 800-722-6227. *E-mail:* admissions@eriebcs.com.
Website: http://www.eriebc.edu/newcastle/.

Erie Institute of Technology
Erie, Pennsylvania

Freshman Application Contact Erie Institute of Technology, 940 Millcreek Mall, Erie, PA 16565. *Phone:* 814-868-9900. *Toll-free phone:* 866-868-3743.
Website: http://www.erieit.edu/.

Everest Institute
Pittsburgh, Pennsylvania

Director of Admissions Director of Admissions, Everest Institute, 100 Forbes Avenue, Suite 1200, Pittsburgh, PA 15222. *Phone:* 412-261-4520. *Toll-free phone:* 888-741-4270. *Fax:* 412-261-4546.
Website: http://www.everest.edu/.

Fortis Institute
Erie, Pennsylvania

Director of Admissions Guy M. Euliano, President, Fortis Institute, 5757 West 26th Street, Erie, PA 16506. *Phone:* 814-838-7673. *Fax:* 814-838-8642. *E-mail:* geuliano@tsbi.org.
Website: http://www.fortis.edu/.

Fortis Institute
Forty Fort, Pennsylvania

Freshman Application Contact Admissions Office, Fortis Institute, 166 Slocum Street, Forty Fort, PA 18704. *Phone:* 570-288-8400.
Website: http://www.fortis.edu/.

Harcum College
Bryn Mawr, Pennsylvania

Freshman Application Contact Office of Enrollment Management, Harcum College, 750 Montgomery Avenue, Bryn Mawr, PA 19010-3476. *Phone:* 610-526-6050. *E-mail:* enroll@harcum.edu.
Website: http://www.harcum.edu/.

Harrisburg Area Community College
Harrisburg, Pennsylvania

- **State and locally supported** 2-year, founded 1964
- **Urban** 212-acre campus
- **Endowment** $32.1 million
- **Coed,** 21,945 undergraduate students, 31% full-time, 63% women, 37% men

Undergraduates 6,882 full-time, 15,063 part-time. Students come from 10 states and territories; 58 other countries; 1% are from out of state; 12% Black or African American, non-Hispanic/Latino; 9% Hispanic/Latino; 2% Asian, non-Hispanic/Latino; 0.2% Native Hawaiian or other Pacific Islander, non-Hispanic/Latino; 0.4% American Indian or Alaska Native, non-Hispanic/Latino; 2% Two or more races, non-Hispanic/Latino; 2% Race/ethnicity unknown; 2% international.
Freshmen *Admission:* 2,077 enrolled.
Faculty *Total:* 980, 33% full-time, 13% with terminal degrees. *Student/faculty ratio:* 22:1.
Majors Accounting and business/management; accounting technology and bookkeeping; administrative assistant and secretarial science; agribusiness; architectural engineering technology; architecture; art; automobile/automotive mechanics technology; banking and financial support services; biology/biological sciences; building/home/construction inspection; business administration and management; business/commerce; cabinetmaking and millwork; cardiovascular technology; chemistry; civil engineering technology; clinical/medical laboratory technology; computer and information sciences; computer and information systems security; computer installation and repair technology; computer science; computer systems networking and telecommunications; construction engineering technology; construction trades; court reporting; crafts, folk art and artisanry; criminalistics and criminal science; criminal justice/law enforcement administration; criminal justice/police science; culinary arts; dental hygiene; design and visual communications; diagnostic medical sonography and ultrasound technology; dietetics; dramatic/theater arts; early childhood education; electrical, electronic and communications engineering technology; electrician; emergency medical technology (EMT paramedic); energy management and systems technology; engineering; engineering technologies and engineering related; environmental science; environmental studies; fire science/firefighting; food service systems administration; general studies; geographic information science and cartography; graphic design; health/health-care administration; health services administration; heating, air

conditioning, ventilation and refrigeration maintenance technology; hospitality administration; hotel/motel administration; human services; international relations and affairs; landscaping and groundskeeping; legal assistant/paralegal; lineworker; management information systems and services related; mass communication/media; mathematics; mechanical engineering/mechanical technology; mechatronics, robotics, and automation engineering; medical/clinical assistant; music management; nuclear medical technology; philosophy; photography; physical sciences; psychology; radiologic technology/science; real estate; registered nursing/registered nurse; respiratory care therapy; sales, distribution, and marketing operations; secondary education; small business administration; social sciences; social work; surgical technology; tourism and travel services management; visual and performing arts; viticulture and enology; web page, digital/multimedia and information resources design.

Academics *Calendar:* semesters. *Degree:* certificates, diplomas, and associate. *Special study options:* academic remediation for entering students, adult/continuing education programs, advanced placement credit, distance learning, double majors, English as a second language, honors programs, independent study, internships, part-time degree program, services for LD students, student-designed majors, study abroad, summer session for credit. *ROTC:* Army (b).

Library McCormick Library plus 6 others with 155,069 titles, 855 serial subscriptions, 8,449 audiovisual materials, an OPAC, a Web page.

Student Life *Housing:* college housing not available. *Activities and Organizations:* drama/theater group, student-run newspaper, Student Government Association, Phi Theta Kappa, African American Student Association, Mosiaco Club, Fourth Estate. *Campus security:* 24-hour emergency response devices and patrols, late-night transport/escort service.

Athletics *Intercollegiate sports:* basketball M/W, soccer M, tennis M/W. *Intramural sports:* basketball M/W, soccer M/W, swimming and diving M/W, tennis M/W, volleyball M/W.

Costs (2013–14) *Tuition:* area resident $4185 full-time, $140 per credit hour part-time; state resident $5850 full-time, $195 per credit hour part-time; nonresident $8775 full-time, $293 per credit hour part-time. *Required fees:* $1170 full-time.

Financial Aid Of all full-time matriculated undergraduates who enrolled in 2011, 4,396 applied for aid, 3,366 were judged to have need, 93 had their need fully met. In 2011, 13 non-need-based awards were made. *Average percent of need met:* 51%. *Average financial aid package:* $6381. *Average need-based loan:* $3265. *Average need-based gift aid:* $2407. *Average non-need-based aid:* $981.

Applying *Options:* electronic application, early admission, deferred entrance. *Application fee:* $35. *Required for some:* high school transcript, 1 letter of recommendation, interview. *Application deadlines:* rolling (freshmen), rolling (transfers).

Freshman Application Contact Mrs. Vanita L. Cowan, Administrative Clerk, Admissions, Harrisburg Area Community College, Harrisburg, PA 17110. *Phone:* 717-780-2694. *Toll-free phone:* 800-ABC-HACC. *Fax:* 717-231-7674. *E-mail:* admit@hacc.edu. *Website:* http://www.hacc.edu/.

Hussian School of Art
Philadelphia, Pennsylvania

Freshman Application Contact Director of Admissions, Hussian School of Art, The Bourse, Suite 300, 111 South Independence Mall East, Philadelphia, PA 19106. *Phone:* 215-574-9600. *Fax:* 215-574-9800. *E-mail:* info@hussianart.edu. *Website:* http://www.hussianart.edu/.

ITT Technical Institute
Dunmore, Pennsylvania

- **Proprietary** 2-year, part of ITT Educational Services, Inc.
- **Coed**

Academics *Calendar:* quarters. *Degree:* diplomas and associate.

Freshman Application Contact Director of Recruitment, ITT Technical Institute, 1000 Meade Street, Dunmore, PA 18512. *Phone:* 570-330-0600. *Toll-free phone:* 800-774-9791. *Website:* http://www.itt-tech.edu/.

ITT Technical Institute
Harrisburg, Pennsylvania

- **Proprietary** 2-year, part of ITT Educational Services, Inc.
- **Coed**

Academics *Degree:* diplomas and associate.

Freshman Application Contact Director of Recruitment, ITT Technical Institute, 449 Eisenhower Boulevard, Suite 100, Harrisburg, PA 17111. *Phone:* 717-565-1700. *Toll-free phone:* 800-847-4756. *Website:* http://www.itt-tech.edu/.

ITT Technical Institute
Levittown, Pennsylvania

- **Proprietary** 2-year, founded 2000, part of ITT Educational Services, Inc.
- **Coed**

Academics *Calendar:* quarters. *Degree:* diplomas and associate.

Freshman Application Contact Director of Recruitment, ITT Technical Institute, 311 Veterans Highway, Levittown, PA 19056. *Phone:* 215-702-6300. *Toll-free phone:* 866-488-8324. *Website:* http://www.itt-tech.edu/.

ITT Technical Institute
Pittsburgh, Pennsylvania

- **Proprietary** 2-year, part of ITT Educational Services, Inc.
- **Coed**

Academics *Calendar:* quarters. *Degree:* diplomas and associate.

Freshman Application Contact Director of Recruitment, ITT Technical Institute, 10 Parkway Center, Pittsburgh, PA 15220-3801. *Phone:* 412-937-9150. *Toll-free phone:* 800-353-8324. *Website:* http://www.itt-tech.edu/.

ITT Technical Institute
Plymouth Meeting, Pennsylvania

- **Proprietary** 2-year, founded 2002, part of ITT Educational Services, Inc.
- **Coed**

Academics *Calendar:* quarters. *Degree:* diplomas and associate.

Freshman Application Contact Director of Recruitment, ITT Technical Institute, 220 West Germantown Pike, Suite 100, Plymouth Meeting, PA 19462. *Phone:* 610-491-8004. *Toll-free phone:* 866-902-8324. *Website:* http://www.itt-tech.edu/.

ITT Technical Institute
Tarentum, Pennsylvania

- **Proprietary** 2-year, part of ITT Educational Services, Inc.
- **Coed**

Academics *Calendar:* quarters. *Degree:* diplomas and associate.

Freshman Application Contact Director of Recruitment, ITT Technical Institute, 100 Pittsburgh Mills Circle, Suite 100, Tarentum, PA 15084. *Phone:* 724-274-1400. *Toll-free phone:* 800-488-0121. *Website:* http://www.itt-tech.edu/.

JNA Institute of Culinary Arts
Philadelphia, Pennsylvania

- **Proprietary** 2-year, founded 1988
- **Urban** campus with easy access to Philadelphia
- **Coed,** 65 undergraduate students, 100% full-time, 45% women, 55% men

Undergraduates 65 full-time. 57% Black or African American, non-Hispanic/Latino; 26% Hispanic/Latino; 3% Asian, non-Hispanic/Latino.

Freshmen *Admission:* 31 enrolled.

Majors Restaurant, culinary, and catering management.

Academics *Calendar:* continuous. *Degree:* associate.

Freshman Application Contact Admissions Office, JNA Institute of Culinary Arts, 1212 South Broad Street, Philadelphia, PA 19146. *Website:* http://www.culinaryarts.com/.

Johnson College
Scranton, Pennsylvania

Freshman Application Contact Ms. Melissa Ide, Director of Enrollment Management, Johnson College, 3427 North Main Avenue, Scranton, PA 18508. *Phone:* 570-702-8910. *Toll-free phone:* 800-2WE-WORK. *Fax:* 570-348-2181. *E-mail:* admit@johnson.edu. *Website:* http://www.johnson.edu/.

Kaplan Career Institute, Broomall Campus

Broomall, Pennsylvania

- **Proprietary** 2-year, founded 1958
- **Small-town** campus
- **Coed**

Academics *Calendar:* quarters. *Degree:* diplomas and associate.
Freshman Application Contact Kaplan Career Institute, Broomall Campus, 1991 Sproul Road, Suite 42, Broomall, PA 19008. *Phone:* 610-353-3300. *Toll-free phone:* 800-935-1857.
Website: http://broomall.kaplancareerinstitute.com/.

Kaplan Career Institute, Franklin Mills Campus

Philadelphia, Pennsylvania

- **Proprietary** 2-year, founded 1981
- **Suburban** campus
- **Coed**

Academics *Calendar:* quarters. *Degree:* diplomas and associate.
Financial Aid Of all full-time matriculated undergraduates who enrolled in 2011, 30 Federal Work-Study jobs (averaging $2050).
Freshman Application Contact Kaplan Career Institute, Franklin Mills Campus, 177 Franklin Mills Boulevard, Philadelphia, PA 19154. *Phone:* 215-612-6600. *Toll-free phone:* 800-935-1857.
Website: http://franklin-mills.kaplancareerinstitute.com/.

Kaplan Career Institute, Harrisburg Campus

Harrisburg, Pennsylvania

- **Proprietary** 2-year, founded 1918
- **Suburban** campus
- **Coed**

Academics *Calendar:* quarters. *Degree:* diplomas and associate.
Freshman Application Contact Kaplan Career Institute, Harrisburg Campus, 5650 Derry Street, Harrisburg, PA 17111-3518. *Phone:* 717-558-1300. *Toll-free phone:* 800-935-1857.
Website: http://harrisburg.kaplancareerinstitute.com/.

Kaplan Career Institute, Philadelphia Campus

Philadelphia, Pennsylvania

- **Proprietary** 2-year
- **Coed**

Academics *Degree:* diplomas and associate.
Freshman Application Contact Admissions Director, Kaplan Career Institute, Philadelphia Campus, 3010 Market Street, Philadelphia, PA 19104. *Toll-free phone:* 800-935-1857.
Website: http://philadelphia.kaplancareerinstitute.com/.

Kaplan Career Institute, Pittsburgh Campus

Pittsburgh, Pennsylvania

- **Proprietary** 2-year, founded 1963
- **Urban** campus
- **Coed**

Academics *Calendar:* continuous. *Degree:* diplomas and associate.
Freshman Application Contact Kaplan Career Institute, Pittsburgh Campus, 933 Penn Avenue, Pittsburgh, PA 15222. *Phone:* 412-261-2647. *Toll-free phone:* 800-935-1857.
Website: http://pittsburgh.kaplancareerinstitute.com/.

Keystone Technical Institute

Harrisburg, Pennsylvania

Freshman Application Contact Tom Bogush, Director of Admissions, Keystone Technical Institute, 2301 Academy Drive, Harrisburg, PA 17112. *Phone:* 717-545-4747. *Toll-free phone:* 800-400-3322. *Fax:* 717-901-9090.

E-mail: info@acadcampus.com.
Website: http://www.kti.edu/.

Lackawanna College

Scranton, Pennsylvania

Freshman Application Contact Ms. Stacey Muchal, Associate Director of Admissions, Lackawanna College, 501 Vine Street, Scranton, PA 18509. *Phone:* 570-961-7868. *Toll-free phone:* 877-346-3552. *Fax:* 570-961-7843.
E-mail: muchals@lackawanna.edu.
Website: http://www.lackawanna.edu/.

Lancaster General College of Nursing & Health Sciences

Lancaster, Pennsylvania

- **Independent** primarily 2-year, founded 1903
- **Urban** campus with easy access to Harrisburg, PA
- **Endowment** $1.0 million
- **Coed,** 1,375 undergraduate students, 37% full-time, 85% women, 15% men

Undergraduates 503 full-time, 872 part-time. 2% are from out of state; 5% Black or African American, non-Hispanic/Latino; 4% Hispanic/Latino; 3% Asian, non-Hispanic/Latino; 0.3% Native Hawaiian or other Pacific Islander, non-Hispanic/Latino; 0.1% American Indian or Alaska Native, non-Hispanic/Latino; 0.1% Two or more races, non-Hispanic/Latino; 3% Race/ethnicity unknown; 25% transferred in.
Freshmen *Admission:* 517 applied, 145 admitted, 367 enrolled. *Test scores:* SAT critical reading scores over 500: 44%; SAT math scores over 500: 57%; SAT critical reading scores over 600: 13%; SAT math scores over 600: 8%; SAT math scores over 700: 1%.
Faculty *Total:* 168, 38% full-time. *Student/faculty ratio:* 8:1.
Majors Cardiovascular technology; diagnostic medical sonography and ultrasound technology; electrocardiograph technology; health/health-care administration; health services/allied health/health sciences; medical radiologic technology; nuclear medical technology; radiologic technology/science; registered nursing/registered nurse; respiratory care therapy; surgical technology.
Academics *Degrees:* certificates, associate, and bachelor's. *Special study options:* accelerated degree program, adult/continuing education programs, advanced placement credit, distance learning, part-time degree program, services for LD students, summer session for credit.
Library Health Sciences Library with 60,590 titles, 17,719 serial subscriptions, 112 audiovisual materials, an OPAC, a Web page.
Student Life *Housing:* college housing not available. *Activities and Organizations:* Student Government Association, Soccer Club, Distance Running. *Campus security:* 24-hour emergency response devices and patrols, late-night transport/escort service. *Student services:* health clinic, personal/psychological counseling.
Athletics *Intramural sports:* cross-country running M(c)/W(c), soccer M(c)/W(c).
Standardized Tests *Required:* SAT or ACT (for admission).
Costs (2013–14) *Tuition:* $18,800 full-time, $425 per credit part-time. Full-time tuition and fees vary according to program. Part-time tuition and fees vary according to program. *Required fees:* $1350 full-time, $250 per term part-time. *Payment plan:* installment. *Waivers:* employees or children of employees.
Applying *Options:* electronic application. *Application fee:* $60. *Required:* minimum 3.0 GPA, 2 letters of recommendation, Official GED transcript may be substituted in lieu of high school transcript. SAT or ACT scores required if graduated from high school within last 2 years. Official transcripts of all institutions attended. *Required for some:* essay or personal statement, high school transcript. *Application deadline:* 2/1 (freshmen). *Notification:* continuous (freshmen).
Freshman Application Contact Admissions Office, Lancaster General College of Nursing & Health Sciences, 410 Lime Street, Lancaster, PA 17602. *Phone:* 800-622-5443. *Toll-free phone:* 800-622-5443. *E-mail:* lgc_admissions@lancastergeneral.org.
Website: http://www.lancastergeneralcollege.edu/content/.

Lansdale School of Business

North Wales, Pennsylvania

Director of Admissions Ms. Marianne H. Johnson, Director of Admissions, Lansdale School of Business, 201 Church Road, North Wales, PA 19454-4148. *Phone:* 215-699-5700 Ext. 112. *Toll-free phone:* 800-219-0486. *Fax:* 215-699-8770. *E-mail:* mjohnson@lsb.edu.
Website: http://www.lsb.edu/.

Laurel Business Institute

Uniontown, Pennsylvania

Freshman Application Contact Mrs. Lisa Dolan, Laurel Business Institute, 11 East Penn Street, PO Box 877, Uniontown, PA 15401. *Phone:* 724-439-4900 Ext. 158. *Fax:* 724-439-3607. *E-mail:* ldolan@laurel.edu. *Website:* http://www.laurel.edu/lbi/.

Laurel Technical Institute

Meadville, Pennsylvania

Freshman Application Contact Admissions Officer, Laurel Technical Institute, 847 North Main Street, Suite 204, Meadville, PA 16335. *Phone:* 814-724-0700. *Fax:* 814-724-2777. *E-mail:* lti.admission@laurel.edu. *Website:* http://www.laurel.edu/lti/.

Laurel Technical Institute

Sharon, Pennsylvania

Freshman Application Contact Irene Lewis, Laurel Technical Institute, 335 Boyd Drive, Sharon, PA 16146. *Phone:* 724-983-0700. *Fax:* 724-983-8355. *E-mail:* info@biop.edu. *Website:* http://www.laurel.edu/lti/.

Le Cordon Bleu Institute of Culinary Arts in Pittsburgh

Pittsburgh, Pennsylvania

Freshman Application Contact Ms. Juliette Mariani, Dean of Students, Le Cordon Bleu Institute of Culinary Arts in Pittsburgh, 717 Liberty Avenue, 19th Floor, Pittsburgh, PA 15222. *Phone:* 412-566-2433. *Toll-free phone:* 888-314-8222. *Fax:* 412-566-2434. *Website:* http://www.chefs.edu/Pittsburgh.

Lehigh Carbon Community College

Schnecksville, Pennsylvania

- **State and locally supported** 2-year, founded 1967
- **Suburban** 254-acre campus with easy access to Philadelphia
- **Endowment** $2.4 million
- **Coed,** 8,880 undergraduate students, 31% full-time, 49% women, 51% men

Undergraduates 2,725 full-time, 6,155 part-time. Students come from 11 states and territories; 15 other countries; 0.3% are from out of state; 5% Black or African American, non-Hispanic/Latino; 18% Hispanic/Latino; 2% Asian, non-Hispanic/Latino; 0.1% American Indian or Alaska Native, non-Hispanic/Latino; 3% Two or more races, non-Hispanic/Latino; 5% Race/ethnicity unknown; 0.2% international; 46% transferred in.

Freshmen *Admission:* 4,566 applied, 4,566 admitted, 2,993 enrolled.

Faculty *Total:* 399, 22% full-time, 5% with terminal degrees. *Student/faculty ratio:* 22:1.

Majors Accounting technology and bookkeeping; aeronautics/aviation/aerospace science and technology; airline pilot and flight crew; animation, interactive technology, video graphics and special effects; art; biology/biological sciences; biotechnology; building/construction site management; business administration and management; business/commerce; chemical technology; computer and information sciences; computer and information systems security; computer programming; computer programming (specific applications); computer systems networking and telecommunications; construction trades; criminal justice/law enforcement administration; criminal justice/safety; drafting and design technology; early childhood education; education; electrical, electronic and communications engineering technology; engineering; fashion/apparel design; game and interactive media design; general studies; geographic information science and cartography; graphic design; health information/medical records technology; heating, air conditioning, ventilation and refrigeration maintenance technology; horticultural science; humanities; human resources management; human services; industrial electronics technology; interior design; legal assistant/paralegal; liberal arts and sciences/liberal studies; manufacturing engineering technology; mathematics; mechanical engineering/mechanical technology; medical/clinical assistant; nanotechnology; occupational therapist assistant; physical sciences; physical therapy technology; psychology; public administration; radio and television broadcasting technology; recording arts technology; registered nursing/registered nurse; resort management; social work; special education; speech communication and rhetoric; sport and fitness administration/management; teacher assistant/aide; veterinary/animal health technology; web page, digital/multimedia and information resources design.

Academics *Calendar:* semesters. *Degree:* certificates, diplomas, and associate. *Special study options:* academic remediation for entering students, advanced placement credit, cooperative education, distance learning, English as a second language, external degree program, honors programs, independent study, internships, part-time degree program, services for LD students, summer session for credit. *ROTC:* Army (c).

Library Rothrock Library with 90,968 titles, 336 serial subscriptions, 7,563 audiovisual materials, an OPAC, a Web page.

Student Life *Housing:* college housing not available. *Activities and Organizations:* drama/theater group, choral group, Phi Theta Kappa, Criminal Justice/Justice Society, Psychology Club, Student Government Association, Teacher Education Student Association (TESA). *Campus security:* 24-hour emergency response devices. *Student services:* personal/psychological counseling.

Athletics Member NJCAA. *Intercollegiate sports:* baseball M, basketball M/W, golf M/W, soccer M, softball W, volleyball W. *Intramural sports:* basketball M/W, golf M/W, table tennis M/W, volleyball M/W.

Standardized Tests *Required for some:* TEAS (for those applying to Nursing Program).

Costs (2012–13) *Tuition:* area resident $2880 full-time, $96 per credit part-time; state resident $6030 full-time, $201 per credit part-time; nonresident $9180 full-time, $306 per credit part-time. *Required fees:* $510 full-time, $17 per credit part-time. *Payment plan:* installment. *Waivers:* senior citizens and employees or children of employees.

Applying *Options:* electronic application. *Required for some:* essay or personal statement, high school transcript, interview. *Application deadlines:* rolling (freshmen), rolling (out-of-state freshmen), rolling (transfers). *Notification:* continuous (freshmen), continuous (out-of-state freshmen), continuous (transfers).

Freshman Application Contact Mr. Louis Hegyes; Director of Recruitment/Admissions, Lehigh Carbon Community College, 4525 Education Park Drive, Schnecksville, PA 18078. *Phone:* 610-799-1575. *Fax:* 610-799-1527. *E-mail:* admissions@lccc.edu. *Website:* http://www.lccc.edu/.

Lincoln Technical Institute

Allentown, Pennsylvania

Freshman Application Contact Admissions Office, Lincoln Technical Institute, 5151 Tilghman Street, Allentown, PA 18104-3298. *Phone:* 610-398-5301. *Website:* http://www.lincolnedu.com/.

Lincoln Technical Institute

Philadelphia, Pennsylvania

Director of Admissions Mr. James Kuntz, Executive Director, Lincoln Technical Institute, 9191 Torresdale Avenue, Philadelphia, PA 19136-1595. *Phone:* 215-335-0800. *Fax:* 215-335-1443. *E-mail:* jkuntz@lincolntech.com. *Website:* http://www.lincolnedu.com/.

Luzerne County Community College

Nanticoke, Pennsylvania

- **County-supported** 2-year, founded 1966
- **Suburban** 122-acre campus with easy access to Philadelphia
- **Coed,** 6,579 undergraduate students, 51% full-time, 59% women, 41% men

Undergraduates 3,335 full-time, 3,244 part-time. 4% Black or African American, non-Hispanic/Latino; 7% Hispanic/Latino; 2% Asian, non-Hispanic/Latino; 0.2% Native Hawaiian or other Pacific Islander, non-Hispanic/Latino; 0.2% American Indian or Alaska Native, non-Hispanic/Latino; 0.9% Two or more races, non-Hispanic/Latino; 6% Race/ethnicity unknown. *Retention:* 55% of full-time freshmen returned.

Freshmen *Admission:* 2,558 applied, 2,558 admitted, 1,722 enrolled.

Faculty *Total:* 489, 24% full-time. *Student/faculty ratio:* 20:1.

Majors Accounting; administrative assistant and secretarial science; airline pilot and flight crew; architectural engineering; architectural engineering technology; automobile/automotive mechanics technology; aviation/airway management; baking and pastry arts; banking and financial support services; biological and physical sciences; building/property maintenance; business administration and management; child-care provision; commercial and advertising art; commercial photography; computer and information sciences; computer and information sciences related; computer graphics; computer programming related; computer science; computer systems networking and telecommunications; computer technology/computer systems technology; court reporting; criminal justice/law enforcement administration; culinary arts; data entry/microcomputer applications; data processing and data processing technology; dental assisting; dental hygiene; drafting and design technology;

drafting/design engineering technologies related; drawing; early childhood education; education; electrical, electronic and communications, engineering technology; electrician; emergency medical technology (EMT paramedic); engineering technology; executive assistant/executive secretary; fire science/firefighting; food technology and processing; funeral service and mortuary science; general studies; graphic and printing equipment operation/production; graphic design; health and physical education/fitness; health/health-care administration; heating, air conditioning, ventilation and refrigeration maintenance technology; horticultural science; hospitality and recreation marketing; hotel/motel administration; humanities; human services; industrial and product design; international business/trade/commerce; journalism; legal assistant/paralegal; liberal arts and sciences and humanities related; liberal arts and sciences/liberal studies; mathematics; medical administrative assistant and medical secretary; painting; photography; physical education teaching and coaching; plumbing technology; pre-pharmacy studies; radio and television broadcasting technology; real estate; registered nursing/registered nurse; respiratory care therapy; social sciences; surgical technology; tourism and travel services management; tourism and travel services marketing.

Academics *Calendar:* semesters. *Degree:* certificates, diplomas, and associate. *Special study options:* academic remediation for entering students, accelerated degree program, advanced placement credit, distance learning, external degree program, internships, part-time degree program, services for LD students, summer session for credit. *ROTC:* Air Force (c).

Library Learning Resources Center plus 1 other with 60,000 titles, 744 serial subscriptions, 3,000 audiovisual materials, an OPAC, a Web page.

Student Life *Housing:* college housing not available. *Activities and Organizations:* student-run newspaper, radio and television station, student government, Circle K, Nursing Forum, Science Club, SADAH. *Campus security:* 24-hour patrols.

Athletics Member NJCAA. *Intercollegiate sports:* baseball M, basketball M/W, cross-country running M/W, golf M/W, soccer M/W, softball W, volleyball W. *Intramural sports:* badminton M/W, basketball M/W, bowling M/W, softball M/W, tennis M/W, volleyball M/W.

Applying *Options:* early admission, deferred entrance. *Application fee:* $40. *Recommended:* high school transcript. *Application deadlines:* rolling (freshmen), rolling (transfers).

Freshman Application Contact Mr. Francis Curry, Director of Admissions, Luzerne County Community College, 1333 South Prospect Street, Nanticoke, PA 18634-9804. *Phone:* 570-740-0337. *Toll-free phone:* 800-377-5222 Ext. 7337. *Fax:* 570-740-0238. *E-mail:* admissions@luzerne.edu. *Website:* http://www.luzerne.edu/.

Manor College
Jenkintown, Pennsylvania

- **Independent Byzantine Catholic** 2-year, founded 1947
- **Small-town** 35-acre campus with easy access to Philadelphia
- **Coed,** 926 undergraduate students, 67% full-time, 77% women, 23% men

Undergraduates 616 full-time, 310 part-time. Students come from 4 states and territories; 2% are from out of state; 28% Black or African American, non-Hispanic/Latino; 6% Hispanic/Latino; 3% Asian, non-Hispanic/Latino; 0.1% Native Hawaiian or other Pacific Islander, non-Hispanic/Latino; 1% Two or more races, non-Hispanic/Latino; 14% Race/ethnicity unknown; 0.1% international.

Freshmen *Admission:* 712 applied, 349 admitted.

Faculty *Student/faculty ratio:* 10:1.

Majors Accounting; business administration and management; business, management, and marketing related; communication and media related; computer programming (specific applications); dental assisting; dental hygiene; education (specific subject areas) related; elementary education; health professions related; human resources management and services related; international business/trade/commerce; legal assistant/paralegal; liberal arts and sciences/liberal studies; marketing/marketing management; psychology; religious education; veterinary/animal health technology.

Academics *Calendar:* semesters. *Degrees:* certificates, diplomas, associate, and postbachelor's certificates. *Special study options:* academic remediation for entering students, adult/continuing education programs, advanced placement credit, distance learning, double majors, English as a second language, honors programs, independent study, internships, part-time degree program, summer session for credit.

Library Basileiad Library with 41,688 titles, 97 serial subscriptions, an OPAC, a Web page.

Student Life *Housing Options:* coed. *Activities and Organizations:* choral group. *Campus security:* 24-hour emergency response devices and patrols. *Student services:* personal/psychological counseling.

Athletics Member NJCAA. *Intercollegiate sports:* basketball M/W, soccer M/W.

Standardized Tests *Required:* SAT or ACT (for admission).

Financial Aid Of all full-time matriculated undergraduates who enrolled in 2009, 35 Federal Work-Study jobs (averaging $3000). 10 state and other part-time jobs (averaging $3600).

Applying *Options:* electronic application, deferred entrance. *Application fee:* $25. *Required:* high school transcript, interview. *Application deadlines:* rolling (freshmen), rolling (transfers). *Notification:* continuous (freshmen), continuous (transfers).

Freshman Application Contact Manor College, 700 Fox Chase Road, Jenkintown, PA 19046. *Phone:* 215-884-2216. *Website:* http://www.manor.edu/.

McCann School of Business & Technology
Pottsville, Pennsylvania

- **Proprietary** 2-year, founded 1897
- **Small-town** campus
- **Coed,** 1,657 undergraduate students

Majors Accounting; business administration and management; computer and information sciences related; computer science; cosmetology; criminal justice/safety; early childhood education; legal assistant/paralegal; massage therapy; medical administrative assistant and medical secretary; medical/clinical assistant; surgical technology.

Academics *Calendar:* quarters. *Degree:* certificates, diplomas, and associate. *Special study options:* advanced placement credit, cooperative education, double majors, internships, part-time degree program, services for LD students, summer session for credit.

Library McCann Main Library plus 2 others with 1,850 titles, 26 serial subscriptions.

Student Life *Housing:* college housing not available. *Activities and Organizations:* Medical Club, Criminal Justice Club, Student Ambassador Club, Marketing Club, IT Club. *Campus security:* controlled dormitory access.

Standardized Tests *Required:* Wonderlic aptitude test (for admission).

Applying *Options:* electronic application. *Application fee:* $40. *Required:* high school transcript, minimum 2.0 GPA, interview, GED or High School Attestation form. *Application deadlines:* rolling (freshmen), rolling (transfers).

Freshman Application Contact Mrs. Amelia Hopkins, Director, Pottsville Campus, McCann School of Business & Technology, 2650 Woodglen Rd., Pottsville, PA 17901. *Phone:* 570-622-7622. *Fax:* 570-622-7770. *Website:* http://www.mccannschool.com/.

Mercyhurst North East
North East, Pennsylvania

Director of Admissions Travis Lindahl, Director of Admissions, Mercyhurst North East, 16 West Division Street, North East, PA 16428. *Phone:* 814-725-6217. *Toll-free phone:* 866-846-6042. *Fax:* 814-725-6251. *E-mail:* neadmiss@mercyhurst.edu. *Website:* http://northeast.mercyhurst.edu/.

Metropolitan Career Center Computer Technology Institute
Philadelphia, Pennsylvania

Freshman Application Contact Admissions Office, Metropolitan Career Center Computer Technology Institute, 100 South Broad Street, Suite 830, Philadelphia, PA 19110. *Phone:* 215-568-7861. *Website:* http://www.careersinit.org/.

Montgomery County Community College
Blue Bell, Pennsylvania

- **County-supported** 2-year, founded 1964
- **Suburban** 186-acre campus with easy access to Philadelphia
- **Coed,** 13,645 undergraduate students, 37% full-time, 56% women, 44% men

Undergraduates 5,013 full-time, 8,632 part-time. Students come from 9 states and territories; 104 other countries; 0.2% are from out of state; 14% Black or African American, non-Hispanic/Latino; 6% Hispanic/Latino; 6% Asian, non-Hispanic/Latino; 0.2% Native Hawaiian or other Pacific Islander, non-Hispanic/Latino; 0.3% American Indian or Alaska Native, non-Hispanic/Latino; 2% Two or more races, non-Hispanic/Latino; 8% Race/ethnicity unknown; 2% international; 4% transferred in. *Retention:* 61% of full-time freshmen returned.

Freshmen *Admission:* 11,557 applied, 11,557 admitted, 3,604 enrolled.

Faculty *Total:* 778, 25% full-time. *Student/faculty ratio:* 20:1.

Majors Accounting; accounting technology and bookkeeping; administrative assistant and secretarial science; architectural drafting and CAD/CADD; art; automobile/automotive mechanics technology; baking and pastry arts; biology/biological sciences; biotechnology; business administration and management; business/commerce; business/corporate communications; CAD/CADD drafting/design technology; child-care and support services management; clinical/medical laboratory technology; commercial and advertising art; communications technologies and support services related; computer and information sciences; computer programming; computer systems networking and telecommunications; criminal justice/police science; culinary arts; dental hygiene; electrical, electronic and communications engineering technology; electromechanical technology; elementary education; engineering science; engineering technologies and engineering related; environmental science; fire prevention and safety technology; health and physical education/fitness; hospitality and recreation marketing; humanities; information science/studies; liberal arts and sciences/liberal studies; management information systems and services related; mathematics; mechanical drafting and CAD/CADD; mechanical engineering/mechanical technology; medical/clinical assistant; medical radiologic technology; network and system administration; physical education teaching and coaching; physical sciences; psychiatric/mental health services technology; psychology; radiologic technology/science; radio, television, and digital communication related; real estate; recording arts technology; registered nursing/registered nurse; sales, distribution, and marketing operations; secondary education; social sciences; speech communication and rhetoric; surgical technology; teacher assistant/aide; tourism and travel services marketing; web/multimedia management and webmaster.

Academics *Calendar:* semesters. *Degree:* certificates and associate. *Special study options:* academic remediation for entering students, accelerated degree program, adult/continuing education programs, advanced placement credit, cooperative education, distance learning, English as a second language, honors programs, independent study, internships, part-time degree program, services for LD students, student-designed majors, study abroad, summer session for credit.

Library The Brendlinger Library/Branch Library Pottstown Campus with 87,136 titles, 378 serial subscriptions, 12,948 audiovisual materials, an OPAC, a Web page.

Student Life *Housing:* college housing not available. *Activities and Organizations:* drama/theater group, student-run newspaper, radio and television station, choral group, student government, Thrive (Christian Fellowship), radio station, Drama Club, African - American Student League. *Campus security:* 24-hour emergency response devices and patrols, late-night transport/escort service, bicycle patrol. *Student services:* health clinic, personal/psychological counseling.

Athletics Member NJCAA. *Intercollegiate sports:* baseball M, basketball M/W, soccer M/W, softball W, volleyball W. *Intramural sports:* badminton M/W, basketball M/W, bowling M/W, cross-country running M/W, football M, racquetball M/W, soccer M/W, table tennis M/W, tennis M/W, volleyball M/W, weight lifting M/W.

Costs (2012–13) *Tuition:* area resident $3360 full-time, $112 per credit hour part-time; state resident $7020 full-time, $224 per credit hour part-time; nonresident $10,680 full-time, $336 per credit hour part-time. *Required fees:* $690 full-time, $23 per credit hour part-time. *Payment plan:* deferred payment. *Waivers:* senior citizens and employees or children of employees.

Financial Aid Of all full-time matriculated undergraduates who enrolled in 2011, 60 Federal Work-Study jobs (averaging $2500).

Applying *Options:* electronic application, early admission, deferred entrance. *Application fee:* $25. *Required:* high school transcript. *Required for some:* interview. *Application deadline:* rolling (transfers). *Notification:* continuous (freshmen), continuous (transfers).

Freshman Application Contact Ms. Penny Sawyer, Director of Admissions and Recruitment, Montgomery County Community College, Blue Bell, PA 19422. *Phone:* 215-641-6551. *Fax:* 215-619-7188. *E-mail:* admrec@ admin.mc3.edu. *Website:* http://www.mc3.edu/.

New Castle School of Trades
Pulaski, Pennsylvania

Freshman Application Contact Mr. James Catheline, Admissions Director, New Castle School of Trades, New Castle Youngstown Road, Route 422 RD1, Pulaski, PA 16143-9721. *Phone:* 724-964-8811. *Toll-free phone:* 800-837-8299. *Website:* http://www.ncstrades.com/.

Newport Business Institute
Lower Burrell, Pennsylvania

Freshman Application Contact Admissions Coordinator, Newport Business Institute, Lower Burrell, PA 15068. *Phone:* 724-339-7542. *Toll-free phone:* 800-752-7695. *Fax:* 724-339-2950. *E-mail:* admissions@ newportbusiness.com. *Website:* http://www.nbi.edu/.

Newport Business Institute
Williamsport, Pennsylvania

Freshman Application Contact Ms. Ashley Wall, Admissions Representative, Newport Business Institute, 941 West Third Street, Williamsport, PA 17701. *Phone:* 570-326-2869. *Toll-free phone:* 800-962-6971. *Fax:* 570-326-2136. *E-mail:* admissions2_NBI@Comcast.net. *Website:* http://www.nbi.edu/.

Northampton Community College
Bethlehem, Pennsylvania

- **State and locally supported** 2-year, founded 1967
- **Suburban** 165-acre campus with easy access to Philadelphia
- **Endowment** $30.3 million
- **Coed,** 11,018 undergraduate students, 42% full-time, 59% women, 41% men

Undergraduates 4,668 full-time, 6,350 part-time. Students come from 24 states and territories; 52 other countries; 2% are from out of state; 11% Black or African American, non-Hispanic/Latino; 18% Hispanic/Latino; 2% Asian, non-Hispanic/Latino; 0.2% Native Hawaiian or other Pacific Islander, non-Hispanic/Latino; 0.3% American Indian or Alaska Native, non-Hispanic/Latino; 2% Two or more races, non-Hispanic/Latino; 2% Race/ethnicity unknown; 0.9% international; 8% transferred in; 2% live on campus.

Freshmen *Admission:* 4,699 applied, 4,699 admitted, 2,267 enrolled.

Faculty *Total:* 697, 17% full-time, 19% with terminal degrees. *Student/faculty ratio:* 22:1.

Majors Accounting technology and bookkeeping; acting; administrative assistant and secretarial science; architectural engineering technology; athletic training; automobile/automotive mechanics technology; biology/biological sciences; biotechnology; business administration and management; business/commerce; CAD/CADD drafting/design technology; chemistry; computer and information systems security; computer installation and repair technology; computer programming; computer science; computer systems networking and telecommunications; construction management; criminal justice/safety; culinary arts; dental hygiene; diagnostic medical sonography and ultrasound technology; early childhood education; electrical, electronic and communications engineering technology; electrician; electromechanical technology; engineering; fine/studio arts; fire science/firefighting; fire services administration; funeral service and mortuary science; general studies; graphic design; heating, air conditioning, ventilation and refrigeration maintenance technology; hotel/motel administration; industrial electronics technology; interior design; journalism; legal administrative assistant/secretary; legal assistant/paralegal; liberal arts and sciences and humanities related; liberal arts and sciences/liberal studies; marketing/marketing management; mathematics; medical administrative assistant and medical secretary; middle school education; physics; quality control technology; radio and television broadcasting technology; radiologic technology/science; registered nursing/registered nurse; restaurant/food services management; secondary education; social work; speech communication and rhetoric; sport and fitness administration/management; teacher assistant/aide; veterinary/animal health technology; web page, digital/multimedia and information resources design.

Academics *Calendar:* semesters. *Degree:* certificates, diplomas, and associate. *Special study options:* academic remediation for entering students, adult/continuing education programs, advanced placement credit, distance learning, English as a second language, honors programs, independent study, internships, off-campus study, part-time degree program, services for LD students, student-designed majors, study abroad, summer session for credit.

Library Paul & Harriett Mack Library with 111,697 titles, 197 serial subscriptions, 11,981 audiovisual materials, an OPAC, a Web page.

Student Life *Housing Options:* coed. Campus housing is university owned. *Activities and Organizations:* drama/theater group, student-run newspaper, radio station, choral group, Phi Theta Kappa, Student Senate, College and Hospital Association of Radiologic Technologies Students (CHARTS), American Dental Hygiene Association (ADHA), International Student Organization. *Campus security:* 24-hour emergency response devices and patrols, controlled dormitory access. *Student services:* health clinic, personal/psychological counseling.

Athletics Member NJCAA. *Intercollegiate sports:* baseball M, basketball M/W, golf M/W, soccer M, softball W, tennis M/W, volleyball W. *Intramural sports:* basketball M/W, cheerleading M(c)/W(c), soccer M/W, volleyball M/W.

Costs (2012–13) *Tuition:* area resident $2550 full-time, $85 per credit hour part-time; state resident $5100 full-time, $170 per credit hour part-time; nonresident $7650 full-time, $255 per credit hour part-time. Full-time tuition and fees vary according to course load. Part-time tuition and fees vary according to course load. *Required fees:* $1020 full-time, $34 per credit hour part-time. *Room and board:* $7676; room only: $4386. Room and board charges vary according to board plan and housing facility. *Payment plan:* installment. *Waivers:* senior citizens and employees or children of employees.

Financial Aid Of all full-time matriculated undergraduates who enrolled in 2012, 159 Federal Work-Study jobs (averaging $1840). 91 state and other part-time jobs (averaging $2000).

Applying *Options:* electronic application, deferred entrance. *Application fee:* $25. *Required for some:* high school transcript, minimum 2.5 GPA, interview, interview required: rad and veterinary. *Recommended:* high school transcript. *Application deadlines:* rolling (freshmen), rolling (out-of-state freshmen), rolling (transfers). *Notification:* continuous (freshmen), continuous (out-of-state freshmen), continuous (transfers).

Freshman Application Contact Mr. James McCarthy, Director of Admissions, Northampton Community College, 3835 Green Pond Road, Bethlehem, PA 18020-7599. *Phone:* 610-861-5506. *Fax:* 610-861-5551. *E-mail:* jrmccarthy@northampton.edu. *Website:* http://www.northampton.edu/.

Oakbridge Academy of Arts
Lower Burrell, Pennsylvania

Freshman Application Contact Matthew Belferman, Admissions Coordinator, Oakbridge Academy of Arts, 1250 Greensburg Road, Lower Burrell, PA 15068. *Phone:* 724-335-5336. *Toll-free phone:* 800-734-5601. *E-mail:* mbelferman@oaa.edu. *Website:* http://oaa.edu/.

Orleans Technical Institute
Philadelphia, Pennsylvania

- **Independent** 2-year
- **Urban** 9-acre campus with easy access to Philadelphia
- **Coed**

Undergraduates 400 full-time, 133 part-time. Students come from 3 states and territories; 5% are from out of state; 49% Black or African American, non-Hispanic/Latino; 11% Hispanic/Latino; 2% Asian, non-Hispanic/Latino; 0.6% Native Hawaiian or other Pacific Islander, non-Hispanic/Latino; 0.2% American Indian or Alaska Native, non-Hispanic/Latino; 0.2% Two or more races, non-Hispanic/Latino; 0.8% transferred in.

Faculty *Student/faculty ratio:* 13:1.

Academics *Calendar:* trimesters. *Degree:* diplomas and associate. *Special study options:* academic remediation for entering students, cooperative education, internships, part-time degree program, summer session for credit.

Student Life *Campus security:* 24-hour emergency response devices.

Standardized Tests *Required:* Wonderlic (for admission).

Financial Aid Of all full-time matriculated undergraduates who enrolled in 2011, 5 Federal Work-Study jobs (averaging $4800). *Financial aid deadline:* 8/1.

Applying *Options:* electronic application. *Application fee:* $125. *Required:* high school transcript, interview.

Freshman Application Contact Mrs. Dorothy Stinson, Admissions Secretary, Orleans Technical Institute, 2770 Red Lion Road, Philadelphia, PA 19114. *Phone:* 215-728-4700. *Fax:* 215-745-1689. *E-mail:* stinsd@jevs.org. *Website:* http://www.orleanstech.edu/.

Pace Institute
Reading, Pennsylvania

Director of Admissions Mr. Ed Levandowski, Director of Enrollment Management, Pace Institute, 606 Court Street, Reading, PA 19601. *Phone:* 610-375-1212. *Fax:* 610-375-1924. *Website:* http://www.paceinstitute.com/.

Penn Commercial Business and Technical School
Washington, Pennsylvania

Director of Admissions Mr. Michael John Joyce, Director of Admissions, Penn Commercial Business and Technical School, 242 Oak Spring Road, Washington, PA 15301. *Phone:* 724-222-5330 Ext. 1. *Toll-free phone:* 888-309-7484. *E-mail:* mjoyce@penn-commercial.com. *Website:* http://www.penncommercial.net/.

Pennco Tech
Bristol, Pennsylvania

- **Proprietary** 2-year, founded 1961, part of Pennco Institutes, Inc.
- **Suburban** 7-acre campus with easy access to Philadelphia
- **Coed**

Undergraduates 245 full-time, 155 part-time. Students come from 6 states and territories; 3% are from out of state; 1% transferred in; 3% live on campus. *Retention:* 78% of full-time freshmen returned.

Faculty *Student/faculty ratio:* 18:1.

Academics *Calendar:* modular. *Degree:* certificates, diplomas, and associate. *Special study options:* academic remediation for entering students, adult/continuing education programs, advanced placement credit, double majors.

Student Life *Campus security:* 24-hour emergency response devices, controlled dormitory access.

Costs (2012–13) *Tuition:* $21,500 full-time. Full-time tuition and fees vary according to class time, course load, and program. Part-time tuition and fees vary according to class time, course load, and program. *Room only:* $4000.

Applying *Application fee:* $100. *Required:* high school transcript, minimum 2.0 GPA, interview, Interview and school visit, exam at campus. *Required for some:* essay or personal statement.

Freshman Application Contact Pennco Tech, 3815 Otter Street, Bristol, PA 19007-3696. *Phone:* 215-785-0111. *Toll-free phone:* 800-575-9399. *Website:* http://www.penncotech.com/.

Penn State Beaver
Monaca, Pennsylvania

- **State-related** primarily 2-year, founded 1964, part of Pennsylvania State University
- **Small-town** campus
- **Coed,** 759 undergraduate students, 84% full-time, 45% women, 55% men

Undergraduates 634 full-time, 125 part-time. 8% are from out of state; 11% Black or African American, non-Hispanic/Latino; 4% Hispanic/Latino; 2% Asian, non-Hispanic/Latino; 0.3% Native Hawaiian or other Pacific Islander, non-Hispanic/Latino; 0.2% American Indian or Alaska Native, non-Hispanic/Latino; 2% Two or more races, non-Hispanic/Latino; 2% Race/ethnicity unknown; 1% international; 4% transferred in; 22% live on campus. *Retention:* 71% of full-time freshmen returned.

Freshmen *Admission:* 670 applied, 585 admitted, 208 enrolled. *Average high school GPA:* 2.94. *Test scores:* SAT critical reading scores over 500: 37%; SAT math scores over 500: 46%; SAT writing scores over 500: 28%; ACT scores over 18: 71%; SAT critical reading scores over 600: 10%; SAT math scores over 600: 15%; SAT writing scores over 600: 7%; ACT scores over 24: 29%; SAT critical reading scores over 700: 1%; SAT math scores over 700: 2%; SAT writing scores over 700: 2%.

Faculty *Total:* 64, 53% full-time, 41% with terminal degrees. *Student/faculty ratio:* 15:1.

Majors Accounting; acting; actuarial science; adult and continuing education administration; advertising; aerospace, aeronautical and astronautical/space engineering; African American/Black studies; agribusiness; agricultural and extension education; agricultural business and management related; agricultural engineering; agricultural mechanization; agriculture; agronomy and crop science; animal sciences; animal sciences related; anthropology; applied economics; archeology; architectural engineering; art; art history, criticism and conservation; art teacher education; Asian studies (East); astronomy; atmospheric sciences and meteorology; biochemistry; bioengineering and biomedical engineering; biological and biomedical sciences related; biological and physical sciences; biology/biological sciences; biology/biotechnology laboratory technician; business administration and management; business/commerce; business/managerial economics; chemical engineering; chemistry; civil engineering; classics and classical languages; communication and journalism related; communication sciences and disorders; comparative literature; computer and information sciences; computer engineering; criminal justice/law enforcement administration; economics; electrical and electronics engineering; elementary education; engineering science; English; environmental/environmental health engineering; film/cinema/video studies; finance; food science; foreign language teacher education; forest sciences and biology; forest technology; French; geography; geological and earth sciences/geosciences related; geology/earth science; German; graphic design; health/health-care administration; history; horticultural science; hospitality administration related; human development and family studies; human nutrition; industrial engineering; information science/studies; international relations and affairs; Italian; Japanese; Jewish/Judaic studies; journalism; kinesiology and exercise science; labor and industrial relations; landscaping and groundskeeping; Latin American studies; liberal arts and sciences/liberal studies; logistics, materials, and supply chain management; management information systems; marketing/marketing management; materials science; mathematics; mechanical engineering;

medical microbiology and bacteriology; medieval and Renaissance studies; mining and mineral engineering; music; natural resources and conservation related; natural resources/conservation; nuclear engineering; organizational behavior; parks, recreation and leisure facilities management; petroleum engineering; philosophy; physics; political science and government; premedical studies; psychology; registered nursing/registered nurse; rehabilitation and therapeutic professions related; religious studies; Russian; secondary education; sociology; soil science and agronomy; Spanish; special education; speech communication and rhetoric; statistics; theater design and technology; toxicology; turf and turfgrass management; visual and performing arts; women's studies.

Academics *Calendar:* semesters. *Degrees:* certificates, associate, and bachelor's. *Special study options:* adult/continuing education programs.

Student Life *Housing Options:* coed, disabled students. Campus housing is university owned. Freshman campus housing is guaranteed.

Athletics Member NJCAA. *Intercollegiate sports:* baseball M, basketball M, softball M/W, volleyball W. *Intramural sports:* basketball M/W, cheerleading M(c)/W(c), cross-country running M/W, football M, golf M/W, soccer M/W, softball M/W, table tennis M/W.

Standardized Tests *Required:* SAT or ACT (for admission).

Costs (2013–14) *Tuition:* state resident $12,474 full-time, $504 per credit hour part-time; nonresident $19,030 full-time, $793 per credit hour part-time. Full-time tuition and fees vary according to course level, degree level, location, program, and student level. Part-time tuition and fees vary according to course level, course load, degree level, location, program, and student level. *Required fees:* $876 full-time. *Room and board:* $9690; room only: $4910. Room and board charges vary according to board plan, housing facility, and location. *Payment plans:* installment, deferred payment. *Waivers:* employees or children of employees.

Financial Aid Of all full-time matriculated undergraduates who enrolled in 2011, 624 applied for aid, 534 were judged to have need, 29 had their need fully met. In 2011, 33 non-need-based awards were made. *Average percent of need met:* 66%. *Average financial aid package:* $10,703. *Average need-based loan:* $4065. *Average need-based gift aid:* $6659. *Average non-need-based aid:* $2144. *Average indebtedness upon graduation:* $35,100.

Applying *Options:* electronic application, early admission, deferred entrance. *Application fee:* $50. *Required:* high school transcript. *Required for some:* interview. *Recommended:* essay or personal statement. *Application deadlines:* rolling (freshmen), rolling (transfers). *Notification:* continuous (freshmen), continuous (transfers).

Freshman Application Contact Admissions Office, Penn State Beaver, 100 University Drive, Monaca, PA 15061. *Phone:* 724-773-3800. *Fax:* 724-773-3658. *E-mail:* br-admissions@psu.edu.
Website: http://www.br.psu.edu/.

Penn State Brandywine
Media, Pennsylvania

- **State-related** primarily 2-year, founded 1966, part of Pennsylvania State University
- **Small-town** campus
- **Coed,** 1,581 undergraduate students, 85% full-time, 44% women, 56% men

Undergraduates 1,338 full-time, 243 part-time. 6% are from out of state; 13% Black or African American, non-Hispanic/Latino; 5% Hispanic/Latino; 9% Asian, non-Hispanic/Latino; 0.1% Native Hawaiian or other Pacific Islander, non-Hispanic/Latino; 0.2% American Indian or Alaska Native, non-Hispanic/Latino; 2% Two or more races, non-Hispanic/Latino; 2% Race/ethnicity unknown; 0.9% international; 4% transferred in. *Retention:* 71% of full-time freshmen returned.

Freshmen *Admission:* 1,279 applied, 1,011 admitted, 368 enrolled. *Average high school GPA:* 3. *Test scores:* SAT critical reading scores over 500: 36%; SAT math scores over 500: 50%; SAT writing scores over 500: 35%; ACT scores over 18: 68%; SAT critical reading scores over 600: 9%; SAT math scores over 600: 15%; SAT writing scores over 600: 6%; ACT scores over 24: 11%; SAT critical reading scores over 700: 1%; SAT math scores over 700: 1%; SAT writing scores over 700: 1%; ACT scores over 30: 4%.

Faculty *Total:* 131, 46% full-time, 47% with terminal degrees. *Student/faculty ratio:* 17:1.

Majors Accounting; acting; actuarial science; adult and continuing education administration; advertising; aerospace, aeronautical and astronautical/space engineering; African American/Black studies; agribusiness; agricultural and extension education; agricultural business and management related; agricultural engineering; agricultural mechanization; agriculture; agronomy and crop science; American studies; animal sciences; animal sciences related; anthropology; applied economics; archeology; architectural engineering; art; art history, criticism and conservation; art teacher education; Asian studies (East); astronomy; atmospheric sciences and meteorology; biochemistry; bioengineering and biomedical engineering; biological and biomedical sciences related; biological and physical sciences; biology/biological sciences; biology/biotech-

nology laboratory technician; business administration and management; business/commerce; business/managerial economics; chemical engineering; chemistry; civil engineering; classics and classical languages; communication and journalism related; communication sciences and disorders; comparative literature; computer and information sciences; computer engineering; criminal justice/law enforcement administration; economics; electrical and electronics engineering; electrical, electronic and communications engineering technology; elementary education; engineering science; English; environmental/environmental health engineering; film/cinema/video studies; finance; food science; foreign language teacher education; forest sciences and biology; forest technology; French; geography; geological and earth sciences/geosciences related; geology/earth science; German; graphic design; health/health-care administration; history; horticultural science; hospitality administration related; human development and family studies; human nutrition; industrial engineering; information science/studies; international relations and affairs; Italian; Japanese; Jewish/Judaic studies; journalism; kinesiology and exercise science; labor and industrial relations; landscape architecture; landscaping and groundskeeping; Latin American studies; liberal arts and sciences/liberal studies; logistics, materials, and supply chain management; management information systems; marketing/marketing management; materials science; mathematics; mechanical engineering; medical microbiology and bacteriology; medieval and Renaissance studies; mining and mineral engineering; music; natural resources and conservation related; natural resources/conservation; nuclear engineering; organizational behavior; parks, recreation and leisure facilities management; petroleum engineering; philosophy; physics; political science and government; premedical studies; psychology; registered nursing/registered nurse; rehabilitation and therapeutic professions related; religious studies; Russian; secondary education; sociology; soil science and agronomy; Spanish; special education; speech communication and rhetoric; statistics; theater design and technology; turf and turfgrass management; visual and performing arts; women's studies.

Academics *Calendar:* semesters. *Degrees:* certificates, associate, and bachelor's. *Special study options:* adult/continuing education programs. *ROTC:* Army (c), Air Force (c).

Student Life *Housing:* college housing not available. *Campus security:* late-night transport/escort service, part-time trained security personnel.

Athletics Member NJCAA. *Intercollegiate sports:* baseball M, basketball M/W, soccer M/W, tennis M/W, volleyball W. *Intramural sports:* basketball M/W, cheerleading M(c)/W(c), golf M/W, ice hockey M(c)/W(c), lacrosse M/W, soccer M/W, softball W(c), tennis M/W, volleyball M(c)/W.

Standardized Tests *Required:* SAT or ACT (for admission).

Costs (2013–14) *Tuition:* state resident $12,474 full-time, $504 per credit hour part-time; nonresident $19,030 full-time, $793 per credit hour part-time. Full-time tuition and fees vary according to course level, degree level, location, program, and student level. Part-time tuition and fees vary according to course level, course load, degree level, location, program, and student level. *Required fees:* $882 full-time. *Payment plans:* installment, deferred payment. *Waivers:* employees or children of employees.

Financial Aid Of all full-time matriculated undergraduates who enrolled in 2011, 1,038 applied for aid, 807 were judged to have need, 30 had their need fully met. In 2011, 101 non-need-based awards were made. *Average percent of need met:* 61%. *Average financial aid package:* $9345. *Average need-based loan:* $3960. *Average need-based gift aid:* $6338. *Average non-need-based aid:* $2237. *Average indebtedness upon graduation:* $35,100.

Applying *Options:* electronic application, early admission, deferred entrance. *Application fee:* $50. *Required:* high school transcript. *Required for some:* interview. *Recommended:* essay or personal statement. *Application deadlines:* rolling (freshmen), rolling (transfers). *Notification:* continuous (freshmen), continuous (transfers).

Freshman Application Contact Admissions Office, Penn State Brandywine, 25 Yearsley Mill Road, Media, PA 19063-5596. *Phone:* 610-892-1200. *Fax:* 610-892-1320. *E-mail:* bwadmissions@psu.edu.
Website: http://www.brandywine.psu.edu/.

Penn State DuBois
DuBois, Pennsylvania

- **State-related** primarily 2-year, founded 1935, part of Pennsylvania State University
- **Small-town** campus
- **Coed,** 704 undergraduate students, 79% full-time, 52% women, 48% men

Undergraduates 554 full-time, 150 part-time. 2% are from out of state; 2% Black or African American, non-Hispanic/Latino; 1% Hispanic/Latino; 0.7% Asian, non-Hispanic/Latino; 0.3% American Indian or Alaska Native, non-Hispanic/Latino; 1% Two or more races, non-Hispanic/Latino; 0.7% Race/ethnicity unknown; 0.5% international; 2% transferred in. *Retention:* 71% of full-time freshmen returned.

Freshmen *Admission:* 439 applied, 386 admitted, 183 enrolled. *Average high school GPA:* 3.06. *Test scores:* SAT critical reading scores over 500: 35%; SAT math scores over 500: 46%; SAT writing scores over 500: 28%; ACT scores over 18: 100%; SAT critical reading scores over 600: 5%; SAT math scores over 600: 13%; SAT writing scores over 600: 6%; SAT critical reading scores over 700: 1%; SAT math scores over 700: 1%; SAT writing scores over 700: 1%.

Faculty *Total:* 79, 58% full-time, 43% with terminal degrees. *Student/faculty ratio:* 11:1.

Majors Accounting; acting; actuarial science; adult and continuing education administration; advertising; aerospace, aeronautical and astronautical/space engineering; African American/Black studies; agribusiness; agricultural and extension education; agricultural business and management related; agricultural engineering; agricultural mechanization; agriculture; agronomy and crop science; animal sciences; animal sciences related; anthropology; applied economics; archeology; architectural engineering; art; art history, criticism and conservation; art teacher education; Asian studies (East); astronomy; atmospheric sciences and meteorology; biochemistry; bioengineering and biomedical engineering; biological and biomedical sciences related; biological and physical sciences; biology/biological sciences; biology/biotechnology laboratory technician; biomedical technology; business administration and management; business/commerce; business/managerial economics; chemical engineering; chemistry; civil engineering; classics and classical languages; clinical/medical laboratory technology; communication and journalism related; communication sciences and disorders; comparative literature; computer and information sciences; computer engineering; criminal justice/law enforcement administration; economics; electrical and electronics engineering; electrical, electronic and communications engineering technology; elementary education; engineering science; English; environmental/environmental health engineering; film/cinema/video studies; finance; food science; foreign language teacher education; forest sciences and biology; forest technology; French; geography; geological and earth sciences/geosciences related; geology/earth science; German; graphic design; health/health-care administration; history; horticultural science; hospitality administration related; human development and family studies; human nutrition; industrial engineering; information science/studies; international business/trade/commerce; international relations and affairs; Italian; Japanese; Jewish/Judaic studies; journalism; kinesiology and exercise science; labor and industrial relations; landscaping and groundskeeping; Latin American studies; liberal arts and sciences/liberal studies; management information systems; marketing/marketing management; materials science; mathematics; mechanical engineering; mechanical engineering/mechanical technology; medical microbiology and bacteriology; medieval and Renaissance studies; metallurgical technology; mining and mineral engineering; music; natural resources and conservation related; natural resources/conservation; nuclear engineering; occupational therapist assistant; organizational behavior; parks, recreation and leisure facilities management; petroleum engineering; philosophy; physical therapy technology; physics; political science and government; premedical studies; psychology; registered nursing/registered nurse; rehabilitation and therapeutic professions related; religious studies; Russian; secondary education; sociology; soil science and agronomy; Spanish; special education; speech communication and rhetoric; statistics; telecommunications technology; theater design and technology; toxicology; turf and turfgrass management; visual and performing arts; wildlife, fish and wildlands science and management; women's studies.

Academics *Calendar:* semesters. *Degrees:* certificates, associate, and bachelor's. *Special study options:* adult/continuing education programs.

Student Life *Housing:* college housing not available.

Athletics Member NJCAA. *Intercollegiate sports:* basketball M, cross-country running M/W, golf M/W, volleyball W. *Intramural sports:* basketball M/W, football M/W, soccer M/W, table tennis M/W, volleyball M/W.

Standardized Tests *Required:* SAT or ACT (for admission).

Costs (2013–14) *Tuition:* state resident $12,474 full-time, $504 per credit hour part-time; nonresident $19,030 full-time, $793 per credit hour part-time. Full-time tuition and fees vary according to course level, degree level, location, program, and student level. Part-time tuition and fees vary according to course level, course load, degree level, location, program, and student level. *Required fees:* $770 full-time. *Payment plans:* installment, deferred payment. *Waivers:* employees or children of employees.

Financial Aid Of all full-time matriculated undergraduates who enrolled in 2011, 529 applied for aid, 482 were judged to have need, 16 had their need fully met. In 2011, 12 non-need-based awards were made. *Average percent of need met:* 63%. *Average financial aid package:* $11,410. *Average need-based loan:* $3919. *Average need-based gift aid:* $6353. *Average non-need-based aid:* $1474. *Average indebtedness upon graduation:* $35,100.

Applying *Options:* electronic application, early admission, deferred entrance. *Application fee:* $50. *Required:* high school transcript. *Required for some:* interview. *Recommended:* essay or personal statement. *Application deadlines:* rolling (freshmen), rolling (transfers). *Notification:* continuous (freshmen), continuous (transfers).

Freshman Application Contact Admissions Office, Penn State DuBois, College Place, DuBois, PA 15801-3199. *Phone:* 814-375-4720. *Toll-free phone:* 800-346-7627. *Fax:* 814-375-4784. *E-mail:* duboisinfo@psi.edu. *Website:* http://www.ds.psu.edu/.

Penn State Fayette, The Eberly Campus
Uniontown, Pennsylvania

- **State-related** primarily 2-year, founded 1934, part of Pennsylvania State University
- **Small-town** campus
- **Coed,** 867 undergraduate students, 78% full-time, 55% women, 45% men

Undergraduates 680 full-time, 187 part-time. 5% are from out of state; 3% Black or African American, non-Hispanic/Latino; 1% Hispanic/Latino; 0.6% Asian, non-Hispanic/Latino; 0.1% Native Hawaiian or other Pacific Islander, non-Hispanic/Latino; 0.2% American Indian or Alaska Native, non-Hispanic/Latino; 2% Two or more races, non-Hispanic/Latino; 0.9% Race/ethnicity unknown; 2% international; 4% transferred in. *Retention:* 69% of full-time freshmen returned.

Freshmen *Admission:* 610 applied, 544 admitted, 224 enrolled. *Average high school GPA:* 3.09. *Test scores:* SAT critical reading scores over 500: 36%; SAT math scores over 500: 45%; SAT writing scores over 500: 26%; ACT scores over 18: 75%; SAT critical reading scores over 600: 6%; SAT math scores over 600: 11%; SAT writing scores over 600: 4%; SAT critical reading scores over 700: 1%; SAT math scores over 700: 2%.

Faculty *Total:* 96, 55% full-time, 35% with terminal degrees. *Student/faculty ratio:* 11:1.

Majors Accounting; acting; actuarial science; adult and continuing education administration; advertising; aerospace, aeronautical and astronautical/space engineering; African American/Black studies; agribusiness; agricultural and extension education; agricultural business and management related; agricultural engineering; agricultural mechanization; agriculture; agronomy and crop science; animal sciences; animal sciences related; anthropology; applied economics; archeology; architectural engineering; architectural engineering technology; art; art history, criticism and conservation; art teacher education; Asian studies (East); astronomy; atmospheric sciences and meteorology; biochemistry; bioengineering and biomedical engineering; biological and biomedical sciences related; biological and physical sciences; biology/biological sciences; biology/biotechnology laboratory technician; biomedical technology; business administration and management; business/commerce; business/managerial economics; chemical engineering; chemistry; civil engineering; classics and classical languages; communication and journalism related; communication sciences and disorders; comparative literature; computer and information sciences; computer engineering; criminal justice/law enforcement administration; criminal justice/safety; economics; electrical and electronics engineering; electrical, electronic and communications engineering technology; elementary education; engineering science; English; environmental/environmental health engineering; film/cinema/video studies; finance; food science; foreign language teacher education; forest sciences and biology; forest technology; French; geography; geological and earth sciences/geosciences related; geology/earth science; German; graphic design; health/health-care administration; history; horticultural science; hospitality administration related; human development and family studies; human nutrition; industrial engineering; information science/studies; international relations and affairs; Italian; Japanese; Jewish/Judaic studies; journalism; kinesiology and exercise science; labor and industrial relations; landscaping and groundskeeping; Latin American studies; liberal arts and sciences/liberal studies; logistics, materials, and supply chain management; management information systems; manufacturing engineering; marketing/marketing management; materials science; mathematics; mechanical engineering; medical microbiology and bacteriology; medieval and Renaissance studies; metallurgical technology; mining and mineral engineering; natural resources and conservation related; natural resources/conservation; nuclear engineering; organizational behavior; parks, recreation and leisure facilities management; petroleum engineering; philosophy; physics; political science and government; premedical studies; psychology; registered nursing/registered nurse; rehabilitation and therapeutic professions related; religious studies; Russian; secondary education; sociology; soil science and agronomy; Spanish; special education; speech communication and rhetoric; statistics; telecommunications technology; theater design and technology; toxicology; turf and turfgrass management; visual and performing arts; women's studies.

Academics *Calendar:* semesters. *Degrees:* certificates, associate, and bachelor's. *Special study options:* adult/continuing education programs. *ROTC:* Army (b).

Student Life *Housing:* college housing not available. *Campus security:* student patrols, 8-hour patrols by trained security personnel.

Athletics Member NJCAA. *Intercollegiate sports:* baseball M, basketball M, softball W, volleyball W. *Intramural sports:* badminton M/W, basketball M/W,

cheerleading M(c)/W(c), equestrian sports M(c)/W(c), football M/W, golf M(c)/W(c), softball M/W, tennis M/W, volleyball M/W, weight lifting M/W.
Standardized Tests *Required:* SAT or ACT (for admission).
Costs (2013–14) *Tuition:* state resident $12,474 full-time, $504 per credit hour part-time; nonresident $19,030 full-time, $793 per credit hour part-time. Full-time tuition and fees vary according to course level, degree level, location, program, and student level. Part-time tuition and fees vary according to course level, course load, degree level, location, program, and student level. *Required fees:* $826 full-time. *Payment plans:* installment, deferred payment. *Waivers:* employees or children of employees.
Financial Aid Of all full-time matriculated undergraduates who enrolled in 2011, 698 applied for aid, 629 were judged to have need, 32 had their need fully met. In 2011, 31 non-need-based awards were made. *Average percent of need met:* 63%. *Average financial aid package:* $10,156. *Average need-based loan:* $3959. *Average need-based gift aid:* $6396. *Average non-need-based aid:* $2479. *Average indebtedness upon graduation:* $35,100.
Applying *Options:* electronic application, early admission, deferred entrance. *Application fee:* $50. *Required:* high school transcript. *Required for some:* interview. *Recommended:* essay or personal statement. *Application deadlines:* rolling (freshmen), rolling (transfers). *Notification:* continuous (freshmen), continuous (transfers).
Freshman Application Contact Admissions Office, Penn State Fayette, The Eberly Campus, 1 University Drive, PO Box 519, Uniontown, PA 15401-0519. *Phone:* 724-430-4130. *Toll-free phone:* 877-568-4130. *Fax:* 724-430-4175. *E-mail:* feadm@psu.edu.
Website: http://www.fe.psu.edu/.

Penn State Greater Allegheny

McKeesport, Pennsylvania

- **State-related** primarily 2-year, founded 1947, part of Pennsylvania State University
- **Small-town** campus
- **Coed,** 635 undergraduate students, 92% full-time, 43% women, 57% men

Undergraduates 582 full-time, 53 part-time. 9% are from out of state; 24% Black or African American, non-Hispanic/Latino; 4% Hispanic/Latino; 2% Asian, non-Hispanic/Latino; 0.2% Native Hawaiian or other Pacific Islander, non-Hispanic/Latino; 3% Two or more races, non-Hispanic/Latino; 1% Race/ethnicity unknown; 5% international; 4% transferred in; 27% live on campus. *Retention:* 75% of full-time freshmen returned.
Freshmen *Admission:* 699 applied, 558 admitted, 201 enrolled. *Average high school GPA:* 3.04. *Test scores:* SAT critical reading scores over 500: 32%; SAT math scores over 500: 47%; SAT writing scores over 500: 25%; ACT scores over 18: 89%; SAT critical reading scores over 600: 6%; SAT math scores over 600: 18%; SAT writing scores over 600: 5%; ACT scores over 24: 44%; SAT critical reading scores over 700: 1%; SAT math scores over 700: 3%.
Faculty *Total:* 62, 61% full-time, 45% with terminal degrees. *Student/faculty ratio:* 13:1.
Majors Accounting; acting; actuarial science; adult and continuing education administration; advertising; aerospace, aeronautical and astronautical/space engineering; African American/Black studies; agribusiness; agricultural and extension education; agricultural business and management related; agricultural engineering; agricultural mechanization; agriculture; agronomy and crop science; animal sciences; animal sciences related; anthropology; applied economics; archeology; architectural engineering; art; art history, criticism and conservation; art teacher education; Asian studies (East); astronomy; atmospheric sciences and meteorology; biochemistry; bioengineering and biomedical engineering; biological and biomedical sciences related; biological and physical sciences; biology/biological sciences; biology/biotechnology laboratory technician; business administration and management; business/commerce; business/managerial economics; chemical engineering; chemistry; civil engineering; classics and classical languages; communication and journalism related; communication sciences and disorders; comparative literature; computer and information sciences; computer engineering; criminal justice/law enforcement administration; economics; electrical and electronics engineering; elementary education; engineering science; English; environmental/environmental health engineering; film/cinema/video studies; finance; food science; foreign language teacher education; forest sciences and biology; forest technology; French; geography; geological and earth sciences/geosciences related; geology/earth science; German; graphic design; health/health-care administration; history; horticultural science; hospitality administration related; human development and family studies; human nutrition; industrial engineering; information science/studies; international relations and affairs; Italian; Japanese; Jewish/Judaic studies; journalism; kinesiology and exercise science; labor and industrial relations; landscaping and groundskeeping; Latin American studies; liberal arts and sciences/liberal studies; logistics, materials, and supply chain management; management information systems; manufacturing engineering; marketing/marketing management; materials science; mathematics; mechanical engineering; medical microbiology and bacteriology; medieval

and Renaissance studies; mining and mineral engineering; music; natural resources and conservation related; natural resources/conservation; nuclear engineering; organizational behavior; parks, recreation and leisure facilities management; petroleum engineering; philosophy; physics; political science and government; premedical studies; psychology; registered nursing/registered nurse; rehabilitation and therapeutic professions related; religious studies; Russian; secondary education; sociology; soil science and agronomy; Spanish; special education; speech communication and rhetoric; statistics; theater design and technology; toxicology; turf and turfgrass management; visual and performing arts; women's studies.
Academics *Calendar:* semesters. *Degrees:* certificates, associate, bachelor's, and master's. *Special study options:* adult/continuing education programs.
Student Life *Housing Options:* coed, disabled students. Campus housing is university owned. Freshman campus housing is guaranteed. *Campus security:* 24-hour patrols, controlled dormitory access.
Athletics Member NJCAA. *Intercollegiate sports:* baseball M, basketball M, softball W, volleyball W. *Intramural sports:* basketball M/W, cheerleading M(c)/W(c), football M/W, ice hockey M(c), racquetball M/W, skiing (cross-country) M(c)/W(c), skiing (downhill) M(c)/W(c), soccer M(c)/W(c), softball M/W, tennis M/W, volleyball M/W.
Standardized Tests *Required:* SAT or ACT (for admission).
Costs (2013–14) *Tuition:* state resident $12,474 full-time, $504 per credit hour part-time; nonresident $19,030 full-time, $793 per credit hour part-time. Full-time tuition and fees vary according to course level, degree level, location, program, and student level. Part-time tuition and fees vary according to course level, course load, degree level, location, program, and student level. *Required fees:* $882 full-time. *Room and board:* $9690; room only: $4910. Room and board charges vary according to board plan, housing facility, and location. *Payment plans:* installment, deferred payment. *Waivers:* employees or children of employees.
Financial Aid Of all full-time matriculated undergraduates who enrolled in 2011, 544 applied for aid, 498 were judged to have need, 24 had their need fully met. In 2011, 24 non-need-based awards were made. *Average percent of need met:* 67%. *Average financial aid package:* $12,082. *Average need-based loan:* $3916. *Average need-based gift aid:* $7587. *Average non-need-based aid:* $2627. *Average indebtedness upon graduation:* $35,100.
Applying *Options:* electronic application, early admission, deferred entrance. *Application fee:* $50. *Required:* high school transcript. *Required for some:* interview. *Recommended:* essay or personal statement. *Application deadlines:* rolling (freshmen), rolling (transfers). *Notification:* continuous (freshmen), continuous (transfers).
Freshman Application Contact Admissions Office, Penn State Greater Allegheny, 4000 University Drive, McKeesport, PA 15132-7698. *Phone:* 412-675-9010. *Fax:* 412-675-9046. *E-mail:* psuga@psu.edu.
Website: http://www.ga.psu.edu/.

Penn State Hazleton

Hazleton, Pennsylvania

- **State-related** primarily 2-year, founded 1934, part of Pennsylvania State University
- **Small-town** campus
- **Coed,** 1,060 undergraduate students, 94% full-time, 45% women, 55% men

Undergraduates 1,000 full-time, 60 part-time. 28% are from out of state; 16% Black or African American, non-Hispanic/Latino; 15% Hispanic/Latino; 4% Asian, non-Hispanic/Latino; 0.1% Native Hawaiian or other Pacific Islander, non-Hispanic/Latino; 0.3% American Indian or Alaska Native, non-Hispanic/Latino; 3% Two or more races, non-Hispanic/Latino; 1% Race/ethnicity unknown; 0.9% international; 4% transferred in; 45% live on campus. *Retention:* 78% of full-time freshmen returned.
Freshmen *Admission:* 1,179 applied, 1,018 admitted, 433 enrolled. *Average high school GPA:* 2.89. *Test scores:* SAT critical reading scores over 500: 35%; SAT math scores over 500: 41%; SAT writing scores over 500: 25%; ACT scores over 18: 93%; SAT critical reading scores over 600: 6%; SAT math scores over 600: 10%; SAT writing scores over 600: 3%; ACT scores over 24: 40%; ACT scores over 30: 7%.
Faculty *Total:* 80, 68% full-time, 45% with terminal degrees. *Student/faculty ratio:* 16:1.
Majors Accounting; acting; actuarial science; adult and continuing education administration; advertising; aerospace, aeronautical and astronautical/space engineering; African American/Black studies; agribusiness; agricultural and extension education; agricultural business and management related; agricultural engineering; agricultural mechanization; agriculture; agronomy and crop science; animal sciences; animal sciences related; anthropology; applied economics; archeology; architectural engineering; art; art history, criticism and conservation; art teacher education; Asian studies (East); astronomy; atmospheric sciences and meteorology; biochemistry; bioengineering and biomedical engineering; biological and biomedical sciences related; biological and physical sciences; biology/biological sciences; biology/biotechnology labora-

tory technician; biomedical technology; business administration and management; business/commerce; business/managerial economics; chemical engineering; chemistry; civil engineering; classics and classical languages; clinical/medical laboratory technology; communication and journalism related; communication sciences and disorders; comparative literature; computer and information sciences; computer engineering; criminal justice/law enforcement administration; economics; electrical and electronics engineering; electrical, electronic and communications engineering technology; elementary education; engineering science; English; environmental/environmental health engineering; film/cinema/video studies; finance; food science; forest sciences and biology; forest technology; French; geography; geological and earth sciences/geosciences related; geology/earth science; German; graphic design; health/health-care administration; history; horticultural science; hospitality administration related; human development and family studies; human nutrition; industrial engineering; information science/studies; international relations and affairs; Italian; Japanese; Jewish/Judaic studies; journalism; kinesiology and exercise science; labor and industrial relations; landscaping and groundskeeping; Latin American studies; liberal arts and sciences/liberal studies; logistics, materials, and supply chain management; management information systems; manufacturing engineering; marketing/marketing management; materials science; mathematics; mechanical engineering; mechanical engineering/mechanical technology; medical microbiology and bacteriology; medieval and Renaissance studies; metallurgical technology; mining and mineral engineering; music; natural resources and conservation related; natural resources/conservation; nuclear engineering; organizational behavior; parks, recreation and leisure facilities management; petroleum engineering; philosophy; physical therapy technology; physics; political science and government; premedical studies; psychology; registered nursing/registered nurse; rehabilitation and therapeutic professions related; religious studies; Russian; secondary education; sociology; soil science and agronomy; Spanish; special education; speech communication and rhetoric; statistics; telecommunications technology; theater design and technology; toxicology; turf and turfgrass management; visual and performing arts; women's studies.

Academics *Calendar:* semesters. *Degrees:* certificates, associate, and bachelor's. *Special study options:* adult/continuing education programs. *ROTC:* Army (b), Air Force (c).

Student Life *Housing Options:* coed. Campus housing is university owned. Freshman campus housing is guaranteed. *Campus security:* 24-hour patrols, late-night transport/escort service, controlled dormitory access.

Athletics Member NJCAA. *Intercollegiate sports:* baseball M, basketball M/W, cheerleading M/W, soccer M, softball W(s), tennis M/W, volleyball M/W. *Intramural sports:* basketball M/W, skiing (downhill) M(c)/W(c), soccer M/W, volleyball M/W.

Standardized Tests *Required:* SAT or ACT (for admission).

Costs (2013–14) *Tuition:* state resident $12,474 full-time, $504 per credit hour part-time; nonresident $19,030 full-time, $793 per credit hour part-time. Full-time tuition and fees vary according to course level, degree level, location, program, and student level. Part-time tuition and fees vary according to course level, course load, degree level, location, program, and student level. *Required fees:* $826 full-time. *Room and board:* $9690; room only: $4910. Room and board charges vary according to board plan, housing facility, and location. *Payment plans:* installment, deferred payment. *Waivers:* employees or children of employees.

Financial Aid Of all full-time matriculated undergraduates who enrolled in 2011, 978 applied for aid, 852 were judged to have need, 26 had their need fully met. In 2011, 61 non-need-based awards were made. *Average percent of need met:* 61%. *Average financial aid package:* $9823. *Average need-based loan:* $3819. *Average need-based gift aid:* $6462. *Average non-need-based aid:* $2301. *Average indebtedness upon graduation:* $35,100.

Applying *Options:* electronic application, early admission, deferred entrance. *Application fee:* $50. *Required:* high school transcript. *Required for some:* interview. *Recommended:* essay or personal statement. *Application deadlines:* rolling (freshmen), rolling (transfers). *Notification:* continuous (freshmen), continuous (transfers).

Freshman Application Contact Admissions Office, Penn State Hazleton, Hazleton, PA 18201-1291. *Phone:* 570-450-3142. *Toll-free phone:* 800-279-8495. *Fax:* 570-450-3182. *E-mail:* admissions-hn@psu.edu. *Website:* http://www.hn.psu.edu/.

Penn State Lehigh Valley
Fogelsville, Pennsylvania

- **State-related** primarily 2-year, founded 1912, part of Pennsylvania State University
- **Rural** campus
- **Coed,** 907 undergraduate students, 80% full-time, 44% women, 56% men

Undergraduates 728 full-time, 179 part-time. 4% are from out of state; 5% Black or African American, non-Hispanic/Latino; 15% Hispanic/Latino; 10% Asian, non-Hispanic/Latino; 0.1% Native Hawaiian or other Pacific Islander,

non-Hispanic/Latino; 2% Two or more races, non-Hispanic/Latino; 2% Race/ethnicity unknown; 0.5% international; 5% transferred in. *Retention:* 81% of full-time freshmen returned.

Freshmen *Admission:* 909 applied, 777 admitted, 225 enrolled. *Average high school GPA:* 2.98. *Test scores:* SAT critical reading scores over 500: 43%; SAT math scores over 500: 58%; SAT writing scores over 500: 43%; ACT scores over 18: 90%; SAT critical reading scores over 600: 11%; SAT math scores over 600: 16%; SAT writing scores over 600: 6%; ACT scores over 24: 30%; SAT critical reading scores over 700: 1%; SAT math scores over 700: 1%; SAT writing scores over 700: 1%; ACT scores over 30: 10%.

Faculty *Total:* 90, 39% full-time, 46% with terminal degrees. *Student/faculty ratio:* 15:1.

Majors Accounting; acting; actuarial science; adult and continuing education administration; advertising; aerospace, aeronautical and astronautical/space engineering; African American/Black studies; agribusiness; agricultural and extension education; agricultural business and management related; agricultural engineering; agricultural mechanization; agriculture; American studies; animal sciences; animal sciences related; anthropology; applied economics; archeology; architectural engineering; art; art history, criticism and conservation; art teacher education; Asian studies (East); astronomy; atmospheric sciences and meteorology; biochemistry; bioengineering and biomedical engineering; biological and biomedical sciences related; biological and physical sciences; biology/biological sciences; biology/biotechnology laboratory technician; business/commerce; business/managerial economics; chemical engineering; chemistry; civil engineering; classics and classical languages; communication and journalism related; communication sciences and disorders; comparative literature; computer and information sciences; computer engineering; criminal justice/law enforcement administration; economics; electrical and electronics engineering; elementary education; engineering science; English; environmental/environmental health engineering; film/cinema/video studies; finance; food science; foreign languages and literatures; forest sciences and biology; forest technology; French; geography; geological and earth sciences/geosciences related; geology/earth science; German; graphic design; health/health-care administration; history; horticultural science; hospitality administration related; human development and family studies; human nutrition; industrial engineering; information science/studies; international business/trade/commerce; international relations and affairs; Italian; Japanese; Jewish/Judaic studies; journalism; kinesiology and exercise science; labor and industrial relations; landscape architecture; landscaping and groundskeeping; Latin American studies; liberal arts and sciences/liberal studies; logistics, materials, and supply chain management; management information systems; management sciences and quantitative methods related; marketing/marketing management; materials science; mathematics; mechanical engineering; medical microbiology and bacteriology; medieval and Renaissance studies; mining and mineral engineering; natural resources and conservation related; natural resources/conservation; nuclear engineering; organizational behavior; parks, recreation and leisure facilities management; petroleum engineering; philosophy; physics; political science and government; premedical studies; professional, technical, business, and scientific writing; psychology; registered nursing/registered nurse; rehabilitation and therapeutic professions related; religious studies; Russian; secondary education; sociology; soil science and agronomy; Spanish; special education; speech communication and rhetoric; statistics; theater design and technology; turf and turfgrass management; visual and performing arts; women's studies.

Academics *Calendar:* semesters. *Degrees:* certificates, associate, and bachelor's (enrollment figures include students enrolled at The Graduate School at Penn State who are taking courses at this location). *Special study options:* adult/continuing education programs. *ROTC:* Army (c).

Student Life *Housing:* college housing not available.

Athletics Member NJCAA. *Intercollegiate sports:* baseball M, basketball M/W, bowling M(c)/W(c), cheerleading M/W, cross-country running M/W, football M(c), golf M(c)/W(c), ice hockey M(c)/W(c), skiing (downhill) M(c)/W(c), soccer M(c)/W, tennis M/W, volleyball M(c)/W. *Intramural sports:* badminton M/W, basketball M/W, football M/W, golf M/W, soccer M/W, volleyball M/W.

Standardized Tests *Required:* SAT or ACT (for admission).

Costs (2013–14) *Tuition:* state resident $12,474 full-time, $504 per credit hour part-time; nonresident $19,030 full-time, $793 per credit hour part-time. Full-time tuition and fees vary according to course level, degree level, location, program, and student level. Part-time tuition and fees vary according to course level, course load, degree level, location, program, and student level. *Required fees:* $876 full-time. *Payment plans:* installment, deferred payment. *Waivers:* employees or children of employees.

Financial Aid Of all full-time matriculated undergraduates who enrolled in 2011, 584 applied for aid, 504 were judged to have need, 14 had their need fully met. In 2011, 44 non-need-based awards were made. *Average percent of need met:* 61%. *Average financial aid package:* $9723. *Average need-based loan:* $4101. *Average need-based gift aid:* $6442. *Average non-need-based aid:* $1838. *Average indebtedness upon graduation:* $35,100.

Applying *Options:* electronic application, early admission, deferred entrance. *Application fee:* $50. *Required:* high school transcript. *Application deadlines:* rolling (freshmen), rolling (transfers). *Notification:* continuous (freshmen), continuous (transfers).

Freshman Application Contact Admissions Office, Penn State Lehigh Valley, 2809 Saucon Valley Road, Fogelsville, PA 18051-9999. *Phone:* 610-285-5000. *Fax:* 610-285-5220. *E-mail:* admissions-lv@psu.edu. *Website:* http://www.lv.psu.edu/.

Penn State Mont Alto

Mont Alto, Pennsylvania

- **State-related** primarily 2-year, founded 1929, part of Pennsylvania State University
- **Small-town** campus
- **Coed,** 1,106 undergraduate students, 75% full-time, 56% women, 44% men

Undergraduates 831 full-time, 275 part-time. 17% are from out of state; 11% Black or African American, non-Hispanic/Latino; 4% Hispanic/Latino; 2% Asian, non-Hispanic/Latino; 3% Two or more races, non-Hispanic/Latino; 1% Race/ethnicity unknown; 0.7% international; 4% transferred in; 29% live on campus. *Retention:* 74% of full-time freshmen returned.

Freshmen *Admission:* 827 applied, 684 admitted, 325 enrolled. *Average high school GPA:* 2.97. *Test scores:* SAT critical reading scores over 500: 36%; SAT math scores over 500: 47%; SAT writing scores over 500: 29%; ACT scores over 18: 91%; SAT critical reading scores over 600: 6%; SAT math scores over 600: 17%; SAT writing scores over 600: 6%; ACT scores over 24: 18%; SAT math scores over 700: 2%.

Faculty *Total:* 108, 53% full-time, 35% with terminal degrees. *Student/faculty ratio:* 13:1.

Majors Accounting; acting; actuarial science; adult and continuing education administration; advertising; aerospace, aeronautical and astronautical/space engineering; African American/Black studies; agribusiness; agricultural and extension education; agricultural business and management related; agricultural engineering; agricultural mechanization; agriculture; agronomy and crop science; animal sciences; animal sciences related; anthropology; applied economics; archeology; architectural engineering; art; art history, criticism and conservation; art teacher education; Asian studies (East); astronomy; atmospheric sciences and meteorology; biochemistry; bioengineering and biomedical engineering; biological and biomedical sciences related; biological and physical sciences; biology/biological sciences; biology/biotechnology laboratory technician; business administration and management; business/commerce; business/managerial economics; chemical engineering; chemistry; civil engineering; classics and classical languages; communication and journalism related; communication sciences and disorders; comparative literature; computer and information sciences; computer engineering; criminal justice/law enforcement administration; economics; electrical and electronics engineering; elementary education; engineering science; English; environmental/environmental health engineering; film/cinema/video studies; finance; food science; foreign language teacher education; forest sciences and biology; forest technology; French; geography; geological and earth sciences/geosciences related; geology/earth science; German; graphic design; health/health-care administration; history; horticultural science; hospitality administration related; human development and family studies; human nutrition; industrial engineering; information science/studies; international relations and affairs; Italian; Japanese; Jewish/Judaic studies; journalism; kinesiology and exercise science; labor and industrial relations; landscaping and groundskeeping; Latin American studies; liberal arts and sciences/liberal studies; management information systems; marketing/marketing management; materials science; mathematics; mechanical engineering; medical microbiology and bacteriology; medieval and Renaissance studies; mining and mineral engineering; music; natural resources and conservation related; natural resources/conservation; nuclear engineering; occupational therapist assistant; occupational therapy; organizational behavior; parks, recreation and leisure facilities management; petroleum engineering; philosophy; physical therapy technology; physics; political science and government; premedical studies; psychology; registered nursing/registered nurse; rehabilitation and therapeutic professions related; religious studies; Russian; secondary education; sociology; soil science and agronomy; Spanish; special education; speech communication and rhetoric; statistics; theater design and technology; toxicology; turf and turfgrass management; visual and performing arts; women's studies.

Academics *Calendar:* semesters. *Degrees:* certificates, associate, and bachelor's. *Special study options:* adult/continuing education programs. *ROTC:* Army (c).

Student Life *Housing Options:* coed, disabled students. Campus housing is university owned. Freshman campus housing is guaranteed. *Campus security:* 24-hour patrols, controlled dormitory access.

Athletics Member NJCAA. *Intercollegiate sports:* basketball M/W, cheerleading M/W, cross-country running M/W, golf M/W, soccer M/W, softball W, tennis M/W, volleyball W. *Intramural sports:* badminton M/W, basketball M/W,

cheerleading M(c)/W(c), racquetball M/W, soccer M/W, softball W, volleyball M/W.

Standardized Tests *Required:* SAT or ACT (for admission).

Costs (2013–14) *Tuition:* state resident $12,474 full-time, $504 per credit hour part-time; nonresident $19,030 full-time, $793 per credit hour part-time. Full-time tuition and fees vary according to course level, degree level, location, program, and student level. Part-time tuition and fees vary according to course level, course load, degree level, location, program, and student level. *Required fees:* $882 full-time. *Room and board:* $9690; room only: $4910. Room and board charges vary according to board plan, housing facility, and location. *Payment plans:* installment, deferred payment. *Waivers:* employees or children of employees.

Financial Aid Of all full-time matriculated undergraduates who enrolled in 2011, 852 applied for aid, 754 were judged to have need, 40 had their need fully met. In 2011, 46 non-need-based awards were made. *Average percent of need met:* 64%. *Average financial aid package:* $10,829. *Average need-based loan:* $3849. *Average need-based gift aid:* $6401. *Average non-need-based aid:* $2946. *Average indebtedness upon graduation:* $35,100.

Applying *Options:* electronic application, early admission, deferred entrance. *Application fee:* $50. *Required:* high school transcript. *Required for some:* interview. *Recommended:* essay or personal statement. *Application deadlines:* rolling (freshmen), rolling (transfers). *Notification:* continuous (freshmen), continuous (transfers).

Freshman Application Contact Admissions Office, Penn State Mont Alto, 1 Campus Drive, Mont Alto, PA 17237-9703. *Phone:* 717-749-6130. *Toll-free phone:* 800-392-6173. *Fax:* 717-749-6132. *E-mail:* psuma@psu.edu. *Website:* http://www.ma.psu.edu/.

Penn State New Kensington

New Kensington, Pennsylvania

- **State-related** primarily 2-year, founded 1958, part of Pennsylvania State University
- **Small-town** campus
- **Coed,** 715 undergraduate students, 78% full-time, 40% women, 60% men

Undergraduates 558 full-time, 157 part-time. 2% are from out of state; 3% Black or African American, non-Hispanic/Latino; 2% Hispanic/Latino; 1% Asian, non-Hispanic/Latino; 0.2% American Indian or Alaska Native, non-Hispanic/Latino; 1% Two or more races, non-Hispanic/Latino; 2% Race/ethnicity unknown; 0.9% international; 7% transferred in. *Retention:* 71% of full-time freshmen returned.

Freshmen *Admission:* 477 applied, 352 admitted, 154 enrolled. *Average high school GPA:* 3.03. *Test scores:* SAT critical reading scores over 500: 44%; SAT math scores over 500: 56%; SAT writing scores over 500: 35%; ACT scores over 18: 67%; SAT critical reading scores over 600: 13%; SAT math scores over 600: 18%; SAT writing scores over 600: 9%; ACT scores over 24: 50%; SAT critical reading scores over 700: 1%; SAT math scores over 700: 5%; SAT writing scores over 700: 1%.

Faculty *Total:* 78, 47% full-time, 44% with terminal degrees. *Student/faculty ratio:* 12:1.

Majors Accounting; acting; actuarial science; adult and continuing education administration; advertising; aerospace, aeronautical and astronautical/space engineering; African American/Black studies; agribusiness; agricultural and extension education; agricultural business and management related; agricultural engineering; agricultural mechanization; agriculture; agronomy and crop science; animal sciences; animal sciences related; anthropology; applied economics; archeology; architectural engineering; art; art history, criticism and conservation; art teacher education; Asian studies (East); astronomy; atmospheric sciences and meteorology; biochemistry; bioengineering and biomedical engineering; biological and biomedical sciences related; biological and physical sciences; biology/biological sciences; biology/biotechnology laboratory technician; biomedical technology; business administration and management; business/commerce; business/managerial economics; chemical engineering; chemistry; civil engineering; classics and classical languages; communication and journalism related; communication sciences and disorders; comparative literature; computer and information sciences; computer engineering; computer engineering technology; criminal justice/law enforcement administration; economics; electrical and electronics engineering; electrical, electronic and communications engineering technology; elementary education; engineering science; English; environmental/environmental health engineering; film/cinema/video studies; finance; food science; forest sciences and biology; forest technology; French; geography; geological and earth sciences/geosciences related; geology/earth science; German; graphic design; health/health-care administration; history; horticultural science; hospitality administration related; human development and family studies; human nutrition; industrial engineering; information science/studies; international relations and affairs; Italian; Japanese; Jewish/Judaic studies; journalism; kinesiology and exercise science; labor and industrial relations; landscaping and groundskeeping; Latin American studies; liberal arts and sciences/liberal studies;

logistics, materials, and supply chain management; management information systems; marketing/marketing management; materials science; mathematics; mechanical engineering; mechanical engineering/mechanical technology; medical microbiology and bacteriology; medical radiologic technology; medieval and Renaissance studies; metallurgical technology; mining and mineral engineering; music; natural resources and conservation related; natural resources/conservation; nuclear engineering; organizational behavior; parks, recreation and leisure facilities management; petroleum engineering; philosophy; physics; political science and government; premedical studies; psychology; registered nursing/registered nurse; rehabilitation and therapeutic professions related; religious studies; Russian; secondary education; sociology; soil science and agronomy; Spanish; special education; speech communication and rhetoric; statistics; telecommunications technology; theater design and technology; toxicology; turf and turfgrass management; visual and performing arts; women's studies.

Academics *Calendar:* semesters. *Degrees:* certificates, associate, bachelor's, and master's. *Special study options:* adult/continuing education programs, external degree program. *ROTC:* Air Force (c).

Student Life *Campus security:* part-time trained security personnel.

Athletics Member NJCAA. *Intercollegiate sports:* baseball M; basketball M/W, cheerleading M/W, golf M/W, softball W, volleyball W. *Intramural sports:* badminton M/W, basketball M/W, bowling M/W, cheerleading M(c)/W(c), football M/W, ice hockey M(c)/W(c), racquetball M/W, skiing (downhill) M(c)/W(c), soccer M/W, softball W, volleyball M/W.

Standardized Tests *Required:* SAT or ACT (for admission).

Costs (2013–14) *Tuition:* state resident $504 per credit part-time; nonresident $793 per credit part-time. Full-time tuition and fees vary according to course level, degree level, location, program, and student level. Part-time tuition and fees vary according to course level, course load, degree level, location, program, and student level. *Payment plans:* installment, deferred payment. *Waivers:* employees or children of employees.

Financial Aid Of all full-time matriculated undergraduates who enrolled in 2011, 521 applied for aid, 447 were judged to have need, 17 had their need fully met. In 2011, 28 non-need-based awards were made. *Average percent of need met:* 64%. *Average financial aid package:* $9992. *Average need-based loan:* $3993. *Average need-based gift aid:* $5931. *Average non-need-based aid:* $1979. *Average indebtedness upon graduation:* $35,100.

Applying *Options:* electronic application, early admission, deferred entrance. *Application fee:* $50. *Required:* high school transcript. *Required for some:* interview. *Recommended:* essay or personal statement. *Application deadlines:* rolling (freshmen), rolling (transfers). *Notification:* continuous (freshmen), continuous (transfers).

Freshman Application Contact Admissions Office, Penn State New Kensington, 3550 Seventh Street Road, New Kensington, PA 15068. *Phone:* 724-334-5466. *Toll-free phone:* 888-968-7297. *Fax:* 724-334-6111. *E-mail:* nkadmissions@psu.edu. *Website:* http://www.nk.psu.edu/.

Penn State Schuylkill

Schuylkill Haven, Pennsylvania

- **State-related** primarily 2-year, founded 1934, part of Pennsylvania State University
- **Small-town** campus
- **Coed,** 867 undergraduate students, 80% full-time, 58% women, 42% men

Undergraduates 696 full-time, 171 part-time. 18% are from out of state; 29% Black or African American, non-Hispanic/Latino; 6% Hispanic/Latino; 1% Asian, non-Hispanic/Latino; 0.2% Native Hawaiian or other Pacific Islander, non-Hispanic/Latino; 0.2% American Indian or Alaska Native, non-Hispanic/Latino; 2% Two or more races, non-Hispanic/Latino; 2% Race/ethnicity unknown; 1% international; 5% transferred in; 32% live on campus. *Retention:* 69% of full-time freshmen returned.

Freshmen *Admission:* 693 applied, 562 admitted, 248 enrolled. *Average high school GPA:* 2.75. *Test scores:* SAT critical reading scores over 500: 21%; SAT math scores over 500: 23%; SAT writing scores over 500: 18%; ACT scores over 18: 75%; SAT critical reading scores over 600: 3%; SAT math scores over 600: 5%; SAT writing scores over 600: 2%; ACT scores over 24: 13%.

Faculty *Total:* 68, 65% full-time, 56% with terminal degrees. *Student/faculty ratio:* 15:1.

Majors Accounting; acting; actuarial science; adult and continuing education administration; advertising; aerospace, aeronautical and astronautical/space engineering; African American/Black studies; agribusiness; agricultural and extension education; agricultural business and management related; agricultural engineering; agricultural mechanization; agriculture; American studies; animal sciences; animal sciences related; anthropology; applied economics; archeology; architectural engineering; art; art history, criticism and conservation; art teacher education; Asian studies (East); astronomy; atmospheric sciences and meteorology; biochemistry; bioengineering and biomedical engineering; biological and biomedical sciences related; biological and physi-

cal sciences; biology/biological sciences; biology/biotechnology laboratory technician; biomedical technology; business/commerce; business/managerial economics; chemical engineering; chemistry; civil engineering; classics and classical languages; clinical/medical laboratory technology; communication and journalism related; communication sciences and disorders; comparative literature; computer and information sciences; computer engineering; criminal justice/law enforcement administration; criminal justice/safety; economics; electrical and electronics engineering; electrical, electronic and communications engineering technology; elementary education; engineering science; English; environmental/environmental health engineering; film/cinema/video studies; finance; food science; forest sciences and biology; forest technology; French; geography; geological and earth sciences/geosciences related; geology/earth science; German; graphic design; health/health-care administration; history; horticultural science; hospitality administration related; human development and family studies; human nutrition; industrial engineering; information science/studies; international business/trade/commerce; international relations and affairs; Italian; Japanese; Jewish/Judaic studies; journalism; kinesiology and exercise science; labor and industrial relations; landscape architecture; landscaping and groundskeeping; Latin American studies; liberal arts and sciences/liberal studies; logistics, materials, and supply chain management; management information systems; management sciences and quantitative methods related; marketing/marketing management; materials science; mathematics; mechanical engineering; medical microbiology and bacteriology; medical radiologic technology; medieval and Renaissance studies; metallurgical technology; mining and mineral engineering; natural resources and conservation related; natural resources/conservation; nuclear engineering; organizational behavior; parks, recreation and leisure facilities management; petroleum engineering; philosophy; physics; political science and government; premedical studies; psychology; registered nursing/registered nurse; rehabilitation and therapeutic professions related; religious studies; Russian; secondary education; sociology; soil science and agronomy; Spanish; special education; speech communication and rhetoric; statistics; telecommunications technology; theater design and technology; turf and turfgrass management; visual and performing arts; women's studies.

Academics *Calendar:* semesters. *Degrees:* certificates, associate, and bachelor's (bachelor's degree programs completed at the Harrisburg campus). *Special study options:* adult/continuing education programs, external degree program.

Student Life *Housing Options:* disabled students. *Campus security:* 24-hour patrols, controlled dormitory access.

Athletics Member NJCAA. *Intercollegiate sports:* basketball M, cross-country running M/W, golf M, soccer M, softball W, volleyball W. *Intramural sports:* basketball M/W, football M, soccer M/W, softball M/W, table tennis M/W, volleyball M/W.

Standardized Tests *Required:* SAT or ACT (for admission).

Costs (2012–13) *Tuition:* state resident $12,474 full-time, $504 per credit part-time; nonresident $19,030 full-time, $793 per credit part-time. Full-time tuition and fees vary according to course level, degree level, location, program, and student level. Part-time tuition and fees vary according to course level, course load, degree level, location, program, and student level. *Required fees:* $770 full-time. *Payment plans:* installment, deferred payment. *Waivers:* employees or children of employees.

Financial Aid Of all full-time matriculated undergraduates who enrolled in 2011, 775 applied for aid, 719 were judged to have need, 28 had their need fully met. In 2011, 20 non-need-based awards were made. *Average percent of need met:* 64%. *Average financial aid package:* $10,749. *Average need-based loan:* $3912. *Average need-based gift aid:* $6796. *Average non-need-based aid:* $2001. *Average indebtedness upon graduation:* $35,100.

Applying *Options:* electronic application, early admission, deferred entrance. *Application fee:* $50. *Required:* high school transcript. *Application deadlines:* rolling (freshmen), rolling (transfers). *Notification:* continuous (freshmen), continuous (transfers).

Freshman Application Contact Admissions Office, Penn State Schuylkill, 200 University Drive, Schuylkill Haven, PA 17972-2208. *Phone:* 570-385-6252. *Fax:* 570-385-6272. *E-mail:* sl-admissions@psu.edu. *Website:* http://www.sl.psu.edu/.

Penn State Wilkes-Barre

Lehman, Pennsylvania

- **State-related** primarily 2-year, founded 1916, part of Pennsylvania State University
- **Rural** campus
- **Coed,** 617 undergraduate students, 87% full-time, 31% women, 69% men

Undergraduates 539 full-time, 78 part-time. 6% are from out of state; 5% Black or African American, non-Hispanic/Latino; 5% Hispanic/Latino; 1% Asian, non-Hispanic/Latino; 0.2% Native Hawaiian or other Pacific Islander, non-Hispanic/Latino; 0.2% American Indian or Alaska Native, non-Hispanic/Latino; 1% Two or more races, non-Hispanic/Latino; 1% Race/ethnicity unknown; 0.7% international; 4% transferred in. *Retention:* 84% of full-time freshmen returned.

Freshmen *Admission:* 472 applied, 387 admitted, 148 enrolled. *Average high school GPA:* 3. *Test scores:* SAT critical reading scores over 500: 44%; SAT math scores over 500: 54%; SAT writing scores over 500: 30%; ACT scores over 18: 83%; SAT critical reading scores over 600: 13%; SAT math scores over 600: 19%; SAT writing scores over 600: 6%; ACT scores over 24: 17%; SAT math scores over 700: 2%.

Faculty *Total:* 58, 57% full-time, 43% with terminal degrees. *Student/faculty ratio:* 14:1.

Majors Accounting; acting; actuarial science; adult and continuing education administration; advertising; aerospace, aeronautical and astronautical/space engineering; African American/Black studies; agribusiness; agricultural and extension education; agricultural business and management related; agricultural engineering; agricultural mechanization; agriculture; agronomy and crop science; animal sciences; animal sciences related; anthropology; applied economics; archeology; architectural engineering; art; art history, criticism and conservation; art teacher education; astronomy; atmospheric sciences and meteorology; biochemistry; bioengineering and biomedical engineering; biological and biomedical sciences related; biological and physical sciences; biology/biological sciences; biology/biotechnology laboratory technician; business administration and management; business/commerce; business/managerial economics; chemical engineering; chemistry; civil engineering; classics and classical languages; communication and journalism related; communication sciences and disorders; comparative literature; computer and information sciences; computer engineering; criminal justice/law enforcement administration; criminal justice/safety; economics; electrical and electronics engineering; electrical, electronic and communications engineering technology; elementary education; engineering science; English; environmental/environmental health engineering; film/cinema/video studies; finance; food science; forest sciences and biology; forest technology; French; geography; geological and earth sciences/geosciences related; geology/earth science; German; graphic design; health/health-care administration; history; horticultural science; hospitality administration related; human development and family studies; human nutrition; industrial engineering; information science/studies; international relations and affairs; Italian; Japanese; Jewish/Judaic studies; journalism; kinesiology and exercise science; labor and industrial relations; landscape architecture; landscaping and groundskeeping; Latin American studies; liberal arts and sciences/liberal studies; management information systems; manufacturing engineering; marketing/marketing management; materials science; mathematics; mechanical engineering; medical microbiology and bacteriology; medieval and Renaissance studies; metallurgical technology; mining and mineral engineering; music; natural resources and conservation related; natural resources/conservation; nuclear engineering; organizational behavior; parks, recreation and leisure facilities management; petroleum engineering; philosophy; physics; political science and government; premedical studies; psychology; registered nursing/registered nurse; rehabilitation and therapeutic professions related; religious studies; Russian; secondary education; sociology; soil science and agronomy; Spanish; special education; speech communication and rhetoric; statistics; surveying technology; telecommunications technology; theater design and technology; toxicology; turf and turfgrass management; visual and performing arts; women's studies.

Academics *Calendar:* semesters. *Degrees:* certificates, associate, and bachelor's (enrollment figures include students enrolled at The Graduate School at Penn State who are taking courses at this location). *Special study options:* adult/continuing education programs. *ROTC:* Army (c), Air Force (c).

Student Life *Housing:* college housing not available.

Athletics Member NJCAA. *Intercollegiate sports:* baseball M, basketball M, cross-country running M/W, golf M/W, soccer M/W, volleyball W. *Intramural sports:* basketball M/W, bowling M(c)/W(c), cheerleading M(c)/W(c), football M, racquetball M/W, softball M, volleyball M(c)/W.

Standardized Tests *Required:* SAT or ACT (for admission).

Costs (2013–14) *Tuition:* state resident $12,474 full-time, $504 per credit hour part-time; nonresident $19,030 full-time, $793 per credit hour part-time. Full-time tuition and fees vary according to course level, degree level, location, program, and student level. Part-time tuition and fees vary according to course level, course load, degree level, location, program, and student level. *Required fees:* $764 full-time. *Payment plans:* installment, deferred payment. *Waivers:* employees or children of employees.

Financial Aid Of all full-time matriculated undergraduates who enrolled in 2011, 491 applied for aid, 420 were judged to have need, 26 had their need fully met. In 2011, 39 non-need-based awards were made. *Average percent of need met:* 65%. *Average financial aid package:* $10,042. *Average need-based loan:* $4051. *Average need-based gift aid:* $6492. *Average non-need-based aid:* $2715. *Average indebtedness upon graduation:* $35,100.

Applying *Options:* electronic application, early admission, deferred entrance. *Application fee:* $50. *Required:* high school transcript. *Required for some:* interview. *Recommended:* essay or personal statement. *Application deadlines:* rolling (freshmen), rolling (transfers). *Notification:* continuous (freshmen), continuous (transfers).

Freshman Application Contact Admissions Office, Penn State Wilkes-Barre, PO PSU, Lehman, PA 18627-0217. *Phone:* 570-675-9238. *Fax:* 570-675-9113. *E-mail:* wbadmissions@psu.edu.
Website: http://www.wb.psu.edu/.

Penn State Worthington Scranton
Dunmore, Pennsylvania

- **State-related** primarily 2-year, founded 1923, part of Pennsylvania State University
- **Small-town** campus
- **Coed**, 1,234 undergraduate students, 80% full-time, 54% women, 46% men

Undergraduates 990 full-time, 244 part-time. 3% are from out of state; 2% Black or African American, non-Hispanic/Latino; 5% Hispanic/Latino; 5% Asian, non-Hispanic/Latino; 0.1% Native Hawaiian or other Pacific Islander, non-Hispanic/Latino; 0.3% American Indian or Alaska Native, non-Hispanic/Latino; 2% Two or more races, non-Hispanic/Latino; 2% Race/ethnicity unknown; 0.4% international; 4% transferred in. *Retention:* 69% of full-time freshmen returned.

Freshmen *Admission:* 722 applied, 591 admitted, 282 enrolled. *Average high school GPA:* 2.84. *Test scores:* SAT critical reading scores over 500: 34%; SAT math scores over 500: 42%; SAT writing scores over 500: 26%; ACT scores over 18: 80%; SAT critical reading scores over 600: 6%; SAT math scores over 600: 9%; SAT writing scores over 600: 5%; ACT scores over 24: 20%.

Faculty *Total:* 99, 52% full-time, 40% with terminal degrees. *Student/faculty ratio:* 16:1.

Majors Accounting; acting; actuarial science; adult and continuing education administration; advertising; aerospace, aeronautical and astronautical/space engineering; African American/Black studies; agribusiness; agricultural and extension education; agricultural business and management related; agricultural engineering; agricultural mechanization; agriculture; agronomy and crop science; American studies; animal sciences; animal sciences related; anthropology; applied economics; archeology; architectural engineering; architectural engineering technology; art; art history, criticism and conservation; art teacher education; Asian studies (East); astronomy; atmospheric sciences and meteorology; biochemistry; bioengineering and biomedical engineering; biological and biomedical sciences related; biological and physical sciences; biology/biological sciences; biology/biotechnology laboratory technician; business administration and management; business/commerce; business/managerial economics; chemical engineering; chemistry; civil engineering; classics and classical languages; communication and journalism related; communication sciences and disorders; comparative literature; computer and information sciences; computer engineering; criminal justice/law enforcement administration; economics; electrical and electronics engineering; electrical, electronic and communications engineering technology; elementary education; engineering science; English; environmental/environmental health engineering; film/cinema/video studies; finance; food science; foreign language teacher education; forest sciences and biology; forest technology; French; geography; geological and earth sciences/geosciences related; geology/earth science; German; graphic design; health/health-care administration; history; horticultural science; hospitality administration related; human development and family studies; human nutrition; industrial engineering; information science/studies; international relations and affairs; Italian; Japanese; Jewish/Judaic studies; journalism; kinesiology and exercise science; labor and industrial relations; landscaping and groundskeeping; Latin American studies; liberal arts and sciences/liberal studies; management information systems; marketing/marketing management; materials science; mathematics; mechanical engineering; medical microbiology and bacteriology; medieval and Renaissance studies; mining and mineral engineering; music; natural resources and conservation related; natural resources/conservation; nuclear engineering; organizational behavior; parks, recreation and leisure facilities management; petroleum engineering; philosophy; physics; political science and government; premedical studies; psychology; registered nursing/registered nurse; rehabilitation and therapeutic professions related; religious studies; Russian; secondary education; sociology; soil science and agronomy; Spanish; special education; speech communication and rhetoric; statistics; theater design and technology; turf and turfgrass management; visual and performing arts; women's studies.

Academics *Calendar:* semesters. *Degrees:* certificates, associate, and bachelor's. *Special study options:* adult/continuing education programs. *ROTC:* Army (c), Air Force (c).

Student Life *Housing:* college housing not available.

Athletics Member NJCAA. *Intercollegiate sports:* baseball M, basketball M/W, cheerleading M/W, cross-country running M/W, soccer M, softball W, volleyball W. *Intramural sports:* basketball M/W, bowling M(c)/W(c), skiing (downhill) M(c)/W(c), soccer M/W, softball M/W, volleyball M/W(c), weight lifting M(c)/W(c).

Standardized Tests *Required:* SAT or ACT (for admission).

Costs (2013–14) *Tuition:* state resident $12,474 full-time, $504 per credit hour part-time; nonresident $19,030 full-time, $793 per credit hour part-time. Full-time tuition and fees vary according to course level, degree level, location, program, and student level. Part-time tuition and fees vary according to course level, course load, degree level, location, program, and student level. *Required fees:* $756 full-time. *Payment plans:* installment, deferred payment. *Waivers:* employees or children of employees.

Financial Aid Of all full-time matriculated undergraduates who enrolled in 2011, 880 applied for aid, 770 were judged to have need, 30 had their need fully met. In 2011, 27 non-need-based awards were made. *Average percent of need met:* 62%. *Average financial aid package:* $9815. *Average need-based loan:* $4047. *Average need-based gift aid:* $6305. *Average non-need-based aid:* $2258. *Average indebtedness upon graduation:* $35,100.

Applying *Options:* electronic application, early admission, deferred entrance. *Application fee:* $50. *Required:* high school transcript. *Required for some:* interview. *Recommended:* essay or personal statement. *Application deadlines:* rolling (freshmen), rolling (transfers). *Notification:* continuous (freshmen), continuous (transfers).

Freshman Application Contact Admissions Office, Penn State Worthington Scranton, 120 Ridge View Drive, Dunmore, PA 18512-1699. *Phone:* 570-963-2500. *Fax:* 570-963-2524. *E-mail:* wsadmissions@psu.edu. *Website:* http://www.sn.psu.edu/.

Penn State York

York, Pennsylvania

- **State-related** primarily 2-year, founded 1926, part of Pennsylvania State University
- **Suburban** campus
- **Coed,** 1,155 undergraduate students, 72% full-time, 43% women, 57% men

Undergraduates 829 full-time, 326 part-time. 10% are from out of state; 9% Black or African American, non-Hispanic/Latino; 7% Hispanic/Latino; 5% Asian, non-Hispanic/Latino; 0.1% American Indian or Alaska Native, non-Hispanic/Latino; 3% Two or more races, non-Hispanic/Latino; 2% Race/ethnicity unknown; 5% international; 4% transferred in. *Retention:* 76% of full-time freshmen returned.

Freshmen *Admission:* 1,329 applied, 1,123 admitted, 300 enrolled. *Average high school GPA:* 2.95. *Test scores:* SAT critical reading scores over 500: 43%; SAT math scores over 500: 54%; SAT writing scores over 500: 33%; ACT scores over 18: 91%; SAT critical reading scores over 600: 10%; SAT math scores over 600: 18%; SAT writing scores over 600: 6%; ACT scores over 24: 36%; SAT critical reading scores over 700: 2%; SAT math scores over 700: 3%.

Faculty *Total:* 103, 50% full-time, 47% with terminal degrees. *Student/faculty ratio:* 14:1.

Majors Accounting; acting; actuarial science; adult and continuing education administration; advertising; aerospace, aeronautical and astronautical/space engineering; African American/Black studies; agribusiness; agricultural and extension education; agricultural business and management related; agricultural engineering; agricultural mechanization; agriculture; agronomy and crop science; American studies; animal sciences; animal sciences related; anthropology; applied economics; archeology; architectural engineering; art; art history, criticism and conservation; art teacher education; Asian studies (East); astronomy; atmospheric sciences and meteorology; biochemistry; bioengineering and biomedical engineering; biological and biomedical sciences related; biological and physical sciences; biology/biological sciences; biology/biotechnology laboratory technician; biomedical technology; business administration and management; business/commerce; business/managerial economics; chemical engineering; chemistry; civil engineering; classics and classical languages; communication and journalism related; communication sciences and disorders; comparative literature; computer and information sciences; computer engineering; criminal justice/law enforcement administration; economics; electrical and electronics engineering; electrical, electronic and communications engineering technology; elementary education; engineering science; English; environmental/environmental health engineering; film/cinema/video studies; finance; food science; foreign language teacher education; forest sciences and biology; forest technology; French; geography; geological and earth sciences/geosciences related; geology/earth science; German; graphic design; health/health-care administration; history; horticultural science; hospitality administration related; human development and family studies; human nutrition; industrial engineering; industrial technology; information science/studies; international relations and affairs; Italian; Japanese; Jewish/Judaic studies; journalism; kinesiology and exercise science; labor and industrial relations; landscaping and groundskeeping; Latin American studies; liberal arts and sciences/liberal studies; logistics, materials, and supply chain management; management information systems; manufacturing engineering; marketing/marketing management; materials science; mathematics; mechanical engineering; mechanical engineering/mechanical technology; medical microbiology and bacteriology; medieval and Renaissance studies; metallurgi-

cal technology; mining and mineral engineering; music; natural resources and conservation related; natural resources/conservation; nuclear engineering; organizational behavior; parks, recreation and leisure facilities management; petroleum engineering; philosophy; physics; political science and government; premedical studies; psychology; registered nursing/registered nurse; rehabilitation and therapeutic professions related; religious studies; Russian; secondary education; sociology; soil science and agronomy; Spanish; special education; speech communication and rhetoric; statistics; telecommunications technology; theater design and technology; toxicology; turf and turfgrass management; visual and performing arts; women's studies.

Academics *Calendar:* semesters. *Degrees:* certificates, associate, bachelor's, and master's (also offers up to 2 years of most bachelor's degree programs offered at University Park campus). *Special study options:* adult/continuing education programs.

Student Life *Housing:* college housing not available.

Athletics Member NJCAA.

Standardized Tests *Required:* SAT or ACT (for admission).

Costs (2013–14) *Tuition:* state resident $12,474 full-time, $504 per credit hour part-time; nonresident $19,030 full-time, $793 per credit hour part-time. Full-time tuition and fees vary according to course level, degree level, location, program, and student level. Part-time tuition and fees vary according to course level, course load, degree level, location, program, and student level. *Required fees:* $764 full-time. *Payment plans:* installment, deferred payment. *Waivers:* employees or children of employees.

Financial Aid Of all full-time matriculated undergraduates who enrolled in 2011, 695 applied for aid, 570 were judged to have need, 37 had their need fully met. In 2011, 61 non-need-based awards were made. *Average percent of need met:* 61%. *Average financial aid package:* $9745. *Average need-based loan:* $3912. *Average need-based gift aid:* $6385. *Average non-need-based aid:* $2555. *Average indebtedness upon graduation:* $35,100.

Applying *Options:* electronic application, early admission, deferred entrance. *Application fee:* $50. *Required:* high school transcript. *Required for some:* interview. *Recommended:* essay or personal statement. *Application deadlines:* rolling (freshmen), rolling (transfers). *Notification:* continuous (freshmen), continuous (transfers).

Freshman Application Contact Admissions Office, Penn State York, 1031 Edgecomb Avenue, York, PA 17403. *Phone:* 717-771-4040. *Toll-free phone:* 800-778-6227. *Fax:* 717-771-4005. *E-mail:* ykadmission@psu.edu. *Website:* http://www.yk.psu.edu/.

Pennsylvania Highlands Community College

Johnstown, Pennsylvania

Freshman Application Contact Mr. Jeff Maul, Admissions Officer, Pennsylvania Highlands Community College, 101 Community College Way, Johnstown, PA 15904. *Phone:* 814-262-6431. *E-mail:* jmaul@pennhighlands.edu. *Website:* http://www.pennhighlands.edu/.

Pennsylvania Institute of Technology

Media, Pennsylvania

Freshman Application Contact Ms. Angela Cassetta, Dean of Enrollment Management, Pennsylvania Institute of Technology, 800 Manchester Avenue, Media, PA 19063-4036. *Phone:* 610-892-1550 Ext. 1553. *Toll-free phone:* 800-422-0025. *Fax:* 610-892-1510. *E-mail:* info@pit.edu. *Website:* http://www.pit.edu/.

Pennsylvania School of Business

Allentown, Pennsylvania

Freshman Application Contact Mr. Bill Barber, Director, Pennsylvania School of Business, 406 West Hamilton Street, Allentown, PA 18101. *Phone:* 610-841-3333. *Fax:* 610-841-3334. *E-mail:* wbarber@pennschoolofbusiness.edu. *Website:* http://www.psb.edu/.

Pittsburgh Institute of Aeronautics

Pittsburgh, Pennsylvania

Freshman Application Contact Mr. Vincent J. Mezza, Director of Admissions, Pittsburgh Institute of Aeronautics, PO Box 10897, Pittsburgh, PA 15236-0897. *Phone:* 412-346-2100. *Toll-free phone:* 800-444-1440. *Fax:* 412-466-5013. *E-mail:* admissions@pia.edu. *Website:* http://www.pia.edu/.

Pittsburgh Institute of Mortuary Science, Incorporated

Pittsburgh, Pennsylvania

Freshman Application Contact Ms. Karen Rocco, Registrar, Pittsburgh Institute of Mortuary Science, Incorporated, 5808 Baum Boulevard, Pittsburgh, PA 15206-3706. *Phone:* 412-362-8500 Ext. 105. *Fax:* 412-362-1684. *E-mail:* pims5808@aol.com.
Website: http://www.pims.edu/.

Pittsburgh Technical Institute

Oakdale, Pennsylvania

- **Proprietary** 2-year, founded 1946
- **Suburban** 180-acre campus with easy access to Pittsburgh
- **Coed,** 1,792 undergraduate students, 100% full-time, 43% women, 57% men
- 84% of applicants were admitted

Undergraduates 1,792 full-time. Students come from 15 states and territories; 18% are from out of state; 9% Black or African American, non-Hispanic/Latino; 1% Hispanic/Latino; 0.6% Asian, non-Hispanic/Latino; 0.2% American Indian or Alaska Native, non-Hispanic/Latino; 3% Two or more races, non-Hispanic/Latino; 21% Race/ethnicity unknown; 13% transferred in; 40% live on campus. *Retention:* 63% of full-time freshmen returned.
Freshmen *Admission:* 2,126 applied, 1,777 admitted, 686 enrolled. *Average high school GPA:* 2.25.
Faculty *Total:* 116, 56% full-time. *Student/faculty ratio:* 28:1.
Majors Architectural drafting and CAD/CADD; business administration and management; computer graphics; computer programming; computer technology/computer systems technology; electrical, electronic and communications engineering technology; electrical/electronics equipment installation and repair; homeland security, law enforcement, firefighting and protective services related; hotel/motel administration; medical/health management and clinical assistant; medical office assistant; surgical technology; web page, digital/multimedia and information resources design.
Academics *Calendar:* quarters. *Degree:* certificates and associate. *Special study options:* academic remediation for entering students, advanced placement credit, cooperative education, distance learning, double majors, internships, services for LD students.
Library Library Resource Center with 10,776 titles, 128 serial subscriptions, 2,036 audiovisual materials, an OPAC.
Student Life *Housing Options:* coed. Campus housing is university owned and leased by the school. Freshman campus housing is guaranteed. *Activities and Organizations:* drama/theater group, choral group, American Society of Travel Agents (ASTA), MEDICS Club, Alpha Beta Gamma (ABG), Drama Club, Direct Connect. *Campus security:* 24-hour emergency response devices and patrols, controlled dormitory access. *Student services:* personal/psychological counseling.
Athletics *Intramural sports:* basketball M/W, soccer M/W, softball M/W, ultimate Frisbee M/W, volleyball M/W.
Costs (2013–14) *Comprehensive fee:* $23,777 includes full-time tuition ($15,524) and room and board ($8253). Full-time tuition and fees vary according to course load and program. No tuition increase for student's term of enrollment. *Room and board:* Room and board charges vary according to housing facility. *Payment plans:* installment, deferred payment. *Waivers:* children of alumni and employees or children of employees.
Applying *Options:* electronic application, deferred entrance. *Required:* high school transcript. *Required for some:* essay or personal statement, certain programs require a criminal background check; some programs require applicants to be in top 50-80% of class; Practical Nursing requires entrance exam. *Recommended:* interview. *Application deadlines:* rolling (freshmen), rolling (out-of-state freshmen), rolling (transfers). *Notification:* continuous (freshmen), continuous (out-of-state freshmen), continuous (transfers).
Freshman Application Contact Ms. Nancy Goodlin, Admissions Office Assistant, Pittsburgh Technical Institute, 1111 McKee Road, Oakdale, PA 15071. *Phone:* 412-809-5100. *Toll-free phone:* 800-784-9675. *Fax:* 412-809-5351. *E-mail:* goodlin.nancy@pti.edu.
Website: http://www.pti.edu/.

Prism Career Institute

Upper Darby, Pennsylvania

Director of Admissions Ms. Dina Gentile, Director, Prism Career Institute, 6800 Market Street, Upper Darby, PA 19082. *Phone:* 610-789-6700. *Toll-free phone:* 800-571-2213. *Fax:* 610-789-5208. *E-mail:* dgentile@pjaschool.com.
Website: http://www.prismcareerinstitute.edu/.

Reading Area Community College

Reading, Pennsylvania

Director of Admissions Ms. Maria Mitchell, Associate Vice President of Enrollment Management and Student Services, Reading Area Community College, PO Box 1706, Reading, PA 19603-1706. *Phone:* 610-607-6224. *E-mail:* mmitchell@racc.edu.
Website: http://www.racc.edu/.

The Restaurant School at Walnut Hill College

Philadelphia, Pennsylvania

- **Proprietary** primarily 2-year, founded 1974
- **Urban** 2-acre campus
- **Coed**
- 97% of applicants were admitted

Undergraduates 402 full-time. Students come from 4 other countries; 29% are from out of state; 14% Black or African American, non-Hispanic/Latino; 4% Hispanic/Latino; 2% Asian, non-Hispanic/Latino; 1% Two or more races, non-Hispanic/Latino; 32% Race/ethnicity unknown; 10% transferred in.
Faculty *Student/faculty ratio:* 22:1.
Academics *Calendar:* quarters. *Degrees:* associate and bachelor's. *Special study options:* internships, part-time degree program.
Student Life *Campus security:* 24-hour emergency response devices and patrols, student patrols, controlled dormitory access.
Standardized Tests *Recommended:* SAT or ACT (for admission).
Costs (2012–13) *One-time required fee:* $200. *Tuition:* $19,050 full-time. *Required fees:* $3675 full-time. *Room only:* $4600. Room and board charges vary according to housing facility. *Payment plans:* installment, deferred payment.
Applying *Options:* electronic application, early admission, early decision, deferred entrance. *Application fee:* $50. *Required:* essay or personal statement, high school transcript, 2 letters of recommendation, interview. *Required for some:* entrance exam. *Recommended:* minimum 2.0 GPA.
Freshman Application Contact Miss Toni Morelli, Director of Admissions, The Restaurant School at Walnut Hill College, 4207 Walnut Street, Philadelphia, PA 19104-3518. *Phone:* 267-295-2353. *Fax:* 215-222-4219. *E-mail:* tmorelli@walnuthillcollege.edu.
Website: http://www.walnuthillcollege.edu/.

Rosedale Technical Institute

Pittsburgh, Pennsylvania

Freshman Application Contact Ms. Debbie Bier, Director of Admissions, Rosedale Technical Institute, 215 Beecham Drive, Suite 2, Pittsburgh, PA 15205-9791. *Phone:* 412-521-6200. *Toll-free phone:* 800-521-6262. *Fax:* 412-521-2520. *E-mail:* admissions@rosedaletech.org.
Website: http://www.rosedaletech.org/.

Sanford-Brown Institute–Pittsburgh

Pittsburgh, Pennsylvania

Director of Admissions Mr. Bruce E. Jones, Director of Admission, Sanford-Brown Institute–Pittsburgh, 421 Seventh Avenue, Pittsburgh, PA 15219-1907. *Phone:* 412-281-7083 Ext. 114. *Toll-free phone:* 888-270-6333.
Website: http://www.sanfordbrown.edu/.

South Hills School of Business & Technology

Altoona, Pennsylvania

Freshman Application Contact Ms. Holly J. Emerick, Director of Admissions, South Hills School of Business & Technology, 508 58th Street, Altoona, PA 16602. *Phone:* 814-944-6134. *Fax:* 814-944-4684. *E-mail:* hemerick@southhills.edu.
Website: http://www.southhills.edu/.

South Hills School of Business & Technology

State College, Pennsylvania

Freshman Application Contact Ms. Diane M. Brown, Director of Admissions, South Hills School of Business & Technology, 480 Waupelani Drive, State College, PA 16801-4516. *Phone:* 814-234-7755 Ext. 2020. *Toll-free phone:* 888-282-7427. *Fax:* 814-234-0926. *E-mail:* admissions@

southhills.edu.
Website: http://www.southhills.edu/.

Thaddeus Stevens College of Technology

Lancaster, Pennsylvania

Director of Admissions Ms. Erin Kate Nelsen, Director of Enrollment, Thaddeus Stevens College of Technology, 750 East King Street, Lancaster, PA 17602-3198. *Phone:* 717-299-7772. *Toll-free phone:* 800-842-3832. *Website:* http://www.stevenscollege.edu/.

Triangle Tech–Greensburg School

Greensburg, Pennsylvania

Freshman Application Contact Mr. John Mazzarese, Vice President of Admissions, Triangle Tech–Greensburg School, 222 East Pittsburgh Street, Greensburg, PA 15601. *Phone:* 412-359-1000. *Toll-free phone:* 800-874-8324. *Website:* http://www.triangle-tech.edu/.

Triangle Tech Inc–Bethlehem

Bethlehem, Pennsylvania

Freshman Application Contact Triangle Tech Inc–Bethlehem, Lehigh Valley Industrial Park IV, 31 South Commerce Way, Bethlehem, PA 18017. *Website:* http://www.triangle-tech.edu/.

Triangle Tech, Inc.–DuBois School

DuBois, Pennsylvania

Freshman Application Contact Terry Kucic, Director of Admissions, Triangle Tech, Inc.–DuBois School, PO Box 551, DuBois, PA 15801. *Phone:* 814-371-2090. *Toll-free phone:* 800-874-8324. *Fax:* 814-371-9227. *E-mail:* tkucic@triangle-tech.com. *Website:* http://www.triangle-tech.edu/.

Triangle Tech, Inc.–Erie School

Erie, Pennsylvania

Freshman Application Contact Admissions Representative, Triangle Tech, Inc.–Erie School, 2000 Liberty Street, Erie, PA 16502-2594. *Phone:* 814-453-6016. *Toll-free phone:* 800-874-8324 (in-state); 800-TRI-TECH (out-of-state). *Website:* http://www.triangle-tech.edu/.

Triangle Tech, Inc.–Pittsburgh School

Pittsburgh, Pennsylvania

Freshman Application Contact Director of Admissions, Triangle Tech, Inc.–Pittsburgh School, 1940 Perrysville Avenue, Pittsburgh, PA 15214-3897. *Phone:* 412-359-1000. *Toll-free phone:* 800-874-8324. *Fax:* 412-359-1012. *E-mail:* info@triangle-tech.edu. *Website:* http://www.triangle-tech.edu/.

Triangle Tech, Inc.–Sunbury School

Sunbury, Pennsylvania

Freshman Application Contact Triangle Tech, Inc.–Sunbury School, 191 Performance Road, Sunbury, PA 17801. *Phone:* 412-359-1000. *Website:* http://www.triangle-tech.edu/.

University of Pittsburgh at Titusville

Titusville, Pennsylvania

- **State-related** 2-year, founded 1963, part of University of Pittsburgh System
- **Small-town** 10-acre campus
- **Endowment** $850,000
- **Coed,** 388 undergraduate students, 81% full-time, 65% women, 35% men

Undergraduates 313 full-time, 75 part-time. Students come from 15 states and territories; 8% are from out of state; 14% Black or African American, non-Hispanic/Latino; 4% Hispanic/Latino; 2% Asian, non-Hispanic/Latino; 2% Two or more races, non-Hispanic/Latino; 2% Race/ethnicity unknown; 4% transferred in; 42% live on campus.

Freshmen *Admission:* 160 enrolled. *Average high school GPA:* 3.1. *Test scores:* SAT critical reading scores over 500: 22%; SAT math scores over 500: 29%; SAT writing scores over 500: 23%; ACT scores over 18: 69%; SAT critical reading scores over 600: 5%; SAT math scores over 600: 4%; SAT writing scores over 600: 4%; ACT scores over 24: 7%.

Faculty *Total:* 59, 42% full-time. *Student/faculty ratio:* 15:1.

Majors Accounting; biology/biological sciences; business/commerce; criminal justice/law enforcement administration; history related; human services; information technology; liberal arts and sciences/liberal studies; management information systems; natural sciences; physical therapy technology; psychology related; registered nursing/registered nurse.

Academics *Calendar:* semesters. *Degree:* associate. *Special study options:* academic remediation for entering students, advanced placement credit, distance learning, internships, part-time degree program, study abroad, summer session for credit.

Library Haskell Memorial Library with 49,256 titles, 126 serial subscriptions, an OPAC.

Student Life *Housing:* on-campus residence required through sophomore year. *Options:* coed, disabled students. Campus housing is university owned. Freshman campus housing is guaranteed. *Activities and Organizations:* drama/theater group, choral group, Phi Theta Kappa, BSU, SAB, Dining Club, Diversity Club. *Campus security:* 24-hour emergency response devices and patrols, late-night transport/escort service, controlled dormitory access. *Student services:* health clinic.

Athletics Member NJCAA. *Intercollegiate sports:* basketball M/W, cheerleading M/W. *Intramural sports:* badminton M/W, basketball M/W, bowling M/W, football M/W, golf M/W, racquetball M/W, softball M/W, table tennis M/W, tennis M/W, volleyball M/W, weight lifting M/W.

Standardized Tests *Required:* SAT or ACT (for admission).

Costs (2013–14) *Tuition:* state resident $10,544 full-time, $439 per credit hour part-time; nonresident $19,918 full-time, $829 per credit hour part-time. Full-time tuition and fees vary according to program. Part-time tuition and fees vary according to program. *Required fees:* $780 full-time. *Room and board:* $9364; room only: $4982. Room and board charges vary according to board plan. *Payment plan:* installment.

Financial Aid Of all full-time matriculated undergraduates who enrolled in 2009, 429 applied for aid, 408 were judged to have need, 23 had their need fully met. In 2009, 10 non-need-based awards were made. *Average percent of need met:* 80%. *Average financial aid package:* $15,305. *Average need-based loan:* $9451. *Average need-based gift aid:* $1992. *Average non-need-based aid:* $39,059.

Applying *Required:* high school transcript, minimum 2.0 GPA. *Required for some:* essay or personal statement, 3 letters of recommendation. *Recommended:* interview.

Freshman Application Contact Mr. Robert J. Wyant, Director of Admissions, University of Pittsburgh at Titusville, 504 E Main St, Titusville, PA 16354. *Phone:* 814-827-4457. *Toll-free phone:* 888-878-0462. *Fax:* 814-827-4519. *E-mail:* wyant@pitt.edu. *Website:* http://www.upt.pitt.edu/.

Valley Forge Military College

Wayne, Pennsylvania

Freshman Application Contact Maj. Greg Potts, Dean of Enrollment Management, Valley Forge Military College, 1001 Eagle Road, Wayne, PA 19087-3695. *Phone:* 610-989-1300. *Toll-free phone:* 800-234-8362. *Fax:* 610-688-1545. *E-mail:* admissions@vfmac.edu. *Website:* http://www.vfmac.edu/.

Vet Tech Institute

Pittsburgh, Pennsylvania

- **Private** 2-year, founded 1958
- **Urban** campus
- **Coed,** 340 undergraduate students
- 62% of applicants were admitted

Freshmen *Admission:* 541 applied, 335 admitted.

Majors Veterinary/animal health technology.

Academics *Calendar:* quarters. *Degree:* associate. *Special study options:* accelerated degree program, internships, summer session for credit.

Freshman Application Contact Admissions Office, Vet Tech Institute, 125 7th Street, Pittsburgh, PA 15222-3400. *Phone:* 412-391-7021. *Toll-free phone:* 800-570-0693. *Website:* http://www.vettechinstitute.edu/.

Westmoreland County Community College

Youngwood, Pennsylvania

- **County-supported** 2-year, founded 1970
- **Rural** 85-acre campus with easy access to Pittsburgh
- **Endowment** $488,371
- **Coed**, 6,571 undergraduate students, 45% full-time, 65% women, 35% men

Undergraduates 2,974 full-time, 3,597 part-time. Students come from 5 states and territories; 0.1% are from out of state; 4% Black or African American, non-Hispanic/Latino; 1% Hispanic/Latino; 0.7% Asian, non-Hispanic/Latino; 0.1% Native Hawaiian or other Pacific Islander, non-Hispanic/Latino; 0.2% American Indian or Alaska Native, non-Hispanic/Latino; 1% Two or more races, non-Hispanic/Latino; 2% transferred in. *Retention:* 56% of full-time freshmen returned.

Freshmen *Admission:* 2,778 applied, 2,778 admitted, 1,681 enrolled.

Faculty *Total:* 521, 16% full-time. *Student/faculty ratio:* 18:1.

Majors Accounting technology and bookkeeping; administrative assistant and secretarial science; applied horticulture/horticulture operations; architectural drafting and CAD/CADD; baking and pastry arts; banking and financial support services; biology/biotechnology laboratory technician; business administration and management; business/commerce; casino management; chemical technology; child-care provision; clinical/medical laboratory assistant; communications systems installation and repair technology; computer and information systems security; computer numerically controlled (CNC) machinist technology; computer programming; computer programming (specific applications); computer support specialist; computer systems networking and telecommunications; corrections; criminal justice/police science; criminal justice/safety; culinary arts; data entry/microcomputer applications; data processing and data processing technology; dental assisting; dental hygiene; diagnostic medical sonography and ultrasound technology; dietetic technology; early childhood education; electrical, electronic and communications engineering technology; family and community services; fire prevention and safety technology; floriculture/floristry management; food service and dining room management; graphic design; health and medical administrative services related; health information/medical records technology; heating, air conditioning, ventilation and refrigeration maintenance technology; homeland security, law enforcement, firefighting and protective services related; hotel/motel administration; human resources management; industrial mechanics and maintenance technology; legal assistant/paralegal; liberal arts and sciences/liberal studies; library and information science; licensed practical/vocational nurse training; machine tool technology; manufacturing engineering technology; mechanical drafting and CAD/CADD; mechanical engineering/mechanical technology; mechatronics, robotics, and automation engineering; medical/clinical assistant; medical insurance coding; medical office assistant; medical transcription; network and system administration; phlebotomy technology; physical science technologies related; pre-engineering; radio and television broadcasting technology; radiologic technology/science; real estate; registered nursing/registered nurse; restaurant, culinary, and catering management; sales, distribution, and marketing operations; special education–elementary school; tourism and travel services management; turf and turfgrass management; web page, digital/multimedia and information resources design; welding technology.

Academics *Calendar:* semesters. *Degree:* certificates, diplomas, and associate. *Special study options:* academic remediation for entering students, adult/continuing education programs, advanced placement credit, cooperative education, distance learning, double majors, English as a second language, honors programs, independent study, internships, off-campus study, part-time degree program, services for LD students, summer session for credit.

Library Westmoreland County Community College Learning Resources Center with 64,000 titles, 250 serial subscriptions, 3,500 audiovisual materials, an OPAC, a Web page.

Student Life *Housing:* college housing not available. *Activities and Organizations:* drama/theater group, choral group, Phi Theta Kappa, Sigma Alpha Pi Leadership Society, Criminal Justice Fraternity, Gay Straight Alliance, SADAA/SADHA. *Campus security:* 24-hour emergency response devices and patrols, late-night transport/escort service. *Student services:* personal/psychological counseling.

Athletics Member NJCAA. *Intercollegiate sports:* baseball M, basketball M/W, bowling M/W, cross-country running M/W, golf M/W, soccer M/W, softball W, volleyball W. *Intramural sports:* basketball M/W, bowling M/W, golf M/W, skiing (downhill) M/W, volleyball M/W, weight lifting M/W.

Costs (2012–13) *Tuition:* area resident $2700 full-time, $90 per credit part-time; state resident $5400 full-time, $180 per credit part-time; nonresident $8100 full-time, $270 per credit part-time. Full-time tuition and fees vary according to course load. Part-time tuition and fees vary according to course load. *Required fees:* $630 full-time, $21 per credit part-time. *Payment plans:* installment, deferred payment. *Waivers:* senior citizens and employees or children of employees.

Applying *Options:* electronic application, early admission. *Application fee:* $15. *Application deadlines:* rolling (freshmen), rolling (transfers). *Notification:* continuous (freshmen), continuous (transfers).

Freshman Application Contact Mr. Andrew Colosimo, Admissions Coordinator, Westmoreland County Community College, 145 Pavillon Lane, Youngwood, PA 15697. *Phone:* 724-925-4064. *Toll-free phone:* 800-262-2103. *Fax:* 724-925-4292. *E-mail:* admission@wccc.edu. *Website:* http://www.wccc.edu/.

The Williamson Free School of Mechanical Trades

Media, Pennsylvania

Freshman Application Contact Mr. Jay Merillat, Dean of Enrollments, The Williamson Free School of Mechanical Trades, 106 South New Middletown Road, Media, PA 19063. *Phone:* 610-566-1776 Ext. 235. *E-mail:* jmerillat@williamson.edu. *Website:* http://www.williamson.edu/.

WyoTech Blairsville

Blairsville, Pennsylvania

Freshman Application Contact Mr. Tim Smyers, WyoTech Blairsville, 500 Innovation Drive, Blairsville, PA 15717. *Phone:* 724-459-2311. *Toll-free phone:* 888-577-7559. *Fax:* 724-459-6499. *E-mail:* tsmyers@wyotech.edu. *Website:* http://www.wyotech.edu/.

Yorktowne Business Institute

York, Pennsylvania

Director of Admissions Director of Admissions, Yorktowne Business Institute, West Seventh Avenue, York, PA 17404. *Phone:* 717-846-5000. *Toll-free phone:* 800-840-1004. *Website:* http://www.ybi.edu/.

YTI Career Institute–Altoona

Altoona, Pennsylvania

Admissions Office Contact YTI Career Institute–Altoona, 2900 Fairway Drive, Altoona, PA 16602. *Website:* http://www.yti.edu/.

YTI Career Institute–Capital Region

Mechanicsburg, Pennsylvania

Admissions Office Contact YTI Career Institute–Capital Region, 401 East Winding Hill Road, Mechanicsburg, PA 17055. *Website:* http://www.yti.edu/.

YTI Career Institute–York

York, Pennsylvania

- **Private** 2-year, founded 1967, part of York Technical Institute, LLC
- **Suburban** campus with easy access to Harrisburg
- **Coed**

Undergraduates 680 full-time. Students come from 9 states and territories; 2% are from out of state; 9% Black or African American, non-Hispanic/Latino; 9% Hispanic/Latino; 1% Asian, non-Hispanic/Latino; 0.3% Native Hawaiian or other Pacific Islander, non-Hispanic/Latino; 0.1% American Indian or Alaska Native, non-Hispanic/Latino; 3% Two or more races, non-Hispanic/Latino.

Faculty *Student/faculty ratio:* 15:1.

Academics *Calendar:* continuous. *Degree:* diplomas and associate. *Special study options:* academic remediation for entering students, advanced placement credit, cooperative education, internships.

Standardized Tests *Required:* ACT COMPASS (for admission).

Costs (2012–13) *One-time required fee:* $50. *Tuition:* $15,000 full-time. Full-time tuition and fees vary according to location and program.

Applying *Application fee:* $50. *Required:* high school transcript, minimum 2.0 GPA, interview. *Recommended:* admissions test.

Freshman Application Contact YTI Career Institute–York, 1405 Williams Road, York, PA 17402-9017. *Phone:* 717-757-1100 Ext. 318. *Toll-free phone:* 800-557-6335. *Website:* http://www.yti.edu/.

PUERTO RICO

The Center of Cinematography, Arts and Television
Bayamon, Puerto Rico

Admissions Office Contact The Center of Cinematography, Arts and Television, 51 Dr. Veve Street, Degetau Street Corner, Bayamón, PR 00960. *Website:* http://ccatmiami.com/.

Centro de Estudios Multidisciplinarios
Rio Piedras, Puerto Rico

Director of Admissions Admissions Department, Centro de Estudios Multidisciplinarios, Calle 13 #1206, Ext. San Agustin, Rio Piedras, PR 00926. *Phone:* 787-765-4210 Ext. 115. *Toll-free phone:* 877-779-CDEM. *Website:* http://www.cempr.edu/.

Huertas Junior College
Caguas, Puerto Rico

Director of Admissions Mrs. Barbara Hassim López, Director of Admissions, Huertas Junior College, PO Box 8429, Caguas, PR 00726. *Phone:* 787-743-1242. *Fax:* 787-743-0203. *E-mail:* huertas@huertas.org. *Website:* http://www.huertas.edu/.

Humacao Community College
Humacao, Puerto Rico

Director of Admissions Ms. Xiomara Sanchez, Director of Admissions, Humacao Community College, PO Box 9139, Humacao, PR 00792. *Phone:* 787-852-2525. *Website:* http://www.hccpr.edu/.

Instituto Comercial de Puerto Rico Junior College
San Juan, Puerto Rico

Freshman Application Contact Admissions Office, Instituto Comercial de Puerto Rico Junior College, 558 Munoz Rivera Avenue, PO Box 190304, San Juan, PR 00919-0304. *Phone:* 787-753-6335. *Website:* http://www.icprjc.edu/.

Ramírez College of Business and Technology
San Juan, Puerto Rico

Director of Admissions Mr. Arnaldo Castro, Director of Admissions, Ramírez College of Business and Technology, Avenue Ponce de Leon #70, San Juan, PR 00918. *Phone:* 787-763-3120. *E-mail:* ramirezcollege@prtc.net. *Website:* http://www.galeon.com/ramirezcollege/.

RHODE ISLAND

Community College of Rhode Island
Warwick, Rhode Island

- **State-supported** 2-year, founded 1964
- **Urban** 205-acre campus with easy access to Boston
- **Coed,** 17,884 undergraduate students, 33% full-time, 60% women, 40% men

Undergraduates 5,857 full-time, 12,027 part-time. Students come from 17 states and territories; 4% are from out of state; 9% Black or African American, non-Hispanic/Latino; 17% Hispanic/Latino; 3% Asian, non-Hispanic/Latino; 0.7% American Indian or Alaska Native, non-Hispanic/Latino; 1% Two or more races, non-Hispanic/Latino; 6% Race/ethnicity unknown; 0.1% international.
Freshmen *Admission:* 6,655 applied, 6,552 admitted, 3,708 enrolled.
Faculty *Total:* 859, 39% full-time. *Student/faculty ratio:* 20:1.

Majors Accounting; administrative assistant and secretarial science; adult development and aging; art; banking and financial support services; biological and physical sciences; business administration and management; business/commerce; chemical technology; clinical/medical laboratory technology; computer and information sciences; computer engineering technology; computer programming (specific applications); computer systems networking and telecommunications; criminal justice/police science; crisis/emergency/disaster management; customer service management; dental hygiene; diagnostic medical sonography and ultrasound technology; dramatic/theater arts; electromechanical technology; engineering; fire science/firefighting; general studies; histologic technician; jazz/jazz studies; kindergarten/preschool education; legal administrative assistant/secretary; legal assistant/paralegal; liberal arts and sciences/liberal studies; licensed practical/vocational nurse training; marketing/marketing management; massage therapy; medical administrative assistant and medical secretary; mental health counseling; music; occupational therapist assistant; opticianry; physical therapy technology; radiologic technology/science; registered nursing/registered nurse; respiratory care therapy; social work; special education; substance abuse/addiction counseling; surveying engineering; web/multimedia management and webmaster.
Academics *Calendar:* semesters. *Degree:* certificates, diplomas, and associate. *Special study options:* academic remediation for entering students, adult/continuing education programs, advanced placement credit, cooperative education, distance learning, double majors, English as a second language, external degree program, honors programs, independent study, internships, off-campus study, part-time degree program, services for LD students, study abroad, summer session for credit. *ROTC:* Army (c).
Library Community College of Rhode Island Learning Resources Center plus 3 others with an OPAC, a Web page.
Student Life *Housing:* college housing not available. *Activities and Organizations:* drama/theater group, student-run newspaper, choral group, Distributive Education Clubs of America, Theater group - Players, Skills USA, Phi Theta Kappa, student government. *Campus security:* 24-hour emergency response devices and patrols. *Student services:* health clinic, personal/psychological counseling.
Athletics Member NJCAA. *Intercollegiate sports:* baseball M(s), basketball M(s)/W(s), golf M/W, soccer M(s)/W(s), softball W(s), tennis M/W, track and field M/W, volleyball W(s). *Intramural sports:* basketball M/W, volleyball M/W.
Costs (2012–13) *Tuition:* state resident $3624 full-time, $165 per credit hour part-time; nonresident $10,256 full-time, $490 per semester hour part-time. Full-time tuition and fees vary according to program. Part-time tuition and fees vary according to course load and program. *Required fees:* $326 full-time, $12 per credit hour part-time, $30 per term part-time. *Payment plans:* installment, deferred payment. *Waivers:* senior citizens and employees or children of employees.
Financial Aid Of all full-time matriculated undergraduates who enrolled in 2011, 500 Federal Work-Study jobs (averaging $2500).
Applying *Options:* deferred entrance. *Application fee:* $20. *Application deadlines:* rolling (freshmen), rolling (transfers). *Notification:* continuous (freshmen).
Freshman Application Contact Community College of Rhode Island, Flanagan Campus, 1762 Louisquisset Pike, Lincoln, RI 02865-4585. *Phone:* 401-333-7490. *Fax:* 401-333-7122. *E-mail:* webadmission@ccri.edu. *Website:* http://www.ccri.edu/.

SOUTH CAROLINA

Aiken Technical College
Aiken, South Carolina

- **State and locally supported** 2-year, founded 1972, part of South Carolina State Board for Technical and Comprehensive Education
- **Rural** 88-acre campus
- **Endowment** $4.1 million
- **Coed**

Undergraduates 1,315 full-time, 1,730 part-time. 10% are from out of state; 33% Black or African American, non-Hispanic/Latino; 2% Hispanic/Latino; 0.6% Asian, non-Hispanic/Latino; 0.3% Native Hawaiian or other Pacific Islander, non-Hispanic/Latino; 0.7% American Indian or Alaska Native, non-Hispanic/Latino; 0.7% Two or more races, non-Hispanic/Latino; 1% Race/ethnicity unknown; 11% transferred in. *Retention:* 23% of full-time freshmen returned.
Faculty *Student/faculty ratio:* 31:1.
Academics *Calendar:* semesters. *Degree:* certificates, diplomas, and associate. *Special study options:* academic remediation for entering students, advanced placement credit, cooperative education, internships, off-campus

study, part-time degree program, services for LD students, summer session for credit.

Student Life *Campus security:* 24-hour emergency response devices and patrols, late-night transport/escort service.

Athletics Member NJCAA.

Costs (2012–13) *Tuition:* area resident $3576 full-time, $149 per credit hour part-time; state resident $3936 full-time, $164 per credit hour part-time; nonresident $9600 full-time, $400 per credit hour part-time. Full-time tuition and fees vary according to course load and reciprocity agreements. Part-time tuition and fees vary according to course load and reciprocity agreements. *Required fees:* $290 full-time, $5 per credit hour part-time, $85 per term part-time. *Payment plans:* installment, deferred payment.

Financial Aid Of all full-time matriculated undergraduates who enrolled in 2011, 48 Federal Work-Study jobs (averaging $3000).

Applying *Options:* electronic application, deferred entrance. *Recommended:* high school transcript.

Freshman Application Contact Ms. Lisa Sommers, Aiken Technical College, PO Drawer 696, Aiken, SC 29802. *Phone:* 803-593-9231 Ext. 1584. *Fax:* 803-593-6526. *E-mail:* sommersl@atc.edu. *Website:* http://www.atc.edu/.

Brown Mackie College–Greenville

Greenville, South Carolina

Freshman Application Contact Brown Mackie College–Greenville, Two Liberty Square, 75 Beattie Place, Suite 100, Greenville, SC 29601. *Phone:* 864-239-5300. *Toll-free phone:* 877-479-8465. *Website:* http://www.brownmackie.edu/greenville/.

See display below and page 362 for the College Close-Up.

Central Carolina Technical College

Sumter, South Carolina

- **State-supported** 2-year, founded 1963, part of South Carolina State Board for Technical and Comprehensive Education
- **Small-town** 70-acre campus with easy access to Columbia, SC
- **Endowment** $1.4 million
- **Coed**

Undergraduates 1,607 full-time, 2,915 part-time. 1% are from out of state; 48% Black or African American, non-Hispanic/Latino; 2% Hispanic/Latino; 0.8% Asian, non-Hispanic/Latino; 0.1% American Indian or Alaska Native, non-Hispanic/Latino; 0.6% Two or more races, non-Hispanic/Latino; 5% Race/ethnicity unknown; 7% transferred in.

Faculty *Student/faculty ratio:* 17:1.

Academics *Calendar:* semesters. *Degree:* certificates, diplomas, and associate. *Special study options:* academic remediation for entering students, accelerated degree program, adult/continuing education programs, advanced placement credit, cooperative education, distance learning, external degree program, independent study, internships, part-time degree program, services for LD students, summer session for credit.

Student Life *Campus security:* 24-hour emergency response devices, student patrols, security patrols parking lots and halls during working hours and off-duty police officers are deployed on main campus during peak hours.

Standardized Tests *Required:* COMPASS/ASSET (for admission). *Required for some:* SAT (for admission), ACT (for admission), SAT or ACT (for admission).

Costs (2012–13) *Tuition:* area resident $3584 full-time, $150 per credit hour part-time; state resident $4178 full-time, $175 per credit hour part-time; nonresident $6232 full-time, $260 per credit hour part-time. Full-time tuition and fees vary according to program. Part-time tuition and fees vary according to program.

Applying *Options:* electronic application. *Required for some:* high school transcript.

Freshman Application Contact Ms. Barbara Wright, Director of Admissions and Counseling, Central Carolina Technical College, 506 North Guignard Drive, Sumter, SC 29150. *Phone:* 803-778-6695. *Toll-free phone:* 800-221-8711. *Fax:* 803-778-6696. *E-mail:* wrightb@cctech.edu. *Website:* http://www.cctech.edu/.

Clinton Junior College

Rock Hill, South Carolina

Director of Admissions Robert M. Copeland, Vice President for Student Affairs, Clinton Junior College, PO Box 968, 1029 Crawford Road, Rock Hill, SC 29730. *Phone:* 803-327-7402. *Toll-free phone:* 877-837-9645. *Fax:* 803-327-3261. *E-mail:* rcopeland@clintonjrcollege.org. *Website:* http://www.clintonjuniorcollege.edu/.

Denmark Technical College

Denmark, South Carolina

- **State-supported** 2-year, founded 1948, part of South Carolina State Board for Technical and Comprehensive Education
- **Rural** 53-acre campus
- **Coed,** 2,003 undergraduate students, 91% full-time, 54% women, 46% men

Undergraduates 1,821 full-time, 182 part-time. 3% are from out of state; 96% Black or African American, non-Hispanic/Latino; 0.2% Hispanic/Latino; 0.0% American Indian or Alaska Native, non-Hispanic/Latino; 0.1% Race/ethnicity unknown; 2% transferred in. *Retention:* 54% of full-time freshmen returned.

Freshmen *Admission:* 701 enrolled.

Faculty *Total:* 49, 69% full-time. *Student/faculty ratio:* 21:1.

Majors Administrative assistant and secretarial science; automobile/automotive mechanics technology; business administration and management; computer and information sciences; criminal justice/law enforcement administration; engineering technology; human services; kindergarten/preschool education.

Academics *Calendar:* semesters. *Degree:* certificates, diplomas, and associate. *Special study options:* academic remediation for entering students, adult/continuing education programs, advanced placement credit, cooperative education, distance learning, independent study, internships, off-campus study, part-time degree program, summer session for credit.

Library Denmark Technical College Learning Resources Center with 18,735 titles, 195 serial subscriptions, 802 audiovisual materials, an OPAC.

Student Life *Housing Options:* men-only, women-only. Campus housing is university owned. Freshman applicants given priority for college housing. *Activities and Organizations:* choral group, Student Government Association, DTC Choir, athletics, Phi Theta Kappa Internal Honor Society, Esquire Club (men and women). *Campus security:* 24-hour patrols, late-night transport/escort service, 24-hour emergency contact line/alarm devices. *Student services:* health clinic, personal/psychological counseling.

Athletics Member NJCAA. *Intercollegiate sports:* basketball M/W, cheerleading W. *Intramural sports:* basketball M/W.

Standardized Tests *Required:* ACT, ASSET, COMPASS, and TEAS (Nursing) (for admission). *Recommended:* SAT or ACT (for admission).

Costs (2013–14) *Tuition:* state resident $2662 full-time; nonresident $5014 full-time. *Room and board:* $3566; room only: $1762.

Financial Aid Of all full-time matriculated undergraduates who enrolled in 2011, 250 Federal Work-Study jobs (averaging $2000).

Applying *Options:* electronic application, early admission, deferred entrance. *Application fee:* $10. *Required:* high school transcript. *Required for some:* essay or personal statement. *Recommended:* SLED Check, TEAS Testing, Drug Test, PPD Test (all requirement for LPN). *Application deadlines:* rolling (freshmen), rolling (out-of-state freshmen), rolling (transfers). *Early decision deadline:* rolling. *Notification:* continuous (freshmen), continuous (out-of-state freshmen), continuous (transfers).

Freshman Application Contact Ms. Kara Troy, Administrative Specialist II, Denmark Technical College, PO Box 327, 1126 Solomon Blatt Boulevard, Denmark, SC 29042. *Phone:* 803-793-5180. *Fax:* 803-793-5942. *E-mail:* troyk@denmarktech.edu.
Website: http://www.denmarktech.edu/.

ECPI College of Technology

Columbia, South Carolina

Admissions Office Contact ECPI College of Technology, 250 Berryhill Road, #300, Columbia, SC 29210. *Toll-free phone:* 866-708-6168.
Website: http://www.ecpi.edu/.

ECPI College of Technology

Greenville, South Carolina

Admissions Office Contact ECPI College of Technology, 1001 Keys Drive, #100, Greenville, SC 29615. *Toll-free phone:* 866-708-6171.
Website: http://www.ecpi.edu/.

ECPI College of Technology

North Charleston, South Carolina

Admissions Office Contact ECPI College of Technology, 7410 Northside Drive, Suite 100, North Charleston, SC 29420. *Toll-free phone:* 866-708-6166.
Website: http://www.ecpi.edu/.

Florence-Darlington Technical College

Florence, South Carolina

Director of Admissions Shelley Fortin, Vice President for Enrollment Management and Student Services, Florence-Darlington Technical College, 2715 West Lucas Street, PO Box 100548, Florence, SC 29501-0548. *Phone:* 843-661-8111 Ext. 117. *Toll-free phone:* 800-228-5745. *E-mail:* shelley.fortin@fdtc.edu.
Website: http://www.fdtc.edu/.

Forrest College

Anderson, South Carolina

- **Proprietary** 2-year, founded 1946
- **Rural** 3-acre campus
- **Coed,** 120 undergraduate students, 72% full-time, 89% women, 11% men

Undergraduates 86 full-time, 34 part-time. Students come from 2 states and territories; 1% are from out of state.

Freshmen *Admission:* 13 enrolled.

Faculty *Total:* 20, 10% full-time, 20% with terminal degrees. *Student/faculty ratio:* 6:1.

Majors Accounting; business administration and management; child-care and support services management; computer installation and repair technology; computer technology/computer systems technology; legal administrative assistant/secretary; legal assistant/paralegal; medical/clinical assistant; medical office management; office management.

Academics *Calendar:* quarters. *Degree:* certificates, diplomas, and associate. *Special study options:* advanced placement credit, cooperative education, double majors, independent study, internships, part-time degree program, summer session for credit.

Library Forrest Junior College Library with 40,000 titles, 225 serial subscriptions, 2,200 audiovisual materials, an OPAC.

Student Life *Housing:* college housing not available. *Campus security:* 24-hour emergency response devices, late-night transport/escort service.

Standardized Tests *Required:* Gates-McGinnity (for admission).

Costs (2013–14) *Tuition:* $8820 full-time, $245 per credit part-time. *Required fees:* $375 full-time. *Payment plan:* deferred payment.

Financial Aid Of all full-time matriculated undergraduates who enrolled in 2012, 98 applied for aid, 97 were judged to have need.

Applying *Required:* essay or personal statement, high school transcript, minimum 2.0 GPA, interview. *Recommended:* minimum 2.5 GPA.

Freshman Application Contact Ms. Janie Turmon, Admissions and Placement Coordinator/Representative, Forrest College, 601 East River Street, Anderson, SC 29624. *Phone:* 864-225-7653 Ext. 210. *Fax:* 864-261-7471. *E-mail:* janieturmon@forrestcollege.com.
Website: http://www.forrestcollege.edu/.

Golf Academy of America

Myrtle Beach, South Carolina

Admissions Office Contact Golf Academy of America, 3268 Waccamaw Boulevard, Myrtle Beach, SC 29579.
Website: http://www.golfacademy.edu/.

Greenville Technical College

Greenville, South Carolina

Director of Admissions Carolyn Watkins, Dean of Admissions, Greenville Technical College, PO Box 5616, Greenville, SC 29606-5616. *Phone:* 864-250-8287. *Toll-free phone:* 800-992-1183 (in-state); 800-723-0673 (out-of-state). *E-mail:* carolyn.watkins@gvltec.edu.
Website: http://www.gvltec.edu/.

Horry-Georgetown Technical College

Conway, South Carolina

Freshman Application Contact Mr. George Swindoll, Vice President for Enrollment, Development, and Registration, Horry-Georgetown Technical College, 2050 Highway 502 East, PO Box 261966, Conway, SC 29528-6066. *Phone:* 843-349-5277. *Fax:* 843-349-7501. *E-mail:* george.swindoll@hgtc.edu.
Website: http://www.hgtc.edu/.

ITT Technical Institute

Columbia, South Carolina

- **Proprietary** primarily 2-year, part of ITT Educational Services, Inc.
- **Coed**

Academics *Degrees:* associate and bachelor's.

Freshman Application Contact Director of Recruitment, ITT Technical Institute, 1628 Browning Road, Suite 180, Columbia, SC 29210. *Phone:* 803-216-6000. *Toll-free phone:* 800-242-5158.
Website: http://www.itt-tech.edu/.

ITT Technical Institute

Greenville, South Carolina

- **Proprietary** primarily 2-year, founded 1992, part of ITT Educational Services, Inc.
- **Coed**

Academics *Calendar:* quarters. *Degrees:* associate and bachelor's.

Financial Aid Of all full-time matriculated undergraduates who enrolled in 2011, 3 Federal Work-Study jobs.

Freshman Application Contact Director of Recruitment, ITT Technical Institute, Independence Corporate Park, 6 Independence Pointe, Greenville, SC 29615. *Phone:* 864-288-0777. *Toll-free phone:* 800-932-4488.
Website: http://www.itt-tech.edu/.

ITT Technical Institute

Myrtle Beach, South Carolina

- **Proprietary** primarily 2-year, part of ITT Educational Services, Inc.
- **Coed**

Academics *Calendar:* quarters. *Degrees:* associate and bachelor's.

Freshman Application Contact Director of Recruitment, ITT Technical Institute, 9654 N. Kings Highway, Suite 101, Myrtle Beach, SC 29572. *Phone:* 843-497-7820. *Toll-free phone:* 877-316-7054.
Website: http://www.itt-tech.edu/.

ITT Technical Institute

North Charleston, South Carolina

- **Proprietary** primarily 2-year, part of ITT Educational Services, Inc.
- **Coed**

Academics *Calendar:* quarters. *Degrees:* associate and bachelor's.

Freshman Application Contact Director of Recruitment, ITT Technical Institute, 2431 W. Aviation Avenue, North Charleston, SC 29406. *Phone:* 843-745-5700. *Toll-free phone:* 877-291-0900.
Website: http://www.itt-tech.edu/.

Midlands Technical College

Columbia, South Carolina

Freshman Application Contact Ms. Sylvia Littlejohn, Director of Admissions, Midlands Technical College, PO Box 2408, Columbia, SC 29202. *Phone:* 803-738-8324. *Toll-free phone:* 800-922-8038. *Fax:* 803-790-7524.
E-mail: admissions@midlandstech.edu.
Website: http://www.midlandstech.edu/.

Miller-Motte Technical College

Charleston, South Carolina

Freshman Application Contact Ms. Elaine Cue, Campus President, Miller-Motte Technical College, 8085 Rivers Avenue, Suite E, Charleston, SC 29406. *Phone:* 843-574-0101. *Toll-free phone:* 800-923-4162. *Fax:* 843-266-3424.
E-mail: juliasc@miller-mott.net.
Website: http://www.miller-motte.edu/.

Northeastern Technical College

Cheraw, South Carolina

Freshman Application Contact Mrs. Mary K. Newton, Dean of Students, Northeastern Technical College, PO Drawer 1007, Cheraw, SC 29520-1007. *Phone:* 843-921-6935. *Toll-free phone:* 800-921-7399. *Fax:* 843-921-1476.
E-mail: mpace@netc.edu.
Website: http://www.netc.edu/.

Orangeburg-Calhoun Technical College

Orangeburg, South Carolina

Freshman Application Contact Mr. Dana Rickards, Director of Recruitment, Orangeburg-Calhoun Technical College, 3250 St Matthews Road, NE, Orangeburg, SC 29118-8299. *Phone:* 803-535-1219. *Toll-free phone:* 800-813-6519.
Website: http://www.octech.edu/.

Piedmont Technical College

Greenwood, South Carolina

Director of Admissions Mr. Steve Coleman, Director of Admissions, Piedmont Technical College, 620 North Emerald Road, PO Box 1467, Greenwood, SC 29648-1467. *Phone:* 864-941-8603. *Toll-free phone:* 800-868-5528.
Website: http://www.ptc.edu/.

Spartanburg Community College

Spartanburg, South Carolina

- **State-supported** 2-year, founded 1961, part of South Carolina State Board for Technical and Comprehensive Education
- **Suburban** 104-acre campus with easy access to Charlotte
- **Coed,** 6,036 undergraduate students, 48% full-time, 60% women, 40% men

Undergraduates 2,868 full-time, 3,168 part-time. Students come from 10 states and territories; 3 other countries; 2% are from out of state; 23% Black or African American, non-Hispanic/Latino; 5% Hispanic/Latino; 3% Asian, non-Hispanic/Latino; 0.1% Native Hawaiian or other Pacific Islander, non-Hispanic/Latino; 0.6% American Indian or Alaska Native, non-Hispanic/Latino; 2% Two or more races, non-Hispanic/Latino; 1% Race/ethnicity unknown; 9% transferred in. *Retention:* 58% of full-time freshmen returned.
Freshmen *Admission:* 1,179 enrolled.
Faculty *Total:* 380. *Student/faculty ratio:* 16:1.
Majors Accounting; administrative assistant and secretarial science; applied horticulture/horticulture operations; automobile/automotive mechanics technology; business administration and management; clinical/medical laboratory technology; computer and information sciences; data processing and data processing technology; drafting and design technology; electrical, electronic and communications engineering technology; engineering technology; heating, air conditioning, ventilation and refrigeration maintenance technology; horticultural science; industrial electronics technology; liberal arts and sciences/liberal studies; machine tool technology; marketing/marketing management; mechanical drafting and CAD/CADD; mechanical engineering/mechanical technology; medical radiologic technology; multi/interdisciplinary studies related; radiation protection/health physics technology; registered nursing/registered nurse; respiratory care therapy; sales, distribution, and marketing operations.
Academics *Calendar:* semesters condensed semesters plus summer sessions. *Degree:* certificates, diplomas, and associate. *Special study options:* academic remediation for entering students, adult/continuing education programs, advanced placement credit, cooperative education, distance learning, English as a second language, part-time degree program, services for LD students, summer session for credit.
Library Spartanburg Community College Library with 40,078 titles, 295 serial subscriptions, an OPAC, a Web page.
Student Life *Housing:* college housing not available. *Activities and Organizations:* drama/theater group, student-run newspaper. *Campus security:* 24-hour emergency response devices and patrols. *Student services:* personal/psychological counseling, women's center.
Standardized Tests *Required for some:* SAT or ACT (for admission).
Applying *Options:* electronic application, early admission. *Application fee:* $25. *Required:* high school transcript, high school diploma, GED or equivalent. *Recommended:* interview. *Application deadlines:* rolling (freshmen), rolling (transfers). *Notification:* continuous (freshmen), continuous (transfers).
Freshman Application Contact Sabrina Sims, Admissions Counselor, Spartanburg Community College, PO Box 4386, Spartanburg, SC 29305. *Phone:* 864-592-4816. *Toll-free phone:* 866-591-3700. *Fax:* 864-592-4564.
E-mail: admissions@stcsc.edu.
Website: http://www.sccsc.edu/.

Spartanburg Methodist College

Spartanburg, South Carolina

Freshman Application Contact Daniel L. Philbeck, Vice President for Enrollment Management, Spartanburg Methodist College, 1000 Powell Mill Road, Spartanburg, SC 29301-5899. *Phone:* 864-587-4223. *Toll-free phone:*

800-772-7286. *Fax:* 864-587-4355. *E-mail:* admiss@smcsc.edu. *Website:* http://www.smcsc.edu/.

Technical College of the Lowcountry
Beaufort, South Carolina

- **State-supported** 2-year, founded 1972, part of South Carolina Technical and Comprehensive Education System
- **Small-town** 12-acre campus
- **Coed,** 2,511 undergraduate students

Undergraduates Students come from 4 states and territories.
Faculty *Student/faculty ratio:* 15:1.
Majors Administrative assistant and secretarial science; business/commerce; child-care provision; civil engineering technology; construction engineering technology; data processing and data processing technology; early childhood education; education; emergency medical technology (EMT paramedic); fire services administration; golf course operation and grounds management; hospitality administration; industrial electronics technology; legal assistant/paralegal; liberal arts and sciences and humanities related; liberal arts and sciences/liberal studies; medical radiologic technology; physical therapy technology; registered nursing/registered nurse.
Academics *Calendar:* semesters. *Degree:* certificates, diplomas, and associate. *Special study options:* academic remediation for entering students, adult/continuing education programs, advanced placement credit, distance learning, part-time degree program, summer session for credit.
Student Life *Housing:* college housing not available. *Campus security:* security during class hours.
Standardized Tests *Required:* ACT ASSET (for admission). *Recommended:* SAT and SAT Subject Tests or ACT (for admission).
Financial Aid Of all full-time matriculated undergraduates who enrolled in 2011, 56 Federal Work-Study jobs (averaging $1700).
Applying *Options:* early admission, deferred entrance. *Application fee:* $25. *Application deadlines:* rolling (freshmen), rolling (transfers).
Freshman Application Contact Rhonda Cole, Admissions Services Manager, Technical College of the Lowcountry, 921 Ribaut Road, PO Box 1288, Beaufort, SC 29901-1288. *Phone:* 843-525-8229. *Fax:* 843-525-8285. *E-mail:* rcole@tcl.edu.
Website: http://www.tcl.edu/.

Tri-County Technical College
Pendleton, South Carolina

Director of Admissions Renae Frazier, Director, Recruitment and Admissions, Tri-County Technical College, PO Box 587, 7900 Highway 76, Pendleton, SC 29670-0587. *Phone:* 864-646-1550. *Fax:* 864-646-1890. *E-mail:* infocent@tctc.edu.
Website: http://www.tctc.edu/.

Trident Technical College
Charleston, South Carolina

- **State and locally supported** 2-year, founded 1964, part of South Carolina State Board for Technical and Comprehensive Education
- **Urban** campus
- **Coed,** 17,224 undergraduate students, 44% full-time, 62% women, 38% men

Undergraduates 7,557 full-time, 9,667 part-time. Students come from 71 other countries; 3% are from out of state; 32% Black or African American, non-Hispanic/Latino; 4% Hispanic/Latino; 2% Asian, non-Hispanic/Latino; 0.3% Native Hawaiian or other Pacific Islander, non-Hispanic/Latino; 0.8% American Indian or Alaska Native, non-Hispanic/Latino; 2% Two or more races, non-Hispanic/Latino; 2% Race/ethnicity unknown; 6% transferred in.
Freshmen *Admission:* 2,962 applied, 2,982 enrolled.
Faculty *Total:* 869, 38% full-time. *Student/faculty ratio:* 21:1.
Majors Accounting; administrative assistant and secretarial science; airframe mechanics and aircraft maintenance technology; automobile/automotive mechanics technology; biological and physical sciences; business administration and management; child-care provision; civil engineering technology; clinical/medical laboratory technology; commercial and advertising art; computer engineering technology; computer graphics; computer/information technology services administration related; computer programming (specific applications); computer systems networking and telecommunications; criminal justice/law enforcement administration; culinary arts; dental hygiene; electrical, electronic and communications engineering technology; engineering technology; horticultural science; hotel/motel administration; human services; industrial technology; legal assistant/paralegal; legal studies; liberal arts and sciences/liberal studies; machine tool technology; marketing/marketing management; mechanical engineering/mechanical technology; medical administrative assistant and medical secretary; occupational therapy; physical therapy; registered nurs-

ing/registered nurse; respiratory care therapy; telecommunications technology; veterinary/animal health technology; web/multimedia management and webmaster; web page, digital/multimedia and information resources design.
Academics *Calendar:* semesters. *Degree:* certificates, diplomas, and associate. *Special study options:* part-time degree program.
Library Learning Resource Center plus 3 others with 113,550 titles, 265 serial subscriptions, 5,659 audiovisual materials, an OPAC, a Web page.
Student Life *Housing:* college housing not available. *Activities and Organizations:* drama/theater group, student-run newspaper, radio station, Phi Theta Kappa, Lex Artis Paralegal Society, Hospitality and Culinary Student Association, Partnership for Change in Communities and Families, Society of Student Leaders. *Campus security:* 24-hour emergency response devices and patrols, late-night transport/escort service. *Student services:* personal/psychological counseling.
Costs (2013–14) *Tuition:* area resident $3834 full-time, $153 per credit hour part-time; state resident $4236 full-time, $170 per credit hour part-time; nonresident $7122 full-time, $290 per credit hour part-time. Full-time tuition and fees vary according to course load. *Required fees:* $100 full-time. *Payment plan:* installment. *Waivers:* senior citizens.
Applying *Options:* electronic application, early admission. *Application fee:* $30. *Required for some:* high school transcript. *Application deadlines:* 8/6 (freshmen), 8/6 (transfers). *Notification:* continuous (freshmen), continuous (transfers).
Freshman Application Contact Ms. Clara Martin, Admissions Director, Trident Technical College, Charleston, SC 29423-8067. *Phone:* 843-574-6326. *Fax:* 843-574-6109. *E-mail:* Clara.Martin@tridenttech.edu.
Website: http://www.tridenttech.edu/.

University of South Carolina Lancaster
Lancaster, South Carolina

Freshman Application Contact Susan Vinson, Admissions Counselor, University of South Carolina Lancaster, PO Box 889, Lancaster, SC 29721. *Phone:* 803-313-7000. *Fax:* 803-313-7116. *E-mail:* vinsons@mailbox.sc.edu. *Website:* http://usclancaster.sc.edu/.

University of South Carolina Salkehatchie
Allendale, South Carolina

Freshman Application Contact Ms. Carmen Brown, Admissions Coordinator, University of South Carolina Salkehatchie, PO Box 617, Allendale, SC 29810. *Phone:* 803-584-3446. *Toll-free phone:* 800-922-5500. *Fax:* 803-584-3884. *E-mail:* cdbrown@mailbox.sc.edu. *Website:* http://uscsalkehatchie.sc.edu/.

University of South Carolina Sumter
Sumter, South Carolina

Freshman Application Contact Mr. Keith Britton, Director of Admissions, University of South Carolina Sumter, 200 Miller Road, Sumter, SC 29150-2498. *Phone:* 803-938-3882. *Fax:* 803-938-3901. *E-mail:* kbritton@usc.sumter.edu.
Website: http://www.uscsumter.edu/.

University of South Carolina Union
Union, South Carolina

- **State-supported** 2-year, founded 1965, part of University of South Carolina System
- **Small-town** campus with easy access to Charlotte
- **Coed,** 500 undergraduate students, 50% full-time, 60% women, 40% men

Undergraduates 250 full-time, 250 part-time.
Freshmen *Admission:* 400 enrolled. *Average high school GPA:* 3.
Faculty *Total:* 38, 26% full-time. *Student/faculty ratio:* 14:1.
Majors Biological and physical sciences; liberal arts and sciences/liberal studies.
Academics *Calendar:* semesters. *Degree:* associate. *Special study options:* part-time degree program.
Library USC UNION CAMPUS LIBRARY plus 1 other.
Student Life *Housing:* college housing not available. *Activities and Organizations:* drama/theater group, student-run newspaper, choral group.
Athletics *Intramural sports:* baseball M(c).
Standardized Tests *Required:* SAT or ACT (for admission).

Costs (2012–13) *Tuition:* state resident $2900 full-time; nonresident $7200 full-time. Full-time tuition and fees vary according to course load, degree level, and student level. Part-time tuition and fees vary according to student level. *Required fees:* $249 full-time, $249 per credit hour part-time. *Payment plan:* deferred payment. *Waivers:* senior citizens.

Financial Aid Of all full-time matriculated undergraduates who enrolled in 2011, 16 Federal Work-Study jobs (averaging $3400).

Applying *Application fee:* $40. *Required:* high school transcript. *Application deadline:* rolling (freshmen).

Freshman Application Contact Mr. Michael B. Greer, Director of Enrollment Services, University of South Carolina Union, PO Drawer 729, Union, SC 29379-0729. *Phone:* 864-429-8728. *E-mail:* tyoung@gwm.sc.edu. *Website:* http://uscunion.sc.edu/.

Virginia College in Spartanburg
Spartanburg, South Carolina

Admissions Office Contact Virginia College in Spartanburg, 8150 Warren H. Abernathy Highway, Spartanburg, SC 29301.
Website: http://www.vc.edu/.

Williamsburg Technical College
Kingstree, South Carolina

Freshman Application Contact Williamsburg Technical College, 601 Martin Luther King, Jr Avenue, Kingstree, SC 29556-4197. *Phone:* 843-355-4162. *Toll-free phone:* 800-768-2021.
Website: http://www.wiltech.edu/.

York Technical College
Rock Hill, South Carolina

Freshman Application Contact Mr. Kenny Aldridge, Admissions Department Manager, York Technical College, Rock Hill, SC 29730. *Phone:* 803-327-8008. *Toll-free phone:* 800-922-8324. *Fax:* 803-981-7237. *E-mail:* kaldridge@yorktech.com.
Website: http://www.yorktech.com/.

SOUTH DAKOTA

Kilian Community College
Sioux Falls, South Dakota

- **Independent** 2-year, founded 1977
- **Urban** 2-acre campus
- **Coed,** 294 undergraduate students, 13% full-time, 67% women, 33% men

Undergraduates 37 full-time, 257 part-time. Students come from 3 states and territories; 2% are from out of state; 12% Black or African American, non-Hispanic/Latino; 3% Hispanic/Latino; 1% Asian, non-Hispanic/Latino; 9% American Indian or Alaska Native, non-Hispanic/Latino; 14% Race/ethnicity unknown; 10% transferred in.

Freshmen *Admission:* 159 applied, 99 admitted, 41 enrolled.

Faculty *Total:* 34, 15% full-time, 18% with terminal degrees. *Student/faculty ratio:* 8:1.

Majors Accounting; American Indian/Native American studies; business administration and management; counseling psychology; criminal justice/law enforcement administration; education; environmental studies; financial planning and services; history; information technology; liberal arts and sciences/liberal studies; medical office management; psychology; social work; sociology; substance abuse/addiction counseling.

Academics *Calendar:* trimesters. *Degree:* certificates and associate. *Special study options:* academic remediation for entering students, advanced placement credit, distance learning, double majors, English as a second language, independent study, off-campus study, part-time degree program, services for LD students, summer session for credit.

Library Sioux Falls Public Library with 78,000 titles, 395 serial subscriptions, an OPAC, a Web page.

Student Life *Housing:* college housing not available. *Activities and Organizations:* Phi Theta Kappa, Students in Free Enterprise (SIFE), Student Leadership. *Campus security:* late-night transport/escort service. *Student services:* personal/psychological counseling.

Costs (2012–13) *Tuition:* $9900 full-time, $275 per credit hour part-time. *Required fees:* $330 full-time, $110 per term part-time. *Payment plan:* installment. *Waivers:* senior citizens and employees or children of employees.

Financial Aid Of all full-time matriculated undergraduates who enrolled in 2011, 31 applied for aid, 31 were judged to have need. 26 Federal Work-Study jobs (averaging $1500). *Average percent of need met:* 61%. *Average financial aid package:* $9000. *Average need-based loan:* $4500. *Average need-based gift aid:* $4500.

Applying *Options:* electronic application, deferred entrance. *Application fee:* $25. *Required:* high school transcript. *Application deadlines:* rolling (freshmen), rolling (out-of-state freshmen), rolling (transfers).

Freshman Application Contact Ms. Mary Klockman, Director of Admissions, Kilian Community College, 300 East 6th Street, Sioux Falls, SD 57103. *Phone:* 605-221-3100. *Toll-free phone:* 800-888-1147. *Fax:* 605-336-2606. *E-mail:* info@killian.edu.
Website: http://www.kilian.edu/.

Lake Area Technical Institute
Watertown, South Dakota

- **State-supported** 2-year, founded 1964
- **Small-town** 40-acre campus
- **Coed,** 1,600 undergraduate students

Undergraduates 1% Black or African American, non-Hispanic/Latino; 1% Hispanic/Latino; 2% American Indian or Alaska Native, non-Hispanic/Latino. *Retention:* 81% of full-time freshmen returned.

Freshmen *Admission:* 1,689 applied, 1,020 admitted.

Faculty *Total:* 97, 98% full-time. *Student/faculty ratio:* 16:1.

Majors Agricultural business and management; agricultural production; aircraft powerplant technology; autobody/collision and repair technology; automobile/automotive mechanics technology; banking and financial support services; biology/biotechnology laboratory technician; carpentry; clinical/medical laboratory technology; computer programming; computer science; construction engineering technology; dental assisting; diesel mechanics technology; drafting and design technology; electrical, electronic and communications engineering technology; electrical/electronics equipment installation and repair; electromechanical technology; emergency medical technology (EMT paramedic); engineering technology; environmental science; human services; licensed practical/vocational nurse training; machine tool technology; manufacturing engineering technology; marketing/marketing management; medical/clinical assistant; occupational therapist assistant; physical therapy technology; robotics technology; sales, distribution, and marketing operations; small business administration; welding technology.

Academics *Calendar:* semesters. *Degree:* diplomas and associate. *Special study options:* academic remediation for entering students, internships, services for LD students.

Library Leonard H. Timmerman Library plus 1 other with 5,000 titles, 128 serial subscriptions.

Student Life *Housing:* college housing not available.

Athletics *Intramural sports:* basketball M/W, softball M/W, volleyball M/W.

Standardized Tests *Required:* ACT (for admission).

Applying *Options:* electronic application. *Application fee:* $20. *Required:* high school transcript. *Required for some:* essay or personal statement, 3 letters of recommendation, interview.

Freshman Application Contact Lake Area Technical Institute, 1201 Arrow Ave, Watertown, SD 57201. *Phone:* 605-882-5284. *Toll-free phone:* 800-657-4344.
Website: http://www.lakeareatech.edu/.

Mitchell Technical Institute
Mitchell, South Dakota

- **State-supported** 2-year, founded 1968, part of South Dakota Board of Education
- **Rural** 90-acre campus
- **Endowment** $1.4 million
- **Coed,** 1,089 undergraduate students, 80% full-time, 34% women, 66% men

Undergraduates 873 full-time, 216 part-time. Students come from 14 states and territories; 6% are from out of state; 0.1% Black or African American, non-Hispanic/Latino; 0.8% Hispanic/Latino; 0.1% Asian, non-Hispanic/Latino; 4% American Indian or Alaska Native, non-Hispanic/Latino; 0.4% Two or more races, non-Hispanic/Latino; 1% Race/ethnicity unknown; 10% transferred in; 9% live on campus.

Freshmen *Admission:* 996 applied, 589 admitted, 367 enrolled. *Average high school GPA:* 2.76. *Test scores:* ACT scores over 18: 71%; ACT scores over 24: 14%.

Faculty *Total:* 83, 86% full-time, 2% with terminal degrees. *Student/faculty ratio:* 13:1.

Majors Accounting and business/management; agricultural mechanics and equipment technology; agricultural production; automation engineer technology; building construction technology; building/property maintenance; business automation/technology/data entry; clinical/medical laboratory technology; computer support specialist; construction trades related; culinary arts; electrician; energy management and systems technology; geographic information science and cartography; heating, air conditioning, ventilation and refrigeration maintenance technology; lineworker; medical/clinical assistant; medical office assistant; medical radiologic technology; network and system administration; radiologic technology/science; radio, television, and digital communication related; small engine mechanics and repair technology; speech-language pathology assistant; telecommunications technology; welding engineering technology.

Academics *Calendar:* semesters. *Degree:* certificates, diplomas, and associate. *Special study options:* academic remediation for entering students, advanced placement credit, cooperative education, distance learning, internships, part-time degree program, services for LD students, summer session for credit.

Library Instructional Services Center with 3,000 titles, 100 serial subscriptions, 300 audiovisual materials, an OPAC.

Student Life *Housing Options:* Campus housing is provided by a third party. *Activities and Organizations:* Student Representative Board, Skills USA, Post-Secondary Agricultural Students, Rodeo Club, Student Veterans Organization. *Student services:* personal/psychological counseling.

Athletics *Intercollegiate sports:* equestrian sports M/W. *Intramural sports:* basketball M/W, bowling M/W, riflery M/W, softball M/W, volleyball M/W.

Standardized Tests *Required for some:* SAT or ACT (for admission), COMPASS.

Costs (2012–13) *One-time required fee:* $999. *Tuition:* state resident $3564 full-time, $99 per credit hour part-time; nonresident $3564 full-time, $99 per credit hour part-time. Full-time tuition and fees vary according to course load and program. Part-time tuition and fees vary according to course load and program. *Required fees:* $2890 full-time, $73 per credit hour part-time. *Payment plan:* installment. *Waivers:* employees or children of employees.

Financial Aid Of all full-time matriculated undergraduates who enrolled in 2011, 765 applied for aid, 693 were judged to have need, 8 had their need fully met. In 2011, 2 non-need-based awards were made. *Average percent of need met:* 51%. *Average financial aid package:* $7046. *Average need-based loan:* $3567. *Average need-based gift aid:* $4202. *Average non-need-based aid:* $475. *Average indebtedness upon graduation:* $6277.

Applying *Options:* electronic application. *Required:* high school transcript. *Required for some:* essay or personal statement, interview. *Recommended:* minimum 2.0 GPA. *Application deadlines:* rolling (freshmen), rolling (out-of-state freshmen), rolling (transfers). *Notification:* continuous (freshmen), continuous (out-of-state freshmen), continuous (transfers).

Freshman Application Contact Mr. Clayton Deuter, Director of Admissions, Mitchell Technical Institute, 1800 East Spruce Street, Mitchell, SD 57301. *Phone:* 605-995-3025. *Toll-free phone:* 800-684-1969. *Fax:* 605-995-3067. *E-mail:* clayton.deuter@mitchelltech.edu. *Website:* http://www.mitchelltech.edu/.

National American University
Ellsworth AFB, South Dakota

Freshman Application Contact Admissions Office, National American University, 1000 Ellsworth Street, Suite 2400B, Ellsworth AFB, SD 57706. *Website:* http://www.national.edu/.

Sisseton-Wahpeton College
Sisseton, South Dakota

Freshman Application Contact Sisseton-Wahpeton College, Old Agency Box 689, Sisseton, SD 57262. *Phone:* 605-698-3966 Ext. 1180. *Website:* http://www.swc.tc/.

Southeast Technical Institute
Sioux Falls, South Dakota

- **State-supported** 2-year, founded 1968
- **Urban** 138-acre campus
- **Endowment** $768,716
- **Coed,** 2,632 undergraduate students, 72% full-time, 52% women, 48% men

Undergraduates 1,901 full-time, 731 part-time. Students come from 11 states and territories; 8% are from out of state; 2% Black or African American, non-Hispanic/Latino; 2% Hispanic/Latino; 0.6% Asian, non-Hispanic/Latino; 0.4% Native Hawaiian or other Pacific Islander, non-Hispanic/Latino; 2% American Indian or Alaska Native, non-Hispanic/Latino; 2% Two or more races, non-Hispanic/Latino; 13% Race/ethnicity unknown; 14% transferred in; 8% live on campus. *Retention:* 56% of full-time freshmen returned.

Freshmen *Admission:* 3,119 applied, 1,324 admitted, 640 enrolled. *Average high school GPA:* 2.7.

Faculty *Total:* 201, 44% full-time, 3% with terminal degrees. *Student/faculty ratio:* 18:1.

Majors Accounting; animation, interactive technology, video graphics and special effects; applied horticulture/horticulture operations; architectural engineering technology; autobody/collision and repair technology; automobile/automotive mechanics technology; banking and financial support services; biomedical technology; building/construction finishing, management, and inspection related; business administration and management; cardiovascular technology; child-care and support services management; child-care provision; civil engineering technology; clinical/medical laboratory science and allied professions related; clinical/medical laboratory technology; commercial and advertising art; computer and information sciences and support services related; computer and information systems security; computer/information technology services administration related; computer installation and repair technology; computer programming; computer programming related; computer software engineering; computer systems networking and telecommunications; computer technology/computer systems technology; construction engineering technology; criminal justice/police science; desktop publishing and digital imaging design; diagnostic medical sonography and ultrasound technology; diesel mechanics technology; electrical, electronic and communications engineering technology; electrical/electronics equipment installation and repair; electromechanical technology; electroneurodiagnostic/electroencephalographic technology; finance; health unit coordinator/ward clerk; heating, air conditioning, ventilation and refrigeration maintenance technology; horticultural science; industrial technology; licensed practical/vocational nurse training; marketing/marketing management; mechanical engineering/mechanical technology; merchandising, sales, and marketing operations related (general); nuclear medical technology; office occupations and clerical services; registered nursing/registered nurse; surgical technology; surveying technology; turf and turfgrass management; welding technology.

Academics *Calendar:* semesters. *Degree:* certificates, diplomas, and associate. *Special study options:* academic remediation for entering students, advanced placement credit, distance learning, double majors, independent study, internships, part-time degree program, services for LD students, summer session for credit.

Library Southeast Library with 10,643 titles, 158 serial subscriptions, an OPAC, a Web page.

Student Life *Housing Options:* coed. Campus housing is provided by a third party. *Activities and Organizations:* VICA (Vocational Industrial Clubs of America), American Landscape Contractors Association. *Campus security:* 24-hour patrols, late-night transport/escort service, controlled dormitory access. *Student services:* personal/psychological counseling.

Athletics *Intramural sports:* basketball M/W, bowling M/W, volleyball M/W.

Standardized Tests *Recommended:* ACT (for admission).

Costs (2013–14) *Tuition:* state resident $3120 full-time, $104 per credit hour part-time; nonresident $3120 full-time, $104 per credit hour part-time. Full-time tuition and fees vary according to program. Part-time tuition and fees vary according to program. *Required fees:* $2670 full-time, $89 per credit hour part-time. *Room and board:* room only: $4650. *Payment plan:* installment.

Financial Aid Of all full-time matriculated undergraduates who enrolled in 2011, 35 Federal Work-Study jobs (averaging $2550).

Applying *Options:* electronic application. *Required:* high school transcript, minimum 2.2 GPA. *Required for some:* interview, background check and drug testing for certain programs. *Application deadlines:* rolling (freshmen), rolling (out-of-state freshmen), rolling (transfers). *Notification:* continuous (freshmen), continuous (out-of-state freshmen), continuous (transfers).

Freshman Application Contact Mr. Scott Dorman, Recruiter, Southeast Technical Institute, Sioux Falls, SD 57107. *Phone:* 605-367-4458. *Toll-free phone:* 800-247-0789. *Fax:* 605-367-8305. *E-mail:* scott.dorman@southeasttech.edu. *Website:* http://www.southeasttech.edu/.

Western Dakota Technical Institute
Rapid City, South Dakota

- **State-supported** 2-year, founded 1968
- **Small-town** 5-acre campus
- **Coed,** 1,019 undergraduate students, 77% full-time, 48% women, 52% men

Undergraduates 785 full-time, 234 part-time. Students come from 11 states and territories; 3% are from out of state; 1% Black or African American, non-Hispanic/Latino; 4% Hispanic/Latino; 0.7% Asian, non-Hispanic/Latino; 0.2% Native Hawaiian or other Pacific Islander, non-Hispanic/Latino; 13% American Indian or Alaska Native, non-Hispanic/Latino; 0.6% Two or more races, non-Hispanic/Latino; 9% Race/ethnicity unknown; 8% transferred in. *Retention:* 67% of full-time freshmen returned.

Freshmen *Admission:* 1,110 applied, 814 admitted, 266 enrolled. *Average high school GPA:* 2.6.

Faculty *Total:* 123, 37% full-time. *Student/faculty ratio:* 18:1.

Majors Accounting; architectural drafting and CAD/CADD; autobody/collision and repair technology; automobile/automotive mechanics technology; business administration and management; computer systems networking and telecommunications; criminal justice/police science; drafting and design technology; electrician; emergency medical technology (EMT paramedic); environmental control technologies related; fire science/firefighting; legal assistant/paralegal; library and archives assisting; medical/clinical assistant; medical transcription; precision metal working related; vehicle maintenance and repair technologies related.

Academics *Calendar:* semesters. *Degree:* certificates, diplomas, and associate. *Special study options:* academic remediation for entering students, advanced placement credit, distance learning, independent study, internships, part-time degree program, services for LD students, summer session for credit.

Library Western Dakota Technical Institute Library with 8,211 titles, 87 serial subscriptions, 133 audiovisual materials, an OPAC, a Web page.

Student Life *Housing:* college housing not available. *Campus security:* 24-hour video surveillance.

Standardized Tests *Recommended:* SAT or ACT (for admission).

Costs (2013–14) *One-time required fee:* $250. *Tuition:* state resident $3564 full-time, $99 per credit hour part-time; nonresident $3564 full-time, $99 per credit hour part-time. Full-time tuition and fees vary according to course load and program. Part-time tuition and fees vary according to course load. *Required fees:* $2887 full-time, $80 per credit hour part-time. *Payment plans:* installment, deferred payment. *Waivers:* employees or children of employees.

Financial Aid Of all full-time matriculated undergraduates who enrolled in 2011, 85 Federal Work-Study jobs (averaging $1400).

Applying *Options:* electronic application. *Application fee:* $20. *Required:* high school transcript, Placement test. *Required for some:* essay or personal statement, 3 letters of recommendation, interview. *Recommended:* minimum 2.0 GPA. *Application deadlines:* 8/1 (freshmen), 8/1 (transfers). *Notification:* continuous until 8/15 (freshmen), continuous until 8/15 (transfers).

Freshman Application Contact Jill Elder, Admissions Coordinator, Western Dakota Technical Institute, 800 Mickelson Drive, Rapid City, SD 57703. *Phone:* 605-718-2411. *Toll-free phone:* 800-544-8765. *Fax:* 605-394-2204. *E-mail:* jill.elder@wdt.edu. *Website:* http://www.wdt.edu/.

TENNESSEE

Anthem Career College

Memphis, Tennessee

Freshman Application Contact Admissions Office, Anthem Career College, 5865 Shelby Oaks Circle, Suite 100, Memphis, TN 38134. *Toll-free phone:* 866-381-5623. *Website:* http://www.anthem.edu/memphis-tennessee/.

Anthem Career College–Nashville

Nashville, Tennessee

Freshman Application Contact Admissions Office, Anthem Career College–Nashville, 560 Royal Parkway, Nashville, TN 37214. *Phone:* 615-902-9705. *Toll-free phone:* 866-381-5791. *Website:* http://anthem.edu/nashville-tennessee/.

Chattanooga College–Medical, Dental and Technical Careers

Chattanooga, Tennessee

Director of Admissions Toney McFadden, Admission Director, Chattanooga College–Medical, Dental and Technical Careers, 3805 Brainerd Road, Chattanooga, TN 37411-3798. *Phone:* 423-624-0077. *Toll-free phone:* 877-313-2373. *Fax:* 423-624-1575. *Website:* http://www.chattanoogacollege.edu/.

Chattanooga State Community College

Chattanooga, Tennessee

- **State-supported** 2-year, founded 1965, part of Tennessee Board of Regents
- **Urban** 100-acre campus
- **Endowment** $6.8 million
- **Coed**

Undergraduates 4,775 full-time, 5,663 part-time. Students come from 23 states and territories; 9 other countries; 11% are from out of state; 18% Black or African American, non-Hispanic/Latino; 2% Hispanic/Latino; 1% Asian, non-Hispanic/Latino; 0.2% American Indian or Alaska Native, non-Hispanic/Latino; 0.4% Race/ethnicity unknown; 210% transferred in.

Faculty *Student/faculty ratio:* 19:1.

Academics *Calendar:* semesters. *Degree:* certificates, diplomas, and associate. *Special study options:* academic remediation for entering students, accelerated degree program, adult/continuing education programs, advanced placement credit, cooperative education, distance learning, double majors, external degree program, honors programs, independent study, internships, part-time degree program, services for LD students, summer session for credit.

Student Life *Campus security:* 24-hour emergency response devices and patrols, late-night transport/escort service.

Athletics Member NJCAA.

Costs (2012–13) *Tuition:* state resident $3555 full-time, $135 per credit hour part-time; nonresident $13,683 full-time, $422 per credit hour part-time. Full-time tuition and fees vary according to course load. Part-time tuition and fees vary according to course load. *Required fees:* $315 full-time.

Applying *Options:* electronic application, early admission, deferred entrance. *Application fee:* $15. *Required for some:* high school transcript, interview. *Recommended:* high school transcript.

Freshman Application Contact Brad McCormick, Director Admissions and Records, Chattanooga State Community College, 4501 Amnicola Highway, Chattanooga, TN 37406. *Phone:* 423-697-4401 Ext. 3264. *Toll-free phone:* 866-547-3733. *Fax:* 423-697-4709. *E-mail:* brad.mccormick@chattanoogastate.edu. *Website:* http://www.chattanoogastate.edu/.

Cleveland State Community College

Cleveland, Tennessee

- **State-supported** 2-year, founded 1967, part of Tennessee Board of Regents
- **Suburban** 83-acre campus
- **Endowment** $6.4 million
- **Coed,** 3,640 undergraduate students, 53% full-time, 62% women, 38% men

Undergraduates 1,920 full-time, 1,720 part-time. Students come from 7 states and territories; 3 other countries; 1% are from out of state; 6% Black or African American, non-Hispanic/Latino; 0.3% Hispanic/Latino; 1% Asian, non-Hispanic/Latino; 0.3% American Indian or Alaska Native, non-Hispanic/Latino; 1% Two or more races, non-Hispanic/Latino; 4% Race/ethnicity unknown; 0.2% international; 5% transferred in.

Freshmen *Admission:* 1,619 applied, 784 admitted, 784 enrolled. *Average high school GPA:* 2.97. *Test scores:* ACT scores over 18: 65%; ACT scores over 24: 10%.

Faculty *Total:* 194, 37% full-time, 14% with terminal degrees. *Student/faculty ratio:* 22:1.

Majors Administrative assistant and secretarial science; business administration and management; child development; community organization and advocacy; criminal justice/police science; general studies; industrial technology; kindergarten/preschool education; liberal arts and sciences and humanities related; liberal arts and sciences/liberal studies; public administration and social service professions related; registered nursing/registered nurse; science technologies related.

Academics *Calendar:* semesters. *Degree:* certificates and associate. *Special study options:* academic remediation for entering students, adult/continuing education programs, advanced placement credit, cooperative education, distance learning, double majors, external degree program, honors programs, independent study, internships, off-campus study, part-time degree program, services for LD students, summer session for credit.

Library Cleveland State Community College Library with 153,456 titles, 1,137 serial subscriptions, 8,142 audiovisual materials, an OPAC, a Web page.

Student Life *Housing:* college housing not available. *Activities and Organizations:* student-run newspaper, choral group, Human Services/Social Work, Computer Aided Design, Phi Theta Kappa, Student Nursing Association, Early Childhood Education. *Campus security:* 24-hour emergency response devices and patrols. *Student services:* personal/psychological counseling.

Athletics Member NJCAA. *Intercollegiate sports:* baseball M(s), basketball M(s)/W(s), softball W(s). *Intramural sports:* archery M/W, basketball M/W, bowling M/W, cheerleading M(c)/W(c), softball W, table tennis M/W, volleyball M/W.

Costs (2012–13) *Tuition:* state resident $3402 full-time, $135 per credit hour part-time; nonresident $14,034 full-time, $557 per credit hour part-time. Full-time tuition and fees vary according to course load. *Required fees:* $269 full-time, $14 per credit hour part-time, $22 per term part-time. *Payment plan:* deferred payment. *Waivers:* senior citizens and employees or children of employees.

Financial Aid Of all full-time matriculated undergraduates who enrolled in 2011, 52 Federal Work-Study jobs (averaging $1025).

Applying *Options:* electronic application, early admission, deferred entrance. *Application fee:* $10. *Required:* high school transcript. *Application deadlines:* rolling (freshmen), rolling (transfers). *Notification:* continuous (freshmen), continuous (transfers).

Freshman Application Contact Mrs. Suzanne Bayne, Assistant Director of Admissions and Recruitment, Cleveland State Community College, P O Box 3570, Cleveland, TN 37320-3570. *Phone:* 423-472-7141 Ext. 743. *Toll-free phone:* 800-604-2722. *Fax:* 423-478-6255. *E-mail:* SBayne@clevelandstatecc.edu.
Website: http://www.clevelandstatecc.edu/.

Columbia State Community College
Columbia, Tennessee

Freshman Application Contact Mr. Joey Scruggs, Coordinator of Recruitment, Columbia State Community College, PO Box 1315, Columbia, TN 38402-1315. *Phone:* 931-540-2540. *E-mail:* scruggs@coscc.cc.tn.us. *Website:* http://www.columbiastate.edu/.

Concorde Career College
Memphis, Tennessee

Freshman Application Contact Dee Vickers, Director, Concorde Career College, 5100 Poplar Avenue, Suite 132, Memphis, TN 38137. *Phone:* 901-761-9494. *Fax:* 901-761-3293. *E-mail:* dvickers@concorde.edu. *Website:* http://www.concorde.edu/.

Daymar Institute
Nashville, Tennessee

Director of Admissions Admissions Office, Daymar Institute, 340 Plus Park Boulevard, Nashville, TN 37217. *Phone:* 615-361-7555. *Fax:* 615-367-2736. *Website:* http://www.daymarinstitute.edu/.

Dyersburg State Community College
Dyersburg, Tennessee

- **State-supported** 2-year, founded 1969, part of Tennessee Board of Regents
- **Small-town** 100-acre campus with easy access to Memphis
- **Endowment** $5.4 million
- **Coed,** 3,590 undergraduate students, 45% full-time, 67% women, 33% men

Undergraduates 1,601 full-time, 1,989 part-time. Students come from 2 states and territories; 2 other countries; 20% Black or African American, non-Hispanic/Latino; 2% Hispanic/Latino; 0.4% Asian, non-Hispanic/Latino; 0.1% Native Hawaiian or other Pacific Islander, non-Hispanic/Latino; 0.5% American Indian or Alaska Native, non-Hispanic/Latino; 1% Two or more races, non-Hispanic/Latino; 1% Race/ethnicity unknown; 6% transferred in. *Retention:* 54% of full-time freshmen returned.

Freshmen *Admission:* 777 enrolled. *Average high school GPA:* 2.69. *Test scores:* ACT scores over 18: 92%; ACT scores over 24: 42%; ACT scores over 30: 1%.

Faculty *Total:* 204, 33% full-time, 8% with terminal degrees. *Student/faculty ratio:* 18:1.

Majors Agriculture; business administration and management; child development; computer and information systems security; criminal justice/police science; education; emergency medical technology (EMT paramedic); health information/medical records technology; health services/allied health/health sciences; information science/studies; liberal arts and sciences/liberal studies; music performance; registered nursing/registered nurse; web page, digital/multimedia and information resources design.

Academics *Calendar:* semesters. *Degree:* certificates and associate. *Special study options:* academic remediation for entering students, adult/continuing education programs, advanced placement credit, distance learning, double

majors, honors programs, independent study, part-time degree program, services for LD students, summer session for credit.

Library Learning Resource Center with 66,892 titles, 35 serial subscriptions, 479 audiovisual materials, an OPAC, a Web page.

Student Life *Housing:* college housing not available. *Activities and Organizations:* drama/theater group, student-run television station, choral group, Psychology Club, Phi Theta Kappa, Student Government, Media Club, Criminal Justice Association. *Campus security:* 24-hour patrols. *Student services:* personal/psychological counseling.

Athletics Member NJCAA. *Intercollegiate sports:* baseball M(s), basketball M(s)/W(s), cheerleading W(s), softball W(s). *Intramural sports:* basketball M/W, soccer M/W, volleyball M/W.

Costs (2012–13) *Tuition:* state resident $3531 full-time, $135 per credit hour part-time; nonresident $13,659 full-time, $590 per credit hour part-time. Full-time tuition and fees vary according to course load. Part-time tuition and fees vary according to course load. *Required fees:* $291 full-time, $146 per term part-time. *Payment plan:* deferred payment. *Waivers:* senior citizens and employees or children of employees.

Financial Aid Of all full-time matriculated undergraduates who enrolled in 2011, 45 Federal Work-Study jobs (averaging $2455). 125 state and other part-time jobs (averaging $1652).

Applying *Required:* high school transcript.

Freshman Application Contact Ms. Josh Caviness, Admissions Counselor, Dyersburg State Community College, Dyersburg, TN 38024. *Phone:* 731-286-3324. *Fax:* 731-286-3325. *E-mail:* jcaviness@dscc.edu.
Website: http://www.dscc.edu/.

Fortis Institute
Cookeville, Tennessee

Director of Admissions Ms. Sharon Mellott, Director of Admissions, Fortis Institute, 1025 Highway 111, Cookeville, TN 38501. *Phone:* 931-526-3660. *Toll-free phone:* 855-4-FORTIS.
Website: http://www.fortis.edu/.

Fountainhead College of Technology
Knoxville, Tennessee

- **Proprietary** primarily 2-year, founded 1947
- **Suburban** 2-acre campus
- **Coed,** 230 undergraduate students, 100% full-time, 13% women, 87% men

Undergraduates 230 full-time. *Retention:* 82% of full-time freshmen returned.

Faculty *Total:* 23, 48% full-time. *Student/faculty ratio:* 9:1.

Majors Communications technology; computer and information systems security; computer engineering technology; computer programming; electrical, electronic and communications engineering technology; health information/medical records technology; information technology; medical insurance coding.

Academics *Calendar:* semesters. *Degrees:* associate and bachelor's. *Special study options:* accelerated degree program, distance learning, double majors, summer session for credit.

Library Library and Resource Center with an OPAC, a Web page.

Student Life *Housing:* college housing not available. *Campus security:* 24-hour emergency response devices.

Standardized Tests *Required for some:* SAT or ACT (for admission).

Costs (2012–13) *Tuition:* $485 per credit hour part-time. Full-time tuition and fees vary according to program. No tuition increase for student's term of enrollment. *Payment plans:* tuition prepayment, installment.

Applying *Required:* high school transcript, interview. *Application deadlines:* rolling (freshmen), rolling (transfers). *Notification:* continuous (freshmen), continuous (transfers).

Freshman Application Contact Mr. Joel B Southern, Director of Admissions, Fountainhead College of Technology, 10208 Technology Drive, Knoxville, TN 37932. *Phone:* 865-688-9422. *Toll-free phone:* 888-218-7335. *Fax:* 865-688-2419. *E-mail:* joel.southern@fountainheadcollege.edu.
Website: http://www.fountainheadcollege.edu/.

ITT Technical Institute
Chattanooga, Tennessee

- **Proprietary** primarily 2-year, part of ITT Educational Services, Inc.
- **Coed**

Academics *Degrees:* associate and bachelor's.

Freshman Application Contact Director of Recruitment, ITT Technical Institute, 5600 Brainerd Road, Suite G-1, Chattanooga, TN 37411. *Phone:* 423-510-6800. *Toll-free phone:* 877-474-8312.
Website: http://www.itt-tech.edu/.

ITT Technical Institute
Cordova, Tennessee
- **Proprietary** primarily 2-year, founded 1994, part of ITT Educational Services, Inc.
- **Suburban** campus
- **Coed**

Academics *Calendar:* quarters. *Degrees:* associate and bachelor's.
Freshman Application Contact Director of Recruitment, ITT Technical Institute, 7260 Goodlett Farms Parkway, Cordova, TN 38016. *Phone:* 901-381-0200. *Toll-free phone:* 866-444-5141.
Website: http://www.itt-tech.edu/.

ITT Technical Institute
Johnson City, Tennessee
- **Proprietary** primarily 2-year
- **Coed**

Academics *Degrees:* associate and bachelor's.
Freshman Application Contact Director of Recruitment, ITT Technical Institute, 4721 Lake Park Drive, Suite 100, Johnson City, TN 37615. *Phone:* 423-952-4400. *Toll-free phone:* 877-301-9691.
Website: http://www.itt-tech.edu/.

ITT Technical Institute
Knoxville, Tennessee
- **Proprietary** primarily 2-year, founded 1988, part of ITT Educational Services, Inc.
- **Suburban** campus
- **Coed**

Academics *Calendar:* quarters. *Degrees:* associate and bachelor's.
Freshman Application Contact Director of Recruitment, ITT Technical Institute, 9123 Executive Park Drive, Knoxville, TN 37923. *Phone:* 865-671-2800. *Toll-free phone:* 800-671-2801.
Website: http://www.itt-tech.edu/.

ITT Technical Institute
Nashville, Tennessee
- **Proprietary** primarily 2-year, founded 1984, part of ITT Educational Services, Inc.
- **Urban** campus
- **Coed**

Academics *Calendar:* quarters. *Degrees:* associate and bachelor's.
Freshman Application Contact Director of Recruitment, ITT Technical Institute, 2845 Elm Hill Pike, Nashville, TN 37214. *Phone:* 615-889-8700. *Toll-free phone:* 800-331-8386.
Website: http://www.itt-tech.edu/.

Jackson State Community College
Jackson, Tennessee
- **State-supported** 2-year, founded 1967, part of Tennessee Board of Regents
- **Suburban** 97-acre campus with easy access to Memphis
- **Endowment** $800,579
- **Coed,** 5,109 undergraduate students

Undergraduates Students come from 7 states and territories; 3 other countries. *Retention:* 49% of full-time freshmen returned.
Faculty *Total:* 306, 32% full-time, 5% with terminal degrees. *Student/faculty ratio:* 21:1.
Majors Agriculture; business administration and management; child development; clinical/medical laboratory technology; computer science; education; general studies; industrial technology; liberal arts and sciences/liberal studies; management information systems; medical radiologic technology; physical therapy technology; registered nursing/registered nurse; respiratory care therapy; science technologies related.
Academics *Calendar:* semesters. *Degree:* certificates, diplomas, and associate. *Special study options:* academic remediation for entering students, adult/continuing education programs, advanced placement credit, cooperative education, distance learning, external degree program, honors programs, independent study, internships, off-campus study, part-time degree program, services for LD students, summer session for credit. *ROTC:* Army (b).
Library Jackson State Community College Library with 56,024 titles, 105 serial subscriptions, 2,128 audiovisual materials, an OPAC, a Web page.
Student Life *Activities and Organizations:* drama/theater group, choral group, Spanish Club, Philosophy Club, Nation Against Genocide, FFA/Agriculture Club, Biology Club. *Campus security:* 24-hour patrols, late-night transport/escort service, field camera surveillance. *Student services:* personal/psychological counseling.
Athletics Member NJCAA. *Intercollegiate sports:* baseball M(s), basketball M(s)/W(s), softball W(s).
Standardized Tests *Required:* SAT or ACT (for admission), COMPASS (for admission). *Recommended:* ACT (for admission).
Financial Aid Of all full-time matriculated undergraduates who enrolled in 2011, 30 Federal Work-Study jobs (averaging $3000). 10 state and other part-time jobs (averaging $3000).
Applying *Options:* electronic application. *Application fee:* $10. *Required for some:* high school transcript. *Application deadlines:* 8/23 (freshmen), 8/23 (out-of-state freshmen), rolling (transfers). *Notification:* continuous (freshmen), continuous (out-of-state freshmen), continuous (transfers).
Freshman Application Contact Ms. Andrea Winchester, Director of Admissions, Jackson State Community College, 2046 North Parkway, Jackson, TN 38301-3797. *Phone:* 731-425-8844 Ext. 484. *Toll-free phone:* 800-355-5722. *Fax:* 731-425-9559. *E-mail:* awinchester@jscc.edu.
Website: http://www.jscc.edu/.

John A. Gupton College
Nashville, Tennessee
- **Independent** 2-year, founded 1946
- **Urban** 1-acre campus with easy access to Nashville
- **Endowment** $60,000
- **Coed,** 138 undergraduate students, 49% full-time, 53% women, 47% men

Undergraduates 67 full-time, 71 part-time. Students come from 3 states and territories; 1% are from out of state; 22% Black or African American, non-Hispanic/Latino; 0.7% American Indian or Alaska Native, non-Hispanic/Latino; 14% transferred in; 11% live on campus.
Freshmen *Admission:* 74 applied, 36 admitted, 32 enrolled.
Faculty *Total:* 13, 15% full-time. *Student/faculty ratio:* 8:1.
Majors Funeral service and mortuary science.
Academics *Calendar:* semesters. *Degree:* diplomas and associate. *Special study options:* part-time degree program.
Library Memorial Library with 4,000 titles, 54 serial subscriptions, a Web page.
Student Life *Housing Options:* coed. Campus housing is university owned. *Campus security:* controlled dormitory access, day patrols.
Standardized Tests *Required:* ACT (for admission).
Costs (2013–14) *Tuition:* $9440 full-time, $295 per semester hour part-time. Full-time tuition and fees vary according to course load. Part-time tuition and fees vary according to course load. *Required fees:* $70 full-time. *Room only:* $3600. *Payment plan:* installment.
Financial Aid *Financial aid deadline:* 6/1.
Applying *Options:* deferred entrance. *Application fee:* $50. *Required:* essay or personal statement, high school transcript, 2 letters of recommendation. *Application deadlines:* rolling (freshmen), rolling (transfers).
Freshman Application Contact John A. Gupton College, 1616 Church Street, Nashville, TN 37203-2920. *Phone:* 615-327-3927.
Website: http://www.guptoncollege.edu/.

Kaplan Career Institute, Nashville Campus
Nashville, Tennessee
- **Proprietary** 2-year, founded 1981
- **Coed**

Academics *Degree:* certificates, diplomas, and associate.
Freshman Application Contact Kaplan Career Institute, Nashville Campus, 750 Envious Lane, Nashville, TN 37217. *Phone:* 615-269-9900. *Toll-free phone:* 800-935-1857.
Website: http://nashville.kaplancareerinstitute.com/.

L'Ecole Culinaire
Cordova, Tennessee
Admissions Office Contact L'Ecole Culinaire, 1245 N. Germantown Parkway, Cordova, TN 38016.
Website: http://www.lecole.edu/memphis/.

Lincoln College of Technology
Nashville, Tennessee
Freshman Application Contact Ms. Peggie Werrbach, Director of Admissions, Lincoln College of Technology, 1524 Gallatin Road, Nashville,

TN 37206. *Phone:* 615-226-3990 Ext. 8465. *Toll-free phone:* 800-228-6232. *Fax:* 615-262-8466. *E-mail:* wpruitt@nadcedu.com. *Website:* http://www.lincolnedu.com/campus/nashville-tn.

Miller-Motte Technical College

Clarksville, Tennessee

Director of Admissions Ms. Lisa Teague, Director of Admissions, Miller-Motte Technical College, 1820 Business Park Drive, Clarksville, TN 37040. *Phone:* 800-558-0071. *E-mail:* lisateague@hotmail.com. *Website:* http://www.miller-motte.edu/.

Motlow State Community College

Tullahoma, Tennessee

- **State-supported** 2-year, founded 1969, part of Tennessee Board of Regents
- **Rural** 187-acre campus with easy access to Nashville
- **Endowment** $4.6 million
- **Coed,** 4,580 undergraduate students, 39% full-time, 62% women, 38% men

Undergraduates 1,791 full-time, 2,789 part-time. Students come from 12 states and territories; 25 other countries; 1% are from out of state; 10% Black or African American, non-Hispanic/Latino; 3% Hispanic/Latino; 2% Asian, non-Hispanic/Latino; 0.1% Native Hawaiian or other Pacific Islander, non-Hispanic/Latino; 0.3% American Indian or Alaska Native, non-Hispanic/Latino; 1% Two or more races, non-Hispanic/Latino; 1% Race/ethnicity unknown; 0.2% international; 7% transferred in.

Freshmen *Admission:* 5,010 applied, 1,512 admitted, 1,065 enrolled.

Faculty *Total:* 236, 37% full-time, 13% with terminal degrees.

Majors Business administration and management; education; general studies; liberal arts and sciences/liberal studies; registered nursing/registered nurse; special education–early childhood; web page, digital/multimedia and information resources design.

Academics *Calendar:* semesters. *Degree:* certificates and associate. *Special study options:* academic remediation for entering students, accelerated degree program, adult/continuing education programs, advanced placement credit, cooperative education, distance learning, double majors, honors programs, independent study, part-time degree program, services for LD students, study abroad, summer session for credit.

Library Clayton-Glass Library with 194,392 titles, 9,411 serial subscriptions, 5,430 audiovisual materials, an OPAC, a Web page.

Student Life *Housing:* college housing not available. *Activities and Organizations:* drama/theater group, choral group, PTK Club, Communication Club, Student Government Association, Art Club, Baptist Student Union. *Campus security:* 24-hour patrols, late-night transport/escort service. *Student services:* personal/psychological counseling.

Athletics Member NJCAA. *Intercollegiate sports:* baseball M(s), basketball M(s)/W(s), softball W(s). *Intramural sports:* badminton M/W, basketball M/W, bowling M/W, golf M/W, tennis M/W, volleyball M/W.

Costs (2013–14) *Tuition:* state resident $3516 full-time; nonresident $13,368 full-time.

Financial Aid Of all full-time matriculated undergraduates who enrolled in 2011, 37 Federal Work-Study jobs (averaging $1883).

Applying *Options:* electronic application, early admission, deferred entrance. *Application fee:* $10. *Required:* high school transcript. *Application deadlines:* 8/13 (freshmen), 8/13 (transfers). *Notification:* continuous (freshmen), continuous (transfers).

Freshman Application Contact Ms. Sheri Mason, Assistant Director of Student Services, Motlow State Community College, Lynchburg, TN 37352-8500. *Phone:* 931-393-1764. *Toll-free phone:* 800-654-4877. *Fax:* 931-393-1681. *E-mail:* smason@mscc.edu. *Website:* http://www.mscc.edu/.

Nashville State Community College

Nashville, Tennessee

Freshman Application Contact Mr. Beth Mahan, Coordinator of Recruitment, Nashville State Community College, 120 White Bridge Road, Nashville, TN 37209-4515. *Phone:* 615-353-3214. *Toll-free phone:* 800-272-7363. *E-mail:* beth.mahan@nscc.edu. *Website:* http://www.nscc.edu/.

National College of Business and Technology

Bristol, Tennessee

Freshman Application Contact National College of Business and Technology, 1328 Highway 11 West, Bristol, TN 37620. *Phone:* 423-878-4440. *Toll-free phone:* 888-9-JOBREADY. *Website:* http://www.national-college.edu/.

National College of Business and Technology

Knoxville, Tennessee

Director of Admissions Frank Alvey, Campus Director, National College of Business and Technology, 8415 Kingston Pike, Knoxville, TN 37919. *Phone:* 865-539-2011. *Toll-free phone:* 888-9-JOBREADY. *Fax:* 865-539-2049. *Website:* http://www.national-college.edu/.

National College of Business and Technology

Nashville, Tennessee

Director of Admissions Jerry Lafferty, Campus Director, National College of Business and Technology, 1638 Bell Road, Nashville, TN 37211. *Phone:* 615-333-3344. *Toll-free phone:* 888-9-JOBREADY. *Website:* http://www.national-college.edu/.

North Central Institute

Clarksville, Tennessee

Freshman Application Contact Dale Wood, Director of Admissions, North Central Institute, 168 Jack Miller Boulevard, Clarksville, TN 37042. *Phone:* 931-431-9700. *Toll-free phone:* 800-603-4116. *Fax:* 931-431-9771. *E-mail:* admissions@nci.edu. *Website:* http://www.nci.edu/.

Northeast State Community College

Blountville, Tennessee

Freshman Application Contact Dr. Jon P. Harr, Vice President for Student Affairs, Northeast State Community College, PO Box 246, Blountville, TN 37617. *Phone:* 423-323-0231. *Toll-free phone:* 800-836-7822. *Fax:* 423-323-0240. *E-mail:* jpharr@northeaststate.edu. *Website:* http://www.northeaststate.edu/.

Nossi College of Art

Goodlettsville, Tennessee

- **Independent** primarily 2-year
- **Urban** 10-acre campus with easy access to Nashville
- **Coed,** 478 undergraduate students, 100% full-time, 56% women, 44% men
- 63% of applicants were admitted

Undergraduates 478 full-time. Students come from 12 states and territories; 1 other country; 12% are from out of state; 20% Black or African American, non-Hispanic/Latino; 4% Hispanic/Latino; 1% Asian, non-Hispanic/Latino; 0.6% Two or more races, non-Hispanic/Latino; 1% Race/ethnicity unknown; 0.2% international. *Retention:* 72% of full-time freshmen returned.

Freshmen *Admission:* 210 applied, 133 admitted.

Faculty *Total:* 37, 16% full-time. *Student/faculty ratio:* 10:1.

Majors Commercial and advertising art; commercial photography; film/video and photographic arts related; graphic design; illustration.

Academics *Calendar:* semesters. *Degrees:* associate and bachelor's. *Special study options:* independent study, internships, services for LD students, summer session for credit.

Library Learning Resource Center with an OPAC.

Student Life *Housing:* college housing not available. *Activities and Organizations:* national fraternities. *Campus security:* campus has a gated entrance, all doors are kept locked.

Applying *Options:* electronic application, early admission. *Application fee:* $100. *Required:* essay or personal statement, high school transcript, interview, portfolio of work is required for Associate or Bachelor of Graphic Art and Design program and the Bachelor of Illustration program.

Freshman Application Contact Ms. Mary Alexander, Admissions Director, Nossi College of Art, 590 Cheron Road, Madison, TN 37115. *Phone:* 615-514-2787 (ARTS). *Toll-free phone:* 888-986-ARTS. *Fax:* 615-514-2788. *E-mail:*

admissions@nossi.edu.
Website: http://www.nossi.edu/.

Pellissippi State Community College
Knoxville, Tennessee

Freshman Application Contact Director of Admissions and Records, Pellissippi State Community College, PO Box 22990, Knoxville, TN 37933-0990. *Phone:* 865-694-6400. *Fax:* 865-539-7217.
Website: http://www.pstcc.edu/.

Remington College–Memphis Campus
Memphis, Tennessee

Director of Admissions Randal Hayes, Director of Recruitment, Remington College–Memphis Campus, 2710 Nonconnah Boulevard, Memphis, TN 38132. *Phone:* 901-345-1000. *Fax:* 901-396-8310. *E-mail:* randal.hayes@remingtoncollege.edu.
Website: http://www.remingtoncollege.edu/.

Remington College–Nashville Campus
Nashville, Tennessee

Director of Admissions Mr. Frank Vivelo, Campus President, Remington College–Nashville Campus, 441 Donelson Pike, Suite 150, Nashville, TN 37214. *Phone:* 615-889-5520. *Fax:* 615-889-5528. *E-mail:* frank.vivelo@remingtoncollege.edu.
Website: http://www.remingtoncollege.edu/.

Roane State Community College
Harriman, Tennessee

Freshman Application Contact Admissions Office, Roane State Community College, 276 Patton Lane, Harriman, TN 37748. *Phone:* 865-882-4523. *Toll-free phone:* 866-462-7722 Ext. 4554. *E-mail:* admissions@roanestate.edu.
Website: http://www.roanestate.edu/.

Southwest Tennessee Community College
Memphis, Tennessee

Freshman Application Contact Ms. Cindy Meziere, Assistant Director of Recruiting, Southwest Tennessee Community College, PO Box 780, Memphis, TN 38103-0780. *Phone:* 901-333-4195. *Toll-free phone:* 877-717-STCC. *Fax:* 901-333-4473. *E-mail:* cmeziere@southwest.tn.edu.
Website: http://www.southwest.tn.edu/.

Vatterott College
Memphis, Tennessee

Admissions Office Contact Vatterott College, 2655 Dividend Drive, Memphis, TN 38132. *Toll-free phone:* 888-553-6627.
Website: http://www.vatterott.edu/.

Volunteer State Community College
Gallatin, Tennessee

- **State-supported** 2-year, founded 1970, part of Tennessee Board of Regents
- **Suburban** 100-acre campus with easy access to Nashville
- **Endowment** $122,153
- **Coed,** 8,177 undergraduate students, 44% full-time, 62% women, 38% men

Undergraduates 3,619 full-time, 4,558 part-time. Students come from 13 states and territories; 10 other countries; 0.8% are from out of state; 9% Black or African American, non-Hispanic/Latino; 3% Hispanic/Latino; 2% Asian, non-Hispanic/Latino; 0.5% American Indian or Alaska Native, non-Hispanic/Latino; 1% Two or more races, non-Hispanic/Latino; 3% Race/ethnicity unknown; 0.4% international; 7% transferred in.
Freshmen *Admission:* 2,132 applied, 2,132 admitted, 1,474 enrolled. *Average high school GPA:* 2.98. *Test scores:* ACT scores over 18: 67%; ACT scores over 24: 12%.

Faculty *Total:* 368, 42% full-time, 13% with terminal degrees. *Student/faculty ratio:* 23:1.
Majors Business administration and management; child development; clinical/medical laboratory technology; criminal justice/police science; education; fire science/firefighting; general studies; health information/medical records technology; health professions related; legal assistant/paralegal; liberal arts and sciences/liberal studies; medical radiologic technology; ophthalmic technology; physical therapy technology; respiratory care therapy; veterinary/animal health technology; web page, digital/multimedia and information resources design.
Academics *Calendar:* semesters. *Degree:* certificates and associate. *Special study options:* academic remediation for entering students, accelerated degree program, adult/continuing education programs, advanced placement credit, distance learning, double majors, English as a second language, honors programs, independent study, internships, part-time degree program, services for LD students, study abroad, summer session for credit.
Library Thigpen Learning Resource Center with 178,186 titles, 156 serial subscriptions, 2,018 audiovisual materials, an OPAC, a Web page.
Student Life *Housing:* college housing not available. *Activities and Organizations:* drama/theater group, student-run newspaper, radio station, choral group, Gamma Beta Phi, Returning Woman's Organization, Phi Theta Kappa, Student Government Association, The Settler. *Campus security:* 24-hour emergency response devices and patrols, late-night transport/escort service. *Student services:* personal/psychological counseling.
Athletics Member NJCAA. *Intercollegiate sports:* baseball M(s), basketball M(s)/W(s), softball W(s).
Standardized Tests *Required for some:* SAT or ACT (for admission).
Costs (2012–13) *Tuition:* state resident $3673 full-time, $135 per credit hour part-time; nonresident $14,305 full-time, $557 per credit hour part-time. Full-time tuition and fees vary according to course load. Part-time tuition and fees vary according to course load. *Required fees:* $271 full-time, $22 per term part-time. *Payment plan:* deferred payment. *Waivers:* senior citizens and employees or children of employees.
Financial Aid Of all full-time matriculated undergraduates who enrolled in 2011, 3,427 applied for aid, 2,615 were judged to have need, 105 had their need fully met. 52 Federal Work-Study jobs (averaging $1622). In 2011, 71 non-need-based awards were made. *Average percent of need met:* 45%. *Average financial aid package:* $5816. *Average need-based loan:* $2854. *Average need-based gift aid:* $4460. *Average non-need-based aid:* $2081.
Applying *Options:* electronic application, early admission, deferred entrance. *Application fee:* $20. *Required:* high school transcript. *Required for some:* minimum 2.0 GPA, interview. *Application deadlines:* 8/25 (freshmen), 8/25 (transfers). *Notification:* continuous (freshmen), continuous (transfers).
Freshman Application Contact Mr. Tim Amyx, Director of Admissions, Volunteer State Community College, 1480 Nashville Pike, Gallatin, TN 37066-3188. *Phone:* 615-452-8600 Ext. 3614. *Toll-free phone:* 888-335-8722. *Fax:* 615-230-4875. *E-mail:* admissions@volstate.edu.
Website: http://www.volstate.edu/.

Walters State Community College
Morristown, Tennessee

Freshman Application Contact Mr. Michael Campbell, Assistant Vice President for Student Affairs, Walters State Community College, 500 South Davy Crockett Parkway, Morristown, TN 37813-6899. *Phone:* 423-585-2682. *Toll-free phone:* 800-225-4770. *Fax:* 423-585-6876. *E-mail:* mike.campbell@ws.edu.
Website: http://www.ws.edu/.

TEXAS

Alvin Community College
Alvin, Texas

- **State and locally supported** 2-year, founded 1949
- **Suburban** 114-acre campus with easy access to Houston
- **Coed,** 5,794 undergraduate students, 27% full-time, 54% women, 46% men

Undergraduates 1,560 full-time, 4,234 part-time. 10% Black or African American, non-Hispanic/Latino; 4% Hispanic/Latino; 5% Asian, non-Hispanic/Latino; 0.3% Native Hawaiian or other Pacific Islander, non-Hispanic/Latino; 2% American Indian or Alaska Native, non-Hispanic/Latino; 1% Race/ethnicity unknown.
Freshmen *Admission:* 1,097 enrolled.
Faculty *Total:* 262, 37% full-time. *Student/faculty ratio:* 17:1.
Majors Accounting; administrative assistant and secretarial science; aeronautics/aviation/aerospace science and technology; art; biology/biological sci-

ences; business administration and management; chemical technology; child development; computer engineering technology; computer programming; corrections; court reporting; criminal justice/police science; drafting and design technology; dramatic/theater arts; electrical, electronic and communications engineering technology; emergency medical technology (EMT paramedic); legal administrative assistant/secretary; legal assistant/paralegal; legal studies; liberal arts and sciences/liberal studies; marketing/marketing management; mathematics; medical administrative assistant and medical secretary; mental health counseling; music; physical education teaching and coaching; physical sciences; radio and television; registered nursing/registered nurse; respiratory care therapy; substance abuse/addiction counseling; voice and opera.

Academics *Calendar:* semesters. *Degree:* certificates, diplomas, and associate. *Special study options:* academic remediation for entering students, accelerated degree program, adult/continuing education programs, advanced placement credit, distance learning, double majors, English as a second language, honors programs, independent study, internships, part-time degree program, services for LD students, student-designed majors, study abroad, summer session for credit.

Library Alvin Community College Library with an OPAC, a Web page.

Student Life *Campus security:* 24-hour patrols, late-night transport/escort service. *Student services:* personal/psychological counseling.

Athletics Member NJCAA. *Intercollegiate sports:* baseball M(s), softball W(s). *Intramural sports:* soccer M(c)/W(c).

Costs (2012–13) *Tuition:* area resident $1008 full-time, $42 per credit hour part-time; state resident $2016 full-time, $84 per credit hour part-time; nonresident $3120 full-time, $130 per credit hour part-time. Full-time tuition and fees vary according to program. Part-time tuition and fees vary according to program. *Required fees:* $414 full-time, $202 part-time. *Payment plan:* installment.

Applying *Options:* electronic application. *Required for some:* high school transcript. *Application deadlines:* rolling (freshmen), rolling (transfers).

Freshman Application Contact Alvin Community College, 3110 Mustang Road, Alvin, TX 77511-4898. *Phone:* 281-756-3531.

Website: http://www.alvincollege.edu/.

Amarillo College
Amarillo, Texas

- **State and locally supported** 2-year, founded 1929
- **Urban** 1542-acre campus
- **Endowment** $29.0 million
- **Coed**

Undergraduates 5% Black or African American, non-Hispanic/Latino; 32% Hispanic/Latino; 3% Asian, non-Hispanic/Latino; 1% American Indian or Alaska Native, non-Hispanic/Latino; 2% Race/ethnicity unknown. *Retention:* 52% of full-time freshmen returned.

Faculty *Total:* 443, 50% full-time.

Majors Accounting; administrative assistant and secretarial science; airframe mechanics and aircraft maintenance technology; architectural engineering technology; art; automobile/automotive mechanics technology; behavioral sciences; biblical studies; biology/biological sciences; broadcast journalism; business administration and management; business teacher education; chemical technology; chemistry; child development; clinical laboratory science/medical technology; commercial and advertising art; computer engineering technology; computer programming; computer science; computer systems analysis; corrections; criminal justice/law enforcement administration; criminal justice/police science; dental hygiene; drafting and design technology; dramatic/theater arts; electrical, electronic and communications engineering technology; elementary education; emergency medical technology (EMT paramedic); engineering; English; environmental health; fine/studio arts; fire science/firefighting; funeral service and mortuary science; general studies; geology/earth science; health information/medical records administration; heating, air conditioning, ventilation and refrigeration maintenance technology; heavy equipment maintenance technology; history; industrial radiologic technology; information science/studies; instrumentation technology; interior design; journalism; laser and optical technology; legal administrative assistant/secretary; liberal arts and sciences/liberal studies; licensed practical/vocational nurse training; machine tool technology; mass communication/media; mathematics; medical administrative assistant and medical secretary; modern languages; music; music teacher education; natural sciences; nuclear medical technology; occupational therapy; photography; physical education teaching and coaching; physical sciences; physical therapy; physics; pre-engineering; pre-pharmacy studies; psychology; public relations/image management; radio and television; radiologic technology/science; real estate; registered nursing/registered nurse; religious studies; respiratory care therapy; rhetoric and composition; social sciences; social work; substance abuse/addiction counseling; telecommunications technology; tourism and travel services management; visual and performing arts.

Academics *Calendar:* semesters. *Degree:* certificates and associate. *Special study options:* academic remediation for entering students, adult/continuing education programs, advanced placement credit, cooperative education, dis-

tance learning, English as a second language, freshman honors college, honors programs, part-time degree program, services for LD students, summer session for credit.

Library Lynn Library Learning Center plus 2 others with 62,076 titles, 24,020 serial subscriptions, an OPAC, a Web page.

Student Life *Housing:* college housing not available. *Activities and Organizations:* drama/theater group, student-run newspaper, radio station, choral group, Student Government Association, College Republicans. *Campus security:* 24-hour emergency response devices, late-night transport/escort service, Campus police patrol Monday through Saturday, 0700 to 2300.

Athletics *Intramural sports:* basketball M/W, soccer M/W, softball M/W, tennis M/W, volleyball M/W.

Costs (2013–14) *Tuition:* area resident $1842 full-time, $77 per semester hour part-time; state resident $2778 full-time, $116 per semester hour part-time; nonresident $4242 full-time, $177 per semester hour part-time. Full-time tuition and fees vary according to course load. Part-time tuition and fees vary according to course load. *Payment plan:* installment. *Waivers:* senior citizens and employees or children of employees.

Financial Aid Of all full-time matriculated undergraduates who enrolled in 2011, 100 Federal Work-Study jobs (averaging $3000).

Applying *Options:* early admission, deferred entrance. *Required:* high school transcript. *Notification:* continuous (freshmen), continuous (transfers).

Freshman Application Contact Amarillo College, PO Box 447, Amarillo, TX 79178-0001. *Phone:* 806-371-5000. *Toll-free phone:* 800-227-8784. *Fax:* 806-371-5497. *E-mail:* askac@actx.edu.

Website: http://www.actx.edu/.

Angelina College
Lufkin, Texas

Freshman Application Contact Angelina College, PO Box 1768, Lufkin, TX 75902-1768. *Phone:* 936-633-5213.

Website: http://www.angelina.cc.tx.us/.

ATI Technical Training Center
Dallas, Texas

Freshman Application Contact Admissions Office, ATI Technical Training Center, 6627 Maple Avenue, Dallas, TX 75235. *Phone:* 214-352-2222. *Toll-free phone:* 888-209-8264.

Website: http://www.aticareertraining.edu/.

Austin Community College
Austin, Texas

- **State and locally supported** 2-year, founded 1972
- **Urban** campus with easy access to Austin
- **Endowment** $4.5 million
- **Coed,** 43,315 undergraduate students, 23% full-time, 56% women, 44% men

Undergraduates 9,905 full-time, 33,410 part-time. 8% Black or African American, non-Hispanic/Latino; 28% Hispanic/Latino; 5% Asian, non-Hispanic/Latino; 0.2% Native Hawaiian or other Pacific Islander, non-Hispanic/Latino; 0.8% American Indian or Alaska Native, non-Hispanic/Latino; 1% Two or more races, non-Hispanic/Latino; 6% Race/ethnicity unknown; 3% international.

Faculty *Total:* 2,060, 30% full-time, 21% with terminal degrees. *Student/faculty ratio:* 19:1.

Majors Accounting technology and bookkeeping; administrative assistant and secretarial science; animation, interactive technology, video graphics and special effects; anthropology; art; automobile/automotive mechanics technology; banking and financial support services; biology/biological sciences; biology/biotechnology laboratory technician; business administration and management; business/commerce; carpentry; chemistry; child development; clinical/medical laboratory technology; commercial and advertising art; commercial photography; computer and information sciences; computer programming; computer systems networking and telecommunications; corrections; creative writing; criminal justice/police science; culinary arts; dance; dental hygiene; diagnostic medical sonography and ultrasound technology; drafting and design technology; dramatic/theater arts; early childhood education; economics; electrical, electronic and communications engineering technology; emergency medical technology (EMT paramedic); engineering; environmental engineering technology; fire prevention and safety technology; foreign languages and literatures; French; general studies; geographic information science and cartography; geography; geology/earth science; German; health and physical education/fitness; health information/medical records technology; health teacher education; heating, ventilation, air conditioning and refrigeration engineering technology; history; hospitality administration; human services; international business/trade/commerce; Japanese; journalism; Latin; legal assistant/paralegal; marketing/marketing management; mathematics; middle school education; music; music management; occupational therapist assistant; philosophy; physical sciences; physical therapy technology; physics; political science and government; pre-dentistry studies; premedical studies; pre-pharmacy studies; pre-veterinary studies; professional, technical, business, and scientific writing; psychology; radio and television; radiologic technology/science; real estate; registered nursing/registered nurse; rhetoric and composition; Russian; secondary education; sign language interpretation and translation; social work; sociology; Spanish; substance abuse/addiction counseling; surgical technology; surveying technology; therapeutic recreation; watchmaking and jewelrymaking; welding technology; writing.

Academics *Calendar:* semesters. *Degree:* certificates and associate. *Special study options:* academic remediation for entering students, accelerated degree program, adult/continuing education programs, advanced placement credit, cooperative education, distance learning, English as a second language, honors programs, independent study, internships, part-time degree program, services for LD students, summer session for credit. *ROTC:* Army (c), Air Force (c).

Library Main Library plus 8 others with 190,539 titles, 52,057 serial subscriptions, 16,875 audiovisual materials, an OPAC, a Web page.

Student Life *Housing:* college housing not available. *Activities and Organizations:* student-run newspaper, Intramurals, Student Government Association (SGA), Phi Theta Kappa (PTK), Center for Student Political Studies (CSPS), Circle K International (CKI). *Campus security:* 24-hour emergency response devices and patrols, late-night transport/escort service. *Student services:* personal/psychological counseling.

Athletics *Intramural sports:* basketball M/W, bowling M/W, golf M/W, soccer M/W, volleyball W.

Costs (2012–13) *Tuition:* area resident $1860 full-time, $62 per credit hour part-time; state resident $6720 full-time, $224 per credit hour part-time; nonresident $9240 full-time, $308 per credit hour part-time. Full-time tuition and fees vary according to course load. Part-time tuition and fees vary according to course load. *Required fees:* $480 full-time, $16 per credit hour part-time. *Payment plan:* installment. *Waivers:* senior citizens and employees or children of employees.

Financial Aid Of all full-time matriculated undergraduates who enrolled in 2012, 5,822 applied for aid, 5,202 were judged to have need. 329 Federal Work-Study jobs (averaging $2103). 34 state and other part-time jobs (averaging $2059). *Average need-based loan:* $1828. *Average need-based gift aid:* $2531.

Applying *Options:* electronic application. *Required:* high school transcript. *Application deadlines:* rolling (freshmen), rolling (transfers).

Freshman Application Contact Ms. Linda Kluck, Director, Admissions and Records, Austin Community College, 5930 Middle Fiskville Road, Austin, TX 78752. *Phone:* 512-223-7503. *Fax:* 512-223-7665. *E-mail:* admission@austincc.edu.
Website: http://www.austincc.edu/.

Blinn College
Brenham, Texas

Freshman Application Contact Mrs. Stephanie Wehring, Coordinator, Recruitment and Admissions, Blinn College, 902 College Avenue, Brenham, TX 77833-4049. *Phone:* 979-830-4152. *Fax:* 979-830-4110. *E-mail:* recruit@blinn.edu.
Website: http://www.blinn.edu/.

Brazosport College
Lake Jackson, Texas

Freshman Application Contact Brazosport College, 500 College Drive, Lake Jackson, TX 77566-3199. *Phone:* 979-230-3020.
Website: http://www.brazosport.edu/.

Brookhaven College
Farmers Branch, Texas

- **County-supported** 2-year, founded 1978, part of Dallas County Community College District System
- **Suburban** 200-acre campus with easy access to Dallas-Fort Worth
- **Coed,** 13,705 undergraduate students, 21% full-time, 59% women, 41% men

Undergraduates 2,889 full-time, 10,816 part-time. Students come from 28 states and territories; 10 other countries; 0.4% are from out of state; 18% Black or African American, non-Hispanic/Latino; 30% Hispanic/Latino; 11% Asian, non-Hispanic/Latino; 0.2% Native Hawaiian or other Pacific Islander, non-Hispanic/Latino; 1% American Indian or Alaska Native, non-Hispanic/Latino; 0.7% Two or more races, non-Hispanic/Latino; 3% Race/ethnicity unknown; 0.5% international; 7% transferred in.

Freshmen *Admission:* 1,648 enrolled.

Faculty *Total:* 545, 24% full-time. *Student/faculty ratio:* 23:1.

Majors Accounting; automobile/automotive mechanics technology; business administration and management; business/commerce; child development; computer engineering technology; computer programming; computer technology/computer systems technology; design and visual communications; e-commerce; education (multiple levels); emergency medical technology (EMT paramedic); executive assistant/executive secretary; general studies; geographic information science and cartography; graphic design; humanities; information science/studies; liberal arts and sciences/liberal studies; marketing/marketing management; music; office management; radiologic technology/science; registered nursing/registered nurse; secondary education; speech communication and rhetoric.

Academics *Calendar:* semesters. *Degree:* certificates and associate. *Special study options:* academic remediation for entering students, adult/continuing education programs, advanced placement credit, cooperative education, distance learning, English as a second language, honors programs, independent study, internships, off-campus study, part-time degree program, services for LD students, student-designed majors, study abroad, summer session for credit.

Library Brookhaven College Learning Resources Center plus 1 other with an OPAC, a Web page.

Student Life *Housing:* college housing not available. *Activities and Organizations:* drama/theater group, student-run newspaper, choral group. *Campus security:* 24-hour emergency response devices and patrols, late-night transport/escort service. *Student services:* health clinic, personal/psychological counseling.

Athletics Member NJCAA. *Intercollegiate sports:* baseball M, basketball M, soccer W, volleyball W. *Intramural sports:* weight lifting M/W.

Standardized Tests *Required:* STAAR test scores or an approved test for Reading, Writing and Math course placement. Test scores used for placement, not admission, purposes. Certain programs require specific tests (for admission).

Costs (2013–14) *Tuition:* area resident $1560 full-time, $52 per credit part-time; state resident $2910 full-time, $97 per credit part-time; nonresident $4590 full-time, $153 per credit part-time. *Payment plan:* installment. *Waivers:* senior citizens and employees or children of employees.

Applying *Options:* electronic application, early admission, deferred entrance. *Required:* high school transcript. *Required for some:* Admission to the nursing program is based on a point system consisting of three parts: (1) HESI score, (2)GPA of prerequisite courses, and (3) completion of support courses. *Application deadlines:* rolling (freshmen), rolling (transfers).

Freshman Application Contact Admissions Office, Brookhaven College, 3939 Valley View Lane, Farmers Branch, TX 75244-4997. *Phone:* 972-860-4883. *Fax:* 972-860-4886. *E-mail:* bhcAdmissions@dcccd.edu.
Website: http://www.brookhavencollege.edu/.

Brown Mackie College– Dallas/Fort Worth
Bedford, Texas

Admissions Office Contact Brown Mackie College–Dallas/Fort Worth, 2200 North Highway 121, Suite 270, Bedford, TX 76021.
Website: http://www.brownmackie.edu/dallas/.

See display on next page and page 356 for the College Close-Up.

Brown Mackie College–San Antonio
San Antonio, Texas

Director of Admissions Director of Admissions, Brown Mackie College–San Antonio, 4715 Fredericksburg Road, Suite 100, San Antonio, TX 78229. *Phone:* 210-428-2210. *Toll-free phone:* 877-460-1714.
Website: http://www.brownmackie.edu/san-antonio.

See display on next page and page 392 for the College Close-Up.

Cedar Valley College
Lancaster, Texas

Freshman Application Contact Admissions Office, Cedar Valley College, Lancaster, TX 75134-3799. *Phone:* 972-860-8206. *Fax:* 972-860-8207.
Website: http://www.cedarvalleycollege.edu/.

Center for Advanced Legal Studies
Houston, Texas

Freshman Application Contact Mr. James Scheffer, Center for Advanced Legal Studies, 3910 Kirby, Suite 200, Houston, TX 77098. *Phone:* 713-529-2778. *Toll-free phone:* 800-446-6931. *Fax:* 713-523-2715. *E-mail:* james.scheffer@paralegal.edu. *Website:* http://www.paralegal.edu/.

Central Texas College

Killeen, Texas

Freshman Application Contact Admissions Office, Central Texas College, PO Box 1800, Killeen, TX 76540-1800. *Phone:* 254-526-1696. *Toll-free phone:* 800-223-4760 (in-state); 800-792-3348 (out-of-state). *Fax:* 254-526-1545. *E-mail:* admrec@ctcd.edu.
Website: http://www.ctcd.edu/.

Cisco College

Cisco, Texas

Freshman Application Contact Mr. Olin O. Odom III, Dean of Admission/Registrar, Cisco College, 101 College Heights, Cisco, TX 76437-9321. *Phone:* 254-442-2567 Ext. 5130. *E-mail:* oodom@cjc.edu.
Website: http://www.cisco.edu/.

Clarendon College

Clarendon, Texas

Freshman Application Contact Ms. Martha Smith, Admissions Director, Clarendon College, PO Box 968, Clarendon, TX 79226. *Phone:* 806-874-3571 Ext. 106. *Toll-free phone:* 800-687-9737. *Fax:* 806-874-3201. *E-mail:* martha.smith@clarendoncollege.edu.
Website: http://www.clarendoncollege.edu/.

Coastal Bend College

Beeville, Texas

Freshman Application Contact Ms. Alicia Ulloa, Director of Admissions/Registrar, Coastal Bend College, Beeville, TX 78102-2197. *Phone:* 361-354-2245. *Toll-free phone:* 866-722-2838 (in-state); 866-262-2838 (out-of-state). *Fax:* 361-354-2254. *E-mail:* register@coastalbend.edu.
Website: http://www.coastalbend.edu/.

The College of Health Care Professions

Houston, Texas

Freshman Application Contact Admissions Office, The College of Health Care Professions, 240 Northwest Mall Boulevard, Houston, TX 77092. *Phone:* 713-425-3100. *Toll-free phone:* 800-487-6728. *Fax:* 713-425-3193.
Website: http://www.chcp.edu/.

College of the Mainland

Texas City, Texas

Freshman Application Contact Ms. Kelly Musick, Registrar/Director of Admissions, College of the Mainland, 1200 Amburn Road, Texas City, TX 77591. *Phone:* 409-938-1211 Ext. 469. *Toll-free phone:* 888-258-8859 Ext. 8264. *Fax:* 409-938-3126. *E-mail:* sem@com.edu.
Website: http://www.com.edu/.

Collin County Community College District

McKinney, Texas

- **State and locally supported** 2-year, founded 1985
- **Suburban** 333-acre campus with easy access to Dallas-Fort Worth
- **Endowment** $4.3 million
- **Coed,** 27,424 undergraduate students, 36% full-time, 56% women, 44% men

Undergraduates 9,755 full-time, 17,669 part-time. Students come from 48 states and territories; 109 other countries; 2% are from out of state; 11% Black or African American, non-Hispanic/Latino; 18% Hispanic/Latino; 8% Asian, non-Hispanic/Latino; 0.3% Native Hawaiian or other Pacific Islander, non-Hispanic/Latino; 0.4% American Indian or Alaska Native, non-Hispanic/Latino; 3% Two or more races, non-Hispanic/Latino; 0.8% Race/ethnicity unknown; 3% international; 9% transferred in. *Retention:* 62% of full-time freshmen returned.
Freshmen *Admission:* 5,091 applied, 5,091 admitted, 5,091 enrolled.
Faculty *Total:* 1,163, 36% full-time, 20% with terminal degrees. *Student/faculty ratio:* 24:1.

Majors Administrative assistant and secretarial science; animation, interactive technology, video graphics and special effects; biology/biotechnology laboratory technician; business administration and management; business automation/technology/data entry; child-care provision; child development; commercial and advertising art; computer and information sciences; computer and information systems security; computer programming; computer systems networking and telecommunications; criminal justice/police science; culinary arts; dental hygiene; drafting and design technology; early childhood education; educational/instructional technology; electrical, electronic and communications engineering technology; electrical/electronics drafting and CAD/CADD; electrical/electronics equipment installation and repair; emergency medical technology (EMT paramedic); engineering technology; environmental engineering technology; fire prevention and safety technology; fire science/firefighting; general studies; health information/medical records technology; Hispanic-American, Puerto Rican, and Mexican-American/Chicano studies; hospitality administration; interior design; kindergarten/preschool education; legal assistant/paralegal; liberal arts and sciences/liberal studies; medical transcription; middle school education; music; music management; real estate; recording arts technology; registered nursing/registered nurse; respiratory care therapy; sales, distribution, and marketing operations; secondary education; sign language interpretation and translation; speech communication and rhetoric; surgical technology; telecommunications technology; web page, digital/multimedia and information resources design.

Academics *Calendar:* semesters. *Degree:* certificates and associate. *Special study options:* academic remediation for entering students, adult/continuing education programs, advanced placement credit, cooperative education, distance learning, English as a second language, honors programs, internships, part-time degree program, services for LD students, summer session for credit. *ROTC:* Air Force (c).

Library Spring Creek Library, Preston Ridge Library, Central Park Library plus 3 others with 178,212 titles, 888 serial subscriptions, 32,095 audiovisual materials, an OPAC, a Web page.

Student Life *Housing:* college housing not available. *Activities and Organizations:* drama/theater group, choral group, Student Government, Phi Theta Kappa, Baptist Student Ministry, National Society of Leadership Success, Political Science Club. *Campus security:* 24-hour emergency response devices and patrols, late-night transport/escort service. *Student services:* personal/psychological counseling.

Athletics Member NJCAA. *Intercollegiate sports:* basketball M(s)/W(s), tennis M(s)/W(s), volleyball W(s).

Costs (2013–14) *Tuition:* area resident $810 full-time, $34 per credit hour part-time; state resident $1830 full-time, $68 per credit hour part-time; nonresident $3480 full-time, $123 per credit hour part-time. *Required fees:* $214 full-time. *Payment plan:* installment. *Waivers:* senior citizens.

Applying *Options:* electronic application. *Required:* high school transcript. *Application deadlines:* rolling (freshmen), rolling (out-of-state freshmen), rolling (transfers). *Notification:* continuous (freshmen), continuous (out-of-state freshmen), continuous (transfers).

Freshman Application Contact Mr. Todd Fields, Registrar, Collin County Community College District, 2800 E. Spring Creek Pkwy., Plano, TX 75074. *Phone:* 972-881-5174. *Fax:* 972-881-5175. *E-mail:* tfields@collin.edu. *Website:* http://www.collin.edu/.

Commonwealth Institute of Funeral Service
Houston, Texas

Freshman Application Contact Ms. Patricia Moreno, Registrar, Commonwealth Institute of Funeral Service, 415 Barren Springs Drive, Houston, TX 77090. *Phone:* 281-873-0262. *Toll-free phone:* 800-628-1580. *Fax:* 281-873-5232. *E-mail:* p.moreno@commonwealth.edu. *Website:* http://www.commonwealth.edu/.

Computer Career Center
El Paso, Texas

Director of Admissions Ms. Sarah Hernandez, Registrar, Computer Career Center, 6101 Montana Avenue, El Paso, TX 79925. *Phone:* 915-779-8031. *Toll-free phone:* 866-442-4197. *Website:* http://www.vistacollege.edu/.

Court Reporting Institute of Dallas
Dallas, Texas

Director of Admissions Ms. Debra Smith-Armstrong, Director of Admissions, Court Reporting Institute of Dallas, 1341 West Mockingbird Lane, Suite 200E, Dallas, TX 75247. *Phone:* 214-350-9722 Ext. 227. *Toll-free phone:* 877-841-3557 (in-state); 888-841-3557 (out-of-state). *Website:* http://www.crid.com/.

Court Reporting Institute of Houston
Houston, Texas

Freshman Application Contact Admissions Office, Court Reporting Institute of Houston, 13101 Northwest Freeway, Suite 100, Houston, TX 77040. *Phone:* 713-996-8300. *Toll-free phone:* 888-841-3557. *Website:* http://www.crid.com/.

Culinary Institute LeNotre
Houston, Texas

- **Proprietary** 2-year
- **Urban** campus
- **Coed,** 403 undergraduate students, 62% full-time, 55% women, 45% men

Undergraduates 248 full-time, 155 part-time. Students come from 6 states and territories; 3 other countries; 6% are from out of state; 22% Black or African American, non-Hispanic/Latino; 40% Hispanic/Latino; 2% Asian, non-Hispanic/Latino; 0.2% Native Hawaiian or other Pacific Islander, non-Hispanic/Latino; 0.5% Two or more races, non-Hispanic/Latino; 1% Race/ethnicity unknown.

Faculty *Student/faculty ratio:* 12:1.

Majors Baking and pastry arts; culinary arts.

Academics *Degree:* associate. *Special study options:* academic remediation for entering students, cooperative education, internships, study abroad.

Library an OPAC.

Student Life *Housing:* college housing not available.

Applying *Application fee:* $50. *Required:* essay or personal statement, high school transcript, minimum 2.0 GPA, interview.

Freshman Application Contact Admissions Office, Culinary Institute LeNotre, 7070 Allensby, Houston, TX 77022-4322. *Phone:* 713-358-5070. *Toll-free phone:* 888-LENOTRE. *Website:* http://www.culinaryinstitute.edu/.

Dallas Institute of Funeral Service
Dallas, Texas

- **Independent** 2-year, founded 1945
- **Urban** 4-acre campus with easy access to Dallas-Fort Worth
- **Coed**

Undergraduates 141 full-time. Students come from 7 states and territories; 11% are from out of state.

Faculty *Student/faculty ratio:* 17:1.

Academics *Calendar:* quarters. *Degree:* certificates and associate. *Special study options:* distance learning, services for LD students.

Student Life *Campus security:* 24-hour emergency response devices.

Applying *Application fee:* $50. *Required:* high school transcript.

Freshman Application Contact Director of Admissions, Dallas Institute of Funeral Service, 3909 South Buckner Boulevard, Dallas, TX 75227. *Phone:* 214-388-5466. *Toll-free phone:* 800-235-5444. *Fax:* 214-388-0316. *E-mail:* difs@dallasinstitute.edu. *Website:* http://www.dallasinstitute.edu/.

Del Mar College
Corpus Christi, Texas

Freshman Application Contact Ms. Frances P. Jordan, Director of Admissions and Registrar, Del Mar College, 101 Baldwin, Corpus Christi, TX 78404. *Phone:* 361-698-1255. *Toll-free phone:* 800-652-3357. *Fax:* 361-698-1595. *E-mail:* fjordan@delmar.edu. *Website:* http://www.delmar.edu/.

Eastfield College
Mesquite, Texas

Freshman Application Contact Ms. Glynis Miller, Director of Admissions/Registrar, Eastfield College, 3737 Motley Drive, Mesquite, TX 75150-2099. *Phone:* 972-860-7010. *Fax:* 972-860-8306. *E-mail:* efc@dcccd.edu. *Website:* http://www.efc.dcccd.edu/.

El Centro College
Dallas, Texas

- **County-supported** 2-year, founded 1966, part of Dallas County Community College District System
- **Urban** 2-acre campus
- **Coed,** 10,101 undergraduate students, 23% full-time, 66% women, 34% men

Undergraduates 2,314 full-time, 7,787 part-time. Students come from 49 other countries; 1% are from out of state; 19% Black or African American, non-Hispanic/Latino; 38% Hispanic/Latino; 3% Asian, non-Hispanic/Latino; 0.0% Native Hawaiian or other Pacific Islander, non-Hispanic/Latino; 0.3% American Indian or Alaska Native, non-Hispanic/Latino; 24% Two or more races, non-Hispanic/Latino; 2% Race/ethnicity unknown; 0.3% international; 74% transferred in. *Retention:* 39% of full-time freshmen returned.

Freshmen *Admission:* 2,962 applied, 2,962 admitted, 1,935 enrolled.

Faculty *Total:* 493, 27% full-time, 8% with terminal degrees. *Student/faculty ratio:* 19:1.

Majors Accounting; apparel and accessories marketing; baking and pastry arts; biotechnology; business administration and management; business automation/technology/data entry; business/commerce; cardiovascular technology; clinical/medical laboratory technology; computer and information systems security; computer/information technology services administration related; computer programming; computer science; culinary arts; data processing and data processing technology; diagnostic medical sonography and ultrasound technology; emergency medical technology (EMT paramedic); executive assistant/executive secretary; fashion/apparel design; health information/medical records administration; information science/studies; interior design; legal administrative assistant/secretary; legal assistant/paralegal; licensed practical/vocational nurse training; medical/clinical assistant; medical radiologic technology; medical transcription; office occupations and clerical services; peace studies and conflict resolution; radiologic technology/science; registered nursing/registered nurse; respiratory care therapy; special products marketing; surgical technology; teacher assistant/aide; web page, digital/multimedia and information resources design.

Academics *Calendar:* semesters. *Degree:* certificates and associate. *Special study options:* academic remediation for entering students, adult/continuing education programs, advanced placement credit, cooperative education, distance learning, double majors, English as a second language, freshman honors college, honors programs, internships, part-time degree program, services for LD students, summer session for credit. *ROTC:* Army (c).

Library El Centro College Library with 77,902 titles, 224 serial subscriptions, 585 audiovisual materials, an OPAC, a Web page.

Student Life *Housing:* college housing not available. *Activities and Organizations:* choral group, Phi Theta Kappa, Student Government, Paralegal Student Association, El Centro Computer Society, Conflict Resolution Society. *Campus security:* 24-hour emergency response devices and patrols, late-night transport/escort service, e-mail and text message alerts. *Student services:* health clinic, personal/psychological counseling.

Costs (2013–14) *Tuition:* area resident $1248 full-time, $52 per credit hour part-time; state resident $2328 full-time, $97 per credit hour part-time; nonresident $3672 full-time, $153 per credit hour part-time. Full-time tuition and fees vary according to program. Part-time tuition and fees vary according to program. *Payment plans:* installment, deferred payment. *Waivers:* senior citizens and employees or children of employees.

Applying *Options:* electronic application, early admission. *Required for some:* high school transcript, 1 letter of recommendation. *Application deadlines:* rolling (freshmen), rolling (transfers).

Freshman Application Contact Ms. Rebecca Garza, Director of Admissions and Registrar, El Centro College, Dallas, TX 75202. *Phone:* 214-860-2618. *Fax:* 214-860-2233. *E-mail:* rgarza@dcccd.edu. *Website:* http://www.elcentrocollege.edu/.

El Paso Community College
El Paso, Texas

- **County-supported** 2-year, founded 1969
- **Urban** campus
- **Coed**

Undergraduates 11,886 full-time, 18,837 part-time. 2% Black or African American, non-Hispanic/Latino; 85% Hispanic/Latino; 0.8% Asian, non-Hispanic/Latino; 0.1% Native Hawaiian or other Pacific Islander, non-Hispanic/Latino; 0.4% American Indian or Alaska Native, non-Hispanic/Latino; 0.7% Race/ethnicity unknown; 2% international.

Academics *Calendar:* semesters. *Degree:* certificates and associate. *Special study options:* academic remediation for entering students, adult/continuing education programs, advanced placement credit, cooperative education, distance learning, English as a second language, external degree program, honors programs, internships, off-campus study, part-time degree program, services for LD students, summer session for credit. *ROTC:* Army (c).

Student Life *Campus security:* 24-hour patrols, late-night transport/escort service.

Athletics Member NJCAA.

Costs (2012–13) *Tuition:* state resident $1848 full-time, $67 per hour part-time; nonresident $2496 full-time, $94 per hour part-time. *Required fees:* $240 full-time, $10 per hour part-time.

Financial Aid Of all full-time matriculated undergraduates who enrolled in 2011, 750 Federal Work-Study jobs (averaging $1800). 50 state and other part-time jobs (averaging $1800).

Applying *Options:* early admission, deferred entrance. *Application fee:* $10.

Freshman Application Contact Daryle Hendry, Director of Admissions, El Paso Community College, PO Box 20500, El Paso, TX 79998-0500. *Phone:* 915-831-2580. *E-mail:* daryleh@epcc.edu. *Website:* http://www.epcc.edu/.

Everest College
Arlington, Texas

Freshman Application Contact Admissions Office, Everest College, 300 Six Flags Drive, Suite 200, Arlington, TX 76011. *Phone:* 817-652-7790. *Toll-free phone:* 888-741-4270. *Fax:* 817-649-6033. *Website:* http://www.everest.edu/.

Everest College
Dallas, Texas

Freshman Application Contact Admissions Office, Everest College, 6080 North Central Expressway, Dallas, TX 75206. *Phone:* 214-234-4850. *Toll-free phone:* 888-741-4270. *Fax:* 214-696-6208. *Website:* http://www.everest.edu/.

Everest College
Fort Worth, Texas

Freshman Application Contact Admissions Office, Everest College, 5237 North Riverside Drive, Suite 100, Fort Worth, TX 76137. *Phone:* 817-838-3000. *Toll-free phone:* 888-741-4270. *Fax:* 817-838-2040. *Website:* http://www.everest.edu/.

Frank Phillips College
Borger, Texas

Freshman Application Contact Ms. Michele Stevens, Director of Enrollment Management, Frank Phillips College, PO Box 5118, Borger, TX 79008-5118. *Phone:* 806-457-4200 Ext. 707. *Fax:* 806-457-4225. *E-mail:* mstevens@fpctx.edu. *Website:* http://www.fpctx.edu/.

Galveston College
Galveston, Texas

Freshman Application Contact Galveston College, 4015 Avenue Q, Galveston, TX 77550-7496. *Phone:* 409-944-1234. *Website:* http://www.gc.edu/.

Grayson County College
Denison, Texas

Freshman Application Contact Tana Adams, Lead Enrollment Advisor, Grayson County College, 6101 Grayson Drive, Denison, TX 75020-8299. *Phone:* 903-463-8627. *E-mail:* hallt@grayson.edu. *Website:* http://www.grayson.edu/.

Hallmark College of Technology
San Antonio, Texas

- **Independent** primarily 2-year, founded 1969
- **Suburban** 3-acre campus
- **Coed,** 356 undergraduate students, 100% full-time, 55% women, 45% men

Undergraduates 356 full-time. Students come from 1 other state; 15% Black or African American, non-Hispanic/Latino; 55% Hispanic/Latino; 0.6% Asian, non-Hispanic/Latino; 0.3% Native Hawaiian or other Pacific Islander, non-Hispanic/Latino; 4% Two or more races, non-Hispanic/Latino; 1% Race/ethnicity unknown.

Freshmen *Admission:* 356 enrolled.

Faculty *Total:* 43, 47% full-time, 7% with terminal degrees. *Student/faculty ratio:* 8:1.

Majors Airframe mechanics and aircraft maintenance technology; aviation/airway management; business administration and management; business automation/technology/data entry; computer systems networking and telecommunications; data processing and data processing technology; electrical, electronic and communications engineering technology; information technology; medical administrative assistant and medical secretary; medical/clinical assistant; medical insurance coding; registered nursing/registered nurse; system, networking, and LAN/WAN management.

Academics *Calendar:* continuous. *Degrees:* certificates, associate, bachelor's, and master's. *Special study options:* accelerated degree program, advanced placement credit, distance learning, internships.

Library Randall K. Williams Virtual Library plus 1 other.

Student Life *Housing:* college housing not available. *Activities and Organizations:* Alpha Beta Kappa Honor Society. *Campus security:* 24-hour emergency response devices.

Standardized Tests *Required:* Wonderlic aptitude test, SAT/ACT is used for entrance to some degree programs (for admission). *Required for some:* SAT or ACT (for admission).

Applying *Application fee:* $110. *Required:* high school transcript, interview, tour, application requirements differ depending on program of enrollment. *Required for some:* essay or personal statement. *Application deadlines:* rolling (freshmen), rolling (transfers). *Notification:* continuous (freshmen), continuous (transfers).

Freshman Application Contact Sal Ross, Vice President of Admissions, Hallmark College of Technology, 10401 IH-10 West, San Antonio, TX 78230. *Phone:* 210-690-9000 Ext. 214. *Fax:* 210-697-8225. *E-mail:* slross@hallmarkcollege.edu.
Website: http://www.hallmarkcollege.edu/.

Hallmark Institute of Aeronautics
San Antonio, Texas

- **Private** 2-year
- **Urban** 2-acre campus with easy access to San Antonio
- **Coed,** 227 undergraduate students, 100% full-time, 7% women, 93% men

Undergraduates 227 full-time. Students come from 1 other state; 10% Black or African American, non-Hispanic/Latino; 49% Hispanic/Latino; 1% Asian, non-Hispanic/Latino; 0.4% Native Hawaiian or other Pacific Islander, non-Hispanic/Latino; 3% Two or more races, non-Hispanic/Latino; 0.4% Race/ethnicity unknown; 2% transferred in.

Freshmen *Admission:* 193 enrolled.

Faculty *Total:* 17, 100% full-time. *Student/faculty ratio:* 17:1.

Majors Aircraft powerplant technology; airframe mechanics and aircraft maintenance technology.

Academics *Calendar:* continuous. *Degree:* diplomas and associate. *Special study options:* academic remediation for entering students.

Library (Virtual Library) plus 1 other.

Student Life *Housing:* college housing not available. *Campus security:* 24-hour emergency response devices and patrols.

Applying *Application fee:* $110. *Required:* high school transcript, interview, assessment, tour, background check. *Application deadlines:* rolling (freshmen), rolling (transfers). *Notification:* continuous (freshmen), continuous (transfers).

Freshman Application Contact Hallmark Institute of Aeronautics, 8901 Wetmore Road, San Antonio, TX 78216. *Phone:* 210-690-9000 Ext. 214.
Website: http://www.hallmarkcollege.edu/programs/school-of-aeronautics/.

Hill College
Hillsboro, Texas

Freshman Application Contact Ms. Diane Harvey, Director of Admissions/Registrar, Hill College, 112 Lamar Drive, Hillsboro, TX 76645. *Phone:* 254-582-2555. *Fax:* 254-582-7591. *E-mail:* diharvey@hillcollege.cc.tx.us.
Website: http://www.hillcollege.edu/.

Houston Community College System
Houston, Texas

- **State and locally supported** 2-year, founded 1971
- **Urban** campus
- **Coed,** 58,476 undergraduate students, 32% full-time, 59% women, 41% men

Undergraduates 18,476 full-time, 40,000 part-time. 2% are from out of state; 31% Black or African American, non-Hispanic/Latino; 31% Hispanic/Latino; 9% Asian, non-Hispanic/Latino; 0.3% Native Hawaiian or other Pacific Islander, non-Hispanic/Latino; 0.2% American Indian or Alaska Native, non-Hispanic/Latino; 1% Two or more races, non-Hispanic/Latino; 2% Race/ethnicity unknown; 10% international; 7% transferred in.

Freshmen *Admission:* 8,726 enrolled.

Majors Accounting; animation, interactive technology, video graphics and special effects; applied horticulture/horticulture operations; automobile/automotive mechanics technology; banking and financial support services; biology/biotechnology laboratory technician; business administration and management; business automation/technology/data entry; business/corporate communications; cardiovascular technology; chemical technology; child development; cinematography and film/video production; clinical/medical laboratory science and allied professions related; clinical/medical laboratory technology; commercial photography; computer engineering technology; computer programming; computer programming (specific applications); computer systems networking and telecommunications; construction engineering technology; cosmetology; court reporting; criminal justice/police science; culinary arts; desktop publishing and digital imaging design; drafting and design technology; emergency medical technology (EMT paramedic); fashion/apparel design; fashion merchandising; fire prevention and safety technology; geographic information science and cartography; graphic and printing equipment operation/production; health and physical education/fitness; health information/medical records technology; histologic technician; hotel/motel administration; instrumentation technology; interior design; international business/trade/commerce; legal assistant/paralegal; logistics, materials, and supply chain management; manufacturing engineering technology; marketing/marketing management; music management; music performance; music theory and composition; network and system administration; nuclear medical technology; occupational therapist assistant; physical therapy technology; psychiatric/mental health services technology; public administration; radio and television broadcasting technology; radiologic technology/science; real estate; registered nursing/registered nurse; respiratory care therapy; sign language interpretation and translation; tourism and travel services management; turf and turfgrass management.

Academics *Calendar:* semesters. *Degree:* certificates and associate. *Special study options:* adult/continuing education programs, part-time degree program. *ROTC:* Army (c), Air Force (c).

Student Life *Housing:* college housing not available. *Activities and Organizations:* drama/theater group, student-run newspaper, television station. *Campus security:* 24-hour emergency response devices and patrols, late-night transport/escort service. *Student services:* personal/psychological counseling.

Applying *Required for some:* high school transcript, interview. *Application deadlines:* rolling (freshmen), rolling (transfers). *Notification:* continuous (transfers).

Freshman Application Contact Ms. Mary Lemburg, Registrar, Houston Community College System, 3100 Main Street, PO Box 667517, Houston, TX 77266-7517. *Phone:* 713-718-8500. *Toll-free phone:* 877-422-6111. *Fax:* 713-718-2111.
Website: http://www.hccs.edu/.

Howard College
Big Spring, Texas

Freshman Application Contact Ms. TaNeal Richardson, Assistant Registrar, Howard College, 1001 Birdwell Lane, Big Spring, TX 79720-3702. *Phone:* 432-264-5105. *Toll-free phone:* 866-HC-HAWKS. *Fax:* 432-264-5604. *E-mail:* trichardson@howardcollege.edu.
Website: http://www.howardcollege.edu/.

ITT Technical Institute
Arlington, Texas

- **Proprietary** primarily 2-year, founded 1982, part of ITT Educational Services, Inc.
- **Suburban** campus
- **Coed**

Academics *Calendar:* quarters. *Degrees:* associate and bachelor's.

Freshman Application Contact Director of Recruitment, ITT Technical Institute, 551 Ryan Plaza Drive, Arlington, TX 76011. *Phone:* 817-794-5100. *Toll-free phone:* 888-288-4950. *Fax:* 817-275-8446.
Website: http://www.itt-tech.edu/.

ITT Technical Institute
Austin, Texas

- **Proprietary** primarily 2-year, founded 1985, part of ITT Educational Services, Inc.
- **Urban** campus
- **Coed**

Academics *Calendar:* quarters. *Degrees:* associate and bachelor's.

Financial Aid Of all full-time matriculated undergraduates who enrolled in 2011, 1 Federal Work-Study job.
Freshman Application Contact Director of Recruitment, ITT Technical Institute, 6330 Highway 290 East, Austin, TX 78723. *Phone:* 512-467-6800. *Toll-free phone:* 800-431-0677. *Fax:* 512-467-6677.
Website: http://www.itt-tech.edu/.

ITT Technical Institute
DeSoto, Texas

- **Proprietary** primarily 2-year
- **Coed**

Academics *Degrees:* associate and bachelor's.
Freshman Application Contact Director of Recruitment, ITT Technical Institute, 921 West Belt Line Road, Suite 181, DeSoto, TX 75115. *Phone:* 972-274-8600. *Toll-free phone:* 877-854-5728.
Website: http://www.itt-tech.edu/.

ITT Technical Institute
Houston, Texas

- **Proprietary** primarily 2-year, founded 1985, part of ITT Educational Services, Inc.
- **Suburban** campus
- **Coed**

Academics *Calendar:* quarters. *Degrees:* associate and bachelor's.
Freshman Application Contact Director of Recruitment, ITT Technical Institute, 15651 North Freeway, Houston, TX 77090. *Phone:* 281-873-0512. *Toll-free phone:* 800-879-6486.
Website: http://www.itt-tech.edu/.

ITT Technical Institute
Houston, Texas

- **Proprietary** primarily 2-year, founded 1983, part of ITT Educational Services, Inc.
- **Urban** campus
- **Coed**

Academics *Calendar:* quarters. *Degrees:* associate and bachelor's.
Freshman Application Contact Director of Recruitment, ITT Technical Institute, 2950 South Gessner, Houston, TX 77063-3751. *Phone:* 713-952-2294. *Toll-free phone:* 800-235-4787.
Website: http://www.itt-tech.edu/.

ITT Technical Institute
Richardson, Texas

- **Proprietary** primarily 2-year, founded 1989, part of ITT Educational Services, Inc.
- **Suburban** campus
- **Coed**

Academics *Calendar:* quarters. *Degrees:* associate and bachelor's.
Financial Aid Of all full-time matriculated undergraduates who enrolled in 2011, 5 Federal Work-Study jobs (averaging $5000).
Freshman Application Contact Director of Recruitment, ITT Technical Institute, 2101 Waterview Parkway, Richardson, TX 75080. *Phone:* 972-690-9100. *Toll-free phone:* 888-488-5761.
Website: http://www.itt-tech.edu/.

ITT Technical Institute
San Antonio, Texas

- **Proprietary** primarily 2-year, founded 1988, part of ITT Educational Services, Inc.
- **Urban** campus
- **Coed**

Academics *Calendar:* quarters. *Degrees:* associate and bachelor's.
Freshman Application Contact Director of Recruitment, ITT Technical Institute, 5700 Northwest Parkway, San Antonio, TX 78249-3303. *Phone:* 210-694-4612. *Toll-free phone:* 800-880-0570.
Website: http://www.itt-tech.edu/.

ITT Technical Institute
Waco, Texas

- **Proprietary** primarily 2-year, part of ITT Educational Services, Inc.
- **Coed**

Academics *Calendar:* quarters. *Degrees:* associate and bachelor's.
Freshman Application Contact Director of Recruitment, ITT Technical Institute, 3700 S. Jack Kultgen Expressway, Suite 100, Waco, TX 76706. *Phone:* 254-881-2200. *Toll-free phone:* 877-201-7143.
Website: http://www.itt-tech.edu/.

ITT Technical Institute
Webster, Texas

- **Proprietary** primarily 2-year, founded 1995, part of ITT Educational Services, Inc.
- **Coed**

Academics *Calendar:* quarters. *Degrees:* associate and bachelor's.
Freshman Application Contact Director of Recruitment, ITT Technical Institute, 1001 Magnolia Avenue, Webster, TX 77598. *Phone:* 281-316-4700. *Toll-free phone:* 888-488-9347.
Website: http://www.itt-tech.edu/.

Jacksonville College
Jacksonville, Texas

Freshman Application Contact Danny Morris, Director of Admissions, Jacksonville College, 105 B.J. Albritton Drive, Jacksonville, TX 75766. *Phone:* 903-589-7110. *Toll-free phone:* 800-256-8522. *E-mail:* admissions@jacksonville-college.org.
Website: http://www.jacksonville-college.edu/.

Kaplan College, Arlington Campus
Arlington, Texas

- **Proprietary** 2-year
- **Coed**

Academics *Degree:* diplomas and associate.
Freshman Application Contact Kaplan College, Arlington Campus, 2241 South Watson Road, Arlington, TX 76010. *Phone:* 866-249-2074. *Toll-free phone:* 800-935-1857.
Website: http://arlington.kaplancollege.com/.

Kaplan College, Beaumont Campus
Beaumont, Texas

- **Proprietary** 2-year
- **Coed**

Academics *Calendar:* continuous. *Degree:* diplomas and associate.
Freshman Application Contact Admissions Office, Kaplan College, Beaumont Campus, 6115 Eastex Freeway, Beaumont, TX 77706. *Phone:* 409-833-2722. *Toll-free phone:* 800-935-1857.
Website: http://beaumont.kaplancollege.com/.

Kaplan College, Brownsville Campus
Brownsville, Texas

- **Proprietary** 2-year
- **Coed**

Academics *Degree:* diplomas and associate.
Freshman Application Contact Director of Admissions, Kaplan College, Brownsville Campus, 1900 North Expressway, Suite O, Brownsville, TX 78521. *Phone:* 956-547-8200.
Website: http://brownsville.kaplancollege.com/.

Kaplan College, Corpus Christi Campus
Corpus Christi, Texas

- **Proprietary** 2-year
- **Coed**

Academics *Calendar:* other. *Degree:* diplomas and associate.
Freshman Application Contact Admissions Director, Kaplan College, Corpus Christi Campus, 1620 South Padre Island Drive, Suite 600, Corpus Christi, TX 78416. *Phone:* 361-852-2900.
Website: http://corpus-christi.kaplancollege.com/.

Kaplan College, Dallas Campus

Dallas, Texas

- **Proprietary** 2-year, founded 1987
- **Coed**

Academics *Degree:* diplomas and associate.
Freshman Application Contact Kaplan College, Dallas Campus, 12005 Ford Road, Suite 100, Dallas, TX 75234. *Phone:* 972-385-1446. *Toll-free phone:* 800-935-1857.
Website: http://dallas.kaplancollege.com/.

Kaplan College, El Paso Campus

El Paso, Texas

- **Proprietary** 2-year
- **Coed**

Academics *Degree:* diplomas and associate.
Freshman Application Contact Director of Admissions, Kaplan College, El Paso Campus, 8360 Burnham Road, Suite 100, El Paso, TX 79907.
Website: http://el-paso.kaplancollege.com/.

Kaplan College, Fort Worth Campus

Fort Worth, Texas

- **Proprietary** 2-year
- **Coed**

Academics *Degree:* diplomas and associate.
Freshman Application Contact Director of Admissions, Kaplan College, Fort Worth Campus, 2001 Beach Street, Suite 201, Fort Worth, TX 76103. *Phone:* 817-413-2000.
Website: http://fort-worth.kaplancollege.com/.

Kaplan College, Laredo Campus

Laredo, Texas

- **Proprietary** 2-year
- **Coed**

Academics *Degree:* diplomas and associate.
Freshman Application Contact Admissions Office, Kaplan College, Laredo Campus, 6410 McPherson Road, Laredo, TX 78041. *Phone:* 956-717-5909. *Toll-free phone:* 800-935-1857.
Website: http://laredo.kaplancollege.com/.

Kaplan College, Lubbock Campus

Lubbock, Texas

- **Proprietary** 2-year
- **Coed**

Academics *Degree:* diplomas and associate.
Freshman Application Contact Admissions Office, Kaplan College, Lubbock Campus, 1421 Ninth Street, Lubbock, TX 79401. *Phone:* 806-765-7051. *Toll-free phone:* 800-935-1857.
Website: http://lubbock.kaplancollege.com/.

Kaplan College, McAllen Campus

McAllen, Texas

Admissions Office Contact Kaplan College, McAllen Campus, 1500 South Jackson Road, McAllen, TX 78503. *Toll-free phone:* 800-935-1857.
Website: http://mcallen.kaplancollege.com/.

Kaplan College, San Antonio Campus

San Antonio, Texas

- **Proprietary** 2-year
- **Coed**

Academics *Degree:* certificates, diplomas, and associate.
Freshman Application Contact Admissions Office, Kaplan College, San Antonio Campus, 6441 NW Loop 410, San Antonio, TX 78238. *Phone:* 210-308-8584. *Toll-free phone:* 800-935-1857.
Website: http://wsan-antonio.kaplancollege.com/.

Kaplan College, San Antonio–San Pedro Area Campus

San Antonio, Texas

- **Proprietary** 2-year
- **Coed**

Academics *Degree:* diplomas and associate.
Freshman Application Contact Director of Admissions, Kaplan College, San Antonio–San Pedro Area Campus, 7142 San Pedro Avenue, Suite 100, San Antonio, TX 78216. *Toll-free phone:* 800-935-1857.
Website: http://nsan-antonio.kaplancollege.com/.

KD Studio

Dallas, Texas

- **Proprietary** 2-year, founded 1979
- **Urban** campus
- **Coed**

Undergraduates 9% are from out of state; 46% Black or African American, non-Hispanic/Latino; 18% Hispanic/Latino; 2% Asian, non-Hispanic/Latino. *Retention:* 69% of full-time freshmen returned.
Faculty *Student/faculty ratio:* 6:1.
Academics *Calendar:* semesters. *Degree:* associate. *Special study options:* cooperative education.
Student Life *Campus security:* 24-hour emergency response devices and patrols.
Applying *Options:* deferred entrance. *Application fee:* $100. *Required:* essay or personal statement, high school transcript, interview, audition.
Freshman Application Contact Mr. T. A. Taylor, Director of Education, KD Studio, 2600 Stemmons Freeway, Suite 117, Dallas, TX 75207. *Phone:* 214-638-0484. *Toll-free phone:* 877-278-2283. *Fax:* 214-630-5140. *E-mail:* tataylor@kdstudio.com.
Website: http://www.kdstudio.com/.

Kilgore College

Kilgore, Texas

- **State and locally supported** 2-year, founded 1935
- **Small-town** 35-acre campus with easy access to Dallas-Fort Worth
- **Coed,** 6,231 undergraduate students, 46% full-time, 62% women, 38% men

Undergraduates 2,858 full-time, 3,373 part-time. Students come from 25 states and territories; 28 other countries; 1% are from out of state; 21% Black or African American, non-Hispanic/Latino; 13% Hispanic/Latino; 0.8% Asian, non-Hispanic/Latino; 0.1% Native Hawaiian or other Pacific Islander, non-Hispanic/Latino; 0.5% American Indian or Alaska Native, non-Hispanic/Latino; 2% Two or more races, non-Hispanic/Latino; 1% Race/ethnicity unknown; 1% international; 7% transferred in; 7% live on campus. *Retention:* 52% of full-time freshmen returned.
Freshmen *Admission:* 1,204 enrolled.
Faculty *Total:* 398, 39% full-time. *Student/faculty ratio:* 17:1.
Majors Accounting technology and bookkeeping; aerospace, aeronautical and astronautical/space engineering; agriculture; architecture; art; autobody/collision and repair technology; automobile/automotive mechanics technology; biological and physical sciences; business administration and management; business/commerce; chemical engineering; chemistry; child-care and support services management; child-care provision; civil engineering; clinical/medical laboratory technology; commercial and advertising art; commercial photography; computer and information sciences; computer installation and repair technology; computer programming; computer systems networking and telecommunications; corrections; criminal justice/law enforcement administration; dance; diesel mechanics technology; drafting and design technology; dramatic/theater arts; electrical, electronic and communications engineering technology; elementary education; emergency medical technology (EMT paramedic); English; executive assistant/executive secretary; fashion merchandising; forestry; general studies; geology/earth science; health teacher education; heating, air conditioning, ventilation and refrigeration maintenance technology; journalism; legal assistant/paralegal; management information systems; mathematics; mechanical engineering; medical radiologic technology; metallurgical technology; multi/interdisciplinary studies related; music; occupational safety and health technology; occupational therapist assistant; operations management; petroleum engineering; physical education teaching and coaching; physical therapy; physical therapy technology; physics; pre-dentistry studies; pre-law studies; premedical studies; pre-pharmacy studies; pre-veterinary studies; psychology; radiologic technology/science; registered nursing/registered nurse; religious studies; social sciences; surgical technology; web/multimedia management and webmaster; welding technology.

Academics *Calendar:* semesters. *Degree:* certificates and associate. *Special study options:* academic remediation for entering students, adult/continuing education programs, advanced placement credit, cooperative education, distance learning, English as a second language, internships, part-time degree program, services for LD students, student-designed majors, summer session for credit.

Library Randolph C. Watson Library plus 1 other with 65,000 titles, 6,679 serial subscriptions, 13,351 audiovisual materials, an OPAC, a Web page.

Student Life *Housing Options:* coed, men-only, women-only. Campus housing is university owned. *Activities and Organizations:* drama/theater group, student-run newspaper, choral group, marching band. *Campus security:* 24-hour emergency response devices and patrols. *Student services:* personal/psychological counseling.

Athletics Member NJCAA. *Intercollegiate sports:* basketball M(s)/W(s), cheerleading M(s)/W(s), football M(s). *Intramural sports:* basketball M/W, football M/W, racquetball M/W, tennis M/W, volleyball M/W.

Costs (2012–13) *Tuition:* area resident $696 full-time, $29 per semester hour part-time; state resident $2304 full-time, $96 per semester hour part-time; nonresident $3456 full-time, $144 per semester hour part-time. *Required fees:* $672 full-time. *Room and board:* $4270. Room and board charges vary according to board plan and housing facility. *Payment plan:* installment. *Waivers:* senior citizens and employees or children of employees.

Financial Aid Of all full-time matriculated undergraduates who enrolled in 2011, 80 Federal Work-Study jobs (averaging $2500). *Financial aid deadline:* 6/1.

Applying *Options:* electronic application, early admission. *Required:* high school transcript. *Required for some:* interview. *Application deadlines:* rolling (freshmen), rolling (out-of-state freshmen), rolling (transfers).

Freshman Application Contact Kilgore College, 1100 Broadway Boulevard, Kilgore, TX 75662-3299. *Phone:* 903-983-8200. *E-mail:* register@ kilgore.cc.tx.us.
Website: http://www.kilgore.edu/.

Lamar Institute of Technology

Beaumont, Texas

Freshman Application Contact Admissions Office, Lamar Institute of Technology, 855 East Lavaca, Beaumont, TX 77705. *Phone:* 409-880-8354. *Toll-free phone:* 800-950-6989.
Website: http://www.lit.edu/.

Lamar State College–Orange

Orange, Texas

Freshman Application Contact Kerry Olson, Director of Admissions and Financial Aid, Lamar State College–Orange, 410 Front Street, Orange, TX 77632. *Phone:* 409-882-3362. *Fax:* 409-882-3374.
Website: http://www.lsco.edu/.

Lamar State College–Port Arthur

Port Arthur, Texas

Freshman Application Contact Ms. Connie Nicholas, Registrar, Lamar State College–Port Arthur, PO Box 310, Port Arthur, TX 77641-0310. *Phone:* 409-984-6165. *Toll-free phone:* 800-477-5872. *Fax:* 409-984-6025. *E-mail:* nichoca@lamarpa.edu.
Website: http://www.lamarpa.edu/.

Laredo Community College

Laredo, Texas

Freshman Application Contact Ms. Josie Soliz, Admissions Records Supervisor, Laredo Community College, Laredo, TX 78040-4395. *Phone:* 956-721-5177. *Fax:* 956-721-5493.
Website: http://www.laredo.edu/.

Le Cordon Bleu College of Culinary Arts in Austin

Austin, Texas

Director of Admissions Paula Paulette, Vice President of Marketing and Admissions, Le Cordon Bleu College of Culinary Arts in Austin, 3110 Esperanza Crossing, Suite 100, Austin, TX 78758. *Phone:* 512-837-2665. *Toll-free phone:* 888-559-7222. *E-mail:* ppaulette@txca.com.
Website: http://www.chefs.edu/Austin.

Lee College

Baytown, Texas

Director of Admissions Ms. Becki Griffith, Registrar, Lee College, PO Box 818, Baytown, TX 77522-0818. *Phone:* 281-425-6399. *E-mail:* bgriffit@ lee.edu.
Website: http://www.lee.edu/.

Lone Star College–CyFair

Cypress, Texas

- **State and locally supported** 2-year, founded 2002, part of Lone Star College System
- **Suburban** campus with easy access to Houston
- **Coed,** 18,906 undergraduate students, 33% full-time, 58% women, 42% men

Undergraduates 6,314 full-time, 12,592 part-time. Students come from 65 other countries; 15% Black or African American, non-Hispanic/Latino; 37% Hispanic/Latino; 9% Asian, non-Hispanic/Latino; 0.3% American Indian or Alaska Native, non-Hispanic/Latino; 3% Two or more races, non-Hispanic/Latino; 5% Race/ethnicity unknown.

Freshmen *Admission:* 3,041 applied, 3,041 admitted, 3,041 enrolled.

Faculty *Total:* 1,041, 19% full-time, 3% with terminal degrees. *Student/faculty ratio:* 27:1.

Majors Accounting; animation, interactive technology, video graphics and special effects; art; biology/biological sciences; business administration and management; chemistry; computer and information sciences; computer science; criminal justice/law enforcement administration; dance; design and visual communications; diagnostic medical sonography and ultrasound technology; dramatic/theater arts; economics; education; electrical, electronic and communications engineering technology; emergency medical technology (EMT paramedic); English; fire science/firefighting; foreign languages and literatures; health information/medical records technology; history; industrial technology; information technology; interdisciplinary studies; language interpretation and translation; logistics, materials, and supply chain management; management science; marketing/marketing management; mathematics; medical radiologic technology; music; office occupations and clerical services; physics; political science and government; psychology; radiation protection/health physics technology; registered nursing/registered nurse; rhetoric and composition; social sciences; speech communication and rhetoric; welding technology.

Academics *Calendar:* semesters. *Degree:* certificates, diplomas, and associate. *Special study options:* academic remediation for entering students, accelerated degree program, adult/continuing education programs, advanced placement credit, cooperative education, distance learning, double majors, English as a second language, honors programs, independent study, internships, part-time degree program, services for LD students, study abroad, summer session for credit.

Library LSC-CyFair Library with an OPAC, a Web page.

Student Life *Housing:* college housing not available. *Activities and Organizations:* drama/theater group, choral group. *Campus security:* 24-hour emergency response devices and patrols, late-night transport/escort service. *Student services:* personal/psychological counseling.

Costs (2013–14) *Tuition:* area resident $960 full-time, $480 per year part-time; state resident $2640 full-time, $1320 per year part-time; nonresident $3000 full-time, $1500 per year part-time. Full-time tuition and fees vary according to program. Part-time tuition and fees vary according to program. *Required fees:* $448 full-time, $192 per year part-time, $64 per year part-time.

Applying *Options:* electronic application, early admission.

Freshman Application Contact Admissions Office, Lone Star College–CyFair, 9191 Barker Cypress Road, Cypress, TX 77433-1383. *Phone:* 281-290-3200. *E-mail:* cfc.info@lonestar.edu.
Website: http://www.lonestar.edu/cyfair.

Lone Star College–Kingwood

Kingwood, Texas

- **State and locally supported** 2-year, founded 1984, part of Lone Star College System
- **Suburban** 264-acre campus with easy access to Houston
- **Coed,** 11,947 undergraduate students, 35% full-time, 65% women, 35% men

Undergraduates 4,147 full-time, 7,800 part-time. Students come from 35 other countries; 17% Black or African American, non-Hispanic/Latino; 24% Hispanic/Latino; 3% Asian, non-Hispanic/Latino; 0.4% American Indian or Alaska Native, non-Hispanic/Latino; 2% Two or more races, non-Hispanic/Latino; 5% Race/ethnicity unknown.

Freshmen *Admission:* 1,481 applied, 1,481 admitted, 1,481 enrolled.

Faculty *Total:* 625, 21% full-time, 5% with terminal degrees. *Student/faculty ratio:* 23:1.

Majors Accounting; administrative assistant and secretarial science; animation, interactive technology, video graphics and special effects; art; biology/biological sciences; business administration and management; chemistry; computer and information sciences; computer engineering technology; computer graphics; computer science; cosmetology; criminal justice/law enforcement administration; dental hygiene; design and visual communications; dramatic/theater arts; economics; education; English; facilities planning and management; foreign languages and literatures; health information/medical records technology; history; humanities; human services; information science/studies; interdisciplinary studies; interior design; kinesiology and exercise science; licensed practical/vocational nurse training; marketing/marketing management; mathematics; medical radiologic technology; music; occupational therapy; philosophy; physics; political science and government; psychology; registered nursing/registered nurse; respiratory care therapy; rhetoric and composition; social sciences; sociology; visual and performing arts; welding technology.

Academics *Calendar:* semesters. *Degree:* certificates and associate. *Special study options:* academic remediation for entering students, accelerated degree program, adult/continuing education programs, advanced placement credit, cooperative education, distance learning, double majors, English as a second language, honors programs, independent study, internships, part-time degree program, services for LD students, study abroad, summer session for credit.

Library LSC-Kingwood Library with an OPAC, a Web page.

Student Life *Housing:* college housing not available. *Activities and Organizations:* drama/theater group, student-run television station, choral group. *Campus security:* 24-hour emergency response devices and patrols, late-night transport/escort service. *Student services:* personal/psychological counseling.

Athletics *Intramural sports:* baseball M.

Costs (2013–14) *Tuition:* area resident $960 full-time, $480 per year part-time; state resident $2640 full-time, $1320 per year part-time; nonresident $3000 full-time, $1500 per year part-time. *Required fees:* $448 full-time, $192 per year part-time, $64 per year part-time.

Financial Aid Of all full-time matriculated undergraduates who enrolled in 2009, 28 Federal Work-Study jobs, 6 state and other part-time jobs. *Financial aid deadline:* 4/1.

Applying *Options:* electronic application, early admission. *Application deadlines:* rolling (freshmen), rolling (transfers).

Freshman Application Contact Admissions Office, Lone Star College–Kingwood, 20000 Kingwood Drive, Kingwood, TX 77339. *Phone:* 281-312-1525. *Fax:* 281-312-1477. *E-mail:* kingwoodadvising@lonestar.edu. *Website:* http://www.lonestar.edu/kingwood.htm.

Lone Star College–Montgomery

Conroe, Texas

- **State and locally supported** 2-year, founded 1995, part of Lone Star College System
- **Suburban** campus with easy access to Houston
- **Coed,** 13,250 undergraduate students, 35% full-time, 63% women, 37% men

Undergraduates 4,655 full-time, 8,595 part-time. Students come from 56 other countries; 12% Black or African American, non-Hispanic/Latino; 24% Hispanic/Latino; 4% Asian, non-Hispanic/Latino; 0.5% American Indian or Alaska Native, non-Hispanic/Latino; 3% Two or more races, non-Hispanic/Latino; 4% Race/ethnicity unknown.

Freshmen *Admission:* 1,965 applied, 1,965 admitted, 1,965 enrolled.

Faculty *Total:* 700, 22% full-time, 6% with terminal degrees. *Student/faculty ratio:* 24:1.

Majors Accounting and business/management; administrative assistant and secretarial science; animation, interactive technology, video graphics and special effects; art; audiovisual communications technologies related; automobile/automotive mechanics technology; biology/biological sciences; biology/biotechnology laboratory technician; business administration and management; CAD/CADD drafting/design technology; chemistry; computer and information systems security; computer programming; computer science; computer software technology; computer systems networking and telecommunications; criminal justice/law enforcement administration; design and visual communications; drafting/design engineering technologies related; dramatic/theater arts; economics; education; emergency medical technology (EMT paramedic); engineering; English; fire science/firefighting; foreign languages and literatures; health information/medical records technology; history; humanities; human services; information technology; interdisciplinary studies; marketing/marketing management; mathematics; medical radiologic technology; music; physical therapy technology; physics; political science and government; psychology; radiation protection/health physics technology; registered nursing/registered nurse; rhetoric and composition; social work; sociology; system, networking, and LAN/WAN management; web/multimedia

management and webmaster; web page, digital/multimedia and information resources design; welding technology.

Academics *Calendar:* semesters. *Degree:* certificates and associate. *Special study options:* academic remediation for entering students, adult/continuing education programs, advanced placement credit, cooperative education, distance learning, double majors, English as a second language, honors programs, independent study, internships, part-time degree program, services for LD students, study abroad, summer session for credit.

Library LSC-Montgomery Library with an OPAC, a Web page.

Student Life *Housing:* college housing not available. *Activities and Organizations:* drama/theater group, student-run newspaper, choral group, Campus Crusade for Christ, Criminal Justice Club, Phi Theta Kappa, Latino-American Student Association, African-American Cultural Awareness. *Campus security:* 24-hour emergency response devices and patrols, late-night transport/escort service. *Student services:* personal/psychological counseling.

Costs (2013–14) *Tuition:* area resident $960 full-time, $480 per year part-time; state resident $2640 full-time, $1320 per year part-time; nonresident $3000 full-time, $1500 per year part-time. *Required fees:* $448 full-time, $192 per year part-time, $64 per year part-time.

Financial Aid Of all full-time matriculated undergraduates who enrolled in 2011, 25 Federal Work-Study jobs (averaging $2500). 4 state and other part-time jobs.

Applying *Options:* electronic application, early admission. *Application deadlines:* rolling (freshmen), rolling (transfers).

Freshman Application Contact Lone Star College–Montgomery, 3200 College Park Drive, Conroe, TX 77384. *Phone:* 936-273-7236. *Website:* http://www.lonestar.edu/montgomery.

Lone Star College–North Harris

Houston, Texas

- **State and locally supported** 2-year, founded 1972, part of Lone Star College System
- **Suburban** campus with easy access to Houston
- **Coed,** 18,756 undergraduate students, 31% full-time, 63% women, 37% men

Undergraduates 5,800 full-time, 12,956 part-time. Students come from 46 other countries; 32% Black or African American, non-Hispanic/Latino; 35% Hispanic/Latino; 5% Asian, non-Hispanic/Latino; 0.2% American Indian or Alaska Native, non-Hispanic/Latino; 2% Two or more races, non-Hispanic/Latino; 6% Race/ethnicity unknown.

Freshmen *Admission:* 2,696 applied, 2,696 admitted, 2,696 enrolled.

Faculty *Total:* 998, 21% full-time, 4% with terminal degrees. *Student/faculty ratio:* 23:1.

Majors Accounting; administrative assistant and secretarial science; animation, interactive technology, video graphics and special effects; anthropology; architecture; art; automobile/automotive mechanics technology; aviation/airway management; biology/biological sciences; business administration and management; CAD/CADD drafting/design technology; chemistry; computer and information sciences; computer science; cosmetology; criminal justice/law enforcement administration; dance; design and visual communications; drafting and design technology; dramatic/theater arts; economics; education; electrical, electronic and communications engineering technology; emergency medical technology (EMT paramedic); engineering; English; finance; foreign languages and literatures; geography; geology/earth science; health information/medical records technology; heating, air conditioning, ventilation and refrigeration maintenance technology; history; hospitality administration; human services; information science/studies; interdisciplinary studies; journalism; kinesiology and exercise science; language interpretation and translation; legal administrative assistant/secretary; legal studies; liberal arts and sciences/liberal studies; management information systems; marketing/marketing management; mathematics; music; pharmacy technician; philosophy; photography; physical education teaching and coaching; physics; political science and government; pre-engineering; psychology; registered nursing/registered nurse; religious studies; respiratory care therapy; rhetoric and composition; sociology; welding technology.

Academics *Calendar:* semesters. *Degree:* certificates and associate. *Special study options:* academic remediation for entering students, adult/continuing education programs, advanced placement credit, cooperative education, distance learning, double majors, English as a second language, honors programs, independent study, internships, part-time degree program, services for LD students, study abroad, summer session for credit.

Library LSC-North Harris Library with an OPAC, a Web page.

Student Life *Activities and Organizations:* drama/theater group, student-run newspaper, choral group, Student Government Association, Phi Theta Kappa, Ambassadors, honors student organizations, Soccer Club. *Campus security:* 24-hour emergency response devices and patrols, late-night transport/escort service. *Student services:* personal/psychological counseling, women's center.

Athletics *Intramural sports:* badminton M/W, baseball M/W, basketball M/W, bowling M/W, football M/W, golf M/W, gymnastics M/W, racquetball M/W, soccer M/W, softball M/W, table tennis M/W, tennis M/W, track and field M/W, volleyball M/W, weight lifting M/W.

Costs (2013–14) *Tuition:* area resident $960 full-time, $480 per year part-time; state resident $2640 full-time, $1320 per year part-time; nonresident $3000 full-time, $1320 per year part-time. *Required fees:* $448 full-time, $192 per year part-time, $64 per year part-time.

Applying *Options:* electronic application, early admission. *Application deadlines:* rolling (freshmen), rolling (transfers).

Freshman Application Contact Admissions Office, Lone Star College–North Harris, 2700 W. W. Thorne Drive, Houston, TX 77073-3499. *Phone:* 281-618-5410. *E-mail:* nhcounselor@lonestar.edu.

Website: http://www.lonestar.edu/northharris.

Lone Star College–Tomball
Tomball, Texas

- **State and locally supported** 2-year, founded 1988, part of Lone Star College System
- **Suburban** campus with easy access to Houston
- **Coed,** 9,454 undergraduate students, 32% full-time, 63% women, 37% men

Undergraduates 3,024 full-time, 6,430 part-time. Students come from 30 other countries; 13% Black or African American, non-Hispanic/Latino; 21% Hispanic/Latino; 5% Asian, non-Hispanic/Latino; 0.4% American Indian or Alaska Native, non-Hispanic/Latino; 2% Two or more races, non-Hispanic/Latino; 5% Race/ethnicity unknown.

Freshmen *Admission:* 1,115 applied, 1,115 admitted, 1,115 enrolled.

Faculty *Total:* 540, 21% full-time, 6% with terminal degrees. *Student/faculty ratio:* 18:1.

Majors Accounting; administrative assistant and secretarial science; animation, interactive technology, video graphics and special effects; art; biology/biological sciences; business administration and management; chemistry; computer and information sciences; computer programming; computer science; criminal justice/law enforcement administration; dance; dramatic/theater arts; economics; education; electrical, electronic and communications engineering technology; engineering; English; finance; foreign languages and literatures; geography; geology/earth science; health information/medical records technology; history; humanities; interdisciplinary studies; kinesiology and exercise science; marketing/marketing management; mathematics; music; occupational therapy; pharmacy technician; philosophy; physics; political science and government; registered nursing/registered nurse; religious studies; rhetoric and composition; sociology; system, networking, and LAN/WAN management; veterinary/animal health technology.

Academics *Calendar:* semesters. *Degree:* certificates and associate. *Special study options:* academic remediation for entering students, adult/continuing education programs, advanced placement credit, cooperative education, distance learning, double majors, English as a second language, honors programs, independent study, internships, part-time degree program, services for LD students, study abroad, summer session for credit.

Library LSC-Tomball Community Library with an OPAC, a Web page.

Student Life *Housing:* college housing not available. *Activities and Organizations:* drama/theater group, student-run newspaper, choral group, Phi Theta Kappa, Occupational Therapy OTA, Veterinary Technicians Student Organization, STARS, Student Nurses Association. *Campus security:* 24-hour emergency response devices and patrols, late-night transport/escort service, trained security personnel during open hours. *Student services:* personal/psychological counseling.

Costs (2013–14) *Tuition:* area resident $960 full-time; state resident $1320 full-time; nonresident $1500 full-time. Full-time tuition and fees vary according to program. Part-time tuition and fees vary according to program. *Required fees:* $448 full-time, $192 per year part-time, $64 per year part-time.

Financial Aid Of all full-time matriculated undergraduates who enrolled in 2011, 34 Federal Work-Study jobs (averaging $3000).

Applying *Options:* electronic application, early admission. *Application deadlines:* rolling (freshmen), rolling (transfers).

Freshman Application Contact Admissions Office, Lone Star College–Tomball, 30555 Tomball Parkway, Tomball, TX 77375-4036. *Phone:* 281-351-3310. *E-mail:* tcinfo@lonestar.edu.

Website: http://www.lonestar.edu/tomball.

McLennan Community College
Waco, Texas

Freshman Application Contact Dr. Vivian G. Jefferson, Director, Admissions and Recruitment, McLennan Community College, 1400 College Drive, Waco, TX 76708. *Phone:* 254-299-8689. *Fax:* 254-299-8694. *E-mail:* vjefferson@mclennan.edu.

Website: http://www.mclennan.edu/.

Mountain View College
Dallas, Texas

Freshman Application Contact Ms. Glenda Hall, Director of Admissions, Mountain View College, 4849 West Illinois Avenue, Dallas, TX 75211-6599. *Phone:* 214-860-8666. *Fax:* 214-860-8570. *E-mail:* ghall@dcccd.edu.

Website: http://www.mountainviewcollege.edu/.

Navarro College
Corsicana, Texas

Freshman Application Contact David Edwards, Registrar, Navarro College, 3200 West 7th Avenue, Corsicana, TX 75110-4899. *Phone:* 903-875-7348. *Toll-free phone:* 800-NAVARRO (in-state); 800-628-2776 (out-of-state). *Fax:* 903-875-7353. *E-mail:* david.edwards@navarrocollege.edu.

Website: http://www.navarrocollege.edu/.

North Central Texas College
Gainesville, Texas

Freshman Application Contact Melinda Carroll, Director of Admissions/Registrar, North Central Texas College, 1525 West California, Gainesville, TX 76240-4699. *Phone:* 940-668-7731. *Fax:* 940-668-7075. *E-mail:* mcarroll@nctc.edu.

Website: http://www.nctc.edu/.

Northeast Texas Community College
Mount Pleasant, Texas

Freshman Application Contact Ms. Sherry Keys, Director of Admissions, Northeast Texas Community College, PO Box 1307, Mount Pleasant, TX 75456-1307. *Phone:* 903-572-1911 Ext. 263. *Toll-free phone:* 800-870-0142. *Website:* http://www.ntcc.edu/.

North Lake College
Irving, Texas

Freshman Application Contact Admissions/Registration Office (A405), North Lake College, 5001 North MacArthur Boulevard, Irving, TX 75038. *Phone:* 972-273-3183.

Website: http://www.northlakecollege.edu/.

Northwest Vista College
San Antonio, Texas

Freshman Application Contact Dr. Elaine Lang, Interim Director of Enrollment Management, Northwest Vista College, 3535 North Ellison Drive, San Antonio, TX 78251. *Phone:* 210-348-2016. *E-mail:* elang@accd.edu.

Website: http://www.alamo.edu/nvc/.

Odessa College
Odessa, Texas

Freshman Application Contact Ms. Tracy Hilliard, Associate Director, Admissions, Odessa College, 201 West University Avenue, Odessa, TX 79764. *Phone:* 432-335-6816. *Fax:* 432-335-6303. *E-mail:* thilliard@odessa.edu.

Website: http://www.odessa.edu/.

Palo Alto College
San Antonio, Texas

Freshman Application Contact Ms. Rachel Montejano, Director of Enrollment Management, Palo Alto College, 1400 West Villaret Boulevard, San Antonio, TX 78224. *Phone:* 210-921-5279. *Fax:* 210-921-5310. *E-mail:* pacar@accd.edu.

Website: http://www.alamo.edu/pac/.

Panola College
Carthage, Texas

- **State and locally supported** 2-year, founded 1947
- **Small-town** 35-acre campus
- **Endowment** $2.4 million
- **Coed,** 2,562 undergraduate students, 44% full-time, 70% women, 30% men

Undergraduates 1,134 full-time, 1,428 part-time. Students come from 23 states and territories; 11 other countries; 8% are from out of state; 22% Black or African American, non-Hispanic/Latino; 7% Hispanic/Latino; 0.7% Asian, non-Hispanic/Latino; 1% American Indian or Alaska Native, non-Hispanic/Latino; 0.4% Two or more races, non-Hispanic/Latino; 1% international; 12% transferred in; 8% live on campus. *Retention:* 39% of full-time freshmen returned.

Freshmen *Admission:* 421 admitted, 474 enrolled.

Faculty *Total:* 140, 46% full-time, 5% with terminal degrees. *Student/faculty ratio:* 19:1.

Majors Administrative assistant and secretarial science; clinical/medical laboratory technology; early childhood education; education; general studies; health information/medical records technology; industrial technology; information science/studies; information technology; medical/clinical assistant; middle school education; occupational therapist assistant; petroleum technology; registered nursing/registered nurse.

Academics *Calendar:* semesters. *Degree:* certificates and associate. *Special study options:* academic remediation for entering students, advanced placement credit, cooperative education, distance learning, English as a second language, part-time degree program, services for LD students, summer session for credit.

Library M. P. Baker Library with 103,639 titles, 31,932 serial subscriptions, 4,870 audiovisual materials, an OPAC, a Web page.

Student Life *Housing Options:* coed. Campus housing is university owned. *Activities and Organizations:* drama/theater group, student-run newspaper, choral group, Student Government Organization, Student Occupational Therapy Assistant Club, Baptist Student Ministries, Texas Nursing Student Association, Phi Theta Kappa. *Campus security:* controlled dormitory access.

Athletics Member NCAA, NJCAA. *Intercollegiate sports:* baseball M(s), basketball M(s)/W(s), volleyball W(s). *Intramural sports:* basketball M/W, football M/W, racquetball M/W, table tennis M/W, volleyball M/W, weight lifting M/W.

Costs (2013–14) *Tuition:* area resident $750 full-time, $67 per semester hour part-time; state resident $1950 full-time, $107 per semester hour part-time; nonresident $2790 full-time, $135 per semester hour part-time. *Required fees:* $1260 full-time. *Room and board:* $4800. *Payment plan:* deferred payment. *Waivers:* employees or children of employees.

Applying *Options:* electronic application, early admission. *Required for some:* high school transcript. *Recommended:* high school transcript. *Application deadlines:* rolling (freshmen), rolling (out-of-state freshmen), rolling (transfers). *Notification:* continuous (freshmen), continuous (out-of-state freshmen), continuous (transfers).

Freshman Application Contact Mr. Jeremy Dorman, Registrar/Director of Admissions, Panola College, 1109 West Panola Street, Carthage, TX 75633-2397. *Phone:* 903-693-2009. *Fax:* 903-693-2031. *E-mail:* bsimpson@panola.edu. *Website:* http://www.panola.edu/.

Paris Junior College
Paris, Texas

- **State and locally supported** 2-year, founded 1924
- **Rural** 54-acre campus
- **Endowment** $14.8 million
- **Coed,** 5,513 undergraduate students, 47% full-time, 60% women, 40% men

Undergraduates 2,567 full-time, 2,946 part-time. Students come from 22 states and territories; 7 other countries; 3% are from out of state; 12% Black or African American, non-Hispanic/Latino; 10% Hispanic/Latino; 0.9% Asian, non-Hispanic/Latino; 0.1% Native Hawaiian or other Pacific Islander, non-Hispanic/Latino; 2% American Indian or Alaska Native, non-Hispanic/Latino; 0.7% Two or more races, non-Hispanic/Latino; 0.1% Race/ethnicity unknown; 0.2% international; 35% transferred in; 4% live on campus. *Retention:* 52% of full-time freshmen returned.

Freshmen *Admission:* 1,072 applied, 1,072 admitted, 1,197 enrolled.

Faculty *Total:* 250, 38% full-time, 8% with terminal degrees. *Student/faculty ratio:* 23:1.

Majors Agricultural mechanization; art; biological and physical sciences; business administration and management; business teacher education; computer engineering technology; computer typography and composition equipment operation; cosmetology; drafting and design technology; education; electrical, electronic and communications engineering technology; elementary education; emergency medical technology (EMT paramedic); engineering; heating, air conditioning, ventilation and refrigeration maintenance technology; information science/studies; liberal arts and sciences/liberal studies; mathematics; medical insurance coding; metal and jewelry arts; radiologic technology/science; registered nursing/registered nurse; surgical technology; welding technology.

Academics *Calendar:* semesters. *Degree:* certificates, diplomas, and associate. *Special study options:* academic remediation for entering students, adult/continuing education programs, advanced placement credit, cooperative education, distance learning, English as a second language, part-time degree program, services for LD students, summer session for credit.

Library Mike Rheudasil Learning Center with 38,150 titles, 404 serial subscriptions, an OPAC.

Student Life *Housing Options:* men-only, women-only. Campus housing is university owned. *Activities and Organizations:* drama/theater group, student-run newspaper, choral group, Student Government Organization, Blends Club for all ethic groups. *Campus security:* 24-hour emergency response devices and patrols, late-night transport/escort service, controlled dormitory access. *Student services:* personal/psychological counseling.

Athletics Member NJCAA. *Intercollegiate sports:* baseball M(s), basketball M(s)/W(s), golf M(s), soccer M(s)/W(s), softball W(s), volleyball W(s). *Intramural sports:* badminton M/W, basketball M, football M, table tennis M/W, tennis M/W, volleyball M/W.

Costs (2013–14) *Tuition:* area resident $1740 full-time, $50 per credit hour part-time; state resident $2670 full-time, $81 per credit hour part-time; nonresident $4080 full-time, $128 per credit hour part-time. Full-time tuition and fees vary according to course load, location, and program. Part-time tuition and fees vary according to course load, location, and program. *Required fees:* $240 full-time. *Room and board:* Room and board charges vary according to board plan and housing facility. *Payment plan:* installment. *Waivers:* employees or children of employees.

Financial Aid Of all full-time matriculated undergraduates who enrolled in 2011, 60 Federal Work-Study jobs (averaging $3800).

Applying *Options:* electronic application, early admission. *Required:* high school transcript. *Application deadlines:* rolling (freshmen), rolling (out-of-state freshmen), rolling (transfers).

Freshman Application Contact Paris Junior College, 2400 Clarksville Street, Paris, TX 75460-6298. *Phone:* 903-782-0211. *Toll-free phone:* 800-232-5804. *Website:* http://www.parisjc.edu/.

Pima Medical Institute
Houston, Texas

Freshman Application Contact Christopher Luebke, Corporate Director of Admissions, Pima Medical Institute, 2160 South Power Road, Mesa, AZ 85209. *Phone:* 480-610-6063. *E-mail:* cluebke@pmi.edu. *Website:* http://www.pmi.edu/.

Ranger College
Ranger, Texas

Freshman Application Contact Dr. Jim Davis, Dean of Students, Ranger College, 1100 College Circle, Ranger, TX 76470. *Phone:* 254-647-3234 Ext. 110. *Website:* http://www.rangercollege.edu/.

Remington College–Dallas Campus
Garland, Texas

Director of Admissions Ms. Shonda Wisenhunt, Remington College–Dallas Campus, 1800 Eastgate Drive, Garland, TX 75041. *Phone:* 972-686-7878. *Fax:* 972-686-5116. *E-mail:* shonda.wisenhunt@remingtoncollege.edu. *Website:* http://www.remingtoncollege.edu/.

Remington College–Fort Worth Campus
Fort Worth, Texas

Director of Admissions Marcia Kline, Director of Recruitment, Remington College–Fort Worth Campus, 300 East Loop 820, Fort Worth, TX 76112. *Phone:* 817-451-0017. *Toll-free phone:* 800-560-6192. *Fax:* 817-496-1257. *E-mail:* marcia.kline@remingtoncollege.edu. *Website:* http://www.remingtoncollege.edu/.

Remington College–Houston Campus
Houston, Texas

Director of Admissions Kevin Wilkinson, Director of Recruitment, Remington College–Houston Campus, 3110 Hayes Road, Suite 380, Houston, TX 77082. *Phone:* 281-899-1240. *Fax:* 281-597-8466. *E-mail:* kevin.wilkinson@remingtoncollege.edu. *Website:* http://www.remingtoncollege.edu/.

Remington College–Houston Southeast

Webster, Texas

Director of Admissions Lori Minor, Director of Recruitment, Remington College–Houston Southeast, 20985 Interstate 45 South, Webster, TX 77598. *Phone:* 281-554-1700. *Fax:* 281-554-1765. *E-mail:* lori.minor@remingtoncollege.edu. *Website:* http://www.remingtoncollege.edu/.

Remington College–North Houston Campus

Houston, Texas

Director of Admissions Edmund Flores, Director of Recruitment, Remington College–North Houston Campus, 11310 Greens Crossing Boulevard, Suite 300, Houston, TX 77067. *Phone:* 281-885-4450. *Fax:* 281-875-9964. *E-mail:* edmund.flores@remingtoncollege.edu. *Website:* http://www.remingtoncollege.edu/.

Richland College

Dallas, Texas

Freshman Application Contact Ms. Carol McKinney, Department Assistant, Richland College, 12800 Abrams Road, Dallas, TX 75243-2199. *Phone:* 972-238-6100. *Website:* http://www.rlc.dcccd.edu/.

St. Philip's College

San Antonio, Texas

- **District-supported** 2-year, founded 1898, part of Alamo Community College District
- **Urban** 68-acre campus with easy access to San Antonio
- **Coed,** 10,710 undergraduate students, 21% full-time, 57% women, 43% men

Undergraduates 2,232 full-time, 8,478 part-time. Students come from 45 states and territories; 11 other countries; 1% are from out of state; 13% Black or African American, non-Hispanic/Latino; 50% Hispanic/Latino; 2% Asian, non-Hispanic/Latino; 0.4% American Indian or Alaska Native, non-Hispanic/Latino; 2% Two or more races, non-Hispanic/Latino; 0.3% international; 10% transferred in.

Freshmen *Admission:* 1,690 enrolled.

Faculty *Total:* 398, 43% full-time, 8% with terminal degrees. *Student/faculty ratio:* 15:1.

Majors Accounting; administrative assistant and secretarial science; aircraft powerplant technology; airframe mechanics and aircraft maintenance technology; art; autobody/collision and repair technology; automobile/automotive mechanics technology; biology/biological sciences; biomedical technology; building/construction finishing, management, and inspection related; business administration and management; CAD/CADD drafting/design technology; chemistry; clinical/medical laboratory technology; computer and information systems security; computer systems networking and telecommunications; computer technology/computer systems technology; construction engineering technology; criminal justice/law enforcement administration; culinary arts; data entry/microcomputer applications; diesel mechanics technology; dramatic/theater arts; dramatic/theater arts and stagecraft related; early childhood education; e-commerce; economics; education; electrical/electronics equipment installation and repair; electromechanical technology; energy management and systems technology; English; environmental science; geology/earth science; health information/medical records technology; heating, air conditioning, ventilation and refrigeration maintenance technology; history; hotel/motel administration; kinesiology and exercise science; legal administrative assistant/secretary; liberal arts and sciences/liberal studies; mathematics; medical administrative assistant and medical secretary; medical radiologic technology; music; natural resources/conservation; occupational safety and health technology; occupational therapist assistant; philosophy; physical therapy technology; political science and government; pre-dentistry studies; pre-engineering; pre-law studies; premedical studies; prenursing studies; pre-pharmacy studies; psychology; respiratory care therapy; restaurant/food services management; rhetoric and composition; social work; sociology; Spanish; system, networking, and LAN/WAN management; teacher assistant/aide; telecommunications technology; welding technology.

Academics *Calendar:* semesters. *Degree:* certificates, diplomas, and associate. *Special study options:* academic remediation for entering students, adult/continuing education programs, advanced placement credit, cooperative education, distance learning, double majors, English as a second language,

honors programs, independent study, internships, off-campus study, part-time degree program, services for LD students, study abroad, summer session for credit. *ROTC:* Army (c).

Library Library plus 1 other with 112,745 titles, 107 serial subscriptions, 11,520 audiovisual materials, an OPAC, a Web page.

Student Life *Housing:* college housing not available. *Activities and Organizations:* drama/theater group, choral group, Student Government, Future United Latino Leaders of Change, Anime. *Campus security:* 24-hour emergency response devices and patrols, late-night transport/escort service. *Student services:* health clinic, women's center.

Athletics *Intramural sports:* basketball M/W, cheerleading M/W, table tennis M/W, volleyball M/W, weight lifting M/W.

Costs (2012–13) *Tuition:* area resident $2008 full-time, $80 per credit hour part-time; state resident $5470 full-time, $195 per credit hour part-time; nonresident $10,660 full-time, $368 per credit hour part-time. Full-time tuition and fees vary according to program. Part-time tuition and fees vary according to program. *Required fees:* $30 full-time, $1 per credit hour part-time. *Payment plan:* installment. *Waivers:* senior citizens and employees or children of employees.

Applying *Options:* electronic application, early admission. *Required:* high school transcript. *Application deadlines:* rolling (freshmen), rolling (transfers). *Notification:* continuous (freshmen), continuous (transfers).

Freshman Application Contact Ms. Penelope Velasco, Associate Director, Residency and Reports, St. Philip's College, 1801 Martin Luther King Drive, San Antonio, TX 78203-2098. *Phone:* 210-486-2283. *Fax:* 210-486-2103. *E-mail:* pvelasco@alamo.edu. *Website:* http://www.alamo.edu/spc/.

San Antonio College

San Antonio, Texas

Director of Admissions Mr. J. Martin Ortega, Director of Admissions and Records, San Antonio College, 1300 San Pedro Avenue, San Antonio, TX 78212-4299. *Phone:* 210-733-2582. *Website:* http://www.alamo.edu/sac/.

San Jacinto College District

Pasadena, Texas

- **State and locally supported** 2-year, founded 1961
- **Suburban** 445-acre campus with easy access to Houston
- **Endowment** $3.2 million
- **Coed,** 28,721 undergraduate students, 30% full-time, 57% women, 43% men

Undergraduates 8,625 full-time, 20,096 part-time. Students come from 44 states and territories; 76 other countries; 1% are from out of state; 9% Black or African American, non-Hispanic/Latino; 44% Hispanic/Latino; 5% Asian, non-Hispanic/Latino; 0.1% Native Hawaiian or other Pacific Islander, non-Hispanic/Latino; 0.3% American Indian or Alaska Native, non-Hispanic/Latino; 2% Two or more races, non-Hispanic/Latino; 7% Race/ethnicity unknown; 1% international; 26% transferred in.

Freshmen *Admission:* 11,631 applied, 11,631 admitted, 5,524 enrolled.

Faculty *Total:* 1,248, 41% full-time, 11% with terminal degrees. *Student/faculty ratio:* 20:1.

Majors Accounting; administrative assistant and secretarial science; agribusiness; agriculture; airline pilot and flight crew; art; autobody/collision and repair technology; automobile/automotive mechanics technology; aviation/airway management; baking and pastry arts; behavioral sciences; biology/biological sciences; biotechnology; business administration and management; business automation/technology/data entry; business/commerce; chemical process technology; chemical technology; chemistry; child development; clinical laboratory science/medical technology; clinical/medical laboratory technology; commercial and advertising art; computer and information sciences; computer and information systems security; computer programming; computer science; construction engineering technology; cosmetology; cosmetology, barber/styling, and nail instruction; criminal justice/police science; culinary arts; dance; design and visual communications; diagnostic medical sonography and ultrasound technology; diesel mechanics technology; digital communication and media/multimedia; drafting and design technology; dramatic/theater arts; education (multiple levels); electrical and power transmission installation; electrical, electronic and communications engineering technology; elementary education; emergency medical technology (EMT paramedic); engineering; engineering mechanics; English; environmental science; film/cinema/video studies; fire prevention and safety technology; fire science/firefighting; food preparation; food service systems administration; foreign languages and literatures; general studies; geology/earth science; health and physical education/fitness; health information/medical records technology; heating, air conditioning, ventilation and refrigeration maintenance technology; Hispanic-American, Puerto Rican, and Mexican-American/Chicano studies; history; institutional food workers; instrumentation technology; interior design; international business/trade/commerce; journalism; kindergarten/preschool education; legal assistant/paralegal; licensed practical/vocational nurse training; management information systems; marine science/merchant marine officer; mathematics; medical administrative assistant and medical secretary; mental health counseling; middle school education; multi/interdisciplinary studies related; music; occupational safety and health technology; optometric technician; philosophy; physical sciences; physical therapy technology; physics; political science and government; psychology; radio and television broadcasting technology; radiologic technology/science; real estate; registered nursing/registered nurse; respiratory care therapy; restaurant, culinary, and catering management; rhetoric and composition; science teacher education; secondary education; social sciences; sociology; speech communication and rhetoric; surgical technology; system, networking, and LAN/WAN management; web/multimedia management and webmaster; welding technology.

Academics *Calendar:* semesters. *Degree:* certificates and associate. *Special study options:* academic remediation for entering students, accelerated degree program, adult/continuing education programs, advanced placement credit, cooperative education, distance learning, double majors, English as a second language, honors programs, part-time degree program, services for LD students, student-designed majors, study abroad, summer session for credit. *ROTC:* Army (c), Air Force (c).

Library Lee Davis Library (C), Edwin E. Lehr (N), and Parker Williams (S) with 283,963 titles, 1,303 serial subscriptions, 2,809 audiovisual materials, an OPAC, a Web page.

Student Life *Housing:* college housing not available. *Activities and Organizations:* drama/theater group, student-run newspaper, choral group, Phi Theta Kappa, Nurses Association, Student Government Association, ABG Radiography, Texas Student Education Association. *Campus security:* 24-hour emergency response devices and patrols, late-night transport/escort service.

Athletics Member NJCAA. *Intercollegiate sports:* baseball M, basketball M(s), cheerleading M(s), golf M, soccer M/W, softball W, tennis M/W, volleyball W(s). *Intramural sports:* basketball M/W, bowling M/W, football M/W, racquetball M/W, table tennis M/W, volleyball M/W, weight lifting M/W.

Costs (2013–14) *Tuition:* area resident $1312 full-time, $43 per credit hour part-time; state resident $2296 full-time, $84 per credit hour part-time; nonresident $3496 full-time, $134 per credit hour part-time. Full-time tuition and fees vary according to course load. Part-time tuition and fees vary according to course load. *Required fees:* $280 full-time. *Payment plan:* installment. *Waivers:* senior citizens.

Applying *Options:* electronic application, early admission. *Required:* high school transcript. *Required for some:* interview.

Freshman Application Contact San Jacinto College District, 4624 Fairmont Parkway, Pasadena, TX 77504-3323. *Phone:* 281-998-6150.
Website: http://www.sanjac.edu/.

South Plains College
Levelland, Texas

- **State and locally supported** 2-year, founded 1958
- **Small-town** 177-acre campus
- **Endowment** $3.0 million
- **Coed,** 9,444 undergraduate students, 46% full-time, 54% women, 46% men

Undergraduates 4,382 full-time, 5,062 part-time. Students come from 21 states and territories; 8 other countries; 4% are from out of state; 10% transferred in; 10% live on campus. *Retention:* 45% of full-time freshmen returned.
Freshmen *Admission:* 3,189 applied, 3,189 admitted, 1,384 enrolled.
Faculty *Total:* 454, 60% full-time. *Student/faculty ratio:* 20:1.
Majors Accounting; administrative assistant and secretarial science; advertising; agricultural economics; agriculture; agronomy and crop science; art; automobile/automotive mechanics technology; biological and physical sciences; biology/biological sciences; business administration and management; carpentry; chemistry; child development; commercial and advertising art; computer engineering technology; computer programming; computer science; consumer merchandising/retailing management; cosmetology; criminal justice/law enforcement administration; criminal justice/police science; data processing and data processing technology; developmental and child psychology; dietetics; drafting and design technology; education; electrical, electronic and communications engineering technology; engineering; fashion merchandising; fire science/firefighting; health/health-care administration; health information/medical records administration; heating, air conditioning, ventilation and refrigeration maintenance technology; industrial radiologic technology; journalism; legal administrative assistant/secretary; liberal arts and sciences/liberal studies; licensed practical/vocational nurse training; machine tool technology; marketing/marketing management; mass communication/media; medical administrative assistant and medical secretary; mental health counseling; music; petroleum technology; physical education teaching and coaching; physical therapy; pre-engineering; real estate; recording arts technology; registered nursing/registered nurse; respiratory care therapy; social work; special prod-

ucts marketing; surgical technology; telecommunications technology; welding technology.

Academics *Calendar:* semesters. *Degree:* certificates and associate. *Special study options:* academic remediation for entering students, accelerated degree program, adult/continuing education programs, advanced placement credit, distance learning, double majors, internships, off-campus study, part-time degree program, services for LD students, study abroad, summer session for credit. *ROTC:* Army (c), Air Force (c).

Library South Plains College Library plus 1 other with 70,000 titles, 310 serial subscriptions, an OPAC.

Student Life *Housing:* on-campus residence required through sophomore year. *Options:* men-only, women-only. Campus housing is university owned. Freshman applicants given priority for college housing. *Activities and Organizations:* drama/theater group, student-run newspaper, radio and television station, choral group, student government, Phi Beta Kappa, Bleacher Bums, Law Enforcement Association. *Campus security:* 24-hour emergency response devices and patrols, controlled dormitory access. *Student services:* health clinic.

Athletics Member NJCAA. *Intercollegiate sports:* basketball M(s)/W(s), cross-country running M(s)/W(s), equestrian sports M(s)/W(s), track and field M(s)/W(s). *Intramural sports:* basketball M/W, cross-country running M/W, football M/W, golf M/W, racquetball M/W, softball M/W, table tennis M/W, tennis M/W, volleyball M/W.

Standardized Tests *Recommended:* ACT (for admission), SAT Subject Tests (for admission).

Costs (2013–14) *Tuition:* area resident $864 full-time, $36 per hour part-time; state resident $1329 full-time, $48 per hour part-time; nonresident $1776 full-time, $64 per hour part-time. *Required fees:* $1250 full-time. *Room and board:* $3100. *Payment plan:* installment.

Financial Aid Of all full-time matriculated undergraduates who enrolled in 2011, 80 Federal Work-Study jobs (averaging $2000). 22 state and other part-time jobs (averaging $2000).

Applying *Options:* electronic application, early admission. *Required:* high school transcript. *Application deadlines:* rolling (freshmen), rolling (out-of-state freshmen), rolling (transfers). *Notification:* continuous (freshmen), continuous (out-of-state freshmen), continuous (transfers).

Freshman Application Contact Mrs. Andrea Rangel, Dean of Admissions and Records, South Plains College, 1401 College Avenue, Levelland, TX 78336. *Phone:* 806-894-9611 Ext. 2370. *Fax:* 806-897-3167. *E-mail:* arangel@southplainscollege.edu.
Website: http://www.southplainscollege.edu/.

South Texas College
McAllen, Texas

Freshman Application Contact Mr. Matthew Hebbard, Director of Enrollment Services and Registrar, South Texas College, 3201 West Pecan, McAllen, TX 78501. *Phone:* 956-872-2147. *Toll-free phone:* 800-742-7822. *E-mail:* mshebbar@southtexascollege.edu.
Website: http://www.southtexascollege.edu/.

Southwest Institute of Technology
Austin, Texas

Freshman Application Contact Director of Admissions, Southwest Institute of Technology, 5424 Highway 290 West, Suite 200, Austin, TX 78735-8800. *Phone:* 512-892-2640. *Fax:* 512-892-1045.
Website: http://www.swse.net/.

Southwest Texas Junior College
Uvalde, Texas

Director of Admissions Mr. Joe C. Barker, Dean of Admissions and Student Services, Southwest Texas Junior College, 2401 Garner Field Road, Uvalde, TX 78801-6297. *Phone:* 830-278-4401 Ext. 7284.
Website: http://www.swtjc.edu/.

Tarrant County College District
Fort Worth, Texas

- **County-supported** 2-year, founded 1967
- **Urban** 667-acre campus with easy access to Dallas-Fort Worth
- **Endowment** $5.8 million
- **Coed,** 50,062 undergraduate students, 35% full-time, 59% women, 41% men

Undergraduates 17,530 full-time, 32,532 part-time. Students come from 39 states and territories; 19% Black or African American, non-Hispanic/Latino; 24% Hispanic/Latino; 6% Asian, non-Hispanic/Latino; 0.2% Native Hawaiian or other Pacific Islander, non-Hispanic/Latino; 0.5% American Indian or

Alaska Native, non-Hispanic/Latino; 0.4% Two or more races, non-Hispanic/Latino; 0.9% Race/ethnicity unknown; 0.9% international.

Freshmen *Admission:* 9,924 applied, 9,924 admitted, 9,924 enrolled.

Faculty *Total:* 1,861, 35% full-time. *Student/faculty ratio:* 28:1.

Majors Accounting; administrative assistant and secretarial science; architectural engineering technology; automobile/automotive mechanics technology; avionics maintenance technology; business administration and management; clinical laboratory science/medical technology; clinical/medical laboratory technology; computer programming; computer science; construction engineering technology; consumer merchandising/retailing management; criminal justice/law enforcement administration; dental hygiene; developmental and child psychology; dietetics; drafting and design technology; educational/instructional technology; electrical, electronic and communications engineering technology; electromechanical technology; emergency medical technology (EMT paramedic); fashion merchandising; fire science/firefighting; food technology and processing; graphic and printing equipment operation/production; health information/medical records administration; heating, air conditioning, ventilation and refrigeration maintenance technology; horticultural science; industrial radiologic technology; legal assistant/paralegal; liberal arts and sciences/liberal studies; machine tool technology; marketing/marketing management; mechanical engineering/mechanical technology; mental health counseling; physical therapy; quality control technology; registered nursing/registered nurse; respiratory care therapy; sign language interpretation and translation; surgical technology; welding technology.

Academics *Calendar:* semesters. *Degree:* certificates and associate. *Special study options:* academic remediation for entering students, adult/continuing education programs, advanced placement credit, distance learning, English as a second language, honors programs, part-time degree program, services for LD students, summer session for credit. *ROTC:* Army (c), Air Force (c).

Library 197,352 titles, 1,649 serial subscriptions, 18,833 audiovisual materials, an OPAC, a Web page.

Student Life *Housing:* college housing not available. *Activities and Organizations:* drama/theater group, student-run newspaper, choral group. *Campus security:* 24-hour emergency response devices and patrols, late-night transport/escort service. *Student services:* health clinic, personal/psychological counseling.

Athletics *Intramural sports:* football M, golf M, sailing M/W, table tennis M, tennis M/W, volleyball M/W.

Costs (2013–14) *Tuition:* area resident $1320 full-time, $55 per credit hour part-time; state resident $2064 full-time, $86 per credit hour part-time; nonresident $4920 full-time, $205 per credit hour part-time. Full-time tuition and fees vary according to course load and program. Part-time tuition and fees vary according to course load and program. *Payment plan:* installment. *Waivers:* senior citizens.

Financial Aid Of all full-time matriculated undergraduates who enrolled in 2011, 12,635 applied for aid, 11,641 were judged to have need. 99 Federal Work-Study jobs (averaging $2053). In 2011, 77 non-need-based awards were made. *Average need-based loan:* $2686. *Average need-based gift aid:* $4350. *Average non-need-based aid:* $1256.

Applying *Options:* electronic application, early admission. *Application deadlines:* rolling (freshmen), rolling (transfers).

Freshman Application Contact Mr. Vikas Rajpurohit, Assistant Director of Admissions Services, Tarrant County College District, 300 Trinity Campus Circle, Fort Worth, TX 76102-6599. *Phone:* 817-515-1581. *E-mail:* vikas.rajpurohit@tccd.edu.

Website: http://www.tccd.edu/.

Temple College
Temple, Texas

- **District-supported** 2-year, founded 1926
- **Suburban** 106-acre campus with easy access to Austin
- **Endowment** $638,964
- **Coed,** 5,547 undergraduate students, 39% full-time, 67% women, 33% men

Undergraduates 2,174 full-time, 3,373 part-time. Students come from 30 states and territories; 9 other countries; 2% are from out of state; 19% Black or African American, non-Hispanic/Latino; 20% Hispanic/Latino; 2% Asian, non-Hispanic/Latino; 0.2% Native Hawaiian or other Pacific Islander, non-Hispanic/Latino; 0.7% American Indian or Alaska Native, non-Hispanic/Latino; 6% Race/ethnicity unknown; 0.1% international; 7% transferred in.

Freshmen *Admission:* 625 applied, 625 admitted, 539 enrolled.

Faculty *Total:* 284, 44% full-time, 15% with terminal degrees. *Student/faculty ratio:* 18:1.

Majors Administrative assistant and secretarial science; art; biology/biotechnology laboratory technician; business administration and management; computer and information sciences; computer programming; computer science; criminal justice/law enforcement administration; criminal justice/police science; data processing and data processing technology; dental hygiene; diag-

nostic medical sonography and ultrasound technology; drafting and design technology; emergency medical technology (EMT paramedic); liberal arts and sciences/liberal studies; licensed practical/vocational nurse training; registered nursing/registered nurse; respiratory care therapy; system, networking, and LAN/WAN management; web/multimedia management and webmaster.

Academics *Calendar:* semesters. *Degree:* certificates and associate. *Special study options:* academic remediation for entering students, adult/continuing education programs, advanced placement credit, cooperative education, distance learning, English as a second language, internships, off-campus study, part-time degree program, services for LD students, study abroad, summer session for credit.

Library Hubert Dawson Library with 58,907 titles, 271 serial subscriptions, 2,900 audiovisual materials, an OPAC, a Web page.

Student Life *Housing Options:* coed, disabled students. Campus housing is provided by a third party. *Activities and Organizations:* drama/theater group, choral group, Baptist Student Ministries, student government, Phi Theta Kappa, Delta Epsilon Chi, Nursing Student Organization. *Campus security:* 24-hour emergency response devices and patrols.

Athletics Member NJCAA. *Intercollegiate sports:* baseball M(s), basketball M(s)/W(s), softball W(s), tennis M(s)/W(s), volleyball W(s).

Costs (2013–14) *Tuition:* area resident $2640 full-time, $88 per semester hour part-time; state resident $4620 full-time, $154 per semester hour part-time; nonresident $7020 full-time, $330 per semester hour part-time. Full-time tuition and fees vary according to course load and program. Part-time tuition and fees vary according to course load and program. *Required fees:* $150 full-time, $24 per course part-time, $48 per term part-time. *Room and board:* $7696. *Payment plan:* installment. *Waivers:* employees or children of employees.

Financial Aid Of all full-time matriculated undergraduates who enrolled in 2009, 116 Federal Work-Study jobs (averaging $2007). 67 state and other part-time jobs (averaging $1119).

Applying *Options:* electronic application, early admission. *Required for some:* high school transcript. *Recommended:* high school transcript. *Application deadlines:* rolling (freshmen), rolling (transfers).

Freshman Application Contact Ms. Carey Rose, Director of Admissions and Records, Temple College, 2600 South First Street, Temple, TX 76504. *Phone:* 254-298-8303. *Toll-free phone:* 800-460-4636. *E-mail:* carey.rose@templejc.edu.

Website: http://www.templejc.edu/.

Texarkana College
Texarkana, Texas

- **State and locally supported** 2-year, founded 1927
- **Urban** 90-acre campus
- **Coed,** 4,111 undergraduate students, 39% full-time, 63% women, 37% men

Undergraduates 1,587 full-time, 2,524 part-time. Students come from 7 states and territories; 27% are from out of state; 23% Black or African American, non-Hispanic/Latino; 5% Hispanic/Latino; 1% Asian, non-Hispanic/Latino; 0.8% American Indian or Alaska Native, non-Hispanic/Latino; 3% Two or more races, non-Hispanic/Latino; 3% Race/ethnicity unknown; 2% live on campus.

Faculty *Total:* 227, 42% full-time. *Student/faculty ratio:* 20:1.

Majors Administrative assistant and secretarial science; agriculture; art; automobile/automotive mechanics technology; biology/biological sciences; business administration and management; business/commerce; chemistry; childcare and support services management; child development; computer and information sciences; cosmetology; criminal justice/law enforcement administration; criminal justice/safety; culinary arts; drafting and design technology; dramatic/theater arts; electrical, electronic and communications engineering technology; emergency medical technology (EMT paramedic); engineering; foreign languages and literatures; heating, air conditioning, ventilation and refrigeration maintenance technology; history; humanities; journalism; liberal arts and sciences/liberal studies; licensed practical/vocational nurse training; marketing/marketing management; mathematics; music; physics; political science and government; real estate; registered nursing/registered nurse; social sciences; substance abuse/addiction counseling; welding technology.

Academics *Calendar:* semesters. *Degree:* certificates and associate. *Special study options:* academic remediation for entering students, adult/continuing education programs, advanced placement credit, cooperative education, part-time degree program, services for LD students, summer session for credit.

Library Palmer Memorial Library with 46,700 titles, 646 serial subscriptions.

Student Life *Housing Options:* Campus housing is university owned. *Activities and Organizations:* drama/theater group, student-run newspaper, radio station, choral group, Black Student Association, Earth Club, Baptist Student Union, 21st Century Democrats, Young Republicans. *Campus security:* 24-hour patrols. *Student services:* personal/psychological counseling.

Athletics Member NJCAA. *Intercollegiate sports:* baseball M(s), golf M/W, softball W(s).

Costs (2012–13) *Tuition:* area resident $1170 full-time, $39 per semester hour part-time; state resident $2430 full-time, $81 per semester hour part-time; nonresident $3600 full-time, $120 per semester hour part-time. Full-time tuition and fees vary according to course load. Part-time tuition and fees vary according to course load. *Required fees:* $660 full-time. *Room and board:* room only: $2000. *Payment plan:* installment. *Waivers:* employees or children of employees.

Financial Aid Of all full-time matriculated undergraduates who enrolled in 2011, 30 Federal Work-Study jobs (averaging $3090).

Applying *Options:* early admission. *Required:* high school transcript. *Recommended:* Interview recommended for nursing program. Must have meningitis vaccine before student can start. *Application deadlines:* rolling (freshmen), rolling (transfers).

Freshman Application Contact Mrs. Linda Bennett, Director of Admissions, Texarkana College, 2500 North Robison Road, Texarkana, TX 75599-0001. *Phone:* 903-838-4541 Ext. 3011. *Fax:* 903-832-5030. *E-mail:* linda.bennett@texarkanacollege.edu. *Website:* http://www.texarkanacollege.edu/.

Texas School of Business, Friendswood Campus

Friendswood, Texas

- Proprietary 2-year
- Coed

Academics *Degree:* diplomas and associate.

Freshman Application Contact Admissions Office, Texas School of Business, Friendswood Campus, 3208 Farm to Market Road 528, Friendswood, TX 77546. *Website:* http://www.friendswood.tsb.edu/.

Texas School of Business, Houston North Campus

Houston, Texas

- Proprietary 2-year
- Coed

Academics *Degree:* diplomas and associate.

Freshman Application Contact Admissions Office, Texas School of Business, Houston North Campus, 711 East Airtex Drive, Houston, TX 77073. *Phone:* 281-443-8900. *Website:* http://www.north.tsb.edu/.

Texas Southmost College

Brownsville, Texas

Freshman Application Contact New Student Relations, Texas Southmost College, 80 Fort Brown, Brownsville, TX 78520-4991. *Phone:* 956-882-8860. *Toll-free phone:* 877-882-8721. *Fax:* 956-882-8959. *Website:* http://www.utb.edu/.

Texas State Technical College Harlingen

Harlingen, Texas

- State-supported 2-year, founded 1967, part of Texas State Technical College System
- Small-town 125-acre campus
- Coed, 5,509 undergraduate students, 43% full-time, 52% women, 48% men

Undergraduates 2,361 full-time, 3,148 part-time. Students come from 18 states and territories; 2 other countries; 0.4% are from out of state; 0.7% Black or African American, non-Hispanic/Latino; 88% Hispanic/Latino; 0.6% Asian, non-Hispanic/Latino; 0.1% Native Hawaiian or other Pacific Islander, non-Hispanic/Latino; 0.1% American Indian or Alaska Native, non-Hispanic/Latino; 1% Two or more races, non-Hispanic/Latino; 1% Race/ethnicity unknown; 0.1% international; 6% transferred in; 5% live on campus.

Freshmen *Admission:* 620 enrolled.

Faculty *Total:* 215, 73% full-time, 2% with terminal degrees. *Student/faculty ratio:* 19:1.

Majors Administrative assistant and secretarial science; agricultural business technology; aircraft powerplant technology; airframe mechanics and aircraft maintenance technology; autobody/collision and repair technology; automobile/automotive mechanics technology; biology/biological sciences; biomedical technology; chemical technology; commercial and advertising art; computer programming; computer systems networking and telecommunications; computer technology/computer systems technology; construction engineering technology; dental hygiene; dental laboratory technology; drafting and design technology; electromechanical technology; emergency medical technology (EMT paramedic); engineering; executive assistant/executive secretary; health information/medical records technology; health services/allied health/health sciences; heating, air conditioning, ventilation and refrigeration maintenance technology; information technology; mathematics; medical/clinical assistant; physics; prenursing studies; surgical technology; teacher assistant/aide; telecommunications technology; tool and die technology; welding technology.

Academics *Calendar:* semesters. *Degree:* certificates and associate. *Special study options:* academic remediation for entering students, adult/continuing education programs, cooperative education, distance learning, double majors, English as a second language, internships, part-time degree program, services for LD students, summer session for credit.

Library Dr. J. Gilbert Leal Learning Resource Center with 23,506 titles, 80 serial subscriptions, 649 audiovisual materials, an OPAC, a Web page.

Student Life *Housing Options:* men-only, women-only, disabled students. Campus housing is university owned. *Activities and Organizations:* student-run newspaper, Student Government Association, VICA (Vocational Industrial Clubs of America), Business Professionals of America. *Campus security:* 24-hour emergency response devices and patrols, late-night transport/escort service, night watchman for housing area. *Student services:* health clinic, personal/psychological counseling, women's center.

Athletics *Intramural sports:* badminton M/W, basketball M/W, football M/W, racquetball M/W, soccer M/W, softball M/W, table tennis M/W, tennis M/W, track and field M/W, volleyball M/W, weight lifting M/W.

Costs (2012–13) *Tuition:* state resident $3240 full-time, $90 per credit hour part-time; nonresident $9144 full-time, $254 per credit hour part-time. Full-time tuition and fees vary according to course load and program. Part-time tuition and fees vary according to course load and program. *Required fees:* $1656 full-time. *Room and board:* $2775; room only: $2175. Room and board charges vary according to board plan and housing facility. *Payment plan:* installment. *Waivers:* senior citizens and employees or children of employees.

Financial Aid Of all full-time matriculated undergraduates who enrolled in 2011, 120 Federal Work-Study jobs (averaging $2400). 15 state and other part-time jobs (averaging $2400).

Applying *Options:* electronic application, early admission, deferred entrance. *Required:* high school transcript. *Application deadlines:* rolling (freshmen), rolling (transfers). *Notification:* continuous (freshmen), continuous (transfers).

Freshman Application Contact Texas State Technical College Harlingen, 1902 North Loop 499, Harlingen, TX 78550-3697. *Phone:* 956-364-4100. *Toll-free phone:* 800-852-8784. *Website:* http://www.harlingen.tstc.edu/.

Texas State Technical College– Marshall

Marshall, Texas

Director of Admissions Pat Robbins, Registrar, Texas State Technical College–Marshall, 2650 East End Boulevard South, Marshall, TX 75671. *Phone:* 903-935-1010. *Toll-free phone:* 888-382-8782. *Fax:* 903-923-3282. *E-mail:* Pat.Robbins@marshall.tstc.edu. *Website:* http://www.marshall.tstc.edu/.

Texas State Technical College Waco

Waco, Texas

Freshman Application Contact Mr. Marcus Balch, Director, Recruiting Services, Texas State Technical College Waco, 3801 Campus Drive, Waco, TX 76705. *Phone:* 254-867-2026. *Toll-free phone:* 800-792-8784 Ext. 2362. *Fax:* 254-867-3827. *E-mail:* marcus.balch@tstc.edu. *Website:* http://waco.tstc.edu/.

Texas State Technical College West Texas

Sweetwater, Texas

Freshman Application Contact Ms. Maria Aguirre-Acuna, Texas State Technical College West Texas, 300 Homer K Taylor Drive, Sweetwater, TX 79556-4108. *Phone:* 325-235-7349. *Toll-free phone:* 800-592-8784. *Fax:* 325-235-7443. *E-mail:* maria.aquirre@sweetwater.tstc.edu. *Website:* http://www.westtexas.tstc.edu/.

Trinity Valley Community College

Athens, Texas

Freshman Application Contact Dr. Colette Hilliard, Dean of Enrollment Management and Registrar, Trinity Valley Community College, 100 Cardinal Drive, Athens, TX 75751. *Phone:* 903-675-6209 Ext. 209.
Website: http://www.tvcc.edu/.

Tyler Junior College

Tyler, Texas

- **State and locally supported** 2-year, founded 1926
- **Suburban** 85-acre campus
- **Coed,** 11,374 undergraduate students, 56% full-time, 58% women, 42% men

Undergraduates 6,344 full-time, 5,030 part-time. Students come from 34 states and territories; 27 other countries; 3% are from out of state; 23% Black or African American, non-Hispanic/Latino; 13% Hispanic/Latino; 1% Asian, non-Hispanic/Latino; 0.1% Native Hawaiian or other Pacific Islander, non-Hispanic/Latino; 0.7% American Indian or Alaska Native, non-Hispanic/Latino; 1% Two or more races, non-Hispanic/Latino; 2% Race/ethnicity unknown; 0.7% international; 6% transferred in; 9% live on campus. *Retention:* 49% of full-time freshmen returned.
Freshmen *Admission:* 2,811 applied, 2,811 admitted, 2,811 enrolled.
Faculty *Total:* 559, 51% full-time, 18% with terminal degrees. *Student/faculty ratio:* 21:1.
Majors Accounting; administrative assistant and secretarial science; art; automobile/automotive mechanics technology; behavioral sciences; biology/biological sciences; business administration and management; chemistry; child development; clinical/medical laboratory technology; commercial and advertising art; computer and information sciences; computer and information sciences related; computer engineering technology; computer graphics; computer programming related; computer science; computer systems networking and telecommunications; criminal justice/law enforcement administration; criminal justice/police science; dance; data entry/microcomputer applications; dental hygiene; dramatic/theater arts; economics; emergency medical technology (EMT paramedic); engineering; environmental science; family and consumer sciences/human sciences; fire science/firefighting; geology/earth science; health/health-care administration; health information/medical records technology; industrial radiologic technology; information technology; legal administrative assistant/secretary; liberal arts and sciences/liberal studies; licensed practical/vocational nurse training; mathematics; medical administrative assistant and medical secretary; modern languages; optometric technician; photography; physical education teaching and coaching; physics; political science and government; psychology; registered nursing/registered nurse; respiratory care therapy; sign language interpretation and translation; social sciences; speech communication and rhetoric; substance abuse/addiction counseling; surgical technology; surveying technology; welding technology.
Academics *Calendar:* semesters. *Degree:* certificates and associate. *Special study options:* academic remediation for entering students, accelerated degree program, adult/continuing education programs, advanced placement credit, distance learning, English as a second language, freshman honors college, honors programs, part-time degree program, services for LD students, summer session for credit.
Library Vaughn Library and Learning Resource Center with 104,000 titles, 10,000 serial subscriptions, an OPAC.
Student Life *Housing Options:* men-only, women-only. Campus housing is university owned. *Activities and Organizations:* drama/theater group, student-run newspaper, choral group, marching band, student government, religious affiliation clubs, Phi Theta Kappa, national fraternities, national sororities. *Campus security:* 24-hour emergency response devices and patrols, controlled dormitory access. *Student services:* health clinic, personal/psychological counseling.
Athletics Member NJCAA. *Intercollegiate sports:* baseball M, basketball M(s)/W(s), football M(s), golf M/W, soccer M(s)/W(s), tennis M(s)/W(s), volleyball W(s). *Intramural sports:* basketball M/W, racquetball M/W, volleyball M/W, weight lifting M/W.
Costs (2013–14) *Tuition:* area resident $900 full-time, $30 per credit hour part-time; state resident $2280 full-time, $76 per credit hour part-time; nonresident $2880 full-time, $96 per credit hour part-time. *Required fees:* $1362 full-time, $39 per credit part-time, $100 per term part-time. *Room and board:* $6400.
Financial Aid Of all full-time matriculated undergraduates who enrolled in 2011, 5,278 applied for aid, 4,434 were judged to have need, 43 had their need fully met. In 2011, 808 non-need-based awards were made. *Average percent of need met:* 63%. *Average financial aid package:* $3698. *Average need-based loan:* $1367. *Average need-based gift aid:* $2388. *Average non-need-based aid:* $979. *Average indebtedness upon graduation:* $13,109.
Applying *Options:* electronic application, early admission. *Required:* high school transcript. *Application deadlines:* rolling (freshmen), rolling (transfers). *Notification:* continuous (freshmen), continuous (transfers).

Freshman Application Contact Ms. Janna Chancey, Director of Enrollment Management, Tyler Junior College, PO Box 9020, Tyler, TX 75711-9020. *Phone:* 903-510-3325. *Toll-free phone:* 800-687-5680. *E-mail:* jcha@tjc.edu. *Website:* http://www.tjc.edu/.

Universal Technical Institute

Houston, Texas

Director of Admissions Director of Admissions, Universal Technical Institute, 721 Lockhaven Drive, Houston, TX 77073-5598. *Phone:* 281-443-6262. *Toll-free phone:* 800-510-5072. *Fax:* 281-443-0610.
Website: http://www.uti.edu/.

Vernon College

Vernon, Texas

Director of Admissions Mr. Joe Hite, Dean of Admissions/Registrar, Vernon College, 4400 College Drive, Vernon, TX 76384-4092. *Phone:* 940-552-6291 Ext. 2204.
Website: http://www.vernoncollege.edu/.

Vet Tech Institute of Houston

Houston, Texas

- **Private** 2-year, founded 1958
- **Suburban** campus
- **Coed,** 239 undergraduate students
- **66%** of applicants were admitted

Freshmen *Admission:* 570 applied, 379 admitted.
Majors Veterinary/animal health technology.
Academics *Degree:* associate. *Special study options:* accelerated degree program, internships.
Student Life *Housing:* college housing not available.
Freshman Application Contact Admissions Office, Vet Tech Institute of Houston, 4669 Southwest Freeway, Suite 100, Houston, TX 77027. *Phone:* 888-884-1468. *Toll-free phone:* 800-275-2736.
Website: http://www.vettechinstitute.edu/.

Victoria College

Victoria, Texas

Freshman Application Contact Ms. Lavern Dentler, Registrar, Victoria College, 2200 East Red River, Victoria, TX 77901-4494. *Phone:* 361-573-3291. *Toll-free phone:* 877-843-4369. *Fax:* 361-582-2525. *E-mail:* registrar@victoriacollege.edu.
Website: http://www.victoriacollege.edu/.

Virginia College in Austin

Austin, Texas

Admissions Office Contact Virginia College in Austin, 6301 East Highway 290, Austin, TX 78723.
Website: http://www.vc.edu/.

Wade College

Dallas, Texas

Freshman Application Contact Wade College, INFOMart, 1950 Stemmons Freeway, Suite 4080, LB 562, Dallas, TX 75207. *Phone:* 214-637-3530. *Toll-free phone:* 800-624-4850.
Website: http://www.wadecollege.edu/.

Weatherford College

Weatherford, Texas

Freshman Application Contact Mr. Ralph Willingham, Director of Admissions, Weatherford College, 225 College Park Drive, Weatherford, TX 76086-5699. *Phone:* 817-598-6248. *Toll-free phone:* 800-287-5471. *Fax:* 817-598-6205. *E-mail:* willingham@wc.edu.
Website: http://www.wc.edu/.

Western Technical College

El Paso, Texas

Freshman Application Contact Laura Pena, Director of Admissions, Western Technical College, 9451 Diana, El Paso, TX 79930-2610. *Phone:* 915-566-

9621. *Toll-free phone:* 800-201-9232. *E-mail:* lpena@westerntech.edu. *Website:* http://www.westerntech.edu/.

Western Technical College

El Paso, Texas

Freshman Application Contact Mr. Bill Terrell, Chief Admissions Officer, Western Technical College, 9624 Plaza Circle, El Paso, TX 79927. *Phone:* 915-532-3737 Ext. 117. *Fax:* 915-532-6946. *E-mail:* bterrell@wtc-ep.edu. *Website:* http://www.westerntech.edu/.

Western Texas College

Snyder, Texas

Director of Admissions Dr. Jim Clifton, Dean of Student Services, Western Texas College, 6200 College Avenue, Snyder, TX 79549. *Phone:* 325-573-8511 Ext. 204. *Toll-free phone:* 888-GO-TO-WTC. *E-mail:* jclifton@wtc.cc.tx.us. *Website:* http://www.wtc.edu/.

Wharton County Junior College

Wharton, Texas

Freshman Application Contact Mr. Albert Barnes, Dean of Admissions and Registration, Wharton County Junior College, 911 Boling Highway, Wharton, TX 77488-3298. *Phone:* 979-532-6381. *E-mail:* albertb@wcjc.edu. *Website:* http://www.wcjc.edu/.

UTAH

Everest College

West Valley City, Utah

Director of Admissions Director of Admissions, Everest College, 3280 West 3500 South, West Valley City, UT 84119. *Phone:* 801-840-4800. *Toll-free phone:* 888-741-4270. *Fax:* 801-969-0828. *Website:* http://www.everest.edu/.

ITT Technical Institute

Murray, Utah

- **Proprietary** primarily 2-year, founded 1984, part of ITT Educational Services, Inc.
- **Suburban** campus
- **Coed**

Academics *Calendar:* quarters. *Degrees:* associate and bachelor's.
Freshman Application Contact Director of Recruitment, ITT Technical Institute, 920 West Levoy Drive, Murray, UT 84123-2500. *Phone:* 801-263-3313. *Toll-free phone:* 800-365-2136. *Website:* http://www.itt-tech.edu/.

LDS Business College

Salt Lake City, Utah

- **Independent** 2-year, founded 1886, affiliated with The Church of Jesus Christ of Latter-day Saints, part of Latter-day Saints Church Educational System
- **Urban** 2-acre campus with easy access to Salt Lake City
- **Coed,** 2,191 undergraduate students, 73% full-time, 47% women, 53% men

Undergraduates 1,589 full-time, 602 part-time. Students come from 37 states and territories; 60 other countries; 45% are from out of state; 0.2% Black or African American, non-Hispanic/Latino; 11% Hispanic/Latino; 1% Asian, non-Hispanic/Latino; 2% Native Hawaiian or other Pacific Islander, non-Hispanic/Latino; 0.5% American Indian or Alaska Native, non-Hispanic/Latino; 4% Two or more races, non-Hispanic/Latino; 3% Race/ethnicity unknown; 13% international; 34% transferred in. *Retention:* 48% of full-time freshmen returned.
Freshmen *Admission:* 878 applied, 820 admitted, 604 enrolled.
Faculty *Total:* 142, 10% full-time, 66% with terminal degrees. *Student/faculty ratio:* 25:1.
Majors Accounting; accounting and business/management; accounting technology and bookkeeping; administrative assistant and secretarial science; business administration and management; entrepreneurship; health information/medical records administration; information technology; interior

design; liberal arts and sciences/liberal studies; medical administrative assistant and medical secretary; medical/clinical assistant; medical office assistant; system, networking, and LAN/WAN management; web page, digital/multimedia and information resources design.
Academics *Calendar:* semesters. *Degree:* certificates and associate. *Special study options:* academic remediation for entering students, adult/continuing education programs, advanced placement credit, internships, part-time degree program, services for LD students, summer session for credit. *ROTC:* Army (c), Air Force (c).
Library LDS Business College Library with 115,920 titles, 121 serial subscriptions, 1,128 audiovisual materials, an OPAC, a Web page.
Student Life *Housing:* college housing not available. *Activities and Organizations:* drama/theater group, choral group. *Campus security:* 24-hour emergency response devices and patrols.
Standardized Tests *Recommended:* SAT or ACT (for admission).
Costs (2013–14) *Tuition:* $3060 full-time, $128 per credit hour part-time. Full-time tuition and fees vary according to course load. Part-time tuition and fees vary according to course load. *Payment plan:* deferred payment. *Waivers:* employees or children of employees.
Applying *Options:* electronic application, deferred entrance. *Application fee:* $35. *Required:* essay or personal statement, high school transcript, interview. *Application deadlines:* rolling (freshmen), rolling (out-of-state freshmen), rolling (transfers). *Notification:* continuous (freshmen), continuous (out-of-state freshmen), continuous (transfers).
Freshman Application Contact Miss Dawn Fellows, Assistant Director of Admissions, LDS Business College, 95 North 300 West, Salt Lake City, UT 84101-3500. *Phone:* 801-524-8146. *Toll-free phone:* 800-999-5767. *Fax:* 801-524-1900. *E-mail:* DFellows@ldsbc.edu. *Website:* http://www.ldsbc.edu/.

Provo College

Provo, Utah

Director of Admissions Mr. Gordon Peters, College Director, Provo College, 1450 West 820 North, Provo, UT 84601. *Phone:* 801-375-1861. *Toll-free phone:* 877-777-5886. *Fax:* 801-375-9728. *E-mail:* gordonp@provocollege.org. *Website:* http://www.provocollege.edu/.

Salt Lake Community College

Salt Lake City, Utah

- **State-supported** 2-year, founded 1948, part of Utah System of Higher Education
- **Urban** 114-acre campus with easy access to Salt Lake City
- **Endowment** $826,231
- **Coed,** 28,967 undergraduate students, 31% full-time, 51% women, 49% men

Undergraduates 9,091 full-time, 19,876 part-time. 2% Black or African American, non-Hispanic/Latino; 12% Hispanic/Latino; 3% Asian, non-Hispanic/Latino; 1% Native Hawaiian or other Pacific Islander, non-Hispanic/Latino; 0.8% American Indian or Alaska Native, non-Hispanic/Latino; 1% Two or more races, non-Hispanic/Latino; 10% Race/ethnicity unknown; 1% international; 4% transferred in.
Freshmen *Admission:* 2,769 applied, 2,769 admitted, 2,769 enrolled.
Faculty *Total:* 1,479, 23% full-time. *Student/faculty ratio:* 21:1.
Majors Accounting technology and bookkeeping; airline pilot and flight crew; architectural engineering technology; autobody/collision and repair technology; avionics maintenance technology; biology/biological sciences; biology/biotechnology laboratory technician; building/construction finishing, management, and inspection related; business administration and management; chemistry; clinical/medical laboratory technology; computer and information sciences; computer science; cosmetology; criminal justice/law enforcement administration; culinary arts; dental hygiene; design and visual communications; diesel mechanics technology; drafting and design technology; economics; electrical, electronic and communications engineering technology; engineering; engineering technology; English; entrepreneurship; environmental engineering technology; finance; general studies; geology/earth science; graphic design; health professions related; heating, air conditioning, ventilation and refrigeration maintenance technology; history; human development and family studies; humanities; industrial radiologic technology; information science/studies; information technology; instrumentation technology; international/global studies; international relations and affairs; kinesiology and exercise science; legal assistant/paralegal; marketing/marketing management; mass communication/media; medical/clinical assistant; medical radiologic technology; music; occupational therapist assistant; photographic and film/video technology; physical sciences; physical therapy technology; physics; political science and government; psychology; public health related; quality control technology; radio and television broadcasting technology; registered nurs-

ing/registered nurse; sign language interpretation and translation; social work; sociology; speech communication and rhetoric; sport and fitness administration/management; surveying technology; teacher assistant/aide; telecommunications technology; welding technology.

Academics *Calendar:* semesters. *Degree:* certificates, diplomas, and associate. *Special study options:* academic remediation for entering students, advanced placement credit, cooperative education, distance learning, double majors, English as a second language, internships, part-time degree program, services for LD students, student-designed majors, study abroad, summer session for credit. *ROTC:* Army (c), Air Force (c).

Library Markosian Library plus 2 others with 152,537 titles, 21,736 serial subscriptions, 20,645 audiovisual materials, an OPAC, a Web page.

Student Life *Housing:* college housing not available. *Activities and Organizations:* drama/theater group, student-run newspaper, radio and television station, choral group, marching band. *Campus security:* 24-hour emergency response devices and patrols, late-night transport/escort service. *Student services:* health clinic, personal/psychological counseling.

Athletics Member NJCAA. *Intercollegiate sports:* baseball M(s), basketball M(s)/W(s), cheerleading M(s)/W(s), soccer M(c)/W(c), softball W(s), volleyball W(s).

Financial Aid Of all full-time matriculated undergraduates who enrolled in 2011, 132 Federal Work-Study jobs (averaging $2567).

Applying *Options:* electronic application, early admission. *Application fee:* $40. *Application deadlines:* rolling (freshmen), rolling (transfers).

Freshman Application Contact Ms. Kathy Thompson, Salt Lake Community College, Salt Lake City, UT 84130. *Phone:* 801-957-4485. *E-mail:* kathy.thompson@slcc.edu. *Website:* http://www.slcc.edu/.

Snow College

Ephraim, Utah

- **State-supported** 2-year, founded 1888, part of Utah System of Higher Education
- **Rural** 50-acre campus
- **Endowment** $6.2 million
- **Coed**

Undergraduates 2,943 full-time, 1,522 part-time. Students come from 34 states and territories; 12 other countries; 6% are from out of state; 1% Black or African American, non-Hispanic/Latino; 3% Hispanic/Latino; 0.5% Asian, non-Hispanic/Latino; 2% Native Hawaiian or other Pacific Islander, non-Hispanic/Latino; 1% American Indian or Alaska Native, non-Hispanic/Latino; 1% Two or more races, non-Hispanic/Latino; 3% Race/ethnicity unknown; 2% international; 2% transferred in. *Retention:* 47% of full-time freshmen returned.

Faculty *Student/faculty ratio:* 19:1.

Academics *Calendar:* semesters. *Degree:* certificates, diplomas, and associate. *Special study options:* academic remediation for entering students, adult/continuing education programs, advanced placement credit, cooperative education, English as a second language, external degree program, honors programs, independent study, part-time degree program, services for LD students, summer session for credit.

Student Life *Campus security:* 24-hour emergency response devices and patrols, student patrols, late-night transport/escort service.

Athletics Member NJCAA.

Standardized Tests *Recommended:* SAT or ACT (for admission).

Financial Aid Of all full-time matriculated undergraduates who enrolled in 2011, 302 Federal Work-Study jobs (averaging $1017).

Applying *Options:* electronic application, early admission. *Application fee:* $30. *Required:* high school transcript.

Freshman Application Contact Ms. Lorie Parry, Admissions Advisor, Snow College, 150 East College Avenue, Ephraim, UT 84627. *Phone:* 435-283-7144. *Fax:* 435-283-7157. *E-mail:* snowcollege@snow.edu. *Website:* http://www.snow.edu/.

VERMONT

Community College of Vermont

Montpelier, Vermont

- **State-supported** 2-year, founded 1970, part of Vermont State Colleges System
- **Rural** campus
- **Coed,** 6,908 undergraduate students, 16% full-time, 68% women, 32% men

Undergraduates 1,078 full-time, 5,830 part-time. Students come from 18 states and territories; 3% are from out of state; 3% Black or African American, non-Hispanic/Latino; 2% Hispanic/Latino; 2% Asian, non-Hispanic/Latino; 0.8% American Indian or Alaska Native, non-Hispanic/Latino; 3% Two or more races, non-Hispanic/Latino; 3% Race/ethnicity unknown.

Freshmen *Admission:* 1,805 applied, 1,140 admitted.

Faculty *Total:* 735, 11% with terminal degrees. *Student/faculty ratio:* 13:1.

Majors Accounting; administrative assistant and secretarial science; art; business administration and management; CAD/CADD drafting/design technology; child development; community organization and advocacy; computer and information sciences; computer science; computer systems networking and telecommunications; criminal justice/law enforcement administration; data entry/microcomputer applications; developmental and child psychology; digital communication and media/multimedia; early childhood education; education; environmental science; graphic design; hospitality administration; human services; industrial technology; information technology; liberal arts and sciences/liberal studies; social sciences; teacher assistant/aide.

Academics *Calendar:* semesters. *Degree:* certificates and associate. *Special study options:* academic remediation for entering students, accelerated degree program, adult/continuing education programs, advanced placement credit, cooperative education, distance learning, double majors, English as a second language, external degree program, independent study, internships, part-time degree program, services for LD students, student-designed majors, study abroad, summer session for credit.

Library Hartness Library plus 1 other with 59,000 titles, 36,500 serial subscriptions, 6,200 audiovisual materials, an OPAC, a Web page.

Student Life *Housing:* college housing not available.

Standardized Tests *Required for some:* ACCUPLACER assessments are required for degree seeking applicants and some continuing education applicants. SAT/ACT scores as well as college transcripts may be used to waive the Accuplacers. *Recommended:* SAT or ACT (for admission).

Costs (2012–13) *Tuition:* state resident $6690 full-time, $223 per credit hour part-time; nonresident $13,380 full-time, $446 per credit hour part-time. *Required fees:* $150 full-time, $50 per term part-time. *Payment plan:* installment. *Waivers:* senior citizens and employees or children of employees.

Financial Aid Of all full-time matriculated undergraduates who enrolled in 2011, 84 Federal Work-Study jobs (averaging $2000).

Applying *Options:* electronic application. *Application deadlines:* rolling (freshmen), rolling (out-of-state freshmen), rolling (transfers). *Notification:* continuous (freshmen), continuous (out-of-state freshmen), continuous (transfers).

Freshman Application Contact Community College of Vermont, 660 Elm St, PO Box 489, Montpelier, VT 05602. *Phone:* 802-654-0505. *Toll-free phone:* 800-CCV-6686. *Website:* http://www.ccv.edu/.

Landmark College

Putney, Vermont

Freshman Application Contact Admissions Main Desk, Landmark College, Putney, VT 05346. *Phone:* 802-387-6718. *Fax:* 802-387-6868. *E-mail:* admissions@landmark.edu. *Website:* http://www.landmark.edu/.

New England Culinary Institute

Montpelier, Vermont

Freshman Application Contact Jan Knutsen, Vice President of Enrollment, New England Culinary Institute, 56 College Street, Montpelier, VT 05602-3115. *Toll-free phone:* 877-223-6324. *Fax:* 802-225-3280. *E-mail:* janknutsen@neci.edu. *Website:* http://www.neci.edu/.

VIRGINIA

Advanced Technology Institute

Virginia Beach, Virginia

Freshman Application Contact Admissions Office, Advanced Technology Institute, 5700 Southern Boulevard, Suite 100, Virginia Beach, VA 23462. *Phone:* 757-490-1241. *Toll-free phone:* 888-468-1093. *Website:* http://www.auto.edu/.

Aviation Institute of Maintenance–Chesapeake

Chesapeake, Virginia

Freshman Application Contact Aviation Institute of Maintenance–Chesapeake, 2211 South Military Highway, Chesapeake, VA 23320. *Phone:* 757-363-2121. *Toll-free phone:* 888-349-5387. *Fax:* 757-363-2044. *Website:* http://www.aviationmaintenance.edu/.

Aviation Institute of Maintenance–Manassas

Manassas, Virginia

Freshman Application Contact Aviation Institute of Maintenance–Manassas, 9821 Godwin Drive, Manassas, VA 20110. *Phone:* 703-257-5515. *Toll-free phone:* 888-349-5387- (in-state); 888-349-5387 (out-of-state). *Fax:* 703-257-5523. *Website:* http://www.aviationmaintenance.edu/.

Blue Ridge Community College

Weyers Cave, Virginia

Freshman Application Contact Blue Ridge Community College, PO Box 80, Weyers Cave, VA 24486-0080. *Phone:* 540-453-2217. *Toll-free phone:* 888-750-2722. *Website:* http://www.brcc.edu/.

Bryant & Stratton College - Richmond Campus

Richmond, Virginia

Freshman Application Contact Mr. David K. Mayle, Director of Admissions, Bryant & Stratton College - Richmond Campus, 8141 Hull Street Road, Richmond, VA 23235-6411. *Phone:* 804-745-2444. *Fax:* 804-745-6884. *E-mail:* tlawson@bryanstratton.edu. *Website:* http://www.bryantstratton.edu/.

Bryant & Stratton College - Virginia Beach

Virginia Beach, Virginia

Freshman Application Contact Bryant & Stratton College - Virginia Beach, 301 Centre Pointe Drive, Virginia Beach, VA 23462-4417. *Phone:* 757-499-7900 Ext. 173. *Website:* http://www.bryantstratton.edu/.

Central Virginia Community College

Lynchburg, Virginia

Freshman Application Contact Admissions Office, Central Virginia Community College, 3506 Wards Road, Lynchburg, VA 24502-2498. *Phone:* 434-832-7633. *Toll-free phone:* 800-562-3060. *Fax:* 434-832-7793. *Website:* http://www.cvcc.vccs.edu/.

Centura College

Chesapeake, Virginia

Director of Admissions Director of Admissions, Centura College, 932 Ventures Way, Chesapeake, VA 23320. *Phone:* 757-549-2121. *Toll-free phone:* 877-575-5627. *Fax:* 575-549-1196. *Website:* http://www.centuracollege.edu/.

Centura College

Newport News, Virginia

Director of Admissions Victoria Whitehead, Director of Admissions, Centura College, 616 Denbigh Boulevard, Newport News, VA 23608. *Phone:* 757-874-2121. *Toll-free phone:* 877-575-5627. *Fax:* 757-874-3857. *E-mail:* admdircpen@centura.edu. *Website:* http://www.centuracollege.edu/.

Centura College

Norfolk, Virginia

Director of Admissions Director of Admissions, Centura College, 7020 North Military Highway, Norfolk, VA 23518. *Phone:* 757-853-2121. *Toll-free phone:* 877-575-5627. *Fax:* 757-852-9017. *Website:* http://www.centuracollege.edu/.

Centura College

North Chesterfield, Virginia

Freshman Application Contact Admissions Office, Centura College, 7914 Midlothian Turnpike, North Chesterfield, VA 23235-5230. *Phone:* 804-330-0111. *Toll-free phone:* 877-575-5627. *Fax:* 804-330-3809. *Website:* http://www.centuracollege.edu/.

Centura College

Richmond, Virginia

Director of Admissions Terry Gates, Director of Admissions, Centura College, 7001 West Broad Street, Richmond, VA 23294. *Phone:* 804-672-2300. *Toll-free phone:* 877-575-5627. *Fax:* 804-672-3338. *Website:* http://www.centuracollege.edu/.

Centura College

Virginia Beach, Virginia

Freshman Application Contact Admissions Office, Centura College, 2697 Dean Drive, Suite 100, Virginia Beach, VA 23452. *Phone:* 757-340-2121. *Toll-free phone:* 877-575-5627. *Fax:* 757-340-9704. *Website:* http://www.centuracollege.edu/.

Dabney S. Lancaster Community College

Clifton Forge, Virginia

- **State-supported** 2-year, founded 1964, part of Virginia Community College System
- **Rural** 117-acre campus
- **Endowment** $3.3 million
- **Coed,** 1,538 undergraduate students, 31% full-time, 54% women, 46% men

Undergraduates 479 full-time, 1,059 part-time. Students come from 8 states and territories; 3% are from out of state; 6% Black or African American, non-Hispanic/Latino; 1% Hispanic/Latino; 0.4% Asian, non-Hispanic/Latino; 0.8% American Indian or Alaska Native, non-Hispanic/Latino; 0.9% Two or more races, non-Hispanic/Latino; 1% Race/ethnicity unknown; 26% transferred in. **Freshmen** *Admission:* 222 enrolled.
Faculty *Total:* 97, 24% full-time. *Student/faculty ratio:* 16:1.
Majors Administrative assistant and secretarial science; biological and physical sciences; business administration and management; computer programming; criminal justice/law enforcement administration; data processing and data processing technology; drafting and design technology; drafting/design engineering technologies related; education; electrical, electronic and communications engineering technology; forest technology; information science/studies; legal administrative assistant/secretary; liberal arts and sciences/liberal studies; medical administrative assistant and medical secretary; registered nursing/registered nurse; wood science and wood products/pulp and paper technology.
Academics *Calendar:* semesters. *Degree:* certificates, diplomas, and associate. *Special study options:* academic remediation for entering students, adult/continuing education programs, advanced placement credit, cooperative education, distance learning, honors programs, independent study, internships, part-time degree program, services for LD students, study abroad, summer session for credit.
Library DSLCC Library plus 1 other with 34,397 titles, 853 serial subscriptions, 1,260 audiovisual materials, an OPAC.

Student Life *Housing:* college housing not available. *Campus security:* 24-hour emergency response devices. *Student services:* personal/psychological counseling.

Athletics *Intercollegiate sports:* basketball M. *Intramural sports:* basketball M/W, bowling M/W, skiing (downhill) M/W, volleyball M/W.

Costs (2013–14) *Tuition:* state resident $2808 full-time, $117 per credit part-time; nonresident $7046 full-time, $294 per credit part-time. *Required fees:* $240 full-time, $120 per year part-time. *Payment plan:* installment.

Applying *Recommended:* high school transcript, interview.

Freshman Application Contact Mrs. Lorrie Wilhelm Ferguson, Registrar, Dabney S. Lancaster Community College, Backels Hall, Clifton Forge, VA 24422. *Phone:* 540-863-2823. *Toll-free phone:* 877-73-DSLCC. *Fax:* 540-863-2915. *E-mail:* lwferguson@dslcc.edu. *Website:* http://www.dslcc.edu/.

Danville Community College
Danville, Virginia

Freshman Application Contact Cathy Pulliam, Coordinator of Student Recruitment and Enrollment, Danville Community College, 1008 South Main Street, Danville, VA 24541-4088. *Phone:* 434-797-8538. *Toll-free phone:* 800-560-4291. *E-mail:* cpulliam@dcc.vccs.edu. *Website:* http://www.dcc.vccs.edu/.

Eastern Shore Community College
Melfa, Virginia

- **State-supported** 2-year, founded 1971, part of Virginia Community College System
- **Rural** 117-acre campus with easy access to Hampton Roads/Virginia Beach, Norfolk
- **Coed,** 1,332 undergraduate students, 17% full-time, 67% women, 33% men

Undergraduates 229 full-time, 1,103 part-time. Students come from 3 states and territories; 2% are from out of state.

Faculty *Total:* 57, 32% full-time, 7% with terminal degrees. *Student/faculty ratio:* 13:1.

Majors Administrative assistant and secretarial science; biological and physical sciences; business administration and management; computer and information sciences and support services related; computer/information technology services administration related; education; electrical, electronic and communications engineering technology; liberal arts and sciences/liberal studies; registered nursing/registered nurse.

Academics *Calendar:* semesters. *Degree:* certificates and associate. *Special study options:* academic remediation for entering students, adult/continuing education programs, distance learning, internships, part-time degree program, services for LD students, summer session for credit.

Library Learning Resources Center plus 1 other with 25,000 titles, 102 serial subscriptions, an OPAC, a Web page.

Student Life *Housing:* college housing not available. *Activities and Organizations:* All Christians Together in Service (ACTS), Phi Theta Kappa, Phi Beta Lambda, The Electronics Club, SNAP Photography Club. *Campus security:* security guards, day and night during classes when the college is in session.

Standardized Tests *Required:* The Virginia Community College System (VCCS) has a placement test designed for and utilized by all schools in its system (for admission).

Financial Aid Of all full-time matriculated undergraduates who enrolled in 2011, 11 Federal Work-Study jobs.

Applying *Options:* electronic application. *Required:* high school transcript, high school diploma. *Application deadlines:* rolling (freshmen), rolling (transfers). *Notification:* continuous (freshmen), continuous (transfers).

Freshman Application Contact P. Bryan Smith, Dean of Student Services, Eastern Shore Community College, 29300 Lankford Highway, Melfa, VA 23410. *Phone:* 757-789-1732. *Toll-free phone:* 877-871-8455. *Fax:* 757-789-1737. *E-mail:* bsmith@es.vccs.edu. *Website:* http://www.es.vccs.edu/.

ECPI College of Technology
Richmond, Virginia

Freshman Application Contact Director, ECPI College of Technology, 800 Moorefield Park Drive, Richmond, VA 23236. *Phone:* 804-330-5533. *Toll-free phone:* 800-986-1200. *Fax:* 804-330-5577. *E-mail:* agerard@ecpi.edu. *Website:* http://www.ecpi.edu/.

Everest College
Arlington, Virginia

Freshman Application Contact Director of Admissions, Everest College, 801 North Quincy Street, Suite 500, Arlington, VA 22203. *Phone:* 703-248-8887. *Toll-free phone:* 888-741-4270. *Fax:* 703-351-2202. *Website:* http://www.everest.edu/.

Fortis College
Norfolk, Virginia

Admissions Office Contact Fortis College, 6300 Center Drive, Suite 100, Norfolk, VA 23502. *Website:* http://www.fortis.edu/.

Fortis College
Richmond, Virginia

Admissions Office Contact Fortis College, 2000 Westmoreland Street, Suite A, Richmond, VA 23230. *Website:* http://www.fortis.edu/.

Germanna Community College
Locust Grove, Virginia

Freshman Application Contact Ms. Rita Dunston, Registrar, Germanna Community College, 10000 Germanna Point Drive, Fredericksburg, VA 22408. *Phone:* 540-891-3020. *Fax:* 540-891-3092. *Website:* http://www.germanna.edu/.

ITT Technical Institute
Chantilly, Virginia

- **Proprietary** primarily 2-year, founded 2002, part of ITT Educational Services, Inc.
- **Coed**

Academics *Calendar:* quarters. *Degrees:* associate and bachelor's.

Freshman Application Contact Director of Recruitment, ITT Technical Institute, 14420 Abermarle Point Place, Suite 100, Chantilly, VA 20151. *Phone:* 703-263-2541. *Toll-free phone:* 888-895-8324. *Website:* http://www.itt-tech.edu/.

ITT Technical Institute
Norfolk, Virginia

- **Proprietary** primarily 2-year, founded 1988, part of ITT Educational Services, Inc.
- **Suburban** campus
- **Coed**

Academics *Calendar:* quarters. *Degrees:* associate and bachelor's.

Financial Aid Of all full-time matriculated undergraduates who enrolled in 2011, 3 Federal Work-Study jobs (averaging $5000).

Freshman Application Contact Director of Recruitment, ITT Technical Institute, 863 Glenrock Road, Suite 100, Norfolk, VA 23502-3701. *Phone:* 757-466-1260. *Toll-free phone:* 888-253-8324. *Website:* http://www.itt-tech.edu/.

ITT Technical Institute
Richmond, Virginia

- **Proprietary** primarily 2-year, founded 1999, part of ITT Educational Services, Inc.
- **Coed**

Academics *Calendar:* quarters. *Degrees:* associate and bachelor's.

Freshman Application Contact Director of Recruitment, ITT Technical Institute, 300 Gateway Centre Parkway, Richmond, VA 23235. *Phone:* 804-330-4992. *Toll-free phone:* 888-330-4888. *Website:* http://www.itt-tech.edu/.

ITT Technical Institute
Salem, Virginia

- **Proprietary** primarily 2-year
- **Coed**

Academics *Degrees:* associate and bachelor's.

Freshman Application Contact Director of Recruitment, ITT Technical Institute, 2159 Apperson Drive, Salem, VA 24153. *Phone:* 540-989-2500. *Toll-*

free phone: 877-208-6132.
Website: http://www.itt-tech.edu/.

ITT Technical Institute

Springfield, Virginia

- **Proprietary** primarily 2-year, founded 2002, part of ITT Educational Services, Inc.

- **Coed**

Academics *Calendar:* quarters. *Degrees:* associate and bachelor's.

Freshman Application Contact Director of Recruitment, ITT Technical Institute, 7300 Boston Boulevard, Springfield, VA 22153. *Phone:* 703-440-9535. *Toll-free phone:* 866-817-8324.
Website: http://www.itt-tech.edu/.

John Tyler Community College

Chester, Virginia

- **State-supported** 2-year, founded 1967, part of Virginia Community College System

- **Suburban** 160-acre campus with easy access to Richmond

- **Coed,** 10,145 undergraduate students, 28% full-time, 58% women, 42% men

Undergraduates 2,820 full-time, 7,325 part-time. 25% Black or African American, non-Hispanic/Latino; 6% Hispanic/Latino; 3% Asian, non-Hispanic/Latino; 0.5% American Indian or Alaska Native, non-Hispanic/Latino; 3% Two or more races, non-Hispanic/Latino; 1% Race/ethnicity unknown; 0.2% international. *Retention:* 51% of full-time freshmen returned.

Freshmen *Admission:* 1,379 enrolled.

Faculty *Total:* 542, 22% full-time. *Student/faculty ratio:* 20:1.

Majors Accounting related; administrative assistant and secretarial science; architectural engineering technology; architectural technology; business administration and management; business administration, management and operations related; business/commerce; child-care provision; computer and information sciences; criminal justice/law enforcement administration; electrical and electronics engineering; engineering; engineering technology; funeral service and mortuary science; general studies; humanities; human services; industrial electronics technology; industrial technology; information technology; liberal arts and sciences/liberal studies; management information systems; mechanical engineering/mechanical technology; mechanical engineering technologies related; mental and social health services and allied professions related; quality control and safety technologies related; registered nursing/registered nurse; visual and performing arts related.

Academics *Calendar:* semesters. *Degree:* certificates and associate. *Special study options:* academic remediation for entering students, adult/continuing education programs, advanced placement credit, distance learning, external degree program, honors programs, off-campus study, part-time degree program, services for LD students, study abroad, summer session for credit. *ROTC:* Army (c).

Library John Tyler Community College Learning Resource and Technology Center with 52,000 titles, 10,150 serial subscriptions, 1,335 audiovisual materials, an OPAC, a Web page.

Student Life *Housing:* college housing not available. *Activities and Organizations:* drama/theater group, choral group, Phi Theta Kappa -TauRho, Phi Theta Kappa - BOO, Art Club, Elements of Life Club, Funeral Services Club. *Campus security:* 24-hour emergency response devices and patrols.

Costs (2012–13) *Tuition:* state resident $2988 full-time, $125 per credit hour part-time; nonresident $7598 full-time, $316 per credit hour part-time. Full-time tuition and fees vary according to course load. Part-time tuition and fees vary according to course load. *Required fees:* $50 full-time, $25 per term part-time. *Payment plan:* installment. *Waivers:* senior citizens.

Applying *Options:* early admission, deferred entrance. *Recommended:* high school transcript. *Application deadline:* rolling (freshmen). *Notification:* continuous (freshmen).

Freshman Application Contact Ms. Joy James, Director of Admission, John Tyler Community College, 13101 Jefferson Davis Highway, Chester, VA 23831. *Phone:* 804-706-5214. *Toll-free phone:* 800-552-3490. *Fax:* 804-796-4362.
Website: http://www.jtcc.edu/.

J. Sargeant Reynolds Community College

Richmond, Virginia

- **State-supported** 2-year, founded 1972, part of Virginia Community College System

- **Suburban** 207-acre campus

- **Coed**

Undergraduates 4,075 full-time, 9,295 part-time. 37% Black or African American, non-Hispanic/Latino; 3% Hispanic/Latino; 4% Asian, non-Hispanic/Latino; 1% American Indian or Alaska Native, non-Hispanic/Latino; 2% Race/ethnicity unknown.

Academics *Calendar:* semesters. *Degree:* certificates and associate. *Special study options:* academic remediation for entering students, adult/continuing education programs, advanced placement credit, distance learning, English as a second language, independent study, internships, off-campus study, part-time degree program, services for LD students, summer session for credit.

Student Life *Campus security:* 24-hour emergency response devices and patrols, late-night transport/escort service, security during open hours.

Financial Aid Of all full-time matriculated undergraduates who enrolled in 2009, 14,628 applied for aid, 11,184 were judged to have need. 64 Federal Work-Study jobs (averaging $2600). In 2009, 121. *Average percent of need met:* 49. *Average financial aid package:* $6950. *Average need-based loan:* $2792. *Average need-based gift aid:* $3400. *Average non-need-based aid:* $891. *Average indebtedness upon graduation:* $3891.

Applying *Options:* electronic application. *Required:* high school transcript. *Required for some:* interview.

Freshman Application Contact Ms. Karen Pettis-Walden, Director of Admissions and Records, J. Sargeant Reynolds Community College, PO Box 85622, Richmond, VA 23285-5622. *Phone:* 804-523-5029. *Fax:* 804-371-3650. *E-mail:* kpettis-walden@reynolds.edu.
Website: http://www.reynolds.edu/.

Lord Fairfax Community College

Middletown, Virginia

Freshman Application Contact Karen Bucher, Director of Enrollment Management, Lord Fairfax Community College, 173 Skirmisher Lane, Middletown, VA 22645. *Phone:* 540-868-7132. *Toll-free phone:* 800-906-LFCC. *Fax:* 540-868-7005. *E-mail:* kbucher@lfcc.edu.
Website: http://www.lfcc.edu/.

Miller-Motte Technical College

Roanoke, Virginia

Admissions Office Contact Miller-Motte Technical College, 4444 Electric Road, Roanoke, VA 24018.
Website: http://www.miller-motte.edu/.

Mountain Empire Community College

Big Stone Gap, Virginia

Freshman Application Contact Mountain Empire Community College, 3441 Mountain Empire Road, Big Stone Gap, VA 24219. *Phone:* 276-523-2400 Ext. 219.
Website: http://www.mecc.edu/.

National College

Charlottesville, Virginia

Director of Admissions Kimberly Moore, Campus Director, National College, 3926 Seminole Trail, Charlottesville, VA 22911. *Phone:* 434-295-0136. *Toll-free phone:* 888-9-JOBREADY. *Fax:* 434-979-8061.
Website: http://www.national-college.edu/.

National College

Danville, Virginia

Freshman Application Contact Admissions Office, National College, 336 Old Riverside Drive, Danville, VA 24541. *Phone:* 434-793-6822. *Toll-free phone:* 888-9-JOBREADY.
Website: http://www.national-college.edu/.

National College
Harrisonburg, Virginia

Director of Admissions Jack Evey, Campus Director, National College, 1515 Country Club Road, Harrisonburg, VA 22802. *Phone:* 540-432-0943. *Toll-free phone:* 888-9-JOBREADY.
Website: http://www.national-college.edu/.

National College
Lynchburg, Virginia

Freshman Application Contact Admissions Representative, National College, 104 Candlewood Court, Lynchburg, VA 24502-2653. *Phone:* 804-239-3500. *Toll-free phone:* 888-9-JOBREADY.
Website: http://www.national-college.edu/.

National College
Martinsville, Virginia

Director of Admissions Mr. John Scott, Campus Director, National College, 905 Memorial Boulevard North, Martinsville, VA 24112. *Phone:* 276-632-5621. *Toll-free phone:* 888-9-JOBREADY.
Website: http://www.national-college.edu/.

National College
Salem, Virginia

Freshman Application Contact Director of Admissions, National College, 1813 East Main Street, Salem, VA 24153. *Phone:* 540-986-1800. *Toll-free phone:* 888-9-JOBREADY. *Fax:* 540-444-4198.
Website: http://www.national-college.edu/.

New River Community College
Dublin, Virginia

Freshman Application Contact Ms. Margaret G. Taylor, Director of Student Services, New River Community College, PO Box 1127, Dublin, VA 24084-1127. *Phone:* 540-674-3600. *Toll-free phone:* 866-462-6722. *Fax:* 540-674-3644. *E-mail:* nrtaylm@nr.edu.
Website: http://www.nr.edu/.

Northern Virginia Community College
Annandale, Virginia

Director of Admissions Dr. Max L. Bassett, Dean of Academic and Student Services, Northern Virginia Community College, 4001 Wakefield Chapel Road, Annandale, VA 22003-3796. *Phone:* 703-323-3195.
Website: http://www.nvcc.edu/.

Patrick Henry Community College
Martinsville, Virginia

Freshman Application Contact Mr. Travis Tisdale, Coordinator, Admissions and Records, Patrick Henry Community College, Martinsville, VA 24115. *Phone:* 276-656-0311. *Toll-free phone:* 800-232-7997. *Fax:* 276-656-0352.
Website: http://www.ph.vccs.edu/.

Paul D. Camp Community College
Franklin, Virginia

- **State-supported** 2-year, founded 1971, part of Virginia Community College System
- **Small-town** 99-acre campus
- **Endowment** $500,000
- **Coed,** 1,579 undergraduate students, 27% full-time, 68% women, 32% men

Undergraduates 426 full-time, 1,153 part-time. Students come from 2 states and territories; 2 other countries; 0.5% are from out of state; 38% Black or African American, non-Hispanic/Latino; 4% Race/ethnicity unknown. *Retention:* 66% of full-time freshmen returned.
Freshmen *Admission:* 597 applied, 597 admitted. *Average high school GPA:* 2.2.
Faculty *Total:* 161, 11% full-time. *Student/faculty ratio:* 16:1.
Majors Administrative assistant and secretarial science; business administration and management; computer technology/computer systems technology; criminal justice/law enforcement administration; data processing and data processing technology; early childhood education; education; industrial technol-

ogy; liberal arts and sciences/liberal studies; registered nursing/registered nurse.
Academics *Calendar:* semesters. *Degree:* certificates and associate. *Special study options:* academic remediation for entering students, adult/continuing education programs, advanced placement credit, cooperative education, distance learning, honors programs, independent study, internships, off-campus study, part-time degree program, summer session for credit.
Library Paul D. Camp Community College Library with 22,000 titles, 200 serial subscriptions, an OPAC.
Student Life *Housing:* college housing not available. *Activities and Organizations:* student-run newspaper, African-American History Club, Phi Beta Lambda, Phi Theta Kappa, Student Government Association, Student Newspaper. *Campus security:* late-night transport/escort service.
Costs (2013–14) *Tuition:* state resident $3965 full-time, $122 per credit part-time; nonresident $9803 full-time, $298 per credit part-time. *Required fees:* $10 per credit part-time.
Financial Aid Of all full-time matriculated undergraduates who enrolled in 2011, 30 Federal Work-Study jobs (averaging $2000).
Applying *Options:* electronic application, deferred entrance. *Required:* high school transcript. *Application deadlines:* rolling (freshmen), rolling (transfers). *Notification:* continuous (freshmen), continuous (transfers).
Freshman Application Contact Mrs. Trina Jones, Dean Student Services, Paul D. Camp Community College, PO Box 737, 100 N College Drive, Franklin, VA 23851. *Phone:* 757-569-6720. *E-mail:* tjones@pdc.edu.
Website: http://www.pdc.edu/.

Piedmont Virginia Community College
Charlottesville, Virginia

- **State-supported** 2-year, founded 1972, part of Virginia Community College System
- **Suburban** 114-acre campus with easy access to Richmond
- **Coed,** 5,693 undergraduate students, 21% full-time, 59% women, 41% men

Undergraduates 1,179 full-time, 4,514 part-time. Students come from 15 states and territories; 14% Black or African American, non-Hispanic/Latino; 4% Hispanic/Latino; 4% Asian, non-Hispanic/Latino; 0.1% Native Hawaiian or other Pacific Islander, non-Hispanic/Latino; 0.3% American Indian or Alaska Native, non-Hispanic/Latino; 3% Two or more races, non-Hispanic/Latino; 2% Race/ethnicity unknown; 0.4% international; 6% transferred in.
Freshmen *Admission:* 718 enrolled.
Faculty *Total:* 74.
Majors Biological and physical sciences; business administration and management; computer and information sciences and support services related; computer programming; computer science; criminal justice/police science; diagnostic medical sonography and ultrasound technology; education; emergency medical technology (EMT paramedic); engineering; general studies; liberal arts and sciences/liberal studies; marketing/marketing management; radiologic technology/science; registered nursing/registered nurse; visual and performing arts.
Academics *Calendar:* semesters. *Degree:* certificates and associate. *Special study options:* academic remediation for entering students, adult/continuing education programs, advanced placement credit, cooperative education, distance learning, English as a second language, honors programs, independent study, internships, part-time degree program, services for LD students, summer session for credit. *ROTC:* Army (c).
Library Jessup Library with 37,261 titles, 139 serial subscriptions, 1,058 audiovisual materials, an OPAC, a Web page.
Student Life *Housing:* college housing not available. *Activities and Organizations:* drama/theater group, student-run newspaper, choral group. *Campus security:* 24-hour emergency response devices and patrols, late-night transport/escort service.
Athletics *Intramural sports:* basketball M/W, golf M/W, soccer M/W, table tennis M/W, tennis M/W, ultimate Frisbee M/W, volleyball M/W, weight lifting M/W.
Costs (2012–13) *Tuition:* state resident $3510 full-time, $117 per credit hour part-time; nonresident $9593 full-time, $294 per credit hour part-time. Full-time tuition and fees vary according to course load. Part-time tuition and fees vary according to course load. *Required fees:* $320 full-time, $11 per credit hour part-time. *Payment plan:* installment. *Waivers:* senior citizens and employees or children of employees.
Financial Aid Of all full-time matriculated undergraduates who enrolled in 2011, 50 Federal Work-Study jobs.
Applying *Options:* electronic application, early admission, deferred entrance. *Required for some:* high school transcript, Admission to programs in Nursing, Practical Nursing, Radiography, Sonography, Surgical Technology, Emergency Medical Services, Health Information Management, and Patient Admissions

Coordination is competitive and/or requires completion of specific prerequisites. *Application deadlines:* rolling (freshmen), rolling (transfers). *Notification:* continuous (freshmen), continuous (transfers).

Freshman Application Contact Ms. Mary Lee Walsh, Dean of Student Services, Piedmont Virginia Community College, 501 College Drive, Charlottesville, VA 22902-7589. *Phone:* 434-961-6540. *Fax:* 434-961-5425. *E-mail:* mwalsh@pvcc.edu.
Website: http://www.pvcc.edu/.

Rappahannock Community College

Glenns, Virginia

- **State and locally supported** 2-year, founded 1970, part of Virginia Community College System
- **Rural** campus
- **Coed,** 3,711 undergraduate students, 100% full-time, 61% women, 39% men

Undergraduates 3,711 full-time.

Majors Accounting; administrative assistant and secretarial science; biological and physical sciences; business administration and management; business administration, management and operations related; criminal justice/law enforcement administration; criminal justice/police science; engineering technology; information science/studies; liberal arts and sciences/liberal studies; registered nursing/registered nurse.

Academics *Calendar:* semesters. *Degree:* certificates, diplomas, and associate. *Special study options:* academic remediation for entering students, adult/continuing education programs, distance learning, honors programs, internships, off-campus study, part-time degree program, services for LD students, summer session for credit.

Library an OPAC, a Web page.

Student Life *Student services:* personal/psychological counseling.

Athletics *Intercollegiate sports:* baseball M, softball W.

Costs (2012–13) *Tuition:* state resident $2808 full-time, $117 per credit hour part-time; nonresident $7046 full-time, $294 per credit hour part-time. Full-time tuition and fees vary according to course load. Part-time tuition and fees vary according to course load. *Required fees:* $281 full-time, $12 per credit hour part-time. *Payment plan:* deferred payment.

Financial Aid Of all full-time matriculated undergraduates who enrolled in 2011, 40 Federal Work-Study jobs (averaging $1015).

Applying *Options:* electronic application, early admission. *Application deadlines:* rolling (freshmen), rolling (transfers). *Notification:* continuous (freshmen), continuous (transfers).

Freshman Application Contact Ms. Felicia Packett, Admissions and Records Officer, Rappahannock Community College, 12745 College Drive, Glenns, VA 23149-0287. *Phone:* 804-758-6740. *Toll-free phone:* 800-836-9381.
Website: http://www.rappahannock.edu/.

Richard Bland College of The College of William and Mary

Petersburg, Virginia

Freshman Application Contact Office of Admissions, Richard Bland College of The College of William and Mary, 11301 Johnson Road, Petersburg, VA 23805-7100. *Phone:* 804-862-6249.
Website: http://www.rbc.edu/.

Southside Virginia Community College

Alberta, Virginia

Freshman Application Contact Mr. Brent Richey, Dean of Enrollment Management, Southside Virginia Community College, 109 Campus Drive, Alberta, VA 23821. *Phone:* 434-949-1012. *Fax:* 434-949-7863. *E-mail:* rhina.jones@sv.vccs.edu.
Website: http://www.southside.edu/.

Southwest Virginia Community College

Richlands, Virginia

- **State-supported** 2-year, founded 1968, part of Virginia Community College System
- **Rural** 100-acre campus with easy access to None
- **Endowment** $8.7 million
- **Coed,** 2,766 undergraduate students, 42% full-time, 60% women, 40% men

Undergraduates 1,159 full-time, 1,607 part-time. Students come from 4 states and territories; 2% are from out of state; 3% Black or African American, non-Hispanic/Latino; 0.8% Hispanic/Latino; 0.8% Asian, non-Hispanic/Latino; 0.1% Native Hawaiian or other Pacific Islander, non-Hispanic/Latino; 0.4% American Indian or Alaska Native, non-Hispanic/Latino; 0.6% Two or more races, non-Hispanic/Latino; 0.3% Race/ethnicity unknown; 0.1% international; 19% transferred in. *Retention:* 57% of full-time freshmen returned.
Freshmen *Admission:* 504 enrolled.
Faculty *Total:* 226, 22% full-time. *Student/faculty ratio:* 16:1.
Majors Accounting related; business administration, management and operations related; business operations support and secretarial services related; child-care provision; computer and information sciences; criminal justice/law enforcement administration; electrical, electronic and communications engineering technology; emergency medical technology (EMT paramedic); liberal arts and sciences/liberal studies; mental and social health services and allied professions related; radiologic technology/science; registered nursing/registered nurse.
Academics *Calendar:* semesters. *Degree:* certificates, diplomas, and associate. *Special study options:* academic remediation for entering students, accelerated degree program, adult/continuing education programs, advanced placement credit, distance learning, double majors, honors programs, internships, off-campus study, part-time degree program, summer session for credit.
Library Southwest Virginia Community College Library with 111,000 titles, 950 serial subscriptions, 1,000 audiovisual materials, an OPAC, a Web page.
Student Life *Housing:* college housing not available. *Activities and Organizations:* choral group, Phi Theta Kappa, Phi Beta Lambda, Intervoice, Helping Minds Club, Project ACHEIVE. *Campus security:* 24-hour emergency response devices and patrols, student patrols, heavily saturated camera system. *Student services:* personal/psychological counseling.
Standardized Tests *Required:* VCCS Math and English Assessments (for admission).
Financial Aid Of all full-time matriculated undergraduates who enrolled in 2011, 150 Federal Work-Study jobs (averaging $1140).
Applying *Options:* electronic application, early admission, deferred entrance. *Required:* high school transcript, interview. *Application deadlines:* rolling (freshmen), rolling (transfers).
Freshman Application Contact Ms. Dionne Cook, Admissions Counselor, Southwest Virginia Community College, Box SVCC, Richlands, VA 24641. *Phone:* 276-964-7301. *Toll-free phone:* 800-822-7822. *Fax:* 276-964-7716. *E-mail:* dionne.cook@sw.edu.
Website: http://www.sw.edu/.

Thomas Nelson Community College

Hampton, Virginia

- **State-supported** 2-year, founded 1968, part of Virginia Community College System
- **Suburban** 85-acre campus with easy access to Virginia Beach
- **Coed,** 10,942 undergraduate students, 34% full-time, 61% women, 39% men

Undergraduates 3,689 full-time, 7,253 part-time.
Faculty *Student/faculty ratio:* 22:1.
Majors Accounting related; automobile/automotive mechanics technology; biological and physical sciences; business administration and management; business administration, management and operations related; business operations support and secretarial services related; CAD/CADD drafting/design technology; child-care provision; computer and information sciences; criminal justice/law enforcement administration; dental hygiene; design and visual communications; emergency medical technology (EMT paramedic); engineering; fire science/firefighting; general studies; industrial electronics technology; industrial technology; information technology; legal assistant/paralegal; liberal arts and sciences/liberal studies; mechanical engineering technologies related; mental and social health services and allied professions related; photography; public administration; registered nursing/registered nurse; social sciences; visual and performing arts related.
Academics *Calendar:* semesters. *Degree:* certificates, diplomas, and associate. *Special study options:* academic remediation for entering students, accelerated degree program, adult/continuing education programs, advanced

placement credit, cooperative education, distance learning, English as a second language, honors programs, internships, off-campus study, part-time degree program, services for LD students, summer session for credit.

Library Thomas Nelson Community College Library with an OPAC, a Web page.

Student Life *Activities and Organizations:* drama/theater group, choral group, Phi Theta Kappa, Student Nurses Association, International Club, Student Government Association. *Campus security:* 24-hour emergency response devices and patrols, late-night transport/escort service. *Student services:* personal/psychological counseling.

Athletics *Intramural sports:* baseball M, basketball M/W, cheerleading W.

Costs (2012–13) *Tuition:* state resident $3735 full-time, $125 per credit hour part-time; nonresident $9498 full-time, $317 per credit hour part-time. *Required fees:* $43 full-time, $22 per term part-time. *Waivers:* senior citizens and employees or children of employees.

Financial Aid Of all full-time matriculated undergraduates who enrolled in 2012, 62 Federal Work-Study jobs (averaging $4800).

Applying *Options:* electronic application, early admission, deferred entrance. *Required for some:* interview. *Recommended:* high school transcript. *Application deadlines:* rolling (freshmen), rolling (transfers). *Notification:* continuous (freshmen), continuous (transfers).

Freshman Application Contact Ms. Geraldine Newson, Sr. Admission Specialist, Thomas Nelson Community College, PO Box 9407, Hampton, VA 23670-0407. *Phone:* 757-825-2800. *Fax:* 757-825-2763. *E-mail:* admissions@tncc.edu.

Website: http://www.tncc.edu/.

Tidewater Community College
Norfolk, Virginia

Freshman Application Contact Kellie Sorey PhD, Registrar, Tidewater Community College, Norfolk, VA 23510. *Phone:* 757-822-1900. *E-mail:* CentralRecords@tcc.edu.

Website: http://www.tcc.edu/.

Virginia College in Richmond
Richmond, Virginia

Admissions Office Contact Virginia College in Richmond, 7200 Midlothian Turnpike, Richmond, VA 23225.

Website: http://www.vc.edu/.

Virginia Highlands Community College
Abingdon, Virginia

Freshman Application Contact Karen Cheers, Acting Director of Admissions, Records, and Financial Aid, Virginia Highlands Community College, PO Box 828, 100 VHCC Drive Abingdon, Abingdon, VA 24212. *Phone:* 276-739-2490. *Toll-free phone:* 877-207-6115. *E-mail:* kcheers@vhcc.edu.

Website: http://www.vhcc.edu/.

Virginia Western Community College
Roanoke, Virginia

- **State-supported** 2-year, founded 1966, part of Virginia Community College System
- **Suburban** 70-acre campus
- **Endowment** $3.0 million
- **Coed,** 8,440 undergraduate students, 30% full-time, 55% women, 45% men

Undergraduates 2,568 full-time, 5,872 part-time. Students come from 9 states and territories; 54 other countries; 2% are from out of state; 14% Black or African American, non-Hispanic/Latino; 3% Hispanic/Latino; 2% Asian, non-Hispanic/Latino; 0.2% Native Hawaiian or other Pacific Islander, non-Hispanic/Latino; 0.4% American Indian or Alaska Native, non-Hispanic/Latino; 2% Two or more races, non-Hispanic/Latino; 0.7% Race/ethnicity unknown; 0.5% international; 4% transferred in. *Retention:* 55% of full-time freshmen returned.

Freshmen *Admission:* 1,245 enrolled.

Faculty *Student/faculty ratio:* 23:1.

Majors Accounting; administrative assistant and secretarial science; art; automobile/automotive mechanics technology; biological and physical sciences; business administration and management; child development; civil engineering technology; commercial and advertising art; computer science; criminal justice/law enforcement administration; data processing and data processing technology; dental hygiene; education; electrical, electronic and communica-

tions engineering technology; engineering; industrial radiologic technology; kindergarten/preschool education; liberal arts and sciences/liberal studies; mechanical engineering/mechanical technology; mental health counseling; pre-engineering; radio and television; radiologic technology/science; registered nursing/registered nurse.

Academics *Calendar:* semesters. *Degree:* certificates and associate. *Special study options:* academic remediation for entering students, advanced placement credit, cooperative education, distance learning, double majors, English as a second language, honors programs, independent study, internships, part-time degree program, services for LD students, summer session for credit.

Library Brown Library with an OPAC, a Web page.

Student Life *Housing:* college housing not available. *Activities and Organizations:* drama/theater group, student-run newspaper. *Campus security:* 24-hour emergency response devices and patrols, late-night transport/escort service. *Student services:* personal/psychological counseling.

Athletics *Intramural sports:* baseball M, basketball M/W.

Costs (2012–13) *Tuition:* state resident $3242 full-time, $135 per credit hour part-time; nonresident $7853 full-time, $327 per credit hour part-time. Full-time tuition and fees vary according to program. Part-time tuition and fees vary according to program. *Payment plans:* installment, deferred payment. *Waivers:* employees or children of employees.

Applying *Options:* electronic application, early admission, deferred entrance. *Required for some:* high school transcript. *Recommended:* high school transcript. *Application deadlines:* rolling (freshmen), rolling (transfers). *Notification:* continuous (freshmen), continuous (transfers).

Freshman Application Contact Admissions Office, Virginia Western Community College, PO Box 14007, Roanoke, VA 24038. *Phone:* 540-857-7231.

Website: http://www.virginiawestern.edu/.

Wytheville Community College
Wytheville, Virginia

- **State-supported** 2-year, founded 1967, part of Virginia Community College System
- **Rural** 141-acre campus
- **Coed,** 3,792 undergraduate students, 36% full-time, 64% women, 36% men

Undergraduates 1,370 full-time, 2,422 part-time. 7% Black or African American, non-Hispanic/Latino; 1% Hispanic/Latino; 0.8% Asian, non-Hispanic/Latino; 0.1% Native Hawaiian or other Pacific Islander, non-Hispanic/Latino; 0.3% American Indian or Alaska Native, non-Hispanic/Latino; 2% Two or more races, non-Hispanic/Latino; 0.4% Race/ethnicity unknown. *Retention:* 59% of full-time freshmen returned.

Faculty *Total:* 216, 20% full-time. *Student/faculty ratio:* 23:1.

Majors Accounting; administrative assistant and secretarial science; biological and physical sciences; business administration and management; civil engineering technology; clinical/medical laboratory technology; corrections; criminal justice/law enforcement administration; criminal justice/police science; dental hygiene; drafting and design technology; education; electrical, electronic and communications engineering technology; information science/studies; liberal arts and sciences/liberal studies; machine tool technology; mass communication/media; mechanical engineering/mechanical technology; medical administrative assistant and medical secretary; physical therapy; registered nursing/registered nurse.

Academics *Calendar:* semesters. *Degree:* certificates, diplomas, and associate. *Special study options:* academic remediation for entering students, adult/continuing education programs, advanced placement credit, distance learning, external degree program, independent study, part-time degree program, services for LD students, summer session for credit.

Library Wytheville Community College Library.

Student Life *Housing:* college housing not available. *Activities and Organizations:* drama/theater group, student-run newspaper. *Campus security:* 24-hour emergency response devices and patrols.

Athletics Member NJCAA. *Intercollegiate sports:* basketball M, volleyball W. *Intramural sports:* golf M/W.

Costs (2013–14) *Tuition:* state resident $3810 full-time, $117 per credit part-time; nonresident $9573 full-time, $294 per credit part-time. *Required fees:* $320 full-time, $10 per credit part-time.

Financial Aid Of all full-time matriculated undergraduates who enrolled in 2011, 125 Federal Work-Study jobs (averaging $2592).

Applying *Options:* early admission. *Required:* high school transcript. *Required for some:* interview. *Application deadlines:* rolling (freshmen), rolling (transfers). *Notification:* continuous (freshmen), continuous (transfers).

Freshman Application Contact Wytheville Community College, 1000 East Main Street, Wytheville, VA 24382-3308. *Phone:* 276-223-4701. *Toll-free phone:* 800-468-1195.

Website: http://www.wcc.vccs.edu/.

WASHINGTON

The Art Institute of Seattle
Seattle, Washington

- **Proprietary** primarily 2-year, founded 1982, part of Education Management Corporation
- **Urban** campus
- **Coed**

Academics *Calendar:* quarters. *Degrees:* diplomas, associate, and bachelor's.
Freshman Application Contact The Art Institute of Seattle, 2323 Elliott Avenue, Seattle, WA 98121-1642. *Phone:* 206-448-6600. *Toll-free phone:* 800-275-2471.
Website: http://www.artinstitutes.edu/seattle/.

See full-page display on page 48 and page 340 for the College Close-Up.

Bates Technical College
Tacoma, Washington

Director of Admissions Director of Admissions, Bates Technical College, 1101 South Yakima Avenue, Tacoma, WA 98405-4895. *Phone:* 253-680-7000.
E-mail: registration@bates.ctc.edu.
Website: http://www.bates.ctc.edu/.

Bellevue College
Bellevue, Washington

Freshman Application Contact Morenika Jacobs, Associate Dean of Enrollment Services, Bellevue College, 3000 Landerholm Circle, SE, Bellevue, WA 98007-6484. *Phone:* 425-564-2205. *Fax:* 425-564-4065.
Website: http://www.bcc.ctc.edu/.

Bellingham Technical College
Bellingham, Washington

Freshman Application Contact Bellingham Technical College, 3028 Lindbergh Avenue, Bellingham, WA 98225. *Phone:* 360-752-8324.
Website: http://www.btc.ctc.edu/.

Big Bend Community College
Moses Lake, Washington

- **State-supported** 2-year, founded 1962
- **Small-town** 159-acre campus
- **Coed,** 1,946 undergraduate students, 71% full-time, 57% women, 43% men

Undergraduates 1,390 full-time, 556 part-time. 1% Black or African American, non-Hispanic/Latino; 34% Hispanic/Latino; 0.9% Asian, non-Hispanic/Latino; 0.1% Native Hawaiian or other Pacific Islander, non-Hispanic/Latino; 0.8% American Indian or Alaska Native, non-Hispanic/Latino; 1% Two or more races, non-Hispanic/Latino; 0.3% Race/ethnicity unknown; 0.4% international; 5% live on campus.
Freshmen *Admission:* 229 enrolled.
Faculty *Student/faculty ratio:* 20:1.
Majors Accounting technology and bookkeeping; agricultural production; airline pilot and flight crew; automobile/automotive mechanics technology; avionics maintenance technology; early childhood education; industrial electronics technology; industrial mechanics and maintenance technology; liberal arts and sciences/liberal studies; licensed practical/vocational nurse training; medical/clinical assistant; medical office management; network and system administration; registered nursing/registered nurse; welding technology.
Academics *Calendar:* quarters. *Degree:* certificates and associate. *Special study options:* academic remediation for entering students, advanced placement credit, cooperative education, distance learning, English as a second language, part-time degree program, services for LD students, summer session for credit.
Library Big Bend Community College Library with 42,647 titles, 115 serial subscriptions, 4,124 audiovisual materials, an OPAC, a Web page.
Student Life *Housing Options:* coed. Campus housing is university owned. *Activities and Organizations:* choral group. *Campus security:* 24-hour emergency response devices, student patrols, late-night transport/escort service, controlled dormitory access, Daytime Security on campus during the week, Student security in dorms four evenings a week, Enhanced Campus Notification System. *Student services:* personal/psychological counseling.
Athletics *Intercollegiate sports:* baseball M, basketball M/W, softball W, volleyball W.

Costs (2013–14) *One-time required fee:* $30. *Tuition:* state resident $3687 full-time, $112 per credit hour part-time; nonresident $4550 full-time, $125 per credit hour part-time. Full-time tuition and fees vary according to course load and program. Part-time tuition and fees vary according to course load and program. *Required fees:* $150 full-time, $5 per credit hour part-time. *Room and board:* $6900; room only: $2700. *Payment plan:* installment. *Waivers:* senior citizens.
Applying *Options:* electronic application, early admission, deferred entrance. *Application fee:* $30. *Required for some:* high school transcript. *Application deadlines:* rolling (freshmen), rolling (transfers). *Notification:* continuous (freshmen), continuous (transfers).
Freshman Application Contact Candis Lacher, Associate Vice President of Student Services, Big Bend Community College, 7662 Chanute Street, Moses Lake, WA 98837. *Phone:* 509-793-2061. *Toll-free phone:* 877-745-1212. *Fax:* 509-793-6243. *E-mail:* admissions@bigbend.edu.
Website: http://www.bigbend.edu/.

Carrington College–Spokane
Spokane, Washington

- **Proprietary** 2-year, founded 1976, part of Carrington Colleges Group, Inc.
- **Coed,** 448 undergraduate students, 100% full-time, 82% women, 18% men

Undergraduates 448 full-time. 2% Black or African American, non-Hispanic/Latino; 5% Hispanic/Latino; 2% Asian, non-Hispanic/Latino; 0.4% Native Hawaiian or other Pacific Islander, non-Hispanic/Latino; 4% American Indian or Alaska Native, non-Hispanic/Latino; 2% Two or more races, non-Hispanic/Latino; 0.7% Race/ethnicity unknown.
Freshmen *Admission:* 60 enrolled.
Faculty *Total:* 28, 39% full-time. *Student/faculty ratio:* 27:1.
Majors Medical administrative assistant and medical secretary; medical office management; medical radiologic technology.
Academics *Degree:* certificates and associate.
Student Life *Housing:* college housing not available.
Applying *Required:* essay or personal statement, high school transcript, interview, Entrance test administered by Carrington College.
Freshman Application Contact Carrington College–Spokane, 10102 East Knox Avenue, Suite 200, Spokane, WA 99206.
Website: http://carrington.edu/.

Cascadia Community College
Bothell, Washington

- **State-supported** 2-year, founded 1999
- **Suburban** 128-acre campus
- **Coed,** 2,834 undergraduate students, 54% full-time, 50% women, 50% men

Undergraduates 1,544 full-time, 1,290 part-time. Students come from 2 states and territories; 1% Black or African American, non-Hispanic/Latino; 8% Hispanic/Latino; 8% Asian, non-Hispanic/Latino; 0.6% Native Hawaiian or other Pacific Islander, non-Hispanic/Latino; 0.3% American Indian or Alaska Native, non-Hispanic/Latino; 8% Two or more races, non-Hispanic/Latino; 10% Race/ethnicity unknown; 4% international; 21% transferred in.
Freshmen *Admission:* 373 enrolled.
Faculty *Total:* 127, 32% full-time. *Student/faculty ratio:* 18:1.
Majors Liberal arts and sciences and humanities related; liberal arts and sciences/liberal studies; science technologies related.
Academics *Calendar:* quarters. *Degree:* certificates and associate. *Special study options:* academic remediation for entering students, accelerated degree program, adult/continuing education programs, advanced placement credit, cooperative education, distance learning, double majors, English as a second language, independent study, internships, off-campus study, part-time degree program, services for LD students, study abroad, summer session for credit.
Library UWB/CCC Campus Library with 73,749 titles, 850 serial subscriptions, 6,100 audiovisual materials, an OPAC, a Web page.
Student Life *Housing:* college housing not available. *Activities and Organizations:* drama/theater group, student-run newspaper. *Campus security:* 24-hour emergency response devices, late-night transport/escort service.
Costs (2013–14) *Tuition:* state resident $3606 full-time, $107 per credit part-time; nonresident $3606 full-time, $279 per credit part-time. Full-time tuition and fees vary according to course load and program. Part-time tuition and fees vary according to course load and program. *Waivers:* senior citizens and employees or children of employees.
Applying *Options:* electronic application. *Application deadlines:* rolling (freshmen), rolling (out-of-state freshmen), rolling (transfers). *Notification:* continuous (freshmen), continuous (out-of-state freshmen), continuous (transfers).

Freshman Application Contact Ms. Erin Blakeney, Dean for Student Success, Cascadia Community College, 18345 Campus Way, NE, Bothell, WA 98011. *Phone:* 425-352-8000. *Fax:* 425-352-8137. *E-mail:* admissions@cascadia.edu.
Website: http://www.cascadia.edu/.

Centralia College

Centralia, Washington

Freshman Application Contact Admissions Office, Centralia College, Centralia, WA 98531. *Phone:* 360-736-9391 Ext. 221. *Fax:* 360-330-7503. *E-mail:* admissions@centralia.edu.
Website: http://www.centralia.edu/.

Clark College

Vancouver, Washington

- **State-supported** 2-year, founded 1933, part of Washington State Board for Community and Technical Colleges
- **Urban** 101-acre campus with easy access to Portland
- **Coed,** 12,314 undergraduate students, 51% full-time, 57% women, 43% men

Undergraduates 6,262 full-time, 6,052 part-time. 4% are from out of state; 2% Black or African American, non-Hispanic/Latino; 8% Hispanic/Latino; 4% Asian, non-Hispanic/Latino; 0.5% Native Hawaiian or other Pacific Islander, non-Hispanic/Latino; 0.7% American Indian or Alaska Native, non-Hispanic/Latino; 7% Two or more races, non-Hispanic/Latino; 6% Race/ethnicity unknown; 0.6% international.

Freshmen *Admission:* 1,844 applied, 1,844 admitted.

Faculty *Total:* 689, 29% full-time, 14% with terminal degrees. *Student/faculty ratio:* 17:1.

Majors Accounting technology and bookkeeping; applied horticulture/horticulture operations; automobile/automotive mechanics technology; baking and pastry arts; business administration and management; business automation/technology/data entry; computer programming; computer systems networking and telecommunications; construction engineering technology; culinary arts; data entry/microcomputer applications; dental hygiene; diesel mechanics technology; early childhood education; electrical, electronic and communications engineering technology; emergency medical technology (EMT paramedic); executive assistant/executive secretary; graphic communications; human resources management; landscaping and groundskeeping; legal administrative assistant/secretary; legal assistant/paralegal; liberal arts and sciences/liberal studies; machine tool technology; manufacturing engineering technology; medical administrative assistant and medical secretary; medical/clinical assistant; radiologic technology/science; registered nursing/registered nurse; retailing; selling skills and sales; sport and fitness administration/management; substance abuse/addiction counseling; surveying technology; telecommunications technology; web/multimedia management and webmaster; welding technology.

Academics *Calendar:* quarters. *Degree:* certificates, diplomas, and associate. *Special study options:* adult/continuing education programs, part-time degree program. *ROTC:* Army (c), Air Force (c).

Library Lewis D. Cannell Library.

Student Life *Housing:* college housing not available. *Campus security:* 24-hour patrols, late-night transport/escort service, security staff during hours of operation.

Athletics *Intercollegiate sports:* baseball M, basketball M(s)/W(s), cross-country running M(s)/W(s), fencing M(c)/W(c), soccer M(s)/W(s), softball W, track and field M(s)/W(s), volleyball W(s). *Intramural sports:* basketball M/W, fencing M/W, soccer M/W, softball M/W, volleyball M/W.

Costs (2012–13) *Tuition:* area resident $4154 full-time, $110 per credit hour part-time; state resident $4544 full-time, $123 per credit hour part-time; nonresident $9389 full-time, $282 per credit hour part-time. Full-time tuition and fees vary according to course load and reciprocity agreements. Part-time tuition and fees vary according to course load and reciprocity agreements. *Payment plan:* installment. *Waivers:* senior citizens and employees or children of employees.

Applying *Options:* electronic application, early admission, deferred entrance. *Application fee:* $20. *Application deadline:* 9/7 (freshmen). *Notification:* continuous (freshmen), continuous (transfers).

Freshman Application Contact Ms. Sheryl Anderson, Director of Admissions, Clark College, Vancouver, WA 98663. *Phone:* 360-992-2308. *Fax:* 360-992-2867. *E-mail:* admissions@clark.edu.
Website: http://www.clark.edu/.

Clover Park Technical College

Lakewood, Washington

Director of Admissions Ms. Judy Richardson, Registrar, Clover Park Technical College, 4500 Steilacoom Boulevard, SW, Lakewood, WA 98499. *Phone:* 253-589-5570.
Website: http://www.cptc.edu/.

Columbia Basin College

Pasco, Washington

Freshman Application Contact Admissions Department, Columbia Basin College, 2600 North 20th Avenue, Pasco, WA 99301-3397. *Phone:* 509-542-4524. *Fax:* 509-544-2023. *E-mail:* admissions@columbiabasin.edu.
Website: http://www.columbiabasin.edu/.

Edmonds Community College

Lynnwood, Washington

Freshman Application Contact Ms. Nancy Froemming, Enrollment Services Office Manager, Edmonds Community College, 20000 68th Avenue West, Lynwood, WA 98036-5999. *Phone:* 425-640-1853. *Fax:* 425-640-1159. *E-mail:* nanci.froemming@edcc.edu.
Website: http://www.edcc.edu/.

Everest College

Vancouver, Washington

Director of Admissions Ms. Renee Schiffhauer, Director of Admissions, Everest College, 120 Northeast 136th Avenue, Suite 130, Vancouver, WA 98684. *Phone:* 360-254-3282. *Toll-free phone:* 888-741-4270. *Fax:* 360-254-3035. *E-mail:* rschiffhauer@cci.edu.
Website: http://www.everest.edu/.

Everett Community College

Everett, Washington

Freshman Application Contact Ms. Linda Baca, Entry Services Manager, Everett Community College, 2000 Tower Street, Everett, WA 98201-1327. *Phone:* 425-388-9219. *Fax:* 425-388-9173. *E-mail:* admissions@everettcc.edu.
Website: http://www.everettcc.edu/.

Grays Harbor College

Aberdeen, Washington

Freshman Application Contact Ms. Brenda Dell, Admissions Officer, Grays Harbor College, 1620 Edward P Smith Drive, Aberdeen, WA 98520-7599. *Phone:* 360-532-9020 Ext. 4026. *Toll-free phone:* 800-562-4830.
Website: http://www.ghc.edu/.

Green River Community College

Auburn, Washington

Freshman Application Contact Ms. Peggy Morgan, Program Support Supervisor, Green River Community College, 12401 Southeast 320th Street, Auburn, WA 98092-3699. *Phone:* 253-833-9111. *Fax:* 253-288-3454.
Website: http://www.greenriver.edu/.

Highline Community College

Des Moines, Washington

- **State-supported** 2-year, founded 1961, part of Washington State Board for Community and Technical Colleges
- **Suburban** 81-acre campus with easy access to Seattle
- **Endowment** $1.4 million
- **Coed**

Undergraduates 3,932 full-time, 2,811 part-time. Students come from 6 states and territories; 50 other countries; 1% are from out of state; 11% Black or African American, non-Hispanic/Latino; 7% Hispanic/Latino; 15% Asian, non-Hispanic/Latino; 1% Native Hawaiian or other Pacific Islander, non-Hispanic/Latino; 0.7% American Indian or Alaska Native, non-Hispanic/Latino; 6% Two or more races, non-Hispanic/Latino; 11% Race/ethnicity unknown; 7% international; 71% transferred in. *Retention:* 57% of full-time freshmen returned.

Faculty *Student/faculty ratio:* 19:1.

Academics *Calendar:* quarters. *Degree:* certificates, diplomas, and associate. *Special study options:* academic remediation for entering students, advanced placement credit, cooperative education, distance learning, English as a second language, freshman honors college, honors programs, independent study, internships, off-campus study, part-time degree program, services for LD students, student-designed majors, study abroad, summer session for credit. *ROTC:* Army (c), Air Force (c).

Student Life *Campus security:* 24-hour emergency response devices and patrols, late-night transport/escort service.

Athletics Member NJCAA.

Costs (2012–13) *Tuition:* $107 per credit part-time; state resident $4000 full-time, $120 per credit part-time; nonresident $4400 full-time, $279 per credit part-time. Full-time tuition and fees vary according to course load and program. Part-time tuition and fees vary according to course load and program. *Required fees:* $75 full-time, $107 per credit part-time, $75 per term part-time.

Applying *Options:* electronic application. *Application fee:* $26.

Freshman Application Contact Ms. Michelle Kuwasaki, Director of Admissions, Highline Community College, 2400 South 240th Street, Des Moines, WA 98198-9800. *Phone:* 206-878-3710 Ext. 9800. *Website:* http://www.highline.edu/.

ITT Technical Institute

Everett, Washington

- **Proprietary** primarily 2-year, part of ITT Educational Services, Inc.
- **Coed**

Academics *Degrees:* associate and bachelor's.

Freshman Application Contact Director of Recruitment, ITT Technical Institute, 1615 75th Street SW, Everett, WA 98203. *Phone:* 425-583-0200. *Toll-free phone:* 800-272-3791. *Website:* http://www.itt-tech.edu/.

ITT Technical Institute

Seattle, Washington

- **Proprietary** primarily 2-year, founded 1932, part of ITT Educational Services, Inc.
- **Urban** campus
- **Coed**

Academics *Calendar:* quarters. *Degrees:* associate and bachelor's.

Freshman Application Contact Director of Recruitment, ITT Technical Institute, 12720 Gateway Drive, Suite 100, Seattle, WA 98168-3333. *Phone:* 206-244-3300. *Toll-free phone:* 800-422-2029. *Website:* http://www.itt-tech.edu/.

ITT Technical Institute

Spokane Valley, Washington

- **Proprietary** primarily 2-year, founded 1985, part of ITT Educational Services, Inc.
- **Suburban** campus
- **Coed**

Academics *Calendar:* quarters. *Degrees:* associate and bachelor's.

Freshman Application Contact Director of Recruitment, ITT Technical Institute, 13518 East Indiana Avenue, Spokane Valley, WA 99216. *Phone:* 509-926-2900. *Toll-free phone:* 800-777-8324. *Website:* http://www.itt-tech.edu/.

Lake Washington Institute of Technology

Kirkland, Washington

Freshman Application Contact Shawn Miller, Registrar Enrollment Services, Lake Washington Institute of Technology, 11605 132nd Avenue NE, Kirkland, WA 98034-8506. *Phone:* 425-739-8104. *E-mail:* info@lwtc.edu. *Website:* http://www.lwtech.edu/.

Lower Columbia College

Longview, Washington

- **State-supported** 2-year, founded 1934, part of Washington State Board for Community and Technical Colleges
- **Rural** 39-acre campus with easy access to Portland
- **Endowment** $12.0 million
- **Coed,** 4,252 undergraduate students, 61% full-time, 63% women, 37% men

Undergraduates 2,579 full-time, 1,673 part-time. Students come from 7 states and territories; 2 other countries; 2% are from out of state; 2% Black or African American, non-Hispanic/Latino; 6% Hispanic/Latino; 2% Asian, non-Hispanic/Latino; 0.1% Native Hawaiian or other Pacific Islander, non-Hispanic/Latino; 2% American Indian or Alaska Native, non-Hispanic/Latino; 2% Two or more races, non-Hispanic/Latino; 9% Race/ethnicity unknown; 11% transferred in. *Retention:* 53% of full-time freshmen returned.

Freshmen *Admission:* 388 enrolled.

Faculty *Total:* 222, 31% full-time. *Student/faculty ratio:* 24:1.

Majors Accounting; accounting technology and bookkeeping; administrative assistant and secretarial science; automobile/automotive mechanics technology; business administration and management; criminal justice/law enforcement administration; data entry/microcomputer applications; diesel mechanics technology; early childhood education; fire science/firefighting; industrial mechanics and maintenance technology; instrumentation technology; legal administrative assistant/secretary; liberal arts and sciences/liberal studies; machine tool technology; medical administrative assistant and medical secretary; medical/clinical assistant; registered nursing/registered nurse; substance abuse/addiction counseling; welding technology.

Academics *Calendar:* quarters. *Degree:* certificates, diplomas, and associate. *Special study options:* academic remediation for entering students, adult/continuing education programs, advanced placement credit, cooperative education, distance learning, English as a second language, external degree program, independent study, internships, part-time degree program, services for LD students, student-designed majors, summer session for credit.

Library Alan Thompson Library plus 1 other with 38,841 titles, 130 serial subscriptions, 4,573 audiovisual materials, an OPAC, a Web page.

Student Life *Housing:* college housing not available. *Activities and Organizations:* drama/theater group, choral group, Phi Theta Kappa, Biological Society, Electric Vehicle Club, American Sign Language Club, Global Medical Brigade. *Campus security:* 24-hour emergency response devices and patrols. *Student services:* personal/psychological counseling.

Athletics *Intercollegiate sports:* baseball M(s), basketball M(s)/W(s), soccer W(s), softball W(s), volleyball W(s).

Costs (2012–13) *One-time required fee:* $30. *Tuition:* state resident $4275 full-time, $115 per credit part-time; nonresident $4813 full-time, $129 per credit part-time. Full-time tuition and fees vary according to course load and reciprocity agreements. Part-time tuition and fees vary according to course load and reciprocity agreements. *Required fees:* $275 full-time, $8 per credit part-time. *Payment plan:* deferred payment. *Waivers:* senior citizens and employees or children of employees.

Financial Aid Of all full-time matriculated undergraduates who enrolled in 2011, 440 Federal Work-Study jobs (averaging $708). 447 state and other part-time jobs (averaging $2415).

Applying *Options:* electronic application. *Application fee:* $14. *Recommended:* high school transcript. *Application deadlines:* rolling (freshmen), rolling (transfers). *Notification:* continuous (freshmen).

Freshman Application Contact Ms. Lynn Lawrence, Director of Registration, Lower Columbia College, 1600 Maple Street, Longview, WA 98632. *Phone:* 360-442-2371. *Toll-free phone:* 866-900-2311. *Fax:* 360-442-2379. *E-mail:* registration@lowercolumbia.edu. *Website:* http://www.lowercolumbia.edu/.

North Seattle Community College

Seattle, Washington

- **State-supported** 2-year, founded 1970, part of Seattle Community College District
- **Urban** 65-acre campus
- **Endowment** $4.4 million
- **Coed**

Undergraduates 1,953 full-time, 4,350 part-time. Students come from 50 states and territories; 39 other countries; 5% are from out of state; 7% Black or African American, non-Hispanic/Latino; 7% Hispanic/Latino; 12% Asian, non-Hispanic/Latino; 1% Native Hawaiian or other Pacific Islander, non-Hispanic/Latino; 0.8% American Indian or Alaska Native, non-Hispanic/Latino; 8% Two or more races, non-Hispanic/Latino; 12% Race/ethnicity unknown; 23% transferred in.

Faculty *Student/faculty ratio:* 20:1.

Academics *Calendar:* quarters. *Degree:* certificates, diplomas, and associate. *Special study options:* academic remediation for entering students, adult/continuing education programs, advanced placement credit, cooperative education, distance learning, English as a second language, external degree program, independent study, internships, part-time degree program, services for LD students, study abroad, summer session for credit. *ROTC:* Army (c).
Student Life *Campus security:* 24-hour emergency response devices, late-night transport/escort service, patrols by security.
Applying *Options:* electronic application, early admission, deferred entrance. *Required:* high school transcript. *Required for some:* essay or personal statement, English/Math Placement Test.
Freshman Application Contact Ms. Betsy Abts, Registrar, North Seattle Community College, Seattle, WA 98103-3599. *Phone:* 206-934-3663. *Fax:* 206-934-3671. *E-mail:* arrc@seattlecolleges.edu.
Website: http://www.northseattle.edu/.

Northwest Indian College

Bellingham, Washington

Freshman Application Contact Office of Admissions, Northwest Indian College, 2522 Kwina Road, Bellingham, WA 98226. *Phone:* 360-676-2772. *Toll-free phone:* 866-676-2772. *Fax:* 360-392-4333. *E-mail:* admissions@nwic.edu.
Website: http://www.nwic.edu/.

Northwest School of Wooden Boatbuilding

Port Hadlock, Washington

Director of Admissions Student Services Coordinator, Northwest School of Wooden Boatbuilding, 42 North Water Street, Port Hadlock, WA 98339. *Phone:* 360-385-4948. *Fax:* 360-385-5089. *E-mail:* info@nwboatschool.org.
Website: http://www.nwboatschool.org/.

Olympic College

Bremerton, Washington

- **State-supported** primarily 2-year, founded 1946, part of Washington State Board for Community and Technical Colleges
- **Suburban** 33-acre campus with easy access to Seattle
- **Coed,** 8,260 undergraduate students

Undergraduates 5% Black or African American, non-Hispanic/Latino; 6% Hispanic/Latino; 8% Asian, non-Hispanic/Latino; 2% American Indian or Alaska Native, non-Hispanic/Latino; 1% international.
Freshmen *Admission:* 3,126 applied, 3,126 admitted.
Faculty *Total:* 472, 26% full-time.
Majors Accounting technology and bookkeeping; administrative assistant and secretarial science; business administration and management; computer systems networking and telecommunications; cosmetology; culinary arts; drafting and design technology; early childhood education; electrical, electronic and communications engineering technology; industrial technology; legal administrative assistant/secretary; medical/clinical assistant; organizational leadership; physical therapy technology; registered nursing/registered nurse; substance abuse/addiction counseling; welding technology.
Academics *Calendar:* quarters. *Degrees:* certificates, diplomas, associate, and bachelor's. *Special study options:* academic remediation for entering students, adult/continuing education programs, advanced placement credit, cooperative education, distance learning, English as a second language, honors programs, independent study, internships, off-campus study, part-time degree program, services for LD students, summer session for credit.
Library Haselwood Library with an OPAC, a Web page.
Student Life *Housing:* college housing not available. *Activities and Organizations:* drama/theater group, student-run newspaper, choral group, Phi Theta Kappa, International Student Club, MESA/STEM club, Armed Services, ASL. *Campus security:* 24-hour emergency response devices and patrols, student patrols, late-night transport/escort service. *Student services:* personal/psychological counseling.
Athletics *Intercollegiate sports:* baseball M(s), basketball M(s)/W(s), cross-country running M/W, golf M/W, soccer M(s)/W(s), softball W(s), track and field M/W, volleyball M/W(s). *Intramural sports:* basketball M/W, table tennis M/W, volleyball M/W, weight lifting M/W.
Costs (2012–13) *Tuition:* state resident $3523 full-time, $107 per credit hour part-time; nonresident $3943 full-time, $120 per credit hour part-time. Full-time tuition and fees vary according to course load and degree level. Part-time tuition and fees vary according to course load and degree level. *Required fees:* $195 full-time. *Payment plan:* installment. *Waivers:* senior citizens.

Financial Aid Of all full-time matriculated undergraduates who enrolled in 2011, 105 Federal Work-Study jobs (averaging $2380). 31 state and other part-time jobs (averaging $2880).
Applying *Options:* electronic application. *Required for some:* high school transcript. *Application deadlines:* rolling (freshmen), rolling (out-of-state freshmen), rolling (transfers).
Freshman Application Contact Ms. Jennifer Fyllingness, Director of Admissions, Outreach and International Student Programs, Olympic College, 1600 Chester Avenue, Bremerton, WA 98337-1699. *Phone:* 360-475-7128. *Toll-free phone:* 800-259-6718. *Fax:* 360-475-7202. *E-mail:* jfyllingness@olympic.edu.
Website: http://www.olympic.edu/.

Peninsula College

Port Angeles, Washington

- **State-supported** primarily 2-year, founded 1961, part of Washington State Community and Technical Colleges
- **Small-town** 75-acre campus
- **Coed**

Undergraduates 1,705 full-time, 1,616 part-time.
Faculty *Student/faculty ratio:* 21:1.
Academics *Calendar:* quarters. *Degrees:* certificates, associate, and bachelor's. *Special study options:* academic remediation for entering students, adult/continuing education programs, advanced placement credit, distance learning, English as a second language, honors programs, internships, part-time degree program, services for LD students, summer session for credit.
Student Life *Campus security:* 8-hour patrols by trained security personnel.
Financial Aid Of all full-time matriculated undergraduates who enrolled in 2011, 30 Federal Work-Study jobs (averaging $3600). 25 state and other part-time jobs (averaging $3600).
Applying *Required for some:* high school transcript.
Freshman Application Contact Ms. Pauline Marvin, Peninsula College, 1502 East Lauridsen Boulevard, Port Angeles, WA 98362. *Phone:* 360-417-6596. *Toll-free phone:* 877-452-9277. *Fax:* 360-457-8100. *E-mail:* admissions@pencol.edu.
Website: http://www.pc.ctc.edu/.

Pierce College at Puyallup

Puyallup, Washington

- **State-supported** 2-year, founded 1967, part of Washington State Board for Community and Technical Colleges
- **Suburban** 140-acre campus with easy access to Seattle
- **Coed,** 13,294 undergraduate students

Undergraduates Students come from 12 other countries.
Faculty *Total:* 600.
Majors Accounting; administrative assistant and secretarial science; business administration and management; computer programming; computer typography and composition equipment operation; criminal justice/law enforcement administration; dental hygiene; electrical, electronic and communications engineering technology; fire science/firefighting; industrial technology; information science/studies; kindergarten/preschool education; liberal arts and sciences/liberal studies; marketing/marketing management; mental health counseling; substance abuse/addiction counseling; veterinary/animal health technology.
Academics *Calendar:* quarters. *Degree:* certificates, diplomas, and associate. *Special study options:* academic remediation for entering students, adult/continuing education programs, advanced placement credit, cooperative education, distance learning, English as a second language, independent study, internships, off-campus study, part-time degree program, services for LD students, study abroad, summer session for credit. *ROTC:* Army (c).
Library 55,000 titles, 425 serial subscriptions.
Student Life *Housing:* college housing not available. *Activities and Organizations:* drama/theater group, student-run newspaper, choral group, Student Life, Phi Theta Kappa, Dental Hygiene Association, Veterinary Technology Association. *Campus security:* 24-hour emergency response devices and patrols, late-night transport/escort service. *Student services:* women's center.
Athletics *Intercollegiate sports:* baseball M(s), basketball M(s)/W(s), soccer M(s), softball W(s), volleyball W(s).
Costs (2012–13) *Tuition:* state resident $2836 full-time, $107 per credit hour part-time; nonresident $3104 full-time, $120 per credit hour part-time. Full-time tuition and fees vary according to course load and location. Part-time tuition and fees vary according to course load and location. *Required fees:* $228 full-time, $9 per credit hour part-time. *Payment plan:* installment. *Waivers:* senior citizens.
Financial Aid Of all full-time matriculated undergraduates who enrolled in 2011, 18 Federal Work-Study jobs (averaging $1889). 55 state and other part-time jobs (averaging $3058).

Applying *Options:* electronic application, early admission. *Application deadlines:* rolling (freshmen), rolling (out-of-state freshmen), rolling (transfers). *Notification:* continuous (freshmen), continuous (out-of-state freshmen), continuous (transfers).

Freshman Application Contact Pierce College at Puyallup, 1601 39th Avenue Southeast, Puyallup, WA 98374. *Phone:* 253-840-8400. *Website:* http://www.pierce.ctc.edu/.

Pima Medical Institute
Renton, Washington

Freshman Application Contact Pima Medical Institute, 555 South Renton Village Place, Renton, WA 98057. *Phone:* 425-228-9600. *Website:* http://www.pmi.edu/.

Pima Medical Institute
Seattle, Washington

Freshman Application Contact Admissions Office, Pima Medical Institute, 9709 Third Avenue NE, Suite 400, Seattle, WA 98115. *Phone:* 206-322-6100. *Toll-free phone:* 800-477-PIMA (in-state); 888-477-PIMA (out-of-state). *Website:* http://www.pmi.edu/.

Renton Technical College
Renton, Washington

Director of Admissions Becky Riverman, Vice President for Student Services, Renton Technical College, 3000 NE Fourth Street, Renton, WA 98056. *Phone:* 425-235-2463. *Website:* http://www.rtc.edu/.

Seattle Central Community College
Seattle, Washington

Freshman Application Contact Admissions Office, Seattle Central Community College, 1701 Broadway, Seattle, WA 98122-2400. *Phone:* 206-587-5450. *Website:* http://www.seattlecentral.edu/.

Shoreline Community College
Shoreline, Washington

Director of Admissions Mr. Chris Linebarger, Director, Recruiting and Enrollment Services, Shoreline Community College, 16101 Greenwood Avenue North, Shoreline, WA 98133-5696. *Phone:* 206-546-4581. *Website:* http://www.shore.ctc.edu/.

Skagit Valley College
Mount Vernon, Washington

Freshman Application Contact Ms. Karen Marie Bade, Admissions and Recruitment Coordinator, Skagit Valley College, 2405 College Way, Mount Vernon, WA 98273-5899. *Phone:* 360-416-7620. *E-mail:* karenmarie.bade@skagit.edu. *Website:* http://www.skagit.edu/.

South Puget Sound Community College
Olympia, Washington

- **State-supported** 2-year, founded 1970, part of Washington State Board for Community and Technical Colleges
- **Suburban** 102-acre campus with easy access to Seattle
- **Coed,** 4,955 undergraduate students, 54% full-time, 58% women, 42% men

Undergraduates 2,693 full-time, 2,262 part-time. Students come from 16 states and territories; 27 other countries; 0.4% are from out of state; 2% Black or African American, non-Hispanic/Latino; 8% Hispanic/Latino; 5% Asian, non-Hispanic/Latino; 0.7% Native Hawaiian or other Pacific Islander, non-Hispanic/Latino; 1% American Indian or Alaska Native, non-Hispanic/Latino; 7% Two or more races, non-Hispanic/Latino; 11% Race/ethnicity unknown; 1% international; 33% transferred in. *Retention:* 59% of full-time freshmen returned.

Freshmen *Admission:* 525 applied, 525 admitted, 538 enrolled.

Faculty *Total:* 263, 33% full-time, 8% with terminal degrees. *Student/faculty ratio:* 18:1.

Majors Accounting; administrative assistant and secretarial science; automobile/automotive mechanics technology; business administration and management; computer and information sciences; computer programming; culinary arts; data processing and data processing technology; dental assisting; drafting and design technology; fire science/firefighting; food technology and processing; horticultural science; information science/studies; kindergarten/preschool education; legal administrative assistant/secretary; legal assistant/paralegal; liberal arts and sciences/liberal studies; licensed practical/vocational nurse training; medical administrative assistant and medical secretary; medical/clinical assistant; registered nursing/registered nurse; welding technology.

Academics *Calendar:* quarters. *Degree:* certificates, diplomas, and associate. *Special study options:* academic remediation for entering students, adult/continuing education programs, advanced placement credit, cooperative education, distance learning, English as a second language, internships, part-time degree program, services for LD students, study abroad, summer session for credit. *ROTC:* Army (c).

Library Library/Media Center plus 1 other with 115,056 titles, 63,122 serial subscriptions, 5,515 audiovisual materials, an OPAC, a Web page.

Student Life *Housing:* college housing not available. *Activities and Organizations:* drama/theater group, student-run newspaper, Building Revolution by Increasing Community Knowledge (BRICK), Christian Club, Welding Club, Automotive Club, Psychology/Sociology Club. *Campus security:* 24-hour emergency response devices and patrols, late-night transport/escort service. *Student services:* personal/psychological counseling.

Athletics *Intercollegiate sports:* basketball M(s)/W(s), soccer M(s), softball W(s).

Financial Aid Of all full-time matriculated undergraduates who enrolled in 2011, 42 Federal Work-Study jobs (averaging $3150). 14 state and other part-time jobs (averaging $4400). *Financial aid deadline:* 6/29.

Applying *Options:* electronic application, early admission, deferred entrance. *Application deadlines:* rolling (freshmen), rolling (out-of-state freshmen), rolling (transfers). *Notification:* continuous (freshmen), continuous (out-of-state freshmen), continuous (transfers).

Freshman Application Contact Ms. Heidi Dearborn, South Puget Sound Community College, 2011 Mottman Road, SW, Olympia, WA 98512-6292. *Phone:* 360-754-7711 Ext. 5358. *E-mail:* hdearborn@spcc.edu. *Website:* http://www.spscc.ctc.edu/.

South Seattle Community College
Seattle, Washington

Director of Admissions Ms. Kim Manderbach, Dean of Student Services/Registration, South Seattle Community College, 6000 16th Avenue, SW, Seattle, WA 98106-1499. *Phone:* 206-764-5378. *Fax:* 206-764-7947. *E-mail:* kimmanderb@sccd.ctc.edu. *Website:* http://southseattle.edu/.

Spokane Community College
Spokane, Washington

Freshman Application Contact Ms. Brenda Burns, Researcher, District Institutional Research, Spokane Community College, Spokane, WA 99217-5399. *Phone:* 509-434-5242. *Toll-free phone:* 800-248-5644. *Fax:* 509-434-5249. *E-mail:* mlee@ccs.spokane.edu. *Website:* http://www.scc.spokane.edu/.

Spokane Falls Community College
Spokane, Washington

Freshman Application Contact Admissions Office, Spokane Falls Community College, Admissions MS 3011, 3410 West Fort George Wright Drive, Spokane, WA 99224. *Phone:* 509-533-3401. *Toll-free phone:* 888-509-7944. *Fax:* 509-533-3852. *Website:* http://www.spokanefalls.edu/.

Tacoma Community College
Tacoma, Washington

Freshman Application Contact Enrollment Services, Tacoma Community College, 6501 South 19th Street, Tacoma, WA 98466. *Phone:* 253-566-5325. *Fax:* 253-566-6034. *Website:* http://www.tacomacc.edu/.

Walla Walla Community College
Walla Walla, Washington

Freshman Application Contact Walla Walla Community College, 500 Tausick Way, Walla Walla, WA 99362-9267. *Phone:* 509-522-2500. *Toll-free*

phone: 877-992-9922.
Website: http://www.wwcc.edu/.

Wenatchee Valley College
Wenatchee, Washington

Freshman Application Contact Ms. Cecilia Escobedo, Registrar/Admissions Coordinator, Wenatchee Valley College, 1300 Fifth Street, Wenatchee, WA 98801-1799. *Phone:* 509-682-6836. *E-mail:* cescobedo@wvc.edu.
Website: http://www.wvc.edu/.

Whatcom Community College
Bellingham, Washington

Freshman Application Contact Entry and Advising Center, Whatcom Community College, 237 West Kellogg Road, Bellingham, WA 98226-8003. *Phone:* 360-676-2170. *Fax:* 360-676-2171. *E-mail:* admit@whatcom.ctc.edu. *Website:* http://www.whatcom.ctc.edu/.

Yakima Valley Community College
Yakima, Washington

Freshman Application Contact Denise Anderson, Registrar and Director for Enrollment Services, Yakima Valley Community College, PO Box 1647, Yakima, WA 98907-1647. *Phone:* 509-574-4702. *Fax:* 509-574-6879. *E-mail:* admis@yvcc.edu.
Website: http://www.yvcc.edu/.

WEST VIRGINIA

Blue Ridge Community and Technical College
Martinsburg, West Virginia

- **State-supported** 2-year, founded 1974
- **Small-town** campus
- **Coed,** 4,317 undergraduate students, 27% full-time, 67% women, 33% men

Undergraduates 1,161 full-time, 3,156 part-time. 5% are from out of state; 15% Black or African American, non-Hispanic/Latino; 3% Hispanic/Latino; 0.8% Asian, non-Hispanic/Latino; 0.2% Native Hawaiian or other Pacific Islander, non-Hispanic/Latino; 0.4% American Indian or Alaska Native, non-Hispanic/Latino; 3% Two or more races, non-Hispanic/Latino; 0.3% Race/ethnicity unknown; 4% transferred in. *Retention:* 54% of full-time freshmen returned.
Freshmen *Admission:* 403 enrolled. *Test scores:* SAT critical reading scores over 500: 45%; ACT scores over 18: 34%; SAT critical reading scores over 600: 10%; ACT scores over 24: 1%.
Faculty *Total:* 169, 35% full-time. *Student/faculty ratio:* 23:1.
Majors Business, management, and marketing related; criminal justice/safety; culinary arts; design and visual communications; electromechanical technology; emergency medical technology (EMT paramedic); fashion merchandising; fire science/firefighting; general studies; information technology; legal assistant/paralegal; office occupations and clerical services; quality control and safety technologies related.
Academics *Degree:* certificates and associate. *Special study options:* academic remediation for entering students, accelerated degree program, adult/continuing education programs, advanced placement credit, double majors, English as a second language, independent study, internships, part-time degree program, services for LD students.
Library Martinsburg Public Library.
Student Life *Housing:* college housing not available. *Activities and Organizations:* drama/theater group, national fraternities. *Campus security:* late-night transport/escort service. *Student services:* personal/psychological counseling.
Standardized Tests *Recommended:* SAT and SAT Subject Tests or ACT (for admission).
Costs (2012–13) *Tuition:* state resident $3120 full-time, $130 per credit hour part-time; nonresident $5616 full-time, $234 per credit hour part-time. Full-time tuition and fees vary according to course load. Part-time tuition and fees vary according to course load. *Waivers:* adult students, senior citizens, and employees or children of employees.

Applying *Options:* deferred entrance. *Application fee:* $25. *Required:* high school transcript. *Required for some:* interview.
Freshman Application Contact Brenda K. Neal, Director of Access, Blue Ridge Community and Technical College, 400 West Stephen Street, Martinsburg, WV 25401. *Phone:* 304-260-4380 Ext. 2109. *Fax:* 304-260-4376. *E-mail:* bneal@blueridgectc.edu.
Website: http://www.blueridgectc.edu/.

Bridgemont Community & Technical College
Montgomery, West Virginia

Director of Admissions Ms. Lisa Graham, Director of Admissions, Bridgemont Community & Technical College, 405 Fayette Pike, Montgomery, WV 25136. *Phone:* 304-442-3167.
Website: http://www.bridgemont.edu/.

Eastern West Virginia Community and Technical College
Moorefield, West Virginia

Freshman Application Contact Learner Support Services, Eastern West Virginia Community and Technical College, HC 65 Box 402, Moorefield, WV 26836. *Phone:* 304-434-8000. *Toll-free phone:* 877-982-2322. *Fax:* 304-434-7000. *E-mail:* askeast@eastern.wvnet.edu.
Website: http://www.eastern.wvnet.edu/.

Everest Institute
Cross Lanes, West Virginia

Freshman Application Contact Director of Admissions, Everest Institute, 5514 Big Tyler Road, Cross Lanes, WV 25313-1390. *Phone:* 304-776-6290. *Toll-free phone:* 888-741-4270. *Fax:* 304-776-6262.
Website: http://www.everest.edu/.

Huntington Junior College
Huntington, West Virginia

Director of Admissions Mr. James Garrett, Educational Services Director, Huntington Junior College, 900 Fifth Avenue, Huntington, WV 25701-2004. *Phone:* 304-697-7550. *Toll-free phone:* 800-344-4522.
Website: http://www.huntingtonjuniorcollege.com/.

ITT Technical Institute
Huntington, West Virginia

- **Proprietary** 2-year, part of ITT Educational Services, Inc.
- **Coed**

Academics *Calendar:* quarters. *Degree:* associate.
Freshman Application Contact Director of Recruitment, ITT Technical Institute, 5183 US Route 60, Building 1, Suite 40, Huntington, WV 25705. *Phone:* 304-733-8700. *Toll-free phone:* 800-224-4695.
Website: http://www.itt-tech.edu/.

Kanawha Valley Community and Technical College
South Charleston, West Virginia

Freshman Application Contact Mr. Bryce Casto, Vice President, Student Affairs, Kanawha Valley Community and Technical College, 333 Sullivan Hall. *Phone:* 304-766-3140. *Fax:* 304-766-4158. *E-mail:* castosb@wvstateu.edu.
Website: http://www.kvctc.edu/.

Mountain State College
Parkersburg, West Virginia

Freshman Application Contact Ms. Judith Sutton, President, Mountain State College, 1508 Spring Street, Parkersburg, WV 26101-3993. *Phone:* 304-485-5487. *Toll-free phone:* 800-841-0201. *Fax:* 304-485-3524. *E-mail:* jsutton@msc.edu.
Website: http://www.msc.edu/.

Mountwest Community & Technical College
Huntington, West Virginia

Freshman Application Contact Dr. Tammy Johnson, Admissions Director, Mountwest Community & Technical College, 1 John Marshall Drive, Huntington, WV 25755. *Phone:* 304-696-3160. *Toll-free phone:* 866-676-5533. *Fax:* 304-696-3135. *E-mail:* admissions@marshall.edu. *Website:* http://www.mctc.edu/.

New River Community and Technical College
Beckley, West Virginia

Director of Admissions Dr. Allen B. Withers, Vice President, Student Services, New River Community and Technical College, 167 Dye Drive, Beckley, WV 25801. *Phone:* 304-929-5011. *E-mail:* awithers@newriver.edu. *Website:* http://www.newriver.edu/.

Pierpont Community & Technical College
Fairmont, West Virginia

Freshman Application Contact Mr. Steve Leadman, Director of Admissions and Recruiting, Pierpont Community & Technical College, 1201 Locust Avenue, Fairmont, WV 26554. *Phone:* 304-367-4892. *Toll-free phone:* 800-641-5678. *Fax:* 304-367-4789. *Website:* http://www.pierpont.edu/.

Potomac State College of West Virginia University
Keyser, West Virginia

- **State-supported** primarily 2-year, founded 1901, part of West Virginia Higher Education Policy Commission
- **Small-town** 18-acre campus
- **Coed,** 1,781 undergraduate students, 81% full-time, 53% women, 47% men

Undergraduates 1,436 full-time, 345 part-time. Students come from 19 states and territories; 2 other countries; 31% are from out of state; 17% Black or African American, non-Hispanic/Latino; 2% Hispanic/Latino; 0.3% Asian, non-Hispanic/Latino; 0.1% Native Hawaiian or other Pacific Islander, non-Hispanic/Latino; 1% American Indian or Alaska Native, non-Hispanic/Latino; 0.3% Two or more races, non-Hispanic/Latino; 0.7% Race/ethnicity unknown; 0.2% international; 3% transferred in; 28% live on campus. *Retention:* 46% of full-time freshmen returned.
Freshmen *Admission:* 1,006 admitted, 729 enrolled. *Average high school GPA:* 2.82. *Test scores:* SAT critical reading scores over 500: 15%; SAT math scores over 500: 21%; ACT scores over 18: 62%; SAT critical reading scores over 600: 3%; SAT math scores over 600: 2%; ACT scores over 24: 15%; ACT scores over 30: 1%.
Faculty *Total:* 95, 44% full-time, 14% with terminal degrees. *Student/faculty ratio:* 25:1.
Majors Accounting; administrative assistant and secretarial science; agricultural business and management; agricultural economics; agricultural mechanization; agricultural teacher education; agriculture; agriculture and agriculture operations related; agronomy and crop science; animal sciences; biological and physical sciences; biology/biological sciences; business administration and management; business/managerial economics; chemistry; civil engineering technology; computer and information sciences related; computer engineering technology; computer programming; computer programming (specific applications); computer science; computer systems networking and telecommunications; criminal justice/safety; data processing and data processing technology; economics; education; electrical, electronic and communications engineering technology; elementary education; engineering; English; forestry; forest technology; geology/earth science; history; horticultural science; hospitality administration; information technology; journalism; kindergarten/preschool education; liberal arts and sciences/liberal studies; mathematics; mechanical engineering/mechanical technology; medical administrative assistant and medical secretary; network and system administration; parks, recreation and leisure facilities management; physical education teaching and coaching; political science and government; pre-engineering; psychology; social work; sociology; wildlife, fish and wildlands science and management; wood science and wood products/pulp and paper technology.
Academics *Calendar:* semesters. *Degrees:* associate and bachelor's. *Special study options:* academic remediation for entering students, adult/continuing

education programs, advanced placement credit, distance learning, double majors, honors programs, independent study, internships, part-time degree program, services for LD students, study abroad, summer session for credit.
Library Mary F. Shipper Library with 51,028 titles, 286 serial subscriptions, 1,253 audiovisual materials, an OPAC.
Student Life *Housing:* on-campus residence required through sophomore year. *Options:* coed. Campus housing is university owned. Freshman applicants given priority for college housing. *Activities and Organizations:* drama/theater group, student-run newspaper, choral group, Community Chorus, Circle K, Agriculture and Forestry Club, Catamounts Against Cancer, Intramural Program. *Campus security:* 24-hour patrols, late-night transport/escort service, controlled dormitory access. *Student services:* health clinic, personal/psychological counseling.
Athletics Member NJCAA. *Intercollegiate sports:* baseball M(s), basketball M(s)/W(s), soccer M/W, softball W(s), volleyball W(s). *Intramural sports:* basketball M/W, football M/W, volleyball M/W.
Standardized Tests *Recommended:* SAT or ACT (for admission).
Financial Aid Of all full-time matriculated undergraduates who enrolled in 2011, 70 Federal Work-Study jobs (averaging $1300).
Applying *Options:* electronic application. *Required:* high school transcript. *Application deadlines:* rolling (freshmen), rolling (transfers).
Freshman Application Contact Ms. Beth Little, Director of Enrollment Services, Potomac State College of West Virginia University, 75 Arnold Street, Keyser, WV 26726. *Phone:* 304-788-6820. *Toll-free phone:* 800-262-7332 Ext. 6820. *Fax:* 304-788-6939. *E-mail:* go2psc@mail.wvu.edu. *Website:* http://www.potomacstatecollege.edu/.

Southern West Virginia Community and Technical College
Mount Gay, West Virginia

Freshman Application Contact Mr. Roy Simmons, Registrar, Southern West Virginia Community and Technical College, PO Box 2900, Mt. Gay, WV 25637. *Phone:* 304-792-7160 Ext. 120. *Fax:* 304-792-7096. *E-mail:* admissions@southern.wvnet.edu. *Website:* http://southernwv.edu/.

Valley College of Technology
Martinsburg, West Virginia

Freshman Application Contact Ms. Gail Kennedy, Admissions Director, Valley College of Technology, 287 Aikens Center, Martinsburg, WV 25404. *Phone:* 304-263-0878. *Fax:* 304-263-2413. *E-mail:* gkennedy@vct.edu. *Website:* http://www.vct.edu/.

West Virginia Business College
Nutter Fort, West Virginia

Director of Admissions Robert Wright, Campus Director, West Virginia Business College, 116 Pennsylvania Avenue, Nutter Fort, WV 26301. *Phone:* 304-624-7695. *E-mail:* info@wvbc.edu. *Website:* http://www.wvbc.edu/.

West Virginia Business College
Wheeling, West Virginia

Freshman Application Contact Ms. Karen D. Shaw, Director, West Virginia Business College, 1052 Main Street, Wheeling, WV 26003. *Phone:* 304-232-0361. *Fax:* 304-232-0363. *E-mail:* wvbcwheeling@stratuswave.net. *Website:* http://www.wvbc.edu/.

West Virginia Junior College–Bridgeport
Bridgeport, West Virginia

- **Proprietary** 2-year, founded 1922, part of West Virginia Junior College-Charleston, WV; West Virginia Junior College-Morgantown, WV; Pennsylvania Institute of Health & Technology-Uniontown, PA; Ohio Institute of Health & Technology, E. Liverpool, OH
- **Small-town** 3-acre campus with easy access to Pittsburgh
- **Coed,** 507 undergraduate students, 100% full-time, 83% women, 17% men

Undergraduates 507 full-time. Students come from 4 states and territories; 0.4% Black or African American, non-Hispanic/Latino; 20% transferred in. *Retention:* 74% of full-time freshmen returned.
Freshmen *Admission:* 507 enrolled. *Average high school GPA:* 2.5.

Faculty *Total:* 19, 53% full-time, 79% with terminal degrees. *Student/faculty ratio:* 15:1.

Majors Business administration and management; computer technology/computer systems technology; dental assisting; medical administrative assistant and medical secretary; medical/clinical assistant; medical insurance coding; pharmacy technician; web/multimedia management and webmaster.

Academics *Calendar:* quarters. *Degree:* associate. *Special study options:* cooperative education, distance learning, independent study, internships, services for LD students, summer session for credit.

Library WVJC Resource Center plus 1 other with an OPAC.

Student Life *Housing:* college housing not available. *Activities and Organizations:* Medical Club, Business Club, Computer Club, Dental Assisting Club, Pharmacy Tech Club. *Campus security:* 24-hour emergency response devices.

Standardized Tests *Recommended:* SAT or ACT (for admission).

Financial Aid Of all full-time matriculated undergraduates who enrolled in 2011, 10 Federal Work-Study jobs.

Applying *Options:* electronic application. *Required:* essay or personal statement, minimum 2.5 GPA, interview, Applicants are required to meet with an Admissions Representative. *Required for some:* 1 letter of recommendation. *Recommended:* high school transcript. *Application deadline:* rolling (freshmen). *Notification:* continuous (freshmen).

Freshman Application Contact Mr. Adam Pratt, High School Admissions Coordinator, West Virginia Junior College–Bridgeport, 176 Thompson Drive, Bridgeport, WV 26330. *Phone:* 304-842-4007 Ext. 112. *Toll-free phone:* 800-470-5627. *Fax:* 304-842-8191. *E-mail:* apratt@wvjcinfo.net. *Website:* http://www.wvjcinfo.net/.

West Virginia Junior College–Charleston

Charleston, West Virginia

Freshman Application Contact West Virginia Junior College–Charleston, 1000 Virginia Street East, Charleston, WV 25301-2817. *Phone:* 304-345-2820. *Toll-free phone:* 800-924-5208. *Website:* http://www.wvjc.edu/.

West Virginia Junior College–Morgantown

Morgantown, West Virginia

Freshman Application Contact Admissions Office, West Virginia Junior College–Morgantown, 148 Willey Street, Morgantown, WV 26505-5521. *Phone:* 304-296-8282. *Website:* http://www.wvjcmorgantown.edu/.

West Virginia Northern Community College

Wheeling, West Virginia

- **State-supported** 2-year, founded 1972
- **Small-town** campus with easy access to Pittsburgh
- **Endowment** $659,426
- **Coed,** 2,505 undergraduate students, 46% full-time, 68% women, 32% men

Undergraduates 1,156 full-time, 1,349 part-time. Students come from 14 states and territories; 24% are from out of state; 5% Black or African American, non-Hispanic/Latino; 0.4% Hispanic/Latino; 0.4% Asian, non-Hispanic/Latino; 0.3% American Indian or Alaska Native, non-Hispanic/Latino; 2% Two or more races, non-Hispanic/Latino; 1% Race/ethnicity unknown; 12% transferred in.

Freshmen *Admission:* 350 applied, 350 admitted, 368 enrolled. *Average high school GPA:* 2.92.

Faculty *Total:* 190, 31% full-time, 3% with terminal degrees.

Majors Administrative assistant and secretarial science; business/commerce; computer programming; criminal justice/police science; culinary arts; executive assistant/executive secretary; general studies; health information/medical records technology; heating, air conditioning, ventilation and refrigeration maintenance technology; hospitality administration; information technology; legal assistant/paralegal; liberal arts and sciences and humanities related; liberal arts and sciences/liberal studies; medical/clinical assistant; medical radiologic technology; multi/interdisciplinary studies related; registered nursing/registered nurse; respiratory care therapy; science technologies related; social work; surgical technology.

Academics *Calendar:* semesters. *Degree:* certificates and associate. *Special study options:* academic remediation for entering students, accelerated degree program, adult/continuing education programs, advanced placement credit, cooperative education, distance learning, double majors, honors programs,

internships, part-time degree program, services for LD students, student-designed majors, summer session for credit.

Library Wheeling B&O Campus Library plus 2 others with 36,650 titles, 188 serial subscriptions, 3,495 audiovisual materials, an OPAC, a Web page.

Student Life *Housing:* college housing not available. *Activities and Organizations:* student-run newspaper, Community Outreach Opportunity Program (COOP). *Campus security:* police officer on staff during the day at Main Campus, security personnel during evening and during night classes.

Athletics *Intramural sports:* basketball M/W, bowling M/W, golf M/W, softball M/W, volleyball M/W.

Standardized Tests *Required for some:* Compass. *Recommended:* Compass.

Costs (2013–14) *Tuition:* state resident $2256 full-time; nonresident $7416 full-time. Full-time tuition and fees vary according to course load, location, program, reciprocity agreements, and student level. Part-time tuition and fees vary according to course load, location, program, reciprocity agreements, and student level. *Required fees:* $390 full-time. *Payment plan:* installment. *Waivers:* adult students, senior citizens, and employees or children of employees.

Applying *Options:* electronic application, early admission, deferred entrance. *Required for some:* high school transcript. *Application deadlines:* rolling (freshmen), rolling (transfers).

Freshman Application Contact Mrs. Janet Fike, Vice President of Student Services, West Virginia Northern Community College, 1704 Market Street, Wheeling, WV 26003. *Phone:* 304-214-8837. *E-mail:* jfike@northern.wvnet.edu. *Website:* http://www.wvncc.edu/.

West Virginia University at Parkersburg

Parkersburg, West Virginia

Freshman Application Contact Christine Post, Associate Dean of Enrollment Management, West Virginia University at Parkersburg, 300 Campus Drive, Parkersburg, WV 26104. *Phone:* 304-424-8223 Ext. 223. *Toll-free phone:* 800-WVA-WVUP. *Fax:* 304-424-8332. *E-mail:* christine.post@mail.wvu.edu. *Website:* http://www.wvup.edu/.

WISCONSIN

Blackhawk Technical College

Janesville, Wisconsin

- **District-supported** 2-year, founded 1968, part of Wisconsin Technical College System
- **Small-town** 84-acre campus
- **Coed,** 2,967 undergraduate students, 44% full-time, 62% women, 38% men

Undergraduates 1,306 full-time, 1,661 part-time. Students come from 2 states and territories; 1% are from out of state; 10% Black or African American, non-Hispanic/Latino; 10% Hispanic/Latino; 1% Asian, non-Hispanic/Latino; 0.2% Native Hawaiian or other Pacific Islander, non-Hispanic/Latino; 0.5% American Indian or Alaska Native, non-Hispanic/Latino; 3% Two or more races, non-Hispanic/Latino; 7% Race/ethnicity unknown. *Retention:* 83% of full-time freshmen returned.

Freshmen *Admission:* 530 enrolled.

Faculty *Total:* 357, 27% full-time, 1% with terminal degrees. *Student/faculty ratio:* 11:1.

Majors Accounting; administrative assistant and secretarial science; business administration and management; clinical/medical laboratory technology; computer and information systems security; computer systems networking and telecommunications; criminal justice/police science; culinary arts; drafting/design engineering technologies related; early childhood education; electromechanical technology; fire prevention and safety technology; fire science/firefighting; heating, air conditioning, ventilation and refrigeration maintenance technology; heating, ventilation, air conditioning and refrigeration engineering technology; human resources management; industrial engineering; industrial technology; legal administrative assistant/secretary; marketing/marketing management; mechanical drafting and CAD/CADD; medical administrative assistant and medical secretary; medical radiologic technology; physical therapy; physical therapy technology; radiologic technology/science; registered nursing/registered nurse; restaurant, culinary, and catering management; web page, digital/multimedia and information resources design.

Academics *Calendar:* semesters. *Degree:* associate. *Special study options:* academic remediation for entering students, accelerated degree program, adult/continuing education programs, advanced placement credit, cooperative education, distance learning, English as a second language, independent study,

internships, part-time degree program, services for LD students, student-designed majors, summer session for credit.
Library Blackhawk Technical College Library with 101,024 titles, 300 serial subscriptions, 5,889 audiovisual materials, an OPAC, a Web page.
Student Life *Housing:* college housing not available. *Activities and Organizations:* student-run newspaper, Student Government, Association of Information Technology Professionals, Criminal Justice, Epicurean Club, Phi Theta Kappa Honor Society. *Campus security:* student patrols.
Costs (2012–13) *Tuition:* state resident $3507 full-time, $117 per credit part-time; nonresident $5261 full-time, $175 per credit part-time. Full-time tuition and fees vary according to course load. Part-time tuition and fees vary according to course load. *Required fees:* $455 full-time, $6 per credit part-time. *Payment plan:* deferred payment. *Waivers:* senior citizens.
Financial Aid Of all full-time matriculated undergraduates who enrolled in 2011, 33 Federal Work-Study jobs (averaging $1150).
Applying *Options:* electronic application. *Application fee:* $30. *Required:* high school transcript. *Application deadlines:* rolling (freshmen), rolling (transfers). *Notification:* continuous (freshmen), continuous (transfers).
Freshman Application Contact Blackhawk Technical College, PO Box 5009, Janesville, WI 53547-5009. *Phone:* 608-757-7713.
Website: http://www.blackhawk.edu/.

Bryant & Stratton College - Milwaukee Campus
Milwaukee, Wisconsin

Freshman Application Contact Mr. Dan Basile, Director of Admissions, Bryant & Stratton College - Milwaukee Campus, 310 West Wisconsin Avenue, Suite 500 East, Milwaukee, WI 53203-2214. *Phone:* 414-276-5200.
Website: http://www.bryantstratton.edu/.

Chippewa Valley Technical College
Eau Claire, Wisconsin

- **District-supported** 2-year, founded 1912, part of Wisconsin Technical College System
- **Urban** 255-acre campus
- **Coed,** 6,086 undergraduate students, 43% full-time, 55% women, 45% men

Undergraduates 2,640 full-time, 3,446 part-time. 2% are from out of state; 1% Black or African American, non-Hispanic/Latino; 2% Hispanic/Latino; 4% Asian, non-Hispanic/Latino; 0.1% Native Hawaiian or other Pacific Islander, non-Hispanic/Latino; 0.7% American Indian or Alaska Native, non-Hispanic/Latino; 2% Two or more races, non-Hispanic/Latino; 5% Race/ethnicity unknown.
Freshmen *Admission:* 1,863 enrolled.
Faculty *Total:* 491, 46% full-time, 7% with terminal degrees. *Student/faculty ratio:* 14:1.
Majors Accounting; administrative assistant and secretarial science; agricultural business and management related; applied horticulture/horticultural business services related; business administration and management; civil engineering technology; clinical/medical laboratory technology; computer programming; computer systems networking and telecommunications; criminal justice/police science; dental hygiene; diagnostic medical sonography and ultrasound technology; early childhood education; electromechanical technology; emergency medical technology (EMT paramedic); health information/medical records technology; heating, ventilation, air conditioning and refrigeration engineering technology; human resources management; legal assistant/paralegal; liberal arts and sciences/liberal studies; marketing/marketing management; medical radiologic technology; multi/interdisciplinary studies related; nanotechnology; physical therapy technology; registered nursing/registered nurse; respiratory care therapy; substance abuse/addiction counseling.
Academics *Calendar:* semesters. *Degree:* certificates, diplomas, and associate. *Special study options:* academic remediation for entering students, accelerated degree program, adult/continuing education programs, advanced placement credit, cooperative education, distance learning, double majors, English as a second language, honors programs, independent study, internships, part-time degree program, services for LD students, student-designed majors, summer session for credit.
Library The Learning Center with an OPAC, a Web page.
Student Life *Housing:* college housing not available. *Activities and Organizations:* Collegiate DECA. *Campus security:* 24-hour emergency response devices, late-night transport/escort service, security cameras. *Student services:* health clinic, personal/psychological counseling.
Standardized Tests *Required:* Compass, Accuplacer (for admission). *Recommended:* ACT (for admission).
Costs (2012–13) *Tuition:* state resident $3524 full-time, $117 per credit part-time; nonresident $5260 full-time, $175 per credit part-time. Full-time tuition

and fees vary according to course load and reciprocity agreements. Part-time tuition and fees vary according to course load and reciprocity agreements. *Required fees:* $291 full-time, $291 per term part-time. *Room and board:* $6452. *Payment plans:* installment, deferred payment. *Waivers:* senior citizens.
Financial Aid Of all full-time matriculated undergraduates who enrolled in 2011, 218 Federal Work-Study jobs (averaging $875).
Applying *Options:* electronic application, early admission, deferred entrance. *Application fee:* $30. *Required for some:* high school transcript. *Application deadlines:* rolling (freshmen), rolling (transfers). *Notification:* continuous (freshmen), continuous (transfers).
Freshman Application Contact Admissions Office, Chippewa Valley Technical College, 620 W. Clairemont Avenue, Eau Claire, WI 54701. *Phone:* 715-833-6200. *Toll-free phone:* 800-547-2882. *Fax:* 715-833-6470. *E-mail:* infocenter@cvtc.edu.
Website: http://www.cvtc.edu/.

College of Menominee Nation
Keshena, Wisconsin

Director of Admissions Tessa James, Admissions Coordinator, College of Menominee Nation, PO Box 1179, Keshena, WI 54135. *Phone:* 715-799-5600 Ext. 3053. *Toll-free phone:* 800-567-2344. *E-mail:* tjames@menominee.edu.
Website: http://www.menominee.edu/.

Fox Valley Technical College
Appleton, Wisconsin

- **State and locally supported** 2-year, founded 1967, part of Wisconsin Technical College System
- **Suburban** 100-acre campus
- **Endowment** $2.1 million
- **Coed,** 10,948 undergraduate students, 27% full-time, 49% women, 51% men

Undergraduates 2,902 full-time, 8,046 part-time. Students come from 15 states and territories; 14 other countries; 1% are from out of state; 2% Black or African American, non-Hispanic/Latino; 3% Hispanic/Latino; 4% Asian, non-Hispanic/Latino; 0.2% Native Hawaiian or other Pacific Islander, non-Hispanic/Latino; 1% American Indian or Alaska Native, non-Hispanic/Latino; 0.4% Two or more races, non-Hispanic/Latino; 6% Race/ethnicity unknown; 0.1% international.
Freshmen *Admission:* 1,396 applied, 1,062 admitted, 1,071 enrolled.
Faculty *Total:* 917, 36% full-time. *Student/faculty ratio:* 11:1.
Majors Accounting; administrative assistant and secretarial science; agricultural/farm supplies retailing and wholesaling; agricultural mechanization; airline pilot and flight crew; autobody/collision and repair technology; automobile/automotive mechanics technology; avionics maintenance technology; banking and financial support services; biology/biotechnology laboratory technician; business administration and management; computer engineering technology; computer programming; computer systems analysis; computer systems networking and telecommunications; criminal justice/police science; dental hygiene; early childhood education; electrical and electronic engineering technologies related; electrical, electronic and communications engineering technology; electromechanical technology; emergency medical technology (EMT paramedic); environmental control technologies related; fire prevention and safety technology; fire protection related; forensic science and technology; graphic and printing equipment operation/production; graphic communications; health information/medical records technology; heavy equipment maintenance technology; hospitality administration; human resources management; instrumentation technology; interior design; logistics, materials, and supply chain management; manufacturing engineering technology; marketing/marketing management; mechanical drafting and CAD/CADD; medical office management; multi/interdisciplinary studies related; natural resources/conservation; occupational therapist assistant; operations management; registered nursing/registered nurse; restaurant, culinary, and catering management; substance abuse/addiction counseling; web/multimedia management and webmaster; welding technology.
Academics *Calendar:* semesters. *Degree:* certificates, diplomas, and associate. *Special study options:* academic remediation for entering students, accelerated degree program, advanced placement credit, cooperative education, distance learning, double majors, English as a second language, independent study, internships, off-campus study, part-time degree program, services for LD students, student-designed majors, study abroad, summer session for credit.
Library William M. Sirek Educational Resource Center with 99,130 titles, 182 serial subscriptions, 6,884 audiovisual materials, an OPAC, a Web page.
Student Life *Housing:* college housing not available. *Activities and Organizations:* student-run newspaper, Student Government Association, Phi Theta Kappa, Culinary Arts, Student Nurses, Post Secondary Agribusiness. *Campus*

security: 24-hour emergency response devices, late-night transport/escort service, 16-hour patrols by trained security personnel. *Student services:* health clinic, personal/psychological counseling.

Athletics *Intercollegiate sports:* basketball M/W, volleyball W. *Intramural sports:* basketball M/W, football M/W, soccer M/W, softball M/W, table tennis M/W, volleyball M/W.

Costs (2012–13) *Tuition:* state resident $3507 full-time, $117 per credit part-time; nonresident $5261 full-time, $175 per credit part-time. *Required fees:* $471 full-time, $16 per credit part-time. *Payment plan:* installment.

Applying *Options:* electronic application, early admission, deferred entrance. *Application fee:* $30. *Required:* high school transcript. *Application deadlines:* rolling (freshmen), rolling (transfers).

Freshman Application Contact Admissions Center, Fox Valley Technical College, 1825 North Bluemound Drive, PO Box 2277, Appleton, WI 54912-2277. *Phone:* 920-735-5643. *Toll-free phone:* 800-735-3882. *Fax:* 920-735-2582.
Website: http://www.fvtc.edu/.

Gateway Technical College
Kenosha, Wisconsin

- **State and locally supported** 2-year, founded 1911, part of Wisconsin Technical College System
- **Urban** 10-acre campus with easy access to Chicago, Milwaukee
- **Coed,** 8,720 undergraduate students, 20% full-time, 61% women, 39% men

Undergraduates 1,717 full-time, 7,003 part-time. Students come from 7 states and territories; 2 other countries; 1% are from out of state; 15% Black or African American, non-Hispanic/Latino; 12% Hispanic/Latino; 1% Asian, non-Hispanic/Latino; 0.1% Native Hawaiian or other Pacific Islander, non-Hispanic/Latino; 0.5% American Indian or Alaska Native, non-Hispanic/Latino; 2% Two or more races, non-Hispanic/Latino; 0.9% Race/ethnicity unknown; 1% transferred in. *Retention:* 64% of full-time freshmen returned.

Freshmen *Admission:* 1,482 enrolled.

Faculty *Student/faculty ratio:* 16:1.

Majors Accounting; administrative assistant and secretarial science; airline pilot and flight crew; applied horticulture/horticultural business services related; applied horticulture/horticulture operations; architectural engineering technology; automobile/automotive mechanics technology; biology/biotechnology laboratory technician; business administration and management; business operations support and secretarial services related; civil engineering technology; computer and information systems security; computer programming; computer support specialist; computer systems analysis; computer systems networking and telecommunications; criminal justice/police science; early childhood education; electrical, electronic and communications engineering technology; electromechanical technology; emergency medical technology (EMT paramedic); fire science/firefighting; graphic design; health information/medical records technology; heating, air conditioning, ventilation and refrigeration maintenance technology; heating, ventilation, air conditioning and refrigeration engineering technology; hotel, motel, and restaurant management; industrial mechanics and maintenance technology; interior design; marketing/marketing management; marketing related; mechanical drafting and CAD/CADD; medical radiologic technology; mental and social health services and allied professions related; multi/interdisciplinary studies related; operations management; physical therapy technology; professional, technical, business, and scientific writing; quality control technology; radio and television broadcasting technology; registered nursing/registered nurse; restaurant, culinary, and catering management; surgical technology; surveying technology; teacher assistant/aide; transportation and highway engineering; water quality and wastewater treatment management and recycling technology; web/multimedia management and webmaster.

Academics *Calendar:* semesters. *Degree:* certificates, diplomas, and associate. *Special study options:* academic remediation for entering students, advanced placement credit, cooperative education, distance learning, double majors, English as a second language, independent study, internships, part-time degree program, services for LD students, student-designed majors, summer session for credit.

Library Library/Learning Resources Center plus 3 others with 46,103 titles, 173 serial subscriptions, 4,438 audiovisual materials, an OPAC, a Web page.

Student Life *Housing:* college housing not available. *Activities and Organizations:* student-run newspaper, radio station, International Club. *Campus security:* 24-hour emergency response devices and patrols, late-night transport/escort service. *Student services:* personal/psychological counseling.

Applying *Options:* electronic application, early admission, deferred entrance. *Application fee:* $30. *Required:* high school transcript. *Application deadlines:* rolling (freshmen), rolling (transfers). *Notification:* continuous (freshmen), continuous (transfers).

Freshman Application Contact Admissions, Gateway Technical College, 3520 30th Avenue, Kenosha, WI 53144-1690. *Phone:* 262-564-2300. *Fax:* 262-564-2301. *E-mail:* admissions@gtc.edu.
Website: http://www.gtc.edu/.

ITT Technical Institute
Green Bay, Wisconsin

- **Proprietary** primarily 2-year, founded 2000, part of ITT Educational Services, Inc.
- **Coed**

Academics *Calendar:* quarters. *Degrees:* associate and bachelor's.

Freshman Application Contact Director of Recruitment, ITT Technical Institute, 470 Security Boulevard, Green Bay, WI 54313. *Phone:* 920-662-9000. *Toll-free phone:* 888-884-3626. *Fax:* 920-662-9384.
Website: http://www.itt-tech.edu/.

ITT Technical Institute
Greenfield, Wisconsin

- **Proprietary** primarily 2-year, founded 1968, part of ITT Educational Services, Inc.
- **Suburban** campus
- **Coed**

Academics *Calendar:* quarters. *Degrees:* associate and bachelor's.

Freshman Application Contact Director of Recruitment, ITT Technical Institute, 6300 West Layton Avenue, Greenfield, WI 53220-4612. *Phone:* 414-282-9494.
Website: http://www.itt-tech.edu/.

ITT Technical Institute
Madison, Wisconsin

- **Proprietary** primarily 2-year, part of ITT Educational Services, Inc.
- **Coed**

Academics *Degrees:* associate and bachelor's.

Freshman Application Contact Director of Recruitment, ITT Technical Institute, 2450 Rimrock Road, Suite 100, Madison, WI 53713. *Phone:* 608-288-6301. *Toll-free phone:* 877-628-5960.
Website: http://www.itt-tech.edu/.

Lac Courte Oreilles Ojibwa Community College
Hayward, Wisconsin

Freshman Application Contact Ms. Annette Wiggins, Registrar, Lac Courte Oreilles Ojibwa Community College, 13466 West Trepania Road, Hayward, WI 54843-2181. *Phone:* 715-634-4790 Ext. 104. *Toll-free phone:* 888-526-6221.
Website: http://www.lco.edu/.

Lakeshore Technical College
Cleveland, Wisconsin

Freshman Application Contact Lakeshore Technical College, 1290 North Avenue, Cleveland, WI 53015. *Phone:* 920-693-1339. *Toll-free phone:* 888-GO TO LTC. *Fax:* 920-693-3561.
Website: http://www.gotoltc.com/.

Madison Area Technical College
Madison, Wisconsin

Director of Admissions Ms. Maureen Menendez, Interim Admissions Administrator, Madison Area Technical College, 1701 Wright Street, Madison, WI 53704. *Phone:* 608-246-6212. *Toll-free phone:* 800-322-6282.
Website: http://madisoncollege.edu/.

Madison Media Institute
Madison, Wisconsin

Freshman Application Contact Mr. Chris K. Hutchings, President/Director, Madison Media Institute, 2702 Agriculture Drive, Madison, WI 53718. *Phone:* 608-237-8301. *Toll-free phone:* 800-236-4997.
Website: http://www.mediainstitute.edu/.

Mid-State Technical College

Wisconsin Rapids, Wisconsin

Freshman Application Contact Ms. Carole Prochnow, Admissions Assistant, Mid-State Technical College, 500 32nd Street North, Wisconsin Rapids, WI 54494-5599. *Phone:* 715-422-5444.
Website: http://www.mstc.edu/.

Milwaukee Area Technical College

Milwaukee, Wisconsin

Freshman Application Contact Sarah Adams, Director, Enrollment Services, Milwaukee Area Technical College, 700 West State Street, Milwaukee, WI 53233-1443. *Phone:* 414-297-6595. *Fax:* 414-297-7800. *E-mail:* adamss4@ matc.edu.
Website: http://www.matc.edu/.

Moraine Park Technical College

Fond du Lac, Wisconsin

- **District-supported** 2-year, founded 1967, part of Wisconsin Technical College System
- **Small-town** 40-acre campus with easy access to Milwaukee
- **Coed,** 6,074 undergraduate students, 18% full-time, 61% women, 39% men

Undergraduates 1,079 full-time, 4,995 part-time. 1% Black or African American, non-Hispanic/Latino; 2% Hispanic/Latino; 0.8% Asian, non-Hispanic/Latino; 0.6% American Indian or Alaska Native, non-Hispanic/Latino; 0.1% Two or more races, non-Hispanic/Latino; 3% Race/ethnicity unknown.
Freshmen *Admission:* 303 enrolled.
Faculty *Total:* 297, 48% full-time. *Student/faculty ratio:* 14:1.
Majors Accounting; administrative assistant and secretarial science; automobile/automotive mechanics technology; business administration and management; chiropractic assistant; clinical/medical laboratory technology; computer programming related; computer support specialist; computer systems networking and telecommunications; corrections; court reporting; culinary arts; early childhood education; electrical and electronic engineering technologies related; electromechanical technology; emergency medical technology (EMT paramedic); graphic design; health information/medical records technology; heating, ventilation, air conditioning and refrigeration engineering technology; hotel/motel administration; human resources management; legal administrative assistant/secretary; legal assistant/paralegal; machine tool technology; marketing/marketing management; mechanical drafting and CAD/CADD; mechanical engineering technologies related; medical radiologic technology; multi/interdisciplinary studies related; office management; registered nursing/registered nurse; respiratory care therapy; structural engineering; substance abuse/addiction counseling; surgical technology; teacher assistant/aide; water quality and wastewater treatment management and recycling technology.
Academics *Calendar:* semesters. *Degree:* certificates, diplomas, and associate. *Special study options:* academic remediation for entering students, accelerated degree program, adult/continuing education programs, advanced placement credit, distance learning, double majors, English as a second language, external degree program, independent study, internships, part-time degree program, services for LD students, student-designed majors, study abroad, summer session for credit.
Library Moraine Park Technical College Library/Learning Resource Center with 41,021 titles, 185 serial subscriptions, 12,025 audiovisual materials, an OPAC, a Web page.
Student Life *Housing:* college housing not available. *Campus security:* late-night transport/escort service, Safety & Security provided between the hours of 5-10 p.m. when students are on campus and will provide late night transportation/escort. *Student services:* personal/psychological counseling.
Standardized Tests *Required:* ACT, ACCUPLACER OR COMPASS (for admission). *Required for some:* ACT (for admission).
Costs (2013–14) *Tuition:* state resident $3688 full-time, $123 per credit hour part-time; nonresident $5442 full-time, $181 per credit hour part-time. Full-time tuition and fees vary according to program. Part-time tuition and fees vary according to program. *Required fees:* $297 full-time, $10 per credit hour part-time. *Payment plans:* installment, deferred payment. *Waivers:* senior citizens.
Applying *Options:* electronic application, deferred entrance. *Application fee:* $30. *Required:* high school transcript, Placement test required for all; Criminal background ground check required for some. *Required for some:* interview. *Application deadlines:* rolling (freshmen), rolling (out-of-state freshmen), rolling (transfers). *Notification:* continuous (freshmen), continuous (out-of-state freshmen), continuous (transfers).
Freshman Application Contact Ms. Karen Jarvis, Student Services, Moraine Park Technical College, 235 North National Avenue, Fond du Lac, WI 54935. *Phone:* 920-924-3200. *Toll-free phone:* 800-472-4554. *Fax:* 920-924-3421.

E-mail: kjarvis@morainepark.edu.
Website: http://www.morainepark.edu/.

Nicolet Area Technical College

Rhinelander, Wisconsin

Freshman Application Contact Ms. Susan Kordula, Director of Admissions, Nicolet Area Technical College, PO Box 518, Rhinelander, WI 54501. *Phone:* 715-365-4451. *Toll-free phone:* 800-544-3039. *E-mail:* inquire@ nicoletcollege.edu.
Website: http://www.nicoletcollege.edu/.

Northcentral Technical College

Wausau, Wisconsin

Director of Admissions Ms. Carolyn Michalski, Team Leader, Student Services, Northcentral Technical College, 1000 West Campus Drive, Wausau, WI 54401-1899. *Phone:* 715-675-3331 Ext. 4285.
Website: http://www.ntc.edu/.

Northeast Wisconsin Technical College

Green Bay, Wisconsin

Freshman Application Contact Christine Lemerande, Program Enrollment Supervisor, Northeast Wisconsin Technical College, 2740 W Mason Street, PO Box 19042, Green Bay, WI 54307-9042. *Phone:* 920-498-5444. *Toll-free phone:* 888-385-6982. *Fax:* 920-498-6882.
Website: http://www.nwtc.edu/.

Rasmussen College Green Bay

Green Bay, Wisconsin

- **Proprietary** primarily 2-year, part of Rasmussen College System
- **Suburban** campus
- **Coed,** 582 undergraduate students

Faculty *Student/faculty ratio:* 22:1.
Majors Accounting; accounting and business/management; business administration and management; clinical/medical laboratory technology; computer and information systems security; computer science; computer software engineering; corrections and criminal justice related; early childhood education; graphic communications related; health/health-care administration; health information/medical records administration; health information/medical records technology; human resources management; human services; legal assistant/paralegal; management information systems and services related; marketing/marketing management; medical administrative assistant and medical secretary; medical/clinical assistant; pharmacy technician; web page, digital/multimedia and information resources design.
Academics *Degrees:* certificates, diplomas, associate, and bachelor's. *Special study options:* academic remediation for entering students, accelerated degree program, adult/continuing education programs, distance learning, double majors, internships, part-time degree program, summer session for credit.
Library Rasmussen College Library - Green Bay with 2,097 titles, 15 serial subscriptions, 138 audiovisual materials, an OPAC, a Web page.
Student Life *Housing:* college housing not available.
Standardized Tests *Required:* Internal Exam (for admission).
Costs (2013–14) *Tuition:* $12,600 full-time. Full-time tuition and fees vary according to course level, course load, degree level, location, and program. Part-time tuition and fees vary according to course level, course load, degree level, location, and program. *Required fees:* $1800 full-time. *Payment plans:* installment, deferred payment. *Waivers:* employees or children of employees.
Applying *Options:* electronic application, early admission, deferred entrance. *Required:* high school transcript, minimum 2.0 GPA. *Required for some:* interview. *Application deadlines:* rolling (freshmen), rolling (transfers).
Freshman Application Contact Susan Hammerstrom, Director of Admissions, Rasmussen College Green Bay, 940 South Taylor Street, Suite 100, Green Bay, WI 54303. *Phone:* 920-593-8400. *Toll-free phone:* 888-549-6755. *E-mail:* susan.hammerstrom@rasmussen.edu.
Website: http://www.rasmussen.edu/.

Southwest Wisconsin Technical College

Fennimore, Wisconsin

Freshman Application Contact Student Services, Southwest Wisconsin Technical College, 1800 Bronson Boulevard, Fennimore, WI 53809-9778. *Phone:* 608-822-2354. *Toll-free phone:* 800-362-3322. *Fax:* 608-822-6019.

E-mail: student-services@swtc.edu.
Website: http://www.swtc.edu/.

University of Wisconsin–Baraboo/Sauk County

Baraboo, Wisconsin

Freshman Application Contact Ms. Jan Gerlach, Assistant Director of Student Services, University of Wisconsin–Baraboo/Sauk County, Baraboo, WI 53913-1015. *Phone:* 608-355-5270. *E-mail:* booinfo@uwc.edu.
Website: http://www.baraboo.uwc.edu/.

University of Wisconsin–Barron County

Rice Lake, Wisconsin

Freshman Application Contact Assistant Dean for Student Services, University of Wisconsin–Barron County, 1800 College Drive, Rice Lake, WI 54868-2497. *Phone:* 715-234-8024. *Fax:* 715-234-8024.
Website: http://www.barron.uwc.edu/.

University of Wisconsin–Fond du Lac

Fond du Lac, Wisconsin

Freshman Application Contact University of Wisconsin–Fond du Lac, 400 University Drive, Fond du Lac, WI 54935. *Phone:* 920-929-1122.
Website: http://www.fdl.uwc.edu/.

University of Wisconsin–Fox Valley

Menasha, Wisconsin

- **State-supported** 2-year, founded 1933, part of University of Wisconsin System
- **Urban** 33-acre campus
- **Coed,** 1,797 undergraduate students, 58% full-time, 52% women, 48% men

Undergraduates 1,037 full-time, 760 part-time. Students come from 3 states and territories; 4 other countries; 1% are from out of state.
Freshmen *Admission:* 1,166 enrolled. *Average high school GPA:* 2.5.
Faculty *Total:* 91, 34% full-time. *Student/faculty ratio:* 20:1.
Majors Liberal arts and sciences/liberal studies.
Academics *Calendar:* semesters. *Degree:* certificates and associate. *Special study options:* academic remediation for entering students, accelerated degree program, adult/continuing education programs, advanced placement credit, cooperative education, distance learning, honors programs, independent study, internships, off-campus study, part-time degree program, services for LD students, study abroad, summer session for credit.
Library UW Fox Library with 30,000 titles, 230 serial subscriptions, an OPAC, a Web page.
Student Life *Housing:* college housing not available. *Activities and Organizations:* drama/theater group, student-run newspaper, radio and television station, choral group, Business Club, Education Club, Earth Science Club, Computer Science Club, Political Science Club. *Campus security:* 24-hour emergency response devices, late-night transport/escort service. *Student services:* personal/psychological counseling.
Athletics Member NJCAA. *Intercollegiate sports:* basketball M/W, golf M/W, soccer M/W, tennis M/W, volleyball M/W. *Intramural sports:* basketball M/W, volleyball M/W, wrestling M(c).
Standardized Tests *Required:* ACT (for admission).
Costs (2012–13) *Tuition:* state resident $5017 full-time; nonresident $12,001 full-time. Full-time tuition and fees vary according to course load and reciprocity agreements. Part-time tuition and fees vary according to course load and reciprocity agreements. *Required fees:* $172 full-time. *Payment plans:* installment, deferred payment. *Waivers:* minority students and senior citizens.
Applying *Required:* essay or personal statement, high school transcript.
Freshman Application Contact University of Wisconsin–Fox Valley, 1478 Midway Road, Menasha, WI 54952. *Phone:* 920-832-2620.
Website: http://www.uwfox.uwc.edu/.

University of Wisconsin–Manitowoc

Manitowoc, Wisconsin

Freshman Application Contact Dr. Christopher Lewis, Assistant Campus Dean for Student Services, University of Wisconsin–Manitowoc, 705 Viebahn Street, Manitowoc, WI 54220-6699. *Phone:* 920-683-4707. *Fax:* 920-683-4776. *E-mail:* christopher.lewis@uwc.edu.
Website: http://www.manitowoc.uwc.edu/.

University of Wisconsin–Marathon County

Wausau, Wisconsin

Freshman Application Contact Dr. Nolan Beck, Director of Student Services, University of Wisconsin–Marathon County, 518 South Seventh Avenue, Wausau, WI 54401-5396. *Phone:* 715-261-6238. *Toll-free phone:* 888-367-8962. *Fax:* 715-848-3568.
Website: http://www.uwmc.uwc.edu/.

University of Wisconsin–Marinette

Marinette, Wisconsin

Freshman Application Contact Ms. Cynthia M. Bailey, Assistant Campus Dean for Student Services, University of Wisconsin–Marinette, 750 West Bay Shore, Marinette, WI 54143-4299. *Phone:* 715-735-4301. *E-mail:* cynthia.bailey@uwc.edu.
Website: http://www.marinette.uwc.edu/.

University of Wisconsin–Marshfield/Wood County

Marshfield, Wisconsin

Freshman Application Contact Mr. Jeff Meece, Director of Student Services, University of Wisconsin–Marshfield/Wood County, 2000 West 5th Street, Marshfield, WI 54449. *Phone:* 715-389-6500. *Fax:* 715-384-1718.
Website: http://marshfield.uwc.edu/.

University of Wisconsin–Richland

Richland Center, Wisconsin

- **State-supported** 2-year, founded 1967, part of University of Wisconsin System
- **Rural** 135-acre campus
- **Coed,** 519 undergraduate students, 56% full-time, 54% women, 46% men

Undergraduates 291 full-time, 228 part-time. 4% Black or African American, non-Hispanic/Latino; 0.6% Hispanic/Latino; 1% Asian, non-Hispanic/Latino; 0.4% American Indian or Alaska Native, non-Hispanic/Latino; 0.6% Race/ethnicity unknown. *Retention:* 58% of full-time freshmen returned.
Freshmen *Admission:* 519 enrolled.
Faculty *Total:* 31, 42% full-time. *Student/faculty ratio:* 17:1.
Majors Biological and physical sciences; liberal arts and sciences/liberal studies.
Academics *Calendar:* semesters. *Degree:* associate. *Special study options:* academic remediation for entering students, adult/continuing education programs, advanced placement credit, distance learning, external degree program, independent study, off-campus study, part-time degree program, services for LD students, study abroad, summer session for credit.
Library Miller Memorial Library with 40,000 titles, 200 serial subscriptions, an OPAC, a Web page.
Student Life *Housing Options:* coed. Campus housing is provided by a third party. *Activities and Organizations:* drama/theater group, choral group, Student Senate, International Club, Campus Ambassadors, Educators of the Future, Gamers Club. *Student services:* personal/psychological counseling.
Athletics *Intercollegiate sports:* basketball M/W, volleyball W. *Intramural sports:* badminton M/W, basketball M/W, football M/W, golf M/W, racquetball M/W, swimming and diving M/W, table tennis M/W, tennis M/W, volleyball M/W.
Standardized Tests *Required:* SAT or ACT (for admission). *Recommended:* ACT (for admission).
Costs (2012–13) *Tuition:* state resident $5272 full-time, $198 per credit part-time; nonresident $12,255 full-time, $489 per credit part-time. Full-time tuition and fees vary according to reciprocity agreements. Part-time tuition and fees vary according to reciprocity agreements. *Required fees:* $439 full-time. *Room and board:* room only: $3500. Room and board charges vary according to board plan. *Payment plan:* installment. *Waivers:* senior citizens.
Applying *Options:* electronic application. *Application fee:* $44. *Required:* high school transcript. *Required for some:* interview. *Application deadlines:* rolling (freshmen), 9/1 (transfers). *Notification:* continuous until 9/1 (freshmen), continuous until 9/1 (transfers).
Freshman Application Contact Mr. John D. Poole, Assistant Campus Dean, University of Wisconsin–Richland, 1200 Highway 14 West, Richland Center, WI 53581. *Phone:* 608-647-8422. *Fax:* 608-647-2275. *E-mail:* john.poole@uwc.edu.
Website: http://richland.uwc.edu/.

University of Wisconsin–Rock County

Janesville, Wisconsin

Freshman Application Contact University of Wisconsin–Rock County, 2909 Kellogg Avenue, Janesville, WI 53546-5699. *Phone:* 608-758-6523. *Toll-free phone:* 888-INFO-UWC.
Website: http://rock.uwc.edu/.

University of Wisconsin–Sheboygan

Sheboygan, Wisconsin

Freshman Application Contact University of Wisconsin–Sheboygan, One University Drive, Sheboygan, WI 53081-4789. *Phone:* 920-459-6633.
Website: http://www.sheboygan.uwc.edu/.

University of Wisconsin–Washington County

West Bend, Wisconsin

Freshman Application Contact Mr. Dan Cebrario, Associate Director of Student Services, University of Wisconsin–Washington County, Student Services Office, 400 University Drive, West Bend, WI 53095. *Phone:* 262-335-5201. *Fax:* 262-335-5220. *E-mail:* dan.cibrario@uwc.edu.
Website: http://www.washington.uwc.edu/.

University of Wisconsin–Waukesha

Waukesha, Wisconsin

- **State-supported** 2-year, founded 1966, part of University of Wisconsin System
- **Suburban** 86-acre campus with easy access to Milwaukee
- **Coed,** 2,115 undergraduate students, 42% full-time, 46% women, 54% men

Undergraduates 891 full-time, 1,224 part-time. Students come from 6 states and territories; 1 other country; 1% are from out of state; 4% Black or African American, non-Hispanic/Latino; 3% Hispanic/Latino; 2% Asian, non-Hispanic/Latino; 0.2% American Indian or Alaska Native, non-Hispanic/Latino; 0.2% Race/ethnicity unknown; 0.4% international; 8% transferred in.
Freshmen *Admission:* 706 applied, 666 admitted, 1,334 enrolled.
Faculty *Total:* 93, 60% full-time, 87% with terminal degrees. *Student/faculty ratio:* 21:1.
Majors Liberal arts and sciences/liberal studies.
Academics *Calendar:* semesters. *Degree:* associate. *Special study options:* academic remediation for entering students, accelerated degree program, advanced placement credit, distance learning, honors programs, internships, off-campus study, part-time degree program, services for LD students, study abroad, summer session for credit.
Library University of Wisconsin-Waukesha Library plus 1 other with 61,000 titles, 300 serial subscriptions, 5,382 audiovisual materials, a Web page.
Student Life *Housing:* college housing not available. *Activities and Organizations:* drama/theater group, student-run newspaper, choral group, Student Government, Student Activities Committee, Campus Crusade, Phi Theta Kappa, Circle K. *Campus security:* late-night transport/escort service, part-time patrols by trained security personnel. *Student services:* personal/psychological counseling.
Athletics Member NJCAA. *Intercollegiate sports:* basketball M/W, golf M/W, soccer M/W, tennis M/W, volleyball W. *Intramural sports:* basketball M, bowling M/W, cheerleading W, football M/W, skiing (downhill) M/W, table tennis M/W, volleyball M(c).
Standardized Tests *Required:* SAT or ACT (for admission).
Costs (2012–13) *Tuition:* state resident $5088 full-time, $215 per hour part-time; nonresident $12,072 full-time, $506 per hour part-time. Full-time tuition and fees vary according to course load and reciprocity agreements. Part-time tuition and fees vary according to course load and reciprocity agreements. *Required fees:* $394 full-time. *Payment plan:* installment. *Waivers:* senior citizens.
Applying *Options:* electronic application, early admission, deferred entrance. *Application fee:* $44. *Required:* high school transcript. *Required for some:* interview. *Recommended:* essay or personal statement, admission interview may be recommended. *Application deadline:* rolling (freshmen). *Notification:* continuous (freshmen).
Freshman Application Contact Ms. Deb Kusick, Admissions Specialist, University of Wisconsin–Waukesha, 1500 North University Drive, Waukesha, WI 53188-2799. *Phone:* 262-521-5200. *Fax:* 262-521-5530. *E-mail:* deborah.kusick@uwc.edu.
Website: http://www.waukesha.uwc.edu/.

Waukesha County Technical College

Pewaukee, Wisconsin

- **State and locally supported** 2-year, founded 1923, part of Wisconsin Technical College System
- **Suburban** 137-acre campus with easy access to Milwaukee
- **Coed,** 10,286 undergraduate students, 20% full-time, 46% women, 54% men

Undergraduates 2,081 full-time, 8,205 part-time. 8% Black or African American, non-Hispanic/Latino; 7% Hispanic/Latino; 2% Asian, non-Hispanic/Latino; 0.2% Native Hawaiian or other Pacific Islander, non-Hispanic/Latino; 0.8% American Indian or Alaska Native, non-Hispanic/Latino; 1% Two or more races, non-Hispanic/Latino; 0.9% Race/ethnicity unknown.
Freshmen *Admission:* 657 enrolled.
Faculty *Total:* 857, 22% full-time. *Student/faculty ratio:* 20:1.
Majors Accounting; administrative assistant and secretarial science; architectural drafting and CAD/CADD; autobody/collision and repair technology; automobile/automotive mechanics technology; business administration and management; business administration, management and operations related; computer and information sciences and support services related; computer programming; computer support specialist; computer systems networking and telecommunications; criminal justice/police science; dental hygiene; digital arts; early childhood education; electrical, electronic and communications engineering technology; electromechanical and instrumentation and maintenance technologies related; emergency medical technology (EMT paramedic); fire prevention and safety technology; graphic communications; graphic design; health information/medical records technology; hotel, motel, and restaurant management; interior design; international marketing; marketing/marketing management; mechanical drafting and CAD/CADD; medical radiologic technology; mental and social health services and allied professions related; multi/interdisciplinary studies related; operations management; physical therapy technology; real estate; registered nursing/registered nurse; restaurant, culinary, and catering management; surgical technology; teacher assistant/aide.
Academics *Calendar:* semesters. *Degree:* certificates, diplomas, and associate. *Special study options:* academic remediation for entering students, adult/continuing education programs, advanced placement credit, cooperative education, distance learning, English as a second language, part-time degree program, services for LD students, student-designed majors, summer session for credit.
Student Life *Housing:* college housing not available. *Campus security:* patrols by police officers 8 am to 10 pm.
Financial Aid Of all full-time matriculated undergraduates who enrolled in 2011, 40 Federal Work-Study jobs (averaging $2400). 100 state and other part-time jobs (averaging $2000).
Applying *Options:* electronic application. *Application fee:* $30. *Required:* high school transcript. *Required for some:* interview. *Application deadlines:* rolling (freshmen), rolling (transfers).
Freshman Application Contact Waukesha County Technical College, 800 Main Street, Pewaukee, WI 53072-4601. *Phone:* 262-691-5464.
Website: http://www.wctc.edu/.

Western Technical College

La Crosse, Wisconsin

Freshman Application Contact Ms. Jane Wells, Manager of Admissions, Registration, and Records, Western Technical College, PO Box 908, La Crosse, WI 54602-0908. *Phone:* 608-785-9158. *Toll-free phone:* 800-322-9982. *Fax:* 608-785-9094. *E-mail:* mildes@wwtc.edu.
Website: http://www.westerntc.edu/.

Wisconsin Indianhead Technical College

Shell Lake, Wisconsin

- **District-supported** 2-year, founded 1912, part of Wisconsin Technical College System
- **Urban** 118-acre campus
- **Endowment** $2.9 million
- **Coed,** 3,596 undergraduate students, 44% full-time, 62% women, 38% men

Undergraduates 1,577 full-time, 2,019 part-time. Students come from 4 states and territories; 1% are from out of state; 0.9% Black or African American, non-Hispanic/Latino; 0.5% Hispanic/Latino; 0.4% Asian, non-Hispanic/Latino; 2% American Indian or Alaska Native, non-Hispanic/Latino; 1% Two or more races, non-Hispanic/Latino; 1% Race/ethnicity unknown. *Retention:* 70% of full-time freshmen returned.
Freshmen *Admission:* 581 enrolled.

Faculty *Total:* 740, 23% full-time. *Student/faculty ratio:* 10:1.

Majors Accounting; administrative assistant and secretarial science; architectural engineering technology; business administration and management; childcare and support services management; computer and information sciences; computer installation and repair technology; computer support specialist; computer systems networking and telecommunications; corrections and criminal justice related; court reporting; criminal justice/police science; early childhood education; emergency medical technology (EMT paramedic); energy management and systems technology; finance; mental and social health services and allied professions related; multi/interdisciplinary studies related; occupational therapist assistant; operations management; web page, digital/multimedia and information resources design.

Academics *Calendar:* semesters. *Degree:* certificates, diplomas, and associate.

Student Life *Housing:* college housing not available. *Student services:* health clinic.

Costs (2013–14) *Tuition:* state resident $3808 full-time, $127 per credit part-time; nonresident $5610 full-time, $187 per credit part-time. Full-time tuition and fees vary according to course load, location, program, and reciprocity agreements. Part-time tuition and fees vary according to course load, location, program, and reciprocity agreements. *Required fees:* $127 per credit part-time. *Room and board:* Room and board charges vary according to housing facility. *Payment plan:* installment.

Applying *Options:* electronic application. *Application fee:* $30. *Application deadline:* rolling (freshmen).

Freshman Application Contact Mr. Steve Bitzer, Vice President, Student Affairs and Campus Administrator, Wisconsin Indianhead Technical College, 2100 Beaser Avenue, Ashland, WI 54806. *Phone:* 715-468-2815 Ext. 3149. *Toll-free phone:* 800-243-9482. *Fax:* 715-468-2819. *E-mail:* Steve.Bitzer@witc.edu.
Website: http://www.witc.edu/.

WYOMING

Casper College
Casper, Wyoming

- **State and locally supported** 2-year, founded 1945
- **Small-town** 200-acre campus
- **Coed,** 4,207 undergraduate students, 46% full-time, 57% women, 43% men

Undergraduates 1,935 full-time, 2,272 part-time. Students come from 37 states and territories; 17 other countries; 10% are from out of state; 2% Black or African American, non-Hispanic/Latino; 5% Hispanic/Latino; 0.6% Asian, non-Hispanic/Latino; 0.3% Native Hawaiian or other Pacific Islander, non-Hispanic/Latino; 0.6% American Indian or Alaska Native, non-Hispanic/Latino; 0.6% Two or more races, non-Hispanic/Latino; 3% Race/ethnicity unknown; 0.9% international; 5% transferred in; 10% live on campus. *Retention:* 61% of full-time freshmen returned.

Freshmen *Admission:* 945 applied, 945 admitted, 712 enrolled. *Average high school GPA:* 3.1. *Test scores:* ACT scores over 18: 75%; ACT scores over 24: 25%; ACT scores over 30: 1%.

Faculty *Total:* 260, 57% full-time, 22% with terminal degrees. *Student/faculty ratio:* 15:1.

Majors Accounting; accounting technology and bookkeeping; acting; administrative assistant and secretarial science; agricultural business and management; agriculture; airline pilot and flight crew; animal sciences; anthropology; art; art teacher education; athletic training; autobody/collision and repair technology; automobile/automotive mechanics technology; biology/biological sciences; business administration and management; business automation/technology/data entry; chemistry; clinical laboratory science/medical technology; computer and information systems security; computer programming; construction management; construction trades; criminal justice/law enforcement administration; crisis/emergency/disaster management; dance; diesel mechanics technology; drafting and design technology; economics; electrical, electronic and communications engineering technology; elementary education; emergency medical technology (EMT paramedic); energy management and systems technology; engineering; English; entrepreneurship; environmental science; fine/studio arts; fire science/firefighting; foreign languages and literatures; forensic science and technology; general studies; geographic information science and cartography; geology/earth science; graphic design; health services/allied health/health sciences; history; hospitality administration; industrial mechanics and maintenance technology; international relations and affairs; journalism; kindergarten/preschool education; legal assistant/paralegal; liberal arts and sciences/liberal studies; machine tool technology; manufacturing engineering technology; marketing/marketing management; mass communication/media; mathematics; mining technology; museum studies;

music; musical theater; music performance; music teacher education; nutrition sciences; occupational therapist assistant; pharmacy technician; photography; physical education teaching and coaching; physics; political science and government; pre-dentistry studies; pre-law studies; premedical studies; pre-occupational therapy; pre-optometry; pre-pharmacy studies; pre-physical therapy; pre-veterinary studies; psychology; radiologic technology/science; range science and management; registered nursing/registered nurse; respiratory care therapy; retailing; robotics technology; social studies teacher education; social work; sociology; speech communication and rhetoric; statistics related; substance abuse/addiction counseling; technology/industrial arts teacher education; theater design and technology; water quality and wastewater treatment management and recycling technology; web/multimedia management and webmaster; web page, digital/multimedia and information resources design; welding technology; wildlife, fish and wildlands science and management; women's studies.

Academics *Calendar:* semesters. *Degree:* certificates and associate. *Special study options:* academic remediation for entering students, accelerated degree program, advanced placement credit, cooperative education, distance learning, English as a second language, honors programs, independent study, internships, off-campus study, part-time degree program, services for LD students, summer session for credit.

Library Goodstein Foundation Library with 128,000 titles, 385 serial subscriptions, an OPAC, a Web page.

Student Life *Housing Options:* coed. Campus housing is university owned. *Activities and Organizations:* drama/theater group, student-run newspaper, choral group, Student Senate, Student Activities Board, Agriculture Club, Theater Club, Phi Theta Kappa. *Campus security:* 24-hour patrols, late-night transport/escort service. *Student services:* health clinic, personal/psychological counseling.

Athletics Member NJCAA. *Intercollegiate sports:* basketball M(s)/W(s), equestrian sports M/W, volleyball W(s). *Intramural sports:* basketball M/W, bowling M/W, football M/W, golf M/W, racquetball M/W, soccer M/W, softball M/W, tennis M/W.

Costs (2012–13) *Tuition:* state resident $1800 full-time, $75 per credit hour part-time; nonresident $5400 full-time, $225 per credit hour part-time. *Required fees:* $432 full-time, $18 per credit hour part-time. *Room and board:* $5530. Room and board charges vary according to board plan and housing facility. *Payment plan:* deferred payment. *Waivers:* senior citizens and employees or children of employees.

Financial Aid Of all full-time matriculated undergraduates who enrolled in 2011, 80 Federal Work-Study jobs (averaging $2000).

Applying *Options:* electronic application, early admission. *Required:* high school transcript. *Application deadlines:* 8/15 (freshmen), 8/15 (transfers). *Notification:* continuous until 8/15 (freshmen), continuous until 8/15 (transfers).

Freshman Application Contact Mrs. Kyla Foltz, Director of Admissions Services, Casper College, 125 College Drive, Casper, WY 82601. *Phone:* 307-268-2111. *Toll-free phone:* 800-442-2963. *Fax:* 307-268-2611. *E-mail:* kfoltz@caspercollege.edu.
Website: http://www.caspercollege.edu/.

Central Wyoming College
Riverton, Wyoming

- **State and locally supported** 2-year, founded 1966, part of Wyoming Community College Commission
- **Small-town** 200-acre campus
- **Endowment** $13.8 million
- **Coed,** 2,164 undergraduate students, 39% full-time, 58% women, 42% men

Undergraduates 838 full-time, 1,326 part-time. Students come from 45 states and territories; 7 other countries; 14% are from out of state; 1% Black or African American, non-Hispanic/Latino; 7% Hispanic/Latino; 0.7% Asian, non-Hispanic/Latino; 0.3% Native Hawaiian or other Pacific Islander, non-Hispanic/Latino; 11% American Indian or Alaska Native, non-Hispanic/Latino; 3% Two or more races, non-Hispanic/Latino; 2% Race/ethnicity unknown; 0.4% international; 5% transferred in; 8% live on campus. *Retention:* 52% of full-time freshmen returned.

Freshmen *Admission:* 478 applied, 478 admitted, 266 enrolled. *Average high school GPA:* 2.99. *Test scores:* SAT critical reading scores over 500: 33%; SAT math scores over 500: 17%; ACT scores over 18: 69%; ACT scores over 24: 20%; ACT scores over 30: 2%.

Faculty *Total:* 152, 32% full-time, 46% with terminal degrees. *Student/faculty ratio:* 16:1.

Majors Accounting; accounting technology and bookkeeping; acting; administrative assistant and secretarial science; agricultural and domestic animal services related; agricultural business and management; American Indian/Native American studies; area studies related; art; athletic training; automobile/automotive mechanics technology; biology/biological sciences; business administration and management; business automation/technology/data entry;

business/commerce; carpentry; child-care and support services management; commercial photography; computer science; computer technology/computer systems technology; criminal justice/law enforcement administration; culinary arts; customer service support/call center/teleservice operation; dental assisting; dramatic/theater arts; early childhood education; elementary education; emergency medical technology (EMT paramedic); engineering; English; environmental/environmental health engineering; environmental science; equestrian studies; fire science/firefighting; general studies; geology/earth science; graphic design; health services/allied health/health sciences; homeland security, law enforcement, firefighting and protective services related; hotel/motel administration; international/global studies; manufacturing engineering; mathematics; medical office assistant; music; occupational safety and health technology; office occupations and clerical services; parks, recreation and leisure; parks, recreation and leisure facilities management; physical sciences; pre-law studies; psychology; radio and television; range science and management; registered nursing/registered nurse; rehabilitation and therapeutic professions related; secondary education; selling skills and sales; social sciences; teacher assistant/aide; theater design and technology; welding technology.

Academics *Calendar:* semesters. *Degree:* certificates, diplomas, and associate. *Special study options:* academic remediation for entering students, adult/continuing education programs, advanced placement credit, cooperative education, distance learning, double majors, English as a second language, honors programs, independent study, off-campus study, part-time degree program, services for LD students, summer session for credit.

Library Central Wyoming College Library with 54,974 titles, 2,940 serial subscriptions, 1,450 audiovisual materials, an OPAC, a Web page.

Student Life *Housing Options:* coed. Campus housing is university owned. *Activities and Organizations:* drama/theater group, student-run radio and television station, choral group, Multi-Cultural Club, La Vida Nueva Club, Fellowship of College Christians, Quality Leaders, Science Club. *Campus security:* 24-hour emergency response devices, late-night transport/escort service, controlled dormitory access. *Student services:* personal/psychological counseling.

Athletics Member NJCAA. *Intercollegiate sports:* basketball M(s)/W(s), equestrian sports M(s)/W(s), volleyball W(s). *Intramural sports:* badminton M/W, basketball M/W, football M/W, rock climbing M/W, skiing (cross-country) M/W, skiing (downhill) M/W, soccer M/W, softball M/W, swimming and diving M/W, table tennis M/W, tennis M/W, ultimate Frisbee M/W, volleyball M/W, weight lifting M/W.

Costs (2013–14) *Tuition:* state resident $1896 full-time, $79 per credit part-time; nonresident $5688 full-time, $237 per credit part-time. Full-time tuition and fees vary according to course load, program, and reciprocity agreements. Part-time tuition and fees vary according to course load, program, and reciprocity agreements. *Required fees:* $672 full-time, $28 per credit part-time. *Room and board:* $4607; room only: $2297. Room and board charges vary according to board plan and housing facility. *Payment plans:* installment, deferred payment. *Waivers:* senior citizens and employees or children of employees.

Financial Aid Of all full-time matriculated undergraduates who enrolled in 2011, 550 applied for aid, 465 were judged to have need. 40 Federal Work-Study jobs (averaging $2291). *Financial aid deadline:* 6/30.

Applying *Options:* electronic application, early admission, deferred entrance. *Recommended:* high school transcript. *Application deadlines:* rolling (freshmen), rolling (out-of-state freshmen), rolling (transfers).

Freshman Application Contact Mrs. Mikal Dalley, Admissions Assistant, Central Wyoming College, 2660 Peck Avenue, Riverton, WY 82501-2273. *Phone:* 307-855-2061. *Toll-free phone:* 800-735-8418. *Fax:* 307-855-2065. *E-mail:* admit@cwc.edu. *Website:* http://www.cwc.edu/.

Eastern Wyoming College

Torrington, Wyoming

Freshman Application Contact Dr. Rex Cogdill, Vice President for Students Services, Eastern Wyoming College, 3200 West C Street, Torrington, WY 82240. *Phone:* 307-532-8257. *Toll-free phone:* 866-327-8996. *Fax:* 307-532-8222. *E-mail:* rex.cogdill@ewc.wy.edu. *Website:* http://www.ewc.wy.edu/.

Laramie County Community College

Cheyenne, Wyoming

- **District-supported** 2-year, founded 1968, part of Wyoming Community College Commission
- **Small-town** 271-acre campus
- **Endowment** $15.6 million
- **Coed,** 5,115 undergraduate students, 41% full-time, 57% women, 43% men

Undergraduates 2,088 full-time, 3,027 part-time. Students come from 40 states and territories; 7 other countries; 12% are from out of state; 3% Black or African American, non-Hispanic/Latino; 10% Hispanic/Latino; 0.7% Asian, non-Hispanic/Latino; 0.3% Native Hawaiian or other Pacific Islander, non-Hispanic/Latino; 1% American Indian or Alaska Native, non-Hispanic/Latino; 0.4% Two or more races, non-Hispanic/Latino; 3% Race/ethnicity unknown; 1% international; 5% transferred in; 4% live on campus. *Retention:* 58% of full-time freshmen returned.

Freshmen *Admission:* 1,582 applied, 1,582 admitted, 401 enrolled. *Average high school GPA:* 3.08. *Test scores:* ACT scores over 18: 68%; ACT scores over 24: 16%; ACT scores over 30: 1%.

Faculty *Total:* 359, 32% full-time, 8% with terminal degrees. *Student/faculty ratio:* 16:1.

Majors Accounting; agribusiness; agricultural business technology; agricultural production; agriculture; anthropology; art; autobody/collision and repair technology; automobile/automotive mechanics technology; biological and physical sciences; biology/biological sciences; business administration and management; business/commerce; chemistry; computer programming; computer science; corrections; criminal justice/law enforcement administration; dental hygiene; diagnostic medical sonography and ultrasound technology; diesel mechanics technology; digital communication and media/multimedia; drafting and design technology; early childhood education; economics; education; emergency medical technology (EMT paramedic); energy management and systems technology; engineering; English; entrepreneurship; equestrian studies; fire science/firefighting; general studies; heating, air conditioning, ventilation and refrigeration maintenance technology; history; homeland security, law enforcement, firefighting and protective services related; humanities; human services; kinesiology and exercise science; legal assistant/paralegal; mass communication/media; mathematics; mechanic and repair technologies related; medical insurance coding; music; physical education teaching and coaching; physical therapy technology; political science and government; pre-law studies; pre-pharmacy studies; psychology; public administration; radiologic technology/science; registered nursing/registered nurse; religious studies; social sciences; sociology; Spanish; speech communication and rhetoric; surgical technology; wildlife, fish and wildlands science and management.

Academics *Calendar:* semesters. *Degree:* certificates and associate. *Special study options:* academic remediation for entering students, adult/continuing education programs, advanced placement credit, cooperative education, distance learning, double majors, English as a second language, honors programs, independent study, internships, off-campus study, part-time degree program, services for LD students, summer session for credit. *ROTC:* Army (c), Air Force (c).

Library Ludden Library plus 1 other with 56,351 titles, 188 serial subscriptions, 5,594 audiovisual materials, an OPAC, a Web page.

Student Life *Housing Options:* coed. Campus housing is university owned. *Activities and Organizations:* drama/theater group, student-run newspaper, choral group. *Campus security:* 24-hour emergency response devices and patrols, late-night transport/escort service, controlled dormitory access. *Student services:* personal/psychological counseling.

Athletics Member NJCAA. *Intercollegiate sports:* basketball M(s), cheerleading M(s)/W(s), equestrian sports M(s)/W(s), soccer M(s)/W(s), volleyball W(s). *Intramural sports:* basketball M/W, equestrian sports M/W, racquetball M/W, rock climbing M/W, skiing (cross-country) M/W, soccer M/W, softball M/W, table tennis M/W, ultimate Frisbee M/W, volleyball M/W.

Costs (2013–14) *Tuition:* state resident $1896 full-time, $79 per credit part-time; nonresident $5688 full-time, $237 per credit part-time. Part-time tuition and fees vary according to course load. *Required fees:* $840 full-time. *Room and board:* $7594; room only: $4648. Room and board charges vary according to housing facility. *Payment plan:* installment. *Waivers:* senior citizens and employees or children of employees.

Applying *Options:* electronic application, deferred entrance. *Required for some:* high school transcript, interview. *Application deadlines:* rolling (freshmen), rolling (out-of-state freshmen), rolling (transfers). *Notification:* continuous (freshmen), continuous (out-of-state freshmen), continuous (transfers).

Freshman Application Contact Ms. Holly Bruegman, Director of Admissions, Laramie County Community College, 1400 East College Drive, Cheyenne, WY 82007. *Phone:* 307-778-1117. *Toll-free phone:* 800-522-2993 Ext. 1357. *Fax:* 307-778-1360. *E-mail:* learnmore@lccc.wy.edu. *Website:* http://www.lccc.wy.edu/.

Northwest College
Powell, Wyoming

- **State and locally supported** 2-year, founded 1946, part of Wyoming Community College System
- **Rural** 124-acre campus
- **Endowment** $8.3 million
- **Coed,** 2,047 undergraduate students, 59% full-time, 60% women, 40% men

Undergraduates 1,201 full-time, 846 part-time. Students come from 38 states and territories; 28 other countries; 21% are from out of state; 0.8% Black or African American, non-Hispanic/Latino; 7% Hispanic/Latino; 0.6% Asian, non-Hispanic/Latino; 0.2% Native Hawaiian or other Pacific Islander, non-Hispanic/Latino; 2% American Indian or Alaska Native, non-Hispanic/Latino; 3% Two or more races, non-Hispanic/Latino; 3% international. *Retention:* 59% of full-time freshmen returned.

Freshmen *Admission:* 452 enrolled.

Faculty *Total:* 194, 41% full-time. *Student/faculty ratio:* 13:1.

Majors Accounting; administrative assistant and secretarial science; aeronautics/aviation/aerospace science and technology; agribusiness; agricultural communication/journalism; agricultural production; agricultural teacher education; animal sciences; anthropology; archeology; art; athletic training; biology/biological sciences; broadcast journalism; business administration and management; business/commerce; CAD/CADD drafting/design technology; chemistry; cinematography and film/video production; commercial and advertising art; commercial photography; criminal justice/law enforcement administration; crop production; desktop publishing and digital imaging design; electrician; elementary education; engineering; English; equestrian studies; farm and ranch management; French; general studies; graphic and printing equipment operation/production; health and physical education/fitness; health/medical preparatory programs related; health services/allied health/health sciences; history; international relations and affairs; journalism; kindergarten/preschool education; liberal arts and sciences/liberal studies; mathematics; music; natural resources management and policy; parks, recreation and leisure; physics; playwriting and screenwriting; political science and government; pre-pharmacy studies; psychology; radio and television; radio, television, and digital communication related; range science and management; registered nursing/registered nurse; secondary education; social sciences; sociology; Spanish; speech communication and rhetoric; veterinary/animal health technology; visual and performing arts related; welding technology.

Academics *Calendar:* semesters. *Degree:* certificates and associate. *Special study options:* academic remediation for entering students, adult/continuing education programs, advanced placement credit, cooperative education, distance learning, double majors, English as a second language, external degree program, independent study, internships, off-campus study, part-time degree program, services for LD students, study abroad, summer session for credit.

Library John Taggart Hinckley Library with 47,375 titles, 59,654 serial subscriptions, 28,531 audiovisual materials, an OPAC, a Web page.

Student Life *Housing:* on-campus residence required for freshman year. *Options:* coed, women-only, disabled students. Campus housing is university owned. Freshman campus housing is guaranteed. *Activities and Organizations:* drama/theater group, student-run newspaper, radio and television station, choral group. *Campus security:* 24-hour emergency response devices and patrols, late-night transport/escort service, controlled dormitory access. *Student services:* health clinic, personal/psychological counseling.

Athletics Member NJCAA. *Intercollegiate sports:* basketball M(s)/W(s), equestrian sports M(s)/W(s), soccer M(s)/W(s), volleyball W(s), wrestling M(s). *Intramural sports:* basketball M/W, football M/W, golf M/W, softball M/W, tennis M/W, ultimate Frisbee M/W, volleyball M/W.

Standardized Tests *Recommended:* SAT or ACT (for admission), ACT COMPASS.

Costs (2012–13) *Tuition:* state resident $1800 full-time, $75 per credit hour part-time; nonresident $5400 full-time, $225 per credit hour part-time. Full-time tuition and fees vary according to course load, location, and program. Part-time tuition and fees vary according to course load, location, and program. *Required fees:* $637 full-time, $21 per credit hour part-time. *Room and board:* $4650; room only: $2070. Room and board charges vary according to board plan and housing facility. *Payment plan:* installment. *Waivers:* children of alumni, senior citizens, and employees or children of employees.

Financial Aid Of all full-time matriculated undergraduates who enrolled in 2011, 115 Federal Work-Study jobs (averaging $2700). 215 state and other part-time jobs (averaging $2700).

Applying *Options:* electronic application. *Required:* high school transcript. *Required for some:* minimum 2.0 GPA. *Recommended:* minimum 2.0 GPA. *Application deadlines:* rolling (freshmen), rolling (out-of-state freshmen), rolling (transfers). *Notification:* continuous (freshmen), continuous (out-of-state freshmen), continuous (transfers).

Freshman Application Contact Mr. West Hernandez, Admissions Manager, Northwest College, 231 West 6th Street, Orendorff Building 1, Powell, WY 82435-1898. *Phone:* 307-754-6103. *Toll-free phone:* 800-560-4692. *Fax:* 307-754-6249. *E-mail:* west.hernandez@northwestcollege.edu. *Website:* http://www.northwestcollege.edu/.

Sheridan College
Sheridan, Wyoming

- **State and locally supported** 2-year, founded 1948, part of Wyoming Community College Commission
- **Small-town** 124-acre campus
- **Endowment** $22.6 million
- **Coed,** 4,236 undergraduate students, 35% full-time, 49% women, 51% men

Undergraduates 1,463 full-time, 2,773 part-time. Students come from 41 states and territories; 7 other countries; 22% are from out of state; 1% Black or African American, non-Hispanic/Latino; 6% Hispanic/Latino; 0.7% Asian, non-Hispanic/Latino; 0.1% Native Hawaiian or other Pacific Islander, non-Hispanic/Latino; 1% American Indian or Alaska Native, non-Hispanic/Latino; 2% Two or more races, non-Hispanic/Latino; 0.5% international; 2% transferred in; 11% live on campus.

Freshmen *Admission:* 584 enrolled.

Faculty *Total:* 197, 51% full-time, 14% with terminal degrees. *Student/faculty ratio:* 18:1.

Majors Administrative assistant and secretarial science; agricultural business and management; agriculture; agriculture and agriculture operations related; art; biological and physical sciences; biology/biological sciences; building construction technology; business/commerce; CAD/CADD drafting/design technology; computer and information sciences; computer and information systems security; criminal justice/safety; culinary arts; dental hygiene; diesel mechanics technology; dramatic/theater arts; early childhood education; electrical and electronic engineering technologies related; elementary education; engineering; English; environmental engineering technology; foreign languages and literatures; general studies; health and physical education/fitness; health services/allied health/health sciences; history; horticultural science; hospitality administration; information science/studies; kinesiology and exercise science; machine tool technology; massage therapy; mathematics; mining technology; multi/interdisciplinary studies related; music; precision production related; psychology; range science and management; registered nursing/registered nurse; secondary education; social sciences; surveying technology; teacher assistant/aide; turf and turfgrass management; web/multimedia management and webmaster; welding technology.

Academics *Calendar:* semesters. *Degree:* certificates and associate. *Special study options:* academic remediation for entering students, accelerated degree program, advanced placement credit, cooperative education, distance learning, double majors, English as a second language, independent study, internships, off-campus study, part-time degree program, services for LD students, summer session for credit.

Library Griffith Memorial Library plus 1 other with 47,882 titles, 98 serial subscriptions, 4,816 audiovisual materials, an OPAC, a Web page.

Student Life *Housing Options:* coed. Campus housing is university owned and leased by the school. *Activities and Organizations:* drama/theater group, student-run television station, choral group, National Society of Leadership and Success, Student Senate, Baptist Collegiate Ministries, Nursing Club, Dental Hygiene Club. *Campus security:* 24-hour emergency response devices, student patrols, controlled dormitory access, night patrols by certified officers. *Student services:* personal/psychological counseling.

Athletics Member NJCAA. *Intercollegiate sports:* basketball M(s)/W(s), cross-country running M(s)/W(s), equestrian sports M(s)/W(s), volleyball W(s). *Intramural sports:* basketball M/W, bowling M/W, football M/W, softball M/W, table tennis M/W, tennis M/W, ultimate Frisbee M/W, volleyball M/W.

Costs (2013–14) *Tuition:* state resident $2678 full-time, $79 per credit part-time; nonresident $6470 full-time, $237 per credit part-time. Full-time tuition and fees vary according to course load and location. Part-time tuition and fees vary according to location. *Required fees:* $896 full-time, $28 per hour part-time. *Room and board:* $6050. Room and board charges vary according to board plan, housing facility, and location. *Payment plans:* installment, deferred payment. *Waivers:* senior citizens and employees or children of employees.

Financial Aid Of all full-time matriculated undergraduates who enrolled in 2011, 92 Federal Work-Study jobs (averaging $1798).

Applying *Options:* electronic application, early admission, deferred entrance. *Required for some:* high school transcript. *Recommended:* high school transcript. *Application deadlines:* rolling (freshmen), rolling (out-of-state freshmen), rolling (transfers). *Notification:* continuous (freshmen), continuous (out-of-state freshmen), continuous (transfers).

Freshman Application Contact Mr. Matt Adams, Admissions Coordinator, Sheridan College, PO Box 1500, Sheridan, WY 82801-1500. *Phone:* 307-674-6446 Ext. 2005. *Toll-free phone:* 800-913-9139 Ext. 2002. *Fax:* 307-674-3373. *E-mail:* madams@sheridan.edu. *Website:* http://www.sheridan.edu/.

Western Wyoming Community College

Rock Springs, Wyoming

Freshman Application Contact Director of Admissions, Western Wyoming Community College, PO Box 428, Rock Springs, WY 82902-0428. *Phone:* 307-382-1647. *Toll-free phone:* 800-226-1181. *Fax:* 307-382-1636. *E-mail:* admissions@wwcc.wy.edu. *Website:* http://www.wwcc.wy.edu/.

WyoTech Laramie

Laramie, Wyoming

Director of Admissions Director of Admissions, WyoTech Laramie, 4373 North Third Street, Laramie, WY 82072-9519. *Phone:* 307-742-3776. *Toll-free phone:* 888-577-7559. *Fax:* 307-721-4854. *Website:* http://www.wyotech.edu/.

CANADA

Southern Alberta Institute of Technology

Calgary, Alberta, Canada

Freshman Application Contact Southern Alberta Institute of Technology, 1301 16th Avenue NW, Calgary, AB T2M 0L4, Canada. *Phone:* 403-284-8857. *Toll-free phone:* 877-284-SAIT. *Website:* http://www.sait.ca/.

INTERNATIONAL

MEXICO

Westhill University

Sante Fe, Mexico

Freshman Application Contact Admissions, Westhill University, 56 Domingo Garcia Ramos, Zona Escolar, Prados de la Montana I, 05610 Sante Fe, Cuajimalpa, Mexico. *Phone:* 52-55 5292-1121. *Toll-free phone:* 877-403-4535. *E-mail:* admissions@westhill.edu.mx. *Website:* http://www.westhill.edu.mx/.

PALAU

Palau Community College

Koror, Palau

- **Territory-supported** 2-year, founded 1969
- **Small-town** 30-acre campus
- **Endowment** $1.3 million
- **Coed**

Undergraduates 463 full-time, 231 part-time. 2% transferred in; 20% live on campus.

Faculty *Student/faculty ratio:* 16:1.

Academics *Calendar:* semesters. *Degree:* certificates and associate. *Special study options:* academic remediation for entering students, adult/continuing education programs, cooperative education, distance learning, double majors, English as a second language, internships, part-time degree program, summer session for credit.

Student Life *Campus security:* 24-hour emergency response devices and patrols, late-night transport/escort service, evening patrols by trained security personnel.

Costs (2012–13) *Tuition:* state resident $2640 full-time, $110 per credit hour part-time; nonresident $3000 full-time, $125 per credit hour part-time. Full-time tuition and fees vary according to course load. Part-time tuition and fees vary according to course load. *Required fees:* $610 full-time, $610 per term part-time. *Room and board:* $3381; room only: $1176.

Financial Aid *Financial aid deadline:* 6/30.

Applying *Options:* early admission, deferred entrance. *Application fee:* $10. *Required:* high school transcript, minimum 2.0 GPA.

Freshman Application Contact Ms. Dahlia Katosang, Director of Admissions and Financial Aid, Palau Community College, PO Box 9, Koror, PW 96940-0009. *Phone:* 680-488-2471 Ext. 233. *Fax:* 680-488-4468. *E-mail:* dahliapcc@palaunet.com. *Website:* http://www.palau.edu/.

College
Close-Ups

THE ART INSTITUTE OF NEW YORK CITY
NEW YORK, NEW YORK

The Art Institute of New York City is one of The Art Institutes, a system of over fifty schools throughout North America dedicated to providing hands-on education in the creative and applied arts. The Art Institute of New York City offers associate degree programs for students interested in pursuing career opportunities from among tomorrow's 10 million jobs in creative fields like design, fashion, and media arts (based on information from the U.S. Bureau of Labor Statistics for job growth between 2012 and 2022).

A focused education from The Art Institute of New York City can help students turn their creative energy into a powerful tool that can make a difference in the world. Students are part of a collaborative and supportive community, where experienced instructors provide the guidance and skills needed to pursue a career in the creative economy.

The Art Institute of New York City is also an important resource for creative industry leaders who value the opportunity provided students to learn by using professional-grade technology to build a portfolio of work to show potential employers after graduation.

Accreditation

The Art Institute of New York City is accredited by the Accrediting Council for Independent Colleges and Schools to award associate degrees. The Accrediting Council for Independent Colleges and Schools is listed as a nationally recognized accrediting agency by the United States Department of Education and is recognized by the Council for Higher Education Accreditation. ACICS can be contacted at 750 First Street NE, Suite 980, Washington, D.C. 20002; telephone: 202-336-6780.

The Art Institute of New York City has received permission to operate from the State of New York Board of Regents State Education Department, 89 Washington Avenue, 5 North Mezzanine, Albany, New York 12234; phone: 518-474-2593.

Academic Programs

Creativity is all around, and with millions of tomorrow's jobs in creative fields, the world needs more creative professionals. No matter which course of study a student chooses, the instructors at The Art Institutes will guide, support, and help students fine-tune their visual thinking and problem solving, so that they can take advantage of the world's growing creative opportunities and put their passion to work. Programs are offered in the areas of design, which focuses on communicating conceptually and helping people connect in living and work spaces; media arts, that centers on utilizing technology to deliver information and entertainment; and fashion, where students learn anything from designing clothes for the runway to running a retail shop.

Associate degree programs are offered in the areas of fashion design, graphic design, and web design and interactive media.

Program availability and degree offerings are subject to change.

Costs

Actual tuition and housing costs will vary depending on program, number of credits enrolled, and living arrangements. Prospective students should contact a Student Financial Services professional at the school for details.

Financial Aid

Financial aid is available for those who qualify. Students who require financial assistance should first complete and submit the Free Application for Federal Student Aid (FAFSA) online at www.fafsa.ed.gov and meet with a financial aid officer. Students may also apply for a number of scholarships focusing on their specific areas of career interest.

Faculty

Faculty members are hands-on creative professionals with proven experience as business leaders and innovators, hosting a learning environment similar to the career world students will face after graduation. Part instructor, part mentor, their mission is to help develop and transform creative potential into high-demand marketable skills.

Student Body Profile

Students come to The Art Institute of New York City from throughout the United States and abroad. The student population includes recent high school graduates, transfer students, and those who have left a previous employment situation to study and train for a new career. Students are creative, competitive, and open to new ideas. They place great value on an education that prepares them for an exciting entry-level position in the arts.

Student Activities

The Art Institute of New York City offers a wide range of professionally related curricular activities in which students can voluntarily participate. Some of these activities are: participation in local charity events, fund-raising events to provide meals and food to the needy, junior membership in faculty-represented organizations, and gallery art and design exhibitions and fashion shows.

Student Support Services provides assistance such as wellness workshops, assistance with study habits and time management, and counseling.

Facilities and Resources

The Art Institute of New York City provides a learning environment with professional-grade technology applicable to each student's course of study. Students have the opportunity to build a portfolio of work that shows potential employers that they are trained to use the software, hardware, or equipment utilized within the industry. Depending upon the course of study, students are immersed in a creative environment—from classrooms to computer labs to studios—focused on relevant, hands-on education designed to prepare them for the real world.

Location

The Art Institute of New York City is located in the SoHo/Tribeca district of New York City. SoHo/Tribeca is recognized as New York's center of contemporary art and creativity. West Broadway, the district's main thoroughfare, is lined with avant-garde boutiques and trend-setting galleries. Lower Manhattan's dining attractions are a culinary melting pot—from health foods to hot dogs, sushi to pastry, salad bars, coffee bars and international bistros—it's all here.

New York City provides a wealth of opportunities for students to explore their creative side, such as Broadway plays, art museums, music halls, and professional sports events.

Admission Requirements

Prospective students should refer to the current academic catalog for full details regarding admission requirements and process.

Application and Information

To obtain an application or make arrangements for an interview or tour of the school, prospective students should contact:

The Art Institute of New York City
11 Beach Street
New York, New York 10013
United States
Phone: 212-226-5500
          800-654-2433 (toll-free)
Fax: 212-966-0706
Website: http://www.artinstitutes.edu/newyork

THE ART INSTITUTE OF SEATTLE
SEATTLE, WASHINGTON

The Art Institute of Seattle is one of The Art Institutes, a system of over fifty schools throughout North America dedicated to providing hands-on education in the creative and applied arts. The Art Institute of Seattle offers bachelor's and associate degree programs as well as non-degree programs for students interested in pursuing career opportunities from among tomorrow's 15 million jobs in creative fields like design, fashion, media arts, and culinary (based on information from the U.S. Bureau of Labor Statistics for job growth between 2012 and 2022).

A focused education from The Art Institute of Seattle can help students turn their creative energy into a powerful tool that can make a difference in the world. Students are part of a collaborative and supportive community, where experienced instructors provide the guidance and skills needed to pursue a career in the creative economy.

The Art Institute of Seattle is also an important resource for creative industry leaders who value the opportunity provided students to learn by using professional-grade technology to build a portfolio of work to show potential employers after graduation.

Accreditation

The Art Institute of Seattle is accredited by the Northwest Commission on Colleges and Universities. Accreditation of an institution of higher education by the Northwest Commission on Colleges and Universities indicates that it meets or exceeds criteria for the assessment of institutional quality evaluated through a peer review process. An accredited college or university is one which has available the necessary resources to achieve its stated purposes through appropriate educational programs, is substantially doing so, and gives reasonable evidence that it will continue to do so in the foreseeable future. Institutional integrity is also addressed through accreditation. Accreditation by the Northwest Commission on Colleges and Universities is not partial but applies to the institution as a whole. As such, it is not a guarantee of every course or program offered, or the competence of individual graduates. Rather, it provides reasonable assurance about the quality of opportunities available to students who attend the institution. Inquiries regarding an institution's accredited status by the Northwest Commission on Colleges and Universities should be directed to the administrative staff of the institution. Individuals may also contact: Northwest Commission on Colleges and Universities, 8060 165th Avenue N.E., Suite 100 Redmond, Washington 98052; telephone: 425-558-4224; www.nwccu.org.

The Art Institute of Seattle is licensed under Chapter 28c.10RCW; inquiries or complaints regarding this or any other private vocational school may be made to the Workforce Training and Education Coordinating Board, 128 10th Avenue SW, P.O. Box 43105, Olympia, Washington 98504-3105; phone: 360-753-5662.

The Associate of Applied Arts in culinary arts degree program is accredited by The Accrediting Commission of the American Culinary Federation Education Foundation.

The interior design program leading to the Bachelor of Fine Arts degree is accredited by the Council for Interior Design Accreditation, 206 Grandville Ave., Suite 350, Grand Rapids, Michigan 49503; www.accredit-id.org.

Academic Programs

Creativity is all around, and with millions of tomorrow's jobs in creative fields, the world needs more creative professionals. No matter which course of study a student chooses, the instructors at The Art Institutes will guide, support, and help students fine-tune their visual thinking and problem solving, so they can take advantage of the world's growing creative opportunities and put their passion to work. Programs are offered in the areas of design, which focuses on communicating conceptually and helping people connect in living and work spaces; media arts, which centers on utilizing technology to deliver information and entertainment; fashion, where students learn anything from designing clothes for the runway to running a retail shop; and culinary, which exposes learners to international cuisines as well as restaurant management techniques.

Associate degree programs are available in the areas of audio production, baking and pastry, culinary arts, fashion design, fashion marketing, graphic design, industrial design technology, interior design, photography, video production, and web design and interactive media.

Bachelor's degree programs are available in the areas of audio design technology, culinary arts management, digital filmmaking and video production, fashion design, fashion marketing, game art and design, industrial design, interior design, media arts and animation, photography, and web design and interactive media.

Diploma programs are offered in the areas of art of cooking, baking and pastry, digital design, digital image management, fashion retailing, residential design, web design and development, and web design and interactive communications.

Program availability and degree offerings are subject to change.

Costs

Actual tuition and housing costs will vary depending on program, number of credits enrolled, and living arrangements. Prospective students should contact a Student Financial Services professional at the school for details.

Financial Aid

Financial aid is available for those who qualify. Students who require financial assistance should first complete and submit the Free Application for Federal Student Aid (FAFSA) online at www.fafsa.ed.gov and meet with a financial aid officer. Students may also apply for a number of scholarships focusing on their specific areas of career interest.

Faculty

Faculty members are hands-on creative professionals with proven experience as business leaders and innovators, hosting a learning environment similar to the career world students will face after graduation. Part instructor, part mentor, their mission is to help develop and transform creative potential into high-demand marketable skills.

Student Body Profile

Students come to The Art Institute of Seattle from throughout the United States and abroad. The student population includes recent high school graduates, transfer students, and those who have left a previous employment situation to study and train for a new career. Students are creative, competitive, and open to new ideas. They place great value on an education that prepares them for an exciting entry-level position in the arts.

Student Activities

The Art Institute of Seattle provides an environment that encourages involvement in a wide variety of activities of an academic and non-academic nature, including clubs and organizations, community service opportunities, and various committees designed to enhance the quality of student life.

Student Support Services provides assistance such as wellness workshops, assistance with study habits and time management, and counseling.

Facilities and Resources

The Art Institute of Seattle provides a learning environment with professional-grade technology applicable to each student's course of study. Students have the opportunity to build a portfolio of work that shows potential employers that they are trained to use the software, hardware, or equipment utilized within the industry. Depending upon the course of study, students are immersed in a creative environment—from classrooms to computer labs to studios—focused on relevant, hands-on education designed to prepare them for the real world.

Location

Water, mountains, culture, music, commerce—and of course, coffee and computers. Seattle, a thriving, forward-thinking, sophisticated city in the shadow of majestic Mount Rainier, is an international port on beautiful Puget Sound that offers the finest in arts and entertainment.

The Art Institute of Seattle is situated on the city's Elliott Bay waterfront, just a few blocks from the Belltown neighborhood and its vibrant restaurants and nightlife, and not far from the famous Pike Place Market, the Olympic Sculpture Park, and other interesting attractions.

Seattle boasts a calendar full of cultural events. From the 24-day Seattle International Film Festival to Hempfest, to book fairs, concerts featuring a diverse range of alternative music, performance poetry, and an abundance of art galleries and artists' studios that are open to the public, there's a wide variety of things to see and do in this city.

As for professional sports, Seattle has them covered with baseball's Mariners and the NFL's Seahawks, along with soccer, ice hockey, and women's basketball teams.

In addition, there are museums, covering everything from Asian culture to maritime history to rock 'n roll. The iconic Seattle Space Needle adds a unique feature to the city skyline. Along with the abundance and variety of fresh seafood and local produce, Seattle has earned a spot as one of the country's true culinary capitals.

The Seattle area is home to an array of globally recognized companies. While Starbucks and Microsoft call Seattle home, the city's other corporate residents include the headquarters of Amazon, Expedia, RealNetworks, Getty Images, Corbis, Nintendo of America, REI, Eddie Bauer, Nordstrom, Brooks Running, Fantagraphics Books, Costco, and Weyerhauser, as well as the offices of Adobe, Facebook, and Google.

Admission Requirements

Prospective students should refer to the current academic catalog for full details regarding admission requirements and process.

Application and Information

To obtain an application, make arrangements for an interview, or tour the school, prospective students should contact:

The Art Institute of Seattle
2323 Elliott Avenue
Seattle, Washington 98121-1642
Phone: 206-448-6600
        800-275-2471 (toll-free)
Fax: 206-269-0275
Website: http://www.artinstitutes.edu/seattle

BAY STATE COLLEGE
BOSTON, MASSACHUSETTS

The College and Its Mission

Founded in 1946, Bay State College is a private, independent, coeducational institution located in Boston's historic Back Bay. Since its founding, Bay State College has been preparing graduates for outstanding careers and continued education.

Bay State College is a small, private college focused on passionate students who want to turn their interests into a rewarding career. The College offers associate and bachelor's degrees in a number of rewarding fields. Everyone at Bay State—from admissions counselors and professors to the career services team—helps to assist, guide, and advise students, from the moment they apply and throughout their careers. Located in Boston's Back Bay, the College offers the city of Boston as a campus, small classes, and one-on-one attention. For students seeking a career in one of the professions offered by Bay State, a degree program at the College could be a strong first step on their career path.

The College offers associate degrees and bachelor's degrees. The educational experience offered through the variety of programs prepares students to excel in the careers of their choice. Personalized attention is the cornerstone of a Bay State College education. Through the transformative power of its core values of quality, respect, and support, Bay State College has been able to assist students with setting and achieving goals that prepare them for careers and continued education.

Recognizing that one of the most important aspects of college is life outside the classroom, the Office of Student Affairs seeks to provide services from orientation through graduation and beyond. Special events throughout the year include a fashion show and a host of events produced by the Entertainment Management Association. Students also enjoy professional sports teams such as the Boston Celtics and Boston Red Sox.

Bay State College's campus experience can be whatever the student chooses it to be. It's not the typical college campus—its residence halls are actually brownstones along Boston's trendy Commonwealth Avenue and Bay State's quad could be Boston Common, the banks of the Charles River by the Esplanade, or Copley Square. That's the advantage of being located in Boston's Back Bay, which is also the safest neighborhood in the city. Students can relax at a favorite coffee shop, bike along the Charles River, ice skate on the Frog Pond, check out the city's nightlife, or take in a ball game at Fenway Park.

Bay State College is accredited by the New England Association of Schools and Colleges and is authorized to award the Associate in Science, Associate in Applied Science, and three Bachelor of Science degrees by the Commonwealth of Massachusetts. Bay State is a member of several professional educational associations. Its medical assisting program is accredited by the Accrediting Bureau of Health Education Schools (ABHES). The physical therapist assistant program is accredited by the Commission on Accreditation in Physical Therapy Education (CAPTE) of the American Physical Therapy Association (APTA).

Academic Programs

Bay State College operates on a semester calendar. The fall semester runs from early September to late December. The spring semester runs from late January until mid-May. A satellite campus is located in Middleborough, Massachusetts.

Bachelor's degrees are offered in criminal justice, entertainment management, fashion merchandising, and management.

Associate degrees are offered in business administration, criminal justice, early childhood education, entertainment management (with a concentration in audio production), fashion design, fashion merchandising, health studies, marketing, medical assisting, nursing, physical therapist assistant studies, retail business management, and hospitality management.

Bay State College also offers courses on-ground and online to working adults in its Evening and Online Division. The courses are offered in eight-week sessions and allow more flexibility for students who must balance work and family commitments while pursuing their education.

Bay State College reviews, enhances, and adds new programs to help graduates remain industry-current in their respective fields.

Off-Campus Programs

Many students cite Bay State's internship program as a turning point for them. Bay State internships allow students to gain hands-on experience and spend time working in their chosen fields. These valuable opportunities can give students an advantage when they apply for positions after they have completed school.

Bay State's Boston location allows the College to offer internships at many well-known companies and organizations. Students are able to apply what they've learned in the classroom and do meaningful work in their field of study. In addition, they build working relationships with people in their chosen profession. For more information on internships, prospective students may contact Tom Corrigan, Director of Career Services, at 617-217-9000.

Costs

Tuition charges are assessed on a per-credit-hour basis and vary depending upon program of study. This provides students with maximum flexibility based on individual financial and academic needs, making a Bay State College education more accommodating and affordable. Rates quoted below by program were for the 2012–13 academic year. Charges are not prorated unless noted. Program flow sheets may require more or less than 30 credits per academic year.

Early childhood education, medical assisting, and health studies: $749 per credit, $22,470 (30 credits). Business, criminal justice, fashion merchandising, fashion design, entertainment management, and hospitality management: $802 per credit, $24,060 (30 credits). Nursing and physical therapy assistant: $821 per credit, $24,630 (30 credits).

Evening students paid $300 per credit. Room and board were $11,800 per year, the application fee was $40, the student services fee was $400 (for day students only), and the student activity fee was $50. The cost of books and additional fees vary by major. A residence hall security deposit of $300 and a technology fee of $250 are required of all resident students.

The fall tuition payment due date is July 1; the spring tuition payment is due December 1.

Financial Aid

Each student works with a personal advocate to thoroughly explain financial options and guide them through the financial aid application process. Many options are available: aid, grants and scholarships, federal programs, and private loans. Bay State College's Financial Aid Department and tuition planners can help students determine what aid may apply. Approximately 85 percent of students receive some form of financial assistance. Bay State College requires a completed Free Application for Federal Student Aid (FAFSA) form and signed federal tax forms. The College's institutional financial aid priority deadline is March 15. Financial aid is granted on a rolling basis.

Faculty

There are 72 faculty members, many holding advanced degrees and several holding doctoral degrees. The student-faculty ratio is 20:1.

Student Body Profile

There are approximately 1,200 students in degree programs in both the day and evening divisions.

Student Activities

Bay State College students participate in a multitude of activities offered by the College through existing student organizations. Students also have the opportunity to create clubs and organizations that meet their interests. Existing organizations include the Student Government Association, Entertainment Management Association, Justice Society, the Criminal Justice Society, DEX, and the Early Childhood Education Club. Students produce an annual talent show as well as an annual fashion show that showcases student work from the College's fashion design program. An annual literary magazine also features the work of students throughout the College.

Facilities and Resources

Advisement/Counseling: Trained staff members assist students in selecting courses and programs of study. A counseling center is available to provide mental and physical health referrals to all students in need of such services. Referral networks are extensive, within a wide range of geographic areas, and provide access to a variety of public and private health agencies.

Specialized Services: The Office of Academic Development at Bay State College is designed to meet and support the various academic needs of the student body and serve as a resource for supplemental instruction, academic plans, learning accommodations, and other types of support. The Office of Academic Development operates on the belief that all students can achieve success in their courses by accessing support services and creating individual academic plans.

The Center for Learning and Academic Success (CLAS) at Bay State College is a key component available to help students achieve academic success. Students come to CLAS to get support in specific subject areas as well as study skills such as note-taking, reading comprehension, writing research papers, time management, and coping with exam anxiety. They utilize CLAS to develop study plans and strategies that positively impact their grades in all subjects. Students can also take advantage of the tutoring and seminars CLAS offers. CLAS's goal is to ensure that students are provided with exceptional academic support in all areas of study.

Career Planning/Placement: For many college students, the transition from student life to professional life is filled with questions and uncharted realities. Bay State College's Career Services Department offers students their own personal career advancement team. The department can help students learn to write a resume and cover letter, use social networks, practice interviewing skills, find the right job opportunity, and learn other career-related functions. Students even receive a Professionalism Grade, which lets future employers know they have what it takes to start contributing on day one. The Career Services Department at is determined to see each student succeed and offers valuable instruction that will serve students throughout their professional careers.

Library and Audiovisual Services: The library is staffed with trained librarians who are available to guide students in their research process. The library's resources include 7,500 books, eighty-five periodical subscriptions, and a dramatically increased reach through its online library resource databases that include ProQuest, InfoTrac, and LexisNexis. In addition, the library provides computer access and study space for students. The library catalog and databases are accessible from any Internet-ready terminal.

First-Year Experience: The First-Year Experience (FYE) is a 1-credit course that is required of all first-year students and takes place during the first three days that students are on campus. FYE combines social activities with an academic syllabus that is designed to ease the transition into the college experience. Through FYE, students have the opportunity to connect with their academic advisers as well as with other students in their academic programs. At the conclusion of FYE, students are on the road to mapping out their personal action plan for success. The plan, designed by students, guided by academic advisers, and revisited each semester, helps students set, monitor, and achieve academic and life goals. It also builds the preparation for lifelong accomplishment.

Location

Located in the historic city of Boston, Massachusetts, and surrounded by dozens of colleges and universities, Bay State College is an ideal setting in which to pursue a college degree. Tree-lined streets around the school are mirrored in the skyscrapers of the Back Bay. The College is located within walking distance of several major league sport franchises, concert halls, museums, the Freedom Trail, Boston Symphony Hall, the Boston Public Library, and the Boston Public Garden. World-class shopping and major cultural and sporting events help make college life a memorable experience.

The College is accessible by the MBTA and commuter rail and bus, and it is near Boston Logan International Airport.

Admission Requirements

Applicants must be a high school graduate, a current high school student working toward graduation, or a recipient of a GED certificate. The Office of Admissions requires that applicants to the associate degree programs have a minimum of a 2.0 GPA (on a 4.0 scale); if available, applicants may submit SAT and/or ACT scores. Applicants to bachelor's degree programs must have a minimum 2.3 GPA (on a 4.0 scale) and must also submit SAT or ACT scores. International applicants must also submit high school transcripts translated to English with an explanation of the grading system, financial documentation, and a minimum TOEFL score of 500 on the paper-based exam or 173 on the computer-based exam if English is not their native language.

The physical therapist assistant studies and nursing programs require a minimum 2.7 GPA (on a 4.0 scale) and the Evening Division has different or additional admission requirements. For more information about these programs, interested students should visit the Web site at http://www.baystate.edu.

A personal interview is required for all prospective students—parents are encouraged to attend. Applicants must receive the recommendation of a Bay State College Admissions Officer.

Application and Information

Applications are accepted on a rolling basis. A $40 fee is required at the time of application. Students are responsible for arranging for their official high school transcripts, test scores, and letters of recommendation to be submitted to Bay State College.

The Bay State College Admissions Office notifies applicants of a decision within one week of receipt of the transcript and other required documents. There is a $100 nonrefundable tuition deposit required upon acceptance to ensure a place in the class; the deposit is credited toward the tuition fee. Deposits are due within thirty days of acceptance. Once a student is accepted, a Bay State College representative creates a personalized financial plan that provides payment options for a Bay State College education.

Applications should be submitted to:

Admissions Office
Bay State College
122 Commonwealth Avenue
Boston, Massachusetts 02116
Phone: 800-81-LEARN (53276)
Fax: 617-249-0400 (eFax)
E-mail: admissions@baystate.edu
Website: http://www.baystate.edu
http://www.facebook.com/baystatecollege
http://twitter.com/baystatecollege

Giving students access is an essential part of a Bay State College education. Students have access to a community of support, experiential learning, faculty with real-world experience, and a dynamic location in the heart of the city.

BROWN MACKIE COLLEGE — AKRON

AKRON, OHIO

BROWN
MACKIE
COLLEGE
AKRON℠

The College and Its Mission

Brown Mackie College — Akron (Brown Mackie College) is one of over twenty-five locations in the Brown Mackie College system of schools (www.brownmackie.edu), which is dedicated to providing educational programs that prepare students to pursue entry-level positions in a competitive, rapidly changing workplace. Brown Mackie College schools offer bachelor's degree, associate degree, diploma, and certificate programs in health sciences, business, information technology, legal studies, and design to thousands of students in the Midwest, Southeast, Southwest, and Western United States.

Brown Mackie College was founded in Cincinnati, Ohio, in February 1927, as a traditional business college. In March 1980, the college added a branch campus in Akron, Ohio. The college outgrew this space and relocated to its current address in January 2007.

Brown Mackie College — Akron is accredited by the Accrediting Council for Independent Colleges and Schools to award associate degrees and diplomas. The Accrediting Council for Independent Colleges and Schools is listed as a nationally recognized accrediting agency by the United States Department of Education and is recognized by the Council for Higher Education Accreditation. ACICS can be contacted at 750 First Street NE, Suite 980, Washington, D.C. 20002; phone: 202-336-6780.

Brown Mackie College — Akron is licensed by the Ohio State Board of Career Colleges and Schools, 30 East Broad Street, 24th Floor, Suite 2481, Columbus, Ohio 43215-3138; phone: 614-466-2752. Ohio registration #03-09-1685T.

The Associate of Applied Science in surgical technology program is accredited by the Commission on Accreditation of Allied Health Education Programs (www.caahep.org) upon the recommendation of the Accreditation Review Council on Education in Surgical Technology and Surgical Assisting (ARC/STSA). The Commission on Accreditation of Allied Health Education Programs is located at 1361 Park Street, Clearwater, Florida 33756; phone: 727-210-2350; www.caahep.org.

The Associate of Applied Science in occupational therapy assistant program is accredited by the Accreditation Council for Occupational Therapy Education (ACOTE) of the American Occupational Therapy Association (AOTA), located at 4720 Montgomery Lane, Suite 200, Bethesda, Maryland 20814-3449; phone: 301-652-AOTA. Graduates of the program will be eligible to sit for the national certification examination for the occupational therapy assistant administered by the National Board for Certification in Occupational Therapy (NBCOT). After successful completion of this exam, the individual will be a Certified Occupational Therapy Assistant (COTA). In addition, most states require licensure in order to practice; however, state licenses are usually based on the results of the NBCOT Certification Examination. Note that a felony conviction may affect a graduate's ability to sit for the NBCOT certification examination or attain state licensure.

The Associate of Applied Science in veterinary technology program has provisional programmatic accreditation granted by the American Veterinary Medical Association (AVMA) through the Committee on Veterinary Technician Education and Activities (CVTEA).

The Associate of Applied Science in medical assisting program is accredited by the Commission of Accreditation of Allied Health Education Programs (www.caahep.org) upon the recommendation of the Curriculum Review Board of the Medical Assisting Education Review Board (MAERB). Commission on Accreditation of Allied Health Education Programs can be contacted at 1361 Park Street Clearwater, Florida 33756; phone: 727-210-2350.

Academic Programs

Brown Mackie College — Akron provides higher education to traditional and nontraditional students through associate degree and diploma programs that can assist them in enhancing their career opportunities, broadening their perspectives through appropriate general education courses, thinking independently and critically, and improving problem-solving abilities.

Each college quarter comprises twelve weeks. Associate degree programs require a minimum of eight quarters to complete. Programs are offered on a year-round basis, providing students with the ability to work uninterrupted toward their degree. Brown Mackie College offers all programs in a unique One Course a Month format. This schedule allows students to focus studies on only one course for four weeks and has proven convenient for students with multiple obligations such as jobs and family.

Associate Degree Programs: The Associate of Applied Business degree is awarded in accounting technology, business management, criminal justice, office management, and paralegal.

The Associate of Applied Science degree is awarded in computer networking and applications, database technology, early childhood education, health care administration, information technology, medical assisting, occupational therapy assistant, pharmacy technology, surgical technology, and veterinary technology.

Diploma Programs: Brown Mackie College offers diploma programs in bookkeeping specialist, criminal justice specialist, general business, medical assistant, medical coding and billing, paralegal assistant, and practical nursing.

The American Medical Technologists (AMT), which offers the certification for Registered Medical Assistant (RMA), accepts the accreditation of Brown Mackie College — Akron. Students will qualify to take the RMA certification examination upon graduating the Brown Mackie College — Akron medical assisting and medical assistant programs. Graduates of the 48 credit-hour medical assistant program are not qualified to take the AMT/RMA exam.

Brown Mackie College — Akron does not guarantee third-party certification. Outside agencies control the requirements for certifications and are subject to change without notice to Brown Mackie College.

Program availability and degree offerings are subject to change.

Costs

Tuition for the 2012–13 academic year was $314 per credit hour and $20 per credit hour for general fees. Tuition for the practical nursing program was $381 per credit hour and $30 per credit hour for general fees. Tuition for the occupational therapy assistant program was $381 per credit hour and $20 per credit hour for general fees. Tuition for the surgical technology program was $360 per credit hour and $20 per credit hour for general fees. The cost of textbooks, if applicable, and other instructional materials varies by program

Financial Aid

Financial aid is available to those who qualify. The college maintains a full-time staff of Student Financial Services Advisors to assist qualified students in obtaining financial assistance. The college participates in several student aid programs. Forms of financial aid available through federal resources include the Federal Pell Grant Program, Federal Supplemental Educational Opportunity Grant (FSEOG) Program, Federal Work-Study Program, Federal Stafford Student Loan Program (subsidized and unsubsidized), and the Federal PLUS Loan Program. Eligible students may also apply for veterans' educational benefits. Students with physical or mental disabilities that are a handicap to employment may be eligible for training services through the state Agency for Vocational Rehabilitation. For further information, students should contact the Student Financial Services Office.

Each year, the college makes available President's Scholarships of $1,000 each to qualifying seniors from area high schools. In order to qualify, a senior must be graduating from a participating high school, have maintained a cumulative grade point average of at least 2.0, and submitted a brief essay. The student's extracurricular activities and community service are also considered. These scholarships are available only to students enrolling in one of the college's degree programs. Students awarded the scholarship must enroll at Brown Mackie College between June and September immediately following their high school graduation. Applications for these scholarships can be obtained from the guidance departments of participating high schools. These applications must be completed and returned to Brown Mackie College by March 31.

The Education Foundation was established in 2000 to offer scholarship support to students interested in continuing their education at one of the postsecondary, career-focused schools in the EDMC system. The number and amount of the awards can vary, depending on the funds available. Scholarship applications are considered every quarter. At Brown Mackie College, applicants must be currently enrolled in an associate or bachelor's degree program and in their fourth quarter or higher (but no further than their second-to-last quarter) at the time of application. Awards are made based on academic performance and potential, as well as financial need. Interested students should contact the college's Student Financial Service Department for additional information.

Faculty

There are 20 full-time and 39 part-time faculty members. The student-faculty ratio is 17:1.

Facilities and Resources

Brown Mackie College provides media presentation rooms for special instructional needs, a library that provides instructional resources and academic support for both faculty members and students, and qualified and experienced faculty members who are committed to the academic and technical preparation of their students. Brown Mackie College is nonresidential; students who are unable to commute daily from their homes may request assistance from the Office of Admissions in locating off-campus housing. The college is accessible by public transportation and provides ample parking, available at no charge.

Brown Mackie College — Akron is fully committed to using eTextbooks and computer tablets in the classroom. Utilizing these tablets to access expanded course material, students are able to increase their acumen for using this technology and further enhance their educational experience. Students have the ability to directly download their eTextbooks to their tablet, eliminating the need to carry heavy, physical textbooks and reducing the overall cost of supplies.

The College is a nonresidential, smoke-free institution.

Location

Brown Mackie College — Akron is located at 755 White Pond Drive in Akron, Ohio.

Admission Requirements

Each applicant for admission is assigned to an Assistant Director of Admissions who directs the applicant through the steps of the admissions process, providing information on curriculum, policies, procedures, and services and assisting the applicant in setting necessary appointments and interviews.

To qualify for admission, each applicant must provide documentation of graduation from an accredited high school or from a state-approved secondary education curriculum or provide official documentation of high school graduation equivalency. All transcripts become the property of Brown Mackie College. Admission to Brown Mackie College is based upon the applicant meeting the stated requirements, a review of the applicant's previous education records, and a review of the applicant's career interests. If previous academic records indicate that the Brown Mackie College education and training programs would not benefit the applicant, the Brown Mackie College reserves the right to advise the applicant not to enroll. Special requirements for enrollment into certain programs are discussed in the descriptions of those programs.

For the most recent information regarding admission requirements, applicants should refer to the current academic catalog.

Application and Information

Applicants must complete and submit an application form along with documentation of graduation from an accredited high school or state-approved secondary education curriculum, or applicants must provide official documentation of high school graduation equivalency. Prospective students can go online to BMCprograms.info for program duration, tuition, fees and other costs, median debt, federal salary data, alumni success, programmatic accreditation, and other important details.

Brown Mackie College is a system of over twenty-five schools located throughout North America. Programs, credential levels, technology, and scheduling options vary by school, and employment opportunities are not guaranteed. Financial aid is available for those who qualify. Administrative offices are located at 625 Eden Park Drive, Suite 1100; Cincinnati, Ohio 45202; phone: 513-830-2000. ©2013 Brown Mackie College. OH Registration #03-09-1685T; #03-09-1686T; #03-09-1687T; #03-09-1688T; #06-03-1781T; AC0150, AC0109, AC0078, AC0045, AC0138, AC0110; Licensed by the Florida Commission for Independent Education, License No. 3206.

For additional information, prospective students should contact:

Senior Director of Admissions
Brown Mackie College — Akron
755 White Pond Drive, Suite 101
Akron, Ohio 44320
Phone: 330-869-3600
Fax: 330-869-3650
E-mail: bmcakadm@brownmackie.edu
Website: http://www.brownmackie.edu/Akron

BROWN MACKIE COLLEGE — ALBUQUERQUE

ALBUQUERQUE, NEW MEXICO

The College and Its Mission

Brown Mackie College — Albuquerque (Brown Mackie College) is one of over twenty-five locations in the Brown Mackie College system of schools (www.brownmackie.edu), which is dedicated to providing educational programs that prepare students to pursue entry-level positions in a competitive, rapidly changing workplace. Brown Mackie College schools offer bachelor's degree, associate degree, diploma, and certificate programs in health sciences, business, information technology, legal studies, and design to thousands of students in the Midwest, Southeast, Southwest, and Western United States.

Brown Mackie College was originally founded and approved by the Board of Trustees of Kansas Wesleyan College in Salina, Kansas on July 30, 1892. In 1938, the college was incorporated as the Brown Mackie School of Business under the ownership of Perry E. Brown and A.B. Mackie, former instructors at Kansas Wesleyan University in Salina, Kansas. Their last names formed the name of Brown Mackie. By January 1975, with improvements in curricula and higher degree-granting status, the Brown Mackie School of Business became Brown Mackie College.

Brown Mackie College — Albuquerque is accredited by the Accrediting Council for Independent Colleges and Schools to award associate degrees and diplomas. The Accrediting Council for Independent Colleges and Schools is listed as a nationally recognized accrediting agency by the United States Department of Education and is recognized by the Council for Higher Education Accreditation. ACICS can be contacted at 750 First Street NE, Suite 980, Washington, D.C. 20002; phone: 202-336-6780.

Brown Mackie College — Albuquerque is licensed by the New Mexico Higher Education Department, 2048 Galisteo Street, Santa Fe, New Mexico 87505-2100; phone: 505-476-8400.

The occupational therapy assistant program is accredited by the Accreditation Council for Occupational Therapy Education (ACOTE) of the American Occupational Therapy Association (AOTA), located at 4720 Montgomery Lane, Suite 200, Bethesda, Maryland 20814-3449; phone: 301-652-AOTA. Graduates of the program will be eligible to sit for the national certification examination for the occupational therapy assistant administered by the National Board for Certification in Occupational Therapy (NBCOT). After successful completion of this exam, the individual will be a Certified Occupational Therapy Assistant (COTA). In addition, most states require licensure in order to practice; however, state licenses are usually based on the results of the NBCOT Certification Examination. Note that a felony conviction may affect a graduate's ability to sit for the NBCOT certification examination or attain state licensure.

The Associate of Applied Science in surgical technology program is accredited by the Accrediting Bureau of Health Education Schools.

The Associate of Applied Science in veterinary technology program has provisional programmatic accreditation granted by the American Veterinary Medical Association (AVMA) through the Committee on Veterinary Technician Education and Activities (CVTEA).

Academic Programs

Brown Mackie College — Albuquerque provides higher education to traditional and nontraditional students through associate degree and diploma programs that assist in enhancing their career opportunities, broadening their perspectives through appropriate general education courses, thinking independently and critically, and improving problem-solving abilities. The college strives to develop within its students the desire for lifelong and continued education.

Each college quarter comprises twelve weeks. Associate degree programs require a minimum of eight quarters to complete. Programs are offered on a year-round basis, providing students with the ability to work uninterrupted toward completion of their programs. The college offers all programs in a unique One Course a Month format. This allows students to focus studies on only one course for four weeks. This schedule has proven convenient for students with multiple obligations such as jobs and family.

Associate Degree Programs: The Associate of Applied Science degree is awarded in accounting technology, architectural design and drafting technology, business management, criminal justice, health care administration, information technology, medical assisting, nursing, occupational therapy assistant, paralegal, pharmacy technology, surgical technology, and veterinary technology.

Diploma Programs: Brown Mackie College — Albuquerque offers diploma programs in accounting, business, criminal justice, medical assistant, and paralegal assistant.

The American Medical Technologists (AMT), which offers the certification for Registered Medical Assistant (RMA), accepts the accreditation of Brown Mackie College — Albuquerque. Students will qualify to take the RMA certification examination upon graduating the Brown Mackie College — Albuquerque medical assisting and medical assistant programs. Graduates of the 48 credit-hour medical assistant program are not qualified to take the AMT/RMA exam.

Brown Mackie College — Albuquerque does not guarantee third-party certification. Outside agencies control the requirements for certifications and are subject to change without notice to Brown Mackie College.

Program availability and degree offerings are subject to change.

Costs

Tuition in the 2012–13 academic year for all associate degree and certificate programs was $324 per credit hour; fees were $25 per credit hour. Tuition for the occupational therapy assistant program was $355 per credit hour; fees were $25 per credit hour. Tuition for the surgical technology program was $339 per credit hour; fees were $25 per credit hour. Tuition for the nursing program was $390 per credit hour; fees were $30 per credit hour. The cost of textbooks, if applicable, and other instructional materials varies by program.

Financial Aid

Financial aid is available for those who qualify. Brown Mackie College maintains a full-time staff of Student Financial Services Advisors to assist qualified students in obtaining the financial assistance they require to meet their educational expenses. Available resources include federal and state aid, student loans from private lenders, and Federal Work-Study opportunities, both on and off college premises.

Each year, the college makes available President's Scholarships of $1,000 each to qualifying seniors from area high schools. In order to qualify, a senior must have graduated from a participating high school, must have maintained a cumulative grade point average of at least 2.0, and submitted a brief essay. The student's extracurricular activities and community service are also considered. These scholarships are available only to students enrolling in one of the college's degree programs. Students awarded the scholarship must enroll at Brown Mackie College — Albuquerque between June and September immediately following their high school graduation. Applications for these scholarships can be obtained from the guidance departments of participating high schools. These applications must be completed and returned to the college by March 31.

The Education Foundation was established in 2000 to offer scholarship support to students interested in continuing their education at one of the postsecondary, career-focused schools in the EDMC system. The number and amount of the awards can vary, depending on the funds available. Scholarship applications are considered every quarter. At Brown Mackie College, applicants must be currently enrolled in an associate or bachelor's degree program and in their fourth quarter or higher (but no further than their second-to-last quarter) at the time of application. Awards are made based on academic performance and potential, as well as financial need. Interested students should contact the college's Student Financial Service Department for additional information.

Faculty

Experienced faculty members provide academic support and are committed to the academic and technical preparation of their students. The college has both full-time and part-time instructors, with a student-faculty ratio of 15:1.

Facilities and Resources

A modern facility, Brown Mackie College — Albuquerque offers more than 35,000 square feet. The college is equipped with multiple computer labs, housing over 100 computers. High-speed access to the Internet and other online resources are available to students and faculty. Multimedia classrooms are outfitted with overhead projectors, VCR/DVD players, and computers.

In 2012, Brown Mackie College — Albuquerque began its transition to using eTextbooks and computer tablets in the classroom. Utilizing these tablets to access expanded course material, students will be able to increase their acumen for using this technology and further enhance their educational experience. Students have the ability to directly download their eTextbooks to their tablet, eliminating the need to carry heavy, physical textbooks and reducing the overall cost of supplies.

Brown Mackie College — Albuquerque is fully committed to using eTextbooks and computer tablets in the classroom. Utilizing these tablets to access expanded course material, students are able to increase their acumen for using this technology and further enhance their educational experience. Students have the ability to directly download their eTextbooks to their tablet, eliminating the need to carry heavy, physical textbooks and reducing the overall cost of supplies.

Brown Mackie College is nonresidential; public transportation and ample parking at no cost are available. The campus is a smoke-free facility.

Location

Brown Mackie College — Albuquerque is conveniently located at 10500 Copper Avenue NE, in Albuquerque, New Mexico.

Admission Requirements

Each applicant for admission is assigned to an Assistant Director of Admissions who directs the applicant through the steps of the admissions process. They provide information on curriculum, policies, procedures, and services and assist the applicant in setting necessary appointments and interviews. To qualify for admission, each applicant must provide documentation of graduation from an accredited high school or from a state-approved secondary education curriculum or provide official documentation of high school graduation equivalency. All transcripts become the property of the college. Admission to the college is based on the applicant meeting the stated requirements, a review of the applicant's previous educational records, and a review of the applicant's career interests. If previous academic records indicate the college's education and training programs would not benefit the applicant, the college reserves the right to advise the applicant not to enroll. Special requirements for enrollment into certain programs are discussed in the descriptions of those programs.

For the most recent information regarding admission requirements, prospective students should refer to the current academic catalog.

Application and Information

Applicants must complete and submit an application form, along with documentation of graduation from an accredited high school or state-approved secondary education curriculum or official documentation of high school graduation equivalency.

Applicants can go online to BMCprograms.info for program duration, tuition, fees and other costs, median debt, federal salary data, alumni success, programmatic accreditation and other important information.

Brown Mackie College is a system of over twenty-five schools located throughout North America. Programs, credential levels, technology, and scheduling options vary by school, and employment opportunities are not guaranteed. Financial aid is available for those who qualify. Administrative offices are located at: 625 Eden Park Drive, Suite 1100; Cincinnati, Ohio 45202; phone: 513-830-2000. ©2013 Brown Mackie College. OH Registration #03-09-1685T; #03-09-1686T; #03-09-1687T; #03-09-1688T; #06-03-1781T; AC0150, AC0109, AC0078, AC0045, AC0138, AC0110; Licensed by the Florida Commission for Independent Education, License No. 3206.

For additional information, prospective students should contact:

Director of Admissions
Brown Mackie College — Albuquerque
10500 Copper Avenue NE
Albuquerque, New Mexico 87123
Phone: 505-559-5200
　　　877-271-3488 (toll-free)
Fax: 505-559-5222
E-mail: bmcalbadm@brownmackie.edu
Web site: http://www.brownmackie.edu/Albuquerque

BROWN MACKIE COLLEGE — ATLANTA
ATLANTA, GEORGIA

The College and Its Mission

Brown Mackie College — Atlanta (Brown Mackie College) is one of over twenty-five locations in the Brown Mackie College system of schools (http://www.brownmackie.edu), which is dedicated to providing educational programs that prepare students to pursue entry-level positions in a competitive, rapidly changing workplace. Brown Mackie College schools offer bachelor degree, associate degree, certificate, and diploma programs in health sciences, business, information technology, legal studies, and design to thousands of students in the Midwest, Southeast, Southwest, and Western United States.

Brown Mackie College — Atlanta is accredited by the Accrediting Council for Independent Colleges and Schools (ACICS) to award associate degrees and diplomas. The Accrediting Council for Independent Colleges and Schools is listed as a nationally recognized accrediting agency by the United States Department of Education and is recognized by the Council for Higher Education Accreditation. ACICS can be contacted at 750 First Street NE, Suite 980, Washington, D.C. 20002; phone: 202-336-6780.

The occupational therapy assistant program is accredited by the Accreditation Council for Occupational Therapy Education (ACOTE) of the American Occupational Therapy Association (AOTA), located at 4720 Montgomery Lane, Suite 200, Bethesda, Maryland 20814-3449; phone: 301-652-AOTA. Graduates of the program will be eligible to sit for the national certification examination for the occupational therapy assistant administered by the National Board for Certification in Occupational Therapy (NBCOT). After successful completion of this exam, the individual will be a Certified Occupational Therapy Assistant (COTA). In addition, most states require licensure in order to practice; however, state licenses are usually based on the results of the NBCOT Certification Examination. Note that a felony conviction may affect a graduate's ability to sit for the NBCOT certification examination or attain state licensure.

The Associate of Applied Science in surgical technology program is accredited by the Accrediting Bureau of Health Education Schools (http://www.abhes.org).

Academic Programs

Brown Mackie College — Atlanta provides higher education to traditional and nontraditional students through associate degree and diploma programs that can assist students in enhancing their career opportunities, broadening their perspectives through appropriate general education courses, thinking independently and critically, and improving problem-solving abilities. Brown Mackie College strives to develop within its students the desire for lifelong and continued education.

Each college quarter comprises twelve weeks. Associate degree programs require a minimum of eight quarters to complete. Programs are offered on a year-round basis, providing students with the ability to work uninterrupted toward their degrees. Brown Mackie College offers all programs in a unique One Course a Month format. This schedule allows students to focus studies on only one course for four weeks and has proven convenient for students with multiple obligations such as jobs and family.

Associate Degree Programs: The Associate of Applied Business degree is awarded in accounting technology, business management, criminal justice, and paralegal. The Associate of Applied Science degree is awarded in early childhood education, health care administration, medical assisting, occupational therapy assistant, pharmacy technology, and surgical technology.

Diploma Programs: Brown Mackie College — Atlanta also offers diploma programs in accounting, business, criminal justice, medical assistant, and paralegal assistant.

The American Medical Technologists (AMT), which offers the certification for Registered Medical Assistant (RMA), accepts the accreditation of Brown Mackie College — Atlanta. Students will qualify to take the RMA certification examination upon graduating the Brown Mackie College — Atlanta medical assisting and medical assistant programs. Graduates of the 48 credit-hour medical assistant program are not qualified to take the AMT/RMA exam.

Brown Mackie College — Atlanta does not guarantee third-party certification. Outside agencies control the requirements for certifications and are subject to change without notice to Brown Mackie College.

Program availability and degree offerings are subject to change.

Costs

Tuition for the 2012–13 academic year was $366 per credit hour and $20 per credit hour for general fees. Tuition for the occupational therapy assistant program was $381 per credit hour and $20 per credit hour for general fees. Tuition for the surgical technology program was $360 per credit hour and $15 per credit hour for general fees. The cost of textbooks, if applicable, and other instructional materials varies by program.

Financial Aid

Financial aid is available to those who qualify. Brown Mackie College — Atlanta maintains a full-time staff of financial aid professionals to assist qualified students in obtaining financial assistance. The college participates in several student aid programs. Forms of financial aid available through federal resources include the Federal Pell Grant Program, Federal Supplemental Educational Opportunity Grant (FSEOG) Program, Federal Work-Study Program, Federal Perkins Loan Program, Federal Stafford Student Loan Program (subsidized and unsubsidized), and the Federal PLUS Loan Program. Eligible students may also apply for state awards and veterans' educational benefits. Students with physical or mental disabilities that are a handicap to employment may be eligible for training services through the state Agency for Vocational Rehabilitation. For further information, students should contact the Brown Mackie College — Atlanta Student Financial Services Office.

Each year, the college makes available President's Scholarships of $1,000 each to qualifying seniors from area high schools. In order to qualify, a senior must be graduating from a participating high school, have maintained a cumulative grade point average of at least 2.0, and submitted a brief essay. The student's extracurricular activities and community service are also considered. The President's Scholarship is available only to students enrolling in one of the college's degree programs. Students awarded the scholarship must enroll at Brown Mackie College — Atlanta between June and September immediately following their high school graduation. Applications for these scholarships can be obtained from the guidance departments of participating high schools. These applications must be completed and returned to the college by March 31.

The Education Foundation was established in 2000 to offer scholarship support to students interested in continuing their education at one of the postsecondary, career-focused schools in the EDMC system. The number and amount of the awards can vary, depending on the funds available. Scholarship applications are considered every quarter. At Brown Mackie College, applicants must be currently enrolled in an associate or bachelor's degree program and in their fourth quarter or higher (but no further than their second-to-last quarter) at the time of application. Awards are made based on academic performance and potential, as well as financial need. Interested students should contact the college's Student Financial Service Department for additional information.

Faculty

There are 4 full-time and 5 part-time faculty members. The average student-faculty ratio is 19:1. Each student has a faculty and student adviser.

Facilities and Resources

Brown Mackie College — Atlanta comprises administrative offices, faculty and student lounges, a reception area, and spacious classrooms and laboratories. Instructional equipment includes personal computers, LANs, printers, and transcribers. The library provides support for the academic programs through volumes covering a broad range of subjects, as well as through Internet access. Vehicle parking is provided for both students and staff members.

Brown Mackie College — Atlanta is fully committed to using eTextbooks and computer tablets in the classroom. Utilizing these tablets to access expanded course material, students are able to increase their acumen for using this technology and further enhance their educational experience. Students have the ability to directly download their eTextbooks to their tablet, eliminating the need to carry heavy, physical textbooks and reducing the overall cost of supplies.

Brown Mackie College is a nonresidential, smoke-free institution.

Location

Brown Mackie College — Atlanta is located at 4370 Peachtree Road NE in Atlanta, Georgia, which is easily accessible from I-285 and the MARTA Brookhaven rail station.

Admission Requirements

Each applicant for admission is assigned to an Assistant Director of Admissions who directs the applicant through the steps of the admissions process, providing information on curriculum, policies, procedures, and services and assisting the applicant in setting necessary appointments and interviews.

To qualify for admission, each applicant must provide documentation of graduation from an accredited high school or from a state-approved secondary education curriculum or provide official documentation of high school graduation equivalency. All transcripts become the property of Brown Mackie College. Admission is based upon the applicant meeting the stated

requirements, a review of the applicant's previous education records, and a review of the applicant's career interests. If previous academic records indicate that the Brown Mackie College education and training programs would not benefit the applicant, the college reserves the right to advise the applicant not to enroll. Special requirements for enrollment into certain programs are discussed in the descriptions of those programs.

For the most recent information regarding admission requirements, applicants should refer to the current academic catalog.

Application and Information

Applicants must complete and submit an application form along with documentation of graduation from an accredited high school or state-approved secondary education curriculum, or applicants must provide official documentation of high school graduation equivalency.

Applicants can go online to BMCprograms.info for program duration, tuition, fees and other costs, median debt, federal salary data, alumni success, programmatic accreditation and other important information.

Brown Mackie College is a system of over twenty-five schools located throughout North America. Programs, credential levels, technology, and scheduling options vary by school, and employment opportunities are not guaranteed. Financial aid is available for those who qualify. Administrative offices are located at: 625 Eden Park Drive, Suite 1100; Cincinnati, Ohio 45202; phone: 513-830-2000. ©2013 Brown Mackie College. OH Registration #03-09-1685T; #03-09-1686T; #03-09-1687T; #03-09-1688T; #06-03-1781T; AC0150, AC0109, AC0078, AC0045, AC0138, AC0110; Licensed by the Florida Commission for Independent Education, License No. 3206.

For additional information, prospective students should contact:

Director of Admissions
Brown Mackie College — Atlanta
4370 Peachtree Road NE
Atlanta, Georgia 30319
Phone: 404-799-4500
         877-479-8419 (toll-free)
Fax: 404-799-4522
E-mail: bmcatadm@brownmackie.edu
Web site: http://www.brownmackie.edu/Atlanta

BROWN MACKIE COLLEGE — BIRMINGHAM

BIRMINGHAM, ALABAMA

The College and Its Mission

Brown Mackie College — Birmingham (Brown Mackie College) is one of over twenty-five locations in the Brown Mackie College system of schools (www.brownmackie.edu), which is dedicated to providing educational programs that prepare students to pursue entry-level positions in a competitive, rapidly changing workplace. Brown Mackie College schools offer bachelor's degree, associate degree, diploma, and certificate programs in health sciences, business, information technology, legal studies, and design to thousands of students in the Midwest, Southeast, Southwest, and Western United States.

Brown Mackie College was originally founded and approved by the Board of Trustees of Kansas Wesleyan College in Salina, Kansas on July 30, 1892. In 1938, the College was incorporated as the Brown Mackie School of Business under the ownership of Perry E. Brown and A.B. Mackie, former instructors at Kansas Wesleyan University in Salina, Kansas. Their last names formed the name of Brown Mackie. By January 1975, with improvements in curricula and higher degree-granting status, the Brown Mackie School of Business became Brown Mackie College.

Brown Mackie College — Birmingham is accredited by the Accrediting Council for Independent Colleges and Schools to award associate degrees and diplomas. The Accrediting Council for Independent Colleges and Schools is listed as a nationally recognized accrediting agency by the United States Department of Education and is recognized by the Council for Higher Education Accreditation. ACICS can be contacted at 750 First Street NE, Suite 980, Washington, D.C. 20002; phone: 202-336-6780.

The occupational therapy assistant program has applied for accreditation to the Accreditation Council for Occupational Therapy Education (ACOTE) of the American Occupational Therapy Association (AOTA), located at 4720 Montgomery Lane, Suite 200, Bethesda, Maryland 20814-3449; phone: 301-652-AOTA. Graduates of the program will be eligible to sit for the national certification examination for the occupational therapy assistant administered by the National Board for Certification in Occupational Therapy (NBCOT). After successful completion of this exam, the individual will be a Certified Occupational Therapy Assistant (COTA). In addition, most states require licensure in order to practice; however, state licenses are usually based on the results of the NBCOT Certification Examination. Note that a felony conviction may affect a graduate's ability to sit for the NBCOT certification examination or attain state licensure.

Academic Programs

Brown Mackie College — Birmingham provides higher education to traditional and nontraditional students through associate degree and diploma programs that assist in enhancing their career opportunities, broadening their perspectives through appropriate general education courses, thinking independently and critically, and improving problem-solving abilities. The college strives to develop within its students the desire for lifelong and continued education.

Each college quarter comprises twelve weeks. Associate degree programs require a minimum of eight quarters to complete. Programs are offered on a year-round basis, providing students with the ability to work uninterrupted toward completion of their programs. The college offers all programs in a unique One Course a Month format. This allows students to focus studies on only one course for four weeks. This schedule has proven convenient for students with multiple obligations such as jobs and family.

Associate Degree Programs: The Associate of Science degree is awarded in architectural design and drafting technology, biomedical equipment technology, business management, graphic design, health care administration, information technology, medical assisting, paralegal, and surgical technology.

The Associate of Applied Science degree is awarded in occupational therapy assistant.

Diploma Programs: The college offers diploma programs in bookkeeping specialist, dental assistant, general business, medical insurance specialist, medical assistant, and paralegal assistant.

The American Medical Technologists (AMT), which offers the certification for Registered Medical Assistant (RMA), accepts the accreditation of Brown Mackie College — Birmingham. Students will qualify to take the RMA certification examination upon graduating the Brown Mackie College — Birmingham medical assisting and medical assistant programs. Graduates of the 48 credit-hour medical assistant program are not qualified to take the AMT/RMA exam.

Brown Mackie College — Birmingham does not guarantee third-party certification. Outside agencies control the requirements for certifications and are subject to change without notice to Brown Mackie College.

Program availability and degree offerings are subject to change.

Costs

Tuition in the 2012–13 academic year for most bachelor's and associate degrees and certificates was $315 per credit hour; fees were $20 per credit hour. Tuition for the surgical technology program was $350 per credit hour; fees were $20 per credit hour. Tuition for the occupational therapy assistant program was $381 per credit hour; fees were $20 per credit hour. The cost of textbooks, if applicable, and other instructional materials varies by program.

Financial Aid

Financial aid is available for those who qualify. Brown Mackie College maintains a full-time staff of Student Financial Services Advisors to assist qualified students in obtaining the financial assistance they require to meet their educational expenses. Available resources include federal and state aid, student loans from private lenders, and Federal Work-Study opportunities, both on and off college premises.

Each year, the college makes available President's Scholarships of $1,000 each to qualifying seniors from area high schools. In order to qualify, a senior must have graduated from a participating high school, must be maintained a cumulative grade point average of at least 2.0, and submitted a brief essay. The student's extracurricular activities and community service are also considered. These scholarships are available only to students enrolling in one of the college's degree programs. Students awarded the scholarship must enroll at Brown

Mackie College — Birmingham between June and September immediately following their high school graduation. Applications for these scholarships can be obtained from the guidance departments of participating high schools. These applications must be completed and returned to the college by March 31.

The Education Foundation was established in 2000 to offer scholarship support to students interested in continuing their education at one of the postsecondary, career-focused schools in the EDMC system. The number and amount of the awards can vary, depending on the funds available. Scholarship applications are considered every quarter. At Brown Mackie College, applicants must be currently enrolled in an associate or bachelor's degree program and in their fourth quarter or higher (but no further than their second-to-last quarter) at the time of application. Awards are made based on academic performance and potential, as well as financial need. Interested students should contact the college's Student Financial Service Department for additional information.

Faculty

Experienced faculty members provide academic support and are committed to the academic and technical preparation of their students. The college has both full-time and part-time instructors, with a student-faculty ratio of 15:1.

Facilities and Resources

A modern facility, Brown Mackie College offers approximately 35,000 square feet of classroom, computer and allied health labs, library, and office space. The college is equipped with multiple computer labs, housing over 100 computers. High-speed access to the Internet and other online resources are available to students and faculty. Multimedia classrooms are outfitted with overhead projectors, VCR/DVD players, and computers.

Brown Mackie College — Birmingham is fully committed to using eTextbooks and computer tablets in the classroom. Utilizing these tablets to access expanded course material, students will be able to increase their acumen for using this technology and further enhance their educational experience. Students have the ability to directly download their eTextbooks to their tablet, eliminating the need to carry heavy, physical textbooks and reducing the overall cost of supplies.

Brown Mackie College is nonresidential and has ample parking at no cost. The campus is a smoke-free facility.

Location

Brown Mackie College — Birmingham is conveniently located at 105 Vulcan Road, in Birmingham, Alabama.

Admission Requirements

Each applicant for admission is assigned to an Assistant Director of Admissions who directs the applicant through the steps of the admissions process. They provide information on curriculum, policies, procedures, and services and assist the applicant in setting necessary appointments and interviews. To qualify for admission, each applicant must provide documentation of graduation from an accredited high school or from a state-approved secondary education curriculum or provide official documentation of high school graduation equivalency. All transcripts become the property of the college. Admission to the college is based on the applicant meeting the stated requirements, a review of the applicant's previous educational records, and a review of the applicant's career interests. If previous academic records indicate the college's education and training programs would not benefit the applicant, the college reserves the right to advise the applicant not to enroll. Special requirements for enrollment into certain programs are discussed in the descriptions of those programs.

For the most recent information regarding admission requirements, prospective students should refer to the current academic catalog.

Application and Information

Applicants must complete and submit an application form, along with documentation of graduation from an accredited high school or state-approved secondary education curriculum or official documentation of high school graduation equivalency.

Prospective students should go online to BMCprograms.info for program duration, tuition, fees and other costs, median debt, federal salary data, alumni success, programmatic accreditation and other important information.

Brown Mackie College is a system of over twenty-five schools located throughout North America. Programs, credential levels, technology, and scheduling options vary by school, and employment opportunities are not guaranteed. Financial aid is available for those who qualify. Administrative offices are located at 625 Eden Park Drive, Suite 1100; Cincinnati, Ohio 45202; phone: 513.830.2000. ©2013 Brown Mackie College. OH Registration #03-09-1685T; #03-09-1686T; #03-09-1687T; #03-09-1688T; #06-03-1781T; AC0150, AC0109, AC0078, AC0045, AC0138, AC0110; Licensed by the Florida Commission for Independent Education, License No. 3206.

For additional information, prospective students should contact:

Director of Admissions
Brown Mackie College — Birmingham
105 Vulcan Road, Suite 100
Birmingham, Alabama 35209
Phone: 205-909-1500
          888-299-4699 (toll-free)
Fax: 205-909-1588
E-mail: bmbirmadm@brownmackie.edu
Web site: http://www.brownmackie.edu/Birmingham

BROWN MACKIE COLLEGE — BOISE
BOISE, IDAHO

The College and Its Mission

Brown Mackie College — Boise (Brown Mackie College) is one of over twenty-five locations in the Brown Mackie College system of schools (www.brownmackie.edu), which is dedicated to providing educational programs that prepare students to pursue entry-level positions in a competitive, rapidly changing workplace. Brown Mackie College schools offer bachelor's degree, associate degree, diploma, and certificate programs in health sciences, business, information technology, legal studies, and design to thousands of students in the Midwest, Southeast, Southwest, and Western United States.

Brown Mackie College — Boise is accredited by the Accrediting Council for Independent Colleges and Schools to award associate degrees and diplomas. The Accrediting Council for Independent Colleges and Schools is listed as a nationally recognized accrediting agency by the United States Department of Education and is recognized by the Council for Higher Education Accreditation. ACICS can be contacted at 750 First Street NE, Suite 980, Washington, D.C. 20002; phone: 202-336-6780.

Brown Mackie College — Boise is registered with the State Board of Education in accordance with Section 33-2403, Idaho Code.

The occupational therapy assistant program is accredited by the Accreditation Council for Occupational Therapy Education (ACOTE) of the American Occupational Therapy Association (AOTA), located at 4720 Montgomery Lane, Suite 200, Bethesda, Maryland 20814-3449; phone: 301-652-AOTA. Graduates of the program will be eligible to sit for the national certification examination for the occupational therapy assistant administered by the National Board for Certification in Occupational Therapy (NBCOT). After successful completion of this exam, the individual will be a Certified Occupational Therapy Assistant (COTA). In addition, most states require licensure in order to practice; however, state licenses are usually based on the results of the NBCOT Certification Examination. Note that a felony conviction may affect a graduate's ability to sit for the NBCOT certification examination or attain state licensure.

The surgical technology program is accredited by the Accrediting Bureau of Health Education Schools, ABHES.

The veterinary technology program has provisional programmatic accreditation granted by the American Veterinary Medical Association (AVMA) through the Committee on Veterinary Technician Education and Activities (CVTEA).

Academic Programs

Brown Mackie College — Boise provides higher education to traditional and nontraditional students through associate degree, and diploma programs that assist in enhancing their career opportunities, broadening their perspectives through appropriate general education courses, thinking independently and critically, and improving problem-solving abilities.

Each college quarter comprises twelve weeks. Associate degree programs require a minimum of eight quarters to complete. Programs are offered on a year-round basis, providing students with the opportunity to work uninterrupted toward completion of their programs. The college offers all programs in a unique One Course a Month format. This allows students to focus studies on only one course for four weeks. This schedule has proven convenient for students with multiple obligations such as jobs and family.

Associate Degree Programs: The Associate of Science degree is awarded in accounting technology, architectural design and drafting technology, bioscience laboratory technology, business management, criminal justice, health care administration, information technology, paralegal, surgical technology, and veterinary technology.

The Associate of Applied Science degree is awarded in occupational therapy assistant.

Diploma Programs: Diploma programs are offered in accounting, business, criminal justice, medical assistant, and paralegal assistant.

The American Medical Technologists (AMT), which offers the certification for Registered Medical Assistant (RMA), accepts the accreditation of Brown Mackie College — Boise. Students will qualify to take the RMA certification examination upon graduating the Brown Mackie College — Boise medical assistant program. Graduates of the 48 credit-hour medical assistant program are not qualified to take the AMT/RMA exam.

Program availability and degree offerings are subject to change.

Costs

Tuition for programs in the 2012–13 academic year was $324 per credit hour, with a general fee of $20 per credit hour applied to instructional costs for activities and services. Tuition for the occupational therapy assistant courses was $381 per credit hour with a $20 per credit fee applied to instructional costs for activities and services. Tuition for the surgical technology courses was $360 per credit hour with a $20 per credit fee applied to instructional costs for activities and services. The cost of textbooks, if applicable, and other instructional materials varies by program

Financial Aid

Financial aid is available for those who qualify. The college maintains a full-time staff of Student Financial Services Advisors to assist qualified students in obtaining financial assistance. The college participates in several student aid programs. Forms of financial aid available through federal resources include the Federal Pell Grant Program, Federal Supplemental Educational Opportunity Grant (FSEOG) Program, Federal Work-Study Program, Federal Perkins Loan Program, Federal Stafford Student Loan Program (subsidized and unsubsidized), and the Federal PLUS Loan Program.

Each year, the college makes available President's Scholarships of $1,000 each to qualifying seniors from area high schools. In order to qualify, a senior must be graduating from a participating high school, must be maintaining a cumulative grade point average of at least 2.0, and must submit a brief essay. The student's extracurricular activities and community service are also considered. The President's Scholarship is available only to students enrolling in one of the college's degree programs. Students awarded the scholarship must enroll at Brown Mackie College — Boise between June and September immediately following their high school graduation. Applications for these scholarships can be obtained from the guidance departments of participating high schools. These applications must be completed and returned to the college by March 31.

The Education Foundation was established in 2000 to offer scholarship support to students interested in continuing their education at one of the postsecondary, career-focused schools in the EDMC system. The number and amount of the awards can vary, depending on the funds available. Scholarship applications are considered every quarter. At Brown Mackie College, applicants must be currently enrolled in an associate or bachelor's degree program and in their fourth quarter or higher (but no further than their second-to-last quarter) at the time of application. Awards are made based on academic performance and potential, as well as financial need. Interested students should contact the college's Student Financial Service Department for additional information.

Faculty

There are 14 full-time and 34 part-time faculty members at the college. The average student-faculty ratio is 15:1. Each student is assigned to a program department chair as an advisor.

Facilities and Resources

Opened in 2008, this modern facility offers more than 40,000 square feet of tastefully decorated classrooms, laboratories, and office space designed to specifications of the college for its business, medical, and technical programs. Instructional equipment is comparable to current technology used in business and industry today. Modern classrooms for special instructional needs offer multimedia capabilities with surround sound and overhead projectors accessible through computer, or DVD. Internet access and instructional resources are available at the college's library. Experienced faculty members provide academic support and are committed to the academic and technical preparation of their students.

Brown Mackie College — Boise is fully committed to using eTextbooks and computer tablets in the classroom. Utilizing these tablets to access expanded course material, students are able to increase their acumen for using this technology and further enhance their educational experience. Students have the ability to directly download their eTextbooks to their tablet, eliminating the need to carry heavy, physical textbooks and reducing the overall cost of supplies.

The campus is nonresidential; public transportation and ample parking at no cost are available.

Location

Brown Mackie College — Boise is conveniently located at 9050 West Overland Road in Boise, Idaho.

Admission Requirements

Each applicant for admission is assigned to an Assistant Director of Admissions who directs the applicant through the steps of the admissions process. They provide information on curriculum, policies, procedures, and services, and assist the applicant in setting necessary appointments and interviews. To qualify for admission, each applicant must provide documentation of graduation from an accredited high school or from a state-approved secondary education curriculum or provide official documentation of high school graduation equivalency. All transcripts become the property of the college.

As part of the admission process, students are given an assessment of academic skills. Although the results of this assessment do not determine eligibility for admission, they provide the college with a means of determining the need for academic support as well as a means by which the college can evaluate the effectiveness of its educational programs. All new students are required to complete this assessment, which is readministered at the end of the student's program so results may be compared with those of the initial administration.

In addition to the college's general admission requirements, applicants enrolling in the occupational therapy assistant program must document one of the following: a high school cumulative grade point average of at least 2.5, a score on the GED examination of at least 57 (557 if taken on or after January 15, 2002), or completion of 12 quarter-credit hours or 8 semester-credit hours of collegiate course work with a grade point average of at least 2.5. Credit hours may not include Professional Development (CF 1100), the Brown Mackie College — Boise course. Students entering the program must also have completed a biology course with a grade of at least a C (or an average of at least 2.0 on a 4.0 scale).

For the most recent information regarding admission requirements, prospective students should refer to the current academic catalog.

Application and Information

Applicants must complete and submit an application form, along with documentation of graduation from an accredited high school or state-approved secondary education curriculum or official documentation of high school graduation equivalency.

Applicants can go online to BMCprograms.info for program duration, tuition, fees and other costs, median debt, federal salary data, alumni success, programmatic accreditation and other important information.

Brown Mackie College is a system of over twenty-five schools located throughout North America. Programs, credential levels, technology, and scheduling options vary by school, and employment opportunities are not guaranteed. Financial aid is available for those who qualify. Administrative offices are located at 625 Eden Park Drive, Suite 1100; Cincinnati, Ohio 45202; phone: 513-830-2000. ©2013 Brown Mackie College. OH Registration #03-09-1685T; #03-09-1686T; #03-09-1687T; #03-09-1688T; #06-03-1781T; AC0150, AC0109, AC0078, AC0045, AC0138, AC0110; Licensed by the Florida Commission for Independent Education, License No. 3206.

For additional information, prospective students should contact:

Director of Admissions
Brown Mackie College — Boise
9050 West Overland Road
Suite 100
Boise, Idaho 83709
Phone: 208-321-8800
    888-810-9286 (toll-free)
Fax: 208-375-3249
E-mail: bmcboiadm@brownmackie.edu
Web site: http://www.brownmackie.edu/Boise

BROWN MACKIE COLLEGE — CINCINNATI
CINCINNATI, OHIO

BROWN
MACKIE
COLLEGE
CINCINNATI℠

The College and Its Mission

Brown Mackie College — Cincinnati (Brown Mackie College) is one of over twenty-five locations in the Brown Mackie College system of schools (www.brownmackie.edu), which is dedicated to providing educational programs that prepare students to pursue entry-level positions in a competitive, rapidly changing workplace. Brown Mackie College schools offer bachelor's degree, associate degree, diploma, and certificate programs in health sciences, business, information technology, legal studies, and design to thousands of students in the Midwest, Southeast, Southwest, and Western United States.

Brown Mackie College — Cincinnati was founded in February 1927 as Southern Ohio Business College. In 1978, the college's main location was relocated from downtown Cincinnati to the Bond Hill–Roselawn area and in 1995 to its current location at 1011 Glendale-Milford Road in the community of Woodlawn.

Brown Mackie College — Cincinnati is accredited by the Accrediting Council for Independent Colleges and Schools to award associate degrees, diplomas, and certificates. The Accrediting Council for Independent Colleges and Schools is listed as a nationally recognized accrediting agency by the United States Department of Education and is recognized by the Council for Higher Education Accreditation. ACICS can be contacted at 750 First Street NE, Suite 980, Washington, D.C. 20002; phone: 202-336-6780.

The Brown Mackie College — Cincinnati Associate of Applied Science degree in surgical technology is accredited by the Commission on Accreditation of Allied Health Education Programs (www.caahep.org), upon the recommendation of the Accreditation Review Committee on Education in Surgical Technology. The Commission on Accreditation of Allied Health Education Programs is located at 1361 Park Street, Clearwater, Florida 33756; phone: 727-210-2350.

The veterinary technology program has provisional programmatic accreditation granted by the American Veterinary Medical Association (AVMA) through the Committee on Veterinary Technician Education and Activities (CVTEA).

The practical nursing diploma program complies with the Ohio Board of Nursing guidelines as set forth in the Ohio Administrative Code, Chapter 4723-5. The program is administered at the following locations: Brown Mackie College — Cincinnati, Brown Mackie College — Findlay, Brown Mackie College — Akron, and Brown Mackie College — North Canton, and all operate under the same approval. The Ohio Board of Nursing is located at 17 South High Street, Suite 400, Columbus, Ohio 43215-3413; phone: 614-466-3947.

Brown Mackie College — Cincinnati is licensed by the Ohio State Board of Career Colleges and Schools, 30 East Broad Street, 24th Floor, Suite 2481, Columbus, Ohio 43215-3138; phone: 614-466-2752. Ohio registration #03-09-1686T.

Brown Mackie College — Cincinnati is regulated by the Board for Proprietary Education Indiana Commission for Higher Education, 101 West Ohio Street, Suite 670, Indianapolis, Indiana 46204; phone: 317-464-4400. Indiana advertising code: AC0150.

Academic Programs

Brown Mackie — Cincinnati provides higher education to traditional and nontraditional students through associate degrees, diploma, and certificate programs that can assist them in enhancing their career opportunities, broadening their perspectives through appropriate general education courses, thinking independently and critically, and improving problem-solving abilities. The college strives to develop within its students the desire for lifelong and continued education.

Each college quarter comprises twelve weeks. Associate degree programs require a minimum of eight quarters to complete. Programs are offered on a year-round basis, providing students with the ability to work uninterrupted toward their degrees. The college offers all programs in a unique One Course a Month format. This schedule allows students to focus studies on only one course for four weeks and has proven convenient for students with multiple obligations such as jobs and family.

Associate Degree Programs: The Associate of Applied Business degree is awarded in accounting technology, business management, computer networking and applications, criminal justice, information technology, and paralegal.

The Associate of Applied Science degree is awarded in architectural design and drafting technology, audio/video production, biomedical equipment technology, early childhood education, health care administration, pharmacy technology, surgical technology, and veterinary technology.

Diploma Programs: Diploma programs are offered in audio/video technician, bookkeeping specialist, criminal justice specialist, general business, medical assistant, paralegal assistant, and practical nursing.

Certificate Program: The college offers a certificate program in computer networking.

The American Medical Technologists (AMT), which offers the certification for Registered Medical Assistant (RMA), accepts the accreditation of Brown Mackie College — Cincinnati. Students will qualify to take the RMA certification examination upon graduating the Brown Mackie College — Cincinnati medical assistant program. Graduates of the 48 credit-hour medical assistant program are not qualified to take the AMT/RMA exam.

Brown Mackie College — Cincinnati does not guarantee third-party certification. Outside agencies control the requirements for certifications and are subject to change without notice to Brown Mackie College.

Program availability and degree offerings are subject to change.

Costs

Tuition for the 2012–13 academic year was $314 per credit hour and $20 per credit hour for general fees. Tuition for the practical nursing program was $381 per credit hour and $30 per credit hour for general fees. Tuition for the surgical technology program was $360 per credit hour and $20 per credit hour for general fees. Tuition for the computer networking and applications program was $314 per credit hour and $25 per credit hour for general fees. The cost of textbooks, if applicable, and other instructional materials varies by program.

Financial Aid

Financial aid is available to those who qualify. Brown Mackie College maintains a full-time staff of Student Financial Services Advisers to assist qualified students in obtaining financial assistance. The college participates in several student aid programs. Forms of financial aid available to qualified students through federal resources include the Federal Pell Grant Program, Federal Supplemental Educational Opportunity Grant (FSEOG) Program, Federal Work-Study Program, Federal Perkins Loan Program, Federal Stafford Student Loan

Program (subsidized and unsubsidized), and the Federal PLUS Loan Program. Eligible students may apply for state awards, such as veterans' educational benefits. Students with physical or mental disabilities that are a handicap to employment may be eligible for training services through the state Agency for Vocational Rehabilitation. For further information, students should contact the Student Financial Services Office.

Each year, the college makes available President's Scholarships of $1,000 each to qualifying seniors from area high schools. In order to qualify, a senior must be graduating from a participating high school, have maintained a cumulative grade point average of at least 2.0, and submitted a brief essay. The student's extracurricular activities and community service are also considered. The President's Scholarship is available only to students enrolling in one of the college's degree programs. Students awarded the scholarship must enroll at Brown Mackie College — Cincinnati between June and September immediately following their high school graduation. Applications for these scholarships can be obtained from the guidance departments of participating high schools. These applications must be completed and returned to the college by March 31.

The Education Foundation was established in 2000 to offer scholarship support to students interested in continuing their education at one of the postsecondary, career-focused schools in the EDMC system. The number and amount of the awards can vary depending on the funds available. Scholarship applications are considered every quarter. At Brown Mackie College — Cincinnati, applicants must be currently enrolled in an associate degree program and in their fourth quarter or higher (but no further than their second-to-last quarter) at the time of application. Awards are made based on academic performance and potential, as well as financial need.

Faculty

There are 20 full-time and 90 part-time faculty members. The average student-faculty ratio is 20:1. Each student has a faculty and student adviser.

Facilities and Resources

Brown Mackie College — Cincinnati consists of more than 57,000 square feet of classroom, laboratory, and office space at the main campus and more than 28,000 square feet at the learning site. Both sites are designed to specifications of the college for its business, computer, medical, and creative programs.

Brown Mackie College — Cincinnati is fully committed to using eTextbooks and computer tablets in the classroom. Utilizing these tablets to access expanded course material, students are able to increase their acumen for using this technology and further enhance their educational experience. Students have the ability to directly download their eTextbooks to their tablet, eliminating the need to carry heavy, physical textbooks and reducing the overall cost of supplies.

Location

Brown Mackie College — Cincinnati is located in the Woodlawn section of Cincinnati, Ohio. The college is accessible by public transportation and provides parking at no cost. For added convenience, the college also holds classes at the Norwood Learning Site at 4805 Montgomery Road in Norwood, Ohio.

Admission Requirements

Each applicant for admission is assigned to an Assistant Director of Admissions, who directs the applicant through the steps of the admissions process, providing information on curriculum, policies, procedures, and services and assisting the applicant in setting necessary appointments and interviews.

To qualify for admission, each applicant must provide documentation of graduation from an accredited high school or from a state-approved secondary education curriculum or provide official documentation of high school graduation equivalency. All transcripts become the property of the college. Admission to the college is based on the applicant meeting the stated requirements, a review of the applicant's previous educational records, and a review of the applicant's career interests. If previous academic records indicate that the college's education and training programs would not benefit the applicant, the college reserves the right to advise the applicant not to enroll. Special requirements for enrollment into certain programs are discussed in the descriptions of those programs.

For the most recent information regarding admission requirements, please refer to the current academic catalog.

Application and Information

Applicants must complete and submit an application form, along with documentation of graduation from an accredited high school or state-approved secondary education curriculum or official documentation of high school graduation equivalency.

Prospective students can go online to BMCprograms.info for program duration, tuition, fees and other costs, median debt, federal salary data, alumni success, programmatic accreditation, and other important details.

Brown Mackie College is a system of over twenty-five schools located throughout North America. Programs, credential levels, technology, and scheduling options vary by school, and employment opportunities are not guaranteed. Financial aid is available for those who qualify. Administrative offices are located at 625 Eden Park Drive, Suite 1100; Cincinnati, Ohio 45202; phone: 513-830-2000. ©2013 Brown Mackie College. OH Registration #03-09-1685T; #03-09-1686T; #03-09-1687T; #03-09-1688T; #06-03-1781T; AC0150, AC0109, AC0078, AC0045, AC0138, AC0110; Licensed by the Florida Commission for Independent Education, License No. 3206.

For additional information, prospective students should contact:

Senior Director of Admissions
Brown Mackie College — Cincinnati
1011 Glendale-Milford Road
Cincinnati, Ohio 45215
Phone: 513-771-2424
        800-888-1445 (toll-free)
Fax: 513-771-3413
E-mail: bmcciadm@brownmackie.edu
Web site: http://www.brownmackie.edu/Cincinnati

BROWN MACKIE COLLEGE — DALLAS/FORT WORTH

DALLAS, TEXAS

The College and Its Mission

Brown Mackie College — Dallas/Fort Worth (Brown Mackie College) is one of over twenty-five locations in the Brown Mackie College system of schools (www.brownmackie.edu), which is dedicated to providing educational programs that prepare students to pursue entry-level positions in a competitive, rapidly changing workplace. The Brown Mackie College family of schools offers bachelor's degree, associate degree, diploma, and certificate programs in health sciences, business, information technology, legal studies, and design to thousands of students in the Midwest, Southeast, Southwest, and Western United States.

Brown Mackie College — Dallas/Fort Worth is accredited by the Accrediting Council for Independent Colleges and Schools to award associate degrees and diplomas. The Accrediting Council for Independent Colleges and Schools is listed as a nationally recognized accrediting agency by the United States Department of Education and is recognized by the Council for Higher Education Accreditation. ACICS can be contacted at 750 First Street NE, Suite 980, Washington, D.C. 20002; phone: 202-336-6780.

Brown Mackie College — Dallas/Fort Worth is approved and regulated by the Texas Workforce Commission, Career Schools and Colleges, Austin, Texas.

Brown Mackie College — Dallas/Fort Worth holds a Certificate of Authorization acknowledging exemption from the Texas Higher Education Coordinating Board Regulations.

Academic Programs

Brown Mackie College — Dallas/Fort Worth provides higher education to traditional and nontraditional students through associate degree and diploma programs that assist them in enhancing their career opportunities, broadening their perspectives through appropriate general education courses, thinking independently and critically, and improving problem-solving abilities. The college strives to develop within its students the desire for lifelong and continued education.

Each college quarter comprises ten to twelve weeks. Associate degree programs require a minimum of eight quarters to complete. Programs are offered on a year-round basis, providing students with the ability to work uninterrupted toward their degrees. The college offers all programs in a unique One Course a Month format. This allows students to focus studies on only one course for four weeks. This schedule has proven convenient for students with multiple obligations such as jobs and family.

Associate Degree Programs: The Associate of Science degree is awarded in accounting technology, architectural design and drafting technology, biomedical equipment technology, business management, computer networking, graphic design, health care administration, information technology, and surgical technology.

Diploma Programs: Brown Mackie College offers a medical assistant diploma program.

The American Medical Technologists (AMT), which offers the certification for Registered Medical Assistant (RMA), accepts the accreditation of Brown Mackie College — Dallas/Fort Worth. Students will qualify to take the RMA certification examination upon graduating the Brown Mackie College — Dallas/Fort Worth medical assistant program. Graduates of the 48 credit-hour medical assistant program are not qualified to take the AMT/RMA exam.

Brown Mackie College — Dallas/Fort Worth does not guarantee third-party certification. Outside agencies control the requirements for certifications and are subject to change without notice to Brown Mackie College.

Program availability and degree offerings are subject to change.

Costs

Tuition for the 2012–13 academic year was $324 per credit hour and general fees were $20 per credit hour, with some exceptions. The surgical technology tuition was $371 per credit hour and general fees were $20 per credit hour. The cost of textbooks, if applicable, and other instructional materials varies by program.

Financial Aid

Financial aid is available to those who qualify. The college maintains a full-time staff of Student Financial Services Advisers to assist qualified students in obtaining financial assistance. The college participates in several student aid programs. Forms of financial aid available through federal resources include Federal Pell Grants, Federal Supplemental Educational Opportunity Grants (FSEOG), Federal Work-Study Program awards, Federal Perkins Loans, Federal Stafford Student Loans (subsidized and unsubsidized), and Federal PLUS loans. Eligible students may apply for veterans' educational benefits. Students with physical or mental disabilities that are a handicap to employment may be eligible for training services through the state Vocational Rehabilitation Agency. For further information, students should contact the college Student Financial Services Office.

Each year, the college makes available President's Scholarships of $1,000 each to qualifying seniors from area high schools. In order to qualify, a senior must have graduated from a participating high school, maintained a cumulative grade point average of at least 2.0, and submitted a brief essay. The student's extracurricular activities and community service are also considered. The President's Scholarship is available only to students enrolling in one of the college's degree programs. Students who receive the scholarship must enroll at Brown Mackie College — Dallas/Fort Worth between June and September immediately following their high school graduation. Applications for these scholarships can be obtained from the guidance departments of participating high schools. These applications must be completed and returned to the college by March 31.

The Education Foundation was established in 2000 to offer scholarship support to students interested in continuing their education at one of the postsecondary, career-focused schools in the EDMC system. The number and amount of the awards can vary, depending on the funds available. Scholarship applications are considered every quarter. At Brown Mackie College applicants must be currently enrolled in an associate or bachelor's degree program and in their fourth quarter or higher (but no further than their second-to-last quarter) at the time of application. Awards are made based on academic performance and potential, as well as financial need. Interested students should contact the college's Student Financial Service Department for additional information.

Faculty

Classes at Brown Mackie College — Dallas/Fort Worth began July 2, 2012. There are 3 full-time and 14 part-time adjunct instructors at the college. The average student-faculty ratio is 14:1. Each student is able to meet and speak with the director of their program.

Academic Facilities

Brown Mackie College — Dallas/Fort Worth offers media presentation rooms for special instructional needs and a library that provides instructional resources and academic support for both faculty members and students.

Brown Mackie College — Dallas/Fort Worth is fully committed to using eTextbooks and computer tablets in the classroom. Utilizing these tablets to access expanded course material, students will be able to increase their acumen for using this technology and further enhance their educational experience. Students have the ability to directly download their eTextbooks to their tablet, eliminating the need to carry heavy, physical textbooks and reducing the overall cost of supplies.

Brown Mackie College — Dallas/Fort Worth is nonresidential; public transportation and ample parking at no cost are available. The campus is a smoke-free facility.

Location

Brown Mackie College — Dallas/Fort Worth is conveniently located at 2200 North Highway 121, Suite 250, in Bedford, Texas.

Admission Requirements

Each applicant for admission is assigned to an Assistant Director of Admissions, who directs the applicant through the steps of the admissions process, providing information on curriculum, policies, procedures, and services and assisting the applicant in setting necessary appointments and interviews. To qualify for admission, each applicant must provide documentation of graduation from an accredited high school or from a state-approved secondary education curriculum or provide official documentation of high school graduation equivalency. All transcripts become the property of the college. Admission to the college is based upon the applicant meeting the stated requirements, a review of the applicant's previous education records, and a review of the applicant's career interests. If previous academic records indicate the college's education and training programs would not benefit the applicant, the college reserves the right to advise the applicant not to enroll. Special requirements for enrollment into certain programs are discussed in the descriptions of those programs.

For the most recent information regarding admission requirements, prospective students should refer to the current academic catalog.

Application and Information

Applicants must complete and submit an application form, along with documentation of graduation from an accredited high school or state-approved secondary education curriculum or official documentation of high school graduation equivalency.

Prospective students can go online to BMCprograms.info for program duration, tuition, fees and other costs, median debt, federal salary data, alumni success, programmatic accreditation, and other important details.

Brown Mackie College is a system of over twenty-five schools located throughout North America. Programs, credential levels, technology, and scheduling options vary by school, and employment opportunities are not guaranteed. Financial aid is available for those who qualify. Administrative offices are located at 625 Eden Park Drive, Suite 1100; Cincinnati, Ohio 45202; phone: 513.830.2000. ©2013 Brown Mackie College. OH Registration #03-09-1685T; #03-09-1686T; #03-09-1687T; #03-09-1688T; #06-03-1781T; AC0150, AC0109, AC0078, AC0045, AC0138, AC0110; Licensed by the Florida Commission for Independent Education, License No. 3206.

For additional information, prospective students should contact:

Director of Admissions
Brown Mackie College — Dallas/Fort Worth
2200 North highway 121, Suite 250
Bedford, Texas 76021
Phone: 817-799-0500
          888-299-4799 (toll-free)
Fax: 817-799-0515
E-mail: bmcdaladm@brownmackie.edu
Web site: http://www.brownmackie.edu/Dallas

BROWN MACKIE COLLEGE — FINDLAY
FINDLAY, OHIO

The College and Its Mission

Brown Mackie — Findlay (Brown Mackie College) is one of over twenty-five locations in the Brown Mackie College system of schools (www.brownmackie.edu), which is dedicated to providing educational programs that prepare students to pursue entry-level positions in a competitive, rapidly changing workplace. The Brown Mackie College family of schools offers bachelor's degree, associate degree, diploma, and certificate programs in health sciences, business, information technology, legal studies, and design to thousands of students in the Midwest, Southeast, Southwest, and Western United States.

Brown Mackie College — Findlay was founded in 1926 by William H. Stautzenberger to provide solid business education at a reasonable cost. In 1960, the college was acquired by George R. Hawes, who served as its president until 1969. The college changed its name from Southern Ohio College–Findlay in 2001 to AEC Southern Ohio College; it was changed again to Brown Mackie College — Findlay in November 2004.

Brown Mackie College — Findlay is accredited by the Accrediting Council for Independent Colleges and Schools to award associate degrees and diplomas. The Accrediting Council for Independent Colleges and Schools is listed as a nationally recognized accrediting agency by the United States Department of Education and is recognized by the Council for Higher Education Accreditation. ACICS can be contacted at 750 First Street NE, Suite 980, Washington, D.C. 20002; phone: 202-336-6780.

The occupational therapy assistant program is accredited by the Accreditation Council for Occupational Therapy Education (ACOTE) of the American Occupational Therapy Association (AOTA), located at 4720 Montgomery Lane, Suite 200, Bethesda, Maryland 20814-3449; phone: 301-652-AOTA. Graduates of the program will be eligible to sit for the national certification examination for the occupational therapy assistant administered by the National Board for Certification in Occupational Therapy (NBCOT). After successful completion of this exam, the individual will be a Certified Occupational Therapy Assistant (COTA). In addition, most states require licensure in order to practice; however, state licenses are usually based on the results of the NBCOT Certification Examination. Note that a felony conviction may affect a graduate's ability to sit for the NBCOT certification examination or attain state licensure.

The Associate of Science in surgical technology program is accredited by the Commission on Accreditation of Allied Health Education Programs (www.caahep.org) upon the recommendation of the Accreditation Review Committee on Education in Surgical Technology.

The Associate of Applied Science in veterinary technology program has provisional programmatic accreditation granted by the American Veterinary Medical Association (AVMA) through the Committee on Veterinary Technician Education and Activities (CVTEA).

Brown Mackie College — Findlay is licensed by the Ohio State Board of Career Colleges and Schools, 30 East Broad Street, 24th Floor, Suite 2481, Columbus, Ohio 43215-3138; phone: 614-466-2752. Ohio registration #03-09-1687T.

Academic Programs

Brown Mackie College — Findlay provides higher education to traditional and nontraditional students through associate degree and diploma programs that can assist them in enhancing their career opportunities, broadening their perspectives through appropriate general education courses, thinking independently and critically, and improving problem-solving abilities. The college strives to develop within its students the desire for lifelong and continued education.

Each college quarter comprises twelve weeks. Associate degree programs require a minimum of eight quarters to complete. Programs are offered on a year-round basis, providing students with the ability to work uninterrupted toward completion of their programs. The college offers all programs in a unique One Course a Month format. This schedule allows students to focus studies on only one course for four weeks and has proven convenient for students with multiple obligations such as jobs and family.

Associate Degree Programs: The Associate of Applied Business degree is awarded in business management, criminal justice, and paralegal. The Associate of Applied Science degree is awarded in occupational therapy assistant, pharmacy technology, surgical technology, and veterinary technology.

Diploma Programs: In addition to the associate degree programs, the college offers diploma programs in criminal justice specialist, dental assistant, general business, medical assistant, paralegal assistant, and practical nursing.

The American Medical Technologists (AMT), which offers the certification for Registered Medical Assistant (RMA), accepts the accreditation of Brown Mackie College — Findlay. Students will qualify to take the RMA certification examination upon graduating the Brown Mackie College — Findlay medical assistant program. Graduates of the 48 credit-hour medical assistant program are not qualified to take the AMT/RMA exam.

Brown Mackie College — Findlay does not guarantee third-party certification. Outside agencies control the requirements for certifications and are subject to change without notice to Brown Mackie College.

Program availability and degree offerings are subject to change.

Costs

Tuition for programs in the 2012–13 academic year was $314 per credit hour, with a general fee of $20 per credit hour. Tuition for the practical nursing diploma program was $381 per credit hour, with a general fee of $30 per credit hour. Tuition for the occupational therapy assistant program was $381 per credit hour, with a general fee of $20 per credit hour. Tuition for the surgical technology program was $360 per credit hour, with a general fee of $20 per credit hour. The length of the program determines total cost. The cost of textbooks, if applicable, and other instructional materials varies by program.

Financial Aid

Financial aid is available to those who qualify. The college maintains a full-time staff of Student Financial Services Advisers to assist qualified students in obtaining financial assistance. The college participates in several student aid programs. Forms of financial aid available through federal resources include the Federal DIRECT Pell Grant Program, Federal Supplemental Educational Opportunity Grant (FSEOG) Program, Federal Work-Study Program, Federal DIRECT Stafford Student Loan Program (subsidized and unsubsidized), the Federal DIRECT PLUS Loan Program, the Ohio College Opportunity Grant (OHCOG), and the Smart Grant. Eligible students may apply for state awards, such as the veterans' educational benefits. Students with physical or mental disabilities that are a handicap to employment may be eligible for training services through the state Agency for Vocational Rehabilitation. For further information, students should contact the college's Student Financial Services Office.

Each year, the college makes available President's Scholarships of $1,000 each to qualifying seniors from area high schools. In order to qualify, a senior must be graduating from a participating high school, have maintained a cumulative grade point average of at least 2.0, and submitted a brief essay. The student's extracurricular activities and community service are also considered. The President's Scholarship is available only to students enrolling in one of the college's degree programs. Students awarded the scholarship must enroll at Brown Mackie College — Findlay between June and September immediately following their high school graduation. Applications for these scholarships can be obtained from the guidance departments of participating high schools. These applications must be completed and returned to the college by March 31.

The Education Foundation was established in 2000 to offer scholarship support to students interested in continuing their education at one of the postsecondary, career-focused schools in the EDMC system. The number and amount of the awards can vary, depending on the funds available. Scholarship applications are considered every quarter. At Brown Mackie College, applicants must be currently enrolled in an associate or bachelor's degree program and in their fourth quarter or higher (but no further than their second-to-last quarter) at the time of application. Awards are made based on academic performance and potential, as well as financial need. Interested students should contact the college's Student Financial Service Department for additional information.

Faculty

There are 27 full-time and 90 part-time adjunct instructors at the college. The average student-faculty ratio is 14:1. Each student is assigned a faculty adviser.

Academic Facilities

Brown Mackie College — Findlay is a nonresidential, smoke-free institution. Although the college does not offer residential housing, students who are unable to commute daily from their homes may request assistance from the Admissions Office in locating housing. Ample parking is available at no additional cost.

Brown Mackie College — Findlay is fully committed to using eTextbooks and computer tablets in the classroom. Utilizing these tablets to access expanded course material, students are able to increase their acumen for using this technology and further enhance their educational experience. Students have the ability to directly download their eTextbooks to their tablet, eliminating the need to carry heavy, physical textbooks and reducing the overall cost of supplies.

Location

Located at 1700 Fostoria Avenue, Suite 100, in Findlay, Ohio, the college is easily accessible from Interstate 75.

Admission Requirements

Each applicant for admission is assigned to an Assistant Director of Admissions, who directs the applicant through the steps of the admissions process, providing information on curriculum, policies, procedures, and services and assisting the applicant in setting necessary appointments and interviews.

To qualify for admission, each applicant must provide documentation of graduation from an accredited high school or from a state-approved secondary education curriculum or provide official documentation of high school graduation equivalency. All transcripts become the property of the college. Admission to the college is based upon the applicant meeting the stated requirements, a review of the applicant's previous educational records, and a review of the applicant's career interests. If previous academic records indicate that the college's education and training programs would not benefit the applicant, the college reserves the right to advise the applicant not to enroll. Special requirements for enrollment into certain programs are discussed in the descriptions of those programs.

For the most recent information regarding admission requirements, please refer to the current academic catalog.

Application and Information

Applicants must complete and submit an application form, along with documentation of graduation from an accredited high school or state-approved secondary education curriculum or official documentation of high school graduation equivalency.

Prospective students can go online to BMCprograms.info for program duration, tuition, fees and other costs, median debt, federal salary data, alumni success, programmatic accreditation, and other important details.

Brown Mackie College is a system of over twenty-five schools located throughout North America. Programs, credential levels, technology, and scheduling options vary by school, and employment opportunities are not guaranteed. Financial aid is available for those who qualify. Administrative offices are located at 625 Eden Park Drive, Suite 1100; Cincinnati, Ohio 45202; phone: 513.830.2000. ©2013 Brown Mackie College. OH Registration # 03-09-1685T; #03-09-1686T; #03-09-1687T; #03-09-1688T; #06-03-1781T; AC0150, AC0109, AC0078, AC0045, AC0138, AC0110; Licensed by the Florida Commission for Independent Education, License No. 3206.

For additional information, prospective students should contact:

Director of Admissions
Brown Mackie College — Findlay
1700 Fostoria Avenue, Suite 100
Findlay, Ohio 45840
Phone: 419-423-2211
          800-842-3687 (toll-free)
Fax: 419-423-0725
E-mail: bmcfiadm@brownmackie.edu
Web site: http://www.brownmackie.edu/Findlay

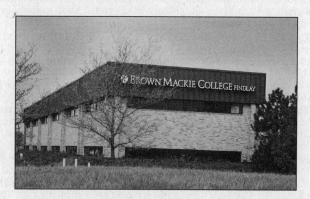

BROWN MACKIE COLLEGE — FORT WAYNE

FORT WAYNE, INDIANA

The College and Its Mission

Brown Mackie College — Fort Wayne (Brown Mackie College) is one of over twenty-five locations in the Brown Mackie College system of schools (www.brownmackie.edu), which is dedicated to providing educational programs that prepare students to pursue entry-level positions in a competitive, rapidly changing workplace. Brown Mackie College schools offer bachelor degree, associate degree, diploma, and certificate programs in health sciences, business, information technology, legal studies, and design to thousands of students in the Midwest, Southeast, Southwest, and Western United States.

Brown Mackie College — Fort Wayne is one of the oldest institutions of its kind in the country and the oldest in the state of Indiana. Established in 1882 as the South Bend Commercial College, the school later changed its name to Michiana College. In 1930, the college was incorporated under the laws of the state of Indiana and was authorized to confer associate degrees and certificates in business. In 1992, the College in South Bend added a branch location in Fort Wayne, Indiana. In 2004, Michiana College changed its name to Brown Mackie College — Fort Wayne.

Brown Mackie College — Fort Wayne is accredited by the Accrediting Council for Independent Colleges and Schools to award associate degrees, diplomas, and certificates. The Accrediting Council for Independent Colleges and Schools is listed as a nationally recognized accrediting agency by the United States Department of Education and is recognized by the Council for Higher Education Accreditation. ACICS can be contacted at 750 First Street NE, Suite 980, Washington, D.C. 20002; phone: 202-336-6780.

The Associate of Science in surgical technology program is accredited by the Accrediting Bureau of Health Education Schools and by the Commission on Accreditation of Allied Health Education Programs (www.caahep.org) upon the recommendation of the Accreditation Review Council on Education in Surgical Technology and Surgical Assisting (ARC/STSA). The Commission on Accreditation of Allied Health Education Programs is located at 1361 Park Street, Clearwater, Florida 33756; phone: 727-210-2350; www.caahep.org.

The Associate of Applied Science in occupational therapy assistant program is accredited by the Accreditation Council for Occupational Therapy Education (ACOTE) of the American Occupational Therapy Association (AOTA), located at 4720 Montgomery Lane, Suite 200, Bethesda, Maryland 20814-3449; phone: 301-652-AOTA. Graduates of the program will be eligible to sit for the national certification examination for the occupational therapy assistant administered by the National Board for Certification in Occupational Therapy (NBCOT). After successful completion of this exam, the individual will be a Certified Occupational Therapy Assistant (COTA). In addition, most states require licensure in order to practice; however, state licenses are usually based on the results of the NBCOT Certification Examination. Note that a felony conviction may affect a graduate's ability to sit for the NBCOT certification examination or attain state licensure.

The Associate of Applied Science in physical therapist assistant program at Brown Mackie College — Fort Wayne is accredited by the Commission on Accreditation in Physical Therapy Education (CAPTE), located at 1111 North Fairfax Street, Alexandria, Virginia 22314; phone: 703-706-3245; e-mail: accreditation@apta.org; www.capteonline.org.

The Associate of Applied Science in veterinary technology program has provisional programmatic accreditation granted by the American Veterinary Medical Association (AVMA) through the Committee on Veterinary Technician Education and Activities (CVTEA).

Brown Mackie College — Fort Wayne is regulated by the Board for Proprietary Education Indiana Commission for Higher Education, 101 West Ohio Street, Suite 670, Indianapolis, Indiana 46204; phone: 317-464-4400. Indiana advertising code: AC-0109.

Academic Programs

Brown Mackie College — Fort Wayne provides higher education to traditional and nontraditional students through associate degree, diploma, and certificate programs that assist them in enhancing their career opportunities, broadening their perspectives through appropriate general education courses, thinking independently and critically, and improving problem-solving abilities. The college strives to develop within its students the desire for lifelong and continued education.

Each college quarter comprises twelve weeks. Associate degree programs require a minimum of eight quarters to complete. Programs are offered on a year-round basis, providing students with the ability to work uninterrupted toward their degrees. The college offers all programs in a unique One Course a Month format. This allows students to focus studies on only one course for four weeks. This schedule has proven convenient for students with multiple obligations such as jobs and family.

Associate Degree Programs: The Associate of Science degree is awarded in accounting technology, business management, criminal justice, health care administration, office management, paralegal, and surgical technology.

The Associate of Applied Science degree is awarded in biomedical equipment technology, health and fitness training, nursing, occupational therapy assistant, physical therapist assistant, and veterinary technology.

Diploma Program: A diploma is awarded in practical nursing.

Certificate Programs: The college offers certificate programs in bookkeeping specialist, criminal justice, fitness trainer, general business, medical assistant, and paralegal assistant.

The American Medical Technologists (AMT), which offers the certification for Registered Medical Assistant (RMA), accepts the accreditation of Brown Mackie College — Fort Wayne. Students will qualify to take the RMA certification examination upon graduating the Brown Mackie College — Fort Wayne medical assistant program. Graduates of the 48 credit-hour medical assistant program are not qualified to take the AMT/RMA exam.

Brown Mackie College does not guarantee third-party certification/licensing exams. Outside agencies control the requirements for certification/licensing and are subject to change without notification to the college.

Program availability and degree offerings are subject to change.

Costs

Tuition in the 2012–13 academic year was $314 per credit hour with fees of $20 per credit hour for all programs except nursing, surgical technology, personal fitness training, occupational therapy assistant studies, and physical therapist assistant studies. Costs for textbooks, if applicable, and other instructional materials vary by program. For the nursing program, tuition was $410 per credit hour; fees were $30 per credit hour. For the surgical technology program, tuition was $360 per credit hour; fees were $20. Tuition for the personal fitness training programs was $324 per credit hour; fees were $30 per credit hour. Textbook expenses are estimated at $400 for the first term, $600 for the second term, and $100 for the third, fourth, and fifth terms. For certain courses in the occupational therapy assistant studies and physical therapist assistant studies programs, tuition was $381 per credit hour; fees were $20 per credit hour.

Financial Aid

The college maintains a full-time staff of Student Financial Services Advisers to assist qualified students in obtaining financial assistance. The college participates in several student aid programs. Forms of financial aid available through federal resources include the Federal Pell Grant Program, Federal Supplemental Educational

Opportunity Grant (FSEOG) Program, Federal Work-Study Program, Federal Perkins Loan Program, Federal Stafford Student Loan Program (subsidized and unsubsidized), and the Federal PLUS Loan Program. Eligible students may apply for Indiana state awards, such as the Frank O'Bannon Grant Program (formerly the Indiana State Grant Program), the Higher Education Award, and Twenty-First Century Scholarships for high school students; for the Core 40 awards; and for veterans' educational benefits. For further information, students should contact the Student Financial Services Office.

Each year, the college makes available President's Scholarships of $1,000 each to qualifying seniors from area high schools. In order to qualify, a senior must have graduated from a participating high school, maintained a cumulative grade point average of at least 2.0, and submitted a brief essay. The student's extracurricular activities and community service are also considered. The President's Scholarship is available only to students enrolling in one of the college's degree programs. Students awarded the scholarship must enroll at Brown Mackie College — Fort Wayne between June and September immediately following their high school graduation. Applications for these scholarships can be obtained from the guidance departments of participating high schools. These applications must be completed and returned to the college by March 31.

The Education Foundation was established in 2000 to offer scholarship support to students interested in continuing their education at one of the postsecondary, career-focused schools in the EDMC system. The number and amount of the awards can vary, depending on the funds available. Scholarship applications are considered every quarter. At Brown Mackie College, applicants must be currently enrolled in an associate or bachelor's degree program and in their fourth quarter or higher (but no further than their second-to-last quarter) at the time of application. Awards are made based on academic performance and potential, as well as financial need. Interested students should contact the college's Student Financial Service Department for additional information.

Faculty

The college has 45 full-time and 80 part-time instructors, with a student-faculty ratio of 15:1. Each student is assigned a faculty adviser.

Facilities and Resources

In 2005, the campus located in a 75,000-square-foot facility at 3000 East Coliseum Boulevard. Record enrollment allowed the institution to triple in size in less than one year. The three-story building offers a modern, professional environment for study. Ten classrooms are outfitted as "classrooms of the future," with an instructor workstation, full multimedia capabilities, a surround sound system, and projection screen that can be accessed by computer, DVD, or VHS equipment. The Brown Mackie College — Fort Wayne facility includes a criminal justice lab, surgical technology labs, medical labs, computer labs, and occupational and physical therapy labs, as well as a library and bookstore. The labs provide students with hands-on opportunities to apply knowledge and skills learned in the classroom. Students are welcome to use the labs when those facilities are not in use for scheduled classes.

Brown Mackie College — Fort Wayne is fully committed to using eTextbooks and computer tablets in the classroom. Utilizing these tablets to access expanded course material, students will be able to increase their acumen for using this technology and further enhance their educational experience. Students have the ability to directly download their eTextbooks to their tablet, eliminating the need to carry heavy, physical textbooks and reducing the overall cost of supplies.

The college is nonresidential; public transportation and ample parking at no cost are available. The campus is a smoke-free facility.

Location

Brown Mackie College — Fort Wayne is located at 3000 East Coliseum Boulevard in Fort Wayne, Indiana. The college facility is accessible by public transportation. Ample parking is provided at no additional charge. For added convenience, the college also operates a learning site at 2135 South Hannah Drive in Fort Wayne.

Admission Requirements

Each applicant for admission is assigned to an Assistant Director of Admissions, who directs the applicant through the steps of the admissions process, providing information on curriculum, policies, procedures, and services and assisting the applicant in setting necessary appointments and interviews. To qualify for admission, each applicant must provide documentation of graduation from an accredited high school or from a state-approved secondary education curriculum or provide official documentation of high school graduation equivalency. All transcripts become the property of the college. Admission to the college is based on the applicant meeting the stated requirements, a review of the applicant's previous educational records, and a review of the applicant's career interests. If previous academic records indicate the college's education and training programs would not benefit the applicant, the college reserves the right to advise the applicant not to enroll. Special requirements for enrollment into certain programs are discussed in the descriptions of those programs.

In addition to the college's general admission requirements, applicants enrolling in the practical nursing program must document the following, which must be completed and a record of proof must appear in the student's file prior to the start of the nursing fundamentals course. No student will be admitted to a clinical agency unless all paperwork is completed. This paperwork is a requirement of all contracted agencies. This paperwork includes records of (1) a complete physical, current to within six months of admission; (2) a two-step Mantoux test that is kept current throughout schooling; (3) a hepatitis B vaccination or signed refusal; (4) up-to-date immunizations, including tetanus and rubella; (5) a record of current CPR certification that is maintained throughout the student's clinical experience; and (6) hospitalization insurance or a signed waiver.

Application and Information

Applicants must complete and submit an application form, along with documentation of graduation from an accredited high school or state-approved secondary education curriculum or official documentation of high school graduation equivalency.

Prospective students can go online to BMCprograms.info for program duration, tuition, fees and other costs, median debt, federal salary data, alumni success, programmatic accreditation, and other important details.

Brown Mackie College is a system of over twenty-five schools located throughout North America. Programs, credential levels, technology, and scheduling options vary by school, and employment opportunities are not guaranteed. Financial aid is available for those who qualify. Administrative offices are located at 625 Eden Park Drive, Suite 1100; Cincinnati, Ohio 45202; phone: 513-830-2000. ©2013 Brown Mackie College. OH Registration #03-09-1685T; #03-09-1686T; #03-09-1687T; #03-09-1688T; #06-03-1781T; AC0150, AC0109, AC0078, AC0045, AC0138, AC0110; Licensed by the Florida Commission for Independent Education, License No. 3206.

For additional information, prospective students should contact:

Director of Admissions
Brown Mackie College — Fort Wayne
3000 East Coliseum Boulevard
Fort Wayne, Indiana 46805
Phone: 260-484-4400
        866-433-2289 (toll-free)
Fax: 260-484-2678
E-mail: bmcfwaadm@brownmackie.edu
Web site: http://www.brownmackie.edu/FortWayne

BROWN MACKIE COLLEGE — GREENVILLE
GREENVILLE, SOUTH CAROLINA

The College and Its Mission

Brown Mackie College — Greenville (Brown Mackie College) is one of over twenty-five locations in the Brown Mackie College system of schools (www.brownmackie.edu), which is dedicated to providing educational programs that prepare students to pursue entry-level positions in a competitive, rapidly changing workplace. Brown Mackie College schools offer bachelor's degree, associate degree, diploma, and certificate programs in health sciences, business, information technology, and legal studies to thousands of students in the Midwest, Southeast, Southwest, and Western United States.

Brown Mackie College was originally founded and approved by the Board of Trustees of Kansas Wesleyan College in Salina, Kansas on July 30, 1892. In 1938, the college was incorporated as The Brown Mackie School of Business under the ownership of Perry E. Brown and A.B. Mackie, former instructors at Kansas Wesleyan University in Salina, Kansas. Their last names formed the name of Brown Mackie. By January 1975, with improvements in curricula and higher degree-granting status, The Brown Mackie School of Business became Brown Mackie College.

Brown Mackie College — Greenville is accredited by the Accrediting Council for Independent Colleges and Schools to award associate degrees and certificates. The Accrediting Council for Independent Colleges and Schools is listed as a nationally recognized accrediting agency by the United States Department of Education and is recognized by the Council for Higher Education Accreditation. ACICS can be contacted at 750 First Street NE, Suite 980, Washington, D.C. 20002; phone: 202-336-6780.

Brown Mackie College — Greenville is licensed by the South Carolina Commission on Higher Education, 1122 Lady Street, Suite 300, Columbia, South Carolina 29201; phone: 803-737-2260. Licensure indicates only that minimum standards have been met; it is not equal to or synonymous with accreditation by an accrediting agency recognized by the U.S. Department of Education.

The occupational therapy assistant program is accredited by the Accreditation Council for Occupational Therapy Education (ACOTE) of the American Occupational Therapy Association (AOTA), located at 4720 Montgomery Lane, Suite 200, Bethesda, Maryland 20814-3449; phone: 301-652-AOTA. Graduates of the program will be eligible to sit for the national certification examination for the occupational therapy assistant administered by the National Board for Certification in Occupational Therapy (NBCOT). After successful completion of this exam, the individual will be a Certified Occupational Therapy Assistant (COTA). In addition, most states require licensure in order to practice; however, state licenses are usually based on the results of the NBCOT Certification Examination. Note that a felony conviction may affect a graduate's ability to sit for the NBCOT certification examination or attain state licensure.

The Brown Mackie College — Greenville Associate of Science in surgical technology program is accredited by the Accrediting Bureau of Health Education Schools.

Academic Programs

Brown Mackie College — Greenville provides higher education to traditional and nontraditional students through associate degree and certificate programs that assist in enhancing their career opportunities, broadening their perspectives through appropriate general education courses, thinking independently and critically, and improving problem-solving abilities. The college strives to develop within its students the desire for lifelong and continued education.

Each college quarter comprises twelve weeks. Associate degree programs require a minimum of eight quarters to complete. Programs are offered on a year-round basis, providing students with the ability to work uninterrupted toward completion of their degrees. The college offers all programs in a unique One Course a Month format. This allows students to focus studies on only one course for four weeks. This schedule has proven convenient for students with multiple obligations such as jobs and family.

Associate Degree Programs: The Associate of Applied Science degree is awarded in accounting technology, business management, criminal justice, health care administration, information technology, medical assisting, nursing, occupational therapy assistant, office management, paralegal, and surgical technology.

Certificate Programs: The certificate is awarded in accounting, business, criminal justice, medical assistant, and paralegal assistant.

The American Medical Technologists (AMT), which offers the certification for Registered Medical Assistant (RMA), accepts the accreditation of Brown Mackie College — Greenville. Students will qualify to take the RMA certification examination upon graduating the Brown Mackie College — Greenville medical assisting and medical assistant programs. Graduates of the 48 credit-hour medical assistant program are not qualified to take the AMT/RMA exam.

Brown Mackie College — Greenville does not guarantee third party certification. Outside agencies control the requirements for certifications and are subject to change without notice to Brown Mackie College.

Program availability and degree offerings are subject to change.

Costs

Tuition in the 2012–13 academic year for most associate degree and certificate programs was $314 per credit hour; fees were $20 per credit hour. Tuition for the nursing program was $410 per credit hour; fees were $30 per credit hour. Tuition for the occupational therapy assistant program was $381 per credit hour; fees were $20 per credit hour. Tuition for the surgical technology program was $360 per credit hour; fees were $20 per credit hour. The cost of textbooks, if applicable, and other instructional expenses vary by program.

Financial Aid

Financial aid is available for those who qualify. The college maintains a full-time staff of Student Financial Services Advisers to assist qualified students in obtaining the financial assistance they require to meet their educational expenses. Available resources include federal and state aid, student loans from private lenders, and Federal Work-Study opportunities, both on and off college premises.

Each year, the college makes available President's Scholarships of $1,000 each to qualifying seniors from area high schools. In order to qualify, a senior must have graduated from a participating high school, maintained a cumulative grade point average of at least 2.0, and submitted a brief essay. The student's extracurricular activities and community service are also considered. The President's Scholarship is available only to students enrolling in one of the college's degree programs. Students awarded the scholarship must enroll at Brown Mackie College — Greenville between June and September immediately following their high school graduation. Applications for these scholarships can be obtained from the guidance departments of participating high schools. These applications must be completed and returned to the college by March 31.

The Education Foundation was established in 2000 to offer scholarship support to students interested in continuing their education at one of the postsecondary, career-focused schools in the EDMC system. The number and amount of the awards can vary, depending on the funds available. Scholarship applications are considered every quarter. At Brown Mackie College applicants must be currently enrolled in an associate or bachelor's degree program and in their fourth quarter or higher (but no further than their second-to-last quarter) at the time of application. Awards are made based on academic performance and potential, as well as financial need. Interested students should contact the college's Student Financial Service Department for additional information.

Faculty

Experienced faculty members provide academic support and are committed to the academic and technical preparation of their students. The college has 9 full-time and 30 part-time instructors, with a student-faculty ratio of 24:1. Each student is assigned a faculty adviser.

Facilities and Resources

A modern facility, Brown Mackie College — Greenville offers nearly 50,000 square feet. The college is equipped with multiple computer labs housing over 100 computers. High-speed access to the Internet and other online resources are available for students and faculty. Multimedia classrooms are outfitted with overhead projectors, VCR/DVD players, and computers.

Brown Mackie College — Greenville is fully committed to using eTextbooks and computer tablets in the classroom. Utilizing these tablets to access expanded course material, students are able to increase their acumen for using this technology and further enhance their educational experience. Students have the ability to directly download their eTextbooks to their tablet, eliminating the need to carry heavy, physical textbooks and reducing the overall cost of supplies.

Brown Mackie College is nonresidential; public transportation and ample parking at no cost are available. The college is a smoke-free facility.

Location

Brown Mackie College — Greenville is conveniently located at Two Liberty Square, 75 Beattie Place, Suite 100, in Greenville, South Carolina.

Admission Requirements

Each applicant for admission is assigned to an Assistant Director of Admissions who directs the applicant through the steps of the admissions process. They provide information on curriculum, policies, procedures, and services and assist the applicant in setting necessary appointments and interviews. To qualify for admission, each applicant must provide documentation of graduation from an accredited high school or from a state-approved secondary education curriculum or provide official documentation of high school graduation equivalency. All transcripts become the property of the college. Admission to the college is based on the applicant meeting the stated requirements, a review of the applicant's previous educational records, and a review of the applicant's career interests. If previous academic records indicate the college's education and training programs would not benefit the applicant, the college reserves the right to advise the applicant not to enroll. Special requirements for enrollment into certain programs are discussed in the descriptions of those programs.

For the most recent information regarding admission requirements, prospective students should refer to the current academic catalog.

Application and Information

Applicants must complete and submit an application form along with documentation of graduation from an accredited high school or state-approved secondary education curriculum or official documentation of high school graduation equivalency.

Prospective students should go online to BMCprograms.info for program duration, tuition, fees and other costs, median debt, federal salary data, alumni success, programmatic accreditation, and other important details.

Brown Mackie College is a system of over twenty-five schools located throughout North America. Programs, credential levels, technology, and scheduling options vary by school, and employment opportunities are not guaranteed. Financial aid is available for those who qualify. Administrative offices are located at 625 Eden Park Drive, Suite 1100; Cincinnati, Ohio 45202; phone: 513-830-2000. ©2013 Brown Mackie College. OH Registration #03-09-1685T; #03-09-1686T; #03-09-1687T; #03-09-1688T; #06-03-1781T; AC0150, AC0109, AC0078, AC0045, AC0138, AC0110; Licensed by the Florida Commission for Independent Education, License No. 3206.

For additional information, prospective students should contact:

Director of Admissions
Brown Mackie College — Greenville
Two Liberty Square
75 Beattie Place, Suite 100
Greenville, South Carolina 29601
Phone: 864-239-5300
         877-479-8465 (toll-free)
Fax: 864-232-4094
E-mail: bmcgrweb@brownmackie.edu
Web site: http://www.brownmackie.edu/greenville

BROWN MACKIE COLLEGE — HOPKINSVILLE

HOPKINSVILLE, KENTUCKY

The College and Its Mission

Brown Mackie College — Hopkinsville (Brown Mackie College) is one of over twenty-five locations in the Brown Mackie College system of schools (www.brownmackie.edu), which is dedicated to providing educational programs that prepare students to pursue entry-level positions in a competitive, rapidly changing workplace. Brown Mackie College schools offer bachelor degree, associate degree, certificate, and diploma programs in health sciences, business, information technology, legal studies, and design to thousands of students in the Midwest, Southeast, Southwest, and Western United States.

Brown Mackie College — Hopkinsville is accredited by the Accrediting Council for Independent Colleges and Schools (ACICS) to award associate degrees and diplomas. ACICS is listed as a nationally recognized accrediting agency by the United States Department of Education and is recognized by the Council for Higher Education Accreditation. ACICS can be contacted at 750 First Street NE, Suite 980, Washington, D.C. 20002; phone: 202-336-6780.

The Associate of Applied Science in occupational therapy assistant program is accredited by the Accreditation Council for Occupational Therapy Education (ACOTE) of the American Occupational Therapy Association (AOTA), located at 4720 Montgomery Lane, Suite 200, Bethesda, Maryland, 20814-3449; phone 301-652-AOTA. Graduates of the program will be eligible to sit for the national certification examination for the occupational therapy assistant administered by the National Board for Certification in Occupational Therapy (NBCOT). After successful completion of this exam, the individual will be a Certified Occupational Therapy Assistant (COTA). In addition, most states require licensure in order to practice; however, state licenses are usually based on the results of the NBCOT Certification Examination. Note that a felony conviction may affect a graduate's ability to sit for the NBCOT certification examination or attain state licensure.

Brown Mackie College—Hopkinsville is licensed by the Kentucky State Board for Proprietary Education and is authorized for operation as a postsecondary educational institution by the Tennessee Higher Education Commission (www.state.tn.us/thec).

Academic Programs

Brown Mackie College — Hopkinsville provides higher education to traditional and nontraditional students through associate degree and diploma programs that can assist them in enhancing their career opportunities, broadening their perspectives through appropriate general education courses, thinking independently and critically, and improving problem-solving abilities.

Each college quarter comprises ten to twelve weeks. Programs are offered on a year-round basis, providing students with the ability to work uninterrupted toward their degrees. Brown Mackie College offers all programs in a unique One Course a Month format. This schedule allows students to focus studies on only one course for four weeks and has proven convenient for students with multiple obligations such as jobs and family.

Associate Degree Programs: Associate degree programs require a minimum of eight quarters to complete. The Associate of Applied Business degree is awarded in accounting technology, business management, criminal justice, and paralegal. The Associate of Applied Science degree is awarded in medical office management and occupational therapy assistant.

Diploma Programs: Brown Mackie College also offers diploma programs in business, criminal justice, medical assistant, and medical coding and billing for healthcare.

The American Medical Technologists (AMT), which offers the certification for Registered Medical Assistant (RMA), accepts the accreditation of Brown Mackie College — Hopkinsville. Students will qualify to take the RMA certification examination upon graduating the Brown Mackie College — Hopkinsville medical assistant program. Graduates of the 48 credit-hour medical assistant program are not qualified to take the AMT/RMA exam.

Brown Mackie College — Hopkinsville does not guarantee third-party certification. Outside agencies control the requirements for certifications and are subject to change without notice to Brown Mackie College.

Program availability and degree offerings are subject to change.

Costs

Tuition for the 2012–13 academic year was $314 per credit hour with a general fee of $20 per credit hour. Tuition for the occupational therapy assistant program was $381 per credit hour, with a general fee of $20 per credit hour. The cost of textbooks, if applicable, and other instructional materials varied by program.

Financial Aid

Financial aid is available to those who qualify. Brown Mackie College — Hopkinsville maintains a full-time staff of financial aid professionals to assist qualified students in obtaining the financial assistance they require to meet their educational expenses. The college participates in several student aid programs. Forms of financial aid available through federal resources include Federal Pell Grants, Federal Supplemental Educational Opportunity Grants (FSEOG), the Federal Work-Study Program, Federal Stafford Student Loans (subsidized and unsubsidized), and the Federal PLUS Program. Students may apply for the College Access Program (CAP) grant. Eligible students may also apply for veterans' educational benefits. Students with physical or mental disabilities that are a handicap to employment may be eligible for training services through the State Vocational Rehabilitation Agency. For further information, students should contact the Brown Mackie College — Hopkinsville Student Financial Services Office.

Each year, the college makes available President's Scholarships of $1,000 each to qualifying seniors from area high schools. In order to qualify, a senior must be graduating from a participating high school, must have maintained a cumulative grade point average of at least 2.0, and must have submitted a brief essay. The student's extracurricular activities and community service are also considered. These scholarships are available only to students enrolling in one of the college's degree programs. Students awarded the scholarship must enroll at Brown Mackie College between June and September immediately following their high school graduation. Applications for these scholarships can be obtained from the guidance departments of participating high schools and must be completed and returned to Brown Mackie College by March 31.

The Education Foundation was established in 2000 to offer scholarship support to students interested in continuing their education at one of the postsecondary, career-focused schools in the EDMC system. The number and amount of the awards can vary, depending on the funds available. Scholarship applications are considered every quarter. At Brown Mackie College applicants must be currently enrolled in an associate or bachelor's degree program and in their fourth quarter or higher (but no further than their second-to-last quarter) at the time of application. Awards are made based on academic performance and potential, as well as financial need. Please contact the colleges Student Financial Service Department for addition information.

Faculty

There are 3 full-time and approximately 15 adjunct instructors. The student-faculty ratio is 12:1.

Facilities and Resources

Brown Mackie College — Hopkinsville occupies a spacious building that has been specifically designed to provide a comfortable and effective environment for learning. The facility comprises approximately 17,100 square feet, including sixteen classrooms, two medical laboratories, an academic resource center, administrative and faculty offices, a bookstore, and a student lounge. Computer equipment for hands-on learning includes six networked laboratories. Medical equipment includes monocular and binocular microscopes, electrocardiograph, autoclave, centrifuge, and other equipment appropriate to hands-on laboratory and clinical instruction.

Brown Mackie College — Hopkinsville is fully committed to using eTextbooks and computer tablets in the classroom. Utilizing these tablets to access expanded course material, students will be able to increase their acumen for using this technology and further enhance their educational experience. Students have the ability to directly download their eTextbooks to their tablet, eliminating the need to carry heavy, physical textbooks and reducing the overall cost of supplies.

Convenient parking is available to all students. Brown Mackie College is a nonresidential, smoke-free institution.

Location

Brown Mackie College — Hopkinsville is conveniently located at 4001 Fort Campbell Boulevard in Hopkinsville, Kentucky.

Admission Requirements

Each applicant for admission is assigned to an Assistant Director of Admissions who directs the applicant through the steps of the admissions process, providing information on curriculum, policies, procedures, and services and assisting the applicant in setting necessary appointments and interviews.

To qualify for admission, each applicant must provide documentation of graduation from an accredited high school or from a state-approved secondary education curriculum or provide official documentation of high school graduation equivalency. All transcripts become the property of Brown Mackie College. Admission to the college is based upon the applicant meeting the stated requirements, a review of the applicant's previous education records, and a review of the applicant's career interests. If previous academic records indicate that the Brown Mackie College education and training programs would not benefit the applicant, the college reserves the right to advise the applicant not to enroll. Special requirements for enrollment into certain programs are discussed in the descriptions of those programs.

For the most recent information regarding admission requirements, please refer to the current academic catalog.

Application and Information

Applicants must complete and submit an application form, along with documentation of graduation from an accredited high school or state-approved secondary education curriculum or provide official documentation of high school graduation equivalency.

Prospective students should go online to BMCprograms.info for program duration, tuition, fees and other costs, median debt, federal salary data, alumni success, programmatic accreditation, and other important details.

Brown Mackie College is a system of over 25 schools located throughout North America. Programs, credential levels, technology, and scheduling options vary by school, and employment opportunities are not guaranteed. Financial aid is available for those who qualify. Administrative office: 625 Eden Park Drive, Suite 1100; Cincinnati, OH 45202; 513-830-2000. ©2013 Brown Mackie College. OH Registration #03-09-1685T; #03-09-1686T; #03-09-1687T; #03-09-1688T; #06-03-1781T; AC0150, AC0109, AC0078, AC0045, AC0138, AC0110; Licensed by the Florida Commission for Independent Education, License No. 3206.

For additional information, prospective students should contact:

Senior Director of Admissions
Brown Mackie College — Hopkinsville
4001 Fort Campbell Boulevard
Hopkinsville, Kentucky 42240
Phone: 270-886-1302
 800-359-4753 (toll-free)
Fax: 270-886-3544
E-mail: bmchoadm@brownmackie.edu
Web site: http://www.brownmackie.edu/Hopkinsville

BROWN MACKIE COLLEGE — INDIANAPOLIS
INDIANAPOLIS, INDIANA

The College and Its Mission

Brown Mackie College — Indianapolis (Brown Mackie College) is one of over twenty-five locations in the Brown Mackie College system of schools (http://www.brownmackie.edu), which is dedicated to providing educational programs that prepare students to pursue entry-level positions in a competitive, rapidly changing workplace. The Brown Mackie College schools offer bachelor's degree, associate degree, diploma, and certificate programs in health sciences, business, information technology, legal studies, and design to thousands of students in the Midwest, Southeast, Southwest, and Western United States.

Brown Mackie College — Indianapolis was founded in 2007 as a branch of Brown Mackie College — Findlay, Ohio.

Brown Mackie College — Indianapolis is accredited by the Accrediting Council for Independent Colleges and Schools to award associate degrees, diplomas, and certificates. The Accrediting Council for Independent Colleges and Schools is listed as a nationally recognized accrediting agency by the United States Department of Education and is recognized by the Council for Higher Education Accreditation. ACICS can be contacted at 750 First Street NE, Suite 980, Washington, D.C. 20002; phone: 202-336-6780.

Brown Mackie College — Indianapolis is regulated by the Board for Proprietary Education Indiana Commission for Higher Education, 101 West Ohio Street, Suite 670, Indianapolis, Indiana 46204; phone: 317-464-4400. Indiana advertising code: AC0078.

The occupational therapy assistant program is accredited by the Accreditation Council for Occupational Therapy Education (ACOTE) of the American Occupational Therapy Association (AOTA), located at 4720 Montgomery Lane, Suite 200, Bethesda, Maryland 20814-3449; phone: 301-652-AOTA. Graduates of the program will be eligible to sit for the national certification examination for the occupational therapy assistant administered by the National Board for Certification in Occupational Therapy (NBCOT). After successful completion of this exam, the individual will be a Certified Occupational Therapy Assistant (COTA). In addition, most states require licensure in order to practice; however, state licenses are usually based on the results of the NBCOT Certification Examination. Note that a felony conviction may affect a graduate's ability to sit for the NBCOT certification examination or attain state licensure.

The Brown Mackie College — Indianapolis practical nursing diploma program is approved by the Indiana State Board of Nursing, 402 West Washington Street, Room W066, Indianapolis, Indiana 46204; phone: 317-234-2043.

Academic Programs

Brown Mackie College — Indianapolis provides higher education to traditional and nontraditional students through associate degree, diploma, and certificate programs that assist them in enhancing their career opportunities, broadening their perspectives through appropriate general education courses, thinking independently and critically, and improving problem-solving abilities. The college strives to develop within its students the desire for lifelong and continued education.

Each college quarter comprises twelve weeks. Associate degree programs require a minimum of eight quarters to complete. Programs are offered on a year-round basis, providing students with the ability to work uninterrupted toward their degrees. The college offers all programs in a unique One Course a Month format. This allows students to focus studies on only one course for four weeks. This schedule has proven convenient for students with multiple obligations such as jobs and family.

Associate Degree Programs: The Associate of Science degree is awarded in business management, criminal justice, health care administration, medical assisting, and paralegal. The Associate of Applied Science degree is awarded in occupational therapy assistant.

Diploma Program: The college offers a diploma program in practical nursing.

Certificate Programs: The college offers certificate programs in bookkeeping specialist, general business, medical assistant, and medical insurance specialist.

The American Medical Technologists (AMT), which offers the certification for Registered Medical Assistant (RMA), accepts the accreditation of Brown Mackie College — Indianapolis. Students will qualify to take the RMA certification examination upon graduating the Brown Mackie College — Indianapolis medical assisting and medical assistant programs. Graduates of the 48 credit-hour medical assistant program are not qualified to take the AMT/RMA exam.

Brown Mackie College — Indianapolis does not guarantee third-party certification. Outside agencies control the requirements for certifications and are subject to change without notice to Brown Mackie College.

Program availability and degree offerings are subject to change.

Costs

Tuition for most programs in the 2012–13 academic year was $332 per credit hour with a general fee of $20 per credit hour. Tuition for the practical nursing diploma program was $381 per credit hour with a general fee of $30 per credit hour applied to instructional costs for activities and services. For the occupational therapy assistant program, the tuition was $381 per credit hour with a general fee of $20 per credit hour.

Financial Aid

Financial aid is available to those who qualify. The college maintains a full-time staff of Student Financial Services Advisers to assist qualified students in obtaining the financial assistance they require to meet their educational expenses. Available resources include federal and state aid, student loans from private lenders, and federal work-study opportunities, both on and off college premises.

Each year, the college makes available President's Scholarships of $1,000 each to qualifying seniors from area high schools. In order to qualify, a senior must be graduating from a participating high school, must be maintaining a cumulative grade point average of at least 2.0, and must submit a brief essay. The student's extracurricular activities and community service are also considered. These scholarships are available only to students enrolling in one of the college's degree programs. Students awarded the scholarship must enroll at Brown Mackie College — Indianapolis between June and September immediately following their high school graduation. Applications for these scholarships can be obtained from the guidance departments of participating high schools. These applications must be completed and returned to the college by March 31.

The Education Foundation was established in 2000 to offer scholarship support to students interested in continuing their education at one of the postsecondary, career-focused schools in the EDMC system. The number and amount of the awards can vary, depending on the funds available. Scholarship applications are considered every quarter. At Brown Mackie College applicants must be currently enrolled in an associate or bachelor's degree program and in their fourth quarter or higher (but no further than their second-to-last quarter) at the time of application. Awards are made based on academic performance and potential, as well as financial need. Interested students should contact the college's Student Financial Service Department for additional information.

Faculty

The college has 24 full-time instructors, 77 adjunct instructors, and 16 lab assistants, with a student-faculty ratio of 12:1. Faculty members provide tutoring and additional academic services to students as needed.

Facilities and Resources

Opened in January 2008, this modern facility offers more than 22,000 square feet of tastefully decorated classrooms, laboratories, and office space designed to the specifications of the college for its business, health-care, and technical programs. The Circle Centre Mall branch learning site boasts 25,000 square feet with 20 lecture rooms, computer labs, 2 medical labs, college store, and more. Instructional equipment is comparable to current technology used in business and industry today. Modern classrooms for special instructional needs offer multimedia capabilities with surround sound and overhead projectors accessible through computer, DVD, or VHS. Internet access and instructional resources are available at the college's library. Experienced faculty members provide academic support and are committed to the academic and technical preparation of their students.

Brown Mackie College — Indianapolis is fully committed to using eTextbooks and computer tablets in the classroom. Utilizing these tablets to access expanded course material, students are able to increase their acumen for using this technology and further enhance their educational experience. Students have the ability to directly download their eTextbooks to their tablet, eliminating the need to carry heavy, physical textbooks and reducing the overall cost of supplies.

Brown Mackie College — Indianapolis is nonresidential; public transportation and ample parking are available at no additional cost.

Location

Brown Mackie College — Indianapolis is conveniently located at 1200 North Meridian Street in Indianapolis, Indiana.

In November 2011 the college opened an innovative branch learning site on Level 4 of Circle Centre Mall located at 49 West Maryland Street in the heart of downtown Indianapolis. Daily shuttle service is provided to and from the main college.

Admission Requirements

Each applicant for admission is assigned to an Assistant Director of Admissions, who directs the applicant through the steps of the admissions process, providing information on curriculum, policies, procedures, and services and assisting the applicant in setting necessary appointments and interviews. To qualify for admission, each applicant must provide documentation of graduation from an accredited high school or from a state-approved secondary education curriculum or provide official documentation of high school graduation equivalency. All transcripts become the property of the college. Admission to the college is based on the applicant meeting the stated requirements, a review of the applicant's previous educational records, and a review of the applicant's career interests. If previous academic records indicate the college's education and training programs would not benefit the applicant, the college reserves the right to advise the applicant not to enroll. Special requirements for enrollment into certain programs are discussed in the descriptions of those programs.

In addition to the college's general admission requirements, applicants enrolling in the practical nursing program must document the following: fulfillment of Brown Mackie College — Indianapolis general requirements; complete physical (must be current to within six months of admission); two-step Mantoux TB skin test (must be current throughout schooling); hepatitis B vaccination or signed refusal; up-to-date immunizations, including tetanus and rubella; record of current CPR certification (certification must be current throughout the clinical experience through health care provider certification or the American Heart Association); and hospitalization insurance or a signed waiver.

For the most recent information regarding admission requirements, please refer to the current academic catalog.

Application and Information

Applicants must complete and submit an application form, along with documentation of graduation from an accredited high school or state-approved secondary education curriculum or official documentation of high school graduation equivalency.

Prospective students should go online to BMCprograms.info for program duration, tuition, fees and other costs, median debt, federal salary data, alumni success, programmatic accreditation, and other important details.

Brown Mackie College is a system of over twenty-five schools located throughout North America. Programs, credential levels, technology, and scheduling options vary by school, and employment opportunities are not guaranteed. Financial aid is available for those who qualify. Administrative offices are located at 625 Eden Park Drive, Suite 1100; Cincinnati, Ohio 45202; phone: 513-830-2000. ©2013 Brown Mackie College. OH Registration #03-09-1685T; #03-09-1686T; #03-09-1687T; #03-09-1688T; #06-03-1781T; AC0150, AC0109, AC0078, AC0045, AC0138, AC0110; Licensed by the Florida Commission for Independent Education, License No. 3206.

For additional information, prospective students should contact:

Director of Admissions
Brown Mackie College — Indianapolis
1200 North Meridian Street, Suite 100
Indianapolis, Indiana 46204
Phone: 317-554-8300
      866-255-0279 (toll-free)
Fax: 317-632-4557
E-mail: bmcindadm@brownmackie.edu
Web site: http://www.brownmackie.edu/Indianapolis

BROWN MACKIE COLLEGE — KANSAS CITY
LENEXA, KANSAS

The College and Its Mission

Brown Mackie College — Kansas City (Brown Mackie College) is one of over twenty-five locations in the Brown Mackie College system of schools (www.brownmackie.edu), which is dedicated to providing educational programs that prepare students to pursue entry-level positions in a competitive, rapidly changing workplace. Brown Mackie College schools offer bachelor degree, associate degree, certificate, and diploma programs in health sciences, business, information technology, legal studies, and design to thousands of students in the Midwest, Southeast, Southwest, and Western United States.

The college was founded in Salina, Kansas, in July 1892 as the Kansas Wesleyan School of Business. In 1938, the college was incorporated as the Brown Mackie School of Business under the ownership of former Kansas Wesleyan instructors Perry E. Brown and A. B. Mackie. It became Brown Mackie College in January 1975.

Brown Mackie College in Lenexa, Kansas is a branch of Brown Mackie College in Salina, Kansas, which is accredited by the Higher Learning Commission and is a member of the North Central Association (NCA), 230 South LaSalle Street, Suite 7-500, Chicago, Illinois 60604-1413; phone: 800-621-7440 (toll free); www.ncahlc.org.

Brown Mackie College in Lenexa, Kansas is approved and authorized to grant the Associate of Applied Science (AAS) degree by the Kansas Board of Regents, 1000 Southwest Jackson Street, Suite 520, Topeka, Kansas 66612-1368.

The occupational therapy assistant program is accredited by the Accreditation Council for Occupational Therapy Education (ACOTE) of the American Occupational Therapy Association (AOTA), 4720 Montgomery Lane, Suite 200, Bethesda, Maryland 20814-3449; phone: 301-652-AOTA. Graduates of the program will be eligible to sit for the national certification examination for the occupational therapy assistant administered by the National Board for Certification in Occupational Therapy (NBCOT). After successful completion of this exam, the individual will be a Certified Occupational Therapy Assistant (COTA). In addition, most states require licensure in order to practice; however, state licenses are usually based on the results of the NBCOT Certification Examination. Note that a felony conviction may affect a graduate's ability to sit for the NBCOT certification examination or attain state licensure.

The veterinary technology program has provisional programmatic accreditation granted by the American Veterinary Medical Association (AVMA) through the Committee on Veterinary Technician Education and Activities (CVTEA).

Academic Programs

Brown Mackie College — Kansas City provides higher education to traditional and nontraditional students through associate degree, diploma, and certificate programs that can assist them in enhancing their career opportunities, broadening their perspectives through appropriate general education courses, thinking independently and critically, and improving problem-solving abilities. Brown Mackie College strives to develop within its students the desire for lifelong and continued education.

In most programs, students can participate in day or evening classes, which begin every month. Programs are offered on a year-round basis, providing students with the ability to work uninterrupted toward completion of their programs. Brown

Mackie College offers all programs in a unique One Course a Month format. This schedule-allows students to focus studies on only one course for four weeks and has proven convenient for students with multiple obligations such as jobs and family.

Associate Degree Programs: The Associate of Applied Science degree is awarded in architectural design and drafting technology, business management, computer software applications, criminal justice, fitness trainer, health care administration, medical assisting, nursing, occupational therapy assistant, and veterinary technology.

Diploma Programs: Brown Mackie College — Kansas City also offers diploma programs in accounting, business, computer aided design and drafting technician, computer software applications, criminal justice, fitness trainer, medical assistant, medical insurance specialist, and paralegal assistant.

Certificate Program: A certificate program is offered in practical nursing.

The American Medical Technologists (AMT), which offers the certification for Registered Medical Assistant (RMA), accepts the accreditation of Brown Mackie College — Kansas City. Students will qualify to take the RMA certification examination upon graduating the Brown Mackie College — Kansas City medical assisting and medical assistant programs. Graduates of the 48 credit-hour medical assistant program are not qualified to take the AMT/RMA exam.

Brown Mackie College does not guarantee third-party certification/licensing exams. Outside agencies control the requirements for certification/licensing and are subject to change without notification to the college.

Program availability and degree offerings are subject to change.

Costs

Tuition for most programs in the 2012–13 academic year was $314 per credit hour and $20 per credit hour for general fees. Tuition for nursing programs was $381 per credit hour with general fees of $30 per credit hour. Tuition for the occupational therapy assistant program was $381 per credit hour with fees of $20 per credit hour. The cost of textbooks, if applicable, and other instructional materials varies by program

Financial Aid

Financial aid is available to those who qualify. Brown Mackie College — Kansas City maintains a full-time staff of financial aid professionals to assist qualified students in obtaining financial assistance. The college participates in several student aid programs. Forms of financial aid available to qualified students through federal resources include Federal Pell Grants, Federal Supplemental Educational Opportunity Grants (FSEOG), Academic Competitiveness Grant, Federal Work-Study Program, Federal Perkins Loans, Federal Stafford Student Loans (subsidized and unsubsidized), Federal Direct Loans (subsidized and unsubsidized), and the Federal PLUS Program. Eligible students may apply for veterans' educational benefits. Students with physical or mental disabilities that are a handicap to employment may be eligible for training services through the state Vocational Rehabilitation Agency. For further information, students should contact the Brown Mackie College — Kansas City Student Financial Services Office.

Each year, the college makes available President's Scholarships of $1,000 each to qualifying seniors from area high schools. In order to qualify, a senior must be graduating from a participating high school, have maintained a cumulative grade point average of at least 2.0, and submitted a brief essay. The student's extracurricular activities and community service are also considered. The President's Scholarship is available only to students enrolling in one of the college's degree programs. Students awarded the scholarship must enroll at Brown Mackie College—Kansas City between June and September immediately following their high school graduation. Applications for these scholarships can be obtained from the guidance departments of participating high schools. These applications must be completed and returned to the college by March 31.

The Education Foundation was established in 2000 to offer scholarship support to students interested in continuing their education at one of the postsecondary, career-focused schools in the EDMC system. The number and amount of the awards can vary, depending on the funds available. Scholarship applications are considered every quarter. At Brown Mackie College, applicants must be currently enrolled in an associate or bachelor's degree program and in their fourth quarter or higher (but no further than their second-to-last quarter) at the time of application. Awards are made based on academic performance and potential, as well as financial need. Interested students should contact the college's Student Financial Service Department for additional information.

Faculty

There are 23 full-time faculty members and 25 adjunct faculty members. The average class student-instructor ratio is 14:1.

Facilities and Resources

In addition to classrooms and computer labs, Brown Mackie College—Kansas City maintains a library of curriculum-related resources, technical and general education materials, academic and professional periodicals, and audiovisual resources. Internet access also is available for research. The college has a bookstore that stocks texts, courseware, and other educational supplies required for courses and a variety of personal, recreational, and gift items, including apparel, supplies, and general merchandise incorporating the Brown Mackie College logo. Hours are posted at the bookstore entrance.

Brown Mackie College—Kansas City is fully committed to using eTextbooks and computer tablets in the classroom. Utilizing these tablets to access expanded course material, students are able to increase their acumen for using this technology and further enhance their educational experience. Students have the ability to directly download their eTextbooks to their tablet, eliminating the need to carry heavy, physical textbooks and reducing the overall cost of supplies.

Brown Mackie College — Kansas City is nonresidential, smoke free, and provides ample parking at no additional cost.

Location

Brown Mackie College — Kansas City is located at 9705 Lenexa Drive in Lenexa, Kansas, just off Interstate 35 at 95th Street in Johnson County. The Olathe course site is located at 450 North Rogers Road, Suite 175, in Olathe, Kansas, just off Interstate 35 and Santa Fe Street in Johnson County.

Admission Requirements

Each applicant for admission is assigned to an Assistant Director of Admissions, who directs the applicant through the steps of the admissions process, providing information on curriculum, policies, procedures, and services and assisting the applicant in setting necessary appointments and interviews.

To qualify for admission, each applicant must provide documentation of graduation from an accredited high school or from a state-approved secondary education curriculum or provide official documentation of high school graduation equivalency. All transcripts become the property of Brown Mackie College — Kansas City. Admission to the college is based upon the applicant meeting the stated requirements, a review of the applicant's previous education records, and a review of the applicant's career interests. If previous academic records indicate that the Brown Mackie College education and training programs would not benefit the applicant, the college reserves the right to advise the applicant not to enroll. Special requirements for enrollment into certain programs are discussed in the descriptions of those programs.

For the most recent information regarding admission requirements, please refer to the current academic catalog.

Application and Information

Applicants must complete and submit an application form, along with documentation of graduation from an accredited high school or state-approved secondary education curriculum or official documentation of high school graduation equivalency.

Prospective students can go online to BMCprograms.info for program duration, tuition, fees and other costs, median debt, federal salary data, alumni success, programmatic accreditation, and other important details.

Brown Mackie College is a system of over twenty-five schools located throughout North America. Programs, credential levels, technology, and scheduling options vary by school, and employment opportunities are not guaranteed. Financial aid is available for those who qualify. Administrative offices are located at 625 Eden Park Drive, Suite 1100; Cincinnati, Ohio 45202; phone: 513-830-2000. ©2013 Brown Mackie College. OH Registration #03-09-1685T; #03-09-1686T; #03-09-1687T; #03-09-1688T; #06-03-1781T; AC0150, AC0109, AC0078, AC0045, AC0138, AC0110; Licensed by the Florida Commission for Independent Education, License No. 3206.

For additional information, prospective students should contact:

Director of Admissions
Brown Mackie College — Kansas City
9705 Lenexa Drive
Lenexa, Kansas 66215
Phone: 913-768-1900
      800-635-9101 (toll-free)
Fax: 913-495-9555
E-mail: bmckcadm@brownmackie.edu
Web site: http://www.brownmackie.edu/KansasCity

BROWN MACKIE COLLEGE — LOUISVILLE
LOUISVILLE, KENTUCKY

The College and Its Mission

Brown Mackie College — Louisville (Brown Mackie College) is one of over twenty-five locations in the Brown Mackie College system of schools (www.brownmackie.edu), which is dedicated to providing educational programs that prepare students to pursue entry-level positions in a competitive, rapidly changing workplace. Brown Mackie College schools offer bachelor degree, associate degree, diploma, and certificate programs in health sciences, business, information technology, legal studies, and design to thousands of students in the Midwest, Southeast, Southwest, and Western United States.

Brown Mackie College — Louisville opened in 1972 as RETS Institute of Technology. The first RETS school was founded in 1935 in Detroit in response to the rapid growth of radio broadcasting and the need for qualified radio technicians. The RETS Institute changed its name to Brown Mackie College — Louisville in 2004.

Brown Mackie College — Louisville is accredited by the Accrediting Council for Independent Colleges and Schools to award associate degrees, diplomas, and certificates. The Accrediting Council for Independent Colleges and Schools is listed as a nationally recognized accrediting agency by the United States Department of Education. Its accreditation of degree-granting institutions is recognized by the Council for Higher Education Accreditation. ACICS can be contacted at 750 First Street NE, Suite 980, Washington, D.C. 20002; phone: 202-336-6780.

Brown Mackie College — Louisville is licensed by the Kentucky Council on Postsecondary Education, 1024 Capital Center Drive, Suite 320 Frankfort, Kentucky 40601.

Brown Mackie College — Louisville is regulated by the Board for Proprietary Education Indiana Commission for Higher Education, 101 West Ohio Street, Suite 670, Indianapolis, Indiana 46204; phone: 317-464-4400. Indiana advertising code: AC0045.

The Associate of Applied Science in veterinary technology program has probationary accreditation by the American Veterinary Medical Association (AVMA) through the Committee on Veterinary Technician Education and Activities (CVTEA). The American Veterinary Medical Association can be contacted at 1931 North Meacham Road, Suite 100, Schaumburg, Illinois, 60173-4360; phone: 800-248-2862.

The Associate of Applied Science in occupational therapy assistant program is accredited by the Accreditation Council for Occupational Therapy Education (ACOTE) of the American Occupational Therapy Association (AOTA), located at 4720 Montgomery Lane, Suite 200, Bethesda, Maryland 20814-3449; phone: 301-652-AOTA. Graduates of the program will be eligible to sit for the national certification examination for the occupational therapy assistant administered by the National Board for Certification in Occupational Therapy (NBCOT). After successful completion of this exam, the individual will be a Certified Occupational Therapy Assistant (COTA). In addition, most states require licensure in order to practice; however, state licenses are usually based on the results of the NBCOT Certification Examination. Note that a felony conviction may affect a graduate's ability to sit for the NBCOT certification examination or attain state licensure

The Associate of Applied Science in surgical technology is accredited by the Accrediting Bureau of Health Education Schools (www.abhes.org). The Accrediting Bureau of Health Education Schools can be contacted at 7777 Leesburg Pike, Suite 314 N. Falls Church, Virginia 22043; phone: 703-917-9503.

The Associate of Science in surgical technology program is accredited by the Commission on Accreditation of Allied Health Education Programs (www.caahep.org), upon the recommendation of the Accreditation Review Council on Education in Surgical Technology and Surgical Assisting (ARC/STSA). The Commission on Accreditation of Allied Health Education Programs is located at 1361 Park Street, Clearwater, Florida 33756; phone: 727-210-2350

Academic Programs

Brown Mackie College — Louisville provides higher education to traditional and nontraditional students through associate degree, and diploma programs that assist in enhancing their career opportunities, broadening their perspectives through appropriate general education courses, thinking independently and critically, and improving problem-solving abilities.

Each college quarter comprises twelve weeks. Associate degree programs require a minimum of eight quarters to complete. Programs are offered on a year-round basis, providing students with the ability to work uninterrupted toward completion of their programs. The college offers all programs in a unique One Course a Month format. This allows students to focus studies on only one course for four weeks. This schedule has proven convenient for students with multiple obligations such as jobs and family.

Associate Degree Programs: The Associate of Applied Business degree is awarded in accounting technology, business management, criminal justice, and paralegal.

The Associate of Applied Science degree is awarded in biomedical equipment technology, electronics, graphic design, health care administration, medical assisting, occupational therapy assistant, pharmacy technology, surgical technology, and veterinary technology.

Diploma Program: The college offers a diploma program in practical nursing.

Certificate Program: The college offers a certificate program in computer networking.

The American Medical Technologists (AMT), which offers the certification for Registered Medical Assistant (RMA), accepts the accreditation of Brown Mackie College — Louisville. Students will qualify to take the RMA certification examination upon graduating the Brown Mackie College — Louisville medical assisting program.

Brown Mackie College — Louisville does not guarantee third-party certification. Outside agencies control the requirements for certifications and are subject to change without notice to Brown Mackie College.

Program availability and degree offerings are subject to change.

Costs

Tuition for most programs in the 2012–13 academic year was $314 per credit hour, and the general fees were $20 per credit hour. The practical nursing diploma program was $381 per credit hour, and the general fees were $30 per credit hour. The surgical technology program was $360 per credit hour, and the general fees were $20 per credit hour. The occupational therapy program was $381 per credit hour, and the general fees were $20 per credit hour. The computer networking certificate program was $314 per credit hour, and the general fees were $25 per credit hour. The length of the program determines total cost. The cost of textbooks, if applicable, and other instructional materials varies by program.

Financial Aid

Financial aid is available for those who qualify. The college maintains a full-time staff of Student Financial Services Advisers to assist qualified students in obtaining financial assistance. The college participates in several student aid programs. Forms of financial aid available through federal resources include the Federal Pell Grant Program, Federal Supplemental Educational Opportunity Grant (FSEOG) Program, Federal Work-Study Program, Federal Perkins Loan Program, Federal Stafford Student Loan Program (subsidized and unsubsidized), and the Federal PLUS Loan Program.

Each year, the college makes available President's Scholarships of $1,000 each to qualifying seniors from area high schools. In order to qualify, a senior must have graduated from a participating high school, maintained a cumulative grade point average of at least 2.0, and submitted a brief essay. The student's extracurricular activities and community service are also considered. The President's Scholarship is available only to students enrolling in one of the college's degree programs. Students awarded the scholarship must enroll at Brown Mackie College — Louisville between June and September immediately following their high school graduation. Applications for these scholarships can be obtained from the guidance departments of participating high schools. These applications must be completed and returned to the college by March 31.

The Education Foundation was established in 2000 to offer scholarship support to students interested in continuing their education at one of the postsecondary, career-focused schools in the EDMC system. The number and amount of the awards can vary, depending on the funds available. Scholarship applications are considered every quarter. At Brown Mackie College, applicants must be currently enrolled in an associate or bachelor's degree program and in their fourth quarter or higher (but no further than their second-to-last quarter) at the time of application. Awards are made based on academic performance and potential, as well as financial need. Interested students should contact the college's Student Financial Service Department for additional information.

Faculty

There are 32 full-time and over 100 part-time faculty members at the college. The average student-faculty ratio is 20:1.

Facilities and Resources

Brown Mackie College — Louisville has more than 69,000 square feet of multipurpose classrooms, including networked computer laboratories, electronics laboratories, veterinary technology labs, medical labs, nursing labs, a resource center, and offices for administrative personnel as well as for student services such as admissions, student financial services, and career-services assistance. In 2009, 6,000 square feet was opened at the Louisville location. Included in this build-out are an occupational therapy lab, a criminal justice lab, additional classrooms, and faculty space. In 2010, 25,000 square feet opened at this location. This build-out included a biomedical equipment lab, additional classrooms, a career services center, and additional faculty/administration space.

Brown Mackie College — Louisville is fully committed to using eTextbooks and computer tablets in the classroom. Utilizing these tablets to access expanded course material, students are able to increase their acumen for using this technology and further enhance their educational experience. Students have the ability to directly download their eTextbooks to their tablet, eliminating the need to carry heavy, physical textbooks and reducing the overall cost of supplies.

Brown Mackie College — Louisville is nonresidential; ample parking at no cost is available. Brown Mackie College is a smoke-free facility.

Location

Brown Mackie College — Louisville is conveniently located at 3605 Fern Valley Road in Louisville, Kentucky. The college has a generous parking area and is easily accessible by public transportation.

Admission Requirements

Each applicant for admission is assigned to an Assistant Director of Admissions, who directs the applicant through the steps of the admissions process, providing information on curriculum, policies, procedures, and services and assisting the applicant in setting necessary appointments and interviews.

To qualify for admission, each applicant must provide documentation of graduation from an accredited high school or from a state-approved secondary education curriculum or provide official documentation of high school graduation equivalency. All transcripts become the property of the college. Admission to the college is based on the applicant meeting the stated requirements, a review of the applicant's previous educational records, and a review of the applicant's career interests. If previous academic records indicate the college's education and training programs would not benefit the applicant, the college reserves the right to advise the applicant not to enroll. Special requirements for enrollment into certain programs are discussed in the descriptions of those programs.

In addition to the college's general admission requirements, applicants enrolling in either the occupational therapy assistant program or the surgical technology program must document one of the following: a high school cumulative grade point average of at least 2.5, a score on the GED examination of at least 57 (557 if taken on or after January 15, 2002), or completion of 12 quarter-credit hours or 8 semester-credit hours of collegiate course work with a grade point average of at least 2.5. Credit hours may not include Professional Development (CF 1100), the Brown Mackie College — Louisville course. Students entering the program must also have completed a biology course with a grade of at least a C (or an average of at least 2.0 on a 4.0 scale).

In addition to the college's general admission requirements, applicants enrolling in the practical nursing program must document the following, which must be completed and a record of proof must appear in the student's file prior to the start of the nursing fundamentals course. No student will be admitted to a clinical agency unless all paperwork is completed. The paperwork is a requirement of all contracted agencies. This paperwork includes records of (1) a complete physical, current to within six months of admission; (2) a two-step Mantoux test that is kept current throughout schooling; (3) a hepatitis B vaccination or signed refusal; (4) up-to-date immunizations, including tetanus and rubella; (5) a record of current CPR certification that is maintained throughout the student's clinical experience; and (6) hospitalization insurance or a signed waiver.

For the most recent information regarding admission requirements, prospective students should refer to the current academic catalog.

Application and Information

Applicants must complete and submit an application form along with documentation of graduation from an accredited high school or completion of state-approved secondary education curriculum or provide official documentation of high school graduation equivalency.

Prospective students may go online to BMCprograms.info for program duration, tuition, fees and other costs, median debt, federal salary data, alumni success, programmatic accreditation, and other important details.

Brown Mackie College is a system of over twenty-five schools located throughout North America. Programs, credential levels, technology, and scheduling options vary by school, and employment opportunities are not guaranteed. Financial aid is available for those who qualify. Administrative offices are located at 625 Eden Park Drive, Suite 1100; Cincinnati, Ohio 45202; phone: 513-830-2000. ©2013 Brown Mackie College. OH Registration #03-09-1685T; #03-09-1686T; #03-09-1687T; #03-09-1688T; #06-03-1781T; AC0150, AC0109, AC0078, AC0045, AC0138, AC0110; Licensed by the Florida Commission for Independent Education, License No. 3206.

For additional information, prospective students should contact:

Director of Admissions
Brown Mackie College — Louisville
3605 Fern Valley Road
Louisville, Kentucky 40219
Phone: 502-968-7191
        800-999-7387 (toll-free)
Fax: 502-357-9956
E-mail: bmcloadm@brownmackie.edu
Web site: http://www.brownmackie.edu/Louisville

BROWN MACKIE COLLEGE — MERRILLVILLE
MERRILLVILLE, INDIANA

The College and Its Mission

Brown Mackie College — Merrillville (Brown Mackie College) is one of over twenty-five locations in the Brown Mackie College system of schools (www.brownmackie.edu), which is dedicated to providing educational programs that prepare students to pursue entry-level positions in a competitive, rapidly changing workplace. Brown Mackie College schools offer bachelor's degree, associate degree, diploma, and certificate programs in health sciences, business, information technology, legal studies, and design to thousands of students in the Midwest, Southeast, Southwest, and Western United States.

Founded in 1890 by A. N. Hirons as LaPorte Business College in LaPorte, Indiana, the institution later became known as Commonwealth Business College. In 1919, ownership was transferred to Grace and J. J. Moore, who successfully operated the college under the name of Reese School of Business for several decades. In 1975, the college came under the ownership of Steven C. Smith as Commonwealth Business College. A second location, now known as Brown Mackie College — Merrillville, was opened in 1984 in Merrillville, Indiana.

Brown Mackie College — Merrillville is accredited by the Accrediting Council for Independent Colleges and Schools to award associate degrees, diplomas, and certificates. The Accrediting Council for Independent Colleges and Schools is listed as a nationally recognized accrediting agency by the United States Department of Education and is recognized by the Council for Higher Education Accreditation. ACICS can be contacted at 750 First Street NE, Suite 980, Washington, D.C. 20002; phone: 202-336-6780.

Brown Mackie College — Merrillville is regulated by the Board for Proprietary Education Indiana Commission for Higher Education, 101 West Ohio Street, Suite 670, Indianapolis, Indiana 46204; phone: 317-464-4400. Indiana advertising code: AC0138.

Brown Mackie College — Merrillville Associate of Science in surgical technology program is accredited by the Commission on Accreditation of Allied Health Education Programs (www.caahep.og) upon the recommendation of the Accreditation Review Committee on Education in Surgical Technology and Surgical Assisting (ARC/STSA). The Commission on Accreditation of Allied Health Education Programs can be contacted at 1361 Park Street, Clearwater, Florida 33756; phone: 727-210-2350.

The Associate of Applied Science in occupational therapy assistant program is accredited by the Accreditation Council for Occupational Therapy Education (ACOTE) of the American Occupational Therapy Association (AOTA), 4720 Montgomery Lane, Suite 200, Bethesda, Maryland 20814-3449; phone: 301-652-AOTA. Graduates of the program will be eligible to sit for the national certification examination for the occupational therapy assistant administered by the National Board for Certification in Occupational Therapy (NBCOT). After successful completion of this exam, the individual will be a Certified Occupational Therapy Assistant (COTA). In addition, most states require licensure in order to practice; however, state licenses are usually based on the results of the NBCOT Certification Examination. Note that a felony conviction may affect a graduate's ability to sit for the NBCOT certification examination or attain state licensure.

Academic Programs

Brown Mackie College — Merrillville provides higher education to traditional and nontraditional students through associate degree, diploma, and certificate programs that assist in enhancing their career opportunities, broadening their perspectives through appropriate general education courses, thinking independently and critically, and improving problem-solving abilities. The college strives to develop within its students the desire for lifelong and continued education.

Each college quarter comprises ten to twelve weeks. Associate degree programs require a minimum of eight quarters to complete.

Programs are offered on a year-round basis, providing students with the ability to work uninterrupted toward completion of their programs. The college offers all programs in a unique One Course a Month format. This allows students to focus on only one course for four weeks. This schedule has proven convenient for students with multiple obligations such as jobs and family.

Associate Degree Programs: The Associate of Science degree is awarded in accounting technology, biomedical equipment technician, business management, criminal justice, health care management, legal studies, medical office management, paralegal, and surgical technology.

The Associate of Applied Science degree is awarded in occupational therapy assistant.

Certificate Programs: The college offers certificate programs in bookkeeping specialist, criminal justice, general business, graphic design assistant, medical assistant, medical billing and coding, medical insurance specialist, and paralegal assistant.

The American Medical Technologists (AMT), which offers the certification for Registered Medical Assistant (RMA), accepts the accreditation of Brown Mackie College — Merrillville. Students will qualify to take the RMA certification examination upon graduating the Brown Mackie College — Merrillville medical assistant program. Graduates of the 48 credit-hour medical assistant program are not qualified to take the AMT/RMA exam.

Brown Mackie College — Merrillville does not guarantee third-party certification. Outside agencies control the requirements for certifications and are subject to change without notice to Brown Mackie College.

Program availability and degree offerings are subject to change.

Costs

Tuition for most programs in the 2012–13 academic year was $314 per credit hour and fees were $20 per credit hour, with some exceptions. For the surgical technology program, tuition was $360 per credit hour and fees were $20 per credit hour. For the occupational therapy assistant program, tuition was $381 per credit hour and fees were $20 per credit hour. The length of the program determines total cost. Textbook fees, if applicable, vary according to program.

Financial Aid

Financial aid is available to those who qualify. The college maintains a full-time staff of Student Financial Services Advisers to assist qualified students in obtaining financial assistance. The college participates in several student aid programs. Forms of financial aid available through federal resources include the Federal Pell Grant Program, Federal Supplemental Educational Opportunity Grant (FSEOG) Program, Federal Work-Study Program, Federal Perkins Loan Program, Federal Stafford Student Loan Program (subsidized and unsubsidized), and the Federal PLUS Loan Program. Eligible students may apply for Indiana state awards, such as the Higher Education Award and Twenty-First Century Scholarships for high school students, the Core 40 awards, and veterans' educational benefits. Students with physical or mental disabilities that are a handicap to employment may be eligible for training services through the state's Bureau of Vocational Rehabilitation. For further information, students should contact the college's Student Financial Services Office.

Each year, the college makes available President's Scholarships of $1,000 each to qualifying seniors from area high schools. In order to qualify, a senior must be graduating from a participating high school, must be maintaining a cumulative grade point average of at least 2.0, and must submit a brief essay. The student's extracurricular activities and community service are also considered. These scholarships are available only to students enrolling in one of the college's degree programs. Students awarded the scholarship must enroll at Brown Mackie College — Merrillville between June and September immediately following their high school graduation.

Applications for these scholarships can be obtained from the guidance departments of participating high schools. These applications must be completed and returned to the college by March 31.

The Education Foundation was established in 2000 to offer scholarship support to students interested in continuing their education at one of the postsecondary, career-focused schools in the EDMC system. The number and amount of the awards can vary, depending on the funds available. Scholarship applications are considered every quarter. At Brown Mackie College, applicants must be currently enrolled in an associate or bachelor's degree program and in their fourth quarter or higher (but no further than their second-to-last quarter) at the time of application. Awards are made based on academic performance and potential, as well as financial need. Interested students should contact the college's Student Financial Service Department for additional information.

Faculty

There are approximately 60 full-time and 25 part-time faculty members at the college, practitioners in their fields of expertise. The average student-faculty ratio is 17:1.

Facilities and Resources

Occupying 26,000 square feet, Brown Mackie College — Merrillville was opened to students in October 1998 in the Twin Towers complex of Merrillville and comprises several instructional rooms, including five computer labs with networked computers and four medical laboratories. The administrative offices, college library, and student lounge are all easily accessible to students. The college bookstore stocks texts, courseware, and other educational supplies required for courses at the college. Students also find a variety of personal, recreational, and gift items, including apparel, supplies, and general merchandise incorporating the college logo. Hours are posted at the bookstore entrance.

Brown Mackie College — Merrillville is fully committed to using eTextbooks and computer tablets in the classroom. Utilizing these tablets to access expanded course material, students are able to increase their acumen for using this technology and further enhance their educational experience. Students have the ability to directly download their eTextbooks to their tablet, eliminating the need to carry heavy, physical textbooks and reducing the overall cost of supplies.

The college is a nonresidential, smoke-free institution.

Location

Brown Mackie College — Merrillville is conveniently located in northwest Indiana at 1000 East 80th Place, Merrillville, in the Twin Towers business complex just west of the intersection of U.S. Route 30 and Interstate 65. A spacious parking lot provides ample parking at no additional charge.

Admission Requirements

Each applicant for admission is assigned to an Assistant Director of Admissions who directs the applicant through the steps of the admissions process, providing information on curriculum, policies, procedures, and services and assisting the applicant in setting necessary appointments and interviews. To qualify for admission, each applicant must provide documentation of graduation from an accredited high school or completion of a state-approved secondary education curriculum or provide official documentation of high school graduation equivalency. All transcripts become the property of the college.

As part of the admission process, students are given an assessment of academic skills. Although the results of this assessment do not determine eligibility for admission, they provide the college with a means of determining the need for academic support as well as a means by which the college can evaluate the effectiveness of its educational programs. All new students are required to complete this assessment, which is readministered at the end of the student's program so results may be compared with those of the initial administration.

In addition to the college's general admission requirements, applicants enrolling in the practical nursing program must document the following, which must be completed, and a record of proof must appear in the student's file prior to the start of the nursing fundamentals course. No student will be admitted to a clinical agency unless all paperwork is completed. The paperwork is a requirement of all contracted agencies. This paperwork includes records of (1) a complete physical, current to within six months of admission, (2) a two-step Mantoux test that is kept current throughout schooling, (3) a hepatitis B vaccination or signed refusal, (4) up-to-date immunizations, including tetanus and rubella, (5) a record of current CPR certification that is maintained throughout the student's clinical experience, and (6) hospitalization insurance or a signed waiver.

For the most recent information regarding admission requirements, please refer to the current academic catalog.

Application and Information

Applicants must complete and submit an application form along with documentation of graduation from an accredited high school or completion of state-approved secondary education curriculum or provide official documentation of high school graduation equivalency.

Prospective students can go online to BMCprograms.info for program duration, tuition, fees and other costs, median debt, federal salary data, alumni success, programmatic accreditation, and other important details.

Brown Mackie College is a system of over twenty-five schools located throughout North America. Programs, credential levels, technology, and scheduling options vary by school, and employment opportunities are not guaranteed. Financial aid is available for those who qualify. Administrative offices are located at 625 Eden Park Drive, Suite 1100; Cincinnati, Ohio 45202; phone: 513-830-2000. ©2013 Brown Mackie College. OH Registration #03-09-1685T; #03-09-1686T; #03-09-1687T; #03-09-1688T; #06-03-1781T; AC0150, AC0109, AC0078, AC0045, AC0138, AC0110; Licensed by the Florida Commission for Independent Education, License No. 3206.

For additional information, prospective students should contact:

Brown Mackie College — Merrillville
1000 East 80th Place, Suite 205M
Merrillville, Indiana 46410
Phone: 219-769-3321
      800-258-3321 (toll-free)
Fax: 219-738-1076
E-mail: bmcmeadm@brownmackie.edu
Web site: http://www.brownmackie.edu/Merrillville

BROWN MACKIE COLLEGE — MIAMI
MIRAMAR, FLORIDA

The College and Its Mission

Brown Mackie College — Miami (Brown Mackie College) is one of over twenty-five locations in the Brown Mackie College system of schools (www.brownmackie.edu), which is dedicated to providing educational programs that prepare students to pursue entry-level positions in a competitive, rapidly changing workplace. Brown Mackie College schools offer bachelor's degree, associate degree, diploma, and certificate programs in health sciences, business, information technology, legal studies, criminal justice, early childhood education, and design to thousands of students in the Midwest, Southeast, Southwest, and Western United States.

Brown Mackie College — Miami, Florida is accredited by the Accrediting Council for Independent Colleges and Schools to award associate degrees and diplomas. The Accrediting Council for Independent Colleges and Schools is listed as a nationally recognized accrediting agency by the United States Department of Education and is recognized by the Council for Higher Education Accreditation. ACICS can be contacted at 750 First Street NE, Suite 980, Washington, D.C. 20002; phone: 202-336-6780.

Brown Mackie College — Miami is licensed by the Commission for Independent Education, Florida Department of Education. Additional information regarding this institution may be obtained by contacting the Commission at 325 West Gaines Street, Suite 1414, Tallahassee, Florida 32399-0400; phone: 888-224-6684 (toll-free). Licensed by the Commission for Independent Education, license no. 3206.

The Brown Mackie College – Miami location is approved by the Florida Board of Nursing to offer the Associate of Science in nursing; 4052 Bald Cypress Way, Bin C-02; Tallahassee, Florida 32399-3252; phone: 850-488-0595; http://www.doh.state.fl.us/mqa/nursing/index.html.

Academic Programs

Brown Mackie College — Miami provides higher education to traditional and nontraditional students through associate degree and diploma programs that assist them in enhancing their career opportunities, broadening their perspectives through appropriate general education courses, thinking independently and critically, and improving problem-solving abilities. The college strives to develop within its students the desire for lifelong and continued education.

Each college quarter comprises twelve weeks. Associate degree programs require a minimum of eight quarters to complete. Programs are offered on a year-round basis, providing students with the ability to work uninterrupted toward their degrees. The college offers all programs in a unique One Course a Month format. This allows students to focus studies on only one course for four weeks. This schedule has proven convenient for students with multiple obligations such as jobs and family.

Associate Degree Programs: The Associate of Science degree is awarded in accounting technology, biomedical equipment technology, business management, computer networking, criminal justice, early childhood education, health care administration, information technology, nursing, and paralegal.

Diploma Program: The college offers diploma programs in criminal justice specialist, medical assistant, medical insurance specialist, and paralegal assistant.

The American Medical Technologists (AMT), which offers the certification for Registered Medical Assistant (RMA), accepts the accreditation of Brown Mackie College — Miami. Students will qualify to take the RMA certification examination upon graduating the Brown Mackie College — Miami medical assistant program.

Brown Mackie College — Miami does not guarantee third-party certification. Outside agencies control the requirements for certifications and are subject to change without notice to Brown Mackie College.

Program availability and degree offerings are subject to change.

Costs

Tuition in the 2012–13 academic year for most programs was $391 per credit hour; fees were $20 per credit hour. For the nursing program, tuition was $410 per credit hour; fees were $30 per credit hour. Textbooks, if applicable, and other instructional materials vary by program.

Financial Aid

Financial aid is available for those who qualify. The college maintains a full-time staff of Student Financial Services Advisers to assist qualified students in obtaining financial assistance. The college participates in several student aid programs. Forms of financial aid available to qualified students through federal resources include the Federal Pell Grant Program, Federal Supplemental Educational Opportunity Grant (FSEOG) Program, Federal Work-Study Program, Federal Perkins Loan Program, Federal Stafford Student Loan Program (subsidized and unsubsidized), Federal PLUS loan program, and Florida State grant program. Eligible students may apply for veterans' educational benefits. Students with physical or mental disabilities that are a handicap to employment may be eligible for training services through the state Agency for Vocational Rehabilitation. For further information, students should contact the Student Financial Services Office.

Each year, the college makes available President's Scholarships of $1,000 each to qualifying seniors from area high schools. In order to qualify, a senior must be graduating from a participating high school, must be maintaining a cumulative grade point average of at least 2.0, and must submit a brief essay. The student's extracurricular activities and community service are also considered. The President's Scholarship is available only to students enrolling in one of the college's degree programs. Students awarded the scholarship must enroll at Brown Mackie College — Miami between June and September immediately following their high school graduation. Applications for these scholarships can be obtained from the guidance departments of participating high schools. These applications must be completed and returned to the college by March 31. Those awarded scholarships will be notified by April 30. A list of participating high schools may be obtained from the campus Admissions Office.

The Education Foundation was established in 2000 to offer scholarship support to students interested in continuing their education at one of the postsecondary, career-focused schools in the EDMC system. The number and amount of the awards can vary, depending on the funds available. Scholarship applications are considered every quarter. At Brown Mackie College, applicants must be currently enrolled in an associate or bachelor's degree program and in their fourth quarter or higher (but no further than their second-to-last quarter) at the time of application. Awards are made based on academic performance and potential, as well as financial need. Interested students should contact the college's Student Financial Service Department for additional information.

Faculty

There are 15 full-time and more than 70 adjunct faculty members at the college. The average student-faculty ratio is 17:1.

Facilities and Resources

The main campus of Brown Mackie College — Miami is conveniently located at 3700 Lakeside Drive, Miramar, Florida. The college occupies more than 40,000 square feet on the first, second, and third floors of the Space Coast building, which is located in central Miramar.

The two nursing labs, as well as multiple computer classrooms, offer students a modern and professional environment for study. A medical assisting lab is used to instruct clinical medical skills. The college offers a computer networking lab as well as biomedical equipment technology lab for hands-on use and repair of equipment. The facility offers an equipped criminal justice lab including a crime scene and computers with facial recognition software. Each student has access to the technology, tools, and facilities needed to complete projects in each subject area. Students are welcome to use the labs when they are not being used for scheduled classes.

The college features a comfortable student lounge as well as a college store offering retail items including iPad accessories, kits specific to programs of study, and college apparel. The onsite library offers multimedia resources including laptop and iPad stations, power towers for convenient connectivity, books, and electronic resources specific to all academic programs offered.

The college offers an additional academic location in downtown Miami on the fifth and sixth floors of the Bayfront Plaza building. This location offers a number of computer classrooms as well as a criminal justice lab with a crime scene and facial recognition software. The downtown location also has an onsite library including laptop and iPad stations, books, and a wealth of electronic resources specific to all academic programs offered. Course delivery at both Brown Mackie College – Miami locations includes on-ground as well as blended courses.

Brown Mackie College — Miami is fully committed to using eTextbooks and computer tablets in the classroom. Utilizing these tablets to access expanded course material, students are able to increase their acumen for using this technology and further enhance their educational experience. Students have the ability to directly download their eTextbooks to their tablet, eliminating the need to carry heavy, physical textbooks and reducing the overall cost of supplies.

The college is a nonresidential, smoke-free institution.

Location

Brown Mackie College — Miami's main campus is located at 3700 Lakeside Drive, Miramar, Florida. There is an additional location in downtown at 100 South Biscayne Boulevard, Miami, Florida.

Admission Requirements

Each applicant for admission is assigned to an assistant director of admissions who directs the applicant through the steps of the admissions process, providing information on curriculum, policies, procedures, and services, and assisting the applicant in setting necessary appointments and interviews. To qualify for admission, applicants must be a graduate of a public or private high school or a correspondence school or education center that is accredited by an agency that is recognized by the U.S. Department of Education or the State of Florida's Department of Education or any of its approved agents, or provides official documentation of high school graduation equivalency. As part of the admissions process applicants must sign a document attesting to graduation or completion and containing the information to obtain verification of such. Official high school transcripts or official documentation of high school graduation equivalency must be obtained within the first term

(90 days) or the student will be withdrawn from the institution following established guidelines for withdrawn students noted in the catalog. Title IV aid will not be dispersed until verification of graduation or completion has been received by the college.

Students seeking entry into the college with a high school diploma completed in a foreign country must provide an original U.S. – equivalency evaluation from an evaluating agency which is a member of the National Association of Credential Evaluation Services (NACES) (http://www.naces.org/) or the Association of International Credential Evaluators, Inc. (AICES) (http://www.aice-eval.org/). The cost of evaluating the foreign transcript is borne by the applicant.

Brown Mackie College — Miami is authorized under Federal law to enroll nonimmigrant students. Applicants seeking entry into the college with a high school diploma completed in a foreign country must provide an original U. S. equivalency evaluation from a recognized evaluating agency. The cost of evaluating the foreign transcript is borne by the applicant.

For the most recent information regarding admission requirements, please refer to the current academic catalog.

Application and Information

Applicants must complete and submit an application form, along with documentation of graduation from an accredited high school or state-approved secondary education curriculum or official documentation of high school graduation equivalency.

Prospective students can go online to BMCprograms.info for program duration, tuition, fees and other costs, median debt, federal salary data, alumni success, programmatic accreditation, and other important details.

Brown Mackie College is a system of over twenty-five schools located throughout North America. Programs, credential levels, technology, and scheduling options vary by school, and employment opportunities are not guaranteed. Financial aid is available for those who qualify. Administrative offices are located at 625 Eden Park Drive, Suite 1100; Cincinnati, Ohio 45202; phone: 513-830-2000. ©2013 Brown Mackie College. OH Registration #03-09-1685T; #03-09-1686T; #03-09-1687T; #03-09-1688T; #06-03-1781T; AC0150, AC0109, AC0078, AC0045, AC0138, AC0110; Licensed by the Florida Commission for Independent Education, License No. 3206.

For additional information, prospective students should contact:

Director of Admissions
Brown Mackie College — Miami
3700 Lakeside Drive
Miramar, Florida 33027-3264
Phone: 305-341-6600
    866-505-0335 (toll-free)
Fax: 305-373-8814
E-mail: bmmiaadm@brownmackie.edu
Web site: http://www.brownmackie.edu/Miami

BROWN MACKIE COLLEGE — MICHIGAN CITY

MICHIGAN CITY, INDIANA

BROWN
MACKIE
COLLEGE
MICHIGAN
CITY℠

The College and Its Mission

Brown Mackie College — Michigan City (Brown Mackie College) is one of over twenty-five locations in the Brown Mackie College system of schools (www.brownmackie.edu), which is dedicated to providing educational programs that prepare students to pursue entry-level positions in a competitive, rapidly changing workplace. Brown Mackie College schools offer bachelor's degree, associate degree, diploma, and certificate programs in health sciences, business, information technology, legal studies, and design to thousands of students in the Midwest, Southeast, Southwest, and Western United States.

Founded in 1890 by A. N. Hirons as LaPorte Business College in LaPorte, Indiana, the institution later became known as Commonwealth Business College. In 1919, ownership was transferred to Grace and J. J. Moore, who successfully operated the college under the name of Reese School of Business for several decades. In 1975, the college came under the ownership of Steven C. Smith as Commonwealth Business College. In 1997, the college relocated to its present site in Michigan City, Indiana. The college was acquired by Education Management Corporation (EDMC) on September 2, 2003, and changed its name to Brown Mackie College — Michigan City in November 2003.

Brown Mackie College — Michigan City is accredited by the Accrediting Council for Independent Colleges and Schools to award associate degrees and certificates. The Accrediting Council for Independent Colleges and Schools is listed as a nationally recognized accrediting agency by the United States Department of Education and is recognized by the Council for Higher Education Accreditation. ACICS can be contacted at 750 First Street NE, Suite 980, Washington, D.C. 20002; phone: 202-336-6780.

Brown Mackie College — Michigan City is regulated by the Board for Proprietary Education Indiana Commission for Higher Education, W462 Indiana Government Center South, 402 West Washington Street, Indianapolis, Indiana 46204; phone: 317-232-1324 or 317-232-6716. Indiana advertising code: AC0138.

The Associate of Science in veterinary technology program has provisional programmatic accreditation granted by the American Veterinary Medical Association (AVMA) through the Committee on Veterinary Technician Education and Activities (CVTEA) 1931 North Meachum Road, Suite 100, Schaumburg, Illinois 60173; phone: 800-248-2862.

Academic Programs

Brown Mackie College — Michigan City provides higher education to traditional and nontraditional students through associate degree and certificate programs that assist in enhancing their career opportunities, broadening their perspectives through appropriate general education courses, thinking independently and critically, and improving problem-solving abilities. Brown Mackie College strives to develop within its students the desire for lifelong and continued education.

Each college quarter comprises twelve weeks. Associate degree programs require a minimum of eight quarters to complete. Programs are offered on a year-round basis, providing students with the ability to work uninterrupted toward their degrees. The college offers all programs in a unique One Course a Month format. This allows students to focus studies on only one course for four weeks. This schedule has proven convenient for students with multiple obligations such as jobs and family.

Associate Degree Programs: The Associate of Science degree is awarded in accounting technology, business management, criminal justice, and veterinary technology.

Certificate Programs: The college offers certificate programs in criminal justice, general business, and medical assistant.

The American Medical Technologists (AMT), which offers the certification for Registered Medical Assistant (RMA), accepts the accreditation of Brown Mackie College — Michigan City. Students will qualify to take the RMA certification examination upon graduating the Brown Mackie College — Michigan City medical assistant program.

Brown Mackie College — Michigan City does not guarantee third-party certification. Outside agencies control the requirements for certifications and are subject to change without notice to Brown Mackie College.

The degree and certificate programs at Brown Mackie College — Michigan City are approved for veteran's training by the Indiana State Approving Agency for Veterans Training.

Program availability and degree offerings are subject to change.

Costs

Tuition in the 2012–13 academic year was $314 per credit hour and fees were $20 per credit hour. Textbook fees, if applicable, vary according to the program.

Financial Aid

The college maintains a full-time staff of Student Financial Services Advisers to assist qualified students in obtaining financial assistance. The college participates in several student aid programs. Forms of financial aid available to qualified students through federal resources include the Federal Pell Grant Program, Federal Supplemental Educational Opportunity Grant (FSEOG) Program, Federal Work-Study Program, Federal Stafford Student Loan Program (subsidized and unsubsidized), and Federal PLUS loan program.

Eligible students may apply for Indiana state awards, such as the Higher Education Award and Twenty-First Century Scholarships for high school students, the Core 40 awards, and veterans' educational benefits. Students with physical or mental disabilities that are a handicap to employment may be eligible for training services through the state's Bureau of Vocational Rehabilitation. For further information, students should contact the Brown Mackie College — Michigan City Student Financial Services Office.

Brown Mackie College — Michigan City is eligible for, and participates in, certain Title IV financial aid programs, state grant programs, and vocational education contracts with private vocational institutions. The college is authorized to enroll students as Vocational Rehabilitation program participants and as Social Security beneficiaries. The college does not participate in the Department of Education's Leave of Absence Program.

Each year, the college makes available President's Scholarships of $1,000 each to qualifying seniors from area high schools. In order to qualify, a senior must be graduating from a participating high school, must be maintaining a cumulative grade point average of at least 2.0, and must submit a brief essay. The student's extracurricular activities and community service are also considered. These scholarships are available only to students enrolling in one of the college's degree programs. Students awarded the scholarship must enroll at Brown Mackie College — Michigan City between June and September immediately following their high school graduation. Applications for these scholarships can be obtained from the guidance departments of participating high schools. These applications must be completed and returned to the college by March 31.

The Education Foundation was established in 2000 to offer scholarship support to students interested in continuing their education at one of the postsecondary, career-focused schools in the EDMC system. The number and amount of the awards can vary, depending on the funds available. Scholarship applications are considered every quarter. At Brown Mackie College, applicants must be currently enrolled in an associate or bachelor's degree program and in their fourth quarter or higher (but no further than their second-to-last quarter) at the time of application. Awards are made based on academic performance and potential, as well as financial need. Interested students should contact the college's Student Financial Service Department for additional information.

Faculty

There are 9 full-time and 31 part-time faculty members at the college. The average student-faculty ratio is 13:1. Each student is assigned a department chair.

Facilities and Resources

In November 2012, the campus relocated to a 29,000-square-foot facility at 1001 East U.S. Highway 20. The new space offers a modern, professional environment for study with a floor plan that features twenty new classrooms with new computers, furniture, audio/visual equipment, and networking equipment for podium additions. The Brown Mackie College — Michigan City facility includes six computer labs, two medical assisting labs, a criminal justice lab, and a veterinary technology lab. The labs provide students with hands-on opportunities to apply knowledge and skills learned in the classroom. Students are welcome to use the labs when those facilities are not in use for scheduled classes. There is a student lounge, a bookstore, and new digital signage in the reception area as well as directional signage throughout the space.

Brown Mackie College — Michigan City is fully committed to using eTextbooks and computer tablets in the classroom. Utilizing these tablets to access expanded course material, students are able to increase their acumen for using this technology and further enhance their educational experience. Students have the ability to directly download their eTextbooks to their tablet, eliminating the need to carry heavy, physical textbooks and reducing the overall cost of supplies.

The college is a nonresidential, smoke-free institution.

Location

Brown Mackie College — Michigan City is conveniently located in northwest Indiana, at 1001 East U.S. Highway 20, Michigan City, 1 mile north of Interstate 94, 2 miles east of the intersection of routes 20 and 421.

Admission Requirements

Each applicant for admission is assigned to an Assistant Director of Admissions, who directs the applicant through the steps of the admissions process, providing information on curriculum, policies, procedures, and services and assisting the applicant in setting necessary appointments and interviews. To qualify for admission, each applicant must provide documentation of graduation from an accredited high school or completion of a state-approved secondary education curriculum or provide official documentation of high school graduation equivalency. All transcripts become the property of the Brown Mackie College.

As part of the admission process, students are given an assessment of academic skills. Although the results of this assessment do not determine eligibility for admission, they provide the college with a means of determining the need for academic support, as well as a means by which the college can evaluate the effectiveness of its educational programs. All new students are required to complete this assessment.

For the most recent information regarding admission requirements, please refer to the current academic catalog.

Application and Information

Applicants must complete and submit an application form along with documentation of graduation from an accredited high school or completion of a state-approved secondary education curriculum or provide official documentation of high school graduation equivalency.

Prospective students can go online to BMCprograms.info for program duration, tuition, fees and other costs, median debt, federal salary data, alumni success, programmatic accreditation, and other important details.

Brown Mackie College is a system of over twenty-five schools located throughout North America. Programs, credential levels, technology, and scheduling options vary by school, and employment opportunities are not guaranteed. Financial aid is available for those who qualify. Administrative offices are located at 625 Eden Park Drive, Suite 1100; Cincinnati, Ohio 45202; phone: 513-830-2000. ©2013 Brown Mackie College. OH Registration #03-09-1685T; #03-09-1686T; #03-09-1687T; #03-09-1688T; #06-03-1781T; AC0150, AC0109, AC0078, AC0045, AC0138, AC0110; Licensed by the Florida Commission for Independent Education, License No. 3206.

For additional information, prospective students should contact:

Director of Admissions
Brown Mackie College — Michigan City
1001 East U.S. Highway 20
Michigan City, Indiana 46360
Phone: 219-877-3100
     800-519-2416 (toll-free)
Fax: 219-877-3110
E-mail: bmcmcadm@brownmackie.edu
Web site: http://www.brownmackie.edu/MichiganCity

BROWN MACKIE COLLEGE — NORTH CANTON

NORTH CANTON, OHIO

The College and Its Mission

Brown Mackie College — North Canton (Brown Mackie College) one of over twenty-five locations in the Brown Mackie College system of schools (www.brownmackie.edu), which is dedicated to providing educational programs that prepare students to pursue entry-level positions in a competitive, rapidly changing workplace. Brown Mackie College schools offer bachelor's degree, associate degree, diploma, and certificate programs in health sciences, business, information technology, legal studies, and design to thousands of students in the Midwest, Southeast, Southwest, and Western United States.

The college opened in the 1980s as the National Electronics Institute. In 2002, the Southern Ohio College took ownership. The following year it became part of the Brown Mackie College family of schools.

Brown Mackie College — North Canton is accredited by the Accrediting Council for Independent Colleges and Schools to award associate degrees and diplomas. The Accrediting Council for Independent Colleges and Schools is listed as a nationally recognized accrediting agency by the United States Department of Education and is recognized by the Council for Higher Education Accreditation. ACICS can be contacted at 750 First Street NE, Suite 980, Washington, D.C. 20002; phone: 202-336-6780.

Brown Mackie College — North Canton is licensed by the Ohio State Board of Career Colleges and Schools, 30 East Broad Street, 24th Floor, Suite 2481, Columbus, Ohio 43215-3138; phone: 614-466-2752. Ohio registration #03-09-1688T.

The Associate of Science in medical assisting program is accredited by the Accrediting Bureau of Health Education Schools.

The Associate of Science in surgical technology is accredited by the Commission on Accreditation of Allied Health Education Programs (www.caahep.org) upon the recommendation of the Accreditation Review Committee on Education in Surgical Technology. The Commission on Accreditation of Allied Health Education Programs can be contacted at 1361 Park Street, Clearwater, Florida 33756; phone: 727-210-2350.

The Associate of Science in veterinary technology program has provisional programmatic accreditation granted by the American Veterinary Medical Association (AVMA) through the Committee on Veterinary Technician Education and Activities (CVTEA).

Brown Mackie College — North Canton is licensed by the Ohio State Board of Career Colleges and Schools, located at 30 East Broad Street, 24th Floor, Suite 2481, Columbus, Ohio 43215-3138; phone: 614-466-2752. Ohio registration #03-09-1688T.

The Associate of Science in surgical technology program is accredited by the Accrediting Bureau of Health Education Schools. (ABHES). The Accrediting Bureau of Health Education Schools may be contacted at 7777 Leesburg Pike, Suite 314, North Falls Church, Virginia 22043; phone: 703-917-9503.

Academic Programs

Brown Mackie College — North Canton provides higher education to traditional and nontraditional students through associate degree and diploma programs that can assist students in enhancing their career opportunities, broadening their perspectives through appropriate general education courses, thinking independently and critically, and improving problem-solving abilities. The college strives to develop within its students the desire for lifelong and continued education.

Each college quarter comprises twelve weeks. Associate degree programs require a minimum of eight quarters to complete. Programs are offered on a year-round basis, providing students with the ability to work uninterrupted toward their degrees. The college offers all programs in a unique One Course a Month format. This schedule allows students to focus studies on only one course for four weeks and has proven convenient for students with multiple obligations such as jobs and family.

Associate Degree Programs: The Associate of Applied Business degree is awarded in accounting technology, business management, computer networking and applications, criminal justice, and paralegal. The Associate of Applied Science degree is awarded in computer networking and applications, health care administration, medical assisting, pharmacy technology, surgical technology, and veterinary technology.

Diploma Programs: The college also offers diploma programs in bookkeeping specialist, computer aided design and drafting technician, criminal justice specialist, general business, medical assistant, paralegal assistant, and practical nursing.

The American Medical Technologists (AMT), which offers the certification for Registered Medical Assistant (RMA), accepts the accreditation of Brown Mackie College — North Canton. Students will qualify to take the Registered Medical Assistant certification examination upon graduating the Brown Mackie College — North Canton medical assisting and medical assistant programs. Graduates of the 48-credit-hour medical assistant program are not qualified to take the AMT/RMA exam.

Brown Mackie College — North Canton does not guarantee third-party certification. Outside agencies control the requirements for certifications and are subject to change without notice to Brown Mackie College.

Program availability and degree offerings are subject to change.

Costs

Tuition for the 2012–13 academic year was $314 per credit hour and $20 per credit hour for general fees. The tuition for the surgical technology program was $360 per credit hour and $20 per credit hour for general fees. The tuition for the practical nursing program was $381 per credit hour and $30 per credit hour for general fees. The cost of textbooks, if applicable, and other instructional materials varies by program.

Financial Aid

Financial aid is available to those who qualify. The college maintains a full-time staff of Student Financial Services Advisers to assist qualified students in obtaining financial assistance. The college participates in several student aid programs. Forms of financial aid available through federal resources include the Federal Pell Grant Program, Federal Supplemental Educational Opportunity Grant (FSEOG) Program, Federal Work-Study Program, Federal Perkins Loan Program, Federal Stafford Student Loan Program (subsidized and unsubsidized), and the Federal PLUS Loan Program. Eligible students may also apply for state awards and veterans' educational benefits. Students with physical or mental disabilities that are a handicap to employment may be eligible for training services through the state Agency for Vocational Rehabilitation. For further information, students should contact the Brown Mackie College — North Canton Student Financial Services Office.

Each year, the college makes available President's Scholarships of $1,000 each to qualifying seniors from area high schools. In order to qualify, a senior must be graduating from a participating high school, must be maintaining a cumulative grade point average of at least 2.0, and must submit a brief essay. The student's extracurricular activities and community service are also considered. The President's Scholarship is available only to students enrolling in one of the college's degree programs. Students awarded the scholarship must enroll at Brown Mackie College — North Canton between June and September immediately following their high school graduation. Applications for these scholarships can be obtained from the guidance departments of participating high schools. These applications must be completed and returned to the college by March 31.

The Education Foundation was established in 2000 to offer scholarship support to students interested in continuing their education at one of the postsecondary, career-focused schools in the EDMC system. The number and amount of the awards can vary, depending on the funds available. Scholarship applications are considered every quarter. At Brown Mackie College, applicants must be currently enrolled in an associate or bachelor's degree program and in their fourth quarter or higher (but no further than their second-to-last quarter) at the time of application. Awards are made based on academic performance and potential, as well as financial need. Interested students should contact the college's Student Financial Service Department for additional information.

Faculty

There are approximately 20 full-time and approximately 35 part-time faculty members. The average student-faculty ratio is approximately 19:1. Each student has a faculty and student adviser.

Facilities and Resources

The college comprises administrative offices, faculty and student lounges, a reception area, and spacious classrooms and laboratories. Instructional equipment includes personal computers, LANs, printers, and LCD projectors. The library provides support for the academic programs through volumes covering a broad range of subjects, as well as through Internet access. Vehicle parking is provided for both students and staff members.

Brown Mackie College — North Canton is fully committed to using eTextbooks and computer tablets in the classroom. Utilizing these tablets to access expanded course material, students are able to increase their acumen for using this technology and further enhance their educational experience. Students have the ability to directly download their eTextbooks to their tablet, eliminating the need to carry heavy, physical textbooks and reducing the overall cost of supplies.

Location

Brown Mackie College — North Canton is located at 4300 Munson Street, NW in Canton, Ohio. The school is easily accessible from I-77 and Route 687 and by the SARTA bus line.

Admission Requirements

Each applicant for admission is assigned to an Assistant Director of Admissions, who directs the applicant through the steps of the admissions process, providing information on curriculum, policies, procedures, and services and assisting the applicant in setting necessary appointments and interviews. To qualify for admission, each applicant must provide documentation of graduation from an accredited high school or from a state-approved secondary education curriculum or provide official documentation of high school graduation equivalency. All transcripts become the property of the college. Admission to the college is based upon the applicant meeting the stated requirements, a review of the applicant's previous education records, and a review of the applicant's career interests. If previous academic records indicate that the college's education and training programs would not benefit the applicant, the college reserves the right to advise the applicant not to enroll. Special requirements for enrollment into certain programs are discussed in the descriptions of those programs.

For the most recent information regarding admission requirements, please refer to the current academic catalog.

Application and Information

Applicants must complete and submit an application form, along with documentation of graduation from an accredited high school or state-approved secondary education curriculum or official documentation of high school graduation equivalency.

Prospective students can go online to BMCprograms.info for program duration, tuition, fees and other costs, median debt, federal salary data, alumni success, programmatic accreditation, and other important details.

Brown Mackie College is a system of over twenty-five schools located throughout North America. Programs, credential levels, technology, and scheduling options vary by school, and employment opportunities are not guaranteed. Financial aid is available for those who qualify. Administrative offices are located at 625 Eden Park Drive, Suite 1100; Cincinnati, Ohio 45202; phone: 513-830-2000. ©2013 Brown Mackie College. OH Registration # 03-09-1685T; #03-09-1686T; #03-09-1687T; #03-09-1688T; #06-03-1781T; AC0150, AC0109, AC0078, AC0045, AC0138, AC0110; Licensed by the Florida Commission for Independent Education, License No. 3206.

For additional information, prospective students should contact:

Director of Admissions
Brown Mackie College — North Canton
4300 Munson Street NW
Canton, Ohio 44718-3674
Phone: 330-494-1214
Fax: 330-494-8112
E-mail: bmcncweb@brownmackie.edu
Web site: http://www.brownmackie.edu/North-Canton

BROWN MACKIE COLLEGE — NORTHERN KENTUCKY
FORT MITCHELL, KENTUCKY

BROWN
MACKIE
COLLEGE
NORTHERN
KENTUCKY™

The College and Its Mission

Brown Mackie College — Northern Kentucky (Brown Mackie College) is one of over twenty-five locations in the Brown Mackie College system of schools (www.brownmackie.edu), which is dedicated to providing educational programs that prepare students to pursue entry-level positions in a competitive, rapidly changing workplace. The Brown Mackie College schools offer bachelor's degree, associate degree, diploma, and certificate programs in health sciences, business, information technology, legal studies, and design to thousands of students in the Midwest, Southeast, Southwest, and Western United States.

The college was founded in Cincinnati, Ohio, in February 1927 as a traditional business college. In May 1981, the college opened a branch location in northern Kentucky, which moved in 1986 to its current location in Fort Mitchell.

Brown Mackie College — Northern Kentucky is accredited by the Accrediting Council for Independent Colleges and Schools to award associate degrees and diplomas. The Accrediting Council for Independent Colleges and Schools is listed as a nationally recognized accrediting agency by the United States Department of Education and is recognized by the Council for Higher Education Accreditation. ACICS can be contacted at 750 First Street NE, Suite 980, Washington, D.C. 20002; phone: 202-336-6780.

Brown Mackie College — Northern Kentucky is regulated by the Board for Proprietary Education Indiana Commission for Higher Education, 101 West Ohio Street, Suite 670, Indianapolis, Indiana 46204; 317-464-4400. Indiana advertising code: AC0150.

Brown Mackie College — Northern Kentucky is licensed by the Ohio State Board of Career Colleges and Schools, located at 30 East Broad Street, 24th Floor, Suite 2481, Columbus, Ohio 43215-3138; phone: 614-466-2752. Ohio registration #06-03-1781T.

Brown Mackie College — Northern Kentucky is licensed by the Kentucky Council on Postsecondary Education, 1024 Capital Center Drive, Suite 320; Frankfort, Kentucky 40601.

The occupational therapy assistant program is accredited by the Accreditation Council for Occupational Therapy Education (ACOTE) of the American Occupational Therapy Association (AOTA), located at 4720 Montgomery Lane, Suite 200, Bethesda, Maryland 20814-3449; phone: 301-652-AOTA. Graduates of the program will be eligible to sit for the national certification examination for the occupational therapy assistant administered by the National Board for Certification in Occupational Therapy (NBCOT). After successful completion of this exam, the individual will be a Certified Occupational Therapy Assistant (COTA). In addition, most states require licensure in order to practice; however, state licenses are usually based on the results of the NBCOT Certification Examination. Note that a felony conviction may affect a graduate's ability to sit for the NBCOT certification examination or attain state licensure.

The Associate of Applied Science in surgical technology program is accredited by the Commission on Accreditation of Allied Health Education Programs (http://www.caahep.org) upon the recommendation of the Accreditation Review Council on Education in Surgical Technology and Surgical Assisting (ARC/STSA).

The Kentucky Board of Nursing has granted conditional approval status for the prelicensure of the practical nursing diploma program at Brown Mackie College — Northern Kentucky. A factor in the decision was based on the graduates' first-time NCLEX pass rate of 75 percent.

Academic Programs

Brown Mackie College — Northern Kentucky provides higher education to traditional and nontraditional students through associate degree, and diploma programs that assist them in enhancing their career opportunities, broadening their perspectives through appropriate general education courses, thinking independently and critically, and improving problem-solving abilities. The college strives to develop within its students the desire for lifelong and continued education.

Each college quarter comprises ten to twelve weeks. Associate degree programs require a minimum of eight quarters to complete. Programs are offered on a year-round basis, providing students with the ability to work uninterrupted toward their degrees. The college offers all programs in a unique One Course a Month format. This allows students to focus studies on only one course for four weeks. This schedule has proven convenient for students with multiple obligations such as jobs and family.

Associate Degree Programs: The Associate of Applied Business degree is awarded in accounting technology, business management, information technology, and paralegal.

The Associate of Applied Science degree is awarded in computer-aided design and drafting technology, health care administration, medical assisting, occupational therapy assistant, pharmacy technology, and surgical technology.

Diploma Programs: The college offers diploma programs in accounting, business, computer software applications, medical assistant, and practical nursing.

The American Medical Technologists (AMT), which offers the certification for Registered Medical Assistant (RMA), accepts the accreditation of Brown Mackie College — Northern Kentucky. Students will qualify to take the RMA certification examination upon graduating the Brown Mackie College — Northern Kentucky medical assisting and medical assistant programs. Graduates of the 48 credit-hour medical assistant program are not qualified to take the AMT/RMA exam.

Brown Mackie College — Northern Kentucky does not guarantee third-party certification. Outside agencies control the requirements for certifications and are subject to change without notice to Brown Mackie College.

Program availability and degree offerings are subject to change.

Costs

Tuition for the 2012–13 academic year was $314 per credit hour and general fees were $20 per credit hour, with some exceptions. The practical nursing program tuition was $381 per credit hour and general fees were $30 per credit hour. The surgical technology tuition was $360 per credit hour and general fees were $20 per credit hour. Tuition for the occupational therapy assistant program was $381 per credit hour and general fees were $20 per credit hour. The cost of textbooks, if applicable, and other instructional materials varies by program.

Financial Aid

Financial aid is available to those who qualify. The college maintains a full-time staff of Student Financial Services Advisers to assist qualified students in obtaining financial assistance. The college participates in several student aid programs. Forms of financial aid available through federal resources include Federal Pell Grants, Federal Supplemental Educational Opportunity Grants (FSEOG), Federal Work-Study Program awards, Federal Perkins Loans, Federal Stafford Student Loans (subsidized and unsubsidized), and Federal PLUS loans. Eligible students may apply for veterans' educational benefits. Students with physical or mental disabilities that are a handicap to employment may be eligible for training services through the state Vocational Rehabilitation Agency. For further information, students should contact the Student Financial Services Office.

Each year, the college makes available President's Scholarships of $1,000 each to qualifying seniors from area high schools. In order to qualify, a senior have graduated from a participating high school, maintained a cumulative grade point average of at least 2.0, and submitted a brief essay. The student's extracurricular activities and community service are also considered. The President's Scholarship is available only to students enrolling in one of the college's degree programs. Students who receive the scholarship must enroll at Brown Mackie College — Northern Kentucky between June and September immediately following their high school graduation. Applications for these scholarships can be obtained from the guidance departments of participating high schools. These applications must be completed and returned to the college by March 31.

The Education Foundation was established in 2000 to offer scholarship support to students interested in continuing their education at one of the postsecondary, career-focused schools in the EDMC system. The number and amount of the awards can vary, depending on the funds available. Scholarship applications are considered every quarter. At Brown Mackie College, applicants must be currently enrolled in an associate or bachelor's degree program and in their fourth quarter or higher (but no further than their second-to-last quarter) at the time of application. Awards are made based on academic performance and potential, as well as financial need. Interested students should contact the college's Student Financial Service Department for additional information.

Faculty

There are 12 full-time and 30 adjunct faculty members. The student-faculty ratio is 12:1.

Facilities and Resources

Brown Mackie College offers media presentation rooms for special instructional needs and a library that provides instructional resources and academic support for both faculty members and students.

Brown Mackie College — Northern Kentucky is fully committed to using eTextbooks and computer tablets in the classroom. Utilizing these tablets to access expanded course material, students are able to increase their acumen for using this technology and further enhance their educational experience. Students have the ability to directly download their eTextbooks to their tablet, eliminating the need to carry heavy, physical textbooks and reducing the overall cost of supplies.

The college is nonresidential; public transportation and ample parking at no cost are available. The campus is a smoke-free facility.

Location

Brown Mackie College — Northern Kentucky is conveniently located at 309 Buttermilk Pike in Fort Mitchell, Kentucky.

Admission Requirements

Each applicant for admission is assigned to an Assistant Director of Admissions, who directs the applicant through the steps of the admissions process, providing information on curriculum, policies, procedures, and services and assisting the applicant in setting necessary appointments and interviews. To qualify for admission, each applicant must provide documentation of graduation from an accredited high school or from a state-approved secondary education curriculum or provide official documentation of high school graduation equivalency. All transcripts become the property of the college. Admission to the college is based upon the applicant meeting the stated requirements, a review of the applicant's previous education

records, and a review of the applicant's career interests. If previous academic records indicate the college's education and training programs would not benefit the applicant, the college reserves the right to advise the applicant not to enroll. Special requirements for enrollment into certain programs are discussed in the descriptions of those programs.

In addition to the college's general admission requirements, applicants enrolling in the practical nursing program must document the following, which must be completed, and a record of proof must appear in the student's file prior to the start of the nursing fundamentals course. No student will be admitted to a clinical agency unless all paperwork is completed. The paperwork is a requirement of all contracted agencies. This paperwork includes records of (1) a complete physical, current to within six months of admission; (2) a two-step Mantoux test that is kept current throughout schooling; (3) a hepatitis B vaccination or signed refusal; (4) up-to-date immunizations, including tetanus and rubella; (5) a record of current CPR certification that is maintained throughout the student's clinical experience; and (6) hospitalization insurance or a signed waiver.

For the most recent information regarding admission requirements, prospective students should refer to the current academic catalog.

Application and Information

Applicants must complete and submit an application form, along with documentation of graduation from an accredited high school or state-approved secondary education curriculum or official documentation of high school graduation equivalency.

Prospective students can go online to BMCprograms.info for program duration, tuition, fees and other costs, median debt, federal salary data, alumni success, programmatic accreditation, and other important details.

Brown Mackie College is a system of over twenty-five schools located throughout North America. Programs, credential levels, technology, and scheduling options vary by school, and employment opportunities are not guaranteed. Financial aid is available for those who qualify. Administrative offices are located at 625 Eden Park Drive, Suite 1100; Cincinnati, Ohio 45202; phone: 513-830-2000. ©2013 Brown Mackie College. OH Registration #03-09-1685T; #03-09-1686T; #03-09-1687T; #03-09-1688T; #06-03-1781T; AC0150, AC0109, AC0078, AC0045, AC0138, AC0110; Licensed by the Florida Commission for Independent Education, License No. 3206.

For additional information, prospective students should contact:

Director of Admissions
Brown Mackie College — Northern Kentucky
309 Buttermilk Pike
Fort Mitchell, Kentucky 41017
Phone: 859-341-5627
    800-888-1445 (toll-free)
Fax: 859-341-6483
E-mail: bmcnkadm@brownmackie.edu
Web site: http://www.brownmackie.edu/NorthernKentucky

BROWN MACKIE COLLEGE — OKLAHOMA CITY

OKLAHOMA CITY, OKLAHOMA

BROWN
MACKIE
COLLEGE

OKLAHOMA
CITY℠

The College and Its Mission

Brown Mackie College—Oklahoma City (Brown Mackie College) is one of over twenty-five locations in the Brown Mackie College system of schools (www.brownmackie.edu), which is dedicated to providing educational programs that prepare students to pursue entry-level positions in a competitive, rapidly changing workplace. Brown Mackie College schools offer bachelor's degree, associate degree, certificate, and diploma programs in health sciences, business, information technology, legal studies, and design to thousands of students in the Midwest, Southeast, Southwest, and Western United States.

Brown Mackie College — Oklahoma City is a branch campus of Brown Mackie College — Salina which is accredited by the Higher Learning Commission and a member of the North Central Association, 230 South LaSalle Street, Suite 7-500, Chicago, Illinois 60604-1413; phone: 800-621-7440 (toll-free); www.ncahlc.org.

This institution has been granted authority to operate in Oklahoma by the Oklahoma State Regents for Higher Education (OSRHE), 655 Research Parkway, Suite 200, Oklahoma City, Oklahoma 73101; phone: 405-225-9100.

The Associate of Applied Science in occupational therapy assistant program has applied for accreditation to the Accreditation Council for Occupational Therapy Education (ACOTE) of the American Occupational Therapy Association (AOTA), located at 4720 Montgomery Lane, Suite 200, Bethesda, Maryland 20814-3449; phone: 301-652-AOTA. Graduates of the program will be eligible to sit for the national certification examination for the occupational therapy assistant administered by the National Board for Certification in Occupational Therapy (NBCOT). After successful completion of this exam, the individual will be a Certified Occupational Therapy Assistant (COTA). In addition, most states require licensure in order to practice; however, state licenses are usually based on the results of the NBCOT Certification Examination. Note that a felony conviction may affect a graduate's ability to sit for the NBCOT certification examination or attain state licensure.

Academic Programs

Brown Mackie College — Oklahoma City provides higher education to traditional and nontraditional students through associate degree programs that can assist students in enhancing their career opportunities, broadening their perspectives through appropriate general education courses, thinking independently and critically, and improving problem-solving abilities. Brown Mackie College strives to develop within its students the desire for lifelong and continued education.

Each college quarter comprises twelve weeks. Associate degree programs require a minimum of eight quarters to complete. Programs are offered on a year-round basis, providing students with the ability to work uninterrupted toward their degrees. Brown Mackie College offers all programs in a unique One Course a Month format. This schedule allows students to focus studies on only one course for four weeks and has proven convenient for students with multiple obligations such as jobs and family.

Associate Degree Programs: The Associate of Applied Science degree is awarded in accounting technology, business management, health care administration, medical assisting, occupational therapy assistant, office management, and paralegal.

The American Medical Technologists (AMT), which offers the certification for Registered Medical Assistant (RMA), accepts the accreditation of Brown Mackie College — Oklahoma City. Students will qualify to take the RMA certification examination upon graduating the Brown Mackie College — Oklahoma City medical assisting program.

Brown Mackie College does not guarantee third-party certification/licensing exams. Outside agencies control the requirements for certification/licensing and are subject to change without notification to the college.

Program availability and degree offerings are subject to change.

Costs

Tuition for the 2012–13 academic year was $314 per credit hour, and $20 per credit hour for general fees. Tuition for the occupational therapy assistant program was $381 per credit hour, and $20 per credit hour for general fees. The cost of textbooks, if applicable, and other instructional materials varies by program.

Financial Aid

Financial aid is available to those who qualify. Brown Mackie College — Oklahoma City maintains a full-time staff of financial aid professionals to assist qualified students in obtaining financial assistance. The college participates in several student aid programs. Forms of financial aid available through federal resources include the Federal Pell Grant Program, Federal Supplemental Educational Opportunity Grant (FSEOG) Program, Federal Work-Study Program, Federal Perkins Loan Program, Federal Stafford Student Loan Program (subsidized and unsubsidized), and the Federal PLUS Loan Program. Eligible students may also apply for state awards and veterans' educational benefits. Students with physical or mental disabilities that are a handicap to employment may be eligible for training services through the state Agency for Vocational Rehabilitation. For further information, students should contact the Brown Mackie College — Oklahoma City Student Financial Services Office.

Each year, the college makes available President's Scholarships of $1,000 each to qualifying seniors from area high schools. In order to qualify, a senior must be graduating from a participating high school, have maintained a cumulative grade point average of at least 2.0, and submitted a brief essay. The student's extracurricular activities and community service are also considered. The President's Scholarship is available only to students enrolling in one of the college's degree programs. Students awarded the scholarship must enroll at Brown Mackie College — Oklahoma City between June and September immediately following their high school graduation. Applications for these scholarships can be obtained from the guidance departments of participating high schools. These applications must be completed and returned to the college by March 31.

The Education Foundation was established in 2000 to offer scholarship support to students interested in continuing their education at one of the postsecondary, career-focused schools in the EDMC system. The number and amount of the awards can vary, depending on the funds available. Scholarship applications are considered every quarter. At Brown Mackie College, applicants must be currently enrolled in an associate or bachelor's degree program and in their fourth quarter or higher (but no further than their second-to-last quarter) at the time of application. Awards are made based on academic performance and potential, as well as financial need. Interested students should contact the college's Student Financial Service Department for additional information.

Faculty

Brown Mackie College — Oklahoma City has 11 full-time and 30 regular adjunct faculty members, with an average student-faculty ratio of 15:1.

Facilities and Resources

Brown Mackie College — Oklahoma City comprises administrative offices, faculty and student lounges, a reception area, and spacious classrooms and laboratories. Instructional equipment includes personal computers, LANs, printers, and transcribers. The library provides support for the academic programs through volumes covering a broad range of subjects, as well as through Internet access. Vehicle parking is provided for both students and staff members.

Brown Mackie College — Oklahoma City is fully committed to using eTextbooks and computer tablets in the classroom. Utilizing these tablets to access expanded course material, students are able to increase their acumen for using this technology and further enhance their educational experience. Students have the ability to directly download their eTextbooks to their tablet, eliminating the need to carry heavy, physical textbooks and reducing the overall cost of supplies.

The college is nonresidential; public transportation and ample parking at no cost are available. The school is a smoke-free facility.

Location

Brown Mackie College — Oklahoma City is located at 7101 Northwest Expressway, Suite 800, in Oklahoma City, Oklahoma.

Admission Requirements

Each applicant for admission is assigned an Assistant Director of Admissions who directs the applicant through the steps of the admissions process, providing information on curriculum, policies, procedures, and services and assisting the applicant in setting necessary appointments and interviews.

To qualify for admission, each applicant must provide documentation of graduation from an accredited high school or from a state-approved secondary education curriculum or provide official documentation of high school graduation equivalency. All transcripts become the property of Brown Mackie College — Oklahoma City. Admission to the college is based upon the applicant meeting the stated requirements, a review of the applicant's previous education records, and a

review of the applicant's career interests. If previous academic records indicate that the Brown Mackie College education and training programs would not benefit the applicant, the college reserves the right to advise the applicant not to enroll. Special requirements for enrollment into certain programs are discussed in the descriptions of those programs.

For the most recent information regarding admission requirements, please refer to the current academic catalog.

Application and Information

Applicants must complete and submit an application form along with documentation of graduation from an accredited high school or state-approved secondary education curriculum, or applicants must provide official documentation of high school graduation equivalency.

Prospective students can go online to BMCprograms.info for program duration, tuition, fees and other costs, median debt, federal salary data, alumni success, programmatic accreditation, and other important details.

Brown Mackie College is a system of over twenty-five schools located throughout North America. Programs, credential levels, technology, and scheduling options vary by school, and employment opportunities are not guaranteed. Financial aid is available for those who qualify. Administrative offices are located at 625 Eden Park Drive, Suite 1100; Cincinnati, Ohio 45202; phone: 513-830-2000. ©2013 Brown Mackie College. OH Registration #03-09-1685T; #03-09-1686T; #03-09-1687T; #03-09-1688T; #06-03-1781T; AC0150, AC0109, AC0078, AC0045, AC0138, AC0110; Licensed by the Florida Commission for Independent Education, License No. 3206.

For additional information, prospective students should contact:

Director of Admissions
Brown Mackie College — Oklahoma City
7101 Northwest Expressway, Suite 800
Oklahoma City, Oklahoma 73132
Phone: 405-621-8000
    888-229-3280 (toll-free)
Fax: 405-621-8055
E-mail: bmcokcadm@brownmackie.edu
Web site: http://www.brownmackie.edu/Oklahoma-City

BROWN MACKIE COLLEGE — PHOENIX

PHOENIX, ARIZONA

BROWN MACKIE COLLEGE PHOENIX℠

The College and Its Mission

Brown Mackie College — Phoenix (Brown Mackie College) is one of over twenty-five locations in the Brown Mackie College system of schools (www.brownmackie.edu), which is dedicated to providing educational programs that prepare students to pursue entry-level positions in a competitive, rapidly changing workplace. The Brown Mackie College schools offer bachelor's degree, associate degree, diploma, and certificate programs in health sciences, business, information technology, legal studies, and design to thousands of students in the Midwest, Southeast, Southwest, and Western United States.

Brown Mackie College — Phoenix was founded in 2009 as a branch of Brown Mackie College — Tucson, Arizona.

Brown Mackie College — Phoenix is accredited by the Accrediting Council for Independent Colleges and Schools to award associate degrees and diplomas. The Accrediting Council for Independent Colleges and Schools is listed as a nationally recognized accrediting agency by the United States Department of Education and is recognized by the Council for Higher Education Accreditation. ACICS can be contacted at 750 First Street NE, Suite 980, Washington, D.C. 20002; phone: 202-336-6780.

Brown Mackie College — Phoenix is authorized by the Arizona State Board for Private Postsecondary Education, 1400 West Washington Street, Room 2560, Phoenix, Arizona 85007; phone: 602-542-5709; http://azppse.state.az.us.

The occupational therapy assistant program is accredited by the Accreditation Council for Occupational Therapy Education (ACOTE) of the American Occupational Therapy Association (AOTA), located at 4720 Montgomery Lane, Suite 200, Bethesda, Maryland 20814-3449; phone: 301-652-AOTA. Graduates of the program will be eligible to sit for the national certification examination for the occupational therapy assistant administered by the National Board for Certification in Occupational Therapy (NBCOT). After successful completion of this exam, the individual will be a Certified Occupational Therapy Assistant (COTA). In addition, most states require licensure in order to practice; however, state licenses are usually based on the results of the NBCOT Certification Examination. Note that a felony conviction may affect a graduate's ability to sit for the NBCOT certification examination or attain state licensure.

The Associate of Science in surgical technology program is accredited by the Accrediting Bureau of Health Education Schools.

Academic Programs

Brown Mackie College provides higher education to traditional and nontraditional students through associate degree and diploma programs that assist in enhancing their career opportunities, broadening their perspectives through appropriate general education courses, thinking independently and critically, and improving problem-solving abilities. The college strives to develop within its students the desire for lifelong and continued education.

Each college quarter comprises twelve weeks. Associate degree programs require a minimum of eight quarters to complete. Programs are offered on a year-round basis, providing students with the ability to work uninterrupted toward completion of their programs. The college offers all programs in a unique One Course a Month format. This allows students to focus studies on only one course for four weeks. This schedule has proven convenient for students with multiple obligations such as jobs and family.

Associate Degree Programs: The Associate of Science degree is awarded in accounting technology, business management, criminal justice, health care administration, information technology, medical assisting, paralegal, and surgical technology.

The Associate of Applied Science degree is awarded in biomedical equipment technology, nursing, and occupational therapy assistant.

Diploma Programs: Brown Mackie College — Phoenix offers diploma programs in biomedical equipment technician, bookkeeping specialist, general business, and medical assistant.

The American Medical Technologists (AMT), which offers the certification for Registered Medical Assistant (RMA), accepts the accreditation of Brown Mackie College — Phoenix. Students will qualify to take the RMA certification examination upon graduating the Brown Mackie College — Phoenix medical assisting and medical assistant programs. Graduates of the 48 credit-hour medical assistant program are not qualified to take the AMT/RMA exam.

Brown Mackie College — Phoenix does not guarantee third-party certification. Outside agencies control the requirements for certifications and are subject to change without notice to Brown Mackie College.

Program availability and degree offerings are subject to change.

Costs

Tuition for programs in the 2012–13 academic year was $314 per credit hour, with a $20 per credit hour general fee applied to instructional costs for activities and services. For the surgical technology program, the tuition was $360 per credit hour with a $20 per credit hour general fee applied to instructional costs for activities. For the occupational therapy assistant program, the tuition was $381 per credit hour with a $20 per credit hour general fee applied to instructional costs for activities. For the nursing program, the tuition was $410 per credit hour with a $30 per credit hour general fee applied to instructional costs for activities. Textbooks, if applicable, and other instructional materials vary by program.

Financial Aid

Financial aid is available for those who qualify. The college maintains a full-time staff of Student Financial Services Advisers to assist qualified students in obtaining financial assistance. The college participates in several student aid programs. Forms of financial aid available to those who qualify through federal resources include the Federal Pell Grant Program, Federal Supplemental Educational Opportunity Grant (FSEOG) Program, Federal Work-Study Program, Federal Perkins Loan Program, Federal Stafford Student Loan Program (subsidized and unsubsidized), and the Federal PLUS Loan Program.

Each year, the college makes available President's Scholarships of $1,000 each to qualifying seniors from area high schools. In order to qualify, a senior must be graduating from a participating high school, must be maintaining a cumulative grade point average of at least 2.0, and must submit a brief essay. The student's extracurricular activities and community service are also considered. The President's Scholarship is available only to students enrolling in one of the college's degree programs. Students awarded the scholarship must enroll at Brown Mackie College — Phoenix between June and September immediately following their high school graduation. Applications for these scholarships can be obtained from the guidance departments of participating high schools. These applications must be completed and returned to the college by March 31.

The Education Foundation was established in 2000 to offer scholarship support to students interested in continuing their education at one of the postsecondary, career-focused schools in the EDMC system. The number and amount of the awards can vary, depending on the funds available. Scholarship applications are considered every quarter. At Brown Mackie College applicants must be currently enrolled in an associate's or bachelor's degree program and in their fourth quarter or higher (but no further than their second-to-last quarter) at the time of application. Awards are made based on academic performance and potential, as well as financial need. Please contact the colleges Student Financial Service Department for addition information.

Faculty

Experienced faculty members provide academic support and are committed to the academic and technical preparation of their students. The college has both full- and part-time faculty members. The average student-faculty ratio is 14:1. Each student is assigned a program director as an adviser.

Facilities and Resources

Brown Mackie College — Phoenix has a variety of classrooms including computer labs housing the latest technology in the industry. High-speed access to the Internet and other online resources are available for students and faculty. Multimedia classrooms provide a learning environment equipped with overhead projectors, TVs, DVD/VCR players, computers, and sound systems.

Brown Mackie College — Phoenix is fully committed to using eTextbooks and computer tablets in the classroom. Utilizing these tablets to access expanded course material, students are able to increase their acumen for using this technology and further enhance their educational experience. Students have the ability to directly download their eTextbooks to their tablet, eliminating the need to carry heavy, physical textbooks and reducing the overall cost of supplies.

The college has a generous parking area and is easily accessible by public transportation. The college is a nonresidential, smoke-free institution.

Location

Brown Mackie College — Phoenix is conveniently located at 13430 North Black Canyon Highway, Suite 190, in Phoenix, Arizona.

Admission Requirements

Each applicant for admission is assigned to an Assistant Director of Admissions, who directs the applicant through the steps of the admissions process, providing information on curriculum, policies, procedures, and services and assisting the applicant in setting necessary appointments and interviews. To qualify for admission, each applicant must provide documentation of graduation from an accredited high school or from a state-approved secondary education curriculum or provide official documentation of high school graduation equivalency. All transcripts become the property of the college.

For the most recent information regarding admission requirements, please refer to the current academic catalog.

Application and Information

Applicants must complete and submit an application form, along with documentation of graduation from an accredited high school or state-approved secondary education curriculum or official documentation of high school graduation equivalency.

Prospective students can go online to BMCprograms.info for program duration, tuition, fees and other costs, median debt, federal salary data, alumni success, programmatic accreditation, and other important details.

Brown Mackie College is a system of over 25 schools located throughout North America. Programs, credential levels, technology, and scheduling options vary by school, and employment opportunities are not guaranteed. Financial aid is available for those who qualify. Administrative office: 625 Eden Park Drive, Suite 1100; Cincinnati, OH 45202; 513-830-2000. ©2013 Brown Mackie College. OH Registration #03-09-1685T; #03-09-1686T; #03-09-1687T; #03-09-1688T; #06-03-1781T; AC0150, AC0109, AC0078, AC0045, AC0138, AC0110; Licensed by the Florida Commission for Independent Education, License No. 3206.

For additional information, prospective students should contact:

Director of Admissions
Brown Mackie College — Phoenix
13430 North Black Canyon Highway, Suite 190
Phoenix, Arizona 85029
Phone: 602-337-3044
　　　866-824-4793 (toll-free)
Fax: 480-375-2450
E-mail: bmcpxadmn@brownmackie.edu
Web site: http://www.brownmackie.edu/Phoenix

BROWN MACKIE COLLEGE — QUAD CITIES

BETTENDORF, IOWA

The College and Its Mission

Brown Mackie College — Quad Cities (Brown Mackie College) is one of over twenty-five locations in the Brown Mackie College system of schools (www.brownmackie.edu), which is dedicated to providing educational programs that prepare students to pursue entry-level positions in a competitive, rapidly changing workplace. Brown Mackie College schools offer bachelor's degree, associate degree, certificate, and diploma programs in health sciences, business, information technology, legal studies, and design to thousands of students in the Midwest, Southeast, Southwest, and Western United States.

Founded in 1890 by A. N. Hirons as LaPorte Business College in LaPorte, Indiana, the institution later became known as Commonwealth Business College. In 1919, ownership was transferred to Grace and J. J. Moore, who successfully operated the college for almost thirty years. Following World War II, Harley and Stephanie Reese operated the college under the name of Reese School of Business for several decades.

In 1975, the college came under the ownership of Steven C. Smith as Commonwealth Business College. A second location, now known as Brown Mackie College — Merrillville, was opened in 1984 in Merrillville, Indiana, and a third location was opened a year later in Davenport, Iowa. In 1987, the Davenport site relocated to Moline, Illinois. In September 2003, the college changed ownership again and the name was changed to Brown Mackie College — Moline in November 2004. In 2010, the college moved to its current location in Bettendorf, Iowa, and changed its name to Brown Mackie College — Quad Cities.

Brown Mackie College — Quad Cities is accredited by the Accrediting Council for Independent Colleges and Schools (ACICS) to award associate degrees and diplomas. ACICS is listed as a nationally recognized accrediting agency by the United States Department of Education and is recognized by the Council for Higher Education Accreditation. ACICS can be contacted at 750 First Street NE, Suite 980, Washington, D.C. 20002; phone: 202-336-6780.

The occupational therapy assistant program is accredited by the Accreditation Council for Occupational Therapy Education (ACOTE) of the American Occupational Therapy Association (AOTA), located at 4720 Montgomery Lane, Suite 200, Bethesda, Maryland 20814-3449; phone: 301-652-AOTA. Graduates of the program will be eligible to sit for the national certification examination for the occupational therapy assistant administered by the National Board for Certification in Occupational Therapy (NBCOT). After successful completion of this exam, the individual will be a Certified Occupational Therapy Assistant (COTA). In addition, most states require licensure in order to practice; however, state licenses are usually based on the results of the NBCOT Certification Examination. Note that a felony conviction may affect a graduate's ability to sit for the NBCOT certification examination or attain state licensure.

Brown Mackie College — Quad Cities is approved and registered by the Iowa College Student Aid Commission (ICSAC) under the authority of Chapters 261 and 261B of the Iowa Code. ICSCA can be contacted at 200 10th Street, fourth floor, Des Moines, Iowa 50309-3609; phone: 877-272-4456 (toll-free); www.iowacollegeaid.gov.

Academic Programs

Brown Mackie College — Quad Cities provides higher education to traditional and nontraditional students through associate degree and diploma programs that can assist them in enhancing their career opportunities, broadening their perspectives through appropriate general education courses, thinking independently and critically, and improving problem-solving abilities. The college strives to develop within its students the desire for lifelong and continued education.

Each college quarter comprises twelve weeks. Programs are offered on a year-round basis, providing students with the ability to work uninterrupted toward the completion of their programs. Brown Mackie College offers all programs in a unique One Course a Month format. This schedule allows students to focus studies on only one course for four weeks and has proven convenient for students with multiple obligations such as jobs and family.

Associate Degree Programs: The Associate of Applied Science degree is awarded in accounting technology, business management, criminal justice, health care administration, information technology, occupational therapy assistant, and paralegal.

Diploma Programs: Brown Mackie College — Quad Cities offers diploma programs in accounting, business, medical assistant, and medical coding and billing.

The American Medical Technologists (AMT), which offers the certification for Registered Medical Assistant (RMA), accepts the accreditation of Brown Mackie College — Quad Cities. Students will qualify to take the RMA certification examination upon graduating the Brown Mackie College — Quad Cities medical assistant program. Graduates of the 48 credit-hour medical assistant program are not qualified to take the AMT/RMA exam.

Brown Mackie College — Quad Cities does not guarantee third-party certification. Outside agencies control the requirements for certifications and are subject to change without notice to Brown Mackie College.

Program availability and degree offerings are subject to change.

Costs

Tuition for the 2012–13 academic year was $314 per credit hour and $20 per credit hour for general fees. Tuition for the occupational therapy assistant program was $381 per credit hour and $20 per credit hour for general fees. Textbook costs, if applicable, vary by program.

Financial Aid

Financial aid is available to those who qualify. Brown Mackie College — Quad Cities maintains a full-time staff of financial aid professionals to assist qualified students in obtaining the financial assistance they require to meet their educational expenses. The college participates in several student aid programs. Forms of financial aid available through federal resources include the Federal Pell Grant Program, Federal Supplemental Educational Opportunity Grant (FSEOG) Program, Federal Work-Study Program, Federal Perkins Loan Program, Federal Stafford Student Loan Program (subsidized and unsubsidized), and Federal PLUS loan program. Eligible students may apply for veterans' educational benefits. Students with physical or mental disabilities that are a handicap to employment may be eligible for training services through the state Agency for Vocational Rehabilitation. For further information, students should contact the Brown Mackie College — Quad Cities Student Financial Services Office.

Each year, the college makes available President's Scholarships of $1,000 each to qualifying seniors from area high schools. In order to qualify, a senior must be graduating from a participating high school, have maintained a cumulative grade point average of at least 2.0, and submitted a brief essay. The student's extracurricular activities and community service are also considered. The President's Scholarship is available only to students enrolling in one of the college's degree programs. Students awarded the scholarship must enroll at Brown Mackie College—Quad Cities between June and September immediately following their high school graduation. Applications for these scholarships can be obtained from the guidance departments of participating high schools. These applications must be completed and returned to the college by March 31.

The Education Foundation was established in 2000 to offer scholarship support to students interested in continuing their education at one of the postsecondary, career-focused schools in the EDMC system. The number and amount of the awards can vary, depending on the funds available. Scholarship applications are considered every quarter. At Brown Mackie College applicants must be currently enrolled in an associate's or bachelor's degree program and in their fourth quarter or higher (but no further than their second-to-last quarter) at the time of application. Awards are made based on academic performance and potential, as well as financial need. Please contact the colleges Student Financial Service Department for addition information.

Faculty

Brown Mackie College — Quad Cities has 4 full-time and 43 regular adjunct faculty members, with an average student-faculty ratio of 12:1.

Facilities and Resources

Brown Mackie College — Quad Cities maintains a library of curriculum-related resources. Technical and general education materials, academic and professional periodicals, and audiovisual resources are available to both students and faculty members. Students have borrowing privileges at several local libraries. Internet access is available for research.

Brown Mackie College — Quad Cities is fully committed to using eTextbooks and computer tablets in the classroom. Utilizing these tablets to access expanded course material, students are able to increase their acumen for using this technology and further enhance their educational experience. Students have the ability to directly download their eTextbooks to their tablet, eliminating the need to carry heavy, physical textbooks and reducing the overall cost of supplies.

The college is a nonresidential, smoke-free institution.

Location

Brown Mackie College — Quad Cities is located at 2119 East Kimberly Road in Bettendorf, Iowa. The college is easily accessible by public transportation, and ample parking is available at no cost.

Admission Requirements

Each applicant for admission is assigned to an Assistant Director of Admissions, who directs the applicant through the steps of the admissions process, providing information on curriculum, policies, procedures, and services and assisting the applicant in setting necessary appointments and interviews.

To qualify for admission, each applicant must provide documentation of graduation from an accredited high school or from a state-approved secondary education curriculum or provide official documentation of high school graduation equivalency. All transcripts become the property of Brown Mackie College — Quad Cities. Admission to the college is based on the applicant meeting the above requirements, a review of the applicant's previous education records, and a review of the applicant's career interests. If previous academic records indicate that the Brown Mackie College education and training programs would not benefit the applicant, the college reserves the right to advise the applicant not to enroll. Special requirements for enrollment into certain programs are discussed in the descriptions of those programs.

Application and Information

Applicants must complete and submit an application form along with documentation of graduation from an accredited high school or state-approved secondary education curriculum, or applicants must provide official documentation of high school graduation equivalency.

Prospective students can go online to BMCprograms.info for program duration, tuition, fees and other costs, median debt, federal salary data, alumni success, programmatic accreditation, and other important details.

Brown Mackie College is a system of over 25 schools located throughout North America. Programs, credential levels, technology, and scheduling options vary by school, and employment opportunities are not guaranteed. Financial aid is available for those who qualify. Administrative office: 625 Eden Park Drive, Suite 1100; Cincinnati, OH 45202; 513-830-2000. ©2013 Brown Mackie College. OH Registration #03-09-1685T; #03-09-1686T; #03-09-1687T; #03-09-1688T; #06-03-1781T; AC0150, AC0109, AC0078, AC0045, AC0138, AC0110; Licensed by the Florida Commission for Independent Education, License No. 3206.

For further information, prospective students should contact:

Director of Admissions
Brown Mackie College — Quad Cities
2119 East Kimberly Road
Bettendorf, Iowa 52722
Phone: 563-344-1500
    888-420-1652 (toll-free)
Fax: 563-344-1501
E-mail: bmcmoadm@brownmackie.edu
Web site: http://www.brownmackie.edu/Quad-Cities

BROWN MACKIE COLLEGE — ST. LOUIS

FENTON, MISSOURI

BROWN
MACKIE
COLLEGE
ST. LOUIS℠

The College and Its Mission

Brown Mackie College — St. Louis (Brown Mackie College) is one of over twenty-five locations in the Brown Mackie College system of schools (www.brownmackie.edu), which is dedicated to providing educational programs that prepare students to pursue entry-level positions in a competitive, rapidly changing workplace. The Brown Mackie College schools offer bachelor's degree, associate degree, diploma, and certificate programs in health sciences, business, information technology, legal studies, and design to thousands of students in the Midwest, Southeast, Southwest, and Western United States.

Brown Mackie College was originally founded and approved by the Board of Trustees of Kansas Wesleyan College in Salina, Kansas on July 30, 1892. In 1938, the college was incorporated as The Brown Mackie School of Business under the ownership of Perry E. Brown and A. B. Mackie, former instructors at Kansas Wesleyan University in Salina, Kansas. Their last names formed the name of Brown Mackie. By January 1975, with improvements in curricula and higher degree-granting status, The Brown Mackie School of Business became Brown Mackie College.

Brown Mackie College — St. Louis is accredited by the Accrediting Council for Independent Colleges and Schools to award associate degrees and certificates. The Accrediting Council for Independent Colleges and Schools is listed as a nationally recognized accrediting agency by the United States Department of Education and is recognized by the Council for Higher Education Accreditation. ACICS can be contacted at 750 First Street NE, Suite 980, Washington, D.C. 20002; phone: 202-336-6780.

The Associate of Applied Science in occupational therapy assistant program is accredited by the Accreditation Council for Occupational Therapy Education (ACOTE) of the American Occupational Therapy Association (AOTA), located at 4720 Montgomery Lane, Suite 200, Bethesda, Maryland 20814-3449; phone: 301-652-AOTA. Graduates of the program will be eligible to sit for the national certification examination for the occupational therapy assistant administered by the National Board for Certification in Occupational Therapy (NBCOT). After successful completion of this exam, the individual will be a Certified Occupational Therapy Assistant (COTA). In addition, most states require licensure in order to practice; however, state licenses are usually based on the results of the NBCOT Certification Examination. Note that a felony conviction may affect a graduate's ability to sit for the NBCOT certification examination or attain state licensure.

The Associate of Science in surgical technology program is accredited by the Accrediting Bureau of Health Education Schools (ABHES).

The Associate of Applied Science in veterinary technology program has provisional programmatic accreditation granted by the American Veterinary Medical Association (AVMA) through the Committee on Veterinary Technician Education and Activities (CVTEA).

Academic Programs

Brown Mackie College — St. Louis provides higher education to traditional and nontraditional students through associate degree programs that assist in enhancing their career opportunities, broadening their perspectives through appropriate general education courses, thinking independently and critically, and improving problem-solving abilities. The college strives to develop within its students the desire for lifelong and continued education.

Each college quarter comprises twelve weeks. Associate degree programs require a minimum of eight quarters to complete. Programs are offered on a year-round basis, providing students with the ability to work uninterrupted toward completion of their programs. The college offers all programs in a unique One Course a Month format. This allows students to focus studies on only one course for four weeks. This schedule has proven convenient for students with multiple obligations such as jobs and family.

Associate Degree Programs: The Associate of Applied Science degree is awarded in accounting technology, biomedical equipment technology, business management, criminal justice, health care administration, information technology, nursing, occupational therapy assistant, paralegal, surgical technology, and veterinary technology.

Certificate Programs: The college offers certificate programs in accounting, biomedical equipment technician, business, criminal justice, medical assistant, and paralegal assistant.

The American Medical Technologists (AMT), which offers the certification for Registered Medical Assistant (RMA), accepts the accreditation of Brown Mackie College — St. Louis. Students will qualify to take the RMA certification examination upon graduating the Brown Mackie College — St. Louis medical assistant program. Graduates of the 48 credit-hour medical assistant program are not qualified to take the AMT/RMA exam.

Brown Mackie College — St. Louis does not guarantee third party certification. Outside agencies control the requirements for certifications and are subject to change without notice to Brown Mackie College.

Program availability and degree offerings are subject to change.

Costs

Tuition in the 2012–13 academic year for most associate degrees and diploma programs was $288 per credit hour; fees were $20 per credit hour. Tuition for the surgical technology program was $339 per credit hour; fees were $20 per credit hour. Tuition for the nursing program was $410 per credit hour; fees were $30 per credit hour. Tuition for the occupational therapy assistant program was $355 per credit hour; fees were $20 per credit hour. The cost of textbooks, if applicable, and other instructional materials varies by program.

Financial Aid

Financial aid is available for those who qualify. The college maintains a full-time staff of Student Financial Services Advisers to assist qualified students in obtaining the financial assistance they require to meet their educational expenses. Available resources include federal and state aid, student loans from private lenders, and Federal Work-Study opportunities, both on and off college premises.

Each year, the college makes available President's Scholarships of $1,000 each to qualifying seniors from area high schools.

In order to qualify, a senior must have graduated from a participating high school, maintained a cumulative grade point average of at least 2.0, and submitted a brief essay. The student's extracurricular activities and community service are also considered. These scholarships are available only to students enrolling in one of the college's degree programs. Students awarded the scholarship must enroll at Brown Mackie College — St. Louis between June and September immediately following their high school graduation. Applications for these scholarships can be obtained from the guidance departments of participating high schools. These applications must be completed and returned to the college by March 31.

The Education Foundation was established in 2000 to offer scholarship support to students interested in continuing their education at one of the postsecondary, career-focused schools in the EDMC system. The number and amount of the awards can vary, depending on the funds available. Scholarship applications are considered every quarter. At Brown Mackie College, applicants must be currently enrolled in an associate or bachelor's degree program and in their fourth quarter or higher (but no further than their second-to-last quarter) at the time of application. Awards are made based on academic performance and potential, as well as financial need. Interested students should contact the college's Student Financial Service Department for additional information.

Faculty

Experienced faculty members provide academic support and are committed to the academic and technical preparation of their students. The college has 12 full-time and 23 part-time instructors, with a student-faculty ratio of 20:1.

Facilities and Resources

A modern facility, Brown Mackie College — St. Louis offers more than 30,000 square feet of educational and administrative space. The college is equipped with multiple computer labs, housing over 200 computers. High-speed access to the Internet and other online resources are available for students and faculty. Multimedia classrooms are outfitted with overhead projectors, VCR/DVD players, and computers.

Brown Mackie College — St. Louis is fully committed to using eTextbooks and computer tablets in the classroom. Utilizing these tablets to access expanded course material, students are able to increase their acumen for using this technology and further enhance their educational experience. Students have the ability to directly download their eTextbooks to their tablet, eliminating the need to carry heavy, physical textbooks and reducing the overall cost of supplies.

The campus is nonresidential. The college has a generous parking area and is easily accessible by public transportation. The campus is a smoke-free facility.

Location

Brown Mackie College — St. Louis is conveniently located at #2 Soccer Park Road in Fenton, Missouri.

Admission Requirements

Each applicant for admission is assigned to an Assistant Director of Admissions who directs the applicant through the steps of the admissions process. They provide information on curriculum, policies, procedures, and services and assist the applicant in setting necessary appointments and interviews. To qualify for admission, each applicant must provide documentation of graduation from an accredited high school or from a state-approved secondary education curriculum or provide official documentation of high school graduation equivalency. All transcripts become the property of the college. Admission to the college is based on the applicant meeting the stated requirements, a review of the applicant's previous educational records, and a review of the applicant's career interests. If previous academic records indicate the college's education and training programs would not benefit the applicant, the college reserves the right to advise the applicant not to enroll. Special requirements for enrollment into certain programs are discussed in the descriptions of those programs.

For the most recent information regarding admission requirements, prospective students should refer to the current academic catalog.

Application and Information

Applicants must complete and submit an application form, along with documentation of graduation from an accredited high school or state-approved secondary education curriculum or official documentation of high school graduation equivalency.

Prospective students can go online to BMCprograms.info for program duration, tuition, fees and other costs, median debt, federal salary data, alumni success, programmatic accreditation, and other important details.

Brown Mackie College is a system of over twenty-five schools located throughout North America. Programs, credential levels, technology, and scheduling options vary by school, and employment opportunities are not guaranteed. Financial aid is available for those who qualify. Administrative offices are located at 625 Eden Park Drive, Suite 1100; Cincinnati, Ohio 45202; phone: 513-830-2000. ©2013 Brown Mackie College. OH Registration #03-09-1685T; #03-09-1686T; #03-09-1687T; #03-09-1688T; #06-03-1781T; AC0150, AC0109, AC0078, AC0045, AC0138, AC0110; Licensed by the Florida Commission for Independent Education, License No. 3206.

For additional information, prospective students should contact:

Director of Admissions
Brown Mackie College — St. Louis
#2 Soccer Park Road
Fenton, Missouri 63026
Phone: 636-651-3290
      888-874-4375 (toll-free)
Fax: 636-651-3349
E-mail: bmcstladm@brownmackie.edu
Web site: http://www.brownmackie.edu/StLouis

BROWN MACKIE COLLEGE — SALINA

SALINA, KANSAS

BROWN
MACKIE
COLLEGE
SALINA℠

The College and Its Mission

Brown Mackie College — Salina (Brown Mackie College) is one of over twenty-five locations in the Brown Mackie College system of schools (www.brownmackie.edu), which is dedicated to providing educational programs that prepare students to pursue entry-level positions in a competitive, rapidly changing workplace. Brown Mackie College schools offer bachelor's degree, associate degree, certificate, and diploma programs in health sciences, business, information technology, legal studies, and design to thousands of students in the Midwest, Southeast, Southwest, and Western United States.

The college was originally founded in July 1892 as the Kansas Wesleyan School of Business. In 1938, the college was incorporated as the Brown Mackie School of Business under the ownership of former Kansas Wesleyan instructors Perry E. Brown and A. B. Mackie; it became Brown Mackie College in January 1975.

Brown Mackie College — Salina is accredited by the Higher Learning Commission and is a member of the North Central Association (NCA), 230 South LaSalle Street, Suite 7-500, Chicago, Illinois 60604-1413; phone 800-621-7440 (toll-free); www.ncahlc.org.

Brown Mackie College — Salina is approved and authorized to grant the Associate of Applied Science (A.A.S.) and Associate of General Studies (A.G.D.) degrees by the Kansas Board of Regents, 1000 Southwest Jackson Street, Suite 520, Topeka, Kansas 66612-1368.

The Associate of Applied Science in occupational therapy assistant program is accredited by the Accreditation Council for Occupational Therapy Education (ACOTE) of the American Occupational Therapy Association (AOTA), located at 4720 Montgomery Lane, Suite 200, Bethesda, Maryland 20814-3449; phone: 301-652-AOTA. Graduates of the program will be eligible to sit for the national certification examination for the occupational therapy assistant administered by the National Board for Certification in Occupational Therapy (NBCOT). After successful completion of this exam, the individual will be a Certified Occupational Therapy Assistant (COTA). In addition, most states require licensure in order to practice; however, state licenses are usually based on the results of the NBCOT Certification Examination. Note that a felony conviction may affect a graduate's ability to sit for the NBCOT certification examination or attain state licensure.

The Associate of Applied Science in veterinary technology program has provisional programmatic accreditation granted by the American Veterinary Medical Association (AVMA) through the Committee on Veterinary Technician Education and Activities (CVTEA).

Academic Programs

Brown Mackie College — Salina provides higher education to traditional and nontraditional students through associate degree, diploma, and certificate programs that can assist them in enhancing their career opportunities, broadening their perspectives through appropriate general education courses, thinking independently and critically, and improving problem-solving abilities. The college strives to develop within its students the desire for lifelong and continued education.

In most programs, students can participate in day or evening classes, which begin every month. Programs are offered on a year-round basis, providing students with the ability to work uninterrupted toward completion of their programs. Brown Mackie College offers all programs in a unique One Course a Month format. This schedule allows students to focus studies on only one course for four weeks and has proven convenient for students with multiple obligations such as jobs and family.

Associate Degree Programs: The Associate of Applied Science degree is awarded in accounting technology, business management, computer aided design and drafting technology, computer networking and applications, criminal justice, health and fitness training, health care administration, medical assisting, nursing, occupational therapy assistant, and veterinary technology. An associate degree in general studies is also offered to create a greater level of flexibility for students who may be unsure of their career choice, who want a more generalized education, or who want to transfer to a baccalaureate program.

Diploma Programs: Brown Mackie College — Salina also offers diploma programs in bookkeeping specialist, general business, computer aided designer/drafter, criminal justice specialist, fitness trainer, general business, medical assistant, medical insurance specialist, and networking specialist.

Certificate Programs: Certificate programs are offered in network engineer specialist and practical nursing.

The American Medical Technologists (AMT), which offers the certification for Registered Medical Assistant (RMA), accepts the accreditation of Brown Mackie College — Salina. Students will qualify to take the RMA certification examination upon graduating the Brown Mackie College — Salina medical assisting and medical assistant programs. Graduates of the 48 credit-hour medical assistant program are not qualified to take the AMT/RMA exam.

Brown Mackie College does not guarantee third-party certification/licensing exams. Outside agencies control the requirements for certification/licensing and are subject to change without notification to the college.

Program availability and degree offerings are subject to change.

Costs

Tuition for the 2012–13 academic year was $314 per credit hour and general fees were $20 per credit hour. Tuition for computer networking was $314 per credit hour and general fees were $25 per credit hour. Tuition for the fitness programs was $324 per credit hour and general fees were $30 per credit hour. Tuition for the nursing programs was $381 per credit hour and general fees were $30 per credit hour. Tuition for the occupational therapy assistant program was $381 per credit hour and general fees were $20 per credit hour. The cost of textbooks, if applicable, and other instructional materials varies by program..

Financial Aid

Financial aid is available to those who qualify. Brown Mackie College — Salina maintains a full-time staff of financial aid professionals to assist qualified students in obtaining financial assistance. The college participates in several student aid programs. Forms of financial aid that are available through federal resources include Federal Pell Grants, Federal Supplemental Educational Opportunity Grants (FSEOG), Academic Competitiveness Grant, Federal Work-Study Program awards, Federal Perkins Loans, Federal Stafford Student Loans (subsidized and unsubsidized), and Federal PLUS loans. Eligible students may apply for veterans' educational benefits. Students with physical or mental disabilities that are a handicap to employment may be eligible for training services through the state Vocational Rehabilitation Agency. For further information, students should contact the Brown Mackie College — Salina Student Financial Services Office.

Each year, the college makes available President's Scholarships of $1,000 each to qualifying seniors from area high schools. In order to qualify, a senior must be graduating from a participating high school, have maintained a cumulative grade point average of at least 2.0, and submitted a brief essay. The student's extracurricular activities and community service are also considered. The President's Scholarship is available only to students enrolling in one of the college's degree programs. Students awarded the scholarship must enroll at Brown Mackie College — Salina between June and September immediately following their high school graduation. Applications for these scholarships can be obtained from the guidance departments of participating high schools. These applications must be completed and returned to the college by March 31.

The Education Foundation was established in 2000 to offer scholarship support to students interested in continuing their education at one of the postsecondary, career-focused schools in the EDMC system. The number and amount of the awards can vary, depending on the funds available. Scholarship applications are considered every quarter. At Brown Mackie College, applicants must be currently enrolled in an associate or bachelor's degree program and in their fourth quarter or higher (but no further than their second-to-last quarter) at the time of application. Awards are made based on academic performance and potential, as well as financial need. Interested students should contact the college's Student Financial Service Department for additional information.

The Merit Scholarship is a college-sponsored scholarship that may be awarded to students who demonstrate exceptional academic ability. To qualify for a Merit Scholarship, an applicant or student must have scored 21 or higher on the ACT or 900 or higher on the SAT. The maximum amount awarded by this scholarship to any student is $500.

Athletic scholarships may be awarded to students who participate in athletic programs that are sponsored by Brown Mackie College — Salina. Current sports are men's baseball, men's and women's basketball, and women's fast-pitch softball. Maximum awards for any applicant or student are determined by the college president. Further information is available from the Athletic Office. Recipients of athletic scholarships must achieve a cumulative grade point average of at least 2.0 by their graduation. Recipients who fail to maintain full-time status or the required grade point average forfeit their awards.

Faculty

There are 21 full-time and 19 adjunct faculty members. The average student-instructor ratio is 15:1.

Facilities and Resources

In addition to classrooms and computer labs, Brown Mackie College — Salina maintains a library of curriculum-related resources, technical and general education materials, academic and professional periodicals, and audiovisual resources. Internet access is also available for research. The college has a bookstore that stocks texts, courseware, and other educational supplies that are required for courses and a variety of personal, recreational, and gift items, including apparel, supplies, and general merchandise incorporating the Brown Mackie College logo. Hours are posted at the bookstore entrance.

Brown Mackie College — Salina is fully committed to using eTextbooks and computer tablets in the classroom. Utilizing these tablets to access expanded course material, students are able to increase their acumen for using this technology and further enhance their educational experience. Students have the ability to directly download their eTextbooks to their tablet, eliminating the need to carry heavy, physical textbooks and reducing the overall cost of supplies.

Location

Brown Mackie College — Salina is located at 2106 South Ninth Street in Salina, Kansas.

Admission Requirements

Each applicant for admission is assigned to an Assistant Director of Admissions, who directs the applicant through the steps of the admissions process, providing information on curriculum, policies, procedures, and services and assisting the applicant in setting necessary appointments and interviews.

To qualify for admission, each applicant must provide documentation of graduation from an accredited high school or from a state-approved secondary education curriculum or provide official documentation of high school graduation equivalency. All transcripts become the property of Brown Mackie College. Admission to the college is based upon the applicant meeting the above requirements, a review of the applicant's previous education records, and a review of the applicant's career interests. If previous academic records indicate that the Brown Mackie College education and training programs would not benefit the applicant, the college reserves the right to advise the applicant not to enroll. Special requirements for enrollment into certain programs are discussed in the descriptions of those programs.

For the most recent information regarding admissions requirements, please refer to the most current academic catalog.

Application and Information

Applicants must complete and submit an application form, along with documentation of graduation from an accredited high school or state-approved secondary education curriculum or official documentation of high school graduation equivalency.

Prospective students can go online to BMCprograms.info for program duration, tuition, fees and other costs, median debt, federal salary data, alumni success, programmatic accreditation, and other important details.

Brown Mackie College is a system of over twenty-five schools located throughout North America. Programs, credential levels, technology, and scheduling options vary by school, and employment opportunities are not guaranteed. Financial aid is available for those who qualify. Administrative offices are located at 625 Eden Park Drive, Suite 1100; Cincinnati, Ohio 45202; phone: 513-830-2000. ©2013 Brown Mackie College. OH Registration #03-09-1685T; #03-09-1686T; #03-09-1687T; #03-09-1688T; #06-03-1781T; AC0150, AC0109, AC0078, AC0045, AC0138, AC0110; Licensed by the Florida Commission for Independent Education, License No. 3206.

For additional information, prospective students should contact:

Director of Admissions
Brown Mackie College — Salina
2106 South Ninth Street
Salina, Kansas 67401
Phone: 785-825-5422
      800-365-0433 (toll-free)
Fax: 785-827-7623
E-mail: bmcsaadm@brownmackie.edu
Web site: http://www.brownmackie.edu/Salina)

BROWN MACKIE COLLEGE — SAN ANTONIO

SAN ANTONIO, TEXAS

The College and Its Mission

Brown Mackie College — San Antonio (Brown Mackie College) is one of over twenty-five locations in the Brown Mackie College system of schools (www.brownmackie.edu), which is dedicated to providing educational programs that prepare students to pursue entry-level positions in a competitive, rapidly changing workplace. The Brown Mackie College schools offer bachelor's degree, associate degree, diploma, and certificate programs in health sciences, business, information technology, legal studies, and design to thousands of students in the Midwest, Southeast, Southwest, and Western United States.

Brown Mackie College was originally founded and approved by the Board of Trustees of Kansas Wesleyan College in Salina, Kansas on July 30, 1892. In 1938, the college was incorporated as the Brown Mackie School of Business under the ownership of Perry E. Brown and A. B. Mackie, former instructors at Kansas Wesleyan University in Salina, Kansas. Their last names formed the name of Brown Mackie. By January 1975, with improvements in curricula and higher degree-granting status, the Brown Mackie School of Business became Brown Mackie College.

Brown Mackie College — San Antonio is accredited by the Accrediting Council for Independent Colleges and Schools to award associate degrees and diplomas. The Accrediting Council for Independent Colleges and Schools is listed as a nationally recognized accrediting agency by the United States Department of Education and is recognized by the Council for Higher Education Accreditation. ACICS can be contacted at 750 First Street NE, Suite 980, Washington, D.C. 20002; phone: 202-336-6780.

Brown Mackie College — San Antonio is approved and regulated by the Texas Workforce Commission, Career School and Colleges, Austin, Texas.

Brown Mackie College — San Antonio holds a Certificate of Authorization acknowledging exemption from Texas Higher Education Coordinating Board regulations.

Academic Programs

Brown Mackie College — San Antonio provides higher education to traditional and nontraditional students through associate degree programs that assist in enhancing their career opportunities, broadening their perspectives through appropriate general education courses, thinking independently and critically, and improving problem-solving abilities. The college strives to develop within its students the desire for lifelong and continued education.

Each college quarter comprises twelve weeks. Associate degree programs require a minimum of eight quarters to complete. Programs are offered on a year-round basis, providing students with the ability to work uninterrupted toward completion of their programs. The college offers all programs in a unique One Course a Month format. This allows students to focus studies on only one course for four weeks. This schedule has proven convenient for students with multiple obligations such as jobs and family.

Associate Degree Programs: The Associate of Science degree is awarded in accounting technology, architectural design and drafting technology, business management, criminal justice, health care administration, information technology, medical assisting, paralegal, pharmacy technology, and surgical technology.

Diploma Programs: Brown Mackie College — San Antonio offers a diploma program in medical assistant.

The American Medical Technologists (AMT), which offers the certification for Registered Medical Assistant (RMA), accepts the accreditation of Brown Mackie College — San Antonio. Students will qualify to take the RMA certification examination upon graduating the Brown Mackie College — San Antonio medical assisting and medical assistant programs.

Brown Mackie College — San Antonio does not guarantee third-party certification. Outside agencies control the requirements for certifications and are subject to change without notice to Brown Mackie College.

Program availability and degree offerings are subject to change.

Costs

Tuition in the 2012–13 academic year for most of the degrees was $324 per credit hour; fees were $20 per credit hour. Tuition for the surgical technology program was $360 per credit hour; fees were $20 per credit hour. The cost of textbooks, if applicable, and other instructional materials varies by program.

Financial Aid

Financial aid is available for those who qualify. The college maintains a full-time staff of Student Financial Services Advisers to assist qualified students in obtaining the financial assistance they require to meet their educational expenses. Available resources include federal and state aid, student loans from private lenders, and Federal Work-Study opportunities, both on and off college premises.

Each year, the college makes available President's Scholarships of $1,000 each to qualifying seniors from area high schools. In order to qualify, a senior must have graduated from a participating high school, must be maintained a cumulative grade point average of at least 2.0, and submitted a brief essay. The student's extracurricular activities and community service are also considered. These scholarships are available only to students enrolling in one of the college's degree programs. Students awarded the scholarship must enroll at Brown Mackie College — San Antonio between June and September immediately following their high school graduation. Applications for these scholarships can be obtained from the guidance departments of participating high schools. These applications must be completed and returned to the college by March 31.

The Education Foundation was established in 2000 to offer scholarship support to students interested in continuing their education at one of the postsecondary, career-focused schools in the EDMC system. The number and amount of the awards can vary, depending on the funds available. Scholarship applications are considered every quarter. At Brown Mackie

College, applicants must be currently enrolled in an associate or bachelor's degree program and in their fourth quarter or higher (but no further than their second-to-last quarter) at the time of application. Awards are made based on academic performance and potential, as well as financial need. Interested students should contact the college's Student Financial Service Department for additional information.

Faculty

Experienced faculty members provide academic support and are committed to the academic and technical preparation of their students. Brown Mackie College — San Antonio has both full-time and part-time instructors, with a student-faculty ratio of 15:1.

Facilities and Resources

A modern facility, Brown Mackie College — San Antonio offers more than 35,000 square feet. The College is equipped with multiple computer labs, housing over 100 computers. High-speed access to the Internet and other online resources are available to students and faculty. Multimedia classrooms are outfitted with overhead projectors, VCR/DVD players, and computers.

Brown Mackie College — San Antonio is fully committed to using eTextbooks and computer tablets in the classroom. Utilizing these tablets to access expanded course material, students are able to increase their acumen for using this technology and further enhance their educational experience. Students have the ability to directly download their eTextbooks to their tablet, eliminating the need to carry heavy, physical textbooks and reducing the overall cost of supplies.

The college is nonresidential; public transportation and ample parking at no cost are available. The college has a generous parking area and is easily accessible by public transportation. The campus is a smoke-free facility.

Location

Brown Mackie College — San Antonio is conveniently located at 4715 Fredericksburg Road in San Antonio, Texas.

Admission Requirements

Each applicant for admission is assigned to an Assistant Director of Admissions who directs the applicant through the steps of the admissions process. They provide information on curriculum, policies, procedures, and services and assist the applicant in setting necessary appointments and interviews. To qualify for admission, each applicant must provide documentation of graduation from an accredited high school or from a state-approved secondary education curriculum or provide official documentation of high school graduation equivalency. All transcripts become the property of the college. Admission to the college is based on the applicant meeting the stated requirements, a review of the applicant's previous educational records, and a review of the applicant's career interests. If previous academic records indicate the college's education and training programs would not benefit the applicant, the college reserves the right to advise the applicant not to enroll. Special requirements for enrollment into certain programs are discussed in the descriptions of those programs.

For the most recent information regarding admission requirements, prospective students should refer to the current academic catalog.

Application and Information

Applicants must complete and submit an application form, along with documentation of graduation from an accredited high school or state-approved secondary education curriculum or official documentation of high school graduation equivalency.

Prospective students can go online to BMCprograms.info for program duration, tuition, fees and other costs, median debt, federal salary data, alumni success, programmatic accreditation, and other important details.

Brown Mackie College is a system of over twenty-five schools located throughout North America. Programs, credential levels, technology, and scheduling options vary by school, and employment opportunities are not guaranteed. Financial aid is available for those who qualify. Administrative offices are located at 625 Eden Park Drive, Suite 1100; Cincinnati, Ohio 45202; phone: 513-830-2000. ©2013 Brown Mackie College. OH Registration #03-09-1685T; #03-09-1686T; #03-09-1687T; #03-09-1688T; #06-03-1781T; AC0150, AC0109, AC0078, AC0045, AC0138, AC0110; Licensed by the Florida Commission for Independent Education, License No. 3206.

For additional information, prospective students should contact:

Director of Admissions
Brown Mackie College — San Antonio
4715 Fredericksburg Road, Suite 100
San Antonio, Texas 78229
Phone: 210-428-2210
    877-460-1714 (toll-free)
Fax: 210-428-2265
E-mail: bmsanadm@brownmackie.edu
Web site: http://www.brownmackie.edu/SanAntonio

BROWN MACKIE COLLEGE — SOUTH BEND

SOUTH BEND, INDIANA

The College and Its Mission

Brown Mackie College — South Bend (Brown Mackie College) is one of over twenty-five locations in the Brown Mackie College system of schools (www.brownmackie.edu), which is dedicated to providing educational programs that prepare students to pursue entry-level positions in a competitive, rapidly changing workplace. The Brown Mackie College schools offer bachelor's degree, associate degree, diploma, and certificate programs in health sciences, business, information technology, legal studies, and design to thousands of students in the Midwest, Southeast, Southwest, and Western United States.

Brown Mackie College — South Bend is one of the oldest institutions of its kind in the country and the oldest in the state of Indiana. Established in 1882 as the South Bend Commercial College, the school later changed its name to Michiana College. In 1930, the school was incorporated under the laws of the state of Indiana and was authorized to confer associate degrees and certificates in business. The college relocated to East Jefferson Boulevard in 1987. In September 2009, Brown Mackie College — South Bend officially opened a new 46,000-square-foot facility at 3454 Douglas Road in South Bend, Indiana.

Brown Mackie College — South Bend is accredited by the Accrediting Council for Independent Colleges and Schools to award associate degrees, diplomas, and certificates. The Accrediting Council for Independent Colleges and Schools is listed as a nationally recognized accrediting agency by the United States Department of Education and is recognized by the Council for Higher Education Accreditation. ACICS can be contacted at 750 First Street NE, Suite 980, Washington, D.C. 20002; phone: 202-336-6780.

Brown Mackie College — South Bend is regulated by the Board for Proprietary Education Indiana Commission for Higher Education, 101 West Ohio Street, Suite 550, Indianapolis, Indiana 46204; phone: 317-464-4400. Indiana advertising code: AC-0110.

The practical nursing diploma program is accredited by the Indiana State Board of Nursing, 402 West Washington Street, Room W066, Indianapolis, Indiana 46204; phone: 317-234-2043.

The Associate of Applied Science in occupational therapy assistant program is accredited by the Accreditation Council for Occupational Therapy Education (ACOTE) of the American Occupational Therapy Association (AOTA), located at 4720 Montgomery Lane, Suite 200, Bethesda, Maryland 20814-3449; phone: 301-652-AOTA. Graduates of the program will be eligible to sit for the national certification examination for the occupational therapy assistant administered by the National Board for Certification in Occupational Therapy (NBCOT). After successful completion of this exam, the individual will be a Certified Occupational Therapy Assistant (COTA). In addition, most states require licensure in order to practice; however, state licenses are usually based on the results of the NBCOT Certification Examination. Note that a felony conviction may affect a graduate's ability to sit for the NBCOT certification examination or attain state licensure.

The Associate of Applied Science in physical therapist assistant program is accredited by the Commission on Accreditation in Physical Therapy Education (CAPTE) of the American Physical Therapy Association (APTA), 1111 North Fairfax Street, Alexandria, Virginia 22314; phone: 703-706-3241.

The Associate of Science in veterinary technology program has provisional programmatic accreditation granted by the American Veterinary Medical Association (AVMA) through the Committee on Veterinary Technician Education and Activities (CVTEA).

Academic Programs

Brown Mackie College — South Bend provides higher education to traditional and nontraditional students through associate degrees, diploma, and certificate programs that assist in enhancing their career opportunities, broadening their perspectives through appropriate general education courses, thinking independently and critically, and improving problem-solving abilities.

Each college quarter comprises twelve weeks. Associate degree programs require a minimum of eight quarters to complete. Programs are offered on a year-round basis, providing students with the ability to work uninterrupted toward completion of their programs. The college offers all programs in a unique One Course a Month format. This allows students to focus studies on only one course for four weeks. This schedule has proven convenient for students with multiple obligations such as jobs and family.

Associate Degree Programs: The Associate of Science degree is awarded in accounting technology, business management, computer software technology, criminal justice, health care administration, information technology, paralegal, and veterinary technology.

The Associate of Applied Science degree is awarded in occupational therapy assistant and physical therapist assistant.

Diploma Program: The college offers a diploma program in practical nursing.

Certificate Programs: The college offers certificate programs in bookkeeping specialist, criminal justice specialist, general business, medical assistant, medical coding and billing, and paralegal assistant.

The American Medical Technologists (AMT), which offers the certification for Registered Medical Assistant (RMA), accepts the accreditation of Brown Mackie College — South Bend. Students will qualify to take the RMA certification examination upon graduating the Brown Mackie College — South Bend medical assistant program. Graduates of the 48 credit-hour medical assistant program are not qualified to take the AMT/RMA exam.

Brown Mackie College — South Bend does not guarantee third-party certification. Outside agencies control the requirements for certifications and are subject to change without notice to Brown Mackie College.

Program availability and degree offerings are subject to change.

Costs

Tuition for programs in the 2012–13 academic year was $314 per credit hour, with a general fee of $20 per credit hour applied to instructional costs for activities and services. Tuition for the practical nursing program was $381 per credit hour, with a general fee of $30 per credit hour applied to instructional costs for activities and services. Tuition for the physical therapist assistant program was $381 per credit hour with a general fee of $20 per credit hour. Tuition for the occupational therapy assistant program was $381 per credit hour with a general fee of $20 per credit hour. Textbooks, if applicable, and other instructional materials vary by program.

Financial Aid

Financial aid is available for those who qualify. The college maintains a full-time staff of Student Financial Services Advisers to assist qualified students in obtaining financial assistance. The college participates in several student aid programs. Forms of financial aid available through federal resources include the Federal Pell Grant Program, Federal Supplemental Educational Opportunity Grant (FSEOG) Program, Federal Work-Study Program, Federal Perkins Loan Program, Federal Stafford Student Loan Program (subsidized and unsubsidized), and the Federal PLUS Loan Program.

Eligible students may apply for Indiana state awards, such as the Frank O'Bannon Grant Program (formerly the Indiana Higher Education Grant) and Twenty-First Century Scholars Program for high school students, the Core 40 awards, and veterans' educational benefits. Students with physical or mental disabilities that are a handicap may be eligible for training services through the state's Bureau of Vocational Rehabilitation. For further information, students should contact the Student Financial Services Office.

Each year, the college makes available President's Scholarships of $1,000 each to qualifying seniors from area high schools. In order to qualify, a senior must be graduating from a participating high school, must be maintaining a cumulative grade point average of at least 2.0, and must submit a brief essay. The student's extracurricular activities and community service are also considered. The President's

Scholarship is available only to students enrolling in one of the college's degree programs. Students awarded the scholarship must enroll at Brown Mackie College — South Bend between June and September immediately following their high school graduation. Applications for these scholarships can be obtained from the guidance departments of participating high schools. These applications must be completed and returned to the college by March 31.

The Education Foundation was established in 2000 to offer scholarship support to students interested in continuing their education at one of the postsecondary, career-focused schools in the EDMC system. The number and amount of the awards can vary, depending on the funds available. Scholarship applications are considered every quarter. At Brown Mackie College, applicants must be currently enrolled in an associate or bachelor's degree program and in their fourth quarter or higher (but no further than their second-to-last quarter) at the time of application. Awards are made based on academic performance and potential, as well as financial need. Interested students should contact the college's Student Financial Service Department for additional information.

Faculty

There are 24 full-time and 36 part-time faculty members at the college. The average student-faculty ratio is 11:1. Each student is assigned a program director as an adviser.

Facilities and Resources

Brown Mackie College — South Bend's new location has a generous parking area and is easily accessible by public transportation. The college's smoke-free, three-story 46,000 square foot building offers a modern, professional environment for study. The facility offers "classrooms of the future," with instructor workstations and full multimedia capabilities that include surround sound and projection screens that can be accessed by computer, DVD, and VHS machines. The new facility includes medical, computer, and occupational and physical therapy labs, as well as a library and bookstore. The labs provide students with hands-on opportunities to apply knowledge and skills learned in the classroom. The veterinary technology lab is 2,600 square feet and includes surgery areas, treatment areas, and kennels.

Brown Mackie College — South Bend is fully committed to using eTextbooks and computer tablets in the classroom. Utilizing these tablets to access expanded course material, students are able to increase their acumen for using this technology and further enhance their educational experience. Students have the ability to directly download their eTextbooks to their tablet, eliminating the need to carry heavy, physical textbooks and reducing the overall cost of supplies.

The college has a generous parking area and is also easily accessible by public transportation. The college is a nonresidential, smoke-free institution.

Location

Brown Mackie College — South Bend is conveniently located at 3454 Douglas Road in South Bend, Indiana.

Admission Requirements

Each applicant for admission is assigned to an Assistant Director of Admissions, who directs the applicant through the steps of the admissions process, providing information on curriculum, policies, procedures, and services; and assisting the applicant in setting necessary appointments and interviews. To qualify for admission, each applicant must provide documentation of graduation from an accredited high school or from a state-approved secondary education curriculum or provide official documentation of high school graduation equivalency. All transcripts become the property of the college.

Admission to the college is based on the applicant meeting the stated requirements, a review of the applicant's previous educational records, and a review of the applicant's career interests. If previous academic records indicate the college's education and training programs would not benefit the applicant, the college reserves the right to advise the applicant not to enroll. Special requirements for enrollment into certain programs are discussed in the descriptions of those programs.

In addition to the college's general admission requirements, applicants enrolling in the occupational therapy assistant (OTA) program must also meet some additional requirements. They must complete COMPASS assessment before the first course is scheduled to determine if transitional courses are needed (minimal scores: reading 75, writing 60, math 51). If minimum scores or better are attained on all three sections the student is scheduled in CF1000–Professional Development. If the student's scores are below the minimum on any

of the sections, the student is advised that they will be placed in transitional course(s). After successful completion of all the required transitional courses, the student will have one opportunity to retake the COMPASS assessment and achieve the minimum score(s). If the student does not successfully obtain the minimum scores in all three sections on the second attempt, the student will not be allowed to continue in the OTA program, but can be considered for another program at Brown Mackie College.

In addition to the college's general admission requirements, applicants enrolling in the physical therapist assistant program must document the following: a minimum high school cumulative grade point average of 3.0 on a 4.0 scale or minimum score of 600 on the GED examination (if taken on or after January 15, 2002) or 60 (if taken before January 15, 2002); a minimum of 12 quarter-credit hours or 9 semester-credit hours of consecutive collegiate coursework with a minimum GPA of 3.0 on a 4.0 scale (may be completed at Brown Mackie College); a biology course in high school or college with a minimum grade of a B (3.0 on a 4.0 scale); and 20 hours (total) of documented observation, volunteer, or employment hours in at least two different physical therapy settings with no less than 8 hours in one setting completed within the past three years.

In addition to the college's general admission requirements, applicants enrolling in the practical nursing program must document the following: fulfillment of Brown Mackie College — South Bend general requirements; complete physical (must be current to within six months of admission); two-step Mantoux TB skin test (must be current throughout schooling); hepatitis B vaccination or signed refusal; up-to-date immunizations, including tetanus and rubella; record of current CPR certification (certification must be current throughout the clinical experience through health-care provider certification or the American Heart Association); and hospitalization insurance or a signed waiver.

For the most recent administration regarding admission requirements, please refer to the current academic catalog.

Application and Information

Applicants must complete and submit an application form, along with documentation of graduation from an accredited high school or state-approved secondary education curriculum or official documentation of high school graduation equivalency.

Prospective students can go online to BMCprograms.info for program duration, tuition, fees and other costs, median debt, federal salary data, alumni success, programmatic accreditation, and other important details.

Brown Mackie College is a system of over twenty-five schools located throughout North America. Programs, credential levels, technology, and scheduling options vary by school, and employment opportunities are not guaranteed. Financial aid is available for those who qualify. Administrative offices are located at 625 Eden Park Drive, Suite 1100; Cincinnati, Ohio 45202; phone: 513-830-2000. ©2013 Brown Mackie College. OH Registration #03-09-1685T; #03-09-1686T; #03-09-1687T; # 03-09-1688T; # 06-03-1781T; AC0150, AC0109, AC0078, AC0045, AC0138, AC0110; Licensed by the Florida Commission for Independent Education, License No. 3206.

For additional information, prospective students should contact:

Director of Admissions
Brown Mackie College — South Bend
3454 Douglas Road
South Bend, Indiana 46635
Phone: 574-237-0774
    800-743-2447 (toll-free)
Fax: 574-237-3585
E-mail: bmcsbadm@brownmackie.edu
Web site: http://www.brownmackie.edu/SouthBend)

BROWN MACKIE COLLEGE — TUCSON
TUCSON, ARIZONA

The College and Its Mission

Brown Mackie College — Tucson (Brown Mackie College) is one of over twenty-five locations in the Brown Mackie College system of schools (www.brownmackie.edu), which is dedicated to providing educational programs that prepare students to pursue entry-level positions in a competitive, rapidly changing workplace. Brown Mackie College schools offer bachelor's degree, associate degree, diploma, and certificate programs in health sciences, business, information technology, legal studies, and design to thousands of students in the Midwest, Southeast, Southwest, and Western United States.

Brown Mackie College was originally founded and approved by the Board of Trustees of Kansas Wesleyan College in Salina, Kansas on July 30, 1892. In 1938, the college was incorporated as The Brown Mackie School of Business under the ownership of Perry E. Brown and A. B. Mackie, former instructors at Kansas Wesleyan University in Salina, Kansas. Their last names formed the name of Brown Mackie. By January 1975, with improvements in curricula and higher degree-granting status, The Brown Mackie School of Business became Brown Mackie College.

Brown Mackie College entered the Arizona market in 2007 when it purchased a school that had been previously established in the Tucson area. That school had an established history in the community and was converted into what is now known as Brown Mackie College — Tucson. The historical timeline of Brown Mackie College — Tucson started in 1972 when Rockland West Corporation first formed a partnership with Lamson Business College. At that time the school was a career college that offered only short-term programs focusing on computer training and secretarial skills. In 1994 the college became accredited as a junior college and began offering associate degrees in academic subjects. The mission was then modified to include the goal of instilling in graduates an appreciation for lifelong learning through the general education courses that became a part of every program.

In 1996 the college applied for and received status as a senior college by the Accrediting Commission of Independent Colleges and Schools. This gave the school the ability to offer course work leading to a Bachelor of Science degree in business administration. Since then the program offerings for bachelor and associate degrees have expanded.

In 1986, the college moved from 5001 East Speedway to the 4585 East Speedway location where it remains today. In 2008, two of the college's three buildings were remodeled which resulted in updated classrooms; networked computer laboratories; new medical, surgical technology, and forensics laboratories; a larger library and offices for student services such as academics, admissions, and student financial services; and a full-service college store. In 2009, the third building was remodeled and provides newer classrooms and a new career services department.

Brown Mackie College — Tucson is accredited by the Accrediting Council for Independent Colleges and Schools to award associate degrees and diplomas. The Accrediting Council for Independent Colleges and Schools is listed as a nationally recognized accrediting agency by the United States Department of Education and is recognized by the Council for Higher Education Accreditation. ACICS can be contacted at 750 First Street NE, Suite 980, Washington, D.C. 20002; phone: 202-336-6780.

Brown Mackie College — Tucson is authorized by the Arizona State Board for Private Post-secondary Education, 1400 West Washington Street, Room 2560, Phoenix, Arizona 85007; phone: 602-542-5709; http://azppse.state.az.us.

The Associate of Science in surgical technology program is accredited by the Accrediting Bureau of Health Education Schools.

The Associate of Applied Science in occupational therapy assistant program is accredited by the Accreditation Council for Occupational Therapy Education (ACOTE) of the American Occupational Therapy Association (AOTA), located at 4720 Montgomery Lane, Suite 200, Bethesda, Maryland 20814-3449; phone: 301-652-AOTA. Graduates of the program will be eligible to sit for the national certification examination for the occupational therapy assistant administered by the National Board for Certification in Occupational Therapy (NBCOT). After successful completion of this exam, the individual will be a Certified Occupational Therapy Assistant (COTA). In addition, most states require licensure in order to practice; however, state licenses are usually based on the results of the NBCOT Certification Examination. Note that a felony conviction may affect a graduate's ability to sit for the NBCOT certification examination or attain state licensure.

Academic Programs

Brown Mackie College — Tucson provides higher education to traditional and nontraditional students through associate degree and diploma programs that assist in enhancing their career opportunities, broadening their perspectives through appropriate general education courses, thinking independently and critically, and improving problem-solving abilities. The college strives to develop within its students the desire for lifelong and continued education.

Each college quarter comprises twelve weeks. Associate degree programs require a minimum of eight quarters to complete. Programs are offered on a year-round basis, providing students with the ability to work uninterrupted toward their degrees. The college offers all programs in a unique One Course a Month format. This allows students to focus studies on only one course for four weeks. This schedule has proven convenient for students with multiple obligations such as jobs and family.

Associate Degree Programs: The Associate of Science degree is awarded in accounting technology, business management, computer networking and security, criminal justice, graphic design, health care administration, medical assisting, and surgical technology.

The Associate of Applied Science degree is awarded in biomedical equipment technology and occupational therapy assistant.

Diploma Program: A diploma is awarded in graphic design assistant, medical assistant, and practical nursing.

The American Medical Technologists (AMT), which offers the certification for Registered Medical Assistant (RMA), accepts the accreditation of Brown Mackie College — Tucson. Students will qualify to take the RMA certification examination upon graduating the Brown Mackie College — Tucson medical assisting and medical assistant programs. Graduates of the 48 credit-hour medical assistant program are not qualified to take the AMT/RMA exam.

Brown Mackie College — Tucson does not guarantee third-party certification. Outside agencies control the requirements for certifications and are subject to change without notice to Brown Mackie College.

Program availability and degree offerings are subject to change.

Costs

Tuition in the 2012–13 academic year for most associate and diploma programs was $344 per credit hour; fees were $20 per credit hour. Tuition for the surgical technology program was $360 per credit hour; fees were $20 per credit hour. Tuition for the occupational therapy assistant program was $381 per credit hour; fees were $20 per credit hour. Tuition for the practical nursing program was $381 per credit hour; fees were $30 per credit hour. Textbooks, if applicable, and other instructional expenses vary by program.

Financial Aid

Financial aid is available for those who qualify. The college maintains a full-time staff of Student Financial Services Advisers to assist qualified students in obtaining the financial assistance they require to meet their educational expenses. Available resources include federal and state aid, student loans from private lenders, and Federal Work-Study opportunities, both on and off college premises.

Each year, the college makes available President's Scholarships of $1,000 each to qualifying seniors from area high schools. In order to qualify, a senior must be graduating from a participating high school, must be maintaining a cumulative grade point average of at least 2.0, and must submit a brief essay. The student's extracurricular activities and community service are also considered. These scholarships are available only to students enrolling in one of the college's degree programs. Students awarded the scholarship must enroll at Brown Mackie College — Tucson between June and September immediately following their high school graduation. Applications for these scholarships can be obtained from the guidance departments of participating high schools. These applications must be completed and returned to the college by March 31.

The Education Foundation was established in 2000 to offer scholarship support to students interested in continuing their education at one of the postsecondary, career-focused schools in the EDMC system. The number and amount of the awards can vary, depending on the funds available. Scholarship applications are considered every quarter. At Brown Mackie College, applicants must be currently enrolled in an associate or bachelor's degree program and in their fourth quarter or higher (but no further than their second-to-last quarter) at the time of application. Awards are made based on academic performance and potential, as well as financial need. Interested students should contact the college's Student Financial Service Department for additional information.

Faculty

Experienced faculty members provide academic support and are committed to the academic and technical preparation of their students. The college has 15 full-time and 35 part-time instructors, with a student-faculty ratio of 12:1. Each student is assigned a faculty adviser.

Facilities and Resources

A modern facility, Brown Mackie College — Tucson offers more than 31,000 square feet. The college is equipped with multiple computer labs housing over 200 computers. High-speed access to the Internet and other online resources are available for students and faculty. Multimedia classrooms are outfitted with overhead projectors, VCR/DVD players, and computers. The college is nonresidential; public transportation and parking at no cost are available.

Brown Mackie College — Tucson is fully committed to using eTextbooks and computer tablets in the classroom. Utilizing these tablets to access expanded course material, students are able to increase their acumen for using this technology and further enhance their educational experience. Students have the ability to directly download their eTextbooks to their tablet, eliminating the need to carry heavy, physical textbooks and reducing the overall cost of supplies.

The college has a generous parking area and is also easily accessible by public transportation.

Location

Brown Mackie College — Tucson is conveniently located at 4585 East Speedway Boulevard in Tucson, Arizona.

Admission Requirements

Each applicant for admission is assigned to an Assistant Director of Admissions who directs the applicant through the steps of the admissions process. They provide information on curriculum, policies, procedures, and services and assist the applicant in setting necessary appointments and interviews. To qualify for admission, each applicant must provide documentation of graduation from an accredited high school or from a state-approved secondary education curriculum or provide official documentation of high school graduation equivalency. All transcripts become the property of the college. Admission to the college is based on the applicant meeting the stated requirements, a review of the applicant's previous educational records, and a review of the applicant's career interests. If previous academic records indicate the college's education and training programs would not benefit the applicant, the college reserves the right to advise the applicant not to enroll. Special requirements for enrollment into certain programs are discussed in the descriptions of those programs.

For the most recent information regarding admission requirements, please refer to the current academic catalog.

Application and Information

Applicants must complete and submit an application form, along with documentation of graduation from an accredited high school or state-approved secondary education curriculum or official documentation of high school graduation equivalency.

Prospective students can go online to BMCprograms.info for program duration, tuition, fees and other costs, median debt, federal salary data, alumni success, programmatic accreditation, and other important details.

Brown Mackie College is a system of over twenty-five schools located throughout North America. Programs, credential levels, technology, and scheduling options vary by school, and employment opportunities are not guaranteed. Financial aid is available for those who qualify. Administrative offices are located at 625 Eden Park Drive, Suite 1100; Cincinnati, Ohio 45202; phone: 513-830-2000. ©2013 Brown Mackie College. OH Registration #03-09-1685T; #03-09-1686T; # 3-09-1687T; #03-09-1688T; #06-03-1781T; AC0150, AC0109, AC0078, AC0045, AC0138, AC0110; Licensed by the Florida Commission for Independent Education, License No. 3206.

For additional information, prospective students should contact:

Senior Director of Admissions
Brown Mackie College — Tucson
4585 East Speedway Boulevard, Suite 204
Tucson, Arizona 85712
Phone: 520-319-3300
Fax: 520-319-3495
E-mail: bmctuadm@brownmackie.edu
Web site: http://www.brownmackie.edu/Tucson

BROWN MACKIE COLLEGE — TULSA
TULSA, OKLAHOMA

BROWN
MACKIE
COLLEGE
TULSA℠

The College and Its Mission

Brown Mackie College — Tulsa (Brown Mackie College) is one of over twenty-five locations in the Brown Mackie College system of schools (www.brownmackie.edu), which is dedicated to providing educational programs that prepare students to pursue entry-level positions in a competitive, rapidly changing workplace. Brown Mackie College schools offer bachelor's degree, associate degree, diploma, and certificate programs in health sciences, business, information technology, legal studies, and design to thousands of students in the Midwest, Southeast, Southwest, and Western United States.

Brown Mackie College — Tulsa was founded in 2008 as a branch of Brown Mackie College — South Bend, Indiana.

Brown Mackie College — Tulsa is accredited by the Accrediting Council for Independent Colleges and Schools to award associate degrees and diplomas. The Accrediting Council for Independent Colleges and Schools is listed as a nationally recognized accrediting agency by the United States Department of Education and is recognized by the Council for Higher Education Accreditation. ACICS can be contacted at 750 First Street NE, Suite 980, Washington, D.C. 20002; phone: 202-336-6780.

This institution is licensed by the Oklahoma Board of Private Vocational Schools (OBPVS), 3700 North Classen Boulevard, Suite 250, Oklahoma City, Oklahoma 73118; phone: 405-528-3370.

This institution has been granted authority to operate in Oklahoma by the Oklahoma State Regents for Higher Education (OSRHE), 655 Research Parkway, Suite 200, Oklahoma City, Oklahoma 73101; phone: 405-225-9100; www.okhighered.org.

The occupational therapy assistant program is accredited by the Accreditation Council for Occupational Therapy Education (ACOTE) of the American Occupational Therapy Association (AOTA), located at 4720 Montgomery Lane, Suite 200, Bethesda, Maryland 20814-3449; phone: 301-652-AOTA. Graduates of the program will be eligible to sit for the national certification examination for the occupational therapy assistant administered by the National Board for Certification in Occupational Therapy (NBCOT). After successful completion of this exam, the individual will be a Certified Occupational Therapy Assistant (COTA). In addition, most states require licensure in order to practice; however, state licenses are usually based on the results of the NBCOT Certification Examination. Note that a felony conviction may affect a graduate's ability to sit for the NBCOT certification examination or attain state licensure.

Academic Programs

Brown Mackie College — Tulsa provides higher education to traditional and nontraditional students through associate degree and diploma programs that assist in enhancing their career opportunities, broadening their perspectives through appropriate general education courses, thinking independently and critically, and improving problem-solving abilities. The college strives to develop within its students the desire for lifelong and continued education.

Each college quarter comprises twelve weeks. Associate degree programs require a minimum of eight quarters to complete. Programs are offered on a year-round basis, providing students with the ability to work uninterrupted toward completion of their programs. The college offers all programs in a unique One Course a Month format. This allows students to focus on only one course for four weeks. This schedule has proven convenient for students with multiple obligations such as jobs and family.

Associate Degree Programs: The Associate of Applied Science degree is awarded in accounting technology, business management, criminal justice, health care administration, information technology, medical assisting, nursing, occupational therapy assistant, paralegal, and surgical technology.

Diploma Programs: Diploma programs are offered in accounting, business, criminal justice, medical assistant, and paralegal assistant.

The American Medical Technologists (AMT), which offers the certification for Registered Medical Assistant (RMA), accepts the accreditation of Brown Mackie College — Tulsa. Students will qualify to take the RMA certification examination upon graduating the Brown Mackie College — Tulsa medical assisting and medical assistant programs. Graduates of the 48 credit-hour medical assistant program are not qualified to take the AMT/RMA exam.

Brown Mackie College — Tulsa does not guarantee third-party certification. Outside agencies control the requirements for certifications and are subject to change without notice to Brown Mackie College.

Program availability and degree offerings are subject to change.

Costs

Tuition for programs in the 2012–13 academic year was $314 per credit hour, with a general fee of $20 per credit hour applied to instructional costs for activities and services. Tuition for the occupational therapy program was $381 per credit hour with a general fee of $20 per credit hour applied to instructional costs for activities. Tuition for the surgical technology program was $360 per credit hour with a general fee of $20 per credit hour applied to instructional costs for activities. Tuition for the nursing program was $410 per credit hour with a general fee of $30 per credit hour applied to instructional costs for activities. Textbooks, if applicable, and other instructional materials vary by program.

Financial Aid

Financial aid is available for those who qualify. The college maintains a full-time staff of Student Financial Services Advisers to assist qualified students in obtaining the financial assistance they require to meet their educational expenses. Available resources include federal and state aid, student loans from private lenders, and Federal Work-Study opportunities, both on and off college premises.

Each year, the college makes available President's Scholarships of $1,000 each to qualifying seniors from area high schools. In order to qualify, a senior must be graduating from a participating high school, must be maintaining a cumulative grade point average of at least 2.0, and must submit a brief essay. The student's extracurricular activities and community service are also considered. These scholarships are available only to students enrolling in one of the college's degree programs. Students awarded the scholarship must enroll at Brown Mackie College — Tucson between June and September immediately following their high school graduation. Applications for these scholarships can be obtained from the guidance departments of participating high schools. These applications must be completed and returned to the college by March 31.

The Education Foundation was established in 2000 to offer scholarship support to students interested in continuing their education at one of the postsecondary, career-focused schools in the EDMC system. The number and amount of the awards can vary, depending on the funds available. Scholarship applications are considered every quarter. At Brown Mackie College, applicants must be currently enrolled in an associate or bachelor's degree program and in their fourth quarter or higher (but no further than their second-to-last quarter) at the time of application. Awards are made based on academic performance and potential, as well as financial need. Interested students should contact the college's Student Financial Service Department for additional information.

Faculty

There are 14 full-time and several adjunct faculty members. The average class size is 14 students. Each student has a faculty and student adviser.

Facilities and Resources

Opened in 2008, this modern facility offers more than 25,000 square feet of tastefully decorated classrooms, laboratories, and office space designed to specifications of the college for its business, medical, and technical programs. Instructional equipment is comparable to current technology used in business and industry today. Modern classrooms for special instructional needs offer multimedia capabilities with surround sound and overhead projectors accessible through computer, DVD, or VHS. Internet access and instructional resources are available at the college's library. Experienced faculty members provide academic support and are committed to the academic and technical preparation of their students.

Brown Mackie College — Tulsa is fully committed to using eTextbooks and computer tablets in the classroom. Utilizing these tablets to access expanded course material, students are able to increase their acumen for using this technology and further enhance their educational experience. Students have the ability to directly download their eTextbooks to their tablet, eliminating the need to carry heavy, physical textbooks and reducing the overall cost of supplies.

The college is nonresidential; public transportation and ample parking at no cost are available.

Location

Brown Mackie College — Tulsa is conveniently located at 4608 South Garnett Road, Suite 110 in Tulsa, Oklahoma.

Admission Requirements

Each applicant for admission is assigned to an Assistant Director of Admissions, who directs the applicant through the steps of the admissions process, providing information on curriculum, policies, procedures, and services and assisting the applicant in setting necessary appointments and interviews. To qualify for admission, applicants must be a graduate of a public or private high school or a correspondence school or education center that is accredited by an agency that is recognized by the U.S. or State of Oklahoma Department of Education or any of its approved agents. As part of the admissions process applicants must sign a document attesting to graduation or completion and containing the information to obtain verification of such. Verification must be obtained within the first term (90 days) or the student will be withdrawn from the institution following established guidelines for withdrawn students noted in the catalog. Title IV aid will not be dispersed until verification of graduation or completion has been received by the college. All transcripts become the property of the college.

Students are given an assessment of academic skills. Although the results of this assessment do not determine eligibility for admission, they provide the college with a means of determining the need for academic support.

For the most recent information regarding admission requirements, please refer to the current academic catalog.

Application and Information

Applicants must complete and submit an application form, along with documentation of graduation from an accredited high school or state-approved secondary education curriculum or official documentation of high school graduation equivalency.

Prospective students can go online to BMCprograms.info for program duration, tuition, fees and other costs, median debt, federal salary data, alumni success, programmatic accreditation, and other important details.

Brown Mackie College is a system of over twenty-five schools located throughout North America. Programs, credential levels, technology, and scheduling options vary by school, and employment opportunities are not guaranteed. Financial aid is available for those who qualify. Administrative offices are located at 625 Eden Park Drive, Suite 1100; Cincinnati, Ohio 45202; phone: 513-830-2000. ©2013 Brown Mackie College. OH Registration #03-09-1685T; #03-09-1686T; #03-09-1687T; #03-09-1688T; #06-03-1781T; AC0150, AC0109, AC0078, AC0045, AC0138, AC0110; Licensed by the Florida Commission for Independent Education, License No. 3206.

For additional information, prospective students should contact:

Senior Director of Admissions
Brown Mackie College — Tulsa
4608 South Garnett Road, Suite 110
Suite 110
Tulsa, Oklahoma 74146
Phone: 918-628-3700
      888-794-8411 (toll-free)
Fax: 918-828-9083
E-mail: bmctuladm@brownmackie.edu
Web site: http://www.brownmackie.edu/Tulsa

CAMDEN COUNTY COLLEGE
BLACKWOOD, NEW JERSEY

The College and Its Mission

Camden County College (CCC) is a fully accredited comprehensive public community college in New Jersey. CCC provides accessible and affordable education. The College offers 100-plus associate degree and occupational certificate programs along with noncredit development courses and customized job training. The College also provides support services students need to transfer for further studies or to begin a career. The College has four primary locations: the main campus in Blackwood, a branch campus in Camden in the University District, the William G. Rohrer Center in Cherry Hill, and other instructional sites including the Regional Emergency Training Center (RETC) in Blackwood and the Technical Institute (TI) in Sicklerville.

The College is one of the largest community colleges in New Jersey and one of the most sophisticated in the nation. Recognized nationally as a leader in technology programs, the College is also regionally acknowledged for nursing and health education and is a vital resource for transfer education, customized training, and cultural events.

The main campus is situated on 320 sylvan acres near Philadelphia and New York, allowing students to take advantage of the cities for recreation, education, and work opportunities.

A capital initiative is transforming many of the facilities and structural amenities on the main campus. The 107,000-square-foot Kevin G. Halpern Hall for Science & Health Education recently opened; roads, athletic fields, and parking have been upgraded. The College is easily accessible from Route 42 via Exit 7B, which leads directly into the College's main entrance.

College housing is not available on campus; however, students may reside at local apartment complexes that are within walking distance of the main campus.

Over 20 student clubs and service organizations, national honor societies, and other activities are available. The College also has a student newspaper, the *Campus Press,* and a radio station.

A variety of athletic activities are offered for both experienced competitors and casual participants. Varsity teams for both men and women compete against other two-year college teams in the New Jersey Garden State Athletic Conference and Region XIX of the National Junior College Athletic Association. Men compete in baseball, basketball, cross-country, golf, and soccer. Women compete in basketball, cross-country, golf, soccer, and softball. Students can use College athletic facilities, including an all-weather quarter-mile track; an athletic center with a weight and fitness room; basketball/volleyball courts; and various outdoor playing fields.

Academic Programs

(http://camdencc.edu/academics/cataloginfo.cfm)

Camden County College offers the following associate degrees: A.A., A.S., A.F.A., and A.A.S., as well as C.T., C.A., and C.P.S. certificates.

The College operates on a fifteen- or thirteen-week semester and offers courses in arts, humanities, social sciences, business, computers, mathematics, health care, and science. Online and hybrid courses are offered. Summer sessions are five, seven, and eight weeks long; online and weekend courses are offered as well. The College's academic calendar is accessible online at www.camdencc.edu.

In general, approximately 60 credits are required to earn an associate degree and about 30 credits for a certificate. The total number of credits required varies by program.

Career programs (A.A.S.) include the following: accounting; addictions counseling; automotive technology (apprentice); automotive technology: GM/ASEP; biotechnology; biotechnology: cell and tissue culture option; biotechnology: forensic science option; CADD: computer-aided drafting and design; computer graphics; computer graphics: game design and development; computer information systems; computer information systems: personal computer option; computer integrated manufacturing/engineering technology; computer systems technology; dental assisting; dental hygiene; dietetic technology; engineering technology: electrical electronic engineering; engineering technology: electromechanical engineering; engineering technology: mechanical engineering; film and television production; finance; fire science technology; fire science technology: administration option; health information technology; health science; health science: certified medical assistant option; health science: surgical technology option; hospitality technology; management; management: business paraprofessional management option; management: small business management option; marketing; massage therapy; medical laboratory technology; office systems technology administrative assistant; office systems technology administrative assistant: information processing option; ophthalmic science technology; paralegal studies; paramedic sciences; paramedic sciences: paramedic educational management option; photonics: laser/electro-optic technology; photonics: laser/electro-optic technology fiber-optic option; preschool teacher education; respiratory therapy; sign language interpreter education; technical studies; veterinary technology; video imaging; and Web design and development.

Transfer programs (A.A./ A.S. /A.F.A.) include computer science (A.A.) and (A.S.); criminal justice (A.S.); early childhood education (A.A.); elementary/secondary education (A.S.); engineering science (A.S.); human services (A.S.); human services: developmental disabilities option (AS); human services: early childhood education option (A.S.); liberal arts and science (LAS) (A.A.); LAS: applied & fine arts option (A.A.); LAS: communications option (A.A.); LAS: photo-journalism track (A.A.); LAS: public relations/advertising track (A.A.); LAS: computer graphics option (A.A.); LAS: electronic publishing track (A.A.); LAS dance option (A.A.); LAS: deaf studies option (A.A.); LAS English option (A.A.); LAS history option (A.A.); LAS: language & culture option (A.A.); LAS: languages & international studies option (A.A.); LAS: law, government & politics option (A.A.); LAS law, government & politics option (A.A.); LAS: music option (A.A.); LAS: photography option (A.A.); LAS: psychology option (A.A.); LAS: speech option (A.A.); LAS: theatre option (A.A.); liberal arts and science (LAS) (A.S.); LAS biology option (A.S.); LAS: business administration option (A.S.); LAS: information systems track (A.S.); LAS chemistry option (A.S.); LAS: environmental science option (A.S.); LAS: food science option (A.S.); LAS: health and exercise science option (A.S.); LAS: mathematics option (A.S.); LAS: nursing: pre nursing option; LAS: physics option (A.S.); LAS: pre-pharmacy option (A.S.); LAS: secondary education in biology option; LAS: secondary education I mathematics option (A.S.); Nursing: Our Lady of Lourdes School of Nursing (A.S.); occupational therapy assistant (A.S.); psychosocial rehabilitation and treatment (A.S.); sport management (A.S.); studio art (A.F.A).

Academic Certificate Programs (C.T.) offered are computer applications programming, computer graphics, computer integrated manufacturing technology, computer programming, computer systems technology, dental assisting, developmental disabilities, film and television production assistant, medical coding, nutrition care manager, office assistant, personal computer specialist, photonics: fiber-optic technical specialist, practical nursing, social services, and Web design development.

Certificate of Achievement Programs (C.A.) include addictions counseling; alternate energy engineering technology; automotive general technician; behavioral health care; CADD: computer-aided drafting and design; computer-aided manufacturing technician; computer science; computerized accounting specialist; crime and intelligence analysis; culinary; educational interpreter training; emergency and disaster management; fine art techniques; food services management; fundamentals of policing; hotel and resort management; industrial controls: precision machining technology; programmable logic controller; instructional aide paraprofessional core; international healthcare; Linux/UNIX administration; massage therapy; meeting and event planning; Microsoft Office specialist; multi-skilled technician; music recording; ophthalmic medical technician; ophthalmic science apprentice; paramedic sciences; personal trainer; relational database management system using ORACLE; and surgical technology.

A Certificate of Postsecondary Study (C.P.S.) is offered in independent skills pathway.

Off-Campus Programs

Camden County College has articulation agreements with regional four-year colleges and universities to offer bachelor's degree completion programs on the CCC campus. One of the largest is a partnership with Rutgers University's College of Nursing in New Brunswick and Newark. More information is available online at www.camdencc.edu.

Credit for Nontraditional Learning Experiences

CCC offers a number of opportunities including evaluating educational experiences approved by the American Council on Education and the Program on Non-Collegiate Sponsored Instruction and validating armed services training among others. More details can be found in the College *Catalog* at www.camdencc.edu.

Costs

For students who enter in September 2013, tuition costs are $104 per credit for in-county residents, $108 per credit for out-of-county residents, and $183 per credit for international students. The general service fee per credit is $28, and the facility fee per credit is $6. Course fees vary depending on courses taken, and hourly instruction fees vary depending on courses taken.

The cost of books and supplies is estimated to be $1600 for one year for a full-time student. Students who choose e-textbooks instead of new books can reduce the cost by up to 50 percent. Students can also save by participating in book rentals and buybacks. Actual costs depend on the specific courses chosen.

Financial Aid

Financial aid comes in the form of scholarships, grants, loans and work-study. Students are required to file a Free Application for Federal Student Aid (FAFSA) as soon as possible after January 1 of each year (the College's school code is 006865), as well as the College's authorization and certification form. Financial aid applications filed by May 1 and completed by June 1 of each year are given priority. Students must be admitted before an offer of financial aid can be made. Additional application information is available at www.camdencc.edu.

Faculty

The student-faculty ratio is 28:1. Faculty members are dedicated to teaching and supporting students throughout the academic year. In addition to the College's advisory staff, some faculty members may assist in providing academic advisement for their field of specialization. Full-time faculty members hold advanced degrees as do adjuncts.

Student Body Profile

Of the College's 21,832 credit students served in the financial year 2012, 75.5 percent are Camden County residents and 95.8 percent are New Jersey residents. Approximately 51.8 percent of the students are Caucasian, 21.3 percent African American, 5.2 percent Asian, 12.5 percent Hispanic, 0.7 percent American Indian/Alaskan native, 0.2 percent Native Hawaiian/Pacific Islander, 2.4 percent are two or more, and 5.8 unknown/not reported. The mean student age is 27.

Academic Facilities

The newly constructed Kevin G. Halpern Hall for Science and Health Education houses state-of-the-art biology, chemistry, and physics labs; a dental hygiene clinic; a café; a health-care education suite with a laboratory, a surgical suite, and patient care for nursing, medical laboratory technology, veterinary technology, and surgical technology students. Additional information is available online at camdencc.edu. The library is located on the Blackwood Campus, and an e-library is located at the Cherry Hill location.

Students on the Camden City Campus have access to the Rutgers University library and gym. CCC offers open-access computer labs, laser labs, automotive facility, vision care facility, and numerous other laboratories. The Otto R. Mauke Community Center houses a cyber café, student activities offices, a cafeteria, and student lounge areas. The facility also contains student support offices including advising, a Barnes & Noble bookstore, and student employment, student transfer, and international student offices. The Papiano Gymnasium hosts a fitness center and variety of indoor and outdoor sports.

Location

The 320-acre main campus is located in Blackwood, New Jersey. The College is easily reached from the interstate highway system, is located a short distance from the PATCO high-speed train line service to and from Philadelphia, and is available via NJ Transit buses. Lincoln Hall's Marlin Art Gallery, Dennis Flyer Memorial Theatre, Little Theatre, and the Madison Connector Building's Civic Hall, home to the Center for Civic Leadership and Responsibility are venues for College, county, and regional communities. The facilities host musical concerts, dance performances, theatrical presentations, lectures, workshops, and community events. The conference center on the Camden City Campus is used by businesses, community, and government organizations. The Regional Emergency Training Center is home to The Camden County College Police Academy and The Camden County College Fire Academy. The Technical Institute provides training in a variety of trades.

Admission Requirements

The College has open enrollment. Students must be 18 years of age. A few selected programs have additional admission criteria. Prospective students should apply online at www.camdencc.edu. The website provides details about the enrollment process. There is no cost to apply to CCC.

Application and Information

Processing of applications for admission each year begins no later than February 15 for the fall semester and no later than October 1 for the spring semester. Rolling admission for a semester occurs through the last day of the semester.

For more information, contact:

Office of Admissions, Records and Registration Services
Camden County College
200 College Drive
Blackwood, New Jersey 08012
Phone: 856-227-7200
Website: http://www.camdencc.edu

One of the many student lounge and study areas at Camden County College.

FASHION INSTITUTE OF TECHNOLOGY
State University of New York
NEW YORK, NEW YORK

The College and Its Mission

The Fashion Institute of Technology (FIT) is New York's celebrated urban college for creative and business talent. A State University of New York (SUNY) college of art, design, business, and technology, FIT is a dynamic mix of innovative achievers, original thinkers, and industry pioneers. FIT balances a real-world-based curriculum and hands-on instruction with a rigorous liberal arts foundation. The college marries design and business and supports individual creativity in a collaborative environment. It offers a complete college experience with a vibrant student and residential life.

With an extraordinary location at the center of New York City—world capital of the arts, business, and media—FIT maintains close ties with the design, fashion, advertising, communications, and international commerce industries. Academic departments consult with advisory boards of noted experts to ensure that the curriculum and classroom technology reflect current industry practices. The college's faculty of successful professionals brings experience to the classroom, while field trips, guest lectures, and sponsored competitions introduce students to the opportunities and challenges of their disciplines.

FIT's mission is to produce well-rounded graduates—doers and thinkers who raise the professional bar to become the next generation of business pacesetters and creative icons.

FIT's four residence halls house 2,300 students in fully furnished traditional or apartment-style accommodations. Various dining options and meal plans are available. Residential counselors and student staff members live in the residence halls, helping students adjust to college life and New York City.

FIT is accredited by the Middle States Commission on Higher Education, the National Association of Schools of Art and Design, and the Council for Interior Design Accreditation.

Academic Programs

FIT serves approximately 10,000 full-time, part-time, and evening/weekend students from the metropolitan area, New York State, across the country, and around the world, offering nearly fifty programs leading to the A.A.S., B.F.A., B.S., M.A., M.F.A., and M.P.S. degrees. Each undergraduate program includes a core of traditional liberal arts courses, providing students with a global perspective, critical-thinking skills, and the ability to communicate effectively. All degree programs are designed to prepare students for creative and business careers and to provide them with the prerequisite studies to go on to baccalaureate, master's, or doctoral degrees, if they wish.

All students complete a two-year A.A.S. program in their major area and the liberal arts. They may then choose to go on to a related, two-year B.F.A. or B.S. program or begin their careers with their A.A.S. degree, which qualifies them for entry-level positions.

Associate Degree Programs: For the A.A.S. degree, FIT offers eleven majors through the School of Art and Design, four through the Jay and Patty Baker School of Business and Technology, and one through the School of Liberal Arts. The A.A.S. programs are accessories design*, advertising and marketing communications*, communication design foundation*, fashion design*, fashion merchandising management* (with an online option), filmmaking, fine arts, illustration, interior design, jewelry design*, menswear, photography, production management: fashion and related industries, textile development and marketing*, textile/surface design*, and visual presentation and exhibition design. Programs with an asterisk (*) are also available in a one-year format for students with sufficient transferable credits.

Bachelor's Degree Programs: Many A.A.S. graduates choose to pursue a related, two-year baccalaureate program at the college. FIT offers twenty-five baccalaureate programs—thirteen B.F.A. programs through the School of Art and Design, ten B.S. programs through the Baker School of Business and Technology, and two B.S. programs through the School of Liberal Arts. The B.F.A. programs

are accessories design, advertising design, computer animation and interactive media, fabric styling, fashion design (with specializations in children's wear, intimate apparel, knitwear, special occasion, and sportswear), fine arts, graphic design, illustration, interior design, packaging design, photography and the digital image, textile/surface design, and toy design. The B.S. programs are advertising and marketing communications, art history and museum professions, cosmetics and fragrance marketing, direct and interactive marketing, entrepreneurship for the fashion and design industries, fashion merchandising management, film and media, home products development, international trade and marketing for the fashion industries, production management: fashion and related industries, technical design, and textile development and marketing.

Liberal Arts Minors: The School of Liberal Arts offers FIT students the opportunity to minor in a variety of liberal arts areas in two forms: traditional subject-based minors and interdisciplinary minors unique to the FIT liberal arts curriculum. Selected minors include film and media, economics, English literature, international politics, Asian studies, and psychology.

Evening/Weekend Programs: FIT's School of Continuing Education and Professional Studies provides evening and weekend credit and noncredit classes to students and working professionals interested in pursuing a degree or certificate or furthering their knowledge of a particular industry, while balancing the demands of career or family. There are nine degree programs available through evening/weekend study: advertising and marketing communications (A.A.S. and B.S.), communication design foundation (A.A.S.), fashion design (A.A.S.), fashion merchandising management (A.A.S. and B.S.), graphic design (B.F.A.), illustration (B.F.A.), and international trade and marketing for the fashion industries (B.S.).

Honors Program: The Presidential Scholars honors program, available to academically exceptional students in all majors, offers special courses, projects, colloquia, and off-campus activities that broaden horizons and stimulate discourse. Presidential Scholars receive priority course registration and an annual merit stipend.

Internships: Internships are a required element of most programs and are available to all matriculated students. Nearly one third of FIT student interns are offered employment on completion of their internships; past sponsors include American Eagle Outfitters, Bloomingdale's, Calvin Klein, Estée Lauder, Fairchild Publications, MTV, and Saatchi & Saatchi.

Precollege Programs: Precollege programs (Saturday Live, Sunday Live, and Summer Live) are available to middle and high school students during the fall, spring, and summer. More than 100 courses provide the chance to learn in an innovative environment, develop art and design portfolios, explore the business and technological sides of many creative careers, and discover natural talents and abilities.

Off-Campus Programs

The study-abroad experience lets students immerse themselves in diverse cultures and prepares them to live and work in a global community. FIT has two campuses in Italy—one in Milan, one in Florence—where students study fashion design or fashion merchandising management and gain firsthand experience in the dynamics of European fashion. FIT also offers study-abroad options in countries like Australia, China, England, France, and Mexico. Students can study abroad during the winter or summer sessions, for a semester, or for a full academic year.

Costs

As a SUNY college, FIT offers affordable tuition for both New York State residents and nonresidents. The 2012–13 associate-level tuition per semester for in-state residents was $2,100; for nonresidents, $6,300. Baccalaureate-level tuition per semester was $2,884 for in-state residents and $7,715 for nonresidents. Per-semester housing costs were $6,119–$6,299 for traditional residence hall accommodations with mandatory meal plan and $5,241–$9,521 for apartment-style accommodations. Meal plans ranged from $1,643 to $2,105 per semester. Textbook costs and other nominal fees, such as locker rental or laboratory use, vary per program. All costs are subject to change.

Financial Aid

FIT offers scholarships, grants, loans, and work-study employment for students with financial need. Overall, two-thirds of full-time, matriculated undergraduate students who complete the federal financial aid application process receive some type of assistance through loans and/or grants. The college directly administers its own institutional grants and scholarships, which are provided by the FIT Foundation.

College-administered funding includes Federal Pell Grants, Federal Perkins Loans, Federal Supplemental Educational Opportunity Grants, Federal Work-Study, and the Federal Family Educational Loan Program, which includes student and parent loans. New York State residents who meet eligibility guidelines may also receive Tuition Assistance Program (TAP) and/or Educational Opportunity Program (EOP) grants. Financial aid applicants must file the Free Application for Federal Student Aid (FAFSA) and should also apply to all available outside sources of aid. Additional documentation may be requested by the Financial Aid Office. Applications for financial aid should be completed prior to February 15 for fall admission or November 1 for spring admission.

Faculty

FIT's faculty is drawn from top professionals in academia, art, design, communications, and business, providing a curriculum rich in real-world experience and traditional educational values. Student-instructor interaction is encouraged, with a maximum class size of 25, and courses are structured to foster participation, independent thinking, and self-expression.

Student Body Profile

Fall 2012 enrollment was 10,052 with 8,199 students enrolled in degree programs. Thirty-six percent of degree-seeking students are enrolled in the School of Art and Design; 43 percent are in the Baker School of Business and Technology. The average age of full-time degree seekers is 23. Forty percent of FIT's students are New York City residents, 23 percent are New York State (non–New York City) residents, and 37 percent are out-of-state residents or international students. The ethnic/racial makeup of the student body is approximately 0.12 percent American Indian or Alaskan, 11.9 percent Asian, 10.25 percent black, 18.09 percent Hispanic, 3.73 percent multiracial, 0.46 percent Native Hawaiian or Pacific Islander, and 55.45 percent white. There are 1,294 international students.

Student Activities

Participation in campus life is encouraged, and the college is home to more than seventy student organizations, societies, athletic teams, major-related groups, and special-interest clubs. Each organization is open to all students who have paid their activity fee.

Student Government: The Student Council, the governing body of the Student Association, grants all students the privileges and responsibilities of citizens in a self-governing college community. Faculty committees often include student representatives, and the president of the student government sits on FIT's Board of Trustees.

Athletics: FIT has intercollegiate teams in cross-country, half marathon, track and field, table tennis, tennis, soccer, swimming and diving, and volleyball. Athletics and Recreation offers a full array of group fitness classes, including aerobics, dance, spin, and yoga at no extra cost. Students can also work out on their own in a 5,000-square-foot fitness center. Open gym activities allow students to participate in both team and individual sports.

Events: Concerts, dances, field trips, films, flea markets, and other events are planned by the Student Association and Programming Board and various clubs. Student-run publications include a campus newspaper, a literary and art magazine, and the FIT yearbook.

Facilities and Resources

FIT's campus provides its students with classrooms, laboratories, and studios that reflect the most advanced educational and industry practices. The Fred P. Pomerantz Art and Design Center houses drawing, painting, photography, printmaking, and sculpture studios; display and exhibit design rooms; a model-making work-shop; and a graphics printing service bureau. The Peter G. Scotese Computer-Aided Design and Communications Center provides the latest technology in computer graphics, design, photography, and animation. Other cutting-edge facilities include a professionally equipped fragrance-development laboratory—the only one of its kind on a U.S. college campus—cutting and sewing labs, a design/research lighting laboratory, knitting lab, broadcasting studio, multimedia foreign languages laboratory, and forty-six computer labs containing Mac and PC workstations.

The Museum at FIT, New York City's only museum dedicated to fashion, contains one of the most important collections of fashion and textiles in the world. The museum, which is accredited by the American Alliance of Museums, operates year-round, and its exhibitions are free and open to the public. The Gladys Marcus Library provides more than 300,000 volumes of print, nonprint, and electronic materials. The periodicals collection includes over 500 current subscriptions, with a specialization in international design and trade publications; online resources include more than 90 searchable databases.

The David Dubinsky Student Center offers student lounges, a game room, a student radio station, the Style Shop (a student-run boutique), a full-service dining hall and Starbucks, student government and club offices, disability services, comprehensive health services and a counseling center, two gyms, a state-of-the-art fitness center, and a dance studio.

Location

Occupying an entire block in Manhattan's Chelsea neighborhood, FIT makes extensive use of the city's creative, commercial, and cultural resources, providing students with unrivaled internship opportunities and professional connections. A wide range of cultural and entertainment options are available within a short walk of the campus, as is convenient access to several subway and bus lines and the city's major rail and bus transportation hubs.

Admission Requirements

Applicants for admission must be either candidates for or recipients of a high school diploma or a General Educational Development (GED) certificate. Admission is based on strength and performance in college-preparatory coursework, and the student essay. A portfolio evaluation is required for art and design majors. Specific portfolio requirements are explained on FIT's website. SAT and ACT scores are required for placement in math and English classes and they are required for students applying to the Presidential Scholars honors program. International applicants whose native language is not English must submit scores from TOEFL or IELTS examinations.

Transfer students must submit official transcripts for admission and credit evaluation. Students may qualify for the one-year A.A.S. option if they hold a bachelor's degree or if they have a minimum of 30 transferable college credits, including 24 credits equivalent to FIT's liberal arts requirements.

Students seeking admission to a B.F.A. or B.S. program must hold an A.A.S. degree from FIT or an equivalent college degree and must meet the prerequisites for the specific major. Further requirements may include an interview with a departmental committee, review of academic standing, and portfolio review for applicants to B.F.A. programs. Any student who applies for baccalaureate-level transfer to FIT from a four-year program must have completed a minimum of 60 credits, including the requisite art or technical courses and the liberal arts requirements.

Application and Information

Students wishing to visit FIT are encouraged to attend a group information session and take a tour of FIT's campus. The visit schedule is available online at fitnyc.edu/visitfit. A virtual tour of the campus can be found at fitnyc.edu/virtualtour. Candidates may apply online at fitnyc.edu/admissions. More information is available by contacting:

Admissions
Fashion Institute of Technology
227 West 27 Street, Room C139
New York, New York 10001-5992
Phone: 212-217-3760
      800-GO-TO-FIT (toll-free)
E-mail: fitinfo@fitnyc.edu
Website: http://www.fitnyc.edu
      http://www.facebook.com/FashionInstituteofTechnology

FIDM/FASHION INSTITUTE OF DESIGN & MERCHANDISING

LOS ANGELES, CALIFORNIA

The Institute and Its Mission

FIDM/Fashion Institute of Design & Merchandising provides a dynamic and exciting community of learning in the fashion, graphics, interior design, digital media, and entertainment industries. Students can launch into one of thousands of exciting careers in as little as two years. FIDM offers two-year and four-year degree programs—Associate of Arts (A.A.), A.A. professional designation, A.A. advanced study, and Bachelor of Science (B.S.).

FIDM offers a highly focused education that prepares students for the professional world. Students can choose from twenty specialized creative business and design majors.

Established in 1969, FIDM is a private college that enrolls more than 7,500 students a year and has graduated nearly 50,000 students. Graduates receive membership in the Alumni Association, which keeps them well connected while providing up-to-the-minute alumni news and information. FIDM alumni chapters can be found in thirty-five locations around the United States, Europe, and Asia.

Career planning and job placement are among the most important services offered by the college. Career assistance includes job search techniques, preparation for employment interviews, resume preparation, virtual portfolios, and job adjustment assistance. FIDM's full-time Career Center department and advisers partner one-on-one with current students and graduates to help them move forward on their career path, within their chosen major. Employers post over 19,000 jobs a year on FIDM's alumni job search site, which is available 24/7 exclusively to FIDM students and graduates. FIDM career advisers connect students to internships and directly to professionals in the industry. FIDM also offers job fairs, open portfolio days, and networking days to allow students to meet alumni and industry leaders face-to-face. Because of the college's long-standing industry relationships, many firms come to FIDM first to recruit its students. Over 90 percent of FIDM graduates in all majors are successfully employed in their field of study within six months of graduation. Some of FIDM's successful graduates include celebrity designers Nick Verreos, Monique Lhuillier, and the co-founder of Juicy Couture, as well as Hollywood costume designer Marlene Stewart.

FIDM's ethnically and culturally diverse student body is one of the factors that attracts students. The current population includes students from more than thirty different countries. The Student Activities Department plans and coordinates social activities, cultural events, and community projects. Student organizations include the ASID student chapter, Cross-Cultural Student Alliance, American Association of Textile Chemists and Colorists, Phi Theta Kappa honor society, and the Alumni Association. The students also produce *FIDM MODE*, the student magazine that promotes awareness about the design industry, current events, and FIDM student life.

FIDM is accredited by the Accrediting Commission for Community and Junior and Senior Colleges of the Western Association of Schools and Colleges (WASC) and the National Association of Schools of Art and Design (NASAD).

Academic Programs

FIDM offers Associate of Arts (A.A.) degree programs, Bachelor's degree programs, Advanced Study programs, and Professional Designation programs. There are 22 specialized creative business and design majors to choose from.

Students can choose from the following Associate of Arts degrees: Apparel Industry Management, Beauty Industry

Merchandising & Marketing, Digital Media, Fashion Design, Fashion Knitwear Design, Graphic Design, Interior Design, Jewelry Design, Merchandise Marketing, Merchandising Product Development, Textile Design, and Visual Communications. All of these programs offer the highly specialized curriculum of a specific major combined with a core general education/liberal arts foundation.

Many FIDM A.A. graduates take their skills to the next level through FIDM's B.S. in Business Management program as well. Only FIDM graduates from A.A. majors are eligible to apply to the Bachelor's program, which is offered at the Los Angeles and San Francisco campuses and available online. Students from all FIDM majors study and collaborate on business projects and take courses in accounting, human resource management, international finance, ethics, leadership, and more, giving them extensive knowledge of managing a business and the creative edge that is a growing necessity in the corporate world. FIDM's unique industry partnerships offer exciting opportunities for students through internships, job fairs events, and informative guest speakers that include companies such as Forever 21, JCPenney, Mattel, NBC Universal, Oakley, Smashbox, and Stila.

Students from other regionally accredited college programs have the opportunity to complement their previous college education by enrolling in FIDM's Professional Designation programs. Students can determine which credits will transfer and receive a personalized schedule toward completion of their professional designation program by consulting with FIDM admissions advisers. FIDM offers professional designation programs in Apparel Industry Management, Beauty Industry Management, Digital Media, Fashion Design, Fashion Knitwear Design, Graphic Design, Interior Design, International Manufacturing and Product Development, Jewelry Design, Textile Design, and Visual Communications. For more information about FIDM transfer programs, students can visit http://fidm.edu/go/admissionstransfer.

FIDM operates on a four-quarter academic calendar. New students may begin their studies at the start of any quarter throughout the year. Detailed information about FIDM majors and curriculum is also available online at http://fidm.edu/en/Majors/.

Department chairs and trained Advisors assist students in selecting the correct sequence of courses to complete degree requirements. The counseling department provides personal guidance and referral to outside counseling services and matches peer tutors to specific students' needs. Individual Development and Education Assistance (IDEA) Centers at each campus provide students with additional educational assistance in the areas of writing, mathematics, computer competency, study skills, research skills, and reading comprehension.

FIDM's eLearning program, which includes the B.S. in Business Management and some classes in other majors, ensures that a student's educational experience can take place anywhere. The online courses are designed to replicate the experience of classes on campus. Students in the eLearning program are granted the same high-quality education as students on campus and have immediate access to valuable campus resources, including the FIDM Library, career advisers, and instructors.

Off-Campus Programs

Internships are available within each major. Paid and volunteer positions provide work experience for students to gain practical application of classroom skills.

FIDM provides the opportunity for students to participate in academic study tours in Europe, Asia, and New York. These tours are specifically designed to broaden and enhance the specialized education offered at FIDM. Participants may earn academic credit under faculty-supervised directed studies. Exchange programs are also available with Esmod, Paris; Instituto Artictico dell' Abbigliamento Marangoni, Milan; Accademia Internazionale d'Alta Mode e d'Arte del Costume Koefia, Rome; St. Martins School of Art, London; College of Distributive Trades, London; and Janette Klein Design School, Mexico City.

Costs

For the 2012–13 academic year, tuition, fees, books, and most supplies started at $27,910, depending on the selected major. First-year application fees range from $225 for California residents to $525 for international students.

Financial Aid

There are several sources of financial funding available to the student, including federal financial aid and education loan programs, California state aid programs, institutional loan programs, and FIDM awards and scholarships. The FIDM Student Financial Services Office and FIDM admissions advisors work one-on-one with students and parents to help them find funding for their FIDM education. More information on FIDM scholarships and financial aid can be found at http://fidm.edu/go/fidmscholarships.

Faculty

FIDM faculty members are selected as specialists in their fields, working professionals with impressive resumes and invaluable industry connections. They bring daily exposure from their industry into the classroom for the benefit of the students. In pursuit of the best faculty members, consideration is given to both academic excellence and practical experience.

Facilities and Resources

FIDM's award-winning campuses feature design studios with computer labs and innovative study spaces, spacious classrooms, imaginative common areas, and state-of-the-industry technology. Computer labs support and enhance the educational programs of the Institute. Specialized labs offer computerized cutting and marking; graphic, interior, and textile design; word processing; and database management.

The FIDM Library goes beyond traditional sources of information. It houses a print and electronic collection of over 2.5 million titles that encompass all subject areas, with an emphasis on fashion, interior design, retailing, and costume. The library subscribes to over 160 international and national periodicals, offering the latest information on art, design, graphics, fashion, beauty, business, and current trends. The FIDM Library also features an international video library, subscriptions to major predictive services, interior design workrooms, textile samples, a trimmings/findings collection, and access to the Internet.

The FIDM Museum & Galleries' permanent and study collections contain more than 12,000 garments from the eighteenth century to present day, including film and theater costumes. One of the largest collections in the United States, it features top designer holdings including Chanel, Yves Saint Laurent, Dior, and Lacroix. The collection also includes items from the California Historical Society (First Families), the Hollywood Collection, and the Rudi Gernreich Collection.

Location

FIDM's main campus is in the heart of downtown Los Angeles near the famed California Market Center and Fashion District. There are additional California campuses in San Francisco, San Diego, and Orange County. A virtual tour of the campuses and their locations is available at http://fidm.edu/en/Visit+FIDM/Launch+Virtual+Tour.

FIDM Los Angeles is nestled at the center of an incredibly vibrant apparel and entertainment hub, surrounded by the fashion, entertainment, jewelry, and financial districts. It is situated next to beautiful Grand Hope Park, a tree-filled oasis amid the hustle and bustle of downtown Los Angeles. Newly renovated by acclaimed architect Clive Wilkinson, FIDM San Francisco stands in the heart of historic Union Square. The country's third-largest shopping area and stimulating atmosphere combined with the industry-based staff and faculty make this campus as incredible as the city in which it is located.

The FIDM Orange County campus is a dynamic visual experience with ultramodern lofts, an indoor/outdoor student lounge, eye-popping colors, and a one-of-a-kind audiovisual igloo. Also designed by world-renowned architect Clive Wilkinson, this campus has received several prestigious architectural awards and has been featured in numerous national magazines.

FIDM San Diego's gorgeous campus overlooks PETCO Park and is near the historic Gaslamp district and the San Diego harbor. FIDM's newest campus is sophisticated, stylish, and tech savvy, reflecting the importance of California's fastest-growing city and its appeal to the global industry.

Admission Requirements

Students are accepted into one of FIDM's specialized Associate of Arts degree programs which offer 16–25 challenging courses per major. Associate of Arts programs are designed for high school graduates or applicants with strong GED scores. These programs offer the highly specialized curriculum of a specific major, as well as a traditional liberal arts/ general studies foundation. Official transcripts from high school/secondary schools and all colleges/universities attended are needed to apply. International students must send transcripts accompanied by official English translations. Three recommendations from teachers, counselors, or employers are also required for admission. FIDM provides a reference request form on its website in the Admissions section under "How To Apply." All references must be sealed and mailed to the school when applying. An admissions essay portion and portfolio/entrance project requirement, which is specific to the student's selected major, are also available on the website's Admissions section under "How To Apply."

For more information on the application process, prospective students can go to www.fidm.edu.

Application and Information

FIDM/Fashion Institute of Design & Merchandising
919 South Grand Avenue
Los Angeles, California 90015
United States
Phone: 800-624-1200 (toll-free)
Fax: 213-624-4799
Website: http://www.fidm.edu
http://www.facebook.com/home.php/#!/FIDMCollege
http://twitter.com/#!/FIDM

FIDM Los Angeles (exterior campus)

Indexes

2012–13 Changes in Institutions

Following is an alphabetical listing of institutions that have recently closed, merged with other institutions, or changed their name or status. In the case of a name change, the former name appears first, followed by the new name.

Academy of Court Reporting (Cleveland, OH): *name changed to Miami-Jacobs Career College.*

ACT College (Arlington, VA): *closed.*

American Academy of Dramatic Arts (New York, NY): *name changed to American Academy of Dramatic Arts–New York.*

Anthem College Aurora (Aurora, CO): *name changed to Anthem College–Aurora.*

Arizona College of Allied Health (Glendale, AZ): *name changed to Arizona College.*

Atlanta Metropolitan College (Atlanta, GA): *name hanged to Atlanta Metropolitan State College.*

Belmont Technical College (St. Clairsville, OH): *name changed to Belmont College.*

College of Health Care Professions (Houston, TX): *name changed to The College of Health Care Professions.*

Colorado Mountain College (Glenwood Springs, CO): *now classified as 4-year college.*

Colorado Mountain College, Alpine Campus (Steamboat Springs, CO): *now classified as 4-year college.*

Colorado Mountain College, Timberline Campus (Leadville, CO): *now classified as 4-year college.*

Creative Center (Omaha, NE): *now classified as 4-year college.*

Darton College (Albany, GA): *name changed to Darton State College.*

East Georgia College (Swainsboro, GA): *name changed to East Georgia State College.*

Everest College (Rancho Cucamonga, CA): *closed.*

Fashion Careers College (San Diego, CA): *closed.*

Fort Belknap College (Harlem, MT): *name changed to Aaniiih Nakoda College.*

Gainesville State College (Gainesville, GA): *merged into a single entry for University of North Georgia (Dahlonega, GA).*

Gordon College (Barnesville, GA): *name changed to Gordon State College.*

Gretna Career College (Gretna, LA): *closed.*

Harrison College (Anderson, IN): *merged into a single entry for Harrison College (Indianapolis, IN) by request from the institution and now classified as 4-year college.*

Harrison College (Columbus, IN): *merged into a single entry for Harrison College (Indianapolis, IN) by request from the institution and now classified as 4-year college.*

Harrison College (Elkhart, IN): *merged into a single entry for Harrison College (Indianapolis, IN) by request from the institution and now classified as 4-year college.*

Harrison College (Evansville, IN): *merged into a single entry for Harrison College (Indianapolis, IN) by request from the institution and now classified as 4-year college.*

Harrison College (Fort Wayne, IN): *merged into a single entry for Harrison College (Indianapolis, IN) by request from the institution and now classified as 4-year college.*

Harrison College (Indianapolis, IN): *now classified as 4-year college.*

Harrison College (Lafayette, IN): *merged into a single entry for Harrison College (Indianapolis, IN) by request from the institution and now classified as 4-year college.*

Harrison College (Muncie, IN): *merged into a single entry for Harrison College (Indianapolis, IN) by request from the institution and now classified as 4-year college.*

Harrison College (Terre Haute, IN): *merged into a single entry for Harrison College (Indianapolis, IN) by request from the institution and now classified as 4-year college.*

Harrison College (Grove City, OH): *now classified as 4-year college.*

Hill College of the Hill Junior College District (Hillsboro, TX): *name changed to Hill College.*

IHM Health Studies Center (St. Louis, MO): *name changed to IHM Academy of EMS.*

Indian River State College (Fort Pierce, FL): *now classified as 4-year college.*

Jackson Community College (Jackson, MI): *name changed to Jackson College.*

Kaplan Career Institute, Dearborn Campus (Detroit, MI): *closed.*

Kaplan Career Institute, ICM Campus (Pittsburgh, PA): *name changed to Kaplan Career Institute, Pittsburgh Campus.*

Kaplan College, Chesapeake Campus (Chesapeake, VA): *closed.*

Kaplan College, Cincinnati Campus (Cincinnati, OH): *closed.*

Kaplan College, Columbus Campus (Columbus, OH): *closed.*

Kaplan College, Midland Campus (Midland, TX): *closed.*

Kaplan College, Milwaukee Campus (Milwaukee, WI): *closed.*

Kaplan College, Northwest Indianapolis Campus (Indianapolis, IN): *closed.*

Kaplan College, Pembroke Pines Campus (Pembroke Pines, FL): *closed.*

Kaplan College, Phoenix Campus (Phoenix, AZ): *closed.*

Kaplan College, Stockton Campus (Stockton, CA): *closed.*

Keiser Career College–Greenacres (Greenacres, FL): *name changed to Southeastern College–Greenacres.*

Lake-Sumter Community College (Leesburg, FL): *name changed to Lake-Sumter State College.*

Lake Washington Technical College (Kirkland, WA): *name changed to Lake Washington Institute of Technology.*

Lamson College (Tempe, AZ): *closed.*

Lincoln College of Technology (Cincinnati, OH): *closed.*

Lincoln College of Technology (Franklin, OH): *closed.*

Lon Morris College (Jacksonville, TX): *closed.*

Metropolitan Career Center (Philadelphia, PA): *name changed to Metropolitan Career Center Computer Technology Institute.*

Metropolitan Community College–Blue River (Independence, MO): *merged into a single entry for Metropolitan Community College–Kansas City (Lee's Summit, MO) by request from the institution.*

Metropolitan Community College–Business & Technology Campus (Kansas City, MO): *merged into a single entry for Metropolitan Community College–Kansas City (Lee's Summit, MO) by request from the institution.*

Metropolitan Community College–Longview (Lee's Summit, MO): *name changed to Metropolitan Community College–Kansas City.*

Metropolitan Community College–Maple Woods (Kansas City, MO): *merged into a single entry for Metropolitan Community*

College–Kansas City *(Lee's Summit, MO) by request from the institution.*

Metropolitan Community College–Penn Valley (Kansas City, MO): *merged into a single entry for Metropolitan Community College–Kansas City (Lee's Summit, MO) by request from the institution.*

Middle Georgia College (Cochran, GA): *now classified as 4-year college and name changed to Middle Georgia State College.*

Montana State University–Great Falls College of Technology (Great Falls, MT): *name changed to Great Falls College Montana State University.*

Nashville Auto Diesel College (Nashville, TN): *name changed to Lincoln College of Technology.*

Nashville State Technical Community College (Nashville, TN): *name changed to Nashville State Community College.*

National College (Bristol, TN): *name changed to National College of Business and Technology.*

National College (Knoxville, TN): *name changed to National College of Business and Technology.*

National College (Nashville, TN): *name changed to National College of Business and Technology.*

National College (Bluefield, VA): *closed.*

Northeast State Technical Community College (Blountville, TN): *name changed to Northeast State Community College.*

Northshore Technical College–Florida Parishes Campus (Greensburg, LA): *name changed to Northshore Technical Community College–Florida Parishes Campus.*

Palm Beach State College (Lake Worth, FL): *now classified as 4-year college.*

Pellissippi State Technical Community College (Knoxville, TN): *name changed to Pellissippi State Community College.*

Penn State Shenango (Sharon, PA): *now classified as 4-year college.*

Platt College (Aurora, CO): *now classified as 4-year college.*

Polk State College (Winter Haven, FL): *now classified as 4-year college.*

Puerto Rico Technical Junior College (San Juan, PR): *closed.*

Remington College–Colorado Springs Campus (Colorado Springs, CO): *closed.*

Remington College–Largo Campus (Largo, FL): *closed.*

St. Johns River Community College (Palatka, FL): *name changed to St. Johns River State College.*

Sanford-Brown College (Fenton, MO): *closed.*

Sanford-Brown College (St. Peters, MO): *closed.*

Sanford-Brown Institute–Wilkins Township (Pittsburgh, PA): *closed.*

Seward County Community College (Liberal, KS): *name changed to Seward County Community College and Area Technical School.*

South Florida Community College (Avon Park, FL): *name changed to South Florida State College.*

South Georgia College (Douglas, GA): *name changed to South Georgia State College.*

State College of Florida Manatee-Sarasota (Bradenton, FL): *now classified as 4-year college.*

State University of New York College of Environmental Science & Forestry, Ranger School (Wanakena, NY): *name changed to State University of New York College of Environmental Science and Forestry, Ranger School.*

Valencia College (Orlando, FL): *now classified as 4-year college.*

Virginia College at Austin (Austin, TX): *name changed to Virginia College in Austin.*

Virginia College at Jackson (Jackson, MS): *name changed to Virginia College in Jackson.*

Waycross College (Waycross, GA): *name changed to South Georgia State College.*

West Virginia Junior College (Charleston, WV): *name changed to West Virginia Junior College–Charleston.*

West Virginia Junior College (Morgantown, WV): *name changed to West Virginia Junior College–Morgantown.*

Westwood College–Houston South Campus (Houston, TX): *closed.*

Associate Degree Programs at Two-Year Colleges

ACCOUNTING
Adirondack Comm Coll (NY)
Alexandria Tech and Comm Coll (MN)
Alpena Comm Coll (MI)
Alvin Comm Coll (TX)
Amarillo Coll (TX)
Anoka-Ramsey Comm Coll (MN)
Anoka-Ramsey Comm Coll, Cambridge Campus (MN)
Arizona Western Coll (AZ)
Bainbridge Coll (GA)
Bakersfield Coll (CA)
Barton County Comm Coll (KS)
Bay State Coll (MA)
Beaufort County Comm Coll (NC)
Berkeley City Coll (CA)
Blackhawk Tech Coll (WI)
Brookhaven Coll (TX)
Burlington County Coll (NJ)
Butte Coll (CA)
Carroll Comm Coll (MD)
Casper Coll (WY)
Central Carolina Comm Coll (NC)
Central New Mexico Comm Coll (NM)
Central Oregon Comm Coll (OR)
Central Wyoming Coll (WY)
Century Coll (MN)
Chemeketa Comm Coll (OR)
Chipola Coll (FL)
Chippewa Valley Tech Coll (WI)
Clark State Comm Coll (OH)
Cleveland Comm Coll (NC)
Clinton Comm Coll (NY)
Coll of Southern Maryland (MD)
Colorado Northwestern Comm Coll (CO)
Comm Coll of Philadelphia (PA)
Comm Coll of Rhode Island (RI)
Comm Coll of Vermont (VT)
Copiah-Lincoln Comm Coll (MS)
Corning Comm Coll (NY)
Cowley County Comm Coll and Area Vocational–Tech School (KS)
Cuyahoga Comm Coll (OH)
Dakota Coll at Bottineau (ND)
Darton State Coll (GA)
Daytona State Coll (FL)
De Anza Coll (CA)
Delaware Tech & Comm Coll, Jack F. Owens Campus (DE)
Delaware Tech & Comm Coll, Stanton/Wilmington Campus (DE)
Delaware Tech & Comm Coll, Terry Campus (DE)
Dutchess Comm Coll (NY)
Eastern Idaho Tech Coll (ID)
Edison Comm Coll (OH)
El Centro Coll (TX)
Elgin Comm Coll (IL)
Elmira Business Inst (NY)
Essex County Coll (NJ)
Fayetteville Tech Comm Coll (NC)
Finger Lakes Comm Coll (NY)
Flathead Valley Comm Coll (MT)
Foothill Coll (CA)
Forrest Coll (SC)
Forsyth Tech Comm Coll (NC)
Fox Valley Tech Coll (WI)
Gateway Tech Coll (WI)
Genesee Comm Coll (NY)
Halifax Comm Coll (NC)
Harford Comm Coll (MD)
Harper Coll (IL)
Hawkeye Comm Coll (IA)
Highland Comm Coll (IL)
Housatonic Comm Coll (CT)
Houston Comm Coll System (TX)

Howard Comm Coll (MD)
Illinois Central Coll (IL)
Illinois Eastern Comm Colls, Olney Central College (IL)
Ivy Tech Comm Coll–Lafayette (IN)
James Sprunt Comm Coll (NC)
Jefferson Comm Coll (NY)
J. F. Drake State Tech Coll (AL)
Johnston Comm Coll (NC)
Kaskaskia Coll (IL)
Kent State U at Ashtabula (OH)
Kent State U at Tuscarawas (OH)
Kilian Comm Coll (SD)
Klamath Comm Coll (OR)
Lakeland Comm Coll (OH)
Lake Michigan Coll (MI)
Lake Superior Coll (MN)
Laramie County Comm Coll (WY)
LDS Business Coll (UT)
Lincoln Land Comm Coll (IL)
Lone Star Coll–CyFair (TX)
Lone Star Coll–Kingwood (TX)
Lone Star Coll–North Harris (TX)
Lone Star Coll–Tomball (TX)
Long Island Business Inst (NY)
Lorain County Comm Coll (OH)
Lower Columbia Coll (WA)
Luzerne County Comm Coll (PA)
Macomb Comm Coll (MI)
Manchester Comm Coll (CT)
Manor Coll (PA)
Massachusetts Bay Comm Coll (MA)
McCann School of Business & Technology, Pottsville (PA)
McHenry County Coll (IL)
Mendocino Coll (CA)
Mesa Comm Coll (AZ)
Metropolitan Comm Coll–Kansas City (MO)
Minnesota West Comm and Tech Coll (MN)
Missouri State U–West Plains (MO)
Mohave Comm Coll (AZ)
Monroe Comm Coll (NY)
Monroe County Comm Coll (MI)
Montcalm Comm Coll (MI)
Montgomery County Comm Coll (PA)
Moraine Park Tech Coll (WI)
Mt. San Antonio Coll (CA)
Nassau Comm Coll (NY)
Niagara County Comm Coll (NY)
Northeastern Jr Coll (CO)
Northeast Iowa Comm Coll (IA)
Northern Essex Comm Coll (MA)
North Hennepin Comm Coll (MN)
North Shore Comm Coll (MA)
NorthWest Arkansas Comm Coll (AR)
Northwest Coll (WY)
Northwest State Comm Coll (OH)
Northwest Tech Coll (MN)
Norwalk Comm Coll (CT)
Oklahoma City Comm Coll (OK)
Oklahoma State U, Oklahoma City (OK)
Onondaga Comm Coll (NY)
Orange Coast Coll (CA)
Ozarks Tech Comm Coll (MO)
Pasadena City Coll (CA)
Pensacola State Coll (FL)
Phoenix Coll (AZ)
Piedmont Comm Coll (NC)
Pierce Coll at Puyallup (WA)
Potomac State Coll of West Virginia U (WV)
Randolph Comm Coll (NC)
Rappahannock Comm Coll (VA)
Rasmussen Coll Aurora (IL)
Rasmussen Coll Bismarck (ND)

Rasmussen Coll Bloomington (MN)
Rasmussen Coll Brooklyn Park (MN)
Rasmussen Coll Eagan (MN)
Rasmussen Coll Fort Myers (FL)
Rasmussen Coll Green Bay (WI)
Rasmussen Coll Lake Elmo/Woodbury (MN)
Rasmussen Coll Mankato (MN)
Rasmussen Coll Moorhead (MN)
Rasmussen Coll New Port Richey (FL)
Rasmussen Coll Ocala (FL)
Rasmussen Coll St. Cloud (MN)
St. Philip's Coll (TX)
San Diego City Coll (CA)
San Diego Mesa Coll (CA)
San Jacinto Coll District (TX)
Schoolcraft Coll (MI)
Scottsdale Comm Coll (AZ)
Seminole State Coll of Florida (FL)
Shawnee Comm Coll (IL)
Sierra Coll (CA)
Southeastern Comm Coll (IA)
Southeast Tech Inst (SD)
South Plains Coll (TX)
South Puget Sound Comm Coll (WA)
South Suburban Coll (IL)
Spartanburg Comm Coll (SC)
Spoon River Coll (IL)
Springfield Tech Comm Coll (MA)
Stark State Coll (OH)
Sullivan County Comm Coll (NY)
Taft Coll (CA)
Tarrant County Coll District (TX)
Terra State Comm Coll (OH)
Tri-County Comm Coll (NC)
Trident Tech Coll (SC)
Tunxis Comm Coll (CT)
Tyler Jr Coll (TX)
U of Pittsburgh at Titusville (PA)
Virginia Western Comm Coll (VA)
Waubonsee Comm Coll (IL)
Waukesha County Tech Coll (WI)
Westchester Comm Coll (NY)
Western Dakota Tech Inst (SD)
Western Iowa Tech Comm Coll (IA)
West Kentucky Comm and Tech Coll (KY)
Wilson Comm Coll (NC)
Wisconsin Indianhead Tech Coll (WI)
Wytheville Comm Coll (VA)
York County Comm Coll (ME)

ACCOUNTING AND BUSINESS/MANAGEMENT
Berkeley City Coll (CA)
Bradford School (OH)
Harrisburg Area Comm Coll (PA)
King's Coll (NC)
LDS Business Coll (UT)
Lone Star Coll–Montgomery (TX)
Mitchell Tech Inst (SD)
Oakland Comm Coll (MI)

ACCOUNTING AND FINANCE
Jackson Coll (MI)

ACCOUNTING RELATED
Dakota Coll at Bottineau (ND)
John Tyler Comm Coll (VA)
Lansing Comm Coll (MI)
Northwest State Comm Coll (OH)
Raritan Valley Comm Coll (NJ)
Southwest Virginia Comm Coll (VA)
Thomas Nelson Comm Coll (VA)

ACCOUNTING TECHNOLOGY AND BOOKKEEPING
Adirondack Comm Coll (NY)
Alamance Comm Coll (NC)

Anne Arundel Comm Coll (MD)
Anoka-Ramsey Comm Coll (MN)
Anoka-Ramsey Comm Coll, Cambridge Campus (MN)
Arapahoe Comm Coll (CO)
Austin Comm Coll (TX)
Big Bend Comm Coll (WA)
Borough of Manhattan Comm Coll of the City U of New York (NY)
Bradford School (OH)
Bradford School (PA)
Bucks County Comm Coll (PA)
Cape Fear Comm Coll (NC)
Carrington Coll California–Pleasant Hill (CA)
Carrington Coll California–San Jose (CA)
Carrington Coll California–San Leandro (CA)
Carrington Coll of California–Citrus Heights (CA)
Casper Coll (WY)
Catawba Valley Comm Coll (NC)
Cayuga County Comm Coll (NY)
Central Maine Comm Coll (ME)
Central Wyoming Coll (WY)
Chemeketa Comm Coll (OR)
Clark Coll (WA)
Coll of Lake County (IL)
Coll of Marin (CA)
Coll of Southern Maryland (MD)
Coll of the Canyons (CA)
Comm Coll of Allegheny County (PA)
The Comm Coll of Baltimore County (MD)
Comm Coll of Beaver County (PA)
Dakota Coll at Bottineau (ND)
Essex County Coll (NJ)
Fiorello H. LaGuardia Comm Coll of the City U of New York (NY)
Fox Coll (IL)
Gadsden State Comm Coll (AL)
Gateway Comm and Tech Coll (KY)
Glendale Comm Coll (AZ)
Goodwin Coll (CT)
Great Falls Coll Montana State U (MT)
Greenfield Comm Coll (MA)
Guilford Tech Comm Coll (NC)
Hagerstown Comm Coll (MD)
Harford Comm Coll (MD)
Harrisburg Area Comm Coll (PA)
Hillsborough Comm Coll (FL)
Holyoke Comm Coll (MA)
Illinois Central Coll (IL)
International Business Coll, Indianapolis (IN)
Ivy Tech Comm Coll–Bloomington (IN)
Ivy Tech Comm Coll–Central Indiana (IN)
Ivy Tech Comm Coll–Columbus (IN)
Ivy Tech Comm Coll–East Central (IN)
Ivy Tech Comm Coll–Kokomo (IN)
Ivy Tech Comm Coll–Lafayette (IN)
Ivy Tech Comm Coll–North Central (IN)
Ivy Tech Comm Coll–Northeast (IN)
Ivy Tech Comm Coll–Northwest (IN)
Ivy Tech Comm Coll–Richmond (IN)
Ivy Tech Comm Coll–Southeast (IN)
Ivy Tech Comm Coll–Southern Indiana (IN)
Ivy Tech Comm Coll–Southwest (IN)
Ivy Tech Comm Coll–Wabash Valley (IN)
James A. Rhodes State Coll (OH)
Jamestown Comm Coll (NY)

Jefferson Comm Coll (NY)
Jefferson State Comm Coll (AL)
J. F. Drake State Tech Coll (AL)
Johnston Comm Coll (NC)
Kennebec Valley Comm Coll (ME)
Kent State U at Ashtabula (OH)
Kent State U at East Liverpool (OH)
Kent State U at Salem (OH)
Kent State U at Trumbull (OH)
Kent State U at Tuscarawas (OH)
Kilgore Coll (TX)
King's Coll (NC)
Lansing Comm Coll (MI)
Lawson State Comm Coll (AL)
LDS Business Coll (UT)
Lehigh Carbon Comm Coll (PA)
Lower Columbia Coll (WA)
Lurleen B. Wallace Comm Coll (AL)
Miami Dade Coll (FL)
Minneapolis Business Coll (MN)
Mohawk Valley Comm Coll (NY)
Montgomery Coll (MD)
Montgomery County Comm Coll (PA)
Mott Comm Coll (MI)
Nassau Comm Coll (NY)
Northampton Comm Coll (PA)
Oakland Comm Coll (MI)
Oakton Comm Coll (IL)
Olympic Coll (WA)
Onondaga Comm Coll (NY)
Owens Comm Coll, Toledo (OH)
Parkland Coll (IL)
Pasadena City Coll (CA)
Pensacola State Coll (FL)
Raritan Valley Comm Coll (NJ)
Red Rocks Comm Coll (CO)
Rogue Comm Coll (OR)
St. Clair County Comm Coll (MI)
St. Louis Comm Coll at Forest Park (MO)
St. Louis Comm Coll at Meramec (MO)
Salt Lake Comm Coll (UT)
San Juan Coll (NM)
Schoolcraft Coll (MI)
Southern State Comm Coll (OH)
South Suburban Coll (IL)
Southwestern Michigan Coll (MI)
Spencerian Coll (KY)
State U of New York Coll of Technology at Alfred (NY)
Tallahassee Comm Coll (FL)
Tompkins Cortland Comm Coll (NY)
Union County Coll (NJ)
Vincennes U (IN)
Westmoreland County Comm Coll (PA)
Wood Tobe–Coburn School (NY)

ACTING
Casper Coll (WY)
Central Wyoming Coll (WY)
Greenfield Comm Coll (MA)
Northampton Comm Coll (PA)

ADMINISTRATIVE ASSISTANT AND SECRETARIAL SCIENCE
Alpena Comm Coll (MI)
Alvin Comm Coll (TX)
Amarillo Coll (TX)
Arkansas State U–Mountain Home (AR)
Austin Comm Coll (TX)
Bainbridge Coll (GA)
Bakersfield Coll (CA)
Barton County Comm Coll (KS)
Beaufort County Comm Coll (NC)
Bevill State Comm Coll (AL)
Bismarck State Coll (ND)
Blackhawk Tech Coll (WI)

Borough of Manhattan Comm Coll of the City U of New York (NY)
Bossier Parish Comm Coll (LA)
Bradford School (PA)
Butte Coll (CA)
Career Tech Coll (LA)
Casper Coll (WY)
Cecil Coll (MD)
Central Carolina Comm Coll (NC)
Central Maine Comm Coll (ME)
Central New Mexico Comm Coll (NM)
Central Oregon Comm Coll (OR)
Central Wyoming Coll (WY)
Century Coll (MN)
Chemeketa Comm Coll (OR)
Chippewa Valley Tech Coll (WI)
Clark State Comm Coll (OH)
Cleveland State Comm Coll (TN)
Clinton Comm Coll (NY)
Cochise Coll, Sierra Vista (AZ)
Colby Comm Coll (KS)
Coll of Lake County (IL)
Coll of the Canyons (CA)
Collin County Comm Coll District (TX)
Comm Coll of Allegheny County (PA)
The Comm Coll of Baltimore County (MD)
Comm Coll of Beaver County (PA)
Comm Coll of Rhode Island (RI)
Comm Coll of Vermont (VT)
County Coll of Morris (NJ)
Cowley County Comm Coll and Area Vocational–Tech School (KS)
Crowder Coll (MO)
Cuyahoga Comm Coll (OH)
Dabney S. Lancaster Comm Coll (VA)
Dakota Coll at Bottineau (ND)
Daytona State Coll (FL)
De Anza Coll (CA)
Denmark Tech Coll (SC)
Eastern Idaho Tech Coll (ID)
Eastern Shore Comm Coll (VA)
Elaine P. Nunez Comm Coll (LA)
Elgin Comm Coll (IL)
Elmira Business Inst (NY)
Essex County Coll (NJ)
Finger Lakes Comm Coll (NY)
Fiorello H. LaGuardia Comm Coll of the City U of New York (NY)
Flathead Valley Comm Coll (MT)
Fox Coll (IL)
Fox Valley Tech Coll (WI)
Gadsden State Comm Coll (AL)
Garden City Comm Coll (KS)
Gateway Tech Coll (WI)
Genesee Comm Coll (NY)
Glendale Comm Coll (AZ)
Greenfield Comm Coll (MA)
Harper Coll (IL)
Harrisburg Area Comm Coll (PA)
Holyoke Comm Coll (MA)
Housatonic Comm Coll (CT)
Hutchinson Comm Coll and Area Vocational School (KS)
Illinois Central Coll (IL)
Illinois Eastern Comm Colls, Frontier Community College (IL)
Illinois Eastern Comm Colls, Olney Central College (IL)
Illinois Eastern Comm Colls, Wabash Valley College (IL)
International Business Coll, Indianapolis (IN)
Jackson Coll (MI)
James A. Rhodes State Coll (OH)
Jamestown Business Coll (NY)
Jamestown Comm Coll (NY)
Jefferson Coll (MO)
Jefferson Comm Coll (NY)
Jefferson State Comm Coll (AL)
J. F. Drake State Tech Coll (AL)
Johnston Comm Coll (NC)
John Tyler Comm Coll (VA)
Kankakee Comm Coll (IL)
Kent State U at Ashtabula (OH)
Kent State U at Salem (OH)
Kent State U at Trumbull (OH)
Kent State U at Tuscarawas (OH)
King's Coll (NC)
Kirtland Comm Coll (MI)
Klamath Comm Coll (OR)
Lakeland Comm Coll (OH)
Lake Michigan Coll (MI)
Lake Region State Coll (ND)
Lansing Comm Coll (MI)
Lawson State Comm Coll (AL)
LDS Business Coll (UT)

Lincoln Land Comm Coll (IL)
Lone Star Coll–Kingwood (TX)
Lone Star Coll–Montgomery (TX)
Lone Star Coll–North Harris (TX)
Lone Star Coll–Tomball (TX)
Lorain County Comm Coll (OH)
Lower Columbia Coll (WA)
Lurleen B. Wallace Comm Coll (AL)
Luzerne County Comm Coll (PA)
Macomb Comm Coll (MI)
Manchester Comm Coll (CT)
McHenry County Coll (IL)
Mendocino Coll (CA)
Mesa Comm Coll (AZ)
Miami Dade Coll (FL)
Mid-Plains Comm Coll, North Platte (NE)
Mineral Area Coll (MO)
Minneapolis Business Coll (MN)
Minnesota West Comm and Tech Coll (MN)
Mohawk Valley Comm Coll (NY)
Monroe Comm Coll (NY)
Monroe County Comm Coll (MI)
Montcalm Comm Coll (MI)
Montgomery County Comm Coll (PA)
Moraine Park Tech Coll (WI)
Moraine Valley Comm Coll (IL)
Mott Comm Coll (MI)
Mt. San Antonio Coll (CA)
Nassau Comm Coll (NY)
Niagara County Comm Coll (NY)
Northampton Comm Coll (PA)
North Dakota State Coll of Science (ND)
Northeast Iowa Comm Coll (IA)
Northern Essex Comm Coll (MA)
North Shore Comm Coll (MA)
NorthWest Arkansas Comm Coll (AR)
Northwest Coll (WY)
Northwest-Shoals Comm Coll (AL)
Northwest State Comm Coll (OH)
Northwest Tech Coll (MN)
Norwalk Comm Coll (CT)
Oakton Comm Coll (IL)
Ocean County Coll (NJ)
Oklahoma City Comm Coll (OK)
Olympic Coll (WA)
Orange Coast Coll (CA)
Oxnard Coll (CA)
Ozarks Tech Comm Coll (MO)
Panola Coll (TX)
Parkland Coll (IL)
Pasadena City Coll (CA)
Paul D. Camp Comm Coll (VA)
Pensacola State Coll (FL)
Phoenix Coll (AZ)
Pierce Coll at Puyallup (WA)
Potomac State Coll of West Virginia U (WV)
Rappahannock Comm Coll (VA)
Raritan Valley Comm Coll (NJ)
Reid State Tech Coll (AL)
Robeson Comm Coll (NC)
St. Philip's Coll (TX)
San Diego City Coll (CA)
San Diego Mesa Coll (CA)
San Jacinto Coll District (TX)
San Juan Coll (NM)
Schoolcraft Coll (MI)
Scottsdale Comm Coll (AZ)
Seminole State Coll of Florida (FL)
Shawnee Comm Coll (IL)
Shelton State Comm Coll (AL)
Sheridan Coll (WY)
Sierra Coll (CA)
Southeastern Comm Coll (IA)
Southern State Comm Coll (OH)
South Plains Coll (TX)
South Puget Sound Comm Coll (WA)
Southwestern Michigan Coll (MI)
Spartanburg Comm Coll (SC)
Spoon River Coll (IL)
Springfield Tech Comm Coll (MA)
Stark State Coll (OH)
Sullivan County Comm Coll (NY)
Taft Coll (CA)
Tallahassee Comm Coll (FL)
Tarrant County Coll District (TX)
Tech Coll of the Lowcountry (SC)
Temple Coll (TX)
Texarkana Coll (TX)
Texas State Tech Coll Harlingen (TX)
Tompkins Cortland Comm Coll (NY)
Trident Tech Coll (SC)
Tunxis Comm Coll (CT)
Tyler Jr Coll (TX)
The U of Akron–Wayne Coll (OH)
Victor Valley Coll (CA)

Vincennes U (IN)
Virginia Western Comm Coll (VA)
Waukesha County Tech Coll (WI)
Westchester Comm Coll (NY)
Western Iowa Tech Comm Coll (IA)
Westmoreland County Comm Coll (PA)
West Virginia Northern Comm Coll (WV)
Wisconsin Indianhead Tech Coll (WI)
Wood Tobe–Coburn School (NY)
Wytheville Comm Coll (VA)

ADULT AND CONTINUING EDUCATION
Cochise Coll, Sierra Vista (AZ)

ADULT DEVELOPMENT AND AGING
Comm Coll of Beaver County (PA)
Comm Coll of Rhode Island (RI)
Dakota Coll at Bottineau (ND)
Fiorello H. LaGuardia Comm Coll of the City U of New York (NY)
Oakland Comm Coll (MI)

ADVERTISING
Dakota Coll at Bottineau (ND)
Fashion Inst of Technology (NY)
Harford Comm Coll (MD)
Mohawk Valley Comm Coll (NY)
Mt. San Antonio Coll (CA)
Parkland Coll (IL)
South Plains Coll (TX)

AERONAUTICAL/AEROSPACE ENGINEERING TECHNOLOGY
Comm Coll of Beaver County (PA)
Delaware Tech & Comm Coll, Jack F. Owens Campus (DE)

AERONAUTICS/AVIATION/ AEROSPACE SCIENCE AND TECHNOLOGY
Alvin Comm Coll (TX)
Cecil Coll (MD)
The Comm Coll of Baltimore County (MD)
Comm Coll of the Air Force (AL)
Lehigh Carbon Comm Coll (PA)
Miami Dade Coll (FL)
Northwest Coll (WY)
Orange Coast Coll (CA)

AEROSPACE, AERONAUTICAL AND ASTRONAUTICAL/SPACE ENGINEERING
Kent State U at Ashtabula (OH)
Kilgore Coll (TX)

AFRICAN AMERICAN/BLACK STUDIES
Lansing Comm Coll (MI)
Nassau Comm Coll (NY)
San Diego City Coll (CA)
San Diego Mesa Coll (CA)

AGRIBUSINESS
Burlington County Coll (NJ)
Butte Coll (CA)
Colby Comm Coll (KS)
Coll of the Desert (CA)
Copiah-Lincoln Comm Coll (MS)
Crowder Coll (MO)
Harrisburg Area Comm Coll (PA)
James Sprunt Comm Coll (NC)
Laramie County Comm Coll (WY)
Mineral Area Coll (MO)
Minnesota West Comm and Tech Coll (MN)
Northeast Iowa Comm Coll (IA)
Northwest Coll (WY)
The Ohio State U Ag Tech Inst (OH)
San Jacinto Coll District (TX)
State U of New York Coll of Technology at Alfred (NY)

AGRICULTURAL AND DOMESTIC ANIMAL SERVICES RELATED
Central Wyoming Coll (WY)

AGRICULTURAL AND FOOD PRODUCTS PROCESSING
Garden City Comm Coll (KS)
Minnesota West Comm and Tech Coll (MN)
Northeast Iowa Comm Coll (IA)

AGRICULTURAL AND HORTICULTURAL PLANT BREEDING
Lake Michigan Coll (MI)

AGRICULTURAL BUSINESS AND MANAGEMENT
Arizona Western Coll (AZ)
Bakersfield Coll (CA)
Barton County Comm Coll (KS)
Bismarck State Coll (ND)
Casper Coll (WY)
Central Wyoming Coll (WY)
Chemeketa Comm Coll (OR)
Clark State Comm Coll (OH)
Cochise Coll, Sierra Vista (AZ)
Colby Comm Coll (KS)
Copiah-Lincoln Comm Coll (MS)
County Coll of Morris (NJ)
Delaware Tech & Comm Coll, Jack F. Owens Campus (DE)
Delaware Tech & Comm Coll, Stanton/Wilmington Campus (DE)
Delaware Tech & Comm Coll, Terry Campus (DE)
Harford Comm Coll (MD)
Highland Comm Coll (IL)
Illinois Central Coll (IL)
Illinois Eastern Comm Colls, Wabash Valley College (IL)
Lake Area Tech Inst (SD)
Lake Region State Coll (ND)
Lansing Comm Coll (MI)
Mesa Comm Coll (AZ)
Miles Comm Coll (MT)
Mt. San Antonio Coll (CA)
North Dakota State Coll of Science (ND)
Northeastern Jr Coll (CO)
The Ohio State U Ag Tech Inst (OH)
Parkland Coll (IL)
Potomac State Coll of West Virginia U (WV)
Santa Rosa Jr Coll (CA)
Shawnee Comm Coll (IL)
Sheridan Coll (WY)
Southeastern Comm Coll (IA)
Spoon River Coll (IL)
Terra State Comm Coll (OH)
Vincennes U (IN)

AGRICULTURAL BUSINESS AND MANAGEMENT RELATED
Chippewa Valley Tech Coll (WI)
Copiah-Lincoln Comm Coll (MS)
Penn State Beaver (PA)
Penn State Brandywine (PA)
Penn State DuBois (PA)
Penn State Fayette, The Eberly Campus (PA)
Penn State Greater Allegheny (PA)
Penn State Hazleton (PA)
Penn State Lehigh Valley (PA)
Penn State Mont Alto (PA)
Penn State New Kensington (PA)
Penn State Schuylkill (PA)
Penn State Wilkes-Barre (PA)
Penn State Worthington Scranton (PA)
Penn State York (PA)

AGRICULTURAL BUSINESS TECHNOLOGY
Copiah-Lincoln Comm Coll (MS)
Laramie County Comm Coll (WY)
The Ohio State U Ag Tech Inst (OH)
Texas State Tech Coll Harlingen (TX)

AGRICULTURAL COMMUNICATION/ JOURNALISM
Northwest Coll (WY)
The Ohio State U Ag Tech Inst (OH)
Santa Rosa Jr Coll (CA)

AGRICULTURAL ECONOMICS
Copiah-Lincoln Comm Coll (MS)
Northeastern Jr Coll (CO)
The Ohio State U Ag Tech Inst (OH)
Potomac State Coll of West Virginia U (WV)
South Plains Coll (TX)

AGRICULTURAL ENGINEERING
Vincennes U (IN)

AGRICULTURAL/FARM SUPPLIES RETAILING AND WHOLESALING
Copiah-Lincoln Comm Coll (MS)
Fox Valley Tech Coll (WI)

Hawkeye Comm Coll (IA)
Illinois Central Coll (IL)
Minnesota West Comm and Tech Coll (MN)
Western Iowa Tech Comm Coll (IA)

AGRICULTURAL MECHANICS AND EQUIPMENT TECHNOLOGY
Butte Coll (CA)
Hutchinson Comm Coll and Area Vocational School (KS)
Illinois Central Coll (IL)
Mitchell Tech Inst (SD)
North Dakota State Coll of Science (ND)
Spoon River Coll (IL)

AGRICULTURAL MECHANIZATION
Clark State Comm Coll (OH)
Fox Valley Tech Coll (WI)
Garden City Comm Coll (KS)
Mesa Comm Coll (AZ)
Metropolitan Comm Coll–Kansas City (MO)
Northeastern Jr Coll (CO)
The Ohio State U Ag Tech Inst (OH)
Owens Comm Coll, Toledo (OH)
Paris Jr Coll (TX)
Parkland Coll (IL)
Potomac State Coll of West Virginia U (WV)
Spoon River Coll (IL)

AGRICULTURAL POWER MACHINERY OPERATION
Guilford Tech Comm Coll (NC)
Hawkeye Comm Coll (IA)
Northeast Iowa Comm Coll (IA)
The Ohio State U Ag Tech Inst (OH)

AGRICULTURAL PRODUCTION
Big Bend Comm Coll (WA)
Delaware Tech & Comm Coll, Jack F. Owens Campus (DE)
Garden City Comm Coll (KS)
Illinois Central Coll (IL)
Illinois Eastern Comm Colls, Wabash Valley College (IL)
Lake Area Tech Inst (SD)
Laramie County Comm Coll (WY)
Lincoln Land Comm Coll (IL)
Miles Comm Coll (MT)
Minnesota West Comm and Tech Coll (MN)
Mitchell Tech Inst (SD)
Northeast Iowa Comm Coll (IA)
Northwest Coll (WY)
Southern State Comm Coll (OH)

AGRICULTURAL TEACHER EDUCATION
Colby Comm Coll (KS)
Northeastern Jr Coll (CO)
Northwest Coll (WY)
The Ohio State U Ag Tech Inst (OH)
Potomac State Coll of West Virginia U (WV)
Spoon River Coll (IL)
Victor Valley Coll (CA)

AGRICULTURE
Arizona Western Coll (AZ)
Bainbridge Coll (GA)
Bakersfield Coll (CA)
Barton County Comm Coll (KS)
Butte Coll (CA)
Casper Coll (WY)
Central New Mexico Comm Coll (NM)
Chipola Coll (FL)
Clark State Comm Coll (OH)
Coll of the Desert (CA)
Copiah-Lincoln Comm Coll (MS)
Cowley County Comm Coll and Area Vocational–Tech School (KS)
Crowder Coll (MO)
Dakota Coll at Bottineau (ND)
Darton State Coll (GA)
Dyersburg State Comm Coll (TN)
Georgia Highlands Coll (GA)
Hutchinson Comm Coll and Area Vocational School (KS)
Jackson State Comm Coll (TN)
Kankakee Comm Coll (IL)
Kaskaskia Coll (IL)
Kilgore Coll (TX)
Klamath Comm Coll (OR)
Laramie County Comm Coll (WY)

Macomb Comm Coll (MI)
Mendocino Coll (CA)
Miami Dade Coll (FL)
Minnesota West Comm and Tech Coll (MN)
Missouri State U–West Plains (MO)
Mt. San Antonio Coll (CA)
Northeastern Jr Coll (CO)
Owensboro Comm and Tech Coll (KY)
Pensacola State Coll (FL)
Potomac State Coll of West Virginia U (WV)
San Jacinto Coll District (TX)
Shawnee Comm Coll (IL)
Sheridan Coll (WY)
Sierra Coll (CA)
Southern State Comm Coll (OH)
South Plains Coll (TX)
State U of New York Coll of Technology at Alfred (NY)
Texarkana Coll (TX)
Vincennes U (IN)

AGRICULTURE AND AGRICULTURE OPERATIONS RELATED
Potomac State Coll of West Virginia U (WV)
Sheridan Coll (WY)

AGROECOLOGY AND SUSTAINABLE AGRICULTURE
Santa Rosa Jr Coll (CA)
State U of New York Coll of Technology at Alfred (NY)

AGRONOMY AND CROP SCIENCE
Chipola Coll (FL)
Colby Comm Coll (KS)
Mesa Comm Coll (AZ)
Minnesota West Comm and Tech Coll (MN)
Northeastern Jr Coll (CO)
The Ohio State U Ag Tech Inst (OH)
Potomac State Coll of West Virginia U (WV)
Shawnee Comm Coll (IL)
Southeastern Comm Coll (IA)
South Plains Coll (TX)
State U of New York Coll of Technology at Alfred (NY)

AIR AND SPACE OPERATIONS TECHNOLOGY
Cochise Coll, Sierra Vista (AZ)

AIRCRAFT POWERPLANT TECHNOLOGY
Colorado Northwestern Comm Coll (CO)
Hallmark Inst of Aeronautics (TX)
Lake Area Tech Inst (SD)
Lansing Comm Coll (MI)
Middlesex Comm Coll (MA)
St. Philip's Coll (TX)
Texas State Tech Coll Harlingen (TX)
Vincennes U (IN)

AIRFRAME MECHANICS AND AIRCRAFT MAINTENANCE TECHNOLOGY
Amarillo Coll (TX)
Comm Coll of the Air Force (AL)
Hallmark Coll of Technology (TX)
Hallmark Inst of Aeronautics (TX)
Ivy Tech Comm Coll–Wabash Valley (IN)
Lansing Comm Coll (MI)
Lincoln Land Comm Coll (IL)
Mohawk Valley Comm Coll (NY)
Mt. San Antonio Coll (CA)
Oklahoma City Comm Coll (OK)
St. Philip's Coll (TX)
Texas State Tech Coll Harlingen (TX)
Trident Tech Coll (SC)

AIRLINE PILOT AND FLIGHT CREW
Big Bend Comm Coll (WA)
Casper Coll (WY)
Central Oregon Comm Coll (OR)
Cochise Coll, Sierra Vista (AZ)
Colorado Northwestern Comm Coll (CO)
Comm Coll of Allegheny County (PA)
Comm Coll of Beaver County (PA)
County Coll of Morris (NJ)
Dutchess Comm Coll (NY)
Fox Valley Tech Coll (WI)
Gateway Tech Coll (WI)

Guilford Tech Comm Coll (NC)
Jackson Coll (MI)
Lake Superior Coll (MN)
Lansing Comm Coll (MI)
Lehigh Carbon Comm Coll (PA)
Luzerne County Comm Coll (PA)
Miami Dade Coll (FL)
Mt. San Antonio Coll (CA)
North Shore Comm Coll (MA)
Orange Coast Coll (CA)
Salt Lake Comm Coll (UT)
San Jacinto Coll District (TX)
Vincennes U (IN)

AIR TRAFFIC CONTROL
Cecil Coll (MD)
Comm Coll of Beaver County (PA)
Comm Coll of the Air Force (AL)
Miami Dade Coll (FL)
Mt. San Antonio Coll (CA)

ALLIED HEALTH AND MEDICAL ASSISTING SERVICES RELATED
Bowling Green State U-Firelands Coll (OH)
Carrington Coll California–San Jose (CA)

ALLIED HEALTH DIAGNOSTIC, INTERVENTION, AND TREATMENT PROFESSIONS RELATED
Forsyth Tech Comm Coll (NC)
Ivy Tech Comm Coll–Wabash Valley (IN)
Union County Coll (NJ)

ALTERNATIVE AND COMPLEMENTARY MEDICINE RELATED
Quinsigamond Comm Coll (MA)

AMERICAN GOVERNMENT AND POLITICS
Oklahoma City Comm Coll (OK)

AMERICAN INDIAN/NATIVE AMERICAN STUDIES
Central Wyoming Coll (WY)
Kilian Comm Coll (SD)

AMERICAN SIGN LANGUAGE (ASL)
Berkeley City Coll (CA)
Burlington County Coll (NJ)
Montgomery Coll (MD)
Oklahoma State U, Oklahoma City (OK)
Quinsigamond Comm Coll (MA)
Santa Rosa Jr Coll (CA)
Sierra Coll (CA)
Union County Coll (NJ)
Vincennes U (IN)

AMERICAN SIGN LANGUAGE RELATED
Union County Coll (NJ)

AMERICAN STUDIES
Bucks County Comm Coll (PA)
Foothill Coll (CA)
Greenfield Comm Coll (MA)
Lansing Comm Coll (MI)
Miami Dade Coll (FL)

ANATOMY
Northeastern Jr Coll (CO)

ANIMAL HEALTH
Miles Comm Coll (MT)

ANIMAL/LIVESTOCK HUSBANDRY AND PRODUCTION
Hawkeye Comm Coll (IA)
Illinois Central Coll (IL)
Jefferson Comm Coll (NY)
The Ohio State U Ag Tech Inst (OH)
Sierra Coll (CA)

ANIMAL SCIENCES
Alamance Comm Coll (NC)
Bakersfield Coll (CA)
Casper Coll (WY)
James Sprunt Comm Coll (NC)
Mt. San Antonio Coll (CA)
Niagara County Comm Coll (NY)
Northeastern Jr Coll (CO)
Northwest Coll (WY)
The Ohio State U Ag Tech Inst (OH)
Potomac State Coll of West Virginia U (WV)
Santa Rosa Jr Coll (CA)

Shawnee Comm Coll (IL)
State U of New York Coll of Technology at Alfred (NY)

ANIMATION, INTERACTIVE TECHNOLOGY, VIDEO GRAPHICS AND SPECIAL EFFECTS
Austin Comm Coll (TX)
Bay State Coll (MA)
Burlington County Coll (NJ)
Cecil Coll (MD)
Coll of Marin (CA)
Coll of the Canyons (CA)
Collin County Comm Coll District (TX)
Elgin Comm Coll (IL)
Finger Lakes Comm Coll (NY)
Forsyth Tech Comm Coll (NC)
Hagerstown Comm Coll (MD)
Houston Comm Coll System (TX)
Illinois Central Coll (IL)
Kirtland Comm Coll (MI)
Lansing Comm Coll (MI)
Lehigh Carbon Comm Coll (PA)
Lone Star Coll–CyFair (TX)
Lone Star Coll–Kingwood (TX)
Lone Star Coll–Montgomery (TX)
Lone Star Coll–North Harris (TX)
Lone Star Coll–Tomball (TX)
McHenry County Coll (IL)
Montgomery Coll (MD)
Oklahoma City Comm Coll (OK)
Pasadena City Coll (CA)
Raritan Valley Comm Coll (NJ)
Red Rocks Comm Coll (CO)
Southeast Tech Inst (SD)
Springfield Tech Comm Coll (MA)
Sullivan Coll of Technology and Design (KY)
Terra State Comm Coll (OH)
Union County Coll (NJ)
Western Iowa Tech Comm Coll (IA)

ANTHROPOLOGY
Austin Comm Coll (TX)
Bakersfield Coll (CA)
Barton County Comm Coll (KS)
Casper Coll (WY)
Cochise Coll, Sierra Vista (AZ)
Coll of the Desert (CA)
Darton State Coll (GA)
Foothill Coll (CA)
Harford Comm Coll (MD)
Lansing Comm Coll (MI)
Laramie County Comm Coll (WY)
Lone Star Coll–North Harris (TX)
Miami Dade Coll (FL)
Northwest Coll (WY)
Orange Coast Coll (CA)
Oxnard Coll (CA)
Pasadena City Coll (CA)
San Diego City Coll (CA)
Santa Rosa Jr Coll (CA)
Vincennes U (IN)

APPAREL AND ACCESSORIES MARKETING
El Centro Coll (TX)
FIDM/The Fashion Inst of Design & Merchandising, Los Angeles Campus (CA)
FIDM/The Fashion Inst of Design & Merchandising, San Diego Campus (CA)
FIDM/The Fashion Inst of Design & Merchandising, San Francisco Campus (CA)

APPAREL AND TEXTILE MANUFACTURING
Fashion Inst of Technology (NY)
Sierra Coll (CA)
Westchester Comm Coll (NY)

APPAREL AND TEXTILE MARKETING MANAGEMENT
Comm Coll of the Air Force (AL)
Sierra Coll (CA)

APPAREL AND TEXTILES
FIDM/The Fashion Inst of Design & Merchandising, Los Angeles Campus (CA)
FIDM/The Fashion Inst of Design & Merchandising, Orange County Campus (CA)
FIDM/The Fashion Inst of Design & Merchandising, San Francisco Campus (CA)
Mt. San Antonio Coll (CA)

APPLIED HORTICULTURE/ HORTICULTURAL BUSINESS SERVICES RELATED
Chippewa Valley Tech Coll (WI)
Dakota Coll at Bottineau (ND)
Forsyth Tech Comm Coll (NC)
Gateway Tech Coll (WI)

APPLIED HORTICULTURE/ HORTICULTURE OPERATIONS
Alamance Comm Coll (NC)
Catawba Valley Comm Coll (NC)
Cecil Coll (MD)
Chemeketa Comm Coll (OR)
Clark Coll (WA)
Coll of the Desert (CA)
Comm Coll of Allegheny County (PA)
The Comm Coll of Baltimore County (MD)
Dakota Coll at Bottineau (ND)
Delaware Tech & Comm Coll, Jack F. Owens Campus (DE)
Fayetteville Tech Comm Coll (NC)
Gateway Tech Coll (WI)
Halifax Comm Coll (NC)
Hawkeye Comm Coll (IA)
Houston Comm Coll System (TX)
Illinois Central Coll (IL)
Kankakee Comm Coll (IL)
Kaskaskia Coll (IL)
Kent State U at Salem (OH)
Lake Michigan Coll (MI)
McHenry County Coll (IL)
Mineral Area Coll (MO)
Montgomery Coll (MD)
St. Louis Comm Coll at Meramec (MO)
Sierra Coll (CA)
Southeast Tech Inst (SD)
Southern Maine Comm Coll (ME)
Spartanburg Comm Coll (SC)
Vincennes U (IN)
Westmoreland County Comm Coll (PA)

APPLIED MATHEMATICS
Northeastern Jr Coll (CO)

AQUACULTURE
Hillsborough Comm Coll (FL)

ARCHEOLOGY
Northwest Coll (WY)

ARCHITECTURAL DRAFTING AND CAD/CADD
Anne Arundel Comm Coll (MD)
Carrington Coll California–San Jose (CA)
Carroll Comm Coll (MD)
Central New Mexico Comm Coll (NM)
Coll of Lake County (IL)
Coll of the Canyons (CA)
Comm Coll of Allegheny County (PA)
The Comm Coll of Baltimore County (MD)
Comm Coll of Beaver County (PA)
Dunwoody Coll of Technology (MN)
Glendale Comm Coll (AZ)
Harper Coll (IL)
Hutchinson Comm Coll and Area Vocational School (KS)
Kaskaskia Coll (IL)
Lake Superior Coll (MN)
Lincoln Land Comm Coll (IL)
Macomb Comm Coll (MI)
Miami Dade Coll (FL)
Montgomery Coll (MD)
Montgomery County Comm Coll (PA)
Oakton Comm Coll (IL)
Oklahoma City Comm Coll (OK)
Owens Comm Coll, Toledo (OH)
Phoenix Coll (AZ)
Pittsburgh Tech Inst, Oakdale (PA)
Sierra Coll (CA)
Southern Maine Comm Coll (ME)
South Suburban Coll (IL)
Sullivan Coll of Technology and Design (KY)
Vincennes U (IN)
Waukesha County Tech Coll (WI)
Western Dakota Tech Inst (SD)
Westmoreland County Comm Coll (PA)
York County Comm Coll (ME)

ARCHITECTURAL ENGINEERING
Luzerne County Comm Coll (PA)

ARCHITECTURAL ENGINEERING TECHNOLOGY
Amarillo Coll (TX)
Arapahoe Comm Coll (CO)
Bakersfield Coll (CA)
Cape Fear Comm Coll (NC)
Catawba Valley Comm Coll (NC)
Central Maine Comm Coll (ME)
Comm Coll of Philadelphia (PA)
Daytona State Coll (FL)
Delaware Tech & Comm Coll, Jack F. Owens Campus (DE)
Delaware Tech & Comm Coll, Stanton/Wilmington Campus (DE)
Delaware Tech & Comm Coll, Terry Campus (DE)
Dutchess Comm Coll (NY)
Erie Comm Coll, South Campus (NY)
Essex County Coll (NJ)
Fayetteville Tech Comm Coll (NC)
Finger Lakes Comm Coll (NY)
Forsyth Tech Comm Coll (NC)
Gateway Tech Coll (WI)
Grand Rapids Comm Coll (MI)
Guilford Tech Comm Coll (NC)
Harper Coll (IL)
Harrisburg Area Comm Coll (PA)
Hillsborough Comm Coll (FL)
Inst of Design and Construction (NY)
John Tyler Comm Coll (VA)
Lansing Comm Coll (MI)
Luzerne County Comm Coll (PA)
Miami Dade Coll (FL)
Monroe County Comm Coll (MI)
Mott Comm Coll (MI)
Mt. San Antonio Coll (CA)
Northampton Comm Coll (PA)
North Dakota State Coll of Science (ND)
Norwalk Comm Coll (CT)
Oakland Comm Coll (MI)
Oklahoma State U, Oklahoma City (OK)
Onondaga Comm Coll (NY)
Orange Coast Coll (CA)
Owens Comm Coll, Toledo (OH)
Penn State Fayette, The Eberly Campus (PA)
Penn State Worthington Scranton (PA)
St. Clair County Comm Coll (MI)
Salt Lake Comm Coll (UT)
San Diego Mesa Coll (CA)
Seminole State Coll of Florida (FL)
Southeast Tech Inst (SD)
Stark State Coll (OH)
State U of New York Coll of Technology at Alfred (NY)
Sullivan Coll of Technology and Design (KY)
Tarrant County Coll District (TX)
Terra State Comm Coll (OH)
Wisconsin Indianhead Tech Coll (WI)

ARCHITECTURAL TECHNOLOGY
Arizona Western Coll (AZ)
Coll of Marin (CA)
Coll of the Desert (CA)
Dunwoody Coll of Technology (MN)
John Tyler Comm Coll (VA)
Lansing Comm Coll (MI)
Onondaga Comm Coll (NY)
St. Louis Comm Coll at Meramec (MO)

ARCHITECTURE
Barton County Comm Coll (KS)
Copiah-Lincoln Comm Coll (MS)
Grand Rapids Comm Coll (MI)
Harrisburg Area Comm Coll (PA)
Howard Comm Coll (MD)
Kilgore Coll (TX)
Lone Star Coll–North Harris (TX)
Pasadena City Coll (CA)
San Diego Mesa Coll (CA)

ARCHITECTURE RELATED
Garden City Comm Coll (KS)
Sullivan Coll of Technology and Design (KY)

AREA STUDIES RELATED
Central Wyoming Coll (WY)

ARMY ROTC/MILITARY SCIENCE
Georgia Military Coll (GA)

ART
Alvin Comm Coll (TX)
Amarillo Coll (TX)
Austin Comm Coll (TX)

Bainbridge Coll (GA)
Bakersfield Coll (CA)
Barton County Comm Coll (KS)
Berkeley City Coll (CA)
Burlington County Coll (NJ)
Butte Coll (CA)
Carroll Comm Coll (MD)
Casper Coll (WY)
Cayuga County Comm Coll (NY)
Central New Mexico Comm Coll (NM)
Central Oregon Comm Coll (OR)
Central Wyoming Coll (WY)
Chipola Coll (FL)
Cochise Coll, Sierra Vista (AZ)
Coll of Lake County (IL)
Coll of Marin (CA)
Coll of the Canyons (CA)
Coll of the Desert (CA)
Comm Coll of Allegheny County (PA)
Comm Coll of Philadelphia (PA)
Comm Coll of Rhode Island (RI)
Comm Coll of Vermont (VT)
Corning Comm Coll (NY)
Cowley County Comm Coll and Area Vocational–Tech School (KS)
Crowder Coll (MO)
Darton State Coll (GA)
De Anza Coll (CA)
Dutchess Comm Coll (NY)
Edison Comm Coll (OH)
Essex County Coll (NJ)
Foothill Coll (CA)
Georgia Highlands Coll (GA)
Gordon State Coll (GA)
Grand Rapids Comm Coll (MI)
Greenfield Comm Coll (MA)
Harper Coll (IL)
Harrisburg Area Comm Coll (PA)
Holyoke Comm Coll (MA)
Housatonic Comm Coll (CT)
Howard Comm Coll (MD)
Kankakee Comm Coll (IL)
Kilgore Coll (TX)
Kirtland Comm Coll (MI)
Lake Michigan Coll (MI)
Lansing Comm Coll (MI)
Laramie County Comm Coll (WY)
Lehigh Carbon Comm Coll (PA)
Lone Star Coll–CyFair (TX)
Lone Star Coll–Kingwood (TX)
Lone Star Coll–Montgomery (TX)
Lone Star Coll–North Harris (TX)
Lone Star Coll–Tomball (TX)
Lorain County Comm Coll (OH)
Mendocino Coll (CA)
Mesa Comm Coll (AZ)
Miami Dade Coll (FL)
Middlesex Comm Coll (MA)
Mohave Comm Coll (AZ)
Mohawk Valley Comm Coll (NY)
Monroe Comm Coll (NY)
Monroe County Comm Coll (MI)
Montgomery Coll (MD)
Montgomery County Comm Coll (PA)
Nassau Comm Coll (NY)
Northeastern Jr Coll (CO)
Northwest Coll (WY)
Norwalk Comm Coll (CT)
Oakland Comm Coll (MI)
Oklahoma City Comm Coll (OK)
Oklahoma State U, Oklahoma City (OK)
Onondaga Comm Coll (NY)
Orange Coast Coll (CA)
Oxnard Coll (CA)
Paris Jr Coll (TX)
Parkland Coll (IL)
Pasadena City Coll (CA)
Pensacola State Coll (FL)
Phoenix Coll (AZ)
St. Philip's Coll (TX)
San Diego City Coll (CA)
San Diego Mesa Coll (CA)
San Jacinto Coll District (TX)
Santa Rosa Jr Coll (CA)
Sheridan Coll (WY)
Sierra Coll (CA)
South Plains Coll (TX)
Spoon River Coll (IL)
Taft Coll (CA)
Temple Coll (TX)
Texarkana Coll (TX)
Tunxis Comm Coll (CT)
Tyler Jr Coll (TX)
Victor Valley Coll (CA)
Vincennes U (IN)
Virginia Western Comm Coll (VA)

ART HISTORY, CRITICISM AND CONSERVATION
De Anza Coll (CA)
Foothill Coll (CA)
Lansing Comm Coll (MI)
Pasadena City Coll (CA)
Santa Rosa Jr Coll (CA)
Terra State Comm Coll (OH)

ARTIFICIAL INTELLIGENCE
Lorain County Comm Coll (OH)
Metropolitan Comm Coll–Kansas City (MO)
San Diego City Coll (CA)
Southeastern Comm Coll (IA)
Sullivan Coll of Technology and Design (KY)

ART TEACHER EDUCATION
Bakersfield Coll (CA)
Casper Coll (WY)
Cochise Coll, Sierra Vista (AZ)
Copiah-Lincoln Comm Coll (MS)
Darton State Coll (GA)
Northeastern Jr Coll (CO)
Parkland Coll (IL)
Pensacola State Coll (FL)
Vincennes U (IN)

ART THERAPY
Vincennes U (IN)

ASIAN STUDIES
Miami Dade Coll (FL)

ASTRONOMY
Gordon State Coll (GA)

ATHLETIC TRAINING
Barton County Comm Coll (KS)
Casper Coll (WY)
Central Wyoming Coll (WY)
Coll of the Canyons (CA)
Comm Coll of Allegheny County (PA)
Foothill Coll (CA)
Lorain County Comm Coll (OH)
Northampton Comm Coll (PA)
Northwest Coll (WY)
Orange Coast Coll (CA)

ATMOSPHERIC SCIENCES AND METEOROLOGY
Comm Coll of the Air Force (AL)

AUDIOLOGY AND SPEECH-LANGUAGE PATHOLOGY
Miami Dade Coll (FL)
Pasadena City Coll (CA)

AUDIOVISUAL COMMUNICATIONS TECHNOLOGIES RELATED
Lone Star Coll–Montgomery (TX)

AUTOBODY/COLLISION AND REPAIR TECHNOLOGY
Bismarck State Coll (ND)
Casper Coll (WY)
Coll of Marin (CA)
Comm Coll of Beaver County (PA)
Corning Comm Coll (NY)
Dunwoody Coll of Technology (MN)
Erie Comm Coll, South Campus (NY)
Fox Valley Tech Coll (WI)
Hawkeye Comm Coll (IA)
Highland Comm Coll (IL)
Hutchinson Comm Coll and Area Vocational School (KS)
Illinois Eastern Comm Colls, Olney Central College (IL)
Kaskaskia Coll (IL)
Kilgore Coll (TX)
Lake Area Tech Inst (SD)
Lansing Comm Coll (MI)
Laramie County Comm Coll (WY)
Lincoln Land Comm Coll (IL)
Mid-Plains Comm Coll, North Platte (NE)
Mineral Area Coll (MO)
North Dakota State Coll of Science (ND)
Oxnard Coll (CA)
Ozarks Tech Comm Coll (MO)
Parkland Coll (IL)
Randolph Comm Coll (NC)
Red Rocks Comm Coll (CO)
St. Philip's Coll (TX)
Salt Lake Comm Coll (UT)
San Jacinto Coll District (TX)
San Juan Coll (NM)

Southeast Tech Inst (SD)
State U of New York Coll of Technology at Alfred (NY)
Texas State Tech Coll Harlingen (TX)
U of Arkansas Comm Coll at Morrilton (AR)
Vincennes U (IN)
Waubonsee Comm Coll (IL)
Waukesha County Tech Coll (WI)
Western Dakota Tech Inst (SD)
Western Iowa Tech Comm Coll (IA)

AUTOMATION ENGINEER TECHNOLOGY
Alexandria Tech and Comm Coll (MN)
Mitchell Tech Inst (SD)
Southwestern Michigan Coll (MI)

AUTOMOBILE/AUTOMOTIVE MECHANICS TECHNOLOGY
Alamance Comm Coll (NC)
Alpena Comm Coll (MI)
Amarillo Coll (TX)
Arapahoe Comm Coll (CO)
Austin Comm Coll (TX)
Bakersfield Coll (CA)
Barton County Comm Coll (KS)
Beaufort County Comm Coll (NC)
Big Bend Comm Coll (WA)
Bismarck State Coll (ND)
Brookhaven Coll (TX)
Butte Coll (CA)
Cape Fear Comm Coll (NC)
Casper Coll (WY)
Catawba Valley Comm Coll (NC)
Central Carolina Comm Coll (NC)
Central Maine Comm Coll (ME)
Central Oregon Comm Coll (OR)
Central Wyoming Coll (WY)
Chemeketa Comm Coll (OR)
Clark Coll (WA)
Cochise Coll, Sierra Vista (AZ)
Coll of Lake County (IL)
Coll of Marin (CA)
Coll of the Canyons (CA)
Coll of the Desert (CA)
The Comm Coll of Baltimore County (MD)
Comm Coll of Beaver County (PA)
Comm Coll of Philadelphia (PA)
Comm Coll of the Air Force (AL)
Corning Comm Coll (NY)
Cossatot Comm Coll of the U of Arkansas (AR)
Cowley County Comm Coll and Area Vocational–Tech School (KS)
Cuyahoga Comm Coll (OH)
Daytona State Coll (FL)
De Anza Coll (CA)
Delaware Tech & Comm Coll, Jack F. Owens Campus (DE)
Delaware Tech & Comm Coll, Stanton/Wilmington Campus (DE)
Denmark Tech Coll (SC)
Dunwoody Coll of Technology (MN)
Eastern Idaho Tech Coll (ID)
Elgin Comm Coll (IL)
Erie Comm Coll, South Campus (NY)
Fayetteville Tech Comm Coll (NC)
Forsyth Tech Comm Coll (NC)
Fox Valley Tech Coll (WI)
Garden City Comm Coll (KS)
Gateway Tech Coll (WI)
Glendale Comm Coll (AZ)
Grand Rapids Comm Coll (MI)
Guilford Tech Comm Coll (NC)
Harrisburg Area Comm Coll (PA)
Hawkeye Comm Coll (IA)
Highland Comm Coll (IL)
Houston Comm Coll System (TX)
Hutchinson Comm Coll and Area Vocational School (KS)
Illinois Central Coll (IL)
Illinois Eastern Comm Colls, Frontier Community College (IL)
Illinois Eastern Comm Colls, Olney Central College (IL)
Ivy Tech Comm Coll–Central Indiana (IN)
Ivy Tech Comm Coll–Columbus (IN)
Ivy Tech Comm Coll–East Central (IN)
Ivy Tech Comm Coll–Kokomo (IN)
Ivy Tech Comm Coll–Lafayette (IN)
Ivy Tech Comm Coll–North Central (IN)
Ivy Tech Comm Coll–Northeast (IN)
Ivy Tech Comm Coll–Northwest (IN)

Ivy Tech Comm Coll–Richmond (IN)
Ivy Tech Comm Coll–Southern Indiana (IN)
Ivy Tech Comm Coll–Southwest (IN)
Ivy Tech Comm Coll–Wabash Valley (IN)
Jackson Coll (MI)
Jefferson Coll (MO)
J. F. Drake State Tech Coll (AL)
Kankakee Comm Coll (IL)
Kaskaskia Coll (IL)
Kilgore Coll (TX)
Kirtland Comm Coll (MI)
Klamath Comm Coll (OR)
Lake Area Tech Inst (SD)
Lake Superior Coll (MN)
Lansing Comm Coll (MI)
Laramie County Comm Coll (WY)
Lincoln Land Comm Coll (IL)
Lone Star Coll–Montgomery (TX)
Lone Star Coll–North Harris (TX)
Lower Columbia Coll (WA)
Luzerne County Comm Coll (PA)
Macomb Comm Coll (MI)
McHenry County Coll (IL)
Mendocino Coll (CA)
Mesa Comm Coll (AZ)
Metropolitan Comm Coll–Kansas City (MO)
Mid-Plains Comm Coll, North Platte (NE)
Mineral Area Coll (MO)
Minnesota West Comm and Tech Coll (MN)
Mohave Comm Coll (AZ)
Monroe Comm Coll (NY)
Montcalm Comm Coll (MI)
Montgomery Coll (MD)
Montgomery County Comm Coll (PA)
Moraine Park Tech Coll (WI)
Moraine Valley Comm Coll (IL)
Mott Comm Coll (MI)
Northampton Comm Coll (PA)
North Dakota State Coll of Science (ND)
Northeastern Jr Coll (CO)
Northeast Iowa Comm Coll (IA)
Northwest Tech Coll (MN)
Oakton Comm Coll (IL)
Oklahoma City Comm Coll (OK)
Oklahoma Tech Coll (OK)
Onondaga Comm Coll (NY)
Oxnard Coll (CA)
Ozarka Coll (AR)
Ozarks Tech Comm Coll (MO)
Parkland Coll (IL)
Pasadena City Coll (CA)
Pensacola State Coll (FL)
Quinsigamond Comm Coll (MA)
Randolph Comm Coll (NC)
Red Rocks Comm Coll (CO)
Rogue Comm Coll (OR)
St. Louis Comm Coll at Forest Park (MO)
St. Philip's Coll (TX)
San Diego City Coll (CA)
San Jacinto Coll District (TX)
San Juan Coll (NM)
Santa Rosa Jr Coll (CA)
Seminole State Coll of Florida (FL)
Shawnee Comm Coll (IL)
Sierra Coll (CA)
Southeastern Comm Coll (IA)
Southeast Tech Inst (SD)
Southern Maine Comm Coll (ME)
South Plains Coll (TX)
South Puget Sound Comm Coll (WA)
Southwestern Michigan Coll (MI)
Spartanburg Comm Coll (SC)
Stark State Coll (OH)
Taft Coll (CA)
Tarrant County Coll District (TX)
Texarkana Coll (TX)
Texas State Tech Coll Harlingen (TX)
Thomas Nelson Comm Coll (VA)
Tri-County Comm Coll (NC)
Trident Tech Coll (SC)
Tyler Jr Coll (TX)
Union County Coll (NJ)
U of Arkansas Comm Coll at Morrilton (AR)
Victor Valley Coll (CA)
Vincennes U (IN)
Virginia Western Comm Coll (VA)
Waubonsee Comm Coll (IL)
Waukesha County Tech Coll (WI)
Western Dakota Tech Inst (SD)
Western Iowa Tech Comm Coll (IA)
Wilson Comm Coll (NC)

AUTOMOTIVE ENGINEERING TECHNOLOGY
Burlington County Coll (NJ)
Central New Mexico Comm Coll (NM)
Comm Coll of Allegheny County (PA)
J. F. Drake State Tech Coll (AL)
Lawson State Comm Coll (AL)
Macomb Comm Coll (MI)
Massachusetts Bay Comm Coll (MA)
Miles Comm Coll (MT)
Northwest State Comm Coll (OH)
Owens Comm Coll, Toledo (OH)
Raritan Valley Comm Coll (NJ)
Springfield Tech Comm Coll (MA)
State U of New York Coll of Technology at Alfred (NY)
Terra State Comm Coll (OH)

AVIATION/AIRWAY MANAGEMENT
Comm Coll of Allegheny County (PA)
Comm Coll of Beaver County (PA)
Dutchess Comm Coll (NY)
Lincoln Land Comm Coll (IL)
Lone Star Coll–North Harris (TX)
Luzerne County Comm Coll (PA)
Miami Dade Coll (FL)
San Jacinto Coll District (TX)

AVIONICS MAINTENANCE TECHNOLOGY
Big Bend Comm Coll (WA)
Cochise Coll, Sierra Vista (AZ)
Comm Coll of the Air Force (AL)
Cuyahoga Comm Coll (OH)
Fox Valley Tech Coll (WI)
Guilford Tech Comm Coll (NC)
Housatonic Comm Coll (CT)
Lansing Comm Coll (MI)
Mt. San Antonio Coll (CA)
Orange Coast Coll (CA)
Salt Lake Comm Coll (UT)
Tarrant County Coll District (TX)

BAKING AND PASTRY ARTS
Bucks County Comm Coll (PA)
Clark Coll (WA)
Culinary Inst LeNotre (TX)
El Centro Coll (TX)
Elgin Comm Coll (IL)
Luzerne County Comm Coll (PA)
Montgomery County Comm Coll (PA)
Mott Comm Coll (MI)
Niagara County Comm Coll (NY)
St. Louis Comm Coll at Forest Park (MO)
San Jacinto Coll District (TX)
Schoolcraft Coll (MI)
State U of New York Coll of Technology at Alfred (NY)
Sullivan County Comm Coll (NY)
Westmoreland County Comm Coll (PA)

BANKING AND FINANCIAL SUPPORT SERVICES
Alamance Comm Coll (NC)
Arapahoe Comm Coll (CO)
Austin Comm Coll (TX)
Barton County Comm Coll (KS)
Catawba Valley Comm Coll (NC)
Central New Mexico Comm Coll (NM)
Cleveland Comm Coll (NC)
Colorado Northwestern Comm Coll (CO)
Comm Coll of Allegheny County (PA)
Comm Coll of Beaver County (PA)
Comm Coll of Rhode Island (RI)
Fayetteville Tech Comm Coll (NC)
Fox Valley Tech Coll (WI)
Harper Coll (IL)
Harrisburg Area Comm Coll (PA)
Houston Comm Coll System (TX)
Illinois Central Coll (IL)
Lake Area Tech Inst (SD)
Lansing Comm Coll (MI)
Luzerne County Comm Coll (PA)
Mohawk Valley Comm Coll (NY)
Northwest State Comm Coll (OH)
Oakton Comm Coll (IL)
Oklahoma City Comm Coll (OK)
Pensacola State Coll (FL)
Phoenix Coll (AZ)
Seminole State Coll of Florida (FL)
Southeast Tech Inst (SD)
State U of New York Coll of Technology at Alfred (NY)
Terra State Comm Coll (OH)

Westmoreland County Comm Coll (PA)

BARBERING
Oklahoma Tech Coll (OK)

BEHAVIORAL ASPECTS OF HEALTH
Darton State Coll (GA)

BEHAVIORAL SCIENCES
Amarillo Coll (TX)
Ancilla Coll (IN)
De Anza Coll (CA)
Glendale Comm Coll (AZ)
Miami Dade Coll (FL)
Monroe Comm Coll (NY)
Orange Coast Coll (CA)
San Diego City Coll (CA)
San Jacinto Coll District (TX)
Santa Rosa Jr Coll (CA)
Tyler Jr Coll (TX)
Vincennes U (IN)

BIBLICAL STUDIES
Amarillo Coll (TX)

BILINGUAL AND MULTILINGUAL EDUCATION
Delaware Tech & Comm Coll, Terry Campus (DE)

BIOCHEMISTRY
Pasadena City Coll (CA)
Pensacola State Coll (FL)
Vincennes U (IN)

BIOENGINEERING AND BIOMEDICAL ENGINEERING
Anoka-Ramsey Comm Coll (MN)
Anoka-Ramsey Comm Coll, Cambridge Campus (MN)
Quinsigamond Comm Coll (MA)

BIOETHICS/MEDICAL ETHICS
Pasadena City Coll (CA)

BIOLOGICAL AND BIOMEDICAL SCIENCES RELATED
Darton State Coll (GA)
Gordon State Coll (GA)
Vincennes U (IN)

BIOLOGICAL AND PHYSICAL SCIENCES
Ancilla Coll (IN)
Burlington County Coll (NJ)
Central Oregon Comm Coll (OR)
Chipola Coll (FL)
Clinton Comm Coll (NY)
Coll of Lake County (IL)
Coll of Marin (CA)
Coll of the Canyons (CA)
Coll of the Desert (CA)
The Comm Coll of Baltimore County (MD)
Comm Coll of Beaver County (PA)
Comm Coll of Rhode Island (RI)
Copiah-Lincoln Comm Coll (MS)
Dabney S. Lancaster Comm Coll (VA)
Eastern Shore Comm Coll (VA)
Elgin Comm Coll (IL)
Finger Lakes Comm Coll (NY)
Georgia Highlands Coll (GA)
Highland Comm Coll (IL)
Howard Comm Coll (MD)
Illinois Eastern Comm Colls, Frontier Community College (IL)
Illinois Eastern Comm Colls, Lincoln Trail College (IL)
Illinois Eastern Comm Colls, Olney Central College (IL)
Illinois Eastern Comm Colls, Wabash Valley College (IL)
Kaskaskia Coll (IL)
Kilgore Coll (TX)
Laramie County Comm Coll (WY)
Lincoln Land Comm Coll (IL)
Lorain County Comm Coll (OH)
Luzerne County Comm Coll (PA)
Massachusetts Bay Comm Coll (MA)
McHenry County Coll (IL)
Metropolitan Comm Coll–Kansas City (MO)
Monroe Comm Coll (NY)
Moraine Valley Comm Coll (IL)
Mt. San Antonio Coll (CA)
Niagara County Comm Coll (NY)
Northeastern Jr Coll (CO)
Northern Essex Comm Coll (MA)
Oakton Comm Coll (IL)

Paris Jr Coll (TX)
Parkland Coll (IL)
Pasadena City Coll (CA)
Penn State Beaver (PA)
Penn State DuBois (PA)
Penn State Fayette, The Eberly Campus (PA)
Penn State Greater Allegheny (PA)
Penn State New Kensington (PA)
Penn State Schuylkill (PA)
Piedmont Virginia Comm Coll (VA)
Potomac State Coll of West Virginia U (WV)
Rappahannock Comm Coll (VA)
Shawnee Comm Coll (IL)
Sheridan Coll (WY)
Sierra Coll (CA)
South Plains Coll (TX)
South Suburban Coll (IL)
Spoon River Coll (IL)
Terra State Comm Coll (OH)
Thomas Nelson Comm Coll (VA)
Trident Tech Coll (SC)
U of South Carolina Union (SC)
U of Wisconsin–Richland (WI)
Victor Valley Coll (CA)
Vincennes U (IN)
Virginia Western Comm Coll (VA)
Waubonsee Comm Coll (IL)
Wytheville Comm Coll (VA)

BIOLOGY/BIOLOGICAL SCIENCES
Alpena Comm Coll (MI)
Alvin Comm Coll (TX)
Amarillo Coll (TX)
Anne Arundel Comm Coll (MD)
Anoka-Ramsey Comm Coll (MN)
Anoka-Ramsey Comm Coll, Cambridge Campus (MN)
Arizona Western Coll (AZ)
Austin Comm Coll (TX)
Bainbridge Coll (GA)
Bakersfield Coll (CA)
Barton County Comm Coll (KS)
Burlington County Coll (NJ)
Butte Coll (CA)
Carl Albert State Coll (OK)
Casper Coll (WY)
Cecil Coll (MD)
Central Oregon Comm Coll (OR)
Central Wyoming Coll (WY)
Cochise Coll, Sierra Vista (AZ)
Coll of Marin (CA)
Coll of the Desert (CA)
Comm Coll of Allegheny County (PA)
Copiah-Lincoln Comm Coll (MS)
Cowley County Comm Coll and Area Vocational–Tech School (KS)
Crowder Coll (MO)
Dakota Coll at Bottineau (ND)
Darton State Coll (GA)
De Anza Coll (CA)
Delaware Tech & Comm Coll, Jack F. Owens Campus (DE)
Delaware Tech & Comm Coll, Stanton/Wilmington Campus (DE)
Essex County Coll (NJ)
Finger Lakes Comm Coll (NY)
Fiorello H. LaGuardia Comm Coll of the City U of New York (NY)
Foothill Coll (CA)
Garden City Comm Coll (KS)
Georgia Military Coll (GA)
Harford Comm Coll (MD)
Harper Coll (IL)
Harrisburg Area Comm Coll (PA)
Hutchinson Comm Coll and Area Vocational School (KS)
Jamestown Comm Coll (NY)
Kankakee Comm Coll (IL)
Lake Michigan Coll (MI)
Lansing Comm Coll (MI)
Laramie County Comm Coll (WY)
Lehigh Carbon Comm Coll (PA)
Lone Star Coll–CyFair (TX)
Lone Star Coll–Kingwood (TX)
Lone Star Coll–Montgomery (TX)
Lone Star Coll–North Harris (TX)
Lone Star Coll–Tomball (TX)
Lorain County Comm Coll (OH)
Macomb Comm Coll (MI)
Mendocino Coll (CA)
Mesa Comm Coll (AZ)
Metropolitan Comm Coll–Kansas City (MO)
Miami Dade Coll (FL)
Middlesex Comm Coll (MA)
Monroe Comm Coll (NY)
Monroe County Comm Coll (MI)
Montgomery County Comm Coll (PA)

Mott Comm Coll (MI)
Northampton Comm Coll (PA)
Northeastern Jr Coll (CO)
North Hennepin Comm Coll (MN)
Northwest Coll (WY)
Oklahoma City Comm Coll (OK)
Orange Coast Coll (CA)
Oxnard Coll (CA)
Pasadena City Coll (CA)
Pensacola State Coll (FL)
Potomac State Coll of West Virginia U (WV)
St. Philip's Coll (TX)
Salt Lake Comm Coll (UT)
San Diego City Coll (CA)
San Diego Mesa Coll (CA)
San Jacinto Coll District (TX)
San Juan Coll (NM)
Santa Rosa Jr Coll (CA)
Sheridan Coll (WY)
Sierra Coll (CA)
South Plains Coll (TX)
Spoon River Coll (IL)
Springfield Tech Comm Coll (MA)
State U of New York Coll of Technology at Alfred (NY)
Taft Coll (CA)
Terra State Comm Coll (OH)
Texarkana Coll (TX)
Texas State Tech Coll Harlingen (TX)
Tyler Jr Coll (TX)
Union County Coll (NJ)
U of Pittsburgh at Titusville (PA)
Victor Valley Coll (CA)
Vincennes U (IN)

BIOLOGY/BIOTECHNOLOGY LABORATORY TECHNICIAN
Austin Comm Coll (TX)
Berkeley City Coll (CA)
Bucks County Comm Coll (PA)
Carrington Coll California–San Jose (CA)
Cleveland Comm Coll (NC)
Collin County Comm Coll District (TX)
County Coll of Morris (NJ)
Delaware Tech & Comm Coll, Jack F. Owens Campus (DE)
Delaware Tech & Comm Coll, Stanton/Wilmington Campus (DE)
Elgin Comm Coll (IL)
Finger Lakes Comm Coll (NY)
Forsyth Tech Comm Coll (NC)
Fox Valley Tech Coll (WI)
Gateway Tech Coll (WI)
Guilford Tech Comm Coll (NC)
Hagerstown Comm Coll (MD)
Hillsborough Comm Coll (FL)
Houston Comm Coll System (TX)
Jamestown Comm Coll (NY)
Kennebec Valley Comm Coll (ME)
Lake Area Tech Inst (SD)
Lone Star Coll–Montgomery (TX)
Massachusetts Bay Comm Coll (MA)
Middlesex Comm Coll (MA)
Minnesota West Comm and Tech Coll (MN)
Monroe Comm Coll (NY)
Montgomery Coll (MD)
North Dakota State Coll of Science (ND)
North Shore Comm Coll (MA)
The Ohio State U Ag Tech Inst (OH)
Randolph Comm Coll (NC)
Salt Lake Comm Coll (UT)
Temple Coll (TX)
Westmoreland County Comm Coll (PA)
Wilson Comm Coll (NC)

BIOLOGY TEACHER EDUCATION
Bucks County Comm Coll (PA)

BIOMEDICAL TECHNOLOGY
Anoka-Ramsey Comm Coll (MN)
Anoka-Ramsey Comm Coll, Cambridge Campus (MN)
Comm Coll of the Air Force (AL)
Delaware Tech & Comm Coll, Terry Campus (DE)
Hillsborough Comm Coll (FL)
Howard Comm Coll (MD)
Miami Dade Coll (FL)
Owens Comm Coll, Toledo (OH)
Parkland Coll (IL)
Penn State DuBois (PA)
Penn State Fayette, The Eberly Campus (PA)
Penn State Hazleton (PA)
Penn State New Kensington (PA)

Penn State Schuylkill (PA)
Penn State York (PA)
Quinsigamond Comm Coll (MA)
St. Philip's Coll (TX)
Schoolcraft Coll (MI)
Southeastern Comm Coll (IA)
Southeast Tech Inst (SD)
Stark State Coll (OH)
Texas State Tech Coll Harlingen (TX)

BIOPHYSICS
Forsyth Tech Comm Coll (NC)

BIOTECHNOLOGY
Alamance Comm Coll (NC)
Borough of Manhattan Comm Coll of the City U of New York (NY)
Bucks County Comm Coll (PA)
Burlington County Coll (NJ)
Cecil Coll (MD)
Central New Mexico Comm Coll (NM)
El Centro Coll (TX)
Essex County Coll (NJ)
Glendale Comm Coll (AZ)
Howard Comm Coll (MD)
Hutchinson Comm Coll and Area Vocational School (KS)
Ivy Tech Comm Coll–Central Indiana (IN)
Ivy Tech Comm Coll–Lafayette (IN)
Ivy Tech Comm Coll–North Central (IN)
Lakeland Comm Coll (OH)
Lansing Comm Coll (MI)
Lehigh Carbon Comm Coll (PA)
Miami Dade Coll (FL)
Montgomery County Comm Coll (PA)
Northampton Comm Coll (PA)
Oakland Comm Coll (MI)
Oklahoma City Comm Coll (OK)
Owensboro Comm and Tech Coll (KY)
Quinsigamond Comm Coll (MA)
Raritan Valley Comm Coll (NJ)
San Jacinto Coll District (TX)
Southern Maine Comm Coll (ME)
Springfield Tech Comm Coll (MA)
Tompkins Cortland Comm Coll (NY)
Vincennes U (IN)

BLOOD BANK TECHNOLOGY
Rasmussen Coll St. Cloud (MN)

BOILERMAKING
Ivy Tech Comm Coll–Southwest (IN)

BOTANY/PLANT BIOLOGY
Pensacola State Coll (FL)
Spoon River Coll (IL)

BROADCAST JOURNALISM
Amarillo Coll (TX)
Bakersfield Coll (CA)
Colby Comm Coll (KS)
Northwest Coll (WY)
Ocean County Coll (NJ)
Oklahoma City Comm Coll (OK)
Pasadena City Coll (CA)

BUILDING/CONSTRUCTION FINISHING, MANAGEMENT, AND INSPECTION RELATED
Central New Mexico Comm Coll (NM)
Coll of Southern Maryland (MD)
The Comm Coll of Baltimore County (MD)
Fayetteville Tech Comm Coll (NC)
Ivy Tech Comm Coll–Northwest (IN)
Lawson State Comm Coll (AL)
Mid-Plains Comm Coll, North Platte (NE)
Mohave Comm Coll (AZ)
Montgomery Coll (MD)
Mt. San Antonio Coll (CA)
Oakton Comm Coll (IL)
Parkland Coll (IL)
St. Philip's Coll (TX)
Salt Lake Comm Coll (UT)
Seminole State Coll of Florida (FL)
Southeast Tech Inst (SD)
Springfield Tech Comm Coll (MA)
Victor Valley Coll (CA)

BUILDING/CONSTRUCTION SITE MANAGEMENT
Coll of the Canyons (CA)
Coll of the Desert (CA)
The Comm Coll of Baltimore County (MD)
Dunwoody Coll of Technology (MN)
Hillsborough Comm Coll (FL)
Lehigh Carbon Comm Coll (PA)

Metropolitan Comm Coll–Kansas City (MO)
North Hennepin Comm Coll (MN)
The Ohio State U Ag Tech Inst (OH)

BUILDING CONSTRUCTION TECHNOLOGY
Central Maine Comm Coll (ME)
Cochise Coll, Sierra Vista (AZ)
Lake Superior Coll (MN)
Mitchell Tech Inst (SD)
North Dakota State Coll of Science (ND)
Red Rocks Comm Coll (CO)
Sheridan Coll (WY)

BUILDING/HOME/CONSTRUCTION INSPECTION
Bucks County Comm Coll (PA)
Chemeketa Comm Coll (OR)
Harrisburg Area Comm Coll (PA)
McHenry County Coll (IL)
North Hennepin Comm Coll (MN)
Oklahoma State U, Oklahoma City (OK)
Orange Coast Coll (CA)
Pasadena City Coll (CA)
Phoenix Coll (AZ)
St. Louis Comm Coll at Forest Park (MO)
South Suburban Coll (IL)
Vincennes U (IN)

BUILDING/PROPERTY MAINTENANCE
Cape Fear Comm Coll (NC)
Century Coll (MN)
Comm Coll of Allegheny County (PA)
Erie Comm Coll (NY)
Guilford Tech Comm Coll (NC)
Ivy Tech Comm Coll–Bloomington (IN)
Ivy Tech Comm Coll–Central Indiana (IN)
Ivy Tech Comm Coll–Columbus (IN)
Ivy Tech Comm Coll–East Central (IN)
Ivy Tech Comm Coll–Kokomo (IN)
Ivy Tech Comm Coll–Lafayette (IN)
Ivy Tech Comm Coll–North Central (IN)
Ivy Tech Comm Coll–Northeast (IN)
Ivy Tech Comm Coll–Northwest (IN)
Ivy Tech Comm Coll–Richmond (IN)
Ivy Tech Comm Coll–Southern Indiana (IN)
Ivy Tech Comm Coll–Southwest (IN)
Ivy Tech Comm Coll–Wabash Valley (IN)
Lincoln Land Comm Coll (IL)
Luzerne County Comm Coll (PA)
Miles Comm Coll (MT)
Mitchell Tech Inst (SD)
Mohawk Valley Comm Coll (NY)
Pensacola State Coll (FL)
Piedmont Comm Coll (NC)

BUSINESS ADMINISTRATION AND MANAGEMENT
Adirondack Comm Coll (NY)
Alamance Comm Coll (NC)
Alexandria Tech and Comm Coll (MN)
Alpena Comm Coll (MI)
Alvin Comm Coll (TX)
Amarillo Coll (TX)
Ancilla Coll (IN)
Anne Arundel Comm Coll (MD)
Anoka-Ramsey Comm Coll (MN)
Anoka-Ramsey Comm Coll, Cambridge Campus (MN)
Arapahoe Comm Coll (CO)
Arizona Western Coll (AZ)
Austin Comm Coll (TX)
Bainbridge Coll (GA)
Bakersfield Coll (CA)
Barton County Comm Coll (KS)
Bay State Coll (MA)
Beaufort County Comm Coll (NC)
Berkeley City Coll (CA)
Berkshire Comm Coll (MA)
Blackhawk Tech Coll (WI)
Borough of Manhattan Comm Coll of the City U of New York (NY)
Bowling Green State U-Firelands Coll (OH)
Brookhaven Coll (TX)
Bucks County Comm Coll (PA)
Burlington County Coll (NJ)
Butte Coll (CA)
Cape Fear Comm Coll (NC)
Career Tech Coll (LA)

Carl Albert State Coll (OK)
Carrington Coll California–Pleasant Hill (CA)
Carrington Coll California–San Jose (CA)
Carrington Coll California–San Leandro (CA)
Carrington Coll of California–Citrus Heights (CA)
Carroll Comm Coll (MD)
Casper Coll (WY)
Catawba Valley Comm Coll (NC)
Cayuga County Comm Coll (NY)
Cecil Coll (MD)
Central Carolina Comm Coll (NC)
Central Maine Comm Coll (ME)
Central New Mexico Comm Coll (NM)
Central Oregon Comm Coll (OR)
Central Wyoming Coll (WY)
Century Coll (MN)
Chemeketa Comm Coll (OR)
Chipola Coll (FL)
Chippewa Valley Tech Coll (WI)
Clark Coll (WA)
Clark State Comm Coll (OH)
Cleveland Comm Coll (NC)
Cleveland State Comm Coll (TN)
Clinton Comm Coll (NY)
Cochise Coll, Sierra Vista (AZ)
Colby Comm Coll (KS)
Coll of Lake County (IL)
Coll of Marin (CA)
Coll of Southern Maryland (MD)
Coll of the Canyons (CA)
Coll of the Desert (CA)
Collin County Comm Coll District (TX)
Comm Coll of Allegheny County (PA)
The Comm Coll of Baltimore County (MD)
Comm Coll of Beaver County (PA)
Comm Coll of Philadelphia (PA)
Comm Coll of Rhode Island (RI)
Comm Coll of Vermont (VT)
Copiah-Lincoln Comm Coll (MS)
Corning Comm Coll (NY)
Cossatot Comm Coll of the U of Arkansas (AR)
County Coll of Morris (NJ)
Cowley County Comm Coll and Area Vocational–Tech School (KS)
Crowder Coll (MO)
Cuyahoga Comm Coll (OH)
Dabney S. Lancaster Comm Coll (VA)
Dakota Coll at Bottineau (ND)
Darton State Coll (GA)
Daytona State Coll (FL)
De Anza Coll (CA)
Delaware Tech & Comm Coll, Stanton/Wilmington Campus (DE)
Delaware Tech & Comm Coll, Terry Campus (DE)
Denmark Tech Coll (SC)
Dutchess Comm Coll (NY)
Dyersburg State Comm Coll (TN)
Eastern Shore Comm Coll (VA)
Edison Comm Coll (OH)
El Centro Coll (TX)
Elgin Comm Coll (IL)
Erie Comm Coll (NY)
Erie Comm Coll, North Campus (NY)
Erie Comm Coll, South Campus (NY)
Essex County Coll (NJ)
Fayetteville Tech Comm Coll (NC)
Finger Lakes Comm Coll (NY)
Fiorello H. LaGuardia Comm Coll of the City U of New York (NY)
Flathead Valley Comm Coll (MT)
Foothill Coll (CA)
Forrest Coll (SC)
Forsyth Tech Comm Coll (NC)
Fox Valley Tech Coll (WI)
Garden City Comm Coll (KS)
Garrett Coll (MD)
Gateway Comm and Tech Coll (KY)
Gateway Tech Coll (WI)
Genesee Comm Coll (NY)
Georgia Highlands Coll (GA)
Georgia Military Coll (GA)
Glendale Comm Coll (AZ)
Goodwin Coll (CT)
Gordon State Coll (GA)
Grand Rapids Comm Coll (MI)
Great Falls Coll Montana State U (MT)
Greenfield Comm Coll (MA)
Guilford Tech Comm Coll (NC)
Hagerstown Comm Coll (MD)
Halifax Comm Coll (NC)
Hallmark Coll of Technology (TX)
Harford Comm Coll (MD)
Harper Coll (IL)
Harrisburg Area Comm Coll (PA)
Hillsborough Comm Coll (FL)
Holyoke Comm Coll (MA)
Housatonic Comm Coll (CT)
Houston Comm Coll System (TX)
Howard Comm Coll (MD)
Illinois Central Coll (IL)
Illinois Eastern Comm Colls, Wabash Valley College (IL)
Ivy Tech Comm Coll–Bloomington (IN)
Ivy Tech Comm Coll–Central Indiana (IN)
Ivy Tech Comm Coll–Columbus (IN)
Ivy Tech Comm Coll–East Central (IN)
Ivy Tech Comm Coll–Kokomo (IN)
Ivy Tech Comm Coll–Lafayette (IN)
Ivy Tech Comm Coll–North Central (IN)
Ivy Tech Comm Coll–Northeast (IN)
Ivy Tech Comm Coll–Northwest (IN)
Ivy Tech Comm Coll–Richmond (IN)
Ivy Tech Comm Coll–Southeast (IN)
Ivy Tech Comm Coll–Southern Indiana (IN)
Ivy Tech Comm Coll–Southwest (IN)
Ivy Tech Comm Coll–Wabash Valley (IN)
Jackson Coll (MI)
Jackson State Comm Coll (TN)
James Sprunt Comm Coll (NC)
Jamestown Business Coll (NY)
Jamestown Comm Coll (NY)
Jefferson Coll (MO)
Jefferson Comm Coll (NY)
Johnston Comm Coll (NC)
John Tyler Comm Coll (VA)
Kankakee Comm Coll (IL)
Kilgore Coll (TX)
Kilian Comm Coll (SD)
Kirtland Comm Coll (MI)
Klamath Comm Coll (OR)
Lakeland Comm Coll (OH)
Lake Michigan Coll (MI)
Lake Region State Coll (ND)
Lake Superior Coll (MN)
Lansing Comm Coll (MI)
Laramie County Comm Coll (WY)
Lawson State Comm Coll (AL)
LDS Business Coll (UT)
Lehigh Carbon Comm Coll (PA)
Lone Star Coll–CyFair (TX)
Lone Star Coll–Kingwood (TX)
Lone Star Coll–Montgomery (TX)
Lone Star Coll–North Harris (TX)
Lone Star Coll–Tomball (TX)
Long Island Business Inst (NY)
Lorain County Comm Coll (OH)
Lower Columbia Coll (WA)
Luzerne County Comm Coll (PA)
Macomb Comm Coll (MI)
Manchester Comm Coll (CT)
Manor Coll (PA)
Massachusetts Bay Comm Coll (MA)
McCann School of Business & Technology, Pottsville (PA)
McHenry County Coll (IL)
Mendocino Coll (CA)
Mesa Comm Coll (AZ)
Metropolitan Comm Coll–Kansas City (MO)
Miami Dade Coll (FL)
Middlesex Comm Coll (MA)
Mid-Plains Comm Coll, North Platte (NE)
Minnesota West Comm and Tech Coll (MN)
Missouri State U–West Plains (MO)
Mohave Comm Coll (AZ)
Mohawk Valley Comm Coll (NY)
Monroe Comm Coll (NY)
Monroe County Comm Coll (MI)
Montcalm Comm Coll (MI)
Montgomery Comm Coll (NC)
Montgomery County Comm Coll (PA)
Moraine Park Tech Coll (WI)
Moraine Valley Comm Coll (IL)
Motlow State Comm Coll (TN)
Mott Comm Coll (MI)
Mt. San Antonio Coll (CA)
Nassau Comm Coll (NY)
Niagara County Comm Coll (NY)
Northampton Comm Coll (PA)
North Dakota State Coll of Science (ND)
Northeastern Jr Coll (CO)
Northeast Iowa Comm Coll (IA)
Northern Essex Comm Coll (MA)
North Hennepin Comm Coll (MN)
North Shore Comm Coll (MA)
NorthWest Arkansas Comm Coll (AR)
Northwest Coll (WY)
Northwest State Comm Coll (OH)
Northwest Tech Coll (MN)
Norwalk Comm Coll (CT)
Oakland Comm Coll (MI)
Ocean County Coll (NJ)
Oklahoma City Comm Coll (OK)
Oklahoma State U, Oklahoma City (OK)
Olympic Coll (WA)
Onondaga Comm Coll (NY)
Orange Coast Coll (CA)
Owensboro Comm and Tech Coll (KY)
Oxnard Coll (CA)
Ozarks Tech Comm Coll (MO)
Paris Jr Coll (TX)
Parkland Coll (IL)
Pasadena City Coll (CA)
Pasco-Hernando Comm Coll (FL)
Paul D. Camp Comm Coll (VA)
Pensacola State Coll (FL)
Phoenix Coll (AZ)
Piedmont Comm Coll (NC)
Piedmont Virginia Comm Coll (VA)
Pierce Coll at Puyallup (WA)
Pittsburgh Tech Inst, Oakdale (PA)
Potomac State Coll of West Virginia U (WV)
Quinsigamond Comm Coll (MA)
Randolph Comm Coll (NC)
Rappahannock Comm Coll (VA)
Raritan Valley Comm Coll (NJ)
Rasmussen Coll Aurora (IL)
Rasmussen Coll Bloomington (MN)
Rasmussen Coll Brooklyn Park (MN)
Rasmussen Coll Eagan (MN)
Rasmussen Coll Fort Myers (FL)
Rasmussen Coll Green Bay (WI)
Rasmussen Coll Lake Elmo/Woodbury (MN)
Rasmussen Coll Mankato (MN)
Rasmussen Coll Moorhead (MN)
Rasmussen Coll New Port Richey (FL)
Rasmussen Coll Ocala (FL)
Rasmussen Coll St. Cloud (MN)
Red Rocks Comm Coll (CO)
Robeson Comm Coll (NC)
Rogue Comm Coll (OR)
St. Louis Comm Coll at Meramec (MO)
St. Philip's Coll (TX)
Salt Lake Comm Coll (UT)
San Diego City Coll (CA)
San Diego Mesa Coll (CA)
San Jacinto Coll District (TX)
San Juan Coll (NM)
Santa Rosa Jr Coll (CA)
Schoolcraft Coll (MI)
Scottsdale Comm Coll (AZ)
Seminole State Coll of Florida (FL)
Shawnee Comm Coll (IL)
Sierra Coll (CA)
Southeastern Comm Coll (IA)
Southeast Tech Inst (SD)
Southern Maine Comm Coll (ME)
Southern State Comm Coll (OH)
South Plains Coll (TX)
South Puget Sound Comm Coll (WA)
Southwestern Michigan Coll (MI)
Spartanburg Comm Coll (SC)
Spoon River Coll (IL)
Springfield Tech Comm Coll (MA)
Stark State Coll (OH)
Sullivan County Comm Coll (NY)
Taft Coll (CA)
Tallahassee Comm Coll (FL)
Tarrant County Coll District (TX)
Temple Coll (TX)
Terra State Comm Coll (OH)
Texarkana Coll (TX)
Thomas Nelson Comm Coll (VA)
Tompkins Cortland Comm Coll (NY)
Tri-County Comm Coll (NC)
Trident Tech Coll (SC)
Tunxis Comm Coll (CT)
Tyler Jr Coll (TX)
Union County Coll (NJ)
The U of Akron–Wayne Coll (OH)
U of Alaska Anchorage, Kenai Peninsula Coll (AK)
Victor Valley Coll (CA)
Vincennes U (IN)
Virginia Western Comm Coll (VA)
Volunteer State Comm Coll (TN)
Waubonsee Comm Coll (IL)
Waukesha County Tech Coll (WI)
Westchester Comm Coll (NY)
Western Dakota Tech Inst (SD)
Western Iowa Tech Comm Coll (IA)
West Kentucky Comm and Tech Coll (KY)
Westmoreland County Comm Coll (PA)
West Virginia Jr Coll–Bridgeport (WV)
Wilson Comm Coll (NC)
Wisconsin Indianhead Tech Coll (WI)
Wytheville Comm Coll (VA)
York County Comm Coll (ME)

BUSINESS ADMINISTRATION, MANAGEMENT AND OPERATIONS RELATED

Anne Arundel Comm Coll (MD)
Berkeley City Coll (CA)
The Comm Coll of Baltimore County (MD)
John Tyler Comm Coll (VA)
Northwest State Comm Coll (OH)
Rappahannock Comm Coll (VA)
Red Rocks Comm Coll (CO)
Southwest Virginia Comm Coll (VA)
Thomas Nelson Comm Coll (VA)
Waukesha County Tech Coll (WI)

BUSINESS AND PERSONAL/FINANCIAL SERVICES MARKETING

Hutchinson Comm Coll and Area Vocational School (KS)

BUSINESS AUTOMATION/TECHNOLOGY/DATA ENTRY

Alpena Comm Coll (MI)
Berkshire Comm Coll (MA)
Bismarck State Coll (ND)
Casper Coll (WY)
Central Wyoming Coll (WY)
Clark Coll (WA)
Coll of Lake County (IL)
Collin County Comm Coll District (TX)
Comm Coll of Allegheny County (PA)
Crowder Coll (MO)
Dakota Coll at Bottineau (ND)
Delaware Tech & Comm Coll, Jack F. Owens Campus (DE)
Delaware Tech & Comm Coll, Stanton/Wilmington Campus (DE)
Delaware Tech & Comm Coll, Terry Campus (DE)
El Centro Coll (TX)
Garrett Coll (MD)
Hallmark Coll of Technology (TX)
Houston Comm Coll System (TX)
Illinois Eastern Comm Colls, Frontier Community College (IL)
Illinois Eastern Comm Colls, Lincoln Trail College (IL)
Illinois Eastern Comm Colls, Olney Central College (IL)
Illinois Eastern Comm Colls, Wabash Valley College (IL)
Ivy Tech Comm Coll–Bloomington (IN)
Ivy Tech Comm Coll–Central Indiana (IN)
Ivy Tech Comm Coll–Columbus (IN)
Ivy Tech Comm Coll–East Central (IN)
Ivy Tech Comm Coll–Kokomo (IN)
Ivy Tech Comm Coll–Lafayette (IN)
Ivy Tech Comm Coll–North Central (IN)
Ivy Tech Comm Coll–Northeast (IN)
Ivy Tech Comm Coll–Northwest (IN)
Ivy Tech Comm Coll–Richmond (IN)
Ivy Tech Comm Coll–Southeast (IN)
Ivy Tech Comm Coll–Southern Indiana (IN)
Ivy Tech Comm Coll–Southwest (IN)
Kaskaskia Coll (IL)
Lake Superior Coll (MN)
Lincoln Land Comm Coll (IL)
Macomb Comm Coll (MI)
Mitchell Tech Inst (SD)
Northeast Iowa Comm Coll (IA)
Northwest State Comm Coll (OH)
Oakland Comm Coll (MI)
Ozarka Coll (AR)
Parkland Coll (IL)
Pasadena City Coll (CA)
St. Louis Comm Coll at Forest Park (MO)
St. Louis Comm Coll at Meramec (MO)
San Jacinto Coll District (TX)
Schoolcraft Coll (MI)
Shawnee Comm Coll (IL)
Waubonsee Comm Coll (IL)
Western Iowa Tech Comm Coll (IA)

BUSINESS/COMMERCE

Anne Arundel Comm Coll (MD)
Anoka-Ramsey Comm Coll (MN)
Anoka-Ramsey Comm Coll, Cambridge Campus (MN)
Arizona Western Coll (AZ)
Arkansas State U–Mountain Home (AR)
Austin Comm Coll (TX)
Berkeley City Coll (CA)
Berkshire Comm Coll (MA)
Bismarck State Coll (ND)
Bossier Parish Comm Coll (LA)
Brookhaven Coll (TX)
Bucks County Comm Coll (PA)
Carl Albert State Coll (OK)
Cecil Coll (MD)
Central Wyoming Coll (WY)
Coll of Marin (CA)
Coll of Southern Maryland (MD)
Coll of the Desert (CA)
The Comm Coll of Baltimore County (MD)
Comm Coll of Beaver County (PA)
Comm Coll of Rhode Island (RI)
Delaware Tech & Comm Coll, Jack F. Owens Campus (DE)
Delaware Tech & Comm Coll, Stanton/Wilmington Campus (DE)
Delaware Tech & Comm Coll, Terry Campus (DE)
Elaine P. Nunez Comm Coll (LA)
El Centro Coll (TX)
Garrett Coll (MD)
Glendale Comm Coll (AZ)
Goodwin Coll (CT)
Greenfield Comm Coll (MA)
Hagerstown Comm Coll (MD)
Harford Comm Coll (MD)
Harrisburg Area Comm Coll (PA)
Hutchinson Comm Coll and Area Vocational School (KS)
Jefferson Coll (MO)
John Tyler Comm Coll (VA)
Kaskaskia Coll (IL)
Kent State U at Ashtabula (OH)
Kent State U at East Liverpool (OH)
Kent State U at Salem (OH)
Kent State U at Trumbull (OH)
Kent State U at Tuscarawas (OH)
Kilgore Coll (TX)
Lansing Comm Coll (MI)
Laramie County Comm Coll (WY)
Lehigh Carbon Comm Coll (PA)
Lincoln Land Comm Coll (IL)
Macomb Comm Coll (MI)
Massachusetts Bay Comm Coll (MA)
Miles Comm Coll (MT)
Mineral Area Coll (MO)
Minnesota West Comm and Tech Coll (MN)
Missouri State U–West Plains (MO)
Montgomery Coll (MD)
Montgomery County Comm Coll (PA)
Moraine Valley Comm Coll (IL)
Mott Comm Coll (MI)
Northampton Comm Coll (PA)
Northwest Coll (WY)
Northwest State Comm Coll (OH)
Ocean County Coll (NJ)
Oklahoma City Comm Coll (OK)
Onondaga Comm Coll (NY)
Owens Comm Coll, Toledo (OH)
Penn State Beaver (PA)
Penn State Brandywine (PA)
Penn State DuBois (PA)
Penn State Fayette, The Eberly Campus (PA)
Penn State Greater Allegheny (PA)
Penn State Hazleton (PA)
Penn State Lehigh Valley (PA)
Penn State Mont Alto (PA)
Penn State New Kensington (PA)
Penn State Schuylkill (PA)
Penn State Wilkes-Barre (PA)

Penn State Worthington Scranton (PA)
Penn State York (PA)
Pensacola State Coll (FL)
Phoenix Coll (AZ)
Quinsigamond Comm Coll (MA)
Raritan Valley Comm Coll (NJ)
Rogue Comm Coll (OR)
St. Clair County Comm Coll (MI)
San Jacinto Coll District (TX)
Schoolcraft Coll (MI)
Shelton State Comm Coll (AL)
Sheridan Coll (WY)
Sierra Coll (CA)
Southern State Comm Coll (OH)
Springfield Tech Comm Coll (MA)
Tech Coll of the Lowcountry (SC)
Terra State Comm Coll (OH)
Texarkana Coll (TX)
Union County Coll (NJ)
U of Arkansas Comm Coll at Morrilton (AR)
U of Pittsburgh at Titusville (PA)
Victor Valley Coll (CA)
Vincennes U (IN)
Westmoreland County Comm Coll (PA)
West Virginia Northern Comm Coll (WV)

BUSINESS/CORPORATE COMMUNICATIONS
Cecil Coll (MD)
Houston Comm Coll System (TX)
Montgomery County Comm Coll (PA)
York County Comm Coll (ME)

BUSINESS MACHINE REPAIR
Comm Coll of Allegheny County (PA)
De Anza Coll (CA)
Ozarks Tech Comm Coll (MO)

BUSINESS, MANAGEMENT, AND MARKETING RELATED
Berkeley City Coll (CA)
Blue Ridge Comm and Tech Coll (WV)
Bucks County Comm Coll (PA)
County Coll of Morris (NJ)
James A. Rhodes State Coll (OH)
Long Island Business Inst (NY)
Manor Coll (PA)
Niagara County Comm Coll (NY)
Tompkins Cortland Comm Coll (NY)

BUSINESS/MANAGERIAL ECONOMICS
Potomac State Coll of West Virginia U (WV)

BUSINESS OPERATIONS SUPPORT AND SECRETARIAL SERVICES RELATED
Gateway Tech Coll (WI)
Southwest Virginia Comm Coll (VA)
Thomas Nelson Comm Coll (VA)

BUSINESS TEACHER EDUCATION
Amarillo Coll (TX)
Bainbridge Coll (GA)
Darton State Coll (GA)
Essex County Coll (NJ)
Mt. San Antonio Coll (CA)
Northeastern Jr Coll (CO)
Northern Essex Comm Coll (MA)
Paris Jr Coll (TX)
Spoon River Coll (IL)

CABINETMAKING AND MILLWORK
Bucks County Comm Coll (PA)
Harrisburg Area Comm Coll (PA)
Ivy Tech Comm Coll–Bloomington (IN)
Ivy Tech Comm Coll–Central Indiana (IN)
Ivy Tech Comm Coll–Columbus (IN)
Ivy Tech Comm Coll–East Central (IN)
Ivy Tech Comm Coll–Kokomo (IN)
Ivy Tech Comm Coll–Lafayette (IN)
Ivy Tech Comm Coll–North Central (IN)
Ivy Tech Comm Coll–Northeast (IN)
Ivy Tech Comm Coll–Northwest (IN)
Ivy Tech Comm Coll–Richmond (IN)
Ivy Tech Comm Coll–Southern Indiana (IN)
Ivy Tech Comm Coll–Southwest (IN)
Ivy Tech Comm Coll–Wabash Valley (IN)

Macomb Comm Coll (MI)
Sierra Coll (CA)

CAD/CADD DRAFTING/DESIGN TECHNOLOGY
Central Oregon Comm Coll (OR)
Century Coll (MN)
Chemeketa Comm Coll (OR)
Comm Coll of Vermont (VT)
Corning Comm Coll (NY)
Delaware Tech & Comm Coll, Stanton/Wilmington Campus (DE)
Dunwoody Coll of Technology (MN)
Elgin Comm Coll (IL)
Erie Comm Coll, South Campus (NY)
Gateway Comm and Tech Coll (KY)
Glendale Comm Coll (AZ)
Harford Comm Coll (MD)
Lake Superior Coll (MN)
Lone Star Coll–Montgomery (TX)
Lone Star Coll–North Harris (TX)
Montgomery County Comm Coll (PA)
Northampton Comm Coll (PA)
Northwest Coll (WY)
Northwest State Comm Coll (OH)
St. Philip's Coll (TX)
Sheridan Coll (WY)
Southern State Comm Coll (OH)
South Suburban Coll (IL)
State U of New York Coll of Technology at Alfred (NY)
Sullivan Coll of Technology and Design (KY)
Thomas Nelson Comm Coll (VA)
Waubonsee Comm Coll (IL)

CARDIOVASCULAR SCIENCE
Forsyth Tech Comm Coll (NC)

CARDIOVASCULAR TECHNOLOGY
Comm Coll of the Air Force (AL)
Darton State Coll (GA)
Delaware Tech & Comm Coll, Stanton/Wilmington Campus (DE)
El Centro Coll (TX)
Forsyth Tech Comm Coll (NC)
Harper Coll (IL)
Harrisburg Area Comm Coll (PA)
Houston Comm Coll System (TX)
Howard Comm Coll (MD)
Kirtland Comm Coll (MI)
Lancaster General Coll of Nursing & Health Sciences (PA)
Orange Coast Coll (CA)
Southeast Tech Inst (SD)
Southern Maine Comm Coll (ME)
Spencerian Coll (KY)

CARPENTRY
Alamance Comm Coll (NC)
Alexandria Tech and Comm Coll (MN)
Arizona Western Coll (AZ)
Austin Comm Coll (TX)
Bakersfield Coll (CA)
Bismarck State Coll (ND)
Central Wyoming Coll (WY)
Comm Coll of Allegheny County (PA)
Comm Coll of Beaver County (PA)
Elaine P. Nunez Comm Coll (LA)
Flathead Valley Comm Coll (MT)
Hutchinson Comm Coll and Area Vocational School (KS)
Ivy Tech Comm Coll–Central Indiana (IN)
Ivy Tech Comm Coll–East Central (IN)
Ivy Tech Comm Coll–Lafayette (IN)
Ivy Tech Comm Coll–North Central (IN)
Ivy Tech Comm Coll–Northwest (IN)
Ivy Tech Comm Coll–Southern Indiana (IN)
Ivy Tech Comm Coll–Southwest (IN)
Ivy Tech Comm Coll–Wabash Valley (IN)
Kaskaskia Coll (IL)
Lake Area Tech Inst (SD)
Lansing Comm Coll (MI)
Metropolitan Comm Coll–Kansas City (MO)
Mineral Area Coll (MO)
Oakland Comm Coll (MI)
San Diego City Coll (CA)
San Juan Coll (NM)
South Plains Coll (TX)
Southwestern Michigan Coll (MI)
State U of New York Coll of Technology at Alfred (NY)

CASINO MANAGEMENT
Lake Michigan Coll (MI)
Westmoreland County Comm Coll (PA)

CERAMIC ARTS AND CERAMICS
Butte Coll (CA)
De Anza Coll (CA)
Oakland Comm Coll (MI)

CHEMICAL ENGINEERING
Alpena Comm Coll (MI)
Burlington County Coll (NJ)
Kilgore Coll (TX)
Monroe Comm Coll (NY)

CHEMICAL PROCESS TECHNOLOGY
San Jacinto Coll District (TX)

CHEMICAL TECHNOLOGY
Alvin Comm Coll (TX)
Amarillo Coll (TX)
Bucks County Comm Coll (PA)
Cape Fear Comm Coll (NC)
Coll of Lake County (IL)
Comm Coll of Allegheny County (PA)
Comm Coll of Beaver County (PA)
Comm Coll of Philadelphia (PA)
Comm Coll of Rhode Island (RI)
Corning Comm Coll (NY)
County Coll of Morris (NJ)
Delaware Tech & Comm Coll, Stanton/Wilmington Campus (DE)
Essex County Coll (NJ)
Guilford Tech Comm Coll (NC)
Houston Comm Coll System (TX)
ITI Tech Coll (LA)
Lansing Comm Coll (MI)
Lehigh Carbon Comm Coll (PA)
Massachusetts Bay Comm Coll (MA)
Mohawk Valley Comm Coll (NY)
Niagara County Comm Coll (NY)
Pensacola State Coll (FL)
Raritan Valley Comm Coll (NJ)
San Jacinto Coll District (TX)
Texas State Tech Coll Harlingen (TX)
Westmoreland County Comm Coll (PA)

CHEMISTRY
Alpena Comm Coll (MI)
Amarillo Coll (TX)
Arizona Western Coll (AZ)
Austin Comm Coll (TX)
Bainbridge Coll (GA)
Bakersfield Coll (CA)
Barton County Comm Coll (KS)
Burlington County Coll (NJ)
Butte Coll (CA)
Casper Coll (WY)
Cecil Coll (MD)
Cochise Coll, Sierra Vista (AZ)
Coll of Marin (CA)
Coll of the Desert (CA)
Comm Coll of Allegheny County (PA)
Comm Coll of Beaver County (PA)
Copiah-Lincoln Comm Coll (MS)
Cowley County Comm Coll and Area Vocational–Tech School (KS)
Dakota Coll at Bottineau (ND)
Darton State Coll (GA)
Essex County Coll (NJ)
Finger Lakes Comm Coll (NY)
Foothill Coll (CA)
Georgia Highlands Coll (GA)
Gordon State Coll (GA)
Grand Rapids Comm Coll (MI)
Harford Comm Coll (MD)
Harper Coll (IL)
Harrisburg Area Comm Coll (PA)
Kankakee Comm Coll (IL)
Kilgore Coll (TX)
Lake Michigan Coll (MI)
Lansing Comm Coll (MI)
Laramie County Comm Coll (WY)
Lone Star Coll–CyFair (TX)
Lone Star Coll–Kingwood (TX)
Lone Star Coll–Montgomery (TX)
Lone Star Coll–North Harris (TX)
Lone Star Coll–Tomball (TX)
Lorain County Comm Coll (OH)
Macomb Comm Coll (MI)
Mendocino Coll (CA)
Metropolitan Comm Coll–Kansas City (MO)
Miami Dade Coll (FL)
Monroe Comm Coll (NY)
Northampton Comm Coll (PA)
North Hennepin Comm Coll (MN)
Northwest Coll (WY)
Oklahoma City Comm Coll (OK)

Orange Coast Coll (CA)
Pasadena City Coll (CA)
Pensacola State Coll (FL)
Potomac State Coll of West Virginia U (WV)
St. Philip's Coll (TX)
Salt Lake Comm Coll (UT)
San Diego Mesa Coll (CA)
San Jacinto Coll District (TX)
San Juan Coll (NM)
Santa Rosa Jr Coll (CA)
Sierra Coll (CA)
South Plains Coll (TX)
Spoon River Coll (IL)
Springfield Tech Comm Coll (MA)
Terra State Comm Coll (OH)
Texarkana Coll (TX)
Tyler Jr Coll (TX)
Union County Coll (NJ)
Vincennes U (IN)

CHEMISTRY RELATED
Vincennes U (IN)

CHEMISTRY TEACHER EDUCATION
Anne Arundel Comm Coll (MD)
Bucks County Comm Coll (PA)
Carroll Comm Coll (MD)
The Comm Coll of Baltimore County (MD)
Harford Comm Coll (MD)
Montgomery Coll (MD)
Vincennes U (IN)

CHILD-CARE AND SUPPORT SERVICES MANAGEMENT
Alexandria Tech and Comm Coll (MN)
Anne Arundel Comm Coll (MD)
Barton County Comm Coll (KS)
Bay State Coll (MA)
Bevill State Comm Coll (AL)
Carroll Comm Coll (MD)
Cayuga County Comm Coll (NY)
Cecil Coll (MD)
Central New Mexico Comm Coll (NM)
Central Oregon Comm Coll (OR)
Central Wyoming Coll (WY)
Chemeketa Comm Coll (OR)
Colby Comm Coll (KS)
Coll of Southern Maryland (MD)
Coll of the Desert (CA)
The Comm Coll of Baltimore County (MD)
Cowley County Comm Coll and Area Vocational–Tech School (KS)
Dakota Coll at Bottineau (ND)
Dutchess Comm Coll (NY)
Erie Comm Coll (NY)
Flathead Valley Comm Coll (MT)
Forrest Coll (SC)
Gadsden State Comm Coll (AL)
Goodwin Coll (CT)
Grand Rapids Comm Coll (MI)
Hagerstown Comm Coll (MD)
Hillsborough Comm Coll (FL)
Holyoke Comm Coll (MA)
Hutchinson Comm Coll and Area Vocational School (KS)
Ivy Tech Comm Coll–Bloomington (IN)
Ivy Tech Comm Coll–Central Indiana (IN)
Ivy Tech Comm Coll–Columbus (IN)
Ivy Tech Comm Coll–East Central (IN)
Ivy Tech Comm Coll–Kokomo (IN)
Ivy Tech Comm Coll–Lafayette (IN)
Ivy Tech Comm Coll–North Central (IN)
Ivy Tech Comm Coll–Northeast (IN)
Ivy Tech Comm Coll–Northwest (IN)
Ivy Tech Comm Coll–Richmond (IN)
Ivy Tech Comm Coll–Southeast (IN)
Ivy Tech Comm Coll–Southern Indiana (IN)
Ivy Tech Comm Coll–Southwest (IN)
Ivy Tech Comm Coll–Wabash Valley (IN)
Jefferson Coll (MO)
Jefferson Comm Coll (NY)
Jefferson State Comm Coll (AL)
Kilgore Coll (TX)
Lawson State Comm Coll (AL)
Lurleen B. Wallace Comm Coll (AL)
Macomb Comm Coll (MI)
Massachusetts Bay Comm Coll (MA)
Minnesota West Comm and Tech Coll (MN)
Missouri State U–West Plains (MO)
Montcalm Comm Coll (MI)

Montgomery County Comm Coll (PA)
Northwest-Shoals Comm Coll (AL)
Northwest State Comm Coll (OH)
Northwest Tech Coll (MN)
Oakland Comm Coll (MI)
Orange Coast Coll (CA)
Pensacola State Coll (FL)
Phoenix Coll (AZ)
Piedmont Comm Coll (NC)
Reid State Tech Coll (AL)
Rogue Comm Coll (OR)
Southeast Tech Inst (SD)
Texarkana Coll (TX)
Tompkins Cortland Comm Coll (NY)
Victor Valley Coll (CA)
Vincennes U (IN)
Wisconsin Indianhead Tech Coll (WI)

CHILD-CARE PROVISION
Alexandria Tech and Comm Coll (MN)
Bucks County Comm Coll (PA)
Coll of Lake County (IL)
Coll of Marin (CA)
Coll of the Canyons (CA)
Collin County Comm Coll District (TX)
Comm Coll of Allegheny County (PA)
Dakota Coll at Bottineau (ND)
Elaine P. Nunez Comm Coll (LA)
Harper Coll (IL)
Hawkeye Comm Coll (IA)
Highland Comm Coll (IL)
Illinois Central Coll (IL)
John Tyler Comm Coll (VA)
Kaskaskia Coll (IL)
Kilgore Coll (TX)
Lakeland Comm Coll (OH)
Lake Region State Coll (ND)
Lansing Comm Coll (MI)
Lincoln Land Comm Coll (IL)
Luzerne County Comm Coll (PA)
McHenry County Coll (IL)
Metropolitan Comm Coll–Kansas City (MO)
Mineral Area Coll (MO)
Montcalm Comm Coll (MI)
Montgomery Coll (MD)
Moraine Valley Comm Coll (IL)
Mott Comm Coll (MI)
Oakton Comm Coll (IL)
Orange Coast Coll (CA)
Parkland Coll (IL)
Pensacola State Coll (FL)
Raritan Valley Comm Coll (NJ)
St. Louis Comm Coll at Forest Park (MO)
St. Louis Comm Coll at Meramec (MO)
San Diego Mesa Coll (CA)
San Juan Coll (NM)
Southeast Tech Inst (SD)
South Suburban Coll (IL)
Southwest Virginia Comm Coll (VA)
Tech Coll of the Lowcountry (SC)
Thomas Nelson Comm Coll (VA)
Trident Tech Coll (SC)
Vincennes U (IN)
Waubonsee Comm Coll (IL)
Western Iowa Tech Comm Coll (IA)
Westmoreland County Comm Coll (PA)

CHILD DEVELOPMENT
Alexandria Tech and Comm Coll (MN)
Alvin Comm Coll (TX)
Amarillo Coll (TX)
Austin Comm Coll (TX)
Bakersfield Coll (CA)
Brookhaven Coll (TX)
Butte Coll (CA)
Carl Albert State Coll (OK)
Central Maine Comm Coll (ME)
Cleveland State Comm Coll (TN)
Colby Comm Coll (KS)
Collin County Comm Coll District (TX)
Comm Coll of Allegheny County (PA)
Comm Coll of Vermont (VT)
Copiah-Lincoln Comm Coll (MS)
Cowley County Comm Coll and Area Vocational–Tech School (KS)
Daytona State Coll (FL)
De Anza Coll (CA)
Dyersburg State Comm Coll (TN)
Edison Comm Coll (OH)
Florida Gateway Coll (FL)
Foothill Coll (CA)
Goodwin Coll (CT)
Housatonic Comm Coll (CT)
Houston Comm Coll System (TX)

Howard Comm Coll (MD)
Illinois Eastern Comm Colls, Wabash Valley College (IL)
Ivy Tech Comm Coll–Central Indiana (IN)
Jackson State Comm Coll (TN)
James A. Rhodes State Coll (OH)
James Sprunt Comm Coll (NC)
Jefferson Comm Coll (NY)
Kennebec Valley Comm Coll (ME)
Mendocino Coll (CA)
Mesa Comm Coll (AZ)
Miami Dade Coll (FL)
Monroe County Comm Coll (MI)
Mt. San Antonio Coll (CA)
Northeastern Jr Coll (CO)
North Shore Comm Coll (MA)
Northwest-Shoals Comm Coll (AL)
Northwest State Comm Coll (OH)
Oklahoma City Comm Coll (OK)
Oxnard Coll (CA)
Pasadena City Coll (CA)
San Jacinto Coll District (TX)
Santa Rosa Jr Coll (CA)
Schoolcraft Coll (MI)
Seminole State Coll of Florida (FL)
Shawnee Comm Coll (IL)
Sierra Coll (CA)
Southeastern Comm Coll (IA)
South Plains Coll (TX)
Spoon River Coll (IL)
Stark State Coll (OH)
Texarkana Coll (TX)
Tyler Jr Coll (TX)
U of Arkansas Comm Coll at Morrilton (AR)
Victor Valley Coll (CA)
Virginia Western Comm Coll (VA)
Volunteer State Comm Coll (TN)
Westchester Comm Coll (NY)
York County Comm Coll (ME)

CHIROPRACTIC ASSISTANT
Barton County Comm Coll (KS)
Moraine Park Tech Coll (WI)

CINEMATOGRAPHY AND FILM/VIDEO PRODUCTION
Bucks County Comm Coll (PA)
Cape Fear Comm Coll (NC)
Coll of Marin (CA)
Glendale Comm Coll (AZ)
Hillsborough Comm Coll (FL)
Houston Comm Coll System (TX)
Lansing Comm Coll (MI)
Mott Comm Coll (MI)
Northwest Coll (WY)
Oklahoma City Comm Coll (OK)
Orange Coast Coll (CA)
Pasadena City Coll (CA)
Pensacola State Coll (FL)
Piedmont Comm Coll (NC)
Raritan Valley Comm Coll (NJ)
Red Rocks Comm Coll (CO)
Western Iowa Tech Comm Coll (IA)

CIVIL DRAFTING AND CAD/CADD
Comm Coll of Allegheny County (PA)
Delaware Tech & Comm Coll, Stanton/Wilmington Campus (DE)
Sullivan Coll of Technology and Design (KY)

CIVIL ENGINEERING
Fiorello H. LaGuardia Comm Coll of the City U of New York (NY)
Kilgore Coll (TX)
Pensacola State Coll (FL)
Vincennes U (IN)

CIVIL ENGINEERING TECHNOLOGY
Arapahoe Comm Coll (CO)
Arizona Western Coll (AZ)
Chemeketa Comm Coll (OR)
Chippewa Valley Tech Coll (WI)
Clark State Comm Coll (OH)
Coll of Lake County (IL)
Comm Coll of Allegheny County (PA)
Copiah-Lincoln Comm Coll (MS)
Delaware Tech & Comm Coll, Jack F. Owens Campus (DE)
Delaware Tech & Comm Coll, Terry Campus (DE)
Erie Comm Coll, North Campus (NY)
Essex County Coll (NJ)
Fayetteville Tech Comm Coll (NC)
Gadsden State Comm Coll (AL)
Gateway Tech Coll (WI)

Guilford Tech Comm Coll (NC)
Harrisburg Area Comm Coll (PA)
Hawkeye Comm Coll (IA)
James A. Rhodes State Coll (OH)
Lakeland Comm Coll (OH)
Lake Superior Coll (MN)
Lansing Comm Coll (MI)
Lorain County Comm Coll (OH)
Macomb Comm Coll (MI)
Miami Dade Coll (FL)
Mineral Area Coll (MO)
Mohawk Valley Comm Coll (NY)
Monroe Comm Coll (NY)
Mt. San Antonio Coll (CA)
Nassau Comm Coll (NY)
North Dakota State Coll of Science (ND)
Northern Essex Comm Coll (MA)
Oklahoma State U, Oklahoma City (OK)
Pensacola State Coll (FL)
Phoenix Coll (AZ)
Potomac State Coll of West Virginia U (WV)
Santa Rosa Jr Coll (CA)
Seminole State Coll of Florida (FL)
Southeast Tech Inst (SD)
Springfield Tech Comm Coll (MA)
Stark State Coll (OH)
Tallahassee Comm Coll (FL)
Tech Coll of the Lowcountry (SC)
Trident Tech Coll (SC)
Union County Coll (NJ)
Virginia Western Comm Coll (VA)
Westchester Comm Coll (NY)
Wytheville Comm Coll (VA)

CLASSICS AND CLASSICAL LANGUAGES
Foothill Coll (CA)
Pasadena City Coll (CA)

CLINICAL LABORATORY SCIENCE/MEDICAL TECHNOLOGY
Amarillo Coll (TX)
Casper Coll (WY)
Chipola Coll (FL)
Cuyahoga Comm Coll (OH)
Darton State Coll (GA)
Georgia Highlands Coll (GA)
Howard Comm Coll (MD)
Monroe County Comm Coll (MI)
Northeastern Jr Coll (CO)
Orange Coast Coll (CA)
San Jacinto Coll District (TX)
Tarrant County Coll District (TX)
Westchester Comm Coll (NY)

CLINICAL/MEDICAL LABORATORY ASSISTANT
Comm Coll of Beaver County (PA)
Delaware Tech & Comm Coll, Jack F. Owens Campus (DE)
Westmoreland County Comm Coll (PA)

CLINICAL/MEDICAL LABORATORY SCIENCE AND ALLIED PROFESSIONS RELATED
Houston Comm Coll System (TX)
Southeast Tech Inst (SD)

CLINICAL/MEDICAL LABORATORY TECHNOLOGY
Alamance Comm Coll (NC)
Alexandria Tech and Comm Coll (MN)
Anne Arundel Comm Coll (MD)
Arapahoe Comm Coll (CO)
Austin Comm Coll (TX)
Barton County Comm Coll (KS)
Beaufort County Comm Coll (NC)
Bismarck State Coll (ND)
Blackhawk Tech Coll (WI)
Carrington Coll–Phoenix Westside (AZ)
Carrington Coll–Tucson (AZ)
Central New Mexico Comm Coll (NM)
Chippewa Valley Tech Coll (WI)
Clark State Comm Coll (OH)
Coll of Southern Maryland (MD)
Comm Coll of Allegheny County (PA)
The Comm Coll of Baltimore County (MD)
Comm Coll of Philadelphia (PA)
Comm Coll of Rhode Island (RI)
Comm Coll of the Air Force (AL)

Copiah-Lincoln Comm Coll (MS)
Dutchess Comm Coll (NY)
Edison Comm Coll (OH)
El Centro Coll (TX)
Elgin Comm Coll (IL)
Erie Comm Coll, North Campus (NY)
Forsyth Tech Comm Coll (NC)
Gadsden State Comm Coll (AL)
Genesee Comm Coll (NY)
Halifax Comm Coll (NC)
Harrisburg Area Comm Coll (PA)
Hawkeye Comm Coll (IA)
Housatonic Comm Coll (CT)
Houston Comm Coll System (TX)
Illinois Central Coll (IL)
Ivy Tech Comm Coll–North Central (IN)
Ivy Tech Comm Coll–Wabash Valley (IN)
Jackson State Comm Coll (TN)
Jefferson State Comm Coll (AL)
Kankakee Comm Coll (IL)
Kaskaskia Coll (IL)
Kilgore Coll (TX)
Lake Area Tech Inst (SD)
Lakeland Comm Coll (OH)
Lake Superior Coll (MN)
Lorain County Comm Coll (OH)
Manchester Comm Coll (CT)
Miami Dade Coll (FL)
Mid-Plains Comm Coll, North Platte (NE)
Minnesota West Comm and Tech Coll (MN)
Mitchell Tech Inst (SD)
Montgomery County Comm Coll (PA)
Moraine Park Tech Coll (WI)
Nassau Comm Coll (NY)
Northeast Iowa Comm Coll (IA)
North Hennepin Comm Coll (MN)
Oakton Comm Coll (IL)
The Ohio State U Ag Tech Inst (OH)
Panola Coll (TX)
Penn State Hazleton (PA)
Penn State Schuylkill (PA)
Phoenix Coll (AZ)
Rasmussen Coll Bismarck (ND)
Rasmussen Coll Green Bay (WI)
Rasmussen Coll Lake Elmo/Woodbury (MN)
Rasmussen Coll Mankato (MN)
Rasmussen Coll Moorhead (MN)
Rasmussen Coll St. Cloud (MN)
St. Louis Comm Coll at Forest Park (MO)
St. Philip's Coll (TX)
Salt Lake Comm Coll (UT)
San Diego Mesa Coll (CA)
San Jacinto Coll District (TX)
San Juan Coll (NM)
Shawnee Comm Coll (IL)
Southeast Tech Inst (SD)
Spartanburg Comm Coll (SC)
Spencerian Coll (KY)
Springfield Tech Comm Coll (MA)
Stark State Coll (OH)
Tarrant County Coll District (TX)
Trident Tech Coll (SC)
Tyler Jr Coll (TX)
Volunteer State Comm Coll (TN)
Westchester Comm Coll (NY)
Wytheville Comm Coll (VA)

CLINICAL/MEDICAL SOCIAL WORK
Halifax Comm Coll (NC)
Piedmont Comm Coll (NC)

COMMERCIAL AND ADVERTISING ART
Alamance Comm Coll (NC)
Alexandria Tech and Comm Coll (MN)
Amarillo Coll (TX)
Austin Comm Coll (TX)
Bismarck State Coll (ND)
Bucks County Comm Coll (PA)
Burlington County Coll (NJ)
Catawba Valley Comm Coll (NC)
Clark State Comm Coll (OH)
Collin County Comm Coll District (TX)
Comm Coll of Allegheny County (PA)
The Comm Coll of Baltimore County (MD)
Comm Coll of the Air Force (AL)
Cuyahoga Comm Coll (OH)
De Anza Coll (CA)
Delaware Tech & Comm Coll, Terry Campus (DE)

Dutchess Comm Coll (NY)
Edison Comm Coll (OH)
Fashion Inst of Technology (NY)
Fayetteville Tech Comm Coll (NC)
FIDM/The Fashion Inst of Design & Merchandising, Los Angeles Campus (CA)
FIDM/The Fashion Inst of Design & Merchandising, Orange County Campus (CA)
FIDM/The Fashion Inst of Design & Merchandising, San Diego Campus (CA)
FIDM/The Fashion Inst of Design & Merchandising, San Francisco Campus (CA)
Finger Lakes Comm Coll (NY)
Glendale Comm Coll (AZ)
Guilford Tech Comm Coll (NC)
Hagerstown Comm Coll (MD)
Halifax Comm Coll (NC)
Housatonic Comm Coll (CT)
James Sprunt Comm Coll (NC)
Jamestown Comm Coll (NY)
J. F. Drake State Tech Coll (AL)
Johnston Comm Coll (NC)
Kilgore Coll (TX)
Lakeland Comm Coll (OH)
Luzerne County Comm Coll (PA)
Macomb Comm Coll (MI)
Manchester Comm Coll (CT)
Metropolitan Comm Coll–Kansas City (MO)
Miami Dade Coll (FL)
Middlesex Comm Coll (MA)
Mid-Plains Comm Coll, North Platte (NE)
Mohawk Valley Comm Coll (NY)
Monroe Comm Coll (NY)
Montgomery Coll (MD)
Montgomery County Comm Coll (PA)
Mt. San Antonio Coll (CA)
Nassau Comm Coll (NY)
Northern Essex Comm Coll (MA)
NorthWest Arkansas Comm Coll (AR)
Northwest Coll (WY)
Norwalk Comm Coll (CT)
Nossi Coll of Art (TN)
Oakland Comm Coll (MI)
Oklahoma City Comm Coll (OK)
Orange Coast Coll (CA)
Owens Comm Coll, Toledo (OH)
Pensacola State Coll (FL)
Phoenix Coll (AZ)
Randolph Comm Coll (NC)
St. Clair County Comm Coll (MI)
San Diego City Coll (CA)
San Jacinto Coll District (TX)
San Juan Coll (NM)
Schoolcraft Coll (MI)
Southeast Tech Inst (SD)
South Plains Coll (TX)
Springfield Tech Comm Coll (MA)
Sullivan County Comm Coll (NY)
Terra State Comm Coll (OH)
Texas State Tech Coll Harlingen (TX)
Tompkins Cortland Comm Coll (NY)
Trident Tech Coll (SC)
Tunxis Comm Coll (CT)
Tyler Jr Coll (TX)
U of Arkansas Comm Coll at Morrilton (AR)
Vincennes U (IN)
Virginia Western Comm Coll (VA)

COMMERCIAL PHOTOGRAPHY
Austin Comm Coll (TX)
Cecil Coll (MD)
Central Wyoming Coll (WY)
Fashion Inst of Technology (NY)
Fiorello H. LaGuardia Comm Coll of the City U of New York (NY)
Hawkeye Comm Coll (IA)
Houston Comm Coll System (TX)
Kilgore Coll (TX)
Luzerne County Comm Coll (PA)
Mohawk Valley Comm Coll (NY)
Montgomery Coll (MD)
Northwest Coll (WY)
Nossi Coll of Art (TN)
Owens Comm Coll, Toledo (OH)
Phoenix Coll (AZ)
Randolph Comm Coll (NC)
Sierra Coll (CA)
Springfield Tech Comm Coll (MA)
Western Iowa Tech Comm Coll (IA)

COMMUNICATION
Foothill Coll (CA)

Gordon State Coll (GA)
Lake Michigan Coll (MI)
Santa Rosa Jr Coll (CA)

COMMUNICATION AND JOURNALISM RELATED
Cayuga County Comm Coll (NY)
Comm Coll of Beaver County (PA)
Gadsden State Comm Coll (AL)
Georgia Highlands Coll (GA)

COMMUNICATION AND MEDIA RELATED
Manor Coll (PA)
Raritan Valley Comm Coll (NJ)

COMMUNICATION DISORDERS SCIENCES AND SERVICES RELATED
Burlington County Coll (NJ)

COMMUNICATION SCIENCES AND DISORDERS
Forsyth Tech Comm Coll (NC)

COMMUNICATIONS SYSTEMS INSTALLATION AND REPAIR TECHNOLOGY
Cayuga County Comm Coll (NY)
Central Maine Comm Coll (ME)
Dutchess Comm Coll (NY)
Erie Comm Coll, South Campus (NY)
Mohawk Valley Comm Coll (NY)
Westmoreland County Comm Coll (PA)

COMMUNICATIONS TECHNOLOGIES AND SUPPORT SERVICES RELATED
Anne Arundel Comm Coll (MD)
Bowling Green State U-Firelands Coll (OH)
Comm Coll of Allegheny County (PA)
Comm Coll of Beaver County (PA)
Montgomery Coll (MD)
Montgomery County Comm Coll (PA)
Ocean County Coll (NJ)

COMMUNICATIONS TECHNOLOGY
Comm Coll of the Air Force (AL)
Daytona State Coll (FL)
Essex County Coll (NJ)
Fountainhead Coll of Technology (TN)
Hutchinson Comm Coll and Area Vocational School (KS)
Illinois Central Coll (IL)
Mott Comm Coll (MI)
Orange Coast Coll (CA)
Owens Comm Coll, Toledo (OH)
Pensacola State Coll (FL)
St. Louis Comm Coll at Forest Park (MO)
Vincennes U (IN)

COMMUNITY HEALTH AND PREVENTIVE MEDICINE
Anoka-Ramsey Comm Coll (MN)
Anoka-Ramsey Comm Coll, Cambridge Campus (MN)

COMMUNITY HEALTH SERVICES COUNSELING
Comm Coll of Allegheny County (PA)
Dutchess Comm Coll (NY)
Erie Comm Coll (NY)
Greenfield Comm Coll (MA)
Illinois Central Coll (IL)
Mott Comm Coll (MI)
Oakland Comm Coll (MI)
Santa Rosa Jr Coll (CA)
Waubonsee Comm Coll (IL)

COMMUNITY ORGANIZATION AND ADVOCACY
Berkshire Comm Coll (MA)
Borough of Manhattan Comm Coll of the City U of New York (NY)
Cleveland State Comm Coll (TN)
Clinton Comm Coll (NY)
Comm Coll of Vermont (VT)
Jefferson Comm Coll (NY)
Lansing Comm Coll (MI)
Mohawk Valley Comm Coll (NY)
State U of New York Coll of Technology at Alfred (NY)
Tompkins Cortland Comm Coll (NY)
Westchester Comm Coll (NY)

COMPARATIVE LITERATURE
Foothill Coll (CA)
Miami Dade Coll (FL)
St. Louis Comm Coll at Meramec
    (MO)

**COMPUTER AND
INFORMATION SCIENCES**
Alexandria Tech and Comm Coll
    (MN)
Alpena Comm Coll (MI)
Anne Arundel Comm Coll (MD)
Arapahoe Comm Coll (CO)
Arizona Western Coll (AZ)
Austin Comm Coll (TX)
Berkeley City Coll (CA)
Berkshire Comm Coll (MA)
Bevill State Comm Coll (AL)
Borough of Manhattan Comm Coll of
    the City U of New York (NY)
Bucks County Comm Coll (PA)
Carl Albert State Coll (OK)
Carroll Comm Coll (MD)
Cayuga County Comm Coll (NY)
Colby Comm Coll (KS)
Coll of Southern Maryland (MD)
Collin County Comm Coll District
    (TX)
The Comm Coll of Baltimore County
    (MD)
Comm Coll of Beaver County (PA)
Comm Coll of Rhode Island (RI)
Comm Coll of Vermont (VT)
Corning Comm Coll (NY)
Cowley County Comm Coll and Area
    Vocational–Tech School (KS)
Dakota Coll at Bottineau (ND)
Darton State Coll (GA)
Delaware Tech & Comm Coll, Jack F.
    Owens Campus (DE)
Delaware Tech & Comm Coll,
    Stanton/Wilmington Campus (DE)
Delaware Tech & Comm Coll, Terry
    Campus (DE)
Denmark Tech Coll (SC)
Dutchess Comm Coll (NY)
Edison Comm Coll (OH)
Erie Comm Coll, North Campus (NY)
Essex County Coll (NJ)
Finger Lakes Comm Coll (NY)
Florida Gateway Coll (FL)
Forsyth Tech Comm Coll (NC)
Gadsden State Comm Coll (AL)
Georgia Highlands Coll (GA)
Glendale Comm Coll (AZ)
Greenfield Comm Coll (MA)
Hagerstown Comm Coll (MD)
Harford Comm Coll (MD)
Harper Coll (IL)
Harrisburg Area Comm Coll (PA)
Hutchinson Comm Coll and Area
    Vocational School (KS)
Ivy Tech Comm Coll–Bloomington
    (IN)
Ivy Tech Comm Coll–Central Indiana
    (IN)
Ivy Tech Comm Coll–Columbus (IN)
Ivy Tech Comm Coll–East Central
    (IN)
Ivy Tech Comm Coll–Kokomo (IN)
Ivy Tech Comm Coll–Lafayette (IN)
Ivy Tech Comm Coll–North Central
    (IN)
Ivy Tech Comm Coll–Northeast (IN)
Ivy Tech Comm Coll–Northwest (IN)
Ivy Tech Comm Coll–Richmond (IN)
Ivy Tech Comm Coll–Southeast (IN)
Ivy Tech Comm Coll–Southern
    Indiana (IN)
Ivy Tech Comm Coll–Southwest (IN)
Ivy Tech Comm Coll–Wabash Valley
    (IN)
Jefferson Comm Coll (NY)
Jefferson State Comm Coll (AL)
J. F. Drake State Tech Coll (AL)
John Tyler Comm Coll (VA)
Kilgore Coll (TX)
Lake Michigan Coll (MI)
Lansing Comm Coll (MI)
Lawson State Comm Coll (AL)
Lehigh Carbon Comm Coll (PA)
Lone Star Coll–CyFair (TX)
Lone Star Coll–Kingwood (TX)
Lone Star Coll–North Harris (TX)
Lone Star Coll–Tomball (TX)
Lurleen B. Wallace Comm Coll (AL)
Luzerne County Comm Coll (PA)
Massachusetts Bay Comm Coll (MA)
Middlesex Comm Coll (MA)
Mid-Plains Comm Coll, North Platte
    (NE)

Miles Comm Coll (MT)
Mohawk Valley Comm Coll (NY)
Montgomery Coll (MD)
Montgomery County Comm Coll (PA)
Mt. San Antonio Coll (CA)
Nassau Comm Coll (NY)
North Dakota State Coll of Science
    (ND)
Northern Essex Comm Coll (MA)
Northwest-Shoals Comm Coll (AL)
Ocean County Coll (NJ)
Owensboro Comm and Tech Coll
    (KY)
Parkland Coll (IL)
Penn State Schuylkill (PA)
Pensacola State Coll (FL)
Phoenix Coll (AZ)
Robeson Comm Coll (NC)
Rogue Comm Coll (OR)
St. Louis Comm Coll at Forest Park
    (MO)
Salt Lake Comm Coll (UT)
San Diego Mesa Coll (CA)
San Jacinto Coll District (TX)
Sheridan Coll (WY)
South Puget Sound Comm Coll (WA)
Southwest Virginia Comm Coll (VA)
Spartanburg Comm Coll (SC)
State U of New York Coll of
    Technology at Alfred (NY)
Sullivan Coll of Technology and
    Design (KY)
Tallahassee Comm Coll (FL)
Temple Coll (TX)
Terra State Comm Coll (OH)
Texarkana Coll (TX)
Thomas Nelson Comm Coll (VA)
Tompkins Cortland Comm Coll (NY)
Tyler Jr Coll (TX)
Victor Valley Coll (CA)
Vincennes U (IN)
Westchester Comm Coll (NY)
West Kentucky Comm and Tech Coll
    (KY)
Wisconsin Indianhead Tech Coll (WI)

**COMPUTER AND
INFORMATION SCIENCES AND
SUPPORT SERVICES RELATED**
Arapahoe Comm Coll (CO)
Bowling Green State U-Firelands Coll
    (OH)
Career Tech Coll (LA)
Cayuga County Comm Coll (NY)
Clark State Comm Coll (OH)
Corning Comm Coll (NY)
Dakota Coll at Bottineau (ND)
Darton State Coll (GA)
Eastern Shore Comm Coll (VA)
Fiorello H. LaGuardia Comm Coll of
    the City U of New York (NY)
Greenfield Comm Coll (MA)
Jackson Coll (MI)
Jefferson Comm Coll (NY)
Middlesex Comm Coll (MA)
Mohawk Valley Comm Coll (NY)
Monroe Comm Coll (NY)
Oakland Comm Coll (MI)
Parkland Coll (IL)
Piedmont Virginia Comm Coll (VA)
Raritan Valley Comm Coll (NJ)
Robeson Comm Coll (NC)
Seminole State Coll of Florida (FL)
Sierra Coll (CA)
Southeast Tech Inst (SD)
Southwestern Michigan Coll (MI)
Stark State Coll (OH)
Sullivan Coll of Technology and
    Design (KY)
Tompkins Cortland Comm Coll (NY)
Union County Coll (NJ)
Waukesha County Tech Coll (WI)
Westchester Comm Coll (NY)

**COMPUTER AND
INFORMATION SCIENCES
RELATED**
Berkeley City Coll (CA)
Central Oregon Comm Coll (OR)
Chipola Coll (FL)
Colby Comm Coll (KS)
Corning Comm Coll (NY)
Daytona State Coll (FL)
Genesee Comm Coll (NY)
Howard Comm Coll (MD)
Lorain County Comm Coll (OH)
Luzerne County Comm Coll (PA)
McCann School of Business &
    Technology, Pottsville (PA)
Metropolitan Comm Coll–Kansas City
    (MO)
Missouri State U–West Plains (MO)

Mohave Comm Coll (AZ)
Monroe Comm Coll (NY)
Monroe County Comm Coll (MI)
Nassau Comm Coll (NY)
North Shore Comm Coll (MA)
Pensacola State Coll (FL)
Potomac State Coll of West Virginia
    U (WV)
Seminole State Coll of Florida (FL)
Stark State Coll (OH)
Tyler Jr Coll (TX)
Westchester Comm Coll (NY)

**COMPUTER AND
INFORMATION SYSTEMS
SECURITY**
Alexandria Tech and Comm Coll
    (MN)
Anne Arundel Comm Coll (MD)
Berkeley City Coll (CA)
Blackhawk Tech Coll (WI)
Casper Coll (WY)
Century Coll (MN)
Cleveland Comm Coll (NC)
Cochise Coll, Sierra Vista (AZ)
Collin County Comm Coll District
    (TX)
The Comm Coll of Baltimore County
    (MD)
Comm Coll of Beaver County (PA)
Cowley County Comm Coll and Area
    Vocational–Tech School (KS)
Dyersburg State Comm Coll (TN)
Edison Comm Coll (OH)
El Centro Coll (TX)
Elgin Comm Coll (IL)
Fayetteville Tech Comm Coll (NC)
Gateway Tech Coll (WI)
Glendale Comm Coll (AZ)
Hagerstown Comm Coll (MD)
Harford Comm Coll (MD)
Harrisburg Area Comm Coll (PA)
Lehigh Carbon Comm Coll (PA)
Lone Star Coll–Montgomery (TX)
McHenry County Coll (IL)
Miles Comm Coll (MT)
Minnesota West Comm and Tech
    Coll (MN)
Montgomery Coll (MD)
Moraine Valley Comm Coll (IL)
Northampton Comm Coll (PA)
North Dakota State Coll of Science
    (ND)
Northwest State Comm Coll (OH)
Norwalk Comm Coll (CT)
Oakland Comm Coll (MI)
Owens Comm Coll, Toledo (OH)
Oxnard Coll (CA)
Quinsigamond Comm Coll (MA)
St. Philip's Coll (TX)
San Jacinto Coll District (TX)
Seminole State Coll of Florida (FL)
Sheridan Coll (WY)
Southeast Tech Inst (SD)
Spoon River Coll (IL)
Springfield Tech Comm Coll (MA)
Sullivan Coll of Technology and
    Design (KY)
Westchester Comm Coll (NY)
Westmoreland County Comm Coll
    (PA)
Wilson Comm Coll (NC)

COMPUTER ENGINEERING
Carroll Comm Coll (MD)
Daytona State Coll (FL)
Northwest State Comm Coll (OH)
Pensacola State Coll (FL)

**COMPUTER ENGINEERING
RELATED**
Daytona State Coll (FL)
Monroe Comm Coll (NY)
Seminole State Coll of Florida (FL)
Stark State Coll (OH)

**COMPUTER ENGINEERING
TECHNOLOGY**
Alvin Comm Coll (TX)
Amarillo Coll (TX)
Bowling Green State U-Firelands Coll
    (OH)
Brookhaven Coll (TX)
Catawba Valley Comm Coll (NC)
Chemeketa Comm Coll (OR)
Comm Coll of Allegheny County (PA)
Comm Coll of Rhode Island (RI)
Cuyahoga Comm Coll (OH)
Delaware Tech & Comm Coll,
    Stanton/Wilmington Campus (DE)
Delaware Tech & Comm Coll, Terry
    Campus (DE)

Forsyth Tech Comm Coll (NC)
Fountainhead Coll of Technology
    (TN)
Fox Valley Tech Coll (WI)
Genesee Comm Coll (NY)
Grand Rapids Comm Coll (MI)
Houston Comm Coll System (TX)
Lakeland Comm Coll (OH)
Lone Star Coll–Kingwood (TX)
Lorain County Comm Coll (OH)
Massachusetts Bay Comm Coll (MA)
Miami Dade Coll (FL)
Middlesex Comm Coll (MA)
Minnesota West Comm and Tech
    Coll (MN)
Monroe Comm Coll (NY)
Monroe County Comm Coll (MI)
Mt. San Antonio Coll (CA)
Northeastern Jr Coll (CO)
Northern Essex Comm Coll (MA)
North Shore Comm Coll (MA)
Northwest State Comm Coll (OH)
Oklahoma City Comm Coll (OK)
Onondaga Comm Coll (NY)
Orange Coast Coll (CA)
Owens Comm Coll, Toledo (OH)
Paris Jr Coll (TX)
Penn State New Kensington (PA)
Potomac State Coll of West Virginia
    U (WV)
Quinsigamond Comm Coll (MA)
San Diego City Coll (CA)
Seminole State Coll of Florida (FL)
Southern Maine Comm Coll (ME)
South Plains Coll (TX)
Springfield Tech Comm Coll (MA)
State U of New York Coll of
    Technology at Alfred (NY)
Sullivan Coll of Technology and
    Design (KY)
Trident Tech Coll (SC)
Tyler Jr Coll (TX)

COMPUTER GRAPHICS
Arizona Western Coll (AZ)
Berkeley City Coll (CA)
Burlington County Coll (NJ)
Carrington Coll California–San Jose
    (CA)
Carroll Comm Coll (MD)
Coll of the Desert (CA)
The Comm Coll of Baltimore County
    (MD)
Cowley County Comm Coll and Area
    Vocational–Tech School (KS)
Daytona State Coll (FL)
De Anza Coll (CA)
Genesee Comm Coll (NY)
Howard Comm Coll (MD)
Lone Star Coll–Kingwood (TX)
Luzerne County Comm Coll (PA)
Metropolitan Comm Coll–Kansas City
    (MO)
Miami Dade Coll (FL)
Missouri State U–West Plains (MO)
Monroe County Comm Coll (MI)
Mt. San Antonio Coll (CA)
Nassau Comm Coll (NY)
Northern Essex Comm Coll (MA)
North Shore Comm Coll (MA)
Orange Coast Coll (CA)
Parkland Coll (IL)
Phoenix Coll (AZ)
Pittsburgh Tech Inst, Oakdale (PA)
Quinsigamond Comm Coll (MA)
Schoolcraft Coll (MI)
Seminole State Coll of Florida (FL)
Shawnee Comm Coll (IL)
Sullivan Coll of Technology and
    Design (KY)
Sullivan County Comm Coll (NY)
Tallahassee Comm Coll (FL)
Trident Tech Coll (SC)
Tyler Jr Coll (TX)

**COMPUTER HARDWARE
ENGINEERING**
Seminole State Coll of Florida (FL)
Stark State Coll (OH)
Sullivan Coll of Technology and
    Design (KY)

**COMPUTER HARDWARE
TECHNOLOGY**
Forsyth Tech Comm Coll (NC)
Oakland Comm Coll (MI)
State U of New York Coll of
    Technology at Alfred (NY)
Sullivan Coll of Technology and
    Design (KY)

**COMPUTER/INFORMATION
TECHNOLOGY SERVICES
ADMINISTRATION RELATED**
Alpena Comm Coll (MI)
Anne Arundel Comm Coll (MD)
Barton County Comm Coll (KS)
Central Carolina Comm Coll (NC)
Cleveland Inst of Electronics (OH)
Clinton Comm Coll (NY)
Corning Comm Coll (NY)
Daytona State Coll (FL)
Dutchess Comm Coll (NY)
Eastern Shore Comm Coll (VA)
El Centro Coll (TX)
Flathead Valley Comm Coll (MT)
Hawkeye Comm Coll (IA)
Hillsborough Comm Coll (FL)
Howard Comm Coll (MD)
Jefferson Comm Coll (NY)
Kent State U at Trumbull (OH)
Oakland Comm Coll (MI)
Owensboro Comm and Tech Coll
    (KY)
Parkland Coll (IL)
Pasadena City Coll (CA)
Seminole State Coll of Florida (FL)
Southeast Tech Inst (SD)
Stark State Coll (OH)
Trident Tech Coll (SC)
Vincennes U (IN)
Western Iowa Tech Comm Coll (IA)

**COMPUTER INSTALLATION
AND REPAIR TECHNOLOGY**
Central Maine Comm Coll (ME)
Coll of Lake County (IL)
Fiorello H. LaGuardia Comm Coll of
    the City U of New York (NY)
Forrest Coll (SC)
Harrisburg Area Comm Coll (PA)
Kilgore Coll (TX)
Montcalm Comm Coll (MI)
Northampton Comm Coll (PA)
Sierra Coll (CA)
Southeast Tech Inst (SD)
Sullivan Coll of Technology and
    Design (KY)
Wisconsin Indianhead Tech Coll (WI)

**COMPUTER NUMERICALLY
CONTROLLED (CNC)
MACHINIST TECHNOLOGY**
Corning Comm Coll (NY)
Westmoreland County Comm Coll
    (PA)

COMPUTER PROGRAMMING
Alvin Comm Coll (TX)
Amarillo Coll (TX)
Austin Comm Coll (TX)
Beaufort County Comm Coll (NC)
Bradford School (PA)
Brookhaven Coll (TX)
Casper Coll (WY)
Catawba Valley Comm Coll (NC)
Central Carolina Comm Coll (NC)
Chippewa Valley Tech Coll (WI)
Clark Coll (WA)
Clark State Comm Coll (OH)
Cochise Coll, Sierra Vista (AZ)
Coll of Southern Maryland (MD)
Collin County Comm Coll District
    (TX)
Copiah-Lincoln Comm Coll (MS)
Dabney S. Lancaster Comm Coll
    (VA)
Daytona State Coll (FL)
De Anza Coll (CA)
Edison Comm Coll (OH)
El Centro Coll (TX)
Essex County Coll (NJ)
Fayetteville Tech Comm Coll (NC)
Fiorello H. LaGuardia Comm Coll of
    the City U of New York (NY)
Florida Gateway Coll (FL)
Forsyth Tech Comm Coll (NC)
Fountainhead Coll of Technology
    (TN)
Fox Valley Tech Coll (WI)
Gateway Tech Coll (WI)
Grand Rapids Comm Coll (MI)
Guilford Tech Comm Coll (NC)
Harper Coll (IL)
Houston Comm Coll System (TX)
Illinois Central Coll (IL)
International Business Coll,
    Indianapolis (IN)
James A. Rhodes State Coll (OH)
Jamestown Comm Coll (NY)
Johnston Comm Coll (NC)
Kilgore Coll (TX)
King's Coll (NC)

Lake Area Tech Inst (SD)
Laramie County Comm Coll (WY)
Lehigh Carbon Comm Coll (PA)
Lincoln Land Comm Coll (IL)
Lone Star Coll–Montgomery (TX)
Lone Star Coll–Tomball (TX)
Lorain County Comm Coll (OH)
Macomb Comm Coll (MI)
Metropolitan Comm Coll–Kansas City (MO)
Miami Dade Coll (FL)
Middlesex Comm Coll (MA)
Mineral Area Coll (MO)
Minneapolis Business Coll (MN)
Mohawk Valley Comm Coll (NY)
Montgomery County Comm Coll (PA)
Mott Comm Coll (MI)
Northampton Comm Coll (PA)
North Dakota State Coll of Science (ND)
Northern Essex Comm Coll (MA)
North Shore Comm Coll (MA)
NorthWest Arkansas Comm Coll (AR)
Northwest State Comm Coll (OH)
Oakland Comm Coll (MI)
Oakton Comm Coll (IL)
Orange Coast Coll (CA)
Parkland Coll (IL)
Pensacola State Coll (FL)
Piedmont Virginia Comm Coll (VA)
Pierce Coll at Puyallup (WA)
Pittsburgh Tech Inst, Oakdale (PA)
Potomac State Coll of West Virginia U (WV)
Rasmussen Coll Fargo (ND)
Red Rocks Comm Coll (CO)
St. Clair County Comm Coll (MI)
St. Louis Comm Coll at Meramec (MO)
San Jacinto Coll District (TX)
Schoolcraft Coll (MI)
Seminole State Coll of Florida (FL)
Sierra Coll (CA)
Southeastern Comm Coll (IA)
Southeast Tech Inst (SD)
Southern State Comm Coll (OH)
South Plains Coll (TX)
South Puget Sound Comm Coll (WA)
Southwestern Michigan Coll (MI)
Stark State Coll (OH)
Tallahassee Comm Coll (FL)
Tarrant County Coll District (TX)
Temple Coll (TX)
Terra State Comm Coll (OH)
Texas State Tech Coll Harlingen (TX)
Vincennes U (IN)
Waubonsee Comm Coll (IL)
Waukesha County Tech Coll (WI)
Westmoreland County Comm Coll (PA)
West Virginia Northern Comm Coll (WV)
Wood Tobe–Coburn School (NY)

COMPUTER PROGRAMMING RELATED
Clark State Comm Coll (OH)
Lorain County Comm Coll (OH)
Luzerne County Comm Coll (PA)
Moraine Park Tech Coll (WI)
Northern Essex Comm Coll (MA)
Pasco-Hernando Comm Coll (FL)
San Diego Mesa Coll (CA)
Seminole State Coll of Florida (FL)
Southeast Tech Inst (SD)
Stark State Coll (OH)
Tyler Jr Coll (TX)

COMPUTER PROGRAMMING (SPECIFIC APPLICATIONS)
Barton County Comm Coll (KS)
Bucks County Comm Coll (PA)
Central Carolina Comm Coll (NC)
Chemeketa Comm Coll (OR)
Coll of Lake County (IL)
Comm Coll of Rhode Island (RI)
Cowley County Comm Coll and Area Vocational–Tech School (KS)
Daytona State Coll (FL)
Essex County Coll (NJ)
Harper Coll (IL)
Hillsborough Comm Coll (FL)
Holyoke Comm Coll (MA)
Houston Comm Coll System (TX)
Kent State U at Ashtabula (OH)
Kent State U at East Liverpool (OH)
Kent State U at Salem (OH)
Kent State U at Trumbull (OH)
Kent State U at Tuscarawas (OH)

Lakeland Comm Coll (OH)
Lansing Comm Coll (MI)
Lehigh Carbon Comm Coll (PA)
Lincoln Land Comm Coll (IL)
Lorain County Comm Coll (OH)
Macomb Comm Coll (MI)
Manor Coll (PA)
Missouri State U–West Plains (MO)
Mohave Comm Coll (AZ)
Monroe County Comm Coll (MI)
Mott Comm Coll (MI)
Northeast Iowa Comm Coll (IA)
Northern Essex Comm Coll (MA)
North Shore Comm Coll (MA)
Orange Coast Coll (CA)
Owens Comm Coll, Toledo (OH)
Parkland Coll (IL)
Pasco-Hernando Comm Coll (FL)
Pensacola State Coll (FL)
Piedmont Comm Coll (NC)
Potomac State Coll of West Virginia U (WV)
Quinsigamond Comm Coll (MA)
St. Louis Comm Coll at Forest Park (MO)
San Diego Mesa Coll (CA)
Schoolcraft Coll (MI)
Seminole State Coll of Florida (FL)
Southern State Comm Coll (OH)
Spoon River Coll (IL)
Springfield Tech Comm Coll (MA)
Stark State Coll (OH)
Sullivan County Comm Coll (NY)
Tallahassee Comm Coll (FL)
Trident Tech Coll (SC)
Victor Valley Coll (CA)
Westmoreland County Comm Coll (PA)

COMPUTER PROGRAMMING (VENDOR/PRODUCT CERTIFICATION)
Lorain County Comm Coll (OH)
Parkland Coll (IL)
Raritan Valley Comm Coll (NJ)
St. Louis Comm Coll at Forest Park (MO)
Seminole State Coll of Florida (FL)
Stark State Coll (OH)
Sullivan Coll of Technology and Design (KY)

COMPUTER SCIENCE
Adirondack Comm Coll (NY)
Amarillo Coll (TX)
Anoka-Ramsey Comm Coll (MN)
Anoka-Ramsey Comm Coll, Cambridge Campus (MN)
Bakersfield Coll (CA)
Barton County Comm Coll (KS)
Borough of Manhattan Comm Coll of the City U of New York (NY)
Burlington County Coll (NJ)
Butte Coll (CA)
Central Oregon Comm Coll (OR)
Central Wyoming Coll (WY)
Century Coll (MN)
Chipola Coll (FL)
Cochise Coll, Sierra Vista (AZ)
Coll of Marin (CA)
Coll of the Canyons (CA)
Coll of the Desert (CA)
Comm Coll of Philadelphia (PA)
Comm Coll of Vermont (VT)
Corning Comm Coll (NY)
Cowley County Comm Coll and Area Vocational–Tech School (KS)
Darton State Coll (GA)
Daytona State Coll (FL)
De Anza Coll (CA)
El Centro Coll (TX)
Essex County Coll (NJ)
Finger Lakes Comm Coll (NY)
Fiorello H. LaGuardia Comm Coll of the City U of New York (NY)
Foothill Coll (CA)
Garden City Comm Coll (KS)
Gordon State Coll (GA)
Grand Rapids Comm Coll (MI)
Harford Comm Coll (MD)
Harper Coll (IL)
Harrisburg Area Comm Coll (PA)
Howard Comm Coll (MD)
Jackson State Comm Coll (TN)
Jefferson Comm Coll (NY)
Lake Area Tech Inst (SD)
Laramie County Comm Coll (WY)
Lone Star Coll–CyFair (TX)
Lone Star Coll–Kingwood (TX)
Lone Star Coll–Montgomery (TX)

Lone Star Coll–North Harris (TX)
Lone Star Coll–Tomball (TX)
Lorain County Comm Coll (OH)
Luzerne County Comm Coll (PA)
Massachusetts Bay Comm Coll (MA)
McCann School of Business & Technology, Pottsville (PA)
Metropolitan Comm Coll–Kansas City (MO)
Miami Dade Coll (FL)
Minnesota West Comm and Tech Coll (MN)
Mohave Comm Coll (AZ)
Mohawk Valley Comm Coll (NY)
Monroe Comm Coll (NY)
Mt. San Antonio Coll (CA)
Nassau Comm Coll (NY)
Niagara County Comm Coll (NY)
Normandale Comm Coll (MN)
Northampton Comm Coll (PA)
Northeastern Jr Coll (CO)
Northern Essex Comm Coll (MA)
North Hennepin Comm Coll (MN)
North Shore Comm Coll (MA)
Oklahoma City Comm Coll (OK)
Onondaga Comm Coll (NY)
Parkland Coll (IL)
Pasadena City Coll (CA)
Pensacola State Coll (FL)
Piedmont Virginia Comm Coll (VA)
Potomac State Coll of West Virginia U (WV)
Quinsigamond Comm Coll (MA)
Salt Lake Comm Coll (UT)
San Diego Mesa Coll (CA)
San Jacinto Coll District (TX)
Santa Rosa Jr Coll (CA)
South Plains Coll (TX)
Springfield Tech Comm Coll (MA)
State U of New York Coll of Technology at Alfred (NY)
Taft Coll (CA)
Tarrant County Coll District (TX)
Temple Coll (TX)
Tyler Jr Coll (TX)
Union County Coll (NJ)
Victor Valley Coll (CA)
Vincennes U (IN)
Virginia Western Comm Coll (VA)
Westchester Comm Coll (NY)

COMPUTER SOFTWARE AND MEDIA APPLICATIONS RELATED
Anne Arundel Comm Coll (MD)
Berkeley City Coll (CA)
Dakota Coll at Bottineau (ND)
Genesee Comm Coll (NY)
Parkland Coll (IL)
San Diego Mesa Coll (CA)
Seminole State Coll of Florida (FL)
Stark State Coll (OH)

COMPUTER SOFTWARE ENGINEERING
Cleveland Inst of Electronics (OH)
Rasmussen Coll Bismarck (ND)
Rasmussen Coll Bloomington (MN)
Rasmussen Coll Brooklyn Park (MN)
Rasmussen Coll Eagan (MN)
Rasmussen Coll Fargo (ND)
Rasmussen Coll Fort Myers (FL)
Rasmussen Coll Green Bay (WI)
Rasmussen Coll Lake Elmo/ Woodbury (MN)
Rasmussen Coll Mankato (MN)
Rasmussen Coll Moorhead (MN)
Rasmussen Coll New Port Richey (FL)
Rasmussen Coll Ocala (FL)
Rasmussen Coll St. Cloud (MN)
Seminole State Coll of Florida (FL)
Southeast Tech Inst (SD)
Stark State Coll (OH)

COMPUTER SOFTWARE TECHNOLOGY
Lone Star Coll–Montgomery (TX)
Miami Dade Coll (FL)
Rogue Comm Coll (OR)

COMPUTER SUPPORT SPECIALIST
Corning Comm Coll (NY)
Gateway Tech Coll (WI)
Lake Superior Coll (MN)
Mitchell Tech Inst (SD)
Moraine Park Tech Coll (WI)
North Dakota State Coll of Science (ND)

Southwestern Michigan Coll (MI)
Waukesha County Tech Coll (WI)
Westmoreland County Comm Coll (PA)
Wisconsin Indianhead Tech Coll (WI)

COMPUTER SYSTEMS ANALYSIS
Amarillo Coll (TX)
Central New Mexico Comm Coll (NM)
Fox Valley Tech Coll (WI)
Gateway Tech Coll (WI)
Glendale Comm Coll (AZ)
Guilford Tech Comm Coll (NC)
Hillsborough Comm Coll (FL)
Hutchinson Comm Coll and Area Vocational School (KS)
Kirtland Comm Coll (MI)
Lakeland Comm Coll (OH)
Oakland Comm Coll (MI)
Oklahoma City Comm Coll (OK)
Pensacola State Coll (FL)
Phoenix Coll (AZ)
Quinsigamond Comm Coll (MA)
Southern State Comm Coll (OH)

COMPUTER SYSTEMS NETWORKING AND TELECOMMUNICATIONS
Adirondack Comm Coll (NY)
Alexandria Tech and Comm Coll (MN)
Alpena Comm Coll (MI)
Anne Arundel Comm Coll (MD)
Anoka-Ramsey Comm Coll (MN)
Anoka-Ramsey Comm Coll, Cambridge Campus (MN)
Austin Comm Coll (TX)
Barton County Comm Coll (KS)
Bismarck State Coll (ND)
Blackhawk Tech Coll (WI)
Borough of Manhattan Comm Coll of the City U of New York (NY)
Bowling Green State U–Firelands Coll (OH)
Bradford School (OH)
Bradford School (PA)
Bucks County Comm Coll (PA)
Cape Fear Comm Coll (NC)
Central Carolina Comm Coll (NC)
Central Oregon Comm Coll (OR)
Century Coll (MN)
Chippewa Valley Tech Coll (WI)
Clark Coll (WA)
Clark State Comm Coll (OH)
Cleveland Comm Coll (NC)
Cochise Coll, Sierra Vista (AZ)
CollAmerica–Flagstaff (AZ)
Coll of Lake County (IL)
Coll of Marin (CA)
Coll of the Canyons (CA)
Collin County Comm Coll District (TX)
Comm Coll of Allegheny County (PA)
The Comm Coll of Baltimore County (MD)
Comm Coll of Beaver County (PA)
Comm Coll of Rhode Island (RI)
Comm Coll of Vermont (VT)
Crowder Coll (MO)
Daytona State Coll (FL)
Delaware Tech & Comm Coll, Stanton/Wilmington Campus (DE)
Delaware Tech & Comm Coll, Terry Campus (DE)
Dunwoody Coll of Technology (MN)
Eastern Idaho Tech Coll (ID)
Edison Comm Coll (OH)
Fayetteville Tech Comm Coll (NC)
Forsyth Tech Comm Coll (NC)
Fox Valley Tech Coll (WI)
Garden City Comm Coll (KS)
Gateway Tech Coll (WI)
Glendale Comm Coll (AZ)
Great Falls Coll Montana State U (MT)
Guilford Tech Comm Coll (NC)
Halifax Comm Coll (NC)
Hallmark Coll of Technology (TX)
Harrisburg Area Comm Coll (PA)
Hawkeye Comm Coll (IA)
Houston Comm Coll System (TX)
Howard Comm Coll (MD)
Hutchinson Comm Coll and Area Vocational School (KS)
Illinois Central Coll (IL)
Illinois Eastern Comm Colls, Lincoln Trail College (IL)

International Business Coll, Indianapolis (IN)
Jefferson Coll (MO)
Kilgore Coll (TX)
King's Coll (NC)
Lakeland Comm Coll (OH)
Lake Superior Coll (MN)
Lansing Comm Coll (MI)
Lehigh Carbon Comm Coll (PA)
Lincoln Land Comm Coll (IL)
Lone Star Coll–Montgomery (TX)
Lorain County Comm Coll (OH)
Luzerne County Comm Coll (PA)
Minneapolis Business Coll (MN)
Minnesota West Comm and Tech Coll (MN)
Montgomery County Comm Coll (PA)
Moraine Park Tech Coll (WI)
Mott Comm Coll (MI)
Nassau Comm Coll (NY)
Northampton Comm Coll (PA)
North Dakota State Coll of Science (ND)
Northern Essex Comm Coll (MA)
Northwest Tech Coll (MN)
Norwalk Comm Coll (CT)
Oklahoma City Comm Coll (OK)
Olympic Coll (WA)
Onondaga Comm Coll (NY)
Oxnard Coll (CA)
Ozarks Tech Comm Coll (MO)
Parkland Coll (IL)
Pasco-Hernando Comm Coll (FL)
Piedmont Comm Coll (NC)
Potomac State Coll of West Virginia U (WV)
Randolph Comm Coll (NC)
Raritan Valley Comm Coll (NJ)
Red Rocks Comm Coll (CO)
Robeson Comm Coll (NC)
St. Louis Comm Coll at Forest Park (MO)
St. Philip's Coll (TX)
Schoolcraft Coll (MI)
Seminole State Coll of Florida (FL)
Shawnee Comm Coll (IL)
Sierra Coll (CA)
Southeast Tech Inst (SD)
Southwestern Michigan Coll (MI)
Stark State Coll (OH)
Sullivan Coll of Technology and Design (KY)
Tallahassee Comm Coll (FL)
Terra State Comm Coll (OH)
Texas State Tech Coll Harlingen (TX)
Trident Tech Coll (SC)
Tyler Jr Coll (TX)
Vincennes U (IN)
Waukesha County Tech Coll (WI)
Westchester Comm Coll (NY)
Western Dakota Tech Inst (SD)
Westmoreland County Comm Coll (PA)
Wilson Comm Coll (NC)
Wisconsin Indianhead Tech Coll (WI)
Wood Tobe–Coburn School (NY)

COMPUTER TECHNOLOGY/ COMPUTER SYSTEMS TECHNOLOGY
Brookhaven Coll (TX)
Cape Fear Comm Coll (NC)
Central Wyoming Coll (WY)
Century Coll (MN)
Chemeketa Comm Coll (OR)
Comm Coll of Allegheny County (PA)
Corning Comm Coll (NY)
Dakota Coll at Bottineau (ND)
Daytona State Coll (FL)
Delaware Tech & Comm Coll, Jack F. Owens Campus (DE)
Delaware Tech & Comm Coll, Terry Campus (DE)
Erie Comm Coll, South Campus (NY)
Forrest Coll (SC)
Hillsborough Comm Coll (FL)
ITI Tech Coll (LA)
James A. Rhodes State Coll (OH)
Jefferson Comm Coll (NY)
Lakeland Comm Coll (OH)
Lake Superior Coll (MN)
Lansing Comm Coll (MI)
Lorain County Comm Coll (OH)
Luzerne County Comm Coll (PA)
Miami Dade Coll (FL)
Minnesota West Comm and Tech Coll (MN)
Montgomery Coll (MD)
Normandale Comm Coll (MN)

Oakland Comm Coll (MI)
Pasadena City Coll (CA)
Pasco-Hernando Comm Coll (FL)
Paul D. Camp Comm Coll (VA)
Pittsburgh Tech Inst, Oakdale (PA)
St. Philip's Coll (TX)
Schoolcraft Coll (MI)
Southeast Tech Inst (SD)
Southern State Comm Coll (OH)
Sullivan Coll of Technology and Design (KY)
Texas State Tech Coll Harlingen (TX)
U of Arkansas Comm Coll at Morrilton (AR)
West Virginia Jr Coll–Bridgeport (WV)

COMPUTER TYPOGRAPHY AND COMPOSITION EQUIPMENT OPERATION
Cuyahoga Comm Coll (OH)
Housatonic Comm Coll (CT)
Metropolitan Comm Coll–Kansas City (MO)
Northern Essex Comm Coll (MA)
Orange Coast Coll (CA)
Paris Jr Coll (TX)
Pierce Coll at Puyallup (WA)

CONSTRUCTION ENGINEERING
Bossier Parish Comm Coll (LA)
Illinois Central Coll (IL)

CONSTRUCTION ENGINEERING TECHNOLOGY
Burlington County Coll (NJ)
Central Maine Comm Coll (ME)
Clark Coll (WA)
Coll of Lake County (IL)
Comm Coll of Allegheny County (PA)
Comm Coll of Philadelphia (PA)
Comm Coll of the Air Force (AL)
Crowder Coll (MO)
De Anza Coll (CA)
Harrisburg Area Comm Coll (PA)
Houston Comm Coll System (TX)
Illinois Central Coll (IL)
Inst of Design and Construction (NY)
Jefferson State Comm Coll (AL)
Lake Area Tech Inst (SD)
Lincoln Land Comm Coll (IL)
Macomb Comm Coll (MI)
Miami Dade Coll (FL)
Mid-Plains Comm Coll, North Platte (NE)
Miles Comm Coll (MT)
Monroe Comm Coll (NY)
North Dakota State Coll of Science (ND)
Norwalk Comm Coll (CT)
The Ohio State U Ag Tech Inst (OH)
Oklahoma State U, Oklahoma City (OK)
Onondaga Comm Coll (NY)
Orange Coast Coll (CA)
Owens Comm Coll, Toledo (OH)
Ozarks Tech Comm Coll (MO)
Pensacola State Coll (FL)
Raritan Valley Comm Coll (NJ)
Rogue Comm Coll (OR)
St. Philip's Coll (TX)
San Diego Mesa Coll (CA)
San Jacinto Coll District (TX)
Seminole State Coll of Florida (FL)
Southeastern Comm Coll (IA)
Southeast Tech Inst (SD)
South Suburban Coll (IL)
State U of New York Coll of Technology at Alfred (NY)
Tallahassee Comm Coll (FL)
Tarrant County Coll District (TX)
Tech Coll of the Lowcountry (SC)
Texas State Tech Coll Harlingen (TX)
Victor Valley Coll (CA)

CONSTRUCTION/HEAVY EQUIPMENT/EARTHMOVING EQUIPMENT OPERATION
Ivy Tech Comm Coll–Southwest (IN)
Ivy Tech Comm Coll–Wabash Valley (IN)
Lansing Comm Coll (MI)

CONSTRUCTION MANAGEMENT
Casper Coll (WY)
Delaware Tech & Comm Coll, Jack F. Owens Campus (DE)
Delaware Tech & Comm Coll, Stanton/Wilmington Campus (DE)
Delaware Tech & Comm Coll, Terry Campus (DE)
Dunwoody Coll of Technology (MN)
Erie Comm Coll, North Campus (NY)
Kankakee Comm Coll (IL)
Klamath Comm Coll (OR)
Lansing Comm Coll (MI)
Northampton Comm Coll (PA)
North Hennepin Comm Coll (MN)
Oakland Comm Coll (MI)
The Ohio State U Ag Tech Inst (OH)
Oklahoma State U, Oklahoma City (OK)
Phoenix Coll (AZ)
Waubonsee Comm Coll (IL)

CONSTRUCTION TRADES
Casper Coll (WY)
Chemeketa Comm Coll (OR)
Harrisburg Area Comm Coll (PA)
Illinois Eastern Comm Colls, Frontier Community College (IL)
Illinois Eastern Comm Colls, Lincoln Trail College (IL)
Ivy Tech Comm Coll–East Central (IN)
Ivy Tech Comm Coll–Northeast (IN)
Ivy Tech Comm Coll–Northwest (IN)
Ivy Tech Comm Coll–Richmond (IN)
Lehigh Carbon Comm Coll (PA)
Northeast Iowa Comm Coll (IA)
Oklahoma State U, Oklahoma City (OK)
Pasadena City Coll (CA)
Red Rocks Comm Coll (CO)
Rogue Comm Coll (OR)
Sierra Coll (CA)
Southern Maine Comm Coll (ME)
Vincennes U (IN)

CONSTRUCTION TRADES RELATED
Arizona Western Coll (AZ)
Central Maine Comm Coll (ME)
Central New Mexico Comm Coll (NM)
Comm Coll of Allegheny County (PA)
Dutchess Comm Coll (NY)
Ivy Tech Comm Coll–East Central (IN)
Ivy Tech Comm Coll–Kokomo (IN)
Ivy Tech Comm Coll–Northeast (IN)
Ivy Tech Comm Coll–Richmond (IN)
Jackson Coll (MI)
Mitchell Tech Inst (SD)
State U of New York Coll of Technology at Alfred (NY)
Tompkins Cortland Comm Coll (NY)
York County Comm Coll (ME)

CONSUMER MERCHANDISING/ RETAILING MANAGEMENT
Clinton Comm Coll (NY)
FIDM/The Fashion Inst of Design & Merchandising, Los Angeles Campus (CA)
FIDM/The Fashion Inst of Design & Merchandising, Orange County Campus (CA)
FIDM/The Fashion Inst of Design & Merchandising, San Diego Campus (CA)
FIDM/The Fashion Inst of Design & Merchandising, San Francisco Campus (CA)
Lorain County Comm Coll (OH)
Monroe Comm Coll (NY)
Niagara County Comm Coll (NY)
Parkland Coll (IL)
South Plains Coll (TX)
Stark State Coll (OH)
Sullivan County Comm Coll (NY)
Tarrant County Coll District (TX)
Westchester Comm Coll (NY)

CONSUMER SERVICES AND ADVOCACY
Pensacola State Coll (FL)
San Diego City Coll (CA)

COOKING AND RELATED CULINARY ARTS
Adirondack Comm Coll (NY)
Bradford School (OH)
Central Oregon Comm Coll (OR)
Columbus Culinary Inst at Bradford School (OH)
Culinary Inst of St. Louis at Hickey Coll (MO)
Miami Dade Coll (FL)
Pensacola State Coll (FL)
State U of New York Coll of Technology at Alfred (NY)

CORRECTIONS
Alpena Comm Coll (MI)
Alvin Comm Coll (TX)
Amarillo Coll (TX)
Austin Comm Coll (TX)
Bakersfield Coll (CA)
Barton County Comm Coll (KS)
Bucks County Comm Coll (PA)
Cayuga County Comm Coll (NY)
Clark State Comm Coll (OH)
Comm Coll of Allegheny County (PA)
De Anza Coll (CA)
Florida Gateway Coll (FL)
Garrett Coll (MD)
Grand Rapids Comm Coll (MI)
Illinois Central Coll (IL)
Illinois Eastern Comm Colls, Frontier Community College (IL)
Illinois Eastern Comm Colls, Lincoln Trail College (IL)
Jackson Coll (MI)
James A. Rhodes State Coll (OH)
Kilgore Coll (TX)
Kirtland Comm Coll (MI)
Klamath Comm Coll (OR)
Lakeland Comm Coll (OH)
Lake Michigan Coll (MI)
Lansing Comm Coll (MI)
Laramie County Comm Coll (WY)
Lorain County Comm Coll (OH)
Metropolitan Comm Coll–Kansas City (MO)
Monroe Comm Coll (NY)
Montcalm Comm Coll (MI)
Moraine Park Tech Coll (WI)
Mt. San Antonio Coll (CA)
Northeastern Jr Coll (CO)
Northwest State Comm Coll (OH)
Oakland Comm Coll (MI)
Owens Comm Coll, Toledo (OH)
Raritan Valley Comm Coll (NJ)
St. Louis Comm Coll at Forest Park (MO)
Sierra Coll (CA)
Southern State Comm Coll (OH)
Sullivan County Comm Coll (NY)
Tunxis Comm Coll (CT)
Vincennes U (IN)
Westchester Comm Coll (NY)
Westmoreland County Comm Coll (PA)
Wytheville Comm Coll (VA)

CORRECTIONS AND CRIMINAL JUSTICE RELATED
Career Tech Coll (LA)
Corning Comm Coll (NY)
Fayetteville Tech Comm Coll (NC)
Northwest State Comm Coll (OH)
Rasmussen Coll Aurora (IL)
Rasmussen Coll Bismarck (ND)
Rasmussen Coll Bloomington (MN)
Rasmussen Coll Brooklyn Park (MN)
Rasmussen Coll Eagan (MN)
Rasmussen Coll Fort Myers (FL)
Rasmussen Coll Green Bay (WI)
Rasmussen Coll Lake Elmo/ Woodbury (MN)
Rasmussen Coll Mankato (MN)
Rasmussen Coll Moorhead (MN)
Rasmussen Coll New Port Richey (FL)
Rasmussen Coll Ocala (FL)
Rasmussen Coll Rockford (IL)
Rasmussen Coll St. Cloud (MN)
Wisconsin Indianhead Tech Coll (WI)

COSMETOLOGY
Bakersfield Coll (CA)
Butte Coll (CA)
Central New Mexico Comm Coll (NM)
Century Coll (MN)
Clary Sage Coll (OK)
Colorado Northwestern Comm Coll (CO)
Comm Coll of Beaver County (PA)
Copiah-Lincoln Comm Coll (MS)
Cowley County Comm Coll and Area Vocational–Tech School (KS)
Garden City Comm Coll (KS)
Guilford Tech Comm Coll (NC)
Houston Comm Coll System (TX)
J. F. Drake State Tech Coll (AL)
Kirtland Comm Coll (MI)
Lone Star Coll–Kingwood (TX)
Lone Star Coll–North Harris (TX)
Lorain County Comm Coll (OH)
McCann School of Business & Technology, Pottsville (PA)
Montcalm Comm Coll (MI)
Northeastern Jr Coll (CO)
Northeast Iowa Comm Coll (IA)
Oakland Comm Coll (MI)
Olympic Coll (WA)
Paris Jr Coll (TX)
Pasadena City Coll (CA)
Randolph Comm Coll (NC)
Red Rocks Comm Coll (CO)
Salt Lake Comm Coll (UT)
San Diego City Coll (CA)
San Jacinto Coll District (TX)
San Juan Coll (NM)
Shawnee Comm Coll (IL)
Southeastern Comm Coll (IA)
South Plains Coll (TX)
Texarkana Coll (TX)
Vincennes U (IN)

COSMETOLOGY AND PERSONAL GROOMING ARTS RELATED
Comm Coll of Allegheny County (PA)
Lorain County Comm Coll (OH)

COSMETOLOGY, BARBER/ STYLING, AND NAIL INSTRUCTION
Pasadena City Coll (CA)
San Jacinto Coll District (TX)

COUNSELING PSYCHOLOGY
Kilian Comm Coll (SD)

COURT REPORTING
Alvin Comm Coll (TX)
Clark State Comm Coll (OH)
Coll of Marin (CA)
Comm Coll of Allegheny County (PA)
Cuyahoga Comm Coll (OH)
Gadsden State Comm Coll (AL)
Harrisburg Area Comm Coll (PA)
Houston Comm Coll System (TX)
Long Island Business Inst (NY)
Luzerne County Comm Coll (PA)
Miami Dade Coll (FL)
Moraine Park Tech Coll (WI)
New York Career Inst (NY)
Oakland Comm Coll (MI)
St. Louis Comm Coll at Meramec (MO)
San Diego City Coll (CA)
South Suburban Coll (IL)
Stark State Coll (OH)
State U of New York Coll of Technology at Alfred (NY)
West Kentucky Comm and Tech Coll (KY)
Wisconsin Indianhead Tech Coll (WI)

CRAFTS, FOLK ART AND ARTISANRY
Harrisburg Area Comm Coll (PA)
Montgomery Comm Coll (NC)

CREATIVE WRITING
Adirondack Comm Coll (NY)
Austin Comm Coll (TX)
Berkeley City Coll (CA)
Coll of the Desert (CA)
Normandale Comm Coll (MN)
North Hennepin Comm Coll (MN)
Tompkins Cortland Comm Coll (NY)

CREDIT MANAGEMENT
Alexandria Tech and Comm Coll (MN)

CRIMINALISTICS AND CRIMINAL SCIENCE
Century Coll (MN)
Harrisburg Area Comm Coll (PA)
Oakland Comm Coll (MI)

CRIMINAL JUSTICE/LAW ENFORCEMENT ADMINISTRATION
Amarillo Coll (TX)
Anne Arundel Comm Coll (MD)
Arapahoe Comm Coll (CO)
Arizona Western Coll (AZ)
Arkansas State U–Mountain Home (AR)
Bainbridge Coll (GA)
Bakersfield Coll (CA)
Beaufort County Comm Coll (NC)
Bucks County Comm Coll (PA)
Casper Coll (WY)
Central Carolina Comm Coll (NC)
Central Maine Comm Coll (ME)
Central Wyoming Coll (WY)
Clark State Comm Coll (OH)
Clinton Comm Coll (NY)
Colby Comm Coll (KS)
Coll of Southern Maryland (MD)
Comm Coll of Philadelphia (PA)
Comm Coll of the Air Force (AL)
Comm Coll of Vermont (VT)
Cossatot Comm Coll of the U of Arkansas (AR)
Cowley County Comm Coll and Area Vocational–Tech School (KS)
Dabney S. Lancaster Comm Coll (VA)
Darton State Coll (GA)
Daytona State Coll (FL)
De Anza Coll (CA)
Delaware Tech & Comm Coll, Jack F. Owens Campus (DE)
Delaware Tech & Comm Coll, Stanton/Wilmington Campus (DE)
Delaware Tech & Comm Coll, Terry Campus (DE)
Denmark Tech Coll (SC)
Finger Lakes Comm Coll (NY)
Flathead Valley Comm Coll (MT)
Florida Gateway Coll (FL)
Gateway Comm and Tech Coll (KY)
Genesee Comm Coll (NY)
Georgia Military Coll (GA)
Goodwin Coll (CT)
Grand Rapids Comm Coll (MI)
Harper Coll (IL)
Harrisburg Area Comm Coll (PA)
Hillsborough Comm Coll (FL)
Housatonic Comm Coll (CT)
Howard Comm Coll (MD)
Jackson Coll (MI)
Jefferson Coll (MO)
Jefferson Comm Coll (NY)
John Tyler Comm Coll (VA)
Kankakee Comm Coll (IL)
Kaskaskia Coll (IL)
Kilgore Coll (TX)
Kilian Comm Coll (SD)
Kirtland Comm Coll (MI)
Lake Michigan Coll (MI)
Laramie County Comm Coll (WY)
Lehigh Carbon Comm Coll (PA)
Lone Star Coll–CyFair (TX)
Lone Star Coll–Kingwood (TX)
Lone Star Coll–Montgomery (TX)
Lone Star Coll–North Harris (TX)
Lone Star Coll–Tomball (TX)
Lower Columbia Coll (WA)
Luzerne County Comm Coll (PA)
Macomb Comm Coll (MI)
Manchester Comm Coll (CT)
Massachusetts Bay Comm Coll (MA)
Mendocino Coll (CA)
Mesa Comm Coll (AZ)
Metropolitan Comm Coll–Kansas City (MO)
Miami Dade Coll (FL)
Middlesex Comm Coll (MA)
Missouri State U–West Plains (MO)
Mohawk Valley Comm Coll (NY)
Monroe Comm Coll (NY)
Montcalm Comm Coll (MI)
Nassau Comm Coll (NY)
Niagara County Comm Coll (NY)
Northern Essex Comm Coll (MA)
North Hennepin Comm Coll (MN)
North Shore Comm Coll (MA)
NorthWest Arkansas Comm Coll (AR)
Northwest Coll (WY)
Northwest State Comm Coll (OH)
Norwalk Comm Coll (CT)
Oakland Comm Coll (MI)
Onondaga Comm Coll (NY)
Owens Comm Coll, Toledo (OH)
Ozarka Coll (AR)
Pasadena City Coll (CA)
Pasco-Hernando Comm Coll (FL)
Paul D. Camp Comm Coll (VA)
Pensacola State Coll (FL)
Piedmont Comm Coll (NC)
Pierce Coll at Puyallup (WA)
Rappahannock Comm Coll (VA)
Raritan Valley Comm Coll (NJ)
Robeson Comm Coll (NC)
St. Philip's Coll (TX)
Salt Lake Comm Coll (UT)
Santa Rosa Jr Coll (CA)
Scottsdale Comm Coll (AZ)
Seminole State Coll of Florida (FL)
Southeastern Comm Coll (IA)
Southern State Comm Coll (OH)
South Plains Coll (TX)
Southwest Virginia Comm Coll (VA)
Spoon River Coll (IL)
Taft Coll (CA)
Tallahassee Comm Coll (FL)
Tarrant County Coll District (TX)
Temple Coll (TX)

Texarkana Coll (TX)
Thomas Nelson Comm Coll (VA)
Tompkins Cortland Comm Coll (NY)
Trident Tech Coll (SC)
Tunxis Comm Coll (CT)
Tyler Jr Coll (TX)
Union County Coll (NJ)
U of Arkansas Comm Coll at Morrilton (AR)
U of Pittsburgh at Titusville (PA)
Virginia Western Comm Coll (VA)
West Kentucky Comm and Tech Coll (KY)
Wytheville Comm Coll (VA)

CRIMINAL JUSTICE/POLICE SCIENCE
Adirondack Comm Coll (NY)
Alexandria Tech and Comm Coll (MN)
Alpena Comm Coll (MI)
Alvin Comm Coll (TX)
Amarillo Coll (TX)
Anne Arundel Comm Coll (MD)
Arkansas State U–Mountain Home (AR)
Austin Comm Coll (TX)
Bakersfield Coll (CA)
Barton County Comm Coll (KS)
Beaufort County Comm Coll (NC)
Blackhawk Tech Coll (WI)
Borough of Manhattan Comm Coll of the City U of New York (NY)
Burlington County Coll (NJ)
Butte Coll (CA)
Cape Fear Comm Coll (NC)
Carrington Coll California–Pleasant Hill (CA)
Carroll Comm Coll (MD)
Cayuga County Comm Coll (NY)
Cecil Coll (MD)
Century Coll (MN)
Chippewa Valley Tech Coll (WI)
Clark State Comm Coll (OH)
Cleveland State Comm Coll (TN)
Clinton Comm Coll (NY)
Cochise Coll, Sierra Vista (AZ)
Colby Comm Coll (KS)
Coll of Lake County (IL)
Coll of Marin (CA)
Coll of the Canyons (CA)
Coll of the Desert (CA)
Collin County Comm Coll District (TX)
Comm Coll of Allegheny County (PA)
The Comm Coll of Baltimore County (MD)
Comm Coll of Beaver County (PA)
Comm Coll of Rhode Island (RI)
Copiah-Lincoln Comm Coll (MS)
Corning Comm Coll (NY)
County Coll of Morris (NJ)
Cowley County Comm Coll and Area Vocational–Tech School (KS)
Cuyahoga Comm Coll (OH)
Daytona State Coll (FL)
De Anza Coll (CA)
Delaware Tech & Comm Coll, Jack F. Owens Campus (DE)
Delaware Tech & Comm Coll, Stanton/Wilmington Campus (DE)
Delaware Tech & Comm Coll, Terry Campus (DE)
Dutchess Comm Coll (NY)
Dyersburg State Comm Coll (TN)
Edison Comm Coll (OH)
Elgin Comm Coll (IL)
Erie Comm Coll (NY)
Erie Comm Coll, North Campus (NY)
Erie Comm Coll, South Campus (NY)
Essex County Coll (NJ)
Finger Lakes Comm Coll (NY)
Fox Valley Tech Coll (WI)
Gadsden State Comm Coll (AL)
Garden City Comm Coll (KS)
Gateway Tech Coll (WI)
Georgia Highlands Coll (GA)
Grand Rapids Comm Coll (MI)
Greenfield Comm Coll (MA)
Hagerstown Comm Coll (MD)
Halifax Comm Coll (NC)
Harford Comm Coll (MD)
Harrisburg Area Comm Coll (PA)
Hawkeye Comm Coll (IA)
Houston Comm Coll System (TX)
Hutchinson Comm Coll and Area Vocational School (KS)
Illinois Central Coll (IL)
James A. Rhodes State Coll (OH)

Jamestown Comm Coll (NY)
Jefferson Coll (MO)
Jefferson State Comm Coll (AL)
Johnston Comm Coll (NC)
Kankakee Comm Coll (IL)
Kent State U at Tuscarawas (OH)
Lakeland Comm Coll (OH)
Lake Region State Coll (ND)
Lansing Comm Coll (MI)
Lawson State Comm Coll (AL)
Lincoln Land Comm Coll (IL)
Lorain County Comm Coll (OH)
Macomb Comm Coll (MI)
McHenry County Coll (IL)
Mendocino Coll (CA)
Metropolitan Comm Coll–Kansas City (MO)
Miami Dade Coll (FL)
Mineral Area Coll (MO)
Minnesota West Comm and Tech Coll (MN)
Mohave Comm Coll (AZ)
Monroe Comm Coll (NY)
Monroe County Comm Coll (MI)
Montgomery Coll (MD)
Montgomery County Comm Coll (PA)
Moraine Valley Comm Coll (IL)
Mott Comm Coll (MI)
Mt. San Antonio Coll (CA)
Normandale Comm Coll (MN)
Northeastern Jr Coll (CO)
North Hennepin Comm Coll (MN)
Northwest-Shoals Comm Coll (AL)
Northwest State Comm Coll (OH)
Oakland Comm Coll (MI)
Oakton Comm Coll (IL)
Ocean County Coll (NJ)
Oklahoma State U, Oklahoma City (OK)
Onondaga Comm Coll (NY)
Owensboro Comm and Tech Coll (KY)
Owens Comm Coll, Toledo (OH)
Piedmont Virginia Comm Coll (VA)
Quinsigamond Comm Coll (MA)
Rappahannock Comm Coll (VA)
Raritan Valley Comm Coll (NJ)
Rasmussen Coll Bloomington (MN)
Rasmussen Coll Brooklyn Park (MN)
Rasmussen Coll Eagan (MN)
Rasmussen Coll Lake Elmo/Woodbury (MN)
Rasmussen Coll Mankato (MN)
Rasmussen Coll St. Cloud (MN)
Red Rocks Comm Coll (CO)
Rogue Comm Coll (OR)
St. Clair County Comm Coll (MI)
St. Louis Comm Coll at Forest Park (MO)
St. Louis Comm Coll at Meramec (MO)
San Jacinto Coll District (TX)
San Juan Coll (NM)
Schoolcraft Coll (MI)
Shawnee Comm Coll (IL)
Sierra Coll (CA)
Southeast Tech Inst (SD)
Southern Maine Comm Coll (ME)
Southern State Comm Coll (OH)
South Plains Coll (TX)
Spoon River Coll (IL)
Springfield Tech Comm Coll (MA)
Temple Coll (TX)
Terra State Comm Coll (OH)
Tyler Jr Coll (TX)
Union County Coll (NJ)
Victor Valley Coll (CA)
Vincennes U (IN)
Volunteer State Comm Coll (TN)
Waubonsee Comm Coll (IL)
Waukesha County Tech Coll (WI)
Western Dakota Tech Inst (SD)
Western Iowa Tech Comm Coll (IA)
Westmoreland County Comm Coll (PA)
West Virginia Northern Comm Coll (WV)
Wisconsin Indianhead Tech Coll (WI)
Wytheville Comm Coll (VA)

CRIMINAL JUSTICE/SAFETY
Alamance Comm Coll (NC)
Ancilla Coll (IN)
Bay State Coll (MA)
Berkshire Comm Coll (MA)
Bismarck State Coll (ND)
Blue Ridge Comm and Tech Coll (WV)

Borough of Manhattan Comm Coll of the City U of New York (NY)
Bossier Parish Comm Coll (LA)
Bowling Green State U-Firelands Coll (OH)
Bucks County Comm Coll (PA)
Carrington Coll California–Pleasant Hill (CA)
Carrington Coll California–San Jose (CA)
Carrington Coll of California–Antioch (CA)
Carrington Coll of California–Citrus Heights (CA)
Catawba Valley Comm Coll (NC)
Central New Mexico Comm Coll (NM)
Century Coll (MN)
Chemeketa Comm Coll (OR)
Cleveland Comm Coll (NC)
Fayetteville Tech Comm Coll (NC)
Fiorello H. LaGuardia Comm Coll of the City U of New York (NY)
Forsyth Tech Comm Coll (NC)
Georgia Highlands Coll (GA)
Glendale Comm Coll (AZ)
Gordon State Coll (GA)
Guilford Tech Comm Coll (NC)
Holyoke Comm Coll (MA)
Ivy Tech Comm Coll–Bloomington (IN)
Ivy Tech Comm Coll–Central Indiana (IN)
Ivy Tech Comm Coll–East Central (IN)
Ivy Tech Comm Coll–Kokomo (IN)
Ivy Tech Comm Coll–North Central (IN)
Ivy Tech Comm Coll–Northwest (IN)
Ivy Tech Comm Coll–Southwest (IN)
Ivy Tech Comm Coll–Wabash Valley (IN)
James Sprunt Comm Coll (NC)
Kent State U at Ashtabula (OH)
Kent State U at East Liverpool (OH)
Kent State U at Salem (OH)
Kent State U at Trumbull (OH)
Kent State U at Tuscarawas (OH)
Lehigh Carbon Comm Coll (PA)
McCann School of Business & Technology, Pottsville (PA)
Monroe County Comm Coll (MI)
Montgomery Comm Coll (NC)
Nassau Comm Coll (NY)
Normandale Comm Coll (MN)
Northampton Comm Coll (PA)
North Hennepin Comm Coll (MN)
NorthWest Arkansas Comm Coll (AR)
Northwest State Comm Coll (OH)
Oregon Coast Comm Coll (OR)
Parkland Coll (IL)
Phoenix Coll (AZ)
Potomac State Coll of West Virginia U (WV)
Randolph Comm Coll (NC)
Sheridan Coll (WY)
South Suburban Coll (IL)
Texarkana Coll (TX)
Westmoreland County Comm Coll (PA)
Wilson Comm Coll (NC)
York County Comm Coll (ME)

CRIMINOLOGY
Genesee Comm Coll (NY)

CRISIS/EMERGENCY/DISASTER MANAGEMENT
Bucks County Comm Coll (PA)
Casper Coll (WY)
Comm Coll of Rhode Island (RI)
Fayetteville Tech Comm Coll (NC)
Flathead Valley Comm Coll (MT)
Montgomery Coll (MD)

CRITICAL INCIDENT RESPONSE/SPECIAL POLICE OPERATIONS
Raritan Valley Comm Coll (NJ)

CROP PRODUCTION
Arizona Western Coll (AZ)
Barton County Comm Coll (KS)
Chemeketa Comm Coll (OR)
Coll of the Desert (CA)
Dakota Coll at Bottineau (ND)
Greenfield Comm Coll (MA)
Illinois Central Coll (IL)
Northeast Iowa Comm Coll (IA)

Northwest Coll (WY)
The Ohio State U Ag Tech Inst (OH)

CULINARY ARTS
Alamance Comm Coll (NC)
Austin Comm Coll (TX)
Bakersfield Coll (CA)
Blackhawk Tech Coll (WI)
Blue Ridge Comm and Tech Coll (WV)
Bossier Parish Comm Coll (LA)
Bradford School (OH)
Bucks County Comm Coll (PA)
Cape Fear Comm Coll (NC)
Central New Mexico Comm Coll (NM)
Central Wyoming Coll (WY)
Clark Coll (WA)
Cochise Coll, Sierra Vista (AZ)
Coll of the Desert (CA)
Collin County Comm Coll District (TX)
Comm Coll of Allegheny County (PA)
Comm Coll of Beaver County (PA)
Comm Coll of Philadelphia (PA)
Culinary Inst LeNotre (TX)
Daytona State Coll (FL)
Delaware Tech & Comm Coll, Stanton/Wilmington Campus (DE)
Delaware Tech & Comm Coll, Terry Campus (DE)
Elaine P. Nunez Comm Coll (LA)
El Centro Coll (TX)
Elgin Comm Coll (IL)
Erie Comm Coll (NY)
Erie Comm Coll, North Campus (NY)
Fayetteville Tech Comm Coll (NC)
Flathead Valley Comm Coll (MT)
Grand Rapids Comm Coll (MI)
Guilford Tech Comm Coll (NC)
Harrisburg Area Comm Coll (PA)
Houston Comm Coll System (TX)
Illinois Central Coll (IL)
Jefferson Coll (MO)
J. F. Drake State Tech Coll (AL)
Kaskaskia Coll (IL)
Luzerne County Comm Coll (PA)
Macomb Comm Coll (MI)
Miami Dade Coll (FL)
Mineral Area Coll (MO)
Mitchell Tech Inst (SD)
Mohave Comm Coll (AZ)
Monroe County Comm Coll (MI)
Montgomery County Comm Coll (PA)
Moraine Park Tech Coll (WI)
Mott Comm Coll (MI)
Niagara County Comm Coll (NY)
Northampton Comm Coll (PA)
North Dakota State Coll of Science (ND)
North Shore Comm Coll (MA)
NorthWest Arkansas Comm Coll (AR)
Oakland Comm Coll (MI)
Olympic Coll (WA)
Orange Coast Coll (CA)
Oxnard Coll (CA)
Ozarka Coll (AR)
Ozarks Tech Comm Coll (MO)
Phoenix Coll (AZ)
Red Rocks Comm Coll (CO)
St. Louis Comm Coll at Forest Park (MO)
St. Philip's Coll (TX)
Salt Lake Comm Coll (UT)
San Jacinto Coll District (TX)
Santa Rosa Jr Coll (CA)
Schoolcraft Coll (MI)
Scottsdale Comm Coll (AZ)
Shelton State Comm Coll (AL)
Sheridan Coll (WY)
Southern Maine Comm Coll (ME)
South Puget Sound Comm Coll (WA)
Sullivan County Comm Coll (NY)
Texarkana Coll (TX)
Trident Tech Coll (SC)
Vincennes U (IN)
Westchester Comm Coll (NY)
West Kentucky Comm and Tech Coll (KY)
Westmoreland County Comm Coll (PA)
West Virginia Northern Comm Coll (WV)
Wilson Comm Coll (NC)
York County Comm Coll (ME)

CULINARY ARTS RELATED
State U of New York Coll of Technology at Alfred (NY)

CUSTOMER SERVICE MANAGEMENT
Alexandria Tech and Comm Coll (MN)
Catawba Valley Comm Coll (NC)
Central Oregon Comm Coll (OR)
Comm Coll of Rhode Island (RI)
Corning Comm Coll (NY)
Delaware Tech & Comm Coll, Stanton/Wilmington Campus (DE)

CUSTOMER SERVICE SUPPORT/CALL CENTER/TELESERVICE OPERATION
Central Wyoming Coll (WY)
Delaware Tech & Comm Coll, Jack F. Owens Campus (DE)
Delaware Tech & Comm Coll, Stanton/Wilmington Campus (DE)
Lansing Comm Coll (MI)
Union County Coll (NJ)

CYBER/COMPUTER FORENSICS AND COUNTERTERRORISM
Catawba Valley Comm Coll (NC)
Harper Coll (IL)

CYBER/ELECTRONIC OPERATIONS AND WARFARE
Oklahoma City Comm Coll (OK)

CYTOTECHNOLOGY
Barton County Comm Coll (KS)

DAIRY HUSBANDRY AND PRODUCTION
Northeast Iowa Comm Coll (IA)
The Ohio State U Ag Tech Inst (OH)

DAIRY SCIENCE
Mt. San Antonio Coll (CA)
The Ohio State U Ag Tech Inst (OH)
State U of New York Coll of Technology at Alfred (NY)

DANCE
Austin Comm Coll (TX)
Barton County Comm Coll (KS)
Casper Coll (WY)
Coll of Marin (CA)
Darton State Coll (GA)
Greenfield Comm Coll (MA)
Kilgore Coll (TX)
Lone Star Coll–CyFair (TX)
Lone Star Coll–North Harris (TX)
Lone Star Coll–Tomball (TX)
Miami Dade Coll (FL)
Nassau Comm Coll (NY)
Northern Essex Comm Coll (MA)
Orange Coast Coll (CA)
Pasadena City Coll (CA)
Raritan Valley Comm Coll (NJ)
San Jacinto Coll District (TX)
Santa Rosa Jr Coll (CA)
Tyler Jr Coll (TX)
Westchester Comm Coll (NY)

DATA ENTRY/MICROCOMPUTER APPLICATIONS
Arizona Western Coll (AZ)
Clark Coll (WA)
Comm Coll of Vermont (VT)
Elgin Comm Coll (IL)
Fiorello H. LaGuardia Comm Coll of the City U of New York (NY)
Glendale Comm Coll (AZ)
Illinois Central Coll (IL)
Lorain County Comm Coll (OH)
Lower Columbia Coll (WA)
Luzerne County Comm Coll (PA)
Montgomery Coll (MD)
North Dakota State Coll of Science (ND)
North Shore Comm Coll (MA)
Northwest State Comm Coll (OH)
Owensboro Comm and Tech Coll (KY)
Parkland Coll (IL)
St. Philip's Coll (TX)
Seminole State Coll of Florida (FL)
Sierra Coll (CA)
Stark State Coll (OH)
Sullivan County Comm Coll (NY)
Tyler Jr Coll (TX)
Westmoreland County Comm Coll (PA)

DATA ENTRY/MICROCOMPUTER APPLICATIONS RELATED

Berkeley City Coll (CA)
Butte Coll (CA)
Lorain County Comm Coll (OH)
Orange Coast Coll (CA)
Pasadena City Coll (CA)
San Diego Mesa Coll (CA)
Seminole State Coll of Florida (FL)
Stark State Coll (OH)

DATA MODELING/WAREHOUSING AND DATABASE ADMINISTRATION

Coll of Marin (CA)
Lansing Comm Coll (MI)
Quinsigamond Comm Coll (MA)
Red Rocks Comm Coll (CO)
Seminole State Coll of Florida (FL)

DATA PROCESSING AND DATA PROCESSING TECHNOLOGY

Alpena Comm Coll (MI)
Bainbridge Coll (GA)
Bakersfield Coll (CA)
Central New Mexico Comm Coll (NM)
Cochise Coll, Sierra Vista (AZ)
Copiah-Lincoln Comm Coll (MS)
Dabney S. Lancaster Comm Coll (VA)
El Centro Coll (TX)
Finger Lakes Comm Coll (NY)
Hallmark Coll of Technology (TX)
Housatonic Comm Coll (CT)
Illinois Central Coll (IL)
Jackson Coll (MI)
Jamestown Comm Coll (NY)
Luzerne County Comm Coll (PA)
Mendocino Coll (CA)
Mesa Comm Coll (AZ)
Metropolitan Comm Coll–Kansas City (MO)
Miami Dade Coll (FL)
Monroe Comm Coll (NY)
Monroe County Comm Coll (MI)
Montcalm Comm Coll (MI)
Mt. San Antonio Comm Coll (CA)
Nassau Comm Coll (NY)
Northern Essex Comm Coll (MA)
NorthWest Arkansas Comm Coll (AR)
Oakland Comm Coll (MI)
Orange Coast Coll (CA)
Paul D. Camp Comm Coll (VA)
Potomac State Coll of West Virginia U (WV)
St. Clair County Comm Coll (MI)
St. Louis Comm Coll at Forest Park (MO)
San Diego City Coll (CA)
San Juan Coll (NM)
Schoolcraft Coll (MI)
Seminole State Coll of Florida (FL)
South Plains Coll (TX)
South Puget Sound Comm Coll (WA)
Spartanburg Comm Coll (SC)
Springfield Tech Comm Coll (MA)
State U of New York Coll of Technology at Alfred (NY)
Taft Coll (CA)
Tallahassee Comm Coll (FL)
Tech Coll of the Lowcountry (SC)
Temple Coll (TX)
Terra State Comm Coll (OH)
Tunxis Comm Coll (CT)
Virginia Western Comm Coll (VA)
Westchester Comm Coll (NY)
Westmoreland County Comm Coll (PA)

DENTAL ASSISTING

Bradford School (PA)
Carrington Coll–Boise (ID)
Carrington Coll California–Pleasant Hill (CA)
Carrington Coll California–San Jose (CA)
Carrington Coll California–San Leandro (CA)
Carrington Coll of California–Antioch (CA)
Carrington Coll of California–Citrus Heights (CA)
Carrington Coll of California–Sacramento (CA)
Central Oregon Comm Coll (OR)
Central Wyoming Coll (WY)
Century Coll (MN)
Coll of Marin (CA)
Comm Coll of the Air Force (AL)
Eastern Idaho Tech Coll (ID)

Foothill Coll (CA)
International Business Coll, Indianapolis (IN)
Lake Area Tech Inst (SD)
Lake Michigan Coll (MI)
Luzerne County Comm Coll (PA)
Manor Coll (PA)
Middlesex Comm Coll (MA)
Mid-Plains Comm Coll, North Platte (NE)
Minnesota West Comm and Tech Coll (MN)
Mohave Comm Coll (AZ)
Mott Comm Coll (MI)
North Dakota State Coll of Science (ND)
Northern Essex Comm Coll (MA)
Northwest Tech Coll (MN)
Pasadena City Coll (CA)
Phoenix Coll (AZ)
Raritan Valley Comm Coll (NJ)
San Diego Mesa Coll (CA)
South Puget Sound Comm Coll (WA)
Union County Coll (NJ)
Westmoreland County Comm Coll (PA)
West Virginia Jr Coll–Bridgeport (WV)

DENTAL HYGIENE

Amarillo Coll (TX)
Austin Comm Coll (TX)
Bakersfield Coll (CA)
Barton County Comm Coll (KS)
Burlington County Coll (NJ)
Cape Fear Comm Coll (NC)
Carrington Coll–Boise (ID)
Carrington Coll California–San Jose (CA)
Carrington Coll–Mesa (AZ)
Carrington Coll of California–Sacramento (CA)
Catawba Valley Comm Coll (NC)
Century Coll (MN)
Chippewa Valley Tech Coll (WI)
Clark Coll (WA)
Colby Comm Coll (KS)
Coll of Lake County (IL)
Collin County Comm Coll District (TX)
Colorado Northwestern Comm Coll (CO)
The Comm Coll of Baltimore County (MD)
Comm Coll of Philadelphia (PA)
Comm Coll of Rhode Island (RI)
Darton State Coll (GA)
Daytona State Coll (FL)
Delaware Tech & Comm Coll, Stanton/Wilmington Campus (DE)
Erie Comm Coll, North Campus (NY)
Essex County Coll (NJ)
Fayetteville Tech Comm Coll (NC)
Foothill Coll (CA)
Fox Valley Tech Coll (WI)
Georgia Highlands Coll (GA)
Grand Rapids Comm Coll (MI)
Great Falls Coll Montana State U (MT)
Guilford Tech Comm Coll (NC)
Hagerstown Comm Coll (MD)
Halifax Comm Coll (NC)
Harper Coll (IL)
Harrisburg Area Comm Coll (PA)
Hawkeye Comm Coll (IA)
Hillsborough Comm Coll (FL)
Illinois Central Coll (IL)
James A. Rhodes State Coll (OH)
Lakeland Comm Coll (OH)
Lake Superior Coll (MN)
Lansing Comm Coll (MI)
Laramie County Comm Coll (WY)
Lone Star Coll–Kingwood (TX)
Luzerne County Comm Coll (PA)
Manor Coll (PA)
Miami Dade Coll (FL)
Middlesex Comm Coll (MA)
Mohave Comm Coll (AZ)
Monroe Comm Coll (NY)
Montgomery County Comm Coll (PA)
Mott Comm Coll (MI)
Normandale Comm Coll (MN)
Northampton Comm Coll (PA)
North Dakota State Coll of Science (ND)
Oakland Comm Coll (MI)
Ocean County Coll (NJ)
Orange Coast Coll (CA)
Owens Comm Coll, Toledo (OH)
Oxnard Coll (CA)
Parkland Coll (IL)

Pasadena City Coll (CA)
Pasco-Hernando Comm Coll (FL)
Pensacola State Coll (FL)
Phoenix Coll (AZ)
Pierce Coll at Puyallup (WA)
Quinsigamond Comm Coll (MA)
Raritan Valley Comm Coll (NJ)
St. Louis Comm Coll at Forest Park (MO)
Salt Lake Comm Coll (UT)
San Juan Coll (NM)
Santa Rosa Jr Coll (CA)
Sheridan Coll (WY)
Springfield Tech Comm Coll (MA)
Stark State Coll (OH)
Taft Coll (CA)
Tallahassee Comm Coll (FL)
Tarrant County Coll District (TX)
Temple Coll (TX)
Texas State Tech Coll Harlingen (TX)
Thomas Nelson Comm Coll (VA)
Trident Tech Coll (SC)
Tunxis Comm Coll (CT)
Tyler Jr Coll (TX)
Union County Coll (NJ)
Virginia Western Comm Coll (VA)
Waukesha County Tech Coll (WI)
Western Iowa Tech Comm Coll (IA)
Westmoreland County Comm Coll (PA)
Wytheville Comm Coll (VA)

DENTAL LABORATORY TECHNOLOGY

Comm Coll of the Air Force (AL)
Erie Comm Coll, South Campus (NY)
Middlesex Comm Coll (MA)
Pasadena City Coll (CA)
Texas State Tech Coll Harlingen (TX)

DENTAL SERVICES AND ALLIED PROFESSIONS RELATED

Gordon State Coll (GA)
Quinsigamond Comm Coll (MA)

DESIGN AND APPLIED ARTS RELATED

County Coll of Morris (NJ)
Howard Comm Coll (MD)
Mohawk Valley Comm Coll (NY)
Niagara County Comm Coll (NY)
Oklahoma City Comm Coll (OK)
Raritan Valley Comm Coll (NJ)
State U of New York Coll of Technology at Alfred (NY)
Tunxis Comm Coll (CT)
Vincennes U (IN)
Westchester Comm Coll (NY)

DESIGN AND VISUAL COMMUNICATIONS

Adirondack Comm Coll (NY)
Blue Ridge Comm and Tech Coll (WV)
Brookhaven Coll (TX)
Cecil Coll (MD)
Chemeketa Comm Coll (OR)
Coll of Marin (CA)
Elgin Comm Coll (IL)
FIDM/The Fashion Inst of Design & Merchandising, Los Angeles Campus (CA)
FIDM/The Fashion Inst of Design & Merchandising, San Diego Campus (CA)
FIDM/The Fashion Inst of Design & Merchandising, San Francisco Campus (CA)
Harford Comm Coll (MD)
Harrisburg Area Comm Coll (PA)
Hutchinson Comm Coll and Area Vocational School (KS)
Ivy Tech Comm Coll–Central Indiana (IN)
Ivy Tech Comm Coll–Columbus (IN)
Ivy Tech Comm Coll–North Central (IN)
Ivy Tech Comm Coll–Southern Indiana (IN)
Ivy Tech Comm Coll–Southwest (IN)
Ivy Tech Comm Coll–Wabash Valley (IN)
Lone Star Coll–CyFair (TX)
Lone Star Coll–Kingwood (TX)
Lone Star Coll–Montgomery (TX)
Lone Star Coll–North Harris (TX)
Nassau Comm Coll (NY)
Northwest State Comm Coll (OH)
Oklahoma City Comm Coll (OK)
Parkland Coll (IL)
Salt Lake Comm Coll (UT)

San Jacinto Coll District (TX)
Thomas Nelson Comm Coll (VA)
York County Comm Coll (ME)

DESKTOP PUBLISHING AND DIGITAL IMAGING DESIGN

Dunwoody Coll of Technology (MN)
Eastern Idaho Tech Coll (ID)
Houston Comm Coll System (TX)
Kankakee Comm Coll (IL)
Northeast Iowa Comm Coll (IA)
Northwest Coll (WY)
Pasadena City Coll (CA)
Southeast Tech Inst (SD)
Sullivan Coll of Technology and Design (KY)
Terra State Comm Coll (OH)
Western Iowa Tech Comm Coll (IA)

DEVELOPMENTAL AND CHILD PSYCHOLOGY

Bakersfield Coll (CA)
Comm Coll of Vermont (VT)
De Anza Coll (CA)
Mendocino Coll (CA)
San Diego City Coll (CA)
South Plains Coll (TX)
Tarrant County Coll District (TX)

DIAGNOSTIC MEDICAL SONOGRAPHY AND ULTRASOUND TECHNOLOGY

Austin Comm Coll (TX)
Bowling Green State U-Firelands Coll (OH)
Cape Fear Comm Coll (NC)
Central New Mexico Comm Coll (NM)
Chippewa Valley Tech Coll (WI)
Comm Coll of Allegheny County (PA)
Comm Coll of Rhode Island (RI)
Darton State Coll (GA)
Delaware Tech & Comm Coll, Jack F. Owens Campus (DE)
Delaware Tech & Comm Coll, Stanton/Wilmington Campus (DE)
El Centro Coll (TX)
Foothill Coll (CA)
Forsyth Tech Comm Coll (NC)
Harper Coll (IL)
Harrisburg Area Comm Coll (PA)
Hillsborough Comm Coll (FL)
Howard Comm Coll (MD)
Jackson Coll (MI)
Kennebec Valley Comm Coll (ME)
Lake Michigan Coll (MI)
Lancaster General Coll of Nursing & Health Sciences (PA)
Lansing Comm Coll (MI)
Laramie County Comm Coll (WY)
Lone Star Coll–CyFair (TX)
Lorain County Comm Coll (OH)
Lurleen B. Wallace Comm Coll (AL)
Miami Dade Coll (FL)
Middlesex Comm Coll (MA)
Montgomery Coll (MD)
Northampton Comm Coll (PA)
Oakland Comm Coll (MI)
Oklahoma City Comm Coll (OK)
Owensboro Comm and Tech Coll (KY)
Owens Comm Coll, Toledo (OH)
Pensacola State Coll (FL)
Piedmont Virginia Comm Coll (VA)
Red Rocks Comm Coll (CO)
San Jacinto Coll District (TX)
Southeast Tech Inst (SD)
Springfield Tech Comm Coll (MA)
Temple Coll (TX)
Union County Coll (NJ)
West Kentucky Comm and Tech Coll (KY)
Westmoreland County Comm Coll (PA)

DIESEL MECHANICS TECHNOLOGY

Alexandria Tech and Comm Coll (MN)
Casper Coll (WY)
Clark Coll (WA)
Comm Coll of Beaver County (PA)
Eastern Idaho Tech Coll (ID)
Hawkeye Comm Coll (IA)
Illinois Central Coll (IL)
Illinois Eastern Comm Colls, Wabash Valley College (IL)
Johnston Comm Coll (NC)
Kilgore Coll (TX)
Klamath Comm Coll (OR)
Lake Area Tech Inst (SD)
Laramie County Comm Coll (WY)
Lower Columbia Coll (WA)

Mid-Plains Comm Coll, North Platte (NE)
Minnesota West Comm and Tech Coll (MN)
North Dakota State Coll of Science (ND)
Oklahoma City Comm Coll (OK)
Oklahoma Tech Coll (OK)
Ozarks Tech Comm Coll (MO)
Raritan Valley Comm Coll (NJ)
Rogue Comm Coll (OR)
St. Louis Comm Coll at Forest Park (MO)
St. Philip's Coll (TX)
Salt Lake Comm Coll (UT)
San Jacinto Coll District (TX)
San Juan Coll (NM)
Santa Rosa Jr Coll (CA)
Shelton State Comm Coll (AL)
Sheridan Coll (WY)
Southeast Tech Inst (SD)
State U of New York Coll of Technology at Alfred (NY)
Vincennes U (IN)

DIETETICS

Bakersfield Coll (CA)
Central Oregon Comm Coll (OR)
Comm Coll of the Air Force (AL)
Harper Coll (IL)
Harrisburg Area Comm Coll (PA)
Miami Dade Coll (FL)
Orange Coast Coll (CA)
Owens Comm Coll, Toledo (OH)
Pensacola State Coll (FL)
South Plains Coll (TX)
Tarrant County Coll District (TX)
Vincennes U (IN)
Westchester Comm Coll (NY)

DIETETICS AND CLINICAL NUTRITION SERVICES RELATED

Cowley County Comm Coll and Area Vocational–Tech School (KS)

DIETETIC TECHNOLOGY

Coll of the Desert (CA)
Fiorello H. LaGuardia Comm Coll of the City U of New York (NY)
Great Falls Coll Montana State U (MT)
Harper Coll (IL)
Miami Dade Coll (FL)
Normandale Comm Coll (MN)
Santa Rosa Jr Coll (CA)
Southern Maine Comm Coll (ME)
Westmoreland County Comm Coll (PA)

DIETITIAN ASSISTANT

Barton County Comm Coll (KS)
Comm Coll of Allegheny County (PA)
Erie Comm Coll, North Campus (NY)
Hillsborough Comm Coll (FL)

DIGITAL ARTS

Corning Comm Coll (NY)
Fiorello H. LaGuardia Comm Coll of the City U of New York (NY)
Harford Comm Coll (MD)
State U of New York Coll of Technology at Alfred (NY)
Waukesha County Tech Coll (WI)

DIGITAL COMMUNICATION AND MEDIA/MULTIMEDIA

Butte Coll (CA)
Century Coll (MN)
Comm Coll of Beaver County (PA)
Comm Coll of Vermont (VT)
Delaware Tech & Comm Coll, Terry Campus (DE)
Finger Lakes Comm Coll (NY)
Laramie County Comm Coll (WY)
Oklahoma City Comm Coll (OK)
Pasadena City Coll (CA)
Raritan Valley Comm Coll (NJ)
Red Rocks Comm Coll (CO)
San Jacinto Coll District (TX)
Santa Rosa Jr Coll (CA)
Sierra Coll (CA)
Southern Maine Comm Coll (ME)
State U of New York Coll of Technology at Alfred (NY)
Sullivan Coll of Technology and Design (KY)
U of Alaska Anchorage, Kenai Peninsula Coll (AK)

DRAFTING AND DESIGN TECHNOLOGY

Alpena Comm Coll (MI)
Alvin Comm Coll (TX)
Amarillo Coll (TX)
Austin Comm Coll (TX)
Bainbridge Coll (GA)
Bakersfield Coll (CA)
Beaufort County Comm Coll (NC)
Bevill State Comm Coll (AL)
Bossier Parish Comm Coll (LA)
Burlington County Coll (NJ)
Butte Coll (CA)
Carrington Coll California–San Jose (CA)
Casper Coll (WY)
Cayuga County Comm Coll (NY)
Central Carolina Comm Coll (NC)
Central Oregon Comm Coll (OR)
Clark State Comm Coll (OH)
Coll of the Desert (CA)
Collin County Comm Coll District (TX)
Comm Coll of Allegheny County (PA)
Comm Coll of Philadelphia (PA)
Copiah-Lincoln Comm Coll (MS)
Cowley County Comm Coll and Area Vocational–Tech School (KS)
Crowder Coll (MO)
Dabney S. Lancaster Comm Coll (VA)
Daytona State Coll (FL)
Delaware Tech & Comm Coll, Jack F. Owens Campus (DE)
Delaware Tech & Comm Coll, Stanton/Wilmington Campus (DE)
Delaware Tech & Comm Coll, Terry Campus (DE)
Finger Lakes Comm Coll (NY)
Gadsden State Comm Coll (AL)
Garden City Comm Coll (KS)
Genesee Comm Coll (NY)
Grand Rapids Comm Coll (MI)
Houston Comm Coll System (TX)
Hutchinson Comm Coll and Area Vocational School (KS)
Inst of Design and Construction (NY)
ITI Tech Coll (LA)
Ivy Tech Comm Coll–Central Indiana (IN)
Ivy Tech Comm Coll–Columbus (IN)
Ivy Tech Comm Coll–Kokomo (IN)
Ivy Tech Comm Coll–Lafayette (IN)
Ivy Tech Comm Coll–Northeast (IN)
Ivy Tech Comm Coll–Northwest (IN)
J. F. Drake State Tech Coll (AL)
Kankakee Comm Coll (IL)
Kilgore Coll (TX)
Lake Area Tech Inst (SD)
Lake Michigan Coll (MI)
Laramie County Comm Coll (WY)
Lawson State Comm Coll (AL)
Lehigh Carbon Comm Coll (PA)
Lone Star Coll–North Harris (TX)
Lorain County Comm Coll (OH)
Lurleen B. Wallace Comm Coll (AL)
Luzerne County Comm Coll (PA)
Macomb Comm Coll (MI)
Massachusetts Bay Comm Coll (MA)
Mesa Comm Coll (AZ)
Metropolitan Comm Coll–Kansas City (MO)
Miami Dade Coll (FL)
Mineral Area Coll (MO)
Mohave Comm Coll (AZ)
Mohawk Valley Comm Coll (NY)
Monroe County Comm Coll (MI)
Montcalm Comm Coll (MI)
Mott Comm Coll (MI)
Mt. San Antonio Coll (CA)
Niagara County Comm Coll (NY)
NorthWest Arkansas Comm Coll (AR)
Northwest-Shoals Comm Coll (AL)
Oakland Comm Coll (MI)
Oklahoma City Comm Coll (OK)
Oklahoma State U, Oklahoma City (OK)
Olympic Coll (WA)
Orange Coast Coll (CA)
Paris Jr Coll (TX)
Pasadena City Coll (CA)
Pasco-Hernando Comm Coll (FL)
Pensacola State Coll (FL)
Red Rocks Comm Coll (CO)
Salt Lake Comm Coll (UT)
San Diego City Coll (CA)
San Jacinto Coll District (TX)
San Juan Coll (NM)
Schoolcraft Coll (MI)

Seminole State Coll of Florida (FL)
Shelton State Comm Coll (AL)
Southeastern Comm Coll (IA)
Southern State Comm Coll (OH)
South Plains Coll (TX)
South Puget Sound Comm Coll (WA)
Southwestern Michigan Coll (MI)
Spartanburg Comm Coll (SC)
Stark State Coll (OH)
Sullivan Coll of Technology and Design (KY)
Taft Coll (CA)
Tarrant County Coll District (TX)
Temple Coll (TX)
Texarkana Coll (TX)
Texas State Tech Coll Harlingen (TX)
U of Arkansas Comm Coll at Morrilton (AR)
Western Dakota Tech Inst (SD)
Wytheville Comm Coll (VA)

DRAFTING/DESIGN ENGINEERING TECHNOLOGIES RELATED

Blackhawk Tech Coll (WI)
Comm Coll of Allegheny County (PA)
Corning Comm Coll (NY)
Dabney S. Lancaster Comm Coll (VA)
De Anza Coll (CA)
James A. Rhodes State Coll (OH)
Kennebec Valley Comm Coll (ME)
Lone Star Coll–Montgomery (TX)
Lorain County Comm Coll (OH)
Luzerne County Comm Coll (PA)
Macomb Comm Coll (MI)
Mt. San Antonio Coll (CA)
Niagara County Comm Coll (NY)
Sullivan Coll of Technology and Design (KY)

DRAMA AND DANCE TEACHER EDUCATION

Darton State Coll (GA)

DRAMATIC/THEATER ARTS

Alvin Comm Coll (TX)
Amarillo Coll (TX)
American Academy of Dramatic Arts–New York (NY)
Anoka-Ramsey Comm Coll (MN)
Anoka-Ramsey Comm Coll, Cambridge Campus (MN)
Arizona Western Coll (AZ)
Austin Comm Coll (TX)
Bainbridge Coll (GA)
Bakersfield Coll (CA)
Barton County Comm Coll (KS)
Bossier Parish Comm Coll (LA)
Bucks County Comm Coll (PA)
Burlington County Coll (NJ)
Central Wyoming Coll (WY)
Clark State Comm Coll (OH)
Cochise Coll, Sierra Vista (AZ)
Coll of Marin (CA)
Coll of the Canyons (CA)
Coll of the Desert (CA)
Comm Coll of Allegheny County (PA)
Comm Coll of Rhode Island (RI)
Cowley County Comm Coll and Area Vocational–Tech School (KS)
Crowder Coll (MO)
Darton State Coll (GA)
De Anza Coll (CA)
Edison Comm Coll (OH)
Finger Lakes Comm Coll (NY)
Fiorello H. LaGuardia Comm Coll of the City U of New York (NY)
Foothill Coll (CA)
Genesee Comm Coll (NY)
Gordon State Coll (GA)
Harrisburg Area Comm Coll (PA)
Howard Comm Coll (MD)
Kilgore Coll (TX)
Lake Michigan Coll (MI)
Lansing Comm Coll (MI)
Lone Star Coll–CyFair (TX)
Lone Star Coll–Kingwood (TX)
Lone Star Coll–Montgomery (TX)
Lone Star Coll–North Harris (TX)
Lone Star Coll–Tomball (TX)
Lorain County Comm Coll (OH)
Manchester Comm Coll (CT)
Mendocino Coll (CA)
Miami Dade Coll (FL)
Mohawk Valley Comm Coll (NY)
Nassau Comm Coll (NY)
Niagara County Comm Coll (NY)
Normandale Comm Coll (MN)
Northeastern Jr Coll (CO)

Northern Essex Comm Coll (MA)
North Hennepin Comm Coll (MN)
Oklahoma City Comm Coll (OK)
Orange Coast Coll (CA)
Pasadena City Coll (CA)
Pensacola State Coll (FL)
Phoenix Coll (AZ)
St. Philip's Coll (TX)
San Diego City Coll (CA)
San Jacinto Coll District (TX)
Santa Rosa Jr Coll (CA)
Scottsdale Comm Coll (AZ)
Sheridan Coll (WY)
Spoon River Coll (IL)
Texarkana Coll (TX)
Tyler Jr Coll (TX)
Victor Valley Coll (CA)
Vincennes U (IN)

DRAMATIC/THEATER ARTS AND STAGECRAFT RELATED

Oakland Comm Coll (MI)
St. Philip's Coll (TX)

DRAWING

Cecil Coll (MD)
De Anza Coll (CA)
Luzerne County Comm Coll (PA)
Northeastern Jr Coll (CO)

EARLY CHILDHOOD EDUCATION

Ancilla Coll (IN)
Anne Arundel Comm Coll (MD)
Arizona Western Coll (AZ)
Arkansas State U–Mountain Home (AR)
Austin Comm Coll (TX)
Barton County Comm Coll (KS)
Big Bend Comm Coll (WA)
Blackhawk Tech Coll (WI)
Bucks County Comm Coll (PA)
Cape Fear Comm Coll (NC)
Carroll Comm Coll (MD)
Catawba Valley Comm Coll (NC)
Central Oregon Comm Coll (OR)
Central Wyoming Coll (WY)
Chippewa Valley Tech Coll (WI)
Clark Coll (WA)
Cleveland Comm Coll (NC)
Cochise Coll, Sierra Vista (AZ)
Coll of Southern Maryland (MD)
Collin County Comm Coll District (TX)
Colorado Northwestern Comm Coll (CO)
The Comm Coll of Baltimore County (MD)
Comm Coll of Vermont (VT)
Corning Comm Coll (NY)
Cossatot Comm Coll of the U of Arkansas (AR)
Delaware Tech & Comm Coll, Jack F. Owens Campus (DE)
Delaware Tech & Comm Coll, Stanton/Wilmington Campus (DE)
Delaware Tech & Comm Coll, Terry Campus (DE)
Fayetteville Tech Comm Coll (NC)
Finger Lakes Comm Coll (NY)
Forsyth Tech Comm Coll (NC)
Fox Valley Tech Coll (WI)
Garrett Coll (MD)
Gateway Comm and Tech Coll (KY)
Gateway Tech Coll (WI)
Georgia Military Coll (GA)
Glendale Comm Coll (AZ)
Gordon State Coll (GA)
Greenfield Comm Coll (MA)
Guilford Tech Comm Coll (NC)
Hagerstown Comm Coll (MD)
Halifax Comm Coll (NC)
Harford Comm Coll (MD)
Harper Coll (IL)
Harrisburg Area Comm Coll (PA)
Highland Comm Coll (IL)
Ivy Tech Comm Coll–Bloomington (IN)
Ivy Tech Comm Coll–Central Indiana (IN)
Ivy Tech Comm Coll–Columbus (IN)
Ivy Tech Comm Coll–East Central (IN)
Ivy Tech Comm Coll–Kokomo (IN)
Ivy Tech Comm Coll–Lafayette (IN)
Ivy Tech Comm Coll–North Central (IN)
Ivy Tech Comm Coll–Northeast (IN)
Ivy Tech Comm Coll–Northwest (IN)
Ivy Tech Comm Coll–Richmond (IN)

Ivy Tech Comm Coll–Southeast (IN)
Ivy Tech Comm Coll–Southern Indiana (IN)
Ivy Tech Comm Coll–Southwest (IN)
Ivy Tech Comm Coll–Wabash Valley (IN)
Jackson Coll (MI)
James Sprunt Comm Coll (NC)
Jamestown Comm Coll (NY)
Jefferson Comm Coll (NY)
Johnston Comm Coll (NC)
Kankakee Comm Coll (IL)
Lake Michigan Coll (MI)
Laramie County Comm Coll (WY)
Lehigh Carbon Comm Coll (PA)
Lincoln Land Comm Coll (IL)
Lower Columbia Coll (WA)
Luzerne County Comm Coll (PA)
McCann School of Business & Technology, Pottsville (PA)
Montgomery Coll (MD)
Montgomery Comm Coll (NC)
Moraine Park Tech Coll (WI)
Mott Comm Coll (MI)
Northampton Comm Coll (PA)
NorthWest Arkansas Comm Coll (AR)
Norwalk Comm Coll (CT)
Oklahoma State U, Oklahoma City (OK)
Olympic Coll (WA)
Owens Comm Coll, Toledo (OH)
Panola Coll (TX)
Paul D. Camp Comm Coll (VA)
Pensacola State Coll (FL)
Randolph Comm Coll (NC)
Rasmussen Coll Aurora (IL)
Rasmussen Coll Bismarck (ND)
Rasmussen Coll Bloomington (MN)
Rasmussen Coll Brooklyn Park (MN)
Rasmussen Coll Eagan (MN)
Rasmussen Coll Fargo (ND)
Rasmussen Coll Fort Myers (FL)
Rasmussen Coll Green Bay (WI)
Rasmussen Coll Lake Elmo/ Woodbury (MN)
Rasmussen Coll Mankato (MN)
Rasmussen Coll Moorhead (MN)
Rasmussen Coll New Port Richey (FL)
Rasmussen Coll Ocala (FL)
Rasmussen Coll Rockford (IL)
Rasmussen Coll St. Cloud (MN)
Red Rocks Comm Coll (CO)
Robeson Comm Coll (NC)
St. Philip's Coll (TX)
Santa Rosa Jr Coll (CA)
Sheridan Coll (WY)
Southern Maine Comm Coll (ME)
Southern State Comm Coll (OH)
Southwestern Michigan Coll (MI)
Springfield Tech Comm Coll (MA)
Tech Coll of the Lowcountry (SC)
Tompkins Cortland Comm Coll (NY)
Tri-County Comm Coll (NC)
U of Alaska Anchorage, Kenai Peninsula Coll (AK)
Vincennes U (IN)
Waukesha County Tech Coll (WI)
Westmoreland County Comm Coll (PA)
Wilson Comm Coll (NC)
Wisconsin Indianhead Tech Coll (WI)

E-COMMERCE

Brookhaven Coll (TX)
Catawba Valley Comm Coll (NC)
Delaware Tech & Comm Coll, Jack F. Owens Campus (DE)
Delaware Tech & Comm Coll, Terry Campus (DE)
Finger Lakes Comm Coll (NY)
Forsyth Tech Comm Coll (NC)
Halifax Comm Coll (NC)
Lansing Comm Coll (MI)
North Dakota State Coll of Science (ND)
Pasco-Hernando Comm Coll (FL)
Piedmont Comm Coll (NC)
St. Philip's Coll (TX)

ECONOMICS

Austin Comm Coll (TX)
Bakersfield Coll (CA)
Barton County Comm Coll (KS)
Casper Coll (WY)
Cochise Coll, Sierra Vista (AZ)
Coll of the Desert (CA)
Copiah-Lincoln Comm Coll (MS)
Darton State Coll (GA)

De Anza Coll (CA)
Foothill Coll (CA)
Georgia Highlands Coll (GA)
Greenfield Comm Coll (MA)
Harford Comm Coll (MD)
Lansing Comm Coll (MI)
Laramie County Comm Coll (WY)
Lone Star Coll–CyFair (TX)
Lone Star Coll–Kingwood (TX)
Lone Star Coll–Montgomery (TX)
Lone Star Coll–North Harris (TX)
Lone Star Coll–Tomball (TX)
Miami Dade Coll (FL)
Northeastern Jr Coll (CO)
Oklahoma State U, Oklahoma City (OK)
Orange Coast Coll (CA)
Oxnard Coll (CA)
Potomac State Coll of West Virginia U (WV)
St. Philip's Coll (TX)
Salt Lake Comm Coll (UT)
Santa Rosa Jr Coll (CA)
Terra State Comm Coll (OH)
Tyler Jr Coll (TX)
Vincennes U (IN)

EDUCATION

Bainbridge Coll (GA)
Bay State Coll (MA)
Bossier Parish Comm Coll (LA)
Bowling Green State U-Firelands Coll (OH)
Bucks County Comm Coll (PA)
Burlington County Coll (NJ)
Carroll Comm Coll (MD)
Cecil Coll (MD)
Central Oregon Comm Coll (OR)
Chipola Coll (FL)
Coll of Southern Maryland (MD)
The Comm Coll of Baltimore County (MD)
Comm Coll of Beaver County (PA)
Comm Coll of Philadelphia (PA)
Comm Coll of Vermont (VT)
Copiah-Lincoln Comm Coll (MS)
Cowley County Comm Coll and Area Vocational–Tech School (KS)
Crowder Coll (MO)
Dabney S. Lancaster Comm Coll (VA)
Dakota Coll at Bottineau (ND)
Dyersburg State Comm Coll (TN)
Eastern Shore Comm Coll (VA)
Edison Comm Coll (OH)
Elaine P. Nunez Comm Coll (LA)
Essex County Coll (NJ)
Garden City Comm Coll (KS)
Garrett Coll (MD)
Genesee Comm Coll (NY)
Georgia Military Coll (GA)
Greenfield Comm Coll (MA)
Hagerstown Comm Coll (MD)
Harford Comm Coll (MD)
Hutchinson Comm Coll and Area Vocational School (KS)
Jackson State Comm Coll (TN)
Kankakee Comm Coll (IL)
Kilian Comm Coll (SD)
Klamath Comm Coll (OR)
Laramie County Comm Coll (WY)
Lehigh Carbon Comm Coll (PA)
Lone Star Coll–CyFair (TX)
Lone Star Coll–Kingwood (TX)
Lone Star Coll–Montgomery (TX)
Lone Star Coll–North Harris (TX)
Lone Star Coll–Tomball (TX)
Lorain County Comm Coll (OH)
Luzerne County Comm Coll (PA)
Miami Dade Coll (FL)
Miles Comm Coll (MT)
Mohave Comm Coll (AZ)
Motlow State Comm Coll (TN)
Northeastern Jr Coll (CO)
Northern Essex Comm Coll (MA)
NorthWest Arkansas Comm Coll (AR)
Northwest State Comm Coll (OH)
Owens Comm Coll, Toledo (OH)
Panola Coll (TX)
Paris Jr Coll (TX)
Paul D. Camp Comm Coll (VA)
Pensacola State Coll (FL)
Piedmont Virginia Comm Coll (VA)
Potomac State Coll of West Virginia U (WV)
St. Philip's Coll (TX)
Schoolcraft Coll (MI)
South Plains Coll (TX)
Spoon River Coll (IL)

Tech Coll of the Lowcountry (SC)
Terra State Comm Coll (OH)
Vincennes U (IN)
Virginia Western Comm Coll (VA)
Volunteer State Comm Coll (TN)
Wytheville Comm Coll (VA)
York County Comm Coll (ME)

EDUCATIONAL/INSTRUCTIONAL TECHNOLOGY
Bossier Parish Comm Coll (LA)
Collin County Comm Coll District (TX)
Comm Coll of the Air Force (AL)
Essex County Coll (NJ)
Ivy Tech Comm Coll–North Central (IN)
Red Rocks Comm Coll (CO)
Tarrant County Coll District (TX)

EDUCATIONAL LEADERSHIP AND ADMINISTRATION
Comm Coll of the Air Force (AL)
Glendale Comm Coll (AZ)

EDUCATION (MULTIPLE LEVELS)
Arkansas State U–Mountain Home (AR)
Brookhaven Coll (TX)
Cayuga County Comm Coll (NY)
Comm Coll of Beaver County (PA)
Delaware Tech & Comm Coll, Jack F. Owens Campus (DE)
Delaware Tech & Comm Coll, Stanton/Wilmington Campus (DE)
Delaware Tech & Comm Coll, Terry Campus (DE)
Onondaga Comm Coll (NY)
San Jacinto Coll District (TX)
U of Arkansas Comm Coll at Morrilton (AR)
Westchester Comm Coll (NY)

EDUCATION RELATED
Corning Comm Coll (NY)
Georgia Highlands Coll (GA)
Guilford Tech Comm Coll (NC)
Kent State U at Salem (OH)
Kent State U at Tuscarawas (OH)
Miami Dade Coll (FL)

EDUCATION (SPECIFIC LEVELS AND METHODS) RELATED
Comm Coll of Allegheny County (PA)
Corning Comm Coll (NY)
Jefferson Coll (MO)

EDUCATION (SPECIFIC SUBJECT AREAS) RELATED
Comm Coll of Allegheny County (PA)
Manor Coll (PA)

ELECTRICAL AND ELECTRONIC ENGINEERING TECHNOLOGIES RELATED
Corning Comm Coll (NY)
Fox Valley Tech Coll (WI)
Kent State U at Ashtabula (OH)
Kent State U at Trumbull (OH)
Kent State U at Tuscarawas (OH)
Lake Region State Coll (ND)
Miami Dade Coll (FL)
Mohawk Valley Comm Coll (NY)
Moraine Park Tech Coll (WI)
North Dakota State Coll of Science (ND)
Onondaga Comm Coll (NY)
Pasadena City Coll (CA)
Sheridan Coll (WY)
Sullivan Coll of Technology and Design (KY)
Terra State Comm Coll (OH)

ELECTRICAL AND ELECTRONICS ENGINEERING
Anne Arundel Comm Coll (MD)
Carroll Comm Coll (MD)
Chemeketa Comm Coll (OR)
Corning Comm Coll (NY)
Fiorello H. LaGuardia Comm Coll of the City U of New York (NY)
Garrett Coll (MD)
John Tyler Comm Coll (VA)
Pasadena City Coll (CA)
Pensacola State Coll (FL)

ELECTRICAL AND POWER TRANSMISSION INSTALLATION
Ivy Tech Comm Coll–Columbus (IN)
Lansing Comm Coll (MI)

Minnesota West Comm and Tech Coll (MN)
Oklahoma State U, Oklahoma City (OK)
Orange Coast Coll (CA)
Piedmont Comm Coll (NC)
Rogue Comm Coll (OR)
San Jacinto Coll District (TX)

ELECTRICAL AND POWER TRANSMISSION INSTALLATION RELATED
Minnesota West Comm and Tech Coll (MN)

ELECTRICAL, ELECTRONIC AND COMMUNICATIONS ENGINEERING TECHNOLOGY
Adirondack Comm Coll (NY)
Alamance Comm Coll (NC)
Alvin Comm Coll (TX)
Amarillo Coll (TX)
Anne Arundel Comm Coll (MD)
Arapahoe Comm Coll (CO)
Austin Comm Coll (TX)
Bainbridge Coll (GA)
Bakersfield Coll (CA)
Beaufort County Comm Coll (NC)
Berkshire Comm Coll (MA)
Bismarck State Coll (ND)
Bowling Green State U–Firelands Coll (OH)
Burlington County Coll (NJ)
Cape Fear Comm Coll (NC)
Casper Coll (WY)
Catawba Valley Comm Coll (NC)
Cayuga County Comm Coll (NY)
Cecil Coll (MD)
Central Carolina Comm Coll (NC)
Central New Mexico Comm Coll (NM)
Central Oregon Comm Coll (OR)
Chemeketa Comm Coll (OR)
Clark Coll (WA)
Clark State Comm Coll (OH)
Cleveland Comm Coll (NC)
Cleveland Inst of Electronics (OH)
Clinton Comm Coll (NY)
Cochise Coll, Sierra Vista (AZ)
Coll of Lake County (IL)
Collin County Comm Coll District (TX)
Comm Coll of Allegheny County (PA)
Comm Coll of Beaver County (PA)
Comm Coll of the Air Force (AL)
Copiah-Lincoln Comm Coll (MS)
County Coll of Morris (NJ)
Crowder Coll (MO)
Dabney S. Lancaster Comm Coll (VA)
Daytona State Coll (FL)
Delaware Tech & Comm Coll, Jack F. Owens Campus (DE)
Delaware Tech & Comm Coll, Stanton/Wilmington Campus (DE)
Delaware Tech & Comm Coll, Terry Campus (DE)
Dunwoody Coll of Technology (MN)
Dutchess Comm Coll (NY)
Eastern Shore Comm Coll (VA)
Edison Comm Coll (OH)
Erie Comm Coll, North Campus (NY)
Essex County Coll (NJ)
Fayetteville Tech Comm Coll (NC)
Foothill Coll (CA)
Forsyth Tech Comm Coll (NC)
Fountainhead Coll of Technology (TN)
Fox Valley Tech Coll (WI)
Gadsden State Comm Coll (AL)
Gateway Tech Coll (WI)
Genesee Comm Coll (NY)
Grand Rapids Comm Coll (MI)
Guilford Tech Comm Coll (NC)
Halifax Comm Coll (NC)
Hallmark Coll of Technology (TX)
Harper Coll (IL)
Harrisburg Area Comm Coll (PA)
Hawkeye Comm Coll (IA)
Hillsborough Comm Coll (FL)
Howard Comm Coll (MD)
Hutchinson Comm Coll and Area Vocational School (KS)
Illinois Central Coll (IL)
ITI Tech Coll (LA)
Ivy Tech Comm Coll–Bloomington (IN)
Ivy Tech Comm Coll–Central Indiana (IN)
Ivy Tech Comm Coll–Columbus (IN)
Ivy Tech Comm Coll–East Central (IN)
Ivy Tech Comm Coll–Kokomo (IN)

Ivy Tech Comm Coll–Lafayette (IN)
Ivy Tech Comm Coll–North Central (IN)
Ivy Tech Comm Coll–Northeast (IN)
Ivy Tech Comm Coll–Northwest (IN)
Ivy Tech Comm Coll–Richmond (IN)
Ivy Tech Comm Coll–Southeast (IN)
Ivy Tech Comm Coll–Southern Indiana (IN)
Ivy Tech Comm Coll–Southwest (IN)
Ivy Tech Comm Coll–Wabash Valley (IN)
Jackson Coll (MI)
James A. Rhodes State Coll (OH)
Jamestown Comm Coll (NY)
Jefferson Coll (MO)
J. F. Drake State Tech Coll (AL)
Johnston Comm Coll (NC)
Kaskaskia Coll (IL)
Kennebec Valley Comm Coll (ME)
Kent State U at Trumbull (OH)
Kilgore Coll (TX)
Kirtland Comm Coll (MI)
Lake Area Tech Inst (SD)
Lakeland Comm Coll (OH)
Lake Superior Coll (MN)
Lehigh Carbon Comm Coll (PA)
Lincoln Land Comm Coll (IL)
Lone Star Coll–CyFair (TX)
Lone Star Coll–North Harris (TX)
Lone Star Coll–Tomball (TX)
Lorain County Comm Coll (OH)
Luzerne County Comm Coll (PA)
Macomb Comm Coll (MI)
McHenry County Coll (IL)
Mesa Comm Coll (AZ)
Metropolitan Comm Coll–Kansas City (MO)
Miami Dade Coll (FL)
Middlesex Comm Coll (MA)
Miles Comm Coll (MT)
Mineral Area Coll (MO)
Mohawk Valley Comm Coll (NY)
Monroe Comm Coll (NY)
Monroe County Comm Coll (MI)
Montcalm Comm Coll (MI)
Montgomery County Comm Coll (PA)
Mott Comm Coll (MI)
Mt. San Antonio Coll (CA)
Northampton Comm Coll (PA)
Northeast Iowa Comm Coll (IA)
Northern Essex Comm Coll (MA)
NorthWest Arkansas Comm Coll (AR)
Northwest State Comm Coll (OH)
Oakland Comm Coll (MI)
Oakton Comm Coll (IL)
Oklahoma City Comm Coll (OK)
Oklahoma State U, Oklahoma City (OK)
Olympic Coll (WA)
Onondaga Comm Coll (NY)
Orange Coast Coll (CA)
Owensboro Comm and Tech Coll (KY)
Owens Comm Coll, Toledo (OH)
Ozarks Tech Comm Coll (MO)
Paris Jr Coll (TX)
Penn State Brandywine (PA)
Penn State DuBois (PA)
Penn State Fayette, The Eberly Campus (PA)
Penn State Hazleton (PA)
Penn State New Kensington (PA)
Penn State Schuylkill (PA)
Penn State Wilkes-Barre (PA)
Penn State Worthington Scranton (PA)
Penn State York (PA)
Pensacola State Coll (FL)
Pierce Coll at Puyallup (WA)
Pittsburgh Tech Inst, Oakdale (PA)
Potomac State Coll of West Virginia U (WV)
Quinsigamond Comm Coll (MA)
Reid State Tech Coll (AL)
Robeson Comm Coll (NC)
Rogue Comm Coll (OR)
St. Clair County Comm Coll (MI)
Salt Lake Comm Coll (UT)
San Diego City Coll (CA)
San Jacinto Coll District (TX)
San Juan Coll (NM)
Santa Rosa Jr Coll (CA)
Schoolcraft Coll (MI)
Scottsdale Comm Coll (AZ)
Seminole State Coll of Florida (FL)
Shawnee Comm Coll (IL)
Shelton State Comm Coll (AL)
Southeastern Comm Coll (IA)
Southeast Tech Inst (SD)

Southern Maine Comm Coll (ME)
Southern State Comm Coll (OH)
South Plains Coll (TX)
South Suburban Coll (IL)
Southwestern Michigan Coll (MI)
Southwest Virginia Comm Coll (VA)
Spartanburg Comm Coll (SC)
Spoon River Coll (IL)
Springfield Tech Comm Coll (MA)
State U of New York Coll of Technology at Alfred (NY)
Sullivan Coll of Technology and Design (KY)
Sullivan County Comm Coll (NY)
Taft Coll (CA)
Tarrant County Coll District (TX)
Terra State Comm Coll (OH)
Texarkana Coll (TX)
Tompkins Cortland Comm Coll (NY)
Tri-County Comm Coll (NC)
Trident Tech Coll (SC)
Victor Valley Coll (CA)
Vincennes U (IN)
Virginia Western Comm Coll (VA)
Waubonsee Comm Coll (IL)
Waukesha County Tech Coll (WI)
Westchester Comm Coll (NY)
Westmoreland County Comm Coll (PA)
Wytheville Comm Coll (VA)

ELECTRICAL/ELECTRONICS DRAFTING AND CAD/CADD
Central New Mexico Comm Coll (NM)
Collin County Comm Coll District (TX)
Dunwoody Coll of Technology (MN)
Middlesex Comm Coll (MA)

ELECTRICAL/ELECTRONICS EQUIPMENT INSTALLATION AND REPAIR
Arizona Western Coll (AZ)
Cape Fear Comm Coll (NC)
Collin County Comm Coll District (TX)
Hutchinson Comm Coll and Area Vocational School (KS)
Lake Area Tech Inst (SD)
Lake Region State Coll (ND)
Macomb Comm Coll (MI)
Orange Coast Coll (CA)
Pittsburgh Tech Inst, Oakdale (PA)
St. Philip's Coll (TX)
Schoolcraft Coll (MI)
Sierra Coll (CA)
Southeast Tech Inst (SD)
State U of New York Coll of Technology at Alfred (NY)
Sullivan Coll of Technology and Design (KY)

ELECTRICAL/ELECTRONICS MAINTENANCE AND REPAIR TECHNOLOGY RELATED
Kennebec Valley Comm Coll (ME)
Mohawk Valley Comm Coll (NY)
Sullivan Coll of Technology and Design (KY)

ELECTRICIAN
Adirondack Comm Coll (NY)
Bevill State Comm Coll (AL)
Cleveland Comm Coll (NC)
Coll of Lake County (IL)
Coll of Southern Maryland (MD)
Comm Coll of Beaver County (PA)
Dunwoody Coll of Technology (MN)
Fayetteville Tech Comm Coll (NC)
Flathead Valley Comm Coll (MT)
Guilford Tech Comm Coll (NC)
Harrisburg Area Comm Coll (PA)
Ivy Tech Comm Coll–Bloomington (IN)
Ivy Tech Comm Coll–Central Indiana (IN)
Ivy Tech Comm Coll–East Central (IN)
Ivy Tech Comm Coll–Kokomo (IN)
Ivy Tech Comm Coll–Lafayette (IN)
Ivy Tech Comm Coll–North Central (IN)
Ivy Tech Comm Coll–Northeast (IN)
Ivy Tech Comm Coll–Northwest (IN)
Ivy Tech Comm Coll–Richmond (IN)
Ivy Tech Comm Coll–Southern Indiana (IN)
Ivy Tech Comm Coll–Southwest (IN)
Ivy Tech Comm Coll–Wabash Valley (IN)
J. F. Drake State Tech Coll (AL)
Kennebec Valley Comm Coll (ME)

Lake Superior Coll (MN)
Lansing Comm Coll (MI)
Lurleen B. Wallace Comm Coll (AL)
Luzerne County Comm Coll (PA)
Minnesota West Comm and Tech Coll (MN)
Mitchell Tech Inst (SD)
Northampton Comm Coll (PA)
Northeast Iowa Comm Coll (IA)
Northwest Coll (WY)
Oakland Comm Coll (MI)
Piedmont Comm Coll (NC)
Randolph Comm Coll (NC)
Red Rocks Comm Coll (CO)
Shelton State Comm Coll (AL)
State U of New York Coll of Technology at Alfred (NY)
Waubonsee Comm Coll (IL)
Western Dakota Tech Inst (SD)
West Kentucky Comm and Tech Coll (KY)
Wilson Comm Coll (NC)

ELECTROCARDIOGRAPH TECHNOLOGY
Delaware Tech & Comm Coll, Stanton/Wilmington Campus (DE)
Lancaster General Coll of Nursing & Health Sciences (PA)
Oklahoma State U, Oklahoma City (OK)

ELECTROMECHANICAL AND INSTRUMENTATION AND MAINTENANCE TECHNOLOGIES RELATED
Cape Fear Comm Coll (NC)
Catawba Valley Comm Coll (NC)
Chemeketa Comm Coll (OR)
Cowley County Comm Coll and Area Vocational–Tech School (KS)
Halifax Comm Coll (NC)
Piedmont Comm Coll (NC)
Randolph Comm Coll (NC)
Red Rocks Comm Coll (CO)
Sullivan Coll of Technology and Design (KY)
Waukesha County Tech Coll (WI)

ELECTROMECHANICAL TECHNOLOGY
Blackhawk Tech Coll (WI)
Blue Ridge Comm and Tech Coll (WV)
Bowling Green State U–Firelands Coll (OH)
Central Maine Comm Coll (ME)
Chippewa Valley Tech Coll (WI)
Comm Coll of Rhode Island (RI)
Delaware Tech & Comm Coll, Terry Campus (DE)
Edison Comm Coll (OH)
Fox Valley Tech Coll (WI)
Gateway Tech Coll (WI)
Guilford Tech Comm Coll (NC)
Kirtland Comm Coll (MI)
Lake Area Tech Inst (SD)
Lansing Comm Coll (MI)
Macomb Comm Coll (MI)
Montgomery County Comm Coll (PA)
Moraine Park Tech Coll (WI)
Northampton Comm Coll (PA)
Oakland Comm Coll (MI)
Quinsigamond Comm Coll (MA)
St. Philip's Coll (TX)
Schoolcraft Coll (MI)
Southeast Tech Inst (SD)
Southern State Comm Coll (OH)
Springfield Tech Comm Coll (MA)
State U of New York Coll of Technology at Alfred (NY)
Tarrant County Coll District (TX)
Texas State Tech Coll Harlingen (TX)
Union County Coll (NJ)

ELECTRONEURODIAGNOSTIC/ELECTROENCEPHALOGRAPHIC TECHNOLOGY
Catawba Valley Comm Coll (NC)
Comm Coll of Allegheny County (PA)
Harford Comm Coll (MD)
Oakland Comm Coll (MI)
Parkland Coll (IL)
Southeast Tech Inst (SD)

ELEMENTARY EDUCATION
Alpena Comm Coll (MI)
Amarillo Coll (TX)
Ancilla Coll (IN)
Anne Arundel Comm Coll (MD)
Arizona Western Coll (AZ)
Bainbridge Coll (GA)

Barton County Comm Coll (KS)
Carl Albert State Coll (OK)
Carroll Comm Coll (MD)
Casper Coll (WY)
Cecil Coll (MD)
Central New Mexico Comm Coll (NM)
Central Wyoming Coll (WY)
Cleveland Comm Coll (NC)
Cochise Coll, Sierra Vista (AZ)
Coll of Southern Maryland (MD)
The Comm Coll of Baltimore County (MD)
Copiah-Lincoln Comm Coll (MS)
Cowley County Comm Coll and Area Vocational–Tech School (KS)
Crowder Coll (MO)
Delaware Tech & Comm Coll, Jack F. Owens Campus (DE)
Delaware Tech & Comm Coll, Stanton/Wilmington Campus (DE)
Delaware Tech & Comm Coll, Terry Campus (DE)
Fayetteville Tech Comm Coll (NC)
Garrett Coll (MD)
Genesee Comm Coll (NY)
Grand Rapids Comm Coll (MI)
Hagerstown Comm Coll (MD)
Halifax Comm Coll (NC)
Harford Comm Coll (MD)
Harper Coll (IL)
Howard Comm Coll (MD)
James Sprunt Comm Coll (NC)
Jamestown Comm Coll (NY)
Kankakee Comm Coll (IL)
Kilgore Coll (TX)
Lake Michigan Coll (MI)
Lansing Comm Coll (MI)
Lorain County Comm Coll (OH)
Manor Coll (PA)
Miami Dade Coll (FL)
Middlesex Comm Coll (MA)
Miles Comm Coll (MT)
Mohawk Valley Comm Coll (NY)
Monroe County Comm Coll (MI)
Montgomery Coll (MD)
Montgomery County Comm Coll (PA)
Niagara County Comm Coll (NY)
Normandale Comm Coll (MN)
Northeastern Jr Coll (CO)
Northern Essex Comm Coll (MA)
Northwest Coll (WY)
Oklahoma City Comm Coll (OK)
Paris Jr Coll (TX)
Parkland Coll (IL)
Pensacola State Coll (FL)
Phoenix Coll (AZ)
Piedmont Comm Coll (NC)
Potomac State Coll of West Virginia U (WV)
Quinsigamond Comm Coll (MA)
San Jacinto Coll District (TX)
San Juan Coll (NM)
Sheridan Coll (WY)
Springfield Tech Comm Coll (MA)
Sullivan County Comm Coll (NY)
Vincennes U (IN)
Wilson Comm Coll (NC)

EMERGENCY CARE ATTENDANT (EMT AMBULANCE)
Barton County Comm Coll (KS)
Carroll Comm Coll (MD)
Delaware Tech & Comm Coll, Stanton/Wilmington Campus (DE)
Illinois Eastern Comm Colls, Frontier Community College (IL)
Waubonsee Comm Coll (IL)

EMERGENCY MEDICAL TECHNOLOGY (EMT PARAMEDIC)
Alvin Comm Coll (TX)
Amarillo Coll (TX)
Arapahoe Comm Coll (CO)
Arizona Western Coll (AZ)
Arkansas State U–Mountain Home (AR)
Austin Comm Coll (TX)
Bakersfield Coll (CA)
Barton County Comm Coll (KS)
Bevill State Comm Coll (AL)
Bismarck State Coll (ND)
Blue Ridge Comm and Tech Coll (WV)
Borough of Manhattan Comm Coll of the City U of New York (NY)
Bossier Parish Comm Coll (LA)
Brookhaven Coll (TX)

Butte Coll (CA)
Casper Coll (WY)
Catawba Valley Comm Coll (NC)
Cecil Coll (MD)
Central Oregon Comm Coll (OR)
Central Wyoming Coll (WY)
Century Coll (MN)
Chemeketa Comm Coll (OR)
Chippewa Valley Tech Coll (WI)
Clark Coll (WA)
Clark State Comm Coll (OH)
Cleveland Comm Coll (NC)
Cochise Coll, Sierra Vista (AZ)
Coll of Southern Maryland (MD)
Collin County Comm Coll District (TX)
Colorado Northwestern Comm Coll (CO)
The Comm Coll of Baltimore County (MD)
Cowley County Comm Coll and Area Vocational–Tech School (KS)
Darton State Coll (GA)
Daytona State Coll (FL)
Delaware Tech & Comm Coll, Jack F. Owens Campus (DE)
Delaware Tech & Comm Coll, Stanton/Wilmington Campus (DE)
Delaware Tech & Comm Coll, Terry Campus (DE)
Dutchess Comm Coll (NY)
Dyersburg State Comm Coll (TN)
Elaine P. Nunez Comm Coll (LA)
El Centro Coll (TX)
Erie Comm Coll, South Campus (NY)
Fayetteville Tech Comm Coll (NC)
Finger Lakes Comm Coll (NY)
Fiorello H. LaGuardia Comm Coll of the City U of New York (NY)
Flathead Valley Comm Coll (MT)
Florida Gateway Coll (FL)
Foothill Coll (CA)
Forsyth Tech Comm Coll (NC)
Fox Valley Tech Coll (WI)
Gadsden State Comm Coll (AL)
Garden City Comm Coll (KS)
Gateway Tech Coll (WI)
Glendale Comm Coll (AZ)
Great Falls Coll Montana State U (MT)
Guilford Tech Comm Coll (NC)
Hagerstown Comm Coll (MD)
Harper Coll (IL)
Harrisburg Area Comm Coll (PA)
Highland Comm Coll (IL)
Hillsborough Comm Coll (FL)
Houston Comm Coll System (TX)
Howard Comm Coll (MD)
Hutchinson Comm Coll and Area Vocational School (KS)
Illinois Central Coll (IL)
Ivy Tech Comm Coll–Bloomington (IN)
Ivy Tech Comm Coll–Kokomo (IN)
Ivy Tech Comm Coll–North Central (IN)
Ivy Tech Comm Coll–Southwest (IN)
Ivy Tech Comm Coll–Wabash Valley (IN)
Jackson Coll (MI)
James A. Rhodes State Coll (OH)
Jefferson Coll (MO)
Jefferson Comm Coll (NY)
Jefferson State Comm Coll (AL)
Kankakee Comm Coll (IL)
Kaskaskia Coll (IL)
Kennebec Valley Comm Coll (ME)
Kent State U at Trumbull (OH)
Kilgore Coll (TX)
Lake Area Tech Inst (SD)
Lake Michigan Coll (MI)
Lansing Comm Coll (MI)
Laramie County Comm Coll (WY)
Lincoln Land Comm Coll (IL)
Lone Star Coll–CyFair (TX)
Lone Star Coll–Montgomery (TX)
Lone Star Coll–North Harris (TX)
Lurleen B. Wallace Comm Coll (AL)
Luzerne County Comm Coll (PA)
Macomb Comm Coll (MI)
McHenry County Coll (IL)
Metropolitan Comm Coll–Kansas City (MO)
Miami Dade Coll (FL)
Mineral Area Coll (MO)
Mohave Comm Coll (AZ)
Mohawk Valley Comm Coll (NY)
Montcalm Comm Coll (MI)
Moraine Park Tech Coll (WI)

Moraine Valley Comm Coll (IL)
Mott Comm Coll (MI)
Mt. San Antonio Coll (CA)
North Dakota State Coll of Science (ND)
Northeastern Jr Coll (CO)
Northeast Iowa Comm Coll (IA)
NorthWest Arkansas Comm Coll (AR)
Northwest-Shoals Comm Coll (AL)
Oakland Comm Coll (MI)
Oklahoma City Comm Coll (OK)
Oklahoma State U, Oklahoma City (OK)
Orange Coast Coll (CA)
Ozarks Tech Comm Coll (MO)
Paris Jr Coll (TX)
Pasco-Hernando Comm Coll (FL)
Pensacola State Coll (FL)
Phoenix Coll (AZ)
Piedmont Virginia Comm Coll (VA)
Quinsigamond Comm Coll (MA)
Red Rocks Comm Coll (CO)
Rogue Comm Coll (OR)
St. Louis Comm Coll at Meramec (MO)
San Diego City Coll (CA)
San Jacinto Coll District (TX)
San Juan Coll (NM)
Santa Rosa Jr Coll (CA)
Schoolcraft Coll (MI)
Scottsdale Comm Coll (AZ)
Seminole State Coll of Florida (FL)
Southeastern Comm Coll (IA)
Southern Maine Comm Coll (ME)
Southern State Comm Coll (OH)
Southwestern Michigan Coll (MI)
Southwest Virginia Comm Coll (VA)
Tallahassee Comm Coll (FL)
Tarrant County Coll District (TX)
Tech Coll of the Lowcountry (SC)
Temple Coll (TX)
Texarkana Coll (TX)
Texas State Tech Coll Harlingen (TX)
Thomas Nelson Comm Coll (VA)
Tyler Jr Coll (TX)
Union County Coll (NJ)
U of Alaska Anchorage, Kenai Peninsula Coll (AK)
Vincennes U (IN)
Waukesha County Tech Coll (WI)
Westchester Comm Coll (NY)
Western Dakota Tech Inst (SD)
Western Iowa Tech Comm Coll (IA)
Wisconsin Indianhead Tech Coll (WI)

ENERGY MANAGEMENT AND SYSTEMS TECHNOLOGY
Casper Coll (WY)
Century Coll (MN)
Clinton Comm Coll (NY)
Comm Coll of Allegheny County (PA)
Corning Comm Coll (NY)
Delaware Tech & Comm Coll, Jack F. Owens Campus (DE)
Delaware Tech & Comm Coll, Stanton/Wilmington Campus (DE)
Delaware Tech & Comm Coll, Terry Campus (DE)
Essex County Coll (NJ)
Great Falls Coll Montana State U (MT)
Harrisburg Area Comm Coll (PA)
Hawkeye Comm Coll (IA)
Illinois Central Coll (IL)
Illinois Eastern Comm Colls, Wabash Valley College (IL)
Lakeland Comm Coll (OH)
Lake Michigan Coll (MI)
Lansing Comm Coll (MI)
Laramie County Comm Coll (WY)
Macomb Comm Coll (MI)
Minnesota West Comm and Tech Coll (MN)
Mitchell Tech Inst (SD)
North Dakota State Coll of Science (ND)
Northeast Iowa Comm Coll (IA)
Northwest State Comm Coll (OH)
Northwest Tech Coll (MN)
Owens Comm Coll, Toledo (OH)
Quinsigamond Comm Coll (MA)
Red Rocks Comm Coll (CO)
St. Clair County Comm Coll (MI)
St. Philip's Coll (TX)
Westchester Comm Coll (NY)
Western Iowa Tech Comm Coll (IA)
Wisconsin Indianhead Tech Coll (WI)

ENGINEERING
Adirondack Comm Coll (NY)
Amarillo Coll (TX)
Anne Arundel Comm Coll (MD)
Arizona Western Coll (AZ)
Austin Comm Coll (TX)
Bakersfield Coll (CA)
Berkshire Comm Coll (MA)
Borough of Manhattan Comm Coll of the City U of New York (NY)
Burlington County Coll (NJ)
Butte Coll (CA)
Carl Albert State Coll (OK)
Casper Coll (WY)
Central New Mexico Comm Coll (NM)
Central Oregon Comm Coll (OR)
Central Wyoming Coll (WY)
Cochise Coll, Sierra Vista (AZ)
Coll of Lake County (IL)
Coll of Marin (CA)
Coll of Southern Maryland (MD)
The Comm Coll of Baltimore County (MD)
Comm Coll of Philadelphia (PA)
Comm Coll of Rhode Island (RI)
Copiah-Lincoln Comm Coll (MS)
Daytona State Coll (FL)
De Anza Coll (CA)
Dutchess Comm Coll (NY)
Elgin Comm Coll (IL)
Erie Comm Coll, North Campus (NY)
Essex County Coll (NJ)
Garden City Comm Coll (KS)
Grand Rapids Comm Coll (MI)
Hagerstown Comm Coll (MD)
Harford Comm Coll (MD)
Harper Coll (IL)
Harrisburg Area Comm Coll (PA)
Highland Comm Coll (IL)
Holyoke Comm Coll (MA)
Howard Comm Coll (MD)
Hutchinson Comm Coll and Area Vocational School (KS)
Illinois Central Coll (IL)
Illinois Eastern Comm Colls, Frontier Community College (IL)
Illinois Eastern Comm Colls, Olney Central College (IL)
Illinois Eastern Comm Colls, Wabash Valley College (IL)
Jamestown Comm Coll (NY)
Jefferson Coll (MO)
Jefferson Comm Coll (NY)
John Tyler Comm Coll (VA)
Kankakee Comm Coll (IL)
Kaskaskia Coll (IL)
Lansing Comm Coll (MI)
Laramie County Comm Coll (WY)
Lehigh Carbon Comm Coll (PA)
Lincoln Land Comm Coll (IL)
Lone Star Coll–Montgomery (TX)
Lone Star Coll–North Harris (TX)
Lone Star Coll–Tomball (TX)
Lorain County Comm Coll (OH)
McHenry County Coll (IL)
Metropolitan Comm Coll–Kansas City (MO)
Miami Dade Coll (FL)
Miles Comm Coll (MT)
Missouri State U–West Plains (MO)
Mohawk Valley Comm Coll (NY)
Montgomery Coll (MD)
Nassau Comm Coll (NY)
Northampton Comm Coll (PA)
North Hennepin Comm Coll (MN)
Northwest Coll (WY)
Oakland Comm Coll (MI)
Oakton Comm Coll (IL)
Ocean County Coll (NJ)
Orange Coast Coll (CA)
Paris Jr Coll (TX)
Pensacola State Coll (FL)
Piedmont Virginia Comm Coll (VA)
Potomac State Coll of West Virginia U (WV)
St. Clair County Comm Coll (MI)
Salt Lake Comm Coll (UT)
San Diego Mesa Coll (CA)
San Jacinto Coll District (TX)
San Juan Coll (NM)
Santa Rosa Jr Coll (CA)
Schoolcraft Coll (MI)
Sheridan Coll (WY)
Sierra Coll (CA)
South Plains Coll (TX)
Springfield Tech Comm Coll (MA)
State U of New York Coll of Technology at Alfred (NY)
Tallahassee Comm Coll (FL)

Terra State Comm Coll (OH)
Texarkana Coll (TX)
Texas State Tech Coll Harlingen (TX)
Thomas Nelson Comm Coll (VA)
Tompkins Cortland Comm Coll (NY)
Tunxis Comm Coll (CT)
Tyler Jr Coll (TX)
Union County Coll (NJ)
Virginia Western Comm Coll (VA)
Waubonsee Comm Coll (IL)

ENGINEERING/INDUSTRIAL MANAGEMENT
Delaware Tech & Comm Coll, Stanton/Wilmington Campus (DE)
Northwest State Comm Coll (OH)

ENGINEERING MECHANICS
San Jacinto Coll District (TX)

ENGINEERING PHYSICS/ APPLIED PHYSICS
Lansing Comm Coll (MI)

ENGINEERING RELATED
Colby Comm Coll (KS)
Macomb Comm Coll (MI)
Miami Dade Coll (FL)
Northwest State Comm Coll (OH)
Southeastern Comm Coll (IA)

ENGINEERING SCIENCE
Corning Comm Coll (NY)
County Coll of Morris (NJ)
Finger Lakes Comm Coll (NY)
Genesee Comm Coll (NY)
Greenfield Comm Coll (MA)
Jefferson Comm Coll (NY)
Manchester Comm Coll (CT)
Monroe Comm Coll (NY)
Montgomery County Comm Coll (PA)
Northern Essex Comm Coll (MA)
North Shore Comm Coll (MA)
Norwalk Comm Coll (CT)
Onondaga Comm Coll (NY)
Parkland Coll (IL)
Raritan Valley Comm Coll (NJ)
Westchester Comm Coll (NY)

ENGINEERING TECHNOLOGIES AND ENGINEERING RELATED
Burlington County Coll (NJ)
Butte Coll (CA)
Carl Albert State Coll (OK)
Coll of Southern Maryland (MD)
Comm Coll of Allegheny County (PA)
The Comm Coll of Baltimore County (MD)
Essex County Coll (NJ)
Hagerstown Comm Coll (MD)
Harrisburg Area Comm Coll (PA)
Kent State U at Tuscarawas (OH)
Middlesex Comm Coll (MA)
Montgomery County Comm Coll (PA)
Mott Comm Coll (MI)
Northwest State Comm Coll (OH)
Ocean County Coll (NJ)
Oklahoma City Comm Coll (OK)
Quinsigamond Comm Coll (MA)
Raritan Valley Comm Coll (NJ)
State U of New York Coll of Technology at Alfred (NY)
Sullivan Coll of Technology and Design (KY)

ENGINEERING TECHNOLOGY
Arapahoe Comm Coll (CO)
Barton County Comm Coll (KS)
Bismarck State Coll (ND)
Bucks County Comm Coll (PA)
Coll of Marin (CA)
Collin County Comm Coll District (TX)
Comm Coll of Beaver County (PA)
Comm Coll of Philadelphia (PA)
Corning Comm Coll (NY)
Cowley County Comm Coll and Area Vocational–Tech School (KS)
Cuyahoga Comm Coll (OH)
Darton State Coll (GA)
De Anza Coll (CA)
Denmark Tech Coll (SC)
Gateway Comm and Tech Coll (KY)
Glendale Comm Coll (AZ)
Harford Comm Coll (MD)
Hillsborough Comm Coll (FL)
Jefferson State Comm Coll (AL)
John Tyler Comm Coll (VA)
Kent State U at Tuscarawas (OH)
Lake Area Tech Inst (SD)
Lorain County Comm Coll (OH)

Luzerne County Comm Coll (PA)
Massachusetts Bay Comm Coll (MA)
Mesa Comm Coll (AZ)
Miami Dade Coll (FL)
Mineral Area Coll (MO)
Mt. San Antonio Coll (CA)
Oklahoma State U, Oklahoma City (OK)
Pasadena City Coll (CA)
Rappahannock Comm Coll (VA)
St. Louis Comm Coll at Forest Park (MO)
Salt Lake Comm Coll (UT)
San Diego City Coll (CA)
San Juan Coll (NM)
Southwestern Michigan Coll (MI)
Spartanburg Comm Coll (SC)
Sullivan Coll of Technology and Design (KY)
Trident Tech Coll (SC)
Tunxis Comm Coll (CT)
Vincennes U (IN)
Westchester Comm Coll (NY)

ENGINE MACHINIST
Northwest Tech Coll (MN)
Tri-County Comm Coll (NC)

ENGLISH
Alpena Comm Coll (MI)
Amarillo Coll (TX)
Arizona Western Coll (AZ)
Bainbridge Coll (GA)
Bakersfield Coll (CA)
Barton County Comm Coll (KS)
Berkeley City Coll (CA)
Borough of Manhattan Comm Coll of the City U of New York (NY)
Burlington County Coll (NJ)
Carl Albert State Coll (OK)
Casper Coll (WY)
Central Wyoming Coll (WY)
Cochise Coll, Sierra Vista (AZ)
Coll of Marin (CA)
Coll of the Canyons (CA)
Coll of the Desert (CA)
Comm Coll of Allegheny County (PA)
Copiah-Lincoln Comm Coll (MS)
Darton State Coll (GA)
De Anza Coll (CA)
Fiorello H. LaGuardia Comm Coll of the City U of New York (NY)
Foothill Coll (CA)
Garden City Comm Coll (KS)
Georgia Highlands Coll (GA)
Gordon State Coll (GA)
Grand Rapids Comm Coll (MI)
Greenfield Comm Coll (MA)
Harford Comm Coll (MD)
Harper Coll (IL)
Hutchinson Comm Coll and Area Vocational School (KS)
Kankakee Comm Coll (IL)
Kilgore Coll (TX)
Lake Michigan Coll (MI)
Lansing Comm Coll (MI)
Laramie County Comm Coll (WY)
Lone Star Coll–CyFair (TX)
Lone Star Coll–Kingwood (TX)
Lone Star Coll–Montgomery (TX)
Lone Star Coll–North Harris (TX)
Lone Star Coll–Tomball (TX)
Mendocino Coll (CA)
Miami Dade Coll (FL)
Mohave Comm Coll (AZ)
Monroe County Comm Coll (MI)
Northeastern Jr Coll (CO)
Northwest Coll (WY)
Orange Coast Coll (CA)
Oxnard Coll (CA)
Parkland Coll (IL)
Pensacola State Coll (FL)
Potomac State Coll of West Virginia U (WV)
Raritan Valley Comm Coll (NJ)
St. Philip's Coll (TX)
Salt Lake Comm Coll (UT)
San Diego City Coll (CA)
San Diego Mesa Coll (CA)
San Jacinto Coll District (TX)
Santa Rosa Jr Coll (CA)
Sheridan Coll (WY)
Sierra Coll (CA)
Spoon River Coll (IL)
Taft Coll (CA)
Terra State Comm Coll (OH)
Vincennes U (IN)

ENGLISH AS A SECOND/FOREIGN LANGUAGE (TEACHING)
Gordon State Coll (GA)

ENGLISH LANGUAGE AND LITERATURE RELATED
Butte Coll (CA)
Mt. San Antonio Coll (CA)

ENGLISH/LANGUAGE ARTS TEACHER EDUCATION
Anne Arundel Comm Coll (MD)
Carroll Comm Coll (MD)
Cecil Coll (MD)
Cochise Coll, Sierra Vista (AZ)
Darton State Coll (GA)
Hagerstown Comm Coll (MD)
Harford Comm Coll (MD)
Montgomery Coll (MD)
Vincennes U (IN)

ENTREPRENEURIAL AND SMALL BUSINESS RELATED
Dakota Coll at Bottineau (ND)
State U of New York Coll of Technology at Alfred (NY)

ENTREPRENEURSHIP
Anne Arundel Comm Coll (MD)
Casper Coll (WY)
Cleveland Comm Coll (NC)
Comm Coll of Allegheny County (PA)
Comm Coll of Beaver County (PA)
Cowley County Comm Coll and Area Vocational–Tech School (KS)
Delaware Tech & Comm Coll, Jack F. Owens Campus (DE)
Delaware Tech & Comm Coll, Terry Campus (DE)
Elgin Comm Coll (IL)
Goodwin Coll (CT)
Great Falls Coll Montana State U (MT)
Harford Comm Coll (MD)
Laramie County Comm Coll (WY)
LDS Business Coll (UT)
Missouri State U–West Plains (MO)
Mohawk Valley Comm Coll (NY)
Montcalm Comm Coll (MI)
Mott Comm Coll (MI)
Nassau Comm Coll (NY)
Northwest State Comm Coll (OH)
Oakland Comm Coll (MI)
Salt Lake Comm Coll (UT)
Schoolcraft Coll (MI)
Southern State Comm Coll (OH)
State U of New York Coll of Technology at Alfred (NY)

ENVIRONMENTAL CONTROL TECHNOLOGIES RELATED
Bismarck State Coll (ND)
Fox Valley Tech Coll (WI)
Hillsborough Comm Coll (FL)
Holyoke Comm Coll (MA)
James A. Rhodes State Coll (OH)
Northwest State Comm Coll (OH)
Westchester Comm Coll (NY)
Western Dakota Tech Inst (SD)

ENVIRONMENTAL DESIGN/ARCHITECTURE
Scottsdale Comm Coll (AZ)

ENVIRONMENTAL ENGINEERING TECHNOLOGY
Austin Comm Coll (TX)
Bakersfield Coll (CA)
Coll of Southern Maryland (MD)
Collin County Comm Coll District (TX)
Comm Coll of Allegheny County (PA)
Comm Coll of Beaver County (PA)
Crowder Coll (MO)
Dakota Coll at Bottineau (ND)
Kent State U at Trumbull (OH)
Lansing Comm Coll (MI)
Massachusetts Bay Comm Coll (MA)
Miami Dade Coll (FL)
Northwest-Shoals Comm Coll (AL)
Onondaga Comm Coll (NY)
Owens Comm Coll, Toledo (OH)
Oxnard Coll (CA)
Salt Lake Comm Coll (UT)
San Diego City Coll (CA)
Schoolcraft Coll (MI)
Sheridan Coll (WY)
Southern Maine Comm Coll (ME)

ENVIRONMENTAL/ENVIRONMENTAL HEALTH ENGINEERING
Central New Mexico Comm Coll (NM)
Central Wyoming Coll (WY)

ENVIRONMENTAL HEALTH
Amarillo Coll (TX)
Comm Coll of the Air Force (AL)
Crowder Coll (MO)

ENVIRONMENTAL SCIENCE
Anoka-Ramsey Comm Coll (MN)
Anoka-Ramsey Comm Coll, Cambridge Campus (MN)
Arizona Western Coll (AZ)
Bucks County Comm Coll (PA)
Burlington County Coll (NJ)
Butte Coll (CA)
Casper Coll (WY)
Central Wyoming Coll (WY)
Coll of the Desert (CA)
Comm Coll of Vermont (VT)
Corning Comm Coll (NY)
Erie Comm Coll, North Campus (NY)
Fiorello H. LaGuardia Comm Coll of the City U of New York (NY)
Gordon State Coll (GA)
Greenfield Comm Coll (MA)
Harford Comm Coll (MD)
Harrisburg Area Comm Coll (PA)
Lake Area Tech Inst (SD)
Lake Michigan Coll (MI)
Montgomery County Comm Coll (PA)
NorthWest Arkansas Comm Coll (AR)
Ocean County Coll (NJ)
The Ohio State U Ag Tech Inst (OH)
St. Philip's Coll (TX)
San Jacinto Coll District (TX)
State U of New York Coll of Technology at Alfred (NY)
Tyler Jr Coll (TX)
Westchester Comm Coll (NY)

ENVIRONMENTAL STUDIES
Berkshire Comm Coll (MA)
Coll of the Desert (CA)
Comm Coll of the Air Force (AL)
Darton State Coll (GA)
De Anza Coll (CA)
Finger Lakes Comm Coll (NY)
Goodwin Coll (CT)
Harford Comm Coll (MD)
Harper Coll (IL)
Harrisburg Area Comm Coll (PA)
Housatonic Comm Coll (CT)
Howard Comm Coll (MD)
Kilian Comm Coll (SD)
Klamath Comm Coll (OR)
Monroe Comm Coll (NY)
Santa Rosa Jr Coll (CA)
Stark State Coll (OH)
Sullivan County Comm Coll (NY)
Westchester Comm Coll (NY)

EQUESTRIAN STUDIES
Central Wyoming Coll (WY)
Colorado Northwestern Comm Coll (CO)
Harford Comm Coll (MD)
Laramie County Comm Coll (WY)
Miles Comm Coll (MT)
Northeastern Jr Coll (CO)
Northwest Coll (WY)
The Ohio State U Ag Tech Inst (OH)
Scottsdale Comm Coll (AZ)
Sierra Coll (CA)

ETHNIC, CULTURAL MINORITY, GENDER, AND GROUP STUDIES RELATED
Coll of Marin (CA)

EXECUTIVE ASSISTANT/EXECUTIVE SECRETARY
Alamance Comm Coll (NC)
Brookhaven (TX)
Cape Fear Comm Coll (NC)
Central New Mexico Comm Coll (NM)
Chemeketa Comm Coll (OR)
Clark Coll (WA)
Comm Coll of Beaver County (PA)
Crowder Coll (MO)
Dakota Coll at Bottineau (ND)
Edison Comm Coll (OH)
El Centro Coll (TX)
Elgin Comm Coll (IL)
Hawkeye Comm Coll (IA)
Hillsborough Comm Coll (FL)
Ivy Tech Comm Coll–Bloomington (IN)
Ivy Tech Comm Coll–Central Indiana (IN)
Ivy Tech Comm Coll–Columbus (IN)
Ivy Tech Comm Coll–East Central (IN)
Ivy Tech Comm Coll–Kokomo (IN)

Ivy Tech Comm Coll–Lafayette (IN)
Ivy Tech Comm Coll–North Central (IN)
Ivy Tech Comm Coll–Northeast (IN)
Ivy Tech Comm Coll–Northwest (IN)
Ivy Tech Comm Coll–Richmond (IN)
Ivy Tech Comm Coll–Southeast (IN)
Ivy Tech Comm Coll–Southern Indiana (IN)
Ivy Tech Comm Coll–Southwest (IN)
Ivy Tech Comm Coll–Wabash Valley (IN)
Jackson Coll (MI)
Kaskaskia Coll (IL)
Kennebec Valley Comm Coll (ME)
Kilgore Coll (TX)
Luzerne County Comm Coll (PA)
Northwest State Comm Coll (OH)
Owensboro Comm and Tech Coll (KY)
Owens Comm Coll, Toledo (OH)
Pensacola State Coll (FL)
Quinsigamond Comm Coll (MA)
St. Clair County Comm Coll (MI)
Schoolcraft Coll (MI)
Southern State Comm Coll (OH)
South Suburban Coll (IL)
Southwestern Michigan Coll (MI)
Springfield Tech Comm Coll (MA)
Terra State Comm Coll (OH)
Texas State Tech Coll Harlingen (TX)
Waubonsee Comm Coll (IL)
West Virginia Northern Comm Coll (WV)
Wilson Comm Coll (NC)

FACILITIES PLANNING AND MANAGEMENT
Comm Coll of Philadelphia (PA)
Lone Star Coll–Kingwood (TX)

FAMILY AND COMMUNITY SERVICES
Glendale Comm Coll (AZ)
Oxnard Coll (CA)
Phoenix Coll (AZ)
Westmoreland County Comm Coll (PA)

FAMILY AND CONSUMER ECONOMICS RELATED
Bakersfield Coll (CA)
Orange Coast Coll (CA)

FAMILY AND CONSUMER SCIENCES/HOME ECONOMICS TEACHER EDUCATION
Copiah-Lincoln Comm Coll (MS)
Vincennes U (IN)

FAMILY AND CONSUMER SCIENCES/HUMAN SCIENCES
Bainbridge Coll (GA)
Butte Coll (CA)
Garden City Comm Coll (KS)
Hutchinson Comm Coll and Area Vocational School (KS)
Mesa Comm Coll (AZ)
Metropolitan Comm Coll–Kansas City (MO)
Monroe Comm Coll (NY)
Mt. San Antonio Coll (CA)
Northeastern Jr Coll (CO)
Orange Coast Coll (CA)
Phoenix Coll (AZ)
Tyler Jr Coll (TX)
Vincennes U (IN)

FARM AND RANCH MANAGEMENT
Alexandria Tech and Comm Coll (MN)
Bismarck State Coll (ND)
Colby Comm Coll (KS)
Copiah-Lincoln Comm Coll (MS)
Crowder Coll (MO)
Hutchinson Comm Coll and Area Vocational School (KS)
Northeastern Jr Coll (CO)
Northwest Coll (WY)

FASHION AND FABRIC CONSULTING
Harper Coll (IL)

FASHION/APPAREL DESIGN
Burlington County Coll (NJ)
Clary Sage Coll (OK)
El Centro Coll (TX)
Fashion Inst of Technology (NY)

FASHION MERCHANDISING
Alexandria Tech and Comm Coll (MN)
Bay State Coll (MA)
Blue Ridge Comm and Tech Coll (WV)
Fashion Inst of Technology (NY)
FIDM/The Fashion Inst of Design & Merchandising, Los Angeles Campus (CA)
FIDM/The Fashion Inst of Design & Merchandising, Orange County Campus (CA)
FIDM/The Fashion Inst of Design & Merchandising, San Diego Campus (CA)
FIDM/The Fashion Inst of Design & Merchandising, San Francisco Campus (CA)
Harper Coll (IL)
Houston Comm Coll System (TX)
Lehigh Carbon Comm Coll (PA)
Metropolitan Comm Coll–Kansas City (MO)
Monroe Comm Coll (NY)
Nassau Comm Coll (NY)
Pasadena City Coll (CA)
Phoenix Coll (AZ)
San Diego Mesa Coll (CA)
Santa Rosa Jr Coll (CA)
Wood Tobe–Coburn School (NY)

FASHION MERCHANDISING
Alexandria Tech and Comm Coll (MN)
Bay State Coll (MA)
Blue Ridge Comm and Tech Coll (WV)
Fashion Inst of Technology (NY)
FIDM/The Fashion Inst of Design & Merchandising, Los Angeles Campus (CA)
FIDM/The Fashion Inst of Design & Merchandising, Orange County Campus (CA)
FIDM/The Fashion Inst of Design & Merchandising, San Diego Campus (CA)
FIDM/The Fashion Inst of Design & Merchandising, San Francisco Campus (CA)
Genesee Comm Coll (NY)
Grand Rapids Comm Coll (MI)
Harper Coll (IL)
Houston Comm Coll System (TX)
Kilgore Coll (TX)
Lansing Comm Coll (MI)
Mesa Comm Coll (AZ)
Metropolitan Comm Coll–Kansas City (MO)
Middlesex Comm Coll (MA)
Monroe Comm Coll (NY)
Mt. San Antonio Coll (CA)
Nassau Comm Coll (NY)
Oakland Comm Coll (MI)
Orange Coast Coll (CA)
Pasadena City Coll (CA)
Phoenix Coll (AZ)
San Diego City Coll (CA)
San Diego Mesa Coll (CA)
Santa Rosa Jr Coll (CA)
Scottsdale Comm Coll (AZ)
South Plains Coll (TX)
Tarrant County Coll District (TX)
Tunxis Comm Coll (CT)
Vincennes U (IN)

FASHION MODELING
Fashion Inst of Technology (NY)

FIBER, TEXTILE AND WEAVING ARTS
FIDM/The Fashion Inst of Design & Merchandising, Orange County Campus (CA)
Mendocino Coll (CA)

FILM/CINEMA/VIDEO STUDIES
Carl Albert State Coll (OK)
Coll of Marin (CA)
De Anza Coll (CA)
Oakland Comm Coll (MI)
Orange Coast Coll (CA)
San Jacinto Coll District (TX)
Tallahassee Comm Coll (FL)

FILM/VIDEO AND PHOTOGRAPHIC ARTS RELATED
Greenfield Comm Coll (MA)
Westchester Comm Coll (NY)

FINANCE
Bakersfield Coll (CA)
Chipola Coll (FL)
Comm Coll of Beaver County (PA)
Comm Coll of Philadelphia (PA)
Comm Coll of the Air Force (AL)
Cuyahoga Comm Coll (OH)

Harper Coll (IL)
James A. Rhodes State Coll (OH)
Kennebec Valley Comm Coll (ME)
Lone Star Coll–North Harris (TX)
Lone Star Coll–Tomball (TX)
Lorain County Comm Coll (OH)
Macomb Comm Coll (MI)
Mendocino Coll (CA)
Mesa Comm Coll (AZ)
Miami Dade Coll (FL)
Monroe County Comm Coll (MI)
Mt. San Antonio Coll (CA)
Northern Essex Comm Coll (MA)
North Hennepin Comm Coll (MN)
NorthWest Arkansas Comm Coll
(AR)
Norwalk Comm Coll (CT)
Oklahoma City Comm Coll (OK)
Salt Lake Comm Coll (UT)
San Diego City Coll (CA)
Scottsdale Comm Coll (AZ)
Seminole State Coll of Florida (FL)
Southeast Tech Inst (SD)
Spoon River Coll (IL)
Springfield Tech Comm Coll (MA)
Stark State Coll (OH)
State U of New York Coll of
Technology at Alfred (NY)
Tallahassee Comm Coll (FL)
Vincennes U (IN)
Westchester Comm Coll (NY)
Western Iowa Tech Comm Coll (IA)
Wisconsin Indianhead Tech Coll (WI)

FINANCIAL PLANNING AND SERVICES
Barton County Comm Coll (KS)
Cecil Coll (MD)
Howard Comm Coll (MD)
Kilian Comm Coll (SD)
Raritan Valley Comm Coll (NJ)

FINE ARTS RELATED
Carl Albert State Coll (OK)
Corning Comm Coll (NY)

FINE/STUDIO ARTS
Amarillo Coll (TX)
Anoka-Ramsey Comm Coll (MN)
Anoka-Ramsey Comm Coll,
Cambridge Campus (MN)
Arizona Western Coll (AZ)
Berkeley City Coll (CA)
Casper Coll (WY)
Cayuga County Comm Coll (NY)
Cecil Coll (MD)
Century Coll (MN)
Comm Coll of Beaver County (PA)
Corning Comm Coll (NY)
County Coll of Morris (NJ)
Elgin Comm Coll (IL)
Fashion Inst of Technology (NY)
Finger Lakes Comm Coll (NY)
Fiorello H. LaGuardia Comm Coll of
the City U of New York (NY)
Foothill Coll (CA)
Greenfield Comm Coll (MA)
Harford Comm Coll (MD)
Harper Coll (IL)
Jamestown Comm Coll (NY)
Lake Superior Coll (MN)
Lansing Comm Coll (MI)
Lincoln Land Comm Coll (IL)
Manchester Comm Coll (CT)
McHenry County Coll (IL)
Niagara County Comm Coll (NY)
Normandale Comm Coll (MN)
Northampton Comm Coll (PA)
Northeastern Jr Coll (CO)
North Hennepin Comm Coll (MN)
Norwalk Comm Coll (CT)
Oklahoma City Comm Coll (OK)
Oxnard Coll (CA)
Phoenix Coll (AZ)
Raritan Valley Comm Coll (NJ)
South Suburban Coll (IL)
Springfield Tech Comm Coll (MA)
Terra State Comm Coll (OH)
Waubonsee Comm Coll (IL)
Westchester Comm Coll (NY)

FIRE PREVENTION AND SAFETY TECHNOLOGY
Anne Arundel Comm Coll (MD)
Austin Comm Coll (TX)
Blackhawk Tech Coll (WI)
Bucks County Comm Coll (PA)
Cape Fear Comm Coll (NC)
Catawba Valley Comm Coll (NC)

Central New Mexico Comm Coll
(NM)
Chemeketa Comm Coll (OR)
Cleveland Comm Coll (NC)
Coll of Lake County (IL)
Coll of Southern Maryland (MD)
Coll of the Canyons (CA)
Collin County Comm Coll District
(TX)
Comm Coll of Allegheny County (PA)
County Coll of Morris (NJ)
Delaware Tech & Comm Coll,
Stanton/Wilmington Campus (DE)
Fayetteville Tech Comm Coll (NC)
Forsyth Tech Comm Coll (NC)
Fox Valley Tech Coll (WI)
Greenfield Comm Coll (MA)
Guilford Tech Comm Coll (NC)
Hillsborough Comm Coll (FL)
Houston Comm Coll System (TX)
Jamestown Comm Coll (NY)
Jefferson Coll (MO)
Jefferson Comm Coll (NY)
Lakeland Comm Coll (OH)
Lake Superior Coll (MN)
Macomb Comm Coll (MI)
Montgomery Coll (MD)
Montgomery County Comm Coll (PA)
Moraine Valley Comm Coll (IL)
Mott Comm Coll (MI)
Ocean County Coll (NJ)
Oklahoma State U, Oklahoma City
(OK)
Onondaga Comm Coll (NY)
Owens Comm Coll, Toledo (OH)
Oxnard Coll (CA)
Pasadena City Coll (CA)
Pensacola State Coll (FL)
Rogue Comm Coll (OR)
San Jacinto Coll District (TX)
Springfield Tech Comm Coll (MA)
Union County Coll (NJ)
Victor Valley Coll (CA)
Waukesha County Tech Coll (WI)
Westmoreland County Comm Coll
(PA)
Wilson Comm Coll (NC)

FIRE PROTECTION RELATED
Fox Valley Tech Coll (WI)

FIRE SCIENCE/FIREFIGHTING
Amarillo Coll (TX)
Arizona Western Coll (AZ)
Bakersfield Coll (CA)
Barton County Comm Coll (KS)
Berkshire Comm Coll (MA)
Blackhawk Tech Coll (WI)
Blue Ridge Comm and Tech Coll
(WV)
Burlington County Coll (NJ)
Butte Coll (CA)
Casper Coll (WY)
Cecil Coll (MD)
Central Oregon Comm Coll (OR)
Central Wyoming Coll (WY)
Chemeketa Comm Coll (OR)
Cochise Coll, Sierra Vista (AZ)
Coll of Southern Maryland (MD)
Coll of the Desert (CA)
Collin County Comm Coll District
(TX)
Comm Coll of Philadelphia (PA)
Comm Coll of Rhode Island (RI)
Comm Coll of the Air Force (AL)
Crowder Coll (MO)
Cuyahoga Comm Coll (OH)
Daytona State Coll (FL)
Delaware Tech & Comm Coll,
Stanton/Wilmington Campus (DE)
Eastern Idaho Tech Coll (ID)
Elgin Comm Coll (IL)
Garden City Comm Coll (KS)
Gateway Comm and Tech Coll (KY)
Gateway Tech Coll (WI)
Glendale Comm Coll (AZ)
Great Falls Coll Montana State U
(MT)
Harper Coll (IL)
Harrisburg Area Comm Coll (PA)
Hutchinson Comm Coll and Area
Vocational School (KS)
Illinois Central Coll (IL)
Illinois Eastern Comm Colls, Frontier
Community College (IL)
Lansing Comm Coll (MI)
Laramie County Comm Coll (WY)
Lincoln Land Comm Coll (IL)
Lone Star Coll–CyFair (TX)
Lone Star Coll–Montgomery (TX)

Lorain County Comm Coll (OH)
Lower Columbia Coll (WA)
Luzerne County Comm Coll (PA)
McHenry County Coll (IL)
Mesa Comm Coll (AZ)
Metropolitan Comm Coll–Kansas
City (MO)
Miami Dade Coll (FL)
Middlesex Comm Coll (MA)
Mid-Plains Comm Coll, North Platte
(NE)
Mineral Area Coll (MO)
Mohave Comm Coll (AZ)
Monroe Comm Coll (NY)
Moraine Valley Comm Coll (IL)
Mt. San Antonio Coll (CA)
Northampton Comm Coll (PA)
Northeast Iowa Comm Coll (IA)
North Shore Comm Coll (MA)
Norwalk Comm Coll (CT)
Oakland Comm Coll (MI)
Oakton Comm Coll (IL)
Oklahoma State U, Oklahoma City
(OK)
Owensboro Comm and Tech Coll
(KY)
Oxnard Coll (CA)
Ozarks Tech Comm Coll (MO)
Pensacola State Coll (FL)
Phoenix Coll (AZ)
Pierce Coll at Puyallup (WA)
Red Rocks Comm Coll (CO)
St. Louis Comm Coll at Forest Park
(MO)
San Jacinto Coll District (TX)
San Juan Coll (NM)
Santa Rosa Jr Coll (CA)
Schoolcraft Coll (MI)
Scottsdale Comm Coll (AZ)
Seminole State Coll of Florida (FL)
Sierra Coll (CA)
Southern Maine Comm Coll (ME)
South Plains Coll (TX)
South Puget Sound Comm Coll (WA)
Southwestern Michigan Coll (MI)
Stark State Coll (OH)
Tarrant County Coll District (TX)
Thomas Nelson Comm Coll (VA)
Tyler Jr Coll (TX)
Victor Valley Coll (CA)
Vincennes U (IN)
Volunteer State Comm Coll (TN)
Waubonsee Comm Coll (IL)
Western Dakota Tech Inst (SD)
Western Iowa Tech Comm Coll (IA)
West Kentucky Comm and Tech Coll
(KY)

FIRE SERVICES ADMINISTRATION
Delaware Tech & Comm Coll,
Stanton/Wilmington Campus (DE)
Dutchess Comm Coll (NY)
Erie Comm Coll, South Campus
(NY)
Jefferson Comm Coll (NY)
Jefferson State Comm Coll (AL)
Mohawk Valley Comm Coll (NY)
Northampton Comm Coll (PA)
NorthWest Arkansas Comm Coll
(AR)
Oxnard Coll (CA)
Quinsigamond Comm Coll (MA)
Tech Coll of the Lowcountry (SC)

FISHING AND FISHERIES SCIENCES AND MANAGEMENT
Central Oregon Comm Coll (OR)
Dakota Coll at Bottineau (ND)
Finger Lakes Comm Coll (NY)

FLORICULTURE/FLORISTRY MANAGEMENT
Dakota Coll at Bottineau (ND)
The Ohio State U Ag Tech Inst (OH)
Santa Rosa Jr Coll (CA)
Westmoreland County Comm Coll
(PA)

FOOD PREPARATION
San Jacinto Coll District (TX)

FOODS AND NUTRITION RELATED
San Diego Mesa Coll (CA)

FOOD SCIENCE
Greenfield Comm Coll (MA)
Miami Dade Coll (FL)
Missouri State U–West Plains (MO)

Normandale Comm Coll (MN)
Orange Coast Coll (CA)
Vincennes U (IN)

FOOD SERVICE AND DINING ROOM MANAGEMENT
Pasadena City Coll (CA)
Westmoreland County Comm Coll
(PA)

FOOD SERVICE SYSTEMS ADMINISTRATION
Bucks County Comm Coll (PA)
Burlington County Coll (NJ)
Comm Coll of Allegheny County (PA)
Harper Coll (IL)
Harrisburg Area Comm Coll (PA)
Mohawk Valley Comm Coll (NY)
Mott Comm Coll (MI)
Pensacola State Coll (FL)
Phoenix Coll (AZ)
San Jacinto Coll District (TX)

FOODS, NUTRITION, AND WELLNESS
Bakersfield Coll (CA)
Bossier Parish Comm Coll (LA)
Butte Coll (CA)
Carl Albert State Coll (OK)
North Shore Comm Coll (MA)
Orange Coast Coll (CA)
Pensacola State Coll (FL)
San Diego Mesa Coll (CA)

FOOD TECHNOLOGY AND PROCESSING
Adirondack Comm Coll (NY)
Copiah-Lincoln Comm Coll (MS)
Luzerne County Comm Coll (PA)
Monroe Comm Coll (NY)
Orange Coast Coll (CA)
Robeson Comm Coll (NC)
Southern State Comm Coll (OH)
South Puget Sound Comm Coll (WA)
Stark State Coll (OH)
Tarrant County Coll District (TX)
Victor Valley Coll (CA)
Westchester Comm Coll (NY)

FOREIGN LANGUAGES AND LITERATURES
Austin Comm Coll (TX)
Casper Coll (WY)
Central Oregon Comm Coll (OR)
Coll of Marin (CA)
Comm Coll of Allegheny County (PA)
Darton State Coll (GA)
Georgia Highlands Coll (GA)
Gordon State Coll (GA)
Grand Rapids Comm Coll (MI)
Hutchinson Comm Coll and Area
Vocational School (KS)
Lake Michigan Coll (MI)
Lansing Comm Coll (MI)
Lone Star Coll–CyFair (TX)
Lone Star Coll–Kingwood (TX)
Lone Star Coll–Montgomery (TX)
Lone Star Coll–North Harris (TX)
Lone Star Coll–Tomball (TX)
Oklahoma City Comm Coll (OK)
San Jacinto Coll District (TX)
Sheridan Coll (WY)
Texarkana Coll (TX)
Vincennes U (IN)

FOREIGN LANGUAGES RELATED
Vincennes U (IN)

FOREIGN LANGUAGE TEACHER EDUCATION
Cochise Coll, Sierra Vista (AZ)

FORENSIC SCIENCE AND TECHNOLOGY
Arkansas State U–Mountain Home
(AR)
Borough of Manhattan Comm Coll of
the City U of New York (NY)
Carroll Comm Coll (MD)
Casper Coll (WY)
Catawba Valley Comm Coll (NC)
Comm Coll of Philadelphia (PA)
Cossatot Comm Coll of the U of
Arkansas (AR)
Darton State Coll (GA)
Fayetteville Tech Comm Coll (NC)
Forsyth Tech Comm Coll (NC)
Fox Valley Tech Coll (WI)
Illinois Central Coll (IL)
Lake Michigan Coll (MI)

Macomb Comm Coll (MI)
Massachusetts Bay Comm Coll (MA)
Phoenix Coll (AZ)
Tompkins Cortland Comm Coll (NY)
Tunxis Comm Coll (CT)
U of Arkansas Comm Coll at
Morrilton (AR)

FOREST RESOURCES PRODUCTION AND MANAGEMENT
Pensacola State Coll (FL)

FORESTRY
Bainbridge Coll (GA)
Bakersfield Coll (CA)
Barton County Comm Coll (KS)
Central Oregon Comm Coll (OR)
Copiah-Lincoln Comm Coll (MS)
Darton State Coll (GA)
Gordon State Coll (GA)
Grand Rapids Comm Coll (MI)
Kilgore Coll (TX)
Miami Dade Coll (FL)
Monroe Comm Coll (NY)
Pensacola State Coll (FL)
Potomac State Coll of West Virginia
U (WV)
Sierra Coll (CA)

FOREST TECHNOLOGY
Central Oregon Comm Coll (OR)
Dabney S. Lancaster Comm Coll
(VA)
Jefferson Comm Coll (NY)
Lurleen B. Wallace Comm Coll (AL)
Montgomery Comm Coll (NC)
Mt. San Antonio Coll (CA)
Penn State Mont Alto (PA)
Pensacola State Coll (FL)
Potomac State Coll of West Virginia
U (WV)

FRENCH
Austin Comm Coll (TX)
Bakersfield Coll (CA)
Coll of Marin (CA)
Coll of the Canyons (CA)
Coll of the Desert (CA)
Copiah-Lincoln Comm Coll (MS)
Lansing Comm Coll (MI)
Mendocino Coll (CA)
Miami Dade Coll (FL)
Northwest Coll (WY)
Orange Coast Coll (CA)
San Diego Mesa Coll (CA)
Santa Rosa Jr Coll (CA)

FUNERAL SERVICE AND MORTUARY SCIENCE
Amarillo Coll (TX)
Arapahoe Comm Coll (CO)
Arkansas State U–Mountain Home
(AR)
Barton County Comm Coll (KS)
The Comm Coll of Baltimore County
(MD)
Fayetteville Tech Comm Coll (NC)
Fiorello H. LaGuardia Comm Coll of
the City U of New York (NY)
Ivy Tech Comm Coll–Northwest (IN)
Jefferson State Comm Coll (AL)
John A. Gupton Coll (TN)
John Tyler Comm Coll (VA)
Luzerne County Comm Coll (PA)
Miami Dade Coll (FL)
Monroe County Comm Coll (MI)
Nassau Comm Coll (NY)
Northampton Comm Coll (PA)
Randolph Comm Coll (NC)
St. Louis Comm Coll at Forest Park
(MO)
Vincennes U (IN)

GAME AND INTERACTIVE MEDIA DESIGN
Cayuga County Comm Coll (NY)
Fayetteville Tech Comm Coll (NC)
Lehigh Carbon Comm Coll (PA)
Oklahoma City Comm Coll (OK)
Red Rocks Comm Coll (CO)
Wilson Comm Coll (NC)

GENERAL STUDIES
Alpena Comm Coll (MI)
Amarillo Coll (TX)
Ancilla Coll (IN)
Arizona Western Coll (AZ)
Austin Comm Coll (TX)
Barton County Comm Coll (KS)
Berkeley City Coll (CA)

Bevill State Comm Coll (AL)
Blue Ridge Comm and Tech Coll (WV)
Bossier Parish Comm Coll (LA)
Brookhaven Coll (TX)
Carroll Comm Coll (MD)
Casper Coll (WY)
Catawba Valley Comm Coll (NC)
Cayuga County Comm Coll (NY)
Cecil Coll (MD)
Central New Mexico Comm Coll (NM)
Central Wyoming Coll (WY)
Chemeketa Comm Coll (OR)
Cleveland Comm Coll (NC)
Cleveland State Comm Coll (TN)
Cochise Coll, Sierra Vista (AZ)
Collin County Comm Coll District (TX)
Colorado Northwestern Comm Coll (CO)
Comm Coll of Allegheny County (PA)
Comm Coll of Beaver County (PA)
Comm Coll of Rhode Island (RI)
Cossatot Comm Coll of the U of Arkansas (AR)
Crowder Coll (MO)
Dakota Coll at Bottineau (ND)
Darton State Coll (GA)
Dutchess Comm Coll (NY)
Elaine P. Nunez Comm Coll (LA)
Forsyth Tech Comm Coll (NC)
Gadsden State Comm Coll (AL)
Garden City Comm Coll (KS)
Gateway Comm and Tech Coll (KY)
Georgia Highlands Coll (GA)
Georgia Military Coll (GA)
Gordon State Coll (GA)
Guilford Tech Comm Coll (NC)
Harford Comm Coll (MD)
Harrisburg Area Comm Coll (PA)
Highland Comm Coll (IL)
Howard Comm Coll (MD)
Illinois Central Coll (IL)
Illinois Eastern Comm Colls, Frontier Community College (IL)
Illinois Eastern Comm Colls, Lincoln Trail College (IL)
Illinois Eastern Comm Colls, Olney Central College (IL)
Illinois Eastern Comm Colls, Wabash Valley College (IL)
Ivy Tech Comm Coll–Bloomington (IN)
Ivy Tech Comm Coll–Central Indiana (IN)
Ivy Tech Comm Coll–Columbus (IN)
Ivy Tech Comm Coll–East Central (IN)
Ivy Tech Comm Coll–Kokomo (IN)
Ivy Tech Comm Coll–Lafayette (IN)
Ivy Tech Comm Coll–North Central (IN)
Ivy Tech Comm Coll–Northeast (IN)
Ivy Tech Comm Coll–Northwest (IN)
Ivy Tech Comm Coll–Richmond (IN)
Ivy Tech Comm Coll–Southeast (IN)
Ivy Tech Comm Coll–Southern Indiana (IN)
Ivy Tech Comm Coll–Southwest (IN)
Ivy Tech Comm Coll–Wabash Valley (IN)
Jackson Coll (MI)
Jackson State Comm Coll (TN)
James Sprunt Comm Coll (NC)
Jefferson State Comm Coll (AL)
John Tyler Comm Coll (VA)
Kankakee Comm Coll (IL)
Kaskaskia Coll (IL)
Kent State U at Ashtabula (OH)
Kilgore Coll (TX)
Kirtland Comm Coll (MI)
Klamath Comm Coll (OR)
Lake Michigan Coll (MI)
Laramie County Comm Coll (WY)
Lawson State Comm Coll (AL)
Lehigh Carbon Comm Coll (PA)
Lincoln Land Comm Coll (IL)
Lurleen B. Wallace Comm Coll (AL)
Luzerne County Comm Coll (PA)
Macomb Comm Coll (MI)
Manchester Comm Coll (CT)
Massachusetts Bay Comm Coll (MA)
McHenry County Coll (IL)
Miami Dade Coll (FL)
Middlesex Comm Coll (MA)
Mineral Area Coll (MO)
Missouri State U–West Plains (MO)
Montcalm Comm Coll (MI)
Motlow State Comm Coll (TN)
Mott Comm Coll (MI)
Nassau Comm Coll (NY)

Niagara County Comm Coll (NY)
Northampton Comm Coll (PA)
Northern Essex Comm Coll (MA)
Northwest Coll (WY)
Northwest-Shoals Comm Coll (AL)
Norwalk Comm Coll (CT)
Oakland Comm Coll (MI)
Ocean County Coll (NJ)
Oklahoma City Comm Coll (OK)
Oklahoma State U, Oklahoma City (OK)
Onondaga Comm Coll (NY)
Oregon Coast Comm Coll (OR)
Owens Comm Coll, Toledo (OH)
Panola Coll (TX)
Parkland Coll (IL)
Phoenix Coll (AZ)
Piedmont Comm Coll (NC)
Piedmont Virginia Comm Coll (VA)
Quinsigamond Comm Coll (MA)
Red Rocks Comm Coll (CO)
Rogue Comm Coll (OR)
Salt Lake Comm Coll (UT)
San Jacinto Coll District (TX)
San Juan Coll (NM)
Schoolcraft Coll (MI)
Shelton State Comm Coll (AL)
Sheridan Coll (WY)
Sierra Coll (CA)
Southwestern Michigan Coll (MI)
Spoon River Coll (IL)
Springfield Tech Comm Coll (MA)
Taft Coll (CA)
Terra State Comm Coll (OH)
Thomas Nelson Comm Coll (VA)
The U of Akron–Wayne Coll (OH)
U of Arkansas Comm Coll at Morrilton (AR)
Volunteer State Comm Coll (TN)
Waubonsee Comm Coll (IL)
West Virginia Northern Comm Coll (WV)
Wilson Comm Coll (NC)

GEOGRAPHIC INFORMATION SCIENCE AND CARTOGRAPHY

Alexandria Tech and Comm Coll (MN)
Austin Comm Coll (TX)
Brookhaven Coll (TX)
Casper Coll (WY)
Harrisburg Area Comm Coll (PA)
Houston Comm Coll System (TX)
Lehigh Carbon Comm Coll (PA)
Mitchell Tech Inst (SD)
Oklahoma City Comm Coll (OK)

GEOGRAPHY

Austin Comm Coll (TX)
Bakersfield Coll (CA)
Cayuga County Comm Coll (NY)
Coll of Marin (CA)
Coll of the Desert (CA)
The Comm Coll of Baltimore County (MD)
Darton State Coll (GA)
Foothill Coll (CA)
Holyoke Comm Coll (MA)
Lake Michigan Coll (MI)
Lansing Comm Coll (MI)
Lone Star Coll–North Harris (TX)
Lone Star Coll–Tomball (TX)
Montgomery Coll (MD)
Orange Coast Coll (CA)
San Diego Mesa Coll (CA)
San Juan Coll (NM)

GEOLOGICAL AND EARTH SCIENCES/GEOSCIENCES RELATED

Burlington County Coll (NJ)
Erie Comm Coll, North Campus (NY)

GEOLOGY/EARTH SCIENCE

Amarillo Coll (TX)
Arizona Western Coll (AZ)
Austin Comm Coll (TX)
Bakersfield Coll (CA)
Barton County Comm Coll (KS)
Casper Coll (WY)
Central Wyoming Coll (WY)
Coll of Marin (CA)
Coll of the Desert (CA)
Georgia Highlands Coll (GA)
Grand Rapids Comm Coll (MI)
Kilgore Coll (TX)
Lake Michigan Coll (MI)
Lone Star Coll–North Harris (TX)
Lone Star Coll–Tomball (TX)
Miami Dade Coll (FL)
Orange Coast Coll (CA)
Pensacola State Coll (FL)

Potomac State Coll of West Virginia U (WV)
St. Philip's Coll (TX)
Salt Lake Comm Coll (UT)
San Jacinto Coll District (TX)
San Juan Coll (NM)
Sierra Coll (CA)
Tyler Jr Coll (TX)
Vincennes U (IN)

GERMAN

Austin Comm Coll (TX)
Bakersfield Coll (CA)
Miami Dade Coll (FL)
Orange Coast Coll (CA)

GERMANIC LANGUAGES

Lansing Comm Coll (MI)

GERONTOLOGY

Genesee Comm Coll (NY)
North Shore Comm Coll (MA)

GLAZIER

Metropolitan Comm Coll–Kansas City (MO)

GOLF COURSE OPERATION AND GROUNDS MANAGEMENT

Harford Comm Coll (MD)
Owens Comm Coll, Toledo (OH)
Tech Coll of the Lowcountry (SC)

GRAPHIC AND PRINTING EQUIPMENT OPERATION/PRODUCTION

Burlington County Coll (NJ)
Central Maine Comm Coll (ME)
Chemeketa Comm Coll (OR)
Erie Comm Coll, South Campus (NY)
Fox Valley Tech Coll (WI)
Houston Comm Coll System (TX)
Luzerne County Comm Coll (PA)
Macomb Comm Coll (MI)
Mineral Area Coll (MO)
Monroe Comm Coll (NY)
Northwest Coll (WY)
Ozarks Tech Comm Coll (MO)
Pasadena City Coll (CA)
San Diego City Coll (CA)
Sullivan Coll of Technology and Design (KY)
Tarrant County Coll District (TX)
Vincennes U (IN)

GRAPHIC COMMUNICATIONS

Clark Coll (WA)
Fox Valley Tech Coll (WI)
Hawkeye Comm Coll (IA)
Oklahoma City Comm Coll (OK)
Piedmont Comm Coll (NC)
Sullivan Coll of Technology and Design (KY)
Waukesha County Tech Coll (WI)

GRAPHIC COMMUNICATIONS RELATED

Carrington Coll California–Pleasant Hill (CA)
Rasmussen Coll Moorhead (MN)
Sullivan Coll of Technology and Design (KY)

GRAPHIC DESIGN

Anne Arundel Comm Coll (MD)
Antonelli Inst (PA)
Arapahoe Comm Coll (CO)
Barton County Comm Coll (KS)
Bradford School (OH)
Bradford School (PA)
Brookhaven Coll (TX)
Burlington County Coll (NJ)
Butte Coll (CA)
Casper Coll (WY)
Cayuga County Comm Coll (NY)
Central Wyoming Coll (WY)
Chemeketa Comm Coll (OR)
Coll of the Canyons (CA)
Comm Coll of Vermont (VT)
Corning Comm Coll (NY)
County Coll of Morris (NJ)
Dunwoody Coll of Technology (MN)
Elgin Comm Coll (IL)
Florida Gateway Coll (FL)
Foothill Coll (CA)
Forsyth Tech Comm Coll (NC)
Fox Coll (IL)
Gateway Tech Coll (WI)
Glendale Comm Coll (AZ)
Great Falls Coll Montana State U (MT)
Harford Comm Coll (MD)

Harrisburg Area Comm Coll (PA)
Highland Comm Coll (IL)
Illinois Central Coll (IL)
International Business Coll, Indianapolis (IN)
Ivy Tech Comm Coll–Southwest (IN)
Jackson Coll (MI)
King's Coll (NC)
Kirtland Comm Coll (MI)
Lake Michigan Coll (MI)
Lansing Comm Coll (MI)
Lehigh Carbon Comm Coll (PA)
Lincoln Land Comm Coll (IL)
Luzerne County Comm Coll (PA)
Minneapolis Business Coll (MN)
Moraine Park Tech Coll (WI)
Moraine Valley Comm Coll (IL)
Mott Comm Coll (MI)
Northampton Comm Coll (PA)
North Hennepin Comm Coll (MN)
Norwalk Comm Coll (CT)
Oakland Comm Coll (MI)
Oakton Comm Coll (IL)
Parkland Coll (IL)
Pasadena City Coll (CA)
Pensacola State Coll (FL)
Phoenix Coll (AZ)
St. Louis Comm Coll at Forest Park (MO)
St. Louis Comm Coll at Meramec (MO)
Salt Lake Comm Coll (UT)
Santa Rosa Jr Coll (CA)
Sierra Coll (CA)
Southwestern Michigan Coll (MI)
Spoon River Coll (IL)
Sullivan Coll of Technology and Design (KY)
Waubonsee Comm Coll (IL)
Waukesha County Tech Coll (WI)
Westmoreland County Comm Coll (PA)
Wood Tobe–Coburn School (NY)

GREENHOUSE MANAGEMENT

Century Coll (MN)
Comm Coll of Allegheny County (PA)
Dakota Coll at Bottineau (ND)
The Ohio State U Ag Tech Inst (OH)

GUNSMITHING

Colorado School of Trades (CO)

HAZARDOUS MATERIALS MANAGEMENT AND WASTE TECHNOLOGY

Barton County Comm Coll (KS)
Butte Coll (CA)
Pensacola State Coll (FL)
Sierra Coll (CA)

HEALTH AIDES/ATTENDANTS/ORDERLIES RELATED

Barton County Comm Coll (KS)

HEALTH AND MEDICAL ADMINISTRATIVE SERVICES RELATED

Barton County Comm Coll (KS)
Carrington Coll California–Pleasant Hill (CA)
Carrington Coll California–San Leandro (CA)
Comm Coll of Beaver County (PA)
Kent State U at Ashtabula (OH)
Kent State U at Salem (OH)
Westmoreland County Comm Coll (PA)

HEALTH AND PHYSICAL EDUCATION/FITNESS

Alexandria Tech and Comm Coll (MN)
Anne Arundel Comm Coll (MD)
Arapahoe Comm Coll (CO)
Austin Comm Coll (TX)
Butte Coll (CA)
Central Oregon Comm Coll (OR)
Cochise Coll, Sierra Vista (AZ)
Coll of Marin (CA)
Coll of the Canyons (CA)
Coll of the Desert (CA)
Comm Coll of Allegheny County (PA)
Comm Coll of Beaver County (PA)
Corning Comm Coll (NY)
Dakota Coll at Bottineau (ND)
Darton State Coll (GA)
Elgin Comm Coll (IL)
Gordon State Coll (GA)
Holyoke Comm Coll (MA)
Houston Comm Coll System (TX)
Illinois Central Coll (IL)

Lake Michigan Coll (MI)
Lansing Comm Coll (MI)
Luzerne County Comm Coll (PA)
McHenry County Coll (IL)
Montgomery County Comm Coll (PA)
Mt. San Antonio Coll (CA)
Northwest Coll (WY)
Raritan Valley Comm Coll (NJ)
San Jacinto Coll District (TX)
San Juan Coll (NM)
Santa Rosa Jr Coll (CA)
Sheridan Coll (WY)
Sierra Coll (CA)
Vincennes U (IN)
Waubonsee Comm Coll (IL)

HEALTH AND PHYSICAL EDUCATION RELATED

Ancilla Coll (IN)
Coll of Southern Maryland (MD)
Corning Comm Coll (NY)
Garden City Comm Coll (KS)

HEALTH AND WELLNESS

Corning Comm Coll (NY)

HEALTH/HEALTH-CARE ADMINISTRATION

Carrington Coll California–Pleasant Hill (CA)
Carrington Coll California–San Jose (CA)
Carrington Coll California–San Leandro (CA)
Carrington Coll of California–Antioch (CA)
Carrington Coll of California–Citrus Heights (CA)
Carrington Coll of California–Sacramento (CA)
Comm Coll of the Air Force (AL)
Essex County Coll (NJ)
Harrisburg Area Comm Coll (PA)
Kent State U at Trumbull (OH)
Luzerne County Comm Coll (PA)
Oakland Comm Coll (MI)
Oklahoma State U, Oklahoma City (OK)
Owens Comm Coll, Toledo (OH)
South Plains Coll (TX)
Terra State Comm Coll (OH)
Tyler Jr Coll (TX)

HEALTH INFORMATION/MEDICAL RECORDS ADMINISTRATION

Amarillo Coll (TX)
Barton County Comm Coll (KS)
Bowling Green State U-Firelands Coll (OH)
Central New Mexico Comm Coll (NM)
Comm Coll of Philadelphia (PA)
Darton State Coll (GA)
Daytona State Coll (FL)
Elaine P. Nunez Comm Coll (LA)
El Centro Coll (TX)
Florida Gateway Coll (FL)
Forsyth Tech Comm Coll (NC)
Georgia Highlands Coll (GA)
Hagerstown Comm Coll (MD)
Illinois Eastern Comm Colls, Lincoln Trail College (IL)
LDS Business Coll (UT)
Metropolitan Comm Coll–Kansas City (MO)
Miami Dade Coll (FL)
Monroe Comm Coll (NY)
Northern Essex Comm Coll (MA)
Oakton Comm Coll (IL)
Oklahoma City Comm Coll (OK)
Pensacola State Coll (FL)
San Diego Mesa Coll (CA)
South Plains Coll (TX)
Stark State Coll (OH)
Tarrant County Coll District (TX)
Terra State Comm Coll (OH)

HEALTH INFORMATION/MEDICAL RECORDS TECHNOLOGY

Anne Arundel Comm Coll (MD)
Arapahoe Comm Coll (CO)
Austin Comm Coll (TX)
Borough of Manhattan Comm Coll of the City U of New York (NY)
Burlington County Coll (NJ)
Carrington Coll California–Pleasant Hill (CA)
Carroll Comm Coll (MD)
Catawba Valley Comm Coll (NC)
Central Oregon Comm Coll (OR)
Chippewa Valley Tech Coll (WI)

Collin County Comm Coll District (TX)
Comm Coll of Allegheny County (PA)
Darton State Coll (GA)
Dyersburg State Comm Coll (TN)
Erie Comm Coll, North Campus (NY)
Fountainhead Coll of Technology (TN)
Fox Valley Tech Coll (WI)
Gateway Tech Coll (WI)
Great Falls Coll Montana State U (MT)
Highland Comm Coll (IL)
Houston Comm Coll System (TX)
Hutchinson Comm Coll and Area Vocational School (KS)
Illinois Eastern Comm Colls, Frontier Community College (IL)
Jamestown Comm Coll (NY)
Kaskaskia Coll (IL)
Kennebec Valley Comm Coll (ME)
Kirtland Comm Coll (MI)
Lehigh Carbon Comm Coll (PA)
Lone Star Coll–CyFair (TX)
Lone Star Coll–Kingwood (TX)
Lone Star Coll–Montgomery (TX)
Lone Star Coll–North Harris (TX)
Lone Star Coll–Tomball (TX)
Montgomery Coll (MD)
Moraine Park Tech Coll (WI)
Moraine Valley Comm Coll (IL)
Mott Comm Coll (MI)
North Dakota State Coll of Science (ND)
Northeast Iowa Comm Coll (IA)
Onondaga Comm Coll (NY)
Owens Comm Coll, Toledo (OH)
Ozarka Coll (AR)
Ozarks Tech Comm Coll (MO)
Panola Coll (TX)
Phoenix Coll (AZ)
Raritan Valley Comm Coll (NJ)
Rasmussen Coll Aurora (IL)
Rasmussen Coll Bismarck (ND)
Rasmussen Coll Bloomington (MN)
Rasmussen Coll Brooklyn Park (MN)
Rasmussen Coll Eagan (MN)
Rasmussen Coll Fort Myers (FL)
Rasmussen Coll Green Bay (WI)
Rasmussen Coll Lake Elmo/Woodbury (MN)
Rasmussen Coll Mankato (MN)
Rasmussen Coll Moorhead (MN)
Rasmussen Coll New Port Richey (FL)
Rasmussen Coll Ocala (FL)
Rasmussen Coll Rockford (IL)
Rasmussen Coll St. Cloud (MN)
St. Clair County Comm Coll (MI)
St. Louis Comm Coll at Forest Park (MO)
St. Philip's Coll (TX)
San Jacinto Coll District (TX)
San Juan Coll (NM)
Schoolcraft Coll (MI)
Shawnee Comm Coll (IL)
Southern Maine Comm Coll (ME)
Southwestern Michigan Coll (MI)
State U of New York Coll of Technology at Alfred (NY)
Tallahassee Comm Coll (FL)
Terra State Comm Coll (OH)
Texas State Tech Coll Harlingen (TX)
Tyler Jr Coll (TX)
Vincennes U (IN)
Volunteer State Comm Coll (TN)
Waubonsee Comm Coll (IL)
Waukesha County Tech Coll (WI)
Westmoreland County Comm Coll (PA)
West Virginia Northern Comm Coll (WV)
York County Comm Coll (ME)

HEALTH/MEDICAL PREPARATORY PROGRAMS RELATED
Darton State Coll (GA)
Edison Comm Coll (OH)
Essex County Coll (NJ)
Gordon State Coll (GA)
Lake Michigan Coll (MI)
Miami Dade Coll (FL)
Northwest Coll (WY)

HEALTH PROFESSIONS RELATED
Berkshire Comm Coll (MA)
Bowling Green State U–Firelands Coll (OH)

Bucks County Comm Coll (PA)
Carl Albert State Coll (OK)
Carroll Comm Coll (MD)
Comm Coll of Allegheny County (PA)
Comm Coll of Philadelphia (PA)
Corning Comm Coll (NY)
Essex County Coll (NJ)
Forsyth Tech Comm Coll (NC)
Gateway Comm and Tech Coll (KY)
Genesee Comm Coll (NY)
Greenfield Comm Coll (MA)
Halifax Comm Coll (NC)
Lakeland Comm Coll (OH)
Manor Coll (PA)
Mendocino Coll (CA)
Miami Dade Coll (FL)
Mineral Area Coll (MO)
Northeastern Jr Coll (CO)
North Shore Comm Coll (MA)
Oakland Comm Coll (MI)
Onondaga Comm Coll (NY)
Orange Coast Coll (CA)
Piedmont Comm Coll (NC)
Salt Lake Comm Coll (UT)
Spoon River Coll (IL)
Terra State Comm Coll (OH)
Volunteer State Comm Coll (TN)

HEALTH SERVICES ADMINISTRATION
Florida Gateway Coll (FL)
Harrisburg Area Comm Coll (PA)

HEALTH SERVICES/ALLIED HEALTH/HEALTH SCIENCES
Ancilla Coll (IN)
Anoka-Ramsey Comm Coll (MN)
Anoka-Ramsey Comm Coll, Cambridge Campus (MN)
Arizona Western Coll (AZ)
Burlington County Coll (NJ)
Carl Albert State Coll (OK)
Casper Coll (WY)
Cecil Coll (MD)
Central Wyoming Coll (WY)
Century Coll (MN)
Dakota Coll at Bottineau (ND)
Dyersburg State Comm Coll (TN)
Essex County Coll (NJ)
Garden City Comm Coll (KS)
Georgia Military Coll (GA)
Goodwin Coll (CT)
Klamath Comm Coll (OR)
Lake Superior Coll (MN)
Northwest Coll (WY)
Quinsigamond Comm Coll (MA)
Raritan Valley Comm Coll (NJ)
Schoolcraft Coll (MI)
Sheridan Coll (WY)
Texas State Tech Coll Harlingen (TX)
York County Comm Coll (ME)

HEALTH TEACHER EDUCATION
Austin Comm Coll (TX)
Bainbridge Coll (GA)
Copiah-Lincoln Comm Coll (MS)
Georgia Military Coll (GA)
Harper Coll (IL)
Howard Comm Coll (MD)
Kilgore Coll (TX)

HEALTH UNIT COORDINATOR/WARD CLERK
Comm Coll of Allegheny County (PA)
Southeast Tech Inst (SD)

HEATING, AIR CONDITIONING, VENTILATION AND REFRIGERATION MAINTENANCE TECHNOLOGY
Amarillo Coll (TX)
Arizona Western Coll (AZ)
Bismarck State Coll (ND)
Blackhawk Tech Coll (WI)
Century Coll (MN)
Coll of Lake County (IL)
Coll of the Desert (CA)
Comm Coll of Allegheny County (PA)
Comm Coll of Beaver County (PA)
Delaware Tech & Comm Coll, Jack F. Owens Campus (DE)
Dunwoody Coll of Technology (MN)
Edison Comm Coll (OH)
Elaine P. Nunez Comm Coll (LA)
Elgin Comm Coll (IL)
Fayetteville Tech Comm Coll (NC)
Gateway Tech Coll (WI)
Grand Rapids Comm Coll (MI)
Guilford Tech Comm Coll (NC)

Harper Coll (IL)
Harrisburg Area Comm Coll (PA)
Illinois Central Coll (IL)
Ivy Tech Comm Coll–Bloomington (IN)
Ivy Tech Comm Coll–Central Indiana (IN)
Ivy Tech Comm Coll–Columbus (IN)
Ivy Tech Comm Coll–East Central (IN)
Ivy Tech Comm Coll–Kokomo (IN)
Ivy Tech Comm Coll–Lafayette (IN)
Ivy Tech Comm Coll–North Central (IN)
Ivy Tech Comm Coll–Northeast (IN)
Ivy Tech Comm Coll–Northwest (IN)
Ivy Tech Comm Coll–Richmond (IN)
Ivy Tech Comm Coll–Southern Indiana (IN)
Ivy Tech Comm Coll–Southwest (IN)
Ivy Tech Comm Coll–Wabash Valley (IN)
Jefferson Coll (MO)
Johnston Comm Coll (NC)
Kankakee Comm Coll (IL)
Kilgore Coll (TX)
Kirtland Comm Coll (MI)
Lansing Comm Coll (MI)
Laramie County Comm Coll (WY)
Lehigh Carbon Comm Coll (PA)
Lone Star Coll–North Harris (TX)
Luzerne County Comm Coll (PA)
Macomb Comm Coll (MI)
Miami Dade Coll (FL)
Mid-Plains Comm Coll, North Platte (NE)
Minnesota West Comm and Tech Coll (MN)
Mitchell Tech Inst (SD)
Mohave Comm Coll (AZ)
Monroe Comm Coll (NY)
Montgomery Comm Coll (NC)
Moraine Valley Comm Coll (IL)
Mt. San Antonio Coll (CA)
Northampton Comm Coll (PA)
North Dakota State Coll of Science (ND)
Orange Coast Coll (CA)
Oxnard Coll (CA)
Ozarks Tech Comm Coll (MO)
Paris Jr Coll (TX)
St. Philip's Coll (TX)
Salt Lake Comm Coll (UT)
San Jacinto Coll District (TX)
Southeast Tech Inst (SD)
Southern Maine Comm Coll (ME)
South Plains Coll (TX)
Spartanburg Comm Coll (SC)
State U of New York Coll of Technology at Alfred (NY)
Tarrant County Coll District (TX)
Texarkana Coll (TX)
Texas State Tech Coll Harlingen (TX)
U of Arkansas Comm Coll at Morrilton (AR)
Waubonsee Comm Coll (IL)
Westmoreland County Comm Coll (PA)
West Virginia Northern Comm Coll (WV)
Wilson Comm Coll (NC)

HEATING, VENTILATION, AIR CONDITIONING AND REFRIGERATION ENGINEERING TECHNOLOGY
Alamance Comm Coll (NC)
Austin Comm Coll (TX)
Bevill State Comm Coll (AL)
Blackhawk Tech Coll (WI)
Chippewa Valley Tech Coll (WI)
The Comm Coll of Baltimore County (MD)
Delaware Tech & Comm Coll, Stanton/Wilmington Campus (DE)
Dunwoody Coll of Technology (MN)
Gadsden State Comm Coll (AL)
Gateway Tech Coll (WI)
Jackson Coll (MI)
J. F. Drake State Tech Coll (AL)
Kennebec Valley Comm Coll (ME)
Macomb Comm Coll (MI)
Miami Dade Coll (FL)
Mineral Area Coll (MO)
Mohawk Valley Comm Coll (NY)
Moraine Park Tech Coll (WI)
Mott Comm Coll (MI)
North Dakota State Coll of Science (ND)
Oakland Comm Coll (MI)

Oakton Comm Coll (IL)
Oklahoma Tech Coll (OK)
Raritan Valley Comm Coll (NJ)
Shelton State Comm Coll (AL)
Springfield Tech Comm Coll (MA)
State U of New York Coll of Technology at Alfred (NY)
Sullivan Coll of Technology and Design (KY)
Terra State Comm Coll (OH)

HEAVY EQUIPMENT MAINTENANCE TECHNOLOGY
Amarillo Coll (TX)
Beaufort County Comm Coll (NC)
Fox Valley Tech Coll (WI)
Highland Comm Coll (IL)
Mesa Comm Coll (AZ)
Metropolitan Comm Coll–Kansas City (MO)
The Ohio State U Ag Tech Inst (OH)
Ozarks Tech Comm Coll (MO)
State U of New York Coll of Technology at Alfred (NY)

HEAVY/INDUSTRIAL EQUIPMENT MAINTENANCE TECHNOLOGIES RELATED
Mineral Area Coll (MO)

HEMATOLOGY TECHNOLOGY
Comm Coll of the Air Force (AL)

HIGHER EDUCATION/HIGHER EDUCATION ADMINISTRATION
Lansing Comm Coll (MI)

HISPANIC-AMERICAN, PUERTO RICAN, AND MEXICAN-AMERICAN/CHICANO STUDIES
Collin County Comm Coll District (TX)
San Diego City Coll (CA)
San Diego Mesa Coll (CA)
San Jacinto Coll District (TX)

HISTOLOGIC TECHNICIAN
Comm Coll of Rhode Island (RI)
Darton State Coll (GA)
Houston Comm Coll System (TX)
Lansing Comm Coll (MI)
Miami Dade Coll (FL)
Mott Comm Coll (MI)
Oakland Comm Coll (MI)

HISTOLOGIC TECHNOLOGY/HISTOTECHNOLOGIST
Delaware Tech & Comm Coll, Stanton/Wilmington Campus (DE)
North Hennepin Comm Coll (MN)
Oakland Comm Coll (MI)
Phoenix Coll (AZ)

HISTORIC PRESERVATION AND CONSERVATION
Bucks County Comm Coll (PA)

HISTORY
Amarillo Coll (TX)
Ancilla Coll (IN)
Arizona Western Coll (AZ)
Austin Comm Coll (TX)
Bainbridge Coll (GA)
Bakersfield Coll (CA)
Barton County Comm Coll (KS)
Burlington County Coll (NJ)
Casper Coll (WY)
Cochise Coll, Sierra Vista (AZ)
Coll of Marin (CA)
Coll of the Canyons (CA)
Coll of the Desert (CA)
Copiah-Lincoln Comm Coll (MS)
Dakota Coll at Bottineau (ND)
Darton State Coll (GA)
De Anza Coll (CA)
Foothill Coll (CA)
Georgia Highlands Coll (GA)
Georgia Military Coll (GA)
Gordon State Coll (GA)
Harford Comm Coll (MD)
Harper Coll (IL)
Kankakee Comm Coll (IL)
Kilian Comm Coll (SD)
Lake Michigan Coll (MI)
Lansing Comm Coll (MI)
Laramie County Comm Coll (WY)
Lone Star Coll–CyFair (TX)
Lone Star Coll–Kingwood (TX)
Lone Star Coll–Montgomery (TX)
Lone Star Coll–North Harris (TX)

Lone Star Coll–Tomball (TX)
Lorain County Comm Coll (OH)
Miami Dade Coll (FL)
Mohave Comm Coll (AZ)
Monroe Comm Coll (NY)
Northeastern Jr Coll (CO)
Northern Essex Comm Coll (MA)
North Hennepin Comm Coll (MN)
Northwest Coll (WY)
Northwest State Comm Coll (OH)
Oklahoma City Comm Coll (OK)
Oklahoma State U, Oklahoma City (OK)
Orange Coast Coll (CA)
Oxnard Coll (CA)
Parkland Coll (IL)
Pasadena City Coll (CA)
Pensacola State Coll (FL)
Potomac State Coll of West Virginia U (WV)
St. Philip's Coll (TX)
Salt Lake Comm Coll (UT)
San Jacinto Coll District (TX)
Santa Rosa Jr Coll (CA)
Sheridan Coll (WY)
Spoon River Coll (IL)
Terra State Comm Coll (OH)
Texarkana Coll (TX)
Vincennes U (IN)

HISTORY RELATED
U of Pittsburgh at Titusville (PA)

HISTORY TEACHER EDUCATION
Bucks County Comm Coll (PA)
Cochise Coll, Sierra Vista (AZ)
Darton State Coll (GA)

HOLISTIC HEALTH
Anoka-Ramsey Comm Coll (MN)
Anoka-Ramsey Comm Coll, Cambridge Campus (MN)
Red Rocks Comm Coll (CO)

HOME FURNISHINGS AND EQUIPMENT INSTALLATION
Illinois Central Coll (IL)

HOME HEALTH AIDE/HOME ATTENDANT
Barton County Comm Coll (KS)

HOMELAND SECURITY
Goodwin Coll (CT)
Harper Coll (IL)
Long Island Business Inst (NY)

HOMELAND SECURITY, LAW ENFORCEMENT, FIREFIGHTING AND PROTECTIVE SERVICES RELATED
Barton County Comm Coll (KS)
Central Wyoming Coll (WY)
Century Coll (MN)
Georgia Military Coll (GA)
Glendale Comm Coll (AZ)
Goodwin Coll (CT)
Lakeland Comm Coll (OH)
Laramie County Comm Coll (WY)
Miami Dade Coll (FL)
NorthWest Arkansas Comm Coll (AR)
Ocean County Coll (NJ)
Onondaga Comm Coll (NY)
Pittsburgh Tech Inst, Oakdale (PA)
Red Rocks Comm Coll (CO)
Schoolcraft Coll (MI)
Westmoreland County Comm Coll (PA)

HORSE HUSBANDRY/EQUINE SCIENCE AND MANAGEMENT
Cecil Coll (MD)
Colby Comm Coll (KS)
Highland Comm Coll (IL)
The Ohio State U Ag Tech Inst (OH)
Santa Rosa Jr Coll (CA)

HORTICULTURAL SCIENCE
Bakersfield Coll (CA)
Butte Coll (CA)
Century Coll (MN)
Clark State Comm Coll (OH)
Dakota Coll at Bottineau (ND)
Lehigh Carbon Comm Coll (PA)
Luzerne County Comm Coll (PA)
Mesa Comm Coll (AZ)
Miami Dade Coll (FL)
Missouri State U–West Plains (MO)
Mt. San Antonio Coll (CA)

The Ohio State U Ag Tech Inst (OH)
Oklahoma State U, Oklahoma City (OK)
Orange Coast Coll (CA)
Potomac State Coll of West Virginia U (WV)
Shawnee Comm Coll (IL)
Sheridan Coll (WY)
Southeast Tech Inst (SD)
South Puget Sound Comm Coll (WA)
Spartanburg Comm Coll (SC)
Tarrant County Coll District (TX)
Trident Tech Coll (SC)
Victor Valley Coll (CA)

HOSPITAL AND HEALTH-CARE FACILITIES ADMINISTRATION
Carrington Coll–Phoenix Westside (AZ)
Illinois Central Coll (IL)
Minnesota West Comm and Tech Coll (MN)

HOSPITALITY ADMINISTRATION
Adirondack Comm Coll (NY)
Alexandria Tech and Comm Coll (MN)
Arizona Western Coll (AZ)
Austin Comm Coll (TX)
Berkshire Comm Coll (MA)
Burlington County Coll (NJ)
Casper Coll (WY)
Central New Mexico Comm Coll (NM)
Chemeketa Comm Coll (OR)
Coll of Southern Maryland (MD)
Coll of the Canyons (CA)
Coll of the Desert (CA)
Collin County Comm Coll District (TX)
Comm Coll of Vermont (VT)
Daytona State Coll (FL)
Fox Valley Tech Coll (WI)
Greenfield Comm Coll (MA)
Harper Coll (IL)
Harrisburg Area Comm Coll (PA)
Hillsborough Comm Coll (FL)
Ivy Tech Comm Coll–East Central (IN)
Ivy Tech Comm Coll–North Central (IN)
Ivy Tech Comm Coll–Northeast (IN)
Ivy Tech Comm Coll–Northwest (IN)
Jefferson Comm Coll (NY)
Jefferson State Comm Coll (AL)
Lakeland Comm Coll (OH)
Lake Michigan Coll (MI)
Lincoln Land Comm Coll (IL)
Lone Star Coll–North Harris (TX)
Massachusetts Bay Comm Coll (MA)
Miami Dade Coll (FL)
Moraine Valley Comm Coll (IL)
Niagara County Comm Coll (NY)
Normandale Comm Coll (MN)
North Shore Comm Coll (MA)
Onondaga Comm Coll (NY)
Pasadena City Coll (CA)
Pensacola State Coll (FL)
Potomac State Coll of West Virginia U (WV)
Quinsigamond Comm Coll (MA)
St. Louis Comm Coll at Forest Park (MO)
San Diego City Coll (CA)
Scottsdale Comm Coll (AZ)
Sheridan Coll (WY)
Sullivan County Comm Coll (NY)
Tech Coll of the Lowcountry (SC)
Terra State Comm Coll (OH)
Union County Coll (NJ)
Vincennes U (IN)
West Virginia Northern Comm Coll (WV)

HOSPITALITY ADMINISTRATION RELATED
Corning Comm Coll (NY)
Holyoke Comm Coll (MA)
Ivy Tech Comm Coll–Central Indiana (IN)
Ivy Tech Comm Coll–East Central (IN)
Ivy Tech Comm Coll–Northeast (IN)
Long Island Business Inst (NY)
Penn State Beaver (PA)

HOSPITALITY AND RECREATION MARKETING
County Coll of Morris (NJ)
Dakota Coll at Bottineau (ND)
Flathead Valley Comm Coll (MT)
Luzerne County Comm Coll (PA)

Montgomery County Comm Coll (PA)
Pensacola State Coll (FL)
San Diego Mesa Coll (CA)

HOTEL/MOTEL ADMINISTRATION
Anne Arundel Comm Coll (MD)
Bakersfield Coll (CA)
Bradford School (OH)
Bradford School (PA)
Cape Fear Comm Coll (NC)
Carl Albert State Coll (OK)
Central Oregon Comm Coll (OR)
Central Wyoming Coll (WY)
Chemeketa Comm Coll (OR)
Coll of the Canyons (CA)
Comm Coll of Allegheny County (PA)
The Comm Coll of Baltimore County (MD)
Comm Coll of Philadelphia (PA)
Comm Coll of the Air Force (AL)
Cowley County Comm Coll and Area Vocational–Tech School (KS)
Daytona State Coll (FL)
Delaware Tech & Comm Coll, Stanton/Wilmington Campus (DE)
Delaware Tech & Comm Coll, Terry Campus (DE)
Essex County Coll (NJ)
Finger Lakes Comm Coll (NY)
Fox Coll (IL)
Genesee Comm Coll (NY)
Guilford Tech Comm Coll (NC)
Harrisburg Area Comm Coll (PA)
Houston Comm Coll System (TX)
International Business Coll, Indianapolis (IN)
King's Coll (NC)
Lansing Comm Coll (MI)
Luzerne County Comm Coll (PA)
Manchester Comm Coll (CT)
Middlesex Comm Coll (MA)
Minneapolis Business Coll (MN)
Mohawk Valley Comm Coll (NY)
Monroe Comm Coll (NY)
Montgomery Coll (MD)
Moraine Park Tech Coll (WI)
Mt. San Antonio Coll (CA)
Nassau Comm Coll (NY)
Northampton Comm Coll (PA)
Northern Essex Comm Coll (MA)
Norwalk Comm Coll (CT)
Oakland Comm Coll (MI)
Orange Coast Coll (CA)
Oxnard Coll (CA)
Ozarks Tech Comm Coll (MO)
Pittsburgh Tech Inst, Oakdale (PA)
St. Philip's Coll (TX)
San Diego Mesa Coll (CA)
Scottsdale Comm Coll (AZ)
Southern Maine Comm Coll (ME)
Southwestern Michigan Coll (MI)
Tompkins Cortland Comm Coll (NY)
Trident Tech Coll (SC)
Union County Coll (NJ)
Vincennes U (IN)
Westmoreland County Comm Coll (PA)
Wood Tobe–Coburn School (NY)

HOTEL, MOTEL, AND RESTAURANT MANAGEMENT
Fayetteville Tech Comm Coll (NC)
Gateway Tech Coll (WI)
Waukesha County Tech Coll (WI)

HOUSING AND HUMAN ENVIRONMENTS
Orange Coast Coll (CA)
Sullivan Coll of Technology and Design (KY)

HOUSING AND HUMAN ENVIRONMENTS RELATED
Comm Coll of Allegheny County (PA)

HUMAN DEVELOPMENT AND FAMILY STUDIES
Bucks County Comm Coll (PA)
Georgia Military Coll (GA)
Orange Coast Coll (CA)
Penn State Brandywine (PA)
Penn State DuBois (PA)
Penn State Fayette, The Eberly Campus (PA)
Penn State Mont Alto (PA)
Penn State New Kensington (PA)
Penn State Schuylkill (PA)
Penn State Worthington Scranton (PA)
Penn State York (PA)
Salt Lake Comm Coll (UT)

HUMAN DEVELOPMENT AND FAMILY STUDIES RELATED
Comm Coll of Allegheny County (PA)
Northwest State Comm Coll (OH)

HUMANITIES
Brookhaven Coll (TX)
Bucks County Comm Coll (PA)
Cayuga County Comm Coll (NY)
Central Oregon Comm Coll (OR)
Clinton Comm Coll (NY)
Cochise Coll, Sierra Vista (AZ)
Coll of Marin (CA)
Coll of the Canyons (CA)
Coll of the Desert (CA)
Comm Coll of Allegheny County (PA)
Comm Coll of Beaver County (PA)
Corning Comm Coll (NY)
Dakota Coll at Bottineau (ND)
De Anza Coll (CA)
Dutchess Comm Coll (NY)
Erie Comm Coll (NY)
Erie Comm Coll, North Campus (NY)
Erie Comm Coll, South Campus (NY)
Finger Lakes Comm Coll (NY)
Garden City Comm Coll (KS)
Harper Coll (IL)
Housatonic Comm Coll (CT)
Jamestown Comm Coll (NY)
Jefferson Comm Coll (NY)
John Tyler Comm Coll (VA)
Lake Michigan Coll (MI)
Lansing Comm Coll (MI)
Laramie County Comm Coll (WY)
Lehigh Carbon Comm Coll (PA)
Lone Star Coll–Kingwood (TX)
Lone Star Coll–Montgomery (TX)
Lone Star Coll–Tomball (TX)
Luzerne County Comm Coll (PA)
Miami Dade Coll (FL)
Mohawk Valley Comm Coll (NY)
Montgomery County Comm Coll (PA)
Mt. San Antonio Coll (CA)
Niagara County Comm Coll (NY)
Northeastern Jr Coll (CO)
Oklahoma City Comm Coll (OK)
Oklahoma State U, Oklahoma City (OK)
Onondaga Comm Coll (NY)
Orange Coast Coll (CA)
Pasadena City Coll (CA)
Salt Lake Comm Coll (UT)
Santa Rosa Jr Coll (CA)
State U of New York Coll of Technology at Alfred (NY)
Terra State Comm Coll (OH)
Texarkana Coll (TX)
Tompkins Cortland Comm Coll (NY)
Victor Valley Coll (CA)
Westchester Comm Coll (NY)

HUMAN RESOURCES MANAGEMENT
Anoka-Ramsey Comm Coll (MN)
Anoka-Ramsey Comm Coll, Cambridge Campus (MN)
Barton County Comm Coll (KS)
Blackhawk Tech Coll (WI)
Cecil Coll (MD)
Chippewa Valley Tech Coll (WI)
Clark Coll (WA)
Comm Coll of Allegheny County (PA)
Comm Coll of Beaver County (PA)
Comm Coll of the Air Force (AL)
Delaware Tech & Comm Coll, Terry Campus (DE)
Edison Comm Coll (OH)
Fayetteville Tech Comm Coll (NC)
Fox Valley Tech Coll (WI)
Goodwin Coll (CT)
Guilford Tech Comm Coll (NC)
Harford Comm Coll (MD)
Hawkeye Comm Coll (IA)
Lansing Comm Coll (MI)
Lehigh Carbon Comm Coll (PA)
Moraine Park Tech Coll (WI)
Moraine Valley Comm Coll (IL)
Rasmussen Coll Bloomington (MN)
Rasmussen Coll Brooklyn Park (MN)
Rasmussen Coll Eagan (MN)
Rasmussen Coll Fargo (ND)
Rasmussen Coll Fort Myers (FL)
Rasmussen Coll Green Bay (WI)
Rasmussen Coll Lake Elmo/ Woodbury (MN)
Rasmussen Coll Mankato (MN)
Rasmussen Coll Moorhead (MN)
Rasmussen Coll New Port Richey (FL)
Rasmussen Coll Ocala (FL)
Santa Rosa Jr Coll (CA)
Waubonsee Comm Coll (IL)

Western Iowa Tech Comm Coll (IA)
Westmoreland County Comm Coll (PA)

HUMAN RESOURCES MANAGEMENT AND SERVICES RELATED
Barton County Comm Coll (KS)
Manor Coll (PA)

HUMAN SERVICES
Alexandria Tech and Comm Coll (MN)
Austin Comm Coll (TX)
Bakersfield Coll (CA)
Berkshire Comm Coll (MA)
Bismarck State Coll (ND)
Bowling Green State U–Firelands Coll (OH)
Burlington County Coll (NJ)
Central Maine Comm Coll (ME)
Century Coll (MN)
Clark State Comm Coll (OH)
Comm Coll of Philadelphia (PA)
Comm Coll of Vermont (VT)
Corning Comm Coll (NY)
Daytona State Coll (FL)
Delaware Tech & Comm Coll, Jack F. Owens Campus (DE)
Delaware Tech & Comm Coll, Stanton/Wilmington Campus (DE)
Delaware Tech & Comm Coll, Terry Campus (DE)
Denmark Tech Coll (SC)
Dutchess Comm Coll (NY)
Essex County Coll (NJ)
Finger Lakes Comm Coll (NY)
Flathead Valley Comm Coll (MT)
Forsyth Tech Comm Coll (NC)
Genesee Comm Coll (NY)
Georgia Highlands Coll (GA)
Goodwin Coll (CT)
Harper Coll (IL)
Harrisburg Area Comm Coll (PA)
Housatonic Comm Coll (CT)
Ivy Tech Comm Coll–Bloomington (IN)
Ivy Tech Comm Coll–Central Indiana (IN)
Ivy Tech Comm Coll–Columbus (IN)
Ivy Tech Comm Coll–East Central (IN)
Ivy Tech Comm Coll–Kokomo (IN)
Ivy Tech Comm Coll–Lafayette (IN)
Ivy Tech Comm Coll–North Central (IN)
Ivy Tech Comm Coll–Northeast (IN)
Ivy Tech Comm Coll–Northwest (IN)
Ivy Tech Comm Coll–Richmond (IN)
Ivy Tech Comm Coll–Southeast (IN)
Ivy Tech Comm Coll–Southern Indiana (IN)
Ivy Tech Comm Coll–Southwest (IN)
Ivy Tech Comm Coll–Wabash Valley (IN)
Jamestown Comm Coll (NY)
Jefferson Comm Coll (NY)
John Tyler Comm Coll (VA)
Lake Area Tech Inst (SD)
Laramie County Comm Coll (WY)
Lehigh Carbon Comm Coll (PA)
Lone Star Coll–Kingwood (TX)
Lone Star Coll–Montgomery (TX)
Lone Star Coll–North Harris (TX)
Lorain County Comm Coll (OH)
Luzerne County Comm Coll (PA)
Manchester Comm Coll (CT)
Massachusetts Bay Comm Coll (MA)
Mendocino Coll (CA)
Metropolitan Comm Coll–Kansas City (MO)
Miami Dade Coll (FL)
Minnesota West Comm and Tech Coll (MN)
Monroe Comm Coll (NY)
Niagara County Comm Coll (NY)
Northern Essex Comm Coll (MA)
Norwalk Comm Coll (CT)
Ocean County Coll (NJ)
Oklahoma State U, Oklahoma City (OK)
Owensboro Comm and Tech Coll (KY)
Parkland Coll (IL)
Pasco-Hernando Comm Coll (FL)
Phoenix Coll (AZ)
Quinsigamond Comm Coll (MA)
Rasmussen Coll Bismarck (ND)
Rasmussen Coll Bloomington (MN)
Rasmussen Coll Brooklyn Park (MN)
Rasmussen Coll Eagan (MN)
Rasmussen Coll Fargo (ND)

Rasmussen Coll Fort Myers (FL)
Rasmussen Coll Green Bay (WI)
Rasmussen Coll Lake Elmo/ Woodbury (MN)
Rasmussen Coll Mankato (MN)
Rasmussen Coll Moorhead (MN)
Rasmussen Coll New Port Richey (FL)
Rasmussen Coll Ocala (FL)
Rasmussen Coll St. Cloud (MN)
St. Louis Comm Coll at Forest Park (MO)
St. Louis Comm Coll at Meramec (MO)
Santa Rosa Jr Coll (CA)
Shawnee Comm Coll (IL)
Southern State Comm Coll (OH)
Stark State Coll (OH)
State U of New York Coll of Technology at Alfred (NY)
Sullivan County Comm Coll (NY)
Trident Tech Coll (SC)
Tunxis Comm Coll (CT)
Union County Coll (NJ)
U of Alaska Anchorage, Kenai Peninsula Coll (AK)
U of Pittsburgh at Titusville (PA)

HYDRAULICS AND FLUID POWER TECHNOLOGY
The Comm Coll of Baltimore County (MD)
Minnesota West Comm and Tech Coll (MN)
The Ohio State U Ag Tech Inst (OH)

ILLUSTRATION
Fashion Inst of Technology (NY)
Oakland Comm Coll (MI)
Oklahoma State U, Oklahoma City (OK)

INDUSTRIAL AND PRODUCT DESIGN
Fiorello H. LaGuardia Comm Coll of the City U of New York (NY)
Kirtland Comm Coll (MI)
Luzerne County Comm Coll (PA)
Mt. San Antonio Coll (CA)
Orange Coast Coll (CA)
Owens Comm Coll, Toledo (OH)

INDUSTRIAL ELECTRONICS TECHNOLOGY
Bevill State Comm Coll (AL)
Big Bend Comm Coll (WA)
Illinois Central Coll (IL)
J. F. Drake State Tech Coll (AL)
John Tyler Comm Coll (VA)
Kankakee Comm Coll (IL)
Lawson State Comm Coll (AL)
Lehigh Carbon Comm Coll (PA)
Lincoln Land Comm Coll (IL)
Lurleen B. Wallace Comm Coll (AL)
Moraine Valley Comm Coll (IL)
Northampton Comm Coll (PA)
Northwest-Shoals Comm Coll (AL)
Northwest State Comm Coll (OH)
Pasadena City Coll (CA)
Randolph Comm Coll (NC)
Shelton State Comm Coll (AL)
Sierra Coll (CA)
Spartanburg Comm Coll (SC)
Sullivan Coll of Technology and Design (KY)
Tech Coll of the Lowcountry (SC)
Thomas Nelson Comm Coll (VA)

INDUSTRIAL ENGINEERING
Blackhawk Tech Coll (WI)
Manchester Comm Coll (CT)
Montcalm Comm Coll (MI)

INDUSTRIAL MECHANICS AND MAINTENANCE TECHNOLOGY
Alexandria Tech and Comm Coll (MN)
Big Bend Comm Coll (WA)
Bismarck State Coll (ND)
Bossier Parish Comm Coll (LA)
Casper Coll (WY)
Chemeketa Comm Coll (OR)
Coll of Lake County (IL)
Elgin Comm Coll (IL)
Gadsden State Comm Coll (AL)
Gateway Tech Coll (WI)
Illinois Eastern Comm Colls, Olney Central College (IL)
Ivy Tech Comm Coll–East Central (IN)
J. F. Drake State Tech Coll (AL)
Kaskaskia Coll (IL)

Kennebec Valley Comm Coll (ME)
Lower Columbia Coll (WA)
Macomb Comm Coll (MI)
Northwest-Shoals Comm Coll (AL)
Northwest State Comm Coll (OH)
San Juan Coll (NM)
Southwestern Michigan Coll (MI)
Sullivan Coll of Technology and Design (KY)
Waubonsee Comm Coll (IL)
Westmoreland County Comm Coll (PA)

INDUSTRIAL PRODUCTION TECHNOLOGIES RELATED
Barton County Comm Coll (KS)
Bismarck State Coll (ND)
Comm Coll of Beaver County (PA)
Essex County Coll (NJ)
Guilford Tech Comm Coll (NC)
Ivy Tech Comm Coll–Central Indiana (IN)
Ivy Tech Comm Coll–East Central (IN)
Ivy Tech Comm Coll–Lafayette (IN)
Ivy Tech Comm Coll–North Central (IN)
Ivy Tech Comm Coll–Northeast (IN)
Ivy Tech Comm Coll–Richmond (IN)
Ivy Tech Comm Coll–Southwest (IN)
Ivy Tech Comm Coll–Wabash Valley (IN)
Kent State U at Trumbull (OH)
Lansing Comm Coll (MI)
Mohawk Valley Comm Coll (NY)
Northwest State Comm Coll (OH)
Oakland Comm Coll (MI)
St. Clair County Comm Coll (MI)
Southwestern Michigan Coll (MI)

INDUSTRIAL RADIOLOGIC TECHNOLOGY
Amarillo Coll (TX)
Bakersfield Coll (CA)
Copiah-Lincoln Comm Coll (MS)
Cowley County Comm Coll and Area Vocational–Tech School (KS)
Cuyahoga Comm Coll (OH)
Daytona State Coll (FL)
Lorain County Comm Coll (OH)
Monroe Comm Coll (NY)
Mt. San Antonio Coll (CA)
Northern Essex Comm Coll (MA)
Orange Coast Coll (CA)
Salt Lake Comm Coll (UT)
San Diego Mesa Coll (CA)
Southeastern Comm Coll (IA)
South Plains Coll (TX)
Tarrant County Coll District (TX)
Tyler Jr Coll (TX)
Virginia Western Comm Coll (VA)

INDUSTRIAL SAFETY TECHNOLOGY
Northwest Tech Coll (MN)

INDUSTRIAL TECHNOLOGY
Arizona Western Coll (AZ)
Bakersfield Coll (CA)
Bismarck State Coll (ND)
Blackhawk Tech Coll (WI)
Bowling Green State U-Firelands Coll (OH)
Bucks County Comm Coll (PA)
Central Oregon Comm Coll (OR)
Clark State Comm Coll (OH)
Cleveland State Comm Coll (TN)
Clinton Comm Coll (NY)
Comm Coll of Allegheny County (PA)
Comm Coll of the Air Force (AL)
Comm Coll of Vermont (VT)
Crowder Coll (MO)
Daytona State Coll (FL)
De Anza Coll (CA)
Edison Comm Coll (OH)
Elaine P. Nunez Comm Coll (LA)
Erie Comm Coll, North Campus (NY)
FIDM/The Fashion Inst of Design & Merchandising, Orange County Campus (CA)
Forsyth Tech Comm Coll (NC)
Gateway Comm and Tech Coll (KY)
Grand Rapids Comm Coll (MI)
Hagerstown Comm Coll (MD)
Highland Comm Coll (IL)
Illinois Central Coll (IL)
Illinois Eastern Comm Colls, Wabash Valley College (IL)
Ivy Tech Comm Coll–Bloomington (IN)

Ivy Tech Comm Coll–Central Indiana (IN)
Ivy Tech Comm Coll–Columbus (IN)
Ivy Tech Comm Coll–East Central (IN)
Ivy Tech Comm Coll–Kokomo (IN)
Ivy Tech Comm Coll–Lafayette (IN)
Ivy Tech Comm Coll–North Central (IN)
Ivy Tech Comm Coll–Northeast (IN)
Ivy Tech Comm Coll–Northwest (IN)
Ivy Tech Comm Coll–Richmond (IN)
Ivy Tech Comm Coll–Southeast (IN)
Ivy Tech Comm Coll–Southern Indiana (IN)
Ivy Tech Comm Coll–Southwest (IN)
Ivy Tech Comm Coll–Wabash Valley (IN)
Jackson State Comm Coll (TN)
James A. Rhodes State Coll (OH)
John Tyler Comm Coll (VA)
Kent State U at Trumbull (OH)
Kent State U at Tuscarawas (OH)
Lake Michigan Coll (MI)
Lincoln Land Comm Coll (IL)
Lone Star Coll–CyFair (TX)
Lorain County Comm Coll (OH)
Macomb Comm Coll (MI)
Manchester Comm Coll (CT)
Mesa Comm Coll (AZ)
Miami Dade Coll (FL)
Mineral Area Coll (MO)
Missouri State U–West Plains (MO)
Monroe Comm Coll (NY)
Monroe County Comm Coll (MI)
Montcalm Comm Coll (MI)
Northwest Tech Coll (MN)
Oakland Comm Coll (MI)
The Ohio State U Ag Tech Inst (OH)
Olympic Coll (WA)
Owens Comm Coll, Toledo (OH)
Ozarks Tech Comm Coll (MO)
Panola Coll (TX)
Parkland Coll (IL)
Paul D. Camp Comm Coll (VA)
Penn State York (PA)
Piedmont Comm Coll (NC)
Pierce Coll at Puyallup (WA)
Red Rocks Comm Coll (CO)
Robeson Comm Coll (NC)
San Diego City Coll (CA)
San Juan Coll (NM)
Schoolcraft Coll (MI)
Seminole State Coll of Florida (FL)
Southeast Tech Inst (SD)
Spoon River Coll (IL)
Stark State Coll (OH)
Thomas Nelson Comm Coll (VA)
Trident Tech Coll (SC)
Waubonsee Comm Coll (IL)

INFORMATION RESOURCES MANAGEMENT
Rasmussen Coll Fort Myers (FL)
Rasmussen Coll New Port Richey (FL)
Rasmussen Coll Ocala (FL)

INFORMATION SCIENCE/STUDIES
Alamance Comm Coll (NC)
Alexandria Tech and Comm Coll (MN)
Alpena Comm Coll (MI)
Amarillo Coll (TX)
Arkansas State U–Mountain Home (AR)
Bainbridge Coll (GA)
Bakersfield Coll (CA)
Barton County Comm Coll (KS)
Beaufort County Comm Coll (NC)
Bossier Parish Comm Coll (LA)
Brookhaven Coll (TX)
Bucks County Comm Coll (PA)
Cayuga County Comm Coll (NY)
Central Carolina Comm Coll (NC)
Central New Mexico Comm Coll (NM)
Clark State Comm Coll (OH)
Cleveland Comm Coll (NC)
Cochise Coll, Sierra Vista (AZ)
Dabney S. Lancaster Comm Coll (VA)
Dakota Coll at Bottineau (ND)
De Anza Coll (CA)
Dutchess Comm Coll (NY)
Dyersburg State Comm Coll (TN)
Elaine P. Nunez Comm Coll (LA)
El Centro Coll (TX)
Essex County Coll (NJ)

Fayetteville Tech Comm Coll (NC)
Forsyth Tech Comm Coll (NC)
Genesee Comm Coll (NY)
Guilford Tech Comm Coll (NC)
Howard Comm Coll (MD)
Jefferson Comm Coll (NY)
J. F. Drake State Tech Coll (AL)
Kaskaskia Coll (IL)
Kirtland Comm Coll (MI)
Lone Star Coll–Kingwood (TX)
Lone Star Coll–North Harris (TX)
Lorain County Comm Coll (OH)
Manchester Comm Coll (CT)
Massachusetts Bay Comm Coll (MA)
Mendocino Coll (CA)
Metropolitan Comm Coll–Kansas City (MO)
Miami Dade Coll (FL)
Monroe Comm Coll (NY)
Montgomery County Comm Coll (PA)
Niagara County Comm Coll (NY)
North Shore Comm Coll (MA)
Norwalk Comm Coll (CT)
Oklahoma State U, Oklahoma City (OK)
Orange Coast Coll (CA)
Ozarka Coll (AR)
Ozarks Tech Comm Coll (MO)
Panola Coll (TX)
Paris Jr Coll (TX)
Parkland Coll (IL)
Penn State DuBois (PA)
Penn State Hazleton (PA)
Penn State Lehigh Valley (PA)
Penn State New Kensington (PA)
Penn State Schuylkill (PA)
Pensacola State Coll (FL)
Pierce Coll at Puyallup (WA)
Rappahannock Comm Coll (VA)
Salt Lake Comm Coll (UT)
Scottsdale Comm Coll (AZ)
Seminole State Coll of Florida (FL)
Shawnee Comm Coll (IL)
Sheridan Coll (WY)
Southeastern Comm Coll (IA)
South Puget Sound Comm Coll (WA)
Spoon River Coll (IL)
Sullivan County Comm Coll (NY)
Tompkins Cortland Comm Coll (NY)
Tunxis Comm Coll (CT)
Union County Coll (NJ)
Victor Valley Coll (CA)
Westchester Comm Coll (NY)
Wytheville Comm Coll (VA)

INFORMATION TECHNOLOGY
Adirondack Comm Coll (NY)
Blue Ridge Comm and Tech Coll (WV)
Burlington County Coll (NJ)
Butte Coll (CA)
Catawba Valley Comm Coll (NC)
Central Carolina Comm Coll (NC)
Clark State Comm Coll (OH)
Cleveland Comm Coll (NC)
Coll of Southern Maryland (MD)
Coll of the Desert (CA)
Comm Coll of Vermont (VT)
Corning Comm Coll (NY)
Dakota Coll at Bottineau (ND)
Daytona State Coll (FL)
Erie Comm Coll, North Campus (NY)
Fayetteville Tech Comm Coll (NC)
Florida Gateway Coll (FL)
Forsyth Tech Comm Coll (NC)
Fountainhead Coll of Technology (TN)
Gateway Comm and Tech Coll (KY)
Georgia Military Coll (GA)
Gordon State Coll (GA)
Great Falls Coll Montana State U (MT)
Guilford Tech Comm Coll (NC)
Halifax Comm Coll (NC)
Hallmark Coll of Technology (TX)
Highland Comm Coll (IL)
Howard Comm Coll (MD)
Illinois Eastern Comm Colls, Frontier Community College (IL)
ITI Tech Coll (LA)
James Sprunt Comm Coll (NC)
Jamestown Comm Coll (NY)
Jefferson Coll (MO)
John Tyler Comm Coll (VA)
Kilian Comm Coll (SD)
LDS Business Coll (UT)
Lone Star Coll–CyFair (TX)
Lone Star Coll–Montgomery (TX)
Lorain County Comm Coll (OH)
McHenry County Coll (IL)

Metropolitan Comm Coll–Kansas City (MO)
Minnesota West Comm and Tech Coll (MN)
Missouri State U–West Plains (MO)
Mohave Comm Coll (AZ)
Monroe Comm Coll (NY)
Monroe County Comm Coll (MI)
Norwalk Comm Coll (CT)
Oakton Comm Coll (IL)
Oklahoma State U, Oklahoma City (OK)
Owensboro Comm and Tech Coll (KY)
Owens Comm Coll, Toledo (OH)
Panola Coll (TX)
Pasco-Hernando Comm Coll (FL)
Piedmont Comm Coll (NC)
Potomac State Coll of West Virginia U (WV)
Randolph Comm Coll (NC)
Raritan Valley Comm Coll (NJ)
Salt Lake Comm Coll (UT)
Seminole State Coll of Florida (FL)
Sierra Coll (CA)
South Suburban Coll (IL)
Stark State Coll (OH)
Sullivan Coll of Technology and Design (KY)
Texas State Tech Coll Harlingen (TX)
Thomas Nelson Comm Coll (VA)
Tri-County Comm Coll (NC)
Tyler Jr Coll (TX)
Union County Coll (NJ)
U of Pittsburgh at Titusville (PA)
West Virginia Northern Comm Coll (WV)
Wilson Comm Coll (NC)

INSTITUTIONAL FOOD WORKERS
James Sprunt Comm Coll (NC)
San Jacinto Coll District (TX)

INSTRUMENTATION TECHNOLOGY
Amarillo Coll (TX)
Cape Fear Comm Coll (NC)
Central Carolina Comm Coll (NC)
Fox Valley Tech Coll (WI)
Hagerstown Comm Coll (MD)
Houston Comm Coll System (TX)
ITI Tech Coll (LA)
Lakeland Comm Coll (OH)
Lower Columbia Coll (WA)
Monroe Comm Coll (NY)
Moraine Valley Comm Coll (IL)
Nassau Comm Coll (NY)
Ozarks Tech Comm Coll (MO)
Salt Lake Comm Coll (UT)
San Jacinto Coll District (TX)
San Juan Coll (NM)

INSURANCE
Comm Coll of Allegheny County (PA)
Mesa Comm Coll (AZ)
Miles Comm Coll (MT)
Nassau Comm Coll (NY)
San Diego City Coll (CA)

INTELLIGENCE
Cochise Coll, Sierra Vista (AZ)

INTERDISCIPLINARY STUDIES
Bowling Green State U-Firelands Coll (OH)
Lone Star Coll–CyFair (TX)
Lone Star Coll–Kingwood (TX)
Lone Star Coll–Montgomery (TX)
Lone Star Coll–North Harris (TX)
Lone Star Coll–Tomball (TX)
North Shore Comm Coll (MA)

INTERIOR ARCHITECTURE
Inst of Design and Construction (NY)
State U of New York Coll of Technology at Alfred (NY)

INTERIOR DESIGN
Alexandria Tech and Comm Coll (MN)
Amarillo Coll (TX)
Arapahoe Comm Coll (CO)
Bakersfield Coll (CA)
Butte Coll (CA)
Cape Fear Comm Coll (NC)
Century Coll (MN)
Clary Sage Coll (OK)
Coll of Marin (CA)
Coll of the Canyons (CA)

Collin County Comm Coll District (TX)
Daytona State Coll (FL)
Delaware Tech & Comm Coll, Terry Campus (DE)
El Centro Coll (TX)
Fashion Inst of Technology (NY)
FIDM/The Fashion Inst of Design & Merchandising, Los Angeles Campus (CA)
FIDM/The Fashion Inst of Design & Merchandising, Orange County Campus (CA)
FIDM/The Fashion Inst of Design & Merchandising, San Diego Campus (CA)
FIDM/The Fashion Inst of Design & Merchandising, San Francisco Campus (CA)
Forsyth Tech Comm Coll (NC)
Fox Valley Tech Coll (WI)
Gateway Tech Coll (WI)
Great Falls Coll Montana State U (MT)
Halifax Comm Coll (NC)
Harford Comm Coll (MD)
Harper Coll (IL)
Hawkeye Comm Coll (IA)
Houston Comm Coll System (TX)
Ivy Tech Comm Coll–North Central (IN)
Ivy Tech Comm Coll–Southwest (IN)
Lansing Comm Coll (MI)
LDS Business Coll (UT)
Lehigh Carbon Comm Coll (PA)
Lone Star Coll–Kingwood (TX)
Mesa Comm Coll (AZ)
Miami Dade Coll (FL)
Monroe Comm Coll (NY)
Montgomery Coll (MD)
Mt. San Antonio Coll (CA)
Nassau Comm Coll (NY)
Northampton Comm Coll (PA)
Norwalk Comm Coll (CT)
Oakland Comm Coll (MI)
Onondaga Comm Coll (NY)
Orange Coast Coll (CA)
Phoenix Coll (AZ)
Randolph Comm Coll (NC)
Raritan Valley Comm Coll (NJ)
Red Rocks Comm Coll (CO)
St. Louis Comm Coll at Meramec (MO)
San Diego City Coll (CA)
San Diego Mesa Coll (CA)
San Jacinto Coll District (TX)
Santa Rosa Jr Coll (CA)
Scottsdale Comm Coll (AZ)
Seminole State Coll of Florida (FL)
State U of New York Coll of Technology at Alfred (NY)
Sullivan Coll of Technology and Design (KY)
Waukesha County Tech Coll (WI)
Western Iowa Tech Comm Coll (IA)

INTERMEDIA/MULTIMEDIA
Coll of the Canyons (CA)
San Diego Mesa Coll (CA)

INTERNATIONAL BUSINESS/TRADE/COMMERCE
Austin Comm Coll (TX)
Central New Mexico Comm Coll (NM)
Foothill Coll (CA)
Forsyth Tech Comm Coll (NC)
Harper Coll (IL)
Houston Comm Coll System (TX)
Lansing Comm Coll (MI)
Luzerne County Comm Coll (PA)
Manor Coll (PA)
Monroe Comm Coll (NY)
Northwest State Comm Coll (OH)
Oakland Comm Coll (MI)
Owens Comm Coll, Toledo (OH)
Pasadena City Coll (CA)
Raritan Valley Comm Coll (NJ)
San Jacinto Coll District (TX)
Stark State Coll (OH)
Tompkins Cortland Comm Coll (NY)
Westchester Comm Coll (NY)

INTERNATIONAL/GLOBAL STUDIES
Berkshire Comm Coll (MA)
Burlington County Coll (NJ)
Central Wyoming Coll (WY)
Macomb Comm Coll (MI)
Oakland Comm Coll (MI)

Pasadena City Coll (CA)
Salt Lake Comm Coll (UT)

INTERNATIONAL MARKETING
Waukesha County Tech Coll (WI)

INTERNATIONAL RELATIONS AND AFFAIRS
Casper Coll (WY)
Coll of Marin (CA)
De Anza Coll (CA)
Georgia Military Coll (GA)
Greenfield Comm Coll (MA)
Harrisburg Area Comm Coll (PA)
Lansing Comm Coll (MI)
Massachusetts Bay Comm Coll (MA)
Miami Dade Coll (FL)
Northern Essex Comm Coll (MA)
Northwest Coll (WY)
Salt Lake Comm Coll (UT)

IRONWORKING
Ivy Tech Comm Coll–Lafayette (IN)
Ivy Tech Comm Coll–North Central (IN)
Ivy Tech Comm Coll–Northeast (IN)
Ivy Tech Comm Coll–Northwest (IN)
Ivy Tech Comm Coll–Southwest (IN)
Ivy Tech Comm Coll–Wabash Valley (IN)

ITALIAN
Coll of the Desert (CA)
Miami Dade Coll (FL)

JAPANESE
Austin Comm Coll (TX)
Foothill Coll (CA)
Lansing Comm Coll (MI)

JAZZ/JAZZ STUDIES
Comm Coll of Rhode Island (RI)
Santa Rosa Jr Coll (CA)

JOURNALISM
Amarillo Coll (TX)
Austin Comm Coll (TX)
Bainbridge Coll (GA)
Bakersfield Coll (CA)
Barton County Comm Coll (KS)
Bucks County Comm Coll (PA)
Burlington County Coll (NJ)
Butte Coll (CA)
Carl Albert State Coll (OK)
Casper Coll (WY)
Cochise Coll, Sierra Vista (AZ)
Coll of the Canyons (CA)
Coll of the Desert (CA)
Comm Coll of Allegheny County (PA)
Comm Coll of Beaver County (PA)
Copiah-Lincoln Comm Coll (MS)
Cowley County Comm Coll and Area Vocational–Tech School (KS)
Darton State Coll (GA)
De Anza Coll (CA)
Georgia Highlands Coll (GA)
Housatonic Comm Coll (CT)
Kilgore Coll (TX)
Lone Star Coll–North Harris (TX)
Lorain County Comm Coll (OH)
Luzerne County Comm Coll (PA)
Manchester Comm Coll (CT)
Miami Dade Coll (FL)
Monroe County Comm Coll (MI)
Mt. San Antonio Coll (CA)
Northampton Comm Coll (PA)
Northeastern Jr Coll (CO)
Northern Essex Comm Coll (MA)
Northwest Coll (WY)
Orange Coast Coll (CA)
Pensacola State Coll (FL)
Potomac State Coll of West Virginia U (WV)
St. Clair County Comm Coll (MI)
St. Louis Comm Coll at Forest Park (MO)
San Diego City Coll (CA)
San Jacinto Coll District (TX)
South Plains Coll (TX)
Taft Coll (CA)
Texarkana Coll (TX)
Vincennes U (IN)
Westchester Comm Coll (NY)

JUVENILE CORRECTIONS
Chemeketa Comm Coll (OR)
Kaskaskia Coll (IL)
Lansing Comm Coll (MI)

KINDERGARTEN/PRESCHOOL EDUCATION
Alamance Comm Coll (NC)

Bainbridge Coll (GA)
Beaufort County Comm Coll (NC)
Bowling Green State U-Firelands Coll (OH)
Carroll Comm Coll (MD)
Casper Coll (WY)
Central Carolina Comm Coll (NC)
Clark State Comm Coll (OH)
Cleveland State Comm Coll (TN)
Collin County Comm Coll District (TX)
Comm Coll of Philadelphia (PA)
Comm Coll of Rhode Island (RI)
County Coll of Morris (NJ)
Cuyahoga Comm Coll (OH)
Daytona State Coll (FL)
Delaware Tech & Comm Coll, Jack F. Owens Campus (DE)
Delaware Tech & Comm Coll, Stanton/Wilmington Campus (DE)
Delaware Tech & Comm Coll, Terry Campus (DE)
Denmark Tech Coll (SC)
Elaine P. Nunez Comm Coll (LA)
Essex County Coll (NJ)
Finger Lakes Comm Coll (NY)
Genesee Comm Coll (NY)
Howard Comm Coll (MD)
Jamestown Comm Coll (NY)
Johnston Comm Coll (NC)
Lorain County Comm Coll (OH)
Manchester Comm Coll (CT)
Mendocino Coll (CA)
Metropolitan Comm Coll–Kansas City (MO)
Miami Dade Coll (FL)
Middlesex Comm Coll (MA)
Mt. San Antonio Coll (CA)
Nassau Comm Coll (NY)
Northeastern Jr Coll (CO)
Northern Essex Comm Coll (MA)
North Shore Comm Coll (MA)
Northwest Coll (WY)
Northwest State Comm Coll (OH)
Orange Coast Coll (CA)
Owensboro Comm and Tech Coll (KY)
Ozarks Tech Comm Coll (MO)
Parkland Coll (IL)
Pierce Coll at Puyallup (WA)
Potomac State Coll of West Virginia U (WV)
Quinsigamond Comm Coll (MA)
Raritan Valley Comm Coll (NJ)
St. Clair County Comm Coll (MI)
San Jacinto Coll District (TX)
Scottsdale Comm Coll (AZ)
Southern State Comm Coll (OH)
South Puget Sound Comm Coll (WA)
Spoon River Coll (IL)
Sullivan County Comm Coll (NY)
Taft Coll (CA)
Tallahassee Comm Coll (FL)
Terra State Comm Coll (OH)
Tompkins Cortland Comm Coll (NY)
Tunxis Comm Coll (CT)
Victor Valley Coll (CA)
Virginia Western Comm Coll (VA)

KINESIOLOGY AND EXERCISE SCIENCE
Barton County Comm Coll (KS)
Carroll Comm Coll (MD)
Central Oregon Comm Coll (OR)
Clark State Comm Coll (OH)
County Coll of Morris (NJ)
Delaware Tech & Comm Coll, Stanton/Wilmington Campus (DE)
Glendale Comm Coll (AZ)
Laramie County Comm Coll (WY)
Lone Star Coll–Kingwood (TX)
Lone Star Coll–North Harris (TX)
Lone Star Coll–Tomball (TX)
Norwalk Comm Coll (CT)
Oakland Comm Coll (MI)
Orange Coast Coll (CA)
Raritan Valley Comm Coll (NJ)
St. Philip's Coll (TX)
Salt Lake Comm Coll (UT)
Santa Rosa Jr Coll (CA)
Sheridan Coll (WY)
South Suburban Coll (IL)

LABOR AND INDUSTRIAL RELATIONS
The Comm Coll of Baltimore County (MD)
San Diego City Coll (CA)

LANDSCAPE ARCHITECTURE
Monroe Comm Coll (NY)

Mt. San Antonio Coll (CA)
San Diego Mesa Coll (CA)

LANDSCAPING AND GROUNDSKEEPING
Cape Fear Comm Coll (NC)
Century Coll (MN)
Clark Coll (WA)
Clark State Comm Coll (OH)
Coll of Lake County (IL)
Coll of Marin (CA)
Coll of the Canyons (CA)
Comm Coll of Allegheny County (PA)
Dakota Coll at Bottineau (ND)
Florida Gateway Coll (FL)
Grand Rapids Comm Coll (MI)
Harford Comm Coll (MD)
Harrisburg Area Comm Coll (PA)
Hillsborough Comm Coll (FL)
Johnston Comm Coll (NC)
Lake Michigan Coll (MI)
Lincoln Land Comm Coll (IL)
Miami Dade Coll (FL)
Oakland Comm Coll (MI)
The Ohio State U Ag Tech Inst (OH)
Owens Comm Coll, Toledo (OH)
Parkland Coll (IL)
Pensacola State Coll (FL)
St. Clair County Comm Coll (MI)
San Juan Coll (NM)
Santa Rosa Jr Coll (CA)
Springfield Tech Comm Coll (MA)

LAND USE PLANNING AND MANAGEMENT
Dakota Coll at Bottineau (ND)

LANGUAGE INTERPRETATION AND TRANSLATION
Cape Fear Comm Coll (NC)
Century Coll (MN)
Cleveland Comm Coll (NC)
Lake Region State Coll (ND)
Lone Star Coll–CyFair (TX)
Lone Star Coll–North Harris (TX)
Oklahoma State U, Oklahoma City (OK)
Terra State Comm Coll (OH)
Union County Coll (NJ)

LASER AND OPTICAL TECHNOLOGY
Amarillo Coll (TX)
Central Carolina Comm Coll (NC)
Central New Mexico Comm Coll (NM)
Monroe Comm Coll (NY)
Springfield Tech Comm Coll (MA)

LATIN
Austin Comm Coll (TX)

LATIN AMERICAN STUDIES
Miami Dade Coll (FL)
San Diego City Coll (CA)
Santa Rosa Jr Coll (CA)

LEGAL ADMINISTRATIVE ASSISTANT/SECRETARY
Alamance Comm Coll (NC)
Alexandria Tech and Comm Coll (MN)
Alvin Comm Coll (TX)
Amarillo Coll (TX)
Arizona Western Coll (AZ)
Bakersfield Coll (CA)
Bismarck State Coll (ND)
Blackhawk Tech Coll (WI)
Bradford School (OH)
Bradford School (PA)
Butte Coll (CA)
Career Tech Coll (LA)
Central Carolina Comm Coll (NC)
Clark Coll (WA)
Cleveland Comm Coll (NC)
Comm Coll of Allegheny County (PA)
Comm Coll of Rhode Island (RI)
Cowley County Comm Coll and Area Vocational–Tech School (KS)
Crowder Coll (MO)
Dabney S. Lancaster Comm Coll (VA)
Delaware Tech & Comm Coll, Jack F. Owens Campus (DE)
Delaware Tech & Comm Coll, Terry Campus (DE)
Edison Comm Coll (OH)
El Centro Coll (TX)
Forrest Coll (SC)
Harper Coll (IL)
Howard Comm Coll (MD)
International Business Coll, Indianapolis (IN)

Jefferson Coll (MO)
Kennebec Valley Comm Coll (ME)
King's Coll (NC)
Kirtland Comm Coll (MI)
Lake Michigan Coll (MI)
Lake Superior Coll (MN)
Lincoln Land Comm Coll (IL)
Lone Star Coll–North Harris (TX)
Lower Columbia Coll (WA)
Manchester Comm Coll (CT)
Metropolitan Comm Coll–Kansas City (MO)
Miami Dade Coll (FL)
Miles Comm Coll (MT)
Minneapolis Business Coll (MN)
Monroe Comm Coll (NY)
Monroe County Comm Coll (MI)
Montgomery Comm Coll (NC)
Moraine Park Tech Coll (WI)
Mt. San Antonio Coll (CA)
Nassau Comm Coll (NY)
Northampton Comm Coll (PA)
Northeastern Jr Coll (CO)
North Shore Comm Coll (MA)
Northwest State Comm Coll (OH)
Oklahoma City Comm Coll (OK)
Olympic Coll (WA)
Pensacola State Coll (FL)
St. Philip's Coll (TX)
San Diego City Coll (CA)
San Diego Mesa Coll (CA)
Shawnee Comm Coll (IL)
South Plains Coll (TX)
South Puget Sound Comm Coll (WA)
Spoon River Coll (IL)
Stark State Coll (OH)
Tallahassee Comm Coll (FL)
Tunxis Comm Coll (CT)
Tyler Jr Coll (TX)

LEGAL ASSISTANT/PARALEGAL
Alexandria Tech and Comm Coll (MN)
Alvin Comm Coll (TX)
Anne Arundel Comm Coll (MD)
Arapahoe Comm Coll (CO)
Austin Comm Coll (TX)
Bevill State Comm Coll (AL)
Blue Ridge Comm and Tech Coll (WV)
Bradford School (OH)
Bradford School (PA)
Burlington County Coll (NJ)
Casper Coll (WY)
Central Carolina Comm Coll (NC)
Central New Mexico Comm Coll (NM)
Chippewa Valley Tech Coll (WI)
Clark Coll (WA)
Clark State Comm Coll (OH)
Coll of Southern Maryland (MD)
Coll of the Canyons (CA)
Collin County Comm Coll District (TX)
Comm Coll of Allegheny County (PA)
The Comm Coll of Baltimore County (MD)
Comm Coll of Rhode Island (RI)
Comm Coll of the Air Force (AL)
Cuyahoga Comm Coll (OH)
Daytona State Coll (FL)
De Anza Coll (CA)
Dutchess Comm Coll (NY)
Eastern Idaho Tech Coll (ID)
Edison Comm Coll (OH)
Elaine P. Nunez Comm Coll (LA)
El Centro Coll (TX)
Elgin Comm Coll (IL)
Erie Comm Coll (NY)
Essex County Coll (NJ)
Fayetteville Tech Comm Coll (NC)
Finger Lakes Comm Coll (NY)
Fiorello H. LaGuardia Comm Coll of the City U of New York (NY)
Forrest Coll (SC)
Forsyth Tech Comm Coll (NC)
Gadsden State Comm Coll (AL)
Genesee Comm Coll (NY)
Georgia Military Coll (GA)
Guilford Tech Comm Coll (NC)
Halifax Comm Coll (NC)
Harford Comm Coll (MD)
Harper Coll (IL)
Harrisburg Area Comm Coll (PA)
Hillsborough Comm Coll (FL)
Houston Comm Coll System (TX)
Hutchinson Comm Coll and Area Vocational School (KS)
Illinois Central Coll (IL)
Illinois Eastern Comm Colls, Wabash Valley College (IL)

International Business Coll, Indianapolis (IN)
Ivy Tech Comm Coll–Bloomington (IN)
Ivy Tech Comm Coll–Central Indiana (IN)
Ivy Tech Comm Coll–Columbus (IN)
Ivy Tech Comm Coll–East Central (IN)
Ivy Tech Comm Coll–Kokomo (IN)
Ivy Tech Comm Coll–Lafayette (IN)
Ivy Tech Comm Coll–North Central (IN)
Ivy Tech Comm Coll–Northeast (IN)
Ivy Tech Comm Coll–Northwest (IN)
Ivy Tech Comm Coll–Richmond (IN)
Ivy Tech Comm Coll–Southeast (IN)
Ivy Tech Comm Coll–Southern Indiana (IN)
Ivy Tech Comm Coll–Southwest (IN)
Ivy Tech Comm Coll–Wabash Valley (IN)
James A. Rhodes State Coll (OH)
Jefferson Comm Coll (NY)
Johnston Comm Coll (NC)
Kankakee Comm Coll (IL)
Kent State U at East Liverpool (OH)
Kent State U at Trumbull (OH)
Kilgore Coll (TX)
King's Coll (NC)
Lakeland Comm Coll (OH)
Lake Superior Coll (MN)
Lansing Comm Coll (MI)
Laramie County Comm Coll (WY)
Lehigh Carbon Comm Coll (PA)
Luzerne County Comm Coll (PA)
Macomb Comm Coll (MI)
Manchester Comm Coll (CT)
Manor Coll (PA)
Massachusetts Bay Comm Coll (MA)
McCann School of Business & Technology, Pottsville (PA)
Miami Dade Coll (FL)
Middlesex Comm Coll (MA)
Minneapolis Business Coll (MN)
Missouri State U–West Plains (MO)
Mohave Comm Coll (AZ)
Montgomery Coll (MD)
Moraine Park Tech Coll (WI)
Mt. San Antonio Coll (CA)
Nassau Comm Coll (NY)
New York Career Inst (NY)
Northampton Comm Coll (PA)
Northern Essex Comm Coll (MA)
North Hennepin Comm Coll (MN)
North Shore Comm Coll (MA)
NorthWest Arkansas Comm Coll (AR)
Northwest State Comm Coll (OH)
Norwalk Comm Coll (CT)
Oakland Comm Coll (MI)
Oxnard Coll (CA)
Pasadena City Coll (CA)
Pasco-Hernando Comm Coll (FL)
Pensacola State Coll (FL)
Phoenix Coll (AZ)
Raritan Valley Comm Coll (NJ)
Rasmussen Coll Aurora (IL)
Rasmussen Coll Bismarck (ND)
Rasmussen Coll Bloomington (MN)
Rasmussen Coll Brooklyn Park (MN)
Rasmussen Coll Eagan (MN)
Rasmussen Coll Fargo (ND)
Rasmussen Coll Fort Myers (FL)
Rasmussen Coll Green Bay (WI)
Rasmussen Coll Lake Elmo/ Woodbury (MN)
Rasmussen Coll Mankato (MN)
Rasmussen Coll Moorhead (MN)
Rasmussen Coll New Port Richey (FL)
Rasmussen Coll Ocala (FL)
Rasmussen Coll Rockford (IL)
Rasmussen Coll St. Cloud (MN)
St. Louis Comm Coll at Meramec (MO)
Salt Lake Comm Coll (UT)
San Diego City Coll (CA)
San Jacinto Coll District (TX)
San Juan Coll (NM)
Santa Rosa Jr Coll (CA)
Seminole State Coll of Florida (FL)
South Puget Sound Comm Coll (WA)
South Suburban Coll (IL)
Sullivan County Comm Coll (NY)
Tallahassee Comm Coll (FL)
Tarrant County Coll District (TX)
Tech Coll of the Lowcountry (SC)
Thomas Nelson Comm Coll (VA)
Tompkins Cortland Comm Coll (NY)
Trident Tech Coll (SC)

Union County Coll (NJ)
Vincennes U (IN)
Volunteer State Comm Coll (TN)
Westchester Comm Coll (NY)
Western Dakota Tech Inst (SD)
Western Iowa Tech Comm Coll (IA)
Westmoreland County Comm Coll (PA)
West Virginia Northern Comm Coll (WV)
Wilson Comm Coll (NC)

LEGAL PROFESSIONS AND STUDIES RELATED
Bucks County Comm Coll (PA)

LEGAL STUDIES
Alvin Comm Coll (TX)
Carroll Comm Coll (MD)
Harford Comm Coll (MD)
Lone Star Coll–North Harris (TX)
Macomb Comm Coll (MI)
Trident Tech Coll (SC)

LIBERAL ARTS AND SCIENCES AND HUMANITIES RELATED
Anne Arundel Comm Coll (MD)
Bucks County Comm Coll (PA)
Cascadia Comm Coll (WA)
Cleveland Comm Coll (NC)
Cleveland State Comm Coll (TN)
Coll of Southern Maryland (MD)
The Comm Coll of Baltimore County (MD)
Corning Comm Coll (NY)
Dakota Coll at Bottineau (ND)
Dutchess Comm Coll (NY)
Elaine P. Nunez Comm Coll (LA)
Fayetteville Tech Comm Coll (NC)
Garrett Coll (MD)
Great Falls Coll Montana State U (MT)
Guilford Tech Comm Coll (NC)
Hagerstown Comm Coll (MD)
Halifax Comm Coll (NC)
Holyoke Comm Coll (MA)
James Sprunt Comm Coll (NC)
Jamestown Comm Coll (NY)
Kennebec Valley Comm Coll (ME)
Kent State U at Ashtabula (OH)
Kent State U at East Liverpool (OH)
Kent State U at Salem (OH)
Kent State U at Trumbull (OH)
Kent State U at Tuscarawas (OH)
Luzerne County Comm Coll (PA)
Minnesota West Comm and Tech Coll (MN)
Mohawk Valley Comm Coll (NY)
Montgomery Coll (MD)
Northampton Comm Coll (PA)
Oakland Comm Coll (MI)
Onondaga Comm Coll (NY)
Piedmont Comm Coll (NC)
Randolph Comm Coll (NC)
Red Rocks Comm Coll (CO)
Southern Maine Comm Coll (ME)
Tech Coll of the Lowcountry (SC)
West Virginia Northern Comm Coll (WV)
Wilson Comm Coll (NC)
York County Comm Coll (ME)

LIBERAL ARTS AND SCIENCES/ LIBERAL STUDIES
Adirondack Comm Coll (NY)
Alamance Comm Coll (NC)
Alexandria Tech and Comm Coll (MN)
Alpena Comm Coll (MI)
Alvin Comm Coll (TX)
Amarillo Coll (TX)
Anne Arundel Comm Coll (MD)
Anoka-Ramsey Comm Coll (MN)
Anoka-Ramsey Comm Coll, Cambridge Campus (MN)
Arapahoe Comm Coll (CO)
Arkansas State U–Mountain Home (AR)
Bainbridge Coll (GA)
Bakersfield Coll (CA)
Barton County Comm Coll (KS)
Beaufort County Comm Coll (NC)
Berkeley City Coll (CA)
Berkshire Comm Coll (MA)
Bevill State Comm Coll (AL)
Big Bend Comm Coll (WA)
Bismarck State Coll (ND)
Borough of Manhattan Comm Coll of the City U of New York (NY)
Bossier Parish Comm Coll (LA)
Bowling Green State U-Firelands Coll (OH)
Brookhaven Coll (TX)
Bucks County Comm Coll (PA)
Burlington County Coll (NJ)
Butte Coll (CA)
Cape Fear Comm Coll (NC)
Carroll Comm Coll (MD)
Cascadia Comm Coll (WA)
Casper Coll (WY)
Catawba Valley Comm Coll (NC)
Cayuga County Comm Coll (NY)
Cecil Coll (MD)
Central Carolina Comm Coll (NC)
Central Maine Comm Coll (ME)
Central New Mexico Comm Coll (NM)
Central Oregon Comm Coll (OR)
Century Coll (MN)
Chemeketa Comm Coll (OR)
Chipola Coll (FL)
Chippewa Valley Tech Coll (WI)
Clark Coll (WA)
Clark State Comm Coll (OH)
Cleveland Comm Coll (NC)
Cleveland State Comm Coll (TN)
Clinton Comm Coll (NY)
Colby Comm Coll (KS)
Coll of Lake County (IL)
Coll of Marin (CA)
Coll of Southern Maryland (MD)
Coll of the Canyons (CA)
Coll of the Desert (CA)
Collin County Comm Coll District (TX)
Colorado Northwestern Comm Coll (CO)
Comm Coll of Allegheny County (PA)
The Comm Coll of Baltimore County (MD)
Comm Coll of Beaver County (PA)
Comm Coll of Philadelphia (PA)
Comm Coll of Rhode Island (RI)
Comm Coll of Vermont (VT)
Copiah-Lincoln Comm Coll (MS)
Corning Comm Coll (NY)
Cossatot Comm Coll of the U of Arkansas (AR)
County Coll of Morris (NJ)
Cowley County Comm Coll and Area Vocational–Tech School (KS)
Crowder Coll (MO)
Cuyahoga Comm Coll (OH)
Dabney S. Lancaster Comm Coll (VA)
Dakota Coll at Bottineau (ND)
De Anza Coll (CA)
Deep Springs Coll (CA)
Dutchess Comm Coll (NY)
Dyersburg State Comm Coll (TN)
Eastern Shore Comm Coll (VA)
Edison Comm Coll (OH)
Elaine P. Nunez Comm Coll (LA)
Elgin Comm Coll (IL)
Erie Comm Coll (NY)
Erie Comm Coll, North Campus (NY)
Erie Comm Coll, South Campus (NY)
Essex County Coll (NJ)
Fayetteville Tech Comm Coll (NC)
Finger Lakes Comm Coll (NY)
Fiorello H. LaGuardia Comm Coll of the City U of New York (NY)
Flathead Valley Comm Coll (MT)
Florida Gateway Coll (FL)
Foothill Coll (CA)
Forsyth Tech Comm Coll (NC)
Gadsden State Comm Coll (AL)
Garden City Comm Coll (KS)
Garrett Coll (MD)
Genesee Comm Coll (NY)
Georgia Highlands Coll (GA)
Goodwin Coll (CT)
Gordon State Coll (GA)
Grand Rapids Comm Coll (MI)
Greenfield Comm Coll (MA)
Guilford Tech Comm Coll (NC)
Hagerstown Comm Coll (MD)
Halifax Comm Coll (NC)
Harford Comm Coll (MD)
Harper Coll (IL)
Hawkeye Comm Coll (IA)
Highland Comm Coll (IL)
Hillsborough Comm Coll (FL)
Holyoke Comm Coll (MA)
Housatonic Comm Coll (CT)
Howard Comm Coll (MD)
Hutchinson Comm Coll and Area Vocational School (KS)
Illinois Central Coll (IL)
Illinois Eastern Comm Colls, Frontier Community College (IL)
Illinois Eastern Comm Colls, Lincoln Trail College (IL)
Illinois Eastern Comm Colls, Olney Central College (IL)
Illinois Eastern Comm Colls, Wabash Valley College (IL)
Ivy Tech Comm Coll–Bloomington (IN)
Ivy Tech Comm Coll–Central Indiana (IN)
Ivy Tech Comm Coll–Columbus (IN)
Ivy Tech Comm Coll–East Central (IN)
Ivy Tech Comm Coll–Kokomo (IN)
Ivy Tech Comm Coll–Lafayette (IN)
Ivy Tech Comm Coll–North Central (IN)
Ivy Tech Comm Coll–Northeast (IN)
Ivy Tech Comm Coll–Northwest (IN)
Ivy Tech Comm Coll–Richmond (IN)
Ivy Tech Comm Coll–Southeast (IN)
Ivy Tech Comm Coll–Southern Indiana (IN)
Ivy Tech Comm Coll–Southwest (IN)
Ivy Tech Comm Coll–Wabash Valley (IN)
Jackson Coll (MI)
Jackson State Comm Coll (TN)
James Sprunt Comm Coll (NC)
Jamestown Comm Coll (NY)
Jefferson Coll (MO)
Jefferson Comm Coll (NY)
Jefferson State Comm Coll (AL)
Johnston Comm Coll (NC)
John Tyler Comm Coll (VA)
Kaskaskia Coll (IL)
Kennebec Valley Comm Coll (ME)
Kent State U at Salem (OH)
Kent State U at Trumbull (OH)
Kent State U at Tuscarawas (OH)
Kilian Comm Coll (SD)
Kirtland Comm Coll (MI)
Klamath Comm Coll (OR)
Lakeland Comm Coll (OH)
Lake Michigan Coll (MI)
Lake Region State Coll (ND)
Lake Superior Coll (MN)
Lansing Comm Coll (MI)
Lawson State Comm Coll (AL)
LDS Business Coll (UT)
Lehigh Carbon Comm Coll (PA)
Lincoln Land Comm Coll (IL)
Lone Star Coll–North Harris (TX)
Lorain County Comm Coll (OH)
Lower Columbia Coll (WA)
Lurleen B. Wallace Comm Coll (AL)
Luzerne County Comm Coll (PA)
Macomb Comm Coll (MI)
Manchester Comm Coll (CT)
Manor Coll (PA)
Massachusetts Bay Comm Coll (MA)
McHenry County Coll (IL)
Mendocino Coll (CA)
Mesa Comm Coll (AZ)
Metropolitan Comm Coll–Kansas City (MO)
Middlesex Comm Coll (MA)
Mid-Plains Comm Coll, North Platte (NE)
Miles Comm Coll (MT)
Mineral Area Coll (MO)
Minnesota West Comm and Tech Coll (MN)
Mohave Comm Coll (AZ)
Mohawk Valley Comm Coll (NY)
Monroe Comm Coll (NY)
Monroe County Comm Coll (MI)
Montcalm Comm Coll (MI)
Montgomery Coll (MD)
Montgomery Comm Coll (NC)
Montgomery County Comm Coll (PA)
Moraine Valley Comm Coll (IL)
Motlow State Comm Coll (TN)
Mott Comm Coll (MI)
Nassau Comm Coll (NY)
Niagara County Comm Coll (NY)
Normandale Comm Coll (MN)
Northampton Comm Coll (PA)
North Dakota State Coll of Science (ND)
Northeastern Jr Coll (CO)
Northeast Iowa Comm Coll (IA)
Northern Essex Comm Coll (MA)
North Hennepin Comm Coll (MN)
North Shore Comm Coll (MA)
NorthWest Arkansas Comm Coll (AR)
Northwest Coll (WY)
Northwest-Shoals Comm Coll (AL)
Northwest State Comm Coll (OH)
Norwalk Comm Coll (CT)
Oakland Comm Coll (MI)
Oakton Comm Coll (IL)
Ocean County Coll (NJ)
Oklahoma City Comm Coll (OK)
Orange Coast Coll (CA)
Oregon Coast Comm Coll (OR)
Owensboro Comm and Tech Coll (KY)
Ozarka Coll (AR)
Ozarks Tech Comm Coll (MO)
Paris Jr Coll (TX)
Parkland Coll (IL)
Pasadena City Coll (CA)
Pasco-Hernando Comm Coll (FL)
Paul D. Camp Comm Coll (VA)
Penn State Beaver (PA)
Penn State Brandywine (PA)
Penn State DuBois (PA)
Penn State Fayette, The Eberly Campus (PA)
Penn State Greater Allegheny (PA)
Penn State Hazleton (PA)
Penn State Lehigh Valley (PA)
Penn State Mont Alto (PA)
Penn State New Kensington (PA)
Penn State Schuylkill (PA)
Penn State Wilkes-Barre (PA)
Penn State Worthington Scranton (PA)
Penn State York (PA)
Pensacola State Coll (FL)
Phoenix Coll (AZ)
Piedmont Comm Coll (NC)
Piedmont Virginia Comm Coll (VA)
Pierce Coll at Puyallup (WA)
Potomac State Coll of West Virginia U (WV)
Quinsigamond Comm Coll (MA)
Randolph Comm Coll (NC)
Rappahannock Comm Coll (VA)
Raritan Valley Comm Coll (NJ)
Red Rocks Comm Coll (CO)
Rogue Comm Coll (OR)
St. Clair County Comm Coll (MI)
St. Louis Comm Coll at Meramec (MO)
St. Philip's Coll (TX)
San Diego City Coll (CA)
San Diego Mesa Coll (CA)
San Juan Coll (NM)
Santa Rosa Jr Coll (CA)
Schoolcraft Coll (MI)
Seminole State Coll of Florida (FL)
Shawnee Comm Coll (IL)
Shelton State Comm Coll (AL)
Sierra Coll (CA)
Southeastern Comm Coll (IA)
Southern State Comm Coll (OH)
South Plains Coll (TX)
South Puget Sound Comm Coll (WA)
South Suburban Coll (IL)
Southwestern Michigan Coll (MI)
Southwest Virginia Comm Coll (VA)
Spartanburg Comm Coll (SC)
Spoon River Coll (IL)
Springfield Tech Comm Coll (MA)
State U of New York Coll of Technology at Alfred (NY)
Sullivan County Comm Coll (NY)
Taft Coll (CA)
Tallahassee Comm Coll (FL)
Tarrant County Coll District (TX)
Tech Coll of the Lowcountry (SC)
Temple Coll (TX)
Terra State Comm Coll (OH)
Texarkana Coll (TX)
Thomas Nelson Comm Coll (VA)
Tompkins Cortland Comm Coll (NY)
Tri-County Comm Coll (NC)
Trident Tech Coll (SC)
Tunxis Comm Coll (CT)
Tyler Jr Coll (TX)
Union County Coll (NJ)
The U of Akron–Wayne Coll (OH)
U of Alaska Anchorage, Kenai Peninsula Coll (AK)
U of Arkansas Comm Coll at Morrilton (AR)
U of Pittsburgh at Titusville (PA)
U of South Carolina Union (SC)
U of Wisconsin–Fox Valley (WI)
U of Wisconsin–Richland (WI)
U of Wisconsin–Waukesha (WI)
Victor Valley Coll (CA)
Vincennes U (IN)
Virginia Western Comm Coll (VA)
Volunteer State Comm Coll (TN)
Waubonsee Comm Coll (IL)
Westchester Comm Coll (NY)
Western Iowa Tech Comm Coll (IA)
Westmoreland County Comm Coll (PA)
West Virginia Northern Comm Coll (WV)
Wilson Comm Coll (NC)
Wytheville Comm Coll (VA)

LIBRARY AND ARCHIVES ASSISTING
Coll of the Canyons (CA)
Illinois Central Coll (IL)
Ivy Tech Comm Coll–Bloomington (IN)
Ivy Tech Comm Coll–Columbus (IN)
Ivy Tech Comm Coll–East Central (IN)
Ivy Tech Comm Coll–Kokomo (IN)
Ivy Tech Comm Coll–Lafayette (IN)
Ivy Tech Comm Coll–North Central (IN)
Ivy Tech Comm Coll–Northeast (IN)
Ivy Tech Comm Coll–Northwest (IN)
Ivy Tech Comm Coll–Richmond (IN)
Ivy Tech Comm Coll–Southeast (IN)
Ivy Tech Comm Coll–Southern Indiana (IN)
Ivy Tech Comm Coll–Southwest (IN)
Ivy Tech Comm Coll–Wabash Valley (IN)
Oakland Comm Coll (MI)
Waubonsee Comm Coll (IL)
Western Dakota Tech Inst (SD)

LIBRARY AND INFORMATION SCIENCE
Copiah-Lincoln Comm Coll (MS)
Grand Rapids Comm Coll (MI)
Mesa Comm Coll (AZ)
Westmoreland County Comm Coll (PA)

LIBRARY SCIENCE RELATED
Pasadena City Coll (CA)

LICENSED PRACTICAL/ VOCATIONAL NURSE TRAINING
Alexandria Tech and Comm Coll (MN)
Alpena Comm Coll (MI)
Amarillo Coll (TX)
Bainbridge Coll (GA)
Barton County Comm Coll (KS)
Big Bend Comm Coll (WA)
Bismarck State Coll (ND)
Butte Coll (CA)
Carrington Coll California–San Jose (CA)
Carrington Coll of California–Antioch (CA)
Carrington Coll of California–Sacramento (CA)
Central Maine Comm Coll (ME)
Central Oregon Comm Coll (OR)
Clark State Comm Coll (OH)
Colby Comm Coll (KS)
Coll of Southern Maryland (MD)
Coll of the Desert (CA)
Comm Coll of Allegheny County (PA)
Comm Coll of Rhode Island (RI)
Dakota Coll at Bottineau (ND)
De Anza Coll (CA)
Delaware Tech & Comm Coll, Jack F. Owens Campus (DE)
Eastern Idaho Tech Coll (ID)
El Centro Coll (TX)
Fiorello H. LaGuardia Comm Coll of the City U of New York (NY)
Flathead Valley Comm Coll (MT)
Grand Rapids Comm Coll (MI)
Great Falls Coll Montana State U (MT)
Harford Comm Coll (MD)
Howard Comm Coll (MD)
Ivy Tech Comm Coll–Southeast (IN)
Jackson Coll (MI)
Jefferson Coll (MO)
J. F. Drake State Tech Coll (AL)
Kirtland Comm Coll (MI)
Lake Area Tech Inst (SD)
Lansing Comm Coll (MI)
Lone Star Coll–Kingwood (TX)
Mid-Plains Comm Coll, North Platte (NE)
North Dakota State Coll of Science (ND)
Northeastern Jr Coll (CO)

Northwest Tech Coll (MN)
Pasadena City Coll (CA)
San Diego City Coll (CA)
San Jacinto Coll District (TX)
Santa Rosa Jr Coll (CA)
Schoolcraft Coll (MI)
Sierra Coll (CA)
Southeastern Comm Coll (IA)
Southeast Tech Inst (SD)
South Plains Coll (TX)
South Puget Sound Comm Coll (WA)
Temple Coll (TX)
Texarkana Coll (TX)
Tyler Jr Coll (TX)
Union County Coll (NJ)
Westmoreland County Comm Coll (PA)

LINEWORKER
Bismarck State Coll (ND)
Coll of Southern Maryland (MD)
Harrisburg Area Comm Coll (PA)
Ivy Tech Comm Coll–Lafayette (IN)
Kennebec Valley Comm Coll (ME)
Minnesota West Comm and Tech Coll (MN)
Mitchell Tech Inst (SD)
Raritan Valley Comm Coll (NJ)

LITERATURE
Oklahoma City Comm Coll (OK)

LITERATURE RELATED
Cayuga County Comm Coll (NY)

LIVESTOCK MANAGEMENT
Barton County Comm Coll (KS)
Miles Comm Coll (MT)
The Ohio State U Ag Tech Inst (OH)

LOGISTICS, MATERIALS, AND SUPPLY CHAIN MANAGEMENT
Ancilla Coll (IN)
Arizona Western Coll (AZ)
Barton County Comm Coll (KS)
Cecil Coll (MD)
Cochise Coll, Sierra Vista (AZ)
Comm Coll of the Air Force (AL)
Edison Comm Coll (OH)
Forsyth Tech Comm Coll (NC)
Fox Valley Tech Coll (WI)
Georgia Military Coll (GA)
Guilford Tech Comm Coll (NC)
Houston Comm Coll System (TX)
Lone Star Coll–CyFair (TX)
Northwest State Comm Coll (OH)
Randolph Comm Coll (NC)

MACHINE SHOP TECHNOLOGY
Cape Fear Comm Coll (NC)
Chemeketa Comm Coll (OR)
Coll of Lake County (IL)
Comm Coll of Allegheny County (PA)
Daytona State Coll (FL)
Fayetteville Tech Comm Coll (NC)
Forsyth Tech Comm Coll (NC)
Guilford Tech Comm Coll (NC)
Ivy Tech Comm Coll–Central Indiana (IN)
Johnston Comm Coll (NC)
Metropolitan Comm Coll–Kansas City (MO)
Orange Coast Coll (CA)
Pasadena City Coll (CA)
Randolph Comm Coll (NC)
Red Rocks Comm Coll (CO)
San Juan Coll (NM)
West Kentucky Comm and Tech Coll (KY)

MACHINE TOOL TECHNOLOGY
Alamance Comm Coll (NC)
Alexandria Tech and Comm Coll (MN)
Amarillo Coll (TX)
Bakersfield Coll (CA)
Casper Coll (WY)
Central Maine Comm Coll (ME)
Clark Coll (WA)
Coll of Marin (CA)
Comm Coll of Beaver County (PA)
Corning Comm Coll (NY)
Cowley County Comm Coll and Area Vocational–Tech School (KS)
De Anza Coll (CA)
Elgin Comm Coll (IL)
Hawkeye Comm Coll (IA)
Hutchinson Comm Coll and Area Vocational School (KS)
Illinois Eastern Comm Colls, Wabash Valley College (IL)

Ivy Tech Comm Coll–Bloomington (IN)
Ivy Tech Comm Coll–Central Indiana (IN)
Ivy Tech Comm Coll–Columbus (IN)
Ivy Tech Comm Coll–East Central (IN)
Ivy Tech Comm Coll–Kokomo (IN)
Ivy Tech Comm Coll–Lafayette (IN)
Ivy Tech Comm Coll–North Central (IN)
Ivy Tech Comm Coll–Northeast (IN)
Ivy Tech Comm Coll–Northwest (IN)
Ivy Tech Comm Coll–Richmond (IN)
Ivy Tech Comm Coll–Southern Indiana (IN)
Ivy Tech Comm Coll–Southwest (IN)
Ivy Tech Comm Coll–Wabash Valley (IN)
Jefferson Coll (MO)
J. F. Drake State Tech Coll (AL)
Johnston Comm Coll (NC)
Kennebec Valley Comm Coll (ME)
Lake Area Tech Inst (SD)
Lake Michigan Coll (MI)
Lake Superior Coll (MN)
Lansing Comm Coll (MI)
Lorain County Comm Coll (OH)
Lower Columbia Coll (WA)
Macomb Comm Coll (MI)
Mineral Area Coll (MO)
Moraine Park Tech Coll (WI)
Mt. San Antonio Coll (CA)
North Dakota State Coll of Science (ND)
Northern Essex Comm Coll (MA)
Northwest State Comm Coll (OH)
Oakland Comm Coll (MI)
Orange Coast Coll (CA)
Ozarks Tech Comm Coll (MO)
San Diego City Coll (CA)
Shelton State Comm Coll (AL)
Sheridan Coll (WY)
Southeastern Comm Coll (IA)
Southern Maine Comm Coll (ME)
South Plains Coll (TX)
Southwestern Michigan Coll (MI)
Spartanburg Comm Coll (SC)
State U of New York Coll of Technology at Alfred (NY)
Tarrant County Coll District (TX)
Trident Tech Coll (SC)
Westmoreland County Comm Coll (PA)
Wytheville Comm Coll (VA)

MAGNETIC RESONANCE IMAGING (MRI) TECHNOLOGY
Lake Michigan Coll (MI)
Lansing Comm Coll (MI)

MANAGEMENT INFORMATION SYSTEMS
Anne Arundel Comm Coll (MD)
Burlington County Coll (NJ)
Carl Albert State Coll (OK)
Carroll Comm Coll (MD)
Cecil Coll (MD)
Central Oregon Comm Coll (OR)
Comm Coll of Allegheny County (PA)
The Comm Coll of Baltimore County (MD)
Comm Coll of the Air Force (AL)
Cossatot Comm Coll of the U of Arkansas (AR)
County Coll of Morris (NJ)
Delaware Tech & Comm Coll, Jack F. Owens Campus (DE)
Delaware Tech & Comm Coll, Stanton/Wilmington Campus (DE)
Delaware Tech & Comm Coll, Terry Campus (DE)
Garrett Coll (MD)
Hagerstown Comm Coll (MD)
Hillsborough Comm Coll (FL)
Jackson State Comm Coll (TN)
John Tyler Comm Coll (VA)
Kennebec Valley Comm Coll (ME)
Kilgore Coll (TX)
Kirtland Comm Coll (MI)
Lakeland Comm Coll (OH)
Lake Region State Coll (ND)
Lake Superior Coll (MN)
Lansing Comm Coll (MI)
Lone Star Coll–North Harris (TX)
Manchester Comm Coll (CT)
Miami Dade Coll (FL)
Moraine Valley Comm Coll (IL)
Nassau Comm Coll (NY)
Normandale Comm Coll (MN)
North Hennepin Comm Coll (MN)
Oakland Comm Coll (MI)

Oklahoma City Comm Coll (OK)
Ozarks Tech Comm Coll (MO)
Pensacola State Coll (FL)
Raritan Valley Comm Coll (NJ)
Red Rocks Comm Coll (CO)
San Jacinto Coll District (TX)
Tallahassee Comm Coll (FL)
Union County Coll (NJ)
U of Pittsburgh at Titusville (PA)
Victor Valley Coll (CA)
York County Comm Coll (ME)

MANAGEMENT INFORMATION SYSTEMS AND SERVICES RELATED
Anne Arundel Comm Coll (MD)
Bowling Green State U–Firelands Coll (OH)
Harrisburg Area Comm Coll (PA)
Hillsborough Comm Coll (FL)
Missouri State U–West Plains (MO)
Mohawk Valley Comm Coll (NY)
Montgomery Coll (MD)
Montgomery County Comm Coll (PA)
Pensacola State Coll (FL)
Rasmussen Coll Aurora (IL)
Rasmussen Coll Bismarck (ND)
Rasmussen Coll Bloomington (MN)
Rasmussen Coll Brooklyn Park (MN)
Rasmussen Coll Eagan (MN)
Rasmussen Coll Fargo (ND)
Rasmussen Coll Fort Myers (FL)
Rasmussen Coll Green Bay (WI)
Rasmussen Coll Lake Elmo/Woodbury (MN)
Rasmussen Coll Mankato (MN)
Rasmussen Coll Moorhead (MN)
Rasmussen Coll New Port Richey (FL)
Rasmussen Coll Ocala (FL)
Rasmussen Coll Rockford (IL)
Rasmussen Coll St. Cloud (MN)

MANAGEMENT SCIENCE
Career Tech Coll (LA)
Delaware Tech & Comm Coll, Stanton/Wilmington Campus (DE)
Lone Star Coll–CyFair (TX)
Pensacola State Coll (FL)

MANUFACTURING ENGINEERING
Central Wyoming Coll (WY)
Lake Michigan Coll (MI)
Penn State Fayette, The Eberly Campus (PA)
Penn State Greater Allegheny (PA)
Penn State Hazleton (PA)
Penn State Wilkes-Barre (PA)
Penn State York (PA)

MANUFACTURING ENGINEERING TECHNOLOGY
Alexandria Tech and Comm Coll (MN)
Alpena Comm Coll (MI)
Bowling Green State U–Firelands Coll (OH)
Casper Coll (WY)
Central New Mexico Comm Coll (NM)
Central Oregon Comm Coll (OR)
Clark Coll (WA)
Coll of the Canyons (CA)
Corning Comm Coll (NY)
Delaware Tech & Comm Coll, Stanton/Wilmington Campus (DE)
Essex County Coll (NJ)
Fox Valley Tech Coll (WI)
Gadsden State Comm Coll (AL)
Garden City Comm Coll (KS)
Gateway Comm and Tech Coll (KY)
Hawkeye Comm Coll (IA)
Houston Comm Coll System (TX)
Hutchinson Comm Coll and Area Vocational School (KS)
Illinois Central Coll (IL)
Illinois Eastern Comm Colls, Wabash Valley College (IL)
Jefferson Coll (MO)
Lake Area Tech Inst (SD)
Lehigh Carbon Comm Coll (PA)
Macomb Comm Coll (MI)
Minnesota West Comm and Tech Coll (MN)
Mott Comm Coll (MI)
Normandale Comm Coll (MN)
North Dakota State Coll of Science (ND)
Northwest Tech Coll (MN)
Oakland Comm Coll (MI)
Oakton Comm Coll (IL)
Oklahoma City Comm Coll (OK)

Owens Comm Coll, Toledo (OH)
Pensacola State Coll (FL)
Quinsigamond Comm Coll (MA)
Raritan Valley Comm Coll (NJ)
Red Rocks Comm Coll (CO)
Rogue Comm Coll (OR)
Schoolcraft Coll (MI)
Sierra Coll (CA)
Sullivan Coll of Technology and Design (KY)
Terra State Comm Coll (OH)
Union County Coll (NJ)
Vincennes U (IN)
Westmoreland County Comm Coll (PA)

MARINE BIOLOGY AND BIOLOGICAL OCEANOGRAPHY
Oregon Coast Comm Coll (OR)
Southern Maine Comm Coll (ME)

MARINE MAINTENANCE AND SHIP REPAIR TECHNOLOGY
Alexandria Tech and Comm Coll (MN)
Cape Fear Comm Coll (NC)
Orange Coast Coll (CA)

MARINE SCIENCE/MERCHANT MARINE OFFICER
San Jacinto Coll District (TX)

MARKETING/MARKETING MANAGEMENT
Adirondack Comm Coll (NY)
Alexandria Tech and Comm Coll (MN)
Alvin Comm Coll (TX)
Arizona Western Coll (AZ)
Austin Comm Coll (TX)
Bainbridge Coll (GA)
Bakersfield Coll (CA)
Barton County Comm Coll (KS)
Blackhawk Tech Coll (WI)
Brookhaven Coll (TX)
Casper Coll (WY)
Cecil Coll (MD)
Central Carolina Comm Coll (NC)
Central Oregon Comm Coll (OR)
Century Coll (MN)
Chippewa Valley Tech Coll (WI)
Cleveland Comm Coll (NC)
Comm Coll of Allegheny County (PA)
Comm Coll of Beaver County (PA)
Comm Coll of Rhode Island (RI)
Cowley County Comm Coll and Area Vocational–Tech School (KS)
Cuyahoga Comm Coll (OH)
Dakota Coll at Bottineau (ND)
De Anza Coll (CA)
Delaware Tech & Comm Coll, Jack F. Owens Campus (DE)
Delaware Tech & Comm Coll, Stanton/Wilmington Campus (DE)
Delaware Tech & Comm Coll, Terry Campus (DE)
Eastern Idaho Tech Coll (ID)
Edison Comm Coll (OH)
Elgin Comm Coll (IL)
Fayetteville Tech Comm Coll (NC)
FIDM/The Fashion Inst of Design & Merchandising, Orange County Campus (CA)
Finger Lakes Comm Coll (NY)
Fox Valley Tech Coll (WI)
Gateway Tech Coll (WI)
Genesee Comm Coll (NY)
Georgia Highlands Coll (GA)
Glendale Comm Coll (AZ)
Harford Comm Coll (MD)
Harper Coll (IL)
Houston Comm Coll System (TX)
Jackson Coll (MI)
James A. Rhodes State Coll (OH)
Kennebec Valley Comm Coll (ME)
Lake Area Tech Inst (SD)
Lakeland Comm Coll (OH)
Lake Michigan Coll (MI)
Lone Star Coll–CyFair (TX)
Lone Star Coll–Kingwood (TX)
Lone Star Coll–Montgomery (TX)
Lone Star Coll–North Harris (TX)
Lone Star Coll–Tomball (TX)
Lorain County Comm Coll (OH)
Macomb Comm Coll (MI)
Manchester Comm Coll (CT)
Manor Coll (PA)
Mesa Comm Coll (AZ)
Metropolitan Comm Coll–Kansas City (MO)
Miami Dade Coll (FL)
Monroe Comm Coll (NY)

Monroe County Comm Coll (MI)
Moraine Park Tech Coll (WI)
Mott Comm Coll (MI)
Mt. San Antonio Coll (CA)
Nassau Comm Coll (NY)
Normandale Comm Coll (MN)
Northampton Comm Coll (PA)
Northeastern Jr Coll (CO)
Northern Essex Comm Coll (MA)
North Hennepin Comm Coll (MN)
North Shore Comm Coll (MA)
Northwest State Comm Coll (OH)
Norwalk Comm Coll (CT)
Oakton Comm Coll (IL)
Orange Coast Coll (CA)
Oxnard Coll (CA)
Pasadena City Coll (CA)
Pasco-Hernando Comm Coll (FL)
Phoenix Coll (AZ)
Piedmont Virginia Comm Coll (VA)
Pierce Coll at Puyallup (WA)
Raritan Valley Comm Coll (NJ)
Rasmussen Coll Bismarck (ND)
Rasmussen Coll Bloomington (MN)
Rasmussen Coll Brooklyn Park (MN)
Rasmussen Coll Eagan (MN)
Rasmussen Coll Fargo (ND)
Rasmussen Coll Fort Myers (FL)
Rasmussen Coll Green Bay (WI)
Rasmussen Coll Lake Elmo/Woodbury (MN)
Rasmussen Coll Mankato (MN)
Rasmussen Coll Moorhead (MN)
Rasmussen Coll New Port Richey (FL)
Rasmussen Coll Ocala (FL)
Rasmussen Coll St. Cloud (MN)
Rogue Comm Coll (OR)
St. Clair County Comm Coll (MI)
Salt Lake Comm Coll (UT)
San Diego City Coll (CA)
San Diego Mesa Coll (CA)
Schoolcraft Coll (MI)
Seminole State Coll of Florida (FL)
Southeast Tech Inst (SD)
South Plains Coll (TX)
Spartanburg Comm Coll (SC)
Springfield Tech Comm Coll (MA)
Stark State Coll (OH)
State U of New York Coll of Technology at Alfred (NY)
Sullivan County Comm Coll (NY)
Tallahassee Comm Coll (FL)
Tarrant County Coll District (TX)
Terra State Comm Coll (OH)
Texarkana Coll (TX)
Trident Tech Coll (SC)
Tunxis Comm Coll (CT)
Union County Coll (NJ)
Vincennes U (IN)
Waukesha County Tech Coll (WI)
Westchester Comm Coll (NY)

MARKETING RELATED
Dakota Coll at Bottineau (ND)
Gateway Tech Coll (WI)

MARKETING RESEARCH
San Diego Mesa Coll (CA)

MASONRY
Comm Coll of Beaver County (PA)
Ivy Tech Comm Coll–Central Indiana (IN)
Ivy Tech Comm Coll–Columbus (IN)
Ivy Tech Comm Coll–East Central (IN)
Ivy Tech Comm Coll–Lafayette (IN)
Ivy Tech Comm Coll–North Central (IN)
Ivy Tech Comm Coll–Northeast (IN)
Ivy Tech Comm Coll–Northwest (IN)
Ivy Tech Comm Coll–Southern Indiana (IN)
Ivy Tech Comm Coll–Southwest (IN)
Ivy Tech Comm Coll–Wabash Valley (IN)
Metropolitan Comm Coll–Kansas City (MO)
State U of New York Coll of Technology at Alfred (NY)

MASSAGE THERAPY
Arizona Western Coll (AZ)
Career Tech Coll (LA)
Career Training Academy, Pittsburgh (PA)
Carrington Coll–Boise (ID)
Carrington Coll California–Pleasant Hill (CA)
Carrington Coll California–San Jose (CA)

Carrington Coll California–San Leandro (CA)
Carrington Coll of California–Antioch (CA)
Carrington Coll of California–Sacramento (CA)
Carrington Coll–Phoenix (AZ)
Central Oregon Comm Coll (OR)
Coll of Southern Maryland (MD)
The Comm Coll of Baltimore County (MD)
Comm Coll of Rhode Island (RI)
Forsyth Tech Comm Coll (NC)
Greenfield Comm Coll (MA)
Ivy Tech Comm Coll–Northeast (IN)
Kennebec Valley Comm Coll (ME)
McCann School of Business & Technology, Pottsville (PA)
Niagara County Comm Coll (NY)
Oakland Comm Coll (MI)
Owens Comm Coll, Toledo (OH)
Phoenix Coll (AZ)
St. Clair County Comm Coll (MI)
Schoolcraft Coll (MI)
Sheridan Coll (WY)
Spencerian Coll (KY)
Springfield Tech Comm Coll (MA)
Vincennes U (IN)
Waubonsee Comm Coll (IL)

MASS COMMUNICATION/ MEDIA
Amarillo Coll (TX)
Ancilla Coll (IN)
Arizona Western Coll (AZ)
Casper Coll (WY)
Chipola Coll (FL)
Coll of Marin (CA)
Coll of the Desert (CA)
Crowder Coll (MO)
De Anza Coll (CA)
Finger Lakes Comm Coll (NY)
Genesee Comm Coll (NY)
Georgia Military Coll (GA)
Grand Rapids Comm Coll (MI)
Harford Comm Coll (MD)
Harrisburg Area Comm Coll (PA)
Laramie County Comm Coll (WY)
Lorain County Comm Coll (OH)
Miami Dade Coll (FL)
Monroe Comm Coll (NY)
Monroe County Comm Coll (MI)
Nassau Comm Coll (NY)
Niagara County Comm Coll (NY)
Oklahoma City Comm Coll (OK)
Orange Coast Coll (CA)
Parkland Coll (IL)
Salt Lake Comm Coll (UT)
South Plains Coll (TX)
Spoon River Coll (IL)
Union County Coll (NJ)
Westchester Comm Coll (NY)
Wytheville Comm Coll (VA)

MATERIALS ENGINEERING
Comm Coll of Beaver County (PA)
Southern Maine Comm Coll (ME)

MATERIALS SCIENCE
Mt. San Antonio Coll (CA)
Northern Essex Comm Coll (MA)

MATHEMATICS
Alpena Comm Coll (MI)
Alvin Comm Coll (TX)
Amarillo Coll (TX)
Anne Arundel Comm Coll (MD)
Arizona Western Coll (AZ)
Austin Comm Coll (TX)
Bainbridge Coll (GA)
Bakersfield Coll (CA)
Barton County Comm Coll (KS)
Borough of Manhattan Comm Coll of the City U of New York (NY)
Bucks County Comm Coll (PA)
Burlington County Coll (NJ)
Butte Coll (CA)
Carl Albert State Coll (OK)
Casper Coll (WY)
Cecil Coll (MD)
Central Oregon Comm Coll (OR)
Central Wyoming Coll (WY)
Cochise Coll, Sierra Vista (AZ)
Coll of Marin (CA)
Coll of the Canyons (CA)
Coll of the Desert (CA)
Comm Coll of Allegheny County (PA)
Comm Coll of Beaver County (PA)
Corning Comm Coll (NY)
Crowder Coll (MO)

Dakota Coll at Bottineau (ND)
Darton State Coll (GA)
De Anza Coll (CA)
Essex County Coll (NJ)
Finger Lakes Comm Coll (NY)
Foothill Coll (CA)
Garden City Comm Coll (KS)
Genesee Comm Coll (NY)
Gordon State Coll (GA)
Harford Comm Coll (MD)
Harper Coll (IL)
Harrisburg Area Comm Coll (PA)
Housatonic Comm Coll (CT)
Hutchinson Comm Coll and Area Vocational School (KS)
Jefferson Comm Coll (NY)
Kankakee Comm Coll (IL)
Kilgore Coll (TX)
Lake Michigan Coll (MI)
Lansing Comm Coll (MI)
Laramie County Comm Coll (WY)
Lehigh Carbon Comm Coll (PA)
Lone Star Coll–CyFair (TX)
Lone Star Coll–Kingwood (TX)
Lone Star Coll–Montgomery (TX)
Lone Star Coll–North Harris (TX)
Lone Star Coll–Tomball (TX)
Lorain County Comm Coll (OH)
Luzerne County Comm Coll (PA)
Macomb Comm Coll (MI)
Mendocino Coll (CA)
Mesa Comm Coll (AZ)
Miami Dade Coll (FL)
Mohave Comm Coll (AZ)
Monroe Comm Coll (NY)
Monroe County Comm Coll (MI)
Montgomery County Comm Coll (PA)
Mt. San Antonio Coll (CA)
Nassau Comm Coll (NY)
Niagara County Comm Coll (NY)
Northampton Comm Coll (PA)
Northeastern Jr Coll (CO)
North Hennepin Comm Coll (MN)
Northwest Coll (WY)
Oklahoma City Comm Coll (OK)
Orange Coast Coll (CA)
Oxnard Coll (CA)
Paris Jr Coll (TX)
Pasadena City Coll (CA)
Pensacola State Coll (FL)
Potomac State Coll of West Virginia U (WV)
St. Philip's Coll (TX)
San Diego City Coll (CA)
San Diego Mesa Coll (CA)
San Jacinto Coll District (TX)
San Juan Coll (NM)
Santa Rosa Jr Coll (CA)
Scottsdale Comm Coll (AZ)
Sheridan Coll (WY)
Sierra Coll (CA)
Spoon River Coll (IL)
Springfield Tech Comm Coll (MA)
Sullivan County Comm Coll (NY)
Taft Coll (CA)
Terra State Comm Coll (OH)
Texarkana Coll (TX)
Texas State Tech Coll Harlingen (TX)
Tyler Jr Coll (TX)
Union County Coll (NJ)
Victor Valley Coll (CA)
Vincennes U (IN)

MATHEMATICS AND COMPUTER SCIENCE
Crowder Coll (MO)

MATHEMATICS AND STATISTICS RELATED
Georgia Highlands Coll (GA)

MATHEMATICS RELATED
Cayuga County Comm Coll (NY)
Corning Comm Coll (NY)

MATHEMATICS TEACHER EDUCATION
Anne Arundel Comm Coll (MD)
Bucks County Comm Coll (PA)
Carroll Comm Coll (MD)
The Comm Coll of Baltimore County (MD)
Darton State Coll (GA)
Delaware Tech & Comm Coll, Jack F. Owens Campus (DE)
Delaware Tech & Comm Coll, Stanton/Wilmington Campus (DE)
Delaware Tech & Comm Coll, Terry Campus (DE)
Harford Comm Coll (MD)

Highland Comm Coll (IL)
Kankakee Comm Coll (IL)
Kaskaskia Coll (IL)
Montgomery Coll (MD)
Moraine Valley Comm Coll (IL)
Vincennes U (IN)

MECHANICAL DRAFTING AND CAD/CADD
Alexandria Tech and Comm Coll (MN)
Blackhawk Tech Coll (WI)
Chemeketa Comm Coll (OR)
Cleveland Comm Coll (NC)
Comm Coll of Allegheny County (PA)
Corning Comm Coll (NY)
Delaware Tech & Comm Coll, Jack F. Owens Campus (DE)
Edison Comm Coll (OH)
Fox Valley Tech Coll (WI)
Gateway Tech Coll (WI)
Hutchinson Comm Coll and Area Vocational School (KS)
Lake Superior Coll (MN)
Lansing Comm Coll (MI)
Macomb Comm Coll (MI)
Montgomery County Comm Coll (PA)
Moraine Park Tech Coll (WI)
Oakland Comm Coll (MI)
Ozarks Tech Comm Coll (MO)
St. Clair County Comm Coll (MI)
Sierra Coll (CA)
Spartanburg Comm Coll (SC)
State U of New York Coll of Technology at Alfred (NY)
Sullivan Coll of Technology and Design (KY)
Vincennes U (IN)
Waukesha County Tech Coll (WI)
Western Iowa Tech Comm Coll (IA)
Westmoreland County Comm Coll (PA)

MECHANICAL ENGINEERING
Cayuga County Comm Coll (NY)
Fiorello H. LaGuardia Comm Coll of the City U of New York (NY)
Kilgore Coll (TX)
Northwest State Comm Coll (OH)
Pasadena City Coll (CA)

MECHANICAL ENGINEERING/ MECHANICAL TECHNOLOGY
Alamance Comm Coll (NC)
Beaufort County Comm Coll (NC)
Bowling Green State U–Firelands Coll (OH)
Cape Fear Comm Coll (NC)
Catawba Valley Comm Coll (NC)
Cayuga County Comm Coll (NY)
Clark State Comm Coll (OH)
Coll of Lake County (IL)
Corning Comm Coll (NY)
County Coll of Morris (NJ)
Delaware Tech & Comm Coll, Stanton/Wilmington Campus (DE)
Edison Comm Coll (OH)
Erie Comm Coll, North Campus (NY)
Finger Lakes Comm Coll (NY)
Forsyth Tech Comm Coll (NC)
Guilford Tech Comm Coll (NC)
Hagerstown Comm Coll (MD)
Harrisburg Area Comm Coll (PA)
Illinois Central Coll (IL)
Illinois Eastern Comm Colls, Lincoln Trail College (IL)
James A. Rhodes State Coll (OH)
Jamestown Comm Coll (NY)
John Tyler Comm Coll (VA)
Kent State U at Trumbull (OH)
Kent State U at Tuscarawas (OH)
Lakeland Comm Coll (OH)
Lehigh Carbon Comm Coll (PA)
Macomb Comm Coll (MI)
Massachusetts Bay Comm Coll (MA)
Mohawk Valley Comm Coll (NY)
Monroe Comm Coll (NY)
Montgomery County Comm Coll (PA)
Moraine Valley Comm Coll (IL)
Mott Comm Coll (MI)
Northwest State Comm Coll (OH)
Oakton Comm Coll (IL)
Onondaga Comm Coll (NY)
Penn State DuBois (PA)
Penn State Hazleton (PA)
Penn State New Kensington (PA)
Penn State York (PA)
Potomac State Coll of West Virginia U (WV)
Schoolcraft Coll (MI)

Southeastern Comm Coll (IA)
Southeast Tech Inst (SD)
Spartanburg Comm Coll (SC)
Springfield Tech Comm Coll (MA)
Stark State Coll (OH)
State U of New York Coll of Technology at Alfred (NY)
Sullivan Coll of Technology and Design (KY)
Tarrant County Coll District (TX)
Terra State Comm Coll (OH)
Trident Tech Coll (SC)
Union County Coll (NJ)
Vincennes U (IN)
Virginia Western Comm Coll (VA)
Westchester Comm Coll (NY)
Westmoreland County Comm Coll (PA)
Wilson Comm Coll (NC)
Wytheville Comm Coll (VA)

MECHANICAL ENGINEERING TECHNOLOGIES RELATED
Comm Coll of Beaver County (PA)
Corning Comm Coll (NY)
Jefferson Comm Coll (NY)
John Tyler Comm Coll (VA)
Mohawk Valley Comm Coll (NY)
Moraine Park Tech Coll (WI)
Terra State Comm Coll (OH)
Thomas Nelson Comm Coll (VA)

MECHANIC AND REPAIR TECHNOLOGIES RELATED
Corning Comm Coll (NY)
Ivy Tech Comm Coll–Bloomington (IN)
Ivy Tech Comm Coll–Columbus (IN)
Ivy Tech Comm Coll–Kokomo (IN)
Ivy Tech Comm Coll–Lafayette (IN)
Ivy Tech Comm Coll–North Central (IN)
Ivy Tech Comm Coll–Northwest (IN)
Ivy Tech Comm Coll–Southwest (IN)
Laramie County Comm Coll (WY)
Macomb Comm Coll (MI)

MECHANICS AND REPAIR
Corning Comm Coll (NY)
Ivy Tech Comm Coll–Bloomington (IN)
Ivy Tech Comm Coll–Central Indiana (IN)
Ivy Tech Comm Coll–Columbus (IN)
Ivy Tech Comm Coll–Kokomo (IN)
Ivy Tech Comm Coll–Lafayette (IN)
Ivy Tech Comm Coll–North Central (IN)
Ivy Tech Comm Coll–Northeast (IN)
Ivy Tech Comm Coll–Northwest (IN)
Ivy Tech Comm Coll–Richmond (IN)
Ivy Tech Comm Coll–Southern Indiana (IN)
Ivy Tech Comm Coll–Southwest (IN)
Ivy Tech Comm Coll–Wabash Valley (IN)
Oakland Comm Coll (MI)
Rogue Comm Coll (OR)

MECHATRONICS, ROBOTICS, AND AUTOMATION ENGINEERING
Harrisburg Area Comm Coll (PA)
Westmoreland County Comm Coll (PA)

MEDICAL ADMINISTRATIVE ASSISTANT AND MEDICAL SECRETARY
Alamance Comm Coll (NC)
Alexandria Tech and Comm Coll (MN)
Alvin Comm Coll (TX)
Amarillo Coll (TX)
Anne Arundel Comm Coll (MD)
Barton County Comm Coll (KS)
Berkeley City Coll (CA)
Bismarck State Coll (ND)
Blackhawk Tech Coll (WI)
Butte Coll (CA)
Carrington Coll–Spokane (WA)
Central Carolina Comm Coll (NC)
Century Coll (MN)
Chemeketa Comm Coll (OR)
Clark Coll (WA)
Clark State Comm Coll (OH)
Coll of Marin (CA)
Comm Coll of Allegheny County (PA)
The Comm Coll of Baltimore County (MD)

Comm Coll of Beaver County (PA)
Comm Coll of Philadelphia (PA)
Comm Coll of Rhode Island (RI)
Crowder Coll (MO)
Dabney S. Lancaster Comm Coll (VA)
Dakota Coll at Bottineau (ND)
Daytona State Coll (FL)
Edison Comm Coll (OH)
Flathead Valley Comm Coll (MT)
Goodwin Coll (CT)
Grand Rapids Comm Coll (MI)
Halifax Comm Coll (NC)
Hallmark Coll of Technology (TX)
Harper Coll (IL)
Hawkeye Comm Coll (IA)
Howard Comm Coll (MD)
Illinois Eastern Comm Colls, Olney Central College (IL)
Jefferson Coll (MO)
Jefferson Comm Coll (NY)
Johnston Comm Coll (NC)
Kennebec Valley Comm Coll (ME)
Kirtland Comm Coll (MI)
Lake Michigan Coll (MI)
Lake Superior Coll (MN)
LDS Business Coll (UT)
Lower Columbia Coll (WA)
Luzerne County Comm Coll (PA)
Manchester Comm Coll (CT)
McCann School of Business & Technology, Pottsville (PA)
Mesa Comm Coll (AZ)
Metropolitan Comm Coll–Kansas City (MO)
Miles Comm Coll (MT)
Minnesota West Comm and Tech Coll (MN)
Monroe County Comm Coll (MI)
Montcalm Comm Coll (MI)
Mt. San Antonio Coll (CA)
Nassau Comm Coll (NY)
Northampton Comm Coll (PA)
Northeastern Jr Coll (CO)
Northern Essex Comm Coll (MA)
North Shore Comm Coll (MA)
Northwest State Comm Coll (OH)
Northwest Tech Coll (MN)
Orange Coast Coll (CA)
Owens Comm Coll, Toledo (OH)
Piedmont Comm Coll (NC)
Potomac State Coll of West Virginia U (WV)
Quinsigamond Comm Coll (MA)
Rasmussen Coll Aurora (IL)
Rasmussen Coll Bismarck (ND)
Rasmussen Coll Bloomington (MN)
Rasmussen Coll Brooklyn Park (MN)
Rasmussen Coll Eagan (MN)
Rasmussen Coll Fargo (ND)
Rasmussen Coll Fort Myers (FL)
Rasmussen Coll Green Bay (WI)
Rasmussen Coll Lake Elmo/ Woodbury (MN)
Rasmussen Coll Mankato (MN)
Rasmussen Coll Moorhead (MN)
Rasmussen Coll New Port Richey (FL)
Rasmussen Coll Ocala (FL)
Rasmussen Coll Rockford (IL)
Rasmussen Coll St. Cloud (MN)
St. Clair County Comm Coll (MI)
St. Philip's Coll (TX)
San Jacinto Coll District (TX)
Scottsdale Comm Coll (AZ)
Shawnee Comm Coll (IL)
Shelton State Comm Coll (AL)
South Plains Coll (TX)
South Puget Sound Comm Coll (WA)
Spoon River Coll (IL)
Springfield Tech Comm Coll (MA)
Terra State Comm Coll (OH)
Trident Tech Coll (SC)
Tunxis Comm Coll (CT)
Tyler Jr Coll (TX)
Western Iowa Tech Comm Coll (IA)
West Virginia Jr Coll–Bridgeport (WV)
Wytheville Comm Coll (VA)

MEDICAL/CLINICAL ASSISTANT
Alamance Comm Coll (NC)
Barton County Comm Coll (KS)
Bay State Coll (MA)
Big Bend Comm Coll (WA)
Bossier Parish Comm Coll (LA)
Bradford School (OH)
Bradford School (PA)
Bucks County Comm Coll (PA)

Career Tech Coll (LA)
Career Training Academy, Pittsburgh (PA)
Carrington Coll–Boise (ID)
Carrington Coll California–Pleasant Hill (CA)
Carrington Coll California–San Jose (CA)
Carrington Coll California–San Leandro (CA)
Carrington Coll of California–Antioch (CA)
Carrington Coll of California–Citrus Heights (CA)
Carrington Coll of California–Sacramento (CA)
Central Carolina Comm Coll (NC)
Central Maine Comm Coll (ME)
Central Oregon Comm Coll (OR)
Clark Coll (WA)
Cleveland Comm Coll (NC)
Coll of Marin (CA)
Comm Coll of Allegheny County (PA)
Cossatot Comm Coll of the U of Arkansas (AR)
Dakota Coll at Bottineau (ND)
De Anza Coll (CA)
Delaware Tech & Comm Coll, Jack F. Owens Campus (DE)
Delaware Tech & Comm Coll, Stanton/Wilmington Campus (DE)
Delaware Tech & Comm Coll, Terry Campus (DE)
Eastern Idaho Tech Coll (ID)
Edison Comm Coll (OH)
El Centro Coll (TX)
Elmira Business Inst (NY)
Flathead Valley Comm Coll (MT)
Forrest Coll (SC)
Forsyth Tech Comm Coll (NC)
Fox Coll (IL)
Goodwin Coll (CT)
Great Falls Coll Montana State U (MT)
Guilford Tech Comm Coll (NC)
Hallmark Coll of Technology (TX)
Harford Comm Coll (MD)
Harper Coll (IL)
Harrisburg Area Comm Coll (PA)
Highland Comm Coll (IL)
International Business Coll, Indianapolis (IN)
Ivy Tech Comm Coll–Central Indiana (IN)
Ivy Tech Comm Coll–Columbus (IN)
Ivy Tech Comm Coll–East Central (IN)
Ivy Tech Comm Coll–Kokomo (IN)
Ivy Tech Comm Coll–Lafayette (IN)
Ivy Tech Comm Coll–North Central (IN)
Ivy Tech Comm Coll–Northeast (IN)
Ivy Tech Comm Coll–Northwest (IN)
Ivy Tech Comm Coll–Richmond (IN)
Ivy Tech Comm Coll–Southeast (IN)
Ivy Tech Comm Coll–Southern Indiana (IN)
Ivy Tech Comm Coll–Southwest (IN)
Ivy Tech Comm Coll–Wabash Valley (IN)
Jackson Coll (MI)
James A. Rhodes State Coll (OH)
James Sprunt Comm Coll (NC)
Jamestown Business Coll (NY)
J. F. Drake State Tech Coll (AL)
Johnston Comm Coll (NC)
Kankakee Comm Coll (IL)
Kennebec Valley Comm Coll (ME)
King's Coll (NC)
Lake Area Tech Inst (SD)
LDS Business Coll (UT)
Lehigh Carbon Comm Coll (PA)
Lower Columbia Coll (WA)
Macomb Comm Coll (MI)
McCann School of Business & Technology, Pottsville (PA)
Miami Dade Coll (FL)
Middlesex Comm Coll (MA)
Minneapolis Business Coll (MN)
Minnesota West Comm and Tech Coll (MN)
Mitchell Tech Inst (SD)
Mohave Comm Coll (AZ)
Mohawk Valley Comm Coll (NY)
Montgomery Comm Coll (NC)
Montgomery County Comm Coll (PA)
Niagara County Comm Coll (NY)
Northwest-Shoals Comm Coll (AL)
Northwest State Comm Coll (OH)
Oakland Comm Coll (MI)
Oklahoma City Comm Coll (OK)

Olympic Coll (WA)
Orange Coast Coll (CA)
Panola Coll (TX)
Pasadena City Coll (CA)
Phoenix Coll (AZ)
Randolph Comm Coll (NC)
Raritan Valley Comm Coll (NJ)
Rasmussen Coll Aurora (IL)
Rasmussen Coll Bismarck (ND)
Rasmussen Coll Bloomington (MN)
Rasmussen Coll Brooklyn Park (MN)
Rasmussen Coll Eagan (MN)
Rasmussen Coll Fort Myers (FL)
Rasmussen Coll Green Bay (WI)
Rasmussen Coll Lake Elmo/Woodbury (MN)
Rasmussen Coll Mankato (MN)
Rasmussen Coll Moorhead (MN)
Rasmussen Coll New Port Richey (FL)
Rasmussen Coll Ocala (FL)
Rasmussen Coll Rockford (IL)
Rasmussen Coll St. Cloud (MN)
St. Clair County Comm Coll (MI)
Salt Lake Comm Coll (UT)
San Diego Mesa Coll (CA)
Santa Rosa Jr Coll (CA)
Southeastern Comm Coll (IA)
Southern Maine Comm Coll (ME)
Southern State Comm Coll (OH)
South Puget Sound Comm Coll (WA)
Southwestern Michigan Coll (MI)
Springfield Tech Comm Coll (MA)
Stark State Coll (OH)
Sullivan County Comm Coll (NY)
Terra State Comm Coll (OH)
Texas State Tech Coll Harlingen (TX)
Tri-County Comm Coll (NC)
Western Dakota Tech Inst (SD)
Westmoreland County Comm Coll (PA)
West Virginia Jr Coll–Bridgeport (WV)
West Virginia Northern Comm Coll (WV)
Wood Tobe–Coburn School (NY)
York County Comm Coll (ME)

MEDICAL/HEALTH MANAGEMENT AND CLINICAL ASSISTANT
CollAmerica–Flagstaff (AZ)
Owens Comm Coll, Toledo (OH)
Pittsburgh Tech Inst, Oakdale (PA)
Terra State Comm Coll (OH)

MEDICAL INFORMATICS
The Comm Coll of Baltimore County (MD)
Mott Comm Coll (MI)

MEDICAL INSURANCE CODING
Barton County Comm Coll (KS)
Berkshire Comm Coll (MA)
Bucks County Comm Coll (PA)
Career Training Academy, Pittsburgh (PA)
Cowley County Comm Coll and Area Vocational–Tech School (KS)
Dakota Coll at Bottineau (ND)
Elmira Business Inst (NY)
Flathead Valley Comm Coll (MT)
Fountainhead Coll of Technology (TN)
Goodwin Coll (CT)
Hallmark Coll of Technology (TX)
Laramie County Comm Coll (WY)
Minnesota West Comm and Tech Coll (MN)
North Dakota State Coll of Science (ND)
Paris Jr Coll (TX)
Spencerian Coll (KY)
Springfield Tech Comm Coll (MA)
Terra State Comm Coll (OH)
Westmoreland County Comm Coll (PA)
West Virginia Jr Coll–Bridgeport (WV)

MEDICAL INSURANCE/MEDICAL BILLING
Carrington Coll–Boise (ID)
Carrington Coll California–Pleasant Hill (CA)
Carrington Coll California–San Jose (CA)
Carrington Coll California–San Leandro (CA)
Carrington Coll of California–Antioch (CA)

Carrington Coll of California–Citrus Heights (CA)
Carrington Coll of California–Sacramento (CA)
Goodwin Coll (CT)
Great Falls Coll Montana State U (MT)
Jackson Coll (MI)
Pasadena City Coll (CA)
Schoolcraft Coll (MI)
Spencerian Coll (KY)

MEDICAL OFFICE ASSISTANT
Alpena Comm Coll (MI)
Barton County Comm Coll (KS)
Central Wyoming Coll (WY)
Dakota Coll at Bottineau (ND)
Harford Comm Coll (MD)
Kankakee Comm Coll (IL)
LDS Business Coll (UT)
Lincoln Land Comm Coll (IL)
Mitchell Tech Inst (SD)
New York Career Inst (NY)
Pasadena City Coll (CA)
Phoenix Coll (AZ)
Pittsburgh Tech Inst, Oakdale (PA)
Schoolcraft Coll (MI)
Terra State Comm Coll (OH)
Westmoreland County Comm Coll (PA)

MEDICAL OFFICE COMPUTER SPECIALIST
Normandale Comm Coll (MN)
Rogue Comm Coll (OR)

MEDICAL OFFICE MANAGEMENT
Arapahoe Comm Coll (CO)
Bay State Coll (MA)
Beaufort County Comm Coll (NC)
Big Bend Comm Coll (WA)
Cape Fear Comm Coll (NC)
Career Tech Coll (LA)
Carrington Coll–Albuquerque (NM)
Carrington Coll–Boise (ID)
Carrington Coll California–San Jose (CA)
Carrington Coll–Mesa (AZ)
Carrington Coll of California–Antioch (CA)
Carrington Coll of California–Sacramento (CA)
Carrington Coll–Phoenix (AZ)
Carrington Coll–Spokane (WA)
Carrington Coll–Tucson (AZ)
Catawba Valley Comm Coll (NC)
Chemeketa Comm Coll (OR)
Cleveland Comm Coll (NC)
Coll of Lake County (IL)
Elaine P. Nunez Comm Coll (LA)
Erie Comm Coll, North Campus (NY)
Fayetteville Tech Comm Coll (NC)
Forrest Coll (SC)
Forsyth Tech Comm Coll (NC)
Fox Valley Tech Coll (WI)
Guilford Tech Comm Coll (NC)
Johnston Comm Coll (NC)
Kilian Comm Coll (SD)
Long Island Business Inst (NY)
Norwalk Comm Coll (CT)
Randolph Comm Coll (NC)
Red Rocks Comm Coll (CO)
The U of Akron–Wayne Coll (OH)
Western Iowa Tech Comm Coll (IA)
Wilson Comm Coll (NC)

MEDICAL RADIOLOGIC TECHNOLOGY
Anne Arundel Comm Coll (MD)
Blackhawk Tech Coll (WI)
Bowling Green State U-Firelands Coll (OH)
Burlington County Coll (NJ)
Cape Fear Comm Coll (NC)
Carolinas Coll of Health Sciences (NC)
Carrington Coll–Phoenix Westside (AZ)
Carrington Coll–Portland (OR)
Carrington Coll–Spokane (WA)
Catawba Valley Comm Coll (NC)
Central New Mexico Comm Coll (NM)
Chippewa Valley Tech Coll (WI)
Coll of Lake County (IL)
Comm Coll of Allegheny County (PA)
The Comm Coll of Baltimore County (MD)
Comm Coll of Beaver County (PA)
Comm Coll of Philadelphia (PA)
Comm Coll of the Air Force (AL)

Dunwoody Coll of Technology (MN)
El Centro Coll (TX)
Erie Comm Coll (NY)
Essex County Coll (NJ)
Fiorello H. LaGuardia Comm Coll of the City U of New York (NY)
Flathead Valley Comm Coll (MT)
Foothill Coll (CA)
Forsyth Tech Comm Coll (NC)
Gateway Tech Coll (WI)
Hagerstown Comm Coll (MD)
Hillsborough Comm Coll (FL)
Holyoke Comm Coll (MA)
Hutchinson Comm Coll and Area Vocational School (KS)
Illinois Eastern Comm Colls, Olney Central College (IL)
Ivy Tech Comm Coll–Central Indiana (IN)
Ivy Tech Comm Coll–Columbus (IN)
Ivy Tech Comm Coll–East Central (IN)
Ivy Tech Comm Coll–Wabash Valley (IN)
Jackson Coll (MI)
Jackson State Comm Coll (TN)
James A. Rhodes State Coll (OH)
Johnston Comm Coll (NC)
Kent State U at Ashtabula (OH)
Kent State U at Salem (OH)
Kilgore Coll (TX)
Lakeland Comm Coll (OH)
Lake Michigan Coll (MI)
Lancaster General Coll of Nursing & Health Sciences (PA)
Lone Star Coll–CyFair (TX)
Lone Star Coll–Kingwood (TX)
Lone Star Coll–Montgomery (TX)
Massachusetts Bay Comm Coll (MA)
Middlesex Comm Coll (MA)
Mitchell Tech Inst (SD)
Mohawk Valley Comm Coll (NY)
Montgomery Coll (MD)
Montgomery County Comm Coll (PA)
Moraine Park Tech Coll (WI)
Mott Comm Coll (MI)
Nassau Comm Coll (NY)
Niagara County Comm Coll (NY)
North Shore Comm Coll (MA)
Oakland Comm Coll (MI)
Owensboro Comm and Tech Coll (KY)
Owens Comm Coll, Toledo (OH)
Parkland Coll (IL)
Penn State New Kensington (PA)
Penn State Schuylkill (PA)
Pensacola State Coll (FL)
St. Philip's Coll (TX)
Salt Lake Comm Coll (UT)
Southern Maine Comm Coll (ME)
Spartanburg Comm Coll (SC)
Tech Coll of the Lowcountry (SC)
Union County Coll (NJ)
Vincennes U (IN)
Volunteer State Comm Coll (TN)
Waukesha County Tech Coll (WI)
West Virginia Northern Comm Coll (WV)

MEDICAL TRANSCRIPTION
Barton County Comm Coll (KS)
Chemeketa Comm Coll (OR)
Collin County Comm Coll District (TX)
Cowley County Comm Coll and Area Vocational–Tech School (KS)
Dakota Coll at Bottineau (ND)
El Centro Coll (TX)
Great Falls Coll Montana State U (MT)
Jackson Coll (MI)
Northern Essex Comm Coll (MA)
Oakland Comm Coll (MI)
Schoolcraft Coll (MI)
Western Dakota Tech Inst (SD)
Westmoreland County Comm Coll (PA)

MEDICATION AIDE
Barton County Comm Coll (KS)

MEDIUM/HEAVY VEHICLE AND TRUCK TECHNOLOGY
Edison Comm Coll (OH)

MEETING AND EVENT PLANNING
Raritan Valley Comm Coll (NJ)
Southwestern Michigan Coll (MI)

MENTAL AND SOCIAL HEALTH SERVICES AND ALLIED PROFESSIONS RELATED
Coll of Southern Maryland (MD)
Gateway Tech Coll (WI)
John Tyler Comm Coll (VA)
Kennebec Valley Comm Coll (ME)
Montgomery Comm Coll (NC)
Southern Maine Comm Coll (ME)
Southwest Virginia Comm Coll (VA)
Thomas Nelson Comm Coll (VA)
Waukesha County Tech Coll (WI)
Wisconsin Indianhead Tech Coll (WI)

MENTAL HEALTH COUNSELING
Alvin Comm Coll (TX)
Comm Coll of Philadelphia (PA)
Comm Coll of Rhode Island (RI)
Comm Coll of the Air Force (AL)
Housatonic Comm Coll (CT)
Illinois Central Coll (IL)
Macomb Comm Coll (MI)
Mt. San Antonio Coll (CA)
Northern Essex Comm Coll (MA)
North Shore Comm Coll (MA)
Pierce Coll at Puyallup (WA)
San Jacinto Coll District (TX)
South Plains Coll (TX)
Tarrant County Coll District (TX)
Virginia Western Comm Coll (VA)

MERCHANDISING
Cuyahoga Comm Coll (OH)

MERCHANDISING, SALES, AND MARKETING OPERATIONS RELATED (GENERAL)
Lake Region State Coll (ND)
Northwest State Comm Coll (OH)
Southeast Tech Inst (SD)
State U of New York Coll of Technology at Alfred (NY)

MERCHANDISING, SALES, AND MARKETING OPERATIONS RELATED (SPECIALIZED)
Bay State Coll (MA)

METAL AND JEWELRY ARTS
Fashion Inst of Technology (NY)
FIDM/The Fashion Inst of Design & Merchandising, Los Angeles Campus (CA)
Flathead Valley Comm Coll (MT)
Paris Jr Coll (TX)

METALLURGICAL TECHNOLOGY
Comm Coll of the Air Force (AL)
Kilgore Coll (TX)
Macomb Comm Coll (MI)
Penn State DuBois (PA)
Penn State Fayette, The Eberly Campus (PA)
Penn State Hazleton (PA)
Penn State New Kensington (PA)
Penn State Schuylkill (PA)
Penn State Wilkes-Barre (PA)
Penn State York (PA)
Schoolcraft Coll (MI)

MIDDLE SCHOOL EDUCATION
Arkansas State U–Mountain Home (AR)
Austin Comm Coll (TX)
Collin County Comm Coll District (TX)
Cossatot Comm Coll of the U of Arkansas (AR)
Darton State Coll (GA)
Delaware Tech & Comm Coll, Jack F. Owens Campus (DE)
Delaware Tech & Comm Coll, Stanton/Wilmington Campus (DE)
Delaware Tech & Comm Coll, Terry Campus (DE)
Erie Comm Coll (NY)
Gordon State Coll (GA)
Miami Dade Coll (FL)
Northampton Comm Coll (PA)
Ozarka Coll (AR)
Panola Coll (TX)
San Jacinto Coll District (TX)

MILITARY STUDIES
Barton County Comm Coll (KS)

MINING TECHNOLOGY
Casper Coll (WY)

Illinois Eastern Comm Colls, Wabash
   Valley College (IL)
Sheridan Coll (WY)

MODERN LANGUAGES
Amarillo Coll (TX)
Barton County Comm Coll (KS)
San Diego City Coll (CA)
Tyler Jr Coll (TX)

**MOTORCYCLE MAINTENANCE
AND REPAIR TECHNOLOGY**
Red Rocks Comm Coll (CO)
Western Iowa Tech Comm Coll (IA)

**MOVEMENT AND MIND-BODY
THERAPIES AND EDUCATION
RELATED**
Moraine Valley Comm Coll (IL)

**MULTI/INTERDISCIPLINARY
STUDIES RELATED**
Alexandria Tech and Comm Coll
   (MN)
Anoka-Ramsey Comm Coll (MN)
Anoka-Ramsey Comm Coll,
   Cambridge Campus (MN)
Bucks County Comm Coll (PA)
Carroll Comm Coll (MD)
Central Maine Comm Coll (ME)
Century Coll (MN)
Chippewa Valley Tech Coll (WI)
Coll of Southern Maryland (MD)
Coll of the Desert (CA)
Cossatot Comm Coll of the U of
   Arkansas (AR)
County Coll of Morris (NJ)
Fox Valley Tech Coll (WI)
Gateway Tech Coll (WI)
Harford Comm Coll (MD)
Hawkeye Comm Coll (IA)
James A. Rhodes State Coll (OH)
J. F. Drake State Tech Coll (AL)
Kilgore Coll (TX)
Lake Superior Coll (MN)
Moraine Park Tech Coll (WI)
Normandale Comm Coll (MN)
North Dakota State Coll of Science
   (ND)
North Hennepin Comm Coll (MN)
Northwest-Shoals Comm Coll (AL)
Oklahoma City Comm Coll (OK)
Raritan Valley Comm Coll (NJ)
San Jacinto Coll District (TX)
Sheridan Coll (WY)
Spartanburg Comm Coll (SC)
Waukesha County Tech Coll (WI)
Western Iowa Tech Comm Coll (IA)
West Virginia Northern Comm Coll
   (WV)
Wisconsin Indianhead Tech Coll (WI)
York County Comm Coll (ME)

MUSEUM STUDIES
Casper Coll (WY)

MUSIC
Adirondack Comm Coll (NY)
Alvin Comm Coll (TX)
Amarillo Coll (TX)
Anoka-Ramsey Comm Coll (MN)
Anoka-Ramsey Comm Coll,
   Cambridge Campus (MN)
Arizona Western Coll (AZ)
Austin Comm Coll (TX)
Bakersfield Coll (CA)
Barton County Comm Coll (KS)
Bossier Parish Comm Coll (LA)
Brookhaven Coll (TX)
Bucks County Comm Coll (PA)
Burlington County Coll (NJ)
Carroll Comm Coll (MD)
Casper Coll (WY)
Central Wyoming Coll (WY)
Century Coll (MN)
Cochise Coll, Sierra Vista (AZ)
Coll of Lake County (IL)
Coll of Marin (CA)
Coll of the Canyons (CA)
Coll of the Desert (CA)
Collin County Comm Coll District
   (TX)
Comm Coll of Allegheny County (PA)
Comm Coll of Beaver County (PA)
Comm Coll of Philadelphia (PA)
Comm Coll of Rhode Island (RI)
County Coll of Morris (NJ)
Cowley County Comm Coll and Area
   Vocational–Tech School (KS)
Crowder Coll (MO)
Darton State Coll (GA)

De Anza Coll (CA)
Elgin Comm Coll (IL)
Essex County Coll (NJ)
Finger Lakes Comm Coll (NY)
Foothill Coll (CA)
Gordon State Coll (GA)
Grand Rapids Comm Coll (MI)
Harford Comm Coll (MD)
Harper Coll (IL)
Holyoke Comm Coll (MA)
Howard Comm Coll (MD)
Jamestown Comm Coll (NY)
Kaskaskia Coll (IL)
Kilgore Coll (TX)
Lake Michigan Coll (MI)
Lansing Comm Coll (MI)
Laramie County Comm Coll (WY)
Lincoln Land Comm Coll (IL)
Lone Star Coll–CyFair (TX)
Lone Star Coll–Kingwood (TX)
Lone Star Coll–Montgomery (TX)
Lone Star Coll–North Harris (TX)
Lone Star Coll–Tomball (TX)
Lorain County Comm Coll (OH)
Manchester Comm Coll (CT)
McHenry County Coll (IL)
Mendocino Coll (CA)
Mesa Comm Coll (AZ)
Miami Dade Coll (FL)
Monroe Comm Coll (NY)
Mt. San Antonio Coll (CA)
Niagara County Comm Coll (NY)
Normandale Comm Coll (MN)
Northeastern Jr Coll (CO)
Northern Essex Comm Coll (MA)
North Hennepin Comm Coll (MN)
Northwest Coll (WY)
Oakton Comm Coll (IL)
Oklahoma City Comm Coll (OK)
Onondaga Comm Coll (NY)
Orange Coast Coll (CA)
Pensacola State Coll (FL)
Raritan Valley Comm Coll (NJ)
St. Philip's Coll (TX)
Salt Lake Comm Coll (UT)
San Diego City Coll (CA)
San Diego Mesa Coll (CA)
San Jacinto Coll District (TX)
Sheridan Coll (WY)
Sierra Coll (CA)
South Plains Coll (TX)
Terra State Comm Coll (OH)
Texarkana Coll (TX)
Victor Valley Coll (CA)
Vincennes U (IN)
Waubonsee Comm Coll (IL)

**MUSICAL INSTRUMENT
FABRICATION AND REPAIR**
Orange Coast Coll (CA)
Western Iowa Tech Comm Coll (IA)

MUSICAL THEATER
Casper Coll (WY)

MUSIC MANAGEMENT
Austin Comm Coll (TX)
Collin County Comm Coll District
   (TX)
Glendale Comm Coll (AZ)
Harrisburg Area Comm Coll (PA)
Houston Comm Coll System (TX)
Orange Coast Coll (CA)
Phoenix Coll (AZ)
Terra State Comm Coll (OH)

MUSIC PERFORMANCE
Adirondack Comm Coll (NY)
Casper Coll (WY)
Comm Coll of the Air Force (AL)
Dyersburg State Comm Coll (TN)
Greenfield Comm Coll (MA)
Houston Comm Coll System (TX)
Lansing Comm Coll (MI)
Macomb Comm Coll (MI)
Miami Dade Coll (FL)
Nassau Comm Coll (NY)
Oakland Comm Coll (MI)
Parkland Coll (IL)
Terra State Comm Coll (OH)

MUSIC RELATED
Carl Albert State Coll (OK)
Cayuga County Comm Coll (NY)
Santa Rosa Jr Coll (CA)
Terra State Comm Coll (OH)

MUSIC TEACHER EDUCATION
Amarillo Coll (TX)
Casper Coll (WY)

Coll of Lake County (IL)
Copiah-Lincoln Comm Coll (MS)
Darton State Coll (GA)
Miami Dade Coll (FL)
Northeastern Jr Coll (CO)
Parkland Coll (IL)
Pensacola State Coll (FL)
Schoolcraft Coll (MI)
Vincennes U (IN)

MUSIC TECHNOLOGY
Foothill Coll (CA)
Owens Comm Coll, Toledo (OH)

**MUSIC THEORY AND
COMPOSITION**
Houston Comm Coll System (TX)
Oakland Comm Coll (MI)

NANOTECHNOLOGY
Chippewa Valley Tech Coll (WI)
Foothill Coll (CA)
Harper Coll (IL)
Lehigh Carbon Comm Coll (PA)
North Dakota State Coll of Science
   (ND)
Oakland Comm Coll (MI)

**NATURAL RESOURCES/
CONSERVATION**
Central Oregon Comm Coll (OR)
Coll of the Desert (CA)
Colorado Northwestern Comm Coll
   (CO)
Dakota Coll at Bottineau (ND)
Finger Lakes Comm Coll (NY)
Florida Gateway Coll (FL)
Fox Valley Tech Coll (WI)
Niagara County Comm Coll (NY)
St. Philip's Coll (TX)
Santa Rosa Jr Coll (CA)
Tompkins Cortland Comm Coll (NY)
Vincennes U (IN)

**NATURAL RESOURCES/
CONSERVATION RELATED**
Greenfield Comm Coll (MA)

**NATURAL RESOURCES
MANAGEMENT AND POLICY**
Butte Coll (CA)
Coll of Lake County (IL)
Finger Lakes Comm Coll (NY)
Hawkeye Comm Coll (IA)
Northwest Coll (WY)
The Ohio State U Ag Tech Inst (OH)
Pensacola State Coll (FL)

**NATURAL RESOURCES
MANAGEMENT AND POLICY
RELATED**
Finger Lakes Comm Coll (NY)
The Ohio State U Ag Tech Inst (OH)

NATURAL SCIENCES
Amarillo Coll (TX)
Foothill Coll (CA)
Miami Dade Coll (FL)
Northeastern Jr Coll (CO)
Orange Coast Coll (CA)
Phoenix Coll (AZ)
Santa Rosa Jr Coll (CA)
U of Pittsburgh at Titusville (PA)
Victor Valley Coll (CA)

**NETWORK AND SYSTEM
ADMINISTRATION**
Big Bend Comm Coll (WA)
Bucks County Comm Coll (PA)
Butte Coll (CA)
Corning Comm Coll (NY)
Dakota Coll at Bottineau (ND)
Genesee Comm Coll (NY)
Houston Comm Coll System (TX)
Kaskaskia Coll (IL)
Lake Superior Coll (MN)
Metropolitan Comm Coll–Kansas
   City (MO)
Mitchell Tech Inst (SD)
Montgomery County Comm Coll (PA)
Northwest State Comm Coll (OH)
Owensboro Comm and Tech Coll
   (KY)
Parkland Coll (IL)
Potomac State Coll of West Virginia
   U (WV)
Seminole State Coll of Florida (FL)
Sierra Coll (CA)
Springfield Tech Comm Coll (MA)
Sullivan Coll of Technology and
   Design (KY)

Tallahassee Comm Coll (FL)
Westmoreland County Comm Coll
   (PA)

NONPROFIT MANAGEMENT
Goodwin Coll (CT)
Miami Dade Coll (FL)
Northwest State Comm Coll (OH)

**NUCLEAR AND INDUSTRIAL
RADIOLOGIC TECHNOLOGIES
RELATED**
Eastern Idaho Tech Coll (ID)

**NUCLEAR ENGINEERING
TECHNOLOGY**
Bismarck State Coll (ND)
Delaware Tech & Comm Coll, Jack F.
   Owens Campus (DE)
Delaware Tech & Comm Coll,
   Stanton/Wilmington Campus (DE)

**NUCLEAR MEDICAL
TECHNOLOGY**
Amarillo Coll (TX)
Central Maine Medical Center Coll of
   Nursing and Health Professions
   (ME)
Comm Coll of Allegheny County (PA)
Comm Coll of the Air Force (AL)
Darton State Coll (GA)
Delaware Tech & Comm Coll,
   Stanton/Wilmington Campus (DE)
Fayetteville Tech Comm Coll (NC)
Forsyth Tech Comm Coll (NC)
Harrisburg Area Comm Coll (PA)
Hillsborough Comm Coll (FL)
Houston Comm Coll System (TX)
Howard Comm Coll (MD)
Lakeland Comm Coll (OH)
Lancaster General Coll of Nursing &
   Health Sciences (PA)
Lorain County Comm Coll (OH)
Miami Dade Coll (FL)
Oakland Comm Coll (MI)
Orange Coast Coll (CA)
Owens Comm Coll, Toledo (OH)
Southeast Tech Inst (SD)
Springfield Tech Comm Coll (MA)
Union County Coll (NJ)
Vincennes U (IN)

**NUCLEAR/NUCLEAR POWER
TECHNOLOGY**
Cape Fear Comm Coll (NC)
Terra State Comm Coll (OH)

NURSING ADMINISTRATION
South Suburban Coll (IL)

**NURSING ASSISTANT/AIDE
AND PATIENT CARE
ASSISTANT/AIDE**
Barton County Comm Coll (KS)
Comm Coll of Allegheny County (PA)
Elaine P. Nunez Comm Coll (LA)
Schoolcraft Coll (MI)

NUTRITION SCIENCES
Casper Coll (WY)
Mohawk Valley Comm Coll (NY)
Santa Rosa Jr Coll (CA)

**OCCUPATIONAL HEALTH AND
INDUSTRIAL HYGIENE**
Niagara County Comm Coll (NY)

**OCCUPATIONAL SAFETY AND
HEALTH TECHNOLOGY**
Anne Arundel Comm Coll (MD)
Central Wyoming Coll (WY)
The Comm Coll of Baltimore County
   (MD)
Comm Coll of the Air Force (AL)
Ivy Tech Comm Coll–Central Indiana
   (IN)
Ivy Tech Comm Coll–Northeast (IN)
Ivy Tech Comm Coll–Northwest (IN)
Ivy Tech Comm Coll–Wabash Valley
   (IN)
Kilgore Coll (TX)
Mt. San Antonio Coll (CA)
NorthWest Arkansas Comm Coll
   (AR)
Oklahoma State U, Oklahoma City
   (OK)
St. Philip's Coll (TX)
San Diego City Coll (CA)
San Jacinto Coll District (TX)
San Juan Coll (NM)

U of Alaska Anchorage, Kenai
   Peninsula Coll (AK)

**OCCUPATIONAL THERAPIST
ASSISTANT**
Austin Comm Coll (TX)
Cape Fear Comm Coll (NC)
Carrington Coll–Phoenix Westside
   (AZ)
Casper Coll (WY)
Comm Coll of Allegheny County (PA)
Comm Coll of Philadelphia (PA)
Comm Coll of Rhode Island (RI)
Darton State Coll (GA)
Daytona State Coll (FL)
Delaware Tech & Comm Coll, Jack F.
   Owens Campus (DE)
Delaware Tech & Comm Coll,
   Stanton/Wilmington Campus (DE)
Erie Comm Coll, North Campus (NY)
Fiorello H. LaGuardia Comm Coll of
   the City U of New York (NY)
Fox Valley Tech Coll (WI)
Goodwin Coll (CT)
Hawkeye Comm Coll (IA)
Houston Comm Coll System (TX)
Illinois Central Coll (IL)
Ivy Tech Comm Coll–Central Indiana
   (IN)
James A. Rhodes State Coll (OH)
Jamestown Comm Coll (NY)
Kaskaskia Coll (IL)
Kennebec Valley Comm Coll (ME)
Kent State U at Ashtabula (OH)
Kent State U at East Liverpool (OH)
Kilgore Coll (TX)
Lake Area Tech Inst (SD)
Lehigh Carbon Comm Coll (PA)
Lincoln Land Comm Coll (IL)
Macomb Comm Coll (MI)
Manchester Comm Coll (CT)
Mott Comm Coll (MI)
North Dakota State Coll of Science
   (ND)
Oakland Comm Coll (MI)
Ocean County Coll (NJ)
Owens Comm Coll, Toledo (OH)
Ozarks Tech Comm Coll (MO)
Panola Coll (TX)
Parkland Coll (IL)
Penn State DuBois (PA)
Penn State Mont Alto (PA)
Quinsigamond Comm Coll (MA)
St. Louis Comm Coll at Meramec
   (MO)
St. Philip's Coll (TX)
Salt Lake Comm Coll (UT)
Shawnee Comm Coll (IL)
South Suburban Coll (IL)
Springfield Tech Comm Coll (MA)
Wisconsin Indianhead Tech Coll (WI)

OCCUPATIONAL THERAPY
Amarillo Coll (TX)
Barton County Comm Coll (KS)
Carrington Coll–Phoenix (AZ)
The Comm Coll of Baltimore County
   (MD)
Lone Star Coll–Kingwood (TX)
Lone Star Coll–Tomball (TX)
Metropolitan Comm Coll–Kansas
   City (MO)
North Shore Comm Coll (MA)
Oklahoma City Comm Coll (OK)
Ozarks Tech Comm Coll (MO)
Quinsigamond Comm Coll (MA)
Stark State Coll (OH)
Trident Tech Coll (SC)

**OCEANOGRAPHY (CHEMICAL
AND PHYSICAL)**
Cape Fear Comm Coll (NC)

OFFICE MANAGEMENT
Alexandria Tech and Comm Coll
   (MN)
Alpena Comm Coll (MI)
Arizona Western Coll (AZ)
Berkeley City Coll (CA)
Brookhaven Coll (TX)
Catawba Valley Comm Coll (NC)
Cecil Coll (MD)
Chemeketa Comm Coll (OR)
Cleveland Comm Coll (NC)
Coll of Marin (CA)
Coll of the Desert (CA)
Comm Coll of Allegheny County (PA)
Comm Coll of the Air Force (AL)
Corning Comm Coll (NY)
Dakota Coll at Bottineau (ND)

Delaware Tech & Comm Coll, Jack F. Owens Campus (DE)
Delaware Tech & Comm Coll, Stanton/Wilmington Campus (DE)
Delaware Tech & Comm Coll, Terry Campus (DE)
Erie Comm Coll, North Campus (NY)
Fayetteville Tech Comm Coll (NC)
Florida Gateway Coll (FL)
Forrest Coll (SC)
Forsyth Tech Comm Coll (NC)
Goodwin Coll (CT)
Guilford Tech Comm Coll (NC)
Halifax Comm Coll (NC)
Howard Comm Coll (MD)
Ivy Tech Comm Coll–Wabash Valley (IN)
Jamestown Business Coll (NY)
Jefferson Comm Coll (NY)
Jefferson State Comm Coll (AL)
Johnston Comm Coll (NC)
Lake Region State Coll (ND)
Lake Superior Coll (MN)
Lansing Comm Coll (MI)
Montgomery Comm Coll (NC)
Moraine Park Tech Coll (WI)
Northwest State Comm Coll (OH)
Oakland Comm Coll (MI)
Owens Comm Coll, Toledo (OH)
Pensacola State Coll (FL)
Piedmont Comm Coll (NC)
Randolph Comm Coll (NC)
St. Clair County Comm Coll (MI)
South Suburban Coll (IL)
Spencerian Coll (KY)
Wilson Comm Coll (NC)

OFFICE OCCUPATIONS AND CLERICAL SERVICES
Alamance Comm Coll (NC)
Blue Ridge Comm and Tech Coll (WV)
Central Wyoming Coll (WY)
Corning Comm Coll (NY)
Dakota Coll at Bottineau (ND)
El Centro Coll (TX)
Gateway Comm and Tech Coll (KY)
ITI Tech Coll (LA)
Jefferson Comm Coll (NY)
Lone Star Coll–CyFair (TX)
Middlesex Comm Coll (MA)
Southeast Tech Inst (SD)

OPERATIONS MANAGEMENT
Alexandria Tech and Comm Coll (MN)
Alpena Comm Coll (MI)
Central Carolina Comm Coll (NC)
Cleveland Comm Coll (NC)
Fayetteville Tech Comm Coll (NC)
Fox Valley Tech Coll (WI)
Gateway Tech Coll (WI)
Hillsborough Comm Coll (FL)
Kilgore Coll (TX)
Macomb Comm Coll (MI)
McHenry County Coll (IL)
Mineral Area Coll (MO)
Oakton Comm Coll (IL)
Owens Comm Coll, Toledo (OH)
Pensacola State Coll (FL)
Stark State Coll (OH)
Terra State Comm Coll (OH)
Waukesha County Tech Coll (WI)
Wisconsin Indianhead Tech Coll (WI)

OPERATIONS RESEARCH
Delaware Tech & Comm Coll, Stanton/Wilmington Campus (DE)

OPHTHALMIC AND OPTOMETRIC SUPPORT SERVICES AND ALLIED PROFESSIONS RELATED
Vincennes U (IN)

OPHTHALMIC LABORATORY TECHNOLOGY
Comm Coll of the Air Force (AL)

OPHTHALMIC TECHNOLOGY
Lakeland Comm Coll (OH)
Miami Dade Coll (FL)
Volunteer State Comm Coll (TN)

OPTICIANRY
Comm Coll of Rhode Island (RI)
Cuyahoga Comm Coll (OH)
Erie Comm Coll, North Campus (NY)
Essex County Coll (NJ)
Hillsborough Comm Coll (FL)
Holyoke Comm Coll (MA)
Raritan Valley Comm Coll (NJ)

OPTOMETRIC TECHNICIAN
Barton County Comm Coll (KS)
Hillsborough Comm Coll (FL)
Raritan Valley Comm Coll (NJ)
San Jacinto Coll District (TX)
Tyler Jr Coll (TX)

ORGANIZATIONAL BEHAVIOR
Phoenix Coll (AZ)

ORGANIZATIONAL LEADERSHIP
Olympic Coll (WA)

ORNAMENTAL HORTICULTURE
Bakersfield Coll (CA)
Coll of Lake County (IL)
Comm Coll of Allegheny County (PA)
Dakota Coll at Bottineau (ND)
Finger Lakes Comm Coll (NY)
Foothill Coll (CA)
Mendocino Coll (CA)
Mesa Comm Coll (AZ)
Miami Dade Coll (FL)
Mt. San Antonio Coll (CA)
Orange Coast Coll (CA)
Pensacola State Coll (FL)
Victor Valley Coll (CA)

ORTHOTICS/PROSTHETICS
Century Coll (MN)
Oklahoma City Comm Coll (OK)

OUTDOOR EDUCATION
Corning Comm Coll (NY)

PAINTING
Luzerne County Comm Coll (PA)

PAINTING AND WALL COVERING
Ivy Tech Comm Coll–Central Indiana (IN)
Ivy Tech Comm Coll–East Central (IN)
Ivy Tech Comm Coll–Lafayette (IN)
Ivy Tech Comm Coll–North Central (IN)
Ivy Tech Comm Coll–Northeast (IN)
Ivy Tech Comm Coll–Northwest (IN)
Ivy Tech Comm Coll–Southwest (IN)
Ivy Tech Comm Coll–Wabash Valley (IN)

PARKS, RECREATION AND LEISURE
Bakersfield Coll (CA)
Central New Mexico Comm Coll (NM)
Central Wyoming Coll (WY)
Coll of the Canyons (CA)
The Comm Coll of Baltimore County (MD)
Comm Coll of the Air Force (AL)
Corning Comm Coll (NY)
Dakota Coll at Bottineau (ND)
Miami Dade Coll (FL)
Monroe Comm Coll (NY)
Mt. San Antonio Coll (CA)
Niagara County Comm Coll (NY)
Northern Essex Comm Coll (MA)
Northwest Coll (WY)
Norwalk Comm Coll (CT)
Onondaga Comm Coll (NY)
Phoenix Coll (AZ)
Red Rocks Comm Coll (CO)
San Diego City Coll (CA)
San Juan Coll (NM)
Sierra Coll (CA)
Taft Coll (CA)
Tallahassee Comm Coll (FL)
Vincennes U (IN)

PARKS, RECREATION AND LEISURE FACILITIES MANAGEMENT
Adirondack Comm Coll (NY)
Arizona Western Coll (AZ)
Bucks County Comm Coll (PA)
Butte Coll (CA)
Central Wyoming Coll (WY)
Coll of the Desert (CA)
Dakota Coll at Bottineau (ND)
Mohawk Valley Comm Coll (NY)
Moraine Valley Comm Coll (IL)
Mt. San Antonio Coll (CA)
Oklahoma City Comm Coll (OK)
Potomac State Coll of West Virginia U (WV)
Santa Rosa Jr Coll (CA)
Tompkins Cortland Comm Coll (NY)

PARKS, RECREATION, LEISURE, AND FITNESS STUDIES RELATED
Anne Arundel Comm Coll (MD)
The Comm Coll of Baltimore County (MD)
Corning Comm Coll (NY)
Dakota Coll at Bottineau (ND)
Tompkins Cortland Comm Coll (NY)

PARTS AND WAREHOUSING OPERATIONS AND MAINTENANCE TECHNOLOGY
Red Rocks Comm Coll (CO)

PEACE STUDIES AND CONFLICT RESOLUTION
El Centro Coll (TX)

PERIOPERATIVE/OPERATING ROOM AND SURGICAL NURSING
Comm Coll of Allegheny County (PA)

PERSONAL AND CULINARY SERVICES RELATED
Mohave Comm Coll (AZ)

PETROLEUM ENGINEERING
Kilgore Coll (TX)

PETROLEUM TECHNOLOGY
Bakersfield Coll (CA)
Panola Coll (TX)
South Plains Coll (TX)
U of Arkansas Comm Coll at Morrilton (AR)

PHARMACY
Barton County Comm Coll (KS)
Lorain County Comm Coll (OH)

PHARMACY TECHNICIAN
Barton County Comm Coll (KS)
Bossier Parish Comm Coll (LA)
Carrington Coll–Boise (ID)
Carrington Coll California–Pleasant Hill (CA)
Carrington Coll California–San Jose (CA)
Carrington Coll California–San Leandro (CA)
Carrington Coll of California–Antioch (CA)
Carrington Coll of California–Citrus Heights (CA)
Carrington Coll of California–Sacramento (CA)
Casper Coll (WY)
Chemeketa Comm Coll (OR)
Comm Coll of Allegheny County (PA)
Comm Coll of the Air Force (AL)
Fayetteville Tech Comm Coll (NC)
Foothill Coll (CA)
Guilford Tech Comm Coll (NC)
Hutchinson Comm Coll and Area Vocational School (KS)
Kirtland Comm Coll (MI)
Lone Star Coll–North Harris (TX)
Lone Star Coll–Tomball (TX)
Mohave Comm Coll (AZ)
North Dakota State Coll of Science (ND)
Oakland Comm Coll (MI)
Rasmussen Coll Aurora (IL)
Rasmussen Coll Bloomington (MN)
Rasmussen Coll Brooklyn Park (MN)
Rasmussen Coll Eagan (MN)
Rasmussen Coll Fort Myers (FL)
Rasmussen Coll Green Bay (WI)
Rasmussen Coll Lake Elmo/Woodbury (MN)
Rasmussen Coll Mankato (MN)
Rasmussen Coll Moorhead (MN)
Rasmussen Coll New Port Richey (FL)
Rasmussen Coll Ocala (FL)
Rasmussen Coll Rockford (IL)
Rasmussen Coll St. Cloud (MN)
Santa Rosa Jr Coll (CA)
Vincennes U (IN)
West Virginia Jr Coll–Bridgeport (WV)

PHILOSOPHY
Arizona Western Coll (AZ)
Austin Comm Coll (TX)
Bakersfield Coll (CA)
Barton County Comm Coll (KS)
Burlington County Coll (NJ)
Cochise Coll, Sierra Vista (AZ)
Coll of the Desert (CA)

Darton State Coll (GA)
De Anza Coll (CA)
Fiorello H. LaGuardia Comm Coll of the City U of New York (NY)
Foothill Coll (CA)
Georgia Highlands Coll (GA)
Harford Comm Coll (MD)
Harper Coll (IL)
Harrisburg Area Comm Coll (PA)
Lake Michigan Coll (MI)
Lansing Comm Coll (MI)
Lone Star Coll–Kingwood (TX)
Lone Star Coll–North Harris (TX)
Lone Star Coll–Tomball (TX)
Miami Dade Coll (FL)
Oklahoma City Comm Coll (OK)
Orange Coast Coll (CA)
Oxnard Coll (CA)
Pensacola State Coll (FL)
St. Philip's Coll (TX)
San Jacinto Coll District (TX)
Santa Rosa Jr Coll (CA)
Sierra Coll (CA)
Vincennes U (IN)

PHLEBOTOMY TECHNOLOGY
Barton County Comm Coll (KS)
Schoolcraft Coll (MI)
Westmoreland County Comm Coll (PA)

PHOTOGRAPHIC AND FILM/VIDEO TECHNOLOGY
Catawba Valley Comm Coll (NC)
Coll of the Canyons (CA)
Daytona State Coll (FL)
Miami Dade Coll (FL)
Oakland Comm Coll (MI)
Oklahoma City Comm Coll (OK)
Pensacola State Coll (FL)
Randolph Comm Coll (NC)
Salt Lake Comm Coll (UT)

PHOTOGRAPHY
Amarillo Coll (TX)
Antonelli Inst (PA)
Bakersfield Coll (CA)
Butte Coll (CA)
Casper Coll (WY)
Cecil Coll (MD)
Coll of the Canyons (CA)
Comm Coll of Philadelphia (PA)
County Coll of Morris (NJ)
Cuyahoga Comm Coll (OH)
De Anza Coll (CA)
Delaware Tech & Comm Coll, Terry Campus (DE)
Foothill Coll (CA)
Harford Comm Coll (MD)
Harrisburg Area Comm Coll (PA)
Howard Comm Coll (MD)
Lansing Comm Coll (MI)
Lone Star Coll–North Harris (TX)
Luzerne County Comm Coll (PA)
Miami Dade Coll (FL)
Mott Comm Coll (MI)
Mt. San Antonio Coll (CA)
Nassau Comm Coll (NY)
Oakland Comm Coll (MI)
Onondaga Comm Coll (NY)
Orange Coast Coll (CA)
Pasadena City Coll (CA)
Red Rocks Comm Coll (CO)
San Diego City Coll (CA)
Scottsdale Comm Coll (AZ)
Sullivan County Comm Coll (NY)
Thomas Nelson Comm Coll (VA)
Tompkins Cortland Comm Coll (NY)
Tyler Jr Coll (TX)

PHOTOJOURNALISM
Pasadena City Coll (CA)
Randolph Comm Coll (NC)
Vincennes U (IN)

PHYSICAL AND BIOLOGICAL ANTHROPOLOGY
Cowley County Comm Coll and Area Vocational–Tech School (KS)

PHYSICAL EDUCATION TEACHING AND COACHING
Alvin Comm Coll (TX)
Amarillo Coll (TX)
Bakersfield Coll (CA)
Barton County Comm Coll (KS)
Bucks County Comm Coll (PA)
Carl Albert State Coll (OK)
Casper Coll (WY)
Clinton Comm Coll (NY)
Copiah-Lincoln Comm Coll (MS)
Crowder Coll (MO)

De Anza Coll (CA)
Dutchess Comm Coll (NY)
Erie Comm Coll (NY)
Erie Comm Coll, North Campus (NY)
Erie Comm Coll, South Campus (NY)
Essex County Coll (NJ)
Finger Lakes Comm Coll (NY)
Foothill Coll (CA)
Genesee Comm Coll (NY)
Harper Coll (IL)
Jamestown Comm Coll (NY)
Kilgore Coll (TX)
Laramie County Comm Coll (WY)
Lone Star Coll–North Harris (TX)
Lorain County Comm Coll (OH)
Luzerne County Comm Coll (PA)
Mendocino Coll (CA)
Miami Dade Coll (FL)
Miles Comm Coll (MT)
Monroe Comm Coll (NY)
Montgomery County Comm Coll (PA)
Niagara County Comm Coll (NY)
Northeastern Jr Coll (CO)
Northern Essex Comm Coll (MA)
North Hennepin Comm Coll (MN)
Orange Coast Coll (CA)
Pensacola State Coll (FL)
Potomac State Coll of West Virginia U (WV)
San Diego City Coll (CA)
San Diego Mesa Coll (CA)
South Plains Coll (TX)
Spoon River Coll (IL)
Taft Coll (CA)
Tyler Jr Coll (TX)
Vincennes U (IN)

PHYSICAL FITNESS TECHNICIAN
Alexandria Tech and Comm Coll (MN)
Lake Region State Coll (ND)

PHYSICAL SCIENCES
Alvin Comm Coll (TX)
Amarillo Coll (TX)
Austin Comm Coll (TX)
Barton County Comm Coll (KS)
Borough of Manhattan Comm Coll of the City U of New York (NY)
Butte Coll (CA)
Carl Albert State Coll (OK)
Central Oregon Comm Coll (OR)
Central Wyoming Coll (WY)
Coll of Marin (CA)
Crowder Coll (MO)
Dakota Coll at Bottineau (ND)
Garden City Comm Coll (KS)
Harper Coll (IL)
Harrisburg Area Comm Coll (PA)
Howard Comm Coll (MD)
Hutchinson Comm Coll and Area Vocational School (KS)
Lake Michigan Coll (MI)
Lehigh Carbon Comm Coll (PA)
Mendocino Coll (CA)
Miami Dade Coll (FL)
Middlesex Comm Coll (MA)
Montgomery County Comm Coll (PA)
Northeastern Jr Coll (CO)
Ozarks Tech Comm Coll (MO)
Phoenix Coll (AZ)
Salt Lake Comm Coll (UT)
San Diego City Coll (CA)
San Diego Mesa Coll (CA)
San Jacinto Coll District (TX)
San Juan Coll (NM)
Spoon River Coll (IL)
Taft Coll (CA)
Victor Valley Coll (CA)
Vincennes U (IN)

PHYSICAL SCIENCES RELATED
Dakota Coll at Bottineau (ND)
Mt. San Antonio Coll (CA)
Schoolcraft Coll (MI)

PHYSICAL SCIENCE TECHNOLOGIES RELATED
Westmoreland County Comm Coll (PA)

PHYSICAL THERAPY
Amarillo Coll (TX)
Barton County Comm Coll (KS)
Blackhawk Tech Coll (WI)
Bossier Parish Comm Coll (LA)
Central Oregon Comm Coll (OR)
Clark State Comm Coll (OH)
Daytona State Coll (FL)
De Anza Coll (CA)
Genesee Comm Coll (NY)

Housatonic Comm Coll (CT)
James A. Rhodes State Coll (OH)
Kilgore Coll (TX)
Metropolitan Comm Coll–Kansas City (MO)
Monroe County Comm Coll (MI)
NorthWest Arkansas Comm Coll (AR)
Oklahoma City Comm Coll (OK)
Seminole State Coll of Florida (FL)
South Plains Coll (TX)
Stark State Coll (OH)
Tarrant County Coll District (TX)
Trident Tech Coll (SC)
Tunxis Comm Coll (CT)
Wytheville Comm Coll (VA)

PHYSICAL THERAPY TECHNOLOGY
Anne Arundel Comm Coll (MD)
Anoka-Ramsey Comm Coll (MN)
Arapahoe Comm Coll (CO)
Austin Comm Coll (TX)
Barton County Comm Coll (KS)
Bay State Coll (MA)
Berkshire Comm Coll (MA)
Blackhawk Tech Coll (WI)
Bradford School (VA)
Carl Albert State Coll (OK)
Carrington Coll–Albuquerque (NM)
Carrington Coll–Boise (ID)
Carrington Coll California–Pleasant Hill (CA)
Carrington Coll–Las Vegas (NV)
Carrington Coll–Mesa (AZ)
Carroll Comm Coll (MD)
Chippewa Valley Tech Coll (WI)
Colby Comm Coll (KS)
Coll of Southern Maryland (MD)
Comm Coll of Allegheny County (PA)
Comm Coll of Rhode Island (RI)
Comm Coll of the Air Force (AL)
Darton State Coll (GA)
Delaware Tech & Comm Coll, Jack F. Owens Campus (DE)
Delaware Tech & Comm Coll, Stanton/Wilmington Campus (DE)
Edison Comm Coll (OH)
Elgin Comm Coll (IL)
Essex County Coll (NJ)
Fayetteville Tech Comm Coll (NC)
Fiorello H. LaGuardia Comm Coll of the City U of New York (NY)
Florida Gateway Coll (FL)
Fox Coll (IL)
Gateway Tech Coll (WI)
Great Falls Coll Montana State U (MT)
Guilford Tech Comm Coll (NC)
Hawkeye Comm Coll (IA)
Houston Comm Coll System (TX)
Howard Comm Coll (MD)
Hutchinson Comm Coll and Area Vocational School (KS)
Illinois Central Coll (IL)
Ivy Tech Comm Coll–East Central (IN)
Jackson State Comm Coll (TN)
Jefferson State Comm Coll (AL)
Kankakee Comm Coll (IL)
Kaskaskia Coll (IL)
Kennebec Valley Comm Coll (ME)
Kent State U at Ashtabula (OH)
Kent State U at East Liverpool (OH)
Kilgore Coll (TX)
Lake Area Tech Inst (SD)
Lake Superior Coll (MN)
Laramie County Comm Coll (WY)
Lehigh Carbon Comm Coll (PA)
Lone Star Coll–Montgomery (TX)
Lorain County Comm Coll (OH)
Macomb Comm Coll (MI)
Manchester Comm Coll (CT)
Massachusetts Bay Comm Coll (MA)
Miami Dade Coll (FL)
Mohave Comm Coll (AZ)
Montgomery Coll (MD)
Mott Comm Coll (MI)
Nassau Comm Coll (NY)
Niagara County Comm Coll (NY)
North Shore Comm Coll (MA)
Oakland Comm Coll (MI)
Oakton Comm Coll (IL)
Olympic Coll (WA)
Onondaga Comm Coll (NY)
Owens Comm Coll, Toledo (OH)
Ozarks Tech Comm Coll (MO)
Penn State DuBois (PA)
Penn State Hazleton (PA)
Penn State Mont Alto (PA)

Pensacola State Coll (FL)
Randolph Comm Coll (NC)
St. Louis Comm Coll at Meramec (MO)
St. Philip's Coll (TX)
Salt Lake Comm Coll (UT)
San Diego Mesa Coll (CA)
San Jacinto Coll District (TX)
San Juan Coll (NM)
Springfield Tech Comm Coll (MA)
Tech Coll of the Lowcountry (SC)
Union County Coll (NJ)
U of Pittsburgh at Titusville (PA)
Vincennes U (IN)
Volunteer State Comm Coll (TN)
Waukesha County Tech Coll (WI)
Western Iowa Tech Comm Coll (IA)
West Kentucky Comm and Tech Coll (KY)

PHYSICIAN ASSISTANT
Barton County Comm Coll (KS)
Cuyahoga Comm Coll (OH)
Foothill Coll (CA)
Georgia Highlands Coll (GA)

PHYSICS
Amarillo Coll (TX)
Arizona Western Coll (AZ)
Austin Comm Coll (TX)
Bakersfield Coll (CA)
Barton County Comm Coll (KS)
Burlington County Coll (NJ)
Butte Coll (CA)
Casper Coll (WY)
Cecil Coll (MD)
Cochise Coll, Sierra Vista (AZ)
Coll of Marin (CA)
Coll of the Desert (CA)
Comm Coll of Allegheny County (PA)
Comm Coll of Beaver County (PA)
Darton State Coll (GA)
De Anza Coll (CA)
Finger Lakes Comm Coll (NY)
Foothill Coll (CA)
Georgia Highlands Coll (GA)
Gordon State Coll (GA)
Harford Comm Coll (MD)
Kankakee Comm Coll (IL)
Kilgore Coll (TX)
Lake Michigan Coll (MI)
Lone Star Coll–CyFair (TX)
Lone Star Coll–Kingwood (TX)
Lone Star Coll–Montgomery (TX)
Lone Star Coll–North Harris (TX)
Lone Star Coll–Tomball (TX)
Lorain County Comm Coll (OH)
Miami Dade Coll (FL)
Monroe Comm Coll (NY)
Northampton Comm Coll (PA)
Northwest Coll (WY)
Oklahoma City Comm Coll (OK)
Oklahoma State U, Oklahoma City (OK)
Orange Coast Coll (CA)
Pensacola State Coll (FL)
Salt Lake Comm Coll (UT)
San Diego Mesa Coll (CA)
San Jacinto Coll District (TX)
San Juan Coll (NM)
Santa Rosa Jr Coll (CA)
Sierra Coll (CA)
Spoon River Coll (IL)
Springfield Tech Comm Coll (MA)
Terra State Comm Coll (OH)
Texarkana Coll (TX)
Texas State Tech Coll Harlingen (TX)
Tyler Jr Coll (TX)

PHYSICS TEACHER EDUCATION
Anne Arundel Comm Coll (MD)
The Comm Coll of Baltimore County (MD)
Harford Comm Coll (MD)
Montgomery Coll (MD)

PHYSIOLOGY
Comm Coll of the Air Force (AL)

PIPEFITTING AND SPRINKLER FITTING
Bakersfield Coll (CA)
Ivy Tech Comm Coll–Bloomington (IN)
Ivy Tech Comm Coll–Central Indiana (IN)
Ivy Tech Comm Coll–Columbus (IN)
Ivy Tech Comm Coll–East Central (IN)

Ivy Tech Comm Coll–Kokomo (IN)
Ivy Tech Comm Coll–Lafayette (IN)
Ivy Tech Comm Coll–North Central (IN)
Ivy Tech Comm Coll–Northeast (IN)
Ivy Tech Comm Coll–Northwest (IN)
Ivy Tech Comm Coll–Richmond (IN)
Ivy Tech Comm Coll–Southern Indiana (IN)
Ivy Tech Comm Coll–Southwest (IN)
Ivy Tech Comm Coll–Wabash Valley (IN)
Oakland Comm Coll (MI)

PLANT NURSERY MANAGEMENT
Coll of Marin (CA)
Comm Coll of Allegheny County (PA)
Miami Dade Coll (FL)
The Ohio State U Ag Tech Inst (OH)

PLASTICS AND POLYMER ENGINEERING TECHNOLOGY
Daytona State Coll (FL)
Grand Rapids Comm Coll (MI)
Lorain County Comm Coll (OH)
Macomb Comm Coll (MI)
Northwest State Comm Coll (OH)
Terra State Comm Coll (OH)

PLATEMAKING/IMAGING
Illinois Central Coll (IL)

PLAYWRITING AND SCREENWRITING
Northwest Coll (WY)

PLUMBING TECHNOLOGY
Arizona Western Coll (AZ)
Comm Coll of Beaver County (PA)
Luzerne County Comm Coll (PA)
Macomb Comm Coll (MI)
Minnesota West Comm and Tech Coll (MN)
North Dakota State Coll of Science (ND)
Northeast Iowa Comm Coll (IA)
Southern Maine Comm Coll (ME)
State U of New York Coll of Technology at Alfred (NY)

POLITICAL SCIENCE AND GOVERNMENT
Arizona Western Coll (AZ)
Austin Comm Coll (TX)
Bainbridge Coll (GA)
Bakersfield Coll (CA)
Barton County Comm Coll (KS)
Casper Coll (WY)
Cochise Coll, Sierra Vista (AZ)
Coll of Marin (CA)
Coll of the Desert (CA)
Darton State Coll (GA)
De Anza Coll (CA)
Finger Lakes Comm Coll (NY)
Foothill Coll (CA)
Georgia Highlands Coll (GA)
Gordon State Coll (GA)
Harford Comm Coll (MD)
Kankakee Comm Coll (IL)
Lake Michigan Coll (MI)
Lansing Comm Coll (MI)
Laramie County Comm Coll (WY)
Lone Star Coll–CyFair (TX)
Lone Star Coll–Kingwood (TX)
Lone Star Coll–Montgomery (TX)
Lone Star Coll–North Harris (TX)
Lone Star Coll–Tomball (TX)
Lorain County Comm Coll (OH)
Miami Dade Coll (FL)
Monroe Comm Coll (NY)
Northern Essex Comm Coll (MA)
Northwest Coll (WY)
Oklahoma City Comm Coll (OK)
Orange Coast Coll (CA)
Oxnard Coll (CA)
Potomac State Coll of West Virginia U (WV)
St. Philip's Coll (TX)
Salt Lake Comm Coll (UT)
San Diego City Coll (CA)
San Jacinto Coll District (TX)
Santa Rosa Jr Coll (CA)
Spoon River Coll (IL)
Texarkana Coll (TX)
Tyler Jr Coll (TX)
Vincennes U (IN)

POLYMER/PLASTICS ENGINEERING
Central Oregon Comm Coll (OR)

POLYSOMNOGRAPHY
Catawba Valley Comm Coll (NC)
Genesee Comm Coll (NY)

PORTUGUESE
Miami Dade Coll (FL)

POULTRY SCIENCE
Crowder Coll (MO)
Delaware Tech & Comm Coll, Jack F. Owens Campus (DE)

PRECISION METAL WORKING RELATED
Northwest State Comm Coll (OH)
Oakland Comm Coll (MI)
Shelton State Comm Coll (AL)
Western Dakota Tech Inst (SD)

PRECISION PRODUCTION RELATED
Jefferson Coll (MO)
Lake Michigan Coll (MI)
Mineral Area Coll (MO)
Mott Comm Coll (MI)
Sheridan Coll (WY)

PRECISION PRODUCTION TRADES
Bucks County Comm Coll (PA)
Mineral Area Coll (MO)
Owensboro Comm and Tech Coll (KY)

PRE-DENTISTRY STUDIES
Austin Comm Coll (TX)
Barton County Comm Coll (KS)
Casper Coll (WY)
Darton State Coll (GA)
Howard Comm Coll (MD)
Kilgore Coll (TX)
Lake Michigan Coll (MI)
Pensacola State Coll (FL)
St. Philip's Coll (TX)
Vincennes U (IN)

PRE-ENGINEERING
Alpena Comm Coll (MI)
Amarillo Coll (TX)
Anoka-Ramsey Comm Coll (MN)
Anoka-Ramsey Comm Coll, Cambridge Campus (MN)
Barton County Comm Coll (KS)
Chipola Coll (FL)
Cleveland Comm Coll (NC)
Coll of the Canyons (CA)
Comm Coll of Philadelphia (PA)
Corning Comm Coll (NY)
Cowley County Comm Coll and Area Vocational–Tech School (KS)
Crowder Coll (MO)
Darton State Coll (GA)
De Anza Coll (CA)
Finger Lakes Comm Coll (NY)
Gordon State Coll (GA)
Housatonic Comm Coll (CT)
Lake Michigan Coll (MI)
Lone Star Coll–North Harris (TX)
Lorain County Comm Coll (OH)
Macomb Comm Coll (MI)
Mesa Comm Coll (AZ)
Metropolitan Comm Coll–Kansas City (MO)
Miami Dade Coll (FL)
Monroe County Comm Coll (MI)
Mt. San Antonio Coll (CA)
Normandale Comm Coll (MN)
Northeastern Jr Coll (CO)
North Hennepin Comm Coll (MN)
North Shore Comm Coll (MA)
Oklahoma City Comm Coll (OK)
Oklahoma State U, Oklahoma City (OK)
Potomac State Coll of West Virginia U (WV)
Randolph Comm Coll (NC)
St. Philip's Coll (TX)
San Diego City Coll (CA)
Southern Maine Comm Coll (ME)
South Plains Coll (TX)
Spoon River Coll (IL)
Taft Coll (CA)
Virginia Western Comm Coll (VA)
Westmoreland County Comm Coll (PA)

PRE-LAW STUDIES
Anne Arundel Comm Coll (MD)
Barton County Comm Coll (KS)
Carl Albert State Coll (OK)
Casper Coll (WY)

Central Oregon Comm Coll (OR)
Central Wyoming Coll (WY)
Darton State Coll (GA)
Foothill Coll (CA)
Garden City Comm Coll (KS)
Kilgore Coll (TX)
Lake Michigan Coll (MI)
Laramie County Comm Coll (WY)
Pensacola State Coll (FL)
St. Philip's Coll (TX)

PREMEDICAL STUDIES
Austin Comm Coll (TX)
Barton County Comm Coll (KS)
Casper Coll (WY)
Central Oregon Comm Coll (OR)
Dakota Coll at Bottineau (ND)
Darton State Coll (GA)
Garden City Comm Coll (KS)
Howard Comm Coll (MD)
Kilgore Coll (TX)
Lake Michigan Coll (MI)
Lansing Comm Coll (MI)
Pensacola State Coll (FL)
St. Philip's Coll (TX)
San Juan Coll (NM)
Springfield Tech Comm Coll (MA)
Vincennes U (IN)

PRENURSING STUDIES
Arizona Western Coll (AZ)
Cleveland Comm Coll (NC)
Dakota Coll at Bottineau (ND)
Edison Comm Coll (OH)
Garden City Comm Coll (KS)
Georgia Military Coll (GA)
Oklahoma State U, Oklahoma City (OK)
Pensacola State Coll (FL)
Randolph Comm Coll (NC)
St. Philip's Coll (TX)
Southwestern Michigan Coll (MI)
Texas State Tech Coll Harlingen (TX)

PRE-OCCUPATIONAL THERAPY
Casper Coll (WY)
Georgia Highlands Coll (GA)
Gordon State Coll (GA)

PRE-OPTOMETRY
Casper Coll (WY)

PRE-PHARMACY STUDIES
Amarillo Coll (TX)
Austin Comm Coll (TX)
Casper Coll (WY)
Central Oregon Comm Coll (OR)
Darton State Coll (GA)
Garden City Comm Coll (KS)
Georgia Highlands Coll (GA)
Gordon State Coll (GA)
Howard Comm Coll (MD)
Kilgore Coll (TX)
Lake Michigan Coll (MI)
Laramie County Comm Coll (WY)
Luzerne County Comm Coll (PA)
Monroe Comm Coll (NY)
Northwest Coll (WY)
Pensacola State Coll (FL)
Quinsigamond Comm Coll (MA)
St. Philip's Coll (TX)
Schoolcraft Coll (MI)
Vincennes U (IN)

PRE-PHYSICAL THERAPY
Casper Coll (WY)
Georgia Highlands Coll (GA)
Gordon State Coll (GA)

PRE-VETERINARY STUDIES
Austin Comm Coll (TX)
Barton County Comm Coll (KS)
Casper Coll (WY)
Dakota Coll at Bottineau (ND)
Darton State Coll (GA)
Garden City Comm Coll (KS)
Howard Comm Coll (MD)
Kilgore Coll (TX)
Lake Michigan Coll (MI)
Pensacola State Coll (FL)
Vincennes U (IN)

PRINTING PRESS OPERATION
Dunwoody Coll of Technology (MN)

PRINTMAKING
De Anza Coll (CA)

PROFESSIONAL, TECHNICAL, BUSINESS, AND SCIENTIFIC WRITING

Austin Comm Coll (TX)
Coll of Lake County (IL)
De Anza Coll (CA)
Gateway Tech Coll (WI)
Oklahoma State U, Oklahoma City (OK)
Southwestern Michigan Coll (MI)

PSYCHIATRIC/MENTAL HEALTH SERVICES TECHNOLOGY

Anne Arundel Comm Coll (MD)
Comm Coll of Allegheny County (PA)
The Comm Coll of Baltimore County (MD)
Fiorello H. LaGuardia Comm Coll of the City U of New York (NY)
Guilford Tech Comm Coll (NC)
Hagerstown Comm Coll (MD)
Hillsborough Comm Coll (FL)
Houston Comm Coll System (TX)
Illinois Central Coll (IL)
Ivy Tech Comm Coll–Bloomington (IN)
Ivy Tech Comm Coll–Central Indiana (IN)
Ivy Tech Comm Coll–Columbus (IN)
Ivy Tech Comm Coll–East Central (IN)
Ivy Tech Comm Coll–Kokomo (IN)
Ivy Tech Comm Coll–Lafayette (IN)
Ivy Tech Comm Coll–Northeast (IN)
Ivy Tech Comm Coll–Northwest (IN)
Ivy Tech Comm Coll–Richmond (IN)
Ivy Tech Comm Coll–Southeast (IN)
Ivy Tech Comm Coll–Southern Indiana (IN)
Ivy Tech Comm Coll–Southwest (IN)
Ivy Tech Comm Coll–Wabash Valley (IN)
Middlesex Comm Coll (MA)
Montgomery Coll (MD)
Montgomery County Comm Coll (PA)
North Dakota State Coll of Science (ND)

PSYCHOLOGY

Amarillo Coll (TX)
Austin Comm Coll (TX)
Bainbridge Coll (GA)
Bakersfield Coll (CA)
Barton County Comm Coll (KS)
Berkeley City Coll (CA)
Bucks County Comm Coll (PA)
Burlington County Coll (NJ)
Carroll Comm Coll (MD)
Casper Coll (WY)
Central Wyoming Coll (WY)
Cochise Coll, Sierra Vista (AZ)
Coll of Marin (CA)
Coll of the Canyons (CA)
Coll of the Desert (CA)
Comm Coll of Allegheny County (PA)
Comm Coll of Beaver County (PA)
Comm Coll of Philadelphia (PA)
Crowder Coll (MO)
Dakota Coll at Bottineau (ND)
Darton State Coll (GA)
De Anza Coll (CA)
Finger Lakes Comm Coll (NY)
Fiorello H. LaGuardia Comm Coll of the City U of New York (NY)
Foothill Coll (CA)
Garden City Comm Coll (KS)
Genesee Comm Coll (NY)
Georgia Highlands Coll (GA)
Georgia Military Coll (GA)
Gordon State Coll (GA)
Harford Comm Coll (MD)
Harper Coll (IL)
Harrisburg Area Comm Coll (PA)
Howard Comm Coll (MD)
Hutchinson Comm Coll and Area Vocational School (KS)
Kankakee Comm Coll (IL)
Kilgore Coll (TX)
Kilian Comm Coll (SD)
Lake Michigan Coll (MI)
Lansing Comm Coll (MI)
Laramie County Comm Coll (WY)
Lehigh Carbon Comm Coll (PA)
Lone Star Coll–CyFair (TX)
Lone Star Coll–Kingwood (TX)
Lone Star Coll–Montgomery (TX)
Lone Star Coll–North Harris (TX)
Lorain County Comm Coll (OH)
Manor Coll (PA)
Mendocino Coll (CA)
Miami Dade Coll (FL)

Mohave Comm Coll (AZ)
Monroe County Comm Coll (MI)
Montgomery County Comm Coll (PA)
Northeastern Jr Coll (CO)
Northwest Coll (WY)
Norwalk Comm Coll (CT)
Oklahoma City Comm Coll (OK)
Oklahoma State U, Oklahoma City (OK)
Oxnard Coll (CA)
Pasadena City Coll (CA)
Pensacola State Coll (FL)
Potomac State Coll of West Virginia U (WV)
St. Philip's Coll (TX)
Salt Lake Comm Coll (UT)
San Diego City Coll (CA)
San Diego Mesa Coll (CA)
San Jacinto Coll District (TX)
San Juan (NM)
Santa Rosa Jr Coll (CA)
Sheridan Coll (WY)
Sierra Coll (CA)
Spoon River Coll (IL)
Terra State Comm Coll (OH)
Tyler Jr Coll (TX)
Vincennes U (IN)

PSYCHOLOGY RELATED

Cayuga County Comm Coll (NY)
U of Pittsburgh at Titusville (PA)

PUBLIC ADMINISTRATION

Barton County Comm Coll (KS)
County Coll of Morris (NJ)
Fayetteville Tech Comm Coll (NC)
Housatonic Comm Coll (CT)
Houston Comm Coll System (TX)
Laramie County Comm Coll (WY)
Lehigh Carbon Comm Coll (PA)
Miami Dade Coll (FL)
Mohawk Valley Comm Coll (NY)
Owens Comm Coll, Toledo (OH)
Scottsdale Comm Coll (AZ)
Tallahassee Comm Coll (FL)
Thomas Nelson Comm Coll (VA)
Westchester Comm Coll (NY)

PUBLIC ADMINISTRATION AND SOCIAL SERVICE PROFESSIONS RELATED

Cleveland State Comm Coll (TN)
Erie Comm Coll (NY)
Oklahoma State U, Oklahoma City (OK)
Onondaga Comm Coll (NY)

PUBLIC HEALTH

Anne Arundel Comm Coll (MD)

PUBLIC HEALTH EDUCATION AND PROMOTION

Berkeley City Coll (CA)
Georgia Military Coll (GA)

PUBLIC HEALTH RELATED

Berkeley City Coll (CA)
Salt Lake Comm Coll (UT)

PUBLIC RELATIONS, ADVERTISING, AND APPLIED COMMUNICATION

Oklahoma City Comm Coll (OK)

PUBLIC RELATIONS, ADVERTISING, AND APPLIED COMMUNICATION RELATED

Comm Coll of Beaver County (PA)
Harper Coll (IL)

PUBLIC RELATIONS/IMAGE MANAGEMENT

Amarillo Coll (TX)
Bismarck State Coll (ND)
Comm Coll of the Air Force (AL)
Crowder Coll (MO)
Glendale Comm Coll (AZ)
Vincennes U (IN)

PURCHASING, PROCUREMENT/ ACQUISITIONS AND CONTRACTS MANAGEMENT

Cecil Coll (MD)
Comm Coll of the Air Force (AL)
De Anza Coll (CA)

QUALITY CONTROL AND SAFETY TECHNOLOGIES RELATED

Blue Ridge Comm and Tech Coll (WV)
Cuyahoga Comm Coll (OH)
Ivy Tech Comm Coll–Lafayette (IN)

Ivy Tech Comm Coll–Wabash Valley (IN)
John Tyler Comm Coll (VA)
Macomb Comm Coll (MI)

QUALITY CONTROL TECHNOLOGY

Central Carolina Comm Coll (NC)
Comm Coll of Allegheny County (PA)
Gateway Tech Coll (WI)
Grand Rapids Comm Coll (MI)
Illinois Eastern Comm Colls, Frontier Community College (IL)
Illinois Eastern Comm Colls, Lincoln Trail College (IL)
Ivy Tech Comm Coll–Lafayette (IN)
James A. Rhodes State Coll (OH)
Lakeland Comm Coll (OH)
Lorain County Comm Coll (OH)
Macomb Comm Coll (MI)
Mesa Comm Coll (AZ)
Metropolitan Comm Coll–Kansas City (MO)
Monroe Comm Coll (NY)
Mt. San Antonio Coll (CA)
Northampton Comm Coll (PA)
Northwest State Comm Coll (OH)
Owens Comm Coll, Toledo (OH)
Salt Lake Comm Coll (UT)
Tarrant County Coll District (TX)

RADIATION PROTECTION/ HEALTH PHYSICS TECHNOLOGY

Lone Star Coll–CyFair (TX)
Lone Star Coll–Montgomery (TX)
Spartanburg Comm Coll (SC)

RADIO AND TELEVISION

Alvin Comm Coll (TX)
Amarillo Coll (TX)
Austin Comm Coll (TX)
Butte Coll (CA)
Central Carolina Comm Coll (NC)
Central Wyoming Coll (WY)
Colby Comm Coll (KS)
Coll of the Canyons (CA)
Daytona State Coll (FL)
De Anza Coll (CA)
Illinois Eastern Comm Colls, Wabash Valley College (IL)
Miami Dade Coll (FL)
Mt. San Antonio Coll (CA)
Northwest Coll (WY)
Onondaga Comm Coll (NY)
Oxnard Coll (CA)
Parkland Coll (IL)
Pasadena City Coll (CA)
San Diego City Coll (CA)
Sullivan County Comm Coll (NY)
Virginia Western Comm Coll (VA)

RADIO AND TELEVISION BROADCASTING TECHNOLOGY

Adirondack Comm Coll (NY)
Arizona Western Coll (AZ)
Borough of Manhattan Comm Coll of the City U of New York (NY)
Cleveland Comm Coll (NC)
Gateway Tech Coll (WI)
Hillsborough Comm Coll (FL)
Houston Comm Coll System (TX)
Lansing Comm Coll (MI)
Lehigh Carbon Comm Coll (PA)
Luzerne County Comm Coll (PA)
Miami Dade Coll (FL)
Mineral Area Coll (MO)
Northampton Comm Coll (PA)
Oakland Comm Coll (MI)
Ozarks Tech Comm Coll (MO)
Parkland Coll (IL)
Pasadena City Coll (CA)
St. Clair County Comm Coll (MI)
Salt Lake Comm Coll (UT)
San Jacinto Coll District (TX)
Schoolcraft Coll (MI)
Springfield Tech Comm Coll (MA)
Tompkins Cortland Comm Coll (NY)
Vincennes U (IN)
Waubonsee Comm Coll (IL)
Westmoreland County Comm Coll (PA)

RADIOLOGIC TECHNOLOGY/ SCIENCE

Adirondack Comm Coll (NY)
Amarillo Coll (TX)
Arizona Western Coll (AZ)
Austin Comm Coll (TX)
Barton County Comm Coll (KS)
Blackhawk Tech Coll (WI)
Brookhaven Coll (TX)

Career Tech Coll (LA)
Carl Albert State Coll (OK)
Carolinas Coll of Health Sciences (NC)
Carrington Coll–Phoenix (AZ)
Casper Coll (WY)
Central Maine Medical Center Coll of Nursing and Health Professions (ME)
Central Oregon Comm Coll (OR)
Century Coll (MN)
Clark Coll (WA)
Cleveland Comm Coll (NC)
Comm Coll of Rhode Island (RI)
County Coll of Morris (NJ)
Delaware Tech & Comm Coll, Jack F. Owens Campus (DE)
Delaware Tech & Comm Coll, Stanton/Wilmington Campus (DE)
El Centro Coll (TX)
Elgin Comm Coll (IL)
Fayetteville Tech Comm Coll (NC)
Foothill Coll (CA)
Forsyth Tech Comm Coll (NC)
Gadsden State Comm Coll (AL)
Gordon State Coll (GA)
Great Falls Coll Montana State U (MT)
Harper Coll (IL)
Harrisburg Area Comm Coll (PA)
Houston Comm Coll System (TX)
Illinois Central Coll (IL)
Jefferson State Comm Coll (AL)
Kankakee Comm Coll (IL)
Kaskaskia Coll (IL)
Kennebec Valley Comm Coll (ME)
Kilgore Coll (TX)
Lake Michigan Coll (MI)
Lake Superior Coll (MN)
Lancaster General Coll of Nursing & Health Sciences (PA)
Lansing Comm Coll (MI)
Laramie County Comm Coll (WY)
Lincoln Land Comm Coll (IL)
Miami Dade Coll (FL)
Minnesota West Comm and Tech Coll (MN)
Mitchell Tech Inst (SD)
Montgomery County Comm Coll (PA)
Moraine Valley Comm Coll (IL)
Northampton Comm Coll (PA)
Northeast Iowa Comm Coll (IA)
Northern Essex Comm Coll (MA)
Oklahoma State U, Oklahoma City (OK)
Paris Jr Coll (TX)
Pasadena City Coll (CA)
Pasco-Hernando Comm Coll (FL)
Piedmont Virginia Comm Coll (VA)
Quinsigamond Comm Coll (MA)
Randolph Comm Coll (NC)
Red Rocks Comm Coll (CO)
St. Louis Comm Coll at Forest Park (MO)
St. Luke's Coll (IA)
San Jacinto Coll District (TX)
Santa Rosa Jr Coll (CA)
Southern Maine Comm Coll (ME)
South Suburban Coll (IL)
Southwest Virginia Comm Coll (VA)
Spencerian Coll (KY)
Springfield Tech Comm Coll (MA)
Union County Coll (NJ)
Virginia Western Comm Coll (VA)
Westmoreland County Comm Coll (PA)

RADIO, TELEVISION, AND DIGITAL COMMUNICATION RELATED

Cayuga County Comm Coll (NY)
Mitchell Tech Inst (SD)
Montgomery County Comm Coll (PA)
Northwest Coll (WY)
Sullivan County Comm Coll (NY)

RANGE SCIENCE AND MANAGEMENT

Casper Coll (WY)
Central Wyoming Coll (WY)
Northwest Coll (WY)
Sheridan Coll (WY)

REAL ESTATE

Amarillo Coll (TX)
Austin Comm Coll (TX)
Bakersfield Coll (CA)
Butte Coll (CA)
Coll of Marin (CA)
Coll of the Canyons (CA)
Collin County Comm Coll District (TX)

Comm Coll of Allegheny County (PA)
Cuyahoga Comm Coll (OH)
De Anza Coll (CA)
Foothill Coll (CA)
Harrisburg Area Comm Coll (PA)
Houston Comm Coll System (TX)
Illinois Central Coll (IL)
Lansing Comm Coll (MI)
Lorain County Comm Coll (OH)
Luzerne County Comm Coll (PA)
Mendocino Coll (CA)
Mesa Comm Coll (AZ)
Montgomery County Comm Coll (PA)
Mt. San Antonio Coll (CA)
Nassau Comm Coll (NY)
Northern Essex Comm Coll (MA)
Oakton Comm Coll (IL)
Red Rocks Comm Coll (CO)
San Diego City Coll (CA)
San Diego Mesa Coll (CA)
San Jacinto Coll District (TX)
Santa Rosa Jr Coll (CA)
Scottsdale Comm Coll (AZ)
Sierra Coll (CA)
Southern State Comm Coll (OH)
South Plains Coll (TX)
Terra State Comm Coll (OH)
Texarkana Coll (TX)
Victor Valley Coll (CA)
Waukesha County Tech Coll (WI)
Westmoreland County Comm Coll (PA)

RECEPTIONIST

Dakota Coll at Bottineau (ND)

RECORDING ARTS TECHNOLOGY

Bossier-Parish Comm Coll (LA)
Collin County Comm Coll District (TX)
Comm Coll of Philadelphia (PA)
Finger Lakes Comm Coll (NY)
Fiorello H. LaGuardia Comm Coll of the City U of New York (NY)
Glendale Comm Coll (AZ)
Guilford Tech Comm Coll (NC)
International Coll of Broadcasting (OH)
Lehigh Carbon Comm Coll (PA)
Miami Dade Coll (FL)
Montgomery County Comm Coll (PA)
Phoenix Coll (AZ)
Schoolcraft Coll (MI)
South Plains Coll (TX)
Springfield Tech Comm Coll (MA)
Union County Coll (NJ)
Vincennes U (IN)
Western Iowa Tech Comm Coll (IA)

REGISTERED NURSING/ REGISTERED NURSE

Adirondack Comm Coll (NY)
Alamance Comm Coll (NC)
Alexandria Tech and Comm Coll (MN)
Alpena Comm Coll (MI)
Alvin Comm Coll (TX)
Amarillo Coll (TX)
Ancilla Coll (IN)
Anne Arundel Comm Coll (MD)
Anoka-Ramsey Comm Coll (MN)
Anoka-Ramsey Comm Coll, Cambridge Campus (MN)
Arapahoe Comm Coll (CO)
Austin Comm Coll (TX)
Bainbridge Coll (GA)
Bakersfield Coll (CA)
Barton County Comm Coll (KS)
Beaufort County Comm Coll (NC)
Berkshire Comm Coll (MA)
Bevill State Comm Coll (AL)
Big Bend Comm Coll (WA)
Bismarck State Coll (ND)
Blackhawk Tech Coll (WI)
Borough of Manhattan Comm Coll of the City U of New York (NY)
Bowling Green State U-Firelands Coll (OH)
Brookhaven Coll (TX)
Bucks County Comm Coll (PA)
Burlington County Coll (NJ)
Butte Coll (CA)
Cape Fear Comm Coll (NC)
Carl Albert State Coll (OK)
Carolinas Coll of Health Sciences (NC)
Carrington Coll–Albuquerque (NM)
Carrington Coll–Boise (ID)
Carrington Coll of California– Sacramento (CA)
Carrington Coll–Phoenix (AZ)

Carrington Coll–Phoenix Westside (AZ)
Carrington Coll–Reno (NV)
Carroll Comm Coll (MD)
Casper Coll (WY)
Catawba Valley Comm Coll (NC)
Cayuga County Comm Coll (NY)
Cecil Coll (MD)
Central Carolina Comm Coll (NC)
Central Maine Comm Coll (ME)
Central Maine Medical Center Coll of Nursing and Health Professions (ME)
Central New Mexico Comm Coll (NM)
Central Oregon Comm Coll (OR)
Central Wyoming Coll (WY)
Century Coll (MN)
Chemeketa Comm Coll (OR)
Chipola Coll (FL)
Chippewa Valley Tech Coll (WI)
Clark Coll (WA)
Clark State Comm Coll (OH)
Cleveland Comm Coll (NC)
Cleveland State Comm Coll (TN)
Clinton Comm Coll (NY)
Cochise Coll, Sierra Vista (AZ)
Colby Comm Coll (KS)
Coll of Lake County (IL)
Coll of Marin (CA)
Coll of Southern Maryland (MD)
Coll of the Canyons (CA)
Coll of the Desert (CA)
Collin County Comm Coll District (TX)
Colorado Northwestern Comm Coll (CO)
Comm Coll of Allegheny County (PA)
The Comm Coll of Baltimore County (MD)
Comm Coll of Beaver County (PA)
Comm Coll of Philadelphia (PA)
Comm Coll of Rhode Island (RI)
Copiah-Lincoln Comm Coll (MS)
Corning Comm Coll (NY)
County Coll of Morris (NJ)
Crowder Coll (MO)
Cuyahoga Comm Coll (OH)
Dabney S. Lancaster Comm Coll (VA)
Dakota Coll at Bottineau (ND)
Darton State Coll (GA)
Daytona State Coll (FL)
De Anza Coll (CA)
Delaware Tech & Comm Coll, Jack F. Owens Campus (DE)
Delaware Tech & Comm Coll, Stanton/Wilmington Campus (DE)
Delaware Tech & Comm Coll, Terry Campus (DE)
Dyersburg State Comm Coll (TN)
Eastern Idaho Tech Coll (ID)
Eastern Shore Comm Coll (VA)
Edison Comm Coll (OH)
El Centro Coll (TX)
Elgin Comm Coll (IL)
Ellis School of Nursing (NY)
Erie Comm Coll (NY)
Erie Comm Coll, North Campus (NY)
Essex County Coll (NJ)
Fayetteville Tech Comm Coll (NC)
Finger Lakes Comm Coll (NY)
Fiorello H. LaGuardia Comm Coll of the City U of New York (NY)
Flathead Valley Comm Coll (MT)
Florida Gateway Coll (FL)
Forsyth Tech Comm Coll (NC)
Fox Valley Tech Coll (WI)
Gadsden State Comm Coll (AL)
Garden City Comm Coll (KS)
Gateway Comm and Tech Coll (KY)
Gateway Tech Coll (WI)
Genesee Comm Coll (NY)
Georgia Highlands Coll (GA)
Glendale Comm Coll (AZ)
Goodwin Coll (CT)
Gordon State Coll (GA)
Grand Rapids Comm Coll (MI)
Greenfield Comm Coll (MA)
Guilford Tech Comm Coll (NC)
Hagerstown Comm Coll (MD)
Halifax Comm Coll (NC)
Hallmark Coll of Technology (TX)
Harford Comm Coll (MD)
Harper Coll (IL)
Harrisburg Area Comm Coll (PA)
Hawkeye Comm Coll (IA)
Highland Comm Coll (IL)
Hillsborough Comm Coll (FL)
Holyoke Comm Coll (MA)
Housatonic Comm Coll (CT)
Houston Comm Coll System (TX)
Howard Comm Coll (MD)
Hutchinson Comm Coll and Area Vocational School (KS)
Illinois Central Coll (IL)
Illinois Eastern Comm Colls, Frontier Community College (IL)
Illinois Eastern Comm Colls, Olney Central College (IL)
Ivy Tech Comm Coll–Bloomington (IN)
Ivy Tech Comm Coll–Central Indiana (IN)
Ivy Tech Comm Coll–East Central (IN)
Ivy Tech Comm Coll–Lafayette (IN)
Ivy Tech Comm Coll–North Central (IN)
Ivy Tech Comm Coll–Northwest (IN)
Ivy Tech Comm Coll–Richmond (IN)
Ivy Tech Comm Coll–Southeast (IN)
Ivy Tech Comm Coll–Southern Indiana (IN)
Ivy Tech Comm Coll–Southwest (IN)
Ivy Tech Comm Coll–Wabash Valley (IN)
Jackson Coll (MI)
Jackson State Comm Coll (TN)
James A. Rhodes State Coll (OH)
James Sprunt Comm Coll (NC)
Jamestown Comm Coll (NY)
Jefferson Coll (MO)
Jefferson Comm Coll (NY)
Jefferson State Comm Coll (AL)
Johnston Comm Coll (NC)
John Tyler Comm Coll (VA)
Kankakee Comm Coll (IL)
Kaskaskia Coll (IL)
Kennebec Valley Comm Coll (ME)
Kent State U at Ashtabula (OH)
Kent State U at East Liverpool (OH)
Kent State U at Tuscarawas (OH)
Kilgore Coll (TX)
Kirtland Comm Coll (MI)
Lakeland Comm Coll (OH)
Lake Michigan Coll (MI)
Lake Region State Coll (ND)
Lake Superior Coll (MN)
Lancaster General Coll of Nursing & Health Sciences (PA)
Lansing Comm Coll (MI)
Laramie County Comm Coll (WY)
Lawson State Comm Coll (AL)
Lehigh Carbon Comm Coll (PA)
Lincoln Land Comm Coll (IL)
Lone Star Coll–CyFair (TX)
Lone Star Coll–Kingwood (TX)
Lone Star Coll–Montgomery (TX)
Lone Star Coll–North Harris (TX)
Lone Star Coll–Tomball (TX)
Lorain County Comm Coll (OH)
Lower Columbia Coll (WA)
Lurleen B. Wallace Comm Coll (AL)
Luzerne County Comm Coll (PA)
Macomb Comm Coll (MI)
Massachusetts Bay Comm Coll (MA)
McHenry County Coll (IL)
Mesa Comm Coll (AZ)
Metropolitan Comm Coll–Kansas City (MO)
Miami Dade Coll (FL)
Middlesex Comm Coll (MA)
Mid-Plains Comm Coll, North Platte (NE)
Miles Comm Coll (MT)
Mineral Area Coll (MO)
Minnesota West Comm and Tech Coll (MN)
Missouri State U–West Plains (MO)
Mohave Comm Coll (AZ)
Mohawk Valley Comm Coll (NY)
Monroe Comm Coll (NY)
Monroe County Comm Coll (MI)
Montcalm Comm Coll (MI)
Montgomery Coll (MD)
Montgomery County Comm Coll (PA)
Moraine Park Tech Coll (WI)
Moraine Valley Comm Coll (IL)
Motlow State Comm Coll (TN)
Mott Comm Coll (MI)
Mt. San Antonio Coll (CA)
Nassau Comm Coll (NY)
Niagara County Comm Coll (NY)
Normandale Comm Coll (MN)
Northampton Comm Coll (PA)
North Dakota State Coll of Science (ND)
Northeastern Jr Coll (CO)
Northeast Iowa Comm Coll (IA)
Northern Essex Comm Coll (MA)
North Hennepin Comm Coll (MN)
North Shore Comm Coll (MA)
NorthWest Arkansas Comm Coll (AR)
Northwest Coll (WY)
Northwest-Shoals Comm Coll (AL)
Northwest State Comm Coll (OH)
Northwest Tech Coll (MN)
Norwalk Comm Coll (CT)
Oakland Comm Coll (MI)
Oakton Comm Coll (IL)
Ocean County Coll (NJ)
Oklahoma City Comm Coll (OK)
Oklahoma State U, Oklahoma City (OK)
Olympic Coll (WA)
Onondaga Comm Coll (NY)
Oregon Coast Comm Coll (OR)
Owensboro Comm and Tech Coll (KY)
Owens Comm Coll, Toledo (OH)
Panola Coll (TX)
Paris Jr Coll (TX)
Parkland Coll (IL)
Pasadena City Coll (CA)
Pasco-Hernando Comm Coll (FL)
Paul D. Camp Comm Coll (VA)
Penn State Fayette, The Eberly Campus (PA)
Penn State Mont Alto (PA)
Penn State Worthington Scranton (PA)
Pensacola State Coll (FL)
Phoenix Coll (AZ)
Piedmont Comm Coll (NC)
Piedmont Virginia Comm Coll (VA)
Quinsigamond Comm Coll (MA)
Randolph Comm Coll (NC)
Rappahannock Comm Coll (VA)
Raritan Valley Comm Coll (NJ)
Robeson Comm Coll (NC)
Rogue Comm Coll (OR)
St. Louis Comm Coll at Forest Park (MO)
St. Louis Comm Coll at Meramec (MO)
St. Luke's Coll (IA)
Salt Lake Comm Coll (UT)
San Diego City Coll (CA)
San Jacinto Coll District (TX)
San Juan Coll (NM)
Santa Rosa Jr Coll (CA)
Schoolcraft Coll (MI)
Scottsdale Comm Coll (AZ)
Seminole State Coll of Florida (FL)
Shawnee Comm Coll (IL)
Shelton State Comm Coll (AL)
Sheridan Coll (WY)
Sierra Coll (CA)
Southeastern Comm Coll (IA)
Southeast Tech Inst (SD)
Southern Maine Comm Coll (ME)
Southern State Comm Coll (OH)
South Plains Coll (TX)
South Puget Sound Comm Coll (WA)
Southwestern Michigan Coll (MI)
Southwest Virginia Comm Coll (VA)
Spartanburg Comm Coll (SC)
Spencerian Coll (KY)
Spoon River Coll (IL)
Springfield Tech Comm Coll (MA)
Stark State Coll (OH)
State U of New York Coll of Technology at Alfred (NY)
Sullivan County Comm Coll (NY)
Tallahassee Comm Coll (FL)
Tarrant County Coll District (TX)
Tech Coll of the Lowcountry (SC)
Temple Coll (TX)
Terra State Comm Coll (OH)
Texarkana Coll (TX)
Thomas Nelson Comm Coll (VA)
Tompkins Cortland Comm Coll (NY)
Tri-County Comm Coll (NC)
Trident Tech Coll (SC)
Tyler Jr Coll (TX)
Union County Coll (NJ)
U of Arkansas Comm Coll at Morrilton (AR)
U of Pittsburgh at Titusville (PA)
Victor Valley Coll (CA)
Vincennes U (IN)
Virginia Western Comm Coll (VA)
Waubonsee Comm Coll (IL)
Waukesha County Tech Coll (WI)
Westchester Comm Coll (NY)
Western Iowa Tech Comm Coll (IA)
West Kentucky Comm and Tech Coll (KY)
Westmoreland County Comm Coll (PA)
West Virginia Northern Comm Coll (WV)
Wilson Comm Coll (NC)
Wytheville Comm Coll (VA)

REHABILITATION AND THERAPEUTIC PROFESSIONS RELATED

Central Wyoming Coll (WY)
Nassau Comm Coll (NY)
Union County Coll (NJ)

RELIGIOUS EDUCATION

Manor Coll (PA)

RELIGIOUS STUDIES

Amarillo Coll (TX)
Barton County Comm Coll (KS)
Cowley County Comm Coll and Area Vocational–Tech School (KS)
Kilgore Coll (TX)
Lansing Comm Coll (MI)
Laramie County Comm Coll (WY)
Lone Star Coll–North Harris (TX)
Lone Star Coll–Tomball (TX)
Orange Coast Coll (CA)
Pensacola State Coll (FL)
Santa Rosa Jr Coll (CA)

RESORT MANAGEMENT

Coll of the Desert (CA)
Lehigh Carbon Comm Coll (PA)

RESPIRATORY CARE THERAPY

Alvin Comm Coll (TX)
Amarillo Coll (TX)
Arkansas State U–Mountain Home (AR)
Barton County Comm Coll (KS)
Berkshire Comm Coll (MA)
Bossier Parish Comm Coll (LA)
Bowling Green State U-Firelands Coll (OH)
Burlington County Coll (NJ)
Butte Coll (CA)
Carrington Coll–Mesa (AZ)
Carrington Coll–Phoenix (AZ)
Casper Coll (WY)
Catawba Valley Comm Coll (NC)
Central New Mexico Comm Coll (NM)
Chippewa Valley Tech Coll (WI)
Cochise Coll, Sierra Vista (AZ)
Collin County Comm Coll District (TX)
Comm Coll of Allegheny County (PA)
The Comm Coll of Baltimore County (MD)
Comm Coll of Philadelphia (PA)
Comm Coll of Rhode Island (RI)
County Coll of Morris (NJ)
Cuyahoga Comm Coll (OH)
Darton State Coll (GA)
Daytona State Coll (FL)
El Centro Coll (TX)
Erie Comm Coll, North Campus (NY)
Essex County Coll (NJ)
Fayetteville Tech Comm Coll (NC)
Foothill Coll (CA)
Genesee Comm Coll (NY)
Goodwin Coll (CT)
Great Falls Coll Montana State U (MT)
Harrisburg Area Comm Coll (PA)
Hawkeye Comm Coll (IA)
Hillsborough Comm Coll (FL)
Houston Comm Coll System (TX)
Illinois Central Coll (IL)
Ivy Tech Comm Coll–Central Indiana (IN)
Ivy Tech Comm Coll–Lafayette (IN)
Ivy Tech Comm Coll–Northeast (IN)
Ivy Tech Comm Coll–Northwest (IN)
Ivy Tech Comm Coll–Southern Indiana (IN)
Jackson State Comm Coll (TN)
James A. Rhodes State Coll (OH)
Kankakee Comm Coll (IL)
Kaskaskia Coll (IL)
Kennebec Valley Comm Coll (ME)
Kent State U at Ashtabula (OH)
Lakeland Comm Coll (OH)
Lake Superior Coll (MN)
Lancaster General Coll of Nursing & Health Sciences (PA)
Lone Star Coll–Kingwood (TX)
Lone Star Coll–North Harris (TX)
Luzerne County Comm Coll (PA)
Macomb Comm Coll (MI)
Manchester Comm Coll (CT)
Massachusetts Bay Comm Coll (MA)
Metropolitan Comm Coll–Kansas City (MO)
Miami Dade Coll (FL)
Mohawk Valley Comm Coll (NY)
Monroe County Comm Coll (MI)
Moraine Park Tech Coll (WI)
Moraine Valley Comm Coll (IL)
Mott Comm Coll (MI)
Mt. San Antonio Coll (CA)
Nassau Comm Coll (NY)
Northeast Iowa Comm Coll (IA)
Northern Essex Comm Coll (MA)
North Shore Comm Coll (MA)
NorthWest Arkansas Comm Coll (AR)
Norwalk Comm Coll (CT)
Oakland Comm Coll (MI)
Oklahoma City Comm Coll (OK)
Onondaga Comm Coll (NY)
Orange Coast Coll (CA)
Ozarks Tech Comm Coll (MO)
Parkland Coll (IL)
Quinsigamond Comm Coll (MA)
Raritan Valley Comm Coll (NJ)
Robeson Comm Coll (NC)
St. Louis Comm Coll at Forest Park (MO)
St. Luke's Coll (IA)
St. Philip's Coll (TX)
San Jacinto Coll District (TX)
San Juan Coll (NM)
Seminole State Coll of Florida (FL)
Shelton State Comm Coll (AL)
Southeastern Comm Coll (IA)
Southern Maine Comm Coll (ME)
Southern State Comm Coll (OH)
South Plains Coll (TX)
Spartanburg Comm Coll (SC)
Spencerian Coll (KY)
Springfield Tech Comm Coll (MA)
Stark State Coll (OH)
Sullivan County Comm Coll (NY)
Tallahassee Comm Coll (FL)
Tarrant County Coll District (TX)
Temple Coll (TX)
Trident Tech Coll (SC)
Tyler Jr Coll (TX)
Union County Coll (NJ)
Victor Valley Coll (CA)
Volunteer State Comm Coll (TN)
Westchester Comm Coll (NY)
West Kentucky Comm and Tech Coll (KY)
West Virginia Northern Comm Coll (WV)

RESPIRATORY THERAPY TECHNICIAN

Borough of Manhattan Comm Coll of the City U of New York (NY)
Career Tech Coll (LA)
Carrington Coll California–Pleasant Hill (CA)
Carrington Coll–Las Vegas (NV)
Carrington Coll–Mesa (AZ)
Carrington Coll–Phoenix Westside (AZ)
Delaware Tech & Comm Coll, Jack F. Owens Campus (DE)
Delaware Tech & Comm Coll, Stanton/Wilmington Campus (DE)
Georgia Highlands Coll (GA)
Hutchinson Comm Coll and Area Vocational School (KS)
Miami Dade Coll (FL)
Mineral Area Coll (MO)
Missouri State U–West Plains (MO)
Northern Essex Comm Coll (MA)

RESTAURANT, CULINARY, AND CATERING MANAGEMENT

Blackhawk Tech Coll (WI)
Coll of Lake County (IL)
Coll of the Canyons (CA)
Comm Coll of Allegheny County (PA)
Cuyahoga Comm Coll (OH)
Delaware Tech & Comm Coll, Stanton/Wilmington Campus (DE)
Elgin Comm Coll (IL)
Erie Comm Coll, North Campus (NY)
Fox Valley Tech Coll (WI)
Gateway Tech Coll (WI)
Hillsborough Comm Coll (FL)
JNA Inst of Culinary Arts (PA)
Lakeland Comm Coll (OH)
Mohawk Valley Comm Coll (NY)
Moraine Valley Comm Coll (IL)

Orange Coast Coll (CA)
Pensacola State Coll (FL)
Raritan Valley Comm Coll (NJ)
San Jacinto Coll District (TX)
Vincennes U (IN)
Waukesha County Tech Coll (WI)
Westmoreland County Comm Coll (PA)

RESTAURANT/FOOD SERVICES MANAGEMENT
Burlington County Coll (NJ)
Fiorello H. LaGuardia Comm Coll of the City U of New York (NY)
Hillsborough Comm Coll (FL)
Northampton Comm Coll (PA)
Norwalk Comm Coll (CT)
Oakland Comm Coll (MI)
Owens Comm Coll, Toledo (OH)
Oxnard Coll (CA)
Quinsigamond Comm Coll (MA)
St. Philip's Coll (TX)
Santa Rosa Jr Coll (CA)

RETAILING
Alamance Comm Coll (NC)
Bradford School (PA)
Bucks County Comm Coll (PA)
Burlington County Coll (NJ)
Butte Coll (CA)
Casper Coll (WY)
Central Oregon Comm Coll (OR)
Clark Coll (WA)
Comm Coll of Allegheny County (PA)
Elgin Comm Coll (IL)
Fox Coll (IL)
Garden City Comm Coll (KS)
Holyoke Comm Coll (MA)
Hutchinson Comm Coll and Area Vocational School (KS)
Illinois Central Coll (IL)
Moraine Valley Comm Coll (IL)
Nassau Comm Coll (NY)
Orange Coast Coll (CA)
Waubonsee Comm Coll (IL)
Wood Tobe–Coburn School (NY)

RETAIL MANAGEMENT
Oakland Comm Coll (MI)

RHETORIC AND COMPOSITION
Amarillo Coll (TX)
Austin Comm Coll (TX)
Bainbridge Coll (GA)
Bakersfield Coll (CA)
Carl Albert State Coll (OK)
De Anza Coll (CA)
Lone Star Coll–CyFair (TX)
Lone Star Coll–Kingwood (TX)
Lone Star Coll–Montgomery (TX)
Lone Star Coll–North Harris (TX)
Lone Star Coll–Tomball (TX)
Mendocino Coll (CA)
Monroe County Comm Coll (MI)
St. Philip's Coll (TX)
San Diego City Coll (CA)
San Diego Mesa Coll (CA)
San Jacinto Coll District (TX)
Sierra Coll (CA)
Spoon River Coll (IL)

ROBOTICS TECHNOLOGY
Casper Coll (WY)
Comm Coll of Allegheny County (PA)
Daytona State Coll (FL)
Dunwoody Coll of Technology (MN)
Illinois Central Coll (IL)
Ivy Tech Comm Coll–Columbus (IN)
Ivy Tech Comm Coll–Lafayette (IN)
Ivy Tech Comm Coll–North Central (IN)
Ivy Tech Comm Coll–Northeast (IN)
Ivy Tech Comm Coll–Richmond (IN)
Ivy Tech Comm Coll–Southwest (IN)
Ivy Tech Comm Coll–Wabash Valley (IN)
James A. Rhodes State Coll (OH)
Kirtland Comm Coll (MI)
Lake Area Tech Inst (SD)
Macomb Comm Coll (MI)
Minnesota West Comm and Tech Coll (MN)
Oakland Comm Coll (MI)
St. Clair County Comm Coll (MI)
Schoolcraft Coll (MI)
State U of New York Coll of Technology at Alfred (NY)
Sullivan Coll of Technology and Design (KY)
Terra State Comm Coll (OH)
Vincennes U (IN)

RUSSIAN
Austin Comm Coll (TX)

SALES AND MARKETING/ MARKETING AND DISTRIBUTION TEACHER EDUCATION
Parkland Coll (IL)

SALES, DISTRIBUTION, AND MARKETING OPERATIONS
Alexandria Tech and Comm Coll (MN)
Anoka-Ramsey Comm Coll (MN)
Anoka-Ramsey Comm Coll, Cambridge Campus (MN)
Burlington County Coll (NJ)
Butte Coll (CA)
Coll of the Canyons (CA)
Collin County Comm Coll District (TX)
Cuyahoga Comm Coll (OH)
Gadsden State Comm Coll (AL)
Greenfield Comm Coll (MA)
Harper Coll (IL)
Harrisburg Area Comm Coll (PA)
Hawkeye Comm Coll (IA)
Lake Area Tech Inst (SD)
Lansing Comm Coll (MI)
Miles Comm Coll (MT)
Montgomery County Comm Coll (PA)
Northeast Iowa Comm Coll (IA)
Northwest Tech Coll (MN)
Oakton Comm Coll (IL)
Owens Comm Coll, Toledo (OH)
Sierra Coll (CA)
Spartanburg Comm Coll (SC)
Western Iowa Tech Comm Coll (IA)
Westmoreland County Comm Coll (PA)

SALON/BEAUTY SALON MANAGEMENT
Mott Comm Coll (MI)
Oakland Comm Coll (MI)
Schoolcraft Coll (MI)

SCIENCE TEACHER EDUCATION
Darton State Coll (GA)
Moraine Valley Comm Coll (IL)
San Jacinto Coll District (TX)
Vincennes U (IN)

SCIENCE TECHNOLOGIES
Harford Comm Coll (MD)

SCIENCE TECHNOLOGIES RELATED
Cascadia Comm Coll (WA)
Cayuga County Comm Coll (NY)
Cleveland State Comm Coll (TN)
Comm Coll of Allegheny County (PA)
The Comm Coll of Baltimore County (MD)
Dakota Coll at Bottineau (ND)
Delaware Tech & Comm Coll, Stanton/Wilmington Campus (DE)
Jackson State Comm Coll (TN)
Klamath Comm Coll (OR)
Oakland Comm Coll (MI)
Red Rocks Comm Coll (CO)
Sullivan County Comm Coll (NY)
Victor Valley Coll (CA)
West Virginia Northern Comm Coll (WV)

SCULPTURE
De Anza Coll (CA)
Schoolcraft Coll (MI)

SECONDARY EDUCATION
Alpena Comm Coll (MI)
Ancilla Coll (IN)
Arizona Western Coll (AZ)
Austin Comm Coll (TX)
Barton County Comm Coll (KS)
Brookhaven Coll (TX)
Carl Albert State Coll (OK)
Cecil Coll (MD)
Central Wyoming Coll (WY)
Collin County Comm Coll District (TX)
Georgia Highlands Coll (GA)
Georgia Military Coll (GA)
Gordon State Coll (GA)
Harford Comm Coll (MD)
Harrisburg Area Comm Coll (PA)
Howard Comm Coll (MD)
Kankakee Comm Coll (IL)
Lake Michigan Coll (MI)
Lansing Comm Coll (MI)

Mohawk Valley Comm Coll (NY)
Montgomery County Comm Coll (PA)
Northampton Comm Coll (PA)
Northwest Coll (WY)
Parkland Coll (IL)
San Jacinto Coll District (TX)
San Juan Coll (NM)
Sheridan Coll (WY)
Springfield Tech Comm Coll (MA)
State U of New York Coll of Technology at Alfred (NY)
Vincennes U (IN)

SECURITIES SERVICES ADMINISTRATION
Vincennes U (IN)

SECURITY AND LOSS PREVENTION
Comm Coll of Beaver County (PA)
Comm Coll of the Air Force (AL)
Illinois Central Coll (IL)
Union County Coll (NJ)
Vincennes U (IN)

SELLING SKILLS AND SALES
Central Wyoming Coll (WY)
Clark Coll (WA)
Coll of Lake County (IL)
Cuyahoga Comm Coll (OH)
Illinois Central Coll (IL)
Lansing Comm Coll (MI)
McHenry County Coll (IL)
Orange Coast Coll (CA)

SHEET METAL TECHNOLOGY
Comm Coll of Allegheny County (PA)
Ivy Tech Comm Coll–Central Indiana (IN)
Ivy Tech Comm Coll–Lafayette (IN)
Ivy Tech Comm Coll–North Central (IN)
Ivy Tech Comm Coll–Northeast (IN)
Ivy Tech Comm Coll–Northwest (IN)
Ivy Tech Comm Coll–Southern Indiana (IN)
Ivy Tech Comm Coll–Southwest (IN)
Ivy Tech Comm Coll–Wabash Valley (IN)
Lake Superior Coll (MN)
Macomb Comm Coll (MI)
Northwest State Comm Coll (OH)
Terra State Comm Coll (OH)
Vincennes U (IN)

SIGN LANGUAGE INTERPRETATION AND TRANSLATION
Austin Comm Coll (TX)
Berkeley City Coll (CA)
Burlington County Coll (NJ)
Coll of the Canyons (CA)
Collin County Comm Coll District (TX)
Comm Coll of Allegheny County (PA)
The Comm Coll of Baltimore County (MD)
Comm Coll of Philadelphia (PA)
Houston Comm Coll System (TX)
Illinois Central Coll (IL)
Lakeland Comm Coll (OH)
Lansing Comm Coll (MI)
Miami Dade Coll (FL)
Mohawk Valley Comm Coll (NY)
Mott Comm Coll (MI)
Mt. San Antonio Coll (CA)
Northern Essex Comm Coll (MA)
Oakland Comm Coll (MI)
Ocean County Coll (NJ)
Oklahoma State U, Oklahoma City (OK)
Phoenix Coll (AZ)
Salt Lake Comm Coll (UT)
Tarrant County Coll District (TX)
Tyler Jr Coll (TX)
Union County Coll (NJ)
Waubonsee Comm Coll (IL)
Wilson Comm Coll (NC)

SMALL BUSINESS ADMINISTRATION
Borough of Manhattan Comm Coll of the City U of New York (NY)
Butte Coll (CA)
Coll of the Canyons (CA)
Colorado Northwestern Comm Coll (CO)
Comm Coll of Beaver County (PA)
Dakota Coll at Bottineau (ND)
Flathead Valley Comm Coll (MT)
Harper Coll (IL)
Harrisburg Area Comm Coll (PA)

Lake Area Tech Inst (SD)
Miles Comm Coll (MT)
Moraine Valley Comm Coll (IL)
North Hennepin Comm Coll (MN)
Raritan Valley Comm Coll (NJ)
Schoolcraft Coll (MI)
Sierra Coll (CA)
South Suburban Coll (IL)
Springfield Tech Comm Coll (MA)
Waubonsee Comm Coll (IL)

SMALL ENGINE MECHANICS AND REPAIR TECHNOLOGY
Alexandria Tech and Comm Coll (MN)
Mitchell Tech Inst (SD)
North Dakota State Coll of Science (ND)

SOCIAL PSYCHOLOGY
Macomb Comm Coll (MI)

SOCIAL SCIENCES
Amarillo Coll (TX)
Arizona Western Coll (AZ)
Burlington County Coll (NJ)
Butte Coll (CA)
Carl Albert State Coll (OK)
Central Oregon Comm Coll (OR)
Central Wyoming Coll (WY)
Clinton Comm Coll (NY)
Coll of Marin (CA)
Coll of the Canyons (CA)
Coll of the Desert (CA)
Comm Coll of Allegheny County (PA)
Comm Coll of Beaver County (PA)
Comm Coll of Vermont (VT)
Corning Comm Coll (NY)
Dakota Coll at Bottineau (ND)
De Anza Coll (CA)
Essex County Coll (NJ)
Finger Lakes Comm Coll (NY)
Foothill Coll (CA)
Garden City Comm Coll (KS)
Georgia Military Coll (GA)
Greenfield Comm Coll (MA)
Harrisburg Area Comm Coll (PA)
Housatonic Comm Coll (CT)
Howard Comm Coll (MD)
Hutchinson Comm Coll and Area Vocational School (KS)
Kilgore Coll (TX)
Lansing Comm Coll (MI)
Laramie County Comm Coll (WY)
Lone Star Coll–CyFair (TX)
Lone Star Coll–Kingwood (TX)
Lorain County Comm Coll (OH)
Luzerne County Comm Coll (PA)
Massachusetts Bay Comm Coll (MA)
Mendocino Coll (CA)
Miami Dade Coll (FL)
Monroe Comm Coll (NY)
Montgomery County Comm Coll (PA)
Mt. San Antonio Coll (CA)
Niagara County Comm Coll (NY)
Northeastern Jr Coll (CO)
Northwest Coll (WY)
Orange Coast Coll (CA)
San Diego City Coll (CA)
San Diego Mesa Coll (CA)
San Jacinto Coll District (TX)
Santa Rosa Jr Coll (CA)
Sheridan Coll (WY)
Sierra Coll (CA)
Spoon River Coll (IL)
Taft Coll (CA)
Terra State Comm Coll (OH)
Texarkana Coll (TX)
Thomas Nelson Comm Coll (VA)
Tyler Jr Coll (TX)
Victor Valley Coll (CA)
Westchester Comm Coll (NY)

SOCIAL SCIENCES RELATED
Berkeley City Coll (CA)
Greenfield Comm Coll (MA)

SOCIAL STUDIES TEACHER EDUCATION
Casper Coll (WY)

SOCIAL WORK
Amarillo Coll (TX)
Austin Comm Coll (TX)
Barton County Comm Coll (KS)
Bismarck State Coll (ND)
Bowling Green State U-Firelands Coll (OH)
Casper Coll (WY)
Central Carolina Comm Coll (NC)
Chemeketa Comm Coll (OR)
Chipola Coll (FL)

Clark State Comm Coll (OH)
Cochise Coll, Sierra Vista (AZ)
Coll of Lake County (IL)
Comm Coll of Allegheny County (PA)
Comm Coll of Rhode Island (RI)
Comm Coll of the Air Force (AL)
Cowley County Comm Coll and Area Vocational–Tech School (KS)
Darton State Coll (GA)
Edison Comm Coll (OH)
Elgin Comm Coll (IL)
Essex County Coll (NJ)
Garden City Comm Coll (KS)
Gordon State Coll (GA)
Harford Comm Coll (MD)
Harrisburg Area Comm Coll (PA)
Holyoke Comm Coll (MA)
Illinois Eastern Comm Colls, Wabash Valley College (IL)
James A. Rhodes State Coll (OH)
Kilian Comm Coll (SD)
Lakeland Comm Coll (OH)
Lawson State Comm Coll (AL)
Lehigh Carbon Comm Coll (PA)
Lone Star Coll–Montgomery (TX)
Lorain County Comm Coll (OH)
Manchester Comm Coll (CT)
Miami Dade Coll (FL)
Monroe County Comm Coll (MI)
Northampton Comm Coll (PA)
Northeastern Jr Coll (CO)
Northeast Iowa Comm Coll (IA)
Northwest State Comm Coll (OH)
Oakton Comm Coll (IL)
Owensboro Comm and Tech Coll (KY)
Potomac State Coll of West Virginia U (WV)
Rogue Comm Coll (OR)
St. Philip's Coll (TX)
Salt Lake Comm Coll (UT)
San Diego City Coll (CA)
San Juan Coll (NM)
Shawnee Comm Coll (IL)
South Plains Coll (TX)
South Suburban Coll (IL)
Southwestern Michigan Coll (MI)
Terra State Comm Coll (OH)
The U of Akron–Wayne Coll (OH)
Vincennes U (IN)
Waubonsee Comm Coll (IL)
West Virginia Northern Comm Coll (WV)

SOCIAL WORK RELATED
Berkeley City Coll (CA)

SOCIOLOGY
Austin Comm Coll (TX)
Bainbridge Coll (GA)
Bakersfield Coll (CA)
Barton County Comm Coll (KS)
Berkeley City Coll (CA)
Burlington County Coll (NJ)
Casper Coll (WY)
Cochise Coll, Sierra Vista (AZ)
Coll of the Canyons (CA)
Coll of the Desert (CA)
Comm Coll of Allegheny County (PA)
Comm Coll of Beaver County (PA)
Darton State Coll (GA)
De Anza Coll (CA)
Finger Lakes Comm Coll (NY)
Foothill Coll (CA)
Georgia Highlands Coll (GA)
Gordon State Coll (GA)
Harford Comm Coll (MD)
Kankakee Comm Coll (IL)
Kilian Comm Coll (SD)
Lake Michigan Coll (MI)
Lansing Comm Coll (MI)
Laramie County Comm Coll (WY)
Lone Star Coll–Kingwood (TX)
Lone Star Coll–Montgomery (TX)
Lone Star Coll–North Harris (TX)
Lone Star Coll–Tomball (TX)
Lorain County Comm Coll (OH)
Miami Dade Coll (FL)
Mohave Comm Coll (AZ)
Northwest Coll (WY)
Oklahoma City Comm Coll (OK)
Orange Coast Coll (CA)
Oxnard Coll (CA)
Pasadena City Coll (CA)
Pensacola State Coll (FL)
Potomac State Coll of West Virginia U (WV)
St. Philip's Coll (TX)
Salt Lake Comm Coll (UT)
San Diego City Coll (CA)
San Diego Mesa Coll (CA)
San Jacinto Coll District (TX)

Santa Rosa Jr Coll (CA)
Spoon River Coll (IL)
Vincennes U (IN)

SOCIOLOGY AND ANTHROPOLOGY
Harper Coll (IL)

SOIL SCIENCE AND AGRONOMY
The Ohio State U Ag Tech Inst (OH)

SOLAR ENERGY TECHNOLOGY
Arizona Western Coll (AZ)
Comm Coll of Allegheny County (PA)
San Juan Coll (NM)

SPANISH
Arizona Western Coll (AZ)
Austin Comm Coll (TX)
Bakersfield Coll (CA)
Berkeley City Coll (CA)
Coll of Marin (CA)
Coll of the Canyons (CA)
Coll of the Desert (CA)
De Anza Coll (CA)
Fiorello H. LaGuardia Comm Coll of the City U of New York (NY)
Foothill Coll (CA)
Lansing Comm Coll (MI)
Laramie County Comm Coll (WY)
Mendocino Coll (CA)
Miami Dade Coll (FL)
Northwest Coll (WY)
Orange Coast Coll (CA)
Oxnard Coll (CA)
Pasadena City Coll (CA)
St. Philip's Coll (TX)
San Diego Mesa Coll (CA)
Santa Rosa Jr Coll (CA)

SPANISH LANGUAGE TEACHER EDUCATION
Anne Arundel Comm Coll (MD)
Carroll Comm Coll (MD)
The Comm Coll of Baltimore County (MD)
Harford Comm Coll (MD)
Montgomery Coll (MD)

SPECIAL EDUCATION
Comm Coll of Rhode Island (RI)
Darton State Coll (GA)
Highland Comm Coll (IL)
Kankakee Comm Coll (IL)
Lehigh Carbon Comm Coll (PA)
Lincoln Land Comm Coll (IL)
Miles Comm Coll (MT)
Moraine Valley Comm Coll (IL)
Normandale Comm Coll (MN)
Pensacola State Coll (FL)
San Juan Coll (NM)
Vincennes U (IN)

SPECIAL EDUCATION (ADMINISTRATION)
Foothill Coll (CA)

SPECIAL EDUCATION–EARLY CHILDHOOD
Motlow State Comm Coll (TN)

SPECIAL EDUCATION–ELEMENTARY SCHOOL
Westmoreland County Comm Coll (PA)

SPECIAL EDUCATION–INDIVIDUALS WITH SPEECH/LANGUAGE IMPAIRMENTS
Chemeketa Comm Coll (OR)

SPECIAL PRODUCTS MARKETING
Copiah-Lincoln Comm Coll (MS)
El Centro Coll (TX)
Metropolitan Comm Coll–Kansas City (MO)
Monroe Comm Coll (NY)
Orange Coast Coll (CA)
San Diego City Coll (CA)
Scottsdale Comm Coll (AZ)
South Plains Coll (TX)

SPEECH COMMUNICATION AND RHETORIC
Adirondack Comm Coll (NY)
Barton County Comm Coll (KS)
Brookhaven Coll (TX)
Bucks County Comm Coll (PA)
Casper Coll (WY)

Central Oregon Comm Coll (OR)
Cochise Coll, Sierra Vista (AZ)
Coll of Marin (CA)
Coll of the Desert (CA)
Collin County Comm Coll District (TX)
Comm Coll of Beaver County (PA)
Edison Comm Coll (OH)
Erie Comm Coll, South Campus (NY)
Fiorello H. LaGuardia Comm Coll of the City U of New York (NY)
Garden City Comm Coll (KS)
Harper Coll (IL)
Hutchinson Comm Coll and Area Vocational School (KS)
Jamestown Comm Coll (NY)
Lansing Comm Coll (MI)
Laramie County Comm Coll (WY)
Lehigh Carbon Comm Coll (PA)
Lone Star Coll–CyFair (TX)
Macomb Comm Coll (MI)
Manchester Comm Coll (CT)
Massachusetts Bay Comm Coll (MA)
Montgomery Coll (MD)
Montgomery County Comm Coll (PA)
Nassau Comm Coll (NY)
Northampton Comm Coll (PA)
Northwest Coll (WY)
Norwalk Comm Coll (CT)
Onondaga Comm Coll (NY)
Pasadena City Coll (CA)
Pensacola State Coll (FL)
Salt Lake Comm Coll (UT)
San Jacinto Coll District (TX)
Tompkins Cortland Comm Coll (NY)
Tyler Jr Coll (TX)

SPEECH-LANGUAGE PATHOLOGY
Lake Region State Coll (ND)
Parkland Coll (IL)

SPEECH-LANGUAGE PATHOLOGY ASSISTANT
Fayetteville Tech Comm Coll (NC)
Mitchell Tech Inst (SD)
Oklahoma City Comm Coll (OK)

SPEECH TEACHER EDUCATION
Darton State Coll (GA)

SPORT AND FITNESS ADMINISTRATION/MANAGEMENT
Adirondack Comm Coll (NY)
Barton County Comm Coll (KS)
Bucks County Comm Coll (PA)
Cayuga County Comm Coll (NY)
Central Oregon Comm Coll (OR)
Clark Coll (WA)
Garrett Coll (MD)
Holyoke Comm Coll (MA)
Howard Comm Coll (MD)
Lehigh Carbon Comm Coll (PA)
Lorain County Comm Coll (OH)
Niagara County Comm Coll (NY)
Northampton Comm Coll (PA)
Salt Lake Comm Coll (UT)
Springfield Tech Comm Coll (MA)
State U of New York Coll of Technology at Alfred (NY)
Sullivan County Comm Coll (NY)
Tompkins Cortland Comm Coll (NY)
Union County Coll (NJ)
Vincennes U (IN)

STATISTICS RELATED
Casper Coll (WY)

STRUCTURAL ENGINEERING
Moraine Park Tech Coll (WI)

SUBSTANCE ABUSE/ADDICTION COUNSELING
Adirondack Comm Coll (NY)
Alvin Comm Coll (TX)
Amarillo Coll (TX)
Anne Arundel Comm Coll (MD)
Austin Comm Coll (TX)
Butte Coll (CA)
Casper Coll (WY)
Central Oregon Comm Coll (OR)
Century Coll (MN)
Chemeketa Comm Coll (OR)
Chippewa Valley Tech Coll (WI)
Clark Coll (WA)
Colby Comm Coll (KS)
Coll of Lake County (IL)
Coll of the Desert (CA)
Comm Coll of Allegheny County (PA)

The Comm Coll of Baltimore County (MD)
Comm Coll of Rhode Island (RI)
Corning Comm Coll (NY)
Delaware Tech & Comm Coll, Stanton/Wilmington Campus (DE)
Delaware Tech & Comm Coll, Terry Campus (DE)
Erie Comm Coll (NY)
Finger Lakes Comm Coll (NY)
Flathead Valley Comm Coll (MT)
Fox Valley Tech Coll (WI)
Gadsden State Comm Coll (AL)
Garden City Comm Coll (KS)
Genesee Comm Coll (NY)
Guilford Tech Comm Coll (NC)
Housatonic Comm Coll (CT)
Howard Comm Coll (MD)
Illinois Central Coll (IL)
Kilian Comm Coll (SD)
Lower Columbia Coll (WA)
Mendocino Coll (CA)
Miami Dade Coll (FL)
Mohave Comm Coll (AZ)
Mohawk Valley Comm Coll (NY)
Moraine Park Tech Coll (WI)
Moraine Valley Comm Coll (IL)
North Shore Comm Coll (MA)
Oakton Comm Coll (IL)
Oklahoma State U, Oklahoma City (OK)
Olympic Coll (WA)
Oxnard Coll (CA)
Pierce Coll at Puyallup (WA)
Shawnee Comm Coll (IL)
Southeastern Comm Coll (IA)
Southern State Comm Coll (OH)
Sullivan County Comm Coll (NY)
Texarkana Coll (TX)
Tompkins Cortland Comm Coll (NY)
Tunxis Comm Coll (CT)
Tyler Jr Coll (TX)
Westchester Comm Coll (NY)

SURGICAL TECHNOLOGY
Anne Arundel Comm Coll (MD)
Austin Comm Coll (TX)
Bismarck State Coll (ND)
Cape Fear Comm Coll (NC)
Career Tech Coll (LA)
Carrington Coll California–San Jose (CA)
Carrington Coll of California–Citrus Heights (CA)
Collin County Comm Coll District (TX)
Comm Coll of Allegheny County (PA)
Comm Coll of the Air Force (AL)
Cuyahoga Comm Coll (OH)
Eastern Idaho Tech Coll (ID)
El Centro Coll (TX)
Fayetteville Tech Comm Coll (NC)
Flathead Valley Comm Coll (MT)
Gateway Tech Coll (WI)
Great Falls Coll Montana State U (MT)
Guilford Tech Comm Coll (NC)
Harrisburg Area Comm Coll (PA)
Illinois Central Coll (IL)
Ivy Tech Comm Coll–Central Indiana (IN)
Ivy Tech Comm Coll–Columbus (IN)
Ivy Tech Comm Coll–East Central (IN)
Ivy Tech Comm Coll–Kokomo (IN)
Ivy Tech Comm Coll–Lafayette (IN)
Ivy Tech Comm Coll–Northwest (IN)
Ivy Tech Comm Coll–Southwest (IN)
Ivy Tech Comm Coll–Wabash Valley (IN)
Kilgore Coll (TX)
Kirtland Comm Coll (MI)
Lakeland Comm Coll (OH)
Lake Superior Coll (MN)
Lancaster General Coll of Nursing & Health Sciences (PA)
Lansing Comm Coll (MI)
Laramie County Comm Coll (WY)
Lincoln Land Comm Coll (IL)
Lorain County Comm Coll (OH)
Luzerne County Comm Coll (PA)
Macomb Comm Coll (MI)
Manchester Comm Coll (CT)
McCann School of Business & Technology, Pottsville (PA)
Mohave Comm Coll (AZ)
Montgomery Coll (MD)
Montgomery County Comm Coll (PA)
Moraine Park Tech Coll (WI)
Nassau Comm Coll (NY)

Niagara County Comm Coll (NY)
Oakland Comm Coll (MI)
Oklahoma City Comm Coll (OK)
Owens Comm Coll, Toledo (OH)
Paris Jr Coll (TX)
Parkland Coll (IL)
Pittsburgh Tech Inst, Oakdale (PA)
Rasmussen Coll Brooklyn Park (MN)
Rasmussen Coll St. Cloud (MN)
San Jacinto Coll District (TX)
San Juan Coll (NM)
Southeast Tech Inst (SD)
Southern Maine Comm Coll (ME)
South Plains Coll (TX)
Spencerian Coll (KY)
Springfield Tech Comm Coll (MA)
Tarrant County Coll District (TX)
Texas State Tech Coll Harlingen (TX)
Tyler Jr Coll (TX)
Vincennes U (IN)
Waukesha County Tech Coll (WI)
Western Iowa Tech Comm Coll (IA)
West Kentucky Comm and Tech Coll (KY)
West Virginia Northern Comm Coll (WV)
Wilson Comm Coll (NC)

SURVEYING ENGINEERING
Comm Coll of Rhode Island (RI)

SURVEYING TECHNOLOGY
Austin Comm Coll (TX)
Bakersfield Coll (CA)
Bismarck State Coll (ND)
Central New Mexico Comm Coll (NM)
Clark Coll (WA)
Coll of the Canyons (CA)
The Comm Coll of Baltimore County (MD)
Delaware Tech & Comm Coll, Jack F. Owens Campus (DE)
Delaware Tech & Comm Coll, Stanton/Wilmington Campus (DE)
Fayetteville Tech Comm Coll (NC)
Flathead Valley Comm Coll (MT)
Gateway Tech Coll (WI)
Guilford Tech Comm Coll (NC)
Lansing Comm Coll (MI)
Macomb Comm Coll (MI)
Mohawk Valley Comm Coll (NY)
Mt. San Antonio Coll (CA)
Oklahoma State U, Oklahoma City (OK)
Penn State Wilkes-Barre (PA)
Phoenix Coll (AZ)
Salt Lake Comm Coll (UT)
Santa Rosa Jr Coll (CA)
Sheridan Coll (WY)
Southeast Tech Inst (SD)
Stark State Coll (OH)
State U of New York Coll of Technology at Alfred (NY)
Sullivan County Comm Coll (NY)
Tyler Jr Coll (TX)
U of Arkansas Comm Coll at Morrilton (AR)
Vincennes U (IN)
Waubonsee Comm Coll (IL)

SYSTEM, NETWORKING, AND LAN/WAN MANAGEMENT
Arapahoe Comm Coll (CO)
Bradford School (OH)
Catawba Valley Comm Coll (NC)
Comm Coll of Beaver County (PA)
Guilford Tech Comm Coll (NC)
LDS Business Coll (UT)
Lone Star Coll–Montgomery (TX)
Lone Star Coll–Tomball (TX)
Metropolitan Comm Coll–Kansas City (MO)
Mineral Area Coll (MO)
Moraine Valley Comm Coll (IL)
Oklahoma City Comm Coll (OK)
St. Louis Comm Coll at Meramec (MO)
St. Philip's Coll (TX)
San Jacinto Coll District (TX)
Temple Coll (TX)

TEACHER ASSISTANT/AIDE
Alamance Comm Coll (NC)
Borough of Manhattan Comm Coll of the City U of New York (NY)
Central Maine Comm Coll (ME)
Central Wyoming Coll (WY)
Century Coll (MN)
Comm Coll of Beaver County (PA)

Comm Coll of Vermont (VT)
Dakota Coll at Bottineau (ND)
El Centro Coll (TX)
Fiorello H. LaGuardia Comm Coll of the City U of New York (NY)
Gateway Tech Coll (WI)
Highland Comm Coll (IL)
Illinois Central Coll (IL)
Illinois Eastern Comm Colls, Lincoln Trail College (IL)
Jefferson Comm Coll (NY)
Kankakee Comm Coll (IL)
Kaskaskia Coll (IL)
Kennebec Valley Comm Coll (ME)
Kirtland Comm Coll (MI)
Lansing Comm Coll (MI)
Lehigh Carbon Comm Coll (PA)
Lincoln Land Comm Coll (IL)
Manchester Comm Coll (CT)
Mesa Comm Coll (AZ)
Miami Dade Coll (FL)
Montcalm Comm Coll (MI)
Montgomery County Comm Coll (PA)
Moraine Park Tech Coll (WI)
Moraine Valley Comm Coll (IL)
Northampton Comm Coll (PA)
Northwest State Comm Coll (OH)
Phoenix Coll (AZ)
St. Clair County Comm Coll (MI)
St. Philip's Coll (TX)
Salt Lake Comm Coll (UT)
San Diego City Coll (CA)
Sheridan Coll (WY)
Southern State Comm Coll (OH)
Southwestern Michigan Coll (MI)
Texas State Tech Coll Harlingen (TX)
The U of Akron–Wayne Coll (OH)
Victor Valley Coll (CA)
Vincennes U (IN)
Waubonsee Comm Coll (IL)
Waukesha County Tech Coll (WI)

TEACHING ASSISTANTS/AIDES RELATED
Terra State Comm Coll (OH)

TECHNICAL TEACHER EDUCATION
Chemeketa Comm Coll (OR)
Mineral Area Coll (MO)

TECHNOLOGY/INDUSTRIAL ARTS TEACHER EDUCATION
Casper Coll (WY)
Central New Mexico Comm Coll (NM)
Cowley County Comm Coll and Area Vocational–Tech School (KS)

TELECOMMUNICATIONS TECHNOLOGY
Amarillo Coll (TX)
Carl Albert State Coll (OK)
Cayuga County Comm Coll (NY)
Central Carolina Comm Coll (NC)
Clark Coll (WA)
Collin County Comm Coll District (TX)
County Coll of Morris (NJ)
Guilford Tech Comm Coll (NC)
Howard Comm Coll (MD)
Illinois Eastern Comm Colls, Lincoln Trail College (IL)
Ivy Tech Comm Coll–North Central (IN)
Ivy Tech Comm Coll–Northwest (IN)
Miami Dade Coll (FL)
Mitchell Tech Inst (SD)
Monroe Comm Coll (NY)
Northern Essex Comm Coll (MA)
Penn State DuBois (PA)
Penn State Fayette, The Eberly Campus (PA)
Penn State Hazleton (PA)
Penn State New Kensington (PA)
Penn State Schuylkill (PA)
Penn State Wilkes-Barre (PA)
Penn State York (PA)
Quinsigamond Comm Coll (MA)
St. Philip's Coll (TX)
Salt Lake Comm Coll (UT)
San Diego City Coll (CA)
Seminole State Coll of Florida (FL)
South Plains Coll (TX)
Springfield Tech Comm Coll (MA)
Texas State Tech Coll Harlingen (TX)
Trident Tech Coll (SC)
Union County Coll (NJ)
Western Iowa Tech Comm Coll (IA)

THEATER DESIGN AND TECHNOLOGY
Carroll Comm Coll (MD)
Casper Coll (WY)
Central Wyoming Coll (WY)
Foothill Coll (CA)
Harford Comm Coll (MD)
Howard Comm Coll (MD)
Lansing Comm Coll (MI)
Nassau Comm Coll (NY)
Normandale Comm Coll (MN)
Pasadena City Coll (CA)
Red Rocks Comm Coll (CO)
San Juan Coll (NM)
Southwestern Michigan Coll (MI)
Vincennes U (IN)

THEATER/THEATER ARTS MANAGEMENT
Harper Coll (IL)
Parkland Coll (IL)

THERAPEUTIC RECREATION
Austin Comm Coll (TX)
Comm Coll of Allegheny County (PA)

TOOL AND DIE TECHNOLOGY
Bevill State Comm Coll (AL)
Dunwoody Coll of Technology (MN)
Gadsden State Comm Coll (AL)
Ivy Tech Comm Coll–Bloomington (IN)
Ivy Tech Comm Coll–Central Indiana (IN)
Ivy Tech Comm Coll–Columbus (IN)
Ivy Tech Comm Coll–East Central (IN)
Ivy Tech Comm Coll–Kokomo (IN)
Ivy Tech Comm Coll–Lafayette (IN)
Ivy Tech Comm Coll–North Central (IN)
Ivy Tech Comm Coll–Northeast (IN)
Ivy Tech Comm Coll–Northwest (IN)
Ivy Tech Comm Coll–Richmond (IN)
Ivy Tech Comm Coll–Southern Indiana (IN)
Ivy Tech Comm Coll–Southwest (IN)
Ivy Tech Comm Coll–Wabash Valley (IN)
J. F. Drake State Tech Coll (AL)
Macomb Comm Coll (MI)
Northwest State Comm Coll (OH)
Oakland Comm Coll (MI)
Owens Comm Coll, Toledo (OH)
Shelton State Comm Coll (AL)
Southwestern Michigan Coll (MI)
Texas State Tech Coll Harlingen (TX)
Vincennes U (IN)

TOURISM AND TRAVEL SERVICES MANAGEMENT
Adirondack Comm Coll (NY)
Amarillo Coll (TX)
Bradford School (OH)
Bucks County Comm Coll (PA)
Butte Coll (CA)
Chemeketa Comm Coll (OR)
Daytona State Coll (FL)
Finger Lakes Comm Coll (NY)
Fiorello H. LaGuardia Comm Coll of the City U of New York (NY)
Genesee Comm Coll (NY)
Harrisburg Area Comm Coll (PA)
Houston Comm Coll System (TX)
Lakeland Comm Coll (OH)
Lansing Comm Coll (MI)
Lorain County Comm Coll (OH)
Luzerne County Comm Coll (PA)
Miami Dade Coll (FL)
Monroe Comm Coll (NY)
Moraine Valley Comm Coll (IL)
Niagara County Comm Coll (NY)
Northern Essex Comm Coll (MA)
North Shore Comm Coll (MA)
San Diego City Coll (CA)
San Diego Mesa Coll (CA)
Sullivan County Comm Coll (NY)
Westmoreland County Comm Coll (PA)

TOURISM AND TRAVEL SERVICES MARKETING
Bay State Coll (MA)
Comm Coll of Beaver County (PA)
Luzerne County Comm Coll (PA)
Montgomery County Comm Coll (PA)
San Diego Mesa Coll (CA)

TOURISM PROMOTION
Comm Coll of Allegheny County (PA)
Jefferson Comm Coll (NY)

TRADE AND INDUSTRIAL TEACHER EDUCATION
Copiah-Lincoln Comm Coll (MS)
Darton State Coll (GA)
Northeastern Jr Coll (CO)
Southeastern Comm Coll (IA)
Victor Valley Coll (CA)

TRANSPORTATION AND HIGHWAY ENGINEERING
Gateway Tech Coll (WI)

TRANSPORTATION AND MATERIALS MOVING RELATED
Cecil Coll (MD)
Mid-Plains Comm Coll, North Platte (NE)
Mt. San Antonio Coll (CA)
Nassau Comm Coll (NY)
St. Clair County Comm Coll (MI)
San Diego City Coll (CA)

TRANSPORTATION/MOBILITY MANAGEMENT
Cecil Coll (MD)
Hagerstown Comm Coll (MD)

TRUCK AND BUS DRIVER/ COMMERCIAL VEHICLE OPERATION/INSTRUCTION
Eastern Idaho Tech Coll (ID)
Mohave Comm Coll (AZ)
Spoon River Coll (IL)

TURF AND TURFGRASS MANAGEMENT
Catawba Valley Comm Coll (NC)
Coll of Lake County (IL)
Coll of the Desert (CA)
Comm Coll of Allegheny County (PA)
Delaware Tech & Comm Coll, Jack F. Owens Campus (DE)
Florida Gateway Coll (FL)
Guilford Tech Comm Coll (NC)
Harford Comm Coll (MD)
Houston Comm Coll System (TX)
Lake Michigan Coll (MI)
The Ohio State U Ag Tech Inst (OH)
Oklahoma State U, Oklahoma City (OK)
Ozarks Tech Comm Coll (MO)
Sheridan Coll (WY)
Southeast Tech Inst (SD)
Westmoreland County Comm Coll (PA)

URBAN FORESTRY
Dakota Coll at Bottineau (ND)
Kent State U at Trumbull (OH)
State U of New York Coll of Technology at Alfred (NY)

URBAN STUDIES/AFFAIRS
Lorain County Comm Coll (OH)

VEHICLE MAINTENANCE AND REPAIR TECHNOLOGIES
Coll of the Desert (CA)
Corning Comm Coll (NY)
Red Rocks Comm Coll (CO)

VEHICLE MAINTENANCE AND REPAIR TECHNOLOGIES RELATED
Central Maine Comm Coll (ME)
Central New Mexico Comm Coll (NM)
Corning Comm Coll (NY)
Guilford Tech Comm Coll (NC)
North Dakota State Coll of Science (ND)
State U of New York Coll of Technology at Alfred (NY)
Victor Valley Coll (CA)
Western Dakota Tech Inst (SD)

VETERINARY/ANIMAL HEALTH TECHNOLOGY
Bradford School (OH)
Carrington Coll California–Pleasant Hill (CA)
Carrington Coll California–San Jose (CA)
Carrington Coll California–San Leandro (CA)
Carrington Coll of California–Citrus Heights (CA)
Carrington Coll of California–Sacramento (CA)
Central Carolina Comm Coll (NC)
Central New Mexico Comm Coll (NM)
Colby Comm Coll (KS)

The Comm Coll of Baltimore County (MD)
County Coll of Morris (NJ)
Cuyahoga Comm Coll (OH)
Delaware Tech & Comm Coll, Jack F. Owens Campus (DE)
Fiorello H. LaGuardia Comm Coll of the City U of New York (NY)
Florida Gateway Coll (FL)
Foothill Coll (CA)
Fox Coll (IL)
Genesee Comm Coll (NY)
Hillsborough Comm Coll (FL)
Holyoke Comm Coll (MA)
International Business Coll, Indianapolis (IN)
Jefferson Coll (MO)
Jefferson State Comm Coll (AL)
Kaskaskia Coll (IL)
Kent State U at Tuscarawas (OH)
Lansing Comm Coll (MI)
Lehigh Carbon Comm Coll (PA)
Lone Star Coll–Tomball (TX)
Macomb Comm Coll (MI)
Manor Coll (PA)
Northampton Comm Coll (PA)
North Shore Comm Coll (MA)
Northwest Coll (WY)
Oakland Comm Coll (MI)
Oklahoma State U, Oklahoma City (OK)
Parkland Coll (IL)
Pierce Coll at Puyallup (WA)
San Diego Mesa Coll (CA)
San Juan Coll (NM)
Shawnee Comm Coll (IL)
State U of New York Coll of Technology at Alfred (NY)
Trident Tech Coll (SC)
Vet Tech Inst (PA)
Vet Tech Inst at Bradford School (OH)
Vet Tech Inst at Fox Coll (IL)
Vet Tech Inst at Hickey Coll (MO)
Vet Tech Inst at International Business Coll, Fort Wayne (IN)
Vet Tech Inst at International Business Coll, Indianapolis (IN)
Vet Tech Inst of Houston (TX)
Volunteer State Comm Coll (TN)
Westchester Comm Coll (NY)

VISUAL AND PERFORMING ARTS
Amarillo Coll (TX)
Berkshire Comm Coll (MA)
Borough of Manhattan Comm Coll of the City U of New York (NY)
Bucks County Comm Coll (PA)
The Comm Coll of Baltimore County (MD)
Dutchess Comm Coll (NY)
Fiorello H. LaGuardia Comm Coll of the City U of New York (NY)
Garden City Comm Coll (KS)
Harford Comm Coll (MD)
Harrisburg Area Comm Coll (PA)
Hutchinson Comm Coll and Area Vocational School (KS)
Kankakee Comm Coll (IL)
Lone Star Coll–Kingwood (TX)
Moraine Valley Comm Coll (IL)
Mott Comm Coll (MI)
Mt. San Antonio Coll (CA)
Nassau Comm Coll (NY)
Phoenix Coll (AZ)
Piedmont Virginia Comm Coll (VA)
Rogue Comm Coll (OR)
Sierra Coll (CA)

VISUAL AND PERFORMING ARTS RELATED
Comm Coll of Allegheny County (PA)
John Tyler Comm Coll (VA)
Northwest Coll (WY)
Thomas Nelson Comm Coll (VA)

VITICULTURE AND ENOLOGY
Chemeketa Comm Coll (OR)
Harrisburg Area Comm Coll (PA)
James Sprunt Comm Coll (NC)
Kent State U at Ashtabula (OH)
Santa Rosa Jr Coll (CA)

VOICE AND OPERA
Alvin Comm Coll (TX)
Oakland Comm Coll (MI)

WATCHMAKING AND JEWELRYMAKING
Austin Comm Coll (TX)

WATER QUALITY AND WASTEWATER TREATMENT MANAGEMENT AND RECYCLING TECHNOLOGY
Casper Coll (WY)
Coll of the Canyons (CA)
Delaware Tech & Comm Coll, Jack F. Owens Campus (DE)
Gateway Tech Coll (WI)
Moraine Park Tech Coll (WI)
Red Rocks Comm Coll (CO)

WEB/MULTIMEDIA MANAGEMENT AND WEBMASTER
Casper Coll (WY)
Clark Coll (WA)
Comm Coll of Beaver County (PA)
Comm Coll of Rhode Island (RI)
Flathead Valley Comm Coll (MT)
Fox Valley Tech Coll (WI)
Gateway Tech Coll (WI)
Illinois Central Coll (IL)
Kaskaskia Coll (IL)
Kilgore Coll (TX)
Kirtland Comm Coll (MI)
Lone Star Coll–Montgomery (TX)
Metropolitan Comm Coll–Kansas City (MO)
Monroe County Comm Coll (MI)
Montgomery County Comm Coll (PA)
Moraine Valley Comm Coll (IL)
Northern Essex Comm Coll (MA)
Oklahoma City Comm Coll (OK)
Red Rocks Comm Coll (CO)
St. Clair County Comm Coll (MI)
San Jacinto Coll District (TX)
Seminole State Coll of Florida (FL)
Sheridan Coll (WY)
Stark State Coll (OH)
Sullivan County Comm Coll (NY)
Temple Coll (TX)
Tompkins Cortland Comm Coll (NY)
Trident Tech Coll (SC)
Vincennes U (IN)
West Virginia Jr Coll–Bridgeport (WV)

WEB PAGE, DIGITAL/ MULTIMEDIA AND INFORMATION RESOURCES DESIGN
Berkeley City Coll (CA)
Bismarck State Coll (ND)
Blackhawk Tech Coll (WI)
Borough of Manhattan Comm Coll of the City U of New York (NY)
Bucks County Comm Coll (PA)
Casper Coll (WY)
Cecil Coll (MD)
Collin County Comm Coll District (TX)
Corning Comm Coll (NY)
County Coll of Morris (NJ)
Dunwoody Coll of Technology (MN)
Dyersburg State Comm Coll (TN)
El Centro Coll (TX)
Glendale Comm Coll (AZ)
Great Falls Coll Montana State U (MT)
Hagerstown Comm Coll (MD)
Harper Coll (IL)
Harrisburg Area Comm Coll (PA)
Hawkeye Comm Coll (IA)
Hutchinson Comm Coll and Area Vocational School (KS)
Illinois Central Coll (IL)
Lake Superior Coll (MN)
Lansing Comm Coll (MI)
LDS Business Coll (UT)
Lehigh Carbon Comm Coll (PA)
Lone Star Coll–Montgomery (TX)
Metropolitan Comm Coll–Kansas City (MO)
Middlesex Comm Coll (MA)
Miles Comm Coll (MT)
Monroe County Comm Coll (MI)
Montgomery Coll (MD)
Motlow State Comm Coll (TN)
Mott Comm Coll (MI)
Niagara County Comm Coll (NY)
Northampton Comm Coll (PA)
North Dakota State Coll of Science (ND)
Northern Essex Comm Coll (MA)
North Shore Comm Coll (MA)
Northwest State Comm Coll (OH)
Norwalk Comm Coll (CT)
Oklahoma State U, Oklahoma City (OK)
Oxnard Coll (CA)
Parkland Coll (IL)

Pasco-Hernando Comm Coll (FL)
Phoenix Coll (AZ)
Pittsburgh Tech Inst, Oakdale (PA)
Quinsigamond Comm Coll (MA)
Raritan Valley Comm Coll (NJ)
Rasmussen Coll Aurora (IL)
Rasmussen Coll Bismarck (ND)
Rasmussen Coll Bloomington (MN)
Rasmussen Coll Brooklyn Park (MN)
Rasmussen Coll Eagan (MN)
Rasmussen Coll Fargo (ND)
Rasmussen Coll Fort Myers (FL)
Rasmussen Coll Green Bay (WI)
Rasmussen Coll Lake Elmo/ Woodbury (MN)
Rasmussen Coll Mankato (MN)
Rasmussen Coll Moorhead (MN)
Rasmussen Coll New Port Richey (FL)
Rasmussen Coll Ocala (FL)
Rasmussen Coll St. Cloud (MN)
Red Rocks Comm Coll (CO)
Schoolcraft Coll (MI)
Seminole State Coll of Florida (FL)
Sierra Coll (CA)
Spoon River Coll (IL)
Springfield Tech Comm Coll (MA)
Stark State Coll (OH)
Sullivan Coll of Technology and Design (KY)
Terra State Comm Coll (OH)
Trident Tech Coll (SC)
Volunteer State Comm Coll (TN)
Waubonsee Comm Coll (IL)
Western Iowa Tech Comm Coll (IA)
Westmoreland County Comm Coll (PA)
Wisconsin Indianhead Tech Coll (WI)

WELDING ENGINEERING TECHNOLOGY
Mitchell Tech Inst (SD)

WELDING TECHNOLOGY
Alamance Comm Coll (NC)
Arizona Western Coll (AZ)
Arkansas State U–Mountain Home (AR)
Austin Comm Coll (TX)
Bainbridge Coll (GA)
Bakersfield Coll (CA)
Beaufort County Comm Coll (NC)
Big Bend Comm Coll (WA)
Bismarck State Coll (ND)
Butte Coll (CA)
Casper Coll (WY)
Central Wyoming Coll (WY)
Chemeketa Comm Coll (OR)
Clark Coll (WA)
Cochise Coll, Sierra Vista (AZ)
Coll of the Canyons (CA)
Comm Coll of Allegheny County (PA)
Comm Coll of Beaver County (PA)
Cowley County Comm Coll and Area Vocational–Tech School (KS)
Dunwoody Coll of Technology (MN)
Eastern Idaho Tech Coll (ID)
Elaine P. Nunez Comm Coll (LA)
Flathead Valley Comm Coll (MT)
Fox Valley Tech Coll (WI)
Garden City Comm Coll (KS)
Grand Rapids Comm Coll (MI)
Great Falls Coll Montana State U (MT)
Hutchinson Comm Coll and Area Vocational School (KS)
Illinois Central Coll (IL)
Jamestown Comm Coll (NY)
Jefferson Coll (MO)
Kankakee Comm Coll (IL)
Kaskaskia Coll (IL)
Kilgore Coll (TX)
Kirtland Comm Coll (MI)
Lake Area Tech Inst (SD)
Lansing Comm Coll (MI)
Lone Star Coll–CyFair (TX)
Lone Star Coll–Kingwood (TX)
Lone Star Coll–Montgomery (TX)
Lone Star Coll–North Harris (TX)
Lower Columbia Coll (WA)
Macomb Comm Coll (MI)
Mid-Plains Comm Coll, North Platte (NE)
Mohave Comm Coll (AZ)
Monroe County Comm Coll (MI)
Montcalm Comm Coll (MI)
Mt. San Antonio Coll (CA)
North Dakota State Coll of Science (ND)
Northwest Coll (WY)
Oakland Comm Coll (MI)
Oklahoma Tech Coll (OK)

Olympic Coll (WA)
Orange Coast Coll (CA)
Owens Comm Coll, Toledo (OH)
Ozarks Tech Comm Coll (MO)
Paris Jr Coll (TX)
Pasadena City Coll (CA)
Red Rocks Comm Coll (CO)
Rogue Comm Coll (OR)
St. Clair County Comm Coll (MI)
St. Philip's Coll (TX)
Salt Lake Comm Coll (UT)
San Diego City Coll (CA)
San Jacinto Coll District (TX)
San Juan Coll (NM)
Schoolcraft Coll (MI)
Shawnee Comm Coll (IL)
Shelton State Comm Coll (AL)
Sheridan Coll (WY)
Southeastern Comm Coll (IA)
Southeast Tech Inst (SD)
South Plains Coll (TX)

South Puget Sound Comm Coll (WA)
Southwestern Michigan Coll (MI)
State U of New York Coll of
  Technology at Alfred (NY)
Tarrant County Coll District (TX)
Terra State Comm Coll (OH)
Texarkana Coll (TX)
Texas State Tech Coll Harlingen (TX)
Tri-County Comm Coll (NC)
Tyler Jr Coll (TX)
Victor Valley Coll (CA)
Waubonsee Comm Coll (IL)
Westmoreland County Comm Coll
  (PA)

**WILDLIFE, FISH AND
WILDLANDS SCIENCE AND
MANAGEMENT**
Barton County Comm Coll (KS)
Casper Coll (WY)
Dakota Coll at Bottineau (ND)

Flathead Valley Comm Coll (MT)
Garrett Coll (MD)
Laramie County Comm Coll (WY)
Mt. San Antonio Coll (CA)
Penn State DuBois (PA)
Potomac State Coll of West Virginia
  U (WV)
Shawnee Comm Coll (IL)

WINE STEWARD/SOMMELIER
Cayuga County Comm Coll (NY)
Niagara County Comm Coll (NY)

WOMEN'S STUDIES
Bucks County Comm Coll (PA)
Casper Coll (WY)
Foothill Coll (CA)
Greenfield Comm Coll (MA)
Northern Essex Comm Coll (MA)
Norwalk Comm Coll (CT)

Santa Rosa Jr Coll (CA)
Sierra Coll (CA)

**WOOD SCIENCE AND WOOD
PRODUCTS/PULP AND PAPER
TECHNOLOGY**
Bakersfield Coll (CA)
Copiah-Lincoln Comm Coll (MS)
Dabney S. Lancaster Comm Coll
  (VA)
Halifax Comm Coll (NC)
Kennebec Valley Comm Coll (ME)
Potomac State Coll of West Virginia
  U (WV)

WOODWORKING
Red Rocks Comm Coll (CO)
Vincennes U (IN)

WORD PROCESSING
Lorain County Comm Coll (OH)

Monroe County Comm Coll (MI)
Orange Coast Coll (CA)
Owensboro Comm and Tech Coll
  (KY)
Seminole State Coll of Florida (FL)
Stark State Coll (OH)
Tallahassee Comm Coll (FL)

WORK AND FAMILY STUDIES
Arizona Western Coll (AZ)

WRITING
Austin Comm Coll (TX)
Berkeley City Coll (CA)
Cayuga County Comm Coll (NY)

ZOOLOGY/ANIMAL BIOLOGY
Dakota Coll at Bottineau (ND)
Garden City Comm Coll (KS)
Northeastern Jr Coll (CO)
Pensacola State Coll (FL)

Associate Degree Programs at Four-Year Colleges

ACCOUNTING
AIB Coll of Business (IA)
American U of Puerto Rico (PR)
Baker Coll of Clinton Township (MI)
California U of Pennsylvania (PA)
Calumet Coll of Saint Joseph (IN)
Central Penn Coll (PA)
Champlain Coll (VT)
Clarke U (IA)
Cleary U (MI)
Coll of Mount St. Joseph (OH)
Colorado Mountain Coll (CO)
Colorado Mountain Coll, Alpine Campus (CO)
Colorado Mountain Coll, Timberline Campus (CO)
Dakota Wesleyan U (SD)
Davenport U, Grand Rapids (MI)
Fisher Coll (MA)
Florida National U (FL)
Franklin U (OH)
Goldey-Beacom Coll (DE)
Harrison Coll, Indianapolis (IN)
Harrison Coll (OH)
Hawai`i Pacific U (HI)
Husson U (ME)
Immaculata U (PA)
Indiana Tech (IN)
Indiana Wesleyan U (IN)
Indian River State Coll (FL)
Inter American U of Puerto Rico, Aguadilla Campus (PR)
Inter American U of Puerto Rico, Bayamón Campus (PR)
Inter American U of Puerto Rico, Fajardo Campus (PR)
Inter American U of Puerto Rico, Ponce Campus (PR)
Inter American U of Puerto Rico, San Germán Campus (PR)
Johnson State Coll (VT)
Lake Superior State U (MI)
Lebanon Valley Coll (PA)
Maria Coll (NY)
Morrisville State Coll (NY)
Mount Aloysius Coll (PA)
Mount Marty Coll (SD)
Muhlenberg Coll (PA)
Palm Beach State Coll (FL)
Point Park U (PA)
Post U (CT)
Potomac Coll (DC)
Rasmussen Coll Appleton (WI)
Rasmussen Coll Blaine (MN)
Rasmussen Coll Land O' Lakes (FL)
Rasmussen Coll Mokena/Tinley Park (IL)
Rasmussen Coll Romeoville/Joliet (IL)
Rasmussen Coll Tampa/Brandon (FL)
Rasmussen Coll Wausau (WI)
Rogers State U (OK)
Saint Mary-of-the-Woods Coll (IN)
Shawnee State U (OH)
Siena Heights U (MI)
Southern New Hampshire U (NH)
State Coll of Florida Manatee-Sarasota (FL)
State U of New York Coll of Agriculture and Technology at Cobleskill (NY)
State U of New York Coll of Technology at Delhi (NY)
Stratford U, Woodbridge (VA)
Sullivan U (KY)
Thomas More Coll (KY)
Tiffin U (OH)
Trine U (IN)
Union Coll (NE)
Universidad del Turabo (PR)
U of Alaska Anchorage (AK)
U of Cincinnati (OH)
The U of Findlay (OH)
U of Rio Grande (OH)
The U of Texas at Brownsville (TX)
U of the Virgin Islands (VI)
The U of Toledo (OH)
The U of West Alabama (AL)
Utah Valley U (UT)
Walsh U (OH)
Webber International U (FL)
Youngstown State U (OH)

ACCOUNTING AND BUSINESS/ MANAGEMENT
AIB Coll of Business (IA)
Kansas State U (KS)

ACCOUNTING AND FINANCE
AIB Coll of Business (IA)

ACCOUNTING RELATED
AIB Coll of Business (IA)
Caribbean U (PR)
Franklin U (OH)

ACCOUNTING TECHNOLOGY AND BOOKKEEPING
American Public U System (WV)
DeVry U, Pomona (CA)
DeVry U, Westminster (CO)
DeVry U, Miramar (FL)
DeVry U, Orlando (FL)
DeVry U, Decatur (GA)
DeVry U, Federal Way (WA)
DeVry U Online (IL)
Ferris State U (MI)
Florida National U (FL)
Gannon U (PA)
Hickey Coll (MO)
Hilbert Coll (NY)
International Business Coll, Fort Wayne (IN)
Kent State U at Geauga (OH)
Lewis-Clark State Coll (ID)
Mercy Coll (NY)
Miami U (OH)
Montana Tech of The U of Montana (MT)
New York City Coll of Technology of the City U of New York (NY)
New York Inst of Technology (NY)
Pennsylvania Coll of Technology (PA)
Polk State Coll (FL)
Post U (CT)
State U of New York Coll of Technology at Canton (NY)
The U of Akron (OH)
U of Alaska Fairbanks (AK)
U of Cincinnati (OH)
U of Rio Grande (OH)
U of the District of Columbia (DC)
The U of Toledo (OH)
Valencia Coll (FL)

ACTING
Pacific Union Coll (CA)

ADMINISTRATIVE ASSISTANT AND SECRETARIAL SCIENCE
American U of Puerto Rico (PR)
Arkansas Tech U (AR)
Baker Coll of Clinton Township (MI)
Ball State U (IN)
Baptist Bible Coll of Pennsylvania (PA)
Campbellsville U (KY)

Caribbean U (PR)
Clarion U of Pennsylvania (PA)
Clayton State U (GA)
Columbia Centro Universitario, Caguas (PR)
Columbia Centro Universitario, Yauco (PR)
Concordia Coll–New York (NY)
Dordt Coll (IA)
EDP U of Puerto Rico (PR)
Faith Baptist Bible Coll and Theological Seminary (IA)
Florida National U (FL)
Harrison Coll, Indianapolis (IN)
Harrison Coll (OH)
Hickey Coll (MO)
Idaho State U (ID)
Indian River State Coll (FL)
Inter American U of Puerto Rico, Bayamón Campus (PR)
Inter American U of Puerto Rico, San Germán Campus (PR)
International Business Coll, Fort Wayne (IN)
Kuyper Coll (MI)
Lamar U (TX)
Lewis-Clark State Coll (ID)
Miami U (OH)
Montana Tech of The U of Montana (MT)
New York Inst of Technology (NY)
Northern Michigan U (MI)
Oakland City U (IN)
Ohio U–Chillicothe (OH)
Palm Beach State Coll (FL)
Rider U (NJ)
State Coll of Florida Manatee-Sarasota (FL)
Sul Ross State U (TX)
Tennessee State U (TN)
Universidad Adventista de las Antillas (PR)
U of Puerto Rico at Ponce (PR)
U of Rio Grande (OH)
U of the District of Columbia (DC)
Washburn U (KS)
Weber State U (UT)

ADULT AND CONTINUING EDUCATION
Fisher Coll (MA)

ADULT AND CONTINUING EDUCATION ADMINISTRATION
Concordia Coll–New York (NY)

ADULT DEVELOPMENT AND AGING
The U of Toledo (OH)

ADVERTISING
Academy of Art U (CA)
Fashion Inst of Technology (NY)
State Coll of Florida Manatee-Sarasota (FL)

AERONAUTICAL/AEROSPACE ENGINEERING TECHNOLOGY
Purdue U (IN)
Vaughn Coll of Aeronautics and Technology (NY)

AERONAUTICS/AVIATION/ AEROSPACE SCIENCE AND TECHNOLOGY
Embry-Riddle Aeronautical U–Worldwide (FL)
Liberty U (VA)
Montana State U (MT)

Ohio U (OH)
Pacific Union Coll (CA)
U of Alaska Anchorage (AK)
U of Cincinnati (OH)
U of the District of Columbia (DC)
Vaughn Coll of Aeronautics and Technology (NY)
Walla Walla U (WA)

AFRICAN AMERICAN/BLACK STUDIES
State Coll of Florida Manatee-Sarasota (FL)
U of Cincinnati (OH)

AGRIBUSINESS
Morehead State U (KY)
Morrisville State Coll (NY)
Southern Arkansas U–Magnolia (AR)
Vermont Tech Coll (VT)

AGRICULTURAL BUSINESS AND MANAGEMENT
Coll of Coastal Georgia (GA)
Indian River State Coll (FL)
Michigan State U (MI)
North Carolina State U (NC)
State U of New York Coll of Agriculture and Technology at Cobleskill (NY)

AGRICULTURAL BUSINESS AND MANAGEMENT RELATED
Penn State Abington (PA)
Penn State Altoona (PA)
Penn State Berks (PA)
Penn State Erie, The Behrend Coll (PA)
Penn State Shenango (PA)
Penn State U Park (PA)
U of Guelph (ON, Canada)

AGRICULTURAL ENGINEERING
Morrisville State Coll (NY)

AGRICULTURAL PRODUCTION
Eastern New Mexico U (NM)
Western Kentucky U (KY)

AGRICULTURE
Morrisville State Coll (NY)
North Carolina State U (NC)
South Dakota State U (SD)
U of Delaware (DE)
U of Guelph (ON, Canada)

AGRICULTURE AND AGRICULTURE OPERATIONS RELATED
Murray State U (KY)
U of New Hampshire (NH)

AGRONOMY AND CROP SCIENCE
State U of New York Coll of Agriculture and Technology at Cobleskill (NY)

AIRCRAFT POWERPLANT TECHNOLOGY
Embry-Riddle Aeronautical U–Daytona (FL)
Embry-Riddle Aeronautical U–Worldwide (FL)
Idaho State U (ID)
Pennsylvania Coll of Technology (PA)
U of Alaska Fairbanks (AK)

AIRFRAME MECHANICS AND AIRCRAFT MAINTENANCE TECHNOLOGY
Kansas State U (KS)
Lewis U (IL)
Northern Michigan U (MI)
Thomas Edison State Coll (NJ)
U of Alaska Anchorage (AK)

AIRLINE FLIGHT ATTENDANT
Liberty U (VA)

AIRLINE PILOT AND FLIGHT CREW
Indian River State Coll (FL)
Kansas State U (KS)
Lewis U (IL)
New England Inst of Technology (RI)
Palm Beach State Coll (FL)
Southern Illinois U Carbondale (IL)
U of Alaska Anchorage (AK)
U of Alaska Fairbanks (AK)
Utah Valley U (UT)

AIR TRAFFIC CONTROL
LeTourneau U (TX)
Lewis U (IL)
Thomas Edison State Coll (NJ)
U of Alaska Anchorage (AK)

AIR TRANSPORTATION RELATED
Thomas Edison State Coll (NJ)

ALLIED HEALTH AND MEDICAL ASSISTING SERVICES RELATED
Clarion U of Pennsylvania (PA)
Florida National U (FL)
Jones Coll, Jacksonville (FL)
National U (CA)
Nebraska Methodist Coll (NE)
Stratford U, Falls Church (VA)
Thomas Edison State Coll (NJ)
Widener U (PA)

ALLIED HEALTH DIAGNOSTIC, INTERVENTION, AND TREATMENT PROFESSIONS RELATED
Ball State U (IN)
Cameron U (OK)
Pennsylvania Coll of Technology (PA)
Thomas Edison State Coll (NJ)

AMERICAN GOVERNMENT AND POLITICS
State Coll of Florida Manatee-Sarasota (FL)

AMERICAN INDIAN/NATIVE AMERICAN STUDIES
Inst of American Indian Arts (NM)

AMERICAN NATIVE/NATIVE AMERICAN LANGUAGES
Idaho State U (ID)
U of Alaska Fairbanks (AK)

AMERICAN SIGN LANGUAGE (ASL)
Bethel Coll (IN)
Idaho State U (ID)
Madonna U (MI)

AMERICAN STUDIES
State Coll of Florida Manatee-Sarasota (FL)

ANIMAL/LIVESTOCK HUSBANDRY AND PRODUCTION
Michigan State U (MI)
North Carolina State U (NC)
Southern Utah U (UT)
U of Connecticut (CT)

ANIMAL SCIENCES
Becker Coll (MA)
State U of New York Coll of Agriculture and Technology at Cobleskill (NY)
Sul Ross State U (TX)
U of Connecticut (CT)
U of New Hampshire (NH)

ANIMAL TRAINING
Becker Coll (MA)

ANIMATION, INTERACTIVE TECHNOLOGY, VIDEO GRAPHICS AND SPECIAL EFFECTS
Academy of Art U (CA)
Colorado Mesa U (CO)
New England Inst of Technology (RI)

ANTHROPOLOGY
Indian River State Coll (FL)

APPAREL AND TEXTILE MANUFACTURING
Fashion Inst of Technology (NY)

APPAREL AND TEXTILE MARKETING MANAGEMENT
U of the Incarnate Word (TX)

APPAREL AND TEXTILES
Indian River State Coll (FL)
Palm Beach State Coll (FL)

APPLIED HORTICULTURE/ HORTICULTURAL BUSINESS SERVICES RELATED
Morrisville State Coll (NY)
U of Massachusetts Amherst (MA)

APPLIED HORTICULTURE/ HORTICULTURE OPERATIONS
Oakland City U (IN)
Pennsylvania Coll of Technology (PA)
Temple U (PA)
U of Connecticut (CT)
U of Massachusetts Amherst (MA)
U of New Hampshire (NH)

APPLIED MATHEMATICS
Central Methodist U (MO)
Clarion U of Pennsylvania (PA)

AQUACULTURE
Morrisville State Coll (NY)

ARCHITECTURAL DRAFTING AND CAD/CADD
Indiana U–Purdue U Indianapolis (IN)
Indian River State Coll (FL)
New York City Coll of Technology of the City U of New York (NY)
Universidad del Turabo (PR)
Western Kentucky U (KY)

ARCHITECTURAL ENGINEERING TECHNOLOGY
Baker Coll of Clinton Township (MI)
Baker Coll of Port Huron (MI)
Bluefield State Coll (WV)
Ferris State U (MI)
Indiana U–Purdue U Fort Wayne (IN)
New England Inst of Technology (RI)
Norfolk State U (VA)
Northern Kentucky U (KY)
State U of New York Coll of Technology at Delhi (NY)
U of Alaska Anchorage (AK)
U of the District of Columbia (DC)
Valencia Coll (FL)
Vermont Tech Coll (VT)
Wentworth Inst of Technology (MA)

ARCHITECTURAL TECHNOLOGY
Pennsylvania Coll of Technology (PA)

ARCHITECTURE
Morrisville State Coll (NY)

ARCHITECTURE RELATED
Abilene Christian U (TX)
New York Inst of Technology (NY)

ART
Coll of Coastal Georgia (GA)
Coll of Mount St. Joseph (OH)
Eastern New Mexico U (NM)
Felician Coll (NJ)
Indiana Wesleyan U (IN)
Kent State U at Stark (OH)
Keystone Coll (PA)
Lourdes U (OH)
Midland Coll (TX)
Northern Michigan U (MI)
Palm Beach State Coll (FL)
Rivier U (NH)
State Coll of Florida Manatee-Sarasota (FL)
State U of New York Empire State Coll (NY)
U of Cincinnati (OH)
U of Rio Grande (OH)
The U of Texas at Brownsville (TX)

ART HISTORY, CRITICISM AND CONSERVATION
Clarke U (IA)
John Cabot U (Italy)
Palm Beach State Coll (FL)
State Coll of Florida Manatee-Sarasota (FL)
Thomas More Coll (KY)

ARTIFICIAL INTELLIGENCE
Lamar U (TX)

ART TEACHER EDUCATION
Indian River State Coll (FL)

ASIAN STUDIES
State Coll of Florida Manatee-Sarasota (FL)

ASTRONOMY
State Coll of Florida Manatee-Sarasota (FL)

ATHLETIC TRAINING
The U of Akron (OH)

AUDIOLOGY AND SPEECH-LANGUAGE PATHOLOGY
U of Cincinnati (OH)

AUDIOVISUAL COMMUNICATIONS TECHNOLOGIES RELATED
AIB Coll of Business (IA)

AUTOBODY/COLLISION AND REPAIR TECHNOLOGY
Idaho State U (ID)
Lewis-Clark State Coll (ID)
New England Inst of Technology (RI)
Pennsylvania Coll of Technology (PA)
Utah Valley U (UT)

AUTOMOBILE/AUTOMOTIVE MECHANICS TECHNOLOGY
Baker Coll of Clinton Township (MI)
Baker Coll of Port Huron (MI)
Colorado Mesa U (CO)
Ferris State U (MI)
Idaho State U (ID)
Indian River State Coll (FL)
Lamar U (TX)
Lewis-Clark State Coll (ID)
Midland Coll (TX)
Montana Tech of The U of Montana (MT)
Morrisville State Coll (NY)
New England Inst of Technology (RI)
Northern Michigan U (MI)
Oakland City U (IN)
Pennsylvania Coll of Technology (PA)
Pittsburg State U (KS)
State U of New York Coll of Technology at Canton (NY)
U of Alaska Anchorage (AK)
U of the District of Columbia (DC)
Utah Valley U (UT)
Walla Walla U (WA)
Weber State U (UT)

AUTOMOTIVE ENGINEERING TECHNOLOGY
Farmingdale State Coll (NY)

Vermont Tech Coll (VT)
Weber State U (UT)

AVIATION/AIRWAY MANAGEMENT
U of Alaska Anchorage (AK)
U of the District of Columbia (DC)
Vaughn Coll of Aeronautics and Technology (NY)

AVIONICS MAINTENANCE TECHNOLOGY
Excelsior Coll (NY)
U of Alaska Anchorage (AK)
U of the District of Columbia (DC)
Vaughn Coll of Aeronautics and Technology (NY)

BAKING AND PASTRY ARTS
The Culinary Inst of America (NY)
Harrison Coll, Indianapolis (IN)
Newbury Coll (MA)
Pennsylvania Coll of Technology (PA)
Southern New Hampshire U (NH)
Stratford U (MD)
Stratford U, Falls Church (VA)
Stratford U, Woodbridge (VA)
Sullivan U (KY)
Valencia Coll (FL)

BANKING AND FINANCIAL SUPPORT SERVICES
Caribbean U (PR)
Harrison Coll, Indianapolis (IN)
Harrison Coll (OH)
Hilbert Coll (NY)
Indian River State Coll (FL)
Utah Valley U (UT)
Washburn U (KS)

BEHAVIORAL SCIENCES
Colorado Mountain Coll (CO)
Colorado Mountain Coll, Alpine Campus (CO)
Granite State Coll (NH)
Lewis-Clark State Coll (ID)
Midland Coll (TX)
Utah Valley U (UT)

BIBLICAL STUDIES
Alaska Bible Coll (AK)
Appalachian Bible Coll (WV)
Barclay Coll (KS)
Bethel Coll (IN)
Briercrest Coll (SK, Canada)
Campbellsville U (KY)
Cincinnati Christian U (OH)
Coll of Biblical Studies–Houston (TX)
Columbia International U (SC)
Corban U (OR)
Covenant Coll (GA)
Dallas Baptist U (TX)
Eastern Mennonite U (VA)
Faith Baptist Bible Coll and Theological Seminary (IA)
Florida Christian Coll (FL)
Grace U (NE)
Houghton Coll (NY)
Howard Payne U (TX)
Kuyper Coll (MI)
Lincoln Christian U (IL)
Maple Springs Baptist Bible Coll and Seminary (MD)
Mid-Atlantic Christian U (NC)
Nyack Coll (NY)
Point U (GA)
Simpson U (CA)
Southeastern Bible Coll (AL)
Southern Methodist Coll (SC)
Trinity Coll of Florida (FL)

BIOCHEMISTRY
Saint Joseph's Coll (IN)

BIOLOGICAL AND BIOMEDICAL SCIENCES RELATED
Alderson-Broaddus Coll (WV)
Roberts Wesleyan Coll (NY)

BIOLOGICAL AND PHYSICAL SCIENCES
Colorado Mountain Coll (CO)
Colorado Mountain Coll, Alpine Campus (CO)
Ferris State U (MI)
Ohio U–Zanesville (OH)
Penn State Altoona (PA)
Penn State Shenango (PA)

State U of New York Empire State Coll (NY)
Trine U (IN)
Valparaiso U (IN)

BIOLOGY/BIOLOGICAL SCIENCES
Cleveland Chiropractic Coll–Kansas City Campus (KS)
Coll of Coastal Georgia (GA)
Colorado Mountain Coll (CO)
Colorado Mountain Coll, Alpine Campus (CO)
Dalton State Coll (GA)
East-West U (IL)
Immaculata U (PA)
Indiana U South Bend (IN)
Indiana Wesleyan U (IN)
Indian River State Coll (FL)
Lourdes U (OH)
Midland Coll (TX)
National U (CA)
Palm Beach State Coll (FL)
Pine Manor Coll (MA)
Presentation Coll (SD)
Rogers State U (OK)
Shawnee State U (OH)
Siena Heights U (MI)
State Coll of Florida Manatee-Sarasota (FL)
State U of New York Coll of Agriculture and Technology at Cobleskill (NY)
Thomas Edison State Coll (NJ)
Thomas More Coll (KY)
Thompson Rivers U (BC, Canada)
U of Cincinnati (OH)
U of New Hampshire at Manchester (NH)
U of Puerto Rico at Ponce (PR)
U of Rio Grande (OH)
The U of Tampa (FL)
Utah Valley U (UT)
Wright State U (OH)
York Coll of Pennsylvania (PA)

BIOLOGY/BIOTECHNOLOGY LABORATORY TECHNICIAN
State U of New York Coll of Agriculture and Technology at Cobleskill (NY)
Weber State U (UT)

BIOLOGY TEACHER EDUCATION
State Coll of Florida Manatee-Sarasota (FL)

BIOMEDICAL TECHNOLOGY
Indiana U–Purdue U Indianapolis (IN)
Penn State Altoona (PA)
Penn State Berks (PA)
Penn State Erie, The Behrend Coll (PA)
Penn State Shenango (PA)
Thomas Edison State Coll (NJ)
U of Arkansas for Medical Sciences (AR)

BIOTECHNOLOGY
Indiana U–Purdue U Indianapolis (IN)
Universidad del Turabo (PR)

BOTANY/PLANT BIOLOGY
Palm Beach State Coll (FL)

BRASS INSTRUMENTS
McNally Smith Coll of Music (MN)

BROADCAST JOURNALISM
Evangel U (MO)
Ohio U–Zanesville (OH)

BUILDING/CONSTRUCTION FINISHING, MANAGEMENT, AND INSPECTION RELATED
John Brown U (AR)
Palm Beach State Coll (FL)
Pratt Inst (NY)
State U of New York Coll of Technology at Delhi (NY)
Weber State U (UT)
Wentworth Inst of Technology (MA)

BUILDING/CONSTRUCTION SITE MANAGEMENT
Utah Valley U (UT)
Wentworth Inst of Technology (MA)

BUILDING CONSTRUCTION TECHNOLOGY
Wentworth Inst of Technology (MA)

BUILDING/HOME/ CONSTRUCTION INSPECTION
Utah Valley U (UT)

BUILDING/PROPERTY MAINTENANCE
State U of New York Coll of Technology at Canton (NY)
Utah Valley U (UT)

BUSINESS ADMINISTRATION AND MANAGEMENT
AIB Coll of Business (IA)
Alaska Pacific U (AK)
Albertus Magnus Coll (CT)
American U of Puerto Rico (PR)
The American U of Rome (Italy)
Anderson U (IN)
Austin Peay State U (TN)
Ball State U (IN)
Bay Path Coll (MA)
Beacon Coll (FL)
Benedictine Coll (KS)
Benedictine U (IL)
Bethel Coll (IN)
California U of Pennsylvania (PA)
Calumet Coll of Saint Joseph (IN)
Cameron U (OK)
Campbellsville U (KY)
Cardinal Stritch U (WI)
Carroll Coll (MT)
Central Penn Coll (PA)
Chaminade U of Honolulu (HI)
Clarion U of Pennsylvania (PA)
Cleary U (MI)
Coll of Coastal Georgia (GA)
Coll of Mount St. Joseph (OH)
Coll of Saint Mary (NE)
Colorado Mountain Coll (CO)
Colorado Mountain Coll, Alpine Campus (CO)
Columbia Centro Universitario, Yauco (PR)
Concordia Coll–New York (NY)
Concordia U (OR)
Concord U (WV)
Corban U (OR)
Dakota State U (SD)
Dakota Wesleyan U (SD)
Dallas Baptist U (TX)
Dalton State Coll (GA)
Davenport U, Grand Rapids (MI)
East-West U (IL)
Edinboro U of Pennsylvania (PA)
EDP U of Puerto Rico (PR)
Excelsior Coll (NY)
Faulkner U (AL)
Fisher Coll (MA)
Five Towns Coll (NY)
Florida National U (FL)
Franklin U (OH)
Geneva Coll (PA)
Goldey-Beacom Coll (DE)
Grantham U (MO)
Harrison Coll, Indianapolis (IN)
Harrison Coll (OH)
Hawai'i Pacific U (HI)
Hilbert Coll (NY)
Husson U (ME)
Immaculata U (PA)
Indiana Tech (IN)
Indiana U of Pennsylvania (PA)
Indiana U–Purdue U Fort Wayne (IN)
Indiana Wesleyan U (IN)
Indian River State Coll (FL)
Inter American U of Puerto Rico, Aguadilla Campus (PR)
Inter American U of Puerto Rico, Bayamón Campus (PR)
Inter American U of Puerto Rico, Fajardo Campus (PR)
Inter American U of Puerto Rico, Ponce Campus (PR)
Inter American U of Puerto Rico, San Germán Campus (PR)
John Cabot U (Italy)
Johnson State Coll (VT)
Jones Coll, Jacksonville (FL)
Jones International U (CO)
Kansas Wesleyan U (KS)
Kent State U (OH)
Keystone Coll (PA)
King's Coll (PA)
Lake Superior State U (MI)
Lebanon Valley Coll (PA)
Lincoln Memorial U (TN)

Lock Haven U of Pennsylvania (PA)
Long Island U–Brooklyn Campus (NY)
Madonna U (MI)
Maria Coll (NY)
Marian U (IN)
Marietta Coll (OH)
McKendree U (IL)
Medaille Coll (NY)
Mercy Coll (NY)
Missouri Baptist U (MO)
Missouri Western State U (MO)
Montreat Coll, Montreat (NC)
Morrisville State Coll (NY)
Mount Aloysius Coll (PA)
Mount Marty Coll (SD)
Mount St. Mary's Coll (CA)
Muhlenberg Coll (PA)
Newbury Coll (MA)
New England Inst of Technology (RI)
Newman U (KS)
New Mexico Inst of Mining and Technology (NM)
Niagara U (NY)
Northwood U, Michigan Campus (MI)
Nyack Coll (NY)
Oakland City U (IN)
Ohio Dominican U (OH)
Ohio U–Chillicothe (OH)
Peirce Coll (PA)
Pennsylvania Coll of Technology (PA)
Point Park U (PA)
Polk State Coll (FL)
Post U (CT)
Potomac Coll (DC)
Providence Coll (RI)
Rasmussen Coll Appleton (WI)
Rasmussen Coll Blaine (MN)
Rasmussen Coll Land O' Lakes (FL)
Rasmussen Coll Mokena/Tinley Park (IL)
Rasmussen Coll Romeoville/Joliet (IL)
Rasmussen Coll Tampa/Brandon (FL)
Rasmussen Coll Wausau (WI)
Regent U (VA)
Rider U (NJ)
Rivier U (NH)
Robert Morris U Illinois (IL)
Rogers State U (OK)
Roger Williams U (RI)
St. Francis Coll (NY)
St. Gregory's U, Shawnee (OK)
St. John's U (NY)
Saint Joseph's U (PA)
Saint Peter's U (NJ)
St. Thomas Aquinas Coll (NY)
Salem International U (WV)
Shawnee State U (OH)
Shaw U (NC)
Siena Heights U (MI)
Southern California Inst of Technology (CA)
Southern New Hampshire U (NH)
State Coll of Florida Manatee-Sarasota (FL)
State U of New York Coll of Agriculture and Technology at Cobleskill (NY)
State U of New York Coll of Technology at Canton (NY)
State U of New York Coll of Technology at Delhi (NY)
State U of New York Empire State Coll (NY)
Stratford U, Falls Church (VA)
Stratford U, Woodbridge (VA)
Taylor U (IN)
Thomas Edison State Coll (NJ)
Thomas More Coll (KY)
Tiffin U (OH)
Trine U (IN)
Tulane U (LA)
Union Coll (NE)
Universidad Adventista de las Antillas (PR)
Universidad del Turabo (PR)
The U of Akron (OH)
U of Alaska Anchorage (AK)
U of Alaska Fairbanks (AK)
U of Arkansas–Fort Smith (AR)
U of Central Arkansas (AR)
U of Cincinnati (OH)
The U of Findlay (OH)
U of Maine at Fort Kent (ME)
The U of Montana Western (MT)
U of New Hampshire (NH)
U of New Hampshire at Manchester (NH)
U of New Haven (CT)

U of Pennsylvania (PA)
U of Pikeville (KY)
U of Rio Grande (OH)
The U of Scranton (PA)
U of the Incarnate Word (TX)
U of the Virgin Islands (VI)
The U of Toledo (OH)
Upper Iowa U (IA)
Utah Valley U (UT)
Valencia Coll (FL)
Vermont Tech Coll (VT)
Villa Maria Coll of Buffalo (NY)
Walla Walla U (WA)
Walsh U (OH)
Wayland Baptist U (TX)
Webber International U (FL)
Wesley Coll (DE)
Western Kentucky U (KY)
Wright State U (OH)
Xavier U (OH)
York Coll of Pennsylvania (PA)
Youngstown State U (OH)

BUSINESS ADMINISTRATION, MANAGEMENT AND OPERATIONS RELATED
AIB Coll of Business (IA)
Columbia Centro Universitario, Caguas (PR)
Embry-Riddle Aeronautical U–Worldwide (FL)
U of Cincinnati (OH)

BUSINESS AUTOMATION/TECHNOLOGY/DATA ENTRY
Baker Coll of Clinton Township (MI)
Colorado Mesa U (CO)
Mercy Coll (NY)
Northern Michigan U (MI)
The U of Akron (OH)
U of Alaska Anchorage (AK)
U of Rio Grande (OH)
U of the District of Columbia (DC)
The U of Toledo (OH)
Utah Valley U (UT)

BUSINESS/COMMERCE
Adams State U (CO)
AIB Coll of Business (IA)
Alderson-Broaddus Coll (WV)
Alvernia U (PA)
American Public U System (WV)
Caribbean U (PR)
Castleton State Coll (VT)
Champlain Coll (VT)
Coll of Staten Island of the City of New York (NY)
Colorado Mountain Coll, Timberline Campus (CO)
Columbia Coll (MO)
Crown Coll (MN)
Ferris State U (MI)
Fisher Coll (MA)
Gannon U (PA)
Granite State Coll (NH)
Hillsdale Free Will Baptist Coll (OK)
Idaho State U (ID)
Indiana U Kokomo (IN)
Indiana U Northwest (IN)
Indiana U South Bend (IN)
Indiana U Southeast (IN)
Kent State U at Geauga (OH)
Limestone Coll (SC)
Lourdes U (OH)
Mayville State U (ND)
Midland Coll (TX)
Mount Vernon Nazarene U (OH)
Murray State U (KY)
New York U (NY)
Northern Kentucky U (KY)
Northern Michigan U (MI)
Pacific Union Coll (CA)
Penn State Abington (PA)
Penn State Altoona (PA)
Penn State Berks (PA)
Penn State Erie, The Behrend Coll (PA)
Penn State Harrisburg (PA)
Penn State Shenango (PA)
Penn State U Park (PA)
Purdue U Calumet (IN)
Saint Leo U (FL)
Saint Mary-of-the-Woods Coll (IN)
Southern Arkansas U–Magnolia (AR)
Southern Nazarene U (OK)
Southwest Baptist U (MO)
Spalding U (KY)
State Coll of Florida Manatee-Sarasota (FL)
Thomas More Coll (KY)
Thomas U (GA)
Troy U (AL)

Tulane U (LA)
U of Alaska Anchorage (AK)
U of Bridgeport (CT)
U of Cincinnati (OH)
U of New Hampshire (NH)
U of Puerto Rico at Ponce (PR)
U of Southern Indiana (IN)
The U of Toledo (OH)
Wright State U (OH)
Youngstown State U (OH)

BUSINESS/CORPORATE COMMUNICATIONS
AIB Coll of Business (IA)

BUSINESS MACHINE REPAIR
Lamar U (TX)

BUSINESS, MANAGEMENT, AND MARKETING RELATED
Ball State U (IN)
Caribbean U (PR)
Five Towns Coll (NY)
Florida National U (FL)
Presentation Coll (SD)
Purdue U North Central (IN)
Sacred Heart U (CT)
Sullivan U (KY)

BUSINESS/MANAGERIAL ECONOMICS
Campbellsville U (KY)
Caribbean U (PR)
Saint Peter's U (NJ)
State Coll of Florida Manatee-Sarasota (FL)

BUSINESS OPERATIONS SUPPORT AND SECRETARIAL SERVICES RELATED
Thomas Edison State Coll (NJ)

BUSINESS TEACHER EDUCATION
Wright State U (OH)

CABINETMAKING AND MILLWORK
Utah Valley U (UT)

CAD/CADD DRAFTING/DESIGN TECHNOLOGY
Ferris State U (MI)
Idaho State U (ID)
Montana Tech of The U of Montana (MT)
Northern Michigan U (MI)
Shawnee State U (OH)
U of Arkansas–Fort Smith (AR)

CANADIAN STUDIES
Thompson Rivers U (BC, Canada)

CARDIOVASCULAR TECHNOLOGY
Mercy Coll of Ohio (OH)
Nebraska Methodist Coll (NE)
New York U (NY)
Polk State Coll (FL)
Valencia Coll (FL)

CARPENTRY
Indian River State Coll (FL)
Liberty U (VA)
Montana Tech of The U of Montana (MT)
New England Inst of Technology (RI)
Southern Utah U (UT)
U of Alaska Fairbanks (AK)

CERAMIC ARTS AND CERAMICS
Palm Beach State Coll (FL)

CHEMICAL ENGINEERING
U of the District of Columbia (DC)

CHEMICAL TECHNOLOGY
Ball State U (IN)
Excelsior Coll (NY)
Ferris State U (MI)
Indiana U–Purdue U Fort Wayne (IN)
Lawrence Technological U (MI)
Midland Coll (TX)
Millersville U of Pennsylvania (PA)
New York City Coll of Technology of the City U of New York (NY)
State U of New York Coll of Agriculture and Technology at Cobleskill (NY)
U of Cincinnati (OH)
Weber State U (UT)

CHEMISTRY
Castleton State Coll (VT)
Central Methodist U (MO)
Clarke U (IA)
Coll of Coastal Georgia (GA)
Dalton State Coll (GA)
Immaculata U (PA)
Indiana U–Purdue U Indianapolis (IN)
Indiana U South Bend (IN)
Indiana Wesleyan U (IN)
Indian River State Coll (FL)
Lake Superior State U (MI)
Lindsey Wilson Coll (KY)
Midland Coll (TX)
Ohio Dominican U (OH)
Palm Beach State Coll (FL)
Presentation Coll (SD)
Siena Heights U (MI)
Southern Arkansas U–Magnolia (AR)
State Coll of Florida Manatee-Sarasota (FL)
Thomas More Coll (KY)
Thompson Rivers U (BC, Canada)
U of Cincinnati (OH)
U of Rio Grande (OH)
The U of Tampa (FL)
U of the Incarnate Word (TX)
Utah Valley U (UT)
Wichita State U (KS)
Wright State U (OH)
York Coll of Pennsylvania (PA)

CHEMISTRY TEACHER EDUCATION
State Coll of Florida Manatee-Sarasota (FL)

CHILD-CARE AND SUPPORT SERVICES MANAGEMENT
Bob Jones U (SC)
Eastern New Mexico U (NM)
Ferris State U (MI)
Mount Vernon Nazarene U (OH)
Nicholls State U (LA)
Pine Manor Coll (MA)
Post U (CT)
Siena Heights U (MI)
Southeast Missouri State U (MO)
State U of New York Coll of Agriculture and Technology at Cobleskill (NY)
Youngstown State U (OH)

CHILD-CARE PROVISION
American Public U System (WV)
Louisiana State U at Alexandria (LA)
Mayville State U (ND)
Pennsylvania Coll of Technology (PA)
Trevecca Nazarene U (TN)
U of Alaska Anchorage (AK)
U of Alaska Fairbanks (AK)

CHILD DEVELOPMENT
Arkansas Tech U (AR)
Evangel U (MO)
Grambling State U (LA)
Indian River State Coll (FL)
Kuyper Coll (MI)
Lamar U (TX)
Lewis-Clark State Coll (ID)
Madonna U (MI)
Midland Coll (TX)
Northern Michigan U (MI)
Ohio U (OH)
Ohio U–Chillicothe (OH)
Polk State Coll (FL)
Southern Utah U (UT)
State Coll of Florida Manatee-Sarasota (FL)
U of the District of Columbia (DC)
Youngstown State U (OH)

CHRISTIAN STUDIES
Crown Coll (MN)
Huntington U (IN)
Oklahoma Baptist U (OK)
Regent U (VA)
Wayland Baptist U (TX)

CINEMATOGRAPHY AND FILM/VIDEO PRODUCTION
Academy of Art U (CA)
New England Inst of Technology (RI)
Pacific Union Coll (CA)
Valencia Coll (FL)

CIVIL ENGINEERING TECHNOLOGY
Bluefield State Coll (WV)
Fairmont State U (WV)
Ferris State U (MI)
Idaho State U (ID)

Indiana U–Purdue U Fort Wayne (IN)
Indiana U–Purdue U Indianapolis (IN)
Indian River State Coll (FL)
Montana Tech of The U of Montana (MT)
New York City Coll of Technology of the City U of New York (NY)
Pennsylvania Coll of Technology (PA)
Point Park U (PA)
State Coll of Florida Manatee-Sarasota (FL)
State U of New York Coll of Technology at Canton (NY)
U of New Hampshire (NH)
U of Puerto Rico at Bayamón (PR)
U of Puerto Rico at Ponce (PR)
U of the District of Columbia (DC)
Valencia Coll (FL)
Vermont Tech Coll (VT)
Youngstown State U (OH)

CLINICAL LABORATORY SCIENCE/MEDICAL TECHNOLOGY
Arkansas State U (AR)
Dalton State Coll (GA)
Ferris State U (MI)
Harrison Coll, Indianapolis (IN)
Lake Superior State U (MI)
Shawnee State U (OH)
Thomas Edison State Coll (NJ)
U of Cincinnati (OH)

CLINICAL/MEDICAL LABORATORY ASSISTANT
U of Alaska Fairbanks (AK)

CLINICAL/MEDICAL LABORATORY SCIENCE AND ALLIED PROFESSIONS RELATED
Youngstown State U (OH)

CLINICAL/MEDICAL LABORATORY TECHNOLOGY
Coll of Coastal Georgia (GA)
Dalton State Coll (GA)
Farmingdale State Coll (NY)
Ferris State U (MI)
The George Washington U (DC)
Indian River State Coll (FL)
Louisiana State U at Alexandria (LA)
Marshall U (WV)
Mount Aloysius Coll (PA)
State U of New York Coll of Agriculture and Technology at Cobleskill (NY)
U of Alaska Anchorage (AK)
U of Rio Grande (OH)
The U of Texas at Brownsville (TX)
Weber State U (UT)
Youngstown State U (OH)

COMMERCIAL AND ADVERTISING ART
Academy of Art U (CA)
Baker Coll of Clinton Township (MI)
Baker Coll of Port Huron (MI)
Colorado Mountain Coll (CO)
Fashion Inst of Technology (NY)
Mercy Coll (NY)
Mitchell Coll (CT)
Mount St. Mary's Coll (CA)
New York City Coll of Technology of the City U of New York (NY)
Northern State U (SD)
Palm Beach State Coll (FL)
Pennsylvania Coll of Technology (PA)
Pratt Inst (NY)
Robert Morris U Illinois (IL)
State Coll of Florida Manatee-Sarasota (FL)
State U of New York Coll of Agriculture and Technology at Cobleskill (NY)
Suffolk U (MA)
U of Cincinnati (OH)
Utah Valley U (UT)
Valencia Coll (FL)
Villa Maria Coll of Buffalo (NY)

COMMERCIAL PHOTOGRAPHY
Academy of Art U (CA)
Fashion Inst of Technology (NY)

COMMUNICATION
American U of Puerto Rico (PR)
Midland Coll (TX)
Thomas More Coll (KY)

COMMUNICATION AND JOURNALISM RELATED
Clarke U (IA)

Immaculata U (PA)
Keystone Coll (PA)
Madonna U (MI)
National U (CA)
Tulane U (LA)
Valparaiso U (IN)

COMMUNICATION AND MEDIA RELATED
Keystone Coll (PA)

COMMUNICATION SCIENCES AND DISORDERS
Ohio U–Chillicothe (OH)

COMMUNICATIONS TECHNOLOGY
AIB Coll of Business (IA)
Colorado Mesa U (CO)

COMMUNITY HEALTH AND PREVENTIVE MEDICINE
Utah Valley U (UT)

COMMUNITY HEALTH SERVICES COUNSELING
State Coll of Florida Manatee-Sarasota (FL)

COMMUNITY ORGANIZATION AND ADVOCACY
State U of New York Empire State Coll (NY)
The U of Akron (OH)
U of Alaska Fairbanks (AK)
The U of Findlay (OH)
U of New Hampshire (NH)

COMPARATIVE LITERATURE
John Cabot U (Italy)
Palm Beach State Coll (FL)

COMPUTER AND INFORMATION SCIENCES
Ball State U (IN)
Caribbean U (PR)
Chaminade U of Honolulu (HI)
Clarke U (IA)
Coll of Mount St. Joseph (OH)
Columbia Coll (MO)
Edinboro U of Pennsylvania (PA)
Fisher Coll (MA)
Indiana Wesleyan U (IN)
Inter American U of Puerto Rico, Fajardo Campus (PR)
Inter American U of Puerto Rico, Ponce Campus (PR)
Jones Coll, Jacksonville (FL)
King's Coll (PA)
Lewis-Clark State Coll (ID)
Lincoln U (MO)
Manchester U (IN)
Midland Coll (TX)
Morrisville State Coll (NY)
National U (CA)
New England Inst of Technology (RI)
New York City Coll of Technology of the City U of New York (NY)
Rogers State U (OK)
St. John's U (NY)
Salem International U (WV)
Southern New Hampshire U (NH)
State Coll of Florida Manatee-Sarasota (FL)
State U of New York Coll of Agriculture and Technology at Cobleskill (NY)
Troy U (AL)
Tulane U (LA)
U of Alaska Anchorage (AK)
U of Arkansas–Fort Smith (AR)
U of Cincinnati (OH)
The U of Tampa (FL)
The U of Texas at Brownsville (TX)
The U of Toledo (OH)
Utah Valley U (UT)
Washburn U (KS)
Webber International U (FL)

COMPUTER AND INFORMATION SCIENCES AND SUPPORT SERVICES RELATED
Colorado Mountain Coll (CO)
Florida National U (FL)
Husson U (ME)
Indiana U–Purdue U Indianapolis (IN)
Pace U (NY)
Palm Beach State Coll (FL)
Potomac Coll (DC)
Utah Valley U (UT)

COMPUTER AND INFORMATION SCIENCES RELATED
Limestone Coll (SC)
Lindsey Wilson Coll (KY)
Madonna U (MI)
State Coll of Florida Manatee-Sarasota (FL)

COMPUTER AND INFORMATION SYSTEMS SECURITY
Davenport U, Grand Rapids (MI)
Florida National U (FL)
Potomac Coll (DC)
St. John's U (NY)
Stratford U, Woodbridge (VA)

COMPUTER ENGINEERING
New England Inst of Technology (RI)
The U of Scranton (PA)

COMPUTER ENGINEERING TECHNOLOGIES RELATED
Thomas Edison State Coll (NJ)
Universidad del Turabo (PR)

COMPUTER ENGINEERING TECHNOLOGY
California U of Pennsylvania (PA)
Colorado Mountain Coll (CO)
Colorado Mountain Coll, Alpine Campus (CO)
Dalton State Coll (GA)
Indiana U–Purdue U Indianapolis (IN)
Indian River State Coll (FL)
Northern Michigan U (MI)
Oakland City U (IN)
State Coll of Florida Manatee-Sarasota (FL)
Universidad del Turabo (PR)
U of Alaska Anchorage (AK)
U of Hartford (CT)
U of the District of Columbia (DC)
Valencia Coll (FL)
Vermont Tech Coll (VT)
Weber State U (UT)

COMPUTER GRAPHICS
Creative Center (NE)
EDP U of Puerto Rico (PR)
Florida National U (FL)
Indiana Tech (IN)
Purdue U Calumet (IN)
State Coll of Florida Manatee-Sarasota (FL)

COMPUTER/INFORMATION TECHNOLOGY SERVICES ADMINISTRATION RELATED
Keystone Coll (PA)
Limestone Coll (SC)
Maria Coll (NY)
Mercy Coll (NY)
Pennsylvania Coll of Technology (PA)
Valencia Coll (FL)

COMPUTER INSTALLATION AND REPAIR TECHNOLOGY
Dalton State Coll (GA)
Inter American U of Puerto Rico, Aguadilla Campus (PR)
Inter American U of Puerto Rico, Bayamón Campus (PR)
Inter American U of Puerto Rico, Fajardo Campus (PR)
Sullivan U (KY)
U of Alaska Fairbanks (AK)

COMPUTER PROGRAMMING
Baker Coll of Port Huron (MI)
Caribbean U (PR)
Castleton State Coll (VT)
Champlain Coll (VT)
Coll of Staten Island of the City U of New York (NY)
Columbia Centro Universitario, Caguas (PR)
EDP U of Puerto Rico (PR)
Florida National U (FL)
Hickey Coll (MO)
Indian River State Coll (FL)
International Business Coll, Fort Wayne (IN)
Limestone Coll (SC)
New England Inst of Technology (RI)
Oakland City U (IN)
Palm Beach State Coll (FL)

State Coll of Florida Manatee-Sarasota (FL)
Stratford U, Falls Church (VA)
U of Arkansas at Little Rock (AR)
Walla Walla U (WA)
Youngstown State U (OH)

COMPUTER PROGRAMMING RELATED
Florida National U (FL)
State Coll of Florida Manatee-Sarasota (FL)
Stratford U, Falls Church (VA)

COMPUTER PROGRAMMING (SPECIFIC APPLICATIONS)
Florida National U (FL)
Indiana U South Bend (IN)
Indiana U Southeast (IN)
Kent State U at Geauga (OH)
Palm Beach State Coll (FL)
U of Alaska Anchorage (AK)
The U of Toledo (OH)
Valencia Coll (FL)

COMPUTER SCIENCE
Alderson-Broaddus Coll (WV)
American U of Puerto Rico (PR)
Calumet Coll of Saint Joseph (IN)
Carroll Coll (MT)
Central Methodist U (MO)
Central Penn Coll (PA)
Coll of Coastal Georgia (GA)
Creighton U (NE)
Dalton State Coll (GA)
Farmingdale State Coll (NY)
Felician Coll (NJ)
Florida National U (FL)
Franklin U (OH)
Grantham U (MO)
Hawai`i Pacific U (HI)
Indian River State Coll (FL)
Inter American U of Puerto Rico, Aguadilla Campus (PR)
Inter American U of Puerto Rico, Bayamón Campus (PR)
Inter American U of Puerto Rico, Ponce Campus (PR)
Inter American U of Puerto Rico, San Germán Campus (PR)
Kansas Wesleyan U (KS)
Lake Superior State U (MI)
Madonna U (MI)
Midland Coll (TX)
Morrisville State Coll (NY)
New England Inst of Technology (RI)
New York City Coll of Technology of the City U of New York (NY)
Oakland City U (IN)
Palm Beach State Coll (FL)
Southern California Inst of Technology (CA)
Southwest Baptist U (MO)
Thomas Edison State Coll (NJ)
Thompson Rivers U (BC, Canada)
Universidad Adventista de las Antillas (PR)
The U of Findlay (OH)
U of Maine at Fort Kent (ME)
U of New Haven (CT)
U of Rio Grande (OH)
U of the Virgin Islands (VI)
Utah Valley U (UT)
Walsh U (OH)
Weber State U (UT)

COMPUTER SOFTWARE AND MEDIA APPLICATIONS RELATED
American Public U System (WV)
Champlain Coll (VT)
International Academy of Design & Technology (FL)

COMPUTER SOFTWARE ENGINEERING
Rasmussen Coll Appleton (WI)
Rasmussen Coll Blaine (MN)
Rasmussen Coll Land O' Lakes (FL)
Rasmussen Coll Tampa/Brandon (FL)
Rasmussen Coll Wausau (WI)
Vermont Tech Coll (VT)

COMPUTER SYSTEMS ANALYSIS
Davenport U, Grand Rapids (MI)
New England Inst of Technology (RI)
The U of Akron (OH)

The U of Toledo (OH)
Valencia Coll (FL)

COMPUTER SYSTEMS NETWORKING AND TELECOMMUNICATIONS
Clayton State U (GA)
Colorado Mountain Coll (CO)
DeVry Coll of New York (NY)
DeVry U, Phoenix (AZ)
DeVry U, Pomona (CA)
DeVry U, Westminster (CO)
DeVry U, Miramar (FL)
DeVry U, Orlando (FL)
DeVry U, Decatur (GA)
DeVry U, Chicago (IL)
DeVry U, Kansas City (MO)
DeVry U, North Brunswick (NJ)
DeVry U, Columbus (OH)
DeVry U, Fort Washington (PA)
DeVry U, Houston (TX)
DeVry U, Irving (TX)
DeVry U, Arlington (VA)
DeVry U, Federal Way (WA)
DeVry U Online (IL)
Florida National U (FL)
Grantham U (MO)
Harrison Coll, Indianapolis (IN)
Hickey Coll (MO)
Idaho State U (ID)
Indiana Tech (IN)
International Business Coll, Fort Wayne (IN)
Montana Tech of The U of Montana (MT)
Pace U (NY)
Robert Morris U Illinois (IL)
Stratford U, Falls Church (VA)
The U of Akron (OH)
U of Alaska Anchorage (AK)

COMPUTER TECHNOLOGY/COMPUTER SYSTEMS TECHNOLOGY
Dalton State Coll (GA)
Harrison Coll, Indianapolis (IN)
Morrisville State Coll (NY)
New England Inst of Technology (RI)
Southeast Missouri State U (MO)
U of Alaska Anchorage (AK)
U of Cincinnati (OH)
Valencia Coll (FL)

COMPUTER TYPOGRAPHY AND COMPOSITION EQUIPMENT OPERATION
Baker Coll of Clinton Township (MI)
Indian River State Coll (FL)
U of Cincinnati (OH)
The U of Toledo (OH)

CONSTRUCTION ENGINEERING TECHNOLOGY
Coll of Staten Island of the City U of New York (NY)
Ferris State U (MI)
Lawrence Technological U (MI)
New England Inst of Technology (RI)
New York City Coll of Technology of the City U of New York (NY)
Pennsylvania Coll of Technology (PA)
Purdue U Calumet (IN)
State Coll of Florida Manatee-Sarasota (FL)
State U of New York Coll of Technology at Canton (NY)
State U of New York Coll of Technology at Delhi (NY)
The U of Akron (OH)
Valencia Coll (FL)
Vermont Tech Coll (VT)

CONSTRUCTION/HEAVY EQUIPMENT/EARTHMOVING EQUIPMENT OPERATION
U of Alaska Anchorage (AK)

CONSTRUCTION MANAGEMENT
U of Alaska Anchorage (AK)
U of Alaska Fairbanks (AK)
U of the District of Columbia (DC)
Vermont Tech Coll (VT)

CONSTRUCTION TRADES
Colorado Mesa U (CO)
Morrisville State Coll (NY)
Northern Michigan U (MI)
Utah Valley U (UT)

CONSTRUCTION TRADES RELATED
John Brown U (AR)
Utah Valley U (UT)

CONSUMER MERCHANDISING/RETAILING MANAGEMENT
Colorado Mountain Coll, Alpine Campus (CO)
Indian River State Coll (FL)
Madonna U (MI)
The U of Toledo (OH)

COOKING AND RELATED CULINARY ARTS
Colorado Mesa U (CO)
Hickey Coll (MO)

CORRECTIONS
Colorado Mountain Coll, Timberline Campus (CO)
Indian River State Coll (FL)
Lake Superior State U (MI)
Lamar U (TX)
Mercyhurst U (PA)
Mount Aloysius Coll (PA)
Polk State Coll (FL)
U of the District of Columbia (DC)
Xavier U (OH)

CORRECTIONS ADMINISTRATION
John Jay Coll of Criminal Justice of the City U of New York (NY)

CORRECTIONS AND CRIMINAL JUSTICE RELATED
Cameron U (OK)
Inter American U of Puerto Rico, Aguadilla Campus (PR)
Inter American U of Puerto Rico, Fajardo Campus (PR)
Rasmussen Coll Appleton (WI)
Rasmussen Coll Blaine (MN)
Rasmussen Coll Land O' Lakes (FL)
Rasmussen Coll Mokena/Tinley Park (IL)
Rasmussen Coll Romeoville/Joliet (IL)
Rasmussen Coll Tampa/Brandon (FL)
Rasmussen Coll Wausau (WI)

COSMETOLOGY
Indian River State Coll (FL)
Lamar U (TX)
Midland Coll (TX)

COUNSELING PSYCHOLOGY
Point U (GA)

CREATIVE WRITING
Inst of American Indian Arts (NM)

CRIMINAL JUSTICE/LAW ENFORCEMENT ADMINISTRATION
American Public U System (WV)
Anderson U (IN)
Arkansas State U (AR)
Bemidji State U (MN)
Boise State U (ID)
Calumet Coll of Saint Joseph (IN)
Campbellsville U (KY)
Castleton State Coll (VT)
Clarion U of Pennsylvania (PA)
Coll of Coastal Georgia (GA)
Colorado Mesa U (CO)
Colorado Mountain Coll (CO)
Colorado Mountain Coll, Timberline Campus (CO)
Columbia Coll (MO)
Dalton State Coll (GA)
Farmingdale State Coll (NY)
Faulkner U (AL)
Fisher Coll (MA)
Florida National U (FL)
Grantham U (MO)
Harrison Coll, Indianapolis (IN)
Harrison Coll (OH)
Hawai`i Pacific U (HI)
Indian River State Coll (FL)
Lake Superior State U (MI)
Lincoln U (MO)
Lock Haven U of Pennsylvania (PA)
Mansfield U of Pennsylvania (PA)
Morrisville State Coll (NY)
National U (CA)
New England Inst of Technology (RI)
Northern Michigan U (MI)
Palm Beach State Coll (FL)

Peirce Coll (PA)
Polk State Coll (FL)
Regent U (VA)
Roger Williams U (RI)
St. John's U (NY)
Salem International U (WV)
Suffolk U (MA)
Thomas U (GA)
Tiffin U (OH)
Trine U (IN)
U of Arkansas–Fort Smith (AR)
The U of Findlay (OH)
U of Maine at Fort Kent (ME)
Utah Valley U (UT)
Valencia Coll (FL)
Washburn U (KS)
York Coll of Pennsylvania (PA)

CRIMINAL JUSTICE/POLICE SCIENCE
Arkansas State U (AR)
Armstrong Atlantic State U (GA)
Caribbean U (PR)
Dalton State Coll (GA)
Ferris State U (MI)
Hilbert Coll (NY)
Husson U (ME)
Idaho State U (ID)
Indian River State Coll (FL)
John Jay Coll of Criminal Justice of the City U of New York (NY)
Lake Superior State U (MI)
Miami U (OH)
Missouri Western State U (MO)
Northern Kentucky U (KY)
Ohio U–Chillicothe (OH)
Palm Beach State Coll (FL)
Rasmussen Coll Blaine (MN)
Rogers State U (OK)
Southern Utah U (UT)
State U of New York Coll of Technology at Canton (NY)
The U of Akron (OH)
U of Arkansas at Little Rock (AR)
U of New Haven (CT)
U of the Virgin Islands (VI)

CRIMINAL JUSTICE/SAFETY
American U of Puerto Rico (PR)
Arkansas Tech U (AR)
Ball State U (IN)
Bethel Coll (IN)
Central Penn Coll (PA)
Colorado Mesa U (CO)
Columbus State U (GA)
Dakota Wesleyan U (SD)
Edinboro U of Pennsylvania (PA)
Fisher Coll (MA)
Florida National U (FL)
Gannon U (PA)
Georgia Regents U (GA)
Harrison Coll, Indianapolis (IN)
Husson U (ME)
Idaho State U (ID)
Indiana Tech (IN)
Indiana U Kokomo (IN)
Indiana U Northwest (IN)
Indiana U–Purdue U Indianapolis (IN)
Indiana Wesleyan U (IN)
Kent State U at Stark (OH)
Keystone Coll (PA)
King's Coll (PA)
Liberty U (VA)
Lourdes U (OH)
Madonna U (MI)
Manchester U (IN)
New Mexico State U (NM)
Northern Michigan U (MI)
Penn State Altoona (PA)
St. Francis Coll (PA)
State Coll of Florida Manatee-Sarasota (FL)
Sullivan U (KY)
Thomas Edison State Coll (NJ)
Thomas More Coll (KY)
U of Cincinnati (OH)
U of Pikeville (KY)
The U of Scranton (PA)
Weber State U (UT)
Xavier U (OH)
Youngstown State U (OH)

CRIMINOLOGY
Chaminade U of Honolulu (HI)
Faulkner U (AL)

CRISIS/EMERGENCY/DISASTER MANAGEMENT
Arkansas State U (AR)

CROP PRODUCTION
North Carolina State U (NC)
U of Massachusetts Amherst (MA)

CULINARY ARTS
The Culinary Inst of America (NY)
Harrison Coll, Indianapolis (IN)
Indian River State Coll (FL)
Keystone Coll (PA)
Newbury Coll (MA)
Nicholls State U (LA)
Oakland City U (IN)
Pennsylvania Coll of Technology (PA)
Purdue U Calumet (IN)
Robert Morris U Illinois (IL)
Southern New Hampshire U (NH)
State U of New York Coll of Agriculture and Technology at Cobleskill (NY)
State U of New York Coll of Technology at Delhi (NY)
Stratford U (MD)
Stratford U, Falls Church (VA)
Stratford U, Woodbridge (VA)
Sullivan U (KY)
The U of Akron (OH)
U of Alaska Anchorage (AK)
U of Alaska Fairbanks (AK)
U of Charleston (WV)
Utah Valley U (UT)
Valencia Coll (FL)

CULINARY ARTS RELATED
Keystone Coll (PA)

DAIRY SCIENCE
Michigan State U (MI)
Morrisville State Coll (NY)
Vermont Tech Coll (VT)

DANCE
Southern Utah U (UT)
Utah Valley U (UT)

DATA ENTRY/MICROCOMPUTER APPLICATIONS
Florida National U (FL)

DATA ENTRY/MICROCOMPUTER APPLICATIONS RELATED
Colorado Mountain Coll (CO)
Colorado Mountain Coll, Alpine Campus (CO)
Florida National U (FL)

DATA MODELING/WAREHOUSING AND DATABASE ADMINISTRATION
American Public U System (WV)

DATA PROCESSING AND DATA PROCESSING TECHNOLOGY
Baker Coll of Clinton Township (MI)
Baker Coll of Port Huron (MI)
Campbellsville U (KY)
Dordt Coll (IA)
Farmingdale State Coll (NY)
Florida National U (FL)
Lamar U (TX)
Miami U (OH)
Mount Vernon Nazarene U (OH)
New York Inst of Technology (NY)
Northern State U (SD)
Palm Beach State Coll (FL)
Polk State Coll (FL)
Saint Peter's U (NJ)
U of Cincinnati (OH)
U of Puerto Rico at Ponce (PR)
The U of Toledo (OH)
Utah Valley U (UT)
Western Kentucky U (KY)
Youngstown State U (OH)

DENTAL ASSISTING
Boston U (MA)
U of Alaska Anchorage (AK)
U of Alaska Fairbanks (AK)
U of Southern Indiana (IN)

DENTAL HYGIENE
Baker Coll of Port Huron (MI)
Coll of Coastal Georgia (GA)
Dalton State Coll (GA)
Farmingdale State Coll (NY)
Ferris State U (MI)
Florida National U (FL)
Indiana U Northwest (IN)
Indiana U–Purdue U Fort Wayne (IN)
Indiana U–Purdue U Indianapolis (IN)
Indiana U South Bend (IN)
Indian River State Coll (FL)

Lamar U (TX)
New York City Coll of Technology of the City U of New York (NY)
New York U (NY)
Palm Beach State Coll (FL)
Pennsylvania Coll of Technology (PA)
Shawnee State U (OH)
State U of New York Coll of Technology at Canton (NY)
Tennessee State U (TN)
Thomas Edison State Coll (NJ)
U of Alaska Anchorage (AK)
U of Alaska Fairbanks (AK)
U of Arkansas for Medical Sciences (AR)
U of Arkansas–Fort Smith (AR)
U of Bridgeport (CT)
U of Cincinnati (OH)
U of Medicine and Dentistry of New Jersey (NJ)
U of New Haven (CT)
Utah Valley U (UT)
Valdosta State U (GA)
Valencia Coll (FL)
Vermont Tech Coll (VT)
Western Kentucky U (KY)
West Liberty U (WV)
Wichita State U (KS)

DENTAL LABORATORY TECHNOLOGY
Boston U (MA)
Florida National U (FL)
Indiana U–Purdue U Fort Wayne (IN)
New York City Coll of Technology of the City U of New York (NY)

DESIGN AND APPLIED ARTS RELATED
Washburn U (KS)

DESIGN AND VISUAL COMMUNICATIONS
Academy of Art U (CA)
Corcoran Coll of Art and Design (DC)
Creative Center (NE)
Inst of American Indian Arts (NM)
U of Cincinnati (OH)
Utah Valley U (UT)

DESKTOP PUBLISHING AND DIGITAL IMAGING DESIGN
Academy of Art U (CA)
Ferris State U (MI)
New England Inst of Technology (RI)

DIAGNOSTIC MEDICAL SONOGRAPHY AND ULTRASOUND TECHNOLOGY
Adventist U of Health Sciences (FL)
Arkansas State U (AR)
Baker Coll of Port Huron (MI)
Ferris State U (MI)
Florida National U (FL)
Keystone Coll (PA)
Mercy Coll of Health Sciences (IA)
Midland Coll (TX)
Nebraska Methodist Coll (NE)
Polk State Coll (FL)
U of Arkansas for Medical Sciences (AR)
U of Charleston (WV)
The U of Texas at Brownsville (TX)
Valencia Coll (FL)

DIESEL MECHANICS TECHNOLOGY
Idaho State U (ID)
Lewis-Clark State Coll (ID)
Midland Coll (TX)
Morrisville State Coll (NY)
Pennsylvania Coll of Technology (PA)
State U of New York Coll of Agriculture and Technology at Cobleskill (NY)
Utah Valley U (UT)
Vermont Tech Coll (VT)
Weber State U (UT)

DIETETICS
Ferris State U (MI)
Life U (GA)
State Coll of Florida Manatee-Sarasota (FL)

DIETETIC TECHNOLOGY
Morrisville State Coll (NY)
Youngstown State U (OH)

DIETITIAN ASSISTANT
Youngstown State U (OH)

DIGITAL ARTS
Academy of Art U (CA)

DIGITAL COMMUNICATION AND MEDIA/MULTIMEDIA
Colorado Mountain Coll (CO)
Florida National U (FL)
Indiana U–Purdue U Indianapolis (IN)
Vaughn Coll of Aeronautics and Technology (NY)

DISABILITY STUDIES
U of Alaska Anchorage (AK)

DIVINITY/MINISTRY
Carson-Newman U (TN)
Florida Christian Coll (FL)
Providence Coll (RI)

DOG/PET/ANIMAL GROOMING
Becker Coll (MA)

DRAFTING AND DESIGN TECHNOLOGY
Baker Coll of Clinton Township (MI)
Baker Coll of Port Huron (MI)
Caribbean U (PR)
Dalton State Coll (GA)
Indian River State Coll (FL)
Kentucky State U (KY)
Lamar U (TX)
Langston U (OK)
LeTourneau U (TX)
Lewis-Clark State Coll (ID)
Lincoln U (MO)
Montana State U (MT)
Morrisville State Coll (NY)
New England Inst of Technology (RI)
Palm Beach State Coll (FL)
Robert Morris U Illinois (IL)
State Coll of Florida Manatee-Sarasota (FL)
The U of Akron (OH)
U of Alaska Anchorage (AK)
U of Alaska Fairbanks (AK)
U of Puerto Rico at Ponce (PR)
U of Rio Grande (OH)
Utah Valley U (UT)
Valencia Coll (FL)
Weber State U (UT)
Wright State U (OH)
Youngstown State U (OH)

DRAFTING/DESIGN ENGINEERING TECHNOLOGIES RELATED
Murray State U (KY)
Pennsylvania Coll of Technology (PA)
Thomas Edison State Coll (NJ)

DRAMATIC/THEATER ARTS
Adams State U (CO)
Clarke U (IA)
Colorado Mountain Coll (CO)
Indian River State Coll (FL)
Midland Coll (TX)
Palm Beach State Coll (FL)
Pine Manor Coll (MA)
State Coll of Florida Manatee-Sarasota (FL)
Thomas More Coll (KY)
Utah Valley U (UT)

DRAMATIC/THEATER ARTS AND STAGECRAFT RELATED
Utah Valley U (UT)

DRAWING
Academy of Art U (CA)
Pratt Inst (NY)

EARLY CHILDHOOD EDUCATION
Adams State U (CO)
Baptist Bible Coll of Pennsylvania (PA)
Bethel Coll (IN)
Boise State U (ID)
Coll of Saint Mary (NE)
Colorado Mountain Coll, Alpine Campus (CO)
Colorado Mountain Coll, Timberline Campus (CO)
Cornerstone U (MI)
Gannon U (PA)
Granite State Coll (NH)
Indiana U South Bend (IN)
Keystone Coll (PA)
Lake Superior State U (MI)
Lincoln Christian U (IL)
Lincoln U (MO)
Lindsey Wilson Coll (KY)

Manchester U (IN)
Maranatha Baptist Bible Coll (WI)
Marian U (IN)
Morrisville State Coll (NY)
Mount Aloysius Coll (PA)
Mount St. Mary's Coll (CA)
Nova Southeastern U (FL)
Oakland City U (IN)
Pacific Union Coll (CA)
Point Park U (PA)
Purdue U Calumet (IN)
Rasmussen Coll Appleton (WI)
Rasmussen Coll Blaine (MN)
Rasmussen Coll Land O' Lakes (FL)
Rasmussen Coll Mokena/Tinley Park (IL)
Rasmussen Coll Romeoville/Joliet (IL)
Rasmussen Coll Tampa/Brandon (FL)
Rasmussen Coll Wausau (WI)
St. Gregory's U, Shawnee (OK)
State U of New York Coll of Technology at Canton (NY)
Sullivan U (KY)
Taylor U (IN)
U of Alaska Fairbanks (AK)
U of Arkansas–Fort Smith (AR)
U of Great Falls (MT)
The U of Montana Western (MT)
U of Southern Indiana (IN)
U of the Virgin Islands (VI)
Washburn U (KS)
Western Kentucky U (KY)
Xavier U (OH)

E-COMMERCE
Colorado Mountain Coll, Alpine Campus (CO)

ECONOMICS
Hawai'i Pacific U (HI)
Immaculata U (PA)
Indian River State Coll (FL)
John Cabot U (Italy)
Palm Beach State Coll (FL)
State Coll of Florida Manatee-Sarasota (FL)
State U of New York Empire State Coll (NY)
Thomas More Coll (KY)
The U of Tampa (FL)

EDUCATION
Alderson-Broaddus Coll (WV)
Central Baptist Coll (AR)
Cincinnati Christian U (OH)
Corban U (OR)
Dalton State Coll (GA)
Florida National U (FL)
Indian River State Coll (FL)
Kent State U (OH)
Lamar U (TX)
Montreat Coll, Montreat (NC)
Morrisville State Coll (NY)
National U (CA)
Palm Beach State Coll (FL)
State U of New York Empire State Coll (NY)
U of Cincinnati (OH)
The U of Montana Western (MT)
U of the District of Columbia (DC)

EDUCATIONAL/INSTRUCTIONAL TECHNOLOGY
Cameron U (OK)

EDUCATION (MULTIPLE LEVELS)
Coll of Coastal Georgia (GA)
Midland Coll (TX)

EDUCATION RELATED
The U of Akron (OH)

EDUCATION (SPECIFIC SUBJECT AREAS) RELATED
National U (CA)

ELECTRICAL AND ELECTRONIC ENGINEERING TECHNOLOGIES RELATED
Lawrence Technological U (MI)
Northern Michigan U (MI)
Pittsburg State U (KS)
Point Park U (PA)
Rochester Inst of Technology (NY)
Thomas Edison State Coll (NJ)
Vaughn Coll of Aeronautics and Technology (NY)
Youngstown State U (OH)

ELECTRICAL AND ELECTRONICS ENGINEERING
Lake Superior State U (MI)
New England Inst of Technology (RI)
Southern California Inst of Technology (CA)
Thompson Rivers U (BC, Canada)
The U of Scranton (PA)

ELECTRICAL AND POWER TRANSMISSION INSTALLATION
Polk State Coll (FL)
State U of New York Coll of Technology at Delhi (NY)

ELECTRICAL, ELECTRONIC AND COMMUNICATIONS ENGINEERING TECHNOLOGY
Bluefield State Coll (WV)
California U of Pennsylvania (PA)
Cameron U (OK)
Dalton State Coll (GA)
DeVry Coll of New York (NY)
DeVry U, Phoenix (AZ)
DeVry U, Pomona (CA)
DeVry U, Westminster (CO)
DeVry U, Miramar (FL)
DeVry U, Orlando (FL)
DeVry U, Decatur (GA)
DeVry U, Chicago (IL)
DeVry U, Kansas City (MO)
DeVry U, North Brunswick (NJ)
DeVry U, Columbus (OH)
DeVry U, Fort Washington (PA)
DeVry U, Houston (TX)
DeVry U, Irving (TX)
DeVry U, Federal Way (WA)
DeVry U Online (FL)
Fairmont State U (WV)
Grantham U (MO)
Idaho State U (ID)
Indiana U–Purdue U Fort Wayne (IN)
Indiana U–Purdue U Indianapolis (IN)
Indian River State Coll (FL)
Inter American U of Puerto Rico, Aguadilla Campus (PR)
Inter American U of Puerto Rico, San Germán Campus (PR)
Kentucky State U (KY)
Lake Superior State U (MI)
Lamar U (TX)
Langston U (OK)
Lawrence Technological U (MI)
New England Inst of Technology (RI)
New York City Coll of Technology of the City U of New York (NY)
Northern Kentucky U (KY)
Northern Michigan U (MI)
Northwestern State U of Louisiana (LA)
Palm Beach State Coll (FL)
Penn State Altoona (PA)
Penn State Berks (PA)
Penn State Erie, The Behrend Coll (PA)
Penn State Shenango (PA)
Pennsylvania Coll of Technology (PA)
Purdue U North Central (IN)
State Coll of Florida Manatee-Sarasota (FL)
State U of New York Coll of Technology at Canton (NY)
Thomas Edison State Coll (NJ)
Universidad del Turabo (PR)
The U of Akron (OH)
U of Alaska Anchorage (AK)
U of Arkansas at Little Rock (AR)
U of Hartford (CT)
U of the District of Columbia (DC)
Utah Valley U (UT)
Valencia Coll (FL)
Vermont Tech Coll (VT)
Youngstown State U (OH)

ELECTRICAL/ELECTRONICS EQUIPMENT INSTALLATION AND REPAIR
Lewis-Clark State Coll (ID)
New England Inst of Technology (RI)
U of Arkansas–Fort Smith (AR)

ELECTRICAL/ELECTRONICS MAINTENANCE AND REPAIR TECHNOLOGY RELATED
Pittsburg State U (KS)

ELECTRICIAN
Liberty U (VA)
Michigan State U (MI)

Pennsylvania Coll of Technology (PA)
Universidad del Turabo (PR)
Weber State U (UT)

ELECTROMECHANICAL TECHNOLOGY
John Brown U (AR)
Midland Coll (TX)
New York City Coll of Technology of the City U of New York (NY)
Northern Michigan U (MI)
Shawnee State U (OH)
Utah Valley U (UT)

ELECTRONEURODIAGNOSTIC/ELECTROENCEPHALOGRAPHIC TECHNOLOGY
DeVry U, North Brunswick (NJ)

ELEMENTARY EDUCATION
Adams State U (CO)
Alaska Pacific U (AK)
Dalton State Coll (GA)
Edinboro U of Pennsylvania (PA)
Ferris State U (MI)
Hillsdale Free Will Baptist Coll (OK)
New Mexico Highlands U (NM)
Palm Beach State Coll (FL)
Rogers State U (OK)
Saint Mary-of-the-Woods Coll (IN)
U of Cincinnati (OH)

EMERGENCY CARE ATTENDANT (EMT AMBULANCE)
Trinity Coll of Nursing and Health Sciences (IL)

EMERGENCY MEDICAL TECHNOLOGY (EMT PARAMEDIC)
Baker Coll of Clinton Township (MI)
Colorado Mesa U (CO)
Colorado Mountain Coll, Timberline Campus (CO)
Creighton U (NE)
EDP U of Puerto Rico (PR)
Idaho State U (ID)
Indiana U–Purdue U Indianapolis (IN)
Indian River State Coll (FL)
Mercy Coll of Health Sciences (IA)
Midland Coll (TX)
Pacific Union Coll (CA)
Pennsylvania Coll of Technology (PA)
Polk State Coll (FL)
Rogers State U (OK)
Saint Joseph's Coll (IN)
Shawnee State U (OH)
Southwest Baptist U (MO)
Spalding U (KY)
State U of New York Coll of Agriculture and Technology at Cobleskill (NY)
Trinity Coll of Nursing and Health Sciences (IL)
The U of Akron (OH)
U of Alaska Anchorage (AK)
U of Arkansas for Medical Sciences (AR)
U of Cincinnati (OH)
The U of Texas at Brownsville (TX)
Valencia Coll (FL)
Weber State U (UT)
Western Kentucky U (KY)
Youngstown State U (OH)

ENERGY MANAGEMENT AND SYSTEMS TECHNOLOGY
Idaho State U (ID)
U of Rio Grande (OH)

ENGINEERING
Coll of Staten Island of the City U of New York (NY)
Ferris State U (MI)
Geneva Coll (PA)
Indian River State Coll (FL)
Lake Superior State U (MI)
Lindsey Wilson Coll (KY)
Palm Beach Atlantic U (FL)
Purdue U North Central (IN)
State Coll of Florida Manatee-Sarasota (FL)
State U of New York Coll of Technology at Canton (NY)
Thompson Rivers U (BC, Canada)
Union Coll (NE)
Utah Valley U (UT)

ENGINEERING/INDUSTRIAL MANAGEMENT
Grantham U (MO)
Purdue U Calumet (IN)

ENGINEERING SCIENCE
National U (CA)
Rochester Inst of Technology (NY)
State U of New York Coll of Technology at Delhi (NY)
U of Pittsburgh at Bradford (PA)

ENGINEERING TECHNOLOGIES AND ENGINEERING RELATED
Arkansas State U (AR)
Rogers State U (OK)
State U of New York Maritime Coll (NY)
Thomas Edison State Coll (NJ)
U of Puerto Rico at Bayamón (PR)
Utah Valley U (UT)

ENGINEERING TECHNOLOGY
Austin Peay State U (TN)
Edinboro U of Pennsylvania (PA)
Excelsior Coll (NY)
Fairmont State U (WV)
Indian River State Coll (FL)
Kansas State U (KS)
Lake Superior State U (MI)
Lincoln U (MO)
McNeese State U (LA)
Miami U (OH)
New Mexico State U (NM)
Northern Kentucky U (KY)
Southern Utah U (UT)
State U of New York Coll of Technology at Delhi (NY)
U of Alaska Anchorage (AK)
The U of Toledo (OH)
Wright State U (OH)
Youngstown State U (OH)

ENGLISH
Calumet Coll of Saint Joseph (IN)
Carroll Coll (MT)
Central Methodist U (MO)
Coll of Coastal Georgia (GA)
Colorado Mountain Coll (CO)
Colorado Mountain Coll, Alpine Campus (CO)
Dalton State Coll (GA)
Felician Coll (NJ)
Hillsdale Free Will Baptist Coll (OK)
Immaculata U (PA)
Indiana Wesleyan U (IN)
Indian River State Coll (FL)
Lourdes U (OH)
Madonna U (MI)
Midland Coll (TX)
National U (CA)
Palm Beach State Coll (FL)
Pine Manor Coll (MA)
State Coll of Florida Manatee-Sarasota (FL)
Thomas More Coll (KY)
U of Cincinnati (OH)
The U of Tampa (FL)
Utah Valley U (UT)
Xavier U (OH)

ENGLISH AS A SECOND/FOREIGN LANGUAGE (TEACHING)
Cornerstone U (MI)
Lincoln Christian U (IL)

ENGLISH LANGUAGE AND LITERATURE RELATED
Presentation Coll (SD)

ENGLISH/LANGUAGE ARTS TEACHER EDUCATION
State Coll of Florida Manatee-Sarasota (FL)

ENTREPRENEURSHIP
Central Penn Coll (PA)
Colorado Mountain Coll, Timberline Campus (CO)
U of Alaska Anchorage (AK)

ENVIRONMENTAL CONTROL TECHNOLOGIES RELATED
Montana Tech of The U of Montana (MT)

ENVIRONMENTAL ENGINEERING TECHNOLOGY
Baker Coll of Port Huron (MI)

New York City Coll of Technology of the City U of New York (NY)
Ohio U–Chillicothe (OH)

ENVIRONMENTAL SCIENCE
Thomas Edison State Coll (NJ)

ENVIRONMENTAL STUDIES
Colorado Mountain Coll, Timberline Campus (CO)
Columbia Coll (MO)
State U of New York Coll of Agriculture and Technology at Cobleskill (NY)

EQUESTRIAN STUDIES
Saint Mary-of-the-Woods Coll (IN)
The U of Findlay (OH)
U of Massachusetts Amherst (MA)
The U of Montana Western (MT)

EXECUTIVE ASSISTANT/EXECUTIVE SECRETARY
U of Arkansas–Fort Smith (AR)
U of Cincinnati (OH)
Western Kentucky U (KY)

EXPLOSIVE ORDINANCE/BOMB DISPOSAL
American Public U System (WV)

FAMILY AND CONSUMER SCIENCES/HOME ECONOMICS TEACHER EDUCATION
State Coll of Florida Manatee-Sarasota (FL)

FAMILY AND CONSUMER SCIENCES/HUMAN SCIENCES
Indian River State Coll (FL)
Mount Vernon Nazarene U (OH)
Palm Beach State Coll (FL)
U of Alaska Anchorage (AK)

FASHION/APPAREL DESIGN
Academy of Art U (CA)
EDP U of Puerto Rico (PR)
Fashion Inst of Technology (NY)
Fisher Coll (MA)
Palm Beach State Coll (FL)
Parsons The New School for Design (NY)
Universidad del Turabo (PR)

FASHION MERCHANDISING
Fashion Inst of Technology (NY)
Fisher Coll (MA)
Harrison Coll, Indianapolis (IN)
Immaculata U (PA)
Indian River State Coll (FL)
LIM Coll (NY)
New York City Coll of Technology of the City U of New York (NY)
Palm Beach State Coll (FL)
Parsons The New School for Design (NY)
Southern New Hampshire U (NH)
The U of Akron (OH)
U of Bridgeport (CT)
U of the District of Columbia (DC)

FASHION MODELING
Fashion Inst of Technology (NY)

FIBER, TEXTILE AND WEAVING ARTS
Academy of Art U (CA)

FINANCE
AIB Coll of Business (IA)
Colorado Mountain Coll, Timberline Campus (CO)
Davenport U, Grand Rapids (MI)
Franklin U (OH)
Harrison Coll, Indianapolis (IN)
Harrison Coll (OH)
Hawai'i Pacific U (HI)
Indiana Wesleyan U (IN)
Indian River State Coll (FL)
Palm Beach State Coll (FL)
Polk State Coll (FL)
Saint Peter's U (NJ)
State Coll of Florida Manatee-Sarasota (FL)
The U of Findlay (OH)
Youngstown State U (OH)

FINE ARTS RELATED
Academy of Art U (CA)
Madonna U (MI)

Pennsylvania Coll of Technology (PA)

FINE/STUDIO ARTS
Academy of Art U (CA)
Adams State U (CO)
Colorado Mountain Coll, Alpine Campus (CO)
Corcoran Coll of Art and Design (DC)
Fashion Inst of Technology (NY)
Inst of American Indian Arts (NM)
Keystone Coll (PA)
Lindsey Wilson Coll (KY)
Madonna U (MI)
Marian U (IN)
New Mexico State U (NM)
Pratt Inst (NY)
State Coll of Florida Manatee-Sarasota (FL)
Thomas More Coll (KY)
U of New Hampshire at Manchester (NH)
Villa Maria Coll of Buffalo (NY)
York Coll of Pennsylvania (PA)

FIRE PREVENTION AND SAFETY TECHNOLOGY
Colorado Mountain Coll, Timberline Campus (CO)
Thomas Edison State Coll (NJ)
The U of Akron (OH)
U of Nebraska–Lincoln (NE)
U of New Haven (CT)

FIRE SCIENCE/FIREFIGHTING
Idaho State U (ID)
Indian River State Coll (FL)
Lake Superior State U (MI)
Lamar U (TX)
Lewis-Clark State Coll (ID)
Madonna U (MI)
Midland Coll (TX)
Palm Beach State Coll (FL)
Polk State Coll (FL)
Providence Coll (RI)
State Coll of Florida Manatee-Sarasota (FL)
U of Alaska Anchorage (AK)
U of Alaska Fairbanks (AK)
U of Cincinnati (OH)
U of the District of Columbia (DC)
Utah Valley U (UT)
Valencia Coll (FL)
Vermont Tech Coll (VT)

FIRE SERVICES ADMINISTRATION
American Public U System (WV)
Columbia Coll (MO)

FISHING AND FISHERIES SCIENCES AND MANAGEMENT
State U of New York Coll of Agriculture and Technology at Cobleskill (NY)

FOOD PREPARATION
Washburn U (KS)

FOODS AND NUTRITION RELATED
U of Guelph (ON, Canada)

FOOD SCIENCE
Lamar U (TX)

FOOD SERVICE SYSTEMS ADMINISTRATION
Inter American U of Puerto Rico, Aguadilla Campus (PR)
Northern Michigan U (MI)
U of New Hampshire (NH)

FOODS, NUTRITION, AND WELLNESS
Indian River State Coll (FL)
Madonna U (MI)
Morrisville State Coll (NY)
Palm Beach State Coll (FL)

FOOD TECHNOLOGY AND PROCESSING
Arkansas State U (AR)
Washburn U (KS)

FOREIGN LANGUAGES AND LITERATURES
Coll of Coastal Georgia (GA)

FOREIGN LANGUAGES RELATED
U of Alaska Fairbanks (AK)

FOREIGN LANGUAGE TEACHER EDUCATION
State Coll of Florida Manatee-Sarasota (FL)

FORENSIC SCIENCE AND TECHNOLOGY
Arkansas State U (AR)
U of Arkansas–Fort Smith (AR)

FORESTRY
Coll of Coastal Georgia (GA)
Indian River State Coll (FL)
U of Maine at Fort Kent (ME)

FOREST TECHNOLOGY
Keystone Coll (PA)
Pennsylvania Coll of Technology (PA)
State U of New York Coll of
  Technology at Canton (NY)
U of Maine at Fort Kent (ME)
U of New Hampshire (NH)

FRENCH
Indian River State Coll (FL)
State Coll of Florida Manatee-
  Sarasota (FL)
Thomas More Coll (KY)
U of Cincinnati (OH)
The U of Tampa (FL)
Xavier U (OH)

FUNERAL SERVICE AND MORTUARY SCIENCE
Ferris State U (MI)
State U of New York Coll of
  Technology at Canton (NY)
U of the District of Columbia (DC)

GAME AND INTERACTIVE MEDIA DESIGN
Academy of Art U (CA)

GENERAL STUDIES
Adventist U of Health Sciences (FL)
AIB Coll of Business (IA)
Alderson-Broaddus Coll (WV)
Alverno Coll (WI)
American Public U System (WV)
Anderson U (IN)
Arkansas State U (AR)
Arkansas Tech U (AR)
Asbury U (KY)
Austin Peay State U (TN)
Averett U (VA)
Baptist Bible Coll of Pennsylvania
  (PA)
Barclay Coll (KS)
Belhaven U (MS)
Bob Jones U (SC)
Butler U (IN)
Calumet Coll of Saint Joseph (IN)
Cameron U (OK)
Castleton State Coll (VT)
Central Baptist Coll (AR)
Chaminade U of Honolulu (HI)
City U of Seattle (WA)
Clearwater Christian Coll (FL)
Coll of Mount St. Joseph (OH)
Colorado Mountain Coll, Timberline
  Campus (CO)
Columbia Coll (MO)
Concordia Coll Alabama (AL)
Concordia U, St. Paul (MN)
Concordia U Texas (TX)
Dakota State U (SD)
Dalton State Coll (GA)
Eastern Connecticut State U (CT)
Eastern Mennonite U (VA)
Fisher Coll (MA)
Friends U (KS)
Grantham U (MO)
Hillsdale Free Will Baptist Coll (OK)
Hope International U (CA)
Idaho State U (ID)
Indiana Tech (IN)
Indiana U Bloomington (IN)
Indiana U Kokomo (IN)
Indiana U Northwest (IN)
Indiana U of Pennsylvania (PA)
Indiana U–Purdue U Indianapolis (IN)
Indiana U South Bend (IN)
Indiana U Southeast (IN)
Indiana Wesleyan U (IN)
John Brown U (AR)
Johnson State Coll (VT)
La Salle U (PA)
Lawrence Technological U (MI)

Lebanon Valley Coll (PA)
Lincoln Christian U (IL)
Lipscomb U (TN)
Louisiana Tech U (LA)
McNeese State U (LA)
Mercy Coll of Ohio (OH)
Miami U (OH)
Mid-Continent U (KY)
Midland Coll (TX)
Monmouth U (NJ)
Morehead State U (KY)
Mount Aloysius Coll (PA)
Mount Marty Coll (SD)
Mount Vernon Nazarene U (OH)
National U (CA)
Newbury Coll (MA)
New Mexico Inst of Mining and
  Technology (NM)
New Mexico State U (NM)
Nicholls State U (LA)
Northern Michigan U (MI)
Northwest Christian U (OR)
Northwestern State U of Louisiana
  (LA)
Northwest U (WA)
Ohio Dominican U (OH)
The Ohio State U at Lima (OH)
Pace U (NY)
Pacific Union Coll (CA)
Peirce Coll (PA)
Point Park U (PA)
Point U (GA)
Presentation Coll (SD)
Regent U (VA)
Rider U (NJ)
Shawnee State U (OH)
Siena Heights U (MI)
Simpson U (CA)
South Dakota State U (SD)
Southern Arkansas U–Magnolia (AR)
Southern Nazarene U (OK)
Southern Utah U (UT)
Southwest Baptist U (MO)
Southwestern Adventist U (TX)
State U of New York Coll of
  Technology at Delhi (NY)
Temple U (PA)
Thompson Rivers U (BC, Canada)
Tiffin U (OH)
Trevecca Nazarene U (TN)
Trinity Coll of Florida (FL)
U of Arkansas at Little Rock (AR)
U of Arkansas–Fort Smith (AR)
U of Bridgeport (CT)
U of Central Arkansas (AR)
U of Cincinnati (OH)
U of Hartford (CT)
U of La Verne (CA)
U of Louisiana at Monroe (LA)
U of Maine at Fort Kent (ME)
U of Mobile (AL)
U of Rio Grande (OH)
U of Wisconsin–Superior (WI)
Utah State U (UT)
Utah Valley U (UT)
Viterbo U (WI)
Weber State U (UT)
Western Kentucky U (KY)
Wichita State U (KS)
Widener U (PA)
Winona State U (MN)
York Coll of Pennsylvania (PA)

GEOGRAPHIC INFORMATION SCIENCE AND CARTOGRAPHY
The U of Akron (OH)

GEOGRAPHY
The U of Tampa (FL)
Wright State U (OH)

GEOGRAPHY RELATED
Adams State U (CO)

GEOLOGICAL AND EARTH SCIENCES/GEOSCIENCES RELATED
Utah Valley U (UT)

GEOLOGY/EARTH SCIENCE
Coll of Coastal Georgia (GA)
Colorado Mountain Coll, Alpine
  Campus (CO)
Midland Coll (TX)
Thompson Rivers U (BC, Canada)
U of Cincinnati (OH)
Wright State U (OH)

GERMAN
State Coll of Florida Manatee-
  Sarasota (FL)

U of Cincinnati (OH)
Xavier U (OH)

GERONTOLOGY
Holy Cross Coll (IN)
Madonna U (MI)
Manchester U (IN)
Ohio Dominican U (OH)
Siena Heights U (MI)
Thomas More Coll (KY)
Washburn U (KS)

GRAPHIC AND PRINTING EQUIPMENT OPERATION/PRODUCTION
Chowan U (NC)
Lewis-Clark State Coll (ID)
New England Inst of Technology (RI)

GRAPHIC COMMUNICATIONS
New England Inst of Technology (RI)
Pennsylvania Coll of Technology (PA)
Walla Walla U (WA)

GRAPHIC COMMUNICATIONS RELATED
U of the District of Columbia (DC)

GRAPHIC DESIGN
Academy of Art U (CA)
Coll of Mount St. Joseph (OH)
Columbia Centro Universitario,
  Caguas (PR)
Corcoran Coll of Art and Design (DC)
Ferris State U (MI)
Hickey Coll (MO)
International Academy of Design &
  Technology (FL)
International Business Coll, Fort
  Wayne (IN)
Madonna U (MI)
Pacific Union Coll (CA)
Parsons The New School for Design
  (NY)
Pratt Inst (NY)
Union Coll (NE)
U of the District of Columbia (DC)
Villa Maria Coll of Buffalo (NY)

HAZARDOUS MATERIALS MANAGEMENT AND WASTE TECHNOLOGY
Ohio U–Chillicothe (OH)

HEALTH AIDE
National U (CA)

HEALTH AND MEDICAL ADMINISTRATIVE SERVICES RELATED
National U (CA)

HEALTH AND PHYSICAL EDUCATION/FITNESS
Coll of Coastal Georgia (GA)
Midland Coll (TX)
Robert Morris U Illinois (IL)
State U of New York Coll of
  Technology at Delhi (NY)
Utah Valley U (UT)

HEALTH AND PHYSICAL EDUCATION RELATED
Pennsylvania Coll of Technology (PA)

HEALTH AND WELLNESS
Howard Payne U (TX)
Presentation Coll (SD)

HEALTH/HEALTH-CARE ADMINISTRATION
Mount St. Mary's Coll (CA)
Park U (MO)
State Coll of Florida Manatee-
  Sarasota (FL)
The U of Scranton (PA)
Washburn U (KS)

HEALTH INFORMATION/MEDICAL RECORDS ADMINISTRATION
AIB Coll of Business (IA)
Baker Coll of Clinton Township (MI)
Baker Coll of Port Huron (MI)
Dalton State Coll (GA)
Indian River State Coll (FL)
Inter American U of Puerto Rico, San
  Germán Campus (PR)
Polk State Coll (FL)

HEALTH INFORMATION/MEDICAL RECORDS TECHNOLOGY
Boise State U (ID)
Dakota State U (SD)
Davenport U, Grand Rapids (MI)
DeVry U, Pomona (CA)
DeVry U, Decatur (GA)
DeVry U, Chicago (IL)
DeVry U, North Brunswick (NJ)
DeVry U, Columbus (OH)
DeVry U, Fort Washington (PA)
DeVry U, Houston (TX)
DeVry U, Irving (TX)
DeVry U Online (IL)
Ferris State U (MI)
Fisher Coll (MA)
Hodges U (FL)
Idaho State U (ID)
Indiana U Northwest (IN)
Louisiana Tech U (LA)
Mercy Coll of Ohio (OH)
Midland Coll (TX)
Missouri Western State U (MO)
Molloy Coll (NY)
National U (CA)
New England Inst of Technology (RI)
Northern Michigan U (MI)
Peirce Coll (PA)
Pennsylvania Coll of Technology (PA)
Rasmussen Coll Appleton (WI)
Rasmussen Coll Blaine (MN)
Rasmussen Coll Land O' Lakes (FL)
Rasmussen Coll Mokena/Tinley Park
  (IL)
Rasmussen Coll Romeoville/Joliet
  (IL)
Rasmussen Coll Tampa/Brandon
  (FL)
Rasmussen Coll Wausau (WI)
U of Arkansas for Medical Sciences
  (AR)
Washburn U (KS)
Weber State U (UT)
Western Kentucky U (KY)

HEALTH/MEDICAL PREPARATORY PROGRAMS RELATED
Immaculata U (PA)
Mount St. Mary's Coll (CA)
Ohio Valley U (WV)
U of Cincinnati (OH)

HEALTH PROFESSIONS RELATED
Arkansas Tech U (AR)
Caribbean U (PR)
Ferris State U (MI)
Fisher Coll (MA)
Lock Haven U of Pennsylvania (PA)
Morrisville State Coll (NY)
Newman U (KS)
New York U (NY)
Northwest U (WA)
Ohio U–Chillicothe (OH)
Point Park U (PA)
Saint Peter's U (NJ)
U of Cincinnati (OH)
U of Hartford (CT)
Villa Maria Coll of Buffalo (NY)

HEALTH SERVICES ADMINISTRATION
Florida National U (FL)

HEALTH SERVICES/ALLIED HEALTH/HEALTH SCIENCES
Fisher Coll (MA)
Florida National U (FL)
Howard Payne U (TX)
Lindsey Wilson Coll (KY)
Mercyhurst U (PA)
Northwest Christian U (OR)
Pennsylvania Coll of Technology (PA)
Pine Manor Coll (MA)
U of Hartford (CT)
U of the Incarnate Word (TX)
Weber State U (UT)

HEALTH TEACHER EDUCATION
Palm Beach State Coll (FL)
State Coll of Florida Manatee-
  Sarasota (FL)

HEATING, AIR CONDITIONING, VENTILATION AND REFRIGERATION MAINTENANCE TECHNOLOGY
Indian River State Coll (FL)
Lamar U (TX)
Lewis-Clark State Coll (ID)

New England Inst of Technology (RI)
Oakland City U (IN)
State U of New York Coll of
  Technology at Canton (NY)
U of Alaska Anchorage (AK)

HEATING, VENTILATION, AIR CONDITIONING AND REFRIGERATION ENGINEERING TECHNOLOGY
Ferris State U (MI)
Liberty U (VA)
Midland Coll (TX)
Northern Michigan U (MI)
Oakland City U (IN)
Pennsylvania Coll of Technology (PA)
State U of New York Coll of
  Technology at Canton (NY)
State U of New York Coll of
  Technology at Delhi (NY)

HEAVY EQUIPMENT MAINTENANCE TECHNOLOGY
Ferris State U (MI)
Pennsylvania Coll of Technology (PA)
U of Alaska Anchorage (AK)

HEBREW
U of Cincinnati (OH)
Yeshiva U (NY)

HISTOLOGIC TECHNICIAN
Indiana U–Purdue U Indianapolis (IN)
Northern Michigan U (MI)
The U of Akron (OH)

HISTOLOGIC TECHNOLOGY/HISTOTECHNOLOGIST
Tarleton State U (TX)

HISTORIC PRESERVATION AND CONSERVATION
Colorado Mountain Coll, Timberline
  Campus (CO)
Montana Tech of The U of Montana
  (MT)

HISTORY
American Public U System (WV)
Clarke U (IA)
Coll of Coastal Georgia (GA)
Dalton State Coll (GA)
Indiana Wesleyan U (IN)
Indian River State Coll (FL)
Lindsey Wilson Coll (KY)
Lourdes U (OH)
Midland Coll (TX)
Palm Beach State Coll (FL)
Regent U (VA)
Rogers State U (OK)
State Coll of Florida Manatee-
  Sarasota (FL)
State U of New York Empire State
  Coll (NY)
Thomas More Coll (KY)
U of Cincinnati (OH)
U of Rio Grande (OH)
The U of Tampa (FL)
Utah Valley U (UT)
Wright State U (OH)
Xavier U (OH)

HOMELAND SECURITY, LAW ENFORCEMENT, FIREFIGHTING AND PROTECTIVE SERVICES RELATED
Idaho State U (ID)
Universidad del Turabo (PR)

HORSE HUSBANDRY/EQUINE SCIENCE AND MANAGEMENT
Michigan State U (MI)
Morrisville State Coll (NY)
Southern Utah U (UT)
U of Guelph (ON, Canada)

HORTICULTURAL SCIENCE
Andrews U (MI)
Morrisville State Coll (NY)
State U of New York Coll of
  Technology at Delhi (NY)
U of Connecticut (CT)
U of Guelph (ON, Canada)

HOSPITAL AND HEALTH-CARE FACILITIES ADMINISTRATION
State Coll of Florida Manatee-
  Sarasota (FL)

HOSPITALITY ADMINISTRATION
AIB Coll of Business (IA)
Colorado Mesa U (CO)

Colorado Mountain Coll, Alpine Campus (CO)
Colorado Mountain Coll, Timberline Campus (CO)
Florida National U (FL)
Lewis-Clark State Coll (ID)
Morrisville State Coll (NY)
New York City Coll of Technology of the City U of New York (NY)
Stratford U (MD)
Sullivan U (KY)
The U of Akron (OH)
U of Cincinnati (OH)
Utah Valley U (UT)
Valencia Coll (FL)
Webber International U (FL)
Western Kentucky U (KY)
Youngstown State U (OH)

HOSPITALITY ADMINISTRATION RELATED
Morrisville State Coll (NY)
Penn State Berks (PA)
Purdue U (IN)
U of the District of Columbia (DC)

HOSPITALITY AND RECREATION MARKETING
State U of New York Coll of Technology at Delhi (NY)

HOTEL/MOTEL ADMINISTRATION
Baker Coll of Port Huron (MI)
Colorado Mountain Coll, Alpine Campus (CO)
Indian River State Coll (FL)
Inter American U of Puerto Rico, Fajardo Campus (PR)
International Business Coll, Fort Wayne (IN)
Palm Beach State Coll (FL)
State U of New York Coll of Agriculture and Technology at Cobleskill (NY)
State U of New York Coll of Technology at Delhi (NY)
Stratford U, Falls Church (VA)
Stratford U, Woodbridge (VA)
The U of Akron (OH)
U of the Virgin Islands (VI)
Valencia Coll (FL)

HUMAN DEVELOPMENT AND FAMILY STUDIES
Mount Vernon Nazarene U (OH)
Penn State Abington (PA)
Penn State Altoona (PA)
Penn State Berks (PA)
Penn State Erie, The Behrend Coll (PA)
Penn State Shenango (PA)
State U of New York Empire State Coll (NY)

HUMAN DEVELOPMENT AND FAMILY STUDIES RELATED
Utah State U (UT)

HUMANITIES
Briercrest Coll (SK, Canada)
Colorado Mountain Coll (CO)
Colorado Mountain Coll, Alpine Campus (CO)
Faulkner U (AL)
Fisher Coll (MA)
Harrison Middleton U (AZ)
Indian River State Coll (FL)
John Cabot U (Italy)
Ohio U (OH)
Ohio U–Chillicothe (OH)
Saint Peter's U (NJ)
State Coll of Florida Manatee-Sarasota (FL)
State U of New York Coll of Agriculture and Technology at Cobleskill (NY)
State U of New York Coll of Technology at Delhi (NY)
State U of New York Empire State Coll (NY)
Thomas More Coll (KY)
Utah Valley U (UT)
Valparaiso U (IN)
Washburn U (KS)

HUMAN RESOURCES DEVELOPMENT
Park U (MO)

HUMAN RESOURCES MANAGEMENT
American U of Puerto Rico (PR)
Harrison Coll, Indianapolis (IN)
Harrison Coll (OH)
King's Coll (PA)
Marian U (IN)
Rasmussen Coll Appleton (WI)
Rasmussen Coll Blaine (MN)
Rasmussen Coll Land O' Lakes (FL)
Rasmussen Coll Tampa/Brandon (FL)
Rasmussen Coll Wausau (WI)
U of Alaska Fairbanks (AK)
The U of Findlay (OH)
The U of Scranton (PA)

HUMAN RESOURCES MANAGEMENT AND SERVICES RELATED
American Public U System (WV)

HUMAN SERVICES
Alaska Pacific U (AK)
Arkansas Tech U (AR)
Baker Coll of Clinton Township (MI)
Beacon Coll (FL)
Bethel Coll (IN)
Caribbean U (PR)
Columbia Coll (MO)
Hilbert Coll (NY)
Indian River State Coll (FL)
Mercy Coll (NY)
Morrisville State Coll (NY)
Mount Vernon Nazarene U (OH)
New York City Coll of Technology of the City U of New York (NY)
Rasmussen Coll Appleton (WI)
Rasmussen Coll Blaine (MN)
Rasmussen Coll Land O' Lakes (FL)
Rasmussen Coll Tampa/Brandon (FL)
Rasmussen Coll Wausau (WI)
State U of New York Empire State Coll (NY)
Thomas Edison State Coll (NJ)
U of Alaska Anchorage (AK)
U of Great Falls (MT)
U of Maine at Fort Kent (ME)
The U of Scranton (PA)
Walsh U (OH)
Wayland Baptist U (TX)

HYDROLOGY AND WATER RESOURCES SCIENCE
Indian River State Coll (FL)
Lake Superior State U (MI)
U of the District of Columbia (DC)

ILLUSTRATION
Academy of Art U (CA)
Creative Center (NE)
Fashion Inst of Technology (NY)
Pratt Inst (NY)

INDUSTRIAL AND PRODUCT DESIGN
Academy of Art U (CA)
Oakland City U (IN)

INDUSTRIAL ELECTRONICS TECHNOLOGY
Dalton State Coll (GA)
Ferris State U (MI)
Lewis-Clark State Coll (ID)
Pennsylvania Coll of Technology (PA)

INDUSTRIAL ENGINEERING
Indiana Tech (IN)

INDUSTRIAL MECHANICS AND MAINTENANCE TECHNOLOGY
Northern Michigan U (MI)
Pennsylvania Coll of Technology (PA)
U of Alaska Anchorage (AK)

INDUSTRIAL PRODUCTION TECHNOLOGIES RELATED
Austin Peay State U (TN)
California U of Pennsylvania (PA)
Clarion U of Pennsylvania (PA)
U of Alaska Fairbanks (AK)

INDUSTRIAL RADIOLOGIC TECHNOLOGY
The George Washington U (DC)
Indian River State Coll (FL)
Lamar U (TX)

Palm Beach State Coll (FL)
Widener U (PA)

INDUSTRIAL TECHNOLOGY
Arkansas Tech U (AR)
Dalton State Coll (GA)
Indiana U–Purdue U Fort Wayne (IN)
Kansas State U (KS)
Millersville U of Pennsylvania (PA)
Murray State U (KY)
New England Inst of Technology (RI)
Southeastern Louisiana U (LA)
Southern Arkansas U–Magnolia (AR)
U of Alaska Anchorage (AK)
U of Puerto Rico at Bayamón (PR)
U of Puerto Rico at Ponce (PR)
U of Rio Grande (OH)
Washburn U (KS)

INFORMATION RESOURCES MANAGEMENT
Rasmussen Coll Land O' Lakes (FL)
Rasmussen Coll Tampa/Brandon (FL)

INFORMATION SCIENCE/STUDIES
Baker Coll of Clinton Township (MI)
Beacon Coll (FL)
Campbellsville U (KY)
Farmingdale State Coll (NY)
Faulkner U (AL)
Goldey-Beacom Coll (DE)
Husson U (ME)
Immaculata U (PA)
Indiana U–Purdue U Fort Wayne (IN)
Indian River State Coll (FL)
Johnson State Coll (VT)
Mansfield U of Pennsylvania (PA)
Newman U (KS)
Oakland City U (IN)
Penn State Abington (PA)
Penn State Altoona (PA)
Penn State Berks (PA)
Penn State Erie, The Behrend Coll (PA)
Penn State U Park (PA)
Polk State Coll (FL)
Saint Peter's U (NJ)
State Coll of Florida Manatee-Sarasota (FL)
State U of New York Coll of Agriculture and Technology at Cobleskill (NY)
State U of New York Coll of Technology at Canton (NY)
Tulane U (LA)
U of Alaska Anchorage (AK)
U of Cincinnati (OH)
U of Pittsburgh at Bradford (PA)
The U of Scranton (PA)
The U of Toledo (OH)
Wright State U (OH)

INFORMATION TECHNOLOGY
Arkansas Tech U (AR)
Cameron U (OK)
Ferris State U (MI)
Florida National U (FL)
Franklin U (OH)
Harrison Coll, Indianapolis (IN)
Indiana U–Purdue U Fort Wayne (IN)
Keystone Coll (PA)
McNeese State U (LA)
Mercy Coll (NY)
New England Inst of Technology (RI)
Peirce Coll (PA)
Point Park U (PA)
Regent U (VA)
Southern Utah U (UT)
Thomas More Coll (KY)
Tiffin U (OH)
Trevecca Nazarene U (TN)
Vermont Tech Coll (VT)
Youngstown State U (OH)

INSTITUTIONAL FOOD WORKERS
Immaculata U (PA)

INSTRUMENTATION TECHNOLOGY
Idaho State U (ID)
U of Alaska Anchorage (AK)
U of Puerto Rico at Bayamón (PR)

INSURANCE
AIB Coll of Business (IA)
Caribbean U (PR)

INTERCULTURAL/MULTICULTURAL AND DIVERSITY STUDIES
Baptist U of the Americas (TX)

INTERDISCIPLINARY STUDIES
Cardinal Stritch U (WI)
Central Methodist U (MO)
John Brown U (AR)
Kansas State U (KS)
Lesley U (MA)
State U of New York Empire State Coll (NY)
Suffolk U (MA)
U of North Florida (FL)

INTERIOR ARCHITECTURE
Villa Maria Coll of Buffalo (NY)

INTERIOR DESIGN
Academy of Art U (CA)
Baker Coll of Clinton Township (MI)
Baker Coll of Port Huron (MI)
Bay Path Coll (MA)
Chaminade U of Honolulu (HI)
EDP U of Puerto Rico (PR)
Fashion Inst of Technology (NY)
Indiana U–Purdue U Fort Wayne (IN)
Indiana U–Purdue U Indianapolis (IN)
Indian River State Coll (FL)
International Academy of Design & Technology (FL)
Montana State U (MT)
New England Inst of Technology (RI)
New York School of Interior Design (NY)
Palm Beach State Coll (FL)
Parsons The New School for Design (NY)
Robert Morris U Illinois (IL)
Weber State U (UT)

INTERMEDIA/MULTIMEDIA
Academy of Art U (CA)

INTERNATIONAL BUSINESS/TRADE/COMMERCE
AIB Coll of Business (IA)
The American U of Rome (Italy)
Potomac Coll (DC)
Saint Peter's U (NJ)
Utah Valley U (UT)

INTERNATIONAL/GLOBAL STUDIES
Briercrest Coll (SK, Canada)
Holy Cross Coll (IN)
Thomas More Coll (KY)

INTERNATIONAL RELATIONS AND AFFAIRS
John Cabot U (Italy)
U of Cincinnati (OH)

ITALIAN STUDIES
John Cabot U (Italy)

JAZZ/JAZZ STUDIES
Five Towns Coll (NY)
State Coll of Florida Manatee-Sarasota (FL)
Villa Maria Coll of Buffalo (NY)

JEWISH/JUDAIC STUDIES
State Coll of Florida Manatee-Sarasota (FL)

JOURNALISM
Indiana U Southeast (IN)
Indian River State Coll (FL)
John Brown U (AR)
Madonna U (MI)
Manchester U (IN)
Morrisville State Coll (NY)
Palm Beach State Coll (FL)
State Coll of Florida Manatee-Sarasota (FL)

JOURNALISM RELATED
Adams State U (CO)
National U (CA)

KEYBOARD INSTRUMENTS
McNally Smith Coll of Music (MN)

KINDERGARTEN/PRESCHOOL EDUCATION
Baker Coll of Clinton Township (MI)
California U of Pennsylvania (PA)
Fisher Coll (MA)

Indian River State Coll (FL)
Keystone Coll (PA)
Maria Coll (NY)
Miami U (OH)
Mitchell Coll (CT)
Mount St. Mary's Coll (CA)
Palm Beach State Coll (FL)
Shawnee State U (OH)
State Coll of Florida Manatee-Sarasota (FL)
Tennessee State U (TN)
U of Cincinnati (OH)
U of Great Falls (MT)
U of Rio Grande (OH)
Wilmington U (DE)

KINESIOLOGY AND EXERCISE SCIENCE
Southwestern Adventist U (TX)
Thomas More Coll (KY)

LABOR AND INDUSTRIAL RELATIONS
Indiana U–Purdue U Fort Wayne (IN)
Rider U (NJ)
State U of New York Empire State Coll (NY)
Youngstown State U (OH)

LABOR STUDIES
Indiana U Bloomington (IN)
Indiana U Kokomo (IN)
Indiana U Northwest (IN)
Indiana U–Purdue U Indianapolis (IN)
Indiana U South Bend (IN)

LANDSCAPE ARCHITECTURE
Academy of Art U (CA)
Keystone Coll (PA)
Morrisville State Coll (NY)
State U of New York Coll of Technology at Delhi (NY)

LANDSCAPING AND GROUNDSKEEPING
Farmingdale State Coll (NY)
Michigan State U (MI)
North Carolina State U (NC)
Pennsylvania Coll of Technology (PA)
State U of New York Coll of Technology at Delhi (NY)
U of Massachusetts Amherst (MA)
Valencia Coll (FL)
Vermont Tech Coll (VT)

LAND USE PLANNING AND MANAGEMENT
Colorado Mountain Coll, Timberline Campus (CO)

LANGUAGE INTERPRETATION AND TRANSLATION
Indian River State Coll (FL)

LATIN AMERICAN STUDIES
State Coll of Florida Manatee-Sarasota (FL)

LAW ENFORCEMENT INVESTIGATION AND INTERVIEWING
U of the District of Columbia (DC)

LAY MINISTRY
Howard Payne U (TX)
Maranatha Baptist Bible Coll (WI)
Southeastern Bible Coll (AL)

LEGAL ADMINISTRATIVE ASSISTANT/SECRETARY
Baker Coll of Clinton Township (MI)
Baker Coll of Port Huron (MI)
Clarion U of Pennsylvania (PA)
Dordt Coll (IA)
Florida National U (FL)
Hickey Coll (MO)
International Business Coll, Fort Wayne (IN)
Lamar U (TX)
Lewis-Clark State Coll (ID)
Palm Beach State Coll (FL)
Shawnee State U (OH)
Sullivan U (KY)
U of Cincinnati (OH)
U of Rio Grande (OH)
U of the District of Columbia (DC)
Washburn U (KS)
Youngstown State U (OH)

LEGAL ASSISTANT/PARALEGAL

American Public U System (WV)
Central Penn Coll (PA)
Clayton State U (GA)
Coll of Mount St. Joseph (OH)
Coll of Saint Mary (NE)
Davenport U, Grand Rapids (MI)
Faulkner U (AL)
Ferris State U (MI)
Florida National U (FL)
Gannon U (PA)
Harrison Coll, Indianapolis (IN)
Hickey Coll (MO)
Hilbert Coll (NY)
Hodges U (FL)
Husson U (ME)
Idaho State U (ID)
Indian River State Coll (FL)
International Business Coll, Fort Wayne (IN)
Jones Coll, Jacksonville (FL)
Lewis-Clark State Coll (ID)
Madonna U (MI)
Maria Coll (NY)
McNeese State U (LA)
Midland Coll (TX)
Missouri Western State U (MO)
Mount Aloysius Coll (PA)
Newman U (KS)
New York City Coll of Technology of the City U of New York (NY)
Peirce Coll (PA)
Pennsylvania Coll of Technology (PA)
Post U (CT)
Rasmussen Coll Appleton (WI)
Rasmussen Coll Blaine (MN)
Rasmussen Coll Land O' Lakes (FL)
Rasmussen Coll Mokena/Tinley Park (IL)
Rasmussen Coll Romeoville/Joliet (IL)
Rasmussen Coll Tampa/Brandon (FL)
Rasmussen Coll Wausau (WI)
Robert Morris U Illinois (IL)
Saint Mary-of-the-Woods Coll (IN)
Shawnee State U (OH)
Southern Utah U (UT)
State Coll of Florida Manatee-Sarasota (FL)
Suffolk U (MA)
Sullivan U (KY)
Tulane U (LA)
The U of Akron (OH)
U of Alaska Fairbanks (AK)
U of Arkansas–Fort Smith (AR)
U of Cincinnati (OH)
U of Great Falls (MT)
U of Hartford (CT)
U of Louisville (KY)
U of the District of Columbia (DC)
Utah Valley U (UT)
Valencia Coll (FL)
Washburn U (KS)
Western Kentucky U (KY)
Widener U (PA)

LEGAL PROFESSIONS AND STUDIES RELATED

Florida National U (FL)

LEGAL STUDIES

Maria Coll (NY)
National U (CA)
St. John's U (NY)
U of Hartford (CT)
U of New Haven (CT)

LIBERAL ARTS AND SCIENCES AND HUMANITIES RELATED

Adams State U (CO)
Ball State U (IN)
Colorado Mesa U (CO)
Dallas Baptist U (TX)
Ferris State U (MI)
Kent State U at Geauga (OH)
Kent State U at Stark (OH)
Marymount Coll, Palos Verdes, California (CA)
Mount Aloysius Coll (PA)
New York U (NY)
Nyack Coll (NY)
Pennsylvania Coll of Technology (PA)
Sacred Heart U (CT)
Southern New Hampshire U (NH)
Taylor U (IN)
U of Hartford (CT)
U of Wisconsin–Green Bay (WI)
U of Wisconsin–La Crosse (WI)
Walsh U (OH)
Wayland Baptist U (TX)

LIBERAL ARTS AND SCIENCES/LIBERAL STUDIES

Adams State U (CO)
Adelphi U (NY)
Alverno Coll (WI)
American U (DC)
American U of Puerto Rico (PR)
The American U of Rome (Italy)
Amridge U (AL)
Arizona Christian U (AZ)
Arkansas State U (AR)
Armstrong Atlantic State U (GA)
Ball State U (IN)
Bard Coll (NY)
Bay Path Coll (MA)
Beacon Coll (FL)
Bemidji State U (MN)
Bethel Coll (IN)
Bethel U (MN)
Boise State U (ID)
Bryn Athyn Coll of the New Church (PA)
California U of Pennsylvania (PA)
Calumet Coll of Saint Joseph (IN)
Cardinal Stritch U (WI)
Charter Oak State Coll (CT)
Chestnut Hill Coll (PA)
Christendom Coll (VA)
Clarke U (IA)
Clayton State U (GA)
Coll of Coastal Georgia (GA)
The Coll of Saints John Fisher & Thomas More (TX)
Coll of Staten Island of the City U of New York (NY)
Colorado Mesa U (CO)
Colorado Mountain Coll (CO)
Colorado Mountain Coll, Alpine Campus (CO)
Colorado Mountain Coll, Timberline Campus (CO)
Columbia Coll (MO)
Columbus State U (GA)
Concordia Coll–New York (NY)
Concordia U (CA)
Concordia U (OR)
Concordia U Texas (TX)
Crossroads Coll (MN)
Dallas Baptist U (TX)
Dalton State Coll (GA)
Dominican Coll (NY)
Eastern New Mexico U (NM)
Eastern U (PA)
East-West U (IL)
Emmanuel Coll (GA)
Endicott Coll (MA)
Excelsior Coll (NY)
Fairfield U (CT)
Fairleigh Dickinson U, Metropolitan Campus (NJ)
Farmingdale State Coll (NY)
Faulkner U (AL)
Felician Coll (NJ)
Ferris State U (MI)
Fisher Coll (MA)
Five Towns Coll (NY)
Florida A&M U (FL)
Florida Atlantic U (FL)
Florida Coll (FL)
Florida National U (FL)
Franklin Coll Switzerland (Switzerland)
Gannon U (PA)
Georgia Regents U (GA)
Grace U (NE)
Granite State Coll (NH)
Hilbert Coll (NY)
Holy Cross Coll (IN)
Houghton Coll (NY)
Indiana State U (IN)
Indiana U Bloomington (IN)
Indiana U Northwest (IN)
Indiana U–Purdue U Indianapolis (IN)
Indiana U South Bend (IN)
Indiana U Southeast (IN)
Indian River State Coll (FL)
Johnson State Coll (VT)
Kent State U (OH)
Kent State U at Stark (OH)
Kentucky State U (KY)
Keystone Coll (PA)
Kuyper Coll (MI)
Lake Superior State U (MI)
Laurel U (NC)
Lewis-Clark State Coll (ID)
Limestone Coll (SC)
Long Island U–Brooklyn Campus (NY)
Louisiana State U at Alexandria (LA)
Lourdes U (OH)
Maria Coll (NY)

Marian U (IN)
Marymount Coll, Palos Verdes, California (CA)
Medaille Coll (NY)
Mercy Coll (NY)
MidAmerica Nazarene U (KS)
Midwestern State U (TX)
Minnesota State U Mankato (MN)
Minnesota State U Moorhead (MN)
Mitchell Coll (CT)
Molloy Coll (NY)
Montreat Coll, Montreat (NC)
Morrisville State Coll (NY)
Mount Aloysius Coll (PA)
Mount Marty Coll (SD)
Mount St. Mary's Coll (CA)
Murray State U (KY)
Neumann U (PA)
New England Coll (NH)
Newman U (KS)
New Saint Andrews Coll (ID)
New York City Coll of Technology of the City U of New York (NY)
New York U (NY)
Niagara U (NY)
Northern Kentucky U (KY)
Northern State U (SD)
Northwestern Coll (MN)
Nyack Coll (NY)
Oakland City U (IN)
The Ohio State U at Marion (OH)
The Ohio State U–Mansfield Campus (OH)
The Ohio State U–Newark Campus (OH)
Ohio U (OH)
Ohio U–Chillicothe (OH)
Ohio Valley U (WV)
Okanagan Coll (BC, Canada)
Palm Beach State Coll (FL)
Penn State Abington (PA)
Penn State Altoona (PA)
Penn State Berks (PA)
Penn State Erie, The Behrend Coll (PA)
Penn State Harrisburg (PA)
Penn State Shenango (PA)
Penn State U Park (PA)
Polk State Coll (FL)
Providence Coll (RI)
Purdue U Calumet (IN)
Quincy U (IL)
Rivier U (NH)
Rocky Mountain Coll (MT)
Rogers State U (OK)
Roger Williams U (RI)
St. Francis Coll (NY)
St. Gregory's U, Shawnee (OK)
St. John's U (NY)
Saint Joseph's U (PA)
Saint Leo U (FL)
Saint Louis Christian Coll (MO)
St. Thomas Aquinas Coll (NY)
Salve Regina U (RI)
Schreiner U (TX)
Southern Polytechnic State U (GA)
Spring Arbor U (MI)
State Coll of Florida Manatee-Sarasota (FL)
State U of New York Coll of Agriculture and Technology at Cobleskill (NY)
State U of New York Coll of Technology at Canton (NY)
Stephens Coll (MO)
Suffolk U (MA)
Thomas Edison State Coll (NJ)
Thomas More Coll (KY)
Thomas U (GA)
Thompson Rivers U (BC, Canada)
Trine U (IN)
Troy U (AL)
Unity Coll (ME)
The U of Akron (OH)
U of Alaska Fairbanks (AK)
U of Arkansas–Fort Smith (AR)
U of Cincinnati (OH)
U of Delaware (DE)
U of Hartford (CT)
U of Maine at Fort Kent (ME)
U of New Hampshire at Manchester (NH)
U of Pittsburgh at Bradford (PA)
The U of South Dakota (SD)
U of the District of Columbia (DC)
U of the Incarnate Word (TX)
The U of Toledo (OH)
U of West Florida (FL)
U of Wisconsin–Eau Claire (WI)
U of Wisconsin–Platteville (WI)
U of Wisconsin–Stevens Point (WI)

U of Wisconsin–Superior (WI)
Upper Iowa U (IA)
Valdosta State U (GA)
Valencia Coll (FL)
Villa Maria Coll of Buffalo (NY)
Waldorf Coll (IA)
Washburn U (KS)
Wesley Coll (DE)
Western Connecticut State U (CT)
Wichita State U (KS)
Winona State U (MN)
Xavier U (OH)
Youngstown State U (OH)

LIBRARY AND INFORMATION SCIENCE

Indian River State Coll (FL)

LICENSED PRACTICAL/VOCATIONAL NURSE TRAINING

Campbellsville U (KY)
Colorado Mountain Coll (CO)
Grace U (NE)
Indian River State Coll (FL)
Inter American U of Puerto Rico, Aguadilla Campus (PR)
Inter American U of Puerto Rico, Ponce Campus (PR)
Inter American U of Puerto Rico, San Germán Campus (PR)
Lamar U (TX)
Lewis-Clark State Coll (ID)
Maria Coll (NY)
Ohio U–Chillicothe (OH)
The U of Texas at Brownsville (TX)
Virginia State U (VA)

LINEWORKER

Pennsylvania Coll of Technology (PA)
Utah Valley U (UT)

LOGISTICS, MATERIALS, AND SUPPLY CHAIN MANAGEMENT

Park U (MO)
Sullivan U (KY)
U of Alaska Anchorage (AK)
The U of Toledo (OH)

MACHINE TOOL TECHNOLOGY

Colorado Mesa U (CO)
Idaho State U (ID)
Lamar U (TX)
Pennsylvania Coll of Technology (PA)

MANAGEMENT INFORMATION SYSTEMS

Arkansas State U (AR)
Columbia Centro Universitario, Yauco (PR)
Husson U (ME)
Inter American U of Puerto Rico, Bayamón Campus (PR)
Johnson State Coll (VT)
Lake Superior State U (MI)
Liberty U (VA)
Lindsey Wilson Coll (KY)
Lock Haven U of Pennsylvania (PA)
Morehead State U (KY)
Ohio U–Chillicothe (OH)
Shawnee State U (OH)
Universidad del Turabo (PR)
U of the Virgin Islands (VI)
Weber State U (UT)
Wright State U (OH)

MANAGEMENT INFORMATION SYSTEMS AND SERVICES RELATED

Harrison Coll, Indianapolis (IN)
Mount Aloysius Coll (PA)
Purdue U North Central (IN)
Rasmussen Coll Appleton (WI)
Rasmussen Coll Blaine (MN)
Rasmussen Coll Land O' Lakes (FL)
Rasmussen Coll Mokena/Tinley Park (IL)
Rasmussen Coll Romeoville/Joliet (IL)
Rasmussen Coll Tampa/Brandon (FL)
Rasmussen Coll Wausau (WI)

MANAGEMENT SCIENCE

Hawai`i Pacific U (HI)
U of Alaska Anchorage (AK)

MANUFACTURING ENGINEERING

New England Inst of Technology (RI)

MANUFACTURING ENGINEERING TECHNOLOGY

Colorado Mesa U (CO)
Edinboro U of Pennsylvania (PA)
Excelsior Coll (NY)
Harrison Coll, Indianapolis (IN)
Lawrence Technological U (MI)
Lewis-Clark State Coll (ID)
Missouri Western State U (MO)
Morehead State U (KY)
New England Inst of Technology (RI)
Pennsylvania Coll of Technology (PA)
Thomas Edison State Coll (NJ)
The U of Akron (OH)
Weber State U (UT)
Western Kentucky U (KY)
Wright State U (OH)

MARINE MAINTENANCE AND SHIP REPAIR TECHNOLOGY

New England Inst of Technology (RI)

MARINE SCIENCE/MERCHANT MARINE OFFICER

Indian River State Coll (FL)

MARKETING/MARKETING MANAGEMENT

AIB Coll of Business (IA)
Baker Coll of Clinton Township (MI)
Central Penn Coll (PA)
Cleary U (MI)
Colorado Mountain Coll, Alpine Campus (CO)
Dalton State Coll (GA)
Harrison Coll, Indianapolis (IN)
Harrison Coll (OH)
Hawai`i Pacific U (HI)
Idaho State U (ID)
Indian River State Coll (FL)
Marian U (IN)
Miami U (OH)
New York City Coll of Technology of the City U of New York (NY)
Palm Beach State Coll (FL)
Polk State Coll (FL)
Post U (CT)
Rasmussen Coll Appleton (WI)
Rasmussen Coll Blaine (MN)
Rasmussen Coll Land O' Lakes (FL)
Rasmussen Coll Tampa/Brandon (FL)
Rasmussen Coll Wausau (WI)
Saint Peter's U (NJ)
Southern New Hampshire U (NH)
State U of New York Coll of Technology at Delhi (NY)
Tulane U (LA)
Universidad del Turabo (PR)
The U of Akron (OH)
U of Cincinnati (OH)
The U of Texas at Brownsville (TX)
Walsh U (OH)
Webber International U (FL)
Wright State U (OH)
Youngstown State U (OH)

MARKETING RELATED

Sullivan U (KY)

MASONRY

Liberty U (VA)
Pennsylvania Coll of Technology (PA)

MASSAGE THERAPY

Columbia Centro Universitario, Caguas (PR)
Harrison Coll, Indianapolis (IN)
Idaho State U (ID)
Morrisville State Coll (NY)

MASS COMMUNICATION/MEDIA

Adams State U (CO)
Inter American U of Puerto Rico, Bayamón Campus (PR)
John Cabot U (Italy)
Palm Beach State Coll (FL)
State Coll of Florida Manatee-Sarasota (FL)
U of Rio Grande (OH)
U of the Incarnate Word (TX)
York Coll of Pennsylvania (PA)

MATHEMATICS

Clarke U (IA)
Coll of Coastal Georgia (GA)
Colorado Mountain Coll (CO)
Colorado Mountain Coll, Alpine Campus (CO)
Creighton U (NE)
Dalton State Coll (GA)

Hawai`i Pacific U (HI)
Idaho State U (ID)
Indiana Wesleyan U (IN)
Indian River State Coll (FL)
Midland Coll (TX)
Palm Beach State Coll (FL)
Shawnee State U (OH)
State U of New York Coll of Agriculture and Technology at Cobleskill (NY)
State U of New York Coll of Technology at Delhi (NY)
State U of New York Empire State Coll (NY)
Thomas Edison State Coll (NJ)
Thomas More Coll (KY)
Thomas U (GA)
Thompson Rivers U (BC, Canada)
Trine U (IN)
U of Cincinnati (OH)
U of Great Falls (MT)
U of Rio Grande (OH)
The U of Tampa (FL)
Utah Valley U (UT)

MATHEMATICS AND COMPUTER SCIENCE
Immaculata U (PA)

MATHEMATICS TEACHER EDUCATION
State Coll of Florida Manatee-Sarasota (FL)

MECHANICAL DRAFTING AND CAD/CADD
Indiana U–Purdue U Indianapolis (IN)
Midland Coll (TX)
New York City Coll of Technology of the City U of New York (NY)

MECHANICAL ENGINEERING
New England Inst of Technology (RI)

MECHANICAL ENGINEERING/MECHANICAL TECHNOLOGY
Bluefield State Coll (WV)
Fairmont State U (WV)
Farmingdale State Coll (NY)
Idaho State U (ID)
Indiana U–Purdue U Fort Wayne (IN)
Lake Superior State U (MI)
Lawrence Technological U (MI)
Miami U (OH)
Morrisville State Coll (NY)
New York City Coll of Technology of the City U of New York (NY)
Penn State Altoona (PA)
Penn State Berks (PA)
Penn State Erie, The Behrend Coll (PA)
Penn State Shenango (PA)
Point Park U (PA)
State U of New York Coll of Agriculture and Technology at Cobleskill (NY)
State U of New York Coll of Technology at Canton (NY)
Universidad del Turabo (PR)
The U of Akron (OH)
U of Arkansas at Little Rock (AR)
U of Rio Grande (OH)
Vermont Tech Coll (VT)
Weber State U (UT)
Youngstown State U (OH)

MECHANICAL ENGINEERING TECHNOLOGIES RELATED
Indiana U–Purdue U Indianapolis (IN)
Purdue U North Central (IN)

MECHANIC AND REPAIR TECHNOLOGIES RELATED
Pennsylvania Coll of Technology (PA)
Thomas Edison State Coll (NJ)
Washburn U (KS)

MECHANICS AND REPAIR
Idaho State U (ID)
Lewis-Clark State Coll (ID)
Utah Valley U (UT)

MEDICAL ADMINISTRATIVE ASSISTANT AND MEDICAL SECRETARY
Baker Coll of Clinton Township (MI)
Baker Coll of Port Huron (MI)
Florida National U (FL)

Indian River State Coll (FL)
Lamar U (TX)
Polk State Coll (FL)
Rasmussen Coll Appleton (WI)
Rasmussen Coll Blaine (MN)
Rasmussen Coll Land O' Lakes (FL)
Rasmussen Coll Mokena/Tinley Park (IL)
Rasmussen Coll Romeoville/Joliet (IL)
Rasmussen Coll Tampa/Brandon (FL)
Rasmussen Coll Wausau (WI)
U of Cincinnati (OH)
U of Rio Grande (OH)

MEDICAL/CLINICAL ASSISTANT
Arkansas Tech U (AR)
Baker Coll of Clinton Township (MI)
Baker Coll of Port Huron (MI)
Central Penn Coll (PA)
Davenport U, Grand Rapids (MI)
Florida National U (FL)
Harrison Coll, Indianapolis (IN)
Harrison Coll (OH)
Hodges U (FL)
Idaho State U (ID)
International Business Coll, Fort Wayne (IN)
Mercy Coll of Health Sciences (IA)
Montana Tech of The U of Montana (MT)
Mount Aloysius Coll (PA)
New England Inst of Technology (RI)
Ohio U–Chillicothe (OH)
Presentation Coll (SD)
Rasmussen Coll Appleton (WI)
Rasmussen Coll Blaine (MN)
Rasmussen Coll Land O' Lakes (FL)
Rasmussen Coll Mokena/Tinley Park (IL)
Rasmussen Coll Romeoville/Joliet (IL)
Rasmussen Coll Tampa/Brandon (FL)
Rasmussen Coll Wausau (WI)
Robert Morris U Illinois (IL)
Sullivan U (KY)
The U of Akron (OH)
U of Alaska Anchorage (AK)
U of Alaska Fairbanks (AK)
U of Cincinnati (OH)
Youngstown State U (OH)

MEDICAL/HEALTH MANAGEMENT AND CLINICAL ASSISTANT
Florida National U (FL)
Lewis-Clark State Coll (ID)
Stratford U, Woodbridge (VA)

MEDICAL INFORMATICS
Montana Tech of The U of Montana (MT)

MEDICAL INSURANCE CODING
Grantham U (MO)
Stratford U, Woodbridge (VA)

MEDICAL INSURANCE/MEDICAL BILLING
Harrison Coll, Indianapolis (IN)
Harrison Coll (OH)

MEDICAL MICROBIOLOGY AND BACTERIOLOGY
Florida National U (FL)

MEDICAL OFFICE ASSISTANT
Hickey Coll (MO)
Lewis-Clark State Coll (ID)
Mercy Coll of Health Sciences (IA)

MEDICAL OFFICE MANAGEMENT
Dalton State Coll (GA)
Presentation Coll (SD)
Sullivan U (KY)
The U of Akron (OH)

MEDICAL RADIOLOGIC TECHNOLOGY
Arkansas State U (AR)
Ball State U (IN)
Bluefield State Coll (WV)
Coll of Coastal Georgia (GA)
Drexel U (PA)
Ferris State U (MI)
Gannon U (PA)
Idaho State U (ID)

Indiana U–Purdue U Fort Wayne (IN)
Inter American U of Puerto Rico, Aguadilla Campus (PR)
Inter American U of Puerto Rico, Ponce Campus (PR)
Inter American U of Puerto Rico, San Germán Campus (PR)
Keystone Coll (PA)
La Roche Coll (PA)
Mercy Coll of Health Sciences (IA)
Mercy Coll of Ohio (OH)
Molloy Coll (NY)
Morehead State U (KY)
Mount Aloysius Coll (PA)
Newman U (KS)
New York City Coll of Technology of the City U of New York (NY)
Northern Kentucky U (KY)
Pennsylvania Coll of Technology (PA)
Shawnee State U (OH)
State Coll of Florida Manatee-Sarasota (FL)
Thomas Edison State Coll (NJ)
Trinity Coll of Nursing and Health Sciences (IL)
The U of Akron (OH)
U of Arkansas for Medical Sciences (AR)
U of Charleston (WV)
U of Cincinnati (OH)
U of New Mexico (NM)
Valencia Coll (FL)

MEDICAL TRANSCRIPTION
U of Cincinnati (OH)

MENTAL AND SOCIAL HEALTH SERVICES AND ALLIED PROFESSIONS RELATED
Clarion U of Pennsylvania (PA)
U of Alaska Fairbanks (AK)
Washburn U (KS)

MERCHANDISING
The U of Akron (OH)

MERCHANDISING, SALES, AND MARKETING OPERATIONS RELATED (GENERAL)
American U of Puerto Rico (PR)
Inter American U of Puerto Rico, San Germán Campus (PR)
Post U (CT)

METAL AND JEWELRY ARTS
Academy of Art U (CA)
Fashion Inst of Technology (NY)

METALLURGICAL TECHNOLOGY
Penn State Altoona (PA)
Penn State Berks (PA)
Penn State Erie, The Behrend Coll (PA)
Penn State Shenango (PA)

MIDDLE SCHOOL EDUCATION
U of Cincinnati (OH)
Wright State U (OH)

MILITARY HISTORY
American Public U System (WV)

MILITARY STUDIES
Hawai`i Pacific U (HI)

MILITARY TECHNOLOGIES AND APPLIED SCIENCES RELATED
Thomas Edison State Coll (NJ)

MINING AND PETROLEUM TECHNOLOGIES RELATED
U of the Virgin Islands (VI)

MISSIONARY STUDIES AND MISSIOLOGY
Faith Baptist Bible Coll and Theological Seminary (IA)
Hillsdale Free Will Baptist Coll (OK)

MULTI/INTERDISCIPLINARY STUDIES RELATED
Arkansas Tech U (AR)
Grantham U (MO)
Miami U (OH)
Montana Tech of The U of Montana (MT)
Ohio U–Chillicothe (OH)

Pennsylvania Coll of Technology (PA)
Providence Coll (RI)
Thomas Edison State Coll (NJ)
The U of Akron (OH)
U of Alaska Fairbanks (AK)
U of Arkansas–Fort Smith (AR)
U of Cincinnati (OH)
The U of Toledo (OH)
Utah Valley U (UT)

MUSEUM STUDIES
Inst of American Indian Arts (NM)

MUSIC
Alderson-Broaddus Coll (WV)
Alverno Coll (WI)
Central Baptist Coll (AR)
Clayton State U (GA)
Five Towns Coll (NY)
Grace U (NE)
Hillsdale Free Will Baptist Coll (OK)
Indian River State Coll (FL)
Midland Coll (TX)
Mount Vernon Nazarene U (OH)
Nyack Coll (NY)
Pacific Union Coll (CA)
Palm Beach State Coll (FL)
State Coll of Florida Manatee-Sarasota (FL)
Thomas More Coll (KY)
Thompson Rivers U (BC, Canada)
U of Rio Grande (OH)
Utah Valley U (UT)
Villa Maria Coll of Buffalo (NY)
York Coll of Pennsylvania (PA)

MUSICAL INSTRUMENT FABRICATION AND REPAIR
Indiana U Bloomington (IN)

MUSIC MANAGEMENT
Ferris State U (MI)
Five Towns Coll (NY)
McNally Smith Coll of Music (MN)
Villa Maria Coll of Buffalo (NY)

MUSIC PERFORMANCE
Five Towns Coll (NY)
State Coll of Florida Manatee-Sarasota (FL)
Villa Maria Coll of Buffalo (NY)

MUSIC RELATED
Academy of Art U (CA)
Alverno Coll (WI)
Five Towns Coll (NY)
Valencia Coll (FL)

MUSIC TEACHER EDUCATION
State Coll of Florida Manatee-Sarasota (FL)
U of the District of Columbia (DC)
Wright State U (OH)

MUSIC TECHNOLOGY
McNally Smith Coll of Music (MN)

MUSIC THEORY AND COMPOSITION
State Coll of Florida Manatee-Sarasota (FL)

NATURAL RESOURCES/CONSERVATION
Colorado Mountain Coll, Timberline Campus (CO)
Morrisville State Coll (NY)
State U of New York Coll of Environmental Science and Forestry (NY)
Suffolk U (MA)

NATURAL RESOURCES MANAGEMENT AND POLICY
Lake Superior State U (MI)
U of Alaska Fairbanks (AK)

NATURAL RESOURCES MANAGEMENT AND POLICY RELATED
U of Guelph (ON, Canada)

NATURAL SCIENCES
Colorado Mountain Coll (CO)
Lourdes U (OH)
Madonna U (MI)
Roberts Wesleyan Coll (NY)
U of Alaska Fairbanks (AK)
The U of Toledo (OH)
Washburn U (KS)

NETWORK AND SYSTEM ADMINISTRATION
Florida National U (FL)
Harrison Coll, Indianapolis (IN)
Palm Beach State Coll (FL)

NUCLEAR ENGINEERING TECHNOLOGY
Arkansas Tech U (AR)
Idaho State U (ID)
Thomas Edison State Coll (NJ)

NUCLEAR MEDICAL TECHNOLOGY
Adventist U of Health Sciences (FL)
Ball State U (IN)
The George Washington U (DC)
Thomas Edison State Coll (NJ)
U of Cincinnati (OH)

NUCLEAR/NUCLEAR POWER TECHNOLOGY
Excelsior Coll (NY)

NURSING EDUCATION
U of the District of Columbia (DC)

NURSING SCIENCE
EDP U of Puerto Rico (PR)
Trinity Coll of Nursing and Health Sciences (IL)
U of Alaska Anchorage (AK)

NUTRITION SCIENCES
U of Cincinnati (OH)

OCCUPATIONAL SAFETY AND HEALTH TECHNOLOGY
Fairmont State U (WV)
Indiana U Bloomington (IN)
Lamar U (TX)
U of Alaska Anchorage (AK)

OCCUPATIONAL THERAPIST ASSISTANT
Adventist U of Health Sciences (FL)
Arkansas Tech U (AR)
Central Penn Coll (PA)
Inter American U of Puerto Rico, Ponce Campus (PR)
Maria Coll (NY)
Mercy Coll (NY)
New England Inst of Technology (RI)
Newman U (KS)
Penn State Berks (PA)
Pennsylvania Coll of Technology (PA)
Polk State Coll (FL)
State Coll of Florida Manatee-Sarasota (FL)
U of Charleston (WV)
U of Louisiana at Monroe (LA)
U of Southern Indiana (IN)
Washburn U (KS)

OCCUPATIONAL THERAPY
Coll of Coastal Georgia (GA)
Keystone Coll (PA)
Palm Beach State Coll (FL)
Shawnee State U (OH)
State Coll of Florida Manatee-Sarasota (FL)

OFFICE MANAGEMENT
Dalton State Coll (GA)
Emmanuel Coll (GA)
Inter American U of Puerto Rico, Aguadilla Campus (PR)
Inter American U of Puerto Rico, Fajardo Campus (PR)
Inter American U of Puerto Rico, Ponce Campus (PR)
Inter American U of Puerto Rico, San Germán Campus (PR)
Maranatha Baptist Bible Coll (WI)
Mercyhurst U (PA)
Miami U (OH)
Shawnee State U (OH)
Sullivan U (KY)
Universidad del Turabo (PR)
The U of Akron (OH)
Washburn U (KS)

OFFICE OCCUPATIONS AND CLERICAL SERVICES
American U of Puerto Rico (PR)
Midland Coll (TX)
Morrisville State Coll (NY)

OPERATIONS MANAGEMENT
Indiana U–Purdue U Fort Wayne (IN)
Indiana U–Purdue U Indianapolis (IN)

OPHTHALMIC LABORATORY TECHNOLOGY
Rochester Inst of Technology (NY)

OPTICAL SCIENCES
Indiana U of Pennsylvania (PA)

OPTICIANRY
New York City Coll of Technology of the City U of New York (NY)

OPTOMETRIC TECHNICIAN
Indiana U Bloomington (IN)
Inter American U of Puerto Rico, Ponce Campus (PR)

ORGANIZATIONAL BEHAVIOR
Hawai`i Pacific U (HI)

ORGANIZATIONAL COMMUNICATION
Creighton U (NE)

ORGANIZATIONAL LEADERSHIP
AIB Coll of Business (IA)
Huntington U (IN)
Point U (GA)

ORNAMENTAL HORTICULTURE
Farmingdale State Coll (NY)
State U of New York Coll of Agriculture and Technology at Cobleskill (NY)
Vermont Tech Coll (VT)

PAINTING
Academy of Art U (CA)
Pratt Inst (NY)

PALLIATIVE CARE NURSING
Madonna U (MI)

PARKS, RECREATION AND LEISURE
Colorado Mountain Coll, Timberline Campus (CO)
State U of New York Coll of Technology at Delhi (NY)

PARKS, RECREATION AND LEISURE FACILITIES MANAGEMENT
Coll of Coastal Georgia (GA)
Colorado Mountain Coll, Alpine Campus (CO)
Colorado Mountain Coll, Timberline Campus (CO)
Indiana Tech (IN)
State U of New York Coll of Technology at Delhi (NY)
Webber International U (FL)

PARKS, RECREATION, LEISURE, AND FITNESS STUDIES RELATED
Southern Nazarene U (OK)

PASTORAL STUDIES/ COUNSELING
Indiana Wesleyan U (IN)
Marian U (IN)

PERCUSSION INSTRUMENTS
McNally Smith Coll of Music (MN)

PERSONAL AND CULINARY SERVICES RELATED
U of Cincinnati (OH)

PETROLEUM TECHNOLOGY
Nicholls State U (LA)
U of Alaska Anchorage (AK)
U of Pittsburgh at Bradford (PA)

PHARMACOLOGY
Universidad del Turabo (PR)

PHARMACY
Indian River State Coll (FL)

PHARMACY, PHARMACEUTICAL SCIENCES, AND ADMINISTRATION RELATED
Universidad del Turabo (PR)

PHARMACY TECHNICIAN
Inter American U of Puerto Rico, Aguadilla Campus (PR)

Rasmussen Coll Appleton (WI)
Rasmussen Coll Blaine (MN)
Rasmussen Coll Land O' Lakes (FL)
Rasmussen Coll Mokena/Tinley Park (IL)
Rasmussen Coll Romeoville/Joliet (IL)
Rasmussen Coll Tampa/Brandon (FL)
Rasmussen Coll Wausau (WI)
Robert Morris U Illinois (IL)
Stratford U, Woodbridge (VA)
Sullivan U (KY)

PHILOSOPHY
Carroll Coll (MT)
Coll of Coastal Georgia (GA)
Indian River State Coll (FL)
Palm Beach State Coll (FL)
State Coll of Florida Manatee-Sarasota (FL)
Thomas More Coll (KY)
U of Cincinnati (OH)
The U of Tampa (FL)
Utah Valley U (UT)

PHLEBOTOMY TECHNOLOGY
Stratford U, Woodbridge (VA)

PHOTOGRAPHIC AND FILM/ VIDEO TECHNOLOGY
St. John's U (NY)
U of Cincinnati (OH)
Villa Maria Coll of Buffalo (NY)

PHOTOGRAPHY
Academy of Art U (CA)
Colorado Mountain Coll (CO)
Corcoran Coll of Art and Design (DC)
International Academy of Design & Technology (FL)
Pacific Union Coll (CA)
Paier Coll of Art, Inc. (CT)
Palm Beach State Coll (FL)
Thomas Edison State Coll (NJ)
Villa Maria Coll of Buffalo (NY)

PHYSICAL EDUCATION TEACHING AND COACHING
Hillsdale Free Will Baptist Coll (OK)
Indian River State Coll (FL)
Palm Beach State Coll (FL)
State Coll of Florida Manatee-Sarasota (FL)
U of Rio Grande (OH)

PHYSICAL SCIENCES
Colorado Mountain Coll, Alpine Campus (CO)
Hillsdale Free Will Baptist Coll (OK)
New York City Coll of Technology of the City U of New York (NY)
Palm Beach State Coll (FL)
Roberts Wesleyan Coll (NY)
U of Cincinnati (OH)
Utah Valley U (UT)

PHYSICAL THERAPY
Coll of Coastal Georgia (GA)
Indian River State Coll (FL)
Palm Beach State Coll (FL)
State Coll of Florida Manatee-Sarasota (FL)

PHYSICAL THERAPY TECHNOLOGY
Arkansas State U (AR)
Arkansas Tech U (AR)
California U of Pennsylvania (PA)
Central Penn Coll (PA)
EDP U of Puerto Rico (PR)
Idaho State U (ID)
Indian River State Coll (FL)
Inter American U of Puerto Rico, Ponce Campus (PR)
Louisiana Coll (LA)
Maria Coll (NY)
Mercy Coll of Health Sciences (IA)
Mercyhurst U (PA)
Missouri Western State U (MO)
Mount Aloysius Coll (PA)
Nebraska Methodist Coll (NE)
New England Inst of Technology (RI)
Penn State Shenango (PA)
Polk State Coll (FL)
Shawnee State U (OH)
Southern Illinois U Carbondale (IL)
State Coll of Florida Manatee-Sarasota (FL)
State U of New York Coll of Technology at Canton (NY)
U of Cincinnati (OH)

U of Evansville (IN)
U of Puerto Rico at Ponce (PR)
Villa Maria Coll of Buffalo (NY)
Washburn U (KS)

PHYSICIAN ASSISTANT
Coll of Coastal Georgia (GA)
State Coll of Florida Manatee-Sarasota (FL)

PHYSICS
Coll of Coastal Georgia (GA)
Dalton State Coll (GA)
Idaho State U (ID)
Indian River State Coll (FL)
Midland Coll (TX)
Rogers State U (OK)
State Coll of Florida Manatee-Sarasota (FL)
Thomas More Coll (KY)
Thompson Rivers U (BC, Canada)
U of the Virgin Islands (VI)
Utah Valley U (UT)
York Coll of Pennsylvania (PA)

PHYSICS TEACHER EDUCATION
State Coll of Florida Manatee-Sarasota (FL)

PIPEFITTING AND SPRINKLER FITTING
New England Inst of Technology (RI)
State U of New York Coll of Technology at Delhi (NY)

PLANT NURSERY MANAGEMENT
Dalhousie U (NS, Canada)

PLANT PROTECTION AND INTEGRATED PEST MANAGEMENT
Dalhousie U (NS, Canada)
North Carolina State U (NC)

PLANT SCIENCES
Michigan State U (MI)
State U of New York Coll of Agriculture and Technology at Cobleskill (NY)

PLASTICS AND POLYMER ENGINEERING TECHNOLOGY
Ferris State U (MI)
Penn State Erie, The Behrend Coll (PA)
Pennsylvania Coll of Technology (PA)
Shawnee State U (OH)

PLAYWRITING AND SCREENWRITING
Pacific Union Coll (CA)

PLUMBING TECHNOLOGY
Liberty U (VA)

POLITICAL SCIENCE AND GOVERNMENT
Adams State U (CO)
Coll of Coastal Georgia (GA)
Dalton State Coll (GA)
Holy Cross Coll (IN)
Immaculata U (PA)
Indian River State Coll (FL)
John Cabot U (Italy)
Midland Coll (TX)
Palm Beach State Coll (FL)
Thomas More Coll (KY)
U of Cincinnati (OH)
The U of Tampa (FL)
The U of Toledo (OH)
Xavier U (OH)
York Coll of Pennsylvania (PA)

POLYSOMNOGRAPHY
Mercy Coll of Health Sciences (IA)

POULTRY SCIENCE
State U of New York Coll of Agriculture and Technology at Cobleskill (NY)

PRECISION METAL WORKING RELATED
Montana Tech of The U of Montana (MT)

PRE-DENTISTRY STUDIES
Coll of Coastal Georgia (GA)
Concordia U Wisconsin (WI)
U of Cincinnati (OH)

PRE-ENGINEERING
Coll of Coastal Georgia (GA)
Colorado Mountain Coll, Alpine Campus (CO)
Columbia Coll (MO)
Indian River State Coll (FL)
Newman U (KS)
Niagara U (NY)
Northern State U (SD)
Palm Beach State Coll (FL)
Polk State Coll (FL)
Siena Heights U (MI)
Southern Utah U (UT)

PRE-LAW STUDIES
Calumet Coll of Saint Joseph (IN)
Ferris State U (MI)
Immaculata U (PA)
Northern Kentucky U (KY)
Thomas More Coll (KY)
U of Cincinnati (OH)
Wayland Baptist U (TX)

PREMEDICAL STUDIES
Coll of Coastal Georgia (GA)
Concordia U Wisconsin (WI)
U of Cincinnati (OH)

PRENURSING STUDIES
Concordia U Wisconsin (WI)
Keystone Coll (PA)
Lincoln Christian U (IL)

PRE-PHARMACY STUDIES
Coll of Coastal Georgia (GA)
Dalton State Coll (GA)
Edinboro U of Pennsylvania (PA)
Ferris State U (MI)
Keystone Coll (PA)
Madonna U (MI)
State Coll of Florida Manatee-Sarasota (FL)
U of Cincinnati (OH)

PRE-THEOLOGY/PRE-MINISTERIAL STUDIES
Eastern Mennonite U (VA)

PRE-VETERINARY STUDIES
Coll of Coastal Georgia (GA)
U of Cincinnati (OH)

PRINTMAKING
Academy of Art U (CA)

PROFESSIONAL, TECHNICAL, BUSINESS, AND SCIENTIFIC WRITING
Florida National U (FL)

PSYCHIATRIC/MENTAL HEALTH SERVICES TECHNOLOGY
Lake Superior State U (MI)
Pennsylvania Coll of Technology (PA)
U of Alaska Anchorage (AK)

PSYCHOLOGY
Beacon Coll (FL)
Central Methodist U (MO)
Coll of Coastal Georgia (GA)
Colorado Mountain Coll (CO)
Dalton State Coll (GA)
Eastern New Mexico U (NM)
Fisher Coll (MA)
Hillsdale Free Will Baptist Coll (OK)
Indiana U–Purdue U Fort Wayne (IN)
Indian River State Coll (FL)
Liberty U (VA)
Marian U (IN)
Midland Coll (TX)
Muhlenberg Coll (PA)
Palm Beach State Coll (FL)
Regent U (VA)
Siena Heights U (MI)
State Coll of Florida Manatee-Sarasota (FL)
Thomas More Coll (KY)
U of Cincinnati (OH)
U of Rio Grande (OH)
The U of Tampa (FL)
Utah Valley U (UT)
Wright State U (OH)
Xavier U (OH)

PUBLIC ADMINISTRATION
Central Methodist U (MO)
Ferris State U (MI)
Florida National U (FL)
Indiana U Bloomington (IN)
Indiana U Northwest (IN)
Indiana U–Purdue U Indianapolis (IN)
Indiana U South Bend (IN)

Point Park U (PA)
State Coll of Florida Manatee-Sarasota (FL)
Universidad del Turabo (PR)

PUBLIC ADMINISTRATION AND SOCIAL SERVICE PROFESSIONS RELATED
Point Park U (PA)
State U of New York Empire State Coll (NY)
The U of Akron (OH)

PUBLIC HEALTH
American Public U System (WV)
U of Alaska Fairbanks (AK)

PUBLIC HEALTH EDUCATION AND PROMOTION
U of Cincinnati (OH)

PUBLIC POLICY ANALYSIS
Saint Peter's U (NJ)

PUBLIC RELATIONS, ADVERTISING, AND APPLIED COMMUNICATION RELATED
John Brown U (AR)

PUBLIC RELATIONS/IMAGE MANAGEMENT
John Brown U (AR)
Xavier U (OH)

PURCHASING, PROCUREMENT/ ACQUISITIONS AND CONTRACTS MANAGEMENT
Mercyhurst U (PA)

QUALITY CONTROL AND SAFETY TECHNOLOGIES RELATED
Lamar U (TX)
Madonna U (MI)
Rochester Inst of Technology (NY)

QUALITY CONTROL TECHNOLOGY
Universidad del Turabo (PR)

RADIATION PROTECTION/ HEALTH PHYSICS TECHNOLOGY
Thomas Edison State Coll (NJ)

RADIO AND TELEVISION
Lawrence Technological U (MI)
Northwestern Coll (MN)
Ohio U–Zanesville (OH)
State Coll of Florida Manatee-Sarasota (FL)
Xavier U (OH)

RADIO AND TELEVISION BROADCASTING TECHNOLOGY
New England Inst of Technology (RI)
New York Inst of Technology (NY)
State Coll of Florida Manatee-Sarasota (FL)

RADIOLOGIC TECHNOLOGY/ SCIENCE
Adventist U of Health Sciences (FL)
Allen Coll (IA)
Baker Coll of Clinton Township (MI)
Champlain Coll (VT)
Colorado Mesa U (CO)
Dalton State Coll (GA)
Fairleigh Dickinson U, Metropolitan Campus (NJ)
Florida National U (FL)
Holy Family U (PA)
Indiana U Kokomo (IN)
Indiana U Northwest (IN)
Indiana U–Purdue U Indianapolis (IN)
Indiana U South Bend (IN)
Keystone Coll (PA)
Lewis-Clark State Coll (ID)
Louisiana State U at Alexandria (LA)
Mansfield U of Pennsylvania (PA)
Midland Coll (TX)
Montana Tech of The U of Montana (MT)
Nebraska Methodist Coll (NE)
Newman U (KS)
Northern Michigan U (MI)
Polk State Coll (FL)
Presentation Coll (SD)
Regis Coll (MA)
State Coll of Florida Manatee-Sarasota (FL)
Trinity Coll of Nursing and Health Sciences (IL)

U of Alaska Anchorage (AK)
U of Arkansas–Fort Smith (AR)
U of Rio Grande (OH)
The U of Texas at Brownsville (TX)
Washburn U (KS)
Widener U (PA)
Xavier U (OH)

RADIO, TELEVISION, AND DIGITAL COMMUNICATION RELATED
Keystone Coll (PA)
Lawrence Technological U (MI)
Madonna U (MI)

REAL ESTATE
American Public U System (WV)
Caribbean U (PR)
Colorado Mountain Coll, Alpine Campus (CO)
Lamar U (TX)

RECORDING ARTS TECHNOLOGY
Columbia Centro Universitario, Caguas (PR)
Indiana U Bloomington (IN)

REGIONAL STUDIES
Arkansas Tech U (AR)

REGISTERED NURSING/ REGISTERED NURSE
Adventist U of Health Sciences (FL)
Alcorn State U (MS)
Arkansas State U (AR)
Arkansas Tech U (AR)
Baker Coll of Clinton Township (MI)
Becker Coll (MA)
Bethel Coll (IN)
Bluefield State Coll (WV)
California U of Pennsylvania (PA)
Campbellsville U (KY)
Cardinal Stritch U (WI)
Castleton State Coll (VT)
Clarion U of Pennsylvania (PA)
Coll of Coastal Georgia (GA)
Coll of Saint Mary (NE)
Coll of Staten Island of the City U of New York (NY)
Colorado Mesa U (CO)
Colorado Mountain Coll (CO)
Columbia Centro Universitario, Caguas (PR)
Columbia Centro Universitario, Yauco (PR)
Columbia Coll (MO)
Dalton State Coll (GA)
Excelsior Coll (NY)
Fairmont State U (WV)
Florida National U (FL)
Freed-Hardeman U (TN)
Gardner-Webb U (NC)
Harrison Coll, Indianapolis (IN)
Idaho State U (ID)
Indiana U Northwest (IN)
Indiana U–Purdue U Indianapolis (IN)
Indian River State Coll (FL)
Inter American U of Puerto Rico, Ponce Campus (PR)
Judson Coll (AL)
Kent State U (OH)
Kent State U at Geauga (OH)
Kentucky State U (KY)
Lamar U (TX)
La Roche Coll (PA)
Lincoln Memorial U (TN)
Lincoln U (MO)
Lock Haven U of Pennsylvania (PA)
Louisiana State U at Alexandria (LA)
Louisiana Tech U (LA)
Maria Coll (NY)
Marshall U (WV)
McNeese State U (LA)
Mercy Coll of Health Sciences (IA)
Mercy Coll of Ohio (OH)
Mercyhurst U (PA)
Miami U (OH)
Midland Coll (TX)
Mississippi U for Women (MS)
Montana Tech of The U of Montana (MT)
Morehead State U (KY)
Morrisville State Coll (NY)
Mount Aloysius Coll (PA)
Mount St. Mary's Coll (CA)
New England Inst of Technology (RI)
New York City Coll of Technology of the City U of New York (NY)

Norfolk State U (VA)
Northwestern State U of Louisiana (LA)
Pacific Union Coll (CA)
Palm Beach State Coll (FL)
Park U (MO)
Penn State Altoona (PA)
Penn State Berks (PA)
Penn State Erie, The Behrend Coll (PA)
Penn State U Park (PA)
Pennsylvania Coll of Technology (PA)
Polk State Coll (FL)
Presentation Coll (SD)
Regis Coll (MA)
Rivier U (NH)
Robert Morris U Illinois (IL)
Rogers State U (OK)
Shawnee State U (OH)
Southern Arkansas U–Magnolia (AR)
Southwest Baptist U (MO)
State Coll of Florida Manatee-Sarasota (FL)
State U of New York Coll of Technology at Canton (NY)
State U of New York Coll of Technology at Delhi (NY)
Sul Ross State U (TX)
Tennessee State U (TN)
Thomas U (GA)
Trinity Coll of Nursing and Health Sciences (IL)
Troy U (AL)
Universidad Adventista de las Antillas (PR)
U of Alaska Anchorage (AK)
U of Arkansas at Little Rock (AR)
U of Arkansas–Fort Smith (AR)
U of Charleston (WV)
U of Cincinnati (OH)
U of Guam (GU)
U of Mobile (AL)
U of North Georgia (GA)
U of Pikeville (KY)
U of Pittsburgh at Bradford (PA)
U of Rio Grande (OH)
The U of South Dakota (SD)
The U of Texas at Brownsville (TX)
U of the Virgin Islands (VI)
The U of West Alabama (AL)
Utah Valley U (UT)
Valencia Coll (FL)
Vermont Tech Coll (VT)
Western Kentucky U (KY)

REHABILITATION AND THERAPEUTIC PROFESSIONS RELATED
National U (CA)
U of Cincinnati (OH)
U of Medicine and Dentistry of New Jersey (NJ)

RELIGIOUS EDUCATION
Cincinnati Christian U (OH)
Dallas Baptist U (TX)
Hillsdale Free Will Baptist Coll (OK)
Kuyper Coll (MI)
Lincoln Christian U (IL)
Oakland City U (IN)
Southern Methodist Coll (SC)

RELIGIOUS/SACRED MUSIC
Briercrest Coll (SK, Canada)
Cincinnati Christian U (OH)
Dallas Baptist U (TX)
Hillsdale Free Will Baptist Coll (OK)
Immaculata U (PA)
Indiana Wesleyan U (IN)
Mount Vernon Nazarene U (OH)

RELIGIOUS STUDIES
Calumet Coll of Saint Joseph (IN)
Concordia Coll–New York (NY)
Corban U (OR)
Global U (MO)
Holy Apostles Coll and Seminary (CT)
Huntington U (IN)
Liberty U (VA)
Lourdes U (OH)
Madonna U (MI)
Mount Marty Coll (SD)
Mount Vernon Nazarene U (OH)
Northwest U (WA)
Palm Beach State Coll (FL)
Presentation Coll (SD)

State Coll of Florida Manatee-Sarasota (FL)
Thomas More Coll (KY)
Xavier U (OH)

RESPIRATORY CARE THERAPY
Boise State U (ID)
Coll of Coastal Georgia (GA)
Dakota State U (SD)
Ferris State U (MI)
Gannon U (PA)
Idaho State U (ID)
Indian River State Coll (FL)
Lamar U (TX)
Mansfield U of Pennsylvania (PA)
Midland Coll (TX)
Molloy U (NY)
Morehead State U (KY)
Nebraska Methodist Coll (NE)
Newman U (KS)
Northern Kentucky U (KY)
Polk State Coll (FL)
Shawnee State U (OH)
State Coll of Florida Manatee-Sarasota (FL)
Thomas Edison State Coll (NJ)
Trinity Coll of Nursing and Health Sciences (IL)
Universidad Adventista de las Antillas (PR)
U of Arkansas for Medical Sciences (AR)
U of Cincinnati (OH)
U of Medicine and Dentistry of New Jersey (NJ)
U of Southern Indiana (IN)
The U of Texas at Brownsville (TX)
U of the District of Columbia (DC)
Valencia Coll (FL)
Vermont Tech Coll (VT)
Washburn U (KS)
York Coll of Pennsylvania (PA)

RESPIRATORY THERAPY TECHNICIAN
Clarion U of Pennsylvania (PA)
Dalton State Coll (GA)
Florida National U (FL)
Northern Michigan U (MI)

RESTAURANT, CULINARY, AND CATERING MANAGEMENT
Arkansas Tech U (AR)
Bob Jones U (SC)
Colorado Mountain Coll, Alpine Campus (CO)
Ferris State U (MI)
State U of New York Coll of Technology at Delhi (NY)
Stratford U (MD)
Sullivan U (KY)

RESTAURANT/FOOD SERVICES MANAGEMENT
American Public U System (WV)
Morrisville State Coll (NY)
Pennsylvania Coll of Technology (PA)
The U of Akron (OH)
Valencia Coll (FL)

RETAILING
American Public U System (WV)
International Business Coll, Fort Wayne (IN)
Weber State U (UT)

RHETORIC AND COMPOSITION
Ferris State U (MI)
Indian River State Coll (FL)
Midland Coll (TX)
State Coll of Florida Manatee-Sarasota (FL)

ROBOTICS TECHNOLOGY
Idaho State U (ID)
Indiana U–Purdue U Indianapolis (IN)
Pennsylvania Coll of Technology (PA)
Purdue U (IN)
U of Rio Grande (OH)

RUSSIAN
Idaho State U (ID)

RUSSIAN, CENTRAL EUROPEAN, EAST EUROPEAN AND EURASIAN STUDIES
State Coll of Florida Manatee-Sarasota (FL)

RUSSIAN STUDIES
State Coll of Florida Manatee-Sarasota (FL)

SALES AND MARKETING/ MARKETING AND DISTRIBUTION TEACHER EDUCATION
Wright State U (OH)

SALES, DISTRIBUTION, AND MARKETING OPERATIONS
AIB Coll of Business (IA)
Clayton State U (GA)
Dalton State Coll (GA)
Inter American U of Puerto Rico, Aguadilla Campus (PR)
The U of Findlay (OH)

SCIENCE TEACHER EDUCATION
State Coll of Florida Manatee-Sarasota (FL)
Wright State U (OH)

SCIENCE TECHNOLOGIES
Washburn U (KS)

SCIENCE TECHNOLOGIES RELATED
Madonna U (MI)
Maria Coll (NY)
Ohio Valley U (WV)
State U of New York Coll of Agriculture and Technology at Cobleskill (NY)
U of Alaska Fairbanks (AK)
U of Cincinnati (OH)

SCULPTURE
Academy of Art U (CA)

SECONDARY EDUCATION
Ferris State U (MI)
Ohio U–Chillicothe (OH)
Rogers State U (OK)
U of Cincinnati (OH)
Utah Valley U (UT)

SECURITIES SERVICES ADMINISTRATION
Davenport U, Grand Rapids (MI)

SECURITY AND LOSS PREVENTION
John Jay Coll of Criminal Justice of the City U of New York (NY)

SELLING SKILLS AND SALES
Inter American U of Puerto Rico, San Germán Campus (PR)
The U of Akron (OH)
The U of Toledo (OH)

SIGN LANGUAGE INTERPRETATION AND TRANSLATION
Cincinnati Christian U (OH)
Mount Aloysius Coll (PA)
U of Arkansas at Little Rock (AR)
U of Louisville (KY)

SMALL BUSINESS ADMINISTRATION
Lewis-Clark State Coll (ID)
The U of Akron (OH)
U of Alaska Anchorage (AK)

SOCIAL PSYCHOLOGY
State Coll of Florida Manatee-Sarasota (FL)

SOCIAL SCIENCES
Briercrest Coll (SK, Canada)
Campbellsville U (KY)
Colorado Mountain Coll (CO)
Colorado Mountain Coll, Alpine Campus (CO)
Faulkner U (AL)
Fisher Coll (MA)
Hillsdale Free Will Baptist Coll (OK)
Indian River State Coll (FL)
Long Island U–Brooklyn Campus (NY)
Midland Coll (TX)
Ohio U–Zanesville (OH)
Palm Beach State Coll (FL)
St. Gregory's U, Shawnee (OK)
Saint Peter's U (NJ)
Shawnee State U (OH)
State Coll of Florida Manatee-Sarasota (FL)

SOCIAL SCIENCES RELATED
Concordia U Texas (TX)

SOCIAL SCIENCE TEACHER EDUCATION
Montana State U (MT)

SOCIAL STUDIES TEACHER EDUCATION
State Coll of Florida Manatee-Sarasota (FL)

SOCIAL WORK
Ferris State U (MI)
Indian River State Coll (FL)
Northern State U (SD)
Palm Beach State Coll (FL)
State Coll of Florida Manatee-Sarasota (FL)
State U of New York Coll of Agriculture and Technology at Cobleskill (NY)
Suffolk U (MA)
U of Cincinnati (OH)
U of Rio Grande (OH)
Wright State U (OH)
Youngstown State U (OH)

SOCIAL WORK RELATED
The U of Akron (OH)

SOCIOLOGY
Coll of Coastal Georgia (GA)
Holy Cross Coll (IN)
Indian River State Coll (FL)
Lourdes U (OH)
Marymount Manhattan Coll (NY)
Midland Coll (TX)
Thomas More Coll (KY)
U of Cincinnati (OH)
U of Rio Grande (OH)
The U of Scranton (PA)
The U of Tampa (FL)
Wright State U (OH)
Xavier U (OH)

SOCIOLOGY AND ANTHROPOLOGY
Midland Coll (TX)

SOIL SCIENCES RELATED
Michigan State U (MI)

SOLAR ENERGY TECHNOLOGY
Pennsylvania Coll of Technology (PA)

SPANISH
Holy Cross Coll (IN)
Immaculata U (PA)
Indian River State Coll (FL)
Midland Coll (TX)
State Coll of Florida Manatee-Sarasota (FL)
Thomas More Coll (KY)
U of Cincinnati (OH)
The U of Tampa (FL)
The U of Texas at Brownsville (TX)
Xavier U (OH)

SPECIAL EDUCATION
Edinboro U of Pennsylvania (PA)
U of Cincinnati (OH)

SPECIAL EDUCATION–INDIVIDUALS WHO ARE DEVELOPMENTALLY DELAYED
Saint Mary-of-the-Woods Coll (IN)

SPECIAL EDUCATION RELATED
Minot State U (ND)

SPECIAL PRODUCTS MARKETING
Indian River State Coll (FL)
Lamar U (TX)
Palm Beach State Coll (FL)

State U of New York Coll of Technology at Delhi (NY)
State U of New York Empire State Coll (NY)
Trine U (IN)
U of Cincinnati (OH)
U of Puerto Rico at Ponce (PR)
U of Southern Indiana (IN)
Valparaiso U (IN)
Wayland Baptist U (TX)

SPEECH COMMUNICATION AND RHETORIC
American Public U System (WV)
American U of Puerto Rico (PR)
Carroll Coll (MT)
Central Penn Coll (PA)
Coll of Mount St. Joseph (OH)
Indiana Wesleyan U (IN)
Presentation Coll (SD)
State U of New York Coll of Agriculture and Technology at Cobleskill (NY)
Thomas Edison State Coll (NJ)
Trine U (IN)
Tulane U (LA)
U of Rio Grande (OH)
Utah Valley U (UT)
Wright State U (OH)

SPORT AND FITNESS ADMINISTRATION/ MANAGEMENT
AIB Coll of Business (IA)
Colorado Mesa U (CO)
Lake Superior State U (MI)
Mount Vernon Nazarene U (OH)
U of Cincinnati (OH)

STATISTICS
State Coll of Florida Manatee-Sarasota (FL)

STRINGED INSTRUMENTS
McNally Smith Coll of Music (MN)

SUBSTANCE ABUSE/ ADDICTION COUNSELING
Indiana Wesleyan U (IN)
Midland Coll (TX)
The U of Akron (OH)
U of Great Falls (MT)
Washburn U (KS)

SURGICAL TECHNOLOGY
Baker Coll of Clinton Township (MI)
Harrison Coll, Indianapolis (IN)
Lincoln U (MO)
Mercy Coll of Health Sciences (IA)
Mount Aloysius Coll (PA)
Nebraska Methodist Coll (NE)
New England Inst of Technology (RI)
Northern Michigan U (MI)
Pennsylvania Coll of Technology (PA)
Presentation Coll (SD)
Robert Morris U Illinois (IL)
Trinity Coll of Nursing and Health Sciences (IL)
The U of Akron (OH)
U of Arkansas for Medical Sciences (AR)
U of Arkansas–Fort Smith (AR)
U of Cincinnati (OH)
Washburn U (KS)

SURVEYING TECHNOLOGY
Indian River State Coll (FL)
Palm Beach State Coll (FL)
Pennsylvania Coll of Technology (PA)
The U of Akron (OH)
U of Alaska Anchorage (AK)

SYSTEM, NETWORKING, AND LAN/WAN MANAGEMENT
Dakota State U (SD)
Midland Coll (TX)
Stratford U, Falls Church (VA)
Sullivan U (KY)

TEACHER ASSISTANT/AIDE
Alverno Coll (WI)
Dordt Coll (IA)
Eastern Mennonite U (VA)
Indian River State Coll (FL)
Lamar U (TX)
Saint Mary-of-the-Woods Coll (IN)
State U of New York Coll of Agriculture and Technology at Cobleskill (NY)
U of Alaska Fairbanks (AK)
Valparaiso U (IN)

TECHNICAL TEACHER EDUCATION
Northern Kentucky U (KY)
Western Kentucky U (KY)

TECHNOLOGY/INDUSTRIAL ARTS TEACHER EDUCATION
State Coll of Florida Manatee-Sarasota (FL)

TELECOMMUNICATIONS TECHNOLOGY
Columbia Coll Hollywood (CA)
Inter American U of Puerto Rico, Bayamón Campus (PR)
New York City Coll of Technology of the City U of New York (NY)
Pace U (NY)
Penn State Shenango (PA)
St. John's U (NY)

TERRORISM AND COUNTERTERRORISM OPERATIONS
American Public U System (WV)

THEATER DESIGN AND TECHNOLOGY
Johnson State Coll (VT)
U of Rio Grande (OH)

THEOLOGICAL AND MINISTERIAL STUDIES RELATED
Lincoln Christian U (IL)

THEOLOGY
Appalachian Bible Coll (WV)
Baptist Missionary Association Theological Seminary (TX)
Creighton U (NE)
Immaculata U (PA)
Marian U (IN)
Missouri Baptist U (MO)
Ohio Dominican U (OH)

THEOLOGY AND RELIGIOUS VOCATIONS RELATED
Anderson U (IN)
Southeastern U (FL)

THERAPEUTIC RECREATION
Colorado Mountain Coll (CO)

TOOL AND DIE TECHNOLOGY
Ferris State U (MI)

TOURISM AND TRAVEL SERVICES MANAGEMENT
Colorado Mountain Coll, Alpine Campus (CO)
Fisher Coll (MA)
Morrisville State Coll (NY)
State U of New York Coll of Technology at Delhi (NY)
Sullivan U (KY)

TOURISM AND TRAVEL SERVICES MARKETING
State U of New York Coll of Agriculture and Technology at Cobleskill (NY)

TRADE AND INDUSTRIAL TEACHER EDUCATION
Cincinnati Christian U (OH)
Murray State U (KY)
State Coll of Florida Manatee-Sarasota (FL)

TRANSPORTATION/MOBILITY MANAGEMENT
Polk State Coll (FL)

TURF AND TURFGRASS MANAGEMENT
Michigan State U (MI)
North Carolina State U (NC)
U of Guelph (ON, Canada)
U of Massachusetts Amherst (MA)

URBAN STUDIES/AFFAIRS
Saint Peter's U (NJ)
U of Cincinnati (OH)

VEHICLE AND VEHICLE PARTS AND ACCESSORIES MARKETING
Pennsylvania Coll of Technology (PA)

VETERINARY/ANIMAL HEALTH TECHNOLOGY
Baker Coll of Port Huron (MI)
Becker Coll (MA)
Colorado Mountain Coll (CO)
Dalhousie U (NS, Canada)
Harrison Coll, Indianapolis (IN)
Hickey Coll (MO)
International Business Coll, Fort Wayne (IN)
Lincoln Memorial U (TN)
Medaille Coll (NY)
Michigan State U (MI)
Morehead State U (KY)
New England Inst of Technology (RI)
Northwestern State U of Louisiana (LA)
Purdue U (IN)
State U of New York Coll of Technology at Canton (NY)
State U of New York Coll of Technology at Delhi (NY)

Sul Ross State U (TX) (continued)
Sul Ross State U (TX)
Thomas Edison State Coll (NJ)
Universidad del Turabo (PR)
U of Cincinnati (OH)
U of Guelph (ON, Canada)
U of New Hampshire (NH)
Vermont Tech Coll (VT)

VISUAL AND PERFORMING ARTS
Pine Manor Coll (MA)

VISUAL AND PERFORMING ARTS RELATED
Valencia Coll (FL)

VITICULTURE AND ENOLOGY
Michigan State U (MI)

VOCATIONAL REHABILITATION COUNSELING
State Coll of Florida Manatee-Sarasota (FL)

VOICE AND OPERA
McNally Smith Coll of Music (MN)

WATER QUALITY AND WASTEWATER TREATMENT MANAGEMENT AND RECYCLING TECHNOLOGY
Colorado Mesa U (CO)
Lake Superior State U (MI)
Western Kentucky U (KY)

WEAPONS OF MASS DESTRUCTION
American Public U System (WV)

WEB/MULTIMEDIA MANAGEMENT AND WEBMASTER
American Public U System (WV)
Indiana Tech (IN)
Lewis-Clark State Coll (ID)
Montana Tech of The U of Montana (MT)

WEB PAGE, DIGITAL/ MULTIMEDIA AND INFORMATION RESOURCES DESIGN
Academy of Art U (CA)
DeVry U, Phoenix (AZ)
DeVry U, Pomona (CA)
DeVry U, Westminster (CO)
DeVry U, Miramar (FL)
DeVry U, Orlando (FL)
DeVry U, Decatur (GA)
DeVry U, Chicago (IL)
DeVry U, Kansas City (MO)
DeVry U, North Brunswick (NJ)
DeVry U, Columbus (OH)
DeVry U, Fort Washington (PA)
DeVry U, Houston (TX)
DeVry U, Irving (TX)
DeVry U, Arlington (VA)
DeVry U, Federal Way (WA)
DeVry U Online (IL)
Florida National U (FL)

International Academy of Design & Technology (FL)
New England Inst of Technology (RI)
Palm Beach State Coll (FL)
Rasmussen Coll Appleton (WI)
Rasmussen Coll Blaine (MN)
Rasmussen Coll Land O' Lakes (FL)
Rasmussen Coll Mokena/Tinley Park (IL)
Rasmussen Coll Romeoville/Joliet (IL)
Rasmussen Coll Tampa/Brandon (FL)
Rasmussen Coll Wausau (WI)
Stratford U, Woodbridge (VA)
Thomas More Coll (KY)
Universidad del Turabo (PR)
Utah Valley U (UT)

WELDING TECHNOLOGY
Excelsior Coll (NY)
Ferris State U (MI)
Idaho State U (ID)
Lamar U (TX)
Lewis-Clark State Coll (ID)
Liberty U (VA)
Midland Coll (TX)
Oakland City U (IN)
Pennsylvania Coll of Technology (PA)
State U of New York Coll of Technology at Delhi (NY)
U of Alaska Anchorage (AK)
Weber State U (UT)

WILDLIFE, FISH AND WILDLANDS SCIENCE AND MANAGEMENT
State U of New York Coll of Agriculture and Technology at Cobleskill (NY)

WOMEN'S STUDIES
Fisher Coll (MA)
Indiana U–Purdue U Fort Wayne (IN)
State Coll of Florida Manatee-Sarasota (FL)

WOOD SCIENCE AND WOOD PRODUCTS/PULP AND PAPER TECHNOLOGY
Morrisville State Coll (NY)

WOODWORKING
Pittsburg State U (KS)
State U of New York Coll of Technology at Delhi (NY)

WORD PROCESSING
Palm Beach State Coll (FL)

WRITING
Carroll Coll (MT)
The U of Tampa (FL)

ZOOLOGY/ANIMAL BIOLOGY
Palm Beach State Coll (FL)

Alphabetical Listing of Two-Year Colleges

In this index, the page numbers of the profiles are printed in regular type, the displays are in *italic*, and the Close-Ups are in **bold**.